Produced Under Supervision of
the PRC State Council Information Office

CHINA ENCYCLOPEDIA

China Encyclopedia Compilation Group

China Intercontinental Press

Chief Advisor: Wang Chen
Chief Planner: Li Bing
Chief Production Supervisor: Guo Changjian
Production Director: Li Xiangping
Chief Editor: Wu Wei
Deputy Chief Editor: Lin Wuhan
Executive Chief Editor: Wu Naitao
Members of Editorial Board: Li Zhihui, Peng Guangqian, Xiao Jiangping, Xue Fukang
Liu Xinshen, Yuan Baoan, Wang Lu, Wang Xianlei
Editor: Qiu Hongyan, Dong Yu

Translators: Wang Guozhen Sun Qiang Zhu Yongmei Gu Xiaohong
English Finalizer: Xue Fukang

Design Manager: Yan Zhijie
Layout by: Liu Peng Shen zhen Wang Gang Yu Hong
Charts by: Zhang Lei
Cover: Xie Jingyi
Printing Manager: Zhang Jianhua
Photos Curtsey of: CFP cnsphoto China Intercontinental Press

Introduction

China Encyclopedia, published both in Chinese and English, provides comprehensive information about China's general situation which will help foreign readers to acquire a better understanding about the country.

China Encyclopedia boasts 20 volumes: Symbols of China, Geography, History, Population, Ethnic Groups, State System, Economy, National Defense, Relations with Foreign Countries, Religion, Science and Technology, Education, Culture, Society, Environmental Protection, Political Parties and Social Organizations, Administrative Division, Judicature, Internet and Sports. The book presents the Chinese history and current status in a concise way and covers the development and change in all the respects of the Chinese society, especially the progress in contemporary China. Readers could see through them the fundamental trend of the social development in China.

China Encyclopedia is intentionally compiled in such a way that it is a more readable book for overseas readers. Each entry is complete with no more than 500 words, and the book contains a great number of photos and charts, plus indexes either by contents or by alphabetical order, making it convenient for readers to pick entries of interest.

China Encyclopedia has thus opened a knowledge gate to China for all the overseas readers.

01 P2 Symbols of China

National Flag of the People's Republic of China...1
National Emblem of the People's Republic of China........1
National Anthem of the People's Republic of China........1
National Day........2
Capital........2

02 P3 Geography

Geographic Location........3
Topography........3
Land Boundary........3
Mainland Coastline........3
Islands........3
Outline of Rivers........4
Exterior and Interior Rivers........4
Yangtze River........4
Yellow River........4
Yarlung Zangbo River........5
Heilongjiang River........5
Pearl River........5
Nujiang River........6
Lancangjiang River........6
Liaohe River........6
Huaihe River........6
Haihe River........6
Grand Canal........6
Outline of Lakes........7
Poyanghu Lake........7
Dongtinghu Lake........7
Hongzehu Lake........7
Taihu Lake........7
Chaohu Lake........7
Qinghaihu Lake........7
Monsoon Climate........8
Temperature........8
Precipitation........8
Temperature Zones........8
Sunlight........8
Natural Resources of China........9
Mineral Resources........9
Metallic Minerals........9
Non-Metallic Minerals........9
Energy Minerals........10
Grassland Resources........10
Inner Mongolia Pasturing Area........10
Xinjiang Pasturing Area........10
Qinghai Pasturing Area........10
Tibet Pasturing Area........10
Forest Resources........11
Natural Forest Conservation Project........11
Project on Converting Cultivated Land to Forest........11
Three-North and Yangtze River Valley Key Forest System Construction Project........11
Wild Animal and Plant Protection and Natural Reserve Construction Project........11
Construction Project of Fast Growing and High Yield Timber Forest Bases........11
Cultivatable Land........12
Wind Power Resources........12
Waterpower Resources........12
Marine Resources........12
Aquatic Products........12
Marine Aquatic Resources........12
Offshore Aquatic Resources........13
Inland Aquatic Resources........13
Organisms Resources........13
Animals........13
Plants........13
Edible Plants........13
Major Rare Animals........14
Pandas........14
Protection of the Pandas........14
Tibetan Antelopes........14
Medicinal Plants........15
Plants of Industrial Utilization........15
Environment Protecting Plants........15
Germplasm Resources........15

03 P16 History

Concise History of China........16
Prehistoric World and Slave Society (1.7 million years ago-476 BC)........16
Peking Man........16
Xia Dynasty (2070-1600 BC)........17
Shang Dynasty (1600-1046 BC)........17
Yin Ruins........17
Western Zhou Dynasty (1046 to 771 BC)........18
Spring and Autumn Period (770-476 BC)........18
Knife Money of the Qi State........18
Sun Wu........18
Warring States Period (475-221 BC)........19
Contention of a Hundred Schools of Thought..19
Confucianism (Confucian School)........19
Confucius (Kong Zi)........19
Mencius (Meng Zi)........20
Taoism (Taoist School)........20
Philosophical Taoism (Daojia) and Religious Taoism (Daojiao)........20
Lao Zi........20
Zhuang Zi........20
Mohist School........21
Legalist School........21
Qin Dynasty (221-206 BC)........21
Emperor Qin Shihuang (259-210 BC)........21
Burning Books and Burying Confucian Scholars Alive........21
Qin Great Wall........22
Han Dynasty (206BC-220 AD)........22
Silk Road........23
Silk Road on the Sea........23
Zhang Heng and Armillary Sphere........23
Cai Lun and the Art of Paper-making........23
Three Kingdoms (220-280)........24
Western Jin Dynasty (265-317)........24
Eastern Jin Dynasty (317-420)........24
Northern and Southern Dynasties (420-589)....24
Qi Min Yao Shu (Essential Techniques for the Peasantry)........25
Zu Chongzhi and π........25
Sui Dynasty (581-618)........25
Tang Dynasty (618-907)........26
Five Dynasties and Ten States (907-960)........26
Song Dynasty (960-1279)........26
Moveable Type........27
Mengxi Bitan (Dream Pool Essays)........27
Yuan Dynasty (1206-1368)........27
Invention of Gunpowder........27
Ming Dynasty (1368-1644)........28
Zheng He's Voyage to Southeast Asia and the Indian Ocean........28
Qing Dynasty (1616-1911)........28
Opium War........28
Republic of China (1912-1949)........29
Revolution of 1911........29
Sun Yat-sen........29
People's Republic of China (founded in 1949)....29

04 P30 Population

1 Percent Sample Census (2005) 30
The Main Datum of the Fifth National Census (2000) 30
Population Growth Rate 30
Population Density 30
Quality of Population 30
Population Distribution 31
Population Structure 31
National Population and Family Planning Commission of China 31
Policies on Population 32
Population Target 32
Population Forecast 32
The Background of the Policies on the Population 32
Starlight Program 32
The Trend of Aging Population 33
The Reasons for the Ageing Trend 33
Composition of the Ethnic Groups 33
Household Registration System 33
Policies on the Equality between Men and Women 34
Women's Employment 34
Women Participating in the Political Affairs 35
Education for Women 35
Protection of Children's Rights and Interests 35
Health Level of the Children 35
Nine-Year Compulsory Education 36
Protection for the Children in Need 36
The Disabled Population 36
Undertakings for the Disabled 36
National Day of Assisting Disabled Persons 36
Themes of Previous National Day of Assisting Disabled Persons 36
China Welfare Fund for the Handicapped 37
Changjiang New Mileage Plan 37

05 P38 Ethnic Groups

Fifty-Six Ethnic Groups 38
Composition of Ethnic Groups 38
Distribution of Ethnic Groups 38
The Han Ethnic Group 39
The Mongolian Ethnic Group 39
The Hui Ethnic Group 39
The Tibetan Ethnic Group 40
The Uygur Ethnic Group 40
The Miao Ethnic Group 41
The Yi Ethnic Group 41
The Zhuang Ethnic Group 41
The Bouyei Ethnic Group 42
The Korean Ethnic Group 42
The Manchu Ethnic Group 43
The Dong Ethnic Group 43
The Yao Ethnic Group 43
The Bai Ethnic Group 44
The Tujia Ethnic Group 44
The Hani Ethnic Group 44
The Kazak Ethnic Group 44
The Dai Ethnic Group 45
The Li Ethnic Group 45
The Lisu Ethnic Group 45
The Va Ethnic Group 45
The She Ethnic Group 46
The Gaoshan Ethnic Group 46
The Lahu Ethnic Group 46
The Shui Ethnic Group 47
The Naxi Ethnic Group 47
The Dongxiang Ethnic Group 47
The Jingpo Ethnic Group 47
The Blang Ethnic Group 48
The Kirgiz Ethnic Group 48
The Tu Ethnic Group 48
The Daur Ethnic Group 49
The Mulam Ethnic Group 49
The Qiang Ethnic Group 49
The Salar Ethnic Group 50
The Tajik Ethnic Group 50
The Maonan Ethnic Group 50
The Gelo Ethnic Group 51
The Xibe Ethnic Group 51
The Achang Ethnic Group 51
The Pumi Ethnic Group 51
The Nu Ethnic Group 52
The Uzbek Ethnic Group 52
The Russian Ethnic Group 52
The Ewenki Ethnic Group 52
The Bonan Ethnic Group 53
The De'ang Ethnic Group 53
The Yugur Ethnic Group 53

The Tatar Ethnic Group 53
The Lhoba Ethnic Group 54
The Jino Ethnic Group 54
The Derung Ethnic Group 54
The Oroqen Ethnic Group 54
The Hezhen Ethnic Group 55
The Moinba Ethnic Group 55
The Jing Ethnic Group 55
Major Ethnic Festivals 56
Spring Festival 56
Corban Festival 56
Fast-Breaking Festival 56
Tibetan New Year 56
Nadam Fair 56
Table of the Festival of Ethnic Minority Groups in China 57
Policies on Ethnic Groups 58
Equality and Unity Among Ethnic Groups 58
Ethnic Regional Autonomy 58
Types of Autonomous Areas for Ethnic Minority Groups 58
Autonomous Areas for Ethnic Minority Groups 58
Organs of Self-Government of Ethnic Autonomous Areas 58
Spoken and Written Languages of the Ethnic Groups 59
Freedom of Religious Belief of Ethnic Minorities 59
Folk Customs of Ethnic Groups 59
Economic Development 59
Self-Government Regulations and Separate Regulations 59
Development of Educational Undertakings 60
Independently Developing Ethnic Culture 60
Development of Ethnic Autonomous Areas...... 60
Special Arrangements for Tibet 60
Improved Transport Conditions in Ethnic Minorities Areas 61
Financial Support for Ethnic Autonomous Areas 61
Ecological Construction and Environmental Protection in Ethnic Autonomous Areas 61
Compulsory Education in Ethnic Autonomous Areas 61
Ethnic Autonomous Areas Encouraged to Open Wider to the Outside World 62
Pairing Off More Developed Areas and Ethnic Autonomous Areas for Aid 62

Special Care for Ethnic Minorities 62
Ethnic Publication 62
Study of the Ethnic Ancient Classics 63
State Ethnic Affairs Commission 63
Cultural Institutions in Ethnic Autonomous Areas 63

06 P64 State System

Legal System 64
The National People's Congress 64
Multi-Party Cooperation System and Political Consultative Conference System 65
Chinese People's Political Consultative Conference (CPPCC) 65
The Organizational Setup of the State 65
Constitution of the PRC 65
President of State 66
Administrative System 66
The State Council 66
The Functions and Powers of the State Council 66
Agencies and Special Commission Directly Under the State Council 66
Websites of the Ministries and Commissions of the State Council 66
Local People's Congresses and Local People's Governments 67
Ethnic Autonomous Regions and Autonomous Organs 67
The Military System 67
The Self-Management System of Villagers 68
The Self-Management System of the Urban Residents 68
The Congress of Workers and Staff 68

07 P69 Economy

General Survey

Five-Year Plans 69
The 10th Five-Year Plan (2001-2005) 69
Economic Growth Rate 69
The 11th Five-Year Plan (2006-2010) 70
Economic Restructuring 70
State Council Office for West Region Development 70
Western Region Development 70
Economic Construction Objective 71
Building an Energy-Efficient Society 71
The National Development and Reform Commission 71
State-owned Assets Supervision and Administration Commission 71
Three Industrial Sectors 72
Industrial Policies 72
Coexistence of Diverse Economic Elements 72
Reform of the State-owned Enterprises 72
Basic Framework of the State-owned Asset Management System 72
All-China Federation of Industry and Commerce 72
Non-Public Ownership Economic Sector 73
Forms of Private Enterprise Organization 73
Haier Group 73
Hope Group 73
Taxation Policies 74
Foreign Taxation in China 74
State Administration of Taxation 74

Agriculture

The General Situation of Agriculture 75
The Import and Export of the Agriculture 75
Township Enterprises 75
Agricultural Industrialization 75
Ministry of Agriculture 75
Spark Program 76
Important Achievements Plan 76
Prairie Fire Program 76
Super Rice Popularization Project 77
Increased Grain Output 77

Industry

Brief Introduction 77
Power Grid Construction 77
Power Industry 77
Clean Energy Sources 78
State Power Grid Corporation of China 78
State Administration of Work Safety 78
Three Gorges Project 79
Three Gorges Transport Hub Situation (2006) 79

The "Most" of the Three Gorges Project 79
The Three Gorges Project Construction Committee 79
Coal Industry 80
Petroleum and Natural Gas Industry 80
Nuclear Power Industry 80
China National Petroleum Corporation 81
China Petrochemical Corporation 81
China National Offshore Oil Corporation 81
Daya Bay Nuclear Power Plant 82
Qinshan Nuclear Power Plant 82
Tianwan Nuclear Power Plant 82
Ling'ao Nuclear Power Plant 82
China National Nuclear Corporation 83
China Nuclear Engineering and Construction Group Corporation 83
Chinese Nuclear Power Research and Design Institute 83
Energy Industry 84
New Energy Resources 84
Machinery Manufacturing Industry 84
Automobile Industry 84
China Machinery Industry Federation 84
China Association of Automobile Manufacturers 85
Aerospace Industry 85
Manned Spacecraft 85
Man-made Satellites 85
Launching Vehicles 85
Satellite Remote-sensing 86
Satellite Telecommunications and Broadcasting 86
Satellite Navigation and Positioning 86
Major Goal of Spaceflight 86
China Academy of Launch Vehicle Technology (CALT) 86
China-Aerospace Science and Industry Corporation 86
Space Science 87
Bilateral Cooperation on the Space Project 87
Multilateral Cooperation in the Space Project .. 88
Cooperation in Space with the United Nations. 88
Cooperation with the Other International Space Organizations 88
Outline of China's Space Science Plan in the 10th Five-Year Plan Period 88
Yang Liwei 88
Policies on International Space Exchanges 89
Activities of Commercial Satellites 89
Posts and Telecommunications 89
Information Industry 90
State Postal Bureau 90
Information Products Export 91
Internet Development 91
Lenovo Group 91
Cooperation with Overseas Partners in Information and Communication 91
High Technology Industry 91

Scientific and Technological Innovation and Incubation System 92
New and Hi-tech Development Zone 92
National Program to Apply Research Fruits to Production 92
China's International Scientific and Technological Cooperation Plan 92
Plan of Revitalizing Trade through Science and Technology 92

Transportation and Communications

Highways 93
Railways 93
China's First Privately-Run Railway 93
ADB-Financed Railway Projects 93
Transportation and Communications 93
Qinghai-Tibet Railway 94
The "Most" of Qinghai-Tibet Railway 94
Ministry of Communications 94
Ministry of Railways 94
Ports 95
System of Civil Aviation 95
Air China Limited 95
China Eastern Airline Holding Company(MU) 95
China Southern Air Holding Company (CZ) 95
Shanghai Airlines Co., Ltd. (FM) 96
Sichuan Airlines Co., Ltd. (3U) 96
Xiamen Airlines Ltd. (MF) 96
Shandong Airlines Group Co., Ltd.(SC) 96
Beijing Capital International Airport 96
Pudong International Airport 97
Guangzhou Baiyun International Airport 97
Hongqiao International Airport 97
Shenzhen Baoan International Airport 97
Chengdu Shuangliu International Airport 98
Hangzhou Xiaoshan International Airport 98
General Administration of Civil Aviation 98

Finance and Insurance

General Survey 99
Financial System 99
Financial Reform 99
State-owned Banks Getting Listed 99
China Banking Regulatory Commission 100
China Banking Association 100
China UnionPay 100
People's Bank of China 100
Bank of China 100
China Construction Bank 101
Industrial and Commercial Bank of China 101
Agricultural Bank of China 101
Shenzhen Development Bank 101
China Minsheng Bank 101
China Development Bank 102
Export-Import Bank of China 102
China Merchants Bank 102
CITIC Industrial Bank 102
Shanghai Pudong Development Bank 102
Agricultural Development Bank of China 103
Bank of Communications 103
China Everbright Bank 103
Industrial Bank 103
Foreign Exchange Management System 104
China's International Balance of Payment Statistics 104
Exchange Rate System 104
History and Status Quo of China's Exchange Rate System 104
The Progress of Renminbi Exchange Rate Reform 104
RMB Exchange Rate Regime 105
Four Phases of Renminbi Exchange Rate Reform 105
State Administration of Foreign Exchange 105
Renminbi 105
Financial Sector's Opening Up 106
Management on the Foreign-funded Banks 106
Laws and Regulations on Supervision and Management on Foreign-Funded Bank 107
Foreign-Funded Banks 107
RMB Business Conducted by the Foreign-Funded Banks 107
Supervision and Management Standard on Chinese-Funded Banks and Foreign-Funded Banks 107
Requirements for Foreign-Funded Banks 107
Operational Procedures for Reorganization of Foreign Banks' Branches 108
Cooperation in International Finance 108
Securities Market 108
China Future Association 108
Capital Markets' Opening Up 109
China's Commitments to the WTO on Opening Its Securities Market 109
China Securities Regulatory Commission 109
Shanghai Stock Exchange 110
Shenzhen Stock Exchange 110
Insurance Industry 110
Insurance Sector's Opening Up 111
Chinese-Funded Insurance Companies' Overseas Investment 111
Export Credit Insurance 111
China Insurance (Holdings) Co.,Ltd. 111
China Ping An Insurance (Group) Co., Ltd. 111
PICC Property and Casualty Co.,Ltd. 111
China Life Insurance (Group) Company 111
China Pacific Insurance (Group) Co., Ltd. 112
China Export and Credit Insurance Corporation 112
China Insurance Regulatory Commission 112

Intellectual Property

Intellectual Property Right Protection 113
Patent Examination System 113
Patent Application and Granting 113
Laws and Regulations on Trademark Protection 113
Trademarks Registration 114
Trademark Registration From Overseas 114
Protecting Well-known Trademark 114
Laws and Regulations on Copyright Protection 114
Cracking Down on Copyright Infringement and Piracy 114
Copyright Administrative Management System 115
Copyright Trade 115
Intellectual Property Rights Protection for Audio and Video Products 115
Scientific Research Institution for Copyright . 115
New Regulation on Network Copyright Protection 116
International Cooperation on Piracy 116
Protection of New Varieties of Agriculture and Forestry Plants 116
New Varieties of Plants 116
Customs Examination System 117
Customs Protection Mechanism 117
Judicial Protection of Intellectual Property Rights 117
China's Accession to International Conventions for the Protection of IPR 118
Guaranteeing the Rights of Foreign Rights Holders 118
International Exchange on IPR 118
System for IPR Protection 118
Laws and Regulations on the Protection of Intellectual Property Rights 119
Related Laws and Regulations 119
China's Action Plan on IPR Protection in 2006 120
Copyright Law 120
Trademark Law 120

Universal Convention on the Protection of Plant Varieties........................... 120
Layout Designs of Integrated Circuits........... 120
China Patent Information Center.................... 120
Copyright Protection Center of China........... 120
Copyright Agency of China (CAC)................ 120
Music Copyright Society of China................. 121
State Intellectual Property Office.................... 121
National Copyright Administration................ 121
General Administration of Press and Publication.................................... 121

Foreign Trade

General Situation of Foreign Trade................ 122
State Trade and Authorized Operation........... 122
Processing Trade... 123
Border Trade.. 123
Service Trade.. 123
Technological Trade...................................... 123
Ministry of Commerce.................................. 123
Overseas Investment...................................... 124
Provisions on Foreign Investment................. 124
International Contracted Projects.................. 124
Relations between China and the World's Economy.. 124
Implementation of the Commitments Made for the Entry into the WTO.................. 124
General Level of Tariff.................................. 125
Non-Tariff Measures and Import-Export Licensing Procedures............. 125
Renaming the Guangzhou Commodities Trade Fair................................ 125
Classified Management of the Import of Electromechanical Products........... 126
Forbidding or Restricting Import of Commodities................................. 126
International Economic and Trade Treaties and Customs..................................... 126
Anti-dumping Policies and Procedures........... 126
Taking the Market Economy Road................ 126
Popularizing the Concept of Market Economy.. 126
Full Market Economy Status......................... 126
Trade Friction.. 126
Opening-up the Telecom Industry.................. 126
Changes of the Telecommunication............... 127
The Opening-up of Commerce...................... 127

The Opening-up Pattern................................. 127
WTO Notification and Consultation Bureau... 127
Top 100 Chain Enterprises............................. 127
General Administration of Customs............... 128
Department of WTO Affairs, Ministry of Commerce.................................. 128
General Survey of Economic and Technological Development Zones................ 128
General Survey of Economic and Technological Development Zones....................................... 128
Export Processing Zone................................. 128
Foreign-related Economic Laws and Regulations.................................... 129
Foreign Trade Law... 129
Rules on Management of Foreign Trade Operators... 129
Rules on Management of Imported and Exported Commodities.................................. 129
Laws and Regulations Governing Inspection of Imported and Exported Commodities......... 129
Laws and Regulations Governing Quarantine of Animals and Plants.................. 129
Laws and Regulations Governing Health Quarantine.. 129
Laws and Regulations on Foreign Exchange Control.. 129
Customs Laws and Regulations..................... 129
Tariff Laws and Regulations.......................... 129
Foreign-related Civil and Commercial Laws.. 129

Utilization of Foreign Funds

Investment in China (2006)........................... 130
Policies on the Foreign Investment................ 130
Regional Policies... 130
Policies Concerning Encouraging Foreign Businessmen to Invest in Central and Western Parts of the Country....... 131
Policies Concerning Encouraging Foreign Businessmen to Invest in the Old Industrial Bases of Northeast China........ 131
Financial Support for the Foreign-invested Enterprises.. 131
Basic Forms of Foreign Direct Investment..... 131
Sino-foreign Joint Venture Enterprise............ 131
Sino-foreign Cooperation Enterprise............. 132
Wholly Foreign Owned Enterprise................ 132
Joint Development... 132
New Investment Forms................................. 132
Laws Concerning Foreign Investment........... 132
Bilateral Investment Protection Agreement.... 132
Bilateral Taxation Agreement........................ 133
Establishing Representative Office in China.. 133
Opening-up of the Service Field.................... 133
Industrial Policies.. 133
China Association of Enterprises with Foreign Investment....................................... 133

08 National Defense P134

National Defense Policy................................ 134
A New Security Concept............................... 134
China's National Defense Policy.................... 134
A Leadership and Administration System for National Defense......................... 135
General Headquarters of the Chinese People's Liberation Army................. 135
General Staff Headquarters............................ 135
Central Military Commission (CMC)............ 135
Ministry of National Defense......................... 135
General Political Department......................... 136
General Logistics Department....................... 136
General Armaments Department.................... 136
Leading Bodies of Armed Services................ 136
Military Area Commands.............................. 136
China's Large-scale Reduction of Military Personnel.. 136
China's Armed Forces................................... 137
Chinese People's Liberation Army................. 137
Active Troops of the PLA............................. 137
Army Flag of the PLA................................... 137
Army Emblem of the PLA............................ 137
Military Rank System of the PLA.................. 137
Reserve Force.. 138
Chinese People's Armed Police Force............ 138
Militia Force.. 138
Difference between Volunteer Military Service System and Mercenary Military Service System... 138
The Military Service System of China........... 139
Administration System for Military Service Work... 139
System of Civil Officers................................ 139
Active Service... 139

Enlistment into Active Service in Peacetime .. 140
Discharge from Active Service and Resettlements 140
Resettlement Policy on Officers and Civil Cadres Transferred to Civilian Work and Discharged Conscripts 140
Reserve Service 140
Reserve Force Building 141
Administration System of Militia Force 141
Military Training on Basic Militia Force 141
Border and Coastal Defense System 141
Building Border and Coastal Defense 141
China's Defense Expenditure 142
Use of Defense Expenditure 142
Maintain Low-level Defense Expenditure 142
Exchanges and Cooperation with Foreign Countries in Science, Technology and Industry for National Defense 143
Major Breakthroughs in Space Technologies for Civil Use 143
The Commission of Science, Technology and Industry for National Defense (COSTIND) 143
Important Progress in Aviation Industry for Civil Use 144
Rapid Growth in Shipbuilding Industry for Civil Use 144
Fifty Years in China's Space Industry 144
Launching Vehicles 145
Manned Spaceflight 145
Man-made Satellites 145
China National Space Administration (China's Space Institution) 145
Chinese PLA Military Academy of Sciences .. 146
National Defense University 146
National University of Defense Technology 146
China's National Defense Education 146
National Defense Education for the Whole People 146
China's International Military Exchanges and Cooperation 147
International Military Academic Exchanges 147
Strategic Consultation and Dialogue 147
Regional Security Cooperation 147
From "Shanghai Five" to Shanghai Cooperation Organization 147
Mutual Confidence and Cooperation between China and ASEAN 148
Signing of Relevant Agreements between China and India 148
International Exchanges and Cooperation in Non-traditional Security Fields 148
PLA Participates in Cooperation in Non-traditional Security Fields 149
Agreements on Disarmament and Confidence-Building Measures between China and Relevant Countries 149
China's Active Participation in UN Peacekeeping Operations 150
Honoring Commitment to International Arms Control and Non-Proliferation 150
China's Basic Position on Issues Related to Arms Control, Disarmament and Non-proliferation. 150
China's Measures in Promoting International Arms Control and Disarmament 150
China's Positive Participation in Other International Multilateral Arms Control Processes 151
China's Position on Nuclear Disarmament Issue 151
China's Policy and Measures on Nuclear Disarmament Issue 151
List of Arms Control, Disarmament and Non-Proliferation Treaties That China Has Joined . 152
China's Fulfilling International Obligations of Non-Proliferation 152
China's Support to Comprehensive Nuclear Test Ban Treaty 153
China's Policy and Position on Banning Biological Weapons 153
China's Efforts in Banning Biological Weapons 153
China's Policy and Position on Banning Chemical Weapons 153
China Makes Effort to Ban Chemical Weapons 153
China's Position on Prevention of Proliferation of Weapons of Mass Destruction (WMD) 153
Settlement on the Chemical Weapons Japan Abandoned in China 154
Developing Relations with Multinational Export Control Mechanisms 154
Conducting Exchanges and Cooperation on Non-Proliferation 154
Promoting the Important Role of the UN in Field of Non-Proliferation 154
Building Legal System on Non-Proliferation Export Control 155
Rigorous Implementation of Laws and Regulations on Non-Proliferation Export Control 155
China's Promotion on Conclusion of a Multilateral Treaty on Mutual No-First-Use of Nuclear Weapons 155
China's Support to Building Nuclear-Weapon-Free Zones 155
Serious Investigation on Suspected Cases of Illegal Export 156
Greater Publicity for Laws and Regulations on Export Control and Education for Enterprises 156
System and Principles on Non-Proliferation Export Control 156
Non-Proliferation Export Control Organs 156
Prevention of Weaponization of and Arms Race in Outer Space (PAROS) 157
Combating the Illicit Trade in Small Arms and Light Weapons (SALW) 157

09 P158 Relations with Foreign Countries

Foreign Policy 158
The Five Principles of Peaceful Coexistence.. 158
Principle of Establishing Diplomatic Relations 159
Ministry of Foreign Affairs 160
Diplomatic Relations 160
Sino-US Relations 160
Sino-Japanese Relations 160
Sino-Russian Relations 160
Sino-European Relations 161
Relations between China and the Surrounding Countries 161
The Chinese People's Association for Friendship with Foreign Countries (CPAFFC) 161
The Chinese People's Institute of Foreign Affairs 161
Relations with ASEAN 162
Relations with Developing Countries 162
Beijing Summit of the Forum on China-Africa Cooperation 162
China and the UN 162
China and APEC 163
China and Shanghai Cooperation Organization 163
China and the WTO 163

10 P164 Religion

Chinese Religion 164
Buddhism in China 164
The Feature of Chinese Buddhism 164
Tibetan Buddhism 165
Tubo Kingdom 165
Princess Wencheng 165
Songtsan Gampo 165
The Six-syllable Prayer 166
Dalai Lama 166
Panchen Lama 166
Living Buddha 166
Lama 166
Yonghegong Lamasery 167
Xuanzang (Tang Seng) 167
Jianzhen 167
Tar Monastery 168
Jokhang Monastery 168
Guangji Temple 168

Fayuan Temple 168
Xihuangsi Temple 168
Lingguang Temple 168
Dabei Temple 168
Dule Temple 168
Linji Temple 168
Puning Temple 169
Chongshan Temple 169
Huayan Temple 169
Xuanzhong Temple 169
Wutaishan Mountain 169
Xuankong Temple 169
Banruo (Prajna) Temple of Shenyang City 169
Ci'en Temple 169
Banruo (Prajna)Temple of Changchun City 169
Kwan-yin Temple of Jilin City 169
Jile Temple 169
Jing'an Temple 169
Chenxiangge Pavilion 169
Jade Buddha Temple 170
Yuanming Schoolroom 170
Qixia Temple 170
Hanshan Temple 170
Lingyanshan Temple 170
Guangjiao Temple (Mahatma Temple) 170
Daming Temple of Yangzhou City 170
Longchang Temple of Jurong County 170
Lingyin Temple of Hangzhou City 170
Jingci Temple of Hangzhou City 170
Seven Towers Temple 170
Putuo Mountain 171
Guoqing Temple 171
Jiuhua Mountain 171
Southern Putuo Temple 171
Kaiyuan Temple 171
Zhanshan Temple 171
White Horse Temple 171
Shaolin Temple 171
Yuelushan Temple 171
Liurong Temple 171
Nanhua Temple 171
Qingyun Temple 171
Guangxiao Temple 171
Wenshu Temple 171
Emeishan Mountain 171
Chinese Buddhist Academies 172
The Research Institute of Buddhism Culture of China 172
Luohan Temple (Arhat Temple) 172
Qianming Temple 172
Yuantong Temple 172
Chongsheng Temple 172
Great Ci'en Temple 172
Great Xingshan Temple 172
Famen Temple 173
Xiangji Temple 173
Buddhist Painting in China 173
Buddhist Sculpture 173

Dunhuang Murals 173
Tangka Paintings 173
Buddhist Association of China 174
Qingzhou Statuary 174
Sichuan Dazu Stone Carvings 174
Taoism in China 175
Ge Hong 175
Lao Zi 175
Zhuang Zi 175
Huashan Mountain 175
Qingchengshan Mountain 175
White Cloud Temple 176
Yongle Palace in Shanxi Province 176
Taiqing Palace of Laoshan Mountain 176
Taiqing Palace of Shenyang City 176
Taoist Temple of Maoshan Mountain 176
Taoist Association of China 176
Islam in China 177
Moslem Pilgrims 177
Baba Mosque of Langzhong City 177
Dongguan Mosque of Xining City 177
Huashi Mosque of Beijing 177
Niujie Mosque of Beijing 177
Yidu Zhenjiao Mosque 178
Islamic Association of China 178
Dongda Mosque of Kaifeng Citys 178
Aitiga Mosque of Kashi (Kashgar) 178
Catholicism in China 178
Qingdao Catholic Church 178
Tianjin Xikai Church 179
Shanghai Old Cathedral 179
Catholic Churches in Beijing 179
Northern Church 179
Eastern Church 179
Western Church 180
St. Michael's Church 180
Dongguantou Church 180
Longzhuang Church 180
Housangyu Village Church 180
Chinese Catholic Organization 180
Protestantism in China 180
Qingdao Christian Church 180
Flower Lane Church in Fuzhou City 181
Shanghai Community Church 181
Haidian Christian Church in Beijing 181
Jinling Xiehe Divinity School 181
China Christian Council 182
Three-Self Patriotic Movement Committee of the Protestant Churches of China 182
Freedom of Religious Belief 182
Religions Should Abide by the Laws 182
All Religions Are Equal 182
Religion Is Separated from Political Power 182
State Protects Normal Religious Activities 182
Theism and Atheism Should Respect Each Other 182
Adopting the Principle of Independence and Self-management 182
Respecting and Protecting Freedom of Religious Belief of Minorities 182
Judicial and Administrative Guarantees and Supervision 183
Registration Procedures of Religious Activities 183
Political Deputies of the Religious Circle 183
International Religious Exchanges 184
Respecting Freedom of Religious Belief of Foreigners in China 184
Protecting Aliens' Exchanges With Respect to Religion 184
Chinese Laws Must Be Observed 184
Handling Aberrant Behavior According to the Law 185
Relations with the Vatican 185
State Administration for Religious Affairs 185

11 P186 Science and Technology

General Survey

The Four Great Inventions of Ancient China 186
Papermaking 186
Gunpowder 186
Compass 186

Printing... 187
Technology Development Today 187
Technology Development in the Present Age... 188

Scientific and Technical Systems

Scientific and Technical Bodies 188
Research and Development Institutions Subject to Higher Schools.............................. 188
Research and Development Institutions Subject to Enterprises 188
Chinese Academy of Sciences 189
Chinese Academy of Agricultural Sciences.... 189
Chinese Academy of Forestry......................... 189
Chinese Academy of Medical Sciences 189

Scientific and Technical Achievements

Significant Scientific and Technical Achievements 190
Biotechnology.. 190
Nano Technological Research Progress.......... 190
Computers Research Progress......................... 191
Material Technological Research Progress..... 191
Rice Technological Research Progress 191
Wild Animal DNA Bank 191
Top 10 Items of Progress in Scientific and Technolog in 2005.................................. 192
China's 10 Most Important Developments in Science and Technology in 2006 192
Top 10 Items of Progress in Science and Technology in 2007 192

Scientific and Technical Awards

Outline of Scientific and Technical Awards.... 194
State Supreme Science and Technology Award 194
China International Science and Technology Cooperation Award...................... 194
National Technical Invention Award............... 195
Scientific and Technical Progress Award 195
Chinese Engineering Science and Technology Guanghua Award......................... 195
State Spark Awards 195
Hua Luogen Mathematics Award................... 195

Science and Technology Programs

State Science and Technology Programs 196
National Key Technologies Research and Development Program 196
863 Program... 196
973 Program... 196
Torch Program.. 196
Spark Program 197

International Cooperation

Scientific and Technical Cooperation between China and Foreign Countries........... 197
Semi-official and Folk Science and Technology Cooperation................................ 197
Technical Trade.. 197
The Human Genome Project........................... 198
Human Brain Project....................................... 198
Global Change Program................................. 198
High Energy Physics Research Program 198
Alpha Magnetic Spectrometer Experiment..... 198
Geospace Double Star Exploration Program .. 198
European Galileo Project............................... 198

Social Sciences

System of Social Sciences 198
Chinese Academy of Social Sciences 199

Famous Scientists

Yuan Longping... 199
Wu Wenjun... 200
Huang Kun 200
Wang Xuan... 200
Jin Yilian 200
Liu Dongsheng... 201
Wang Yongzhi 201
Ye Duzheng.. 201
Wu Mengchao 201
Li Zhensheng 201
Min Enze.. 201
Wu Zhengyi.. 202
The Ministry of Science and Technology 202
National Natural Science Foundation of China 202
China Association for Science and Technology (CAST)...................................... 202

12 P203 Education

Development of Education 203
Imperial Civil Examination System................ 203
Baguwen (Eight-part Essay) 203
Education in Modern China........................... 204
Educational Management System................... 204
Outlays for Education 205
Education System... 205
Basic Education 205
Pre-School Education (Early Childhood Education).......................... 205
Primary and Secondary Education................. 205
Implementation of 9-Year Compulsory Education.................................. 205
The Ministry of Education 206
China National Institute for Educational Research...................................... 206
Educational System (Basic Education) 206
Teaching Materials for Primary and Middle Schools 206
After-School Education.................................. 207
Rural Compulsory Education......................... 207
Project Hope... 207
Spring Bud Project... 207
Special Education... 208
Disabled Receiving Higher Education........... 208
Vocational Training for the Disabled 208
Legal Protection 208
Aid-Study System 208
Vocational Education 209
General Higher Education.............................. 209
Entrance Examination for Universities and Colleges 209
Entrance Examination for Post-Graduate Students................................. 209
Examination for Obtaining Certificate........... 210
Project 211 210
National Teaching Experimental Demonstration Centers of Higher Institutions......................... 210
Higher Education System 210
Graduate Education and Academic Degrees System... 210
Post-Doctorate System................................... 211
State Yangtze Scholar Award Program (Cheung Kong Scholars Program).................. 211
People's Education Press................................ 211
China Academic Degrees and Graduate Education Development Center (CDGDC) 212
Tsinghua MBA Program 212
Adult Education 212
Education for Illiteracy 212
Higher Education for Adults.......................... 213

Subjects of the National Adult College Entrance Examination (NACEE) 213
China Education Development Foundation 213
Self-Taught Higher Education Examination 214
Private Education 214
Laws and Regulations on Privately-Run Education 214
China Adult Education Association (CAEA) 214
Xi'an Translation University 215
Beijing Oriental University 215
Independent Colleges 215
Outline of Ethnic Education 215
Ethnic Minority Education 215
Policies of Ethnic Education 216
Modern Distance Education 216
Distance Education for Primary and Middle Schools in Rural Areas 216
Radio and Television Universities 217
China Central Radio and Television University 217
China Education and Research Network 217
China Education Television 217
China Central Audio-Visual Education Center 218
China Education Satellite Broad Band Transmission Network Platform 218
Modern Distance Education in Zhejiang University 218
Modern Distance Education in Peking University 218
Teachers 218
System of Education Master Degree (EMD) 219
Normal Education 219
Teachers' Law of the PRC 219
International Exchanges and Cooperation 220
Bilateral Governmental Cooperation Programs 220
Exchanges between the Overseas Students 220
China Provides Educational Aid to Developing Countries 220
AFS Intercultural Programs in China 220
AFS Exchanges and Activities in China 221
Studying Abroad 221
Chunhui Program 221
China Educational Associations for International Exchange 221
Qualification of applicants for the Chinese Government Scholarship 222
Application Documents for Chinese Government Scholarships 222
Education for Overseas Students in China 222
Classification of Overseas Students 222
Scholarships for International Student 223
Chinese Government Scholarships 223
Application Approach and Time for the Chinese Government Scholarships 223
Annual Review of the Chinese Government Scholarship 223
China Scholarship Council 224
Choice of Higher Learning Institutions and Specialty 224
China/UNESCO-The Great Wall Fellowship 224
Distinguished International Students Scholarship Scheme 224
HSK Winner Scholarship Scheme 224
Chinese Culture Research Fellowship Scheme 224
Short-term Scholarship for Foreign Teachers of Chinese Language 225
Language Used in Teaching 225
Visa Application and Registration in China 225
Transfer Service for Chinese Government Full-Scholarship Students 225
Applications for Study in China of Non-Government Scholarship Students 225
Applications for Short-term Course and Visa Application 226
Expenses for Self-Supporting Overseas Students 226
Entrance Examination and Assessment 226
Short-term Courses for Foreigners 227
Preparatory Education in Chinese for International Students in China 227
Necessary Preparations 227
Affairs for Entering to China and Admission 227
China-EU Student Exchange Scholarships Program 228
Teaching Chinese as a Foreign Language 228
Chinese Proficiency Test (HSK) 228
Sphere of Application of HSK 228
The Chinese Proficiency Test (HSK) Overseas Exam Sites Distribution 229
Chinese Language Proficiency Certificate 229
Confucius Institute 229
Sino-African Education Minister Forum 229
The 111 Project (Program of Introducing Overseas Talents in Disciplines to Universities) 229
China Europe International Business School (CEIBS) 230
Peking University 230
Tsinghua University 231
Renmin University 231
University of International Business and Economics 231
Central Conservatory of Music 232
University of Science and Technology of China 232
China University of Mining and Technology 232
China University of Political Science and Law 233
Beijing Language and Culture University 233
Beijing Normal University 233
Beijing Jiaotong University 234
Zhejiang University 234
Wuhan University 234
Shandong University 235
Tianjin University 235
Dalian University of Technology 236

Fudan University 236
Sichuan University 236
Harbin Institute of Technology 237
Tongji University 237
Jilin University 237
Xiamen University 237
Nankai University 238
Nanjing University 238
Huazhong University of Science and Technology 238
East China Normal University 239
Xi'an Jiaotong University 239
Lanzhou University 239
Sun Yat-sen University 239
Northeast Forestry University 240
Shanghai University of Finance and Economics 241
Shanghai Jiaotong University 241

13 Culture P242

Language

Chinese 242
Pronunciation of Chinese 242
Chinese Pinyin 242
Language Policy 242
Use of the Chinese Language 242
Syntax of Chinese Language 243
Mandarin and Dialects 243
Chinese Characters 243
Evolution of Chinese Characters 243
Number of Chinese Characters 244
Word-formation of Chinese Characters 244
Grapheme of Chinese Characters 244
Dictionaries 244
Chinese Characters and Names 245

Chinese Characters and Couplets.................... 245
Chinese Characters and
Chinese Seal Cutting....................................... 245
Commonly Used Chinese Characters 245
Spread of Chinese 245

Calligraphy and Painting

Calligraphy.. 246
Same Origin of Calligraphy and Painting....... 246
Evolution of Calligraphy................................. 246
Inscriptions on Tortoise Shells and
Animal Bones.. 247
Bronze Inscriptions... 247
Greater Seal Script.. 247
Lesser Seal Script.. 247
Official Script.. 248
Cursive Script.. 248
Running Script.. 248
Regular Script... 248
Print Hand... 249
Xi'an Stele Forest.. 249
Wang Xizhi... 249
Wang Xianzhi.. 250
Ouyang Xun.. 250
Yan Zhenqing.. 250
Plaque.. 250
Huai Su.. 251
Liu Gongquan 251
Mi Fu... 251
Zhao Mengfu... 251
Zheng Xie.. 251
Wu Changshuo.. 252
China Calligraphers Association..................... 252
Traditional Chinese Painting........................... 252
Usual Subjects in Traditional
Chinese Paintings.. 252
Figure Painting.. 252
Landscape Painting... 253
Flower-and-Bird Painting 253
Cliff Painting... 253
Silk Painting.. 253
Gu Kaizhi and Scroll Painting 253

Colored Painting (Gongbi) and Water-Ink
Painting (Xieyi)... 253
Dunhuang Murals.. 254
Wu Daozi, Sage in Chinese Painting 254
Imperial Painting Academy of the
Song Dynasty.. 254
Zhang Zeduan and the Qingming Festival by the
Riverside 254
The Yongle Palace Mural............................... 254
Prints 255
The Four Great Painters of the Yuan Dynasty and
Chinese Landscape Painting 255
Eight Eccentric Painters of Yangzhou............ 255
Chinese Artists' Association........................... 256
Four Treasures of the Study 256
Brush 256
Ink 256
Paper 257
Ink Stone 257
Writing Utensils in the Study......................... 257
Development of Chinese Oil Painting 258
Development of Chinese Cartoons 258
Development of Modern Lian Huan Hua
(Linked Serial Pictures) 258
Rong Bao Zhai 259
Duo Yun Xuan.. 259
Shen Xue Ren Gallery 259
China National Art Academy......................... 259

Music

Brief History of Folk Music........................... 260
Folk Musical Instruments 260
Xun... 260
Sheng.. 260
Xiao.. 261
Flute 261
Guanzi 261
Hulusi... 262
Bawu 262
Huqin.. 262
Erhu.. 262
Gaohu... 262
Banhu 263
Zhuihu 263
Matouqin (Horse-head Fiddle)....................... 263
Liuqin... 263
Dongbula.. 264
Pipa 264
Spring Moon Light on the
Flowers by the River...................................... 264
Ruan 264
Guqin.. 264
Shi Jing (The Book of Poetry) 265
Official Conservatory in the Han Dynasty...... 265
Se... 265
Tanbu'er.. 265

Pipa of Dong Ethnic Group............................. 265
Yangqin (Dulcimer) 266
Konghou... 266
Bianzhong (Chime Bells)................................ 266
Zeng Houyi Bells 266
Qing.. 266
Gong... 267
Drum 267
Chu Ci (Songs of Chu).................................... 267
Folk Songs 268
Xinjiang Folk Song Region 268
Folk Song Region with Primitive Culture 268
Tibetan Folk Song Region 268
Semi-Agriculture and Semi-Pasturing
Folk Song Region 268
Grassland Folk Song Region 269
Han Folk Song Region................................... 269
Folk Song Region with Hunting Culture 269
Modern Folk Songs.. 269
Modern Chinese Music.................................. 270
Modern Symphonic Music............................. 270
Contemporary Development of
Symphonic Music 270
Symphony Orchestra of the China
National Opera House.................................... 270
Beijing Symphony Orchestra......................... 270
China Philharmonic Orchestra........................ 271
China National Symphony Orchestra 271
Shanghai Symphony Orchestra....................... 271
Chinese Musicians Association...................... 271

Drama

Introduction to Chinese Drama 272
Chinese Dramatists Association...................... 272
Local Operas 273
Beijing Opera 274
Brief History of Beijing Opera 274
Roles in Beijing Opera................................... 274
Types of Facial Make-up in Beijing Opera..... 274
Schools of Beijing Opera 275
Major Schools of Beijing Opera 275
Performances of Beijing Opera....................... 275
Mei Lanfang.. 275
Classical Lists of Beijing Opera Items............ 276
Beijing Opera: A Fork in a Road.................... 276
Beijing Opera: Autumn River 276

Beijing Opera: Entering the Palace for the Second Time............................ 276
Beijing Opera: Yu Tangchun.......................... 276
Beijing Opera: The Drunken Concubine 276
Beijing Opera: Conqueror Xiang Yu Bids Farewell to His Concubine................ 276
Beijing Opera: Mu Guiying Takes Command 277
Beijing Opera: Suo Lin Nang 277
Beijing Opera: Zhaojun Goes to the Border Area.. 277
Beijing Opera: Hongniang............................ 277
Beijing Opera: Qin Xianglian........................ 277
Beijing Opera: White Snake.......................... 277
Beijing Opera: Have the Aid of East Wind..... 277
Beijing Opera: Empty-City Strategy.............. 277
Beijing Opera: Xu Ce Runs in the City.......... 277
Beijing Opera: Chisang Town........................ 277
Beijing Opera: Wild Boar Forest.................... 278
Beijing Opera: Create Serious Disturbance in the Heavenly Palace 278
Beijing Opera: Gathering of Heroes.............. 278
Beijing Opera: Yang Silang Visits His Mother 278
Beijing Opera: Dragon and Phoenix Is a Good Omen............................... 278
Art of Quyi... 279
Performances of Quyi.................................... 279
Danxian.. 279
Xiangsheng.. 279
Er'renzhuan.. 279
Dagu and Gushu.. 280
Yangzhou Pinghua (Storytelling in Yangzhou Dialect)... 280
Pingshu.. 280
Kuaiban and Kuaishu..................................... 281
Early Drama... 281
Modern Drama... 281
Professional Drama Troupes.......................... 281
Contemporary Drama..................................... 282
Realistic Play Writers..................................... 282
Open Dramatic World.................................... 282
China National Huaju Opera Troupe............. 282
China National Youth's Art Theater............... 282
Beijing People's Art Theater.......................... 283
China National Children's Art Troupe........... 283
Central Experimentary Huaju Opera Troupe.. 283
Shanghai People's Art Theater....................... 283
Central Academy of Drama........................... 283
Shanghai Theater Academy........................... 283

Traditional Artware

Traditional Artware.. 284
Bronze Ware... 284
Simuwu Rectangular Ding Tripod................. 284
Horse Stepping on a Swallow........................ 284
Jade Ware... 284
Jade Production... 285
Chinese Cloisonné... 285
Modern Cloisonné.. 285
Lacquer Ware... 285
Development of Lacquer Ware...................... 285
Wax Printing... 286
Paper-Cuts... 286
Abundant Folk Paper Cuts............................. 286
Embroidery.. 287
Xiangxiu (Hunan Embroidery)...................... 287
Shuxiu (Sichuan Embroidery)........................ 287
Yuexiu (Guangdong Embroidery).................. 287
Suxiu (Suzhou Embroidery).......................... 287
Furniture.. 288
Ming Dynasty Style Furniture....................... 288
Qing Dynasty Style Furniture........................ 288
Porcelain.. 288
Jingdezhen Porcelain.................................... 288
Yixing Baccaro Teapot.................................. 289
Primitive Sculpture....................................... 289
Carving.. 289
Bamboo Carving.. 289
Wood Carving.. 289
Tooth and Horn Carving................................ 289
Terracotta Warriors....................................... 290
Stone Carving.. 290
Stone Lion... 290
Stone Horse Stepping on a Hun Soldier......... 290
Yungang Grottoes.. 291
Mogao Grottoes... 291
Longmen Grottoes... 291
Maijishan Grottoes.. 291
Giant Stone Buddha at Leshan....................... 291
Clay Sculptures... 291
Colored Sculptures in the Jin Temple............ 292
Fengxiang Painted Clay Figurines................. 292
Huishan Clay Figurines................................. 292
Gaomi Clay Figurines.................................... 292
Clay Figurine Master Zhang.......................... 293
Dough Sculpture.. 293
Shanxi Dough Sculptures.............................. 293
Shandong Jinan Dough Sculptures................ 293
Shandong Langzhuang Dough Sculptures...... 293
Butter Sculptures... 294
Making of Chinese Kites............................... 294
Brief History of Chinese Kites...................... 294
Folk Chinese New Year Painting.................. 294
New Year Wood Block Paintings.................. 294
Taohuawu New Year Woodblock Prints........ 295
Yangliuqing New Year Woodblock Prints..... 295
Mianzhu New Year Woodblock Prints.......... 295
Zhuxianzhen New Year Woodblock Prints..... 295
Wuqiang New Year Woodblock Prints........... 295
Foshan New Year Woodblock Prints.............. 295
Manual Weaving.. 295
Straw Weaving.. 295
Bamboo and Rattan Weaving........................ 295
Chinese Knots... 295

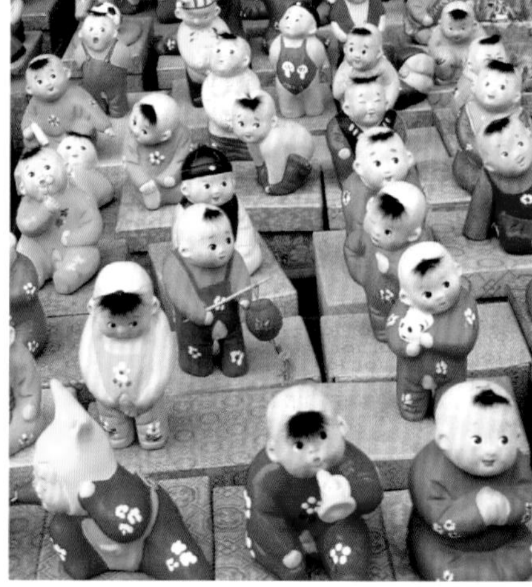

Museums

Museums.. 296
National Museum of China............................ 296
Palace Museum.. 296
Exhibition of Cultural Treasures of the Palace.....296
Cultural Treasures in the Palace..................... 297
Protection on Cultural Treasures of the Palace.... 297
Capital Museum... 297
Tianjin Historical Museum............................ 298
Hebei Museum... 298
Shanxi Museum... 298
Inner Mongolia Museum................................ 298
Liaoning Museum.. 298
Jilin Museum... 299
Heilongjiang Museum.................................... 299
Shanghai Museum.. 299
Zhejiang Museum.. 299
Anhui Museum... 300
Fujian Museum.. 300
Jiangxi Museum... 300
Shandong Museum... 300
Henan Museum.. 301
Hubei Museum... 301
Hunan Museum.. 301
Guangdong Museum...................................... 301
Museum of Guangxi Zhuang Autonomous Region...................................... 301
Chongqing Museum....................................... 302
Sichuan Museum.. 302
Guizhou Museum... 302
Yunnan Museum.. 302

Tibet Museum 303
Shaanxi History Museum 303
Gansu Museum 303
Qinghai Museum 303
Museum of Ningxia Hui Autonomous Region ... 304
Museum of Xinjiang Uygur Autonomous Region 304
Hong Kong Museum 304
Macao Museum 304
Military Museum of the Chinese People's Revolution 305
Beijing Natural History Museum 305
Museum of Chinese Science and Technology 305
China National Museum of Fine Arts 305
Geological Museum of China 305
Ancient Bells Museum at the Great Bell Temple 306
China's Museum of Stamps 306
China Sports Museum 306
International Friendship Museum 306
Relic Hall of Chinese Buddhism Books 307
Dingling Museum 307
Chinese Aviation Museum 307
Beijing Planetarium 307
Beijing Ancient Observatory 307
Cultural Palace of the Ethnic Groups 308
China Modern Literature Museum 308
Tianjin Natural History Museum 308
Tianjin Folklore Museum 308
Shenyang Palace Museum 308
Shanghai Museum of Natural Sciences 309
Museum of Medical History in the Shanghai College of Traditional Chinese Medicine 309
Suzhou Steles Museum 309
China Tea Museum 309
China National Silk Museum 309
Museum of the Hemudu Site 310
Huqing Yutang Museum of Traditional Chinese Medicine 310
Xiamen Overseas Chinese Museum 310
Museum of Ocean Transportation History in Quanzhou 311
Jingdezhen Ceramics Museum 311
Nanyang Museum of Han Dynasty Stone Carving 311
Suizhou Zeng Houyi Tomb Relics Display Hall 311
Museum of the Former Site of Ancient Tonglushan Copper Mine 312
Mawangdui Han Tombs Relics Display Hall in Changsha 312
Mawangdui Han Tombs 312
Guangxi Ethnic Relics Center 312
Zigong Salt History Museum 313
Zigong Dinosaur Museum 313
Sanxingdui Museum 313
China's Museum of the Three Gorges of the Yangtze River 313
Qin Terracotta Army Museum 313
Maolin Museum 314
Qianling Museum 314
Banpo Museum in Xi'an 314
Shaanxi Geological Museum 314
Hong Kong Space Museum 314
Taipei Palace Museum 315
Taipei Insect Science Museum 315
Taiwan Museum of Natural Science 315
Private Museums 316
Ancient Pottery Civilization Museum 316
Guanfu Classic Art Museum 316
Sihai Pots Museum 316
Jianchuan Museum 316

China's Intangible Cultural Heritage

The Intangible Cultural Heritage 317
Significance of Safeguarding Intangible Cultural Heritage 317
General Survey of China's Intangible Cultural Heritage 317
Brief History of China's Protection for Intangible Cultural Heritage 317
Goal and Guiding Principle of Protecting of Intangible Cultural Heritages 318
Intangible Cultural Heritage List 318
Masterpieces of Oral and Intangible Heritage of Humanity 318
Legislation on Intangible Cultural Heritage Protection 319
Transmitter of Intangible Cultural Heritage.... 319
Salvaging Intangible Cultural Heritage 319
Intangible Cultural Heritage in China 319
Emblem of Intangible Cultural Heritage 319
National Intangible Cultural Heritage List 320
China's Intangible Cultural Heritages 320
International Cooperation 320
China Intangible Cultural Heritage Protection Center 320

Folk Literature

Ancient Song of Miao People 320
Bu Luo Tuo 320
Zhe Pama and Zhe Mima 321
Mu Pa Mi Pa Poetry Legend 321
Ke Dao Narrative Poetry 321
The Legend of the White Snake 321
Butterfly Lovers 322
Legend of Meng Jiangnv 322
The Story of Dong Yong and the Seventh Fairy Maiden 322
The Tale of Xishi 322
The Tale of Monk Jigong 323
Ulabun Biographical Singing and Talking 323
Hexi Baojuan 323
The Folklore of Gengcun Village 323
Folklore of Wujiagou Village 324
Folklore of Xiabaoping Township 324
Zouma Town Folklore 324
Guyuyan Folk Stories 324
Kharchin and Eastern Inner Mongolia Folklore 324
Tan Zhenshan's Folk Stories 325
Hejian Song Poem 325
Wu Ballad 325
Ballads of Liu Sanjie 325
The Tune of Four-Season Production 326
The Epic of Manas 326
The Epic of Janggar 326
The Heroic Epic of King Gesar 326
The Legend of Ashima 327
Larenbu and Jimensuo 327
Story Song of She People 327
Qinglinsi Conundrum 327

Folk Music

Zuoquan Blossom Tune 328
Hequ Folk Song 328
The Urtiin Duu or "Long Song" of the Mongolian People 328
The Hoomii of the Mongolian People 328
Dangtu Folk Song 328
Chaohu Folk Song 329
Folk Song of the She Ethnic Group 329
Xingguo Mountain Song 329
Xingshan Folk Song 329
Sangzhi Folk Song 330
Meizhou Hakka Mountain Song 330
Zhongshan Xianshui Song 330
Yazhou Folk Song 330
Danzhou Tunes 331
Shizhu Tujia Luo'er Tune 331
Song of the Bashan Back-Carriers 331
Folk Song of the Lisu Ethnic Group 331
Ziyang Folk Song 332
Folk Song of the Yugur Ethnic Group 332
Hua'er 332

Tibetan Lagzhas 333
Liaozhai Liqu 333
Jingzhou Miao Geteng 333
Chuanjiang Haozi 333
Nanxi Haozi 334
Mudong Mountain Song 334
Northern Sichuan Weeding Drum-Gong Singing 334
The Dong Grand Song 334
The Pipa Song of the Dong Ethnic Group 335
Hani Multi-Voice-Part Folk Song 335
Yi Seaweed Singing 335
Napo Zhuang Folk Song 335
Lishui Boatmen Haozi 336
Chinese Guqin Art 336
Qiang Flute Performance and Manufacture 336
Horse-head Stringed Instrument Music of Mongolia 337
Mongolian Sihu Music 337
Art of Suona Horn 337
Liaoning Wind and Percussion Ensemble 338
Jiangnan Sizhu 338
Haizhou Wuda Gongdiao Music 338
Shengzhou Wind and Percussion Music 339
Zhoushan Gong and Drum Music 339
Shifan Music 339
Southwestern Shandong Guchuiyue 339
Bantou Tunes 340
Yichang Sizhu 340
Zhijiang Folk Wind and Percussion Music 340
Guangdong Music 340
Chaozhou Music 341
Guangdong Hanyue Music 341
Chuida Music 341
Laiziluogu at Liangping 341
Tujia Daliuzi 342
Percussion and Wind Music in Hebei Province 342
Weifeng Gong and Drum in South Shanxi Province 342
Jiangzhou Drum Music 343
Shangdang Bayinhui Music 343
Jizhong Sheng and Pipe Music 343
Twelve Copper Drum Melodies 343
Xi'an Drum Music 344
Lantian Puhua Water Fair Music 344
Folk Musical Instruments of Hui Ethnic Group 344
Wenshui Guzi 344
Jing Music at Beijing Zhihuasi Temple 345
Wutaishan Mountain Buddhist Music 345
Qianshan Mountain Temple Music 345
Taoist Music of Xuanmiaoguan Taoist Temple 346
Wudangshan Mountain Taoist Music 346
Nanyin Music 346
Quanzhou Beiguan Music 347
Xinjiang Uygur Muqam Art 347

Folk Dances

Jingxi Taiping Drum Dance 348
Yangge 348
Jingxing Lahua 348
Dragon Dance 348
Lion Dance 348
Flowery Drum Lantern Dance 349
Nuowu Dance 349
Yingge 349
Stilt Dance 350
Yongxin Shield Dance 350
Yicheng Flowery Drum Dance 350
Quanzhou Breast Clapping Dance 350
Ansai Waist Drum Dance 350
Luochuan Biegu Drum Dance 351
Lanzhou Taiping Drum Dance 351
Yuhang Rolling Lantern Dance 351
Tujia Hand Wielding Dance 351
Tujia Sayeryo Dance 352
Xianzi Dance 352
Guozhuang Dance 352
Raba Dance 352
Cham of Tashilhungpo Monastery in Xigaze . 352
Reed Panpipe Dance of Miao Ethnic Group ... 353
Korean Nongle Dance 353
Wooden Drum Dance 353
Bronze Drum Dance 353
Peacock Dance of Dai Ethnic Group 354
Daur Lurigele Dance 354
Mongol Andai Dance 354
Xiangxi Drum Dance of Miao Ethnic Group .. 354
Xiangxi Maogusi Dance Drama of Tujia Ethnic Group 355
Firewood Gathering Dance of Li Ethnic Group 355
Ka-Si-Da-Wen Dance 355
Zhou Dance 355
Lisu Song-Dance Achi-Mugua 356
Gourd Panpipe Dance of Yi Ethnic Group 356
Tobacco Case Dance of Yi Ethnic Group 356
Jino Bass Drum Dance 356
Shannan Chamgocho Dance 356
Wutu Dance of Tu Ethnic Group 357
Eagle Dance of the Tajik Ethnic Group 357

Traditional Operas

Kunqu Opera 358
Liyuan Opera 358
Puxian Opera 358
Chaozhou Opera 359
The Yiyang Melody 359
The Qingyang Melody 359
Gaoqiang 359
The Xinchang Melody 360
Ninghai Pingdiao 360
Yong'an Daqiang Opera 360
Siping Opera 361
Sichuan Opera 361
Xiang Opera 361
Guangchang Meng Opera 361
Zhengzi Opera 362
Qinqiang 362
Handiao Guangguang 362
Jin Opera 363
Puzhou Bangzi 363
Beilu Bangzi 363
Shangdang Bangzi 364
Hebei Bangzi 364
Henan Opera 364
Wanbang 365
Huaibang 365
Dapingdiao 365
Yue Melody 365
Beijing Opera 366
Anhui Opera 366
Han Opera 366
Handiao Erhuang 366
Taining Meilin Opera 367
Minxi Han Opera 367
Baling Opera 367
Jinghe Opera 367
Cantonese Opera 367
Gui Opera 368
Yihuang Opera 368
Luantan 368
Shijiazhuang Sixian 369
Yanbei Shuahai'er 369
Lingqiu Luoluoqiang 369
Liuzi Opera 369
Daxian Opera 369
Min Opera 370
Shouning Beilu Opera 370
Xiqin Opera 370
Gaojia Opera 371
Wanwan Melody 371
Sipingdiao 371
Pingju Opera 371
Wu'an Pingdiao Laozi 371
Yue Opera 372
Shanghai Opera 372

Suzhou Opera ... 372
Yangzhou Opera ... 373
Lu Opera ... 373
Hubei Opera ... 373
Jingzhuo Flower-drum Opera ... 373
Huangmei Opera ... 374
Shangluo Flower-drum ... 374
Sizhou Opera ... 374
Liuqin Opera ... 374
Gezai Opera ... 375
Tea-picking Opera ... 375
Five-tone Opera ... 375
Maoqiang ... 375
Quju Opera ... 376
Quzi Opera ... 376
Yangge Opera ... 376
Daoqing Opera ... 377
Hahaqiang ... 377
Er' rentai ... 377
Baizi Opera ... 377
Huachao Opera ... 377
Caidiao ... 378
Lantern Opera ... 378
Flower-lantern Opera ... 378
Yigougou ... 378
Tibetan Opera ... 379
Shannan Menba Opera ... 379
Zhuang Opera ... 379
Dong Opera ... 380
Bouyei Opera ... 380
Yi Cuotaiji ... 380
Dai Opera ... 380
Mulian Opera ... 381
Gong-and-drum Mixed Opera ... 381
Nuo Opera ... 381
Anshun Dixi ... 382
Shadow Play ... 382
Puppetry ... 382

Quyi (Chinese Folk Art Forms)

Suzhou Pingtan ... 383
Yangzhou Pinghua (Storytelling in Yangzhou Dialect) ... 383
Fuzhou Pinghua ... 383
Shandong Dagu ... 383
Xihe Dagu ... 383
Dongbei Dagu ... 384
Muban Dagu ... 384
Laoting Dagu ... 384
Lu'an Dagu ... 384
Jingdong Dagu ... 385
Jiaodong Dagu ... 385
Heluo Dagu ... 385
Wenzhou Guci ... 385
Northern Shaanxi Shuoshu ... 386
Fuzhou Chi Yi ... 386
Nanping Nanci ... 386
Shaoxing Pinghu Tune ... 386
Lanxi Tanhuang ... 387
Xianxiao ... 387
Henan Zhuizi ... 387
Shandong Qinshu ... 387
Luogushu ... 388
Shaoxing Lianhua Lao ... 388
Lanzhou Guzi (Drum Song) ... 388
Yangzhou Qingqu (Yangzhou Ditty) ... 388
Jinge Songs ... 389
Changde Silk String ... 389
Yulin Folk Songs ... 389
Tianjin Shidiao ... 389
Xinjiang Quzi ... 390
Dragon Boat Songs ... 390
Basin-Beating Song ... 390
Hanchuan Shanshu Story-Telling ... 390
Dongshan Talking and Singing ... 391
Er'renzhuan ... 391
Fengyang Huagu (Flower Drum) ... 391
Dazuigu (Comic Dialogue) ... 391
Xiaorehun (Small Gong Story-Telling) ... 391
Shandong Kuaishu ... 391
Wulige'er ... 392
Wuqin of the Daur Ethnic Group ... 392
Yimakan Story-telling of the Hezhen Ethnic Group ... 392
Mosukun of the Oroqen Ethnic Group ... 392
Zhangha of the Dai Ethnic Group ... 393
Aites of Kazak Ethnic Group ... 393
Bayin Singing of the Buyei Ethnic Group ... 393

Acrobatics and Sports

Wuqiao Acrobatic ... 394
Liaocheng Acrobatics ... 394
Tianqiao Banner Stunts ... 394
Diabolo Spinning ... 394
Uygur Darwaz ... 395
Ningde Huotong Xianshi (Thread-controlled Puppet Lion) ... 395
Shaolin Kungfu ... 395
Wudang Wushu (Martial Arts) ... 395
Hui (Ethnic Group) Heavy Sword Wushu ... 396
Cangzhou Wushu ... 396
Tai Chi Boxing ... 396
Xingtai Mei Hua Quan ... 396
Tengpai Battle Array of Shahe ... 397
Korean See-Saw and Swinging ... 397
Daur Field Hockey ... 397
Mongolian Wrestling ... 397
Cuju ... 398

Folk Fine Arts

Yangliuqing New Year Woodblock Prints ... 398
Wuqiang New Year Woodblock Prints ... 398
Taohuawu New Year Woodblock Prints ... 399
Zhangzhou New Year Woodblock Prints ... 399
Yangjiabu New Year Woodblock Prints ... 399
Gaomi New Year Rubbing-Ash Prints ... 399
Zhuxianzhen New Year Woodblock Prints ... 400
Tantou New Year Woodblock Prints ... 400
Foshan New Year Woodblock Prints ... 400
Liangping New Year Woodblock Prints ... 401
Mianzhu New Year Woodblock Prints ... 401
Fengxiang New Year Woodblock Prints ... 401
Naxi Ethnic Group Dongba Paintings ... 401
Tibetan Ethnic Group Tangka Paintings ... 402
Hengshui Neihua Paintings ... 402
Paper-cuts ... 402
Guxiu Embroidery ... 402
Suxiu (Suzhou Embroidery) ... 403
Xiangxiu (Hunan Embroidery) ... 403
Yuexiu (Guangdong Embroidery) ... 403
Shuxiu (Sichuan Embroidery) ... 403
Miaoxiu (Miao Embroidery) ... 403
Tu Ethnic Group Panxiu (Bowl Embroidery) . 403
Shui Maweixiu (Horse Tail Embroidery) ... 403
Tiaohua (Cross-Stitch) ... 404
Qingyang Xiangbao (Perfume Sachets) Embroidery ... 404
Ivory Carving ... 404
Yangzhou Jade Carving ... 404
Xiuyan Jade Carving ... 405
Fuxin Agate Carving ... 405

Luminous Cup Carving.................................. 405
Bronze and Stone Seal Carving 405
Qingtian Stone Carving.................................. 406
Quyang Stone Carving.................................... 406
Shoushan Stone Carving................................ 406
Hui'an Stone Carving..................................... 406
Three Carving Arts of Huizhou (Wuyuan)...... 407
Linxia Brick Carving 407
Tibetan Ethnic Group King Gesar
Painted Rock Carving 407
Chaozhou Wood Carving............................... 407
Ningbo Cinnabar and Gold Lacquer
Wood Carving 408
Leqing Box Wood Carving 408
Dongyang Wood Carving............................... 408
Zhangzhou Wood Puppet Head Carving......... 409
Pingxiang Xiangdong Nuo Drama Masks 409
Bamboo Carving 409
Clay Sculptures 409
Tar Monastery Butter Carving 409
Dengcai (Lanterns)... 410
Shengzhou Bamboo Weaving 410
Regong Art 410

Traditional Handicraft Skills

Yixing Zisha Ceramic
Making Skill... 411
Jieshou Painted Pottery Firing and
Manufacturing Skills...................................... 411
Shiwan Pottery Sculpture Skills..................... 411
Li Ethnic Group Primitive Pottery
Shaping Skills 411
Dai Ethnic Group Slow-wheel
Pottery Manufacturing Skills 412
Uyghur Ethnic Group Earthen Pottery Molding,
Firing and Production Skills 412
Yaozhou Kiln Ceramic Firing and
Manufacturing Skills...................................... 412
Longquan Celadon Firing and
Manufacturing Skills...................................... 413
Cizhou Kiln Firing and Manufacturing Skills 413
Jingdezhen Porcelain Handicraft Skills 413
Songjin (Brocade of Song Dynasty)
Weaving Skills 414
Dehua Porcelain Sculpture
Firing and Manufacturing Skills 414
Chengcheng Yaotou Ceramic
Firing and Manufacturing Skills 414
Nanjing Yunjin (Cloud Brocade) Wooden
Loom Handicraft Weaving Skills................... 415
Suzhou Kesi (Silk Tapestry with Cut Designs)
Weaving Skills 415
Shujin (Sichuan Brocade) Weaving Skills 415
Wunijing Handicraft Cotton Weaving Skills .. 415
Tujia Ethnic Group Brocade Weaving Skills .. 416
Li Ethnic Group Traditional Cotton
Weaving Dyeing and Embroidery Skills......... 416

Zhuang Ethnic Group Embroidery Skills 416
Tibetan Ethnic Group Woolen Bangdian (Apron)
and Qiadian (Rug) Weaving Skills................. 417
Tibetan Ethnic Group Gyaya
Carpet Making Skills 417
Uyghur Ethnic Group Decorated Carpet and
Cloth Weaving and Printing Skills................. 417
Nantong Indigo Blue Cloth Decoration and
Printing Skills... 417
Miao Ethnic Group Batik Cloth Dyeing Skills418
Bai Ethnic Group Bandhnu Skills.................. 418
Xiangshanbang Traditional Architectural and
Building Skills 418
Hakka Tulou (Stockade) Building Skills 418
Jingdezhen Traditional Porcelain Kiln and
Workshop Building Skills 419
Dong Ethnic Group Timber Architecture
Building Skills 419
Yuping Flute Making Technique.................... 419
Miao Compound Folk Footed House
Architectural and Building Skills................... 420
Suzhou Imperial-Kiln Golden
Brick Manufacturing Skills............................ 420
Miao Ethnic Group Pan-Pipes Making Skills. 420
Yangcheng Pig Iron Production Skills 420
Nanjing Gold Foil Beating Technique 421
Longquan Precious Sword Forging Skills 421
Zhang Xiaoquan Scissors Forging Skills........ 421
Wuhu Iron Picture Production Skills 422
Miao Ethnic Group Silver Jewelry
Making Skills... 422
Achang Ethnic Group Husa Knife
Making Skills... 422
Bao'an Ethnic Group Waist Dagger
Making Skills... 422
Cloisonné Making Skills................................ 423
Juyuanhao Bow and Arrow Making Skills 423
Ming-Style Furniture Making Skills.............. 423
Mongol Ethnic Group Leleche
(All-Purpose Steppe Vehicle) Making Skills . 424
Lhasa Jiami Waterwheel
Grain Milling Techniques 424
Lanzhou Yellow River Waterwheel
Manufacturing Techniques............................ 424
Wan'an Compass Making Skills..................... 424
Carved Lacquerware Skills 424
Pingyao Buffed Lacquerware
Lacquering Skills 425
Yangzhou Lacquerware Lacquering Skills 425
Tiantaishan Dried Lacquer
Gunny Fetus Skills... 425
Fuzhou Bodiless Lacquerware
Lacquering Skills 426
Xiamen Lacquer Line Carving Skills 426
Chengdu Lacquerware Skills 426
Maotai Spirits Distilling Skills....................... 426
Luzhou Laojiao Spirits Distilling Skills 427
Xinghuacun Fen Chiew Spirits
Distilling Skills 427
Shaoxing Yellow Wine Distilling Skills.......... 427
Qingxu Super-Mature Vinegar
Distilling Skills 427
Zhenjiang Hengshun Fragrant Vinegar
Distilling Skills 428
Wuyi Yancha (Cliff Tea) 428
Zigong Well Salt Drilling Skills..................... 428
Qianshan Liansi Paper Making Skills............ 428
Bark Paper Making Skills 429
Dai and Naxi Ethnic Handicraft
Paper-Making Skills....................................... 429
Tibetan Ethnic Group Paper-Making Skills.... 429
Uyghur Ethnic Group Mulberry
Paper Making Skills....................................... 429
Xuan Paper Making Skills 430
Bamboo Paper Making Skills 430
Huzhou Writing Brush Making Skills............ 430
She Ink-stone Making Skills.......................... 431
Huizhou Ink Making Skills............................ 431
Duan Ink-stone Making Skills 431
Jinxing Ink-stone Making Skills.................... 431
Carved Block Printing Skills 432
Wood-block Water-color Print Making Skills 432
Jinling Carved Sutras Printing Skills 432
Fan Making Skills.. 432
Theater Costumes and Props Making Skills ... 433
Birch Bark Making Skills 433
Dege Sutra-printing House Tibetan Carved
Block Printing Skills...................................... 433
Li Ethnic Group Tapa Making Skills 434
Hezhen Ethnic Group Fish-skin Making Skills.....434
Liuyang Fireworks Production Skills 434
Li Ethnic Group Wood-Drilling Skills for Fire ...434
Kite Making Skills 435
Cool-Tea Compounding................................ 435

Traditional Chinese Medicine (TCM)

Cognitive Methods of TCM on Human Life and Disease 435
TCM Culture of Huqingyutang 436
Traditional Chinese Medicine (TCM) 436
Processing Techniques of Chinese Materia Medica 436
TCM Culture of Tongrentang 437
Traditional Methods of Preparation of Formulas of TCM 437
Acupuncture and Moxibustion 437
Bone-Setting of TCM 438
Tibetan Medicine 438

Folk Customs

Spring Festival 438
Tomb Sweeping Festival 438
Dragon Boat Festival 438
Chinese Valentine's Day 439
Mid-Autumn Festival 439
Double Ninth Festival 439
Ha Festival of Jing Minority 439
Water Splashing Festival of Dai Minority 440
Westward Moving Festival of the Xibe Minority 440
Torch Festival of Yi Minority 440
Munao Singing Party of Jingpo Minority 440
March Third Festival of Li Minority 441
Fire God Sacrifice of Oroqen Minority 441
King Pan Festival of Yao Minority 441
Ma Guai Festival of Zhuang Minority 442
Yifan Festival of Mulam Minority 442
Redemption of the Vows of Maonan Minority ... 442
Waer Ezu Festival of Qiang Minority 442
Guzang Festival of Miao Minority 443
Duan Festival of Shui Minority 443
Chabai Song Festival of Bouyei Minority 443
Sister Festival of Miao Minority 444
Kaquewa Festival of Drung Minority 444
Fairy Festival of Nu Ethnic Group 444
Sama Festival of Dong Ethnic Group 444
Gelo Mao Dragon Festival 445
Sword Pole Festival of Lisu Minority 445
Water-drawing Festival and Sowing Festival of Tajik Minority 445
Nadun Festival of Tu Minority 445
Festival of Discharging Water at Dujiang Weirs 446
Shoton Festival 446
Confucius Grand Ceremony 446
The Sacrificial Ceremonies in the Yellow Emperor's Mausoleum 447
Emperor Yan's Mausoleum Ceremony 447
Sacrificial Ceremony to Genghis Khan 447
Sacrificing Ceremony for Mazu 447
The Taihao Fuxi's Fiesta 448
The Sacrificial Ceremonies for Nvwa 448
Sacrificial Ceremonies for Dayu 448
Aobao Worshipping 448
Raosanling Festival of the Bai Ethnic Group in Dali 449
Changdian Temple Fair 449
Regong Sixth Lunar Month Gathering 449
Chrysanthemum Fair in Xiaolan 449
Shuagetang Festival of the Yao Ethnic Group 450
Gewei of the Zhuang Ethnic Group 450
Slope Gatherings of the Miao in Rongshui County 450
Nadam Fair 450
Uygur Duolong Maxrap 450
Qinhuai Lantern Fair 451
Xiushan Festive Lantern 451
Quanfeng Festive Lantern 451
Taishan Shigandang Customs 451
Shehuo Activities 452
Ordos Wedding 452
Wedding Customs of the Tu Ethnic Group 452
Wedding Customs of the Salar 452
Huji Story-Telling Gathering 453
Majie Story-telling Gathering 453
Medicine Market in Anguo 453
Bronze Drum Custom of Zhuang Ethnic Group 453
Couplet Custom 454
Costume of Women in Luzhi Water Town, Suzhou 454
Costume of Women in Hui'an 454
Costumes of Miao Ethnic Group 454
Costume of the Hui Ethnic Group 455
Costume of the Yao Ethnic Group 455
The Twenty-Four Solar Terms 455
Nvshu, or Women's Script 455
Shuishu 455

Literature

Development of Literature 456
Hundred Schools of Thought 456
The Four Books and the Five Classics 456
Articles of Hundred Schools 456
Dao De Jing 456
Lunyu (The Analects of Confucius) 457
Mengzi (The Book of Mencius) 457

Zhuang Zi (The Book of Zhuang Zi) 457
Zhou Yi (Changes of Zhou, also called Yi Jing) 457
Shang Shu (The Book of History) 457
Baguwen (Eight-part Essay) 457
Li Sao (The Poem on Departure) 457
Qu Yuan 457
Yuefu (Han Music Bureau) Poetry 458
Shi Ji (The Records of the Great Historian).... 458
Sima Qian 458
Tang Poetry 458
Song Ci (Lyric Poetry) 459
Li Bai 459
Du Fu 459
Su Shi 459
Tao Yuanming 459
Dramas of the Yuan Dynasty 460
Sanqu Songs 460
Zaju 460
Supernatural Stories 460
Wen-yen Chinese 460
Vernacular 460
Strange Tales from the Liaozhai Studios 460
Jin Ping Mei (The Golden Lotus) 461
Tang Xianzu 461
Guan Hanqing 461
Cao Xueqin 461
Pu Songling 461
Four Famous Chinese Classics 462
A Dream of Red Mansions 462
The Romance of the Three Kingdoms 462
Outlaws of the Marsh 462
Pilgrimage to the West 462
Internet Literature 463
Pizi (Hooligan) Literature 463
China Federation of Literary and Art Circles (CFLAC) 463
China Writers Association 463
Internet Website of Today Writers 463
China Modern Literature Museum 464
Chinese Novel Union 464
Important Literature Awards in China 464
Mao Dun Literature Award 464
Lu Xun Literature Award 464
Lao She Literature Award 464
Cao Yu Dramatic Literature Award 464
Yao Xueyin Full-Length Historical Novels Award 464

Film and Television

General Survey of Movie............................... 465
Movie in China 465
The First Group of Cinemas 465
The First Film 465
The First Film Studio..................................... 465
Golden Rooster Awards 466
Hundred Flowers Awards 466
Ornamental Column Awards.......................... 466
Shanghai International Film Festival 466
Changchun Film Festival............................... 466
Zhuhai Film Festival...................................... 466
Beijing Student Film Festival 466
Hong Kong International Film Festival.......... 466
Hong Kong Film Awards 466
Hong Kong Film Critics Society Awards........ 467
Hong Kong Film Golden Bauhinia Awards 467
Taipei Film Festival 467
Golden Horse Film Festival........................... 467
The First Generation of Chinese Directors..... 467
The Second Generation of Chinese Directors. 467
The Third Generation of Chinese Directors.... 467
The Fourth Generation of Chinese Directors.. 468
The Fifth Generation of Chinese Directors..... 468
New Year's Day Films.................................... 468
Major Film Studios in China.......................... 468
Changchun Film Studio 468
Xi'an Film Studio... 468
Tianshan Film Studio..................................... 469
Beijing Film Studio.. 469
August First Film Studio................................ 469
Shanghai Film Studio..................................... 469
Shanghai Film Dubbing Studio...................... 469
Shanghai Animation Film Studio................... 469
Agricultural Film Studio of China................. 469
Beijing Film Academy................................... 470
Film Production Industry............................... 470
Film Distribution Industry 470
Film Projection Industry 470
Song of the Fisherman 471
Red Sorghum 471
Honored Film: Hibiscus Town....................... 471
Honored Film: Spring Festival....................... 471
Honored Film: Farewell My Concubine......... 471

Architecture and Gardens

Chinese Architecture...................................... 472
Characteristics of Traditional Architecture..... 472
Influence on Traditional Chinese
Architecture from Yi Jing (Changes of Zhou) 472
City Walls in Beijing...................................... 472
City Walls in Xi'an... 472
City Walls in Pingyao 472
The Great Wall... 473

The Forbidden City (Gu Gong)...................... 473
Taihedian (Hall of Supreme Harmony)........... 473
Color of the Forbidden City.......................... 474
Wenshou 474
Dougong (Bracket Set) 474
Huabiao (Ornamental Column)...................... 474
The Temple of Heaven.................................. 474
Shejitan Altar (Altar of Land and Grain)........ 475
Taimiao (Royal Ancestral Temple) 475
Wenmiao (The Confucian Temple)................ 475
Architecture of Chinese Gardens................... 476
Southern Private Gardens 476
Jichang Garden.. 476
Zhuozheng Garden... 476
Wangshi Garden.. 476
Ge Garden 477
Northern Private Gardens 477
Gongwangfu Garden..................................... 477
Imperial Gardens of the Ming and
Qing Dynasties.. 478
The Summer Palace 478
Yuanming Garden 478
The Imperial Summer Villa of Chengde......... 479
Traditional Residences.................................. 479
Beijing's Siheyuan... 479
Courtyard Residence in North China............. 479
The Southern Tianjing
(Small Courtyard) Residence......................... 479
Zhejiang's "13-roomed" Residence 480
Free-Style Residence in South China 480
Cave Dwelling in Northwest China............... 480
Hakka Group Houses.................................... 481
Wu Feng Lou (Five Phoenix Tower).............. 481
Tu Lou (Earthen Tower)................................ 481
Wei Long Wu (Dragon-Encircled House)....... 481
Bridges and Architecture............................... 482
Zhaozhou Bridge... 482
Luoyang Bridge 482
Anping Bridge... 482
Guangji Bridge.. 482
Lugou Bridge 483
Chinese Towers and Pavilions 483
Yueyang Tower 483
Huanghe Tower... 483
Tengwang Pavilion.. 484
Pagoda (Bao Ta).. 484
Dayan Pagoda 484
Wooden Pagoda in Ying County.................... 484
Iron Pagoda in Kaifeng................................. 485
Three Pagodas in Dali................................... 485
Sutra Columns... 485
Mausoelum.. 486
Qinshihuang Mausoleum 486
Guanzhong Eighteen Mausoleums 486
Ming Xiaoling Mausoleum............................ 486
Ming Dynasty Tombs.................................... 487
Changling Mausoleum.................................. 487
The Architectural Art of Uygur Ethnic Group 488
Bangke Building (Tower).............................. 488
Aitiga Mosque in Kashgar 488
Turpan Emin Mosque.................................... 488
The Architectural Art of Tibetan Buddhism.... 488
Jokhang Monastery 489
The Potala Palace.. 489
Xili Tu-Zhao in Hohhot 489
Monasteries of Dai Ethnic Group.................. 490
The ManSuman Monastery in Xishuangbanna490
Storm-Proof Bridges of Dong Ethnic Group .. 490
Drum Towers of Dong Ethnic Group............. 490
Modern Chinese Architecture 491
Nanjing Road Architecture in Shanghai 491
Bund Architecture in Shanghai...................... 491
Constructions in Concession in Tianjin 491
Quanyechang Mall in Tianjin........................ 492
Thirteen Hongs in Guangzhou....................... 492
Shamian in Guangzhou................................. 492
Ba Da Guan in Qingdao................................ 492
Contemporary Chinese Architecture.............. 493
The Great Hall of the People 493
The Ethnic Groups Cultural Palace................ 493
Beijing Workers' Stadium 493
Fragrant Hill Hotel.. 493
National Grand Theater................................. 494
The Oriental Pearl TV Tower........................ 494
Shanghai Jinmao Building 494
Commune by the Great Wall......................... 494
National Stadium 494
National Aquatics Center.............................. 494

14 Society P495

Life Consumption

General Living Standard 495
Economic Data 495
People's Health Level 495
Gross Amount of Consumption 496
Residents' Income 496
Residents' Savings 496

Residents' Expenditure 496
Catering Consumption 496
Household Consumption on Major Food 497
Green Food 497
Green Food Standard 497
Grade A Green Food 497
The Mark of Green Food 497
Grade AA Green Food (equated with "organic food") 498
Garment Consumption 498
The Sun Yat-sen Suit 498
Qipao 498
Occupational Garments 498
Housing Consumption 499
Welfare Distribution of Houses 499
Housing Security System 499
Housing Accumulation Fund System 499
Economically Affordable Housing 500
Housing Distribution System Reform 500
Low-Rental Housing System 500
Housing of Rural Residents 500
Consumption Boom on Home Decoration 500
Automobile Consumption 501
Urban Public Transportation 501
Information Consumption 501
China Consumers' Association 502
Consumption by Card 502
Bank Card 502
Online Shopping 502

Cuisine

Chinese Cuisine 503
Lu Cai (Shandong Cuisine) 503
Classical Shandong Cuisine 503
Chuan Cai (Sichuan Cuisine) 503
Classical Sichuan Cuisine 503
Huai-Yang Cuisine 503
Classical Huai-Yang Cuisine 504
Yue Cai (Guangdong Cuisine) 504
Classical Guangdong Cuisine 504
Min Cai (Fujian Cuisine) 504
Classical Fujian Cuisine 505
Su Cai (Jiangsu Cuisine) 505
Classical Jiangsu Cuisine 505
Zhe Cai (Zhejiang Cuisine) 505
Classical Zhejiang Cuisine 505
Hui Cai (Anhui Cuisine) 505
Classical Anhui Cuisine 506
Xiang Cai (Hunan Cuisine) 506
Classical Hunan Cuisine 506
Islamic Cuisine 506
Classical Islamic Cuisine 506
Time-Honored Restaurants of China 507
Quanjude 507
Fangshan Restaurant 507
Bianyi Workshop (Cheap Workshop) 507
Duyichu 507
Hongbinlou 508
Fengzeyuan 508
Donglaishun 508
Barbecue Wan 508
Barbecue Ji 508
Tongchunyuan 509
Quyuan Restaurant 509
Emei Restaurant 509
Gongdelin 509
Old Zhengxing 509
Ma Xiangxing Restaurant 510
Taotaoju Restaurant 510
Goubuli Restaurant 510
Famous Chinese Tea 510
Green Tea 510
China's Tea Culture 510
West Lake Longjing (Dragon Well Tea) 511
Huangshan Maofeng 511
Biluochun (Green Spring Snail Tea) 511
Mengding Ganlu 511
Lu Yu 511
Cha Jing (Classic of Tea) 512
Taiping Houkui 512
Xinyang Maojian 512
Liu'an Guapian 512
Lushan Yunwu Tea 512
Black Tea 512
Zhengshan Souchong 513
Qimen Gongfu Tea 513
Oolong Tea 513
Ti Kuan Yin 513
Wuyi Yancha (Cliff Tea) 513
Dark Tea 513
Pu'er Tea 514
Yellow Tea 514
Junshan Silver Needles 514
White Tea 514
Compressed Teas 514
Scented Teas 514
Mongolian Tea with Milk 514
The Three-Course Tea of the Bai Ethnic Minority 515
Tibetan Buttered Tea 515
Gongfu Tea 515
Tea Served in a Set of Cups 516
Big-bowl Tea 516
Tea House 516
The Art of Wine in China 517
Custom of Drinking Wine 517
Guizhou Moutai Wine 517
Wuliangye Wine 517
Luzhou-flavor Laojiao 517
Xifeng Spirit 517
Xinghua Cun Fen-flavor Spirit 518
Shaoxing Jiafan Wine 518
China Cuisine Association 518

Traditional Customs

Traditional Festivals 518
Spring Festival 518
La Yue (the 12th Lunar Month) and Laba Porridge 519
Spring Festival Customs 519
Spring Festival Foods 519
Staying Up All Night 519
Paying New Year's Calls 520
Visiting Temple Fairs 520
Spring Transportation 520
The Lantern Festival 520
Tomb Sweeping Festival 520
Dragon Boat Festival 520
Chinese Valentine's Day 520
Mid-Autumn Festival 520
Double Ninth Festival 520
Lunar Calendar 521
The Twenty-Four Solar Terms 522
Beginning of Spring 523
Rain Water 523
Waking of Insects 523
Spring Equinox 523
Pure Brightness 523
Grain Rain 523
Beginning of Summer 523

Grain Fills 523
Grain in Ear 523
Summer Solstice 523
Slight Heat 523
Great Heat 523
Beginning of Autumn 523
Limit of Heat 523
White Dew 523
Autumnal Equinox 523
Cold Dew 523
Frost's Descent 523
Beginning of Winter 523
Slight Snow 523
Great Snow 523
Winter Solstice 523
Slight Cold 523
Great Cold 523
Twelve Zodiac Animals 524
Rat 524
Horse 524
Ox 524
Ram 524
Tiger 524
Monkey 524
Rabbit 525
Rooster 525
Dragon 525
Dog 525
Snake 525
Pig 525

Marriage and Family

The Origin of Chinese Surnames 526
The Characteristics of China's Surname 526
Marriage and Family 526
Marriage Registration System 526
Vision of Love 526
Changes in Wedding 526
Self-determination in Marriage 527
Equality of Husband and Wife 527
Marriage Consultation 527
Unmarried Group 527
Upsurge in Divorce 527
Custom of Child-bearing and the Pattern of Providing for the Aged 527
The Law of the PRC on Marriage 528
The Ministry of Civil Affairs 528
Trend of Change in Family Structure 528
Traditional Mode of Family 528
Core Family 528
Empty Nest Family 529
DINK Family 529
One Child 529
Homosexuality 529

Healthcare

Survey Data on Health 530
Health System 530
Chinese Center for Disease Control and Prevention 530
Mother and Child Health Care 530
Prevention and Health Care 531
Hospital Classification Management 531
Plans on Public Health Emergencies 531
Community-based Health Network 531
Rural Health System 531
Law of the PRC on Prevention and Treatment of Infectious Diseases 531
Law of the PRC on the Prevention and Treatment of Occupational Diseases 531
Maternity Leave 532
Blood Donation without Payment 532
Hematopoietic Stem Cell Donation 532
Prevention and Cure of Severe Acute Respiratory Syndrome (SARS) 532
Prevention and Cure of Bird Flu 532
Prevention and Control of Acquired Immune Deficiency Syndrome (AIDS) 533
Traditional Chinese Medicine 533
Basic Theory of TCM 533
Yin and Yang Theory 533
The Theory of the Five Elements 533
TCM History 533
Theory of Directing One's Strength 534
Theory of Internal Organs of the Body 534
Theory of Channels (Meridians and Collaterals) 534
Diagnostic Methods in TCM 534
Massage 534
History of Chinese Herbal Medicine 534
Chinese Herbal Medicine 535
Shennong Bencao Jing (Shennong Emperor's Classic of Materia Medica) 535
Tibetan Medicine 535
Basic Theory of Tibetan Medicine 535
Medication of Tibetan Medicine 535
Tongrentang Pharmacy 536
Mongolian Medicine 536
The Basic Theory of Mongolian Medicine 536
Phlebotomy of Mongolian Medicine 536
Uygur Medicine 536

The Uygur Style in Making Medicine 536
Hui Medicine 537
Huang Di Nei Jing (Yellow Emperor's Canons of Internal Medicine) 537
Shanghan Zabinglun (Discourse on Fevers and Miscellaneous Illness) 537
Zhenjiu Jiayi Jing (Jiayi Canon on Acupuncture and Moxibustion) 537
Maijing (Pulse Classic) 537
Yong'antang Pharmacy 537
Qianjin Yaofang (Prescriptions for Emergencies) 538
Bencao Gangmu (Compendium of Materia Medica) 538
Tongren Shuxue Zhenjiu (Illustrated Manual of the Bronze Man Showing Acupuncture and Moxibustion Points) 538
Furen Daquan Liangfang (Complete Dictionary of Effective Prescriptions for Women) 538
Huihui Yaofang (Hui Medical Preparation) 538
Xiyuan Jilu (Collected Writings on the Washing Away of Wrongs) 538
Ministry of Health 539
State Food and Drug Administration 539
State Administration of Traditional Chinese Medicine (SATCM) 539

Employment

Employment Circumstances 540
Basic Employment Situation 540
Unemployment and Registered Unemployment Rate 540
Proactive Employment Policy 540
Coordination Mechanism of Labor Relations 541
Protecting Laborers' Employment Rights 541
Employment System 541
Employment of the Rural Workforce 541
Training for Employment of Rural Labor Forces 542
Safeguarding the Legal Rights and Interests of Rural Migrant Workers 542

Making Experiments in Development and Employment of Rural Workforce 542
Women's Employment 542
Promoting the Employment of Young People..... 542
Helping Disabled People to Find Employment... 543
The Employment License for Foreign Employees 543
Establishing a Vocational Training System..... 544
Pre-Employment Training.............................. 544
Strengthening Labor Skill Training 544
Technical School 544
Reemployment Service Centers...................... 545
Vocational Skills Certification 545
Vocational Skill Competitions 545

Social Security

Social Security System 545
Social Relief... 545
Social Welfare 545
Special Care and Placement............................ 545
Community Service 545
Old-age Insurance System 546
Basic Medical Insurance System for Urban Employees 546
Industrial Injury Insurance............................. 546
Unemployment Insurance System 546
Labor Law of the People's Republic of China 546
Childbirth Insurance System........................... 548
Minimum Living Standard Security System... 548
Minimum Standard of Living for Cities in China.. 548
Security System of Minimum Wage 548
Poverty Alleviation in Rural Areas 548
Poverty Alleviation by Development.............. 549
China Foundation for Poverty Alleviation...... 549
The State "Eight Seven" Program for Poverty Alleviation..................... 549
Program of Development for Poverty Alleviation in China's Rural Areas (2001—2010) 549
NGO Project on Poverty Alleviation 550
Rural Endowment Insurance........................... 550
National Student Loans.................................. 550
Public Charity and Welfare Organizations...... 550
China Charity Federation (CCF)..................... 550
Red Cross Society of China 550
China Association of Social Workers.............. 551
China Soong Ching Ling Foundation 551
China Association for NGO Cooperation 551
China Youth Development Foundation........... 551
Guidelines on Philanthropy Development in China (2006-2010) 551
Project Hope.. 551
Regulations on Foundation Administration 552
China Children and Teenager's Fund (CCTF)..... 552
Spring Bud Project.. 552
Enkon Projec.. 552
China Education Development Foundation.... 552
Volunteers.. 552
Community Volunteers 552
Volunteer 552
Youth Volunteers 552
China International Rescue Teams................. 553
Regular Social Donation 553
Aiding Disabled People 553
Child Social Welfare 554
The Guarantee of Rights and Interests of the Old.. 554
Starlight Program 554

Leisure Activity and Entertainment

The Level of Leisure Activity......................... 554
Tourism 554
Fitness 555
TV Audience Rating.. 555
Box Office.. 555
E-life 555
Museum Visiting.. 555
Collection among Common Chinese 555
Pop Music 555
Bars 556
Book Bars... 556
Legal Holidays 556
New Year's Day.. 556
International Working Women's Day 556
Tree-planting Day (China Arbor Day)............ 556
International Labor Day 556
Chinese Youth Day.. 556
International Children's Day 556
Army Day... 557
Teacher's Day 557
National Day 557

15 P558 Environmental Protection

Environmental Protection in China................. 558
Environmentally-Friendly Society.................. 558
Prevention and Control of Industrial Pollution558
Treatment of Major Polluted Areas................. 558
Prevention and Control of Water Pollution in Key Drainage Areas 558
Control of Air Pollution 559
Motor Vehicle Pollution Prevention................ 559
Control of Pollution in the Bohai Sea 559
Urban Planning and Environment.................. 559
Environment and Investment 560
City Appearance and Environment 560
Water Environment of Three Gorges Reservoir Area 560
Green Olympics 560
Comprehensive Control of the Rural Environment... 560
Development of New-energy Projects in Rural Areas.................................. 561
Financial Budget for Environmental Protection 561
State Scientific and Technological Program for Environmental Protection 561
Technology of Environmental Pollution Control... 562

Environmental Protection Industries.............. 562
Environmental Certification System.............. 562
Public Participation in Environmental Legislation............................. 562
All-China Environmental Award 563
Environmental Label....................................... 563
China Association of the Environmental Protection Industry................. 563
China Environmental Consultative Committee... 563
Non-governmental Environmental Protection Organization 564
Development of Non-Governmental Environmental Protection Organizations........ 564
Action of "Air Conditioner at 26°Centigrade".... 564
Friends of Nature (FON)................................ 564
Types of ENGO.. 564
Distribution of ENGO..................................... 565
Environmental Protection Popularization....... 565
Publication of Environmental Information..... 565
Global Village of Beijing (GVB).................... 565
Safeguarding Public Environmental Rights and Interests... 566
Stockholm Convention.................................... 566
Chinese Regulations on POPs........................ 566
Chinese Investigation on POPs...................... 566
Implementation of Stockholm Convention..... 566
Recycling Economy.. 566
China Environmental Monitoring Station....... 567
China Cleaner Production Portal 567

All China Environmental Federation 567
Online NGO Name List of the Environment .. 567
China Environmental Protection Foundation .. 567
Target of the Recycling Economy 568
Pilot Areas Conducting the Recycling Economy 568
Achievements of Recycling Economy 568
Renewable Energy 568
Extended Producer Responsibility System 568
Biological Fuel 569
Prospects for Bio-Fuel 569
Wind Power Industry 569
Development of Wind Power Industry 569
Policies on Renewable Energy 569
World Bank Aid 570
Utilizing Imported Recyclable Resources 570
Recycling Scrapped Products 570
Guidelines for the Recycling Industry 570
Medium and Long-Term Development Plan for Recyclable Energy 570
Work Committee for Imported Recyclable Energy 570
Building an Energy-Efficient Society 571
Plan of Energy Conservation 571
Alternative Energy 571
Key Sectors for Energy Conservation 571
The One-Watt Plan 572
China Green Lights Project 572
Key Projects for Energy Conservation 572
Activities to Save Energy 572
Activities to Save Water 573
Raw Material Conservation 573
Using Land Resources in an Efficient Way..... 573
Strengthening Comprehensive Utilization of Resources 573
Economic Use of Water for the Olympic Venue 573
Law of the PRC on Conserving Energy 573
Provisions on the Administration of Energy Conservation for Civil Buildings 574
Strengthened Comprehensive Consumption of Wood Resources 574
Wood Saving and Substitution 574
Seawater Utilization 574
Resource-Saving Enterprises: the China National Building Material Group Corporation (CNBM) and the China National Materials Industry Group 575
Energy-Saving Enterprise: China Huaneng Group 575
Energy-Saving Enterprise: Baosteel Group 575
UNIDO International Solar Energy Center for Technology Promotion and Transfer (ISEC-UNIDO) 575
Special Planning of Seawater Utilization 576
Nuclear and Radiation Environment 576
Laws and Regulations on Nuclear Safety and Radiation Environment 576
China Energy Conservation Investment Corporation 576
Nuclear Safety and Radiation Environment Monitored and Controlled According to the Law 577
Monitoring Network of Radiation Environment 577
National Environmental Protection Standards System 577
Law of the PRC on the Prevention and Control of Radioactive Pollution 577
Nuclear and Radiation Safety Center, MEP.... 578
Environmental Impact Assessment 578
Active Prevention of Environmental Accidents 578
Management of Industrial Hazardous Wastes. 578
Environmental Laws and Regulations 578
Cleaner Production Promotion Law 578
Environmental Impact Assessment of the Qinghai-Tibet Railway 578
Environmental Impact Assessment Law 579
Catalogue of Toxic Chemicals China Bans or Strictly Restricts 579
Law of the PRC on the Prevention and Control of Environmental Pollution by Solid Waste 579
Laws and Regulations for Prevention and Control of Hazardous Wastes 579
Regulations on Environmental Protection for Local Areas 579
Export Policies for Environmental Protection Purpose 580
More Effective Measures Taken to Implement the Law on Environmental Protection 580
Forestation 580
Converting Cultivated Land to Forest 580
Nationwide Tree-planting Campaign on a Voluntary Basis 580
Natural Forest Conservation Project 581
Forest Health 581
Majiang Demonstration Area in Guizhou 581
Xinfeng Demonstration Area in Jiangxi 581
Foping Demonstration Area in Shaanxi 581
Lijiang Demonstration Area in Yunnan 581
Badaling Demonstration Area in Beijing 581
The Protection of Pastures 582
Land Protection 582
Water and Soil Conservation 582
Desertification 582
Sand Prevention and Control 583
Prevention and Remedying Desertification Under Local Conditions 583
Sandstorms 583
Sandstorm Prevention System 583
State Forestry Administration 583
Prevention and Treatment of Sandstorm Sources in the Beijing-Tianjin Area 584
Marine Environment 584
Marine Environment Protection 584
Reducing and Controlling Land-sourced Pollutants 585
National Action Program Protecting the Marine Environment from Land-Based Activities 585
Regulation for the Administration on Prevention and Control of Damage to Marine Environment by Pollution from Marine Construction Projects 585
The Marine Nature Reserve 585
Snakes Island-Laotieshan Mountain Nature Reserve 586
National-level Rare Birds Nature Reserve in Yancheng City 586
Nanji Islands Marine Nature Reserve 586
Nature Reserve of Woods from Submerged Forest in Shenhu Bay 586
Nature Reserve of Green Turtles in Huidong Port 587
Nature Reserve of National-level Mangrove Forest Ecology in Shankou 587
State Oceanic Administration 587
Hepu Dugong Nature Reserve 588
Sanya Coral Reefs Nature Reserve 588
Tianjin Seacoast and Wetland National-level Nature Reserve 588
Management Regulations on Marine Nature Reserves 588
Rank-based System of the Marine Nature Reserve 588
Conservation of Biodiversity 588
The Rescue Project Concerning Endangered Plants 588
Rescue Project Relating to Endangered Wildlife Animals 589
Conversation for Wildlife Plants Resources ... 589
National-Level Key Laboratory of Satellite Marine Environment Dynamics 589
Wetland Protection 590
China's Action on Wetland Protection 590
Yinchuan National Wetland Park 590
Hong Kong Wetland Park 590
High Mountain Wetland: Maoershan Mountain 590
Wetland International-China 590
Eco-functional Protection Area 590
Geothermal Resources 591
Dinghushan Mountain National Nature Reserve 591

Huanglong National Nature Reserve 591
Gaoligongshan Mountain
National Nature Reserve 591
Changbaishan Mountain National
Nature Reserve 591
Logo of the National Forest Park 592
Logo of the Nature Reserve of China 592
Environment Websites 592
Scenic Areas and Places of Historical Interest.. 592
Nature Reserves 592
Xilinguole National Nature Reserve 594
Xishuangbanna National Nature Reserve 594
Maolan National Nature Reserve 594
Shennongjia National Nature Reserve 594
Baishuijiang National Nature Reserve 595
Wuyishan Mountain National Nature Reserve ... 595
Fanjingshan Mountain National
Nature Reserve 595
Tianmushan Mountain National
Nature Reserve 595
Wolong National Nature Reserve 595
Bogeda Peak National Nature Reserve 596
Jiuzhaigou National Nature Reserve 596
Fenglin National Nature Reserve 596
Zhangjiajie Nature Reserve 597
Lushan Mountain Nature Reserve 597
Xianghai Nature Reserve 597
Zhalong Nature Reserve 597
Poyanghu Lake Nature Reserve 597
East Dongtinghu Lake Nature Reserve 597
Qinghaihu Lake Bird Islet Nature Reserve 597
Dongzhaigang Nature Reserve 598
Chinese Alligator Nature Reserve 598
Tian'ezhou White-Flag Dolphin
Nature Reserve 598
Songshan Mountain Nature Reserve 598
Paleocoastal Nature Reserve 598
Ke'erqin Nature Reserve 598
Guniujiang Nature Reserve 598
Dafeng David's Deer Nature Reserve 598
Huaping Nature Reserve 599
Hoh Xil Nature Reserve 599
Taibaishan Mountain Nature Reserve 599
Altun Mountain Nature Reserve 599
Motuo Nature Reserve 599
National Nature Reserve 599
Regulatory System on Nature Reserves 599
Development-Restricted Zone 600
Development-Prohibited Zone 600
Development-Restricted Zones 600
Headwaters Zone 600
Flood Storage Zone 601
Major Water Conservancy Zone 601
Windbreak and Sand-Dune Fixation Zone 601
Major Fishing Waters 602
Standards for Eco-Industrial Parks 602
Eco-Industrial Park Development 602
Ecological Conservation in Rural Areas 602
Establishment of Ecological Villages 603
Safe Drinking Water Program in Rural Areas. 603
International Environmental Cooperation 603
Multi-lateral Environmental Cooperation 603
Negotiations on International Conventions and
Accomplishment of Relevant Duties 604
Regional Environmental Cooperation 604
International Cooperation for
Sandstorm Prevention 604
National Action Plan for Comfortable Life and
Environmental Protection in Rural Areas 604
Acid Deposition Monitoring in East Asia 605
Cooperation in Greater Mekong Sub-region for
Environmental Protection 605
Environmental Cooperation
with Other Regions 605
Bilateral Environmental Cooperation 605
China Council for International Cooperation on
Environment and Development 605
International Cooperation on
Nuclear Safety 606
Utilization of Foreign Investments for
Environmental Protection 606
Award of "Green Chinese
Personage of a Year" 606
Green Chinese Personage of Year 2007 (List) 607

16 P608

Political Parties and Social Organizations

Political Parties

Political Party System 608
The Communist Party of China 608
Democratic Parties 608
Revolutionary Committee of the
Chinese Kuomintang 609
United Front Work Department of the
CPC Central Committee 609
China Democratic League 610
China National Democratic
Construction Association (CNDCA) 610
China Association for Promoting Democracy 610
Chinese Peasants and Workers
Democratic Party 610
China Zhi Gong Dang 610
Jiusan Society 610
Taiwan Democratic
Self-Government League 610

Social Organizations

Chinese People's Association for Friendship with
Foreign Countries (CPAFFC) 611
All-China Federation of
Trade Unions (ACFTU) 611
Communist Youth League of China 611
All-China Women's Federation 611
Logo of All-China Women's Federation 611
All-China Federation of
Industry and Commerce 612
China Federation of Literary and Art Circles 612
China Association for
Science and Technology 612
All-China Federation of Returned
Overseas Chinese (AFROC) 612
China Writers Association 612

China Law Society 613
China Council for the Promotion of International Trade 613
All-China Journalists Association 613
China Disabled Persons' Federation 614
China Welfare Fund for the Handicapped 614
Logo of China Disabled Persons' Federation 614

17 P615 Administrative Division

General Information

Administrative Division System 615
Municipalities Directly Under the Central Government 615
Beijing Municipality 615
Shanghai Municipality 616
Tianjin Municipality 616
Chongqing Municipality 617
Hong Kong Special Administrative Region 617
Macao Special Administrative Region 617
Taiwan Province 617

Northeast China

Heilongjiang Province 619
Jilin Province 619
Liaoning Province 620

North China

Inner Mongolia Autonomous Region 620
Hebei Province 620
Shanxi Province 621

South China

Guangdong Province 621
Hainan Province 621
Guangxi Zhuang Autonomous Region 622

East China

Shandong Province 622
Anhui Province 623
Zhejiang Province 623
Fujian Province 624
Jiangsu Province 624
Jiangxi Province 624

Central China

Hunan Province 625
Hubei Province 626
Henan Province 626

Southwest China

Yunnan Province 626
Guizhou Province 627
Sichuan Province 627
Tibet Autonomous Region 628

Northwest China

Shaanxi Province 628
Gansu Province 629
Ningxia Hui Autonomous Region 629
Qinghai Province 629
Xinjiang Uygur Autonomous Region 630

18 P491 Judicature

Judicial System 631
Investigation System 631
Acceptance and Establishment of Cases 631
Procedures for Criminal Investigations 631
Ministry of Public Security 631
Supreme People's Procuratorate 632
Compulsory Measures System 632
Evidence System 632
Procuratorial System 632
Functions and Powers of the People's Procuratorates 633
Public Procurators 633
China Prosecutor Society 633
Qualifications for a Public Procurator 634
Participating in International Anti-Corruption Cooperation 634
International Association of Anti-Corruption Authorities 634
Juridical System 634
The Supreme People's Court 635
Higher People's Court 635
Intermediate People's Court 635
People's Court at the Grassroots Level 636
Special People's Court 636
Military Courts 636
Maritime Courts 636
Railway Courts 636
Forest Courts 636
Open Trials 636
Defense System 637
Withdrawal System 637
Collegiate System 637
The Court of Second Instance Being That of Last Instance 637
Judges System 637
Presenting a Petition and Retrial 637
Judicial Committee 637
Trial Organs 637
Jail System 638
Prison Categories 638
Execution of Penalties 638
Prison Administration 638
Lawyer System 639
Lawyer Qualification 639
Law Practice Application 639
Law Firms 639
Business of Law Firms 640
Rights of Lawyer 640
Obligations of Lawyers 640
All-China Lawyers Association 640
Chinese Lawyers' website 640
Legal Duties of Lawyers 641
Notary System 641
Scope of Business of Notary Office 641
The Effect of Notarization 641
Notarization Procedures 642
Arbitration System 642
Fundamental Principles of Arbitration 642
Arbitration Organs 642
Foreign-Related Arbitration 643
Arbitration Tribunal 643
Arbitrators 643
System of Trial or Arbitration 643
Mediation System 643
People's Mediation Committee 644
People's Mediator 644
Mediation Procedure 644
Methods of Mediation 644
State Compensation System 644
Administrative Compensation 644
Judicatory (Criminal) Compensation 645
Methods of Compensation 645
Foreign-Related Compensation 645
Legal Aid System 645
Scope of Legal Aid 646
Structure of Legal Aid Institutions 646
Implementing Subjects and Fund Sources in Legal Aid 646

Liabilities in Legal Aid 646
National Judicial Examination 646
Five-year Legislation Plan 646
China's Police System 647
China's Rank System of Police 647
The Ministry of Justice 647
Money Laundering Law 647

19 P648 Internet

General Survey of Internet

Key Dates in the Internet Development of China 648
Number of IP Address in China 648
Number of Chinese Domain Names 648
Number of Websites in China 648
China's International Bandwidth 648
Access Methods of Internet Users in China 649
Internet Penetration Rate in China 649
Gender Structure of Chinese Internet Users 649
Age Structure of Chinese Internet Users 649
Structure of Chinese Internet Users in Terms of Education Level 649
Structure of Chinese Internet Users in Terms of Profession 649
Equipment of Chinese Internet Users for Connection to the Internet 649
Home Surfing Equipment in China 649
Internet Access Expenses in China 649
Duration of Surfing Online 650
Application of Internet in China 650
China's Internet Industry 650
Network Advertising 650
Views of Chinese Internet Users 650
Computer World 650
China Information World 650
Computer Newspaper 650
China Internet Weekly 650
China Internet Network Information Center .. 650
Data Center of the China Internet (DCCI) 651
Internet Society of China 651

E-Government

Introduction to E-Government of China 652
Governmental Portal Website 652
Website of the National People's Congress 652
Website of the National Committee of the Chinese People's Political Consultative Conference (CPPCC) 652
Website of the Chinese Government 652
Websites of Local Governments 653
godpp.gov.cn 654
Chinahumanrights.org 654

Electronic Commerce

Introduction to E-Commerce of China 654
Electronic Commerce Mode 654

Major Websites for Individual Trade

Taobao.com 655
PaiPai.com 655
Dangdang.com 655
EachNet 655
Liba.com 655
7cv.com 655
Joyo 655

Major website on B2B Electronic Commerce

Alibaba.com 656
Made-in-china.com 656
hc360.com 656

Main Travel Reservation Websites

Online Travel Reservation 656
Travel Search Engine 656
Instant Hotel Reservations 656
B2B and B2C Tourism Electronic Commerce Platform 657
Ctrip.com 657
eLong, Inc. 657
Easytour.com.cn 657

Electronic Payment Websites

Introduction to Electronic Payment 657
Alipay 657
Tenpay.com 658
99Bill Corporation 658
E-Bank Online (Beijing) Technology Co., Ltd. 658

Online Banking

China's Online Banking Development 659
Laws and Regulations Relating to Online Banking 659
The Electronic Signature Law of the PRC 659
Measures for the Administration of Electronic Certification Services 659
Several Opinions of the State Council on Accelerating Development of E-Commerce 659
Websites of China's Banks 659

Search Engines

Introduction to Search Engine 660
Main Comprehensive Search Websites 660
Baidu 660
Google 660
China Yahoo! 660
Sogou.com 661
Soso.com 661
3721.com 661
Fkee.com 661
Website Navigation 265.com 661
Vertical Search 661
Main Website Navigation Websites 661
Qunar.com 662
So.01hr.com 662
Smarter.com 662
Qihoo.com 662
Douban.com 662
Isoshu.com 662
Shangsou.com 662
Mapabc.com 662
Mapbar.com 663
Local Search 663
Categories of Local Searches 663
Koubei.com 663
Dianping.com 663
58.com 663
Kijiji.cn 663
Kooxoo.com 663
52tong.com 664
Ddmap.com 664
51ditu.com 664

Online Media

Online Media 664
Zgjx.cn 664

News Websites

People's Daily Online 664
Xinhuanet.com 664

China.com.cn 664
CRI Online 665
Chinadaily.com.cn 665
CCTV.com 665
China Economic Net 665
Youth.cn 666
Cnr.cn 666
Chinanews.com 666
Gmw.cn 666
Cyol.net 666
Legaldaily.com.cn 666
China Military Online 666
Chinataiwan.org 667
China Tibet Online 667
Eastday.com 667
Qianlong.com 667
Enorth.com.cn 667
www.southcn.com 667
Wenweipo.com 668
ifeng.com 668

Comprehensive Portal Website

Comprehensive Portal Website 668
QQ 668
SINA 668
Sohu 669
Netease 669
China Yahoo! 669

Other Information Websites

www.rayli.com.cn 669
Military Affairs Channel of China.com 669

Internet Services

Instant Messaging

Instant Messaging 670
Tencent's QQ 670
MSN 670
Sina UC, UTalk 670
Popo.163.com 670
Sohu's soq.com 670
Yahoo! Messenger 671
GTalk 671
Skype 671
Fetion 671
PICA 671

E-Mail Services

E-Mail Services 671
Individual E-Mail 671
Enterprise E-mail 672
126 Mail 672
Netease Mail 672
Yahoo! Mail 672
QQ Mail 672
Sohu Mail 672
Sina Mail 672

Internet Education

Internet Education in China 672
Free Email Addresses 672
Internet Education Users 673
Size of Internet Education Market 673
Internet Education Industry 673
Categories of Internet Education 673
Stepping Stones in Internet Education 673

Network Security

Personal Network Security 673
Main Threats to Personal Network Security 674
Trojan Industry 674
Personal Network Security Products in China 674
Rising 674
Kaspersky 674
360 Safe 674

Daily Life Services

Financial and Economic Category

Introduction to Financial and Economic Websites 675
Main Financial and Economic Websites in China 675
Eastmoney.com 675
Business.sohu.com 675
Finance.sina.com 675
Hexun.com 675
Jrj.com 675
Cnfol.com 675
Stockstar.com 675
10jqka.com 676
Stock.163.com 676

Auto Category

Introduction to Auto Websites 676
Autohome.com 676
CHE168 676
PCauto.com.cn 676
Xcar.com.cn 676

Real Estate Consultation Category

Real Estate Websites 676
Main Real estate websites 677
Soufun.com 677
Goufang.com 677
Homhow.com 677

IT Information Category

Main IT Information Websites 677
Yesky.com 677
IT168 677
Zol.com 677
Main IT websites 677
Pchome.net 678
Pcpop.com 678

Health Category

Main Health Websites 678
39.net 678
Xyxy.net 678

Online Recruitment Category

China Online Recruitment 678
Main Online Recruitment Websites 678
ChinaHR.com 678
51job.com 678
Alliance's Zhaopin.com 679
JOB36 679
Tkzp.com 679

Photography Category

Main Photograph Websites 679
Photograph Websites with Greater Fame 679
Dpnet.com.cn 679
Xitek.com 679
Fengniao.com 679
Xiangshu.com 680
Photofans.cn 680
POCO 680

Digital Entertainment

Online Games

Online Games Industry in China 680
Main Online Game Websites 680
9you.com 680
Xy2.163.com 680
Shengda online 681
Tiancity.com 681
The9.com 681
Ourgame.com 681
17game.com 681

Games Information

Main Game Information Websites 681
uuu9.com 681
Sohu's 17173.com 682
92wy.com 682
PCgames 682
Tkgame.com 682

Online Music

China's Online Music Development 682
Fenbei.com 682
5fad 682
9sky.com 682
Music Website 682

Online Video

China Online Video Development 683
Mop's wideband movie & TV (itv.mop.com) ... 683
Vnet.cn 683
Bbvod.net 683
Ku6.com 683
Video Websites with More Visits 683
Main Video Sharing Websites 683
56.com 684
6rooms.com 684
Youku 684
Tudou.com 684

Digital Journals

Development of China's Digital Journals 684
Digital Journal Platforms 684
ZBOX 684
Xplus 684
Moker.com.cn 684
ZCOM 684

Basic Web2.0 Application (Friend-making, Blog, Online Community)

Brief Introduction of Web2.0 Application in China 685

Blog Website

Development of China Blog Website 685
Poco.cn 685
Bokee.com 685
51.com 685
QQ Zone 685

Original Literature

Main Original Literature Websites 686
Cmfu.com 686
Readnovel.com 686
Xxsy.net 686

Online Community

Development of China's Online Community .. 686
Main Online Community Websites 686
Mop 686
Zhanzuo.com 686
Tianya Virtual Community 686
Xiaonei.com 687
Teein 687
Daqi.com 687
Xici.net 687
ChinaRen community 687

Witkey

Development of China's Witkey 688
Witkey main websites 688
Witkey.com 688
Task China 688
Witkey China 688
Zhubajie.com 688
Witkeysky.com 688

Friendship

Development of China's Friend-Making Websites 688
Wangyou.com 688
360quan.com 688
9158.com 689
Ipart.cn 689
Love21cn.msn.com 689
Jiayuan.com 689
Marry5.com 689
Tianji.com 689
Integrated Friend-making Websites 689
Websites for Dating and Making Friends 689

Chapter Laws and Regulations

Laws

Brief Introduction of the Electronic Signature Law of the PRC 690
Brief Introduction of the Decision of the Standing Committee of the NPC on Preserving Computer Network Security 690
Brief Introduction of the Measures for the Administration of Internet Information Services 690
Brief Introduction of the Regulations on Protection of the Right of Communication through Information Network 691

Administrative Regulations

Brief Introduction of the Regulations on the Administration of Business Sites of Internet Access 691
Protection Measures for the Right Owners 691
Notifying and Removing Procedures for Dealing with Tortuous Dissension 691
Restrictions on the Rightful Owner's Right of the Communication of Information on a Network 692
Provisions on the Legal Responsibilities of Network Service Providers 692
Brief Introduction of the Administration of China Internet Domain Names Procedures 692
Brief Introduction of the Measures for Administration of E-mail Service on Internet .. 693
Brief Introduction of the Measures for the Administration of Electronic Certification Services 693
Brief Introduction of the Administration of Internet News Information Services Provisions 693
Brief Introduction of the Regulations on Administration of Internet-based Audio-Video Program Services 693

20 Sports P694

General Introduction

Introduction to Sports Development in China 694
Traditional Sports 694
Constrution of Sports Teams 694
Training System of Competitive Sports 694
Sports Events Practiced in China 695
Mode of Development 695
The Three-Tier Training System 695
"Olympic Glorious Program" 695
China and Olympics 696
Influence of Olympics on China's Physical Culture 696
The Olympic Badge 696
Successful Bid for 2008 Olympics 696
Olympic Day Run 696
International Sports Exchange 697
The Anti-Doping Work 697
Laws on Anti-Doping 697
Legal Documents on Anti-Doping 697
The First Olympic Gold of Hong Kong SAR .. 697

Beijing Olympic Mascots 697
Changes in Sports Development 698
Sports Goods Industry 698
Sports Entertainment Industry 698
Professionalization of Sports 698
Breakthroughs (2006) 698
The 11th Five-Year Plan on Physical Culture and Sports 698

Sports History

Ancient Sports 699
Baixi (A Hundred Acrobatics) 699
Sports Murals 699
Bingxi (Games on Ice) 699
Ancient Acrobatics 699
Ancient Horsemanship 699
Modern Sports (1860-1949) 699
Jing Wu Athletic Association 699
Regional Games 700
Provincial and Municipal Games 700
Far Eastern Championship Games 700
Early Experiences of Olympic Activities 700
The Law of the Republic of China on Physical Culture and Sport Issued in 1929 700
Early Spread of Olympic Education 701
Early Relationship between the IOC and China 701
The First Chinese IOC Member 701
Accession to the Olympic Family 701
The First Olympic Bid 701
Kong Xiangxi 701
Wang Zhengting 701
Dong Shouyi 701
Debut at the Olympics 702
Liu Changchun 702
China's Participation at Berlin Olympic Games 702
China's Participation at the 14th London Olympic Games 702
China's Participation in the Olympics from 1932 to 1948 702
Introduction of Modern Weightlifting into China 702
China National Amateur Athletic Federation 702
China Young Men's Christian Association 702
The First Chinese Champion in Race Walk 703
The First Baseball Team 703
The First Chinese Overseas Student of Sports 703
The First National Games 703
The First Bodybuilding Contest 703
The First Woman Doctor of Sport Studies 703
The First Boxing Champion 703
The Earliest Sports Textbook 703

Contemporary Sports

Ping Pong Diplomacy 704
The People's Republic of China and the IOC 704
The Mode of Olympics 704
Xu Heng 704
He Zhenliang 704
Lu Shengrong 705
Wu Jingguo 705
The 26th World Table Tennis Championships 705
Games of the New Emerging Forces 705
The Nationwide Fitness Plan 705
Legislation Related to Sports 706
The Insurance Scheme 706
Construction of Sports Facilities 706
Multi-Sport Competitions 706
The National Physique Monitoring 706
Sports Activities for the Public 707
Nationwide Fitness Week 707
Public Sports Organizations 707
Sports Population 707
Timetable for Public Sports Activities 707
Community Sports 707
Sports for the Working People 707
Sports for Senior Citizens 707

Social Sports Coaching Center 708
Social Sports Instructors 708
Sports for Women 708
Sports for the Young 708
College Physical Education Syllabus 708
Sports for Children 708
Grade System of Social Sports Instructors 709
Public Health-Building Goes Hand in Hand with the Olympics 709
Locomotive Sports Association of China 709
Sports in Rural Areas 709
Farmers' Swimming Competition 709
Set Exercises to Radio Music 709
Selection of Disabled Athletes 710
International Sports Events for the Disabled 710
Special Olympic Games 710
Special Olympic Games in China 710
Sports for the Disabled 710
Military Sports 710
Events for the Disabled 711
Sports for Ethnic Minorities 711
Traditional Sports Games of Ethnic Minorities 711
Characteristics of Traditional Sports of Ethnic Minorities 711
Women Administrators of Sports 712
First Chinese Woman to Win the Olympic Badge 712
Cross-Straits Athletes—Competing in the Same Arena 712
The First Olympic Medal 712
The First World Champion 712
The First World Record 712
Sports Documentary Film 712
The Olympic Cup 712

Major Events

The National Games 713
The 1st National Games 713
The 2nd National Games 713
The 3rd National Games 713
The 4th National Games 713
The 5th National Games 713
The 6th National Games 713
The 7th National Games 713
The 8th National Games 714
The 9th National Games 714
The 10th National Games 714
The National Winter Games 714
The 1st National Winter Games 714
The 3rd National Winter Games 715
The 4th National Winter Games 715
The 5th National Winter Games 715
The 6th National Winter Games 715
The 7th National Winter Games 715
The 8th National Winter Games 715
The 9th National Winter Games 715
The 10th National Winter Games 715
The National Sports Meeting 715
The 1st National Sports Meeting 715
The 2nd National Sports Meeting 715
The 3rd National Sports Meeting 716
National Games for the Disabled 716
The 1st National Games for the Disabled 716
The 2nd National Games for the Disabled 716
The 3rd National Games for the Disabled 716
The 4th National Games for the Disabled 716
The 5th National Games for the Disabled 716
The 6th National Games for the Disabled 716

National Traditional Ethnic Sports Games 717
The 1st National Traditional Ethnic Sports Games 717
The 2nd National Traditional Ethnic Sports Games 717
The 3rd National Traditional Ethnic Sports Games 717
The 4th National Traditional Ethnic Sports Games 717
The 5th National Traditional Ethnic Sports Games 718
The 6th National Traditional Ethnic Sports Games 718
The 7th National Traditional Ethnic Sports Games 718
National City Games 718
The 1st National City Games 718
The 2nd National City Games 718
The 3rd National City Games 718
The 4th National City Games 719
The 5th National City Games 719
National Farmers' Games 719
National University Games 719
Summer Olympic Games 719
The 15th Olympic Games in Helsinki 719
The 23rd Summer Olympics in Los Angeles 719
The 24th Summer Olympics in Seoul 720
The 25th Summer Olympics in Barcelona 720
Achievements at the 25th Olympics Games 720
The 26th Summer Olympics in Atlanta 720
Achievements at the 26th Olympics 720
The 27th Summer Olympics in Sydney 721
Achievements at the 27th Olympics 721
The 28th Summer Olympics in Athens 721
Achievements of Chinese Taipei Athletes at the Olympiad 721
Achievements of Hong Kong Athletes at the Olympiad 721
"Ice Break" of Swimming in Olympics 721
The First Olympic Gold 721
The 29th Summer Olympics in Beijing 722
Records of Gold Medals on the 29th Olympic Games 722
List of Gold Medals of the Chinese Delegation in Beijing 2008 Olympic Games 722
The Winter Games 723
The 13th Winter Games 723
The 14th Winter Games 723
The 15th Winter Games 723
The 16th Winter Games 723
The 17th Winter Games 723
The 18th Winter Games 723
The 19th Winter Games 723
The 20th Winter Games 723
China at Paralympics 724
The 7th Paralympics 724
The 8th Paralympics 724
The 9th Paralympics 724
The 10th Paralympics 724
The 11th Paralympics 724
The 12th Paralympics 724
The 13th Paralympics 724
Universiade 724
The 9th Universiade 724
The 19th Universiade 724
The 20th Universiade 725
The 21st Universiade 725
The 22nd Universiade 725
The 23rd Universiade 725
Chinese Athletes at the Universiade 725
Asian Games 725
The 1st Asian Games 725
The 7th Asian Games 725
The 8th Asian Games 726
The 9th Asian Games 726
The 10th Asian Games 726
The 11th Asian Games 726
The 12th Asian Games 726
The 13th Asian Games 726
The 14th Asian Games 726
The 15th Asian Games 727
Asian Winter Games 727
The 1st Asian Winter Games 727
The 2nd Asian Winter Games 727
The 3rd Asian Winter Games 727
The 4th Asian Winter Games 727
The 5th Asian Winter Games 727
East Asian Games 728
The 1st East Asian Games 728
The 2nd East Asian Games 728
The 3rd East Asian Games 728
The 4th East Asian Games 728
World Championships and Games for the Disabled 729
Far East and South Pacific Games for the Disabled (FESPIC Games) 729
Asia-Africa Table Tennis Friendship Invitational 729
World Table Tennis Championships 729
The 1st China International Table Tennis Open Championships 729
Table Tennis World Cup 729
Gymnastics World Cup 730
Volleyball World Cup 730
The 11th World Women's Volleyball Championship 730
The 1st FIFA World Championships of Women's Football 730
World Military Pentathlon Championships (WMPC) 730
ISF World Gymnasiade 730
Beijing International Marathon 730
Beijing International Wushu Invitational 730

Sports Events

Sports Events 731

Baseball

Baseball for the Youth 731
Professionalization of Baseball in China 731
Chinese Baseball Association (CBA) 731

Sailing

China Club Challenge Match 732
China Sailboat and Sailboard Sport Association 732

Sailboard

Hosting International Sailboard Events 732
Promoting Sailboard as a Sport in China 732
The First Chinese World Champion of Sailboard 732
The First Chinese Olympic Champion in Sailboard 733

Fencing

World Wheelchair Fencing Championships 733
World Fencing Championships 733
China's First Fencing Champion 733
Dong Zhaozhi 733
Wang Haibin 734

Wang Lei ... 734
Wu Hanxiong ... 734
Tan Xue ... 734
Chinese Fencing Association ... 734

Weightlifting

Men's Weightlifting ... 734
Achievements of Weightlifting at the Olympics ... 734
World Weightlifting Championships ... 735
Women's Weightlifting ... 735
Weightlifting Reserve ... 735
China's First Weightlifting World Champion ... 735
China's First Olympic Champion in Weightlifting ... 735
Chen Jingkai ... 735
Cai Wenyi ... 735
Chen Weiqiang ... 736
Yao Jingyuan ... 736
Zeng Guoqiang ... 736
He Zhuoqiang ... 736
Tang Lingsheng ... 736
Xing Fen ... 736
Zhang Guozheng ... 736
Zhan Xugang ... 737
Chen Xiaomin ... 737
Yang Xia ... 737
Chen Yanqing ... 737
Ding Meiyuan ... 737
Lin Weining ... 737
Tang Gonghong ... 737
Shi Zhiyong ... 737
Liu Chunhong ... 738
Chinese Weightlifting Association (CWA) ... 738

Basketball

National Basketball Events ... 738
The Chinese Women's Basketball Team ... 738
The Chinese Men's Basketball Team ... 739
The Men's Basketball World Championship ... 739
The CBA League ... 739
A Decade of CBA ... 739
The First Foreign Basketball Player in CBA League ... 740
The First Chinese Basketball Player in NBA ... 740
The North Star Program ... 740
Mou Zuoyun ... 740
Qian Chenghai ... 740
Yang Boyong ... 740
Jiang Xingquan ... 740
Li Yaguang ... 740
Song Xiaobo ... 740
Cong Xuedi ... 741
Zheng Haixia ... 741
Gong Xiaobin ... 741
Hu Weidong ... 741
Li Xin ... 741
Mengke Bateer ... 742
Wang Zhizhi ... 742
Sui Feifei ... 742
Yao Ming ... 742
Yi Jianlian ... 742
Chinese Basketball Association ... 743
Chinese University Basketball Association ... 743

Softball

Softball Players ... 743
Women's Softball World Championship ... 743
Chinese Softball Association ... 743
The 11th Women's Softball World Championship ... 744
Li Minkuan ... 744
Li Nianmin ... 744

Equestrianism

The First National Equestrian and Polo Game ... 745
The Chinese Equestrian Association ... 745

Volleyball

The Early Development of the Chinese Volleyball ... 745
Modern Development of the Chinese Volleyball ... 745
The Splendid Period of the Chinese Volleyball ... 745
The Current State of the Chinese Volleyball ... 746
Becoming a Member of the International Volleyball Federation ... 746
The Chinese Women's Volleyball Team ... 746
The Volleyball League ... 746
Deng Ruozeng ... 747
Yuan Weimin ... 747
Chen Yuxin ... 747
Sun Jinfang ... 747
The First Time to Participate in the Volleyball World Championship ... 747
Lang Ping ... 748
Lai Yawen ... 748
Zhang Yuehong ... 748
Feng Kun ... 748
Zhao Ruirui ... 748
"Three Consecutive Titles" of the Women's Volleyball Team ... 748
The "Five Consecutive Titles" of the Women' Volleyball Team ... 748

Beach Volleyball

The Chinese Volleyball Association ... 749
History of the Chinese Beach Volleyball ... 749
The Chinese Beach Volleyball Team ... 749
Tian Jia ... 749
Wang Fei ... 749

Canoe/Kayak

The Development of Canoe/Kayak Sports in China ... 750
The First Canoe/Kayak World Champion ... 750
Meng Guanliang ... 750
Yang Wenjun ... 751
Chinese Canoeing Association ... 751

Table Tennis

Debut of Table Tennis in China ... 751
Development of Table Tennis in China ... 751
Cultivation System of Table Tennis Players in China ... 751
Techniques Innovation ... 752
China's Performance in Table Tennis Competitions ... 752
The Latest Rankings of Table Tennis Championships ... 752
Chinese Table Tennis Club Super League ... 752
Popularity of Table Tennis Sport in China ... 752
The First Table Tennis Grand Slam Winner in the World ... 753
First Swaythling Cup ... 753
First Marcel Corbillon Cup ... 753
First WTTC Held in China ... 753
First Zdenek Haydusek Prize ... 753
First Clean Sweep of Championships ... 753
The St. Bride Vase Forever in China ... 753
First Table Tennis Referee ... 753
First Table Tennis Champion at the Olympic Games ... 753
China National Junior Table Tennis Open ... 753
Table Tennis as an Olympic Sport ... 754
Overseas Chinese Table Tennis Players ... 754
Fu Qifang ... 754

Qiu Zhonghui 754
Rong Guotuan 754
Xu Yinsheng 754
Zhang Xielin 755
Zhuang Zedong 755
Li Furong 755
Zheng Minzhi 755
Liang Geliang 755
Ge Xin'ai 755
Zhang Deying 755
Lu Yuansheng 756
Chen Xinhua 756
Cai Zhenhua 756
Cao Yanhua 756
Tong Ling 756
Ni Xialian 756
He Zhili 756
Wang Tao 757
Chen Jing 757
Ma Wenge 757
Qiao Hong 757
Ding Song 757
Deng Yaping 757
Kong Linghui 758
Liu Guoliang 758
Li Jun 758
Wang Nan 758
Wang Liqin 758
Ma Lin 759
Zhang Yining 759
Wang Hao 759
The Current ITTF Members in the CTTA 759
Chinese Table Tennis Association 759

Field Hockey

The Chinese Women's Field Hockey Team 760
Achievements of the Chinese Field Hockey Team in 2006 760
Chinese Field Hockey Association 760

Boxing

The Chinese Boxing Association 761
Three visits of Ali to China 761
The Performance of Chinese Boxing 761
The Start of Professional Boxing 761
World Boxing League 761
Zou Shiming 761

Judo

The First Chinese Judo World Champion 762
Zhuang Xiaoyan 762
Sun Fuming 762
Yuan Hua 762
Xian Dongmei 762
Tang Lin 762
Chinese Judo Association 763

Rowing

Development of Rowing Sport in China 763
The First Gold Medal in Rowing 763
The First Rowing Game in Asian Games 763
Liang Sanmei 764
Chinese Rowing Association 764

Shooting

First Skeet World Champion Team 764
China's First World Record in Shooting 764
Popularity of Shooting 764
Development of Shooting 764
Rifle 764
Clay-shooting 764
Pistol 765
Running Target 765
Dong Xiangyi 765
Wu Lanying 765
Feng Meimei 765
Wu Xiaoxuan 765
Xu Haifeng 765
Wang Yifu 765
Gao E 766
Li Yuwei 766
Zhang Shan 766
Li Duihong 767
Tan Zongliang 767
Jia Zhanbo 767
Tao Luna 767
Chen Ying 767
Cai Yalin 767
Li Jie 768
Yang Ling 768
Ren Jie 768
Du Li 768
Zhu Qinan 769
Chinese Shooting Association 769

Archery

The First Archery World Champion in China 769
Li Shulan 769
Meng Fanai 769
Li Lingjuan 769
He Ying 770
Chinese Archery Association 770

Handball

The First Female Handball Referees with International Class A Certificate 770
The First Olympic Handball Medal 771
Chinese Handball Association (CHA) 771

Chinese Wrestling

Freestyle Wrestling 771
Greece-Roman Wresting 771
World Wresting Championships (2005) 771
World Wresting Championships (2006) 772
China Women's Wresting Team 772
Sheng Zetian 772
Wang Xu 772
Chinese Wrestling Association 772

Taekwondo

National Public Taekwondo Championships 773
Chen Shixin 773
Chen Zhong 773
Luo Wei 773
Wu Jingyu 773
Chinese Taekwondo Association 773

Gymnastics

Floor Exercise 774
Pommel Horse 774
Parallel Bars 774
Horizontal Bar 774
The Booming Years of Gymnastics in China 774
The 7th Gymnastics World Cup 774
Rings 775
Vault 775
Uneven Bars 775
Balance Beam 775
Performance in Asian Games 775
Major Events of Gymnastics in 2006 775
The first Gymnastics World Cup for Chinese Athletes 775
The First World Gymnastics Championship for Chinese Gymnasts 775
The First Olympic Championship in Men's Gymnastics Team Competition 775
The First Championship in Gymnastics Team Competition in World Championships 775
The First Gymnastics World Champion 776
Drills Named After Chinese Athletes 776
Li Yuejiu 776

Huang Yubin 776
Li Ning 777
Ma Yanhong 777
Lou Yun 777
Li Xiaoshuang 777
Huang Xu 778
Yang Wei 778
Li Xiaopeng 778
Xing Aowei 778
Teng Haibin 778
Cheng Fei 778
Chinese Gymnastics Association 778

Rhythmic Gymnastics

China's Performance in Rhythmic Gymnastics in Asia 779
China's Performance in Rhythmic Gymnastics in the World 779
Zhong Ling 779
China Student Aerobics and Rhythmic Gymnastics Association 779

Trampoline

Huang Shanshan 780

Acrobatics

World Championships of Acrobatics 780
Zhu Haiying 780
Chinese Trampoline and Acrobatic Gymnastics Association 780

Track and Field

The Holding of International Track and Field Competitions 780
International Communication 780
Ma Family Army 781
Athletic Skills 781
Sprint 781
Middle and Long-Distance Running 781
Marathon 781
Steeplechase 781
Hurdles 782
Relays 782
Race Walk 782
The First Female Marathon Champion 782
The First Chinese Woman Athletics World Champion 782
The First World Group Champion in Women's Race Walk 783
High Jump 783
Pole Vault 783
Shot Put 783
Discus Throw 783
Hammer Throw 783
The First Chinese Woman to Throw Farther Than 21m .... 783 
Hu Hongfei 784
Huang Jian 784
Wang Kui 784
Yang Chuanguang 784
Lou Dapeng 784
Zheng Fengrong 784
Javelin Throw 784
Long Jump 784
Triple Jump 784
Heptathlon and Decathlon 784
Chen Jiaquan 785
Ni Zhiqin 785
Ji Zheng 785
Ma Junren 785
Zou Zhenxian 785
Li Meisu 785
Zhu Jianhua 785
Huang Zhihong 785
Sui Xinmei 785
Tian Yumei 786
Wang Xiuting 786
Xu Demei 786
Yan Hong 786
Chen Yueling 786
Xiao Yehua 786
Qu Yunxia 786
Zhao Yongsheng 786
Cai Weiyan 786
Li Zewen 786
Liu Dong 787
Sun Caiyun 787
Wang Junxia 787
Wang Liping 787
Huang Xiaoxiao 787
Liu Xiang 787
Qi Haifeng 787
Shi Dongpeng 788
Xing Huina 788
Chinese Athletics Association 788

Triathlon

China Triathlon Sports Association 788

Tennis

Evolution of Tennis Skills 788
The First World Tennis Champion 789
The First Tennis Players Participating in Olympic Games 789
The First Time to Hold International Tennis Tournament 789
The First Time to Win Asian Women's Tennis Group Champion 789
The First Olympics Tennis Gold Medal 789
2006 China Open 789
Li Ting 789
Sun Tiantian 789
Li Na 790
Zheng Jie 790
Peng Shuai 790
Chinese Tennis Association 790

Modern Pentathlon

The Track Record of Pentathlon (2006) 790
Chinese Modern Pentathlon Association 791

Swimming

Current Strength of Chinese Swimming Team ... 791
The First Chinese Woman to Set World Swimming Record 791
The First Olympics Swimming Medal 791
The First Olympics Gold Medal 791
The First World Record Setter of Men's Breaststroke 791
Freestyle Swimming 792
Backstroke 792
Breaststroke 792
Butterfly Swimming 792

Individual Medley 792
Relay Swimming 792
Synchronized Swimming 792
Lin Li 792
Qian Hong 793
Yang Wenyi 793
Zhuang Yong 793
Jiang Chengji 793
Chen Hua 793
Luo Xuejuan 793
Qi Hui 794
Wu Peng 794

Diving

The First Time to Become an Asian Diving Giant 794
The First Time to Participate in IFNA Diving World Cup 794
The First Team Title at World Cup 794
The First Olympics Diving Champion 794
The First Diving World Champion 794
Xu Yiming 794
Shi Meiqin 795
Gao Min 795
Xiong Ni 795
Sun Shuwei 795
Fu Mingxia 795
Tian Liang 796
Peng Bo 796
Guo Jingjing 796
Hu Jia 796
Wu Minxia 796
Lao Lishi 796
Li Ting 796
China Swimming Association 797

Water Polo

Water Polo 797

Badminton

Chinese Women Badminton 797
Chinese Badminton Team 797
The First Time to Participate in All England Open Badminton Championships 798
World Mixed Team Badminton Championships 798
Winning Thomas Cup for the First Time 798
Winning Uber Cup for the First Time 798
The First Badminton Olympics Gold Medal .. 798
The First Time to Sweep All Titles of World Badminton Championships 798
The Sweeping of All Three Cups 798
Chen Fushou 798
Tang Xianhu 799
Han Jian 799
Li Yongbo 799
Tian Bingyi 799
Yang Yang 799
Li Lingwei 799
Ye Zhaoying 799
Zhang Ning 799
Chinese Badminton Association 800
Zhang Jun 800
Chen Hong 800
Gao Ling 800
Huang Sui 800
Gong Ruina 800
Xie Xingfang 801
Lin Dan 801

Cycling

The Track Record of the Chinese Cycling Team 801
Tour of China 801
Professional Development of Cycling Event .. 802
Transfer of Foreign Transfer in Chinese Cycling Event 802
The First National Cycling Tournament 802
The First Asian Cycling Champion 802
The First Time to Break Asian Cycling Record 802
The Best Track Record of Mountain Bike (2006) 802
Jiang Yonghua 802
Ma Yanping 802
Li Meifang 803
Chinese Cycling Association 803

Football

The First National Football Tournament 803
The Earliest Football Organization 803
The First Time to Be Qualified for FIFA World Cup in 2001 803
Women's Football 803
Major Events of Chinese Football 803
Chinese Fans 804
The First National Women's Invitational Tournament 804
The Track Record of Women's Football 804
IMG Promotes the Reform of Chinese Football 804
Chinese Football Association Premier League (Group A) 804
The Rules for Chinese Super League 805
The First Bunch of Footballs to Join Foreign Teams 805
The First FIFA Women's of the Year 805
Li Huitang 805
Li Fenglou 805
Xu Fang 805
Fan Zhiyi 805
Golden Ball Award and Golden Boot Award of China 805
Sun Wen 806
Yang Chen 806
Li Tie 806
Sun Jihai 806
Ma Xiaoxu 806
Chinese Football Association 806

Events in Olympic Winter Games

Events in Olympic Winter Games 807

Ice Hockey

Chinese Ice Hockey Association 807

Skating

Speed Skating 807
The First Participation in Speed Skating World Championships-Ladies 807
The First Speed Skating World Champion 807
The First Best World Performance 808
The First to Be Punished Due to Doping 808
Short Track Speed Skating 808
The First World Champion of Short Track Speed Skating 808
Wang Jinyu 808
Luo Zhihuan 808
Wang Xiuli 808
Ye Qiaobo 808
Zhao Hongbo 809
Li Jiajun 809
Yang Yang 809
Chen Lu 809
Yang Yang 809
Wang Chunlu 809
Shen Xue 810
Li Chengjiang 810
Figure Skating 810
The First World Champion in Figure Skating 810
The Track Record of Chinese Skating Team (2006) 810
The First ISU Referee 810
Ice Dancing 810
Chinese Skating Association 810

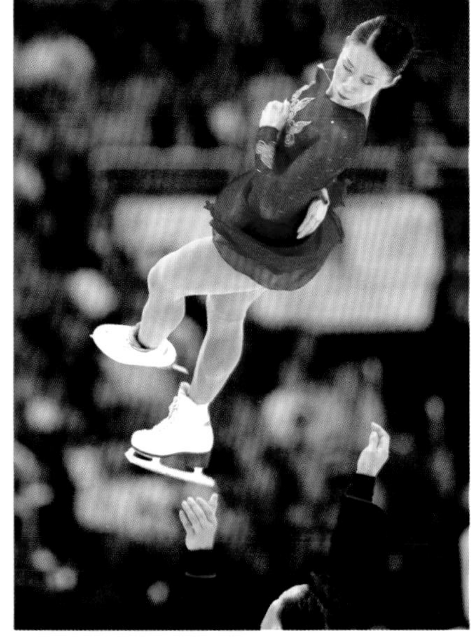

Skiing

Chinese Ski Association 811
Alpine Skiing 811
Cross-Country Skiing 811
Freestyle Skiing 811
Yu Shumei 811
Xu Nannan 811
Han Xiaopeng 811

Modern Biathlon

Modern Biathlon 812

Curling

Curling 812

Non-Olympic Events

Karate 812
Squash 812
Sanshou 812
Kendo 812
China Kendo Competitions 812
Golf 813
Volvo China Open 813
Golf Tournaments 813
Zhang Lianwei 813
Model Ships 813
Achievements of the Chinese Model Ship Building Team 813
Aeromodeling 814
First Chinese World Champion in Model Aeronautics 814
First Chinese Team Gold Medal at the World Aeromodeling Championships 814
Aero Sports Federation of China 814
Hu Shenggao 814
Pu Haiqing 814
Zhou Jianming 814
Lu Weifeng 814
Chinese Marine Model Association 814
Zhu Younan 815
Parachuting 815
The First Parachuting WR 815
The First Women's All Round Parachuting World Champion 815
Jia Chengxiang 815
He Jianhua 815
Mei Yan 815
Chen Li 815
Li Rongrong 815
Motorcycling 815
The MotoGP Chinese Grand Prix 815
Sepak Takraw 815
Automobile Sports 816
China Rally Championship 816
China Circuit Championship 816
China Karting Championship 816
China Circuit Cross-Country Championship 816
China Cross-Country Championship 816
International Events 816
China's Performance in Auto Sports 817
Racing Referee 817
Mountaineering 817
First Ascent Up Vinson Massif 817
First Ascent of Mt. Qomolangma via the North Ridge 817
Chinese Mountaineering Association 817
Aero Sports 818
Radio Sports 818
Chinese Radio Sports Association 818
The First Woman to Reach the Summit of Mt. Qomolangma from the North Ridge 818
The First Chinese Mountains Open to Foreign Climbers 818
Wang Fuzhou 818
Cross-Country Orienteering 819
Water Skiing 819
Motor Boat 819
F1 Powerboat World Championship China Grand Prix 819
Chinese Motorboat Association 820
Water Motorcycling 820
Gliding 820
Paragliding Record 820
Fin Swimming 820
Zheng Shiyu 820
Cheng Chao 820
Shen Jiliang 821
Ping Yali 821
Zhao Tiliang 821
Lin Haiyan 821
Sports Activities and Events for Athletes With Visual or Mobility Impairment 821
Sport Activities and Events for Deaf People 821
Sport Activities and Events for Mentally Defective Persons 821
Wang Juan 822
Wu Bin 822
Li Yansong 822
China Sports Association for the Disabled 822
China Sports Association of the Mentally Retarded People 822
China Sports Association for the Deaf Persons 822
Mass Sports 822
Group Callisthenics 822
Bowling 823
Winter Swimming 823
Car Modelling 823
Multi-bowls 823
Angling 824
Dart 824
Extreme Sports 824
Zhang Jian 824
Bodybuilding 824
First Women Bodybuilding Champions 825
World Top Professional Bodybuilding Stars Performed in China for the First Time 825
Callisthenics 825
Dance Sport 825
Roller Skating 825
Hot Air Balloon 826
Croquet 826
Non-Professional Diving 826
Bridge 827
The First Bridge Masters 827
Women's Bridge Team of China 827
Rock Climbing 827
Billiards 827
Ding Junhui 828
China Billiards & Snooker Association (CBSA) 828
Go (weiqi) 828
Chinese Go Association 828

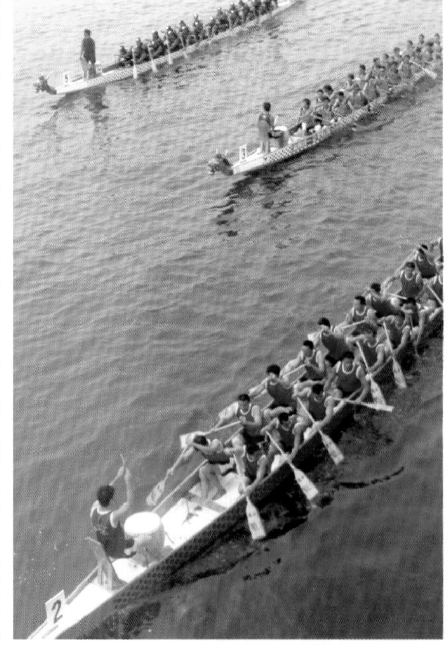

The First Female 9-dan Go (weiqi) in the World .828
National Go Ranking Match ... 828
The First Generation of National Gos ... 828
Nie Weiping ... 829
Ma Xiaochun ... 829
Chang Hao ... 829
Chinese Chess ... 829
The First Big Chessboard ... 829
Hu Ronghua ... 829
The First English Version of Chinese Chess Manual ... 830
Lu Qin ... 830
Chess ... 830
Chinese Chess Association ... 830
The First Title of Asian Chess Team Championship ... 830
Ye Jiangchuan ... 830
Liu Shilan ... 831
Xie Jun ... 831
Zhu Chen ... 831
Xu Yuhua ... 831
Racing Pigeon ... 831
Zhao Xue ... 832
Folk Sports ... 832
Wushu ... 832
The Origin of the Word "Wushu" ... 832
Set Exercises ... 833
Sanda Exercises ... 833
Wushu Competition Rules ... 833
Wushu Athletes Ranking Standards ... 833
The First Wushu Team of China Performing in the Olympics ... 833
The First China International Wushu Festival 834
Chinese Wushu Walking Toward the World ... 834
The First Wushu School Recruiting Overseas Students ... 834
Zhao Changjun ... 834
Liang Rihao ... 835
Rope Skipping ... 835
Tug-of-war ... 835
Lion Dance ... 835
Dragon Boat ... 835

Sports Institutions

General Administration of Sport of China ... 836
All-China Sports Federation ... 836
Chinese Olympic Committe ... 836
Hong Kong Olympic Committee ... 836
Macao Olympic Committee ... 836
Chinese Taipei Olympic Committee ... 837
China Sports Foundation ... 837
China Doping Control Center ... 837
Hong Kong Sports Association for the Mentally Handicapped ... 837
Federation of University Sports of China ... 837
China Sports Association of the Elder ... 837
China Farmer Sports Association ... 838

Physical Education

Beijing Xiannongtan Athletics Technology School ... 838
Beijing Sport University ... 838
Shanghai University of Sport ... 838
Wuhan Institute of Physical Education ... 839
Chengdu Sport University ... 839
Xi'an Physical Education University ... 839

Sports Facilities

Stadium & Gymnasium ... 839
Contemporary Sports Constructions Written into the World Architecture History ... 839
The First Large Comprehensive Stadium ... 839
Capital Stadium ... 840
Beijing International Tennis Center ... 840
Beijing University Students' Gymnasium ... 840
Beijing Shooting Gallery ... 840
Shanghai Gymnasium ... 840
Shanghai Stadium ... 841
Kunming Sports Training Base ... 841
Anyang Aero Sports School ... 841
Yabuli Snow Sports Training Base ... 841
National Olympic Sports Center ... 841
Guangdong Olympic Center Stadium ... 842
National Stadium ... 842
National Gymnasium ... 842
Olympic Village ... 842
National Aquatics Center ... 842
National Conference Center ... 842
Olympic Park ... 842
Olympic Rowing-Canoeing Park ... 843
Qingdao International Sailing Ship Center ... 843
Hong Kong Olympic Equestrian Venues ... 843
China Sports Museum ... 843

Comprehensive Sports Information

Sports Economy ... 844
Sports Industries ... 844
Sports Goods ... 844
Sports Goods Exhibitions ... 844
Sports Market ... 845
Sports Goods Retailing ... 845
Olympic Stamps ... 845
The First Miniature Sheet Pingpong Stamp ... 845
The First Set of Sports Stamps ... 845
The First Set of Chinese Ancient Sports Stamps ... 845
The First National Sports Stamps Exhibition . 846
Licensed Olympic Postcards ... 846
The First Silver Commemorative Coin ... 846
Sports Lottery ... 846
The Earliest Sports Lottery ... 847
Sports Collection ... 847
Sports Media ... 847
New Sports ... 847
The First Sports Encyclopedia ... 847
The First Sports Dictionary ... 848
The First English Sports Magazine ... 848
The Earliest Modern Sports Publication ... 848
The First National Sports Publishing House ... 848
Attending the International Olympic Film Festival ... 848
Titan Sports Media ... 848
Sports Festivals ... 848
Sports Information Websites ... 848

Index P850

CHINA

ENCYCLOPEDIA

Symbols of China

National flag of the People's Republic of China

National Flag of the People's Republic of China

The National Flag of the People's Republic of China is a red flag with five stars, with red symbolizing revolution and the five stars in yellow meaning bright future on the red land. The PRC Law on National Flag stipulates that the national flag must reach the top end of the flagpole when being hoisted, and it should not get down to the land when being lowered. The Tian'anmen Square is the symbol of the People's Republic of China. Every day, when the sun rises or sets, a ceremony will be held to hoist or lower the national flag of the People's Republic of China and the armed police will escort the national flag to/from the Square.

National emblem of the People's Republic of China

National Emblem of the People's Republic of China

The national emblem of the People's Republic of China is composed of the national flag, Tian'anmen, a cogwheel and ears of wheat and rice. The ears of wheat and rice, five stars, Tian'anmen and cogwheel are in gold color, and the base of the part within the round ring and the hanging ribbon are in red. Gold and red are traditional colors of China, symbolizing auspiciousness and happiness; the Tian'anmen symbolizes the undaunted anti-imperialist and anti-feudalist national spirit of the Chinese people; the cogwheel and ears of rice and wheat symbolize the working and peasant classes; and the five stars represent the national unity of the people under the leadership of the Communist Party of China.

National Anthem of the People's Republic of China

China's national anthem, *March of the Volunteers*, was written in 1935 by Tian Han, a famous modern playwright and set to music composed by Nie Er, a great revolutionary composer. Its lyrics are as follows:

Arise, ye who refuse to be slaves;
With our very flesh and blood
Let us build our new Great Wall!
The peoples of China are in the most critical time,
Everybody must roar his defiance.
Arise! Arise! Arise!
Millions of hearts with one mind,
Brave the enemy's gunfire,
March on!
Brave the enemy's gunfire,
March on! March on! March on, on!

The song was originally called *March of Volunteers*, and the theme song of the film called *Sons and Daughters of the Storm.* The film tells of the history: in the 1930s when Japan invaded northeast China, the Chinese nation was on the brink of the national collapse, and many Chinese bravely went to the front of war of resistance against Japan.

Music score of the national anthem of the People's Republic of China

Tian'anmen Square on the National Day

The *March of the Volunteers* was decided upon as the provisional national anthem of the People's Republic of China on September 27, 1949, at the First Plenary Session of the First Chinese People's Political Consultative Conference (CPPCC); and on December 4, 1982, the National People's Congress decided it as the official national anthem.

National Day

October 1 each year is the National Day of the People's Republic of China.

On December 2, 1949, the forth session of the Committee of the Central People's Government passed the Resolution on the National Day of the People's Republic of China. The full text of the resolution is as follows:

The First CPPCC National Committee adopted at the First Session on October 9, 1949 the Proposal of Suggesting the Government to Determine October 1 as the National Day of the People's Republic of China in Place of the Old National Day on October 10, which was sent to the Central People's Government for endorsement and implementation.

The Committee of the Central People's Government thinks that the proposal is in accordance with the historical fact and represents the will of the people, and decides to adopt it.

The Committee of the Central People's Government now declares: From 1950, October 1 of each year shall be the National Day of the People's Republic of China, the great day the People's Republic of China declared its foundation in 1949.

Capital

On September 27, 1949, it was ultimately decided at the First Plenary Session of the CPPCC National Committee that Beiping be the capital of the People's Republic of China and, beginning on this day, Beiping be renamed Beijing.

As the capital of the People's Republic of China, Beijing is one of the four municipalities directly under the Central Government (others are Shanghai, Tianjin and Chongqing). Beijing is China's political, scientific and culture center, as well as the center for international exchanges. Beijing is the famous historical and cultural city of China.

Beijing lies in the north of the North China Plain, covering an area of 16,808 square km. It is 43.5 meters above sea level, and has a population of 16 million. Under its jurisdiction are 16 districts and 2 counties.

Beijing is located in the warm temperature zone and has a continental climate. It has four distinct seasons. Winter in Beijing is dry and cold, and sometimes will be sandy and windy; summer is wet and rainy. The temperature of January is 4 degrees Centigrade below zero; that of July is 26 degrees Centigrade. Late April to early June, and late August to the end of November are the best time to visit Beijing.

Geography

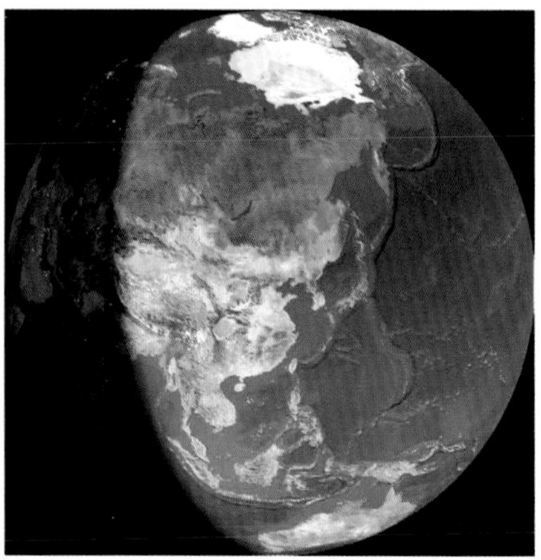

Statellite image map

Geographic Location

Facing the largest ocean of the world, the Pacific Ocean, China is located on the eastern edge of the Eurasian Continent, which is also the biggest continent in the world. On the whole, the terrain step by step descends from west to east; the broad continental shelf combines the Chinese continent with the basin of the Pacific Ocean.

Located in the Northern Hemisphere, the central and eastern part of Asia, and lying on the western side of the Pacific Ocean, China extends furthest east in a southeasterly direction and west in a northwesterly direction. It covers a land area of 9.60 million square km, accounting for nearly one-fourth of the Asian continent and one-fifteenth of the world's continental area, a little smaller than that of the total of Europe, and ranking third in the world behind Russia and Canada. The sea area of China, consisting of the Bohai, Yellow, East China and South China seas, as well as the Pacific Ocean on the eastern side of Taiwan, is 4.73 million square km, about one-third of that of the land area. The Bohai Sea is the continental sea of China.

The longitudinal and latitudinal span of China is large. It begins at the confluence of the Heilongjiang and Wusulijiang Rivers (135° 03'E) in the east and extends to the eastern bank of Kala Lake on the Pamirs Plateau (73°22'E) in the west, making a longitudinal difference of nearly 62 degrees, a span of about 5,200 km in distance and a time difference of over four hours. From the south, it stretches from the southernmost island of Zengmu Ansha in the South China Sea (3°51'N) to the main channel of the Heilongjiang River north of Mohe County (53°34'N), with about 50 degrees and 5,500 km in between.

Topography

China has a terraced terrain, which descends from the west to the east step by step, as well as various landforms, of which mountains account for 33.3 percent; plateaus, 26 percent; basins, 18.8 percent; plains, 12 percent; and hills, 9.9 percent. From west to east, the whole topography can be divided into three terraces. The first, or the highest, terrace is the Qinghai-Tibet Plateau, composed of high mountains and plateaus and known as the "roof of the world", with an average elevation of over 4,000 meters. The second terrace, including mountain areas, plateaus and basins, extends eastward from the Qinghai-Tibet Plateau to the Greater Hinggan Mountains, Taihangshan Mountains, Wushan Mountain, Wulingshan Mountain and Xuefengshan Mountain, averaging 1,000 to 2,000 meters above sea level. The expansive plains and hills constitute the third terrace, averaging 500 to 1,000 meters above sea level. The third terrace continues into the sea, forming the shallow-sea continental shelf. It is generally not deep, and descends slowly. It is rich in marine resources.

Land Boundary

China's land boundary extends for 22,800 km. It is contiguous to 14 countries: Democratic People's Republic of Korea in the east, Russia in the northeast, Mongolia in the north, Russia and Kazakhstan in the northwest, Kyrgyzstan, Tajikistan, Afghanistan, and Pakistan on the west, India, Nepal, and Bhutan to the southwest, and Myanmar, Laos, and Vietnam in the south. It also has six neighbors across the sea, from north to south, the Republic of Korea, Japan, the Philippines, Brunei, Malaysia and Indonesia.

Mainland Coastline

The mainland coastline of China from the mouth of the Yalu River to Beilunhe River totals 18,000 km. Adding in the many islands, China's total coastline stretches for about 30,000 km. Along the coast are many fine bays and port cities including, in order from north to south, Dalian, Qinhuangdao, Tianjin, Yantai, Qingdao, Lianyungang, Nantong, Shanghai, Ningbo, Wenzhou, Fuzhou, Xiamen, Guangzhou, Zhanjiang and Beihai; of these, Shanghai is the biggest city of China. The neritic continental shelf of China is among the most extensive in the world, including the entire Bohai Sea and Yellow Sea, the main body of the East China Sea and part of the South China Sea, abundant in mineral resources and with great development value.

Islands

With a total area of about 80,000 square km, over 5,000 islands are scattered over China's vast seas, of which Taiwan Island is the biggest, covering 35,800 square km; the next is Hainan, with a land area of nearly 33,500 square km; both are provinces for administrative purposes. The third largest is Chongming Island near Shanghai occupying over 1,000 square km. In addition, there are also some strategically-important islands, like the Changshan archipelago, Miaodao archipelago, Zhoushan archipelago, Penghu archipelago, Diaoyu islands, and Dongsha islands, Zhongsha islands, Nansha islands in the South China Sea. These have been a part of the territory of China since ancient times. The four straits from north in turn are the Bohai Strait, Taiwan Strait, Bashi Strait and Qiongzhou strait.

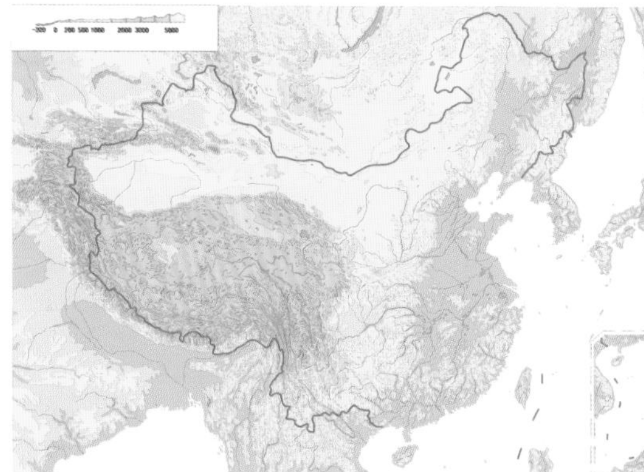

Topographic map of China

Outline of Rivers

The total length of China's rivers is approximately 220,000 km. At least 1,500 of the rivers have a drainage area of over 1,000 square km. The total annual runoff volume reaches 2.7115 trillion cubic meters, roughly equal to that of Europe. The major rivers almost all derive from the Qinghai-Tibet Plateau; therefore the fall is great, the water resources are very abundant, totaling 680 million kW, which leads the world.

With a total length of 6,300 km and a drainage area of 1.809 million square km, the Yangtze River is the biggest waterway in China and also the main artery for inland water transportation.

The Yellow River is the second biggest river, stretching 5,464 km. The Yellow River valley, covering 752,000 square km, is the birthplace of ancient Chinese civilization, so there are many cultural relics.

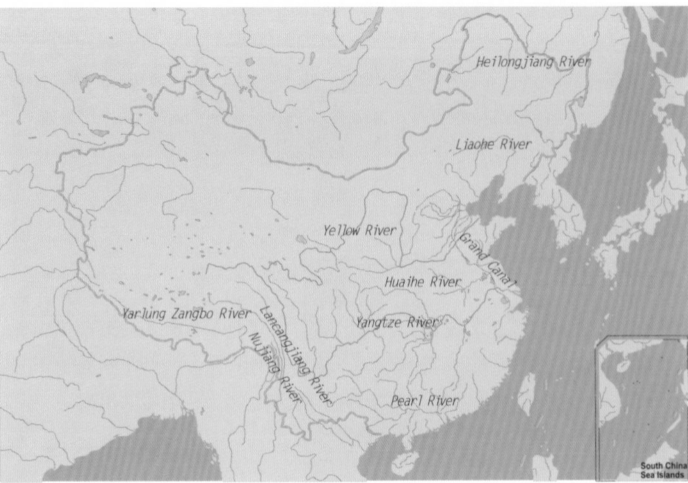

Sketch map of major Chinese rivers

There is also a man-made waterway, the Grand Canal, running from Beijing in the north to Hangzhou in the south. Totaling about 1,800 km, the canal was first carved out in the fifth century BC. With several improvements over the centuries, it became a major channel of transportation for the various dynasties. In ancient times, the goods and materials of the south were shipped to the north through it, while the emperors could use it to travel to the Jiangnan—the area south of the Yangtze River. Today, the section in the south is still in service.

Yangtze River

From its source on Geladandong peak of the Tanggula Mountain Range on the Qinghai-Tibet Plateau and southwestern part of Qinghai Province, the Yangtze River (or Changjiang) snakes eastwards for 6,300 km, spanning 11 provinces, autonomous regions and municipalities, namely Qinghai, Sichuan, Tibet, Yunnan, Chongqing, Hubei, Hunan, Jiangxi, Anhui, Jiangsu and Shanghai, before finally pouring into the East China Sea. It is not only the longest river in China but in all of Asia and the third longest in the world. It drains over 1.8 million square km, one-fifth of the total area of the country; and yearly delivers about a trillion cubic meters of water to the sea, more than one-third of China's total. The river powers its way through the Qinghai-Tibet Plateau, Hengduan mountain areas, Yunnan-Guizhou Plateau, Sichuan Basin, and the middle and lower reaches on the plains. Most regions along its route have a warm and humid climate.

The Wuxia Gorge among the Three Gorges on the Yangtze River

The Yangtze River, together with the Yellow River, is taken as a symbol of the Chinese nation.

Close to 100 million cubic meters of Yangtze River water empties into the sea. The river has a total fall of 5,800 meters; and the water power resources reach 268 million kW , equal to the total of the US, Canada, and Japan combined; moreover, its runoff volume accounts for as much as 37 percent of the nation's total. The Yangtze Three Gorges Project (TGP), under construction and attracting world attention, will be able to ultimately generate 84.9 billion KWh of electricity a year, which can not only greatly relief the present strained situation of China's electricity supply but also relieve suffering along the Yangtze Valley from floods and waterlogging.

Yellow River

The Yellow River (Huanghe), with a total length of 5,464 km, is the second longest river in China. It originates from the northern piedmont of the Bayanhar Mountain Range in the central part of Qinghai Province, loops north and then bends south, meandering across nine provinces, i.e. Qinghai, Sichuan, Gansu, Ningxia, Inner Mongolia, Shaanxi, Shanxi, Henan and Shandong and finally emptying into the Bohai Sea. On its way, it is replenished by over 30 main branches as well as numerous streams, draining an area of 750,000 square km. The river's middle reaches flow through the Loess Plateau collecting a large amount of mud and sand, making it the river with the largest such content in the world and contributing the yellow color that gives the river its popular name.

• Exterior and Interior Rivers

The drainage area of the exterior rivers that flow to the sea accounts for 64 percent of the country's total land area. The Yangtze River, Yellow River, Heilongjiang River, Pearl River, Liaohe River, Haihe River and Huaihe River pour into the Pacific Ocean; the Yarlung Zangbo River in Tibet runs east until it debouches into the Indian Ocean; the Erqis River flows north across the national boundary and finally exits into the Arctic Ocean. The catchment area of interior rivers which either feed inland lakes or disappear into the desert or salt marshes make up about 36 percent of China's total land area. The longest, at 2,179 km, is the Tarim River in southern Xinjiang.

Hukou Waterfall, Yellow River

In ancient times, it was far warmer in the Yellow River Valley than today. The loess soil then favored cultivation for its loose texture and thus could support a growing population. Five thousand years ago, there appeared the Yangshao Culture in the middle and lower reaches, over 1,000 of whose relics have been found in Henan, Shanxi, Shaanxi, Gansu and Qinghai. The items unearthed include stoneware, bone-ware, pottery etc uniquely featuring red surface and colored strips. Hence the other name of the Yangshao Culture is Painted-Pottery Culture. Archaeological finds show that the oldest civilized country was already established in the middle and lower reaches of the Yellow River 3,000 years ago. The Yellow River Valley, and the Tigris-Euphrates Valley, Nile Valley, Ganges Valley together enabled the emergence of various ancient advanced civilizations. The Yellow River is always taken as the mother river of the Chinese nation.

The Yellow River Valley has fertile land accounting for nearly one-fourth of the nation's total, abundant resources and beautiful scenery; the population it feeds makes up a quarter of the national total.

Yarlung Zangbo River

The Yarlung Zangbo River, with the highest altitude in the world, is located in Tibet Autonomous Region. Belonging to the Indian Ocean water system, the river finds its source on the Gyaimanezong Glacier in the northern foothills of the Himalayas and then flows from west to east across the southern section of the Tibet Plateau. After running across Mailing, it then turns to north and east before sharply flowing south entering India at Baxika, where its name changes to the Brahmaputra River. Finally, it joins the Ganges River before debouching into the Indian Ocean from the Bay of Bengal. The total length of the Yarlung Zangbo River is 2,057 km; its annual runoff volume close to 139.5 billion cubic meters, ranking third in China; the average elevation of the river valley is over 4,000 meters; and its drainage area of 240,480 square km ranks fifth in China.

The total drop of the Yarlung Zangbo River within China is over 5,400 meters, so it is the most precipitous river in China. The river boasts extremely abundant water power resources as well as fine development conditions. The total reserves of water power exceed 110 million kW, roughly accounting for one-sixth of China's total, of which that of its trunk stream comes to nearly to 80 million kW, ranking second. If calculated according to the water power reserves per unit of river length or unit of valley area, the Yarlung Zangbo River ranks first in China. At present, China has preliminarily constructed several hydroelectric and hydropower engineering projects on some of the river's medium and small branches, but the full potential has yet to be tapped.

Heilongjiang River

The Heilongjiang River, the Sino-Russian boundary river, flows across the northern part of northern China. Its headstream is composed of two sources, the northern and the southern. The northern source, the Shilka River originates from the eastern foothills of the Mountain Kent in the Mongolia, while the southern source Argun River is derived from the western slope of China's Greater Hingan Mountains. After the convergence of the two sources at Xiluoguhe Village, Mohe County, China, the river becomes the Heilongjiang River that runs east and finally empties into the Sea of Okhotsk. The Heilongjiang River runs across China, Russia and Mongolia. With a total length of 4,370 km, this river is the 11th largest in the world. Its drainage area reaches 1.843 million square km, ranking 10th largest in the world. The drainage area within China accounts for 48 percent of the total. Ships under 3,000 tons can navigate the whole river freely.

Among some 200 branches, the Songhuajiang River is the largest, totaling 1,657 km from Changbaishan Tianchi Lake to the estuary and draining an area of nearly 550,000 square km. Its annual runoff volume is 79.85 billion cubic meters. The Wusulijiang River is another major branch, with a length of 905 km and a drainage area of 187,000 square km; the runoff volume is 63 billion cubic meters. The Heilongjiang River is blocked by ice for nearly a half year.

The river's waterpower resources are relatively large, totaling about 32 million kW and it also produces various fish with high economic value. With the rapid development of Sino-Russian commerce in recent years, China has successively opened seven ports for trade with Russia. The freight in 2007 alone was 11.5 million tons, so these ports every year bring considerable economic benefits to the two sides.

Pearl River

The Pearl River is the third largest river in China as well as the largest in the south of China. Tracing its source in the east of Yunnan Province, the Pearl River runs for 2,214 km through Yunnan Province, Guizhou Province, Guangxi Zhuang Autonomous Region and Guangdong Province to the South China Sea with a drainage area within China of 442,500 square km. It mainly consists of Xijiang [West

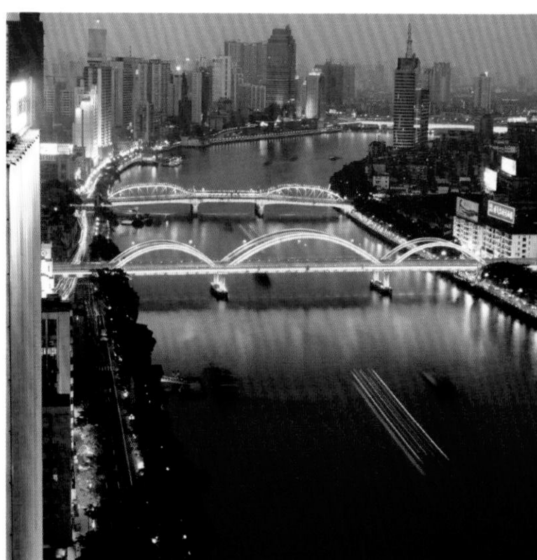
Pearl River

River], Beijiang [North River] and Dongjiang [East River], which form a large water network and converge at the Pearl River Delta. Of them, the Beijiang, and Dongjiang are roughly distributed within Guangdong Province.

Nujiang River

The Nujiang River is one of China's important rivers flowing from north to south. With a total length of 2,816 km and a drainage area of 324,000 square km, it takes its source at the Baskwo Mountain of the Tanggula Mountain Range in Tibet Autonomous Region, tumbling through Tibet Autonomous Region and Yunnan Province and into Myanmar, with the changed name Salween River, at last pouring in the Andaman Sea of Indian Ocean at the Moulmein.

With a rich annual runoff volume and a great drop height, the Nujiang River has abundant hydroelectric resources, the waterpower reserve reaching nearly 35.5 million kW. In addition, there are also rich mineral resources in the Nujiang valley, such as copper, iron, lead, tin, coal, crystal, sulfur, graphite, isinglass, etc.

Lancangjiang River

The Lancangjiang River is the longest river flowing from north to south in China. Its source is Zhaqu of Guangguori Peak of the Tanggula Mountain Range in Qinghai Province. Only after it reaches Qamdo of Tibet does its name change to the Lancang River. The river runs south until it leaves China and becomes the Mekong River that flows out into the ocean in the southern delta region of Vietnam. As the largest river in the Southeast Asia, the Lancangjiang has a total length of 2,354 km and a drainage basin area of 165,000 square km.

The drop height of the Lancangjiang River is up to 4,600 meters with the average gradient ratio of 2.2 per thousand. The waterpower resources in the trunk steam are estimated at 27 million kW, which is of great developmental potential.

Liaohe River

Being one of the important rivers in northern China, the Liaohe River is called the Mother River by the people of Liaoning Province. Originating in Guangtou Mountain of the Qilaotu Range in Hebei Province, the Liaohe River flows for 1,394 km through Hebei, Inner Mongolia, Jilin and Liaoning provinces and at last empties into the Bohai Sea, draining an area of 201,600 square km. Generally taking on a dendritic shape, the gathering system is much wider from west to east than from north to south. In the drainage basin, mountainous terrain accounts for 48.2 percent, hills 21.5 percent, plains 24.3 percent and sand hills six percent.

The river carries a high sediment load, only next to the Yellow River and the Haihe River. Some 20.98 million tons of sediment enter the river channel each year.

Huaihe River

The Huaihe River is one of the major rivers in Eastern China. The Huaihe River Valley originates from Tongbai Mountain and Funiu Mountain, bordering the upper reaches of the Yangtze River, with the Dabie Mountains and Jianghuai hills in the south, and the upper reaches of the Yellow River and Yimengshan Mountain. From east to west, the valley is 700 km long and from south to north 400 km wide with a total drainage area of 270,000 square km. The Huaihe River Valley consists of the Huaihe water system and the Sishui-Yishui-Shuhe water system, the former covering 190,000 square km and the latter 80,000 square km.

In addition the Huaihe River valley involves several large lakes, such as the Hongzehu Lake, Nansihu Lake, Luomahu Lake, Gaoyouhu Lake etc. Of them, Hongzehu Lake, with a storage capacity of 13 billion cubic meters, is the largest freshwater lake in this valley as well as the fourth largest in China.

▲ Grand Canal

The history of excavating canals in China can be traced back to the Spring and Autumn Period in the fifth century BC. Many artificial waterways were successively constructed, which to a large extent facilitated the allocation of goods and materials and as well improving transportation. Among them, the Beijing-Hangzhou Grand Canal, with a history of over 2,000 years, enjoys the finest reputation equal to that of the Great Wall and it has played an important role in connecting north and south. With a total length of about 1,800 km and first built in the Sui Dynasty (581-618), the canal starts from Beijing, and then runs through Tianjin, Hebei, Shandong, Jiangsu and Zhejiang until it reaches Hangzhou. It also connects the Yangtze, Yellow, Huaihe, Haihe, and Qiantang river systems. Even today, the section in Jiangsu and Zhejiang still serves as an important transportation line. The annual freight volume, after that of the Yangtze River, ranks second in inland waterway transportation in China. Other purposes of the canal refer to irrigation, flood control, drainage of waterlogged land etc.

Haihe River

The Haihe River is one of the great rivers in North China. The five rivers (the North Canal, Yongdinghe River, Daqinghe River, Ziyahe River and the South Canal) from north, west and south converge at Tianjin City to form the Haihe River. The Haihe River Valley starts from the western Taihangshan Mountain, reaches the eastern Bohai Sea and borders the Yellow River in the south and the southern edge of the Inner Mongolian Plateau in the north. It spans Beijing, Tianjin, Hebei Province, Shanxi Province, Shandong Province, Henan Province, Liaoning Province and Inner Mongolia Autonomous Region, draining an area of 317,800 square km, accounting for 3.3% of the country's total, of which mountain areas make up nearly 54.1 percent and plains about 45.9 percent.

Haihe River in Tianjin

Poyanghu Lake

Poyanghu, located in the north of Jiangxi Province and on the southern bank of the Yangtze River, is China's largest freshwater lake, with an area of about 2,933 square km, an average length of 170 km, a maximum depth of 29.19 meters. The water of the lake is mainly supplied by surface supply and rainfall on the lake's surface. Besides, a few rivers, like the Ganjiang River, Fuhe River, Xinjiang River, Raohe River and Xiushuihe River are interconnected with the lake.

Dongtinghu Lake

Dongtinghu, the second largest freshwater lake of China, is located in the southern section of the middle reaches of the Yangtze River and in the north of Hunan Province. The total lake area reaches 18,000 square km and the storage volume ten to twenty billion cubic meters. Its main branches include the Xiangjiang, Zishui, Yuanshui and Lishui rivers.

Hongzehu Lake

Located in the alluvial plain in the middle reaches of the Huaihe River and in the western part of Hongze County, Jiangsu Province, Hongzehu is the fourth largest freshwater lake in China. It is shallow, the depth usually within four meters with the deepest place only reaching 5.5 meters. The total lake area covers 2,069 square km. Main branches include the Huaihe, Suihe, Bianhe and Anhe rivers.

A white egret flying above the Hongzehu Lake

Taihu Lake

Located in the border area of Jiangsu and Zhejiang provinces or the southern part of the Yangtze River Delta, the Taihu Lake is the largest lake in the eastern coastal area and the third largest freshwater lake in China. It covers a total area of 3,100 square km with nearly 2,420 square km of water area. Dongruxi River is the main river emptying into this lake.

Chaohu Lake

With an area of 753 square km, Chaohu is the fifth largest freshwater lake and is located in the central area of Jianghuai Hills in Anhui Province. The lake originates in the Ying Mountain and Huoshan Mountain and is connected with the Fenglehe, Hangbuhe and Zhaohe.

Qinghaihu Lake

Qinghaihu Lake Bird Islet

Qinghaihu Lake, the huge expanse of deep, salty water receives its name, literally "Blue Sea" in Mongolian, from the vastness of its azure-colored water. Lying in the Qinghaihu Lake Basin in the northeast of Qinghai Province, it is the largest inland lake and the largest saltwater lake in China. It stretches 105 km in length, with a width of 63 km and a maximum depth of 38 meters. The lake's catchment area reaches 29,661 square km; the surface of the lake is 3,196 meter above the sea level. The lake water mainly comes from surface runoff and rainfall on its surface. Over 40 rivers flow into the lake, including the Buha, Bagewulan and Cetang rivers, of which the Buha is the largest. In recent years, with great climatic changes, the water level has dropped by 80-100 meters, and its surface area also has dwindled by nearly one-third compared to the original.

Outline of Lakes

China has many lakes. According to statistics, there are more than 2,800 natural lakes, each with a surface area of over one square km, and over 130 lakes each more than 100 square km. Moreover, there are also a large number of artificial lakes (reservoirs). Most of China's large freshwater lakes, including Poyanghu, Dongtinghu, Taihu, Hongzehu etc, are distributed in the middle and lower reaches of the Yangtze River, while large salty lakes are mainly found on the Qinghai-Tibet Plateau like Qinghaihu Lake, Nam Co Lake and Qilinhu Lake. Of these lakes, Poyanghu, covering 3,583 square km, is the largest freshwater lake in China; with an area of 4,583 square km, Qinghaihu Lake on the Qinghai-Tibet Plateau is the largest saltwater lake.

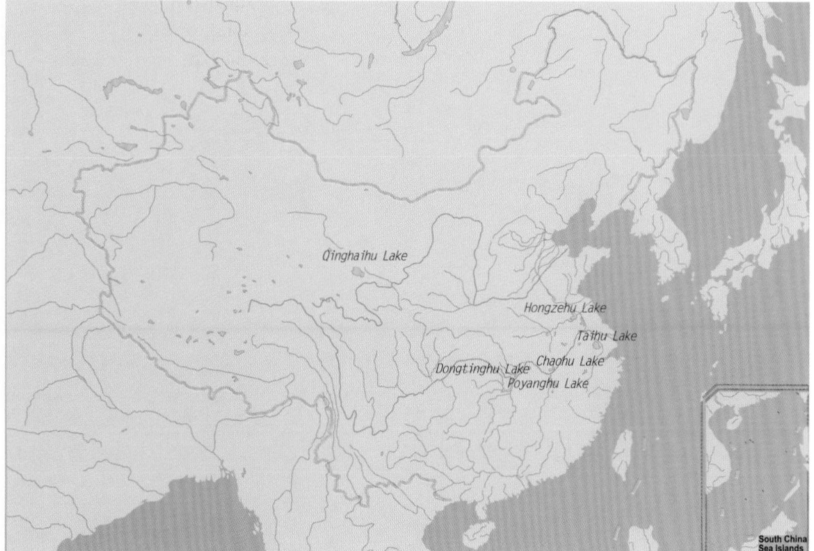

Sketch Map of Major Chinese Lakes

Monsoon Climate

China has various combinations of temperature and precipitation and hence diversified types of climate due to its vast territory, large latitudinal span, great differences in topography, diverse landforms and mountain trends.

With an extensive area under the alternate influence of winter and summer monsoon, China is regarded as a region having the most typical monsoonal climate. Compared with other areas of the same latitude in the world, China has a lower temperature in winter but a higher one in summer. The difference of temperature in a year is remarkable and precipitation is concentrated in summer. Therefore the climate in China is the continental monsoon type.

In summer and autumn, the southeast coastal areas often suffer from tropical storms—typhoons. Typhoons (the result of the evolution of tropical storms) are most frequent from June to September.

In spring and winter, the dry and cold winter monsoon sweeps down from Siberia and the Mongolian Plateau, when cold waves may come into being if the monsoon is especially strong and the temperature drops sharply. This, then, may result in disasters like chills, gusts, sand storms and frost.

Temperature

The Mohe area of Heilongjiang Province at the northernmost tip of China (north of 53° N) features a cold temperate climate, while Zengmu Ansha in Hainan Province at the southernmost end, only 400 km away from the equator, is dominated by the equatorial climate. So, the temperature difference from north to south is rather dramatic.

In winter, the zero degrees Centigrade-isotherm runs across the Huaihe River, Qinling Mountains and the southeastern verge of the Qinghai-Tibet Plateau. The areas to the north of the line (including the North, northwestern areas and the Qinghai-Tibet Plateau) have a temperature below zero degrees Centigrade, of which that in Mohe, Heilongjiang Province is below minus 30 degrees Centigrade; in contrast, the regions south of the line see a temperature above zero degree Centigrade: that in Sanya, Hainan Province even exceeds 20 degree Centigrade. So we can say, a warm South, a cold North, and a big difference between the two mark the winter temperature distribution of China.

In summer, the nationwide temperature is high, and temperature difference is small between the north and the south. Except the Qinghai-Tibet Plateau and the Tianshan Mountains, the temperature of most areas of China is above 20 degrees Centigrade and that in many southern areas tops 28 degrees Centigrade. In the Turpan Basin, Xinjiang, the temperature

Children playing on the Tian'anmen Square in the intermittent rain

in July averages 32 degrees Centigrade; it is the heart of hotness in the Chinese summer.

Precipitation

Most parts of China under the influence of the oceanic warm-moist airflow; precipitation is plentiful but is unevenly distributed both regionally and seasonally.

The regional distribution can be described as follows: the 800-mm isohyet runs along the Huaihe River-Qinling Mountains-Qinghai-Tibet Plateau line; and that of 400-mm along the Greater Hinggan Mountains-Zhangjiakou-Lanzhou-Lhasa-southeast edge of the Qinghai-Tibet Plateau line. Rainfall in the Tarim Basin is less than 50 mm and in some areas is even below 20 mm. The annual precipitation in Tuokexun in the Turpan Basin averages 5.9 mm, so this place is known as the "Drought Extremity". Contrarily, some areas in the southeast of China receive an annual precipitation of over 1,600 mm; this number may reach 3,000 in the eastern mountainous areas of Taiwan Province and average 6,000 in Huoshaoliao in the northeast part. The highest volume there comes to 8,408 mm, so it's the reputed "Rain Extremity" of China.

Temperature Zones

There are various other types of climate due to China's vast territory. Temperature zones from south to north appear in this order: tropical zone, subtropical zone, warm temperate zone, temperate zone, and frigid temperate zone, of which the subtropical zone, warm temperate zone and temperate zone account for 70.5 percent. In addition, there is also a special alpine frigid zone dominating the Qinghai-Tibet Plateau. The Leizhou Peninsula, Hainan Province, Taiwan Province, and the southern part of Yunnan Province in the South controlled by high temperature and plentiful rainfall witness no winter. The middle and lower reaches of the Yangtze River valley and the Yellow River valley are endowed with four distinct seasons. Heilongjiang in northeast China is freezing and has abundant snow. The climate of the vast northwestern areas of China features rare precipitation, cold winter, hot summer, and dramatic temperature changes. In southwestern areas, there are continuous high mountains and deep gorges, where, with rising altitude, various climates can be seen from warm and moist to alpine frigidness. Besides, other types of climate, such as alpine climate, plateau climate, basin climate, forest climate, grassland climate and desert climate coexist in China due to the complicated topography and a great disparity in elevation.

Sunlight

China generally lies north of the Tropic of Cancer. In winter, the angle of incidence of sunlight is small; the time span is short; therefore, the heat quantity is low and becomes lower and lower with the increase of latitude. In summer, the sun rays directly shine on the Northern Hemisphere, so the heat quantity is high by and large; moreover, the duration of the sunshine is long.

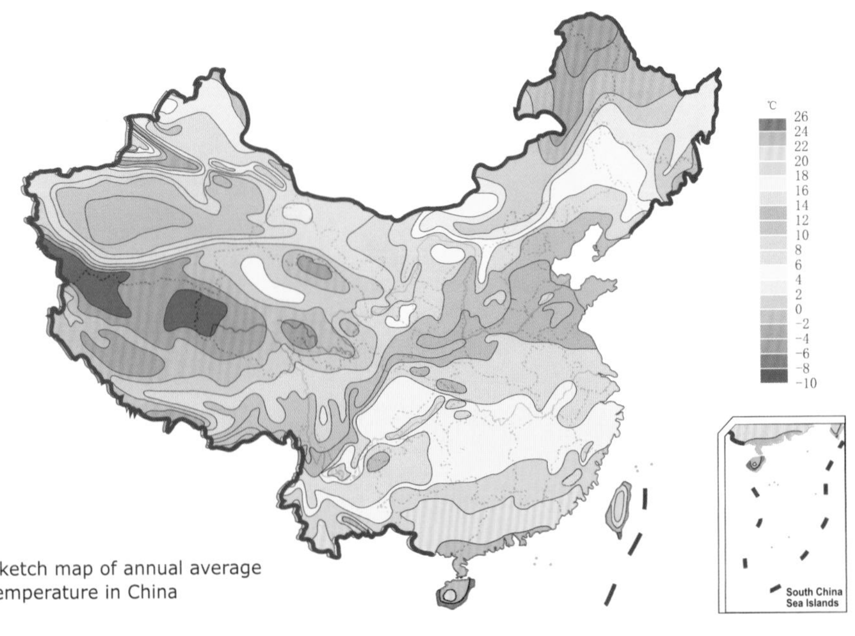

Sketch map of annual average temperature in China

Natural Resources of China

China is one of the biggest possessors of natural resources and in producing resource-consuming products. It has been realizing its economic development goal mainly by relying on the development of its own resources. China feeds 22 percent of the world's population with less than 10 percent of the world's arable land; it supplies 95 percent of the national primary energy needs, 80 percent of industrial raw materials, and over 70 percent of agricultural production materials. In addition, the development and utilization of marine resources is becoming the new growth point of the national economy. But, on the other hand, exploding population, comparative deficiency in resources, and heavy pollution of the environment have become restricting factors for further economic and social development. At present, verified mineral resources account for 12 percent of the world's total, which is next only to the US and Russia. However, the resources per capita represent only 58 percent of the world average, and occupy 53rd place.

Petrochemical enterprises based in Daqing

Mineral Resources

China is rich in mineral resources. To date, geologists have found 171, the reserves of 159 of which have been confirmed, including 10 energy-related minerals, like oil, natural gas, coal, uranium and terrestrial heat etc; 54 metallic minerals, such as iron, manganese, copper, aluminum, lead and zinc; 92 non-metallic minerals, for example, graphite, phosphorus, sulfur and sylvite; and three liquid minerals, such as groundwater, and mineral water. At present, over 92 percent of the primary energy, 80 percent of industrial raw materials, and over 70 percent of agricultural production materials come from these resources.

In 2007, there were 208 large and medium-sized production areas of mineral resources, including 50 of energy-related minerals, 73 of metallic minerals; 82 of non-metallic minerals, and three of liquid minerals. Reserves of 77 have been proved, including 1.21 billion tons of oil, 697.4 billion cubic meters of natural gas and 40.6 billion tons of raw coal.

Metallic Minerals

China has a full variety of metallic minerals that have abundant reserves and are distributed widely; 54 kinds of metallic minerals have proven reserves. Of them, there are 1,834 iron ore mining areas with proven reserves of 46.3 billion tons, ranking fifth in the world; 213 manganese ore mining areas with proven reserves of 566 million tons, ranking third in the world; chromium resources have only total reserves of 10.78 million tons, however; there are totally 357 million tons of titanium in the country's ilmenite ore, ranking first in the world; 25.96 million tons of navajoite, ranking third; 910 copper ore mining areas with total reserves of 62.43 million tons, ranking seventh; over 700 lead-zinc ore mining areas with an estimated 35.72 million tons of lead and 93.84 million tons of zinc, ranking fourth; 310 bauxite mining areas with reserves of 2.27 billion tons, ranking seventh; nearly 100 nickel ore mining areas with reserves of 7.84 million tons, ranking ninth; 150 cobalt ore mining areas with reserves of 470,000 tons; 252 tungsten ore mining areas with reserves of 25.29 million tons, ranking first; 293 tin ore mining areas with reserves of 4.07 million tons, ranking second; 222 molybdenum ore mining areas with reserves of 8.40 million tons, ranking second; 103 hydrargyrum ore mining areas with reserves of 81,400 tons, ranking third; 111 antimony ore mining resources with reserves of 2.78 million tons, ranking first; 35 platinum ore mining resources with reserves of 310 tons; 1,265 gold ore mining resources with reserves of 4,265 tons, ranking seventh; 569 silver ore mining resources with reserves of 116,500 tons, ranking sixth; 13 strontium ore mining resources with reserves of 32.90 million tons, ranking second; more than 60 rare earth resources mining resources with reserves of 90 million tons, ranking first.

Non-Metallic Minerals

China has a full variety of non-metallic minerals, abundant in reserves and distributed widely. There are 92 non-metallic minerals with proven reserves. Of them, there are 27 magnesite mining areas with total proven reserves of 3 billion tons, ranking first; 230 fluorite mining areas with total proven reserves of 108 million tons, ranking third; 327 saggar mining areas with total proven reserves of 2.1 billion tons; over 760 sulfur mining areas with total proven reserves of 1.493 billion tons, ranking second; over 100 mirabilite mining areas with total proven reserves of 10.5 billion tons, ranking first; 103 barite mining areas with total proven reserves of 360 million tons, ranking first; 150 salt mining areas with total proven reserves of 407.5 billion tons; 28 potassium salt mining areas with total proven reserves of 456 million tons; 63 boron mining areas with total proven reserves of 46.7 million tons, ranking fifth; 412 phosphorite mining areas with total proven reserves of 15.2 billion tons, ranking second; 23 diamond mining

China ranks third in the world in the coal ensured reserves.

The Xilingol Grassland in Inner Mongolia Autonomous Region

♦ Inner Mongolia Pasturing Area

The Inner Mongolian Prairie is China's largest pastureland, and the home of Sanhe horses, Sanhe cattle etc. This prairie, with an area of 0.88 billion hectares or 67 percent of the land area of the autonomous region and 22 percent of the nation's total grassland, is one of the best preserved in the world with the most varied types of meadows, and is also an important ecological barrier in the north of China.

A series of measures have been taken by the Inner Mongolia Autonomous Region to preserve and construct grasslands, such as banning grazing, taking land out of circulation through rotational grazing, grassland fencing, and a balanced system of fodder and livestock. In the most recent five years, the ecological environment of the prairie has improved: grassland with lean vegetation has decreased by 50 percent and that with lush vegetation has increased by 56 percent.

♦ Xinjiang Pasturing Area

The Xinjiang pasturing area, with rich types of meadows and an available natural grassland area of 0.48 billion hectares, is one of the five major pastures in China. However, owing to overgrazing and irrational land utilization, by the end of the last century, 80 percent of the grazing land in the region began to retrogress; for nearly one-third, the decline was very serious and the Taklamakan Desert and the surrounding areas of Lake Aibi became a source of sandstorms, imposing great influence on the ecological environment of the northwest and North China.

Since 2003, Xinjiang has implemented a project in 22 counties north and south of the Tianshan Mountain, banning grazing or imposing a rotational grazing system and sealing mountains. To date, the project has converted 310.87 million hectares of grazing land for grassland, with obvious ecological benefits. During the 11th Five-Year Plan (2006-2010), Xinjiang will convert 0.13 billion hectares of grazing land for grassland; newly build 200 million hectares of cultivated fodder land; and protect and improve about 670,000 hectares of natural mowed pasture in order to compensate for the lessened livestock raising capacity.

♦ Qinghai Pasturing Area

Qinghai is one of the five major livestock breeding centers in China. July is the month seeing flocks of sheep and cows

♦ Tibet Pasturing Area

The Tibet Pasturing Area, one of the five major livestock breeding centers in China, has natural grasslands covering over 82 million hectares, roughly 25 percent of the national total; the livestock carrying capacity comes to more than 24 million head. In recent years, with climate warming and the increase of population and the sharp growth of livestock, the contradiction between grass and livestock in Tibet has emerged, and overgrazing has accelerated the degeneration and desertification of Tibet's grasslands. In order to protect the weak grassland resources, Tibet has put into practice the "Natural Grasslands Construction and Preservation Project" since 2001. By now, the desertification and degeneration of Tibet's grasslands has been efficiently halted and the ecological environment has greatly improved.

areas with total proven reserves of 4,179 kg; 91 graphite mining areas with total proven reserves of 173 million tons, ranking first; 31 wollastonite mining areas with total proven reserves of 132 million tons, ranking first; 43 talc mining areas with total proven reserves of 247 million tons, ranking third; 45 asbestos mining areas with total proven reserves of 90.61 million tons, ranking third; 169 mica mining areas with the total proved reserves of 63.1 thousand tons; 169 gypsum mining areas with total proven reserves of 57.6 billion tons; 1,124 cement limestone mining areas with total proven reserves of 48.9 billion tons; 189 glass siliceous raw materials production areas with total proven reserves of 3.8 billion tons; 354 diatomaceous earth mining areas with total proven reserves of 385 million tons, ranking second; 208 kaolin mining areas with total proven reserves of 1.43 billion tons, ranking first; 86 bentonite resource mining areas with total proven reserves of 2.46 billion tons, ranking first; 180 granite mining areas with total proven reserves of 1.7 billion cubic meters; 123 marble mining areas with total proven reserves of 1 billion cubic meters.

Energy Minerals

China is abundant in energy-related minerals covering an extensive variety and having a widespread distribution. They also are a significant part of China's mineral resources. Coal, oil and natural gas respectively account for 93 percent and 95 percent of China's primary energy. There are ten kinds of energy minerals with proven reserves, i.e., coal, oil, natural gas, oil shale, stone coal, uranium, thorium, and terrestrial heat. Of them, there are 5,345 coal mining areas with total reserves of 1.0025 trillion tons, ranking third in the world; 32 oil production areas with total proven reserves of 18.14 billion tons, ranking eleventh; 70 trillion cubic meters of natural gas with 0.7060 trillion exploitable cubic meters, ranking twenty-first. There are widespread terrestrial heat resources, amounting to the energy of 1.3711 trillion tons of coal equivalent within the superficial scope within 2,000 meters of the surface; 64 oil shale mining areas with reserves of 31.5 billion tons; and 93 stone coal mining areas with reserves of 4.256 billion tons.

Grassland Resources

Grasslands in China cover an area of 400 million hectares, or 41.7 percent of national territory, ranking second in the world. Natural grasslands are the main body. Some 84.4 percent of the grasslands are distributed in the west with an area of nearly 331 million hectares.

Now, China has 263.32 million hectares of grazing land of various types suitable for various domestic animals to graze in different seasons.

The area of grazing land accounts for one-fourth of China's total land area, one of the largest in the world. Natural grasslands are mainly distributed in the expanse west and north of the Greater Hingan Mountains-Yinshan Mountain-the eastern foot of the Qinghai-Tibet Plateau line; cultivated grasslands lie mainly in the southeastern areas, interspersed with arable lands and forests.

Forest Resources

The Greater Hinggan Mountains: The biggest and most important pine forest in China. The mountain stretches for 1,400 km and is 300 km wide; 62 percent of the area is covered by forests with a total of 15 million hectares.

The Lesser Hinggan Mountains: having a forest area of 11 million hectares, it is a major provider of timber, producing one-fifth of the country's total.

The Changbaishan Mountains: located in the east of Jilin Province with a forest area of over 10 million hectares. The great variety of flora species makes it a peculiar colorful forest museum, identified by UNESCO as an International Biosphere Protection Zone.

The Xishuangbanna Tropical Forest: lying on the southern tip of Yunnan Province, it is the biggest reserve of natural flora, being the realm of 4,000 higher plants, including 100 rare tree as well as some economic trees, like the rubber tree, oil palm, coconut palm and cinchona.

The Shennongjia Virgin Forest: located in the northwest of Hubei Province with a forest area of 0.5 million hectares. It is well known for its mysterious savages.

The Wuyishan Mountain: lying in the northwest of Fujian Province with the best-preserved primeval forests in southeast China with a forest area of 57,000 hectares.

The Forest of Taiwan: located in the east of Taiwan Province. The large number of camphor trees account for two-thirds of the world's natural camphor production. In addition, red junipers in the A-Lee Mountain are 60 meters tall and 3,000 years old.

Protection Forest System: In order to resist the attack of sandstorms and prevent soil and water loss, China has established many protection forests, such as the Three-North (the west of Northeast China, the north of North China and the northwestern areas) Protection Forest System, the Upper-Middle Yangtze River Protection Forest System, the Coastal Protection Forest System, the Taihangshan Forestation Program, the Plain Greening Project etc. Of them, the Three-North Protection Forest System, claimed as the "world's largest ecological project", aims to set up a 7,000km-long "Green Wall" with a scope of about 260 million hectares, or one-fourth of the continental areas of China.

♦ Natural Forest Conservation Project

The project is to solve the issue of restoration of natural forest resources and realize a harmonious development of ecological construction, economy and society of forest zones thorough banning commercial logging of natural forests of the upper-middle Yangtze River and Yellow River valleys and greatly reducing the output of timber in the key forest zones in Northeast China and Inner Mongolia. In the seven years since the implementation of this project, it has cumulatively completed forestation of bald mountains totaling 4.3282 million hectares, and newly cultivated forest land by sealing mountains of 8.8496 million hectares. The supervision forest area maintains about 90 million hectares per year, and the cumulative volume of timber saved reaches 130.825 million cubic meters (calculated according to 32.054 million cubic meters in 1997, the starting year of the project) and the stock volume of forest saved comes to 252.0713 million hectares. In the influential areas of the project, the forest resources keep increasing, the area of soil and water loss decreasing, along with growing efficiency of ecological management.

♦ Project on Converting Cultivated Land to Forest

The project is to settle the problem of water and soil loss in some key areas by converting cultivated slope land and desertified tillable land back to forest. In the six year since its launching, the project has finished the forestation of 17.342 million hectares, including 7.8345 million hectares of forestland converted from tillable land and 9.5075 million hectares of forestland developed on barren mountains and wasteland. In the project areas, the forest resources grow steadily and the area of the land suffering from soil and water loss has been reduced. The initial effect of control over desertified land has been achieved.

♦ Three-North and Yangtze River Valley Key Forest System Construction Project

This project has the largest coverage among all the protection forest system construction projects, aiming at combating the desertification in the Three-North areas (northeast, North, northwest China) as well as settling various ecological issues in some other areas. Of them, in the four years since the carrying out of the fourth stage, it has constructed an area of 2.715 million hectares and cumulatively completed forestation of 1.5031 million hectares, cultivated forest of 1.2119 million hectares by sealing mountains. The completed portions make up 28.58 percent of the total. Since the implementation of the second phase of the five protection forest projects in the Yangtze River Valley etc, a forested area of 1.2893 million hectares has been established, 20.08 percent of the total in this phase.

♦ Wild Animal and Plant Protection and Natural Reserve Construction Project

This project is mainly to preserve wild animals and plants, diversity among living things, and wetland resources by saving rare species and restoring typical ecological systems. Since the start in 2001, a total of 763 nature reserves have newly been set up, equivalent to 83.9 percent of the total quantity in the past 50 years. The total number now amounts to 1,672 covering 119 million hectares, or 12.4 percent of national territory. These reserves contains 85 percent of China's continental ecological system types, 85 percent of the species of wild animals and plants and 65 percent of higher plant species, effectively protecting the main habitats of over 300 key species of wild animals and the main distribution areas of more than 130 key species of wild plants.

♦ Construction Project of Fast Growing and High Yield Timber Forest Bases

This project is to solve the problem of timber supply, reducing the pressure on the protection and development of forest resources brought about by the demand for timber, and guaranteeing the construction of the other five ecological projects. Since its launch in 2002, the project has newly built or rebuilt 334,500 hectares of fast growing and high yield timber forests, efficiently pushing forward the harmonious development of the forestry industry and some timber-consuming industries like paper-making, easing the contradictions between timber supply and demand and promoting the change from decimating natural forests to cutting down planted forests.

Cultivatable Land

China now has total cultivatable land of 122.5 million hectares, ranking fourth in the world, but representing a per capita figure of only 0.094 hectares. This land is mainly concentrated on the Northeast Plain, the North China Plain, the Middle-Lower Yangtze River Plain, the Pearl River Delta and the Sichuan Basin. The fertile black soil of the Northeast Plain, with an area of more than 350,000 square km, abounds in wheat, corn, sorghum, soybeans, flax and sugar beet. The

The per capita arable land area in China is only 0.094 hectares.

deep brown topsoil of the North China Plain teems with wheat, corn, millet and cotton. The Middle-Lower Yangtze Plain's flat terrain and many lakes and rivers make it especially suitable for the production of paddy rice and freshwater fish, hence its title of "land of fish and rice". This area also produces large quantities of tea and silk. The purplish soil of the warm and humid Sichuan Basin, known as the "land of plenty", is green with crops in all the four seasons, including paddy rice, rape and sugarcane. The Pearl River Delta abounds with paddy rice gathered 2 or 3 times a year.

Wind Power Resources

China is abundant in wind power resources thanks to it vast territory and long coastline. According to an estimate of the Chinese Academy of Meteorological Sciences, the average density of wind power of China is 100W/m^2; the total reserves of wind power are about 3.226 billion kW; the reserves of terrestrial wind power that can be developed and utilized reach 253 million kW (according to the data from instruments 10m above the surface); and that of maritime wind power totals 750 million kW.

China's wind power resources are mainly distributed in the southeast coastal areas as well as the surrounding islands, Xinjiang, Inner Mongolia, Hexi Corridor of Gansu, Northeast China, northwest areas, North China, and Qinghai-Tibet Plateau. Totally there are about 4,000 hours a year when the wind speed exceeds 3 meter/second while in some areas; the speed may surpass 7 meter/second. The value for development and utilization is huge.

Waterpower Resources

The total reserves of China's freshwater resources are 2.8 trillion cubic meters, ranking sixth in the world. However, the resources per capita are only a quarter of the world average, ranking 88th. Moreover, the waterpower resources are unevenly distributed, with those in southeast being much greater than those in the northwest. According to data released by the National Development and Reform Commission, by 2005, there were 3,886 rivers each with theoretical waterpower reserves of over 10 thousand kW and the theoretical electricity contained in these resources amounts to 6.0829 trillion kWh.

There are several distinct characteristics:

First, uneven regional distribution; in general, those in the west are more than in the east and resources are comparatively concentrated in the southwestern areas.

Second, uneven seasonal distribution; the disparity of runoff is great between dry seasons and flood seasons.

Third, the concentration of waterpower resources in big rivers like the Jinshajiang, Yalongjiang, Daduhe and Lancangjiang make centralized development and large-scaled output available.

Marine Resources

China has an abundance of ocean resources: 18,000 km of continental coastal line, over two million square km of continental shelf, over 7,000 islands and about three million square km of maritime area under its jurisdiction. The oceanic area per capita is 0.0027 square km, one-tenth of the world average. China's ratio of ocean to continent is 0.31:1, ranking 108th among the world's coastal countries.

The total number of oceanic species is 20,278, accounting for over 25 percent of the world total, among which 700 can be made into medicine and more than 2,500 are marine animals and fish worth catching, including 84 kinds of cephalopoda, 90 kinds of prawns and 685 kinds of crabs. Moreover there are more than 70 fishing grounds. To date, China has set up 38 commercial maritime oil fields with 900 million tons of crude oil and 250 billion cubic meters of natural gas so far obtained. There are 13 kinds of beach placers with 1.527 billion tons of reserves. The developable coastal tide power is about 21.7931 million kW, generating 62.436 billion kWh of electricity each year; the total

China enjoys rich energy sources and mineral resources.

installed capacity of ocean thermal energy is 13.28 trillion kW; the theoretical power of wave energy is 62.8522 million kW; that of tidal current energy 13.9485 million kW; and ocean salinity energy 125 million kW. China's sea salt production ranks first in the world, accounting for 30 percent of the global total. Thanks to 10 years of efforts, China has successfully determined a 75,000-square km multi-metal nodule mine in the international seabed of the Pacific Ocean, and gained preferential rights to explore this area when the opportunities of commercial mining mature.

Aquatic Products

China has a vast water area and its aquatic products are of great diversity, large quantity and high exploitative value. Roughly, China's aquatic products can be divided into the following five categories: fish, crustaceans, mollusks, algae and mammals, of which fish are most abundant. China has about 2,400 fish species among the world's 3,000 identified kinds, of which marine fish account for three-fifths and the rest are freshwater types. They all feature abundance, fast growing, strong fertility and complementary capacity and wide adaptability, laying strong material foundation for the domestic fishing industry. The total volume of China's aquatic products reached 12.18 million tons in 1990, ranking third in the world. The aquatic resources can be categorized into three parts: marine, offshore and inland aquatic resources.

Marine Aquatic Resources

The production of marine aquatic resources constitutes 57.75 percent of the total aquatic resources, dominated by fish. China has 1,700 species of marine fish, 300 of which are regarded as economic, including 60 to 70 species of high yield. Besides, there are 2,000 species of coastal algae, 300 kinds of shrimps and crabs, and 200 species of economic mollusks. In the sea areas of the Yellow Sea and the Bohai Sea live 250 types of fish, where the fishery output makes up

Bumper fish harvest

27.9 percent of the national total; small yellow croakers, ling, Pacific herring are particularly rich. With over 440 species of fishes, the East China Sea is the largest production area of four types of economic fishes, namely hairtail, large and small yellow croaker and cuttlefish. The fishery output in this area accounts for 51.8 percent of the total. The South China Sea Area is home of nearly one thousand species of fishes, especially tuna, bonito, dorado, shark, sea turtle, hawksbill etc; despite a great variety, the output here, only accounts for 20.3 percent of the national total.

Offshore Aquatic Resources

Because of years of over-fishing, the offshore aquatic resources of China have shown a continuous decline, with shrinking output and smaller fish. In recent years, China has taken a series of measures to increase aquatic resources in the offshore areas of the Baihai Sea, East China Sea and South China Sea, such as releasing fry and laying artificial reefs. Certain effects have been achieved. Currently, China has bred more than 60 species of fish, shrimps, shellfish and algae, including kelp, oyster, pearl oyster, abalone, laver, prawn, sea cucumber, scallop, mullet etc. In 1990, the total aquatic products totaled 1.624 million tons, ranking number one in the world.

Inland Aquatic Resources

China is one of the most advanced countries in inland aquaculture. There are over 800 fishes in the inland water areas, including 40 to 50 species regarded as economic that account for 10 percent of world total fish production. The output of shrimp, crab and shellfish makes up only 3.2 percent of the total production of freshwater fishery. The top-four freshwater fishes are black carp, grass carp, silver carp and bighead carp. The carp, golden carp, bream, blunt-snout bream, marsh shrimp, mitten crab and freshwater mussel are also species of high economic value. Of them, carp account for about 50 percent of the total freshwater fish species in China; silurid fishes and loach fishes for 25 percent; and other freshwater fishes for 25 percent. The northern areas are rich in some cold-resistant species like salmon, grayling, pike, and turbot; the northwestern plateau in drought and saltiness resistant fishes like loach and gymnocypris przewalskii in Qinghaihu Lake; the Yellow River-Yangtze River plain, the center of China's freshwater fishes, in carp; South China as well as southwestern areas in carps, loach, and silurid.

Organisms Resources

With a vast territory and complex geographical conditions, China has a great diversity of organisms, ranking eighth in the world and first in the Northern Hemisphere. According to statistics, the number of the species of higher plants in China reaches 30,000, or 10 percent of the world's total, including 250 gymnosperms; that of vertebrates 6,266, 14 percent of the world total, among which 1,258 are birds and 3,862 fish. Of these species, 667 species of the vertebrates can only be found in China, such as the giant panda, the golden-haired monkey, Yangtze River dolphin, Yangtze alligator and Milu deer. The species of specially-owned higher plants of China are 17,300, such as the Cathay silver fir, golden larch and dove-tree.

Animals

Among those countries with the greatest diversity of wildlife, China has more than 6,266 species of vertebrates, 10 percent of the world total. Among them, 500 are beasts and 1,258 are birds; 320 reptiles; 210 amphibians; and 3,862 fishes. Many species are peculiar to China, including such rare animals as the giant panda, golden-haired monkey, Yangtze River dolphin, white-lipped deer, takin, brown-eared pheasant, Yangtze alligator, red-crowned crane etc; while the red-crowned crane in Northeast China, the golden pheasant in Sichuan, Shaanxi, and Gansu, the blue peacock in Yunnan and Tibet as well as black paradise flycatcher, whooper swan, and antipodes green parrot are also China's rare birds; there are also some rare species of butterflies in Taiwan, Yunnan, Sichuan etc.

The Chinese Government, aware of the important role animals play in the natural environment and national economy, has made a series of laws and regulations to protect animal resources and save those species on the verge of vanishing, severely cracking down illegal hunting and establishing an accepted concept of protecting animals in society.

Plants

China's abundance of plants ranks third in the world, just next to Malaysia and Brazil. There are 3,148 genera and 27,150 species of plants, ranking third, of which 2,411 species can be utilized as economic resources. China's plant species involve almost all the major plants that grow in the northern hemisphere's frigid, temperate and tropical zones, including 32,000 higher plants. Among the 25,000 species of seed plants, over 200 are gymnosperms, accounting for 25 percent in the world; and there are nearly 3,000 genera of angiosperms; more than 7,000 species of woody plants, including 2,800-odd tree species. The metasequoia, gingko, golden larch etc, found only in China, are reputed to be "living fossils" in the world.

Many kinds of cultivated plants plus a variety of original plants gives China its position as one of the most abundant countries in plant resources. From an economic angle, there are about 1,000 timber plants, over 300 amyloid plants, over 600 oil plants, 90-plus vegetable plants, more than 4,000 medicinal plants, 300-odd fruit plants and over 500 fiber plants, as well as some reputed ornamental plants like the plum blossom, orchid, chrysanthemum and peony.

Edible Plants

Edible plants can be divided into those that can be eaten directly and those indirectly, or into seven categories, i.e., amyloid and glucide plants, protein plants, oil plants, vitamin plants, beverage plants, edible perfume and pigment plants, and vegetable feed. Of them, amyloid and glucide plants are the major species of wild plants, including acorn, yam, taro, fern, root of kudzuvine, water chestnut etc; glucide plants include the longan, lychee, persimmon, dates, Grosvenor momordica etc; protein plants include the leaf protein, edible fungus, Chlorella vulgaris, Winged bean, Parkia etc. About 1,000 wild oil plants with over 15 percent of oil, 300 with over 20 percent, and 100 or so that can be eaten, can be found in China, including cleidiocarpon, cucurbita foetialissma, hazelnut etc; fiber plants are mostly wild, like Chinese gooseberry, star fruit, sea buckthorn, hawkthorn, crab apple etc; beverage plants include tea, cocoa, coffee as well as some local ones like white tea, chamomile tea, honeysuckle etc; edible perfume and pigment plants involve traditional edible pigment like Indian madder, safflower, curcuma etc and traditional seasonings, such as Bunge prickly ash, aniseed, Chinese cinnamon etc; and vegetable feed and bait refer to the leaves and seeds of most grasses and legumes, like wild bananas, Broussonetia papyrifera leaves, Quercus aquifolioides etc.

Major Rare Animals

There are 335 species of rare wild animals in the Catalogue of Wild Animals under Special Protection in China released by the State Council in 1989, with 97 under State first-class protection and 238 under second-class protection. Of all the rare species, over 160 are only found in China, such as the panda, golden monkey, takin, white-lipped deer, white-fin dolphin, brown-eared pheasant, black-necked crane, Chinese Alligator, giant salamander and Chinese sturgeon.

Red-crowned Crane

♦ Pandas

The black-and-white panda is a mammal belonging to the bear family, with a Latin name of Ailuropoda melanoleucas. Living in arrow bamboo forests, they mainly eat bamboo leaves, shoots and stems, and occasionally some small animals and birds' eggs. They prefer moderate temperatures. The pandas are by nature solitary animals, with males and females meeting only during the breeding season. Although their hearing and eyesight are poor, their sense of smell is quite good. Despite having huge and clumsy-looking bodies, they are good at climbing and swimming. As a tame animal, with a weak defensive capacity, they are more susceptible to predatory attack from natural enemies. Distributed in the mountain ranges around the Sichuan Basin in central and western China, pandas are only found in China and treated as a national treasure.

As a remaining representative of ancient animals, the panda is the oldest among the present animals, nicknamed as a "living fossil".

In terms of physical appearance, pandas look like bears and cats, but they differ from them. In terms of diet, they used to be carnivores. However, with the changes of the living environment, they became vegetarians almost completely dependent on bamboo. As ancient and rare species, the panda is of significant value in scientific research.

Giant pandas in Wolong, southwestern China's Sichuan

♦ Protection of the Pandas

The panda is under State first-class protection in China as an endangered species. The government attaches great importance to its protection. As early as 1962, the State Council issued a circular ordering protection of wild animals. Today, 32 nature reserves have been set up mainly to protect pandas in Sichuan Province, Gansu Province and Shaanxi Province. The total area is 10,550 square km, occupying 81.2 percent of the total distribution area. After 1992, no migration into the nature reserves has been allowed while any local residents from former times have been moved out. In 1998, the Central Government adopted laws to forbid the felling of natural forest. And no individuals are allowed to possess guns. To some extent, these measures have effectively protected pandas and their habitations and reduced the damage caused by humankind. In 1961, the World Wide Fund For Nature adopted the panda as the symbol on its flag and badge.

♦ Tibetan Antelopes

Tibetan antelope, Bovidae Pantholops hodgsoni, are distributed in China's Qinghai Province, Tibet Autonomous Region and Xinjiang Uygur Autonomous Region They are unique to Qinghai-Tibet Plateau and enjoy State first-class protection. Trade in them is banned under the International Trade of Endangered Species (CITES). Adults have a body length of 135centimetres, shoulder height 80 centimeters, body weight 45-60 kilograms, a healthy and strong body; the fore-part of their heads has a broad and long pattern with thickset lips. For males, the horns are long and straight with glossy color, but females have no horns. Other features are broad noses with slight bulge, short tails, rich and thick fur covering the whole body except the lower part of limbs and tails in light brown color. They roam freely over the vast Qinghai-Tibet Plateau covering 880,000 square km at an elevation of 4,000 to 5,300 meters, and deserts, ice-source areas of frozen soil, lakes and swamps, such as Wutang in northern Tibet, Qinghai Hox Hil and Xinjiang Aerjinshan Mountain, a desolate no-man's land. Tibetan antelopes are the most outstanding among artiodactyls, with pretty body, aggressive character, agile movements, great resistance to high altitudes with low oxygen and frigid cold.

Medicinal Plants

The medicinal plants in China fall into medicinal herbs and pesticidal plants, of which the former have over 5,000 species, including 400 common ones, like ginseng, eucommia, Chinese goldthread, liquorice etc, some of which have been cultivated and made into medicine; the latter include nearly 500 species like pyrethrum, Millettia pachycarpa Benth, derris etc. In addition, phytohormone like Cyanotis arachnoides P.E can be used as pesticide.

Plants of Industrial Utilization

Plants of industrial utilization fall into seven categories: timber, fiber, tan, essential oil, ester gum, industrial grease and vegetable dye. Forests in China are deficient and unevenly distributed so timber resources are also lacking. From now, China will make efforts in developing some fine fast-growing tree species like the paulownia, fir and poplar. China now has 190 major species of fiber plants, such as the stems and leaves of monocotyledon plants like gramineae, freesia, the cattail family, agavaceae, palm family, and the roots, stems, bark, plumule of fruits of the elm, mulberry, nettle, ceiba etc. These materials can be used in the textile, paper-making and weaving industry. Larch, spruce and hemlock etc, all contain rich tannin sources used as tanning agents or in medicine. Essential oil plants are the major sources of perfume and essences. There are over 60 such species among China's seed plants, such as the Litsea pungens Hemsl, camphor tree, citronella, vanilla etc. Vegetable gum resources indicate the plants rich in rubber, ebonite, resin, water soluble polysaccharide etc. Those forming important raw materials in the rubber industry include pinaceae plants, the bean family, Cyamopsis tetragonoloba, acacia farnesiana etc. There are about 300 industrial grease plants with grease content over 20 percent, industrial grease trees accounting for more than 50 percent, such as the tung tree, sumach, tallow tree etc. Tung oil and raw lacquer are both China's traditional exports. Industrial vegetable dyes include morin, hematoxylin, and curcuma etc.

Traditional chinese medicinal materials

Environment Protecting Plants

Environment protecting and improving plants refer to wind proofing and sand-shifting control plants, those maintaining water and soil and greening barren mountains, those efficient in nitrogen fixation and soil improvement, those greening and beautifying and protecting the environment, and those supervising and resisting pollution. Of them, wind proofing and sand-shifting control plants include the horsetail beefwood, cord grass, and eucalyptus of various kinds; those maintaining water and soil and greening barren mountains include hedge acacia, cassia, rain tree, butter tree as well as woody oleiferous plants; those efficient in nitrogen fixation and soil improvement involve the alder, iodine weed, purple common perilla, sesbania, milkvetch, azolla etc; those greening and beautifying and protecting environment include turf, roadside trees, ornamental flowers, potted landscape etc; those supervising and resisting pollution include the iodine weed, water hyacinth etc. Besides what is mentioned above, forests play a very important role in purging environment and algae also has the effect of purifying water.

Germplasm Resources

China boasts 27,000 species of higher plants, most of which are beneficial to humankind. Various beneficial plants belong to different families, genera, and species; usually there are a large amount of closely related ones, among which cross breeding may be conducted and new quality offspring may appear. Variations may also occur among those plants having been cultivated for long and then they take on various germplasm characteristics. In recent years, owing to the damage caused by the irrational development of natural vegetation and severe pollution in some areas, some species of plants have been on the verge of disappearing while the loss of germplasm is irreversible. Therefore it's a priority to establish the germplasm storage of beneficial plants.

Vast stretch of forest in the Greater Hinggan Mountains in autumn

History

Concise History of China

China, with a documented history in ancient writings of nearly 4,000 years, is among the four great ancient civilizations. A fossil anthropoid, known as "Yuanmou Man", unearthed in northern Yunnan Province proves there were human beings living in the land as long ago as 1.7 million years. Surviving through the long primitive society and slave society, China entered a feudal society mode in about the fifth century BC. The slave society endured from the founding of the Xia Dynasty in the 21st century BC, through the Shang Dynasty and the Western Zhou Dynasty, to the final stages of the Spring and Autumn Period. Starting from 475 BC, during the Warring States Period, a feudal society evolved that lasted through the Qin, Western Han, Eastern Han, Three Kingdoms, Western and Eastern Jin, Sui, Tang, Five Dynasties, Song, Liao, Jin, Yuan and Ming until the early stages of the final Qing Dynasty. The Opium War in 1840 launched an era in which the imperialist powers encroached on Chinese territory and the country declined into a semi-feudal and semi-colonial society. The Revolution of 1911 toppled the feudal autocratic monarchy that had lasted for over 2,000 years, but the country still remained in a semi-feudal and semi-colonial state. In 1919, the May 4th Movement marked the commencement of the New Democratic Revolution, which, after 28 years' struggle led by the CPC, founded in 1921, at last gained victory. On October 1, 1949, the People's Republic of China was founded.

Prehistoric World and Slave Society (1.7 million years ago-476 BC)

• Peking Man

In 1927, anthropoid fossils and the relics of anthropoid activities were found in Longgushan, Zhoukoudian of Beijing. After many large-scale excavations, partial craniums, lower jaws, teeth and limb bones were discovered. Compared with Lantian Man, the physique of Peking Man had evolved: the thickness of the skull became thinner and the brain volume increased, more approximate to the average level of modern man. Moreover, his forehead protruded a little; the eye ridge was smaller; the mouth retracted a bit; and the occiput was narrow and long. But, judging from the skulls, the primitive features were still manifest. The stature of men averaged 1.62 meters and that of women 1.52 meters, a little lower than modern times. In the caves they once lived in were found a large amount of chipped stone implements and stone chips, dozens of animal fossils, charcoal, and ashes. Tests showed Peking Man dated back 700,000 years ago.

The land of China witnessed the earliest vestiges of human civilization in the world. China's earliest primitive human discovered so far is known as "Yuanmou Man", a fossil anthropoid unearthed in Yuanmou in Yunnan Province, who lived approximately 1.7 million years ago. The "Peking Man", discovered in the Zhoukoudian area in the suburbs of present-day Beijing, lived about 700,000 years ago. Peking Man was able to walk upright, make and use simple tools, and knew how to make fire. By the Neolithic Age, about 10,000 years ago, people had begun cultivating rice and millet with farming tools, as revealed by the relics found in the ruins of Hemudu in Yuyao, Zhejiang Province, and Banpo, near Xi'an City.

Imperial rule began with the Xia Dynasty in 2070 BC. The center of Xia lay in the western areas of present-day Henan Province and the southern areas of present-day Shanxi Province with a sphere of influence that even reached the northern and southern areas of the Yellow River. It was in this period that a slave society came into being, which was further developed during the ensuing Shang and Western Zhou (11th century -771 BC) dynasties. Then followed the Spring and Autumn (770-476 BC) and Warring States (475-221 BC) periods, acknowledged as the transitional stage from a slave to feudal society, when the royal power declined.

About 5,000 years ago, Chinese knew copper-smelting techniques; and 3,000 years ago, in the Shang Dynasty, ironware was used. Besides, there appeared white pottery and painted pottery; the textile industry was also advanced, including the appearance of the earliest jacquard weaving techniques in the world. By the Spring and Autumn Period, the steel-making technique had been mastered. This era also saw the emergence of a "hundred schools of thought", which produced a galaxy of great philosophers such as Lao Tzu, Confucius, Mencius and the military strategist Sun Wu, all of whom had significant and far-reaching influence on later ages.

Discovery of the black pottery ware with pig patterns of the Hemudu Culture in the lower reaches of the Yangtze River is of great importance for the archaeological work on the New Stone Age.

Xia Dynasty (2070-1600 BC)

As the first slave dynasty in Chinese history, the Xia Dynasty (2070-1600 BC) was said to have begun with the reign of Qi, the son of the Great Yu. With its capital located in Anyi (north of Xia County in mid-west Shanxi Province), the Xia was ruled by the descendants of the Xiahou tribe. Altogether, there were 16 kings in 13 generations.

Formed on an alliance of closely-related tribes led by the Xiahou, the Xia Dynasty carried out a system of hereditary monarchy and aristocracy. Noble organizations at different levels kept their original consanguinity and were strictly restricted to different surnames. The king of the Xia practiced enfeoffment of his lords. With patriarchy as the core of the social system, the nobles were divided into different levels according to positions in the family hierarchy and the degrees of kinship between clans.

The Xia established its own army and penal code Yu Xing. The Xia also created China's first calendar to number the years and days by the Heavenly Stems and Earthly Branches. At that time, people had been able to determine months according to the directions in which the Big Dipper pointed. *Xia Xiao Zheng* , kept in the *Elder Dai' Book of Rites*, is an important extant document regarding the Xia calendar, which records the movements of the sun, moon and stars and the weather in line with the 12 lunar months of a year and also the seasonable farming and political affairs. This document, to a certain extent, reflects the development of agriculture in Xia, leaving an invaluable record of the earliest scientific knowledge in ancient China.

Shang Dynasty (1600-1046 BC)

The Shang Dynasty (1600 -1046 BC) was the second slave dynasty in Chinese history. With its first capital established in Bo, the Shang moved its center of activities several times, finally settling in Yin (present-day Xiaotun in Anyang County, Henan Province) under the kingship of Pan Geng. The Shang Dynasty is also called the Yin Dynasty, consisting of 31 kings in 17 generations.

The Shang basically followed the system of hereditary monarchy with the younger brother succeeding the elder one at first, and gradually developing into the lineal eldest-son succession system in the later period. This laid an important foundation for the patriarchal clan system adopted by the following Zhou Dynasty. The Shang is famous for its augury and the existing Jiaguwen (inscriptions on animal bones and tortoise shells) is a witness to this. The rule of the kings of Shang was limited to a small central area, with surrounding areas belonging to princes of the royal family and other tribes. At that time, the centralization of state power had not yet been developed.

The Shang Dynasty inherited the tradition of astronomical phenomena observation. Many inscriptions on animal bones and tortoise shells discovered in Yin ruins record astronomical phenomena, including the description of the solar and lunar eclipses, stars, and the earliest record of new stars in the world. Based on the Xia calendar, the Shang used a lunar calendar that was combined with the solar year through the addition of an intercalary month once every few years to make up the difference between a year of 12 lunar months and a solar year. The number of days in a month was fixed at 30 for a long month and 29 for a short one. The intercalary month was added at the end of the year as the 13th month. This is the origin of an intercalary month in Chinese history, which laid down the foundation for the traditional Chinese calendar.

Yin Ruins: the site of the capital city of the late Shang Dynasty

Sets of musical instruments have been unearthed in Yin ruins, including pottery Xun (an egg-shaped wind instrument), stone Qing (chime stone), copper bell, copper cymbals and drum etc. One big stone Qing with an embossment of a staring tiger was discovered in a tomb in Wuguan Village in Anyang. It is the earliest large musical instrument found to date and also a piece of sculpture with high artistic value.

• Yin Ruins

The ruins of Yin are located beside the Yellow River in the northwest suburbs of Anyang city in Henan Province. It was the site of the capital city of the late Shang Dynasty, which controlled China from the end of the 14th to the 11th century BC - that is to say, from the time Pan Geng moved the capital to Yin until the immoral King Zhou was overthrown, Yin had remained as the Shang Dynasty's political, economic and cultural center. The discovery of this site came about because oracle bones were unearthed, and then stolen, at the beginning of 20th century. Excavation started to be carried out in 1928. The discovery and excavation of Yin ruins was ranked first in China's selection of 100 most important archaeological discoveries in the 20th century. In 1961 it became a key national cultural relic site under State protection. The Yin Ruins Museum was built in 1987. On July 13, 2006, the Yin ruins were added to UNESCO's World Heritage List.

The currently verified ruins covers an area of 24 square km, with a length of 10km from east to west and a width of 6.4 km from south to north. Since many ruins and tombs are concentrated in the site, most of the unearthed bronze ware and oracle bones of the Shang Dynasty were found here. Up to now, more than 5,000 different characters have been excavated from this site, including some 1,700 that are recognizable. It is the facts recorded by the oracle bone inscriptions that enabled China's written history to be pushed back to the Shang Dynasty. In addition, modern Chinese characters evolved from the oracle inscriptions. And the research on inscriptions on bones and tortoise shells has led to the birth of a new branch of knowledge. Besides, the Simuwu Tripod, which was unearthed in the east of the royal tomb area, is the most important bronze ware ever found in the world.

Oracle Bone Inscription of the Shang Dyanasty excavated from the Yin Ruins.

Western Zhou Dynasty (1046-771 BC)

This was a dynasty following the Shang Dynasty. Historically, the Zhou Dynasty is divided into Western (1046-771 BC) and Eastern (770-256 BC) Dynasties (see the Spring and Autumn Period).

Zhou was originally a dependent state of the Shang Dynasty. Zhou grew strong and extended its power during the reign of King Wen and King Wu. King Wu staged an attack at Muye to topple the Shang Dynasty and establish the Zhou Dynasty, which is known as the Western Zhou in Chinese history. Agriculture, economy, religion, education and arts continued to prosper in the period of the Zhou, especially rites, which not only inherited those of the Shang but also added new innovations. In the early Zhou, to put an end to the popular extravagant practices of the late Shang, the ruler prohibited people from excessive drinking, which can be seen from Shang Shu-Imperial Mandate on Wine to the inscriptions on the Da Yu Ding. In addition, many wine vessels popular in the Shang Dynasty vanished during the Western Zhou. The oracle-bone divination method continued to prevail; unearthed oracle bones are similar to those of the Shang in shape and material. So, it's obvious that certain links exist between the divination methods in the Shang and Western Zhou.

In the final stages of the Western Zhou, the intensification of internal contradictions and the contention for land and political power within the ruling class speeded dynastic collapse. Uprisings shook the ruling class to its very foundations. In 771 BC, King You was killed by the Quan Rong tribe, bringing about the fall of the Western Zhou Dynasty.

• Knife Money of the Qi State

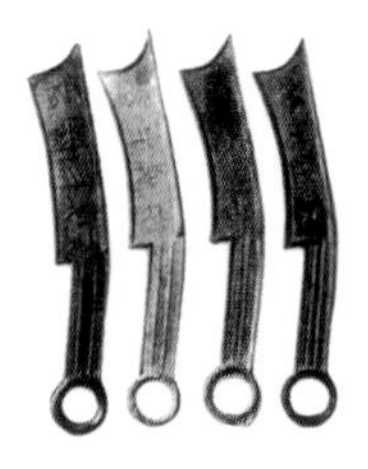

During the Shang and Zhou Dynasties, people mainly used seashell as the intermedia of trade, in addition with metal tools such as knife, shovel and plough as well as jade pieces and rings. In the late Western Zhou Dynasty (1046-771 BC), due to constant development of trade, these intermedias failed to meet the needs of the growing business situation. Hence, financial currency came into being. In the Eastern Zhou Dynasty (770-256 BC), the social economy prospered unprecedentedly. Various mental currencies emerged in succession, of which the knife money prevalent in the Kingdoms of Qi and Yan were of a relatively important kind.

Sun Wu

Sun Wu (535 BC- ?) was an outstanding military strategist and theorist in the Spring and Autumn Period and was addressed respectfully as Sun Zi or Sun Wu Zi later. His book, *The Art of War*, made an in-depth analysis of the waging of war. For the first time, the issues regarding the overall situation of war were elaborated in a book on military theory. More importantly, this book revealed a universal principle for war, that is, knowing oneself and knowing the enemy is the key to winning all battles. In addition, there are many other ideas still valuable today. As a great writing on military strategy, it has exerted wide and deep influence on later generations.

Spring and Autumn Period (770-476 BC)

The Spring and Autumn Period was a transitional time full of turbulence in Chinese history, with the decline of the patriarchal clan system, enfeoffment system and traditional cultural pattern of the Western Zhou, as well as the gestation of a new social system.

During this period, vassal states no longer obeyed orders from the king of Zhou and fought with each other for their own interests. Some powerful states united with other vassal lords by invoking the slogan "loyalty to the King of Zhou" and fought against the anti-Zhou states and others. During the annexation of the vassal states, Duke Huan of the Qi, Duke Wen of the Jin, Duke Mu of the Qin, Duke Xiang of the Song and Duke Chu of the Zhuang, known as the Five Overlords of the Spring and Autumn Period, in turn emerged to hold supreme state power.

From the social structure to the political system, great changes took place during the late Spring and Autumn Period. The cultural and educational systems were no exceptions. At that time persistent social upheavals gradually broke the monopoly of culture and literature held by members of the nobility. To educate and foster more scholars and officials, private schools became a trend. This led to the emergence of Confucius, who created the Confucian school by refining various literary materials in history.

The animal-head-shaped pottery, of the Spring and Autumn Period (770-476 BC)

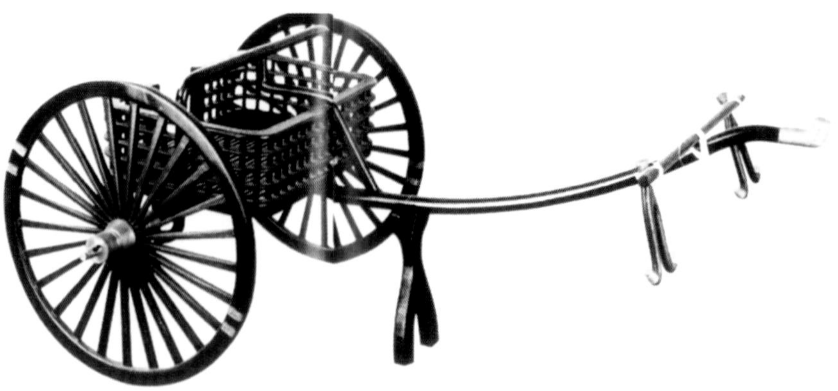

Chariot During the Spring and Autumn Period (770-476 BC)

Warring States Period (475-221 BC)

With the destruction of old traditions and systems and the establishment of new ones, the Warring States Period (475-221 BC) saw greater and sharper social changes than the previous time. In the domain of philosophy there emerged an unprecedented hundred schools of thought. All statesmen noticed these changes and took the initiative to carry out political reforms and expand their power. The historical trend of unification of the country became increasingly visible.

After years of annexation among the vassal states, only seven powerful states, namely Qi, Chu, Yan, Han, Zhao, Wei and Qin, were left. By the year of 221 BC, Qin finally ended the turbulent era and conquered the other six powerful states one by one to establish national unity.

Agriculture, industry and economy developed during the Warring States Period. The increasing popularity of iron tools marked a revolutionary innovation in production and the development of social productive forces.

Book cover of the *Spring and Autumn Annals*

Contention of a Hundred Schools of Thought

This emerged during the Spring and Autumn Period (770-476 BC) and the Period of Warring States (475-221 BC), an era of great cultural and intellectual expansion.

This was a time of turbulence and transition in ancient China. The radical social transformation brought changes into the relations between vassal states. Representative figures from different social classes emerged and voiced their opinions on the social realities. Hence, the situation of "hundred schools of thought contending" emerged as the times demanded. Of all the schools of thought, the most influential ones included Confucianism, Mohism, Taoism and Legalism; but, there were other schools like Yin-Yang, Eclectics, Logicians, Coalition persuaders, Militarism etc. Among these schools, there were politicians, philosophers, sophists and special scholars. Some of them publicized their doctrines so as to serve State rulers, such as those of Confucianism, Legalism and Mohism; some just wanted to express their ideas on politics and society, such as Laozi and Zhuang Zi of Taoism. This period was an unprecedented era of cultural prosperity in Chinese history, equal to the golden age of Greek philosophy. The culture and thought in this period laid a solid cultural foundation for the following feudal era, exerting deep influences on Chinese ancient culture.

♦ Confucianism (Confucian School)

As one of the most important schools of thought in the Spring and Autumn Period and Warring States Period, Confucianism or the Confucian School referred to the masters of various ceremonies like a wedding ceremony, a funeral etc in the early days and developed into a system of ideology with the core of humanity or benevolence later. Confucianism, a mainstream school of thought in ancient China, always took the leading role in China's feudal society since the Han Dynasty. Even today, it still works as the foundation of mainstream thought among Chinese people. Confucianism produced a far-reaching impact on China, East Asia and even the whole world.

Confucius(551-479 BC) was the founder of Confucian School. Among his theories, benevolence was considered as the cornerstone, while propriety was just the norm of institutions and behavior that embodied benevolence. Mencius (372-289 BC) was a representative of the Confucian School in the middle phase of the Warring States Period. He repeatedly promoted the policy of benevolence, treating the people as more important than the rulers. Xunzi (313-238 BC), another representative of the Confucian School, advocated the policy of making a country rich and building up its military power. He was a great publicist for the state of Qin.

Confucius (Kong Zi)

Confucius (551-479 BC) or Kong Zi, lived in Zouyi of Lu State (present Qufu City in Shandong Province) during the later part of the Spring and Autumn Period. His surname is Kong, his given name Qiu, and his social name Zhongni. Confucius was a thinker, political figure, educator, and founder of the Confucian School. His thoughts have exerted huge influence on culture, psychology, ethical codes etc of the Chinese nation. In the wider world, Confucius is also treated as an influential thinker.

Confucius spent half of his life doing teaching. During the period, he created teaching methods which proved to be effective. Based on this, he created a whole set of educational system. Moreover, he set forth a whole series of educational thinking which came down history. He was a good example for others to emulate. The statement he made during his life was gathered and compiled into a book titled *Lunyu* (*The Analects of Confucius*) by his disciples.

It was said that he had over 3000 students, of which there were 72 talents. Among those, many did a lot of success. He played an important role to politics then, especially for the spread of Confucian thought and the formation and development of Confucianism.

Picture of Confucius giving lecture

• Mencius (Meng Zi)

Mencius (Meng Zi) (372-289 BC), named Ke, was a noted thinker in the Chinese history and a representative figure of the Confucian school during the Warring States Period. One of his teachers was Zi Si, grandchild of the Confucian school. Inheriting the doctrine of Confucianism, Mencius brought it to great heights of development. Mencius finally became a Confucian master next only to Confucius. In the Chinese history, the two great men were mentioned together as Con-Men. Mencius taught at home and announced "a man of noble character has three happy things", and one of them "is to have the talents of the world educated". During his lifetime, he visited various states. Later Mencius visited all the different states. As monarchs attached importance to political tactics, it was very hard for his doctrines to be accepted by them.

♦ Taoism (Taoist School)

As one of the most important schools of thought in the Spring and Autumn Period and Warring States Period, Taoism focused on the Chinese character "Dao" (Tao, or the Way). According to Taoism, Dao is the origin of the universe, the basis of all existing things, the law governing their development and change. This sparked much debate on metaphysics in China, and made a prominent contribution to Chinese culture.

The Taoist School was founded by Lao Zi (Lao Tzu). The most important pre-Han Taoist text was Lao Zi (Lao Tzu), also known as *Tao Te Ching (Classic of the Way and Its Power)*, which put forward a dialectical view: Good fortune follows upon disaster; Disaster lurks within good fortune. Nature should be allowed to take its own course without human interference. He also advocated the ideal small realm with a small population.

Zhuang Zhou, or Zhuang zi (Zhuangtse), was a Taoist representative in the Warring States Period. His magnum opus is Zhuang zi (Zhuangtse), in which he named the Tao as the origin of the universe. He believed that all things were in a state of constant change and there was no rule of right and wrong. In his mind, life was but a dream and only the perishing of all could lead to final peace for society.

In Chinese history, Taoism as a school of thought evolved into a religious culture not long after its birth. However, it permeated every aspect of society. Taoism has also spread widely in the West and had impacts on both Arthur Schopenhauer's voluntarism and pessimism doctrine and Martin Heidegger's existentialism to some extent. In addition, the simplicity and truth and non-action advocated by Taoism have also been accepted by many people in the West.

Philosophical Taoism (Daojia) and Religious Taoism (Daojiao)

Philosophical Taoism (Daojia) refers to a school of thought in Chinese philosophy; Daojiao, however, refers to Taoism as a religion. The former can be traced back to the period of pre-Qin Dynasty (4000-221 BC). In the Eastern Han Dynasty (25-220) it began to have relationships with deity worship. The core of Taoism is Tao or the Way, which was inherited in an innovative way by Taoists. Laozi, the founder of Daojia, was worshipped as Tai Shang Lao Jun – the deity and ancestor of Daojiao. Meanwhile, *Dao De Jing (Tao Te Ching)* and *Zhuang Zi (Zhuangtse)*, the classics of Daojia, formed the principal and most important canon of Daojiao.

Taoism is an indigenous traditional religion of China, with the highest ideal of gaining immortality. Taoists believe in both Tao as well as in deities and immortals, by which they have influence on their followers. To achieve the goal, one must practice Taoism both inside and outside one's physical existence, in other words, one must cultivate the self both spiritually and physically and do good deeds to acquire more virtue. In this way, one could enter the world of immortals and escape death.

Lao Zi

Lao Zi (Lao Tzu) (570-470 BC), with the surname of Lee and the given name of Er, was also called Bo Yang. He was believed to live in the Spring and Autumn Period, and was a founder of Taoism. In Daoism Lao Zi is held as the Most Exalted Lord Lao. He advocated "govern by doing nothing that is against nature." He was said to have created the book *Lao Zi* which is also called *Tao Te Ching* (*Classic of the Way and Its Power*). The book shows the height of the Chinese philosophy formed during the Spring and Autumn Period. Lao Zi, also a naturist who held that Man should follow the force of the nature, advocated a society of a small country with a small population and no communications with neighboring countries. He was very much concerned with efforts to cope with and eliminate social conflicts. He thought Man's behavior came from the natural nature and spontaneous nature of Tao; and the political power should not interfere with the life of the populace.

Portrait of Lao Zi

Zhuang Zi

Zhuang Zi (Zhuangtse) (369-286 BC), with the given name of Zhuang Zhou, was another representative of Taoist school of thought after Lao Zi, as well as an excellent litterateur and philosopher. He inherited and carried forward Lao Zi's thought.

Both Lao Zi and Zhuang Zi stood for "govern by doing nothing that is against nature" and a small country with a small population. He proposed the all-in-one idea, and believed that everything in the universe originates from the same thing, and it is an integral whole in various forms. He was in the belief that one should not pursue official posts and benefits, a philosophy and value which modern intellectuals may follow.

Zhuang Zi (Zhuangtse) is his major works, which include *Neipian* (inner section), *Waipian* (outer section) and *Zapian* (mixed section). It is generally believed that *Neipian* was written by Zhuang Zi himself, but other two were mostly done by his pupils and his other followers.

♦ Mohist School

The Mohist School was one of the most important of the schools of thoughts involved in the contention of hundred of schools of thoughts. It was founded by Mozi (468-376BC), whose propositions diametrically opposed those of Confucianism. Master Mo proposed esteeming talent and he objected to hereditary official titles. He called for a smashing of the old hierarchical concepts although through peaceful means. He brought about the concept of "universal love" encompassing all human beings in equal degree. Certainly, this was just a fantasy.

♦ Legalist School

As one of the most important schools of thought in the Spring and Autumn Period and Warring States Period, Legalism advocates governing the state by law and abolishing the hereditary system. Earlier legalists were Li Kui, Wu Qi, Shang Yang and Shen Buhai. Later, Han Fei became the great integrator of absolutism and centralization of State power.

Han Fei (280-233 BC) was born in a rich family in the state of Han. In *Han Fei Zi*, a book he wrote after synthesizing the thoughts of earlier legalists, he put forward a theory on rule by law integrating law, strategies and power. Of them, law was the basis, strategies were the means to an end in political struggle and power was the strength and high position. Only by gaining command of all three could a ruler establish a powerful centralized country. Han Fei's theory was applied by Qin and also became official learning in the Qin Dynasty, playing an important role in unification of China by Emperor Qin Shihuang.

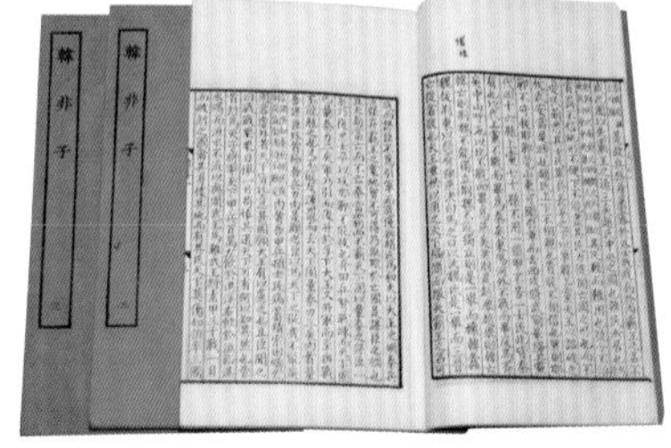

Book cover of the *Han Fei Zi*

Qin Dynasty (221-206 BC)

The Qin Dynasty enjoyed a short life of only 15 years after the First Emperor Qin Shihuang finally unified China in 221 BC, only for the dynasty to be subverted in 206 BC.

After the unification of China, Emperor Qin Shihuang set up a tyrannical centralized system of rule. He abandoned the enfeoffment inherited from old. Acting on the advice of Li Si, the Prime Minister, he adopted a system of prefectures and counties, making the nomination of local officials a right held by the Central Government. At first, there were 36 prefectures, later increased to 46. Taking three councilors and nine heads as the core, the central political system systemized and synthesized the bureaucratic establishments of the Warring States Period. Officeholders would be checked by reports on their annual work. In addition, the Qin Dynasty also standardized the language and written characters, furthering enhancing the development of a national culture and economy; with the purpose of resisting the Hun, the dynasty built the world famous Great Wall based on the city walls of Qin, Yan, and Zhao. This lies further north than the existing Ming Great Wall and is longer in length.

The ruin of the Qin Dynasty was mainly due to its cruel legalist rule. It quickly collapsed under the weight of peasant uprisings.

The Qin Dynasty (221-206 BC) was the first completely unified, multi-ethnic and centralized feudal system established by Emperor Qin Shihuang. He unified characters, weights and measures and currency, and established the system of prefectures and counties. Qin half-liang coin: Its shape was adopted until the 20th century.

Terracotta Warriors and Horses of the Qin Dynasty (221-206 BC)

Burning Books and Burying Confucian Scholars Alive

The event of burning books and burying Confucian scholars alive took place in the Qin Dynasty. In 213 BC, a high-level minister Chun Yuyue opposed the system of prefectures and counties and suggested giving feudal titles and land etc to the descendants of the nobility according to ancient system. Prime Minister Li Si strongly refuted the argument, and at the same time, insisted that Confucian scholars

Emperor Qin Shihuang (259-210 BC)

In 221 BC, Emperor Qin Shihuang ended the Warring States Period that had lasted for over 250 years and established the first unified and centralized multi-ethnic feudal state in Chinese history, namely the Qin Empire. He also unified the characters of the written language, the system of measures and weights, and the currency, and initiated the system of prefectures and counties. The framework of the feudal country he established lasted for over 2,000 years. In just a dozen or so years, he organized more than 300,000 people to build the 5,000km-long Great Wall in the north. Emperor Shihuang even began to build his own grandiose mausoleum while still alive. In 1974, the discovery of terracotta warriors and horses that had guarded the Mausoleum of Qin Shihuang for two millennia stunned the world. Some 8,000 vivid and life-sized terracotta warriors, horses and chariots have been uncovered, which some call the eighth wonder of the ancient world.

be forbidden to censure current affairs using ancient standards and rebuke politics with their private learning. Adopting the advice of Li Si, Emperor Qin Shihuang ordered the burning of the historical records of other states except those of Qin, as well as the *Book of Songs* and Shang Shu etc, which were privately owned and did not belong to the imperial library. Anyone who dared to talk about the *Book of Songs* and *Shang Shu* would be beheaded; and whoever praised the past and denounced the existing policies, would be killed together with all his family members. Private learning was banned and the only way to learn the laws and regulations was study with authorized officials. These measures invited great scholarly discontent. The next year, many alchemists and Confucian scholars started to condemn the emperor. As a result, over 460 of them were buried alive following an investigation by the Emperor.

Bronze Chariot and Horses unearthed from the Mausoleum of Emperor Qin Shihuang

Qin Great Wall

After Emperor Qin Shihuang unified China, he sent forces led by General Meng Tian to suppress the Hun and recaptured much land. In order to guard against further Hun attacks, Meng Tian led soldiers to build the world-renowned Great Wall.

In the Warring States Period (475-221 BC), many states built imposing city walls as their main fortifications. The states of Qin, Zhao and Yan all built long sections of wall to resist Hun invasion. But it was only in the Qin Dynasty that Meng Tian connected the separate walls to form a unified defensive system on the northern border. It took about nine years to finish the wall, stretching from Lintao (in the eastern part of today's Gansu Province) in the west to Liaodong (in today's Jilin Province) in the east.

Further construction and extensions were made in many successive dynasties. In terms of both length and quality, the later Great Wall was better than that originally made in Qin. The Ming Dynasty attached most importance to renovating the Great Wall, which, with a total length of 6,300 km, started from Jiayuguan Pass in today's Gansu Province in the west and finished in Yalujiang River in the northeast. Its height varied from five to ten meters and watch houses were built every 130 meters. Many beacon towers were constructed as well, so that, if invasion threatened, hay blended with wolf feces would be burned in the daytime, creating a huge plume of smoke that rose high in the air. At night, firewood combined with sulfur would create a blaze that could be seen many miles away and the warning passed on down the chain.

We can see the remains of the Qin Wall today, such as the purple wall known as Purple Pass near Datong in Shanxi Province and again some ten kilometers west of Minxian County in Gansu Province. The famous Badaling section of the wall in Beijing that we see today was built in the Ming Dynasty.

Han Dynasty (206 BC-220 AD)

The Han Dynasty (206 BC-220 AD) is divided into two historical periods: Western Han (206 BC-25 AD) and Eastern Han (25-220) dynasties.

In 206 BC, Liu Bang established the powerful Han Dynasty (Western Han). During it, agriculture, handicrafts and commerce all flourished, and the population reached 50 million. During the most prosperous period, Emperor Wudi (Liu Che, reigned 140-87 BC) expanded the territory from the Central Plains to the Western Regions (present-day Xinjiang and Central Asia). He dispatched Zhang Qian twice as his envoy to the Western Regions, and, in the process, pioneered the route known as the "Silk Road" from Chang'an (today's Xi'an, Shaanxi Province), through Xinjiang and Central Asia, and on to the Mediterranean coast. China's colorful silk goods were traded to the West along the Silk Road, giving the route its popular name. As contacts between East and West intensified, Buddhism spread to China in the first century AD. In 105, an official named Cai Lun invented a technique for making fine paper, leading to a revolution in the writing materials available to human beings.

Jade horse of the Han Dynasty (206 BC-220 AD)

• Silk Road

The Silk Road refers to the commercial route linking the Central Plains and the Western Regions (including most parts of today's Xinjiang Uygur Autonomous Region and parts of Central and West Asia). It was pioneered by Zhan Qian, a renowned diplomat and explorer in the Han Dynasty, when he was sent to establish diplomatic relations with the Western Regions by Emperor Han Wudi (reigned 140 – 87 BC). As an overland trade route, the Silk Road started from Chang' an, capital of the Western Han Dynasty, (today's Xi'an, Shaanxi Province), went west through Gansu Province and Xinjiang and reached Central and West Asia. However, the road did not stop here. Connecting with the overland routes in the countries around the Mediterranean Sea, it went on to the farther places like South Asia, Europe and even North Africa. Numerous splendid silk products from China were carried Westward via the route, thus creating its nickname. At that time, only China grew mulberries and raised silkworms to make silk products.

The Silk Road brought constant exchanges between the hinterland of China and the West. Chinese textile products, papermaking technique and some art crafts were introduced to the West as a result. Meanwhile, Western music, dancing, painting, astronomy, calendar and Buddhism were introduced into China.

Yumenguan Pass in Dunhuang: an important pass on the Silk Road

• Silk Road on the Sea

The Marine Silk Road refers to the marine trading route between China and other regions in the world. In the ancient times, apart from being transported to the Central Asia, West Asia, Africa and Europe along the land traffic through the Asian-European Continent, China's silk was shipped to various parts of the world in an endless stream along the sea routes. Therefore, after the silk road on the land was first used by German geographer Ferdinand von Richthofen, some scholars extended the meaning of the term by naming the sea routes between eastern and western regions as the Marine Silk Road. Later, China's well-known pottery and porcelain were shipped to various countries along this sea routes while the western aromatic drugs were shipped back to China, so some scholars also called the sea routes as the ceramic road or Aromatic Drug-Ceramic Road.

According to the historical records, the Marine Silk Road began during the reign of Han Emperor Wudi and flourished during the Tang and Song dynasties. The ancient Chinese traders began to ship chinaware, silk and cloth textiles and other commodities to European countries along a trading route extending from ports in present-day Guangdong and Fujian provinces, via South China Sea, to the Persian Gulf and Red Sea while the European businessmen brought the woolen fabrics, glassware and ivory to China.

Zhang Heng and Armillary Sphere

Zhang Heng (78-139) was a famous scientist of the Eastern Han Dynasty. He was appointed as the Taishiling, an officer in charge of chronometer, calendar and weather forecast.

In his book *Ling Xian*, he also drew the first complete star chart in China with terms like equator, ecliptic, south and north poles etc, showing 2,500 stars. In 117, he made the world's first armillary sphere [basically, a skeletal celestial sphere with a model of the Earth or, later, of the Sun placed in the center, for teaching purposes]. driven by the dripping of a copper kettle, which fell into two spheres. It could rotate, with the marks of the south and north poles, the equator, ecliptic, 24 solar terms and the sun, the moon, and stars etc. The position and the situation of appearing and disappearing of the stars and planets were all in accordance with reality.

In 132, he invented the seismoscope for detecting earthquakes, cast of refined copper and in the shape of a wine vessel with eight dragons whose heads faced in eight directions. There was a copper ball in each dragon's mouth, beneath all of which was a copper frog. When an earthquake occurred, a ball would fall out of a dragon's mouth into a frog's mouth. In this way, the time as well as the direction of the earthquake could be recorded instantly.

Besides, Zhang Heng invented a South Pointing Chariot, wrote over 30 works and papers on topics related to science, philosophy and literature, making prominent contributions in these fields. In memory of his outstanding achievements in science and technology, a crater on the far side of the moon was named "Zhang Heng Crater" by international astronomers.

• Cai Lun and the Art of Paper-making

Cai Lun (61-121) was born in Songyang, Guiyang Prefecture (today's Songyang of Hunan Province). Cai earnestly summarized the experiences of previous generations and improved the papermaking technology. He used bark, flax, linen thread oddments and fish nets to make quality paper, which became known as "Cai Lun paper". Holding office for 46 years, Cain Lun was an influential figure in politics, but his major contribution lay in his development of the art of papermaking, one of the four great inventions of ancient China (along with the compass, gunpowder and the printing press), that have made invaluable contribution to world civilization by helping promote the transmission and exchanges of the world's scientific knowledge and culture.

Jute paper and bark paper were the two mainstays of Chinese paper for 1,200 years from the Han Dynasty and were a must for the rapid development of Chinese culture. By the third or fourth century, paper had replaced bamboo slips and silk as the sole writing material, boosting transmission and development of China's technology and culture.

Three Kingdoms (220-280)

The Three Kingdoms Period, where rival states of the Wei, Shu and Wu existed in tripartite confrontation, lasted approximately from 220-280.

The three kingdoms strived to develop under each regime. After overthrowing the Eastern Han (25-220) and establishing the Wei Kingdom (220-265) , Cao Pi adopted a system of nine ranks of officials recommended by appointed governmental officials, which became the tool doe monopoly by the gentry and was replaced by the imperial examination system in the Sui Dynasty (581-618). This system also formed a foundation for powerful and influential families to rule the country.

In the Shu Kingdom (221-263), Emperor Liu Bei and Prime Minister Zhuge Liang actively promoted the development of the local economy, such as the mass production of the Shu brocade. Zhuge staged several northern expeditions, all of which, however, failed because of the great disparity in strength. He died on his sickbed in the cantonment during the last expedition. The Wu Kingdom (222-280) also attached importance to economic development; its shipbuilding technology was at a high level.

After the Western Jin Dynasty (265-317) upset the Wei Kingdom, the country gradually became unified. In 280, the Western Jin defeated the Wu and unified a China that had remained divided since the end of the Eastern Han Dynasty.

Western Jin Dynasty (265-317)

In 265, Sima Yan dethroned the Wei Emperor and established the Jin Dynasty, known as the Western Jin historically. Although the Western Jin survived for a mere 52 years, it ended the split created during the Three Kingdoms Period and reunified China (in 280 Sima Yan destroyed the Wu Kingdom), providing an opportunity for social and economic development with temporary stability.

The Western Jin Dynasty witnessed fast economic and cultural development. This period also turned out many classics, such as the *Mai Jing (Pulse Classic)* by the prestigious doctor Wang Shuhe; the Yu Gong Map by geographer Pei Xiu; and *Records of the Three Kingdoms* by Chen Shou. Apart from publishing some literary classics, the Xuan Xue School and Xian Xue School popular during the Three Kingdoms Period also continued to spread.

Celadon Sheep of the Western Jin Dynasty (265-317)

Eastern Jin Dynasty (317-420)

After the downfall of the Western Jin, Sima Rui, Emperor Wudi of the Jin, restored the Jin Dynasty in Jiankang (present-day Nanjing City, Jiangsu Province), historically known as the Eastern Jin Dynasty.

In 383, the ruler of the former Qin state in the north launched an attack on the Eastern Jin, hence the reputed Feishui Battle. Although the Eastern Jin army defeated the former Qin troops, the victory of the northern expeditionary force could not save the Eastern Jin from falling due to internal conflicts and rival contention for power. In 420, General Liu Yu deposed the Emperor of the Eastern Jin, and took over the throne and replaced the Eastern Jin with the Song Dynasty among the Southern Dynasties.

Silk Shoes of the Eastern Jin Dynasty (317-420)

Although the Eastern Jin occupied a small territory, it achieved many great cultural successes. During this period, the Xuan Xue School and Taoism also enjoyed greater influence. At the same time, literature, painting and calligraphy also reached a higher level.

In northern China, the upper classes of many minority groups and bureaucratic Han landlords successively set up their own regimes one after another. Altogether, there were 16 states that emerged during the 130 years—from the establishment of the Han State by Liu Yuan to the reunification of the northern part by the Northern Wei. This period was historically called the Sixteen States.

Northern and Southern Dynasties (420-589)

During the Northern Dynasty, the Northern Wei was split into the Eastern Wei and Western Wei. Later, the Eastern Wei was replaced by the Northern Qi, which then was conquered by the Northern Zhou. The Western Wei also was overthrown by the Northern Zhou. The Southern Dynasty refers to four successive dynasties, namely the Song, Qi, Liang and Chen.

The Southern and Northern dynasties witnessed the spread of the Xuan Xue School, where the troubled times provided a large latitude for the development of various schools of thought. During the period, literature, especially poetry, reached a very high level. At the same time, foreign exchanges also prospered, spreading from Japan and Korea in the east to Central Asia and Daqin (the Roman Empire), together with vast areas in Southeast Asia.

The Southern and Northern dynasties proved to be a period of national amalgamation most notable for the cultural exchanges between north and south. Although the chaos caused by war produced great sorrow and sufferings, it also created some advantages.

Celadon Lotus-Flower-shaped Wine Vessel of the Southern Dynasty (420-589)

• Qi Min Yao Shu (Essential Techniques for the Peasantry)

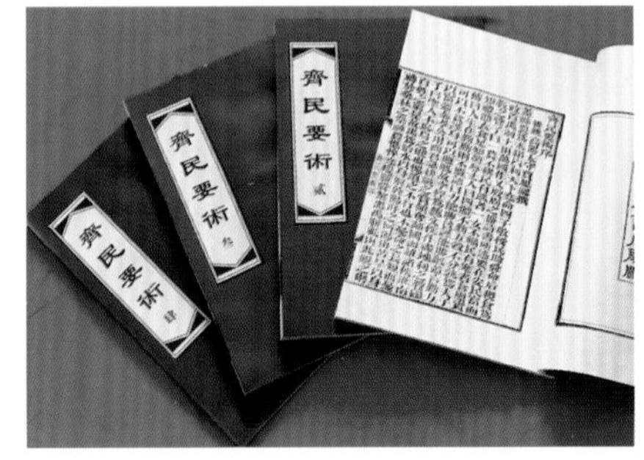

The agricultural masterpiece *Qi Min Yao Shu* (*Essential Techniques for the Peasantry*) by the agriculturalist Jia Sixie (477-538) living in the Northern Wei Dynasty is a classic in the agricultural history of China.

With 10 volumes consisting 92 chapters totaling 110,000 characters and quoting over 160 kinds of documents, this book set up a comparatively complete agricultural system, featuring a rational and practical division on agricultural categories. It introduced many steps of intensive and meticulous farming, such as seed selection, pre-soaking, fertilization, rotation of crops etc; imparted some planting experience of cereals, vegetable, fruit trees, and forests; and recorded the breeding techniques of livestock, fowl, fishes, silkworm etc. It elaborately and clearly touched every aspect of agricultural production from the processing of agricultural and sideline products, brewing, the disease prevention and cure of livestock and fowl. This agricultural system was inherited by later agricultural books.

The book in the Tang Dynasty was introduced to Japan; today, there exist over 20 versions in various languages in the world. Its towering scientific contents had far-reaching (618-907) influence on the agricultural production of both that time and later ages. This is the most comprehensive and systematic agricultural encyclopedia of the time and also the earliest agricultural classic in the world.

• Zu Chongzhi and π

Zu Chongzhi (429-500) was a very eminent mathematician and astronomer in ancient China.

On the basis of the achievements made by his predecessors, Zu worked out the numerical value of π--between 3.1415926 and 3.1415927; he got an approximation of π in the form of a fraction, being 3.141929, if six places of decimals were taken. This fraction was the one that approached most closely to π if the numerator and denominator were restricted to 1,000.

In mathematics, besides the computation of π, another major contribution of Zu as well as his son Zu Geng (another mathematician of China) was his putting forward the formula for computation of the volume of a sphere, equaling 4/3π× r3. In research, they even drew upon the axiom of two solids with the same sectional area at the same height having the same volume, which was not known in Europe until the 17th century through the work of the Italian mathematician Cavalieri. In order to commemorate the contributions of Zu Chongzhi, some foreign mathematical historians have proposed that π be called the rate of Zu.

Sui Dynasty (581-618)

The Sui Dynasty (581-618), a typical, short-lived dynasty, endured for only 37 years, from Yang Jian, known as Emperor Wendi who set up the Sui Dynasty in 581 to Yang Guang, Emperor Yangdi, who was hanged in 618. However, the Sui enjoyed a significant historical status because it established many policies that were later adopted by the Tang Dynasty (618-907). According to Chinese history books, the Tang Dynasty was an extension of the Sui and Chinese history books often use the combination "Sui-Tang" to refer to them.

Yang Jian, Sui Emperor Wendi, contributed most during this period. He conducted the reform of official system, abolished the six-officials system adopted by the Northern Zhou and replaced it with three ministries and six boards—a system that was retained by the Tang and acquired by Japan during its reform. The Sui Emperor also implemented the system of imperial examinations, hailed as a great achievement that was more impartial and reasonable than the previous system.

Emperor Yangdi's reputation in history not only lies in his constructing the Grand Canal, but also in his tyranny. His cruelty aroused the indignation of the masses. He was at last hanged in Jiangdu, which marked the end of the Sui Dynasty.

The Bronze Tiger-shaped Tally of the Sui Dynasty (581-618)

Tang Dynasty (618-907)

The Tang Dynasty is known as the most prosperous dynasty in Chinese history. It can be divided into two periods: early and late, with the eight-year An Lushan-Shi Siming Rebellion as the turning point. The early period was a golden age, while the latter was a period of decline. After Emperor Gaozu founded the Tang Dynasty, Li Shimin, Emperor Taizong, finally unified the whole of China over a 10-year period. During his reign, Emperor Taizong invested all his efforts in consolidating his regime, contributing to unparalleled prosperity in Chinese history. The period was known as the Administration of Zhen Guan; the empire was the world leader in politics, economy and culture. A golden age, a peaceful period called Kai Yuan Sheng Shi (the flourishing age of Kaiyuan) occurred during the reign of Emperor Xuanzong.

Wenyuan Tujuan (Scroll Painting of Wenyuan) by Han Huang of the Tang Dynasty (618-907)

A three-color glazed pottery of performers on a camel and engraved presswork of the Tang Dynasty (618-907)

During the early period, economic growth and political stability provided a favorable environment for the development of culture, art and foreign relations. In the field of literature, Tang poetry was unparalleled and exceptional achievements were also made in other fields.

The late Tang period was marred by political turmoil with continuous peasant uprisings.

Five Dynasties and Ten States (907-960)

The Five Dynasties (907-960) refers to the five states founded on China's Central Plains. During this period, there were 10 other small kingdoms, all of which (except the Northern Han) were located to the south of the Qinling Mountains and the Huaihe River. The states of the two minority regimes, Liao and the Western Xia, also coexisted with these states, but they were seldom mentioned in Chinese history books, which generally focused on the Han ethnic group.

During a period of chaos, tyrants and merciless officials run amuck; continuous wars persisted and heavy taxes were imposed. During this period, the famous cities of Chang'an and Luoyang were destroyed. The tumultuous period was also characterized by the tendency towards a single, central authority, which paved the way to ending the prolonged divisions by the Northern Song. Achievements during this period included the technological development of gunpowder, manufacturing and printing. In literature, ci or poem became the most popular poetic form during the Five Dynasties.

Song Dynasty (960-1279)

The Song Dynasty lasted for 319 years from its establishment by the Chenqiao Mutiny staged by Zhao Kuangyin, who became Emperor Taizu, to its being replaced by the Yuan Dynasty in 1279. Although of longer duration, it did not have the historical influence of the Tang Dynasty.

Usually it is divided into two phases: the Northern Song Dynasty (960-1127) and the Southern Song Dynasty (1127-1279). The Northern Song Dynasty concurrently confronted the Liao, Xia, Jin dynasties, while the Southern Song Dynasty was feeble and content to retain a part of the sovereignty.

After the Northern Song Dynasty unified the north, the economy and culture both developed. Overseas trade prospered; and literature, art, architecture all advanced to a new level.

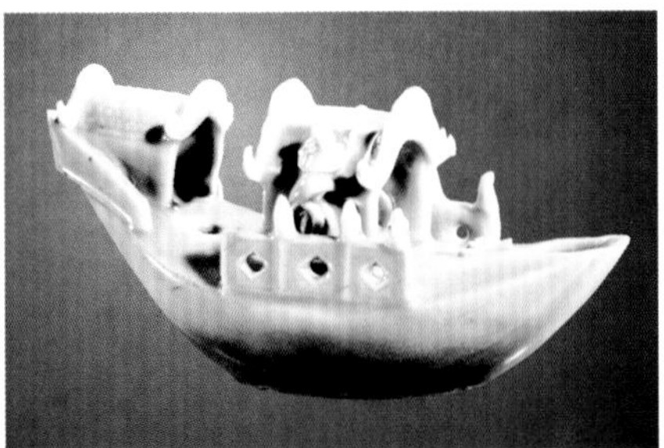

A Boat-shaped Inkstone, produced in Longquan Kilns of the Song Dynasty (960-1279)

After the Northern Song Dynasty was toppled down by the northern Jin Dynasty, the Southern Song Dynasty was happy to occupy the lower reaches of the Yangtze River; the ambition of launching northern expeditions never came into the mind of the ruler. The expeditions launched by Yue Fei, a famous anti-Jin hero were adopted to safeguard the existing territory alone. At last, the abuse of power of the Prime Minister Jia Sidao accelerated ruin.

• Moveable Type

Bi Sheng (?-about 1051), an inventor in the Northern Song Dynasty, invented the moveable type. The invention was the first of its kind in the world. He was a worker with a printing workshop, specializing in hand printing. *Mengxi Bitan* by Shen Kuo of the Song Dynasty recorded the printing art as created by Bi Sheng.

China is the country that first developed printing. In the early stages, people carved characters and drawing lines on wooden boards and coated them with ink before printing. This method, generally called engraving, remains in use in today's water color block printing pictures.

After the 11th century, with the development of social productivity, many reforms and inventions took place in printing. During the Qingli reign (1041) of the Song Dynasty, Bi Sheng initiated clay moveable type, making the printing of books more convenient. According to *Mengxi Bitan* by Shen Kuo, Bi first carved characters on glutinous clay pieces, which, after being baked hard, became movable characters. Before typesetting, he would coat a film of turpentine blended with paper ash on an iron board with an iron frame; the movable types were successively arranged on it. Then, he used heat to make the turpentine fuse a little; subsequently, he pressed the type-bearing board with another flat iron board. The clay characters then were firmly stuck to the iron board, which could be printed like the engraving type. Movable types could be used many times, were more economic and convenient than engraving the whole plate. The moveable type printing is better than carved printing board printing because it consumed less materials and labor power, and the printing speed was faster. As a result, the printing method spread far and wide, and gradually further improved through invention of wood, lead, tin and copper letter printing.

• Mengxi Bitan (Dream Pool Essays)

Shen Kuo (1031-1095) was born in Qiantang (today's Hangzhou) in Zhejiang. He produced the world-famous scientific masterpiece *Menxi Bitan* (Dream Pool Essays) in his late years.

This book served as an essential record of Shen's social and scientific activities throughout his whole life, referring to over 600 articles, including astronomy, calendar, mathematics, physics, chemistry, biology, geography, geology, literature, history, archaeology, music and art etc. Of them, over 200 belonged to science and technology, recording many of his inventions, discoveries and penetrating judgments. The book for the first time mentioned the problem of magnetic variation definitely.

Mengxi Bitan is not only is an academic treasury of ancient China but also an outstanding part of the world's cultural history. Yoshio Mikami, a Japanese mathematician, once remarked that Shen Kuo was second to none in the history of mathematics. Dr. Lee Joseph, the famous English expert in the history of science, took this book as the coordinate of Chinese history of science.

Yuan Dynasty (1206-1368)

Temujin of Mongolia founded the empire in 1206. In 1271, Kubilai designated the national title as Yuan. In 1279, Yuan Dynasty destroyed the Southern Song Dynasty.

The Yuan Dynasty ended the 370-year period of disunity following the downfall of the Tang Dynasty and paved the way for lasting unification through the Ming-Qing period.

During the Yuan Dynasty, economic and cultural exchanges were frequent among different ethnic groups, and the Hui ethnic group came into being. The Yuan had an extremely vast territory, drawing a basic outline of the present Chinese territory.

The Yuan regime can be roughly divided into three periods. The early period began from the reign of Kublai Khan, Yuan Emperor Shizu, until 1294. During this period rulers adopted laws from the Han ethnic group and initiated political, economic and cultural systems to promote social development.

The middle years (1307 to 1323) marked a period of decline. During this period, social conflicts and the competition for imperial power became intensive and continuous uprisings spread all around the country.

From 1329, the late-Yuan period began. Peasant uprisings accelerated the decline of the regime. Zhu Yuanzhang joined a peasant force and later took command to defeat other forces and rebuild the dynasty of the Han ethnic group, namely the Ming Dynasty.

A Lotus Petal-shaped Glass Tray of the Yuan Dynasty (1206-1368)

• Invention of Gunpowder

Gunpowder, one of the four great inventions of ancient China, was created by ancient Taoist alchemists during the process of smelting operations. Available materials show that gunpowder should be invented during the Tang Dynasty (618-907). The black gunpowder was adopted for military purpose when "flying fire" (namely flying arrows) was used in fighting in late Tang Dynasty. The technology of gunpowder-making matured during Song (960-1279) and Yuan (1206-1368) Dynasties, the military applications of gunpowder became common when various types of light and heavy gunpowder weapons appeared. During the Ming Dynasty (1368-1644), a kind of under-water bomb was invented.

During the Yuan Dynasty (1206-1368), the methods of powder-making and fire cannon-making were introduced to Europe. In 1327, the gunpowder formula was found in Europe.

Ming Dynasty (1368-1644)

With a total of 16 emperors, the Ming Dynasty lasted 276 years. Zhu Yuanzhang, Ming Emperor Taizu, carried out a comprehensive reform of previous political, military and other systems. Zhu grasped the political, military and judicial powers in his own hands, pushing feudal centralization to a high level. This was naturally carried on in the Qing Dynasty. In the early Ming, the nation's economy soon recovered and progressed to its highest level.

Stone inscription of the Ming Dynasty (1368-1644) on the Xianzhang Peak of the Wuyishan Mountain

The golden age of the Ming Dynasty thrived under Emperor Chengzu's reign, known as the Yongle period (after 1402). During this period, foreign relations were further strengthened via Zheng He's voyage to Southeast Asia and the Indian Ocean. The Ming regime also strengthened its relations with ethnic minority groups, among which economic and cultural exchanges were promoted further. Its jurisdiction extended to the inside and outside of the Xingan Mountains, Tianshan Mountains and Tibet.

When Emperor Yingzong ascended to the throne in 1436, the Ming Dynasty began to decline. At the same time, the Nüzhen ethnic group of the northeast became powerful and finally overthrew the Ming Dynasty during a storm of peasant uprisings. Emperor Chongzhen hanged himself at the foot of the Coal Hill behind the imperial palace in Beijing.

Golden Crown worn by Zhu Yijun, Emperor Shenzong of the Ming Dynasty (1368-1644)

History

• Zheng He's Voyage to Southeast Asia and the Indian Ocean

Zheng He (1371-1433) also known as Sanbao, which means "Three Treasures") was a eunuch officer of Ming Dynasty. On July 11, 1405, on order of the Ming emperor, leading a huge fleet of more than 240 ships manned by over 27,400 men, Zheng He set sail on a long voyage. During the journey, his ships visited more than 30 countries in the Western Pacific and Indian Ocean, which helped strengthen the friendship between China and Southeast Asia and East Africa. From 1405 to 1433, Zheng He traveled to the Western seas eight times. Each time they set sail from Liujiagang Harbor near Suzhou of Jiangsu Province. Zheng He passed away on the homeward leg of his last voyage in 1433. In Zheng He's fleets, there was a ship with a length of 44.4 zhang (ancient Chinese measurement) and a width of 18 zhang, which would mean 151.18 meters long and 61.6 meters wide. Such a vessel was the biggest of its kind in the world at that time. Moreover, the compass and celestial navigation technology were both used by Zheng He's armada during their voyages.

Qing Dynasty (1616-1911)

The Qing Dynasty was established in 1616. Originally called Later Jin, it changed the title into Qing in 1636 and entered the Shanhaiguan Pass in 1644. After the Opium War of 1840, the Qing became a semi-colonial and semi-feudal society, which can be divided into two periods.

Throughout the reigns of Emperor Kangxi, Yongzheng and Qianlong, the Qing reached its peak. This was known as the Kang Qian Sheng Shi (flourishing age from Kang to Qian, 1662-1795). During this period, Emperor Kangxi recaptured Taiwan and put down the rebellion of the Zhun Ga'er tribe. With a vast territory, the Qing gradually gained stability, which enabled a steady development of the economy, culture, industry and commerce.

In the beginning of the 19th century, the Qing Dynasty began to decline. During this period, Britain imported a large amount of opium into China. Although the Qing Government once tried to ban opium, it became the fuse for the British to stage the Opium War in 1840. This led to the signing of the *Sino-British Treaty of Nanjing*, as well as the successive various unequal treaties between the Qing and Britain, United States, France, Russia, Japan etc. that humiliated the nation and led to the forfeits of sovereignty.

After the Opium War, with the opening of more and more coastal trade ports, China's sovereignty increasingly was encroached upon by foreign powers. Under such humiliating circumstances, patriots never ceased to pursue independence. Uprisings led by Sun Yat-sen finally toppled the Qing Dynasty and set up the Republic of China.

Furnishings inside the the Palace of Heavenly Purity of the Forbidden City

♦ Opium War

The Opium War (1840-1842), also called the Anglo-Chinese War, was the most humiliating defeat China ever suffered. From the last stage of the 18th century, the English kept trafficking opium into China. This trade had produced, quite literally, a country filled with drug addicts and the outflow of a large amount of silver. In 1838, Lin Zexu was appointed the Imperial Commissioner at Guangzhou to suppress opium trafficking. In June 1839, he took action to destroy all the existing stores of opium, about 1.15 million kg, captured from the foreign merchants. With the pretense of protecting trade relations, the English sent warships to attack in 1840. The Qing Government began to waver and compromise, leaving only a part of army and people jointly resisting the invaders. Besides making trouble and invading coastal areas of Guangdong, Fujian, Zhejiang, the British also seized Wusong, penetrated the Yangtze River as far as Nanjing. Finally, in August 1842, the Qing Government was forced to agree to an inglorious peace with the signing of the *Sino-British Treaty of Nanjing*. From then on, China was reduced to a semi-colonial country.

Republic of China (1912-1949)

Towards the end of the Qing Dynasty, the Revolution of 1911 broke out. On January 1, 1912, Sun Yat-sen took the oath of office in Nanjing and declared the establishment of the Republic of China—a provisional government of the republic. The period from the formation of the Provisional Government until 1949 was known as the Republic of China period when the country experienced three shifts in government: Sun Yat-sen's Provisional Government (January-March 1912) in Nanjing, the Northern Warlords Government (1912-1928) in Beijing and the Kuomintang Government in Nanjing (1928-1949). Shifts in power were frequent during the rule of the Northern Warlords—from Yuan Shikai to Duan Qirui, and later to Cao Kun and Zhang Zuolin.

The Chinese Communist Party was founded in 1921 and later twice cooperated with the Kuomintang. The first cooperation, from 1924 to 1927, was when the two parties launched the joint Northern Expeditionary War. The second cooperation, from 1937 to 1945, involved the main task of driving out Japanese invaders. During the two periods of cooperation, the parties broke up on two occasions, declaring war on each other: namely, the First National Revolutionary War from 1927 to 1937, and the War of Liberation from 1946 to 1949.

In 1949, the Kuomintang Government was defeated and moved to Taiwan, marking the end of the Republic of China on the mainland.

• Revolution of 1911

The Revolution of 1911 occurred in the Chinese Xinhai Year (according to the sexagenary cycle of Chinese calendar) under the reign of Qing Emperor Xuangtong. Hence it is called Xinhai Revolution in Chinese. It put an end to the some 2,000-year-old feudal rule in China, and led to the establishment of the Republic of China.

In a narrow sense, the Revolution of 1911 refers to a period of history from October 10, 1911 when the Wuchang Uprising broke out to January 1, 1912 when Sun Yat-sen inaugurated as the Provisional President of the Republic of China. In a broad sense, this revolution is the successive revolutionary movements that broke out in China in the later Qing Dynasty and overthrew the Qing rule in the country.

Sun Yat-sen

Dr. Sun Yat-sen (1866-1925) was the forerunner of the democratic revolution in China. He was born as Sun Wen (also known as Yat-sen) in Xiangshan County (now Zhongshan City) of Guangdong Province on November 12, 1866. When in exile in Japan for his involvement in the anti-Qing movement, Dr. Sun changed his name as Nakayama Shō (a Japanese name meaning the Woodcutter of the Middle Mountain). People usually addressed him as Mr. Sun Zhongshan.

In 1905 Sun Yat-sen established the Revolutionary Alliance in Tokyo. For the first time, he put forward his famous "Three People's Principles"—Nationalism, Democracy, and People's Livelihood. The establishment of the Revolutionary Alliance was a great stimulant for the development of China's democratic revolution and made preparations for the breakout of the 1911 Revolution both ideologically and organizationally. On October 10, 1911, the Wuchang uprising gained a great victory, and Sun Yat-sen was elected as provisional president. After the swearing-in ceremony on January 1, 1912, he engaged in organizing the provisional government of the Republic of China. On February 12, 1912, Xuantong (Poyi), the last emperor of Qing Dynasty, was forced to abdicate, thus putting an end to the 2,000-year long feudal monarchy in China. The founding of the Republic of China was a great event in the modern Chinese history.

However, on February 13, Sun Yat-sen was also forced to resign from the post of provisional president. Of the various reasons for Sun's resignation, the major ones were the pressure from Western imperialism and domestic feudalism, as well as lack of unity in the revolutionary group. After that, Sun Yat-sen still dedicated himself to publicize and develop his "Three People's Principles" and organized the Kuomintang in 1912. On March 12, 1925 he died of liver cancer in the Peking Union Medical College Hospital.

People's Republic of China (founded in 1949)

On October 1, 1949, the People's Republic of China was formally founded.

At the beginning of the PRC, the Chinese Government successfully carried out land reform in rural areas involving over 90 percent of the total national agricultural population, and 300 million farmers were granted approximately 47 million hectares of land. Amazing achievements were made during the First Five-Year Plan period from 1953 to 1957. The average annual growth rate of the national income reached over 8.9 percent. China established basic industries necessary for full industrialization hitherto non-existent domestically, producing airplanes, automobiles, heavy machinery, precision machinery, power-generating equipment, metallurgical and mining equipment, high-grade alloy steel and non-ferrous metals.

The ten years from 1957 to 1966 was the period when China started large-scale socialist construction. The nation's total industrial fixed assets, if calculated on the basis of original price, quadrupled between 1956 and 1966 and the national income increased by 58 percent by comparable prices. The output of major industrial products increased by several or even a dozen times. Large-scale agricultural capital construction and technical transformation got underway.

Unfortunately, the "cultural revolution", which lasted for ten years (May 1966-October 1976), resulted in the State and its people suffering the most serious setbacks and losses since the founding of the PRC.

October 1976 marked the end of the "cultural revolution" and the beginning of a new era in Chinese history. In 1979, China instituted a guiding policy of "reform and opening to the outside world", and the focus was shifted to modernization. Major efforts were made to reform the economic and political systems. China step by step established a road with Chinese characteristics, a road that would lead to socialist modernization.

The Oil Painting "The Founding Ceremony of New China"

Population

♦ 1 Percent Sample Census (2005)

At the end of 2005, China conducted a 1 percent sample census nationwide (excluding Hong Kong, Macao and Taiwan). The survey took the nation as the primary framework and provinces, autonomous regions and municipalities as the secondary framework, using stratified, multi-phased, and cluster probability proportionate sampling as the methodology. The results showed that, at midnight on November 1, 2005, the population stood at 1.30628 billion, and would probably hit 1.30756 billion at the end of the year.

The average life expectancy has reached 71.8 years, five years above the world average and seven years longer than that of developing countries and regions.

The composition of China's population: males: 51.53 percent, females: 48.47 percent; people aged 0-14: 20.27 percent; aged 15-59: 68.70 percent; aged above 60:11.03 percent; urban residents: 42.99 percent; and rural residents: 57.01 percent.

♦ The Main Datum of the Fifth National Census (2000)

According to the No.2 communiqué of the fifth national census publicized by the National Bureau of Statistics on April 2, 2001, China had a population of 1.29533 billion. The total population of the 31 provinces, autonomous regions and municipalities (excluding Jinmen and Mazu islands of Fujian Province, hereafter) and servicemen on the mainland of China was 1.26583 billion; the population of Hong Kong SAR was 6.78 million; the population of Macao SAR was 440,000; the population of Taiwan Province and of Jinmen, Mazu and a few other islands of Fujian Province was 22.28 million.

Population Growth Rate

Compared with the population of 1.13368 billion from the fourth census (conducted at zero hour on July 1, 1990), the total population increased by 132.15 million persons in 2000 when the fifth census was conducted, or an increase of 11.66 percent over the period of 10 years and four months. The average annual growth was 12.79 million, or a rate of 1.07 percent, a decline of four per thousand points compared with that at the end of the 1980s.

At the end of 2007, the national population reached 1.32129 billion, or 55.46 million more than that of 2000. This demonstrates the remarkable effects of the family planning policy. Not only was China able to effectively control excessive population growth, but it also entered a development period characterized by a low fertility rate.

Population Density

China is one of the most populous countries in the world, with 135 people per square km. This population, however, is unevenly distributed. The eastern coastal areas are densely populated, with more than 400 people per square km; in the central areas, over 200; and in the sparsely populated plateaus in the west, there are less than 10 people per square km.

Quality of Population

The average life expectancy has risen from 35 years before the founding of New China in 1949 to 73.0 years in 2007; maternal mortality has fallen from 1,500 per 100,000 in the early 1950s to 36.6 per 100,000 in 2007, and infant mortality from 200 per 1,000 before the founding of New China to 10.7 per thousand in 2007; mortality of children up the age of five has fallen from 250-300 per 1,000 in the early 1950s to 18.1 per 1,000 in 2007.

Composition of Population in 2007

Unit: Percentage (%)

The general level of the scientific and cultural quality of China's population remains low, mainly as follows: First, the crude illiteracy rate of the population was a great deal higher than that of developed countries. Second, the crude rate of people attending colleges was much lower than developed countries. Third, the average

China's population has exceeded 1.3 billion, accouting for about one-fifth of the world's total.

Results of Five National Censuses

Content	1953	1964	1982	1990	2000
Total population(in million persons)	59435	69458	100818	113368	126583
Males	30799	35652	51944	58495	65355
Females	28636	33860	48874	54873	61228
Gender ratio	107.56	105.46	106.3	106.9	106.74
Populations of nationalities (in million persons)					
Han	54728	65456	94088	104248	115940
Proportion in total population (%)	93.94	94.24	93.32	91.96	91.59
Minority nationalities	3532	4002	6730	9120	10643
Proportion in total population (%)	6.06	5.76	6.68	8.04	8.41
Proportions of people of different age brackets in total population (%)					
0–14 years	36.28	40.69	33.59	27.69	22.89
15–64 years	59.31	55.75	61.50	66.74	70.15
65 Years and older	4.41	3.56	4.91	5.57	6.96

Note:
1. All the censuses include men and women on active duty or Chinese People' s Liberation Army.
2.The national population figure of 1953 includes people surveyed, whereas figures for the population of nationalities and urban and rural populations do not include people surveyed indirectly.

number of years of formal education was less than that not only in developed countries but also the world average level (11 years). Moreover, there exist conspicuous differences in education level between the urban and rural areas.

Population Distribution

At the end of 2007, the urban population stood at 593.79 million, about 44.9 percent of the total population, and those living in rural areas totaled 727.50 million, or 55.1 percent. Compared with the fifth census conducted in 2000, the proportion of urban population rose by 7.87percentage points. In recent years, due to actively stepping up the process of urbanizing and industrial structure upgrading, and carrying out a development strategy of cities bringing along the countryside and industry feeding back to agriculture, the rate of urbanization has increased by more than one percentage point. In 2005, China had a mobile population of over 147 million; compared with the fifth census, the transit population increased by 2.96 million.

Population Structure

In 2007, of the Chinese population, 256.60 million persons were in the age group of 0-14, accounting for 19.4% percent of the total population; 911.29 million persons in the age group of 15-59, accounting for 69.0% percent and 153.40 million persons in the age group of 60 and over, accounting for 11.6% percent (of which 106.36 million persons in the age group of 65 and over, accounting for 8.1% percent.). Compared with the results of the fifth census in 2000, the share of people in the age group of 0-14 fell by 3.49% percentage points, and that for people aged 60 and over was up by 1.33 percentage points (that for people aged 65 and over was up by 1.14 percentage points). The aforementioned figures showed:

First, the current social age-dependency ratio of China's population is relative low, the proportion of the working-age population is large and the labor force resources rich, which gives impetus to the rapid development of the economy. But the enormous working-age population imposes great pressure on employment.

Second, the proportion of the people at the age of 65 or above has exceeded seven percent. According to the international standard, China has become an aging society. The aging of China is characterized

Tibet, in western China, covers 1.22 million square km. Population density there averages a bit more than two persons per square km.

Logo of the "China's Population and Family Planning"

♦ National Population and Family Planning Commission of China

The National Population and Family Planning Commission of China was founded on March 6, 1981, according to the decision made by the 17th Meeting of the Standing Committee of the Fifth National People's Congress. As a standing organ under the State Council, the Commission is in charge of the national family planning program. Its missions are to formulate plans and policies on population development; propose guidelines and policies for the national family planning program; organize and draft laws and regulations related to population and family planning; and engage in strategic and foreseeing research on important issues, such as population scale, trends, quality and structure so as to promote the integrated approach to the population and family planning and promote balanced and sustainable development between the economic society and population.

Address: No.14 Zhichun Lu, Haidian District, Beijing
Website: http://www.chinapop.gov.cn/index.html

by rapid speed, large scale and getting old before getting rich, which produces great influence on the social development.

Third, in sex composition, 680.48 million persons or 51.5 percent were males, while 640.810million persons or 48.5 percent were females. The sex ratio (female=100, the proportion of male to female) was 106.19, a fall of 0.55 compared with the fifth census.

Policies on Population

The basic requirements of family planning are late marriage and late childbearing, having fewer but healthier babies, especially one child per couple. But a flexible family planning policy is adopted for rural people and ethnic minorities. In rural areas, couples may have a second baby in exceptional cases, but must wait several years after the birth of the first child.

Family planning has been promoted as one of the basic State policies, and it is the strictest population policy in the world. Since its implementation in 1978, at least 300 million births have been averted, according to the annual bearing level (the birth rate is 3.34 percent), which postponed China's arrival at the 1.2 billion population-level by nine years.

Population Target

The National Population Development Strategy Research Report, the most authoritative report of this kind, was released on January 1, 2007. The report

A happy family

made clear the strategic goals of national population development. These are to keep the population within 1.36 billion by 2010, and to markedly improve population quality. By 2020, China's population is to be held within 1.45 billion, with a significantly improvement in quality. After reaching its peak number of 1.5 billion in mid-century, China will witness a gradual decrease in population. At the same time, per capita income of the Chinese people is expected to be equal to that of moderately developed countries, with an overall improvement in population quality and health level.

♦ The Background of the Policies on the Population

When the People's Republic of China was founded in 1949, the population numbered 541.67 million. Owing to China's stable society, rapid development of production, improvement in medical and health conditions, insufficient awareness of the importance of population growth control and shortage of experience, the population grew rapidly, reaching 806.71 million in 1969. Since the 1970s, China has implemented a policy of family planning to control population growth. By 2006, the annual rate of population growth had decreased to 12.09 per thousand. Now China's population reproduction has basically been turned around into one characterized by low rates of birth, death and natural increase.

Population Forecast

According to the forecast of the China Population Information Research Center, in 2010, the population of China will total 1.377 billion, of which, 927 million will be of working age, and the population over 60 will reach 173 million; the natural growth rate will be 8.17 per thousand points. In 2050, the population will reach 1.522 billion. Of the total, the working-age population will total 939 million and the aging population over 60 will stand at 438 million, with a negative growth of 2.56 per thousand points. Negative population growth is expected to appear in the 2040s.

According to a UN forecast in 2005, in 2010, the total population of China will reach 1.373 billion, and those aged 65 and over will account for 8.1 percent. In 2050, the figures will be 1.478 billion and 22.6 percent.

• Starlight Program

In June 2001, the Ministry of Civil Affairs started the national "Starlight Program of Community Welfare Services for the Elderly" (Starlight Program for short) to cope with the ageing problem. The aim of the program is to, in two to three years, use more than 6 billion Yuan raised through issuance of lotteries to finance the repair of the welfare service establishments and activity centers in the urban areas, and the construction of the Home for the Aged in the rural areas. The welfare service facilities network for the elderly that is gradually being developed will comprise of supervisory stations provided by the residential committees of the communities, while individual streets will have service centers and villages and towns homes for the aged; counties and cities will also provide service centers. Meanwhile, a few demonstration comprehensive social welfare institutions should also be built. The services will gradually cover the aspects of support, family visit, emergency aid, day care, health services and recreational activities and so on.

By 2004, the program was completed and 32,000 Starlight families for the elderly were formed, involving a total investment of 13.485 billion Yuan, including 1.4 billion Yuan from the welfare lotteries of the Ministry of Civil Affairs and 2.6 billion Yuan from local welfare lotteries.

China's Aged Population in the Age Group of 60 and above Accounting for about One-Fifth that of the World

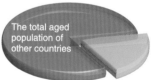

The total aged population of other countries

The number of China's aged population in the age group of 60 and above having amounted to 150 million

China's aged population

China's population aged at and above 60 accounting for over 11 percent of the total population of China

The Trend of Aging Population

According to the national one percent sample population census in 2005, the population aged from zero to 14 stood at 265 million, 20.27 percent of the total; population aged from 15 to 59 was 897 million, 68.70 percent; population aged over 60 was 144 million, 11.03 percent of the total, including 100.45 million people who were over 65, or 7.69 percent. Compared with the fifth national population census in 2000, the number of people aged from zero to 14 decreased 2.62 percent and the number of people over 60 increased 0.76 percent. Population aged over 65 increased 0.73 percent. Experts predict that, in the next 50 years, the number of aged people is expected to increase at an average speed of 3.2 percent annually. By 2040, the population aged over 60 will reach 400 million, or about 26 percent of the total population. That means there will have one elderly person for every three to four persons in the total population and in big cities, it will be one to two or three.

By the end of 2006 people aged 65 years or older in China numbered 96.27 million, 7.9 percent of the national population.

Elderly persons are watching opera in the park.

♦ The Reasons for the Ageing Trend

The first reason is that the average life expectancy has been prolonged. In 1957 it was 57 years, rising about 65 years in the mid-1970s and 68.9 years in 1985. With the development of the economy, the average life expectancy of China is expected to further increase.

The second factor is the decline of the birth rate. Since the 1970s, the great adjustment of the population policies has made the birth rate decline sharply. It decreased from 38 per thousand in 1965 to 17.8 per thousand in 1985, namely declining from five or six babies born by every couple on average to about two.

The migration of the population also contributes to regional ageing. The young and strong people in less developed area float to the developed areas, which cause the ageing of the former. According to authoritative sources, in the five to 10 years to come, China's transit population will increase at an annual average rate of 5 million, reaching about 160 million in 2010.

Composition of the Ethnic Groups

According to the 1 percent sample survey of the Chinese population conducted in 2005 and released on March 16, 2006, of the people enumerated in the 31 provinces, autonomous regions and municipalities and servicemen on the mainland, 1.1829 billion persons, or 90.56 percent, belonged to the Han ethnic group, and 123.33 million persons, or 9.44 percent, were of various national minorities. Compared with the 5th population census in 2000, the population of the Han people increased by 23.55 million persons, or 2.03 percent, while the population of various national minorities increased by 16.9 million persons, or 15.88 percent.

Household Registration System

Since the 1950s, the Chinese household registration system has undergone three stages of change: the first stage was before 1958, when there was free migration; the second was from 1958 to 1978, when movement was strictly checked; and the third was after 1978, a semi-open period.

Before 1958, China had no strict administrative system of household registration and people could migrate freely. On January 9, 1958, however, the government promulgated the first household registration system, namely the Regulations of the People's Republic of China on the Household Registration, which was passed by the Standing Committee of the National People's Congress. It established a comparatively complete household registration system, including seven items of population registration system, namely permanent residence, temporary residence, birth, death, immigration, settling in and variation. The regulation strictly restricted the influx of rural people into urban areas and population fluxion between cities.

On July 22, 1998, the State Council released the documents, making "four items of reforms" on the registered residence management system:

Young people of various ethic groups in their ethnic wedding clothes attend the wedding ceremony for ethnic youths at the Great Wall.

1. Implementing the policy that it is voluntary to decide whose household registration the baby will follow, the mother's or the father's. As for minors, who are required to settle in the urban areas with their father, it is possible to gradually solve their settlement in urban areas, and the children who haven't reach school age should gain preferential settlement.

2. Relaxing the household registration policies on the separation problem of couples. As for the citizens who have lived for certain years in their spouse's city, they are allowed to register there on a voluntary base.

3. As for the males in the age group of over 60, and the females in the age group of over 55, if they have no children nearby and need to go to live with their children in urban areas, they can do so.

4. As for citizens who invest, run enterprises and purchase commercial houses and the lineal relatives living with them, whoever has a legal fixed residence, job and source of income and has lived for a certain number of years in accordance with the regulations of the local government, are allowed to settle in the city.

On March 30, 2001, the State Council approved and issued the Opinions on Promoting the Reform of Household Residential Registration System in Small Cities and Towns. At the end of 2005, a total of 22.755 million rural people went through residential registration.

Policies on the Equality between Men and Women

The Constitution of the People's Republic of China clearly stipulates, "Women enjoy equal rights with men in all spheres of life, political, economic, cultural and social, including family life. The State protects the rights and interests of women, applies the principle of equal pay for equal work for men and women and trains and selects cadres from among women. Marriage, the family and mother and child are protected by the State. Violation of the freedom of marriage is prohibited. Maltreatment of old people, women and children is prohibited."In line with the principles established by the Constitution, New China has promulgated over 10 fundamental laws, including the Marriage Law, Electoral Law, Law of Inheritance, Civil Law and Criminal Law. The State Council and various ministries and commissions under it have enacted over 40 administrative decrees and regulations. Local governments have devised more than 80 local regulations and rules. All the legislation includes clear provisions on the protection of the rights and interests of women. No law in China contains clauses that discriminate against women. The Chinese Government also enacted the China Outline for Development of Women (1995-2000) and the China Outline for Development of Women (2001-2010), which made clear the major goals and tasks for development of women.

Besides establishing a series of laws, the Chinese Government also actively takes part in the activities in the field of international human rights of women. It has signed the Law on International Human Rights and various international documents concerning women and takes the responsibility and obligation to promote their human rights. In 1980, China signed the Convention on the Elimination of All Forms of Discrimination against Women, submitting the convention implementation report to the international institution on time; in 1985, China signed the Nairobi Forward-looking Strategies for the Advancement of Women; and in 1990, it joined the Convention concerning Equal Remuneration for Men and Women Workers for Work of Equal Value.

Women's Employment

The Constitution of the PRC, the Labor Laws of the PRC, and the Law of the PRC on Safeguarding Women's Rights and Interests all contain special provisions for safeguarding women's rights to employment. The state protects women's equal right with men to work, eliminates sexual discrimination in employment, adopts the principle of equal pay for equal work for both sexes, and guarantees special labor protection for women employees during menstruation, pregnancy, confinement and nursing. In May 2001, the Chinese Government promulgated The Program for the Development of Chinese Women (2001-2010), which set the goal of promoting women's employment.

With the country's sustained, rapid economic growth, and the development of industries and trades suitable for women's employment, the female population employed has continuously grown, and the fields of employment for them have kept expanding. To support the reemployment of laid-off women, especially older women, governments at all levels have actively developed and expanded trades and fields suitable for women to work in, and have adopted more flexible forms of employment to provide them with job opportunities according to their needs. Government-run public job agencies provide laid-off and unemployed women gratis consultancy on policy matters, job vacancy information, vocational guidance and job referral services, and actively carries out vocational skill training for them. In China, employed females now account for some 44 percent of the total number of employees compared to the global average of 34.5 percent.

The principle of equal pay for equal work for men and women is basically in

Women members of the CPPCC

place. Workers in the same industries, doing similar kinds of work and having the same technical skills, receive the same pay regardless of sex. The government provides comprehensive protective measures for employed women. The government has established a maternity insurance plan, with the premiums paid for by enterprises, instead of individual employees. This has created a favorable environment for women to participate equally in competition for employment. According to a survey, 85.3 percent of child-bearing female workers and staff members in urban areas enjoy a three-month paid maternity leave, while some units have extended this to six months. Female workers during their pregnancy and lactation period have their work load and work time reduced. Most State-owned enterprises where women predominate have established gynecological clinics, rest rooms for pregnant women, breastfeeding rooms, nurseries and kindergartens.

Happy life in Kindergarten

Women Participating in the Political Affairs

Nine women have acted as national leaders, including one who became vice-president of China and honorary president. Women cadres form 9.9 percent of the total cadres at and above province level. The number of women mayors, vice mayors and prefecture administrators is some 300. Among the 5,500 deputies and commissioners of the People's Congress and the Political Consultative Conference at all levels, 970 are women. Of the deputies to various National People's Congresses, the proportion of women deputies always surpassed 20 percent.

Education for Women

Since the founding of the People's Republic of China in 1949, the education level of Chinese women has been much improved. The illiteracy rate has fallen continuously, with more and more women receiving higher education. At the end of 2006, the child enrolment of primary schools reached 99.27 percent, compared to 20 percent in 1949, and the gross enrolment of middle schools was 97 percent. Girl students of ordinary primary schools, middle schools and high schools made up 46.82 percent, 47.33 percent and 46.43 percent of the total number of students. In 2005, university and postgraduate school girl students made up 47.08 percent and 43.39 percent of the total. All these show there was impressive increase in the number of female who receive high school education.

Protection of Children's Rights and Interests

The government has successively promulgated a series of laws concerning children's survival, protection and development. With the Constitution as the core, these provisions include the Criminal Law, General Principles of Civil Law, Marriage Law, Education Law, Compulsory Education Law, Law on the Protection of Disabled Persons, Law on the Protection of Juveniles, Law on the Protection of Women's Rights and Interests, Law on Health Protection of Mothers and Infants, Law on the Prevention and Control of Infectious Diseases, and the Law on Adoption, in addition to a great number of other relevant regulations and measures. Formulated according to the Constitution, the relevant laws include comprehensive and systematic provisions on children's right to life, survival and development, as well as basic health and health care. Provisions also address children's family environment and care, education, free time and cultural activities and the special protection of disabled children. It is specified that criminal acts, such as maltreating, abandoning and killing children, as well as stealing, abducting and trafficking, kidnapping, selling and buying of children, should be severely punished.

The State Council has set up a Working Committee for Women and Children. Both the central and local government departments involving education, pubic health, culture, public security, physical culture and civil administration have set up functional organs to take charge of children's work. Some mass organizations also perform many tasks to guarantee the development of the work concerning children in China.

China actively participated in working out the UN Convention on the Rights of Children, which formally became effective in China as of April 1, 1992.The government has undertaken and conscientiously fulfilled all the obligations specified in the convention.

Health Level of the Children

In 1949, the mortality rate of the Chinese children was 200 per thousand, and that of the early 1990s was 50.2 per thousand. In 2007, it fell to 10.7 per thousand; the mortality rate of the pregnant and lying-in women in 1949 was 1,500 per 100,000, decreasing to 94.7 per 100,000 in 1989 and 36.6 per 100,000 in 2007.

There are some 3,000 women and children's health institutions, and the planned immunization coverage rate reached over 98 percent; poliomyelitis has been eliminated.

The nutritional level of Chinese children has gradually improved. Now, it is rare to find cases of serious malnutrition caused by shortage of food or cases of serious vitamin-A deficiency. China also vigorously develops and promotes breastfeeding, constructs baby-friendly hospitals and basically popularizes salt iodization.

Nine-Year Compulsory Education

More than 97 percent of the areas carried out the nine-year compulsory education, with the enrolment rate reaching about 99.27 percent for primary school children (compared to 20 percent before 1949), and 97 percent for middle school students. The net primary school enrollment rate for girls was 99.29 percent, exceeding for the first time the rate for boys by 0.04 percentage point. With the exception of a few provinces in west China, gender differences have almost completely disappeared in the majority of provinces. And the illiteracy rate of young and middle-aged people fell to below 4 percent.

In October 1989, the China Youth Development Foundation initiated the Hope Project in Beijing. It provides grant-in-aid as long-term financial assistance to children in poor areas who dropped out because of straitened family circumstances, thus enabling them to return to school. In some poor rural areas, it also helps build or repair schoolhouses and buy teaching aids, stationery and books. At the end of 2006, about 3.2 billion Yuan was raised to aid more than 2.9 million poverty-stricken students in the rural areas, build some 10,000 Hope schools for the dropouts and poor students.

Protection for the Children in Need

China now has some 200 children welfare institutions. And close to 600 comprehensive welfare institutions are complete with departments of children. They adopt more than 66,000 orphans. In addition, China has some 10,000 rehabilitation centers, stations and classes, and some 120 rescue and protection centers for street children. More and more disabled children have been accepted in the compulsory education system and the total enrollment of disabled children reached some 700,000, while many children dropping out of school gained assistance. In addition to government investment, the Communist Youth League of China and the National Women's Union also raised more than two billion Yuan through the "Hope Project" and "Spring Buds Program", giving financial assistance to more than 3 million person/times of children dropping out of school.

The Disabled Population

Given the excessively large population base, the disabled has become a large group in the Chinese society. According to the second national sample survey in 2006, the number of the disabled in China reached 82.96 million, an increase of 21.32 million from the 1987 figure of 51.64 million, or 6.34 percent of the national population. Also according to the National Family Planning Commission, the disabled population in China is 60 million and there will be an increase of about 1 million disabled babies born each year.

Undertakings for the Disabled

Thanks to the efforts made by the government to implement the 10th Five-Year Plan (2001-2005), about 6.42 million people with a disability have been recuperated to varying degrees. Great attention has been paid to the prevention of deformity, and various prevention measures such as the iodine supplement for people in special need and the check of new-born babies have been put into effect, which all reduce the occurrence of deformity.

By the end of 2005, the compulsory education enrolment rate of disabled children increased to 80 percent. With education above high school level has developed stably and 90 percent of disabled examinees who reach the required standard in university entrance examinations have entered the higher schools. The number of vocational

National Day of Assisting Disabled Persons

According to the Article 48 of the Law of the PRC on the Protection of Disabled Persons, the third Sunday of May each year is National Day of Assisting Disabled Persons. This was started in the same year when the Law of the PRC on the Protection of Disabled Persons was put into force on May 15, 1991. The themes each year are decided according to the major duty of the disabled cause of the year. Different activities were conducted according to different themes, such as One Helps Another for Warmth, Volunteers' Help for the Handicapped, Building Families for the Handicapped and Being Friends to Them. On the day, all kinds of assistance and help will be provided to the disabled. To fix the National Day of Assisting Disabled Persons by legislation is an important measure to foster the society to help the disabled and advance the consciousness of all the people to assist them.

♦ Themes of Previous National Day of Assisting Disabled Persons

1st in 1991: Publicize the Law on Protection of Disabled Persons
2nd in 1992: Building Families for the Handicapped and Being Friends to Them
3rd in 1993: Aid and Common Progress
4th in 1994: We are together --Love for the Far East and South Pacific Games Federation for the Disabled
5th in 1995: One Helps Another for Warmth
6th in 1996: Preventing Handicapped Diseases and Building up the Physique
7th in 1997: Assist the Handicapped and Self Reliance
8th in 1998: Aid the Poor and Relieve Poverty
9th in 1999: Obstacle-Free and Help Cataract Patients to See Again
10th in 2000: Volunteers' Help for the Handicapped
11th in 2001: Publicize the Law on Protection of Disabled Persons in the New Century
12th in 2002: Help Disabled People in the Grass-roots to Work, and Guarantee Their Basic Live
13th in 2003: Develop the Cause of the Handicapped, and Realize Common Wealth Together
14th in 2004: Assist Our Brothers and Sisters--the Handicapped
15th in 2005: Equal Working Opportunities for the Disabled People
16th in 2006: True Understanding and Sincerely Love
17th in 2007: Guaranteeing the rights and interests of the disabled and building a harmonious society jointly

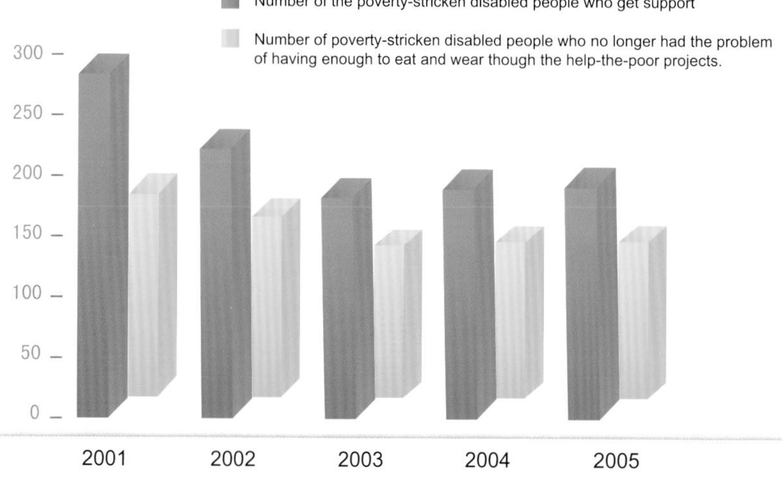

education and training institutions for the disabled has reached 1,000 and 2.5 million disabled people have gained such kind of training.

While disabled people work in the welfare enterprises, individual employment and voluntary employment organizations have become more and more popular. There were more than 4 million disabled people who have been employed in cities and towns, and 17 million in the rural areas.

The State takes the work of helping disabled people into the general plan for helping the poor, and has established a special plan of helping the handicapped at the same time. Through various social security measures, 4 million handicapped in poverty have gained basic living guarantees at the end of 2005.

The cultural and sports life of the handicapped have become increasingly rich. The special arts and sports fit for the handicapped have gained development, and the China Handicapped Art Group has successively visited America and Japan and so on. Disabled athletes have gained over 600 gold medals in major international sports events.

A shot of the National Professional Skill Competition for the Disabled

♦ China Welfare Fund for the Handicapped

China Welfare Fund for the Handicapped (CWFH) is an independent national non-profit charity organization. It was founded in Beijing on March 15 in 1984.

The governing board of directors of CWFH is composed of over 110 individuals from all walks of society. Mr. Deng Pufang is current President of CWFH. The Secretariat Division acts as CWFH's executive body in charge of its daily activities.

Since its establishment with the banner of humanitarianism, adhering to the principle of 'From the society and for the undertaking for disabled', CWFH has so far raised funds amount to 480 millions RMB yuan, of which 280 millions already used in advancing progress in areas such as rehabilitation, education, employment, culture and sports development for disabled persons and benefiting them practically. For its outstanding achievements, the United Nations presented to CWFH the United Nations Peace Passenger Citation in 1988, and to Mr. Deng Pufang a Special Award for UN Decade of Disabled Persons.

• Changjiang New Mileage Plan

In 1991, Dr. Li Ka Shing and his company donated HK$100 million to support the formulation and implementation of the China's 8th Five-Year Plan for the Undertakings of the Disabled (1991-1995). The fund was used to finance eight projects in urgent need of the disabled. Thanks to efforts thus made, 1.07 people suffering from cataract recovered eyesight, some 40,000 suffering from low-eyesight adopted visual aids, some 60,000 deaf-mute children started to speak, 360,000 suffering from polio sequelae received surgical operation, 100,000 mentally retarded children received effective training, 67 million people took iodic pills for the prevention of mental handicap, and 30 provincial-level comprehensive service facilities set up for the disabled.

Ethnic Groups

Fifty-Six Ethnic Groups

China is a unitary multi-ethnic country. To date, 56 ethnic groups have been identified and recognized by the Central Government. The population of the Han ethnic group accounts for the majority. As the population of the other 55 ethnic groups is relatively small, they are customarily referred to as "ethnic minorities". According to statistics collected in the fifth national census, in 2000, the population of all minorities totaled 106.43 million, accounting for 8.41 percent of the national total.

China's ethnic groups are scattered across the country but some live in individual concentrated communities in small areas.

A happy gathering during the National Day celebration

Composition of Ethnic Groups

China is a multi-ethnic nation of 56 ethnic groups. As the majority of the population (90.56 percent or 1.18295 billion) belongs to the Han ethnic group, the remaining 55 ethnic groups are customarily referred to as ethnic minorities. A sample survey conducted among one percent of the total population in 2005 showed that 123.33 million people belonged to these groups, accounting for 9.44 percent of the total population.

Eighteen ethnic minorities have a population of over one million, namely the Zhuang, Manchu, Hui, Miao, Uygur, Yi, Tujia, Mongolian, Tibetan, Bouyei, Dong, Yao, Korean, Bai, Hani, Li, Kazakh and Dai. Of these, the Zhuang ethnic group has the largest population, numbering 16.179 million. There are 17 ethnic groups with a population of between 100,000 and one million, namely the She, Lisu, Gelo, Lahu, Dongxiang, Va, Shui, Naxi, Qiang, Tu, Xibe, Mulam, Kirgiz, Daur, Jingpo, Salar and Maonan. There are 20 ethnic groups with a population of between 10,000 and 100,000, namely Blang, Tajik, Pumi, Achang, Nu, Ewenki, Jing, Jino, De'ang, Uzbek, Russian, Bonan, Moinba, Oroqen, Derung, Tatar, Hezhen, Gaoshan (excluding the Gaoshan ethnic group in Taiwan) and Lhoba. The Lhoba ethnic group, at 2,965, has the smallest population.

Distribution of Ethnic Groups

The Han people can be found throughout the country, mainly on the middle and lower reaches of the Yellow River, the Yangtze River and the Pearl River Valleys, and the Northeast Plain. The 55 ethnic minorities, though fewer in number, are also scattered over vast areas and can be found in approximately 64.3 percent of the national territory, but mainly distributed in the border areas of northeast, north, northwest and southwest China. For historical and geographical reasons, there is a great disparity in population density between the minorities-inhabited areas and the Han-inhabited ones, including the hinterland and coastal areas. For instance, the population density of the Tibet Autonomous Region is 1.73 persons per square km. In general, the population distribution of China's ethnic minorities has two characteristics:

First, living together over vast areas but also some living in compact communities in small areas; the population of the ethnic minorities is mainly concentrated on various provinces and autonomous regions of southwest, northwest and northeast of China. The ethnic minorities inhabit five autonomous regions, namely Inner Mongolia, Xinjiang, Tibet, Guangxi and Ningxia, 30 autonomous prefectures, 120 autonomous counties (banners) and over 1,200 ethnic townships. But Han people also live in the aforementioned areas, while people of many minorities are found in the Han-inhabited areas. In the past two decades, the population of the minorities living in a scattered way has increased rapidly.

Second, although the regions inhabited by ethnic minorities in compact communities are large, their population is concentrated in western part and border areas of China.

The statistics collected in the 2000 census showed that all the ethnic people are distributed in the 30 provinces and autonomous regions and that the people of 29 ethnic groups can be found in every province and autonomous region in China. Eleven provinces and autonomous regions are home to the people of the 56 ethnic groups, accounting for 35.5 percent of the total number of national provinces and autonomous regions. Although the regions inhabited by ethnic minorities in compact communities are large, their population is concentrated in the western part and border areas of China. China has a land frontier of more than 20,000 km, near which the ethnic minorities live.

The Han Ethnic Group

Population:115,940

A Han children

With a long history, the Han ethnic group has the largest population in the world. According to the Fifth National Census in 2000, there were 1,159.4 million Han, constituting 91.59 percent of China's total population. The distribution of Han people around China is characterized by density in the east and sparseness in the west. Sichuan Province has the largest number of Han people, followed by Shandong, Henan, Jiangsu, Guangdong, and Hunan provinces. Tibet Autonomous Region has the smallest number of Han people.

The Chinese language used by the Han ethnic group belongs to the Sino-Tibetan language family. After thousands of years of interaction and evolution, the modern Chinese language can be classified into nine dialects, resulting in a linguistic situation with complex Chinese dialects and a communication barrier between the south and north. The modern common language of the Han ethnic group is based on the Northern Dialect and takes Beijing phonetics as the standard. The system of Han characters is one of the oldest in the world, with a history of around 6,000 years; these square characters evolved gradually from Jiaguwen (inscriptions on bones or tortoise shells of the Shang Dynasty (16-11th Century BCE) and Jinwen (inscriptions on bronze). This system has altogether more than 40,000 characters including about 7,000 in common use. The system of Han characters is viewed as one of the international common languages.

The Han ethnic group has created much outstanding literature and arts with distinctive characteristics. In various fields of politics, military affairs, philosophy, economics, history, natural sciences, literature and arts, it has produced numerous representative figures and works with profound influence. The ancient medicine of the Han ethnic group is called "Zhong Yi (traditional Chinese medicine)" and is an important part of traditional Chinese medicines.

Since ancient times, the Han ethnic group has held an attitude of absorbing various religions. Destiny worship and ancestor worship are the major traditional concepts. In history, some Han people believed in Taoism and Buddhism; while the introduction of Christianity into China in more recent times attracted adherents.

The Han ethnic group has many festivals, including the Spring Festival, Tomb-Sweeping Day, Dragon-Boat Festival, Lantern Festival and Mid-Autumn Festival. The Spring Festival is also celebrated as the lunar New Year. It is a traditional festival of the Han people for thousands of years and is the most ceremonious. When celebrating the New Year, people will keep awake on New Year's Eve and pay a New Year's call on the first day of the first lunar month.

The Mongolian Ethnic Group

Population: 5,813,947

These live mainly in the Inner Mongolia Autonomous Region. Some are distributed in the Mongolian autonomous prefectures or counties in Xinjiang, Qinghai, Gansu, Heilongjiang, Jilin, Liaoning. There are also some scattered in provinces, municipalities and regions such as Ningxia, Hebei, Sichuan, Yunnan and Beijing. Having their own spoken and written language, belonging to the Mongolian group of the Altaic language family, Mongolians use three dialects: Inner Mongolian, Barag-Buryat and Uirad. The Mongolian script was created in the early 13th century on the basis of the script of Huihu, which was revised and developed a century later into the form used today.

In the past, Mongolians lived on the hunting and herding. They are still good at riding and shooting, but gradually settled down according to the season, having different encampments in winter and summer. On level land along the rivers available for cultivation, the Mongolian people have developed a culture incorporating livestock raising and agricultural cultivation.

The traditional medicine of the Mongolian people has a long history formed by the Mongolian's summarizing of their experiences. In terms of diagnosis, it includes watching, questioning and touching methods. It consists of treatment ways such as giving tonic, perspiration, vomit and recuperation. It mainly uses patent medicine to cure diseases and combines food therapy, moxibustion, skin therapy, spring therapy, needling and bleeding therapy, and massage.

A Mongolian woman

The famous Mongolian astronomer, mathematician and geographer Ming Antu (1692-1765) wrote a four-volume mathematical work, *A Quick Method for Determining Segment Areas and Evaluation of the Ratio of the Circumference of a Circle to Its Diameter*, making him the first person to calculate the circumference ratio by an analytical method, thus laying a solid foundation for the development of Chinese mathematics.

The Hui Ethnic Group

Population: 9,816,802

A Hui girl

The Hui ethnic group can be found in most parts of the country, but they live mainly in Ningxia Hui Autonomous Region and Gansu, Qinghai, Henan, Hebei, Shandong and Yunnan provinces.

The name Hui is an abbreviation for "Huihui". The Hui are an ethnic group that finds its origins from a number of other ethnic groups at home or abroad in the course of development. The introduction of Islam into China and its development was vital for the group to come into being. Late in the Ming Dynasty, they gradually spoke the Han language only, while maintaining certain Arabic and Persian phrases.

The Hui have made great achievements in the fields of culture, science and technology. During the Yuan Dynasty, they not only introduced and spread the achievements of Western Asia in astronomy, medicine, architecture and music, but also made outstanding contributions to China in learning and spreading the science, culture and technology of the Han. It was via Hui businessmen that China's major inventions such as paper-making, compass and powder were introduced and spread into Europe. Hui medicine is also fairly famous. Hui leech craft is good at chirurgery and use of drugs. Hui physicians collected and re-edited many prescriptions and compiled five volumes of *Ruizutang Medicinal Preparations*.

The Hui are Muslims and the Islamic Arabic and Persian culture has had a deep influence on the lifestyle of the Hui people. For instance, soon after birth, an infant is given a Huihui name by an Ahung (Imam); wedding ceremonies must be witnessed by Ahung and a deceased person must be cleaned with pure water. Two major festivals are Fast-Breaking and the Corban Festival.

The Tibetan Ethnic Group

Population: 5,416,021

The Tibetan ethnic group is distributed over the vast Qinghai-Tibetan Plateau. Most Tibetans live in Tibet Autonomous Region, the Haibei, Huangnan, Hainan, Guoluo and Yushu Tibetan prefectures and Haixi Mongolian-Tibetan Autonomous Prefecture of Qinghai Province, the Gannan Tibetan Autonomous Prefecture and Tianzhu Tibetan Autonomous County of Gansu Province, the Aba Tibetan Prefecture, Gyangze Tibetan Prefecture and Ili Tibetan Autonomous County of Sichuan Province and the Diqing Tibetan Autonomous Prefecture of Yunnan Province. The Tibetan language belongs to the Tibetan branch of the Tibetan-Myanmar language group of the Chinese-Tibetan language family. According to geographical divisions, it has three major local dialects: U-kang, Kang and Amdo dialect. The Tibetan script, an alphabetic system of writing, was created in the early 7th Century using some elements of Sanskrit. Through three revisions, it is developed and used in all areas inhabited by Tibetans to this day.

The Tibetan people cherish a brilliant culture. As early as the 7th Century, Tibetan documents were being published, including wood slips, paper or leather rolls and metal and stone carvings. The Tubo Kingdom believed in Buddhism and set up special scriptural translation workshops. The engraved block printing technique was introduced from other parts of China in the Song Dynasty. Tibetans' rich literature and writing can compare favorably with those of the Han. The two Tibetan collections of Buddhist scriptures known as the Ganggyur and the Danggyur were compiled in the Yuan Dynasty. In addition, there are works on philosophy, written language, medicine and calendaring, as well as novels, poetry, operas, biographies, stories and fables.

Tibetan women

Tibetans are also good dancers and singers. The tap dance is most typically Tibetan. Most of the musical instruments were introduced from the hinterland. In the past, all performers were men. Wearing masks, they danced and sang to the accompaniment of various musical instruments. The eight best known plays such as the Princess Wencheng are liked by the masses, making the Tibetan opera a famous operatic style in China.

Zanba, roasted qingke barley or pea meal mixed with buttered tea, is the staple food of Tibetans. The Tibetan herdsmen regard beef and mutton as their staple food. Lamas may eat meat. Tibetan houses are often built with stones or earth on elevated sunny sites near a water source. Buildings have a flat roof and many windows, being two or three stories high. Inside the house, boards are used in making the floors. People in pastoral areas camp in tents made of canvas or woven with yak hair. The yak is a big and long-haired animal unique to the Qinghai-Tibet Plateau and capable of withstanding harsh weather and carrying heavy loads. Known as the "Boat of the Plateau", the yak is a major means of transport.

The Tibetan New Year is the most important festival. People in their holiday best extend greetings to each other. The Saka Dawa Festival falls on the fifteenth day of the fourth Tibetan month, and celebrates the birth of Sakyamuni and the arrival of Princess Wencheng in Lhasa. This festival involves a wide range of activities. When the harvest is in sight in July, the farmers carrying sutras on their back walk around the field to pray for a good harvest. From the midsummer to the autumn harvest, Tibetan families in all areas have the habit of going on a journey and picnicking for several days on end.

Most Tibetans follow Lamaism. The 25th day of the tenth lunar month is the death anniversary of the founder of Yellow sect Zongkapa, when the monks and nuns gather and recite sutras in his memory. In addition, different sects in different areas also hold some mass activities. The Yellow sect practices the Living Buddha Reincarnation System. When a Grand Living Buddha dies, his disciples are required to choose a child successor by divination, and seeking over a wide area, to be his reincarnation or "soul boy".

Tibetan Buddhism, also called Lamaism, was introduced into the Tubo Kingdom in the fifth century. In 978, Tibetan Buddhism was grouped into many sects including Nyingma Sect (the Red sect), Sagya Sect (the spotted sect), Gagyu Sect (the white sect) and Getang Sect (meaning sect commandments).

The Uygur Ethnic Group

Population: 8,399,393

Folk artists of the Uygur ethnic group performing

The Uygur ethnic group live mainly in the Xinjiang Uygur Autonomous Region, especially south of Tianshan Mountain. A small number are found in in Hunan Province. According to the fifth census in 2000, the Uygur ethnic group has a population of 8,399,393 people. Their language belongs to the Turkic group of the Altaic system. In ancient times, they used the Huihe script. After Islam was introduced in the 11th century, the old Uygur script based on Arabic was in common use. After the founding of the People's Republic of China, a new Latinized script was created. However, use the old Uygur script resumed in the early 1980s.

Uygur literature is very rich in style and subject matter, such as the epic Kutadolu Biliq (Blessings and Wisdom) passed down to this day. The oral literature by laboring people is also rich and colorful. The tales of Avanti are loved by the people still. The Uygurs are known for their skill in singing and dancing. On festive days and at gatherings of friends and relatives, they love to sing and dance. The "Twelve Mukams" is an epic comprising more than 340 classic songs and folk dances. After liberation, this musical treasure, which was on the verge of being lost, was collected, studied and recorded. There are a dozen varieties of Uygur musical instruments, including dap (tambourine), dutar and rawap.

The government has attached great importance to the work of investigating and preserving Uygur medicine and putting it into common clinical use. In this regard, special study institutions have been set up, which have compiled works involving medicine history, the theoretical basis, leech craft, drugs in common use, folk prescriptions, internal medicine, chirurgery, gynecology, pediatrics and enswathement.

The Uygur farmers' staple food is Nang (a kind of crisp baked pie), noodles, Zhuafan, tea and milk. Zhuafan is an important food for guests. Baked meat, Nang, steamed stuffed bun and dumpling are their favorite foods. Melons and fruits also play an important role.

The major festivals include the Fast-Breaking Festival, Corban Festival (Korban Festival and Sacrificial Animal Festival), and Noluzi Festival. The Corban Festival is celebrated ceremoniously. During the festival, every family believing in Islam needs to fry Yousazi food and most of the families butcher sheep and cock. On that day, the Uygur people, men or women, young or old, in their holiday best exchange visits and festive greetings.

The Miao Ethnic Group

Population: 8,940,116

Miao girls

The Miao live mainly in the provinces and autonomous regions of Guizhou, Hunan, Yunnan, Sichuan, Guangxi, Hubei and Hainan. In southeast Guizhou and provincial common boundary areas of Hunan, Hubei, Sichuan and Guizhou, there are some larger compact communities. In other areas, the Miao live together with other ethnic groups. The little Miao village is comprised of the several or a dozen families while the largest one has hundred or even a thousand families. According to the fifth census in 2000, the Miao has a population of 8,940,116.

The Miao language belongs to the Miao branch of the Miao-Yao language group of the Chinese-Tibetan language family. As the Miao constantly migrated for several thousand years, the Miao language has been divided into three main dialects in China-one based in western Hunan, one in eastern Guizhou and the other in Sichuan, Yunnan and part of Guizhou. In addition, the dialect in Sichuan, Yunnan and part of Guizhou also was grouped into seven sub-dialects. Before the founding of the People's Republic of China, they had no uniform written script. In 1956, the government organized experts in the Chinese and Miao language to create a Latin alphabet-based script, which is now in common use.

The Miao have created a variety of colorful arts and crafts, including cross-stitch work, embroidery, brocade, batik, paper-cuts and jewelry casting. Their batik technique dates back 1,000 years. Their diversified traditional jewelry, including bracelet, chaplet, headgear, plastron and silver dress, featuring the elaborately chiseled patterns, also enjoy good reputation.

Different Miao communities celebrate different festivals. Even the same festivals may fall on different dates. In southeast Guizhou and Rongshui County in Guangxi, the Miao New Year festival is celebrated on "Rabbit Day" or "Ox Day" of the 9th to 11th lunar calendar. The festivities include such activities as beating drums, dancing to the music of a lusheng (a wind instrument), horse racing, and bull-fighting. In counties near Guiyang, people dressed in their holiday best gather at the city's largest fountain on the 8th day of the 4th lunar month to play lusheng and flute and sing of the legendary hero, Yanu. In many areas, the Miao have Dragon Boat festivals and Flower Mountain festivals (on the 5th day of the 5th lunar month), Tasting New Rice festivals (between the 5th and 6th lunar month when the rice ripens), Pure Brightness and the Beginning of Autumn festivals. In Yunnan, "Stepping over Flower Mountains" is a popular festivity for the Miao every year, becoming a traditional mass entertainment festival of the group.

The Yi Ethnic Group

Population: 7,762,286

The Yi ethnic group has a long history and old culture. They are mainly distributed over the provinces of Sichuan, Yunnan and Guizhou, and northwest of the Guangxi Zhuang Autonomous Region. The Yi compact community includes the Liangshan Yi Autonomous Prefecture in Sichuan Province, the Chuxiong Yi Autonomous Prefecture and the Honghe Hani-Yi Autonomous Prefecture of Yunnan Province, and Bijie Prefecture and Liupanshui Prefecture of Guizhou Province. The Yi language belongs to the Yi branch of the Tibetan-Myanmar language group of the Chinese-Tibetan Language Family, and the Yi speak six dialects. The Yi used to have an ideographic syllabic script called Nangwen, which was thought to be a syllabic script. The Trial Scheme on Standardization of the Yi Language formulated in 1975 regularized 819 Yi Characters and was carried out in the Liangshan Yi Autonomous Prefecture in Sichuan Province.

A Yi woman

Many hand-written copies in the Yi language, which recorded their long history and rich culture, were handed down in the Yi areas. As many as one thousand copies covering philosophy, history, literature and religion have been discovered, which have been successively translated, edited and published. In addition, there are some casting coppers and steles in the Yi language, and colorful oral literature. The works in the Yi language retain abundant information about medicine. The group follows the lunar calendar.

The Yi people are good at singing and dancing. All kinds of traditional tunes are often performed, such as mountain climbing tune, door entering tune, guest receiving, toasting tune, marrying tune and keening tunes. Their musical instruments include Huluseng, Mabu, Bawu, kouxian, yu-kin, flute, sanxian, serial bells, bronze drum and flat drum. The traditional arts consist of coating with lacquer, making silver decoration, embroidery, carving and painting. They coat their bowls, plates, pots, cups, armor, shields, arrow canisters, saddles, halters, yu-kin and kouxian with black, red or yellow lacquer.

Yi women are skilled at embroidery. They usually embroider the beautiful patterns on the scarf, Charwa sleeves, front of the garments, trouser cuff, small bag for tobacco and waistband.

The important festivals of the Yi include "the Torch Festival", "the New Year of the Yi" and "Singing and Dancing Festival". "The Torch Festival," held around 24th or 25th of the sixth lunar month, is the grandest festival. During the festival, everyone wears their best clothes and livestock are slaughtered to offer sacrifice to the spirit tablet for the deceased. At night, people carry torches and walk around their houses and fields. After making their rounds, everyone gathers around bonfires, singing and dancing, or watching horse racing and wrestling all night.

The Zhuang Ethnic Group

Population: 16,178,811

The Zhuang is the largest minority group. Most live in Guangxi Zhuang Autonomous Region and Wenshan Zhuang-Miao Autonomous Prefecture. The Zhuang language belongs to the Zhuang-Dai branch of the Zhuang-Dong language group of the Chinese-Tibetan language family. Tushu Square Words,

A Zhuang girl

ancient Zhuang characters based on Chinese appeared in the Southern Song Dynasty, but never became popularized. Only a few people were able to use the characters in making out the names of places, editing folk songs and keeping records of the affairs. In 1955, a Latinized writing system was created with government help and put into operation. In 1982, the Zhuang script was revised and is now widely used.

The Zhuang's ancestors painted numerous frescoes on precipices in the Guangxi Zhuang Autonomous Region. There are more than 60 spots at which frescoes have been found, stretching over 200 km along the Minjiang River and Zuojiang River. The patterns carved include figures and beasts. They were drawn in the middle of the precipices on both banks of the river with the blind bends and dangerous shoals, 30 to 40 meters from the water surface. It was difficult to climb to the spot to create them. Questions, such as when the frescoes were painted, their meaning, how to climb the precipices, and the tools and materials that were used, continue to be studied.

The Zhuang have a history of more than 2,000 years of casting and using a bronze drum. So far, most of the Zhuang-inhabited counties have unearthed such drums of different dynasties in different designs and sizes. The surface of the drums is round and flat while the body is hollow in the middle without a bottom. The tops and sides of the drums are decorated with designs in relief. The bronze drums unearthed in Guogailing of Tiandong County and belonging to the Warring States Period, and those which were excavated in Gui County and Xilin County from the Western Han Dynasty, reach a fairly advanced level in terms of smelting and molding technology.

Zhuang brocade is a handicraft enjoying good reputation. Woven in unique decorative patterns with natural cotton warp and dyed velour weft, the brocade wears well for quilt covers. Zhuang brocade was produced as early as the Tang and Song dynasties. In the Qing Dynasty, production extended all over the Zhuang-inhabited areas.

The Bouyei Ethnic Group

Population: 2,971,460

Most Bouyei people live in South Guizhou and Southwest Guizhou Bouyei-Miao autonomous prefectures, and Anshun and Guiyang cities. Others are distributed in the Southeast Guizhou Miao-Dong Autonomous Prefecture, Tongren Prefecture, Zunyi City, Bijie Prefecture, Liupanshui City of Guizhou Province, Luoping of Yunnan Province, and Ningnan and Huili of Sichuan Province. According to statistics collected in the fifth national census, the population of the Bouyei ethnic group totaled 2,971,460. The Bouyei language belongs to the Zhuang-Dai branch of the Zhuang-Dong language group of the Chinese-Tibetan language family, having close relations with the Zhuang language. The dialect of the northern Zhuang area is similar to the Bouyei language in the counties of Wangmo, Dushan, Anlong and Xingshan. In the past, the Bouyei had no written language and used Han characters instead. After 1949, the government helped create a Bouyei writing system based on Roman script.

In the light of the national ethnic policy, ethnic regional autonomy is carried out in the Bouyei area. The Qiannan Bouyei-Miao Autonomous Prefecture, the Qianxinan Bouyei Autonomous Prefecture, the Zhenning Bouyei-Miao Autonomous County, Ziyun Miao Autonomous County, and Guanling Bouyei-Miao Autonomous County were established.

The Bouyei build their villages near the mountains and water. Their houses are two-storied structures with local characteristics with the upper floor for family living and the ground floor for livestock and storage of firewood and grass. Their batik enjoys a great reputation, featuring simple hues and beautiful patterns. Now, batik has become one of their best-selling handicrafts in Japan and various parts of the world. Knitted ware such as Libo Bamboo Mat and Pingtang Bamboo Hat are famous. Besides the Spring Festival, Dragon Boat Festival and Mid-Autumn Festival, the Bouyei people also celebrate the "Eighth Day of the Fourth Month" and "Sixth Day of the Sixth Month". The former is also called "Ox King Festival". During this festival, each family steams glutinous rice that has been dyed in five different colors. After sacrificing to their ancestors, they feed half of the rice to their oxen, which are then allowed to rest for the remainder of the day. The latter called Genchan in the Bouyei language is the grandest festival for the group.

The Korean Ethnic Group

Population: 1,923,842

People of the Korean ethnic group are distributed mainly in Heilongjiang, Jilin and

Dancers of the Korean ethnic group

Liaoning provinces. Others are scattered in Inner Mongolian Autonomous Region and large and medium-sized cities in the hinterland, such as Beijing, Shanghai, Hangzhou, Guangzhou, Chengdu, Jinan, Xi'an and Wuhan. Members of this minority living in the Yanbian Korean Autonomous Prefecture of Jilin Province speak and write in Korean, while those living in other parts of the country usually speak Chinese.

The Yanbian Korean Autonomous Prefecture of Jilin Province was set up on September 3, 1952 and the Changbai Korean Autonomous County was established in 1958. Several dozen Korean Autonomous townships also were set up in the various areas where Korean people congregate.

The people of the Korean ethnic group are especially good at singing and dancing. During festivals or the breaks in work, they like to express their feelings by singing and dancing. If a happy event takes place in a family, they will celebrate with song and dance.

Korean sports have their own characteristics. Wrestling is an old sport and entertainment activity, while football is especially popular among men of the Korean ethnic group. Every village sets up its own football team. In recent years, some women's football teams have appeared. During festivals and holidays, all kinds of sports dominated by football will be held. As a result, the Yanbian area has become a famous "land of football". Women of the Korean ethnic group are fond of playing on seesaws and swings. Rice and millet are staple foods. To these they add piccalilli or spiced pickled vegetables, which are indispensable to everyday meals. They also like to eat Dagao, cold noodles, pickled soup, capsicum and dog meat.

Korean festivals are similar to those of the Han people, and include Spring Festival, Pure Brightness Festival, Dragon Boat Festival and Mid-Autumn Day. Besides these, they have three important festivals celebrated in their families-a baby's one-year birthday, a senior citizen's 60th birthday (Huijia Festival) and a couple's 60th wedding anniversary (Huihun Festival). At the latter two events, children, relatives, friends and neighbors will congratulate the elderly person or the couple and extend their good wishes.

The Manchu Ethnic Group

Population: 10,682,263

Manchu girls

For historical reasons, the Manchu people are scattered in various areas of China. Most of them live in Liaoning Province. Manchu autonomous counties and township have been set up for the Manchu people to live. According to census in 2000, the Manchu has a population of 10,682,263. The Manchu have their own script and language, which belongs to the Manchu branch of the Manchu-Tungusic group of the Altaic language family. Manchu letters were created in the 16th century on the basis of Mongolian letters. Later, the "circle" and "dot" were added to the introduced Mongolian letters, called the Manchu characters with the circles and dots or New Machu characters. The original characters were called the Machu characters without circles and dots. With more and more Manchu settling in the Central Plains and Han people moving to outside the Shanhaiguan Pass since the Qing Dynasty, the economic and cultural exchange between Han and Manchu became more and more frequent and the Manchu gradually adopted the Han language. Today, only elders in remote Machu-inhabited villages of Heilongjiang Province still know and can use their ancestral language.

The Manchu people have also added splendor to Chinese culture. *Shu Li Jing Yun (Essence of Mathematics and Physics), Li Xiang Kao Cheng (A Study of Universal Phenomena)* and *Huang Yu Quan Lan Tu (Complete Atlas of the Empire)* with the Qing Emperor Xuanye as the chief compiler are of high scientific significance. *Man Wen Lao Dang (Ancient Archives in Manchu), Man Wen Tai Zu Shi Lu (A Manchu Biography of the Founding Emperor)* and *Yi Yu Lu (Stories of Exotic Lands)* by Tu Lichen are among the famous works written in the early years of the dynasty. In addition, there are a large number of works in the study of the Manchu language such as *Qing Wen Qi Meng (Primer of Manchurian), Qing Wen Dian Yao (Fundamentals of Manchurian)* and *Qing Wen Jian.*

While the Manchu language was enriched in vocabulary, efforts were made by the Manchu to translate important works of the Han people into their own language. Along with government documents, such great works as The Three Kingdoms, The Western Chamber, A Dream of Red Mansions, Flowering Plum in the Vase and Strange Tales from a Lonely Studio all had their Manchu versions.

Important festivals of the Manchu are similar to those of the Han people, including the Spring Festival, Lantern Festival, Dragon Boat Festival and Mid-Autumn Festival.

The Dong Ethnic Group

Population: 2,960,293

The Dong is distributed in Guizhou Province, Hunan Province, and the Guangxi Zhuang Autonomous Region. The Dong language belongs to the Dong-Shui branch of the Zhuang-Dong language group of the Chinese-Tibetan language family. It consists of northern and southern dialects. With no written script of their own, they used Chinese. A Dong written language on the basis of the Latin alphabet was created in 1958.

The Dong people cherish rich and colorful culture and arts. The populated areas of the Dongs are regarded as the "Hometown of poems and the sea of songs." The rhythm of Dong poems is strict and rigorous, with varied subjects. The poems and lyrics narrate the origin of humans, ethnic migration and customs, and are of precious value in providing historical data. There is much beautiful music. Dong opera, dating back to early in the 19th century, evolved from the narrative genre of talking and singing, with simple gait and honest movements on stage and varied arias. The Dong people are good at architecture. The drum tower and the roofed bridge in the Dong villages, with ingenious structures and varied styles, are typical of this skill. The drum towers are mortised with high quality wood without a single nail, a single clinch bolt or any other iron pieces. They have several stories, ranging from three to fifteen. The delicately wrought protruding eaves look as if the structure is ready to leap. The pagoda-shaped drum tower is the symbol of a clan or a village, as well as the center of celebration activities. Wood, stone arches, stone slabs and bamboo are all used in erecting the roofed bridges which the Dong have dubbed "wind and rain" bridges. Roofed with tiles engraved with flowers, it has on its sides five large pagoda-like, multi-tier pavilions beautifully decorated with carvings. The covered walkway has railings and benches for people to sit and enjoy the scenery. The Chenyang "Wind and Rain" Bridge in Sanjiang County is the most famous, having been listed as a key cultural relic under national protection.

The Dong people

The important festivals of the Dong include Spring Festival, Ox Worshiping Festival (on the eighth day of the fourth lunar month or the sixth day of the sixth lunar month) and New Rice-Tasting Festival (in the seventh lunar month). In some areas, the Dong also celebrate the Dong New Year in the lunar tenth or eleventh month. Because of their contact with other ethnic groups, they also enjoy the Pure Brightness Festival, Dragon Boat Festival, Mid-Autumn Festival, and Double Ninth Festival.

The Yao Ethnic Group

Population: 2,637,421

The Yao ethnic group lives mainly in the mountainous areas in the Guangxi Zhuang Autonomous Region, Hunan, Yunnan, Guangdong and Guizhou provinces. The Yao people have their own language, whose branches are very complicated. It differs greatly between areas, making communication difficult in that tongue. They speak the Chinese or Zhuang language in general. Having no the written script, they use Chinese characters.

Yao music and dance, such as folk songs, come from work and religion. The famous long drum dance and bronze drum dance is performed when they offer sacrifice to the Pangwang and Milotu. A dozen dances prevail among the common people such as lion dance, and grass-made dragon dance. The Panwang Song featuring a complicated aria has 24 varieties of names of the tunes. The production song and toasting song have a slow and joyful air, the bitter song and dirge are characterized by a sorrowful, deep melody and the love song is lively and affecting. Yao arts include printing and dyeing, cross-stitch work, embroidery, brocade, articles made of bamboo, carving, painting and casting, featuring diversified style and rich meaning. Of these, batik and cross-stitch work are most famous.

The Yao began to record their own history and compile all kinds of ancient books by learning Chinese character as early as the Tang and Song dynasties. So far, a great deal of ancient books and records including the famous historical documentary

Millenium Migration and numerous religious scriptures, songbooks and genealogy are preserved among the common people in the Yao area, a great contribution to national history and culture.

Millenium Migration provides precious information for the study of Yao history. The Yao people living in different areas have differing religious beliefs. Some worship nature, some their ancestors, some the totem, and others practice wizardry and Taoism. The latter actually plays an important role in the life of the Yao people. A set of sacrificial rites during a funeral is held follow the Taoist form mixed with some primitive religion.

The Bai Ethnic Group

Population: 1,858,063

A Bai gril

The Bai ethnic group is a minority living in the border areas of southwestern China. Most live in concentrated communities in the Dali Bai Autonomous Prefecture of Yunnan Province; the rest are scattered in Lijiang, and Kunming of Yunnan Province and Bijie of Guizhou Province, Liangshan of Sichuan Province and Sangzhi County of Hunan Province. The Bai speak a language belonging to the Tibetan-Myanmar group of the Chinese-Tibetan language family. Most speak their own language, but Chinese is widely used.

Bai architecture, engraving and painting enjoy good reputation all over the world. The three pagodas at Chongsheng Temple in Dali were built during the Tang Dynasty. Its 16-storey main tower is 60 meters high and elaborate. Figurines in the Shibaoshan Grottoes in Jianchuan County are lifelike, possessing both the common features of figure creation in China and the unique flavor of the Bai ethnic group and occupying a high position in China's stone inscription art history.

The "March Fair" falls between the fifteenth and twentieth day of the third lunar month, and is a grand Bai festival. It is celebrated at the foot of Diancangshan Mountain to the west of Dali City. Originally, it was religious activity to rally and pay homage, but it gradually evolved into a grand merchandise trade fair. Now, the "March Fair" has developed into one involving trade of merchandise from different regions, as well as performances of traditional sports and dance. Another important event is the "Torch Festival", held on the 25th day of the sixth lunar month by the Bai to usher in a bumper harvest and to bless the people with good health and fortune. On that evening, a torch is lit at the doorway of every family home, and a large torch decorated with red-green paper banners with auspicious words written on them is lit at the entrance to the village. Villagers, holding aloft torches, walk around in the fields for a whole week.

The Tujia Ethnic Group

Population: 8,028,133

The Tujia ethnic group mainly live in west Hunan, west Hubei and Sichuan provinces. They speak a language belonging to an independent language branch of the Tibetan-Myanmar language group of the Chinese-Tibetan language family. They have no written script so commonly use Chinese characters. Now, the majority of Tujia speak Chinese. About 200,000 Tujia along the valley of the Youshui River (originating from Hefeng Mountain in Hubei Province and emptying into the Yuanshui River in Hunan Province) still use the Tujia language and some of them are also proficient in Chinese.

Long historical development has created a colorful culture and unique customs. The Tujia Exorcising Opera, a kind of local opera, can be called a "Living Fossil" of Chinese opera. The Tujia area in Tongren of Guizhou preserves Tan opera and frequently stages performances, attracting the attention of experts at home or abroad.

Tujia houses are usually of two stories, with the ground floor for storage and livestock and the second floor used as family living quarters. The girls' bedrooms are where they weave, embroider, spin and make shoes. Such kind of houses, featuring good ventilation and being damp proof, are both safe and sanitary, and not only overcome the restrictions imposed by uneven topography in the mountainous areas, but also make full use of the space.

The Eighth Day of the Fourth Lunar Month, the Sixth Day of the Sixth Lunar Month, and the New Year of Tujia People are the most important festivals. New Year of the Tujia People, also called the Gannian Festival, comes one day earlier than the New Year's Eve of the Han people, namely the 20th day of the 12th lunar month, and is the most ceremonious festival of the Tujia people. The Small New Year of the Tujia people falls on the 28th day of the 12th lunar month. They have various beliefs including ancestor worship.

The Hani Ethnic Group

Population: 1,439,673

The Hani people mainly live in the Ailaoshan mountain area along the lower reaches of the Lishejiang River and western side of the Honghe River of southwestern Yunnan. Their language belongs to the Yi branch of the Tibetan-Myanmar language group of the Chinese-Tibetan language family. They have no script of their own. In 1957, the government departments helped them to create a script based on the Latin alphabet.

During the past several thousand years, the Hani people constantly opened up terraced field to grow rice and millet and reclaim slopes to plant tea trees. Terraced fields of hundreds of steps are found on the Ailaoshan Mountain. The Hani-inhabited Nanru Hills in Xishuangbanna are one of the country's main producers of the famous Pu'er tea. The Hani people plant hemp, and cotton, providing materials for self-weaving and self-dying. Gejiu City, capital of Honghe Prefecture, is the well-known "capital of tin". According to the *History of Han Dynasty Geographical Records*, tin was first produced there some 2,000 years ago.

The traditional festivals of the Hani people include the Tenth Lunar Month Festival and the Sixth Lunar Month Festival. The Hani regard the first day of the tenth lunar month as the beginning of the year. The Tenth Lunar Month Festival, like the Spring Festival of the Han, lasts 5-6 days and even 15 days in some areas. The Sixth Lunar Month Festival called Kuzhazha in the Honghe area falls on the 24th day of the sixth lunar month, lasting 3-6 days. Like their Han neighbors, the Hani who live in the Honghe area celebrate the Spring, Dragon Boat and Mid-Autumn festivals.

The Kazak Ethnic Group

Population: 1,250,458

According to the fifth census in 2000, the Kazak ethnic group has a population of

Kazak old ladies at work

1,250,458. They live mainly in Ili Kazak Autonomous Prefecture, Mori Kazak Autonomous County and Barkol Kazak Autonomous County in Xinjiang Uygur Autonomous Region. A few are also distributed in the Aksai Kazak Autonomous County in Gansu Province and the Haixi Mongolian, Tibetan and Kazak Autonomous Prefecture in Qinghai Province. The majority, however, are concentrated in Xinjiang. The Kazak language belongs to the Kepuchark language branch of the Turkic language group of the Altaic language family. The ancestors of the Kazaks once used Erhun-Yenisei script and Huihu script. A new Latinized written form was created in 1959.

After 1949, the Central Government made great efforts to develop industry in the Kazak area. It invested in building the famous Kalamayi oil field, the Dushanzi oil field, Ili Oil Mill, Bruchin Flour Mill, Tacheng Flour Mill, Altay Flour Mill and Altay Hydroelectric Power Plant. Ala Mountain pass in Ili Kazak Autonomous Prefecture is the western pass of the second Euro-Asia Continental Bridge in China.

The important festivals include the Corban Festival and Rozha Festival. They also celebrate the Noruz Festival, which falls in the first lunar month. On that day, they pay New Year's calls on each other as the Han people see off the old and welcome in the new during the Spring Festival. During the festivals, they also hold the activities such as Sheep Grabbing, horse racing and "girl-running-after-boy". Most of them believe in Islam but some herdsmen still retain vestiges of Shamanism.

The Dai Ethnic Group

Population: 1,158,989

The Dai live mainly in the Xishuangbanna Dai Autonomous Prefecture, Dehong Dai-Jingpo Autonomous Prefecture, Gengma Dai-Va Autonomous Prefecture and Menglian Dai-Lahu-Va Autonomous County of Yunnan Province. According to the fifth census in 2000, its population is 1,158,989. The intermontane plain where they live boasts a subtropical climate. The Dai language belongs to the Zhuang-Dai branch of the Zhuang-Dong language group of the Chinese-Tibetan language family. They have an alphabetic script which varies from place to place. In the 1950s, thus was reformed.

The Dai have their own calendar starting in 638. There are books in Dai script for calculating solar and lunar eclipses, historical documents and a rich variety of literary works covering poetry, legends, stories and fables. They have about 500 long epics, which is unequaled among all the ethnic groups in China. They cover many themes and are rich in content.

The Dai people are good singers and dancers. The Peacock Dance performed to the

Water-Splashing Festival unique to the Dai people

accompaniment of the elephant-foot drum and gongs is well-known at home or abroad. The carving and paintings are fine and elegant. The magnificent pagodas and the bamboo bridges over the rivers represent their unique architectural art.

Buddhism exerts great influence on the daily of the Dai people. Dai festivals, closely related to religious activities, included the "Door-Closing" festival in the mid sixth lunar month, the "Door-Opening" festival in the mid-ninth lunar month, and the "Water-Splashing" festival ten days after the Pure Brightness Festival by the lunar calendar. "Door-Closing" started three months of intensive religious activities. "Door-Opening" marked the beginning of normal life. "Water-Splashing", still held every year, is the most important festival, during which the Dais splash water on one another, and hold dragon boat races and pray for auspiciousness.

The Li Ethnic Group

Population: 1,247,814

The Li ethnic group live mainly in Hainan Province. According to the fifth census in 2000, its population is 1,247,814. Dialects vary according to geographical division; many also speak Chinese. A new Latinized Li script was created in 1957.

The brocade technique of the Li people is most noted among their arts. As early as the Tang and Song Dynasties, their skill in spinning and weaving exceeded that of the Han. The Li brocade and Li sheets they weave are well-known. They use all kinds of tools to produce colorful brocade, quilt, sheet, skirts and lace through a set of production process of ginning cotton, spinning, dyeing, weaving and embroidering. The "Yazhou Quilt" and "double-sides embroidery" are famed for their refinement, bright colors and ethnic characteristics. In addition, the Li have a tradition of dainty and delicate woodcraft and bine weaving.

The Lisu Ethnic Group

Population: 634,912

The Lisu ethnic group lived mainly in the Nujiang Lisu Autonomous Prefecture of Yunnan Province. The rest are scattered in Sichuan Province. The Lisu language belongs to the Yi branch of the Tibetan-Myanmar language of the Chinese-Tibetan language family. The Lisu people have long used three kinds of written script. The first is the alphabetic writing created by Western missionaries. The second is the syllabic script created by Wang Renbo, a Lisu farmer in Weixi County. The third is the new script created on the basis of the Latin alphabet, which was put into operation in the Nujiang Lisu Autonomous Prefecture.

The Lisu people are good singers and dancers. During wedding ceremonies, while building houses or during the harvest season, they sing and dance as much as they like. In the course of production and labor, they have created a great deal of music with ethnic characteristics and living inspiration, including production songs, house-building songs, harvesting songs and marriage escaping songs. The poems are usually consisted of seven lines, with both sound and sense strictly matching in two poetic lines. Poems and music both are formed regularly. All the poems can be sung as lyrics. They are sung, to the accompaniment of a lute, Sixian and kouxian. They dance with vigorous movements and strong rhythm.

The Lisu have created a rich and colorful oral literature. Numerous folktales narrate the myths and legends, the origin of humans and mountains.

Before 1950, the Lisu people used the nature calendar. They divided a year into ten season months, i.e. flowering month, bird-tweedling month, burning volcano month, hungry month, collecting month, harvesting month, wine-cooking month, hunting month, the New Year spending month and house-building month. The main festivals include the hot spring bathing fair, harvesting festival and the Lunar New Year.

The Va Ethnic Group

Population: 396,610

The Va people live in Yunnan Province. The Va-inhabited areas are situated on the undulating southern Nushan Mountains. Traditionally, this area was called the Ava hilly region. The Va language belongs to the Va branch of the Mon-Khmer group of the Austroasiatic language family. It is divided into three dialects, namely Parok, Ava and Va, each containing many idioms. They have no written script. Before the founding of the People's Republic of China in 1949, British and American missionaries created a kind of written Va script to transmit the Christianity, which was so coarse that it was hardly used. After the founding of the PRC, the government sent experts to investigate the Va language and create a Latinized written script in 1957.

The Va people have rich and colorful oral literature, covering the naissance of the human, the subsistence of everything on earth, marriage and funeral customs, production and daily life, a unique and wonderful flower among the literary arts of the ethnic minorities. Oral literature includes myths, legends, stories, poems, riddles and proverbs. Of these, the stories with animals or animals and humans as the protagonists are characterized by a rich theme and profound morality. It is not certain that cliff fresco groups, discovered in the Cangyuan area since 1965 were drawn by ancestors of the Va, but the contents have a close relationship with their history and customs. There are cliff frescos at 10 sites, concentrated halfway up the hill along the Mengshenghe River, for about dozens of km around. Of them, the fresco of a village scene is similar to the villages in the center of the Ava Mountain in the 1950s in structure and layout, and with a history of about 3,000 years.

Most Va villages were built on hilltops or slopes. Some villages in the area have a history of several hundred years and embrace 300 to 400 households. Most houses are constructed with bamboo and straw and are usually two stories. The upper floor is for family accommodation while the ground floor is reserved for livestock. The furnishings are very simple. The rooms also have fireplaces necessary for warming, offering sacrifice or heating the livestock feed.

The She Ethnic Group

Population: 709,592

The She ethnic group is among those with a relatively small population in China. More than 90 percent of the She live in the vast mountainous areas of Fujian and Zhejiang provinces, but some are scattered throughout Jiangxi, Guangdong and Anhui provinces. The fifth census conducted in 2000 revealed that the She population was 709,592. They speak a language belonging to the Miao-Yao language group of the Chinese-Tibetan language family. The She language is similar to the Hakka dialects with small differences in pronunciation. With no written language, they use Chinese characters.

She ethnic people on way to a singing contest

Most of the costumes of the She people are cyanine and made of self-woven flax. They like to wear jackets decorated with lace on their collars, cuffs and garment fronts. In some areas, women wear shorts year-round. When they do so, they wrap their legs. The young girls like to twine red wool thread with the hair into a long braid and coil it on top of the heads. The married women wear a phoenix coronet, namely a slender and fine bamboo wrapped with a handkerchief of red damask silk.

The traditional festivals of the She include the Dragon Festival in the fourth lunar month, the Seventh Day of the Seventh Lunar Month, the Beginning of Autumn, the Mid-Autumn Festival, the Double-Ninth Festival and the Spring Festival. In addition, the fifth day of the second lunar month, the fifth day of the seventh lunar month and the fifth day of the eighth month are the days for ancestor worship. Their religious belief includes ancestor worship and totemism. They attached great importance to the former.

The Gaoshan Ethnic Group

Population: about 400,000

The Gaoshan ethnic group is a minority living in Taiwan Province. The majority of them live in mountain areas and the flat valleys running along the east coast of Taiwan Island, and on the Isle of Lanyu. The Taiwan authority calls them "compatriots living in mountainous areas". According to the geographical and language division, the Gaoshan includes the Amei people, Taiya people, Paiwan people, Bunong people, Lukai people, Beinan people, Cao people, Saiya People and Yamei People. In addition, there are more than 100,000 Pingpu people assimilated by the Han. Historically, the Pingpu people consist of 10 clans scattered over the western, northern and southwestern parts and coast of Taiwan. As they lived together with the Han people for a long time and accepted their culture, they have been in a hypostatic union with the Han since the 19th century. According to fifth national census data, there were 4,461 Gaoshan on the mainland. The Gaoshan do not have their own script, and their spoken language belongs to the Indonesian group of the Malay/Polynesian language family. Their speech differs according to place.

The wood carving of the Gaoshan is of a unique style drawn from the original arts of the pacific areas. The wood carving by Paiwan people is the most famous. They carve couchant human figures, human heads, snake, deer and combinations of geometric patterns on their houses, weapons and household utensils. The carving, featuring the rough artistry of wielding the knife, and simple and unsophisticated sculpting, pays attention to strong color contrasts and an exaggerated method of painting realistically. The carving decorations by the Paiwan people have been collected by people at home or abroad. In addition, the Yamei people carve and decorate their fishing boats.

The important festivals of the Gaoshan people include Fertility Cult celebrated by Taiya people during the last ten days of the third lunar month when spring sowing ends, the Safety Cult by Bunong people on the fourth day of the fourth lunar month, Ali Ancestor Cult by the Pingpu people on the 16th day of the ninth lunar month, Harvest Cult by the Cao, Lukai and Amei peoples on the 15th day of the eighth lunar month, Bamboo Pole Cult by the Paiwan people on the 25th day of the tenth lunar month, Monkey Cult and Hunting Cult by the Beinan people in the 11th lunar month, and Flying Fish Cult by the Yamei people. Their traditional festivals have sacrificial connections. During the festivals, in addition to singing and dancing, and feasting, they also hold sports games, cultural exhibition and entertainment activities.

The Lahu Ethnic Group

Population: 453,705

The Lahu ethnic group lives in the mountainous area of southwestern Yunnan Province. They are mainly distributed in Simao and Lincang prefectures in the valley of the Lancangjiang River, while others reside in the neighboring Xishuangbanna Dai Autonomous Prefecture, Honghe Hani-Yi Autonomous Prefecture and the Yuxi area. Nearly 80 percent of the Lahu inhabit the areas to the west of the Lancangjiang River. The Lahu language belongs to the Yi branch of the Tibetan-Myanmar language group of the Chinese-Tibetan language family. Due to long years of contacts and exchanges with the neighboring Han and Dai people, most of the Lahu also speak Chinese and the Dai language. In the past, the Latin alphabet invented by Western priests was in use in some parts. In 1957, a script was created for them based on the original alphabet. Lahu men wear a collarless jacket buttoned on the right side, baggy long

A Lahu girl

trousers, and a black turban. The women wear a long robe with slits down the legs. Around the collar and slits are sewn broad strips of colored cloth with beautiful patterns and studded with silver ornaments. Women's headdresses extend down the back and reach the waist. The houses of the Lahu are the pile-styled, incline-roofed, storied buildings made from bamboo and wood. Those for a small family are either square or elliptical. The large-sized building of bamboo and wood is set up with 12 to 21 piles, and generally partitioned into some rooms.

The traditional festivals of the Lahu People include Spring Festival, Dragon-Boat Festival, Torch Festival and New Rice Tasting Festival. The Spring Festival is the grandest one for the Lahu. Before it, every family pounds rice and makes Baba balls. During the festival, the Lahu people, men and women, old and young, dress in their holiday best, pay a call on each other, and then dance. Their Torch Festival is also interesting. On that day, people light pine torches and young men and women in their holiday best sing and dance around bonfires.

The Shui Ethnic Group

Population: 406,902

The majority of Shui live in compact communities in Guizhou Province. Some Shui have their homes in the Guangxi Zhuang Autonomous Region. The Shui language belongs to the Dong-Shui branch of the Zhuang-Dong language group of the Chinese-Tibetan language family. The Shui use Chinese in their daily lives.

The Shui boast a treasure house of colorful oral literature and art. Their literature includes poetry, legends, fairy tales and fables while industrial arts consist of paper-cut, embroidery, printing and dyeing, and carving. Folk songs are rich in form and content. They are used to express feelings by poetry, including long narrative poems and extemporaneous ballads, which reflect rich content. The copper drum is the Shui traditional musical instrument. During festivals, they dance the "Copper Drum Dance" to add to the fun.

The Shui usually dress in black and blue. Men wear long gowns, short jackets and black turbans. Women wear collarless blue blouses, black trousers and aprons, all of which are embroidered. They usually wear their hair in buns. On festive occasions, the females put on skirts and a variety of silver earrings, necklaces and bracelets. The houses of the Shui are constructed of wood. Historically, they were of the fenced building type, while, now, bungalows form the majority.

The Shui have their own calendar which basically follows the lunar calendar of the Han people. However, there is one big difference, that is, the Shui treat the first day of the 8th lunar month as the end of the previous year and the first day of the 9th lunar month as the New Year's Day. The four special Hey days--from the end of the eighth lunar month to the tenth lunar month--are the "duan" holidays, the grandest festival for the Shui. "Jie duan" in Shui language is similar to the Spring Festival of the Han. They hold activities such as horse racing, bronze drum dance and Lusheng dance and feast. Some Shui also celebrate the Mou Festival which falls in the ninth lunar month. They also celebrate the Pure Brightness Festival, Dragon Boat Festival, the Sixth Day of the Sixth Lunar Month and the Sunjingxi Festival, the 15th Day of the Seven Lunar Month.

The Naxi Ethnic Group

Population: 308,839

Most Naxi live in concentrated communities in the Lijiang Naxi Autonomous County in Yunnan Province, Sichuan Province and the Tibet Autonomous Region. The Naxi language belongs to the Yi branch of the Tibetan-Myanmar language group of the Chinese-Tibetan language family. As the Naxi people have come into closer contact with the Han, oral and written Chinese have become an important means of communication in Naxi society. They had already created pictographic characters called the "Dingbat" script and a syllabic writing known as the "Geba" script. However, they were difficult to master. With these scripts they recorded a lot of beautiful folklore, legends, poems and religious classics. In 1957, the government helped the Naxi design an alphabetic script.

The Naxi pictographic characters created more than 1,000 years ago were used by Dongba followers to write the "Dongba Scripture", thus the name of "Dongba script". Early in the 13th century, they also created a syllabic writing known as the "Geba" script. The "Dongba Scripture," a religious work of the Naxi, provides precious data for the study of Naxi social and historical development, language and script, and religious belief.

New Century is a collective creation by the Naxi people. It is a famous long epic depicting the creation of the world and struggle with nature, singing of labor and reflecting the loyal love between man and a girl. Youpei and Xianghuitiao are literary works using the romanticist technique and with unique ethnic style.

The Naxi people are good at singing and dancing. During breaks in labor or at festivals, mass singing and dancing is often performed. Of musical compositions, the beautiful flute tune, kouxian tune, dance are most popular. "Baishaxiyue" and "Lijiangguyue" are two famous large-scale classical musical compositions.

Their traditional festivals include the "Farm-Tool Fair" in the first lunar month, "God of the Rain Festival" (now, the Goods and Materials Fair) in the third lunar month and "Mule and Horse Fair" in the seventh lunar month. There are also the Spring Festival, Pure Brightness Festival, Dragon Boat Festival, Mid-Autumn Festival and Torch Festival-all being the same as those of the Han.

People of the Naxi ethnic group performing the ancient Naxi music in Lijiang ancient town, Yunnan Province

The Dongxiang Ethnic Group

Population: 513,805

The Dongxiang ethnic group dwell mainly in Dongxiang Autonomous County of Linxia Hui Autonomous Prefecture, and the rest are scattered in the city of Lanzhou, Guanghe, Hezheng and Linxia counties, and Ili Prefecture of Xinjiang Uygur Autonomous Region. The Dongxiang language belongs to the Mongolian group of the Altaic language family. Most Dongxiang people also speak Chinese. Without a written script of their own, they use Chinese characters.

The characteristics of the clothes of this ethnic group are embodied in the headwear. Men often wear white or black brimless cap called a "hao cap" while the women wear a silk-knit veil whose colors vary according the age of the woman. Young or newly-married girls wear a green veil, middle-aged women a cyan one, and old women a white one. The veil is long, down to the waist, and covers all the hair. Now, some young women do not wear the veil any more for working convenience, but a white cap.

The Dongxiang are Muslims. Their important festivals are similar to those of other ethnic groups believing in Islam, namely the Fast-Breaking Festival, and Corban Festival. During the latter, people gather in the mosques to recite the Koran, praise the sages and narrate stories of Mahomet's life.

The Jingpo Ethnic Group

Population: 132,143

The Jingpo live mainly in Yunnan Province. The Jingpo speak a language belonging to the Jingpo branch of the

Jingpo dancers

Tibetan-Myanmar family of the Chinese-Tibetan language system. They also speak the Zaiwayu language belonging to the Myanmar branch. They have their own Jingpo Latinized script.

In the long course of production and practice, the Jingpo people have created a rich culture and colorful art. In literature, they have rich oral works involving new century, historical legends and folktales. What's more, they combine them with the music to create a genre of talking and singing. Their musical instruments include wooden drum, ox horn, flute, vertical bamboo flute, Kouxian, gongs, cymbals, elephant-foot drum and small sanxian.

Jingpo are good singers and dancers. Group dancing, their major dancing form, reflects their life, work, wars and sacrificial rites. It sometimes involves more than 1,000 people, their singing, vigorous and firm drumbeat and steps reverberate through the nearby mountain valleys.

Most of the paintings are related to primitive religion. Carving consists of simple round carving and bamboo woodcarving. All kinds of linsey-woolsey [coarse linen fabric] are decorated with the beautiful patterns with ethnic characteristics. The configuration and pattern of the silver jewelry reach a higher level.

Jingpo men cover their head with white or black turbans and wear a black jacket and trousers or white jacket and black trousers. Jingpo men going out invariably wear long knives and carry elaborately-embroidered bags. Jingpo women usually wear black jackets and red self-knitted skirt. Matching the dress is the dark red vine-made waist hoop and leg hoop and a woolen shin guard. Women like wearing all kinds of silver ornaments.

Jingpo people have traditionally lived in thatched cottages of bamboo and wood with a gambrel roof. The cottages, oblong in shape, have two stories; the lower floor, about one meter above the ground, is for keeping animals, while the upper floor is the living quarters. In the middle of every room is a fireplace, around which people sleep on thin bamboo-strip-woven mats. Doors are set up on both sides. Strangers are forbidden from passing through the back door. Every seven or eight years, cottages have to be rebuilt. Rebuilding, with the help of all villagers, is completed in several days and a grand inauguration ceremony is then held.

The Blang Ethnic Group

Population: 91,882

The Blang people live mainly in Yunnan Province. Their language belongs to the Va-De'ang branch of the Mon-Khmer language group of the Austroasiatic language family. Some can speak Chinese, Dai and Va languages. They have no written script and some use the Chinese and Dai script.

The Blang has a rich store of folk tales and ballads transmitted orally. Their songs and dances show the strong influence of their Dai neighbors. Elephant-leg drums, cymbals and three-stringed plucked instruments provide musical accompaniment for dancing. People in the Blang Mountain area revel in their energetic "knife dance"; young people like a courting dance called the "circle dance". For the Blang in the Nujiang area, New Year's Day and weddings are occasions for dancing and singing, often lasting the whole night.

Blang men wear collarless jackets with buttons down the front and loose black trousers. They wear turbans of black or white cloth. Blang women, like their Dai sisters, wear tight collarless jackets and red-and-green striped or black skirts. They tie their hair in a bun and cover it with layers of cloth. Their staple diet consists of rice, maize and beans. They prefer their food sour and hot. Drinking wine and smoking tobacco are their main pastimes. Blang women like chewing betel nut and regard teeth dyed black with betel-nut juice as beautiful. The Blang live in two-storied balustraded bamboo houses. The ground floor is for keeping domestic animals while the upper floor is the living quarters.

Most of the Blang people follow the Hinayana branch of Buddhism and worshiped ancestors in the past. They celebrate the door-opening and door-closing festivals, and hold activities such as "offering sacrifice to the Buddha" and "heaping sands".

The Kirgiz Ethnic Group

Population: 160,823

The Kirgiz people are distributed mainly in the south of Xinjiang Autonomous Region. The majority live in the Kizilsu Kirgiz Autonomous Prefecture and the rest are found in Ili, Tacheng, Aksu and Kashgar. A small percentage lives in Heilongjiang Province.

Most Kirgiz people speak the Kirgiz language, which belongs to the Turkic group of Altaic language family, and has a written form based on Arabic letters. The Kirgiz people in the south of Xinjiang speak Uygur, while those in the north of Xinjiang speak Kazak. Some Kirgiz people living in Fuyu County of Heilongjiang Province speak Chinese and Mongolian.

In the southeast of the Kirgiz Autonomous Prefecture there are oases near the Tarim Basin. The Kirgiz people inhabited the mountainous areas. There are natural pastures in the gorges and along the rivers. Their livestock include sheep, horse, camel, cattle, yak and donkey. They also engage in agricultural production.

The Kirgiz originally practiced the totemism. Their famous totems are snow leopard and ox. In addition, they also believe in the Goddess Woma; they also practice ancestor worship and worship heavenly gods. They prayed towards the south, worshipped the sun and thought Mars threatening. During the Qing Dynasty, Kirgiz became Sunni Muslims. Some Kirgiz follow Shamanism and Tibetan Buddhism.

The important festivals include the Rozah Festival, the Corban Festival and Norooz Festival; during festivals, men and women wear new clothes and treat their relatives and friends to tea, fruit and sumptuous dinners.

The Tu Ethnic Group

Population: 241,198

A shot of the Tu festival

The Tu ethnic group lives in areas in the east of Qinghai Province. The majority of the Tu have their homes in the Huzhu Tu Autonomous County and other areas of Qinghai Province. Others are scattered in the Tianzhu Tibetan Autonomous County in Gansu Province. The language of the Tu people belongs to the Mongolian language group of the Altaic language family. In the past, Chinese characters were in common use. A new Tu written system based on the Latin alphabet is now in trial use.

The close relations exist between the Tu and Mongolian ethnic groups. Popular legends among the Tu of Huzhu Autonomous County have it that their ancestors were Mongolian soldiers under one of Genghis Khan's generals by the name of Gerilite (Geretai).

Most villages are located at the foot of hills and near rivers. Every household has the courtyard, inside which there is the livestock shed, and outside which there is lavatory, kale yard and threshing floor. Their flat-roofed houses include the main hall in the middle, and bedroom and shrine room at the two sides. The kang in the bedroom is connected with the kitchen range. The ridgepoles, beams, doors and windows are carved with colorful patterns, symbolizing abundant flocks and herds, and a bumper harvest.

The Tu people used to practice Animism while some were the followers of Taoism. After the Yuan and Ming dynasties many turned to Lamaism, but the folk religious belief remained unchanged. There are over 40 monasteries of that religion, such as Youning Monastery and Guanghui Monastery, in the Tu area. Youning Monastery produced many famous monks. The monastery is the center of Buddhist activities, contributing to the development and spread of Buddhist culture.

The Daur Ethnic Group

Population: 132,394

The Daur live mainly in the Inner Mongolia Autonomous Region and Heilongjiang Province. The rest are found in the Tacheng area in the Xinjiang Uygur Autonomous Region. They speak a language belonging to the Mongolian language group of the Altaic language family. Without a written language of their own, they mainly use Chinese. A few can also speak Manchu, Mongolian and Kazak.

The Daur people mainly engage in agriculture. Their rich diet includes corn, vegetables, wild animals, wildfowl, livestock, poultry and fish.

As early as the Liao Dynasty, the Daur people created big and small Khitan characters, which were later lost because of limited use. But they did not stop their pursuit of culture and committed themselves to learning the Manchu, Chinese, Kazak and Uygur languages. In the Qing Dynasty, they set up the schools for teaching Manchu. Early in the 20th century, they also worked hard to create a written script of their own and these efforts continue to this day.

The literary works of the Daur people not only reflect their life in agricultural production and herding, hunting and fishing, but also preserve the litany and lyrics of Shamanism. The women do well in the folk fine arts, toy making, embroidery and paper cuts passed down from generation to generation. The traditional hockey sport of the Daur people has achieved great development in recent years. Some Daur athletes have become leading players of the national hockey teams. The Daur area enjoys the reputation as the "land of the hockey".

The Mulam Ethnic Group

Population: 207,352

The Mulam ethnic group is mainly found in the Luocheng Mulam Autonomous County of the Guangxi Zhuang Autonomous Region, while the rest are scattered in counties together with the Zhuang, Han, Yao, Miao, Dong, Maonan, Shui and other ethnic groups. Their language is similar to the Maonan, Dong and Shui languages. Many speak Chinese and some speak Zhuang language. The Chinese written script is in common use.

The Mulam are good at singing folk songs, an art style in which they sing of the production, life and sentiments and pass on scientific and cultural knowledge.

Mulam houses consist of three rooms, usually one-storied, with mud walls and tiled roofs. Inside, the ground is dug away to form a coal-fired cooking pit. Rice, maize and potatoes are the staple diet. It is taboo to eat cats or snakes. Their favorite color is deep blue. During the Qing Dynasty, Mulam women still wore tube-shaped skirts while they now wear jackets buttoned down the front and long trousers. They wear their hair in plaits or coiled bun. Women's jewelry includes earrings, bracelets and finger rings. Men wear Chinese-style costumes with large buttons down the front.

The Mulam celebrate many festivals every year. Among the special ones, for example, the third day of the third month is the Puowang Festival (also called Children's Festival), when villages hold sacrificial activities. The eighth day of the fourth lunar month is the "Ox Festival", when the oxen are given a rest, and a sacrifice is offered to the Ox God. On the fifth day of the fifth lunar month, the Dragon Boat Festival is celebrated. Unlike the Han and Zhuang Dragon Boat Festivals, the Mulam used to carry a paper boat into the fields and a Shaman would chant spells to drive away insects and ensure good harvests. The 15th day of the eighth lunar month is the Youth Festival, when young people gather to conduct Zuopo youth social activities. They also celebrate the Yifan Festival generally every year, with a grand ceremony every three years. The festival falls on the auspicious day after the Beginning of Winter. During the triennial grand ceremony, the village as a unit slaughter pigs and sheep to offer sacrifice to their ancestral temple, and then dramas, lion and dragon dances, and folk songs are performed.

A Mulam gril

The Qiang Ethnic Group

Population: 306,072

Qiang grils

The Qiang live mainly in the Aba Tibetan Autonomous Prefecture of Sichuan Province. Maowen Qiang Autonomous County is the largest home to the Qiang. The Qiang language belongs to the Tibetan-Myanmar language family of the Chinese-Tibetan language system, being divided into northern and southern dialects. Qiang living in Chibusu District of Maowen County and Heishui County speak the northern dialect while those living in the remaining Qiang-inhabited areas use the southern dialect. The Qiang do not have a written script of their own; owing to their close contact with Han people, many Qiang people speak Chinese.

The Qiang have created unique culture and arts. Folk songs and folktales are rich in content and vivid in words. Folk songs include bitter song, carol, love song, toasting song and festival song. Folktales such as the Creation of World, Battle between the Qiang and the Ge and Missing the Red Army Day and Night are the precious literary and historical data. Of the Qiang dances, the Gorzhuang Tiaoshalang is the most popular. The "armor dance" performed when conducting sacrificial rites contains full-bodied ethnic characteristics. They dance, to the accompaniment of the Qiang flute-a kind of old clarinet with two tubes and Liushengzan, small gong, hand bell, suona and sheepskin drum. The Qiang also are famous for their exquisite architecture which includes the Diaolou (a kind of building), rope bridges, plank roads, well and weirs. Of Qiang handcrafts, cross-stitch work, embroidery and woolen fabric and carpet weaving are the most outstanding. As early as the Ming and Qing Dynasties, embroidering prospered in the Qiang area. Later, the cross-stitch technique was taken up by the Qiang women. Other stitches include flat embroidering. The patterns come from nature, a symbol of good luck.

The Salar Ethnic Group

Population: 104,503

The Salar people live on the edge of the Qinghai-Tibet Plateau. They are distributed mainly in the Xunhua Salar Autonomous County and contiguous Gandan Township of the Hualong Hui Autonomous County in Qinghai Province, and some villages of the Shishan Baonan, Dongxiang and Salar Autonomous County of Gansu Province. According to the fifth census in 2000, the Salar has a population of 104,503. The Salar language belongs to the western Hun branch of the Turkic language group of the Altaic language family. Most of them are able to speak Chinese and Tibetan. Having no written script of their own, they generally use Chinese script.

Their style of singing includes Salar song, banquet song, Hua'er (flowers) and other folk songs. During wedding ceremonies, the Salar perform "Camel Dances" in groups of four, featuring simple movements and slow rhythm. Their single musical instrument is the horse's hoof-shaped Kouxian stringed instrument made of copper or silver and often played by women.

Salar women are skilled at embroidery and paper cuts especially for window decoration. Their architecture is embodied in the building and decoration of the mosques, which, influenced by the style of those of hinterland, are constructed with the classical temple structure and upturned eaves, a combination of mosque architecture and classical architecture.

The Salar people are Muslims. Their major festivals include the Fast-Breaking Festival, Corban Festival and Maolude Festival. In addition, the Salar people also celebrate some special festivals of their own. For example, Bailete Night Festival is celebrated in the evening of the 15th day before the month of fasting, when all the households invite the Imams to their homes to recite scriptures. The Fatima Festival falls on the 12th day of the month of fasting in memory of the daughter of Mohammed--Fatima. In general, only adult women join the celebration activities. The Gater Festival also called "Lesser Fast-Breaking Festival" comes on the 27th day of the month of fast, when Kumsen as a unit make Meiren Rice, and steamed stuffed bun and invite the Imam and Manla to their homes to recite scriptures, making preparation for the fast-breaking. Deeply influenced by Islam, the customs and habits as practiced among the Salar are roughly the same as those of the Hui that live nearby.

The Tajik Ethnic Group

Population: 41,028

The Tajik people live mainly in the Taxkorgan Tajik Autonomous County of the Xinjiang Uygur Autonomous Region. The Tajik language belongs to the Pamir branch of the Iranian group of the Indo-European language family. The Tajik living in Shache can also speak the Uygur language and many can write it.

The Tajik, in the past, had no written script, so these literary works were passed down orally. The famous poems such as the Tercel, White Eagle, Smart Precious Stone, Varied and the LikesirWater Bird , belonging to Markamo, are the major works. The legends including the Muztag Mountain and the Ancestor of the Datong People are vivid and affecting.

The Tajik people are good at singing and dancing. Their music is divided into the playing and singing song, the singing and dancing song, the song of holding a sheep in mouth, love song and religious song. The musical instruments include Nayi (a short flute made of eagle wing bone) and two types of plucked seven-string instruments. Many of their dances imitate the hovering tercel. The Tajiks also have unique opera consisting of song and dance drama and modern drama, characterized by vivid words, humorous movements and profound implied meaning. The song and dance drama is very famous with high artistry. Their handcrafts include embroidery, weaving and Buhua cloth pasted patterns.

Tajiks follow both the Shia and Sunni forms of Islam. There are a few mosques in the Tajik areas, but Tajik Muslims do not fast or go on pilgrimage. The masses worship only during festivals.

A Tajik gril

The ethnic and religious festivals of Tajik people include the Corban Festival, Spring Festival, Paluti Festival, Rozha Festival Festival, Sowing Festival and Water Diverting Festival), each with their own ethnic characteristics. For example, Spring Festival falls in March when the grass is budding. Every family will clean up their home. Early on the morning of the festival, a child of the family will lead one cow into the main room of the house and make it walk in a circle. The master sprays some flour on its back and gives it some pancake and then it is led out. Then, families will exchange visits and festival greetings. Women in their holiday best, standing at the door, will spray flour on the left shoulder of guests to wish them happiness.

The Maonan Ethnic Group

Population: 107,166

The Maonan ethnic group is one of the minorities living the mountainous areas with small population. They are found mainly in Guangxi. According to the fifth census in 2000, its population is 107,166. The Maonan language belongs to the Dong-Shui branch of the Zhuang-Dong language group of the Chinese language family. Living together with the Han and Zhuang people for a long time, most of them speak the languages of both. They have no written script of their own and the Chinese script is in common use.

Maonan carving and weaving have unique styles. Their articles made of bamboo are exquisite. The famous flowery bamboo hats, also called, are woven with extremely thin bamboo strips decorated with patterns. The wooden false faces they carve are lively and vivid. Their stelae are carved with the lifelike dragon, phoenix, Kylin, celestial crane, longevity pine and geometrical patterns, earning praise from neighboring ethnic groups. The Nanmu villagers in the central and southern part of Huanjiang County have mastered the unique skill in making silver jewelry, handed down through generations. The silver bracelet, silver necklace and silver Kylin and Five Successful Children decoration for caps, featuring simple and beautiful patterns and exquisite workmanship, are popular with girls.

Their houses with tiled roof and mud walls are two storied with a flat roof in front. The upper floor is for family accommodation while the ground floor is reserved for livestock and storage. They preserve the characteristics of bamboo-wood-structure architecture.

Their costumes are similar to those of the Han. Male or female like to wear blue and cyan jackets with buttons down the front. The women wear the jacket with buttons on the right, edged with colored embroidery, and braids with a wispy bun. They often wear bracelets and silver medals, especially colored bamboo caps.

Maonan people are very hospital, with guests always invited to dine with the senior members of the families.

The Gelo Ethnic Group

Population: 579,357

The Gelo ethnic group is an old one living in the mid Yunnan-Guizhou Plateau. Most of the Gelo live in dispersed clusters of communities in about 20 cities or counties. The rest have their homes in the Guangxi Zhuang Autonomous Region and Yunnan Province.

Because Gelo people live in such scattered communities, the Gelo language differs greatly between them. Even Gelo-speaking people within one county are unable to converse with each other. Now only a few can still speak the language belonging to the Chinese-Tibetan language family. Which branch and language group it belongs to are not determined. For this reason, the language of the Han, or Chinese, has become their common language, though many Gelo have learned three or four languages from other people in their communities, including the Miao, Yi and Bouyei. They have no the written script so Chinese characters are in common use.

A Xibe man

The Gelo believe in polytheism and worship ancestors. They have a number of taboos. On the first day of the first lunar month, for example, they did not allow themselves to sweep floors, carry water, cook raw food, pour water in front of their house and go to the fields for labor. The Spring Festival is the grandest occasion. From the first day to the 15th day of the first lunar month, all kinds of entertainments need to be performed. "Flower Dragon" and "Bamboo-Strip Egg" are two unique games. "Flower Dragon," in fact, is a ball of woven bamboo. Inside are bits of broken porcelain and coins, thus knocking together to produce a sound. People gather on the hillsides, and play it in pairs. Men or women, and old or young can take part. "Bamboo-Strip Egg" is also a ball, but larger and stuffed with rice straw.

Apart from these traditional entertainments, all kinds of ball games and singing and dancing programs are held, making the cultural life of the masses richer and more colorful. On the first day of the tenth lunar month, the Gelo celebrate the Ox King Festival. On this day they cook two pieces of big glutinous rice pounded into paste, hang them on the ox horns, pull it to the waterside, let it see its shadow and feed it with the two pieces of the big glutinous rice thoroughly pounded.

The Xibe Ethnic Group

Population: 188,824

The Xibe ethnic group is one of minorities with a small population. They live in Liaoning Province, the Xinjiang Uygur Autonomous Region, Jilin Province and Beijing. The Xibe living in Xinjiang speak the Xibe language, belonging to the Manchu branch of the Tungu-Manchu language group of the Altaic language family whereas those in the Northeast China usually speak Chinese and Mongolian. They have their own script.

Xibe literature is rich and colorful, including folklore, folktales, ballads, banquet songs, myths, fables and legends. Long narrative poems such as Suixiang Song, Song of Kashi Gar and Song of the Three States, and Letter from Huipoka in prose and epistolary style have profound influence among the Xibe people. The Xibe people excel at singing and dancing. Their songs featuring beautiful rhythm are zealous. Their Belun dance is the most famous. Their musical instruments include the Dongbuer, the Reed Flute and the Maken (harmonica). The industrial arts such as embroidery are also rich and colorful. There are all kinds of entertainment and sport activities such as toxophily (archery), horse racing, wrestling and swinging. Many excellent Xibe archers have emerged through the ages to dominate national sports meetings.

Although the Xibe festivals are similar to those of the Han and Manchu such as the Spring Festival, Dragon Boat Festival, and Pure Brightness Festival, the specific celebrations are quite different. For example, during the Dragon Boat Festival they hold the activities including water splashing, sheep grabbing in the mouth and horse racing. In addition, large-scale activities on the eighteenth day of the fourth lunar month commemorate the day a Xibe tribe migrated westwards to Xinjiang.

The Achang Ethnic Group

Population: 33,936

The Achang ethnic group is mainly distributed in Longchuan and Lianghe counties of Dehong Dai-Jingpo Autonomous Prefectures of Yunnan Province. There are also a small number of them scattered in Yingjiang, Luxi, and Ruili, and Longling and Tengchong counties of Baoshan Prefecture. According to statistics collected in the fifth national census, the population of the Achang ethnic group totaled 33,936. The Achang speak a language belonging to the Myanmar branch of Tibetan-Myanmar language group of Chinese-Tibetan family and divided into three dialects, namely Lianghe, Longchuan and Luxi. They have no written script and habitually speak the Chinese and Dai language. Historically the Achang ethnic group had a close relation with the Jingpo, Han, Dai and Bai ethnic groups.

Achang girls

In the Achang-inhabited area, the agriculture and handicraft industry are more developed. Hualasa tobacco is famous in western Yunnan and even sold to neighboring Myanmar. The "Achang Knife", a necessary production tool, enjoys a high reputation among people in the border areas between Yunnan and Myanmar. Economic crops such as sugar cane and tea leaves and handicrafts such as embroidery and knitting are also well-known.

Most Achang in the Hulasa area believe in Hinayana form of Buddhism. Every year, they regularly celebrate religious festivals such as "Close the Door Festival", "Open the Door Festival" and "Burn Firewood Pagoda". Their major celebrations, including Festival Visiting, Denwolo, Huijie Festival, New Rice Tasting Festival, Water Splashing Festival, "Close the Door Festival" and "Open the Door Festival", are similar to those of the neighboring Dai people. In addition, there are the Torch Festival, Change Yellow Sheet, Burn Firewood Pagoda and Flower Watering Water.

The Pumi Ethnic Group

Population: 33,600

The Pumi are concentrated in Yunnan Province. Some live in Sichuan Province. They speak a language belonging to the Tibetan-Myanmar language group of the Chinese-Tibetan language system. Pumi once wrote with Tibetan characters, this was not widely popularized. Now most use Chinese.

Pumi are good singers and dancers.

A Pumi man

Singing contests in which partners sing ballads in an antiphonal style are a feature of wedding ceremonies and holidays. In addition, they also sing the short tunes covering the love and life of youth. They also like to sing folk songs of the Naxi, Bai and Han. There are many folk tales and stories among the Pumi. They dance to the flute and Lusheng, incorporating in their movements and gestures depictions of their work as farmers, hunters and weavers.

The Pumi festivals include the Large New Year's Day, the Spring Festival, Large 15th Day Festival and the New-Grain Tasting Festival. In some places the Pumi also celebrate the Pure Brightness Festival and the Dragon Boat Festival. For the Spring Festival, all the families of the same clan offer sacrifices to the Gozhuang dance. Then, they have sumptuous meals and hold horse racing and shooting contests.

The Nu Ethnic Group

Population: 28,759

The Nu live mainly in Yunnan Province's Bijiang, Fugong and Gongshan counties. Others are found in Lanping and Weixi counties. The Nu people speak a language belonging to the Tibetan-Myanmar language group of the Chinese-Tibetan language family. These dialects differ so much from each other that people from different areas cannot communicate. Without a written script of their own, most use Chinese characters.

The Nu people are fond of singing and dancing, and their dance forms are very rich. Most imitate the movements of animals, such as Monkey Dance, Cock Dance, Magpie Dance and Bird King Dance. Some depict living scene and reflect the production activity, such as Gozhuang Circle Dance, Clothes Washing Dance, Autumn Harvest Dance and Wheat Reaping Dance. In addition, there are Lute Dance and Heel Dance. Their dances are smart and trenchant with bright rhythm. Whether happy or sorrowful, Nu people express their sincere feelings in singing and dancing. For example, at wedding banquets, elders sing the Wedding Song divided into the Genesis, Courtship, the Shepherding, Hair Cutting and Escorting the Bride to the Groom's House and other chapters.

The Nu still retain remnants of their original religion. They believe in animism and nature worship. Some Nu are followers of Lamaism and Christianity.

The Uzbek Ethnic Group

Population: 12,370

Most live in Yining, Tacheng, Kashi, Urumqi, Shache, and Yecheng of Xinjiang Uygur Autonomous Region, but some are scattered in the various cities throughout the country. They speak a language belonging to the Western Hun branch of the Turki language group of the Altaic language family. They widely use the Uygur language.

The Uzbeks build their houses in different designs. Some have round attics, and most are rectangular adobe houses with flat roofs. These wood and mud structures have thick walls with beautifully patterned niches. Patterns are also carved on wooden pillars.

Both men and women wear skull caps with bright colored embroidery in unique patterns. Men wear button-less robes tied with a triangular embroidered girdle. Women wear broad and pleated dresses without girdles. Uzbek men usually wear leather boots and overshoes with low-cut uppers. Women's embroidered shoes are very beautiful and unique in design. Now, more and more Uzbeks like wear the clothes combining fashion and ethnic custom.

Like other ethnic groups in Xinjiang who are Muslims, Uzbeks are not allowed to drink alcohol and eat pork, dog, donkey and mule meat. They like mutton, beef, horse meat and dairy products. Crusty pancake and tea with milk are standard fare for all three meals of the day. "Naren", a mixture of minced cooked meat, onion and sour milk, dressed with gravy and pepper, is a table delicacy reserved for guests. It is absolutely forbidden to take off one's hat at the table and even visit other homes in shorts and vest.

Historically, Islam exerted great influence on the Uzbek people in regard to politics, economy, culture and daily life. Since the 18th century, they have built many magnificent mosques in Kashi, Shache, Ili and Chitai. The important festivals include Fast-Breaking and the Corban Festival.

The Russian Ethnic Group

Population: 15,609

The Russian people, descendents of immigrants from Tsarist Russia, are scattered around Ili, Tacheng, Altay and Urumqi in the Xinjiang Uygur Autonomous Region. They use their own language and written script, which belongs to the Slavic group of the Indo-European language family.

A Russian gril

The Russian people originally believed in polytheism (animism) while in modern times they turned to the Orthodox Eastern Church. After 1949, China carried out a policy of freedom of religious belief. Most Russians in China are the followers of the Orthodox Eastern Church; some follow Catholicism. Their major festivals include Easter, Christmas Day and Baptism Day. The followers of the Orthodox Eastern Church celebrate Christmas Day on January 7, and the celebration lasts three days.

The Ewenki Ethnic Group

Population: 30,505

The Ewenki ethnic group is distributed in the Inner Mongolia Autonomous Region and Nahe County of Heilongjiang Province, where they live together with Mongolian, Daur, Han and Oroqen. The Ewenki Autonomous Banner is where they live in compact communities. The Ewenki language belongs to the Tungu branch of the Manchu-Tungu language group of the Altaic language family. It is comprised of three dialects. There is no written script. Mongolian and its written form are used in pasturing areas, while Chinese and its written form are used in farming area and areas near mountains.

The Ewenki people have a rich folk literature historical legends, myths, stories, proverbs and riddles, vivid and affecting.

A Ewenki gril

These literary works came into being at different times but all reflected practical life. For example, the Legend of the Origin of Human Beings depicts the migration history of humans, ancient life and the natural atmosphere.

In the daily life of the Ewenki people, the birch bark occupies a certain position. The tools for hunting, fishing and milking are made from it. It is used to make dishes, dresses and personal adornments, containers, houses and fencing. It is even used to wrap corpses. These birch bark wares, portable and practical, are decorated with patterns of flowers, grass, trees, mountains, birds, fish and cliffs, which mainly come from daily life and productive activities. The making of these wares can be called "birch bark culture" with unique ethnic style. At the age of seven or eight, girls begin to learn techniques of various handicrafts, such as carving, incusing, painting and collage which are passed down from generation to generation.

The Bonan Ethnic Group

Population: 16,505

The Bonan people live mainly in Jishishan Bonan, Dongxiang and Salar Autonomous County and a few of them are found in various counties of the Linxia Hui Autonomous Prefecture and Xunhua County of Qinghai Province. The people in compact communities speak the Bonan language belonging to the Mongolian language group of the Altaic language family. Most of them also speak Chinese and use the Chinese writing system.

In the course of development, the Bonan people have created rich and colorful culture and arts. Folktales, poems and proverbs are popular among the common Bonan people, most of which narrate the ethnic history and the simple love between young men and girls. They are the good singers and dancers. The majority of them can sing the folk song-Bonan Hua'er (flowers). The unique folk song consists of such tunes as Bao'anling, Jiaohuling and Liuliusan. The singers often perform using impromptu verses.

Their dance absorbs some characteristics of Tibetan dance with bright rhythm and lively movements. The men like to play traditional stringed and woodwind instruments. They have rich modeling arts. The women are skilled at paper-cuts. On the wooden ware, household utensils and handles of Bonan knives are carved unique patterns or painted with colorful drawings.

The Bonan people are mainly Sunni Muslims divided into two different sects-the Old and the New. With the exception of the Spring Festival and several ethnic minority festivals, almost all their festivals are Islamic ones, such as the Fast-Breaking Festival, Corban Festival and Maolude Festival.

The De'ang Ethnic Group

Population: 17,935

The De'ang people are widely distributed in the Dehong Dai-Jingpo Autonomous Prefecture, Zhengkang, Gengma, Yongde, Baoshan and Lancang counties of Yunnan Province, covering an area of 30,000 square km. They live together with the Jingpo, Va and Han in most of the villages. According to fifth national census data, the population of the De'ang ethnic group totaled 17,935. The De'ang language belongs to the Va-De'ang branch of the Mon-Khmer language group of the Austro-Asiatic language family, including three dialects namely "Bolei", "Rumai" and "Ruchin". The group has no written script.

The De'ang people are skilled in colorful embroidery, architecture and carving arts. Now, some exquisite architectural relics by the De'ang are preserved in some places. The sites of the De'ang Queen Palace, De'ang City, De'ang Road and Stone Arch Bridge are representative of their ancient architectural skills. Examples of their art include De'ang waist hoops, eardrops, silver bracelets, silver cigarette cases and clothes decorated with patterns, including symmetrical bands, birds, tigers, flowers and grass.

The De'ang follow the Hinayana form of Buddhism. Most villages have monasteries populated by bonzes and young monks. The De'ang in different areas are followers of different sects. In some areas, they are allowed to raise pigs or chickens, while in other localities they are forbidden to kill creatures, even if wild beasts destroy their crops. During the religious festivals and the anniversary of the death of their ancestors, they do not engage in productive labor. Besides Buddhism, they also worship the ghosts and gods of the original religion.

The festivals of the De'ang include the Water Splashing Festival, the Closing-Door Festival, the Opening-Door Festival, and Burn Firewood Pagoda, most of which have a religious coloring.

The Yugur Ethnic Group

Population: 13,719

Nearly 90 percent of Yugur people live in the Yugur Autonomous County of southern Gansu Province, with the rest living in the Huangnipu Yugur Autonomous Township of Jiuquan City in Gansu Province. According to the fifth census in 2000, the Yugur ethnic group had a population of 13,719. Three languages are now used by the Yugur people: the western Yugur language (also called Raohul), a Turkic branch of the Altaic language family, used by the Yugur people who live in the western part of the Su'nan Yugur Autonomous County; the eastern Yugur language (also called Engle), a Mongolian branch of the Altaic language family, used by the Yugur people living in the eastern part of the autonomous county; and Chinese. They don't have their own written character and Chinese characters are widely used.

Yugur people greeting visitors wire wine

Although the written script of the Yugur has been lost, they have a rich literary tradition handed down orally, such as folk tales, legends, fables, ballads, epics and proverbs. Their folk songs feature uniquely simple yet graceful tunes, singing of labor and love. In recent years, some scholars have investigated the Yugur folk songs. They found that some folk songs, like cradle songs, still preserved intact the tunes of Hun folk songs from 2,000 years ago, which were passed on to the Tile Huihe people-ancestors of the Yugur by the Hun. They are skilled at plastic arts. They weave beautiful patterns on bags, carpets and so on. Women are good embroiderers, and the variety of patterns embroidered are lively and vivid.

Most Yugur people believe in the Gelug Sect of Lamaism.

The Tatar Ethnic Group

Population: 4,890

The Tatar are scattered in the Xinjiang Uygur Autonomous Region. Most of them are concentrated in Yining, Tacheng and Urumqi. The Tatar language belongs to western Hun branch of Turkic language group of the Altaic language system. Because the Tatars mix freely in Xinjiang with the Uygurs and Kazaks, the languages and written scripts of these two minorities also are in common use among Tatar people.

The Tatars' educational development began in the late 19th century when Tatar clerics opened schools in several areas such as Yining and Tacheng. Besides the religious courses, these schools taught arithmetic and Chinese language. The Yining Tatar School, set up in 1941, was one of the earliest modern schools for ethnic minorities in Xinjiang. There are many Tatar intellectuals.

Early in the 1930s, the Tatar people set up their own Tatar drama troupe giving performances which were popular among various ethnic people. They have various

A Tatar man

musical instruments including the "Kunie" (vertical wooden flute with two holes), the "Kebisi" (a kind of harmonica) and the two-stringed violin. When singing and dancing they are accompanied by the accordion and mandolin. Tatar dances are lively and cheerful. Men use many leg movements, such as squatting, kicking and leaping. Women move their waists and arms more. Their dance styles incorporate features of the Uygur, Russian and Uzbek dances, but also have their own unique characteristics.

Most of Tatars are Muslims. The Islamic culture exerts influence on them in terms of life and customs. They must conduct religious activities in light of the stipulated time and procedures. For example, they recite Nemaz scriptures five times a day and go to the mosque and worship every Friday. The major festivals of the Tatar people include the Fast-Breaking Festival, Corban Festival and the Sapan Festival (also called the Plough Head Festival). Especially the Sapan Festival, which falls on 20-25 June every year, a break time during the busy farming season, are very grand. During this time, the Tatar people, singing and dancing, hold all kinds of sporting games to celebrate.

The Lhoba Ethnic Group

Population: 2,965

The Lhoba have their homes mainly in Luoyu and neighboring Zayu, Mainling, Medog and Lhunze in the southeastern part of the Tibet Autonomous Region.The Lhoba living in northern Medog County speak Tibetan, while the rest use the Lhoba language belonging to the Tibetan-Myanmar language group of the Chinese-Tibetan language family. But there is a great discrepancy in dialects between different areas.

The dress of different clan members varies. Men in northern Luoyu wear black knee-length jackets of sheep's wool and drape a piece of wild cattle skin over their shoulders. They wear helmet-like hats either made from bearskin or woven from rattan laced with bearskin. The brim of the hat is covered with a bearskin circle with hair and a rectangular black bearskin hanging from the back. Women wear self-woven short jackets and skirts made of sheep's wool, flax and cotton. Both men and women go barefoot and have long hair. They wear a variety of ornaments.

The Lhoba people believe in animism. They believe that the world is filled with spirits which dominate their lives, control nature, cause disasters and bestow happiness.

The Jino Ethnic Group

Population: 20,899

According to the fifth census in 2000, the Jino ethnic group has a population 20,899. Most of the them live in Jino Township of Jinhong County in the Xishuangbanna Dai Autonomous Prefecture of Yunnan Province, and the rest are scattered in the neighboring mountainous areas. They speak a language belonging to the Yi branch of Tibetan-Myanmar language group of the Chinese-Tibetan language family but have no written script.

The men usually wear collarless white jackets with buttons down the front and round colored light ray patterns on the back, and white or blue trousers made of flax or cotton. Women, as a rule, prefer the cloak-shaped, peaked cap, short collarless, button-less jackets decorated with seven colors patterns, the triangular-shaped, embroidered apron with round silver decorations, and short black skirts rimmed in red and opened at the front. The houses of the Jino were the tilted storied building made of bamboo in the past. With the improvement in people's living standards, the solid and fireproof building of bamboo with the stake, stone-base and tile-roof has replaced thatched-roof ones.

The Derung Ethnic Group

Population: 7,426

The Derung live mainly in the Dulong River valley of the Gongshan Derung and Nu Autonomous County of the Nujiang Lisu Autonomous Prefecture of Yunnan Province. Their language belongs to the Tibetan-Myanmar group of the Chinese-Tibetan language family. Similar to the language of the Nu people, their neighbors, it does not have a written form.

The Derung people are fond of singing and dancing. When conducting such activities as working, reaping, hunting, building house, proposing and celebrating festivals, they like to sing so as to express their pleasure, anger, sorrow and joy. They dance to the accompaniment of the kouxian, gong, flute and skin drum. The kouxian is played by women. When singing and dancing they drink wine generally. Every adult man or woman can sing or dance off the cuff. They often dance with the male group facing the female in rows or in a circle. The dancers with the sword or bow, or hand in hand, perform lively movements.

Both women and men like to have their upper chest wrapped with a long piece of gunny from the left armpit to the right shoulder, which is fastened with straw ropes or bamboo needles, leaving the left shoulder uncovered. The traditional house of the Derung people-made of logs or bamboo-comprise a large, oblong room which serves as their common quarters where two or more fireplaces are set up. The fireplaces are symmetrically arrayed on the both sides of the room or put at the four corners. The fireplace for the parents is placed at the upper part. Each fireplace in the house symbolizes one small family unit. Once a man marries, a new fireplace will be set up in the large house. The married sons, instead of separating from their parents, will settle down in the house built for them beside the large house.

The Oroqen Ethnic Group

Population: 8,196

According to the fifth census in 2000, the Oroqen ethnic group has a population of 8,196. They are found mainly in Oroqen Autonomous Banner, Butha Banner and Moli Daur Autonomous Banner of Hulun Buir League of the Inner Mongolian Autonomous Region, and the counties of Huma of Heilongjiang Province. The Oroqen language belongs to the Tungu branch of the Tungu-Manchu language group of the Altaic family. Since there is no written language they usually use Chinese.

An Oroqen woman

The Oroqen live mainly in the Great Hinggan Mountains at an altitude of 500 to 1,500 meters, belonging to the high and cold mountainous areas. The luxuriant Hinggan Mountains are home to the wild beasts such as deer, roe, elk, tiger, leopard, wild boar, bear, fox, lynx and otter. All kinds of fish multiply in the rivers. The fine hunting environment has provided the Oroqen people with a source of the food and clothing. Xianrenzhu, meaning "house supported by wooden poles", was the traditional dwelling of the Oroqen people. It is a conical wooden shanty made of 30 poles. The covering varies according to the season. In summer, it is enclosed with stitched birch bark while in winter the skins of wild animals are used. The houses are simply furnished and easy to dismantle.

The Oroqen Autonomous Banner and several Oroqen townships were set up in places where the formally normadic Oroqen live in compact communities on October 1, 1951.

The Hezhen Ethnic Group

Population: 4,640

The Hezhen ethnic group lives mainly in Heilongjiang Province. The fifth census in 2000 shows it has a population of 4,640. Their language, which belongs to the Manchu branch of the Manchu-Tungu group of the Altaic family, has no written form. Ancient Hezhen people kept records of important affairs by carving notches on wood or bamboo slips. Because they have lived together with the Han for a long time, they speak Chinese.

The Hezhen people cherish rich and colorful folk literature. The most popular Yimakan is a genre of folk talk and singing literature with libretto rhyming. The longer ones can be talked and sung for days on end, most of which narrate the stories of heroes and their revenge, the rise and decline of the ethnic group and pure love.

Embroidery is a highly developed art among the Hezhen. They often embroider the clouds, grass, butterfly, geometrical and floral patterns on their clothes, shoes, caps and bedding made of fish skin or hides. The floral patterns women embroider on the front of the garments, capes, caps and trouser legs with colored thread are most beautiful. Colorful embroidered-patterns such as the "Chanticleers Holding Flowers in Their Mouth" and "Gaily Decorated Basket and Lotus Root" are characterized by novel and unique pictorial composition.

The Hezhen people used to believe in Shamanism and practiced animism. They worship their ancestors and nature. They believe that the sun, moon, mountains and rivers are dominated by the gods, so they worship them.

The Moinba Ethnic Group

Population: 8,923

A Moinba festival

The Moinba are scattered in the Menyu area, in the southern part of Tibet Autonomous Region. In the mid-19th century, some who could not bear the oppression and exploitation under the feudal serfdom, moved east to the Medog area. Their language belongs to the Tibetan branch of the Tibetan-Myanmar language group of the Chinese-Tibetan language family. Many of them can speak Tibetan. Without a written script, they use the Tibetan script.

The Moinba people have the rich oral literature. Especially they are good at the creation of poetry. Of the diversified oral literature, there are toasting songs called Sama reflecting their life, customs, psychology, desires, love songs called Gyalu reflecting the pure love between young men and women, and well-wishing songs called Dongsanba. The opera of the Moinba people evolved from folk dances. Influenced by Tibetan Buddhism to certain extent, most plays follow the theme of comeuppance, advising people to do good works and punishing the vicious. The ethnic group is good at singing and dancing. They dance, boldly and in an unconstrained way, accompanied by a flute with four holes.

In Menyu area, men and women prefer to wear Pulu woolen robes with aprons and brown-topped, saffron-brimmed caps with a gap in the front or black yak hair hats. They wear soft-soled leather boots, which are sewn with red or black pulu. Women usually wear white aprons, a string of white, red and green beads, earrings, rings and bracelets. People in Medog County dress differently; women as well as men wear short or long jackets, and the women wear long striped skirts and various kinds of jewelry such as earring and rings.

The Moinba's staple food includes rice, maize, millet and buckwheat. They like to eat butter, Zanba (roasted qingke barley) and chili, and are addicted to smoking and drinking wines. Their homes are two-or three-story, herringbone-shaped houses of wood with bamboo or straw roofs. The second and third floors are used for living quarters and the first for livestock.

The Moinba people believe in Lamaism but some follow the primitive religion. They practice the Tibetan calendar. The New Year according to this is the most important festival for the Moinba. In July, they also celebrate the Ongko Festival.

The Jing Ethnic Group

Population: 22,517

The Jing live in the Guangxi Zhuang Autonomous Region. The Jing language is similar to Vietnamese. Now the Cantonese dialect and Chinese (Putonghua) are in common use.

The Jing people cherish rich and colorful folk literature and art with a strong ethnic style. Their singing arts have unique characteristics, covering narrative epics and Chinese ancient poetry. The "Jing Opera" also called "Chao Opera" has unique ethnic characteristics. The Duxianqin (single-stringed instrument) is a pleasant-sounding ethnic musical instrument unique to the Jing people.

Traditional Jing houses reflect ancient architecture, with wooden pillars, bamboo and mud forming the walls and a thatched roof; they are easy to move. Nowadays, however, they use bricks and stones to build their houses with a tiled roof.

Some Jing elderly women wear their own ethnic costume, namely tight-fitting, collarless short blouses buttoned in front with narrow sleeves plus a diamond-shaped top apron and broad black or brown trousers. When going out, they put on another white long gown, like the cheongsam and with long slit up the sides, and wear a chopping-block-shaped bun. A few women still retain the tradition of dying their teeth black.

The Changha Festival is the most magnificent festival of the Jing. Varying from place to place, the festival date is not fixed. The activities can last three days and nights.

A Jing gril

Major Ethnic Festivals

People in China celebrate various festivals and almost every ethnic group has its own. Typical examples are the Spring Festival for Han people, New Year Festival according to the Tibetan Calendar for Tibetan people, Water-Splashing Festival for Dai people, Torch Festival for Yi People, Temple and Trade Fair in March for Bai people, Singing Carnival for Zhuang people and Naidam Fair for Mongolian people. In addition, some local governments have set up traditional festivals for minority people as legal festivals, such as New Year Festival according to the Tibetan Calendar and Corban Festival. In the meantime, the people of the ethnic minorities, like the Han, celebrate Spring Festival, Mid-Autumn Festival and Dragon Boat Festival.

Spring Festival

(See P518)

Corban Festival

Corban is a traditional annual festival for Muslims. It is celebrated on the 10th day of the 12th month according to Islamic calendar and is the common festival celebrated by Chinese ethnic minorities that believe in Islam, including Hui, Uygur, Kazak, Uzbek, Tajik, Tartar, Kirgiz, Salar, Dongxiang and Bonan. Before Corban, all Islamic families clean their houses and are busy making various cakes for the festival. On the morning of Corban, they put on their best clothes after taking a bath and listen to the Imam's interpretation of the Koran in the mosques. Most families butcher sheep, camels or oxen and distribute them to relatives, friends and guests. Corban also provides a good opportunity for conversation during which many Muslims get together and share mutton, cakes, melons and fruits with others. In addition, Uygur people in Xinjiang hold large-scale singing and dancing performance and Kazak, Kirgiz, Tajik and Uzbek people stage various games to celebrate the festival, including sheep-hunting, horse racing and wrestling.

Fast-Breaking Festival

Fast breaking is in the beginning of the tenth month according to Islamic calendar and serves as the common festival celebrated by some Chinese ethnic minorities, including Hui, Uygur, Kazak, Uzbek, Tajik, Tartar, Kirgiz, Salar, Dongxiang and Bonan. The ninth month according to the Islamic calendar is called Ramadan when Muslims fast during the day and can only eat after dark. In the evening when the bells in the mosques ring, people suspend their fasting and begin to have their meal.

The activities marking the festival of fast breaking constitute a great occasion, and it is a common practice for Muslims to paint their houses, clean up their yard, and have a haircut and bathe before the festival. Fast breaking is also the day favored by many young lovers to hold their weddings.

Tibetan New Year

During the Tibetan New Year, the Tibetan people visit their relatives and friends and exchange New Year greetings and the good wishes to each other, saying "Tashi Delek" which means auspiciousness or luck.

The New Year Festival according to the Tibetan Calendar is the most important and glamorous festival for Tibetans. It usually lasts for 15 days. Tibetans begin preparing for New Year's Day early in the twelfth month. Before the Tibetan New Year, each household makes "qiema" (a wooden measure for grain), expressing the wish for a good harvest and auspiciousness in the coming year. They will also make "kasai" (fried twisted dough sticks) in various forms, which look golden and taste crispy, and "luoguo" (a kind of food made of butter in the shape of sheep's head), signifying thriving domestic animals and abundant life. In addition, they offer dried or fresh fruits, butter and brick tea to Buddha.

On the day before the New Year, all the families clean their houses, hang up new curtains, put up new streamers on the roof, draw signs on the door with the lime powder, symbolizing perpetuity. On New Year's Eve, all family members get together for a big dinner. They will eat "gutu," made of beef and mutton, turnip and flour lumps. What is interesting is that some stones, coins, pepper, charcoal and wool are wrapped in the flour lump. What people eat stands for their fortune and the state of their heart in the coming year. The stones stand for a cruel heart, wool soft heart, charcoal for the scorpion, and coins prosperity.

On the first day of the first month, the Tibetan people lock themselves in. On the second day, they venture out to visit their relatives and friends and exchange New Year greetings and the good wishes to each other, saying "Tashi Delek" which means auspiciousness or luck. They also engage in singing and dancing and Tibetan opera performances. On the 15th day, religious rituals are conducted in most Tibetan-inhabited areas.

Nadam Fair

Nadam Fair is a traditional festival for Mongolians in Inner Mongolia Autonomous Region, Gansu Province, Qinghai Province and Xinjiang Uygur Autonomous Region. It is often held in July and August when the grasslands are beautiful and the herds are stout and strong, and it lasts for several days. The Nadam Fair in Xilingol League is the most representative. "Nadam" means "entertainment and games" in Mongolian, expressing gladness at the harvest.

Nadam Fair is divided into three categories in scale—the mass, medium and small ones. The large one lasts 7-10 days, in which 512 wrestlers and 300 horses will participate; the medium 5-7 days, in which 256 wrestlers and 100-150 horses will take part; and the small 3-5 days, in which 64 or 125 wrestlers and 30 or 50 horses will participate.

In the Yuan Dynasty, Genghis Khan paid more attention to cultivating the Mongolian to be brave and smart and with an indomitable spirit. Wrestling, horse riding and archery, the "three skills", were regarded as the main content of the training for improving the quality of soldiers and people. When Genghis Khan led the Mongolian cavalry to victory in the Western Region, a grand Nadam Fair was held. From then on, it became a traditional festival for celebrating victory in battle, offering sacrifices to the banner, get-togethers among the various leagues and banners and worshipping the Aobao.

At the Nadam Fair, not only traditional wresting, horse racing and archery competitions, but also camel racing, playing Mongolian chess and other activities are conducted. On the sidelines, people will meet relatives, make new friends, banqueting by eating mutton with the hands. The young girls and men will sing and dance, adding florid color to the beautiful grassland.

Horse racing on the Naidam Fair on the Hulunbuir Grassland, in Inner Mongolia Autonomous Region

Festivals of Ethnic Minority Groups in China

Ethnic Group	Name of Festival	Main Activities	Date (Lunar Calendar)
Yi	Torch Festival	Playing with torches, wrestling, bull fight, singing and dancing performance	24th day of the sixth lunar month
	Ikebana Festival	ikebana, antiphonal singing	Eighth day of the second lunar month
	Costume Festival	Singing and dancing, in beautiful costumes	28th day of the third lunar month
	Tiger Festival	Tiger dance	Eighth to 15th day of the first lunar month
	Michi Festival	Rite of offering sacrifice to gods	
	Mouding Third Lunar Month Fair	Materials exchange, folk singing and dancing performance	27th to 29th day of the third lunar month
Bai	Dali Third Lunar Month Fair	Materials exchange, horse racing, singing and dancing performance	15th day to 21st day of the third lunar month
	Girl's Festival	Singing and dancing	15th day of the first lunar month
	Raosanling	Offering sacrifice to gods or ancestors, planting rice seedling	23rd to 25th day of the fourth lunar month
	Rice-seedling Planting Festival	Offering sacrifice to gods or ancestors, planting rice seedling, antiphonal singing	Spring
	Torch Festival	Lighting torches, dragon boat race, and singing	25th day of the sixth lunar month
	Shibaoshan Song Meeting	Temple fair, antiphonal singing	End of the seventh lunar month
	Pear Flower Meeting	Picnic in pear orchard	When the pear flowers are in bloom
	Guardian Worship Festival	Offering sacrifice to gods or ancestors, singing and dancing, Dongjing music	Differs between villages
Dai	Water Splashing Festival	Dagon boat race, water splashing, singing and dancing	Middle 10 days of the fourth lunar month
	Dragon Seeing-off Festival	Offering sacrifices to gods or ancestors, singing and dancing	In January of the Gregorian calendar
	Door-Closing Festival	Buddha pagoda, singing and dancing	Middle ten days of July
	Door-Opening Festival	Village Visits, Auspicious Courting, singing and dancing	Middle ten days of October
Hani	Amatu	Offering sacrifices to gods or ancestors, singing and dancing, Street Feasting	Dragon Day of the second lunar month
	"Kuzhazha" (New Year's Day in the Sixth lunar month)	Swinging, wrestling, singing and dancing	24th day of the sixth lunar month
	Limazhu Festival	Singing and dancing, wrestling	Third lunar month
	Locust Capturing Festival	Capturing locusts to eat	24th day of the sixth lunar month
	Girl's Festival	Swinging, singing and dancing	Fourth day of the second lunar month
	Dragon Worshiping/ New Rice Festival	Performing Gong, cowskin drum, Bawu, Sixian instrument	Second day of the second lunar month
	Misuzha Festival	Swinging, singing and dancing	
	Miao'aina Festival	Bonfire, singing and dancing	First ten days of the fifth lunar month
Miao	Flower Mountain Festival	Pole climbing, lusheng, singing and dancing	First lunar month
Lisu	Hot Spring Bathing Festival	Hot spring bath, singing race	Second day of the first lunar month
	Heshi Festival	Having a reunion dinner, shooting race	First to 15th day of the first lunar month
	Sword-Pole Festival	Climbing sword-pole, Fire Sea, Bag Throwing, singing and dancing	Eighth day of the second lunar month
Naxi	Mila (Bangbang) Festival	Picnic, horse racing, singing and dancing, farm tools exchange	Eighth day of the second lunar month
	Sando Festival	Offering sacrifice to gods or ancestors, antiphonal singing, bullfight	25th day of the sixth lunar month
	Mule and Horse Fair	Materials exchange, recreation and sports performance	Middle ten days of the first and seventh lunar month
	Heaven Worship	Offering sacrifice to gods or ancestors	Spring sacrifice in the first lunar month/Autumn sacrifice in the seventh lunar month
	Seventh Lunar Month Fair	Materials exchange, recreation and sports performance	Middle ten days of the seventh lunar month
	Dragon Worship Festival	Materials exchange, recreation and sports performance	15th day of the first lunar month
Lahu	Kuzha Festival (New Year's Day)	Elephant-foot drum dance, antiphonal singing	End of the third month or the beginning of the fourth month in the Dai calendar
	Calabash Festival	Bonfire, singing and dancing	Tenth day of the tenth lunar month
	Sun God Worship	Offering sacrifice to gods or ancestors, singing and dancing	Beginning of Summer
Va	Lamugu Festival	Offering sacrifice to gods or ancestors, singing and dancing	Gerui month in the Va calendar/ December

Ethnic Group	Name of Festival	Main Activities	Date (Lunar Calendar)
Blang	Gangyong Festival	Offering sacrifice to gods or ancestors, singing and dancing	Fourth and ninth months
Drung	Kaquwa (New Year's Day)	Offering sacrifice to gods or ancestors, Ox Butchering, singing and dancing	11th or first lunar month
Jingpo	Munaozongge Dancing Party	Offering sacrifice to gods or ancestors, singing and dancing	First lunar month
Nu	New Year's Day	Ancestor worship, earth worship, singing and dancing	From the 12th lunar month to the tenth day of the first lunar month of the ensuing year
	Flower Festival	Collecting fresh flowers, singing and dancing	15th day of the third lunar month
Achang	Huijie	White Elephant, elephant-foot drum dance	Middle ten days of the ninth lunar month
Pumi	New Year's Day	Swinging, horse racing, singing and dancing	Sixth day of the 12th lunar month
	Walking-Around-Mountain	Visiting mountains, singing and dancing	Fifth day of the fifth lunar month
Tibetan	Grassland Festival /Tibetan New Year	Horse racing, picnic, Guozhuang dance	First lunar month
	Hua'er Meeting	Antiphonal singing	14th day of the sixth lunar month
	Sorcerer's Dance	Offering sacrifice to gods or ancestors, singing and dancing	New Year's Eve in the Tibetan calendar
	Horse Racing	Horse racing	Fifth day of the fifth lunar month
Hui	Corban Festival	Group visiting, butchering some cattle and sheep	Tenth month in the Hui calendar
	Fast-breaking Festival	Worshiping, reciting sutras, singing and dancing	Sixth lunar month
	Rozha Festival	Food reduction	23rd day of the fifth lunar month
	Animal Butchering Festival	Butchering some cattle and sheep, offering sacrifice to gods or ancestors	The10th and 12th months in the Hui calendar
	Maolude Festival		12th day of the third month of the Islamic calendar
Jino	Temaoke Festival	Singing and dancing, village visiting, throwing peg-top	First month in the Jino calendar
Yao	Panwang Festival	Offering sacrifice to gods or ancestors, singing and dancing	29th day of the fifth lunar month
	Ganba Festival	Bronze drum dance	Last ten days of the lunar 12th month
	Xijiu Festival	Singing and dancing	20th day of the fifth lunar month
	Danu (Never Forget the Past) Festival	Singing and dancing, Wushu, ball game	29th day of the fifth lunar month
	Getang Festival	Singing for courtship	16th day of the tenth lunar month
	Daogao Festival	Bull fight	16th day of the tenth lunar month
	Guests-Entertained-With-Large-Meat Festival	In memory of Shimu Miluyuan with three children	29th day of the fifth lunar month
	Bird Driving Festival	Antiphonal singing	First day of the second lunar month
	Girl's Fair	Materials exchange, folk singing and dancing performance	First fair after the Spring Festival
Zhuang	Longduan Festival	Opera performance, sideshows, singing and dancing	Sixth lunar month
	Liulang Festival	Like the Spring Festival	First day of the sixth or seventh lunar month
Bouyei	Tiaoyue	Materials exchange, folk singing and dancing performance	13th to 15th day of the second lunar month
	Third Day of the Third Lunar Month	Materials exchange, folk singing and dancing performance	Third day of the third lunar month
	Sixth Day of the Sixth Lunar Month	Materials exchange, folk singing and dancing performance	Sixth day of the sixth lunar month
	Tiaohuahui Festival	Performing on ethnic minority musical instruments	First to 21st day of the first lunar month
Shui	Shui Festival	Like the Spring Festival	First day of the sixth lunar month
De'ang	Water Splashing Festival	Water splashing, singing and dancing	Seventh day of the Pure Brightness Festival
	De'ang Ethnic Festival		
Manchu	Manchurian Festival	Ancestor worship, singing and dancing	13th day of the lunar month
Mongolian	Luban Festival	Offering sacrifice to gods or ancestors, singing and dancing	Second day of the fourth lunar month
Uygur	Sayile Festival	Recreation	Fifth, sixth, seventh or eighth lunar month
	Snow Festival	Recreation activities	First snow of each winter

Policies on Ethnic Groups

The policies of the Chinese Government in handling the ethnic problems include the following basic principles:

◇ Equality and unity among ethnic groups
◇ Self-government of ethnic groups
◇ Developing the economy and culture of ethnic groups
◇ Training ethnic cadres
◇ Respecting and developing spoken and written languages of ethnic minorities

Equality and Unity Among Ethnic Groups

Equality and unity among ethnic groups as the basic principle and policy for resolving ethnic problems have been clearly defined in the Constitution and relevant laws.

The policy of equality among ethnic groups in China includes the following principles:

All ethnic groups are equal regardless of their size.

All ethnic groups enjoy equal rights not only in the fields of law and national political life, but also in the field of social life such as economy, culture, education, spoken and written language, customs and habits, and religious belief. On the one hand, no ethnic group enjoys any special privileges, but, on the other hand, the equal rights and interests of the ethnic minorities are protected.

In order to help all ethnic groups enjoy their equal rights, small and weak ethnic groups should be given more help to protect their interests. Equality among ethnic groups stipulated in the Constitution and laws is guaranteed. Moreover, measures are taken to help the backward ethnic groups realize their full rights.

All ethnic groups must perform their related obligations. There is neither obligation without rights, nor rights without obligation. While enjoying their full rights, all ethnic groups should also take up their responsibility of guaranteeing national equality, unity and national unification.

Ethnic Regional Autonomy

To solve the problems of ethnic minorities, different systems have been adopted by various multi-ethnic countries around the world, and what China practices is the system of ethnic regional autonomy. This means that, under the unified leadership of the State, organs of self-government are established for the exercise of autonomy and regional autonomy is practiced in areas where people of ethnic minorities live in compact communities. China's adoption of ethnic regional autonomy is an institutional arrangement based on its own historical development, cultural characteristics, ethnic relations and distribution of ethnic groups, as well as other specific conditions, which accord with the common interests of all ethnic groups and their demands for development. Both the Constitution and the Law on Ethnic Regional Autonomy contain clear stipulations on ethnic regional autonomy and its implementation. The system of ethnic regional autonomy is a basic political system of China.

Types of Autonomous Areas for Ethnic Minority Groups

Autonomous areas are divided into three types. (1) Autonomous areas are established where people of one ethnic minority live in concentrated communities, such as the Tibet Autonomous Region; (2) autonomous areas are established within a larger autonomous area where people of one or several ethnic minorities with a smaller population live in concentrated communities, such as the Kazak, Kirgiz, Mongolian, and Hui autonomous prefectures, and the Xibo and Tajik Autonomous counties in Xinjiang Uygur Autonomous Region; (3) autonomous areas are established where people of two or more ethnic minorities live in concentrated communities, such as the Dehong Dai-Jingpo Autonomous Prefecture in Yunnan Province and the Longsheng multi-ethnic groups Autonomous County in the Guangxi Zhuang Autonomous Region.

Autonomous Areas for Ethnic Minority Groups

Now, China has established 155 ethnic autonomous areas, including five autonomous regions, 30 autonomous prefectures and 120 autonomous counties (banners). Of the 55 ethnic minorities, 44 have their own autonomous areas. The population of ethnic minorities implementing regional autonomy accounts for 71 percent of the total population of ethnic minorities. There are 1,173 autonomous townships in places equivalent to townships where ethnic minorities live in compact communities, as a supplement to the autonomous areas. Of the 11 ethnic minorities for which regional autonomy is not implemented because their populations and habitats are relatively small, nine have set up autonomous townships.

The five ethnic autonomous regions are the Inner Mongolian, Ningxia Hui, Tibet, Xinjiang Uygur, Guangxi Zhuang Autonomous Regions.

Organs of Self-Government of Ethnic Autonomous Areas

In accordance with the Constitution and the Law on Ethnic Regional Autonomy, the organs of self-government of ethnic autonomous areas are the people's congresses and people's governments of autonomous regions, autonomous prefectures and autonomous counties. In addition to exercising the functions and powers of local State organs at the corresponding level, they also exercise the power of autonomy. Firstly, they independently manage the internal affairs of their ethnic groups in their autonomous areas. Among the chairpersons or vice-chairpersons of the standing committees of the people's congresses of all 155 autonomous areas in China, there are citizens of the ethnic group or groups exercising regional autonomy in the area concerned. The chairperson of an autonomous region, the prefect of an autonomous prefecture and the head of an autonomous county are all citizens of the ethnic group or groups exercising regional autonomy in the area concerned. In the working departments of the self-government organs in these autonomous areas, a rational proportion of officials from the ethnic group or groups exercising regional autonomy

Five Autonomous Regions

Names	Founding time	Capital	Area (Square Km)	Population(December 2007) (10,000 people)
Inner Mongolia Autonomous Regions	May 1,1947	Huhhot	1197547	2405.06
Xinjiang Uygur Autonomous Region	October 1,1955	Urumqi	1655826	2095.19
Guangxi Zhuang Autonomous Region	March 15,1958	Nanning	237693	5002
Ningxia Hui Autonomous Region	October 25,1958	Yinchuan	62818	610.25
Tibet Autonomous Region	September 1,1965	Lhasa	1228400	284.15

as well as members of other minorities living in the area concerned are appointed in accordance with the law. At present, minority officials total more than 2.9 million nationwide.

Meanwhile, through electing deputies to the National People's Congress from their own ethnic group, minorities exercise the right to manage State affairs. From the 1st National People's Congress to the present day, the proportion of deputies of ethnic minorities among the total number of deputies in every NPC has been higher than the proportion of their populations in the national total in the corresponding periods. For example, in the 10th National People's Congress there are 415 deputies of ethnic minorities, accounting for 13.91 percent of the total number of deputies, 5.5 percentage points higher than the proportion of their population. Every ethnic group has its own NPC deputy or deputies. Ethnic groups with a population of more than one million have members in the NPC Standing Committee.

Spoken and Written Languages of the Ethnic Groups

Soon after New China was founded in 1949, the State helped a dozen ethnic minorities improve or create their own written languages. By the end of 2003, 22 ethnic minorities used 28 written languages. With the assistance of the State and efforts of the ethnic autonomous areas, by 2003, a total of 4,787 titles of books in ethnic minority languages had been published, totaling 50.34 million copies. There were also 205 magazines and 88 newspapers in such languages, totaling 7.81 million copies and 131.30 million copies, respectively. In China, the spoken and written languages of ethnic minorities are widely used in the fields of law and justice, administration, education, political and social life, and other areas. When important meetings, such as the CPC National Congress, NPC and CPPCC Sessions, are held, the documents of the meetings are available in Mongolian, Tibetan, Uygur, Kazak, Korean, Yi and Zhuang, and simultaneous interpretation in those languages are also provided.

According to the rules and regulations of the autonomous regions, one or more languages shall be used by the autonomous institutions. In areas where several languages are used, the language of the ethnic group which follows the regional autonomy shall be used as the major language. Inner Mongolia, Xinjiang, Tibet and other ethnic autonomous regions have all enacted rules and regulations on the use of ethnic languages.

Freedom of Religious Belief of Ethnic Minorities

Most people of ethnic minorities hold religious beliefs. In some ethnic groups, the majority of the people are adherents to a certain religion. For example, most Tibetans believe in Tibetan Buddhism, while the Hui and Uygur peoples are followers of Islam. Organs of self-government in autonomous areas, in accordance with the provisions of the Constitution and relevant laws, respect and guarantee freedom of religious belief of ethnic minorities, and safeguard all legal and normal religious activities of people of ethnic minorities. By the end of 2003, there were 1,700 sites in Tibet for Buddhists to conduct religious activities, and some 46,000 resident monks and runs; there were 23,900 mosques and 27,000 clerical personnel in the Xinjiang Uygur Autonomous Region. All religious activities are conducted normally, and the freedom of religious belief of ethnic minorities is fully respected and guaranteed.

Folk Customs of Ethnic Groups

Organs of self-government of autonomous areas guarantee the rights and freedom of all ethnic minorities to retain their traditional folkways and customs in daily life or when conducting social activities. These include respecting the habits and customs of minority people, respecting and showing special consideration for their festivals, ensuring the supply of special foods, supporting and ensuring the production and supply of special items, and respecting their marriage and funeral customs. Meanwhile, the ethnic minorities are encouraged to adopt new, scientific, civilized and healthy customs in daily life, as well as in marriage and funerals.

Economic Development

Organs of self-government of autonomous areas may, in accordance with legal provisions and the characteristics of local economic development, rationally adjust the relations of production or economic structure of their areas. Under the guidance of State planning, they independently arrange local capital construction projects, depending on the local financial and material resources, and other conditions. They manage local enterprises and institutions independently. Ethnic autonomous areas can engage in foreign trade in accordance with State provisions. They can also open ports for foreign trade after obtaining approval from the State Council. Autonomous areas enjoy State preferential policy treatment in their foreign trade. All ethnic autonomous areas have formulated their own plans, goals and measures for economic and social development by following the guidance of the overall State plan for national economic and social development, while at the same time taking into consideration local conditions.

Organs of self-government of autonomous areas are bound to protect and improve the local environment, and prevent and deal with pollution and other public hazards. They determine, in accordance with legal provisions, the right to own and use pastures and forests within their autonomous area. They manage

▲ Self-Government Regulations and Separate Regulations

The Law on Regional Ethnic Autonomy stipulates, "Besides enjoying the same rights as enjoyed by other local state organs, people's congresses in autonomous areas have the right to formulate self-government regulations and other separate regulations in light of the particular political, economic and cultural conditions of the ethnic group in that autonomous area." The Law of the PRC on Legislation stipulates: "Self-government regulations and separate regulations may contain provisions which have been flexibly altered on the basis of existing laws or administrative regulations to suit the particular conditions of the ethnic group." It also stipulates: "Wherever self-government regulations and separate regulations have made flexible alterations to existing laws, administrative regulations or local laws and regulations, the self-government regulations and separate regulations shall be applicable in that autonomous area." According to the Law on Regional Ethnic Autonomy: "If the resolutions, decisions, orders and directives of State organs at higher levels are not suitable for the particular situation of an autonomous area, the organs of self-government may report the matter to the higher state organs concerned, asking for permission to flexibly carry out, or halt the carrying out, of those resolutions, decisions, orders and directives." By the end of 2003, ethnic autonomous areas had formulated 133 self-government regulations and 384 separate regulations. In light of the particular situation in each area, ethnic autonomous areas have made flexible alterations or provide supplementary regulations to 68 provisions in such laws as the Marriage Law, Inheritance Law, Election Law, Land Law and Grassland Law.

The Qinghai-Tibet Railway is open to traffic on the morning of July 1, 2006. The first train departing from Lhasa to Beijing is running across the Lhasa River Bridge in Lhasa, Tibet.

♦ Special Arrangements for Tibet

The Central Government has always been attaching great importance to economic and social development of the Tibetan Autonomous Region, which also enjoys support from other parts of China. In 1980, the Central Government decided to introduce the rehabilitation policy in Tibet and removed the agricultural tax. In 1984, the policies of "long-term household land use and independent management" and "long-term private ownership of livestock and independent management" have been adopted in the agricultural and pastoral areas of Tibet by the Central Government. In 2001, the State introduced 50 preferential policies and defined 117 projects to strengthen the aid to Tibet. In 2004, the State Council again arranged 6.4 billion Yuan to be used for improving the infrastructure such as transport and the production and living conditions of the farmers and herders. In November 2006, the State Council introduced 40 new preferential policies to push ahead with the economic and social development of Tibet.

The State has made special arrangements for infrastructure construction and the development of basic industries in Tibet. From 1984 to 1994, a total of 43 projects were constructed, with investment from the Central Government and assistance from nine inland provinces and municipalities, totaling 480 million Yuan. From 1994 to 2001, some 30 projects were constructed with a total direct investment of 3.9 billion Yuan from the Central Government, and 32 projects were completed with investment, totaling 960 million Yuan, from the more developed areas in the east. During the period of the 10th Five-Year Plan (2001-2005), the Central Government invested 31.2 billion Yuan in 117 projects in Tibet alone.

In 2006, Tibet's GDP reached 29.005 billion Yuan, and its per-capita share surpassed 10,000 Yuan for the first time in history.

and protect local natural resources by law. They have the priority, in accordance with legal provisions and the unified plans of the State, in developing and using the natural resources available to them. For instance, the Sichuan Aba Tibetan and Qiang Autonomous Prefecture has taken full advantage of Jiuzhaigou and Huanglong, two World Natural Heritage sites within its borders, to develop a tourist industry. While developing such industry, special attention is paid to the protection of the two sites.

Organs of self-government of autonomous areas have the right to manage local financial matters. All financial revenue belonging to ethnic autonomous areas under the State financial system can be used by the organs of self-government without any restrictions. According to stipulations of the State, financial budgetary expenditure of autonomous areas should include some amounts held as reserve funds, the proportion of which to the total expenditure is higher than those in other areas. In the process of managing financial budgets, organs of self-government of autonomous areas are independent in arranging and using the extra amounts in their revenue or funds saved from their expenditure. In implementing State tax laws, in addition to projects that enjoy tax reduction or exemption with State approval, organs of self-government of autonomous areas can grant tax reduction and exemption to projects that need encouragement and preferential treatment from local revenue.

The Sichuan Liangshan Yi Ethnic Group Autonomous Prefecture built an expressway with capital in terms of the State bonds, thus paving the way the locals to develop their economy.

Development of Educational Undertakings

Organs of self-government of autonomous areas determine the educational plan, the establishment of schools, school system, the forms by which schools are run, curricula, language of teaching and method of enrollment, in accordance with the principles concerning education and legal provisions of the State. Public ethnic primary and middle schools that provide boarding and allowances to most students are established in pastureland and mountainous regions where families normally have financial difficulties and live in scattered locations to ensure that the students can complete their compulsory education. Schools (classes) and other educational institutions whose students are predominantly from ethnic minority families should, if possible, use textbooks printed in their own languages, and lessons should be taught in those languages. Chinese language courses are be offered at different times of the primary school period depending on the particular situation, to propagate the use of Putonghua (standard Chinese).

Independently Developing Ethnic Culture

Organs of self-government of autonomous areas independently develop cultural undertakings with ethnic characteristics, including literature, art, news, publishing, broadcasting, movies and television programs. They organize relevant departments to collect, edit, translate and publish historical and cultural books. They protect scenic spots and historical sites, valuable cultural relics and other important items of the local cultural heritage, and inherit and carry forward the traditional culture of the ethnic group(s). By 2005, China had 31 world cultural and natural heritage sites. Two of the cultural heritage sites, namely the Potala Palace in Lhasa and the Old Town of Lijiang; and three of the natural heritage sites, namely Jiuzhaigou Valley Scenic and Historic Interest Area, Huanglong Scenic and Historic Interest Area and the scenic spot of Three Parallel Rivers, are located in ethnic autonomous areas. In addition, the Dongba classical documents of the Naxi ethnic group are included in the World Memory Heritage List.

Development of Ethnic Autonomous Areas

To accelerate the development of China's western regions and ethnic autonomous areas, the government launched a grand strategy for the development of Western China in 2000, which covers five autonomous regions, 27 autonomous prefecture and 83 of the 120 autonomous counties (banners). In addition, three other autonomous prefectures are allowed to enjoy preferential policies that the State has adopted for the Western regions. During the

The grand strategy for the development of Western China launched in 2000 play an important role in promoting the economic and social development of the ethnic autonomous areas.

five years since the launching of the strategy, the construction of 60 important projects has begun, with a total investment of 850 billion Yuan. They play an important role in promoting the economic and social development of the ethnic autonomous areas.

When making arrangements for infrastructure construction and exploitation of resources in ethnic autonomous areas, the Central Government appropriately raises the proportion of investment and loans from policy banks, and grants the local areas reduction or exemption from supplementary funding according to their different conditions. Starting in the period of the First Five-Year (1953-1957), the government arranged a batch of key construction projects in ethnic autonomous areas, including the Baotou iron and steel base in Inner Mongolia, Qingtongxia Hydropower Station in Ningxia, petroleum exploration in Xinjiang and major highways linking Sichuan and Tibet, Qinghai and Tibet, Xinjiang and Tibet, and main railway lines linking Baotou and Lanzhou, Lanzhou and Xining, and Lanzhou and Urumqi. In the 1990s, larger transport facilities were constructed, including the railway line between Zhongwei in Ningxia and Baoji in Shaanxi, and the Nanjiang Railway and Tacheng Airport in Xinjiang. Since 2000, the State has assisted ethnic autonomous areas to further convert their resource advantages into economic advantages by investing in the construction of a number of key projects, such as the West-East Natural Gas Transmission Project, West-East Power Transmission Project and Qinghai-Tibet Railway.

A shot of the Qinghai-Tibet Railway

Improved Transport Conditions in Ethnic Minorities Areas

Since 1999, the government has launched large-scale transport infrastructure construction programs intended to benefit all ethnic autonomous regions, such as "Outlet Highways for Impoverished Counties," "Asphalt Roads to Every County in Western China" and "Inter-County and Rural Highways." Roads in rural areas and county-level roads totaling 225,000 km have been built or renovated, with a total investment of almost 100 million Yuan. This has markedly improved the formerly backward transport conditions in some areas inhabited by ethnic minorities.

Financial Support for Ethnic Autonomous Areas

With the development of the national economy and the growth in financial revenue, governments at all levels have gradually increased transfer payments from the exchequer to ethnic autonomous areas. Through ordinary transfer payments from the exchequer, special-purpose transfer payments, transfer payments according to preferential policies regarding ethnic minorities, and other ways, the central government has increased the financial input for ethnic autonomous areas to promote their economic development and social progress, and gradually reduce the gap between them and the more developed areas. The Chinese government has established some special-purpose funds, including the "Subsidy for Ethnic Minority Areas" established since 1955, and the "Stand-by Fund for Ethnic Minority Areas" in 1964. Moreover, it has also adopted some preferential policies, such as raising the proportion of reserve funds for ethnic minority areas, to help develop their economies and raise living standards. In the period 1980-1988, the central budget provided a set-quota subsidy system with a yearly increase of 10 percent to Inner Mongolia, Xinjiang, Guangxi, Ningxia and Tibet autonomous regions, as well as Yunnan, Guizhou and Qinghai provinces, which have large numbers of ethnic-minority inhabitants. In 1994, the government introduced a structural reform of its financial management with the focus on a system of sharing tax revenue between the central and local authorities, but the policies of providing subsidies and special appropriations to ethnic minority areas were maintained. While adopting the method of transitional transfer payments in 1995, the government tilted its policy towards the ethnic minority areas by adding special provisions concerning the policy of transfer payments to ethnic minority areas, covering Inner Mongolia, Xinjiang, Guangxi, Ningxia and Tibet autonomous regions, Yunnan, Guizhou and Qinghai provinces and some autonomous prefectures of ethnic minorities in other provinces.

Ecological Construction and Environmental Protection in Ethnic Autonomous Areas

All the four key areas and four key projects included in the National Ecological Environment Construction Plan of the Chinese government are in ethnic minority areas. The "Natural Forest Protection Project" and the projects for converting farming land to forests and pasture are mostly in ethnic minority areas. Nearly half of the 226 national nature reserves are located in those areas, including the Zoige Wetland Nature Reserve in Sichuan and the Xishuangbanna Nature Reserve in Yunnan. In addition, the central government has launched the "Project for Comprehensive Improvement of the Environment of the Tarim Basin" in Xinjiang and the "Project of Protection of the Source of the Three Rivers" in Yushu Tibetan Autonomous Prefecture of Qinghai, and attaches great importance to the ecological improvement of the karst areas in southern China.

Compulsory Education in Ethnic Autonomous Areas

The State helps ethnic autonomous areas universalize nine-year compulsory education and develop diverse forms of education. Ethnic autonomous areas are key target areas for the State's plans to basically universalize nine-year compulsory education and basically eliminate illiteracy among the young and middle-aged population. The "Compulsory Education Project for Impoverished Areas" launched by the State is also geared to the ethnic minority areas in Western China. Furthermore, the State

Lijiang ancient town: the beautiful hometown of the Naxi people

also establishes institutes of higher learning and opens classes and preparatory courses for ethnic minority students. Institutes of higher learning and polytechnic schools have lowered admission standards for ethnic minority students, and give special preference to applicants from ethnic minorities with a very small population. So far, there are 13 institutes of higher learning for ethnic minorities in China. In more developed areas there are middle schools for ethnic minorities and ethnic minority classes in ordinary middle schools enrolling ethnic minority students. To enhance training for high-level backbone personnel from ethnic minorities, the government decided, on an experimental basis, to enroll 2,500 students for Master's and PhD programs from ethnic minority areas in 2005, and the goal of 2007 was to enroll 5,000, thus making the total number of such students reach 15,000.

Ethnic Autonomous Areas Encouraged to Open Wider to the Outside World

The State grants more decision-making power to production enterprises in ethnic autonomous areas in managing foreign trade, encourages them to export local products and implement preferential border trade policies. It encourages and supports the ethnic autonomous areas to give full play to their geographical and cultural advantages in expanding their opening to and cooperation with neighboring countries. In 1992, the government launched its frontier opening-up strategy, designating 13 open cities and 241 first-grade open ports, and establishing 14 border economic and technological cooperation zones, most of which are in ethnic autonomous areas.

Pairing Off More Developed Areas and Ethnic Autonomous Areas for Aid

The government encourages better-off areas and ethnic groups to help those that are not well-off yet in order to attain common prosperity. Since the end of the 1970s, it has organized the more developed areas along the eastern coast to provide corresponding aid to western areas and help ethnic minority areas develop their economies and public services. In 1996, corresponding assistance was made more specific: Beijing is to assist Inner Mongolia; Shandong, Xinjiang; Fujian, Ningxia; and Guangdong, Guangxi. As regards Tibet, it receives assistance from all the other areas of the country. From 1994 to 2001, 15 assistance-providing provinces, and ministries and commissions under the State Council gave assistance gratis for the construction of 716 projects, with the input of funds totaling 3.16 billion Yuan (excluding investment from the central government). During the 10th Five-Year Plan (2001-2005), Tibet received assistance and grants totaling 1.062 billion Yuan from all over the country for the construction of 71 projects (again, excluding central funding).

Special Care for Ethnic Minorities

Respecting the customs of ethnic minorities, and to meet their needs for special necessities in production and living, the State has adopted a special policy for their trade and production of necessities. In 1963, it introduced preferential policies for ethnic minority enterprises in profit retention, self-owned funds and price subsidies. In June 1997, it promulgated a new preferential policy for ethnic minorities' trade and production of necessities for them, which provided that, during the period of the Ninth Five-Year Plan (1996-2000), the People's Bank of China would set aside 100 million Yuan every year for loans with discounted interest for the construction of trade networks for ethnic minorities and technological renovation of enterprises designated to turn out necessities for ethnic minorities. It also stipulated that State-owned trade businesses and grass-roots supply and marketing cooperatives below the county level (not including counties) would be exempt from value-added tax in ethnic minority areas. By the end of 2003, there were 1,378 designated manufacturers of special necessities for ethnic minorities in China, which enjoyed preferential policies concerning working capital loan rates, technological renovation loans with discounted interest, and reduction of and exemption from taxes. Considering the importance of special necessities such as tea in the everyday life of some ethnic minorities, the State established a brick-tea reserve system during the period of the Eighth Five-Year Plan (1991-1995), to guarantee a stable supply. In 2002, the Measures for Administration of National Brick-Tea Reserve were formulated, providing for the management of the reserve of brick-tea raw materials and products, and credit support to units that store the relevant materials. It also provided that the central exchequer should pay the interest on the loans used for the reserve of brick-tea materials.

Ethnic Publication

From the 1950s to the 1980s, the central authorities organized over 3,000 experts and scholars to compile and publish five series of books on ethnic minorities, totaling 403 volumes and over 90 million Chinese characters. The series are: *The Ethnic Minorities in China*, A *Series of Books on the Brief History of the Ethnic Minorities in China*, *A Series of Books on the Brief Record of the Languages of the Ethnic Minorities in China*, *A Series of Books on the Survey of Autonomous Areas of Ethnic Minorities in China*, and *A Collection of Research Materials on the Societies and Histories of the Ethnic Minorities in China*. Over 500,000 copies have been distributed. Today, each of the 55 ethnic minorities in China has its own brief written history.

The 55 ethnic minorities in China, except for the Chinese-speaking Hui and Manchu, each have their own language. The Mongolian, Tibetan, Uygur, Korean and Yi languages have coded character sets and national standards for fonts and keyboard. Software in the Mongolian, Tibetan, Uygur and Korean languages can be run in the Windows system, and laser photo-typesetting in these languages has been realized. Applied software in languages of ethnic minorities are emerging one after another, and some achievements have been made in research into the OCR (optic character recognition) of languages of ethnic minorities and machine-aided translation.

At present, there are 32 publishing houses of various kinds in China that have publications in ethnic minority languages, where the number of ethnic languages being used exceeded 20, the kinds of publications over 4,000, and the total copies of publications beyond 50 million. Upon more than 50 years of development, a complete national minority publishing system incorporating publishing, printing and delivering services has been established, with a relatively high coverage rate. This basically safeguards that: every ethnic minority may find due publishing houses producing publications in its native language, and that every minority language has its own publications in the language.

Of the 37 ethnic minority publishing houses, 31 publish books in 21 ethnic minority languages including Mongolian, Tibetan, Uygur, Zhuang and Korean. Picture shows books in Uygur language at the Xinhua International Book Town in Urumqi of Xinjiang.

Study of the Ethnic Ancient Classics

The state has set up special institutions to collect, assort, translate and study in an organized and programmed manner the three major heroic epics of China's ethnic minorities, i.e., *Gesar* (an oral Tibetan epic), *Jangar* (a Mongolian epic) and *Manas* (an epic of the Kirgiz people). In the past decade, the State has appropriated over 30 million Yuan for the collation and publishing of 160 volumes of the *Buddhist Tripitaka* in the Tibetan language. It has also earmarked a large amount of funds for the renovation of the Drepung, Sera and Ganden monasteries in Tibet, Kumbum Monastery in Qinghai, and Kizil Thousand-Buddha Caves in Xinjiang, and many other key national cultural relics. From 1989 to 1994, the State invested 55 million Yuan and 1,000 kg of gold in the first-stage renovation of the Potala Palace in Lhasa, and in 2001, 330 million Yuan for the second-stage renovation.

♦ State Ethnic Affairs Commission

State Ethnic Affairs Commission is one of the ministries and commissions under the Central Government to be founded earliest. On October 22, 1949, the Ethnic Affairs Commission under the central people's government was established. At the first meeting of the NPC in 1954, the Ethnic Affairs Commission under the central people's government was changed to the Ethnic Affairs Commission of the PRC, but it was abolished on June 22, 1970 and only restored in 1978 at the first meeting of the fifth NPC. Since then, it has been a department under the State Council.

The State Ethnic Affairs Commission practices the commissioner system. All its pluralistic members' units take their own responsibility according to their work division and make concerted efforts to research and solve the problems related to ethnic work.

Units of State Ethnic Affairs Commission's include the State Planning Commission, State Economic and Trade Commission, Ministry of Education, Ministry of Science and Technology, Ministry of Finance, Ministry of Personnel, Ministry of Land and Resources, Ministry of Railways, Ministry of Communications, Ministry of Information Industry, Ministry of Agriculture, Ministry of Foreign Trade and Economic Cooperation, Ministry of Culture, Ministry of Public Health, People's Bank of China, State Administration of Taxation, State Administration of Radio, Film and Television, The Press and Publications Administration, General Administration of Sports, and the Office of Poverty Alleviation and Development under the State Council.

Address: No.252 Taiping Qiao Avenue, West District, Beijing
Website: http:// www.seac.gov.cn

♦ Cultural Institutions in Ethnic Autonomous Areas

With the assistance of the State and efforts of the ethnic autonomous areas, so far, the ethnic autonomous areas have set up some 9,000 cultural institutions, 513 art performance troupes, 188 performance places, 566 libraries, 163 museums, 81 mass art centers, 642 cultural centers and 6,894 cultural stations. The ethnic autonomous areas had 122 radio broadcasting organizations with 73 radio stations and 523 radio transmitting stations, broadcasting in 15 ethnic minority languages; 111 TV broadcasting organizations with 94 TV stations and 830 TV transmitting stations, broadcasting in 11 ethnic minority languages. There were also 254,900 satellite radio and TV receiving and relaying systems.

Books in Uygur language in the Xinhua International Book Store in Urumqi

State System

Legal System

The main body of legal system in China belongs to the mainland legal system, consisting of seven legal categories—the Constitution and relevant laws such as civil law and business law, administrative law, economic law, social law, criminal law, procedure law of litigation and non-litigation procedural law. The legal system in China, from high to low ones, covers the Constitution (adopted and modified by the National People's Congress), basic laws (adopted and modified by the National People's Congress, such as the Criminal Law), general or common laws ("the laws other than those which should be adopted by the National People's Congress", and they should be adopted and modified by the NPC Standing Committee), administrative regulations (adopted and modified by the State Council), regional regulations (adopted and modified by the Standing Committees of People's Congresses in provinces and municipalities directly under the Central Government, and the Standing Committees of People's Congresses in some cities also enjoying the power to formulate administrative regulations), autonomous regulations (adopted and modified by the Standing Committees of People's Congresses of ethnic groups autonomous regions), and departmental regulations (a kind of low-level rules effective within the department, adopted by various ministries, commissions, administrations, bureaus, and offices under the State Council and approved by the State Council).

Since the reform and opening up in late 1978, China's socialist legal system construction has entered a brand-new stage. The National People's Congress amended the PRC Constitution comprehensively in 1982. This was followed with four major amendments to the Constitution. In addition, the NPC and its Standing Committee enacted more than 200 pieces of laws still enforced today and made more than 200 decisions with regard to the law. The local People's Congresses and their Standing Committees have also formulated more than 7,500 pieces of regulations still in effect today. The People's Congresses of the autonomous regions worked out some 600 pieces of regulations on autonomous government and individual rules and regulations. They cover the political, economic, social and other fields. They combine to form a relatively complete set of legal system in the country.

The National People's Congress

The NPC, the highest organ of State power, consists of deputies elected by all the provinces, autonomous regions, municipalities directly under the Central Government, special administrative regions and the armed forces. It exercises legislative power and makes decisions on important issues of national political life. Its main functions and powers include: amending the Constitution and supervising its implementation; enacting and amending basic laws governing criminal offences, civil affairs, State organs and other matters; examining and approving national economic and social development plans and reports on their implementation; examining and approving State budgets and reports on their implementation; approving the setting up of provinces, autonomous regions and municipalities directly under the Central Government and deciding the founding and the systems of the special

Schematic Drawing of the Organizational Structure of the NPC

Schematic Drawing of the Organizational Structure of the NPC
The Standing Committee of the NPC
The Meeting of the Chairmen of the Standing Committee
Special committees
the General Affairs Office, Legislative Work Committee and Budget Committee
Deputy Credential Examination Committee

administrative regions; making decisions on matters of war and peace; electing and choosing the leadership of the highest organs of State, i.e., electing the members of the Standing Committee of the NPC, the State President and Vice-President, deciding on the premier and other members of the State Council, and electing the chairman and other members of the Central Military Commission, the President of the Supreme People's Court and the Procurator-General of the Supreme People's Procuratorate. The NPC has the power to recall any of the aforementioned

Conference hall for the National People's Congress

Constitution of the PRC

Since the founding of the People's Republic of China in 1949, four constitutions have been formulated, in 1954, 1975, 1978 and 1982. The present 1982 Constitution contains four chapters in addition to the Preamble. These are: "General Principles", "The Fundamental Rights and Duties of Citizens", "The Structure of the State" and "The National Flag, the National Anthem, the National Emblem and the Capital", totaling 138 articles. Revisions and amendments to some articles were adopted by the National People's Congress in 1988, 1993, 1999 and 2004. The 2004 Constitutional Amendments added such contents as promoting the harmonious development of the material, political and spiritual civilizations, building and improving the social security system, protecting private property and safeguarding human rights and so on.

The NPC is elected for a term of five years and usually meets annually. When the NPC is not in session its Standing Committee exercises the highest State power. The NPC Standing Committee is composed of a chairman, vice-chairmen, a secretary-general and other members.

Multi-Party Cooperation System and Political Consultative Conference System

China is a country of many ethnic groups and many political parties. Before the State adopts important measures or makes decisions on major issues with a bearing on the national economy and the people's livelihood, the Communist Party of China (CPC), as the party in power, consults with representatives of all ethnic groups, political parties and democrats without party affiliation, and all other social sectors. This system of multi-party cooperation and political consultation led by the CPC is the basic political system in China.

Multi-party cooperation and political consultation take two principal forms: (1) The Chinese People's Political Consultative Conference (CPPCC); (2) consultative conferences and forums participated in by people from non-Communist parties and democrats without party affiliation at the invitation of the CPC Central Committee and local Party committees. The CPC Central Committee routinely invites leaders of the democratic parties and representative personages without party affiliation to consultative conferences, small-scale meetings and forums at which CPC leaders inform the participants of major events, hear their opinions and suggestions, and discuss State affairs with them. In addition to these consultation meetings, the central committee of the democratic parties may submit suggestions in writing to the CPC Central Committee.

Members of the democratic parties and personages without party affiliation form an appropriate proportion among deputies to the NPC, the Standing Committee and the special committees of the NPC. Through their activities in the people's congresses, they reflect the wishes of the people, participate in decision-making on major issues and in the formulation of laws, and supervise government work. In 2003, when the new term of office began, 176,000 members of the democratic parties and personages without party affiliation were elected deputies to people's congresses at various levels. Among them, seven are vice-chairpersons of the NPC Standing Committee and 50 are members of the NPC Standing Committee; 41 are vice-chairpersons of the standing committees of provincial-level people's congresses and 462 are members of such standing committees; and 352 are vice-chairpersons of the standing committees of municipal-level people's congresses and 2, 084 are members of such standing committees.

Conference hall for CPPCC

Multi-party cooperation and political consultative conference form the major part of China's socialist democratic system.

Chinese People's Political Consultative Conference (CPPCC)

The CPPCC is neither a State organ nor an ordinary civic organization. It is a widely representative, patriotic united front organization of the Chinese people. It has a National Committee and provincial (autonomous regional and municipal) and county (city) level local committees. The CPPCC National Committee consists of representatives of the CPC, democratic parties, people without party affiliation, people's organizations, ethnic minorities and other social strata, compatriots from Taiwan, Hong Kong and Macao, returned overseas Chinese, and specially invited individuals. The CPPCC is elected for a term of five years, its current Chairman being Jia Qinglin. In addition to attending a plenary session of the CPPCC once a year, CPPCC National Committee members are invited to attend the NPC and fully air their views as non-voting delegates, so as to exercise the functions of political consultation, democratic supervision and participation in the deliberation and administration of state affairs. When the committee is not in session, special activities for committee members are organized, including inspection tours of various localities. Consultative discussions are held on significant issues relating to major policies, the people's livelihood and united front work. Democratic supervision is exercised over the work of State organs and the fulfillment of the Constitution and laws through the offering of opinions, proposals and criticisms.

The Organizational Setup of the State

The State organs of the PRC include:

Organs of State power—the NPC and the local people's congresses;

President of State;

State administrative organs—the State Council and the local people's governments;

State leading military organ—the Central Military Commission;

State judicial organs—the Supreme People's Court, local people's courts and special people's courts;

State procuratorial organs-the Supreme People's Procuratorate, local people's procuratorates and special people's procuratorates.

President of State

The President and Vice-President of the People's Republic of China are elected at the National People's Congress which also enjoys the power to remove them. The term of office of the State President and Vice-President is the same with each National People's Congress; and they can be in the same office for at most two terms.

In combination with the NPC Standing Committee, the President of the PRC exercises his or her functions and powers as the head of State. The President, pursuant to decisions of the NPC or its Standing Committee, promulgates laws, appoints and removes members of the State Council, issues orders, receives foreign diplomatic representatives on behalf of the PRC, dispatches and recalls plenipotentiary representatives abroad, and ratifies or abrogates treaties and important agreements reached with foreign states.

Administrative System

The Chinese Constitution stipulates that the State Council, the Central People's Government, of the PRC is the executive body of the highest organ of State power. The State Council is responsible and reports on its work to the NPC. Local people's governments at various levels are the executive bodies performing the same functions at local level and they accept the unified leadership of the State Council.

The State Council

The State Council is composed of the Premier; Vice-Premiers; State Councilors; Ministers in charge of Ministries; Ministers in charge of Commissions; Auditor-General; and the Secretary-General. The Premier has overall responsibility for the State Council. The term of office of the State Council is the same as that of the National People's Congress. The Premier, Vice-Premiers and State Councilors can serve no more than two consecutive terms. The establishment, dissolution or merger of ministries and commissions of the State Council shall be proposed by the Premier and decided by the NPC or, when the Congress is not in session, by its Standing Committee.

At present there are 27 departments directly under the State Council: Ministry of Foreign Affairs, Ministry of National Defense, National Development and Reform Commission, Ministry of Education, Ministry of Science and Technology, Ministry of Industry and Information Technology, State Ethnic Affairs Commission, Ministry of Public Security, Ministry of State Security, Ministry of Supervision, Ministry of Civil Affairs, Ministry of Justice, Ministry of Finance, Ministry of Human Resources and Social Security, Ministry of Land and Resources, Ministry of Environmental Protection, Ministry of Housing and Urban-Rural Development, Ministry of Transport, Ministry of Railways, Ministry of Water Resources, Ministry of Agriculture, Ministry of Commerce, Ministry of Culture, Ministry of Health, National Population and Family Planning Commission, People's Bank of China, and National Audit Office.

The Functions and Powers of the State Council

The State Council exercises the following functions and powers:To adopt administrative measures, enact administrative rules and regulations and issue decisions and orders in accordance with the Constitution and the law;To submit proposals to the National People's Congress or its Standing Committee;To formulate the tasks and responsibilities of the ministries and commissions of the State Council, to exercise unified leadership over the work of the ministries and commissions and to direct all other administrative work of a national character that does not fall within the jurisdiction of the ministries and commissions;To exercise unified leadership over the work of local organs of State administration at various levels throughout the country, and to formulate the detailed division of functions and powers between the Central Government and the organs of State administration of provinces, autonomous regions, and municipalities directly under the Central Government;To draw up and implement the plan for national economic and social development and the budget;To direct and administer economic affairs and urban and rural development as well as the affairs of education, science, culture, public health, physical culture and family planning;To direct and administer civil affairs, public security, judicial administration, supervision and the building of national defense and other related matters;To conduct foreign affairs and conclude treaties and agreements with foreign states;To alter or annul inappropriate orders and directives issued by the ministries or commissions;To approve the geographic division of provinces, autonomous regions and municipalities directly under the Central Government, and to approve the establishment and geographic division of autonomous prefectures, counties, autonomous counties, and cities;To decide on the imposition of martial law in parts of provinces, autonomous regions, and municipalities directly under the Central Government;To examine and decide on the size of administrative organs and, in accordance with the law, to appoint or remove administrative officials, train them, appraise their performance and reward or punish them;And to exercise such other functions and powers as the National People's Congress or its Standing Committee may assign to it.

Agencies and Special Commission Directly Under the State Council

Under the State Council there are some directly subordinate agencies, administrative offices and institutions in charge of some trades, systems, and affairs of some aspects. These organizations are inferior to the Ministries, Commissions, People's Bank and National Audit Office. Their administrative heads are not included into the staffing of the State

Websites of the Ministries and Commissions of the State Council

Ministry of Foreign Affairs	www.fmprc.gov.cn
National Development and Reform Commission	www.sdpc.gov.cn
Ministry of Education	www.moe.edu.cn
Ministry of Science and Technology	www.most.gov.cn
State Ethnic Affairs Commission	www.seac.gov.cn
Ministry of Public Security	www.mps.gov.cn
Ministry of Supervision	www.mos.gov.cn
Ministry of Civil Affairs	www.mca.gov.cn
Ministry of Justice	www.legalinfo.gov.cn
Ministry of Finance	www.mof.gov.cn
Ministry of Human Resources and Social Security	www.mohrss.gov.cn
Ministry of Land and Resources	www.mlr.gov.cn
Ministry of Housing and Urban-Rural Development	www.mohurd.gov.cn
Ministry of Environmental Protection	www.mep.gov.cn
Ministry of Railways	www.china-mor.gov.cn
Ministry of Communications	www.moc.gov.cn
Ministry of Industry and Information Technology	www.miit.gov.cn
Ministry of Water Resources	www.mwr.gov.cn
Ministry of Agriculture	www.agri.gov.cn
Ministry of Commerce	www.mofcom.gov.cn
Ministry of Culture	www.ccnt.gov.cn
Ministry of Public Health	www.moh.gov.cn
State Family Planning Commission	www.chinapop.gov.cn
People's Bank of China	www.pbc.gov.cn
State Auditing Administration	www.audit.gov.cn

Council and they are appointed or removed by the Premier, which is decided by the Standing Conference of the State Council.

(1) Agencies directly under the State Council: General Administration of Customs; State Administration of Taxation; State Administration for Industry and Commerce; General Administration of Quality Supervision, Inspection and Quarantine; State Administration of Radio, Film and Television; General Administration of Press and Publication (National Copyright Administration); General Administration of Sport; State Administration of Work Safety; National Bureau of Statistics; State Forestry Administration; State Intellectual Property Office; National Tourism Administration; State Administration for Religious Affairs; Counselors' Office of the State Council; Government Offices Administration of the State Council; and National Bureau of Corruption Prevention.

(2) Special Commission directly under the State Council: State-owned Assets Supervision and Administration Commission of the State Council.

(3) Administrative offices of the State Council: Overseas Chinese Affairs Office of the State Council, Hong Kong and Macao Affairs Office of the State Council, Legislative Affairs Office of the State Council, and Research Office of the State Council.

(4) Institutions directly under the State Council: Xinhua News Agency, Chinese Academy of Sciences, Chinese Academy of Social Sciences, Chinese Academy of Engineering, Development Research Center of the State Council, National School of Administration, China Seismological Bureau, China Meteorological Administration, China Banking Regulatory Commission, China Securities Regulatory Commission, China Insurance Regulatory Commission, State Electricity Regulatory Commission, National Council for Social Security Fund, and National Natural Science Foundation.

In addition, under the State Council there are Taiwan Affairs Office, Information Office, and State Archives Administration.

Local People's Congresses and Local People's Governments

Reflecting existing national administrative divisions, there are people's congresses and people's governments at all levels-in provinces, autonomous regions and municipalities directly under the Central Government, in counties and cities, in townships and towns.

Local people's congresses are the local organs of State power. They have the power to decide on important affairs in their respective administrative areas. The people's congresses of provinces, autonomous regions and municipalities directly under the Central Government have the power to formulate local regulations. Local people's governments are local administrative organs of the state. Working under the unified leadership of the State Council, they are responsible to and report on their work to the people's congresses and their standing committees at the corresponding level and to the organs of State administration at the next higher level. They have overall responsibility for work within their respective administrative areas.

The members of the local governments at all levels are elected or appointed in line with laws by the people's congresses and standing committees at the same level. They are elected for a term of five years.

Ethnic Autonomous Regions and Autonomous Organs

In accordance with the Constitution, under unified national leadership, self-government is exercised in areas where ethnic minorities are concentrated. The organs of self-government of national autonomous areas are the people's congresses and the people's governments of autonomous regions, autonomous prefectures and autonomous counties. Self-government cannot be exercised in towns where ethnic minorities are concentrated as they are small and restrained by economic conditions. These are named ethnic groups townships, but the people's congresses and people's governments there are not organs of self-government.

The organs of self-government of national autonomous areas are at the same time part and parcel of the local organs of State power. The people's governments of the national autonomous areas are local organs of State administration under the unified leadership of the State Council and are subordinate to it. Therefore, they are the same in establishment, terms of office and organization as ordinary local organs of State.

The organs of self-government of autonomous regions, prefectures and counties exercise the functions and powers of local organs of state as specified in the Constitution. At the same time, they exercise the power of autonomy within the limits of their authority as prescribed by the Constitution, the Law of the People's Republic of China on Regional National Autonomy and other laws and implement the laws and policies of the State in the light of the existing local situation. The people's congresses of the national autonomous areas have the power to enact regulations on the exercise of autonomy and other separate regulations in the light of the political, economic and cultural characteristics of the ethnic group or the ones in the areas concerned. All revenues accruing to the national autonomous areas under the financial system of the State are managed and used by the organs of self-government of those areas on their own. The organs of self-government of the national autonomous areas may, in accordance with the military system of the State and practical local needs and with the approval of the State Council, organize local public security forces for the maintenance of public order.

The Military System

The armed forces of the PRC are composed of the PLA, both active and reserve components, Chinese People's Armed Police Force and the militia. The active components of the PLA comprise the State's standing army, which mainly undertakes the task of national defense, and helps to maintain social order. The Chinese People's Armed Police Force undertakes tasks for maintenance of security and social order entrusted by the State. Militiamen, under the command of military organs, perform combat service support and defensive operations, and help to maintain social order. The PLA, comprised of the Army, Navy, Air Force and Second Artillery Force, is organized in seven military area commands nationwide.

Deputies to the NPC from various areas are taking group photo in front of the Great Hall of the People.

The Self-Management System of Villagers

The villagers committees established among rural residents on the basis of their place of residence are mass organizations of self-management at the grass-roots level. They have been widely established since the adoption of the household contract responsibility system with remuneration linked to output in 1980s. The 1982 Constitution stipulates the name, nature, task and organization of villagers committees. The Organic Law of the Villagers Committees of the People's Republic of China (For Trial Implementation) was adopted at the 23rd Meeting of the Standing Committee of the Sixth National People's Congress on November 24, 1987. In light of the relevant provisions of the Organic Law of the Villagers Committees, villagers committees exercise the following functions and duties: to manage public affairs and social services in the village; to mediate civil disputes, promote unity and mutual assistance with other villages and family harmony; to help the people's government and public security organs maintain public and social order; to convey residents opinions and the demands of villagers.

Villagers committees shall be established on the basis of the distribution of the villagers and the sizes of the population and on the principle of facilitating self-government by the masses. Villagers committees shall generally be established in natural villages; several natural villages may jointly establish a villagers committee; a large natural village may establish several villagers committees. A villagers committee shall be composed of 3-7 members, including the chairman, the vice-chairman (vice-chairmen) and the members. The villagers committees shall, when necessary, establish sub-committees for people's mediation, public security, public health and other matters. Rules and regulations for a village and villagers pledges shall be drawn up by the villagers assembly through discussion in light of local conditions, reported to the people's government of a township, ethnic township or town for the record, and implemented under the supervision of the villagers committee. The rules and regulations for a village and villagers' pledges shall not contravene the Constitution, the laws or the regulations.

The Self-Management System of the Urban Residents

The residents committees established among urban residents on the basis of their place of residence are mass organizations of self-management at grassroots level. The Organic Regulations of the Urban Residents Committees was adopted at the 4th Meeting of the Standing Committee of the First National People's Congress on December 31, 1954. The regulations were again promulgated on January 19, 1980. In light of the regulations, residents committees were first established in municipal districts and cities not divided into districts. Neighborhood committees were later set up in towns and places where township governments were located. The Organic Law of Urban Residents Committees of the People's Republic of China was adopted at the 11th Meeting of the Standing Committee of the Seventh National People's Congress. In light of the Organic Law, residents committees exercise the following functions and duties: to manage public affairs and social services in its area; to mediate civil disputes; to help maintain public order; to help the people's government and its agencies do the work in public health, family planning and juvenile education and so on; to convey residents opinions and demands and make suggestions to the people's government or its agencies.

Residents committees shall be established on the basis of the distribution of the residents and the sizes of the population and on the principle of facilitating self-government by the masses. A residents committee shall be generally established on the basis of 100-700 households. A residents committee shall be composed of 5-9 members, including the chairman, the vice-chairman (vice-chairmen) and the members. They are elected by all the residents with the right to vote or representatives from every household. The residents committees shall, when necessary, establish sub-committees for people's mediation, public security, public health and other matters.

The Congress of Workers and Staff

The congress of workers and staff is a basic system ensuring the democratic management of an enterprise or public institution by its workers and staff members. The democratic right as master of an enterprise enjoyed by all the members of an enterprise or public institution is largely exercised through the system of congress of workers and staff. There are related stipulations on the system of congress of workers and staff in China's Constitution, the Law on Industrial Enterprises of Public Ownership, Labor Law, Trade Union Law, and the Regulations Concerning the Congress of workers and Staff in Publicly Owned Industrial Enterprises. According to these related laws, the congress of workers and staff has five functions and rights: the right to

The election of the Urban Residents Commisstee of Yuetan Street, Beijing is being held at expiration of office terms.

deliberate and make suggestions on the plan and scheme of the enterprise's production management and development; the right to examine and adopt important regulations and rules on wages, bonus, labor protection, punishments and rewards; the right to deliberate and decide on important matters concerning workers' and staff members' life and material benefits; the right to appraise and supervise the administrators and leaders of the enterprise; and the right to recommend or elect the head of a factory.

The congress of workers and staff enjoys broad mass support in China, and among its representatives are not only workers but also technological staff, managerial personnel and other members. It can represent all workers and staff in the democratic management of an enterprise. While the conference is in recess, the committee of the trade union of the enterprise functions as its work organ and takes care of the day-to-day work of the congress. By the end of 2004, 1.732 million enterprises and public institutions had established trade unions and 369,000 had set up the conferences of workers and staff, covering 78.364 million employees. In addition, 316,000 had introduced the system of making their affairs public, covering 70.612 million employees. Now, 52.8 percent of the publicly owned enterprises with trade union organizations have set up conferences of workers and staff, covering 35.026 million employees and accounting for 72.9 percent of the employees in publicly owned enterprises with trade union organizations; 32.6 percent of the non-publicly owned enterprises with trade union organizations have introduced the system of congress of workers and staff, covering 27.87 million employees and accounting for 46.7 percent of the employees in non-publicly owned enterprises with trade union organizations.

Economy

General Survey

Five-Year Plans

The Five-Year Plan for National Economic and Social Development is part of the national economic development plan and aims to provide a detailed program for key national construction projects, the distribution of productivity and a significant proportion of the national economic sectors, as well as setting some long-term goals and directions for the development of the national economy. The First Five-Year Plan was launched in 1953, playing the mandatory rule to the national economic development. In 2006, China changed the Five-Year Plan to the Five-Year Program which is of guidance role to the national economic development. Now the country has progressed to the 11 Five-Year Plans and Five-Year Programs. The only periods without such a plan since the founding of the PRC in 1949 were the initial rehabilitation period from 1949 to 1952 and the readjustment period from 1963 to 1965.

The first Five-Year Plan: 1953—1957
The second Five-Year Plan: 1958—1962
The third Five-Year Plan: 1966—1970
The fourth Five-Year Plan: 1971—1975
The fifth Five-Year Plan: 1976—1980
The sixth Five-Year Plan: 1981—1985
The seventh Five-Year Plan: 1986—1990
The eighth Five-Year Plan: 1991—1995
The ninth Five-Year Plan: 1996—2000
The tenth Five-Year Plan: 2001—2005
The eleventh Five-Year Program: 2006—2010

The 10th Five-Year Plan (2001-2005)

The 10th Five-Year Plan (2001-2005) provided the guidelines for China to move into the new century by setting the main development goals. The gross domestic product averaged annual growth of 8.8 percent; GDP per capita topped 10,000 Yuan; the increase in the consumer price index [inflation] was held at a steady 1.4 percent; 43.68 million people in townships got new jobs; the registered urban

Economic Growth Rate

China is one of the countries with the greatest growth potential in the world. According to the National Bureau of Statistics of China, since 2003, China's GDP has been increasing at an annual rate of 10 percent.

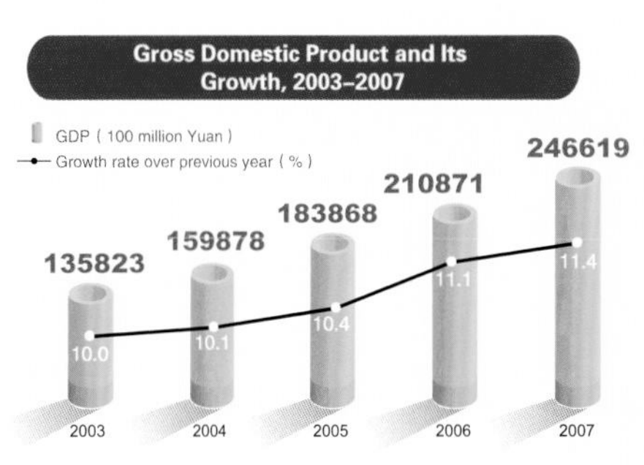

Major indicators of the economic and social development in the 11th Five-Year Plan period

Category	Indicators	2005	2010	Annual growth rate (percent)	Attribute
Economic growth	GDP (1000 billion Yuan)	18.2	26.1	7.5	Anticipated
	Per Capita GDP (Yuan)	13985	19270	6.6	Anticipated
Economic structure	Ratio of Added Value of Service Industry (percent)	40.3	43.3	[3]	Anticipated
	Employment Ratio of Service Industry (percent)	31.3	35.3	[4]	Anticipated
	Ratio of Expenditures on R&D to GDP (percent)	1.3	2	[0.7]	Anticipated
	Urbanization Rate (percent)	43	47	[4]	Anticipated
Population, resources and environment	Total Population(10000 people)	130756	136000	<8‰	Obligatory
	Reduction of Energy Consumption per Unit GDP (percent)			[20]	Obligatory
	Reduction of Water Consumption per Unit Industrial Added Value (percent)			[30]	Obligatory
	Efficient Utilization of Agricultural Irrigation Water	0.45	0.5	[0.05]	Anticipated
	Comprehensive Utilization Rate of Industrial Solid Wastes (percent)	55.8	60	[4.2]	Anticipated
	Total Cultivated Land (100 million hectares)	1.22	1.2	-0.3	Obligatory
	Reduction of Total Major Pollutions Emission Volume (percent)			[10]	Obligatory
	Forest Coverage (percent)	18.2	20	[1.8]	Obligatory
Public services and life quality	Average Schooling Years of Citizens (year)	8.5	9	[0.5]	Anticipated
	Population Covered by Basic Pension in Urban Areas (100 million people)	1.74	2.23	5.1	Obligatory
	Coverage of the New Rural Cooperative Healthcare System (percent)	23.5	>80	>[56.5]	Obligatory
	Newly Increased Urban Employment in Five Years (10,000 people)			[4500]	Anticipated
	Rural Labor Force Transferred in Five Years (10,000 people)			[4500]	Anticipated
	Registered Urban Unemployment Rate (percent)	4.2	5		Anticipated
	Per Capita Disposable Income of Urban Households (Yuan)	10493	13390	5	Anticipated
	Per Capita Net Income of Rural Households (Yuan)	3255	4150	5	Anticipated

Note: Figures of GDP and urban resident income are of 2005 price: those in [ ] are accumulative figures in five years; major pollutants refers to sulfur dioxide and COD.

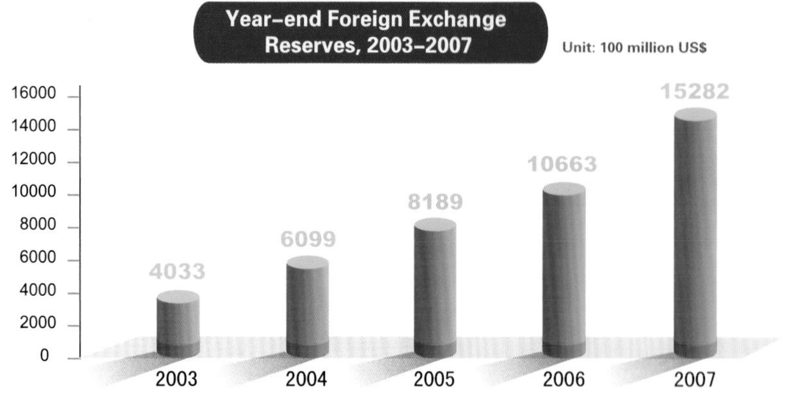

unemployment rate was controlled within five percent; in 2005, the total volume of foreign trade reached US$1.4 trillion, 1.9 times more than at the end of the Ninth Five-Year Plan and ranking third in the world; financial revenue increased to over three trillion Yuan in 2005 from 1.34 trillion Yuan in 2000; the per capita disposable income of urban residents and the per capita net income of the rural residents increased by 9.7 percent and five percent respectively. Meanwhile, important headway was made in the strategic adjustment of the economic structure and a favorable turn appeared in the agriculture industry especially in grain production. Construction of basic industries such as the energy, transportation and important raw materials etc, and infrastructure was speeded up. Compared with the end of the Ninth Five-Year Plan, the installed capacity for power generation increased from 319 million kW to over 500 million kW; the length of expressways increased from 16,300 km to 40,000 km; the length of railways in operation increased from 68,700 km to 75,000 km. The high technology sector also saw great development. The reform process continued to be implemented and especially in some important aspects and key sectors, great breakthroughs were achieved in improving the socialist market economy system. With the further opening-up, foreign trade gained great progress. It was estimated to have used US$270 billion of foreign capital cumulatively in the five-year period. New headway was made in diverse social causes. China's economic strength, comprehensive national power and international status were all enhanced in a remarkable way.

The 11th Five-Year Plan (2006-2010)

The 11th Five-Year Plan attaches great importance to the following six items: accelerating the conversion of the economic growth style; adjusting and optimizing the industrial structure; solving problems related to rural areas, farmers' livelihood and agriculture; boosting healthy urbanization; promoting regional concerted development and practically strengthening the construction of a harmonious society.

♦ State Council Office for West Region Development

In January 2000, in order to speed up the grand strategic decision-making process for middle and western regional development and strengthen the organization and leadership in this regard, the State Council decided to set up a leading group for such development.

The main functions and responsibilities of the office of the leading group of the State Council for western region development are: Firstly, study and set forth the development strategies, programming, great issues and the suggestions on related policies, laws and regulations, and promote the fast, sustainable and healthy development of the regional economy. Secondly, work out and put forward suggestions on rural economic development, key infrastructure construction, eco-environment protection and construction, resource development and the layout of the major projects of the western regions, organize and coordinate the implementation of the program of the conversion of cropland to forest and grassland.

Address: No. 38 Yuetan Nanjie, Xicheng District, Beijing
Website: http://www.chinawest.gov.cn

Economic Restructuring

Economic restructuring is one of the main aspects of China's reform. In the first 30 years after the founding of the PRC, the Chinese government carried out a system of planned economy, and targets and quotas for various spheres of economic development were all set by the special planning committees of the State. Factories produced goods according to State plans, and farmers planted

Economy

• Western Region Development

China's western region involves 10 provinces, autonomous regions and a municipality directly under the Central Government such as Gansu, Guizhou, Ningxia, Qinghai, Shanxi, Sichuan, Tibet, Xinjiang, Yunnan and Chongqing, covering 64 percent of the country's land area and containing 22.8 percent of the total population. The region is rich in mineral resources and enjoys advantages in terms of energy (including water energy), tourism and land resources.

In 2000, China started its western region development campaign. The government offered preferential policies to the region in terms of capital input, investment, internal and external opening-up, development of science and education, and human resources. Efforts were made to build projects including those in the fields of communications, water works, energy, telecommunications, education, healthcare and special industries.

During the 11th Five-Year Plan, the State will implement the "ten projects for new country construction" in Western China. The projects include the basic grain ration construction, regional marketable grain construction, construction of characteristic advantageous primary products production base, water-conservation demonstration project, the project for drinking water safety in rural areas, project on poverty relief and resettlement, project on rural resources, rural roads construction, project on medical sanitation and family planning services in rural areas and the promotion project for the farmers in western areas to establish a business.

In light of the resource advantages of various areas, the State also plans to gradually build ten characteristic advantageous agricultural products production bases such as ones for cotton, sugar crops, tobacco leaf, fruits, flowers, tea, potatoes, livestock products, special forestry products and herbal medicines.

crops also according to State plans. Commercial departments replenished and sold their stocks according to State plans, and the qualities, quantities and prices of the goods were all fixed by planning departments. On the one hand, this system contributed to the stable, planned development of China's economy, but on the other it also limited the development of the economy and sapped its vitality. The economic restructuring began first in the rural areas in 1978 and shifted to the cities in 1984. After ten-odd years of reform and opening-up, in 1992 the Chinese government formulated a policy to establish a socialist market economy.

The main aspects of the economic structural reform are as follows: The development of diversified economic elements will be encouraged while keeping the public sector of the economy in the dominant position. To meet the requirements of the market economy, the operations of State-owned enterprises should be changed so that they fit in with the modern enterprise system. A unified and open market system should be established in the country so as to link the rural and urban markets, and the domestic and international markets, and to promote the optimization of the allocation of resources. The function of managing the economy by the government should be changed so as to establish a complete macro-control system mainly by indirect means. A distribution system in which distribution according to work is dominant while giving priority to efficiency with due consideration to fairness should be established. This system will encourage some people and some places to become rich first, and then they may help other people and places to become rich too. A social security system, suited to China's situation, for both rural and urban residents shall be worked out so as to promote overall economic development and ensure social stability.

Economic Construction Objective

China's overall economic construction objectives were clearly stated in the Three Step Development Strategy set out in 1987: Step One--to double the 1980 GNP and ensure that everyone had enough food and clothing — was attained by the end of the 1980s; Step Two — to quadruple the 1980 GNP by the end of the 20th century — was actually achieved in 1995; Step Three is to increase per-capita GNP to the level of medium-developed countries by the middle of the 21st century, at which point the Chinese people will be fairly well-off and modernization will have been basically realized.

In 2007, China raised its new development goals: On the basis of optimizing the structure, increasing efficiency, reducing consumption and protecting the environment, China quadruples its 2000 GDP in 2020.

Building an Energy-Efficient Society

The Chinese Government presses ahead with the construction of an energy-efficient society. Taking economical use of energy as the State policy, it works hard to effect a fundamental change in the economic growth mode by boosting the use rate of resources, stressing economical use of energy, water, land, materials and other resources, seeking to develop a recyclable economy, speeding up structural readjustment, and promoting technological progress. The aim is to gradually form a sound economic growth and consumption mode featuring economical consumption of energy and high production of resources, recyclable use of resources so as to achieve a sustainable socio-economic development.

Statistics show that per capita fresh water of China is only one-fourth of that of the world level; per capita arable land is less than 40 percent of the world average; per capita proven available reserves of coal stand at 62 percent of the prevailing world average; per capita proven available reserves of oil are only seven percent of the global figure; meanwhile, resource consumption is much higher than the world average. Unit resources of the main products in the power, iron, colored metal, petrochemical, building materials, chemical, light and textile industries is 40 percent higher than that of the international advanced level. The GDP realized by consuming each ton of resources is only 30 percent of the world average. In order to vigorously encourage various regions to save resources and raise their resource utilization

♦ The National Development and Reform Commission

The National Development and Reform Commission (NDRC) is a macroeconomic management agency under the State Council, which studies and formulates policies for economic and social development, maintains a balance of economic aggregates and guides overall economic system restructuring. Its predecessor was the State Planning Commission (SPC), founded in 1952. This was renamed the State Development Planning Commission (SDPC) in 1998. After merging with the State Council Office for Restructuring the Economic System (SCORES) and part of the State Economic and Trade Commission (SETC) in 2003, the SDPC became the NDRC.

Address: No.38, Yuetan Nanjie, Xicheng District, Beijing
Website: http://sdpc.gov.cn

♦ State-owned Assets Supervision and Administration Commission (SASAC)

This manages State-owned enterprises, supervising and administrating the assets of enterprises directly under the jurisdiction of the central government (not including financial enterprises).

The main functions and responsibilities are: authorized by the State Council, in accordance with the Company Law and other administrative regulations, SASAC performs the responsibility as the investor, guides and promotes reform and restructuring of State-owned enterprises; supervises the preservation and increase in the value of State-owned assets for enterprises under its supervision, and enhances the management of assets; promotes the establishment of a modern enterprise system in SOE's, and perfects corporate governance; and propels the strategic adjustment of the structure and layout of the State economy; dispatches supervisory panels to some large enterprises on behalf of the State; takes charge of daily management of the supervisory panels; appoints and removes top executives of enterprises, and evaluates their performances through legal procedures, either granting reward or inflicting punishment based on performance; oversees a corporate executive selection system in accordance with the requirements of a socialist market economic system and modern enterprise system, and perfects an incentives and restraints system for corporate management; supervises and administers the preservation and increase in the value of State-owned assets under the supervision of SASAC through auditing with appropriate assessment criteria; safeguards the rights and interests of the investor of State-owned assets; drafts laws, administrative regulations for the management of State-owned assets and draws up related rules; directs and supervises the management work of local State-owned assets according to law.

Address: No.26, Xidajie, Xuanwu District, Beijing
Website: http:// www. sasac.gov.cn

efficiency, the Government implemented a GDP Resources Consumption Index Report in 2006. At the end of June, China will jointly publicize each region's resource consumption and resource consumption rate per 10,000 Yuan of GDP, as well as the resource consumption for each 10,000 Yuan of industrial added value and the power consumption per 10,000 Yuan of GDP generated for all industrial enterprises above the scale of the previous year (GDP and the industrial added value adopt the comparable price of 2000).

In February 2005, the National People's Congress reviewed and passed the Law of the People's Republic on Renewable Energy, which states clearly the responsibilities and obligations of governments at all levels, enterprises and consumers in the development and utilization of the renewable energy sources, and puts forward a series of related policies and measures at the same time. The National Development and Reform Commission drafted the Mid- and Long-Term Development Program of Renewable Energy, setting forward the development objectives, strategic layout, construction emphases and safeguard measures in this regard by 2020.

Three Industrial Sectors

As is normal, China has divided its economic activities into three industrial sectors each of which involves several trades: the primary industry covering agriculture (including forestry, animal husbandry and fishery); secondary industry, including excavating, manufacturing, power, water and heat supply, and the building industry; the tertiary sector includes various trades other than those in the primary and secondary industries, such as services as well as government institutions.

Industrial Policies

The Chinese Government uses five categories of industrial policies to promote and realize the goal for structural readjustment.

The first category involves supportive industrial policies that play an important role in improving national competitive power and industrial upgrading. Thus, the State will support the development of these trades and enterprises by means of injecting capital, financial discounting, issuing bonds and changing debt into stock.

The second category industrial policies are those worked out to give preferential treatment in taxation to the traditional industry and strategic industries to be upgraded.

The third category refers to competitive industrial policies. Other than trades concerning national security, naturally-monopolized trades, trades providing important public products and services, as well as pillar industries and key enterprises in high-tech industries, most trades, enterprises and products come within the scope of competitive industries. For the competitive industries, the State will create a fair, just and transparent policy environment in terms of fair investment and taxation policies, rigorous technical quality standards, standardized anti-monopoly laws and regulations and quick market information service, so as to realize the survival of the fittest.

The fourth category is called restrictive industrial policies. These involve products whose manufacture causes environmental pollution, with backward technical level and with supply seriously exceeding demand, so as to resolutely eliminate them.

The fifth category is called protective industrial policies. Aiming at agriculture, the service industry and the young industries, the protective industrial policies are adopted within the framework of the WTO regulations to help protect the safety of industries.

Coexistence of Diverse Economic Elements

Before 1978, State-owned and collectively-owned enterprises represented 77.6 percent and 22.4 percent respectively of China's exclusively public-ownership economy. The policy of reform and opening-up helped promote the common development of various economic sectors. Individual and private enterprises and enterprises with foreign, Hong Kong, Macao or Taiwanese investment have mushroomed.

According to official statistics, by the end of 2006, the number of State-owned enterprises and State joint ownership enterprises had reached 26,101; that of private enterprises stood at 4.947 million, an increase of 15 percent more than that of 2005, or 57.4 percent of the national total; and that of enterprises with foreign investment had risen to 594,000.

Reform of the State-owned Enterprises

Reform of State-owned enterprises has always been a major part of China's economic restructuring. Since the foundation of the State-owned Assets Supervision and Administration Commission, it has been working hard to push introduction of a modern enterprise system. Efforts were made to reorganize enterprises directly under the Central Government departments concerned. Now, these enterprises number 161. The State works to ensure proper proportion of State assets in key trades and fields which are of direct bearing to State safety and the lifeline of the national economy, such as national military industry, oil, petrochemical industry, power, telecommunication, civil aviation, shipping, and development of major mineral ores. In the meantime, efforts were made to increase sales of products of enterprises directly under the Central Government departments, increase their profits, and conduct the shareholding system reform of the State-owned enterprises.

Basic Framework of the State-owned Asset Management System

The State-owned Assets Supervision and Administration Commission (SASAC) exercises direct leadership over the local State-assets supervision and administration commissions in the 31 provinces (autonomous regions and municipalities directly under the Central Government) and the Xinjiang Production and Construction Corps with a view to forming a system in the field of State-assets supervision and administration. According to the Interim Measures for the Supervision and Administration of State-Owned Assets of the Enterprises, the SASAC has worked out and promulgated 16 regulations and more than 40 standard documents in regard to enterprise restructuring, the transformation of property rights, assets evaluation, achievements examination, financial supervision, and so on. The State-owned assets supervision and administration institutions of various areas have also promulgated more than 1,000 local laws and regulations and a legal system for assets management has basically

♦ All-China Federation of Industry and Commerce

The All-China Federation of Industry and Commerce (ACFIC) was established in 1953. It is a people's organization and non-governmental chamber of commerce composed of non-public economic personages in Chinese industry and commercial circles.

Pursuant to the laws, the ACFIC builds up its organizations and framework in accordance with the national divisions of administrative areas. The ACFIC is responsible for conducting the work of local federations of industry and commerce and non-governmental chambers of commerce. With 3,119 local organizations at and above county level, ACFIC now has formed a nationwide network. Its membership consists of corporate, group and individual members. Each local member is also a member of the ACFIC. By the end of June 2006, there were 1.97 million ACFIC members. ACFIC has established far-ranging connections with chambers of commerce of over a hundred nations.

Address: No.93, Beiheyan Street, Beijing
Website: http://acfic.org.cn

come into being. The SASAC implemented annual evaluation of management achievements and the tenure examination for the principal of each enterprise, and preliminarily regulated salary management. The commissions of various areas also implemented achievements examinations of the financial contribution enterprises successively and actively probed diverse methods for promoting efficiency and methods of examination. A basic responsibility system for the preservation and increase of the value of the State-owned assets has been formed.

Non-Public Ownership Economic Sector

At the end of 2006, there were 4.947 million registered private enterprises, an increase of 15 percent over the end of 2005. Accounting for 57.4 percent of the total number of Chinese enterprises, it has already become an enterprise colony with the largest quantity and proportion. The registered capital of the private enterprises was 7,500 billion Yuan, an increase of 22 percent. The number of registered private industrial and commercial businesses reached 25.76 million, an increase of 3.8 percent; their capital reached 651.5 billion Yuan. The non-public ownership economy had become the main impetus for the growth of the national economy. During the 10th Five-Year Plan, the individual and private economy of China increased many times faster than the national economy, rising to more than a third of the GDP from less than one-thousandth in 1979, and the investment of the non-public ownership economy accounted for 50 percent of the fixed assets of the entire society. According to statistics, of 40 major industrial sectors, the non-public ownership economy accounted for over 50 percent in 27, and over 70 percent in other parts of the industries, becoming a major engine for development of the industries concerned.

Forms of Private Enterprise Organization

Currently, there are mainly four forms of organization of private enterprises in China, namely those with sole private proprietorship, private partnership enterprise, private limited liability company and private shareholding limited company, which respectively have their own applicable scope and fields and together have promoted the development of the private sector in recent years. The private limited liability company is the main form of organization, leading the various private enterprises in four key indicators—number of enterprises, number of employees, paid-in capital and business income.

Haier Group

The private enterprise, Haier Group is the fourth largest home appliance manufacturer, and Haier is one of the brands with highest value. It has more than 240 divisions and has set up localization design centers, manufacturing bases and trading companies in more than 30 countries. The number of its employees around the world surpasses 50,000. It mainly engages in four sectors, namely science and technology, industry, trade and finance. In 2006, its global turnover reached 103.9 billion Yuan.

Since 2002, Haier has led the list of most valued brands of China. The 16 leading products of Haier such as refrigerators, air conditioners, washing machines, water heaters, computers, mobile phones and integrated furniture and so on are granted the title of famous brand of China. Haier refrigerators and washing machines have been recognized as the first group of China's international famous brands by the General Administration of Quality Supervision, Inspection and Quarantine. Haier was recognized as the leader among "the ten world level brands of China" by the Financial Times of Britain. Haier has already entered the group of the world-known brands, with its influence rising with the expansion of its global market.

Haier's innovative management principles, such as Haier's OEC management model, "market-chain" management and "individual goal combination" – a system of assigning incentives-based responsibility to staff to ensure the quality of products delivered to their customers – have gained high recognition among international management institutes. Haier business case studies are included in the text books of Harvard University, the University of Southern California, Lausanne Management College, European Business College and Kobe University.

So far, the Haier Group has applied for 6,189 patents (including 819 invention patents) and owns 589 software intellectual property rights, upon which, Haier has also presided over or participated nearly a hundred State standard constitution and redaction work, of which, Haier's safe care water heater technology and Haier dual drive washing machine technology have been included in the IEC standard proposal.

Website: http://www.haier.com/cn/index.asp

A refrigerator plant of Hair Group in South Carolina, the US.

Hope Group

At the beginning of the 1980s, four brothers, Chen Yuxin (Liu Yongmei), Liu Yongyan, Liu Yongxing and Liu Yonghao started a business from the commonest animal breeding industry in rural areas. Through development over 20 years, they have become the "Chinese Fodder King", owning nearly a hundred enterprises and realizing an annual sales income of more than eight billion Yuan. It becomes the typical representative of new rising enterprises in China.

The Hope Group has been assessed as "the leading enterprise among the 500 largest private enterprises" by the State Administration for Industry and Commerce and the China Enterprise Evaluation Association, and selected as the enterprise with the largest private assets on the Chinese mainland by the American Forbes Magazine for three successive years from 1994. The board chairman of the New Hope Group, Liu Yonghao takes the post of president of the Hope Group now, holding a quarter of the shares. As a comprehensive group engaged in industrial operations and strategic investment, the New Hope Group is listed as a National Leading Enterprise for Agriculture Industrialization by nine national ministries and has been selected among the "500 Largest Enterprises in China" for three years.

Website: http://www.newhopegroup.com

Taxation Policies

Since 1994, China has practiced a financial system based on a separate tax system; and according to the principle of unifying the rights of finance and work, it has divided rationally the financial revenue of the central and local administrations. The central government, through the system of tax rebate and transfer payments regulates the financial revenue of various regions.

The aforementioned taxes are not to be collected from every enterprise, unit or individual. Generally speaking, industrial and commercial enterprises should pay value added tax; communications and transport, construction and installation, financial and insurance and service enterprises should pay relevant industrial tax and profit-making enterprises should pay enterprise income tax. Besides, enterprises producing goods for consumption that should be taxed should pay consumption tax; mining enterprises should pay resources tax; enterprises engaged in fixed asset investment should pay fixed asset investment orientation regulated tax, enterprises should pay stamp tax for their production, business accounts and contracts signed with others, and enterprises owning houses and cars should pay housing tax and car use tax. Citizens with an income surpassing a certain limit should pay individual income tax. According to tax regulations, some taxpayers can enjoy tax exemption or reduction.

Foreign Taxation in China

Among the current taxation laws and administrative regulations published in China, there are 15 taxes applicable to the enterprises with foreign investment, foreign enterprises and foreigners in China now. They are VAT, Consumption Tax, Vehicle Axquisition Tax, Customs Duties, Business Tax, Income Tax on Enterprises with Foreign Investment and Foreign Enterprises, Individual Income Tax, Land Appreciation Tax, Urban Real Estate Tax, Resource Tax, City and Township Land Use Tax, Deed Tax, Vehicle and Vessel Tax, Vessel Tonnage Tax and Stamp Duty.

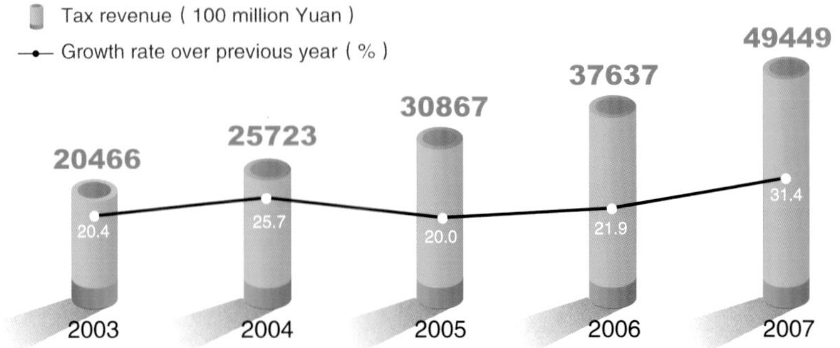

♦ State Administration of Taxation

The main functions and responsibilities of the State Administration of Taxation include: drafting the protocol of the laws and regulations on taxation and working out the specific implementation measures; putting forward suggestions on the taxation policies and reviewing them and reporting to the leadership together with the Ministry of Finance, and constituting the practical measures; taking part in macroeconomic policies, apportioning the taxation right between the Central Government and local entities and offering advice on improving the system of tax distribution; studying the general level of tax and putting forward suggestions on macro-control by taxation; drawing out and supervising the regulations on implementing the taxation business; directing the levy and management of local tax; organizing reforms in the management system of the tax levy; working out the levy management system; supervising and inspecting the implementation of the laws, regulations, guidelines and policies on taxation; carrying out the management of the levying of the central tax, share tax, agricultural tax and the fund designated by the State; creating a long-term program of taxation and the annual tax income plan; explaining the levy and management in the course of the implementation of the laws and regulations and the common problems on taxation; organizing detailed proceedings such as the reduction and exemption of the industrial and commercial tax and reduction and exemption of the agricultural tax in condition of unusual disasters; developing international exchanges and cooperation with regard to taxation; taking part in the international negotiations regarding foreign tax and initially signing and implementing the related agreement and convention; and handling the taxation of the imports and exports products and export tax refund business.

Address: No. 5 Yangfangdian Xilu, Haidian District, Beijing
Website: http://www.chinatax.gov.cn/function.jsp

The Existing Taxation System of China

Kinds of taxation	Contents
Turnover tax	Value-added tax, consumption tax, business tax
Income tax	Enterprise income tax, foreign-invested enterprise and foreign enterprise income tax, and individual income tax
Resources tax	Resources tax, and city and town land use tax
Special purpose tax	City maintenance and construction tax, arable land use tax, fixed assets investment orientation regulating tax, and land value-added tax
Property tax	Housing property tax, urban real estate tax, and inheritance tax (not yet collected)
Social taxes	Car and boat use tax, car and boat license tax, stamp tax, contract tax, securities trading tax, slaughter tax, and banquet tax
Customs duty	

07 Economy

Agriculture

The General Situation of Agriculture

China is a country with a large population but less arable land. With only seven percent of the world's cultivated land, China has to feed a fifth of the world's population. Therefore, agriculture is an important issue and draws wide attention.

This sector has developed rapidly since reforms in the rural areas began in 1978. The major reforms were: the household contract responsibility system, which restored to farmers the right to use land, arrange farm work and to dispose of their output; canceling the State market monopoly of agricultural products, and price controls over most agricultural and ancillary products; abolishing many restrictive policies, allowing farmers to develop diversified business and set up township enterprises so as to fire their enthusiasm for production. The reforms emancipated and developed rural productive forces, promoted the rapid growth of agriculture - particularly in grain production - and the optimization of the agricultural structure. The achievements have been remarkable.

The Import and Export of the Agriculture

Since China's entry into the WTO, the agricultural industry has developed fast. After five years of WTO membership, of the 15 kinds of agricultural products whose trade volume accounts for 85-90 percent of the total agricultural trade volume, eight saw a rise in exports and a fall in imports. They include aquatic products, vegetables, fruits, coffee and cereals. Before China's accession to the WTO, China had to import cereals in large quantities; in the few years after China's accession to the WTO, China cut its import of rice, wheat, corn and other cereals, and even exported some of these.

One of the main reasons was that, according to the promises made in order to gain WTO membership, import customs duty on agricultural products was cut drastically until China became one of the countries with the lowest rate in the world. The agricultural industry of China was weak, and the international competitiveness of its products was very poor, creating a "green barrier" to export expansion.

♦ Ministry of Agriculture

The main functions and responsibilities of the Ministry of Agriculture include: creating the development strategy and mid- and long-term development plans for agriculture and the rural economy and organizing implementation after authorization; working out agricultural development programming and supervising implementation; studying industrial policies of agriculture and directing the rational readjustment of the industrial structure of agriculture, reasonable deployment of agricultural resources and the improvement of product quality; putting forward suggestions on the policies with regard to the readjustment of prices and duties for agricultural means of production and agricultural products, credit and taxation policies for rural areas and agricultural financial subsidies; organizing the drafting of the protocols of the laws and regulations of the various agricultural industries such as the planting industry, animal husbandry, fishery and township enterprises and so on.

Address: No.1 South of Agricultural Exhibition Hall, Chaoyang District, Beijing
Website: http://www.agri.gov.cn

Township Enterprises

Township enterprises are run by farmers in rural areas. Thanks to the rural reforms and the process of the agricultural science and technology, huge gains have been made in agricultural efficiency, so huge numbers of rural laborers have been emancipated from the land, thus laying the foundations for the development of farmer-run township enterprises whose competitively priced goods and services sell well across China. Through long-term development, the township enterprises have already become the main strength of the county-regional economy and the most dynamic increase point in the national economy. Currently, 30 percent of the GDP, 45 percent of the added value of industry and 34 percent of exports come from township enterprises. Among enterprises with the annual turnover surpassing 10 million Yuan, 65 percent had set up research and development institutes, creating 38.6 percent of the added value from all township enterprises. A number of famous enterprises with independent innovative ability and intellectual property right have come into being. Township enterprises are involved in many sectors, such as industry, agricultural product processing, transportation and communications, construction, commerce and catering.

Agricultural Industrialization

Enlarging the operational scale of agricultural industrialization and raising the modernized level of agriculture in an all-round way is an important part of heightening the international competitiveness of Chinese agriculture. Hence, over 3 billion Yuan has been invested in the cause. Since 2003, the State has set up six types of demonstration projects for the industrialization of modern agro-technology, so as to promote the use of advanced technology for agricultural

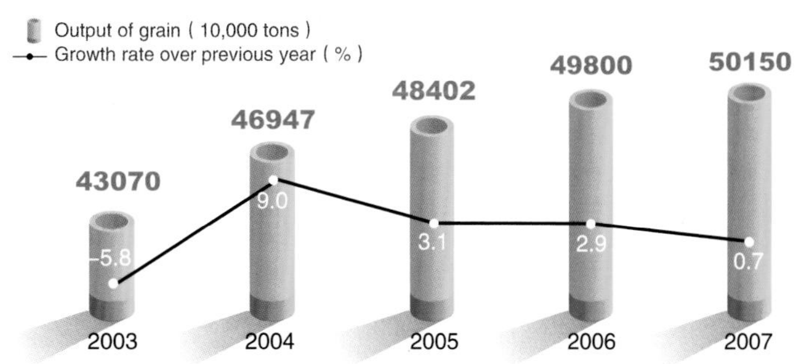

• Spark Program

The specialization and commercialization of agricultural production enabled farmers increasingly to understand the importance of technology, hence arousing the desire to introduce science into rural areas. At the beginning of 1986, the government authorized the "Spark Program", which drew inspiration from an old proverb that "a single spark can start a prairie fire". The main content was: supporting a large number of advanced applicable technological projects that made use of rural resources, required little investment but could take effect quickly, setting up a group of demonstration enterprises as science and technology forerunners, promoting the healthy development of township enterprises and readjusting rural industry and the product structure; developing modern equipment applicable in rural areas and township enterprises and organizing batch production; cultivating a number of rural technological and managerial personnel and farmer entrepreneurs; and developing high yield, quality and efficient agriculture and accelerating the construction of a rural socialization service system and the development of a rural economy of scale.

Website: http://www.cnsp.org.cn/ndbg/ndbg.htm

• Important Achievements Plan

In March 1987, the Chinese Government launched the "Important Achievements Plan". Focusing on improving economic benefits, the program applied existing scientific research results and advanced technologies comprehensively to scope production to realize stable output, high yield, low consumption and high benefits. The operational items of the program refer to the popularization of advanced applicable scientific research results and advanced technologies of the planting industry, animal husbandry, fisheries and agricultural machinery industry and so on. All the scientific research results and advanced technologies that can add output value, improve quality, raise working benefits, decrease consumption, reduce cost, lighten labor intensity, heighten resource utility, benefit environmental protection and produce increased economic, social and ecological benefits and be suitable to be applied on a large scale, can be included.

The program is one of the most important projects for popularization of agricultural technologies. Through its implementation, practical technologies for the planting industry were popularized in 106 million hectares of land, with an added output of 42 billion kg of grain, 1.2 billion kg of lint and 800 million kg of aquatic products, scientifically breeding 500 million domestic animals and birds and 800,000 hectares of fish breeding. Meanwhile, it had trained all levels and all kinds of scientific and technological personnel for one million person/times and farmers for 400 million person/times.

• Prairie Fire Program

The Prairie Fire Program was carried out from 1988 by the State Education Committee, aiming to accelerate the development of rural education reform and promote development of the rural economy and social progress. It is the plan of the "Spark Program" and "Important Achievements Plan", which cultivates agricultural technology qualified persons and creates a base for development.

The main tasks include: on the base of eliminating illiteracy, popularizing compulsory education and vigorously developing occupational education and adult education, fully exerting the relative advantages of intellect and advantages of all levels and all kinds of schools in rural areas; actively developing education in practical technology and managerial knowledge closely connected with local construction; cultivating large number of new type rural economic builders; initiatively cooperating with the departments of agriculture and science and technology to promote activities mainly aimed at popularizing local applicable technologies, such as experiment demonstration, technology training and information services and so on; and promoting the development of agriculture and rural construction.

The objective of the program: changing a situation where rural education was alienated from reality, and popularizing efficient agricultural technologies by way of developing various forms of vocational education to improve the quality and production skills of farmers and enhance their scientific and technological consciousness and commodity economy conception, so that agriculture can develop further.

Combine harvester is reaping the wheat in the field.

production and enhance foreign earnings from exports of farm products. These projects include industrialization of breeding and cultivation of excellent new varieties and fine strains; high-efficiency, eco-friendly planting and aquatic breeding technology; water-saving and precision technologies; downstream processing of agricultural and ancillary products; pollution-free inputs (e.g., fertilizer and fodder) and the establishment of an agricultural information platform. The "downstream processing of main agricultural products project" was listed as an important sci-tech project during the 2000-2005 period. It aims at developing key technologies and equipment for downstream processing of staple agricultural products, research into integrated quality control systems and the quick testing of agro-product technology and equipment. Once completed, some of China's technological aspects will meet advanced international standards. Meanwhile, "dairy industry development" and "water-saving agriculture" projects have been listed among the 12 important sci-tech application programs initiated by the Ministry of Science and Technology.

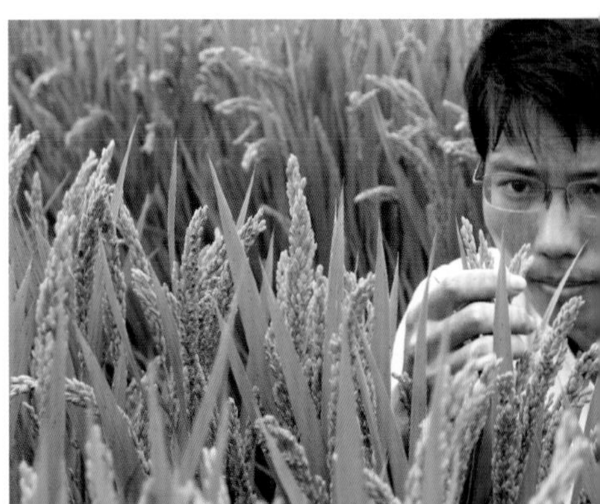

Research and development personnel of the research institute of agricultural sciences are observing and analyzing the way paddy is growing.

Harvesting

Super Rice Popularization Project

In 2005, China set up the super rice popularization project. From the birth of the first super rice breed, Shennong 265 in 1996, more than 30 superior breeding materials were invented and 28 new strains were cultivated. The average yield of per mu in the one hundred mu demonstration field surpassed 700 kg, with one small area achieving over 800 kg. From 1998, super rice was popularized in 14.7 million hectares cumulatively, and, in 2005 alone, it was planted in 4 million hectares with an added yield of around 9.2 billion kg.

Increased Grain Output

Through the combination of high technology and normal technologies, China has made a series of important achievements in the cultivation of fine breeds, highly efficient planting, soil fertility, clean production and prevention and control of major plant diseases and insect pests, which provided strong scientific and technological support for the stable increase of grain output, a sustainable rise on farmers' incomes and safeguarding national grain security. Through projects such as the "scientific and technological project on harvesting grain", China integrated and innovated a number of key common technologies, and set up a 8 million hectares of experimental demonstration fields covering the 12 grain-producing provinces of the Northeast Plain, North China Plain and the middle and lower reaches of the Yangtze River. Grain output per unit increased over 10 percent on the basis of the average output per unit in the first three years, cumulatively producing another 5.16 million tons of grain.

Increase in Output of Main Farm Products

Unit: 10,000 tons

Title	Output	Percent increase over the previous year
Grain	50150	0.7
Summer grain	11534	1.3
Early rice	3196	0.3
Autumn grain	35420	0.6
Oil-bearing crops	2461	-4.2
Cotton	760	1.3
Sugar crops	11110	11.4
Cured tobacco	239	-3.9
Tea	114	10.9

Industry

Brief Introduction

Since China initiated the policy of reform and opening up in late 1978, China's industry has always maintained high growth.

Power Grid Construction

Now, China's power industry has entered a new era featuring large generating units, large power plants, large power grids, ultra-high voltage and automation. The main power grids now cover all the cities and most rural areas, with 500- kV grids beginning to replace 220-kV grids for inter-provincial and inter-regional transmission and exchange operations. An international advanced automated control system with computers as the mainstay is universally adopted.

Power Industry

China's technology equipment level of the power industry has achieved or approached the international advanced level. Currently, China produces mainly 300,000 kW and 600,000 kW generating sets. The 600,000 kW and 900,000 kW supercritical units have been put into production and the domestically-developed million kW ultra-supercritical units will also been put into production. Through introducing international advanced technology, the power equipment produced in China such as the 300,000 kW large scales circulating fluidized bed boiler power equipment, 9F-grade combined circulating gas turbine, 600,000 kW pressurized water reactor nuclear power station and 700,000 kW water-turbine unit of the Three Gorges have already become competitive

Statistical Bulletin Complete List of China's Power industry in 2007

Name of the index	Unit	2007	Growth rate over previous year (±、%)
Installed generating capacity	10,000 Kilowatt	71329	14.4
Hydropower	10,000 Kilowatt	14526	11.5
Thermal power	10,000 Kilowatt	55442	14.6
Nuclear power	10,000 Kilowatt	885	29.2
Wind Power	10,000 Kilowatt	403	94.4
Generating capacity	100 million Kilowatt-hour	32559	14.4
Hydropower	100 million Kilowatt-hour	4867	17.6
Thermal power	100 million Kilowatt-hour	26980	13.8
Nuclear power	100 million Kilowatt-hour	626	14.1
Wind Power	100 million Kilowatt-hour	56	95.2
Utilized hours of the power plants with an installed generating capacity of 6,000 Kilowatt or above	Hour	5011	-187
Hydropower	Hour	3532	139
Thermal power	Hour	5316	-296
Nuclear power	Hour	7737	-69
The standard coal consumption of supplying power by power plants with an installed generating capacity of 6,000 Kilowatt or above	Gram/Kilowatt-hour	357	-10

Output of Major Industrial Products and Their Increase Rate in 2007

Products	Unit	Output	Percent increase over the previous year
Yarn	10000 tons	2000.0	14.7
Cloth	100 million meters	660.0	10.3
Chemical fiber	10000 tons	2390.0	15.3
Sugar	10000 tons	1271.4	34.0
Cured tobaccco	100 million pieces	21413.8	5.9
Color TV	10000	8433.0	0.7
Household refrigerator	10000	4397.1	24.5
Household air-conditione	10000	8014.3	17.0
One-time energy production	100 million tons of standard coal	23.7	7.0
Crude coal	10000 tons	25.36	6.9
Crude oil	100 million tons	1.87	1.1
Natural gas	100 million cubic meters	693.1	18.4
Power generation	100 million kwh	32777.2	14.4
Of this:Thermal	100 million kwh	27218.3	14.9
Hydralulic	100 million kwh	4828.8	10.8
Rough steel	10000 tons	48966.0	16.8
Steels	10000 tons	56894.4	21.3
Ten kinds of non-ferrous metals	10000 tons	2350.8	22.7
Of them: Refined copper (copper)	10000 tons	344.1	14.6
Electrolytic aluminium	10000 tons	1228.4	32.6
Alumina	10000 tons	1945.3	46.7
Cement	100 million tons	13.6	9.9
Sulphuric acid	10000 tons	5500.0	9.3
Soda	10000 tons	1771.8	13.6
Sodiumhydroxide	10000 tons	1759.3	16.4
Ethene ethylene	10000 tons	1047.7	11.4
Chemical fertilixers(100 percent)	10000 tons	5786.9	8.3
Power generator	10000 kW	12991.0	11.1
Automobile	10000	888.7	22.1
Of this:Car	10000	479.8	24.0
Large and medium-sized tractor	10000	20.3	1.9
Integrated circuit	100 million pieces	411.6	22.6
Program controlled exchange	10000 lines	5387.1	-27.2
Mobile phone	10000	54857.9	14.3
Micro computer	10000	12073.4	29.3

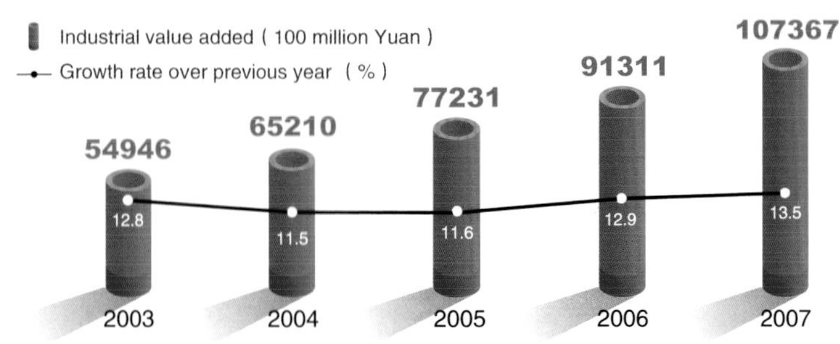

♦ State Power Grid Corporation of China

The corporation was founded on December 29, 2002 as a State-owned corporation. Its core business is to build and operate power grids. With a registered capital of 200 billion Yuan and a service area covering 26 provinces, autonomous regions and municipalities directly under the jurisdiction of the Central Government, which equals 88 percent of national territory.

Website: http://www.sgcc.com.cn/

♦ State Administration of Work Safety

This is an institution directly under the jurisdiction of the State Council in charge of the supervision and administration of work safety. It is also the office institution of the State Council Work Safety Committee.

Its main functions and responsibilities include: studying and putting forward suggestions on grand policies and measures with respect to work safety; supervising, inspecting, directing and harmonizing the work for promoting work safety between the related departments of the State Council and the people's governments of each province, autonomous regions and the municipalities directly under the Central Government; organizing the work safety inspection and special supervision of the State Council; taking part in the research work of related departments regarding work safety in the aspects of industrial policies, investment and scientific and technological development and so on; organizing the investigation of major accidents; organizing emergency rescue efforts in grave accidents; directing and harmonizing the national administration and law enforcement work with regard to work safety; handling the conferences and important activities held by the State Council Work Safety Committee and supervising the implementation of its decisions.

Under regulations of the State Council, it also governs the State Administration of Coal Mine Safety and comprehensively supervises and manages coal mine safety work.

Address: No. 21 Hepingli Beijie, Dongcheng District, Beijing

Website: http://www.chinasafety.gov.cn/

internationally in performance to price ratio. Meanwhile, 500 kV alternating and direct current transmission and transformer equipment produced by domestic manufacturers has become the core of the national grid, but there still exists a certain gap with the international advanced level in some aspects, such as the manufacture of the equipment of the one-mega kW nuclear power plant.

Clean Energy Sources

As a clean and recyclable energy source, hydropower has developed fast. In September 2004, the installed capacity broke through 100 million kW, accounting for 25 percent of the total capacity of the country and leading the world. Meanwhile, the development of nuclear energy and other renewable energy sources were also given due importance. By the end of 2006, the installed capacity of thermal power and hydropower accounted for 77.82 percent and 20.67 percent in total installed generating capacity. During the 11th Five-Year Plan, large power generating units as well as nuclear and wind power generators will enjoy a larger share in total. In 2006, China released the rules and regulations for the implementation of the Law on Recyclable Energy.

Three Gorges Project

The full name of the Three Gorges Project is Yangtze River Three Gorges Water Conservancy Hinge Project, composed of one concrete gravity type dam, discharge sluice, one hydropower station, one permanent ship lock and one ship lift. The construction of the Three Gorges includes dam, workshops of the hydropower station and buildings for navigation. The dam has a total length of 3,035 meters and a height of 185 meters. In front of the hydropower station are the 700,000 kW turbine generator units, with total installed capacity of 1,820 kWh and annual generated power of 84.7 billion kWh. The buildings for navigation lie on the left bank, and the permanent buildings for navigation contain two-way continuous locks and one first grade vertical ship lift.

The project was divided into three phases. The first phase lasted five years (1992-1997), with the main projects including building the cofferdam and digging the open channel. The concrete vertical cofferdam and the temporary ship locks (120 meters high) on the left bank were completed, and the permanent ship locks on the left bank, ship lift and part boulder dam on the left bank begun. The second phase lasted six years (1998-2003), and the main tasks were building the second phase cofferdam and the establishment of the power station on the left bank, installing the generator units and completing the construction of the permanent ship lock and ship lift. The third phase was due to last six years (2003-2009), and the main tasks are to construct the dam and power station on the right bank, and complete the installation of the total generator units. The Three Gorges Reservoir is 600 km long and 2,000 meters wide at most, with an area of 10,000 square km. It is a quiet, gorge-type reservoir.

Panorama of the Three Gorges Dam

Three Gorges Transport Hub Situation (2006)

According to the China Three Gorges Corporation, the ship locks of the Three Gorges, which went into trial operation in 2003, ran well over the years, with 14.75 million tons of goods transport in 2003, 43.09 million tons of goods in 2004, 43.94 million tons of goods in 2005, and 50.24 million tons in 2006. In all, it ran 8,050 times, with 56,400 ships passing and a total of 1.62 million passengers carried.

The "Most" of the Three Gorges Project

The Three Gorges Project is the largest water conservancy hinge project, whose many indices have set new records in China and for the world's water conservancy projects.

Some 75 years passed from the earliest proposal to the formal start, which makes it the hydro engineering project with the longest discussion time in the world.

From the first reconnaissance in the early 1940s and the comprehensive and systemic design and research between the 1950s and the 1980s, the Three Gorges Project accumulated vast basic data and research results, which make it the water project with the largest amount of preliminary work.

The construction issue of the Three Gorges Project has aroused the widest attention both at home and abroad, and it is the only water engineering project that has been reviewed and voted on by China's

♦ The Three Gorges Project Construction Committee

In order to ensure the smooth proceeding of the Three Gorges Project, in January 1993, the State Council founded the State Council Three Gorges Project Construction Committee as the highest decision-making body handling the construction and population relocation work.

There are two institutions under the jurisdiction of the Three Gorges Project Construction Committee. The first is the office of the State Council Three Gorges Project Construction Committee, taking charge of the daily work. The second is the China Yangtze River Three Gorges Project Development Corporation, which is an economic entity assuming sole responsibility for its profits or losses and conducting autonomous management. It is the legal entity (owner) of the Three Gorges Project, being responsible for the construction and operations, the management and use of the funds and the payment of debt in accordance with the policies set up by the State and the preliminary design of the project.

By June 2006, The State Council Three Gorges Project Construction Committee had held 15 plenary sessions, making decisions with regard to the major issues in the course of the construction and the transmission and transformer project and the relocation of communities within the reservoir area to ensure smooth progress in the construction.

Website: http://www.3g.gov.cn/

highest organ of State power, the National People's Congress.

The total storage capacity of the Three Gorges Project is 39.3 billion cubic meters, and the flood control capacity is 22.15 billion cubic meters. The peak discharge is between 27,000 to 33,000 cubic meters per second, making it the water project with the most remarkable flood control efficiency.

The total installed capacity of the hydropower station of the Three Gorges is 18.2 million kW and the annual generated electricity is 84.68 billion kWh. It is the largest power station in the world.

The back water of the Three Gorges Reservoir can improve 650 km of navigation routes on the upper Yangtze River, increasing the shipping tonnage limitation of the Yichang-Chongqing sector from the current 3,000 to 10,000 tons, and the one-way traffic ability from 10 million to 50 million tons; through the adjustment of the reservoir, the navigation depth of the shallow water below Yichang City will also be increased, so it is the hydro project with the most remarkable shipping benefits.

The Three Gorges Project has a total width of 2,335 meters including the non-overflow dam on both banks. The single items of the project are as follows: the length of the spillway section of the dam: 483 meters; the generator units of the hydro station: 700,000 kW×26 units; dual-way five-step ship lock + ship lift. No matter whether the single item or collectively, it is the water project with the largest construction scale.

The main constructions used 125 million cubic meters of earth-rock filling, 26.43 million cubic meters of concrete and 593,000 tons of steel. This makes it the largest water works in the world.

The deepest depth of the deep water cofferdam is 60 meters, the monthly earth-rock filling volume 1.7 million cubic meters, the monthly concrete placing volume 554,000 cubic meters and the annual concrete placing volume 5.43 million cubic meters, which all set world records, so it is the project with the strongest construction intensity in water conservancy.

The dam runoff of the Three Gorges Project reached 9,010 cubic meters per second and the largest peak discharge guided by the construction was 79,000 cubic meters per second. It is the hydro project with the largest runoff volume during construction.

The largest sluice capacity of the flood gate of the Three Gorges Project is 100,000 cubic meters per second, which leads the world.

The dual-way five-step lock with the total water head of the Three Gorges Project is the internal river lock with the most steps and highest water head.

The efficient size of the ship lift of the Three Gorges is 120 x 18 x 3.5 meters, with a gross weight of 11,800 tons; the largest lift of 113 meters and navigation tonnage of 3,000 tons. The ship lift leads the world in scale and difficulty.

By the end of 2009, the number of people relocated from the reservoir areas of the Three Gorges Project should finally reach 1.13 million, the largest number of any construction project.

Coal Industry

Starting in the 1980s, China invested hugely into creating a number of large-scale modern coalmines. China now has the ability to design, construct, equip and administer 10m-ton opencast coalmines and large and medium-sized mining areas. China's coal washing and dressing technologies and abilities have constantly improved and coal liquefaction and underground gasification have been introduced. In 2006, output of crude coal was 2.38 billion tons, an increase of 8 percent over the previous year.

Petroleum and Natural Gas Industry

Petroleum and natural gas are important energy resources. For seven years running from 1997 to 2003, annual crude oil output exceeded 160 million tons, and the annual production of oil was 184 million tons in 2006, ranking fifth in the world. Oil industry development has accelerated the growth of local economies and related industries, such as the machinery manufacturing, iron and steel industries, transport and communications. The output of natural gas in 2006 reached 59.5 billion cubic meters. With the sustainable and fast growth of the Chinese economy, especially the vigorous development of the automobile and aviation industries, there has been a huge upsurge in oil consumption. In the past few years, the average annual increase speed of oil consumption has been above 6 percent. Dependence on foreign oil was 36 percent in 2003, and close to 50 percent in 2006. Currently, China has surpassed Japan to become the second largest oil-importer.

Nuclear Power Industry

China has three nuclear power plants—the Zhejiang Qinshan Nuclear Power Plant, the Guangdong Daya Bay Nuclear Power Plant and the Jiangsu Tianwan Nuclear Power Plant; they have a combined generating capacity of 8.7 million kW. At the end of 2006, 10 nuclear-power generators with a capacity of 7.88 million kW were in operation, having generated 53.082 billion kwh of electricity, or 2.2 percent of the national total which, however, stays lower than the world average.

Qinshan and Daya Bay Nuclear Power Plants have operated safely for 10 years, and there have no major accidents in the construction and operation of them, or in the production of nuclear fuels. The release of radioactive materials from the plants has never produced any perceivable change in the environmental radioactive background level. The second phase of the Qinshan Nuclear Power Plant and the No.1 unit of Ling'ao Nuclear Power Plant have also been put into commercial operation. Another four units are under construction and due to be phased in over a three-year period.

The fast development of the economy and the objective of building a well-off society generate huge energy demand. Furthermore, China's shortage of energy sources also intensifies the demand. Currently, nuclear-power-generated electricity only accounts for two percent of the national total. The government plans that, by 2020, the nuclear power generation capacity will reach 40 million kW, accounting for four percent of total installed capacity. It means that around 30 one MkW nuclear power units are required to be constructed. Hence, China is a huge market for nuclear power.

China has adopted safety measures in the light of the related regulations of the International Atomic Energy Agency. The nuclear power plants are completely built in line with international criteria. Experts of the State Environmental Protection Administration and so on all strictly review the construction of the nuclear power plants according to international norms and standards. The nuclear power plants are open to public inspection.

Under the framework of the Treaty on the Non-Proliferation of Nuclear Weapons, China has actively and practically developed extensive international cooperation. Up to now, it has established exchanges, cooperation and trade relations with over 40 countries. The aforementioned Daya Bay Nuclear Power Plant, Ling'ao Nuclear Power Plant and the third-phase Qinshan Nuclear Power Plant are all the important results of Sino-foreign cooperation.

♦ China National Petroleum Corporation

The corporation(CNPC) is one of the world's leading integrated energy companies. It is a State holding company whose business operations cover a broad spectrum of upstream and downstream activities, oil gas field technical services, and oil materials equipment manufacturing and supply. CNPC ranks 7th among the world's top 50 petroleum companies.

The corporation provides society with over 2.19 million barrels of crude oil and 2.8 billion cubic feet of natural gas a day, and processes 1.8 million barrels of crude oil daily.

It actively takes part in the international cooperation through its sole subsidiary, China National Oil and Gas Exploitation and Development Corporation, covering the aspects of oil and gas exploration, development and production, oil refining and chemical storage and transportation and distribution and so on. CNPC boasts strong technical service strength, providing 46 countries with engineering technical services such as well drilling through its subsidiary, China National International Engineering Technology Corporation. The corporation has preliminarily formed five oil and gas production and development zones in African, Central Asia, the Middle East, South America and Southeast Asia respectively. It has 4.5 billion tons of proven oil geological reserves and 650 million tons of residual available reserves, with annual crude oil production capacity being 35 million tons and the natural gas production capacity of four billion cubic meters. By the end of 2006, it had oil and gas assets in 26 countries.

Website: http://www.cnpc.com.cn

♦ China Petrochemical Corporation

China Petrochemical Corporation (SINOPEC Group) is a super-large petroleum and petrochemical entity incorporated in July 1998 on the basis of the former China Petrochemical Corporation. SINOPEC Group is a national company solely invested in by the State, is a State-authorized investment organization, and is an organization authorized to hold State controlling interests or shares in companies. The President of SINOPEC Group is its legal representative. Headquartered in Beijing, SINOPEC Group has a registered capital of 104.9 billion Yuan.

China Petroleum and Chemical Corporation (SINOPEC Corp.), a company controlled by SINOPEC Group, issued H-shares and A-shares respectively in October 2000 and August 2001, and has been listed on the Hong Kong, New York, London and Shanghai stock markets. By the end of 2005, SINOPEC Corp. had issued a total of 86.7 billion shares, with 71.23 percent of them held by SINOPEC Group, 6.19 percent held by the State Development Bank and State assets management companies, 19.36 percent held by foreign investors and 3.23 percent owned by domestic investors.

SINOPEC Group's key business activities include: industrial investment and portfolio management; the exploration, production, transportation (including pipeline transportation), marketing and comprehensive utilization of oil and natural gas; oil refining; the wholesale trade in gasoline, kerosene and diesel; the production, marketing, storage and transportation of petrochemicals and other chemical products; the design, construction and installation of petroleum and petrochemical engineering projects; the overhaul and maintenance of petroleum and petrochemical equipments; the manufacturing of electrical and mechanical equipments; research, development, application and consultation services on technology, information and alternative energy products; the import and export of commodities and technologies both for the Group and as a proxy (with the exception of those commodities and technologies that are either banned by the State or to be carried out by State-designated companies).

Employees from Zhongyuan Oilfiels Petrochemical Company, a unit of Sinopec, are assembling the equipments of the Saudi Arabia's Well Drilling project for which the Sinopec won the bid.

Website: http:// www.Sinopecgroup.com/

♦ China National Offshore Oil Corporation

China National Offshore Oil Corporation (CNOOC) is the third largest State-owned oil company and the dominant offshore oil and gas producer in China. It takes charge of the exploitation of the offshore oil and natural gas within the maritime areas of China. The company was incorporated in 1982, with a registered capital of 50 billion Yuan. Headquartered in Beijing, it has 37,000 employees.

Through vigorous assets acquisition and cooperative development, the oil and gas assets of CNOOC are also widely distributed in Australia, Southeast Asia, Africa and the Caspian Sea area. The corporation has become the largest offshore oil and gas producer in Indonesia.

The three shareholding enterprises of CNOOC listed both in domestic and foreign stock markets, namely China National Offshore Oil Corporation, China National Oil Field Service Co., Ltd., and Offshore Oil Engineering Co., Ltd. maintain favorable performance in terms of perfect and transparent governance, strong profit-making capacity and growth ability.

Website: http://www.cnooc.com.cn

Daya Bay Nuclear Power Plant

Primary reactor in the Daya Bay Nuclear Power Plant

Guangdong Daya Bay Nuclear Power Plant lies in Malingjiao, Dakeng Village on the bank of Daya Bay in the east of Shenzhen City, 50 km from Hong Kong. There is no capable fault within 20 km scope of its location, so it is in the area with comparatively stable crustal conformation.

Daya Bay Nuclear Power Plant is the first large one-MkW commercial NPP, having two sets of 984,000 kW pressurized-water reactor nuclear power units. It was approved by the State Council in December 1982, and started construction in August 1987 and was completed and put into commercial operation in May 1994. It is the largest large-scale nuclear power construction project, which is jointly invested in by Guangdong Nuclear Power Investment Co., Ltd. and Hong Kong Nuclear Power Investment Co., Ltd. China National Nuclear Corporation holds 45 percent of the shares.

In more than 10 years since it began operation, Daya Bay Nuclear Power Plant has gained favorable achievements with its various technological economic indices reaching the international advanced level In 2004, on the safe operation challenge contest of the same units organized by Electricité de France (EDF), Daya Bay Nuclear Power Operation Management Co., Ltd. gained three number ones in the aspects of "safe operating record", "industrial safety" and "radioactive protection". In 2005, the average capability factor and the load factor of the two units of Daya Bay Nuclear Power Plant were 89.86 percent and 89.62 percent.

By the end 2006, the cumulative electricity provided to the grid by Daya Bay Nuclear Power Plant reached 169.6 billion kWh including 115.8 billion kWh sent to Hong Kong.

Qinshan Nuclear Power Plant

Qinshan Nuclear Power Plant is of 300,000 kW confined water pile type, designed, constructed and operated independently for the first time in China. It is located in Haiyan County, Zhejiang Province. China National Nuclear Corporation holds 100 percent of the shares and Qinshan Nuclear Power Corporation takes charge of its operation and management.

Construction of the Qinshan Nuclear Power Plant was started on March 20, 1985 and was incorporated in power network and began to generate electricity on December 15, 1991. It made China the 7th country capable of designing and building nuclear power stations by itself after America, Britain, France, the former Soviet Union, Canada and Sweden.

Qinshan Nuclear Power Plant was put into commercial operation in April, 1994, and passed inspection in July 1995. In the sixth, seventh and eighth fuel cycles from 2002 to 2005, Qinshan Nuclear Power Plant successively created the best record of its kind in China by operating continuously at full power for 331 days, 443 days and 448 days respectively. It is rare internationally to reach this level of performance for a prototype reactor. In the comprehensive index evaluation of the WANO performance norm of 2002, Qinshan Nuclear Power Plant reached the world median level of the confined water pile nuclear power plant in advance. For 14 years of operation, it has run safely and stably with favorable achievements and no radioactive pollution has been found due to its operation.

Tianwan Nuclear Power Plant

Tianwan Nuclear Power Plant is a high-tech cooperative project between China and Russia, and the largest technological and economical cooperation project of the two countries to date. Listed as key nuclear project in the Ninth Five Year Plan, it is constructed by China National Nuclear Corporation and located in Tianwan, Lianyun District, Lianyungang City, Jiangsu Province. The layout of the plant is designed according to the four one-MW nuclear power units, and has scope for an additional two to four units. In the first phase, two Russian AES-91 pressurized-water reactor nuclear power units were due to be built. The installed capacity is 2x1.06 million kW and the design life is 40 years. The annual average load factor is no less than 80 percent and annual generated electricity amounts to 14 billion kWh.

As the owner of the project, Jiangsu Nuclear Power Corporation is mainly responsible for the construction and operation of Tianwan NPP. The corporation consists of the following three shareholders: China National Nuclear Corporation (50 percent), China Power Investment Corporation

Tianwan Nuclear Power Plant

(30 percent) and Jiangsu Guoxin Asset Management Group (20 percent).

The construction of Tianwan Nuclear Power Plant started on October 20, 1999. On May 12, 2006, the No.1 unit was successively incorporated in the power network for the first time, in the course of which, various technological indices of the plant were confirmed as meeting design requirements. The No.2 unit succeeded in being connected with the power grid. After being put into commercial operation, the two units will add 2.12 million kW to the power network of eastern China, providing safe, dependable, clean and high-efficient energy resources.

Ling'ao Nuclear Power Plant

The first phase of the Ling'ao Nuclear Power Plant is the second largest commercial nuclear power plant built in Guangdong Province since the operation of Daya Bay Nuclear Power Plant. It is constructed and run by Ling'ao Nuclear Power Corporation. China National Nuclear Corporation holds 45 percent of its shares.

The first phase has two pressurized-water reactor nuclear power units with installed capacity of 990,000 kW. The principal part of the project was started in May 1997 and put into commercial operation in January 2003, and passed State inspection on July 16, 2004.

Ling'ao Nuclear Power Plant

In 2005, compared with the nine achievement indices of its same kind of WANO in 2004, seven indices of Ling'ao Nuclear Power Plant surpassed the world medium level and one achieved advanced level. On February 20, 2005, the first phase of Ling'ao Nuclear Power Plant realized over 1,000 successive days without any industrial accident. In 2005, the average capability factor and the load factor of the two units of the first phase were 87.16 percent and 86.63 percent. By June 2006, the cumulative electricity amount contributed to the network reached 53.088 billion kWh. It had repaid US$1.371 billion of principle and interest of the loan for capital construction, accounting for 27.99 percent of total repayments and interest.

In the second phase of Ling'ao Nuclear Power Plant, it is planned to build two one-MW pressurized-water reactor nuclear power units. In March 2004, the second phase of Ling'ao Nuclear Power Plant was listed as one of the nuclear power independent projects of the State; in July 2004, the State Council approved its construction; in December 2005, it was formally started; the two units will go into commercial operation in 2010 and 2011 respectively.

♦ China National Nuclear Corporation

China National Nuclear Corporation is an extra-large exclusively State-owned enterprise approved by the State Council on July 1, 1999.

The corporation has complete nuclear scientific and technological industrial system, mainly being responsible for nuclear materials, nuclear power, nuclear fuel, and radioactive waste, prospecting and exploitation of uranium ores, scientific research development, construction, production and management of nuclear power and its related aspects such as the nuclear instruments and equipments, isotopes and the application of nuclear technology. It has scientific and technological economic exchanges with more than 40 countries. Currently, CNNC consists of over 100 member units and 20 academicians.

Through more than 50 years' development, CNNC has set up complete nuclear scientific and technological industrial system special to China, and is the main investor and owner of the nuclear power plants already operating or under construction, the main body of technical exploitation of the nuclear power development, the exclusive supplier of nuclear fuel and the most important facilitator of nuclear power operational technology. It assumes the key tasks of nuclear power plant operations and the guarantee of safety technology.

Website: http://www.cnnc.com.cn

♦ China Nuclear Engineering and Construction Group Corporation

This is a State authorized investment institution and the asset management body approved by the State Council, as well as one of the ten military industrial corporations of the science and technology industry of national defense. The main business of the corporation is the "military industrial project, nuclear power project, the utility of nuclear energy and research and service of nuclear engineering technologies". The engineering construction represented by national defense projects and nuclear power projects and the advanced reactor technology industrialization represented by the technology of the high temperature air cooling reactor and low temperature heating reactor are the core business of the corporation.

The corporation successively completes the construction of all the nuclear weapons research and production bases and the production establishments of the nuclear fuel, and takes charge of the various national defense science and technology projects of diverse military engineering industries such as aviation, spaceflight, weapons and so on. In the aspect of the peaceful utilization of atomic energy, the corporation has undertaken construction of all the nuclear power plants in China such as the first, second and third phases of Qinshan Nuclear Power Plant, Daya Bay Nuclear Power Plant, Ling'ao Nuclear Power Plant and Tianwan Nuclear Power Plant and so on and the Chashma Nuclear Power Plant of Pakistan exported by China. It has accumulated construction experience of many kinds of nuclear reactors, gained many breakthroughs in construction technologies, formed a number of autonomous intellectual properties and grasped the building ability of one-MW nuclear power plants. In 2005, the corporation also gained the building contracts for the second phase project of Ling'ao Nuclear Power Plant, the second phase extension project of Qinshan Nuclear Power Plant and the second phase project of Chashma Nuclear Power Plant of Pakistan.

Website: http://www.cnecc.com

♦ Chinese Nuclear Power Research and Design Institute

Chinese Nuclear Power Research and Design Institute was founded in 1958, being the largest comprehensive base engaged in the research, design, experiment and operation of nuclear reactors in China and the cradle of the nuclear power projects of China.

The institute independently designed and built the first pressurized-water reactor nuclear power unit, the first high throughout project testing reactor and the first impulse reactor successively in China; completed the important experimental research for the first phase of Qinshan Nuclear Power Plant; developed and produced various types of fuel elements for reactors, some of them exported to foreign countries; undertook the design of the reactor of the second phase of Qinshan Nuclear Power Plant and the refrigerant system of the reactors, and related scientific research breakthroughs and experiments of the project. It is carrying out research and development of advanced pressurized-water reactors. Chengdu nuclear power experimental research base of the institute has more than 10 large scale nuclear power experimental equipments, which makes the nuclear power experimental research of China close to or achieving advanced world level.

Website: http://www.npic.ac.cn

Energy Industry

China is the second largest energy consumption market, close to the US. The consumption is concentrated in the coastal area with developed economy. With regard to the regional distribution of energy resources, these are distributed more in the north and less in south, and rich in west and poor in east. The coal, water and oil and gas are mainly distributed in the north, south and west and under the sea respectively. The annual GDP of the provinces, municipalities directly under the Central Government and autonomous regions in the coastal areas accounts for 70 percent of the national total, but the energy resources in those areas occupy less than 20 percent. Hence, large quantities of energy resources have to be transported from other areas in the country or imported. The contradiction between the distribution of the energy resources and the economic layout determines that China's energy resources flow from west to east and from north to south, and the coastal provinces and cities face shortages of energy resources.

With the fast development of China's economy, the energy resources issue has become a strategic problem influencing national security. One highest institution taking charge of China's energy industry, the national energy leading group, has been set up.

New Energy Resources

To relieve the shortage of energy supplies that fetters China's economic growth, the country is developing new energy resources, such as wind, solar, geothermal, and tidal power. Its abundant wind energy resources create the potential for mass-produced wind power. It is expected to reach 20 million kW by 2020. Given northern China's rich wind energy resources, the wind power industry has attracted domestic and overseas investment and Asia's largest wind power station, with an investment of 10 billion Yuan and a capacity of one million kW, will be completed in Inner Mongolia before 2008. Meanwhile, in western China, with a radiation flux of three kWh per day, solar energy has been widely utilized. Asia's largest demonstration base for solar heating and cooling technologies in Yuzhong County, Gansu Province, has become the training center of applied solar technologies for developing countries.

Machinery Manufacturing Industry

China's machinery manufacturing industry can provide complete sets of large advanced equipment, including large gas turbines, large pump storage groups, and nuclear power sets, ultra-high voltage direct-current transmission and transformer equipment, complete sets of large metallurgical, fertilizer and petrochemical equipment, urban light rail transport equipment, and new papermaking and textile machinery. Chinese machinery products have become the mainstay of exports, leading the way each year from 1996 to 2004.

In 2006, the machinery industry realized a total volume of exports and imports of US$2833.971 billion. Machinery products exported were valued at US$142.359 billion; and imports reached US$141.612 billion.

Major electrical machinery exported were (in order of export value) automatic data processing equipment (US$126.05 billion), telecommunications equipment (US$68.835 billion), household electrical appliances an consumer goods (US$64.19 billion), electronic components (US$40.35 billion) and electrical devices (US$34.27 billion). These made up 60.7 percent of the export volume of electrical products exported.

Major electrical machinery imported in 2006 were (in order of export value) electronic components (US$138.05 billion), automatic data processing equipment and parts (US$40.71 billion), electrical devices (US$33.4 billion), telecommunications equipment (US$22.27 billion), and automobile and parts (US$20.65 billion). They made up 57.4 percent of the value of electrical machinery imported in the year.

Automobile Industry

Since the 1990s, the automobile industry developed steadily as a key sector, with output increasing from 514,000 in 1990 to 8.882 million in 2007. The produce and sale rate of enterprises above designated size in automobile industry ranged from 97.08 percent to 97.81 percent. The total number of motor vehicles for civilian use reached 56.97 million (including 13.99 million tri-wheel motor vehicles and low-speed trucks) by the end of 2007, of which, private-owned vehicles numbered 35.34 million. The proportion of China's sales volume of automobiles in the world surpasses 10 percent. Automobiles, a high-class consumer durable with the lowest rate of ownership, now shows the fastest retail growth rate of any commodity in China. The output of the automobiles increased three times in five years, ranking from third in the world, compared to the eighth in the world in the past. In 2006, the exports of China's vehicle industry amounted to 25 billion Yuan, and the imports stood at 19 billion Yuan. The load-carrying vehicle still ranked first among the exports of China's vehicles, with the export amount and value accounting for 45.3 percent and 31.7 percent of China's total, respectively. Currently, there are more than 800 joint venture or cooperative enterprises for automobiles and parts, with the cumulative capital reaching US$96 billion. The automobile industry has completely realized the promises made before entry into the WTO, and has become an increasingly important component of the world automobile industry.

♦ China Machinery Industry Federation

This is the national social economic organization of the machinery industry, having legal person qualification of a social organization. The main membership consists of national special associations and regional associations, intermediary organs, and comprehensive enterprises. It now has more than 120 direct members and 77,800 indirect members of each branch of China's machinery industry.

The website of China Machinery Industry Federation is the only website of the machinery industry licensed to operate as an internet content provider (ICP) of the State. It provides domestic and foreign enterprises with "one stop" information and consultancy services and assists domestic and foreign enterprises to construct and maintain their websites.

Website: http:// www.cmif.gov.cn

♦ China Association of Automobile Manufacturers

This is an institution engaged in the production and operation of automobiles, motorcycles, parts and components and related industries. It is the legal national industrial guild and the self-disciplining and non-profit social organization not restricted by department, regions and types of ownership. It has the legal person qualification of a social organization and accepts the business direction and supervision of the related State departments such as the Ministry of Civil Affairs. Its functions and responsibilities include: undertaking government commissions, assisting government departments to handle the industrial work and putting forward policies and suggestions for the government; providing information and related consultancy services for the industry and actively maintaining the benefit of the industry and the legal rights and interests of members; and organizing and developing the grand activities of the industry.

It is a member of the International Organization of Motor Vehicle Manufacturers (OICA), and has set up friendly relations with international organizations of the vehicle industry and the associations of automobile manufacturers of many countries.

Website: http:// www.caam.org.cn

On 21:10 September 25, 2008, the Shenzhou VII spacecraft was launched at Jiuquan Satellite Launch Center.

Aerospace Industry

As the fifth country to develop and launch an independent man-made satellite, and the third to master satellite recovery technology, China ranks high in many important technological fields, including satellite recovery, the carrying into space of multiple satellites by one rocket, rocket technology, and the launch, testing and control of stationary-orbit satellites. Great achievements have been made in remote-sensing satellites, communications satellites, and in manned space experiments.

Manned Spacecraft

On November 20-21, 1999, China's first unmanned experimental spacecraft - "Shenzhou" was successfully launched. October 15-16, 2003 saw the successful launch and recovery of the first manned spacecraft "Shenzhou V", which made China the third country to independently develop and deploy manned space flight technology. "Shengzhou VI", carrying two astronauts, successfully accomplished its flight on October 12-17, 2005, during which space experimental activities with human involvement took place for the first time.On September 25 to 28, 2008, the Shenzhuo VII manned spaceship fulfilled the two-day manned space flight of three persons and realized the space extravehicular activity. China has become the third country mastering the technologies of space extravehicular activity in the world.

Man-made Satellites

Over the past five years, China has independently developed and launched 22 different types of man-made satellites, upgrading its overall level in this field markedly. On the basis of the four satellite series initially developed, China has developed two more satellite series, to bring the total to six -- the recoverable remote-sensing satellites, "DFH" (Dongfanghong, or The East is Red) telecommunications and broadcasting satellites, "FY" (Fengyun, or Wind and Cloud) meteorological satellites, "SJ" (Shijian, or Practice) scientific research and technological experiment satellites, "ZY" (Ziyuan, or Resources) Earth resource satellites, and "Beidou" (Plough) navigation and positioning satellites. In addition, the oceanic satellite series will come into being soon. China has speeded up the implementation of the plan to establish "a constellation of small satellites for environment and disaster monitoring and forecasting." Research and development of the payload of some new, high-performance satellites have been successful, and many application satellites have begun regular operation. The Fengyun Iand Fengyun II meteorological satellites have been listed by the World Meteorological Organization in the international satellite series for meteorological services. Important breakthroughs have been made in key technologies related to the common platform for big geostationary orbit satellites. Periodical achievements have been made in the research and development of large-capacity telecommunications and broadcasting satellites. Substantial progress has been made in the research and development, and application of small satellites.

China has made known-to-the-world achievement in satellite launching technology. Since China launched its first artificial earth satellite in the 1960s, China has made and launched 26 satellites, including 11 recoverable satellites. China's satellite technology is up to the internationally advanced level. Picture shows launching pads at the Jiuquan Launching Site of China, which has been used many times.

Launching Vehicles

China has independently developed the "Long March" rocket group, containing 12 types of launching vehicles capable of launching satellites to near-earth, geo-stationary and sun-synchronous orbits, with the launch success ratio of 90 percent. It will manufacture the new generation launching rocket group. Important breakthroughs have been made in key technologies of the new-generation launching vehicles. Research and development of the 120-ton thrust liquid-oxygen/kerosene engine and the 50-ton thrust hydrogen-oxygen engine are proceeding smoothly. China has set up three launching sites—in Jiuquan, Xichang and Taiyuan, being the world-famous modernized launching sites. On October 24, 2007, China sent the Chang'e-1 satellite into the orbit with the Long March III-A carrier rocket. The successful launching of the Chang'e-1, the first lunar probe developed by China, marks a step forward in the moon probing project.

China plans to spend seven or eight years developing a new-generation of large carrier rocket, called "Long March V", to be used for launching a space station. It expected to increase the payload capacity of China's "Long March Series" carrier rockets from 9 tons to 25 tons.

♦ China Academy of Launch Vehicle Technology (CALT)

Founded in 1957, China Academy of Launch Vehicle Technology is the cradle of China's spaceflight undertaking, developing the "Long March" launching rocket brand with the independent intellectual property right in internationally high-tech industries. It has 10 institutions, two entity units, two production plants, a workers hospital, two sole subsidiaries, one company listed in Hong Kong, and some share holding or joint venture companies. With the total assets of 18 billion Yuan and staff of 22,000, China Academy of Launch Vehicle Technology (CALT), also known as the First Academy of CASC, set up the its office in the USA, Germany, Russia, Hong Kong, Macao and other countries and regions. It is China's largest base for the research, design and production of launching vehicles and manned spacecrafts.

Website: http://www.calt.com

♦ China-Aerospace Science and Industry Corporation

Under the direct administration of the State Council, China-Aerospace Science and Industry Corporation is one of the biggest enterprises solely owned by the State. Within CASIC, four divisions have been established, including six large-scale academies, over 180 enterprises and institutions with nearly 100,000 employees in total, among which 40 percent are technicians and engineers of different specialties.

Taking missile weapon system as its foundation, CASIC also lays great emphasis on the development of information technology for military and civil purposes, satellite exploration and application, energy, environmental protection and equipment complex, etc. It has produced for the nation a large number of good performance missile weapon systems of different types, and greatly improved the defense force of our nation and the equipment of our army. The successful launch of "Aerospace Tsinghua 1" satellite marks the considerable progress that CASIC has made in the fields of mini satellite and solid launch vehicle. The various aerospace products of high performance are now indispensable components in Long March launch vehicles and manned space flight project.

Website: http://www.casic.com.cn

Satellite Remote-sensing

The fields and scale where satellite remote-sensing is used have been constantly expanded. Breakthroughs have been made in a large number of key application technologies; infrastructure facilities have been strengthened; the technological level and operational capabilities of the application system have been notably improved; and a national satellite remote-sensing application system has taken shape. China has built and improved the National Remote-Sensing Center, National Satellite Meteorology Center, China Resources Satellite Application Center, National Satellite Oceanic Application Center and China Remote-Sensing Satellite Ground Station, as well as satellite remote-sensing application and certification institutes of relevant State departments, provinces and cities. An optical remote-sensing satellite radiation caliberation station has also been completed and put into operation. Many remote-sensing products and services are provided by using data resources obtained from observation of the Earth by both Chinese and foreign satellites of multiple wavelengths of wide scope and long duration. Satellite remote-sensing application systems have been put into regular operation in many important fields, particularly in meteorology, mining, surveying, agriculture, forestry, land mapping, water conservancy, oceanography, environmental protection, disaster mitigation, transportation, and regional and urban planning. They are playing an important role in the nationwide land resources survey, ecological construction and environmental protection, as well as in major State projects, such as the South-North Water Diversion Project, the Three Gorges Project and the Project to Transmit Natural Gas from West to East.

Satellite Telecommunications and Broadcasting

At present, China has five registered satellite telecommunication companies, 9 satellites on orbit, and 342 transponder units, and open 25,000 national bilateral circuits. By the end of 2005, China had more than 80 international and domestic telecommunications and broadcasting Earth stations, and 34 satellite broadcasting and TV link stations. Dozens of departments and some large corporations have established altogether some 100 satellite specialized communication networks and more than 50,000 Very Small Aperture Terminals (VSAT). The programs of 12 channels of CCTV, 32 line broadcasting of the Central People's Broadcasting Station and international station, and the broadcasting and TV programs of 31 provinces, autonomous regions and municipalities directly under the Central Government are transmitted by the satellites. The percentage of coverage of satellite TV and broadcasting reached 94.18 percent and 92.92 percent, respectively. The development and application of satellite radio and TV broadcasting services has increased the coverage and improved the quality of the programs all over China, particularly in the vast countryside. Satellite telecommunications and broadcasting technologies play an irreplaceable role in the projects "to give every village access to broadcasting and TV" and "to give every village access to telephones." A satellite tele-education broadband network and a satellite tele-medicine network have been established. As a member of the International Maritime Satellite Organization, China has established a maritime satellite communication network covering the whole world, ranking it among the advanced countries in the application of international mobile satellite communication.

China's satellite simulation TV programs will be stopped, making the satellite broadcasting and TV transmitting welcoming the digital times.

Satellite Navigation and Positioning

China has implemented several major related projects, one of which is called "industrialization of satellite navigation and positioning applications." By employing domestic and foreign navigation and positioning satellites, China has made great progress in the development, application and services of satellite navigation and positioning technologies. The range and fields where satellite navigation and positioning are applied are being continuously expanded and the size of the national market for satellite navigation and positioning doubles every two years. Satellite navigation and positioning technologies have been widely used in transportation, basic surveying and mapping, project surveys, resources investigation, earthquake monitoring, meteorological exploration, oceanic surveys, and so forth.

Major Goal of Spaceflight

—To develop non-toxic, pollution-free, high-performance, low-cost and powerful thrust carrier rockets of the new generation, eventually increasing the carrying capacity of near-Earth orbiters to 25 tons, and that of geostationary orbiters to 14 tons; develop in an overall way the 120-ton thrust liquid-oxygen/kerosene engine and the 50-ton thrust hydrogen-oxygen engine; and increase the reliability and adaptability of the present "Long March" carrier rockets.

—To start and implement a high-resolution Earth observation system; develop and launch new-type solar-synchronous orbit and geostationary-orbit meteorological satellites, oceanic satellites, Earth resources satellites, small satellites for environmental protection and disaster monitoring and forecasting; and to start research into key technologies of new-type remote-sensing satellites, including stereo mapping satellites. To form an all-weather, 24-hour, multi-spectral, differential-resolution Earth observation system for stable operation, and achieve stereoscopy and dynamic monitoring of the land, atmosphere and sea.

—To make an overall plan for the development of a satellite remote-sensing ground system, and an application system; to integrate and improve the present satellite remote-sensing ground system, establish and improve a national satellite remote-sensing data center, and set up and improve supporting facilities for quantitative application, including a remote-sensing satellite radiation calibration station, and preliminarily materialize the common sharing of remote-sensing data to serve the public good; to set up a satellite environmental application institute and a satellite disaster-mitigation institute, forming several important application systems; and to make breakthroughs in major satellite remote-sensing application fields.

—To develop and launch geostationary orbit telecommunications satellites and direct TV broadcasting satellites with long operating life, high reliability and large capacity; and to develop satellite technologies for live broadcast, broadband multi-media, emergency telecommunications, and telecommunications and broadcasting for public service. To continuously develop and improve the service functions of satellite telecommunications and broadcasting, and increase value-added services in the field of satellite telecommunications and broadcasting; to actively accelerate the commercialization of satellite telecommunications and broadcasting, and expand the industrial scale of telecommunications and broadcasting satellites and applications.

—To improve the "Beidou" navigation satellite test system, and launch and implement the "Beidou" navigation satellite system project; to develop independently application technologies and products in applying satellite navigation, positioning and timing services, and set up a standard positioning service supporting system and popular application terminus related to satellite navigation and positioning, expanding the application fields and market.

—To develop and launch new-technology test satellites, conduct more spaceflight experiments of new technologies, materials,

Shenzhou-1 Spacecraft

apparatus and equipment, enhance the independent research and development level, and increase product quality and reliability.

—To develop and launch the "breeding" satellite, and promote integration of space technology and agricultural breeding technology and expand the application of space technology in the field of agricultural science research.

—To develop scientific satellites, including space telescope and new-type recoverable satellites; to conduct basic research in the fields of space astronomy, space physics, micro-gravity science, and space life science, and make important and original achievements in these fields; and to strengthen the ability to monitor the space environment and space debris, and initially set up a space environment monitoring and warning system.

—To enable astronauts to engage in extravehicular operations and conduct experiments on spacecraft rendezvous and docking; and to carry out research on short-term manned and long-term autonomously orbiting space laboratories, and carry out follow-up work of manned spaceflight.

—To develop a lunar-orbiting probe, make breakthroughs in developing basic technologies for lunar exploration, and develop and launch China's first lunar probe satellite "Chang'e I" for lunar science and lunar resources exploration; and to carry out final-period work for the lunar exploration project.

—To increase the comprehensive experimental ability and returns of spacecraft launching sites, optimize the layout, and enhance the reliability and automation level of the facilities and equipment of the sites.

—To advance the technology and capability of TT and C network, enlarge the coverage rate of the network, and acquire the ability to satisfy the basic demand for deep-space exploration.

Space Science

Sun-Earth space exploration: In cooperation with the European Space Agency (ESA), China has carried out the Double Star Satellite Exploration of the Earth's Space Plan. Together with the four space exploration satellites of the ESA, China's satellites completed the world's first joint, synchronous six-point exploration of the Earth's space, obtaining important data. Advance research into exploration of the lunar and the solar systems was also conducted.

Micro-gravity scientific experiments and space astronomical observation: China has carried out many items of experimental research in such fields as space life science, space materials science and micro-gravity science by using the "Shenzhou" spacecraft and recoverable satellites. It has also conducted trial tests of mutant crop breeding and high-power astronomical observation in space, and scored important achievements.

Space environment research: China has conducted research into space environment monitoring and forecasting, and made important progress in the observation, reduction and forecasting of space debris. It now has the ability to make forecasts of the space environment on a trial basis.

Bilateral Cooperation on the Space Project

Over the past five years, China has signed cooperation agreements on the peaceful use of outer space and space project cooperation agreements with Argentina, Brazil, Canada, France, Malaysia, Pakistan, Russia, Ukraine, the ESA and the European Union Committee, and has established a space cooperation sub-committee or joint commission mechanisms with Brazil, France, Russia and Ukraine. It has signed space cooperation memoranda with the space organizations of India and Britain, and has conducted exchanges with space-related bodies of Algeria, Chile, Germany, Italy, Japan, Peru and the United States.

China continues to collaborate with Brazil on the Earth resources satellite program. Following the successful launch of the Sino-Brazil Earth Resources Satellite 02 in October 2003, the Chinese and Brazilian governments signed supplementary protocols on the joint research and manufacturing of satellites 02B, 03 and 04, and on cooperation in a data application system, maintaining the continuity of data of Sino-Brazil Earth resources satellites and expanding the application of such satellites' data regionally and globally.

China and France have developed extensive space exchanges and cooperation. Under the mechanism of the Sino-French Joint Commission on Space Cooperation, the

Yang Liwei

On October 15, 2003, the "Shenzhou V" manned spacecraft was successfully sent aloft from the Jiuquan Launching Center, China's first of its kind. Yang Liwei (1965-), became China's first spaceman. He graduated from high school in 1983 and began to learn to fly in the Eighth Flight Institute of the Air Force. In 1987, after graduating he eventually amassed 1,350 hours of flight experience and was appraised as a first-class pilot. In 1996, China began to recruit astronauts from the military, which offered a good opportunity to Yang and he eventually became part of the first batch of recruits for the space program.

China's first spaceman Yang Liwei in the recovery capsule

exchanges and cooperation between the two countries have made important progress in space science, Earth science, life science, satellite application, and satellite TT and C.

The space cooperation between China and Russia has produced marked results. Within the framework of the Space Cooperation Sub-Committee of the Committee for the Regular Sino-Russian Premiers' Meeting, a long-term cooperation plan has been determined. In addition, exchanges and cooperation in the sphere of manned spaceflight have been carried out, including astronaut training.

China has worked hard on space exchanges and cooperation with Ukraine. Under the mechanism of the Sino-Ukrainian Joint Commission on Space Cooperation, the two countries have determined various cooperation plans.

China and the ESA have carried out the Sino-ESA Double Star Satellite Exploration of Near Space. China's relevant departments and the ESA have implemented the "Dragon Program," involving cooperation in Earth observation satellites, having so far conducted 16 remote-sensing application projects in the fields of agriculture, forestry, water conservancy, meteorology, oceanography and disasters.

Multilateral Cooperation in the Space Project

In October 2005, the representatives of China, Bangladesh, Indonesia, Iran, Mongolia, Pakistan, Peru and Thailand signed the Asia-Pacific Space Cooperation Organization (APSCO) Convention in Beijing, and, in June 2006, Turkey signed the Convention as well. APSCO will be headquartered in Beijing. This marks a significant step towards its official establishment.

China continues to promote the Asia-Pacific Region Multilateral Cooperation in Small Multi-Mission Satellites Project. Together with Bangladesh, Iran, the Republic of Korea, Mongolia, Pakistan and Thailand, China has started the joint research, manufacture and application of small multi-mission satellites.

Cooperation in Space with the United Nations

China takes a positive part in activities organized by the United Nations Committee on the Peaceful Use of Outer Space (UN COPUOS) and its Scientific and Technical Subcommittee and Legal Subcommittee. China has acceded to the "Treaty on Principles Governing the Activities of States in the Exploration and Use of Outer Space, Including the Moon and Other Celestial Bodies", "Agreement on the Rescue and Return of Astronauts, and on the Return of Objects Launched into Outer Space", "Convention on International Liability for Damage Caused by Space Objects" and "Convention on the Registration of Objects Launched into Outer Space", and strictly fulfils its responsibilities and obligations. China actively participates in the relevant activities organized by the UN COPUOS to implement the recommendations made by the Third United Nations Conference on the Exploration and Peaceful Uses of Outer Space (UNISPACE III). In particular, China, alongside Canada and France as co-chairs, has propelled the work of the space-system-based disaster mitigation and disaster management of the Action Team (AT-7) involving 40 member States of COPUOS and 15 international organizations, and has actively taken part in the work of an ad hoc expert group to study the possibility of creating a coordination mechanism for disaster mitigation and management. China has acceded to a disaster mitigation mechanism consisting of space organizations from different countries in the light of the Charter on Cooperation to Achieve the Coordinated Use of Space Facilities in the Event of Natural or Technological Disasters. China has also collaborated with the Multilateral Cooperation Secretariat of the Asia-Pacific Space Cooperation Organization and the UN, to host training courses and symposia on space technology applications, and has provided financial support for these activities. China has also taken part in a program promoting the application of space for sustainable development in Asia and the Pacific organized and implemented by the UN Economic and Social Commission for Asia and the Pacific.

Cooperation with the Other International Space Organizations

China has actively participated in activities organized by the Inter-Agency Space Debris Coordination Committee, started the Space Debris Action Plan, and strengthened international exchanges and cooperation in the field of space debris research. It has participated in the relevant activities organized by the Committee on Earth Observation Satellites (CEOS). In addition, China has taken part in the relevant activities of the International Telecommunications Union (ITU), World Meteorological Organization (WMO), International Astronautical Federation (IAF), and Committee on Space Research (COSPAR).

Outline of China's Space Science Plan in the 10th Five-Year Plan Period

Five major detailed development goals for China's space science from 2006 to 2010:

—Space astronomy and solar physics field. Observe and research the Sun and black hole to have more knowledge of the fixed star evolvement and the universe evolvement course; conduct the multi-waveband space astronomy observation of and research on the celestial bodies in various measures and arrangements; independently develop and launch the astronomical satellites to make China in the world advanced level in some aspects of astronomy observation.

—Sun-Earth space physics field. Know the occurrence and development of Sun-Earth space weather, make great efforts to make marked progress in the exploration for the whole action in the Sun-Earth space chain change course, and establish the space weather forecast pattern according with the actual needs to provide the scientific basis for the establishment of space weather guarantee system for safeguarding the spaceflight, communication national safety; conduct research in advance on the "Kuafu" project concept on the basis of "double star" plan to perfect China's independent satellite plan for space physics and space environment exploration.

—Solar system exploration and research field. Conduct the research on the moon resources distribution law and utilization; have an understanding of the earth space environment and formation and evolvement of various solid parts inside the earth by means of comparative research on the earth and other planets; develop the scientific research on the earth-alike planets, especially the earth-moon system; make an active exploration for the moon and make the plan for the deep space exploration with the priority given to the Mars on the basis of lunar looping exploration, and actively participate in the relevant international cooperation.

—Micro-gravity science field. Promote the development of high technologies such as the biological engineer and new materials, and the basic research on the gravitation theory and life science according to the goals set in the national scientific and technological strategy and the key problems about the manned spaceflight; as early as possible launch the first micro-gravity science satellite and the first space life science experiment satellite.

—Space life science field. Develop the experiment platform series on the space life science and biological technologies by continuing to use the return satellite resources, strengthen the construction of research bases for them, and continue to try for the space experiment opportunities at home and abroad as best as one can to carefully choose a batch of major subjects with good basis, high show and originality to study.

Policies on International Space Exchanges

The government has adopted the following policies with regard to developing international space exchanges and cooperation:

—Adhering to the principle of independence and taking the initiative in our own hands, carrying out active and practical international cooperation in consideration of the overall, rational utilization of domestic and international markets and resources to meet the needs of the national modernization drive.

—Supporting activities regarding the peaceful use of outer space within the framework of the United Nations; supporting all inter-governmental activities for promoting the development of space technology, space application and space science as well as those conducted between non-governmental space organizations.

—Attaching importance to space cooperation in the Asia-Pacific region, and supporting other regional space cooperation around the world.

—Reinforcing space cooperation with developing countries, and valuing space cooperation with developed countries.

—Encouraging and endorsing the efforts of domestic scientific research institutes, industrial enterprises, institutions of higher learning, as well as social organizations to develop international space exchanges and cooperation in different forms and at different levels under the guidance of relevant State policies, laws and regulations.

Activities of Commercial Satellites

China launched a communications satellite "APSTAR VI" into orbit in April 2005. In December 2004, it had signed a commercial contract for a communications satellite with Nigeria, providing in-orbit delivery service, while in November 2005, it signed a commercial contract for a communications satellite with Venezuela, providing in-orbit delivery service and associated ground application facilities.

At 8:00pm on April 12, 2005, Beijing time, China successfully put the communication satellite "Asia-Pacific-VI" made by French Alcatel Company into the orbit with "Long March-III-B" Carrier Rocket at Xichang Satellite Launch Center.

Children at an international cartoon festival

Posts and Telecommunications

A national postal network has taken shape in China, with Beijing and other major cities as the centers, linking all cities and rural areas. As for the telecommunications network, a basic transmission network featuring large capacity and high speed is now in place. At the end of last century, China completed construction of the optical fiber network which covers all of the capitals of provinces and autonomous regions and more than 90 percent of the counties and cities. Every provincial or autonomous regional capital, with the exception of the Tibetan capital Lhasa, is connected by at least two optical cables. In economically-advanced coastal and inland areas, optical cable has reached villages, towns, urban communities, and high-rise buildings, thus becoming the main technology for transmitting information. All provinces in the country have set up satellite ground stations, with the satellite receiving lines reaching some 20,000 and the

Surfing the web has constituted a part of many people's life.

digital micro-wave lines more than 60,000 km. Meanwhile, China has participated in the construction of a number of international land and sea-bed optical cables, such as the China-Japan, China-ROK, and Asia-Europe sea cables, as well as Asia-Europe and China-Russia land optical cables. China initiated the construction of the 27,000-km Asia-Europe optical cable, the world's longest land optical cable system, passing through 20 countries in its journey from Shanghai to Frankfurt in Germany. So far, China has established telecommunication business relations with more than 200 countries and regions in the world.

Now, the public data telecommunications network has taken initial shape, with group data exchange, digital data, Internet, multimedia telecoms, and frame relay networks as the mainstay. Covering over 90 percent of counties and cities in China, it is among largest public data telecommunications networks in the world. Radio and TV networks continue to develop rapidly.

Information Industry

At present, China has set up an information and communication basic network covering the whole country and leading to the world with advanced technologies and multiple services, with the scale and technical level of the network ranking top in the world. The total number of China's telephone subscriber reached 912 million and the number of Internet user totaled 210 million. China's telephone subscribers and Internet subscribers accounted for a quarter and a tenth of the world's total, respectively. In recent years, the government has been actively pushing ahead the development of rural communications and the construction of rural informatization by organizing and implementing the project "to give every village access to telephones. At present, 98.8 percent of administrative villages have such access, and a batch of websites involving agriculture have been completed, providing diversified services such as agricultural technologies, commerce and labor services for the farmers.

There are an increasing number of farmers in China turning towards the agricultural industrialization.

The Growth of China's Internet Users

Unit: 100 million persons

The number of China's Internet users

2004.12	2005.6	2005.12	2006.6	2006.12	2007.6	2007.12
0.94	1.03	1.11	1.23	1.37	1.62	2.10

♦ State Postal Bureau

The State Postal Bureau, a government agency and a public utility enterprise as well, administers the postal industry and manages postal enterprises nationwide. It undertakes the responsibilities of administrative management to protect the interests of the State and the rights of customers, the construction and operation of the national postal network and the delivery of universal postal services. The State Postal Bureau has offices in all the provinces, autonomous regions and municipalities which serve as public utility enterprises and, with the authorization of the State Postal Bureau take charge of the administration of the local postal sector.

The functions of the SPB are mainly as follows: to formulate the development strategies and policies for China Post; to draw up the postal laws and regulations, work out rules of postal administration and release rules of postal services; to regulate the postal market and philatelic market in accordance with the law, maintain the order of the postal industry, secure the postal network and facilities and protect State interests and customer rights; to formulate policies on postal tariffs, map out the standards of postal services and supervise the quality of postal services; to issue postage vouchers; to join international postal organizations on behalf of the State, handle international affairs concerning postal services and conduct cooperation and exchanges with other postal services in the world; to manage the postal projects under construction, the joint ventures and cooperative projects developed with other postal services as well as research projects.

Address: No.131 Xuanwumen West Avenue, Xicheng District Beijing
Website: http://www.chinapost.gov.cn

lenovo 联想

♦ Lenovo Group

In 1984, not long after PCD was founded, 11 computer scientists in Beijing, China also had a vision—to create a company that would bring the advantages of information technology to the Chinese people. With 200,000 Yuan (US$25,000) in seed money and the determination to turn their research into successful products, the 11 engineers and researchers set up shop in a loaned space—a small, one-story bungalow in Beijing. The company they founded, Legend, opened a new era of consumer PCs in China. Since it was established, the company has affected the lives of millions of Chinese: It first introduced PCs to households and promoted PC usage by establishing retail shops nationwide. It also developed the pioneering Legend Chinese Character Card that translated English operating software into Chinese characters, and achieved breakthroughs like PCs with one-button access to the Internet. In 2003, Lenovo introduced a self-developed collaborative application technology, which heralds the important role Lenovo is going to play in the 3C era (computer, communications and consumer electronics). These and other market-leading personal computing products catapulted Legend to a leadership position in China for eight consecutive years with over 25 percent market share.

By 1994, Legend shares were being traded on the Hong Kong Stock Exchange; four years later, it produced its one-millionth personal computer. In 2003, Legend changed its brand name to Lenovo, taking the "Le" from Legend, a nod to its heritage, and adding "novo," the Latin word for "new," to reflect the spirit of innovation at the core of the company. The company name changed from Legend to Lenovo a year later.

Lenovo's executive headquarters are in Purchase, New York, with two principal operations centers in Beijing and Raleigh, NC. Its sales network spreads out over the world including its own sales organizations, plus those of its cooperative partners. The company employs more than 19,000 people worldwide. Its research and development centers are distributed in Beijing, Shenzhen, Xiamen, Chengdu and Shanghai, Tokyo and Raleigh.

Website: http://www.lenovo.com.cn/

Information Products Export

Electronic information product exports formed a complete system including communications equipment, computers, home appliances, electronic components, and software. The growth rate of exported mobile phones, optical communication equipment, digitally controlled telephone switchboards, color television sets, liquid crystal displays, routers, notebook computers, and cable equipment exceeded 30 percent. Approximately US$4 billion of software was exported, up 40 percent over 2004. At present, the proportion of China's exports and imports of electronic and information products in the world's total exceeded 15 percent. The imports and exports of several products ranked first in the world market, of which those of mobile phone accounted for 47 percent of the world's total, computer 40 percent and color TV set 48 percent.

Internet Development

China's Internet market makes steady progress amidst a quiet surface. According to CNNIC's 21st Statistical Report on the Development of China's Internet Business, by December 2007, netizens in China ranked second in the world, reaching 210 million, next only to the United States (215 million). In terms of Internet business entities, Internet services enterprises topped 13,000. Service providers such as Sina, Shanda and Tencent have risen as a fresh force. As for Internet application services, new Web2.0 applications such as blog and Witkey were gradually accepted by numerous netizens. Their user numbers grew by 200 percent or even over 1000 percent.

Cooperation with Overseas Partners in Information and Communication

In recent years, China has strengthened the exchange and cooperation in the fields of information and communications, actively introduced the foreign capital, technologies and equipments, enhanced its own independent innovation capacity, opened up the international market, enlarged the products exports and made marked achievements. China's telecommunication service has been available in more than 200 countries and regions and the countries and regions opening mobile telecommunication roaming service with China have reached over 200. China's electronic information products have been sold to more than 100 countries and regions, and over 400 telecommunication operation enterprises applied China-made communication equipments.

In the basic telecommunications field, China TeleCom, China Netcom, China Mobile and China Unicom has been listed overseas.

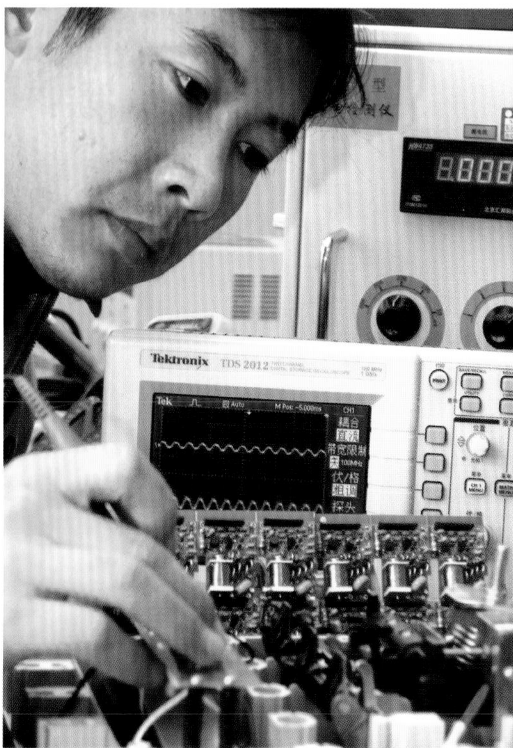

The Hi-tech industry contributes more to economic growth.

High Technology Industry

The native scientific and technological enterprises of China have also started to scramble for the high end scientific and technological products market monopolized by foreign rivals, instead of being the manufacturers of low and middle end products. The information communication enterprises represented by Lenovo Group, Huawei and ZTE Corporation and so on and the high technology manufacturers such as Haier, Kelon and TCL and so on have gained increased world market share depending on core patents. A number of enterprises with great strength have taken part in the establishment of domestic and foreign standards with regard to mobile communications, digital TV and information appliances and so on. For example, the third generation mobile communication standard developed independently by the Datang Telecom Technology Co. Ltd. has already been established as an international standard by the International Telecommunication Union. This is the most influential international standard established by a Chinese enterprise so far.

The high technology industry plays an increasingly special role in foreign trade. In recent years, the contribution rate of exports of the high-tech products has surpassed 30 percent. Since the establishment of the State-class high-tech development zone in 1991, 54 State-class high-tech development zones have made markedly achievements. Their total income of the zones in technology, industry and trade will maintain the annual average increase of 30 percent, and the economic aggregate of them accounted for more than 20 percent of China's industrial added-value and exports. This played increasingly important role in the structure and optimization of exports. The quantity of the telephone and internet users and the scale of the electronic information product manufacturers ranked first, second and third respectively in the world. The innovative ability of the high-tech industry represented by the electronic information product manufacturing industry had been further enhanced, which had already developed from the introduction and absorption period to the independent innovation period. Great breakthroughs were made in core technologies such as the third generation mobile communication, digital TV and the next generation internet and so on. China has seen the construction of a large number of national project centers and technology centers of enterprises, creating the foundations for great-leap-forward development.

Scientific and Technological Innovation and Incubation System

On the basis of introducing the successful experience of foreign incubators, China's high-tech incubation service center is a social service organization established according to national conditions with the view to promoting the transform of Scientific and technological achievements, incubate high-tech enterprises and entrepreneurs, providing necessary service for the incubation and development of Scientific and technological enterprises and driving their rapid growth. With all kinds of Scientific and technological enterprise incubators as the core, it constantly establishes and improves its relevant facilities and organizations to offer many kinds of service needed for incubation and development, including R&D, information, financing, trade, law, voucher, financial affairs, evaluation, human resources, international exchange and training, property rights and technology transfer. A scientific and technological innovation and incubation system has thus taken initial shape with Chinese Characteristics.

National Program to Apply Research Fruits to Production

The National Program to Apply Research Fruits to Production, introduced with the endorsement of the State Council, is aimed at mobilizing and organizing the broad masses of the scientists and technical personnel and the social forces to help apply scientific and technological research fruits to industrial and agricultural production for better benefits, faster economic growth and social development. For this purpose, efforts will be made to rely on the advanced research fruits to solve major, thorny and "hot" problems plaguing the further development of industry and agriculture, and new industries as well.

China's International Scientific and Technological Cooperation Plan

The key fields of China's international Scientific and technological cooperation are as follows during the 11th Five-Year Plan:

First, to give priority to cooperation in technology related to energy, water resources and environmental protection so as to solve key bottleneck problems restricting the development of the national economy.

Second, to strengthen Scientific and technological cooperation in an all-round way with the bio-technological cooperation as the breakthrough to focus on ensuring the safety of food, optimizing the structure of agricultural products and increasing the health level of people.

Third, to promote the development of information, new materials and advanced manufacturing technologies and enhance independent innovative capacity in manufacturing major equipment and products through international Scientific and technological cooperation in the field of industrial technology updates.

Fourth, to make great efforts to promote international cooperation in the basic sciences and cutting-edge technology so as to produce innovative achievements in the key fields with their own advantages.

Plan of Revitalizing Trade through Science and Technology

Establishing export bases for new and high-tech products in selected high-tech industrial development zones is an important part of the government's plan for developing trade through science and technology. The first designated export bases, selected because of their rapid overall development, rich talent, excellent equipment, and rapidly growing export of high-tech products, include the Beijing Zhongguancun Science and Technology Park and high-tech industrial development zones in Tianjin, Shanghai, Heilongjiang, Jiangsu, Anhui, Shandong, Hubei, Guangdong, Shaanxi, Dalian, Xiamen, Qingdao and Shenzhen. The Pearl River Delta, the Yangtze River Delta and the Round-the-Bohai Sea region have the greatest concentration of such export bases; consequently export volumes of new and high-tech products from these areas account for over 80 percent of the national total.

New and Hi-tech Development Zone

China has built up thousands of new and high-tech development zones and carried out relevant preferential policies, with a view to promoting industrialization of sci-tech research results. In the 53 State-level new and high-tech development zones, a great many sci-tech research results have been put into production. Over 30,000 were identified as high-tech enterprises in these zones, 20 of which had annual production worth over 10 billion Yuan, more than 200 over five billion Yuan, and 3,000 over 100 million Yuan. In these zones, the average growth in major economic indicators has been maintained at 60 percent per annum for 13 years running, and they have become important engines of national economic growth.

A total of 53 State-level new and high-tech development zones can be found in Beijing, Wuhan, Nanjing, Shenyang, Tianjin, Xi'an, Chengdu, Weihai, Zhongshan, Changchun, Harbin, Changsha, Fuzhou, Guangzhou, Hefei, Chongqing, Hangzhou, Guilin, Zhengzhou, Lanzhou, Shijiazhuang, Jinan, Shanghai, Dalian, Shenzhen, Xiamen, Hainan, Suzhou, Wuxi (including Yixing Environmentally-friendly Industrial Park), Changzhou, Foshan, Huizhou, Zhuhai, Qingdao, Weifang, Zibo, Kunming, Guiyang, Nanchang, Taiyuan, Nanning, Urumchi, Baotou, Xiangfang, Zhuzhou, Daqing, Luoyang, Baoji, Jilin, Mianyang, Baoding, Anshan and Yangling Agricultural High-tech Industrial park, respectively.

Transportation and Communications

Highways

The aim of the National Expressway Network Plan approved by the State Council in early 2005 is an expressway system connecting all provincial capitals with Beijing and with each other, linking major cities and important counties. The network will have a total length of about 85,000 km, including seven originating in Beijing; the Beijing-Shanghai, Beijing-Taipei, Beijing-Hong Kong-Macao, Beijing-Kunming, Beijing-Lhasa, Beijing-Urumchi, and Beijing-Harbin expressways. At present, half of the aforementioned projects have started construction.

By the end of 2007, China had 3.58 million kilometers of highways (including 5.39 million kilometers of highways. China's national highways skeleton system will be completed in 2008. At that time, Beijing, Shanghai and all municipalities and provincial capitals will be connected with highways, chiefly expressways. Over 200 cities will be connected in the network.

Beijing-Tianjin Inter-City High-speed Railway

Railways

According to the Mid- and Long-Term Railway Network Plan examined and approved by the State Council in January 2004, by 2020 the length will reach 100,000 km, including 12,000 km of passenger-only lines, so that China's railway network will not only be expanded on a large scale, but also make a qualitative leap in standards and level. Efforts are being made to raise fund at home and abroad for the construction of the nine passenger lines and parts of section of the newly-built railways with priority given to passenger transport. These sections mainly involve nine railway lines, i.e. Wuhan-Guangzhou, Zhengzhou-Xi'an, Shijiazhuang-Taiyuan, Hefei-Nanjing, Hefei-Wuhan, Beijing-Tianjin, Wenzhou-Fuzhou, Fuzhou-Xiamen, and Ningbo-Wenzhou Railways with the accumulated construction mileage of 3,220 km and total investment of 300 billion Yuan. After the express passenger railway network is formed, it will cover 12 of cities with populations of more than two million, namely Beijing, Tianjin, Harbin, Shanghai, Nanjing, Wuhan, Guangzhou, Xi'an, Changchun, Dalian and Changchun, and link eight provincial capital cities or traffic hubs, i.e. Shijiazhuang, Zhengzhou, Changsha, Jinan, Xuzhou, Hangzhou, Nanchang and Macao. On a global basis, China's rail transport volume is one of the world's largest, having six percent of the world's operating railways and carrying 25 percent of the total railway workload. China also leads in terms of the growth rate of transport volume and in the efficient use of transport equipment.

China's First Privately-Run Railway

China's first private railway emerged finally. In 2006, The Shenzhen Zhongji Industrial Group Co. Ltd., a private enterprise, bought the property of Luoding City's 62-km railway at the price of 48.16 million Yuan. The Luoding Railway Corp. and Shengzhen Zhongji Industrial Group Co. Ltd. has reached the property transfer agreement that the latter buys the 100 percent of the property of Luoding City's 62-km railway at the floor price of 48.16 million Yuan through auction, under the conditions of being responsible for the former's 790 million Yuan of liability. The buyer promised that it would construct the 76-km Luoding-Cenxi Railway with the total investment of 1.5 billion Yuan. At present, the Luoding Railway only leads to the Chunwan Station of Sanshui-Maoming Railway westward, a typical dead end railway. Luoding Railway, once extending to Cenxi of Guangxi Zhuang Autonomous Region according to original plan, would serve as an shortcut channel linking the Pearl River Delta with Guangxi Zhuang Autonomous Region.

ADB-Financed Railway Projects

Since 1989, the cumulative mileage of railway projects for which loans were provided by the Asian Development Bank has reached more than 6,600 km. So far, 13 single-track, double-track and electrified railway construction projects were financed with loans totaling US$2.637 billion. Of them, there are six State-owned railway projects, receiving

Transportation and Communications

Freight Traffic by All Means of Transportation and the Growth Rates in 2007

Item	Unit	Volume	Increase over 2006 (%)
Total freight traffic	100 million tons	225.3	10.7
Railways	100 million tons	31.4	9.0
Highways	100 million tons	162.8	11.0
Waterways	100 million tons	27.3	9.7
Civil aviation	10 000 tons	401.8	15.0
Pipelines	100 million tons	3.8	17.9
Freight turnover	100 million ton-km	99180.5	11.8
Railways	100 million ton-km	23797.0	8.4
Highways	100 million ton-km	11257.6	15.4
Waterways	100 million ton-km	62182.2	12.1
Civil aviation	100 million ton-km	116.4	23.5
Pipelines	100 million ton-km	1827.3	27.4

Passenger Traffic by All Means of Transportation and the Growth Rates in 2007

Item	Unit	Volume	Increase over 2006 (%)
Total passenger traffic	100 million persons	223.7	10.5
Railways	100 million persons	13.6	8.0
Highways	100 million persons	205.8	10.6
Waterways	100 million persons	2.4	9.6
Civil aviation	10 000 persons	18576.2	16.3
Passenger flows	100 million person-kilometers	21530.3	12.2
Railways	100 million person-kilometers	7216.3	9.0
Highways	100 million person-kilometers	11445.0	13.0
Waterways	100 million person-kilometers	77.3	5.0
Civil aviation	100 million person-kilometers	2791.7	17.8

loans of US$1.78 billion. In addition, three ADB-financed railway construction projects have entered a preparatory phase with the estimated loan scale standing at US$850 million. Of the ADB-financed railways, the mileage of State-owned main lines reached 4,600 km and that of local railways 2,000 km. Currently, ADB-financed railways occupy an increasingly important position in China's railway network, thus giving impetus to national economic development.

Qinghai-Tibet Railway

Qinghai-Tibet Railway

On February 8, 2001, the State Council approved the construction of the Qinghai-Tibet Railway. This extends about 2,000 km from Xining, capital of Qinghai Province, to Lhasa in the Tibet Autonomous Region, passing by many famous scenic spots such as Qinghai Lake, Kunlunshan Mountain, Hox Xil, the Three Rivers Sources, Northern Tibetan Grassland and the Potala Palace, a tourism line full of mysterious color. The Golmud-Lhasa section zigzags 1,142 km with 34 stations; many stations are complete with sightseeing platforms. The trains linger at 3-5 stations with such platforms for the passengers to enjoy the beautiful scenery. The railway also runs through areas where passengers see the migration of Tibetan antelopes but also rare wild animals such as Tibetan wild donkeys and gazelles under State protection.

The project was completed with success achieved in fighting permafrost and scarcity of oxygen and also in protecting the environment.

♦ Ministry of Communications

The ministry's major functions are as follows: formulation of national laws, regulations, policies and development strategies for highway and waterway transportation, and supervision of their enforcement and implementation; formulation of master development plans and mid- and long-term development plans for highway and waterway transportation, and supervision of their implementation; provision of data and statistics concerning highway and waterway transportation; coordination and control of the transportation of cargoes of national importance, and the transportation of cargoes and passengers for emergency purposes; organization of the implementation of priority national highway and waterway construction projects; provision of national guidelines on restructuring economic systems in highway and waterway transportation; maintenance of fair competition in the transportation sector; guiding the transportation sector to optimize its structure for coordinated development; organization of the construction and maintenance of highways and highway facilities, and levying of relevant fees; administration of the industries of automobile maintenance and repair, driver training and of the running of driving schools; organization of the construction and maintenance of waterway infrastructure and levying of relevant fees; administration of waterway safety; survey of vessels and facilities at sea; prevention of pollution by vessels; safeguarding sea navigation; rescue and salvage at sea; telecommunications and navigation services for vessels; administration of the shipping industry; dredging of navigation channels; administration of the utilization of coastlines in the construction of ports and port facilities; formulation of national policies on science and technology in transportation; formulation of national technical standards and specifications, organization of major research and development programs, and promotion of technological advances in the transportation sector; provision of national guidelines for higher education, adult education and occupational education in this sector; inter-governmental cooperation in highway and waterway transportation; provision of national guidelines in the utilization of foreign investment in this sector; international cooperation involving international organizations in the transportation sector; promotion of international economic and technological exchanges and cooperation in transportation; overall leadership and guidance to public security authorities in the shipping and port industries.

Address: No.11 Jianguomennei Avenue, Beijing
Website: http://www.moc.gov.cn/

♦ Ministry of Railways

The ministry's core functions are: to draft the strategy of development, policy and statutes of the railway industry, make uniform rules and regulations and supervise their execution; to draw up the development plan for the railway industry, and produce an annual plan and provide guidance for its implementation; take charge of the administration of railway construction, organize and manage large and medium-sized construction projects; draft the industry's technological policies, standards and management regulations, and organize important research on new technology and products and evaluate their achievements; promote and guide reform; take charge of financial work, arrange the use of national construction funds and capital, and manage the expenditure of the railways industry; take charge of supervision of railway safety; be responsible for the foreign affairs of Chinese Railways and other international communications and economic cooperation.

Address: No.10 Fuxing Road, Beijing
Website: http://www.china-mor.gov.cn/

The "Most" of Qinghai-Tibet Railway

The Qinghai-Tibet Railway is the world's highest railway. Some 960 km of track are located 4,000 meters above sea level and the highest point is at the pass of Tanggula Mountain with an elevation of 5,072 meters.

The line is the world's longest plateau railroad, extending 1,956 km across Gobi and desert, swamp and wetlands, perpetually snow-covered mountains and grassland. The newly completed Golmud-Lhasa section crosses the Kunlun and Tanggula mountain ranges.

About 550 km of track runs on permafrost, the longest section among the world's plateau railways. Kunlun Mountain Tunnel, running 1,686 meters at an elevation of 4,767 meters, is the world's longest plateau tunnel built through permafrost. Fenghuoshan Tunnel on the Qinghai-Tibet Plateau is the world's most elevated tunnel on permafrost, with the rail level set at 4,905 meters above sea level.

Shipping pier of Tianjin Port

Ports

China's coastal ports enable the transportation of coal, containers, imported iron ore, grain; roll-on-roll-off operations between the mainland and offshore islands; and deep-water access to the sea. In port construction, China concentrated on the construction of a group of deep-water container wharves at Dalian, Tianjin, Qingdao, Shanghai, Ningbo, Xiamen and Shenzhen, thus laying the foundations for creation of major container hubs. The coal transportation system has been further strengthened with the construction of a number of coal wharves. In addition, wharves handling crude oil and iron ore imports have been reconstructed or expanded. By the end of 2007, there were 14 ports, i.e. Shanghai port, Ningbo-Zhoushan Port, Qinhuangdao Port, Dalian Port, Shenzhen Port, Guangzhou Port, Tianjin Port, Qingdao Port, Suzhou Port, Nanjing Port, Rizhao Port, Nantong Port, Yingkou Port and Yantai Port, whose annual capacity of freight handling exceeded 100 million tons. Of them, Shanghai Port handled the freight of 492 million tons each year, continuing to rank first in the world. Waterway transportation accounted for 60 percent of total freight turnover and 90 percent of the total foreign trade freight amount.

China has ranked first in the world in the port handling capacity and container handling capacity for three straight years.

System of Civil Aviation

At present, 15 Chinese airline companies were offering flights to 88 cities in 43 countries, providing passengers with 1,300 regular round-trip flights a week. There are also 204 regular round-trip cargo flights every week. Meanwhile, 90-odd overseas airline companies from some 50 countries operated flights to 31 Chinese mainland cities, providing passengers with over 1,260 regular round-trip flights and some 300 regular round-trip cargo transport flights every week.

Adjustments and improvements were also carried out in the CAAC's policy of industrial regulation. For example, market access was further liberalized and private capital investment allowed for airline operations. The control over air route entry, flight scheduling and establishment of operations bases were relaxed, as was control over prices. With regard to enterprise reform, some airlines and airports were reorganized as joint-stock companies and successfully listed on the stock market.

In the five years since China's accession to the WTO, China signed bilateral air transport agreements with 40 countries. By the end of 2006, China signed such agreements with aviation companies of 108 countries. With regard to the expansion of traffic rights, experiments were made to open traffic rights for both passenger and cargo flights in such places as Hainan, Nanjing and Xiamen. New regulations concerning the policy of foreign investment in the civil aviation industry were promulgated; the proportion of foreign investment and other restrictions were considerably relaxed. In 2004, China became a first-class council member of the International Civil Aviation Organization.

Air China Limited

Aeroplane of Air China

On December 15, 2004, Air China Limited ("Air China" for short) was listed in Hong Kong (stock code 0753) and London (trading code AIRC). Air China is the only airline company carrying the national flag. It has the first rank of brand value among domestic airline companies (the value of the brand was evaluated in 2006 at 18.896 billion Yuan), and it holds the leading position in passenger and freight transport and related services etc. Air China takes responsibility for flights by Chinese national leaders who go abroad for visits and foreign leaders and governmental leaders for their China visits. The headquarter of Air China is located in Beijing, and it also has several branch companies such as Southwest, Zhejiang, Chongqing, Inner Mongolia, Tianjin, Guizhou, Tibet branch, Shanghai base and South China base. It also owns a project technology branch company, business plane subsidiary, Ameco, China International Freight Transport Airline Co. Ltd. and Beijing Air Food Company. Up to the end of December 2005, Air China, with a fleet of 176 planes, predominantly from the Boeing and Airbus range, operated 4,160 scheduled flights each week to 70 domestic cities and another 36 cities in 22 countries and regions.

Website: http://www.airchina.com.cn/

China Eastern Airline Holding Company(MU)

China Eastern Airline is one of the three largest State-owned airlines in China. Its present scale was formed by annexing Northwest Airlines and integrating with Yunnan Airlines in 2002. Headquartered in Shanghai, its flights cover most cities across China and connect with Asia, Europe, Australia and North America. The group has registered capital of 2.558 billion Yuan, total assets of 51.699 billion Yuan and 35,000 employees. It possesses 168 large and middle-sized transport aircraft and operates 450 domestic and foreign flights per week. China Eastern Airlines Corporation Limited is the first airline company listed in Hong Kong, New York and Shanghai with registered capital of 480 million Yuan.

Website: http://www.ce-air.com

China Southern Air Holding Company (CZ)

Headquartered in Guangzhou, China Southern Airlines Co. Ltd. is a main air transportation business of China Southern Air Holding Company. The logo features a blue vertical tail fin adorned by the brilliant red kapok. It is also known as number one among all Chinese airlines for the number of aircrafts, widely distributed flight routes and annual volume of passengers. China Southern Airlines has 13 branches located throughout the country, including Beijing, Dalian, Hainan, Henan, Hubei, Hunan, Heilongjiang, Jilin, Northern, Shenzhen, Xinjiang, Sanya and Zhuhai Helicopter Company. Five holding subsidiaries are located in Guangxi, Guizhou, Shantou, Xiamen and Zhuhai with 17 domestic sales and ticket offices situated in major cities such as Beijing, Guangzhou and Shanghai. As China's largest airline, China Southern Airlines has 38 International offices located in major metropolitan markets around the world, including Amsterdam, Ho Chi Minh City, Los Angeles, Paris, Singapore, Seoul, Sharjah, Sydney and Tokyo. By the end of May, 2006, China Southern Airlines operated 259 aircraft, including Boeing 777, 747, 757, 737 and Airbus A330, 321, 320, 319, and 300. Some 600 flight routes take passengers to more than 142 large and medium-sized cities around the world, thus forming an air route network with Guangzhou and Beijing as the center, covering the whole of China, spreading to Asia and linking with Europe, America and Australia.

Website: http://www.cs-air.com/cn

Shanghai Airlines Co., Ltd. (FM)

Aeroplane of Shanghai Airlines

Established in 1985, Shanghai Airlines Co., Ltd. is the first commercial airline with multi-investment in China. On October 11, 2002, it was officially listed on the Shanghai Stock Exchange.

The company operates a fleet of 48 aircraft, including Boeing 737, 757, 767, CRJ, Hawker, MD-11 and others. With an extensive domestic route network, it has also opened numerous international routes from Shanghai to Japan, Thailand, Vietnam, Cambodia, Macao, and other countries and regions. It has more than 140 international and domestic air routes to over 60 large and medium-sized cities.

Shanghai Airlines has launched routes from Shanghai to Germany, Thailand, Japan, Hong Kong, Macao and other countries and regions. For a long time, it has conducted wide commercial cooperation with nearly 50 cooperative partners. Emphasis was laid on cooperating with members of the Star Alliance, the world's largest civil aviation alliance.

Website: http://www.shanghai-air.com

Sichuan Airlines Co., Ltd. (3U)

The restructuring of Sichuan Airlines Co. Ltd. was completed on August 29, 2002. As the holding company, Sichuan Airlines initiated and combined the multiple investment entities into one complex unit with different shares held respectively by Sichuan Airlines Group, China Southern Airlines Co. Ltd., Shanghai Airlines Corp, Ltd., Shandong Airlines Co. Ltd., and Chengdu Gingko Restaurant Ltd. The corporate business network has spread into different regions in various forms of trades and systems of ownership. The corporate headquarters are located near Chengdu Shuangliu International Airport in Sichuan Province. The Chongqing branch is situated next to Jiangbei International Airport in Chongqing.

The company boasts 30 modern aircrafts, including A320 series and Emb-145 manufactured by Airbus Industries and Embraer of Brazil respectively. Sichuan Airlines has opened more than 130 domestic routes that link some 40 cities in a network covering 200,000 km. On May 12, 2005, it opened a Chongqing-Hong Kong air route, the first regional one, and on August 20 Chengdu-Lhasa route.

Website: http://scal.com.cn

Xiamen Airlines Ltd. (MF)

Aeroplane of Xiamen Airlines

Xiamen Airlines Ltd. was founded on July 25, 1984 as the first joint-stock local company in China. It adopts the manager responsibility system under a directorate. Now the shareholders are China South Airline Co. Ltd. (60 percent) and Xiamen Construction and Development Co. Ltd. (40 percent).

Xiamen Airlines provides domestic and international passenger and cargo services from Fujian Province and other designated regions approved by CAAC to neighboring countries or regions. It is the sales agent of other airlines, and it engages in many diversified businesses such as aircraft maintenance, air catering, hotel management, tourism, advertising, import and export trade, etc. From Xiamen, Fuzhou, Jinjiang, Wuyishan, Hangzhou and Nanchang, as its main hubs, it now operates approximately 100 domestic and international routes for passengers and cargo to the major cities in China and East Asia. The airline has ticketing offices located in more than 40 domestic and international cities.

Xiamen Airlines' Engineering and Maintenance Department has been audited by CAAC for its maintenance capability, and approved for accomplishing a wide range of maintenance tasks on various aircraft and other specialized services.

Website: http://www.xiamenair.com.cn/

Shandong Airlines Group Co., Ltd. (SC)

Shandong Airlines Group Co, Ltd. is a group company engaging in air transportation and relevant industries controlled by 12 shareholders such as Air China Limited and Shandong Province Economic Development and Investment Company. On March 12, 1994, SDA was approved by the China Civil Aviation Bureau, Shandong provincial government. The headquarters is located in Jinan, capital of Shandong,

Subordinate enterprises are: Shandong Airlines Co. Ltd. (a listed company), Shandong Taikoo Aircraft Engineering Ltd. (Sino-foreign joint venture), Shandong International Aviation Training Ltd., Shandong Airlines Rainbow Jet Ltd., Shandong Xiangyu Aviation Technology Service Co. Ltd., Shandong Linyi Airport Management Ltd., Shandong Rainbow Air Advertisement Co. Ltd., and Shandong Airlines Dandinghe Hotel. It has formed a business pattern combining air transportation, aircraft maintenance, aviation training, hotel management, tourism and advertising.

Shandong Airlines Co, Ltd., controlled by Shandong Airlines Group and listed on the Shenzhen Stock Exchange, mainly deals with the air transportation side. At present, it has 40 various kinds of aircrafts including Boeing-737-800 and CRJ-700, with more than 220 routes and 1,000 flights every week to 50 large and medium-sized cities in China. It has also opened routes to Hong Kong, Macao, Singapore, South Korea and other neighboring countries and regions. It has established flying bases in Jinan, Qingdao, Yantai, Beijing, Chengdu and Shenzhen.

Website: www.shandongair.com.cn

Beijing Capital International Airport

Beijing Capital International Airport is located in the northeast of Beijing 25.35 km from Tiananmen Square, the city center. It is not only an aviation gateway of Beijing and a window for international communications, but also a radial center for the national civil aviation network. The number of passengers of the Beijing Capital International Airport has been on the increase.

Beijing Capital International Airport, under the administrative control of Civil Aviation Administration of China (CAAC), officially opened on March 2, 1958. With the development of civil aviation business and the increasing volume of passenger and cargo transportation, it has been continuously expanded. Passenger Terminal 1, covering an area of 60,000 square meters, and auxiliary facilities, including parking apron and car parks, officially went into service on January 1, 1980. Terminal 1

Beijing Capital International Airport

was designed to serve 60 flights daily and 1,500 passengers at peak hours. Terminal 2, covering an area of 336,000 square meters and equipped with State-of-the-art facilities, officially went into operation on November 1, 1999. This can handle 26.5 million passengers a year and 9,210 passengers an hour at peak times. Terminal 3 went into service on February 29, 2008. It is armed with high-speed transmission and automatic luggage handling system, and other state-of-the-art technology. Beijing Capital International Airport is expected to handle 60 million passengers, attaining the goal set for 2015 seven or eight years ahead of time.

Due to the excellent geographical location and service facilities, 11 domestic and 55 foreign airlines are participating in the operations. More than 5,000 scheduled flights per week are available to 88 cities in China and 69 cities abroad.

Website: http://www.bcia.com.cn

Pudong International Airport

Pudong International Airport is located on the oceanfront on the southern shore of the Yangtze River, covering an area of 40 square km. It is about 30 km from the city center, and about 40 km from Hongqiao International Airport.

Phase I was completed and opened for traffic in September 1999. This had one 4E South-North runway (4000m×60m), two parallel taxiways, an 800,000 square meter apron, 76 aircraft positions and 50,000 square meters of cargo warehousing. It is equipped with advanced navigation, communications, surveillance, weather and logistics systems.

Pudong International Airport, Shanghai

The terminal building of Pudong International Airport is composed of two parts, i.e. main building and long terminal concourse, both three-story structures, and connected by two passages. The building covers an area of about 280,000 square meters, with 13 luggage conveyor belts and 28 boarding bridges; the area of food and drinks facilities and other leased service facilities covers 60,000 square meters.

Currently, Phase 1 can accommodate an average of over 300,000 aircraft movements and 36.5 million passengers per year. A second terminal was due in service in 2008.

Currently, Pudong International Airport has accommodated an average of 500-plus aircraft movements per day, approximately 60 percent of the total aircraft movements in Shanghai. It is used by about 50 domestic and foreign airlines, connecting with over 73 international and regional destinations and 62 domestic destinations.

Website: http://www.shanghaiairport.com

Guangzhou Baiyun International Airport

Established in the 1930s, Guangzhou Baiyun International Airport is one of the three large hub airports on the Chinese mainland with decisively important status.

The new Guangzhou Baiyun International Airport, with a total investment of 19.8 billion Yuan, was formally put into operation on August 5, 2004. Covering an area of 15 square km, the airport is the first in China designed and built to the hub concept. The two parallel runways in the first phase of the construction were built to navigation grade 4E. The terminal area was designed to accommodate a projected passenger turnover of 25 million in 2010. Covering an area of 320,000 square meters, the first phase of the terminal complex is the biggest of its kind in China and all its equipment and facilities are up to the international standard. Baiyun Airport has set up business relations with 33 airlines and opened more than 110 air routes to over 100 cities at home and abroad. It handles nearly 30 types of aircraft. China Southern Airlines and Shenzhen Airlines are based there.

Website: http://www.baiyunairport.com

Hongqiao International Airport

Hongqiao International Airport is located in the western suburbs of Shanghai, only 13 km from the city center.

Hongqiao International Airport has one runway (3400m×57.6m) and one taxiway, about 486,000 square meters of apron and a total of 66 aircraft positions. Its advanced infrastructure facilities and various navigation, communication and security systems can accommodate all kinds of aircraft. After the airport authority successfully transferred international and regional flights from Hongqiao to Pudong Airport, the former has retained its standby capacity for landings of international flights, while handling domestic services.

The terminal of Hongqiao International Airport covers an area of 82,000 square meters, with 15 waiting halls, 18 VIP lounges and 15 luggage-conveyor belts. Currently, Hongqiao accommodates an average of over 300 aircraft movements per day.

Website: http://www.shanghaiairport.com

Shenzhen Baoan International Airport

Shenzhen Baoan International Airport (SZX), graded 4E is situated on a coastal plain on the eastern bank of Pearl River Delta Area. The airport is operational 24 hours a day in accordance with the standard of large international airports and is suitable for jumbo jets for both passengers and cargo, with one runway (3400m×45m) and a taxiway. The total area of airfield is 588,000 square meters, and the total area of the waiting hall is 146,000 square meters. It can meet the needs of an annual passenger throughput of 15 million and annual cargo disposal of 700,000 tons.

Opened on October 12th 1991, Shenzhen Baoan International Airport is the first modern international transportation hub combining air, road and sea transportation in a single facility in China. It enjoys convenient surface transportation facilities that provide excellent transfer capacity. It is close to the Airport-He'ao Expressway, No.107 National Highway and Guangzhou-Shenzhen Expressway that link Hong Kong, Macao, Dongguan, Huizhou, Zhongshan, Zhuhai and Guangzhou. The airport authorities also own Fuyong Ferry Terminal, which is able to accommodate cargo and passenger ships shuttling between Hong Kong, Macao and Zhuhai. With an average of 107 daily flights to 80 domestic and overseas destinations, it became an international airport on May 16th, 1993, and became the fourth largest airport in China in 1996. From January to November of 2006, Shenzhen Airport's accumulated passenger transport capacity reached 16.6708 million person time, freight capacity 592,700 tons, and the going off and landing airplanes 154,300. According to ACT statistics, the passenger transport capacity of Shenzhen airport was ranked 81st in the world, and the freight capacity was 37th. It joined the list of the world's top 100 influential airports in 2004.

Established in May 1989, Shenzhen Airport Co. Ltd. mainly takes charge of the operations, management and construction of Shenzhen airport. After changing its name to Shenzhen Airport (Group) Co. Ltd., the shares of "Shenzhen Airport" were traded on the Shenzhen Stock Exchange from April 20, 1998. At present, advertising, land transport and property management are also included in the main business activities.

Website: http://www.szairport.com

Chengdu Shuangliu International Airport

Chengdu Shuangliu International Airport is located in the central section of Shuanxi Plain and is 16km southwest of the center of Chengdu City. It is an important aviation hub and distribution center of passengers and cargo in the southwestern region. It houses over 20 units, including Southwestern Civil Aviation Administration of China, China International Airlines Southwest Division, Sichuan Airlines, etc. The airport is connected with the urban district via expressway.

Large-scale expansion was conducted from 1994 to 2001 with total investment of 2.8 billion Yuan so that the flight area reached Class 4E. The runway was extended to 3,600 meters and could handle aircraft up to Boeing 747-400. Moreover, the runway was

Chengdu Shuangliu International Airport

incorporated with PCLS II. The newly built departure building covering an area of 82,000 square meters incorporated a three-parallel-porch design, with separate areas for arrival and departure and domestic and foreign travel It can accommodate an hourly capacity of 3,500 passengers.

The airport invested 380 million Yuan to build an international departure building of 39,000 square meters in 2003 and this was completed and put into use on September 28, 2004. People now find a modern airport with the largest scale, sound facilities and complete functions in the western region.

Website: http://www.cdairport.com

Hangzhou Xiaoshan International Airport

Hangzhou Xiaoshan International Airport

Hangzhou Xiaoshan International Airport is a key trunk airport, a tourist city airport, an international regular-flight airport as well as an airport maintaining standby capacity for flights diverted from Shanghai Pudong International Airport. The airport is built on the southern shore of the Qiantangjiang River in Xiaoshan District and is 27 km from downtown Hangzhou. On December 30, 2000, the construction of new airport was completed and opened for traffic. In March 2004, the airport officially became an international airport after passing State-level quality appraisal.

Phase 1 of the airport was designed to handle aircraft as large as the Boeing 747-400, and serve eight million passengers and handle 110,000 tons of cargo a year. The facilities of the flight areas meet the 4E standard required by the International Civil Aviation Organization. It has one runway 3,600 meters long and 45 meters wide. The passenger terminal was designed to handle 3,600 passengers at peak hours and covers 100,000 square meters (including an underground parking area of 22,000 square meters). The apron occupies 340,000 square meters of land and there are 12 parking spaces and 18 departure gates. It is equipped with the aircraft berth navigation system and the double-circle aircraft pipeline refueling system. Maintenance facilities are certified to perform B-Check on all types of aircraft and C-Check on Boeing 737 and Boeing 757 aircraft. The airport also has the complete power supply, water supply, energy sources and environmental protection facilities. All kinds of equipment, vehicles and operating system adopt world-level advanced products and technologies.

Website: http://www.hzairport.com

♦ General Administration of Civil Aviation

Its major functions are: to study and put forward the guiding principles, policies and strategies for the development of the civil aviation industry, draft civil aviation laws and regulations and supervise their implementation, promote and guide the structural reform of the civil aviation industry and corporate reform; draw up plans for the industry's medium and long-term development, carry out macro-control over the industry, and be responsible for comprehensive statistics of the whole industry; formulate policies, rules and regulations to ensure civil aviation safety, and supervise flight and ground safety, formulate criteria for accidents and incidents, and investigate and handle these as provided; formulate civil aviation flight standards and administrative rules and regulations, carry out operational certification and continuous supervision and inspection of civil aircraft operators, be responsible for the management of credentials for civil pilots and flight dispatchers, examine and approve the flight procedures and minimum operational requirements for airports, and take charge of the civil aviation sanitary tasks; formulate standards and rules and regulations on aircraft airworthiness administration, take charge of aircraft type certification, production licensing, airworthiness certification, nationality registration, maintenance licensing and qualification regulation of maintenance personnel and ensure such supervision and inspection are carried out in a continuous manner; formulate the standards, rules and regulations on air traffic management, draw up airspace plans, be responsible for the construction and management of civil air routes, air traffic management and air traffic controllers' qualification regulations, and supervise civil aviation navigation communications, aeronautical information and aeronautical meteorology; and so on.

Website: http://www.caac.gov.cn

Finance and Insurance

Logo of China UnionPay on the Bank Card

General Survey

In China, a financial system that features regulation and supervision by the central bank, takes the State banks as the main body, divides the work of policy finance and commercial finance, and boasts of cooperation and functional mutual-complementarity among financial institutions of various ownerships, has basically taken shape.

According to CBRC statistics, as of the end of September 2007, domestic assets of banking institutions in China (in both renminbi and foreign currencies) totaled 50.62 trillion Yuan, an increase of 20.3 percent year on year. Of the total, the assets of the State-owned commercial banks, joint-stock commercial banks, urban commercial banks and other financial institutions reached 27.46 trillion Yuan, 6.88 trillion Yuan, 3.09 trillion Yuan and 13.18 trillion Yuan, respectively, up 17.0 percent, 34.6 percent, 27.7 percent and 19.0 percent over the previous year.

The total domestic liabilities (in both renminbi and foreign currencies) reached 47.84 trillion Yuan, rising 19.4 percent year on year. Of the total, the liabilities of the State-owned commercial banks, joint-stock commercial banks, urban commercial banks and other financial institutions stood at 25.89 trillion Yuan, 6.58 trillion Yuan, 2.92 trillion Yuan and 12.45 trillion Yuan, respectively, up 16.3 percent, 33.2 percent, 25.8 percent and 18.2 percent.

In China, a financial system that features regulation and supervision by the central bank, takes the State banks as the main body, divides the work of policy finance and commercial finance, and features cooperation and functional mutual complementary among financial institutions of various ownership, has basically taken shape

Financial System

China's present financial system includes the following institutions:

Central Bank: People's Bank of China

State-owned Commercial Banks: Industrial and Commercial Bank of China, Agriculture Bank of China, Bank of China, China Construction Bank

Joint Stock Commercial Banks: Bank of Communications, Citic Industrial Bank, China Everbright Bank, Shenzhen Development Bank, Shanghai Pudong Development Bank, China Merchants Bank, China Minsheng Bank, Fujian Industrial Bank, Guangdong Development Bank, Huaxia Bank

Policy Banks: China Development Bank, Export-Import Bank of China, Agricultural Development Bank of China

Main Non-banking Financial Institutions: People's Insurance Company of China, credit union and cooperative banks, China International Trust and Investment Corp., State Administration of Foreign Exchange, foreign-funded banks and financial institutions with foreign investment.

Financial Reform

For the past few decades, the People's Bank of China has exercised the functions and powers of a central bank, as well as handling industrial and commercial credits and savings business; it was neither the central bank in the true sense nor a commercial entity conforming to the law of the market economy. But, since reform and opening-up began in 1979, China has carried out a series of significant reforms.

In 1984, the People's Bank of China stopped handling credit and savings business, and began formally to exercise central bank functions and powers by conducting macro-control and supervision over the nation's banking system. In 1994, the Industrial and Commercial Bank of China, the Bank of China, the Agricultural Bank of China and the China Construction Bank were transformed into State-owned commercial banks; three policy-related banks were founded, namely, the Agricultural Development Bank of China, the National Development Bank and the China Import and Export Bank. In 1995, the Commercial Banking Law was promulgated, creating the conditions for forming a commercial banking system and organizational structure, and providing a legal basis for changing the specialized State banks to State-owned commercial banks. Since 1996, the financial organizational system has gradually been perfected; the wholly State-owned commercial banks have been transformed into modern financial enterprises handling currencies; over 120 shareholding medium and small-sized commercial banks have been set up or reorganized; and securities and insurance financial institutions have been further standardized and developed. April 2003 saw the formal establishment of the China Banking Regulatory Commission (CBRC). Since then, a financial regulatory system has been formed in which CBRC, China Securities Regulatory Commission (CSRC) and China Insurance Regulatory Commission (CIRC) work in tandem, each body having its own clearly defined responsibilities.

State-owned Banks Getting Listed

October 27, 2006 was of epochal significance for China's capital market and banking sector. On that day, the Industrial and Commercial Bank of China (ICBC), one of the four major State-owned banks, completed the biggest IPO on the global capital market, beginning an initial public offering of A-shares on the Shanghai Stock Exchange and H-shares on the Hong Kong Stock Exchange. With the P/E rate of 22 and the P/B rate of 2.23, the shares of ISBC were successfully issued, thus setting the securities issuing record of eight "firsts". After ISBC was listed, its total market value broke through the one trillion Yuan mark, thus being the largest of its kind in Chinese stock market history. Before this, the Communications Bank and the China Construction Bank issued H-shares, the Bank of China first issued H-shares and then A-shares, and ICBC issued A-shares and H-shares simultaneously, a great step forward in the reform of State-owned commercial banks.

On December 11 of the same year, the Regulations of the PRC on Management Over Foreign-Invested Banks went into force. It marked China's efforts to honor its words made for the accession to the WTO. It also shows China's banking industry opens wider to the outside world.

♦ China Banking Regulatory Commission

The major functions of the China Banking Regulatory Commission(CBRC) are: to formulate supervisory rules and regulations governing the banking institutions; to authorize the establishment, changes, termination and business scope of banking institutions; to conduct on-site examination and off-site surveillance of banking institutions, and take enforcement actions against rule-breaking behavior; to conduct fit-and-proper tests on senior managerial personnel of banking institutions; to compile and publish statistics and reports of the banking sector in accordance with relevant regulations; to provide proposals on the resolution of problems in deposit-taking institutions in consultation with relevant regulatory authorities; be responsible for the administration of the supervisory boards of the major State-owned banking institutions; and other functions delegated by the State Council.

Address: No.15 Jingrong Avenue, Xicheng District Beijing
Website: http://www.cbrc.gov.cn

♦ China Banking Association

China Banking Association (CBA), founded in May 2000, is a non-profit, non-governmental organization, approved by the China Banking Regulatory Commission (CBRC) and registered at the Ministry of Civil Affairs, with group legal person status. According to CBA rules, all national banking institutions and overseas financial institutions in China with legal person status that recognize and abide by the CBA Articles of Association, upon approval by CBRC, may apply to join CBA. All municipal banking associations that recognize and abide by the CBA Articles of Association, and are registered at the departments of civil affairs, upon approval by the CBRC, may apply to join CBA and become a candidate member.

The Association has 68 members, including policy banks, State-holding commercial banks, joint stock commercial banks, city commercial banks, asset management companies, China Government Security Depository Trust and Clearing Company, China Postal Savings and Remittance Bureau, rural commercial banks, rural cooperatives and rural credit unions, as well as 34 associate members, including banking associations in various provinces including autonomous regions and municipalities directly under the Central Government.

The CBA set up five professional committees, namely Law Work Committee, Self-Discipline Work Committee, Banking Personnel Qualification Authentication Committee, Rural Cooperative Financial Work Committee and Syndicated Loan and Exchange Professional Committee

The mission of CBA is to promote the common interests of its members through its guiding principle of self-discipline, rights protection, coordination and service so as to safeguard the rights and interests of the banking sector, maintain market order, enhance the overall qualities of banking professionals, improve services provided to its members, and promote sound development of the banking sector.

Website: http://www.china-cba.net/

China UnionPay

China UnionPay Co. Ltd., a Shanghai-based national association of card-issuing banks, authorized by the People's Bank of China, was set up on 26 March 2002. With the registered capital of 1.65 billion Yuan, CUP is made up of more than 80 banks and financial institutions.

The functions of China UnionPay are: to establish and run a unified national cross-bank bankcard information switch network; to provide advanced electronic payment technologies and specialized services related to cross-bank bankcard information switch; to formulate operational regulations and technical standards for cross-bank bankcard transactions, and to coordinate and arbitrate cross-bank bankcard business disputes; to manage and operate the CUP brand.

The establishment of CPU has rapidly promoted the cross-network use of bank cards. By the end of 2004, China had realized cross-regional and cross-bank use of bank cards, covering 684 cities including all the prefecture-level cities and 300 developed county-level cities. According to China UnionPay Co. Ltd., the number of countries accepting UnionPay card reached 24 by the end of 2006.

Website: http://www.chinaunionpay.com

People's Bank of China

Under the guidance of the State Council, the PBC formulates and implements monetary policy, prevents and resolves financial risks, and safeguards financial stability.

The PBC was established on December 1, 1948 based on the consolidation of the former Huabei Bank, Beihai Bank and Xibei Farmers Bank. In September 1983, the State Council decided the PBC should function as a central bank. The Law of the People's Republic of China on the People's Bank of China passed by the Third Plenum of the Eighth National People's Congress on March 18, 1995 legally confirmed this status.

The PBC performs the following major functions: issuing and enforcing relevant orders and regulations; formulating and implementing monetary policy; issuing Renminbi and administering its circulation; regulating inter-bank lending market and inter-bank bond market; administering foreign exchange and regulating inter-bank foreign exchange market; regulating gold market; holding and managing official foreign exchange and gold reserves; managing the State treasury; maintaining normal operation of the payment and settlement system; guiding and organizing anti-money laundering work of the financial sector and monitoring relevant fund flows; conducting financial statistics, surveys, analysis and forecasts; participating in international financial activities in the capacity of the central bank; performing other functions specified by the State Council; administering the State Administration of Foreign Exchange.

Website: http://www.pbc.gov.cn/

Bank of China

The Bank of China, founded in 1912, is renowned not just for the most extensive international network but also for its greatest advantage in international financial operations.

On July 14, 2004, Bank of China became the sole banking partner of the Beijing 2008 Olympic Games.

The first bank in China to extend its presence to Asia, Europe, Australia, Africa, South America and North America, BOC currently has 12,967 domestic institutions and 559 overseas ones, forming a global network for financial services. In Hong Kong and Macao, BOC is also the local issuing bank.

Website: http://www.boc.cn/cn/static/index.html

China Construction Bank

China Construction Bank Co. Ltd. is a joint venture commercial bank involved in long and medium-term credit business, and offering all-round commercial bank products and services. On August 24, 2006, China Construction Bank Co. Ltd. (0939.HK) and the US Bank signed the agreement in Hong Kong and the Construction Bank purchased 100 percent of shares of the US Bank Co. Ltd., a wholly-funded branch of the US Bank in Hong Kong.

Headquartered in Beijing, it has an extensive network that covers most parts of the country. Headquartered in Beijing, it has an extensive network of approximately 13,847 branch outlets as of June 30, 2006. There are two joint-venture subsidiaries in China and overseas branches in Hong Kong, Singapore, Frankfurt, Johannesburg and Seoul; representative offices in New York and London. It has 300,000 staff and workers.

Website: http://www.ccb.com

Industrial and Commercial Bank of China

Industrial and Commercial Bank of China Limited (ICBC) is currently the largest bank in China.

On October 28, 2005, ICBC was officially transformed from a State-owned commercial bank into a shareholding company and renamed Industrial and Commercial Bank of China Limited. The new entity has a registered capital of 248 billion Yuan and 248 billion in shares with a face value of 1 Yuan. The Ministry of Finance and Central SAFE Investments Limited are its two shareholders holding 124 billion shares respectively.

Through financial restructuring, issuance of long-term subordinate bonds and asset portfolio optimization, ICBC has substantially improved its capital management and, in turn, its capital adequacy.

On January 27, 2006, ICBC entered into strategic investment and cooperation agreement with Goldman Sachs Group, Allianz Group and American Express Limited and acquired an investment of US$3.782 billion. On June 19, 2006, ICBC signed a strategic investment and cooperation agreement with the governing board of the All-China Social Security Fund, which agreed to inject 18.028 billion Yuan by buying ICBC's newly-issued shares. ICBC also enjoys a multi-dimensional shareholding structure. On October 27, 2006, ICBC completed the largest IPO on the security market, it's A and H shares listed in the Shanghai and Stock Exchanges and the Hong Kong Joint Stock Exchanges.

Website: http://www.icbc.com.cn/index.jsp

Agricultural Bank of China

The Agricultural Bank of China is one of China's largest state-owned commercial banks.

This was founded in August 1951 with the task of handling appropriated agricultural financial funds and providing long-term agricultural loans with a repayment period of one year or more according to the national plan, and to support the development of rural credit cooperation.

As one of the four large State-owned commercial banks, ABC is an important component of China's financial system. It has become one of the biggest banks in the country. Abroad, it is listed as one of the World Top 500 companies by Fortune.

Website: http://www.abchina.com

Shenzhen Development Bank

Shenzhen Development Bank is the first joint stock company listed on the Shenzhen Stock Exchange (000001 SSE), with total assets of 229.2 billion Yuan. It has set up 238 outlets in 18 major cities with more than 7,000 staff. Public shares account for 72 percent, while the American company Newbridge Capital owns 17.9 percent.

On December 28, 1987, Shenzhen Development Bank, the first commercial bank to offer shares to the public, was founded in Shenzhen, a frontline city where China initiated the reform and opening up program. The establishment of SDB marks the beginning of the growth of China's stock markets.

SDB was established on the basis of conducting joint stock reconstruction of six rural credit cooperatives. Since then, it has operated according to the modern commercial bank mode, and was the first commercial bank exercising asset-liability ratio management in China.

Website: http://www.sdb.com.cn/

China Minsheng Bank

Founded on January 12, 1996 in Beijing, China Minsheng Banking Corp., Ltd. ("Minsheng") is the first national joint-stock commercial bank in China with stocks mainly held by non-State-owned enterprises – 85 percent of capitalization totaling 1.38 billion Yuan.

Minsheng listed its A-shares (600016) on the Shanghai Stock Exchange on December 19, 2000, and it also issued 4 billion Yuan of convertible corporate bonds on March 18, 2003. On November 8, 2004, Minsheng successfully issued 5.8 billion Yuan of subordinate bonds in the inter-bank bond market, the first commercial bank to do so by private placement. On October 26, 2005, it became the first commercial bank accomplishing shares merger reform, establishing a successful model in China's capital market reform.

Minsheng has established 20 main branches in Beijing, Guangzhou, Shanghai, Shenzhen, Wuhan, Dalian, Hangzhou, Nanjing, Chongqing, Xi'an, Fuzhou, Ji'nan, Taiyuan, Shijiazhuang, Chengdu, Ningbo, Tianjin, Kunming, Quanzhou and Suzhou, and a direct-reporting sub-branch in Shantou, Guangdong Province. It has an aggregate of banking outlets of more than 240 and also has correspondent relations with 749 overseas banks in 78 countries and regions.

Website: http://www.cmbc.com.cn

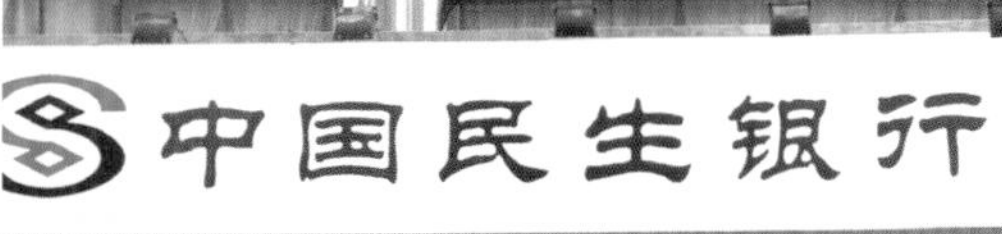

China Minsheng Banking Corp., Ltd. is a national joint-stock commercial bank primarily held by non-public-owned enterprises.

China Development Bank

China Development Bank, founded in March 1994, is under the direct jurisdiction of the State Council. At present, it has 32 branches and four representative offices across the country. CDB follows conscientiously China's macroeconomic policies and carried out its macro-control functions in support of national economic development and strategic structural readjustment. CDB has been a major player in long-term financing for key projects and supportive construction in infrastructure, and basic and pillar industries vital to the development of the national economy.

Website: http://www.cdb.com.cn/web/

Export-Import Bank of China

Established in 1994 and solely owned by the central government, the Export-Import Bank of China (China Eximbank) is a State policy bank under the direct leadership of the State Council. Its international credit ratings are compatible to national sovereign ratings. At present, the Bank has eight business branches, five domestic representative offices and two overseas representative offices - one for Southern and Eastern Africa and the other in Paris. It has established an agency relationship with 140 foreign banks worldwide.

The main mandate of the Bank is to implement State policies in industry, foreign trade and economy and finance to provide policy financial support so as to promote the export of Chinese mechanical and electronic products, complete sets of equipment and high- and new-tech products, to support Chinese companies with comparative advantages to "go global" for offshore construction contracts and overseas investment projects, to develop and strengthen relations with foreign countries, and to enhance Sino-foreign economic and technological cooperation and exchanges.

Website: http://www.eximbank.gov.cn

China Merchants Bank

Founded on April 8, 1987 in Shenzhen, China Merchants Bank is the first shareholding commercial bank wholly owned by corporate legal entities. Since its establishment, the bank has undergone capital enlargement three times, and launched an IPO with 1.5 billion common shares in March 2002 on the Shanghai Stock Exchange (Stock trading Code: 600036). It is the first listed company passing external auditing appraisal based on international accounting standards. On September 2006, it also issued successfully 2.2 billion H shares, and was listed on the Hong Kong Stock Exchange (Stock trading Code: 3968). On October 5, 2006, it exercised the over-allotment option, issuing 2.42 billion H shares in total. At present, the total assets of China Merchants Bank stand above 800 billion Yuan, and it is ranked 114th on the "world 1,000 banks" by the British financial journal The Banker.

China Merchants Bank is a share-holding commercial bank wholly owned by corporate legal entities.

After 18 years of development, China Merchants Bank has made a successful transitioned to a national commercial bank with certain scale and influence from a regional bank located in Shekou, Shenzhen. The bank has been building up its business network and organizational structure throughout China and overseas markets. China Merchants Bank has set up branches in more than 30 major cities in China as well as in HKSAR with a total business network over 400. In addition, it has a US Representative Office in New York. At present, CMB has established correspondent relations with over 1,000 banks in more than 80 countries and regions.

Website: http://www.cmbchina.com/

CITIC Industrial Bank

CITIC Industrial Bank, founded in 1987, is one of China's first batch of joint-stock commercial banks in the progress of reform and opening-up. In 1987, its Industrial Bank cooperated with the US HP Securities Investment Co., Ltd. to successfully lease passenger planes for Chinese civil aviation. In May 1992, it and American Express Company cooperated to set up the first foreign exchange ATM in China. In March 1994, it signed an agreement on money transfers for payment with the American Express Company, being the first providing this service in China. In April 1995, it provided a State-owned enterprise with a loan of US$9.93 million for its project of exporting production lines to foreign countries, for the first time in the form of export buyer's credit. In November 1995, together with US Lehman Brothers, it helped underwrite the "little dragon bonds" of US$200 million issued by US Ford Motor Company, setting an example for China's financial institutions to underwrite bonds by foreign companies.

At present, CITIC Industrial Bank has set up branches in Shanghai, Shenzhen, Dalian, Nanjing, Qingdao, Hangzhou, Guangzhou, Chengdu, Zhengzhou, Chongqing, Fuzhou, Wuhan, Tianjin, Changsha, Kunming, Shenyang, Xi'an and Shijiazhuang. And it has also established an agent relationship with more than 700 banks from over 70 countries.

Website: http://www.ecitic.com/

Shanghai Pudong Development Bank

The headquarters of Shanghai Pudong Development Bank is located in Shanghai.

Shanghai Pudong Development Bank, SPDB, incorporated on January 9, 1993 with the approval of the People's Bank of China (28th, August, 1992), is a joint-stock commercial bank headquartered in Shanghai.

It launched a 400 million A-share offer on September 23,1999 on the Shanghai Stock Exchange, becoming the first shareholding commercial bank to list with both central bank and China Securities Regulatory Commission approval since the enforcement of the "Company Law", "Commercial Bank Law" and "Securities Law". The registered capital was 2.41 billion Yuan and it was listed on the Shanghai Stock Exchange on November 10, 1999 (stock code 600000).

The bank has set up 26 branches and

sub-branches and 350 banking outlets in Shanghai, Beijing, Tianjing, Chongqing, Hangzhou, Nanjing, Guangzhou, Shenzhen, Kunming, Zhengzhou, Dalian, Jinan, Xi'an, Chengdu, Shenyang, Wuhan, Taiyuan, Changsha, Harbin, Nanchang, Ningbo, Suzhou, Wenzhou, Qingdao and Wuhu etc.

Website: http://www.spdb.com.cn

Agricultural Development Bank of China

Agricultural Development Bank of China (ADBC) is a State-owned agricultural policy bank under the direct administration of the State Council.

Its mission is to promote development of agriculture and rural areas through the following activities: to raise funds for agricultural policy businesses based on State credibility in accordance with the laws, regulations, and policies; and to undertake agricultural policy credit businesses specified by the central government; and to serve as an agent for the State treasury to allocate special funds for supporting agriculture. ADBC exercises independent business accounting, break-even operation and enterprise management.

ADBC is guided and supervised by the People's Bank of China and China Banking Regulatory Commission. Based in Beijing, it has set up 30 provincial branches, 329 branches at the magistrate level, 1606 sub-branches at the county level, and three business offices. Currently, ADBC has no branches in Tibet.

Its major businesses of ADBC are as follows:

1. Loans for procurement, reserves and marketing of grain, edible oil and cotton in conformity with the State Council's plan.

2. Special loans for the national reserve of meat, sugar, tobacco and wool.

3. Disbursement of the central government's subsidies for the aforementioned agricultural products; maintaining special accounts for grain risk funds jointly established by central and provincial-level governments, and make disbursements.

4. Loans to the processing enterprises for processing grain, cotton and edible oil

5. Loans to flagship enterprises in the areas of grain, cotton and edible oil industry

6. Accepting deposits from policy-oriented corporate and institutional customers maintaining accounts with ADBC.

7. Settlement for policy-oriented corporate and institutional customers keeping accounts with ADBC.

8. Issuance of financial bonds.

9. Intermediary business including serving as an insurance agent.

10. International settlements for policy-oriented enterprises under import and export account, foreign exchange deposits, foreign exchange remittance, and foreign exchange inter-bank lending, foreign exchange dealing as agent, and foreign exchange purchase and sale.

11. Other business approved by the State Council or the People's Bank of China.

Website: http://www.adbc.com.cn

Bank of Communications

Founded in 1908, Bank of Communications (BOCOM) is one of four oldest banks in China and one of the early note-issuing banks. In 1958, while the Hong Kong Branch continued to operate, the mainland business of BOCOM was merged with the People's Bank of China and the People's Construction Bank of China. BOCOM was restructured on July 24, 1986 with approval from the State Council and began operation anew on April 1, 1987, thus becoming China's first State-owned shareholding commercial bank. Its head office was in Shanghai.

On June 23, 2005, BOCOM was listed in Hong Kong, becoming the first China-based commercial bank of its kind to get listed outside the mainland.

BOCOM has a nationwide and internationally-oriented structure and business network, with branches and outlets in developed regions, central cities and international financial centers. On the Chinese mainland, there are altogether 95 branches including 28 provincial branches, seven of which come directly under the head office, and 60 sub-branches under provincial banking jurisdiction. There are 140 cities where sub-branches (there are 45 county-level sub-branches without independent accounting in addition to the 95 sub-branches previously referred to) with a total of 2,610 BOCOM outlets in operation. BOCOM has set up branches in New York, Tokyo, Hong Kong, Singapore and Seoul as well as representative offices in London and Frankfurt. It has established correspondent relations with about 900 banks in more than 100 countries and regions. BOCOM has a staff of nearly 60,000.

The bank is the fifth largest commercial bank in China, ranking 89th among 1,000 large banks in the world in terms of total assets.

Website: http://www.bankcomm.com/jh/cn

China Everbright Bank

Established in August 1992, China Everbright Bank (CEB) completed joint-stock reform in January 1997, thus becoming the first nation-wide joint-stock commercial bank with the State as controlling shareholder and equity investment from international financial institutions.

China Everbright Bank had established over 370 banking offices in 36 major cities throughout 23 provinces, autonomous regions and municipalities directly under the Central Government throughout the country.

Website: www.cebbank.com

Industrial Bank

Founded in August 1988, headquartered in Fuzhou City, capital of Fujian Province, Industrial Bank is one of the first batch of joint-stock commercial banks approved by the State Council and the People's Bank of China. As of June 30, 2006, its registered capital hit 3.999 billion Yuan, and the number of shareholders reached 147, of which, the top ten were as follows: Financial Bureau of Fujian Province, Hang Seng Bank Limited, Tetrad Ventures Pte Ltd., China National Cereals, Oils and Foodstuffs (Group) Corporation, International Finance Corporation, China Electronic Information Industry Group Corporation, Shanghai Baosteel Group Co, Ltd., Fujian Tobacco Company, Shanghai Guoxin Investment and Development Co., Ltd., and Sept-Wolves Investment Co., Ltd.

According to the list of "Top 100 Chinese Banks" released by the British magazine The Banker, in June 2006, Industrial Bank ranked first among all the domestic commercial banks in terms of average return on capital and 10th in terms of tier one capital and total assets respectively. According to the list of "Top 1000 World Banks" released by The Banker in July of same year, the bank ranked 297th in terms of tier 1 capital and ranked 164th in terms of total assets; it was the first time for it to be listed among top 200 world banks.

Industrial Bank has opened 31 branches and 338 sub-branches in main domestic cities including Beijing, Shanghai, Guangzhou, Shenzhen, Nanjing, Hangzhou, Tianjin, Shenyang, Zhengzhou, Jinan, Chongqing, Wuhan, Chengdu, Xi'an, Fuzhou, Xiamen, Taiyuan, Kunming, Changsha, Nanchang, Hefei, Ningbo, Wenzhou, Dongguan, Foshan, Wuxi and so on. Financial Markets, Credit Card Center, Asset Custody Department, VIC (Very Important Clients) Department, Investment Banking Department and Retail Banking Headquarters have been established in Beijing and Shanghai. At present, the bank has set links with more than 800 corresponding banks worldwide.

Website: http://www.cib.com.cn

Foreign Exchange Management System

On December 1, 1996, China formally accepted Article 8 of the Agreement on International Currencies and Funds, and realized the Renminbi's convertibility under the current account ahead of schedule. It implemented the verification and writing-off system for export collection in 1991 and for import payment in 1994.

Conducting the management of authorization and registration of foreign loans is an important part of China's management policies on foreign loans, as well as the important means for it to maintain the reasonable structure and scale of foreign loans and avoid risk. In accordance with the relevant regulations on foreign loan statistics and monitoring, all the institutions (including foreign-invested enterprises) in the territory of China, after obtaining loans from foreign countries, should register them with the foreign exchange administrative departments. The State Administration of Foreign Exchange and its branches should fulfill the functions of supervising foreign loan registration and monitoring statistics according to law.

On May 10, 2007, Renminbi's exchange rate against the US dollar hit the 7.7 Yuan mark to reach a new level. Picture shows the list of exchange rate quotations in an international hotel

China's International Balance of Payment Statistics

The international balance of payment statistics are an important part of China's macro-economy monitoring system, which mainly reflects the basic situation and trends on the economic exchanges between China and other countries and provides important information for making macro-economic decisions. In 1980, China began to compile an international balance of payments sheet and, in 1985, it started make this public. In 1996, it began to implement the Procedures for Reporting Balance of International Payments. On the basis of reporting balance of payments between financial institutions, it also launched the four reporting works on direct investment, securities investment, profit/loss of financial institutions' assets abroad and exchange. Now, it has set up a complete, scientific reporting and statistical systems for balance of payments. Reporting and forecasting has increasingly played an important role in China's macro-economic control system.

Exchange Rate System

China operates a unified foreign exchange system and the State Administration of Foreign Exchange Control exercises its functions and powers on foreign exchange control.

It continues reforms so as to ensure the exchange rate better reflects market trends. In the course of reform, the government needs to take the nation's actual conditions into account and step towards the objectives of establishing a managed exchange rate regime based on the market. The exchange rate is no longer pegged to the single US dollar, but rather, in light of the actual conditions of China's foreign economic development, a basket of major currencies. In light of domestic and the foreign economic and financial situation, and based on market supply and demand, changes are calculated in the multilateral exchange rate indexes in a rational and balanced level.

Posted rate released by the bank each day

Exchange Rate and State Exchange Reserves

Year	Month	RMB/US$100	RMB/100 Japanese Yen	RMB/ HK$100	National foreign exchange reserves(US$100 million)
2006	1	806.68	7.0071	104.04	8451.80
	2	804.93	6.8264	103.73	8536.72
	3	803.50	6.8519	103.55	8750.70
	4	801.56	6.8441	103.34	8950.40
	5	801.52	7.1947	103.37	9250.20
	6	800.67	6.9904	103.14	9411.15
	7	799.10	6.9064	102.80	9545.50
	8	797.33	6.8824	102.54	9720.39
	9	793.68	6.7788	101.99	9879.28
	10	790.32	6.6474	101.52	10096.26
	11	786.52	6.7043	101.06	10387.51
	12	782.38	6.6726	100.64	10663.44
2007	1	778.98	6.4644	99.85	

China is reforming the RMB exchange rate regime.

History and Status Quo of China's Exchange Rate System

Before 1994, China had both a fixed exchange rate system and a double-track exchange rate system. After their merger in 1994, China instituted a managed floating exchange rate system based on market supply and demand. Enterprises and individuals bought foreign exchange from and sold it to the bank according to regulations; inter-bank transactions were conducted in the foreign exchange market to form a rate. The central bank set down a fixed exchange rate floating limit and maintained the stability of the exchange rate through regulating the market. Practice has proved that this exchange rate regime conformed to China's national condition, and made positive contributions to the sustained and rapid development of the economy and maintaining the financial stability of the regional and even the world economy.

Before 1997, the RMB exchange rate rose on the basis of stability, and people at home and abroad had growing confidence in the RMB. Later, however, due to the Asian financial crisis, and in order to prevent a deepening crisis possibly caused by alternate currency devaluations among neighboring Asian countries and regions, China, as a large responsible country, took the initiative to narrow the RMB exchange rate floating scope. Along with the gradual weakening impact of the Asian financial crisis, in recent years, China's economy has experienced sustained, steady and rapid development, economic structural reform has witnessed continuous deepening, new progress has been made in the financial field, foreign exchange control has been further relaxed, foreign exchange market construction has undergone constant development in depth and breadth—all helping to create conditions for improving the RMB exchange rate formation mechanism.

The Progress of Renminbi Exchange Rate Reform

Before the initiation of China's reform and opening up in 1979, China instituted the fixed floating exchange rate, with the RMB overvalued for a long time.

From 1981, it instituted a multiple exchange rate with the official fixed price calculated according to method of a weighted mean of a basket of currencies.

From 1981 to 1984, the official fixed price and the internal trade settlement price coexisted.

Starting from January 1, 1985, the internal trade settlement price was abolished, and the single exchange rate was re-instituted with one US dollar to 2.7963 Yuan. On July 5, 1986, the exchange rate of the US dollar against the RMB was adjusted to 3.7036 Yuan.

On December 26, 1989, the exchange rate of the US dollar against the RMB was adjusted to 4.7221 Yuan, and adjusted again on November 14, 1990 to 5.2221 Yuan. Depreciation of RMB exerted huge impact on the operation of the macro-economy. On January 1, 1994, China reformed its exchange rate system and instituted a managed floating exchange rate system. One US dollar exchanged for 8.70 Yuan and China's foreign exchange reserves went up by a large amount.

From 1994 to 1996, severe currency inflation, a great deal of capital inflow, and the Asian financial crisis occurred in succession, so that the Renminbi exchange rate came under huge pressure. After 1997, the Renminbi exchange rate always floated within a narrow scope with a not less than 120 points, and did not fluctuate along with the change of macro-economic basic conditions.

From 2003, international society strongly called for Renminbi revaluation amid much controversy. On July 21, 2005, the People's Bank of China announced that the exchange rate would be adjusted to 8.11 Yuan per US dollar from that date.

RMB Exchange Rate Regime

The PBOC issued a notice on July 21, 2005, stating that:

1. Starting from July 21, 2005, China would undertake reform by moving into a managed floating exchange rate regime based on market supply and demand with reference to a basket of currencies. The RMB would no longer be pegged to the US dollar and the RMB exchange rate regime would be improved with greater flexibility.

2. The central bank would announce the closing price of a foreign currency such as the US dollar traded against the RMB in the inter-bank foreign exchange market after the closing of the market on each working day, and create a central parity for trading on the following working day.

3. The exchange rate of the US dollar against the RMB would be adjusted to 8.11 Yuan on July 21, 2005.

4. The daily trading price of the US dollar against the RMB in the inter-bank foreign exchange market would continue to be allowed to float within a band of around 3 per thousand around the central parity published by the PBOC, while the trading prices of other currencies against the RMB would be allowed to move within a certain band announced by the bank.

The People's Bank of China would make adjustment to the RMB exchange rate band when necessary according to market development as well as the economic and financial situation, with more flexibility based on market condition with reference to a basket of currencies. The PBOC is responsible for maintaining the basic stability of the RMB exchange rate at an adaptive and equilibrium level, so as to promote the basic equilibrium of the balance of payments and safeguard macroeconomic and financial stability.

Four Phases of Renminbi Exchange Rate Reform

From 1979 to 1984, the Renminbi experienced the shift from the single exchange rate to multiple rate, and then to single rate.

From 1985 to 1993, the official fixed price and the adjustment price at swap centers coexisted and Renminbi experienced a shift from a listed single rate to actual multiple rate again.

In 1994, China instituted a managed floating exchange rate system.

In 2005, improved the system based on market supply and demand.

◆ Renminbi

The Renminbi(RMB) is the legal tender of China, issued and controlled by the People's Bank of China in a unified way. The basic unit of Renminbi is the Yuan, divided into 10 Jiao, which is further divided into 10 Fen. The current issue of bank notes includes 100, 50, 20, 10, 5 and 1 Yuan notes. In order to improve printing techniques and the anti-counterfeiting technological level, upon approval by the State Council, the People's Bank of China issued the 5th set of 2005-edition RMB, including 100, 50, 20, 10 and 5 Yuan of paper money and 0.1 Yuan of stainless steel coins.

Commemorative currencies are a sort of Renminbi with special themes and a limit in the issuing quantity. They are grouped into common commemorative coin and precious metal commemorative coin. The People's Bank of China issued the first common commemorative coins in 1984. Subjects include events, meetings, characters and animals and involve politics, law, sports, education, environmental protection, finance and so on.

♦ State Administration of Foreign Exchange

The State Administration of Foreign Exchange (SAFE) has the following functions:

Designing and implementing the balance of payments (BOP) statistical system in conformity with international standards, developing and enforcing the BOP statistical reporting system, and collecting relevant data to compile the BOP Statement; analyzing the BOP and foreign exchange positions, providing policy proposals with the aim of achieving an equilibrium BOP position, and conducting feasibility study on the convertibility of the Renminbi on the capital account; drafting rules and regulations governing foreign exchange market activities, overseeing market conduct and operations, and promoting the development of the foreign exchange market; analyzing and forecasting foreign exchange supply/demand positions and providing the People's Bank of China with propositions and references for the formulation of exchange rate policy; promulgating regulatory measures governing foreign exchange transactions on the current account and supervising the transactions accordingly; monitoring and regulating foreign exchange account operations both in China and abroad; supervising and monitoring foreign exchange transactions on the capital account, including inward and outward remittances and payments; managing the nation's foreign exchange reserves in accordance with relevant rules and regulations; drafting foreign exchange administration rules, examining domestic entities' compliance with them, and penalizing institutions engaging in illegal practices; participating in relevant international financial activities.

Address: Huarong Building, No.18 Fucheng Road, Haidian District, Beijing
Website: http://www.safe.gov.cn/

Financial Sector's Opening Up

After its accession to the WTO, China faithfully honored its WTO commitments and took a series of opening-up measures on its own initiative.

It is provided in relevant regulations that a Chinese branch of a foreign bank, a wholly foreign-funded bank or a joint-venture bank is defined as an operational foreign-funded bank. Subject to approval, its permitted scope of business covers deposit-taking, loan-making, clearing, custodial services and insurance agency business. Additionally, such a bank can apply to conduct local currency business as long as it is in business and profitable for a certain period of time and has fulfilled some other prudential requirements. At the same time, the foreign-funded banks are allowed to engage in derivatives trading, QFII custodian services, personal wealth management, offshore banking services on an agency basis (QDII), electronic banking, etc. In general, the range of products and services offered by foreign-funded banks has expanded over the years. The foreign-funded banks are now permitted to engage in over 100 categories of business activities. As of end-September 2006, 25 Chinese cities were opened to the RMB business by foreign-funded banks, of which five cities were opened one year ahead of the schedule. A total of 111 foreign-funded banks are now permitted to undertake RMB business.

Apart from establishing branches, wholly foreign-funded bank and joint venture bank, foreign financial institutions with good credit are encouraged to join China's commercial banks through share purchasing and equity participation, becoming cooperative partners of Chinese-funded banks.

The CSRC has approved the establishment of 13 Sino-foreign equity joint venture fund management companies, and started to formally handle the application for establishment of joint venture fund management companies with a maximum 49 percent foreign share; the CIRC declared that: from December 11, 2004, foreign insurance companies could handle health insurance, group insurance, life insurance and annuity insurance businesses; regional restrictions on establishing wholly foreign-funded insurance institutions were canceled and the proportion of the foreign share in joint venture insurance agencies was allowed to reach 51 percent. Besides seriously fulfilling WTO commitments, taking into account the actual requirements in conducting economic and financial reform, the government has also promoted the progress of capital project convertibility on its own initiative, canceling or reducing the restriction on the large capital projects.

Management on the Foreign-funded Banks

After its accession to the WTO, China took a series of opening-up measures on its own initiative. The number of the foreign-funded banks has increased markedly and their business scope and operating areas have enlarged constantly. Foreign-funded banks were allowed to conduct Renminbi business for Chinese citizens; the geographical restriction has been canceled along with other non-prudence restrictions on business and China now gives national treatment to foreign-funded banks.

The banking sector has been opened wider to the outside world in an gradual way.

In a bid to honor China's WTO commitments, further promoting banking sector opening up and supervision by law, and thereby ensuring safe and sound operations of the banking system, the government amended the Regulations of the People's Republic of China (PRC) on Administration of Foreign-Funded Financial Institutions (original regulation) and renamed them the Regulations of the PRC on Administration of Foreign-Funded Banks (new regulations). These were promulgated on November 11, 2006 in the form of the State Council Decree and became effective on December 11, 2006.

The new regulations consist of 73 articles. In comparison with the original, the amendments mainly fall into five categories, i.e. the amendments made with a view to honoring China's WTO commitments, amendments made with a view to strengthening prudential supervision, amendments made with a view to integrating the supervisory requirements applying to Chinese and foreign banks, amendments made with regard to the application scope of the regulations and those made with a view to embodying China's regional economic development strategy. The new regulations fully embody China's commitments to opening up the banking sector in an all-round manner, and removed all the non-prudential restrictions on foreign-funded banks. Foreign banks are allowed to choose the form of presence in China based on their own business strategies and on a voluntary basis. In line with international practice, foreign-funded banks incorporated in China are allowed to conduct full RMB business, and will be regulated under the same supervisory standards with Chinese banks. In other words: they enjoy full national treatment.

Moreover, the foreign bank branches are also allowed to apply for converting themselves into locally incorporated banks at any point in time based on their own choice and their own business strategies. The Chinese branches of foreign banks, apart from engaging in foreign

China implemented the self-determining opening measures among the foreign-funded banks.

exchange business and RMB business, are also allowed to take RMB time deposits from domestic citizens with each transaction of no less than1 million Yuan. These provisions, which are also prudential requirements, are designed to improve the efficiency and adequacy of supervision. As a result, foreign bank branches will enjoy simplified business authorization procedures and less operating capital requirements, while their operating costs and business scope are expected to remain the same.

Laws and Regulations on Supervision and Management on Foreign-Funded Bank

In recent years, the government has amended and promulgated a series of laws and regulations governing banking institutions and their business activities. Thus, a legal framework for banking regulation and supervision has taken shape, featuring three categories of legislation: namely, laws, regulations and government rules. The major legislation includes the Law of the PRC on Banking Regulation and Supervision, the Law of the PRC on Commercial Banks, Regulations of the PRC on Administration of Foreign-funded Financial Institutions, Rules for Implementing the Regulations of the PRC on Administration of Foreign-funded Financial Institutions, and the Rules Governing the Representative Offices of Foreign Financial Institutions in the PRC. Such a legal framework provides a solid foundation for the continuous opening up of the Chinese banking sector.

Meanwhile, the government attaches great importance to mitigating the risks arising in the process of opening up through prudential supervision. By drawing upon international supervisory standards and best practices, China has endeavored to create a fair and transparent supervisory environment, and has made notable progress in integrating the supervisory standards and requirements for both local and foreign banks. China also keeps improving its processes and procedures for the supervision of foreign-funded banks, including adopting a risk assessment system, together with the systems of ROCA and SOSA for the supervision of foreign bank branches. In addition, China has endeavored to strengthen the trans-border supervision through supervisory cooperation agreements.

Foreign-Funded Banks

The Chinese banking sector has been developing and has gradually opened along with the overall economic reform and opening up. Starting in certain regions, banking sector opening has rolled out to cover the entire country. At the same time, it has extended from foreign currency business to local currency activities, from foreign residents and enterprises to local customers. In the process, foreign banks have been growing steadily in numbers and asset scale, and the range of products and services permitted to foreign banks has expanded progressively. Meanwhile, the foreign banks are encouraged to forge business and equity partnerships with the local banks, thus become an important component of the domestic banking sector.

When China authorized establishment of the first foreign-funded bank, Chinese-funded banks and foreign-funded banks have constantly cooperated. In the first phase, such cooperation concentrated on the cooperation in businesses such as capital lending, settlement and note discounting. In the second phase, cooperation developed into the equity field. Foreign financial institutions may become shareholders of the Chinese-funded financial institutions. A single institution may purchase 20 percent of the Chinese financial institution's total, with a ceiling for total foreign involvement of 25 percent. These Chinese-funded banks include not only State-owned large-sized banks and joint venture banks, but also commercial banks, and banks not only in the developed eastern and coastal regions but also inland and western region, taking on diversified characteristics.

RMB Business Conducted by the Foreign-Funded Banks

A foreign bank branch, after completing the registration with the administrative department for industry and commerce, may receive a time deposit of not less than 1 million Yuan for each time from Chinese citizens within the territory of China. The existing wholly foreign-funded banks and Chinese-foreign joint venture banks, with the approval by the China Banking Regulatory Commission, may offer RMB business for Chinese Citizens within the territory of China. The China Banking Regulatory Commission will establish a green examination and approval channel for foreign bank branches intending to convert into wholly foreign-funded banks and apply to offer RMB business for Chinese Citizens within the territory of China. If they meet the relevant conditions, the application can be approved within three months.

Supervision and Management Standard on Chinese-Funded Banks and Foreign-Funded Banks

The business of acting as an agent for insurance companies is added to the business scope of the foreign-funded bank, so that it is the same as a Chinese-funded bank in business scope. The wholly foreign-funded bank or Chinese-Foreign joint venture bank and its branches are treated the same as a Chinese-funded bank and its branches in their registered capital and operating capital. A branch of a wholly foreign-funded bank or a Chinese-foreign joint venture bank may, with authorization, conduct business within the business scope of its parent bank. The wholly foreign-funded bank or the Chinese-Foreign joint venture bank and the Chinese-funded bank implement the same provisions such as loan classification, information disclosure, preparatory deposit and affiliated trade. The wholly foreign-funded bank or the Chinese-Foreign joint venture bank is treated the same as a Chinese-funded bank in managing the qualification of directors and senior managerial personnel. The Implementing Rules for the Regulations on the Administration of Foreign Funded Banks made the relevant provisions on the qualification of the senior managerial personnel of the foreign bank and added the provisions on qualification of the directors. A foreign bank that has already established an operational foreign-funded bank within the territory of the People's Republic of China cannot establish a new representative office if it has already maintained a representative office.

Requirements for Foreign-Funded Banks

According to relevant stipulations, the business permit of the branches of the foreign banks is divided into two tiers: First, a foreign bank branch conducting all types of foreign exchange business must have an operating capital of no less than 200 million Yuan or an equivalent amount in convertible currencies. Second, a foreign bank branch conducting all types of foreign exchange business and RMB businesses of a foreigner or Chinese-Foreign joint venture institutions and receiving a time deposit of not less than 1 million Yuan each time from Chinese citizens within the territory of China, must have an operating capital of no less than 300 million Yuan or an equivalent amount in convertible currencies. Besides the two tiers, the wholly foreign-funded bank or the Chinese-Foreign joint venture bank also conducts third tier business, i.e. all the foreign exchange business and all the RMB businesses. No matter what tier of business it conducts, the wholly foreign-funded bank or the Chinese-Foreign joint venture bank and its branch are treated the same as a Chinese-funded bank and its branches in regard to the minimum registered capital and operating capital, namely, one billion Yuan and 100 million Yuan.

Operational Procedures for Reorganization of Foreign Banks' Branches

On the basis of commitments, a wholly foreign-funded bank or a Chinese-foreign joint venture bank is treated the same as a Chinese-funded bank in business scope. A branch of a wholly foreign-funded bank or a Chinese-foreign joint venture bank may, with authorization, conduct business within the business scope of its parent, without applying by itself. If a foreign bank changes its branches established within the territory of China into a wholly foreign-funded bank solely funded by its parent bank, it may maintain one branch undertaking foreign exchange wholesale business. A foreign bank that coverts its existing branch within the territory of China into a wholly foreign-funded bank solely funded by its parent bank may choose to covert the operating capital of the original branch into the registered capital of the proposed wholly foreign-funded bank, or to transfer the operating capital back to the parent bank. This proposed wholly foreign-funded bank may continue to conduct all the business for which the original branch was authorized. A wholly foreign-funded bank or a Chinese-foreign joint venture bank is given a certain grace period in achieving the assets-to-liabilities ratio.

The operational procedures for the reorganization of the foreign bank branch into the locally incorporated bank are as follows: first, establishing the wholly foreign-funded bank and changing the original foreign bank branch into a branch of a wholly foreign-funded bank must be conducted simultaneously. If it needs to maintain one branch undertaking foreign exchange wholesale business, it may also apply simultaneously. Second, if the foreign bank applies for maintaining one branch undertaking foreign exchange wholesale business, the assets, liabilities, rights and interests of the original foreign bank branch should be partitioned, defining the assets, liabilities, rights and interests that are inherited by the foreign bank branch undertaking foreign exchange wholesale business and the wholly foreign-funded bank established in the same city, respectively. Third, if a foreign bank branch is changed into a wholly foreign-funded bank, it can apply to conduct all the RMB business when seeking approval for reorganization.

Cooperation in International Finance

All China's commercial banks have set up branches overseas, and started international credit business. The Bank of China ranks first in the number and scale of overseas outlets. In 1980, China resumed membership of the World Bank, and returned to the International Monetary Fund. In 1984, it started business contacts with the Bank for International Settlements. In 1985, China formally joined the African Development Bank and, in 1986, formally became a member of the Asian Development Bank.

Broad international exchanges and cooperation were conducted at different levels. Economic and financial policy dialogues between China and the G7 countries were increased. As President of the G20 and the BIS Asian Consultative Council and a new member of the G30, China promoted high-level dialogue in international and regional macro-economic and financial policies. Regional cooperation achieved material progress, particularly, in the introduction of the second Asian Bond Fund, propelling the development of regional bond markets. Under the 10+3 currency swap framework, China signed follow-up agreements with Japan, Korea and Indonesia and increased the total swap volume. Agreements between the PBC and seven central banks of neighboring countries, including Russia and Mongolia were reached to settle border trade in national currencies. RMB businesses were gradually and steadily promoted in Hong Kong and Macao SAR.

Securities Market

China exercises centralized and unified supervision and management system. The Chinese Securities Supervision and Management Commission is the management authority for securities market.

China has only two stock exchanges at present: Shanghai Stock Exchange and Shenzhen Stock Exchange. Business includes independently-operated buying and selling, purchase and sales on a commission basis, and subscription and marketing of valuable securities. Valuable securities listed on the stock exchanges mainly include: (1) various kinds of bonds issued by the State; (2) various kinds of construction bonds issued by the provincial governments or local people's governments at the provincial level; (3) various kinds of bonds issued by financial institutions; (4) corporate bonds issued openly in various places of the country; stock and various kinds of beneficial equity vouchers.

At present, securities companies and trust and investment companies have all set up operational institutions in big and medium-sized cities in China, which are called securities trading offices, for people to buy and sell various kinds of listed securities.

The Company Law of the People's Republic of China and the Securities Law of the People's Republic of China were put in force on January 1, 2006. The amended company law and securities law, on the basis of summing up the practice of many years and in light of the changes and operational laws of China's current economy and life, adjusted, supplemented and modified the regulations of former laws to a large extent and made improvements and innovations in the relevant regulations.

♦ China Future Association

This was founded on December 29, 2000 with its registered address and standing body in Beijing. Its main functions are: to formulate futures conduct rules, professional ethics criteria, and self-discipline regulation and be responsible for supervising their enforcement; to educate and urge the members to implement national laws, regulations and rules, criteria and regulations on futures trading; to protect the legitimate rights and interests of the members, collect their ideas and suggestions and report them to the CSRC the national relevant departments and actively help members conduct business smoothly; to intercede regarding any dissension over futures trading between members and between them and their customers and accept complaints about illegal activities; be responsible for organizing the training and qualification exam of the personnel engaging in futures trading, issuing the qualification certificate, and making an annual survey on the personnel engaging in futures business; to enhance the professional ethics level; to actively conduct the investigation and research and research into futures trading theory, and organize the members to exchange ideas; to report the situation and problems in the course of development of the futures market to the relevant legislature and supervision departments.

At present, CFA consists mainly of futures brokerage companies as its institutional members and futures exchanges as its special members. Institutional member are futures brokerage companies approved and audited by CSRC and special members are futures exchanges approved and audited by CSRC.

Website: http://www.cfachina.org

Capital Markets' Opening Up

In 2006, the Chinese Government enlarged the scope of opening up its capital markets, allowing foreign investors to make medium and long-term strategic investments in the listed companies that have completed share allocation reform. The revised Measures for Administration of Investment in Domestic Securities by Qualified Foreign Investment Institutional Investors (QFII) was implemented, which relaxes the qualification conditions and the lock-up period of the remitted capital, gives some convenience to QFII in opening an account and investing, and improves the supervision and management system, especially the information disclosure system. These measures show that China's opening up of capital markets has entered a new phase. Up to now, China has fulfilled commitments to WTO on opening up its securities market.

China's Commitments to the WTO on Opening Its Securities Market

The Chinese Securities Regulatory Commission (CSRC) announced its obligations in regard to the securities industry to the World Trade Organization (WTO) on 11th December 2001. The announcement mainly deals with the following:(1) foreign securities organizations can deal in B share transactions directly and do not require the involvement of a Chinese intermediary party; (2)foreign securities organization's representative office in China can be a special member of all China securities exchanges; (3) allowing foreign organizations to set up joint venture companies for carrying on the business of securities investment management funds in China. However, the level of foreign participation should not exceed 33 percent and the level of foreign participation cannot exceed 49 percent within three years after entering WTO; (4) within three years of entering the WTO, foreign security investment companies are allowed to establish joint venture companies with less than 1/3rd foreign interest and the company can participate in the underwriting of A shares, underwriting and dealing in transaction relating to B and H shares, government and corporate bonds and also the establishment of investment funds (without involving any local intermediary companies). A shares are those carrying a face value denominated in RMB and listed within the territory of China while H shares are shares carrying a face value denominated in HKD, issued by domestically by China's enterprises and listed in Hong Kong. Thus far, China has performed its commitments it made for entry into the WTO years ago.

♦ China Securities Regulatory Commission

The development of securities markets in China since the commencement of the opening and reform of China inevitably led to the establishment of a centralized market regulatory body. The establishment of the State Council Securities Commission (SCSC) and the China Securities Regulatory Commission (CSRC) in October 1992 marked the formation of this regulatory body. The SCSC is the State authority responsible for exercising centralized market regulation. The CSRC is the SCSC's executive branch responsible for conducting supervision and regulation of the securities markets in accordance with the law. In April 1998, pursuant to the State Council Reform Plan, the SCSC and the CSRC were merged to form one ministry-rank unit directly under the State Council. Both the power and the functions of the CSRC have been strengthened after the reform. A centralized securities supervisory system was thus established.

Its major responsibilities are: Studying and formulating policies and development plans regarding securities and futures markets; drafting relevant laws and regulations on securities and futures markets; and working out relevant rules on securities and futures markets; supervising securities and futures markets and exercising vertical power of authority over regional and provincial supervisory institutions of the market; overseeing the issuance, trading, custody and settlement of equity shares, convertible bonds, and securities investment funds; approving the listing of corporate bonds; and supervising the trading activities of listed government and corporate bonds; supervising the listing, trading and settlement of domestic futures contracts; and monitoring domestic institutions engaged in overseas futures businesses in accordance with relevant regulations; supervising the behavior of listed companies and their shareholders who are liable for relevant information disclosure in securities markets; supervising securities and futures exchanges and their senior management in accordance with relevant regulations, and securities associations in the capacity of the competent authorities; supervising securities and futures companies, securities investment fund managers, securities registration and settlement companies, futures settlement institutions, and securities and futures investment consulting institutions; approving, in conjunction with the People's Bank of China, the qualifications of fund custody institutions and supervising their fund custody business; formulating and implementing rules on the qualification of senior management for the aforementioned institutions; and granting qualification of the people engaged in securities and futures-related business;

Address: Focus Building A 19,Jin Rong Street,West District,Beijing
Website: http://www.csrc.gov.cn

Stock holders paying attention to the stock market

♦ Shanghai Stock Exchange

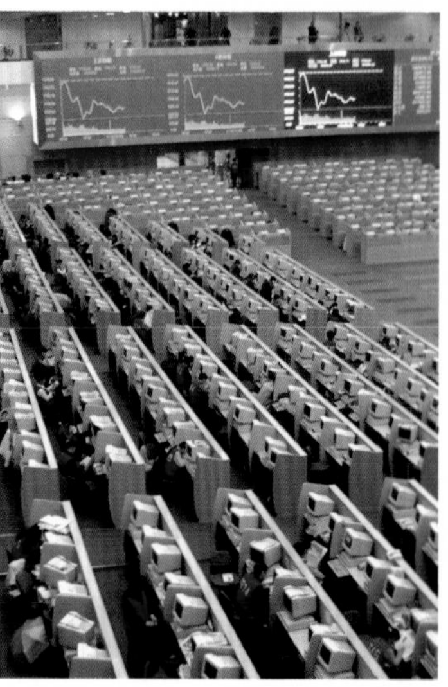

The Shanghai Stock Exchange (SSE) was founded on November 26, 1990 and began operating on December 19 of the same year. It is a non-profit-making membership institution directly governed by the China Securities Regulatory Commission (CSRC). The SSE bases its development on the principle of "legislation, supervision, self-regulation and standardization" to create a transparent, open, safe and efficient marketplace. The SSE endeavors to realize a variety of functions: providing a marketplace and facilities for securities trading; formulating business rules; accepting and arranging listings; organizing and monitoring securities trading; regulating members and listed companies; managing and disseminating market information.

Trading on the SSE is processed through an electronic centralized competitive bidding procedure. All trading orders are openly declared through a mainframe computer. The mainframe will then automatically complete transaction on the principle of price and time precedence. At present, the mainframe can process 29 million trades and complete 16,000 trades every second.

After several years' operation, the SSE has become the most pre-eminent stock market in China's mainland in terms of number of listed companies, number of shares listed, total market value, tradable market value, securities turnover in value, stock turnover in value and the T-bond turnover in value. A large number of companies from key industries, infrastructure and high-tech sectors have not only raised capital, but also improved their operational mechanism through listing on Shanghai stock market.

Address: 528 South Pudong Road, Shanghai
Website: http://www.sse.com.cn

♦ Shenzhen Stock Exchange

The Shenzhen Stock Exchange (SSE) was founded on December 1, 1990. It is a self-discipline management membership institution directly governed by the China Securities Regulatory Commission (CSRC). The SSE is committed to the construction of a multi-tier securities market to create a transparent, open, safe and efficient marketplace. The SSE endeavors to realize a variety of functions: providing marketplace and facilities for the securities trading; formulating business rules; accepting and arranging listings; organizing and monitoring securities trading; regulating members and listed companies; managing and disseminating market information; and other functions authorized by the CSRC.

As one of the two stock exchanges on the mainland, Shenzhen Stock Exchange grows together with China's securities market. For the past 15 years, it has successfully set up a stock market covering the whole country in a new city by using modern technological conditions. It has played an important role in establishing the modern enterprise system, promoting the adjustment of economic structure, optimizing the resources allocation and transmitting the knowledge on the market economy.

With the approval of the State Council and authorization of the CSRC, in May 2004, the SSE launched a second board, providing a platform for medium and small-sized enterprises to directly raise funds in the capital market.

Address: No.5045 Shennan East Road, Shenzhen
Website: http://www.szse.cn

Insurance Industry

The Insurance Law of 1985 and the founding of the CIRC in 1988 provided the legal basis and specific rules for the operation of the insurance market. At present, apart from export credit insurance companies dealing with policy business, all China-funded insurance companies adopt the joint stock system. PICC Property and Casualty Company Limited, China Life Insurance (Group) Co. and China Ping An Insurance (Group) Co. have been listed on foreign exchanges.

On December 11, 2004, the transitional period after China's entry into the WTO ended and China fulfilled its commitments on fully opening up its insurance sector. At present, there are no restrictions except that the foreign-funded insurance enterprise cannot deal with the legal insurance business and should take the qualified form when establishing life insurance branches. The China Insurance Regulatory Commission has acceded to the International Association of Insurance Supervisors and International Association of Annuity Supervisors. In October 2006, the 13th Annual Conference of the International Association of Insurance Supervisors was successfully held in Beijing, and present at the meeting were the representatives of the insurance supervision institutions from 94 countries and regions. At present, China has singed the Memorandum of Understanding on Insurance Supervision Cooperation with the US, Germany, Singapore, South Korea, Hong Kong and Macao and other countries and regions.

At present, there are 110 insurance institutions in China, including eight insurance groups and holding companies, 42 property and casualty insurance companies, 54 life insurance companies, six reinsurance companies and ten insurance assets management companies. It has 2,331 professional insurance medium institutions, 143,000 insurance agencies and 2.015 million insurance sellers.

Foreign-funded insurers have seen relatively steady development in China.

Insurance Sector's Opening Up

At present, foreign-funded insurance enterprises have established branch institutions and offered services in 14 provinces, autonomous regions and municipalities. Shanghai and Beijing have the most foreign-funded institutions, totaling 26 respectively. In addition, 10 foreign-funded insurance enterprises set up 12 branches in four cities in Central and Western China, four foreign-funded insurance enterprises set up five branches in three cities in Northeast China, an old industrial base. The premium of the foreign-funded insurance enterprises in Beijing, Shanghai, Shenzhen and Guangdong, the four areas which opened up earlier and in which the foreign-funded insurance enterprises are concentrated, accounted for 18.15 percent, 18.62 percent, 10.73 percent and 9.68 percent of local market shares. It can be said that foreign-funded insurance maintained steady development in China's market.

Chinese-Funded Insurance Companies' Overseas Investment

As China's insurance market opened further to the foreign insurance companies, Chinese-funded insurance companies also made marked progress in their overseas financing and investment. PICC Property and Casualty Company Limited (PICC), China Life Insurance Company Limited and Ping An Insurance (Group) Company of China were listed successively in overseas markets. In addition, China-funded insurance companies have set up 43 insurance operation organizations and nine insurance representative offices in Southeast Asia, Europe and North America.

Export Credit Insurance

Export credit insurance has fully played an active role in encouraging exports and investment, supporting the adjustment of the industrial structure and promoting transformation of the trade growth mode. It has provided the collection guarantee for exports and investments, insurance support for enterprise foreign trade and investment projects and financing convenience for enterprises. It has also supported the export of agricultural products and high-tech products. Export credit insurance company and Chinese or foreign-funded banks conducted the cooperation in trade financing, providing the export enterprises with the fund support.

China Insurance (Holdings) Co.,Ltd.

The predecessor of China Insurance (Holdings) Company Limited was China Insurance Corp, which was founded in Shanghai in 1931. In 1998, in light of the decisions by the State Council, China People's Insurance (Group) Company was repealed, and its overseas operational institutions were incorporated into the China Insurance Corp. China Insurance Corp and the Hong Kong China Insurance (Group) Co., Ltd. of the former China People's Insurance (Group) Company Hong Kong and Macao Holding Company exercised the managerial mode of "two names, one management". On August 20, 2002, the company was renamed China Insurance (Holdings) Company Limited

Besides insurance, its business also includes enterprise annuity, investment, securities, financing and fund management. It has more than 20 subsidiaries mainly distributed in China's mainland, Hong Kong, Macao, Europe and Southeast Asia.

Website: http://www.chinainsurance.com

China Ping An Insurance (Group) Co., Ltd.

The Company was founded in 1988 and is headquartered in Shenzhen. Ping An is listed on the HKSE with the stock name of "Ping An of China" [stock number 2318].

The Group is the holding company of the following subsidiary companies: Ping An Life Insurance Company of China, Ltd. (Ping An Life), Ping An Property and Casualty Insurance Company of China, Ltd. (Ping An Property and Casualty), Ping An Annuity Insurance Company of China, Ltd., Ping An Asset Management Co., Ltd., Ping An Health Insurance Company of China, Ltd., China Ping An Insurance Overseas (Holdings) Limited and China Ping An Trust and Investment Co., Ltd., which holds an equity interest in Ping An Bank Limited and Ping An Securities Company, Ltd.

Ping An and its subsidiaries provide various financial services, including insurance and investment management to over 37 million retail customers and approximately two million corporate customers. The Company has over 200,000 sales agents, 40,000 staff and over 3,000 branch offices. Ping An Life is the second largest life insurance company in China in terms of gross written premiums and policy fees, while Ping An Property and Casualty is the third largest company in its sector.

Website: http://www.pa18.com

PICC Property and Casualty Co.,Ltd.

PICC Property and Casualty Company Limited

PICC Property and Casualty Company Limited is the largest non-life insurance company in China's mainland initiated by PICC Holding Company. The latter injected all of its commercial insurance operations, together with related assets, liability and subsidiaries into PICC P and C. It is a leading P and C insurance company in China, with superiority in network and professionals. The company has set up an extensive nationwide network comprising more than 4,500 local branch offices in 31 provinces, autonomous regions and municipalities with some 80,000 official staff.

Website: http://www.e-picc.com.cn/

China Life Insurance (Group) Company

China Life Insurance (Group) Company is China's large-sized financial and insurance enterprise headquartered in Beijing. The group is made up of China Life Insurance Co. Ltd., China Life Insurance Asset Management Co. Ltd., China Life Insurance (Overseas) Co. Ltd., and China Life Property and Casualty Insurance Co. Ltd. and Insurance Profession College.

China Life Insurance Co. Ltd. was founded in accordance with the PRC Company Law on June 30, 2003 with a registered address in Beijing. It was listed on the NYSE and HKSE on December17 and 18, 2003, being

China Life Insurance (Group) Company and its subsidiaries constitute the largest commercial insurance group in China.

the first Chinese life insurance company listed overseas and setting the record of the world's largest financing scale for that year. According to the statistics released by the China Insurance Regulatory Commission, the company's market share in the first six months of 2006 reached 49.4 percent.

China Life Insurance (Group) Co. and its subsidiaries make up the biggest commercial insurance company in China. They form the largest institutional investor in China's capital market. It is also the only insurance enterprise ranking among the world's top 500 enterprises in China's mainland.

Website: http://www.e-chinalife.com

China Pacific Insurance (Group) Co., Ltd.

China Pacific Insurance (Group) Co., Ltd., an investment and holding group with its head office in Shanghai, was developed in accordance with the stipulation on the separation of its property and life insurance sectors on the basis of the former China Pacific Insurance Co., Ltd. formed in April 1991.

Domestically, CPIC Group is the majority stake-holder of China Pacific Property Insurance Co., Ltd. and China Pacific Life Insurance Co., Ltd., two specialized insurance operations. At present, the two subsidiaries have a well-established service network with 5,469 business branches across the country. Overseas, CPIC Group fully owns China Pacific (America) Services Inc. in the US, China Pacific Insurance (H.K.) Co., Ltd. in Hong Kong, and representative offices in London and New York respectively. CPIC Group also formed a joint venture with ING called Pacific-Antai Life Insurance Co., Ltd.

Since 1995, CPIC Group has more than once been ranked among the 200 global insurance giants by S and P: 48th in 1999 and 45th in 2000. The rate of the company's bad assets maintains the lower level across the country.

Website: http://www.cpic.com.cn

China Export and Credit Insurance Corporation

China Export and Credit Insurance Corporation (SINOSURE) is the only policy-oriented Chinese insurance company specializing in export credit insurance. It started operation on December 18, 2001. The company has a registered capital of four billion Yuan which came from the Export Credit Insurance Risk Fund as arranged by the State fiscal budget. Headquartered in Beijing, SINOSURE has built a service network of 12 branches and seven business offices nationwide and a representative office in London.

SINOSURE is mandated, in accordance with the Chinese government's diplomatic, foreign trade, industrial, fiscal, and financial policies, to promote Chinese exports and foreign investments, especially the export of high-tech or high added-value capital goods, by means of export credit insurance, export financing facilitation, information, and receivables management services.

SINOSURE offers coverage against political risks and commercial risks. Political risks include restrictions on transfer and remittance of foreign exchanges, expropriation, nationalization and war, etc. Commercial risks include credit risks on the part of buyers (default, bankruptcy and rejection of goods) and credit risks on the part of buyer's banks (e.g. the issuing bank or confirming bank in the case of L/Cs).

Website: http://www.Sinosure.com.cn

♦ China Insurance Regulatory Commission

The China Insurance Regulatory Commission (CIRC), established on November 18, 1998, is authorized by the State Council to conduct administration, supervision and regulation of the domestic insurance market, and to ensure the industry operates stably in compliance with law.

Major Responsibilities:

(1) CIRC formulates policies, strategies and plans regarding the development of the insurance industry, drafts relevant laws and regulations regarding insurance supervision and regulation, and makes relevant rules for the industry.

(2) It examines and approves the establishment of insurance companies and their branches, insurance groups and insurance holding companies; approves, in conjunction with relevant authorities the establishment of insurance asset management companies; examines and approves the establishment of representative offices by overseas insurance organizations within the territory of the PRC; examines and approves the establishment of insurance intermediaries such as agencies, brokerages, loss-adjusting companies and their branches; examines and approves the establishment of overseas insurance organizations by domestic insurance and non-insurance organizations; examines and approves the merger, split, alteration and dissolution of insurance organizations; decides whether or not to take over an insurance company or designates an organization to take it over; organizes or participates in the bankruptcy and liquidation process of insurance companies.

(3) It examines and confirms the qualifications of senior managerial personnel in all insurance-related organizations; establishes the basic qualification standards for insurance practitioners.

(4) It examines and approves the clauses and premium rates of insurance lines related to the public interests, statutory insurance lines and newly developed life insurance lines; files the insurance clauses and premium rates of the other insurance lines.

(5) It supervises the solvency and market conduct of insurance companies according to law; manages the insurance security fund, and monitors the insurance guarantee deposits; formulates rules and regulations on insurance fund management on the basis of laws and relevant policies of the State, and supervises insurance fund management according to law.

Address: No.15 Finance Street, Xicheng District, Beijing
Website: http://www.circ.gov.cn/

Intellectual Property

Intellectual Property Right Protection

The Chinese government has always attached great importance to the protection of Intellectual Property Rights. In 2004, the Chinese Government established the State IPR Protection Work Team consisting of 12 ministries and departments such as the Supreme People's Court, Supreme People's Procuratorate, Ministry of Commerce, Ministry of Public Security, State Administration for Industry and Commerce, the State Intellectual Property Office, and General Administration of Customs. In order to adapt to the new situation after entering the WTO, the government sorted out the relevant laws and regulations on IPR on a large scale. At present it has set up an improved the legal system for IPR protection. In addition, it has also amended or abolished numerous regulations or documents on IPR not conforming to WTO requirements.

China has constituted the Law Enforcement and Coordination Mechanism on IPR and the Mechanism of Regular Communication and Coordination with Foreign Invested Enterprises covering the whole country. It has also launched nationwide special campaigns and publicity and education activities for IPR protection, thus enhancing the people's consciousness of protecting IPR. In the meantime, China has actively participated in various activities held by international organizations regarding IPR. It has established the China-EU Dialogue Mechanism on Intellectual Property, China-US Intellectual Property Protection Working Group, China-Japan-South Korea Bilateral or Triangular Dialogues and Cooperation Mechanisms on IPR. The Chinese Government has also conducted various exchanges and cooperation on IPR protection with other countries or regions like Brazil and Mexico. Through these efforts, the atmosphere of respecting and protecting IPR is being formed in the whole society.

Patent Examination System

On April 1, 1985, the Patent Law of the People's Republic of China went into effect. Following that, China promulgated several patent-related laws and regulations, such as the Rules for the Implementation of the Patent Law, the Regulations on Patent Commissioning, the Procedures for the Administrative Enforcement of Laws Concerning Patents, and Regulations on the Implementation of Customs Protection of Patent Rights. China has twice made revisions to the Patent Law in the light of the requirements of social and economic development so as to enable it to improve continuously.

China has established a relatively complete and independent patent examination system. On January 1, 1994, China became a member State of the "Patent Cooperation Treaty". The China Patent Office is the agency dealing with cases involving the Patent Cooperation Treaty, performing international patent searches and preliminary examinations. Meanwhile, China has established a fairly comprehensive system for patent work. Relevant departments of the State Council and local governments have established patent administrative organs in accordance with the provisions of the "Patent Law." China now has more than 5,000 people working in patent agencies, and a service system mainly providing patent commissioning, patent information, patent technology transfer intermediary and patent technology evaluation services has taken initial shape.

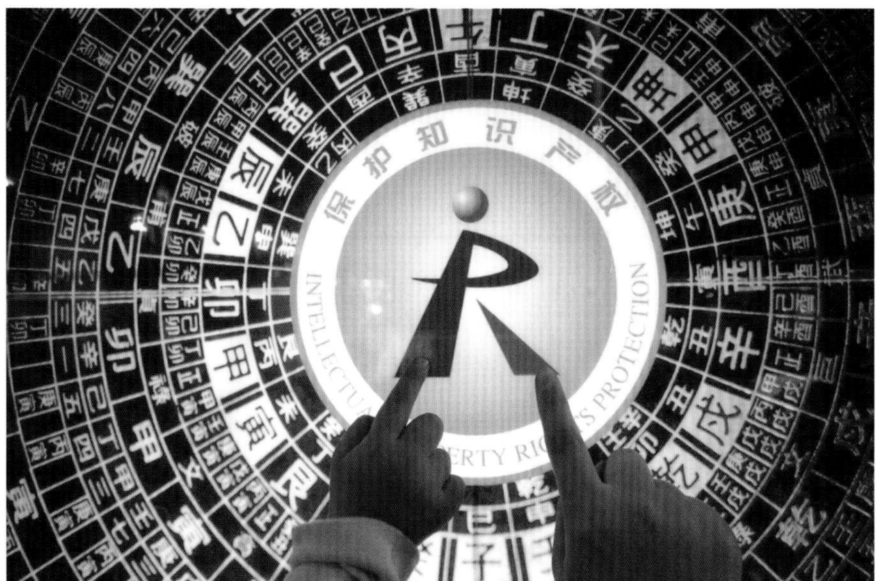

Logo of Intellectual Property Right Protection

China has accepted hundreds of thousands of patent applications.

Patent Application and Granting

Since 1985 the State Intellectual Property Office handled patent applications with an average annual increase of 18.9 percent. Domestic applications and those from other countries accounted for 82 percent and 18 percent respectively. Patent applications in China had exceeded two million by March 17, 2004. It took China 15 years for patent applications to reach the first 1 million, but only four years for the second 1 million. As of the end of 2006, the accumulated number of patent applications in China has passed the 3 million mark to reach 3.334 million.

Laws and Regulations on Trademark Protection

The "Trademark Law" went into effect on March 1, 1983. The government promulgated the "Rules for the Implementation of the Trademark Law" in March 1983 and, in 1988, revised the law for the first time. In February 1993, the Standing Committee of the National People's Congress (NPC) made the first revision to the "Trademark Law" to include service trademarks in the work of trademark protection, strengthen efforts to crack down on trademark infringement and counterfeiting, and improve trademark registration procedures. In July 1993, the government revised the "Rules for the Implementation of the Trademark Law" for the second time to bring collective trademarks and certification trademarks within the scope of legal protection, and added to it provisions on the protection of "trademarks well known to the public."

In October 2001, the NPC Standing Committee made revisions to the "Trademark Law" for the second time to include three-dimensional trademarks and color combination trademarks and offer greater protection to well-known trademarks. The revised "Trademark Law" also stipulates that the trademark system shall be used to protect geographical names, judicial examination shall be added for the certification process of trademark rights, and greater efforts made to crack down on trademark infringement and counterfeiting, thus bringing the relevant provisions of the "Trademark Law" in line with the principles of the WTO's "Agreement on Trade-related Aspects of Intellectual Property Rights". In August 2002, the government again revised the "Rules for the Implementation of the Trademark Law" and renamed it "Regulations for the Implementation of the Trademark Law."

In accordance with the provisions of the "Trademark Law" and the "Regulations for the Implementation of the Trademark Law," the State Administration for Industry and Commerce formulated or revised several administrative rules and regulations, including the "Trademark Assessment Rules", "Provisions on the Recognition and Protection of well-known Trademarks", "Procedures for the Management and Registration of Collective Trademarks and Certification Trademarks", "Procedures for the Implementation of the Madrid Agreement for the International Registration of Trademarks" and "Procedures for the Administration of the Printing of Trademarks".

Trademarks Registration

As improvements are made in the legal system concerning trademarks and as the general public's awareness about trademarks is heightened, applications for trademark registration in China have soared in recent years. The number of applications for all kinds of trademarks and trademark registration maintained first place in the world for four straight years.

In 2006, there were more than 700,000 trademark registration applications handled by TMO, and 260,000 examined and approved. For three years running, the number of Chinese trademark applications examined by TMO stayed at more than 470,000, and the number of trademark registrations and applications reached more than 310,000.

Anyone can log on the TMO website (http://www.ctmo.gov.cn or http://sbj.saic.gov.cn) to check out the information on trademark registration.

Trademark Registration From Overseas

As the investment environment in China is constantly improved, especially after China joined the WTO, both the number of applications for trademark registration from foreigners and the number of registered foreign trademarks have kept increasing. China become the country with the most applications for territorial extension among the federation of the Madrid Agreement Concerning the International Registration of Marks.

Protecting Well-known Trademark

Tongrentang—the No.1 renowned trademark among Chinese pharmaceutical industry

China has actively fulfilled its obligations to protect internationally well-known trademarks since it joined the "Paris Convention for the Protection of Industrial Property." In handling cases involving objections and disputes over ownership of trademarks as well as trademark management, the State Administration for Industry and Commerce has certified many well-known trademarks, effectively protecting according to law the legitimate rights and interests of owners of foreign and Chinese well-known trademarks. Meanwhile, administrative organs of industry and commerce at all levels regard the protection of well-known trademarks as their priority and have made greater efforts to protect them. They have severely cracked down on all kinds of illegal acts that have infringed the rights and interests of well-known trademarks.

Laws and Regulations on Copyright Protection

China's legal system for copyright protection was gradually established in the 1990s, with the implementation of the "Copyright Law" as a hallmark in this process. In recent years, China has revised the "Copyright Law." It has also promulgated a number of regulations with legal effect, such as "Regulations on the Protection of Computer Software", "Regulations for the Implementation of the Copyright Law", "Procedures for the Implementation of Administrative Sanctions Concerning Copyright" and "Regulations on the Collective Management of Copyright". The promulgation and implementation of these legal documents have laid a solid legal foundation for copyright protection. At present, China has formed a three-level copyright administrative management system: the State Copyright Bureau, copyright bureaus at the provincial level and the prefectural (city) level. Governments of various provinces, autonomous regions and municipalities directly under the central government have constantly consolidated their copyright administrative management departments and made improvements to the system of copyright administrative management and law enforcement.

Cracking Down on Copyright Infringement and Piracy

The copyright administrative management departments have always maintained the pressure on copyright infringement and piracy. They have launched several campaigns to crack down on pirated discs, textbooks, reference books, software, illegal duplication and selling of audio-video products, selling of smuggled audio-video products and Internet infringement practices with positive achievements. Copyright administrative management departments at all levels confiscated pirated copies, accepted infringement cases and resolved many of them. These included the investigation and punishment of two Chinese enterprises that had infringed the copyright of the Microsoft Corporation.

In 2005, a total of 9,644 cases were received, and 9,380, or 97 percent, were resolved by various levels of copyright administrative authorities across the country. And in the year, more than 107 million items of different kinds of pirated products were confiscated. Of them, more than 19.08 million were pirated books, about 1.14 million were pirated periodical magazines, 65.87 million were pirated audio-video products, 13.01 million were pirated electronic publications, 7.74 million were pirated software discs, and 90,000 were other kinds of pirated products. The five regions where the more pirated products were confiscated were Guangdong, Hubei, Jiangsu, Beijing and Shandong.

Copyright Administrative Management System

While establishing and improving its copyright legal system and strengthening its copyright administrative management, China also attaches great importance to the establishment of a copyright public service system. At present, China has established a copyright public management and service system consisting of copyright collective management organs, copyright agencies, copyright protection associations, professional associations and organizations of copyright holders. In 1988, the Copyright Agency of China was established. In 1990, the Copyright Research Society of China was established and its name was changed to the Copyright Society of China in 2002. In 1993, the China Copyright Society of Works of Music was established. And in 1998, the Copyright Protection Center of China was established. At present, writers' associations, such as China Federation of Literary and Art Circles, China Writers' Association and China Film Association as well as professional associations of book publishers, producers of audio-video products and software developers have established their own copyright protection organizations. Copyright societies have been established in more than 20 provinces (autonomous regions, and municipalities directly under the central government) and some major cities. Preparatory work is underway to establish China's collective copyright management organizations of written works and audio-video products.

According to the agreement on joining the WTO in the negotiation and the stipulation of China's laws, China's publication industry will not be opened up, but the Chinese Government permit the cooperation of copyright and single product. Now, many international famous publication companies have the copyright cooperation projects in China and there are 51 varieties of newspapers and periodicals which have been approved to be published with the Sino-foreign cooperative copyright, including 25 scientific and technological varieties, 25 life varieties and one business variety.

Copyright Trade

In 2006, China made great breakthrough in copyright exporting. At the Beijing International Book Fair, China signed 1,096 contracts on copyright exporting and 891 on copyright importing, with the rate between them being 1.23 to 1. At the Frankfurt Book Exhibition, China also imported 1,936 copyrights, 205 and 682 more than the last one.

In the second half year of 2004, China launched the "China Book International", which includes subsidizing the translation fee, encouraging the foreign publishers and publishing institutions to translate and publish China's books, and presenting the books on China to the foreign libraries. In 2005, "China Book International" subscribered agreements of 179 kinds of books with financial support of 3 million Yuan with over 10 publishers in Britain, France and other countries. In 2006, this plan increased the subsidizing capital and more than 1,000 kinds of books were incorporated into the list of book recommended by this plan. The foreign publishing institutions who purchase or are presented with the copyrights from the Chinese publishing institutions get the translation fee subsidization.

Intellectual Property Rights Protection for Audio and Video Products

Persistent piracy of audio and video products, in spite of repeated bans, is a problem of international significance. The Chinese government attaches great importance to IPR protection for audio and video products, treats crackdown on piracy of audio and video products as an important task in IPR protection and has made continuous efforts to carry it out. In recent years, China has gradually established a complete system for the management of audio and video products, which mainly includes an IPR protection system, audio and video business license system, exclusive publication right system, duplication authorization system, SID code system, censorship system for imported audio and video products, the system of awards for informants, the system of uniform anti-counterfeit labels for audio and video products, the system of registration and filing of audio and video products in storehouses, and the system of inspection of, report on and keeping the public informed of illegal audio and video products.

In August 1994, the government promulgated the "Regulations on the Administration of Audio and Video Products", amended in December 2001. In accordance with the relevant laws and regulations, including the "General Principles of the Civil Law", "Copyright Law", "Criminal Law" and "Regulations on the Administration of Audio and Video Products", the Press and Publication General Administration, Ministry of Culture, General Administration of Customs and Ministry of Commerce respectively and jointly issued a series of administrative regulations,

♦ Scientific Research Institution for Copyright

◎Intellectual Property Center of China Academy of Social Sciences

Address: No.15 Shatan Beijie, East District, Beijing
Website: http://www.iolaw.org.cn

◎College of Intellectual Property of Peking University

Address: Law Building, Peking University, Beijing
Website: http://162.105.148.89/index.asp

◎Intellectual Property Teaching and Research Center of Renmin University of China

Address: No.59, Zhongguancun Street, Haidian District, Beijing
Website: http://www.cnlawschool.com/introduce/

The Chinese government treats crackdown on piracy of audio and video products as an important task in IPR protection.

such as the "Regulations on the Administration of Publication of Audio and Video Products", "Measures for the Administration of Wholesale, Retail and Renting of Audio and Video Products", "Measures for the Administration of Import of Audio and Video Products" and "Measures for the Administration of China-Foreign Cooperative Distribution Enterprises of Audio-video Products", providing both legal and administrative groundwork for the business and protection of audio and video products.

The "Regulations on the Administration of Audio and Video Products" provides for the division of functions in the administration of the industry. It clearly assigned the administration of audio-video products' production, publication and duplication to the Press and Publication General Administration; and that of wholesale, retail, renting, showing and import of audio-video products to the Ministry of Culture. Following the lead of the central government, local governments have also readjusted their administrative systems in this regard. So far, China has initially established market management networks at the central, provincial, prefectural and county levels. In most areas, investigation squads have been set up to keep watch on cultural markets, including the market for audio and video products.

New Regulation on Network Copyright Protection

Starting from July 1, 2006, China implemented the Regulation on Protection of the Right to Network Dissemination of Information. This regulation clarified ambiguities on the protection of copyright regarding network dissemination of information and strengthened protection. There are 27 articles in the regulation, obviously increasing the scope of protection. As for the hot online film downloading issues: it stipulated: The copyright administrative department will issue a warning to anyone who commits any of the following acts of infringement, and confiscate any illegal earnings and the devices or components mainly used to bypass or overcome the technical measures; if the case is serious, the copyright administrative department may also confiscate such equipment as computers used to provide the network service, and impose a fine of less than 100,000 Yuan:

-Intentionally avoiding or destroying the technical measures, or intentionally providing technical services to others to do so;

-Providing qthers with works, performances, or audio-visual recordings through the information network and obtaining economic benefits. As to whether a network service provider that provides searching or linking services to a service object contributes to the crime, the new regulation gives a definite explanation. Jiang Zhipei, presiding judge for Intellectual Property Right Office of the Supreme People's Court, noted that it covers such activities as providing uploading service and dissemination, or linking and search services.

International Cooperation on Piracy

At the end of 2006, a Memorandum of Understanding on the Establishment of a Coordination Mechanism for Online Copyright Protection was signed in Beijing by the National Copyright Administration of China (NCA) and the Motion Picture Association, Business Software Alliance, Association of American Publishers and Britain-based Publishers Association.

According to this, all sides will strengthen and improve the authentication of copyright authorization, and keep in close contact on cracking down on transnational online piracy and copyright infringement on a regular basis under the framework of the Cooperative Mechanism of Network Copyright Protection. The American and British sides will provide timely lists of their member companies to the NCA, which will pursue the protection of their movies, software, video and audio products and written works. They will also provide information on pirated activities that harm the copyright of their member companies. The NCA will investigate reported cases and, if proven, provide details of illegal activities to judicial departments. Cooperation on publicity and training will be enhanced and regular meetings will be held to exchange views on anti-piracy issues, according to the memorandum.

Protection of New Varieties of Agriculture and Forestry Plants

On October 1, 1997, the government began implementing the "Regulations on the Protection of New Varieties of Plants", greatly expanding the scope of IPR protection in China. To supplement the implementation of the "Regulations on the Protection of New Varieties of Plants", the Chinese government has in succession promulgated and implemented such regulations as the "Rules for the Implementation of the Regulations on the Protection of New Varieties of Plants (Agriculture)", "Rules for the Implementation of the Regulations on the Protection of New Varieties of Plants (Forestry)", "Regulations on Agency of New Agricultural Plant Variety Rights", "Regulations on Handling Cases of Infringement of New Agricultural Plant Variety Rights", and "Regulations of the Ministry of Agriculture on the Work of the Reexamination Board for New Varieties of Plants", providing legal guarantees for the rapid development of new varieties of plants.

The government has set up the Office of Protection of New Varieties of Plants and the Reexamination Board for New Varieties of Plants at the Ministry of Agriculture and State Forestry Administration, respectively, forming an institutional protection system combining examination and approval agencies, law-enforcement organizations, intermediary service organizations and other rights protection organizations. Meanwhile, a technological support system has been established, which includes the Center for the Preservation of Breeding Materials of New Varieties of Agricultural Plants, Center for Testing of New Varieties of Plants and its 14 sub-centers, and the Center for the Testing of New Varieties of Forest Plants and its five sub-centers and two molecule determination labs. To ensure scientific and authoritative examination of plant variety rights, and drawing on the international standards for testing new varieties of plants, the relevant authorities have, based on the actual conditions of China, formulated guides for testing 57 new varieties of plants, including corn, rice, poplar and peony, of which 18 have been promulgated and implemented as national or industrial standards.

New Varieties of Plants

According to the provisions of the 1978 Act of the UPOV Convention, each member State of the Union shall apply the botanical genera and species which must or may be protected to at least ten genera or species in all within three years from the date of the entry into force of this convention; to at least 18 genera or species in all within six year and to at east 24 genera or species in all within eight years. In the past seven years, the protected plants released by the Ministry of Agriculture have reached 62 genera or species, and there were another 78 genera or species released by the State Forestry Administration, making China's botanical genera and species which must or may be protected reach 140, far exceeding the lowest limitation required by the Convention.

The foreign countries have had more understanding of China's system for the protection of new varieties of plants. Applying the plant variety rights in China has been the choice of the increasing plant breeders at home and abroad and the number of plant variety right applications increase by 40 percent each year on average.

List of International Conventions on IPR China Has Acceded

Name of Treaty	Date of Accession
Convention Establishing the World Intellectual Property Organization	Member state since June 3,1980
Paris Convention for the Protection of Industrial Property	Member state since March 19, 1985
Treaty on Intellectual Property in Respects of Integrated Circuits	Member state since 1989
Madrid Agreement Concerning the International Registration of Marks	Member state since October 4, 1989
Bern Convention for the Protection of Literary and Artistic Works	Member state since October 15, 1992
Universal Copyright Convention	Member state since October 30, 1992
Convention for the Protection of Producers of Phonograms against Unauthorized Duplication of their Phonograms	Member state since April 30, 1993
Patent Cooperation Treaty	Member state since January 1, 1994
Nice Agreement Concerning the International Classification of Goods and Service for the Purposes of the Registration of Marks	Member state since August 9, 1994
Budapest Treaty on the International Recognition of the Deposit of Microorganism for the Purpose of Patent Procedure	Member state since July 1, 1995
Locarno Agreement Establishing an International Classification for Industrial Design	Member state since September 19, 1996
Strasbourg Agreement Concerning the International Patent Classification	Member state since June 19, 1997
International Convention for the Protection of New Varieties of Plants	Member state since April 23, 1999
Agreement of World Trade Organization on Trade-related Aspects of Intellectual Property Rights	Member state since December 11, 2001

Customs Examination System

In September 1994, China began to carry out border protection of IPR. At present, Chinese customs houses have established a complete system of IPR-related law enforcement measures, which includes such links as examination of customs declaration bills and certificates, inspection of imported and exported goods, detention and investigation of right-infringing goods, punishment of illegal importers and exporters, and disposal of right-infringing goods.

In October 1995, China promulgated and implemented its first ever Regulations on the Protection of Intellectual Property Rights by the Customs, and began to establish its system of IPR customs protection in accordance with WTO rules. In 2000, the NPC Standing Committee amended the "Customs Law of the People's Republic of China," defining the functions of IPR customs protection from the legal perspective. In December 2003, the Chinese government promulgated the revised "Regulations on the Protection of Intellectual Property Rights by the Customs," which strengthened customs' power in investigating and dealing with rights-infringing goods, reduced the burden on the proprietors of intellectual properties in seeking customs protection, and defined the functions of the customs and the judicial and other administrative organizations. Later, the General Administration of Customs formulated the Measures for Implementation of the revised regulations, which clearly provided for such issues mentioned in the revised regulations as keeping business secrets, filing of international registered trademarks, collecting and returning of security deposit, and the payment of relevant fees by the proprietors. In September 2004, the government promulgated the Regulations on Implementation of Administrative Penalties, which clearly provided administrative penalties for infringements on IPR in import and export. The Interpretations on Several Issues in Practical Application of Laws in Criminal Cases of Infringement on Intellectual Property Rights was promulgated by the Supreme People's Court and the Supreme People's Procuratorate in December 2004, which further stipulated the criminal responsibilities of agencies importing or exporting rights-infringing goods. By then, a legal system for IPR customs protection geared to the needs of economic and social development had been basically established.

Social Service Institution for Copyright

Institutions	Address	Post Code	Telephone
Beijing Copyright Protection Association	#24 Building A, No.11 Community, Heping Street, Chaoyang District, Beijing	100013	010-84251190
Tianjin Copyright Protection Association	No.31, Heiniuchengdao, Hexi District, Tianjin City	300211	022-28335745
Shanghai Copyright Protection Association	No.5, Shaoxing Road, Shanghai City	200020	021-64339268
Guangxi Zhuang Autonomous Region Copyright Protection Association	No.53 Jinhu Road, Nanning City	530021	0771-5516071
Sichuan Province Copyright Protection Association	No.21 Guihua Alley, Chengdu City	610015	028-6636481
Inner Mongolia Autonomous Region Copyright Protection Association	No.15 Laogangfang Street, New Town, Hohhot City	010050	0471-4913671
Heilongjiang Copyright Protection Association	No.68 Senglin Street, Daoli District, Harbin	150010	0451-4614852
Jilin Province Copyright Protection Association	No.124 Renmin Street, Changchun	130021	0431-5644760
Anhui Province Copyright Protection Association	No.1 Yuejin Road, Hefei City	230063	0551-284650
Shaanxi Province Copyright Protection Association	Room 1318, News Press Building, No.147 Beida Street, Xi'an City	710003	029-87205031
Dalian Copyright Protection Association	No.1 Yuren Alley, Huayuan Square, Xigang District, Dalian City	116001	0411-3645450
Shangdong Province Copyright Protection Society	Comprehensive Building, No.1 Shengfuqianjie, Jinan City	250011	0531-6061783
Liaoning Province Copyright Protection Society	No.108 Beiyi Road, Heping District, Shenyang	110001	024-23872188
Henan Province Copyright Protection Society	No.73 Nongye Road, Zhengzhou City	450002	0731-5714182
Guizhou Province Copyright Association	No.289 Zhonghua North Road, Guiyang	550001	0851-6830647
Jilin Province Copyright Protection Center	No.4646 Renmin Avenue, Changchun City	130021	0431-5644760
Beijing Copyright Protection Center	Rm.505, Bld.-B, Haoyuan Building, Jia-88 Caihuying Dongjie, Fengtai District, Beijing	100054	010-63332130

Customs Protection Mechanism

China has established and improved its law enforcement mechanism for IPR customs protection. First, it has established a central filing system. As long as IPR proprietors have filed their rights with the General Administration of Customs, the port customs have the power to detain imported or exported goods that infringe on the filed IPR. Second, a model combining active protection with passive protection is implemented in law enforcement. Besides detaining import or export goods suspected of IPR infringement, the customs can also investigate and deal with illegal import and export of right-infringing goods within the scope of their powers and duties. Third, law enforcement organizations have been founded and improved, and the building of IPR law enforcement teams enhanced. By the end of 2004, all the customs houses directly under the General Administration of Customs had set up relevant departments for the management of IPR protection, and 11 of them had set up special organizations for IPR protection. Some customs houses with adequate conditions had stationed liaison officers on site. A system of IPR law enforcement has taken shape on three levels, namely, the General Administration of Customs, customs houses directly under it, and grass-roots customs posts.

Judicial Protection of Intellectual Property Rights

In 2005, people's courts at each level across China comprehensively enhanced the IP judicial protection, brought trial functions fully into play and severely punished IP crimes in accordance with the law. The number of IP-related civil, administrative and criminal cases that people's courts accepted and concluded during the year increased continuously.

By the end of 2005, the number of the Intermediate People's courts with the

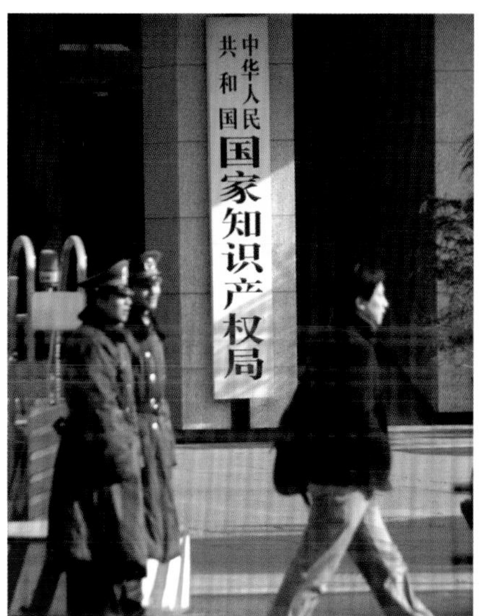

State Intellectual Property Office is the competent authority in charge of patent affairs and the coordinating authority for foreign-related intellectual property issues.

appropriate jurisdiction over patents, new varieties of plants and layout designs of integrated circuits in first instance had respectively reached 51, 37 and 43 across the country.

Apart from the cases directly covering foreign companies and citizens, China's courts also handled a great deal of wholly-funded enterprises and "the Sino-foreign joint ventures, Sino-foreign cooperative enterprises and foreign-funded enterprises."

These cases coverage had also extended from covering trademark, copyright and patent right to internet copyright, network domain, provisional measures before suit, new plant varieties, identification of famous brands, design of integrated circuit layout, folk literature and art, geographical signs, non-infringement acknowledgement, franchise contracts and anti-monopoly.

China's Accession to International Conventions for the Protection of IPR

While improving its legal system, China, since the 1980s, has acceded one after another to the major international conventions and agreements for the protection of IPR. Since 1980, when China first acceded to the Convention Establishing the World Intellectual Property Organization, it has acceded successively to the Paris Convention for the Protection of Industrial Property, Treaty on Intellectual Property in Respect of Integrated Circuits, Madrid Agreement Concerning the International Registration of Marks, Bern Convention for the Protection of Literary and Artistic Works, Universal Copyright Convention, Convention for the Protection of Producers of Phonograms against Unauthorized Duplication, Patent Cooperation Treaty, Nice Agreement Concerning International Classification of Goods and Services for the Purposes of Registering Marks, Budapest Treaty on the International Recognition of Deposit of Microorganisms for the Purposes of Patent Procedure, Locarno Agreement Establishing an International Classification for Industrial Design, Strasbourg Agreement Concerning the International Patent Classification, International Convention for the Protection of New Varieties of Plants and the WTO'S Agreement on Trade-Related Aspects of IPR (See Table 2 for information about China's accession to international conventions for the protection of IPR).

During the process of accession, China has always been active in such activities as prescribed by them, and it has won worldwide recognition for its sincere attitude of adhering to these conventions, treaties and agreements as well as its ability to undertake the international responsibilities.

Furthermore, China is also considering acceding to other international treaties. An example is that it has set about to draft and amend relevant laws in order to accede to the WIPO Copyright Treaty (WCT) and the WIPO Performances and Phonograms Treaty (WPPT).

Guaranteeing the Rights of Foreign Rights Holders

China's laws on IPR protection stipulate that any foreigner shall be treated according to the agreements that China has signed with his country, any international conventions that both countries concluded or on the principle of reciprocity. China's relevant law, regulations and other measures guarantee national treatment and most-favored-nation treatment of the foreign rights holders in all the aspects of IPR protection, which accords with the TRIPS Agreement in an all-round way.

International Exchange on IPR

In recent years, China has held talks, and engaged in exchanges and cooperation with other countries, international organizations and foreign-invested enterprises in the field of IPR. At the suggestion of the United States, starting in 2003, China and the US have held a round-table conference on IPR every year, and reached agreement on many IPR-related issues. In 2004, China and Europe held their first round of talks on IPR in Beijing. Initial agreement was reached between the two sides on matters of cooperation related to IPR. Relevant Chinese departments have established good cooperative relations with corresponding departments in several countries, and international organizations such as World Intellectual Property Organization and International Union for the Protection of New Varieties of Plants. In September 2003, a mechanism was established for regular contact and coordination between relevant Chinese departments and foreign-invested enterprises. Under the mechanism, a meeting is held every three months to solicit comments and suggestions from the foreign-invested enterprises on issues related to IPR protection.

China had also witnessed a lot of exchange with Japan, the Republic of Korea, ASEAN, Germany, Britain, Austria, Spain, Russia and Hong Kong, and had actively participated activities sponsored by WIPO, APEC as well as other regional or other multi-side conference. China had played active roles in Doha Development Agenda and other efforts solving IP issues.

System for IPR Protection

In its practice of IPR protection, a two-way parallel protection mode, namely, administrative and judicial protection, has emerged in China. Several departments are assigned the duty to protect IPR, such as the State Intellectual Property Office, State Administration for Industry and Commerce, Press and Publication General Administration, State Copyright Bureau, Ministry of Culture, Ministry of Agriculture, State Forestry Administration, Ministry of Public Security, General Administration of Customs, Supreme People's Court and Supreme People's Procuratorate. To further strengthen IPR protection, in 2004, China established the State IPR Protection Work Team headed by a vice-premier of the State Council, responsible for planning and coordinating the work regarding IPR protection throughout the country. Its office, located in the Ministry of Commerce, handles the routine work of the team.

At present, the formulation and enforcement of the policies on IPR protection is in charge of different departments. The State Intellectual Property Office is responsible for the approval of patents. The Marks Office under the State Administration for Industry and Commerce is responsible for the registration of marks. The Copyright Office is responsible for the formulation of policies on copyright. The Ministry of Industry and Information Technology is responsible for the dealing with improper competition including business secret protection. MIIT is responsible for the administrative protection of drugs. The General Administration of Customs is responsible for the enforcement of border measures. The Ministry of Agriculture and State Administration of Forestry is responsible for the protection of new varieties of plants. The Ministry of Information Industry is responsible for the protection of integrated circuit chart design. The General Administration of Quality Supervision, Inspection and Quarantine and State Administration for Industry and Commerce is responsible for cracking down the counterfeit behaviors. Other institutions such as press and publication institutions, people's court and public security organs also participate in the IPR protection work.

Laws and Regulations on the Protection of Intellectual Property Rights

China has established a relatively complete system of laws and regulations covering a wide range of subjects in line with generally accepted international rules. Since the 1980s, the State has promulgated and put into effect a number of laws and regulations covering the major contents in IPR protection. These include the Patent Law of the PRC, Trademark Law of the PRC, Copyright Law of the PRC, Regulations on the Protection of Computer Software, Regulations on the Protection of Layout Designs of Integrated Circuits, Regulations on the Collective Management of Copyright, Regulations on the Management of Audio-Video Products, Regulations on the Protection of New Varieties of Plants, Regulations on the Protection of Intellectual Property Rights by the Customs, Regulations on the Protection of Special Signs, and Regulations on the Protection of Olympic Logos. China has also promulgated a series of relevant rules for the implementation of these laws and regulations, and their legal interpretation. As a result, the system of laws and regulations on IPR protection in China has been continuously improved. In 2001, around the time when China was admitted into the WTO, in order to provide effective legal protection to IPR, the country made comprehensive revisions to the laws and regulations regarding IPR protection and their legal interpretation. While more emphasis is given to promoting the progress of science and technology and innovation with regard to legislative intent, content of rights, standards of protection and means of legal remedy, the revisions brought the laws and regulations into conformity with the WTO's Agreement on Trade-related Aspects of Intellectual Property Rights and other international rules on IPR protection.

The Chinese Government pays more attention to spreading the knowledge on intellectual property among the public.

◆ Related Laws and Regulations

Regulations on the Protection of the Right of Communication through Information Network (2006)

Copyright Collective Management Regulations (2005)

Administrative Measures on Internet Copyright Protection (2005)

Regulation of the People's Republic of China on the Customs' Protection of Intellectual Property Right (2004)

Regulations for Approbation and Protection of Well-known Trademark (2003)

The Supreme Court's Explanation of Certain Legal Problems on the Trial of Cases Concerning Disputes over Computer Network Copyright (2003)

The Registration Method of Computer Software Copyright (2002)

The Supreme Court's Explanation of Certain Legal Problems on the Trial of Cases Concerning

Civil Disputes over Copyright (2002)

Regulations on the Protection of Olympic Symbols (2002)

Regulation on the Implementation of the Copyright Law of the People's Republic of China (2002)

Copyright Law of the People's Republic of China (2001)

Patent Law of the People's Republic of China (2001)

Regulations on the Protection of Computer Software (2001)

Regulations on the Reward of Publishing the Written Work (1999)

Measures for Administration of Setting up Permanent Representative Institution in China by the Foreign Copyright Authentication Institution (1996)

Measures for the Registration of the Copyrights Contract of Pledge (1996)

Interim Measures for the Administration of the External Agency of Copyrights (1996)

Administrative Regulations on Special Marks (1996)

Notice Regarding the Registration of Contracts for Publishing the Foreign Audiovisual Products (1995)

Interim Provisions of the Standard of Paying Author's Remuneration When Recording the Published Works with Consent by Law (1993)

Interim Provisions of the Standard of Paying Author's Remuneration When Performing Published Works with Consent by Law (1993)

Law of the PRC against Unfair Competition (1993)

Provisions on the Implementation of the International Copyright Treaty (1992)

China's Action Plan on IPR Protection in 2006

On March 8, 2006, China's Action Plan on IPR Protection 2006 (hereinafter referred to as the "Action Plan") was introduced, showing that China will further strengthen the IPR protection.

The Action Plan covers 4 major areas: trade mark, copyright, patent and import and export, The Action Plan covers 9 areas: legislation, law enforcement, mechanism building, propaganda, training and education, international communication and cooperation, promoting business self discipline, services to right holders, and subject research.

In line with the Action Plan, in 2006 China drafted, formulate and revise 17 laws, regulations, rules and measures relating to trademark, copyright, patent and customs protection, and draft, improve and revise 6 judicial interpretations. The IPR law enforcement efforts included 7 dedicated campaigns such as the "Mountain Eagle", "Sunshine" and "Blue Sky", 8 regular enforcement initiatives and 20 specific measures. The government is going to establish a long standing mechanism constituting 11 parts, including a service center for reporting and complaining IPR violations and publicizing law enforcement statistics, and 18 specific measures. 7 approaches and 39 measures were adopted to raise the general public's awareness of IPR protection. 21 IPR training programs will be organized under the Project of Training Thousands of IPR Personnel. The focus of IPR related international exchanges and cooperation were on legislation, trade mark, copyright, patent and customs protection, which will be facilitated through 19 exchange and cooperation activities, out of which 7 were between China and the US. With a view to improving enterprises' consciousness and awareness of IPR protection, 3 initiatives were launched, including the convening of a conference on enterprises' IPR protection and proprietary innovation. Twelve specific measures covering 9 areas were put in place to better serve the right holders. Besides, countermeasure oriented research were conducted in 5 fields to strengthen IPR protection.

Copyright Law

The Copyright Law, which was promulgated in 1990, established the basic copyright protection system in China together with the Implementing Rules of the Copyright Law (amended on October 27,2001), the Provisions on the Implementation of the International Copyright Treaty (25 September 1992) and other related laws and regulations. In principle, this system was in compliance with international IPR treaties and practices.

Trademark Law

The Trademark Law, its implementing rules and other relevant laws, administrative regulations and departmental rules constitute the existing trademark legal system in China. The objective of these laws is to provide protection to rights-holders in line with international conventions and prevailing practice regarding IPR embodied both in the regulations on the substance and procedures for trademark registration and in the protection of trademark exclusive rights.

Universal Convention on the Protection of Plant Varieties

China is a party to the 1978 text of the Universal Convention on the Protection of Plant Varieties ("UPOV"). In March 1997, the State Council formulated and promulgated the Regulation on the Protection of New Plant Varieties, thus offering protection for new plant varieties in a sui generis form consistent with the requirements of the TRIPS Agreement.

Layout Designs of Integrated Circuits

China was among the first countries to sign the 1989 Treaty on Intellectual Property in Regard to Integrated Circuits. The specific Regulation on the Protection of Layout Designs of Integrated Circuits was issued in April 2001 and effective from 1 October 2001.

♦ China Patent Information Center

The State Intellectual Property Office grants the rights to manage and use the patent database and the right to offer comprehensive services to the China Patent Information Center. As the national-level large-sized patent information service institution, it provides rapid and high quality service to customers in China and abroad relying on its latest, most complete patent information resources, the information collecting and service network covering nationwide, and the advanced information processing technologies.

Address: No.6 Tucheng Road West, Jimen Bridge, Haidian District, Beijing
Website: http://www.cnpat.com.cn/aboutus/

♦ Copyright Protection Center of China

The Copyright Protection Center of China (CPCC) is a social copyright management and social service organization. The purpose of CPCC is, in accordance with the Copyright Law of the PRC and other relevant laws and regulations, to safeguard the legal rights and interests of copyright owners and relevant parties of such rights, to encourage the creation and dissemination of various published works, to bring about the prosperity of science and culture, and to promote the development of China's copyright business and copyright industry.

Under the CPCC, established in Beijing in September 1998, are the PPA and NCAC decided that the Copyright Agency of China (CAC), the Software Registration Center of China (SRCC) (deregistered), the Remuneration Collection and Distribution Center for the Use of Copyright of China (RCDCUCC) (deregistered), and the Editorial Office of Copyright Journal (now named China Copyright) shall be put under the uniform management of CPCC.

Major work of the CPCC are: (1) handle copyright issues on commission; (2) get copyright registered; (3) remuneration for copyright; (4)legal service for copyright; (5) examination and determination of copyright; (6) be responsible for making preparation for the formation of the collective management organs for language work, fine arts and photo copyrights; (7) offer information concerning copyright and gather and issue such information; (8) compile and publish Copyright journal; (9) publicize legal knowledge on copyright and train people involved in copyright work; (10) establish the national office to coordinate the work related to anti-pirates, and gather and issue information on work by various localities in this regard; (11) offer service to protection of copyright; and (12) handle other work related to copyright as authorized by the national copyright bureau.

Address: 5F, Wuhua Building, 4A Chegongzhuang Dajie, Beijing
Website: http://www.ccopyright.com

♦ Copyright Agency of China (CAC)

Set up in 1988, CAC is the first national copyright agency in China and the biggest one that has represented the greatest varieties of copyright in our country. Since its foundation in 1998, CAC has been put under the uniform management of CPCC according to the decision of PPA and NCAC. Its primary responsibility is to transfer and license copyright, to provide legal consultation and protection regarding copyright issues, and to collect and distribute the remuneration for the use of copyright. At present, CAC has cooperated with many major domestic and oversea agencies and publishers from Taiwan, Hong Kong, Macao, Russia, US, UK, Germany, France, Japan,

Italy, Australia, Ukraine, Georgia, Brazil, etc., and has established long-standing friendly cooperation relations. It has established a whole set of scientific, standardized and efficient mode of operation and management, acting as agent and signing more than 5 000 copyright trade contracts and has accumulated very rich resources of authors, works and users as well as information of internal and external publication and copyright.

Address: Jia-7 Xirongxi Hutong, Xicheng District, Beijing

♦ Music Copyright Society of China

The MCSC was established on December 17, 1992 by the Chinese Musicians' Association and the National Copyright Administration of China. It is the only officially recognized, non-profit social organization of collective administration of music copyright in China, specially guaranteeing the legal rights and interests of composers, lyrics writers and other copyright owners.

Its functions are as follows: conducting the registration and archive management of the music copyright owner and musical works; collecting royalties that the user of the musical works pays according to law and granting the use of a permission certificate; regularly allotting the usage fees to the music copyright owner; bringing forward the legal negotiation on the conduct of infringing music copyright; developing publicizing activities on music copyright protection. Authorized by the State Copyright Office, the society also assumes the work of collecting and distributing royalties for music works that have gained legal permission. Through signing contracts with the foreign organizations of such kind, it can act as agent to manage and exercise the copyright of foreign music works within China.

The music copyright owner with Chinese nationality, including composer, lyrics writer, adaptor, inheritor of music writer, and the publisher and recorder who has gained the music copyright, can apply to be a member. So far, the society has some 2,500 members and manages over 14 million music works.

The society acceded to the International Confederation of Authors and Composers Societies in May 1994. Under the framework of CISAC it has concluded agreements for reciprocal representation with similar organizations in 36 countries and regions, and incorporated the list of its members and the information of their works into the CAE (International composer, Author, and Educator List) and WWL (World Works List), thus incorporating the works of China's music copyright owners into the International Recognition System. Once any Chinese work is used overseas, its rights and interests can be protected in a timely way.

Address: Floor 5 Jingfang Building, No.33 Dongdan Santiao, Beijing
Website: http://www.mcsc.com.cn

♦ State Intellectual Property Office

With the approval of the State Council, the Patent Office of the People's Republic of China (CPO, the predecessor of SIPO), was founded in 1980 to protect intellectual property rights, encourage invention and creation, help popularize inventions and their exploitation, promote progress and innovation in science and technology, and meet the needs of socialist modernization. In 1998, with the restructuring of the government agencies, CPO was renamed SIPO and became a government institution directly under the State Council. It is the competent authority in charge of patent affairs and the coordinating authority for foreign-related intellectual property issues.

Address: No.6 Tucheng Road West, Jimen Bridge, Haidian District, Beijing
Website: http://www.sipo.gov.cn

♦ National Copyright Administration

The National Copyright Administration is the highest organ of its kind in the country. Set up in 1985, it operates directly under the State Council. It and the General Administration of Press and Publication belong to the same unit.

The main functions and responsibilities:

1. Implement the laws and regulations on copyright and work out the methods concerning the administrative management of the copyright;

2. Investigate and deal with the major cases of the copyright infringement in the country;

3. Authorize the establishment of the collective management institution of copyright, foreign-related agency and supervise and direct their work;

4. Administer the use of works with copyright

5. Take charge of the foreign-related administrative work on copyright

Address: No.85 Dongsi Nandajie, Beijing
Website: http://www.ncac.gov.cn

♦ General Administration of Press and Publication

The main functions and responsibilities are: drafting the protocols of laws and regulations concerning the press and publications sector, study and draw up the principles and policies of the press and publications industry and work out rules on industry management and copyright protection and the key managerial measures, and organize their implementation and supervision; formulate developmental goals for the press and publication industry, namely the objective of macroscopic control and industrial policies; take part in drafting economic policies and related macroeconomic adjustment measures; examine and approve new publishing units (including book publishing houses, audiovisual publishing house and electronic publishing houses, press offices and periodicals offices and so on) and the general issuing units of the publications (including books, newspaper, periodicals, audiovisual products and electronic publications and so on); examine and approve the replication unit of audiovisual products and electronic publication, the journalism group and the collective management and foreign-related agencies and so on; approve the establishment of Sino-foreign joint venture enterprises and Sino-foreign cooperative enterprises in the press and publications industry; implement supervision and management on press and publishing activities (including the publishing, printing or copying and issuing of the publication); investigating and dealing with illegal publications and activities against the laws and regulations of the publishing, printing, copying and issuing units; supervise and manage the printing industry; studying policies of macroscopic readjustment and control and laws and regulations and direct their implementation; investigate and deal with illegal publishing activities and publications; drafting the principles, policies and plans for eliminating pornography and illegal publications in the publication market and coordinate centralized activities of eliminating pornography and illegal publications in the publications market and the investigation and disposal of the major and key cases, and so on.

Address: No.85 Dongsi Dajie South, Dongcheng District, Beijing
Website: http://www.gapp.gov.cn

Foreign Trade

General Situation of Foreign Trade

According to the requirements of the market economy, and in line with its obligations as a WTO member, China is establishing a stable and transparent economic management system, and creating a fair and transparent legal environment. The newly revised Foreign Trade Law of the PRC, which became effective on July 1, 2004, is the basic law guiding China's foreign economic exchanges and trade, as well as the legal basis establishing an economic and trade management system, and the basis for China to establish its foreign economic cooperation management system and for the government to wield its power in the economic and trade fields. And on this basis, a series of supporting measures and rules have been promulgated.

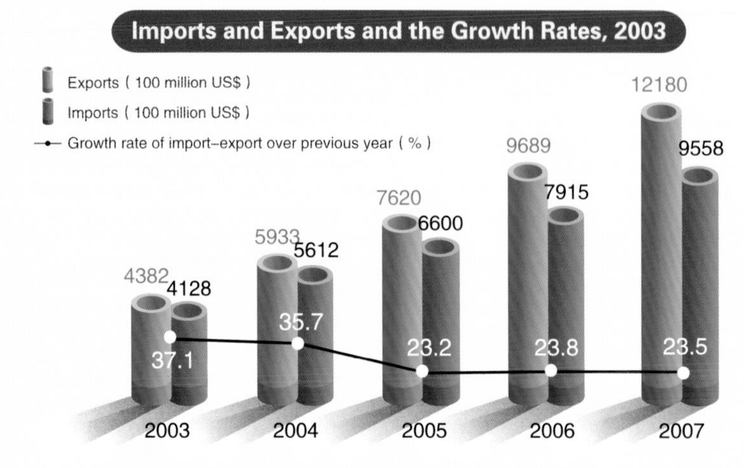

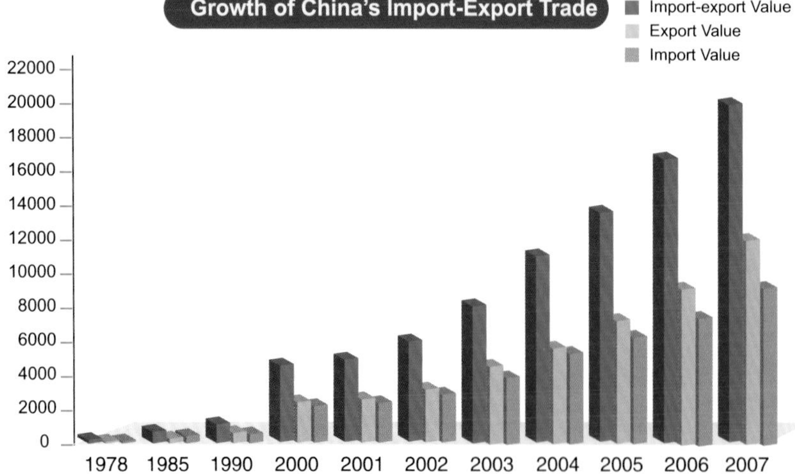

Top 10 Import Sources in 2006

Unit:US$100 million

Rank	Country (Region)	Jan.-Dec.	Increase ± percent	Share ± percent	Change in Share ± percent
	Total Value	7916.1	20.0	100.0	0.0
1	Japan	1157.2	15.2	14.6	-0.6
2	EU	903.2	22.7	11.4	0.2
3	ROK	897.8	16.9	11.3	-0.3
4	ASEAN	895.3	19.4	11.3	-0.1
5	Taiwan	871.1	16.6	11.0	-0.3
6	U.S.A.	592.1	21.8	7.5	0.1
7	Australia	193.2	19.3	2.4	-0.1
8	Russia	175.5	10.5	2.2	-0.2
9	Saudi Arabia	150.8	23.2	1.9	0.0
10	Brazil	129.2	29.3	1.6	0.1

Note: Ranking by total imports and exports.

Top 10 Export Markets in 2006

Unit:US$100 million

Rank	Country (Region)	Jan.-Dec.	Increase ± percent	Share ± percent	Change in Share ± percent
	Total Value	9690.7	27.2	100.0	0.0
1	U.S.A.	2034.7	24.9	21.0	-0.4
2	E.U.	1819.8	26.6	18.8	-0.1
3	Hong Kong	1553.9	24.8	16.0	-0.3
4	Japan	916.4	9.1	9.5	-1.5
5	ASEAN	713.1	28.8	7.4	0.1
6	ROK	445.3	26.8	4.6	0.0
7	Taiwan	207.4	25.3	2.1	-0.1
8	Russia	158.3	19.8	1.6	-0.1
9	Canada	155.2	33.1	1.6	0.1
10	India	145.8	63.2	1.5	0.3

Note: Ranking by total imports and exports.

Top 10 Trading Partner

Unit:US$100 million

Rank	Country (Region)	Jan.-Dec.	Increase ± percent	Share ± percent	Change in Share ± percent
	Total Value	17606.9	23.8	100.0	0.0
1	E.U.	2723.0	25.3	15.5	0.2
2	U.S.A.	2626.8	24.2	14.9	0.0
3	Japan	2073.6	12.5	11.8	-1.2
4	Hong Kong	1661.7	21.6	9.4	-0.2
5	ASEAN	1608.4	23.4	9.1	-0.1
6	ROK	1343.1	20.0	7.6	-0.3
7	Taiwan	1078.4	18.2	6.1	-0.3
8	Russia	333.9	14.7	1.9	-0.1
9	Australia	329.5	20.9	1.9	0.0
10	India	248.6	32.9	1.4	0.1

Note: Ranking by total imports and exports.

State Trade and Authorized Operation

China practices State trade over eight categories of commodities that have a bearing on the national economy and people's livelihood, namely grain, cotton, vegetable oil, edible sugar, crude oil, finished oil, fertilizer and tobacco, and exerts State trade management on the export of tea, rice, maize, soybean, tungsten ores, ammonium paratungState, tungsten products, coal, crude oil, finished oil, silk, unbleached silk, cotton, cotton yarn, cotton woven fabrics, stibium ores, stibium oxide, stibium products and silver.

Non-governmental enterprises are allowed to handle import and export of a certain amount of goods under State trade management.

To safeguard import and export order, foreign economic and trade departments under the State Council may exert authorized operation and management within a specific time limit, that is, authorizing some companies to undertake import and export business of certain products as proxies.

Enterprises or other organizations that are not on the list of State trade enterprises and authorized enterprises cannot engage in State trade management, and import and export of commodities whose operation and management are authorized.

Processing Trade

Processing trade business (including processing with purchased materials and processing with imported materials) is usually examined and approved by the foreign economic and trade departments at provincial level or below. But for processing of edible sugar, cotton, vegetable oil, wool, natural rubber and crude oil which are under State overall balance management, the processing enterprise must apply for examination and approval by the foreign economic and trade department of the province where it is registered.

Chinese Customs exerts systematic management over processing trade according to the classification of commodities. Commodities forbidden from the processing trade refer to those whose import is forbidden by the Foreign Trade Law, and those goods which the customs could not exert bonded inspection; restricted commodities refer to those with a large price gap between the domestic and the international markets, and sensitive commodities; allowed commodities refer to products other than the aforementioned types.

Chinese Customs exerts systematic administration over enterprises engaged in processing trade, and keeps a close eye on the list of these enterprises.

♦ Ministry of Commerce

The main functions and responsibilities of the Ministry of Commerce include: to formulate development strategies, guidelines and policies of domestic and foreign trade and international economic cooperation, draft laws and regulations governing domestic and foreign trade, economic cooperation and foreign investment, devise implementation rules and regulations; to study and put forward proposals on harmonizing domestic legislations on trade and economic affairs as well as bringing Chinese economic and trade laws into conformity with multilateral and bilateral treaties and agreements; to formulate development plans for domestic trade, study and put forward proposals on reforming the commercial distribution system, fosteR&Develop urban and rural markets, promote the restructuring of the commercial distribution sector and the improvement of such modern distribution modalities as chain store operation, modern logistics and e-commerce; to research into and formulate policies for regulating the market operation and distribution order, breaking up market monopoly and regional blockage, to set up and improve an integrated, open, competitive and orderly market system; to monitor and analyze market activities and commodity supply and demand, organize the adjustment of market supply of main consumer goods and regulation of the distribution of major means of production; to study on and work out measures for the regulation of import and export commodities and compile a catalogue thereof, organize the implementation of import and export quota plan, decide on quota quantity and issue licenses; to draft and implement import and export commodity quota tendering policies; to formulate and execute policies concerning trade in technology, State import and export control, and policies encouraging the export of technology and complete set of equipment; to push forward the establishment of foreign trade standardization system; to supervise technology import, equipment import, export of domestic technologies subject to State export restriction and re-export of imported technologies, and to issue export licenses pertaining to nuclear non-proliferation; to study, put forward and implement multilateral and bilateral trade and economic cooperation policies, be responsible for multilateral and bilateral negotiations on trade and economic issues, coordinate domestic positions in negotiating with foreign parties, and to sign the relevant documents and monitor their implementation; to establish multilateral and bilateral intergovernmental liaison mechanisms for economic and trade affairs and organize the related work; to handle major issues in country-specific economic and trade relationships, regulate trade and economic activities with countries without diplomatic relationship with China. In line with the mandate, to handle the relationship with the WTO on behalf of the Chinese government, undertake such responsibilities under the framework of the WTO as multilateral and bilateral negotiations, trade policy reviews, dispute settlement, and notifications and inquires.

Address: No.2 Chang'an Jie East, Beijing
Website: http://www.mofcom.gov.cn/

Border Trade

China supports and encourages development of border trade, and administers it in two ways as the follows:

—Market trading with foreign countries by border residents, which refers to the activities of exchange of commodities by border residents within with a definite value or amount allowed at open or designated country fairs within 20 km of the border. For import of commodities (only limited to articles for daily use) with daily value per capita below 3,000 Yuan, import tax and import linked VAT will be exempted; but for imports exceeding 3,000 Yuan, import tax and import linked VAT will be imposed on the excess.

—Small amount border trade, which refers to the small trading activities of licensed Chinese enterprises with enterprises and other trade organization of neighboring countries through designated inland border ports.

Service Trade

Transportation, tourism, and other commercial services were still the top three items, with total revenue and expenditure scale accounting for four-fifths of the total service trade.

China's service imports and exports still concentrated on tourism and transportation. Among the service industries with high added value, the exports of computer information service, consulting and advertisement and publicity accounted for 3 percent, 9 percent and 2 percent of the total service exports.

Technological Trade

Introducing foreign advanced technology constitutes a major means China adopted during the reform and opening up to upgrade its technologies. According to the Ministry of Commerce, in 2007 China signed 9,773 contracts for the introduction of foreign advanced technology, valued at US$25.42

billion, an increase of 15.6 percent from the previous year. This includes US$19.41 billion for technology fees, or 76.4 percent of the contract value. This marks a historic high.

China introduces mainly complete sets of equipment and key technologies, plus technological services. China imports these mainly from Japan, the United States and EU. The same period saw China begin to export its advanced technology although the work is small.

Foreign advanced technology are introduced mainly by foreign-invested businesses and State-owned enterprises, as well as privately and collectively owned ones.

Electronics as well telecommunications equipment manufacturing, railway transport and transport are the major sectors which introduce foreign advanced technology.

EU was the biggest import source of China's technology import.

Value of technology import by foreign investment enterprises surpassed that of State-owned enterprises.

Major fields of technology import were electronic and telecommunication equipments manufacture, railway transportation and manufacture of transport equipment.

Overseas Investment

Chinese enterprises have made investment in over 160 countries and regions in the world and the fields of their investment cover nearly all business sectors, from export trade, catering business, processing, to distribution network, air logistic service, natural resources exploitation, manufacturing, and research and development.

Multinational mergers and acquisitions are in full swing. Compared with the past, most Chinese enterprises now prefer ODI through mergers and acquisitions. Last year, China made 4.7 billion US dollars of overseas direct investment by merging with or acquiring foreign enterprises, accounting for 37 percent of the total ODI figure.

At present, the total assets of Chinese overseas enterprises (non-financial) exceeded US$200 billion, annual sales of them exceeded US$150 billion and annual profits reached US$17.7 billion.

Provisions on Foreign Investment

In October 2004, the Ministry of Commerce issued the Provisions on the Examination and Approval of Investment to Run Enterprises Abroad, which clearly set forward the principle that "the State shall help and encourage relatively competitive enterprises with various forms of ownership to invest in running enterprises abroad". There are regulations covering enterprises with various forms of ownership to ensure all enjoy equal treatment.

Transportation accounts for most part of the income and expenses of the service trade.

The ministry also promulgated the Provisions on the Examination and Approval of Investment to Run Enterprises Abroad in 2005, abolishing the examination and verification of the feasibility research report and defining the contents required to be examined and verified by the commercial departments in charge at different levels. The contents cover seven aspects such as the investment environment of the country in which the investment is to be made, the security condition, political and economic relations with China, the foreign investment guiding policies of China, the rational layout of the countries (regions), the obligations of carrying out relevant international agreements and guaranteeing the legal interests and rights of the enterprises.

International Contracted Projects

Encouraged by the State policy of "go global", more and more enterprises started to go abroad, with the number and the strength of the overseas project-contracting enterprises increasing constantly. The number of the enterprises with the business qualification of foreign contracted projects and the cooperation of labor services has reached more than 1,600, and there are 1,100 enterprises that have actually engaged in the foreign contracted projects and cooperation in labor services. In 2004, 49 Chinese enterprises contracting projects abroad had entered the list of the top 225 international contractors in the world.

The distribution of the industries in which China's contracted projects overseas are changed a little. The projects still concentrated on such fields as the housing building, transportation, electronic communication, petrochemical and electric power. What worths mentioning is that China's contracted projects made great progress in the new high-tech industries such as electronic communication and environmental protection as the international market demand of these industries increased and the strength of China's relevant industries was stronger.

Relations between China and the World's Economy

China's GDP accounts for less than 4 percent of the world total, but it contributes over 10 percent to world economic growth; the foreign trade of China is less than 6 percent of the world total, but it is contributing 12 percent to the world's trade growth.

From the aspect of the supply, the high quality and cheap products of China reduce the expenses of the importing country and advance the benefit level to consumers. This is particularly true in the United States. A Morgan Stanley report showed that, in the decade to 2005, Chinese products had helped American consumers save more than US$600 billion, with the saving in 2004 alone reaching about US$100 billion.

From the aspect of demand, since its entry into the WTO, China's annual imports have surpassed US$500 billion and helped create or maintain more than 10 million foreign jobs.

From the aspect of investment, an investigation showed that, currently, two-thirds of foreign funded enterprises in China have realized a payoff, and 40 percent of multinational enterprises have achieved profits higher than their global average.

Implementation of the Commitments Made for the Entry into the WTO

In order to implement the commitments made to achieve entry into the WTO, in 2000 and 2001, the National People's Congress amended the Law of the PRC on Chinese-Foreign Joint Ventures and the Law of the PRC on Chinese-Foreign Cooperative Enterprises and the implementation rules, and abolished articles in regard to foreign-funded enterprises maintaining a foreign exchange balance, local content requirements, achievement of a certain level of exports and the record of the production plan. Meanwhile, complete clearance and adjustment was made in the laws and regulations on foreign investment; amendments were also made in regard to contents not in accordance with WTO rules. With regard to the service trade, China had promulgated around 40 laws and regulations covering finance, insurance, trade, distribution, logistics, commerce, communications, tourism and transportation and so on, basically performing on time the promises for opening the service trade.

Since entry, China has observed the rules of the WTO and abided by the promises it originally made so that its market has become more open and standard. According to these promises, China has reduced customs duties year after year, and completely abolished non-tariff measures in 2005. China has also opened up the foreign trade management right, opened the service trade market, enhanced the protection of intellectual property and seriously performed the transparency obligation.

General Level of Tariff

According to China's commitments, its overall tariff level decreased from 14 percent to about 10 percent by 2005. Tariffs on industrial products fell from 13 percent to 9.3 percent; and on agricultural products from 19.9 percent to 15.5 percent. Implementation of tariff concession for agricultural products ended in 2004, while that of tariff concession for 98 percent of industrial products ended in 2005. Tariff concessions for some chemical products will end in 2008. From the January 1, 2005, China abolished most non-tariff measures and the overall tariff level decreased to 9.9 percent.

From July 1, 2006, according to its commitments, China further cut the import tariff rate of automobile parts and components. The customs duty on complete vehicles such as cross-country vehicles and small passenger cars fell from 28 percent to 25 percent, and that of automobile components such as bodies, batholiths, gasoline engines with medium and low cubic capacity fell from 13.8 percent ~16.4 percent to 10 percent. This completed the commitments on the tariff reduction of vehicles and components. At the same time, in the light of the relevant agreement of the China-ASEAN Free Trade Zone, China also reduced tariffs on more than 2,800 commodities originally produced in the Philippines. In order to promote international cooperation and development and help the developing countries, and especially the least-developed countries, to speed up their development, China began to give tariff-free treatment on some commodities of Angola, Yemen, Maldives, Samoa and Vanuatu. Moreover, according to the Supplementary Agreement on the Closer Economic Partnership Agreement between Mainland and HK and Mainland and Macao, China also gave tariff-free treatment on the fourth group of commodities originally produced in Hong Kong and Macao and completed the standard recognition of the place of origin.

Landing-waiters are checking the import and export license.

Non-Tariff Measures and Import-Export Licensing Procedures

China abolished non-tariff measures governing 400-plus tariff codes before January 1, 2005, including quota and license, and the products involved included automobiles, electromechanical products, natural rubber and color sensitive materials.

Starting from January 1, 2005, China abolished import quotas on automobiles and key parts and disc production equipment. Thus, all import quotas imposed on ordinary commodities have been removed, and the government has only retained its import quota licensing management over three specific commodities of chemicals under State control, toxic chemicals and ozone-consuming materials. With the addition of other ordinary commodities freed of control previously, import quota licensing management on ordinary commodities has now been completely removed. This indicates that any enterprise with independent foreign trade rights may apply to import ordinary commodities.

This is the fourth time for China to reduce the number of commodities under management of import quota licensing. Starting from January 1, 2002, it removed import quota management on 14 kinds of ordinary commodities, reducing the number under management to 12. Then, it further reduced to number of eight in 2003 and to two in 2004. Finally, it 2005, the number was reduced to zero.

The List of the Enterprises with Best Brands of Export Commodities

Address	Website
Chunlan (Group) Corporation	www.chunlan.com
Sichuan Chonghong Electrical Appliance Corporation	www.changhong.com
Hisense Group Corporation	www.hisense.com
Nanjing Panda Electronics Group Corporation	www.chinapanda.com
Shandong Xiaoya Group Corporation	www.xiaoyagroup.com
Wuxi Little Swan Corporation	www.littleswan.com
Henan Xinfei Electric Appliance Corporation	www.xinfei.com
Hefei Meiling Corporation	www.meiling.com
Hefei Rongshida Group Corporation	www.rsd.com.cn
Shanghai Fenghuang Import and Export Corporation	www.china-fair.com/2cpzl/sh/shfenghuang
China Jialing Industrial Corporation Group)	www.jialing.com.cn
Construction Industrial (Group) Corporation	www.jianshe.com.cn
Shandong Jincheng Group Corporation	www.jincheng.com
China Qingqi Group Corporation	www.chinaqingqi.net
Shanghai Xingfu Motorcycle General Factory	www.xingfumotor.com
Shenyang Dawn Garments Group Corporation	www.dawn-garments.com
Zhejiang Silk Import and Export Corporation	www.zhejiang-silk.com
Ningbo Youngor Import and Export Corporation	www.youngorgroup.com
Jiangsu Soho International Group Corporation (the original Jiangsu Silk Import and Export Group Corporation)	www.meetsoho.com
Ningbo Shanshan Group Corporation	www.shanshan.com
Ningbo Veken Group Corporation	www.veken.com
Hubei Mailyard Import and Export Trade Corporation	www.globalsources.com/mailyard.com
Jiangsu Sainty Corporation	www.saintycorp.com
Hero (Group) Corporation	www.hero.com.cn
Yantai Polaris Horologe (Group) Corporation	www.asia.globalsources.com
Nanjing International Gifts Corporation	www.porcelaindoll.com
Jiangsu Light Industrial Products Import and Export Group Corporation	www.jslgroup.com
Fujian Light Industrial Products Import and Export Corporation	www.fjlight.com
Zhejiang Wanxiang Group Corporation	www.wanxiang.com.cn
Changchai Corporation	www.changchai.com.cn
White Dove (Group) Corporation	www.white-dove.com (English) www.whitedove.com.cn (Chinese)
The Shandong National Cereals, Oils and foodstuffs Import and Export Corporation of China	www.ceroilfood-shandong.com
China Beijing Tongrentang (Group) Corporation	www.tongrentang.com

• Renaming the Guangzhou Commodities Trade Fair

For the past half-a-century, the Guangzhou Fair has enjoyed an honorary name of "the first fair of China" and acted as a "weather vane" for the country's foreign trade. The official name was changed from "China Export Fair" to "China Import and Export Fair" beginning

The renaming of the event represents China's hard efforts to realize a basic balance between imports and exports. In the "11th Five-Year Plan of Commercial Development" promulgated by the Ministry of Commerce not long before, it was also set forward that the drive for more foreign trade would undergo a major change in thinking towards this basic balance.

Classified Management of the Import of Electromechanical Products

China exerts classified management over the import of electromechanical products under the category of forbidden, restricted and automatic import licensing. For electromechanical products whose imports are restricted, if it is quantitative restriction, quota management applies; if there is no quantitative restriction, such products are called specified electromechanical products, and licensing management will apply. To import specified products, the procurement must be conducted by way of international bidding.

Forbidding or Restricting Import of Commodities

China forbids or restricts import of certain commodities, including weapons, ammunition and explosives, narcotics, narcotic drugs, pornographic materials, and food, drugs and animals and plants that do not meet the technical standards stipulated in Chinese regulations.

International Economic and Trade Treaties and Customs

China has signed bilateral trade agreements or treaties with more than 100 countries and regions, in which the two sides have defined the general principles for trade, while import and export of commodities have been left to the trading companies of the two countries to handle. All payments are made in cash, except for few countries where account settlement is adopted.

Meanwhile, China has participated in many treaties concerning international trade, and accepted and adopted many internationally prevailing practices, regulations or demonstration rules. Such international practices as "Explanatory General Rule of International Commercial Terminology", "Warsaw-Oxford Rules 1932", "Uniform Rules for CT Document", "Uniform Customs and Practice of Documentary Credits" and the "Uniform Rules for Collections" play an important role and influence in China's foreign-related economic and trade activities.

Anti-dumping Policies and Procedures

For imports of commodities by way of dumping or with subsidy that have resulted in substantial damage or threaten such damage to established industries in China, or have constituted physical obstacles to established industries in China, competent governments will, according to the "Anti-Dumping Regulations of the PRC" and "Anti-Subsidy Regulations of the PRC", adopt anti-dumping or anti-subsidy measures.

The Ministry of Commerce is in charge of handling anti-dumping applications, organizing anti-dumping investigations and publicizing the investigation results; according to its investigations and rulings, it puts forward proposals on collecting anti-dumping duties.

In line with the proposal of MOC, the Customs Duties Commission of the State Council decides whether to collect such duties along with the amount and time frame for collection.

The General Administration of Customs is in charge of implementation of anti-dumping measures.

Taking the Market Economy Road

The director-general of the WTO, Pedro Lamy, has said that China's entry to the WTO strengthened the world's multilateral trade system and China had already become one of the most important members. He said that: "Generally speaking, the achievement of China is A+".The stable and forceful growth of China's economy provided broad market opportunities for the countries of the world, brought huge business opportunities for investors and gives great impetus to the economic growth of the world especially that of Asia.

WTO experts have analyzed that China's entry helped promote economic development through trade. At the same time, the economic development also powerfully accelerated the improvement of the market economic system, and accordingly further promoted reforms sought by the government. Entry promoted reform by opening-up and created the internal impetus towards reform. It was said that when China entered into WTO, it amended and abolished more than 2,000 laws, administrative regulations and rules at central government level as well as many local laws and regulations. The newly-established laws and regulations such as the Legislation Law and Procedural Statute on Establishing the Administrative Laws and Regulations promoted further institutionalization and standardization. The Administrative Licensing Law seeks stricter and more concrete requirements on the transparency of governmental behavior.

Popularizing the Concept of Market Economy

For the five years after entering the WTO, with the development of the trade and the easing of trade friction, Chinese officials and domestic enterprises gradually learned and applied the international trade rules to protect themselves and their consciousness and ability in this regard were also enhanced. The concept that the WTO advocated had gradually been perceived by the Chinese people, and the WTO principles such as transparency and non-discriminatory principles had been universally adopted by the foreign trade enterprises of China. The statistical data of the Ministry of Commerce showed that, when facing more and more anti-dumping prosecutions, China also instituted more anti-dumping prosecutions against other countries, vigorously safeguarding domestic industrial safety.

Full Market Economy Status

On November 6-7, 2006, Mali and Gabon successively admitted the full market economy status of China, bringing to 64 the number of countries to do this. The Ministry of Commerce says that, among the 31 countries and areas where China had already launched anti-dumping investigation, 21 had admitted China's full market economic status. Main trade partners such as the US and European Union, which had not admitted China's full market economic status, did set up corresponding working systems with China.

Trade Friction

With the enlargement of the volume of trade, the price of the export products of China went down constantly with the trade condition also increasingly worsening. The latest data of WTO showed that although the anti-dumping cases in the world continued to decline, those towards China increased day by day.

The trade friction condition faced by China has new features: firstly the friction turned from specific cases to the system; secondly, the friction field gradually expanded from the trade in goods to services and from labor-intensive products to other products, and the industry upgraded from the traditional agriculture and textile and automobiles and so on to high technology industries such as electronic information, communications, aircraft manufacture and biotechnology and so on; thirdly, it enlarged from anti-dumping to various trade protection means, adopting the diverse technological trade barrier means including the special protection article 337 intellectual property investigation, quality, technology, health and environmental protection standards and so on; fourthly, it spread from the developed countries to the developing countries. Currently, the number of the anti-dumping cases launched by the developing countries such as India, Brazil and Turkey towards China accounted for 60 percent of the total.

Since China's accession to the WTO, China has adopted rules and regulations for 24 sectors involving anti-dumping, anti-subsidy, guarantee measures, and investigation into trade barriers, forming a fairly complete legal framework.

Opening-up the Telecom Industry

According to the opening-up route map of the communications market regulated for entry into the WTO, China was required to enlarge the maximum foreign share from 33 percent to 49 percent. On January 1, 2002, it promulgated and implemented the Administrative Regulation on Foreign Investment in Telecommunication

Enterprises, according to which, foreign investors could engage in basic telecommunications business and value-added telecommunications business. In the light of the General Agreement on Trade in Services of the WTO, the foreign capital was able to enter the Chinese telecommunications market in the form of joint venture and provide related telecommunications service. In the course of the opening-up of the telecommunications market, China attached more importance to the opening-up in regard to mobile voice and data services, adhering to the gradual opening-up principle, namely opening the value-added telecommunications business first, and then the data and mobile communications and lastly the basic telecommunications business. China would abolish the regional restrictions around 2007 on mobile voice and data services of the basic telecommunications service and other domestic and international business, and the proportion of the foreign capital would be allowed up to 49 percent.

Changes of the Telecommunication

Since the entry into WTO, the opening-up of China's telecommunication industry has not only enabled the industry to develop rapidly but also benefited the public. Currently, it is a very common thing that urban residents of China own a mobile phone; but, in the rural and western areas, more and more people have improved their life through communication means. Not only does China but also the world benefit from its entry into the WTO. By January 1, 2005, all the 256 categories of information technological products had become free of customs duty and other taxes and non-tariff measures were also abolished. In

♦ WTO Notification and Consultation Bureau

The main functions of WTO Notification and Consultation Bureau are: performing the notification obligation undertaken by China in the WTO; implementing the related incumbency of the WTO consultation sites of China; undertaking the relevant affairs of the review system on WTO policies; taking charge of the related work of the transitional review system; taking charge of the technological aid relating to the WTO; undertaking the publicizing and training work relating to the WTO; setting up and managing the databank of Chinese economic and trade policies; taking charge of setting up the notification and consultation liaison sites in the country and directing their work.

Address: No.2 Chang'an Jie East, Beijing

China will open its telecommunications market to the outside world in an gradual way in accordance with its WTO commitments.

the telecommunications business field, China strictly adheres to its commitments in regard to business scope, regional scope, the schedule for opening and the stock rights proportion open to the outside world.

The Opening-up of Commerce

The commerce and trade industries of China opened earlier than other sectors. In 1989, the first KFC fast food restaurant opened in Shanghai. According to commitments to the WTO, China abolished the restrictions in regard to region, shareholdings and so on in 2004. In 2005 alone, the MOC approved 1,027 foreign invested commercial enterprises.

Although in the whole country, the total retail amount of the social commodities only occupied 3 percent, but in major cities like Shanghai, Beijing, Guangzhou, Xiamen and Dalian, foreign-invested stores gathered together to open and increased rapidly. Taking Shanghai as an example, currently the foreign invested enterprises have gained a major presence in various industrial modalities such as large-scale comprehensive supermarkets, shopping centers, convenience stores, family furniture shops, catering, and distribution and so on.

The Opening-up Pattern

The government decided to carry out reform of economic system in 1978, namely, implementing the policy of opening to the outside world in a planned way and step by step. Starting from 1980, the country set up five special economic zones in Shenzhen, Zhuhai and Shantou in South China's Guangdong Province, Xiamen in East China's Fujian Province and the southernmost Hainan Province. In 1984, it opened 14 coastal cities to foreign investors: Dalian, Qinhuangdao, Tianjin, Yantai, Qingdao, Lianyungang, Nantong, Shanghai, Ningbo, Wenzhou, Fuzhou, Guangzhou, Zhanjiang and Beihai. After 1985, the country designated more areas as economic areas open to foreign investment, including the Yangtze River delta, the Pearl River delta, South Fujian Province delta, Shandong Peninsular, Liaodong Peninsular, Hebei and Guangxi, thus forming an economic open zone along the coastal line. In 1990, the

Hong Kong Gome Electrical Appliance

• Top 100 Chain Enterprises

In 2001, China Chain Store and Franchise Association declared the list of the "top 100 chain enterprises of China"; the number of the enterprises each with annual sales income surpassing 14 billion Yuan reached 13. The data of this association also showed that the total retail amount of the social commodities sold in chain stores had already exceeded 10 percent of that of China.

From the list of the "top 100 chain enterprises of China" in the five years, it can be seen that domestic commercial enterprises play a predominant role. The president of Gome Electric Appliances Corporation, Huang Guangyu, noted in 2005, that the number of stores operated by his company throughout the country had increased from 180 to 460. That year saw the complete opening-up of the retail industry for the first time. Depending on abundant capital, management, IT and purchase advantages, a group of multinational giants of the retail industry such as Wal-Mart, Carrefour, METRO and B and Q and so on entered China, which directly challenged domestic companies. For the five years after the entry into WTO, the domestic sector featured a fast increase in scale due primarily to competition. The entry of the foreign capital brought about not only fierce competition, but also introduced advanced management concepts, administrative style and marketing technology and so on, which greatly accelerated the modernization of Chinese commerce. In recent years, the new type industrial modalities such as the chain supermarkets, convenience stores, big-box outlets, shopping centers, dime stores and brand direct sales plazas and so on also appeared, and various management styles such as chain, league and franchise management and so on were also quickly adopted. The domestic leading cities such as Shanghai and so on only spent more than ten years to complete the industrial modality evolution process that took 50 years in developed countries.

♦ General Administration of Customs

China Customs is a government agency that supervises and manages all arrivals and departures from the customs territory of the PRC. China Customs exercises a vertical and three-tiered management structure. The top tier is the General Administration of Customs (i.e. the headquarters in Beijing). The middle tier is composed of the Guangdong Sub-Administration of Customs (in charge of seven customs regions located in Guangdong Province), two supervisory offices (Tianjin and Shanghai), 41 customs regions and two customs educational institutions. The third tier refers to the 562 customs houses or offices under those 41 Customs regions. In addition, it has established overseas offices or based officials in Brussels, Moscow, Washington D.C. and Hong Kong. Its staff numbers over 48,000 (including anti-smuggling police).

According to the Customs Law of the PRC and other relevant laws and regulations, China Customs mainly undertakes four essential tasks: to control inward and outward means of transportation, goods and articles; to collect customs duties, taxes and related charges; to combat smuggling; to compile customs statistics and handle other customs matters. Accordingly, China Customs mainly performs seven functions: clearance operations, revenue collection, processing trade and bond operations, customs statistics compilation, audit-based control, counter-smuggling and port management.

Address: No.6 Jianguo Mennei Dajie, Dongcheng District, Beijing
Website: http://www.customs.gov.com

♦ Department of WTO Affairs, Ministry of Commerce

The main functions and responsibilities are: deal with relations with the WTO on the behalf of China, taking charge of multilateral and bilateral negotiation under the WTO framework WTO including drafting the negotiation scheme, harmonizing the stand and opinions of the related departments of the State Council in the course of negotiations; taking part in the activities of the WTO on the behalf of the Chinese Government and undertaking reviews of the foreign economic trade policies of China in the WTO; putting forward opinions and suggestions in accordance with the regulations and requirements of the WTO in the course of working out the laws, regulations and policies by China; harmonizing and unifying the stand of the bilateral negotiations between the WTO and other international economic and trade organizations and the regional economic and trade organizations that China participates in, and putting forward opinions and suggestions on the aforementioned negotiation scheme; implementing the obligations of circulating the policies, laws and regulations on trade and investment undertaken by China in the WTO and taking charge of the circulation work between governments; undertaking the standard management work of the import and export trade and organizing and harmonizing the research, investigation, statistics and comment work on the foreign technological trade barrier and the corresponding disposals.

Address: No.2 Chang'an Jie East, Beijing
Website: http://www.sms.mofcom.gov.com

government decided to develop and open the Pudong New Area in East China's Shanghai Municipality, opening wider to the outside the cities along the Yangtze River, forming a Yangtze River open zone with Pudong as the head. Since 1992, the country again decided to open a number of cities along the borders, opened capital cities of provinces and autonomous regions in the inland areas, and set up 15 bonded zones, 52 State-class economic and technological development zones and 53 high-tech industry and development zones in some large and medium-sized cities. The moves helped the country to form an all-round, multi-level and wide-ranging pattern of opening to the outside world integrating coastal, riparian, border and inland areas. As these areas adopt different preferential policies; they have served as windows and played a radiation role in developing an export-oriented economy, generating foreign exchange earnings by exporting products and importing advanced technologies.

Economic and Technological Development Zones

China's first group of 14 National Economic and Technological Development Zones (NETDZ) were approved by the State Council and established from 1984 to 1988. An economic and technological development zone should greatly introduce urgently-needed advanced technologies, establishing Sino-foreign equity joint ventures, Sino-foreign contractual joint ventures, solely foreign-invested enterprises and Sino-foreign contractual research institutes, developing joint production, research and design, developing new technologies, manufacturing high-grade products, increasing exports, providing new-type materials and key components to the inland area, and spreading new techniques and technologies and scientific managerial experience. Some development zones should be turned into international carrying trade bases.

The original intention in setting up the national development zones was very clear. The NETDZ's main function was to develop industry and absorb foreign capital. The supporting policies were also made mainly for industrial development. The zones became testing areas for China's industrial modernization.

General Survey of Economic and Technological Development Zones

Building State-level economic and technological development zone was the grand strategic move of China's opening-up. For 20 years, the economic and technological zones of China constantly developed from the coastal areas to the hinterland. From January to September of 2006, the industrial output value, exports and actually utilized foreign investment of 54 national-class development zones, covering 842 square kilometers approved by the State Council, accounted for 9.51 percent, 15.88 percent and 25.4 percent of China's total, respectively. The average industrial output value, exports and actually utilized foreign investment per square kilometer stood at 2.422 billion Yuan, US$116 million and US$12 million, respectively, up 23.74 percent, 24.43 percent and 11.95 percent over the previous year. Their development level improved further.

Export Processing Zone

In order to promote the development of processing trade and standardize the management of the processing trade, the State changed the processing trade from the distribution type to a comparatively concentrated one and provided the enterprises with a looser management environment to encourage the enlargement of the foreign trade exports. On April 27, 2000, the State Council formally approved the setting up of the export processing zones.

Since May 2000, the State Council had authorized 59 export processing zones, and 42 of them have been put into operation. At present, the total volume of foreign trade of the export processing zones accounts for over 8 percent of the national processing trade; in areas such as Shanghai and Jiangsu Province where the export processing zones are densely distributed, the trade volume accounted for 32 percent and 15 percent respectively.

Main Export Processing Zones

City	Address	Website
Beijing	Beijing Tianzhu Export Processing Zone	www.chinabaiz.com
Hebei	Qinhuangdao Export Processing Zone	www.qetdz.com.cn
Liaoning	Dalian Export Processing Zone	www.dlftz.gov.cn
Tianjin	Tianjin Export Processing Zone	www.teda.gov.cn
Anhui	Wuhu Export Processing Zone	www.weda.gov.cn
Shandong	Yantai Export Processing Zone	www.yantaiepz.gov.cn
	Weihai Export Processing Zone	www.whckigq.51.net
Jiangsu	Kunshan Export Processing Zone	www.ketd.gov.cn
	The Export Processing Zone of Suzhou Industrial Park	www.sipac.gov.cn
	Wuxi Export Processing Zone	www.wnd.gov.cn
	Nantong Export Processing Zone	www.netda.com
Shanghai	Shanghai Songjiang Export Processing Zone	www.sjepz.com
	Jinqiao Export Processing Zone	www.goldenbridge.sh.cn
Zhejiang	Hangzhou Export Processing Zone	www.hetz.gov.cn/chinese/ckjgq/tzys.asp
	Ningbo Export Processing Zone	www.nftz.gov.cn/
Fujian	Xiamen Export Processing Zone	www.xmckjgq.com/www/nv/
Henan	Zhengzhou Export Processing Zone	www.zzepz.gov.cn
Guangdong	Guangzhou Export Processing Zone	www.getdd.com.cn/get-x/
	Shenzhen Export Processing Zone	www.szgiz.gov.cn/epz/cn/index.htm
Hubei	Wuhan Export Processing Zone	www.wuhan114.com.cn/wuhan114/wsxh/touzi/03.htm
Jilin	Huichun Export Processing Zone	www.hcexport.com/
Sichuan	Chengdu Export Processing Zone	www.scepz.gov.cn/
Shaanxi	Xi'an Export Processing Zone	www.xetdz.com.cn/jsp/index07-02.jsp
Chongqing	Chongqing Export Processing Zone	www.cetz.com/test/ck.htm

Foreign-related Economic Laws and Regulations

After entering the WTO, the government seriously performed its commitments and constantly accelerated the opening-up. In the light of the commitments to the WTO, China successively promulgated laws, regulations and rules of more than 30 open markets covering dozens of fields such as finance, distribution, logistics, tourism and architecture and so on, lowered the admission standard of related industries, and cleared and amended about 3,000 laws, regulations and rules of departments. It basically perfected the legal system of the opening-up of the service trade and formed a new pattern of the complete opening-up of the service trade. Up to the present, China has established a complete foreign trade legal system with the "Foreign Trade Law of the PRC" at the core.

Foreign Trade Law

This became effective on July 1, 2004 as the basic law for standardizing foreign trade activities. Foreign trade covers the import and export of goods, technologies and the international trade in services. This law applies to foreign trade as well as protection of intellectual property rights. It regulates that the State shall apply the foreign trade system on a uniform basis and maintains a fair and free foreign trade order in accordance with law. The PRC promotes and develops trade ties with other countries and regions, signs or participates in such regional economic and trade agreements as CUA and FTA, and joins in regional economic organizations on the principle of equality and mutual benefit. Under the international treaties or agreements to which it is a contracting or participating party, the PRC grants other contracting or participating parties, under the principles of mutual advantage and reciprocity, most-favored-nation treatment or national treatment within the field of foreign trade. In the event that any country or region applies discriminatory prohibitions, restrictions or other like measures against the PRC in regard to trade, the latter may adopt countermeasures.

Rules on Management of Foreign Trade Operators

Besides the stipulations of Foreign Trade Law, this is also covered by the Regulations on Management of Qualification of Importers and Exporters.

Rules on Management of Imported and Exported Commodities

This is primarily covered by the Regulations of the PRC on the Management of Imported and Exported Commodities. Other important rules are: Measures on the Management of Goods Export Licenses and Measures on the Management of Goods Import Licenses and the corresponding catalogue of goods with import and export licenses, Regulations of the People's Republic of China for the Environmental Management on the First Import of Chemicals and the Import and Export of Toxic Chemicals and the implementing rules, Interim Regulations for Environmental Protection on Import of Wastes and so on.

Laws and Regulations Governing Inspection of Imported and Exported Commodities

This mainly involves the Law of the PRC on Commodity Inspection and implementing regulations.

Laws and Regulations Governing Quarantine of Animals and Plants

This mainly involves the Law of the PRC on Entry and Exit of Animal and Plant Quarantine and implementing regulations.

Laws and Regulations Governing Health Quarantine

This mainly involves the Frontier Health and Quarantine Law of the PRC and implementing regulations, Food Hygiene Law of the PRC and Measures on the Management of Pharmaceutical Imports, and so on.

Laws and Regulations on Foreign Exchange Control

The basic law is the Regulations of the PRC on the Foreign Exchange System. Other major rules and regulations: Circular of the People's Bank of China on Further Reforming the Foreign Exchange System, Regulations on Foreign Exchange Sales, Purchase and Payment, and Measures on Management of Foreign Exchange Settlement under the Current Account, and so on.

Customs Laws and Regulations

This mainly involves the Customs Law of the PRC, Regulations of the PRC on the Customs Protection of Intellectual Property Rights, and Regulations of the PRC on the Inspection Conducted by Customs, and so on.

Tariff Laws and Regulations

Regulations of the PRC on Import and Export Duties

Foreign-related Civil and Commercial laws

As China opens wider to the outside world, the country is increasingly paying attention to legislation of foreign-related civil and commercial laws. The Law of the PRC on Economic Contracts Concerning Foreign Interests was promulgated on March 21, 1985. This is the first legislation concerning economic and trade contracts in China. On April 21, 1986, the General Provisions of Civil Law were promulgated, an important step for China in the field of civil and commercial legislation.

Utilization of Foreign Funds

Investment in China (2006)

By the end of 2006, China has more than 590,000 foreign-invested enterprises with the actually utilized foreign investment exceeding US$700 billion. As the China's environment for utilizing foreign investment improved increasingly and the attraction for the foreign investment increased, China has exceeded the USA for the first time as the first choice place for the multinationals S and D center according to the survey report released by the UN Trade and Development Conference.

The foreign investment in the east and west China increased faster, making the area distribution imbalanced in this regard.

The growth of the wholesale and retail trade in attracting the FDI was fastest. The real estate industry was in the second place.

The top ten countries and regions in the amount actually invested in Chinese mainland were in turn: China Hong Kong (US$20.233 billion), British Virgin Islands (US$11.248 billion), Japan (US$4.598 billion), South Korea (US$3.895 billion), the US (US$2.865 billion), Singapore (US$2.26 billion), Chinese Taiwan (US$2.136 billion), Cayman Islands (US$2.095 billion), Germany (US$1.979 billion), and Samoa (US$1.538 billion). The total investment of them accounted for 83.86 percent of China's actually utilized foreign investment in the non-financial field, and 83.96 percent of China's total.

Policies on the Foreign Investment

According to the commitment to the WTO, in 2002, the government readjusted the Indicative Catalog of Industries for Foreign Investment, enlarged the opening-up field and encouraged foreign businessmen to invest in high technology and high added value fields. In August 2004, the government promulgated the newly-amended Catalog of Advantaged Industries for Foreign Investment in Central and Western China, and further encouraged foreign businessmen to invest in the areas. In June 2005, the government issued the Implementation Opinions of the General Office of the State Council On Further Promoting the Expanding of Opening up to the Outside World of the Old Industrial Bases in Northeast China, and created more advantageous conditions for foreign businessmen to increase their investment in the region.

Regional Policies

China's opening to the outside world first started in eastern coastal areas, and then pushed to the inland areas in stages. Eastern China boasts a sound investment environment and more preferential policies as most of the reform measures and polices were first carried there. The country's five special economic zones, 14 coastal open cities and Shanghai Pudong New Area are all in the eastern part of the country. Up to now, most of the foreign-funded enterprises are located in these areas, with very few in central and west parts of the country.

In recent years, as the country has moved its focus on economic development strategy westward, the government has worked out policies and measures to support development of central and western China, and has increased investment in the areas to step up construction of infrastructure facilities for water conservancy, transportation and communications. While supporting East China to develop capital- and technology-intensive industries and export-oriented production, the government has made active efforts to direct and encourage foreign businesses to invest in the more remote hinterland.

Top Ten Countries and Regions that have the Largest Actual Amount of Investment in Mainland China

Unit: (US$100 million)

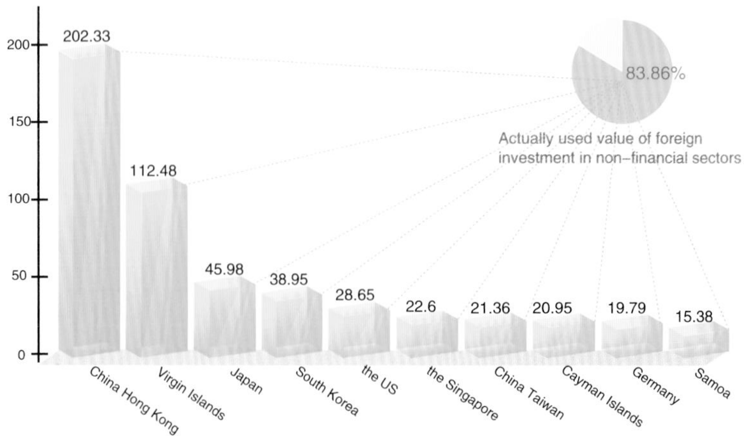

Qianmen Store, the first store set up by the KFC

07 Economy

Fujian Dehua Hiap Huat Koyo Toki Ceramic Co., Ltd. —a wholly foreign-funed enterprise

Policies Concerning Encouraging Foreign Businessmen to Invest in Central and Western Parts of the Country

—Drafting and promulgating the Catalog of Advantaged Industries for Foreign Investment in Central and Western China. Projects listed in the catalog enjoy the policies under the encouragement category of the Indicative Catalog of Industries for Foreign Investment.

—Foreign-invested enterprises under the encouragement category launched in central and western parts of the country can enjoy a 15 percent reduction of corporate income tax for three years after the expiration of the implementation period of the existing tax preferential policy.

—Foreign-funded enterprises launching new investment projects in central and western parts can enjoy corresponding preferential treatment for foreign-funded enterprises on condition that they have a foreign-funded contribution exceeding 25 percent.

—Pilot work in areas and projects permitted by the State for opening to foreign investment can be conducted in central and western areas spontaneously in principle.

—Foreign-funded enterprises from coastal areas are permitted to operate foreign-funded enterprises and domestic capital enterprises on contract management terms in central and western China.

Policies Concerning Encouraging Foreign Businessmen to Invest in the Old Industrial Bases of Northeast China

Like the western development strategy, the government is now working on rejuvenating northeast China, which is an important strategic measure in economic development. It encourages foreign investors to invest in the process of transformation of the former heavy industrial base in the northeast. To further promote participation of foreign investors in transformation of State-owned enterprises, learn from foreign advanced technology and management experience and realize rational allocation of resources, the government produced Interim Regulations on Foreign Enterprises Investing in and Acquiring Domestic Enterprises, encouraging the use of the method of transnational merger and acquisition generally used internationally to attract foreign funds, allowing foreign enterprises to acquire domestic enterprises by purchase of stock rights, and simplifying related examination and approval procedures. At the same time, governments of the three provinces, Liaoning, Jilin and Heilongjiang, in Northeast China have announced preferential policies to attract foreign investment according to actual conditions in the area.

Financial Support for the Foreign-invested Enterprises

1. Foreign-invested enterprises (FIE) which need to raise part of the funds for production and operation can apply for loans from banks in China according to the domestic laws and regulations, and enjoy the same treatment as domestic capital enterprises in terms, interest rates and service charges. Foreign-investment enterprises can borrow money directly from foreign banks so long as they complete the related foreign debt registration procedure, and the borrowed foreign exchange funds are reported to the State Administration of Exchange Control (SAEC) for record.

2. When FIE raise funds domestically, Chinese commercial banks are permitted to become the guarantor of stockholders' rights as entrusted by foreign companies. FIE are permitted to apply for Renminbi loans from designated Chinese banks in the form of exchange hypothecation. All foreign exchange funds of FIE can be used as hypothecation. Overseas financial institutions or foreign financial institutions in China can provide credit security for Renminbi loans under exchange hypothecation. The government has canceled the special restriction on registration procedures under exchange hypothecation and guarantee items, and special restrictions on providing credit grades for foreign banks for exchange guarantee. Renminbi loans with foreign shareholder guarantee and exchange guarantee shall be issued in conformity with industry policy, which can be used to satisfy the need of fixed asset investment and working funds, but not allowed to be used for exchange purchase.

3. The country has set up a special industrial investment fund to make up the present shortage of share capital of the Chinese side when FIE make additional investments. At the same time, Chinese commercial banks are allowed to issue a certain proportion of share capital loans to Chinese shareholder under the prerequisite of the additional share capital of foreign shareholders in Sino-foreign joint venture and cooperation enterprises being available at the same time.

4. The country permits FIE to provide hypothecation to overseas branches of Chinese banks with the overseas assets of foreign investors to get loans from branches at home and abroad of Chinese commercial banks.

5. FIE which have met the requirement can apply for floating shares on China's A-share and B-share stock markets.

6. The country provides insurance service in such fields as political risk, performance and guarantee to foreign investors investing in areas of State priority support including energy and transportation by following a steady and proactive principle.

Basic Forms of Foreign Direct Investment

China's utilization of foreign funds is generally divided into two parts, namely direct Investment form and other investment forms. The most used form is the direct investment, covering Sino-foreign joint venture enterprise, Sino-foreign cooperation enterprise, wholly foreign owned enterprise and joint development. Other investment forms cover compensation trade and processing and assembling.

Sino-foreign Joint Venture Enterprise

Sino-foreign joint venture enterprises also called equity joint venture enterprises, are launched in China by foreign companies, enterprises and other economic organizations and individuals in cooperation with Chinese companies, enterprises and other economic organizations. They feature joint investment and operation, and risk and profit and loss sharing. The contributions of various partners in the joint venture are converted into certain stakes, with the foreign partner required to make a contribution of no less than 25 percent.

The Sino-foreign joint venture enterprise is a form first and most often used in utilization of FDI. It has taken the lion's share in the country's utilization of foreign funds.

Sino-foreign Cooperation Enterprise

The Sino-foreign cooperation enterprise, also called a contract cooperation enterprise, is an enterprise launched in China by foreign companies, enterprises and other economic organizations in cooperation with Chinese companies, enterprises and other economic organizations by joint investment or providing cooperative conditions. The rights and obligations of the various sides are defined in the contract they sign. Foreign cooperation partners usually provide all or most of the funds while the Chinese side provides land, buildings, equipment and facilities, and a certain amount of funds in some cases.

Wholly Foreign Owned Enterprise

The wholly foreign owned enterprise refers to one founded by foreign companies, enterprises, other economic organizations and individuals in China according to related laws and regulations with all the investment by self-owned funds. According to the foreign enterprise law, founding a foreign enterprise in China is required to be good for national development and meet at least one of the following conditions: adopting advanced world technology and equipment; and exporting all or most of the products. Such an enterprise is generally launched in the form of a limited company.

Joint Development

Join development is a short cut for onshore and offshore petroleum exploitation and development. It is one of the economic cooperation forms generally used in the world in the field of development of natural resources. It has the features of high risk, and high investment and potential yield. Joint development is generally divided into three stages, namely, exploitation, development and production. Compared with other methods, joint development forms a very small proportion in the total use of foreign investment.

New Investment Forms

1. BOT: China has started using BOT in launching infrastructure facilities projects.

2. Investment company: the Ministry of Foreign Economic Relations and Trade issued the Interim Regulation on Foreign Businesses Investing in Investment Companies in April 1995 in a bid to encourage big overseas companies to launch their series investment plans.

3. Foreign-invested equity company: This can be founded by sponsorship or placement. Existing foreign-invested companies of limited liability can apply to become equity companies.

4. Acquisition and merger: Transnational acquisition and merger have become a main form of direct foreign investment. At present, China is studying and drafting related policies.

Laws Concerning Foreign Investment

Laws and regulations concerning foreign-invested enterprises include three basic laws and their implementation bylaws, namely, the Law on Sino-Foreign Joint Venture Enterprises of the PRC, the Law on Sino-Foreign Cooperation Enterprises of the PRC, and the Law on Foreign Capital Enterprises of the PRC. Foreign-invested companies of limited liability are adaptable to the Corporate Law of the PRC and related stipulations in the above legal documents. The contracts of foreign-invested enterprises come under China's Contract Law.

Chinese-foreign jointly developed QHD32-6 Oilfield

Chinese and foreign businessmen are talking at the foreign investment fair.

China had ten new and amended economic laws and regulations becoming effective on June 1, 2004. Changes and stipulations made in the laws and regulations concerning foreign businesses mainly include:

—Abolishing regional restriction for foreign commercial enterprises in wholesale services: According to the Administration Rules on Foreign Companies Investing in the Commercial Sector issued in April 2004, foreign companies, enterprises and other economic organizations and individuals shall abide by the rules in founding foreign-funded commercial enterprises and operations.

—Allowing foreign businesses to set up shipping enterprises in China. The Administrative Regulations Concerning Foreign Companies Investing in the International Shipping Industry standardizes the administration of foreign-invested enterprises engaging in international ocean shipping services in China and the subsidiary operation business concerning international ocean shipping.

—In order to keep abreast of the revised Foreign Trade Law, the State Council, starting from April 15, 2004, amended the Anti-Dumping Regulations, the Anti-Subsidy Law and the Safeguard Measures Rules. After the amendments, the three major trade relief documents became effective on June 1.

Bilateral Investment Protection Agreement

Since 1982, China has signed investment protection agreements with 106 countries, including Britain, Germany, France, Japan, Australia and the Republic of Korea (ROK), of which more than 50 percent have become effective.

According to China's laws, investment protection agreement is in the scope of international treaty which has stronger legal force than that of domestic legislation.

Bilateral Taxation Agreement

To solve the taxation issue with other countries, starting from September 1983, the government has signed all-round agreements on double tax avoidance and tax evasion prevention with such countries as Japan and France. By the end of 2004, China had signed agreements on double taxation with 85 countries, of which 76 have become effective.

Establishing Representative Office in China

Application for setting up permanent representative organs in China by foreign enterprises shall be approved by the following departments according to features of different sectors:

1. Trade, manufacturing and cargo shipping agent firms report to the Ministry of Commerce for approval;
2. Banking, securities and insurance companies report to the country's supervision and administration commission of banking, securities and insurance industries for approval;
3. Ocean shipping and ocean shipping agent firms report to the Ministry of Communications for approval.
4. Air transportation report to the Civil Aviation Administration of China (CAAC) for approval.
5. Other industries report to competent commissions, ministries and administrations of the Chinese Government on the basis of different business features of the industries.

Opening-up of the Service Field

On December 11, 2004, except for a few exceptional products, commercial circles abolished the restrictions on the number, regional distribution and shareholding proportion of foreign-invested enterprises, and began to shift to complete opening-up.

In 2005, there are the businessmen from 81 countries and regions such as Hong Kong, the US, Japan, South Korea, and Taiwan Province who invested in China's commercial field. The total amount of the top ten countries and regions in China's commercial field accounted for 78.75 percent of the total in this regard. Calculated by the contracted foreign investment, the provinces or cities which attracted the most foreign investment in the commercial field were Tianjin, Shanghai, Liaoning and Guangdong.

Industrial Policies

With the endorsement of the State Council, the National Development and Reform Commission and the Ministry of Commerce jointly issued the Indicative Catalog of Industries for Foreign Investment (2007 revision) which went into effect on December 1, 2007. The new Catalog cover five aspects: (1) Opening wider to the outside world and striving for industrial upgrading. For the manufacturing industry, foreign businesses are encouraged to invest in high and new industries, equipment manufacturing and production of new raw and semi-finished materials. For the service industry, the Catalog shows the Chinese effort to honor words it made for WTO accession. In the meantime, it says efforts will be made to open wider to the outside world. New encouraging contents include "contracted service" and "modern logistics", and it has also cut the number of categories restricted or prohibited. Foreign businesses are not encouraged to invest in traditional manufacturing sector where domestic technology is mature and domestic factories boast good production capacity. The Catalog makes it clear the restrictive items apply to foreign-invested businesses. (2) Economizing the use of resources and protecting the environment. Foreign businesses are encouraged to invest in development of circular economy, clean production, recyclable energy and protection of eco-environment, as well as the comprehensive utilization of resources. The Catalog includes some new items for this purpose. Foreign businesses are not encouraged to invest in major mineral resources which China is in short or could no re-produce. Foreign businesses are not allowed to invest in minerals prospecting and exploitation; they are restricted or prohibited to be involved in undertaking projects featuring high consumption of raw materials and energy and causing serious pollution. (3) Readjusting the policy geared to encourage pure exports. Given the fact that China enjoyed big favorable balance and the fast increase in foreign exchange reserves, China suspends implementation of the policy geared to purely encourage exports. (4) Promoting coordinated regional development. In coordination with the western region development, the rise of central China and the rejuvenation of the old industrial bases in northeast China, the revised Catalog does not include any items to be undertaken only in central and west China. (5) Defending national economic security. Some industries related to national economic security strategy or are sensitive shall be opened in a prudent way; related items shall be adjusted for further development.

Ningbo Export Processing Area

♦ China Association of Enterprises with Foreign Investment

Founded in November 1987 in Beijing upon registration at the Ministry of Civil Affairs, the China Association of Enterprises with Foreign Investment (CAEFI), is a nationwide non-profit social entity reporting to the Ministry of Commerce mainly composed of companies in the territory of the Chinese mainland with foreign investment or investment from Hong Kong, Macao, Taiwan and overseas compatriots.

Website: http//: caefi.mofcom.gov.cn

National Defense

National Defense Policy

China sticks to the peaceful development road and pursues a national defense policy which is purely defensive in nature.

The fundamental targets and major tasks of China's national defense policy are defined as follows:

——Upholding national security and unity, and ensure the interests of national development. This includes guarding against and resisting aggression, defending against violation of China's territorial sea and air space, and borders; opposing and containing the separatist forces for "Taiwan independence" and their activities, taking precautions against and cracking down on terrorism, separatism and extremism in all forms.

——Achieving the all-round, coordinated and sustainable development of China's national defense and armed forces. China pursues a policy of coordinated development of national defense and economy and builds up a modernized national defense conforming to the situation of China and the world military developing trend.

——Enhancing the performance of the armed forces with informationization as the major measuring criterion. The PLA pursues a strategy of strengthening itself by means of science and technology, and works to enhance the defending and war fighting capabilities under the condition of informationization.

——Implementing the military strategy of active defense.

——Pursuing a self-defensive nuclear strategy. China's nuclear strategy is subject to the state's nuclear policy and military strategy. Its fundamental goal is to deter other countries from using or threatening to use nuclear weapons against China. China remains firmly committed to the policy of no first use of nuclear weapons at any time and under any circumstances. It unconditionally undertakes not to use or threaten to use nuclear weapons against non-nuclear-weapon states or nuclear-weapon-free zones, and stands for the comprehensive prohibition and complete elimination of nuclear weapons.

——Fostering a security environment conducive to China's peaceful development.

The copper,gold plated peace pigeon presented by the UN Secretary-general Javier Perez de Cuellar to Chinese leader Deng Xiaoping in May 1987

China maintains military contacts with other countries on the basis of the Five Principles of Peaceful Coexistence, and develops cooperative military relations that are non-aligned, non-confrontational and not directed against any third party.

A New Security Concept

To foster a long-term stable, secure and reliable international peaceful environment, China persists in advocating a new security concept featuring mutual trust, mutual benefit, equality and coordination. The new security concept was first formally proposed on the speech entitled Make a Joint Endeavor to Build a Fair and Reasonable International Order by Chinese leader on the Duma of Russian Federation on April 23, 1997. In nature the new security concept is to exceed unilateral security category and pursue common security on the basis of mutual benefit and cooperation.

Mutual trust means to exceed different ideologies and social systems, throw away the thought of cold war and power politics, and not to be suspicious or hostile to others. Every country should often make dialogue and notification with each other on its security defense policy and significant activities.

Mutual benefit means to comply with the objective requirements of social development in the time of globalization, respect each other's security interests, and create conditions for each other on the basis of realizing its own security interests and realize common security.

Equality means that every country, no matter how it is big, small, powerful or weak, is a member of the international community, should respect and treat each other equally, should not intervene other country's internal affairs, and promote the democratization of the international relationship.

Coordination means to solve disputes by means of peaceful negotiation and conduct wide and profound cooperation on the security issues concerned by all to eliminate hidden troubles and prevent war and conflict.

The Chinese Government considers that the cooperation mode of the new security concept should be flexible and diversified, including multilateral security system with comparatively strong binding force, multilateral security dialogue with the nature of forum, bilateral security negotiation targeting at enhanced mutual trust, and non-governmental security dialogue with academic nature. To accelerate the integration of economic interests is also one of the effective ways to maintain security.

China's National Defense Policy

☆ Upholding national security and unity, and ensure the interests of national development.

☆ Achieving the all-round, coordinated and sustainable development of China's national defense and armed forces.

☆ Enhancing the performance of the armed forces with informationization as the major measuring criterion.

☆ Implementing the military strategy of active defense.

☆ Pursuing a self-defensive nuclear strategy.

☆ Fostering a security environment conducive to China's peaceful development.

♦ Central Military Commission (CMC)

The CMC of the PRC directs China's armed forces. It has the following functions and powers: deciding on the military strategy and operational guidelines of the armed forces, directing and administering the building of the PLA, submitting proposals related to national defense to the NPC or its Standing Committee, formulating military regulations, issuing decisions and orders, deciding on the structure and organization of the PLA, appointing and removing, training, evaluating, and rewarding and punishing members of the armed forces, approving systems and development programs and plans for weaponry and armaments, and exercising other functions and powers as prescribed by law.

The CMC is composed of the chairman, vice-chairmen and several members; the CMC chairman has overall responsibility for its work; the NPC elects the chairman of the CMC of the PRC and, upon nomination by the chairman, decides on the choice of all other members of the CMC. The tenure of the CMC is the same with that of the NPC; and the CMC chairman is responsible for the NPC and its Standing Committee. Under the leading of the CMC, the PLA consists of the leadership organizations such as headquarters, armed services, arms of the services, and military area commands; and in the Chinese People's Armed Police Force there is a General Headquarters.

♦ Ministry of National Defense

The Ministry of National Defense (MND) is the military department under the State Council of the PRC for directing and administering the national defense building. All the military work charged by the government is decided by the State Council and implemented by the MND or by the name of the MND. The MND is responsible for both the State Council and the CMC. Its concrete work is handled respectively by the General Staff Headquarters, the General Political Department, the General Logistics Department and the General Armaments Department. It is prescribed by the Constitution of the PRC of 1982 that the NPC decides on the choice of the minister of the MND upon the domination of the Premier of the State Council; and when the NPC is in recess, the Standing Committee decides on the choice upon the domination of the Premier of the State Council.

A Leadership and Administration System for National Defense

China's armed forces are under the leadership of the Communist Party of China (CPC). The Central Military Commission (CMC) of the CPC and that of the People's Republic of China (PRC) are completely the same in their composition and in their function of exercising leadership over the armed forces. The CMC chairman has overall responsibility for its work.

The National People's Congress (NPC) elects the chairman of the CMC of the PRC and, upon nomination by the chairman, decides on the choice of all other members of the CMC. The NPC decides on war and peace and exercises other functions and powers relating to national defense as prescribed by the Constitution. When the NPC is in recess, its Standing Committee decides on the proclamation of a state of war, decides on the general or partial mobilization of the country, and exercises other functions and powers relating to national defense as prescribed by the Constitution. The president of the PRC, in pursuance of the decisions of the NPC and its Standing Committee, may proclaim a state of war, issue mobilization orders, and exercise other functions and powers relating to national defense as prescribed by the Constitution.

The State Council directs and administers national defense building in the following areas: making national defense development programs and plans, formulating principles, policies and administrative regulations for defense building, administering defense expenditure and assets, directing and administering national defense scientific research and production, directing and administering work related to mobilization of the national economy, mobilization of people's armed forces, people's air defense and national defense traffic, directing and administering the work of supporting the military and giving preferential treatment to families of servicemen and martyrs, as well as the resettlement of servicemen discharged from active service. It also directs national defense education and, jointly with the CMC, the building of the Chinese People's Armed Police Force (PAPF) and the militia, the work concerning enlistment and reserve service, and the administration of border, coastal and air defenses, and exercises other functions and powers relating to national defense building as prescribed by law. Under the State Council are the Ministry of National Defense (MND) and other departments concerning national defense building.

The CMC directs and exercises unified command of China's armed forces. It has the following functions and powers: deciding on the military strategy and operational guidelines of the armed forces, directing and administering the building of the PLA, submitting proposals related to national defense to the NPC or its Standing Committee, formulating military regulations, issuing decisions and orders, deciding on the structure and organization of the PLA, appointing and removing, training, evaluating, and rewarding and punishing members of the armed forces, approving systems and development programs and plans for weaponry and armaments, and exercising other functions and powers as prescribed by law.

The PLA's General Staff Headquarters, General Political Department, General Logistics Department and General Armaments Department are departments of the CMC respectively responsible for military, political, logistical and armaments work.

General Headquarters of the Chinese People's Liberation Army

The general headquarters of the PLA is composed of the General Staff Headquarters, the General Political Department, the General Logistics Department and the General Armaments Department, respectively responsible for military, political, logistical and armaments work.

General Staff Headquarters

The General Staff Headquarters, a military functional department under the CMC, is the leading unit of the work of all the armed forces in China. It organizes and directs the development of China's armed forces, and organizes and commands their military operations. Under it are departments in charge of operations, intelligence, communications, military training and arms, adjutant and force structure, mobilization, electronic countermeasures, Army aviation, foreign affairs, etc.

Its main functions and powers are to put forward proposals on major issues of military building and operations, organize and exercise strategic command, formulate programs, rules and regulations for military work, and organize and direct war preparations, as well as military training and mobilization.

♦ Military Area Commands

Military area commands (theaters of war) are military organizations set up according to the administrative divisions of the State, geographical locations, strategic and operational directions, and operational tasks. They are CMC-appointed organs for commanding joint theater operations. They direct the military, political, logistical and armaments work of the troops under them. Under a military area command are the headquarters, the political department, the joint logistics department and the armaments department. A military area command is mainly in charge of formulating programs and plans for combat readiness and operations of troops in the theater and for the reserve force buildup of the theater, organizing and commanding joint theater operations involving different services and arms, and providing joint logistical support. At present, the PLA has seven military area commands, namely, Shenyang, Beijing, Lanzhou, Jinan, Nanjing, Guangzhou and Chengdu. Under a military area command are combined Army corps, units of various Army arms, logistical support units and provincial military commands (garrison commands at the same level).

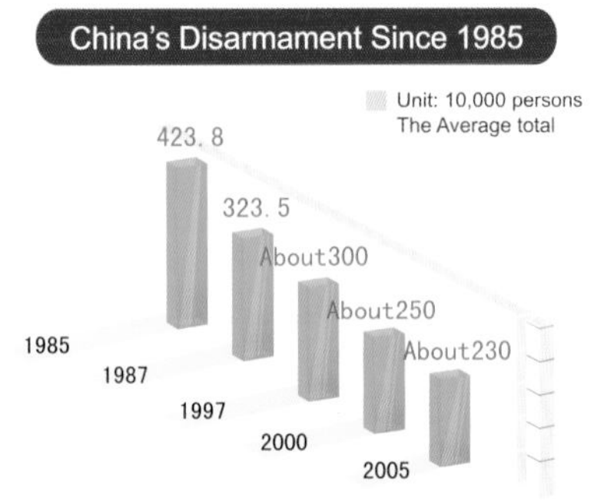

• China's Large-scale Reduction of Military Personnel

China has pursued a national defense policy that is defensive in nature. Under the premise of ensuring national security interests, China has always kept the quantity and size of its armed forces at the minimum level necessary for maintaining national security and has for many times taken the initiative to adopt unilateral disarmament.

In the period from the end of May to early June in 1985, China made decision to downsize its military personnel by 1 million. The emphasis was put upon cutting headquarters, armed services and arms of services, large military area commands, bodies of the Commission of Science, Technology and Industry for National Defense (COSTIND), and units directly under the command of COSTIND; canceling and combining some military colleges; reducing the number of positions of deputies at all levels and transferring 76 kinds of posts in organs and troops from the shoulders of officers to soldiers; transferring Armed Police Troops and the people's armed forces departments of counties (cities and municipal districts) to regional organizational system; and reorganizing all the armored forces, artillery forces, antiaircraft artillery troops and some field engineer force, and reserved Army to a group army. The work of reduction and reorganization was almost completed at the beginning of 1987.

In September 1997, China decided to once again downsize its military personnel by 500,000. In this reduction, more than 200,000 officers in troops were demobilized and transferred to civilian work.

In 2003 China decided to further cut down the number by 200,000 within two years. Of this, 170,000 officers were cut down, its military size was cut down to the level of 2.3 million, and the proportion taken by the Army in the armed forces was reduced to the minimum in the history.

The wide scope and magnitude of China's unilateral disarmament in such a relatively short period of time are rarely seen in the history of international arms control and disarmament.

General Political Department

The General Political Department administers the armed forces' Party work, and organizes their political work. Under it are departments in charge of Party affairs, personnel, publicity, security, discipline inspection, civil-military affairs, etc. Its main responsibilities are to ensure the armed forces' compliance with and implementation of the lines, principles and policies of the Party and the Constitution and laws of the State, draw up general and specific policies for political work, formulate rules and regulations for political work, and make arrangements for, supervise and provide guidance to the political work of the armed forces.

General Logistics Department

The General Logistics Department administers the logistical work of the whole army. Under it are departments in charge of financial matters, quartermaster materials and petroleum, oils and lubricants, health administration, military transportation, capital construction and barracks, auditing, etc. Its main responsibilities are to formulate programs, rules and regulations for logistical construction, deploy logistical forces, organize logistical mobilization and provide logistical support, carry out the application, allocation, budgeting and final accounting of military expenditure, and conduct material procurement.

General Armaments Department

The General Armaments Department administers the provision of armaments for the armed forces. Under it are departments in charge of overall planning, armaments for all services and arms, procurement for Army's military equipment R and D, general-purpose equipment support, electronic information infrastructure, etc. Its main responsibilities are to formulate strategies, programs and plans, policies, and rules and regulations for equipment development, organize equipment R and D, experimentation, procurement, combat service, maintenance and support, and administer the PLA's funds for equipment buildup.

Leading Bodies of Armed Services

The Army has no independent leading body, and the leadership of it is exercised by the four general headquarters/departments (i.e. General Staff Headquarters, General Political Department, General Logistics Department and General Armaments Department).

The Navy, Air Force and Second Artillery Force direct the military, political, logistical and armaments work of their respective troops, and take part in the command of joint operations.

The Navy organizes and commands maritime operations conducted independently by its troops or in support of maritime operations. There are three fleets under the Navy, namely, the Beihai Fleet, Donghai Fleet and Nanhai Fleet. Each fleet has flotillas, aviation divisions, etc. under its command.

The Air Force organizes and commands air operations conducted independently by itself or with Air Force personnel as the main fighting force, as well as air defense operations in the capital area. It has an air command in each of the seven military area commands of Shenyang, Beijing, Lanzhou, Jinan, Nanjing, Guangzhou and Chengdu, respectively.

The Second Artillery Force organizes and commands its own troops in case of launching nuclear counterattacks with strategic missiles and conducting operations with conventional missiles. Under it are missile and training bases, and relevant support troops.

China's Armed Forces

China's national armed forces are composed of Chinese People's Liberation Army (active units and reserve units), Chinese People's Armed Police Force and militia. The PLA currently has 2.3 million troops and the PAPF has 660,000 troops.

Chinese People's Liberation Army

The Chinese People's Liberation Army, the major body of armed forces in China, consists of active units and reserve units and was born on August 1, 1927. In 1985, 1997 and 2003, China announced that it would cut the size of the PLA by one million, 500,000 and 200,000 persons, respectively. The PLA currently has 2.3 million troops. The active units are the standing army of the state, composed of the Army, Navy, Air Force and Second Artillery Force and their major tasks are conducting defending and operation, as well as helping keep the social order according to laws. The CMC exercises unified command of Chinese armed forces and building guidance through the General Staff Headquarters, General Political Department, General Logistics Department and General Armaments Department.

Active Troops of the PLA

The active troops of the PLA are composed of the Army, Navy, Air Force and Second Artillery Force.

By different duties and armaments, the Army consists mainly of the following arms: infantry, armored forces, artillery, engineering, communications, anti-chemical, and so on. The system of the Army is usually organized in the order of corps (group army), division (brigade), regiment, battalion, company, platoon, and squad.

The Chinese Marine Corps are conducting tactical training under high temperature.

The Navy is organized by fleet, navy base and maritime garrison commands. There are three fleets under the Navy, namely, the Beihai Fleet, Donghai Fleet and Nanhai Fleet. Navy

♦ Army Flag of the PLA

The red army flag of the PLA is stitched with a golden five-pointed star and two characters of "八一" (August 1), representing that since the Nanchang Uprising on August 1, 1927, the PLA had eventually won the victory of Chinese revolution under the leadership of the Chinese Communist Party after long and hard struggle. The army flag is mainly used on such occasions as ceremony, inspection, ceremonious assembling and parade, etc.

♦ Army Emblem of the PLA

The army emblem of the PLA is the symbol and sign of the PLA. Servicemen must take good care of army emblem and stick up for the dignity of the army emblem. The design of the army emblem of the PLA is composed of a five-pointed star and the characters of "八一" (August 1). The five-pointed star is red and its out edge and the characters of "八一" are golden. The army emblem is usually used on cap emblem, collar band, shoulder mark, certificate of merit, vehicles, naval ships, aircrafts, important buildings and platform on conference, etc.

♦ Military Rank System of the PLA

In 1955 China began to adopt the military rank system which was set up on the basis of traditional military rank system in China and referring to that of the Soviet Union, the DPRK and other countries. In 1965 that military rank system was abolished. Till 1988 the PLA announced to resume military rank system and "adopt a new military rank system". After several times of revision, the current military rank system of active force of the PLA was set up according to Regulations of the Military Ranks of Officers of the Chinese People's Liberation Army in 1994. In the system there are 10 grades in 3 categories: general officer: general, lieutenant general, and major general; field officer: senior colonel, colonel, lieutenant colonel, and major; and junior officer: captain, first lieutenant, and second lieutenant.

According to the prescription of Reserve Officers Law of the People's Republic of China in 1995, the military ranks for the officers in reserve service are divided into 8 grades in 3 categories: major general; senior colonel, colonel, lieutenant colonel, and major; and captain, first lieutenant and second lieutenant.

The Guard of Honor of the Chinese People's Liberation Army (PLA)

bases are usually subordinate to fleets and have maritime garrison commands and flotillas under their command. In terms of armaments and missions in battle, the Navy can be divided into surface ship units, submarine troops, aviation divisions, navy coastal defense forces, and marine corps, etc.

The Air Force is composed of military area commands, (corps) division, regiment (stations) and brigade. In terms of armaments and missions in charge, the Air Force can be divided into aviation troops, antiaircraft artillery troops, ground-to-air missile troops, airborne troops and radar troops, etc.

The Second Artillery Force of the PLA is composed of the ground-to-ground strategic nuclear missile force, the conventional operational-tactical missile force, and the support units. Under the direct command of the CMC, it is to launch the strategic nuclear counterattack in self-defense and carry out fire assaults with conventional missiles.

Reserve Force

The reserve force of the PLA, built up in 1983, is a force composed by prescriptive system and organization with active servicemen as skeleton and reserve personnel as foundation. The reserve force carries out uniform organization, each division, brigade and regiment is granted with unit designation and army flag, executes the regulations and rules of the PLA, is in the arrangement of the PLA and under the command of provincial military area commands (garrison commands) at peacetime, and in wartime after mobilization is under the command of designated active troops or conducts wartime duties individually; conducts peacetime training as provided for in relevant regulations, assists in maintaining order when necessary pursuant to the law, and activates its units in wartime in observance of the state's mobilization order. The officers and soldiers of the reserve force wear armband with the letter "Y".

Armed police

Chinese People's Armed Police Force

As a component of China's armed forces and subordinate to the State Council, the PAPF was built up on June 19, 1982 and is under the dual leadership of the State Council and the CMC. The PAPF adopts a system of integrating uniform direction and administration and commanding at different levels. The PAPF has an independent budgetary status in the financial expenditure of the state.

The PAPF consists mainly of the internal security force and forces guarding gold mines, forests, water and electricity supply, and communications. The border security, firefighting and security guard forces are also components of the PAPF. The total number of personnel of the PAPF is 660,000 currently. The PAPF General Headquarters is the leading and commanding organ of the PAPF.

The PAPF executes the Military Service Law of the People's Republic of China and rules, regulations and relevant laws of the PLA, and enjoys the same treatment with the PLA. In peacetime, the PAPF is tasked to perform guard duties, handle emergencies, combat terrorism, and participate in and support national economic development. In wartime, it assists the PLA in defensive operations.

The PAPF gold mine force has completed 38 geological prospecting projects in a dozen provinces and autonomous regions, and found some rich gold deposits. In the past two years, the PAPF forest force has put out 552 forest or prairie fires, protecting valuable natural resources. The PAPF water and electricity force has taken part in the construction of 21 key national projects, including the Qinghai-Tibet Railway, the West-East Natural Gas Transmission Project, the South-North Water Diversion Project, and major hydropower projects. The PAPF communications force is responsible for the maintenance of the Xinjiang-Tibet Highway and the Sichuan-Tibet Highway, and has undertaken the construction of national high-grade highways, extra-long tunnels and bridges. Those projects built by the PAPF communications force are all up to standards.

Militia Force

The militia force is an armed mass organization not separated from production, is the force in support of the PLA and is a component of the armed forces in China. The work of militia force is administered by General Staff Headquarters. Under the command of military organs, in wartime the militia force is tasked to assist standing army in battle, do battle independently, support guarantee to battle service for standing army, and supply replacement, and in peacetime it is tasked to perform guard duties, emergency rescue and disaster relief operations and maintain social order. The militia force is composed of ordinary militia and skeleton militia; and the latter one includes emergency-handling units, infantry units, specialized technical units and units geared to the needs of job. At present, China has 10 million skeleton militia troops. In recent years emphasis has been put upon quality building as to militia cause, and the size of infantry units has been cut down, the proportion of specialized technical units has been enlarged and the building of antiaircraft artillery, ground artillery, missile, communications, engineering, anti-chemical, reconnaissance, information and other specialized technical units has been strengthened particularly.

• Difference between Volunteer Military Service System and Mercenary Military Service System

There is a fundamental difference between the volunteer military service adopted by China and the mercenaries military service system (also named volunteer military service) adopted by the United Kingdom, United States and other western countries. As to Chinese volunteer military service system, citizens at the expiration of two-year compulsory service are transferred to first term of volunteer service according to the demands of the army and the free will of the individual and the examination of the organization. There is no contract on legal procedure, and there is no and it is impossible to appear parity between non-commissioned officers and troops on their rights and obligations; salary system is adopted on non-commissioned officers in view of enhancing treatment on soldiers, solving their actual difficulties and making them serve the army with heart set at rest.

As to the mercenary military service system adopted by Western countries, although in form of volunteer enlistment, they will sign contract substantially. They publicize the conditions and treatment for military service and then adopt the methods similar to recruiting workers by enterprises to enlist soldiers, and any person (including foreigners) meeting the qualification can be enlisted as mercenaries.

The Military Service System of China

The military service system is the system stipulated by the State on the participation of citizens into armed organizations or on their assumption of military duties and reception of military training. It is prescribed in Amendment to Military Service Law of the People's Republic of China enacted in 1998, "China practices a military service system which combines conscripts with volunteers and a militia with a reserve service."

(1) System of Conscripts and Volunteers

Citizens have the obligation to enlist in the army. Male citizens who reach the age of 18 by December 31 each year are eligible for enlistment for active service. Those who are not enlisted that year remain eligible for enlistment until the age of 22. Female citizens may also be enlisted, if necessary.

Conscripts in the active service are doing their duties for the State. And the State will implement favorable policies on their family members.

The term for conscripts in the active service is 2 years. At the expiration, conscripts can be changed to volunteers.

(2) System of Militia and Reserve Service.

The militia is a component of armed forces and is the assistant and supporting force of the PLA. And the reserve service is the service taken by citizens outside of the army.

At the time of retiring from active service, conscripts and volunteers who meet the qualification for reserve service are confirmed as in the reserve service for soldiers; and after passing examinations, those who meet the qualification for officers are in the reserve service for officers.

Soldiers out of active service and personnel having received military training who have not reach the age of 28 and the personnel participating in military training are organized as primary militia; other male citizens from the age of 18 to 35 who meet the qualification of military service are organized as ordinary militia.

(3) Military Training System. Skeleton militia who have not enlisted in the army and from the age of 18 to 20 participate into the military training of 30 to 40 days; specialized technical militia have a prolonged training time according to actual demands.

The military training for soldiers in reserve service is undertaken in militia organizations or independently.

Officers for reserve service participate in a military training of 3 to 6 months in the period of taking reserve service.

Students at higher colleges and universities and senior high schools must receive basic military training.

Administration System for Military Service Work

China practices an administration system of unified leadership and graded responsibility for military service work. Under the leadership of the State Council and the CMC, the Ministry of National Defense assumes responsibility for the military service work throughout the country. The military area commands are responsible for the military service work in their respective areas in accordance with the directions of the Ministry of National Defense. The provincial commands (garrison commands), sub-commands (garrison commands) and the people's armed forces departments of counties, autonomous counties, cities and municipal districts concurrently act as the military service organs of the people's governments at corresponding levels and are responsible for the military service work in their respective areas under the leadership of the military organs at higher levels and the people's governments at corresponding levels. The government organs, public organizations, enterprises and institutions and the people's governments of townships, ethnic townships and towns accomplish their military service work in accordance with the provisions of the Military Service Law. Professional work concerning military service is handled by the people's armed forces departments, or by the designated departments where there are no people's armed forces departments.

System of Civil Officers

The civil officers of the PLA are servicemen in active service who are assigned with posts at and above junior specialized technician or at and above the grade of clerical personnel and are not conferred military ranks, and they are a component of state's team of cadres.

In terms of work quality, civil officers can be divided into specialized technical civil cadres and non-specialized technical civil officers.

The organization of civil officers covers: some specialized technical cadres in fields of scientific research, engineer technology, medical treatment, teaching, press, publishing, books, archives, cultural art, and sports, and some cadres in charge of administrative affairs and service and guarantee in such units as organs, colleges and schools, and hospitals.

The treatment on civil cadres is almost the same with that on officers in active service.

According to stipulation, military ranks are not conferred on civil cadres, and they do not wear army uniform but uniform dress, and wear unified badges and shoulder marks and collar marks for civil cadres.

♦ Active Service

Active service is the principal form in which Chinese citizens perform their military service obligations. The citizens in active service in the PLA are servicemen in active service, consisting of officers in active service, civil cadres and soldiers in active service.

Officers in active service are the servicemen who hold posts at or above the platoon level or junior specialized technical level, and are conferred corresponding military ranks. They are classified as operational, political, logistics, armaments and specialized technical officers. The Law of the PRC on Officers in Active Service stipulates that the main sources of officers in active service are: graduates of schools or academies in the military, who are originally selected to study there from among outstanding soldiers and graduates of regular secondary schools; graduates of regular institutions of higher learning; civil cadres in the military; and specialized technicians and other persons recruited from outside the military. In war, soldiers, enlisted reserve officers, and persons in non-military departments may be directly appointed as active officers as needed.

Soldiers in active service are composed of conscripts based on compulsory military service (referred to as conscripts) and volunteers based on volunteer military service (referred to as non-commissioned officers). Non-commissioned officers are chosen from conscripts who have completed their terms of active service, and may be recruited from citizens with professional skills in non-military organizations. The term of service for conscripts in active service is two years. A system of active service for different terms is adopted for non-commissioned officers. The first two terms are three years each, the third and fourth terms four years each, the fifth term five years, and the sixth term nine years or longer. Non-commissioned officers are divided into two categories: specialized-technical and non-specialized-technical. The term of active service for the former ranges from the first to the sixth, and the latter and women non-commissioned officers serve, in principle, only the first term.

♦ Enlistment into Active Service in Peacetime

The number of conscripts enlisted into active service in China every year, and the requirements and time for their enlistment are prescribed by order of the State Council and the CMC. The provinces, autonomous regions and municipalities directly under the Central Government make arrangements for enlistment in their respective areas in accordance with the enlistment order of the State Council and the CMC. Enlistment in peacetime usually takes place once a year. The Military Service Law of the PRC stipulates that male citizens who reach the age of 18 by December 31 each year are eligible for enlistment for active service. Those who are not enlisted that year remain eligible for enlistment until the age of 22. Female citizens may also be enlisted, if necessary. Male citizens reaching the age of 18 before December 31 should register for military service before September 30 of the same year. Citizens who meet the required conditions for active service are enlisted into active service after gaining approval from the military service organs of their own counties, autonomous counties, cities or municipal districts. If a citizen qualified for enlistment is the only supporter of his or her family or is a student in a full-time school, his or her enlistment may be postponed. Citizens who are kept in custody for investigations, legal proceedings or trials, or who are serving sentences or are under criminal detention or surveillance may not be enlisted.

Discharge from Active Service and Resettlements

Active officers who have reached the maximum age limit for peacetime active service should be discharged from active service. Those who have not yet reached the maximum age limit or have not served the minimum term limit for peacetime active service may be discharged from active service in special circumstances after gaining approval. Soldiers who have completed their term of active service should be discharged from active service. The state makes proper arrangements for officers and civil cadres who have been discharged from active service. The main modes of arrangement are transference to civilian work, demobilization and retirement. Transference to civilian work is the principal mode of arrangement for officers and civil cadres discharged from active service. Administrative organs for resettlement of officers and civil cadres who have been transferred to civilian work or have retired, are set up at the national level and at the level of the province (autonomous region or municipality directly under the Central Government), and, if necessary, corresponding organs may be set up at the level of the city (prefecture). The General Political Department is responsible for the overall administration of the PLA resettlement work for officers and civil cadres who have been transferred to civilian work or have retired.

Resettlement Policy on Officers and Civil Cadres Transferred to Civilian Work and Discharged Conscripts

Efforts have been made to implement the Provisional Measures for Resettlement of Officers and Civil Cadres Transferred to Civilian Work and related regulations and policies, providing for execution of the resettlement mode to civilian work, whereby the state planned assignment of jobs and posts is combined with finding jobs by oneself. Officers at the level of division or regiment or at battalion-level with 18 years of military service (including civil cadres at the corresponding levels and specialized technical officers who enjoy corresponding status) can either be assigned civilian jobs according to the unified plan or choose to find jobs by themselves. Those at or below the battalion level with less than 18 years of military service are assigned civilian work under the unified plan. The Party committees and governments are responsible for arranging jobs and posts for officers and civil cadres transferred to civilian work. Those who choose to find jobs by themselves may seek assistance from the government in their job-finding and are entitled to a monthly-paid service-discharge pension for life long with exemption from income tax. Officers and civil cadres transferred to civilian work may settle at their native places or the places where they were enlisted, or settle at the places where their spouses lived before moving to accompany the servicemen or where they were married. When they meet the required conditions, they may also settle at the places where their parents, their spouses' parents, their spouses or their children are permanent residents, or at the places where their troops are stationed. When conscripts have been discharged from active service, the people's

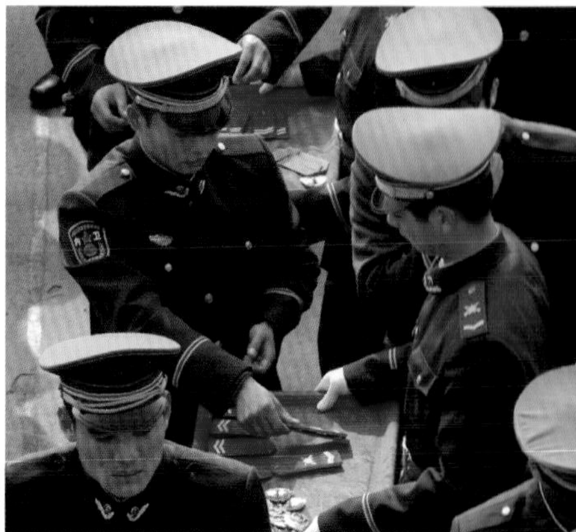
Soldiers retired from army return to their hometown.

government of the county where they were enlisted makes appropriate arrangements for them, depending on whether they are from the countryside or city and whether they have received any awards for meritorious service. Non-commissioned officers are resettled and arranged as transference to civilian work, demobilization, or retirement from active service according to their terms of service.

Reserve Service

Reserve service is divided into reserve service for officers and reserve service for soldiers. Citizens registered for reserve service are reservists. Reserve officers are chosen mainly from officers and civil cadres who have been discharged from active service, soldiers who have been discharged from active service, cadres of the people's armed forces departments and the militia, graduates from non-military institutions of higher learning, and other citizens who meet the qualifications of reserve officers. Reserve officers who hold posts in reserve forces, or are pre-regimented to active forces are reserve officers of Category One, and the other reserve officers are in Category Two. Reserve officers are classified as operational, political, logistics, armaments, and specialized technical officers and their posts are classified as division, regiment, battalion, company and platoon levels, and for specialized technical officers, as senior, intermediate and junior levels. The military ranks for reserve officers are divided into eight grades in three categories: reserve major general; reserve senior colonel, colonel, lieutenant colonel and major; reserve captain, first lieutenant and second lieutenant. Reserve soldiers range in age from 18 to 35. On the basis of age and military qualities, they are classified into Category One and Category Two.

Reserve Force Building

As a component of the PLA, the reserve force receives priority in the building of the defense reserve. The reserve force is organized according to the unified organization of the army with servicemen in active service as skeleton and officers and soldiers in reserve service as base. After more than two decades of building, the reserve force has developed to an important reserve composed of the reserve units of the Army, Navy, Air Force and Second Artillery Force from unitary Army. The reserve force is under dual leadership of the army and local Party committees and governments. In peacetime reserve units of the Army are under the leadership of provincial military area commands (garrison commands), and the reserve units of the Navy, Air Force and Second Artillery Force are under the dual leadership and administration of provincial military area commands (garrison commands) and active service army. In wartime after mobilization the reserve units are under the command of active service army.

Administration System of Militia Force

The militia force in the whole country is under the unified leadership of the State Council and the CMC. The provincial military area commands (garrison commands), sub-military area commands (garrison commands) and people's armed forces departments of counties, autonomous counties, cities, and municipal districts are responsible for the militia work of their corresponding levels. The people's armed forces departments of township, ethnic townships, towns, and streets are responsible for the militia work of their corresponding levels. The militia work of enterprises and institutions is handled by the people's armed forces departments established in them, or by the designated departments or personnel where there are no people's armed forces departments.

Military Training on Basic Militia Force

Basic militia ranging from the age of 18 to 22 participate in the military training of 30 to 40 days, and the training period for specialized technical soldiers is prolonged according to actual demands. With the approval from the CMC, the assignment of military training on national militia is made known to lower levels by General Staff Headquarters. The military training on militia is mainly undertaken in militia military training bases within the administrative regions of county level, and specialized technical soldiers training centers and people's armed force schools are established in some provinces and cities.

♦ Building Border and Coastal Defense

China has promulgated the Law on National Defense, the Law on the Territorial Sea and the Contiguous Zone, the Law on the Exclusive Economic Zone and the Continental Shelf and other relevant laws and regulations, and updated its border and coastal defense policies and regulations pursuant to international laws and practices, to manage its border and sea areas in conformity with the law. China endeavors to strengthen its border and coastal defense, administration and control, and build a modern border and coastal defense force featuring joint military-police-civilian efforts in defense and administration.

China pursues a good-neighborliness policy, and works to enhance friendship and partnership with its neighbors. It calls for settling boundary and maritime demarcation issues with countries concerned in a fair and equitable manner, and through consultations on the basis of equality. China has signed land border treaties or agreements with Myanmar and 11 other neighboring countries, thus resolving boundary issues left from history with these countries; it is currently negotiating with India and Bhutan to settle boundary issues with those two countries respectively. Since 1996, China has set up bilateral consultation mechanisms on the law of the sea with the Republic of Korea and Japan, to exchange views on maritime demarcation and cooperation. In 2004, the Agreement between China and Vietnam on the Demarcation of the Beibu Gulf officially entered into force.

China actively promotes border and coastal defense cooperation with its neighbors, strengthens border and coastal defense contacts in different fields and at various levels, and handles in an appropriate manner border- and coastal-defense-related issues with countries concerned. In 2005, the Agreement on Joint Patrols by the Navies of China and Vietnam in the Beibu Gulf was signed, and China respectively signed with the Philippines and Indonesia the Memorandum of Understanding on Maritime Affairs Cooperation and the Memorandum of Understanding on Maritime Cooperation. In July 2006, China and India reopened the border trade route at Nathu La Pass, which links China's Tibet with Sikkim, India. China's border and coastal defense forces, acting strictly in accordance with international law and the agreements and understandings signed by China with its neighbors, have established and improved mechanisms for talks and meetings with their counterparts in the neighboring countries, and conduct law enforcement and anti-terrorism cooperation to jointly maintain peace and stability in border areas and related sea areas.

Border and Coastal Defense System

China's border and coastal defense is under the unified leadership of the State Council and the CMC, and practices an administration system of sharing responsibilities between the military and the local authorities. The State Commission of Border and Coastal Defense, composed of the relevant departments of the State Council and the PLA, and under the dual leadership of the State Council and the CMC, guides and coordinates China's border and coastal defense. All military area commands, as well as border and coastal provinces, prefectures and counties have commissions to guide and coordinate border and coastal defense within their respective jurisdictions.

The PLA is the main force for defending China's borders and coasts. The PLA border defense force has a three-level structure, namely, regiment, battalion and company. The PLA coastal defense force has a five-level structure, namely, division, brigade, regiment, battalion and company. In 2003, the PLA border defense force took over the defense of the China-DPRK border and the Yunnan section of the China-Myanmar border from the border public security force, thus enabling the state to integrate land border defense and administration. The border public security force is tasked with safeguarding security and maintaining social order in border and coastal areas. Within the border public security force there are contingents in provinces (autonomous regions or municipalities directly under the central government), detachments, groups, border police substations and frontier inspection stations in border and coastal areas, border inspection stations in open ports, and marine police force in coastal waters.

China's Defense Expenditure

The budget and final accounts of defense expenditure is examined and approved by National People's Congress. China practices a strict system of financial appropriation of defense funds.

Since the 1990s, to safeguard its sovereignty, security and unity, and to keep pace with the global revolution in military affairs, China has gradually increased its defense expenditure on the basis of its economic development. This increase, however, is compensatory in nature, and is designed to enhance the originally weak defense foundation. It is a moderate increase in step with China's national economic development. In the 1980s, China began to shift the focus of its work to economic development. At that time, it was decided that national defense should be both subordinated to and serve the country's overall economic development. As a result, national defense received a low input, and was in a state of self-preservation.

Use of Defense Expenditure

China's defense expenditure covers not only the active forces, but also the militia and reserve forces. Also covered by the defense expenditure are costs to support part of the retired officers, education of servicemen's children and the national economic development, as well as other social expenses. China's defense expenditure is primarily used for the following purposes:

(1) Increasing salaries and allowances of military personnel and improving their living conditions. Along with the growth of China's economy and the steady improvement of the people's life, the salaries and allowances of military personnel and the pensions of retired officers are increased accordingly. The insurance, medical, housing and other benefits are also increased. Subsidies are being increased, too, to compensate for regional and post differences, and the living conditions of the troops stationed in hardship areas are being improved.

(2) Increasing investment in weaponry and equipment and infrastructure. The PLA is accelerating its informationization drive, increasing the expenses on procurement and maintenance of weaponry and equipment, upgrading the military infrastructure, and increasing input for improving the facilities for border and coastal defense troops.

(3) Supporting the training of military personnel. The PLA is increasing input into education and training through both military educational institutions and regular institutions of higher learning. It is also increasing subsidies for professionals with outstanding performance and incentives for experts, and increasing the budget for the employment of contract civilians.

(4) Compensating for price rise. As the prices of oil, building materials and staple and non-staple foodstuffs rise, the PLA accordingly increases the expenses on military petroleum, oils and lubricants and defense engineering, and raises the boarding subsidies.

(5) Increasing expenses for international cooperation in non-traditional security fields.

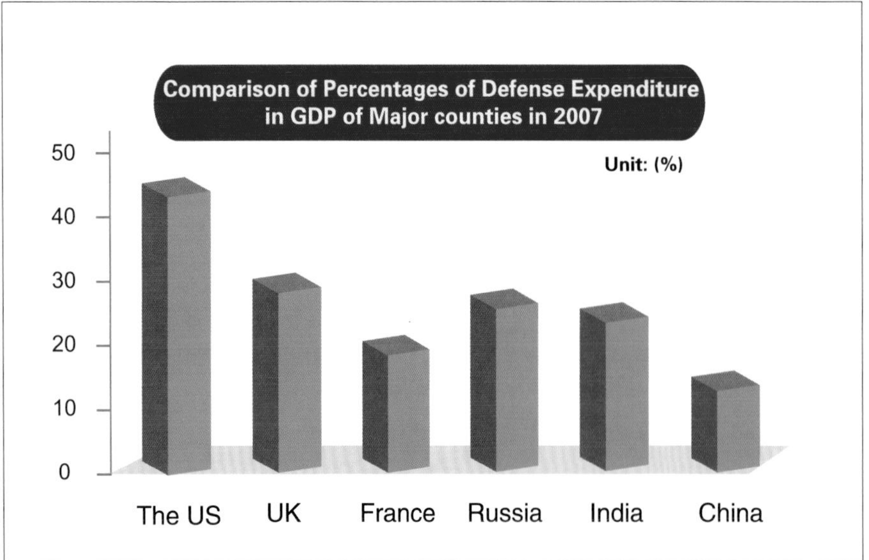

Maintain Low-level Defense Expenditure

China has always been paying attention to the control on size of defense expenditure and makes reasonable arrangement on defense expenditure according to the principle of coordinate development of national defense building and economic construction. Since the adoption of the opening up policy, Chinese Government has had a strict control on defense expenditure to concentrate force on economic construction. From 1979 to 2004 the share of China's defense expenditure in its state financial expenditure in the same period showed the trend of decreasing, 17.37 percent in 1979 and 7.76 percent in 2004, and the decreasing rate is nearly 10 percentage points from 1979 to 2004. The total amount of China's defense expenditure is low compared with that of other countries in the world, so is the share of the defense expenditure in GDP and state financial expenditure. In 2005 the annual defense expenditure of China is 247.496 billion Yuan, with the shares of 1.35 percent and 7.29 percent in its GDP and State financial expenditure respectively. China's defense budget was 283.829 billion Yuan in 2006.

In most years since the 1990s, the growth rates of China's defense expenditure are lower than that of the state's financial expenditure. But both the total amount and per-serviceman share of China's defense expenditure is low compared with those of some other countries, particularly major powers. In 2005, China's defense expenditure equaled 6.19 percent of that of the United States, 52.95 percent of that of the United Kingdom, 71.45 percent of that of France and 67.52 percent of that of Japan. China's defense expenses per serviceman averaged 107,607 Yuan, amounting to 3.74 percent of that of the United States and 7.07 percent of that of Japan.

Exchanges and Cooperation with Foreign Countries in Science, Technology and Industry for National Defense

Since the foundation of the Commission of Science, Technology and Industry for National Defense (COSTIND) in 1982, China has signed 107 relevant international treaties and agreements with some international organizations and governments, established channels for cooperation and exchanges with more than 110 countries and regions, and developed commercial exchanges with more than 80 countries and regions.

China's capability of peaceful use of nuclear energy has been enhanced distinctively and the hot issues related to nuclear power have been handled appropriately. By now China has signed 70 international treaties and agreements in the field of nuclear energy, undertaken 54 assisting projects of foreign technical cooperation, and improved the technology and level of peaceful use of nuclear energy of China through the exchanges and interactive activities of more than a thousand person times. China participated in the ITER negotiation.

China has signed 16 inter-governmental or inter-institutional agreements on peaceful use of space with 13 countries and space institutions and established cooperative relationship with more than 40 countries and international organizations. China takes an active part in the UN activities of peaceful use of space and started Chinese "space fragments action plan". China endeavors to promote the establishment of Asia-Pacific Space Cooperation Organization. China has undertaken fruitful space cooperation with some countries such as France, Brazil, European Space Bureau, Russia, Nigeria and Venezuela. Sino-France Space Cooperation Combined Commission has been established. CBERS (China-Brazil Earth Resource Satellite)-01 and 02 have been launched successfully. "Earth Space Double Satellites Probe Project", the first cooperation with European Space Bureau, has achieved success. A wide exchange and cooperation has been undertaken with Russia. Agreements on in-orbit delivery of communication satellites have been sighed with Nigeria and Venezuela and the satellites for civil use have realized the entirety export. Asia-Pacific VI communication satellite manufactured by French Alcatel Space Co. was launched successfully.

Distinctive achievements have been

Major Breakthroughs in Space Technologies for Civil Use

Since October 1996, China has succeeded in 41 space launches. The successful launching of the "Shenzhou V" spaceship in October 2003 sent China's first astronaut into space. In October 2005, China successfully launched the Shenzhou VI spacecraft carrying two astronauts, which returned as scheduled.

The key technological problems for the new generation of carrier rockets have been tackled. China has successfully launched various application satellites, including SSO (Sun Synchronous Orbit) and GEO (Geostationary Orbit) meteorological satellites, the HY-1 oceanographic satellite and CBERS (China-Brazil Earth Resource Satellite). The R and D of a DMEC (Disaster Monitoring and Environmental Control) satellite constellation, a large GEO satellite platform and a new generation of SSO meteorological satellites is going on smoothly. A lunar probe project was officially started in January 2004. On October 24, 2007, the Long March 3A sent the Chang'e-1 lunar probe into the orbit. The Chang'e-1 is China's first lunar probe developed in China. Its successful probing to the moon some 380,000 km away marks a new success China has made in lunar orbiting exploration.

♦ The Commission of Science, Technology and Industry for National Defense (COSTIND)

The Commission of Science, Technology and Industry for National Defense (COSTIND), established on May 10, 1982, was founded on the combination of Commission of Science and Technology for National Defense of the PLA (founded on October 16, 1958, a leading organ in charge of operation for unified organization of army's strategic nuclear weapon research, trial-manufacture, experiment, determination and supervision on manufacture), Office of Industry for National Defense under the State Council (founded on November 29, 1961, an office for the State Council to administer industry for national defense), and the Commission of Science, Technology and Armaments of CMC (founded on November 14, 1977, a leading organ in charge of the unified leading on scientific and technical research and industrial production for national defense). As one of the 29 ministries and commissions under the State Council, COSTIND is mainly responsible for organizing and administering the supervision on the stipulation and implementation of plans, policies, standards and laws and regulations related to science, technology and industry for national defense.

Concretely speaking, the COSTIND has the major functions defined as follows:

(1) Research and study out the guidelines, policies, laws and regulations related to the development of science, technology and industry for national defense and the civilian use of military technology; and formulate administrative rules for science, technology, industry and trades for national defense;

(2) Organize the optimization and adjustment on the structure, distribution and capability of the science, technology and industry for national defense; and organize military and industrial enterprises and institutions to carry out strategic re-organization;

(3) Research and formulate the annual program for R and D, production, investment on fixed assets and usage of foreign capitals in the science, technology and industry for national defense;

(4) Organize and coordinate the R and D, production and building of the science, technology and industry for national defense to ensure the demands of armament supply;

(5) Study out policies and developing plans for the production and technology in industries of nuclear, space, aviation, shipbuilding and weaponry, and execute administration on the industries;

(6) Organize and administer the foreign exchanges and cooperation in field of science, technology and industry for national defense;

(7) Organize and coordinate the exchanges and cooperation on atomic energy with other governments and international organizations in the name of CAEA; and

(8) Organize and coordinate the exchanges and cooperation on space activities with other governments and international organizations in the name of CNSA.

Address: Jia 8, Fucheng Rd, Haidian District, Beijing
Website: http://www.costind.gov.cn/n435777/index.html

made in space cooperation with great growth in cooperation level and quality. HC120 helicopter of 1.5 tons jointly manufactured by China and France has realized batch production and delivery, and the ERJ145 jet feeder liner jointly manufactured by China and Brazil has realized small batch production and delivery. Progress has been made in the marketing of aircrafts for civil use, and Xinzhou 60 aircraft with independent intellectual property has been delivered to users in batch; 32 aircrafts have been exported and delivered, including 5 to Zimbabwe and Laos.

Distinct effects have been realized in the introduction of technology for shipbuilding use and export of ships has achieved outstanding success. Exchanges and dialogue have been strengthened with OECD and Shipbuilding Workgroup of OECD; and bilateral dialogue mechanism has been established with the governmental departments in charge of shipbuilding in Japan, The Republic of Korea and EU. At present, the export of civilian ships has a share of 12 percent in the international market, ranking third in the world.

Important Progress in Aviation Industry for Civil Use

The aviation industry for civil use has made important headway in the R and D of feeder liners and general-purpose aircraft. ARJ21, a new jet feeder liner with 70 seats, is being independently developed, and is scheduled for delivery in 2008. The Y-12E general-purpose aircraft for use in high-temperature and plateau conditions and the Z-11 and Z-9 helicopters have all received airworthiness certificates and been put on the commercial market. The newly developed "Xiaoying 500" general-purpose plane made its first flight in 2003. The ERJ145 jet feeder liner jointly manufactured by China and Brazil has been delivered to users. An agreement has been formally signed on the building of an assembly line in China for the EC120 helicopter jointly developed by China, France and Singapore. Subcontracting business for the manufacture of foreign aircraft parts has been developing steadily, and begun to be integrated into the large-scale circulation system of the international aviation industry.

The "Dapenghao" liquid natural gas (LNG) ship manufactured by China is delivered to the ship-owner at the Hudong-Zhonghua Shipbuilding plant, in Shanghai in 2008.

On March 30, 2007, the ARJ21 regional jet which China enjoys independent intellectual property right began to be assembled in Shanghai. The first such plane will be available at the end of 2007.

Rapid Growth in Shipbuilding Industry for Civil Use

The shipbuilding industry for civil use has witnessed sustained rapid growth, with an output ranking third in the world for many years. In 2003, China's accomplished shipbuilding output, newly received orders and on-hand orders amounted to 6.41 million DWT, 18.95 million DWT and 26.23 million DWT respectively, accounting for a world market share of 11.8 percent, 18.9 percent and 17.7 percent respectively. Products manufactured by the shipbuilding industry for civil use have been exported to more than 90 countries and regions. The R and D and designing capability of the shipbuilding industry for civil use has been remarkably raised. It can now build and repair large ships, and has made new breakthroughs in building high-tech ships.

Fifty Years in China's Space Industry

In 2006 China's space industry welcomed its 50th anniversary since its foundation. China is unflinching in taking the road of peaceful development, and always maintains that outer space is the common wealth of mankind. While supporting all activities that utilize outer space for peaceful purposes, China actively explores and uses outer space. In the past 50 years China's space industry has made great strides in the development of three great fields, namely space technology, space applications and space science.

China has formed a reliable innovation system for scientific research and production and brought up an innovation team with good quality and excellent technology. The missiles manufactured by China independently form an effective strategic deterrence and defensive and counterattacking method and build up a solid iron barrier to safeguard State's sovereignty and security. By September 2006 China's "Long-March" rocket group has accomplished 90 launches and has accomplished 48 continuous and successful launches since October 1996, with a world leading security and reliability. The 70 satellites manufactured and launched by China are widely applied in various fields such as economy, science and technology, cultural education and national defense building.

The Chang'e-1 lunar probe launched successfully in 2007 is the first lunar probe China developed. The on-going lunar probe project of China started the deep space probe of China and will promote China's space industry to a new and higher stage.

Furthermore, the space science and technologies have been widely applied in various fields such as economy, science and technology, society and national defense building and have obtained distinct social and economic benefits. Satellite remote-sensing has been widely applied in meteorology, mining, surveying, agriculture, forestry, land, water conservancy, oceanography, environmental protection, seismology, traffic, and region and urban planning, and has played an important role in state's land resource investigation, ecological protection, the West-East Natural Gas Transmission Project, the South-North Water Diversion Project, the Three-Gorge Project and other grand projects; the development and application of satellite TV broadcasting enhanced the effective coverage range and quality of the broadcasting and TV in the whole country, especially in the broad rural areas, satellite telecommunications played an irreplaceable role in the project of "each village having access to telephone", and the broad-band multi-media education satellite transmission network and satellite remote medical treatment network have been established initially; and satellite navigation and positioning technology has been widely applied in such fields as communications, land survey, engineering survey, resource investigation, earthquake monitoring, meteorological monitoring and oceanographic monitoring.

Launching Vehicles

In past decades, after generations' unremitting endeavor, "Long-March" rocket group has experienced the course of starting from scratch, from single-satellite launching to multi-satellite launching, and from satellite launching to manned spaceship launching, had the capability to launch different types of satellites in different orbits, obtained outstanding achievements around the world, occupied a share in the international market of commercial satellite launching service, and become one of the few high-tech products with independent intellectual property and strong international competitive force. By September 2006, China has accomplished 90 launches and successfully sent more than 70 domestic large, medium and small-sized satellites to space, including 6 no-man spaceships, and created considerable economic benefits by sending 28 foreign-made satellites successfully to space.

Since launching its first man-made satellite in the 1960s, China has successfully launched 22 home-made satellites, including 11 return satellite. Photo shows the satellite launching tower at the Jiuquan Satellite Launch Center.

Manned Spaceflight

Manned spaceflight. On November 20 and 21, 1999, China launched and retrieved the first "Shenzhou" unmanned experimental spacecraft. It then launched three more "Shenzhou" unmanned experimental spacecrafts not long afterwards. On October 15 and 16, 2003, it launched and retrieved the "Shenzhou V" manned spacecraft, China's first of its kind. Having mastered the basic technologies for manned spacecraft, China became the third country in the world to develop manned spaceflight independently. From October 12 to 17,2005, the "Shenzhou VI" manned spacecraft completed a five-day flight with two astronauts on board. This was the first time for China to have men engage in experiments in space, another major achievement in the sphere of manned spaceflight.

On September 25 to 28, 2008, the Shenzhuo VII manned spaceship fulfilled the two-day manned space flight of three persons and realized the space extravehicular activity. China has become the third country mastering the technologies of space extravehicular activity in the world.

• Man-made Satellites

(See P85)

The Shenzhou VI manned spacecraft is sucessfully launched.

♦ China National Space Administration (China's Space Institution)

China National Space Administration, founded on April 22, 1993 with the approval of the Central Government, was established on the base of Ministry of Space Industry. The major functions of China National Space Administration are defined as follows: research and study out state's policies and laws and regulations related to space; research and formulate state's space developing program and plan and industrial standards; organize argumentation and examine and approve projects on important space scientific and technological activities; supervise and coordinate the implementation of important space scientific and technological projects; and take charge of exchanges and cooperation in field of space with other countries and international organizations.

Address: Jia 8, Fucheng Rd., Haidian District, Beijing
Website: http://www.cnsa.gov.cn

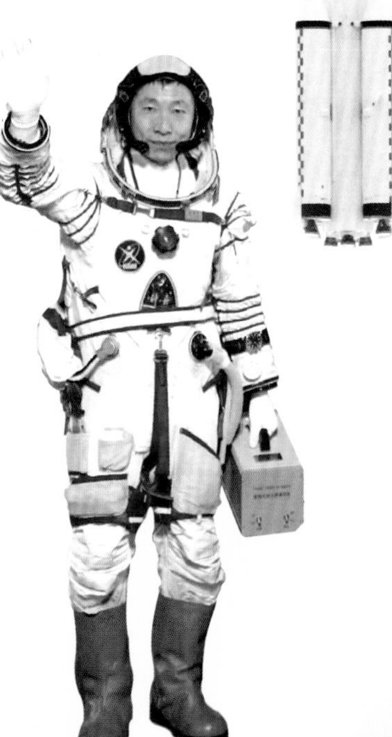

China's first spaceman Yang Liwei

♦ Chinese PLA Military Academy of Sciences

As an institute in charge of military science research under the leadership of the CMC, the Chinese PLA Military Academy of Sciences is the center of military science research in the army, the organ of planning and coordinating the work of military science research in the army, and the assistant of the CMC and General Headquarters in guiding the army construction and battles in the academic level. Its basic tasks include research on military basic theories and significant issues related to national defense building and army building; formulating and amending rules, regulations and other military laws in the army; providing strategic suggestions opinions for the CMC and General Headquarters; and administration on the military science research in the army. Through originative scientific research, the Academy offers high-quality scientific research fruits and provides service to both decision-making by the CMC and General Headquarters and army building and battles. It was founded in 1956.

Address: Qinglongqiao, Haidian District, Beijing

♦ National Defense University

The National Defense University of the PLA is the highest military university in the People's Republic of China and is directly under the leadership of the CMC. Its major tasks are cultivating senior commanders and senior staff officers and academic research personnel for the Army, Navy and Air Force, taking charge of research on issues related to strategic and modernization of national defense, and acting as consultant for decision-making by the CMC and General Headquarters. Previously the National Defense University was Red Army School and Anti-Japanese Army and Government School during revolutionary war-time and Institute of Military, Politics and Logistics after the foundation of new China. In 1985 the National Defense University was founded in Beijing and is located at northwest suburb of Beijing.

Address: Jia-3, Hongshankou, Haidian District, Beijing

♦ National University of Defense Technology

As a comprehensive university, the National University of Defense Technology takes on the important tasks of cultivating senior talents in science and engineering technology for modernization of national defense and researching on key technologies of national defense. Previously the university was Institute of Military Engineering in founded in 1953 in Harbin. In 1970 the major body of the institute moved to Changsha and the institute was transformed to the National University of Defense Technology. In April 1999 the University combined Changsha Artillery Institute, Changsha Engineer Institute and Changsha Politics Institute and was reorganized to a new National University of Defense Technology. The University is one of the first group of key universities receiving special expenditure from the central government.

Students of the PLA University of National Defnse

Address: Shangdalong, Kaifu District, Changsha City, Hunan Province

Website: http://www.nudt.edu.cn/

China's National Defense Education

China's governments and relevant departments at all levels undertake various types of national defense education and enhance the whole people's national defense concept in accordance with National Defense Education Law. The work related to national defense education has formed a good situation with attention from the government, the social support and participation by the whole people. The State has established National Defense Education Office, and each province, autonomous region, municipality and the majority of cities and counties have established national defense education leading organs and offices. Twenty-six provinces, autonomous regions and municipalities have formulated or amended National Defense Education Regulations, and the State National Defense Education Office has organized the draft of national defense education outline.

Mititary training for college freshmen

National Defense Education for the Whole People

The State undertakes the national defense education for the whole people with importance attached to government officials, young students and militia and reserve force personnel. The national defense education is included into the academic studying plan for government officials, and such methods as special lectures, "military day" in military camps, and short-term training are adopted to strengthen the consciousness of performing national defense responsibility of government officials. The national defense education is included into the schools' teaching courses of all grades and kinds, and young students receive education on national defense knowledge and patriotism. Some middle and primary schools undertake activities of juvenile military schools with the subject of national defense education. The national defense education on militia and reserve force personnel is mainly combined with political education, organizational rectification, and military training. All the places across China make use of important festivals, commemoration days and the occasion of enlisting servicemen to hold exhibitions, speeches, performances, knowledge contest, military summer camps and other national defense education activities. Columns or programs of national defense education are established at large in medias such as newspaper, broadcasting, TV and internet. Nine provinces and municipalities have opened newspapers and publications for national defense education, and more than 30 regions have opened national defense education webs.

China's International Military Exchanges and Cooperation

Adhering to the purposes and principles of the UN Charter, China persists in developing friendly relations and strengthening cooperation with other countries on the basis of the Five Principles of Peaceful Co-existence, and devotes itself to promoting international security dialogues and cooperation of all forms. The Chinese People's Liberation Army carries out state's foreign policy, and develops cooperative military relations that are non-aligned, non-confrontational and not directed against any third party. Chinese PLA actively develops international military exchanges and cooperation, and has created a military diplomacy that is all-directional, multi-tiered and wide-ranging.

China has established military ties with over 150 countries and military attaché offices in 107 countries. A total of 85 countries have military attaché offices in China.

China actively undertakes institutionalized defense and security consultations. At present China has established the consultation mechanism for security and institutionalized defense with some major powers such as the United States, Russia, Japan, Australia, the United Kingdom and France, and the mechanism has expanded to some neighboring countries such as Mongolia, Thailand, Vietnam, and Philippine, as well as some regional powers such as South Africa and Italy.

Chinese PLA has held bilateral or multilateral counter-terrorism military exercises with state members of Shanghai Cooperation Organization such as Kyrgyzstan, Russia, and Kazakhstan. The PLA held joint military exercises with Russia. The PLA held bilateral military exercises on land or maritime search and rescue with neighboring countries such as Pakistan, India and Thailand, and held maritime search and rescue exercises with the United Kingdom, France, Australia and the United States. Naval ships from Thailand, the United States, Canada, Australia, New Zealand, the United Kingdom, the Republic of Korea, France, Singapore and Peru have paid port visits to China. PLA naval ships have visited Pakistan, India, Thailand, the United States, Canada and the Philippines.

China actively participates in the peacekeeping operations led by the UN. Since 1990, China has sent 5,915 military personnel to participate in 16 UN peacekeeping operations. Since 2000, China has sent 893 peacekeeping police officers to seven mission areas. At present, China has 1,487 military peacekeeping personnel serving in nine UN mission areas and the UN Department of Peacekeeping Operations. China also has a total of 180 peacekeeping police officers in Liberia, Kosovo, Haiti and Sudan.

The PLA has actively participated in the international disaster relief operations conducted by the Chinese Government. It has set up an emergency command mechanism, sent personnel to join specialized rescue teams, provided equipment, and assisted in mission-oriented training. In the past two years, PLA personnel have joined China's international rescue teams in international rescue operations after the Indian Ocean tsunami and the earthquakes in Pakistan and Indonesia. They have conducted search and rescue operations for people in distress, treatment of the sick and injured and prevention of epidemics, and assisted the Chinese Government in providing relief materials to disaster-stricken countries.

International Military Academic Exchanges

The PLA has held increasingly active military academic exchanges with foreign countries, and some scientific research institutes such as Academy of Military Science have conducted wide academic exchanges with foreign counterparts. The PLA has continued to expand exchanges of military students with its foreign counterparts. In recent years it has sent more than 1,000 military students to more than 20 countries. Nineteen military colleges and universities have established exchanging relationship at interscholastic level with the counterparts in 25 countries such as the United States and Russia. In the past two years, over 2,000 military personnel from more than 140 countries have come to China to study in military schools, including military officers from 44 countries who participated in the International Symposium Courses hosted by the PLA National Defense University. Since 2005 China has held senior military officers seminars with Latin American countries, Arabic Countries, Germany and France, Institutionalized Defense Security Forum of Shanghai Cooperation Organization and Sino-ASEAN Asia-Pacific Security Issues seminars, etc.

Strategic Consultation and Dialogue

In recent years China has strengthened the bilateral and multilateral strategic consultations and dialogues with some countries in fields of security and defense and accelerated the mutual confidence, exchanges and cooperation. At present China has established consultation mechanism for security and defense with some major powers such as the United States, Russia, Japan, Australia, the United Kingdom, and France, and the mechanism has expanded to some neighboring countries such as Mongolia, Thailand, Vietnam, Philippines, etc., as well as regional powers such as South Africa and Italy.

China and Russia have established a meeting mechanism for senior leaders to exchange opinions on important issues. The armies of China and Russia established consultation mechanism in 1997. The senior military leaders of the two countries exchange visits frequently. China and the United States have maintained consultation in such fields as non-proliferation, counter-terrorism and bilateral military security cooperation. In recent years China and the United States have held several rounds of vice-foreign-ministerial level consultations on strategic security, multilateral arms control and non-proliferation, the vice-national-defense-ministerial level defense consultation, the counter-terrorism consultations and the financial counter-terrorism consultation.

Regional Security Cooperation

China pursues a foreign policy of building a good-neighbor relationship and partnership with its neighbors, trying to create an amicable, secure and prosperous neighborhood, and vigorously pushing forward the building of a security dialogue and cooperation mechanism in the Asia-Pacific region.

China stands for peace talks for the solution of international conflicts. Picture shows the six-party talks on the nuclear issue in North Korea, which was held in Beijing and attended by China, North Korea, the United States, South Korea, Japan and Russia.

From "Shanghai Five" to Shanghai Cooperation Organization

On April 26, 1996, the heads of states of China, Russia, Kazakhstan, Kyrgyzstan and Tajikistan signed the Agreement on Confidence-Building in the Military Field along the Border Areas in Shanghai Exhibition Center, which opened prelude for mechanism of "Shanghai Five" and established the basis for Shanghai Cooperation Organization (SCO) founded 5 years later. In June 2001 heads of states of "Shanghai Five" met for the sixth time in Shanghai, and Uzbekistan joined "Shanghai Five" with a completely equal status. Then heads of the six states held the first summit meeting and signed the Declaration on Establishment of the Shanghai Cooperation Organization, and the SCO was formally founded. In the conference they also signed Shanghai Convention on Combating Terrorism, Separatism and Extremism.

Since its establishment the SCO has set up a relatively complete organizational structure and laid a sound legal basis, and

The first meeting of Ministers of Economy and Trade of SCO member states took place in Shanghai on May 28, 2002.

successfully initiated cooperation in security, economic, human culture and other fields. The Shanghai Convention on Combating Terrorism, Separatism and Extremism and the Agreement of State Parties of the Shanghai Cooperation Organization on the Regional Counter-terrorism Agency took effect in 2003. In pursuance of the convention and agreement, the SCO held meetings of chief procurators and ministers of defense, and conducted joint counter-terrorism military exercises. The SCO Secretariat and regional counter-terrorism agency were formally inaugurated in Beijing and Tashkent in January 2004. The Tashkent Summit Meeting of the SCO signed the Tashkent Declaration and the Agreement on Cooperation in Combating Illegal Turnover of Narcotic and Psychotropic Substances and the Precursors Thereof in June 2004. The SCO also set up the mechanism of regular meetings between security committee secretaries of its state members to strengthen security and cooperation.

Mutual Confidence and Cooperation between China and ASEAN

China attaches importance to the role of ASEAN Regional Forum (ARF) and supports its development of confidence-building measures. China will submit annual security prospect reports every year to the ARF. As early as in November 2002, China and ASEAN signed the Declaration on the Conduct of the Parties in the South China Sea (DOC), which showed all parties' common desire to maintain stability and carry out cooperation in this region. The parties concerned undertook to resolve their territorial and jurisdictional disputes by peaceful means, refrain from taking any actions that would complicate or escalate disputes, promote mutual trust through dialogues between defense officials and voluntary notification of joint military exercise, and actively carry out cooperation in the fields of marine environmental protection, marine scientific research, safety of navigation and communication at sea, search and rescue operation and combating transnational crimes. In December 2004, China and ASEAN held the Senior Officials Meeting on the Implementation of the DOC, at which important consensus was reached on launching the South China Sea cooperation and the decision was made on the establishment of a Joint Working Group for the implementation of the DOC. In August 2005, the first meeting of the Joint Working Group was convened in the Philippines.

Since 1997, China has hosted two Inter-sessional Meetings on Confidence-building Measures (CBMs) of the ARF and undertaken eight CBMs programs, including Training Courses on Chinese Security Policies, Seminar on Military Logistics Support and Seminar on Strengthening Cooperation in the Field of Non-traditional Security Issues. China supports gradual expansion of defense officials' participation in the ARF. At the ARF's Tenth Meeting of Foreign Ministers in 2003, China put forward the proposal of convening a meeting on security policies, and in November 2004, the first ARF Security Policy Conference was held in Beijing. From 2005 to 2006, China has, within the ARF framework, hosted the Seminar on Enhancing Cooperation in the Field of Non-traditional Security Issues, sponsored the ARF Seminar on Non-proliferation of Weapons of Mass Destruction with the United States and Singapore, held the Fifth and Sixth ARF Inter-sessional Meetings on Disaster Relief with Indonesia, and held the Fourth ARF Inter-sessional Meeting on Counter-terrorism and Transnational Crime with Brunei. At the ARF's Thirteenth Meeting of Foreign Ministers in July 2006, China put forward the proposals of promoting mutual confidence, respecting characters of diversity, and handling well the relationship between ARF and other mechanisms.

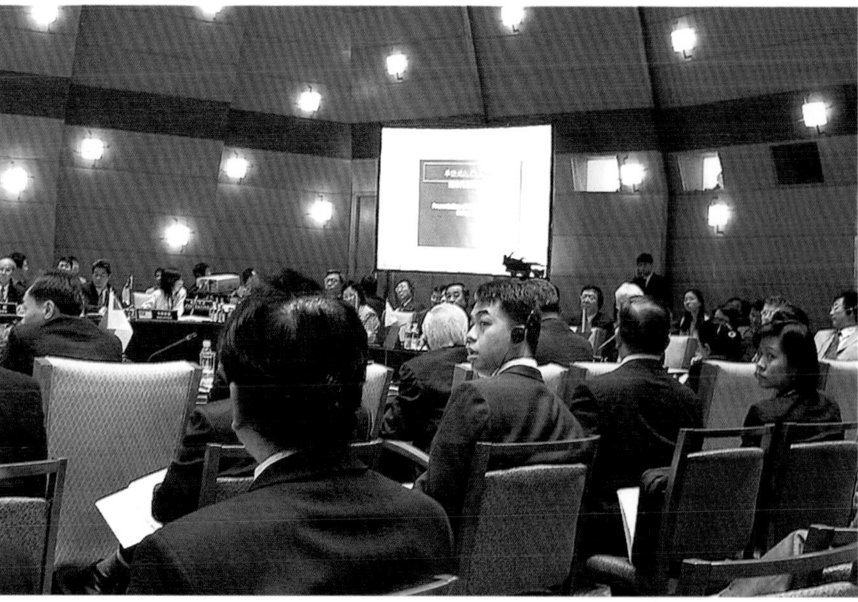
China and the ASEAN have gradually conducted cooperation in the non-traditional security field. Photo shows a special conference on SARS issue convened by China and the ASEAN.

Signing of Relevant Agreements between China and India

In September 1993, China and India signed the Agreement on the Maintenance of Peace and Tranquility along the Line of Actual Control in the China-India Border Areas. In November 1996, the two countries signed the Agreement on Confidence-Building Measures in the Military Field along the Line of Actual Control in the China-India Border Areas. In April 2005, the two countries signed the Protocol on Modalities for the Implementation of Confidence-Building Measures in the Military Field along the Line of Actual Control in the China-India Border Areas, which is an agreement on the concrete implementing approaches of relevant clauses in the Agreement signed in 1996. The signing and implementation of these agreements have played important and positive roles in maintaining peace and tranquility in the China-India border areas, promoting the friendly relations between the two countries and facilitating the peaceful resolution of the border issue.

International Exchanges and Cooperation in Non-traditional Security Fields

Since 1970s and 1980s, the security concept with military security as core has been called as "traditional security concept", the military threats as "traditional security threats", and the security threats other than military threats as "non-traditional security threats". Compared to traditional security, the meaning of non-traditional security covers a wider and more complicated range, including such fields as politics, economy, military, culture, science and technology, information and ecological environment, etc. The non-traditional security issues mainly include terrorism, armament proliferation, ecological environment security, economic crisis, resource shortage, spreading of sickness, food security, information security, science and technology security, economic security, illegal emigration, smuggle and drug trafficking, organizational crimes, piracy and money laundering, etc. Since the beginning of energy crisis in 1970s, Non-traditional Security Strategy has been holding a greater and greater proportion in world security strategy, and has been promoted to an important position equal to Traditional Security.

China has paid more and more attention to the non-traditional security issues. In May 2002, China promulgated the Document Concerning China's Stand in Strengthening Cooperation in Non-Traditional Security Fields. On November 8, 2002, the wording that "threats from traditional security and non-traditional security are interwoven" appeared for the first time in the report of the Sixteenth National Congress of the Communist Party of China. In the China's National Defense of 2002 promulgated on December 20 of the same year, it was stressed once again that prevention against non-traditional security issues is the assignment of China's national defense.

Cooperation in non-traditional security fields within the frameworks of ASEAN and China (10 + 1) and ASEAN and China, Japan and the Republic of Korea (10 + 3) has developed gradually in recent years. In November 2002, leaders of China and ASEAN signed the Joint Declaration between China and ASEAN on Cooperation in Non-Traditional Security Fields. In April 2003, leaders of China and ASEAN held a special meeting in Bangkok, Thailand, on SARS and issued a joint declaration. In January 2004, the two sides signed the Memorandum of Understanding between China and ASEAN on Cooperation in Non-Traditional Security Fields. China initiated and participated in the first ministerial meeting between ASEAN and China, Japan and the Republic of Korea on combating transnational crimes held in Bangkok, Thailand, in January 2004, and submitted a concept paper. The meeting agreed to set up a cooperation mechanism between ASEAN and China, Japan and the Republic of Korea for combating transnational crimes, and adopted the First Joint Communiqué of the ASEAN plus Three Ministerial Meeting on Combating Transnational Crimes.

Since 2002 China's PLA has held a series of exercises in non-traditional security fields with foreign counterparts.

PLA Participates in Cooperation in Non-traditional Security Fields

The PLA has taken an active part in cooperation in non-traditional security fields such as joint counter-terrorism, maritime search and rescue, combating piracy, and cracking down on drug production and trafficking. In 2002 China and Kyrgyzstan held counter-terrorism exercise on land. The ministers of defense of China, Kazakhstan, Kyrgyzstan, Russia and Tajikistan signed the Memorandum of the Ministries of National Defense of the SCO Member Countries on Holding the "Joint-2003" Counter-terrorism Exercise in May 2003. The armed forces of the five countries successfully conducted the first multilateral counter-terrorism exercise in the vicinities of Ucharal in Kazakhstan and Yining in China's Xinjiang Uygur Autonomous Region within the framework of the SCO in August 2003. The armed forces of China and Pakistan conducted Friendship-2004, a joint counter-terrorism exercise, in the border area between the two countries in August 2004. The Chinese navy conducted joint maritime search-and-rescue exercises off the Chinese coast with visiting Pakistani navy in October and Indian navy in November 2003. It also held joint maritime search-and-rescue exercises with French navy in March, British navy in June, and Australian navy in October in 2004 in the Yellow Sea area. In November and December 2005, the PLA Navy held joint maritime search and rescue exercises with its Pakistani, Indian and Thai counterparts, respectively. In September 2006, China and Tajikistan conducted the "Cooperation-2006" joint counter-terrorism military exercise. In September and November 2006, the Chinese Navy and the US Navy conducted joint maritime search and rescue exercises in the offshore waters of San Diego and in the South China Sea. In December 2006, China and Pakistan held the "Friendship-2006" joint counter-terrorism military exercise. In the past two years, the PLA has sent observers to military exercises held by Turkey, Thailand, Pakistan, India, the US and Australia. In September 2005, the PLA invited 41 military observers and military attachés from 24 countries to attend the "Northern Sword-2005" maneuvers organized by the Beijing Military Area Command.

♦ Agreements on Disarmament and Confidence-Building Measures between China and Relevant Countries

Agreement Between the Government of the People's Republic of China and the Government of the Republic of India on the Maintenance of Peace and Tranquility Along the Line of Actual Control in the China-India Border Areas (signed in September 1993)

Agreement Between China and Russia on the Prevention of Dangerous Military Activities (signed in July 1994)

Joint Statement by the President of the People's Republic of China and the President of the Russian Federation on No-First-Use of Nuclear Weapons and Detargeting of Strategic Nuclear Weapons Against Each Other (signed in September 1994)

Agreement on Confidence-Building in the Military Field Along the Border Areas Among China, Kazakhstan, Kyrgyzstan, Russia and Tajikistan (signed in April 1996)

Agreement on Confidence-Building Measures in the Military Field Along the Line of Actual Control in the China-India Border Areas (signed in November 1996)

Agreement on the Mutual Reduction of Military Forces in the Border Areas Among China, Kazakhstan, Kyrgyzstan, Russia and Tajikistan (signed in April 1997)

Agreement Between the Ministry of National Defense of the PRC and the Department of Defense of the USA on Establishing a Consultation Mechanism to Strengthen Military Maritime Safety (signed in January 1998)

Declaration on the Conduct of the Parties in the South China Sea (signed in November 2002)

Protocol Between the Government of the People's Republic of China and the Government of the Republic of India on Modalities for the Implementation of Confidence-Building Measures in the Military Field Along the Line of Actual Control in the China-India Border Areas (signed in April 2005)

China's Active Participation in UN Peacekeeping Operations

China has consistently supported and actively participated in the peacekeeping operations that are consistent with the spirit of the UN Charter. It maintains that the UN peacekeeping operations should abide by the purposes and principles of the UN Charter and other universally recognized principles governing peacekeeping operations. Since its first dispatch of military observers to the UN peacekeeping operations in 1990, China has sent 5,915 military personnel to 16 UN peacekeeping operations. Eight Chinese servicemen lost their lives and dozes wounded in UN peacekeeping operations. Since 2000 China has sent 893 peacekeeping police officers to seven UN peacekeeping task areas. At present 1,487 peacekeeping servicemen are working in nine UN peacekeeping task areas. China also has a total of 180 peacekeeping police officers in Liberia, Kosovo, Haiti and Sudan.

Honoring Commitment to International Arms Control and Non-Proliferation

A preparatory office has been established at the PLA General Armaments Department. With the support of the Ministry of Foreign Affairs, the Ministry of Health, the State Environmental Protection Administration, the China Earthquake Administration and other government departments, this office is responsible for setting up 11 monitoring stations in China as part of the international monitoring system, and formulating their administrative regulations and detailed rules for the implementation of the CTBT. Two primary seismological monitoring stations have been set up in Hailar and Lanzhou, respectively, and three radionuclide stations have been set up in Beijing, Guangzhou and Lanzhou, respectively. The surveying of the two sites for two infrasound stations in Beijing and Kunming has been completed, and construction is scheduled to start soon. The China National Data Center and the Beijing Radionuclide Laboratory have been built, and are now in trial operation.

China supports multilateral efforts aimed at enhancing the effectiveness of the Biological Weapons Convention. It has attended the review conferences, annual meetings of State Parties and meetings of the Ad Hoc Group of Governmental Experts in an active and responsible manner. China has also submitted in a timely fashion to the United Nations declarations regarding confidence-building measures under the Convention.

China honors in good faith its obligations

Chinese riot police patroling around the International Airport of Port-au-Prince, Haiti

under the Chemical Weapons Convention. It has promptly and completely submitted all the annual declarations, subsequent declarations regarding newly discovered chemical weapons abandoned by Japan in China and the annual national programs related to protective purposes. It has also received more than 100 on-site inspections by the Organization for the Prohibition of Chemical Weapons. The PLA is working, in strict compliance with the Convention, to ensure the smooth management and operation of the "single small-scale facility" and the "10kg Schedule I Chemical Synthesis Laboratory." China and Japan have held 42 rounds of bilateral consultations to accelerate the destruction of the chemical weapons abandoned by Japan in China. China has assisted Japan in 24 on-site verifications, and recovered over 3,100 chemical weapons abandoned by Japan. At the request of Japan, China has taken into temporary custody the recovered Japanese-abandoned chemical weapons confirmed by Japan. These chemical weapons will be destroyed by Japan in the future.

China fully honors its obligations under the amended Landmine Protocol to the Convention on Certain Conventional Weapons. The PLA keeps its troops fully informed of China's obligations, and has implemented the technical standards and limitations specified in the Protocol. It has carried out a general check of all the anti-personnel landmines that do not meet the standards of the Protocol, and has destroyed several hundred thousand old landmines in a planned way. China has made technical modifications to usable anti-infantry landmines in inventory to make them conform to the technical standards of the Protocol. China continues to take an active part in international demining operations. In the period September-December 2005, Chinese military demining experts worked in Thailand to train demining personnel and give on-site instructions. China also provided Thailand with demining equipment.

China is firmly opposed to the proliferation of weapons of mass destruction and their means of delivery. It supports the United Nations in playing its due role in non-proliferation. China is a party to all international treaties on non-proliferation and related international organizations. It has established a complete legal regime for controlling the export of nuclear, biological and chemical weapons, missiles and other related sensitive items and technologies, and all defense items. China follows strict procedures in approving exports, to ensure effective export control.

China's Basic Position on Issues Related to Arms Control, Disarmament and Non-proliferation

In recent years, some positive progress has been made in the fields of international arms control, disarmament and non-proliferation, but the proliferation of weapons of mass destruction (WMD) and their means of delivery and other issues have become major factors affecting the international security situation. The Chinese Government maintains that the international community should safeguard the international regime of arms control, disarmament and non-proliferation treaties, promote its universality and reinforce its effectiveness and authority; that it should persist in multilateralism and give full play to the role and influence of the multilateral arms control, disarmament and non-proliferation treaty organs; that it should strive to meet the challenges brought about by the proliferation of WMD through political and diplomatic means on the basis of the existing international laws; and that it should address both the symptoms and root causes and adopt comprehensive measures, which means that it should take into consideration security threats such as proliferation of WMD while not neglecting the social and economic root causes of such threats.

China retains the minimum nuclear deterrent force with nuclear submarine being the major target of development.

China's Measures in Promoting International Arms Control and Disarmament

China has always attached importance to and been supportive of international efforts in the arms control and disarmament field. To oppose arms races and strive for disarmament has been an important part of China's foreign policy ever since the founding of the People's Republic of China. China has successively joined and faithfully implemented relevant international arms control and disarmament treaties. It has actively participated in important activities in the field of arms control and disarmament, including relevant discussions and negotiations in the UN and relevant international agencies, putting forward many reasonable and feasible proposals in this regard in a serious effort to promote the international arms control and disarmament process. In August 2003, China announced that it accepted the amended mandate of the Ad Hoc Committee on the Prevention of an Arms Race in Outer Space (PAROS) in the Five Ambassadors' Proposal, and is ready to participate in reaching consensus through consultation on the Five Ambassadors' Proposal on the Program of Work. It hopes that the other parties concerned would give positive response. China supports the Conference on Disarmament in its efforts to start substantive work on the following four topics: nuclear disarmament, the Fissile Material Cut-off Treaty (FMCT), security assurances to non-nuclear-weapon states, and prevention of an arms race in outer space. China consistently stands for complete prohibition and thorough destruction of nuclear weapons. It always pursues a policy of no first use of nuclear weapons, and undertakes unconditionally not to use or threaten to use nuclear weapons against non-nuclear-weapon states or nuclear-weapon-free zones. China did not and will never engage in a nuclear arms race with any other country. It supports the international community in its efforts to start substantive discussions on nuclear disarmament. China supports an early conclusion of the FMCT through negotiations. In the current situation, the importance and urgency of providing security assurances for non-nuclear-weapon states has become more prominent. China supports the negotiation and conclusion of an international legally binding instrument on this issue. China is the only country among the five nuclear weapon states to commit itself not to use or threaten to use nuclear weapons against non-nuclear-weapon states or nuclear-weapon-free zones. China appeals to the four other nuclear weapon states to make the same commitment.

The China Arms Control and Disarmament Association is a nation-wide non-profitable, non-governmental organization in China in the area of arms control, disarmament and non-proliferation.

China's Positive Participation in Other International Multilateral Arms Control Processes

In the other international multilateral arms control processes, China favors discussions on and settlement of issues such as "terrorism and WMD," "radioactive weapons" and "observance of international treaties on disarmament, arms control and non-proliferation" within multilateral arms control framework. It has taken an active part in the multilateral efforts to enhance the effectiveness of the Biological Weapons Convention (BWC), thus assuming a positive role in maintaining and pushing forward the multilateral arms-control process in the biological field. China supports the efforts of the ASEAN countries, the Central Asian countries and other neighboring countries to establish nuclear-weapon-free zones and has reached agreement in principle with the ASEAN countries on the Protocol to the Southeast Asia Nuclear-Weapon-Free Zone Treaty, and participated in the consultations between the five nuclear weapon states and the Central Asian countries on the Central Asian Nuclear-Weapon-Free Zone Treaty and its protocol. It also participated in the First (Disarmament) Committee sessions of the UN General Assembly, the UN Disarmament Commission meetings, the preparatory committee sessions for the 2005 Review Conference of the Parties to the Treaty on the Non-Proliferation of Nuclear Weapons (NPT), and the sessions of the Conference of the States Parties to the Chemical Weapons Convention (CWC) and its first review conference.

China's Position on Nuclear Disarmament Issue

It is the shared aspiration of the international community as well as the goal of China to thoroughly destroy nuclear weapons and free the world from such weapons. China maintains that nuclear-weapon states should take the following measures to further promote nuclear disarmament process: 1, an international legal instrument on the complete prohibition and thorough destruction of nuclear weapons should be concluded at an early date. 2, Nuclear disarmament should be a just and reasonable process of gradual reduction toward a downward balance. The two countries possessing the largest nuclear arsenals bear special and primary responsibilities for nuclear disarmament. They should earnestly comply with the treaties already concluded on reduction of nuclear weapons and further reduce their nuclear arsenals in a verifiable and irreversible manner so as to create conditions for achieving the ultimate goal of complete and thorough nuclear disarmament. 3, Before the goal of complete prohibition and thorough destruction of nuclear weapons is achieved, nuclear-weapon states should commit themselves to no first use of nuclear weapons and undertake unconditionally not to use or threaten to use nuclear weapons against non-nuclear-weapon states or nuclear-weapon-free zones. 4, Nuclear-weapon states should abandon the policies of nuclear deterrence based on the first use of nuclear weapons and reduce the role of nuclear weapons in their national security. 5, Nuclear disarmament measures, including intermediate measures, should follow the guidelines of maintaining global strategic balance and stability and undiminished security for all. And 6, The Conference on Disarmament (CD) in Geneva should reach an agreement on program of work soon so as to begin at an early date negotiations on the Fissile Material Cut-off Treaty (FMCT) and to establish Ad Hoc Committees and start substantive work on such issues as nuclear disarmament and security assurances to non-nuclear-weapon states.

China's Policy and Measures on Nuclear Disarmament Issue

As a nuclear-weapon state, China has never evaded its due responsibilities and obligations in nuclear disarmament. China has always stood for the complete prohibition and thorough destruction of nuclear weapons. Right after its first nuclear test in 1964, the Chinese Government issued a statement, solemnly proposing to the governments of all countries the convocation of a world summit to discuss the issue of complete prohibition and thorough destruction of nuclear weapons. China has persistently exercised the utmost restraint on the scale and development of its nuclear weapons. China has conducted the smallest number of nuclear tests among the five nuclear-weapon states. China has never taken part and will never take part in any nuclear arms race. China has never deployed nuclear weapons outside its own territories. In the 1990s, China closed down a nuclear weapon research and development base in Qinghai Province. China's development of nuclear weapons has always been for the purpose of self-defense. Since the first day when it came into possession of nuclear weapons, the Chinese Government has solemnly declared that it would not be the first to use such weapons at any time and in any circumstance. Whether confronted with the nuclear threat and nuclear blackmail during the Cold War, or faced with the great changes that have taken place in the international security environment after the Cold War, China has always stayed true to its commitment. China's policy in this regard will remain unchanged in the future.

♦ List of Arms Control, Disarmament and Non-Proliferation Treaties That China Has Joined

In the Nuclear Field

Additional Protocol II to the Treaty for the Prohibition of Nuclear Weapons in Latin America and the Caribbean (signed in August 1973, the instrument of ratification deposited in June 1974).
Additional Protocols II and III to the South Pacific Nuclear-Free Zone Treaty (signed in February 1987, the instrument of ratification deposited in October 1988).
Agreement Between the People's Republic of China and the International Atomic Energy Agency for the Application of Safeguards in China (signed in September 1988, effective since September 1989).
Convention on the Physical Protection of Nuclear Material (acceded in February 1989).
Treaty on the Prohibition of the Emplacement of Nuclear Weapons and Other Weapons of Mass Destruction on the Seabed and the Ocean Floor and in the Subsoil Thereof (acceded in February 1991).
Treaty on the Non-Proliferation of Nuclear Weapons (acceded in March 1992).
Convention on Nuclear Safety (signed in 1994, ratified in April 1996).
Protocols I and II to the African Nuclear-Weapon-Free Zone Treaty (signed in April 1996, the instrument of ratification deposited in October 1997).
Comprehensive Nuclear Test Ban Treaty (signed in September 1996).
Protocol Additional to the Agreement Between the People's Republic of China and the IAEA for the Application of Safeguards in China (signed in December 1998, entered into force in March 2002).

In the Chemical Field

Convention on the Prohibition of the Development, Production, Stockpiling and Use of Chemical Weapons and on Their Destruction (signed in January 1993, the instrument of ratification deposited in April 1997).

In the Biological Field

Protocol for the Prohibition of the Use in War of Asphyxiating, Poisonous or Other Gases, and of Bacteriological Methods of Warfare.
Convention on the Prohibition of the Development, Production and Stockpiling of Bacteriological (Biological) and Toxin Weapons and on Their Destruction (acceded in November 1984).

In the Conventional Field

Convention on Prohibitions or Restrictions on the Use of Certain Conventional Weapons Which May Be Deemed to Be Excessively Injurious or to Have Indiscriminate Effects and Protocols I-III (signed in September 1981, the instrument of ratification deposited in April 1982; the amended Article 1 of the Convention ratified in June 2003, the instrument of ratification deposited in August 2003).
Amended Protocol on Prohibitions or Restrictions on the Use of Mines, Booby-Traps and Other Devices Annexed to the Convention on Prohibitions or Restrictions on the Use of Certain Conventional Weapons Which May Be Deemed to Be Excessively Injurious or to Have Indiscriminate Effects (Amended Protocol II) (the instrument of ratification deposited in November 1998).
Protocol on Blinding Laser Weapons Annexed to the Convention on Prohibitions or Restrictions on the Use of Certain Conventional Weapons Which May Be Deemed to Be Excessively Injurious or to Have Indiscriminate Effects (Protocol IV) (the instrument of ratification deposited in November 1998).
Protocol Against the Illicit Manufacturing of and Trafficking in Firearms, Their Parts and Components and Ammunition, Supplementing the United Nations Convention Against Transnational Organized Crimes (signed in December 2002).

In Other Fields

The Antarctic Treaty (acceded in June 1983).
Treaty on Principles Governing the Activities of States in the Exploration and Use of Outer Space, Including the Moon and Other Celestial Bodies (instrument of accession deposited in December 1983).
Convention on Registration of Objects Launched into Outer Space (acceded in December 1988).
Convention on the Prohibition of Military or Any Other Hostile Use of Environmental Modification Techniques (acceded in June 2005).

China's Fulfilling International Obligations of Non-Proliferation

Since joining the Treaty on the Non-Proliferation of Nuclear Weapons (NPT) in 1992, China has faithfully honored all its obligations and dedicated itself to maintaining and enhancing the universality, effectiveness and authority of the NPT. China remains committed to promoting the three goals of the NPT, namely, non-proliferation of nuclear weapons, nuclear disarmament and peaceful uses of nuclear energy. China joined the International Atomic Energy Agency (IAEA) in 1984. In 1988, China signed the Agreement between the People's Republic of China and the IAEA for the Application of Safeguards in China, and voluntarily placed its civilian nuclear facilities under the IAEA safeguards. China signed with the IAEA the Protocol Additional to the IAEA Safeguards Agreement in 1998, and in early 2002 formally completed the domestic legal procedures necessary for the entry into force of the Additional Protocol, thus becoming the first nuclear-weapon state to complete the relevant procedures. In November 1991, the Chinese Government announced that it would, on a continuing basis, notify the IAEA of China's export to or import from non-nuclear-weapon states of any nuclear material of over one effective kilogram. In July 1993, China formally undertook that it would voluntarily notify IAEA of all its import and export of nuclear material as well as its export of nuclear equipment and related non-nuclear material. In May 1996, China pledged not to provide assistance, including nuclear export and personnel and technical exchanges and cooperation, to nuclear facilities of non-nuclear-weapon states not under the IAEA safeguards. At present, acceptance of the IAEA full-scope safeguards by importing countries has been set by China as the precondition for nuclear export.

China's Support to Comprehensive Nuclear Test Ban Treaty

China firmly supports the Comprehensive Nuclear Test Ban Treaty (CTBT). China has made significant contributions to the conclusion of the Treaty and was among the first to sign it. In July 1996, the Chinese Government declared a moratorium on nuclear test, and has all long honored such commitment. China supports the early entry into force of the CTBT and hopes that all countries will sign and ratify it at an early date. Meanwhile, China appeals to nuclear-weapon states and other relevant countries to maintain the moratorium on nuclear test before the CTBT comes into force. Currently, China is working vigorously on its domestic legal procedures for the ratification of the CTBT, and has established competent national agency to prepare for its implementation. China has actively participated in the work of the CTBT Preparatory Commission and all previous Conferences on Facilitating the Entry into Force of the CTBT. The China National Data Center and the Beijing Radionuclide Laboratory have been built, and are now in trial operation. China supports the early start of the negotiation of a treaty on the prohibition of the production of fissile material for nuclear weapons or other explosive devices on the basis of a comprehensive and balanced program of work to be reached by the CD in Geneva.

China's Policy and Position on Banning Biological Weapons

Against the backdrop of increased threat of bio-terrorism and prominence of bio-security issue, it is of great realistic significance to continue to explore and formulate measures to strengthen the effectiveness of the Biological Weapons Convention (BWC) under the framework of this Convention. China holds that the international community should take the following actions: 1, encourage more countries to accede to the BWC and urge all its States Parties to fulfill their obligations in a comprehensive and faithful manner. 2, maintain and facilitate the multilateral process aimed at enhancing the effectiveness of the BWC and explore and formulate concrete measures through full consultations. And 3, encourage more countries to submit to the UN declarations on confidence-building measures regarding the BWC.

China's Efforts in Banning Biological Weapons

China suffered a lot from the use of biological and chemical weapons by foreign countries in history. China supports the efforts by the international community to ban biological and chemical weapons and has actively participated in the negotiations of relevant treaties or protocols. China has taken concrete actions to promote the process undertaken by the international community to achieve complete prohibition and thorough destruction of biological and chemical weapons. China acceded to the BWC in 1984, and has always supported and actively participated in the multilateral endeavors aimed at strengthening the effectiveness of the Convention. China strictly fulfills its obligation under the BWC and has promulgated a series of laws and regulations to exercise strict control over export of dual-use biological agents and related equipment and technologies. China has actively participated in the BWC Review Conferences and submitted reports on compliance with the BWC. Since 1988, China has submitted to the UN its annual declarations on the confidence-building measures pursuant to relevant decisions of the Review Conferences. China has also played an active role in the negotiations on a protocol to the BWC as well as in the annual meetings of the States Parties and meetings of the experts.

China's Policy and Position on Banning Chemical Weapons

The Chemical Weapons Convention (CWC) is the first international legal instrument for complete prohibition and thorough destruction of a whole category of WMD with strict verification mechanism. It has set a successful example for multilateral arms control and non-proliferation efforts. To ensure full implementation of the CWC, China maintains: 1, Chemical weapon possessors should double their efforts to complete the destruction of their chemical weapons at an early date in strict accordance with the CWC and subject themselves to effective supervision by the Organization for the Prohibition of Chemical Weapons (OPCW). 2, It is imperative to further improve and optimize verification measures, allocate inspection resources in a fair and equitable manner and improve its cost-effectiveness. 3, Continuously promote the universality of the CWC. And 4, The country concerned should fulfill its obligations under the Convention and honor its commitments, start at an early date the substantive destruction process for the chemical weapons it abandoned in China so as to destroy those weapons completely and thoroughly as soon as possible.

China Makes Effort to Ban Chemical Weapons

China actively participated in negotiations for the Convention to Ban Chemical Weapons, and worked and works hard to implement tasks listed in it. China has also promulgated a series of laws, issued categories subject to control, thus forming an effective management with regard to production, management, use and import/export of chemicals attached to the Convention. China and other signatory countries maintain close contacts in the field of chemicals attached to the Convention, and clarify import and export figures in a timely manner, and strictly implement stipulations of the Convention on transfer chemicals to non-signatory countries. It has promptly and completely submitted all the annual declarations, subsequent declarations regarding newly discovered chemical weapons abandoned by Japan in China and the annual national programs related to protective purposes. It has also received more than 100 on-site inspections by the Organization for the Prohibition of Chemical Weapons.

China's Position on Prevention of Proliferation of Weapons of Mass Destruction (WMD)

Proliferation of WMD and their means of delivery is conducive neither to world peace and stability nor to China's security. China firmly opposes proliferation of WMD and their means of delivery. China believes that proliferation of WMD has complicated root causes. In order to prevent their proliferation, an integrated approach must be adopted to address both the symptoms and the root causes. 1, all states should devote themselves to building a global security environment of cooperation and mutual trust, seeking universal improvement of international relations and achieving security for all. This is the best way to eliminate the danger of proliferation as well as the prerequisite for a smooth non-proliferation process. 2, all states should resort to political and diplomatic means to solve the proliferation problem. Non-proliferation means should help maintain and promote international security. Proper solutions to proliferation issues should be sought out through dialogue instead of confrontation, and through cooperation instead of pressuring. 3, full scope should be given to the central role of the UN and other international organizations. The existing non-proliferation mechanism should be strengthened and improved under the framework of international law and on the basis of equal and universal participation of all countries and democratic decision-making. And 4, a balance should be struck between non-proliferation and peaceful uses. The legitimate rights of each state to peaceful uses should be guaranteed while proliferation activities under the pretext of peaceful uses should be prevented.

Developing Relations with Multinational Export Control Mechanisms

China values the important role of the multinational export control mechanisms in the field of non-proliferation. China has conducted active dialogues and exchanges with these mechanisms, learning from and drawing on their useful experience and practices for its own reference. In October 1997, China joined the Zangger Committee. In June 2004, China joined the Nuclear Suppliers Group and is now managing export control in strict accordance with the rules and list of the Group. In February and May 2004, China held two rounds of dialogues with the Missile Technology Control Regime (MTCR) in Paris and Beijing respectively, exchanging views on export control regimes, control lists and law-enforcement in the missile field as well as China's membership in the MTCR. In September 2004, China officially submitted its application for membership of the MTCR. China also keeps contacts and exchanges with the Australia Group. The two sides held two rounds of consultations in March 2004 and March 2005 respectively, during which views were exchanged on the non-proliferation situation in the biological and chemical field, implementation of the CWC and the BWC, operation of the Australia Group and China's non-proliferation policy and export control measures. In April 2004 and May 2005, China held two rounds of dialogues with the Wassenaar Arrangement in Vienna, exchanging views on the principles of export control on conventional weapons and related dual-use items and technologies, the control list and "the best practice". The two sides agreed to hold regular dialogues in the future.

Conducting Exchanges and Cooperation on Non-Proliferation

China attaches importance to and actively participates in bilateral exchanges and cooperation on non-proliferation, whereby it is able to draw on the useful experience and practices of other countries in this field. China has maintained consultations and exchanges with Australia, France, Germany, Japan, the Republic of Korea, Pakistan, Russia, the UK, the US and the EU. In December 2004, China and the EU signed the Joint Declaration on Non-Proliferation and Arms Control, in which the two sides confirm that China and the EU are major strategic partners in the fields of disarmament and non-proliferation, and define the priority areas for cooperation in this regard. China has also, in strict compliance with its non-proliferation policies and export control laws and regulations, worked with relevant countries to crack down on proliferation activities through information exchange and law-enforcement cooperation. China supports the role of relevant regional organizations and mechanisms in the field of non-proliferation, and has participated in relevant exchanges and dialogues in a constructive manner, exploring effective ways to address non-proliferation issues at the regional level. China has participated in the initiatives of the ARF to strengthen non-proliferation efforts. China, in cooperation with the US and Singapore, held an ARF seminar on non-proliferation in 2006. China is ready to keep contact and coordination with other parties to jointly promote the regional non-proliferation process.

Promoting the Important Role of the UN in Field of Non-Proliferation

As a permanent member of the UN Security Council, China supports the important role played by the UN in the field of non-proliferation in further consolidating international consensus and deepening international cooperation. In early 1992, the UN Security Council issued a Presidential Statement, defining the proliferation of WMD as a threat to international peace and security. China played a constructive role in drafting the Statement. In April 2004, the UN Security Council adopted Resolution 1540 unanimously. As the first resolution specifically on non-proliferation adopted by the Security Council, it is conducive to promoting and enhancing international cooperation on the basis of existing international laws, and to properly addressing the problem of acquisition and trafficking of WMD, their means of delivery and the related materials by non-state actors. China actively participated in the consultations on

China and Japan cooperated to recover the chemical weapons left by retreating Japanese troops during World War Two in Ning'an Northeast China's Heilongjiang Province.

♦ Settlement on the Chemical Weapons Japan Abandoned in China

Today, large quantities of chemical weapons abandoned by Japan during World War II still remain on Chinese soil, which pose a grave threat to the lives and property of the Chinese people and to the ecological environment. According to statistics, by now the chemical weapons abandoned by Japan during its aggression in China have been found in 60 spots in 14 provinces (autonomous regions) in China, among which Harbalin in Jilin has the largest quantity, about 400,000 chemical cannonballs according to the exploration by Chinese and Japanese experts. In accordance with *Convention on the Prohibition of the Development, Production, Stockpiling and Use of Chemical Weapons and on Their Destruction,* which became formally effective in 1997, Japan should completely destroy all the chemical weapons it abandoned in China before April 2007.

In 1999 after negotiation the governments of China and Japan signed the Memorandum of Understanding on the Destruction of the Chemical Weapons Abandoned by Japan in China. In the same year Chinese Government set up an office in Ministry of Foreign Affairs to handle the issues and relevant affairs related to the chemical weapons abandoned by Japan. The governments of China and Japan have held 42 negotiations to promote the process of destroying the chemical weapons abandoned by Japan.

Currently, relevant work of disposing the chemical weapons abandoned by Japan has moved from the phase of theoretical research and experiment to that of construction and implementation. The two sides have reached agreement on issues like the destruction technologies and location of destruction facility. Specific environmental standards have, by and large, been worked out. The preparatory work for the excavation and recovery of the chemical weapons abandoned by Japan and construction of the destruction facility is currently under way as planned.

the Resolution, put forward many constructive proposals and made important contributions to its adoption. In October 2004, China submitted its national report on implementation of the Resolution in accordance with the provisions of the Resolution, which introduced in detail measures taken by the Chinese Government to prevent and combat proliferation activities by non-state actors in the areas of legislation, law-enforcement and international cooperation.

Building Legal System on Non-Proliferation Export Control

Effective export control serves as an important means to pursue the non-proliferation goal. As a country with certain capacity in industry, science and technology, China has adopted highly responsible policies and measures in this regard. After years of endeavor, China has completed a transition in its non-proliferation export control from an administrative pattern to one based on law with relevant measures basically in line with common international practices. Since the mid-1990s, China has gradually set up a comprehensive legal system for export control of nuclear, biological, chemical, missile and other sensitive items and technologies as well as all military products. The Chinese Government has promulgated the Regulations of the PRC on the Control of Nuclear Export and the Regulations of the PRC on the Control of Nuclear Dual-Use Items and Related Technologies Export in the nuclear field; the Regulations of the PRC on the Export Control of Dual-Use Biological Agents and Related Equipment and Technologies, the Regulations of the PRC on the Administration of the Controlled Chemicals together with the Detailed Rules for the Implementation of the Regulations, the Controlled Chemicals List and the Measures on the Export Control of Certain Chemicals and Related Equipment and Technologies in the biological and chemical field; the Regulations of the PRC on the Export Control of Missiles and Missile-Related Items and Technologies in the missile field; and the Regulations of the PRC on the Administration of Arms Export in the arms export field.

♦ China's Promotion on Conclusion of a Multilateral Treaty on Mutual No-First-Use of Nuclear Weapons

China has been actively promoting the conclusion of a multilateral treaty among nuclear-weapon states on mutual no-first-use of nuclear weapons against each other. In January 1994, China formally presented a draft text of the Treaty on the No-First-Use of Nuclear Weapons to the other four nuclear-weapon states. At the same time, China worked vigorously for arrangements among nuclear-weapon states on mutual no-first-use of nuclear weapons and mutual detargeting of nuclear weapons at each other. In September 1994, China and Russia declared that they would not be the first to use nuclear weapons against each other and would not target their strategic nuclear weapons at each other. In June 1998, China and the US declared the detargeting of their nuclear weapons against each other. In May 2000, China, together with the other four nuclear-weapon states, the France, Russia, the United Kingdom and the United States, issued a joint statement declaring that their nuclear weapons are not targeted at any country. Ever since the first day when it came into possession of nuclear weapons, China has committed unconditionally not to use or threaten to use nuclear weapons against non-nuclear-weapon states or nuclear-weapon-free zones. In April 1995, the Chinese Government made a statement, reiterating its unconditional provision of negative security assurances to all non-nuclear-weapon states, and at the same time undertaking to provide these countries with positive security assurances. In 2000, China and other nuclear-weapon states issued a joint statement, reaffirming their security assurance commitment made in Resolution 984 of the UN Security Council in 1995. China calls upon the other nuclear-weapon states to unconditionally provide positive and negative security assurances to all non-nuclear-weapon states, and to conclude, through negotiations, an international legal instrument to this end at an early date.

♦ China's Support to Building Nuclear-Weapon-Free Zones

China respects and supports the efforts by relevant countries and regions to establish nuclear-weapon-free zones or WMD-free zones on the basis of consultations among themselves and voluntary agreements in light of actual regional conditions. China believes that nuclear-weapon states should respect the status of nuclear-weapon-free zones and assume corresponding obligations. Proceeding from this position, China has signed and ratified Protocol II of the Treaty for the Prohibition of Nuclear Weapons in Latin America and the Caribbean, Protocols II and III of the South Pacific Nuclear-Free Zone Treaty and Protocols I and II of the African Nuclear-Weapon-Free Zone Treaty. China supports the efforts by the ASEAN countries and the five Central Asian countries to establish nuclear-weapon-free zones and is ready to sign relevant protocols as early as possible after the countries concerned have reached agreement on the texts. China supports endeavors to establish nuclear-weapon-free and WMD-free zones in the Middle East and hopes to see its early realization. China respects and welcomes Mongolia's status as a nuclear-weapon-free country. China supports denuclearization of the Korean Peninsula. China has acceded to the Antarctic Treaty, the Treaty on Principles Governing the Activities of States in the Exploration and Use of Outer Space, Including the Moon and Other Celestial Bodies and the Treaty on the Prohibition of the Emplacement of Nuclear Weapons and Other Weapons of Mass Destruction on the Seabed and the Ocean Floor and in the Subsoil Thereof, and has undertaken corresponding obligations.

Rigorous Implementation of Laws and Regulations on Non-Proliferation Export Control

The Chinese Government attaches great importance to law enforcement and has adopted a series of effective measures to ensure the implementation of laws and regulations on export control. In November 2002, the MOFCOM formulated the Measures on the Administration of Export Registration for Sensitive Items and Technologies. In December 2003, the MOFCOM and the GAC jointly formulated the Provisional Measures on the Administration of Export Licenses on Sensitive Items and Technologies. In January 2004, the MOFCOM and the GAC jointly launched a computer control system for the export of sensitive items and technologies by connecting within the same network different agencies that approve and issue the license with the supervision branch of the Customs. This has greatly enhanced the capacity to supervise and control the export of sensitive items and technologies. Based on control lists for nuclear, biological, chemical and missile exports, the MOFCOM and the GAC jointly compiled the

Export Licensing Catalogue of Sensitive Items and Technologies

covering 658 items and technologies, of which 34 percent have had their customs code determined. China's Customs also extensively apply high-tech equipment in various links in the process of supervision and control of customs clearance, which has significantly upgraded the capacity of on-site law enforcement and efficiency of examination. Relevant competent authorities on export control have set up a "national expert supporting system for export control" that engages experts from nuclear, biological, chemical and missile fields to assist competent authorities in making correct and scientific judgments on relevant items during the process of export examination and approval.

Serious Investigation on Suspected Cases of Illegal Export

In non-proliferation export control, the Chinese Government adheres to the principle of enforcing the law strictly and punishing all offenders. For any suspected case of illegal export of sensitive items and technologies, competent authorities carry out careful investigation and handle it according to law. Since the end of 2002, the Chinese Government has dealt with scores of cases of various types concerning illegal export of sensitive items and technologies. Competent authorities have put the companies involved in these cases on a "watch list" so as to prevent the recurrence of similar activities. In May 2004, the Chinese Government established an inter-agency contingency mechanism for export control and spelt out in detail the responsibilities, division of labor and work procedures of relevant export control departments in dealing with emergency cases in this respect. This has provided an institutional safeguard for swift and effective handling of such cases.

Greater Publicity for Laws and Regulations on Export Control and Education for Enterprises

The Chinese Government attaches importance to educating and training law enforcement officials for export control, especially those at the grass-roots level, so as to raise their policy awareness and capability to exercise export control according to law. After the release of relevant laws and regulations on export control, the MOFCOM carried out comprehensive training programs on policies, laws and regulations for commerce officials at local levels. In places prone to cases of illegal export, the MOFCOM also holds, on non-regular basis, special training courses on policies, laws and regulations and law-enforcement of export control. In May 2004, the GAC, jointly with relevant organs in charge of non-proliferation export control, conducted training programs for on-site customs officials across the country on policies, laws and regulations with regard to the export control of sensitive items and technologies. The Chinese Government has taken various measures to make the legislation on export control known to enterprises, with a view to raising their awareness and self-discipline to abide by the law. Major measures include: to publish the full text of laws and regulations on export control on the websites of competent government departments; to get export enterprises familiarized, by organizing regular training courses and lectures and distributing pamphlets, with policies, laws and regulations on export control as well as the procedures for export examination and approval to ensure that the enterprises implement them in real earnest and run their business according to law; to set up a hotline to timely clear up doubts or questions from the enterprises; and to investigate and punish illegal exporters and make them public.

System and Principles on Non-Proliferation Export Control

China's legislation on export control widely embraces such international practices as licensing system, end-user and end-use certification, list control and "catch-all" principle. In order to reduce the risk of proliferation, relevant regulations also stipulate that nuclear exports and the export of controlled chemicals and military products can only be handled by a few trading companies designated by the Government. All regulations spell out in detail penalty measures for illegal exports. The scope of control of the aforementioned regulations is basically identical with international practices. For example, in the nuclear field, the control list tallies completely with those of the Zangger Committee and the Nuclear Suppliers Group and will undergo constant adjustments corresponding to changes made to them; in the biological and chemical field, the lists are basically the same as those of the Australia Group; and the missile list also conforms by and large with the annex to the MTCR. In real practice, the competent export control departments of the Chinese Government may also exercise, on an ad interim basis, export control according to law on items and technologies not on these lists. In addition, the Foreign Trade Law of the PRC, the Customs Law of the PRC, the Criminal Law of the PRC, the Administrative Punishments Law of the PRC, the Regulations of the PRC on the Import and Export Control of Goods and the Regulations of the PRC on the Import and Export Control of Technologies also provide a legal basis for China's non-proliferation export control.

Non-Proliferation Export Control Organs

China's non-proliferation export control involves many of the government's functional departments. So far, a mechanism for a clear division of responsibility and coordination has been established among these departments. China's nuclear export comes under the control of the state Administration of Science, Technology and Industry for National Defense (SASTIND), in coordination with other relevant government departments. Arms export, including the export of missiles, and facilities and key equipment used directly for the production of missiles, is under the control of the SASTIND and the relevant department under the Ministry of National Defense, in coordination with other government departments concerned. The export of nuclear dual-use items, dual-use biological agents, certain chemicals, and the missile-related dual-use items and technology for civilian use is under the control of the Ministry of Commerce (MOFCOM), in coordination with other government departments concerned. Among them, the export of nuclear dual-use items and missile-related dual-use items and technologies is subject to examination by the MOFCOM, in coordination with the SASTIND. The export of dual-use biological agents and technologies related to animals and plants is subject to examination by the MOFCOM, in coordination with the Ministry of Agriculture if needed. The export of dual-use biological agents and technologies related to humans is subject to examination by the MOFCOM, in coordination with the Ministry of Health if needed. The export of equipment and technologies related to dual-use biological agents and of equipment and technologies related to certain chemicals is subject to examination by the MOFCOM, in coordination with the National Development and Reform Commission (NDRC) if needed. The export of controlled chemicals is subject to examination by the National Development and Reform Commission, in coordination with the MOFCOM. The export of sensitive items and related equipment and technologies that relate to foreign policy is subject to examination by the above-mentioned competent departments, in coordination with the Ministry of Foreign Affairs. Where the export items entail significant impact on national security and public interests, the competent departments shall, jointly with other relevant departments, submit the case to the State Council and the Central Military Commission for approval. The General Administration of Customs (GAC) is responsible for supervision and control of the export of the above-mentioned items and technologies, and it also participates in investigating and handling cases of illegal

exports. The Customs have the authority to question whether the items from the exporters are sensitive items and technologies, and to request the exporters to follow regulations and apply to competent government departments either for export license or for relevant certificates to show that the exports are not controlled items.

Prevention of Weaponization of and Arms Race in Outer Space (PAROS)

China has been vigorously calling for attention and efforts by the international community to prevent an arms race in and the weaponization of outer space. China stands for the establishment of an Ad Hoc Committee on PAROS by the CD in Geneva to negotiate an international legal instrument on PAROS. As a first step, the CD should set out to conduct substantive work on the issue of PAROS at an early date. In 2000, China submitted to the CD a working paper entitled "China's Position on and Suggestions for Ways to Address the Issue of Prevention of an Arms Race in Outer Space at the Conference on Disarmament," pointing out that PAROS should be one of the top priorities on the CD's agenda, and proposing the reestablishment of the Ad Hoc Committee to negotiate an international legal instrument in this regard. In June 2002, China, Russia, Belarus, Indonesia, Syria, Vietnam and Zimbabwe submitted to the CD a joint working paper entitled "Possible Elements for a Future International Agreement on the Prevention of Deployment of Weapons in Outer Space, the Threat or Use of Force against Outer Space Objects," putting forward specific proposals on the major elements for the future international legal instrument, which has gained wide support from many countries. In August 2004, China and Russia jointly distributed two thematic papers at the CD, entitled "Existing International Legal Instruments and the Prevention of the Weaponization of Outer Space" and "Verification Aspects of Prevention of an Arms Race in Outer Space." In March 2005, China and Russia, together with the UN Institute for Disarmament Research and the Simons Foundation of Canada, successfully hosted an international conference in Geneva on "Safeguarding Outer Space Security: Prevention of an Arms Race in Outer Space". In June 2005, China and Russia jointly distributed a thematic paper at the CD, entitled "Definition Issues Regarding Legal Instruments on the Prevention of Weaponization of Outer Space."

Combating the Illicit Trade in Small Arms and Light Weapons (SALW)

China supports multilateral efforts to combat the illicit trade in SALW and has actively participated in the relevant work within the UN framework. China played a constructive role in the negotiation of the Firearms Protocol and signed the Protocol in December 2002. China supports and actively participated in the negotiation of the UN Instrument on Identifying and Tracing Illicit SALW. It has earnestly implemented the UN Program of Action on SALW and has submitted its national reports in a timely manner. In April 2005, China hosted an international workshop on SALW in Beijing, which was co-sponsored with the UN, Japan and Switzerland. Firmly combating illegal activities in the field of SALW is of great importance to maintaining regional peace, stability and development, fighting terrorism and cracking down upon such transnational organized crimes as drug-trafficking and smuggling. China stands for greater efforts at the national, regional and international levels to seek a comprehensive solution in this regard.

Laws and Regulations of China on Non-Proliferation Export Control

	Laws and Regulations	Date
In the Nuclear Field	Regulations of the PRC on the Control of Nuclear Export	promulgated in September 1997, revised in June 2001
	Regulations of the PRC on the Control of Nuclear Dual-Use Items and Related Technologies Export	promulgated in June 1998
	Measures on the Administration of Approval for Transfer and Transit of Nuclear Items (For Trial Implementation)	promulgated in January 2000
In the Biological Field	Regulations of the PRC on the Export Control of Dual-Use Biological Agents and Related Equipment and Technologies	promulgated in October 2002
In the Chemical Field	Regulations of the PRC on the Administration of Controlled Chemicals	promulgated in December 1995
	Controlled Chemicals List	promulgated in May 1996, supplemented in June 1998
	Detailed Rules for the Implementation of the Regulations of the PRC on the Administration of Controlled Chemicals	promulgated in March 1997
	List of New Chemicals Controlled in Category 3	promulgated in June 1998
	Measures on the Export Control of Certain Chemicals and Related Equipment and Technologies	promulgated in October 2002
In the Missile Field	Regulations of the PRC on the Export Control of Missiles and Missile-Related Items and Technologies	promulgated in August 2002
In the Arms Export Field	Regulations of the PRC on the Administration of Arms Export	promulgated in October 1997, amended in October 2002; the Military Products Export Control List promulgated in November 2002
Sensitive Items	Measures on the Administration of Export Registration for Sensitive Items and Technologies	promulgated in November 2002
	Provisional Measures on the Administration of Export Licenses on Sensitive Items and Technologies	promulgated in December 2003
	Export Licensing Catalogue of Sensitive Items and Technologies	promulgated in December 2003
Other Related Laws and Regulations	Foreign Trade Law of the PRC	promulgated in May 1994, amended in April 2004
	Administrative Punishments Law of the PRC	promulgated in March 1996
	Customs Law of the PRC	promulgated in January 1987, amended in July 2000
	Amendments to the Criminal Law of the PRC	promulgated in December 2001
	Regulations of the PRC on the Import and Export Control of Technologies	promulgated in December 2001
	Regulations of the PRC on the Import and Export Control of Goods	promulgated in December 2001
	Regulations of the PRC on the Control of Nuclear Dual-Use Items and Related Technologies Export (Revised)	Promulgated on January 26, 2007

Relations with Foreign Countries

Foreign Policy

China unswervingly pursues an independent foreign policy of peace. The fundamental goals are to maintain world peace and propel common development. The main content is:

—Conforming to the historical trend and maintaining the common interests of all humanity. China is ready to work together with the international community to actively facilitate global multi-polarization, promote harmonious coexistence of various forces, maintain the stability of the international community, boost the development of economic globalization with the orientation of realizing common prosperity, seek advantages and avoid disadvantages, so as to benefit all countries, especially the developing ones.

—Establishing a new international political and economic order that is fair and rational. Politically all countries should mutually respect and consult one another instead of one imposing its will on others; economically, countries should complement one another and pursue common development instead of creating a polarization of wealth; culturally, countries should learn from each other and work for common prosperity, instead of excluding cultures of other nations; in the security field, countries should trust one another, work together to maintain security, foster a new security concept featuring mutual trust, mutual benefit and co-ordination on an equal footing, resolve their disputes and conflicts peacefully through consultation and not resort to the use or the threat of force. China opposes all forms of hegemony and power politics. China will never seek hegemony and never go in for expansion.

—Maintaining the diversity of the world and advocating democracy of international relationships and diversification of developmental models. Countries having different civilizations and social systems and taking roads to development should respect one another and draw upon each other's strong points and should develop side by side by seeking common ground while shelving differences. The affairs of each country should be left to the people of that country to decide. World affairs should be determined by all countries concerned through consultations on the basis of equality.

—Fighting against terrorism in all forms. It is imperative to strengthen international cooperation in this regard, address both the symptoms and root causes of terrorism, prevent and combat terrorist activities and work hard to eliminate terrorism at the root.

—Improving and developing relations with developed countries. China advocates that countries should surmount their differences in social systems and ideology, respect one another, seek common ground and shelve differences and enhance their mutually beneficial cooperation. Their disputes should be appropriately solved through dialogue on the basis of the Five Principles of Peaceful Coexistence.

—Cementing friendly ties with neighbors and persisting in building a good-neighborly relationship and partnership with them and promoting regional cooperation.

—Enhancing solidarity and cooperation with other third world countries, increasing mutual understanding and trust and strengthening mutual help and support. China will enlarge the areas of cooperation and seek to make them more fruitful.

—Taking an active part in multilateral diplomatic activities and playing a major role in the United Nations and other international or regional organizations. China will support other developing countries in their efforts to safeguard their legitimate rights and interests.

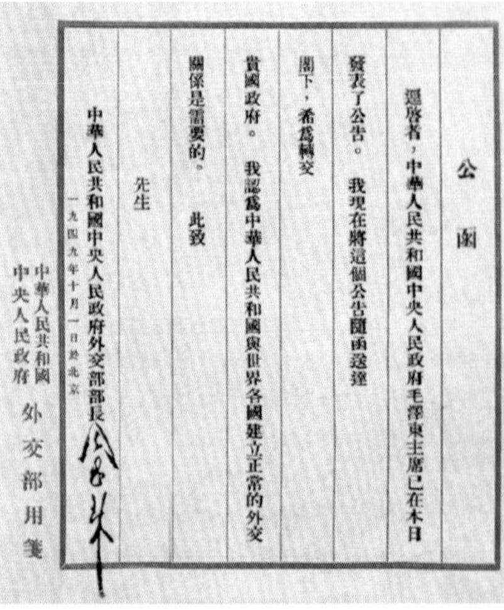

公函

逕啓者，中華人民共和國中央人民政府毛澤東主席已在本日
發表了公告。我現在將這個公告隨函送達
閣下，希爲轉交
貴國政府。我認爲中華人民共和國與世界各國建立正常的外交
關係是需要的。此致

先生

中華人民共和國中央人民政府外交部部長 周恩來
一九四九年十月一日於北京

中華人民共和國 中央人民政府 外交部用箋

After the founding of the New China in 1949, then Foreign Minister Zhou Enlai wrote letters attached to which was the proclamation the People's Central Government to governments of various countries, saying that the New China is willing to establish regular foreign relations with various countries.

The Five Principles of Peaceful Coexistence

In 1953, Premier Zhou Enlai, based on Mao Zedong Thought regarding peaceful coexistence among countries with them all, big or small, being treated as equal, first put forward the Five Principles of Peaceful Coexistence with India and Burma [Myanmar] in 1954. The Five Principles have since been recognized universally. The main contents are mutual respect for territorial integrity and sovereignty, mutual non-aggression, non-interference in each other's internal affairs, equality and mutual benefit, and peaceful coexistence. The Five Principles were incorporated in the preface of the Agreement on Trade and Transportation between India and China's Tibet Region in April, 1954. On June 25, 1954, Premier Zhou Enlai visited India, and on June 28, he and his Indian counterpart issued a joint declaration, reaffirming the Five Principles of Peaceful Coexistence as the main guide for diplomatic relations.

When handling relations between countries, China persistently follows the Five Principles of Peaceful Coexistence, and stresses that social system, ideology and values should not be regarded as criteria. In 1982, the Five Principles of Peaceful Coexistence were

In June 2004, more than 90 political personages and senior scholars from 13 countries met in Beijing to hold an international symposium to mark the 50th anniversary of the introduction of the Five Principles of Peaceful Coexistence.

written into the Constitution of the PRC. Now, the Five Principles serve as a basic principle for China to establish and develop friendly relations with all countries in the world.

Principle of Establishing Diplomatic Relations

The Chinese Government, on October 1, 1949, i.e. the day when the PRC was founded, proclaimed solemnly that "the Government is the sole legitimate government representing the People's Republic of China. Any foreign government ready to conform to the principles of equality, mutual benefit and mutually respect territory and sovereignty is welcome to establish diplomatic relations with our Government."

It is a basic principle of China's diplomacy to maintain its sovereignty over Taiwan. There is only one China in the world and Taiwan is an inalienable part of Chinese territory. Any country, which has established diplomatic relations with China, must make clear that it severs all diplomatic relations with the Taiwan authority and admits the Government of PRC is the only legitimate government of China. The Chinese Government will never tolerate any country to pursue plots like "two Chinas" or "one China one Taiwan", nor tolerate countries with formal diplomatic relations with China establishing any form of official relations with Taiwan.

Date of China Establishing Diplomatic Relations with Other Countries

(Ranking in the sequence of Asia, Africa, Europe, America and Oceania. Countries of the same continent take the English alphabetical order of the shortened form of its country name).

	Name of Countries	Date of Establishing Diplomatic Relations
Asia	Afghanistan	1955.1.20
	Armenia	1992.4.6
	Azerbaijan	1992.4.2
	Bahrain	1989.4.18
	Bengladesh	1975.10.4
	Brunei	1991.9.30
	Cambodia	1958.7.19
	Cyprus	1971.12.14
	North Korea	1949.10.6
	East Timor	2002.5.20
	Georgia	1992.6.9
	India	1950.4.1
	Indonesia	1950.4.13
	Iran	1971.8.16
	Iraq	1958.8.25
	Israel	1992.1.24
	Japan	1972.9.29
	Jordan	1977.4.7
	Kazakhstan	1992.1.3
	Kuwait	1971.3.22
	Kirghizia	1992.1.5
	Laos	1961.4.25
	Lebanon	1971.11.9
	Malaysia	1974.5.31
	Maldives	1972.10.14
	Mongolia	1949.10.16
	Burma	1950.6.8
	Nepal	1955.8.1
	Oman	1978.5.25
	Pakistan	1951.5.21
	Palestine	1988.11.20
	Philippine	1975.6.9
	Qatar	1988.7.9
	South Korea	1992.8.24
	Saudi Arabia	1990.7.21
	Singapore	1990.10.3
	Sri Lanka	1957.2.7
	Syria	1956.8.1
	Tajikistan	1992.1.4
	Thailand	1975.7.1
	Turkey	1971.8.4
	Turkmenistan	1992.1.6
	United Arab Emirates	1984.11.1
	Uzbekistan	1992.1.2
	Viet Nam	1950.1.18
	Yemen	1956.9.24
Africa	Algeria	1958.12.20
	Angola	1983.1.12
	Benin	1964.11.12
	Botswana	1975.1.6
	Burundi	1963.12.21
	Cameroon	1971.3.26
	Cape Verde	1976.4.25
	Central Africa	1964.9.29
	Comorin	1975.11.13
	Congo (with Kinshasa as the capital)	1961.2.20
	Congo (with Brazzaville as the capital)	1964.2.22
	Cote d'Ivoire	1983.3.2
	Djibouti	1979.1.8
	Egypt	1956.5.30
	Equatorial Guinea	1970.10.15
	Eritrea	1993.5.24
	Ethiopia	1970.11.24
	Gabon	1974.4.20
	Ghana	1960.7.5
	Guinea	1959.10.4
	Guinea-Bissau	1974.3.15
	Kenya	1963.12.14
	Lesotho	1983.4.30
	Liberia	1977.2.17
	Libya	1978.8.9
	Madagascar	1972.11.6
	Mali	1960.10.25
	Mauritania	1965.7.19
	Mauritius	1972.4.15
	Morocco	1958.11.1
	Mozambique	1975.6.25
	Namibia	1990.3.22
	Niger	1974.7.20
	Nigeria	1971.2.10
	Rwanda	1971.11.12
	Senegal	1971.12.7
	Seychelles	1976.6.30
	Sierra Leone	1971.7.29
	Somalia	1960.12.14
	South Africa	1998.1.1
	Sudan	1959.2.4
	Tanzania	1964.4.26
	Togo	1972.9.19
	Tunis	1964.1.10
	Uganda	1962.10.18
	Zambia	1964.10.29
	Zimbabwe	1980.4.18
Europe	Albania	1949.11.23
	Andorra	1994.6.29
	Austria	1971.5.28
	White Russia	1992.1.20
	Belgium	1971.10.25
	Bosnia and Herzegovina	1995.4.3
	Bulgaria	1949.10.4
	Croatia	1992.5.13
	Czech Republic	1949.10.6
	Denmark	1950.5.11
	Estonia	1991.9.11
	Finland	1950.10.28
	France	1964.1.27
	Germany	1972.10.11
	Greece	1972.6.5
	Hungary	1949.10.6
	Iceland	1971.12.8
	Ireland	1979.6.22
	Italy	1970.11.6
	Latvia	1991.9.12
	Liechtenstein	1950.9.14
	Lithuania	1991.9.14
	Luxemburg	1972.11.16
	Macedonia	1993.10.12
	Malta	1972.1.31
	Moldova	1992.1.30
	Monaco [1]	1995.1.16
	Netherlands	1972.5.18
	Norway	1954.10.5
	Poland	1949.10.7
	Portugal	1979.2.8
	Romania	1949.10.5
	Russia	1949.10.2
	San Marino	1971.5.6
	Serbia and Montenegro [2]	1955.1.2
	Slovakia	11949.10.6
	Slovenia	1992.5.12
	Spain	1973.3.9
	Sweden	1950.5.9
	Switzerland	1950.9.14
	Ukraine	1992.1.4
	U.K.	1972.3.13
Americas	Antigua and Barbuda	1983.1.1
	Argentina	1972.2.19
	The Bahamas	1997.5.23
	Barbados	1977.5.30
	Bolivia	1985.7.9
	Brazil	1974.8.15
	Canada	1970.10.13
	Chile	1970.12.15
	Colombia	1980.2.7
	Cuba	1960.9.28
	Dominica	2004.3.23
	Ecuador	1980.1.2
	Grenada	1985.10.1
	Guyana	1972.6.27
	Jamaica	1972.11.21
	Mexico	1972.2.14
	Peru	1971.11.2
	Saint Lucia	1997.9.1
	Surinam	1976.5.28
	Trinidad and Tobago	1974.6.20
	U.S.	1979.1.1
	Uruguay	1988.2.3
	Venezuela	1974.6.28
Oceania Islands of Pacific Oceans	Australia	1972.12.21
	Cook Islands	1997.7.25
	Fiji	1975.11.5
	Micronesia	1989.9.11
	New Zealand	1972.12.22
	Papua New Guinea	1976.10.12
	Samoa	1975.11.6
	Tonga	1998.11.2
	Vanuatu	1982.3.26

[1] On January 16, 1995, China established formal consul relations with Monaco.

[2] On January 2, 1955, China established diplomatic relations with Federal People's Republic of Yugoslavia (later renamed the Socialist Federal Republic of Yugoslavia). On April 27, 1992, the Federal Republic of Yugoslavia proclaimed its foundation. The Chinese embassy to the former Yugoslavia was changed to the embassy to the Federal Republic of Yugoslavia, and the ambassador to the former Yugoslavia was changed to ambassador to the Federal Republic of Yugoslavia. On February 4, 2003, the Federal Republic of Yugoslavia changed its name to Serbia and Montenegro.

♦ Ministry of Foreign Affairs

This is the competent department in charge of dealing with representations between countries and consulate and overseas Chinese affairs. Foreign affairs offices are established in all provinces, autonomous regions, and municipalities directly under the Central Government, in charge of the foreign affairs of the locality and under the leadership of the Ministry of Foreign Affairs. The ministry set up commissioner's offices in the Special Administration Regions, an organization which deals with foreign affairs concerned with the SAR under the administration of the Central Government, and serves as a communication channel between the SAR Government and the Central Government on such diplomatic issues.

Address: No.2 Nan Dajie, Chaoyangmen, Chaoyang District, Beijing
Website: http://www.mfa.gov.cn/chn/default.htm

Ministry of Foreign Affairs is located at the Chaoyangmen, Chaoyang District, Beijing.

Diplomatic Relations

Up to November 25, 2005, China has established diplomatic relations with 167 countries.

Sino-US Relations

In February 1972, President Richard Nixon of the United States visited China. The two sides published the Sino-US Joint Communiqué, known as the Shanghai Communiqué, marking the ending of over two decades of separation between the two nations. On December 16, 1978, the two governments issued the Joint Communiqué of the United States of America and the People's Republic of China on the Establishment of Diplomatic Relations simultaneously. The US Government accepted the three principles on establishing diplomatic relations proposed by the Chinese Government, namely severing diplomatic relations with Taiwan, evacuating troops from Taiwan and abolishing its treaty relationship with the Taiwanese authority of Chiang Kai-shek. The two countries established formal diplomatic relations on January 1, 1979, signaling a milestone in the history of the bilateral relations. Thereafter, Sino-US relations entered a new stage.

The establishment of diplomatic relations between China and US opened a path for exchanges and cooperation between the two countries. Amid the twists and turns over the past more than three decades, Sino-US relations have continued developing. The two countries conduct regular mutual visits between the top leaders and consultations between high-ranking officials of the two sides. Meanwhile, the two countries have seen continuing development of exchanges and cooperation in the field of economy and trade, science and technology, culture, education and military. Both China and the US are large countries with tremendous influence in the world. The two sides have important shared strategic interests in the fields of economy and trade, security, public sanitation, energy and environment protection, as well as many significant international and regional issues. In particular, the economic and trade cooperation of mutual benefit and win-win between the two sides not only benefits people of the two countries and promotes economic growth in Asia-Pacific region and even the world as a whole, but also serves as an important foundation for the relations between the two countries.

The Taiwan problem is the largest obstacle to the healthy development of Sino-US relations. The Chinese leaders have constantly proposed that it is the core interests of China to maintain the country's sovereignty and territorial integrity. China's stand on North Korea makes the US side further understand the sensitivity of Taiwan problem, reaffirm that the US adheres to the "One-China Policy" on many occasions, complies with the Joint Communiqué and does not support any words and deeds that change the status quo of Taiwan unilaterally and proclaim the independence of Taiwan.

Sino-Japanese Relations

On October 2, 1971, China put forward "the three principles for the restoration of relations between China and Japan": the People's Republic of China is the sole legitimate government representing China; Taiwan is an inalienable part of China; and the "Peace Treaty between Japan and Chiang Kai-shek" is illegal and invalid, and must be abolished. On September 25, 1972, the Japanese Prime Minister Kakuei Tanaka visited China at the invitation of the Chinese Premier Zhou Enlai. On September 29, both the Chinese and Japanese governments issued the Sino-Japanese Joint Statement. The restoration of diplomatic relations between the two countries was thus achieved. Over the past 30 years, tremendous development has been achieved in the field of politics, economy, culture, education and civilian exchanges, bringing significant improvements for the interests to the two countries and their people, as well as boosting the peace and development in the region and the world.

A stele erecting in the Sino-Japanese Friendship cherry forest, Xuzhou, Jiangsu Province

Sino-Russian Relations

On October 2, 1949, China established diplomatic relations with the Soviet Union. In August 1991, Soviet Union was dissolved. On December 27 of the same year, China and Russia signed an understanding on diplomatic relations between China and the former Soviet Union. In 2001, the Sino-Russia strategic partnership of cooperation entered a new level. The two sides have deepened their mutual trust in political terms and high level contacts have become frequent. In 2001, the two heads of state signed the Treaty of Good-Neighborliness and Friendly Cooperation between the People's Republic of China and Russia, and issued a joint declaration confirming the peaceful ideology featuring long-term friendship in the form of law.

On March 21, 2006, Russian President Putin visited China, highlighting that the Sino-Russia strategic partnership of cooperation had moved to a new stage with great repercussions for maintaining world peace. The heads of state signed the Joint Sino-Russia Statement. The two Governments altogether signed 22 documents on cooperation, involving the fields of politics, diplomacy, energy and finance. President Putin and President Hu Jintao attended the opening ceremony of the "Year of Russia" together. Thereafter, 207 activities were scheduled to be held in succession, covering all fields of exchanges and cooperation between the two countries. In order to enhance mutual understanding between the two peoples, the leaders identified 2006 as "Year of Russia" in China and 2007 as the "Year of China" in Russia. This is the first such event in the history of Sino-Russia relations, and an important step to implementing the principles and spirit of the Treaty of Good-Neighborliness and Friendly Cooperation.

The recent years has seen ever closer

Mark of the 2007 Year of China in Russia

bilateral economic and trade relations and economic and technological cooperation. The two countries also hold frequent exchanges and cooperation in the field of culture, science and technology and education.

China and Russia share a boundary of some 4,370 km and there are boundary issue left over from history. The two sides, based on the current boundary treaty and according to the recognized guidelines of international law and in line with the spirit of equal coordination and mutual understanding and mutual concession, have solved all their border problems for good through years of negotiation.

Sino-European Relations

On May 6, 1975, China and the European Economic Community established formal relations. On November 11, 1983, China established formal relations with the European Coal and Steel Community and the European Atomic Energy Community. Thus China established diplomatic relations with EU as a whole. In recent years, Sino-Europe relations have enjoyed rapid development. In 2001, the two sides decided to establish an all-round partnership. In 2003, after the sixth contact between leaders of the two sides, they reached consensus of developing an all-round strategic partnership.

On October 13, 2003, China issued the 'China EU Policy Paper', which is the first one ever aimed at a certain region issued publicly. Up to now, the EU has issued five policy papers on China, namely Long-term Policy for China-Europe Relations (1955), EU's New Strategy Toward China (1966), Building a Comprehensive Partnership with China (1998), the EU-China Towards China: Implementation of the 1998 Communication and Future Steps for a More Effective EU Policy (2001), A Maturing Partnership—Shared Interests and Challenges in EU-China Relations (2003).

In 1994, China and Europe signed a political dialogue agreement. In June 2002, the two sides reached a new political dialogue agreement. In 1998, annual contact mechanism between the leaders was set up and there have been eight summits so far.

Since the establishment of diplomatic relations between China and Europe, all the previous presidents of European Community (EU) and the present secretary-general and concurrently High Representative for the Common Foreign and Security Polity, Javier Solana, have visited China. Many Chinese leaders have visited the EU headquarters in Brussels.

China and EU have a shared political foundation of comprehensive cooperation: both sides can respect the culture of the other side and carry out an equal dialogue on any disputes. The two sides have the same or similar views on current significant international issues; for example, both sides advocate democracy in international relations and multi-polarization, oppose unilateralism and power politics. In the war against terrorism, both sides stand for the authoritative role of the UN, striking at the roots of terrorism as well as its harmful effects, and oppose excessive use of force. In economic cooperation, both sides look after each other's interests and achieve a win-win situation.

Relations between China and the Surrounding Countries

China earnestly implements the policy of "friendship and partnership with neighboring countries" and the policy of "fostering a harmonious, secure, and prosperous neighborhood", takes "peace, security, cooperation and prosperity" as the objective of its Asian policy, and actively promote good-neighbor relations and regional cooperation. At present, China has solved .boundary issues left over from history with most neighboring countries. Some specific problems with few countries are being solved through peaceful consultation.

Each year, the Chinese leaders will visit some Asian countries, and a lot of leaders from other Asian countries visit China. The frequent high profile visits enhance mutual understanding, and consolidate and promote the friendly and cooperative relations.

In the international arena, China and other Asian countries coordinate positions and support each other. They stick to the "one-China" policy, and China supports their just activities in maintaining national sovereignty and opposing big power hegemonism.

China has established a strategic partnership with many Asian countries. In Oct 2003, China's adherence to the Treaty of Amity and Cooperation in Southeast Asia as a non-ASEAN country has further enhanced mutual trust and strengthened the political and legal foundation for developing bilateral relations.

China has constantly worked to strengthen the efforts of creating bilateral friendship, actively advance regional cooperation, appropriately respond to hot issues and emergencies, and promote regional peace, stability and prosperity. China adheres to the aim of equality, mutual benefit, cooperation and win-win in regional cooperation, and realizes its own interests while expanding common interests with the surrounding countries.

♦ The Chinese People's Association for Friendship with Foreign Countries (CPAFFC)

This is a national people's organization engaged in non-governmental foreign affairs in China. The organization's purpose is the promotion of friendship between Chinese and other peoples throughout the world, promotion of international cooperation, maintenance of world peace and promotion of development together. Representing the Chinese people, it makes contacts and promotes exchanges with friendly organizations and people all over the globe. In line with the Five Principles of Peaceful Coexistence, it works hard to carry out a peaceful foreign policy and undertakes multi-level, all-round non-governmental friendly foreign affairs. Supported by the Chinese Government and all social circles, it has already set up friendly cooperation relations with 550 non-governmental organizations and social organizations in 130 countries.

The association,called (CPAFFC) for short, was co-founded on May 3, 1954 by 10 national social organizations. It was originally named the Chinese People's Association for Culture with Foreign Countries and renamed as the Chinese People's Association for Culture and Friendship with Foreign Countries in 1966, before gaining its present name in 1969. It has branches in all the provinces, autonomous regions and municipalities directly under the Central Government as well as some cities, districts or counties.

The CPAFFC convenes a national council session, at which the chairman, vice chairman and secretary-general are elected, and the standing committee chosen.

Address: No.1 Taijichang Dajie, Dongcheng District, Beijing
Website: http://www.cpaffc.org.cn

♦ The Chinese People's Institute of Foreign Affairs

The Chinese People's Institute for Foreign Affairs (CPIFA) was founded in December 1949. Its remit is to engage in studies on the world situation, international issues and foreign policies, and to carry out exchanges with statesmen, scholars, noted personages, relevant research institutions and social organizations of various countries, with a view to enhancing mutual understanding and friendship between the Chinese people and the people of all other countries, promoting the establishment and development of friendly relations and cooperation between China and other countries and making contributions to peace and development of the world.

Address: No.71, Nanchizi Dajie, Dongcheng District, Beijing
Website: http://www.cpifa.org/index.htm

Relations with ASEAN

In 2004, the relations between China and ASEAN entered a new stage. In June, China and the ten countries of ASEAN held an official conference in Qingdao, reaching a consensus that ASEAN and the permanent representative of China to the UN should conduct regular consultations for realizing an East Asia Community, the long-term objective of cooperation among East Asian countries, through the current cooperative mechanism of "ten plus three", and support the convening of an East Asia Summit at a proper time. In July, the Minister of Foreign Affairs, Li Zhaoxing, attended the ASEAN-China, Japan and South Korea Ministerial Meeting in Jakarta, PMC and ARF. At the end of November, Chinese Premier Wen Jiabao attended the 8th ASEAN-China, Japan and South Korea, ASEAN-China and the 6th China, Japan and South Korea Summit, which were held in Vientiane, proposing the basic policy of "equality, mutual trust, cooperation and win-win" which guides the long-term development of bilateral relations. During the meetings, the two sides published a Joint Declaration on Strategic Partnership for Peace and Prosperity, and signed a series of documents including China-ASEAN Framework Agreement on Comprehensive Economic Cooperation and Agreement on Dispute Settlement Mechanism of the Framework Agreement on Comprehensive Economic Co-operation between the People's Republic of China and the Association of Southeast Asian Nations. In January 2005, Premier Wen Jiabao headed for Jakarta for the ASEAN Special Meeting on issues in the aftermath of earthquake and tsunami.

Relations with Developing Countries

China is the largest developing country in the world. It is the cornerstone of China's foreign policy to consolidate and develop cooperation with developing countries. China makes great efforts to strengthen cooperation with the massive developing countries, boost South-South cooperation and establish new international order featuring fair and rational treatment. At the beginning of 2004, President Hu Jintao conducted state visits to Egypt, Gabon and Algeria, during which "China-Arab Countries Cooperation Forum" was set up, consolidating and expanding the mutually beneficial and cooperative relations with Arab countries in all fields. In November, President Hu Jintao visited Brazil, Argentina, Chile and Cuba of Latin America, laying a solid foundation for the long-term stable and comprehensively friendly cooperation with the four countries. Minister of Foreign Affairs, Li Zhaoxing, also paid official visits to Sudan, Comoros, and Uganda.

Leaders of the developing countries visit China quite frequently. Leaders from Surinam, Papua New Guinea, Yemen, Mozambique, Madagascar, Burundi, Syria, Argentina, Fiji, Kuwait, Mali, Namibia, Jordan, Bahamas, Central Africa Republic, Gabon, Vanuatu, Ethiopia, Venezuela and Mauritius, visited China in succession from the beginning of 2004 to the end of January 2005.

China engages in promoting South-South cooperation and "South-North dialogue, exploring new fields and new approaches for developing mutual beneficial cooperation with developing countries, further provides assistance in its power so as to help developing countries to overcome difficulties and strengthen their independent capability of development. China also provides preferential duties to the most undeveloped countries in Asia and Africa, and has remitted 1.3778 billion Yuan of debt incurred by 38 Asian and African countries. It actively promotes the establishment of the China-Africa and China-Arab Cooperation Forum and strengthens collective dialogue and cooperation between developed and developing countries.

Beijing Summit of the Forum on China-Africa Cooperation

Logo of the Forum on China-Africa Cooperation

The Forum on China-Africa Cooperation serves as a platform of collective consultation and dialogue between China and African countries with whom China has friendly ties, and a cooperative mechanism for South-South cooperation. In October, 2000, the 1st Ministerial Conference was convened in Beijing.

The Beijing Summit convened in October 2006 was the 3rd Ministerial Conference of China-Africa Forum. The forum aims at pragmatic cooperation, strengthening consultation and expanding cooperation. Mutual benefits on an equal basis is another principal, which advocates political dialogue and economic and trade cooperation so as to promote mutual progress and achieve common development. At the summit, Chinese President Hu Jintao proposed eight measures on promoting cooperation between China and Africa:

1. Strengthen China's assistance to Africa.

2. Provide $US3 billion of preferential loans and $US2 billion of preferential buyer's credits to Africa in the next three years.

3. Set up a China-Africa development fund to reach US$5 billion in stages to encourage and support Chinese enterprises to invest in Africa.

4. Build a conference center for the Organization of African Union to support African countries in their efforts to strengthen themselves through unity and support the process of African integration.

5. Cancel debt in the form of all the interest-free government loans that matured at the end of 2005 owed by the heavily-indebted poor countries and the least developed countries in Africa that have diplomatic relations with China.

6. Further open up China's market to Africa by increasing from 190 to over 440 the number of export items receiving zero-tariff treatment from the least developed countries in Africa having diplomatic ties with China.

7. Establish three to five trade and economic cooperation zones in Africa in the next three years.

8. Over the next three years, train 15,000 African professionals; send 100 senior agricultural experts to Africa; set up 10 special agricultural technology demonstration centers in Africa; build 30 hospitals in Africa and provide 300 million Yuan of grants, and building 30 malaria prevention and treatment centers to fight malaria; dispatch 300 youth volunteers to Africa; build 100 rural schools in Africa; and increase the number of Chinese government scholarships to African students from the current 2,000 to 4,000 per year by 2009.

China and the UN

On April 25, 1945, representatives from 50 countries including China convoked the conference of the United Nations in San Francisco. On June 25, the UN Charter was adopted. On June 26, after China, France, Soviet Union, Britain, US and a majority of the signatory countries submitted the authorization letter, the Charter came into effect automatically. Thus, the UN was founded.

The UN is the most important inter-governmental international organization. China is one of the founders of the UN. However, for some time after the founding of New China, it was barred from the UN and it took 22 years for it to resume its legitimate seat. At the 26th UN General Assembly held on October 25, 1971, Resolution No. 2758 was adopted with an overwhelming majority of 76 votes for the proposal, 35 against and 17 abstentions, which "restores all China's lawful right in the UN and expels delegates of the Kuomintang from the UN and all its organizations". On November 15, 1971, the Chinese delegation attended the UN Assembly for the first time and received a warm welcome. Thereafter, all the major bodies of the UN restored China's membership. Chinese is also listed as one of the working languages of the UN.

China is a founding member of the UN and holds a permanent seat on its Security Council. It is China's belief that the UN plays an irreplaceable role in international affairs. While rendering consistent support to the proposed UN reforms, China has repeatedly affirmed its position on the principle and direction of the reforms. The Chinese Government issued the Position Paper on the UN Reforms in June 2005, coming up with a complete, systematic summarization of its stance on UN reforms in an official paper for the first time. The four-part paper gives an overall picture of China's stance on issues such as development, security, the rule of law, human rights and democracy and the strengthening of the world body.

China stresses that the reforms of UN should serve the interests of the entire international community. It puts development in less developed countries, especially the impoverished ones, on top of the agenda and has made suggestions in this respect. China stands for safeguarding the leading role of the Security Council and the sovereignty of developing countries. With regard to human rights, China attaches importance to national sovereignty while endorsing the Security Council's initiatives to resolve massive humanitarian crises and backs the reform of the UN's human rights agency.

Participation in UN Peacekeeping Operations China is committed to, and takes an active part in, peacekeeping operations that conform to the UN Charter. It holds that these missions should earnestly abide by the purpose of the UN Charter and universally recognized peacekeeping principles. It stands for carrying out reforms in UN peacekeeping operations to further enhance its efficacy.

China filed a formal application to join the UN Special Committee on Peacekeeping Operations in September 1988. It sent five military observers to the UN Truce Supervision Organization--the world body's earliest observer mission--in April 1990, marking its first-ever participation in a UN peacekeeping operation. Between 1992 and 1993, China dispatched a regiment of 800 engineering corps in two groups to the UN Transitional Authority in Cambodia, the first time it has sent regularly organized non-combat troops to a UN peacekeeping mission. To date, it has offered more than 4,100 man-hours of peacekeeping to 14 UN missions. Of these, 3,000 went into peacekeeping units, while 900 were accounted for by personnel serving as military observers and staff officers.

In its participation in UN peacekeeping operations, China is guided by the following three principles that have been universally recognized in the UN for the past 50 years: gaining the approval of the country or party concerned before carrying out peacekeeping operations, keeping neutral and using force only for self-defense.

China and APEC

Emblem of the APEC

In January 1989, the Asia-Pacific Economic Cooperation Organization (APEC) was founded. According to the Memo of Understanding reached by China and the APEC, in November 1991, China acceded to the APEC as a sovereign state, and Taipei of China and Hong Kong (renamed "Hong Kong of China" since July 1, 1997) acceded to the APEC as regional economies.

Since its entrance to APEC, China actively participates in all kinds of activities, creating a favorable external environment for China's reform and opening up, as well as promoting the development of bilateral relations between China and other members of APEC. Since 1993, the Chinese President has attended the annual Informal APEC Economic Leaders' Meetings, and put forward China's claims, principles and stance with clear aims, playing a positive and constructive role for the success of the meeting. In 2001, China succeeded in staging an Informal APEC Economic Leaders' Meeting in Shanghai.

China holds that APEC is an organization with economic forum features that should engage in regional economic cooperation. China maintains that "APEC mode" should be the approach and principle of APEC cooperation. This mode acknowledges the diversity, and emphasizes the principles of independence, free will, coordination for consensus, flexibility and progressive proceeding.

China supports advancing the process of liberalization of trade and investment on the basis of following the principle of opening up and non-discrimination, so as to promote the sound development of the multilateral trade system. China upholds the long-term goal of realizing regional liberalization of trade and investment within the scope of APEC, and boosting the process of liberalization of trade and investment with practical actions.

China attaches great importance to economic and technological cooperation, believing that economic and technological cooperation and the liberalization of trade and investment should be closely combined and mutually promote each other's development, so as to make the two wheels of the APEC operate simultaneously. Since China's accession to APEC, it has played an important role in promoting economic and technological cooperation.

China and Shanghai Cooperation Organization

In June 2001, the heads of state of China, Russia, Kazakhstan, Kyrgyzstan, Tajikistan and Uzbekistan met in Shanghai, and signed a Declaration on the Establishment of the Shanghai Cooperation Organization as a new regional multilateral cooperation organization on the basis of the "Shanghai Five-country mechanism". The purpose of the organization is to strengthen mutual trust and good neighborliness among the members, encourage effective cooperation in the fields of politics, economy and trade, science and technology, culture, education, energy, communication and environment protection

The 5th anniversary of the Shanghai Cooperative Organization was celebrated in June 2006.

among the membership, make concerned efforts to maintain world and regional peace, security and stability, and establish a new international economic and political order featuring democratic, fair and rational. It was agreed to set up the secretariat in Beijing.

As one of the initiators and an active force behind the Shanghai Cooperation Organization, China actively participates in all activities within the framework and puts forward a lot of constructive opinions and principles, making a great contribution to its development.

China and the WTO

The predecessor of the World Trade Organization (WTO) was the General Agreement on Tariffs and Trade (GATT) that came into effect in 1948. The main purpose is to coordinate trade relations between contracting parties, promote liberalization of trade in the world and strengthen the stability and transparency of the trade environment. The headquarters of the WTO is located in Geneva, Switzerland. By April 16, 2006, the WTO had 149 members.

As a contracting party, China had a long relationship with the GATT. However, the course of the restoration of membership faced many twists and turns. Since July 10, 1986 when China officially submitted its application it took 15 years before the 4th Ministerial Conference of the WTO made a decision to admit China on November 10, 2001. During that period China gradually implemented the market economic system and integrated with international trading rules while expediting the pace of reform and opening up so as to become integrated in the world economic mainstream. China has only achieved substantial progress in terms of promoting market economic reform, but also made great breakthroughs in the depth and scale of opening up based on its own needs and in line with the requirements of the WTO rules. Since access to the WTO, China has adopted a series of actions to honor its commitments in the fields of trade in goods and services, IPR, investment and transparency. In 2006, WTO Secretary-General Lamy deemed that China had done a great job in its fulfillment of its WTO commitments and was performing its duties in real earnest.

Religion

Chinese Religion

China is a country with a great diversity of religious belief. The main religions are Buddhism, Taoism, Islam, Catholicism and Protestantism. Chinese citizens may freely choose and express their religious beliefs, and make clear their religious affiliations. According to incomplete statistics, there are over 100 million followers of various religious faiths, more than 85,000 sites for religious activities, some 300,000 clergy and over 3,000 religious organizations throughout China. In addition, there are 74 religious schools and colleges run by religious organizations for training clerical personnel.

—Buddhism has a history of 2,000 years in China. Currently, there are some 13,000 Buddhist temples and about 200,000 Buddhist monks and nuns. Among them are 120,000 lamas and nuns, more than 1,700 Living Buddhas, and some 3,000 monasteries of Tibetan Buddhism and nearly 10,000 Bhiksu and senior monks and more than 1,600 monasteries of Pali Buddhism.

—Taoism, native to China, has a history of more than 1,700 years. There are over 1,500 Taoist temples and more than 25,000 Taoist priests and nuns.

—Islam was introduced into China in the seventh century. Nowadays, there are 10 national minorities, including those for the Hui and Uygur, with a total population of 18 million, who follow Islam. Their 30,000-odd mosques are served by 40,000 Imams and Akhunds.

—Catholicism was introduced into China intermittently in the seventh century, but it was not spread widely until after the Opium War in 1840. At present, China has four million Catholics, 4,000 clergy and more than 4,600 churches and meeting houses.

—Protestantism was first brought to China in the early 19th century and spread widely after the Opium War. There are about 10 million Protestants, more than 18,000 clergy, more than 12,000 churches and 25,000-some meeting places throughout China.

China has the following national religious organizations: Buddhist Association of China, Taoist Association of China, Islamic Association of China, Chinese Patriotic Catholic Association, Chinese Catholic Bishops' College, Three-Self Patriotic Movement Committee of the Protestant Churches of China, and China Christian Council. Religious leaders and leading organs of the various religious bodies are selected and ordained in accordance with their own regulations.

Religious organizations in China run their own affairs and set up religious schools, publish religious classics and periodicals, and run social services according to their own needs. As in many other countries, China practices the principle of separating religion from education; religion is not a subject taught in mainstream schools in China, although some institutions of higher learning and research institutes do teach or conduct research into religion. The various religious schools and institutes set up by the different religious organizations teach religious knowledge in line with their own needs. All normal clerical activities conducted by the clergy and all normal religious activities held either at sites for religious activities or in believers' own homes in accordance with usual religious practices, such as worshipping Buddha, reciting scriptures, going to church, praying, preaching, baptism, monk-hood initiation, fasting, celebrating religious festivals, observing extreme unction, and holding memorial ceremonies, are protected by law as the affairs of religious bodies and believers themselves and may not be interfered with.

In China, all religions have equal status and co-exist in tranquility; religious disputes are unknown. Religious believers and non-believers respect each other, are united and have a harmonious relationship. This shows, on the one hand, the influence of traditional Chinese compatibility and tolerance, and, on the other hand, the fact that since the founding of the People's Republic of China in 1949, the Chinese Government has formulated and carried out the policy of freedom of religious belief and established a politico-religious relationship that conforms to China's national conditions.

Buddhism in China

Buddhism came into being in ancient India between the 6th and 5th centuries BC. Its founder, Siddhartha Gautama, left home and became a Buddhist at the age of 20. Later, he was respectfully addressed as "Buddha", meaning "the person with full awareness", so the religion is called "Buddhism".

Buddhism was introduced from India around the first century BC. After long development and evolution, it was divided into Han (Chinese) Buddhism, Tibetan Buddhism (popularly known as Lamaism) and Pali Buddhism (also known as Hinayana, or Lesser Vehicle). The believers of Han Buddhism are mainly of Han ethnic group; Tibetan Buddhism is basically the religion of ethnic minorities such as Tibetan, Mongolian, Yugur, Moinba and Tu and so on, mainly being popular in Tibet, Inner Mongolia and Qinghai Province with a total of about 7.6 million believers. Pali Buddhism is basically the religion of such ethnic minorities as Dai, Blang, De'ang and Va, mostly distributing in Xishuangbanna Dai Autonomous Prefecture, Dehong Dai Jingpo Autonomous Prefecture and Simao Region in Yunnan Province, with the number of believers surpassing 1.5 million.

Currently, there are more than 13,000 Buddhist temples with about 200,000 monks and nuns. Of them, Tibetan Buddhism has about 120,000 lamas and nuns, over 1,700 living Buddhas and more than 3,000 monasteries. Pali Buddhism has nearly 10,000 monks, nuns and elders, and more than 1,600 monasteries. In areas inhabited by the Han people, 142 Buddhist temples are under State-level protection. The three language families of Buddhism have altogether 19 colleges/schools at the primary, secondary and senior levels, including 14 in Han, four in Tibetan and one in Pali. There are Buddhist websites on the Internet, such as China Buddhism Online (www.fjnet) and China Buddhism Information Network (www.buddhism.com.cn).

The Feature of Chinese Buddhism

The feature of Chinese Buddhism lies in the coexistence of Mahayana Buddhism and Hinayana Buddhism as well as the concomitance of Exoteric and Esoteric Buddhism. Buddhism was initiated in India, developed in China and further expanded to Japan and Korea. However, Buddhist doctrinal classification itself never played any crucial role in Indian Buddhism as it did in China. Indian Buddhists were threatened by the values and socio-political structures of the Indian society dominated by Hinduism and Islam and vanished between 9th century and 10th century in India while Buddhism were developed rapidly in China so that China became the true homeland of Buddhism all over the world.

Another feature of Chinese Buddhism is that Mahasanghika Buddhism plays an important role. Most Chinese Buddhists take Mahasanghika Buddhism as their religion except people living near Thailand, whose religion is Theravada Buddhism as well as people living in Tibet whose religion is the Esoteric Buddhism.

The third feature of Chinese Buddhism is that it has ten sects. Some hierarchs founded new sects according to different canons including Tiantai Sect, Garland Sect, Three Sutra Sect, Reality Sect, Lotus Sect, Vinaya, Zen and Esoteric Buddhism.

Tibetan Buddhism

Tibetan Buddhism contains elements of Indian Buddhism, Han Buddhism and the Tibetan Bon Religion but with its own unique features.

Regarding its tenets, it is compatible and inclusive. In the hinterland of the Han ethnic group, the two sects of the Buddhism namely exotic Buddhism and esoteric Buddhism are incompatible, but in Tibetan area, the two coexist and their relationship was eventually basically conciliated. The basic Tibetan tenet is: in order to disentangle the soul, people should discard all happiness and enjoyment in life and strictly adhere to the canons, recite sutras, pray and cultivate themselves intensely. Meanwhile, there are also some contents of the Bon Religion. From its early penetration of Tibet, Buddhism assimilated some religious rituals and divinities from the Bon Religion to create a worship highlighting the similarities between the two religions so as to gain support and tolerance. Furthermore, the sutra wheel used in the daily rituals of the Tibetan Buddhism is also the result of the combination of the mysticism of the Buddhism and the sorcery of the Bon Religion. Esoteric Buddhism is devolved from father to son, and so, in Tibetan Buddhism, monks are allowed to marry and engage in other work beyond the religious affairs except those of the Yellow Sect. In addition, Tibetan Buddhist monks are also allowed to eat meat, eggs, shallots and garlic and so on, all of which practices differ greatly from the Buddhism of the Han ethnic group.

Tibet is one of China's ethnic autonomous regions, and the Tibetans mostly believe in Tibetan Buddhism. Since the 1980s, the Central Government has allocated more than 200 million Yuan in special funds for the maintenance and reconstruction of the famous Potala Palace and the Jokhang, Tashilhungpo and Samye monasteries. The State has also established special funds to support the work of compiling and publishing the Tripitaka in the Tibetan language and other major Tibetan Buddhist classics as well as the work of establishing the Advanced Buddhism College of Tibetan Language Family of China in Beijing and the Tibet College of Buddhism in Lhasa. At present in Tibet, there are over 1,700 places for Buddhist activities and a total of 46,000 resident monks and nuns. Small prayer halls or shrines are virtually universal in the homes of believers, and pilgrims coming to Lhasa number well over one million each year. Believers performing Buddhist rituals, and prayer wheels and Mani rocks carved with Buddhist sutras can be found all over the Tibet Autonomous Region. In addition, religious activities during the annual Shoton Festival and the traditional practice of circling Mount Kangrinboqe in the Year of the Horse and circling Nam Co [Lake] in the Year of the Sheep along pilgrim paths have been carried on and respected by society at large.

• Tubo Kingdom

The Tubo Kingdom (7th century-9th century) was an ancient kingdom established on the Qinghai-Tibet Plateau. It lasted for more than 200 years from the reign of Songtsan Gampo to that of Dharmo; it was the first regime founded in the history of Tibet.

Painting of Princess Wencheng's Going into Tibet

Princess Wencheng

Princess Wencheng (623-680), called Princess Gyamo Sahan in Tibetan, was a royal family niece of the Emperor Taizong of the Tang Dynasty (618-907). She was the second wife of Songtsan Gampo, king of the Tubo Kingdom whose first wife came from the present-day Nepal.

Songtsan Gampo, a hero in the history of Tibetan ethnic group, unified the Tibetan area, established the Tubo Kingdom and became the tsampo (king) of the kingdom. During the 14th year of Tang Zhenguan Emperor (640), he dispatched his Chief Minister Gar Tongsten to pay respects and a tribute of 5,000 taels of gold and hundreds of pieces of precious treasures to Tang Emperor Taizong. The Tang emperor agreed to let the Tubo king marry his niece, Princess Wencheng.

Princess Wencheng lived in Tubo for approximately 40 years and was much respected by people there. She made great contribution to the Tubo Kingdom. She worked out blueprints for construction of the Jokhang Monastery and the Ramoche Monastery. This made it possible for the Han's techniques with regard to milling, weaving and spinning, pottery making, paper making and wine brewing to be introduced to the Tubo. The ancient classics on poems, farming, Buddhism, history and calendaring, which she had brought to Tubo, promoted the development of the region's economic and cultural development. This helped strengthen the friendly relations between the Han and Tibetan peoples. The golden statue of Sakyamuni she brought to Tubo is still worshipped by the Tibetan people today.

Songtsan Gampo

Songtsan Gampo (617-650) is the famous Tsampo (king) in the history of Tibet, as well as the founder of Tubo Kingdom. He is the most important and well-known king of Tibet. He united the separate tribes on the Tibet Plateau and established the Tubo Kingdom. Songtsan Gampo adopted a series of effective measures to consolidate the unification of Tibet: Moving the capital to Lhasa and building the Potala Palace; dividing Tibet into six major administrative areas; promoting Buddhism; creating the writing script; seeking better ties with the Tang Dynasty (618-907) and Nepal by marring Princess Wencheng of the Tang and Princess Bhributi of Nepal, and having the Jokhang Monastery and the Ramoche Monastery built; unifying the measuring system; encouraging reclamation of wasteland; protecting the water resources; building paths zigzagging through mountains to promote the development of trade, and so on. These played an important role to promoting the development of the economy, culture, Buddhism, and medicine in Tubo. The Tibetan people respected Songtsan Gampo as the reincarnation of Kwan-yin (Goddess of Mercy) and he was also worshipped as one of the three major Princess of Dharma. The other two are Trisong Desten and Tritsu Desten.

The Six-syllable Prayer

The Six-syllable Prayer, also known as Mani Incantation, is a most favored and chanted incarnation of Tibetan Buddhism. The six Tibetan syllables, written mostly in Sanskrit or Tibetan, can be found on the colored drawings and the patterns on the ceiling in the Tibetan religious buildings, even on the doorframes and religious wares used by Tibetan people. The six syllables are pronounced in Chinese "Weng, Ma, Ni, Ba, Mi, Hong" respectively. In Tibetan, it pronounces "Om Mani Pad-me Hun".

Tibetan Buddhism holds that the Six-syllabe Prayer is the cream of all Tibetan classics. And hence they recite it repeatedly year on year. The Tibetan believe reciting the prayer will help dispel the evil and bring them luck. Tibetan monks and old herders recite it almost every minute. An important Summons Ceremny, known as the Mani Grand Summons Ceremony, is held in the Tibetan Buddhist monasteries every year.

The Six-syllable Prayer

Dalai Lama

Dalai Lama is one of the supreme heads of the Gelug Sect of Tibetan Budhism, and enjoys high prestige in areas where Tibetan Buddhism dominates. The word "Dalai" comes from the Mongolian Language, meaning the sea, while the Lama means "master" in Tibetan. "Dalai Lama" generally means "ocean of wisdom". It was the honorific title the Mongol Ata Khan bestowed to the Gelug Sect leader Soinam Gyamco at the end of the 16th century. In 1653, Qing Emperor Shunzhi bestowed the title of Dalai Lama to the 5th Dalai. From then on, the honorific title became hereditary. In the Tibetan Buddhist areas, the Dalai Lama was the supreme abbot of the three major monasteries (Zhaibung, Sera, and Gandain Monasteries of Tibetan Buddhism), and he also took charge of the political affairs in the Lhasa area. The Tibetans generally regard the Dalai Lama as the incarnate of the Goddess of Mercy.

Panchen Lama

Panchen Lama is one of the two supreme hierarchs of the Gelug Sect of the Tibetan Buddhism. "Pan" is a Sanskrit word (Pandit meaning great knowledge) and "chen" is a Tibetan meaning " big". Panchen is held as the incarnation of Amitabha.

The title "Panchen" was also bestowed by a local leader of Mongolia. In the 17th century, a Mongolian force controlled Tibetan areas, and in order to gain the support of the Gelug Sect with great influence in the region and further develop the religion of the sect, the Mongolian leader bestowed the tile on Norsang Qoigyi, fourth generation disciple of the famous leader of Gelug Sect, Tsongkapa. In 1713, Emperor Kangxi of Qing Dynasty also formally conferred on him the title of "Panchen Erdeni", which hence established the status of Panchen in Tibetan Buddhism. Thereafter, the title of Panchen was conferred by the Central Government and became a system. In the Tibetan Buddhist area, the Panchen is the supreme hierarch and Living Buddha of the Tashilhungpo Monastery and its affiliated monasteries. He also takes charge of the political affairs in the Tsang. In the light of the theory of the Tibetan Buddhism, he is the reincarnation of Bodhisattva Manjusri.

Living Buddha

A Living Buddha is a very special phenomenon in Tibetan Buddhist areas, which has become a great thing in the culture and the life of the people there. Living Buddha means reincarnation or body in Tibetan, the people who believe in Tibetan Buddhism deem that the soul is eternal, and after the body dies, the soul will transmigrate into other lives, which might be people, deities, ghosts and animals and so on, which is "transmigration". The Living Buddhas are at the peak of this transmigration. However, there is no such concept in the Buddhism practiced by the Han ethnic group. With regard to the religious system, the Living Buddhas came into being in order to solve the problem of finding an heir among the religious sects. In the early times, the lamas of the Tibetan Buddhism were allowed to marry and have children, so there was no such problem. But in the 13th century, the Gelug Sect became popular and later assumed a predominant status, and it banned marriage and procreation. In order to solve the heir problem, they began to adopt the inventive system of " reincarnation". That is to say, when a senior monk died, they will find and confirm a newly born infant as his reincarnation, which is repeated from generation to generation. The Living Buddhas are divided into four grades.

Considering the special place of the Grand Living Buddhas in Tibetan Buddhism of past generations in Tibetan social life, the Ming (1368-1644) and Qing (1616-1911) dynasties gradually brought the identification of the reincarnated soul under the jurisdiction of the Central Government and into the framework of State laws and statutes. In 1792, the Qing government issued an order that the reincarnation of the Grand Living Buddhas above the rank of Hutogtu be determined through drawing lots from a golden urn, which later developed into a historical institution and was accepted as a permanent religious ritual in Tibetan Buddhism. The "soul boy" confirmed through lot-drawing from the golden urn as the reincarnation of a Grand Living Buddha must be reported to the Central Government for approval prior to his official enthronement. The lot-drawing may be dispensed with under special circumstances, but this must also be reported for advance governmental approval. The practice not only upholds the central government's supreme authority and the sovereignty of the State, but religiously displays the "decision by Sakyamuni's Dharma" as well. Since 1792, in the reincarnation system of the Grand Living Buddhas of Tibetan Buddhism, over 70 "soul boys" have been identified by confirmation through lot-drawing from the golden urn and with the approval of the Central Government. Thus, it has become a religious ritual and historical convention of Tibetan Buddhism, and is the key to safeguarding the normal order of Tibetan Buddhism.

Lama

Lama is the appellation used by people outside Tibetan Buddhism. But, in fact, within Tibetan Buddhism, the appellations of the lamas are discriminative and their status and grade differ greatly. So, it is not accurate to generalize by calling them lama, which originated from the Tibetan word meaning teacher. They are the senior monks of advanced learning and noble morality and have certain longevity and religious degree, becoming a teacher of exemplary virtue and able to direct the people in religious cultivation. From this aspect, they are different from the common monks. In Tibetan, the common monks are called "Drakpa" and the Tibetan people only call such people as Dalai, Panchen and other Living Buddhas as "lama".

In the minds of the Tibetan people, the common people can only approach the Buddhas in the Heaven through the lamas and then reach nirvana. Because the lama is the important intermediary, they enjoy extremely lofty status. However, in the ar eas of Han ethnic group, the people always call the monks of Tibetan Buddhism as lama, and the monks in the Buddhist temples in the areas of Han "Heshang" (Chinese characters meaning monks).

Yonghegong Lamasery

Yonghegong Lamasery lies in the northeast of Beijing and is one of the State key cultural relic protected units. It has the largest scale among its counterparts in Beijing and enjoys world fame. In 1983, it was designated as the national key monastery of Buddhism in the Han areas by the State Council. It originally was the mansion of the Emperor Yongzheng of the Qing Dynasty before he mounted the throne and was built in the 33rd year (1694) of the reign of Emperor Kangxi. It was always called as "the mansion of the prince" and changed into Xanadu in the third year of Yongzheng's reign. After Yongzheng died, in order to place his coffin in the palace, the green colored glazes were changed into yellow ones and hence Yonghegong Lamasery became a palace-like monastery. Both Emperor Yongzheng and Emperor Qianlong believed in Lamaism and in order to strengthen good relations with the Tibetan leadership, the government of Qing Dynasty began large scale construction to create a Tibetan Buddhist monastery. The Yonghegong Lamasery covers an area of 66,400 square meters and has more than 1,000 rooms. The layout includes the Tianwang Hall, Yonghegong Hall and the Yongyoudian Hall lying along the central axis from south to north. There is a huge statue of Buddha in the lamasery. Rising 26 meters high, it was sent by religious leaders of Tibet. The building features the national characters of the Han, Manchu, Mongolians and Tibetans and is one of the rare important places of interest in the country.

Thousands of figures of Buddhas and abundant Buddhist classical cultural relics are preserved in the Yonghegong Lamasery. Large quantities of precious cultural relics are also displayed such as the "five hundred of Arhats mountain", the "woodcarving Buddha niche of spun gold wood" and the 18 meter-high "great Buddha of sandalwood", which are praised as the "three wonders" of the Lamasery. There were originally four study palaces, namely Medicine Palace, Mathematics Palace, Exotic Buddhism Palace and Esoteric Buddhism Palace. Lamas learned medicine, Buddhism, calendar and Buddhist sutra knowledge there

Yonghegong Lamasery, Beijing

Xuanzang (Tang Seng)

Xuanzang (602-664), also known as Tang Sanzang or Tang Seng, became a monk at the age of 12. He absorbed in the study of the Sacred Books from India and mastered Buddhist doctrines and principles. Xuanzang set off from Chang'an (today's Xi'an City of Shaanxi Province) on his journey to the west in 629. He traveled along what we now know as the Silk Road including the Xinjiang Autonomous Region, Central Asia and so on and eventually reached India. He studied Buddhist sutras from eminent monks of a Buddhist temple in the largest Buddhist State in northeast India. In 645 Xuanzang returned to Chang'an with canons, Buddha statues, relics and so on.

It took 17 years for Xuanzang to go to and from his destination which is some 25,000 km. He and his disciples spent 19 years to translate Buddhist sutras. They translated 75 volumes of Buddhist classics into Chinese. People of later generations refer to him as one of the four major translators in China. Most of his translated works are on Idealism and Xuanzang is therefore regarded as the founder of Idealism in the country. His efforts made Xi'an one of the Buddhist centers in the world then. Many of his disciples include people hailing from Japan and Korea.

Xuanzang's *Report of the Regions West of Great Tang*, with 12 volumes, provided important information about India. This made him China's first Indian Hand.

Xuanzang was the greatest Buddhist scripture translator in the Chinese history of Buddhism. He also took pains to lecture on Buddhism. His disciples were numerous in number. All these made Chang'an one of the Buddhist centers in the world. Many from Japan and the Republic of Korea studied from Xuanzang and returned to spread Buddhism in their own countries.

Jianzhen

Jianzhen (688-763) was born in Yangzhou City, Jiangsu Province. He was a Chinese Vinaya master and the founder of Japanese Vinaya (a discipline sect). Jianzhen became a monk in the Dayun Temple in Yangzhou at the age of 14 and left for Chang'an in 709 to study. He returned to Yangzhou's Daming Temple in 715 and in 733 he became the temple abbot and had some 40,000 followers.

At the invitation of Japanese monks studying in China, Jianzhen decided to go to Japan to spread Vinaya in 742. He tried five times to cross the sea to Japan but failed due to heavy storms. The extreme conditions of his attempts rendered him blind by the time he succeeded in his sixth endeavor in 754. Japanese highly respected Jianzhen. The Mikado showed his welcome at Jianzhen's arrival and invited him to teach at the Tōdaiji Temple. Jianzhen was also responsible for the establishment of such temples as Toshodaiji where he taught and spread Vinaya. From then on, the Japanese Vinaya came into being and Jianzhen was the founder.

Jianzhen and his disciples were not only proficient in Vinaya but also familiar with the doctrines of the Tiantai Sect of Buddhism. Among the canons they had taken to Japan most were about Tiantai Sect. Thus they were also the pioneers of Tiantai Sect to Japan.

respectively, with the term lasting for more than ten years. The lamas learning Buddhism would spend more than 30 years from entry to graduation. The Yonghegong Lamasery is now not only a holy place of Buddhism, but also the treasury of the culture and art of the Han, Tibet, Mongolia and Manchu ethnic groups.

Tar Monastery

Tar Monastery in Huangzhong County of Qinghai Province is one of the six main monasteries of the Gelug Sect of Tibetan Buddhism. It was originally built in order to commemorate the birthplace of the great master Zongkapa of Tibetan Buddhism and the founder of the Gelug Sect.

Tar Monastery lies in the Lotus Flower Mountain in Huangzhong County of Qinghai Province, and is one of the six main monasteries of the Gelug Sect of Tibetan Buddhism. It was designated as a national key cultural relic in the 1960s. It was built along the mountain in 1529, comprising 11 palaces and other buildings, altogether more than 9,300 rooms. The whole monastery covers an area of nearly 400,000 square meters. It is not only famous in the world for its majestic architecture art, but is also a treasury of the religion, culture and art of Tibetan Buddhism. It was originally built in order to commemorate the birthplace of the great master Zongkapa of Tibetan Buddhism and the founder of the Gelug Sect. It always enjoyed great support by the government, and many of its leaders gained title and largesse from the emperor, which helped the monastery to grow in scale. Tar Monastery blends the traditional architectural art and techniques of the Tibetan and Han ethnic groups, the former dominating.

The fame of Tar Monastery partly stems from three artistic wonders: the ghee flowers, frescos and barbules. In 1986, Qinghai Tibetan Buddhist College, the first institution of higher learning in Qinghai Province was founded there.

Jokhang Monastery

Located in the center of the old city of Lhasa, Jokhang Monastery is one of the religious holy places of Tibetan Buddhism and the one with the longest history in Tibet as well as a Chinese key cultural relic protected unit. It was built as early as 647.

Large quantities of precious Buddhist cultural relics are preserved, with the golden Sakyamuni figure taken by the Princess Wencheng being the most famous. Jokhang Monastery is the most brilliant extant architecture built in the Tufan Period as well as the earliest construction of clay and wood in Tibet, which also inaugurates the Tibetan level land style layout of the monastery. Through numerous repairs and enlargements over the centuries, it finally came into being with its existing majestic scale, covering an area of more than 25,100 square meters.

In front of the Jokhang Monastery stands a stele, more than three meters high, named "the alliance stele of Tang and Fan". It was built in 823 to confirm friendly communications between the Han and Tibetan. Behind the stele is a sapless willow, which is said to have been planted by Princess Wencheng and called the "Tang willow". The monastery is mainly composed of one broad outdoor courtyard; on the walls of the corridors around the yard frescos are drawn, earning it the name of "thousand Buddhas corridor". On the two sides of the courtyard are the Yaksa Palace and Dragon Boat Palace and behind it is the "Juekang" Buddha Palace, which is the main building of the Jokhang Monastery.

The monastery houses many Buddhas and holy articles for believers to worship. Sakyamuni Hall in the center of the great sutra hall is a holy place in the minds of pilgrims and is the center of the main activities of turning prayer wheels.

Guangji Temple

Located with the Fuchengmen Nei Dajie Street of Beijing, it was said to have been founded in the Jin period (1115-1234). Now, it is the site of the Buddhist Association of China.

Fayuan Temple

Located at the southern tip of the Jiaozi Hutong Lane of Beijing, it was built in the 19th year (645) of the Zhenguan period of the Tang Dynasty by Li Shiming (Tang Emperor Taizong). It is the oldest extant temple in Beijing. Now, it is the site of the Chinese Buddhist Academy and the Buddhist Books and Culture Relics Museum of China.

Xihuangsi Temple

Located at the Huangsi Dajie Street outside Andingmen of Beijing, it was a monastery of the Gelug Sect of Tibetan Buddhism built in the ninth year of Qing Dynasty Emperor Shunzhi (1652) for the Dalai Lama and Panchen Erdeni. Inside the temple is the Qing Jing Hua Cheng Ta—the tomb dagoba for the 6th Panchen Erdeni. It is one of the four Diamond dagobas in Beijing.

Now the temple is home to the China Tibetan Language Higher Institute of Buddhism which enrolls Living Buddhas and eminent monks from Tibet, Inner Mongolia and some other areas each year for study.

Lingguang Temple

Located in Badachu Park, Cuiweishan Mountain, Shijingshan District, Beijing, the Lingguang Temple is renowned for its tooth relic of the Buddha and as a place for Chinese and foreign Buddhists to worship. It once had a Zhaoxian Pagoda, which was ruined by the cannon fire of the Eight Power Allied Forces in 1900. Later, the tooth relic of Buddha was found in the stone Buddhas niche in the base of the pagoda. In order to protect it, The Buddhist Association of China built a new octagonal close-eaves brick pagoda.

Dabei Temple

Located at.26 Tianwei Lu, Heibei District, Tianjin, the Dabei Temple is well-preserved. It was built during the reign of the Emperor Kangxi (1662-1772), for enshrining and worshiping Dabei (Great Compassion) Kwan-yin Bodhisattva (also called Qian Shou Kwan-yin). It is now the site of the Tianjin Buddhist Association and the main place for Buddhists to hold religious activities.

Dule Temple

Situated in Jixian County of Tianjin, is a famous ancient Buddhist architecture. It was initially built in Tang Dynasty (618-907) and rebuilt in the second year of Tonghe Regime of Liao Dynasty (984). The two-storied wooden Kwan-yin Pavilion is twenty-three meters high with three stories and so well designed with 24 different joggle joints that it has withstood several earthquakes and remains sound to this day. The pavilion contains a standing statue of the Guanyin Bodhisattva with the heads of ten small Buddhas above it. The 16-meter statue is known as the "Eleven-face Guanyin ", one of the largest painted clay sculptures in China.

Linji Temple

It also named Linji Tower Temple. Located in Zhengding County seat, Hebei Province, it was built in the second year (540) of the reign of Emperor Xiaojing in the Eastern Wei of the Northern Dynasties. In 854, Master Yixuan, the founder of the Linji Sect of Buddhism, lived there and, after he died, the tower was built. It is the important ancestral court of the Linji Sect of China and Japan.

Puning Temple

This is located by the Liehe River to the north of the mountain resort of Chengde in Hebei Province. It is called Dafo (Great Buddha) Temple because there is a great Buddha statue carved out of wood and plated with gold. It was built by the Siweit of the Mongolian ethnic group in the 20th year of the reign of Qing Emperor Qianlong (1755) after a Tibetan monastery. It is a major lamasery of great importance to the Mongolian Buddhism. The Puning Temple features unique architecture style combining that of a Chinese Buddhist temple and Tibetan monastery. It is on the World Cultural Heritage list in 1994. The temple is the largest place for Tibetan Buddhists to hold religious activities in north China.

Chongshan Temple

Located in the southeast of Taiyuan City, Shanxi Province, the Chongshan Temple was built in the Tang Dynasty (618-907). It is now the site of the Buddhist Association of Shanxi Province.

Huayan Temple

Situated in the southwest of Datong, Shanxi Province, Huayan Temple, named after the Huayan Scripture (Buddha-Wisdom or Anuttara-samyak-sambodhi) of the Huayan Sect of Buddhism, is a complex of the Upper Shanghuayan Temple (Upper Huayan Temple) and the Xiahuayan Temple (Lower Huayan Temple). It is a famous temple in Shanxi Province.

Xuanzhong Temple

Situated on Shibishan Mountain 10 km northwest of Jiaocheng County, Shanxi Province, the temple is one of the cradles of the Pure Land Sect of Buddhism. Built in 472 during the Northern Wei Dynasty (386-534), it is held as a Buddhist temple of origin by the Pure Land Sect of Buddhism of Japan [Jodo Shinshu] and other sects of the system. It is influential both at home and abroad.

Wutaishan Mountain

Situated in the northeast of Wutai County, Shanxi Province, this is leading one among the four major Buddhist mountains in China. Legend has it that Wenshu Bodhisattva dwelt in the temple of Wutaishan Mountain to perform rites to save the souls of the dead. There are 47 temples in the area. The famous ones include Xiantong Temple, Tayuan Temple, Bodhisattva Peak, Nanshan Temple, Dailuo Peak, Guangji Temple, Wanfo Temple (Ten Thousand Buddha Temple). Wutaishan Mountain is the only holy place both for

Wutaishan Mountain in Shanxi

Chinese Buddhism and Lamaism, where Han, Mongolian and Tibetan Buddhists perform Buddhist rites.

Xuankong Temple

Located in Hunyuan County, about 65 km southeast of Datong City, Shanxi Province, the temple with a 1,400-year history was founded during the Northern Wei period in the 6th century. It has been influenced by Buddhism, Confucianism and Daoism. It reflects the syncretic element of Chinese religious and philosophical tradition, and is the only temple incarnating the thought of the three religions united as one. It was on Hengshan Mountain with its halls supported with beams inserted into the cliffs, about 50 meters above the ground and connected by plank roads. The whole structure seems to be like a castle suspended in the air.

Xuankong Temple on Hengshan Mountain

Banruo (Prajna) Temple of Shenyang City

It was founded by the Buddhist monk Gulin in the early Qing Dynasty, and is the main temple of Shenyang City. It is now the site of the Buddhist Association of Liaoning Province.

Ci'en Temple

It was founded in the second year (1628) during the reign of Tiancong in Qing Dynasty (16061911), and is the famous temple in northeast China. It is the site of the Buddhist Association of Shenyang.

Banruo (Prajna)Temple of Changchun City

Located at the northeastern corner of the People's Square in Changchun City, it was built in 1922, and is the largest Buddhist temple of Changchun City. It is now the site of the Buddhist Association of Jilin Province and the one of Changchun City.

Kwan-yin Temple of Jilin City

Located at Xiangyang Jie Street of Chuanying District of Jilin City, it is the only Kwan-yin temple which faces north. Built in the 35th year (1770) of the reign of Qing Dynasty Emperor Qianlong, it is now the religious activities center for Buddhists in Jilin City. It is influential among Buddhists in the northeast China and Hong Kong.

Jile Temple

Located at the end of the Dongdazhi Jie Street in Nangang District, Harbin City, it was built in 1923. It is one of the four major temples in northeast China. The three others are the Banru Temple in Changchun, Ci'en Temple in Shenyang, and Lengyan Temple in Yingkou.

Jing'an Temple

Located at Nanjing Xilu Road of Shanghai City, it was built during the Chiwu Period (238-251) of the Kingdom of Wu of the Three Kingdoms and is the famous old historical temple both at home and abroad. The China Buddhist General Association, China's first national Buddhist association, was inaugurated here in 1912.

Chenxiangge Pavilion

Also called Ciyun Chanyuan, it was located at 29 Chenxiangge Lu Road, Shanghai City. Built as a nunnery in the 28th year (1600) during the reign of Emperor Wanli of the Ming Dynasty, it was the preaching place for the late honorary president of the Buddhist Association of China, Master Yingci.

Jade Buddha Temple

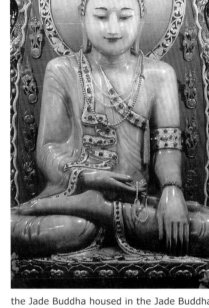

the Jade Buddha housed in the Jade Buddha Temple in Shanghai.

Located at 170 Anyuan Lu Road, it was built in the eighth year (1882) during the reign of Guangxu in Qing Dynasty. It houses the Burma emerald preaching and nirvana statues of Sakyamuni. It is now the site of the Buddhist Association of Shanghai City.

Yuanming Schoolroom

Located at 434 Yan'an Xilu Road of Shanghai City, it is the most important of its kind in the city. It was founded by the late first president of the Buddhist Association of China, Master Yuanying in 1934, and has certain influence among Buddhists residing in Southeast Asia and compatriots of Hong Kong and Macao.

Qixia Temple

Located in the Qixiashan Mountain 22 km northeast of Nanjing, Jiangsu Province, the temple, it is one of the four Buddhist monasteries in China. Built in the seventh year (489) during the reign of Yongming of the Southern Qi, it was where China's Buddhist Three Treaties were born. On December 31 each year, the Qixia Temple will organize ritual for followers to listen to the New Year bells.

Hanshan Temple

Located at Fengqiao Town five km away from Changmen west of Suzhou, Jiangsu Province, it was built during the reign of Tianjian of Liang during the Southern Dynasty (502-519). It is said that the senior monks of the Tang Dynasty, Hanshan and Shide, worked as abbot of the temple. Hence the temple named after him- Hanshan Temple. The poem *Soliloquy at Cold Mountain Temp le* written by the poet Zhangji of the Tang Dynasty is the chant of the temple winning universal praise. Tourists from Japan and South Korea love to hear New Year bells at nights of the New Year's Day and the Spring Festival.

Lingyanshan Temple

It was located in the Lingyangshan Mountain, Mudu Town 15 km southwest of Suzhou. In the end of the Eastern Jin (317-420), Luyuan (a military leader) donated his mansion as a temple. In modern times, Master Yingguang spent his late years here. It is a site for performance of the rites of the Pure Land Sect, influential both at home and abroad in modern times. At the end of 1980, the Lingyanshan Branch of the China Buddhist College was created here.

Guangjiao Temple (Mahatma Temple)

It was built in the second year (669) during the reign of Emperor Gaozong in Tang Dynasty on Langshan Mountain in the southern suburbs of Nantong City, Jiangsu Province. The monks have managed the temple very well. There are thousands of believers coming here for worship on the 13th day of the 7th Chinese lunar month each year, which is the birthday of Mahastha-maprapta Bodhisattva, and the 3rd day of the 3rd Chinese lunar month, the birthday of Sangha (monastic order). Buddhist circles in Hong Kong, Macao, Taiwan have intercommunion with the temple increasingly. Buddhists from Japan, the US and Singapore also come to worship the Mahastha-maprapta Bodhisattva. The vegetable dishes in the Guangjiao Temple are well known.

Daming Temple of Yangzhou City

Located at Zhongfeng of the Shugang Scenic Area on the northwestern outskirts of Yangzhou, Jiangsu Province, the temple was built during the reign of Daming of the Southern Dynasty (457-464). During the Kaiyuan reign (mid-8th century) of Tang Dynasty, the famous accomplished monk Jianzhen acted as its abbot. Between 743 and 754, he made 11 attempts to cross the sea to propagate Buddhism in Japan; the first six failed due to bad weather but he succeeded on the seventh. It is a famous extant temple in the history of Sino-Japan Buddhist relations, with profound and extensive influence at home and abroad.

Daming Temple in Yangzhou City

Longchang Temple of Jurong County

The temple, also called Huijulu Temple, lies in Baohua Mountain of Jurong County, Jiangsu Province. Emperor Shenzhong of Ming Dynasty conferred on it the title of "Holy Country-Defending Longchang Temple". In the summer of 1992, the temple held its first water-land ritual ever since 1949. The ritual, lasting for seven days, attracted some 1,200 Buddhists from Hong Kong, Taiwan, Jiangsu and Shanghai.

Lingyin Temple of Hangzhou City

Located northwest of the West Lake of Hangzhou, Zhejiang Province, it is said that the temple was built by the senior Indian Monk Huili in the third year (328) of the reign of Xianhe in the Eastern Jin, and it is a famous temple of the Chan Sect. With a history of some 1,670 years, it was listed as one of the five mountains of the Chan Sect in the Song Dynasty (960-1279). The ancient Japanese monk Saicho studied there, so it closely related with Japanese Buddhism.

Jingci Temple of Hangzhou City

Located in the Nanpingshan Mountain south of the West Lake of Hangzhou, Zhejiang Province, it was built in the first year (954) during the reign of Xiande of the Later Zhou Dynasty. It is one of the five mountains of the Chan Sect, having profound historical relations with the Rinzai-shu [Linji in Chinese] and Soto [Caodong in Chinese] sects of Japanese Zen Buddhism. Behind the temple lies the grave tower of senior Monk Rujing, teacher of the founder of the Caodong sect, ancestral Master Daoyuan [Dongshan Liangjie]. It is a place where Rinzai and Soto sect members yearn to worship.

Seven Towers Temple

Located in the Jiangdong District of Ningbo City, Zhejiang Province, it was built in 858, and is the famous old Buddhist temple with long history in the east of Zhejiang Province and now the site of the Buddhist Association of the Ningbo City.

Putuo Mountain

The Putuo Mountain is one of the four famous mountains of Chinese Buddhism, having historical relations with the Caodong and Linji sects. Puji Temple, Fasoka Temple and Huiji Temple are the three principal temples of Futuo Mountain. Bodhisattva Kwan-Yin expounded Buddhist doctrines here.

Guoqing Temple

Guoqing Temple of Tiantai County Which located in the southern part of Tiantaishan Mountain of Tiantai County, was built in 598. China's Tendai Sect and the Shingon Sect of Japanese Buddhism both regard Guoqing Temple as an ancestral home.

Jiuhua Mountain

Located in Qingyang County, Chizhou city, Anhui Province, Jiuhua Mountain is one of the four major Buddhist mountains in China. It is the ritual venue for Ksitigarbha. During the peak period of Buddhism, the mountain was home to more than 300 temples. Now, there are 93 temples open to the public. They include nine at the State level and 30 at the provincial level. They hold some 10,000 statues of Buddha. Most famous temples include the Huacheng Temple, Ganlu Temple, Diyuan Temple, and Tiantai Temple.

Southern Putuo Temple

Located in southeast of Xiamen City, Fujian Province, it was built in the late period (between the end of 9th century and early 10th century) in the Tang Dynasty, and exercises great influence both at home and abroad.

Kaiyuan Temple

Located in Xijie Street of Quanzhou, Fujian Province, it was founded in 685, and is the famous temple of the southern Fujian Province. With magnificent architecture and rare scale among domestic temples, it is well-known both at home and abroad and has great influence on Buddhists in Taiwan and in other countries. The Japanese Obaku Zen often sends its believers here to worship and some Japanese Buddhists can recite Buddhist sutras even in southern Fujian dialect.

Zhanshan Temple

Located in Taipingshan Mountain of Qingdao, Shandong Province, it was built during the period from 1932 to 1935. It originally ran the Zhanshan Buddhist College and trained many monks. Hence, many Zhanshan Temples are built overseas with extensive influence.

White Horse Temple

Located in eastern Luoyang, Henan Province, it was built in 68 or the 11th year of the reign of Emperor Yongping of the Eastern Han Dynasty; it was the first after the introduction of Buddhism in China. Two monks from India Kasyapamatanga and Dharmaranya translated the first Chinese Sutra, the Forty-Two Chapter Sutra here. Their graves are located here.

Shaolin Temple

Shaolin Temple

Located in the Songshan Mountain of Dengfen County, Henan Province, it was built in 496, and the founder of the Chan Sect, Bodhi Dharma, established himself here, making the temple the common ritual venue for all the Chan sects with profound influence both at home and abroad. Shaolin Temple was named for the location in the woody forest (lin in Chinese) of Shaoshishan Mountain. Shaolin Temple is famous for its Chan Sect and Wushu (martial arts).

There was supposed to be a Shaolin Temple in Fujian Province, South Shaolin Temple. But the latter does not exist now so arguments continue about its location. Candidates include Putian Shaolin Temple, Quanzhou Shaolin Temple and Fuqing Shaolin Temple.

Yuelushan Temple

Located in the Yulushan Mountain on the western bsank of the Xiangjiang River in Changsha City, it was built in 268 and is known as "the first doctrine- expounding ground in Hunan Province".

Liurong Temple

Located in Guangzhou City of Guangdong Province, Liurong Temple was built in 537, and was where Huineng, the sixth ancestor of the Chan Sect in the Tang Dynasty, expounded doctrine. It is now the site of the Buddhist Association of Guangzhou City.

Nanhua Temple

Located in Qujiang County of Shaoguan city, Guangdong Province, it was built in 504, and was another place where Huineng, expounded doctrines. There exist the figure of Huineng and the statues of the 500 Arhats carved in Song Dynasty. Hence the Nanhua Temple is known as the ancestral temple of the Zan.

Qingyun Temple

Located in the Dinghushan Mountain northeast of Zhaoqing City, Guangdong Province, it was one of the four major temples in area south of the Qinling Mountains. It was built by the senior monk Zhichang of the Tang Dynasty. Another Tang Dynasty monk Jianzhen stopped there while on his way to Japan and his Japanese disciple Rongrui died there. In 1963, in order to commemorate Sino-Japanese culture exchanges and the historical friendship among Buddhists of the two countries, the Buddhist Association of China set up a monument for Rongrui.

Guangxiao Temple

Located in Guangxiao Lu Road of Guangzhou City, the Guangxiao Temple is the oldest and largest temple south of Qinling Mountains, with a history of over 1,700 years. It is a cradle of communications between Chinese and Indian culture. Since the founding of the temple, many eminent monks from China and abroad visited to preach. The construction scale of the temple is grand. It holds the important position in Buddhist history in establishing a unique construction style and genre in southern China.

Wenshu Temple

Located at the northwestern part of Chengdu City, it was built during the Sui Dynasty (581-589) (then named Xingxiang Temple). It is also one of the famous four cultivation temples of the Chan Sect and now houses the Buddhist Association of Sichuan Province.

Emeishan Mountain

Located in Emei City of Sichuan Province, Emeishan Mountain is one of the four famous mountains of Chinese Buddhism, which regards it as the place for the Puxian Bodhisattva to perform rites to save the souls of the dead. It features steep topography and beautiful scenery. There are some 26 temples among the mountains, especially Baoguo Temple, Wannian Temple and Fuhu Temple, with many Buddhist ceremonies being held. The Leshan Giant Buddha is on the World Cultural and Natural Heritage list of UNESCO as of December 6, 1996.

♦ Chinese Buddhist Academies

The Chinese Buddhist Academy cultivates especially talented persons for Chinese Buddhism. It was set up in Beijing in 1956 in Fayuan Temple. Under the leadership of the Buddhist Association of China, the committee of the academy takes charge of teaching and administration. The monk students come from temples throughout the country. It has an undergraduate and specialty courses and set up a research department in 1961. In the next year, it set up Tibetan classes with the students coming from Tibet, Sichuan, Qinghai and Yunnan Provinces. In the first 10 years, it trained over 300 monks, many becoming abbots or administrators of temples of various places, while a few engaged in further Buddhist research. It ceased operating in 1966 but resumed in 1980, setting up one class for a two-year specialty course. In 1982, it started two classes for the undergraduate course and set up branch academies in Lingyanshan Mountain of Suzhou City and Xixiashan Mountain of Nanjing; other areas subsequently set up their own Buddhist academies and training classes. Currently, the Shanghai Buddhist Academy, Sichuan Buddhist Academy for Nuns, Fujian Buddhist Academy, Xiamen Southern Putuo Buddhist Academy and the Buddhist training classes in various areas have enrolled students.

In addition, there are the Hongci Buddhist Academy of Beijing Guangji Temple, Chinese Buddhist Academy of Fayuan Temple, Chinese Buddhist Academy of Ruiying Temple, Bolin Buddhist Academy of Bolin Temple, Henan Buddhist Academy of Kaifeng City, Jiuhua Buddhist Academy of Jiuhua Mountain of Anhui Province, Anhui Buddhist Academy of Yingjiang Temple of Anqing City, Nanhai Buddhist Academy of Putuo Mountain of Zhejiang Province, Wulin Buddhist Academy of Hangzhou City, Weishan Buddhist Academy of Ningxiang of Hunan Province, Fajie Academy of Changshu City of Jiangsu Province, Juehai Buddhist Academy of Taixian County (later renamed as Guangxiao Buddhist Academy), Qingliang Academy of Qingliang Temple of Changzhou City, the Buddhist Academy of Tianning Temple, Zhulin Buddhist Academy of Zhenjiang City, Jiaoshan Buddhist Academy, Lingyanshan Buddhist Academy of Suzhou City, Gushan Buddhist Academy of Fuzhou of Fujian Province, Lingdong Buddhist Academy of Chaozhou Kaiyuan Temple of Guangdong Province, and the Shanghai Buddhist Academy of Yufo Temple and the Buddhist Academy of Jing'an Temple of Shanghai and so on.

♦ The Research Institute of Buddhism Culture of China

On April 23, 1987, the Research Institute of Buddhism Culture of China was formally founded in the Beijing's Guangji Temple, site of the Buddhist Association of China. The President of the Buddhist Association of China and Vice President of the Chinese People's Political Consultative Conference, Zhao Puchu, took the post of honorary president of the institute. The present president is Wu Liming, the proprietor of the Chuanshan Society of Hunan Province.

The main work of the institute is:

1. Publication. Buddhist Culture is a bi-monthly publication.

2. Publishing. The research institute publishes the Chinese Buddhist Culture Series (the "great series" for short). It edits 12 kinds of book series and publishes the Small Chinese Buddhist Culture Series (the "small series " for short), covering research in the aspects of philosophy, literature, language, poems, arts, architecture, painting, calligraphy, music, folk-customs, chronometers, calendar, astrology, catering, tea culture and gardening and so on; comparative research between Buddhism and Taoism, Judaism, Christianity, Islam, Brahmanism and Hinduism and so on; researches into related aspects of Western philosophers such as Nietzsche, Schopenhauer, Kant and Hegel; and research of the relations between Buddhism and the various sects of the modern Western philosophy. It publishes Popular Reading Matters of Chinese Buddhist Culture covering such areas as the popular notations of the sutras, vinaya and Abhidharma and teaching support materials for Buddhist academies.

3. Translating the sutras, and setting up sutra translating houses, which engage in translating the Theravada Buddhism Tripitaka into Chinese, Tibetan Tripitaka into Chinese and vice versa as well as the translation of world famous Buddhist books.

4. Reading and editing teaching materials. On behalf of primary, secondary and senior Buddhist academies, it reads and edits the courses, teaching outline, teaching books and support materials and so on.

5.Tutoring graduate students. The graduates of the Buddhist Academy of China can continue to study in the research institute through examination and gain the degree title equal to master or even doctor. The institute has a staff of famous professors for this purpose.

Luohan Temple (Arhat Temple)

It was built during the period from 1064 to 1067, and is a famous temple of the Chan Sect in Chongqing City, as well as the headquarters of the Buddhist Association of Chongqing. It is an important temple of the Linji Sect of the Chan, the place for Daoyi, the eighth generation head of the Chan Sect to become a monk and preach when he was old.

Qianming Temple

Located in Guiyang City, it was built during the reign of Chongzhen (1628-1644) at the end of the Ming Dynasty and is famous in Guizhou Province as well as the site of the Buddhist Association of Guiyang City.

Yuantong Temple

Located in downtown Kunming City, it was built in the Tang Dynasty, and has a history of some 1,200 years. It is the oldest temple of Yunnan Province, and houses the provincial Buddhist Association.

Chongsheng Temple

Also named the Santa Temple (Three Pagodas Temple), it is 1.5 km north of the ancient town of Dali of Yunnan Province. Dali is renowned as a Buddhist kingdom and is one of areas with relative advanced Buddhist culture. Chongsheng Temple was built during the period from 713 to 741, and was the Royal Temple of the Nanzhao and Dali kingdoms. It was ruined by earthquakes and wars. The temple was rebuilt in 2005.

Great Ci'en Temple

Located in the southern suburb of Xi'an City, Shaanxi Province, it was built in 648 or the 22nd of the year of the reign Tang Dynasty Emperor Taizong. With a history of some 1,350 years, it was the place for the senior Buddhist Monk Tang Xuanzang to translate Buddhist sutras. He set up the Faxiang Sect. The Japanese Buddhist Hosso School takes this temple as its ancestral one. Inside the temple is the famous Great Geese Pagoda.

Great Xingshan Temple

Located south of Xi'an City, Shaanxi Province, it was built during the period from 265 to 289, and was the national site for translating Buddhist sutras in the prosperous period of the Sui (581-618) and Tang (618-907) Dynasties. It was the birthplace of Tantric Buddhism, hence held as the ancestral temple of Tantric Buddhism. It is the site of the Buddhist Association of Xi'an.

Famen Temple

Famen Temple, with a history of over 1,700 years, lies in Famen Town, Fufeng County, Xi'an City of Shaanxi Province. It was a royal temple in the Tang Dynasty. An underground palace was discovered in April 1987. Many precious treasures of the Tang Dynasty were unearthed in the underground palace of which, the four relics of Buddhas finger bone have been appraised to have belonged to Sakyamuni. The finger bone relics of Sakyamuni in the temple, together with tooth relic in Lingguang Temple in Beijing and the Dalada Maligawa in Kandy of Sri Lanka, are unique sarira (relics) of Sakyamuni in the world. There are 11 steles with important historical value and over 600 volumes of Buddhist sutras, of which, the Pilu Tripitaka printed in Song Dynasty (960-1729), the Puning Tripitaka and Guhya Canon printed in Yuan Dynasty (1206-1368), are extraordinarily precious versions.

On November 9, 1988, Famen Temple was reopened to the public after renovation. The new pagoda is 47 meters high with 13 stories. There are eight niches respectively form the second floor to the 12th floor. The relics of Buddhas finger bone are preserved in the underground palace. The Famen Temple Museum lies to the west.

Xiangji Temple

Located in Chang'an County of Xi'an City, Shaanxi Province, it was built in 706 and is one of the cradles of the Pure Land Sect of Buddhism, especially by Japanese followers of the sect. On May 14, 1980, the 1,300th anniversary of the death of Master Shandao of the Pure Land Sect, a delegation of over 2,000 Japanese Buddhists came to the Xiangji Temple for commemorative activities.

Buddhist Painting in China

Record of the Chinese Buddhist painting appeared in the reign of Emperor Mingdi (58-75) of the Eastern Han Dynasty. However, Chinese Buddhist painting did not enter into a prosperous period until the Wei and Jin (265-420), Southern and Northern Dynasties Period (386-581). Representative artists of Buddhist paintings of this period were Dai Kui, Gu Kaizhi, Cao Zhongda, Zhang Zengyao. Representative painting works included Five-Generation Buddha by Dai Kui, the Portrait of Vimalakirti by Gu Kaizhi and Jade Buddha sent by Lion Kingdom (today's Sri Lanka) were three masterpieces of Buddhist paintings. The painting style of the early and mid Tang Dynasty (618-907) represented by Wu Daozi and Zhou Fang was famed for vivid murals in temples. Wu Daozi was good at painting Buddha figures, long murals in particular. He painted murals on walls of three hundred rooms in Chang'an and Luoyang cities. He was capable of painting glory, pillars and beams in just one stroke, and was appraised as Holy Painter ". His representative work was Diyu Bianxiang (The Palace of the Hell). The Picture of Six Buddhas painted by Wu Daozi and Lu Lengjia is a famous extant Buddhist painting.

Painting Indian Monk in Red and the Portrait of Amitabha by Zhao Mengfu, as well as Arhats, Sakyamuni Buddhist Meeting by Ding Yunpeng in the Yuan Dynasty (1206-1368) are all famous paintings.

Buddhist Sculpture

The formal record for Chinese Buddhist sculpture appeared after 200. The first definite record of Buddhist sculpture in Chinese history was made in the Three Kingdoms Period (220-280), which records that there is a golden bronze figure of Buddha in Futu Ancestral Hall.

The extant golden bronze figure of Buddha built in the fourth year (338) of the Jianwu reign of the Latter Zhao Dynasty is the earliest Buddha with definite record in China. It also indicates that individual Buddhist sculptures with a fixed model had been popular by then in China.

Once introduced into China, figures of Buddha in India were altered according to Chinese aesthetic conception and standard. Figures of Buddha in the early stage of Buddhist sculpture featured a full round face, fat and strong body and calm expression. After Emperor Xiaowen (467-499) succeeded to the throne, he carried out a policy to promote the customs of Han nationality and moved his capital to Luoyang City. Figures of Buddha, influenced by the style of "elegance and delicacy", featured a thin face and elegant bearing, which was a combination of the styles of the Southern Wei (420-589) and Northern Wei (386-581) dynasties with Longmen Grottoes as the representative.

Dunhuang Murals

In the vast desert in Northwest China, there is about 25 km to the southwest of the city of Dunhuang in Gansu Province. This is where the famous Dunhuang Murals were found in the Mogao Grottos.

Construction of the Mogao Grottos began in 366 and reached a peak in the Tang Dynasty. By Empress Wuzetian's reign in the Tang Dynasty, more than 1,000 grottos had been hewn out of the mountain slopes. Work continued in each new dynasty, and it was not finished until the Yuan Dynasty. Today, on the conglomerate cliffs some 7,000 caves with 492 grottos remain extant in Dunhuang. The complex contains the earliest carved grotto in China. No other grottos in China have experienced a longer period of construction and have a greater size and richer content.

Dunhuang Grottos include 552 grottos such as Mogao Grottos, West Thousand-Buddha Cave, and Anxi Yulin Grottos, with over 50,000 square meters of murals of past dynasties. It is a grotto group with the most murals in both China and the whole world, with abundant contents. Dunhuang Murals constitute the major part of Dunhuang art. They have huge scale, rich contents and exquisite techniques. They can be classified into the following sorts: 1) paintings of

• Tangka Paintings

Tangka (transliteration from Tibetan language) means the special painting scroll of Tibetan Buddhism mounted with colored satin. Tangka can be found in any Tibetan monastery, worship hall, monk dormitory and even houses of followers, since it is the symbol of Buddhists and the objects for kowtowing and worshiping. Tangka enjoys high artistic value and is a marvelous spectacle in Tibetan culture.

According to different materials, Tangka falls into two categories. One is made of silk and is called gos-thang; the other is achieved with pigment and is called bris-thang. The subject matters of Tangka are much diversified, including religious themes, social history and life custom, and even astronomy, calendar and traditional Tibetan medicine.

Most Tangkas are drawn on cloth or paper. Special rite must be held for artistic monks or painters before they began their work on a selected auspicious day. The monk or painter recites sutras while preparing the materials.

The pigments used in Tangka come from opaque minerals and plant dyes. In addition, some animal glues and cattle bile are added into the pigments according to specific proportions. In this way, the Tangka can last for several thousand years without any fading.

In addition, there is another Tangka art (called as Gaoxiu Tangka), but it is at the brink of being lost. In the whole Tibetan region, such Tangka s can only be found in the Kumbum Monastery. As to such Tangkas, colorful silk satins are cut into various sceneries and figures of Buddha with wool or cotton filling so that the central part humps up. Then, the surface is embroidered with silk threads. Such Tangka therefore presents the third dimension to viewers.

♦ Buddhist Association of China

The Buddhist Association of China was established in Guangji Temple in Beijing on June 3, 1953 and it is the united organization of Buddhists of different ethnic group in China.

The Buddhist Association of China works to bring together Buddhists of different ethnic groups in the whole country, develop the good traditions of Buddhism, cultivate Buddhist talents, carry out research into Buddhism history and dogma, protect and renovate Buddhist cultural relics, maintain famous mountains and big temples, promote friendly exchanges and cultural communication and organize Buddhists to contribute their services for modernization construction, unification of the country and the cause of world peace. Its top institution is the National Congress.

In the recent yeas, there have been many Buddhist temples rebuilt around the country, including Yonghegong Lamasery and Fayuan Temple in Beijing, Yufo Temple and Longhua Temple in Shanghai, Lingyan Temple of Suzhou City and Xixia Temple of Nanjing City in Jiangsu Province, Lingyin Temple of Hangzhou City and Guoqing Temple of Tiantai County in Zhejiang Province, Nanhua Temple in Guangdong Province and Yongquan Temple in Gushan Mountain of Fujian Province as well as many monasteries in Tibet, which have been reopened for religious activities. The Chinese Buddhist Academy is responsible for Buddhist education and academic study. Two branches such as the Lingyanshan Buddhist Academy of Suzhou City and Xixiashan Buddhist Academy of Nanjing have been set up. Buddhist Academies were founded respectively in Shanghai, Fujian, Sichuan, Gansu and Tibet. The Jinling Buddhism Publishing House was reopened in Nanjing. The Chinese Museum of Buddhist Classics and Cultural Relics was founded in Beijing for unearthing, rubbing, sifting, researching and printing the Fangshan Shijing (Stone Buddhist Sutras of Fangshan). Communications between China and foreign Buddhist circles have increased. The Buddhist Association of China has appointed delegates to attend the World Conference of Religions for Peace (WCRP) and Asia Conference on Religion and Peace (ACRP). The Buddhist Association of China has friendly contacts with Buddhists around the world but especially Japanese Buddhists. Since 1995, the Buddhist Association of China has sponsored nine China-Japan-South Korea Buddhist exchange conferences. The Buddhist Association of China with the China Religious Culture Communication Association (CRCCA) sponsored the first World Buddhist Forum April 13-16, 2006.

Address: Guangji Temple, Fucheng Mennei, Beijing

The Buddhist Association of China was based in Guangji Temple in Beijing.

Buddha's. There are 933 pictures expounding Buddhist doctrines and 12,208 Buddha statues of various expressions only in Mogao Grottos; 2) paintings of sutras. The way of painting was usually employed to manifest the profound contents of Buddhist sutras, which is called "change in appearance"; 3) subjects about traditional national fables; 4) figure paintings of donors. They are the figures of people who believed in Buddhism and donated to the construction of the grottos; 5) decorative designs and paintings; 6) paintings about Buddhist stories; 7) landscape paintings.

As to these aforementioned, except for decorative designs, they usually have plots, especially paintings of sutras and paintings of stories, and reflect a great deal of social reality. Therefore, the murals in Dunhuang Grottos constitute not only art but also history. Like other religious arts, Dunhuang Murals different from non-religious paintings in style.

Qingzhou Statuary

Qingzhou Statuary, located in the site of Longxing Temple in Qingzhou County of East China's Shandong Province, was discovered in October 1996. The batch statues excavated feature a large number, a good variety, elaborate design and colorful paintings and have drawn great interest from the circles of academy, religion, art and the whole society. It was listed as one of the Ten Great Chinese Archaeological Discoveries in 1996.

These 400 carved statues were produced in the period from the Northern Wei Dynasty (386-534) to the Northern Song Dynasty (960-1127). The number of such statues made in the Northern Dynasty (420-589) is the greatest. The statues, with their exquisite engraving and outstanding craftsmanship, still show the original varied postures and colors and features of that time, although they have been seriously damaged. It's even more valuable because some colored gold leaves gilded on the surface of many of the statues still remain there, providing a rare chance for people to see the real looks of these carved statues. Among the figures of Buddha in Longxing Temple there are a number of statues of Vairocana Buddha. The Buddha's body is painted with the scenarios of doctrine teaching, images of Flying Apasas, the Hell and so on. Paintings and sculptures were blended together. The Buddhist statues in Longxing Temple are rich in models and patterns. Some clothes on the statues are of densely pleated silk, some are pure and translucent clothes. Bodhisattvas in Longxing Temple feature complicated clothes and wear pearl and jade adornments. The Flying Asparas assume a prominent sitting posture with music instrument in hands, flying in sky.

Qingzhou Statuary

Sichuan Dazu Stone Carvings

Dazu Stone Carvings

Dazu Stone Carvings is situated in Dazu County of Chongqing City in Sichuan Province, which is reputed as the Homeland of Stone Carvings. Dazu Stone Carvings was cut originally in 649 during the Yonghui reign of the Tang Dynasty (618-907), flourished in the Song Dynasty (960-1279) and expanded in the Ming (1368-1644) and Qing dynasties (1616-1911). Finally, a large-scale collection of stone carvings came into being. Dazu Stone Carvings is as famous as Yungang Grottoes, Longmen Grottoes, and Mogao Grottoes. Dazu Stone Carvings include over 100,000 statues in more than 70 sites. Among Dazu stone carvings, quite a few are related to religious beliefs with more than 50,000 Buddhist, Taoist and Confucian statues. Along with the statues, there are all kinds of sutra, eulogy, inscriptions, event records, totaling more than 150,000 characters. These inscriptions and epigraphs are of great academic value and provide plenty of vivid materials for research on politics, economy, religious art, customs, and social life of the Song Dynasty.

Taoism in China

Painting of Laotze's Teaching Scripture

Taoism originated in China in the 2nd century with a history of more than 1800 years. The founder of the Chinese Taoism was commonly regarded as the "Five Whorls of Rice Daoist", Zhang Daoling (34-157) called "Celestial Master Zhang" during the Eastern Han period (25-220). Primarily, Taoism represented the oppressed peasants who wished to alter the society and establish an Ideal Kingdom where all people were equal. Through reform by religious leaders like Ge Hong, Taoism was very popular from the 7th to the 14th centuries, and became one of three major schools of thought in China's feudal society along with Confucianism and Buddhism. Since the 12th century, Taoism gradually evolved into two major sects—Quanzhen Taoism (Way of Completeness and Truth) and Zhengyi Taoism (Way of Orthodox Unity).

The ideological system of Taoism or Daoism covers a wide range of contents. Generally speaking, it evolved into a religious culture by basing itself on ancient religious beliefs surrounding the worship of heaven and ancestors prevalent in the Spring and Autumn Period (770 BC-476 BC) an the Warring States Period (475 BC-221 BC), and was theoretically based on the thoughts of Yellow Emperor and Lao Zi. Taoism worships the birth of the universe, and nature.

As there are no strict rituals and rules for becoming a Taoist, statistics on believers are not available. Currently, there are more than 2,500 Taoist temples (with 21 listed as major ones) in the country with the number of Taoist monks and nuns being over 25,000.

Taoism exerts great influence to China's social life to a varied degree. Sects of Taoism own their own way of martial arts and qigong (deep breathing exercises). Taoist martial arts stress soft attack and gain mastery by striking only after the enemy has struck. This reflects the theory of Taoism. Some of its movements, such as Taijiquan (shadowy boxing), have been adopted by the public in daily morning exercises. Taoist qigong is a major school of Chinese qigong.

Taoist way of keeping fit is a development of the jing-luo theory of the Classics of Internal Medicine Taoists such as Ge Hong an Tao Hongjing also made contribution to the traditional Chinese medicine.

Lao Zi

(See P20)

Zhuang Zi

(See P20)

Huashan Mountain

Huashan is also called as Taihuashan Mountain, and one of the five sacred mountains of China. It lies in Huayin County of Shaanxi Province and is famous for its steepness. Not only is it the famous scenic spot, but also the holy place of Taoism, which takes it as the fourth celestial grotto. From remote antiquity, it has been a place for worshiping deities, and many Taoists went there for self-cultivation. It is said that many deities came into being there. Lao Zi is supposed to have been there and his stove to make elixirs is said to still exist there.

From the third century, due to the prevalence of Tianshi Taoism, the Huashan Mountain attracted many persons to mediate. Henceforward, large numbers of Taoists also came to Huashan Mountain to build a series of Taoist temples, and especially in the Ming Dynasty, the Taoist force of Huashan Mountain was in its prime. Because of the steepness of the mountain slopes, it is extremely hard to construct any building, so the Taoist temples appear more grand and miraculous. Currently, the well preserved Taoist temples on Huashan Mountain include Yuquan Temple (built in 11th century), Dongdao Temple (built in 1714) and Zhenyue Temple (built in the Yuan Dynasty), all of which are key Taoist temples designated by the State Council.

Huashan Mountain, a holy mountain of Taoism, is famous for its steepness.

Qingchengshan Mountain

Qingchengshan Mountain is the cradle of the Chinese Taoism and the fifth of the ten celestial grottoes of Taoism in the country. Qingchengshan Mountain lies to the west of Chengdu City of Sichuan Province. With soaring peaks and boundless luxuriant forest and green trees, the mountain enjoys the appellation of "the quietest place under the sun". Qingchengshan Mountain boasts many places of interest, various old architectures and numerous poems, paintings and articles of celebrities through the ages as well as wonderful scenes and magical legends. The Taoist temple takes the Tianshi Grotto as the core, including Jianfu Palace, Shangqing Palace, Ancestral Palace, Yuanming Palace, Yuqing Palace and Chaoyang Grotto and so on. Qingcheng Mountain has been a place for litterateurs to retire and cultivate their arts

Painting of Gehong's Making Pills of Immortality (by Li Run)

Ge Hong

Ge Hong (283-363) was born into an eminent noble family with generations of high posts. But when he was 13, his father's death brought his family into difficulties, and thereafter, he lived an ordinary life. When Ge Hong was young, he read some Taoist works, and great interest was aroused in him in the Taoist arts for longevity. At the age of 18, he formally became a pupil of an outstanding Taoist, from whom he learned a great deal of Taoist knowledge. When he was 21, a rebellion broke out. After his master went to live in seclusion in a big mountain and had never been seen again ever since, Ge Hong was conferred the title of general for leading the troops in quelling the insurrection. After that, he went to Guangzhou to be an officer there. As he increasingly felt the dark side of the human society at the officialdom, he decided to resign from office and specially practice Taoism. Finally he wrote a book Baopuzi. Later, he was repeatedly invited by the imperial government to be an official, but he declined with thanks.

Of the books Ge Hong had created, Baopuzi exerted great influence on the eventual formation and the later prosperity of Taoism.

since ancient times. The corridors, bridges and pavilions are of special style mostly with the original wood as the supporting poles, the bark of the trees as roofs, the branches as the supporting bow and the roots as the cover, simple but elegant.

White Cloud Temple

White Cloud Temple is one of the most famous holy places of Taoism, lying outside the Xibian Gate of Beijing and built in 739. Its original name was "Temple of Heavenly Eternity". It is the ancestral place of the Longmen School of Complete Perfection Sect of Taoism and the biggest Taoist building in Beijing, known as the "first temple under heaven".

The most extant buildings of the White Cloud Temple were rebuilt during the Qing Dynast. The main buildings are divided into the middle, the eastern and the western line, and the rear court, being of magnificent scale and complete layout. There exist respectively six main halls, namely the Hall of the Luminous Officials, the Jade Emperor Palace, the Hall of Ancient Disciplines, the Hall of the Patriarch Qiu, and the Three Pristine Ones' Pavilion with the Sutra House being to the east of it; along the eastern line there are the Hall of the South Pole, the Big Dipper Pavilion, the Tower of the Revered Mr. Luo and so on; and in the western line there are the Hall of Patriarch Lu, the Eight Immortals Hall, Yuanjun Hall, Yuancheng Palace, the Twelve Animals' Cliff and the Twenty-four Pieties Cliff and so on. The White Cloud Temple preserves large quantities of cultural relics, with the most famous being the "three treasures", namely the Taoist Canon of Zhengtong Era of the edition of the Ming Dynasty, the sitting statue of Lao Zi of the Tang Dynasty and stone inscriptions of the Book of Dao and its Virtue the Book of Secret Correspondences written by Zhao Mengfu, a great calligrapher of the Yuan Dynasty. Currently, the White Cloud Temple houses the Taoist Association of China.

Yongle Palace in Shanxi Province

Yongle Palace, located in Yongji County of Shanxi Province and later moved to Ruicheng County of Shanxi Province, was built for honoring Lu Dongbin, the Chinese famous initiator of Taoism. It is the oldest Taoism Palace extant. It was built in the Tang Dynasty and rebuilt in the third year of Zhongtong (1262) of the Yuan Dynasty. The present structures, including the Mountain Gate on the central line, Wuji Gate, Chunyang Hall and Chongyang Hall fully retain the architectural style and features of the Yuan Dynasty. The murals in the Yongle Palace, totaling 960 square meters, are painting masterpiece of the Yuan Dynasty.

Taiqing Palace of Laoshan Mountain

Taiqing Palace lies in Laoshan Mountain of Qingdao City of Shandong Province. Laoshan Mountain is a famous scenic area covering 300 square km that has been a holy place of Taoism since ancient times.

Taiqing Palace has the longest history, the most profound influence and largest scale among the Taoist buildings of Laoshan Mountain. It was built in 140 and reached a certain scale due to the efforts of several famous Taoists in 905; later, there more and more buildings were added. In the Yuan Dynasty, it became the Taoist temple of the Complete Perfection Sect and gained vigorous support from the imperial court, so its status rose quickly and was ranked second only to the White Cloud Temple. In the Ming Dynasty (1368-1644), the famous Taoist Zhang Sanfeng studied there. Laoshan Mountain is also linked with the great ancient novel Short Stories on the Supernatural, with much content drawn from the mountain. It is said the writer Pu Songling lived there for a long time.

Taiqing Palace mainly comprises the Three Official Palace, Palace of Three Practices of Purification and Three Emperors Palace, totaling 147 rooms. There is also a famous "spring of divine water". Taoists of this school attach great importance to preserving their health and practicing qigong.

Taiqing Palace of Shenyang City

Located in Shenyang City, Liaoning Province, it is the biggest Taoist building in the northeast area and a famous one belonging to the Longmen Branch of the Complete Perfection Sect. In 1983, the palace was designated as a national key Taoist temple by the State Council. The disciple of the eighth generation of the Longmen Sect, Guo Shouzhen, founded it in 1663. Originally called "Three Religions Hall", it houses statues of Lao Zi, Confucius and Buddha, which incarnated the thought of the Complete Perfection Sect of "the three religions united as one". Undergoing many cycles of repair, it was renamed "Taiqing Palace" in 1779.

After 1949, its abbot was elected the first president of the Taoist Association of China. Currently, there are a certain number of Taoists living a normal religious life there. Now it is the site of the Liaoning and Shenyang branches of the China Taoist Association.

Taoist Temple of Maoshan Mountain

Maoshan Mountain lies in Jirong County of Jiangsu Province and is a famous Taoist mountain, which was called "the first blissful realm" and "the eighth heavenly grotto" in history. It is also the cradle of the Shangqing, Lingbao and Maoshan sects, holding high status in the history of Taoism. In 1983, it was listed as the national key temple of Taoism by the State Council. As early as 153,

Taiqing Palace on Laoshan Mountain

Maoshan Mountain became a famous Taoist mountain. Subsequently, there were many Taoist masters who held activities there, which made it more and more influential. In the Song Dynasty (960-1279), Maoshan Mountain entered its prime time, when a large number of Taoist temples were built with government support and it became gradually the place where the doctrines of the Orthodox One Sect were expounded. At the end of the Qing Dynasty, there were more than 700 large and small buildings, mainly composed of Taiyuan Palace and Jiuxiaowanfu Palace with many precious cultural relics and sutras including the four treasures. Furthermore, the religious rites and music of the temples in Maoshan Mountain are extremely characteristic and important materials to study Taoist culture.

White Cloud Temple is the ancestral place of the Longmen School of Complete Perfection Sect of Taoismits. It houses the Taoist Association of China.

♦ Taoist Association of China

The Taoist Association of China was founded in April 1957, and it is a patriotic religious group and religious administration organization uniting all Taoists in the country, with its location in White Cloud Temple.

The association carries out policies for freedom of religious belief, maintain the valid rights and interests of Taoists, promote and develop Taoism, spread Taoist culture and abide by social morality, inherit and carry forward the good traditions of Taoism and enhance Taoist self-construction.

The association holds it national conference every five years.

Website:http://www.taoist.org.cn

Islam in China

Islam spread out quickly from its founding in Mecca in the early seventh century. Within the space of 10 years it united all Arabs under its banner and began outward expansion. The Arab Empire covered parts of Asia, Africa and Europe and made Islam a worldwide religion. Islam now has a billion believers worldwide, and more than 40 countries take it as their national religion. Especially in many Asian and African countries, Islam has far-reaching influence on the social politics and culture.

Islam was introduced to China from Arabia in two ways in the middle of the 7th century: from Dunhuang via the Silk Road, and from Guangzhou and Quanzhou via the Marine Silk Road. There are two major sects, Sunni and Shiite, with Chinese followers primarily belonging to the former. The vast majority of the 10 ethnic minorities of Hui, Uygur, Tatar, Kirgiz, Kazak, Uzbek, Tajik, Dongxiang, Salar and Bonan, totaling more than 20 million people, are Muslims, and most of them live in Xinjiang Uygur Autonomous Region, Ningxia Hui Autonomous Region, and Gansu, Qinghai and Yunnan provinces. Currently, there are more than 30,000 mosques in China with 40,000-plus imams and akhunds.

Moslem Pilgrims

The Chinese government respects and protects Moslem freedom of religious belief as well as their folk customs. The government departments concerned have provided special pilgrimage-related services for Moslem pilgrims, to the acclaim of the latter. Since the 1980s the number of Chinese Moslems going to Mecca on pilgrimages has exceeded 40,000. In the Xinjiang Uygur Autonomous Region alone, there are now 23,788 mosques, with more than 26,000 clergymen, and in the Ningxia Hui Autonomous Region, there are more than 3,500 mosques, with 5,000 clergymen. Different kinds of religious activities are normally held and the freedom of religious belief of ethnic-minority people is fully respected and protected. Out of full consideration for the dietary habits and funeral rites of those ethnic-minority people who believe in Islam, the Chinese government has enacted regulations on the production of halal food and opened Moslems-only cemeteries.

Baba Mosque of Langzhong City

The Baba Mosque is one of the famous mosques in China. It is also called the Jiuzhao Pavilion, Baoning Mosque, and Panlong Mountain Qubbah. It is located on Panlong Mountain near Langzhong City, Sichuan Province.

It was originally the graveyard of a famous Islamic leader and scholar. His followers built a series of buildings here, and these were later expanded with the help and support of the government. A building complex composed of Chinese and Islamic architecture finally came into being. The mosque covers an area of 13,000 square meters. The temple gate is a wood-and-stone construction. There are tablets and carved patterns on it. Embossments carved on the entrance wall are rare artworks. There are sermon rooms and worship halls outside the cemetery. In the mosque there are lots of cultural relics, most of which are epigraphs. The mosque is still the main congregating place for Dagongbei Menhuan, one of the main sects of Islam in China.

Dongguan Mosque of Xining City

The Dongguan Mosque is one of the four great mosques in Northwest China. It is located at Dongguan Street of Xining City, Qinghai Province.

The extant mosque was established at the beginning of the Ming Dynasty. It has undergone several destructions and reconstructions in history. The existing buildings were rebuilt in 1913, expanded in 1946, and renovated in 1979. The mosque buildings combine traditional Chinese architecture with the Islamic architectural forms. In the middle of the courtyard stands the main worship hall, which takes up an area of 1,136 square meters and is of brick-and-wood construction. There are the imam's room, students' dormitories, bathrooms and steles in the mosque, too. The Qinghai Aheng Islam College is located here.

Huashi Mosque of Beijing

The Huashi Mosque is one of the famous mosques in Beijing. It has a long history, and is located on the southern side of Huashi Street in Chongwen District.

It was first built in the early years of the Ming Dynasty (1368-1644) and underwent several repairs and expansions. The largest building in the mosque is the main worship hall. There are three open halls in front of the main worship hall, and they cover a total area of about 500 square meters. The fourth storey is the vault with hexagonal clerestories. Originally, lections of the Koran were carved on the wall. The mosque is the main congregating place of Muslims in Beijing.

Niujie Mosque of Beijing

Located in Niujie Street of Xuanwu District, Niujie Built in the year 996 of the Song Dynasty, renovated in the year 1442 in the Ming Dynasty and completely rebuilt in the 35th year (1696) of the reign of Emperor Kangxi of the Qing dynasty, the mosque has been renovated and redecorated in recent years. Niujie Mosque represents the integration of Chinese architecture and the Arabic architecture style. It can accommodate more than 1,000 Muslims for worship. There are some important cultural relics and tablets with inscriptions preserved in the mosque. Among them, there are two tablets with Arabic inscriptions and a tablet both with Chinese and Arabic inscriptions carved in 1496, named the Memorial for the Emperor Bestowing the Mosque. They are important tangible information for the study of Islamic history. There are Koran scriptures and woodcarvings both in Arabic and Persian characters and incense burners of the Ming and Qing Dynasties.

Baba Mosque in Langzhong City, southwestern China's Sichuan Province was originally the graveyards of the imams of the past dynasties.

Dongguan Mosque in Xining City, northwestern China's Qinghai Province.

Yidu Zhenjiao Mosque

The Yidu Zhenjiao Mosque is one of the famous ancient mosques in China. It is located in Yidu County, Qingzhou City, ancient capital of Shandong Province. It is also called Qingzhou Zhenjiao Mosque.

The mosque was established in 1302 by descendent of Bo Yan, Prime Minister of the Yuan Dynasty, and was rebuilt several times. The whole mosque is divided into three parts. It has a planar and symmetrical layout, and it is a typical traditional Chinese building complex. The gate features the traditional Chinese architectural style with three Chinese characters that mean mosque on it. Many tablets and couplets are hung on the mimbar. Inside, there are steles recording the history of the mosque and Islamic rites. The worship hall is composed of the front hall, main hall and rear hall. The Yidu Zhenjiao Mosque is the activity center for Muslims living in eastern Shandong Province.

♦ Islamic Association of China

The Islamic Association of China was founded on May 11, 1953 in Beijing. It is the national religious group of Chinese Muslims, working to maintain the legal rights and interests of Muslims in all ethnic groups of the country, and encourage Muslims of all ethnic groups to take part in the construction of material and spiritual civilization. Its highest institute is the National Congress.

The Islamic Association of China prints the Koran and other Islamic classics. It founded China Islamic Institute to foster Imams, Mullahs and religious persons with ability. The association has collected and arranged classics and cultural relics, and has carried out the study of Islamic history and doctrine. It owns the Beijing Muslim Classics Service Center, which publishes Chinese Muslim in Chinese (bimonthly) and Uygur languages (quarterly). The association organizes Muslims to go on pilgrimage to Mecca each year.

Website:http://www.chinaislam.net.cn

Dongda Mosque of Kaifeng City

The Dongda Mosque is one of the most famous mosques in China. It is located at Kaifeng City, Henan Province.

The existing mosque is the one rebuilt in 1846. It faces east and covers an area of 6,600 square meters. It is composed of three major parts, and is a good example of traditional Chinese construction. The main buildings include two gates, a pavilion, a sermon room, a water room, a main hall and so on. Some tablets written by celebrities are hung on the first gate. Tablets and couplets are also hung on the second gate. On both sides there are aisles carved with inscriptions. There are the water hall and the pavilion in the courtyard inside the gate. The main hall is very large and has many steles in it. There are lots of cultural relics preserved in the mosque, most of which are epigraphs. It is the largest mosque in Kaifeng City.

Aitiga Mosque of Kashi (kashgar)

The Aitiga Mosque is located at Aitiga Square in Kashi of the Xinjiang Uygur Autonomous Region. It is the largest mosque in Xinjiang. It is said that it was first built in 1462 (864 in the Islamic Calendar).Originally it was a small mosque, but it underwent much reconstruction and expansion. A tall gate and minarets form a symmetrical architecture. The octagonal gate has two porticoes leading to the courtyard, one on each side. In the courtyard, there is a pool containing limpid water. There are 158 carved columns arranged in a grid pattern, supporting the ceiling of the main worship hall, which can accommodate more than 6,000 people. The ceiling is richly decorated.

Catholicism in China

Roman Catholicism, Eastern Orthodox Church and Protestantism are the three major sects of Christianity. In China, Catholicism is called Tianzhu Jiao (Religion), because its Chinese believers called God Tianzhu (God of Heaven).

Foreign missionaries first came to China for preaching in the 7th century when the Catholic Church sent the Franciscan Bishop of Monte Corvino. He arrived in 1294, and was allowed to preach in the capital (Beijing) of the Yuan Dynasty. This marked the official entry of Catholicism into China but, with the downfall of the Yuan Dynasty, the movement was suspended. After the First Opium War (1840-1842), Catholicism began to move into China again. Its activities suffered during the chaotic "cultural revolution" (1966-1976). During the ongoing reform and opening up period, it won new life. Currently, Chinese Catholics have 100 dioceses with close to five million followers. There are 5,000 churches open to the public throughout the country, together with 12 seminaries. Every year, about 50,000 people are baptized in Catholic churches. Since 1981, the Chinese Catholic Church has trained and consecrated more than 1,500 priests. Of them, over 100 have been sent to seminaries in the United States, France, Britain, Belgium, Italy, Germany, the Philippines, the Republic of Korea and other countries, some of them obtaining a Master's or Doctor's degree before returning to China. The Chinese Catholic Church has its own publishing organs, which have printed more than three million copies of the Bible and other religious works. Influential Catholic churches in the country are St. Mary of the Immaculate Conception Cathedral (Xuanwumen Church) in Beijing, the Church of St. Michael in Qingdao, the Church of St. Joseph (Xikai Cathedral) in Tianjin, Hongjialou Church in Jinan and Sheshan Church in Shanghai. Its national organizations are the China Patriotic Catholic Association and the China Catholic Biship Group.

Qingdao Catholic Church

The Qingdao Catholic Church was built in the early 1930s and is the largest example of Gothic architecture in Qingdao as well as a masterpiece of Christian architecture. The church is located to the east of flourishing Zhongshan Road of the seashore city. With two huge crosses, the high red spire stands towers over the buildings set off by the surrounding flowers and trees.

The construction of the church began in 1932 and ended in 1934. Covering an area of 2470 square meters, the church is built of yellow granites and ferroconcretes, and the facade is carved with concise and graceful patterns. The grand and sober windows are half arciform with fluent lines. A huge rosace is set up on the gate. There are red-tiled bell towers over 56 meters high on each side of the main entrance with a cross more than 4.5 meters high. Inside each tower, four great bells are hung whose sound can be heard miles away. Behind the entrance, there is a roomy and bright hall over 18 meters high, which can accommodate more than 1,000 people. Soft light passes through the rosace. Two ambulatories stand on both east and west sides of the hall. There are two large altars and four small altars behind the hall. The icon painted on the hall's vault and the dazzling lamps fill the church with religious atmosphere.

The religious activities are numerous. Masses are held every Sunday with a big attendance. During the Easter and Christmas which are the major activities of Catholicism, the church holds grand activities.

Tianjin Xikai Church

The Xikai Church, also called the French Church, is a famous Catholic church in Tianjin City.

The existing buildings were constructed by French Catholics in 1914 and 1917. They follow the European style, adopting French Romanesque architectural technique. It has a long cross-shaped layout. There are three tall towers standing at the apexes of a triangle, at the front and the back of the church. The pedestals of the towers are built by laying yellow and red bricks, with emerald cyrtostyle spires at the top. There are semicircular arched windows below the eaves. The inner walls are complete with rich colored frescoes. The Xikai Church is the largest of its kind in Tianjin, and it can accommodate many adherents. Now it is still the local center of Catholic activities.

Tianjin Xikai Church

Shanghai Old Cathedral

The Shanghai Old Cathedral is the oldest church in the city. At the end of the Ming Dynasty, a famous Chinese scientist, Xu Guangqi, who was a Shanghai native, took an important position in the government. As the most reputable person in Shanghai, he was baptized in Nanjing and became a Catholic in 1603. Then, the number of people who followed him and believed in Catholicism increased rapidly in Shanghai. Subsequently, the adherents in Shanghai built a Catholic church near Xu's residence. Guo Jujing, the first missionary to Shanghai, served as the priest. Due to their eminent contribution to the compilation of the calendar for the government, a plaque which reads "Emperor Praises the Holy Catholic" was hung in the church in 1622. The descendants of Xu Guangqi cooperated with foreign missionaries to build a Catholic church in 1633, which was called the Old Cathedral afterwards. Besides the chapel, there is an observatory for observing celestial phenomena and doing astronomical research. Because the government banned Catholicism in 1724, the chapel of the Old Cathedral was built into a temple for Guan Yu (an ancient hero of China), and the observatory was renovated into the Jingye College. One hundred years later, the government agreed to return all the lands of the Old Cathedral. The French Catholic Church rebuilt the church at the original address and named it Jingyi Church, but people still call it the Old Cathedral.

Xujiahui Cathedral is the largest Catholic church in Shanghai with a long history. It has a high status among Chinese adherents. The church was established in 1904. Its formal name is St. Ignatius Cathedral.

Catholic Churches in Beijing

Beijing was among the first centers involved in the propagation of Catholicism.

Missionaries, mainly Jesuits, built churches in the city. At present, there are eight Catholic churches that belong to the Beijing parish. They are the Eastern Church, Western Church, Southern Church, Northern Church, St. Michael's Church, Nangangzi Church, Pingfang Church and Dongguantou Church. Nine other churches are in the suburbs.

The churches in Beijing resemble Western ones in terms of architectural style. Most of them are of Romanesque and Gothic styles. most Catholic churches in Beijing face south (facing east mostly in the West), according to Chinese custom of making important buildings face southward. Because of the ascending trend brought about by the towering Gothic spire and forceful pointed arches inside enabling the priest's voice to reverberate through the building in impressive style, Gothic architecture gained special favor among church builders.

Catholicism embraces the Madonna. There are Virgin Mary hills or Virgin Mary pavilions constructed outside each Catholic church. These so-called hills are rockeries that are peculiar to Chinese gardens.

Northern Church

The Northern Church, formerly located at Canchikou near Zhongnanhai of Beijing, was opened in 1703, and torn down in 1887 due to the expansion of the latter. It was later rebuilt in Xishiku, inside Xi'anwumen, with 450,000 taels of silver provided by the Qing government. One floor was added to the church in a renovation carried out in 1900, so that it became the majestic and beautiful church that we see today. The Northern Church is a typical Gothic structure. Four tall spires, three peaked arch entrances and rosace make the facade dignified and gorgeous. The church looks more pure white and upright with surrounding pines and cypresses. On both sides of the church front, there stand two Chinese pavilions with yellow glaze on the roof. There is a stele inscribed personally by Emperor Qianlong inside each pavilion. These constructions, one high and one short, are arranged skillfully. The statuaries of saints on both sides of the main entrance are unique among the churches in Beijing. After the restoration in 1985, the church became the most ornate church in Beijing.

Eastern Church

The Eastern Church, located on the famous Wangfujing Street in Beijing, was first established in 1655, and was the apartment Qing Emperor Shunzhi granted to two foreign priests. They built a small church on the open ground. Later, the church was ruined in

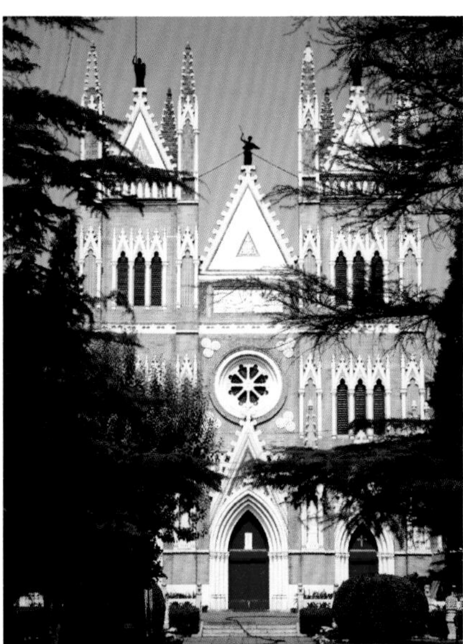

Xishiku Church (northern hall)

earthquakes and wars several times. It was rebuilt in 1904. After the restoration in 1980, it was reopened. Because of the geographical position, the Eastern Church faces West. It follows the Romanesque style. The strong pilasters and one high and two low vaults present a massive appearance. In order to achieve the expansion of Wangfujing, Beijing Municipal Government set aside 130 million Yuan for the restoration of the whole church.

Western Church

The Western Church, located on the southern side of Xizhimen Nei Street in Beijing, is the youngest church among these four churches. The Western Church was first established in 1723 and restored in 1912. Because the pharmaceutical factory beside it has not been moved yet, it nearly cannot be seen from the street. But delicate Collins pillars and Gothic peaked arch inside the church make it grand, elegant and solemn.

Eastern Church

♦ Chinese Catholic Organization

Chinese Patriotic Catholic Association is a mass group formed by Conversus Shenzhang of Chinese Catholic Church and founded in the July 1957 in Beijing with the original name Chinese Patriotic Catholic Association of Conversus. The purpose of the Chinese Catholic Patriotic Association is: to unite all the clergy and Catholics, to carry forward patriotism, to obey the Constitution, laws, regulations and policies, to actively participate in socialist modernization construction of the homeland, to promote friendly communications with international Catholics, to fight against imperialism and hegemonism, to safeguard world peace, and to assist the Government in implementing the policy of freedom of religious belief. Its highest institute is the Congress of Chinese Patriotic Catholic Association, and a National Congress is held every four years in Beijing.

The Chinese Catholic Bishops' College is the leading institute of Chinese Catholic administration, set up in 1980.

St. Michael's Church

St. Michael's Church in Dongjiaomin Alley was first built in 1901. Dongjiaomin Alley was a special zone for foreigners during the late years of the Qing Dynasty, and almost all embassies were built here. St. Michael's Church was especially built for foreigners living here, and it belongs to Beijing parish now. Its entrance is in the south, and the whole building follows typical Gothic style. Three main peaked spires and several spire ornaments bring out the best in each other.

Dongguantou Church

Dongguantou Church is the smallest of the eight Catholic churches in Beijing city. It is located in Dongguantou Village of Fengtai District in southeastern Beijing. The time when it was first built is not known. There used to be an ordinary one-storey house, which was torn down in 1991, and a new church was built on the same site. The style of the church reflects the architect's inspiration, the facade is proportional, and the two warped cornices resemble flying wings and show its individuality.

Longzhuang Church

Longzhuang Church is located in Tongzhou, a suburb of Beijing. There used to be an old church. Local people said that it had been there for more than 100 years, but the exact time cannot be confirmed. In 1998, the Longzhuang Church was rebuilt in the west of the village. It is a red brick construction and faces south. The towering spire points to the blue sky, making the church look most spectacular.

Housangyu Village Church

Housangyu Village Church is located in Mentougou, a suburb of Beijing, and is the capital's oldest Catholic church. According to historical records, it was originally a small church built in 1334, with stone-carved poodles in front of it and carved with eight Chinese characters Zhen Zai Ji Li, Huai Lin De Yi (bringing good luck to the house and lofty morals to the world).

Housangyu Village Church was expanded in 1896, and rebuilt in 1988. With the grand view of mountains, the towering white spire looks striking and splendid. In line with the mountain shape, a winding road was constructed towards the Virgin Mary Hill at the mountainside, which presents a unique view.

Protestantism in China

Protestantism arrived in China as early as the Tang Dynasty in the form of Jingjiao (Nestorianism). However, due to its failure to out down roots in Chinese society and culture, it never achieved significant development and almost disappeared several times. After the Opium War (1840-1842), there were more Protestants, rising to over 700,000 just before the founding of the People's Republic of China in 1949. During the "cultural revolution" (1966-1976), church activities were suspended. They resumed in 1979, followed by the founding of the Chinese Christian Council in 1980.

Over two decades, Protestantism has developed well. Approximately 50,000 churches are now open to the public. The number of Chinese Protestants has surpassed 16 million with over 18,000 clergymen, more than 12,000 churches and over 25,000 accessible sites for Christian activities. At present, there are 18 seminaries and Bible schools throughout the country, and nearly 5,000 graduates are serving in churches or seminaries all over China. The Three-Self Patriotic Movement Committee of the Protestant Churches of China and the Chinese Christian Council have published and distributed approximately 30 million copies of the Bible, 14 million copies of the Psalms (new edition). They also have their own website Chinese Protestant Church (www.chineseprotestantchurch.org).

Qingdao Christian Church

Qingdao Christian Church is a famous religious structure in Qingdao City, Shandong Province. It is a good example of German castle-like architecture, which consists of a bell towel and an auditorium. It is made of granite. The bell tower is 39.1 meters high, and on its top floor visitors can see the sea far away. The auditorium is capacious and bright, and can hold more than 1,000 people.

Originally, this church was the place where the local German community gathered together and worshiped. In 1897, after Germany took possession of the Jiaozhou Area, the Berlin branch of the German Lutheran Church sent a missionary to Qingdao City. He chose a location between the viceroy's official residence and the government office building and began to build a church. It was originally called the German Worship Church. In 1925, it was sold to the Association of American Lutheran Churches,

Christian Church at the Jiangsu Lu, Qingdao

and became the venue of religious activities for foreigners in the neighborhood. After 1949, the church became the primary venue of religious activities for Chinese Christians. With the amalgamation of the oriental and Western cultures in recent years, Christianity has become an influential religion, and the religious services here are numerous.

Flower Lane Church in Fuzhou City

The Flower Lane Church is located at Dongjiekou of Fuzhou City, the capital of Fujian Province, also called "Rongcheng City". It is one of the most important Christian churches in Fuzhou City, and an activity center of the Flower Lane Christian Church as well as a hub of churches in Fujian Province and Fuzhou City.

Following the founding of New China in 1949, the Chinese church terminated its relationship with foreign churches and no services were conducted during the Cultural Revolution. On October 28, 1979, the Flower Lane Church resumed religious services and became the first church in Fuzhou to hold a regular service after the "cultural revolution". Consequently, it became the most popular rendezvous of Fuzhou churches and was renamed from Shang You Tang to the Flower Lane Church by conforming to its location. The church has received 3,000 person/times of visits from 40 countries and regions for international fellowship, being the exchange center between Fujian Christian circles and overseas religious organizations. Up to now, the Flower Lane Church has eleven social-work departments and about a thousand social workers. And it has more than 10,000 adherents of different age and from different professions.

During the Lord's Day, over 4,000 adherents gather in two congregations. More than 2,000 are attracted to the large worship every weekend night.

Shanghai Community Church

Shanghai Community Church is located on Hengshan Road in Shanghai. It is the largest Christian church in the city. Some American residents established a church at Donghu Road in 1920. At first, most Christians who worshiped there were American. In 1923, citizens of different countries living in Shanghai raised funds and began the construction of a new church at Hengshan Road. It was finished in 1925 and called the Shanghai Community Church. Christians of different denominations worshiped here thereafter. It imitated English style and was constructed with red bricks. The door of the church faces the north, and the interior is quadrate. It has corridors, aisles and a pointed vault. Originally the Shanghai Community Church was the dedicated church for expatriates, but later some Chinese Christians of high social status worshiped here. After 1949, the services were completely taken over by Chinese priests.

Shanghai Community Church has 1,400 seats. It boasts a high-standard choir. Every month a musical gathering is held in the church. Many overseas personages have visited the church. Among them there were US President Jimmy Carter and Archbishop Desmond Tutu, the Nobel Peace Prize Laureate.

Haidian Christian Church in Beijing

Formerly called the Haidian Chinese Christian Church, this is located in Haidian District of Beijing. It was subordinate to the Beijing Methodist Church. In 1922, Qi Guodong, a graduate from Yanjing Seminary, was appointed to run the church. In 1927,

Haidian Christian Church

a directorate composed of 12 directors was established. To meet the requirements of increasing congregations and with the effort of worshipers and the directors, 4,600 silver dollars was raised in 1933 and the current church was established in June. Qi Guodong became the pastor and the regular congregation swelled to about 500. Haidian Christian Church also devoted itself to charity work. For instance, Qi established the Peiyuan Primary School in 1929, adding a middle school to it in 1932. He established the Peiyuan, Peide, and Peishan cross-stitch factories with the Charity Association for Women and Children of Yanjing University and created job opportunities for 200 jobless women in 1932; established a retirement home and a hospital of obstetrics and gynecology to serve the residents in Haidian District for free. For historical reasons, services were halted for a while, but the church reopened on May 12, 1985. Now, the church is listed among the renovation plan of western Zhongguancun. A new Haidian Church will be built according to the plan.

Jinling Xiehe Divinity School

Students in the Jinling Xiehe Divinity School are studying the course on the History of Christian Thought.

Jinling Xiehe Divinity School is the national Protestant training center, located in Nanjing of Jiangsu Province, and it got the name because Nanjing was called Jinling in ancient times. In November 1952, it was founded by the Three-Self Patriotic Movement Committee of the Protestant Churches of China and composed of the 12 Protestant divinity schools in Eastern China. In 1962, Yanjing Xiehe Divinity School also joined, but it suspended class from 1966 to 1980 due to the Cultural Revolution (1966-1976) and only resumed teaching in February 1981. Its aim is to train teaching and administrative staff and divinity researchers to be the ones who love

both the country and the religion, adhere to the orientation of "three self (self-government, self-support and self-propagation)" and develop in an all-round way of spirit, virtue, wisdom, physical status and companionship, have superior achievements with regard to spiritual knowledge and are good at uniting believers, and can serve the Protestant churches in the country. It has already a history of 50 years under the leadership of the Bishop Ding Guangxun as well as the principal of the school. It has set up the four-year undergraduate course, three-year postgraduate course and the three-year Bible courses taught by correspondence. From 1995, it began granting a master's degree (for postgraduates) and bachelor's degree (for college graduates) of divinity. The students come from the churches throughout the country, recommended by them and selected by examination (including interviews). Today, various schools have had some 5,000 students. The Record of Jinling Xiehe Divinity Records is published.

♦ China Christian Council

Founded in October 1980, the China Christian Council is the national religious administration institute of Chinese Protestantism. It provides services for all the churches and followers in the country for religious work, such as publishing Bibles, the Psalms and other religious books, discussing the systems and ceremonies to be adopted by Chinese Christianity, educate Christians of the whole country to respect each other and unite in Christian belief. Its supreme organ is the National Conference of China Catholicism held every four years by the council together with the Three-Self Patriotic Movement Committee. The council is headquartered in Shanghai.

♦ Three-Self Patriotic Movement Committee of the Protestant Churches of China

Three-Self Patriotic Movement Committee of the Protestant Churches of China is a patriotic organization of Chinese Protestants founded in August 1954. Its highest institute is the National Congress of Chinese Christianity held every five years with the China Christian Council to choose its National Committee which then elects a Chairman, vice-chairman, secretary-general and standing commissioner. It is located in Shanghai.

Freedom of Religious Belief

Every citizen enjoys the freedom to believe or not to believe in any religion. Within a religion, every Chinese citizen has the freedom to believe in any denomination. These freedoms should be respected and protected. Those are the basic contents. According to the Constitution, both believers and non-believers enjoy equal rights and obligations. No State organ, public organization or individual may compel citizens to believe or not to believe in any religion; nor may they discriminate against citizens who either. Any behavior contrary to this requirement and that tampers with the legal rights and interests of religious circles should be firmly corrected. On the other hand, it is required to insist on unification of rights and obligations. The freedom of religious belief is not equal to religious activities facing no restrictions. The personnel of the religious circle and believers should first be the citizens of the People's Republic of China and place the basic interests of the State and the people in first position and assume the obligation of abiding by the Constitution, laws, regulations and policies.

Religions Should Abide by the Laws

Religions should hold their activities in line with the Constitution, laws and policies. When citizens enjoy freedom of religious belief, they have the obligation to observe the Constitution and laws. No State organ, public organization or individual may damage the legal rights and interests of religious circles and interfere with their normal religious activities. But nobody can use religion to breach the social order and harm the health of citizens, nor utilize religion to oppose the leadership of the Party and the socialist system and destroy the unification of the country and the solidification of the ethnic group.

All Religions Are Equal

Regardless of the number of believers and influence, Buddhism, Taoism, Islam and Christianity are equal and none of them may take predominance. The Government treats all of them equally without discrimination.

Religion Is Separated from Political Power

In light of this principle, no one may utilize religion to interfere with State administration, judicature, school education and social public education, marriage and family planning and so on. The regime of the State may also not be used to push forward or forbid one religion.

State Protects Normal Religious Activities

The State protects all normal religious activities in line with the Constitution, laws and policies. Religious organizations in China run their own affairs independently and set up religious schools, publish religious classics and periodicals, and run social services according to their own needs. Normal religious activities held in registered sites for religious activities or in the homes of the believers according to religious habit are protected by law, and no one may interfere with them. The State protects the legal rights and interests of religious groups and the rights of religious teaching and administrative staff to run their affairs.

Theism and Atheism Should Respect Each Other

No one may publicize atheism in sites for the religious activities, nor hold debate with regard to theism or atheism. No religious organizations and believers may preach, propagandize, publicize theism, and send religious handbills and other religious books and periodicals without the authorization of the relevant administrative department of the government.

Adopting the Principle of Independence and Self-management

Chinese religious affairs and organizations shall not be intervened in and controlled by foreign forces. It is a common principle abided by all the religions in China. Chinese religious organizations carry out self-government, self-support and self- propagation in adherence to the principle of independence and self-management, which do not oppose friendly exchanges with their counterparts in other countries on the basis of complete equality and mutual respect. An organization may accept foreign assistance and donations without the conditions of interfering with Chinese domestic affairs, including religious affairs.

Respecting and Protecting Freedom of Religious Belief of Minorities

China is a united multi-ethnic nation. The Chinese government pursues a policy of equality, unity and mutual assistance among all ethnic groups, respects and protects the right to freedom of religious belief and the folk customs of the ethnic minorities. The Law of

Confucianism, Taoism, and Buddhism are one, a painting portraying the founders of Buddhism, Taoism and Confucianism—Confucius, Taotze and Sakyamuni—laughing by a river stream like discussing scriptures, thus reflecting the thoughts "three religions amalgamated into one."

the People's Republic of China on National Regional Autonomy stipulates: "Organs of self-government in ethnic regional autonomous areas protect the right to freedom of religious belief of the citizens of all ethnic groups."

The Chinese government pays special attention to the religious beliefs and the protection of the cultural heritage of minorities. Special programs have been carried out to survey, collect, classify, study and publish the cultural heritages — including religious cultures — and folk arts of all the ethnic groups. In addition, the State has made huge investments in the maintenance and reconstruction of temples, mosques and other religious facilities of important historical and cultural value in ethnic-minority areas.

Judicial and Administrative Guarantees and Supervision

With respect to judicial guarantees, China stipulates clearly the penalties for the infringement of citizens' right to freedom of religious belief. For instance, Article 251 of the Criminal Law states: "State personnels who unlawfully deprive citizens of their freedom of religious belief and infringe upon the customs and habits of minority ethnic groups, when the circumstances are serious, are to be sentenced to not more than two years of fixed-term imprisonment or criminal detention". In the Decisions on the Standards for Filing Directly Received Cases of Infringement Upon Citizens' Democratic and Personal Rights and Those of Malfeasance, it is stipulated that a people's Procuratorate shall place on file a case in which a State functionary illegally deprives anyone of his or her legitimate freedom of religious belief — such as by interfering in normal religious activities, forcing a believer to give up his/her membership of a religion or compelling a citizen to profess a certain religion or adherence to a certain religious sect — and in which the offense is of an abominable nature and has brought about serious consequences and undesirable effects. A people's Procuratorate shall also put on record cases of illegally closing or destroying lawful religious sites and other religious facilities. In recent years, the Chinese judiciary has tried several cases of infringing upon relevant laws of the State and seriously hurting the religious feelings of certain believers, and has meted out punishments to the persons responsible.

With regard to administrative guarantees, governments at different levels have set up religious affairs departments to administer and supervise the implementation of the laws and statutes pertaining to religion and to put the policy ensuring freedom of religious belief into effect. These departments cannot interfere in the internal affairs of religious organizations.

Registration Procedures of Religious Activities

In China religious organizations and sites for religious activities must register with the government in accordance with the law, which is the case in some other countries as well. Applications for such registration must meet the following basic requirements: a permanent site and name; regular attendance; a management organization composed of adherents to the relevant religion; clerical personnel for officiating over religious activities or personnel with qualifications stipulated in the regulations of various religions; management regulations and lawful income. Government departments shall defer the registration or only approve temporary registration of religious sites that cannot completely satisfy these basic requirements or who have prominent management problems. Government departments shall not permit the registration of, for example, sites for religious activities illegally occupying land or violating city planning rules, which have been set up without authorization or which promote superstitious activities, such as exorcising evil spirits under the pretext of religious activities. Once a site for religious activities is properly registered it has legal status and its lawful rights and interests shall be protected. If these are infringed, the organization in charge of the site is entitled to seek administrative and legal protection by appealing to the relevant government organ or taking the case to a people's court. There is no registration requirement for, to quote from Chinese Christians, "house services", which are mainly attended by relatives and friends for religious activities such as praying and Bible reading.

Political Deputies of the Religious Circle

People's congresses at different levels, which are organs through which the people exercise their power, and the Chinese people's

Buddha's relic shows up in Hong Kong, with the worship ceremony attracting Hong Kong citizens.

political consultative conferences at different levels, which are playing an important role in the political and social life of the State, shall supervise the implementation of the policy and laws relating to the freedom of religious belief. There are about 17,000 religious personages who are deputies to people's congresses or members of political consultative conferences at different levels. On behalf of religious circles they participate in the discussions of important State and social affairs at the people's congresses and political consultative conferences, and offer comments, suggestions and criticisms, or submit proposals and motions relating to the government's work on religion.

In March 2008, the leaders of China's five major relgions met in Beijing to attend the 5th plenary meeting of the Second Committee of the China Committee on Religion and Peace. From right to left: Rev Cao Shengjie, former President of China Christian Council, Liu Bonian, vice chairman of the Catholic Patriotic Association of China, Most Venerable Sheng Hui, vice-president of the Buddhist Association of Chinaall religions in China, Master Ren Farong, president of China Taoist Association, Master Yi Cheng, head of the Buddhist Association of China (BAC), and Imam Chen Guangyuan, President of the Islamic Association of China.

International Religious Exchanges

Religion is a worldwide phenomenon and the five Chinese religions have historical and wide relation with foreign countries, playing an important role in cultural exchanges. At present, Chinese religious organizations maintain friendly contacts with other religious organizations and personnel in more than 70 countries and regions. Since the 1980s, the contacts with the religious organizations of foreign countries have been constantly strengthened and great friendly international exchanges have gradually increased.

Chinese religious organizations also take part in international affairs: the Buddhist Association of China is a member of "International Friendship Association of Buddhism"; the China Christian Council officially participated in the "World Council of Churches" in 1992; the Islamic Association of China took part in "The Highest World Mosque Council of the Islamic Union".

The different religions have wide exchanges with corresponding ones abroad, for example, Chinese Buddhist circles have close contacts with surrounding countries such as Thailand, Korea, Japan, Burma, Sri Lanka and Vietnam. In recent years, the tooth relic of Buddha has been worshiped in Thailand, Burma and Sri Lanka and the religious circles of Thailand have set up periodical system of Buddhist exchanges with Tibet. Invited by some countries in Western Europe and North America, Chinese religious organizations have made visits, not only getting to know about the local religions but also enhancing the understanding of the local people about Chinese religion.

Respecting Freedom of Religious Belief of Foreigners in China

The Chinese Government respects the freedom of religious belief and the normal religious activities of foreigners in China, mainly in the following aspects: 1. The Chinese Government respects all the foreigners in China, no matter if they believe or not believe in any religion, or whether there is such a religion in China. 2. In the areas open to the aliens in China, they may participate in religious activities at recognized sites for religious activities. 3. They may invite Chinese clerical personnel to conduct such religious rituals as baptism, weddings, funerals and prayer meetings. 4. The aliens may bring with them printed religious matter, audio-visual religious material and other religious articles for personal use while entering Chinese territory. 5. More and more large-scale international conferences, sports contests and cultural and academic exchanges have been held in China and the joint-venture or the foreign-invested companies increasingly appear in China, so in order to meet the demand of the collective religious life of aliens, upon application and with the agreement of the department of religious affairs at or above county level, sites for religious activities or provisional sites for aliens to hold religious activities may be designated.

Protecting Aliens' Exchanges With Respect to Religion

The Chinese Government protects aliens' friendly contacts and cultural and academic exchanges with Chinese religious circles with respect to religion, mainly in the following aspects: 1. The Chinese Government supports and protects international cultural and academic exchanges with respect to religion. 2. Aliens may also preach at the invitation of Chinese religious bodies at or above provincial level. 3. As for the religious sutras, books and periodicals and audio-visual religious materials taken by aliens to take part in the religious cultural and academic exchanges, if they completed the procedures required by customs regulations, they may receive certification by the governmental department of religious affairs. 4. As for sending students to study abroad for cultivating religious teaching staff and the foreign student enrolled by China's religious colleges, this should be handled by China's related regulations. No foreign or international religious organization and their institutes in China are allowed to enroll students abroad in China without permission; aliens may study or teach in Chinese Religious Colleges upon invitation.

Chinese Laws Must Be Observed

Aliens within Chinese territory should observe Chinese laws and maintain the social public interests of China. No one is allowed to use religion to interfere in Chinese domestic affairs. No alien is allowed to interfere with Chinese religious affairs, carry printed religious matter and audio-visual religious materials beyond rational use for themselves into China, set up religious organization and offices and rites for religious activities in China, run religious schools, develop followers among Chinese citizens and depute religious teaching and administrative personnel, and conduct other missionary activities.

China Philharmonic Orchestra joined by the Shanghai Opera House chorus performed in the Vatican for Pope Benedict XVI on the evening of May 7, 2008.The orchestra played WA Mozart's Requiem and Chinese folk songs such as , accompanied by the Shanghai Opera House Chorus at the Paul VI Audience Hall in Vatican City. This is the first time the orchestra has made an appearance in the Vatican.

Handling Aberrant Behavior According to the Law

As for the aliens who hold the religious activities that do not adhere to the PRC Regulations Concerning Religious Activities of Foreigners in and Outside China, once discovered, the departments of religious affairs at or above the county level have the right to take action; as for those who break the regulation on the control of the entry and exit of the aliens or harm public security, the public security organ may impose penalties according to the related law and regulation; and as for those who commit a criminal offence, the judicial organ will investigate their criminal responsibility.

Relations with the Vatican

The Chinese government has consistently adhered to a peaceful foreign policy of independence and is willing to improve the relations with the Vatican. However, such improvement requires two basic conditions: First, the Vatican must end its so-called diplomatic relations with Taiwan and recognize that the government of the People's Republic of China is the only legal government in China and that Taiwan is an inalienable part of China's territory. Second, the Vatican must not interfere in China's internal affairs on the pretext of religious affairs. In the first place, the relationship between China and the Vatican is one between two countries. Therefore, only when the relations between the two countries improve can religious issues be discussed. Whether the relations between China and the Vatican change or not, the Chinese government will, as always, support Chinese Catholicism which holds aloft the banner of patriotism, sticks to the principle of independence and self-management, and stands for selection and ordination of bishops by itself.

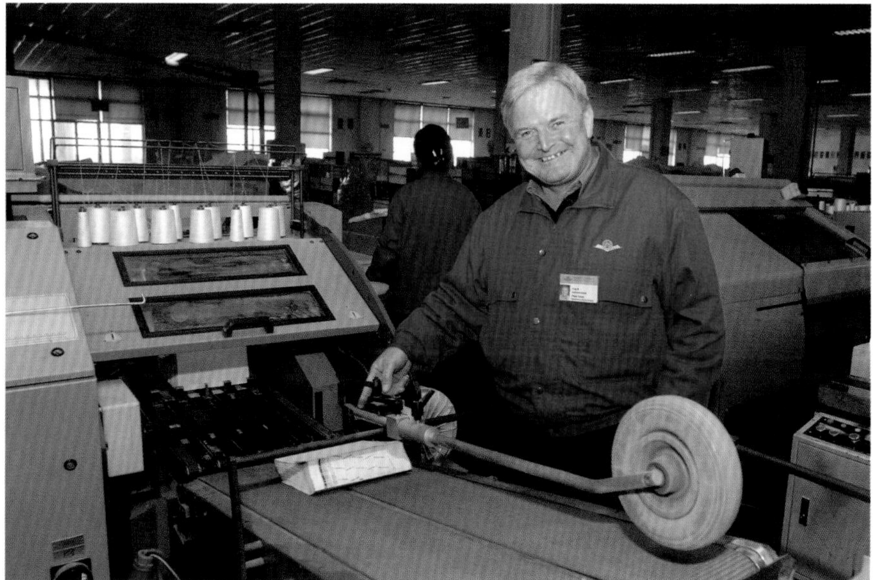

Amity Printing Co., Ltd., founded in 1986, is a joint venture between Amity Foundation and the United Bible Societies, the printing of Bibles and other religious books.

♦ State Administration for Religious Affairs

This is the functional department of the State Council to take charge of the religious affairs, with its main functions including: protecting the freedom of citizens in religious belief in line with the law, the legal rights of religious groups and sites for religious activities, religious teaching and administrative personnel to run normal religious affairs, and the normal religious activities of the believers; investigate the state of religion both at home and abroad and study religious theory problems; draft laws and regulations with respect to religion; conduct research and constitute the rules of the department and the detailed policies with respect to religious work; administer and supervise the implementation of the law, regulations and policies with regard to religion; direct and promote religious activities within the law, regulation and policies, and deal with persons who use religion to cover illegal activities; organize and supervise the propagandizing and education work of the religious policies and legal system; support the personnel of the religious circle to conduct self education in patriotism, socialism and advocacy of national unification and the solidification of ethnic groups; unite and mobilize believers to serve for the reforms and economic construction; help religious groups to cultivate, educate teaching and administrative staff and run religious schools; handle the affairs of religious groups in need of assistance or coordination from the government; direct the work of the departments of religious affairs of the local people's government and assist it to deal with the important problems; support and help religious circles to develop the friendly exchanges with foreign counterparts especially as well as Hong Kong, Macao and Taiwan and so on.

Address: No.44 Houhai Beiyan, Xicheng District, Beijing
Website: http://www.sara.gov.cn

Science and Technology

General Survey

The Four Great Inventions of Ancient China

Chinese science and technology has a long history, and has contributed a lot to the development of humankind. Up to the mid-16th century, China was the technological center of the world. In astronomy, for example, the phenomenon of a solar eclipse had been recorded in an inscription on animal bones and tortoise shells 3,300 years ago.

Kao Gong Ji (Records on Industries) written at the time of the Warring States Period (475 BC-221 BC) contained an exact record of copper-tin alloy, which had six different ingredients. Early in the Western Han Dynasty (206 BC-25 AD), papermaking had been invented in China; around 105AD, after Cai Lun, a Chinese scientist, improved the technology, papermaking spread quickly. By the time of 3rd century, porcelain appeared in China, and soon spread to Persia, and eventually spread throughout Europe by 1470. Gunpowder was invented in the Tang Dynasty, and was firstly used as a means of waging war in the 9th century. During the Song Dynasty (960-1279), the Chinese inventions of the compass and movable type printing were in extensive use. By the mid-15th century, the Compendium of *Materia Medica* (a book on Chinese herbal medicine) became the most successful work of Ancient Chinese medicine. By this time, the Four Great Inventions of Ancient China were known and admired in much of the world.

The Policy of Exclusion begun during the Ming Dynasty (1368-1644) blocked the development and spread of modern technology in China. The gap widened between China and advanced countries in the world.

Papermaking

Papermaking is one of the famous four ancient inventions of China.

Portrait of Cai Lun (61-121)

Before the "Cai Hou paper" invented by Cai Lun in the Eastern Han Dynasty, embryonic papermaking skills already existed in China. The ancient paper found in the Fang Matan, the western Han dynasty tomb, at Tianshui in Northwest China's Gansu province is the earliest example found so far. Similar paper was also excavated in Luobubo in Xinjiang and Baqiao of Xi'an of North China's Shaanxi province. But this paper was crude, were made from flax or cotton. In 105, however, Cai Lun, a eunuch, after summarizing his predecessors' experiences, improved the technology.

Early in the 7th century, during the late Sui Dynasty and the early Tang dynasty, papermaking spread to Korea and Japan. In the other direction, it spread to Samarkand in Central Asia and then on to the Arab world via Baghdad in the 8th century and then on to Damascus and Cairo by the 10th century, Morocco by the 11th century, India by the 13th, and Italy by the 14th century. Many Italian cities built papermaking factories at that time and thus became an important papermaking based in Europe. From there, the technology reached Germany and England, and then to Russia and the Netherlands in the 16th century. It went to the United Kingdom in the 17th century, and Canada in the 19th century. The invention and spread of papermaking drastically cut the cost of writing materials and helped popularize knowledge among the common people.

Gunpowder

Gunpowder is another of the Four Great Inventions of Ancient China.

The invention of gunpowder had a close relationship with the advanced ancient workmanship of the smelting industry. People began to gain a lot of chemistry knowledge related to the nature of different minerals during the process of smelting. Although the exact date of invention still remains unknown, based on the historical materials, gunpowder first appeared before the Tang Dynasty (618-907). People used to call it black powder due to its color. By the end of the Tang Dynasty, gunpowder began to be used by the military. The earliest weapon using it was called "fly fire", which was actually a rocket. During the Song and Yuan dynasties, the military applications of gunpowder became common, and many other weapons like "fire cannon", "rocket", "missile" and "fireball" appeared. In the Ming Dynasty, a landmine controlled by gears and a torpedo timed by a blasting fuse were introduced.

In the Yuan Dynasty (1206-1368), the method of powder-making was introduced to Europe, bringing about a revolution in weapon manufacturing, as well as stratagems and tactics on the battlefield. It also had some big influence on the society and economy of Europe.

Compass

The compass is the third of the Four Great Inventions of Ancient China.

Early in the Spring and Autumn Period (770-476 BC) and the Warring States Period

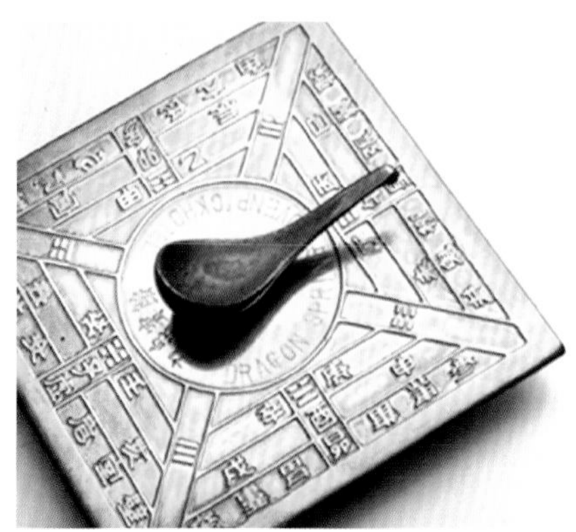

Compass

(475-221 BC), while mining iron ore, people chanced upon a magnetite that had a special quality. In the Warring States Period, people began to made a tool for discerning directions by the magnetite — Si Nan (South pointer). Si Nan was spoon-or ladle-shaped, and was place on the middle of a flat, smooth plate. The operator turned the handle to run the spoon, and when it stopped the handle pointed south.

By the time of the early Northern Song Dynasty (960-1127), people devised a way to magnetize iron needles, by rubbing them with magnetite. It was formally named a needle compass (the magnetite needle is affected by the magnetic pole, and has an angle of 11 degrees. So the North and South showed by the magnetite needle is actually the direction of the magnetic pole). There were various ways to make a compass. The most exact way was to place a needle on an orientation-marked box, thus the compass was also called a box and needle. Since the Song Dynasty, ships had been equipped with a compass. By the end of the 12th century, this invention spread to Europe by Arabia, which was very important for the European navigators when discovering the New World.

Printing

Printing is the fourth of the Four Great Inventions of Ancient China.

Around the early 7th century, block printing first appeared in the Tang Dynasty. The text was first written on paper and glued face down onto a polished wooden plate. Characters would be carved out to make a printing plate, which was then smeared with ink. After placing a sheet of paper on the plate, this was then firmly brushed to produce the printed images. Block printing first took a lot of energy and materials, but showed high efficiency and quantity thereafter. As far as we know, the earliest block printing book was the *Diamond Sutra* printed in the year 868. It was discovered at Dunhuang Cave in fine condition.

In the Northern Song Dynasty (960-1127), a talented worker named Bi Sheng invented movable type printing. Bi Sheng carved individual characters on identical pieces of fine clay; then the block was hardened by fire. When printing, the individual characters were arranged in the order of the text, then glued to a plate. The plate was then heated and pressed with board, and printed with ink. When the printing was finished, the pieces were put away for future use. Movable type spread fast, for it took less time, materials, and energy than block printing. Based on clay type, type made of wood, lead, tin and copper gradually appeared.

typographic block

Technology Development Today

Early in the 20th century, there was no modern technology in China and across the whole country no more than 10 persons understood calculus. By the early of the 21st century, the gap in the research and development of high technologies between China and the leading world level has been distinctly reduced; over 60 percent of the technologies have attained or approached the advanced international level, including atomic energy technology, spatial technology, high energy physics, biological technology, computer technology, information technology, etc. On October 15, 2003, Shenzhou V manned spaceship was launched successfully making China the third country mastering manned space flight technology in the world. According to the lunar probe program started from February 2004, China launched unmanned moon crafts in 2007 and will conclude the undertaking of collecting moon soil samples by 2020.

Beginning in 2002, China turned to seek scientific innovation and achieve technological development. According to the State development plan, by 2010, China will have built a new system for scientific innovation and achieve world advanced level with regard to construction of scientific and technological bases. China will try to have impressive development in scientific innovation. Expanses in scientific research and experiment will make up 2 percent of GDP. By 2020, China is set to build a fairly sound innovation system and the said proportion will reach 3 percent. By then, China will be among the world advanced level in terms of science and technology.

Electronic Information industrial base, the National Torch Program

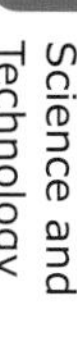

Technology Development in the Present Age

China now have a sizable S and T workforce totaling 32 million people, with 1.05 million persons engaged in research and development each year, and this puts China in the first and second places in the world respectively. Since 1997, the number of scientific papers authored by China to be included in the SCI index has increased by 19 percent annually, ranking fifth in the world. In addition, Chinese scientists have caught world attention with their accomplishments in manned space flights, nanotechnology, hematopoietic stem cells, non-linear optical materials, quantum ICT, parallel computation technology, ultra-intense and ultra-short lasers, and other high-tech fields.

For example, through years of concerted efforts by Professor Yuan Longping, the "Father of Hybrid Paddy Rice", and other agricultural scientists, the per-unit output of crops has increased continuously. Although the Chinese population increased by some 270 million in the last two decades, the annual per-capita grain supply for the Chinese people has jumped from 300 kg to 400 kg. In some major construction projects such as the world's largest Three Gorges Hydroelectric Project and highest altitude Qinghai-Tibet Railway, a great number of technological snags have been overcome, thus ensuring the smooth implementation of the projects. During the past decade, the Chinese high-tech sector has maintained a high rate of growth and become a principal driver for China's economic progress and restructuring. In the area of public health, by depending heavily on scientific and technological advances, the Chinese Government has successfully contained the spread of major epidemics like SARS and Avian Influenza. In addition, systematic research and development have been organized on a number of new drugs with proprietary IPR and on diagnostic and treatment technologies to combat serious life-threatening diseases. In the area of disaster prevention and mitigation, new approaches and models have been developed, thus effectively upgrading the forecast level for such natural disasters as earthquake and severe climatic conditions.

Speaking of international cooperation, China has established ties with 152 countries and entered into inter-governmental S and T cooperation with 96 countries. China has participated in the Global Earth Observation System of Systems (GEOSS), Human Genome Program, Ocean Drilling Program, Galileo Program, and ITER program.

Scientific and Technical Systems

Scientific and Technical Bodies

Like many other countries, scientific research bodies in China consist of two major types: independent bodies and bodies subject to universities or enterprises. In China the independent scientific research bodies are mainly subsidized by the government. At present, there are some 2,000 independent scientific research bodies, including about 500 national bodies.

The scientific research bodies in China can be divided into three kinds: fundamental, application and public welfare. The fundamental scientific research bodies are mainly the Chinese Academy of Sciences and those relevant research institutes subject to universities. The application scientific research bodies were formerly subject to various industrial departments, but now have been reformed to be high-tech enterprises mostly. Public welfare research bodies are mainly those in charge of fundamental research and producing social benefits in such fields as agriculture and weather services.

Research and Development Institutions Subject to Higher Schools

Like many other countries in the world, the research work undertaken by higher schools in China constitutes a very important part in many scientific research fields, research in fundamental theories of natural sciences and human studies in particular.

In recent years, research involving applied basic theories has made great progress. A group of famous universities like Tsinghua University, Peking University, Zhejiang University and Fudan University hold a leading position in research well known across the world.

During cooperation with other research institutes and enterprises, a particular development mode has come into being—undertaking scientific research in universities, bringing those scientific achievements back to industries, i.e. solving problems in production practice by theory, and then bringing them back to produce products with a competitive edge in the markets and transform scientific research achievements into commodities satisfying market demand.

Higher colleges and universities have advantages in integrating multi-subjects, combining various personnel and accessing information by many means. At present, in higher colleges and universities, there are 100 State key laboratories, occupying a comparatively large proportion in total State key laboratories; and there are more than 1,000 research institutes and centers focusing on applied research and technical development, including 23 State engineering research centers and 10 State engineering technical research centers. The projects of the National Natural Science Foundation undertaken by higher schools occupy nearly two-thirds of all those projects. In projects of the 863 Program which follow and develop high and new technologies, higher schools are also charged with nearly a hundred subjects in such fields as biotechnology, information technology, new materials, new energy technology and automation technology, a third of the total projects. The number of theses published by scientific research personnel in higher schools in China and abroad occupies about 60 percent of the total theses in China. The Awards of National Natural Science obtained by them, and the National Invention Awards and Scientific and Technical Progress Awards obtained by them occupy about one-third and a quarter respectively of the total awards in China. Of all national duties of tackling key problems in science and technology, higher schools bear 14 percent according to the amount of project funds.

Research and Development Institutions Subject to Enterprises

During the period of a planned economy, the scientific research resources in China were mainly distributed over independent scientific research institutions and the work of scientific research was also mainly undertaken by independent scientific research institutions and higher schools. With the adoption of scientific and technical system reform, the scientific research bodies in China have realized the strategic transformation from independent scientific research institutions to enterprises.

In order to promote the industrial technology of the nation, the Chinese government has adopted a series of measures to support the construction of research and development centers of experimental enterprises and plans to take five to ten years to build up R and D centers of international leading level in those experimental enterprises, promote a group of original R and D fruits of international frontline level and offer useful references and applications for domestic enterprises.

The study plot of the Chinese Academy of Agricultural Sciences in downtown Beijing growing the wheat

Chinese Academy of Sciences

Founded in November 1949 in Beijing, it is a leading academic institution and comprehensive research and development center in natural science, technological science and high-tech innovation.

Under CAS, there are five academic divisions (Division of Mathematics and Physics, Division of Chemistry, Division of Life Sciences and Medicine, Division of Earth Sciences, Division of Technological Sciences), as well as 11 branches (in Shenyang, Changchun, Shanghai, Nanjing, Wuhan, Guangzhou, Chengdu, Kunming, Xi'an, Lanzhou, and Xinjiang), 84 research institutes, one university, two graduate schools, four documentation and information centers, three technical supporting units and two press and publication units, which are distributed over 20 provinces and municipalities.

CAS possesses a group of high-level S and T talents, including 256 present academicians, 39.8 percent of the total academicians, and 53 academicians of the Chinese Academy of Engineering, 8.6 percent of its total academicians. In CAS, there are 37,000 professional and technical personnel, including 14,000 seniors, 14,000 at medium level and 7,500 junior personnel. There are over 20,000 present post-graduate students and over 1,000 present post-doctorate personnel.

Website: http://www.cas.cn

Chinese Academy of Agricultural Sciences

As a national research institute of agricultural sciences, the Chinese Academy of Agricultural Sciences (CAAS) bears the duty of research and development in significant fundamental studies, applied fundamental studies, applied research and high-tech industries. Under CAAS, there are 39 research institutes (centers), one graduate school, and one Agricultural ScienceTech Press. Of the 39 research institutes, 16 are involved in crop planting, 10 focus on animal husbandry and veterinary practice, eight carry out research on economics and environmental resources and five are devoted to agricultural engineering, high and new agro- technology. A total of 24 research institutes are distributed over 16 provinces, autonomous regions and municipalities.

CAAS possesses two State key opening laboratories, 20 ministry key laboratories, six State crop improving centers, 27 State and ministry quality supervision, inspection and testing centers, one national-level crops germplasm resource bank, 11 national crop germplasm and sub-peripheral wild resources gardens, and 26 experimental farms.

Website: http://www.caas.net.cn

Chinese Academy of Forestry

Chinese Academy of Forestry (CAF) was founded in 1958. Now, CAF has 11 research institutes, four research and development centers, and four forestry experimental centers which are distributed over 11 provinces, autonomous regions and municipalities in China. CAF has established two State engineering (technology) research centers, and eight ministry key opening laboratories. The research undertaken by CAF includes: development of forests, forestry eco-environment and protection, resource management, wood processing and utilization, chemical processing of forest products, resource insects, forestry economy, S and T information, etc.

Website: http://www.forestry.ac.cn

Chinese Academy of Medical Sciences

Chinese Academy of Medical Sciences (CAMS) was founded in 1956 and is the only national medical science academic center and comprehensive science research institute. Under CAMS, there are over 20 research institutes, including the Institute of Clinical Medical Sciences, Institute of Basic Medical Sciences, Institute of Cardiovascular Diseases, Institute of Materia, Institute of Medical Information and Library, Institute of Oncology, Institute of Pharmaceutical Biotechnology, and Institute of Microcirculation, etc.; in addition to seven hospitals, four colleges and five subsidiary hospitals.

Website: http://www.cams.ac.cn

Scientific and Technical Achievements

Significant Scientific and Technical Achievements

China has achieved satisfactory results in term of high technology. The successfully developed Dawning 4000A High-Performance Computer keeps ahead in the performance-price ratio and performance-power waste in the world, making China the world's third which is able to manufacture and apply 10000-billion-time commercial high-performance computer after the US and Japan. The Dragon Chip-2 was developed, making China one who masters the core technology with its own independent intellectual property right in the field of 64-bit high-performance CPC chip. The successfully developed Galaxy Kylin Operating System with high security and high usability provides the important support for China's information security. The 100nm high-density plasma etching recorder and high spud angle ion implanter was successfully developed and entered market and the development of Mask Aligner will be completed in the near future. These major new results narrow the gap between China and the advanced countries in terms of major integrate circuit equipment manufacturing technology.

China has completed the performance examination of its independently developed hybrid vehicles and pure eletromotion auto, which have been put into service in some cities. Its independently developed high-temperature gas cooled reactor occupied an important position in the research and development of new generation nuclear energy system. Hefei Superconducting Tokamak Nuclear Fusion Experimental Device provides new experimental environment and conditions for solving the future energy problem. The 600 MW Supercritical Thermal Generating Unit has been basically manufactured domestically; the 700 MW Hydropower Unit that China and foreign countries jointly designed has been used in the Three Gorges Project; and the key equipments of the 1 million kW class Nuclear Power Plant have been manufactured domestically.

At present, China has developed some 220 varieties of super-quality hybrid rice combination successively, making China keep ahead in terms of super rice breeding technology in the world. The Recombinant Human Ad-p53 Injection has become the world's first commercially licensed gene therapy drug; Tailuo, a drug for Type II Diabetes, was successfully developed, which changed the history in which China did not have its own independent intellectual property right in the drug for diabetes. The new anti-AIDS medicine Sifuvirtide developed by China on its own has become China's first biotechnological drug gaining a US patent. In addition, China has completed phase I clinical trial of avian influenza vaccine, and made great progress in the therapeutic hepatitis B vaccine. These great S and T fruits enhanced China's capacity of dealing with the major diseases.

Since the 1980s, China has reached the world advanced level in such fields as super-conductor research, BEPC, Petroleum Water-Flooding Throughput New Craft, KM4 solar simulator studies, emulate technology, air motive studies, atomistic manipulating and processing, robot development, genetically modified crops studies, etc.

By now, Chinese scientists have finished one percent of genome mapping of the Human Genome Project, and constructed successfully the whole physical mapping of rice genome for the first time in the world; China has for the first time located and cloned the genes causing genetic diseases such as GJB3, Type-II opalescent dentin; the quantum information field error avoiding code is viewed as the "most exciting achievement" in the quantum information field by the international community; Shenzhou VI manned space ship was launched and returned to earth successfully. Chang E Moon Probe was launched successfully and has sent clear pictures of the Moon.

A cloned goat from the somatic cell of a genetically modified goat was born from the clone of the somatic cell of a grown genetically modified female goat.

Biotechnology

A cloned goat from the somatic cell of a genetically modified goat was born from the clone of the somatic cell of a grown genetically modified female goat. The first genetically modified tube cattle was born and testing showed it carried the human serum albumin gene. A kind of human endostatin gene was selected and cloned from the human liver gene library located in the basement membranes that line the blood vessels of a tumor with the peculiar quality of being able to repress the proliferation and growth of endothelium in tumor vessels. The WSBV genome of prawns was identified and the genome library was constructed and 1,500 clone sections of virus genome were identified by separating and purifying a full set of WSBV genome DNA; the sequence identified by them holds 90 percent of the full length.

Nano Technological Research Progress

New progress has been made in the research of hydrogen storage carbon nanotubes. The research staff of CAS Institute of Metallurgy used the hydrogen arc synthesis method by which a kind of single-walled nanotubes with comparatively high purity and large diameter can be synthesized in mass and semi-continuously. They have also initially probed the characteristic of storing hydrogen by means of home-made single-walled nanotubes in macroscopic amount and it is found that the hydrogen storage capacity of single-walled nanotubes at room temperature can reach four percent of the quality percentage, and some hydrogen can be released at room temperature and normal pressure.

In 2001, the first super fine nanometer nickel production line was officially put into production in Ningbo of Zhejiang Province.

Computers Research Progress

Breakthroughs have been obtained in the research of high-powered computers. The super-servers, "DAWN"1000A, "DAWN"2000-I, "DAWN"2000-II and "DAWN" 3000, have been developed successfully one by one, putting China step in an internationally leading position in parallel computers and super-servers. The research in nitride blue organic light emitting devices has reached the internationally advanced level; PN Junction can be made on GaN materials, which realized electrically-driven blue organic light emission, making China the only country mastering this technology in the world. The breakthrough in 10Gb/sSDH transport system and dispersion accommodation key technology also made China one of the few countries mastering and being able to offer 10Gb/s technology in the world.

Paddy in autumn

Material Technological Research Progress

Chinese scientists, for the first time, placed a molecule of Carbon 60 on the surface of silicon and acquired the inside electron cloud distribution of Carbon 60 molecule in different orientations under sample central and side pressure by means of LTSTM, and confirmed uniquely the orientation of the Carbon 60 molecule on a silicon surface by calculating and simulating the image of quantum mechanics' first principle. By an experiment, six new nuclides with only about 1-second half life period were synthesized for the first time near the proton drip-line according to theoretical prediction in light rare earth elements.

Dragon Chip II: home-made high-performance all-purpose processor chip

Rice Technological Research Progress

According to relevant data, at present rice serves as the indispensable daily food for three billion people around the world, and two billion people in Asia get their 80 percent of their heat from rice. Plenteous rice harvests can make a gigantic contribution to social development, averting famine, death and political turbulence.

Since the 1970s, Chinese rice scientists, represented by Professor Yuan Longping, have obtained great breakthroughs in the breeding technology of hybrid rice, which has a profound influence on production in developing countries.

Since the 1990s, China has been sending rice specialists to Bangladesh, India, Indonesia, Myanmar, Vietnam, etc. to conduct training on relevant knowledge about various kinds of hybrid rice and offer technical services to them. At present, many developing countries have started to apply and promote Chinese rice technologies. According to United Nations statistics, by the end of 2001, outside China, high-yield hybrid rice has been planted on about 800,000 hectares of fields. Many developing countries think it is a good idea to solve their grain supply problems by applying breeding technology to increase the yield of rice of per unit area.

Wild Animal DNA Bank

In 2002, the highest prize in research field of world biological diversity was awarded to an Asian scientist for the first time, with Chinese scientist Zhang Yaping being so honored. The "Biological Diversity Leading Award" is awarded every three years to scientists who have made great contributions to research into global biological diversity. Zhang Yaping is the Deputy Director-General of CAS Kunming Animal Research Institute and Director-General of Professional Commission of Animal Heredity of Chinese Heredity. For more than 10 years, he devoted himself to the research in animal evolutionary history and heredity diversity, clarified evolution enigma of some important animal varieties in their molecular system, and made joint efforts with other colleagues to construct the largest wild animal DNA bank in China. In the view of the award appraisal committee, the work helped unveil the relationship between heredity diversity and species facing extinction, offering a scientific basis for creating effective protection plans, and offering new information for confirming the origin of major domestic animals in China, research in gene diversity of different nationalities and unveiling the history of human expansion and movement.

• Top 10 Scientific and Technoloical Achievements for 2005

China's Top 10 scientific and technology achievements for 2005 were selected, according to votes from 570 academicians of both the Chinese Academy of Science and the Chinese Academy of Engineering. They were:

Shenzhou-V manned spaceship completed its first mission.

Qinghai-Tibet railway went into operation.

China's first generic 64-bit CPU chip was accredited.

Chinese Antarctic Expedition Team surmounted the peak of Dome A Icecap, the highest icecap peak in Antarctica.

The Flora of China, showing the most detailed picture of China's plants, was published.

Chinese scientists realized the self-spinning of a single molecule for the first time.

Chinese scientists re-measured the height of Mt. Qomolangma at 8,844.43 meters.

China's scientific continental drilling reached a depth of 5,158 meters.

A nanotechnology-based drug carrier, which could travel through vessels, was developed.

The digital virtual man with the highest resolution, also known as the VCH-M1, was invented.

On March 24, 2006, five overseas scientists received awards for international cooperation in science and technology in 2005 from the Chinese Government. Pictured here is Dr. Nevile Agnes, a cultural relic protection expert from the United States.

• China's 10 Most Important Developments in Science and Technology in 2006

Organized by the Work Bureau of the CAS Members of the Chinese Academy of Sciences and the Work Bureau of the CAE Members of the Chinese Academy of Engineering, 565 CAS and CAE Members voted on the candidate news recommended by the CAS and CAE Members, S and T personnel and S and T pressman, which resulted in the birth of top 10 most significant developments in science and technology in China in 2006.

1. Significant achievements in Next Generation Internet (NGI) technology

2. Largest natural gas field discovered in northeast Sichuan

3. China builds first full superconducting experimental Tokamak fusion device

4. Chemical Reaction Resonance at Quantum resolution

5. First "green corridor" in Taklamakan Desert completed

6. First round-the-world oceanic expedition successful

7. Significant progress made in vaccine for Hepatitis B

8. Crucial breakthrough in renovation of electron positron collider

9. China fulfills quantum teleportation of two-particle system

10. Remote Sensing Satellite-1 successfully launched

On September 28, 2006, the first experimental device for the total super conducting non-toroidal Tokamak atomic fusion, designed and manufactured entirely by China, succeeded in its first discharge experiment. The picture shows the experimental device for the total super conducting Tokamak EAST atomic fusion.

• Top 10 Items of Progress in Science and Technology in 2007

Hosted by the Academicians Working Bureau of Chinese Academy of Sciences, Division Working Bureau of Chinese Academy of Engineering, and Science Times Media Group, 547 academicians of CAS and CAE voted to select the Top 10 news items of scientific and technical progress of China and Top 10 news items of scientific and technical progress of the world in 2007 based on nominations by academicians, scientific and technical personnel, and scientific and technical journalists. The results were published on January 20, 2008 in Beijing.

1. Successful Launch of Chang'e-1 and Obtaining Clear Selenographic Pictures

At 18:05 on October 24, 2007, a Long March 3A launch vehicle carrying the first lunar satellite of China, Chang'e-1, and was launched successfully from Xichang Satellite Launch Center. On November 7, after successful application of the third perilune brake, Chang'e-1 entered a working orbit 200 km from the moon on a 127-minute orbital cycle. From there, it started comprehensive scientific exploration to the moon and sent back the data and clear lunar surface to Earth 380,000 km away. On November 26, the first lunar surface picture was published to demonstrate China's first success in lunar exploration.

The moon probe project is the third milestone in China's space activities after the man-made earth satellite and manned spaceflight and enabled China to become one of only a handful of countries with the capability of launching deep space probes.

2. Successful Manufacture of Super Oil Driller

China National Petroleum Corporation (CNPC) announced on November 16, 2007 that China's first 12,000-m super oil driller with independent intellectual property rights was manufactured successfully by Baojin Oilfield Machinery Co., Ltd. of CNPC. It is China's first land-use 12,000-m driller driven by alternating current with frequency conversion, and also the super oil driller with the most advanced technology in the world. Before, only the United States had produced a 12,000-m analog-controlled driller driven by direct current.

3. Significant Progress in Research of Cancer Treatment

The task team led by Liang Wei and Hang Haiying, researchers of the Institute of Biophysics of CAS, published a research treatise on penetration in tumors with nanoassemblies of chemotherapy medicines in the Journal of the National Cancer Institute on July 4, 2007. This novel nanocarrier - 10 to 20-nm nanoassemblies of polyethylene glycol–phosphatidylethanolamine (PEG-PE) containing doxorubicin - can improve the drug's accumulation in tumors and its penetration into deep histiocytes, enhancing its anti-tumor activity with low toxicity. In addition, the Journal of the National Cancer Institute published the research results on potential targets of cancer treatment by the Chen Yan Research Team of the Institute for Nutritional Sciences, Shanghai Institute for Biological Science, CAS.

This research discovered a novel Raf-1 regulator, revealed for the first time the paradigm of spatial regulation of Raf-1, and indicated a new mechanism of inhibiting the ERK signaling pathway on Golgi apparatus. It pointed to new ways for researching the molecular mechanism of hyperplasia of tumor cells and treating cancer.

4. Realization of Six-photon Schrodinger Cat

Pan Jianwei, Yang Tao, Lu Chaoyang and other members of the National Laboratory for Physical Sciences in Microscale at the University of Science and Technology of China created successfully the largest photonic Schrodinger cat in the world and a cluster state that can be used directly for quantum computation, setting two world records in the fields of entanglement of photons and quantum computation. This research achievement was published as a cover title in Nature Physics of the United Kingdom. The editor appraised that "it is the most advanced experimental work so far in the field of photics quantum computation" and "is an outstanding achievement and has paved the way to quantum computation, quantum error correction and studies of fundamental problems in quantum mechanics."

5. Discovery of Zoic Resting Egg Fossil from 632 Million Years Ago

A team of scientists led by Yin Leiming, researcher of Nanjing Institute of Geology and Paleontology, CAS, made great progress in the studies of early fossil embryos and discovered the earliest zoic resting egg fossil so far. This result was published on Nature of the United Kingdom. This discovery offered a reliable record of the earliest zoolith so far, moving the original time of animals back to 632 million years ago and establishing the presence of zooliths 50 million years earlier.

6. The First Regional Jet with Independent Intellectual Property Rights Rolls off the Production Line

On September 28, 2007, assembly of the new regional jet ARJ21 was finished by Shanghai Aircraft Manufacturing Factory to the Institute of Aircraft Strength of China Aviation Industry Corporation I. Eight aviation industrial units participated in the research and manufacture of this new-generation regional jet with novel digital design and independent intellectual property rights.

The successful manufacture of ARJ21 indicated China had, for the first time, gone through the whole course of research and manufacture of parts and final assembly to join the ranks the world's civil aircraft manufacturing powers.

7. Discovery of the Largest Bird-like Dinosaur Fossil in the World

Specialists of Institute of Vertebrate Paleontology and Paleoanthropology, CAS, announced on June 13, 2007 that a gigantic theropod fossil had been discovered in Erenhot City, Inner Mongolia Autonomous Region and was the largest bird-like dinosaur fossil so far found in the world. This fossil was discovered by Chinese scientists in the rocks deposited from about 80 million years ago in the Erlian Basin in Inner Mongolia. Its body is about eight meters long and its standing height exceeds five meters. Its body can be compared with the famous tyrannosaurus. It weighs about 1,400 kg and it is named Gigantoraptor erlianensis. A series of the research results were published and recommended as a key treatise by Nature of the United Kingdom.

8. Discovery of Breakdown of the Born-Oppenheimer Approximation in F+ D Reaction

The Born-Oppenheimer approximation is an effective and common fundamental way in the studies of molecular physics, quantum chemistry, and quantum physics and can be used to build molecular dynamic models in simple chemistry or physics. But some scientists including Yang Xueming from the Dalian Institute of Chemical Physics, CAS, discovered that the Born-Oppenheimer approximation would break down in the important chemical laser system, F+D reaction, with low collision energy. This important experimental result is supported powerfully by precise theoretical computation. This achievement was published on Science magazine of the United States. This new discovery solved a difficult problem in the research field of chemical dynamics existing for a long time and was a breakthrough with significant academic meaning in the dynamics studies of nonadiabatic course.

9. Construction of the First Wild Biological Germplasm Resource Bank

China Southwest Wild Biological Germplasm Resource Bank, the first State significant project of scientific engineering, was constructed in Kunming Institute of Botany, CAS, by the academy and Yunnan Province. This germplasm resource bank will be built into a top-grade wild biological germplasm conversation installation and scientific research platform with significant influence in the world. The constructed resource bank includes seed bank, botanic vitro germplasm bank, DNA bank, animalcule seed bank, animal germplasm bank, information center, and botanic germplasm resource bank. It will collect and conserve 190,000 trunks of germplasm resource in 19,000 categories. Nature of the United Kingdom published the launch of the project. This germplasm resource bank can provide technical support for protection, research and reasonable use of China's wild biological germplasm resource.

10. New Breed of Soybeans Created a High Yield Record of 5,577 kg Per Hectare

Researcher Wang Lianzheng, former President of Chinese Academy of Agricultural Sciences and a famous soybean breeding scientist in China, supervised the breeding of a new variety of soybean with high yield and oil content, "Zhonghuang No.35". On an experimental field of Crop Institute, Xinjiang Academy of Agricultural Reclamation, this new variety of soybean has a yield of 5,577 kg/ hectare with the actual crop area of 0.08 hectares. In August 2006, Zhonghuang No.35 passed national examination and approval with a yield is 3,076.5 kg/ hectare in the regional experimental field. It was then planned to plant it in the summer in Hebei, Shandong, Beijing, and Tianjin in the Huang-Huai-Hai area, and in spring in Liaoning, Hebei, Shaanxi, Ningxia and Gansu. This variety has oil content as high as 23.45 percent, conforming to the current national policy of supporting the production of oil plants.

Scientific and Technical Awards

Outline of Scientific and Technical Awards

The Chinese government issued Temporary Regulations on the Scientific Bonus of the Chinese Academy of Sciences early in 1955 and decided to grant awards to significant S and T achievements; in 1984, the government established the Scientific and Technical Progress Award. In May 1999, it established five prizes: National Supreme Scientific and Technical Award, National Natural Science Award, National Technical Invention Award, National Scientific and Technical Progress Award and PRC International Scientific and Technical Cooperation Award. These awards will be granted once a year when the National Scientific and Technical Awarding Conference is held and President of China will present the awards.

Some local governments and non-governmental institutions also established independent scientific and technical awards. In addition, some domestic and foreign enterprises, institutions, social associations and other social organizations and individuals make use of non-governmental financial funds or raise funds by themselves to establish scientific and technical awards aimed at individuals in charge of scientific and technical research activities, helping inspire scientists' enthusiasm in conducting scientific and technical innovation and invention. At present, the awards approved by national departments in charge include the Dupont Science and Technology Innovation Award, Li Siguang Geological Science Award, Zhan Tianyou Civil Engineering Award, GM Foundation-NSFC Science and Technology Achievement Award in China and CAS-Bayer Research Awards for Young Scientists, etc.

State Supreme Science and Technology Award

State Supreme Science and Technology Award is the highest honor for Chinese scientists and technology personnel. Set up in 1999, the award system holds an annual presentation ceremony. Its laureates are chosen from scientists as follows: people who have made a significant contribution to cutting-edge scientific research and science and technology development; helped create massive economic returns or social benefits through technology innovations; helped turn scientific achievements into productive force; and helped realize high-tech industrialization. The winner will be presented with a certificate and a five-million Yuan bonus by the President of the PRC. Of the bonus, 4.5 million Yuan is set aside as a fund for his chosen area of research.

Previous Winners:

Year	Winners	
2000	Yuan Longping	Wu Wenjun
2001	Wan Xuan	Huang Kun
2002	Jin Yilian	
2003	Liu Dongsheng	Wang Yongzhi
2004		
2005	Ye Duzheng	Wu Mengchao
2006	Li Zhensheng	
2007	Min Enze	Wu Zhengyi

China International Science and Technology Cooperation Award

The PRC International Science and Technology Cooperation Award was established by the State Council. The idea is to reward foreign scientists, engineering technical staff, science and technology management staff and organizations who have made great contributions in cooperation and exchanges in science and technology with China to promote scientific and technical progress, strengthening cooperation and friendship in science and technology fields between China and foreign countries, and Chinese scientific and technical undertakings. The award is the only one of its kind used to award foreigners, foreign organizations only.

This award is appraised once a year and has no grades. The number of winners will be less than 10. They will get certificates issued by the State Council but no bonus. By 2006, a total of 42 foreign specialists have won this award.

Previous Winners:

2007: Geophysics scientist Ph.D Li Xiangyang (UK), materials science and engineering scientist Ph.D. Liu Jinchuan (USA), and biologist Ph.D. Peter Grus (Germany), geoscientist N.L.Dorbolezv (Russia), and International Rice Research Institute.

2006: Martin Atkins, and Ingemar Ernberg.

2005: Wolf-Dieter Dudenhausen, Evert Jacobsen, Mu Ming Poo, Neville Agnew and David G. Evans.

2004: Daniel Vasella, Kenneth W. Gentle, Corrado Clini, Richard Chang and Kenji Ekuan.

2003: Shing-Tung Yau, Jueregen Voegele, Mizushima Yutaka, Elio Matacena, Nobert Angert, Robert Degeilh, Joseph H. Hamilton (USA), Yunzhen Cao (USA) and Hirano Toshisuke (Japan).

2001: Kuroda Yoshimasu, Huanyu Mao, Bjorn Erik Wilhelm Nordenstrom, Charles Y. Yang, Micheal Petzet and Jose Israel Vargas.

2000: Gurdev Sigh Khush and Wolfgang K.H. Panofsky.

1999: Ishimoto Seiihi and Jose Alberto De Camargo.

1998: Sabourin Jean and J.L.Lions.

A ceremony was held on May 9, 2007 in Beijing to honor the recipients of China International Science and Technology Cooperation Award for 2006. Wan Gang, Chinese Minister of Science and Technology, in behalf of the Chinese Government, presented the medal and certificate to Dr. Martin Atkins, a British expert in chemical engineering.

1997: Ieoh Ming Pei, Jean Pierre Lebrun and Arthur Slmim.

1996: G.S.Bushgens, Samuel.C.C.Ting and Uli Schwarz.

1995: Hara Shoich, Hauesser, Joseph Needham, Chen Ning Yang, Tsung Dao Lee, and Shing Shen Chern.

National Technical Invention Award

National Technical Invention Award is granted to scientific and technical personnel who have made significant technical inventions in products, craft, materials and relevant systems by applying scientific and technical knowledge. This award consists of first and second prizes; it is appraised once a year and the certificates and bonuses issued by the State Council.

Scientific and Technical Progress Award

The National Scientific and Technical Progress Award is mainly given for following four kinds of achievements:

First, some new scientific and technical achievements that are originating innovations, with advanced level in their own industries, have significant economic or social benefits after being proved in practice, and are applied to socialist modernization construction.

Second, some achievements which have made an innovative contribution to promoting, transferring and applying present scientific and technical achievements and have obtained significant economic or social benefits.

Third, some scientific and technical achievements adopting new technologies that have made an innovative contribution and obtained significant economic or social benefits in significant engineering construction, significant equipment development and technical transformation in enterprises.

Fourth, some work results which have made an innovative contribution and obtained special and distinctive benefits in science and technology management, standards, metrology, and science and technology information.

This award was established in 1984 and consists of three grades. Besides certificates and medals, winners can also get bonuses respectively. As to those projects with special contribution, a top grade award can be granted after being approved by the State Council. In accordance with levels, this award can be divided into two grades: State and province (ministry and commission). Only those items of second prize of provincial award or above can apply for the State award. In addition, those items applying for Scientific and Technical Progress Award cannot apply for other science and technology awards.

Chinese Engineering Science and Technology Guanghua Award

This aims at Chinese engineers and scientists of outstanding achievements who have made a great contribution to engineering science and technology and management.

This award was established by joint funds contributed by President Yin Yanliang of Taiwan RuenTex Group, Mr. Chen Youhao, President Du Junyuan of Silicon Integrated Systems Corp., and Zhu Guangya, Vice-Chairman of Chinese People's Political Consultative Conference and academician of two Chinese Academies. Since the first award in 1996, 55 engineers and scientists have gained recognition. The highest bonus is 1 million Yuan, the highest amount in the Chinese engineering science and technology fields. All Chinese engineers and scientists living in Taiwan, Hong Kong, Macao and foreign countries whoever has made great contribution and outstanding achievements in engineering science and technology and management can be nominated.

In 2002, the board of directors for the first time established the "Guanghua Achievement Award" with a bonus of 1 million Yuan to reward people who have made great contribution and achievements in fields of engineering science. It is also the highest award established by non-governmental forces in Chinese engineering field.

State Spark Awards

To encourage the implementation of the "Spark Program", promote scientific and technical progress in medium and small-sized enterprises, township-owned enterprises and villages, and develop vigorously the local economy, the State established the Spark Awards in 1987, including Spark Science and Technology Award, Spark Talent Training Award, Spark Management Award, Spark Excellent Youth Award and Spark Model Enterprise Award. Winners can be units, collective organizations and individuals. The awards are divided into two grades: State and provinces and municipalities.

According to the regulations, the Spark Talent Science and Technology Award is granted to those accomplishing projects developing, promoting or applying advanced technologies, offering guidance and a model for others and with economical investment, fast action and considerable economic benefits. The Spark Training Award is granted to those making a great contribution to training special technical talents. The Spark Management Award is granted to those making a great contribution to the organization and management of the "Spark Program". The Spark Excellent Youth Award is granted to young people who have made outstanding achievements in developing the local economy vigorously. The Spark Model Enterprise Award is granted to those advanced enterprises that play a role of leading and being a model in developing the local economy vigorously. But if any project made or developed by an enterprise results in serious environmental pollution, damage of valued resources and destruction of biological balance, this enterprise is ineligible.

Each province, autonomous region and municipality appraises the Spark awards of their levels and reports to the State Science and Technology Commission. It is the State Spark Awards Appraising Commission under State Science and Technology Commission that takes charge of the appraisal, approval and granting of State Spark Awards. Spark Awards are appraised once a year and the form of the reward and the bonus amount is decided by the appraising unit.

Hua Luogen Mathematics Award

On November 4, 1992, the first award ceremony took place in Beijing. To mark the outstanding contribution made by world famous mathematician Hua Luogeng and accelerate the development of Chinese mathematics, Hunan Education Publishing House contributes funds and holds the award ceremony jointly with the Chinese Mathematics Society The award is appraised every two years. According to the regulations, it is to reward Chinese mathematicians' outstanding contribution over a long period to the development of Chinese mathematics. Winners are often aged 50 to 70. The mathematicians who won this award all have considerable academic level.

Founded in 1992, The Hua Luogeng Mathematics Prize has been granted eight times. Each time, it selected two winners and awarded each 25,000 Yuan.

Previous Winners:

Year	Winners	
1992	Chen Jingrun	Lu Qikeng
1995	Gu Chaohao	Wan Zhexian
1997	Yang Le	Zhou Yulin
2000	Wang Yuan	Ding Xiaqi
2002	Jiang Boju	Gong Sheng
2003	Lu Ruquan	Shi Zhongci
2005	Ma Zhiming	Jiang Lishang
2007	Li Daqian	Yan Jiaan

Science and Technology Programs

State Science and Technology Programs

Since the 1980s, China has promoted continuously a series of macro programs to develop scientific and technical research aiming to enhance generally and strategically comprehensive science and technology competitiveness in 21st Century China. Of them, the National Key Technologies Research and Development Program, 863 Program and 973 Program constitute the main body of State science and technology programs, and Spark Program and Torch Program also play an important role in enhancing the strength of science and technology.

National Key Technologies Research and Development Program

The National Key Technologies Research and Development Program was implemented in 1982 and was the largest science and technology program in the 20th century. It aims at the major field of national economic construction, solving problems related to orientation and integration in national economic and social development, and involves such fields as agriculture, electronic information, energy, transportation, materials, resource prospecting, environmental protection, and health care. This program is the science and technology program with the largest investment, the most involved staff and the greatest influence in the national economy among all Chinese science and technology programs, and tens of thousands of scientific researchers from thousands of scientific research institutions are involved. During the 10th Five-Year Plan (2001-2005), the Key Technologies R and D Program arranged and supported 210 major projects, priority projects and guidance projects, covering agriculture, information, automation, raw material, energy and transportation, resources and environment, medicine and public welfare sectors. Thanks to this, much headway has been made in key technologies comprehensively applied and beneficial for society. They include those concerning technical renovation and upgrading of traditional industries, boosting the sustainable social progress and upgrading people's livelihood.

863 Program

In March 1986, the High-Tech Research and Development Program (863 Program for short) appeared publicly after long discussions by hundreds of Chinese scientists. The 863 Program at present involves 20 subjects in eight fields, Biotechnology, Aerospace, InfoTech, Laser, Automation, Energy, Materials and Marine. In the process of carrying out the 863 Program, the function of the government is to conduct macro-regulation and control and offer services for scientific research. The major orientation of scientific research is decided by scientists after negotiation, and specific projects are also decided by a professional commission, whose members have the function of closely following the development of frontline scientific research in the world, submitting investigation and research reports in their own fields and confirming new orientations for research. Another distinctive character of the 863 Program is that the achievements can be industrialized very fast.

Thanks to efforts made in the past 20 years, the National High-Tech R and D Program, also known as the 863 Program, laid a solid foundation for the birth, development and industrialization of China's high-tech industry. During these years, with an accumulated allocation of 33 billion Yuan, 150,000 experts, 500-plus research centers, 300-plus universities and colleges and nearly 1,000 businesses have engaged in research and development of this program. According to statistics, the program generated 120,000 research papers and 8,000 international or domestic patents. It also helped formulate over 1,800 national or industrial regulations.

On January 5, 2006, the first 50 km "TJ-1" unmanned remote sensing high-speed monitoring system in China, one of the key science and technology achievements of the State 863 Program, was successfully developed in Qingdao.

973 Program

The 973 Program is the National Program on Key Basic Research Projects. Since its implementation in 1998, this program has mainly involved major scientific issues in agriculture, energy, information, resources and environment, population and health, materials and related fields. It involves multi-discipline comprehensive research and offers a theoretical and scientific basis for solving issues. This program encourages excellent scientists to aim at scientific frontline and major scientific and technical issues and conduct key basic research in those key fields with great influence on economic and social development. This program reflects the national objective and offers powerful scientific and technical support to solve the major issues in the Chinese economic and social development in the 21st Century.

The National Basic Research Program of China, namely the 973 Program, was launched in 1998. Up to 2005, the program organized 229 projects covering agriculture, energy, information, resources and environment, population and health care and raw material sectors, as well as some comprehensive or interdisciplinary courses. With the passage of time, the fruitful results of this program play an important role in the socio-economic development. This program is also a driving force for the development of nano-science, life science, informatics and other research sectors. It helped create some home-bred achievements as follows:

Carbon nanotubes are produced from ionized plasma and template synthesis-one of the four major production measures widely adopted by international experts.

Research on non-linear optical crystals, laying the foundation for the fourth generation illuminating source.

The production and control of the five-photon entanglement realized in the world for the first time, which was rated as the Top 10 achievements in physics in 2004 by the American Physical Society (APS) and the European Physical Society (EPS), thanks to efforts made in the quantum information and telecommunications sector.

In the meantime, as the basic research levels in the field of population and health care are remarkably enhanced, and many major problems have been solved. Some new drugs with curative effects for major diseases were invented, such as Schiperine for Alzheimer's disease, anti-cancer drugs Salvicine and Lidamycin, which are under phase-III clinical trials; Schiperine has completed phase-II clinical trials in more than 30 European hospitals.

In 2006, the "973 Program" approved establishment of 70 projects, launching the four major scientific research plans—research into protein, quanta regulation, nanotechnology, and development and propagation.

Torch Program

The Torch Program is the most important high-tech industry program in China, starting in August 1988. As a national guidance program, it involves the following contents: organizing and implementing a group of high-tech product development projects with advanced technical level both for the domestic and foreign markets and with good economic benefits; constructing a group of high-tech industrial development zones across China; and probing into some management system and operational mechanisms that adapt to high-tech industry development. This program puts emphasis on projects in such fields as new materials, biotech, electronic information, technical integration of mechanics and electronics, and new energy and energy-saving technologies. Different from the 863 Program, the Torch Program aims at turning scientific achievements into production by establishing some service centers that help people start their own businesses, also known as incubators. As of the end of 2005, there have been 534 S and T business incubator facilities in China, including 137 national-level ones. There have been 40,639 businesses under incubation, accounting for one-third of the medium and small-sized S and T businesses. The accumulated number of the graduated S and T businesses has reached 15,931, with 3,319 newly graduated in 2003. Various business incubator facilities occupied the total area of 19.699 million square meters. The businesses under incubation gained 10,926 authorized patents, including 3,949 invention patents. The annual total income of the businesses under incubation in technology, industry and trade reached 162.54 billion Yuan and created more than 710,000 job opportunities. Some 50 graduated businesses were listed at home or abroad. The number of China's incubators ranks second next to the US, while the area of incubator facilities and the number of businesses under incubation have ranked first in the world. Since the program began, 100 service centers have been allocated among 53 development zones, which are cradles for many high-tech giants in China, including Founder, Lenovo and Stone. Important Scientific and Technical Achievements

Spark Program

(See P76)

International Cooperation

Scientific and Technical Cooperation between China and Foreign Countries

Up to now, China has established scientific and technical cooperation with 152 countries and regions, of which, 96 have signed scientific and technical cooperation agreements, and has entered more than 1,000 international scientific and technical cooperation organizations. The international scientific and technical cooperation and exchanges conducted by non-governmental organizations are most active. The Chinese Science and Technology Association and its societies have entered 244 international science and technology organizations, more than 290 person/times of Chinese scientists have assumed posts of executive directors of executive committee (council) or above of international science and technology organizations, and some 280 person/times of Chinese scientists shoulder the leadership posts in professional commissions of international organizations; over 250 scientists from the Chinese Academy of Sciences hold posts in international science organizations; the National Natural Science Foundation has signed cooperation agreements and memorandum of understanding with science foundation organizations in 36 countries.

Semi-official and Folk Science and Technology Cooperation

Under the promotion, demonstration and encouragement of science and technology cooperation between Chinese government and other countries, Chinese semi-official and folk science and technology cooperation and exchanges have also made considerable progress. Exchanges between scientific research institutions, between schools of higher learning, between science and technology academic organizations, between enterprises, between cities and between individual scientists are also very active.

By the end of 2003, the Chinese National Natural Science Foundation had signed 58 cooperation agreements with science foundations and scientific research institutions in 38 countries and regions, actively supporting international science and technology cooperation.

CAS has established scientific and technical cooperation with more than 60 countries and regions, and signed more than 80 cooperation agreements of academic grade and nearly 1,000 cooperation agreements of institutional grade. It holds about 100 international and bi-lateral conferences every year; nearly 400 scientists hold posts in more than 400 international science organizations and institutions. CAS has also established a group of united laboratories, youth scientists groups and partner groups and trans-subject research centers with some famous foreign institutions.

The Ministry of Education says the nation's top 16 schools of higher learning alone have established cooperation and exchange programs with nearly 2,500 colleges, institutes, scientific research institutions, international organizations and enterprises in more than 100 countries and signed more than 1,500 scientific and technical projects cooperation agreements.

The Chinese Science and Technology Association has established exchanges and cooperation with folk science and technology bodies and organizations in more than 30 countries and regions and signed 52 bilateral exchanges and cooperation agreements. As a representative of Chinese science and technology circles, the CSTA is the member of some international science and technology organizations such as ICSU and WFEO.

China actively encourages foreign research and development institutions to establish cooperative R and D institutions with Chinese bodies or independent R and D institutions in China. Since the American multinational HP established the first R and D institution in China, trans-national corporations have followed the trend. In 1998, Microsoft also established its research institution in China. By 2004, five such R and D institutions have been established with total investment of US$2 billion. Motorola, the world famous communications corporation, has established 18 R and D centers in China with the total investment of about US$150 million.

Technical Trade

Introduction of technologies has become an important method to enhance the industrial technical level fast since the adoption of reform policies in China. According to the Ministry of Commerce, some 10,538 contracts were signed in 2006 to import advanced technologies. The contract volume of US$22.02 billion was 5.6 percent higher than the previous year. Some US$14.76 billion, or 67 percent of the total contractual value, was technology-related expenditure.

The methods adopted for technology import includes proprietary technologies, technology consultation, technology services and especially technology introduction accompanied by a full set of equipment. At present, the sources of Chinese technology introduction are increasingly diversified, but Japan, the United States and the European Union still serve as the main sources. However, technology import remains weak.

The export of Chinese high-tech products is increasingly active. In 2005, the import and export amount of Chinese high-tech products for the first time exceeded US$400 billion and reached US$415.96 billion, an increase of 27.2 percent from the year before and occupying 29.2 percent of total Chinese foreign trade. The proportions held by electronic products and computer products in high-tech products import and export respectively stand at 50 percent and broke through the US$100 billion barrier for the first time. Among the import of Chinese high-tech products, the top three kinds are electronic, computer and communication products, of which, the import amount of integrated circuits in the first 11 months reached US$72.4 billion, up 33.1 percent and occupying 40.9 percent of the total import amount of Chinese high-tech products.

The Human Genome Project

In the "Chinese Human Genome Project" involving US, UK, French, Japanese and Chinese scientists, China took charge of the identifying of one percent and determined 384 million bases. On June 26, 2000, the Human Genome Project Center made a joint announcement that the draft human genome mapping was successful.

Human Brain Project

The involved countries include the United States, the United Kingdom, Germany, France, Sweden, Norway, Switzerland, Australia, Japan and China, and the European Union also participates in the organization as a formal member. It aims at organizing and bringing into line the scientists of neurology and informatics in the world to do research and develop and protect the brain. Chinese scientists will cooperate with International Neuroinformatics Network and Database and establish Chinese particular neuroinformatics platform, electronic network and information database.

Global Change Program

This program includes four research programs, i.e. IGBP, IHDP, WCRP and DIVERSITE. The Chinese scientists involved have made great contribution already to global research.

High Energy Physics Research Program

Chinese scientists have participated in the Large Hadron Collider Program of CERN. A Chinese expert group took part in the development and data analysis of the ATLAS detector, construction of the CMS detector and magnet components, and the preparation of some analytical software and physical research.

Alpha Magnetic Spectrometer Experiment

This experiment is a large-scale international cooperative scientific experiment project led by Professor Ding Zhaozhong, a Chinese-American physical scientist and winner of the Nobel Award for Physical Science. The objective is to search in space for antiparticles and dark matter and observe high-energy astronomical phenomena. Scientists from more than 10 countries such as the United States, China, Russia, Germany and France took part in this program. Chinese scientists developed the permanent magnet, a core component of the magnetic spectrometer. From June 2 to 12, 1998, the Alpha Magnetic Spectrometer was carried by the American space shuttle Discovery and conducted the first space flight successfully. It collected a great amount of data to help determine the origin of the galaxy.

Geospace Double Star Exploration Program

This is a cooperative program between relevant Chinese departments and the European Space Agency. The major scientific objective is to explore the time and space changing laws of electromagnetic field and energy particles in two near-Earth magnetic fields, i.e. the near-equator region and the near-polar region. On the early morning of December 30, 2003, a Long March II SM Carrier Rocket carried the first satellite of this program, i.e. TC-1 (Exploration-1), into space.

European Galileo Project

In March 2002, the European Union formally launched its "Galileo" global navigation satellite system for civilian use. On September 18, 2003, the Chinese Ministry of Science and Technology initialed *A Cooperation Agreement on Galileo Satellite Navigation* in Beijing with DG Energy and Transport of the EU. According to the agreement, China and the EU will conduct cooperation in such fields as satellite navigation technology, industrial manufacturing, services and marketing, products standardization and frequency.

Social Sciences

System of Social Sciences

In China, five great systems undertake research in social sciences, i.e. Chinese Academy of Social Sciences, regional academies of social sciences, higher colleges and universities, research units subject to the Chinese Communist Party schools and government departments, and research units subject to the military. According to incomplete statistics, the total staff involved in all fields of social sciences numbers more than 100,000.

Founded in 1977, Chinese Academy of Social Sciences is the highest academic research institution in China. It is engaged in innovative theoretical exploration and policy research with the advantages of complete subjects, concentration of talents and abundant resources, and shoulders the duty of enhancing the level of human social sciences in China. Under this academy, at present there are 31 research institutes, 45 research centers and more than 3,200 scientific and technical staff including 1,700 senior professional personnel. The Chinese Academy of Social Sciences possesses a group of professional specialists and scientists well known in both domestic and international academic circles and with profound academic attainments, as well as middle-aged and young scientific and technical staff as the backbone in research of academic theories.

In recent years, regional research institutions of social sciences have made considerable progress as well and all provinces, autonomous regions and municipalities have established institutions in different scales.

The departments of social sciences and human studies in higher schools across China constitute an important research base of social sciences, possessing more than 60,000 teachers. Most of them also do some research besides teaching. Many higher colleges and universities have also established some special research institutions. According to incomplete statistics, there are about 130 research institutes in social sciences and more than 4,000 full-time research staff.

The Chinese Academy of Social Sciences

♦ Chinese Academy of Social Sciences

The Chinese Academy of Social Sciences, established on May 5, 1977, is the highest academic institution and comprehensive research center in the field of philosophy and social science. It grew out of the Department of Philosophy and Social Sciences, Chinese Academy of Sciences. Comprising 34 research units, it works on research related to the economy, law, philosophy, archaeology, history, literature, language, ethnic group and religious issues. Chen Kuiyuan is its current president.

It provides scientific achievements to society in the form of books, scientific papers, research reports, translated works and compiled documents. Since it was established, it has published 4,293 books, 54,517 scientific papers, 7,268 research reports, 2,787 translated books and 16,108 translated scientific papers, as well as numerous reference books and popular books. It also has sifted a large number of ancient books, completing their collation and annotation. Annually, it produces 300 scientific books, 3,890 papers and 510 research reports

Address: No.5 Jianguomennei Dajie,Beijing
Website: http://www.cass.net.cn

Famous Scientists

Yuan Longping

Yuan Longping(1930-), a Chinese agriculturalist, was born in 1930. He is currently an academician of the Chinese Academy of Engineering, Director General of China National Hybrid Rice Research and Development Center and Hunan Hybrid Rice Research Center, as well as the chief advisor to the UN Food and Agricultural Organization. Yuan was a pioneer in hybrid rice research in China and was also the first person developing hybrid rice successfully in the world. The achievements of Yuan Longping not only greatly solve food shortage in China but also provided a solution to worldwide starvation. In the world, hybrid rice is regarded as the fifth invention after China's Four Major Inventions, and is acclaimed as the "Second Green Revolution". He was rewarded with eight international awards, such as Gold Medal Award for the Outstanding Inventor of the United Nations World Intellectual Property Organization, Science Prize of United Nations Educational, Scientific and Cultural Organization, Rank Prize for Agronomy and Nutrition of the United Kingdom, a United States award for helping solving the starvation problem plaguing the world, Medal of Honor for Food Security and Sustainable Development of the United Nations Food and Agriculture Organization, and the Fukui International Koshihikari Rice Prize of Japan. he is the first Chinese scientist to win China's highest scientific development award.

Yuan Longping started research into

Yuan Longping

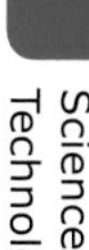

hybrid rice in 1964. At the beginning, he discovered male-sterile rice. Then he brought forward a plan of Three-Line Seedling of Rice and carried out experiments on farmland. Yuan made his breakthrough in 1973 and became the first person to develop indica hybrid rice. The new technology was tested in many areas of South China in 1974 and 1975 with good effects, and was then extended to wider areas from 1976. Since then, China became the first country capable of producing hybrid rice. It is testified by productive practice that in same conditions the yield of hybrid rice exceeds that of ordinary rice by 20 to 30 percent, and even 50 percent. This earned him the title of "Father of Hybrid Rice". In 1980 the technology of indica hybrid rice was transferred to the United States as the first patent in Chinese agriculture.

Many of Yuan's theses and works have won awards, of which, Male Sterility of Rice and Strategy of Hybrid Rice Breeding are viewed as epoch-making works publicly by academic circle and are significant breakthrough on traditional classic theories. His work, Breeding and Cultivation of Hybrid Rice, was rewarded first prize of the National Excellent Book Award in 1993 and was listed as one of the "Top Ten Works Promoting Chinese Science and Technology Advance".

On April 25, 2006, Yuan Longping was chosen by the National Academy of Sciences of the US as a foreign associate. He is the first Chinese agricultural expert to win election to the Academy.

Wu Wenjun

Wu Wenjun (1919-) a famous mathematician, is honorary director of the Research Institute of System Science at the Chinese Academy of Sciences. He was awarded the State Supreme Science and Technology Award in 2000. After graduating from Shanghai Jiaotong University in 1940, he completed his PhD at the University of Strasbourg. He made a significant contribution to the Topology, automatic inference and mathematics mechanization. His achievements have been adopted in various forms of symbolic calculation software. Especially in the field of the characteristic classes and the embedding classes, the fruitful results he produced are still applied to help develop cutting-edge symbolic calculation software.

Huang Kun

Huang Kun (1919-2005) as a member of the Chinese Academy of Science, Huang was a renowned Solid-state physicist. He joined the Chinese Academy of Sciences Semiconductor Institute in 1955. In 1980, he was elected as the foreign member by the Royal Swedish Academy of Sciences. He became the member of the Third World Academy of Sciences (TWAS) in 1985. He predicted X-ray diffuse scattering due to crystal defects in crystalline lattice in 1947, which was honored as the Huang Diffusion. In 1950, he and A. Rhys established the "Huang-Rhys Theory", the quantum theory on radiative and non-radiative multiphonon transition processes. As Pekka put forward the same idea, it is also known as the "Huang-Pekka theory". He proposed the coupling vibration mode between the phonon and electromagnetic waves in crystal and the relevant basic equations (called the Huang equation). In 1984, he won an award in theoretical physics from the University of Notre Dame, and the honor as outstanding international scholar from the Central American Association of State Universities. He was awarded the State Supreme Science and Technology Award in 2001.

Wu Wenjun

Wang Xuan

Wang Xuan

Wang Xuan (1937-2006), Father of Laser Photo Typesetting Technology, was member of Chinese Academy of Sciences and member of the Chinese Academy of Engineering, professor with Peking University, and Chairman of the Board of Directors of the Founder (Hong Kong) Group Corp. It was the research institution led by Wang Xuan which invented the Chinese character laser-photo-typesetting system, bidding farewell to traditional letterpress printing. This laid a solid foundation for computerized work of journalism and publishing houses. Han Chinese characters printing thus bade farewell to the traditional printing method, hence known as the "second invention of the Chinese characters printing." In 1975, he presided over and succeeded in developing the computerized Chinese characters laser photo typesetting system. In 1988, the New Technology Co. of Peking University promoted the Beida Fangzheng system, which was followed by the promotion of the newspaper large screen composing system, computerized management of reporting and editing process, and journalist comprehensive business network. In 1992, he succeeded in developing the world's first Chinese character color laser-photo-typesetting system, which was adopted by more than 1,000 newspapers and more than 6,000 printing houses. Some of the large foreign companies have to give up their endeavor in the Chinese characters laser-photo-typesetting field in China. Chinese technology of Chinese character laser-photo-typesetting now leads the world. It won the highest State scientific invention award in 2001.

Jin Yilian

Jin Yilian (1929-), is a computer scientist from the Chinese Academy of Engineering, one of the pioneers in the development of high performance computers, also dubbed "the father of the high performance computer". He is the director of the National Research Center of Parallel Computer Engineering and Technology. In 2002, he was presented with the State Supreme Science and Technology Award.

Liu Dongsheng

Liu Dongsheng (1917-), an environment geologist, is the member of the Chinese Academy of Science and the Third World Academy of Sciences (TWAS). He is also the researcher of the Institute of Geology and Geophysics, Chinese Academy of Science. He has made great achievements during the past 60 years, in the field of Chinese ancient vertebrates, quaternary geology, environmental science and geology, investigations on the Qinghai-Tibet plateau and in the polar region. Thanks to his contributions, especially his pioneering work on loess soil, China leads the world in the field of global change in ancient times. In 2002, he was awarded the Tyler Prize for Environment. In 2003, he was presented with the State Supreme Science and Technology Award.

Wang Yongzhi

Wang Yongzhi (1932-) graduated from the Moscow Aviation Institute in 1961, Wang is a carrier rocket expert. He is an academician of the Chinese Academy of Engineering and the fifth president of the Chinese Academy of Launch Vehicle Technology. He was appointed as chief designer of China's manned spaceflight program in 1992. He is also the member of the International Academy of Astronautics and the foreign associate of the Russian Academy of Sciences (RAS). He is the chief designer and advocate of the bounding technology applied in the Long March II carrier rockets, China's first launch vehicle. In 2003, he was awarded the State Supreme Science and Technology Award.

Ye Duzheng

Ye Duzheng(1916-), a researcher and academician of the Chinese Academy of Science, is a leading name in the world meteorological community. He made great contributions to studies on global temperature change, atmosphere generation circulation and climate. He also put forward a new theoretical system on global change. He has worked on dynamic meteorology, plateau meteorology, ocean-atmosphere relations, energy dispersion in the atmosphere and global change research, publishing six books and 90-plus research papers. For his distinguished work, he won the first-class prize of the National Natural Sciences Award for Contributions to General Circulation of East Asia in 1987, and China's top science and technology award in 2005.

Wu Mengchao

Wu Mengchao(1922-) is a liver and gallbladder specialist and member of the Chinese Academy of Science. Wu is generally considered as the "father of Chinese hepatobiliary surgery". He also turned out to be a famous surgeon in the field of abdominal surgery. In the 1960s, he created an anus excision method of intermittent liver gate blocking at normal temperature, and successfully completed the first middle lobectomy of the liver. Since then till 1980s, he has conducted 1,019 operations of liver lobectomy, with a success rate of 97 percent. The quantity and quality of his operations combine to make him the leading role among his counterparts in the world. His books entitled *Clinical Research in Surgical Operation of Liver Diseases* helped win the first-class National Science and Technology Progress Award in 1986. He won the State Supreme Science and Technology Award in 2005.

Member Wu Mengchao (middle) and his disciples giving free medical consultation

Li Zhensheng

Li Zhensheng (1931-), a geneticist and an expert on wheat breeding, is a CAS Member and a Member of the Academy of Sciences for Developing World, and now holds the post of the research fellow of the Institute of Genetics and Developmental Biology and the Chairman of the Scientific Committee of the State Key Laboratory of Plant Cell and Chromosome Engineering.

Li Zhensheng has engaged in the research on the hybridization between wheat and couch grass and chromosome engineering breeding for a long time. He developed a new system for blue-grained wheat and chromosome engineering breeding, opening a new road for the application of the wheat chromosome engineering breeding and making great contribution to the increase of China's grain. He is equally famous with Yuan Longping, the father of hybrid rice. And they have the honorific title of "Yuan in South China and Li in North China"

Min Enze

Min Enze (1922-) , is a scientist subject in petrochemical catalyst. He was graduated from the Department of Chemical Industry, the Central University in 1946 and obtained the Ph.D. degree in the Ohio University in the United States in 1951. He serves as the commissioner of the Academic Commission of SINOPEC Research Institute of Petroleum Processing, and senior engineer. In 1960s he developed successfully phosphate diatomaceous polymer catalyst, platinum reforming catalyst, globule silica-alumina cracking catalyst, and micro-spherical silica-alumina cracking catalyst which have all been put into production in built-up factories. In 1970s and 1980s he led the research, development, production and application of molybdenum-nickel-phosphor hydrogenation catalyst, carbon monoxide combustion improver, and semi-synthetic zeolite cracking catalyst. After 1980 he guided the oriented basic researches of new catalyst materials and new chemical reaction projects including non-crystalline alloy, supported heteropoly acid, nano molecular sieve, magnetically stabilized fluidized bed, and suspension catalytic distillation, and has developed successfully such new techniques as hexanolactam magnetically stabilized fluidized bed hydrogenation and alkylation of suspension catalytic distillation. In 1990s he served as the master of "environment-friendly petrochemical catalyst chemistry and reaction project", a significant basic research project of the "Ninth Five-Year Plan" sponsored by the State Natural Science Fund Commission. He entered in the field of green chemistry, guided the development of the whole green-manufacture technologies of chemical fiber monomer hexanolactam that has been industrialized and obtained great economic and social benefits. In recent years he has been guiding the development of biologic oil refinery producing biological diesel oil and chemical products from biomass renewable resources, and put it to industrialization. In 1980 he was elected as academician of Chinese Academy of Sciences. In 1993 he was elected as academician of the Third World Academy of Sciences. In 2007 he won the Highest State Science and Technology Award.

Wu Zhengyi

Wu Zhengyi, (1916-), is a botanist. He was graduated from the Department of Biology, Tsinghua University. He serves as the researcher and honorable president of Kunming Institute of Botany, Chinese Academy of Sciences. In 2007 he won the Highest State Science and Technology Award. He demonstrated the three great historical origins of Chinese floras and 15 geographical elements. He proposed the standpoint that the south and southwest of China in the region of latitude 20 to 40 degrees north is the key region for the origination and development of southern paleo-continent, northern paleo-continent, and paleo-Mediterranean Sea floras. He supervised the publication of two-million-characters Chinese Vegetation that is an important scientific material for relevant subjects of botany and the production of agriculture, forestry and animal husbandry. He organized and led the investigation of vegetal resources in China and especially in Yunnan Province and pointed out the formation of the useful materials of plants is related in some degree with the distribution regions and formation history of plant species sources. He compiled some national and regional botanic records. In recent time he has proposed the concept of "East-Asian Flora" and regards it as one of the oldest botanic regions. He also proposed the theory of "multiple-floras —multiple-periods—multiple-regions" on the origin of angiosperm. In 1955 he was elected as academician of Chinese Academy of Sciences. After 1980 he started to serve as life-time foreign member of the American Society of Plant Biologists, honorable member of Swedish Geo-botany Association, and communication member of former Soviet Union Botany Association. In 1997 he was elected as member of the International Union for Conservation of Nature (IUCN).

The Ministry of Science and Technology

The Ministry of Science and Technology is the highest governmental organ administering scientific and technology work around the country. Its main responsibilities are to put forward macro-administrative strategy for science and technology development, as well as guidelines, policies and laws and regulations for the science and technology to promote social-economic development; conduct research on major issues of promoting economic development by science and technology; study and determine the major and priority areas for the science and technology development; and promote the building of the national science and technology innovation system and improve the national science and technology innovation capacity.

Address: No.15 B Fuxing Road, Haidian District, Beijing

Website: http://www.most.gov.cn

♦ National Natural Science Foundation of China

The National Natural Science Foundation of China (NSFC), established on February 14, 1986, is an affiliated institution of the State Council. As a part of the national innovation system, its major responsibilities are to support basic research, uphold free exploration and play the guiding role in national natural science development. It establishes a funding system to support talented professionals in China, which comprises the National Science Fund for Fostering Talents in Basic Science, the Young Scientists Fund, the National Science Fund for Distinguished Young Scholars and the Science Fund for Creative Research Groups. The Central Government has stepped up its efforts in pooling more resources for the NSFC. It allocated 2.695 billion Yuan for the fund in 2005, compare to 80 million Yuan in 1986. Thanks to this, NSFC's ability to sponsor scientific projects has been strengthened.

Website: http://www.nsfc.gov.cn

♦ China Association for Science and Technology (CAST)

In September 1958, the China Association for Science and Technology (CAST) was formerly established. CAST works on popularization and development of science and technology. It covers natural science, technology, engineering and related sectors. Its network comprises 167 national societies, 31 provincial-level associations, numerous local and basic research institutes, as well as 4.3 million members.

Its main responsibilities are to:

Conduct academic exchanges to inspire ideas of scientists and promote development of science and technology;

Advocate a scientific spirit, popularize scientific knowledge, scientific thinking and methods, safeguard the dignity of science and technology, promote advanced technology, carry out education of science and technology among young people, help raise the population quality;

Reflect the comments and suggestions of scientific and technology personnel, protect their legal rights and interests, organize them participate into the formulation of policies, laws and regulations related to science and technology, as well as political consolation, decision-making and democratic supervision of State affairs;

Award and promote the distinguished scientific and technology personnel;

Provide consulting services, set forth suggestions to the government, promote the science and technology achievements turning into productive force, accept program evaluation and scientific achievements examination and issue professional titles;

Carry out international non-governmental scientific and technological exchanges, promote cooperation with international individuals and institutions; and Provide continuous education and training.

CAST and its national societies have joined 240 international non-governmental science and technology organizations. Some 100-plus Chinese scientists work in these organizations. CAST also maintains good exchanges and cooperation with non-governmental organizations in Hong Kong, Macao and Taiwan.

Website: http://www.cast.org.cn

Education

Development of Education

Through thousands of years of development, school education appeared in China in the Xia Dynasty (2070—1600 BC).

Confucius (551-479 BC) was worshipped by the Chinese as a great thinker and education initiated private schools some 2000 years ago, making it possible for the ordinary people to have access to education.

Education during the feudal dynasties was conducted mainly to train officials. Confucian classics were used for the education and the imperial examinations were held in China on the regular basis for the selection of officials.

Modern school did not appear in China until the 1860s when foreign languages, military and technical schools were run. At that time, the Qing Government also sent people to study in France and Britain.

When the People's Republic of China was founded in October 1949, the PRC Ministry of Education was founded one month later. China has developed a complete educational system composed of pre-school education, primary, middle, high school and university/college education. It branches into daily education, after-work education and on-duty training.

China's educational undertakings have been undergoing reform which was initiated in an all-round way in the mid-1980s. A basic framework of education law and regulations has been set up. In the 1990s, "developing China through science and education" has become the basic policy of China. In the 21st century, China works to establish an educational mechanism and system for people of different age groups and doing different work to receive diversified form of socialized education.

Traditional thread binding *Analects of Confucius* offered to the crown princes of the Ming Dynasty for study.

Confucian Temple in Qufu, Shandong Province

Imperial Civil Examination System

Imperial examination was a system to select officeholders through examinations in ancient China. To put it simple, imperial examination was a system of choosing the best talents through holding examinations at regular time by government. Lasting for 1,300 years, the system started in 605 in the Sui Dynasty, got full development in the Tang Dynasty and was not abolished until 1905 during the Qing Dynasty .

Differing from the Western education system of teaching knowledge under different disciplines, the content of the imperial examination included poems, Confucian classics, and articles of ancient talents, such as the remarks and the strategy of country's management.

During the Ming and Qing dynasties, formal imperial examinations consisted of three levels: provincial, metropolitan and final imperial examination.

The system of imperial examination had a huge influence on China's society and culture and directly resulted in a stratum of "scholar-bureaucrat" disregarding family status and created by examination. Some countries neighboring China in Asia such as Viet Nam, Japan and Korea also introduced this system to choose talents.

Baguwen (Eight-part Essay)

Baguwen refers to the eight-part stereotyped writing specifically for imperial examinations in the Ming (1368-1644) and Qing (1616-1911) dynasties, which requires four couples of parallel sentences with each sentence in accordance with tonal patterns and rhyme schemes. The "gu" in the middle of Baguwen means antithetical parallelism.

In the Sui and Tang dynasties (581-907), China adopted the system of promoting officials through imperial examinations. This made it possible for ordinary scholars to get promotion. The imperial examinations featured poems, which made it hard to tell which was the best. As a result, during the Ming and Qing dynasties , poems made way for Baguwen.

The general features of Baguwen were as follows: firstly, all the titles for examinations were from original texts of *The Four Books (The Analects of Confucius, Mencius, The Great Learning, The Doctrine of the Mean)* and *The Five Classics*; secondly, the content had to be in accordance with the commentary of Chinese ancient philosophers; thirdly, there was a fixed format for the structure of the article. Parts played different roles, including Puoti (first two sentences giving the theme in the essay), Chengti (follow the last part, explain the theme in four or five sentences), Qijiang (begin to explain the theme in details in several sentences), Ruti (the last part of beginning of the article, continue from the preceding and introduce the following), Qigu (start argumentative writing, using four to five separate sentences or eight to nine parallel sentences, which should maintain a rhythm, following a pattern of Zhonggu (the core of the article), Hougu (complements the last part or slows down the tone), Sugu (in two parallel sentences, highlight the keys), Dajie (the ending part of the article in separate sentences). Baguwen had certain limitations and stringent requirements in terms of writing, including the number of words, punctuation and format. It is precisely because of the restrictive requirement for the topics, content and format that Baguwen was eventually considered to have destroyed the creativity and independent ideas of intellectuals. People of later generation refer to articles which are empty in terms of contents but pays high attention to the format as Baguwen.

Education in Modern China

As a country with such a large population, China has numerous educatee. At present there is a population of more than 200 million in diversified schools of different grades to receive full-time education.

The education in China covers the stages of infant education, primary education, middle-school education and college and university education. As to the nine years which from the primary school to junior middle school, the government implements compulsory education and the students at this stage of compulsory education need not pay tuition but the hundreds of Yuan book fees and incidental expenses every year.

The popularization rate of compulsory education in China has reached more than 90 percent. The illiterate rate of the young dropped to less than 5 percent. At present, some 250 million people have received elementary, primary and high school education, a figure that means twice the world level. The net enrolment rate of primary schools reached 98.9 percent and that for middle schools was 94.1 percent. In future years, the Chinese government will give prominence to the development of compulsory education in rural areas and the higher education and hopes that all children can receive education at schools and some world-top universities can be established soon in China.

The education in China gives priority to public education initiated by governments. In recent years the non-government funded education has got some development but on the whole it cannot yet be a match for public schools in respect of educational scale and level.

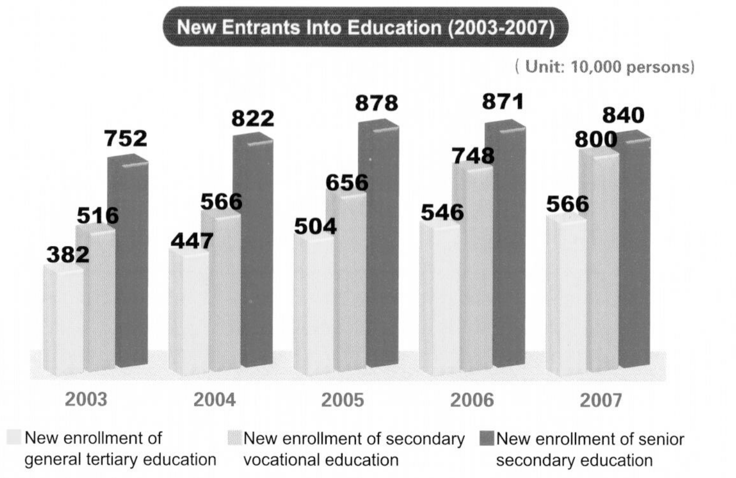

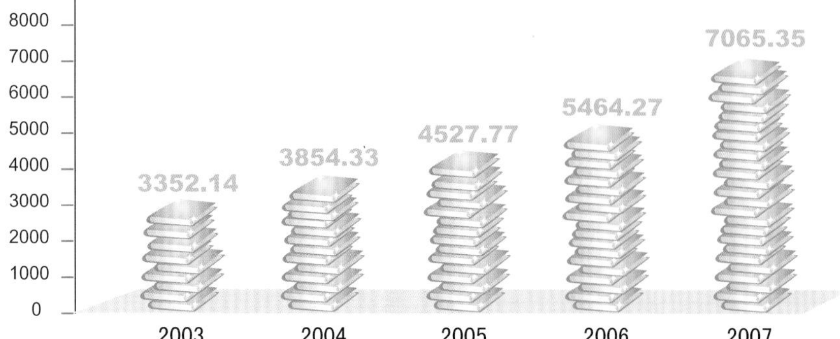

Educational Management System

China follows the system for the schools to be run mainly by the government and also by various social sectors. At present, the elementary education is run mainly by the local governments; higher education by the Central Government and provincial (autonomous regional and municipal) governments, with various social sectors also getting involved in the endeavor. Vocational education and adult education are run mainly by various trades, enterprises, government institutions an social sectors but under the unified management of the Government.

The Ministry of Education is the highest

organ in term of management over education in the country. It is in charge of following the laws and regulations of the Central Government, and enacting rules and regulations concerning educational work. It also oversees the development of educational undertakings, and coordinates educational work of various departments.

Since 1978, China has successively constituted Regulations on Academic Degrees, Compulsory Education Law of the PRC, Teachers Law of the PRC, Law of the PRC on the Protection of Minors, Education Law of the PRC, Regulations on Teacher's Qualification, Higher Education Law of the PRC, and more than 10 other educational administrative regulations. Within the limits of its functions and powers, the Ministry of Education has constituted over 2,000 educational administrative regulations to promote educational development at different levels and types.

Outlays for Education

As to outlays for education, priority is given to funds appropriated by national finance and outlays for education are raised by multiple channels. At present the schools directly under the central government get their outlays from central financial appropriation, the schools under regional governments get their outlays from regional financial appropriation, the schools run by township and village governments in rural areas and by enterprises get their outlays mainly from the initiators and the central government gives proper subsidies, and the schools run by social bodies and prominent personages get their outlays from money-raising by the initiators (through charge from students, subscriptions from society and so on). Besides, the state encourages all the schools at different grades to develop work-study program and increase some incomes by offering service to the society to improve the situations in schools. In addition, to guarantee the input in education from all levels of governments,

Education Law of the People's Republic of China stipulates that the increase in financial appropriation on education funds from all levels of governments should be higher than the increase in financial regular incomes.

Education System

The education system in China consists of basic education, secondary vocational and technical education, regular higher education and education for adults.

Basic Education

Basic education refers to pre-school, primary and regular secondary education (including junior and senior secondary school). Primary education lasts five to six years. Junior secondary education lasts three or four years. Regular senior secondary education lasts three years. China has implemented the nine-year compulsory education approach, including primary and secondary level education.

Pre-School Education (Early Childhood Education)

Pre-school education is an important component of education in China. In urban areas, pre-school education is mainly kindergartens of between one and three years, which could be full time, part-time, boarding or hourly-basis. In rural areas, pre-school education is mainly nursery classes and kindergartens of one year attached to the primary school, and funded by the village government. In addition, according to local conditions, in remote and poor areas, besides the normal pre-school education, there is irregular education in various forms such as multi-classes for different aged children, game groups, children activity centers and mobile services called "caravans", activity centers for mother and child, family aid centers, and pastoral areas mobile kindergartens. According to the areas of learning and activities, per-school education is divided into five aspects of health, society, science, language and arts. In addition, it includes practice of painting, arts and crafts.

The State has also formulated regulations and rules concerning the qualification of kindergarten teachers and the assessment of their performance. At present, the normal schools devoted to the training of kindergarten teachers and the discipline of pre-school education have made big strides and a training system of pre-school teachers at considerable scale has taken shape.

Primary and Secondary Education

In China, primary and secondary education takes 12 years to complete, divided into primary, junior secondary and senior secondary stages. Primary education lasts either five or six years with the former accounting for 35 percent of the total enrollment and the latter 65 percent. At junior secondary stage, most have three years of schooling with a tiny part undergoing four years. Almost 98 percent of students are enrolled in the former schools. The nine-year schooling in primary and junior secondary schools pertains to compulsory education. General senior secondary education lasts three years.

In 2007, there are some 320,000 primary schools in China. The school-age children enrollment rate of primary school reaches 99.49 percent.

There are totally 59,400 middle schools (300 vocational junior schools). The gross enrollment rate of junior middle schools is 98 percent.

National high school education (including ordinary senior high schools, vocational high schools, ordinary secondary vocational schools, worker skills schools, adult high schools and adult secondary specialized schools) develops fast. A total of 31,300 senior high schools are operating. The gross high school enrollment rate reaches 66 percent.

Implementation of 9-Year Compulsory Education

The "Compulsory Education Law of the PRC" promulgated in April 1986 provides for a nine-year period. Regardless of gender, ethnic group and race, any child reaching the age of six should enter primary school and receive compulsory education. In area where middle school education is basically popularized, primary school graduates may enter middle schools located close to their home. But middle school graduates have to pass examinations organized by local education departments to enter high schools.

The China Education Reform and Development Program issued by the Chinese Government in 1994 defines that the nine-year compulsory education shall be completed in three stages: Economically developed area, moderately development area, and economically underdeveloped area. To this end, in the summer of 1995, the Ministry of Education and the Ministry of Finance organized to undertake compulsory education project in the poverty-stricken area. It covers 21 provinces, autonomous regions and municipalities directly under the Central Government, with funds involved totaling 11.6 billion Yuan.

All walks of life support the nine-year compulsory education. The Hope Project and the Spring Bud Program, initiated by the China Youth Development Foundation and the China Children's Fund respectively, have made contribution in this regard.

The first day of the new semester

Educational System (Basic Education)

The school year of primary and secondary school is divided into two semesters. The school year of primary schools comprises 38 weeks of teaching with an additional week in reserve and 13 weeks for holidays. The school year for junior secondary schools comprises 39 weeks for teaching with an additional week in reserve and 12 weeks for holidays. The school year for senior secondary schools comprises 40 weeks of teaching with one or two weeks in reserve and 11 weeks for holidays. A five-day week has been implemented in primary and secondary schools.

In the autumn of 1993, primary and junior secondary schools began to implement the "Teaching Scheme (Curriculum) for Full-time Primary and Secondary Schools (Pilot)", and this scheme includes the arrangement of subjects and syllabus. According to the scheme, subjects are divided into two categories: State-arranged subjects and locally-arranged, with the latter determined by the authorities of provincial-level governments in the light of local realities and needs.

The current curriculum of senior secondary schools consists of two parts: subjects courses and activities. Subjects taught in senior secondary schools are divided into obligatory ones and optional ones. Activities include out-class activities and practice activities.

Throughout compulsory education, students are required to take end-of-term examinations and tests of some kind at the end of each semester, school year and before graduation. In primary schools, Chinese language and mathematics are the required examination subjects for graduation, while the other subjects are check-up subjects. In secondary schools, the graduation examination subjects are determined within the scope of the general subjects taught in the graduating class set by the State, while the students' performance in other subjects are only checked up.

Teaching Materials for Primary and Middle Schools

In 1950, the Ministry of Education formulated curriculum standards for primary schools. Afterwards, in 1956, 1963, 1978

♦ The Ministry of Education

The Ministry of Education is a department under the State Council, responsible for educational undertakings and language work.

The ministry's main missions are: to draft relevant educational rules and regulations; to formulate the policy of educational structural reform as well as the emphases, structure and speed of educational development, and to direct and coordinate the implementation of this work. To manage in accordance with relevant regulations educational aids and loans from abroad. To investigate and put forward the establishment of standards, basic teaching requirements and basic teaching documents for secondary and primary schools; to organize the examination and approval of unified teaching materials for secondary and primary schools; to direct the pedagogical reform of secondary education and types of education lower than that level; and to organize the supervision and evaluation of the implementation of nine-year compulsory schooling and the eradication of illiteracy among young and middle-aged adults; to manage regular higher education, postgraduate education, tertiary vocational education and adult higher education, higher education offered by social forces, as well as the State-administered examinations for self-taught adult learners seeking tertiary qualifications and continuing education; to plan and direct the educational work for the minority nationalities, to coordinate the educational aids to the minority areas; to oversee teachers' work all around the country; to formulate guidelines and policies for Chinese students studying abroad and international students studying in China; to plan, coordinate and direct the work of teaching Chinese as a foreign language; to direct the work of Chinese educational institutions abroad; to be responsible for coordinating the educational cooperation and exchanges with Hong Kong SAR, Macao SAR and Taiwan district; to be responsible for the coordination between the UNESCO National Commission of the PRC and UNESCO itself for cooperation and exchanges in education, science, technology, culture and other sectors; to be responsible for keeping in touch with the head office, Asia-pacific office and Beijing office of UNESO; to be responsible for connecting with China's permanent delegation to UNESO and to supervise its work.

Address: No.37 Damucang Hutong, Xidan, Beijing

Website: http://www.moe.edu.cn

♦ China National Institute for Educational Research

The main missions of CNIER which was set up on January 26, 1957 are: to conduct research into basic education, higher education, vocational education and adult education and the theoretical and practical issues arising from educational reforms and development; to conduct research on developmental strategies of education, educational policy and educational management; to conduct research on rural education, moral education, school physical education, health and art education and comparative education as well. To conduct experiments related to the reform of teaching; to summarize and disseminate results of research so as to provide theoretical guidance, a scientific basis, consultation service, and operational designs for educational reforms and development; to take the responsibility for the formulation of national plans for educational research and the monitoring of national key projects commissioned by the leader team of the national education formulation; To conduct research projects commissioned by the Ministry of Education and its departments; to conduct research on curriculum and teaching materials for basic education and to provide advices and consultation for the Ministry of Education on the guiding principles and policies of basic education curriculum and teaching materials; to compile teaching materials for primary and secondary schools; to promote the development of key disciplines stressing the originality, aim and relevance of basic research.; to carry out international educational exchanges and cooperation; to undertake the collection, selection and dissemination of references and other information on education; to develop a joint graduate program on pedagogy.

Address:No.46 Sanhuan Zhonglu, Haidian District, Beijing

Website: www.cnier.ac.cn/Index.html

and 1986, four conservative sets of syllabi of subjects taught in primary and secondary schools were formulated, and eight sets of school textbooks were compiled and published by the People's Education Press for nationwide use in compliance with the requirements set in these syllabi.

As China is a vast country with significant regional disparities in economics, and social development, it is quite understandable that the conditions of different schools vary greatly, and consequently it is desirable to develop multiple sets of textbooks at various levels to meet the needs of different localities and with their own specific characteristics and styles. For this reason, in 1986, the former SEC (State Education Commission) adopted a policy of diversifying the preparation and production of school textbooks under the condition that unified basic requirements must the complied with. In areas where conditions permit, regional educational departments, educational institutions, experts, scholars and individual teachers are encouraged to compile textbooks for subjects taught in primary and junior secondary schools in compliance with the basic requirements set forth in the syllabi of nine-year compulsory education. As a result, different sets of textbooks will compete with each other bringing a radical change to the old practice in which only one set of textbooks was used throughout the whole country and promoting the prosperous development of school textbooks. Up to 1998, more than 2,000 different sets of textbooks had been provided to meet needs of local areas. In addition, a lot of reference and manuals for teachers, illustrated booklets, atlas for school use, wall charts, slides and audio-visual materials for classroom instruction or doing homework and computer software have been produced to complement and supplement textbooks. Many supplementary teaching materials with local color and flavor have been produced in many localities to meet the needs of local economic and cultural development.

After-School Education

Children may take part in the scientific, cultural, and recreational activities organized by children's palaces, children's clubs, scientific and technological centers for teenagers, activity centers of children and youth and other similar institutions. They number some 10,000 in China.

After-school education, through rich and colorful extracurricular activities and competitions organized in the light of the age and interests of children, such as music, sports, drawing, Gong fu, computer, stage performances, aircraft, ship and motor vehicle models, exhibitions of small inventions and handicraft making, literary writing, summer and winter camping and so on, are used to mould student temperament and their willpower.

Rural Compulsory Education

Between 2006 and 2010, the government planned to gradually incorporate all expenditures for rural compulsory education into the public finance system and establish a mechanism to guarantee funding that divides specific tasks between central and local governments and assigns each a proportion of the burden. On the basis of clear delineation of responsibilities of each level, sharing of the burden by central and local governments, increased government spending, stronger financial guarantees and systematic, step-by-step implementation, the objective is to implement reform in two years and optimize it in three.

New budget allocations from all levels of government from 2006 to 2010 for rural compulsory education will amount to 218.2 billion Yuan, including 125.8 billion Yuan from the Central Government and 92.4 billion from local governments. The government also implemented a new mechanism for maintaining and renovating rural primary and secondary school buildings throughout the country.

The policy of "two exemption and one subsidy" has been applied to 36 million rural students in China. This policy refers to the exemptions of tuition and school fees and subsidy for dormitory fee. It works to make sure that the poor students can enter into the school, afford the school fees and keep studying" and help them to finish school at best.

Project Hope

Project Hope is a public welfare undertaking initiated and organized by the China Youth Development Foundation (CYDF). Its mission: by non-governmental channels, to enlist extensive financial resources from home and abroad, and to establish a fund, so as to assist dropout students and those at risk of dropping out to continue schooling in China's rural areas, to improve educational conditions, and promote basic education development in poverty-stricken areas.

Project Hope has become the largest and most influential non-governmental welfare campaign in China. In the 17 years since its founding, the CYDF had raised over 3.2 billion Yuan in donations, helped 2.9 million children from poverty-stricken rural families return to school and complete their elementary, secondary, and higher education respectively, built over 12,700 Hope primary schools, and, In addition, Project Hope funds had enabled over 30,000 village primary school teachers to receive further training. Project Hope has changed the fate of a large number of drop-out schoolchildren, improved their conditions in the poverty-stricken areas, aroused the whole society to become aware of the need to give priority to the development of education, and promoted the development of basic education in many ways.

• Spring Bud Project

The Spring Bud Project was organized and implemented by the China Children and Teenagers Fund (CCTF) in 1989. It is a public welfare undertaking to help female dropouts to return to school in poverty-stricken areas. Funds needed come from donations from various units and individuals.

In 1989, CCTF launched "Assistance Fund for Girl Students", which aimed to aid girls in poverty areas who were deprived of education to return to school, it was renamed "Spring Bud Project" and, later, "Spring Bud School" and "Spring Bud Girl Class" were set up. CCTF also set up "Spring Bud Practical Skill Training Special Fund" to help the girls support themselves economically and get rich with the agricultural practical skills they learnt in the "Spring Bud School". By 2007, the "Spring Bud Project" had received 600 million Yuan in donations, aided girls in some 30 provinces and cities, set up more than 600 "Spring Bud Schools", and opened more than 5,000 "Spring Bud Classes". The number of the dropout girl students receiving aid from CCTF reached 1.7 million person-times, the number of the women and girls receiving various practical skills training reached 416,000 person-times. The "Spring Bud Project" has become one of the social public welfare brand enjoying the highest popularity and reputation.

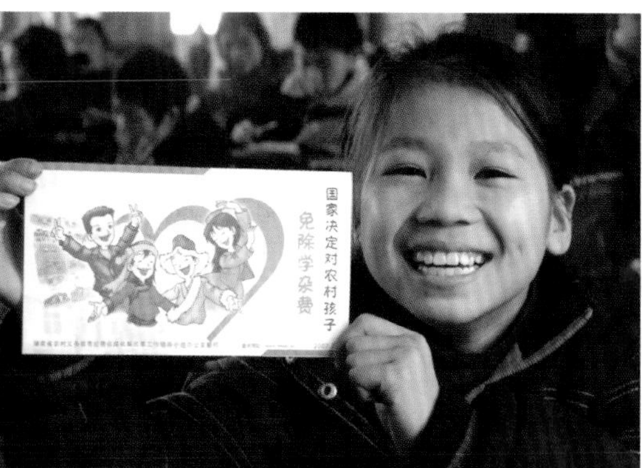

The Chinese Government shall exempt the tuition and other fees for rural students receiving compulsory education. This will be funded by the Central and local finances according to proportion.

Aid-Study System

During the nine-year period of compulsory education, the program of "two exemptions and one allowance" is being extended. Students from lower income families receive subsidies for their higher education divided into different types, "honor, loan, aid, subsidies and free". During senior secondary education, students also benefit from the secondary vocational subsidy system.

The program of "two exemptions and one allowance" is exemption from paying for textbooks, exemption from paying miscellaneous education-related fees and allowances for room and board for the children of poor rural families living at schools while receiving compulsory education. The aim is to ensure that, during the period of compulsory education, students from poverty-stricken families in rural areas enjoy the "two exemptions and one allowance" to prevent students dropping out because of economic difficulties.

Some 20 billion Yuan has been approved in the seven years since the National Subsidy Loan scheme was launched. In 2005, 330,000 students were enabled to participate in higher education through this "green channel", accounting for 44 percent of the total number of poverty-stricken students. For higher education, China has basically established a diversified subsidy system, including scholarships, student loans, work while study, special subsidies to meet difficulties, free study and fee remission.

Central finances provides 800 million Yuan in each of the years to subsidize poor students in secondary vocational schools. Thanks to this and aid given by local governments, schools and through community funding, hundreds of thousands of new students of secondary vocational schools benefited in some way.

Special Education

According to the popular interpretation in the international society, special education refers to the education targeting "children having special demands" on studies (including the handicaps in studies of reading, writing, composing and calculating, handicaps in feelings and emotions, handicap in speaking, puzzle in action, obstacle in association, problems in mental health, weakness and sickness in body, etc.). In China the special education usually refers to a narrow sense, i.e. the education targeting children having handicaps in physical and mental health.

There are about 6 million disabled children in China. According to the type of disability and education targets, the concerned education departments adopt two ways of general education and special education for disabled children. General education includes special education classes attached to ordinary primary schools and absorbing children with disabilities to learn in regular classes. Such enrollment of children with disabilities and accepting special education students in school accounted for 67.11 percent and 64.88 percent of the number of special education enrollment and total number of students in school respectively. The schools implementing special education include those for blind children, schools for children with severe hearing problems and schools for mentally handicapped children. The period of special schooling is generally nine years. The pupils enter the school at 7 to 9 years of age, and leave by 18.

At present in China the special education is run mainly by ministry and departments of education, as well as by departments of civil administration, departments of health, departments of handicapped associations and social powers as supplementary. An educational system of pre-school education, basic education, middle education and higher education is coming into being for handicapped.

Disabled Receiving Higher Education

The disabled began to receive higher education 20 years ago. In 1985, with the help of the Ministry of Education, Ministry of Health, Ministry of Civil Affairs, and China Welfare Fund and the Shandong government, Binzhou Medical College set up the first undergraduate degree department in the country to recruit youth with disabilities for s five-year clinical training program. Currently, there are four specialized colleges to recruit students with disabilities located in Tianjin, Beijing and Binzhou, The new

Ma Di, a deaf-mute child aged 7, is trained to speak in a special education school.

students of Binzhou Medical College need to take the national college entrance examination. The other three colleges are different. The new students' admission is by taking a special exam of their own. There are about 200 students with disabilities graduating from these four colleges each year. Other disabled graduates who receive higher education are from formal institutions of higher education.

Vocational Training for the Disabled

There are more than 1,000 vocational teaching and training institutions for disabled persons at the provincial, prefectural and county levels, nearly some 2,200 ordinary vocational educational training institutions receive disabled for vocational training; and there were over 150 vocational educational training institutions offering the medium-level school diplomas. About 2.6 million disabled persons have received the vocational education and training, thus enhancing their abilities.

Legal Protection

In the 1980s, the Ministry of Education put educating the disabled into the compulsory education plan. Some important laws, including the 1982 Constitution [amended in 1988, 1993, 1999 and 2004], Law on the Protection of Disabled Persons, Law on Compulsory Education and the Education Law, provide general principles and special articles on education of people with disabilities. The Regulations of Education for the Disabled set out the requirements for pre-school education, compulsory education and vocational education of people with disabilities.

In the 1990s, the administrative education department conducted step by step a series of studies on educating and training disabled children, including those with autism and severe mental handicap. In some places, the ordinary kindergarten and pre-school classes of primary schools have paid special attention to enrolling children with disabilities. Beside compulsory education, technical and vocational training are widespread for the blind, deaf-mutes and the mentally handicapped children. Large and medium-sized cities and economically developed areas have achieved nine-year compulsory education for children with these disabilities. In the last decade, the secondary technical education for the blind, deaf and physically handicapped youth, high schools for blind or deaf youth and higher education for the disabled have been developing apace. The Ministry of Education stipulates that, in general admission of ordinary colleges and universities, secondary schools and technical schools, no institution shall reject any student on the basis of disability and must provide youth with disabilities with equal opportunities for and access to higher education.

Vocational Education

Vocational education is provided at three levels: junior secondary, senior secondary and tertiary. In addition, vocational education includes job orientation and training and on-the-job training. It plays an important role in lifelong education, comprising higher vocational technology institutions, secondary technical schools, skilled worker schools, vocational high schools, job orientation and training centers, adult technical training schools and other social training organs.

China's first Vocational Education Law was promulgated and implemented in 1996, which provided a legal guarantee for development and improvement of vocational education.

The system of vocational education consists of education in vocational schools and vocational training. Besides theoretical classroom teaching, vocational technical education teaching includes some practical teaching, such as experiments, training, social studies, specializing in the production of labor, graduation practice (or major operations). The teaching achieves integration of teaching, production practice, application and popularization of science and technology.

Vocational education forms a pattern mainly through government-run schools but also encouraging participation by the whole of society.

Students in a vocational technical school are receiving the training on technique of dismantling and reassembling the engine of the car.

General Higher Education

The general higher education system in China comes in various forms, which combines both degree and non-degree education and integrates college education, undergraduate education, graduate education, doctoral education. The types of universities in China include regular colleges and universities, higher vocational schools, radio and television universities and adult colleges and universities. The schooling period of colleges is 2-3 years; the period for undergraduate education at universities is usually four years, or five years for medicine In addition, a small number of engineering institutions require five years of study. Graduate education lasts two-three years, while doctoral education lasts three years.

Since 1981, China has adopted the degree system divided into bachelor's, master's and doctorate levels.

In China public universities and colleges are the major one among all universities and colleges, and researching and integrated universities are concentrated in regular public universities and colleges. In recent years the non-government funded universities and colleges have got fast development into a large scale, but in respect of running levels, there is a distance between them and public universities and colleges with high prestige.

Entrance Examination for Universities and Colleges

Entrance examination for universities and colleges is divided into regular one and the one for adults. It is the standard for examinee to have the qualification to select and enter a university or college. In regular meaning the entrance examination is the regular one, so is it in this item. Before 2003 the time for the entrance examination was in July and since 2003 the time has been changed to June 7 and it lasts for 2 or 3 days. In recent years some provinces and municipalities have started to hold the examination for twice a year, adding one in January.

At present the entrance examination in China is called as "3+X", "3" referring to the subjects of Chinese, mathematics and foreign language, and "X" referring to the different subjects as options; in some places it represents integrated examination for liberal arts or integrated examination for science, naming the students registered for liberal arts enter the integrated examination for liberal arts and the students registered for science enter the integrated examination for science; and in other places it has a wider meaning that examinee can select the subjects from options of physics, chemistry, biology, history and so on according to the demands from the specialized subject and university or college registered by examinee.

Since its appearance, the entrance examination for universities and colleges has attracted great attention in the society, but, in recent years, with the enlarging of enrolling scale and the increase in enrolling rate, examinee and their parents have less pressure. However, at the time of the entrance examination every year, it is still the focus in the society.

Since 2001 the entrance examination has abolished the restriction on age and marriage situation, and any one with the nationality of mainland China and the proper education background can enter the examination.

Entrance Examination for Post-Graduate Students

Entrance examination for post-graduate students refers to the entrance examination held by all universities or research institutions to enroll post-graduate students and consists of two levels, the one for masters and the one for doctors.

In China the entrance examination for post-graduate students with master's degree

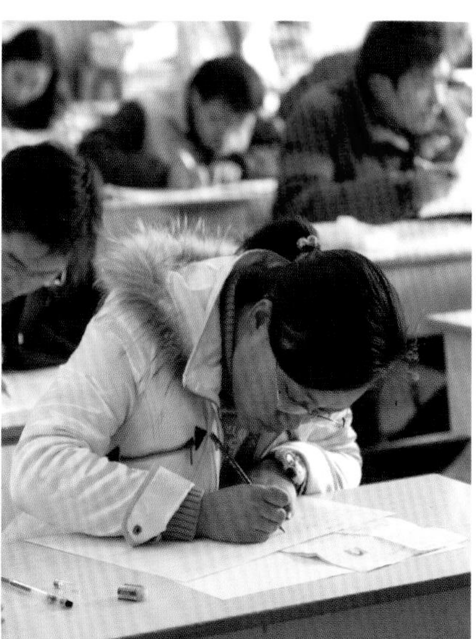

The national entrance examination for postgraduate students

consists of two parts, i.e. written examination and interview. As to written examination, the examinations for common subjects are assigned by the Ministry of Education and a bottom line of marks for enrollment is confirmed, for example, the examinee registered for liberal arts must enter the examinations for politics and foreign language and the examinee registered for science must enter the examinations for politics, foreign language and mathematics; and the examinations for specialized subjects are assigned by universities or research institutions in respect of subjects, contents and enrollment marks for the subjects. The examinee attaining the enrollment marks of the written examination will be required to enter interview, and the universities or research institutions will select their students according to the marks of written examination and interview.

The entrance examination for post-graduate students with doctor's degree is mainly held by universities and research institutions. The examinee with master's degree and registered for his or her original subject need to enter the written examination of foreign language and two or three other specialized subjects as well as interview. The examinee registered for subjects other than his or her original one or with the status having the same educational level basis with those with master's degree need to enter the written examination of five or six subjects as well as interview.

Examination for Obtaining Certificate

Besides the examinations for formal schooling, there are many kinds of examinations for obtaining various certificates in China and these examinations are considered to have the ability to enhance the "abilities" of obtaining employment and prove the working ability or materialize his or her technique ability.

At present the examinations for obtaining certificate with large number of examinee in China mainly include examination of certificating foreign language level, examination of certificating computer level, examination of certificating grades in music and dancing, and examinations of various certified practitioners in such fields of law, accountant and so on. In addition, with the increasing internationalization in economic development in China, some international examinations for occupation qualification and level also enter China.

The examinations for obtaining certificates in China are mainly divided into several grades to represent different levels possessed by people, so many such examinations are not finished once and examinee need to study continuously to enhance their level.

"I passed the Sports Dancing Technique Rank Examination."

Project 211

Project 211 was set in motion in 1997 as the government's new endeavor to strengthen about 100 institutions of higher education and key disciplinary areas as a national priority for the 21st century. The project primarily looks at the overall conditions of universities, key disciplines and public service system of higher education.

The public service system: To build a China Education and Research Network and information service systems covering key disciplines and a higher education literature security system; initially form a digital information platform for Chinese higher education benefiting all universities in the country.

After the completion of the Information and Computer phase of "project 211" at Tsinghua University, nearly 10,000 network computers came into being, and an electronic library and a highly efficient supporting CD-ROM database retrieval system was established in the library. The resulting computer laboratory was the first large-scale facility of its kind in China. The "experimental economics" construction projects of key disciplines in Beijing's Renmin University, based on the penetration of literary arts and sciences and sharing resources, built up a common computer platform and electronic laboratory, and set up the most advanced research and teaching environment in the social science field in the country. As a result, it raised the utilization rate of resources. Peking University built a first-class geological museum in Asia, with an archives area of 1,200 square meters. As a result, the geological department collected a great many specimens of minerals, rocks and ancient extinct life. This helped provided the most basic data and academic environment for study, research and academic exchanges in the geological field.

National Teaching Experimental Demonstration Centers of Higher Institutions

The Ministry of Education started construction and accreditation work of national teaching experimental demonstration centers of higher institutions in May 2005. These centers are being built in three batches between 2005 and 2007. They cover physics, chemistry, biology, mechanical, machinery, electronics, computer, medical, economic management, media and integrated disciplines such as an engineering training center.

National teaching experimental demonstration centers of higher institutions are required to have an advanced teaching system, content and method, advanced teaching group and equipment, advanced laboratory construction model, advanced management system and operation mechanism and notable features of experimental teaching.

Higher Education System

For a long period after the founding of New China in 1949, the State implemented a planned economic system, which provided free schooling for all students of higher learning. Training was funded by the State, who then allocated jobs to graduates. From the mid-1980s, the State adopted the policy of reform and opening up, gradually switching from a planned to a market economy. Universities and colleges began trials in charging part of the tuition fee from all students. By 1997, Universities and colleges all charged freshmen fees. A system of helping students in financial difficulties was established, including scholarships, student loans, work-while-studying, special difficulties aid and exempting and reducing the tuition fees. Employment of graduates was transformed from solely State allocation to one in which graduates could independently choose the profession under the career guidance of the State. This, to a certain extent, helped the universities to set up a rational disciplines structure, in which teaching met society's demand for qualified personnel.

Graduate Education and Academic Degrees System

The graduate school is an important part of training high-level personnel and resolving the important issues of science and technology in China. Currently, 56 graduate schools approved by the Ministry of Education provide 76 percent of the doctors and 55 percent of the master's degree holders nationwide. The graduate school plays an important role in the development of China's graduate education and high-level scientific research.

The post-graduate degree award ceremony

The Regulations of the PRC on Academic Degrees were promulgated in 1980. Its implementation promoted colleges and universities and research institutions to establish a relatively complete system for granting degrees and for postgraduate training. The Interim Measures for Implementation of the Regulations of the PRC on Academic Degrees was approved by the State Council in 1981. This established the academic degree system comprising of three levels of undergraduate degree, master's degree and doctorate degree, so that the development of graduate education entered an orderly stage. In 1985, the State approved the establishment of post-doctoral mobile stations; in October 1985, the first batch of 102 post-doctoral mobile stations was established in 73 universities and research institutions.

Since 1991, in order to meet the need for highly qualified specialists of different backgrounds for industry and the requirements of economic and social development, the Degrees Committee of the State Council approved the establishment of the Master of Business Administration (MBA), master's degree in architecture, master's degree in law and Master of Public Administration (MPA), and other such professional degrees. This is an important part of China's reform of the system of academic degrees. A total of 33 colleges and universities were formally approved by the State to establish graduate schools in 1995. This helped to maintain a high level force in scientific research and teaching in basic subjects.

Post-Doctorate System

The Post-Doctorate system of China was created by the late Deng Xiaoping, based on Nobel Prize laureate Lee Tsung-Dao's recommendations, and was approved and established by the Ministry of Education 22 years ago. As a world power, China has to take the lead in training a numbers of senior personnel. It is a just a step in the process of training to get a doctorate degree. Young doctorate holders gradually mature only after working in a lively academic environment and then experiencing years of training to work independently. Therefore, in some universities and research institutions, some special posts should be set up for those selected for the newly acquired doctorate and let them engage in post-doctoral study to widen their knowledge. This will result in them further developing their abilities of independent work, and turn them into high-caliber professionals.

Since 1995, China has begun to carry out trial postdoctoral work in some enterprises. In some enterprises with strong funding who are advanced in technology and strong in research conditions, post-doctoral research stations have been set up to meet their needs for high-level personnel. The enterprises and units established by the research stations jointly recruit and train post-doctorate candidates.

At present, China has approved over 140 enterprises to establish post-doctoral stations. This approach is designed to promote the integration of production, study and research, and accelerate the production and transformation of scientific and technological achievements, and form a national technological innovation system with enterprises as the main body.

At present, nearly 7,000 people work in postdoctoral research stations. Another 7,000 postdoctoral researchers have already completed the process.

State Yangtze Scholar Award Program (Cheung Kong Scholars Program)

The State Yangtze Scholar Award Program (Cheung Kong Scholars Program) was jointly established by the Ministry of Education and Mr. Li Ka-shing, a Hong Kong entrepreneur. Its main objective is to further improve China's higher education and China's academic research level. The program contains two items of practicing professorships by special appointment and Yangtze Scholar Achievement Award (Cheung Kong Achievement Award). The first batch of investment from Cheung Kong (Groups) leaded by Mr. Li Ka-shing was HK$60 million, with counterpart funding by the Ministry of Education, used for practicing professorships by special appointment. Another HK$10 million was donated from Mr. Li Ka-shing for establishment of the Yangtze

♦ People's Education Press

Founded in 1950, the People's Education Press (PEP) is a specialized publishing house directly under the leadership of the Ministry of Education. It undertakes overall tasks of research, compilation, publishing, and distributing teaching materials for elementary education, and various other textbooks and educational books. Over the past 50 years, the Press has presided over and participated in designing the curriculum standards for all subjects in primary and secondary schools. PEP has successfully researched, written, compiled and published ten series of primary and secondary school textbooks used nationwide. Altogether more than 30,000 kinds of publications have been published with a total circulation of 60 billion volumes.

As one of the largest education publishing house in China, PEP published the first set of textbook used nationwide in 1951. According to the needs of economic development and national education reform, PEP has been compiling and writing new textbooks. At the beginning of new century, under the spirit of basic education curriculum reform and all kinds of curriculum standards, according to the plan of the Ministry of Education, PEP wrote and published experimental textbooks for compulsory education and general high school under the curriculum standards. The Ministry of Education approved this new, 10th set of teaching materials, and they were tested in schools in pilot areas in autumn 2001 and 2004 respectively. The set of teaching materials are being compiled and revised and will be published soon.

PEP not only publishes primary and secondary school textbooks, but also books for pre-school, teacher training, adult education, vocational education, special education and nationality education as well as educational theory and Chinese as a Foreign Language.

The China Educational Publications Import and Export Corporation, one of the top four corporations of its kind in China, is mainly involved in the business of importing and exporting books, periodicals (including e-periodicals) and other publications.

Website: http://www.pep.com.cn

Scholar Achievement Award (Cheung Kong Achievement Award).

During the first phase of the program, the Ministry of Education was to establish 300 to 500 professorships by special appointment among the national key disciplines at tertiary institutions within three to five years. Its main function was to clearly define the duties and terms of employment. And further to employ the best and brightest young minds at home and aboard who would be leaders and masters in their fields by the higher institutions admitted to special professors appointment, so as to attain the world level in key branches of learning improve China's standard of education and intellectual competitiveness. The recommended candidates selected by the universities, after passing the assessment of an expert commission, could then be hired by the universities. The professors employed could receive a special stipend of 100,000 Yuan in addition to the regular remuneration offered by the university in accordance with State guidelines. Professors who achieve outstanding academic distinction or make a commendable contribution have a chance to win the annual Cheung Kong Achievement Award, of which the highest prize is 1 million Yuan for one person and the second highest prize is 500,000 Yuan for each of three persons.

China Academic Degrees and Graduate Education Development Center (CDGDC)

This is an administrative department directly under the Ministry of Education, operating under the joint leadership of ministry and The Academic Degrees Committee of the State Council (ADCSC). CDGDC is a non-profit agency with independent qualification of a legal entity. CDGDC was established on July 2, 2003.

Functions of the CDGDC:

To engage in scientific research into academic degrees and graduate education, providing counseling for the Ministry of Education and The Academic Degrees Committee of the State Council in formulating policies concerned; to undertake the task of evaluating and appraising academic degrees and graduate education, entrusted by the Ministry of Education and the Academic Degrees Committee of the State Council [when necessary, CDGDC has the authority to independently conduct similar tasks entrusted by any social establishment]; to undertake the task of test paper setting and test administration for the two types of examinations: the national tests for the equivalently qualified master (doctorate) degree applicants, and the national entrance examinations for the professional master degree applicants in part-time study programs; to engage in research into the degree equivalency between China and foreign countries, mainland China and its special regions of Hong Kong, Macao, and Taiwan, providing counseling for reciprocal degree acknowledgement agreements in this area. Empowered by the government, CDGDC can sign cooperation agreements concerning degree and graduate education evaluation and acknowledgement with nongovernmental and unofficial organizations. It also provides services for degree and related materials accreditation, authentication and consulting.

Tsinghua MBA Program

The Tsinghua MBA program is one of the earliest and most prestigious of such programs in the PRC, and is the largest, most influential and grand brand among MBA programs in the country. It was launched in 1991. Currently, among students enrolled between 1991 and 2005, a total of 4,072 gained an MBA. The graduates have gained management positions at all levels in middle or large-scale enterprises, foreign companies and private enterprises, and have been making great efforts for the development of the national economy.

Tsinghua MBA program adopts the training model of the general equals the specific. The elective courses of MBA exceed 200, covering six major categories of business administration, financial and finance, business innovation and entrepreneurial management, e-commerce, financial analysis, management control and international business management.

Tsinghua MBA program emphasizes organic unity of internationalization and localization. The university actively promotes exchange activities with world-class business colleges, absorbs the world's advanced management teaching content and teaching methods in an all-round way. Tsinghua MBA program has cooperated with Sloan School of Management at MIT for a long time. The university has also invited a large number of senior management personnel to give lectures or practical courses for MBA students.

Adult Education

Adult education provides various types and levels of education for adults, including school education, literacy courses and so on.

Adult education consists of degree and non-degree education programs. Degree education is provided at several levels for adults: universities with undergraduate courses, colleges with specialized courses, specialized secondary, junior and senior secondary education, etc. The schools include adult institution of higher education, evening university, correspondence college, self-taught higher education examination, radio and TV university, and adult secondary school. Non-degree education consists of literacy courses, training on applied technologies for farmers, in-service training, certificate of course completion in a single subject, occupational certificate and continuing education. Since the adult education pioneered the use of distance education, it has the most students in China and make once in one's life schooling possible to be lifelong learning.

By the end of 2006, a total of 48.70 million persons (the repeated ones are not counted) and 180 million person times have participated in the self-taught examination. About 7.3 million people obtained the university/college degrees and 29 million the non-degree certificates. This means one out of every 30 persons participated in the self-taught examination.

Education for Illiteracy

Since the foundation of New China in 1949, "eradicating illiteracy among 80 percent of the total population" has been an important task for the Central Government, and a corresponding movement on wiping out illiteracy has been launched throughout the country. From 1949 to 1998, a total of 203 million people completed basic literacy courses. The number of adult illiterates declined from above 80 percent in 1949 to below 15 percent in 1998 and the rate of young and middle-aged illiterates dropped to below five percent.

By the 1990s, the content of illiteracy education has progressed from only reading and counting to practical technical training, civic education and culture life education. According to the sample survey by the Ministry of Education, by 2000, the illiteracy rate of the young and middle-aged dropped below 5 percent in 23 provinces (autonomous regions and municipalities). The figure reached the country's basic standard of eradicating young and middle-aged illiteracy at that stage. In

With a child on back, the female members of illiteracy eradicating class come to attend class.

"Graduating!"

2007, a total of 9.578 million people completed basic literacy courses and the illiteracy rate of young and middle-aged was brought below 4 percent. Hence, China achieved two goals of long-term development while halving the number of illiterates and halving the number of poverty-stricken people.

Higher Education for Adults

Higher education for adults is a part of higher education of China. Job training at a higher level and continuing education after colleges and universities are keystones of higher education for adults.

For selecting qualified entrants, higher education for adults requires applicants to take the National Adult College Entrance Examination. The examination includes three levels: upgrading program from college to university, upgrading program from senior high school to university, and higher technical and vocational program. The examination is held Saturday and Sunday of the second week in October every year.

Nowadays, China's higher education institutions for adult include higher education schools for adults (e.g. evening universities, correspondence colleges and part-time colleges), radio and TV universities and self-taught higher education examination. Higher education for adults mainly offers the educational opportunities for on-job people. Now, the largest learning patterns in higher education for adult are Radio and TV universities and self-taught higher education examination. By the end of 2007, there were a total of 413 higher education institutions for adults throughout the country.

Subjects of the National Adult College Entrance Examination (NACEE)

In respect of the upgrading program from senior high school to university or the higher technical and vocational program, the subjects of the NACEE are designed respectively by arts or science. The common subjects of the NACEE are Chinese, mathematics and foreign language, in which, mathematics includes mathematics for arts and mathematics for science; foreign languages include English, Japanese and Russian. Examinees select one of foreign languages in the examination according to the requirement of different schools. In addition to above three common subjects, the examinees need to take an examination of specialized basic courses, specifically, "physics and chemistry" for comprehensive science or "history and geography" for comprehensive arts. The Ministry of Education designs the exam papers.

In terms of the upgrading program from college to university, there are three common subjects in the NACEE. Two of them are politics and foreign language, and the other is a specialized basic course that needs to be decided by the corresponding discipline. Depending on the number of local examinees, the admission office of higher education for adults at provincial level decides if they need to organize the examination of non-English language and designs papers by themselves. In addition to this, the other papers of subjects of the NACEE are designed by the Ministry of Education.

The maximum score on each paper of the NACEE is 150. The length of examination is 120 minutes for each subject for both the upgrading program from senior high school to university and the higher technical and vocational program, and 150 minutes for the upgrading program from college to university.

♦ China Education Development Foundation

China Education Development Foundation, the first national education foundation, was founded on March 30, 2006. It is devoted to raising money widely from home and abroad, undertaking regular national activities of helping students and teaching and other relevant activities, subsidizing students from poor families to finish their education, and helping some poor regions to solve the special difficulties in the course of reforming and developing educational cause.

To fund students from poor families to complete their studies;

To help students from low-income families of Hong Kong, Macao, Taiwan, who study in the mainland, finish their studies;

To support the reform and development of education in poor areas with special difficulties;

To award individuals and units who have made great contributions to China's education reform and development;

To receive enthusiastic support and funding, property donations and technical assistance for China's education from the government, organizations and individuals at home and abroad;

To possible receive generous donations from both home and abroad through a variety of channels;

To conduct the aid programs appointed or commissioned by Chinese Government or all kinds of support and finance projects concerned education or related to education;

To accept the commission of other funds entrusted by funding institutions at home and abroad to manage using for China's education; to carry out exchange and cooperation activities with the domestic and international foundations.

Website: http://www.cedf.org.cn

Self-Taught Higher Education Examination

This combines a self-taught pattern and national test. From the beginning of the reform and opening up in 1978, young people's interests in study soared as never before and the heavy demand of society for specialized talents was also unprecedented. In 1981, in order to open the door to adults willing to learn, Chinese educational staff drew on the educational experiences of foreign countries and designed the authoritative self-taught higher education examination characterized by openness and ease. The examination mainly focuses on the specialized courses while making the undergraduate courses subsidiary. In addition to the subjects and courses of the national uniform examination, special self-taught courses are designed by the particular needs of rural areas, the middle and western regions of China and minority areas.

Private education changed the traditional educational pattern mainly depending on the government, by increasing the overall supply of education. The picture shows a privately0run school in Shanghai City.

Private Education

China is a country of great civilization with a long history of private education. Some 2,400 years ago, in the Spring and Autumn Period (770-476 BC), Confucius began to run his private school. Private education with a "hundred schools of thought", represented by Confucianism, Mohist, Taoism and Legalism, was shaped in the Warring States Period (475-221 BC). Since then, private education has been playing a big role in passing on Chinese civilization.

The State Council issued Regulations on the Running of Educational Institutions with Social Resources in 1997. This is the first administrative regulation for standardizing private schools. It marks that emergence of private education onto a new stage for managing and running schools by law. The national education meeting, held in the summer of 1999, focused on striving to develop private education and decided that over the 10th Five-Year (2001-2005) plan, the educational pattern would focus on running State-run schools while seeking the joint development of State-run and privately-run schools.

Private education changed the traditional educational pattern mainly depending on the government, increasing the overall supply of education.

Laws and Regulations on Privately-Run Education

By the end of 2002, the Law of the PRC on Promotion of Privately-Run Schools was issued, marking the fundamental establishment of China's private education system. Taking the Constitution as the parent law and the *Education Law* as the basic law, the legal system now consists of the Law of the PRC on Promotion of Privately-run Schools, the Regulations of the PRC on Academic Degrees, the Compulsory Education Law of the PRC, the Higher Education Law of the PRC and the Vocational Education Law of the PRC, as well as related administrative regulations issued by the State Council, rules issued by the Ministry of Education and local regulations issued by local administrative departments.

♦ China Adult Education Association (CAEA)

China Adult Education Association (CAEA) is a mass and academic social group organized voluntarily by various educational groups and staff of adult education. Approved by the Ministry of Education in April 1981, it is registered with the Ministry of Civil Affairs.

The work scope of the CAEA is as follows:

Through publicizing the significance and function of adult education, the CAEA mobilizes various social circles to care for and support the work of adult education. Through planning, organizing, harmonizing and evaluating adult education, CAEA seeks to popularize the fruits and experiences of adult education research, and provide counseling of decision-making for educational service departments. Through training with the help of other departments, CAEA seeks to raise the levels of the cadres of adult education and researchers in terms of their theoretical, political and professional quality. CAEA edits and publishes educational magazines, newspapers and materials on adult education. It seeks to strengthen contacts and co-operation with international adult education associations, develop international academic exchanges between the adult education associations and the staff of adult education in any other country and region. It seeks to develop various continuing education and vocational training programs for adults, and provide other supporting services.

Website: http://www.caea.org.cn

Xi'an Fanyi University—one of ten major privately-run universities in China

♦ Xi'an Translation University

In 1987, beginning with only one rented classroom and office, Ding Zuyi, the present principal, set up the privately-run Xi'an Translation University. Now, there are 40,000 full-time students living on campus, with 60,000 graduates of undergraduate and specialized courses. The university now offers nearly 60 subjects.

In 2005, with the approval of the Ministry of Education, the university mainly focused on degree education at undergraduate level while offering vocational and technical education and self-taught examination at university and college level outside the plan of official enrollment subsidiary. It covers Arts, Laws, Science, Business and Fine Arts.

The university has under it five secondary colleges and a fine arts department, containing almost 60 subjects at undergraduate and college level. The five secondary colleges are International Relations College, Foreign Languages College, Communications and Engineering College, Economy and Management College and Translation College.

♦ Beijing Oriental University

Established in 1984, this is a privately-run, full-time university covering many subjects. As one of the earliest privately-run universities, it was approved by Beijing educational authority to be one of the first pilot universities of diploma examination in1993.

It consists of 10 colleges, offering more than 60 subjects for more than 3,600 students enrolled at university and college level. The 10 colleges are the School of Business, School of International Logistics, School of Tourism and Hospitality, School of Modern Arts, School of Computer Science, School of Building Engineering, School of Arts and Legal Studies, School of Foreign Languages, School of International Language and Culture and College of Continuing Education. The university provides a full service for students with well-equipped teaching and living facilities. With strict management, the teaching strength and graduation rate are in the front ranks of privately-run universities.

♦ Independent Colleges

Independent colleges are secondary colleges at undergraduate level run by regular universities according to a new model of education. They are also private institutions of higher education combining the advantages of regular universities and social funds. As independent legal entities, these colleges have independent teaching and financial management, and the qualification for enrollment and issuing diplomas. Because of their private educational system, the independent colleges charge higher fees than regular universities, usually over 10,000 Yuan a year.

According to the country's related educational rules, independent colleges have the qualification of issuing a degree certificate. For example, if they meet the requirements, graduates of Kede College of Capital Normal University can obtain the degree certificate issued by the latter. In addition, according to the certain ratio governed by related policies and regulations, the students enrolled in specialized courses can take the National Adult College Entrance Examination organized by the provincial educational authorities in their graduation year. On the basis of their examination results, qualified students can continue their education at undergraduate level.

Outline of Ethnic Education

Ethnic education is an entire educational system ranging from fundamental to higher education, from general education to vocational and adult education. It includes preschool classes, primary schools, middle schools and universities run by the autonomous regions, as well as the ethnic primary schools, ethnic middle schools, ethnic technical secondary schools and ethnic colleges developed outside the autonomous regions but mainly enrolling students of ethnic groups.

People of ethnic groups live far from each other on a vast land. This is why the various forms of running a school are different according to their conditions. In basic education, the forms include: independent minority primary and middle schools, minority classes in key primary and middle schools, female classes and girls' schools in mountainous regions where Islam prevails or with a low enrollment rate for girls, and primary schools for herders, morning and evening classes, classes every other day and contracting teaching units in scattered settlements in mountainous and pastoral regions. As for higher education, institutes for minorities are specially set up and minority classes are held in ordinary colleges and universities.

Ethnic Minority Education

The Chinese language has been commonly used for economic and cultural exchanges and social intercourse in China, a multi-ethnic country. According to the PRC Law on National Regional Autonomy and the Compulsory Education Law, it is clearly stipulated that in schools and classes where students of an ethnic group constitute the majority, the spoken and written language used by the specific ethnic group may be adopted together with the commonly used language in China. Those who do not have their own written languages may use the commonly used language in China with their own language supporting the teaching. Meanwhile, it is also provided that "the State promotes the national use of Putonghua (common speech based on Beijing Pronunciation) and prescriptive words." These two acts formulate bilingual teaching in ethnic schools. Regions occupied by ethnic groups have formulated the bilingual education principle of mastering both Chinese and their own languages.

China is a unified country with 56 ethnic groups with the Han forming the majority of the population. Handicapped by many factors, including natural conditions, social environment and traditional culture, regions occupied by ethnic groups lagged behind in development and had a weak educational foundation. The Central Government has implemented the policies of ethnic equality, ethnic unity and prosperity for all ethnic

The pupils of Lhoba ethnic group

groups. Laws and regulations have been issued to grant and respect the rights to independently develop education in autonomous regions. In addition, special policies are put forward to support ethnic education, a move that helps the ethnic groups to enjoy rapid development from the former weak foundations. People of some ethnic groups who used to lag behind in social development now have access to college education, and some have even got doctorates. Besides, some academicians in Chinese Academy of Sciences and Chinese Academy of Engineering are also from minority ethnic groups. The education of ten ethnic groups has already been developed above the national average level.

Policies of Ethnic Education

According to the Law of the PRC on Regional National Autonomy, it is stipulated that schools mainly enrolling students of ethnic groups should use textbooks written in their own language, if possible, and give lectures in their own languages. High-grade students in primary schools or middle school students should have access to Chinese lessons, and the nationally-used Putonghua should be taught to them.

Except that the Manchu and Hui ethnic groups have already accepted Chinese as their language, the other 53 ethnic groups all have their own language, of which more than 20 have their own script. These ethnic written languages have all been serving the education to varying degrees. In China, more than 10,000 schools carry out the bilingual teaching in 21 ethnic written languages, and thus 60 ethnic languages and 29 written languages are used for bilingual teaching. Each year, more than 100 million textbooks of some 3,500 kinds in ethnic written languages are published.

Apart from the regular annual education expenditure allocated by national finances, subsidies for ethnic education also play a role. Since 1990, the Central Government has been allocating 20 million Yuan as subsidies for ethnic education each year. In 1995, a special fund began to be appropriated for compulsory education in poverty-stricken regions with 3.9 billion Yuan invested by the Central Government and 10 billion Yuan coming from local counterpart funds. Of these, 2.2 billion Yuan was invested to nine provinces and autonomous regions dominated by minority ethnic groups. Since the 1990s, the government has spent nearly $200 million in developing basic education in nine provinces and autonomous regions with concentrations of ethnic minority groups and nearly 200 minority counties in Hubei, Hunan, Gansu, Hebei, Heilongjiang and Hainan etc. This move has improved the situations of schools for basic education in poverty-stricken minority areas.

Modern Distance Education

Since the 1990s, with the development of computers and network technology, modern distance education has come into being.

In October 1998, the satellite broadcasting of modern education began aiming mainly at basic education especially in poverty-stricken area. At the beginning, it broadcast for 12 hours every day, and the first class was Satellite English Class for middle school students.

In 1996, Tsinghua University took the lead to introduce modern distance education, or network education. So far, the Ministry of Education has approved 66 common colleges, universities and China Central Radio and TV University to launch a pilot modern distance education.

At the beginning of 1999, the Ministry of Education began to implement the Plan for the 21st Century Education Rejuvenation Actions with the Modern Distance Education Project as a key construction project. Depending on the China Education and Research Network and satellite TV network, the Modern Distance Education Project is to upgrade the original equipment, build a high speed transmission network and high-medium speed regional network of the China Education and Research Network, combine satellite digital video broadcasting with the China Education and Research Network to set up the distance education system, and build the Central Educational Resource Center and the Central Educational Resource Database. All these efforts will help to form the mode of modern distance education and its perfect service system. Satellite TV education serves students dearly in mountainous areas, sea islands, pastures and other areas with fierce conditions.

Sixty-six common colleges and universities have set up 2,027 after-school learning centers, a trial that effectively promotes China's modern distance education to develop by leaps and bounds. Thus, a school management system of modern distance education in colleges and universities has basically been formed, comprising 66 common colleges and universities, nearly 2,000 after-school learning centers and nationwide Radio and TV Universities.

Distance Education for Primary and Middle Schools in Rural Areas

The three modes include 20,594 disk broadcasting areas, 49,598 satellite receiving stations and 6,934 computer classrooms.

The basic configurations of these three modes were:

Mode 1: disk broadcasting areas

TV sets, DVD players and disks of all grades in teaching units provided for the teaching units according to the readjustment of rural schools; students taught and tutored by playing disks.

Mode 2: satellite receiving stations

Satellite receiving system, computers, TV sets, DVD players and disks for all-six grades provided for central primary schools in counties. Numerous fine educational resources can be rapidly received via China Education Broadcasting Satellite transfer system (CEBsat). Meanwhile, disk broadcasting areas are also covered. One or two multi-media classrooms are set in line with the number of students.

Mode 3: computer classrooms

Satellite receiving system, network computer classrooms, multi-media classrooms, disk players and disks are provided for rural middle schools. Apart from all the functions described in mode 2, students can also enjoy a preliminary network environment. Each school is equipped with a computer classroom holding 30 terminals and a multi-media classroom.

Radio and Television Universities

These are a kind of distance education facility. Courses are taught via television although some liberal arts courses are taught mainly by radio. These universities are open to the whole society. All the students should take the entrance examination and, on the basis of competitive selection, those with a better performance can be enrolled. At present, there are 43 Radio and Television Universities and 600 branches broadcasting lessons via microwave network.

China Central Radio and Television University

Directly affiliated to the Ministry of Education, China Central Radio and Television University is a new-type university adopting nationwide distance open education via multi-medias including radio, television, textbooks, audiovisual teaching materials, courseware, and network. Preparations began to make for the establishment of the university in February 1978, and it formally opened on February 6 1979.

Now there are six departments, such as rhetoric, finance, engineering, teacher-training, foreign languages, agriculture and medicine, continuing education colleges, August 1 College, PLA General Staff College, College of Education for the Disabled, Tibet College, China Television Normal College, China Liaoyuan Radio Broadcast and Television School, and China Central Radio and Television Secondary Vocational School. Ten unified subjects are set for all students, including science, engineering, medicine, liberal arts, laws, economics, management, education and history. Based on these unified courses and the diploma-less education set in China Central Radio and Television University, other universities have appeared operating on similar lines. Among the derived courses, those that are also compulsory courses offered by China Central Television and Radio University account for no less than 60 percent in terms of credits. At present, there are more than 580 majors offered. At the end of the 20th century, China Central Radio and Television University was listed as one of the ten giant universities engaged in distance learning in the world.

China Central Radio and Television University

China Central Radio and Television University, as a member of AAOU and ICDE, has established a good exchange and cooperative relationship with Hong Kong, Macao, Taiwan and many countries including US, Canada, British, France, Germany, Japan, South Korea, Thailand, India, Singapore, Australia, New Zealand, Egypt and South Africa.

Website: http://www.crtvu.edu.cn

China Education and Research Network

CERNET is supported by the Central Government and directly managed by the Ministry of Education. As the largest national public network, CERNET is built and operated by Tsinghua University and other colleges and universities. It is also a national academic internet backbone.

Established in 1994, CERNET is the first IPv4 backbone network. By December 2003, the transmission rate of CERNET backbone and regional networks had reached 2.5Gbps and 155Mbps, respectively, covering nearly more than 200 cities in 31 provinces. CERNET's own optic fiber network had reached 20,000 km in length and its independent international export-links had exceeded 800M.

It has 10 regional centers and 38 provincial units. CERNET is the basic platform of Chinese educational informationization connecting 1,300-odd universities, educational organizations and scientific research institutes and more than 15 million users.

It is also the test base for research on the next generation internet. In 2000, DRAGONTAP, the switching center of China's next generation high speed internet, was established at the network center of CERNET. This is the first time for China to achieve the interconnection with the international next generation internet. March 2004 saw the opening of the trial network of CERNET2, China's first IPv6 backbone network. This is also the largest pure IPv6 network in the world.

Website: http:// www.edu.cn

China Education Television

China Education Television (CETV) formally began broadcasting on October 1, 1986. On October 1, 1987 it was renamed as China Education Television, CETV for short. CETV, affiliated to the Ministry of Education, is an important national professional organization of public opinion on television news. It is also one of the mainstream media with educational influence, and a distance educational platform with the largest potential.

It now boasts five channels and a platform of China educational satellite broad-band transmission network.

CETV-1 is a comprehensive channel servicing the capacity building of human resources

CETV-2 is a continuous educational channel, mainly broadcasting the modern distance educational courses of China Central Radio and Television University.

CETV-3 serves teenagers and communities in Beijing

CETV-air classroom channel mainly provides services for rural primary and middle schools, teacher training and farmers' education.

CETV-early education professional channel mainly provides professional information on the healthy grown-up of 0-to-8-year-old children.

China educational satellite broad-band transport network mainly transmits 12 sets of broadcast in the form of IP data for 13 organizations including colleges, universities, rural primary and middle schools, farmers and warrant officers' distance education.

Website: http://www.cetv.edu.cn

China Central Audio-Visual Education Center

China Central Audio-Visual Education Center, also called Basic Education Resource Center of the Ministry of Education, was founded in 1978 directly under the Ministry of Education. It is an independent incorporated public institution engaged in educational technology.

Presently, it is actively participating in the implementation of modern distance education in rural primary and middle schools. It provides nearly 80,000 schools concerned with distance educational resources via satellite and network for free, and offers them technical services including acceptance registration. Besides, it also carries out and has made achievements in many projects such as distance education of United Nations Children's Fund (UNICEF), the Sino-Canada enhancement of the development of fundamental education capability in Western China, the MoE-IBM innovative teaching of fundamental education, and the projects cooperated with US World Links.

China Central Audio-Visual Education Center emphasizes educational technology while training different kinds of people in various forms. It has provided training for more than 100,000 people, advancing the theory and practice on educational technology of the Director of China Central Audio-Visual Education Center at all levels, people with expertise and primary and middle school teachers.

China Education Satellite Broad Band Transmission Network Platform

China Education Satellite Broad Band Transmission Network Platform was formally put into operation in October 2000. It integrates visual and audio broadcasting in the form of IP data together, building the largest distance education professional service network with satellite interactive functions. It is the major front-end broadcasting platform of the pilot modern distance education for farmers. At present, it broadcasts five sets of TV programs and 12 sets of IP programs, mainly servicing the key national projects including rural primary and middle schools' modern distance education project, farmers' modern distance education project, warrant officers' in-service training, health network projects and credentials education. Now, many new media technologies are being integrated to build the largest learning platform in the world including digital TV, Direct Broadcasting Satellite (DBS), IPTV, mobile TV, handset TV and office-building TV.

Modern Distance Education in Zhejiang University

Zhejiang University is one of the four universities chosen to carry out the pilot modern distance education, and also one of the test units that Ministry of Public Health approved for national distance medical education. Since the beginning of enrollment in 1998, Zhejiang University has established a distributed distance education comprehensive running platform applying satellite communication and multi-network integration based on satellite networks, Internet, digital broad band networks and cable television networks. It has formed its unique modern distance education and the corresponding management pattern, and cultivated the first graduates with a Bachelor degree with the help of distance education. Taking the advantages of its subjects and depending on 129 off-campus distance education centers in 18 provinces and cities, Zhejiang University has established an on-line base for talent cultivation with the form of high school education promoted to undergraduate courses and professional training promoted to undergraduate course education. Its majors concern science, engineering, medicine, liberal arts, management, laws and agriculture. Currently, there are 30,000-odd students receiving credential education in Zhejiang University.

Website: http://sce.zju.edu.cn

Modern Distance Education in Peking University

Modern distance education in Peking University combines satellite communications with the computer network. Satellite digital broadcasting transmits the lectures delivered by professors mainly for classroom teaching, while the Internet transmits the courseware, Q and A and assignments for after-class learning. Students can attend lectures and study in an assigned teaching center, and can also, if conditions permit, use the network to study exclusively.

Peking University is in charge of drawing up the teaching plan and organizing the teachers in each institution and department to give lectures. Then, depending on the live broadcasting classroom, these lectures are transmitted via satellite. Nine off-campus distance education centers are set in eight provinces and cities for students to watch the lectures. Meanwhile, students can also choose a lecture to learn by request, and make use of the computer network to communicate with teachers in Peking University in order to discuss questions and thus get answers. The teaching center with the video conferencing system has been built for students and teachers to enjoy real-time communications.

The tuition fee for network education is generally some 10 percent lower than that for common higher education. Currently, students in Peking University have to pay 4,800-5,200 Yuan per year as the tuition fee, but those receiving network education only pay 3,000-4,500 Yuan per year.

Teachers

At present, there are 12 million teachers in China, with one teacher teaching an average of 20 students.

In January 1985, the Standing Committee of the NPC passed a resolution that September 10 would be designated as Teachers' Day. In 1986, professional titles of the teachers in schools of all kinds were listed as professional technical posts. The Teachers' Law of the PRC, promulgated in 1994, stipulates teachers' rights, obligations, legal position, treatment and management system in a more systematic way.

The teacher qualification system in China includes academic credential criteria as well as political behavior, professional ethics and teaching ability. Teachers cannot be employed unless they have obtained an accepted qualification. The employed teachers should be approved by educational administrations above the county level.

In-service teachers in primary and middle schools, if qualified, need to receive further training on a five-year cycle. The training is handled by 35 Teachers Training Centers of Higher Education, 240 colleges of education and 2,088 colleges of further education. In colleges and universities, according to the requirements of the teachers of different levels, the Ministry of Education makes the overall arrangements for teachers to attend the classes of advanced training for tutors, short-term seminars, pre-service training classes, classes for a master or doctor degree aiming at those with equal education, classes of advanced training for backbone teachers, single-subject classes of advanced training, senior seminars for domestic visiting scholars, academic vacations and overseas advanced training. With the overall improvement of teachers' academic credentials, the training for teachers in colleges and universities has turned to focusing on updating knowledge and comprehensively enhancing teacher quality.

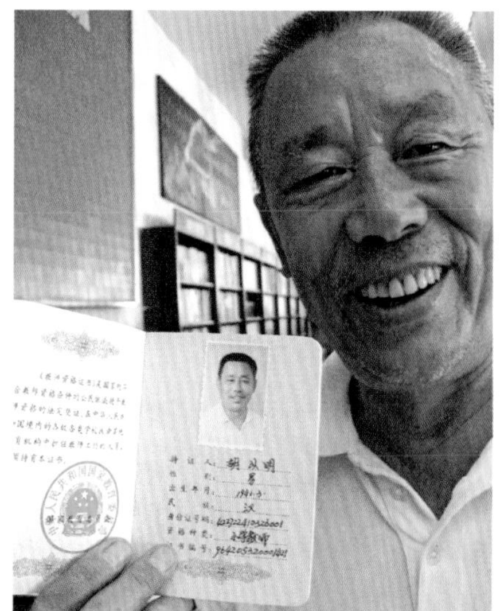

A teacher showing his own Teacher Certificate

System of Education Master Degree (EMD)

Since April 1996, China has begun to set EMD on a trial basis.

As a new type of education to obtain a degree, EMD is a professional degree with the occupational background as a teacher. It differs from a Master's degree in Education in terms of the basis for setting the degree, concrete cultivated targets, cultivation patterns, levels and methods. EMD has been playing a significant role in cultivating high-level talents for fundamental education and management. Some specialists in educational circles see this as a milestone in the history of education in China.

Since 1996, when there were only 16 test units, the number of cultivated colleges and universities has grown to 49, covering all the provinces, autonomous regions and municipalities directly under the Central Government except Hainan, Tibet, Macao and Hong Kong. At first, only in-service teachers in common high schools and administrative staff were enrolled; then in 1997, it also included full-time teachers in common middle schools and administrative staff; from 1999 to 2001, other kinds of teachers were added including full-time teachers in secondary schools who taught foundation courses, training-researching teachers with the post of a middle school teachers, primary school teachers and training-researching teachers or employees with the post of a middle school teachers in cities at or above the county level; in 2002, kindergarten teachers were allowed to apply for the entrance examination; in 2003, the enrolled students were extended to administrative staff in governmental educational departments with the post of kindergarten, primary and middle school teachers.

Normal Education

Normal education includes pre-service education for new teachers' training and in-service education for training teacher in active service. Normal education is mainly given by independent normal schools of all kinds.

Financed by the government, normal education is given the priority for development. Over a long period, the government has allocated special subsidies to improve the conditions for normal schools of all kinds. What's more, World Bank loans have been utilized to equip 50 normal colleges with four years' schooling, 106 specialized higher normal schools with two or three years schooling and 72 colleges of education. Funds from UNICEF and UNDP have been used to equip 203 common secondary normal schools (including kindergarten teachers and teachers of special education) and colleges of further education (training centers). Correspondingly, local funding has also increased for normal education.

Normal education integrates pre-service and in-service education together depending on modern educational technology and information transmission. For a long time to come, China's normal education system will continue to exist independently. Its objects are to take the initial step to establish the continuing educational system for primary and middle school teachers and headmasters, educate primary and middle school teachers to advance their academic credentials. Thus primary and middle school teachers can be cultivated in a diversified way.

中华人民共和国教师法
教师资格条例

• Teachers' Law of the PRC

According to the Teachers' Law of the PRC, "All Chinese citizens, who abide by the Constitution and laws, take a keen interest in education, have sound ideological and moral character, possess a record of formal schooling as stipulated in this Law or have passed the national teachers' qualification examinations, have educational and teaching ability may, after being evaluated as qualified, obtain qualifications as teachers." Moreover, to obtain qualifications for a teacher in a primary school, one shall be a graduate of a secondary normal school or upwards; to obtain qualifications for a teacher in a junior middle school, one shall be a graduate of a specialized higher normal school, or other colleges or universities with two or three years' schooling or upwards. Citizens without the records of formal schooling for teachers' qualifications as stipulated in this Law who apply for teachers' qualifications must pass the national teachers' qualification examinations. The national teachers' qualifications examination system is prescribed by the State Council. If a citizen who possesses a record of formal schooling as stipulated in this law, or who has passed the national teachers' qualification examinations, the departments concerned should evaluate and give approval in accordance with the requirements provided for in this law. Those with qualifications for teachers taking up their first teaching appointment undergo a probationary period. Those who have been deprived of political rights or subjected to fixed-term imprisonment or even more severe punishment for intentional crimes are not be allowed to obtain qualifications for teachers; and those who have already obtained qualifications for teachers must forfeit them.

International Exchanges and Cooperation

China has been carrying out the official international exchanges and cooperation in terms of education with United Nations Children's Fund (UNICEF), United Nations Development Program (UNDP) and United Nations Fund for Population Activities (UNFPA). Besides, China also cooperates with some other regional organizations including APEC, Asia-Europe Foundation (ASEF), Asia Development Bank (ADB) and Organization for Economic Cooperation and Development (OECD) etc.

Since the beginning of 1980s, China has undertaken a comprehensive exchange and cooperation with the organizations mentioned above in the fields of pre-school education, basic education, higher education, normal education, vocational education, distance education, textbooks for primary and middle school students, teaching aids, population education, population research in universities, and the development in human resources.

Bilateral Governmental Cooperation Programs

Now, the major bilateral cooperation programs of the Chinese Government include: The Australia-China (Chongqing) Vocational Education and Training Project (ACCVETP); the China-Canadian Strengthening Capacity in Basic Education in Western China Program (SCBEWC); the China-US Fulbright Program, US-China Friendship Volunteers, US-China E-language Learning System, Canada-China Scholarly Exchange program, Australia Asia Awards and The China-New Zealand Aid Scholarship.

Multilateral cooperation programs undertaken include: cooperation with UNICEF for strengthening educational arrangement and management, adjusting the educational content and process, long-distance education and advancing the elementary education in poor areas, collaboration with the UNDP in strengthening basic education in poor areas with the emphasis on girls, working together with APEC (Asia-Pacific Economic Cooperation) in developing effective schools, improvement of school management and enhancement of educational quality.

Exchanges between the Overseas Students

China has the largest number of overseas students in the world and also receives a large number of foreign students. With the fast development of teaching Chinese as a second language, China has been strengthening the international academic interchanges and implemented the multilateral intelligent cooperation and exchanges with the United Nations and other international organizations.

In 2006, "The Second Forum of the Deans of Chinese and Canadian Agricultural Universities" sponsored by Ministry of Education of PRC and Agriculture and Agri-Food Canada was held in Northwest Sci-Tech University of Agriculture and Forestry in Shaanxi.

The US, Canada, Australia, New Zealand are major destination countries for Chinese students to study. Now, Chinese students in these countries account respectively for more than 200,000 in US, 35,000 in Canada, 25,000 in Australia and 20,000 in New Zealand. Most of them study at their own expense. In recent years, an increasing number of foreign students have come to study in China as well.

China Provides Educational Aid to Developing Countries

In accordance with the government plan, China will further increase its aid in education to developing countries in the following aspects:

Firstly, arrange more school presidents and teachers of developing countries to be trained in China. The number of them is to be increased from 500 to 1,500 annually.

On November 30, 2006, Antipoverty Issue Research Class, one of the projects for external assistance of China completed. Some 41 students from 33 developing countries in the world finished their half-a-month study and investigation. Two students from Africa showed their Certificate of Completion on the Closing Ceremony.

Secondly, provide US$1 million in aid to the African Competence Construction Center and Children and Women Educational Center of UNESCO and conduct specialized research and training together.

Thirdly, aid to build up 100 rural schools in developing countries and provide these schools with needed facilities to meet their development needs for three years.

Fourthly, receive more overseas students in China and increase the chances of the Governments' scholarship. The Chinese Government has been providing scholarships to more than 6,700 foreign students annually. Two-thirds of them come from the developing countries. Moreover, since 2006 it has increased the number of recipients to 10,000 people annually and moderately raised the standard of scholarships.

Fifthly, increase educational aid to developing countries suffering from serious natural disasters such like earthquake, tsunami and hurricane.

AFS Intercultural Programs in China

AFS is an international, non-governmental, non-profit organization that provides intercultural interchanges around the world.

In 1957, AFS conducted interchanges between international middle-school students instead of the previous project hosting middle-school students studying in America.

In 1965, it began to carry out its Visiting Teacher Program. Its headquarters was located in New York. It has set up branches in 54 countries in the world.

CEAIE (China Education Association for International Exchange) is the only channel for AFS to conduct programs in China. AFS China office mainly shoulders the major task of coordinating the overall development of the AFS project in China, communication with the International AFS organization and other AFS branches, guiding the work of offices in different provinces and cities of the sending and hosting project, annual teachers' interchanges and short-term training projects of foreign teachers.

Since 1981 when China introduced the AFS project of middle-school teachers interchanges, some 1,000 teachers from 29 provinces, autonomous regions and municipalities directly under the Central Government have been sent to attend one-year-long cultural interchanges in nine countries including Asia, Oceania, North America and Europe. These teachers made conspicuous progress in language and the cultural understanding.

AFS Exchanges and Activities in China

In 1997, China sent the first group of students to foreign countries. AFS China has sent hundreds of students to some 30 countries to attend one-year-long cultural interchange activities.

The returning students continued their study in high schools. Many of them have become college students in domestic or foreign universities. A large number of the returning students have become volunteers of AFS, working diligently with the aim of the further development for AFS in China.

Since 2002, China has unveiled the host project and has received hundreds of foreign students.

These foreign students live with Chinese volunteer host families and study in local middle schools. They have been warmly received by Chinese families and established sincere friendship with the Chinese common people. As peace envoys, they play an active role in strengthening the non-governmental interchanges between China and other countries.

♦ China Educational Associations for International Exchange

China Education Association for International Exchange (CEAIE) is China's nationwide non-profit organization conducting international educational exchanges. CEAIE has a full commitment to developing exchanges and cooperation between the Chinese educational community and other parts of the world, promoting the advancement of education, culture, science and technology, and strengthening understanding and friendship among the peoples of all countries and regions in the world.

As its basic missions, CEAIE extensively conducts exchanges and cooperation by working together with educational and research institutions, academic bodies, exchange organizations, schools, enterprises, foundations and individuals in other countries and regions who are enthusiastic for supporting educational development on the basis of the principles of equality and friendship.

CEAIE and its local EAIE constitute the non-governmental network for Chinese international educational exchange. As the center of this network, CEAIE provides professional guidance and coordination to its 145 member institutions, local educational associations for international exchange in 31 provinces, autonomous regions and municipalities as well in 11 other cities. So far, CEAIE has established long-term working relationships with over 170 educational organizations in 53 countries and regions.

Now, CEAIE serves as the major significant platform for international educational cooperation and exchanges between non-governmental organizations of China and other countries. China has accumulated the working experience of participating and conducting the bilateral and multilateral international educational cooperation and interchanges in an extensive, overall and high-level way.

Address: Yifu Conference Center, No. 160 Fuxingmennei Dajie Xicheng District, Beijing
Website: http://www.ceale.edu.cn

Studying Abroad

China decided to increase the number of overseas students in 1978 and in the same year sent more than 800 overseas students with funding provided by the government. They specialized in natural science in some 20 countries including the US, UK, France, German, Japan and Canada. Since 1981, China has the self-funded students studying abroad, covering almost all disciplines.

From 1978 to the end of, some 1,067 million Chinese went to study abroad, and 275,000 came back.

At present, there are 792,000 Chinese people overseas for educational purposes, including 583,000 studying abroad, or engaged in cooperative research or academic visits.

In recent years, with the fast development of the Chinese economy, many overseas students choose to return to China and seek the opportunities for their further development. At the same time, there have been an increasing number of Chinese people who work abroad or achieve a permanent residence card to go back to China to attend the short-term academic conference or for giving lectures or for cooperative research. Many of them take full advantage of their professional knowledge to make a contribution to China.

Returned students favour the large-sized state-owned enterprises in job hunting.

Chunhui Program

To finance Chinese students studying abroad to return to work in China for a short period of time, the Ministry of Education earmarks special funds under the Chunhui Program.

Major recipients: People who have studied abroad and have gained a doctorate and have made remarkable academic achievements in their profession (including those who have got permanent residence or those qualified oversea students re-entering China).

Main aid form: provide a one way air-ticket to China

Main aiding scope includes: people engaged in science and research cooperation, academic interchanges and international conferences, organizing short-term symposiums, lectures, giving training and jointly guiding doctorate candidates, introducing technology for poverty eradication and development, participating in the technological renovation of State-owned large or medium size enterprises, and other short-term activities in China approved by the Ministry of Education or the Embassy (Consulate).

Aiding subjects, directions, projects and conferences of the Chunhui Program are annually arranged to meet the needs of China, mainly focusing on the cooperation and interchanges between universities and colleges directly under the Ministry of Education with the universities and institutions in the China's western regions.

Education for Overseas Students in China

Receiving and training foreign students is the important part of Chinese interchanges and cooperation with other countries. Now there are more than 400 universities and colleges recruiting overseas students from 160 countries and regions. The students who are not receiving a Chinese Government scholarship account for some 90 percent of the total. International students in the past tended to study in China not for degrees, but now more and more students are studying for their Bachelor's, Master's and Doctor's degree in China.

Foreign students in China mainly study in such subjects as Chinese, Chinese culture, Chinese history, traditional Chinese medicine and other subjects with Chinese characters, and in recent years the subjects for them expand to law, finance and economics, accounting and science and engineering.

The Chinese government is adopting measures to enlarge the scale of foreign students in China, for example, permitting foreign students to live in residents' families outside of campus so that they can contact common people in China and have further knowledge about China; and giving lessons in both English and Chinese in the stage of post-graduate students to attract students with lower Chinese level.

Classification of Overseas Students

Overseas students include language students, undergraduates, Master's degree candidates, Doctoral degree candidates, general advanced student, senior advanced students, research scholars and short-term course trainees of various kinds. The subjects for overseas students in China are mainly Chinese, Chinese culture, Chinese history, Traditional Chinese Medicine (TCM) and other majors with Chinese characteristics. In recent years, law, finance and economics, accounting and science and engineering courses have also been incorporated.

Depending on the different classification of overseas students, different teaching methods and training measures are adopted in China's universities.

Junior college student: teaching is arranged in line with the Chinese educational system teaching plan; and the length of schooling is two to three years. The overseas students attend classes together with Chinese students and will be awarded college diploma after passing the examination.

Language advanced student: holding a diploma equivalent to high school in China or above and taking remedial course of Chinese in China. The length of learning is generally one to two years. Certificate of study will be issued at the end of the training course.

Undergraduate: teaching is arranged in line with the Chinese educational system teaching plan; and the length of schooling is four to five years. The overseas students attend classes together with Chinese students. At the same time, some selective courses will be reduced while offering some new courses based on different conditions of the overseas students. Bachelor's degree will be awarded after passing the examination and finishing their thesis.

Master's degree candidate: teaching is arranged in line with the Chinese educational system and teaching plan for Master's degree candidates, and the length of schooling is two to three years. Under the guidance of the tutor, the overseas student will be awarded a degree after studying all the required courses, passing the examination, finishing a graduate thesis and passing the thesis defense.

Doctorate degree candidate: teaching is arranged in line with the Chinese educational system and teaching plan for Master's degree candidates, and the length of schooling is three years. Under the guidance of the tutor, the overseas student will be awarded a Doctoral degree after studying all required courses, passing the examination, finishing a doctoral thesis and passing the thesis defense.

General advanced student: students will attend classes together with Chinese students

Qualification of applicants for the Chinese Government Scholarship

1) Non-Chinese citizens in good health;

2) Requirements on the educational background and age of the applicants:

a. Applicants for Bachelor's degree shall hold high school diploma with excellent grades under the age of 25;

b. Applicants for Master degree shall hold Bachelor's degree under the age of 35;

c. Applicants for Doctoral degree shall hold Master's degree and be under the age of 40;

d. Applicants for the Chinese advanced students shall hold high school diploma or above and be under the age of 35;

e. Applicants for general scholars must have completed at least two years of undergraduate studies and be under the age of 45;

f. Applicants for senior scholars must have Master's or higher degree or hold academic title of associate professor or higher and be under the age of 50.

Application Documents for Chinese Government Scholarships

The applicants must provide the following documents:

1. Application Form for Chinese Government Scholarship (printed by the China Scholarship Council)

2. Notarized highest diploma and school report card; if applicants are university students or already employed, they should also provide documents of being university students or on-post employees.

3. Photocopy of Foreigner Physical Examination Form (printed by Chinese quarantine authority and only for those whose period of studies in China lasts up to six months).

4. A study or research plan written in Chinese or English (no less than 200 words).

5. Applicants for Master's or Doctoral degree studies and senior scholars must submit two letters of recommendation by professors or associate professors. Applicants who apply in China for Master's or Doctoral degree studies must submit the Admission Notice of the Chinese institution.

6. Relevant musical work for applicants applying for one of the music majors.

7. Those applying for undergraduate studies for science, technology, agronomy and medicine should submit the results of the Test of Mathematics, Physics and Chemistry held by the Chinese embassy or the transcript of their senior high school studies in their home countries. Those applying for undergraduate studies for economics and management should submit the results of the Test of Mathematics held by the Chinese embassy. Those who have been in China applying for undergraduate studies should submit the transcript of the entrance examination and Admission Notice of the Chinese institution.

8. Applicants for Chinese Culture Research Scholarship should submit the list of papers and publications.

according to their majors or selecting the courses like Chinese students, or they will be offered courses separately. The length of schooling is one to two years. Certificate of study will be issued at the end of the training course.

Senior advanced student: students will be provided with a tutor according to the subject they choose. Universities will assist them to arrange social investigation and visiting related to their subject. The length of schooling is one to two years. Certificate of study will be issued at the end of the training course.

Research scholar: scholars will be provided with teaching according to their subject. It mainly focuses on the research by the scholar himself (or herself). Universities will assist them to arrange social investigation and visiting related to their subject and negotiated beforehand. The time of research will be decided according to the needs of subject research.

The Chinese universities encourage foreign students to come to China for studying Doctoral and Master's degree, and welcome graduated overseas students who have returned to their own countries to come to China again for further study. Some universities offer courses to these students in their own languages.

Scholarships for International Student

The Chinese Government has established a series of scholarship schemes to sponsor international students and scholars to undertake studies and research in Chinese higher learning institutions.

The Ministry of Education is responsible for the provision of the scholarships, and entrusts the China Scholarship Council (CSC) to administer the recruitment of international students and the routine management of the program.

The international students under the Chinese Government scholarship Programs will be placed in Chinese higher learning institutions appointed by the Ministry of Education. There are over 300 specialties in science, technology, agronomy, medicine, economics, laws, management, education, history, liberal arts and philosophy available.

Chinese Government Scholarships

These were established by the Ministry of Education in accordance with educational exchange agreements or understandings reached with the governments of other countries, education organs, institutions and relevant international organizations to provide both full scholarships and partial scholarships to international students and scholars. The scheme supports students who come to study in China as undergraduates, postgraduates, Chinese language students, general advanced students and senior advanced students. Applicants may apply for the scholarship through the competent authorities, appointed institutions or the Chinese Embassy (Consulate General) in their home countries. The application period usually falls between February and April each year.

Full scholarship: A Chinese Government full scholarship includes tuition fee, fee for basic learning materials, accommodation, living allowance, fee for outpatient medical service, Comprehensive Medical Insurance of Foreign Students in China, a one-off settlement subsidy and a one-off inter-city travel allowance.

Partial scholarship: One or some items of the full scholarship

International traveling expenses: Applicants are expected to meet their own international travel costs unless it is set otherwise in bilateral agreements or arrangements.

Application Approach and Time for the Chinese Government Scholarships

Details on the application procedures should be obtained directly from the dispatching organization in the applicant's home country. The applicants can lodge application with the government departments concerned in their own countries which are in charge of studying abroad affairs or the local Chinese embassy. The application period usually lasts from early January to mid-April.

Annual Review of the Chinese Government Scholarship

In accordance with the Measures for the Annual Review of Chinese Government Scholarship Status, international scholarship students who have been approved to study in China for more than one year must participate in this process. The institutions will undertake to review comprehensively such aspects of the scholarship students as academic record, learning attitude, lecture attendance, conduct, rewards and punishment etc.. Those who pass the Annual Review will be qualified to enjoy the scholarship for the following academic year. Those who fail will have their scholarship for the following academic year suspended or terminated. Please refer to the attached Measures for the Annual Review of Chinese Government Scholarship Status for details.

CSC will send the List of Enrolled Students, Admission Notice and Application Form for Study in China (JW201) to the relevant dispatching authorities by July 31, so as to have these documents forwarded to the students. Students under Chinese Government Scholarship Program should apply for a visa to study in China at the Chinese Embassy or Consulate General with the valid ordinary passport, Visa Application for Study in China (JW201), Admission Notice, Foreigner Physical Examination Form (only for those whose study period is above six months), and come to the institutions in China for registration with these documents.

More foreigners come to China to learn Chinese now.

Choice of Higher Learning Institutions and Specialty

Applicants for Chinese Government Scholarships must choose their host institutions and specialties from among the institutions of higher education designated by the Ministry of Education. Please check the Directory of the Chinese Institutions Admitting International Students under Chinese Government Scholarship Program or the website of CSC (http://www.csc.edu.cn) for details.

China/UNESCO-The Great Wall Fellowship

This is a full scholarship scheme set up by the Ministry of Education for candidates recommended by UNESCO. Only general scholar candidates and senior scholar candidates are eligible. Applicants may apply to the UNESCO National Committee in the applicant's home country. The application period usually lasts from February to April each year.

Distinguished International Students Scholarship Scheme

This is a full scholarship or partial scholarship established by the Ministry of Education for the purpose of financing good students of good character that have been recruited or students pursuing a Master's or Doctoral degree to facilitate them to finish their study. Applicants may apply to CSC for the scholarship through the recommendation of their present or other recruitment institutions. The application time usually falls from April to June each year.

HSK Winner Scholarship Scheme

This is a full scholarship established by the Ministry of Education for those who achieve excellent results in Chinese Proficiency Test (HSK) abroad to study Chinese language in China for no more than one year. The age limit is 40.The applicants must submit an application to the Chinese embassy (consulate general) in their own countries or the sponsor of the test - the China Scholarship Council. The application time usually falls from February to April each year.

Chinese Culture Research Fellowship Scheme

This was established by the Ministry of Education to sponsor overseas experts and scholars engaging in research of Chinese culture to conduct short-term research in China. The applicants should be supervised by a Chinese supervisor or cooperate with Chinese professors in the appointed Chinese institutions of higher education to carry out their research and the length of research is no more than five months. The applicants should be under the age of 55, hold a Doctoral degree or have academic title of associate professor or higher, and have published or issued monographs or a thesis on the Chinese language, culture or history. The applicants should be recommended by Chinese higher learning institutions, organizations or the Chinese embassy (consulate general) in their home country. Applicants may apply to CSC through the Chinese diplomatic missions or Chinese intercollegiate institutions at any time.

Learning Chinese calligraphy

♦ China Scholarship Council

This is a non-profit corporate entity directly under the Ministry of Education.

The aims of the council are: in line with the State laws, regulations and related policies and guidelines, to take charge of the organization, financing and management of affairs related to studying abroad for Chinese citizens and foreign citizens studying in China, so as to facilitate exchanges in terms of education, science and technology and culture and economic and trade cooperation between China and other countries, strengthen the friendship and mutual understanding between China and other peoples, and promote China's socialist construction and the cause of world peace.

Financing comes from a special fund within the national fund plan for studying abroad. At the same time, the council also accepts donations and sponsorship from domestic and overseas friendly personages, businesses, social organizations and other organizations.

The tasks of the council are to manage the affairs related to studying abroad by legal and economic means; manage and use national funds for studying abroad, decide related financing projects and their approach, stimulate administrative regulations, and bring the usage benefits of the fund into full play; to be entrusted with the management of bilateral, multilateral or single scholarships, accept consignment by domestic and foreign organizations, institutions and individuals for the management of education exchanges and scientific and technological cooperation, finance the projects beneficial to China's education cause and friendly foreign relations; strive for donations abroad, expand the sources of funding and increase fund accumulation; establish contact with related organizations home and abroad, and conduct exchanges and cooperation.

Address: No.9 Chegongzhuang Dajie, Xicheng District, Beijing

Website：http://www.csc.edu.cn

Short-term Scholarship for Foreign Teachers of Chinese Language

This was established by the Ministry of Education for financing full-time teachers of various countries engaging in teaching the Chinese language to come to China for short-term research. The courses include four weeks of classroom instruction and two weeks of teaching tour that can be attended voluntarily. The applicants should be under the age of 50, hold a Bachelor's degree or above and have engaged in Chinese teaching for more than three consecutive years. The applicants should submit the application via the Chinese embassy (consulate general) in their home country to the China Scholarship Council. The application time usually falls from February to April.

Language Used in Teaching

Chinese institutions of higher education generally use Chinese as the instructional language. Applicants with no command of Chinese are generally required to take Chinese language courses for 1-2 years before pursuing their major studies. In some institutions, some courses set for general advanced students, senior advanced students and postgraduate students can be conducted in English.

Visa Application and Registration in China

1. Visa Application

Students under Chinese Government Scholarship Program should apply for a visa at the Chinese Embassy or Consulate General with the original documents and one set of photocopies of the admission notice, Visa Application for Study in China (JW201) and Foreigner Physical Examination Form and a valid ordinary passport. Those whose study period in China is above six month needs to apply for an "X" visa, and those who stay in China for up to six months should apply for an "F" visa. The scholarship students must enter China with the original copies of the aforementioned documents. Whoever comes to China with other types of passports, visas or without the original documents will not be able to register with the institution, nor will they be able to apply for residence permit in China.

2. Registration

International students must register with the institution at the time specified in the admission notice. Those who are unable to register on time must seek permission from the institution directly. Those who fail

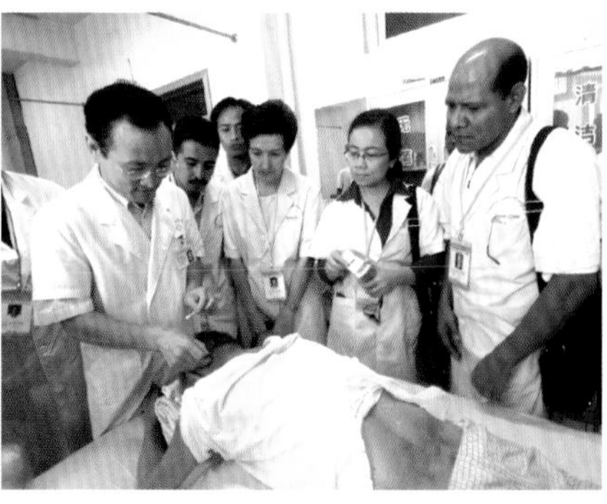

Some 40 students from Brazil, Belarus, Cuba and other countries attend the five-week training course on clinical application of Chinese acupuncture and moxibustion as well as massage technology.

to register on time without the prior consent of the institution will be considered as voluntarily giving up the enrollment and the scholarship will automatically be withdrawn.

3. Health Verification and Residence Registration

Health verification: Scholarship holders who are to stay in China for more than six months are requested to bring their passports, admission notice, and the original copies of the Foreigner Physical Examination Form and the Blood Test Report to the local quarantine office within the set time to have their medical examination verified. International students whose Foreigner Physical Examination Form do not meet the requirement will have undergo the examination again. Those who refuse to re-take the medical examination or are diagnosed as suffering from diseases that bar them from entering China under the laws and regulations will be required to leave. The costs of the medical examination and the international travel should be borne by themselves.

Residence registration: After health verification, scholarship holders must apply for a residence permit from the local police authority within 30 days of their arrival along with their passports, admission notice and Foreigner Physical Examination Form.

Transfer Service for Chinese Government Full-Scholarship Students

1. The CSC entrusts Beijing Language and Culture University to set up a Transfer Service Station for Chinese Government Full-Scholarship Students, which will provide free transfer service to new full-scholarship students who have to make a stopover in Beijing between August 25th and September 18th. The embassies in China or Chinese diplomatic missions concerned should give the Transfer Service Station one week warning in advance of the arrival date as well as full travel details. (The official address of the Transfer Service Station for Chinese Government Scholarship Students is: Department of International Students, Beijing Language and Culture University, No. 15 Xueyuan Lu, Haidian District, Beijing, 100083; Tel: 0086-10-82303706, Fax: 0086-10-82303087)

2. Those who arrive in Beijing before or after the aforementioned period or who have to make a stopover in cities other than Beijing will need to make their own arrangements to reach their universities. The universities will reimburse the cost of a hard-berth railway ticket between the port of entry and the city where the university is located.

Applications for Study in China of Non-Government Scholarship Students

Approach: 1. Inter-governmental exchanges: processed in accordance with the bilateral governmental agreement. 2. Inter-university exchanges: processed in accordance with the inter-university agreement. 3. Recommended by institutions: recommended by foreign universities, educational institutions and friendly organizations through China's competent institutions or directly to the Chinese universities concerned. 4. Individual application: students apply through China's relevant institutions or to the Chinese universities concerned directly.

Procedures: 1. Preparing application materials; 2. filling in Application Form for Study in China in accordance with requirements of the Chinese side; 3. Foreigner Physical Examination Form; 4. notarized diploma, curriculum and school report card; 5. Applicants for Master's or Doctoral degree studies and senior scholars must submit two letters of recommendation by professors or associate professors. 6. Applicants at their own expenses are requested to provide a certificate of a link-person in China and expenses guarantee in addition to the above materials. The materials must be in Chinese or in English or attached translation of this kind of words. Applicants may ask the Chinese embassy, consulate general or universities for the forms concerned.

Period for application: applicants for inter-governmental exchanges program should apply from February 1 to April 30. They should apply through competent departments responsible for dispatching overseas students. Applicants for inter-university exchanges programs who want be enrolled in the spring should apply from September 15 to December

15 of the previous year; and those who want to be enrolled in autumn should apply from February 15 to May 15 of the same year. Regulations may vary among different universities. General Rules for Admission and Application Form for Study can be obtained by asking relevant universities.

Applications for Short-term Course and Visa Application

Foreign universities and friendly organizations that plan to come to China for short-term courses may directly ask for Recruitment Procedures for Foreign Applicants from the Chinese universities concerned and negotiate the affairs relating to running classes. Individuals who apply for short-term courses may also directly contact the relevant Chinese universities and institutions.

Applicants must carefully fill in Application Form for Short-term Study for Foreigners printed by the Chinese higher learning institutions. And they should be in good health and between the age of 16 and 60.

Applicants who are admitted by the relevant universities should apply for an "F" visa at the Chinese Embassy or Consulate General with Admission Notice and Application Form for Study in China (JW202) and register at the university within the regulated period.

Expenses for Self-Supporting Overseas Students

For the convenience of self-supporting applicants for study in China in establishing a proper budget for expenditure, hereafter is an introduction to the charges of various universities of China. Detailed information about the real standard of charge may be referred to Recruitment Procedures for Foreign Applicants of various universities.

Arts: US$1,700-3,200 for undergraduates, Chinese advanced student and general advanced student; US$2,200-3,700 for Master's degree students and senior advanced students; US$2,700-4,200 for Doctoral degree students; US$350-1,200 per month for short-term students.

Science, engineering, agronomy, physical education and art: US$1,800-6,400 for undergraduate and general advanced students; US$2,500-7,400 for Master's degree students and senior advanced students; US$2,900-8,400 for Doctoral degree students; US$350-1,200 per month for short-term students.

Application fee: US$50-100

Accommodation fee: US$2-3 per bed/day (two students sharing a room with public toilet and bathroom), expenses for other standard rooms are decided by their quality.

Teaching materials fee: US$30-50 for arts and science; engineering, agronomy, medicine, physical education and art charge a higher rate.

Boarding fee: US$40-60 per month for a student eating in the international student dining room per month and US$20-30 per month for a student eating at Chinese student dinning room.

Entrance Examination and Assessment

Applicant language students and advanced students in China will be recruited on a selective basis according to their diploma.

Arts undergraduates will be recruited on a selective basis after taking the entrance examination or assessment with their diploma, and medium C-level certificate of the HSK test.

Undergraduates of science, engineering, agronomy and medicine will be recruited on a selective basis after taking the entrance examination or assessment with their diploma, and junior C-level certificate of the HSK test.

Master's degree applicants should take the entrance examination or assessment of the Chinese universities concerned with the Bachelor's degree, curriculum and school report card as well as two letters of recommendation by associated professors or higher. After studying in China and passing the examinations of the studied courses, they are eligible to write a thesis, or they will complete the course as advanced students. Applicants who are studying in China must take the unified entrance examination for postgraduates. University graduating students in China complying with the conditions of studying for a Master's degree while exempted from the examination will be recruited in accordance with the Method of Postgraduate Candidates Exempted from Admission Examination.

Doctoral degree applicants should take the entrance examination or assessment of the Chinese universities concerned along with providing the Master's degree, curriculum and school report card as well as two letters of recommendation from associated professors or higher. After studying in China and passing the examinations of the studied courses, they are eligible for writing their thesis, or they will complete the course as advanced students. Applicants who are studying in China should take China's unified entrance examination for postgraduates. Master's degree students in China complying with the conditions of studying for a Doctoral degree in advance may do so in accordance with the relevant regulations.

Applicants for undergraduates, Master's degree and Doctoral degree of institutions of art shall provide photos and a record of their art work and letter of recommendation of teachers.

Graduated overseas students from China enjoy priority in recruitment when studying in China again.

Self-supporting applicants for study in China will be recruited on a selective basis according to the result of examination or assessment organized by relevant universities.

Learning Chinese Kungfu (Martial arts)

Short-term Courses for Foreigners

Subjects include language, arts, calligraphy, economics, architecture, laws, Traditional Chinese Medicine (TCM), acupuncture, art and physical education. Short-term courses are available throughout the year. Some 200 universities accept short-term students.

Chinese language short-term course: conducted by comprehensive universities, institutions of arts and normal universities. Recruiting objects are foreign middle school students, members of friendly organizations, company staff and other personnel with a strong interest in Chinese culture. According to the Chinese level of the students, teaching is divided into three levels, namely junior, medium and senior.

Chinese culture course: teaching China's politics, economy and trade, foreign relations and traditional culture. The class is conducted in Chinese, English or provided with interpreter. Teaching is also combined with visiting plants, rural areas, residence district and places of interest.

TCM course: conducted by local TCM hospitals, including acupuncture, massage and internal medicine. Recruiting targets are foreign TCM physicians, acupuncturist, undergraduates and postgraduates of medical institutions who know Chinese or English. The teaching method is instruction in the classroom combined with clinical practice.

Law course: teaching Constitution, Civil Law and Economic Law of China as well as related laws and regulations concerning joint ventures. Teaching is combined with visiting law offices, informal discussions with law workers and auditing the hearings of case in the court.

Painting and calligraphy course: teaching theories and skills of Chinese calligraphy, traditional Chinese paintings (landscape, flower-and-bird, and figure).

Ancient architecture course: teaching the development history and the engineering technology of Chinese ancient architecture, visiting ancient structures and gardens of various styles with Chinese characteristics.

Cuisine course: teaching the features and cooking methods of various styles of cuisine. Each student has the opportunity for personal practice.

Physical training course: teaching traditional Chinese martial art, breathing exercise and modern sports. The teaching content may vary between different classes according to the needs of the organizer.

Preparatory Education in Chinese for International Students in China

Chinese is the major teaching language for international students in Chinese universities. Books, periodicals, and reference materials in university libraries and archives are mostly in Chinese. International students have to have a command of Chinese to a certain level in order to finish their studies smoothly. Undergraduates of science and engineering are admitted according to their diplomas, academic record credentials, and the primary stage C-level credentials for the HSK test. Undergraduates of liberal arts, history, philosophy and medicine are admitted according to their diplomas, academic record credentials, and the medium stage C-level credentials for the HSK test.

Undergraduates who didn't learn Chinese or whose Chinese proficiency doesn't meet the needs of subject studies before coming to China, have to learn basic Chinese for one or two school years upon arrival. Visiting students and graduate students taught directly in foreign languages still need to pick up some Chinese for convenience in daily life and study.

♦ Necessary Preparations

China is located in East Asia facing the Pacific Ocean on the east, with a terrain descending from west to east. Most of its areas lie in the northern temperate zone, and the continental monsoon climate is common across the country. In winter, the south-north temperature variations are large with the difference in the January temperature in Guangzhou, southern China and Harbin, northeastern China as much as 35 degrees Celsius on average. It's cold in winter, especially in areas north of the Qinling Mountains and the Huaihe River. So you have to wear heavy clothing outside. In summer, the temperature variations are not to so large, with the difference in temperature in Guangzhou and Harbin being only about five degrees Celsius on average. Skin protection against the strong sun is recommended. In spring and autumn, most of China enjoys a temperate climate, bright sunshine, and charming scenery. Light clothing is all right in most of places. Don't forget to buy health insurance and personal accident insurance.

You should ask for the approval of the accepting school for your family to accompany you, otherwise you will have to find lodgings for them by yourself. According to Chinese laws and regulations, international students are not allowed to obtain employment permit during study time.

♦ Affairs for Entering to China and Admission

International students should hold regular passports and come to China within the validity period of their visa. According to Chinese laws, international students must go through inspection procedures, border and customs checks for health and security checkup records for foreigners at the relevant departments within the due time, upon arrival.

Border check: International students generally should choose the nearest port of entry to their university. When entering China, they should undergo border checks and hand in their passport for visa check. Those holding an X visa should be registered within 24 hours for temporary accommodation procedures and within 30 days after entering obtain residence permission from the local public security department.

Customs check: When enter China, foreign students should complete a "passenger baggage declaration", and declare their carrying baggage to the customs.

Health check: When they enter China, foreign students should complete a "visitors' health declaration form" and show the "medical examination records of foreigners" or vaccination certificates along with the admission notice of the school. Those who fail to provide the required health records must undergo a fresh heath check by local Chinese health quarantine entities. Those who are then confirmed as healthy can then proceed to go through the procedures of residence and enrollment.

Admission: All foreign students who are allowed to register should report to the school within the period listed on the admission notice. If unable to report on time, they should obtain prior permission for the delay, otherwise they may no longer be eligible for entry. After foreign students finish registering at the school, they should go through the procedures for lodging, health quarantine, and registration fee and residence formalities.

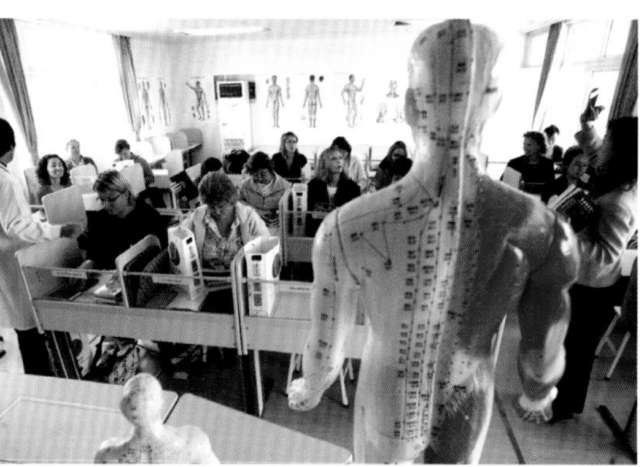

A group of foreign women are learning knowledge on traditional Chinese medicine at the international basic class on Chinese acupuncture and moxibustion, massage and skin scraping.

China-EU Student Exchange Scholarships Program

China and the EU have recognized that the strengthening of educational cooperation serves as the social and cultural foundation for the sustainable development of a comprehensive strategic partnership. In order to constantly meet the needs of young students learning Chinese and seeking to understand Chinese culture, China announced a five-year scheme to encourage students from European Union (EU) countries to learn Chinese. As from 2007, the government will provide 100 scholarships per year for young students. The scholarships will not affect bilateral students exchange arrangements with the 25 EU member countries.

Teaching Chinese as a Foreign Language

Teaching Chinese as a Foreign Language (TCFL) began in 1950, when Tsinghua University set up a training course for students from Eastern Europe, the first group received since the founding of the PRC in 1949. This training course is China's first specialized institution for teaching Chinese as a foreign language. In 1952, in line with agreements between governments, Zhu Dexi, a famous Chinese linguist and some others went to Bulgaria to teach Chinese. This was the first time for New China to send teachers abroad for this purpose. Ever since then, the government and relevant departments have made great efforts to promote TCFL. From 1961 to 1964, four groups of teachers received special training for teaching Chinese abroad, and they become the backbone of TCFL of China. In 1962, with the approval of the State Council, the Higher Preparatory School for Foreign Students was set up, later renamed Beijing Language College in summer 1965. It became a regular base for TCFL in China. Since the early 1960s, to carry out the agreements between governments, China successively sent teachers to foreign countries to teach Chinese, including such African countries as Egypt, Mali and Congo, and Asian countries as Cambodia and Yemen, as well as France in Europe. Since 1978, with the implementation of the reform and opening up policy, the overall national strength of China has enjoyed remarkable improvement, and the TCFL drive has accordingly entered a new era of vigorous development. In July, 1987, with the approval of the State Council, the State Leading Group for TCFL was established, involving the State Education Commission (now the Ministry of Education), Ministry of Foreign Affairs, Ministry of Culture, Foreign Affairs Office of the State Council (renamed the Information Office), Overseas Chinese Affairs Office of the State Council, the State Administration of Radio, Film and Television, the Press and Publication Administration, as well as the State Language Commission. In 1998, the leading group made adjustments to add three new member groups, namely, the State Development Planning Commission, the Ministry of Finance as well as the Ministry of Foreign Trade and Economic Cooperation. This is an indication of the government's emphasis on TCFL.

Up to now, there are more than 330 colleges offering Teaching Chinese as a Foreign Language (TCFL) programs in China, receiving about 40,000 foreign students to learn Chinese every year. There are TCFL programs of various types and levels, and a systematic teaching series and network of TCFL have been completed. There are almost 5,000 teachers of TCFL in China. In order to ensure their quality, the Guidelines for Teacher Qualification Evaluation of TCFL were promulgated in 1990, launching the teacher qualification certificate system of TCFL. More than 2,000 teachers have obtained the certificate so far. In 1992, the State Education Commission (Ministry of Education) promulgated the Guidelines for Chinese Proficiency Test (HSK). There are 36 examination sites in China and 35 abroad.

Since 1983, Beijing Language and Culture University (formerly Beijing Language College), Beijing Foreign Studies University, Shanghai Foreign Studies University, and East China Normal University successively offered bachelor degree programs of TCFL, aimed to train professional TCFL teachers. Some higher education institutions began to recruit students for master's degree programs of TCFL in 1986. In 1999, with the approval of the State Council, the first doctoral program of TCFL was set up in Beijing Language and Culture University.

Chinese language teachers from Russia are conducting warm discussion.

Chinese Proficiency Test (HSK)

Chinese Language Proficiency Test (HSK) is a national standardized test of the Chinese language level of non-native speakers (including foreigners, overseas Chinese and members of minority ethnic groups in China). It was established by the Beijing Languages College (Beijing Language University) in 1984, and was approved and examined by experts in 1990. And it was promoted overseas in 1991, and defined as a national examination by order No. 21 of the Commission of Education in 1992. Now, HSK has become a complete examination system including HSK (Basic), HSK (Elementary-intermediate), HSK (Advanced). By December 2005, a cumulative total of about one million people from more than 120 countries (including candidates from the minority ethnic groups) have participated in the examination. HSK is held annually at home and abroad. Examinations are held at designated points every June and October.The Office of Chinese Language Council International (Hanban) introduces the HSK Winners' Scholarship and the Chinese Bridge HSK Scholarship. Those with the scholarship may study in China for school year, one term or one year.

Sphere of Application of HSK

HSK (Basic) targets beginners who have studied Modern Chinese for 100-800 hours (including those with equivalent Chinese level). HSK (Elementary-intermediate) aims at elementary and intermediate learners who have studied Modern Chinese for 400-2,000 hours (including those with equivalent Chinese level). HSK (Advanced) aims at those who have studied Modern Chinese for over 3,000 hours (including those with equivalent Chinese level).

HSK are standardized tests to measure general language skills. It is based on any particular textbook or handbook, so there is no need for candidates to prepare specific materials for the examination. To understand the HSK Chinese language proficiency examinations requirement, candidates should carefully read the Chinese Language Proficiency Test Program, which comes is accompanied by a guide book, sample paper and answers, HSK vocabulary list and CD of the listening part of sample paper.

The Center of Chinese Proficiency Test (HSK) in Beijing Language and Culture University provides advice and services for people at home and abroad.

Websites: http://www.hsk.org.cn
http://www.blcu.edu.cn

The Chinese Proficiency Test (HSK) Overseas Exam Sites Distribution

Asia: Japan (Tokyo, Osaka, Kyoto, Nagoya, Fukuoka, Kanazawa, Sapporo, Kobe, Hiroshima); South Korea (Seoul, Taegu, Taejon, Busan,Kwungiu); Singapore (Singapore); Philippines (Manila); Malaysia (Kuala Lumpur); Thailand (Bangkok, Lampang); Vietnam (Ho Chi Minh City and Hanoi); Myanmar (Yangon); Indonesia (Jakarta, Surabaya, Bandung, Medan);

Oceania: Australia (Sydney, Melbourne); New Zealand (Auckland, Wellington, Christchurch);

North America: United States (Michigan, Houston, New York); Canada (Vancouver, Edmonton, Montreal, London, Toronto);

Europe: France (Paris, Bordeaux,, Marseilles, Rennes); Italy (Milan, Venice); Germany (Hanover); the United Kingdom (London); Russia (Moscow, Vladivostok); Finland (Helsinki); Austria (Vienna); Sweden (Lund); Denmark (Aarhus); Belgium (Ghent); Hungary (Budapest).

Chinese Language Proficiency Certificate

Chinese Language Proficiency Certificate takes effect in following affairs: of (l) providing certification of those who have reached required level of Chinese when they are involved in enrollment of the universities and colleges or when applying to attend the test of graduate degree programs in China; (2) providing certification for those who have studied the required Chinese lessons and mastered the relevant level of Chinese or could be excused from a required Chinese Lesson; (3) providing proof of the level of Chinese language as the basis for employers hiring staff.

Confucius Institute

Aimed at promoting friendly relations with other countries and enhancing the understanding of the Chinese language and culture as well as providing good learning conditions, the National Office for Teaching Chinese as a Foreign Language set up the "Confucius Institute", whose major activities includes Chinese teaching in countries that have the needs and conditions. At the same time, the "Confucius Institute Headquarters" has been established in Beijing.

The English name of this institute is "Confucius Institute' in honor of the famous thinker, educator and philosopher in Chinese history. His doctrine has a very important influence throughout the world. To name this

Logo of Confucius Institute

institute after him shows the longevity and profundity of Chinese language and culture. It also embodies the development trend of the integration of Chinese language and culture into the world in the new century.

The "Confucius Institute Headquarter" is to be established in Beijing and enjoys an independent legal person status. Its branches, the "Confucius Institute" will be set up abroad, with a Chinese name "XX孔子学院" (XX being the name of city where the institute is located and an English name "Confucius Institute in XX". Names in other languages will be translated from English.

The "Confucius Institute" is a non-profit public institute, usually with an independent legal person status, with a mission of promoting Chinese language and culture and supporting local Chinese teaching. It abides by the local laws and regulations and is subject to supervision and inspections from the local educational administrative authorities.

The locality of the "Confucius Institute" should be a rather busy business district where there is a large flow of people and a very convenient transportation system. The headquarters provides a teaching pattern and curriculum products as the main teaching resources for all the branches. Each branch in their teaching and evaluation work follows a unified set of quality certification systems and standards for teaching, testing and training. The "Confucius Institute" mainly offers training for special purposes for the public and professional training for Chinese teachers. All these training programs fall into the category of non-degree education. The teaching focus is applied Chinese. The headquarters also cooperates with universities in setting up on-campus Chinese centers to support degree programs like the Chinese language major and Chinese as a public course as well as research centers in the field of China studies.

Sino-African Education Minister Forum

China is the largest developing country and Africa is the continent containing the most developing countries, so the two areas share similar historical development experiences and a wide range of common interests. Especially in the field of education, the general level of development in China and in most countries in Africa is still relatively backward. In the process of developing education, they have to face common challenges and shoulder common tasks of development, and there is much to learn from each other through exchanges and cooperation. China has accumulated experiences for reference in the area of education for all African countries.

At the Sino-African Education Ministerial Forum held in 2006 in Beijing, there were ministers of education from

• The 111 Project (Program of Introducing Overseas Talents in Disciplines to Universities)

The 111 project (Program of Introducing Overseas Talents in Disciplines to Universities) is to aim at introducing and gathering more than 1,000 overseas academic talents to China. As a result, to form outstanding faculty groups and high-level research teams equipped with about 100 world-class academic innovation bases. The project will make efforts to create achievements in scientific research and enhance the overall research level and higher international status of China. The overall objective of 111 Project is to aim at the forefront of international developments in disciplines, as well as considering the real conditions of key discipline of higher learning universities and institutions round the state. The project will keep the national key discipline a foundation, keep the science research centers in all levels of national, provincial, ministry and commission level a platform, and to seek the talents from research centers in universities and institutions which rank the top 100 in the world. Each academic innovation base should employ at least 10 that kind of talents, including at least one academic super master, at least three academic core persons, and no fewer than six academic core persons doing short-term academic exchanges in China.

Overseas talents are required to follow the timetable drawn up by the Ministry of Education. Each academic master must work at least one month cumulatively every year, while each academic core person must work at least three month cumulatively every year. Generally there is one core person remaining at the base. The number of academic core persons exchanging in short-term should not be fewer than six persons or times.

Benin, Egypt, Republic of Congo, Kenya, South Africa, Nigeria, Mali, Guinea, Mauritius, Sudan, Ethiopia, Rwanda, Algeria, Mozambique, Tanzania, Djibouti, Mauritania, Senegal and Cameroon, as well as officials from the Chinese ministries of education, foreign affairs, finance, and commerce and UNESCO. With the theme of "Education development strategy of African countries and international exchanges and cooperation", the ministers conducted dialogues and exchanges. The issues involved were strategic planning and basic policy of developing compulsory education in developing countries, developing direction and development model of vocational and technical education, the training and professional development of teachers in primary and secondary schools, higher education quality protection mechanisms and measures and successful models of Sino-African exchange and cooperation in education. The holding of this forum brought new ideas to educational development and opened up various new areas for cooperation.

China Europe International Business School (CEIBS)

China Europe International Business School (CEIBS) was established in November 1994. The school is a non-profit joint venture established under an agreement between concerned departments of the Chinese Government and the European Union. CEIBS is the leading China-based international business school. Its main objective is to contribute to the economic development of the country and its business communities. It does this first in China by offering to MBA students, EMBA students, managers and senior executives of companies operating in (Executive Education students) or planning to enter China, the latest knowledge and a thorough understanding of current practices in international management, helping participants to adapt them successfully to their own business environment. The curriculum and degree of China Europe International Business School have been accredited by EQUIS and the Degree Committee of the State Council. Since 2001, China Europe International Business School has been successively listed among the world top 100 business schools rated by the prestigious British Financial Times newspaper. This makes CEIBS third in Asia, second only to Hong Kong University of Science and Technology and the Chinese University of Hong Kong in Asia. CEIBS was particularly eye-catching in that it was the only school from the Chinese mainland in the top 100.

China Europe International Business School's mission is to train its senior management personnel involved in China-based international business having the ability to fit to the global trend of economic integration, and enjoying international competitiveness of participating in international cooperation and with a strong will to assist China's economic development, and promote China's integration into the world economy.

In 2005, its EMBA program was ranked 13th in the world by the Financial Times , the fourth year to be listed among the top 50 worldwide.

In 2006, its MBA program was ranked the 21st in the world and first in Asia by the same newspaper.

Peking University

Peking University, the former Jing Shi Da Xue Tang (Metropolitan University) of the Qing Dynasty, opened in 1898. The Metropolitan University was then not only the most prestigious institution of higher learning but also the highest administrative organization of education in China. In 1912, it was renamed "Peking University", becoming a comprehensive university comprising departments of both liberal arts and sciences and emphasizing the teaching and research of basic sciences, and has been bringing numbers of talents for the country.

Peking University

According to incomplete statistics, among the teachers there are not only nearly 400 academicians of the Chinese Academy of Sciences and academicians of Chinese Academy of Engineering, and a number of influential professors in the field of humanities and social sciences enjoying world fame, but also a host of creative young and middle-aged experts who have been working at the forefront of teaching and research. Since the beginning of the reform and opening up, Peking University entered an unprecedented period of fast development and great construction, becoming one of two key universities of the national "211 Project" aimed at turning about 100 Chinese universities into exceptionally high quality academic institutions in the new century.

Peking University is situated in the western suburbs of Beijing, covering an area of 2,661,581 square meters. At last count, it had 16,073 faculty and staff and 29,617 students. The university has 221 specialties for master's candidates, 199 specialties for doctoral candidates, 100 specialties for undergraduates, and 139 specialties for 35 post-doctoral research. Peking University ranks first in the country in terms of academicians of the Chinese Academy of Sciences, State key laboratories and national key disciplines.

Address: No.5 Haidian Lu, Haidian District, Beijing
Website: http://www.pku.edu.cn

Tsinghua University

"Qing Hua Yuan", the main part of Tsinghua University, is located in the northwestern suburbs of Beijing, a private garden in Ming Dynasty that became part of the royal garden of Yuanmingyuan in the reign of Emperor Kangxi of the Qing Dynasty, named Yichunyuan; it was renamed Yichunyuan and Jinchunyuan during the reign of Emperor Daoguang and Qing Hua Yuan in the reign of Emperor Xianfeng.

Tsinghua University covers areas of 356 hectares, with a building area of 1.68 million square meters. Tsinghua University, with the garden-like landscape surrounding with many kinds of buildings, has inspired and motivated generations of students. It was established in 1911 originally as "Tsinghua Xuetang," a preparatory school for students to be sent by the government to study in American universities. The school was renamed "Tsinghua School" in 1912, becoming the "National Tsinghua University" in 1928.

Currently, Tsinghua is developing into a comprehensive university at a breathtaking pace with a complete curriculum that includes science, engineering, literary arts, law, medical, economics, management and arts. The university consists of 48 departments distributed in 12 schools, including the schools of science, architecture, civil engineering, mechanical engineering, information science and technology, humanities and social sciences, economics and management, law, arts and design, public policy and management, applied technology, and medical.

The educational philosophy of Tsinghua has so far cultivated 100,000-plus students. They include many outstanding scholars, eminent entrepreneurs and great statesmen remembered and respected by their fellow Chinese. Hence, to study at Tsinghua is the dream of many Chinese youths. Presently, Tsinghua has over 25,000 full time students, including 14,000 undergraduates, 7,400 master's degrees candidates and 3,700 doctoral candidates.

Address: Tsinghua University, Haidian District, Beijing
Website: http://www.tsinghua.edu.cn

Tsinghua University

Renmin University

Renmin University (People's University) is a famous comprehensive and a national key university that emphasize the humanities and social sciences, and management science. It was established in 1950, based on the former Northern Shaanxi Public College founded in 1937 in Yan'an, and later renamed North China Union University and University of North China.

Through 60 years of prudent and dedicated efforts, with undergraduate education as the base as well as an emphasis on postgraduate education, supplemented by adult education courses and online learning, it has formed a multi-dimensional structure and multi-level system in education and research. The university has become an important teaching and research base in the areas of the humanities, social sciences, and management science in China. It has a Graduate School which is responsible for the administration of postgraduate students. There are 11 schools of different disciplines, 13 departments and 12 college level research centers and tens department level research institutes and centers. The university has 41 undergraduate degree disciplines, seven second-undergraduate degree disciplines, 75 master's-degree programs, 45 Ph.D. programs, 14 of which are national key disciplines, or 20 percent of total of national literary arts key academic disciplines. In addition, the university has seven post-doctoral stations, including philosophy, theoretical economics, applied economics, law, sociology, history, business management; five national literary arts bases for personnel training in basic disciplines and scientific research, including philosophy, Chinese language and literature, history, Marxist theory and the ideological and political education, and economics. The university's research work ranks first in many disciplines: law school, economics school, management science school, philosophy school, history school and school of literature. Renmin University has worked hard to develop new disciplines such as information science and computer science, to enhance the arts and the science, to strive to be regarded as a comprehensive university with distinctive features and completely discipline structure.

Address: No.59 Zhongguancun Dajie, Haidian District, Beijing
Website:http://www.ruc.edu.cn

University of International Business and Economics

The University of International Business and Economics (UIBE) was founded in 1951 and focuses on assisting the country's rapid development and is a renowned institution at home and abroad. UIBE has more than 1,600 faculty and staff, including 656 full-time teachers and over 30 foreign experts as guest professors every year.

UIBE consists of 11 academic schools and one department. It has a School of Graduate Studies, School of international Studies and School of Physical Education. Among the 22 undergraduate, 16 two year long bachelor, 13 master's and doctoral programs, and two national bases for social sciences, UIBE offers, international trade, international economic law, English language and international business management courses that have been designated as key programs providing specialty advantages. UIBE's high level of professional education was recognized in 1988 by New York Public University when UIBE became one of the first universities authorized to carry out the latter's MBA program. The university has become one of bases of training senior officers of economic management in China, and there are 12 of this kind of training institute entrusted by the government or jointly commissioned with foreign countries. Academic publication plays an important role in the scientific research of international business and economics in China. There are ten research centers, including the World Trade Organization Research Center, World Trade Training and Research Center, Economic Studies, Research Center for Transnational Corporations, etc. The university produces eight academic journals, among them

International Business, Japanese Studies and Research, International Trade and Financial Science are important influences in the academic area. It publishes over 100 books every year and enjoys high reputation among the universities presses nationwide.

At present, UIBE has a total enrollment of more than 20,000 students, including all kinds of undergraduates and graduate students totaling over 8,000 (6,000 undergraduates and 2,000 graduate students). In addition, it has 1,400 students continuing their study in their spare time, and over 1,000 international students.

Address: No. 12 Huisin Dongjie, Chaoyang District, Beijing
Website: http://www.uibe.edu.cn

Central Conservatory of Music

Central Conservatory of Music was founded in 1950, and moved to Beijing from Tianjin in 1958. It is the only national key high art college in China.

Since its founding, it has evolved a complete system of pedagogy embracing courses of all levels starting from elementary classes up to postgraduate programs for master's and doctoral degrees. The conservatory has now departments offering undergraduate programs of study in composition, conducting, music education, musicology, voice and opera, piano, orchestral instruments, and traditional instruments for a period of four to five years; and other teaching departments including a basic education department, continuing education department, attached middle school and attached primary school. All these departments provide hundreds of professional music courses. It also equipped with the Institute of Music, violin making research center, center of modern electronic music, voice research center, musical therapy center, music education center of modern distance learning and the music community. It integrates research, creation and performance. It is a model both for the formation of a National Music Center to further develop the nation's musical traditions, creativity and performance level.

Now, the teaching and administrative staff totals 562, of which there are 278 full-time teachers, including 19 tutors of a doctoral students, 98 tutors of master's students, among whom there are 69 holding senior titles, and 119 with the title of vice-senior. The current enrolled students number is 1,665, including 538 undergraduates, 223 many kinds of students studying for degrees of all levels, 22 doctorate students, 52 master's degree students, 30 international students, 214 continuing educated students, and 586 primary and middle school students.

Address: No. 43 Baojia Jie, Xicheng District, Beijing
Website: http://www.ccom.edu.cn

University of Science and Technology of China

University of Science and Technology of China (USTC) is a key new type of comprehensive university established by the Chinese Academy of Sciences (CAS). It has become a national key university of science and technology, with emphasis on being at the forefront of science and high and new technology. It was founded in Beijing in September 1958, and was moved to Hefei City, capital of Anhui Province at the beginning of 1970.

USTC possesses nine schools, 23 departments, Special Class for Gifted Youngsters, Experimental Class for the Teaching Reform, Graduate School, School of Management (Beijing), Software School, School of Network Education, and School of Continuing Education. The Higher Graduate School of USTC was set up by the university and Chinese Academy of Sciences, branches being located in Suzhou City and Shanghai. The university offers 43 undergraduate specialties, 17 first-category Ph.D. degree programs,89 second-category Ph.D. degree programs, 105 second-category master's degree specialties. USTC also boasts three professional master's degree specialties of MBA, MPA and Master of Engineering, 17 post-doctoral mobile stations, 45 specialties for the post-doctoral mobile stations. The university is the key base for the education of the Ph.D. students within the CAS. USTC has three national bases for basic scientific research and the training of the talented teaching personnel in mathematics, physics and mechanics. USTC has 19 national key disciplines including basic mathematics, 19 provincial key disciplines including calculate mathematics. The university also boasts of three national research institutions of the National Synchrotron Radiation Lab, the State Key Lab for Fire Science and the National High Performance Computing Center (in Hefei City). The university has six CAS key labs of Bond-selective Chemistry, Structure Analysis, Structural Biology, Internal Friction and Defects in Solids, Quantum Information, and Mechanical Behavior and Design of Materials. The university also has some key scientific research institutions such as the CAS Research Center for Thermal Safety Engineering and Technology, and three provincial key laboratories.

The University has more than 1,100 faculty and staff numbers, 330 professional numbers, 22 CAS and CAE academicians, one academician of the Third World Science Institute, 312 tutors of doctoral students, 432 professors (including research fellows and professorial-level senior engineers), 564 associate professors (including vice-research fellows, senior engineers and senior technicians), and 110 post-doctoral fellows. It has concluded agreements of cooperation and exchange with around 100 universities and research institutions in more than 30 nations and regions. Around 300 international experts and scholars visit USTC every year for lecturing and collaborative research.

Address: No. 96 Jinzhai Lu, Hefei, Anhui Province
Website: http://www.ustc.edu.cn

China University of Mining and Technology

China University of Mining and Technology (CUMT) is well-established as a national university directly under the control of the Ministry of Education. After more than 90 years of growth, it has fully developed in the fields of engineering, sciences, liberal arts and management with engineering as its core. The university also successfully passed the preliminary qualification assessment for the "211 Project" and was included in the priority project for the development of national key universities.

The curriculum includes engineering, sciences, liberal arts and management with coal mining as its major discipline. CUMT main campus is located in Xuzhou City with 15 schools and one department with 49 undergraduate programs, and a Beijing campus with eight schools. There are five top disciplines for M.A. and Ph.D. candidates. There are 31 doctoral programs, 70 master's-degree programs and nine programs open to post-doctoral applicants. CUMT boasts seven national key disciplines, five provincial key disciplines and seven professorial-posts under the "State Yangtze Scholar Award Program".

CUMT has made great achievements in scientific research in the past 10 years. Over 7,000 different kinds of scientific research projects have been undertaken, including over 600 at national level (including over 90 national tasks, over 540 national natural science fund projects, and six national social science fund projects). Recently, the university has made efforts to cultivate qualified students meeting international needs. It has established academic exchanges and cooperation with nearly 50 universities and institutes from other countries, such as the US, UK, Germany, etc. It has hosted many international academic conferences.

CUMT boasts two beautiful campuses occupying an area of 120 hectares (main campus in Xuzhou is 100 hectares and Beijing campus 20 hectares.), and a building area of over 700,000 square meters (over 470,000 square meters in the main campus in Xuzhou and over 220,000 square meters in the Beijing campus). CUMT has excellent facilities. The library holds 1.69 million volumes. The university is equipped with advanced teaching and research laboratories, of which two are listed as State laboratories and seven as provincial key laboratories. And it boasts analysis and test center, rock mechanics and ground control center, CWS preparation centers, caving mining center and other institutes, centers and laboratories.

Address: Jiefang Nan Lu, Xuzhou City, Jiangsu Province
Website: http://www.cumt.edu.cn

China University of Political Science and Law

After half a century of development, CUPL has become a key multi-disciplinary university directly under the Ministry of Education with legal education as its major discipline, centered on the fostering of the political science, sociology, economics, management, literature, philosophy and other major disciplines.

It is the only higher education institution in China that offers courses in all the secondary disciplines of law. There are now 12 schools (departments), namely, Law School, Civil, Commercial and Economical Law School, International Law School, Criminal Judicial School, Politics and the Public Managerial School, Commercial School, School of Humanities and School of Foreign Languages. Today, over 21,325 students are currently studying in CUPL with a teaching staff of more than 1400, including 342 professors and associate professors, 92 doctorate tutors and 140 master's tutors. It is notable that the teaching and research areas of its legal faculty cover almost all the third-class disciplines of law.

In the past 50 years, it has supplied society with more than 10,000 political and legal talents of high qualification, most of whom have played important roles either in various government (judicial) agencies or economic entities or as the country's scholarship mainstays. It is estimated that, among all social service sectors nationwide, a tenth of the judicial staff and personnel of higher education are from CUPL.

The university has all along been committed to the application of its research achievements to the nation's legislative program and other practices. From the drafting of the 1954 Constitution to the promulgation of the Basic Law of the Special Administrative Region of Hong Kong, CUPL staffs have devoted themselves to the enactment and implementation of almost every major law of the country. Since it was rehabilitated in 1978, over 1,000 CUPL staffs have participated in the deliberation and drafting work of the nation's major legislations.

The university is the country's chief law exchange center. It has established various relations of regular exchanges and cooperation with more than 50 universities in 25 countries or regions. It is currently home to over 400 overseas students from 14 countries or regions.

Address: No.25 Xitucheng Lu, Haidian District, Beijing
Website: http://www.cupl.edu.cn

Beijing Language and Culture University

BLCU was established in 1962. It is the only international university in China with its main task set as the teaching of the Chinese language and culture to foreign students. Meanwhile it also undertakes the tasks of teaching foreign languages as well as Chinese, computer science and technology, finance and accountancy to Chinese students, providing training courses for teachers specialized in teaching Chinese as a foreign language, and offering pre-departure language training to candidates intending to go abroad. Since its establishment, the university has trained hundreds of thousands of foreign students who are proficient in Chinese and familiar with the Chinese culture, from over 160 countries and regions. Now, there are about 6,000 foreign students and over 2,000 Chinese studying every year.

Beijing Language and Culture University was the first teaching institution in China to provide degrees for overseas students. It is strong in its faculty and most influential in teaching Chinese as a foreign language and Chinese culture. It comprises the College of Chinese Language Studies, College of Foreign Languages, College of Intensive Chinese Studies, College of Humanities and Social Science (College of Teacher Training), College of Continuing Education, College of Information Science (Institute for Information Management and Technology), International Business School, Network Education College

Dormitory of Beijing Language and Culture University

(technical training centers), Physical Education Department, Chinese as a Foreign Language Research Center, Language Research Institute, Language Comparative Research Center and the Chinese Proficiency Test Center. The structure of disciplines is completely, from the short-term education, intensive education for undergraduates, master's degree study, to doctoral education, covering every academic levels, which are variety and available for all kinds of students.

The university has followed suit, developing partnerships with over 100 universities from 20 countries in the world, including Japan, the US, Italy, Germany, France, Pakistan, Tunisia, South Korea, Egypt, Australia, etc. Every year, the university receives hundreds of visiting experts, professors and celebrities, and sends more than 100 teachers and scholars to study or visit aboard. The university hosts some international academic conferences in different subjects annually. Joint teaching centers have been established in some other provinces and cities of the country, including Beijing, Tianjin, Shandong, etc. Overseas branch schools have been set up in South Korea, Singapore and Japan as remarkable results of education extension. And all this helps in accumulating experiences for further improvement.

Address: No. 15 Xueyuan Lu, Haidian District, Beijing
Website: http://www.blcu.edu.cn

Beijing Normal University

Beijing Normal University was the earliest established teacher-training university in China, which grew out of the Faculty of Education of Metropolitan University. It was renamed Beijing Normal University in 1923 and has become a most influential and important education and research base.

It comprises 48 bachelor's degree programs, 97 master's degree programs, 53 doctorate degree programs, and eight first level disciplines authorized to confer master's and Ph.D. degrees. The number of Ph.D. degree discipline ranks seventh in the country. The university has 16 national key disciplines and seven national bases for personnel training in basic disciplines and scientific research, six key research centers for humanities and social sciences of the Ministry of Education. It became a "national base for life sciences research and talent cultivation" authorized by the Ministry of Education in 2002. There is one national key laboratory, one national professional laboratory, six key laboratories of the Ministry of Education. In addition, it has one engineering works center under the ministry, one online research center, and one the institute of proteomics in Colleges and Universities of the Ministry of Education. The university has six provincial key disciplines, five provincial key laboratories, and two provincial engineering technical research centers. It is one of the innovation bases of science and technology in China. In 2001, it was allowed to build the Beijing Science and Technology University Park, and, in the following year, it was allowed to build a National Science and Technology University Park. Beijing Normal University has nearly 1,200 full time teachers. It has taken an active part in international academic exchanges and cooperation with more than 100 overseas universities and international organizations from over 30 countries and regions.

Address: No. 19 Xinjiekou Dajie, Beijing
Website: http://www.bnu.edu.cn

Beijing Jiaotong University

Beijing Jiaotong University (BJTU) is one of oldest key universities after the founding of the PRC. It is one of the first key universities authorized by the central government to confer master's and doctoral degrees, and to cultivate international students. BJTU was selected as one of the first universities listed in the "211 Project", and one of 52 universities allowed to set up a graduate school.

BJTU has developed into a multidisciplinary key university, featuring with stratified discipline structure of engineering, management, economics, science and humanities. The university is characterized information and communications, management and economic studies. Today, besides Graduate School and School of Continuing Education, the university has other schools, namely: School of Electronic and Information Engineering, School of Computer and Information Technology, School of Economics and Management, School of Traffic and Transportation, School of Civil Engineering and Architecture, School of Mechanical and Dynamical Engineering, School of Electrical Engineering and Electrical Power Studies, School of Sciences, School of Humanities and Social of Sciences, and what's more, there are three schools of vocational education and two on-the-job training centers for managerial personnel and technicians. It handles five State key disciplines, including Communications and Information System, Signals and Information Processing, Traffic Information Engineering and Control, Traffic and Transportation Programming and Management and Discipline of Industrial Economies. Besides, there are 15 ministerial key disciplines, 48 graduate programs, two special discipline master's degree programs (Master of Engineering and MBA), four first class Ph.D. programs, 21 second class doctoral programs and six post-doctoral scientific research stations. There are five disciplines granted the right to establish chairs under the State Yangtze Scholars Award Program. The university has set up graduate degree programs in a variety of first class academic fields.

Address: No. 3 Shangyuancun, Haidian District, Beijing
Website: http://www.njtu.edu.cn

Zhejiang University

Zhejiang University is a key national university with a long history. Its former Qiushi College was founded in 1897, one of the earliest institutions of higher learning founded by Chinese on their own. After more than 100 years of construction and development, with its solid foundation and strong, distinctive features, it has become a first level comprehensive university with a greater impact in the international research-based.

Zhejiang University is a key comprehensive university whose fields of study cover 11 branches of learning, namely philosophy, literature, history, education, science, economics, law, management, engineering, agriculture and medicine. The university now has 110 specialties for undergraduate studies and 39 post-doctoral stations, and it is entitled to confer master's degrees in 262 programs and doctoral degrees in 179 programs. In addition, it is entitled to confer first level doctorates and master's degrees in 31 programs and 10 clinical doctorate-level academics and other professional master degree authorized programs, including Master of Clinical Medicine, MBA, Master of Construction, Master of Law, Master of Engineering, Master of Agricultural Development, Master of Public Administration (MPA), Master of Oral Medicine and Master of Public Health and special master's degree promoting classes for teachers. Under its administration there are 12 national key laboratories, two national engineering research centers, three national engineering technology centers, two national humanity social and science key research centers, eight national teaching personnel training bases, three national basic courses teaching bases, one national base of education in cultural qualities for college students, one national IC personnel training base and one national model software college.

The university is rich in teaching resources. Among its 8,400 staff members and workers, there are 12 members of the Chinese Academy of Sciences, eight members of the Chinese Academy of Engineering, over 1,100 full professors and over 2,400 associate professors. At present, the total number of full-time students has reached over 40,000, including more than 16,000 undergraduates, nearly 10,700 postgraduates working for master's degrees and over 5,000 Ph.D. candidates. There are 26,000 two-year students and undergraduate students, over 800 international students, and also nearly 3,200 students taking courses for a professional master's degree, and over 29,000 students in degree and non-degree programs in on-the-job training, and over 16,000 remote network students.

Address: No. 38 Zheda Lu, Hangzhou City, Zhejiang Province
Website: http://www.zju.edu.cn

Wuhan University

Wuhan University grew out of Ziqiang Institute founded in 1893 by Zhang Zhidong, Governor of Hubei and Hunan Provinces in the late Qing Dynasty after his memorial to the throne was approved. Later, it changed its name several times before it was named National Wuhan University in July 1928. During the past 100-odd years, it has gradually developed a fine school spirit and study style of its own and has made many achievements through its courageous reform, opening up, and advancing in every aspect.

The campus is located between a lake and mountains. There are large traditional and modernized teaching buildings surrounded by many old trees. It is one of most beautiful universities in the world.

Entering to the new century, the university has vast developmental prospects with its rational structure of multiple disciplines and special characterizes. The university is a natural whole with the eleven disciplines of philosophy, economics, law, education, literature, history, science, engineering, agriculture, medicine and management. It has six departments of humanities science, social science, natural science, engineering, information sciences and medical science, and 30 colleges and three first level attached hospitals. It has 105 undergraduate programs, and has been authorized by the State Council to set up graduate schools. There are 22 first level and 143 second class disciplines authorized to confer Ph.D. degrees and 217 disciplines to

Wuhan University in winter

confer master's degrees. In addition, there are 20 disciplines have been evaluated as State-level key disciplines, and 20 listed as "211 Project" key disciplines, and 22 with chairs under the State Yangtze Scholar Award Program. Wuhan University is strong in scientific research. It has three national key laboratories, two national engineering technical research centers, eight national professional laboratories and key laboratories under the Ministry of Education and engineering research centers. In addition, it has six national key bases for the humanities and society science research, eight national bases for personnel training in basic disciplines and scientific research, one national base of education in cultural qualities for college students and 23 post-doctorate circulation stations. The university has established academic cooperation and exchanges with over 300 universities from over 60 countries, including exchange agreements with over 200 universities.

Address: Luojiashan Mountain, Wuhan, Hubei Province
Website: http://www.whu.edu.cn

Shandong University

Shandong University is one of the oldest and most prestigious universities in China. It was founded in 1901 and is the second national university established soon after Jingshi University (Metropolitan University). The Ministry of Education has approved it as a "national key comprehensive university."

Shandong University consists of 30 colleges and a graduate school. Courses are offered in 10 main academic disciplines: philosophy, economics, law, education, literature, history, natural sciences, engineering, management, and medicine. The university has six national key disciplines, eight national key laboratories, 41 provincial key disciplines and technology research centers; one national fundamental science personnel development bases and 10 provincial engineering technical development centers, four national bases for personnel training in basic disciplines and scientific research, one national base of education in cultural qualities for college students, three national key bases for humanity and social science research. There are 13 first class doctoral degree programs, 118 second class doctoral degree programs, 15 post-doctorate mobile stations and 199 master's degree programs. In addition, there are seven professional master's degree programs in law, business management, engineering, clinical medicine (including doctorate and master's degree), public health, dentistry and public administration respectively.

Shandong University embraces an abundance of scientific research facilities and favorable study environment. Over 121 experimental labs, teaching and research facilities hold equipment worth 600 million Yuan. The university has a building area of 1.4 million square meters. The university library houses a collection of over four million volumes.

It has established a broad international network for educational cooperation and has signed exchange agreements with over 50 universities from over 40 countries, including the US, Canada, Japan, France, Germany, Britain, Russia, Israel, and Australia. The university is active in academic cooperation and exchanges with over 100 educational and research institutions worldwide.

Address: No. 27 Shanda Nanlu, Ji'nan City, Shangdong Province
Website: http://www.sdu.edu.cn

Tianjin University

Tianjin University was established on 2nd October, 1895 with the name of "Peiyang University", and became one of the first national key universities in China in 1959.

Tianjin University is considered a comprehensive university with a core of engineering developing with science. Its disciplines include economics, management, humanities, law and education, and its curriculum is developed with a rational structure. The university has 15 academic schools, including School of Mechanical Engineering, School of Precision Instruments and Optoelectronics Engineering, School of Electric Engineering and Energy, School of Electronic Information Engineering, School of Civil Engineering, School of Architecture, School of Chemical Engineering, School of Material Science and Engineering, School of Management, School of Science, School of Social Science and Foreign Languages, School of Pharmaceutical Science and Technology, School of Environmental Science and Engineering, School of TV and Film and School of Agriculture and Biological Engineering. It provides 51 undergraduate specialities, 92 master's degree programs, 54 doctorate degree programs and 17 post-doctoral research centers. In addition, there are 17 engineering specialities. It is authorized to confer the professional master's degree (MBA and MPA). The university has 12 first-level disciplines authorized to confer Ph.D. degrees, 13 national key disciplines, which include fluid mechanics, optical engineering, measuring and testing techniques and instruments, material processing engineering, power machinery and engineering, electric power system and automation, measuring and testing techniques and automatic device, architectural design and theory, port, coastal and offshore engineering, chemical engineering, biochemical engineering, industrial catalysis and management science and engineering. Besides, it has 17 provincial key disciplines, which include engine combustion, chemistry and technology and sophisticated testing equipment. It also has three national key laboratories, one national engineering center, two national key research centers for the promotion of scientific and technological achievements, seven ministerial and commission-level engineering centers for experiments and research development.

Address: No. 92 Weijin Lu, Nankai District, Tianjin
Website: http://www.tju.edu.cn

Dalian University of Technology

Dalian University of Technology (DUT) formally was the Technology College of Dalian University, founded in April, 1949, and renamed the Dalian University of Technology in 1988. It became national key university, and set up its graduate school in 1986.

There are a total of 32,113 students of all kinds, including 9,259 full time graduate students, 16,300 undergraduates, 3,603 students at the school of continuing education and 170 overseas students. There are 3,069 faculty and staff, including 1,415 full-time teachers, and 19 academicians of the Chinese Academy of Sciences and the Chinese Academy of Engineering (including 10 employed by both). The university has a graduate school and 17 colleges with 29 departments.

DUT has developed into a comprehensive university, covering natural sciences, economics, management, social science and applied liberal arts, with the science and engineering sectors remaining its major fields. It has nine national key disciplines, 26 provincial key disciplines, 12 specially-appointed professors under the State Yangtze Scholar Award Program, 16 post-doctoral mobile station, 14 first level doctoral degree programs, 73 second level doctoral degree programs, 115 master degree programs, and two degree authorized subjects, MBA and Master of Engineering. The university provides 45 undergraduate subjects and three second undergraduate subjects.

It has four national key laboratories, one key laboratory under the Ministry of Education, three national technical centers, three national training centers, two provincial and ministerial engineering (technical) research centers, 35 separate research centers or colleges, and 60 research institutes. Since 1978, a total of 842 research projects have been rewarded, including 122 at national level, 352 at provincial or ministerial level. At present, DUT is active in academic exchanges and cooperation and has signed agreements with more than 108 institutions of higher education and scientific research in more than 20 countries and regions and over 50 big or medium- sized companies.

Address: No. 2 Linggong Lu, Ganjingzi District, Dalian, Liaoning Province
Website: http://www.dlut.edu.cn

Fudan University

Fudan University was founded in 1905 and has now become a national multi-disciplinary university with the widest coverage of disciplines, including humanities, social sciences, natural sciences, science and technology and scientific management. Fudan has 15 full-time colleges, including School of humanities, School of Foreign Languages, School of Journalism, School of Law, School of Economics and Management, Faculty of Engineering Science and Technology, College of Life Science, Shanghai Medical College, School of Public Health, College of Pharmacy, College of Nursing, College of Information Science and Engineering, Institute of International Relations and Public Affairs College. Fudan has 72 departments offering 60 undergraduate programs, 22 first-level doctorate programs and 112 second-level doctorate programs, 166 graduate disciplines, six degrees authorized, seven arts education key scientific research bases, nine national basic education research and teaching training bases and 25 post-doctoral research centers, 40 national key disciplines approved by the Ministry of Education. The number of national key disciplines ranks third in the country.

Logo of the Fudan University

Fudan now has an enrollment of 25,000 full-time degree candidates. Another 11,000 are studying at the schools of Continuing Education and Online Education. Besides, Fudan's population of foreign students ranks second in the country, reaching 1,650 today. It has a faculty of over 2,100 full-time teachers and researchers, including 1,300 full professors and associate professors, 25 academicians of the Chinese Academy of Sciences and the Chinese Academy of Engineering, 600 doctoral advisors, 26 chair professors under the Cheungkong Scholars Program, and two lecture professors, three distinguished professors of Fudan University, 10 invited chair professors, six chief scientists of Project 973 and 25 "Young and Middle-Aged Experts Nationally Acknowledged for Their Outstanding Achievements".

Fudan University has been one of most influential international academic centers, extensive working with international institutes, and actively taking part in academic exchanges. It has set up cooperative ties with more than 200 universities and research institutions from nearly 30 countries and regions in the world. There are more than 300 internationally-renowned scholars who received honorary doctorates, honorary professors and consultant professors and so on.

Address: No. 220 Handan Lu, Shanghai
Website: http://www.fudan.edu.cn

Sichuan University

Sichuan University (SCU) is one of the biggest national multi-disciplinary universities with the widest coverage of disciplines and the largest scale of operation in Western China. It has 28 discipline-related colleges and one sports department, including the Graduate School, School of Overseas Education, School of Continuing Education of Literature, National Model Software College and Network Education College, covering 11 disciplines of literature, science, engineering, medicine, management, financial, law, historiography, philosophy, agriculture and teachers training. There are 15 key disciplines at national level, 29 key disciplines at the provincial and ministerial level. It has 138 disciplines to grant doctor's degrees, 224 master's programs, seven specialized degree programs, 109 undergraduate programs and 21 post-doctoral stations. Besides, it has four national bases for personnel training in basic disciplines and scientific research, and one teaching base for engineering courses and one national base of education in cultural qualities for college students. SCU has a current student population of more than 43,800, of which 30,172 are full time undergraduates, 10,392 graduate and special discipline degree students, 2,740 doctoral students, 412 international students and 106 Hong Kong, Macao and Taiwan students. Besides, there are over 20,000 part time higher educated students and over 20,000 remote network education students.

There are two national key labs by function, six national engineering centers, 52 provincial key labs, four key research bases for humanities and social sciences, and four clinical research bases at the national level. SCU has undertaken a considerable number of national, ministerial and regional major research projects, and has made many achievements in liberal arts, historiography, math, agriculture materials, chemical, light industry, engineering, hydroelectricity, mechanics, textile, medicine, basic and clinical research sciences, which are rated first class in China and bear significant international influence.

The library holds about 4.8341 million volumes. The University Museum is the only one of its kind in China with a comprehensive collection of over 40,000 cultural relics and over 600,000 animal and plant specimens, ranking first in the country. The University Stadium is well- equipped. Other sub-divisions available are Campus Web Center, Analytic and Testing Center, University Archive Establishment, University Press, National Foreign Language Examination Center, Intensive Language Training Center. So far, the university has published 37 academic periodicals for domestic and overseas subscribers. It has set up exchanges and cooperation with over 100 famous universities and institutes of over 42 countries and regions in the world.

Address: Moziqiao Bridge, Chengdu, Sichuan Province

Website:http://www.scu.edu.cn

Harbin Institute of Technology

Founded in 1920, Harbin Institute of Technology (HIT), with science, engineering and research as its core, and encompassing management and liberal arts, has developed into an open, scientific research and multi-disciplinary nationally famous university. It now has 60 undergraduate, 85 master's and 57 doctoral programs, 15 post-doctoral mobile stations, and four national teaching bases. Among all these disciplines and programs, there are 14 special discipline master's and doctor's degree programs, 18 national key disciplines, 22 national and provincial (ministerial) key laboratories. The HIT faculty has enormous potential including over 3,020 teachers, including 18 academicians of the Chinese Academy of Sciences and/or the Chinese Academy of Engineering, 378 tutors of doctoral students, 629 professors, and 1,112 associate professors.

For years, Harbin Institute of Technology has taken the lead among universities in China to innovate scientific research and has consistently undertaken large-scale and highly sophisticated national projects. It has developed its discipline advantages of overlapping, cross-linking and army-civilian joint usage. The university attaches great importance to international exchanges and cooperation, and has increased funding, invited experts to give lectures and sent talents aboard for training and scientific research, as well as enrolling international students to study. Currently, the university has established extensive exchanges and co-operation with more than 300 influential universities and scientific research institutions in over 40 countries.

Address: No. 92 Xidazhijie Street, Nangang District, Harbin, Heilongjiang Province

Website: http://www.hit.edu.cn

Tongji University

Tongji University was established in 1907. Its predecessor, Tongji German Medical School, was founded by Erich Paulus, a German doctor in Shanghai. The name Tongji suggests cooperating by riding the same boat.

It has a School of Sciences, School of Architecture and Urban Planning, School of Civil Engineering, Mechanical School, School of Environmental Science and

Landmark building of the Tongji University—the Monument to the National Tongji University

Engineering, School of Material Science and Engineering, School of Electronics and Information Engineering, School of Traffic and Transportation, Medical School, School of Liberal Arts and Law, School of Foreign Languages, School of Economics and Management, School of Software Engineering and School of Ocean and Earth Science. In addition, there are the Institute of Further Education, Institute of Higher Technology, Institute of Vocational and Technical Education, Institute of E-Education, Women's College, Institute of Automobile Marketing and Sino-German Institute which is authorized by Chinese and German governments to run postgraduate courses. There are also Sino-France institutes of management involving cooperation with the High-Tech Group of the University of Paris. The university now has over 50,000 students at all levels from certificate and diploma courses to bachelor's degrees, master's, PhD programs and post doctoral attachments. There are over 4200 academic staff for teaching and/or research. The university offers diverse courses in its 81 Bachelor's Degrees, seven special discipline Master's degree programs, 141 Master's, 58 PhD programs and 13 post doctoral mobile stations. As one of the state leading centers for scientific research, the university has 15 State, departmental and provincial level key laboratories and engineering research centers. It has four university hospitals and three attached schools.

Address: No. 1239 Siping Lu, Shanghai

Website: http://www.tongji.edu.cn

Jilin University

Jilin University is a leading national university under the direct jurisdiction of the Ministry of Education. Covering 11 disciplines, including philosophy, economics, law, literature, education, history, science, engineering, agriculture, medicine, and management, it offers a variety of degree programs. It has now 115 undergraduate programs, 234 master's programs, 140 doctoral programs, seventeen post-doctoral programs and sixteen State key disciplines. Besides, there are 12 special discipline degree programs, and eight national bases for basic science research and talent cultivation. There are 62,764 full-time students among whom 3,316 are doctoral students and 10,614 are graduate students.

Jilin University has several hundred modern laboratories for research, including five key research bases for humanities and social sciences, five national key laboratories, seven key laboratories sponsored by the Ministry of Education and 11 by other ministries for the development of basic science. At present there are 5,824 faculty members, with 14 members of Chinese Academy of Science and Chinese Academy of Engineering, 1,011 full professors, 1,286 associate professors and 623 tutors of doctoral students.

It has eight campuses in five districts occupying 533 hectares. The new campus in Zhuhai city occupies 333 hectares with a first phase construction area of 125,000 square meters. The Library holds 4.9 million books and is designated as a library for UNESCO, UNIDO and the World Bank. It also serves as the Comprehensive Information Center of Liberal Arts of the Education Ministry, the only Foreign Scientific Text Book Center in Northeast China, and the National Humanities and Social Science Higher Education Books Import Center.

The university has established exchange and cooperation ties with more than 100 universities, colleges, and research institutes in over 40 countries/districts.

Address: No. 119 Jiefangda Lu, Changchun, Jilin Province

Website: http://www.jlu.edu.cn

Xiamen University

It was founded in 1921 by Tan Kah Kee, the well-known patriotic overseas Chinese leader and was the first university in China founded by an overseas Chinese. At present it is the only key comprehensive university directly affiliated with the Education Ministry in any of the five special economic zones. Xiamen University has 19 schools containing 36 departments and 66 undergraduate programs. Thirteen subjects have been assessed as "national key disciplines", eight subjects listed among the State key disciplines in the "211 Project" in the Ninth Five-Year Plan, and 11 subjects listed among State key disciplines in the" 211 Project" in the 10th Five-Year Plan; ten subjects are considered as "provincial key disciplines". In addition, there are five national base of training basic disciplines, one State key laboratory, six provincial key laboratories and research centers, four State key liberal arts research bases and 12 post-doctoral research centers.

Xiamen University has over 4,500 staff, including 1,743 full-time faculty and professional researchers, 16 whom are academicians of CAS and CAE (eight academicians of CAS, one academician of CAE, and eight adjunct academicians). Moreover, seven faculty members are on the State Council's Academic Degree Appraisal Committee. There are 262 tutors of doctoral students and 14 experts who have made outstanding contributions to the State. The university now has a total enrollment of over 25,000 full-time students, including 15,813 undergraduates, 7,387 master's and 1,060 doctoral candidates, 847 international students and 426 students from Hong Kong, Macao and Taiwan. In addition, the university has over 6,000 overseas correspondence students.

The university has established inter-university cooperative ties with 69 institutions of higher education outside mainland China. By establishing academic ties with 24 universities and colleges, 63 research institutes and 34 media outlets in Taiwan, Xiamen University has become one of the universities in mainland China most actively engaged in educational, scientific, and cultural exchanges with Taiwan.

Address: Xiamen University, Fujian Province
Website: http://www.xmu.edu.cn

Nankai University

Nankai University was founded in 1919 by famous patriotic educators in Chinese modern history, Mr. Zhang Boling and Mr. Yan Xiu. It occupies an area of 1.46 million square meters with a floor space up to 900,000 square meters. The total collection of the university library reaches over 2.9 million volumes. Besides its main campus, Nankai University also has campuses in Yingshui Lu, Teda College, Financial Engineering College in Shenzhen and a Graduate School in Yunnan Province.

It is considered a comprehensive university with a complete curriculum that includes the humanities, natural sciences, technology, management, life sciences, medical sciences and the arts. The university believes in the equal importance of science and the liberal arts, laying a strong foundation with practical and creative characteristics. It has 18 faculties, including a Graduate School, China APEC Institute, School for Continuing Education, Advanced Vocational School and Modern Distance Education School. Nankai University offers 67 undergraduate specialties, 116 Master's programs, 75 Doctoral programs, 10 first-class doctoral degree programs, 13 Post-Doctoral research stations. Besides, there are 18 national key specialties, 13 provincial and municipal key specialties, two national key labs, four provincial and municipal key labs, one national engineering center, eight national bases for basic science research and talents cultivation, one base for cultural quality education and four key research bases for humanities and social sciences under the Ministry of Education. The university has been active in structuring disciplines to meet the demands of producing talents and 21st Century economic development and social progress.

Nankai University

The university has a complete education system for producing undergraduates, postgraduates on master's and doctoral programs and post-doctoral researchers. Currently, it has an enrollment of 28,023 students, including 10,762 undergraduates, 1,144 two-year program undergraduates, 4,406 master's candidates, 1,609 doctoral candidates, 876 foreign students, 7,618 part-time students and 1,608 students on distance education program and 143 post-doctoral researchers.

Nankai University is a center for both education and academic research. A large number of achievements have been made. The number of SCI theses ranks in the top ten among Chinese universities. The number of national social science projects and those under the Ministry of Education, the funds allocated and the awarded achievements are all in an advanced position nationally. The university has established exchanging and collaborative relationships with more than 100 foreign universities and academic institutions.

Address: No. 94 Weijin Lu, Tianjin
Website: http://www.nankai.edu.cn

Nanjing University

Nanjing University was found in 1902 and has gradually developed multi-disciplinary programs in humanities, social sciences, natural sciences, technological sciences, life sciences, modern engineering and management. At present, it has 17 schools with 45 departments. It runs 70 undergraduate programs, 169 master's programs, five professional master's programs; 16 primary disciplines for doctoral degrees, and 102 Ph.D. programs as well as 18 post-doctoral stations. In addition, it has 28 national key disciplines, 10 provincial key disciplines, and seven national key laboratories. It also houses 11 national training bases for the research and teaching personnel in basic sciences and liberal arts, and three bases for humanities and social sciences research appraised by the Ministry of Education. Among the 2,000 teaching faculty, there are 636 full professors, including 23 academicians of the Chinese Academy of Sciences, three academicians of the Chinese Academy of Engineering, three academicians of the Third-World Academy of Sciences, and one academician of the Russian Academy of Sciences. There are two premier scientists for the "National Key Development Program in Basic Research", and also 18 middle-aged and young scholars nationally appraised for remarkable contributions, 58 winners of National Outstanding Youth Fund, 25 specially-appointed professors of the Yangtze Scholars Award Program, and 510 Ph.D. supervisors. At present, the university has over 37,000 students, including 8,600 Ph.D. and mater's candidates.

Nanjing University is one of the most active universities in China in international academic exchanges. Since 1979, it has set up links with more than 100 universities and institutions in nearly 20 countries, employed over 1,800 foreign scholars to teach and give lectures, held more than 120 international conferences, and more than 2,500 teachers have been sent aboard to pursue higher degrees and conduct research. In the meantime, more than 5,400 international students have studied at this university.

Address: No. 22 Hangkou Lu, Nanjing, Jiangsu Province
Website: http://www.nju.edu.cn

Huazhong University of Science and Technology

Huazhong University of Science and Technology is one of largest key comprehensive universities in China. It is scattered over 400 hectares of land. It has nine faculties: philosophy, economics, law, education, literature, science, engineering, medicine and management. It offers 63 undergraduate programs, 200 master's programs, 139 doctoral programs and 17 post-doctoral research centers. A number of other leading research centers are located here, three national engineering research centers, five national leading and specialized laboratories, and seven departmental level key laboratories. The university has more than 4,000 full time teachers, of which five academicians of the Chinese Academy of

Sciences, eight academicians of the Chinese Academy of Engineering, 511 tutors of doctoral candidates, 751 professors and 1,211 associate professors. The number of resident students is over 60,000 of whom more than 10,000 are graduate students, over 340 are international students.

Huazhong emphasizes fostering students' pioneering spirit and practical abilities and producing top talents as well. The university implements some measures, such as arranging the tutors for the best students, main subjects accompanying selected subjects, gaining both undergraduate degrees and undergraduate and master's link up training and other measures. It has established relations with around 100 foreign universities, research institutes, hospitals and companies.

Address: No. 1037 Luoyu Lu, Hongshan district, Wuhan, Hubei Province
Website: http://www.hust.edu.cn

East China Normal University

East China Normal University (ECNU) was founded in October 1951. It is situated in the Putuo District of Shanghai. Known as a "garden university", the campus is beautiful and the buildings combine European architecture and Chinese traditional style. The university has 15 full-time schools with 35 departments offering 55 undergraduate programs. It also has six State key programs, nine Shanghai provincial level key programs (covering 13 second level programs), of which one Shanghai provincial level top key program, one State key laboratory, three key laboratory under the Ministry of Education, two key laboratories under Shanghai and five key research bases for humanities and social sciences approved by the Ministry of Education. Besides, the training center of secondary school masters under the Ministry of Education is the only national base on training management for the key high school masters from some provinces.

The Graduate School offers nine first-level doctoral programs, 73 second-level doctoral programs, 118 Master's programs (including Master's Degree of Education, MPA and software engineering), and has 10 mobile post-doctoral research stations. In addition, the university has a Web School of Education and College of Continuing Education. Among the total staff of over 4,100, there are nearly 1,400 full-time teachers, including six national academicians and nearly 1,100 professors and associate professors, many of whom enjoy high reputation in their respective academic circles. In addition, the university has 32,000 students of all kinds, of which 18,000 are full-time, including 13,000 undergraduates, 4,000 graduate students and over 1,000 international students.

Address: No. 3663 Zhongshan, Beilu, Shanghai
Website: http://www.ecnu.edu.cn

Xi'an Jiaotong University

Xi'an Jiaotong University

The predecessor of Xi'an Jiaotong University was Nanyang Public University founded in Shanghai in 1896; it was renamed Jiaotong University in 1921. Xi'an Jiaotong University is presently a comprehensive university with the science as its major discipline, in combination with engineering, medicine, economy, management, liberal arts and law. It has 23 colleges (schools) and three affiliated hospitals for teaching. There are over 3,200 full-time teachers, including over 300 tutors of a doctoral graduate student and around 1,600 professors and associate professors.

The university has 32,766 full-time students, including 10,714 doctoral and graduate degree students. There are 65 undergraduate disciplines, 157 graduate programs and 102 doctoral programs. The university has 20 State key programs and 14 programs of the State Yangtze Scholar Award Program. It boasts six professional master's degree stations of engineering, medicine, MBA, MPA, and 18 post-doctoral research stations. The university has five State key laboratories, four national leading and specialized laboratories, one national engineering research center, four key laboratories under the Ministry of Education, one engineering center under the Ministry of Education, two key laboratories under the Ministry of Health, and 13 Shaanxi provincial level key science development and research centers, and one of the most efficient computer centers located in western China.

The university has established inter-school collaboration with over 100 universities and research institutes of more than 20 countries and regions, including the US, Britain, Japan and Germany. University alumni are all over the world. Each year it has academic exchanges and other activities involving around 1,500 people (times) from around the world. The university covers 3,465 hectares.

Address: No. 28 Xianning Xilu, Xi'an, Shaanxi Province
Website: http://www.xjtu.edu.cn

Lanzhou University

Lanzhou University was founded in 1909. There are 61 undergraduate disciplines, including physics, chemistry, biology, geography, history, national basic theoretical research and personnel training, a total of 89 master's-degree programs, two special discipline degree programs, 40 Ph.D. programs, five post-doctoral research centers, six national key academic disciplines and 15 provincial and departmental key academic disciplines are available. There are eight disciplines with special programs to accept visiting scholars. There are 35 research institutions, 84 laboratories, two key national laboratories, two key laboratories of the Ministry of Education, two national humanities and social science research bases. Currently there are nearly 23,000 students of all kinds, including 2,231 graduate students and 9,274 undergraduates.

Lanzhou University has around 2,000 faculty, special and technical staff, including over 700 professors and associate professors, 117 tutors of doctoral candidates, 480 tutors of graduate students, six academicians of the Chinese Academy of Science and Engineering; five faculty members of Lanzhou University are seated on the State Council's Academic Degree Appraisal Committee. There are also seven experts who have made outstanding contributions to the nation, seven winners of National Outstanding Youth Foundation and eight talented persons who gained the Cross-Century award.

The university is active in developing international educational cooperation through the international exchange of post-graduate students, visiting scholars and scientific research cooperation with universities and organizations in more than 30 foreign countries and regions including US, Japan, UK, France, Germany, Australia, Canada, Russia and Hong Kong.

Address: No. 222 Tianshuinan Lu, Lanzhou,Gansu Province
Website: http://www.lzu.edu.cn

Sun Yat-sen University

This is a name-brand institution of higher education with fine traditions in teaching and learning. In 1924, Dr. Sun Yat-sen, a great leader of the 20th century, founded this university personally, and inscribed in his own handwriting the school motto of "Study extensively; Enquire accurately; Reflect carefully; Discriminate clearly; Practice earnestly." It is a comprehensive university including the humanities, social sciences, natural sciences, technical science, medical science, pharmacology and management science. There are 21 schools and colleges, including the School of Humanities, Lingnan College, School of Foreign Languages, School of Law, School Political Science and Public Administration, School of Business, School of Education, School of Communication and Design, School of Mathematics and Computer Science, School of Physics and Engineering, School of Chemistry and Chemical Engineering, School of Geology and Planning, School of Environmental Science and Project, School of Life Science, School of Information Science and Technology, Sun Yat-sen Medical College, School of Fundamental Medicine, School of Public Health, Guanghua School of Stomatology, Nursing School, School of Pharmacology, as well as the Department of Earth Science, the Graduate School, School of Software, School of Network Education and College of Continuing Education, etc.

The university offers a wide variety of subject areas and complete disciplines. In the programs of graduate studies, there are 17 disciplines leading to doctorates and master's degrees, 137 specialties leading to a doctorate, 196 specialties leading to a master's degree; in addition, there are 11 branches of study leading to professional degrees, which are: Doctorate in clinical medicine, MBA, MPA, Master of Judicial Studies, Master of Computer Technology, Master of Environmental Projects, Master of Software Engineering, Master of Electronic and Communications Engineering, Master of Clinical Medicine, Master of Oral Medicine and Master of Public Health. The university has nine post-doctorate research floating stations of Chinese language and literature, history, mathematics, physics, chemistry, biology, fundamental medical science, clinical medical science, management, public management, philosophy, environmental science and engineering; 20 key disciplines at the national level and 31 key disciplines at Guangdong provincial level. In undergraduate education, there are 80 specialties in undergraduate programs, with six national bases of fundamental sciences research and training, such as philosophy, Chinese language and literature, history, physics, chemistry and biology, and nine undergraduate specialties of name-brand specialties at the provincial-level.

Sun Yat-sen University has abundant qualified faculty members. The university has the right to evaluate and confer the titles of full professor and associate professor. There are 12,230 faculty and staff members, of whom more than 500 are Ph. D. candidate supervisors, nearly 650 are full professors and over 1,010 are associate professors. The university has a batch of laboratories and research bases with advanced standards and complete facilities. The library has a collection of 4.34 million volumes. In addition to the traditional services of circulation of books and periodicals, X-copying and quick printing, it also offers various forms of electronic information service, such as internet browsing, database retrieval on compact disk, network database retrieval, DIALOG retrieval on line, UnCover service of special subjects and electronic document transmission. The library of Sun Yat-sen University has been assigned by the Ministry of Education as the center for storing documents of higher education in Southern China, one of the seven centers in the higher education document guarantee system in China.

Sun Yat-sen University is active in international academic exchanges. It has established academic exchanges with more than 100 well-known universities, academic institutes and societies in the US, Canada, Japan, Australia, Britain, France and Germany, and has signed exchange agreements with 40 of them.

Address: No. 135 Xingang Xilu, Guangzhou, Guangdong Province
Website: http://www.zsu.edu.cn

Sun Yat-sen University

Northeast Forestry University

Northeast Forestry University (NEFU) was established in 1952 and is located in Harbin, the center of the largest State-owned forestry region. The campus covers more than 100 hectares, and the university has three teaching scientific research and practice bases with a total area of 33,000 hectares, including Maoershan National Forest Park, Liang Shui State-Level Nature Reserve and Harbin Forest Demonstration Base for Northern Cities.

NEFU is presently a comprehensive university with forestry as its major discipline in combination with science, engineering, economy, management, liberal arts and law. The University at present comprises 16 colleges and two departments. It is running five post-doctoral stations, three first-level doctoral degree programs and 29 doctoral degree programs, 51 master's degree programs, four special discipline master's degree programs and 56 undergraduate programs. The university has six national and 19 provincial and departmental key academic disciplines. NEFU is the largest national higher forestry university with the most disciplines in the country.

There are more than 18,300 students of all kinds. Among 2314 teaching and administrative staff, there are 923 full-time teachers with one academician of the Chinese Academy of Engineering and five specially invited academicians, 160 professors and five members from the Discipline Evaluation Group of the State Council Diploma Evaluation Committee. More than 50 professors hold important positions in academic organizations both in China and abroad and more than 100 guest professors, domestic and overseas, are invited, too.

The university has the key Forest Plant Ecology Laboratory of the Ministry of Education, and four key laboratories of the Ministry of Forestry including a wood science and engineering laboratory. Besides the three bases in Maoershan, Liangshui and Harbin, it also includes 20 economic units like the Engineering Survey and Design Academy, which provide important conditions for the scientific research and the improvement in quality of instruction.

It has established cooperative relations with 43 universities and institutions in more than 20 countries and regions and carried out academic exchanges with more than 100 academic groups, and invited more than 500 foreign culture and education scholars to teach at the university.

Address: 26 Hexing Lu, Dongli District, Harbin, Heilongjiang Province
Website: http://www.nefu.edu.cn

Shanghai University of Finance and Economics

Shanghai University of Finance and Economics (SUFE) is a highly prestigious institute of higher learning. SUFE's history can be traced back to the fall of 1917 when a commerce program was established at the Nanjing Advanced Normal School. Based on theoretical economics with a focus on applied economics and management science, SUFE's approach is multidisciplinary, utilizing elements of finance, economics, management, law, liberal arts and science. The university has a contingent of 544 high level full-time teachers among whom there are 49 tutors of doctoral candidates, 277 professors and associate professors.

SUFE has three post-doctoral stations, 20 Ph.D. programs, 27 master's-degree programs (including MBA) and 25 undergraduate programs. Many dynamic national-level and university-level research centers serve as important think tanks. Among the most renowned are those covering the history of economic theory, accounting, finance and national humanities and social sciences, the Institute of Accounting and Finance, and the national training base of accounting and financial economics, and seven provincial-level key disciplines of accounting, financial, statistics, industrial economics, banking, international trade and business administration.

There are 17,000 students, including over 1,700 doctoral and graduate degree students, more than 6,100 undergraduates, 850 higher vocational students, over 8,000 adult-education students and more than 300 international students. SUFE also positively cultivates economic and management specialties for doctoral, master's and undergraduate students from Hong Kong, Macao and Taiwan regions who now total 100. The university's total area is 339,781.62 square meters divided into three campuses.

The university has embraced internationalization and regularly collaborates with such institutions as the World Bank's Economic Development Institute (EDI), the International Monetary Fund (IMF), and the United Nations Development Program (UNDP) as well as more than 30 universities from other countries and regions such as the US, UK, Japan, Netherlands, Australia, Canada, Russia, the Philippines, Vietnam, Hong Kong, and Taiwan. The University also works with international professional organizations such as the UK's Association of Chartered Certified Accountants (ACCA), Canada's Certified General Accountants (CGA), the USA's Life Office Management Association (LOMA), the UK's Chartered Insurance Institute (CII) and the British Insurance Actuary Association (BIAA) to establish and operate professional testing and training centers. Actively developing inter-university exchanges and joint programs is a SUFE priority. It has established long-term cooperative and exchange relationships with 20 institutions of higher education in 10 countries. SUFE was one of the first universities approved by the Academic Degree Office of the State Council to offer joint Chinese/International MBA programs jointly with Webster (USA) and Southampton (UK) Universities.

Address: No. 777 Guoding Lu, Shanghai
Website: http://www.shufe.edu.cn

Shanghai Jiaotong University

Shanghai Jiaotong University (SJTU) formerly the Nanyang Public School was founded in 1896. It is one of the oldest universities in China. Through its century-long history, it has inherited the old tradition of "high starting points, solid foundation, strict requirements and extensive practice," which has nurtured more than 100,000 outstanding figures, including a number of prominent politicians, social activists, entrepreneurs, scientists, professors and technical specialists. And it has made significant contributions to the thriving prosperity of the nation and the development of science and technology. It has developed solid foundations in science and engineering, along with other subjects such as management, agriculture, liberal arts, laws, and so on. It is a key university in China and a number of its disciplines have been advancing towards first class status in the world, such as communications and electronic systems, naval architecture and ocean engineering, automatic control, composite materials, and metal plasticity processing. A batch of burgeoning branches of learning occupies an important position in the country, such as large-scale integrated circuit, computer science, optical fiber technology and systems engineering.

SJTU has 20 schools, two directly affiliated departments and four non-academic schools of Continuing (Adult) Education,

Shanghai Jiao Tong University

Online Learning, International Education, and a Vocational School. There are 60 undergraduate programs, 146 master's-degree programs, 18 first-level doctorate authorized stations, 93 second-level doctorate authorized stations, 21 post-doctoral stations, which cover the subjects of science, engineering, management, agriculture, liberal arts, financial, laws, and education. Besides, there are four State teaching bases of physics, science mathematics, undergraduate culture and qualified education and life science and technology, 16 State key doctorate programs, nine Shanghai province level key doctorate programs, four State key laboratories, six ministry-level key (opening) laboratories, two national engineering research centers and one national technology transmission center.

SJTU boasts more than 2,170 professors, including 580 full professors and 840 associate professors, of which eight are academicians of CAS and 14 are academicians of CAE. There are 568 tutors of doctoral students, 23 professors of the Yangtze Scholars Award Program, 22 winners of National Science Fund for Distinguished Young Researchers and 11 winners of Young College Teacher Award. The proportion of doctoral degree professors reaches 44 percent. SJTU always focuses on high technology and key national research projects. In recent years, annual research projects have exceeded 1,500.

The school conducts cooperation with international counterparts in education, science and technology. Thus far, it has established ties with some 100 famous universities in over 20 countries and regions. They join hands in setting up joint labs, conducting personnel training, and organizing research in science. The school employs more than 20 internationally famous scholars as honorary professors, including Nobel prize winners such as Yang Chen Ning, Tsung-Dao Lee and Samuel Chao Chung Ting, and some 100 noted scholars as advisors or professors.

Address: No.1954 Huashan Lu,Shanghai
Website: http://www.sjtu.edu.cn

Culture

Language

Chinese

As one of the most commonly used languages in the world, Chinese belongs to the Sino-Tibetan family, which is one of the seven language systems. Chinese is the most important member in the whole language family. Apart from China, Chinese is also used in Singapore, Malaysia and some other countries.

The different languages used in the 56 ethnic groups in China belong to five different language families: Sino-Tibetan, Altai, Austronesian, Indian and Aryan. Among China's 55 minority ethnic groups, only the Hui and Manchu use Chinese as their main tongue; the other 53 minority ethnic groups use their own languages. According to statistics, there are more than 80 languages in China.

Chinese is the common language of the Han ethnic people, which accounts for over 90 percent of the population. It is one of the six working languages of United Nations.

The standard pronunciation of Chinese evolved from the official pronunciation of Northern China in the past few hundred years, namely Beijing pronunciation. It is called Mandarin on the Chinese Mainland, National Language in Taiwan, and simply Chinese in Singapore and Malaysia.

Pronunciation of Chinese

The syllables of Chinese are divided into initial consonant, compound vowels (sometimes with a terminal "n" or "ng"), and tone. The first letter is the initial consonant, the rest of the syllable is compound vowel, and tone is the level of the syllable.

In Chinese, tone is used to distinguish different words. For instance, "汤 (tang —), 糖 (tang /), 躺 (tang V), 烫 (tang \ )" have the same initial consonant [t], and the same [aŋ] as compound vowels (phonetic symbol in the square brackets). But the meaning differs with the varying tones. Orally, they are four different word elements (the smallest unit of meaning that a word can be divided into); in writing, they refer to four completely different characters. Tone is a format of how high or low a sound is of a syllable in speaking. Beijing pronunciation has four tones: the high and level tone, the rising tone, Shangsheng tone, the falling tone.

Guoyu Zhuyinzimu (Pinyin to National Language Conversion Table) is a collection of Pinyin letters based on the grapheme of Chinese characters, which emerged from the Ministry of Education in 1918. The table combines the main vowel and tail vowel, it continues to be used in Taiwan. On the mainland, Hanyu Pinyin Fangan (the Chinese Pinyin Project) was released in 1958, with Latin letters.

Chinese Pinyin has taken place of the Wade-Gilles System since 1978.

Chinese Pinyin

On February 11th 1958, the Hanyu Pinyin Fangan was passed during the 5th Session of the 1st National People's Congress. The Law of the PRC on National Common Language and Character confirmed Hanyu Pinyin as spelling tool and phonetic notation of the national common language and characters. Hanyu Pinyin Fangan became the international standard for the spelling of Chinese names.

Language Policy

According to the principle that all the ethnic groups are equal in the PRC, the government persists in the equality of languages and actively maintains diversification and their harmonious use. The Constitution, the Law of the PRC on Regional National Autonomy, the Law of the PRC on the National Common Language and Characters, the Education Law of the PRC, the Compulsory Education Law of the PRC, and many other laws all confirm the equality and coexistence of languages used by different ethnic groups; discrimination against language in any format is forbidden; every ethnic group is entitled to use and develop their own language and characters; the government encourages different ethnic groups to learn languages and characters from each other; it also persists in the spread of mandarin and the standard Chinese characters.

Use of the Chinese Language

According to the data in "The investigation on the use of Chinese Language and Characters" issued on Dec. 26, 2004, the population using mandarin as the main means of communication accounted for 53.06 percent, dialects for 36.38 percent and minority languages for 5.46 percent. The population using standard characters in daily writing accounted for 95.25 percent and the number who could use Pinyin was 68.32 percent.

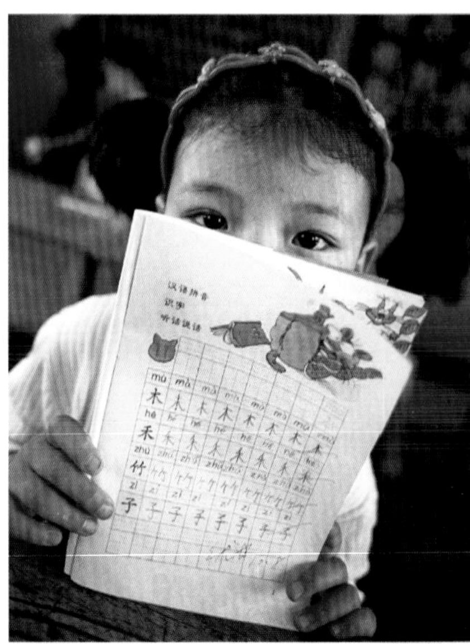

Pingyin and Chinese character

Syntax of Chinese Language

Most of the morphemes in Chinese are monosyllabic. Different morphemes can be combined as phrases [马 (horse) + 路(road) = 马路(street); 开(on) + 关(off) = 开关 (switch or on-off)]. Some morphemes can be considered as phrases themselves [手(hand); 洗(wash)], while some cannot, they have to be joined with other morphemes to become compound words [民—人民(the people); 失—丧失(lose)]. Disyllable words take the largest proportion in modern Chinese, and most of the disyllable words are made in the compound way mentioned above.

When compared with the Indo-European language family, Chinese has some important characteristics in syntax. One of the most obvious differences is that Chinese has no change in form. There are mostly two instances. Firstly, in the Indo-European language family, postfix can be added to verbs and adjectives to change only the syntax (transform into nouns) but not the meanings, for instance, -ness, -ation, -ment, in English. But there is no such device in Chinese. Secondly, there are finite and non-finite verbs in the former (infinitive, participle, gerund), but not in Chinese.

Chinese has an important characteristic in word order, namely all the modifiers should be in front of the modified elements. Thus, it is inadvisable to have long and complex modifiers in Chinese. When translating foreign languages into Chinese, the postpositive modifiers should be pre-posed. If there are too many modifiers, it will be difficult to organize sentences.

Chinese Characters

From grapheme, every Chinese character is a unique block-shaped character. As the root of the ancient culture, Chinese characters have undergone a long process of change, simple at first, then complex and finally brief today.

Chinese characters are only kind of the most ancient characters to survive in general use. In the world, there were originally ancient Sumerian and ancient Egyptian letters. However, the two disappeared successively and only Chinese characters remain extant. The population using Chinese characters is the most throughout the world.

Chinese is the common language of the Han people, as well as all the ethnic groups in China. A total of 21 ethnic groups had their own script before the PRC was founded in 1949. After that, government constituted different projects to develop characters for people of the Zhuang, Buyi, Yi, Miao, Hani, Lisu, Naxi, Tong, Wa, and Li minorities.

China has been coordinating and simplifying the modern Chinese characters ever since the 1950s. Standards like the First Chart of the Variant Characters, the Project of Chinese Character Simplification, the Final List of Simplified Characters, the List of Modern Chinese Characters, and the List of Common Modern Chinese Characters were constituted. And the Law of Character and Language for Common Use in the PRC confirmed the national place of Chinese characters. Standard Chinese characters are those that have been simplified and some inherited characters that are not simplified.

Mandarin and Dialects

There are standard language (mandarin) and dialects in modern Chinese.

Mandarin takes Beijing pronunciation as the standard, Northern pronunciation as basal dialects, and classic modern colloquialism as syntax criterion. The Law of the PRC on the National Common Language and Characters came out Oct. 31, 2000 confirming mandarin as the national common language.

China is a country with a vast territory and large population, so the situation in dialects is complex. Usually, Chinese dialects are cursorily divided into official and unofficial dialects. The official dialects are distributed over the northern area of the Yangtze River, the area between Jiujiang and Zhenjiang along the south bank of the Yangtze River, as well as Hubei, Sichuan, Yunnan and Guizhou provinces. There are north-official, Jianghuai-official, southwest-official regions. The similarity among official dialects is comparatively higher. People from Harbin in northern China have no difficulty in communication with people living in Kunming, Yunnan Province, in south China, though the two cities are thousands of km apart. The unofficial dialects are mainly distributed over southeast China, including Wu-dialect (south of Jiangsu province, greater part of Zhejiang Province), Gan-dialect (greater part of Jiangxi Province), Xiang-dialect (greater part of Hunan Province, northern part of the Guangxi Zhuang Autonomous Region), Yue-dialect (greater part of Guangdong Province, southeast part of the Guangxi Zhuang Autonomous Region), Min-dialect (Fujian Province; Taiwan; Chaozhou, Shantou of Guangdong Province; Hainan), Kejia-dialect (eastern and northern part of Guangdong Province, western part of Fujian Province, southern part of Jiangxi Province, Taiwan). The region of the unofficial dialects is smaller than that of the official dialects, but the differences among the former are more obvious; people using different unofficial dialects have great difficulty understanding each other. It is difficult to communicate even within a same region of the unofficial dialects (Wu-dialect in the southern part of the Jiangnan area and Wu-dialect in southern part of Jiangsu Province; dialect in Fuzhou and dialect in Xiamen, which are both within Fujian Province, for example).

Evolution of the Chinese characters

Evolution of Chinese Characters

Chinese script is the most unique writing systems in the world. It was quite advanced early in the 14th century.

Chinese characters originated from drawings and signs. It is difficult to determine the specific time when Chinese characters emerged. The oldest characters we see today are the scripts on the tortoise shells and animal bones of the Shang Dynasty (17th - 11th century BC) and scripts carved on bronze ware. Characters of the Shang Dynasty were much developed, so Chinese characters might have emerged long before the dynasty, perhaps as early as in the New Stone Age about 4,000 to 5,000 years ago.

Many simple signs and drawings were found carved on excavated earthenware. These signs, dating back to some 6,000 years ago, were considered as the seeds of later Chinese characters by most archaeologists and philologists. Chinese characters thus accumulated over time to become a canonical writing system. According to research, the primordial characters appeared during the middle stage of the New Stone Age. It took about 2,600 years to evolve into a primary system (known in Chinese as Jiaguwen (inscriptions on bones or tortoise shells of the Shang Dynasty that existed from 16th BC-11th BC), or inscriptions carved on animal bones or tortoise shells).

Number of Chinese Characters

The Chinese language has a large vocabulary; as for the total number of characters; perhaps nobody can give an exact figure. From records in ancient books about the Chinese characters and words, we can see their development in terms of numbers.

Dictionaries like Cangjie, Boxue, Yuanli, which were written in the Qin Dynasty (221-206 BC) showed that there were altogether 3,300 characters at that time. Xunzhuanpian compiled by Yang Xiong of the Han Dynasty (206 BC-220AD) collected 5,340 characters. *Kangxi Zidian (Dictionary of Emperor Kangxi)* compiled by Zhang Yushu in 1716, the most recent dictionary developed in the Qing Dynasty, included more than 47,000 characters.

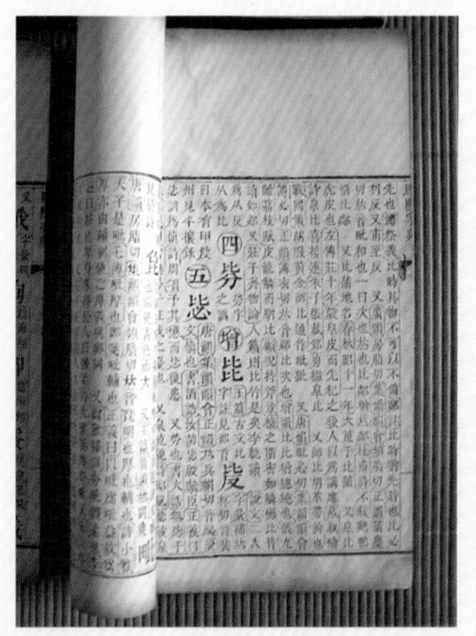

Kangxi Zidian (Kangxi Dictionary)

• Dictionaries

The first dictionary in the East might be considered as the *Erya*, which came out before the Han Dynasty.

From 30 to 124, *Shuowenjiezi* (Elucidations of the Signs and Explications of the Graphs) edited by Xushen of the Eastern Han, established the basic part of Bushou (traditionally recognized components (or radicals) of Chinese characters). *Shuowenjiezi* (Elucidations of the Signs and Explications of the Graphs) was remarkable among all the ancient character books.

The first formal dictionary *Kangxi Zidian* (Kangxi Dictionary) came out in 1716.

Zhonghua Dazidian (Zhonghua Great Dictionary) was printed by Zhonghua publishing house in 1915.

With the passage of time, dictionaries with more and more characters came into being. Zhonghua Zihai (Dictionary of China) compiled by Lengyulong, included 85,000 characters. But most of the characters in this dictionary are "dead characters", namely those abolished from the written language of today.

If there are several ten thousands of Chinese characters, no one would like to learn Chinese anymore. However, according to statistics, the thirteen books (Yijing, Shangshu, Zuozhuan, Gongyangzhuan, Lunyu, Mengzi and so on) have 589,283 characters in number, and the number of the different ones is 6,544. Which means, knowledge of about six or seven thousand of characters are necessary for most common purposes.

Word-formation of Chinese Characters

Traditionally, Chinese characters mainly have four ways of formation:

Pictographs: characters describing the shape of an object by lines, as long as the object truly exists and has exact shape to represent. For instance, the character"日" (the sun), "月"(moon) "木"(wood), and "水"(water). But there are also many objects and phenomena that cannot be shaped, thus there are only a few of pictographs among Chinese characters.

Indicatives: refer to characters that employ a kind of sign to indicate certain meaning, sometimes are on the base of pictographs. For instance, "上"(up), "下"(down), "刃"(blade).

Ideatives: these are characters formed by combining simple elements, which are usually characters themselves, to provide new meanings.

Harmonics: these involve two categories, namely characters formed with a component indicating the pronunciation and a component indicating the meaning. For instance, "想"(think), "枫"(maple), "湖"(lake). Harmonics are very useful, and more than 80 percent of Chinese characters are formed in this way.

Grapheme of Chinese Characters

From antiquity to modern times, the grapheme of the Chinese character had changed a lot. Jiaguwen (inscriptions on bones or tortoise shells of the Shang Dynasty that existed from 1600-1046 BC), Jinwen (inscriptions on ancient bronze objects), Zhuanshu (seal character), Lishu (official script), Kaishu (regular script) took about 3000 years for the evolvement. Jiaguwen (inscriptions on bones or tortoise shells of the Shang Dynasty was a script carved on tortoise shells and animal bones in the Shang Dynasty; Jinwen (inscriptions on ancient bronze objects) is a kind of inscription carved on bronze ware, which was used in the Zhou Dynasty (1046-771 BC), and was also called Zhongdingwen. Zhuanshu (seal character) appeared in the Qin Dynasty (221-206 BC); Lishu (official script) belonged to the Qin and Han Dynasty (221 BC-220 AD); and Kaishu (regular script) has been used from the Eastern Han Dynasty (206 BC-25AD) until today, and has become the general standard.

Writing with brush has become a craft

From the processes, we can tell that the final trend for developing Chinese character is to simplification. It prefers simple to complex, standardizing not only the grapheme but also the amount. The problem that Chinese characters are difficult to identify and write out is being improved gradually.

The "Simplified Characters" published in 1986 contain 2,200 simplified Chinese characters (including the characters that have their side parts simplified).

qiáo	10画			木		
桥	桥梁 石桥 桥洞 过桥					
	一	十	才	木	木丿	木𠂉
	木𠂉丿	木夭	木夭丿	桥		

huā	7画			艹		
花	花卉 鲜花 花生 花样					
	一	十	艹	艹丿	艹亻	艹亻丿
	花					

Pingyin and strokes of Chinese character

13 Culture

Chinese Characters and Names

In ancient times, one's surname, first name, and style (字) were always closely related to identity, status, family and occupation. Not everyone had both a family name and first name, or style (字).

Family name was a product of matriarchy, a symbol of one's family line. The first name was a symbol to distinguish status. It was developed on the basis of the surname.

There is almost no difference between one's surname and first name today.

Style (字) was actually derived from name, and they were closely connected. People could guess the one's style from his name or vice versa while talking, and the visual impression in writing was also great; it showed the connection between name and style. For instance, Kongli, took Boyu as style; Jiyun, took Xiaolan as style; and Hongwu, took Tongsheng as style.

Today, apart from a few clerisies, Chinese use no style. According to Zhongguoxingshi Huibian (Gallery of Chinese Surnames), there are about 5,730 Chinese surnames (including the single surname and the complex surname) presently.

Chinese Characters and Couplets

The couplet, also called Pillar Posters or Antithetical Couplet, is a pair of lines of poetry that are usually rhymed. It can deliver profound meaning by simple language, level and oblique tones and antithesis. It is a derivative of Chinese characters and literature and is unique in the Chinese culture.

The couplet evolved from rhymed sentences in the poems of eight lines, and kept some of the poem's characteristics. Like the eight-line poem, the couplet has level and oblique tones and antithesis. The upper line should have a level tone, and the lower line should have an oblique tone. The format is easy to control. There are couplets of four characters, five characters, six, seven, eight, nine, ten, or even dozens of characters. Some of the couplets in ancient architecture had hundreds of characters.

Whether for description or expression, the author should be an expert in summary. In this way, he would perfectly show not only the characters, as well as his spirit.

Pillar Posters are couplets pasted on pillars of ancient architecture. It is a unique format of Chinese culture. It firstly appeared in the Five Dynasties (907-960), and became common in the Ming (1368-1644) and Qing (1616-1911) Dynasties .

Chinese Language Proficiency Test

Chinese Characters and Chinese Seal Cutting

As an art form born out of the combination of calligraphy (mainly seal script) and carving (chiseling and casting), Chinese seal cutting is a unique format of Chinese characters. Seal cutting has a history of 500 years since the Ming and Qing Dynasties .

Ancient seal-cutting as an art that existed as early as the Spring and Autumn Period (770-476 BC) and the Warring States Period (475-221 BC) with its unique style and high degree of artistry, laying a solid foundation for the seal-cutting art.

Seal cut during the Western Han Dynasty (206BC-25 AD)

Commonly Used Chinese Characters

In May 2006, the Ministry of Education and the National Language and Character Committee issued China's first "Green Book" entitled China Report on Language and Life (2005).

The research involved 15 newspapers, 13 TV stations, and three kinds of on-line media. It drew on more than 890,000 text files, and over 900 million words, among which there were 732 million Chinese characters.

According to the research, the media use 8,225 different Chinese characters in all. Compared with the List of Modern Chinese Characters in Common Use, in the top 2,500 characters used with high frequency of this research, 357 were not in the First-Class Common Characters (2,500 characters in all); in the top 3,500, 398 were not in the List of Modern Chinese Characters in Common Use (3,500 characters in all). Compared with the List of Current Modern Chinese Characters (7,000 characters in all), 615 were not listed. What's more, 244 characters from the List of Current Modern Chinese Characters didn't appear in this research. These "disappeared ones" involved some Chinese characters in original complex form, in variant form, in old weights and measures, and in dialects.

Spread of Chinese

With the opening-up of China in the 1970s, a "Chinese fever" appeared in the world; a second such wave has now emerged in the new century. The block-shaped characters seem to have broken through the "most complex and difficult" crust.

The five-year action program called the Han Chinese Bridge was confirmed by the State Council in 2004. This was the first time for the Chinese government to confirm and actualize a project of spreading Chinese to the world.

The first Confucius Institute abroad appeared in Seoul in November 2004. The Chinese government wishes to spread Chinese into the international community via the Confucius Institute. Kong Zi (511-479 BC), an ideologist, politician, and educationalist in late stage of the Spring and Autumn Period in China, was the father of Confucianism. His name in English is "Confucius", which means clever person. According to its tenet, the Confucius Institute has the responsibility to spread Chinese in local society, to train Chinese teachers for all sorts of organizations, to hold Chinese tests, and to provide authentication for Chinese teachers. Up to September 2006, China had built up 108 Confucius Institutes and 12 Confucius classrooms in 46 countries and regions. The introduction given by the Leading Group for the International Promotion of Han Chinese shows these 108 Confucius Institutes are mostly distributed over Asia, Europe, and North America. Besides, there are six in Africa and three in Oceania. The Confucius Institute is becoming an international brand and stage for the spread of Chinese culture and Chinese teaching.

According o statistics, there are more than 30 million people learning Chinese abroad.

The result of this research told people that Chinese is not that difficult to learn, even it is totally different from the characters used in the West. For among those high frequently used characters, the top 518 occupy 80 percent of the daily language. One can read 90 percent of the publication if one knows more than 900 characters and over 10,000 phrases. A total of 2,315 Chinese characters will account for 99 percent of daily use.

Calligraphy and Painting

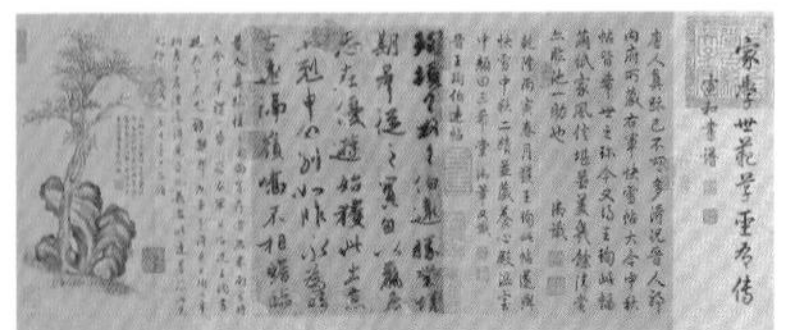

• Same Origin of Calligraphy and Painting

Chinese characters were evolved gradually from paintings and symbols and the art of calligraphy originated from the writing and evolvement of Chinese characters. For centuries, there were great calligraphers who became the representatives of calligraphy arts and styles in their times. The love of calligraphy has been passed down to today.

Different from oil painting in the West, traditional painting of China has its own special expression. There is a very close relationship between calligraphy and traditional Chinese paintings. At the beginning, the same tools were used for painting and writing—brush and xuan paper, and both painting and writing was mainly composed of lines; but calligraphy only used black ink while painting used various colors, so calligraphy and painting were often mentioned together although with calligraphy placed first, that is "calligraphy and painting" (shuhua). On most occasions, calligraphy and painting is combined together as an art. Painters would often leave space on their paintings for writing a poem or some words with poetic flavor related to the scenery in painting for added interest. If this poem was created by the painter, it was more idyllic.

In modern China, calligraphy and painting remain very active. In art museums such as Chinese Art Gallery individual painting exhibitions or associate exhibitions are held constantly, and, every year, Chinese paintings are sent abroad for exhibition. Besides traditional Chinese paintings, oil paintings, prints, watercolor paintings and other Western styles of paintings have developed well in China. Some painters combine the skills of traditional Chinese paintings and Western paintings.

Calligraphy

Calligraphy is the writing art of Chinese characters, and formed a special constructive art as well.

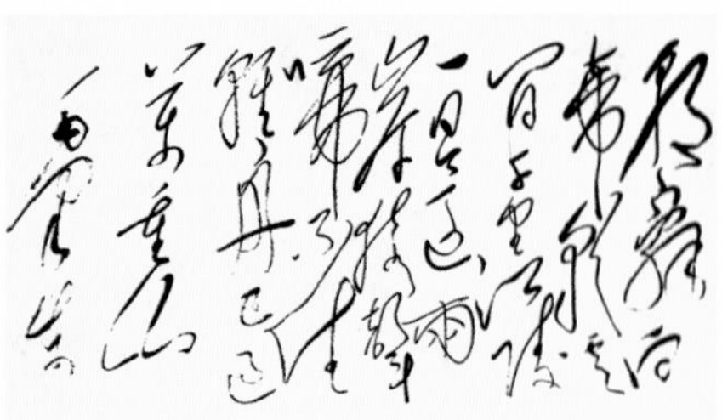

Li Bai's poem *Sailing Downstream for Jiangling* written by Chairman Mao in the cursive hand, with smooth, bold strokes, expresses the artistic conception of "Yet monkeys are still calling on both banks behind me; To my boat these ten thousand mountains away."

Calligraphy refers to the marks left on white paper by flexible and changeable brush movements and water ink that creates a black and white structure with rich meaning. Calligraphy is a constructive art. The brush of a calligrapher is extension of his fingers, and the quickness, slowness, swiftness and the pause and transition of the brush is controlled by him subjectively, serving as the abstraction of his sentiment and feelings. Calligraphy is also an expressive art. It can reflect subtly the living experience, knowledge, cultivation and personality of a calligrapher through his works, and there are always such sayings as "the way characters are written forms a portrait of the person who writes them", and "calligraphy is painting by the heart". Calligraphy can also be used to write epigraphs and tablets with inscriptions, so it is an applied art. In China, it is an art with the most devotees and learners.

Like music, calligraphy has rhythm as an important factor. The strokes of Chinese characters expressed on paper show a distinct rhythm by thickness, thinness, lightness, heaviness, square, round, curve, straight line, slowness, quickness, different shade and different wetness, just like the continuously changing and moving rhythm of music. Both can reflect the surging emotions of the calligraphers (and the musicians).

Evolution of Calligraphy

The origin of Chinese characters is very early and, according to historical records, it was somewhere during the period between the later half of the second and fourth centuries, namely between Wei and Jin Dynasties that followed the Han Dynasty, that Chinese calligraphy came into being as an aesthetic sense derived from written Chinese characters.

Oracle Bone Inscription of the Shang Dyanasty excavated from the Yin Ruins, Anyang, Henan Province in 1899.

Chinese characters are square. Each character occupies a square space on paper. According to statistics, there are 3,500 Chinese characters in common use and about 90,000 in total. Chinese people use these characters that occupy almost the same space and have different appearance as the instrument to exchange and record information. It can be imagined how fine and ingenious structure each Chinese character has to show various appearances in a small square and be easy to distinguish.

Western alphabetic words are absolutely different from Chinese characters; the former has twenty or thirty letters, more than the basic strokes of a single Chinese character, but their line mode follows only three rules, namely, straight line, arc and spot. Particularly, no matter how many letters each alphabetic word is composed of, these letters are arranged from left to right. It is very difficult for them to show various interests and charms of orderliness, unevenness, different density and being strewn at random by various combination and

13 Culture

construction methods of strokes.

The styles of scripts of various words in the world usually consist of two or three kinds, such as regular script and cursive script, while there are around 10 common styles of Chinese calligraphy. The styles experienced an evolution through Jiaguwen (inscriptions on tortoise shells and animal bones), Guwen or Jinwen (bronze inscriptions), Dazhuan or Zhouwen (greater seal script), Xiaozhuan (lesser seal script), Lishu (official script) or Bafen (official script), Caoshu (cursive script), Xingshu (running hand), and Kaishu (regular script), etc.

Inscriptions on Tortoise Shells and Animal Bones

In the Shang Dynasty (1600-1046 BC), people practiced divination using tortoise shells and animal bones. They inscribed the date of divination, name of the diviner, and the results of the divination beside the divination symbols. This kind of record is named divination words by scholars, and such words are Jiaguwen (inscriptions on tortoise shells and animal bones). The discovery of Jiaguwen occurred in a region around Xiaotun Village in Anyang County, Henan Province, and they were determined to be relics from the period between the move of Emperor Pangeng of the Shang Dynasty to Yin and the death of Emperor Zhou, namely the mid-14th century to the mid-11th century BC, or some 3,000 years ago.

There is a very interesting story passed down about the discovery of Jiaguwen: in 1899 (the 25th reign year of Emperor Guangxu, Qing Dynasty), Wang Yirong, a priest handling sacrificial wine in the Imperial College in Beijing, sickened with malaria and sought the aid of doctors and medicines from all around. Later, he sent for an imperial physician. The latter gave him a prescription after feeling his pulse, and one element of the prescription was dragon bone, a traditional Chinese medicine usually used by physicians to tone up the kidney. Wang Yirong immediately sent members of his family to get the medicines from a pharmacy. After they returned, Wang opened the pack of medicine and examined it carefully. He noticed what appeared to be Chinese characters on the dragon bone, which were shapeless and twisted, like Zhuanwen, but at that time unknown. He immediately acknowledged that this "dragon bone" was not some common medicinal material, and he sought information from the pharmacy as to the origin of the "dragon bones". He learned that almost all the "dragon bones" were supplied to Beijing by merchants from Anyang, Henan. Originally, medicine merchants collected tortoise shells as a traditional Chinese medicine. So, the sickness of Wang Yirong resulted in the world-famous discovery of Jiaguwen.

Jiaguwen is the earliest Chinese written script preserved until today. It has about 4,500 individual characters and about a third can be identified. The basic vocabulary, basic grammar and basic forms of characters are consistent with the later Chinese language.

Bronze Inscriptions

Jinwen (inscriptions on ancient bronze objects) are a kind of characters inscribed on bronze ware during the Yin and Zhou Dynasties. Bronze ware is the alloy of copper and stannum. China entered the Bronze Age as early as the Xia Dynasty (2070-1600 BC) when the smelting and production of bronze ware became highly developed. Because before the Zhou Dynasty people had called bronze as gold (Jin), the inscriptions on bronze ware became known as "Jinwen" or "Jijin Wenzi". Furthermore, these characters are also called "Zhongdingwen" as the characters on Zhong (bell) and Ding (tripod) were the most common among all the bronze ware.

Jinwen was used during the period from early Shang Dynasty (1600-1046 BC) to the conquering of the Six Kingdoms by Qin, more than 1,200 years. According to the records of Book on Jinwen by Rong Geng, the number of Jinwen (inscriptions on ancient bronze objects) characters totaled 3,722, of which about 2,420 can be identified.

The numbers of characters in inscriptions on bronze ware differed and the contents were also different, mainly speaking highly of the merits of ancestors and princes and marquises, as well as some important historical events. For example, on the famous Duke Mao Ding, there were 497 characters and the content covered a wide range of subjects reflecting the social life at that time.

Different from Jiaguwen which were thin lines, mostly straight lines and square in their turning points, Jinwenfeatured thick lines and mostly bent lines and ball-like forms.

Inscriptions on the ancient bronze ware

Jinwen characters were unearthed continuously as early as the Han Dynasty and started to be researched by scholars. Jinwen is the principal material for research into the ancient history of China.

Greater Seal Script

Zhouwen is also called Dazhuan (greater seal script).

Elucidations of the Signs and Explications of the Graphs included more than 220 Zhouwen characters. Modern scholar Wang Guowei has noted that "these characters featured balanced left and right parts and slightly complicated structures; much fewer were pictographic and more showed rounded lines and square turns."

During the Sui and Tang Dynasties, ten stone tablets were found in Tianxing County (present-day Fengxiang County in Shaanxi Province). These seemed like steamed bread with high feet, or like a drum, so they were named as "Shigu" (stone drums). On each stone were inscribed a 60 to 70-word poem each line of which consists of four words. Textual research shows that these stone drums were from the late years of the Spring and Autumn Period and the early years of the Warring States Period. Shiguwen (scripts inscribed on stone tablets) on these tablets were all poems paying a tribute to Emperor Qin. Shiguwen form the earliest stone-inscribed characters preserved today.

Three stones carved with inscriptions were discovered in the Northern Song Dynasty, and contents were all a malediction from the ruler of Qin to the ruler of Chu. People of later generations called these inscriptions Zhouchuwen (Script of Malediction to Chu).

Zhouwen, Shiguwen, Zhouchuwen and part of the bronze inscriptions in the Qin State all belonged to the same style and are collectively called Zhouwen or Dazhuan. Zhouwen, characterized by shapely strokes and compact structure, was officially prescribed as standard script of that time and was used for a long period.

Lesser Seal Script

According to *Shuowenjiezi* (Elucidations of the Signs and Explications of the Graphs), Xiaozhuan (lesser seal script) was a style of script developed from the scripts of Dazhuan. Cultural relics of the Qin Dynasty show that Xiaozhuan gradually evolved from Dazhuan, and the two do not have any clear demarcation in time. Some characters of Dazhuan were comparatively complicated and difficult to write, which could not comply with the demands on characters for social development, so, starting from the Spring and Autumn

Period, characters became more simplified, and the pace of simplification obviously picked up in the Warring States Period. Persons simply collected and arranged the characters of Xiaozhuan, which had been popular in the community, to create a standard calligraphy popularized through the whole society.

Examples of Xiaozhuan of the Qin Dynasty are Taishan Keshi (stone inscription on Mount Tai), Langya Keshi (stone inscription on Langya Terrace), Yishan Keshi (stone inscription on Yishan Mountain), Kuaiji Keshi (stone inscription on Kuaijishan Mountain), etc., as well as numerous Qinliang (measuring instruments of the Qin Dynasty), Qinquan (scale of the Qin Dynasty) and Zhaoban (imperial edict inscription).

Elucidations of the Signs and Explications of the Graphs included 9,353 Xiaozhuan characters. Xiaozhuan plays a special role in the development history of Chinese characters and is the bridge between ancient and modern characters.

Official Script

Lishu (official script) comprises second-generation basic-form characters appearing later than Zhuanshu (seal character). It was mainly used in the Han Dynasty. The shapely strokes of Zhuanshu (seal character) were changed to unshapely ones, the pictographic and indicative elements of Zhuanshu (seal character) characters were reduced or disappeared entirely; the types of strokes of Lishu (official script) were also less than Kaishu (regular script). Furthermore, Lishu (official script) is characterized by being round in shape, different from other styles of calligraphy which are mostly in high and elongated shape. Li calligraphy has an ancient flavor, but it is easy to identify.

Lishu (official script) includes three types—Qin Li (Lishu of the Qin Dynasty), Han Li (Lishu of the Han Dynasty) and Bafen calligraphy. Qin Li refers to the simplified characters adopted for use during the reign of Qin Emperor Shihuang. By the time of the Han Dynasty, the calligraphy in daily life was Lishu (official script) but its shape and handwriting saw much development. Xinli (a new style) emerged during the middle period of the Eastern Han Dynasty. It is solemn and elegant. In the fourth year of Emperor Xiping's reign (175), stone scripts in the style of Xinli were set up in the highest seat of learning of that time and that style became the State standard script. The style of that calligraphy after the Wei Dynasty was called Bafen.

The simplified Chinese characters popular in the Qin Dynasty emerged before Qin Emperor Shihuang unified China. According to archeological findings, characters on some weapons, lacquer ware and pottery from the Qin State during the Warring States Period were simplified Chinese characters created by craftsmen of that time. The strokes of these Chinese characters were omitted and tended to have more straight lines and less turns. They were the embryonic form of Lishu (official script).

The Stele of Zhang Qian, the famous inscriptions on a tablet in an official script during the Han Dynasty, is collected in the Dai Temple on the Taishan Mountain, Shandong Province. Its style is powerful, old and strong.

There is a saying about the naming of Lishu (official script) that, as this style of calligraphy was very popular among inferior officials, bailiffs, craftsmen and slaves, it was called "Lishu" (Chinese characters used by slaves and persons in servitude).

The changing of Chinese characters from Zhuanshu (seal character) to Lishu (official script) is called "Li Change". Li Change is an important turning point in the development history of Chinese characters. The forms and shapes after the Li Change were mostly close to the Chinese characters used today.

Cursive Script

Caoshu (cursive script) is characterized by sketchy and quick-writing forms of characters, often distorted or cursive, and some strokes or parts are even simplified. So, it is difficult to write or identify characters of Caoshu.

In theory, any character can be written in Caoshu style. For instance, many characters of inscriptions on bronze wares were in crabbed writing. However, Caoshu in literature refers to a specific style developed from a sketchy handwriting of Qin Li (official script in the Qin Dynasty).

Caoshu in the early period retained most features of Lishu (official script) and was called Zhangcao (a coarse style formed by breaking up the forms of Lishu). From the later period of the Eastern Han Dynasty to the Wei and Jin Dynasties, Caoshu got rid of traces of Lishu (official script) strokes, and employed a large number of running strokes, and was called Jincao (the modern cursive script). By the Tang Dynasty, Caoshu had developed further, was written in a lively and vigorous way and was called Kuangcao (crazy cursive script).

Some simplified Chinese characters used today, such as Dong (东, east), Wei (为, for), Chang (长, long), Shu (书, book), Zhuan (专, expert), etc., are originally forms of Caoshu.

Because Caoshu uses lots of running strokes and only has the outline of the characters for amazingly quick handwriting, it is illegible to most readers and this naturally affects its function of communication. Therefore, though Caoshu came into being comparatively early, it didn't become a common written form within any State. However, it has been always loved by many people as one kind of calligraphy art. Famous Caoshu calligraphers include Zhang Zhi, Zhang Xu and Huai Su and so on.

Running Script

Xingshu (running script) is a style lying between cursive script and regular script. No matter which type, characters of Lishu (official script) and Kaishu (regular script) must be carefully written with distinguishable strokes, which takes a little time. So, when writing down something not very important, people often did it in a little more unrestricted, sketchy and faster way, while retaining the forms of regular scripts at the same time; then, Xingshu came into being. Since the Six Dynasties, Xingshu has served as the major form of handwriting characters.

Xingshu is characterized by the appropriate employment of cursive hand and omission of strokes while retaining the forms and shapes of Kaishu (regular script). There are no strict handwriting rules for Xingshu; Xingkai refers to the style with more features of Kaishu (regular script) than Caoshu, and Xingcao refers to the style with more features of Caoshu than Kaishu (regular script).

Masterpieces of Xingshu passed down include *Preface to the Orchid Pavilion Collection* by Wang Xizhi, which was reputed to be the leading Xingshu Work. Unfortunately, the original was not handed down, and the one we see today is, therefore, only a copy. Due to the high level of skill of the copier, however, the copy retains the beautiful, neat style of the original. Scripts for Memorizing a Nephew by Yan Zhenqing is lively and vigorous with various shapes, and is acknowledged as the second most important Xingshu Work.

Regular Script

Kaishu (regular script) is a style of script with little change from Lishu (official script). It came into being at about the end of the Eastern

• Print Hand

Today Songti, Fangsongti, Kaiti and Heiti are mainly used in typography and computers. Songti was the general print hand in the Song Dynasty (960-1279) when movable type printing was invented. It was based on the styles of scripts adopted by calligraphers Ouyang Xun (557-641) and Ouyang Tong (?-691), father and son in the Tang Dynasty. In the Ming Dynasty, with a little amelioration (mainly unifying the thickness of strokes to thin horizontal strokes and thick vertical strokes), it became the major print hand still called Songti. Fangsongti is the imitation of Songti, but all the strokes of the former one are thin. Kaiti is a kind of print hand that is the closest to handwriting style. In recent years, other Kaiti styles of characters have been put into use in typography and computers, of which one is "Shuti characters" on the basis of the calligraphy of Shu Tong (1906-1998), a famous modern calligrapher.

Han Dynasty and developed to a certain level in the Jin Dynasty. Kaishu (regular script) retains the structure of Lishu (official script), but omitting its wave-rising-strokes, and changing the flat-round shape of Lishu (official script) to almost a square shape. Later generations often call Chinese characters "square characters" in respect of Kaishu (regular script).

Since the Six Dynasties, this kind of new style was called Zhenshu (real script) and Zhengshu (regular script). In the Tang Dynasty, this style saw great development. The reason for the naming of Kaishu (regular script) might be that people could learn from and imitate this kind of script as their model (Kai).

Kaishu (regular script) is characterized by level horizontal stroke and straight vertical stroke, regular with a tight structure and fluent strokes, and it is beautiful in forms. Calligraphers in the history produced many masterpieces that have been handed down. Ouyang Xun, Liu Gongquan, Yan Zhenqin and Zhao Mengfu developed Kaishu (regular script) to its peak with their unique styles, and they were called the Four Masters of Kaishu (regular script).

Because Kaishu (regular script) is easier to write than Lishu (official script) and easier to recognize than Caoshu, it has taken the former's place and become a general font ever since the Wei and Jin dynasties. In the Song Dynasty, the development of typography helped create Songti—a kind of calligraphy specially for typing based on Kaishu (regular script).

♦ Xi'an Stele Forest

Xi'an Stele Forest is located at the old site of Wen Miao in Sanxue Street, Xi'an City, Shaanxi Province, namely inside Shaanxi Province Museum. It is a centralized site of steles established for saving the inscriptions of Shi San Jing engraved in 836 (reign of Emperor Kaicheng of the Tang Dynasty) and in 1090 (Reign of Emperor Yuanyou of the Northern Song Dynasty). As the steles are as numerous as trees in a forest, it is called "Stele Forest".

Xi'an Stele Forest used many materials in various shapes as carriers, such as stones, bamboos, woods, metals, etc. The calligraphy works of those famous calligraphers of past dynasties are shown in accordance with their different times and schools. In the stele forest, there are seven large-scale showrooms, eight galleries, and eight stele pavilions, where more than 2,300 tablet inscriptions have been collected from the Han, Wei, Sui, Tang, Song, Yuan, Ming and Qing dynasties. It is a place where steles were saved the earliest and it is the largest "stone book bank". It is not only a centralized place of tablet inscriptions of Chinese ancient cultural books and records, but also a gathering place of famous calligraphy art treasures of past dynasties.

Many inscriptions there are of the value as rare historical materials; some can make up and correct the losses and errors of historical books and records, and some can serve as precious materials for research into the history of exchanges between Chinese and foreign cultures as well as regional history. For example, *the Stele on Prevalence of Daqin Jing Religion in China* was unearthed from Zhouzhi County, Shaanxi Province and was moved to the Stele Forest in 1907 (the 33rd year of Emperor Guangxu's reign). It is 353 cm high and 103 cm wide. It was engraved in the second year of the reign of Tang Emperor Dezong and recorded the introduction of the Jing Religion, a Christian sect, in the Tang Dynasty, to China in both Chinese characters and Syriac words. In addition, *the Stone Pillar of the Tuoluoni Sutra* Written Jointly by China and Nepal records the friendly exchanges between the Tang Dynasty of China and Nepal. *The Stele on Guangzhi Sanzang of the Tang Dynasty* recorded the experience of an Indian monk in China and the apprentice relationship after the introduction of the "True Word" Sect into Japan.

The comparatively intact preservation of the Stele Forest until today owes much to the contribution made by Bi Yuan, in imperial inspector of Shaanxi Province in the reign of Emperor Qianlong in the Qing Dynasty. In 1555 (the 34th year of the Jiajing Reign in the Ming Dynasty) a serious earthquake with an intensity of eight degrees occurred in Shaanxi and a large number of steles in the Stele Forest were broken. In 1772, Bi Yuan and his colleagues went to the Stele Forest to inspect and found ruins of houses and many steles lying among the grass and rubble. The deserted scene filled him with astonishment and he was heart-struck. Under Bi's leadership, workers repaired the houses, restored the steles, compiled a directory, organized an exhibition of stone inscriptions, established managing institutions and record-keeping system, and re-built and protected the Stele Forest.

The Xi'an Stele Forest was listed as one of the first group of protected units of key cultural relics in China.

Wang Xizhi

Wang Xizhi (303-361, or 321-379) was a calligrapher of the Eastern Jin Dynasty. He was a native of Shandong Province and served as a Right Army General and an imperial officer called Kuaiji, hence his other name—Wang Youjun. He was born in family of good blood in the Jin Dynasty. At the age 12, he learned the technique of writing calligraphy from his father and studied calligraphy from a famous female calligrapher of that time, Mrs. Wei. Later he visited many famous mountains and widely gathered together the good qualities of others' calligraphy.

Chunhua Pavilion Script by Wang Xizhi

The style of scripts of Wang Xizhi is obviously characterized by exquisite hand and changeable structures. The greatest achievement of Wang Xizhi is the adding and omission of ancient styles and changing the simple styles of the Han and Jin Dynasties to exquisite and beautiful forms of calligraphy. In a word, Wang Xizhi brought the handwriting of Chinese characters to a realm of paying attention to techniques and charm from practical usage, which is actually the awakening of calligraphy art and indicates that calligraphers can not only find the beauty of calligraphy but also express it. Almost all later generations of calligraphers have copied the standard models of Wang Xizhi's works, so he is honored as the calligraphy sage. His Kaishu (regular script) works include *Le Yi Lun*, *Huang Ting Jing*, *Dong Fang Shuo Hua Zan*, etc. His Xingshu and Caoshu works are honored as those of the "Sage of Caoshu Calligraphy". Original examples of Wang Xizhi's handwriting are rarely seen today and most of the works we can see now are copies of his works by others, such as *Shi Qi Tie*, *Xiaokai Le Yi Lun*, *Huang Ting Jing*, *Kong Shi Zhong Tie*, *Lan Ting Xu* (copy by Feng Chengsu), *Kuai Xue Shi Qing Tie*, *Yuan Huan Tie*, *Yi Mu Tie* and *Sheng Jiao Xu* of Tang Monk Huairen Collection, etc.

Wang Xianzhi

Wang Xianzhi (344-386), also named Wang Zijin, was the seventh son of Wang Xizhi. He served as a high-ranking government official, Zhong Shuling, hence his other name, Wang Daling. As a small boy, Wang Xianzhi studied calligraphy under his father and Zhang Zhi at the same time. He was good at all styles and was particularly accomplished in writing Xingshu and Caoshu. Wang Xizhi had seven sons and one daughter, and his seven sons were all good at calligraphy, among whom the youngest son, Wang Xianzhi, was the most outstanding. He was good at all styles and was especially accomplished in Xingshu and Caoshu. His handwriting was handsome, heroic and vigorous. In calligraphy history, he was equally famous as his father, Wang Xizhi, and two of them are called together "Two Wang's".

Ouyang Xun

Ouyang Xun (557-641) was a native of Hunan Province. He was a calligrapher of the Tang Dynasty. Ouyang Xun could read books at a glance of several lines and read Confucian classics and historical records widely. In calligraphy, he learned from Wang Xizhi at first, and later his style changed gradually. His style was vigorous and had its uniqueness, called the "Ou Style" by later generations. He was incomparable at that time and was one of the Four Great Calligraphers of the Early Tang Dynasty. When obtaining copies of his calligraphy, people would view them as models, so his calligraphy had a great influence on later generations. Ouyang Xun's Kaishu (regular script) was known for its rigorous and grand strokes as well as its unique order and structure. "Thirty-Six Laws of Ouyang Strokes" handed down through later generations created methods of stroke structure of his Kaishu (regular script) calligraphy, providing great enlightenment to later generations. His famous tablet inscriptions include *Jiuchenggong Liquan Ming*, *Huadusi Bei*, *Huangfudan Bei*, *Wenyanbo Bei*, etc. His Xingshu scripts include *Zhang Han*, *Bu Shang* and *Meng Dian*, etc. He compiled a hundred volumes of Collection of *Literature and Art*.

Yan Zhenqing

Also known as Yan Qingchen, Yan Zhenqing (709-785) was a native of Shandong Province and was hailed as a representative calligrapher of the Tang Dynasty. He served as prefect of Pingyuan and was called Yan Pingyuan. When he was a small boy, he learned from Chu Suiliang, and later he studied the technique of handwriting under Zhang Xu. He absorbed the traits of the Four Great Calligraphers of the Early Tang Dynasty, collected the concepts of Zhuanshu (seal character), Lishu (official script) and the works of the Northern Wei Dynasty, and was accomplished in the creation of robust and grand Yanti (Yan style) Kaishu (regular script), creating a Kaishu (regular script) model of the Tang Dynasty. His Kaishu (regular script) changed the thin and hard style to thick and vigorous style with grand strokes, firm and stern strength, symbolizing the flourishing Tang Empire. As already noted, his style is called as Yanti, and he and another famous calligrapher, Liu Gongquan, were called "Yan Liu", with a reputation of "Yan Strokes and Liu Strength".

Yan style calligraphy had a profound influence on the later development of calligraphy art. Many famous calligraphers after the Tang Dynasty absorbed experiences from the successful changes adopted by Yan Zhenqing. Especially in Xingshu and Caoshu, some famous calligraphers set up their unique styles by studying from Yan Zhenqing on a base of studying the Two Wang's. Masterpieces of Yan Zhenqing include *Wuxing Ji*, *Luzhou Ji*, *Linchuan Ji*, etc. Many of his scripts had been handed down, such as *Yanqinli Bei*, *Yuancishan Bei*, *Yanjiamiao Bei*, and *Magu*

Painting of Yan Lugong Writing the Scripture—describing Tang calligraphist Yan Zhenqing writing the scriptures.

• Plaque

Plaque is a kind of calligraphic work written or engraved on wooden boards usually hung on a door lintel or wall. The art of plaque inscription blends the art of language and literature, and the arts of calligraphy, engraving and lacquer decoration of China and it is a cultural artwork of distinctive Chinese style.

When visiting scenic spots in China, people can see one after another exquisite plaques of unique styles everywhere, such as on mountains, along rivers, in gardens, pavilions, palaces and monasteries, or passes, stations, wharfs, and even ancient stores along flourishing business streets. They speak highly of merit and express ambitions, add a touch that brings a work of art to life and express emotions on viewed scenes.

Xiantan Ji. His handwriting scripts handed down include *Jizhi Wengao*, *Liuzhongshi Tie*, *Zishu Gaoshen Tie*, etc.

Huai Su

Huai Su (725-782) was a native of Hunan Province. He was well known for "crazy Caoshu" and was called a "Caoshu sage" in the history. When he was a small boy, Huai Su became a monk. During free time from reading sutras, he loved calligraphy very much. He worked hard at copying, collecting banana leaves as a brush, using wooden boards as paper. After the boards were pierced through, leaves were exhausted, and brushes were bare with only the top left, his wielding was like running dragons and snakes, his paper was covered with cloud and mist, and many nobilities and celebrities wanted to befriend this crazy monk. Yan Zhenqing was also fond of him, exchanged techniques with him day and night, and gained many benefits. Huai Su was self indulgent and loved drinking alcohol. When he became excited after drinking, he would write calligraphy on anything he could find, such as the inside wall of the monastery, clothes and utensils. According to his own words, "drinking alcohol can mould temperament and writing Caoshu can express ambition." He was equally famous with another famous calligrapher, Zhang Xu, and the two were often called "crazy Zhang and drunken Su". The Caoshu works of Huai Su were vigorous in style and natural in brush wielding, like pouring rain and whirlwinds. Although random and changeable, his calligraphy had its own laws. Huai Su and Zhang Xu formed two peaks of Tang Dynasty calligraphy and in the history of Caoshu. His masterpieces include Zixu Tie, *Kusun Tie*, *Shiyu Tie*, *Shengmu Tie*, *Lunshu Tie*, *Dacao Qianwen*, *Xiaocao Qianwen*, etc. Among them, *Shiyu Tie* is especially thin in shape, vigorous in strength and stern.

Liu Gongquan

Liu Gongquan (778-865) was a native of Shaanxi Province. When he was a small boy, he was fond of study and at the age of 12 he could make sentimental or descriptive compositions. Being accomplished in calligraphy, he took the fancy of Emperor Muzong of the Tang Dynasty and was selected as a scholar of the Imperial Academy. The calligraphy of Liu Gongquan is the most well known for Kaishu (regular script). He was equally famous with Yan Zhenqing and the two together were called "Yan-Liu". His calligraphy technique could parallel that of the masters in Wei and Jin dynasties as well as the early Tang Dynasty. Affected by Yan Zhenqing, he created his unique Liu style between the vigorous and charming calligraphy of Jin Dynasty and the natural, graceful and grand calligraphy of Yan. His calligraphy can compare favorably with vigorous and grand calligraphy of Yan Zhenqing, and they were honored as "the muscle of Yan and bone of Liu" by later generations.

Many of Liu Gongquan's masterpieces have been handed down. His tablet inscriptions include *Jingangjing Keshi, Xuanmita Bei, Fengsu Bei*, etc. *Jingangjing Keshi, Xuanmita Bei and Shencejun Bei* are the representatives of his Kaishu (regular script) style. His Xingshu works include *Fu Shen, Shi Liu Ri, Ruxiang Tie*, etc. These works were still characterized by the style of the Wang family, being tightly knit and natural. His other calligraphy works include *Mengzhao Tie, and Wang Xianzhi Song Li Tie Ba. Mengzhao Tie* is stored in the Museum of the Imperial Palace. His works were inscribed into *Sanxitang Fa Tie*.

Mi Fu

Mi Fu (1051-1108) was a native of Shanxi Province and later moved to Xiangyang. He was also called "Mi Xiangyang". According to historical legends, he was very strange, loved to dress in clothes of the Tang Dynasty, had a mania for cleanliness, and called stones as "brothers" and worshipped them endlessly; so, he was called "Crazy Mi". At the age of six he could read up a hundred poems, at seven he started to study calligraphy, at 10 he started to write tablet inscriptions, at 21 he stepped into official circles. As to calligraphy, his style was handsome, unrestrained and strictly abiding by the laws. He also created a unique technique in landscape painting, "clouds and mountains of Mi". He was good at using "hazy" inks for misty scenes in the south of the lower reaches of the Changjiang River, and using strong ink, burned ink, horizontal dots and dot clusters as layers of mountain tops, which are called "Mi dots".

Zhao Mengfu

Zhao Mengfu (1254-1322) was a native of Zhejiang Province. He was one of the most outstanding painters in the Yuan Dynasty, as well as one of the most distinguished calligraphers. He had wide influence in the history of Chinese calligraphy and painting. He was a noble of a downfallen imperial family of the Song Dynasty. Under the Yuan Dynasty, he was appointed to an official position. In addition to his comprehensive knowledge of poems, calligraphy, painting and composition, he was worthy of the position as leader of the Yuan Dynasty in terms of painting. He called for restoring ancient ways in the painting and writing and imitating Tang Dynasty styles. His calligraphy was best in Kaishu (regular script) and Xingshu, gathering together the good qualities of the calligraphy works of the Jin and Tang dynasties. His style is called "Zhao Ti" (style of Zhao).

Zheng Xie

Zheng Xie (1693-1765) had a style name of Banqiao. He was a native of Xinghua, Jiangsu. He served as county magistrate in Shandong Province. Before and after serving as an official, he lived in Yangzhou and made his living through calligraphy and painting. He was accomplished in painting orchid, bamboo, stone, pine, chrysanthemum, etc. He painted orchid and bamboo for over 50 years and his achievements in this aspect were most outstanding. He learned techniques from Xu Wei, Shi Tao and Bada Shanren, etc., and created his unique style, sparse and bright in form and shape and vigorous and highly abrupt in style. He was skillful at calligraphy.

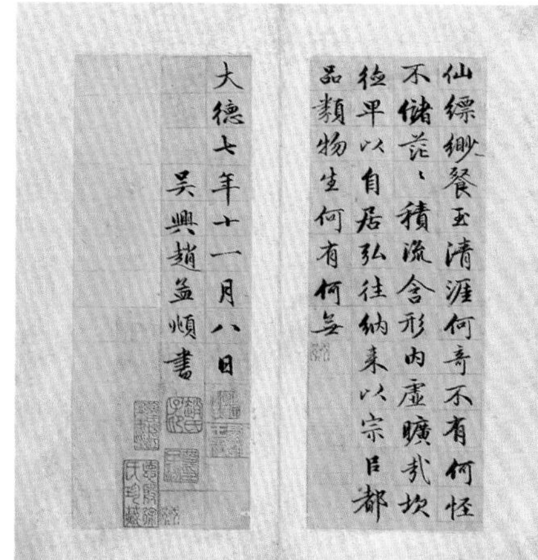

Calligraphy Works by Zhao Mengfu in the running script style

He intermixed Bafen, Kaishu (regular script), Xingshu, and Caoshu, and called his unique style "Liufenban Shu". He blended calligraphy styles and painting. In regard to inheriting traditional ways, he proposed that "70 percent of the traditional ways should be learned and 30 percent should be cast away," and "ancient ways cannot be rigidly adhered to." He paid attention to the originality of art and diversification of styles, namely "before painting, do not set up a standard, and after painting, do not leave a standard", which can still be used as reference. His poems were sincere and interesting and were loved by the common people. He could also make prints and his works include Collected Works of Zhen Banqiao, Printed Volumes of Mr. Banqiao, etc. He had a celebrated dictum, "it is hard to muddle", which covers abundant philosophical theories and was passed down to later generations.

Wu Changshuo

Wu Changshuo (1844-1927) was a famous calligrapher, painter and seal cutting artist in the latter period of the Qing Dynasty. He was originally named Wu Junqing, and his literary name was Changshuo and his style names were Foulu, Kutie, etc. He was a native of Anji, Zhejiang. When he was a small boy, he loved creating calligraphy and cutting seals under his father's influence. He studied Kaishu from Yan Lugong at first and then from Zhong Yuanchang; he studied Lishu from Chinese stone inscriptions; he studied Zhuanshu from Shiguwen (inscriptions on drum-shaped stones), and his style was influenced by Deng Shiru and Zhao Zhiqian at first, and later he blended and harmonized various styles in copying Shigu. In regard to Xingshu, Wu Changshuo studied the sloping styles of Huang Tingjian and Wang Duo, and the orderly ways of Huang Daozhou, and under the influence of the calligraphy of the Northern Stele and Zhuanshu, his works showed violent ups and downs and vigorous styles. At the age of 31, he moved to Suzhou, traveling often between Jiangsu and Zhejiang. He read many stele inscriptions, royal seals, calligraphy and painting works, and gained broad knowledge. Later, he settled in Shanghai and collected various works widely, and his skills in poems, calligraphy, painting and seal were promoted all together. In his old age, his style became very outstanding and he became a master of that time.

Calligraphy by Wu Changshuo

♦ China Calligraphers Association

The China Calligraphers Association was founded on May 9, 1981. At present, there are over 6,000 members. It has 31 branch associations across the country.

Under the China Calligraphers Association, there are the following committees: Academic Committee, Examination Committee, Creation Committee, Calligraphy Education Committee, Seal Cutting Committee, International Exchanges Committee, Rights and Interests Guarantee Committee, Engraving Committee, Authentication Committee, Picture Mounting Art Committee, Hand Pen Committee, Edition and Publication Committee, Art Development Committee, etc.

The China Calligraphers Association publishes the following journals: China Calligraphy, a monthly; and Calligraphy Communication, a bimonthly.

Traditional Chinese Painting

Ancient Chinese paintings can be traced back to as early as 5,000 to 6,000 years ago, when ancient people began to use minerals to draw simple pictures resembling animals, plants, and even human beings on rocks and produce drawings of amazing designs and decorations on the surface of pottery; later, they engraved numerous and mysterious designs and pictures on bronze containers. However, only a few of the works have survived to give us some small appreciation of the appearance of ancient paintings. The earliest drawings that have been preserved were produced on paper and silk and were burial articles with a history of over 2,000 years.

Early Chinese paintings fall into several categories, such as figure paintings, landscapes, and flower-and-bird paintings. European paintings, introduced into China in the 17th century, were called "Western paintings" to distinguish them from the traditional local works that were called "the Chinese paintings".

Chinese paintings are the mainstream of oriental painting art and comprise a unique system in world fine arts circles. Chinese paintings differ greatly from Western paintings in such aspects as content, forms and ways of expression.

Usual Subjects in Traditional Chinese Paintings

In Chinese paintings, figures, landscapes, flowers and birds are the major and usual subjects. They can be compared roughly to the three subjects of European paintings, i.e. figures, scenery and still life. Figure paintings, landscape paintings and flower-and-bird paintings are all important schools of traditional paintings and works that have been handed down are especially vivid.

Figure Painting

Ample evidence can be found in fine-art archeology that paintings with people as the subject were the earliest category of Chinese paintings. Dating back to the primitive age, people drew pictures of human beings and animals on walls and rocks with white stalks, red bauxite or charcoal. However, figure painting did not fully develop until 1,500 years ago, i.e. the time of Wei, Jin and Southern and Northern dynasties, when Gu Kaizhi (348-409), the famous painter and art theorist, asserted that more attention should be paid not only to the external shapes of figures, but also the internal quality, i.e. the spirit and temperament. Hereafter, this argument was accepted by artists and critics and taken as an established rule guiding future works. Figure paintings prospered in the early period of the development of Chinese paintings.

Landscape Painting

As the most important and most influential category, landscape paintings, usually taking images of natural scenery, such as mountains or rivers, as the subjects, developed quickly in the Tang Dynasty (618-907). Then, masters in landscape paintings emerged in great numbers with endless masterpieces. Landscape painting could prosper because of its deep roots in Chinese traditional culture. Chinese philosophers in ancient times believed in the "unity of human beings and heaven", which means that human beings can feel nature and therefore should be in a harmonious relationship with it. Even serving as an official or a businessman, a person would long for mountains, rivers, and forests; being close to and blending in with nature became the greatest wish of Chinese litterateurs. Chinese painters tended to integrate their feelings and dreams into the natural scenery in way that also aroused the aspirations and imagination of viewers. In ancient China, the majority of painters specialized in landscapes.

Flower-and-Bird Painting

With flowers and grass, bamboo and rocks, birds and beasts, and worms and fish as the major subjects, flower-and-bird paintings are greatly admired. The most frequently seen pictures feature a combination of the two. Flower-and-bird paintings display a special temperament and interest for art lovers. The genre came into being earlier than landscape painting. Originally designed for craftwork, flower-and-bird painting eventually established itself as an independent school in the Tang Dynasty. What's more, considered sublime and elegant by literati in ancient China, plum, orchid, bamboo, and chrysanthemum (mei, lan, zhu, ju) are the prime objects painted, which represent the high moral quality of literati free from vulgarity.

Lotus Out of Water

Cliff Painting

There is a wide distribution of cliff paintings in Sichuan, Yunnan, Guizhou and Fujian provinces in the south and the Yinshan Mountain, Heihe River and Altai in the north. In the southern region, a fiery blood-red color was usually employed to show scenes of offering sacrifice to the ancestors and production and daily living activities, with strong visual effects; in the northern region, such subjects as hunting, the pastoral nomadic way of life, wars and dances were usually portrayed.

Silk Painting

This is a kind of painting produced on the silk. In 1949, a painting on white silk was unearthed in a tomb of the Chu Kingdom of the Warring States Period (475-221 BC) in the southeastern suburb of Changsha in Hunan Province. This painting is named Human, Dragon and Phoenix Painting. It is the earliest traditional Chinese painting found so far. The painting was executed about 2,300 years ago on a piece of white silk used as a banner in traditional Chinese funerals. Although it is blotched and indistinct, the outlines are still eligible.

Twenty-four years after the Human, Dragon and Phoenix Painting was discovered, another silk painting was found, also in a tomb of the Chu Kingdom nearby. It depicts a man wearing a thick hat, holding a rein in one hand and a sword in the other, and riding a dragon boat. It is named the Dragon Boat Riding Painting. The figures in the Dragon Boat Riding Painting are rendered more realistically. These examples show that there were already varied painting styles in the Warring States Period. Some tended to be realistic, others more decorative. Paintings on silk developed to a high level during this period, an advance that laid the foundation for meticulous Chinese painting.

Before paper was invented, paintings on silk continued to develop. By the Western Han Dynasty (206 BC-25 AD), they had become richer in content and color, smoother and more forceful in brush strokes, and the depiction of figures had become more vivid.

Gu Kaizhi and Scroll Painting

Gu Kaizhi (344-405) was born in Jiangsu Province. He served as a government officer when he was young, and toured many beautiful places. He had a sense of humor, and was also adept at writing poems and essays. He was called a "superb scholar, superb painter and superb crazy man" by people of that time. Chinese art history abounds in anecdotes about him.

Once, a temple, Waguan Temple, was planned for Jiankang, the capital of that time (present-day Nanjing), but the monks and the abbot could not collect enough money for the construction. While they were worrying about

Tang lady(part)

• Colored Painting (Gongbi) and Water-Ink Painting (Xieyi)

In terms of drawing skills, Chinese paintings can be categorized into two styles: colored paintings and water-ink paintings.

Also known as "fine-stroke" paintings, colored paintings have a neat and careful style; they draw the outline of things in clear and neat lines full of expressive force, pay attention to details and then apply strong and bright colors. Thanks to the use of mineral dyes, the original colors can be fully maintained and the paintings will not fade as time goes by. As a whole, the paintings are pretty and bright, with strong decorative effect. Colored paintings, which manifest in themselves majestic splendor and unparalleled sublime airs, were widely welcomed among the painters serving in royal courts.

In contrast, water-ink paintings, also called "thick-stroke" paintings, are supposed to convey spiritual resonance with strokes as simple as possible, instead of attaching much importance to realistic subjects. Exaggerated forms, such as generalization and hyperbole as well as rich imagination, are employed to express the painters' feelings. Therefore, water-ink painting works have some characters of improvisation, and the random and casual occurrence of unexpected effects. It is relatively difficult to make a copy of a water-ink painting. Almost all were made by water and ink, showing simple and elegant appearance. These works occupy a very large proportion in later-day Chinese painting circles.

In the development history of Chinese paintings, the early (pre-12th century) works were all colored paintings. Most of the middle and later-day works were water-ink paintings. In regard to their originators, those of colored paintings were mostly professional painters or artisans, while those of water-ink paintings were mostly literary people.

Part of the Painting of *Beauties Wearing Flowers* (Tang Dynasty)

the funds, a young man came and said he would donate a large amount of money, a million qian. The abbot did not believe him, thinking that he was boasting. The young man suggested drawing a picture of Vimalakirti (a lay Buddhist in legend who believed in Buddhism but stayed at home) on a wall and collecting money from those who came to see him at work. For three consecutive days, thousands of people crowded the Waguan Temple to see the young man painting the Buddhist. When he finally added the eye lines, the Buddhist seemed to come alive, and the viewers cheered and applauded the young man's artistry. The money needed for the consummate construction of the temple had exceeded 1 million qian. The young painter was Gu Kaizhi.

Gu Kaizhi also made great advances in summarizing painting theories. His theoretical works included *Painting Thesis* and *Notes on Painting Yuntai Mountain*. He paid considerable attention to the vivid expressions of the figures to show their spirit. His Graphic Theory later became a basic theory for traditional Chinese painting. According to historical records, Gu Kaizhi created more than 70 paintings. It is a pity that there are only copies of his three existing scroll paintings, *Nushi Zhen Painting, Luoshen Appraisal Painting and Lienu Renzhi Painting*. These are the earliest examples of scroll paintings.

Dunhuang Murals

(See P173)

Wu Daozi, Sage in Chinese Painting

In Chinese art history, three people are treated as sages. They are the calligraphy sage Wang Xizhi of the Jin Dynasty, the poet sage Du Fu of the Tang Dynasty and the painting sage Wu Daozi, also of the Tang Dynasty.

The birth year of Wu Daozi is unknown. As far as we know, his active living period was in Kaiyuan and Tianbao periods (713-755). Born in Henan Province, Wu studied hard and was talented; he earned himself a good reputation as a painter by the time he was 20. Emperor Xuanzong of the Tang Dynasty invited him to become an imperial painter. As an imperial painter, he was not allowed to paint except on the emperor's orders. It was a big restriction, but, on the other hand, life in court provided the best conditions for living and artistic creativity.

Wu's character was unrestrained, direct and indifferent to trivial matters. It is known that he always drank when painting. Wu Daozi created many art works in his life. According to records, he painted over 300 murals in monasteries and corridors and more than 100 scrolls. Many of them were on Buddhist and Taoist topics but he also drew landscape, flowers and birds, and animals. Unfortunately none of them have been preserved. There is a Song Dynasty copy of his *The Songzi Tianwang Painting* (also called *Painting on the Birth of Sakyamuni*). This demonstrates Wu Daozi's basic painting style. His strokes were full of changes and vigor, expressing the internal world of the characters. Wu used simple colors or none at all.

Imperial Painting Academy of the Song Dynasty

Imperial painting academies were first established in the Five Dynasties by the Western Shu (891-965) and Southern Tang (937-975). They were under the direct administration of the imperial government. Painters of the academies, holding the status of "Hanlin" and "Shizhao", enjoyed the same treatment as literary court officials, wore official clothes and received salaries from the government. The academies gathered the most excellent painters in the country. Their tasks were to draw portraits for the nobles, and when important social events occurred, they were required to record them in paintings.

The Song Dynasty united China again in 960 and expanded the imperial painting academy. All the great painters from the Five Dynasties applied for posts in the Song Dynasty Imperial Painting Academy, and it became the creative center of painting of the time. The abbot of the Zhaoying Palace of the Yuqing Temple selected painters to draw murals and over 3,000 painters came for the selection examination.

Zhang Zeduan and the Qingming Festival by the Riverside

The famous *Qingming Festival by the Riverside* (preserved in Beijing Imperial Palace Museum) is a long colored painted scroll produced by Zhang Zeduan, a painter of the Song Dynasty. This painting portrays noisy street scenes of the capital of the Northern Song Dynasty during the Qingming Festival (for mourning the ancestors). It is a great and rare realistic painting and provides vivid visual information about business, handicrafts, architecture and transportation tools in the big metropolis of the Northern Song Dynasty. It has an important value as historical literature and has the most copies by later-generation painters in the history of Chinese painting.

Zhang was a native of Shandong Province. Later he became a painter of the Imperial Painting Academy of the Northern Song Dynasty. Though there aren't many historical records of him, his name is remembered simply because of this great art work.

Many ancient Chinese paintings contain the seals and signatures of both the painter and the collector. But the Qingming Festival painting is covered with innumerable signatures and seals, indicating it had been in the hands of many private and official collectors. The painting survived many calamities and historical shifts and was handed down to the present day; some collectors even sacrificed their lives in order to preserve this art treasure.

Qingming Festival by the Riverside is a long colored painted scroll with a length of 528 cm and a height of 24.8 cm. People of the time kept the custom of going to street fairs at Qingming to do business, just like fairs at festivals today. The painting has complicated scenes with rigorous structures. It can be divided into three parts: scenes of the suburbs, the Bian River and the city streets. There are over 550 human figures, some 60 animals, 20 wooden boats, 30 rooms and pavilions, and about 20 vehicles of various kinds. Few ancient pictures have such rich content. What is more, all the figures and detailed scenes of the painting are arranged rationally, and the relations between sparseness and density, complication and simplicity, movement and stillness, and meeting and parting are dealt with perfectly, creating an effect of bustle and complexity that still remains well-ordered.

The Yongle Palace Mural

The Yongle Palace Mural in Pinglu County of Shanxi Province on the northern bank of the Yellow River is a treasure of Chinese murals.

The Sanqing Hall is the main hall of the Yongle Palace. Paintings were drawn inside and outside its alcoves and on the walls. The mural in the hall covers a total space of 403.34 square meters, and it decorates the hall like a relief sculpture. Records show the mural was drawn in 1325, the second year of Emperor

Zhaoyuan Drawing is a part of mural paintings in the Sanqing Hall of Yongle Palace, representing highest achievement of the mural painting art of the Yuan Dynasty.

Taiding of the Yuan Dynasty, and it has retained its original beauty even after the wear-and-tear of several hundred years.

The mural in the Sanqing Hall portrays Taoist scenes of gods worshiping Heaven, with portraits of eight 3-meter-tall Taoist gods on the eastern, western and northern walls and on the two sides of the alcoves. Surrounding the gods are some 280 immortals who stand in long rows on four tiers; they include solemn emperors, elegant angels, deities, and kings, powerful and valiant marshals and Hercules, and handsome and pretty immortal boys and girls. Some of them are talking, some listening, some looking around or pondering. This grand, solemn and vivid scene makes viewers feel involved personally in the scene.

The figures portrayed in the Yongle Palace Mural represent fully the characteristics of traditional Chinese painting. The painters used simple, fluid and forceful strokes to depict the various expressions of living creatures of different ages and characteristics. The clothes of the major gods in the mural are painted bright red with some use of golden powder, but the basic color is green, which imparts religious solemnity and tranquility. The 280 immortals in eight groups are drawn with varied expressions to avoid boredom and repetition, which reveals the masterly structure technique and ingenuity of the painters.

The murals in the Yongle Palace have rich contents and show exquisite technique, and they are developed from the figure painting styles of the Tang and Song dynasties. Though the murals depict fairy stories, the figures in the paintings are realistic instead of abstract and have strong personalities. The painters, whose signatures appear on the murals— Ma Junxiang, Ma Qi and Zhang Zunli—were ordinary folk artisan-painters with no personal records in art history, but their excellent works are forever recorded in painting history.

• The Four Great Painters of the Yuan Dynasty and Chinese Landscape Painting

In Chinese painting history, painters of the same period or region are sometimes mentioned together to serve as representatives and are titled with numbers. The Four Great Painters of the Yuan Dynasty(1206-1368) refer to Huang Gongwang, Ni Zan, Wu Zhen and Wang Meng, whose works represent a peak in the history of Chinese landscape paintings.

Landscape is an important branch of traditional Chinese painting. In early Chinese paintings, mountains and forests were drawn very small as embellishments for the human figures. But in the Spring Travel Painting, drawn by Zhan Ziqian in the Sui Dynasty, mountains and water became the main theme. The landscape painting developed to a more mature stage in the Tang Dynasty, and there came green mountain and river painting and splashed-ink landscapes. Landscape painting reached a peak in the Song Dynasty and it was characterized by emphasis on imitating nature and was very realistic. From this basis, the Four Great Painters of the Yuan Dynasty pushed landscape painting to new heights.

The Four Great Painters of the Yuan Dynasty were very careful with brush stroke techniques in order to show developed artistic ideas, and their works have great aesthetic values. Their works had a big influence on the development of landscape painting in the later Ming and Qing dynasties.

• Eight Eccentric Painters of Yangzhou

This refers to a group of painters active in Yangzhou painting circles during the Qing Dynasty (1616-1911) , who had an innovative spirit. In fact, at that time, there were actually 16 or 17 painters active at the time, so "eight" is not a fixed number. According to the earliest records, they included Jin Nong, Huang Shen, Zheng Xie, Li Shan, Li Fangying, Wang Shishen, Gao Xiang and Luo Pin. Their paintings did not follow the old brushstroke conventions, making them look strange compared with other paintings of the time. In addition, these painters were proud and uncontrolled and had bold personalities; thus their title of Eight Eccentric Painters. Many of their works used flower and birds as their subjects in water-ink painting style in a refreshing style.

Ink Bamboo Paiting by Zheng Xie

Prints

Print is an important category of Chinese fine arts. Ancient prints mainly referred to woodblock prints, as well as a few copperplate prints and colored multi-block prints. The special qualities of prints, woodblock and knife-cutting, means this art holds an independent artistic value and position in the history of Chinese arts.

A preface picture of the famous "Xiantong" edition of the Vajracchedika-prajaaparamita-sutra (Diamond Sutra), it is the earliest extant woodblock printed "book" in China with an exact date. According to its preface, it was produced in 868. Works of prints of the Tang Dynasty and Five Dynasties have been found in Northwest China and Southern China. Most of these works are elegant with primitive simplicity and vivid cutting. Religious sutras are the major subjects and contents. Figure of Sakyamuni, a colored multi-block print of the Liao Dynasty, is the earliest extant colored multi-block print in China and boasts great significance in world art history. Due to practical demands, copperplate prints appeared in the Song Dynasty and were often employed to print paper currency and advertisements. The block-printed edition of Pinghua of the Yuan Dynasty was the predecessor of the interlink prints in today's China. Due to the improvement of printing techniques and folk literature, the development of block prints reached its peak in the Ming and Qing dynasties. Along with the development of commerce and the handicraft industry and the increasing demand for rich cultural life by urban people, the thriving dramatic literature became the engine for the growth of book publication and block-printed "books" with illustrations.

With unique development, Chinese ancient prints form a kind of art with special characteristics in history. To the best of their ability, prints reveal the flavor of wood by using the natural color of the subject. Along with crafty utilization of the "black-leaving" method, forms of the subjects in prints are processed by special methods to achieve some special artistic effects. The employment of watercolor printing on an engraved block can make large pieces in relief produce strong artistic effects.

♦ Chinese Artists' Association

The Chinese Artists' Association was founded on July 21, 1949 in Beijing. The first chairman was Xu Beihong, a famous painter. It has enrolled 8,153 in total, 7,072 at present.

It established branches in all provinces, autonomous regions, and municipalities (except for Taiwan Province); since 1990, these have become group members of the association.

The association admits people with outstanding achievements in fine arts creation, fine arts comment, research in fine arts history and artistic design, centralizes the artists and scholars with achievements and influence in China, and is the only State-level fine arts organization in China with integration of all categories of fine arts.

It is in charge of organizing and instructing artists in China to conduct artistic creation and academic research, handles the organization, implementation, appraisal and award-giving of important exhibitions in China, holds national large-scale fine arts exhibitions and various academic exhibitions, publishes academic publications, conducts academic discussion, and makes efforts to promote the development and prosperity of the Chinese fine arts cause. It is active in developing exchanges around the world, holds and participates in various international fine arts exhibitions, receives foreign artists to China and organizes Chinese artists to visit foreign countries, conducts various exchanges with foreign artistic circles, and strengthens the friendship and cooperation with artists around the world.

It publishes *Fine Arts*, a monthly.

Website: http://www.caan.cn/index.html

Four Treasures of the Study

The tools and materials for Chinese calligraphy and painting are mainly composed of brush, paper, ink and ink stone, commonly referred to as the "Four Treasures of the Study".

Besides Chinese characters, Four Treasures of the Study serve as another special condition for the forming of Chinese calligraphy and painting arts. Hu brush, Hui ink, Xuan paper and Duan ink stone are recognized as the ones with superior quality.

Brush

Brushes are the major writing tool for both calligraphy and painting, special to China. A brush of the Spring and Autumn Period (770-476 BC) was unearthed from Second Tomb of Zenghou" in Suizhou, Hubei Province, the earliest found so far.

A brush is made of animal hair clustered on a bamboo or wooden shaft and it is soft and flexible. After dipping in ink, it will also engender capillary action: the ink will run down if the brush touches paper with force, but will be retained if the brush is lifted a little; such capillary action is produced by over a hundred hair bubbles. It also makes brushes have unique charm when expressing the special flavor of calligraphy and painting. Modern people often use purple hair brush, wolf hair brush, goat hair brush and blended hair brush.

Purple hair brush is made of the hair on the back of the neck of a wild rabbit. Rabbit hair is tough and is good for writing vigorous and square characters. Calligraphers often think highly of it. But as only the hair on the back of the neck can be adopted, this being not very long means such a brush cannot write large characters on tablets.

A wolf hair brush, as the name denotes, is made of wolf hair. In the past this kind of brush was really made of wolf hair, but today hair of weasel is used. Only the hair on top of weasel's tail can be used. It is tough and has the similar disadvantages with purple hair brush.

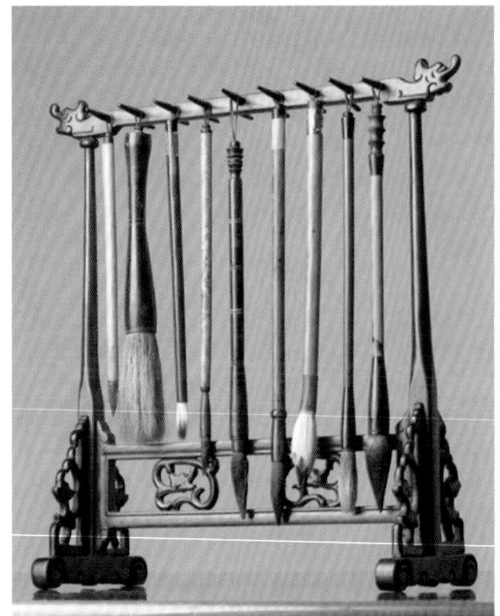

Writing brush holder and writing brushes

Goat hair brush is made of the beard and tail hair of blue goats or yellow goats. Calligraphy pays attention to vigor of strokes, and goat hair is soft without a sharp edge, therefore writing with it is "soft without bones" and calligraphers of past dynasties rarely used it. From the early Qing Dynasty, however, goat hair became popular. As the people in the Qing Dynasty paid attention to smoothness and connotation and they would not reveal talents or publicize themselves, only soft and plump goat hair could satisfy such demands. Goat hair is cheap and facile and is longer, so it can write large characters of above half-a-foot high.

Blended hair brush is made of two or more kinds of hair. Its quality is in accordance with the proportion of blending. Some are tough, some are soft. It is cheap and labor-saving, and possesses good qualities of all types.

Ink

The traditional ink for calligraphy and painting by Chinese people is also special. It is ground out by a square or round column ink stick on an ink stone with added water. The raw material for producing ink is tung oil smoke, coal smoke or pine smoke, added with animal glue and perfume. Though sticky, it is fluent when writing. It is also characterized by never fading, so the ink color of ancient calligraphy masterpieces can still retain their freshness today.

The ink color was only black originally, but as the wielding has differences in shade, depth, dryness and lightness, it can produce various colors on paper and especially in the minds of viewers.

Chinese painting pays much attention to the ink which is classified into "oil smoke" and "pine smoke". The former one is made of tung oil or added by burned smoke; the latter is made of smoke by burning pine branches. The former is characterized by black and bright color with luster; and the latter is characterized as dark without luster. Oil smoke is frequently used in Chinese painting. When expressing subjects without luster, such as black butterfly and black velvet, people will also use pine smoke. The ink for Chinese painting is often processed into an ink stick. The ink color is the standard for choosing a stick. The best one has livid purple light, the next a black light, and the worst one a red and yellow light or has white pigments. Clean water is needed to grind the ink stick, which must be balanced in the hand during the grinding or rubbing process. Press hard and rub lightly, slowly and evenly against the ink slab until a thick, liquid-ink forms; the ink for use must be fresh and made on site, and the ink which has been ground early and laid aside for a long time is called overnight ink and cannot be adopted.

Paper

Paper, compass, powder and typography are called the four great inventions in China. Even today, when machine-made paper is popular, some man-made paper by traditional methods still has an irreplaceable role and has special glory.

The raw material for paper making is mostly plant fiber of bamboo and wood. The fiber of wood is flexible and the paper made of it has strong power to absorb ink; and the fiber of bamboo is hard and crisp and the paper made of it has poor power to absorb ink. The paper for calligraphy and painting often includes Xuan paper, Maobian paper, Yuanshu paper and Lianshi paper.

Xuan paper is named after Xuancheng, Anhui Province. The paper is soft, fine textured, white, close, hard to be damaged when folded, and suitable for calligraphy and painting. It can produce clear layers of ink flavor, has special functions of infiltration, moistening ink and one-time absorption. Ink and the color on paper can show distinctive styles of void and real scenes in calligraphy and painting. In addition, being able to resist aging, moth attack, heat and light, the paper can be preserved for a long time and has the honorable tiles of "pretty thousand-year paper" and "king of paper".

Maobian paper refers to a kind of "bamboo" paper and is produced in all places producing bamboo in south China. Tender bamboos are used as raw material, retted and fermented by lime, pounded to pulp, added with proper yellow dye not glue, and manufactured to paper by handwork curtains. Maobian paper is tender, soft, and with good flexibility, has some yolk color and strong power of absorbing water. Adapting to writing and printing, it can absorb ink dry easily and the writing on it will not change for a long period.

Yuanshu paper is made of bamboo pulp. The paper is poor in quality but has a good quality of absorbing water. It is yolk yellow and is often used as exercise books for pupils to practice Dakai and Xiaokai characters.

Lianshi paper is made of tender bamboos. It is boiled by an alkalified method, bleached to pulp, and manufactured to paper by handwork curtains. The paper is thin and even, white as suet jade, and proper for both calligraphy and painting. It is often used to make high-grade handwork presswork, such as rubbings from stone inscriptions, letter paper and base paper for a fan face, etc.

Ink Stone

Making calligraphy or painting with a brush dipped with ink needs brush, ink and ink stone.

Ink stone is a tool for grinding ink. It should be exquisite, moist, easy to expand the ink, and the ink made by it must be fine, even and without broken bits. Ink stones can be classified into stone, pottery, brick and jade types, and the most famous ones are Duan ink stone produced in Guangdong Province and Shezhou ink stone produced in Anhui Province. It is fine to have the one with good stone quality, deep pool, bigger shape with cover, being able to expand ink fast and not easy to volatilize water.

Duanxi ink stone (usually called Duan ink stone) is listed as the leader among the four great ink stones in China. It was first made in the early Tang Dynasty and has a history of over 1,300 years. Duanxi ink stone has many varieties in stone quality and design. It has elegant shape and color which is unparalleled by other ink stones. Duan ink stone is good at getting the ink down and not damaging the brush.

Chengni ink stone is a pottery ink stone whose predecessor was an ancient pottery slab. Taohe ink stone is produced in Lintao River in Zhuoni County, Gansu Province. As Taohe river stones are soaked and eroded by river water, the stone has fine quality, close texture, is able to expand ink without damaging the brush and can become wet when people exhale. Shezhou ink stone is produced in the Longweishan, Wuyuan, Anhui Province. Shezhou ink stone has a special advantage that "it can become glittering again after clearing long-preserved ink", which means that though used for a long time and full of ink paste, it can become clean immediately after being washed. Shezhou ink stone has advantages of "being rough but not pausing the brush and smooth but not rejecting ink". In addition, Shezhou ink stone is different from Duan ink stone; the former is good in expanding ink to write big characters, and the latter is fine and glossy and absorbing ink to write small characters.

• Writing Utensils in the Study

In a study, besides brush, ink, paper and ink stone, there are some other utensils which are also indispensable members of the utensil family for Chinese calligraphy and painting. They usually include:

seal and seal box

Brush holder: it is also called a brush case and brush stand and is used for standing brushes. It is often in the shape of peaks and brushes can be placed in the concave. There are also brush holders in the shape of human figures and animals, and in particular, natural old roots and branches are excellent.

Brush pot: It is made of various materials, such as pottery, jade, bamboo, wood, lacquer. Some are round, some are square, and some are in shape of plants or other subjects.

Brush cleaning article: After being used, a brush can be cleaned in it to wash out the residual ink. It is often in the shape of a bowl, or petal or other subjects.

Ink bed: In the process of grinding ink, it is a place for laying the ink stick temporarily as the place for grinding the ink is wet.

Ink box: it is used to store ink sticks. It is often a damp-proof lacquer box. On the lacquer surface, there are always designs in gold, and some lacquer surfaces are inlaid with spiral and thin designs.

Paper-weight: Also called a book-weight. It is used to press the paper or book so as to keep a flat surface. It is often in the shape of various animals.

Water pouring article: It is used to pour water onto the ink stone for grinding. It is often in the shape of a round or square kettle with a mouth, and it is also in shape of a toad and heaven chicken for avoiding evils.

Ink stone water container: Used to store water for grinding ink.

Ink stone box: it is used to store the ink stone. The best ones are made of rosewood, ebony, valve nanmu and lacquer.

Seal: it is used to print on calligraphy and painting works. There are name seals and idle seals. It is often made of Shoushan stone, Qingtian stone, Changhua stone, etc., as well as bronze, jade and ivory.

Seal box: It is also called ink pad and pad and used to place ink paste. It is often made of pottery and jade, and in a round or square shape. It has a cover and a body.

Development of Chinese Oil Painting

After a long period of learning, absorbing and growing, oil painting has become a recognized part of Chinese painting.

In 1601, an Italian Jesuit missionary Matteo Ricci, along and other Westerners, came to China to preach and brought with them some European oil paintings.

After the Opium War of 1840, more religious and commercial paintings entered China from the West, exerting some distinctive influence on Chinese painting styles.

In 1909, Zhou Xiang established the Chinese and Western Fine Arts School and, later, the Scenery Painting School, in Shanghai to teach Western painting techniques, the first attempt to teach Western fine arts in China.

Li Shutong, the earliest Chinese artist to learn painting techniques in Japan, returned home in 1910 after finishing his studies. Then, he was engaged to teach fine arts in Tianjin, Hangzhou and Nanjing. He was the first to promote drawing of the human body and the techniques of using plaster casts. He also organized seminars on Western painting in the schools.

In 1912, Liu Haisu and Wu Shiguang founded the Shanghai Academy of Fine Arts, renamed the Shanghai Junior College of Fine Arts in 1919. It was the first regular fine arts school in China. Later, many more fine arts schools were founded and to promote oil painting.

In the 1950s, the Chinese Government sent students in various groups to the former Soviet Union and the socialist countries of Eastern Europe to learn fine arts. Painters of the former Soviet Union and Rumania were also invited to teach in Beijing and Hangzhou. Russian techniques had profound influence on the development of modern oil painting in China.

In the early 1960s, in terms of oil painting teaching, the Oil Painting Seminar held by Luo Gongliu and three studios organized by Wu Zuoren, Dong Xiwen and Luo Gongliu respectively in the Central Academy of Fine Arts were founded with dynamic effect on the teaching of oil painting.

After the adoption of the opening and reform policy in 1978, Chinese oil painting entered a new stage. A large group of young painters emerged to look at life and art with a brand-new sense. They absorbed the forms and concepts of Western modern painting and make bold artistic experiments. As a result, the long-time shortcomings of the humdrum and relatively poor appearance of Chinese oil paintings began to undergo rectification.

Development of Chinese Cartoons

In the history of modern painting in China, the cartoon is one of the most active genres with outstanding achievements.

In ancient China, there appeared satirical paintings that possessed the features of the cartoon, but they did not grow into an independent painting style until the early of 20th century. At that time, it had various names such as caricature, emblem, fashionable painting, humorous painting, laughing painting or funny painting.

In 1925, with the publication of 'Zikai's Cartoons' by Feng Zikai in *Literature Weekly*, the name of Man Hua (cartoon) began to be formally used. His new paintings illustrating ancient poems and cartoons on children's naivety and childishness gained much favor. This led to the founding of the Cartoon Association by Ding Song and Zhang Guangyu.

In the 1930s, Chinese cartoon creation reached its peak and a large number of such publications emerged in Shanghai. Ye Qianyu's cartoon series *Mr. Wang* and *Unofficial History of Xiao Chen in Beijing* had great social influence.

In the contemporary era, humorous and scientific cartoons are universally welcomed. In 1979, the cartoon supplement *Satire and Humor* of the *People's Daily* began publication and cartoon papers were created one after another in various places, and cartoon academies and seminars also appeared. In 1984, cartoons appeared in the Sixth National Exhibition of Fine Arts Works for the first time as an independent painting style. The important fruits of research into cartoon theories include the *Random Talk on Cartoons* by Shen Tongheng, *How Do I Think of and Paint Cartoons* by Hua Junwu, *Humor, Satire, and Cartoon* by Fang Cheng, *History of China's Cartoon* by Bi Keguan and Huang Yuanlin, and others. In 1986, the Cartoon Committee of the Chinese Artists' Association was founded.

Development of Modern Lian Huan Hua (Linked Serial Pictures)

The first *Lian Huan Hua* in China, the *Romance of the Three Kingdoms*, using lithography, was published by the Shanghai Literature Publishing House in 1899. After the 1920s, among the cultural enlightenment movement and the development of publishing, *Lian Huan Hua* gradually became popular. This genre is also known as *Xiao Ren Shu* (children's book) in Beijing and *Tu Hua Shu* (picture book) in Shanghai. In 1925, when *Pilgrimage to the West* was published by Shanghai World Publishing House, its name was fixed as *Lian Huan Hua* (linked serial pictures).

In the 1920s, bookstalls promoting *Lian Huan Hua* appeared on the streets of Shanghai and enjoyed much custom. At that time, *Lian Huan Hua* was mainly compiled and painted according to classical stories, dramas and films, for example, the *Romance of the Three Kingdoms* painted by Zhu Run Studio in Shanghai, which attached importance to dramatic authenticity.

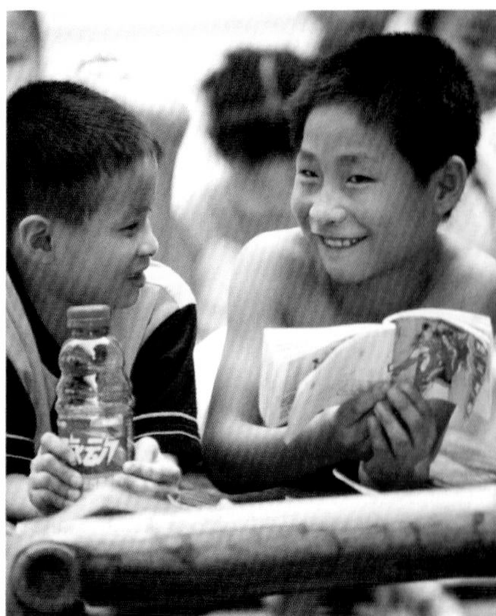

The original memory of the Pictorial Times

From 1949 to 1956, more than 10,000 kinds of new *Lian Huan Hua* were published with a total run of 260 million copies. These creations elevated the literary scripts to an important position and changed the old way of random compiling and painting by originators. In terms of figure painting, importance was attached to the expression of personal characteristics. At the same time, the shortcomings of old *Lian Huan Hua* in copying and imitating the figures in dramas and films were corrected.

From 1957 to 1965, the voluminous *Lian Huan Hua* such as *Outlaws of the Marsh (Shui Hu Zhuan)*, *Romance of the Three Kingdoms (San Guo Yan Yi)* and *Biography of Yue Fei (Yue Fei Zhuan)* were published one after another. *Lian Huan Hua* also began to enter the field of international cultural exchange, for example winning the gold prize at the Leipzig International Books Exhibition in 1959.

From 1983 to 1984, more than 1.5 billion copies were published, followed by the appearance of *Lian Huan Hua* papers. The themes became more varied. Such famous classical literary works as the *Dream of the Red Mansion (Hong Lou Meng)* and *Pilgrim to the West (Xi You Ji)* and the works of Chinese and foreign writers such as Lu Xun, Guo Moruo, Mao Dun, Ba Jin, Lao She, Shakespeare, Victor Hugo, Balzac, Maxim Gorky, Mark Twain and Hans Christian Andersen were also painted. Meanwhile, a large number of *Lian Huan Hua* introducing scientific, cultural and historical knowledge also appeared.

In order to promote further development, *Chinese Study of Comic Books* was founded in May 1983.

Rong Bao Zhai

Rong Bao Zhai is a world-renowned old-brand shop of calligraphy and painting works. It was founded in 1672. It is situated at Liulichang Xi Jie, Hepingmen Wai in Beijing. It is a tall, richly ornamented building in the ancient style.

Rong Bao Zhai has long housed many treasures of the study. There are Baizitu ink of Cheng Jun Fang of the Ming Dynasty (1368-1644), palace brush pen with colored brush and gold lacquer of the Qing Dynasty (1616-1911), paper used in palace, crystal inkpad box, etc. In particular, there is a Tianhuang stone with the weight of 4,275 g, heaviest in the world.

In its business, Rong Bao Zhai attaches importance to the collection of treasures of calligraphy and painting works. And it is honored as a "civilian Imperial Palace." For many years it has collected widely both ancient treasures and the works of modern and contemporary famous masters. There are some cultural relics of first State grade such as the remnant of the famous *Tiaoxi Poem* by Mi Fu. It is one of the units with the most varied cultural relics in Beijing.

In Rong Bao Zhai, wood-block water printing, a unique and ancient hand-printing technology in China, is kept alive. The copies of traditional Chinese paintings printed by this way look genuine. No other printing methods today can compare with this method.

Address: No.19, Liulichang Xi Jie, Beijing

Duo Yun Xuan

In 1900, a new shop emerged in Shanghai, Duo Yun Xuan. While dealing with the four treasures of the study, Duo Yun Xuan gradually has developed its two characteristic businesses: first, on a base of the tradition of making letter paper by itself, it has developed the copying technology of wood water printing. After a long period of artistic exploration, it has formed its special artistic style especially in showing the painting style and charm of freehand water-ink painting. Secondly, it collects old calligraphy and painting works and has saved a large number of State key cultural relics and art treasures. It prints large-sized paper and silk-copied Chinese calligraphy and painting works by complex printing procedures.

In 1978, Shanghai Calligraphy and Painting Publishing House was founded on the base of Duo Yun Xuan. Now Duo Yun Xuan is engaged in two businesses: the publishing business of Shanghai Calligraphy and Printing Publishing House and the cultural operations of Duo Yun Xuan. In terms of publishing, it is the unique professional fine arts publishing house in China dealing with artistic books such as Chinese painting, calligraphy and seal-cutting. There are seven editing rooms in it, i.e. wood-block water printing, traditional Chinese painting, calligraphy, seal cutting, fine arts, New Year's Painting, and textbooks. In its sales department situated at Nanjing Lu in the downtown area of Shanghai, there are sales hall, art gallery and purchasing room for original calligraphy and painting works. It is not only a famous art gallery where calligraphers, painters and seal cutters often do academic exchanges and learn from each other by exchanging skills, but also a characteristic shop dealing with collecting and operating ancient and modern original calligraphy and painting works, sutra stele rubbings and articles for use in study. There are various stored treasures involving all the past dynasties.

Address: No. 422, East Nanjing Lu, Shanghai, China

Shen Xue Ren Gallery

Shen Xue Ren Gallery is a professional fine arts gallery founded by Shen Xueren PhD, a painter of Weifang, Shandong Province. It covers an area of 1,200 square meters.

This gallery holds exhibitions of famous painters regularly. It is also promoted as the first on-line gallery for collectors. Shen Xue Ren Gallery has become one of the large professional fine arts galleries with good service and elegant favor in China.

This gallery has established its branches in Beijing, Qingdao, Zibo, Suzhou, Harbin, Xi'an, Tangshan, Jinan and Jinzhong. In June 2002, it was appraised as a five-star gallery by the Calligraphy and Painting Art Center of the Chinese Cultural Union. In 2004, it was appraised as one of the Top 10 Galleries in China by the Chinese Collectors' Association.

Website: http://www.sxr-gallery.com

Excellent paintings are exhibited for sale in the west gallery of Rong Bao Zhai.

Painters in the China National Academy paint or sketch from nature in countryside.

♦ China National Art Academy

China National Art Academy, originally named Research Institute of Traditional Chinese Painting, was founded in 1981. It was founded for researching, inheriting and carrying forward the excellent traditions of the art of traditional Chinese painting. This academy often invites nationally-renowned artistic critics and artists to give lectures and paint and hold various exhibitions on art research and fine arts works of traditional Chinese painting.

China National Art Academy is a beautiful building complex imitating the style of Suzhou garden. Inside the courtyard the ancient tower, small bridge, running water, bended corridor, corridor, and grassland are artfully combined with the exhibition halls with particular design and 48 studios, which offer a good environment for the research and creation by artists and the exhibition and exchanges of artistic works.

Under China National Art Academy, there are such departments as creation research department and exhibition halls. There are more than 20 professional creators and academic researchers, as well as the Academy Affairs (Art) Committee of China National Art Academy organized by more than 50 national-renown painters or theorists of traditional Chinese painting such as Wu Zuoren, Ye Qianyu, Liu Haisu, He Haixia, Huang Zhou, Li Keran, Liu Boshu, Cai Ruohong, Guan Shanyue, Cui Zifan, Tian Shiguang, Zhang Ding, Wu Guanzhong, Huang Yongyu, Ya Ming and Xie Zhiliu.

Since its foundation, a great deal of precious art information of artists of elder generations have been collected and arranged. The art storage has been enriched continuously. It hosted and organized China Exhibition of International Water-Ink Paintings, Academic Seminar on Traditional Chinese Painting, the Work Conference of the Academy and other large-sized art researching activities. Its publications include the painting magazine of Research of Traditional Chinese Painting, series of books of Research on Traditional Chinese Painting, Newsletter of Research Institute of Traditional Chinese Painting, and large-sized albums Engraved Stones of the Three Gorges and Modern Chinese Art Academies.

Website: http://www.zhggjhy.com

Music

Brief History of Folk Music

Mural painting in the Tomb of Su Sisheng--there are five persons in the right murals, of whom three kneel in the front row holding clarinet, seven-stringed Qin and Konghou in hands respectively and two stand in the back row, one playing vertical flute and one directing.

Based on carbon 14 testing of 16 bone flutes unearthed from a Neolithic site in Wuyang County, Henan Province, the history of Chinese music can be traced back to seven or eight thousand years ago. The distribution of the sound holes on the flutes indicates Chinese music at that time had reached a very high level.

During the 1,200-odd years from the Qin and Han dynasties to the Tang Dynasty, dances and grand music were the major forms of Chinese music. With the advent of the Sui and Tang dynasties, the situation changed; temple fairs held by Buddhist monasteries became the place for civil music activities and restaurants also held frequent activities of intoning poems. In the Song Dynasty, the places for performing music and dances included brothels, amusement parks, opera houses and teahouses, and there came into being various music performance forms such as zaju (poetic drama set to music) and nanxi (southern drama). After the Song Dynasty, "literati music" also saw great development along with "civil music", and with priority given to qin music, musical instruments such as pipa (lute), zheng (zither), dizi (flute) and xiao (vertical flute) also achieved further development. In the Ming and Qing dynasties, entertainments such as talking and singing and operas increasingly matured with abundant artistic variety, such as tanci (fiddle ballads), dagu (story-telling with drum accompaniment), paizi qu (tune music) and kunqu opera, further promoting musical art at that time. Musical instruments slowly developed further in the Qing Dynasty; the stringed bowed instruments such as the huqin (two-stringed bowed instrument) played a more and more important role in accompanying operas and playing tuttis with plucked string instruments and blowing instruments.

Xun

The xun is one of the oldest musical instruments in China, with a history of approximately 7,000 years.

Originally, it was mainly employed in royal music. It is said that the xun originated from the hunting tool of the stone meteor. In ancient times, people often tied a stone or mud ball to a rope that was then used for hunting wild birds and animals. Some of the balls were hollow, and so made many sounds when thrown. Most people found these hollow balls enjoyable and learned how to blow air into them. Gradually, the stone meteor became the musical instrument known as the xun. On top of the xun, there is a blowing hole, the bottom of the xun is flat and sound holes are distributed over the sides. Initially it had only one sound hole, but afterwards gained more. Finally, at the end of the 3rd century BC, a six-holed model appeared.

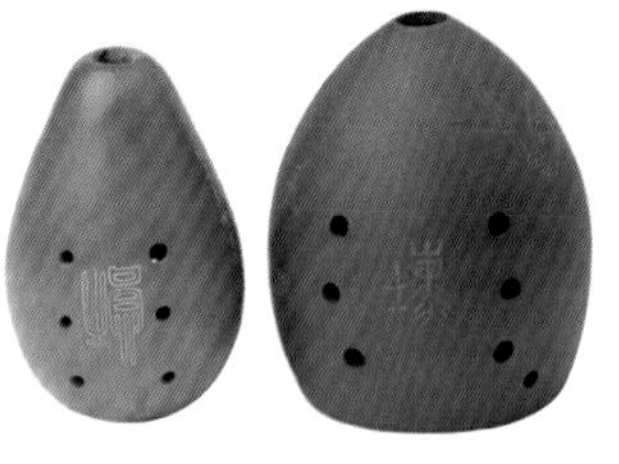
Xun

Chinese musicians have been trying to imitate the ancient earthen xun since the end of the 1930s. Professor Chenzhong of the Tianjin Conservatory of Music created a new version with nine holes on basis of the ancient pear-shaped six-holed model. It is made of purple earth in Yixing, Jiangsu. The nine-holed xun not only has kept the original form and tones, but also has expanded its range and become louder. It can play musical scales and semitones, and as a result, it became capable of playing many tunes. In addition, the tone color is unsophisticated, pure, deep and solemn with unique characteristics. The nine holes are arranged in an order complying with the playing habits of modern people, instead of the original free order, which is convenient for performing solo, tutti or accompaniment.

The birth of the nine-holed earthen xun indicates the resumption of the vital force of ancient xun. Zhao Liangshan from the Song and Dance Ensemble of Hubei Province later developed another new type with ten holes, which is suitable for high octave performances, which was not possible before.

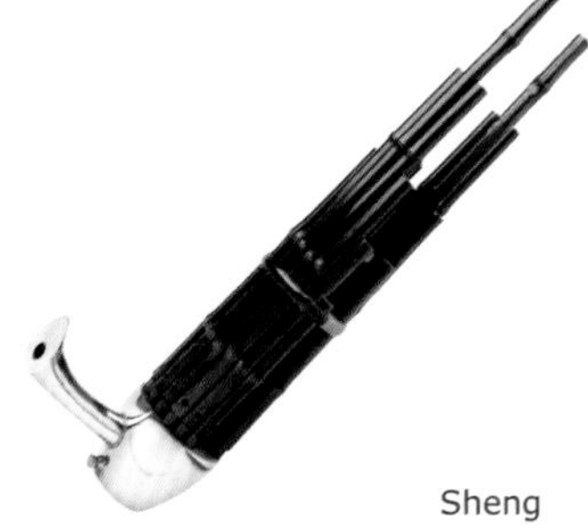
Sheng

• Folk Musical Instruments

Folk musical instruments are an indispensable part of Chinese music. With development spread over thousands of years, numerous varieties of instruments and abundant songs have appeared and can be classified into tutti instruments and solo instruments. The former include gong and drum, suona horn, erhu (two-stringed fiddle), pipa (lute), yangqin (hammered dulcimer), sanxian (three-stringed musical instrument), dizi (flute), sheng (wind instrument), xiao (vertical flute), etc.; the latter include guqin (seven-stringed qin), pipa, erhu, banhu, dizi and zheng, etc.

Sheng

The sheng was a wind instrument played in ancient China. It is the earliest musical instrument with the adoption of a free reed and has played an active role in promoting the development of Western musical instruments. In 1978, Paosheng, the earliest sheng forms, were found in Sui County, Hubei Province in a royal tomb of Zeng Houyi dating back more than 2,400 years.

A sheng sounds bright and sweet in tone, the alto of which is clear, the mediant (middle tone) soft, and the bourdon (low tone) deep and loud. Among the traditional piped instruments, the sheng is the only instrument capable of performing harmonies. When performing tutti with other instruments, the sheng can play a role of tempering the tone color and enriching the sound of the orchestra. Sometimes in grand ethnic orchestras, alto, mediant, and bourdon tones must be played together.

The cup-shaped dou is made of calabash, and the reed holder is made of wood. A dozen bamboo pipes in shape of horse's hoof are arranged on top of the dou. After the Tang Dynasty, performers began to make wooden dou. Later, the dou was made of copper and the reed was also made of copper instead of bamboo. There are different types of sheng in different places due to the long history of the sheng. In recent years, instrument designers and musicians in China have attempted continuous improvements of the instrument. They have made various new types such as expanding-range sheng and adding-keys sheng, and the original disadvantages such as a narrow range, inflexible switching of the tones, and slow performing ability have been enhanced, bringing new life to the sheng.

Xiao

The xiao, a Chinese vertical flute also called dongxiao, has been popular among Chinese people for thousands of years. It is proper to start with the history of the paixiao, however. During the early period of the paixiao's development thousands of years ago, people began to call it xiao. While performing, people found that it gave out high and low tones if there were holes of differing distances between each other. In this regard, the dongxiao of many holes and single pipe gradually took the place of the paixiao containing several pipes.

Its structure is quite simple, and is very much like the flute. It is usually made of purple bamboo, yellow and withered bamboo or white bamboo. The pipe is a little longer than the flute. The top is sealed by bamboo with a mouth, and there are five sound holes on the frontal side and one hole at the back. Besides, there are other three or four sound-releasing and sound-assisting holes at the lower back of the pipe, designed to adjust and smooth the tunes and raise the volume. There are various types of xiao, such as zizhu dongxiao, yuping xiao and jiujie xiao familiar to people.

Chui Xiao Shinv (Maid of Honour Playing the Xiao (a vertical bamboo flute)) by Tang Yin of the Ming Dynasty

A xiao sounds soft and graceful. The bourdon (low tone) is deep and of unique characteristic when playing feebly and the mediant (middle tone) is mellow and graceful. The performance skills are basically the same as that of the flute, but less flexible. For that reason, it is only suitable to play slow and peaceful lyrics instead of fast and flowery contents, which helps convey feelings and draws a beautiful picture of nature. The xiao has a rich expressive force. People may play the xiao solo, in ensemble and in concert, as well as part of some folk musical instrumental music such as that with stringed and woodwind instruments south of the lower reaches of the Changjiang River, and especially the music of Fujian and Guangdong provinces. In addition, people also play the xiao in folk music and as an accompaniment to local dramas.

Flute

The flute is highly popular with Chinese. Due to extensive use of bamboo, it is also called zhudi (bamboo flute).

The gnarls in the long bamboo pipe have been eliminated. There are one blowing hole, one affiliated hole and six sound holes. The blowing hole is the first hole of the flute, where the air is blown in to produce sounds. Next is the affiliated hole, which is covered by the membrane of the bamboo or bulrush. The air makes the membrane vibrate, which can produce clear and smooth tones.

Although the structure of the flute is very simple, it has a development history of 7,000 years. During the reign of Emperor Wudi of the Han Dynasty in the 1st century BC, the flute was also called hengchui (blowing horizontally). From the seventh century onwards, the flute was improved and the addition of the membrane covering created much progress in its expressive force so that performing techniques developed to a high level. With the development of free verse of the Song Dynasty and the music of the Yuan Dynasty, the flute became the main accompaniment, and was also indispensable in folk and ethnic dramas.

The flute has a rich performance spectrum. Not only can it play loud and sonorous tunes, but also cheerful dancing music and quiet songs. In addition, it can imitate various sounds in nature such as the twittering of birds. Besides, there are many kinds of flutes, such as quid, bangdi, fixing-tune flute, flute with keys, yupingdi, seven-holed flute and eleven-holed flute, which form

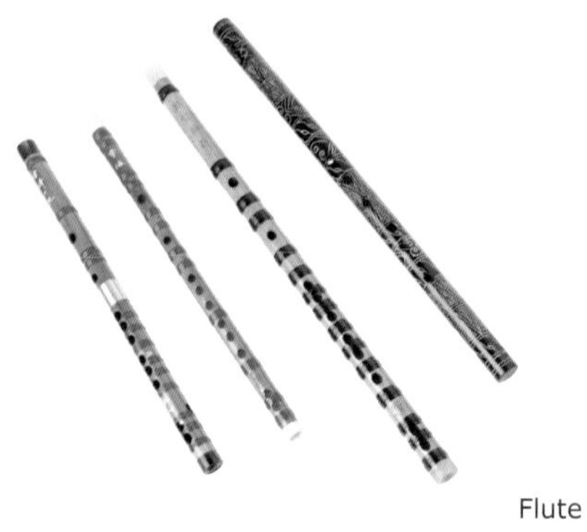

Flute

two schools, the southern school and northern school, with widely different styles.

Besides bamboo flute, there are jade flute, porcelain flute, iron flute, copper flute, etc. There are various performing techniques with rich expressive force.

Guanzi

The guanzi is a double-reed musical instrument with a long history. It developed in ancient Persia (today's Iran). In the Western Han Dynasty, some 2,000 years ago, the guanzi had already been very popular for a time in China's Xinjiang region. Later, it was introduced into the hinterland and performance levels greatly improved. Today, northern people frequently play the guanzi.

The structure is very simple, as it is made of only three parts, pipe whistle, qinzi and column-shaped pipe body. It is widely used in solo, concert, and accompaniment. In some music of Northern China, the guanzi has played a very important role. The performance varies, with performers able to execute roulade, glissando, slipping, aspirating, and flowery tongue tune (types of notes) as well as some unique skills such as beating tune, striding tune, rinsing tune and teeth tune. Besides hand finger skills, a performer can make high and low tones depending on the depth of the whistle in the mouth. Performers, depending on the rounding of their mouth, can imitate human voices and animal sounds.

Besides abundant performing skills, there are various kinds and different sizes of guanzi, such as the small, middle-sized and large guanzi, double-reed guanzi and guanzi with keys. The big one is about 33 cm long, the middle 24.5 cm and the small 18 cm. The big one is four levels lower than the small one and has loud and sonorous tone color. It often plays a role of leading the performance in northern orchestras.

The tone of the guanzi is loud, clear and melodious with unique characteristic and has strong imitating and expressive force. The instrument can be used widely in local dramas, folk wind instrument ensemble and monastery music, etc.

Hulusi

It is a wind instrument popular in some ethnic groups like the Dai and Yi ethnic group. The instrument adopts half a calabash as its sound box into which three bamboo pipes of different length are inserted and combined. A copper reed of peaked-tongue shape is embedded in the part of a pipe that is inserted into the calabash. The middle bamboo pipe is a little longer with seven sound holes and it is the major pipe; performers can make the other two bamboo pipes produce two successive bourdons to compose various chords. It has graceful and soft tone and is often used to play solo and tutti.

Hulusi

Tone of Hulusi is a piece of music popular among the Achang ethnic group living in the basin of the Dayingjiang River in Yunnan. Young people there like to play it as a love offering. The instrument is also popular with other ethnic groups.

Bawu

The bawu has a very special tone color and is the wind instrument used by some ethnic groups like the Yi, Miao and Hani. It looks like a flute. The pipe is made of bamboo or wood, and there are eight sound holes and, on one side, there is a blowing hole with a peaked-tongue-shaped copper reed (the blowing hole is not on the same plane with the sound holes). Performers play it horizontally and make quiet sounds by vibrating the reed.

In recent years many performers have made improvements, adding sound keys, enlarging the range and making the sound louder.

Erhu

The erhu, one type of huqin, is a very famous stringed instrument in China. Its history can be traced back to the Tang Dynasty. It was welcomed among the ethnic people of northwestern China. The erhu has long been the instrumental accompaniment in traditional dramas.

The erhu's structure is quite simple. There is a slim neck about 80 centimeters long, on the surface of which two strings are fixed. In addition, there is a cup-shaped box and a bow made of horsehair. While performing, the musician is usually seated, with the instrument and bow held in the left and right hand respectively. The range consists of three octaves. It can play solo, as well as accompaniment in dancing and singing, dramas, and talking and singing. In ethnic orchestras, the erhu even plays the leading role, just as the violin does in Western orchestras. The tone of the erhu has a rich performance spectrum and is close to the human voice, so the erhu is a musical instrument capable of singing and is called "the Chinese violin". The somewhat melancholic tone is good at conveying sad emotions.

The erhu is highly popular with Chinese because of its simple design, low cost and graceful tone. A large number of erhu musical works have been passed down from ancient times. Especially since the 1930s, Mr. Liu Tianhua created and played many famous erhu musical pieces, such as *Liang Xiao (A Pleasant Night), Guangming Xing (Bright Tour), Kongshan Niaoyu (Tranquil Mountain with Birds' Singing),* etc. The most famous erhu musical work should be *Erquan Yingyue (Moon Image Reflected in the Erquan Springs)*, created by Mr. Hua Yanjun, a blind Chinese folk musician. This musical piece is widely known in China and has also stepped into the musical halls of the world and has earned the praise and favor from the audiences. The Japanese conductor Seiji Ozawa was brought to tears by the music. He said: "The heartbroken feeling is absolutely suitable to describe the sense. People should kneel down while listening to the music."

Gaohu

The gaohu developed from the erhu and it is closely linked to Cantonese music.

This is usually performed with folk instruments in regions of Guangdong. It originated from local dramas and folk music. Around the 1920s, the Cantonese musician and performer Lu Wencheng made great improvements to the erhu. He changed the silk strings to steel ones, and raised the tones. When performing, he put the box between his legs. This erhu with clear and bright tone became known as the gaohu and soon became the leading instrument in Cantonese music.

The materials, construction technique and structure of the gaohu are similar to that of the erhu. The biggest difference is the box; that of the gaohu is thin. Designers had few limits in making the instrument. Some designers

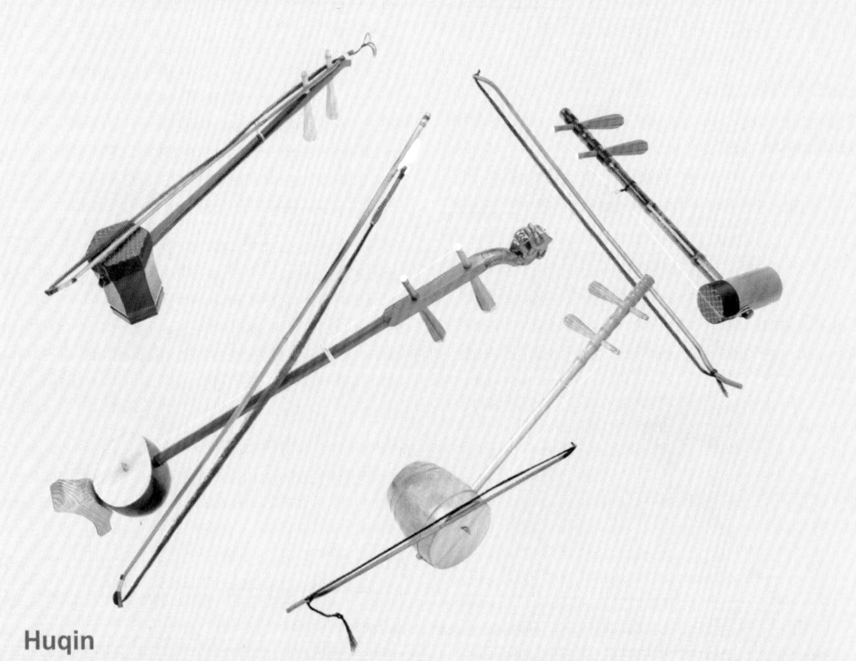

Huqin

Just as its name implies, the huqin was introduced from the Hu tribe in the Western Regions, instead of being a local product of China. In the Tang Dynasty, there was a Xi Tribe living in northern China that had a musical instrument called the xiqin. Later, as "the xiqin is originally the musical instrument of the hu people", its name was changed to "huqin". In the Song Dynasty, there appeared the "horsetail huqin". From the Qing Dynasty onwards, the huqin developed to more than ten varieties, erhu, zhonghu, sihu, gaohu, jinghu, zhuihu, banhu, etc. These instruments play an important role in Chinese folk music.

changed the round box into a flat round one, which raised the volume. Some changed it to a three-stringed instrument, which expanded the range to five levels down.

The gaohu has a clear and bright sound. Along with this characteristic, the full-bodied bass part has been given great prominence. As a rule, the gaohu is given a highly valued seat in Chinese ethnic orchestras. In addition, it is especially good at performing lyrical, lively and flowery rhythms as it has a very rich performance spectrum. For that reason, it is often used to perform the accompaniment of theme songs according to emotional demands.

Banhu

The banhu has a history of more than 300 years. It is called banhu because its box is made of pieces of wood flock bonded together. Compared to other instruments of the huqin family, the banhu is characterized by loud volume and clear tone. It is especially good at expressing loud and sonorous, fevered, enthusiastic and hot emotions, but is also graceful and soft.

At first, the banhu was popular mainly in northern China. It was frequently used as the major accompaniment in many local operas and musical performances such as Hebei Bangzi (a local opera in Hebei), Pingju, Henan and Shanxi opera. The way the banhu is used in such performances, however, varies from place to place with different styles and unique local coloring.

In recent decades, musicians and instrument designers have made great efforts to improve their skills. Many new types of banhu have been created. Among the new members are the mediant banhu, alto banhu, three-stringed banhu, bamboo banhu, Shanxi opera banhu and so on.

Along with improvements in manufacturing, performance skills have also been improved. The banhu has become an indispensable part of ethnic bands in China, and is also a solo-performing instrument with strong local flavor. It is often used to perform accompaniment for ethnic operas and singing and dancing as well as plain singing.

Zhuihu

The zhuihu (Bowed String Instrument), also known as zhuiqin or zhuizi, is adapted from the small sanxian (three-stringed instrument). It can be used to perform solo and tutti. Since zhuihu has a wide diapason, a soft sound and relatively high sound volume, different from other instrument, performers can use it to imitate the voice, singing and talking of human and cries of birds and animals.

There is a legend about its origins. In the Qing Dynasty, Emperor Kangxi banned all opera performances in the Forbidden City and artists had to earn a living on the street. One day, an artist's small sanxian was bitten by mice and the covering leather of the sound box was holed. In order not to miss a chance to perform, the artist used a thin tung wooden piece to replace the leather and used a bow from the huqin to play the sanxian. Thus was a musical instrument that can not only play music but also imitate human voice was generated and it was later called the zhuihu.

Matouqin (Horse-head Fiddle)

The matouqin is a Mongolian instrument. It is called horse-head fiddle because the top of the pole is carved in the shape of a horse's head. The instrument has a long history, and it was quite popular with Mongolian people during the early period of the 13th century. The resonance box resembles the echelon and the top of the pole is carved in the shape of a horse head, which is the basic form of the matouqin. The particular strings, which are made of scores of long horsehair combined together, are fixed with silk. The sound produced by the rubbing with a horsetail bow on horsehair strings is sweet, deep and pleasant, unique among Chinese and foreign stringed instruments.

The early performers made the instruments themselves. They could only be played inside due to their low volume. Later designers made improvements on the traditional instrument. The range was expanded, and the improved matouqin is characterized by clear and bright tone on a base of its original soft and deep tone. With those improvements, the new instrument could be performed on stage and outdoors and, can be played by both rubbing and plucking the strings, becoming one of the main solo instruments in Mongolian music.

In addition, there are also newly-made large and medium-sized organs. Their performing skills are like that of the cello and contrabass (double bass) in the West. The matouqin family has a complete range of alto, mediant and bourdon and can enrich Chinese ethnic music. It is worth mentioning that people can still find Mongolian designs on these newly made instruments displaying traditional style and elegance. In appearance, a well-made matouqin is a piece of exquisite artistry.

Liuqin

The liuqin is a plucked musical instrument belonging to the pipa category. It is named liuqin or liu ye qin because it is made from the wood of the willow tree and also its appearance is similar to the willow leaf. The look and structure of a liuqin resemble that of a pipa. The structure of the earliest liuqin was very simple. Its appearance is so rustic and localized that the Chinese people gave it the very affectionate name of tu pipa, in which the Chinese character tu means rustic and simple. The tu pipa has been very popular in Shandong, Anhui, and Jiangsu provinces in Eastern China. It is played as accompaniment of local operas.

Not only does the liuqin have a similar appearance and structure to the pipa, but also is played in the same way but performers should use a plectrum to pluck the strings. While playing the instrument, the musician should sit straight, holding the instrument at a slant in the left hand before the chest, and press the strings. The plectrum is held between the thumb and the index finger of the right hand. The posture looks very graceful.

In recent decades, musicians and workers have invented new types of liuqin—the three-stringed liuqin and the four-stringed alto liuqin. In the former, the strings and music poles were increased. Most importantly, the shaft of the Chinese sorghum (a kind of plant) was replaced by bamboo, and the strings were made of steel instead of silk. These changes greatly improved the qualities of the liuqin and gave it rich expressive force and it began to be played solo instead of purely accompaniment as before.

Today, the liuqin has been played in all kinds of music performances in China. In folk bands, due to unique sound effects, it is often used to play the high pitch part of the main rhythm. Because the tone is not easily covered and mixed by the sound of other musical instruments, it sometimes plays a very important role in highlight performances. In addition, the liuqin has the sound effect of the stringed mandolin instrument, so it can generate a special flavor when played together with Western bands.

Matouqin (horse-head fiddle)

Dongbula

The dongbula is an ancient stringed musical instrument of the Kazak ethnic group. In Turkic language, the name dongbula has special meanings; "dong" describes the sound of the music, and "bula" means to fix the strings. The dongbula has a very long history and was popular in Xinjiang as early as the 3rd century BC.

The body of the dongbula is made of wood, and looks like an enlarged spoon. The earliest forms were simple to make. The artist cuts an entire piece of wood into the shape of a spoon, mounts a faceplate, and then draws two pieces of sheep intestines as strings, and finally fits it onto nine tambours at the end of the handle. The dongbula is an indispensable accompanying instrument for Kazak folk singers.

The dongbula can be played solo or in ensemble and accompaniment and has a rich expressive force. The performing mode is the same as other plucked instruments. The musician should hold it on a slant in the left hand before the chest, and press the strings with the index finger and thumb, while using the middle finger and thumb of the right hand to pluck. Through the various ways of performing, listeners may have vivid images of gurgling springs, the clear twittering of birds, joyful flocks of sheep, and horses with beating hooves.

The Kazak people are playing the Dongbula.

• Spring Moon Light on the Flowers by the River

Spring Moonlight on the Flowers by the River is one of the most famous Chinese traditional music works. It had been popular among ordinary people before the year 1875, with a history of more than 1,000 years, and has since become one of the masterpieces in the treasury of Chinese classical music.

It was originally named as *Flutes and Drums at Dusk* (or *Xunyang Pipa)*, and was a pipa solo. Later, it was adapted to tutti form and named *Xunyang Moonlight (or Xunyang Music)*. Then, it was renamed as *Spring Moonlight on the Flowers* by the River by Zheng Jinwen in 1930. The music has traditional flavor, gentle, sweet and pleasant, and is highly appraised by both Chinese and foreign audiences.

According to the description, at dusk, when the moon climbs up to the eastern mountain, the moonlight by the river in the spring is secluded and tranquil, the water surface ripples with green waves, and the afterglow of the setting sun on the river surface is peaceful and intoxicating. A misty and melodious musical sound of playing the xiao and the drum is passed dimly from a canoe far away. People become intoxicated in this idyllic scene.

The melody is divided into 10 small sections and each section has a title: bells and drums on the river tower, moon climbing up to the eastern mountain, wind back to crooked river, tiers of flower shadows, deep water and high clouds, fisherman's song at dusk, whirling water beating the shore, sound of paddle accompanying distant rapids, the creak of an oar of a returning canoe, coda.

Pipa

This is named after two kinds of performing methods. It was extremely popular in the Tang Dynasty with frequent competitions that helped raise performance skills.

There are numerous pipa works that can be classified into literary music, military music and large music. The literary music gives priority to expressing emotions, the tone is clear, soft, exquisite and light, and the representative works include: *Chunjiang Huayue Ye* (Spring Moon Light on the Flowers by the River), and *Feihua Diancui*, *Hangong Qiuyue*. Military music is mostly straightforward, bold and unconstrained, and the works include: *Shimian Maifu* (Surrounded on All Sides), *Bawang Xiejia* (The Overlord Doffs His Armor) and so on, which describe ancient war scenes. Large music is mostly lively and delightful and is relatively flexible and free.

Owing to long history, a large number of music works and performance skills have been accumulated. In 1818, *Huaqiuchao Pipa Scores* was formally published in China collecting a dozen ancient music works. In 1929, Shen Hao, descendant of "Pudong School" of pipa, made conclusion on the performance technique of pipa and compiled *Yangzhengxuan Pipa Scores*.

A modern famous pipa musician Liu Dehai made improvements on the performance technique, composed pipa works including *Little Sisters on the Grassland*, a famous pipa concerto, and initiated a new way for performing the pipa.

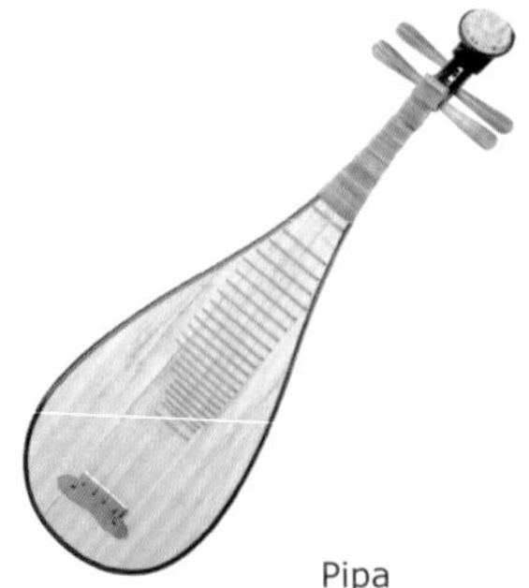

Pipa

Ruan

The ruan is a stringed musical instrument. Its form is very simple and it is made up of the head, the handle and the body. The head is usually decorated with some traditional Chinese bone-carved artwork such as the dragon and ruyi (an S-shaped ornamental object). There are four tuning gauges on the two sides. The body is an oblate resonance box created by gluing together a faceplate, backplate and frameplate. The structural theory, materials, and performing skills are quite similar to those of the pipa.

In recent years, Chinese musicians have made many improvements, developing an alto, mediant, tenor (big) and bourdon ruan.

The alto ruan, which is loud and clear, plays the role of performing the theme in the band.

The tone of the mediant ruan is quiet and soft, full of poetic flavor. It is used to perform the cantus and episodes in concerts, producing appealing effects. It is abundant in rhythmic variations while performing the accompaniment. If more than two mediant ruans are used to play harmony in separate sections in a band, the effect will be much more full-bodied.

The big ruan is five levels lower than the mediant ruan. It is similar to the cello. When used in a band, it often incorporates the mediant ruan in octachord, which may strengthen its sound effect and is suitable for setting off the lyrical rhythm. While performing the solo and chords, it may intensify the rhythm and set off the ardent and unrestrained effects of the music. The bourdon ruan sounds deep, similar to a contrabass.

Guqin

This is the oldest plucked musical instrument in China with a history of more than 3,000 years. It is a musical instrument with the greatest standing in ancient China and headed the list of four subjects scholars trained themselves in, i.e. guqin, chess, calligraphy and painting.

Its tone is vigorous and deep with floating notes. It has strong Chinese ethnic characteristics. The performance technique is complicated and has some special skills such

Ruan

as glissando, rubbing, and harmonious notes, with a rich performance spectrum. The guqin is a typical musical instrument for solo and is seldom used in any other way. In ancient times, it was often used as an accompanying instrument for literati intoning poems.

The late guqin musician Guan Pinghu (1897-1967) once played a gupin musical piece, *Liu Shui* (Running Water), which was included on a golden disc carried into outer space by a US satellite. He made an outstanding contribution in both performance and research.

Yangguan Sandie is a well-known guqin musical piece and it is also named *Yangguan Melody*. It first appeared in *Zheying Shezi Piano Scores* in 1491. The song created for qin piano performance was based on a poem by Wang Wei (699-759). Wang's poem was sung widely in the Tang Dynasty and was later adapted for qin piano performance. It is still performed today, expressing the bitter feeling when people are to part. It also shows the care for friends.

Painting of Cout Ladies Tuning Qin and Sipping Tea

Se

The se is a plucked stringed musical instrument frequently used for accompaniment in ancient China. According to *Rites*, the se was always employed to accompany singing in the rituals of village drinking, village shooting and entertainment. In the Wei, Jin and Southern and Northern dynasties, it was often used to accompany harmony, and, in the Sui and Tang dynasties, it was often used to accompany qingyue. The se is similar to the qin in shape, but it has no cord symbol. It has 25 strings, each of which has a music pole to adjust the length of the string and fix the pitch. It is usually tuned according to the five-tone scale, but the seven-tone scale can be achieved by pressing strings to raise a semitone.

In ancient times, the se was frequently used to play ensemble with the qin and the sheng. It can play arpeggio, consonance, chord and rapid rhythm. It can also be played with such skills as rubbing and glissando.

• Shi Jing (The Book of Poetry)

Shi Jing (The Book of Odes) is one of the important sources of Chinese literature and the earliest collection of Chinese poetry, containing 305 poems from a period of nearly 500 years from the early times of the Western Zhou Dynasty to the mid-Spring and Autumn Period (770-476 BC). The sources of the poems can be divided into three kinds: "offered poems", when the Emperor of Zhou held court, officials offered him poems for giving advice or praise; "collected poems", when the musical officials of the Zhou Court or all vassal states toured towns and villages to collect poems popular among common people; and, accompanied songs, used in rites of offering sacrifice to gods and at banquets, which were created by musical officials and some "professional" musicians such as Wu and Shi in the court.

Painting of Songs of Bin (part)-this part depicts the scenes of picking up mulberry leaves, ploughing, drinking, watching dance and paying a formal visit, which is described in *The Book of Songs*.

Accordingly, these poems belong to different sorts in Shi Jing: those originating from the masses belonged to Feng music which refered to local music of various vassal states, while Ya music refered to court music and was also called "imperial music". Those presented to the Zhou emperors naturally belonged to Ya music. Song music referred to songs and dancing music with relaxed rhythm mainly used in rites of offering sacrifice. Ya and Song were solemn and long, and Feng, also named "State Feng", bright and vivid, so it seemed that the former belonged to imperial courts and the latter to the folk. The book widely reflects all aspects of social life at the time.

It is characterized by realistic means to reflect factually the social life, and working life at that time.

• Official Conservatory in the Han Dynasty

Most of the folk songs in the Han, Wei and Six Dynasties (206 BC-420 AD) were preserved in the official conservatory, and the Official Conservatory in the Han Dynasty is actually a collection of folk songs in the regions along the Huaihe River, the lower reaches of the Yangtze River and the middle and the lower reaches of the Yellow River. At that time, there appeared narrative songs, such as Peacock's Flying to Southeast, and Mulan was Enlisted , which mostly reflected the sufferings inflicted on people by wars and family tragedies under the feudal ethnic code. These stories were passed down from previous generations and are known to almost everyone. They have profound effect as they not only have the form of folk songs but also became famous lists of operas. The folk songs in the Official Conservatory had the words processed and compiled and the music was processed by a famous musician Li Yannian in the Han Dynasty. It is accompanied by traditional stringed and woodwind instruments and is called xianghe (in step with each other) songs.

Tanbu'er

The tanbu'er is one of the plucked musical instruments of the Uygur ethnic group. It is said that there were folk artists in the 15th century who were masters of the instrument. The instrument has a small sound box in the shape of a calabash. The handle is long with five steel strings which are tuned in four or five tones. The two outer strings play rhythm and the middle string and the two inner strings play consonance of various accompanying figures. The instrument has a pure tone and large volume and is often used for playing solo and instrumental ensemble. When performing, musicians hold the organ on a slant on the right leg, with the sound box close to the belly, left hand holding the instrument and pressing strings and the right hand plucking them with a plectrum. Traditional music works include *Aochamo, Linpart and Sharpa.*

Pipa of Dong Ethnic Group

This is often used for accompaniment in Dong songs. It is popular among Dong-inhabited areas in Guizhou, Guangxi and Hunan provinces. Every village of Dong ethnic group has drum towers. On festivals and leisure times, everyone will enjoy themselves, playing the pipa to accompany songs and sing in antiphonal style. Singers of the Dong ethnic group often use it to accompany themselves when singing pipa songs.

The pipa of the Dong ethnic group is composed of head, handle, tuning gauge, resonance box and strings. The size of the pipa varies in different areas and it can be classified into large, medium and small types. The large type has a soft and deep tone, the medium a bright and sweet tone and the small one a silvery and pleasant tone. When performing, musicians hold the instrument and press the strings with the left hand and pluck them with a small ox horn or bamboo-made plectrum held in the right hand. Besides solo and ensemble, it can also accompany singing and dancing.

Yangqin (Dulcimer)

Yangqin (Dulcimer)

The dulcimer is a string-beaten musical instrument with a clear tone and rich expressive force, that can be played solo or in concert and accompaniment for story-telling, talking and singing, and dramas. It is very important in folk and ethnic bands.

The dulcimer is made of wood. The body is its resonance box and is shaped like a butterfly, and so it is also called the butterfly dulcimer. While performing, players put it on a wooden frame and hold two bamboo sticks with elasticity in both hands to knock the strings.

The performance range and tones of dulcimer are changeable. The bourdon part is deep, the mediant pure, and the alto bright. The instrument is good at producing fast rhythms to express lively, resilient, relaxing and joyous feelings.

The instrument has a history of more than four hundred years in China. During this period, instrument designers in China have created new types of dulcimer, such as sound-changing dulcimer, tone-switching dulcimer, zheng dulcimer and the electronic dulcimer.

After years of development, the dulcimer has carried with it traditional and ethnic features, which can be found in its manufacture, performance and musical creations.

Konghou

The konghou is an ancient plucked stringed instrument also called a "Chinese harp". There are three kinds: one is played lying flat and one upright, while the third is the phoenix-headed konghou.

As early as the Spring and Autumn and Warring States periods (770-221 BC), there appeared rudiments of the konghou played lying flat in the Chu Kingdom in southern China.

The konghou played upright, also called hukonghou, upright-head konghou and standing konghou, was introduced from Persia by the Western Region in the Eastern Han Dynasty (25-220) and became popular in the Sui and Tang dynasties. It was generally played in rites and ceremonies.

The phoenix-headed konghou was originally "Weina", a bow-shaped harp in India, and was introduced from India to the Central Plains of China in the Eastern Jin Dynasty (317-420).

The konghou, with its sweet tone and wide diapason, can be used to play not only cantos but also chords and has many advantages in both solo and tutti performances. It was an indispensable instrument in China's ancient royal courts. From bas-reliefs in the Yungang Grottoes of Datong and Dunhuang murals we can see figures playing the konghou.

Bianzhong (Chime Bells)

Chime bells, or bianzhong, were an important percussion instrument in ancient China. Chime bells are divided into one or more groups in which there are dozens of big and small bells, each with a different tone. Although the forms of the bells are different, as they developed in different years, there are fine designs on all of them.

As early as 3,500 years ago, in the Shang Dynasty, there existed serial bells, which were made up of three bells. Over time, the number of bells increased. The ancient instrument was used in royal performances, and was not popular among the people. During wars, royal meetings, and sacrifices, the chimes would be played.

In ancient China, chime bells were an exclusive musical instrument for the upper class. It was regarded as the symbol of power and social class. Recently, ancient bells have been discovered in royal tombs in Yunnan, Shanxi, Hubei, and other provinces. The most remarkable ancient bell set is Zenghouyi bells found in the tomb of Zeng Houyi in Sui County in Hubei Province.

Qing

The qing is the oldest percussion instrument. It is designed finely, and carries with it an ancient flavor. It was first used in folk music and dancing activities. Later, like another ancient musical instrument called the bianzhong, it was used to play some graceful music when the ancient rulers sent troops to war and offered sacrifices. In terms of where and how it was performed, the instrument is divided into two groups. One, called teqing, was performed when the emperors held a memorial ceremony for the

• Zeng Houyi Bells

In the huge tomb of Zeng Houyi, who was a "Zeng Kingdom" duke with the family name of "Yi" around 400 BC, there is a chamber particularly for musical instruments buried with the dead. Among the instruments found was a qin, a zheng, a five-stringed musical instrument, five se, a sheng and a hanging drum. The other instruments found were bianqing, jian drum, paixiao, se, and bao drum. The most distinguished among them were Zeng Houyi bells – the gem of ancient Chinese Art.

The Zeng Houyi bells are a three-tiered set of 65 refined bronze bells. These are arranged in turn on a carpenter's-square-shaped tung wood shelf. On each bell's body there were engraved inscriptions in the style of Jin Zhuan with more than 2,800 characters recording many musical terms and including "made by Zeng Houyi".

The musical range of the Zeng Houyi bells is more than five octaves, and the structure of musical scale is similar to the seven-tone scale of the modern C Major, only next to modern piano. It can produce five-tone, six-tone and seven-tone scale music. It is presumed by modern scholars that this set of bells can carry the main melody as well as the harmony.

Zeng Houyi bells have the most unearthed bells, the largest scale and a good state of preservation. It is honored as a miracle in human cultural history. The bells have a clear, bright, melodious and pleasant sound and can produce rhythm like singing, so they are also called "singing bells".

In 1982, Wuhan Ethnic Instrument Designing Factory and Wuhan Fine Apparatus Foundry Mill produced a set of new bells based on the Zeng Houyi bells. A series of innovations were adopted to satisfy the demands of scenic performance and modern music. The three-tiered set of bells has 24 bells, each of which can produce two tones.

gods and ancestors. The other, called bianqing, was composed of a group of qings and was hung on a wooden shelf for playing. It was mainly used in royal music performances.

In August 1978, a royal tomb more than 2,400 years old, the tomb of Zeng Houyi, was discovered in Sui County, Hubei Province. More than a 120 ancient instruments and cultural relics with ancient Chu cultural characteristics were dug out, such as the bianzhong, qin, se, xiao, drum, etc. There were altogether 32 Zeng Houyi bianqing pieces, which were hung in upper and lower lines on a bronze qing shelf. They were made of limestone, bluestone, and boulder. The sound was bright and clear. It was a pity that most of them were broken, and so cannot produce any sound. In 1980, the museum of Hubei Province and the Wuhan Institute of Physics worked together to duplicate the Zeng Houyi bianqing. The sounds produced by the new ones were basically the same as the originals. The tones were moving and graceful.

In 1983, the Dance and Sing Ensemble of Hubei Province created a set of stone-made bianqing with 32 single pieces. In September 1984, an ethnic instrument-designing factory and a boulder sculpture mill in Suzhou developed a set of jade bianqing with 18 single pieces.

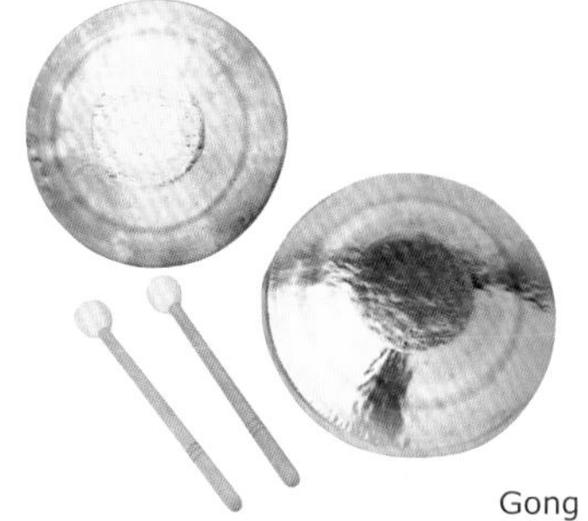
Gong

Drum

Gong

The gong is a traditional Chinese percussion instrument playing a very important role in ethnic music. It is widely used not only in ethnic performances, folk concerts, dramas, operas, and singing and dancing, but also in celebrations, boat races, lion dances, labor races and harvest festivities.

The gong comes from melted copper. The structure is quite simple; it is shaped like a circular arc and is fixed to the frame on four sides. The performers use wooden sticks to strike the middle of the gong, which makes the instrument vibrate to produce sound.

The ethnic groups in Southwest China were the first to play the instrument. Around the 2nd century BC, the gong gradually became popular nationally because of strengthened cultural exchanges. At that time, the copper gong was widely used in wars. Ancient military leaders often used this instrument to command their armies. In a military term in ancient China, Mingjin Shoubing (beating Jin to withdraw troops), "Jin" is another name of the ancient copper gong.

Over a long period, about 30 kinds of gongs developed, due to the instrument's popularity in different areas and occasions. The big and small gongs are the most commonly used. In grand musical performances, the big gong is often used to enhance atmosphere and strengthen the rhythm. In dramas, it is used to add romance and give prominence to the characters' personality. The small gong is widely used as well, especially in Peking Opera, pingju (a local opera in North and Northeast China), bangzi opera, flower-drum opera and many other local operas, as well as folk art forms, dramas, pipe and percussion instrument performances, and folk dancing.

Drum

The drum is a percussion instrument frequently used in China. From the perspective of culture relics these days, the drum has an estimated history of 3,000 years. The drum is widely used in various kinds of activities, such as ethnic music, operas, folk art forms, singing and dancing, boat races, lion dances, and festivals and laboring competitions.

The drum has a quite simple structure made up of the drum skin and body. The drum skin is the sound producer and is usually made of animal hide, and it covers the drum frame. The sounds are produced through vibration when a person strikes or taps on the skins. In China, there are many kinds o f drums including yaogu (indicating drums tied to the waist, with gu meaning drum), dagu, tonggu, and huapengu.

The yaogu is big in the middle and small at the two ends, shaped like a canister. The two ends are covered with cow skin or the skin of a mule. There are two rings on one side of the drum body, tied with a rope. There are four yaogu specifications, but none with fixed tones. They sound clear, and are often used to perform accompaniments for folk dancing. While performing, dancers usually hang the drum on the waist, holding drumsticks in both hands.

The taipinggu is popular in the three provinces in Northeastern China, Inner Mongolia, Shaanxi, Gansu, Hebei and Anhui provinces, and is a characteristic musical instrument frequently used by Han, Man and Mongolian ethnic groups. The shape of the drum varies among different ethnic groups; it is elliptical in Man ethnic group, round, peach-shaped and oblate in Han ethnic group, and oblate in Mongolian ethnic group. The taipinggu is more than a musical instrument. People will beat the drum while dancing. They hold the drum handle high in the left hand, shaking it in various directions, and hold a small whip in the right hand to beat the drum. There are solo dance, double dance and group dance. Especially on festivals such as the Spring Festival and Festival of Lanterns, the drum can produce a very joyful atmosphere.

• Chu Ci (Songs of Chu)

This is a folk song collection compiled by a great poet Qu Yuan based on ancient wu songs along the middle reaches of the Yangtze River. It appeared in the fourth century BC. It is full of ancient myths, legends and fancies. It started to adopt the expressive means of romanticism, developed the four-word folk songs in the *Book of Poetry* to "sao"-style songs with free sentence form and changeable rhyming endings, and has strong regional color. *Li Sao (The Poem on Departure)* by poet Qu Yuan is the outstanding representative of *Chu Ci*.

Folk Songs

Folk songs have been widely popular among people for many generations. It is a musical form with the most typical popular style. With distinctive ethnic characteristics and local color, they are the crystallization of group wisdom through continuous enrichment in circulation. Owing to a long history, broad terrain, great population and numerous ethnic groups, there are a tremendous number of folk songs in China. According to statistics, there are more than 300,000 folk songs collected in all regions.

Shijing (the Book of Poetry) is the first poetry collection in China and unveils the social life of ethnic groups and the common people in the Zhou Dynasty. With profound and rich accumulation of culture, it shows the initial grand achievement of Chinese ancient poems. Later, the "official conservatory" in the Han Dynasty played an important role in recording and promoting folk songs. Against the background of absorbing surrounding ethnic music through external cultural exchanges, in the Tang Dynasty, Chinese folk songs had a flourishing vital force. From the Song Dynasty to the Ming and Qing dynasties, many folk ditty types had become popular, such as haozi (work song), tian'ge (field song), shan'ge (mountain song), xintianyou (Shanxi local melody), hua'er (a folk song popular in Gansu, Qinghai and Ningxia provinces), etc. In history, folk songs have had many different titles, such as xiaoqu (ditty), liqu (popular songs), xiaoling (short lyric), suqu (folk song), shici (time songs), and shan'ge which was usually used to refer various folk songs in the Ming and Qing dynasties.

Semi-Agriculture and Semi-Pasturing Folk Song Region

This covers the areas along the upper reache of the Yellow River including Gansu, Qingha and Ningxia provinces where Han, Hui, Tuzu Salar, Bonan, Dongxiang, Tibetan and Yugu ethnic groups live. Since ancient times it has bee dominated by a semi-agriculture and semi-pasturin culture. In history, it was a key link on the "Si Road". Owing to early exchanges between easter and western cultures and long blending of multip ethnic groups, a type of song jointly held by eig ethnic groups came into being, namely Hua'er. Th folk songs include "domestic songs" and "fie songs"; the former covers various drinking song banquet songs, little words and yangge, and th latter includes various mountain songs and herdin songs such as Hua'er. Field songs can only be sun outdoors. "Hua'er" is a representative style and ha loud, sonorous, and long tunes, deep and swe tones and a straightforward and unsophisticate style. All these ethnic groups sing songs in Chines and each ethnic group has its own supplementar words. The famous songs include *Climbing u High Mountains to Look over Level Land.*

Xinjiang Folk Song Region

This folk song region is located in Xinjiang and is represented by the folk songs of the Uygur and Kazak ethnic groups. It was influenced by Islamic traditional culture in Central Asia and is close to Arabic music and culture. Uygurs are good at singing and dancing. Their folk songs are divided into four kinds: love, labor, historical and living customs. Uygur folk songs cover three kinds of musical systems, i.e. Chinese, Arabic and European music. It has a Chinese folk song tune with the most prominent multiple sources. Many of their folk songs are combined with dance and have vivid and interesting styles. The folk songs well known to China and foreign countries include *Alabenhan, A Half Moon Climbing Up, Daban Town, Giving me a Rose*, etc. The Kazak ethnic group is mainly located in northern Xinjiang and is engaged in herding. Their folk songs are of three main kinds: folk songs with fixed words and songs (including herding songs, hunting songs, love songs and religious songs, etc.), folk songs with improvisational words (including mountain songs, fishing songs and riddle songs), and custom songs (including wedding songs, crying songs for marring daughters, songs for delivering the bride, etc.). Of them, love songs comprise the largest number and most of them express the sufferings and blessing on the separation of lovers. Kazak folk songs cover the Chinese and European musical systems. The Chinese musical system is mostly gong tone and yu tone (two of the five notes of the ancient Chinese five-tone scale). The famous ones include Mayila, Awaiting Me Till Morning, etc.

Tibetan Folk Song Region

This covers the Tibetan Autonomous Region and Tibetan-inhabited areas in Qinghai and Sichuan provinces. The folk songs include mountain songs (herding songs), labor songs, love songs, custom songs and sutras reading tune. Most of the performance activities of folk songs are related to Buddhist festivals and many of the folk songs are combined with dancing, such as Nangma, Tuishie, Gorshie and Guozhuang dances. The music belongs to the Chinese musical system and the folk songs carry rich plateau characteristics and strong rhythm. The famous ones include *On the Golden Hill in Beijing*, etc. This was originally an arrow song (hunting song) and at first it was popular in the southeastern forests in Tibet. But now it has become a new folk song popular across China.

Folk Song Region with Primitive Culture

This covers minor ethnic group areas such Yunnan, Guizhou and Guangxi provinces. More than twenty different ethnic groups live in this region. The songs have ancient cultural characteristic of different levels and special social functions. The folk songs are mostly the combination of "poems, singing and danc with complex and variable contents, and there are folk songs of different historical stages. As many ethnic groups do not have a written language, folk songs se as an important method for recording history, spreading knowledge and conducting social activities and have become an indispensable part of their daily life. representative folk songs in this region are the folk songs of multiple voice parts. Most ethnic groups have two-voice and three-voice-part folk songs. The folk sc are divided into "big songs" and "little songs". Dong, Buyi and Zhuang ethnic groups are the most famous for big songs, which include male voice, female v and children's voices; male big songs often have strong rhythm and bright tune, and female big songs often have free rhythm and smooth and soft tunes. Little sc include two-voice-part songs and single-voice-part songs. They are mostly about love and are sung quietly by youth. In addition, there are ancient songs and thos Miao ethnic group have the longest history. The content is about the creation of sky and earth, the origin of human beings and the cause for traveling far. The tur appropriate for reciting and singers are mostly elders. Big songs of Dong ethnic group became famous across China in the 1950s and there are other representa songs such as *Sweet-Scented Osmanthus Blossoming* and *Honorable Men Coming, Axi Dancing Moon Songs*, etc.

Grassland Folk Song Region

This folk song region is mainly located in present Inner Mongolia Autonomous Region and is represented by Mongolian folk songs. The Mongolian ethnic group has always had the title of "musical ethnic group" and "poetic ethnic group". Their folk songs can be divided into two kinds: long tune and short tune. The long tune folk songs are mainly popular in the eastern herding areas and the areas to north of Yinshan Mountain. They are characterized by fewer words, long tunes, full of decoration, loudness and free rhythm, reflecting the vigor of the broad grasslands and the breadth of vision of herders. Herding songs, homesick songs and praising songs belong to this genre. The famous ones include Vast Grassland and Herding Song, etc. The short tune is mainly popular in the western and southern semi-agricultural and semi-pasturing areas. They are characterized by short structures and neat rhythm, and many narrative songs, love songs and wedding songs belong to this genre. The famous ones include Senji Dema, Little Yellow Horse, etc. The common characteristic of grassland folk songs is the reflection of grassland herders' emotions and character, simple, honest, bright, enthusiastic, bold and unconstrained.

Folk Song Region with Hunting Culture

This mainly covers the areas along the Great and Small Xing'an Mountains in northeast China and is represented by the folk songs of the Oroqen ethnic group (including Evenk, Hezhen, Daur and Manchu). Before 1949, the Oroqen ethnic group still had many marks of primitive society. It is a ethnic group that loves singing and dancing. In the past, they made a living by hunting. On returning from a successful hunt and during ethnic festivals, they would sing and dance in celebration. Their folk songs include three main types: mountain songs, singing and dancing songs and Saman tune. Their mountain songs are divided into long tune and short tune; long tune is loud, sonorous and vigorous with free rhythm and short tune is stable in tune and neat in rhythm. Singing and dancing songs are mostly in the form of one leading and others joining. Saman tune is sung when inviting gods, when sorcerer's dance in a trance, offering sacrifice to ancestors and holding funerals; the tune is in form of reciting and one leading with others joining. Oroqen folk songs are in five-tone scale and are mostly gong-tone and yu-tone songs. One of their favorite folk songs is *Ehulan Tehulan*, a song in praise of nature. In addition, *Oroqen Little Songs* is also well-known in China.

Han Folk Song Region

The Han ethnic group has various types of folk songs and in terms of social function, they can be divided into labor songs, mountain songs, xiaodiao (ditty), field songs, fishing songs, tea-picking songs, yangge (including lantern songs), custom songs, children's songs, and cradle songs.

The Han folk song region covers a very broad area, from cold northern parts to the southern subtropics and from the northwestern plateau and southwestern plateau to the coastland plain in the east. The language spoken in the different places is Chinese but each place has its own dialect; large differences exist among east, west, south and north, and the folk songs in different places have different characteristics. On the other hand, the Han ethnic group is also distributed in northern grasslands, northwestern semi-agricultural and semi-pasturing and southwestern plateau multiple ethnic groups folk song regions with the population of over ten million respectively, so some parts of the folk song regions overlap.

South China Sea Islands

Modern Folk Songs

In the late period of the Qing Dynasty in the mid-19th Century, China entered a period of semi-feudalism and semi-colonialism. In that period appeared many collections of folk songs compiled by literati, such as Kejia Shan'ge by Huang Zunxian, Wu Songs by Feng Menglong, Cantonese Ballads by Li Diaoyuan, and Music Left by White Snow by Hua Guangsheng. Due to individual preference, these folk song collections lay particular stress on folk lyrics and many are popular even today. Worthy of mention is Liaozhai Popular Songs by a famous folk litterateur Pu Songling in the Qing Dynasty, which selected more than fifty folk song tunes popular in the late Ming Dynasty and early Qing Dynasty. Some of these songs are still sung by folk artists today. They are very rare and give us insights into life three or four hundred years ago.

With the foundation of the People's Republic of China in 1949, a great number of folk songs emerged to reflect the new life of people. They were not only new in subject, but also more open and bright in musical style, full of positive ardor and optimism. As the social economy and cultural development of all ethnic groups were not balanced before, some of them still have no written language, and folk songs are still their major art form indispensable in their lives and most of the folk songs still retain the form of combining "poem, singing and dancing". By comparison, due to the fast development of drama and talking and singing, the activities of performing folk songs in the Han ethnic group are not as active as those of other ethnic groups, and the coastland areas do not have so many folk songs as inland areas.

Modern Chinese Music

In the 20th century, the cultures of East and the West fused and tens of thousands of musical works embodying the spirit of the times emerged. Besides vast achievements accomplished in song creation, Chinese music also presented historical progress in many fields such as symphony, chorus, opera, piano, violin, etc., and a number of works with artistic quality and national characteristics were created.

In the past two decades or so, Chinese musicians and musical performance troupes have widely participated in various international musical exchanges and competitive activities and many people have attained excellent results beyond anything seen before. They have made their mark all over the world, and at the same time introduced Chinese musical culture with its excellent traditions to the international community; they have also introduced some excellent foreign musical arts, and musical thought and theories into China. In order to enrich the musical life of common people and enhance their attainments, some large-scale musical festivals have been held regularly, such as "Spring of Shanghai", "Chorus Festival of Beijing" and "Musical and Flower Festival of Goat City", etc. In addition, amateur musical performance activities by common people are also very active, such as "Fresh May Flowers" in Beijing, "October Singing Festival" in Shanghai, "School Musical Festival" in Fujian, etc., and are all held at regular intervals.

Modern Symphonic Music

As early as in 1923, Xiao Youmei composed the orchestral piece New Raiment of Rainbow and Feather Dance, and, in 1929, Huang Zi created Nostalgia. Following these, the representative works of Chinese symphonic music in the first half of the 20th century are generally considered to be Metropolitan Fantasy by Huang Zi, Taiwan Dance composed by Jiang Wenye in his early days, Ma Sicong's First Symphony, Xian Xinghai's National Liberation Symphony and the New China Suite written by Ding Shande.

In the period 1949-1956, folk and mythological elements became prominent, the musical vocabulary was often directly connected with that of folk tunes, and the overall style was one of lyricism, color and strong elements of folklore. The esthetic conception was programmatic. During the period, the representative works included Wang Yunjie's First Symphony, Li Huanzhi's Spring Festival Suite, Ding Shande's Xinjiang Dance, Shi Yongkang's symphonic poem, Story of the Yellow Crane, and Dance of the Yao People by Liu Tieshan and Mao Ruan, etc.

Symphonic Performance in the National Centre for the Performing Arts

From 1957 to 1962, symphonic creation accelerated. According to incomplete data, more than 80 such works were performed in public and published, of which the most influential and successful was the violin concerto Liang Zhu by He Zhanhao and Chen Gang. Other representative works of this period were Ding Shande's Long March Symphony, Wang Yunjie's Second Symphony , known as The Anti-Japanese War, Xin Huguang's symphonic poem Gada Plum Forest, Qu Wei's symphonic poem Monument to the People's Heroes and Zhu Jianer's Festival Overture, etc.

From 1963 to 1966, the representative works of symphonic music included Lu Qiming's Ode to the Red Flag, the piano concerto Yellow River, and the string symphony Moon Image Reflected in the Erquan Springs, rearranged by Wu Zuqiang based on the original composition by Abing with richness and depth and a lingering melody.

After 1976, the representative works of this period include Liu Dunnan's piano concerto Mountain Forest, Zhu Jianer's Fantasia Symphony, Wang Xilin's Yunnan Tone Poem, Chen Peixun's second symphony, titled Qingming Sacrifice, and Zhang Qianyi's symphonic picture Northern Forest, etc.

Contemporary Development of Symphonic Music

In the period 1982-1989, a group of young composers introduced modern Western musical techniques into symphonic creation. Some elderly and middle-aged composers also joined the ranks of the New Wave, and a new high point was reached. The major symphonic composers and works produced in this period were Du Mingxin's fantasia symphony *God of the Luo River*, Tan Dun's *Piano Concerto*, Qu Xiaosong's *Mong Dong*, as well as works by Ye Xiaogang, Chen Yi, Guo Wenjing, He Xuntian, Zhou Long, Xu Shuya, Mou Hong and so on. No matter who was the composer and no matter which technique he used, they all displayed a basic esthetic tendency: an increase in non-programmatic conception and untitled music; more skillful stereophonic and symphonic composition; a more intrinsic and profound pursuit and expression of national style; and more pronounced dramatic, tragic and philosophical elements. All this showed that Chinese composers were acquiring a surer grasp of the rules of symphonic creation.

Symphony Orchestra of the China National Opera House

It is one of the famous symphony orchestras in China and has performed scores of Chinese and foreign operas, such as world-famous works like *La Traviata, Madame Butterfly, Rigoletto, Carmen, Turandot, The Marriage Of Figaro, Cavalleria Rusticana*, and Chinese operas *Liu Hulan, Song Of Grassland, Ngari Goli,* and *Marco Polo*.

Besides operas, the symphony orchestra often gives performance of symphonic pieces by composers such as Beethoven, Tchaikovsky, Brahms, Mahler, Debussy, Stravinsky Igor, George Gershwin, and Shostakovich. The symphony orchestra has given cooperative performance with world-famous violinist David Oistrakh, tenors Luciano Pavarotti and Jose Carreras and the soprano Montserrat Caballe. In June 2001 the symphony orchestra took part in the performance of the "Three Great World-Famous Tenors Forbidden City Concert" in Beijing. The symphony orchestra has visited the former Soviet Union, Japan, Finland, Singapore, Hong Kong, Macao, and Taiwan to give performances and is well known to the world for its trained and skillful operatic performances.

As the preferred orchestra for opera performances in the Macao International Musical Festival, the symphony orchestra has been invited there on eight successive occasions and performed with artists from around the world with such operas as *The Barber of Seville, Turandot, Falstaff, Il Trovatore, Tosca, Carmen, Masked Ball, Der Fliegende Hollander [Flying Dutchman], Aida*, etc., winning recognition from artists all around the world.

Beijing Symphony Orchestra

This is one of the famous symphony orchestras in China and was set up in October 1977.

Since its establishment, the orchestra has staged many famous works by foreign and

Chinese composers. Since the 1990s, it has entered a professional orbit and started to plan an annual calendar according to the musical seasons. In addition to Mr. Tan Lihua, who serves as chief art director and conductor, the orchestra often invites famous foreign and Chinese conductors and solo performers to work with it in concerts offering a broad range of works and various styles. The orchestra performs more than 80 times every year. In addition, it has on many occasions participated in large-scale foreign cultural exchange activities as representative of China and its capital city, toured China and given performance in Yugoslavia and the Republic of Korea.

The orchestra has appeared alongside many foreign and Chinese famous symphony orchestras including Russian National Symphony Orchestra and the Australian ABC Symphony Orchestra.

China Philharmonic Orchestra

The China Philharmonic Orchestra (CPO), a State-grade symphony orchestra, was established on the basis of the China Broadcasting Symphonic Orchestra.

The CPO has held many concerts, staging a large number of Chinese and foreign symphony masterpieces. The orchestra's first musical season ran from September 2001 to July 2002, offering a rich repertoire of works from different periods and styles. Among the highlights was the world premiere of the Philip Glass Concerto for Cello and Orchestra, and performances of Gustav Mahler's *Das lied von der Erde*, Hector Berlioz's *La Damnation de Foust*, and Du Mingxin's Symphonic Peking Opera *Female Generals from the Yang Family*, composed especially for the CPO. In October 2002, under the leadership of Yu Long, the CPO presented the PRC premiere of Mahler's *Symphony No.8* and Symphony of a *Thousand* with more than 800 foreign and Chinese musicians, which became a historic performance event in modern Chinese music. In its 2002-2003 season, the highlights also included "the Immortal Beethoven" series; under the leadership of chief art director Yu Long and several other conductors, the CPO performed all of Beethoven's symphonies and concertos and most of the composer's overtures in nine concerts with the cooperation of excellent musicians from home and abroad, which left supreme impression in minds of the audience, in particular for its vigorous interpretation of Beethoven's Symphony No.9

The China Philharmonic Orchestra gave performance at the Beijing Concert Hall.

The 2003-2004 season saw the completion of the orchestra's huge musical project-Mahler symphony cycle — stretching over three seasons and offering all of Mahler's symphonies to the Chinese audience. The CPO also marked the centenary of Dvorak's death with special performances of his works.

China National Symphony Orchestra

China National Symphony Orchestra is one of the first-class professional symphony orchestras in China. It was previously known as the Central Philharmonic Society, which was established in 1956. In 1996, it changed its name to China National Symphony Orchestra. Mr. Tang Muhai, an internationally famous conductor, is the chief art director and chief conductor viewed as one of the internationally influential Chinese conductors of modern times. In the past 20 years, he has been active on the international stage and has served as chief conductor of several famous symphony orchestras at various times. The orchestra possesses a group of trained players with exquisite techniques including many winners of Chinese and international musical competitions who still retain the high-level performance tradition of the orchestra.

The orchestra also possesses a chorus with a similar long history whose members are all graduates from Chinese higher conservatories. Since its winning of the gold cup in the World Youth Festival Choral Competition in the 1950s, the chorus has always represented the highest level of Chinese choral art.

In the past half century, the orchestra has successfully played a large number of symphony works from home and abroad, including many enjoying their Chinese premiere. The live programs of the concerts by the orchestra are often broadcast to the world by radio and TV, and it has also made a number of recordings with the French Gramophone Corp. and Philips Corp.

Shanghai Symphony Orchestra

With a longtime high reputation, the Shanghai Symphony Orchestra is one of the oldest in China and even in Asia and has broad influence within China. Its predecessor, the Shanghai Public Orchestra was established in 1879.

Since 1949, the orchestra has played more than 4,000 concerts. In the past 10 years, it has also staged more than 600 chamber concerts and been involved in performances of such world classical operas as *Aida, Der Fliegende Hollander, Don Carlos, Faust, Cavalleria Rusticana, La Traviata,* and *The Magic Flute* with the Florence Opera House in Italy, the Royal Opera House at Covent Garden in London, the Dusseldorf Opera House in Germany, Paris Opera House in France, Zurich Opera House in Switzerland, etc.

The China National Symphony Orchestra performing symphonic fantasy *Farewell My Concubine* at the Chicago Symphony Hall.

The orchestra has participated in the China Art Festival, China Shanghai International Art Festival, "Spring of Shanghai" International Musical Festival, Beijing International Musical Festival, Hong Kong Art Festival, Macao International Musical Festival, North Korea "Spring of April" Art Festival, etc. and has won many prizes. It has played for the Shanghai APEC and also at the World Fair. The orchestra pays much attention to the performance of works by Chinese composers, including those of "new generation" composers active around the world such as Tan Dun, Chen Qigang, Sheng Zongliang, Zhou Long, Chen Yi, Huang Anlun, Xu Shuya, Qu Xiaosong, and Ye Xiaogang. The orchestra is done much to popularize the symphonic works of Chinese representative composer Zhu Jianer, recording everyone and participating in the planning and publishing of the Collection of Symphonic Works by Zhu Jianer

♦ Chinese Musicians Association

This national professional musicians organization was established in July 1949 and was originally called the "China National Musical Works Association" of which Mr. Lu Ji was the president. Now, the association has more than 8,000 members across China.

The branches of the association include: Chinese Traditional Musical Academy, Chinese National Orchestral Academy, Chinese Ethnic Groups Vocal Music Academy, Chinese Musical History Academy, Chinese Musical Culture Academy, Nie Er Xian Xinghai Academy and Chinese Symphony Fans Academy.

The publications include: *People's Music* (bi-monthly), *Musical Creation* (quarterly), *Songs* (monthly), *Publication of Words* (bi-monthly), and *Children's Music* (bi-monthly).

Website: http://www.chinama.org.cn/

Drama

Introduction to Chinese Drama

Chinese drama mainly includes traditional operas and stage plays. Operas are China's inherent and traditional form of drama, while stage plays were introduced from the West in the 20th century.

Chinese classical dramas constitute an important part of the national culture and also take a special position in world drama circles along with Greek tragicomedy and the Sanskrit dramas of India.

The formation of dramas can be traced back to the Qin and Han dynasties, but they did not take shape until the Song and Yuan dynasties. The first mature dramas should be zaju of the Yuan Dynasty. After over 800 years of prosperous development, dramas at present belong to more than 360 types. In the longdevelopment, Chinese classical dramas have experienced four basic forms: Southern Drama of the Song and Yuan dynasties, Zaju of the Yuan Dynasty, Saga of the Ming and Qing dynasties, local dramas of the Qing Dynasty and modern dramas.

Stage plays in China have a history of only a hundred years. With the introduction from the West, it was called "cultural new dramas" during the period from early 20th century to the May 4th Movement of 1919, and this kind of early stage play still had the characteristics of old dramas. After 1919, Western dramas were introduced in their original form and were called "new dramas". Since 1928, this form of art has been called "Hua Ju" (stage plays).

♦ Chinese Dramatists Association

The Chinese Dramatists Association was established on July 24, 1949 and it is a people's society organized by dramatists from all ethnic groups in China. The association is a group member of China Federation of Literary and Art Circles.

At the end of 2005, the association has nearly 12,700 members who are all playwrights, directors, actors and actresses, stage artists, musicians, drama theorists and critics, drama educationalists, administrators. The association has 34 group members.

The dramatic activities held by the association include China Drama Festival, China International Drama Festival, BeSeTo (China, South Korea and Japan) Drama Festival, China Yingshanhong Folk Drama Festival, Campus Drama Festival, Playlet Artistic Festival, National Drama and Sketch Competition, etc.

The association has established a biannual national award—China Drama Award, including six sub-categories, i.e. Mei Flower Performance Award, Cao Yu Play Script Award, Excellent List Award, Playlet and Sketch Award, Campus Drama Award and Academic Critical Award. In 2005, the association established the "Mei Flower Award Artistic Troupe".

The association has established friendly ties with dramatic circles in more than 20 countries in the world. In 1981, the association joined the International Dramatists Association and established the Chinese Center of International Dramatists Association. In 1999, the Asian-Pacific Center of International Dramatists Association was founded in Seoul, Korea and the Chinese Dramatists Association became a member. In 1994, China, South Korea and Japan jointly founded the BeSeTo Drama Festival to be held in turn by the three countries; the first was held in Seoul. In 2003, the Chinese Dramatists Association established Sino-Japan Drama Friendship Award.

Website: http://www.chinatheatre.org/

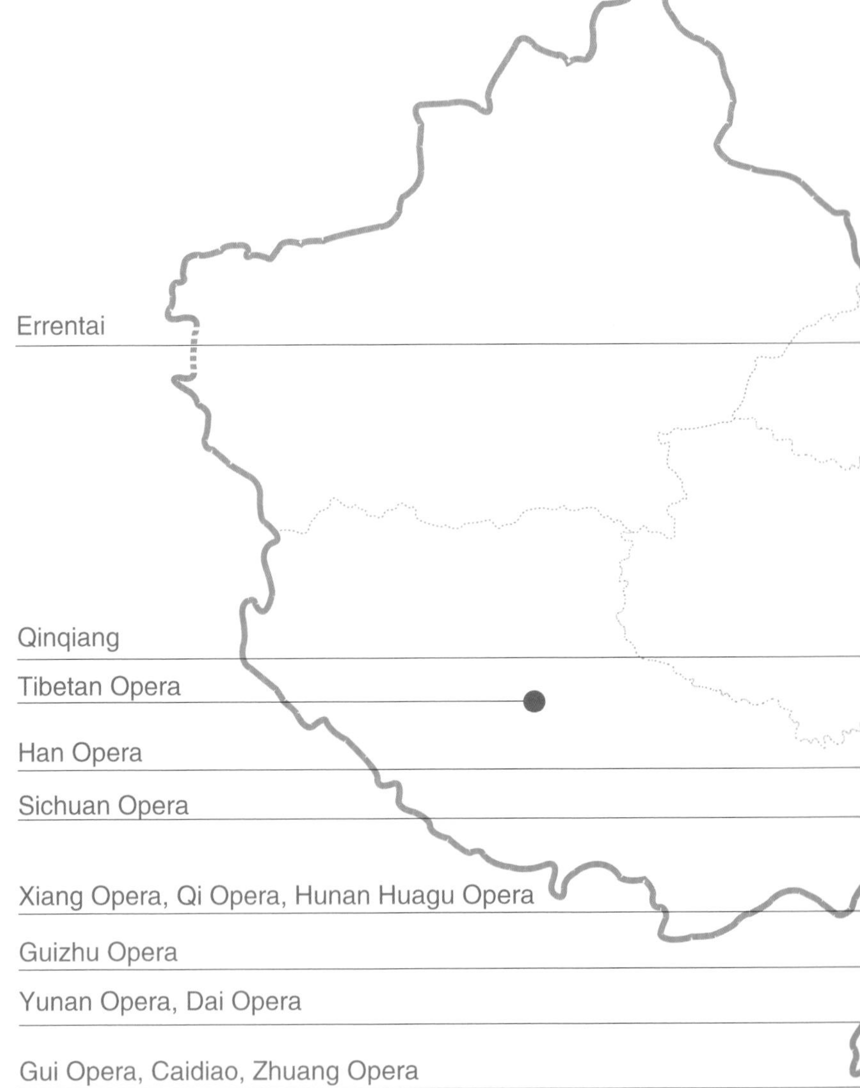

Local Operas

On the basis of inheriting traditions, Chinese local operas have undertaken reform and innovation continuously. The active local operas include Yueju Opera, Huangmei Opera, Sichuan Opera, Yuju Opera, Cantonese Opera, Tibetan Opera, etc.

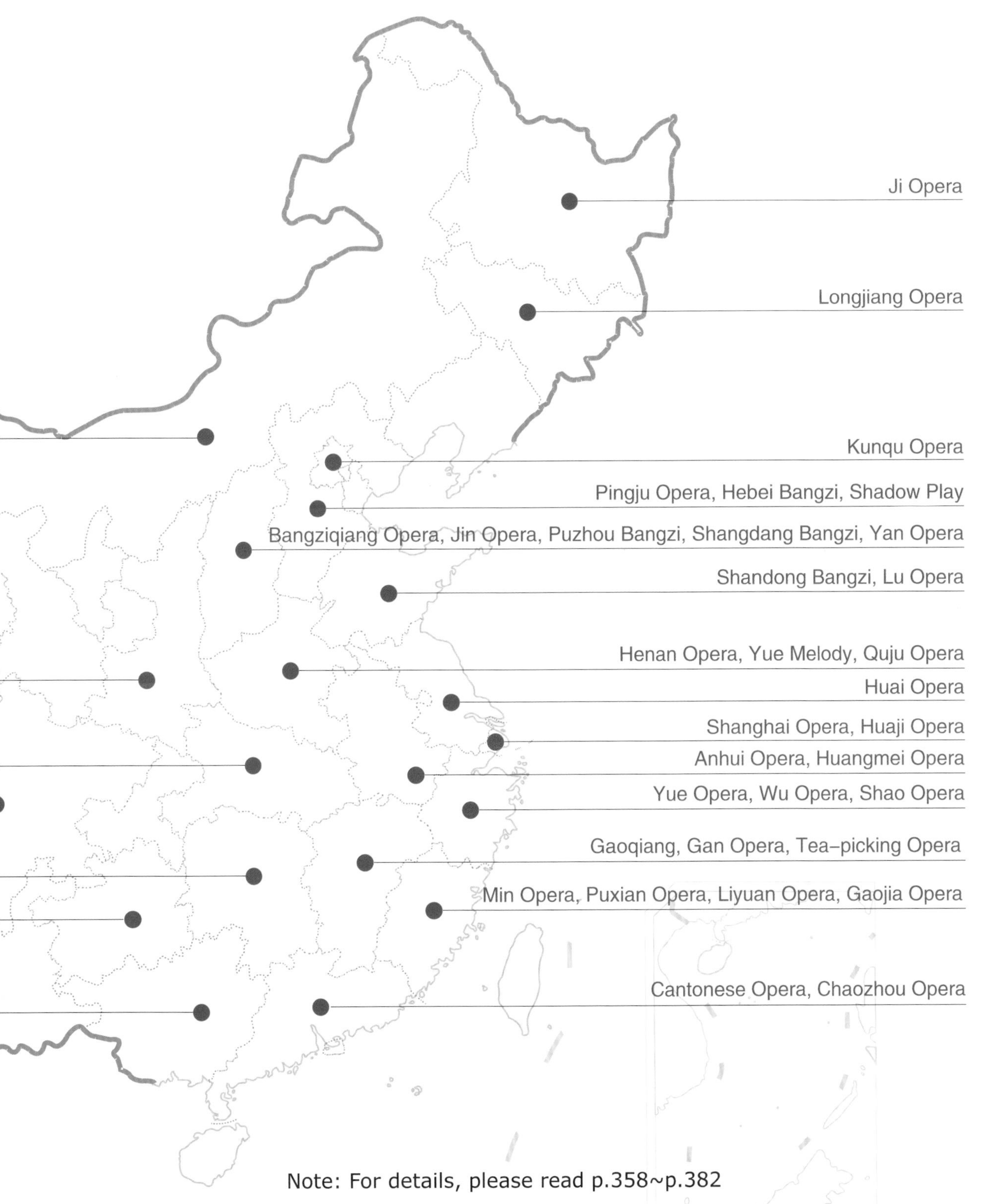

Note: For details, please read p.358~p.382

13 Culture

Beijing Opera

Beijing opera is also called "Pihuang" and two basic tunes, namely "Xipi" and "Erhuang", comprise its musical materials. It also utilizes some local little tunes (such as Liuziqiang and Chuiqiang, etc.) and Kunqu tunes. It came into being around 1840 in Beijing and was prevalent in 1930s and 1940s when it was called "national opera". Today it is still a great opera with national influences. It has complete roles and grand momentum and is a representative of modern Chinese operas.

Beijing Opera is a performance art of singing, speaking, acting, acrobatics and dancing. Formality-based performance styles are used to narrate stories, describe figures and express such emotions as happiness, anger, sorrow, joy, surprise, fear and grief. The characters can be divided into four roles: sheng (man), dan (woman), jing (man), and chou (man and woman). The figures are divided into the loyal and the treacherous, the beautiful and the ugly and the good and the evil. Each figure is distinctive and vivid. The face of a performer is painted with some colour to symbolize his or her personalities, qualities, role and fate. This is a significant feature of Beijing Opera and the key to understanding the plots. A red face has a commendatory meaning and represents the loyal and brave people.

The musical instruments for the Beijing Opera are classified into two kinds, wind and stringed instruments and there is also percussion. The bamboo flute and the erhu are the major wind and stringed instruments respectively. Percussion is often used to set off the dancing movements of the performers and to exaggerate the atmosphere in fighting.

The Beijing Opera performance system named after Mei Lanfang has been viewed as a representative of the oriental opera performance style and along with the Stanislavsky and Brecht performance styles they are called the three great performance styles in the world. Beijing Opera is an important representation of the traditional culture of the Chinese nation and its many artistic elements are used as symbols of traditional Chinese culture.

Sheng, Dan, Jing and Chou: Four character types in Peking Opera

13 Culture

Brief History of Beijing Opera

Beijing Opera has a history of 200 years and is derived from several old local operas, especially Anhui Opera, which was very popular in southern China in the 18th century. In 1790, the first Anhui Opera troupe performance was held in Beijing to celebrate the Emperor's birthday. Later, some other Anhui Opera troupes performed in Beijing. Anhui Opera troupes were good at absorbing the acting styles of other types of opera. Beijing accumulated many local operas, which made Anhui Opera improve quickly.

At the end of the 19th century and the beginning of the 20th century, Beijing Opera was finally formed, and became the biggest of all operatic styles in China. There are more than 1,300 traditional plays, some 400 presented frequently.

It is widely acknowledged that the end of the 18th century was the most flourishing period in its development. During this time, there were lots of performances not only in folk places, but also in the palace. The mutual influence between palace and non-government places promoted Beijing Opera's development. From the 1920's to the 1940's was the second flourishing period of Beijing Opera. The symbol of this period was the emergence of lots of style schools. The four most famous were "Mei" (Mei Lanfang 1894-1961), "Shang" (Shang Xiaoyun 1900-1975), "Cheng" (Cheng Yanqiu 1904-1958), and "Xun" (Xun Huisheng 1900-1968). Every school had its groups of actors and actresses who were very active.

Today, the Beijing Chang'an Opera House offers performances of Beijing Opera throughout the year and holds international competitions every year that attract many fans from various countries, which has done much to create links with foreign cultures.

Roles in Beijing Opera

All the figures on the stage of Beijing opera are divided into four basic roles according to gender and characters: the male (sheng) and female (dan) roles, the painted-face role (jing), and the comic role (chou). Every role has its own specifications regarding the performance process, make-up and costume, and makes a specific contribution to the play.

In the history of Beijing Opera there have always been special groups of performers such as male Dan, female Laosheng, and female Hualian.

The sheng (adult male role) is divided into Laosheng, Wusheng and Xiaosheng according to ages and bearing.

The dan (female role) is divided into "qing yi, hua dan, wu dan, hua shan, lao dan" and "cai dan".

The jing (painted-face role) means all kinds of painted-faces and acts as the male role that has a particular personality or appearance.

The mo role also belongs to the lao sheng category, except that he is much older and a scatterbrain with a low social status.

The chou (comic face, which means clown) always acts as a wise and funny but folk-chivalrous man, or a man who has low social status. Although listed as number four, the chou plays a role of setting off the leading actors. But in the development history of Chinese opera, it appeared earlier than other roles, hence the saying that "there can be no opera without a chou role".

Types of Facial Make-up in Beijing Opera

This is a special make-up method with national characteristics, and each historical figure or some type of figures has a general make-up method. It is generally believed that facial make-up originated from artificial masks.

Specific colors of facial make-up in Beijing Opera are put on the actors' faces to symbolize the personalities, characteristics, and fate of the roles. Red faces have positive meanings, symbolizing brave, faithful, and wise men, such as Guan Yu, Jiang Wei, and Chang Yuchun. Black faces usually symbolize fiery, just, brave and impertinent men, such as Bao Zhen, Zhang Fei and L Kui. Yellow faces symbolize ferocious and atrocious men such as Yuwen Chengdu and Dian Wei. Blue and green faces symbolize forthright and irritable men such as Dou Erdun and Ma Wu. White faces usually symbolize treacherous court officials and bad men, such as Cao Cao and Zhao Gao, etc.

The coloring and making-up methods of facial make-up in Beijing Opera can be classified into three kinds: rubbing, applying and drawing. The original role of facial make-up was to magnify the position of the five sensory organs and facial lines of characters in plays so as to symbolize the nature, mentality and physiology of the figures and serve the whole plot. But, later, with further development, facial make-up became fussier instead of simple, exquisite instead of rude, profound instead of superficial and deep instead of shallow. The facial make-up itself has become a design art with national characteristics.

Mei Lanfang performing the Beijing Opera *The Drunken Concubine*

▲ Mei Lanfang

Mei Lanfang (1894-1961) was one of the most prominent Beijing Opera artists. He began studying opera when he was eight, and began to perform on the stage at the age of 11. In his more than 50 years of performing, Mei created and developed many acting phases of the Dan role, such as dancing, singing, make-up, and costumes, all of which helped him form his own style. In 1919, Mei led the opera troupe to Japan, which was the first time that China began to spread the art of Beijing Opera overseas. In 1930, he led a troupe to the United States and gained great success and significant recognition. In 1934, he was invited to visit Europe, and received much attention from the European opera world.

Schools of Beijing Opera

It is natural to form different schools in various art forms, such as expressive, abstract, impressionism and stream of consciousness.

Schools of Beijing Opera are named after actors as Beijing Opera is a performance art with the leading role as the focal point. Actors study and inherit the performance skills of precursors and form different artistic opinions by combining their own qualities, interests, physical characteristics and artistic accomplishments, and then create performance methods with their own special characteristics. After frequent performances, they can gain acknowledgement from the audience and form artistic movements and schools of their own.

The formation of Beijing Opera schools usually covers the following three situations: first, collect the strong points of various masters, learn from other's strong points to offset one's own weaknesses, incorporate items of diverse nature and do not simply inherit the artistic legacy of some school founder or descendant. Second, possess a special and systematic theoretical basis and means of artistic creation in performance satisfying audience demands and win understanding and acceptance from the audience through frequent practice. Third, build up creative performance troupes with leading roles as the core and form uniform styles in playwriting, actors, composition, music and costume.

Major Schools of Beijing Opera

As at the beginning it was Laosheng that dominated and there were many different schools, such as those of Tan Xinpei, Yu Shuyan (1890-1943), Yan Jupeng (1890-1942), Gao Qingkui (1890-1940), Ma Ma Lianliang, Qi of Zhou Xinfang (1895-1975), Yang Baosen (1909-1958), Xi Xiaobo (1910-1977), etc. Of these, the "Four Great Xusheng" refers to the concise and bright Yu, mild and pretty Yan, vigorous and forceful Gao and natural and elegant Ma schools.

With the rise of the dan role, there emerged the solemn and profound Mei School (initiator Mei Lanfang), strong and fluent Shang school of Shang Xiaoyun (1900-1975), deep and implicit Cheng school of Cheng Yanqiu (1904-1958), the natural and unvarnished Xun school of Xun Huisheng (1900-1968), who are called "Four Great Famous Dan". In addition, there is a Zhang school initiated by Zhang Junqiu (1920-1997).

Honored as "No.1 Famous Character of Modern Xiaosheng", Ye Shenglan (1914-1978) formed his special performances style after middle age and initiated the most influential Xiaosheng school in modern times. Yang Xiaolou (1878-1938)and Gai Jiaotian (1888-1971), playing the role of Wusheng, also formed their distinctive artistic schools.

In the role of Jing, there are the Jin school of Jin Shaoshan (1889-1948) and Qiu school of Qiu Shengrong (1951-1971), etc. Although the schools of the Chou role are not obvious due to various inherent restrictions, the Xiao school of Xiao Changhua (1878-1976) of Wenchou and the Ye school of Ye Shengzhang (1912-1966) of Wuchou are recognized by audiences.

At the peak, there were scores of schools in Beijing Opera. The initiators of each had their own special tone color and charm in performances and music for voice.

Performances of Beijing Opera

The basic performance skills of Beijing Opera include "singing, reciting, dance movements, and special acrobatic movements."

The singing of Beijing Opera is fundamentally different from the Western vocal music system and it is almost impossible to express Beijing Opera through it. The types of singing are not classified according to different ranges but to the different roles by the gender, age, identity, status, character, tone color and singing methods. Each special role has its own phonetic and singing methods. For example, Laodan sings in a real way and Qingyi sings in falsetto. Beijing Opera is an art of vocalization at first and it is different from other operas in its vocal music. Anyone who learns to appreciate the fluctuant music and aesthetic feelings of the music in Beijing Opera steps into a higher realm of appreciation.

"Reciting" refers to spoken parts of figures, which plays a role of narrating in Beijing Opera. It attaches particular importance to reciting and there was once a saying that "reciting weighs a thousand jin and singing weighs four liang". It means that it is naturally not easy to sing with charm, but it is much more difficult to recite with charm and this needs endeavor in conjecture and polish. Reciting symbolizes the civility and elegance of classical Beijing Opera art.

"Dance movements" and "special acrobatic movements" are employed by actors to express figures and illustrate circumstances. There are virtually no realistic stage props in Beijing Opera, so actors have to make full use of body language to create the right effect. Both "dance movements" and "special acrobatic movements" pay attention to the dancing beauty of postures and movements. In Beijing Opera, there are many plays involving acrobatic fighting; they might be bare-handed or use small or long weapon props while wearing heavy costumes and boots with thick bottoms, to dazzle the audience.

Acrobatic fighting performance in the Beijing Opera *Romance of the Iron Bow*

Classical Lists of Beijing Opera Items

There are about 1,300 traditional plays passed down from the early times. Since the 1950s, nearly 100 new plays have been added. There are plays focusing on the art of singing, acrobatic fighting, dance movements and acrobatic movements, and plays of various schools; there are playlets, series of plays, and highlights from some plays; and there are ancient costume plays, modern fashionable plays, newly compiled historical plays and revolutionary modern new operas, etc.

Plays focusing on the art of singing win over the audience by brilliant vocalization; plays focusing on dance movements provide exquisite performances; plays focusing on acrobatic fighting are vehement and fierce; singing and dancing playlets are easy and lively; the series of plays have numerous figures, grand scale and complex plots; highlights from some plays condense the essence of the longer works; plays of various schools have extraordinary splendor and distinctive character, and modern plays emphasize the quality of times and are close to real life.

Lists of Beijing Opera plays have flexible and free structure, strong dramatic and theatrical quality, rich performance skills on stage and are very exotic. Of these,

A Fork in a Road, Autumn River, Entering the Palace for the Second Time, Yu Tangchun, The Drunken Concubine, Conqueror Xiang Yu Bids Farewell to His Concubine, Mu Guiying Takes Command, Zhaojun Goes to the Border Area, Hongniang, Qin Xianglian, Empty-City Strategy, Have the Aid of the East Wind, Xu Ce Runs in the City, White Snake, Chisang Town, Wild Boar Forest, Gathering of Heroes, Yang Silang Visits his Mother, Dragon and Phoenix is a Good Omen, and Create Serious Disturbance in the Heavenly Palace are widely known. Every artistic school has its own popular representative lists.

Beijing Opera: A Fork in a Road

This is an acrobatic fighting play and it is often offered on overseas stages by various troupes. As it attaches importance to dance movements and special acrobatic movements instead of the art of singing, it is easy to break through the linguistic barrier when appreciating Beijing Opera. In this play, the audience can learn not only the basic rules of acrobatic fighting but also the fictitious skills in Beijing Opera. The plot is very simple: a man playing a Wusheng role hurries to a village inn to protect a "painted-face". In the evening, he mistakes the host of the inn, played by a Wuchou, and two fight in the dark; the play, in fact, emphasizes this aspect. The stage lighting is sufficient, but the two figures behave as if they are fighting in the pitch dark through exaggerated movements, although they do not actually strike each other; in fact, although they kick out their legs fiercely, they do not hit the opponent but instead tables and wooden stools to the delight of the audience.

The props on the stage are very simple, comprising only a table and two chairs. Sometimes, the table serves as the table for dining and drinking and sometimes it becomes the bed for the Wusheng. There is no door, but, if one is needed in the story, then a Wuchou carrying a broadsword will use movements that suggest he is opening the door.

Beijing Opera: Autumn River

Among the operas without acrobatics introduced to overseas audiences, Autumn River can be viewed as a leader. Famous actors of the dan role have performed this highlights play. In the play, a young Taoist nun chases after her lover to a river bank. Her heart is burning with impatience while an old helmsman interrogates her. After several complications, the helmsman at last helps the Taoist nun catch up with her lover. An old man and a young girl, an impatient one and a relaxed one, set off each other, full of wit. The stage props are very concise. The audience, having watched the play, says: "The unique paddle in the hands of the helmsman make people feel as if the stage is moving like water." As the operas without acrobatics pay attention to the character's psychology, foreign audience who do not understand the words can still clearly comprehend the exquisite performances of the actors; an expression in the eyes and the gait are both interesting.

Beijing Opera: Entering the Palace for the Second Time

This long-lasting highlights play is performed by Laosheng, painted-face and Qingyi. Any excellent actor of the three roles will give a definitive performance. There are only three people on the stage: an imperial concubine who has lost her husband, a civil official and a military officer. In singing, they discuss which official is loyal to his sovereign and who should take charge of the State. There are not many movements and they are not complicated. In the view of some Western people, this is almost a typical "opera". If the audience can appreciate the beauty of the vocal music, their appreciation level can be promoted to a new level.

Beijing Opera *Entering the Palace for the Second Time*

Beijing Opera: Yu Tangchun

This is not only a play for beginners of Qingyi in Beijing Opera, but also one with the widest prevalence. In the play, a famous female performer Su San (also named Yu Tangchun) meets with Wang Jinlong, the son of a noble and they swear to get married. Su San is swindled and sold by a procuress to a businessman Shen Yanlin as his concubine. Shen's wife has a jealous hatred for the newcomer and brings a false charge against her, saying Su San killed her husband. While taking her to the local authoritie3s, an escorting official Chong Gongdao adopts her as his daughter. After becoming an official, Wang Jinlong takes charge of this case and clears Su San of her false charge, and the two are reunited. The leading characters of the play are performed by Qingyi, Xiaosheng and Chou. The play has several highlights covering almost all the varieties of Xipi tune of the dan role, and the two highlights of Su San is Sent Under Escort and Three Officials Make Joint Trial are particularly wonderful and popular. Mei, Shang, Cheng, Xun and Zhang Junqiu are all good at performing this play.

Beijing Opera: The Drunken Concubine

This single-act play with singing and dancing is one of the classical lists of plays of Mei school. Mei Lanfang plays Yang Yuhuan. At the first performance of this play, Mei made reforms and innovations in various aspects of traditional performances, putting a great deal of effort into designing postures and movements, changing the traditional words. This play tells a love story between Emperor Xuanzong (685-762) of the Tang Dynasty and his Consort Yang. One day, Emperor Xuanzong arranged a meeting with Yang at the Hundred Flower Pavilion to enjoy a flower viewing, but actually went to meet another consort. Yang waits at the Hundred Flower Pavilion for a long time. Downhearted, she starts drinking until she falls unconscious, later awaking filled with both remorse and resentment. In this play, there are many dance movements and Mei sought beautiful postures for each movement. He played a dazzling, charming, soft Consort Yang who is also dignified, natural and graceful. On each foreign tour, Mei offered this performance and, even when in his sixties, continued to play the role in the Beijing Jixiang Opera House and other places.

Beijing Opera: Conqueror Xiang Yu Bids Farewell to His Concubine

Mei Lanfang cooperated with Yang Xiaolou, a leading Wusheng, in 1921 to create the play, and Mei played Yu's concubine and Yang played the overlord of the Chu Kingdom. The premiere was well received and became a

Yu Ji in the Beijing Opera *Conqueror Xiang Yu Bids Farewell to His Concubine*

representative one of Mei school. It tells a story from about 2,000 years ago when Chu, a fierce and powerful person of the times, was defeated and besieged. His beautiful concubine, danced for him to divert his thoughts and then she killed herself with a sword. Chu was overcome with grief and followed suit. The last love song is about being parted forever by death, but it is full of heroic spirit. Mei played an inspiring concubine who sang in a plaintive voice, sorrowful, sweet and touching. In the play, importance is attached to both singing and dancing and the "sword dancing" arranged by Mei is a splendid scene. Today, the role of Chu is often played by a painted-face.

Beijing Opera: Mu Guiying Takes Command

This was the last new play rehearsed by Mei Lanfang, and premiered in 1959. Mei played a heroine who attached most importance to the national situation and who, in her old age, led her troops into battle. Mei played the role of Mu Guiying in old age, a role that combines Qingyi and Daomadan and requires great force and skill. Mei, then in his sixties, played a dignified, gentle but powerful woman with heroic bearing and created a brilliant figure of a female commander who enjoys popular confidence. This play has become one of the classics of the Mei school.

Beijing Opera: Suo Lin Nang

This is a representative work of Chen Yanqiu in middle age. Cheng played a kind woman of a rich family, who obtained gratitude and help as she had helped others unconsciously. Cheng brought his art of singing into full play and his postures were very charming. Since the 1980s, this play has been welcomed by audiences and is one of the most famous of the Cheng school.

Beijing Opera: Zhaojun Goes to the Border Area

This is a representative work of Shang Xiaoyun in early times and has been inherited by descendants of the Shang school. Shang played a princess living over 1,000 years ago who married with King of the Hun in order to safeguard her country. The play is not long. It only shows how she departed from her country to go far away and the songs describe what she saw on the way. Shang designed skillful postures for her, combining both singing and dancing. The performances of the Shang school are characterized by vigor, power and beauty that are prominent in this play.

Beijing Opera: Hongniang

This comes from a classical play, Romance of the West Chamber. In the play, the leading role is not the hostess but a maid Hongniang who tries to make a match between her mistress and her lover. The maid is lively, pretty and enthusiastic. She redresses the scales everywhere and is much favored by audiences. The play is one of the early representative works of Xun Huisheng, and is a classic of the Xun school, which is good at creating the role of beautiful young ladies in small families and rosebuds that is perfectly embodied in this play.

Beijing Opera: Qin Xianglian

It is also entitledThe Story of Chen Shimei and is one of the most popular plays staged by Chinese opera. It is a tragedy about a coldhearted man who became an official and abandoned his wife, who had suffered much with him. It was originally a traditional play of the black-headed Jing role, and Jin Shaoshan and Qiu Shenrong were both good at performing it. After being adapted in 1953, the play became a famous one of the Zhang (Junqiu) school. Zhang played the suffering woman Qin Xianglian who was abandoned by her husband, played for a long time by Ma Lianliang; Qiu Shengrong played the righteous and strict judge Bao Zheng, and the arrangement of roles is a marvel. The play was filmed in 1963 and is very popular.

Beijing Opera: White Snake

This is an old fairy tale that first became a Kunqu opera. A famous modern playwright, Tian Han, created a Beijing Opera version. The play is fluent, precise and complete. There are both lively and breathtaking acrobatic fighting and graceful dancing, and touching singing and elegant words. The play tells a story of a white snake spirit who had practiced asceticism for 1,000 years and came down to earth. She met Xu Xian, the young owner of a drug store in Hangzhou. They fell in love and soon married. However, they were persecuted by a rascally monk named Fa Hai. To safeguard her marriage, the white snake suffered much and finally she was buried under the Leifeng Pagoda. In the premiere in 1950s, Du Jinfang, an excellent descendant of Mei school and a famous Xiaosheng Yu Zhenfei played the roles of the couple. The image of the white snake on the stage is pretty and elegant, and the vocal music is sweet, fluent and very touching. The play is now famous at home and abroad.

Beijing Opera: Have the Aid of East Wind

This highlights play of Laosheng is one of the representative works of Ma Lianliang. It tells of a famous and wise strategist in the period of the Three Kingdoms, Zhuge Liang. As he was good at the ancient art of observing the sky, he could work out the date of the arrival of the east wind in winter before a great battle. He made use of this to spread fire that destroyed the enemy camp. The vocal music of Ma school is well embodied in this play.

Beijing Opera: Empty-City Strategy

This is a play of Laosheng and is part of the repertoire of the Tan school. It is another story of Zhuge Liang, a military strategist of the period of the Three Kingdoms who was stayed calm in the face of danger when the enemy was camped just outside the city wall and there was no soldier defending the city. Zhuge Liang on stage is not only sagacious and scrupulous, but also exhibits graceful and touching vocal tones in a skillful performance.

Beijing Opera: Xu Ce Runs in the City

This is a play of Laosheng and is one of the representative works of Zhou Xinfang (Qi school). Zhou played a kind minister who hurried to the imperial court to report to the Emperor about the victory of justice. He was running while singing and recalling the origin of the event. The plot is very simple and is almost a display of dancing. But it is impossible for dancing itself to describe the character and happiness of the figure. Zhou's performances are vigorous, his voice is raucous and powerful and he is good at embodying a righteous man. His art of singing and movements has a perfect embodiment in this play.

Beijing Opera: Chisang Town

This is a classical play of the Qiu school. Qiu Shengrong is the most influential painted-face actor in the 20th century. He initiated a full-bodied singing way of painted-face in Beijing Opera. He attaches importance to both sentiment and music for the voice. His representative works include both operas

focusing on the art of singing and those focusing on both singing and movements. He is especially good at playing Bao Gong.

Chisang Town reflects the tender feelings of an upright and honest official Bao Zheng. Qiu's performances involve meticulous care and flawless artistry. The story is about Bao Zheng who handled a case impartially. He beheaded his nephew who took bribes and perverted the law. Bao Zheng's brother's wife came to Chisang Town to denounce him, while Bao Zheng explained the cardinal principles of righteousness to her and convinced her. The opera is good at antiphonal singing between painted-face and Laodan.

Beijing Opera: Wild Boar Forest

This comes from the Chinese classical novel Outlaws of the Marsh and was originally a play of Wusheng. In 1950, Yuan Shihai, a famous painted-face actor, and Li Shaochun, a famous Wusheng actor, adapted the play according to the performances of Yang Xiaolou and it was made into a film. It has been part of the repertoire of Jing and Wusheng roles in recent decades. Yuan Shihai played Lu Zhishen, a Robin Hood-type figure, and Li Shaochun played Lin Chong, a drillmaster of the imperial guard. The two people brought their skills of singing, reciting, dancing and special acrobatic movements into full play and their performances are much appreciated.

Beijing Opera: Create Serious Disturbance in the Heavenly Palace

This comes from Journey to the West and is a traditional play of Wusheng. In the opera, there are many brilliant skills of Wusheng. It was originally the representative work of Yang Xiaolou and later Li Wanchun and Li Shaochun were very good at it. This monkey opera familiar to Chinese and foreign audiences tells a story about the handsome monkey king Sun Wukong who ascends to the heaven or descends to earth to challenge the decrepit and arbitrary reigning force. Sun Wukong is wise and full of strategies, is not afraid of power and acts with courage and determination. He reflects a heroic image of resisting power by the weak.

Beijing Opera: Gathering of Heroes

This is a play of about the period of the Three Kingdoms with the cooperative performances of Sheng, Jing and Chou roles. The play tells the story of when the troops of Sun Quan (Wu Kingdom) and Cao Cao (Wei Kingdom) confronted each other, and Sun Quan and Liu Bei (Shu Kingdom) joined forces to defeat Cao Cao. The identity and characters of figures in the play are different from each other and they stage a battle of wits. The play has a concise and touching plot.

In the 1950s, Tan Fuying, Laosheng of Tan school and grandson of Tan Xinpei, playing a honest civil official of Wu Kingdom, Lu Su), Ma Lianliang (Laosheng of the Ma school, playing Zhuge Liang, the wise strategist of the Shu Kingdom), Xiao Changhua (Chou, playing Jiang Gan, a treacherous man who was induced to capitulate to Cao Cao), Ye Shenglan (Xiaosheng of Ye School, playing Zhou Yu, a famous general of Wu Kingdom who was a self-conceited person relying on his own talents), Qiu Shengrong (painted-face of the Qiu school, playing Cao Cao, a white face who achieves high position by unscrupulous scheming), and Yuan Shihai (painted-face, playing Huang Gai, an old general of the Wu Kingdom who staged the ruse of inflicting an injury on himself to win the confidence of the enemy) constitute an excellent combination and their performances are still favored by people today.

Beijing Opera: Yang Silang Visits His Mother

This is a classical great play attaching importance to both Sheng and Dan. It tells a story of when the Song Dynasty (907-1279) was engaged in battle with the state of Liao (960-1125). Yang Yanhui (Yang Silang), a Song general, was captured by Liao but concealed his identity to marry Princess Tiejing of Liao. Fifteen years later, Yang Silang's younger brother and his mother led troops against Liao, which made Silang miss his relatives. But constrained by the battle situation, the mother and son could not meet. Princess Tiejing stole an arrow-shaped token and helped Silang to pass through the barrier to visit his mother. After a hasty meeting, the mother, son and brothers had to part again. At the beginning of the opera, the act of "Sitting in the Hall" can be appreciated as a single highlights play, and the excellent aria in it gives opera fans a detailed explanation. In the play, in the situation of mother facing son in the battle, Silang who missed his mother exposed his real identity to his wife, the princess of the enemy state. A Laosheng and a Qingyi sing graceful and touching arias.

Beijing Opera: Dragon and Phoenix Is a Good Omen

This is a great long-lasting and classical play. It has complete roles and several famous actors often make joint efforts to play the same role, mostly Sheng and Dan, and many sections can be played individually, such as Ganlu Temple, Returning to Jingzhou, Reed Catkins Marsh, etc. It tells a story from the Three Kingdoms period. Liu Bei did not want to give back Jingzhou after holding it for so long, so Sun Quan and Zhou Yu planned to conduct a sex-trap using Sun's sister Shangxiang. Liu Bei turned their trick against them and obtained a beautiful wife instead. In the past, all the most excellent actors of Beijing Opera could perform the play. At the end of the play, the hero and heroine have a satisfactory reunion after suffering a great deal of hardship and many twists of fate. During the Spring Festival every year, the play is performed for luck.

Beijing Opera *Yang Silang Visits His Mother*

Art of Quyi

Quyi is a general name for a variety of spoken and sung arts dating back to ancient China. It became a special art form after undergoing a long period of development and evolution from oral literature and songs.

Research has shown that there are 400 forms of Quyi that are popular in different parts of China. Although each has its own background, they all have original folk features, broad mass appeal, and similar artistic characteristics.

Traditional xiangsheng performance

Performances of Quyi

"Spoken and sung" forms are the dominating forms of Quyi performances. Spoken forms are Xiangsheng or comic cross talk, Pingshu, and Pinghua. Sung forms include Jingyun Dagu, Danxian Paiziqu, Yangzhou Qingqu, Northeast Dagu, Wenzhou Dagu, Jiaodong Dagu, and Hubei Dagu. Some are half sung and half spoken (sometimes called Yunsongti), including Shandong Kuaishu, Kuaibanshu, Luoguhu, Pingxiang Chunluo, and Sichuan Jinqianban. Others combine singing with speech with or without musical accompaniment, such as, for example, Shandong Qinshu, Xuzhou Qinshu, Enshi Yangqin, Wuxiang Qinshu, Anhui Qinshu, Guizhou Qinshu and Yunnan Yangqin. Yet another is a type combining recitation, singing, dancing, and walking. Examples are Errenzhuan, Shibuxia, lianhualuo, Ningbo Zoushu, Fengyang hop, Chedeng and Shangluo Huagu. Because Quyi arts tell stories and express emotions mainly through speech and song, their language must be lively, precise, simple and colloquial, suitable for speaking and singing, and easy to memorize and recite fluently.

Unlike plays or operas, where the artists' costumes express fixed roles, a Quyi item usually needs only one or two people who may take several roles each. Quyi artists are able to play characters of every description, and to tell various kinds of stories through speech and singing. Quyi arts have the special feature of being simple and effortless to prepare for performances. There are one or two people and a minimum of stage props – all that is needed is one or two musical instruments or a special gavel (used to calm or alert the audiences), a fan for Pingshu, a pair of bamboo clappers for Kuaibanshu or nothing at all for Xiangsheng. Performers can give shows wherever they go, enjoying more direct interaction with the audience compared with plays and operas.

Danxian

Danxian (monochord) originated in Beijing and is also called Danxianpaiziqu. It is an art of talking and singing. Beijing Danxian is accompanied on a stringed instrument and an octagonal drum; the performer sings and plays the drum at the same time. The octagonal drum is a small percussion instrument popular among Manchu people. It is covered with snakeskin, and there are holes on seven of the eight sides. Two brass strips are attached to each hole. When the storyteller shakes the drum, the brass strips resound.

There are more than 100 Danxian items. Numerous famous performers had formed their special singing styles. The most famous four schools include Rong, Chang, Xie and Tan.

Danxian gets its themes mostly from famous Chinese novels –Strange Tales of Liaozhai, Strange Tales New and Old, and Outlaws of the Marsh. Some reflect the lifestyles of people at different periods of history. Danxian has developed further over the past few decades. New programs were written and performed, while changes were made in vocal music and performance. A duet of male and female voices was introduced.

Xiangsheng

Xiangsheng (Comic Dialogue) is one of the most humorous, highly satirical, popular and influential types of Quyi.

There are three forms of Xiangsheng. The earliest form was performed by one person, and was called Dankou Xiangsheng. Its contents were mostly jokes and humorous stories. Later, Duikou Xiangsheng or "cross talk", performed by two people, appeared. One man was called Dougen, and the other Penggen. The performers of Duikou Xiangsheng create jokes to give people enlightenment. According to different themes there are different types. When A is the primary talker while B chimes in, this is called Yitouchen (heavy-at-one-end). A program with two people arguing about something is called Zimugen. Recitals and narration are called Guankouhuo, and imitations of opera songs and words are called Liuhuo. The third form of Xiangsheng performed by three or more people is called Qunkou Xiangsheng. It calls for one artist to say funny things, while others chime in. Of the three forms, cross talk is the most popular and widespread and is the dominant form.

The performances of Xiangsheng attach importance to "talking, imitating, being funny and singing", so performers must be articulate, good at imitating various people, objects and musical effects, and adept in making jokes, i.e. Doubaofu (exposing funny things). Meanwhile, they must have a good voice so as to learn various operas' vocal music and popular songs. As the performances of Xiangsheng depend totally on oral skills, the four aforementioned basic skills must be grasped. But, in reality, performers have their own individual genius and style.

Er'renzhuan

This is a form of song-and-dance duet, also known as Bengbeng. It originated in the three provinces of Northeast China – Liaoning, Jilin and Heilongjiang. It is a favorite of people and especially farmers in the region. It is a lively form of Quyi that involves story telling, singing, dancing and walking with a history of some 200 years. The script is written in popular language easy to understand, humorous, and rich in local lifestyle and flavor. The vocal music is based on that of northeastern folk songs and yangge, with a blend of the northeast

Er'renzhuan (a song-and-dance duet popular in the Northeast China)

Dagu, Lianhualao, Ping, and Hebei Bangzi performances. The singing is high-spirited and of an explosive type, sincere and moving. The dancing is derived from the great yangge in Northeast China and combines folk dancing and acrobatic movements, as well as the technique of waving fans or silk handkerchiefs.

There are three kinds of errenzhuan. The most important is the duet sung by a Chou (clown) and a Dan (actor playing a woman's role). It is part song, part dance, and part storytelling. The most prominent items include *The Western Bower and The Blue Bridge*. The second type is a solo called Danchutou, in which the player sings and dances, such as Hong Yue'e Had a Dream. In the third type the actors sing in roles, as in an opera. This is called Lachangxi. An example is *Lord Bao Gong Makes an Apology*.

Er'renzhuan is rich in vocal music, and some 300 Qupai (musical scores) are known to this genre. About 50-60 are rendered repeatedly during performances. The most famous Qupai include *Huhuqiang, Labapaizi, Wenhaihai, Wuhaihai and Hongliuzi*.

Dagu and Gushu

Dagu and Gushu are terms that denote the same category of Qu under the heading of Quyi. They chiefly consist of Jingyun Dagu, Xihe Dagu, Meihua Dagu, Yueting Dagu, Northeastern Dagu, Beijing Qinshu, Henan Zhuizi and Wenzhou Guci. They are popular in townships and rural areas as well as in cities in Northern China.

Dagu and Gushu are always performed in this way: One person beats a drum or plays clappers, accompanied by one or more musicians. The chief instrument is the sanxian (three-stringed lute), which is indispensable. There are also the sihu, pipa, and dulcimer. The drum beaten by the storyteller is referred to as the shugu (story telling drum), which is oblong in shape with animal hides on both ends. It is placed on a rack, which may be high or low, as required by different kinds of Quyi. The drum is beaten with a bamboo stick. The clappers (ban) are of two kinds: one is made of two pieces, usually of hardwood, and the other consists of two pieces of what are called half-moon copper or steel strips, also called "mandarin duck" clappers.

Jingyun Dagu performance

The script is referred to as Guci and has basically seven or ten words per line. The story can be short, medium or long. The short stories are in song form, without narrative. The medium and long stories require both singing and narrative, hence their performance is referred to as "singing the Dagushu" while the performance of short stories is referred to as "singing the Dagu". The music of Dagu is the Banqiangti, which mainly originated from folk music and local ballads in the locality where the particular type of Dagu is popular. The storyteller sings in the local dialect. The difference in vocal music is the chief distinction between different kinds of Dagu.

Yangzhou Pinghua (Storytelling in Yangzhou Dialect)

Yangzhou Pinghua is a kind of Quyi performed by telling stories with musical accompaniment in Yangzhou dialect.

Yangzhou Pinghua was created in the late Ming Dynasty and flourished in the middle of the Qing Dynasty. Artistically, Yangzhou Pinghua is good at exquisite description, well-organized structure, the beginning and end echoed; it excels in rich figures and vivid language.

It is usually performed by one narrator who only tells stories without singing accompaniment. But sometimes, the dialogue is interspersed with singing when there are two actors involved. The language function is exerted to a full extent, with exquisite storytelling, lifelike gestures and careful characterization. It requires a simple performance using the mouth, hands, body, steps, facial expression and eye contact, one person, one table, one fan and xingmu (small wood block used by a storyteller to strike the table before him to draw audience attention). This can exaggerate complicated characters and make the stories sound exciting. In addition, Yangzhou Pinghua is characterized by minor movement, excellent use of eye and facial expressions and stress on feelings residing therein. As a result, it forms a unique technique of expression.

Yangzhou Pinghua boasts local features. Usually, it depicts various folk customs of the past in detail full of jesting and buffoonery. It is divided into public talking (guanbai) and private talking (sibai). Public talking (guanbai) is to differentiate and show characters and imitate the dialect of different characters. It is designed according to the specific characteristics of different roles. Private talking (sibai) is Yangzhou dialect. It is used in narration for expressing character insight, coupled with comments.

Yangzhou Pinghua has rich traditional programs, with more than 20 stories preserved and catalogued. *Outlaws of the Marshes and the Romance of the Three Kingdoms* are representative.

Pingshu

Pingshu (story-telling) is a Quyi art form of oral storytelling. The aesthetic purport of the performance relies on both the telling and playing of stories and the comment on human relationships, praise and disparagement on rights and wrongs, and the explanation on anecdotes of the persons and events in the stories. The art of Pingshu is popular in northern China.

As to the performance of the Pingshu, in early times performers wore a traditional gown and sat behind a table, with a folded fan and a gavel. By the mid-l920s, these props had all disappeared, with the performer appearing only in a standing position in a gown or any other kind of clothes.

The programs of the Pingshu are mostly voluminous stories and the contents are mostly about the alternation of past dynasties and heroic expeditions and knight-errantry. By the mid-1920s, there appeared medium stories with shorter length and short stories suitable for evening party performances, but voluminous stories are still the leading form.

Pingshu (storytelling) performance

Kuaiban and Kuaishu

Zhang Zhikuan performing the Kuaibanshu

Kuaishu and Kuaiban are both Quyi art forms and storytelling and singing with theatrical rhyming. However, they have slight differences.

According to region, dialect and storytelling style, there are different types of Kuaishu, such as Renqiu Zhubanshu popular in Shandong Province, Luogushu popular in the suburbs of Shanghai, Kuaibanshu originated and popular in Tianjin. Shandong Kuaishu, popular all across China, is the most famous and influential one.

According to different prevalence regions, dialects and storytelling styles, there are also different types of Kuaiban, such as Shulaibao (a kind of clapper ballad), Shuoguzi, Shaanxi Kuaiban, etc.

Both Kuaishu and Kuaiban have a very simple form. The actor usually stands to recite and sing, accompanied by the playing of a small percussion instrument held in one hand. The items performed by one, two, or three or more actors are called solo, cross-rhymed dialogue and group-rhymed dialogue respectively. The impromptu clapping instruments differ according to the types of melody. For instance, the Shandong Kuaishu performer holds two small crescent-shaped bronze pieces in one hand, the manipulation of which is called Yuanyangban. For Shulaibao or Kuaiban, two pairs of bamboo clapping instruments are used, a big and small pair, the former composed of two bamboo pieces and the latter of five pieces held together by string. While performing, the actor talks and sings accompanied by clappers in each hand. The actor often beats the clappers between sections and creates various beating effects to amuse the audience.

Early Drama

Drama was introduced to China from foreign countries in the early 20th century.

Diplomats sent to the West on missions were the first to be exposed to Western drama. Later, with the opening of coastal ports in China to foreign trade, some Western missionaries and foreign emigrants poured into China, and Shanghai became the major place of habitation for them. In 1866, foreign emigrants established the first Western-style opera house in Shanghai, Lanxin Great Opera House.

In 1899, Chinese students of St. John's College in Shanghai rehearsed and played a new drama, *Ugly Stories of Officialdom*. The performance differed greatly from traditional operas, but some of the plots were borrowed from traditional operas, which established the foundation for later plays.

In general, drama historians deem the Spring Willow Society's performance of *La Dame aux Camelias and Uncle Tom's Cabin* in 1907 in Tokyo as the beginning of modern Chinese drama. In the spring of 1907, the Spring Willow Society initiated by Li Shutong and Ouyang Yuqian performed the third act of Alexander Dumas's famous play *La Dame aux Camelias* in Tokyo. In their performances, "they talk completely in spoken dialog without any reciting or singing, and there are monologues and asides". This kind of performance mode can be deemed as drama. Before long, they adapted Harriet Beecher Stowe's *Uncle Tom's Cabin* into a stage play. The division into acts, telling the story with dialogue and activities plus true-to-life stage characters, confirmed the birth of an unprecedented dramatic form in China. Later, this form was labeled modern Chinese drama.

Modern Drama

Since the 1920s, there have appeared plays with realistic and expressionistic themes. Initiators of the new drama had a special love for plays of the Norwegian playwright Ibsen. His *A Doll's House* had a great influence on Chinese youth living under the feudalistic arranged marriage system, and Nora became their idol. Under the influence of the play, a group of characters leaving home were created in such plays as *An Important Event in Life* by Hu Shi, *Shrew* by Ouyang Yuqian, *Life of New People* by Xiong Fuxi, *Zhuo Wenjun*, a historical play by Guo Moruo, which are all called "Nora plays". These show the realistic character of Chinese modern drama in the initial period.

The Western trend of thoughts of expressionistic plays also attracted Chinese playwrights and its method of exploring human mentality was extraordinarily attractive. Hong Shen in his *Hades Zhao* presented a Chinese soldier, Zhao Da, who took money obtained by dubious means to flee away to a dark forest. He felt very frightened and suffered from a tortured soul and unreal images in a tangled web.

Through many transitions Western drama was established in China finally. New plays were continuously created, various groups emerged to present dramas led by some great directors, drama education became established and amateur theatrical groups flourished. There also appeared a group of famous playwrights such as Cao Yu, Zhang Pingqun and Jin Yan.

Professional Drama Troupes

Different from the drama troupes in the 1920s, in the 1930s, there appeared professional troupes for drama performances. Among them, the China Travel Troupe was the most famous. The troupe offered performances of both dramas adapted from foreign famous novels and the new plays created by Chinese playwrights, and cultivated a group of performing talents for modern drama. In addition, the Shanghai Amateur Dramatic Association and Shanghai Amateur Experimental Troupe were also large-scale professionalized troupes at that time. They offered performances of dramas such as *Romeo and Juliet, Great Thunderstorm, The Wildness and Imperial Envoy*, etc.

During that period, China had its own excellent directors, such as Hong Shen, Zhang Pengchun, Ying Yunwei, Tang Huaiqiu and Zhang Min, etc. And there emerged a group of excellent actors, such as Jin Shan, Zhao Dan, Jin Yan, Bai Yang and Tang Ruoqing, etc. The general level of stage art had made people look at it with new eyes.

During World War II, drama circles organized dozens of performance groups for resisting Japanese invasion and saving the country, and went around China to promote the spirit of resistance. They created many short and popular performances, such as street plays, teahouse plays, parade plays and puppet plays. The famous street plays such as *Put down Your Whip* exposed the crimes of Japan's aggression. During the period of the Anti-Japanese War, Chongqing became the temporary capital and most of the performance troupes and performers moved there. In October 1938, the First Dramatic Festival was held; 25 performance groups were organized to perform on the streets and in towns, and resisting-enemy dramas were performed for seven continuous nights, which is honored as an unprecedented event in the history of Chinese modern drama.

China National Huaju Opera Troupe produced its first play-the drama *The Dawns Hera Are Quiet* adopted from the works of the former Soviet Union after its founding.

Contemporary Drama

After the founding of the People's Republic of China in 1949, the development of Chinese modern drama also entered a new historical stage, and the past folk troupes began to change into professional and orderly artistic troupes under government direction. In terms of performances, the Stanislavsky performance style was introduced from the Soviet Union, a group of excellent plays emerged and performance schools with Chinese characteristic gradually came into being.

Later a group of works emerged, symbolizing the peak of the development of modern drama in new China, such as *Teahouse* by Lao She and *Guan Hanqing* by Tian Han.

Teahouse, published in 1957, not only marks the peak of Lao She's dramatic creativity but also is a milestone in dramatic creation in China. The play covers three "dynasties", a span over 50 years, and gives vivid description of 70 figures. With supreme artistic generalization and strong national manner, historical contents and living flavor, the play composes an epic magnificent scene. The general director Jiao Juyin (1905-1975) also made great contribution to the success of the play. Today, *Teahouse* is still in the repertoire of the Beijing People's Art Theater.

In 1958, Tian Han created *Guan Hanqing*, a symbol in the creative development of Chinese historical plays. *Guan Hanqing* was made to mark the 700th birth anniversary of *Guan Hanqing*, a famous litterateur and the great dramatist in 13th century China. Tian Han composed a song praising *Guan Hanqing* in poetic words, sentiment and conception.

Beijinger–a drama masterpiece by Cao Yu

In addition, there were a group of other influential plays, such as *The Second Spring, Sentinels under Neon Lights, A Young Generation, Never Forget, Advance Courageously in the Rip Tide, Great Wall on the South China Sea*, etc.

Open Dramatic World

With the breaking of the closed situation in China and the continuous enlargement of opening up, the dramatic world also welcomed a new situation of wide exchanges with foreign circles. Chinese drama enlarged exchanges by invitation; inviting foreign troupes to perform in China or inviting foreign playwrights and directors to rehearse with their Chinese colleagues. Many foreign plays were translated into Chinese.

Modern drama performances and exchanges abroad become more frequent. *Teahouse*, *No. 1 Building in China*, *Dead Water with Tiny Billows*, *Home*, and *Guan Hanqing* have been performed overseas, for example.

The dramatic festivals, special performances and academic seminars for remembering foreign dramatists such as Shakespeare, Ibsen and O'Neill are the most representative events reflecting the open characteristics of Chinese drama. Among them, the "Shakespeare Dramatic Festival" held many times is the most representative and has strengthened the exchanges and cooperation in dramatic culture between China and foreign countries.

China National Huaju Opera Troupe

The troupe performs on behalf of China. It was founded on December 25, 2001 on the basis of the China Youth Art Troupe and the Central Experimentary Huaju Opera Troupe.

Address: No.45, Mao'er Hutong, Di'anmeng, Beijing
Website: http://www.ntcc.com.cn

♦ Realistic Play Writers

Cao Yu (1910-1996) showed his talents again during World War II. He wrote multi-act plays Metamorphosis and People of Beijing, and adapted Ba Jin's novel Home into a modern drama successfully. These are all representative works of promoted realism in Chinese modern drama. The techniques of Cao Yu became more mature and gave more profound themes and richer implications to his plays.

Wu Zuguang (1917-) showed his talent during Anti-Japanese War and revealed his strong poetic sense and vigorous style of writing. His representative work *Returning at Night of Wind and Snow* tells the tragedy of the life of a noted actor of Beijing Opera, Wei Liansheng. On the surface it is a love tragedy, but actually it reflects humanistic thoughts.

Song Zhide (1914-1956) created *Fog Chongqing* in 1940 and became famous after the performance. The play describes the actual life of a group of youths and the social decadence and darkness in Chongqing in wartime, and also criticizes the wavering and compromises of the petit bourgeoisie.

Chen Baichen (1908-1994)'s *Picture of Winning Promotion*, a political irony play, is the highest representative work of modern Chinese ironical comedy. It referred to the comedic conception of Imperial Envoy and the shaping of clowns in traditional Chinese operas, and exposed and sneered incisively and vividly at the corruption of the official system, infestation of evil persons and the vulgar and infamous social reality.

Lao She (1899-1966) created *Remnant Fog* in 1939, satirizing the social reality in the official circles in Chongqing at that time. Lao She's comedies intended to clear away the "remnant fog" under the situation of the Anti-Japanese War and exposed corruption in power. The figures in the play have distinctive characters and the words are lively and fresh.

China National Youth's Art Theater

The troupe is a State class theater. It has since performed close to 200 full-length opera items and 80 one-part ones. Most of these are close to life. Modern dramas include *Press-ganging, Watching Chang'an in the West*, and *Lei Feng*; historical operas include *Qu Yuan* and *Guan Hanqing*; and foreign operas include *Pavel Korchagin, Imperial Commissioner, Biography of Galilei* and *Merchant of Vennice*.

Address: No.71, Beijige Xantiao, Dongcheng District, Beijing

Beijing People's Art Theater is performing the Teahouse by Lao She in New York, the US..

Beijing People's Art Theater

Beijing People's Art Theater is famous around the world and its works represent the highest level of Chinese modern drama.

It was founded in 1952 and Cao Yu became the first president. In more than 50 years it has gradually formed its special performance system and style with Chinese national characteristics. It possesses a series of excellent dramas such as *Longxu Ditch* and *Teahouse* by Lao She, *Cai Wenji* by Guo Moruo, *Death of a Noted Actor* and *Guan Hanqing* by Tian Han, *Thunderstorm* and *Sunrise* by Cao Yu, and subsequent *Absolute Signal*, *Nirvana of Gou Er Ye, No.1 Building in China*, etc. Beijing People's Art Theater holds an open view and has offered performances of a great many foreign famous plays of various schools and styles.

Beijing People's Art Theater formed a directors' group, backed by a group of excellent performance artists. Chief director Jiao Juyin formed his directors' school in the 1950s and 1960s, and his merits cannot be neglected.

Players of the Central Experimentary Huaju Opera Troupe are performing the King Richard III-a famous drama by Shakespeare.

In the past 20 years, the theater has promoted more than 80 new plays, resumed performing 12 original repertoires and almost every performance has a capacity audience.

Address: No.22 Wangfujing Dajie, Beijing
Website: http:// www.bjry.com

China National Children's Art Troupe

This troupe, set up in June 1956, is directly under the Ministry of Culture. It has since its founding performed some 130 Chinse and foreign operas specialized for children. One of these is *Malanhua*. It was held as a milestone in the children's operas. Other works performed included *Children Selling Newspapers*, *New Garments of the Emperor* and *Blue Bird*.

Address: No.64, Dong'anmen Dajie, Dongcheng District, Beijing
Website: http:// www.ntcc.com.cn

Central Experimentary Huaju Opera Troupe

The troupe was set up in September 1956. Its first head is Ouyang Yuqian, the founder of the Chinese Huaju operas and a noted educator. The troupe has over the past 50 years performed many items of different styles and schools.

Address: No.Jia-45, Mao'er Hutong, Di'anmen, Dongcheng District, Beijing

Shanghai People's Art Theater

The Shanghai People's Art Theater, a Chinese modern drama troupe, was organized in 1950. After more than 30 years of artistic practices, Shanghai People's Art Theater has cultivated its own writers, directors, stage artists, and a large number of performers, mainly including the playwrights Wang Lian and Sha Yexin, directors Huang Zuolin, Luo Yizhi, and Yang Cunbin, and performers Gao Zhongshi, Qiao Qi, and Lu Fu. This Theater has held two terms of school to cultivate performers, established a perfect stage art workshop, and made contribution to the cultivation of human resources for modern drama.

Address: No.288 Anfu Lu, Shanghai

Central Academy of Drama

The Central Academy of Drama Theater is the highest school of drama education in China, a world famous art academy, the center of education and research in drama, film and TV in China, the Asian Theater Education Center and the important base of training and practicing drama, film and TV. Formally founded in April 1950, this Academy's predecessors are Yan'an Lu Xun Art College, Art College of North China University, and Nanjing State Drama College. Many famous film actors and actresses in China graduated from this Academy, such as Gong Li, Zhang Ziyi and Jiang Wen.

Address: 39, Dongmianhua Hutong, Dongcheng District, Beijing
Website: http://www.chntheatre.edu.cn/

Shanghai Theater Academy

Shanghai Theater Academy is a higher art academy specialized in cultivating drama artists in China. Along with Central Academy of Drama Theater in the north, it is also the highest school of Chinese drama. Established in 1945, this Academy's predecessor is Shanghai Municipal Experimental Drama School. The famous dramatist Mr. Xiong Foxi is the first president and is the president with the longest tenure. The Experimental Theater of this Academy has a capacity of 999 and is one of the important large-scale art performance places in Shanghai and the appointed performing place of Shanghai International Art Festival. In addition, this Academy has the following performing theaters:

Black Box Drama Laboratory: it gets the name as the inside space is all black, and Black Box is the nickname for small experimental theater in the international drama circle. It has a strong flexibility and suits for the performance of experimental works.

New Experiment Space: the original building is the studio of China Film Company in 1930s which is the birthplace of early films in China. After rebuilding in 2000, it maintains the red brick wall on outside and the inside is a well-equipped new-type small theater. It suits for various experimental dramas and lectures and reports.

Small Theater: Since 1950s all the graduate performances have been given here. It is a new modern medium-sized theater.

Address: 630, Huashan Rd., Shanghai
Website: http://www.sta.edu.cn/

Traditional Artware

Traditional Artware

China has rich and colorful traditional artware with national style and local characteristics. This comes in a wide variety, such as sculpture, embroidery, lacquerware, artistic porcelain, weaving, printing and dyeing, cloisonné, carpet, clay sculpture, etc. Chinese traditional arts and crafts have a long history, some in many sorts, with masterly skills and rich technical and cultural implications and influencing various aspects of social life.

Bronze Ware

The Shang Dynasty rulers treasured fine-shaped bronze ware, especially bronze sacrificial vessels. They handed them down to later generations and were only used for important events or sacrificial ceremonies. Many of the vessels were inscribed with words describing the slave owner's power, orders, battle achievements, awards and sacrificial rites so his descendants could know about his life. The inscription on Duke Mao's Ding is the longest known and comprises 497 characters of rich historical record, involving sacrificial ceremonies, instructive mandate, imperial edict, and descriptions of expeditions and lawsuits. The number of ding owned by rulers reflected their social position, and the vessels' weight symbolized the breadth of' power and even the rise and decline of imperial power.

Much of the bronze ware of the Shang Dynasty was decorated with animal patterns, also called taotie patterns. Taotie is an imaginary and mysterious animal with horns, paws and tail that was greedy and impossible to satiate. The imaginary creature was, in reality, an exaggerated combination of a cow, tiger and sheep. Later decorations on bronzeware had changed to ring and ripple patterns from taotie and kui patterns. The vessels began to have lids, handles and ears; the three-dimensional animal patterns that had then appeared were carved on these parts.

From their fertile imagination, ancient Chinese slaves created the splendid traditional Chinese bronze ware culture. The beautiful and complicated patterns on the ware reveal the craftsmen's wisdom and superb skills. They also reflect the essential concepts of Chinese Slave Society and are a witness of this history.

• Simuwu Rectangular Ding Tripod

In 1939, a huge bronze tripod called ding in Chinese, which was an ancient cooking vessel with two loop handles and three or four legs, was unearthed in Anyang, Henan Province. It is now preserved in the China National Museum.

This is the biggest and heaviest bronze sacrificial vessel in ancient China. The total height is 1.33 m, the opening is 1.10 m long and 0.79 m wide, and the whole ding weighs 832.84 kilograms. The body has great depth and level bottom, and there are leaf arris on the corners of the opening. There are two standing ears on the side of the opening, four column feet under its belly, and kui and animal patterns with clouds and thunder patterns as the base on four sides of the body; the middle part is plain. On the side face of the ears are engraved patterns of two tigers eating a man's head. On top of the Ding's feet there are animal face patterns and on the middle part there are leaf arris. Analysis has found the ding contains 84.77 percent of bronze, 11.64 percent of stannum, and 2.79 percent of lead. It represents the highest achievement of the Shang Dynasty in casting technique and bronze artistry. According to archeologists, the King of the Shang Dynasty asked for the ding to be made to commemorate his mother, which explains the name. With its huge shape, heavy weight and solemnity, the ding is a typical representative of highly-developed bronze culture in ancient China. Not only is it the biggest one among the unearthed bronze ware in China, but also a rare elaborate work among bronze ware in the world.

Dings were used in Chinese primitive society as cooking utensils. At first they were made of pottery clay. Then, as metallurgy emerged and developed, the material was changed to bronze at the end of the Shang Dynasty about 3,000 years ago. By that time, dings undergone a functional change to become sacrificial vessels and the symbol of their owners' power and wealth. Bronze ware of the Shang Dynasty formed a special model series. The vessels include the ding, the ge, which is an ancient cooking tripod with hollow legs, the zun, a wine vessel used in ancient times, and the hu, a type of pot. Musical instruments include the nao (big cymbal), ling (bell), and the drum and chimes imitating woodenware. In addition, there are also weapons and chariots and horses. Of all the bronze ware, it is the vessels that display the greatest variety.

Horse Stepping on a Swallow

There is another famous representative sculpture of the Han Dynasty, the statue of a Horse Stepping on a Swallow.

This ancient bronzeware, unearthed in an Eastern Han Dynasty tomb in Wuwei County, Gansu Province, in 1969, was made around 220 and it is 34.5 cm high and 41 cm long. It has a lively action and accurate proportions. The positioning of its four legs strictly conforms to that of a living horse and is highly praised by many local and foreign archeologists and artists. The horse is raising its head, neighing and galloping forward with one foot treading on a flying swallow. According to analysis of its mechanics, Horse Stepping on a Swallow finds a center of gravity in the swallow to give the statue its stability. The romantic image of the swallow sets off the powerful bearing and swiftness like the wind of the horse, providing a rich imaginative experience for viewers. The statue of Horse Stepping on a Swallow is a unique product among Chinese bronzeware.

Jade Ware

Jade is a rare colorful and hard stone, and it is usually polished and carved to make jade ware. There is a proverb in China that "without being polished and carved, a jade cannot become jade ware". It originally means that a jade stone can become an invaluable treasure after being processed; through extension, it also means that children can become persons of ability only by cultivation and education.

Chinese jade ware has a long history. Jade objects of the Liangzhu Culture of the Neolithic Age were unearthed in Zhejiang Province, and they appear delicate and beautiful. Jade ware production skills greatly improved in the Shang and Zhou dynasties, and jade objects of that time include production tools, weapons, daily utensils, ornaments and sacrificial vessels. They had reached a very high level.

In the Zhou Dynasty, jade was imbued by the ruling class with the concepts of benevolence, righteousness, etiquette, faithfulness, wisdom and courage. Thus, jade ware was not only ornamental, but also a symbol of social virtue and order. In the Han Dynasty, jade ware moved from noble families into ordinary people's homes. Their shapes assumed a more realistic style, although some parts were still very decorative. After the Han Dynasty, jade ware was mainly used as decorations for appreciation and display or every day items.

Jade Production

Some very large and brilliant jade ware pieces were made in the Qing Dynasty(1616-1911). The Dayu Controlling Water jade ware conserved in Gugong (Imperial Palace) Museum, for example, weighs about five tons, and its production took 18 years from preparing materials to completion. With social development, the themes and models of jade ware became increasingly common, such as the very popular Guanyin Bodhisattva, the lion mother and son, and the child with lotus leaf, and designs with good omen occupying an increasingly larger proportion.

Jade production is a complicated process involving material selection, design of the pattern, grinding and polishing. The principal jade objects include jewelry, handicrafts and miniature landscapes. Jade handicrafts have the highest artistic quality, including jade figurines of court ladies, children, old men and Buddha's, jade flowers and birds of three friends of winter (plum blossom, bamboo and pine), four men of virtue (plum blossom, orchid, bamboo and chrysanthemum), and magpie on branches of plum blossom, and jade animals and utensils such as horses, elephants, oxen, sheep, lions, tigers and dragons, kylin, bixie, and oxen zun, lion zun, incense-burners, smoking stoves, and vases.

Jade ware is mostly produced in Beijing, Shanghai, Guangzhou, Yangzhou of Jiangsu Province and Liaoning Province. Jade ware made in different places has a different appearance and style. Beijing jade ware is bold, elegant and dignified. Shanghai jade ware is made in imitation of ancient style bronze ware. Guangzhou jade ware absorbs many Western artistic techniques and looks fresh, natural and unrestrained. Yangzhou jade ware has fluid lines and a transparent quality. The jade-making skills of all these regions have been handed down through for many generations and have formed their distinct characteristics overtime.

Chinese Cloisonné

Cloisonné is one of the famous special art works in China. Also called "bronze inlaid enamel", it is a traditional handicraft. When making the cloisonné, one sticks the pattern on the bronze body by oblate and thin brass wires, and then fills in the inlay pattern by enamel glaze material in different colors; the final procedure is the firing, polishing and gilding.

Cloisonné originated in the Yuan Dynasty and prevailed during the Jingtai period (1450-1457) of the Ming Dynasty. As blue was the most used color, it is also called Jingtai blue. In olden times, cloisonné ware was especially for use by imperial nobles, symbolizing power and position. At present, the varieties include normal cloisonné and flowery-wires cloisonné. The former one divides into golden cloisonné and blue cloisonné, and the latter divides into golden, silver and blue flowery-wires.

Cloisonné

Cloisonné is completely hand-made. The production process is very exquisite, including more than ten procedures such as making the bronze body, sticking in the wires, filling in the blue, firing the blue, polishing and gilding; of these, sticking the wires and filling in the blue are the most complicated and meticulous techniques. The technique of cloisonné employs not only bronze crafts, but also porcelain and enameling crafts, and also incorporates traditional painting and carving techniques, a great combination of Chinese traditional arts. Cloisonné has a beautiful shape, brilliant designs and bright colors; it boasts high artistic value.

Modern Cloisonné

Today, besides traditional decorative objects, such as stoves, ding, pots, three-dimensional animals, candleholders, six-petal vases, plum blossom vases and Chinese flowering crabapple vases, a great number of practical articles of cloisonné have been developed, such as various vases, jugs, plates, bowls, smoking sets, lamps and lanterns, stationery, tea sets, hangings, tables, stools, folding screens, award cups, etc. These various types of cloisonné have new and beautiful shapes and strong national artistic styles. In addition, on a base of the special technique of sticking the wires, cloisonné handicraftsmen also absorb the methods of drawing outlines and adding shading in Chinese traditional painting, which produce more lively designs. The enamel glaze material has more than 80 kinds of colors compared to the original 30 kinds, and some new colors have been created such as coral red, bright red, bean green, milky white, lake blue, star gold, malachite green, etc., which make the cloisonné artwork become more brilliant.

Lacquer Ware

Lacquer ware is a traditional artwork in China, and its shapes and patterns show a strong national style. In ancient times, lacquer ware was mostly utilitarian, such as daily utensils, furniture and woodenware. In terms of production methods, there are shell inlay and engraving.

There is a kind of varnish tree which has mucilage beneath its rind. The mucilage can be used to write or brush the surface of utensils for protection and beauty.

The production of lacquer ware is a complicated process, and is labor-intensive and time consuming. There are various lacquer ware types, for decorating both furniture, utensils, stationery and artwork and musical instruments, funeral goods and weapons. The lacquer ware is usually coated black and decorated with red designs or coated red and decorated with black designs. Gold, silver, tin and wood can all serve as materials for lacquer ware. In the Song Dynasty, gold and silver were usually used to make lacquer ware decorated with red designs especially for imperial usage.

The patterns on the lacquer ware are simple lines or complicated pictures, depending on the function, or to strengthen the vigor and force of human beings or animals in the design. The contrast between the black and red colors creates a special bright and beautiful artistic effect. The black and red pictures, with magnificent and colorful artistic styles in a musical sense, are often found on the lacquer ware.

Development of Lacquer Ware

Chinese began to make lacquer ware about 7,000 years ago. In 1978, red lacquer bowls and tubes were found in the Hemudu Culture Relics site in Yuyao, Zhejiang Province. According to chemical and spectral analysis, the coatings were natural lacquers.

After the Xia Dynasty, the variety of lacquer ware increased, and the craft began to flourish in the Warring States Period. The scale of lacquer ware production had already become very large. It was one of the main economic resources of the time, and there were specific officials in charge of its production.

In the Han Dynasty lacquer ware mainly used black and red colors. Lacquer ware reached its heyday in this period with a growing range of products. Meanwhile, many new crafting

Carved lacquerware—one of China's lacquerware

techniques and decorative methods were also developed such as multiple colors, engraving with needles, copper buttons, sticking gold slices, hawksbill pieces, inlay and piling lacquer.

In the Qing Dynasty, imperial lacquer ware was even more incomparable. Both materials and crafting techniques had reached a peak of perfection, and the products were magnificent and extraordinarily exquisite. In terms of folk lacquer ware, the ones made in southern China were the most exquisite.

The modern craft of lacquer ware is mainly distributed in Beijing, Jiangsu Province, Yangzhou, Shanghai, Sichuan Province, Chongqing, Fujian Province, Pingyao in Shanxi Province, Dafang in Guizhou Province, Tianshui in Gansu Province, Yichun in Jiangxi Province and Fengxiang in Shaanxi Province. Among them, Beijing carved lacquerware is made by coating a wooden body or bronze body with scores or even a hundred layers of lacquer decoration and then doing relief carving. Vermilion is the major color and the style is magnificent. Lacquer ware of Yangzhou, Jiangsu Province is characterized by inlaid shell. Under the shining light, it is very exquisite. The lacquer ware separated from body in Fujian Province is characterized by bright color, light weight, beautiful appearance, being waterproof and heat-resistant, acid- and alkali-resistant. Sichuan lacquer ware is mostly made with a technique of coating lacquer by pushing to glaze or filling after carving. In addition, there are lacquer wire decoration in Xiamen and filling after carving in Tianshui.

Wax Printing

Laran, wax printing, called laxie in ancient time, is honored as one of the Three Great Printing Techniques in ancient China, along with jiaoxie tie-dyeing and jiaxie (hollow printing).

Wax printing might be called actually "wax-prevention dyeing". It is a way of decorating natural fiber fabric such as sack cloth, silk, cotton and wool by covering parts of it with a coat of dissolved beeswax and then dyeing it in an indigo blue dye vat at an appropriate temperature. As the beeswax can resist water, the parts covered by the wax resist the dye and retain their original hues. After dyeing, the beeswax is heated until it dissolves and beautiful designs appear on the fabric due to the wax protection. "Ice patterns" are the soul of wax printing, resulting from uneven infiltration of dye into folded and split beeswax and are usually designs with abstract effects.

As an old prevention dyeing craft in China, wax printing has a very long history. As early as in the Qin and Han dynasties, the ancestors of the ethnic minorities Miao, Yao, and Bouyei in southwest China had grasped the technique.

This ancient craft is still popular in ethnic minorities in Guizhou and Yunnan provinces, such as Bouyei, Miao, Gelao, Shui, Tu, and Yi. The artistic styles and application ranges and parts are different, depending on different ethnic customs and aesthetic characteristics. For example, in Zhenning City, Guizhou Province, the wax printing of the Bouyei ethnic minority is mostly of a single color (blue cloth with white decorations), and the designs are mostly the patterns of dragon prawn, whorl, ripple, chain, etc. on collars, sleeves and skirts. Among the Miao ethnic minority, the wax printing adds red, green and yellow colors; painting red or green on flowers' pistils and leaves, or adding slim bands in red, yellow and green on some parts of blue-and-white skirts, or decorating red cloth with white designs. They are all extraordinarily pretty.

Paper-Cuts

The art of the paper cut is one of the folk art forms in China with the widest popularity, the most distinctive regional style and the richest historical and cultural implications. It is widely prevalent in rural areas, where the folk people still greatly appreciate paper cut works. Most of them are rural women who cut a piece of hand-made jute paper with simple and primitive scissors and form this art form with a powerful expressive force inheriting developments over two thousand years. The special value of paper cuts depends on the primitive tools and materials, original expressive force, common creators and wide practicality.

Paper cuts are used as decorations on windows, doors, walls, roofs, lanterns and at weddings, Spring Festival celebrations and funerals. The emergence and prevalence of paper cuts have close links with traditional Chinese festivals and customs in rural areas. For instance, window, door and lantern paper cuts are put up during Spring Festival and the Lantern Festival. In the rural areas in northern China, at Spring Festival, farmers usually stick white paper on the windows of their houses and then paste green and red paper cuts on them; hanging paper cuts are stuck to the doors and roofs. On the evening of the Lantern Festival, paper cuts are pasted onto lanterns to add to the festive atmosphere. To celebrate a new marriage, paper cuts are put on the furniture, daily utensils and many places in the wedding chamber. They are also pasted in rooms to celebrate birthdays and to commemorate the departed at funerals. When fixing up rooms, people often paste paper cuts on walls and roofs. Generally speaking, paper cuts are pasted in courtyards, rooms and on everyday goods to decorate the domestic environment and to add a cheerful atmosphere.

Paper-cut works are cut or engraved on paper, so they must be hollowed out. Therefore all the lines of paper-cuts in relief must be connected and all the lines of paper-cuts in intaglio must be broken. If some lines are broken, the whole work will break and will not form a picture. It is an important feature of paper-cuts art. Paper-cuts

♦ Abundant Folk Paper Cuts

Chinese paper cuts are rich in content and wide in implication, and are reflected entirely in folk culture. They are used as decorations on windows, kang, cave ceilings, and the totemic door-god, on daily utensils such as vats, urns, and porcelains, the patterns for embroidery on clothes, hats, shoes, pillows, and bellyband. There are paper cuts for tiger pillows, baby pillows and fish pillows implying babies are born by totemic mothers. There are paper cuts of "yin-yang fish", "fish biting lotus" and "lotus giving birth of babies", implying increased offspring in marriage customs. There are paper cuts of the "tree of life" implying immortal souls and eternal life in funeral customs. On festivals, there are paper cuts of "bowls bottom up" and "mouse biting sky open" implying heaven and earth are intersected, everything starts to burgeon, and there is a harvest in corns. In the first lunar month, paper cuts of "spring cattle door-god" are pasted on doors for welcoming spring and preparing for plowing. On Tomb-Sweeping Day, the paper cuts of "fuotuo" are inserted on tombs of ancestors (Manchu minority). During the dragon boat festival in the fifth lunar month, the paper cuts of "loving tiger" are pasted to get rid of evils and disasters. In the Miao minority, there are god figures paper cuts on sacrificial ceremonies for ancestors and gods by killing cattle and paper cuts of "peach blossom cave" on sacrificial ceremonies, dancing and dramas for gods and goddesses. There are too numerous types of paper cuts to mention one by one.

Though their production require only very simple skills and are in simple shapes, their contents are rich and reveal many local Chinese customs and reflect numerous folk art forms in rural areas. An understanding of paper cuts is a good beginning to appreciate other aspects of Chinese folk arts.

Today in the world many countries have paper cuts produced by individual professional artists, but folk paper cuts by common people are rarely seen. Europe and America do not have folk paper cuts by common people, and among the "Four Great Cultures" of the ancient world, only in China can one find the folk paper cut art by common people, which is one of the cultural relics urgently demanding rescue and protection.

pay much attention to lines.

In terms of structure, paper-cuts are different from other paintings. It is hard for them to show three-dimensional space and overlapping of scenes and images. It mainly depends on the relations of images in content and mostly makes use of combination. Due to exaggerated and transformed shapes, it can also use some rules of a picture and convey symmetry, evenness, balance, combination and sequence. It can arrange the sun, moon, stars, flying birds, and clouds in the same picture with buildings, people and animals on Earth.

Embroidery

Embroidery consists of pulling colored threads through a background material with embroidery needles to stitch colored patterns that have been previously designed on the base material. The adoption of different needling methods has resulted in different embroidery styles and technique schools. Chinese embroidery had already reached a high level early in the Qin and Han dynasties, and was one of the important products transported along the ancient Chinese Silk Road. The four famous Chinese embroidery styles are Hunan embroidery of Hunan Province in central China, Shu embroidery of Sichuan Province in western China, Guangdong embroidery of Guangdong Province in southern China and Suzhou embroidery of Jiangsu Province in eastern China.

Xiangxiu (Hunan Embroidery)

Hunan embroidery is well known for its time-honored history, excellent craftsmanship, unique style and numerous varieties. The earliest piece of Hunan embroidery was unearthed at the No 1 Tomb of Mawangdui, Changsha City of the Han Dynasty. The weaving technique was almost the same as that in modern times. In the Qing Dynasty, it became a major handicraft in the urban and rural areas of Changsha. On a base of folk embroidery in Hunan Province, Hunan embroidery was developed by absorbing strong points of Suzhou and Guangdong embroidery. In its long development, Hunan embroidery absorbed the characteristics of traditional Chinese paintings and formed its own unique characteristics. Hunan embroidery experienced its heyday early in the 20th century, even surpassing Suzhou embroidery.

Hunan embroidery products use loose colorful threads to embroider the pattern. Besides the needling methods of "converging needling" and "scattered needling", there is an original method of "mixed needling". The stitches are not neat. The various colored threads are mixed together, showing a gradual change in color with a rich and harmonious tone. Designs on Hunan embroidery mostly derive from traditional Chinese paintings of landscapes, human figures, flowers, birds and animals. The designs are lively and vivid. The most common designs are lions and tigers. The tigers appear strong and bold, revealing their power and menace. Hunan embroidery won the best award in the Torino World Fair in Italy in 1912 and the First Award in the Panama World Fair in 1933. Hunan embroidery is known abroad as the ideal embroidery.

Modern Hunan embroidery uses pure silk, hard satin, soft satin, gauze and nylon as its material, which is connected with colorful silk threads and floss. Hunan embroidery crafts include valuable works of art, as well as materials for daily use.

Shuxiu (Sichuan Embroidery)

Also called Chuan embroidery, Shu embroidery is the general name for embroidery products in areas around Chengdu, Sichuan Province. It has a long history. As early as the Han Dynasty, Shuxiu was already famous. The central government even designated an office in Chengdu for its administration. In the Jin Dynasty Shu embroidery was called the treasure of Shu. It experienced its peak development in the Song Dynasty (960-1279), ranking first in handicraft, production and excellence. In the mid-Qing Dynasty, a Shuxiu industry was formed and in every county the government established a special office, "quangong (persuading needlework) office", to encourage production of Shu embroidery.

Influenced by the geographical environment, customs and cultures in the long development, Shuxiu has formed its own unique characteristics: precise, smooth, bright, neat, scattered designs, vigorous, simple, mellow and vivid.

Soft satin and colorful threads are the major materials. There are 122 needling methods in 12 categories. The common methods include faint needling, spreading needling, rolling needling, intercepting needling, mixed needling, sand needling and covering needling. Its needling characteristics lie in "the even stitches, bright threads, closeness and softness in texture, and both centrifugal and centripetal needling".

The designs on Shuxiu cover a wide range, including flowers, grass, trees, birds, animals, landscapes, fish, worms and human figures. Its products are various and include such utilitarian items as quilt covers, pillowcases, cushions, table cloths, scarf, handkerchief, dresses and shoes, besides screen covers for viewing. It is an excellent artwork with both appreciation value and practicability.

Yuexiu (Guangdong Embroidery)

Also called Guang embroidery, Yuexiu is a general name for embroidery products of the regions of Guangzhou, Chaozhou, Shantou, Zhongshan, Fanyu and Shunde in Guangdong Province. According to historical records, in the first year of Yongzhen's reign (805) during the Tang Dynasty, a girl named Lu Meiniang in Nanhai County, Guangdong Province embroidered seven volumes of the Fahua Buddhist Scripture on a piece of thin silk some 33 cm long. And so, Yuexiu became famous around the country. The prosperous Guangzhou Port in the Song and Yuan dynasties promoted the development of Yuexiu, which began to be exported. Craftsmen originally used peacock feathers twisted together as the embroidering thread to stitch the ornamental designs, brilliant with gold and green colors; and horsetail was used to stitch the outline to make the work more expressive.

Influenced by various ethnic folk arts, Yuexiu formed its own unique characteristics in the long development on a base of incorporating things of diverse nature and achieving mastery through comprehensive employment. Yuexiu embroidery is famous for well-rounded arrangement, exuberant patterns, vivid scenes and bright colors of red and green. It is the most distinguished by the first attribute. The space is filled with landscapes, grass and tree roots. It is crowded and compact.

Yuexiu embroidery has five main characteristics: first, threads are varied. Second, colors are bright with strong contrasts and brilliant effects. Third, gold thread is often used to serve as pattern outlines. Fourth, decorative patterns are numerous, well-rounded and vivid. The subjects have local colors such as a hundred birds worshipping the phoenix and fish and shrimps in the sea. Fifth, embroidery artisans are mostly men. The embroidered pictures are mainly of dragons and phoenixes, flowers and birds, and ancient themes with full composition, neat designs, strong decorative quality, and strong and contrasting colors. The embroidery works are neat and smooth, and gold and silver cushion embroidery creates a magnificent three-dimensional effect. The needling methods are characterized by "even stitches, clear texture, and all-around and neat stitches". Yuexiu is divided into floss, thread and gold-and-silk thread types which are used to produce costumes, decorations for halls, connected curtains, colored hangings, hanging curtain and crafts for daily use. Yuexiu includes the Guang and Chao branches which have different stitching styles.

Suxiu (Suzhou Embroidery)

Suzhou embroidery is the general name for embroidery products in areas around Suzhou, Jiangsu Province. The craft, which dates back to the Three Kingdoms Period, became a sideline of people in the Suzhou area during the Ming Dynasty after continuous development over many generations. At that

Suzhou embroidery—"May you always get more than you wish for"

time, there appeared the situation of "every family raising silkworms and embroidering". Well known for its smoothness and delicateness, Suzhou embroidery won Suzhou the title of "City of Embroidery" in the Qing Dynasty. In the mid and late Qing Dynasty, Suzhou embroidery experienced further development involving works of double-sided embroidering. In the 1930s, the irregular embroidery technique was created in the Zhengze Girl's Vocational School in Danyang. In 1957, the Embroidery Research Institute was established in Suzhou. Now, the needling methods have climbed from 18 to more than 40 at present.

Suzhou embroidery has been known for its delicacy and elegance since ancient times. The thin thread is divided into up to 48 strands that are barely visible to the naked eye. Suzhou embroidery is usually characterized by pretty designs, careful composition, meticulous embroidering, lively stitches, and elegant color, with strong local flavor. Its stitching is smooth, neat, thin, dense, harmonious, brilliant, round and even. The embroidery surface is smooth, the edges of designs are neat, the stitches are exquisite and the thread is thin, the coloring is harmonious, the color is bright and brilliant, the texture is round and smooth, and the lines are dense, exquisite and even. In terms of types, Suzhou embroidery works can be divided into odd cuts, costume and hanging curtain, with qualities of decoration and practicability. Of these, double-sided embroidery has the same pattern on both sides and uses the same or different embroidering methods that do not show the joins in the stitches. The double-faced embroidery The Cat is one of the representative works. Artisans divide an embroidery thread as thin as a hair to two, four, twelve and forty-eight strands of thin thread, and tens of thousands of thread knots and ends are hidden without a trace. The naughty and lively bearing of the cat can be shown on both faces. It is most difficult to embroider the cat's eyes. Artisans need more than 20 kinds of threads to embroider the fiery and vivid eyes.

Furniture

Furniture is both a daily necessity and a handicraft. Chinese furniture has a long history. Lacquered wooden beds appeared early in the Warring States Period. They were very low with handrails on all sides. Furniture was popularized in the Song Dynasty with numerous varieties.

As a handicraft, the most refined and beautiful of ancient Chinese furniture was made in the Ming Dynasty.

• Ming Dynasty Style Furniture

The craftsmen took over from Song Dynasty furniture traditions and formed the Ming Dynasty style of furniture with its own characteristics.

An important feature is that the items are beautifully shaped. The furniture is light with a sense of stability, simple with exposure of sentiment, and round and fluent in lines and shape. The size and proportion of the different parts adhere to aesthetic principles and also take practical use into consideration.

Most Ming Dynasty furniture was made of rare fine timbers, such as rosewood, pear wood, red sandalwood, catalpa wood, and black wood. Sometimes, nanmu, walnut and elm were used. Woods from southern China are hard with fine grain, and their colors are usually very deep. All these qualities played an important role in creating the proper shapes, structures and appearance. Owing to this use of rare materials, combine a sense of reality and natural beauty, and it has an artistic effect of looking hard, smooth, plain and clean.

The third important characteristic of the Ming Dynasty furniture is that it was made with consummate skill. It combined round and square, wide and narrow, thick and thin patterns and lines for contrast to form a unique structure. All parts of the furniture were pieced together with no visible joints. The outline is natural and fluid. The surface was polished with wax to make it look bright, smooth and clean and to reveal the natural beauty of the rare fine timbers.

Pieces of this style of furniture have been handed down as beautiful handicrafts because of their beautiful shapes and exquisite technical craftsmanship. Later furniture connoisseurs and collectors have summarized 16 characteristics and eight taboos of Ming Dynasty furniture making. The 16 characteristics include simple, natural, bold, dignified, elegant, transpose and clean, and the taboos include complicated, fat, disordered and stagnant.

Qing Dynasty Style Furniture

Compared to Ming Dynasty style furniture, Qing Dynasty style furniture showed a vogue of seeking magnificence and trivial carving. This is because, at that time, "Guangdong style furniture" was prevalent and the imperial courts of the Qing Dynasty followed and promoted the fashion.

Instead of the simple and unsophisticated style of Ming Dynasty style furniture, that of the Qing Dynasty style pursued luxuriance and magnificent decoration. The furniture of the style is characterized by thick, heavy and huge shapes.

Porcelain

In China, the origins of pottery craft can be traced back to the period of 4,500 to 2,500 BC. In view of the developing history of Chinese pottery and porcelain, pottery and porcelain refers to two categories.

Chinese porcelain derived from pottery. The primitive porcelain originated more than 3,000 years ago. By the Song Dynasty, famous porcelain and kilns spread over most places in China and the porcelain industry reached its heyday. At that time Jun kiln, Ge kiln, Guan kiln, Ru kiln and Ding kiln were honored as the "Five Great Kilns". The blue and white porcelain produced in Jingdezhen (capital of porcelain), Jiangxi Province in the Yuan Dynasty became the representative of porcelain. After its emergence, blue and white porcelain became fashionable and was listed as the No.1 traditional famous porcelain in Jingdezhen.

The colorful porcelain is one of the great inventions of ancient China, and the English word of "China" also has the meaning of porcelain, which fully reflects that the exquisite and unsurpassed Chinese porcelain can definitely be viewed as the representation of China.

Jingdezhen Porcelain

Famous for producing blue and white porcelain, Jingdezhen is located in the Changjiang river valley in northeastern Jiangxi Province. It is a mountain city with green hills, clear water and quiet and beautiful scenery. Jingdezhen abounds in porcelain clay and kaolin mineral resources and started to produce the porcelain used by the imperial court in the Song Dynasty.

Blue and white porcelain leads among the four great traditional types of porcelain in Jingdezhen, which also include blue and white exquisite porcelain, delicate colored porcelain and color glaze porcelain. Besides the four great types, there are sculpture porcelain, thin-body porcelain and five-color porcelain, etc.

Flat black and white porcelain flask with sea water and dragon patterns produced in the reign (1426-1436) of Emperor Xuande of the Ming Dynasty, a treasure of such porcelains during the period, is collected in the Palace Museum in Beijing.

Blue and white porcelain has a white base with blue design. The best blue and white porcelains were made in Jingdezhen during the Yuan Dynasty. Its emergence is of epochal significance in porcelain history. The glaze of blue and white porcelain is transparent and the base is thin and light. Blue designs are applied to the white body of the porcelain, making it appear elegant, fresh and full of vigor. Blue and white porcelain wares include plates, vases, censers, kettles, pots, bowls and cups, which have complicated designs on their heavy bodies. By the Yuan Dynasty, porcelain had been exported to Japan, Korea, the Philippines, Thailand, India, Turkey, Iran and some parts of Europe and the Americas; they have become treasures in many state museums.

Blue and white exquisite porcelain is exquisite, bright, limpid, gentle and elegant. The green and transparent exquisite porcelain and elegant and verdant blue and white porcelain set off each other, and are honored as "gems of the world".

Delicate colored porcelain has the strongest decorative quality. It shows a quality of being delicate and gentle as arsenic is added in the coloring materials as emulsion and it is bright as an enamel mirror. The decoration applied to the surface of the porcelain draws on the technique of Chinese traditional painting, with gentle colors, beautiful lines, vivid images and three-dimensional effect.

Thin-body porcelain is a special craft existing over a long period. The body is thin as a cicada's wings and light as floating clouds. Under shining milk-white lights, it is transparent with a shadow effect, and the fish on the surface seem to be swimming in water, partly hidden and partly visible, extraordinarily beautiful.

Yixing Baccaro Teapot

Lying in the east of Jiangsu Province, Yixing is well known for its Zisha (Baccaro) Teapot. This is made from the unique clay in the region, which is fine and contains high iron content, producing fine porcelain without glaze mostly red brown, light yellow and blackish purple.

Zisha porcelain was first produced in the Song Dynasty and became popular by the middle of the Ming Dynasty, when people began brewing tea instead of just adding boiling water, thus raising the requirement for the teapot. In practice, people found that the Zisha teapot could produce a mellow flavor. The body of the teapot can absorb some fragrance of the tea and retain it for a long time. The longer the teapot is used, the better the flavor. The Zisha teapot has no glaze or bright color; the plainness fits the aesthetic views and tastes of the literati, so it became prevalent around the country and experts in its production also emerged as time passed.

From the Zhengde reign to the Wanli reign (1506-1619) in the Ming Dynasty, the masters of the Zisha Teapot making made a great contribution to the improvement and development of the production techniques. Their works were rare at that time and there are few extant. At that time, the Zisha craft absorbed the characteristics of the bronze craft in shapes and were also of the same style with the furniture. Focusing on practical use, the Zisha teapots in the Ming Dynasty mainly adopted geometrical designs, simple but harmonious. The simple appearance, thick lines, harmonious proportions and rough grain of the clay highlight the plainness as well as the elegance. The patterns uphold primitive simplicity and elegance. Blemishes can always be found on the surface of the vessels because of the underdeveloped techniques at that time. The colors of the vessels are always liver-red, reddish brown and purple gray because of the materials used and the firing time.

Primitive Sculpture

Ancient Chinese people living along the Yellow and Yangtze rivers began to make pottery and clay figures towards the end of the Primitive Society Period. People living along the upper and middle reaches of the Yellow River left numerous excellent pottery sculptures. In 1975, a beautifully-shaped pottery eagle tripod was unearthed in a tomb of Miaodigou type of the Yangshao culture in Shaanxi Province. Its exquisite shape earned much praise. An Owl Kettle had its top made in the shape of an owl's head, which might have had a totemic meaning. The lid or mouth of some of these utensils assumes the shape of a human head or animal or bird figures with a naive and attractive appearance.

The pottery figures of the Yellow River region were used as utensils of both decorative and practical value, while, in the Yangtze River region, the pottery animal sculptures were very small and made purely for amusement. Some small hand-molded pottery animal figures of the Qujialing culture in Hubei Province and the Hemudu culture in Zhejiang Province have been unearthed. They were made in the shape of birds, pigs, fish and other creatures. Similar small animal pottery sculptures have also been found among relics along the Yellow River.

Carving

Carving art in China has a long history, and the human figures, animals and plants produced are perfect in form and vivid in expression, with exquisite craftsmanship. Modern carving in China can be divided into bamboo, wood, tooth (ivory), stone (brick), and horn (rhinoceros horns), with different techniques and artistic styles.

Bamboo Carving

Bamboo carving refers to carving various decorative designs and Chinese characters on bamboo utensils or carving bamboo roots into various articles for display. Bamboo carving became an art form from the Six Dynasties and flourished in the Ming and Qing dynasties. From the mid-Ming Dynasty, Jiading and Jinling areas in south of the lower reaches of the Yangtze River, which teemed with bamboo, became carving centers. In the Qing Dynasty, two carving methods appeared, namely "peel then carve" and "carve then peel".

Wood Carving

With various woods and roots as materials, wood carving is an important category in the traditional carving crafts. Wood carving has the longest history. At the site of Hemudu Culture, with a history of about 7,000 years, wood-carved fish were unearthed as the earliest material object in the history of Chinese wood-carving. In the Song Dynasty, deep red wood-carving works were popular and most of the materials were woods with a close texture, such as boxwood and sandalwood. In the Yuan and Ming dynasties, due to fast development of overseas commerce, there appeared more varieties of wood and many were hard woods imported from foreign forests, which encouraged the long development of wood-carving craft.

Tooth and Horn Carving

Generally speaking, this refers to objects carved out of animal teeth and horns, although within collectors' circles, it refers specifically to works carved out of ivory and rhinoceros horn. Ivory is naturally beautiful, white and soft, and rhinoceros horn carving is famous for its rarity and great value. The tooth and horn carving in China date back to pre-historical times. Dozens of ivory carvings were excavated from the site of Hemudu Culture. During the Shang and Zhou dynasties, tooth carving gradually prospered. By the Tang and Song Dynasties, tooth and horn carving was much more sophisticated. In the Ming Dynasty, the carving became very popular, while the carving style tended to be simple and smooth.

• Terracotta Warriors

In 1974, Vault 1 of the Terracotta Army of Emperor Qinshihuang was unearthed in Xiyang Village, Lintong County of Shaanxi Province. The terracotta warriors were arranged in an orderly combat formation and about 6,000 were unearthed.

The terracotta figures were found in a big vault, with a black brick floor, supported by column frames and covered by timber, reed mats and earth. There comprise soldier figures, wooden war chariots, and clay horses. The in situ Vault 1 museum has over 500 clay soldiers, all powerful and life-like. The museum displays less than one-twentieth of the warriors contained in the entire area.

The figures in the tomb were not cast from a single mould; they were sculptured individually and are, therefore, great artistic treasures. Each looks imposing and is well-proportioned. Although their clothes and hairstyles are similar, their facial expressions are all different. Some are smiling with a look of age and experience; some appear pure, lively and innocent; others look high spirited while still others seem to be gazing fixedly at something. The different expressions and gestures of soldiers are vividly captured in these figures. From the facial shape of some of them, we can even guess the region of their birth. The crafting technique of the terracotta warriors is superb. The armor and helmets create a sense of good hard quality, the suits look smooth and soft and their pleats are sharply defined. Even the nails, puncheons and holes are complete on the suits and the hair and beards of the soldiers are carefully detailed. The fat and strong war horses are in high spirits with lifted ears and divided mane.

The making of the warrior figures combined hand sculpting and molding techniques. The sculptors used coarse clay as the inner base, covered the base with fine clay, fired the resulting figure in a kiln and then applied color. Because of the different aesthetic approaches of the different artists and the varied production techniques, the figures took on great variety of expression and gesture.

Stone Carving

The material of stone carving is hard with close texture; the usage is wide and it is durable, so people like to use it. The art can show its best side in stone memorial archways, stone leak windows, stone railings, stone pole bases and various stone-made furniture and sculptures for display. The carving methods include line cutting, shallow relief, deep relief, semi-circular cutting, hollowing out, penetrating, etc. The selection of carving methods depends on different stone materials and the knife is used like a pen. The composition depends on the proficiency and practical experience of the manipulator.

Stone Lion

The lion is known as the king of animals. The earliest stone lion was discovered in front of an Eastern Han Dynasty tomb, Gaoze Tomb, in Ya'an, Sichuan Province. The stone lions in front of Liang Chao Tomb in Jurong County of Jiangsu Province are 1,400 years old. Those in the Tangshun Tomb in Shenyang City of Shaanxi Province were built by the Tang Empress, Wu Zetian, for her mother in the family name of Yang. They are the most representative of all existing stone lions. From the Ming Dynasty, stone lions were placed in front of palaces, government buildings, temples and even some rich family mansions to display power. Later, stone lion designs were carved as an indispensable decoration on architectural features such as door lintels, eaves and railings. Beijing now has many stone lions made during the Ming and Qing dynasties. These lions do not seem powerful and wild, but rather are kind and gentle, not tiring of appreciation.

On the well-known Lugou Bridge built in the Jin Dynasty, there are 140 engraved stone columns on each side. Each column has a lively stone lion on its top, and nine small stone lions are hidden under it. The smallest one is only some centimeters long making it hard to establish an accurate count of all the stone lions on the bridge. In 1961, however, archeologists numbered each one and calculated there were altogether 485 stone lions.

Among Chinese folk, the lion has become a symbol of bravery, power and good luck. Figures of the lion were not used exclusively by the royal families in imperial arts as were the dragon and the phoenix. They are popular among the people and a pair of small stone lions is commonly seen in front of the gates of ordinary family homes.

Stone Lion

Stone Horse Stepping on a Hun Soldier

During Emperor Wudi's reign (156-87 BC), to subdue the ethnic Hun invaders in the north, the emperor sent troops to fight them. The commander of the imperial forces, Huo Qubing, was a young man who had the title of Piaoqi General (an ancient title of high military office), who defeated the Hun army six times in the Qilian Mountain area and made brilliant military achievements. Unfortunately, Huo died at the age of 24. A big tomb in the shape of the Qilian Mountain was built to commemorate him. Stone carvings of humans and animals decorated the front of the tomb.

These stone sculptures are now exhibited in the annexes built beside the tomb. They are the earliest and best-preserved stone carvings found in China, and also have great artistic value in the history of world sculpture.

One of the most excellent among the many stone carvings of domesticated and wild animals in the tomb is the Horse Stepping on a Hun Soldier. The horse depicted in the sculpture is Huo Qubing's own mount. Huo had ridden this horse into battle and it became a symbol of him. The stone horse is 1.68 meters high and 1.90 meters in length. It has an imposing appearance, and has one foot on a Hun soldier. The soldier on the ground holds a bow in his hand and has an agonized expression on his

Stone carving *Horse Stepping on a Xiongnu Soldier*

13 Culture

face as he draws his last breath. The sculpture of a man and a horse sums up Huo Qubing's immense military contribution to it. The horse appears brave, strong, placid and firm. The Hun soldier under its feet, although facing the sky in the panicked last moment of his life, retains a fierce expression. He still holds his weapon, as if putting up a desperate last ditch struggle. The spare but accurate carvings of the sculpture, especially the deep lines on the horse's leg, hip, head and neck, convey a sense of movement and make the animal appear very powerful. This stone carving combined traditional round cutting, relief and line cutting skills, retaining the natural beauty of the stone yet revealing the artistic excellence of the carving.

Yungang Grottoes

In 460, the Wuzhou mountain valley in Datong, Shanxi Province reverberated with the sound of iron hammers beating rocks. A monk was directing hundreds of thousands of workers to undertake a grand project, carving stones and rocks to make sculptures. The monk, Yu Yao, was ordered by the Emperor Wencheng of the Northern Wei Dynasty to supervise the historic project. At that time Buddhism had extremely vigorous power and most of the Northern Wei rulers were adherents. The digging of the grotto and making of sculptures went on for some 30 years. The grotto extends for about one km from east to west. Today there are 53 individual grottoes with 51,000 statues.

The statues include Buddha, Bodhisattvas, guardian deities and young children. They show variety of expression and the movement and drapery was carved with refined and consummate skill. The decorative patterns with high achievements in the Yungang Grottoes are also very attractive, adding to the religious atmosphere and setting off the subject. The brilliant and dense decoration on each grotto gate demonstrates the majesty and prosperity of the ruling class of the time. The Yungang Grotto complex introduced foreign Buddhist art imagery and, at the same time, drew on the legacy of the powerful Han Dynasty artistic traditions. The grottoes emphasize the statues in their entirety and reveal their inner spirit and great strength. Being the early focus of Buddhism during the Northern Wei Dynasty, the Yungang Grotto complex had great influence on grotto art development in other Chinese areas.

Mogao Grottoes

The Mogao Grottoes in the Hexi Corridor in Gansu Province are composed of conglomerate rock that cannot be carved, so colored sculptures made of clay dominate; some stand singly, others are in groups. The Buddha statues are usually set in the center, surrounded by followers, Bodhisattvas, gods and Hercules on two sides. These followers number three at least and 11 at most. The biggest Buddha statue is 33 meters high, and the smallest only 10 cm. The statues are surrounded by beautiful murals depicting Buddhist stories.

Longmen Grottoes

The Longmen Grottoes are situated on both banks of the Yi River in Luoyang, Henan Province. They were carved from the Northern Wei to the Song dynasties. There are over 2,100 grottoess with some 100,000 statues. Two caves, Guyang and Binyang, contain the most representative statues. The Sakyamuni statue in the Guyang Cave sits cross-legged with a smile on his round face. The Buddha's on both sides appear solemn. On the walls of the cave are three rows of big niches and hundreds of small niches. The patterns on the lintels and top of these niches are elegant and enigmatic. The main Buddha in the Binyang Cave has a long face and nose; he is smiling. Three fingers of his left hand curve downward, and his right hand is stretched forward, which indicates he is explaining Buddhist scriptures. In front of the Buddha are two mighty stone lions; on two sides are two followers, Anada and Kasaya, and two Bodhisattva, Bodhisattva of Wisdom and Samantabhadra. The roof of the cave is carved with lotus flowers surrounded by white clouds, and the Flying Asparas dance in the clouds. On the front wall and the two side walls in south and north are four tiers of exquisite relief carvings.

Maijishan Grottoes

These are situated in Maiji Mountain, southeast of Tianshui County in Gansu Province. The mountain, which is shaped like a haystack, gets its name from the Chinese word for haystack. Construction of the Maijishan Grottoes went on from the Northern Wei until the Qing dynasties. But because of earthquakes and erosion by wind and water, about one-third of the grottoes have crumbled into ruins. Only 194 grottoes with about 7,800 clay and stone statues and some 1,300 square meters of murals are preserved. Clay statues in the Maijishan Grottoes include round carvings, deep reliefs, paste carvings and wall carvings. The thousands of round carvings are very vivid and full of interest. They range from the 16-meter big Buddha to a small 10cm sculpture, and from holy Buddha to calves under the "golden and silver feet" of the gods. The Buddha statues in the Maijishan Grottoes are humanized with strong living flavor.

Giant Stone Buddha at Leshan

A 70-meter-high giant stone Buddha lies in the beautiful Leshan Mountain at the confluence of the Dadu, Qingyi and Minjiang rivers. Ten people together can sit in the Buddha's hair bun and the space in his ear can hold two people standing. The two feet of the Buddha are nearly 33 meters away from each other. Two people lying head to head and linking hands are shorter than his toe, and the crown of an ordinary person's head does not reach the top of his foot. The stone Buddha in its entirety can only be viewed from the other side of the river.

The giant stone Buddha is properly shaped with accurate proportions, a full-bodied and strong figure, a solemn expression and a strong vigor with concise expressive methods. It is amazing that ancient Chinese artists and workers could make such a big statue with the simple tools they had at that time. They were great talents with considerable creative spirit.

The project was finally completed in 803. The gilded and colored giant Buddha is beautiful and glorious. The colors on its body provide a good contrast and harmonize with the surrounding environment, making it look more approachable yet at the same time powerful, dignified and worthy of respect. To protect the giant Buddha, a seven-story pavilion was built into the mountain as a covering.

The Giant Stone Buddha in Leshan is the largest stone Buddha in the world, built over a total of more than 90 years. Here the mountain is a statue of Buddha and the Buddha is a mountain.

Clay Sculptures

Clay sculptures and pottery both belong to the earliest sculpting forms of humans. Both make use of almost the same materials and sculpting methods, the major difference lying in that the former should be dried in the shade while the latter should be put into a kiln for baking.

Clay sculpture is an old and common folk art in China. The clay is kneaded mainly into images of figures and animals, either painted or left plain.

Chinese clay sculpture can be traced back to the Neolithic Age some 4,000 to 10,000 years ago. The pottery pigs and sheep unearthed from the Hemudu Cultural Sites in Zhejiang were about 6,000 to 7,000 years old. Until the Qing Dynasty, there were two schools of clay sculpture in south and north: in the north there was Tianjin Clay Figurine Zhang, and in the south there was Wuxi Huishan Clay Figurine. Clay Figurine Zhang refers to Zhang Changlin in Tianjin whose works are very realistic. The shapes, expressions, colors and decorations of all figures are lively. Huishan clay figurine can be divided into two kinds: one is "clay shua huo" for enjoying children and "Da'afu" is the typical work. The image is well-rounded, lively, vigorous and concise with bright and vehement colors and strong local flavors. The other is "hand-kneaded drama figures". Such clay figurines pay attention to expression. The images are somewhat exaggerated, the expressions exquisite, colors pure, simple and profound. In addition, Shaanxi Fengxiang and Suzhou Huqiu are also important and famous production areas of folk clay sculptures.

The clay must be prepared carefully. Usually artisans select glutinous and smooth clay. It is beaten, knocked, kneaded, and inserted with cotton wool, paper or honey. Artisans find a piece of prepared clay and make use of carving, sculpturing and kneading to shape a good image. After being modified, polished and dried, the finished work emerges. The last procedure is coloring. There is a saying that "30 percent sculpture and 70 percent painting". The themes for clay sculptures and pottery ware include birds, animals, fish, insects, fairy tales, figures in dramas, fruits, etc.

Colored Sculptures in the Jin Temple

At the foot of the Xuanweng Mountain to the southwest of Taiyuan, Shanxi Province, lies the famous Jin Temple with its great cypress tree dating to the Zhou Dynasty, the "Never Old Spring" that has run for thousands of years, the fish-pond flying girder rarely seen in the world, the Goddess Hall built in the Northern Song Dynasty and the Xian Temple constructed in the Jin Dynasty. But it is the colored sculptures in the Goddess Temple that arouse most attention.

There are now 43 colored sculptures in the Goddess Hall. Except the small ones on each side of the Goddess, which were added later, the sculptures were all created in the Song Dynasty. The statue of the Goddess sits in the middle of the hall inside a canopy. Wearing a phoenix crown, she sits cross-legged on a square wooden seat with a peaceful and kind expression. One hand is held in front of her chest, the other one lies on her leg. Her fingers are hidden inside the sleeves of her long gown which drape down to the seat. The entire statue looks poised and dignified. Other figures in the temple include four eunuchs and a few female servants in men's clothes. The rest are all women servants wearing clothes of the late Tang Dynasty and the following Five Dynasties; some are in long robes, some in short shirts and long skirts.

Colored sculptures of the maidservants in the Goddess Hall, the Jin Temple

The female servant sculptures have distinctive characters and represent women of different temperament and personality. Some are smiling and greeting each other, some are whispering with each other; all, however, have fine features and calm expressions. These sculptures were carved so vividly that one can almost feel their breath and hear their whispered words beside them. We see that Song Dynasty sculptors paid great attention to revealing the inner world of their figures.

Fengxiang Painted Clay Figurines

The craft of making painted clay-figurines of Fengxiang, Shaanxi Province can date back to the Western Zhou Dynasty prior to the Qin Dynasty, and has a prevalent history of more than 3,000 years. They are the oldest clay-figurines with the most representative national characteristics in China.

According to archaeologists, the painted decorative designs of Fengxiang's figurines were different from those on bronze ware of the Western Zhou Dynasty. The images typically included flowers, birds, fish, insects, as well as auspicious birds and beasts, and are relics of ancient totemic and phallic worship, and offerings to the gods, reflecting cultural characteristics of ancient China.

Fengxiang painted clay figurines have strong local living flavor. The contents involve human figures, animals and plants, most of which are hollow round sculptures and some are hanging articles in the mode of reliefs. The production technique was simple. Clay was mixed with pulp to make molded mud. After making the molds, craftsmen turned them into bases and dried them. Then they applied white bottom powder before coloring, painting and glazing. The colors of Fengxiang figurines are extremely bright, and with intensive contrasts. With a black outline, they are primarily scarlet, green and yellow, which give people a bright and striking feeling. The figurines have a wide-range of subjects, including facial makeup for dramas, designs with good omens, folklore, historical stories, rural life and others.

Fengxiang's clay-figurines have become one of the Shaanxi's important travel souvenirs. The former US president Bill Clinton and his wife viewed this set of "unique crafts" when they visited China in June 1998. After receiving the painted clay-figurines, leaders of UNICEF praised them as the best gifts for children. Visitors to Shaanxi Province will always bring some pieces back as souvenirs.

Huishan Clay Figurines

Huishan clay figurine Da A Fu (male)

As a contrast and coordinator of Clay Figurine Zhang, Huishan clay figurines in Wuxi, Jiangsu Province emerged very early and there is no way to establish the exact time.

In the slack seasons, nearly all families in Huishan make clay figurines, and there is a saying since ancient time that "each family is good at sculpting and is able to paint". With Spring Festival approaching, many people sell clay figurines in trays at temple and market fairs. It is also an income for villagers. Huishan clay figurines include fine and coarse ones. Coarse figurines are made from molds and produced in large numbers. However, fine figurines are made by hand with exquisite production in the shapes of figures in operas, spring oxen, tigers, Da A Fu, the God of Longevity and so on. Generally speaking, Huishan clay figurines are short in stature, full with big heads, and their facial expressions are vividly depicted. Craftsmen pay particular attention to colored painting and there is a saying that "bases hold 30 percent and painting holds 70 percent."

Bright red, yellow, green and blue colors are often applied to them to make them more distinct and beautiful. The works of Clay Figurine Zhang are delicate and elegant, while those of Huishan clay figurines are bright and colorful.

One piece particularly familiar and favored by common people of Huishan clay figurines is Huishan Da A Fu, a plump child who is created to express people's yearning for a good life.

Gaomi Clay Figurines

Gaomi (a place in Shandong) clay figurines have a history of 400 years. In the Long Qing and Wan Li periods of the Ming Dynasty, farmers in Gaomi designed a kind of skyrocket, named "Guozihua" (or Nidunzi) in clay to sell. People put powder into the clay idols and after being fired, the idols were collected by people as decorations. Finally there appeared more varieties of clay figurines in the shapes of various animals, such as the tiger, lion, monkey, dog, cat, chicken, duck and other animals and some figures in legends such as "White Snake", "Sun Wukong" and "Niulang and Zhinu". They are painted with various colors to make them vivid.

Gradually, the figurines were no longer the appendages of fireworks, but developed into a kind of independent handicraft. In Qian Long's reign of the Qing Dynasty, they are added with musical effects and actions in some parts. There are always people selling clay toys on temple fairs. At present, Gaomi clay sculptures have become a folk art and is protected and often exhibited in foreign countries.

• Clay Figurine Master Zhang

Clay Figurine Master Zhang in Tianjin is one of the most famous representatives of Chinese folk colored sculptures. It was a kind of school of colored sculptures in northern China and was initiated by Zhang Mingshan in the late Qing Dynasty. Zhang was born into a poor family in Tianjin. He learned from his father how to make clay figurines at a very young age to help feed the family. Zhang was clever, deft and full of imagination. He carefully observed people of different industries in market fairs and various characters in theaters, and molded figurines stealthily in his sleeves. His clay figurines were very vivid and expressive and were soon well known in the surrounding area. Zhang not only inherited the legacy of traditional skills but also incorporated skills from other art forms such as painting, opera and Chinese folk wood engravings. After decades of hard work, he created more than 10,000 clay figurines during his life, and his unique handicrafts became famous both at home and abroad. His works are of great zest to the viewers.

Dough Sculpture

Written records on Chinese dough sculptures date back to the Han Dynasty. After several thousand years of inheritance and development, dough sculptures became a part of Chinese culture and folk arts, and also objects for study in history, archeology, folk arts, sculpture and aesthetics. In terms of style, dough sculptures in the Yellow River Valley are simple, crude, unconstrained and profound, while those in the Yangtze River Valley are delicate, exquisite and polished.

Dough sculptures are small figurines in various shapes molded from glutinous rice flour with colors. They are popular wedding and birthday gifts. They are also considered appropriate for prayer and memorial ceremonies and sacrificial offerings. Farmers place steamed dough sculptures before spirit tablets. Of these, the dough sculptures in shape of pig head are called "big offerings", in addition to flower steamed dough sculptures, flower and fruits steamed dough sculptures, gift steamed dough sculptures and steamed toys. The art of dough sculptures is characterized by "printing, molding, inlaying and rolling" (the procedures for making sculptures). Materials and tools used in making dough sculptures are very simple, mainly including white flour, scissors, a kitchen knife, comb, Chinese dates and Bunge prickly ash. With well-leavened dough, kneaded according to the set pattern, one can produce a vivid dough sculpture.

In Shaanxi and Hebei provinces, people also call dough sculptures "dough flowers" and "new year steamed bread", and this old custom runs through festivals. From the New Year's Eve to the fifteenth day of the first lunar month, there is a tradition of giving gift dough sculptures among villagers. In the east of Guanzhong, Shaanxi Province almost all women are masters of making gift dough sculptures and those senior women have superb skills.

Shanxi Dough Sculptures

Shanxi dough sculpture is a kind of folk artwork. The form, usage and color have a close relationship with local customs and activities, and are in a continuous process of change. In Xinjiang County and Xiangfen County in the south of Shanxi Province, people pay attention to the coloration of dough sculptures which are brilliant and unique. In the Huozhou area, people pay attention to the simplicity and elegance of dough sculptures instead of decoration and coloration. In Xinzhou and Dingxiang, dough sculptures give priority to sculpting and coloration is supplementary. The colors alternate with the native color of dough.

Best-quality flour is the material for Shanxi dough sculptures and the production has the procedures of kneading, molding, steaming and coloring. Generally speaking, the shapes are exaggerative and vivid, the colors are bright and decent, and the styles are rough, simple and concise, with distinctive folk and local characteristics.

Shandong Jinan Dough Sculptures

Jinan dough sculptures are one of the handicrafts with the most distinctive regional characteristics. Li Junxing, a famous old craftsman of Jinan dough sculptures, once went around China with a burden on his shoulder and even went to dozens of countries in Southeast Asia, Europe and Middle East. In his old age, Li Junxing was invited to the Jinan Institute of Handicrafts to teach his skills. He trained two generations of dough sculptures craftsmen and women and formed the special styles of Jinan dough sculptures.

Jinan dough sculptures have bright color with exquisite techniques. With the help of a knife, comb, and needle, artisans use their fingertips to twiddle, knead, and entwine the dough into vivid figures with lively costume and expressions. They are especially good at sculptures of Chinese opera figures in ancient costume.

Shandong Langzhuang Dough Sculptures

Langzhuang is located in Guan County, in the northwest of Shandong Province. In this small village, there are 30 or 40 families and every family member can make dough sculptures. The big Langzhuang dough sculptures are about 15 centimeters high and a small one is only six centimeters. The subjects cover a wide range, such as the 12 animals of the zodiac, historical legends, fairy tales, operas, animals, birds, flowers, fish, insects, vegetables, fruits, etc. Langzhuang dough sculptures usually use leavened dough made of polished wheat and are very simple. Sculpted shapes are produced by molding, kneading and

Lang Xiucai, aged 72, a folk artist from Langzhuang Village, Guan County, Shandong Province, is bringing color to the dough figurine produced by himself.

sticking, use a knife and comb to make details and decoration, color and glue are applied after steaming and drying. The accomplished dough sculptures have a shiny surface and are not easy to desiccate. Langzhuang dough sculptures are mostly oblate suitable for placing flat, hanging and drying. The colors are bright and pure. Besides the dominant pinkish red, yellow and green, there are a little white powder and cobalt-blue for decoration. At last, black ink is used to draw the outline meticulously. The sculptures give a feeling of being lively and colorful. In the patterns, the golden fish and babies are lovely and interesting with exaggerated and concise shapes. The dominant colored pieces feature meticulous painting of facial features of babies and scales of fish.

Butter Sculptures

Butter Sculptures in the Labrang Monastery

As a unique art in Tibetan culture, these sculptures have their origin in the area's indigenous Bon religion and are considered one of the three exotic treasures of Tibetan art.

Butter sculptures are a kind of butter-molded craftwork where the major raw material is butter. The solid material, which is soft and pure with a faint scent, can be molded into vivid, bright, and exquisite craftworks. The craftworks are made in the temperature below freezing, mostly during the three months of the winter.

It was hundreds of years ago that the butter sculpture art was introduced to Ta'er Monastery in Qinghai, birthplace of the Gelug Sect of Tibetan Buddhism. In the beginning, butter sculptures were simple and the techniques were rough. Later, two institutions were set up in the Ta'er Monastery to train monks specializing in this art. With a passion for Buddha and the arts, the monks worked hard and learned from each other to overcome their own weaknesses, thus enriching the art in terms of pattern and content. Their exquisite skills even surpassed those of some monasteries in Tibet where the art originated and were honored as an exotic treasure by the public. A butter sculptures museum was established in Ta'er Monastery.

Styles of butter sculptures vary greatly and cover a wide range of contents. Mostly, they center on Buddhism, historic stories, personal biographies, flowers, grass, trees, birds, beasts, and human figures.

Making of Chinese Kites

The workmanship of Chinese kites can be summarized in four points: structuring, paperhanging, color drawing and flying, called the "four skills" for short. Structuring includes selecting and chopping bamboo, which is then bent and joined to form the frame. Paperhanging includes selecting material, cutting out, paperhanging, and cutting away or adding material as needed. Color drawing includes composing picture, outlining, dyeing (or coloring), and decorating. Flying includes selecting a site and the right weather, choosing the kite, launching it into the air, adjusting the line, and controlling the kite.

To make a kite, bamboo strips should be structured to the frame and then the paper or silk should cover it. The structure must be symmetrical so that a kite has the same area to withstand the wind pressure on two sides. The paper or silk for paperhanging must be regular and clean. The painting on the kite must have an effect of clarity when looked at far into the distance and reality when looking close. When flying kites, the angle of lifting the line must be adjusted according to the wind force.

• Brief History of Chinese Kites

Kites were invented by the Chinese people over 2,000 years ago. Every year, when the spring comes, Chinese people will fly kites, with the implication of reaching yang qi. Henan and Shandong provinces where people worship the sun and birds are the birthplaces of Chinese kites. In Kaifeng, Henan Province there are still preserved the prototypes of kites.

Chinese kites can be divided mainly into two categories, "hard-winged" and "soft-winged". The wings of "hard-winged" kites have good wind-catching effect and can fly very high. The "soft-winged" kites can fly far away, but not high. In terms of shapes, besides traditional birds, animals, insects and fish, there have appeared some new types in the shape of human figures. In the past the kites were all white, but later people started to paint on them.

China has a large territory. As a traditional culture and folk art, the kite has formed a unique style in different regions during its development, among which the most famous ones are the styles of Beijing, Tianjin, Weifang in Shangdong Province, Sichuan and Guangdong Province.

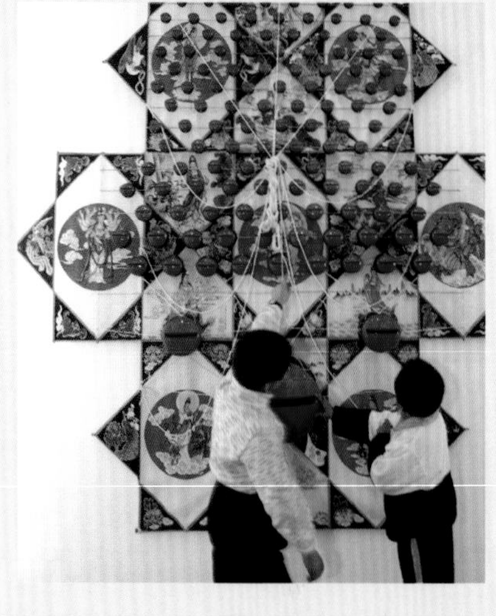

Folk Chinese New Year Painting

New Year's Paintings are a type of picture pasted on walls and doors during the Spring Festival, Chinese lunar New Year. According to the folk custom, as the Spring Festival approaches, every family will clean its rooms and courtyards and paste New Year's Paintings in the bedroom, and on the windows, doors, walls and stoves and in the Buddha niches to add to the New Year atmosphere.

Folk New Year's Painting was basically an art of Chinese farmers. The natural and simple images in the paintings frankly expressed their desires. Most of the New Year's Paintings are decorative, colorful and interesting as they have consecutive plots. Modern New Year's Paintings have gradually become a common and popular art form prevalent among the populace. They reflect real life as the major theme and are welcomed by common people.

There are many types of New Year's Paintings. The Gate Gods are pasted on doors and, according to their roles, there are the main gate god, secondary gate god, back gate god and wing room gate god. There are also New Year's Paintings of the God of the Stove, the Village God and the God of Wealth, and even the God of Vehicles and Horses. "Zhongtang" is pasted in the reception room, "Moon Light" is pasted beside windows, and "Doufang" is pasted on boxes, cabinets or dou. In a word, at Spring Festival time, colorful New Year engravings of various types are put in every corner of the room and courtyard, expressing the wishes of the hosts and imparting a strong festival atmosphere.

New Year Wood Block Paintings

Before the emergence of modern printing technology, New Year's Wood Block Paintings were the only way to produce pictures in large amounts. The making of New Year's Wood Block Paintings include the following procedures, drawing drafting, engraving the wood block, printing, coloration and processing by hand. Painters will finish the outline draft, color effect draft and several pieces of color separation drafts. Then, engravers will paste the drafts in reverse on a pear wood block and engrave strictly according to the drafts. In engraving, the lines must be vigorous, fluent and vivid, and the tracks must be as thin as a hair, so engravers must have superb skills. Then, they will engrave different color blocks according to different color drafts for printing. Printers will place the engraved wood block on a table, fasten the main engraved block and piles of paper, print out the ink draft of the main block, change the main block to different color blocks, and print them out one by one. The printing must be accurate. In terms of color, yellow is made of the flower of the Japanese pagoda tree, crimson is made of saffron wood, blue is made of indigo, and black is made of the smoke from the bottom of boilers. Later, the imported "pinkish red" and "light malachite green" were introduced, which were brighter. There is another type of wood block painting with semi-printing and semi-painting by hand. The wood block printing only serves as the base, and the face, head, hands and other parts of figures should be painted by hand with colors. There is a high requirement on the painting of the head, face, brows and eyes. The face paintings by old craftsmen are very handsome and vivid, and the painting integrates the traditional skills of Chinese colored painting and water-ink painting, with very vivid strokes.

The famous New Year's Wood Block Paintings printing workshops include Yangliuqing in Tianjin, Taohuawu in Suzhou, and those in Mianzhu in Sichuan Province, in Linfen and Xinjiang in Shanxi Province, in Zhuxian Town in Henan Province, in Tantou, Longhui in Hunan Province, in Wei County, Pingdu and Liaocheng in Shandong Province, in Wuqiang in Hebei Province, in Zhangzhou in Fujian Province, in Foshan in Guangdong Province and in Fengxiang in Shaanxi Province. They are listed in the famous ranks of folk Chinese New Year's Paintings by their unique styles.

Taohuawu New Year Woodblock Prints

(See P399)

Yangliuqing New Year Woodblock Prints

(See P398)

Mianzhu New Year Woodblock Prints

(See P401)

Zhuxianzhen New Year Woodblock Prints

(See P400)

Wuqiang New Year Woodblock Prints

(See P398)

Foshan New Year Woodblock Prints

(See P400)

Manual Weaving

Manual weaving is a traditional folk craft in China. Obviously, the craft is carried out by hand with the help of materials in strips to create the weaving activities. It is very common in daily life, such as the hair braids of girls, willow-woven hats, tying shoelace in butterfly knots - the basic and simplest methods of manual weaving. It has rich contents and it is easy to use materials, such as cord, wool, iron wire, electrical wire, scrip, decorative strips, etc. It is economical and substantial, and can not only improve physical agility but also enrich daily life.

Straw Weaving

Like old coarse cloth, straw weaving has a history of thousands of years in Shandong Province and is a traditional handicraft. The materials are the straw of wheat, corn peel, leaf of cattail and other natural things.

Modern people propose to "return to nature", which adds much more value to straw weaving. The products include tables, stools, utensils, straw sandals, and handicrafts, etc.

Bamboo and Rattan Weaving

Bamboo and rattan have good flexibility and plasticity. Bamboo slices and rattan strips can be bent by steaming, firing or grooving, and can then be formed into various designs. When full of water, rattan materials are very tender and after being dried, they are very hard, so they are vigorous when twining, flexible and easy to bend at random for processing and shaping. Hence bamboo basketry furniture has elegant and fluent lines and rich shapes.

Bamboo and rattan weaving is mainly used to make unique furniture. At present the production of bamboo and rattan furniture in China is basically a manual craft. Workers will bend the materials and nail the framework, craftsmen will weave, and then workers will conduct later processing such as singeing, polishing, dyeing and spray painting. Bamboo and rattan weaving has gradually formed a set of weaving shapes with exquisite lines and elegant compositions. Craftsmen can work out products with various shapes and rich modes according to a blueprint and samples. Manual work can give bamboo and rattan furniture rich individuality and various shapes, but production is limited.

bamboo and rattan furniture

• Chinese Knots

Traditional Chinese decorative knots, also known as Chinese knots, are typical local manual weaving arts of China. Chinese knots date back to ancient times when rope knots were not only the necessity of people's daily life but also played an important role of recording history. Long ago, people began to use rope patterns to decorate utensils, which injected aesthetic contents. Besides this, knots also became important parts of ancient dresses and adornments.

The weaving process of Chinese knots is very complex. Each basic knot is woven by a single cord from head to end, and the knots have different names according to their shapes. Finally, different basic knots are combined with decoration. Then, an exquisite and brilliant craftwork emerges with rich cultural implications and good wishes.

Museums

Museums

The historical cultural relics and rare treasures of ancient China were mostly collected in the secret buildings of imperial and noble families, impossible for the public to see. Modern Chinese museums started from the Westernization Movement in the early part of the 20th century. After imperial rule was ended by the Revolution of 1911, common people had the opportunity to step into the imperial halls to appreciate the cultural treasures created by their ancestors. In the past two or three decades, Chinese museums have also seen much development; old museums were rebuilt or expanded, new museums emerged, the collection of treasures was enriched, exhibitions and shows were renovated and the force of archeological research was strengthened.

At present, there are some 1,510 museums altogether in China. With the addition of the special museums of non-governmental organizations, there are more than 2,000 museums, collecting more than 20 million items and staged more than 8,000 exhibitions each year.

By 2015, another 1,000 museums will be built and almost every city above medium size will have one.

National Museum of China

The National Museum of China was inaugurated on February 28th, 2003. With the task of archaeological excavation, collection, research and exhibition, it systematically and comprehensively collects the treasured antiquities reflecting Chinese history through the ages up to modern times. Through permanent displays and special exhibitions, the museum presents and publicizes the spectacular history and magnificent culture of China, and introduces brilliant world civilizations to visitors from home and abroad. The National Museum of China has a collection of 610,000 items now, with a professional team and first-class equipment for antique conservation and repair.

As a State-level academic institute, the National Museum of China frequently organizes various international and national academic seminars, welcomes visiting scholars from home and abroad to conduct joint research or exchange research programs.

In recent years, the field archaeological team has worked on many large-scale excavations, including one of the city sites of the Shang Dynasty at Yuanqu, Shanxi Province, the comprehensive multi-subject archaeological excavation and study of Yingchiban Village Site in Henan Province, and the large-scale investigative excavation of the Taoist sites of the Han Dynasty at Kongwangshan, Lianyungang, Jiangsu Province. The museum has the only professional underwater archaeology institute in China with its own training base. In the four sea areas around China, i.e. Bohai, Yellow, East China and South China seas, it has conducted several investigations and excavations of historical shipwrecks. By dint of remote sensing and aerial photography, the Remote Sensing and Aero-photographic Archaeological Research Center has taken an archaeological survey of the Old City of the Han and Wei Dynasties in Luoyang, and the ancient tomb group at Qishan, as well as the ancient city ruins at Chifeng, Inner Mongolia.

Address: No. 16 East Chang'an Avenue, Dongcheng District, Beijing
Website: http://www.nationalmuseum.cn

Palace Museum

The Palace Museum was established on the foundations of the imperial palace that was the ritual center of two dynasties, the Ming and the Qing, and their collections of treasures. Designated by the State Council as one of China's foremost protected monuments in 1961, the Palace Museum was also made a UNESCO World Heritage Site in 1987.

It is a location endowed with cosmic significance by ancient China's astronomers. Correlating the emperor's abode, which they considered the pivot of the terrestrial world, with the Pole Star (Ziweiyuan), which they believed to be at the center of the heavens, they called the palace the Purple Forbidden City. The Forbidden City was built up in 1420 by the third Ming emperor Zhu Di who, upon usurping the throne, determined to move his capital north from Nanjing to Beijing. In 1911 the Qing dynasty fell to the Republican Revolution of 1911. The last emperor, Puyi, was expelled from the palace in 1924.

It covers an area of 720,000 square

♦ Exhibition of Cultural Treasures of the Palace

Besides conservation and restoration of the original displays in three great halls, three back palaces and six west palaces, the museum has opened galleries to display bronzes, porcelain, crafts, paintings and calligraphy, jewelry, and clocks to expand the scope of its exhibitions. A number of thematic shows have been held in galleries devoted to temporary exhibitions; in recent years these have included such acclaimed ones as "A Comparison of Authentic and Counterfeit Paintings and Calligraphy", "Genuine and Imitation Examples of Ancient Porcelain and Materials from Ancient Kilns", "The Art of Packaging at the Qing Court" and "Selections from the Finest Acquisitions of the Last Fifty Years". Traveling exhibitions have also graced various provincial museums and museums abroad. An increasing number of exhibitions have been mounted in countries such as Britain, the US, France, former Soviet Union, Germany, Austria, Spain, Australia, Japan and Singapore, among others. All of them have aroused great interest and admiration and made it possible for foreign people to learn the long history and brilliant national culture and art of China.

The number of visitors to the Palace Museum has risen along with the growth of tourism, in the last decade reaching six to eight million a year. It is obvious that people have a longstanding interest on the Palace Museum.

Besides receiving visitors directly, the Palace Museum organizes the edition and publication of various publications touching on both the architecture of its buildings and its vast cultural holdings. Those published large-scale works include *Famous Historical Paintings in the Palace Museum Collection, Selected Porcelain from the Palace Museum Collection, National Treasures, Palaces of the Forbidden City, Daily Life in the Forbidden City, A Collection of National Treasures,* and *The Complete Palace Museum Collection* (in 60 volumes, of which 18 have been published so far). There are also two periodicals, *The Palace Museum* and *The Forbidden City*.

meters. Each of the four sides is pierced by a gate, the Meridian Gate (Wu men) on the south and the Gate of Spiritual Valor (Shenwumen) on the north, both used as entrances and exits by tourists today. Once inside, visitors will see a succession of halls and palaces spreading out on either side of an invisible central axis. It is a magnificent sight, the buildings' glowing yellow roofs against vermilion walls, not to mention their painted ridges and carved beams, all contributing to the sumptuous effect.

Address: No.4 Jingshan Qianjie, Beijing
Website: http://www.dpm.org.cn

Cultural Treasures in the Palace

According to a 28-volume inventory, *Check Report by Committee Dealing with Issues on Imperial Family of Qing Dynasty*, published in 1925, the treasure trove left by the Qing numbered more than 1.17 million items including sacrificial vessels and ancient jade artifacts from the earliest dynasties; paintings and calligraphy from the Tang, Song, Yuan and Ming dynasties; porcelain from the Song and Yuan; a variety of enamelware and lacquer ware, gold and silver ornaments; relics in bamboo, wood, horn and gourds; religious statues in gold and bronze; as well as numerous imperial robes and ornaments, textiles, and furniture. In addition, there were countless books, literary works and ancient records. All these were divided into separate collections of antiquities, library materials and historical documents and placed under teams to sort and collate. Exhibition halls were opened to display some of the treasures, while writers and editors worked away at publishing information about the materials.

During World War II, to protect the treasures in the palace from destruction or plundering by the Japanese invaders, the museum authorities decided to evacuate the collection to the south. Over four frantic months between February and May 1933, the most important pieces in the collection were packed into 13,427 crates and 64 bundles and sent to Nanjing where a branch of the Palace Museum was established. In early 1949, the defeated Nationalists selected relics to fill 2,972 crates for shipping to Taiwan. A rival Palace Museum was set up in Shih Lin, Taipei to display these antiquities. Most of what remained were gradually returned to the Palace Museum in Beijing, involving more than 10,000 crates, although to this day 2,221 crates remain in safe-keeping in storage in Nanjing.

Protection on Cultural Treasures of the Palace

In the last few decades, a comprehensive rehabilitation program was launched, and, in time the broken, leaking and crumbling palace buildings were repaired and redecorated and looked resplendent once more. All the tall buildings were equipped with lightning conductors, while modern systems of fire protection and security and high-pressure fire mains were installed.

After more than a decade of painstaking efforts, some 710,000 relics from the Qing palace were retrieved. At the same time, through national allocations, requisitions and private donations, more than 220,000 additional pieces of cultural significance were added, making up for such omissions from the original Qing collection as colored earthenware from the Stone Age, bronzes and jades from the Shang and Zhou dynasties, pottery tomb figurines from the Han Dynasty, stone sculptures from the Northern and Southern Dynasties, and tri-color glazed pottery from the Tang Dynasty. The ancient paintings, scrolls and calligraphy added to the collection were particularly spectacular. These included, from the Jin Dynasty, Lu Ji's cursive calligraphy *A Consoling Letter* (Ping fu tie), Wang Xun's *Letter to Boyuan* (Bo Yuan tie) and Gu Kaizhi's *Goddess of the Luo River* (Luo shen fu tu); from the Sui Dynasty, Zhan Ziqian's *landscape hand scroll Spring Outing* (You chun tu) ; from the Tang Dynasty, Han Huang's *Five Oxen* (Wu niu tu), Du Mu's *Song of the Courtesan Zhan Haohao* (Zhang haohao shijuan) ; from the Five Dynasties, Gu Hongzhong's *The Night Revels of Han Xizai* (Han Xizai yeyan tu); from the Song Dynasty, Li Gonglin's *Painting after Wei Yan's Pasturing Horses* (Lin Wei Yan mu fang tu), Guo Xi's *Dry Tree and Rock, Level Distance Landscape* (Ke shi pingyuan tu), and Zhang Zeduan's *Qingming Festival by the Riverside* (Qingming shang he tu)—all masterpieces without exception. There have been further exertions in recent years to acquire such works as Zhang Xian's Landscape with Poems (Shi yong tu) from the Song Dynasty, Nai Xian's *Ancient Poem on South of the City* (Cheng nan yong gu shi) from the Yuan Dynasty, Shen Zhou's *landscape handscroll After Huang Gongwang's Dwelling in the Fuchun Mountains* (Fang Huang Gongwang fuchun shan ju tu) of the Ming Dynasty, and Shi Tao's *Calling Wen Yuke* (Gao hu Yu ke tu) from the Qing Dynasty.

Capital Museum

The Capital Museum, a large comprehensive museum in Beijing, was formally opened in October 1981.

In past decades, the Capital Museum has widely collected 250,000 cultural treasures, including bronze ware, ceramics, paintings and calligraphy, stone inscriptions, coins, jade ware, seals, embroidery, articles of bamboo, wood, tooth and horn, Buddhist statues, stationery, folk artware, etc; some of the only extant copies.

The Capital Museum stages regular exhibitions, exhibitions of fine artistic collections and temporary exhibitions. Regular exhibitions include "Ancient Capital Beijing: History and Culture", "Ancient Capital Beijing: Urban Construction" and "Old Stories of Beijing: Exhibition of Old Beijing Folk Customs". Exhibitions of fine artistic collection include Exhibition of Fine Artistic Collection of Ancient Chinaware, Exhibition of Fine Collection of Ancient Beijing Bronze Art, Exhibition of Fine Artistic Collection of Ancient Calligraphy, Exhibition of Fine Artistic Collection of Ancient Paintings, Exhibition of Fine Artistic Collection of Ancient Jade Ware, Exhibition of Fine Artistic Collection of Ancient Buddha Statues and Exhibition of Fine Artistic Collection of Gadgets. Temporary exhibitions serve as a stage to study and appreciate the exchange relations between cultures of Beijing and the other regions and that of China and the world.

Address: 16, Fuxingmenwai Dajie, Xicheng District, Beijing
Website: http://www.capitalmuseum.org.cn

The Palace Museum

Tianjin Historical Museum

Tianjin Historical Museum was founded in 1952. It has a collection of more than 100,000 cultural relics of ancient China, including more than 400 first-grade items, and more than 100,000 stored books. The collection includes Jiaguwen (inscriptions on bones or tortoise shells of the Shang Dynasty) originally preserved by Wang Yirong and Wang Xiang, inscriptions and jade decoration of the Warring States Period, patterned bronze belt of Western Zhou Dynasty originally preserved in "Baochuzhai", "Dianbang" broken knife money of the Warring States Period, and other rare and exquisite items. The most precious unearthed cultural relics are a Xian Yu jade tablet of the prefect of Yanmen dating back to 166 (the eighth year of the Yanxi period of the Eastern Han Dynasty) unearthed in 1973 near Lancheng in Wuqing County, Tianjin. It is a completely preserved tablet of the Han Dynasty with the most characters in China. The museum also has a collection of local folk custom relics.

The museum has nine display and exhibition halls, covering an area of 7,000 square meters. The major displays include Ancient History of Tianjin and Modern History of Tianjin. Besides the basic displays, the museum also organizes some temporary exhibitions of cultural relics, such as Exhibition of Currencies of Various Dynasties, Exhibition of Postal History and the Stamps of China, Exhibition of the Evolution of Chinese Characters, and Exhibition of the General History of China. The cultural treasures of the museum have been exhibited in foreign countries many times.

Address: No.4 Guanghua Lu, Hedong District, Tianjin

Hebei Museum

Hebei Museum, a provincial comprehensive museum, was founded in 1953. At present, it has a collection of 150,000 cultural relics, including more than 360 first-grade pieces (six of which are State-level cultural relics). Among the collections are some very famous treasures such as those unearthed from Mancheng Lingshan Tombs of Liu Sheng, Duke Jing of Zhongshan of the Western Han Dynasty, and his wife, including jade burial suits sewn with gold thread that are the first and the best-preserved jade burial suits of the Han Dynasty found in Chinese archaeological excavation. Ceramic cultural relics are the special treasures of the museum, particularly the products of three famous kilns in Hebei, i.e. Xing Kiln, Ding Kiln and Cizhou Kiln, which have different styles and characteristics. The museum also has a group of kiln-stored ceramics of the Yuan Dynasty, unearthed from Baoding. More than a thousand works of painting and calligraphy from the Song Dynasty to modern time form a classical collection, including those of famous persons and masters. There is a collection of more than 50,000 books mostly rare editions of the Ming and Qing dynasties.

The cultural relics in the museum have been exhibited in nearly 40 foreign countries and regions many times. Meanwhile the museum has established cooperative relationship in exchanges and human resource training with the German museum and Japan's Tottori Prefectural Museum.

Address: Dongzhongshan Lu, Shijiazhuang, Hebei Province
Website: http://www.hebeimuseum.org

Shanxi Museum

The Shanxi Museum formally opened in October 1919, and is one of the museums built earlier and with comprehensive local chronicles in China.

The museum has collected more than 100,000 historical relics and natural science specimens, of which 443 items are first grade, including the well-known stone-tower and bronze ware group of Fang State culture in the north of the Yin and Shang dynasties represented by a dragon-shaped wine vessel, founding bronze ware of Jin State, Houma Mengshu (a great number of jade pieces of armistice unearthed from ruins of the Jin State in Houma, Shanxi in 1965), the Zun (a kind of wine vessel used in ancient times) of Hu Fuwen of the Han Dynasty, sculptures of the Northern Dynasty, fired porcelain in local kilns in the Song and Jin dynasties, Wang Yuantoa's painting of Bamboo and Golden Pheasant from the Yuan Dynasty, the best-preserved landscape paintings from the Ming Dynasty, folk artworks of the Ming and Qing dynasties.

The basic exhibition is arrayed in the east and west wings and the main hall of the Confucian Temple. On display in a total space of 2,000 square meters are 1,000 relics.

The museum is a modern one relying on ancient architecture, and the exhibition area is full of modern equipment while retaining its special ancient architectural style. The multi-function illumination system in the galleries, the rigorous technical security network, the computer management of relic files and the complete service equipment offer much convenience to visitors. The cultural treasures of the museum have been exhibited in foreign countries such as the US, Japan, Italy, France, Spain, Canada, Singapore and Australia.

Address: East Shangguan Alley, Taiyuan, Shanxi Province

Inner Mongolia Museum

The Inner Mongolia Museum was built in 1957. It is a white building with a white sculpture of a running courser on the top, which is the typical architectural style of the Mongolian ethnic group. The museum covers an area of 5,000 square meters, with 3,500 square meters for exhibition halls.

It has more than 56,000 cultural relics, of which more than 630 are first-grade, including the historical relics of ancient ethnic groups in the north such as the Hun, Xianbei, Khitan, and Mongolian.

The museum is a topographical museum. Those rare unearthed cultural relics obtained by archaeological investigation and excavation are a great characteristic of it. Its treasures include an eagle-shaped golden coronet of the Hun of the Warring States Period 7.1cm in height and weighing 192 grams, and a set of golden coronet strips (consisting of three pieces) weighing 1,022.4 grams, which was combined by three pieces of semicircular gold bars. These two items were unearthed in Aluzideng in Hanggin Qi, Ih Ju League in 1972. In addition, an incense burner of the Yuan Dynasty 42.7cm high was unearthed in a kiln in Baita village in the eastern suburb of Hohhot in 1970, which was inscribed with characters meaning "an incense burner made by Xiao Song on the fifteenth day of the ninth lunar month of the year of Jiyou".

Address: No.2, Xinhua Jie, Hohhot City, Inner Mongolia Autonomous Region
Website: http://www.chnmuseum.com

Liaoning Museum

Liaoning Museum is a historical and artistic museum at provincial level that brings together 112,000 items, including unearthed and the handed-down historical and artistic cultural relics in the Liaoning area. There is a large-scale collection system consisting of 17 categories, namely archeological materials, paintings and calligraphy, engraving, pottery and porcelain, silk embroidery, dresses and adornments, bronze ware, currencies, lacquer ware, cloisonné, furniture, life existing in prehistoric or geological periods, ancient maps, cultural relics of ethnic minorities, tortoise shells, and inscriptions on tablets, covering a period from the Paleolithic Age to modern times. The most representative and influential pieces include excellent works of paintings and calligraphy of the Jin, Tang, Song and Yuan dynasties, silk tapestry with cut designs and embroidery of the Song, Yuan, Ming and Qing dynasties, jade ware of the Hongshan Culture, cave-reserved bronze ware of the Shang and Zhou dynasties, pottery and porcelain of the Liao Dynasty, inscriptions on tablets of past dynasties, woodblock prints of the Ming and Qing dynasties, ancient maps, and currencies of past dynasties recorded by Collection of Ancient Coins by Li Zuoxian of the Qing Dynasty. There are many rare treasures such as Four Pieces of Cursive Hand Calligraphy by Zhang Xu of the Tang Dynasty and A Cursive Calligraphic Work of a Thousand Characters by Emperor Huizong of the Song Dynasty, Picture of A Maid Wearing Flowers by Zhou Fangzhi of the Tang Dynasty, Picture of Waiting for the Ferry at Mountain Pass in Summer by Dong Yuan of the Five Dynasties, and Picture of Hidden Forestry and Distant Peak by Li Cheng of the Song Dynasty, Diamond Sutra finished in the second year of Zhenming period of Liang of the Five Dynasties, Picture of Yifeng in the Yuan Dynasty, Picture of Purple Mythical Bird, a silk tapestry with cut designs of the Song Dynasty, Picture of Camellia, a silk tapestry with cut designs by Mi Kerou, Picture of Singing Birds on Qiuying Water Pavilion, a silk tapestry with cut designs of the Ming Dynasty, Picture of Riding on a Crane in a Fairy Place, an embroidery of the Song Dynasty, and Hair Embroidery Figures by Qixianglou of Gu Family of the Ming Dynasty. The abundant and rich porcelain of the Liao Dynasty are also one of the special collections. In terms of maps, Jiubiantu (a map of nine sides) by Xu Lun of the Ming Dynasty and Complete Map of the World by Li Madou are both the only copies extant.

Address: No.363 Shifudalu, Shenhe District, Shenyang City, Liaoning Province

Jilin Museum

The display area in the museum is 2,000 square meters and the exhibits are mainly historical cultural relics and natural resources of Jilin Province; the historical relics date from the Paleolithic Age to the Qing Dynasty.

The museum has a collection of nearly 80,000 items, including unearthed and handed-down cultural relics, paintings and calligraphic works of the various dynasties and nature specimens. The most characteristic relics are those of Wuhuan, Xianbei, Gaogouli, Bohai Sea and Liao and Jin times.

Among the exhibits, armor, plate decorations, pottery kettles, harnesses, porcelain, and copper mirrors have strong local ethnic characteristics. The important ones include helmets, gold-plated bronze plate decorations in shape of deity animals and agate bead neck jewelry unearthed from tombs of Xianbei of the Han Dynasty in Yushu, Gaogouli yellow-glaze four-handled pottery kettle, white jade handled cup, gold-plating copper harness, mural paintings copies and book of rubbings of steles of King Haotai unearthed from Ji'an, tombstones of Bohai Princess Zhenhui unearthed from Liudingshan, Dunhua, Bohai gold strip decorations unearthed from Helong, and copies of mural paintings in the tomb of Princess Zhenxiao, copper mirrors with inscriptions of Qidan of the Liao Dynasty, purple glaze printing bowls of the Ding kiln of Jin Dynasty, white glaze engraved dragon patterns plates, copper mirrors and copper official seals, etc.

Most of the paintings and calligraphic works of various dynasties exhibited in the museum are the real works of famous masters. Among the 144 items of first-class collection, there are 106 painting and calligraphic works, such as Painting with Two Written Poems of Zhongshan and Songlao of Spring Scenes in Dongting by Su Shi of the Northern Song Dynasty, Hundred-Flower Painting by Yang Jieyu of the Southern Song Dynasty, Painting of Wenji Returning to Han by Zhang of Jin Dynasty (originally named Painting of Wenji Returning to Han by a man of the Song Dynasty), Painting of Returning to a Village by He Cheng of the Yuan Dynasty, Copying Li Longmian's Painting of Nine Songs by Zhang Wo of the Yuan Dynasty, Painting of Zhou Jintang and Records of Zhou Jintang by Dong Qichang of the Ming Dynasty, Copying Zhang Shengwen's Painting of World Origin by Ding Guanpeng of the Qing Dynasty and many others. There is also a rich collection of works of famous painters in modern time, such as Wu Changshuo, Qi Baishi, Xu Beihong, Zhang Daqian and Pu Xinshe. There is also a collection of elaborate works of fan surfaces with paintings and calligraphy and finished fans in the Ming and Qing dynasties and in past 100 years.

Address: No.90 Renmin Dajie, Changchun City, Jilin Province
Website: http://www.jlmuseum.org/

Heilongjiang Museum

Heilongjiang Museum is a comprehensive museum at provincial level. It is located in the center of Harbin City and covers a building area of more than 7,000 square meters. The main building was built in 1904 in the style of classical Russian buildings. The exhibition area is 3,000 square meters, and the storage area about the same.

The museum collects more than 107,400 cultural relics and specimens, including 55 first-grade collections and one first-grade specimen. In addition, there are more than 40,000 books. There are many natural specimens, such as more than 70,000 specimens of rocks, minerals, soil, animals, plants and fossils of life existing in prehistoric and geological periods. There are more than 30,000 historical cultural relics, cultural relics of ethnic groups and paintings. There are abundant cultural relics of the Jin Dynasty and Hezhe ethnic group. As to paintings and calligraphy, modern ones are dominant and the collection of works by Pan Tianshou, a famous maestro, occupies a larger proportion. The collection in the museum is also characterized by the early representative works of woodblock prints of the Great Northern Wilderness.

The basic exhibitions in the museum include Exhibition of Historical Cultural Relics of Heilongjiang Province, Exhibition of Animals and Exhibition of Ancient Animals.

Address: No.50 Hongjun Avenue, Harbin, Heilongjiang Province

Shanghai Museum

Shanghai Museum

As a large museum of ancient Chinese art, Shanghai Museum possesses a collection of 120,000 precious works. Its rich and high-quality collection of ancient Chinese bronzes, ceramics, painting and calligraphy is especially celebrated in the world.

Shanghai Museum was founded in 1952 and it has 11 galleries and three special temporary exhibition halls. Visitors will see the Gallery of Ancient Chinese Bronze Ware, Gallery of Ancient Chinese Ceramics, Gallery of Ancient Chinese Jade Ware, Gallery of Ancient Chinese Sculptures, Gallery of Chinese Cash of Past Dynasties, Gallery of Chinese Paintings of Past Dynasties, Gallery of Ancient Chinese Furniture, Gallery of Chinese Seals of Past Dynasties, Gallery of Ancient Chinese Calligraphy, and Gallery of Chinese Crafts of Ethnic Minorities.

Shanghai Museum has conducted exchanges with many famous museums abroad. In recent years it has organized such exhibitions as "Exhibition of French Marseilles Art from 18th to 19th Century", "King of the Sun Louis XIV: Exhibition of Treasures on the Versailles Palace", "Light of Gemstone: Exhibition of US Scott Treasured Gemstone", "From Paul Cezanne to Jackson Pollock, Exhibition of Excellent Painting Works of the New York Modern Art Museum", and "Art and Empire, Exhibition of Treasures in the British Museum", etc.

In the underground part of Shanghai Museum, there is a Chinese traditional imitation landscape garden court with unique characteristics. Although underground, the architecture and the environment seem to be in the open air, as it is the only one among museums in China.

Address: No. 201 Renmin Lu, Shanghai
Website: http://www.shanghaimuseum.net

Zhejiang Museum

Originally built up in 1929, Zhejiang Museum was first named "West Lake Museum" and is one of the earliest comprehensive museums built by Chinese. It houses more than 100,000 cultural relics, including items of Hemudu Culture of the Neolithic Age such as lacquer bowls, wooden ware, bone ware and ivory products; items of Liangzhu Culture such as jade ware, satin pieces and sackcloth; items of the Yue State during the Spring and Autumn Period and the Warring States Period such as various bronze weapons, bronze farm tools, painted pottery and primitive porcelain; a group of samples of all the celadon kilns from the Eastern Han to the Ming Dynasty; a great number of ancient and modern paintings and calligraphy such as a religious color-painted picture of Pure Land of the Tang Dynasty, half of the picture scroll Dwelling in Fuchun Mountains by Wang Gongwang of the Yuan Dynasty (another half is preserved in Taiwan), and works of Zhejiang painters and calligraphers of the Ming and Qing dynasties. There are more than 3,700 works of Huang Binhong, a master of landscape painting.

Zhejiang Museum

Zhejiang Museum's cultural treasures are displayed all the year around in the Gallery of Historical Relics, Gallery of Paintings and Calligraphy, Gallery of Celadon, and Gallery of Craftwork. Meanwhile the Gallery of Selected Works periodically promotes various high-quality special exhibitions introduced from other places in China and foreign areas.

The museum has held hundreds of displays and exhibitions, including Zhejiang Cultural Relics Exhibition, Hemudu Culture Exhibition, Hangzhou Historical Sites Displays, Zhejiang Folk Craftwork Exhibition, Zhejiang Celadon Exhibition, Zhejiang Unearthed Cultural Relics Exhibition, and Zhejiang Ancient Paintings and Calligraphy Exhibition, and commemorative exhibitions. The museum also organized exhibitions of selected treasures with local characteristics in Germany, France, Japan, the US and Singapore.

Address: No.25 Gushan Lu, Hangzhou, Zhejiang Province
Website: http://www.zhejiangmuseum.com

Anhui Museum

The Anhui Museum was founded in 1956. It has a collection of cultural relics of nearly 230,000 pieces and the most precious ones include bronze ware of the Shang and Zhou dynasties, coins of Chu State, stone statues of the Han Dynasty, four treasures of the study, gold and silver articles of the Yuan Dynasty, Xin'an paintings and calligraphy, sculptures of Huizhou, ancient rare editions and Huizhou contract documents.

A highlight of the exhibition is the bronze ware of the Shang and Zhou dynasties unearthed in Anhui Province, such as an exceptional Shang bronze pot in the shape of an animal with lotus petals unearthed from the Cai Marquis Tomb of the Spring and Autumn Period, which is large and 80 cm high with a lotus-petals hollowed-out cover, double ear-handles in the shape of animals on the neck and four feet in the shape of animals, a rare art treasure from the Spring and Autumn Period. The Chu Ding (ancient cooking bronze vessel), which is 113 cm high, 87 cm of diameter at the mouth, and weighs 400 kilograms, is the biggest and heaviest extant one of its kind since the Zhou Dynasty, only secondary to the famous Simuwu Ding of the Shang Dynasty. A precious blue and white porcelain stake of 20.2 cm high and bowl of 13.9 cm high, unearthed in 1963 from a Susong County tomb dating from 1087 (the second year of the Yuanyou period in the Northern Song Dynasty), is a rare treasure among blue and white porcelains of Jingdezhen and rare standard instrument of porcelain of the Song Dynasty.

Luxie Painting (Reed and Crab Painting) by Liang Zaibang of the early Qing Dynasty is a gem in the art of iron painting.

Address: Anqing Lu, Hefei, Anhui Province
Website: http://www.ahm.cn/

Fujian Museum

Fujian Museum is a comprehensive museum at provincial level housing more than 50,000 cultural relics and specimens, including more than 360 items of first grade. Most are handed-down artworks, unearthed relics and revolutionary cultural relics. The important ones include gold-plating bronze lion stove made by five generations of kings of the Min kingdom, "rabbit hair cup" from the Song Dynasty, silk dresses and adornments unearthed from tomb of Huang Sheng of the Southern Song Dynasty, iron mace of Li Gang, a famous general of the Song Dynasty resisting the Jin, standing figure of Kwan-yin sculpted by He Chaozong, a craftsman of porcelain sculptures of the Ming Dynasty, paintings and calligraphy of Huang Daozhou, Dong Qichang, Shen Zhou, Wu Bin and Huang Shen in the Ming and Qing dynasties, personal letters of Lin Zexu and Yan Fu, letter of Lin Juemin, a martyr in Huanghuagang, stamps issued by the Soviet established in the region in the civil war, and silver seals of Fujian Province Soviet Executive Committee.

Address: Inside Xihu Park, Fuzhou City, Fujian Province

Jiangxi Museum

Jiangxi Museum covers an area of four hectares, with a building area of 35,000 square meters and an exhibition area of 13,000 square meters.

The museum houses nearly 100,000 cultural treasures of ancient, modern and contemporary times in Jiangxi; more than 40,000 volumes of ancient traditional thread binding books and books on history, art and culture, and an academic periodical, Southern Cultural Relics.

The exhibitions in the historical section of Jiangxi Museum include Brilliant Culture in Jiangxi, Ancient Bronze Ware n Jiangxi and Hakka Folk Customs in Jiangxi. The exhibitions in the natural science museum include Origin of Life, which reveals the evolutionary process of life from simple forms to complex ones and from lower to higher forms by detailed words, pictures and rare fossil specimens. These include rare ancient mammals such as Platybelodon, Chilotherium, and deer's head, and many invertebrates with strange shapes such as a 2.2-meter-long ichthyosaur fossil.

Address: No.99 Xinzhou Lu, Nanchang, Jiangxi Province
Website: http:// www.jxmuseum.cn/jxbwg/jxbwg.htm

Shandong Museum

The museum has a collection of more than 140,000 historical relics, 130,000 documents of modern times, and over 8,000 natural specimens. The historical relics dominate and the relics of pre-historic times include skull and teeth fossils of Yiyuan ape man of 400,000 or 500,000 years ago. The Neolithic Age relics include exquisite colored-pottery, white pottery and eggshell black pottery of the Dawenkou Culture and Longshan Culture. There are more than 5,000 pieces of Jiaguwen (inscriptions on bones or tortoise shells) of the Shang Dynasty, and Shandong is one of the provinces with the largest collection of these. The well-known ones include Yachou bronze battleaxe and Zuxin rectangle ding of the Shang Dynasty, sacrificial food vessels and wine vessels of the Western Zhou Dynasty, Gongsun kettle of the Spring and Autumn and the Warring States Period, such bronze ware as Guozi ding. The bamboo slips of the Western Han Dynasty such as The Art of War by Sun Tzu and The Art of War by Sun Bin are listed as ten great archaeological findings of the 20th century in China. Among the nearly thousand cultural relics unearthed from tombs of Zhu Tan, King of Luhuang in the Ming Dynasty, the most famous ones are stringed-plucked instruments of the Tang Dynasty, paintings of the Song Dynasty and jewelry and jade ware. In addition, the fossil specimens of ancient life such as Shanwang Shandong bird and huge Shandong dragon are rare ones among natural specimens.

Address: No. 14 Jingshiyi Lu, Jinan, Shandong Province
Website: http://www.sdmuseum.com

Henan Museum

Henan Museum is one of the significant museums with a long history, advanced displays and exhibitions, modern equipment and particular architecture in China. At present, it has a collection of more than 130,000 cultural treasures, including more than 5,000 of first and second grade. The most representative ones include prehistoric cultural treasures, bronze ware of the Shang and Zhou dynasties, ceramics of various dynasties and jade ware.

The museum has continuously promoted such displays as Light of Henan Ancient Culture, Changes over Hundreds of Years in the Central Plains, Ancient Stone Carving Art in Henan, Ancient Jade Ware in Henan, Ancient Architecture in Henan, Bronze Ware of Chu State, Craftwork Treasures of the Ming and Qing Dynasties, and the World of Dinosaur. In particular, Light of Henan Ancient Culture is a large display with the largest scale, the most advanced technology and the richest contents in the past 70 years in the museum. The exhibition halls cover an area of more than 3,200 square meters and exhibits more than 1,000 pieces cultural relics, including bronze ware of the Shang, Zhou, the Spring and Autumn Period and the Warring States Period, the primitive porcelain of the Shang Dynasty, tri-color glazed pottery of the Tang Dynasty, architectural models of the Han Dynasty (articles for the dead), and lacquer ware and dinosaur eggs.

Address: No.8 Nongye Lu, Zhengzhou, Henan Province
Website: http://www.chnmus.net

Hubei Museum

The Hubei Museum, established in 1953, is a provincial comprehensive museum that houses a collection of more than 200,000 pieces, including 812 of first grade and 16 State-level cultural relics. Among all its exhibits, the most prominent are its abundant unearthed relics, including pottery, porcelain, bronze ware, lacquer and wooden ware, inscribed bamboo slips, weapons, ancient musical instruments, gold and jade items, ancient paintings and calligraphy, and ancient coins, etc. A large number of treasures of the Qujialing Culture, Chu State history and ancient musical instruments are the most precious, for instance, the sword of King Goujian of the Yue State unearthed in Jiangling, Fuchai spear of the King of Wu State, and Zeng Houyi Bells excavated in Sui County.

The displays include the excavations from the Zeng Houyi Mausoleum. The exhibits include Zeng Houyi bells, bronze ritual vessels, etc. In the museum, there is a special performance hall to play famous ancient Chinese and foreign musical works by the replica bells and chime stones. "Music and Dance of Chime Bells" arranged by the museum according to archaeological research has been offered in foreign places more than 20 times.

Address: 156, Donghu Lu, Wuchang, Wuhan, Hubei Province
Website: http://www.hubeimuseum.net

Hunan Museum

This museum covers an area of 51,000 square meters with a construction area of 29,000 square meters. It is the largest comprehensive historical and artistic museum in Hunan Province, being opened in February 1956.

The museum contains a collection of more than 110,000 objects, including 763 of first grade. Its exhibits consist of stone implements of the Neolithic Age, pottery, bronze ware of the Shang and Zhou dynasties, relics from the Chu State, relics from Mawangdui Western Han Tomb, Xiangyin and Yuezhou celadon produced from the Eastern Han to the Sui and Tang dynasties, Changsha tri-color glazed pottery of the Tang Dynasty, facsimiles of Wang Xizhi's Prologue to the Orchid Pavilion Collection of the Tang Dynasty and the handwriting of Wang Fuzhi, the great thinker in the period between the end of the Ming Dynasty and the early Qing Dynasty. The most excellent ones include a rectangular ding with human face patterns, big cymbals with elephant patterns, and wine vessels in the shape of an elephant of the Li Tomb unearthed from Ningxiang, wine vessels in the shape of a pig from Xiangtan and bronze ware of the Shang Dynasty, and more than 3,000 treasures and a female corpse unearthed from three Mawangdui Western Han Tombs in Changsha. One of the most fascinating finds from the tomb is a 2.05-meter-long T-shaped silk picture found in the Mawangdui No.1 Han Tomb, supposedly a banner for raising the soul to heaven. It describes scenes in heaven, on earth and underground, integrating fairy tales and reality. A total of 28 long-lost ancient silk books with more than 120,000 characters were unearthed in the Mawangdui Lao Zi, Zhou Yi, Jing Fa, Unrestrained Letters from Home in the Warring States Period (Zhanguo Zongheng Jiashu), Stories of the Spring and Autumn Period (Chunqiu Shiyu), Five-Star Astrology (Wu Xing Zhan), Sundry Findings on Astronomy and Meteorology (Tianwen Qixiang Zazhan), Fifty-Two Prescriptions (Wushi'er Bingfang), etc. most of which are of great medicinal, astronomical, philosophical and historical value.

The regular displays of the museum include the Display of Historical Relics of Hunan and the Display of Mawangdui Han Tomb, the Exhibition of Paintings of the Ming and Qing Dynasties Collected by the Museum, the Exhibition of Ancient Ceramics, the Exhibition of Bronzeware of the Shang and Zhou Dynasties, and Ten Great Archaeological Findings in Hunan Province.

Hunan Museum

Address: No.50 Dongfeng Lu, Changsha, Hunan Province
Website: http://www.hnmuseum.com

Guangdong Museum

The Guangdong Museum is devoted to the collection of cultural relics in the province. It boasts more than 130,000 pieces (sets), including over 300 of national first grade, over 25,000 geological relics, specimens and fossils, and tens of thousands of books. The most treasured are a picture of the Ink Dragon by Chen Rong of the Song Dynasty, a Monkey King Ink-Slab of the Qing Dynasty and white-glazed Sakyamuni Statuary of 1068 (first year of the Xining Period in the Northern Song Dynasty).

The museum has co-organized several temporary exhibitions with other museums such as Fung Ping Shan Museum and the Art Museum of the Chinese University of Hong Kong in Hong Kong and a Macao museum in Macao, including Pottery and Porcelain of Shiwan, Calligraphy in Guangdong in the Ming and Qing Dynasties, Unearthed Cultural Relics of Pre-Qin Times in Guangdong, Paintings and Calligraphy of Su Liupeng, Porcelains Unearthed in the Tang Kiln of Guangdong, Cultural Relics of the Jin and Tang Dynasties Unearthed in Guangdong, and so on.

In 2003, the provincial government of Guangdong decided to build the new Guangdong Museum in Zhujiang New Town of Guangzhou. The new museum has a historical folk-custom, art, and nature forming three major displays, including Gallery of History, Gallery of Nature and Gallery of Art, in addition to an advanced displays and exhibition system, collection management system, education and comprehensive service system, business and scientific research system, security system and administration system.

Address: No. 215 Wenming Lu, Dongshan District, Guangzhou Province
Website: Http://www.gdmuseum.com

Museum of Guangxi Zhuang Autonomous Region

The Museum of Guangxi Zhuang Autonomous Region has a collection of more than 50,000 cultural relics, including 152 first-grade and 1,791 second-grade pieces. The most precious are a bronze You (small-mouthed wine vessel) of the Shang Dynasty and a phoenix lamp of the Western Han Dynasty.

Guangxi Zhuang Autonomous Region is one of the important areas in the distribution of ancient bronze drums, with rich and complete varieties, so the museum has become the one with the largest bronze drum collection in the world, totaling more than 360. Of these, a bronze drum of Beiliu type with the diameter of 165 cm and weight of 299 kg is honored as the "king of bronze drums".

In addition, the museum has a collection of hand-operated adzes of 800,000 years ago, a mysterious big stone shovel from the Neolithic Age, a bronze You of the Shang Dynasty, wooden slips with more than 370 characters from the Han Dynasty, lacquer-painted bronze basin and canister painted with fairy tales, bronze horse 115.5 cm high, bronze ox with vivid expression, a bronze phoenix lamp that can dispel smoke, and goat-horn-handle bronze bell, bronze ding of Yue style, bronze granary with railings and other unearthed cultural relics with rich local characteristics. The museum also has a collection of many books including more than 30,000 volumes of rare thread binding ancient books.

Address: 34, Minzu Lu, Nanning, Guangxi Zhuang Autonomous Region
Website: http://www.gxmuseum.com

Chongqing Museum

Chongqing Museum was opened in 1951. The exhibition area covers about 3,000 square meters, with more than 100,000 cultural relics and more than 100,000 various rare books and materials. The treasures of important historical and artistic value include more than 500 stone implements of the Paleolithic Age in Sichuan Province, more than 1,000 cultural relics of the Ba and Shu kingdoms, more than 100 figure stones and bricks of the Han Dynasty, more than 4,000 pieces of pottery and porcelain of famous kilns of past dynasties, and more than 5,000 paintings and calligraphies of famous artists since the Song and Yuan dynasties. In addition, there are cultural relics of ethnic groups in southwest China, including more than 5,000 handicrafts of the Qiang, Tibetan, Yi, Miao and Tujia ethnic groups.

Famous unearthed cultural relics include figure bricks, painted figures and stone and pottery tomb figurines of the Han Dynasty in Sichuan, and relics in the emperor's mausoleum of Ming Yuzhen, founder of the Daxia Kingdom at the end of the Yuan Dynasty. As to cultural relics handed down from ancient times, there are systemic collections of paintings and calligraphies of famous artists since the Song Dynasty, porcelain works of famous kilns of past dynasties, Baccaro ware of the Ming and Qing dynasties, currencies of past dynasties, inscriptions on tablets of past dynasties, jade ware, bamboo, tooth and bone ware, silk and cultural relics of ethnic groups in southwest China. The museum also collects more modern cultural relics that can illustrate important historical courses in Sichuan and Chongqing, such as the Taiping Heavenly Kingdom, litigation against foreign churches in the late Qing Dynasty in Chongqing, opening ports and setting passes, Shuzhong Tongmenghui, secret activities of the Chinese Communist Party in Sichuan, and Chongqing's role as temporary capital during the Anti-Japanese War.

Address: No.72 Zhengjie, Pipashan, Yuzhong District, Chongqing

Sichuan Museum

The Sichuan Museum was opened in 1941. It has a collection of more than 160,000 cultural relics, over 2,000 of them first or second class. The collection has distinctive local characteristics. For example, the bronze ware of the Shang and Zhou dynasties such as gold chime bells inscribed with patterns of fields and brooks in Fulin, bronze inscribed with patterns of entwined dragon and taotie (a mythical ferocious animal), bronze inscribed with patterns of animal face and elephant head, embedded bronze kettle for enjoying a feast and battle and a lot of bronze weapons of many shapes and various patterns. A human face stone baldric of the Neolithic Age unearthed in Daxi, Wushan County in eastern Sichuan Province has a history of more than 5,000 years. The material is a piece of natural elliptical black stone 6 cm long and 3.6 cm wide, and the front and back faces are both engraved with double eyes, nose and mouth of a human face. A bronze sword 62cm long produced in the Warring States Period excavated in Dongsunba, Ba County in Chongqing City has no case and the handle is prolate, the body and the handle of the sword was forged at once in the shape of willow leaf, hence the name of "willow leaf sword". The sword was engraved with patterns all over such as tiger stripes on both sides of the sword back. These patterns and designs are a precious reference to the study of Bashu Culture. In the cultural relics of the Han Dynasty, figure bricks and figure stones involve a wide range of subjects covering farming, salt making, chariot and war-horse, dance and fairy tales; various pottery tomb figurines represented by talking and singing tomb figurines are elaborate works of pottery sculptures of same dynasty. As to the cultural relics of the period from the Southern and Northern Dynasties to the Tang Dynasty, the excellent ones include hundreds of Buddha images unearthed from Wanfo Temple in Chengdu and a lot of cultural relics unearthed from tombs former kings of Shu State.

The paintings and calligraphic works collected by the museum are characterized by large quantity and exquisite quality, and the sutras of the Tang Dynasty, works of famous people of the Song and Yuan dynasties, and more than 180 pieces of Zhang Daqian's works of copying mural paintings of Dunhuang Grottoes are all unique.

Address: 3, Fourth section of Southern Renmin, Chengdu City, Sichuan Province

Guizhou Museum

Guizhou Museum is a comprehensive museum at provincial level. It opened in 1958 and covers an area of 19,300 square meters. It houses more than 60,000 cultural relics and specimens. The unearthed cultural relics include front teeth and premolars of Tongzi Ape-man, a human fossil of the Paleolithic Age, mandible and thighbone of Xingyi Ape-man, skull and maxilla and mandible of Chuandong Ape-man, fossils of extinct mammals, various typical stone implements and typical bone ware, and non-wattle dagger and dagger patterns of the Warring States Period, iron swords with bronze handle, inner model of sword handle, bronze axe in drum shape, and bronze ding, which are viewed as representatives of Yelang bronze ware culture by academic circles. The collected treasures include lacquer cups with ears on two sides and lacquer meal plates (both have long inscriptions) unearthed from a Han tomb in western Guizhou, bronze drum with Jingdu patterns in "Shizhaishan Style", bronze hooks in the shape of a giant salamander and cattle head, bronze bath plates counting the years, wine vessel with bronze handle, and large-scale bronze vehicles and horses, etc.

Cultural relics of ethnic minorities are one of the important collections of the museum. Besides more than 1,000 works of embroidery, wax printing, cross-stitch work, brocade, and silver ornaments, the typical treasures include tallies with marriage records of the Miao ethnic group, wine vessels with engraving of animal designs of Miao ethnic group, women's lined coats with lacework on green satin and adornments of silver bells and silver pendants of the Miao, Eight-Diagram dragon robe of ruler of the Yi ethnic group, hand-written copy of Brief Records of Six Ancestors in the Yi written language, grave stone-engraved "bronze drum" of the Shui ethnic group.

Address: Beijing Lu, Guiyang City, Guizhou Province

Yunnan Museum

This opened in 1951 and now houses over 50,000 cultural relics, including about 30,000 historical items (nearly 10,000 pieces of bronze ware), 7,200-odd revolutionary relics, about 10,000 ethnic relics and over 4,400 handicrafts. The collections are mainly from archeological findings, and the cultural relic works team of the museum has undertaken more than a hundred excavations on ancient tombs and sites in the province, unearthing some 20,000 items. In the museum, there are nearly a hundred excellent items, such as two pieces of human teeth fossil excavated in Yuanmou in

1965, which has a history of 1.7 million years and is the earliest human fossil excavated in Asia so far. It is an important scientific source for research into the evolution from ape to human. In addition, there is the Yunleiwen Bronze Drum (earliest extant bronze drum) and goat's horn-shaped three-button chime bells of the Spring and Autumn Period unearthed from an ancient tomb group in Wanjiaba, and a house-shaped bronze coffin of the Warring States Period unearthed from ancient tombs of Dabona, and so on. The paintings and calligraphy works include Painting Scroll of Travel in Xishan Mountain by Guo Xi of the Northern Song Dynasty, Painting Scroll of Visiting Dai by Shan River by Huang Gongwang of the Yuan Dynasty, Poem Script Given to Monk Jizu Shanmiao as a Gift by Xu Xiake of the Ming Dynasty, Painting Scroll of Wugaoshan Mountain by Shi Dandang of the Ming Dynasty, and Painting of Du Shaoling Riding a Horse by Qian Feng of the Qing Dynasty.

The regular displays include History of Yunnan Slave Society, Records of Scenery and Articles of Minor Ethnic Groups in Yunnan, and Exhibit of Dresses and Adornment of Minor Ethnic Groups in Yunnan showing the dresses and adornment of 22 minority ethnic groups such as the Dai, Bai, Naxi, Hani, Lahu, Jingpo, Blang, De'ang, Lisu, Primi, Va, Nu, Derung, Achang, and Jino, and Kucong people, and most of the collections retain the primitively simple style of the dresses and adornment of all such groups.

Address: No.2 Wuyi Lu, Kunming City, Yunnan Province
Website: http://www.ktb.com.cn/tour/kunming/bwg

Tibet Museum

The Tibet Museum was formally opened in October 1999 and promoted a basic display of the history and culture of Tibet. The designs of the display give prominence to the national styles of Tibetans, such as Tibetan-style architectural structures in the entrance hall, decorations on door head and girders, chapter and ceiling decorated with cylindrical flags, cloth and fragrant cloth in the display hall, and purple copper eight-lucky-item designs embedded in display cabinets, which give a full play to the artistic and cultural atmosphere of Tibet.

The display of History and Culture of Tibet covers the main historical trends, politics, religion, culture and arts, and folk relics in Tibet. The display shows the long history and profound culture of Tibet comprehensively and directly. Numerous historical relics reveal the fact that "Tibet is an indivisible part of China's territory".

The Museum exhibits more than 1,000 rare cultural relics, involving four subjects, i.e. Prehistoric Culture, Indivisible History, Culture and Arts, and Folk Customs. Among them, Culture and Arts are divided into eight units, namely Development and Evolution of the Writing Style of Tibetan Characters, Books and Other Literature in the Tibetan Language, Tibetan Drama, Tibetan Musical Instruments, Tibetan Medicine, Tibetan Chronometer and Calendar, Sculptural Art, and Tangka Art, which give a comprehensive description of Tibetan culture and arts flourishing over thousands of years. The exhibits are have been gathered by cultural relics protection organizations since the foundation of the People's Republic of China, and most of them are rarely seen in the world, serving as detailed historical evidence for researching Tibetan cultural history. For instance, a tangka silk tapestry with cut designs, Immobile Figure of Ming Emperor, given by officials of the Song Dynasty is invaluable, and excellent Buddha figures of the Grand Warrior Attendant of Power and Benevolent Rule and Buddha of Infinite Longevity imply the craft, wisdom and aesthetic sentiment of the Tibetan people.

Address: southeast corner of the Norbu Lingka in Lhasa, Tibet Autonomous Region
Website: http://www.tibet.cn/tibetzt/xzbwg

Shaanxi History Museum

Shaanxi Province is one of the important regions where Chinese first lived and Chinese culture was created and developed. Thirteen feudal dynasties in Chinese history, such as Zhou, Qin, Han and Tang, built their capitals there. Rich cultural relics and deep cultural accumulation form a unique historical and cultural scene in Shaanxi Province, and Shaanxi History Museum is an art palace displaying history and culture of Shaanxi and ancient culture of China.

Shaanxi History Museum opened on June 20, 1991. The museum has a building area of nearly 60,000 square meters, cultural relic storerooms of 8,000 square meters, and exhibition halls of 11,600 square meters with a collection of 370,000 relics. Most are unearthed articles and can be divided into 22 categories, such as stone implements, bone ware, bronze ware, pottery tomb figurines, ceramics, tri-color glazed pottery from the Tang Dynasty, jade ware, bronze mirrors, gold and silver ware, mural paintings, seals, paintings and calligraphy, cash, bricks and tiles and other architectural materials, etc.

"Shaanxi Bronze Ware Treasures Exhibition" and "Shaanxi Pottery Tomb Figurines of Past Dynasties Exhibition" are the two special exhibitions promoted by Shaanxi History Museum for the first time. The exhibition hall covers an area of more than 2,600 square meters with more than 600 relics displayed. As to the Shaanxi Bronze Ware Treasures Exhibition, it displays treasures in five aspects, namely category and usage, inscriptions on tablets and calligraphy, shapes and adornments, funerary objects and cave storage, and founding craft of bronze ware. The Shaanxi Pottery Tomb Figurines of Past Dynasties Exhibition is divided into five stages according to period, namely Qin and Han dynasties, Wei, Jin, and Southern and Northern Dynasties, Sui and Tang dynasties, Song and Yuan dynasties, and Ming Dynasty, and displays the development course of pottery tomb figurines of Shaanxi and China.

Address: No. 70 Yanta Lu, Xi'an, Shaanxi Province
Website: http://www.sxhm.com

Gansu Museum

Gansu Museum is a comprehensive museum at provincial level housing 75,000 cultural relics, ranging from natural specimens to historical, revolutionary and national heritage items, of which more than 110 are of first class importance, including Gansu color-painted pottery, the Galloping Horse of Wuwei that is accompanied by an impressive array of chariots and carriages unearthed from a tomb of Han Dynasty in Leitai, bamboo slips on medication of the Han Dynasty, and Illustration Sutra to Parents Kindness Repaid finished in the second year of the Chunhua period of the Northern Song Dynasty, etc.

The natural specimens include those of China specific animals such as panda, golden monkey and red-crowned crane. Historical relics occupy two-thirds of all the treasures. The most representative ones are various colored potteries of the Neolithic Age, wood slips and wood carving of the Han Dynasty, Buddhist statues from the Sixteen States Period to the Tang Dynasty, and sutras, etc. The museum has a display area of more than 7,500 square meters and has five large exhibition halls.

The Hall of Historical Relics exhibits about 1,500 unearthed relics, including colored pottery objects, excavations from the Silk Road of the Han and Tang dynasties, Buddhist art and other objects related to cultural exchanges between China and the West from the Sixteen States Period to the Sui and Tang dynasties.

The Hall of Jiayuguan Murals of Wei and Jin Period displays over 60 murals on tomb bricks.

The Hall of the Yellow River Ancient Elephants exhibits a 4-meter-tall and 8-meter-long fossil of the Yellow River Xiphodon mammoth, the largest and best-preserved remains of its kind in the world.

Address: Qilihe, Lanzhou, Gansu Province

Qinghai Museum

Qinghai Museum opened to public in September 1986. There are four basic exhibition halls, namely Prehistoric Culture of Qinghai, Ethnic Cultural Relics of Qinghai, Tibetan Buddhism Art in Qinghai, and Strange Stones at the Head of the Yellow River, where the long cultural history and folk customs and practices of the region are displayed collectively and systematically.

There are more than 30,000 cultural relics covering all the past dynasties, including stone implements made in the Paleolithic Age, stone implements, bone ware, pottery and bronze ware of the Neolithic and Bronze Age, bronze seals, bronze tomb figurines, bronze mirrors, inscriptions on tablets, written sutras, wooden tomb figurines, bronze bells, and Persian silver coins of the Han and Tang dynasties, paper currency and stone sculptures of the Yuan Dynasty, and porcelain and paintings and calligraphies of the Ming and Qing dynasties. The ethnic cultural relics include bronze seals of ethnic characters, ethnic dresses and adornments, imperial mandates for the entitlement of local officials of ethnic minorities by the Ming and Qing dynasties, and religious artworks such as Buddhist sutras, Buddha figures, Tangka, and musical instruments used in the Buddhist mass.

The Museum has held the Exhibition of Historical Relics of Qinghai, displaying over 1,000 relics, to express the process of the historical development in Qinghai from the Neolithic Age to the later feudal society, the Exhibition of Relics Related to the Relationship between Tibetans and the Han, the Exhibition of Relics Related to Buddhism Introduced from Tibet, and the Exhibition of Coins and Currencies through the Ages. The Exhibition of Relics Related to Buddhism Introduced from Tibet was once also held in Hong Kong.

The museum compiled Selected Historical Materials Related to Ancient Passages between Tang and the Barbarians and a picture album of the Buddhist Art Introduced from Tibet.

Address: East of Xinning Square in Xining City, Qinghai Province

Museum of Ningxia Hui Autonomous Region

The Museum of Ningxia Hui Autonomous Region was built up in 1973. It has collected over 10,000 cultural relics, of which 45 are Class One, including the ink-stick unearthed from Ya'ergou Han tomb in Guyuan County, and the gold-plated copper bull unearthed from a Western Xia tomb. The overwhelming majority of the relics collected were obtained from archeological survey and field excavation with the exception of a small quantity of collected items and the items left through the ages. The basic exhibitions are the Historical Relics, Folk Custom Relics of Hui Ethnic group and Handed-Down Cultural Relics. The most distinctive cultural relics include animal bronze plates of northern grassland culture, gold-inlaid gold, silver and bronze sheep of the Western Han Dynasty, stone door leaves of Huxuanwu of the Tang Dynasty, gold-plated bronze bull, large stone horses dogs, columns carved with dragons, stone dragon heads, and large glazed Chiwen (an ornament at either end of the roof ridge of a Chinese-style house) of Western Xia, engraved porcelain, flat kettles and Tangka of Western Xia, and gold-plated bronze Buddha figures of the Yuan and Ming dynasties.

The displays include Display of Historical Relics in Ningxia, Display of Historical Relics of Western Xia, Display of the Folk Custom Relics of Hui Ethnic group, Helanshan Rock Paintings Exhibition, etc.

Address: No.2 Jingning Street, Yinchuan, Ningxia Hui Autonomous Region

Museum of Xinjiang Uygur Autonomous Region

The Museum of Xinjiang Uygur Autonomous Region

The Museum of Xinjiang Uygur Autonomous Region was built in 1959. The museum has a collection of 40,000 cultural relics covering regional history, including nearly 400 State-first-grade cultural relics.

These include fabrics of silk, wool, cotton, and hemp fiber (including brocade, damask, damask silk, gauze, plain thin silk, thin silk, printing and dyeing, embroidery and many other silk fabrics of the Han and Tang dynasties); written books and bamboo slips in different languages (Han and Uygur); wooden sculptures and clay tomb figurines of the Jin and Tang dynasties; human figure and flowers and birds paper-paintings or silk-paintings; bronze ware with characteristic of Scythian culture; and dresses and adornments and craftworks of all ethnic groups in Xinjiang. In addition there are some fossils of life existing in prehistoric times and specimens of ancient corpse. Mummy of Loulan Beauty, unearthed from delta of Tiebanhe River north of old Loulan City in 1980, is the earliest (having a history of more than 3,800 years) and the best-preserved mummy unearthed in Xinjiang.

The Museum has two basic displays: Restoring the Splendor of Yesteryears in the Western Region, the Display of Xinjiang Historical Relics and the Display of Xinjiang Folklore and has two medium-sized exhibitions: A Wonder of Imperishable Dead: Exhibition of Xinjiang Ancient Mummies and Monument of History: Exhibition of Revolutionary Relics in Xinjiang.

Address: No.132 Xibei Lu, Saybagh District, Urumqi, Xinjiang Uygur Autonomous Region
Website: http://www.xjmuseum.com

Hong Kong Museum

This used to be the Hong Kong Art Gallery and Museum. Later, it was divided into the Hong Kong Artwork Exhibition Hall and the Hong Kong Museum. The museum opened to the public in 1975.

The basic exhibitions cover natural history and human development in Hong Kong, displaying mainly the development process of Hong Kong in the past 6,000 years. The exhibitions are divided into three parts: an introduction to the natural environment; unearthed relics, ancient stone carvings and ancient kilns to reflect human activities in the area; and the process of Hong Kong development from a small fishing village into a metropolis.

The Museum has collected over 45,000 cultural relics, falling into four categories, namely, archeology, local history, the history of folk customs and natural history. The most well known collections in the archeological category are the items collected by the two Fathers, Fr R.Maglioni and another one; the main collections in the category of the local history are historical photographs, the earliest taken in the 1860s; the collections among the history of folk customs are the models of a Chinese traditional junk, the fishing equipment, traditional farm tools and articles of everyday use; and the collections of the natural history are mainly the rocks and minerals from various parts of the world, and the butterflies and mollusks frequently seen in Hong Kong.

The Hong Kong Museum frequently holds lectures on special topics to introduce the local archeology, folk customs and natural history so as to improve public knowledge and enjoyment.

Address: Buildings S61 and S62, Kowloon Park, Haiphong Road, Tsim Sha Tsui, Kowloon, Hong Kang

Macao Museum

This opened on April 18, 1998.

As far as the thematic areas are concerned, they are divided into three main groups corresponding to each one of the three floors of the building.

Genesis of the Macao Region (floor 1): The territory's origins are presented from the prehistoric age until the mid-17th Century, the golden era of Macao as an important Asian and European commercial port.

Popular Arts and Traditions in Macao (floor 2): The themes focus on the ethnographic and anthropological areas, outlining the colorful socio-cultural characteristics of traditional Macao, such as traditional rites and festivals, daily life, traditional handicrafts and typical industries, etc.

Contemporary Macao (floor 3): This presents the more representative aspects of contemporary Macao until its return to China.

In an ancient subterranean room existing in the interior of the fortress is a permanent exhibition about the history of the actual Monte fortress from the date of its construction by the Jesuit Fathers, at the beginning of the 17th century, until its transformation into a Museum in 1998.

Address: No.112 Front of Macao Museum, Macao
Website: http://www.macaumuseum.gov.mo

Military Museum of the Chinese People's Revolution

The Military Museum of the Chinese People's Revolution is a comprehensive museum on China's military history. Located on Beijing's Fuxing Road, the museum was opened on August 1, 1960.

It has a collection of more than 120,000 pieces of historical relics about China's ancient and modern military history. There are many precious relics such as daggers of the Xue state during the Spring and Autumn Period, Hunnish iron swords during the Eastern Han Dynasty, blunderbuss of 1351, iron cannon set on Weiyuan barbette in Humen during Opium War, the seal of Zuo Zongtang, anchors of Zhenyuan warship of the Beiyang Navy, the record of the first class of Huangpu Military Academy, the telescopes used by Mao Zedong and Zhou Enlai, the gun used by Zhu De in the Nanchang Uprising, the steel seal of Central Military Commission of Soviet Republic of China, iron chain of Luding Bridge, scene of a battle during the Long March, the command sword given to Song Zheyuan by Zhang Xueliang, the command sword given to Chinese government by a commander-in-chief of the Japanese army invading China, the copper-made nameplate of the military warship Chongqing, the aircraft and tanks having participated in the parade marking the founding of the People's Republic of China, the earliest training plane of the air force of the Chinese People's Liberation Army, the aircraft piloted by Wang Hai, a hero of the air force of the Chinese People's Volunteer Army In Korea, and aircraft returned to the mainland from Taiwan by Xu Tingze, and so on. In addition, there are 45,000 historical photos, 67,000 books and literatures and 4,500 artworks.

Address:No.9 Fuxing Lu, Haidian District,Beijing

Beijing Natural History Museum

The Beijing Natural History Museum opened in 1958. It houses nearly 80,000 items covering paleontology, zoology, botany and human evolution. Some fossils are rare treasures, such as those of the flesh-eating Yongchuan dinosaur, acanthoid-nose Qingdao dinosaur, Yang dinosaur with parrot-beak-like mouth, and well-preserved dinosaur eggs and footmarks. Among them, the flesh-eating Yongchuan dinosaur of the late-Jurassic Period is about eight meters long and four meters high, the plant-eating acanthoid-nose Qingdao dinosaur of the late-Cetacean Period is 6.62 meters long and 4.9 meters high, and plant-and-insect-eater Yang dinosaur with parrot-beak-like mouth of early-Cetacean Period is only 70 centimeters long. There are also some rare collections obtained by foreign exchanges, such as fossils of large Moa's from New Zealand, sloth tree otter, echidna and lyrebird from Australia and Latiman from Africa, which have important academic value in explaining biological evolution.

Specimen collected in the Beijing Natural History Museum

The specimens are classified into different systems and the methods of zoology, filmstrip and video are adopted to explain biological evolution from low to high and from water-based to land-based ones. In the Hall of Paleontology are displayed a Hechuan Mamenxi dinosaur 22 meters long that lived 140 million years ago and Xu Lufeng dinosaur six meters long and two meters high living 180 million years ago, as well as a Yi dinosaur, a flying reptile, and Yu dinosaur, a reptile living in the sea, which became extinct at the same time with the main dinosaurs. In the Halls of Zoology and Botany, the systemic evolution of modern biology is used to explain how the various species of today were formed after a long evolutionary process. The displays of rare zoology and botany in severe danger of extinction arouse people's attention on the need to protect biological diversity. In the Hall of Human Evolution, materials related to paleoanthropology, anthropology, anatomy and archaeology explain the origin and development of mankind.

Address:No.126Tianqiao Nandajie, Chongwen District, Beijing
Website: http://www.bmnh.org.cn

Museum of Chinese Science and Technology

Located at No.1 Middle Section of the 3rd Northern Ring Road in Beijing, this is a large national museum of science and technology. The displays are separated into halls of electromagnetism, mechanics, heat, anthropological-reaction, acoustics, optics, nuclear technology and information technology, such as a large-scale device of showing 600,000v high voltage static electricity. The high-tech exhibits include a staged showing of a superconducting experiment and high-precision platform conducting several types of mechanical air-floating experiment.

The museum theater is the first OMNOMAX one in China where the audience can appreciate high-tech films. It adopts double spherical surfaces with a screen of 27 meters in diameter, and the six-way, four-track vertical acoustics and super-field-of-vision ensure viewers can hardly distinguish the edges of the screen and feel they are participating in the actual events. After its opening, such American films as Grand Canyon, Solaris, and Savanna have been screened.

The museum has established periodical information exchanges with the museums of science and technology in other countries in North America, Europe and Southeast Asia and Japan; personnel have also exchanged visits with their overseas counterparts.

Address: No.1 Beisanhuan Zhonglu,Beijing
Website: http://www.cstm.org.cn

China National Museum of Fine Arts

The China National Museum of Fine Arts is the largest museum of fine arts in China.

The museum collects more than 60,000 fine arts works, including elaborate works of modern and contemporary times and some foreign works of fine arts, besides some ancient paintings. The works cover traditional Chinese painting, oil painting, woodblock painting, sculptures, New Year painting, comic strips, picture posters, caricatures, sketch painting, illustration, watercolor painting, lacquer painting and other excellent works of different time characters and artistic styles, and folk artworks such as puppets, shadow play, paper-cutting, kites, clay toys and embroidery.

In addition to the perennial displays and joint displays with other museums, the museum also organizes short-term exhibitions of various types of fine arts (including ancient art and folk fine arts exhibitions). Meanwhile, to strengthen international artistic exchanges, it often introduces foreign exhibitions of fine arts and the collections in the museum are often shown abroad. The museum holds more than 100 domestic and foreign exhibitions every year.

Address: No.1 Wusi Lu, Dongcheng District, Beijing
Website: http://www.ccnt.com.cn

Geological Museum of China

This covers an area of over 11,000 square meters and houses more than 200,000 specimens of rock, minerals and paleontology. It is a geological museum famous in both Asia and the world for its large collection and numerous treasures.

In 2004 the renovated museum was reopened. It has 4,500 square meters for displays classified into the Hall of Earth, Hall of Mineral Rocks, Hall of Diamonds, Hall of Prehistoric Biology, and Hall of Territorial Resources. The Hall of Prehistoric Biology is divided into several units such as emergence of life, outbreak of life, great biological extinction, and emergence of mankind. In the displays of the new museum, modern scientific and high-tech methods are adopted to make the shows more active and the Hall of Mineral

Rocks is constructed on a huge modeled rock, unique in the world. The Hall of Territorial Resources shows a large-scale digital map of the beautiful landscape of China. To encourage audience participation, the museum also introduced many interactive items integrating education and enjoyment, such as model of seabed expansion, making of relief map, digital model of continental drift, differentiation of minerals and evaluation of gems.

The museum has a very abundant collection and the rare treasures include a huge Shandong dinosaur, the highest and best-preserved dinosaur fossils in the world, a series of fossils of primitive birds such as "Chinese dinosaur bird", "king of crystal", being the largest single crystal (3.5 tons) in the world, the "king of cinnabar", being the largest cinnabar single crystal in China, teeth fossils of Yunnan Yuanmou man, the earliest discovered such fossils in China, stoneware, stone beads, bone needles and bone decorations excavated in sites of the Upper Cave Man in Zhoukoudian in Beijing, Guangdong malachite geode, Hunan fragrant-flower stone crystal and orpiment crystal cluster, Guizhou king of vermilion, Shandong gem-grade diamond of 28.061 carats, Qinghai natural gold bullion with the weight of 3,561.407 grams, and Henan silk-like natural silver. In addition, gem-grade diamond specimens created in kimberlite from Botswana and a natural platinum piece from the United States are also conserved.

Address: No.15 Yangrou Alley, Xisi, Beijing
Website: htttp://www.bjmuseumnet.org/museum/dizhi/one.htm

Ancient Bells Museum at the Great Bell Temple

The Ancient Bells Museum is located in Beijing's Great Bell Temple. The temple was originally named Juesheng Temple and was first built in the 11th year (1733) of Emperor Yongzheng's reign, and was a site where Qing emperors prayed for rain. As it houses a huge Buddhist bell made in the Yongle period of the Ming Dynasty, it was commonly called "Great Bell Temple". In March 1980, the Storage Bureau of the Cultural Relics of the Great Bell Temple was set up. In October 1985, the Ancient Bells Museum was built.

This museum houses more than 400 ancient bells with a full variety, such as Yue Bell (chime), Chao Bell (bell set in the imperial court), Fo Bell (bell set in Buddhist temples), Dao Bell (bell set in Taoist temples) and Jingang Bell (Tibetan Bell). Among them, six belong to Class One collections. There are 222 ancient bells and 192 small bells and the highest is about seven meters and the smallest is palm-sized. The oldest is the Chime Bells of the West Zhou Dynasty.

The most precious one is Yongle Big Bell, which was cast around 1420 according to the order of Emperor Chengzu, Zhu Di, of the Ming Dynasty, and is 6.75 meters high and 3.3 meters in diameter. Its weight is approximately 46.5 tons. More than 100 kinds of Buddhist Inscriptions in Chinese and Sanskrit cover the interior and exterior with more than 230,000 words in total; the ringing of the bell can be heard 40 to 50 km away and the sound is very melodious and euphonious; the big bell is hung only by a small pierced-in nail and its acoustic performance and mechanical construction have an important value for scientific research; the craftsmanship is excellent, the alloy proportion of bronze is scientific and reasonable, and it was cast once by traditional Chinese crafts. It called the "King Bell" for five reasons (oldest bell, the most Buddhist Inscriptions, the farthest distance it can be heard, the best mechanical construction and excellent craftsmanship). On New Year's Day, Spring Festival and other important celebration times, the bell will be struck.

Coolections in Beijing Ancient Bells Museum at the Great Bell Temple

Address: No.Jia-31 Western Section of the North 3rd Ring Road, Haidian District, Beijing

China's Museum of Stamps

China's Museum of Stamps contains two exhibition halls in east and west and covers an area of 500 square meters. Besides basic displays, the Museum holds specialized exhibitions several times a year. It has a collection of nearly 200,000 varieties of Chinese and foreign stamps and the total number of all stamps is close to 100 million. Among the collections, the first set of Haiguan Dalong (huge dragon of the customs) stamps issued in 1878, the stamp of Red Printing with Smaller Characters of Additional One Yuan Stamped issued in 1897, the first Black Penny stamp in the world issued in 1840 in Great Britain, the first set of 46 stamps issued by the Republic of China in 1912 with the characters of Temporary Neutrality stamped, and the stamp of Red Postage of Southwestern Jiangxi issued in 1930 are valuable historic relics.

The main composition of the Museum collections is the archives of the postal service run by the customs, the State postal service and the postal delivery department for issuing stamps since 1878 and the various kinds of stamps issued by the aggressive organs of imperialism in China; the archives of the Government of the Northern Warlords, the Nanjing KMT Regime and the local regimes for issuing stamps since the first year of the Republic of China in 1912; the archives of the puppet regimes in the Northeastern China, North China, Mongolia and Xinjiang for issuing various kinds of stamps; the various kinds of stamps issued during the period of the Revolutionary War of the Chinese People, by the various revolutionary base areas and liberated areas since 1930 and part of the archives; the various kinds of stamps issued by the Ministry of Post and Telecommunications, the archives, the original postal service maps, the original engraved plates, the artworks of the well-known domestic artists, and the stamp information materials collected from all fields or donated to the state by patriotic personages since the founding of the People's Republic of China; the stamps obtained from the exchanges with over 200 countries and regions in the world through the Universal Postal Union and the member nations of the Union; and the foreign and domestic philatelic books, books of fine arts, books of historic relics and other important books and information materials related to postal service and stamps.

Address: No.2 Dongdajie (East Avenue), Xuanwumen, Xuanwu District, Beijing

China Sports Museum

(See P843)

International Friendship Museum

This museum is devoted to the collection of gifts received by State and Party leaders of New China through diplomatic activities. It is subordinate to the State Cultural Relics Bureau.

The museum is in charge of investigation, collection, storage and research on important international gifts. At present, it has collected nearly 20,000 gifts from more than 170 states and regions that can be classified into more than 30 categories and hundreds of kinds. The gifts with important political meaning and important historical value are the precious cultural relics left from modern friendly exchanges between China and foreign countries and are closely related to the important events and figures. The gifts with supreme economic value and collection value are rare treasures such as some precious fossils and animal and plant specimens. The collections in the museum are both diplomatic gifts and foreign artworks or precious fossils specimens, which creates the special quality of the museum and the distinctive characteristic and styles different from other museums.

Address: Inside Bolin Temple, No.1 Xilou Alley, Yonghegong Avenue, Dongcheng District, Beijing
Website: http://www.friendshipmuseum.com

Relic Hall of Chinese Buddhism Books

The Relic Hall of Chinese Buddhism Books, located inside Fayuan Buddhist Temple, with a history of 1,300 years in Beijing, is a museum of religious relics that was founded in 1980.

The Hall has collected 2,100 relics, including 34 of Class One. In the Dabei (Infinite Mercy) Hall behind the main hall of the Temple is the Show Room of Different Editions of the Buddhist Sacred Literature through the Ages. On display are the scriptures handwritten by people in the Tang Dynasty, the scriptures written by the people in the Five Dynasties, the edition of Kaibaozang, Sixizang, Qishazang of the Song Dynasty, the edition of Zhaochengzang of the Jin Dynasty, the edition of Puningzang of the Yuan Dynasty, the edition of Nanzang, Beizang and Jiaxingzang and the only edition of Wulinzang of the Ming Dynasty in the world, with a part missing, and the edition of Longzang of the Qing Dynasty. Also on display are the Beiye scripture (Buddhist scripture written on talipot palm) in Sanskrit and the scriptures in the scripts of ethnic minority groups such as Xixia, Huihu, Dai, Tibet and Mongolian. On the second floor of the Cangjinglou (a building for storing Buddhist scriptures) are the precious collection of the Beizang, Jiaxingzang and the Longzang of the Qing Dynasty as well as the rubbings of the Tripitaka in Tibetan and the complete Fangshan Stone Scripture (Buddhist scripture inscribed on stone found at Fangshan in the Beijing suburbs). On the first floor is the Show Room of Buddha Statues through the Ages. Facing the entrance is a 7.4-meter long sleeping Buddha, the biggest wooden sleeping Buddha in Beijing left from the Ming Dynasty. On both sides are shown a pottery Chuang (a pillar inscribed with Buddha's name of Buddha's scriptures) and a pottery pagoda, made during the Five Dynasties, unearthed from a Liao pagoda at Beizheng Village in Fangshan in 1977. Around the room are shown the Buddha statues left from the Eastern Han Dynasty, Three Kingdoms, Northern Wei, Northern Qi, Sui Dynasty, Tang Dynasty, Five Dynasties, Song Dynasty, Liao Dynasty, Jin Dynasty, Yuan Dynasty, Ming Dynasty and Qing Dynasty with different materials, such as bronze, iron, stone, wood, clay, brick, pottery, porcelain, ivory, and colored glaze. The most precious of these Buddha statues are the Arhat from the Song Dynasty, the Bronze Guanyin (Goddess of Mercy) from the Yuan Dynasty, and the Fahua tri-colored glazed porcelain Guanyin and the cast-bronze Guanyin with one thousand hands and one thousand eyes from the Ming Dynasty. The Buddha statues left from different dynasties and made with different materials, a superb collection of beautiful exhibits in one hall, are of great artistic value.

Address: No.7 Fayuansi Qianjie, Xuanwu District, Beijing

Dingling Museum

This is the tenth mausoleum of the famous thirteen mausoleums of the Ming Dynasty in Beijing in which is buried Emperor Shenzong, Zhu Yijun, 13th emperor of the Ming Dynasty and his two empresses, Xiaoduan and Xiaojing. Zhu Yijun, with the title of Wanli, ascended the throne at the age of ten in 1572, and reigned for 48 years, longest in the Ming Dynasty.

The Dingling mausoleum was prepared in 1584 and completed in 1590, covering an area of 18 hectares. The main body consists of a stone bridge, stele pavilion, mausoleum gate, Long'en gate, Long'en Hall, Ming building, treasure town and underground palace on the center line. The surface buildings were destroyed by fire several times, so the only relics come from the Ming building, treasure town and underground palace. The museum is a key unit under State cultural relic protection and was listed as a World Heritage Site in 2003.

The collections in the museum are all relics unearthed from the underground palace and are displayed in Long'en Hall of Changling mausoleum, including colorful silk products, brilliant gold and silver ware, invaluable jewel and jade ware and exquisite blue-and-white porcelain. The group of relics are precious materials for research on imperial life and craftwork in the Ming Dynasty. Among the funerary objects unearthed, the most attractive are emperor's and phoenix coronets which are woven by very fine gold thread and inlaid with two gold dragons playing with a pearl. The entwined dragons have their feet bent or stretched and look vigorous. The coronets are 24 cm high with a mouth diameter of 20.5 cm and 826 grams weight. The phoenix coronet was worn by empresses when they paid respect at temples or attended court ceremonies, and was made from lacquered bamboo thread as the base and decorated with flowery-silk gold dragon, jade phoenix and flowers composed by pearls and gems; the dragon and phoenix hold pearls in their mouths, the flowery-silk gold dragon seems to be climbing the clouds and riding the mist under jade green clouds, and the jade green phoenix raises its head and tail and spreads its wings to fly; on the back of the coronets are three colorful phoenix tails; and one phoenix coronet is inlaid with more than 150 gems and more than 5,000 pearls.

Address: Special Zone of Thirteen Mausoleums, Changping District, Beijing
Website: http://www.chnmuseum.com/dl

Chinese Aviation Museum

Located at the foot of Datangshan Mountain in Changping District of Beijing, the Chinese Aviation Museum is China's first large-scale aviation museum, and the largest gallery of aviation treasures in Asia. Currently, it boasts a collection of 163 aircraft of 91 kinds and more than 600 types of armament such as missiles, radars, ack-ack and so on.

Address: Datangshanxia, Xiaotangshan Town, Changping District, Beijing

Beijing Planetarium

Beijing Planetarium

Located on Xizhimenwai Avenue in Beijing, the Beijing Planetarium is devoted to spreading astronomical knowledge by simulated showing of artificial star fields, holding astronomical exhibitions, editing and publishing books on astronomy and organizing such activities as public astronomical observation.

The Planetarium contains two parts, old and new. The former one was first built in 1955 and the installations include the Hall of Astronomical Phenomena, Hall of Exhibition, Movie and Television Reporting Hall and Public Astronomical Observatory. The Hall of Astronomical Phenomena has 600 seats and in the center is a homemade large-scale planetarium projector which is a complete system showing astronomical phenomena by scores of specific projectors around the wall. Four or five programs about astronomical phenomena are shown daily (except Monday and Tuesday when the Planetarium is closed) such as Trip to the Meta Galaxy. The major open installations in the new facility include a digital astro-theater, 3D vivid astronomical showing theater, 4D vivid theater, astronomical exhibition hall, sun observatory, public observatory and astronomical classroom, etc.

Address: No.138 Xizhimenwai Dajie, Beijing
Website: http://www.bjp.org.cn

Beijing Ancient Observatory

The Beijing Ancient Observatory is an ancient-castle-like gray high platform. At the time of building in the Yuan Dynasty by Guo Shoujing (1231-1316, an astronomer, water conservancy scientist and mathematician) it was named as "Sitian Platform", but in the Qing Dynasty it became the "Observatory".

For nearly 500 years up to 1929, observations of astronomical phenomena took place on the platform, which is the longest historical record of observation on the same spot among the extant observatories in the world. On the high observatory are displayed eight exquisite large-scale bronze observation instruments of the Qing Dynasty, while inside are some ancient architectural structures such as Ziwei Palace, east and west wing-rooms, and the hall of shadow cast by the sun.

On display is the exhibition of "Chinese Ancient Achievements in Astronomy", and the very precious exhibits include Suzhou stone carving star chart and the astronomical picture engraved on the ceiling of Longfu Temple; the former one was painted in 1247with 1,434 stars and was recognized as one of the best star charts in the world; the latter was made during the Jingqin period of the Ming Dynasty, but in view of the words beside the picture, it might have been made in the Tang Dynasty. In the Ziwei Palace and the east wing-room located in the courtyard surrounded by ancient trees are exhibited "Lingtai instruments", introducing sites of Chinese Lingtai (ancient name for observatory), extant ancient observatories and the transformation in the making of astronomical instruments. In the west wing-room are displayed more than 150 kinds of Chinese calendars. In the hall of shadow cast by the sun are displayed ancient clepsydras and modern astronomical clocks and watches. On top of the ancient observatory are set eight bronze observation instruments in the arrangement prevailing in the Qianlong period of the Qing Dynasty, including equatorial transit instrument, ecliptic transit instrument, celestial globe, age limit instrument, horizontal rotation instrument, quadrant instrument, altazimuth, and Jiheng Fuchen instrument (an ancient astronomical instrument).

The Beijing Ancient Observatory is under the management of the Beijing Planetarium and is a key unit under State cultural relic protection.

Address: No.2 Biaobei Alley, East of Jianguomen, Dongcheng District, Beijing

Cultural Palace of the Ethnic Groups

The Cultural Palace of the Ethnic Groups has an architectural area of over 30,000 square meters and is a high-rise tower building with Chinese national style. The Palace collects more than 30,000 relics about ethnic minorities dresses and adornments and artware, which have abundant contents and involve a very wide range of ethnic groups in Tibet, Xinjiang, Inner Mongolia, Guangxi, Ningxia, Yunnan and Guizhou, covering both the 56 modern ethnic groups in China and the ancient ethnic groups active in history for a while, such as the Hun, Dangxiang, Khitan, and Dian. There are also abundant religious relics of various sects, which are important material objects for research on religious issues. The collections also include sutras, classics, files, edicts, contracts and letters in different national languages.

In the Museum the important national historical relics include a color-painted six-string plucked instrument with double sound boxes and dragon-like head of the Tang Dynasty, the drum and zither brought by Princess Wencheng to Tibet, iron high-top helmet and cuirass of the Yuan Dynasty, the jade axe given by Kublai Khan, Wensu garrison nameplate of the Western Xia regime, the silver rewarding plate of chancellors of the Qing court to Tibet, and weapons such as pikes, shields and self-made guns used by Tibetan people in the war resisting Britain aggressors.

On the ground floor of the Palace there is a library with a precious collection of nearly 400,000 volumes of books and literature in 24 national languages such as Han, Mongolian, Tibetan, Korean, Uygur, and Kazak. Many of them are block-printed editions, manuscripts, gold and silver hand-copied books, illustrated books, Beiye scripture (Buddhist scripture written on the talipot palm) and inscriptions of rubbings, such as the gold hand-copied sutras in Tibetan of the Qianlong reign of the Qing Dynasty and the pure gold hand-copied Tripitaka of the Ming Dynasty.

Address: No.49 Fuxingmennei Dajie, Beijing
Website: http://www.bjmuseumnet.org/museum/mzwhg/one.htm

China Modern Literature Museum

(See P464)

Tianjin Natural History Museum

The Tianjin Natural History Museum is one of the largest natural science museums in China, housing about 380,000 exhibits, of which 200 modeled specimens are listed as State first-grade ones. Among the paleo-biology specimens, prominence is given to vertebrates, and the museum has a full collection of fossils rarely seen in the world. In plant specimens, there is a large collection of low-plant fungus specimens, as well as the specimens of foreign moss rarely seen in China. There are also specimens of some French high plants. In the animal section, there are many invertebrate and insect modeled specimens. The museum also specializes in the systemic collection of insect wings and eyes, and has many mollusk and spider specimens.

Address: Machang Road, Hexi District, Tianjin

Reappearance of the Traditional bridal chamber showed in the Tianjin Folklore Museum

Tianjin Folklore Museum

Located in the center of the Ancient Culture Street in Tianjin, this museum has collected more than 2,000 pieces of folklore relics and opened the basic displays focusing on the folklore and customs of Tianjin. The exhibits include the introduction on the rise and changes undergone of Tianjin City, Tianhou Palace and Imperial Union, wall bricks of Tianjin in the Ming Dynasty, water transportation model of the Qing Dynasty, various folklore models (such as wedding ceremonies and dresses, etc.), and folk artworks such as New Year Painting of Yangliuqing, kites, brick reliefs, clay sculptures, velvet flowers, paper cuts and weaving, and folk dramatic art. In addition, the museum has established models of various businesses, such as stores, pawnshop and herbal medicine shop, which show the traditional folklore culture of Tianjin from different angles.

It holds traditional dramatic performances and folk Huahui performances in the ancient theater or square during important festivals.

Address: No. 80 Guwenhua Jie, Nankai District, Tianjin

Shenyang Palace Museum

This is an imperial historical and artistic museum and one of two imperial palace building groups preserved in China.

The Shenyang Imperial Palace was built in 1625 (10th year of the Tianming period of Later Jin Dynasty) and the construction was finished in 1636 (first year of Qing Emperor Chongde). The palace was built and used by the founding emperor of the Qing Dynasty, Nurhachi, and the second emperor, Emperor Taiji. After the Manchu moved their court to Beijing, Shenyang Imperial Palace became the accompanying capital palace mainly for emergency use.

The museum has more than 20 courtyards with 80 various buildings such as Royal Ancestral Temple and palaces engraved with dragon and phoenix patterns and more than 300 rooms, covering an area of 60,000 square meters, the layout of which has special Manchu architectural style. In the museum, there is a collection of more than 10,000 pieces mostly imperial cultural relics, such as swords used by Nurhachi and broadsword and chairs with deer horns used by Emperor Taiji. The Museum now has 30-odd exhibition halls, including the Restored Palace Display, Palace Relics Display, Artworks of the Ming and Qing Dynasties and Exhibitions of the Qing Emperors' Life, etc.

Address: No.171 Shenyang Lu, Shenhe District, Shenyang, Liaoning Province
Website: http://www.chnmuseum.com

Shanghai Museum of Natural Sciences

The Shanghai Museum of Natural Sciences is one of the largest of its type in China, covering an area of 12,880 square meters. It has an abundant collection of specimens and books and documents. Besides accepting the specimens of the former Asian Cultural Union Shanghai Museum initiated by British residents of the city and some natural specimens of the China Museum initiated by the French, the museum has obtained various natural specimens by collecting, purchasing, receiving gifts and exchange. The museum houses more than 200,000 pieces of various specimens, including more than 62,000 animal specimens, more than 135,000 plant specimens, more than 1,700 paleo-biological specimens, more than 700 specimens of the Neolithic and Paleolithic ages, and more than 1,700 mineral and rocks specimens. These specimens include some modeled specimens and newly-recorded specimens first discovered in China, as well as rare biological specimens particular to China, and fossils 600 million years ago. The museum also has a collection of over 60,000 volumes of various books and documents in Chinese and foreign languages for scientific research and education.

The museum has an area of 5,700 square meters for basic displays classified into four parts, namely History of Paleo-animals, History of Human Evolution, Evolution of Animals and Evolution of Plants.

It also holds exhibitions of "Chinese Mummies of Various Dynasties", "Total Solar Eclipse in Yunnan in 1980", "Rare Animals", "Gems", "Eugenics and Nurture", "Biological Project", "Antarctic Investigation and Knowledge", and "Milu, a Special Animal in China".

Address: No.260 Xilu, Shanghai

Museum of Medical History in the Shanghai College of Traditional Chinese Medicine

This is the earliest special museum of medical history in China. It used to be the Medical History Museum of the Chinese Medical Association, founded in 1938, and was affiliated to Shanghai College of Traditional Chinese Medicine in 1959.

The museum covers an area of 344 square meters, 230 square meters of which is used for exhibition. It has collected 10,062 historical relics, of which the precious ones are the Bianshi (a stone acupuncture needle used in ancient times) from the Neolithic Age, pottery shards from the Qin Dynasty, gilded bronze censer from the Han Dynasty, pottery bone ash jar from the Jin Dynasty, large pottery gourd for holding herbal medicine from the Ming Dynasty, bronze human figure for learning acupuncture from the Qing Dynasty and various editions of ancient medical books, such as Zhenghe Bencao (Zhenghe Materia Medica), Bencao Gangmu (Compendium of Materia Medica) and Chifengsui (a special book on qigong, a system of deep breathing exercises) from the Ming Dynasty.

The museum has published Stories of Medical History, Index of Medical History Papers in Chinese, Literature Index of Chinese Medical History in Foreign Languages and the Traditional Chinese Pharmacy (in English).

Address: No.530 Lingling Lu, Shanghai

Suzhou Steles Museum

The Suzhou Steles Museum, located inside the Confucian Temple at Renmin Road of Suzhou City in Jiangsu Province, was opened on July 10, 1985. The museum boasts over 1,000 steles, including the stele of the Astronomical Map of the Song Dynasty, the stele of the Geographical Map, the stele of the Pingjiang Map and the stele of Song Emperor Shaoyuan, as well as the stele called On Strike Tablet, the stele of Guoyun Lou Standard Tablet and the stele of Man Tablet. In addition, there are other stele inscriptions depicting the development of commerce and agriculture in the late Ming and Qing dynasties and standard tablets of the Qing Dynasty. The museum also houses steles and rubbings in all districts and counties in Suzhou City and in other parts of the area south of the Yangtze River, and is a research center of stele materials in South China.

Address: No.45 Renmin Lu, Suzhou, Jiangsu Province

China Tea Museum

Located near the beautiful West Lake in Hangzhou, the museum opened in October 1990. The exhibition halls are divided into five parts, namely history of tea-growing, the varieties and distribution of tea in China, events related to tea, various tea utensils and tea-drinking habits.

In the Hall of History of Tea-Growing, some exhibits such as Table of Milestones in the History of Tea-Growing, and a great number of pictures and real objects are used to give a detailed explanation on the development of tea-growing in China from Shen Nong first discovering the effects of tea after tasting hundreds of kinds of leaves up to developments in the period of Republic of China. In the Hall of the Varieties and Distribution of Tea, more than 300 kinds of excellent tea samples in six varieties, namely green tea, black tea, oolong dark tea, white tea, scented tea and compacted tea are displayed with colored scenery pictures of all tea producing areas. The Hall of Events Related to Tea gives prominence to the technical knowledge about tea growing, picking, processing, preservation and drinking, and the pictures of large-scale modern tea plantations and the models of modern tea factories are displayed. In the Hall of Tea Utensils are displayed more than 200 various and excellently-made tea utensils including bowls, small cups, bottles, pots, and cups from primitive society to modern times. There are celadon bowls of Yue kiln, black-glaze small cups of Jianzhou kiln in the Song Dynasty, teapots of Yaozhou kiln in the Ming Dynasty, bowls with double-dragon covers for imperial use in the Imperial Palace, Baccaro teapots made by Chen Yongjun, a famous craftsman in the Qing Dynasty, and various Baccaro teapots covered with tin and inlaid with jade. In the Hall of Tea-drinking Habits, tea-drinking scenes in five different regions are shown to reflect the strong Chinese national customs and practice.

Address: Shuangfeng Village, Longjing Road, Hangzhou City, Zhejiang Province
Website: http://www.teamuseaum.cn

China National Silk Museum

China National Silk Museum, opened in February 1992, is located at the foot of Lianhua Peak of Yuhuangshan Mountain in Hangzhou City. It is a museum dedicated to reflect over 5,000 years of silk development in China. The museum has 6,100 square meters for displays

Part of the Head of the Zhang Silk Weaving Machine of the Ming Dynasty displayed in the China National Silk Museum

and consists of the Prelude Hall, Relics Hall, Folk Custom Hall, Silkworm Hall, Silk Manufacturing Hall, Weaving Hall, Dying Hall and Modern Achievements Hall, displaying over a thousand relics, samples, pictures, machines and modern exhibits.

In the Relics Hall, there are some precious excavated silk articles, including a piece of the remains of the earliest silk ever found in the world unearthed in Xingyang, Henan Province – Luo silk, which is about 5,630 years ago; another piece unearthed in Qianshanyang, Zhejiang Province, which is the earliest by far discovered in the Yangtze basin and has a history of about 4,700 years; the remained silk marks on bronze ware unearthed in Xingang, Jiangxi Province, Han Dynasty brocade unearthed along the ancient "Silk Road", silk products of the Jin and Tang dynasties, silk tapestry with cut designs of the Song Dynasty, and damask silk clothing, tough silk clothing and silk robes of the Song and Yuan dynasties. The silk and brocade products and silk tapestry with cut designs and embroidery works of the Ming and Qing dynasties manifest a new historical stage of silk manufacturing in China. The brocade robe embroidered with crimson land, colorful clouds and golden dragon of Emperor Qianlong of the Qing Dynasty and the yellow brocade robe embroidered with clouds and dragons for emperors holding court in the Ming Dynasty are unsurpassed works.

The Modern Achievements Hall gives an introduction of the latest developments in modern silk manufacturing and scientific development in China and shows a hopeful future of China's silk culture.

Address: No.73-1,YuhuangshanLu, Hangzhou, Zhejiang Province
Website: http://www.chinasilkmuseum.com

Museum of the Hemudu Site

Pottery unearthed from the Hemudu Site

This is the site of an early Neolithic Age settlement in southern China, covering an area of about 40,000 square meters. It is about 3.7 meters deep and wide in stacks, and consists of four cultural layers and traces back to the period between about 7,000 and 3,500 years BC according to Carbon 14 testing. In 1982, the museum was listed as key unit under State cultural relic protection.

Opened in May 1993, the Museum of the Hemudu Site contains two parts, namely excavation site and unearthed relics exhibition hall, and covers an area of 26,000 square meters with the architectural area of 163 square meters.

On display are more than 3,000 unearthed relics and remnants of animals and plants, wooden components and tens of thousands of broken pottery shards, including human-grown rice grains, pottery pieces with carbonized rice, pottery pieces with rice fringe designs, bone spade-like plough, wooden components with tenon, ivory "bird-shaped round sculpture", ivory sculpted butterfly-like ware with designs of sun, jade, jade pendant of semi-circular shape, bone whistle, bone hairpins and other relics.

The artworks for decoration of Hemudu people on display include jade pendants of semi-circular shape, pipes and pearls made of fluorite and jade for body decoration, as well as a group of wooden sculpted fish, pottery heads, pigs, sheep and fish, and utensils with bird-body and dagger-shape and butterfly-like ware with designs of the sun made of ivory.

Address:Hemudu Town, Yuyao City, Zhejiang Province
Website: http://www.hemudusite.com

Huqing Yutang Museum of Traditional Chinese Medicine

This was built on the original site of the ancient Huqing Yutang Chinese Medicine Mill and Shop, covering an area of 2,700 square meters. The museum contains five parts, namely exhibition hall, workshop of traditional Chinese medicine, outpatient service for regimen and health care, business hall and restaurant of food cooked with medicinal herbs.

Huqing Yutang was called the "medicine repository south of the lower reaches of the Yangtze River" and equally enjoyed fame with Tongrengtang in Beijing in line with the saying, "Qingyutang in the south and Tongrentang in the north". Huqing Yutang was founded by Hu Xueyan, a businessman of the late Qing Dynasty, in 1874. The construction of Huqing Yutang adopted the strong points of other excellent and grand pharmacies and integrates the garden architectural style in southern China. It took use of superior timbers

Huqing Yutang Museum of Traditional Chinese Medicine

such as gingko and fragrant camphor, and it is a wooden construction of late Qing style integrating business practicability and artistic appreciation. It is a key unit under State cultural relic protection.

Basic displays in the museum include the History of Traditional Chinese Medicine, History of the Huqing Yutang and Samples of Chinese Herbal Medicines and Patent Medicines. Among the collections, the most precious are medicinal materials unearthed from the Mawangdui Han Tomb in Changsha, Hunan Province, Hemudu Site of Yuyao, Zhejiang Province, the Liangchu Culture of Zhejiang, and a Song sunken ship in Quanzhou of Fujian Province; some hundred-year-old medicinal production tools such as oak bed, copper ship, big stone mortar, pestle, and balance; some vessels such as bronze milling stove with animal patterns of the Han Dynasty, Xuande stove of the Ming Dynasty, and ceramics and tin jugs of the Qing Dynasty; and precious production tools such as gold shovels and silver boilers for elaborate abstraction with high quality and a horizontal tablet inscribed with "Jie Qi" ("Against Deception") by Hu Xueyan at the beginning of the practice. Besides, there is a simulated workshop of traditional Chinese medicines where visitors can work personally and learn directly the production situation of traditional Chinese medicines in olden times.

Address: No.95 Dajingxiang, Shangcheng District, Hangzhou, Zhejiang Province

Xiamen Overseas Chinese Museum

It is the only comprehensive museum that highlights the history of overseas Chinese and has a wide and profound influence on overseas Chinese.

It has three exhibition halls, namely History of Overseas Chinese, Cultural Relics and Nature. In addition, the Hall of Relics of Motherland's History and the Hall of Nature also house more than 6,000 cultural relics and natural specimens, most of which were collected by Mr. Tan Kah-kee, including many precious cultural relics such as pottery, bronze ware, ancient coins, ancient paintings and calligraphy works, and ancient sculptures of various dynasties, foreign artware, pottery and glass vessels, paintings and calligraphy works and animal specimens; some are Class One State cultural relics. There are also animal and plant specimens of Southeast Asia given by overseas Chinese, such as Australian sunflower parrot, hornbill, Thailand tapir, Indonesian bird of paradise, sloth monkey, orangutan, Singapore tiger, Malaysian big crocodile (four meters long), and so on.

Address: No.493 Southern section of Siming Road, Xiamen City, Fujian Province

Museum of Ocean Transportation History in Quanzhou

This museum opened in July 1959. A new museum was built up by the East Lake in Quanzhou in 1990, containing three exhibition halls, namely "Quanzhou and Ancient Ocean Transportation", "Quanzhou Religious Stone Inscriptions" and "Quanzhou Ceramics for Export". Along with "Quanzhou Bay Ancient Ships Exhibition Hall", which is still in Kaiyuan Temple, the museum covers a total area of 35,000 square meters and nearly 4,000 square meters are for exhibition.

In the Museum the most important exhibit is a Houzhu Bay ship of the Song Dynasty unearthed in 1974. The remains are 24.2 meters long and 9.15 meters wide and have 13 cabins. This is one of the important findings in the history of Chinese natural science. On the right of the hall, there is a display hall of unearthed cultural relics of ocean ships, containing the accompanying relics of Quanzhou Bay Houzhu ship and Fashi ancient ship, another ship of the Song Dynasty unearthed in 1982, and a 1:10 model of Quanzhou Bay ancient ships of the Song Dynasty. The exhibits are accompanied by displays on ship-building and navigation.

The museum houses more than 3,000 items including scores of first and second grade. Among these treasures, the special and precious ones are unearthed relics of ancient ships and religious stone inscriptions. In addition, there are some precious cultural relics about the history of overseas Chinese and foreign cultural relics such as Spanish silver coins, which reflect the flourishing of ancient ocean transportation in Quanzhou.

Address: In East Lake Tourist Culture Region of Quanzhou City, Fujian Province
Website:http://travel.qz.fj.cn

Jingdezhen Ceramics Museum

Ceramics production in Jingdezhen can be traced back more than 1,700 years, but the Kangxi, Yongzhen and Qianlong reigns of the Qing Dynasty were periods of greatest prosperity in the history of ceramics production there. In addition to those famous ceramics of former dynasties, there are original ones such as ancient color, pink color, plain color, hard-jade color, enamel color and blue-and-white porcelain that is called "porcelain inlaid with glass" by foreign people, as well as precious colored glaze such as "Langyao red", "drunk beauty" and "Sanyang Kaitai".

The Jingdezhen Ceramics Museum was opened in October 1984 and houses more than 5,000 pieces of cultural relics including more than 100 of first grade. Most of the pieces are products of government porcelain kilns, the porcelains from the Yuan Dynasty and the samples showing the processing technique of celadon of the Yuan Dynasty. The precious ones include a celadon pillow with the pattern of dragon and tiger from the Song Dynasty which combines the technique of piercing and picking-up; a celadon vase with the pattern of plums left from the Yuan Dynasty which is one of the best among the celadon products left from the Yuan Dynasty; and a celadon big plate of Xuande reign of the Ming Dynasty, 72 cm in diameter, with the pattern of a sea animal, which is a special product produced from the imperial porcelain kiln at that time.

Methods of porcelain production are also shown.

Address: Fengshushan Scenic Spot, West of Jingdezhen City, Jiangxi Province
Website: http://www.travel-jx.com/jdz/bwg.htm

Nanyang Museum of Han Dynasty Stone Carving

The Nanyang Museum of Han Dynasty Stone Carving is a museum in China specialized in collection, display and research of Han Dynasty stone carvings. Situated in the suburbs of Nanyang City in Henan Province, the museum opened in October 1935. It has a collection of over 1,500 stone carvings, of which 150 are of first grade.

Han Dynasty stone carvings are both building materials in the tombs of the Han Dynasty and stone carving artworks with knife as the pen and stone as the base. The contents and structures of the stone carvings differ between various development periods. In early times, the stone carvings had sparse composition and monotone contents, mostly seen in statues and pavilions. In the middle period, the stone carvings had abundant contents and various subjects covering wide knowledge and paid attention to the decorations on space. In the later period, the composition became simpler designs.

Xu Ahqu Tomb Stone Carving of 170 AD is one of the precious treasures in the Museum. It is a rare and particular stone carving epitaph in Chinese ancient society, being 109 centimeters wide and 69 centimeters high.The appearance is divided into two parts, the upper one showing the scene of enjoyment of the tomb master before his death, and the lower one showing the scene of dancing and drama. On the left of the stone carving is the epitaph recording the story of Xu Ahqu that "just at the age of five, he passed away" and the sorrowful funeral ceremony held by his family. In the inscription, there are six lines of words and the longest line has 23 words, being 136 words in total.

Nanyang Han Dynasty stone carvings are held up as "purely indigenous art" by art circles and as "the first artistic ferment time in China" by academic circles.

Address: Suburban Area, Nanyang, Henan Province

Suizhou Zeng Houyi Tomb Relics Display Hall

The Suizhou Zeng Houyi Tomb Relics Display Hall is located in the Hubei Museum. Zeng Houyi tomb was the tomb of the duke named Yi of Zeng (Sui) state in the early time of the Warring States period; it was excavated in 1978. The tomb contains various exquisite relics. Many kinds of musical instruments were unearthed, such as sheng (a reed pipe wind instrument), xiao (vertical flute), bells, drums, qing (chime stone), qin (seven-stringed plucked instrument) and se (25-stringed plucked instrument). The most distinguished among them are 65 sets of chime bells, including 19 Niuzhong (button bells), 45 Yongzhong (handle bells) and 1 Bozhong. Today the set of bells can play many kinds of ancient and modern music with a broad range and graceful tone. In the Hubei Museum there is an exhibition hall especially for the set of chime bells and there are regular performances.

In Zeng Houyi tomb bronze ware treasures, there is a double-layer bronze plate with charcoal on the under layer and fishbone on the upper layer, which was actually a chafing dish more than 2,000 years ago. As to two pieces of utensils containing ice unearthed from the Zeng Houyi tomb, one piece contains two articles: the outer is a square utensil containing ice and the inside is a square pot, connected together by a buckle at the bottom. The pot contains wine and the outer utensil contains ice, so people could drink chilled wine in summer just like their modern counterparts.

Hubei was the center of Chu State culture and both the Chu weapons and elaborate works of other states were unearthed from the Chu tomb, such as the sword of Goujian, Duke of Yue state. The body is covered with rhombic dim designs and the edge is shaped with fresh color, chilling sense and pressing momentum. In addition, there are other superior relics such as a sword and lance of Duke Fu Chai of Wu state.

Address: No. 88 East Lake Road, Wuchang District, Wuhan City, Hubei Province
Website: http://www.hubeimuseum.net

Silk paintings unearthed from the Mawangdui Han Tombs

• Mawangdui Han Tombs

From 1972 to early 1974, Chinese archaeological workers unearthed three tombs of the Western Han Dynasty in Changsha that are among the most important archaeological finding in the 20th century in China. They excavated more than 3,000 cultural treasures and a well-preserved female corpse. The exquisitely wrought and bright lacquer ware indicates the highly developed state of lacquer craftsmanship at the time; brilliant and soft silk shows the astonishing achievements in textile technology; romantic and mysterious silk paintings describe humankind's ideas of the mysterious heaven and the aspiration for longevity; silk books with fragrant ink smell inherited the knowledge and wisdom of earlier generations; the female corpse was named "Corpse of Mawangdui" by medical experts and became an academic term for corpses of the same kind.

Mawangdui Han Tombs are an encyclopedia of rich and profound contents, covering various aspects such as politics, economy, science and technology, culture, religion, folk customs and habits, and noble features, and are a window to society at the beginning of the Han Dynasty 2,100 years ago. The exhibition displays the female corpse and the preserved internal organs in the basement, the restored huge coffin rim, and No.3 and No.2 tombs preserved in situ in Mawangdui. The unearthed relics from Mawangdui Han Tombs and other cultural treasures have been exhibited in many provinces and cities in China, as well as to Japan, the US and Hong Kong.

Museum of the Former Site of Ancient Tonglushan Copper Mine

This is located over the excavation site of an ancient mine of the Spring and Autumn Period. After archaeological excavation, hundreds of mining vertical shafts, inclined shafts and blind shafts of different structures and supported with different wooden structures were found dating from different periods from the Western Zhou Dynasty to the Western Han Dynasty, as well as more than a thousand various kinds of production tools. In addition, 17 vertical furnaces for copper melting from the Song Dynasty have been excavated.

Entering the gate of the museum and rounding the huge slab of malachite, you will see an exhibition hall of 1,100 square meters. There are over 100 well-preserved vertical shafts, flat lanes, blind shafts and inclined shafts; crisscrossed lanes; piles of wooden structures standing in the wall rock; winding drainage works and wooden flumes; and various kinds of mining tools such as copper adze, copper pick, copper axe, wooden scoop, bamboo baskets, ropes and wooden hooks scattered in lanes, bringing the ancient miners back to life.

The geological cross section around the dado of the exhibition hall, which was restored by use of minerals and rock powders and traditional ramming technology in China, and the site are an integrated whole. In the east of the exhibition hall, a section of vertical shaft and flat lane are restored by use of modern building materials according to the supporting methods and structures of the Spring and Autumn Period, and visitors can enter and climb inside to have a taste of the real life of miners more than 2,000 years ago.

Address: Tonglushan Town, Daye County, Huangshi City, Hubei Province

Mawangdui Han Tombs Relics Display Hall in Changsha

The Mawangdui Han Tombs Relics Display Hall where are displayed some of the 3,000 relics unearthed from tomb No.3 of Li Cang, Chancellor of Changsha state in the early Western Han Dynasty, tomb No.1 of Li Cang's wife, Xin Zhui and the tomb of their son.

On display are the lacquer ware unearthed from the three tombs, which are still well preserved and with bright colors even after being buried for more than 2,000 years. In ancient China, there was a saying about silk products that they were "is as thin as cicada's wings and as light as mist", and the two pieces of unearthed white silk clothing are really like cicada's wings, weighing 48 and 49 grams respectively. There are more than 20 kinds of unearthed silk books containing over 100,000, including the first and second silk editions of Lao Zi and Unrestrained Letters from Home in the Warring States Period (Zhanguo Zongheng Jiashu), Stories of the Spring and Autumn Period (Chunqiu Shiyu), Five-Star Astrology (Wu Xing Zhan), most of which are long-lost ancient books of important academic value. Three maps of the silk books are also very precious and reflected the fact that Chinese mapping had reached a considerable level.

In the Mawangdui Han Tombs Relics Display Hall, visitors can not only learn of the daily life and rituals and customs of royal families in the Han Dynasty, but also gain knowledge of the politics, economy, military affairs, culture and scientific technology of the early Western Han Dynasty.

Address: No. 3 Dongfeng Road, Changsha City, Hunan Province

Guangxi Ethnic Relics Center

The Guangxi Ethnic Relics Center is adjacent to the Museum of the Guangxi Zhuang Autonomous Region. Completed in 1988, the center covers an area of 24,000 square meters. It is a unique outdoor museum and is the extension of the indoor displays of the folklore relics of the Museum of the Guangxi Zhuang Autonomous Region.

At the gate, facing visitors is a huge bronze drum with the history of more than 2,700 years. Guangxi was the major region producing and using bronze drums in ancient times and more than 1,400 bronze drums have been unearthed in China, among which Yunleiwen Bronze Drum unearthed in Shuichong'an in Yuanjing Town, Guangxi is the largest extant the world. It has a diameter of 165 cm, a height of 67.5 cm and a weight of more than 300 kg. Bronze drums are a special musical instrument cast by an alloy of bronze and tin and used as tools by ancient Zhuang people when dancing for enjoyment, offering sacrifice to their gods or training troops for battle.

The center brings together the different folklore and customs of various ethnic groups scattered in Guangxi. Unique architecture of various minorities such as Ganlan of the Zhuang ethnic group, bamboo buildings of the Yao ethnic group, houses projecting over the water of the Miao ethnic group, houses in caves of the Maonan ethnic group, and drum towers and storm-proof covered bridges of the Dong ethnic group, are all displayed here, standing in a dense forest on hills or on grassland beside hills and water. Inside these buildings, daily use articles and handicrafts are also on display, as well as the demonstration of making the handicrafts. In those workshops of different ethnic groups, there are shows of traditional ways of pressing oil, grinding rice, making paper, making pottery, squeezing sugar and fetching water by waterwheel. On ethnic festivals there are various performances of national art. Visitors can drink oil tea of the Dong ethnic group.

Address: Minzu Dadao, Nanning, Guangxi Zhuang Autonomous Region

Zigong Salt History Museum

This is located at the Fuxihe riverside at the foot of Longfengshan mountain in the central district of Zigong city, Sichuan Province. Opened in 1959, the museum collects historical books, literature and archives about well-salt development, including 1,322 real objects and tools. Among these items, there are 503 pieces of ancient Chinese well-salt drilling and repair tools, the only ancient well-salt drilling tools group preserved well in China at present. The museum houses well-salt business contracts and well register and account books from the reign of Qing Emperor Qianlong to the Republic of China, which are of great value for research on the scientific and technical history and social economy of that era.

The Display of the Well-Salt Production Technological Development shows the evolution and development of well-salt production technologies in well drilling, salt collection, natural gas exploitation and salt making and demonstrates the ancient well-salt production techniques with drilling technology as the core. In the display there is a well drilling mechanical structure powered by a human peddling that can dig through rocks at the bottom of wells using iron bits and drills at a depth of more than 1,000 meters; there are more than 10 kinds of drilling bits for various rocks. All these real objects are important cultural relics in the history of well drilling in the world.

Address: No. 107 Jiefang Lu, Ziliujing District, Zigong, Sichuan Province

Zigong Dinosaur Museum

Zigong Dinosaur Museum, located at Dashanpu in Zigong City, in the middle of the rich Tuojiang river drainage area in Sichuan Province, is the first dinosaur museum built on a hidden site of dinosaur fossils in China. Covering an area of 25,000 square meters, it opened in 1986.

Zigong is not only the famous salt capital in China, but also an important dinosaur fossils producing area in China. There are more than 50 sites of dinosaur fossils in different layers and a large number of dinosaur fossils and other ancient vertebrate fossils living at the same time as dinosaurs have been unearthed. Among the dinosaur fossils sites in Zigong, Dashanpu has the most concentrated fossils, which are not only of great number and variety but also well preserved. In the region of nearly 3,000 square meters more than 100 dinosaurs' fossils have been excavated including more than 30 complete or comparatively complete skeletons; for researchers the finding of complete skulls is particularly valuable. In addition, fossils of the flying Yi dinosaur and snake-neck dinosaur have been unearthed. At present, only 20 percent of all the dinosaur fossils excavated in the world belong to the Jurassic Era, mostly late Jurassic, and there is a lack of fossils belonging to early and middle periods, which was a key time in the evolution of dinosaurs. In Zigong, however, especially the dinosaur fossils in Dashanpu belong mainly to the early and middle periods of the Jurassic Era.

Dinosaur Fossil collected in the Zigong Dinosaur Museum

The US magazine National Geographic once described Zigong Dinosaur Museum as the best dinosaur museum in the world.

Address: No. 238 Dashanpu, Zigong, Sichuan Province
Website: http://www.zdm.com.cn

Sanxingdui Museum

Sanxingdui Museum is one of the most outstanding site museums from the Neolithic Age to the Shang and Zhou dynasties in China.

Sanxingdui site covers an area of 12 square meters. The most concentrated and richest stacks are in four villages, Sanxing, Rensheng, Zhenwu, and Huilong.

The relics unearthed from Sanxingdui have influenced world thinking to a great extent. In 1986, the thousand-plus precious relics of jade ware, bronze ware and jade ware unearthed from the two large sacrificial pits of the Shang Dynasty at Sanxingdui proved that Sanxingdui was the site of the capital of the ancient Shu State over 3,000 years ago.

The relics unearthed from Sanxingdui include pottery, jade ware, bronzeware and gold ware, and the most special is bronze ware of very high historical, artistic and scientific value.

The museum has a primitively simple appearance with a triangle spire rising to the sky that can been seen from far away.

Address: Beside the Yazihe River, West of Guanghan City, Sichuan Province

Address: Xiyazi Heban, Guanghan, Sichuan Province
Website: http://www.sxd.cn

China's Museum of the Three Gorges of the Yangtze River

This is a product of the world-famous water conservancy project at the Three Gorges of the Yangtze River. The Three Gorges Project will submerge the cultural relics in 1,087 spots, 752 of which are in the region of Chongqing. Among the 752 spots, 246 have ground cultural relics and 506 have underground cultural relics. As to the latter, 68 scientific and research institutes in China have completed 338 projects since 1997, involving excavation of more than 60,000 square meters and have obtained a great number of precious relics and samples; they have completed 92 projects on saving surface relics, 44 projects related to on-the-spot protection, and 47 projects related to moving relics elsewhere such as protection of the Baiheliang Inscription, Zhangfei Temple and Shibao Village. The museum was built in Chongqing to protect relics of the Three Gorges, involving cataloguing, protection and scientific preservation, as well as carrying out research and exhibition.

Address: No.230 Renmin Road, Yuzhong District, Chongqing
Website: http://www.3gmuseum.cn

Qin Terracotta Army Museum

In 1974, a huge vault of terracotta warriors of Emperor Qin Shihuang was excavated nearby Xi'an, a capital in ancient China. To better protect the treasure house of history and culture, a large-scale hangar-like exhibition hall was built over Pit 1 with a vaulted steel structure. The building is 230 meters long, 72 meters wide and 22 meters high. The museum was opened in 1979.

In the exhibition hall of Pit 1, visitors can see more than 1,000 terracotta warriors that have been unearthed and restored, and another 5,000 warriors that are undergoing the process. This oblong phalanx, facing east, contains 210 warriors as the vanguard in the front three lines, followed by 38 columns of foot soldiers alternating with horse-chariots.

Address: Qinling Town, Lintong County, Xi'an City, Shaanxi Province

Address: Qinling Town, Lintong County, Xi'an City, Shaanxi Province
Website: http://www.bmy.com.cn

Maolin Museum

Located in Xingping County, Shaanxi Province, this is the mausoleum of Emperor Wudi of the Han Dynasty, Liu Che. Built in 139 BC, the mausoleum is a key unit under State cultural relic protection. It covers an area of more than 50,000 square meters with an architectural area of more than 7,600 square meters.

There are two exhibition halls, the east one displaying precious relics unearthed from Yangxin mausoleum and the west displaying historical relics of the Western Han Dynasty. The two halls house 320 relics of the Western Han Dynasty, including some rare treasures such as large jade knocker-holder, bronze clepsydra of the Western Han Dynasty, gold-gilded horse, incense burner upon gold and silver-gilded bamboo, and white jade pig.

The museum houses more than 3,500 relics at present, most of which are from the early Western Han Dynasty with articles ranging from those for the dead to daily-use utensils. With a distinctive style of the Western Han Dynasty, the relics provide a comprehensive view of the life and customs in the regions at that time.

Among the collections, there are some special and rare ones, such as iron tools for the ancient punishment of shaving off the hair or gripping the neck of a criminal, large rear works of the crossbar with front sight and graduation, nude pottery idol, candlestick and other utensils in unique shapes of owl and bear, large pottery watercourse tube, hollow bricks with designs and eaves tiles with character designs such as "Shanglin", "Tunzhai Liuchi", "yangmang Wuyin", "Changle Weiyan", "Changsheng Wuji" and designs of 12 characters. The relics are displayed by turn in the halls.

Address: Xingping County, Shaanxi Province
Website: http://mlbwg.8u8.com

Qianling Museum

This is the joint mausoleum of the Tang Emperor Gaozong (Li Zhi) and his consort, Empress Wu Zetian. It's the most representative and best-preserved mausoleum among the 18 Tang mausoleums known today. It is a large scale covering 2.4 million square meters.

The ground settings in the Qianling mausoleum are mainly exquisite stone carvings, and have a history of more than 1,200 years. These stone carvings gather on both sides of Sima Way before the mausoleum.

According to historical literature, several accompanying mausoleums were distributed in an area of about 40 km around the Qianling mausoleum and had various tri-colored tomb figures and ceramics. On the walls and ceilings of mausoleum passages, caves, paved path to the main tomb and tomb chambers are painted with murals, including Painting of Maids reflecting the parasitical life of royal families, pictures reflecting the architectural style of the Tang Dynasty, and Painting of Playing Ball and Painting of Envoys reflecting the cultural exchanges and friendly communications between China and the world.

Though having suffered from grave robbers, these accompanying mausoleums still have a great number of precious relics for excavation, including tri-colored tomb figures and nearly 300 pieces of gold, jade, bronze, iron and tin ware unearthed from the mausoleum of Princess Yongtai, remnants of Ou-style intaglio books for sorrow in jade quality filled with gold, and colored and gilded horses and tomb figures with armor and different clothes unearthed from the mausoleum of Prince Yide, and tomb figures of civilian officials and warriors each over one meter high and colored animal sculptures for protecting the tomb unearthed from the mausoleum of Prince Zhanghuai.

Address: Qian County, Shaanxi Province
Website: http://www.chnmusum.com/js/sxql.htm

Banpo Museum in Xi'an

Some five km east of Xi'an in Shaanxi Province, there is a modern building with round vault, the famous Banpo Museum in Xi'an.

The Banpo site was found in 1953 to the north of the Banpo Village. It is a village site from the matrilineal clan commune period of the primitive Neolithic Age and was buried underground for more than 6,000 years. The Institute of Archaeology of the Chinese Academy of Sciences undertook five large-scale scientific excavations on the site, involving an area of 10,000 square meters. On the site of archaeological excavation, the first museum was built in 1958.

The museum houses more than 30,000 relics including more than 200 first-grade ones. Among the collections, there are about 3,000 pieces of stoneware, 14,000 pieces of pottery ware, more than 3,700 pieces of articles of other quality, more than 200 bone samples and over 200 paleo-biological fossils and early human fossil specimens.

Address: 1, Banpo Road, East Suburb of Xi'an City, Shaanxi Province
Website: http://www.taxitour.com/bpdm.htm

Shaanxi Geological Museum

The Shaanxi Geological Museum is a provincial-level comprehensive museum of geological science that was opened to the public in 1981. There are five exhibition halls, namely, the Exhibition Hall of Stratum Rocks, Exhibition Hall of Minerals, Exhibition Hall of Mineral Products, the Exhibition Hall of Mineral Deposits, and Exhibition Hall of Ancient Vertebrate. The museum has collected over 4,500 samples, 2,500 of which are on display at any time.

On display in the Exhibition Hall of Stratum Rocks are mainly the stratum cross sections of the main re4sources of the province, such as coal, oil and bauxite; cross section of the Cambrian System at Luonan, which is listed as one of the major historical sites under provincial protection; and the cross section of the graptolite in the medium and lower Silurian stratums at Wafangdian. Also on display in this hall are 523 rock samples of various kinds found in Shaanxi. The volcanic rock, granite, bedrock and super bedrock displays are of great research value and economic significance. A total of 1,546 samples are on display in the three exhibition halls covering minerals, mineral Products and mineral deposits, and include the main ores and minerals commonly seen in Shaanxi, the mineral resources and the locations with their reserves explored and 407 special samples of minerals of other provinces and regions such as Yue'ertan turquoise of Baihe County of Shaanxi Province and Hujingshi (tiger eye stone) of Shangnan used for arts and crafts, as well as samples and data on the major ore deposits. The rare mineral samples include the native gold, "Goutoujin", weighing 747 grams, diamond, aquamarine, agate and wood fossils. Included in the display in the Exhibition Hall of Ancient Vertebrates are the Hanjiang Chinese Elephant (a Class One collection under State protection) found in 1984 and named after the location where it was excavated.

Address: Outer Yanta Road of Hepingmen, Xi'an City, Shaanxi Province

Hong Kong Space Museum

The Hong Kong Space Museum, located at the center of Jianshazui in Kowloon, is one of the most famous planetariums in Asia. The construction was completed in 1980. Covering an area of 8,000 square meters, the museum comprises two wings – east and west. The east wing has an egg-shaped dome structure, beneath which are the Space Theater and the Exhibition Hall. The west wing houses the Hall of Sun Science. The Space Theatre, which has a velarium with a diameter of 23 meters and

Hong Kong Space Museum

can seat 316 people, is one of the largest space theaters in the world. The astrological projector can project over 8,000 fixed stars, the Moon, as well as the five major planets, namely Venus, Jupiter, Mercury, Mars, and Saturn, to the velarium. Boasting the first OMNIMAX film projector in the eastern hemisphere, the Hong Kong Space Museum was also the first planetarium in the world to possess a fully automated control system at its Space Theatre. The six-track acoustics system has scores of loudspeakers with very fine effects.

The Exhibition Hall introduces ancient and modern astronomy. The ancient astronomy displays include the record made by Chinese astronomers in 1054 about the observation of a supernova in Taurus, which is precious material for research on celestial bodies, as well as ancient astronomical sites in the West, such as the stelae group in the United Kingdom, the pyramids in Egypt, Nazca Plain in Peru, and Dunhuang star chart, one of the oldest extant ancient star charts, and various ancient astronomical instruments. The modern astronomy displays introduce the development of rockets and the exploration technology of modern space besides common astronomical phenomena, and shows models of the space shuttle, airtight cabin of a spaceship and Vanguard 10.

Address: No.10 Salisbury Road, Tsim Sha Tsui, Kowloon Peninsula, Hong Kong
Website: http://www.lcsd.gov.hk

Taipei Palace Museum

Taipei Palace Museum

The Taipei Palace Museum is located in the northwest of Taipei City. Its construction followed the style of the Beijing Palace Museum. In this grand building, there is a collection of 620,000 items of historical and cultural art treasures.

The construction of the museum started in 1962 and was finished in mid-1965. More than 240,000 relics originally belonged to Beijing Palace Museum and most of them are excellent works, which were transported to Taiwan in 3,824 boxes in 1949, including bronze ware and jade ware of the Shang and Zhou dynasties, calligraphy works since the Jin and Tang dynasties, famous paintings since the Tang and Song dynasties, porcelain of famous kilns, bamboo ware, and rare editions of books since the Song and Yuan dynasties, files of the Qing Dynasty, and sculptures, jade ware, lacquer ware, enamel, etc. The various pieces are all remarkable treasures of China.

Among these treasures, the most outstanding is the Maogong Ding of the Western Zhou Dynasty unearthed from Qi County, Shaanxi Province in 1850, a national treasure. The ding is 53.8 cm high and the diameter of the mouth is 47.9 cm. It has three feet and two rising ears. The patterns are simple and the shape is of primitive simplicity. In the inscription inside the ding, there are 491 characters, the most among all bronze ware.

In the museum, there is a collection of paintings and calligraphy works of a large number of famous masters, such as Painting of Demounting Helmet by a famous painter Li Gonglin (1049-1106) of the Song Dynasty, Painting of Wenji Returning to Han by Chen Juzhong (a painter of the Southern Song Dynasty), Spring Dawn in the Palace of the Han by Qiu Ying (ca. 1509-1551, a painter of the Ming Dynasty), Shaded by Weeping Foliage in Summer by Wang Hui (1632-1717, a painter at the beginning of the Qing Dynasty), Travel in Xishan Mountain by Fan Kuan (ca. 950-1027, a painter of the Song Dynasty), Painting of Early Spring by Guo Xi (1023-ca. 1085, a painter of the Song Dynasty), Tablet of Rapid Snow and Occasional Sun by Wang Xizhi (ca. 303-361, a calligrapher of the Jin Dynasty), etc. All the paintings and calligraphy works have precise and exquisite strokes and clear, vigorous and natural signs.

There are 20,000 exhibits for regular showing in the museum and they are renewed every three months. In every ten years, all the treasures can be displayed by stages.

Address: 221, Second Section of Zhishan Road, Double Brooks outside of Shilin, Taipei City, Taiwan Province
Website: http://www.npm.gov.tw

Taipei Insect Science Museum

The Taipei Insect Science Museum, located at Chenggong High School of Taipei City, is one of the largest of its type in Asia. Covering an area of over 600 square meters, the museum was completed in 1971.

The museum collects insect specimens from all over the world, 50,000 in total. In addition, it has also collected ecological films and slides of the insects in Taiwan Province, the sound recording of insect chirpings and folk handicrafts related to insects. On display in the exhibition hall are around 30,000 insect exhibits in 10,000 varieties, kept in the 600-odd boxes, including a rare specimen of hermaphroditic butterfly. The museum has also made a 3-D model of the Butterfly Valley area in Taiwan. Ecological films and photos of butterflies are played and shown in the museum and live insects are sometimes displayed in spring and summer.

The luxurious parlor of the museum in Chinese classic style is known as an insect palace with its decoration of 16,000 specially processed specimens of butterfly and insects decorated from the ground to the ceiling.

Address: Jinan Road, Zhongzheng District, Taipai City, Taiwan Province

Taiwan Museum of Natural Science

Located in Taizhong City, this is the first museum of science in Taiwan Province; it opened to the public in four stages from 1986 to 1993.

The museum features four exhibition halls, namely Scientific Center, Life Science, Global Environment, and Chinese Science and Technology, and four theaters of space, 3D, environment and bird's-eye view. Among them, the Exhibition Hall of Chinese Science and Technology introduces science, agriculture, astronomy, shipbuilding, navigation, and the spiritual life of Chinese people, etc. The theaters are all installed with computer-controlled systems and state-of-the-art audio-visual equipment, and provide various types of latest knowledge to visitors.

After the opening, the museum has been receiving nearly 3 million visitors on average every year. In 1999, the government of Taizhong City handed over a park of 4.96 hectares nearby to the museum to be converted into an arboretum, creating a greenhouse of tropic rain forest and collecting more than 700 kinds of original plants in Taiwan Province.

Address: No.1 Kuanchian Road, Northern District, Taichung City, Taiwan
Website: http://www.nmns.edu.tw

Private Museums

The State collection of cultural relics has been found to fall behind the social need in China. As a result, private museums emerge to cope with the need. Following the promulgation of the revised PRC Law on Protection of Cultural Relics in October 2002, the Rules for the Implementation of the said law was issued, which established the legal status of non-governmental collection of cultural relics.

China's first private museum was born in the late 1980s in Guangdong Province. In the ensuing 20-odd years, the number of private museums has risen to close to 380.

Ancient Pottery Civilization Museum

This is one of the first group of private museums set up in the mainland. It was created by collector Lu Dongzhi in 1996. Major exhibits include potteries of the Zhou, Qin, Han and Tang Dynasties, bricks and tiles of the Warring States period, Qin and Han Dynasties, and others, totaling some 3,000 unearthed cultural relics.

The museum covers an area of 400 square meters, and exhibts close to 600 pieces of relics of four categories including colored pottery places for fish and animals, and bricks and tiles. The pottery places for fish and animals are composed of about 100 pieces of the Majiayao, Qijia, Tangwang and Xingdian Cultures unearthed from Gansu, Qinghai and Ningxia; they date back to 5,000 years. Pottery tiles and bricks totaling 140 pieces are of the Warring States period and the Eastern Han Dynasty. Clay stamped with seals total 175 pieces, making the museum the most important of its kind in China. Ancient potteries totaling 130 pieces were of the Zhou, Han and Tang Dynasties, spanning 2,000 years.

Address: No.12 Youan Mennei Xijie (Daguanyuan Northern Gate), Xuanwu District, Beijing
Website: http://www.gtbwg.com

Guanfu Classic Art Museum

This is China's first private museum in Beijing. Opened on January 18, 1997, the museum was initiated by Ma Weidu, a cultural relics collector. The museum is composed of six halls including those for oil paintings, ancient family utensils, ancient potteries, ancient doors and windows, ancient calligraphy and paintings, and ancient industrial art works. They mainly include some 50 pieces of the late Ming Dynasty. In addition, the museum also displays ancient furniture, carpets and garments of the Ming and Qing Dynasties. It features art appreciation and historical research. Its Hangzhou an Xiamen branches opened in 2001 and 2005 respectively.

The museum and the activities venue cover an areas of 2,800 square meters. The museum is resounded with music played with piano, impressing the visitors of being a home furnished with everything left behind from history.

Guan Fu Classic Art Museum which shows classic furniture and silver objects

The museum often plays host to China Ancient Art Show and Cultural Art Exchanges. In the meantime, it partakes knowledge and skills with regard to examining real cultural relics to the public. Exhibits are renewed on the regular basis. It is staffed with guides. Visitors are happy also to enjoy piano playing and tea available by the windows. They are free to touch the exhibits, which makes it different from others.

Address: No.18 Zhangwanfen Jinnanlu, Dashanzi, Chaoyang District, Beijing
Website: http://www.guanfumuseum.org.cn/

Sihai Pots Museum

The museum is created in 1984 by Xu Sihai, a pot collector an red pottery artist. It was opened to the public on December 18, 1992. After repeated removal, it is now housed in the 100-Buddha Garden, which was privately owned and covers some 3.3 hectares. The museum has a collection of some 1,000 pieces of pots and kettles, including those made by Hui Mengcheng of the Ming Dynasty, and Chen Hongyuan, Shao Daheng, Chen Mansheng and Feng Gui of the Qing Dynasty.

In addition, the museum displays colored potter of the New Stone Age, glazed pottery of the Qin and Han Dynasties, blue porcelain of the Western Jin Dynasty, tri-color porcelain of the Tang Dynasty, and red pottery of the Ming and Qing Dynasty. They come of water kettles, tea pots and wine vessels. It is a show of China's 5,000-year history of pots and kettles.

The museum is also complete with pottery making workshop, kiln equipment, store, and research office.

Address: No.322 Xingguo Lu, Xuhui District, Shanghai

Jianchuan Museum

This museum was set up in 2005 by Fan Jianchuan in Anren Town of Sichuan, it displays three categories of cultural relics—those of the War of Resistence Against Japan, "cultural revolution", and folks collection. It now collects some 1.5 million pieces, including 14 confirmed by the National Cultural Relics Bureau as State Class I ones. It shows cultural relics of US troops who were in aid of China during the War of Resistence Against Japan, including letters and documents. It also displays relics belonging to the KMT troops during the War of Resistence Against Japan, including those of Chiang Kai-shek, Chiang Weikuo and some other KMT generals and leaders. It also shows art works prevalent during the "cultural revolution" (1966-1976).

Address: Anren Town, Dayi County, Chengdu City, Sichuan Province
Website: http://www.jc-museum.cn

Jianchuan Museum

China's Intangible Cultural Heritage

The Intangible Cultural Heritage

The Convention for the Safeguarding of the Intangible Cultural Heritage was adopted by UNESCO on October 17, 2003. According to its definition, "intangible cultural heritage" means the practices, representations, expressions, knowledge, skills - as well as the instruments, objects, artifacts and cultural spaces associated therewith - that communities, groups and, in some cases, individuals recognize as part of their cultural heritage. This intangible cultural heritage, transmitted from generation to generation, is constantly recreated by communities and groups in response to their environment, their interaction with nature and their history, and provides them with a sense of identity and continuity, thus promoting respect for cultural diversity and human creativity.

Intangible cultural heritage includes the following:

(a) Oral traditions and expressions,

(b) Performing arts,

(c) Social practices, rituals and festive events,

(d) Knowledge and practices concerning nature and the universe,

(e) Traditional craftsmanship.

Significance of Safeguarding Intangible Cultural Heritage

"Intangible cultural Heritage" means the unique and salient culture and customs created and built during the long history of humanity, which reveals the differences between them that produce the diversity of cultural expression.

The Convention on the Protection and Promotion of the Diversity of Cultural Expressions passed by UNESCO on October 20, 2005 emphasizes that "culture takes diverse forms across time and space and that this diversity is embodied in the uniqueness and plurality of the identities and cultural expressions of the peoples and societies making up humanity," and "cultural diversity creates a rich and varied world, which increases the range of choices and nurtures human capacities and values, and therefore is a mainspring for sustainable development for communities, peoples and nations."

In recent years, many countries have attached great importance to protection of their intangible cultural heritage. Due to the high-speed development of the world economy, science and technology and the information communications in the era of globalization, intangible cultural heritage is greatly influenced to impairment, even extinction. Therefore, it is necessary for the development of the nation, ethnic group and society to safeguard the intangible cultural heritage, as well as the necessary requirements for the sustainable development of the world civilization and the human society.

General Survey of China's Intangible Cultural Heritage

China is home to 56 ethnic groups. In its history, people of these groups created abundant intangible cultural heritage with their wisdom and imagination, such as the art of Kunqu Opera, the art of Peking Opera, the art of Guqin, the art of Xinjiang Muqum, the Mongolian art of the Urtiin Duu, and traditional Chinese Medicine and Chinese Herbal Medicine.

In the past five or six years, work on protection of intangible cultural heritage has entered the period of system integrity from the past practice of single project. The goal is to rally efforts from all walks of life and gradually establish a full-fledged system with Chinese characteristics, so that precious and endangered intangible cultural heritage of great historical, cultural and scientific value can be effectively protected, promoted and carried forward. The goal is gradually realized through the following works: to attach much importance on participation in international cooperation, for instance, to apply for the "Masterpieces of the Oral and Intangible Heritage of Humanity" and to intensify development of laws and regulations in this regard; to implement diversity in protection, including general investigation of the project, establishment and implementation of laws and regulations on the protection, establishment of the inventory system of intangible cultural heritage at national, provincial, municipal and county levels; to protect transmission channels; to strength the protection of cultural heritage and the cultural and ecological areas of minority ethnic groups and to develop a series of exhibitions, performances and theoretical research in this respect.

Brief History of China's Protection for Intangible Cultural Heritage

The concept of intangible cultural heritage is fairly new, but China actually has a long history of protecting it. Such protection used to be known as "Protection of Traditional and Folk Culture" or "Protection of Ethnic and Folk Culture". The explicit expression should be "the protection of traditional and folk culture of ethnic groups". China, as a united multi-ethnic country, attaches great importance to the protection and transmission of the culture of various ethnic groups and has done much good work since the founding of the PRC in 1949.

In modern Chinese history, there have been several large-scale protection movements. Early in the last century, around the time of the "May 4th" Movement, some educated and cultured people started to collect and study folk ballads. Later on, many scholars carried out cultural investigations among the people or in the areas where ethnic groups were concentrated.

Since the founding of the PRC in 1949, the Chinese Government has sought to rescue and protect ethnic and folk culture. It has supported a large batch of cultural workers to collect a lot of traditional and folk cultural and arts data of ethnic groups in rural areas and the remote areas. These efforts saved valuable and endangered items from extinction, which were transmitted and preserved as masterpieces.

Since 1979, the Ministry of Culture, State Ethnic Affairs Commission and China Federation of Literary and Art Circles has jointly worked on compilation of 'Ten Collections of China's Folk and Ethnic Culture and Arts' and on general investigation and research. The range of general investigation included 10 fields in five categories such as opera, folk music, folk dance, quyi (folk vocal art forms rich in local flavor, including ballad singing, story-telling, comic dialogues, clapper talks, cross talks, etc) and folk literature. As a result, an abundance of data was collected.

In 2003, the Ministry of Culture, the Ministry of Finance, State Ethnic Affairs Commission and China Federation of

Literary and Art Circles jointly launched the project of the protection of intangible cultural heritage, especially folk and ethnic culture. From 2003 to 2020, a complete mechanism and system is being established. In terms of scale, it is the largest cultural protection movement in Chinese history.

On March 26, 2005, the General Office of the State Council promulgated the Recommendations on Intensifying the Protection of Intangible Cultural Heritage in China. These identified the goal and the guiding principle of the protection work. The goal is to unite the efforts of all walks of life and gradually establish a full-fledged system with Chinese characteristics on the protection of intangible cultural heritage, so that precious and endangered intangible cultural heritage of great historical, cultural and scientific value can be effectively protected, promoted and carried forward. The guiding principle is summarized as "protection as priority, primacy in rescue, rational utilization, and inheritance for development. The relationship between protection and utilization should be correctly treated, the authenticity and integrity of the protection of intangible cultural heritage should also be adhered to. Rational utilization can be conducted on the premise of effective protection, and misunderstanding, distortion or misuse of intangible cultural heritage should be prevented. Based on scientific identification, effective measures should be adopted to make intangible cultural heritage acknowledged, respected and promoted by the whole society."

On May 20, 2006, the State Council promulgated the first national 'Intangible Cultural Heritage List', containing 518 items in 10 categories such as: folk literature, folk music, folk dance, traditional opera, quyi, acrobatics and sports, literature arts, traditional craftsmanship, traditional medicine and the folk customs.

A graded protection mechanism will be adopted for the protection of intangible cultural heritage, including criteria for the identification of intangible cultural heritage masterpieces. An inventory system at national, provincial, municipal and county levels will be established after scientific assessment. For China, to establish the inventory system of intangible cultural heritage is to perform its obligations after accession to the UNESCO Convention. The State Council will identify and proclaim national masterpieces of intangible cultural heritage, and provincial, municipal and county-level masterpieces will be identified and proclaimed by corresponding governments and be reported for reference to governments at higher levels.

Goal and Guiding Principle of Protecting of Intangible Cultural Heritages

On March 26, 2005, the General Office of the State Council promulgated the Opinions on Intensified Protection of Intangible Cultural Heritages in China. These identified the goal and the guiding principle of the protection work. The goal is to unite the efforts of all walks of life and gradually establish a full-fledged system with Chinese characteristics on the protection of intangible cultural heritage, so that precious and endangered intangible cultural heritage of great historical, cultural and scientific value can be effectively protected, promoted and carried forward. The guiding principle is summarized as "protection as priority, primacy in rescue, rational utilization, and inheritance for development. The relationship between protection and utilization should be correctly treated, the authenticity and integrity of the protection of intangible cultural heritage should also be adhered to. Rational utilization can be conducted on the premise of effective protection, and misunderstanding, distortion or misuse of intangible cultural heritage should be prevented. Based on scientific identification, effective measures should be adopted to make intangible cultural heritage acknowledged, respected and promoted by the whole society."

Intangible Cultural Heritage List

On May 20, 2006, the State Council promulgated the first national 'Intangible Cultural Heritage List', containing 518 items in 10 categories, such as folk literature, folk music, folk dance, traditional opera, quyi, acrobatics and sports, literature arts, traditional craftsmanship, traditional medicine and the folk customs.

A graded protection mechanism will be adopted for the protection of intangible cultural heritage, including criteria for the identification of intangible cultural heritage masterpieces. An inventory system at national, provincial, municipal and county levels will be established after scientific assessment. For China, to establish the inventory system of intangible cultural heritage is to perform its obligations after accession to the UNESCO Convention. The State Council will identify and proclaim national masterpieces of intangible cultural heritage, and provincial, municipal and county-level masterpieces will be identified and proclaimed by corresponding governments and be reported for reference to governments at higher levels.

Artisans are making the Yangliuqing New Year pictures using the traditional technique.

Masterpieces of Oral and Intangible Heritage of Humanity

On November 1997, UNESCO passed the resolution of establishment of the "Masterpieces of Oral and Intangible Heritage of Humanity"at its 29th general conference. According to the resolution, UNESCO would proclaim such masterpieces every two years, based on the submission of each member state. Only one item can be selected each time per country. The criteria used in the selection process is masterpieces of intangible cultural heritage with outstanding value, representing the creation of genius, or the popular traditional culture expression with outstanding value in terms of history, art, ethnogeny, sociology, linguistics and literature. If the expression or the cultural space exceeds the political boundary, the concerned States can jointly submit the same item, which will not be counted as their own quota.

The Chinese Government has attached much importance to protection of intangible cultural heritage, and actively participated in safeguarding work. Thanks to these efforts, the art of Chinese Kunqu Opera, the art of Guqin, the art of Xinjiang Uyghur Muqum and the Mongolian art of the Urtiin Duu, jointly submitted with the People's Republic of Mongolia, were included in masterpiece list.

Legislation on Intangible Cultural Heritage Protection

In 1997, the State Council promulgated the Provisions on the Protection of Traditional Arts and Crafts. Since 1998, the Ministry of Culture and Committee of Education, Science, Culture, Health and Sports of National People's Congress have been actively engaged in the research and investigation of domestic and foreign legislations and on this basis organized the drafting of the Law of the PRC on Protection of Folk and Ethnic Traditional Culture (Draft). In light of the basic spirit of the UNESCO Convention for the Safeguarding of the Intangible Cultural Heritage, the draft law has been renamed as the Law of the PRC on the Protection of Intangible Cultural Heritage. At present, a legislative leadership panel composed of personnel from the National People's Congress, Department of Publicity of the CPC Central Committee and Ministry of Culture has been established to further work on the draft law. The promulgation of the Recommendations on Intensifying the Protection of Intangible Cultural Heritage in China by the General Office of the State Council will surely inject new impetus into the process of legislation. In addition, statutes on the protection of folk and ethnic traditional culture were also promulgated by Yunnan, Guizhou, Fujian provinces and Guangxi Zhuang Autonomous Region. In some places, local regulations on the protection of specific forms of folk and ethnic traditional cultural expression were also developed.

Transmitter of Intangible Cultural Heritage

Transmitters are those who have mastered some kind of intangible cultural heritage and developed some technique and skills that can be passed on to others. On June 5, 2007, the Ministry of Culture proclaimed the list of "the first proclamation of the representative transmitter of national intangible cultural heritage" (226 persons). These were engaged in folk literature, traditional sports and recreation. For identified transmitters at national level, the State has the regulations that the responsible body (institutions) is in charge of carrying out protection measures. These measures include: to help them to resume the "master-apprentice system", to open the skills teaching and training course (or base), to bring the skills into schools, and to offer finance aid for the transmitters in their daily living.

Salvaging Intangible Cultural Heritage

In the mid-20th century, the Chinese Government organized large numbers of cultural personnel for investigation and study of traditional cultural heritage and a lot of intangible cultural heritage on the verge of extinction was salvaged. In 1979, the Ministry of Culture, State Ethnic Affairs Commission and China Federation of Literary and Art Circles jointly proposed the compilation of the 'Ten Collections of China's Folk and Ethnic Culture and Arts'. By the end of 2004, a total of 298 provincial volumes had been completed, with 224 volumes totaling about 400 million words already published. Through this huge project, a lot of artistic resources have been preserved and the project was universally lauded as a modern "Great Wall" of cultural undertakings. In 1997, the State Council promulgated the Provisions on the Protection of Traditional Arts and Crafts, in which explicit criteria of traditional arts and crafts are laid out and national assessment institutions established. As a result, a great variety of traditional arts and crafts were preserved and more than two hundred people were nominated as "masters of traditional arts and crafts" by national assessment institutions. China also set up the Steering Committee on the Rejuvenation of Beijing Opera and the Steering Committee on the Rejuvenation of Kunqu Opera. In 2007, special funds were allocated to implement the "project on the rescue, protection and support of Kunqu Opera". Meanwhile, a number of villages and towns with time-honored traditions and ethnic uniqueness were nominated as "home of folk art" and "home of unique art" so that the awareness of protecting traditional cultural heritage in the whole society was raised and documentation, research and development of intangible cultural heritage at different localities bolstered.

Intangible Cultural Heritage in China

Many traditional folk customs and festivals have come into being in China through thousands of years. Some are included in the list of the first proclamation of the national intangible cultural heritage: the Spring Festival, Qingming (Tomb Sweeping) Festival, Duanwu (Dragon Boat) Festival, Double Seventh Festival, Mid-Autumn Festival, Double Ninth Festival (a time to protect against danger by climbing high places), and some festivals of minority ethnic groups. All festivals contain deep cultural contents and symbolic meaning. The activities of thanking god paying homage to the ancestors, reuniting of the family, meeting and visiting friends, relaxation and entertainment are observed on each festival. And for each participant, it is a chance to brush up the national and ethnic culture memory.

In 2006, China decided to establish the system of "Intangible Cultural Day". In 2007, the second such day was honored in some places with an abundance of cultural activities. The idea of Intangible Cultural Heritage and its protection has gradually become rooted in the common people. Some concerned departments have adopted measures to bring performance arts into the city and onto the stage that were previously hidden in the mountains and fields. The performance succeeded in representing uniqueness in style and character and its grassroots charm to audiences far away from the realistic and original scene.

• Emblem of Intangible Cultural Heritage

The outer part of the emblem is a ring, a symbol of eternal circulation, and the inner part is a square, which symbolize the circular heaven and the square earth - an ancient Chinese belief about the composition of the universe. The fish pattern in the centre, one of the earliest patterns ancient Chinese painted on earthenware, forms a Chinese character, "文," which refers to culture. The fish, which is associated with water, symbolizes the sustainable conservation and development of ICH. The character "文" embraced in an abstract pattern of hands, signifies joint efforts to safeguard and salvage ICH and our spiritual homeland.

National Intangible Cultural Heritage List

In recent years, many efforts have been made in protection work, following the principle of "giving priority to protection, putting rescue in first place, rational utilization, and succession and development". On May 20, 2006, the State Council approved and proclaimed the first National Intangible Cultural Heritage List of 518 items of 10 categories. China also established an intangible cultural heritage protection system at four levels: national, provincial, city (prefecture) and county (town).

Candidates for recognition as national masterpieces of intangible cultural heritage must meet the following criteria:

1) Possessing outstanding value as a masterpiece of the cultural creativity of the Chinese nation;

2) Rooted in the cultural traditions of communities concerned and passed down from generation to generation, possessing distinctive local flavors;

3) Conducive to the affirmation of cultural identity of the Chinese people, instrumental to the enhancement of social cohesion, national solidarity and social stability, constituting important bond of cultural exchange;

4) Excellence in the application of traditional techniques and skills, demonstration of superb qualities;

5) Possessing unique values as testimony to the living cultural traditions of the Chinese nation;

6) Bearing great significance in the cultural inheritance of the Chinese nation, and facing the risk of disappearing due to social change or lack of protective measures.

♦ International Cooperation

In 2000, UNESCO launched the application for of "Masterpieces of the Oral and Intangible Heritage of Humanity", China has actively taken part in the application and submitted a candidate list. In October 2003, the 32nd session General Conference passed the Convention for the Safeguarding of Intangible Cultural Heritage. In August 2004, with approval by the Standing Committee of the National Peoples Congress, China became one of the first countries to accede to the convention.

To date, the Chinese art of Kunqu, Guqin, the Xinjiang Uyghur Muqam and the Urtiin Duu (Mongolian traditional long song) submitted jointly with Mongolia have been accepted. China is one of the counties with the most included items.

China's Intangible Cultural Heritages

On May 20, 2006, the State Council promulgated the first national Intangible Cultural Heritage List, containing 518 items in 10 categories such as folk literature, folk music, folk dance, traditional opera, quyi, acrobatics and sports, literature arts, traditional craftsmanship, traditional medicine and the folk customs.

♦ China Intangible Cultural Heritage Protection Center

The functions of the center are: carrying out concrete tasks for safeguarding works concerned with national intangible cultural heritage, offering policy information, organizing and developing a general investigation, guiding the implementation, carrying out theory research, holding seminars, exhibitions and the public welfare activities, exchanging, introducing and publicizing achievements and experiences, and organizing the issue of reports on research achievements and training.

The center has established "China Intangible Cultural Heritage Website • China Intangible Cultural Heritage Digital Museum" In addition, it has launched a series of books on China's Intangible Cultural Heritage.

Address: No. Jia 1 Huixin Beili, Chaoyang District, Beijing

Folk Literature

Ancient Song of Miao People

Applicant: Taijiang and Huangping Counties, Guizhou Province

Miao people mainly live in the southwest provinces of China, and the drainage area of the Qingshui River in the southeast region of Guizhou has the largest population of Miao. A kind of poetry legend, mainly about the genesis of the world and the Miao people, is very popular in these areas, and people call it the "ancient song". *Ancient Song of Miao People* is the only non-religious epic passed down in China, as well as an encyclopedia combining the history, ethics, folk-customs, dress and personal adornment and architecture and climate of the Miao.

The content of this ancient song is rich and colorful, and covers the birth of the world, the genesis of mankind and all of Earth's creatures, a flood in ancient times, the migrations of the Miao, their social system, and the day-to-day life in ancient times. The song brings together all the ancient Miao legends. It is divided into four parts, Creation of the World, Song of Maple, Great Flood and Crossing Mountains and Peddling. The epic, containing 15,000 verses, has been passed down orally.

Because the Miao people have no written language of their own, the singing of the epic has the function of passing on the group's history to each succeeding generation. Therefore, there are some strict taboos about its performance. It is usually sung on formal occasions such as sacrifices, weddings, funerals, family parties, feasts and festivals. Most of the singers are elders and necromancers. A feast is an important occasion at which ancient songs are sung. When the epic is sung, the guest and host sit face to face, questioning and answering in the form of a dialogue. The singing lasts several days and nights and up to half a month. The tune is full of power and grandeur, but is somewhat bleak.

Bu Luo Tuo

Applicant: Tianyang County, Guangxi Zhuang Autonomous Region

Bu Luo Tuo is a mythological character in the Zhuang people's oral literature regarded as the creator. The Bu Luo Tuo, in poetic form, vividly depicts the creation of the world, the sun, moon, stars, fire and growing of rice, and relates the origin of human beings, all kinds of crops, livestock and living customs of people in ancient times. This epic fervidly describes the great achievements of Bu Luo Tuo, ancestor of the Zhuang people who is both a god and a man, in creating the human race and all of nature. The poem containing 10,000 verses has been passed down orally in Tianyang County in Guangxi Zhuang Autonomous Region.

From the Ming Dynasty, the Bu Luo Tuo has been preserved in the form of the ancient Zhuang written language, part of which has been turned into a religious scripture. The hand-written copy of the Scripture Poem of Bu Luo Tuo was completely written in this way. The poem reflects the five-word style of Zhuang rhyming poetry. In terms of content, it combines myth, religion, ethics and folk customs with profound thought in an involved and abstruse way. After being polished for over 1,000 years, the epic is concise and fine in language and rhythm. It also preserves many parts of the ancient Zhuang language and religious language.

Bu Luo Tuo vividly relates the basic emergence of the Zhuang during the primitive period, showing they had engaged in agricultural production. For example, the section on creation of rice depicts the scenes of plowing, harrowing and hoeing the field. Descriptions of planting, livestock-raising, archery, customs and habits, are of great research value.

Zhe Pama and Zhe Mima

Applicant: Lianghe County, Yunnan Province

Zhe Pama and Zhe Mima is a voluminous poetic mythology of the Achang ethnic group. Nowadays, it survives mainly among Achang people in Lianghe County of the Dehong-Dai-Jingpo Autonomous Prefecture of Yunnan Province in both poetic song and colloquial forms.

The stories recount how the ancestors of the Achang people created the world, brought the floods under control, produced humankind, conquered the devil and finally brought peace to the world. They are not only the supreme gods in charge of ritual activities, but also the protectors of the Achang people. Zhe Pama and Zhe Mima reflects the transformation of human society from matrilineal to patrilineal form. The Salt Goddess Myth in the story is a "living fossil" of the nomadic culture of ancient ethnic groups in southwest China. The Zhe Pama and Zhe Mima is a monument to Achang people's culture.

In order to be grateful to Zhe Pama and Zhe Mima who created the world, patched up the sky, got rid of evils and saved the human race, Achang people conduct lion dancing, elephant dance, double dragon and sacrificial dances when the early spring comes or blows.

Mu Pa Mi Pa Poetry Legend

Applicant: Simao City, Yunnan Province

The Mu Pa Mi Pa is a voluminous poetic genesis mythology popular among the Lahu people. It is the oral literature of the Lahu ethnic group around Langcang Lahu Autonomous County of Simao City of Yunnan Province. Mu Pa Mi Pa, a transliteration from Lahu language, means "creation of the world".

The poem has 17 sections and 2,300 lines in total. It discusses the creation of the world, and the living conditions of human beings in ancient times. Full of dense, mystic ideas on original religion, it shows the evolution of the family, marriage and traditional ethics of the Lahu ethnic group, at the same time revealing the historical process of development of social productivity of the people, and explains the historical evolution of the means of production from nomadic hunting to nomadic farming and then settled farming.

Mu Pa Mi La is mainly sung by the "Ga Mu Ke" (man who can sing the poem) and the 'Mo Ba' (the emcee of the ritual), but can also be sung by many people in accompaniment or in trolling form. Its lyrics are simple and concise, and its rules and forms are regular. The tone is beautiful, nut varying between regions.

Ke Dao Narrative Poetry

Applicant: Shibing County, Guizhou Province

Ke Dao, a poem about the Miao people's marriage rites and a record of their history, is also called Ke Mu, which literally means 'wood engraving' in Chinese or the Miao Marriage Song. It is one kind of toasting song of the Miao people popular in Shibing County. Its contents are engraved onto round wood sticks that people hold in their hand while singing. It is popular in Feiyun Grand Canyon, in Yangliutang Town of Shibing County of Guizhou Province. Ke Dao is the only remaining system of engraving wood with marks to chronicle events, preserved by the Miao people as one of the oldest tools of written language.

The Miao Marriage Song reflects the marriage under the power of mother's brother. It, in the form of toasting song, recorded the origin, deduction, development and advancement of the marriage customs of the Miao people. Experts on ethnic groups and folklore regard it as a living fossil of important value for research into the development history of the Miao.

Leifeng Pagoda is well-known for the legend Madam White Snake spreading for 1,000 years. With a mysterious color, it is a beautiful scenic spot among West Lake scenic areas, as well as a must see place in Hangzhou.

Ke Dao was mainly made from the maple, pear tree and bamboo, with a total of 27 squares, in each of which a simple mark was recorded. The song is sung in the repeated and antiphonal style.

Ke Dao is made up of five-word style poems, narrating the old marriage customs of the Miao. The marks engraved on the sticks are not complicated. Among all the ancient songs of the Miao, Ke Dao is the longest and most popular toasting song, consisting of more than 10,000 lines. Ancestors of the Miao first engraved strange marks on a short stick representing the list of the Marriage Song. The stick can be easily carried, hence the name "song stick".

The Legend of the White Snake

Applicant: Zhengjiang City, Jiangsu Province; Hangzhou City, Zhejiang Province

The Legend of the White Snake, one of the four great folktales of China, originated in Zhenjiang, has a history of more than 1,000 years. Its characters such as White Maiden, Xu Xian, Abbot Fa Hai, and Xiaoqing express the aspiration for human liberation. With a great deal of ancient traditional customs preserved, it possesses the richest information on Chinese folk-customs and culture.

The Legend of the White Snake, also called the Legend of the White Maiden, and the Legend of Leifeng Tower, is one of the four representative tales of the Han people, which narrates how the White Snake turned into the White Maiden (Bai Suzhen) after 1,000 years of Buddhist practice goes with the Black Snake, who has turned into another beautiful maiden, (Xiao Qing) to the West Lake in Hangzhou. There, the former meets Xu Xian, a salesclerk of a drugstore, marries him, but then suffers interference from Abbot Fa Hai, and the story ends in tragedy and death.

It was created during the Tang (618-907) and Five Dynasties (907-960), completed in the Southern Song Dynasty (1127-1279) and was adapted into poetic drama set to music and script for story-telling in the Yuan Dynasty (1206-1368). White Maiden in the Leifeng Pagoda, a novel written in the style of a script for oral story-telling compiled by Feng Menglong of the Ming Dynasty, is the earliest and relatively complete version.

During the Ming and Qing Dynasties, folk oral literature works were adapted into other literature and art forms. The Tale of White Snake has been the classic subject of stories, songs, novels, story-telling script, drama, fiddle ballads in Chinese southern dialects, films, TV shows, animation, dance performances and strip cartoons. Its influence is not only felt in China, but also in countries like Japan, Korea, Vietnam and India.

Butterfly Lovers

Declarers: Jiangsu, Zhejiang, Shandong, and Henan Provinces

The still of the new version Yueju Opera *Liang Shanbo and Zhu Yingtai (Butterfly Lovers)*

The Butterfly Lovers, another of the four major folktales of China exerting global impact, is often known as the "Oriental Romeo and Juliet". It originated in the Eastern Jin Dynasty about 1,600 years ago, and was then passed down from generation to generation. It has been the source material of literature and art forms such as oral story, novel, script, folk art forms, Chinese traditional opera, symphony, ballet, opera, TV play and movie.

The story narrates the story of Zhu Yingtai, from Zhujiazhuang Village of Shangyu County. Zhu Yingtai assumes a male identity so she may travel to study in Hangzhou. On the way, she meets Liang Shanbo, a scholar from Kuaiji also going to study in Hangzhou, and they join forces. A deep relationship develops during their three years of study. Zhu Yingtai finishes her study early and returns home. Two years later, having discovered that Zhu Yingtai is a girl, Liang Shanbo goes to Shangyu to look for her and then informs his parents of his intention to marry her. Unfortunately, Zhu Yingtai had long been affianced by her parents to a son of the Ma Family. Learning of this, Liang Shanbo goes into decline and finally dies. In the second year after Liang's death, Zhu Yingtai passes his tomb on her way to be wed in a storm. Learning of the identity of the tomb occupant, Zhu is filled with sadness. She climbs the mountain where the tomb is located to offer sacrifice and pray for the soul of the dead person .Her actions move Heaven and Earth. The tomb of Liang Shanbo abruptly opens and Zhu Yingtai leaps into it to her death. Later, the twin souls turn into dancing colorful butterflies.

Legend of Meng Jiangnv

Applicant: Zibo City, Shandong Province

This has been passed around most areas of China in literature and art forms such as story, ballad, poem and Chinese traditional opera over a period of more than 2,500 years.

In those days, the Emperor ordered the gathering up of vast numbers of young people to build the Great Wall to keep out foreign invaders. Considering that it would be very cold in north China in winter, Meng Jiangnv determined to carry winter clothing to her laboring husband. Unfortunately, by the time she reached the Great Wall, she found he was already dead. Hearing the bad news, she cried her heart out causing part of the wall to collapse.

The cries of Meng Jiangnv shocked Heaven and even changed the customs of the Qi State. Middle-aged or old women around present-day Zibo City still express their emotion and mourning with the traditional crying song of Meng Jiangnv on special occasions.

The story of Meng Jiangnv crying at the Great Wall is an important part of the ethnic traditional culture exerting much impact on the development of all folk literature.

Meng Jiangnv

The Story of Dong Yong and the Seventh Fairy Maiden

Applicant: Wangrong County, Shanxi Province, Dongtai City of Jiangsu Province, Wuzhi County of Henan Province, Xiaogan City of Hubei Province

When Dong Yong, born in the early Eastern Han Dynasty, was 18 years old, his father died of serious illness. Dong Yong, whose family circumstances were very poor, sold himself to a local landlord named Fu as a servant to raise funds to bury his father. The filial piety of Dong Yong deeply moved not only local people, but also the seventh daughter of the Jade Emperor of Heaven. The Fairy Maiden secretly came down to the human world and married Dong Yong. Then the couple went to the landlord's home to do manual work.

Dough sculptures of the Dong Yong and the Seventh Fairy Maiden

The Seventh Fairy Maiden heard that the Jade Emperor of Heaven, learning of her action, had ordered to return to Heaven immediately, otherwise he would cause great damage for Dong Yong. Not wishing to see this happen, she told Dong Yong the truth of her action and then returned to the clouds and leaving him extremely bitter.

The story of Dong Yong and the Seventh Fairy Maiden expresses the wish of people for lasting stability and peace. The love story corresponds to the inner emotions of people and is much loved for its combination of the supernatural conceit and ordinary life.

The Legend of Dong Yong widely circulated across China passed down from one generation to the next for 2,000 years, and has formed the basis of some local legends. Among the ancient books and records, there are numerous versions through much development and evolution. It has also been adapted into many operas. The earliest is the *Note of Brocade* of the Ming Dynasty, and the most famous is the Huangmei Opera telling the love story of a Heavenly Maid with an ordinary man.

The Tale of Xishi

Applicant: Zhuji City, Zhejiang Province

Xishi, the first of the Four Great Beauties of China, serves as the symbol of beauty in Chinese traditional culture.

Zhuji, the birthplace of the Tale of Xishi, located in central northern Zhejiang Province, was the capital of Yue State during the Spring and Autumn Period, when The Tale of Xishi originated. It was earliest recorded by both Mozi and Mencius, and passed down orally gradually becoming richer in content.

With the war between Wu and Yue states as the historical background, the tale sings the praises of the beautiful and kind Xishi who is willing to sacrifice her life for the country.

The important value of the Tale of Xishi lies in the following aspects: in terms of literature, it has provided a theme for many forms of literature. In terms of history, it provides valuable data on the history and culture of the two ancient states, playing an important role in researching the history of the Spring and Autumn Period. In the term of aesthetics, Xishi is beautifully from physically and mentally, reflecting the fine taste of Chinese people.

The Tale of Xishi has a long history of more than 2,500 years. It has also spread to South Korea, Japan, Southeast Asian countries like Singapore and Chinese-inhabited areas of other foreign countries. In addition to being passed down orally, the Tale of Xishi has been also made into dramas and plays.

The Tale of Monk Jigong

Applicant: Tiantai County, Zhejiang Province

The tale of Jigong is folk oral literature that evolved from the story of Daoji, a Zen Buddhist hierarch in the Southern Song Dynasty (1127-1279). It circulated originally in Tiantai County of Zhejiang Province but later spread to other parts of the country.

During the Six Dynasties, Sui and Tang Dynasties, there were many legends about an Arhat or insane monk circulating in Tiantai County. In the early Southern Song Dynasty, Daoji, born in Tiantai County, pretended to be insane in order to be able to help the people. During the Ming and Qing Dynasties, his story became widely known across the country.

The tale of Jigong, based on a real historical figure, emphasizes supernaturalism, embodies historical Zen thought and the Arhat religion, covers all aspects of life, and reflects the passions of the people. Common people like Jigong, because he cared about others, and defended them against injustice.

Over 800 years, the tale has been an endless literary resource. His story was also made into novels, paintings, sculptures, movies, and TV plays. Meanwhile, the tale, as a unique cultural phenomenon has been imprinted on minds of the people and can play a role in enhancing national morals and ethos.

Ulabun Biographical Singing and Talking

Applicant: Jilin Province

Changbai Mountain in southeastern Jilin Province is a vast, beautiful and supernatural area that was inhabited by ancestors of the Manchu people. Ulabun, or biography in the Manchu language, is an ancient folk art of singing and talking about Manchu heroic legends. In olden days, venerable elders of a Manchu tribe performed the "Ulabun" in their spare time, at holidays and worship ceremonies. The elders had to purify themselves and burn incense before the performance to pay their respects to the ancestors. They then sang and talked to the accompaniment of bells, drums, and other musical instrument.

Ulabun has independent plots and a complete structural system, showing the historical picture and colorful folk customs of the past 1,000 years. Its contents cover historical facts such as the meeting and parting of the clans, ancient expeditions, rise and fall of clans, heroic deeds, ancient sacrifices and the history of the ethnic group. It is actually an epic of the ethnic group in north China. Ulabun Biographical Singing and Talking was regarded as forming the living regulations of the ethnic group with grand religious coloring.

Ulabun lives on in the memories of the history of the Manchu people and their ancestors. Some contents found in books are rare, while other material makes up for the lack of historical recorded materials in north China, forming precious materials for the research into the history of the ethnic group, history of border area, anthropology, sociology and folklore.

Hexi Baojuan

Applicant: Liangzhou District, Wuwei City, and Suzhou District, Jiuquan City, Gansu Province

Hexi Baojuan (literally, Volumes of Treasure) is a type of popular folk literature based on Buddhist teachings when visiting monks told stories from Buddhism classics during the Tang and Song dynasties. It adopted the structure of Buddhism classics in Dunhuang, an artistic treasure trove with 492 grottoes of some 45,000 square meters of murals and 2,415 painted clay figures. Influenced by the script for story-telling, novel, modes of ancient Chinese music and traditional operas, its content covers Confucianism, Buddhism, Taoism and other mystic religions and contains non-religious stories about historical figures, folk myths and legends. There are more than 100 kinds of Hexi Baojuan, with themes about punishing evil and wrongdoings and advocating benevolence and filial piety. They were narrated and sung at temple fairs, recreational venues and in courtyards during the slack season or Spring Festival.

Baojuan circulates in oral and written forms. The stories are very long, the shortest being about 5,000 or 6,000 words, while the longest one contains 80,000-90,000 words. The local people consider that making a copy of Baojuan is a means of accumulating merits and virtues. Literate people who are willing to copy may keep the copied versions or present them to relatives and friends. Those who are not literate will invite others to copy to avoid evil. There are many woodcut and lithographic Baojuan.

Baojuan circulated in the Ming and Qing dynasties. In rural areas of present-day Hexi Prefecture of Gansu Province, Baojuan still has a vigorous life force. Around the Spring Festival and in the slack season, the activities of "Xuanjuan" (reading the volume) are conducted, thereby conserving a great number of versions mainly hand-written copies.

Now, more than 700 kinds of Hexi Baojuan have been collected. After removing repetitions, there are 110 items most of which come from the Central Plains.

The Folklore of Gengcun Village

Applicant: Gaocheng City, Hebei Province

Gengcun Village, under the jurisdiction of Chang'an Town of Gaocheng City of Hebei Province, is located in the Jizhong Plain. It is a small village that is home to around 280 households with 86.67 hectares of cultivated land.

The folk culture of Gengcun Village is a cultural phenomenon unique to Gaocheng City. Historically, Gengcun Village was located on the main road between Yangquan of Shanxi Province and Dezhou in Shandong Province. The bazaar and temple fairs here attracted believers and merchants from surrounding areas. The merchants brought with them not only all kinds of commodities but also stories and ballads. Gengcun villagers who went outside to trade, travel or fight also brought back stories and legends from different areas. Therefore, the place became a commodity and folk literature distribution center.

The all-inclusive folk tales in Gengcun Village contain myths on the creation of the world, legends of famous scenic spots, legends about historical figures and historical facts, and, later, stories of the Republic of China, the anti-Japanese war, liberation war and new living and new characters after liberation. Folk tales in Gengcun Village form a historic chain covering more than 170 counties (cities) of over 20 provinces, autonomous regions and municipalities directly under the Central Government, which form a relatively complete unofficial history of past dynasties of China.

In order to collect and arrange these tales, 10 large-scale general investigation teams were formed together working for 15 years. Some 11 collections of tales and special collections of tales containing 12 million words have been published. The Folk Culture in Gengcun Village with 4.55 million words, published in August 1999, is a collection of folk tales, ballads, proverbs and research fruits, and even an important work of significance in developing the treasury of folk culture.

Folklore of Wujiagou Village

Applicant: Danjiangkou City, Hubei Province

Wujiagou Village, under the jurisdiction of the Liuliping Town in western Danjiangkou City of Hubei Province, covers an area of 3.9 square km. It contains 223 households totaling 871 people, half of the adults being able to tell stories. The folklore there can be divided into six categories of myths, legend, stories, fables, jokes and fairy tales. Folklore Collection of Wujiagou Village is in two volumes containing 760,000 words. In the 1980s, over 1,000 folklore stories and some 1,000 folk songs were identified in the village, so it became 'A Village of Folklore'. In addition to folklore, there are many proverbs, riddles and two-part allegorical sayings. The Folklore of Wujiagou Village is called "a jewel of the nation" and a "living fossil" of Chinese folk culture.

The all-inclusive folktales in Wujiagou contain myths on the creation of the world, and stories of modern society and political and interesting news. The history of the place and its families is revealed through the tales.

Wujiagou, is a common and yet special phenomenon of folk culture containing Jingchu culture and Taoist culture, as well as a special form of village culture in China. Influenced by the Taoism of Wudang Mountain, the historical and folk culture of Wujiagou Village has formed a system with its own style and characteristics.

Folklore of Xiabaoping Township

Applicant: Yiling District, Yichang City, Hubei Province

Xiapuping Township of Yiling District of Yichang City of Hubei Province lies in mountains on the northern bank of Xiling Gorge of Yangtze River.

The folk literature here underwent a period of fusion of the ancient Jingchu culture and Bashu culture. There are over 2,000 folk stories circulating in Xiabaoping Township where almost all the persons can tell stories; according to a survey, over 100 people can tell at least 50, and more than 20 people with a repertoire of 100. Four people can tell over 200 stories and a 67-year-old peasant named Liu Defang from Tanjiaping Village has a fund of over 400 stories and can sing funeral songs totaling over a million words, shadow play operas, mountain songs and other folk songs. He has been named as China Folklore Master by the Chinese Folk Literature and Art Association.

Most tales have bright local features and high cultural quality and are the epitome of the folk literature in the areas around the Three Gorges Dam-Yiling district of Yichang City with high academic and appreciation value.

The tales are grouped into five categories, myth, historical stories, life-related tales, stories about clever people and folk jokes. The folktales have bright characteristics. Especially in the term of form, there are many with verses and couplets. They are told by combined speaking and singing, riddling and gestures.

Zouma Town Folklore

Applicant: Jiulongpo District, Chongqing City

Zouma Town lies in Jiulongpo District of Chongqing City, in which a kind of folk story orally created and passed down by those who make their living driving horses and known as Zouma (horse trotting) stories. The exact year of their origin is obscure but they prospered early in the Qing Dynasty. The stories then underwent synchronous development. The ancient town always attracted the traveling merchants, whose visits enabled the exchange of folktales.

Zouma Town Folklore has rich content in many types with many storytellers. It includes myths, legends about places, plants and animals, legends related to folk customs and stories on life. These stories contain rich cultural information. For example, the legend of dragons and snakes, the totem of the Ba people, is the important heritage of the ancient Ba culture. When the three collections of the Chinese Folk Literature were compiled in the 1980s, the list of some 10,915 folktales was collected and recorded, of which 9,714 have been finished. In addition, some 3,000 folk songs, 4,000 proverbs and 4,000 two-part allegorical sayings and common sayings have also been recorded. There were about 316 storytellers in the whole town, of whom two can tell 1,000 stories and three between 500 and 1,000.

Guyuyan Folk Stories

Applicant: Dawa County, Liaoning Province

Before the 1930s, there were many people coming to the mouth of the Liaohe River every Spring to catch fish and shrimps and returning to their own native place in the autumn. These people were called the "Yuyan Tribe". Unable to tackle the open seas, they traveled like migratory birds along the river banks to catch their prey. They created a great number of stories, fishing songs, and proverbs called "Guyuyan". These have disappeared now except along the Liaohe River. Guyuyan Folk Stories are known as a living fossil of ancient human fishing and hunting activities.

Guyuyan Folk literature circulating in Erjiegou, the mouth of the Liaohe River, include "Guyuyan" ancestral worship, "Guyuyan" sea god worship, "Guyuyan" dragon king worship, "Guyuya" sacrifice and celebration, and the origin and evolution of "Guyuyan" tools.

This folk literature, with bright living characteristics of Yuyan and inheriting primitive culture, shows the history, living customs, traditions, religion and cultural creation in an all-around way. In form, Guyuyan Folk Literature, short in length, with simple plots and primitive contents, has undergone few cultural changes.

Kharchin and Eastern Inner Mongolia Folklore

Applicant: Kharchin Mongolian Autonomous County, Liaoning Province

This is a kind of oral folklore circulating in Kharchin Mongolian Autonomous County. The storytellers, through narration and singing, have passed down the culture of the Mongolian people, featuring a fusion of grassland and farming culture in Eastern Inner Mongolia. There is no written language so it lives solely in people's memory.

Eastern Inner Mongolia folk literature includes folktales, legends, myths and folk songs. There are some expatiating on the philosophy of the remote ancestors of Mongolian people, such as worship of all things on earth like the Sun, Moon, and stars; tales about hunting and herding, such as archery, horse riding, milking and living in a Yurt; some tales describe farming, such as growing crops, chopping firewood and raising chickens and ducks. They express the passion and aspiration of the Mongolian people in farming production.

The tales that have been collected and recorded so far include all types of stories, and at the same time with their particular historic, local and artistic characteristics make clear to all that Eastern Inner Mongolia folk literature with rich content and wide themes is a precious cultural heritage of the Mongolian people and China.

Eastern Inner Mongolia folk literature works include 891 folktales, 213 ballads and 110 proverbs which have been included in five volumes of *Pearl of the Aomolun River* which is divided into sections on legends, stories, ballads and proverbs.

Tan Zhenshan's Folk Stories

Applicant: Xinmin City, Liaoning Province

Tan Zhenshn, a legendary storyteller, is the only individual in China included into the state-class intangible culture heritage list. Photo shows Tan Zhenshan is telling his neighbors' children stories.

Tan Zhenshan, a famous folktale teller whose ancestral home is in Hebei Province, was born in Taipingzhuang Village, Luojiafang Township, Xinmin City, Liaoning Province on the 10th day of the 11th month of 1925 in the traditional calendar. The village became home to people who migrated from Shandong, Henan and Hebei Provinces during the reign of Emperor Xianfeng of Qing Dynasty. The folktales recited by Tan cover legends, ghost stories, tales of historical figures and jokes. These stories were passed down basically by the families. Tan Zhenshan has lived and labored on the black earth for 80 years and has told stories in the fields, sitting on beds, at the street corner and in front of the gate for more than 70 years.

Tan Zhenshan's Folk Stories are passed down mainly orally. He can tell 1,000 stories, which is very rare in China and even in the world. His simple style is good at capturing listener attention and creating a good atmosphere. With high narration technique, he does not give prominence to the physical romance, but pays attention to tone and expressions. He is good at narrating devious and moving plots

The stories reflect in an all-round way the production, living, knowledge, wisdom, ideals and wishes of the people engaging in farming in the plains of the Lihe River drainage area, ands are of important cultural and historical value. Tan Zhenshan is rare among Chinese storytellers. Over the past 20 years, many famous and influential storytellers have passed away, So Tan Zhenshan is one of the very few oral litterateurs still living. He is the first individual in China named as a natural heritage and the sole storyteller to travel abroad.

Hejian Song Poem

Applicant: Hejian City, Hebei Province

Hejian City lies in the center of Jizhong Plains in the central southern Hebei Province. *Hejian Song Poem*, with its roots in *Shi Jing*, or the *Book of Songs*, is a typical representative of the pre-Qin dynasty oral literature kept alive by Shijing and other villages in Hejian County. Hejian Song Poem is a kind of old art form integrating folk literature and music that is now an important part of modern *Shi Jing* culture. It has been orally passed down for generations. During the slack season, the older generation get together to create poems in accordance with the old rhyming requirements with the accompaniment of Erhu, Zheng, a Chinese zither with 25 strings, and other musical instruments.

Wu Ballad

Applicant: Suzhou City, Jiangsu Province

Wu Ballad refers to folk songs like mountain songs, ditties and work songs sung in the Wu dialect in areas using this dialect, including southern Jiangsu Province, Northern Zhejiang Province, Shanghai, and other areas in the lower reaches of the Yangtze River. Legend has it that the king of the Zhou Dynasty sent his eldest son to found a capital in Wuxi in the 13th Century BCE, where he encouraged singing among local people. Hence, Wu Ballad has a long history of 3,000 years.

The area to the south of the lower reaches of the Yangtze River has a great treasury of folk songs. From the perspective of musical form, the Wu Ballad is divided into two categories, short song and long narrative song.

It includes two parts: song and ballad. The former refers to the mountain songs and folk songs, while the latter refers to doggerel verse. From the perspective of content, it includes love songs, labor songs, political songs, ritual songs and children's songs.

The Wu Ballad is sung orally among common people, which is the basic way of its artistic expression. The singers sing without instrumental accompaniment.

People in the lower Yangtze River area tend to be bright, gentle and soft, with fine sensibility so that the folk songs appear mild, roundabout, implicative, touching, and tortuous. They are sung in a low voice in the Wu dialect, taking on the beauty of Yin softness.

The love song of the Wu Ballad, represented by the Song of Midnight, is mild, roundabout, and implicative, giving a sense of "water". The expression of emotion is long, which circles in the minds of people.

Ballads of Liu Sanjie

Applicant: Yizhou City, Guangxi Zhuang Autonomous Region

Liu Sanjie (which translates as "third sister in the Liu family") is a legendary figure among the Zhuang people. The earliest legend may be found in the "Sanmei Mountain", volume 98 by Wang Xiangzhi

The Yufengshan Mountain in Guangxi Zhuang Autonomous Region, a place where Liu Sanjie, the Zhuang singer immortal, spreads the mountain songs, rides on a fish to the Heaven, and becomes celestial being.

in the Southern Song Dynasty. There were more books recording the legends and songs about her in the Ming and Qing dynasties. Many stories and songs about her are passed down orally among the Zhuang people.

According to legend, Liu Sanjie was born in 703. From childhood, she was so smart and good at singing that she was regarded as the "magic girl". At the age of 12, she was already famous for her extraordinary talent at improvising songs. Later, she taught singing in the neighboring areas. An endless stream of people came to sing with her in antiphonal style, and this could last from one to five days; at last, they had no words left to say and withdrew quietly. Her talent was much and eventually she was murdered by rogues in Liuzhou. Liu Sanjie was considered as the "Goddess of Song". Yizhou, the most representative area for her ballads, is recognized as her hometown.

The Ballads of Liu Sanjie are grouped in seven categories, songs of daily life, production songs, love songs, ritual songs, riddle songs, story songs and ancient genesis songs. The Third Day of the Third Month, the largest song festival in Zhuang inhabited areas, also called "the Festival of Immortals of Song", is a time when common people commemorate Liu Sanjie.

The Tune of Four-Season Production

Applicant: Honghe Hani-Yi Autonomous Prefecture, Yunnan Province

The Tune of Four-Season Production, the summary of the experience in farming in the famous Hani terrace, profoundly shows the whole process of the labor in the four seasons, breeding seed-rice, casting seedling, transplanting seedling, trashing rice and shipping the rice to the granaries. The Hani people living in Burma, Vietnam, Laos, Thailand and other southeast Asian countries also sing this old song. The Tune of Four-Season Production is comprised of five parts: the preface, third month of winter, third month of spring, third month of summer and third month of autumn, and has higher artistic value.

The Tune of Four-Season Production, known as Haba in the Hani language, which means "walking along the road that the ancestors created", is the mother of folk poems of the Hani ethnic group. It is sung without any performance movements or instrumental accompaniment. Its tone is very simple, unsophisticated, solemn, and slow. It has been preserved from being handed down orally over the centuries.

The song is structurally tight, easy to understand and can be both recited and sung. The language is lively and similar to real life. It has a long history, and not only shows the Hani's agricultural skills, but also their social ethics.

The Epic of Manas

Applicant: Kizilsu Kirgiz Autonomous Prefecture, and the Folk Litterateur and Artists' Association of the China Federation of Literary and Art Circles, Xinjiang Uygur Autonomous Region

The Epic of Manas is a traditional heroic epic poem of the Kirgiz people and one of the three major epics of the ethnic minorities. Manas is the name of the hero, a legendary Kirgiz leader and the embodiment of force, braveness and wisdom. This epic recounts the stories of Manas and seven generations of descendants who led the Kirgiz people in fighting bravely against cruel rulers from other races, eventually winning their freedom and happiness.

The Epic of Manas, originating in the 9th-10th centuries, has been polished by Kirgiz singers during the process of being circulated and has absorbed the wisdom of the ethnic group, thus having high artistry and strong ethnic characteristics. In addition, the epic also circulated in Central Asian countries like Kyrgyzstan, Kazakhstan, and Northern Afghanistan.

There are dozens of major war scenes vividly described. The color of the hair of the horse of the generals has over 30 varieties, let alone the descriptions of all kinds of weapons.

The Epic of Manas, an ethnic folk epic, is recited by specialists called Manaschi. Inviting a Manaschi to sing it during festivals has been a traditional custom of Kirgiz people. Over the past few centuries, without libretto and musical score, it has been passed down orally and translated into Russian, Chinese, Turkic, Japanese, English and Kazakh language. The United Nations designated the year 1995 as the "the Year of International Manas".

The Epic of Janggar

Applicant: Xinjiang Uygur Autonomous Region, Buke Sai'er Mongolia Autonomous County, Bo'er Tala-Mongolian Prefecture, Bayin Guoleng Mongolia Autonomous Prefecture, Folk Artists and Litterateur Association of China Federation of Literary and Art Circles in Xinjiang

The Epic of Janggar is a monumental work of ethnic folk literature originating from the voluminous heroic epic popular in the Ulat tribe of Mongolia in the Western Regions during the Song, Yuan and Ming Dynasties as well as one of the three major epics of the ethnic minorities. The epic that has been created and passed down orally for generations has retained its original state without amendment.

The Epic of Janggar, originating in about the 13th century, tells how a heroic group represented by Janggar successfully fought for their homeland named Bamba which is beautiful, strong and peaceful. The epic, with the military campaigns led by Janggar as the main thread, depicted the magnificent mountains and rivers and lush grassland of Bamba, singing of the braveness, honesty and selflessness of Janggar and showing the goodness, industry and wisdom of herders. It is mainly circulated orally and in scripts.

The Epic of Janggar, with its unique artistic charm, took root in the fertile soil of THE Mongolian people. From its birth, it was sung by Gyanggarchi, which means the folk artists specializing in singing the Epic of Janggar in Mongolian language, and passed down to this day through them. Gyanggarchi are respected by the herders for their pre-eminent memories and rich knowledge.

In 1771, arrangement of the Epic of Janggar began, which was originally conducted dispersedly by Mongolian aristocracy living in Xinjiang. The number of the chapters of different versions ranges from 12 to 32. As for how many chapters the *Epic of Janggar* has, *Chinese Literature: the Great Encyclopedia of China* says, "There are 60 versions collected, each containing 100,000 verses."

The Heroic Epic of King Gesar

Applicant: Tibet, Inner Mongolia, Sichuan Province, Yunnan Province, Gansu Province, Qinghai Province, and Xinjiang Uygur Autonomous Region, and The Gesar Study Office of Chinese Academy of Social Sciences

The Epic of Gesar or King Gesar, one of the three major epics of ethnic minorities, circulated mainly orally among the groups such as Tibetan, Mongolian, Tu, Yugu, Naxi and Pumi living on the Qinghai-Tibet Plateau. It narrates how King Gesar descends to the human world to rid it of demons, curb the strong, support the weak, unite all tribes and at last return to Heaven.

The longest epic in the world and an oral epic unusually shared by many ethnic groups, this is the crystallization of grassland nomadic culture, representing the highest achievements of folk culture and oral narrative art of the ancient Tibetan and Mongolian people. Many wandering singers performed it and passed it on.

At present, there are about 100 versions of King Gesar, each containing 500,000 verses. In length, it surpasses the total verses of the several famous epics in the world. There are about 100 Tibetan, Mongolian and Tu artists who can sing and narrate it and are both disseminators and creators of the epic. With the acceleration of modern processes, and because some artists are old and weak, the epic is on the verge of extinction.

The Legend of Ashima

Applicant: Shilin Yi Autonomous County, Yunnan Province

This is a classic love legend of the Sani people, one branch of the Yi ethnic group. Ashima, a smart, kind and beautiful girl falls in love with a brave, simple and honest young sheepherder called Ahei. Unfortunately Azhi, the son of the local tribal chief, imprisons Ashima to force her to marry him, but she refuses. Ahei hurries to rescue her and a jealous Azhi then creates a flood to drown the two lovers. Ashima turns into a stone elephant stationed in the rock forest.

The Stone Forest in Yunnan Province, a place where the touching Ashima Legendary took place

The story mainly circulates in areas inhabited by Sani people in Shilin Yi Autonomous County, Yunnan Province. The Legend of Ashima is called "Song of Our ethnic group" by the Sani people. The legend may be sung or recited on any occasion like weddings, funerals, and sacrifices. Though it is a narrative poem, the plot is not complicated. The Sani People sing its 1,560 verses to express their own emotion.

Larenbu and Jimensuo

Applicant: Huzhu Tu Autonomous County, Qinghai Province

This folk literature work narrates a tragic love story of a poor man named Larenbu, and Jimensuo daughter of the slave owner, with lively images, solemn and stirring languages and in storytelling and singing form. Larenbu and Jimensuo is a long folk poem of the Tu ethnic group, most widely spread among the Tu people with the most influence and known as the Butterfly Lovers of the Tu ethnic group. It was created and sung in the Tu dialect, and passed down orally among the Tu people and remains a living oral literature form.

The whole poem is composed of eight chapters comprised of singing and storytelling. It's one of the best-loved love songs of the Tu people. There are different versions in different areas. Larenbu and Jimensuo is sung mainly in antiphonal style, but differs from general antiphonal singing including questions and answers. The tune is unique, with a clear structure and arrangement is evident.

The story also reflects the shift of Tu people from a nomadic lifestyle to an agricultural one and is remarkably valuable for historical research.

Story Song of She People

Declarer: Xiapu County, Fujian Province

The Story Song originated in Bailukeng Village, Hounan Town, Xiafu County, Fujian Province about 100 to 200 years ago. This is a village where the She ethnic people are most densely gathered together and ethnic culture has deep roots; it is known as the First Village of Eastern Fujian Province. In the beginning, some singers of the She ethnic group who were able to be 识字adopted chapter stories and the story-telling lyrics of the Han people into their own songs in oral and written forms. Later, on the basis of the popular heroic stories of She people, some story song works were created in accordance with the lifestyle, thinking processes and language characteristics of She ethnic group, such as Gaohuang Song, Liqi Song, Zhong Liangbi, the Story of the White Snake, Ten Sages Song, Zhong Jingqi, and Lan Tian Jade. The Story Song, based on long stories, is a unique folk art and cultural carrier that the She ethnic people have created.

It is divided into four categories of ballad, novel song, traditional mountain song and modern mountain song, and shows the history of the She ethnic group in accordance with the emergence of the four categories.

It is the most representative cultural form of the She ethnic group and art form in Eastern Fujian Province, holding an important position in the history of culture and history of literature of the She people Today, 130 handwritten copies and oral songbooks remain.

Qinglinsi Conundrum

Applicant: Yidu City, Hubei Province

Qinglinsi Village lies in Gaobazhou Town in Hubei Province. The area has a long history and unique geography. People in the village are good at creating and guessing riddles. They are so crazy about them that almost every person can riddle. The villagers, young or old, male or female, can have a competition over their best works at any time. According to research, 15 percent of the village population has mastered 30 to 100 riddles, and five percent have mastered over 100.

In recent years this unique cultural phenomenon has attracted academic and expert attention from all over the country. Experts think it integrates entertainment, interest and knowledge, and is an important reference for research into the Chinese Folk literature, folklore and local records. Relevant departments has successively compiled and published six specials such as the Collection of Qinglinsi Riddles, Collection of Qinglinsi Riddles (continuation), Collection of Qinglinsi Riddles (selection), Collection of Qinglinsi Riddle Songs, The Qinglinsi Riddle Village of Hubei Province of China, and the Collection of Riddles on weddings, and set up an organization for the rescue and protection of Qinglinsi Riddles. The riddle songs been listed into the local teaching materials for elementary and middle schools in Yichang City. There are around 5,000 riddles in many types, including riddles on articles, things and words. Many of the riddles have higher cultural and artistic quality.

Folk Music

Zuoquan Blossom Tune

Applicant: Zuoquan County, Shanxi Province

Zuoquan County is located in the western parts of the Taihangshan Mountain in eastern Shanxi Province.

The Blossom Tune is a kind of mountain song, and is widespread throughout the area of the Taihangshan Mountain (East Mountain). Its lyrics are simple, but moving, and mostly consist of two phrases which echo each other. The rhythm is based on seven notes, with frequent shifts to express the highs and lows of the singers'emotions, thus creating an inspired piece of folk music.

Why is it called a Blossom Tune? Because the lyrics express the conception that not only plants but also tools, even stones, can blossom. For the Zuoquan people it becomes a metaphor by which they may express their pursuit of beauty.

The Zuoquan people love singing the Blossom Tune, and it is a feature of their daily life. Most of its variations express love in one form or another, and the people are quite unembarrassed about expressing their love in song.

Ever since the 1940s, music historians have been collecting the folk songs of Zuoquan County, and in the last half century or so have identified and recorded over 100 songs. Representative of these are *The Red Peach Blossom and The White Apricot Blossom, Dating one's Lover, Wanting to Kiss one's Lover* and *The Homelands Return to Every Family*.

Hequ Folk Song

Applicant: Hequ County, Shanxi Province

The Hequ Folk Song is widespread throughout Hequ County and northwestern Shanxi Province, as far as the junction of Shanxi and Shaanxi Provinces and Inner Mongolia Autonomous Region. Located on the floodplains of the Yellow River, Hequ County has poor transportation and barren land, and experiences extremes of drought and flood, inuring its local population to a lifetime of hardship and toil. Due to this special geographical environment, many people go to Daqingshan and Hetao in Inner Mongolia, to seek work as casual or long-term laborers. Their songs of lament describe separation, loneliness, and sadness.

The Hequ Folk Song is rich in content, speaking of every aspect of the singer's day to day life. The lyrics are naturalistic and deeply felt, and are often in the local dialects. The melodies are vivacious and have a wonderful aesthetic quality. Rhythm is free, and incorporates colloquial grace notes. So the Hequ Folk Song is typical of mountain folk song tradition.

The Hequ Folk Song is, in fact, a sort of encyclopedia, in the musical pages of which one can gain an idea of the whole society and life of Hequ County. Developed over countless generations, it is a living tradition, always truly representing the spirit of the people who sing it, while at the same time being a vital cultural link with a past that might otherwise recede entirely away.

The Urtiin Duu or "Long Song" of the Mongolian People

Applicant: Inner Mongolia Autonomous Region

Mongolian singers are singing the Urtiin Duu (long song).

The Urtiin Duu or "Long Song" of the Mongolian people is closely linked with the grassland they inhabit and the nomadic life they lead. Bearing witness to the history of the Mongolian ethnic group, is an expression of their day to day life, their hopes and aspirations. In November 2005, the Urtiin Duu was included by UNESCO in its third catalog of "Masterpieces of Oral and Intangible Heritage of Humanity".

The Urtiin Duu or "Long Song" is one of the two major forms of Mongolian songs, the other being the 'Short Song" (or Bogino Duu), and has existed for as long as the Mongolian people themselves. It is traditionally sung with few words and long, rolling notes Given its antiquity, we cannot be absolutely sure of its origins, but by placing it within the context of the musical culture of the Mongolian people as a whole, we can make the reasonable assumption that is a kind of folk song created by the nomadic tribes of north China whilst taking care of their herds, relaxing on the plains, or celebrating their various festivals. Its lyrics consist of two sentences, and within them the singers incorporate their own history and the beauties of their environment, including the grassland, horses, camels, cattle, sheep, vast blue skies, white clouds, rivers and lakes.

The Urtiin Duu is a lyrical chant, characterized by an abundance of musical ornamentation, falsetto notes, an extremely wide vocal range, and a free compositional form. The *Norgula* (literally tranliterated from the Mongolian word, grace note) is quite unique.

Meanwhile, the "Llong Song" retains its position as standard-bearer of the Mongolian culture as distributed throughout the Inner Mongolia Autonomous Region of China and the Mongolian Republic, and is much valued by both.

The Hoomii of the Mongolian People

Applicant: Inner Mongolia Autonomous Region

Hoomii is a kind of supernatural singing art, developed over a period of more than 800 years by the Mongolian people. Also known as'Throat-singing', it was widespread among the Mongolians of ancient times. Using the special technique of sounding, one person may simultaneously perform two voice parts, between which there is a range of six octaves. Hoomii is the outcome of the centuries-long development of Mongolian music, over which time the Mongolian people have made great progress in terms of knowing and mastering the laws of acoustics. Also known as "The Sound of Nature", Hoomii is unique among the Chinese folk songs of all the various ethnic groups.

Hoomii can be heard all across the Xilin Gol and Hulun Buir grasslands, as well as in Hohehot of the Inner Mongolian Autonomous Region and those Mongolian-inhabited areas by the Altai in Xinjiang Uygur Autonomous Region. It can even be heard as far away as gthe steppes of Russia.

Hoomii, one of the oldest art forms of the Mongolian ethnic group, has preserved many of its original elements, especially in regard of the primitive style of singing. It is a kind of long-reverberating echo in the deep and collective memory of the Mongolian people, being closely bound up with their history and culture.

Dangtu Folk Song

Applicant: Ma'anshan City, Anhui Province

Dangtu County is located on the eastern border of Anhui Province and on the east bank of the lower reaches of the Yangtze River.

Over many many years, the people of Dangtu County have created a great number of oral literary works inspired by their daily life, chief amongst which is the widely-known Dangtu Folk Song. With its wonderful melody and brisk rhythm, it is unique to the watery margins south of the lower reaches of the Yangtze River, although its popularity has spread all across the county. It is encompasses a number of variations, and its lyrics cover pretty much all the aspects of Dangtu social life. In addition, there are a number of folk songs specific to the plains, the hills and the mountains.

Those popular in Dagongyu are haozi, ox song, and dance tune; those most prevalent in Bowang and Huyang are the boat song, fishing song and lantern song; and those we find in Caishi and Xinqiao along the Yangtze River include the seedling song, antiphonal song and door song. Dangtu Folk Songs are an expression of the daily lives and occupations of the local people, in addition to which they are of important aesthetic value, exerting a significant influence on the local culture through their uniqueness, charm of language, and narrative style. Dangtu folk songs are part of an oral tradition, being passed from performer to performer, and each of which is part of the treasurey of local music and language.

Chaohu Folk Song

Applicant: Chaohu City, Anhui Province

Chaohu City, in Central Anhui Province, home to the Hexian County Ape-man Site, is one of the birthplaces of Chinese culture.

Along with the ancient history of Chaohu City itself, the Chaohu Folk Song has undergone an evolution from the simple to the more complicated and from having one form to several. Dating back to the Northern Song (1127-1279) and Yuan (1206-1368) Dynasties, it is the most traditional folk music in Chaohu City, as well as being representative of folk songs in the area between the Yangtze and Huaihe Rivers. It is also an excellent example of Chinese folk music culture. Chaohu people love singing and writing folk songs, and wherever they go turn the sights and sounds around them into song. Chaohu folk songs are grouped into three categories—haozi, mountain song and ditty.

Over the past few years, cultural historians have collected more than 1,000 primitive Chaohu folk songs. Representative works include the *Dialogue Between The Daughter and Her Brother's Wife*, and *Singing Yangtze*, as well as the ever-popular rural folk dances, *Sister Liu* and *Frightening Hawk*. To this day, the composing and singing of Chaohu folk songs goes on.

Folk Song of the She Ethnic Group

Applicant: Ningde City, Fujian Province

The She ethnic group mainly live in the eastern part of Fujian Province and the north of

The Shes hold the song festival on the 3rd day of the 3rd lunar month.

Zhejiang Province.

This ethnic group has a long history. The Chinese character meaning slash-and-burn cultivation, was adopted as its name back in the time of the late Southern Song Dynasty. The She ethnic group has its own customs and language, of which singing mountain songs is an important part. All the people, men and woman, old and young, are good at singing. With no written language, the She people have passed down their culture and music by oral transmission.

The folk songs of the She people are rhyming compositions in either a four- or seven-character format. Each song consists of four sentences, the first of which has three or five characters. They can be sung solo, or else in the form of antiphonal singing and chorus. The catagories into which they fall include narrative songs, songs celebrating local customs, labor songs, seasonal songs, epic songs, revolutionary songs, children's songs and miscellaneous songs. The mountain song without accompaniment is a particular favorite of the She people

The period from the 15th day of the 8th lunar month to the 3rd day of the 3rd lunar month of the following year is traditionally the season when the She people sing. Especially during the 1st lunar month, and the 3rd day of the 3rd lunar month, the 15th day of the 8th lunar month, the 9th day of the 9th lunar month and any other holidays, the She people always visit their relatives and friends in groups, and hold a splendid song festival. These are the best times to hear and appreciate the folk songs of the She ethnic group.

The Folk Songs of the She ethnic group are an important part of their traditional culture. Most have been preserved in the memories of the She people themselves, and are passed down from generation to generation, although some copies have been hand-written in the Chinese language. The principle song, consisting of 112 poems, records and narrates the legends of the She people. It is a special treasure, handed down from ancient times and representing a culture spanning many hundreds of years.

Xingguo Mountain Song

Applicant: Xingguo County, Jiangxi Province

Xingguo County is in the south of Jiangxi Province under the jurisdiction of Ganzhou City. Some 95 percent of its population is made up of the Hakka people, whose ancestors are said to have migrated from the Central Plains.

Xingguo Mountain Song is a blend of the culture of the Central Plains and the local aboriginal culture. With its unique style, flexible form, changeful techniques, lively language and wonderful rhythms, it has been sung for hundreds of years, becoming a bright jewel in the crown of Chinese folk arts. Xingguo was named as the "Town of Mountain Song—a Chinese Folk Art" by the Ministry of Culture.

The song is fluent, with a great freedom in its music, and is redolent of local color. There is a tone of "Aiyalai" at the beginning of the song, with its rhythm extending on the alto, acting as a bold and unrestrained introduction. Xingguo Mountain Song is wide-ranging in content, featuring, in addition to love and daily labor, historic stories, legends and current affairs. Some are improvised, whereas others follow a pre-set narrative and can be very long.

Xingguo Mountain Song has deep roots in the culture of the Hakka people, covering various aspects of their life and presenting the listener with a wealth of information about their world. In a sense, one might describe it as an historical scroll painting depicting the life and history of the Hakka people. The great works include *Embroidered Bag* and *Eulogizing the Eight Immortals*.

Xingshan Folk Song

Applicant: Xingshan County, Hubei Province

Xingshan Folk Songs are widespread in various towns and townships of the Xinshan County of Hubei Province and the neighboring areas to the east, south and north of the County. In recognition of its unique style it has been officially named "Xingshan Folk Song" by the Ministry of Culture.

According to textual research, the Xingshan Folk Song has a continuous history of more than 800 years. However, there are no written records of the original music or lyrics, which present difficulties in performance. It has a special interval between the major and minor third, which cannot be found in the standard intervals of modern music, and has hence been given the name 'the third interval of Xingshan'. The style of song itself also goes by the name of "third interval folk song with Xingshan features." It can be sung by everybody, men or women, young or old, in the villages of Xinshang County. Its variations are grouped into the haozi, mountain song, field song, lantern song, ditty, local custom song and daily life song. Even the tears of lovelorn young girls have been set to music

With a history of more than 2,000 years, Xingshan Folk Song has attracted the attention of experts and scholars in the musical world, and has been described as the "living fossil of Bachu Ancient music", proving that Chinese ancient folk art is not lost and that its ethnic music continues to thrive. Its unique features give it an enormous value in the research of the history of Chinese ancient music and the way in which that music has been passed down.

Xingshan Folk Song was traditionally accompanied by the Xingshan Gong and the Drum for Pulling Up Weeds (also the Xingshan Drum for Funerals). With changing times, however, these implements have ceased to be part of the workers'daily lives, and it is estimated that some 90 percent of the folk artists who still use the Xingshan Gong and the Drum for Pulling Up Weeds are above 90 years old.

Sangzhi Folk Song

Applicant: Sangzhi County, Hunan Province

Sangzhi County is located in the northwest of Hunan Province. Sangzhi Folk Song, having its roots in the productive labor practised during the primitive farming period, is simple, coarse, unconstrained and full of humor.

Sangzhi folk songs are grouped as follows: mountain songs, ditties, and ritual songs, covering a broad spectrum of traditional folk songs. With their precise structure, diversified tunes, and unique harmonies, they are redolent of ethnic style and full of local color. They reach their artistic height by the manner in which they incorporate atmosphere and reveal the innermost emotions of the singer.

These singers like to perform songs which combine vocal technique with the lyrics, ethnic language and rustic features. While singing, they are adept at expressing different thoughts and emotions. Representative works of the Sangzhi Folk Song such as *Walnut Blossoms All in a Line, Flowers that Blossom in All Seasons, Hanging a Lamp over the Door* and *Sipping Slowly the Tea Made With Cold Water are classics* in the great treasury of Chinese folk song.

According to literary sources, there are a total of 10,000 Sangzhi folk songs. They have been put into different categories and adapted over the years. They include 1,400 mountain songs, 129 flower lantern airs, 200 ditties, over 100 work songs, and 66 local custom songs, containing more than 500,000 words.

The Sangzhi Folk Song is the product of the geographical environment and the close or half-close subsistence state unique to Sangzhi County. There are many recorded ballads mirroring the primitive religion of this area. The three-sentence-format lyrics are of great interest to scholars and historians, for they provide precious information and specific examples of ethnic tradition for those researching the diversification of the Chinese folk song, and reflect the simple philosophy of the Sanzhi people.

Meizhou Hakka Mountain Song

Applicant: Meizhou City Guangdong Province

A girl ensemble from Meizhou, Guangdong Province sing the Ballad of Hakka Meeting Guests without accompaniment.

Hakka Mountain Song is the most illustrious branch of Chinese folk music, featuring such a wide transmission and so great an influence that other folk traditions despair of comparison. It is the ballad sung by the Hakka farmers in mountain villages of their homeland.

Meizhou Hakka Mountain Song is the folk tune that approximately five million people in the territory of Meizhou City sing in the Hakka dialect, and serves as the oral literature of the entire Hakka population. It is widespread in the Hakka-inhabited area of northeastern Guangdong Province and has been carried everywhere that Hakka people have settled.

The Meizhou Hakka Mountain Song has been passed down through generations. It is a blend of the culture of the Central Plains and the aboriginal culture of Meizhou. Its lyrics are very poetic and similar to the Zuzhi Ci, with elements of Guofeng and Wu Songs.

Meizhou Hakka Mountain Song originated in the Tang Dynasty (618-907) and has a history of more than 1,000 years. As the most independent of the famous Chinese folk songs, it has over 100 varieties of aria, and 200 other distinct folk ditties. It is characterized by its loud, fluent and slightly undulating tone, narrow range, free rhythm, and diversified meter. From a cultural perspective, the Hakka Mountain Song is not stagnant, but develops with the times, representing contemporary fashions and thought.

Zhongshan Xianshui Song

Applicant: Zhongshan City, Guangdong Province

Xianshui Song is a kind of folk music that the people living in the Zhujiang Delta have sung for generations. With its simple melodies, it is easy to remember and perform. Those people who can speak Cantonese are able to sing the Xiangshui Song. The people living in Tanzhou of Zhongshan City in Guangdong Province have developed the habit of singing in an antistrophic style, competing with each other musically while they harvest the fields or cast their fishing nets. Especially during wedding and funeral ceremonies, they sing improvisationally, their performance heightened by the feelings engendered by the occasion. With its long history, Xianshui Song is popular throughout Tanzhou of Zhongshan City, and the traditional way of singing has been maintained. For example, when sung in the Zhongshan dialect of the Cantonese it includes the purely ornamental words "Alie" and "A", and the ornamental sentences "Mei Hao Alie" and "Di Hao Alie". Performances are improvised.

Xianshui Songs are divided into long and short. Most of the traditional examples are love songs.

Xianshui Song is closely linked with the daily life of the people living on the water, and takes its basic rhythm from the rocking of a boat or the rippling of the waves. It mainly features regular rhythms, with the eighth and sixteenth notes used in turn. To meet the needs of language and feeling, a form of syncopation has been developed, so that the irregular rhythms are made to change in the contraposition, thus giving a beautiful and smooth effect. When people listen to the Xianshui songs it is as though they see thousands of boats competing.

Yazhou Folk Song

Applicant: Sanya City, Hainan Province

Yazhou Folk Song refers to a kind of ballad with its unique and precise poetic metre sung in a dialect unique to the countryside of Xiliuli of ancient Yazhou, and surrounding areas. One of the principle genres of folk songs in Hainan Province, it is popular in Sanya, Huangliu of Ledong County and the territory of the ancient Yazhou, where it continues to be sung to this day. Without over-elaborate verbal effects, the performers still manage to infuse the melodies with passion, and, in unpretentious language, vividly express their deep love of life.

Yazhou Folk Song features many themes and is subsequently rich in content. Its lyrics, in the seven-character style, cover human history, the love of nature, day to day work, social activities and all the other various aspects of life. They feature no less than 100 narrative poems, each of which is a litery gem in the folk history of Yazhou. With wonderful, sweet-sounding melodies, Yazhou Folk songs are grouped into the haozi, the peddling tune, heartthrob tune, and lamenting tune. Representative songs include *Seeing Boyfriends Off*, *Liang Song*, *Zhang Song*, and

Meng Lijun.

Yazhou Folk Song is grouped into four categories— long ballads, life-long ballads, short songs and liberally improvised call-and-response songs. The singers of the call-and-response songs have a great capacity for immediate improvisation, and are happy to perform all through the night.

Danzhou Tunes

Applicant: Danzhou City, Hainan Province

Danzhou Tunes are actually a combination of folk song and dance widespread in Danzhou City of Hainan Province, known as "The Wonderful Flower Flourishing in Southern China". They originated from the northern part of Danzhou during the Western Han Dynasty. Danzhou has been named "the home-town of Chinese folk art" by the Ministry of Culture in recognition of its various musical and artistic forms.

The words of Danzhou Tunes are in the Danzhou dialect. With a lucid and lively rhythm, beautiful melody, and impassioned feeling, Danzhou Tunes may simply be sung or else might accompany a dance. They feature antiphonal singing by the male and female choruses, who themselves blend song and dance. They offer an excellent example of the heritage of folk culture.

There is no fixed time or occasion for performances. Singing might spontaneously break out on the mountains or in the valleys during the slack season in farming or on holidays, the young men and women holding impromptu vocal competitions. However, the yearly Mid-Autumn Danzhou Tunes Day is traditional, with thousands of people participating in song. When singing, the men and women usually stand face to face in two rows or a ring, and dance hand in hand with their bodies swaying in time to the music. Danzhou Tunes feature wonderful melodies and beautiful accompanying dance movements. Usually, during the song, the men pose questions and the girls respond. The whole performance has salient local features and a unique artistic style.

Danzhou Tunes have many airs in common use, and from these, with some changes, new melodies are composed. Over 600 tunes have been collected over the past few years. Representative works include *Loyal to Love No Matter What*, *Our Beautiful Motherland*, *Three Moments When I Missed Thee*, and *Dull Drumbeats*

The Danzhou Municipal Government has designated the 15th day of the 8th lunar month as the "Mid-Autumn Danzhou Tunes Day" in order to help preserve traditional Danzhou Tunes in a practical way.

Shizhu Tujia Luo'er Tune

Applicant: Shizhu Tujia Autonomous County, Chongqing

Shizhu Tujia Autonomous County of Chongqing City is located where the Wulingshan Mountains and the Yangtze River meet. Shizhu Tujia Luo'er Tune gets its name from the "Luo'er" of the Tujia mountain dialect. Most of the lyrics are in seven-character, four-sentence style. They are easy to understand, mirroring the life, labor, folk-customs, emotions, religious beliefs and other aspects of the Tujia people's daily lives, and also record their manners and customs, revealing the overall evolution of their unique ethnic culture.

Shizhu Tujia Luo'er Tune has a simple rhythm, the range of which is within a given scale. With relatively little ornamention, the tunes are smooth and undulating, making them quite easy to master. Some are traditional; others improvised. They are of great value to those conducting research into the history of Bayu, as well as their interest purely as art.

Over the years, Shizhu Tujia Luo'er Tune has become an independent genre within the folk song tradition, featuring a rich and diversified content, simple and lilting melody, and a full-bodied local flavor. It includes songs celebrating life, love, and the mountains where its singers make their home. There are antiphonal songs, humorous songs, haozi and other varieties. Of the numerous individual works, of special mention is *The Sun Rises Happily*, which is sung all over the country.

Song of the Bashan Back-Carriers

Applicant: Bazhong City, Sichuan Province

Song of the Bashan Back-Carriers can be dated back 3,000 years, and originated in the territory of Bashan City in the northeastern part of Sichuan Province.

Bazhong City, located in a remote mountainous area, was, before the advent of modern transport, an out-of-the-way place, to and from which supplies and trading goods were carried on the backs of porters, who thus became known as "Back Carriers". The song they sang while taking a rest on the mountain paths is that which we still know as the *Song of the Bashan Back-Carriers*. It was traditionally sung by a leading singer, with the other resting porters joining in the chorus.

The lyrics of the song are mainly in the seven-character format. They are intended to be humorous, are all improvised. Loud yet melodious, with a bullish and bold style, the song ends with an exaggerated coda of signing and groaning, expressive of the weariness caused by carrying heavy loads up the mountain tracks. *The Song the of Back-Carriers* is an excellent example of a folk song based on the daily lives of its original singers. During the Qin and Han Dynasties, an ancient route for carrying rice ran through the territory of Bazhong City, connecting Chang'an (Xi'an) with Chengdu. It was this line of communication that the first Back-Carriers enlivened with their song, the song itself being a musical embodiment of the spirit and culture of the Bashan people, without reference to which no meaningful history of their culture would be complete. It bears excellent witness to their natural conditions and social customs. A representative work is the one entitled *Climbing Slowly Up the Slopes With a Heavy Loads on My Back*.

Folk Song of the Lisu Ethnic Group

Applicant: Yunnan Province

Lisu people mainly live in Nujiang Lisu Autonomous Prefecture and Weixi Lisu Autonomous County of Yunnan Province. They have their own language, which belongs to the Yi branch of the Tibetan-Burmese language family, itself included within the Chinese and Tibetan language family.

The Lisu people love to sing, and their folk songs, characterized by their rich melodies, are both simple and moving. Most of the traditional dances are performed in groups. Some imitate the movements of animals, whereas others represent the Lisu people's daily work and recreation. In fact, the Lisu people have always had a tradition of singing while going about their day to day tasks, and are particularly well-known for their love songs.

The folk songs of the Lisu ethnic group can be grouped into four categories according

Two Lisu women singing the guest-meeting song to welcome the guests

to the quality of the melody. The first is the Mogua air, suitable to be sung by the middle-aged and elders of the village. Loud and sonorous, it is mainly used as the basis of the Ancient Song, Production Tune, House-Building Tune and Funeral Song. Second is the love song, that can be performed by either young men or girls. After the leading singer sings the introduction, all the other people present take up the tune while making all kinds of dance movements. Every song ends with the "Yalayi" with its warm and tender melody. Third is the category of Sorrowful Songs, used to express pain, grief and indignation. Its lyrics relate tales of misfortune, such as lovers having to part for ever. Fourth is a short song used to express yearning for absent friends or lovers. With a lively and melodious tune, it is suitable for expressing emotion and is particularly popular with young girls.

The folk songs of the Lisu ethnic group are well-diversified. They can be sung and enjoyed by all the people, young or old. When out in the open air, climbing the mountains and or walking through the fields, people improvise songs to give voice to their feelings. The music varies in tempo, so as to express gladness, contentment or sorrow.

Ziyang Folk Song

Applicant: Ziyang County, Shaaxi Province

Ziyang Folk Song is the general term for the folk songs that are produced in, and widespread throughout, the territory of Ziyang County of Shaanxi Province. It is the representative genre of the folk songs of southern Shaanxi Province. Combining vivid lyrics and wonderful melodies, it has both general artistic value and a specifically local style.

The Ziyang Folk Song genre is rich in haozi, mountain songs, simple ditties, local songs, and songs telling of local customs, but are officially all grouped within the first three categories. There are over a dozen kinds of tunes. Overall, they are suitable for expressing and reflecting the complicated feelings of the singer's character. They are also very representative of the style of folk songs popular in southern Shaanxi Province.

The Labor Haozi is the cornerstone of the Ziyang Folk Song, while The Boatman's Haozi is, in its turn, the most popular of the Labor Haozi, holding an important position among the Ziyang people with its rough and bold style and complicated and changeful melodies. The category of Mountain Songs refers to all kinds of mountain and steppe songs with the exception of Labor Haozi. Most of them are the expression of love. The ditty, like the mountain song, has numerous variations and is widely sung. It features an exquisite, fluent tune within a narrow range. Its narrative (non-improvised) lyrics are full of individual feeling.

Of the 5,028 songs identified in Ziyang, 828 have been compiled into a book and printed. They include all the types discussed above, of which some representative examples are *Boyfriends Are Singing the Mountain Songs*, *Washing Clothes* and *Bamboo on Nanshan Mountain*.

Folk Song of the Yugur Ethnic Group

Applicant: Su'nan Yugur Autonomous County , Gansu Province

Yugur girls festivaly singing and dancing

The Yugur people represent an ethnic minority group living along the Silk Road, and originating from the Huigur who lived a nomadic life in the reaches of the Erhun River in the Tang Dynasty (618-907). It has a population of 10,569.

The Yugur people use two varieties of language. One is called Shohor, belonging to the Turkic language family of Altai phylum and being closely related to the Uygur and Kazak languages, which also belong to the same language family. The other is Angar, which shares many features with the Mongolian language, to which linguistic family it also belongs. Because the original Yugur written language was lost many years ago, the ethnic culture and history of the Yugur people has been passed down by their folk singers throughout successive historical periods. Therefore, the folk music of the Yugur is very developed. It also incorporates some characteristics of the songs of the ancient Tingling, Turks and Huigurs. They are very similar to the folk songs of Hungary.

Folk music works of the Yugur ethnic group are quite simple in structure, reflecting the ancient ways of production and daily life (such as walking through the fields, breast-feeding puppies, drinking wine, and harvesting the grass), and the singers'customs and habits. The rules and forms of its lyrics have a quite significant amount in common with the folk songs in the Turkish language and the folk songs of the Mongolian people as recorded in ancient literary sources. They share many features of both these ancient languages, and thus provide a fascinating and historically valuable link with the past.

Folk Song of the Yugur Ethnic Minority Group is divided under the headings "Narrative Songs", "Love Songs" and "Labor Songs" according to its theme and content, and also into popular tunes, *haozi*, ditties, banqueting songs, toasting songs, felt-rolling songs and pup-breast-feeding songs in terms of its type and function.

As at the time of writing, Su'nan County has collated more than 310 of the Yugur ethnic people's traditional songs.

Hua'er

Applicant: Gansu Province, Qinghai Province and Ningxia Hui Autonomous Region

Hua'er, literally meaning flower, is a unique form of love song found among the ethnic minorities of Gansu and Qinghai Provinces and Ningxia Hui and Xinjiang Uygur Autonomous Regions. It is specific to the Muslim religeon. With a vast number of separate lyrics and high literary value, it is known as the Soul of Northwest China. The Hui people particularly hold this kind of song in high regard, and have appointed themselves its creators, singers, preservers and disseminators.

With a long history, rich content, various forms and exquisite melodies, Hua'er boasts an intense ethnic flavor characterised by the direct, intensely masculine style typical of the plateau. Some are narratives, whereas others are

Hua'er is a unique form of folk song mainly prevailing among the ethnic minorities in Gansu, Qinghai, Ningxia and Xinjiang. Photo shows a folk singer singing.

extemporised expressions of emotion. Some are in the four-sentence format, while others are six-sentence pieces. Some are sung solo, others in unison. Hua'er has enjoyed a great reputation ever since the time of the Emperor Qianlong's reign during the Qing Dynasty. The Han, Tibetan, Hui, Tu and Salar people living in the northwest of China will all sing the Hua'er whenever the opportunity presents itself, whether working in the fields, climbing the mountainside, fixing tools, or even riding in the bus.

Influenced by the different cultures of the various ethnic groups in Northwest China, there emerged many different genres and art styles across the region. The Ningxia Hua'er, for example, has more than 30 distinct airs. During the 6th and 7th lunar months, the grand Hua'er meetings will be held in Gansu and Qinhai Provinces, Ningxia Hui Autonomous Region and Xindu, attracting enthusiasts from various areas. The number of the participants can range from thousands to tens of thousands. There are 10 venues for holding the grander hua'er meeting Just in Ningxia Hui Autonomous Region alone there are 10 venues designated for these grand assemblies of music lovers.

Tibetan Lagzhas

Applicant: Hainan Tibetan Autonomous Prefecture, Qinghai Province

Lagzhas are a kind of mountain song indigenous to the Tibetan-inhabited areas in Qinghai, Gansu and Sichuan Provinces where people speak the Amdo dialect. They were born of the Tibetan mountain songs. Thanks to the division of the three Tibetan-inhabited areas in the 7th century, Lagzhas spread widely throughout the Amdo-speaking world.

In content they are love songs, by means of which the young Tibetan men and girls can pour out their hearts. With a long history, they are widely sung in Hainan Tibetan Autonomous Prefecture of Qinghai Province. The annual Lagzhas competition gives prominence to the featuring of Hainan's Lagzhas, well-known in the Tibetan-inhabited area of Qinghai Province. Traditionally, their lyrics tell of first meeting, first love, developing acquaintance, true love, and finally the sorrow of parting. It is lively, wonderful and touching in form. More than just love songs, in fact, they touch upon the economy, politics, culture and history of the Tibetan-inhabited areas, and help to preserve the simple and rustic lifestyle of ancient times.

These songs are not intended to be sung at home or in the village, but rather out in the boundless open-air of the mountains and steppes. They feature circumlocutory and lyric tunes, with developed lento and free rhythm. With no great changes in rhythm, they are made moving by the quality of the singing. Without fixed lyrics, they are improvised according to the emotion of the moment. Also, many poems of the 6th Dalai Lama Cangyang Gyamco have been set to music.

Lagzhas, with their long history, are synchronous with the process of the development of the Tibetan ethnic group, bearing witness to its creativity and inspiration. It is of extremely important value for the research into the anthropology, ethnology and folklore of the region and its people.

Liaozhai Liqu

Applicant: Zibo City, Shandong Province

Liaozhai Liqu is an ancient folk song widespread in Zibo City of Shandong Province. The Pu Family and their descendants were its inheritors. Pu Songling (1640-1715), a literary master during the Qing Dynasty, set his own librettos to the already extant tunes that were popular at the time. These works, written in the Zibo dialect, and combining singing and spoken dialogue, are similar to contemporary local opera. Pu Songling wrote an anthology of Strange Stories from a Chinese Studio, hence the name Liaozhai Liqu or Pu Songling Liqu.

In his later years, Pu Songling completed 15 Liqu, and used more than 50 named tunes. They include Playing with a Child, Red Lotus and Piled Broken Bridge.

Most Liqu are an expression of the daily life of the farmers, whereas others draw their subject matter from myth, historic events, love stories and legends. The language is that of the common people, and introduces folk proverbs and two-part allegorical sayings, with a humorous, lively and interesting style. Liaozhai Liqu, which reached the high-water mark of their development about 300 years ago, have always been associated with the Qing Dynasty, and is unique to Shandong Province. With its unique charm, it has helped to promote the development of other arts (opera, for example). Its stories have formed the dramatic basis of the Wuyinxi, Liuzi, Sichuan, Peking, Qinqiang and Hebei Bangzi Operas.

Jingzhou Miao Geteng

Applicant: Jingzhou Miao–Dong Autonomous County, Hunan Province

Qiuli of Jingzhou County is located in southwestern Hunan Province at the junction of the Hunan and Guizhou Provinces. About 20,000 Miao people live there.

Geteng of the Miao ethnic group is a kind of multi-voice-part chorus, which evolved from the sounds of nature. In the old Miao-inhabited villages, due to the beautiful natural environment and simple yet joyful life, the ancestors of the Miao people had a special interest in the harmony of nature, such as the warbling of birds, the sound of the cicada, running water and the rustlings of the forest, all of which produced a mental association from which they composed high and low overlapping tunes by imitating the harmony of the natural world. Since then, Geteng of the Miao ethnic group has been passed down from generation to generation, and has become known as the living fossil of primitive folk songs.

Geteng of the Miao ethnic group in Jingzhou County may be divided under the headings of tea song, toast song, meal song, mountain song, and fetching-water song. Its lyrics, in the seven-character, four-sentence style, incorporate historical legend, sacrifice ritual, production, labor, marriage, and love. The Mountain Song, Fetching-water song, and Tea Song are representative of these Geteng songs. They are sung in the local dialect of the Miao people.

Chuanjiang Haozi

Applicant: Chongqing City and Sichuan Province

Chuanjiang Haozi is the song that the boatmen near the Three Gorges sing when towing a boat upstream, sculling and oaring. It is an important form of Labor Song.

When, in olden days, the wooden boats were taken upstream or across dangerous shoals they had to be towed. Chuanjiang Haozi is a kind of folk song featuring a solo leading singer and a group of responding singers. The 1,000-km section of the Yangtze River from Yibin City to Yichang City, known as Chuanjiang River, with its treacherous shoals, numerous reefs and turbulent current, presents a multitude of hardships and dangers. Chongqing City and eastern Sichuan Province serve as the main cradle of the Chuanjiang Haozi, as well as the center from which it has subsequently been passed down.

The leader of the song is called the Haozi Head, who commands the other sailors by changing the pace or volume of his singing, and is thus much respected by the boatmen.

Haozi, Work Songs have a long history. Their rhythms are closely connected with those of different forms of labor, and are classified as forest work songs, agricultural work songs, boatman work songs, fisherman work songs, construction work songs, transportation work songs, and workshop work songs, as well as others.

Nanxi Haozi

Applicant: Qianjiang District, Chongqing

Nanxi Haozi is widespread in Qianjiang District of Chongqing City, and can be dated back to the Tang Dynasty (618-907). Its embryonic form was the labor haozi and mountain song haozi that the Tujia people sang to recover from fatigue and pep themselves up during rest breaks in their work. Haozi is sung by no less than seven people. They include a leading singer, two or three tenors, and several basses, but all follow the same tune.

When young men and girls sing it is nine times out of ten in antiphonal style, while a similar proportion of the mountain songs are love songs. With their improvised lyrics, Nanxi haozi are sung without the accompaniment of musical instruments, and have been passed down for generations by oral teaching, i.e. there is no written notation. Each singer is free to respond to what he or she sees around them, or how they feel in their hearts. A mountain song is commenced by one person, and then taken up by others.

The content of the Nanxi Haozi, relating as it does to the history, geography and folklore of the Tujia ethnic group, offers us a wealth of ancient historical and cultural information. At the time of writing, there are just 10 old men who can really sing the pure form of Nanxi Haozi, of whom the oldest is 78 years old and the youngest 58.

Mudong Mountain Song

Applicant: Banan District, Chongqing

Mudong Mountain Song is a genre of mountain songs specific to the people in Mudong Town of Banan District of Chongqing City. Its origins can be traced back to ancient Bayu song and dance, which gradually evolved into the Mudong Mountain Song as we now know it.

Mudong Mountain Songs are highly representative of Bayu folk songs as a whole. They have their roots in the daily labor of field and slope, and possess a unique style. In addition to reflecting labor practices, refreshing the singers when they are tired, staving off boredom, and promoting social contactrelationship, they have the important function of expressing the singers' ideas, feelings and spiritual beliefs. Mudong Town is located among the hills, so mountain songs are a way for the young men and women to express their love.

In addition to singing mountain songs while working, living and engaging in folk-custom activities, the people in Mudong Town also used to hold some traditional musical get-togethers to celebrate specific events, typical of which were seedling-pulling-out song meeting, wedding song meeting, funeral song meeting, thrashing song meeting, hot pickled mustard tuber song meeting, crab song meeting, fish-catching song meeting, cow-browsing song meeting, and children's song meeting.

At present, more than 1,000 Mudong Mountain Songs have been collected. The manner in which they are sung is quite diverse —some are performed solo, others in unison. When singing the second section in the seven—character sentences, the voice should be suddenly lifted for several minutes from the fourth character, creating an interesting musical effect, and producing an end note with a lasting aftersound.

Northern Sichuan Weeding Drum-Gong Singing

Applicant: Qingchuan County, Sichuan Province

Weeding Drum-Gong Singing is part of a folk culture widespread in the countryside around the mountainous areas of northern Sichuan Province. It is a kind of mountain song that people sing while pulling out the weeds from the corn and yellow bean fields in June or August. Weeding Drum-Gong Singing has the function of not only ensuring the weed-pulling-out is done quickly and thoroughly, but also relaxes the laborers during the course of what can be back-breaking work.

When pulling out the weeds, the laborers of several or even dozens of households assemble and stand in a row along the hillside. One person sounds a gong, another beats a drum to heighten the morale of the workers and set them weeding at the same pace, also setting the rhythm for their singing. Throughout the day, gong, drum and singing duties are rotated, and during the whole of this time, from morning to evening, not a song is repeated. The persons who beat the gong or drum are drawn from the most respected elders of the village, or are selected from the most prospective of the younger men. They are called Gelang and Lianshou or Tongluo. The day's work begins at 8:00 a.m. with the first strike of the gong, which is carried ahead of the rest of the working party. If any person is observed to lag behind when the weeding is in progress, the Gelang will come up behind him and strike the gong as loudly as possible. This usually has the desired result!

Some lyrics for these songs exist in manuscript; others, in the seven- or ten-character-format, have been passed on orally. Weeding Drum-Gong Singing includes seven beats, nine beats, 12 beats and beats called Huapaizi. The tune and libretto are grouped into the seven-character and ten-character music style. There are also five-character lyrics, as well as traditional and improvised librettoes.

The Dong Grand Song

Applicant: Liping County, Guizhou Province

One of the ethnic minority groups of China, the Dong people are said to be the descendants of the ancient Guyue society, with a history of more than 2500 years. Mainly distributed in Guizhou, Hunan, Guangxi and Hubei Provinces, they have a population of 2.6 million.

Without their own written language, the Dong people have passed down their history and expressed their life-view by oral transmission. The Grand Song, untranscribed and only available to the ear and the heart, is the folk music specific to the Dong ethnic group. The fact that we can appreciate it today we owe to the traditional "song class" of the Dong villages. In addition to offering an enlightened education, these song classes produce a level of choral singing in its students that is unmatched anywhere else in the world. Such has been the training ground for generations of Dong Grand Song choruses.

A performance of these Grand Songs requires at least three people. It is a polyphonic folk song with its own unique multiple vocal parts and neither has instrumental accompaniment nor a conductor. Imitating the sounds of nature such as the trilling of birds and the murmering of flowing water is a salient feature of its composition. The performers sing of the natural world, of their daily labors, love and human companionship, creating a harmonic bridge themselves and the world around them. The Grand Song is sung when the whole village gather together or another clan pay a visit. It is absolutely central to the culture of the Dong people, and to some extent can be said to express and reflect their very soul.

Dong Grand Song is one of the Chinese folk music arts with completely recognisable local features. The polyphonic chorus with its own unique multiple vocal parts is rare among both Chinese and foreign folk songs.

The Dongs in Guizhou singing the Dong Grand Song

The Pipa Song of the Dong Ethnic Group

Applicant: Rongjiang County and Liping County, Guizhou Province

The pipa of the Dong ethnic group is a plucked string instrument that is a favorite of their musicians. It is used to accompany their songs, and is particularly popular in the Dong-inhabited areas of Guizhou, Guangxi and Hunan Provinces and Autonomous Region. The singer plays the pipa to accompany him- or herself, hence the name Pipa Song. With a round sound box, long neck, and four strings of steel wire, it is different from the pipas we find elsewhere, producing a particularly sweet and agreeable, clear and melodious sound.

In the Dong-inhabited areas, it seems that every one is able to play the pipa and sing the Pipa Song. The latter is a real gem in the culture of the Dong ethnic group. It is believed that its tunes can exceed 100 varieties, divided into the major and minor. In addition to its role of accompaniment, the pipa can also be used to play the introduction and 过门.

Whilst playing, the performer usually sits or walks. The instrument may accompany not only the lyric love song and ditty, but also narrative songs. It is loved by the Dong young men and girls, who are adept at simultaneously singing and playing. It can be performed solo or used to accompany the Dong Opera.

Dong Pipa Songs in Wan Village are the most elaborate works of Dong Music. Over the past 300 years, they have been sung and passed down for generations through oral teaching.

Hani Multi-Voice-Part Folk Song

Applicant: Yunnan Province

Puchuan of Azhahe Township in Yunnan Province is the birthplace of the Hani Multi-Voice-Part Folk Song. The origin of the multi-voice-part music "*Mountain Song—Growing Seedlings*" cannot be researched. According to some surveys, however, it is the ancient traditional folk song of the Hani ethnic group. Over the past thousands of years, "*Mountain Song—Growing Seedlings*" has developed as a result of farming labor. In Puchun, girls above 16 years old and middle-aged and old women can sing this type of song. The Hani people, with their age-old dependence on the soil of mountain terraces, pay particular attention to the seedling-growing season, during which, as one mountain song fades away, another rises in its place.

Hani multi-voice-part folk songs express the labor expended on, and the love felt for, their gardens, as well as the beautiful scenery they create. Representative works include *Mountain Song—Growing Seedlings* and the

Hani girls heartily singing

Love Song. They may be performed to the accompaniment of musical instruments or else with only vocal backing. There are a number of occasions when the Hani multi-voice-part folk song is heard, including when people are gathered on mountain terraces, or on hillside forests, or on village holidays. The musical instruments are made by the folk singers themselves. The rising wording, themed libretto and vocal accompaniment constitute in themselves a fascinating lyric style. Multi-voice-part folk songs show obvious ethnic and local features in the terms of their structure, composition, and range, color, and combination of melody.

These songs are important, for they contain all the musical wisdom and talent of the Hani people, and give them the opportunity to display their performing skills . In a recent field survey, relevant experts were able to collect the primitive Hani multi-voice-part folk songs with eight vocal parts, which, being very rare, have significant historic, scientific and artistic value.

Yi Seaweed Singing

Applicant: Honghe Hani–Yi Autonomous Region, Yunnan Province

Yi Seaweed Singing is a genre of folk songs specific to the Yi ethnic group and well-known both at home and abroad. The name is derived from the hydrophytic herb known as "seaweed" , which grows in the local Yilonghu Lake. The song was created by the Yi people in the process of their labor and living, and evolved out of the mountain songs that the young men and girls of the Yi ethnic group sang while expressing their love in the mountains, steppes, and fields, and also by the lake-shore. Since its emergence, it has been sung in those areas centered on the Yilonghu Lake.

In form and development, the Yi Seaweed Singing was deeply influenced by the culture brought by the Han people who migrated to this area during the Ming (1368-1644) and Qing (1616-1911) Dynasties. In the local chronicles written after the Qing Dynasty, there are many records and poems regarding seaweed signing. A complete performance, with its long length, and complicated melody and structure, takes the form of a great suite consisting of many musical parts and combining the vocal solo, antiphonal singing, led chorus, unison, tutti and other singing forms. A representative song is *The Brother Sings for his Sister to Learn*.

Seaweed singing is unique among the musical varieties of the ethnic groups. It is a kind of folk song in the antiphonal style. There is a singer leading the chorus, and others provide vocal accompaniment. It features a wide range, and an attractive rhythm.

Its lyrics are written in Chinese, although its melody preserves the musical traditions of the Yi ethnic group, the latter characterized by the exquisite and variable rhythm and long-flowing melody. It is mainly accompanied by the tetrachord or blown-into tree leaves, but does not employ a regular instrumental music. It is generally sung or spoken with a clear and rich tone, incorporating the skills of improvisation.

Napo Zhuang Folk Song

Applicant: Napo County, Guangxi Zhuang Autonomous Region

Napo Zhuang (also called "black costume" Zhuang) is unique to the Zhuang people. With a population of 51,800, the Zhuang derive their alternate name from the black clothes they favor. Their coats and trousers are dyed with a solution prepared from the indigo leaf. They mainly live in Napo County of Guangxi Zhuang Autonomous Region on the China-Vietnam border. The Napo Zhuang Folk Song has been sung by them for generations. Over the years, the "black costume" Zhuang have managed to preserve their simple, complete and (ironically) colorful folk songs, which are known as the living fossils of the Zhuang people.

The "black costume" Zhuang have a special talent for singing and dancing. In their villages in Napo County, almost everybody, from three-year-old children to 70-year-old grandparents, are able to perform the guest-greeting dance, black spear dance, wedding dance and other ancient Zhuang dances, accompanied by the appropriate traditional music. Their lovely-sounding mountain songs can even develop into the two-voice-part ensemble, with delightful melodies.

"Nidiya", meaning "Okay" in the Napo Zhuang language, is often incorporated into their folk songs as a sort of refrain. "Nidiya" mountain songs, characterised by clear melodies and unique artistic charm, have become the touchstone of traditional Zhuang music.

Napo Zhuang Folk Song features dependence on folk customs, consistent style of performance, rich content and a certain (yet deeply attractive) primitive quality. It is the living heritage of the ancient ballads of the Zhuang people.

The mountain songs of the "black costume" Zhuang that have come down to us may be grouped into six distinct categories according to their content and inspiration, and include more than 160 suites with a combined total of approximately one million characters. That the Song has survived and been passed down to this day is due to the well-developed tradition of oral teaching, and to which thanks must go to the singer-teachers responsible.

Lishui Boatmen Haozi

Applicant: Lixian County, Hunan Province

Lixian County is located in northern Hunan Province on the west bank of the Dongtinghu Lake. Due to its special geographical environment, the passage of goods and supplies depended on line-haul along the water-ways. The laborers along the Lishui, Censhui and Daohe Rivers in the territory of Lixian County traditionally lived by this method of transport. Once, there were approximately 1,000 boats plying these routes, each manned by a minimum crew of 20 sailors. While drawing the towline against the current, the boatmen sang a unique haozi evolved from an ancient ditty intended to concentrate their efforts, revive their spirits, and set a unified pace.

Lishui boatmen haozis have no fixed libretto, so they can quite easily passed on from one generation the next. These haozis are improvised by different people in different places. Though intended as popular tunes for the common people, they are still capable of expressing an heroic spirit combined with no lack of artistic charm. The lyrics consist mainly of five or seven-character sentences. They are sung by a leading singer and subsequently taken up by a chorus. In addition, there are many haozi which are sung for the boat owners and their guests.

The haozis that the boatmen created and sang, adapting each to the various currents against which they sailed, are, as one might suppose, diversified in character. The Lishui haozis are grouped under four headings—the flat, the lower, allegretto, and adagiettos. The flat, also called "Huhai", is sung by the boatmen while sculling over tranquil waters; the "lower aria" is compact in rhythm and fast in speed, and is sung while the boat is running in deep water. Allegretto, also known as the "loud aria", is the haozi sung by the boatmen while sculling and fighting to keep the vessel afloat against a swollen current. The adagietto is the haozi sung by the boatmen while sculling in the deep water, with an appropriate steady rhythm and balanced tone.

Chinese Guqin Art

Applicant: Chinese Academy of Art

The Chinese zither has existed for over 3,000 years and represents China's foremost solo musical instrument tradition. It produces varying sounds by a combination of strings and a wooden resonator and, until the early part of the last century, was known as the guqin. Chinese guqin Art has had a great impact upon Chinese musical, aesthetic, socio-cultural and ideological history. It is one of the main representatives of the ancient Chinese spirit. In November 2003, the Chinese zither was included in UNESCO's second list of the "Oral and Intangible Culture Heritage of Humanity."

Even before the Qin Dynasties, the zither enjoyed great popularity. The version in common use today has preserved the shape of those made after the Wei and Jin Dynasties. It is typically 110 centimeters long, with a head and tail 17 centimeters and 12 centimeters wide respectively, although guqins can come in a whole range of sizes from big to small. The number of strings can vary from five, nine, ten, twelve, or even as many as twenty, although

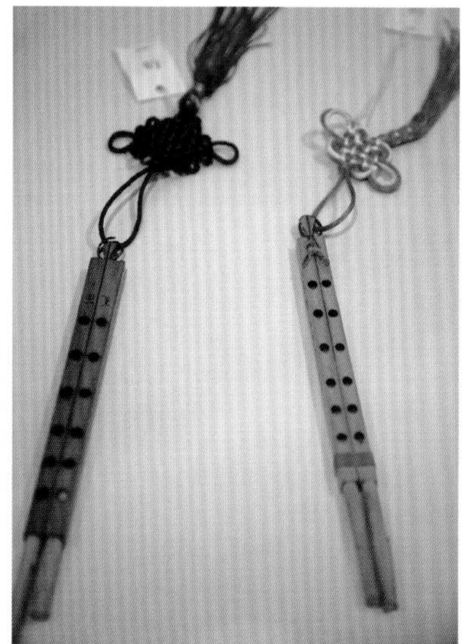

Qiang flute—a traditional musical instrument

Qiang Flute Performance and Manufacture

Applicant: Maoxian County, Sichuan Province

The Qiang flute is an old single-reed wind instrument, with a history of more than 2,000 years. It prevails in the communities inhabited by the Qiang ethnic group in the Aba Tibetan Autonomous Prefecture in north Sichuan Province. Without a written language, successive generations of these people have passed down their history and culture orally, a process in which the Qiang flute has provided an important channel for the communication and inheritance of the ethnic culture. It features a characteristic temperament, individual timbre, and requires skill in playing, and is rare among the ethnic musical instruments of China.

The flute is played from one end, with two pipes producing the same pitch. Its timbre is silvery and resounding and sounds a little doleful, which is fully expressed in the Tang verses,

"A Tartar under the willows is lamenting on his flute;
spring never blows to him through the Yumenguan Pass".

and is hence most suitable for the solo performer. Of course, it can also be used to accompany singing and dancing. Qiang people often play it to express sentiments of various kinds. Common tunes include those called *Zheliu Ci*, *Sixiang Qu* and *Shalang Qu* in Chinese.

Mention of the Qiang flute can often be found in the poems of the Tang (618-907), Song (960-1279), Yuan (1206-1368) and Ming (1368-1644) Dynasties, and such a kind of musical instrument still exists in the areas inhabited by the Qiang ethnic group in the Maowen Qiang Autonomous County and Heishui County in Sichuan Province. Usually, the straight and tough arrow bamboo, with its long cylindrical tubes, is used to manufacture the Qiang flute; such bamboo features a moderate and even thickness and dense fibres, thus will not easily split. The length, thickness and size of the bamboo tubes combined decide the accuracy in pitch. The distances between the stops must be exactly equal, or the accuracy in pitch will vary from one to the other.

It is a pity that now, after several thousand years of history, there are all together less than ten persons skilled at making and playing the Qiang flute.

the most familiar is the one called The Seven-Stringed Qin.

From the Tang Dynasty onwards, musicians developed a special way of playing the instrument. This way used both hands to alter the position of string and peg, but maintained a constant pitch. The musical notes are based on the radicals in Chinese characters, plus some numbers, with the addition of some simplified characters, hence the name Simplified Character Music. 150 separate guqin compositions using this simplified character system have been passed down to us. Thus a great number of ancient musical works have been preserved, forming a unique and precious music treasury.

An independent and complete system has taken shape in terms of the way the guqin is played, how its music is notated, its history, its conventions, and its aesthetics, all of which in combination are known as Guqin Learning. With a content both profound and wide-ranging, it is an excellent representative of Chinese traditional music, mirroring China's philosophy, history and literature.

Horse-head Stringed Instrument Music of Mongolia

Applicant: Inner Mongolia Autonomous Region

The Horse-head Stringed Instrument, so called for the hors's head carved at its fingering end, is a bow instrument in common use among the Mongolian communities in Inner Mongolian, Liaoning, Jilin, Heilongjiang, Gansu and Xinjiang provinces and autonomous regions. It evolved from the huqin in the Tang and Song Dynasties and was passed down among the common people during the reign of Genghis Khan.

The Horse-head Stringed Instrument is a typical representative of the music and life of the Mongolian people. In terms of its shape, material composition, tone color, and the way in which it is played, it fully reflects the historic state of Mongolian nomadic life.

Mongolian youth playing the Matouqin (horse-head fiddle)

The body of the instrument, made of the wood, is about one meter long. Its sound box, also made of wood, is echelon, and covered with either horse or sheep skin. On each side of the top of its pole is installed a tuning peg. The bow is made of rattan (bamboo) and horsetail; the strings are two bundles of horsetails. The bow brushes the strings so as to create a soft, sweet sound. It can be played as a solo instrument, or as part of an ensemble. According to the style of performing, there are a number of categories into which its music can be divided. The horse-head stringed instrument is not only played on grand and official occasions, but also during the ordinary village people's ceremonies such as weddings and parties.

The horse-head stringed instrument produces the best music for the accompaniment of Mongolian love songs. On a wider note, it can also express the whole exterior life of the Mongolian people, the seemingly endless grasslands, howling winds, sorrowful hearts, the riotous thundering of horses' hooves, and tranquil pastoral scenes. Thus it is much respected in Mongolian culture.

Mongolian Sihu Music

Applicant: Inner Mongolia Autonomous Region

The Mongolian *sihu* is another musical instrument with distinctive local features. Similar in shape to the sihu popular in the Han-inhabited areas, it is made from rosewood. The resonance box, octagonal in shape, is covered with the skin of a boa constrictor or an ox. The *sihu* has been played in the Mongolian-inhabited areas since the 13th century.

Known as the "Hou Le" or "Huer" in Mongolian, the Sihu is one of the most traditional musical instruments that can be heard on the Inner Mongolian Prairie, accompanying both singing or chanting, and has formed a musical backdrop for the daily lives of many generations. But how is this ancient instrument faring today?

Mongolian *sihu* is grouped into three categories—the alt, mediant and bass. The alt sihu, clear and loud in tone color, is used for solo and ensemble performances. The mediant sihu, with its fruity tone color, is particularly good for playing lyrical music. It is used to accompany the Wuligar, a traditional combination of talking and singing of the Horqin people. They play an important role in the cultural life of the Mongolian people. Representative works include *Hurrying along on One's Journey*, and *The Snaky Grapevine*. The Mongolian *sihu*, featuring many many years of rich cultural accumulation, a deeply expressive force, unique technique, and a simple and melodious rhythm, is a wonderful product of a people who engage in semi-nomadic farming and herding, and is of incalculable value in research into the history, culture, folk customs, and social exchanges of those people.

After the Yuan Dynasty (1271-1368), the *sihu* art began to be widely spread, becoming fashionable in the Han-inhabited areas of the Inner Mongolian Autonomous Region, Liaoning, Jilin, Heilongjiang Provinces and north China, exerting a far-reaching impact upon the folk art combining talking and singing as practised by the Han. Tongliao, in the hinterland of the Horqin Grasslands, is the place where the art of the *sihu* continues to prosper.

Art of Suona Horn

Applicant: Qinyang City of Henan Province and Qingyang City of Gansu Province

Old men in northern Shaanxi Province playing Suona at the Hukou Waterfall.

Customarily called "Laba (horn)", *suona* is a kind of folk musical instrument widely prevalent in China since it first arrived here around the 3rd century. In the fresco featuring a singing and dancing scene found in Grotto 38 of the Kizil Grottoes in Baicheng, Xinjiang, there are suona-playing images. In the Jin (1115-1234) and Yuan (1206-1368) Dynasties, suona was introduced to the Central Plains of China.

Suona is composed of five parts: whistle, flaring horn, wooden pipe, Qingzi pipe and bowl. The wooden pipe, which has eight sound holes, has a copper Qingzi pipe on its upper end and a bowl on the lower end. A flaring horn and a reed whistle cover the Qingzi pipe.

The art of *suona* is rich and varied. In leading or accompanying an instrument ensemble or cooperating with gong and drum, *suona* produces a unique artistic effect. With its bold and vigorous tunes, it is most appropriate for the creation of a lively and joyous atmosphere and spectacular scenes. On the other hand, *suona* is also quite capable of profoundly and exquisitely expressing human sensibilities, as well as vividly imitating the sounds of insects and birds.

The *suona* solos mostly find their sources in folk songs, ditties, local operas and dramas, all of which feature a strong local and folk flavor. Its traditional melody *One Hundred Birds Singing in Homage to the Phoenix* won the silver medal at the Folk Music Contest of the Fourth World Youth Festival in the early 1950s.

The Qingyang *Suona* features a wide variety of tunes, simple rhythms, and a unique style, and can be played on its own rather than as part of an ensemble. More than 1,200 tunes have been collected and recorded, of which, a total of 496 have been included in the *Folk Instrumental Music Collection in Qingyang Area*. In the light of their sources and evolution, these tunes can be divided into the traditional tunes (comparatively high in the degree of instrumental music), variations on folk songs, and the tunes of local operas. *Pihong Guahua* (meaning having red silk draped over one's shoulders and flowers pinned to one's chest) is a representative piece.

Liaoning Wind and Percussion Ensemble

Applicant: Liaoning Province

The Liaoning Wind and Percussion Ensemble began with pipe-wind music to which was added suona music in the Ming (1368-1644) and Qing (1616-1911) Dynasties, and matured into its final form during the middle period of the Qing Dynasty. Regarding repertoire, it maintains a few tunes of the Tang (618-907) and Song (960-1279) Dynasties, though the majority belong to the Yuan (1206-1368), Ming and Qing Dynasties. So far as structure is concerned, the form of the tune is extremely precise; each kind has a specific musical construction, with fairly strict regulation. From the perspective of the tone of some tunes, we can say that it was obviously influenced by the music of the northern ethnic minority groups such as the Khitan and Nuchen.

Liaoning Wind and Percussion Ensemble mainly include the *suona* and pipe-wind music; both are independent, with different musical styles and special tunes. The *suona* music, mainly performed by *suona* horn, occupies a prominent place, and its application and influence exceed those of the pipe-wind music. The latter is principally played by single or double pipes and the reed pipe wind instruments.

Each ensemble has its own pedigree, relying on folk customs and centered on family troupes. They follow the ancestral teaching that, "The master shall impart his wisdom orally to the apprentice and make him or her have a true understanding".

Such ensembles are prevalent across Liaoning Province, especially in the southern areas such as Haicheng, Niuzhuang, Nantai, Anshan and Shenyang, and have exerted a profound influence on the music of this kind in various places throughout northeastern China.

Jiangnan Sizhu

Applicant: Jiangsu Province, Shanghai

Jiangnan sizhu is a general term referring to the traditional instrumental music which is prevalent in south Jiangsu, west Zhejiang and Shanghai. The instruments used are mainly the traditional Chinese stringed and woodwind instruments such as *erhu, yangqin, pipa, sanxian, qinqin*, flute and *xiao*. However, such music totally differs in style from the rural to the urban areas. That of the latter features an elegant and flowery style and various grace notes, and enjoys wide popularity; whereas that of the former usually adopts the gong and drum to create a warm atmosphere, and overall is simpler in style.

As a representative of the Jiangnan culture, Jiangnan sizhu dates back to the late Ming Dynasty , reaching the high point of its development in the late Qing Dynasty and enjoyng a golden period in the Republic of China . Thanks to the efforts of sizhu masters to recompose and reprocess both folk and classical music over the course of many generations, it has gradually developed certain generic characteristics, and remains prevalent in both rural and urban areas south of the lower reaches of the Yangtze River.

The instruments used in Jiangnan sizhu fall into three categories. The first includes *erhu, zhonghu, pipa, sanxian, yangqin* and *qinqin*; the second consists of *dizi, xiao* and *sheng*; and the third contains *ban, bangu* and *pengling*. An ensemble ranges from three or four to as many as nine or ten musicians, each of whom, though a virtuoso on one instrument, is also capable of playing others. The flexible and concise structure of the ensemble has enabled to flourish in rural areas.

An aged folk music band playing the Jiangnan stringed and woodwind music *Zhong hua liu ban*

In performance, all the musical instruments bring their peculiarities into full play and cooperate with each other, creating a multi-part music with a rich and strong expressive force. It finds its fullest and most distinct expression in the performance of *Zhonghua Liuban* (*Moderately Ornamented Six Beats*). It is regarded as "Chinese style chamber music".

Haizhou Wuda Gongdiao Music

Applicant: Lianyungang City, Jiangsu Province

The so-called Gongdiao refers to the five notes of the ancient Chinese five-tone scale.

Haizhou is the ancient name of Lianyungang City. Haizhou Wuda Gongdiao Music has been prevalent in Lianyungang City and its surrounding areas for several hundred years. Wuda Gongdiao refers to a type of verse based on five major tunes, namely Ruanping, Dieluo, Lidiao, Nandiao, and Boyang. It is a kind of folk art lying somewhere between the opera and quyi, which can be adopted to express various stories and emotions.

As one of the important folk arts of Jiangsu in the Ming and Qing Dynasties, Haizhou Wuda Gongdiao originated from the "short lyric" of the Ming Dynasty and derived rich nourishment from the local folk songs and dialects, forming a unique style and at the same time achieving popularity among the ordinary people. It has been a long-standing custom for local people to sing in verse. After the Ming Dynasty , Wuda Gongdiao gradually took shape and reached maturity, its popularity increasing due to the development of the river transportation of salt. Located on the border of Jiangsu and Shandong Provinces, Haizhou was a melting pot of northern Chinese dialects and southern Yangzi River and Huai River dialects. Over time, verse songs from both northern and southern China came together here and took root. Since there was not much traffic in very ancient times, folk tunes and melodies were able to be passed down and kept intact without being diluted by other musical forms.

Some verses from the Ming Dynasty such as those named *Jisheng Cao, Shanpo Yang* and *Da Zaogan* in Chinese, managed to remain intact. Some ancient music, such as *Matou Tune,* that had disappeared in Jiangsu and Zhejiang Provinces has now been rediscovered in Haizhou, with the lyrics being basically same as those used for *Baixue Yiyin*

(*Historical Tune for White Snow*). Some tunes that require a high degree of performance skill are still being sung there.

Shengzhou Wind and Percussion Music

Applicant: Shengzhou City, Zhejiang Province

Shengzhou wind and percussion instrumental music originated from folk activities at temple fairs, during which such musical instruments as gong, drum, *erhu*, *jinghu*, *sanxian*, cymbals, *suona* and trombone were used. It is recorded that, as early as the Spring and Autumn (770-476 BC) and Warring States (475-221 BC) Periods, there were celebrations and temple fairs. The custom was passed down over the centuries, and in the mid-Ming Dynasty, every village had temples and memorial temples in which were theater stages.

From 1949 until the 1980s, Shengzhou folk music underwent changes that led to the formation of two major schools, the east village school, and the west village school. The latter is represented by Changle Town Farmers' Band. It is performed with gongs, drums and other wind and percussion instruments. The wind instruments are played in an unusual way. The musicians breathe in instead of out, thus making the music louder and more penetrating. The former school, represented by the Huangze Farmers' Band, is mainly accompanied by stringed instruments, and is much more soft and tender. The repertoires are mainly folk tunes and traditional music.

Shengzhou music is both the foundation and an important component of Yue opera, exerting an important influence on the arias and their accompanying music.

Zhoushan Gong and Drum Music

Applicant: Zhoushan City, Zhejiang Province

The Zhoushan Gong and Drum Music has its source in sailing. Alongside the shore, it was performed to attract people onto the boat, and during the subsequent voyage it helped to amuse the passengers. Also, in the case of fog at sea, it sent out a signal to other boats. The Ming and Qing Dynasties saw the Zhoushan Gong and Drum Music develop into a kind of high-level art featuring a complete set of musical instruments and richly varied repertoire. There were professional and semi-professional performing troupes. With a strong local flavor of the island communities, Zhoushan Gong and Drum Music is appropriate to the bold and straightforward character of the fishermen of the East China Sea and expresses the awesome majesty of the ocean, plus the joyful holiday atmosphere at the beginning and end of a voyage. It also reflects the unique marine culture and historical features of a certain period of Zhoushan.

The basic instruments include gong, drum, cymbals and suona horn, sometimes accompanied by strings and woodwinds, and all combining to produce loud music with an insistent, bold and unrestrained rhythm and an extremely warm atmosphere.

Technically it is catagorised as wind and percussion instrumental music, utilising a complete range of musical instruments of this kind. The two major ones are the Pailuo, made up of 13 gongs, and the Paigu, consisting of five drums. Unique in performing style, they create a bright contrast in volume and possess a wonderfully rich sound.

The traditional tunes include *Zhoushan Drum and Gong*, *Preface of the Eight Immortals*, *Happy Fishing Family*, *Shadiao* and *Sound of the Tide*, which have been listed in the *Chinese Folk Instrumental Music Collection: Zhejiang Volume.* There are also many tunes that have been recorded on disc.

Shifan Music

Applicant: Fujian Province

As the major kind of local music of Fuzhou, Shifan Music is famous for its ten musical instruments made of silk, bamboo, leather, wood and gold. The performance stresses the second half beat; the music reaches above an octave, featuring a straightforward style.

The instruments consist of flute, douguan, yehu (coconut-string lute), yunluo (a set of ten gongs), langchuan (tambourine), large and small gongs and large and small cymbals, plus the qinggu drum. As the Shifan Music developed and evolved, sheng (a reed pipe wind instrument) and wooden fish were added. Due to their extreme antiquity, these musical instruments are regarded as living fossils, of which the langchuan and douguan have been recorded in the Book of Music written by Chen Liang, a musician of the Northern Song Dynasty in Fujian Province. The songs are mostly about the relationships between man, nature and society, expressive of a certain artistic conception and also including the retelling of old legends.

People sit inside or walk around outside to perform the music. In the past, Shifan Music was mainly performed on the occasion of normal folk activities such as weddings and funerals, as well as during ceremonies to welcome the deities, and in these cases the performers would play the music while walking on the streets. Each instrument features a distinct timbre and a strong penetrating power. With the time beaten to the steps, the rhythm sounds alternately gentle and urgent. When the climax is reached, the music can be heard quite clearly several kilometers away.

Southwestern Shandong Guchuiyue

Applicant: Jiaxiang County, Shandong Province

Southwestern Shandong Guchuiyue (percussion and wind music) is mainly played on the *suona* horn and is typically represented by Jiaxiang Guchuiyue. The genre is mainly distributed in Jining, Zaozhuang and Heze Cities and their surrounding areas in Shandong Province. With regard to function, it is divided into performance music, sacrificial music and drum-worshiping music. The copper-pipe *suona* horn is unique to the mid-south Shandong percussion and wind music. The Southwestern Shandong Guchuiyue is traditionally performed during holidays, weddings, funerals and other folk activities, being the most important and representative part of the Shandong percussion and wind music. Jiaxiang County has the reputation throughout China of being the "hometown of *suona* horn" .

According to custom, an ensemble led by a suona horn and accompanied by flute, *sheng*, small cymbals and drum is called a "single big flute (*suona* horn being customarily regarded as a big flute)". If the leading instruments are two suona horns accompanied by small cymbals, yunluo gong, wangluo gong and drum, the ensemble is called "a pair of big flutes". There is also a genre where the ensemble is made up mostly of tin flutes, named "Kaxi" in Chinese.

The professional and semi-professional bands who perform this kind of percussion and wind music can easily be found in the rural and urban areas of southwestern Shandong Province. They are mostly comprised of families or close relatives, and most usually practise hairdressing as their day to day trade. On the occasion of weddings, funerals, festivals or other celebrations, they will be invited to give performances which can last for several days. Southwestern Shandong Guchuiyue constitutes an indispensable part of the folk music of that region.

During its long history, the Southwestern Shandong Guchuiyue has developed a rich variety of musical genres and dynamic melodies. There have been literally hundreds of bands practising this kind of music, made up of thousands of musicians with consummate performing skills. It boasts a total of more than 300 tunes, of which representative ones include One Hundred Birds Singing in Homage to the

Phoenix, *One Flower, Wind Blowing Snow and Carrying a Wedding Sedan Chair* and also those named *Liuzi Kaimen* and *Da Hetao* in Chinese.

Bantou Tunes

Applicant: Nanyang City, Henan Province

Henan Bantou Tunes originated in the Song Dynasty (960-1279) and are regarded as the "foundation" of Chinese ethnic music. Collectively they are one of the four major tunes of China, the other three being Fujian Nanyin Music, Jiangnan Sizhu and Guangdong Music. It is a rare tune in Henan Province, let alone in China.

It was played in Nanyang as a sort of curtain-raiser to the main performance, with a view to attracting people and also entertaining those who had taken their seats earlier. Subsequently, it developed into a comparatively independent tune, which could be performed both prior to the major tune or during the main performance in order to establish changes in atmosphere.

Composed by the accompanying players of the major tunes, Bantou Tunes were originally derivatives of those melodies and were principally played on the *sanxian*, *zheng* and *pipa*. Subsequently, they gradually developed into an independent form of instrumental music and incorporated more musical instruments, such as *zhuihu*, *erhu*, *jinghu* and *dongxiao*. As a result, it became a kind of music in its own right, which could be played either solo or in accompaniment.

In the late Qing Dynasty and the early Republic of China, Nanyang Bantou Tunes was extremely popular and each bandsman could play a number of tunes. The players came from various social classes, which laid the foundation for the popularization of Bantou Tunes.

These tunes are divided into those of quick and those of slow tempo. The latter feature one accented beat followed by one unaccented, and are mostly plaintive and grave; the former have only accented beats and are brisk and fluent. Characterized by their wide register, bright timbre and beautiful musical sound, such musical instruments as *zheng* and *sanxian* are particularly suitable for expressing the exquisite and euphemistic flavor of the Bantou Tunes, most of which sound melodious and brisk.

Yichang Sizhu

Applicant: Yichang City, Hubei Province

Yichang Sizhu is unique to the folk instrumental music of Yichang in Hubei. It is mainly played on the stringed and woodwind instruments, with the addition of some percussion, so is also known as "Xiyue (fine music)". It prevails in the eastern parts of Yichang, especially in the Yaqueling area of Yichang. Due to its exquisite, euphemistic, auspicious and elegant flavor, Yichang Xiyue is widely performed at both folk celebrations and grand ceremonies.

Yichang Stringed and Woodwind music *Yiling Stringed and Woodwind Music*

"Si" and "Zhu" together constitute two of the eight categories of the musical instruments of the Zhou Dynasty . "Si" refers to the stringed instruments and "Zhu" to the woodwinds made of bamboo. The term Sizhu thus refers to an ensemble performed by the aforesaid two kinds of musical instruments together, featuring exquisite style and sounding both brisk and melodious.

With a profound cultural tradition, Yichang Sizhu has a history of some 200 years, representing seven generations of musicians and more than 60 songs. There are now at least 60 bands featuring 700-odd musicians in Yaqueling Town.

The basic characteristics of the Yichang Sizhu are as follows. Firstly, it is performed at weddings, funerals and other folk activities. Secondly, the instruments employed are mainly strings and woodwinds. Thirdly, its tunes are those which bring out the best qualities of the instruments themselves. Fourthly, it is graceful in melody and exquisite in expression, and, combined with a light percussion music, gives the overall impression of elegance and freshness. Lastly, it boasts a flowery rhythm over standard beats, and is entirely characteristic of local folk songs.

The make-up of a typical Jiangnan Sizhu band is representative of the Sizhu bands as a whole. Commonly utilised musical instruments include *xiao*, *sheng*, *erhu*, *zhonghu*, *pipa*, *yangqin*, small *sanxian*, clappers and jigu drum.

Zhijiang Folk Wind and Percussion Music

Applicant: Zhijiang City, Hubei Province

Folk music in Zhijiang is usually performed on a variety of instruments, such as percussion, silk string, horn and others.

A large number of folk percussion instruments, such as the clay drum and bell, unearthed from the site of the primitive Guanmiaoshan Village in Zhijiang City demonstrate that there were such instruments 6,000 years ago in the Yangtze River valley. The clay bell is similar to the sand rammer in shape and principle.

The extant scores show that the folk wind and percussion music in Zhijiang area is characterized by a bright rhythm and a rough and unconstrained flavor in west Hubei, and a graceful rhythm and fluent tune in the Jianghan Plain. Zhijiang folk music focuses on the complete combination of its ten musical instruments. Also, it incorporates musical elements of the local shan'ge (mountain song), tiange (farmland song), wujuzi (five sentences), and other folk songs. The skill and style that gradually formed contain a strong local flavor. Meanwhile, it boasts various genres, a rich repertoire, and innovation in its continuing development.

Through years of such development, the folk wind and percussion music in Zhijiang has become completely identified with the common and practical folk culture and customs of the region. It is usually performed at weddings, funerals and other celebrations and is accompanied by dances.

Guangdong Music

Applicant: Guangzhou City and Taishan City, Guangdong Province

Guangdong music, also known as Cantonese music, is prevalent in the Pearl River Delta and has a history of 100-odd years. Its forerunner was principally the interlude music and accompanying ditties, which developed into a kind of instrumental music which could be played independently.

It adopts many grace notes in performance; various musical instruments

Guangzhou Ethnic Philharmonic playing the Guangdong music Higher and Higher

combine to produce a unique timbre and style. Gaohu, also called yuehu and nanhu,.is the leading instrument, also used for solos.

Stressing a simplicity of structure, Guangdong is a form of what is known in the Western classsical tradition as program music. It depicts scenes and objects and expresses feelings through the richness of its music, wide register, and variable artistic interpretations. Hence, it features a strong local flavor and boasts a very special aesthetic charm. With regard to structure, it mostly consists of many short and individual tunes rather than interrelated movements.

The period from the 1920s to the 1930s witnessed the high point of the Guangdong music in terms of popularity and development, based on its reinterpretation of the traditional tunes of earlier times, thus creating a large number of new folk pieces. This further developed and improved the Guangdong music in the aspects of rhythm, mode, structure and performance style.

There are more than 500 extant tunes with both title and score. Representative of these are *Rain on the Plantain Leaves, Thunder in Drought, Double Hatred, Triratna Buddha, Rising Step by Step, The Autumn Moon on the Calm Lake, Joy and Peace* and *Dragon Boat Racing.*

Being light, soft, flowery and exquisite, with the fresh, fluent and melodious Lingnan style, the widely influential Guangdong music is deeply loved by ordinary people and can be heard all over the world where Chinese communities have been established.

Chaozhou Music

Applicant: Chaozhou City and Shantou City, Guangdong Province

Chaozhou music prevails in the Chaozhou and Shantou areas of Guangdong Province and among the people from those areas both at home and abroad. The ancient music of the central plains flowed into these lands, and was later combined with the local music and operas, assimilating the melodic style of such genres as Yiyang Tune, Kunqu Opera, Shanxi Opera, Handiao Tune, Daodiao Tune and Faqu Tune, resulting finally in what we know as Chaozhou music.

The music can be traced back to a common origin, beginning with the ancient rhythmics in musical theory and practice. It is divided into five categories: gong and drum music led by *suona* horn; flute music mainly played on *sheng*, *xiao*, windpipe and flute; tone-poem music led by *sanxian* and accompanied by other plucked and stringed instruments; shrine music played on ritual implements used in Buddhist services and led by *suona* and fife; and especially fine music played on *pipa*, *sanxian* and *zheng*. It is an extremely rare ancient form that has retained its original soul despite being some 1,000 years old. Flexible in performing style, it has the depth to paint magnificent and moving scenes, but is also full of brisk and melodious tunes.

The Chaozhou music features a simple and elegant flavor, and sounds melodious. It includes many of the ancient tunes of the Nanyin tradition, and as such has aroused international attention. The "two-four system tablature" is a fairly old score unique to Chaozhou music. In its combination of instruments, playing techniques, and variations it boasts a particular organization, structure and aesthetic basis; hence it is upheld as an extremely precious cultural heritage.

Guangdong Hanyue Music

Applicant: Dabu County, Guangdong Province

With a history of more than 1,000 years, Guangdong Hanyue Music enjoys great popularity among ordinary people, and is equally famous as the Cantonese and Chaozhou music. It is mainly prevalent in east Guangdong Province, west Fujian Province, South Jiangxi Province and Taiwan, and also among the Hakka people in southeast Asia. It originated when the Hakka people moved south from the central plains and has retained elements of their central plains music, while at the same time blending with local musical elements.

It can be divided into five categories: silk string music (the most common) led by *touxian* or *tihu* and accompanied by *yangqin*, *sanxian*, flute and *yehu*; qingyue music (also called Confucian music, and favored by intellectuals) generally performed by *guzheng*, lute, *yehu* and *dongxiao*; big gong and drum music (generally performed during the folk activities of welcoming deities, and also the traditional festivals of the Hakka such as the Lantern Festival) led by *suona* and accompanied by various gongs, big drums and big and small cymbals; zhongjunban music (mainly performed by professional or semi-professional folk groups as honor music at weddings and funerals) mainly played by *suona* and accompanied by percussion instruments and several silk stringed instruments; and temple music (used in religious rituals) mainly played by suona and accompanied by percussion instruments and several silk stringed instruments.

Guangdong Hanyue Music has an archive of 600-odd excellent traditional tunes of various flavors and modes as well as a range of performing styles.

Chuida Music

Applicant: Chongqing

Chuida Music of the Jielong Town of Banan District in Chongqing City is a kind of instrumental folk music closely connected with local customs and traditions. It formally came into being during the late Ming Dynasty (in mid-17th century) and underwent great development over the next 400 years.

The Jielong Chuida falls into three major categories, which are wind and percussion music, gong and drum music, and wind and percussion singing ensembles, containing a total of 983 melodies. The tunes of Jielong Chuida mainly include those called *Dahao Pai*, *Zhao Pai*, *Jiangjun Ling*, *Shuilong Yin*, *Nan Luo*, *Liuyao Ling* and *Feng Ru Song* in Chinese. It is universally acknowledged that the folk wind and percussion music of this mountainous village is of a very high artistic standard.

The wind and percussion bands of Jielong Town feature various musical instruments, principle among which are the suona, gongs and drums. Additionally, there are also bell, flute, *qin* and horn, as well as such stringed instruments as *erhu* and violin.

The Banan District now has 260-plus bands containing some 2,000 musicians. There are 26 traditional musical instruments above 100 years old, four of which go back to at least the 18th Century. These bands often give performances at weddings, funerals and birthday ceremonies.

Jinqiao Chuida Music is a kind of folk wind and percussion music of the Wansheng District in Jinqiao Town of Chongqing City. It originated during the Song and Yuan Dynasties, and has a history of over 700 years. Its major musical instruments include *suona*, drum, gong and cymbals. The music typically features a pure, clear, silvery and brisk timbre, regular time, and a loud volume with a wide range and penetrating force. The most remarkable piece of Jinqiao chuida is known as "The Sound of Wind and Horses", recreating the hoofbeats of thousands of horses galloping across the plains.

Laiziluogu at Liangping

Applicant: Liangping County, Chongqing City

Laiziluogu (Laizi Gong and Drum), with a history of over 1,000 years, is a kind of folk instrumental music popular in Liangping County of Chongqing City. It is deeply rooted in the people's daily life and is performed at weddings, funerals, birthday ceremonies, opening ceremonies and various other festivals. The annual Liangping Gong and

Drum Performance for Spring Festival has become a folk custom passed down through successive generations. In addition, people also perform it impromptu in the courtyard, on the flatlands, or in the fields around their villages.

There are six kinds of percussion instruments in the ensemble, which, according to the different preludes of the gong and drum, attend to their own duties, producing clear, loud and melodious tunes.

A good example is provided by the gong and drum prelude to the *Eighteen Laizi*. In the performance, a total of 18 separate tunes are required to be played in a row. Three pieces form one group, totaling six groups; the first set is led by a horse gong, the second by a cymbal, and the third by a big gong. The ensemble consists of five people playing the six kinds of instruments, one of whom plays both the horse gong and hook gong. Though influenced by the inherited style of the families who form each band, the playing method of the gong and drum prelude differs in neighboring areas. However, the *Eighteen Laizi* has a uniform standard even when played by scores of bands throughout Liangping County.

Tujia Daliuzi

Applicant: Xiangxi Tujia and Miao Autonomous Prefecture, Hunan Province

"Daliuzi" is the kind of folk instrumental ensemble most prevalent in the areas inhabited by the Tujia ethnic group and has a long history. As an artistic form unique to the Tujia people, it boasts numerous tunes, requiring exquisite degrees of skill to produce a rich rendering force.

Deeply rooted in the life of the local people, the Tujia Daliuzi is present at all kinds of festivals and celebrations, in particular the traditional Sheba Day of the Tujia ethnic group. The Daliuzi ensemble is harmoniously composed of liuzi gong, head cymbal, second cymbal and horse gong, and gives full play to each of them. There are generally three or four people in one ensemble, which is why it is referred to as "three-person liuzi" or "four-person liuzi". If there are five people, a suona horn is added to increase the gaiety of the music.

Tujia Daliuzi Performance

A daliuzi band is comprised of five people, respectively playing drum, gong, hook gong and double cymbals (including the head cymbal and second cymbal, which are also known as Shangxia Shou in Chinese). With their unique timbre, the double cymbals present a sharp contrast: one is high, but the other low; one clear, the other raucous. Various timbres can be produced by beating the cymbals at various points of their surface, or at different speeds, or with different degrees of force. The daliuzi takes its musical themes from nature, and can imitate the billowing echoes of the mountain and the gurgling of running water, and well as the sounds made by birds and other animals. During a performance a great deal of assistance and cooperation is required from each member of the ensemble.

There are two kinds of score - civil and martial. The former is used at weddings and funerals; whereas the latter is played during the performance of playing lanterns (lion or dragon dances).

Percussion and Wind Music in Hebei Province

Applicant: Yongnian County and Funing County, Hebei Province

This kind of music is played by a combination of percussion and wind instruments, and has always been an important part of China's musical history. Originally, drum, horn, *xiao* and *jia* were played in the ensemble, which also had sung lyrics to accompany the tune.

The Yongnian Percussion and Wind Music is the most representative of its genre in southeast Hebei Province, as well as being one of the most influential kinds of instrumental folk music. It is mainly categorized into wind music, percussion music and kaxi opera. There are more than 200 tunes under 50-odd names, many of which are unique to Yongnian. Its style is straightforward, bright and lively, and is characteristic of the local color. Common tunes include *One Flower, The Passion for Taihang, Little Donkey Herd, Dadeng Dian, Carrying a Wedding Sedan Chair* and *Big Donkey Herd*. It is chiefly passed down through families.

The Funing percussion and wind music boasts various playing modes and requires a range of unique skills. The performance is warm and humorous and has a strong local flavor. Deeply loved by the ordinary people, it is mainly heard at weddings, funerals and festivals, and is also used to accompany folk dances. It is inherited through generations of families, relatives of nominal kinship and sworn brothers, and from master to apprentice, among which there have been many practitioners of great fame and rare talent. Different kinds of *suona* of various individual shapes are used as the lead instrument, the sounds from which are emphasised by the player's body movements. Moreover, "kawan bowls" are also employed as musical instruments during productions of kaxi opera, as well as harmonicas and other common musical instruments.

Weifeng Gong and Drum in South Shanxi Province

Applicant: Linfen City, Shanxi Province

Weifeng Gong and Drum refers to an old collective folk percussion art, originating in the Linfen area of the Shanxi Province over 4,000 years ago. It was initially performed during sacrificial ceremonies, and later at Spring Festival, harvest celebrations, parades and other festive occasions. Its original musical instruments include eight flat gongs, one drum, two nao cymbals, two bo cymbals and one douluo gong. The performance has been described as "majestic", thus getting the name "Weifeng (a Chinese word with the same meaning)".

In the past, a Weifeng Gong and Drum Team, also known as Yitang in Chinese, was fairly small in size, generally with no more than 14 performers. Two of them would beat a drum; two hold nao cymbals; two strike bo cymbals; and eight beat gongs. Because of these eight gongs, it was also known by the Chinese name "Bamian Weifeng". Today, the number of performers has increased to between four and five hundred, the greater number of drums and gongs proportionally amplifying the sound. The majestic feature of Weifeng gong and drum performance finds full expression in the arrangement and playing method of the instruments, as well as in the overall organization, performance and costumes of the teams.

In the performance as favored in most parts of Pingyang, a big round drum is carried by the drummer on his arm. The other mode of performance takes the form of a parade, in which a regular formation is maintained. The drum serves as the leader of the orchestra, under which the gongs are used as major instruments while the nao cymbals and bo cymbals are played alternately with two voice parts.

The Weifeng gong and drum performance

has a complete set of varied gong-drum beats, namely gong-drum tablature, which is able to express various feelings and create different effects. It is the standard principle of the gong-drum performance. Usually the folk players read the tablature, which has its own unique musical notation, as swiftly as a classical musician might read a score. Even now, some rural gong and drum teams still follow this primitive form of musical notation.

Jiangzhou Drum Music

Applicant: Xinjiang County, Shanxi Province

The Jiangzhou (the old name of Xinjiang) Drum Music, also known outside the Province as Jiangzhou Big Drum, refers to the gong-drum music and wind and percussion music popular in Xinjiang County.

Xinjiang County has a tradition of drum music, the performance of which constitutes the principle part of the village recreational activities and constitutes the most popular item in the program of local folk art performance. Having assimilated thousands of years of the traditional culture along the Yellow River, the Jiangzhou Drum Music is straightforward, simple, generous, vigorous and unconstrained in style. Employing gongs, cymbals and wind and stringed instruments, and especially giving full play to each part of the drum, the music uses a rich and varied language to present the listener with vivid images of persons, animals and objects, or even a complete story. It has been hailed as the "leading wonder" of the three major forms of the drum music of Shanxi, and as a "national treasure" in China's overall art of traditional drum music.

Jiangzhou Drum Music originated during the Qin Dynasty (221 BC-206 BC), and became popular in the Ming (1368-1644) and Qing (1616-1911) Dynasties, during which it gained a high reputation for magnificence and loudness. There are many extant tunes, among which, the *King of Qin Breaks the Battle Array* is the most famous.

The Huaqiao drum is the most representative in Jiangzhou drum music. One ensemble consists of different kinds of drums, and at present there are more than ten preserved drumming skills that give full play to different parts of the drum as well as the drumsticks and drum frame. They are all unique to Jiangzhou Drum Music. There are three genres of music, and each of them have different melodies. Should one be interested in developing one's appreciation of this musical tradition, it is advisable to try and attend performances of the Jiangzhou Drum Music given during the folk art performance at Spring Festival, generally reckoned as the grandest of its kind.

Shangdang Bayinhui Music

Applicant: Jincheng City, Shanxi Province

Shangdang Bayinhui Music is a kind of wind and percussion folk music prevalent in the Changzhi and Jincheng areas in Shanxi Province, with a history of more than 2,000 years. Bayinhui is the term used to describe a folk band, usually employing eight kinds of musical instruments such as drum, gong, cymbals, *sheng*, *xiao*, flute and *guan*; hence the name Bayinhui. Bayinhui literally translates as "eight instrument group".

Shangdang Bayinhui is a spontaneous gathering of players, which occurs during various local occasions, principally temple fairs, festivals, weddings and funerals.

In the course of its formation and development, it has assimilated the very best aspects of imperial music, temple music, opera, folk songs and ditties, thus forming an easy-going and generous flavor over and above its finer details. After introducing a new piece of music, no matter what kind it may be, Bayinhui transforms its tune and uses other kinds of instrument to play it, always retaining something which sounds reasonable and rhythmic. However, it never fails to maintain its own ethnic flavor, one that has been scrupulously abided by for generations. The fundamental musical elements of the local operas and folk songs unique to Bayinhui music have never undergone any material change.

The musical instruments are divided into the civil and martial kind. The former include *suona*, *sheng*, *xiao*, bamboo flute and *huqin*; the latter are mainly wind and percussion instruments such as the big drum, big gong, small cymbals and slit drum, which are backed by various stringed instruments. They combine harmoniously, with the loud and sonorous percussion rhythms underscored by gentle and delicate singing. The performance thus given is straightforward and unconstrained, unique in flavor, and deeply cherished by the local people.

Jizhong Sheng and Pipe Music

Applicant: Hebei Province

Jizhong Sheng and Pipe Music, known by the common name of "concert music" , is popular on the Jizhong Plain. It is led by a pipe and accompanied by *sheng*, hence the name. Sometimes gongs, flute and other percussion instruments such as drum and cymbals are also used. Sheng and Pipe Music falls into three categories: the suite, the ditty and the single-set percussion. The suite, with its long length and complicated structure, is the major part of this musical tradition. Each village on the Jizhong Plain has their own band that performs on special occasions such as sacrificial ceremonies and funerals.

All of the performers are farmers, who spend their working days in agricultural labor. But almost every night, except in the busiest part of the agricultural year, they get together to practise and play. Besides the purpose of simple and relaxing self-entertainment, it is also performed on the occasion of folk ceremonies (the farmers will perform free in their native village, but will ask for payment if invited to other villages). At the time of the Lantern Festival (falling on the fifteenth day of the first lunar month), the performance reaches its climax, and the band of each village will be invited on a friendly footing to perform in a neighboring village. They begin their performance on the road, and are greeted at their destination by the letting-off of firecrackers and the sound of gongs and drums. What a jolly scene!

Twelve Copper Drum Melodies

Applicant: Zhenning Bouyei and Miao Autonomous County and Zhenfeng County, Guizhou Province

Beating the Bouyei bronze drums to celebrate the auspiciousness

Within the family, the copper drum is perceived as an heirloom and also a symbol of the unity between that family and their religion. In Bouyei areas, almost each village has one or several copper drums. Sometimes, one family keeps possession of one drum, other times, several families with the same surname share one. Usually, the drum is preserved by the elder, or at least someone of high prestige within the family.

The Bouyei copper drum is one of the ancient percussion instruments of the Bouyei ethnic group and is a precious part of their ethnic cultural heritage. It is made of copper and bronze, and when played is usually accompanied by suona, skin drum, cymbals, gongs or other percussion instruments. It basically maintains the performing style of the ancient musical instruments and features a style unique to the Bouyei ethnic group. As these people do not possess a written language, the drumming tradition is passed down orally from one generation to the next.

There are 12 melodies played on the Bouyei copper drum on the occasion of celebrations and sacrificial ceremonies. They include the pied magpie melody, flower scattering melody, the melodies for worshiping drum and ancestors, the three, six and nine part melodies, the sacrificial melody and the festive melody.

The major instrument for playing these old tunes is, of course, the copper drum itself, but it can be accompanied by the skin drum, gong and cymbals. The sounds thus produced are simultaneously powerful, genial and touching. Each village, perhaps even each family if it has many members, will have someone who can beat the correct time on the copper drum.

As an important part of the regional culture of the Bouyei ethnic group, this type of drum has always been connected with the life and cultural style of its people. Over the course of a long long history, many of China's ancient musical instruments have disappeared and are completely lost to us. The copper drum musical culture of the Bouyei people, however, remains wonderfully intact.

Xi'an Drum Music

Applicant: Shaanxi Province

Xi'an Drum Music is a large-scale folk ensemble combining wind instruments with gongs and drums, prevalent in Xi'an (called Chang'an in ancient times) and its surrounding areas.

Xi'an Drum Music consists of various forms, including folk music, imperial music, dramatic music and religious music. It has continuously followed the most traditional performance style and structure, has never ceased to use traditional instruments, and has maintained the original names of tunes and scores. These scores still in use are the ancient hand-written half-word manuscripts, some of which date back to the Ming Dynasty (1368-1644). Comprehensively, Xi'an Drum Music retains the tunes of the Tang (618-907), Song (960-1279), Yuan (1206-1368), Ming and Qing (1616-1911) Dynasties; hence it is a musical phylogeny of China.

The performing styles are divided into the Buddhist, Taoist and vulgar genres, each varying in effectiveness and skill. The drum music of the Taoist genre is graceful and elegant, and features a high level of skill; that of Buddhist genre is warm and straightforward and full of the flavor of life; and that of the vulgar genre is mostly performed in rural areas and assimilates many of the elements of folk music. However, the music of all genres is played when either walking or sitting down around a table. The latter is a sort of suite, combining many tunes and various kinds of percussion music, and which lasts for two hours or so. However, the music played when walking gives priority to the melody, and is accompanied by rhythm instruments. It is mostly performed as part of a street parade or at temple fairs.

There are some 100 extant scores of Xi'an Drum Music, incorporating 3,000-odd tunes under 1,200-plus names, plus more than 40 suites.

Lantian Puhua Water Fair Music

Applicant: Lantian County, Shaanxi Province

Lantian Puhua Water Fair Music is a kind of wind and percussion folk music that is used for Buddhist and sacrificial ceremonies, and which has been prevalent in the Puhua Town of Lantian County in Shaanxi Province for over 1,000 years. It began at the time of the Sui Dynasty (581-618) and reached prominence during the Tang Dynasty, from the imperial music of which it evolved, spreading rapidly and blending with the folk music of the ordinary people, although maintaining a flavor of the rich Dynastic style.

The "water and land fair" was generally abbreviated to "water fair". It was a kind of sacrificial activity held during the dry season, when all the villagers prayed for rain, and the music thus became known as "water fair music".

Lantian Puhua Water Fair Music can be performed when walking or sitting down. Because of its somber tone, it is never used at festivals or weddings. Simple, elegant and delicate, it is in marked contrast to the music of Shaanxi opera, which is rough and vehement. Tunes commonly performed include those called *Qingjiang Song*, *Xiao Quzi*, *San Lianzi*, *Ba Ban*, *Gong Diao* and *Laoding Gang* in Chinese. They have survived to the present day by being passed down by monks and folk musicians.

Historically, the water music was mainly played during folk temple fairs, ceremonies of praying for rain, large sacrificial activities, and the Buddhist or Taoist rites for the deliverance of those who swim in the water or inhabit the dry land. On such occasions, its lovely melodies would be heard among the vast and mighty processions attendant upon these ceremonies. It was also performed as a part of the sacrificial entertainment at the time of the New Year.

Folk Musical Instruments of Hui Ethnic Group

Applicant: Ningxia Hui Autonomous Region

Over a long-term period of cultural development and practice, the Hui ethnic group in Ningxia inherited and passed on the ancient primordial musical instruments of Ningxia and of the northwestern frontier fortresses, in the process of which, those musical instruments evolved into those which the Hui ethnic group called wawu, mimi and kouxian. The Hui virtuoso is able to produce the most wonderful music with crossed quivering fingers on the high-pitched wawu; and few other instruments can produce anything to compare. Hui instruments are usually made in the shape of an ox head or a lamb, and are decorated with traditional Hui-style patterns as well as Arabic characters. They are easy to play and carry, and, due to the beautiful sounds they are capable of producing, are passed down from one generation to the next by the Hui people of Ningxia.

The young Hui men and women of Qinghai have a particular affection for, and are adept at playing, the musical instrument called the "mimi". It is made from a bamboo tube as thick as the third finger of their hand. With six sounding holes, it bears a marked resemblance to the flute, but is played from its end. When spring comes, a kind of melodious "mimi" music can be heard on the river banks, across the fields, in the marketplace, or at the temple fairs.

The Kouxian is a kind of small musical instrument especially loved by Hui girls. It is usually made of yellow steel, red copper or white silver. A Hui woman, wearing a red veil and playing the kouxian, is a well-known cultural representation of the Hui ethnic group in Ningxia.

Wawu is another kind of musical instrument favored by the Hui people. It is small in size and is made from the solid and durable yellow mastic which was called "xun" in ancient times. It is capable of playing some simple and gentle tunes. If a young man plays the "ox head-shaped xun" outside the house of a girl, and if she responds by playing the kouxian, then they will go out on a date!

Wenshui Guzi

Applicant: Wenshui County, Shanxi Province

Wenshui Guzi is a kind of old percussion instrumental folk ensemble, the members of which are people of Yuecun Village in Wenshui County. It came into being during the Jiajing Period of the Ming Dynasty, and

Master Benxing (left), an old artistic monk of the 26th generation of the Zhihua Temple, and the one of 27th generation playing the music in Beijing.

therefore has a history of some 500 years. Originally, it was a kind of divine drum used for sacrifice and when praying for rain. On the one hand, it has maintained this staus; on the other hand, guzi has been absorbed into the people's daily customs and has become the honor music of those ceremonies welcoming deities and guests. Over the course of history, it has gradually evolved into a kind of folk art indispensable to the people of Yuecun Village when holding festivals, giving folk art performances and celebrating harvests.

Guzi music is made using small and large cymbals and drums. Different combinations of instruments, unique playing methods, and various gestures employed during the performance result in idiographic sound effects. The major musical instrument for Wenshui Guzi is a tailor-made small cymbal with a diameter of some 20 cm at its outside edge and a diameter of 16 cm across its bowl, which is rare among percussion instruments. About three kg in weight, the small cymbal produces intense and vigorous tunes.

Wenshui Guzi is rich in sound effects. According to the ability of the player, it can reproduce the shock of a thunderclap, the rumble of thunder, the whistle of the wind, and the sudden flash of lightning, giving its listeners the overall impression of a terrific storm.

Jing Music at Beijing Zhihuasi Temple

Applicant: Beijing

Jing music is a classical combination of the melodies, lively folk music and imperial marches of the Tang and Song Dynasties. It arrived on the scene just as the music of these Dynasties reached an apex in regard of score, phonation, tune and development of its musical instruments. The most important of these were wind instruments such as pipe, sheng and flute, accompanied by such percussion instruments as gong, drum, musical stone and cymbals. In 1446, the Zhihuasi Temple was completed and imperial music was introduced, which was subsequently transformed into Buddhist music by the artist monks. That the Jing music has maintained its conservative and strict ways of inheritance and practice, passed down from one generation to the next without interruption is a rare thing that should be prized.

But, in fact, the Jing music is remarkably well preserved. It has been recorded in *gongchipu* (a type of traditional Chinese musical notation) with a definite chronological record. Also it has characteristic musical instruments and tunes, as well as player-monks who have inherited it from previous generations.

The music features distinct artistic characteristics. It is of a grand, simple and elegant style, with an extensive and standardised tune structure. Moreover, it is rich in playing skills and boasts a wide range of repertoire.

The Jing music has all together 300-odd tunes. But unfortunately, there are only 48 actual scores left to us. A band formed to play this music is usually comprised of nine players and 14 musical instruments.

Wutaishan Mountain Buddhist Music

Applicant: Wutai County, Shanxi Province

The Wutaishan Mountain, situated in the northeast of Shanxi Province, is one of the four major Buddhist mountains in China. It is the exclusive Buddhist sanctuary of both Han Buddhism (called "Green Temple") and Tibetan Buddhism (called "Yellow Monastery"). Buddhist music was introduced to the Wutaishan Mountain during the Northern Wei (386-534) Dynasty and became an important part of the Buddhist tradition there.

The music can be divided into that of the Han or the Tibetan Buddhist tradition. Influenced by its ethnic background, the latter features bright and cheerful tunes and local flavor, uninhibited by any strict rules; it is pretty much localised in the Wutaishan Mountain area. However, the Han Buddhist music stresses the adherence to a standard with an elegant and peaceful style, and has spread far from the slopes from where it originated. The musical instruments employed for the Buddhist music of both kinds are generally the same, including both percussion and woodwind.

The Wutaishan Mountain Buddhist Music derived from that of India, assimilating along the way elements of the ancient traditional music of China, thus becoming a fair representative of the northern Buddhist musical tradition. The Tang Dynasty saw the increasing collectivization and standardization of Buddhist rituals, during which time, the Buddhist music entered its golden period. Many kinds of singing styles, such as solo, unison and in-the-round, came into being. During the transition period of the Yuan and Ming Dynasties, musical instruments were introduced to the Wutaishan Mountain, which greatly accelerated the development of the artistic quality of the Buddhist rituals in this part of the world.

Buddhist music can be either vocal or instrumental. The former refers to the singing of various sutras, including the four modes of ensemble, and recitation; the latter covers the part-tunes of sutra recitation and is used to play some ditties. It is the finest expression of shrine music on the Wutaishan Mountain.

Qianshan Mountain Temple Music

Applicant: Anshan City, Liaoning Province

Qianshan Mountain lies 20 km to the southeast of Anshan City, Liaoning Province, and is one of the best-known scenic spots in China. It is the sanctuary of both Buddhism and Taoism, and its shrine music celebrates and honors both.

The Buddhist music of the Qianshan Mountain originated from various activities held in the mountainside temples, and developed along with them. Thanks to constant assimilation of the local folk music, plus that of the Indian Buddhist tradition, it reached maturity and remained pure in form during the period from 1115 to 1911. It is comprised of sutra chanting and instrumental music. The latter is mainly played on wind instruments, the sound production of which is similar to that of the sheng and other woodwinds popular in south Liaoning Province. The traditional tunes of sutra chanting belong to the northern tradition. Although experts all agree that this music has a very long history, no-one is exactly sure when it began.

The Buddhist music features a lively rhythm, loud and sonorous tonality, bold and straightforward tunes, and expresses heated emotion. It carries the strong religious flavor one would obviously expect, but combined with a distinct local color. With regard to the singing style, there are principally solos, choruses, and rhythmical chants.

Buddhist music is played on ethnic wind instruments such as *sheng*, pipe and flute, and the equally traditional percussion instruments such as drum and cymbals, plus those gongs that can be found in any temple. It is divided into the "cymbal ritual tune", the "chanting tune" and various forms of instrumental music. Currently, there are only a few lay Buddhists who are still able to play the traditional *sheng* and woodwind instruments. Most tunes have been lost, and now there are less than 20 in existence.

With a history of over100 years, the Taoist music of the Qianshan Mountain boasts fluent tunes, a large number of which are particularly melodious and all of which are colored by the religeous philosophies of the composers. It is played on wind instruments such as *xiao*, flute, pipe and *sheng*, alongside such percussion instruments as the drum and wooden fish, and complemented by those musical instruments used in Taoist ceremonies.

Taoist Music of Xuanmiaoguan Taoist Temple

Applicant: Suzhou City, Jiangsu Province

Located on Guanqian Jie in Suzhou City, the original Xuanmiaoguan Taoist Temple was first founded in the second year (276) of the Xianning Period of the Western Jin Dynasty. The structure we see now, erected during the Song Dynasty (960-1279) is the largest extant building of wooden construction in the whole area south of the Yangtze River.

As the most venerable of all the Taoist temples in Suzhou, it has also become a center for the theory and practise of studying and playing Taoist music. The temple monks are famous for playing the civil form of their music, which dates back to the Western Jin Dynasty (265-317), and has inherited the ancient traditions of worship, as well as assimilating elements of ceremonial and sacrificial music. It has also been influenced by Jiangnan music, Kunqu opera and Wu ballads, all of which combine to produce a unique style.

The Suzhou Taoist music requires the skillful playing of such instruments as the flute, with its alternately rapid, moderate and slow solos, and the drums, woodwinds and percussion instruments which also are used in Buddhist music. When played as part of the Taoist sacrificial ceremony, there is a bass drum solo, a further leading solo played on the sanxian, and then one tune repeated four times.

This music inherits the tradition of the old Imperial court, with a delicate overlay of religious and folk traditions, and still uses the gongchipu (a type of traditional Chinese musical notation). Its tunes are both simple and elegant, and are intended to entertain the deities during religious ceremonies, being slow, gentle and deep. The Taoists' devotional beliefs and yearning for an imaginary place of peace and serenity find full expression in their music.

Wudangshan Mountain Taoist Music

Applicant: Wudangshan Special Zone, Shiyan City, Hubei Province

Situated in Shiyan City in north Hubei Province, the Wudangshan Mountain has always been an ideal place for Taoists, and their magnificent buildings can be found all over its slopes.

The Taoist Music, also known as "Fashi Music (as used in religious ceremonies)" and "Daochang Music (the sort used in Taoist rites)", is a combination of the excellent folk culture of the Qinling and Bashan areas and the Imperial music of the Tang Dynasty (618-907) to Ming Dynasty (1368-1644). Usually, song, dance and music are performed together.

This music not only maintains the features of the "Rhythm of Ten Directions" , as formulated by the Sect of Complete Reality, but also blends in the music of various other sects. It has a wide range of tunes which are played on a correspondingly wide range of instruments, and falls into three categories: the one for self-cultivation of the Taoist in the morning and evening; the one for the Taoist sacrificial ceremony, held to release souls from purgatory so as to prevent disasters here on earth; and the one for memorial ceremonies, which are held on the third day of the third lunar month, the ninth day of the ninth lunar month, the fifteenth day of the seventh lunar month, and on the ceremony of consecration.

Nanyin Music

Applicant: Quanzhou City and Xiamen City, Fujian Province

Also known as "Quanzhou Nanyin", Nanyin Music is considered to be one of the most ancient musical art forms in China. It combines the elegant music of the Central Plains from the Tang Dynasty with what is best of the verses popular in Yuan Dynasty (1206-1368), in addition to elements of Yiyang tune and Kunqu opera, all blended with the folk music of south Fujian Province. The resulting

Chinese Taoist music is of long standing.

mix is a kind of wonderful music featuring beautiful and gentle melodies and touching and profound rhythms. Featuring a unique ethnic style, strong local flavor and pretty tunes, it is easy to learn and sing, thus enjoying great popularity in both south Fujian Province and overseas.

Nanyin Music is a unique system comprised of three major parts, called "Zhi", "Pu" and "Qu". The "Zhi" refers to a kind of suite with lyrics, score and specific directions for fingering the lute. There are all together 49 major suites, each of which is composed of several tunes in the same mode. Though there are lyrics, they are seldom sung, being more often simply a guideline for the character of the instrumental music. The "Pu" is a kind of programmatic instrumental suite. There are 16 major suites in total. The "Qu" refers to a type of verse accompanied by a background of instrumental music.

The major musical instrument of Nanyin is *dongxiao*, also known as "Chiba". It somewhat resembles the Tang *xiao* and is characterised by its deep and vigorous tones. Usually, the singer (also holding a clapper) is placed at the center of the performers, with the *pipa* and *sanxian* on the right and *dongxiao* and *erxian* on the left. Its gongchipu (a type of traditional Chinese musical notation) is of an independent system.

It boasts more than 2,000 tunes of both instrumental and vocal music, including the Qingshang tunes of the Jin Dynasty, tunes of the Tang Dynasty, tunes for religious rites, Yan music, Buddhist music, and the music for poems and operas composed during the Song Dynasty. The Nanyin is sung in the ancient standard dialect of Quanzhou, maintaining the phonology of the ancient Chinese language of the Central Plains. When being sung, it stresses the distinctiveness of these antique characters, both in its lyrics and in the arrangement of its rhythm.

Maqam Performance in Qiemo County, Xinjiang at the Noruz Festival.

Quanzhou Beiguan Music

Applicant: Quanzhou City, Fujian Province

More than 300 years ago, Beiguan Music was introduced to Quanzou from Beijing, Tianjin and the areas along the Yangtze and Huaihe Rivers. Since Nanyin music was already popular, the local people called this new form Beiguan for the purpose of differentiation.

Beiguan is a form of traditional stringed and woodwind music. There are Beiguan clubs in Taiwan, Singapore, and Malaysia.

It is divided into two kinds: qu (vocal music) and pu (instrumental music). Qu mostly originates from the tunes popular in the areas along the Yangtze River and Huaihe River during the Ming and Qing Dynasties. Pu derives from the music of Guangdong, the stringed and woodwind music south of the Yangtze River, and from the tradition of Peking Opera. The lyrics are mostly narratives and expressions of feeling, often with "oho" inserted at the ends of the sentences, and are sung to the accompaniment of a mandarin. At the beginning of a tune or at the end of a verse or stanza, singers often introduce a percussion instrument to add some luster to the performance.

Singers often raise one octave during their recital, and also incorporate some of the vocal methods of the Puxian Opera in Fujian Province plus those of the traditional Nanyin, adding volume, vigor, flexibility, and giving strength to the melody. In the qu performance, only clappers and wooden fish are used to play accented beats. A connected series of several pieces characterises the performance, and there are also tunes formed by changing the beats of the clappers.

The musical instruments upon which Beiguan is played are principally the stringed and woodwind instruments indigenous to the region south of the Yangtze River, with the addition of those used in the Puxian Opera in Fujian Province and the traditional Nanyin folk songs. Besides the jinghu and flute, there are also home-made instruments unique to the singers themselves. A band usually has seven or eight members, although there can be more than ten. On festival days, the Beiguan performers will dress up and join in with such activities as forming processions and welcoming deities.

Xinjiang Uygur Muqam Art

Applicant: Xinjiang Uygur Autonomous Region

The Xinjiang Uygur Muqam Art of China is the general term for a variety of Muqam practices widespread in the communities inhabited by the Uygur ethnic group in Xinjiang. It is a large and comprehensive collection of songs, dances and music which can be found in 19 countries and regions across Central, South, West and North Asia. Xinjiang lies in the eastermost of these parts of the world and thus gained maximum benefit from the "Silk Road", that historical artery linking Europe and Asia, for its music and dance are the product of cross-cultural communication between East and West. In November 2005, Xinjiang Uygur Muqam Art was listed in the third group of the "Masterpieces of the Oral and Intangible Heritage of Humanity" by UNESCO.

In the modern Uygur language, Muqam means principle, criterion and tune. A full musical suite is comprised of 12 muqams, each consisting of naqma (set of songs), dastan (narrative poems) and maxrap (folk songs and dances). The performance of each muqam lasts about two hours, and includes between 20 or 30 songs and tunes. Hence, it takes over 40 hours to play in full. The Muqam art boasts variety, a complex rhythmical structure, and a number of memorable tunes. With a vivid musical imagery and language, deep and slow classical narrative songs, warm and bright folk dance music, and fluent and melodious set of narrative songs, it has few rivals in artistic achievement.

The songs contain mottoes, admonitions, rural slang and folk stories. Some are in folk ballad form, others more purely lyrical.

Folk Dances

Jingxi Taiping Drum Dance

Applicant: Mentougou District, Beijing

It first appeared in Beijing during the Ming Dynasty and became common during the following Qing Dynasty. After it spread to Mentougou District during the late-Qing Dynasty, the dance was performed in many villages by people of all ages. The dance is especially popular from the twelfth lunar month and the first month of the following year; people dance to express their hopes for peace and prosperity. The performance of Taiping Drum not only adds luster to festivals, but also reflects festival customs in the Beijing area.

The dance is usually accompanied by a Taiping Drum, which is a round single-faced drum with a handle hung with several small tinkling metal rings. Its face is mounted with goat skin or brown paper, ornamented with several red pompons around the rim. Holding the drum in the left and drumstick in the right hand, people beat out the rhythm with a metallic sound.

Integrating sports, amusement and improvisation, Taiping Drum is a typical folk dance of the Han ethnic group in Beijing area. To perform the Jingxi Taiping Drum Dance, groups of people sway together from the waist while constantly beating each side of the drum or rim. Each village differs in playing method.

Yangge

Applicants: Hebei, Liaoning, Shandong and Shaanxi Provinces

Yangge originated from rice planting and farming. It also has some connections with ancient eulogistic songs sung in sacrifices to the God of Farming. During its development, it incorporated much from farming songs, folk songs, folk wushu (martial arts), acrobatics and traditional operas. By the Qing Dynasty, it had spread across the country.

With a long history, Yangge is one of the most representative folk dances in China. It is a unique collective art combining song and dance. Yangge dancers usually dress up as characters from history, myth, legend or from real life. They are skilled at changing the movements with the rhythm of drumbeats. The rich and varied movements and postures of the dancers combined make it popular among the masses.

Yangge Dance Performance in Northeast China

Yangge is now performed by teams in various places, with the number of performers ranging from two or three to several hundred. Corresponding to the roles, there are such props as handkerchief, umbrella, stick, drum and scourge for them to use. The accompanying musical instruments include suona horn, gong and drum. Yangge is performed in the street, alleyway or public square, creating a magnificent scene and warm atmosphere, On grand festivals such as New Year, Yangge teams are organized to extend regards to people in both urban and rural areas. Moreover, different villages will also send their Yangge teams to pay a visit and compete in singing and dancing of this kind.

Jingxing Lahua

Applicant: Jingxing County, Hebei Province

This is a kind of folk art, popular in and unique to Jingxing County. Originating in the Ming Dynasty, it prevails in folk festivals, temple fairs, celebrations and sacrificial ceremonies.

It is of distinct artistic feature, stressing the movements and actions of shoulder, wrist, arms, legs and feet. Main props are vase, colorful umbrellas and fans, scourge and board. The umbrella represents favorable weather; the board peace throughout the year; the scourge civil and military administration; and the vase safety and happiness.

Lahua is a kind of collective dance that can be performed on the street or in a theatre. The former features simple formation and incomplete dance, but the latter has a complete performance and various formations in which the performing skills are given full play. The number of participants is usually a multiple of six.

Jingxing Lahua features independent musical accompaniment, which combines the flavors of Chuige Song in Hebei and temple and palace music. It is in perfect coordination with the connotative, vigorous and generous style of Lahua dances. The palm gong is one of the characteristic instruments.

Dragon Dance

Applicants: Zhejiang, Guangdong and Sichuan Provinces, and Chongqing

This is a kind of folk dance of the Han ethnic group. It gets its name from the dancers holding a dragon-shaped prop. The image of the dragon originates from the ancient totem of China and is regarded as the symbol of the nation. The dragon was supposed to be capable of making rain as well as eliminating disasters and bringing good fortune.

Dancing Dragon

It is called "Dancing Dragon" or "Dragon-Lantern Dance" in some places and is widely spread in Guangdong, Zhejiang, Sichuan, Chongqing, Hubei, Hunan and Shanxi provinces. The dance is usually performed on the first day (Spring Festival) and fifteenth day (Lantern Festival) of the first lunar month, as well as the second day (Dragon Head-Raising Day) of the second lunar month in some places.

The dragon-shaped prop comprises a head, body and tail. The long body is framed with iron wires covered with paper or cloth. The tubular sections of the body are connected and then painted. After the head, body and tail are made, candles are placed in the middle of each section and wooden handles installed underneath for players to hold when performing.

In a performance, each player holds a handle and waves it to make the whole dragon fly in the air. At night, the candles inside it are lit, supplemented with fancy lanterns and lotus flower-shaped lanterns. Meanwhile, fireworks and firecrackers are also set off.

Lion Dance

Applicants: Hebei, Shanxi, Zhejiang and Guangdong Provinces

Lion Dance is a kind of comprehensive folk art combining martial art, acrobatics and drama.

The lion's head is framed with bamboo splints and mounted with colored paper and cloth. The body is made with colored cloth. Finally, it is set up with mobile eyes, ears and mouth.

The Lion Dance boasts a long history performed everywhere in China on festivals and ceremonies fully expressing people's joy. The lion is an auspicious animal in the eyes of the Chinese so the dance expresses people's wish for good luck and no disasters or evils.

The lion played by two persons is known as a senior lion, while the junior has only one person. The player, dressed as a knight, holds a pompon to dance accompanied by a big gong, drum, suona horn and reed pipes. The lion dance has civil and military versions. The civil lion performs interesting actions, such as snatching at and playing with a ball, wallowing, lapping hair and titillating. The military lion sets great store by acrobatics, including climbing, stepping on the ball, crossing a teeterboard and walking on staggered stilts. Through the long-term development, the lion dances of various places differ with each in style and character. The Beijing area stresses the technique in making the lion's head. The heavier the head, the stricter the required skill; the head weighs as much as 45 to 50 kg. The Lion Dance of Hebei Province emphasizes high jumping; the lion can jump up to the top of the five overlapped old-fashioned square tables and then somersault down to the ground. In the Lion Dance of Guangdong Province climbing is an important skill; the lion can climb up to towering pole to pick up the pompon.

Flowery Drum Lantern Dance

Applicant: Anhui Province

This is a kind of folk art combining song, dance and drama. It boasts a unique artistic style and rich artistic language. The dance movement is energetic, simple, bright, passionate and generous; the performing style has strong local flavor. Its music originates from folk songs, featuring a wide range of subjects and a changeable rhythm, elated, intense or gentle. It is the most representative and touching folk dance of the Han ethnic group.

The Flowery Drum Lantern Dance is mostly performed in rural areas during the period between the autumn harvest and following spring plowing, especially at temple fairs and the Spring Festival. It is usually comprised of dance, song, playlet and gong and drum performance; dance forms its principal part.

The dance is a typical folk art performed on a square. Accompanied by gong and drum, it uses such props as folding fan, handkerchief and colored umbrella, expressing happiness after the harvest through graceful movements, folk songs and ditties.

The performer playing the male part is called "Gu Jiazi", featuring vigorous and straightforward movements and a lot of flips and acrobatics; the one playing the female part is called "Lahua", employing a handkerchief, fan and umbrella and beating the flowery drum when singing and dancing. The performance usually takes place on a square decorated with colorful lanterns at night in rural areas, thus the name "Flowery Drum Lantern Dance".

The movements are changeable comparable with other folk dances in degree of vehemence, complication and accurate and exquisite expression of feelings. The gong and drum have distinct features producing a complex accompaniment. In the original performance of the dance, the lantern song and dance appeared alternately.

Flower drum lantern dance is popular in the reaches of the Huaihe River, known as the representative dance of the Han and the "Orient Ballet".

Nuowu Dance

Applicant: Jiangxi Province

Nuowu Dance is a kind of dance in the Nuoji Sacrificial Ceremony, which had its origin in totem worship of primeval times. It became a kind of fixed sacrificial ceremony for exorcising plague and demons.

Customarily called "Ghost Drama", Nuowu Dance is usually performed from the first to the sixteenth day of the first lunar month. The extant Nuowu Dance is mainly distributed in Jiangxi, Anhui, Guizhou, Guangxi, Shandong, Henan, Shaanxi, Hubei, Fujian, Yunnan and Guangdong provinces.

This folk dance with a long history has two performing styles. One is performed by the four leading actors; the performers wear a hat-shaped mask on their face, while a hide covers the body, and hold a dagger and guilder in the hands. They utter a sound in pronunciation of the Chinese character "nuo" constantly. The other style is performed by a group of 12 persons, each featuring red hair and painted skin and holding a long scourge made of hemp to make a sound. Meanwhile, they call loudly the names of the deities especially for eating evils and fierce animals. They also dance to musical accompaniment accordingly.

Attractive Nuo dance

The performer usually wears a mask to play a part of a deity or a historical figure. Hence, a huge pedigree of Nuo deities has come into being. "The performer is a human being without mask; while he or she becomes a deity when wearing a mask".

The accompanying musical instruments are simple, usually being percussion instruments such as drum and gong. The organization performing Nuowu Dance is called "Nuoban Troupe", with usually eight to 10 members and strict rules. The dance usually appears in the climactic part in the Nuoji Sacrificial Ceremony. Nuowu Dances in various places are rich in content, with integrated functions for worship and recreation.

Yingge

Applicant: Guangdong Province

Yingge is a kind of folk dance performed on a square, combining dance, southern-style boxing and acting of dramas. Grand and heroic in vigor and warm in atmosphere, it prevails in Guangdong and Fujian Provinces. It is performed by males in praise of heroes.

It is said to have a history of some 300 years, originating from the martial arts custom of local people or the stories of The Water Margin. The dance is usually performed on festivals; the number of performers is even, ranging from 12 to 108. Each performer holds a pair of colored wood sticks, knocking them in different ways in line with the drumbeat and shouts. They walk in the dance. The performance is divided into front and back parts: the former includes the performance of gong and drum and Yingge Dance; the latter embraces various characteristic playlets and adept programs.

The basic movement of Yingge Dance is playing the sticks. Each performer holds a pair of round short wooden sticks (diameter 10 cm, length 20 cm). They squat in the posture of riding a horse and then move the legs sideways, knocking with one stick against the other up and down and on the left and right. The rhythm of Yingge varies from fast to moderate or slow, with many shifts. The Yingge Dance features manly virility. At the climax, shouts and trumpet calls resound through the air.

The folk art features characteristic regional flavor. The word "Yingge" reminds one the Chaoshan area in Guangdong Province. Puning in the Chaoshan area is the "hometown of Yingge Dance". The Yingge of Puning combines dance, southern-style boxing and acting of dramas in the most outstanding way.

Stilt Dance

Applicants: Shanxi, Liaoning and Gansu Provinces

Stilts have long been popular for play and entertainment. There are various kinds: high stilt, medium stilt and running stilt. The height of the stilt ranges from less than 0.67 meters to 3.3 meters, but averages about one meter.

Stilt Dance, also known as "Stilt Yangge", gets the name from the fact that the performer dances on stilts in a way demanding great skill. Since it is performed on stilts, it can be appreciated at a distance. The performance proceeds freely without the restriction of a stage. Deeply loved by the masses, it is a kind of folk dance widely prevalent in China.

Stilt Yangge Performance

The dance is usually performed by a team, with 10-plus to scores of members. The performer mostly plays the part of a character in some ancient myth or historical story, with the costume imitating those in traditional operas. Common props include fan, handkerchief, crabstick, sword and spear. The performing style is divided into two kinds called "Caijie" and "Liaochang". The latter refers to a stilt team dancing, mostly a male and a female performer dancing as a pair, sometimes accompanied with songs. The accompanying musical instruments are categorized into two kinds. Take the Beijing-Tianjin Stilt Dance, for example. It is accompanied by two waist drums and two hand gongs. The players dance and at the same time beat the instruments to accompany the whole team. The other kind is a percussion instrument such as bass drum and top cymbal, whose large sound volume serves as a foil to the warm atmosphere.

Yongxin Shield Dance

Applicant: Yongxin County, Jiangxi Province

This is a kind of comprehensive folk art combining martial arts, acrobatics, dance and music. With a history of some 150 years, it is popular in Longyuankou and Yange Towns.

After the mid-19th Century Taiping Rebellion collapsed, some officers and soldiers of the Taiping Army stranded in Yongxin continued to drill. Subsequently, some people practicing martial arts improved on the drill and gradually developed it into a folk dance of great value in appreciation, fitness and recreation.

The Shield Dance has traditional, stately and stirring performing styles. It features rapidly changing actions. The performer is required to master the eight-character knack of "pushing, shielding, striking, withstanding, compelling, dodging, falling and rolling".

Nine performers wrap their heads with a towel and wear a short dark gown with buttons down the front and white brims, black trousers with tight cuffs, leg wrappings and straw sandals. One performer holding a steel fork with rings plays the part of an officer or a trooper of the enemy; others hold a shield in one hand and a sword in the other. All of them are doughty and martial.

The dance is simple in content, including fighting between two corps in various formations.

The accompanying music is also unique, mostly produced by folk percussion instruments. Some places adopt stringed and wind instrumental music; some employ a special kind of musical instrument called "Na Zi" in Chinese, featuring a wiry and elated sound.

Yicheng Flowery Drum Dance

Applicant: Yicheng County, Shanxi Province

This boasts a rich performing styles, lively and bright rhythm and great vigor. Through more than 1,000 years, it has evolved into a characteristic folk dance spread to Shaanxi, Inner Mongolia, Tianjin and Henan, and so on. The flowery drum is hung close to the chin declining from the right to the left, slanting in front of the chest or on the waist.

Performers carry several such flowery drums on the body and play them in different ways. They can also jump up onto parallel bars raised by two persons to perform freely to great audience acclaim. In Yicheng, almost everybody can play the flowery drum.

There are mainly two kinds of performing styles. One is a parade performance at grand festival featuring slow movements and gentle rhythm, usually performed together with folk art performances such as Yangge. The other is a stage performance, which is also divided into two kinds. One kind occurs in the process of parade performance. If there are dense crowds, the parade will stop to show off some unrivalled skills; the other kind is performed on a square usually accompanied with folk songs led by the drummer and female actress.

Quanzhou Breast Clapping Dance

Applicant: Quanzhou City, Fujian Province

This is one of the most representative folk dances in Fujian Province, mainly in Fuqiao and Jiangnan in south Fujian and Quanzhou and Jinmen. It is comparatively simple in style and can be performed by one or two persons at will.

The dance is traditionally performed by males. Performers wear a grass hoop on the head are have a bare torso and feet. The actions include clapping, clamping and stamping with single rhythm. They pull in the waist and throw out the chest. Sometimes, they jump, squat or shake the head in a straightforward, simple, humorous and ardent style.

The basic movement is clapping in seven places. First, clap the hands in front of the chest and then the left and right sides, left and right elbows and left and right legs. The performers jump in line with bowed steps and shake the head to form a unique weaving movement. The dance appears free, natural, smart and humorous. It proceeds by repeating the movements.

The grass hoops they wear are in the shape of snake, which maintains the ancient snake totem of the Minyue Tribe in the Qin and Han dynasties. The performing style also retains the custom of the primitive dance of the tribe.

Ansai Waist Drum Dance

Applicant: Ansai County, Shaanxi Province

This is a unique kind of large-scale folk dance with a 2,000-year history.

The dance was originally used to promote soldiers' morale and pass on information. The virility of the men living on the Loess Plateau finds full expression in the high-frequency drumbeats, vigorous steps, rapidly changing array and loud whoops.

The action of turning around while beating the drum is a key point. It is required to be vigorous to fulfill the combination

Common people play the Ansai Waistdrum to celebrate Chinese traditional Lantern Festival in Yan'an, Shaanxi Province.

13 Culture

and change of the series of actions such as squatting, kicking and jumping in fixed time.

The Waist Drum Dance is also divided into civilian and military kinds. The first stresses writhing and the second playing the drum. The movement of the dance is fast, ever-changing, natural, bright and fluent, combining both firm and gentle elements. It has evolved into a blend of dance, martial art, gymnastics, percussion and wind instrumental music and folk songs, becoming richer in both content and form and worthier of appreciation and performing.

The dance is mostly performed collectively, with the number of performers ranging from dozens to over a hundred. The performance stresses overall effect, requiring orderly movements and standard array. Besides the drumbeats of the performers, the dance is sometimes accompanied by a folk band with such musical instruments as drum, small cymbals and gong.

Luochuan Biegu Drum Dance

Applicant: Luochuan County, Shaanxi Province

Luochuan Biegu Drum Dance

This dance mainly prevails in Luochuan County of Shaanxi Province. In Shaanxi dialect, the Chinese character "Bie" refers to jumping, which is characteristic of this dance. Uniquely, it completes various kinds of movements in jumping. The performer hangs an oblate drum with a diameter of some 50 cm in front of the abdomen, jumping and playing at the same time.

Luochuan was contended for by the states of Qin, Jin and Wei during the Warring States Period (475-221 BC), containing part of the Great Wall built then and a beacon tower. The Biegu Drum Dance is supposed to have evolved from the battle array; it is a folk dance reflecting ancient warfare. The dance contains elements of sacrificial activity.

The drummers, dressed as warriors, wrap their head with a red towel, put four flags on their back, tie a skirt to the waist and wind their legs with leggings. The drum is hung from the waist, and the drummers hold a red and a white drumstick, while playing and jumping. Other performers add to the noise with big cymbals and small gongs. It is mostly performed by a large group up to 100 on a square. The dance features unique steps and strict and ever-changing formations.

On Spring Festivals, each village in Luochuan County organizes a Biegu Drum Dance Team, with drummers drawn from each family. They parade in the village to pay a New Year Call from door to door and celebrate the harvest. In addition, the dance team serves as a characteristic indispensable honor guard for the sacrificial ceremony held in the temple.

Lanzhou Taiping Drum Dance

Applicant: Lanzhou City, Gansu Province

With a history of more than 600 years, Lanzhou Taiping Drum Dance is one of the folk performances loved by the people in the area as a celebration of peace at New Year. At grand ceremonies, the performance is a climax of the whole activity. The clangorous and vigorous drumbeats contain the strong flavor of northwest China with artistic charm.

The traditional Taiping Drum is a fairly regular cylinder 70 cm long and with a diameter of about 45 cm. The drum is made of wood wrapped with thick and solid cowhide. The body of the drum is painted red or black, with designs of lions playing with an embroidered ball and two dragons playing with a pearl. The rims are decorated with lacework comprised of 卐-shaped designs; the drumheads are painted with the design of the Eight Diagrams. Two hoops are nailed on either end for fastening the straps. The strap is long enough to reach from the shoulder to the knee of the drummer so it can be thrown in any direction.

Numerous drummers dance vigorously in order and harmony, playing the drum while jumping, rising and turning around. It looks like ten thousand horses galloping ahead.

Yuhang Rolling Lantern Dance

Applicant: Yuhang District of Hangzhou City in Zhejiang Province

This is a folk dance of the Han ethnic group prevailing in the Yuhang and Haiyan areas along the banks of the Qiantangjiang. With a history of 800-odd years, it is usually performed on festivals and lantern fairs.

The lantern is woven with half-centimeter-thick bamboo strips, varying in size. The large-sized lantern has a diameter of more than one meter and a weight of some 50 kg. A small ball-shaped lantern woven with bamboo strips is installed in the center, in which a red or black candle is lit. The lantern with red candle is regarded as "civilian lantern"; the one with a black candle as a "martial lantern".

Basically, the dance has nine sets of 27 movements such as rolling the lantern around the waist and raising it high. The performance proceeds in certain order and always ends with the action of "opening the lotus flower". Male performers generally employ a large lantern with a black candle in it, which can be played by different performers. Accompanied with gongs and drums, the performance is extremely brilliant at night.

In activities like temple fairs, the Rolling Lantern Dance usually appears in front of the parade because the performers roll the lantern in all directions so that people around will give way; hence, it plays a role in clearing the way.

Tujia Hand Wielding Dance

Applicant: Xiangxi Tujia and Miao Autonomous Prefecture of Hunan Province

The Tujia Hand Wielding Dance is a folk dance of the Tujia ethnic group, prevailing in the Yongshun, Longshan and Baojing areas of Hunan Province and the area collectively inhabited by the Tujia ethnic group on the border between Hubei and Sichuan provinces. It is a ritual collective dance held in front of the Temple of King Tu. It originated in the late Tang Dynasty as a sacrificial activity.

In Tujia areas, there is special place for dancing the Hand Wielding Dance called the "Hand Wielding Hall", which is also a place for worshiping the spirit tablets of ancestors. From the third to the fifteenth day of the first lunar month, sacrificial activity will be held there, with the Hand Wielding Dance as main content.

The ground of the "Hand Wielding Hall" is paved with stone slabs, flat and smooth. A high cassia tree, pine or cypress stands in the middle, hung with red lanterns above a big gong and drum. One person plays the gong and drum; while dancers form a line to circle the tree.

The dance is divided into large and small Hand Wielding. The former is mainly performed for sacrifice once every three or five years, with several thousand participants. The latter is adopted for common festival activities, with dozens or several hundred participants.

The movements of the dance include the "single wielding", "double wielding" or "whirl wielding", embodying various sacrificial rituals and actions of work and combat, such as putting the palms together, going down on one's knees, sitting cross-legged, playing with a sword or stick, surrounding and crossing a mountain or a river. They are concise and straightforward, full of primitive flavor.

Tujia Sayeryo Dance

Applicant: Changyang Tujia Autonomous County, Hubei Province

Changyang Tujia Sayeryo is a kind of sacrificial dance of the Tujia ethnic group in the middle reaches of the Qingjiang for soothing the spirit of the dead with pleasant song and dance.

"Sayeryo" is held in the mourning room established in the main hall. A bass drum mounted with cowhide is placed on the left side of the coffin. The man playing the drum is called "drum master"; he is also in charge of leading the chorus. Dancers join in the chorus while dancing, and they are known as the "song master". Usually, there are one or two pairs. If the space is not enough for more dancers, they can dance in the yard outside the main gate.

The tune sung by the drum master is the melody of folk songs familiar to local people, and he sings in accordance with popular content or impromptu.

"Sayeryo" uses the male ottava alta in tune and a kind of old special third in tone which only exists in the Xingshan area on the northern bank of the Three Gorges and cannot be found in other kinds of songs. It is similar to the style of Songs of Chu in terms of structure. It also carries some flavor of ancient songs for worshiping deities in the states of Ba and Chu.

Xianzi Dance

Applicants: Sichuan Province and Tibet Autonomous Region

Xianzi is a kind of Chinese violin unique to Tibetans, customarily played by males. Accompanied by this instrument, Xianzi Dance is a comprehensive Tibetan art combining song, dance and music. It prevails in eastern Tibet and Tibetan communities in Yunnan, Sichuan and Qinghai provinces as self-entertainment.

It can be divided into three kinds of content. The first is for welcoming guests, extending acknowledgment and praising each other; the second kind is for respecting seniors and loving the hometown; the third is for expressing love and pure and sincere friendship.

There is no fixed venue for the dance, which can be performed in the courtyard, on the flat roof or in the house by anyone. At festivals or grand assemblies, people will get together to form a circle, with one side leading the chorus and the other repeating it alternately. Hence, a unique antiphonal style of singing emerges.

Males play the Xianzi; females dance and play with a long colored sleeve. The song and dance vary in line with the rhythm of the Xianzi. The performance features various tunes, rich lyrics and many changes in step. The male and female teams form separate semicircles, coming together and parting in turn while singing. With regard to movements, males stress stamping to show a bold and straightforward beauty; females mainly show a gentle beauty by wielding their long sleeves.

Wielding colored sleeves is a basic characteristic of Xianzi dance; and stooping every three steps is one of the basic movements of the dance.

Guozhuang Dance

Applicants: Tibet Autonomous Region, Qinghai and Yunnan Provinces

Guozhuang Dance, also known as "Zhuo", refers to the Tibetan Circle Dance. As one of the three major folk dances of Tibetans, it is found in Qamdo and Nagqu of Tibet, Aba and Ganzi of Sichuan, Diqing of Yunnan and Tibetan communities in Qinghai and Gansu provinces.

It is a kind of joyful dance. On festivals, people, old or young, will dance cheerfully. Especially when there is a wedding or the Spring Festival or the Dragon Boat Festival arrives, people will dance throughout the night.

It is a collective dance without accompaniment. The males and females form separate semicircles. The steps are divided into "Guozhuo (walking)" and "Kuwu (turning)". Performers dance and sing antiphonally at the same time. The dance proceeds slowly at first and then gets faster and the dancers' gestures more pronounced as they forming large or small circles and sometimes create a design of "dragon swaying the tail".

The Guozhuang Dance is divided into large and small versions. The first is a ceremonial dance mostly performed when scriptures are chanted or for welcoming guests. It has strict requirements. For example, the leading dancer should be designated in advance, mostly being a saintly male senior; and dress is unified. Moreover, with certain procedure, it features steady steps and restrained movements and postures expressing honor and sincerity. The small Guozhuang Dance is for self-entertainment. There is no restriction on the leading dancer. In regard to content, it mainly expresses love, work and nature. Hence, it is lively, free and easy.

Guozhuang Dance of the Tibetan

Raba Dance

Applicant: Tibet Autonomous Region

A dancing performance staged by the Tibetan artists known as "Raba", the Raba Dance is an artistic form centered on bell and drum and integrating singing, comic dialogue, dancing, qigong, acrobatics and Raba drama. It has a comparatively fixed set of procedures, comprising 12 programs; the whole set lasts five hours.

Raba originally meant folk artists. The dance named after them is free and lively in style. A female plays a hand drum and male shakes a bass bell in echo, thus the name "Bell and Drum Dance". Sometimes, they whirl constantly on a single foot.

The rhythm of the bell and drum is distinct, changing with the tune and emotion. At the climax, the movements are extremely vigorous. The male whirls on one feet like a tercel; the female, holding the bow-shaped drumstick over her head, turn round cheerfully like a peacock spreading its tail. The dance demands high skill, brisk at first and vigorous at the climax.

It was originally staged to pray for a good harvest, village security, the thriving of the domestic animals and elimination of disasters. The performers need long-term training in the aspects of singing, dancing and playing musical instruments.

The bell and drum are important components of the dance. There are nine kinds of drumbeats, which dictate the style of performance.

Cham of Tashilhungpo Monastery in Xigaze

Applicant: Tibet Autonomous Region

"Cham" is a kind of ritual dance held in the Buddhist monasteries in Tibet for exorcising demons and rewarding deities. It is performed by masked lamas accompanied by such musical instruments as drum. "Cham" refers to dancing for deities held on grand Buddhist festivals. The mask in Cham constitutes an important part of Tibetan mask art.

"Sermo Cham" is that of the Gelug Sect of Tibetan Buddhism, performed by the lamas of the Tashilhungpo Monastery in the Xigaze area of Tibet in the eighth month according to Tibetan calendar. In Tibetan language, "Sermo" refers to appreciating and "Cham" large scale. Together, it means appreciating large-scale Cham.

As a kind of sacrificial activity in monasteries, Cham is unique in style. It is staged in the courtyard of the monastery, with characteristic masks, props and garments. The whole activity involves solo, pairs or group dance. Its performance order, decoration, structure of the performers and props are closely designated. All the characters involved carry the image of Buddha. Hence, their movements and postures are eccentric.

Cham is accompanied by wind and percussion instruments. The band mainly plays bass drum and top cymbal. The latter is the directing musical instrument of Cham. Lamas who play the top cymbal are required to master the whole process and movements of Cham because the performers take their cue from him. The band usually plays on the terrace. Lamas also chant scriptures by the left side of the monastery gate.

Reed Panpipe Dance of Miao Ethnic Group

Applicant: Guizhou Province

This is prevalent among Miao people in southeast Guizhou Province, performed by both sexes and all ages.

It is a traditional folk dance in which males play the reed panpipe and at the same time, conduct the movements of crotch, knee and ankle; hence the name Reed Panpipe Dance. Its basic steps are "exploring the way". Dancers raise their left foot and rotate it in a semicircle and then put the foot down again, before doing the same with the right foot, and so on.

In the past, the dance was performed at weddings or funerals or when a house was completed, besides sacrificial activities. Subsequently, it appeared at festivals and in the celebration for the harvest and traditional social activities held by young people. In content, there are five kinds: self-entertainment, custom, performance, sacrifice and etiquette. It plays an important role in the social life of Miao People.

The Reed Panpipe Dance for self-entertainment is most prevalent, and there are no restrictions on gender or age, hence attracting many participants. It usually takes place on the lawn, embankment or mountain slope. There are two kinds of common performing styles. In one, males playing a small reed panpipe and females each holding a flowery handkerchief form separate circles to surround dancers playing large reed panpipes. They perform a circle dance briskly in line with the rhythm. In regard to the other kind, at least one pair of reed panpipe players is chosen to lead the dance, with other people (mostly female) follow them to form a circle and dance. Their movements vary in line with the tunes.

Korean Nongle Dance

Applicants: Liaoning and Jilin Provinces

This is popular among Korean communities in Jilin, Heilongjiang and Liaoning provinces. It is a folk art mixing music, dance and singing.

Usually, there are two forms. One is a scenario-related performance staged in the form of dance and mummery; the other is a mass performance containing rich traditional dances and staged at the beginning of the New Year and in celebrating the harvest. The dance team commonly comprises 60 members. They raise the banner inscribed with "Agriculture Is the Foundation of the Country", emphasizing agriculture as the base and farming as pleasure.

Nongle Dance comprises 12 parts all together, including the "tabour dance" performed by young men; "making a human pyramid" staged by children; traditional "flat drum dance" performed by a large number of people; "long drum dance" performed by males or females; "fan dance" originating from the ancient witch dance; the "crane dance"; and "Xiangmao Dance" performed by males. The "Xiangmao Dance", in which the young male dancers swing a 20-meter-long colored ribbon, arouses a great response from audiences.

The men run and jump in line with the warm and cheerful drumbeats, fully showing their virility. In the female solo dance with a flat drum, the actress should not only show her varied, adept drum playing skills, but also dance vigorously, gracefully and smartly.

Happy dance loved by farmers of the Korean ethnic group

Wooden Drum Dance

Applicants: Guizhou and Yunnan Provinces

This is a kind of folk dance for worship prevalent among the Miao, Yi and Va ethnic groups in southwest China. The drum is made from a hollow tree trunk. The Wooden Drum Dance is a part of a large sacrificial activity involving the whole tribe. The wooden drum is regarded as the tribal symbol and the activity obviously embodies ancestor and nature worship, with distinct characteristics of primitive culture.

The Wooden Drum Dance of the Miao ethnic group in the Taijiang County of Guizhou Province features concise movements and rich combinations to honor ancestors and describe group's origins and geographic environment. The dance moves steadily to a climax. Each scenario has distinct arrangement with natural transitions. Performers sing and dance at the same time, swinging their arms and stamping in 2/4 time. The movements are straightforward and bold. In the Year of the Ox, the Wooden Drum Dance will be performed in combination with the sacrifice of an ox and other grand festival activities.

The Wooden Drum Dance is also performed by the Va ethnic group in Cangyuan of Yunnan Province during festivals and ceremonies. On the occasion, everyone wearing new clothes performs a circle dance to thunderous drumbeats around the house of the wooden drum. They bow to show their respect to the wooden drum. All the performers move slowly counter-clockwise, swinging their arms, walking and stamping their feet. The dance is accompanied by songs of the drummer and performers mainly narrating the history of the ethnic group, sacrifice, work, production and life.

Bronze Drum Dance

Applicant: Wenshan Zhuang and Miao Autonomous Prefecture, Yunnan Province

This is one of the old dances most prevalent and influential among the Zhuang and Yi people of the Wenshan Zhuang and Miao Autonomous Prefecture of Yunnan Province. It has its origins in nature and ancestor worship. The Yi hold that the bronze drum is the soul of the universe and people's wishes can be passed to the God and the ancestors through beating it and performing the Bronze Drum Dance. However, the Zhuang ethnic group believes beating the bronze drum and dancing can exorcise demons and offer prayers for safety.

The drummer beats the bronze drum rhythmically as the performers dance and change formation. There are six to seven kinds of characteristic movements, each differing in steps and tempo In the collective dance, young people form either a circle, semicircle, row, column, cross and square. The dance features vigorous steps, straightforward and agile movements and postures. At the climax, drummers often shout cheerfully and excitedly. The high spirits and touching scene fully express the bold, unconstrained and simple character of the local people.

The Bronze Drum Dance of the Miao ethnic group is mostly performed on grand festivals. The bronze drum is put up in the center of the venue and beaten by one drummer. Another person holds a special wooden barrel behind the bronze drum, beating the barrel in tune with the drumbeats to strengthen the effect of the tones. There is no limit on the number of performers, which usually surpasses one thousand.

The Bronze Drum Dance of the Yao ethnic group is spectacular. On festivals, many drums are placed in a row, each with its own drummer beating and dancing at the same time. In the center there is a large wooden drum more than 60 cm in diameter leading the performance.

Peacock Dance of Dai Ethnic Group

Applicant: Ruili City, Yunnan Province

This is the most famous traditional performance among the folk dances of the Dai, who regard the peacock as the symbol of happiness and auspiciousness. Of the various Dai dances, the Peacock Dance is the most popular and familiar. It is also one of the dances with largest change and fastest development.

Yang Liping, noted Chinese dancer, performs Peacock Dance

The dance boasts a long history and is included in religious rituals. On festivals such as the annual Water-Splashing Festival, Door-Closing Festival and Door-Opening Festival, Dai people will get together to beat a bass gong and elephant-foot drum and perform the graceful Peacock Dance.

The dance mostly imitates a peacock running down the hill, wandering in the forest, drinking at a spring, playing, pulling, spreading and shaking its wings, resting on a branch and flying. It features implicit emotions, rich dance language and sculptural postures. The performer mostly maintains a squatting posture. Each joint of body will bend, forming a unique three-curvature posture. It also has many hand shapes and movements, which present different concepts of beauty and artistry even in the same posture and step. The Peacock dance has strict procedures and requirements as well as standard positions and steps. Each movement is accompanied by a corresponding drumbeat.

The elephant-foot drum is the important instrument for the dances of Dai. From very young to very old, every person of the ethnic group can beat it.

Daur Lurigele Dance

Applicants: Morin Dawa Daur Autonomous Banner, Inner Mongolia and Harbin City, Heilongjiang Province

In communities of the Daur ethnic group in Inner Mongolia, Lurigele Dance is the general designation for folk dances, mostly performed by women for self-entertainment purposes. Lurigele refers to "burning" or "flourishing" in Chinese and means "having a dance" by extension in the Daur language. The dance has its origin in early hunting times when their ancestors lived around a bonfire in the remote mountains.

The performers are mainly young women and girls. The males seldom perform it, mostly being spectators. At the outset, one pair of performers dance and then others join in up to the climax. Accompanied by melodious and slow tunes, dancers begin to swing their hands slowly and move airily, like walking in embroidered shoes on ice. After a while, the rhythm becomes loud and sonorous, in line with which, the steps speed up and movements grow more vigorous. The arms are swung like hammers. One performer puts a hand on the waist and brandishes the other hand to the next person, the action repeated alternately so that it looks like they are fighting. The stubbornness of the Daur women finds full expression in the "fighting", which also brings about the dance climax. Then a third performer will join them to relax the atmosphere. The movements gradually slow down and go back to the initial stage before winding up again.

Mongol Andai Dance

Applicant: Huret Banner, Inner Mongolia Autonomous Region

Known as a living fossil of Mongol dance, this is a primitive dance prevails in the surrounding areas of Tongliao City in Inner Mongolia. It originated from the Huret Banner and came into being in the late Ming Dynasty and early Qing Dynasty.

It is usually performed on festivals or in leisure time, with one leading singer and hundreds of people of both sexes and all ages echoing the refrain and dancing. It is for self-entertainment purposes and features a distinct ethnic character and strong flavor of living, pleasant and simple to learn. The libretto is created at will. The dance has no restrictions on time and venue and is suitable for everybody to join. The performers are only required to swing a ribbon and mark time to echo the leading singer.

The traditional Andai Dance is usually accompanied with songs. The movements are slow and in line with the rhythm. When climax is reached, performers become vigorous and high-spirited. "Marking time", "stamping", "swinging the ribbon" and forming a circle at will are the basic steps. In the development of the Andai Dance, Mongolian people added lots of folk songs, and congratulations and eulogies. The dance is organically combined with the songs and talking, gradually forming scores of melodies.

Over some 400 years, the Andai Dance, characterized by "inherent folk qualities", has gradually become the most popular dance of Mongol religious rituals and at the grand Nadam Fair. According to historical records of Huret Banner, one Andai Dance lasted for as many as some 40 days. It leads the folk dances in China in scale and number of participants.

Xiangxi Drum Dance of Miao Ethnic Group

Applicant: Xiangxi Tujia–Miao Autonomous Prefecture, Hunan Province

This is the most unique dancing art among Miao. During Spring Festival or grand festivals, villagers in Xiangxi gather to conduct a drum dance contest.

Xiangxi Drum Dance has many characteristics. Firstly, it is rich in movements and postures. In line with the emotion, it can be divided into beating drum, stepping on the drum. In expressing the idea of work, it performs the actions of plowing, transplanting rice seedlings and harvesting paddy; in expressing ways of life, it has actions of washing face and doing up the hair; and it imitates the buffalo scrubbing the back, the monkey beating the drum and cat washing its face. Secondly, in regard to performing style and number of performers, there are the drum dances performed by two persons, an empty-handed male, two females or one female, the drum dance performed by one person or more in imitation of the monkey are for celebrating reunion and New Year. Thirdly, the placement of the drum differs in various places. The drum may be placed flat, slanting or upright. Fourthly, the music for the dance has strong ethnic flavor and the costumes are also characteristic.

Performers dance vigorously while beating the drum. In line with the bright rhythm, drummers beat the drum with both hands alternately. Meanwhile, they jump with one foot and then the other in turn, swinging the body ceaselessly.

Miao people beat the drum on the eighth day of the fourth lunar month, around the Spring Festival and in grand activities such as hurrying up to the autumn, celebrating harvest, holding a wedding ceremony or welcoming guests. It is a special way to express emotion.

Xiangxi Maogusi Dance Drama of Tujia Ethnic Group

Applicant: Xiangxi Tujia-Miao Autonomous Prefecture, Hunan Province

Maogusi prevails in the area of Tujia ethnic group in Xiangxi of Hunan Province, referring to hunters with hairs over the entire body in Tujia language. Maogusi Dance has its origin from a Tujia sacrificial ceremony and is an old dance in Xiangxi still performed.

The dance mainly presents the different aspects of the ancestors "hairy people". Performers put couch grass or straw all over their body to depict the production activities of their ancestors such as fishing, hunting and farming with miming and other artistic techniques similar to drama. It combines dance and drama performance.

Maogusi Dance is of primitive simplicity and unique in form and style. The most obvious distinction is the costume made of grass and bark. Wearing it, performers seem to be simple and unsophisticated, full of primitive flavor. In dialogue, performers are required to change their tone so the audience find it hard to recognize their real identity.

Throughout, performers should speak Tujia language and sing Tujia songs. They have rude and humoristic actions and weird and foolish postures. In addition, with the costume, they realistically represent the behavior and ideas of their ancestors, Though the Tujia have no written language, Maogusi Dance has been passed down from generation to generation and been improved along the way.

The Li Firewood-Gathering Dance in Sanya, Hainan Province

Firewood Gathering Dance of Li Ethnic Group

Applicant: Sanya City, Hainan Province

This is the most representative kind of folk dance of the Li ethnic group. It originates from funeral customs in the ancient Yazhou area (present-day Sanya City of Hainan Province).

The dance has a complete set of props and performing skills. Two square timbers are placed parallel on which several long wrist-thick bamboo poles lie crossways. Performers hold one end of the pole in each hand, producing rhythmic sound by collision between the bamboo poles and between pole and plank. They can sit, squat or stand to do it. Dancers, in line with the sound, jump nimbly in the instantaneous space between the poles, imitating working actions of people and movements and animal sounds naturally and gracefully.

Due to the peculiarity of the dance in props, rhythm and performing skill as well as its strong nature of entertainment and athletics, it spread quickly all over the Li-inhabited areas in Hainan Province and became a famous kind of dance for the group. With the change of times, the custom of dancing the Firewood Gathering Dance gradually evolved into a kind of fitness activity with cultural flavor.

Ka-Si-Da-Wen Dance

Applicant: Heishui County, Sichuan Province

"Ka-Si-Da-Wen" is the dialect of Heishui. "Kasida" refers to armor and "Wen" means "wearing". The dance mainly prevails in the Heishuihe Valley. Performers dance in armor.

According to research, the dance was originally staged before the soldiers went out to battle, and functioned as a ceremony to pray for good luck. It has developed into a singing and dancing performance at festivals and ceremonies. The dance features much vigor and huge scale. With respect to music, it features two vocal parts, which is hard to be found in the music of other ethnic groups.

Scores of warriors wear the armor made of yak hide and leather helmet or round cap inserted with the tail feather of a pheasant, stalk or oxtail, hang numerous copper bells on the shoulder and hold a sword, dagger, spear or powder shotgun. After walking around the square for several circles, they constantly change the formations and stage graceful, sonorous, mutual-active and touching songs and dances to embody the martial spirit of the ancient Tibetan warriors. Accompanied with shouting, the movements of the warriors include swinging the arms, turning round, raising the leg, swaying, shaking the armor, shooting toward the sky and brandishing arms. Subsequently, scores of women sing melodious and euphemistical folk songs with multi-voice parts along with the warrior team, bringing back the atmosphere of solacing the relatives and inspiring morale. Both the male and female movements proceed in slow songs and fast dance, obviously carrying the flavor of equine culture and at the same time, expressing strong visual and aural effects.

Zhou Dance

Applicant: Jiuzhaigou County, Sichuan Province

This refers to an auspicious mask dance, customarily known as "Auspicial Facial Mask Dance". The dance has its sources from the animism of the white-horse people in primeval times. It is a mix of Diqiang and Tibetan culture, with a hint of sacrifice. It is only performed on grand festivals.

The performers, wearing a wood-carved mask, each sing and dance festively. Drum, cymbals and copper horn are the major musical instruments. It is the most important entertainment activity for white-horse people, with a view to worshipping deities, praying for security, exorcising demons and preventing evil. It also expresses the wish of the white-horse Tibetan people for harmoniously living with wild animals. In line with the bold and vigorous sounds of drums and horns, performers turn round anti-clockwise with quick short steps and imitate the actions of various birds and animals.

The dance is usually performed by seven, nine or 11 persons. The leading dancer wears a lion's head-shaped mask; others put on the masks in the shape of the heads of ox, tiger, dragon, leopard, snake and cock as well as two little ghosts and two big ghosts respectively in accordance with custom. It is of extremely great value in studying the origin, development, evolvement and formalization of the primitive animal-imitating dance.

The dance combines the shuffle of circle dance and tiptoe jumping basically. The basic movements include small and quick steps, squat steps and turning round while jumping right and left. In combination with the rough and mysterious movements of the upper limbs, the performance vividly presents the form of the animals imitated and embodies the unique taste of the white-horse people.

Lisu Song-Dance Achi-Mugua

Applicant: Weixi Lisu Autonomous County, Yunnan Province

This refers to the "song and dance of the goat" or "song in imitation of baa", prevailing in the Weixi Lisu Autonomous County of the Diqing Tibetan Autonomous Prefecture in Yunnan Province. It is a traditional local folk song and dance for self-entertainment purposes. Historically, Weixi was isolated; Lisu people seldom had communications with the outside world. Production was basically a mix of farming and animal husbandry. Goats could be found in every household. The dance vividly embodies traditional production and life as well as thoughts and emotions of the Lisu people.

Usually, a male team and a female team form a semi-circle or a straight column respectively to dance and sing. The movements are in imitation of the goat's actions, including swinging, twisting and stamping the feet, swaying the upper body right and left, leaning forward and looking up and back.

There are more than 10 methods of performing the dance. It has no musical instruments. Each song begins with a tune without libretto, like a quivery and melodious baa. Each team has a leading singer; others sing in chorus. The libretto is rich in content, from the ancient myths and legends to present-day production and life, with additional improvised content. If the lead singers are well-matched, the song will last for several days and nights.

Gourd Panpipe Dance of Yi Ethnic Group

Applicant: Wenshan Zhuang–Miao Autonomous Prefecture, Yunnan Province

This is a kind of old folk dance of the Yi ethnic group prevailing in the Wenshan Zhuang-Miao Autonomous Prefecture of Yunnan Province.

Hualuo people constitute one branch of the Yi, totaling more than 2,000 persons. They have their own spoken language but no written language. Uniquely, when one male plays the gourd panpipe, women will stand in rows and begin to dance to the tune. They constantly swing in an "S" shape from head to toe. The movements are brisk and simple.

The gourd panpipe players lead the dance. As soon as they hear the sound, women will stand shoulder to shoulder in pairs and dance hand in hand gracefully. The music features slow rhythm and steady cadence. No matter how the formation changes, the team should constantly proceed to the right or anti-clockwise.

Hualuo people boast unique technique in making the gourd panpipe. They insert bamboo or copper reeds into the root segments of five bamboo tubes different in length and then put them into a gourd. The tubes have sound holes at the side; the shortest tube also has a sound hole; and the longest one is covered with a small gourd to strengthen resonance.

On grand festivals, all people of the village gather. Women, in full dress, form a circle to dance to the accompaniment of the gourd panpipe.

Tobacco Case Dance of Yi Ethnic Group

Applicant: Honghe Hani–Yi Autonomous Prefecture, Yunnan Province

This is a kind of mass folk dance of the Nisupo Branch of the Yi ethnic group in Yunnan. It developed in the Yuan and Ming dynasties and entered a golden period in the Qing Dynasty and Republic of China. Accompanied by tetrachord, dancers, holding a round wooden tobacco case formerly containing tobacco in their hand, dance while flipping the bottom of the case with a brisk rhythm, thus creating a warm atmosphere. The dance enjoys great popularity among the Yi people. Both children and the elderly love to dance it.

The Tobacco Case Dance relates closely to the life of the Yi ethnic group. It is said that the dance had no props at the outset and unified the rhythm by clapping hands to lead the dance in order. Subsequently, someone flipped the tobacco case containing yellow sun-cured tobaccos for amusement, but unexpectedly producing pleasant sound. Hence, flipping the tobacco case was adopted in the dance to replace the clapping movement. Through generations, the dance became richer and richer and developed into the present one.

Characteristically, the dance is a skillful and harmonious combination with changing formations. At the beginning, the leading dancer embarks on playing the tetrachord and dancing at the same time. Others begin to flip the tobacco case and dance to the tune in a straightforward but chic manner. They stand in rows or form circles, holding two tobacco cases in either hand and swinging the arms back and forth rhythmically. They flip the cases on each downbeat and at the same time, conduct the movements of hands and feet. The tetrachord plays the role in leading the dance and serves as the accompaniment. In general, the dance has a melodious tune, distinct tempo, brisk rhythm and disciplinary tone.

Jino Bass Drum Dance

Applicant: Jinghong City, Yunnan Province

Jino is an ethnic minority in Yunnan Province. The Bass Drum Dance is a folk dance with long history and profound influence. The Jino have their own myth of creation. They regard it as their "Ancestry Chart" and worship and commemorate it with song, dance and sacrificial ceremonies. It serves as a vivid historical subject, class and teaching material. According to the myth, their ancestors came from the Bass Drum, which becomes a divine object.

The Bass Drum has a length of some one meter and a diameter of 40 to 50 cm. It is mounted with ox hide on both drumheads. It is forbidden to beat the drum at ordinary times. Only on the Temok Festival and when worshiping the deity called "Tieluo Momo" can it be beaten and the Bass Drum Dance performed.

The dance has a complete set of rituals. Before dancing, villagers kill a piglet and chicken to offer them in front of the bass drum as a sacrifice. Then, seven seniors do obeisance, one of whom reads the sacrificial words to pray that the bass drum will bring people auspiciousness and safety. After the ceremony, one person holds drumsticks in either hand to beat the drum and dance, accompanied by small cymbal players, singers and dancers. The lyrics mostly relate to the history, morals and custom of the Jino people.

Its main movements include bending the legs, raising the hands and turning around. Dancers first stand naturally and hold the drumsticks at ease. Secondly, they stretch the left foot and let the heel down to the ground, bend the left knee and shake the two legs at the same time. Thirdly, they raise the drumstick in the left hand over the head and hang the right hand down, then reverse the motion, turn around and then switch posture.

Shannan Chamgocho Dance

Applicant: Tibet Autonomous Region

This is a kind of waist drum dance. In Tibetan, "Gocho" refers to circle dance. As a comparatively special art in the traditional dance-related culture of Tibetan ethnic group,

Shannan Chamgocho Dance with strong rhythm

the magic, magnificent and charming dance not only is deeply loved by Tibetan people but also attracts other ethnic groups in China as well as foreigners. It is one of the oldest extant items of the traditional dance-related culture of various nations in the world.

Two bands are tied onto the drum. One of them is tied around the waist and the other around of the base of the thigh, thus fixing the round drum on end on the left side of the waist. The array of the performance is basically round; performers are divided into leading dancers and collective dancers. There are two to six leading dancers, who, without the waist drum, are in charge of prompting the correct sequence of actions, controlling the speed of rhythm. Their movements are of strong rhythm; and their postures basically same to those of the collective dancers but less difficult. The collective dancers beat the drum and at the same time dance to the drumbeats. They brandish the long plait into the "∞" and "o" shapes. The movements are straightforward, bold, vigorous, martial and rich in rhythm and change.

Wutu Dance of Tu Ethnic Group

Applicant: Tongren County, Qinghai Province

Wutu defines a unique, local culture prevalent among the Tu ethnic group of Leduhu Village in Tongren County, Qinghai Province. Held every year from the fifth to 20th days of the 11th lunar month, the activities include a series of ceremonial procedures as follows: reciting Buddhist scriptures for a life free of danger, dispelling diseases and exorcizing evils, and seeking pleasure together with divine beings. At the outset of the ceremony, stripped to the waist and tattooed with tigers, a team of men will perform a sort of dance from door to door in the village. The dancers are also named "Wutu", an equivalent to "tiger" in the dialects of an ancient ethnic group. The dance is centuries old.

Local people regards the 20th day of the 12th lunar month as a "black day", on which, demons and ghosts will come out to do bad deeds. Hence, people perform the Wutu Dance which imitates the actions of tiger to exorcize evils and safeguard peace.

The language and rhythm of the dance is comparatively simple. Since dancers hold a two-meter-long stick, the movements of the upper body and hands are fairly simple. Legs also act in line with the development and change of the mood of dance. It is an embodiment of the primeval animal imitating dance in the modern folk activities of Tu ethnic group. The animal imitating dance relates closely to the hunting life of the primitives; it is also the most common and representative dance among the primeval dances. Wutu Dance has become an important part of folk sacrificial activity. It is performed only for exorcizing evils and praying for safety. It is a remnant of animism in folk art.

Wutu Festival is a traditional festival that Tu people in Nianduhu Village, Huangnan Prefecture, Qinghai Province celebrate. The young men with white tiger patterns drawn on their bare upper body go to the villagers' households while singing and dancing, thus praying blessing for them.

Eagle Dance of the Tajik Ethnic Group

Applicant: Tashikurgan Tajik Autonomous County, Xinjiang Uyghur Autonomous Region

This stems from the totem worship of the Tajik ancestors for the eagle in the bad environment of the Pamirs. The accompanying musical instruments are eagle flute and hand drums made from the wing bones of an eagle. The dance mainly imitates the eagle flying and whirling. It is mainly performed by males but sometimes by both males and females. On festivals and weddings, all dance it together.

There is no limit on the venue where it is performed. People can dance it everywhere if there is an interest. The eagle flute is unique to Tajik ethnic group, with a clear sound that is loud and pleasant. The hand drum is the major musical instrument. Two women beat one hand drum with various kinds of drumbeats, which is rare among other ethnic groups.

The dance is rapid and demands high skill. Usually, performers dance in pairs. They can perform freely in two or three groups or in a pair with the opposite sex. Mostly, a man invites another man to dance together. Extending gently the arms, they first proceed slowly along the rim, like eagles flying and whirling. Subsequently, the rhythm becomes fast; two men begin to play, sometimes walking fast shoulder to shoulder, sometimes jumping and parting. Then, they whirl and rise steeply, bringing the dance to an end.

Tajik Eagle Dance

Traditional Operas

Kunqu Opera

Applicants: Chinese Academy of Arts, Jiangsu Province, Zhejiang Province, Shanghai City, Beijing City and Hunan Province

Kunqu Opera originated in Kunshan, Jiangsu Province some 600 years ago. Kunqu Opera is regarded as the "grandfather and teacher of all operas" in China. Many local operas have assimilated various aspects from Kunqu Opera. In May 2001 the Chinese art of Kunqu Opera was selected into the first group of "representative works of the oral and intangible heritages" declared by UNESCO in Paris and China became one of the first 9 countries that received this honour.

At the end of the Yuan Dynasty and early Ming Dynasty Southern Opera spread to Kunshan, Jiangsu and gave birth to a new opera, Kunshanqiang, which added the combination of local music, dances and dialect. Since their beginning Chinese operas have been performed on stage and spread around the country in this way. As time passed they witnessed many changes in music and performances. Since its inception few changes have occurred in Kunqu Opera and it has maintained many of the traditional features and an abundant list of plays, so it is called the "living fossil" opera.

The bamboo flute is the major musical instrument used as accompaniment in Kunqu Opera. Other instruments used include the sheng (a reed pipe), the xiao (a vertical bamboo flute), the suona (a Chinese oboe), the sanxian (a Chinese trichord instrument) and the pipa (a plucked string instrument) along with some percussion instruments. The performances of Kunqu Opera have their own special system and style. It is characterized by strong lyrics, minute actions and an artful and harmonious combination of singing and dancing.

The Kunqu Opera *Peony Pavilion*

Its representative plays include *Pipa Ji* (*The Tale of Pipa*), *Mudan Ting* (*The Peony Pavilion*), *Changsheng Dian* (*The Longevity Palace*), *Mingfeng Ji* (*The Tale of Mingfeng*), *Yuzan Ji* (*The* Tale *of the Jade Hairpin*), *Hongli Ji* (*The Record of the Red Pear*), *Shuihu Ji* (*The Tale of the Waterside*), *Lan Ke Shan, Shiwu Guan* (*Fifteen Strings of Copper Coins*). The former three plays have the remains of a complete music score or notes of a musical score. After the middle of the Qing Dynasty Kunqu Opera was performed in Zhezi Opera and more than 400 Zhezi Opera plays have been kept.

Liyuan Opera

Applicant: Quanzhou City, Fujian Province

As a rare local opera in China, Quanzhou Liyuan Opera preserves the features of the Southern Opera during the Tang and Song dynasties. Rooted in Quanzhou, the opera spread to Taiwan and Southeast Asia along with the Quanzhou people. Liyuan (pear garden) is another name for a theatrical troupe in ancient China. Liyuan Opera originated from Quanzhou during the Song and Yuan dynasties and has a history of more than 800 years and is honoured as a "living fossil of ancient Southern Opera."

The performance of a Liyuan Opera has very strict and minute details that are called the "eighteen-step rules". There are strict regulations on the movement of the hands, the eyes, the body and steps in each performance. For example, "the hands are raised up to the height of the eyebrow, parted at the navel and cupped under the lower jaw." The psychological portrayal of ancient figures is especially minute and vivid. The roles followed the old system of Southern Opera during the Song and Yuan dynasties. In the early days there were only seven roles but later more roles were created. The music of Liyuan Opera is beautiful and pleasant. The extant music for voices mostly originated from Daqu and Faqu folk songs during the Tang and Song dynasties and later absorbed the music of other operas, hence the Quanqiang tune. The musical instruments used include the suona, xiao, sanxian, southern pipa, drum and clappers.

Today there are still many plays from the Southern Opera of the Song and Yuandynasties performed in Liyuan Opera. It has preserved many ancient dialects in its phonology. The Quanzhou dialect is the standard local dialect and is used for most of the tunes. Attention is also paid to the different figure positions and local colours and local dialect and ancient pronunciations are still preserved in some plays.

The costumes are simple and unadorned except for those of the dan (female role). Performers usually wear sleeveless jackets and skirts and do not play the flowing-water sleeve style. The Xiaodan (young girl) wears underpants with a wrap. The sleeves for the other roles such as the sheng (male role), the wai (man), the laodan (old man), the jing (painted-face role) and the chou (comic-face clown) are very short, so there is no performance of the flowing-water sleeve style.

Puxian Opera

Applicant: Putian City, Fujian Province

Puxian Opera is one of the Chinese operas with the longest history. It also has the oldest form of performance, the richest plays and the most characteristic art. It is popular in the two counties of Putian and Xianyou and other neighbouring Xinghua dialect counties such as Hui'an, Fuqing and Yongtai in Fujian.

The performance of Puxian Opera is unvarnished and elegant and many movements show an influence from puppetry. The roles in Puxian Opera followed the old form of Southern Opera. In the beginning there were only seven roles of sheng, dan, tiesheng, zedan, liangzhuang (jing), mo (older man) and chou and the opera was commonly called the "seven-role theatrical troupe." Puxian Opera has a profound musical tradition and an abundance of range of voices and there are still remnants of Southern Opera from the Song and Yuan dynasties. The music of the opera is mainly Xinghua music that combines Puxian folk songs, Buddhist music, ci and qu of the Song and Yuan dynasties and daqu singing and dancing. It is performed in the dialect and is music with strong local colour and flavour.

The Lili (a Tartar pipe) was used during imperial dinners during the Tang Dynasty and as an accompaniment for ci music of the Song Dynasty and was the major musical instrument in early Southern Opera. Today only Puxian Opera is still using this old musical instrument. It is a very important symbol for both the early Southern Opera and the traditional music of Puxian Opera.

There are more than 5,000 traditional plays in Puxian Opera and some 80 of them have remained like the originals or have similar plots to those of the Southern Opera from the Song and Yuan dynasties. Among them are included *Qin Tiao* (the *Plectrum*), *After the Reunion, Chuncao is Rushed into the Hall, and the Number One Scholar and Beggar.*

Chaozhou Opera

Applicants: Shantou City and Chaozhou City, Guangdong Province

The Chaozhou Opera

Chaozhou Opera, mainly popular in the Chaozhou dialect regions, is an old local opera performed in the Chaozhou dialect. It is found mainly in east Guangdong, south Fujian, Taiwan, Hong Kong and Southeast Asia.

The formation and development of Chaozhou Opera has a history of more than 430 years. It is a branch of the Southern Opera of the Song and Yuan dynasties. As well as gradually evolving from the Southern Opera of the Song and Yuan dynasties, it absorbed the strong points of the Yiyang, Kunqu, Pihuang and Bangzi operas. It also combined the local folk music such as Chaozhou and finally forged its own special artistic form and style.

Chaozhou Opera has complete roles. Sheng, dan, jing and chou have their respective roles. The performance is minute and vivid. The movements and acting have both precise formalities and freedom. Attention is paid to the play of skills. The performance skills of chou and huadan (a young girl serving as a maid) are especially lively with style and local colour.

In terms of performance, the roles of sheng, dan and chou in Chaozhou Opera have the strongest local characters. Sao Chuang Hui, a sheng-dan play, is regarded as a typical representative story of dancing and singing among Chinese operas. The role of chou in Chaozhou Opera is divided into ten types and the fan skills of one type of chou are famous around China.

Chaozhou Opera has its own system and special styles. The score for the opera is mainly a normal musical tune with an accented-beat tune with the former predominant. Till today it still reserves certain forms of vocal accompaniment, such as one sings and others accompany, two or three people sing the same tune and everyone sings together the chorus and the end. Its score for voices is characterized by a mild, sweet tone and lyrics with many lengthened and turned sounds. Other performers backstage will sing in unison when the performer on stage sings the crescendo. This phenomenon is rarely seen in other operas and is a feature of Chaozhou Opera.

The Yiyang Melody

Applicant: Yiyang County, Jiangxi Province

Yiyang style melody, an old Chinese opera tune, once shared fame with Haiyan, Kunshan and Yuyao melodies in the history of Chinese operas. They were known as the Four Great Melodies. When the Southern Opera from Zhejiang was introduced to Jiangxi at the end of the Southern Song (1127-1279) Dynasty, it gave birth to a brand new local style melody in Yiyang with the combination of the local dialect, folk music and local customs. The new melody was called the Yiyang Melody after where it originated.

The Yiyang Melody has its own special characteristics in terms of singing forms and styles. It is sung without the accompaniment of musical instruments but uses the gong and drum for rhythm and working up the stage atmosphere. In the Yiyang Melody the accompaniment of big drums and gongs is closely combined with loud, sonorous music for voices, forming a noisy and rough music style. The Yiyang Melody is also characterized by "one singing and others accompanying", i.e. vocal accompaniment. One performer starts the music and several others follow. Such form has continuous development with the different demands for its performance. It can not only play up the stage atmosphere but also emphasize the expression of words, help portray figures, describe the environment in the play and narrate the plots. So, it has become an important form of artistic expression and has a strong artistic inspiration.

At its most popular the Yiyang Melody could be found all around China and had many Gaoqiang varieties and branches derived from it. As the mother of Gaoqiang, the Yiyang Melody has left branches and remnants in different Chinese operas. So, the Yiyang Melody is also regarded as the originator of Gaoqiang Opera in China and the head of the Four Great Melodies in China.

The Qingyang Melody

Applicants: Qingyang County of Anhui Province and Hukou County of Jiangxi Province

The Qingyang Melody was named after its place of origin, Qingyang County. During the Jiajing Period (1522-1566) of the Ming Dynasty, the Yiyang Melody spread to Qingyang and gave birth to the Qingyang Melody after being combined with the local dialect and folk songs. This new melody broke the musical structure of linked music tunes, developed Gundiao, created the singing method with the combination of qiang and gun and pushed Chinese opera melodies to a new height.

The performance of the Qingyang Melody is accompanied only by the big drum, big cymbal and big gong instead of wind instruments. The vocal solo is combined with vocal accompaniment and one person sings accompanied by others. Meanwhile Gundiao is used in the singing and the music for voices is blended with the Gun monologue and Gun singing, so the Qingyang Melody is good at narration. The music for voices is flexible and varied, the language is popular and easy to understand and the plasticity and expressive force of the opera tunes are enhanced greatly. The Qingyang Melody inherited the old role system of the ancient Southern Opera. It has seven roles of sheng, dan, jing, mo, chou, wai and tie and later two more roles of xiao and fu were added. A theatre show without acrobatics is often performed in the style of a fighting play. It is very amusing and interesting with a forceful and joyful atmosphere. Such acrobatics as tumbling from a high platform and jumping through fire hoops are often performed as interludes. Various paper masks are also used in the Qingyang Melody style and are very characteristic in terms of stage art.

The music for voices in the Qingyang Melody is flexible. The opera language is popular and easy to understand and the plasticity and expressive force of opera tunes are enhanced greatly. Later on it spread from South Anhui to Fujian, Hunan, Sichuan, Henan, Shanxi and Shandong and was in vogue for a while and directly or indirectly influenced the formation and development of the Hui, Beijing, Jiangxi, Sichuan and Huangmei operas. In particular, it became the basis for the formation of the Beijing Opera when Four Great Anhui Theatrical Troupes came to Beijing.

Gaoqiang

Applicants: Zhejiang, Anhui, Fujian and Hunan Provinces

In terms of Chinese opera melodies, the Yiyang Melody of the Ming Dynasty and the Qingyang Melody of later time were the origin of various melodies, such as the Gaoqiang of Jiangxi Opera, the Qingxi of Hubei, the Gaoqiang of Sichuan Opera, the Jingqiang of Beijing and other types of Gaoqiang such as those of Changsha, Changde, Qiyang and Chenhe in Hunan Province. Most of the types of Gaoqiang followed the features of the Yiyang Melody i.e. without any accompaniment of stringed and wind instruments and the beating of time by gongs and drums, and one person singing and others accompanying. After hundreds of years of change some Gaoqiang operas witnessed great changes. For example, in the Chenhe Gaoqiang of Hunan the suona takes the place of the voice for accompaniment and it is very interesting; in the Xiwu and Songyang Gaoqiang of Zhejiang, a small-size orchestra is included but the drums, gongs, and vocal accompaniment are still preserved, so that singing without accompaniment, instrument accompaniment and vocal accompaniment appear in turns to enrich the expressive force of the music. In the scores of recent years Sichuan, Hunan and Jiangxi operas have included orchestral accompaniment and have tended to become diverse in form.

There are hundreds of melodies for Gaoqiang and their names still follow those of the Southern and Northern operas. Compared to the melodies of the Kunqu Opera, there are great differences in tone, rhythm, melody, circling method and syntax. In addition to the five-tone scale of Southern Opera, some Gaoqiang operas also adopt a seven-tone scale. The original form of Gunchang singing is still used but it has been developed. All the Gaoqiang operas have vocal accompaniment while other systems of melodies do not have and its vocal accompaniment is varied; the accompaniment after each word, the accompaniment after a whole sentence, bass major singing with high accompaniment, high major singing with bass accompaniment, compact singing with loose accompaniment, loose singing with compact accompaniment, singing before accompaniment or accompaniment before singing. They play an important role in expressing the inner thoughts of figures, playing up the atmosphere and setting off the environment.

The Xinchang Melody

Applicant: Xinchang County, Zhejiang Province

The Xinchang Melody, one of the old opera melodies, is regarded as the only remains of the Yuyao Melody, one of the Four Great Melodies of the Southern Opera during the Ming Dynasty.

The music of the Xinchang Melody can be divided into two parts, theatrical singing music and spectacle music. The theatrical singing music is composed of two parts, the libretto and music for voices. The libretto of the melody is precise. There are many plays and more than 360 traditional plays still remain.

The Xinchang Melody music has three characteristics: vocal accompaniment, continuous clapping and solo without accompaniment. In this case, the vocal accompaniment is not "one singing and others accompanying", nor a chorus backstage but is an accompaniment in an ordered form and layers according to the psychology and environment of the figures in the play. When a performer sings on stage, others backstage will accompany or follow the end of the music for one or several words or repeat the words at the end one beat slower and in a different melody. It is a pure human vocal accompaniment and the melody of each sentence tends to descend gradually. It is astonishing that the same sentence of a libretto can show an artistic effect by means of the vocal accompaniment, something which is unreachable for other operas.

There was originally no orchestral accompaniment only percussion. Later, due to the impact of Kunqu and Luantan operas, bamboo flutes and banhu (a Chinese stringed instrument) were adopted for accompaniment in a few Zhezi plays. The band accompanying the melody is very simple. Only six people take charge of the clappers and small gongs.

The Xinchang Melody has no music score. It is very strange. The old artists of former generations accumulated a set of simple symbols as notes beside the libretto of ancient hand-copied scripts. They look like earthworms and are called "earthworm notes". Artists can sing in a specific tone according to the noted music and the different notes.

Ninghai Pingdiao

Applicant: Ninghai County, Zhejiang Province

Ninghai Pingdiao is an important branch of Zhejiang opera melodies. Due to its low tone it belongs to Siping (a note of the Chinese scale) and so it is called Pingdiao. It mainly concerns Gaoqiang (Pingdiao) and also performances of Kunqiang and Luantan.

The music and performance of Ninghai Pingdiao are characteristic. The music is mainly in the style of Qupai and the male and female voices are combined. Generally the sound of laosheng is loud and sonorous and is mostly nasal. The sound of xiaosheng is vigorous and forceful and is mostly falsetto. The sound of jing is rough and powerful and has a large range of vocal vibration. A performer on stage sings and others backstage accompany. In the case of a lengthened tune the word at the end of the sentence will be broken into several pieces. Ninghai mandarin is the standard language for the monologue. The sound is very loud and attractive.

Ninghai Shuaya is a unique form of acrobatics used in the performance of Ninghai Pingdiao and has been around for more than 100 years. Four, eight or ten wild boar tusks are held in the mouth. Sometimes they are popped out or pierce the nose or swing in all directions and break through the nose in pairs. In particular the performer can sing, dance, read and do acrobatics with two tusks inside the mouth all the times.

The Shuaya is an amazing performance. There are three kinds of musical instruments for singing, acting and beat. The percussion has rules for accompanying the music; the rhythm is slow and it is suitable for xiaosheng

"Ninghai Shuaya" performance with a history of more than 100 years

(young man) and huadan. The suona is the only wind instrument. It is used for giving an accurate scale, guiding the connection between well known tunes and playing up the atmosphere when performers are entering or leaving the stage or major actions occur and changing positions.

Yong'an Daqiang Opera

Applicant: Yong'an City, Fujian Province

Daqiang Opera which is honoured as a "living opera fossil" is also known as Damenqiang. Yong'an Daqiang Opera was formed during the middle of the Ming Dynasty and is a branch of the Yiyang Melody. There is a saying that "big gongs and drums are used for a full-scale opera and a big voice is used to sing Gaoqiang," and this applies to Daqiang Opera.

A theatrical troupe for Daqiang Opera is usually 15 people and the musical instrument accompaniment includes the gong, drum, cymbals, suona and clappers. The props on stage are very simple. In a performance there is only one table and two chairs on stage. Performers are usually dressed in simply costumes or just do not wear costumes. Only red, black and white are used for make-up. Then they wear a special "beard cover" and go to the table for the performance. This is the symbolic costume of Daqiang Opera. The drummers sit on a chair, beat the drum and sing all the time to accompany the performer.

The music is linked tunes with ups and downs and a loud and sonorous sound. In the music there are more words and fewer melodies. The sound is rough and loud, unvarnished and straightforward. The vocalization mainly depends on one big voice with a combination of big and small voices. In a performance the people backstage make vocal accompaniment continuously and feature the Yiyang Melody, "one starting the singing and others accompanying", is retained. The libretto mainly adopts the form of ci and the phonology belongs to Zhongzhou. Gongs and drums are the important instruments used in Daqiang Opera music.

The actions, stage dispatch and stage artistic forms are all remains of the operas from the Ming Dynasty and are first-hand materials for studying Chinese opera history, cultural history and social history.

Siping Opera

Applicants: Pingnan County and Zhenghe County, Fujian Province

Siping Opera is derived from the Yiyang Melody, one of the Four Great Melodies popular in the middle of the Ming Dynasty . During the Jiajing Period (1522-1566) it was popular in Huizhou (She County in Anhui Province). At the end of the Ming Dynasty and the early part of the Qing Dynasty, it spread to Zhenghe deep in the mountains of northeast Fujian Province. It is preserved in its original appearance in Yangyuan of Zhenghe County and Longtan of Pingnan County.

There are many traditional plays in Siping Opera such as *Jing Chai Ji* (The *Record of a Bramble Hairpin*) and *Bai Tu Ji* (The *Record of a White Rabbit*). It belongs to the Gaoqiang system. The music is unvarnished, rough, fresh, sweet, elegant and attractive. The accompaniment at the end of a sentence is sung in the lengthened tune style. The monologue is read in "local mandarin" which is a language between mandarin and the local dialect and which is commonly called "reading in orthography." The original Siping plays which remain only have light-tone and accent marks without any musical score. There is only a tone score. The music has been passed down completely in the oral tradition for generations. The roles were completed during the Yongzheng Period (1723-1735) of the Qing Dynasty. In terms of performance, the role of sheng stresses elegance, dan minuteness, jing roughness and chou humoristic. They are the special performing styles of Siping Opera. The performing actions of the roles include jumping, moving, rolling and beating and their speed is in harmony with that of the drum beat. There are precise formulas stipulated for the hands and feet actions of the different roles. In the performance the drum is the major performing instrument and such percussion as cymbals and clappers serve as foils. It has inherited the ancient tradition of Yiyang Melody, "one performer sings clearly while others accompany."

On the ninth day of the second lunar month and the sixth day of the eighth lunar month every year the Siping Troupe from Yangyuan Town give a performance of Siping Opera for three days and nights.

Sichuan Opera

Applicants: Sichuan Province and Chongqing City

The Sichuan Opera *Jinshan Temple*

Sichuan Opera is another great characteristic of Sichuan culture. Based on the local Chedeng Opera during the Qianlong Period (1736-1795) of the Qing Dynasty, it absorbed and combined the music of various places such as Jiangsu, Jiangxi, Anhui, Hubei, Shaanxi and Gansu and this gave birth to Sichuan Opera which is sung in the Sichuan dialect and includes the five tunes of Gaoqiang, Huqin, Kunqiang, Dengxi and Tanxi. Gaoqiang of Sichuan Opera has many songs, the music is beautiful and attractive and it is very characteristic. It is the major singing form of Sichuan Opera. It is an ottava-alta style singing without music accompaniment but with percussion and vocal accompaniment.

The vocal accompaniment in Sichuan Opera can be classified into leading the tune, joining the tune, chorus, accompanying and ensemble. It is meaningful and attractive. The language of Sichuan Opera is lively, vivid, humorous and full of local colour. It also has a strong living flavour, and broad mass basis.

There are hundreds of plays which are frequently seen on stage. Sichuan Opera features a complete set of singing, acting and acrobatics, humorous narration and the accompaniment of musical instruments as foils. "Face changing," "spitting fire" and "flowing-water sleeves" have developed a school of their own in Sichuan Opera which is very interesting along with freehand actions in formality.

Facing-changing is one of the special performing skills in Sichuan Opera. It is a romantic way to express the inner thoughts and emotions of the figures in plays. According to actual demands, performers paint different masks of facial make-up on different materials such as wood, paper, cloth, silk and rubber in advance and which are well prepared for changing. While moving his head a performer can change one mask and within a short breath a performer can change five or six masks, which is an astonishing sight for audiences.

There five roles in Sichuan Opera, i.e. xiaosheng, dan, sheng, hualian and chou. Each role has its special systematic formality for skills and the most characteristic performance is in the roles of sheng, chou and dan.

Xiang Opera

Applicant: Hengyang City, Hunan Province

It is one of the local operas in Hunan Province with Changsha and Xiangtan as its active centres. It was once called "Changsha Xiang Opera" and it involves four tunes, i.e. Gaoqiang, Dipaizi, Kunqu and Luantan.

In the performance of Xiang Opera, the Gaoqiang large-size plays shown sequentially on stage pay attention to skills and acrobatics. Xiang Opera combines acrobatics and wushu. For example, the big play Mu Lian attaches importance to such acrobatics as the human pyramid and pole-climbing. With the introduction of the Qingyang tune, the focus is shifted from big gongs and drums to small gongs and drums. The opera prefers singing to acting. There is a strong life-style flavour and there are few formal actions. For example, Pipa Ji (The Record of Pipa) and Jin Yin Ji (The Record of the Gold Seal) still retain the significant, simple and unvarnished style. With the introduction of Kunqiang the performance got further developed. It absorbed the feature of singing while dancing in Kunqiang and attached equal importance to singing and acting and the performance on stage became vivid and varied. At the end of the Qing Dynasty, Beijing Opera came to Changsha and 18 Beijing Opera artists participated in the performance of a Xiang Opera on the same stage. The artists of the Xiang Opera learned the skills of acrobatics from the Beijing Opera artists and absorbed huaqiang from Beijing Opera, which further enriched the performances of Xiang Opera.

There four roles in Xiang Opera, i.e. sheng, dan, jing and chou. Each role has its branches with their special skills.

There are colourful plays in Xiang Opera. The total number of plays is around 1,150.

Guangchang Meng Opera

Applicant: Guangchang County, Jiangxi Province

Guangchang Meng Opera, popular within Guangchang County, Jiangxi Province, is an opera focusing on the theme that Meng Jiangnu cried at the Great Wall and her cry made the Great Wall fall down. It is commonly called Meng Opera. It originated from the early part of the Ming Dynasty and thus has a history of more than 500 years. The singing style of Meng Opera is Gaoqiang. After textual research by experts, its music for voices is the remains of Haiyan Melody which was the head of the Four

Great Tunes during the Ming Dynasty.

Meng Opera is performed only once a year in the first lunar month for such activities as praying to the gods and offering sacrifice to ancestors of clans. As a clan opera offering sacrifice to gods and ancestors, Guangchang Meng Opera has some performing customs. Guards of honour carry flags and weapons to clear the way, all the musical instruments play at the same time and dragon lanterns and mussel shell lanterns accompany the performance. The participants can be as many as 1,000. It is a very joyful style of opera.

Guangchang Meng Opera is in the style of qupai (names of tunes to which qu are composed) and sung in gaoqiang. One performer sings while others accompanying the latter half of the tail sentence. It also features "mixed singing."

There are two folk theatrical troupes of Guangchang Meng Opera singing different plays in different tunes but they have the same story about Meng Jiangnu crying at the Great Wall and making it fall down. Chibi Sangria Meng Opera, regarded as the play of the Yuan Dynasty, is performed over two nights. It has 64 scenes and needs nine hours to give the full performance. Only one part is performed in a night. Dalubei Liujia Meng Opera, regarded as the play of the Ming Dynasty, started from the Wanli Period (1573-1620) of the Ming Dynasty. It is performed over three continuous nights, has 69 scenes and needs 11 hours to complete the full play.

Among the folk people in China the story about Meng Jiangnu crying at the Great Wall is well known and there are various plays or performances of singing and talking about it but it is believed that the whole play of Meng Jiangnu of the Southern Opera was lost. In Ganzhu, Guangchang County, the whole Southern-Opera play Meng Jiangnu Sending Winter Clothing performed in Chixi Zhengjia Village and the romantic play The Record of the Great Wall performed in Dalubei Liujia Village, both named as Meng Opera, have a history of around 500 and 400 years respectively.

Zhengzi Opera

Applicant: Lufeng City, Guangdong Province

Zhengzi Opera, also called Zhengyin Opera, got its name as it is sung in the language of Zhongzhou Mandarin (which is called Zhengyin or Zhengzi in southern Fujian and Chaozhou). At the beginning of the Ming Dynasty a branch of the Southern Opera was introduced to eastern Guangdong Province and mainly rooted in Hailufeng. Later it spread to Hong Kong, Macao, Taiwan and Southeast Asia.

Zhengzi Opera is an old and rare opera with a variety of tunes. The main tunes include Zhengyi qu and Kunqu and there are some mixed qu and ditties. Big wind and stringed instruments made from the agave shell are the major accompanying instruments in Zhengyin qu, along with the sanxian and zhuxian (bamboo stringed instruments). Kunqu and mixed qu are accompanied mainly by bamboo flute and suona.

Zhengzi Opera has a simple and unvarnished style and grand momentum. It is good at performing linked plays. There are two kinds of traditional plays, i.e. plays of singing and acting and plays of acrobatics. There are more than 170 traditional plays of singing and acting which are good at the minute expression of emotions. There are more than 2,000 traditional plays of acrobatics (outline plays) without written play books which have none or little music for voices and beating instruments are used to set off the hot and vehement atmosphere. There are many excellent performances of shaking back flags, shaking muscles, shaking artificial whiskers, running cloth horses and showing southern-school wushu. Most are war-gown and armour plays about political and military struggles.

Traditionally Zhengzi Opera has 12 roles of hongmian (red face), wumian (black face), baimian (white face), laosheng (mature, middle-aged man), wusheng (fighting man), baishan (white fan), zhengdan (main female role), huadan (young girl), shuaizhu (commander-in-chief), gongmo (middle-aged man of low social status), po (old woman) and chou (clown). Some of the roles have facial make-up. In Zhengzi Opera there are more than 200 different designs of facial make-up, such as facial hair, tortoise eyes, eagle beak, tiger eyes, etc.

Qinqiang

Applicant: Shaanxi Province

Qinqiang (Shaanxi opera) is the most popular opera in Shaanxi, Gansu, Qinghai, Ningxia and Xinjiang in northwest China. As the Chinese jujube trunk (bangzi) is used as the rhythmic musical instrument in the opera, it is also known as Bangzi Opera.

Originating from the ancient folk singing and dancing in Shaanxi and Gansu, Qinqiang grew and developed well in Chang'an, the political, economic and cultural center in ancient China and finally came into being after many generations. Since the Zhou Dynasty the central Shaanxi Plain has been called Qin, hence the name of Qinqiang for this very old opera. "It came into being during the Qin Dynasty (221-206 BC), became polished during the Han Dynasty (206 BC – 220 AD), flourished during the Tang Dynasty (618-907), was completed during the Yuan Dynasty (1206-1368), matured during the Ming Dynasty (1368-1644) and became popular during the Qing Dynasty (1616-1911). After these stages of development, it has changed into a grand opera."

The Shaanxi Opera (Qinqiang) *Chopping Open the Mountain to Save the Mother*

Qinqiang features "vehement, vigorous, solemn, stirring plots and straight ups and downs in a big voice." The performance of Qinqiang is simple, unvarnished, rough and bold with exaggeration. "Singing while roaring" in Qinqiang is viewed as one of the ten great strange things in the central Shaanxi Plain. It has its special styles in facial make-up, posture, costume, acrobatics (spitting and blowing fire and walking on stilts) and language and sound. It has formed its own school of performance and has four major roles of sheng, dan, jing and chou and each of them is divided into 13 styles.

Qinqiang qupai has six categories of instruments, suona, haidi (a very big bamboo flute), sheng, Kunqu and Taoqu. The major musical instrument is the banhu fiddle that has a high-pitched and clear sound. The stringed-instrument players often have an important position in the theatrical troupe of Qinqiang and sit in the middle of the front stage.

Handiao Guangguang

Applicant: Hanzhong City, Shaanxi Province

Handiao Guangguang, popular in the region along Hanzhong and Ankang in southern Shaanxi Province, is a Bangzi Opera combining Qinqiang and local dialect and folk music. It came into being at the end of the Ming Dynasty when Qinqiang was introduced to the region of Hanzhong. Its music for voices and pronunciation and rhythm in monologues is based on the dialect in Hanzhong (the language in the area of the Hanshui River). As beating the Bangzi produces the sound "guang, guang", the opera is also called Handiao Guangguang. As it has many common points with Qinqiang in the major rhythm modes, melody structure and musical instruments, it is also named as "southern Qinqiang" and "Handiao Qinqiang."

The music for voices of Handiao

Guangguang not only shows the beauty of the loud, sonorous, and vehement sound of Qinqiang but also reflects the elegance and softness in the local music in southern Shaanxi Province. The music for the voices of the dan role is loud and sonorous and that of the painted faces is often sung in falsetto with a lengthened end sound. It is known as the "pairing of the old and young." The musical accompaniment in Handiao Guangguang is divided into two kinds, one for singing and acting plays and one for plays with acrobatics. For the former one, the banhu fiddle is the major musical instrument accompanied by jinghu, haidi and sanxian; and for the latter one, percussion instruments are mainly used such as the pointed drum, the flat drum, the hooked gong, cymbal, bangzi, yazi and wooden fish.

The performance of Handiao Guangguang requires large-scaled exaggeration. It has many special acrobatics such as "trussing barrels," "changing face," and "hiding fire," and many specific postures with weapons, sticks and tuck toss.

Handiao Guangguang has many different plays and the number of traditional plays is about 700 including 560 book plays and 170 Zhezi plays.

Jin Opera

Applicant: Shanxi Province

Jin Opera (Shanxi Opera) is one of the four great Bangzi operas in Shanxi Province. At the beginning of the Qing Dynasty Puzhou Bangzi was introduced to Jinzhong (center of Shanxi). With the combination of Qitai yangge and Jinzhong folk songs, it evolved to Jin Opera after the participation of Shanxi merchants and local literati. After several changes it spread and became popular in centre and northern Shanxi as well as some parts in Inner Mongolia, Hebei and northern Shaanxi provinces.

Jin Opera has the common features of Bangzi opera, being vigorous, vehement and rough, in the music for voices and performances and also has some specific mellow styles. Therefore it can represent both vehement historical stories and common folk lives. Owing directly to the artistic combination of roughness and exquisiteness Jin Opera is popular with many audiences.

Jin Opera features sweet and fluent rhythm, beautiful, mellow and amiable melody and clear monologue and has the strong local flavour of the Jinzhong region and its specific styles. Jin Opera pays a lot of attention to the methods of antiphonal and round singing with two or more persons to bring the artistic features of its tune into play. For example, in Zhong Bao Guo, the figures with the big painted faces, xusheng (male figures with beard) and zhengdan (main female figures) sing in round to tell about past stories and exchange current emotions.

Puzhou Bangzi

Applicants: Linfen City and Yuncheng City, Shanxi Province

"Puzhou Bangzi" is one of the four great Bangzi in Shanxi Province and evolved from Shan-Shaan Bangzi, although some claim it actual was the origin of the latter. Bangzi, also named Bangban, is a kind of percussion instrument. Bangzi Opera got its name due to the use of the Bangzi for rhythm.

Puzhou Bangzi came into being in Puzhou, between Shanxi, Shaanxi and Henan provinces, at the end of the Ming Dynasty and early Qing Dynasty. It is mainly popular in southern Shanxi and in some parts of Shaanxi, Henan, Gansu and Qinghai provinces. It is one of the oldest Bangzi operas in China.

Bangzi melody is the major music for voices in Puzhou Bangzi and other tunes include Kunqu, Chuiqiang and folk songs. The melody of Puzhou Bangzi features a high-pitched voice, rapid beat, and straight ups and downs and it is good at expressing vehement emotions. The music of Puzhou Opera is good at expressing enthusiasm. Because of the lifestyle, language and tone among local people, Puzhou Opera tune has a changeable melody, a high-pitched starting voice and a combination of big and small voices. So Puzhou Bangzi is always famous for its vehemence and roughness. The accompanying bands are classified into two kinds, i.e. those for singing and acting and those for acrobatics. The banhu is the major instrument used for singing and acting, assisted by the bamboo flute, a two-stringed instrument, the sanxian and the erhu. The musical instruments for acrobatics include the banhu, zaobang, maluo and cymbals and there are various gongs and drums.

The performance of Puzhou Bangzi has a long history and deep traditions and it is vehement, bold, unrestrained, vigorous, natural, comfortable, lively, implicative and minute. It pays attention to acting and is good at using acrobatics to represent figures. It has many performance skills with a high degree of difficulty and worthy of appreciation. There are more than 30 kinds of special acrobatics and its cap wing skills, beard skills, lingzi (long pheasant tail feathers worn on warriors' helmets) skills, tip skills, whip skills, chair skills and fan skills are well known across China.

The Shanxi Jin Opera *Fengtai Pass*

Beilu Bangzi

Applicant: Xinzhou City, Shanxi Province

Beilu Bangzi got its name as it came into being and is popular in northern Shanxi. Zhonglu Bangzi (Jin Opera), Shangdang Bangzi, Puzhou Opera and Beilu Bangzi are together known as the four great Bangzi operas in Shanxi. It is one of the most influential operas in northern China.

Beilu Bangzi came into being in the middle of the 16th century and reached maturity early in the 19th century during the Jiaqing (1796-1820) and Daoguang (1821-1850) periods of the Qing Dynasty. For three hundred years Beilu Bangzi has been popular in northern Shanxi, Inner Mongolia, Zhangjiakou, Baotou and Hohhot for its vehement frontier style.

The roles in Beilu Bangzi are divided into three main categories (xusheng, zhengdan, and hualian), three small categories (xiaosheng, xiaodan, and xiaochou) and minor roles. Plays are mainly about historical themes and a few of them reflect folk lives. The performances are famous for the combination of strict formality and life flavour and the combination of boldness and exquisiteness.

Many artists created many florid ornaments in the singing, which add emotional colours to the vehement music and full plateau style. There are various tunes played by suona, sixian (silk stringed instrument) or sheng respectively. Some originate from folk songs and others are directly transplanted from Buddhist music. The traditional accompaniment instruments are divided into two categories for plays of singing and acting and plays of acrobatics respectively. The musical instrument for plays of singing and acting include banghu, erxian (two-stringed instrument), sanxian (three-stringed instrument), sixian (four-stringed instrument), sheng, bamboo flute and suona and those for plays of acrobatics include bangu (a kind of drum), maluo (a kind of gong), and bangzi. The music of Beilu Bangzi features vehemence, vividness, ease, steadiness, and roughness. With the combination of the local folk songs, Kekeqiang, a singing style of its own, came into being with distinctive local characters.

Shangdang Bangzi

Applicant: Jincheng City, Shanxi Province

Shangdang Bangzi, one of the four great Bangzi Operas in Shanxi Province, is popular in south-eastern Shanxi. During the Daoguang Period (1821-1850) it was known as a local opera. Bangzi is the main melody in Shangdang Bangzi which became popular during the middle and later Qianlong Period (1736-1795) of the Qing Dynasty.

Shangdang Bangzi originated from the end of the Ming Dynasty (1368-1644). Its tone is loud, sonorous, broad, rough, simple and unvarnished. There are various tunes and the sound is strong. Its representation is straight, vehement and vivid by rough lines and outlines. Attention is paid to singing and saying. Of about 400 traditional plays, those reflecting ancient heroes, loyal officials and generals, aggression by foreign invaders and punishment of traitors are in the majority. Many plays are meaningful and full of strong patriotism.

The basic skill of Shangdang Bangzi is "sanba". When applying the skill, a performer will raise his head up and throw his chest out, being steady and powerful. But heavy feet and stiff buttocks are the deficiencies of the posture and the protruding buttocks are not handsome. The role of xusheng is the most outstanding, followed by jing, qingyi (young female figure) and wuxiaosheng (young fighting man). Shangdang Bangzi is rough and healthy. The gaits and postures are unvarnished and old, the music is loud, sonorous, sweet and lively, the tunes are varied and each tune has its specific musical instruments.

The music of Shangdang Bangzi is mostly derived from folk music. In the 200 original tunes of music in Shangdang Bangzi, most of them are folk music, folk ditties and music under governmental control in ancient times.

Based on statistics there are more than 700 traditional plays in Shangdang Bangzi.

Hebei Bangzi

Applicant: Hebei Province

Hebei Bangzi is the most representative local opera in Hebei Province and has a history of about 200 years. It is an important branch of Bangzi Opera. It came into being during the Jiaqing (1796-1820) and Daoguang (1821-1850) periods in the Qing Dynasty and was popular across Hebei Province. It involves the features of Shanxi and Shaanxi Bangzi Operas and today it is popular mainly in Hebei, Beijing, Tianjin, and some parts in Shandong and Northeast China.

The artistic characters of Hebei Bangzi are mainly reflected by plays, music and performance. Its facial make-up, dress and the appearance of the performers are specific in a few plays, but those in most plays are the same as in Beijing Opera. It has no distinctive opera feature.

The music of Hebei Bangzi has always been loud, sonorous, vehement, solemn and stirring and can make audiences feel hot in their ears, sad in their hearts and impassioned and forceful.

Hebei Bangzi opera *Lin Chong is Exiled for Penal Servitude* performed by a three-year-old child strikes the eye. He has delicate features and sings with a clear and rich tone, showing his solid art of singing.

The performance of Hebei Bangzi pays much attention to formality and the performance of the figures' emotions, feelings, personalities and features is accomplished by some kind of formality. In performances some acrobatics are often used and this is frequently seen in short plays of acrobatics. The performance formality of Hebei Bangzi is generally the same as that of Beijing Opera but is more exaggerated and bolder than Beijing Opera in terms of concrete application. Hence it's rough, vehement and unrestrained showing style. There is no standard criterion on the application of very-difficult acrobatics and different performers perform in different ways.

The traditional plays mostly use materials from the historical stories of the Yin, Zhou, Spring and Autumn Period, Warring States Period, Western and Eastern Han, Three Kingdoms, Sui, Tang, Song, Yuan, Ming, Qing and the early period of the Republic of China. In the traditional plays the words and sentences are popular and the language is mostly the local dialect in Hebei with a strong local flavour. The words lack embellishment and the texts of some plays are rough.

Henan Opera

Applicant: Henan Province

Henan Opera, also called Henan Bangzi, is an extremely important branch of the Bangzi Operas in China and favoured widely by many people. It is mainly popular in Henan Province and is spread across China. It has a history of over a hundred years. As early as the Qianlong Period (1736-1795) in the Qing Dynasty it became an influential local opera in Henan Province. Henan Opera has absorbed the popular music, quyi, singing and talking and ditties in Henan and become straightforward, pure, abundant, exquisite and full of local flavours.

Henan Opera has good singing melodies. The Datan melody is arranged at the key points in plots. The music is fluent, the rhythm is distinctive and words are colloquial. The pronunciation is clear, the tune is used with ease and verve and the singing is easy for audiences to understand. It shows its specific artistic charm. First of all Henan Opera is full of vehement and unrestrained vigour and is good at showing grand scenes and has a strong emotional force. Secondly, it has a strong local flavour and is unvarnished, popular, natural and close to the lives of the common people. Thirdly, it has a distinctive and strong rhythm, sharp-pointed conflicts, complete story plots

The Henan Opera Opera *Judge Bao*

and figures with distinctive characters.

Henan Bangzi Opera pays attention to singing and acting. It includes the customs and habits in Henan and integrates the lives and actions of the people. In Henan Opera the gongs and drums have a loud sound, the sixian has a high-pitched sound and singing is predominant while the monologue has a lesser part and the male figures hop and the females walk on stage. During festivals many people gather together to watch the opera and relax in its atmosphere.

There are about 1,000 traditional plays for Henan Opera and most of them drew materials from historical stories and novels.

Wanbang

Applicant: Neixiang County, Henan Province

Wanbang, a rare local opera, grew up and is popular in Nanyang and the surrounding areas in south-western Henan. On the whole it retains the elite style of Henan Bangzi in early times and its original music. Its music is beautiful and the style is specific. It has a history of more than 300 years.

In terms of stories these are mainly positive and tragic reflecting the stories about the royal court, battles and legal cases. In terms of music, it has its own specific style and the music is variable. The gongs and drums used in percussion in Wanbang are similar to other operas but the percussion style in the beginning, middle and end of the music are specific.

Wanbang shows the vehemence of Shaanxi Bangzi, the neatness of music from the Central Plain and the sweetness and pureness of Hubei music. Falsetto is used for ottava alta tunes without words to set off emotions. This is a stunt of Wan melody and has a unique artistic value.

Wanbang has many melodies, vehement music and a loud and unrestrained sound. Male figures use a full voice to sing, being rough, bold, unrestrained and clear. In particular, the ottava alta coloratura in female singing is clear, bright and sweet and sounds like a bird singing with the accompaniment of chirping played by stringed instruments. It is the main character of the opera and can be called a stunt.

Huaibang

Applicant: Qinyang City, Henan Province

Huaibang, a rare and old local opera in Henan Province, originated from the old Huaiqing Prefecture (Qinyang today) and took the name Huaibang.

As early as 800 years ago Huaiqing Prefecture had become a place with many opera artists and schools. Huaibang was a specific local opera in Huaiqing Prefecture. In ancient times when serious drought occurred people would offer sacrifice to the gods and organize some artists to sing around a table without dressing up or a stage to pray for rain. Later it gradually evolved into a stage performance with all the costumes and make-up.

The specific Huaibang has a unique style in performance. On the whole the music, monologue, musical accompaniment, posture and acrobatics of Huaibang are rough, unrestrained, bold, vehement and heart-quaking. Equal attention is paid to singing and acting and the performers sing while dancing which give audiences an intense impression. Huaibang belongs to the system of Northern Bangzi and its melody and monologue are both based on the dialect of the ancient Huaiqing Prefecture. It also has the distinctive features of the local language.

The Chinese jujube bang is used for beating the rhythm in the singing of Huaibang opera. Stringed instruments are the main accompaniment used in Huaibang. These include the daxian (sharp-pointed xian), banhu, erhu, yueqin, yangqin, cello and violin. Percussion is also a major force in the music of Huaibang. In the acrobatic scenes of Huaibang, most performers can apply wushu actions naturally into the performance of the opera, which is unique in the drama circle of China.

Based on incomplete statistics, there are nearly 300 plays in Huaibang and most of them are positive plays about loyalty to country, battles and weeding out the wicked and letting the law-abiding citizens live in peace.

Dapingdiao

Applicant: Puyang County, Huaxian County and Yanjin County, Henan Province

Dapingdiao, originated from middle of the Ming Dynasty and has a history of more than 500 years. The music of Dapingdiao belongs to the system of Bangzi Operas. Its tone is lower than Shandong Bangzi, Henan Bangzi and Hebei Bangzi, so it is called Pingdiao or Dapingdiao. In terms of musical mode and structure, it is the same as Henan Opera mostly and in terms of artistic style, it is rougher and more vehement than Henan Opera. Dapingdiao has had a great influence in a wide region to the north of the Yellow River and gradually three branches came into being, i.e. Donglu Pingdiao, Xilu Pingdiao and Hedong Pingdiao.

Dapingdiao has a simple and unvarnished performance, beautiful music and frequent usage of acrobatics and specific musical instruments. There are 16 kinds of extant unique music in four categories, 38 styles of tune, 10 styles of percussion, 630 plays passed down in oral form (including 180 oral copybooks), 15 styles of special posture acrobatics and four kinds of specific musical instruments.

The music of Dapingdiao is the same as that of Shandong Bangzi on the whole, but the former one often uses real voices in pronunciation and very high-pitched falsetto in the ending. The major accompanying instruments include the daxian, erxian, sanxian, dabang and dahao. In terms of roles in Dapingdiao the black face and the red face are the main parts and form an important feature of the opera. Its performance is grand in momentum and scenery. Equal attention is paid to singing, acting and speaking. It is rough, bold, unrestrained, gentle and firm.

Yue Melody

Applicant: Zhoukou City, Henan Province

Yue Melody, one of the local operas in Henan Province, has an elegant, pure and simple music with various metres such as slow, medium, rapid and free.

After the formation of Yue Tune, there were three forms of performance: shadow-play Yue Tune, puppetry Yue Tune and Yue Tune full-scale opera. Till today these three forms are still popular in rural areas in northern Hubei province, west Anhui province and Nanyang of Henan province.

The main accompanying instruments for the scenes of singing and acting are the trunk, the sixian and the yueqin. In the early 20th century the shaft of the yueqin(a plucked string instrument) gradually became short and the pitch also changed. These compose the three major instruments for accompanying the Yue Melody. Other accompanying instruments which may be found include the bamboo flute, the sanxian, the suona and the sheng. The accompanying instruments for the scenes of acrobatics mainly include the guban, hand cymbals, big gong and small gong as well as the hall drum and bass gong. Sometimes many different percussion instruments with sound effects are also included to enrich its presentation.

In terms of libretto the Yue Melody has a very strict structure of traditional opera with fewer librettos and more monologues and the words and sentences used are comparatively elegant and profound. The music is based on certain tunes and pitches. Most of the modern plays are adaptations of singing-and-talking stories and novels. There are more librettos and fewer monologues and the words are colloquial. When singing, performers often use their real voices as the major one and a falsetto as an assistant. During the Qing Dynasty the characters of all the roles were men so it was easy to adopt the same tone and tune. After the 1920s some female characters were brought in and it adopted the Yue Tune style that men and women sing in the same tone but different tunes.

Beijing Opera

Applicants: China National Peking Opera Company, Beijing City, Tianjin City, Liaoning Province, Shandong Province, and Shanghai City

(See P274)

Anhui Opera

Applicants: Anhui Province and Wuyuan County, Jiangxi Province

Anhui Opera, one of the source operas for Beijing Opera, is an important local opera and mainly popular in Anhui Province and Wuyuan County in Jiangxi Province.

Anhui Opera has a broad space for figures in plays to pour out their inner accumulated melancholy and anger and is full of narration. The range of music is extraordinarily broad and feels both rough and fine.

Anhui Opera is a colourful performance art. The scenes of singing and acting combine singing and dancing and are sweet and exquisite. The scenes of acrobatics are rough and vehement with profound wushu and the actors are good at falling down and throwing themselves from heights on stage. It pays attention to sculpture style beauty of postures and striking a pose on stage and to the images of figures and the momentum of the scenes. Wushu on the flat, high stage is the most outstanding in Anhui Opera. In terms of flat stage, "kicking with a single foot", "kicking singly with crossed legs" and the "flying cross" are extraordinarily breathtaking. In terms of stage height the performers usually somersault over three tables and some even somersault over seven tables.

The large and small suona are often used as accompanying instruments in Anhui Opera and the momentum is very grand along with the accompaniment of big gongs and drums.

There are many plays written for Anhui Opera including about 1,404 traditional plays and 753 of them can be seen performed. The contents are various such as disputes between various states, great events in court, fairy tales and living folk stories. Most of the plays are in written-copy form and have a long history. Many or the original play books have been lost.

Anhui Opera has a history of more than 300 years and once played an important role in the development of Chinese operas. It not only gave birth to Beijing Opera, but also has close relations with scores of local operas across China.

The Anhui Opera *Flooding the Enemy's Troops*

Han Opera

Applicant: Wuhan City, Hubei Province

It is one of the local operas in Hubei Province and popular in the drainage areas of the Yangtze River and Hanshui River in Hubei and some places in the neighbouring areas such as Henan, Hunan, Shaanxi and Sichuan provinces. There are more than 660 traditional plays and most of them are about historical stories and folk legends.

Han Opera has a loud, sonorous, vehement, bright and fluent music. The rhythm is flexible and changeable with strong plasticity and wide usage. The music in Han Opera also includes some ditties and folk songs with sweet, lively tunes and a distinctive rhythm. It is often used in small-scale operas full of comedy colours and has a strong live flavour. Han Opera has various tunes. There are more than 400 traditional singing and instrument-playing tunes. Based on features and usage range, the tunes are divided into seven categories and they are martial music, ceremony music, banquet music, object music, wedding music, funeral music and god music.

In Han Opera gongs and drums are indispensable. There are various beating methods; heavy, light and continuous beating. A continuous beat is accompanied by maluo with a strong rhythm and vehement atmosphere.

Handiao Erhuang

Applicant: Ankang City, Shaanxi Province

Handiao Erhuang uses two flutes as accompanying instruments. As a flute has the huang (reed) made of bamboo, it is also called the "erhuang."

Handiao Erhuang is a local opera in southern Shaanxi Province and came from the mountain songs, folk songs and ditties in the drainage area of the Hanshui River. The tone used is the dialect in Hanzhong. It is similar with Han Tune in Hubei Province. It has good scenes of singing and acting and has a strong flavour of the Bashan Mountain. The tune is elegant, music is sweet, monologue is gentle, words are humorous, performance is exquisite, pure, simple and natural and the singing and speaking have significant tones of the dialect in the Bashan Mountain with Sichuan tones in the majority. The measures are divided into upper and lower melodies; the former one is often used to express sorrowful, dismal and resentful emotions and the latter one is often used to express free, happy, bright and unrestrained emotions.

Handiao Erhuang has various traditional plays. In Ankang there are more than 1,200 plays, including 420 book-plays and 517 Zhezi plays that have been unearthed and compiled correctly.

The performance of Handiao Erhuang is exquisite. Real and false voices are used together and the music is sweet and melodious. The performers of sheng and laodan often use their real voices to sing and dan performers use falsetto voices to sing. The real and false voices are used in turns according to the demands of the plots, forming sweet and bitter music. The huqin, erhu, yueqin, sanxian, ruan, suona, flute, and trumpet are used to accompany the scenes of singing and acting, and the yaban, bangzi, baogu (a kind of drum), pointed drum, gong and cymbals are used to accompany the scenes of acrobatics.

There are various facial make-ups in Handiao Erhuang which are nicer than those of Beijing Opera and Qinqiang. Now about 450 kinds of facial make-ups have been collected. Many facial make-ups were painted with animals, plants, stars, weapons, characters, designs and religious symbols. The same figure will be dressed up with different facial make-ups in structures and colours according to specific scenes. They are very meticulous and vivid.

Taining Meilin Opera

Applicant: Taining County, Fujian Province

Meilin Opera got its name as it was born in Meilin Township, Taining County, Northern Fujian Province.

Meilin Opera, commonly known as Tuxi Opera, is one of the local operas in Fujian Province. During the Qianlong (1736-1795) and Jiaqing (1796-1820) periods in the Qing Dynasty, Hui Tune spread to Taining by Zhejiang and Jiangxi. With the combination of local dialects, folk ditties and Taoist music, a special opera came into being. The monologue is spoken in local mandarin, the music is beautiful, the roles are complete, the performance is straightforward and the singing, acting, reading and acrobatics all possess distinctive features.

Meilin Opera is straightforward, simple and unvarnished with great ups and downs. The music is sound and sonorous and both large and small voices are used in singing. The librettos are mostly in the form of long and short sentences and the end often has the lengthened tune somolar to folk songs. These are the special features of Meilin Opera. Gongs and drums are important parts of Meilin Opera music. A theatrical troupe is usually composed of 15 persons. The props on stage are very simple – one table and two chairs. Only three colours red, black and white are used for costumes.

The roles are complete in Meilin Opera and have a strict and distinctive drama formula. The performance is simple, unvarnished and precise and has the characteristic movements similar to ancient "amusement gods" and puppetry. There are many traditional acrobatics in Meilin Opera, such as "face changing", "making trouble", "stepping down high stage", etc. There are more than 330 traditional plays including 130 with collected records in Meilin Opera.

Minxi Han Opera

Applicant: Longyan City, Fujian Province

Minxi Han Opera is one of the major local operas in Fujian Province. It originated during the Qianlong Period (1736-1795) in the Qing Dynasty and has a history of more than 200 years. It is a local opera with specific styles with the combination of the Hakka dialect and folk music in west Fujian and is mainly popular in west Fujian (Minxi), east Guangdong, south Jiangxi and south Fujian provinces with influences in Taiwan and Southeast Asia.

The monologue and librettos in Minxi Han Opera are based on mandarin and have a special rhythm with the combination of the Minxi dialect. Its facial make-up is mainly represented by two roles of jing and chou. The role of jing has the most facial make-up and red jing and black jing have 80 traditional facial make-up types in two sets. Each role has its traditional basic skills and some wushu acrobatics are specific in Minxi Han Opera.

The accompanying music and scores for gongs and drums are extremely various and distinctively different from other operas. There are more than 300 accompaniment music pieces and more than 100 wind instrument music pieces. In addition there is a lot of Han music plus some folk ditties and folk instrumental music pieces from southwest Fujian and Chaoshan in Guangdong, which were adapted by Minxi Han Opera artists and enriched the opera music. There are more than 100 sets of scores for gongs and drums.

The instruments diaogui and dasuluo are characteristic of this opera. The Diaogui looks like an ox horn and is also named an ox-horn xian. It has a high pitch and a silvery sound and is the leading musical instrument in Minxi Han Opera. The Dasuluo has a diameter of about 80 cm and a weight of eight to nine kg. It is huge in size and the sound is simple, elegant, slow and melodious.

Baling Opera

Applicant: Yueyang City, Hunan Province

Baling Opera, one of the important operas in Hunan Province, has tanqiang as the major tune and also has kunqiang, zaqiang and ditties. It is mainly popular in Yueyang, Yiyang, Changde, Xiangxi and Changsha in Hunan Province and some places in neighbouring Hubei and Jiangxi provinces.

Baling Opera is sung in the Zhongzhou tone and Hubei and Hunan tones with the combination of the northern Hunan dialect. Attention is paid to the description of figures. There is a complete set of traditional performance formulae and the artistic style is straightforward, simple, meticulous and vivid. The performance has the "eight inner skills" of happiness, anger, sorrow, joy, sadness, worry, hate and astonishment to depict figures' mentality and express figures' emotions and the "eight outer skills" of using hands, legs, body, neck, moustache, wings, long pheasant tail feathers on helmets, fans and flowing-water sleeves.

Baling Opera pays attention to the expression of the eyes especially and there are more than thirty common expressions in the eyes such as looking forward, sidelong glance, happy eyes, angry eyes and sorrowful eyes. The monologue in Baling Opera includes common yunbai (orderly and rhythm monologue) and xibai (monologue), as well as dialects in Beijing, Jiangsu, Sichuan, Anhui and Shanxi to reflect the regional features and social status and qualities of figures.

In the plays about fighting in Baling Opera the artists of past generations adopted and created many acrobatics such as light skills, soft bar, fork throwing, chair throwing, getting through a knife circle, getting through a fire circle, turning somersaults over tables, the human pyramid and flags down the wind. These fighting skills are deeply related to folk wushu and acrobatics.

There are about 370 traditional plays for Baling Opera. They mainly draw materials from historical novels and the scripts for story-telling reflect the political and military struggle themes in past dynasties.

Jinghe Opera

Applicant: Li County, Hunan Province

Lizhou Jinghe Opera is an opera popular in north-western Hunan and Jingzhou and Shashi in Hubei Province. It got its name as it is most popular in the Jinghe River section of the Yangtze Basin.

The music of Jinghe Opera is divided into northern and southern types. The northern type is loud, sonorous and vehement and evolved from Qinqiang. The southern type is gentle, colourful and evolved from Hubei melody and Anhui melody.

In Jinghe Opera the music is loud and grand and performers use different voices for different roles. Xusheng mostly uses a side voice and a hoarse voice, xiaosheng and dan use a falsetto voice and xiaohualian and laodan use their real voices. The monologue is spoken in Lizhou mandarin and a few plays are sung in Beijing, Sichuan, Jiangsu and Shanxi mandarin.

Jinghe Opera is good at fighting plays. It has many traditional plays and more than 500 plays are preserved today including about 450 complete plays and 60 scattered zhezi plays. These plays mostly drew materials from zaju (poetic drama), legends, novels and folk stories of the Yuan and Ming dynasties.

Cantonese Opera

Applicants: Guangzhou City and Foshan City of Guangdong Province, the Home Affairs Bureau of Hong Kong Special Administration Region and the Cultural Affairs Bureau of Macao Special Administration Region

Cantonese Opera, also known as Guangdong full-scale opera, is a performance art combining singing, acting, reading, fighting, musical accompaniment, dressing on stage and abstract body shapes.

The music and words of Cantonese Opera are popular and many vivid and lively dialect words are used in the opera and it is especially vivid in its monologues. Cantonese Opera widely absorbs the local arts in Guangdong

The Cantonese Opera *Madam White Snake*

Province such as music, embroidery, ivory carving, porcelain and ash sculpture. It fully reflects the regional cultural traditions among people in Guangdong, has influences over the whole world and has a strong cultural cohesion among Chinese people around the world.

In the aspect of music, Cantonese Opera absorbed the folk music elements and reflective ways in Guangdong to serve the plots. Some music pieces in Cantonese Opera came from the famous Guangdong music. In early times the musical instruments used in Cantonese Opera included the erxian, tiqin, yueqin, vertical and bamboo flutes, sanxian, gong, cymbals and drums with simple tunes. After maturing the Cantonese Opera used more than forty kinds of musical instruments and even accepted western musical instruments such as the saxaphone and violin to perfect musical effects. It was rarely seen in drama circles at that time, showing the innovative spirit in Lingnan (south of the Five Ridges in Guangdong and Guangxi provinces) operas.

The roles in Cantonese Opera are divided into wenwusheng, xiaosheng, zhengyin huadan, erbang huadan, chousheng and wusheng. The performance of Cantonese Opera is simple and straightforward and has some specific acrobatics. The fighting plays are based on the southern wushu skills and the use of targets, hand bridge, shaolin boxing and chair skills and high-stage skills with a high degree of difficulty are all excellent. In Cantonese Opera the make-up is simple and the colours are strong and brilliant. Brilliant and exquisite Guangdong embroidery is often used in the dresses and there are strong local characters.

Gui Opera

Applicant: Guangxi Zhuang Autonomous Region

Gui Opera, one of the major operas in Guangxi, is commonly called Gui Drama or Gui Troupe Drama. It is sung in the Guilin dialect and is exquisite, vivid and lively. Performers make use of expressions on faces and body postures to express emotions and attach importance to the live performance to create figures. Even most of the fighting plays are performed with singing and acting. It is popular in Guilin City, Liuzhou City, Hezhou City, Hechi City and some mandarin areas in Wuzhou City in Guangxi and spreads to southern Hunan Province and the northwest corner of Guangdong Province.

Gui Opera absorbs the tunes and performing styles of Qi Opera, Beijing Opera and Kunqu. It attaches equal importance to singing, acting, reading and dancing and is especially good at exquisite singing and vivid acting. The music of Gui Opera is loud, sonorous, solemn and stirring. It is characterized by the unique music accompaniment of gongs and drums and the singing accompaniment of human voices. Wind and stringed instruments are unnecessary. Gui Opera is sung in the Guilin dialect and the tune is sweet with orderly rises and falls in the music. The performance is simple, unvarnished and meticulous and the music is sweet, clear and bright with strong local flavours.

The current roles of Gui Opera include sheng, dan, jing and chou. The limits for roles are often broken when performers act the figures in modern plays. The performers with corresponding conditions will act out figures according to the characters of the figures in plays.

Yihuang Opera

Applicant: Yihuang County, Jiangxi Province

Yihuang Opera, originated from Yihuang County, Jiangxi Province, has a history of more than 300 years and is one of the large-sized classical operas in place. Its main melody, Yihuang Melody, is the predecessor of "erhuang melody" in Beijing Opera, Jiangxi Opera, Han Opera and Anhui Opera. It got its name as it was created in Yihuang County. Yihuang is also known as the hometown of opera. As early as the middle of the Ming Dynasty (1368-1644) it had become the center of local operas in Jiangxi.

Yihuang Opera has many traditional plays with distinctive characters. Most of them are complete plays with vivid plots. The division of roles is meticulous, the music is simple and unvarnished and the words are colloquial. The performance is straightforward and rough and the singing, acting, reading and fighting compose a set of precise and flexible formulae. The musical accompaniment of the huqin has a strong local colour. It is much different from Beijing Opera and Jiangxi Opera and it is suitable to reflect on the different figures with various characters and the plays of different times with different contents.

The music of Yihuang Opera is primitive and straightforward. Laosheng and laodan use real voices, xiaosheng uses both big and small voices and the end sound often rises by ottava alta. Men and women sing in the same tune and tone. The melody is simple and unvarnished. There are a few starting and falling sounds but they are very short. Performers sing the tune on the base of the pronunciation of the words often close to the spoken language. The tune range is not wide and the music often runs within a six-degree scale.

In the performance of Yihuang Opera, the singing, reading, acting and fighting have strict formulae and each action must follow rules. For example, the action of "qiba" made by a military officer "raising up two hands to support the sky" should adopt the different postures of "dragon claws" or "tiger claws" according to the different status of the figures.

Luantan

Applicants: Taizhou City and Pujiang County, Zhejiang Province

The *Qinglong Pass,* a traditional play of Taizhou Luantan (thruming). The acrobatic fighting of the Taizhou Luantan (thruming) has a beauty of hideousness.

Luantan has loud, sonorous and vehement music. Performers are required to sing in real voices, so the primitive, bold and straightforward characters are preserved. (Luan refers to a skill and frequency of plucking.)

Taizhou Luantan came into being towards the end of the Ming Dynasty and the early part of the Qing Dynasty and is popular in Taizhou, Wenzhou, Ningbo, Shaoxing, Jinhua and Lishui. Taizhou Luantan has many melodies. Luantan is the major melody and there are other melodies such as Kunqu, Gaoqiang, Hui tune, Cidiao and Tanhuang. It is one of the rare operas with mixed melodies. The language on the stage is the combination of the melody of the Central Plain and the local mandarin in Taizhou. It is full of local tunes and is colloquial and unique. The accompanying instruments are divided into those for singing and acting plays and those for fighting plays. The former one is classified into two kinds, wind and stringed instruments and suona and the latter one is classified into gongs and drums for exaggerating the atmosphere and those for performing. In the aspect of performance, Taizhou Luantan has many acrobatics such as "shuaya" and "double horsing" which have been famous for a long time. There are more than 300 plays in Taizhou Luantan.

Pujiang Luantan came into being in the middle of the Ming Dynasty and got its name as it originated in Pujiang County in the center of Zhejiang. In the period between the end of the Southern Song Dynasty to the middle of the Ming Dynasty, Pujiang Luantan became popular among the people in the form of a singing and talking art. In the middle of the Ming Dynasty Pujiang Luantan changed to performing on stage from just singing while sitting on chairs. The music of Pujiang Luantan is magnificent, fluent and comfortable and it reflects vehement, loud, sonorous, solemn, stirring and gloomy emotions. The performance of Pujiang Luantan is characterized by performing fighting plays with singing and acting and performing singing and acting plays by fighting. It is rough, forceful and full of local flavours and is unique in its performances of acrobatics and fighting. There are about 300 plays in Pujiang Luantan.

Shijiazhuang Sixian

Applicant: Shijiazhuang City, Hebei Province

Shijiazhuang Sixian, one of the old specific operas in Hebei Province, is one of the rare local operas in China. It is popular in most places in Hebei Province and in the east of Shanxi province and the region of Yanbei.

Shijiazhuang Sixian came into being based on popular music in the Ming and Qing dynasties. The music is unique. It is sung in real voices. The melody rises high and steeply. Performers lengthen the end sound in a falsetto voice. The melody then goes down gradually. It is vehement, melodious, bold and unrestrained. Sixian music belongs to the melody of xiansuo (a kind of stringed instrument). There are more than 500 various musical pieces and more than 100 accompanying musical pieces.

The performance of Sixian Opera inherited the legacy of puppetry. Later it changed to performing on stage with real performers. They created different figures with various characters using different postures, actions, facial expressions and finger movements. They used many exaggerated movements and adopted stiff and straightforward puppet-like actions. Later performers made use of acrobatics (such as playing with plates, bowls, whips, fans, handkerchiefs, cap wings and moustaches) and facial make-up as well as real props of swords and spears in the form of "shehuo" (a folk art performance given on traditional or religious festivals) to give performances. In addition, it learned from the other sister arts of Kunqu, Beijing Opera and Hebei Bangzi.

The orchestras of Sixian are divided into those for singing and acting plays and those for fighting plays. The former one includes xiansuo, yueqin, big sanxian, small sanxian and "sijia xian" and the latter one includes bangu (a kind of small drum), big shailuo (a kind of gong), big cymbals and deaf cymbals. The roles of Sixian are divided into sheng, dan, jing and chou. The performance is vehement, rough, bold and unconstrained. The actions are much exaggerated and the acting of the figures is vivid and exquisite with strong local flavours.

Yanbei Shuahai'er

Applicant: Datong City, Shanxi Province

Shuahai'er, also known as Kekeqiang, is a local favourite opera in Datong. It has a long history of more than 600 years. The most distinctive character of the opera is the using of the rear voice in singing. This sound is produced from the part under the throat and sounds simple and honest. The singing and musical accompaniment are tuneful, which is another significant character of Shuahai'er.

The strong character of Shuahai'er is collectively reflected by its unique singing style and lively performance. For the operas in the traditional singing style performers use rear voices, similar to the style of Buddhist singing. Before each sung sentence, performers often use "Keqiang", which is rarely seen in opera, so it is also named Kekeqiang. The performances absorbed the folk dancing in yangge. This is very vivid with most parts of the singing and dancing. The performance of the role of chou is very humorous and specific. There are many tragedies in their operas and there are often plays with importance attached to the role of chou in the tragedies. The performance is vivid and interesting and is very popular among the local people.

Lingqiu Luoluoqiang

Applicant: Lingqiu County, Shanxi Province

Luoluoqiang is an opera popular in Lingqiu County and neighbouring parts of Shanxi Province. Only one performer sings front stage and others accompany back stage with the sound of "luoluo yo-yo", hence the name of Luoluoqiang.

Lingqiu Luoluoqiang has distinctive local characteristics. The plays have strong living flavours. The stage lines are vivid, lively and colloquial. Most of the parts are singing and talking and it uses the art of singing and talking. The band doest not accompany the singing with lengthened tunes and only accompanies the end sound and pauses after the short interludes. Performers have a large space for singing. They can sing or talk with a rapid or slow rhythm and with loud and low sounds. Their pronunciation is extraordinarily clear. It is most characteristic that the male figures sing in a falsetto in ottava alta which reflects the marks of the old tunes. Performers sing and dance with different steps and postures and this is full of living flavour which is the performing formula especially for the role of dan in Luoluoqiang.

Liuzi Opera

Applicant: Shandong Province

Liuzi Opera is popular in Shandong, Henan, northern Jiangsu, southern Hebei and northern Anhui provinces. It evolved from the folk ditties and popular music in the Central Plain during the Yuan and Ming dynasties. Its major singing and talking tune "liuzi" is colloquial and influential, so it is called Liuzi Opera.

The performance of Liuzi Opera is rough, bold and straightforward with special styles. The design of the figures' actions is vivid with strong living flavours. For example, when military officer performers step on the stage, they must kick out their legs, fly their feet and strike a pose on the stage. When they become angry they jump up on both feet to show their temper. When fighting with each other they often use real swords and spears.

The accompanying instruments in Liuzi Opera include the bamboo flute, sheng (a reed pipe wind instrument) and sanxian. While accompanying, the instruments often play together in a single melody to follow the music. The melody played by the bamboo flute is basically the same as the singing tune and the sheng and sanxian may be interchangeable. When playing the short interludes the bamboo flute gives improvisation and composes the compound tune with the sheng and sanxian.

Liuzi Opera covers various old tunes popular during the Ming and Qing dynasties. More than 600 music pieces are preserved and they have an important value that is very important in the study of northern operas and verses of the Yuan Dynasty.

Daxian Opera

Applicants: Hua County and Puyang County, Henan Province

Daxian Opera uses a tin flute as its major musical instrument and also uses the sanxian and sheng. The jianzihao and sirenshan accompany the music intermittently. It is very specific. The sanxian is used to start the music for singing, hence the name of Xian opera. As it originated from the imperial palace, the word "da" (great) was added to the name to show its dignity. Therefore, it got the name of "Daxian

Daxian Opera is the Liyuan Opera performed in the court. With a history of more than 1,000 years, it is viewed as a "living fossil" among operas. Photo shows the Daxian Opera Troupe performing in Puyang, Henan Province.

Opera". The tin flute is the particular musical instrument inherited from the ancestors of Daxian Opera.

Daxian Opera is an old and rare opera with mixed tunes. With Kaifeng and Puyang as the centres it is popular in north-eastern Henan, southern Hebei and south-western Shandong provinces. The performances of Daxian Opera are very particular. It is based on Hong boxing and plum blossom boxing. The actions are extremely exaggerated. When walking on stage, performers often push their hands in a circle and stride. The hands are raised up above the head and the performers are good at flying feet. In particular, maojing, wusheng and wudan often come onto the stage in jumps. Most of the plays are about loyal and treacherous people in past dynasties and about eliminating local tyrants. There were originally more than 500 plays including many original scripts of zaju (poetic drama) from the Yuan Dynasty.

The performers often raise the music to ottava alta for the end sound. The monologue is often read in rhyme and accompanied by the sanxian. During the fighting plays the big cymbals and tuba are used to set off the intense and vehement atmosphere. The rhythms in the music have great leaps. Real voices are used together with falsetto. The musical range is wide, deep and vigorous. The music for plays of singing and acting is exceedingly sentimental, sweet and exquisite and the music for plays about fighting sounds like fighting with weapons and the whinnying of battle horses and is stirring and vehement. The music for plays of singing and acting has orderly rises and falls and shows different stages of happiness, anger, sorrow and joy. The music for plays about fighting is accompanied by cymbals, gongs and drums, has steep rises along with the rhythm and at the same time is simple and vigorous.

In the aspects of plays, music and performance Daxian Opera basically preserved the primitive features and allows people to feel the music left by the army plays of the Tang Dynasty, daqu of the Tang and Song dynasties and the zaju of Song and Yuan dynasties.

Min Opera

Applicant: Fuzhou City, Fujian Province

Min Opera, also known as Fuzhou Opera, has a history of more than 400 years. It heads the five great operas in Fujian Province and is the only extant opera sung and read in the Fuzhou dialect. The music has a strong local character and is high-spirited, bold, unrestrained, sweet, moving, bright and lively. It is widely performed in Fuzhou-dialect regions. It is popular in the centre, east and north of Fujian Province and has spread to Taiwan and south-eastern Asia.

Douqiang is the major melody in Min Opera. The musical structure is regular and precise, the melody is sweet and exceedingly sentimental, the style is elegant, the lengthened tune is frequently heard and the accompanying sounds are "ah and oh". In singing both the men and the women use their real voices and the music is vehement, vigorous, simple and rough as well as sweet and exquisite.

The monologues in Min Opera have absorbed many local children's songs, slang, proverbs and two-part allegorical sayings.

In early times the roles in Min Opera were very simple, including only three roles of sheng, dan and chou and the opera was called the "three small opera". Later with the absorption of the roles in Anhui and Beijing operas these roles became complete.

There are more than 1,000 traditional plays in Min Opera and most of them drew materials from folk legends, historical stories and zaju.

Fujian Opera *Wang Lianlian performed* by Lin Ying, a well-known Fujian Opera artist, is full of remarkable voice and emotions.

Shouning Beilu Opera

Applicant: Shouning County, Fujian Province

Beilu Opera, commonly known as Fujian Luantan, is the local opera combined with Luantan which was introduced to Fujian in the middle of the Qing Dynasty. It was popular in northern, central and eastern Fujian and has a history of more than 300 years and is a rare opera representing Luantan tune during the Qing Dynasty.

The music of Beilu Opera has a sweet melody, bright rhythm, fluent music and features narration. Its monologues and words in singing are in mandarin and this is the outstanding character of Beilu Opera. In the hundreds of years of performance, Beilu Opera has acquired a set of performances favoured by most audiences. All the role figures make use of body language to express the figures' qualities and psychology and push forward the plot. The intensification of the postures and actions and the showing of the figures' psychology are closely combined with the music. The singing and acting are in harmony. There are many performing styles combining singing and dancing and acting and fighting which enrich the expressive force of the operas.

The music of Beilu Opera is not as sweet and elegant as Kunqu but it expresses a lot of emotions and shows exquisiteness in its roughness. The rhythm is variable, the melody rises and falls constantly and the music is lively and forceful. It preserves the primitive style of accompaniment from backstage. There are many traditional plays in Beilu Opera and it is said that 105 plays are frequently shown.

Xiqin Opera

Applicant: Haifeng County, Guangdong Province

Xiqin Opera, also called Luantan Opera, is popular in Haifeng, Lufeng and Chaoshan in Guangdong Province, southern Fujian Province and Taiwan.

Xiqin Opera is straightforward, bold, vehement and heated in its performance. It is good for fighting plays and the fighting skills are based in southern wushu. The singing and monologues in Xiqin Opera follow the melody of Zhongzhou. Men and women sing in different styles to the same tune. Men use their real voices and women use falsetto. The orchestras are divided into those for plays of singing and acting and for plays of fighting. The musical instruments of the former one include the touxian, erxian, sanxian, yueqin, suona and haotou and the musical instruments for fighting plays include gongs, drums and other percussion instruments.

Gaojia Opera

Applicants: Quanzhou and Xiamen Cities, Fujian Province

Quanzhou's Gaojia Opera *Seeing Guan Fu Off* narrates a pair of lovers from Quanzhou and Taiwan reluctant to leave

Gaojia Opera came from the costume parade acting as Liangshan heroes and wushu skills. It was popular in rural areas at the end of the Ming Dynasty and early Qing Dynasty and is a local opera with the largest area and audiences in southern Fujian. It is well known in Jinjiang, Quanzhou, Xiamen, Longxi and other Minnan dialect areas and Taiwan.

The plays in Gaojia Opera are divided into three kinds, "daqi plays" (royal-court plays and fighting plays), "young girl's bedroom plays" and "chou and dan plays." Most of them are about fighting, chou and dan and legal case plays and a few are sheng and dan plays. There are more than 900 traditional plays. Most of them came from Beijing Opera, puppetry and hop-pocket play, and a few of them came from Liyuan plays and some of them were created by artists according to historical stories and folk legends.

Gaojia Opera has an outstanding regional character. It is sung in the Minnan dialect to the Quanzhou melody. Performers sing in southern styles and play southern music. It is a big opera worthy of appreciation and carries many good points of local culture. The performance of puppetry chou created in the opera is rarely seen in other operas. It is lively and humorous and dancing plays a major part. It is of a high aesthetic value.

Looking at the different aspects of Gaojia Opera, some came from Liyuan Opera and puppetry play and others came from Yiyang Melody, Hui Opera and Beijing Opera. In early times the operas had no fixed scripts and the performers made doggerel verse according to the plots. They were free in singing and acting and there was no fixed stage position for them. Also the length of the performance was not fixed. The music for Gaojia Opera came mostly from southern music and puppetry play but the rhythm and melody is interchangeable. Performers use real voices to sing and their singing is vigorous and high-spirited as well as sweet and exquisite.

Wanwan Melody

Applicant: Xiaoyi City, Shanxi Province

This is a local opera in Shaanxi Province. The wanwan and yueqin are the major musical instruments used and other accompanying instruments include the erxian, huqin, biangu (side drum), bangzi, majun and suona. The wanwan is beaten for the rhythm of the music, so it is called Wanwan Melody

The music of Wanwan melody is exquisite, quiet and easy to listen to. It can express the complex emotions of various figures in the various roles of sheng, dan, jing and chou.

Wanwan tune uses the traditional formula of Chinese operas in the aspect of performance and absorbed the actions of figures in shadow plays. In Wanwan melody different roles sing in the same key but men and women sing different tunes. The performers sing in different ways to express the various emotions and different qualities of the figures being portrayed. The performers of xusheng should be old and steady, those of chou should be humorous and those of xiaodan should be moving and sweet and they often sing in falsetto. So, on the stage Wanwan melody is the most suitable for plays with female leading roles and modern plays without a division of roles.

There are many plays in Wanwan melody and about 240 plays have been copied and published.

Sipingdiao

Applicants: Shangqiu City and Puyang City, Henan Province

Sipingdiao is a singing and talking art. It evolved from the northern Jiangsu flower-drum and os popular in the border areas of Henan, Shandong, Jiangsu and Anhui provinces.

Sipingdiao is good for singing and is full of folk flavours. The music is mellow and full, sweet and touching and liked by most people. In the past it absorbed some tunes of Ping, Yue and Lu operas and by means of many performances it gave birth to a particular style of simple rhythm and beautiful music and it is lyrical, touching and very steady (siping bawen), so it is called Sipingdiao.

Sipingdiao is based on flower-drum music and it absorbed artistic nutrition from other sister operas and formed its own strong local characters. The female sound is both simple and sweet and the male sound is vehement, high-spirited, vigorous and tender. The original features of singing and talking are preserved.

Most of the plays in Sipingdiao are "three small plays" (xiaosheng, xiàodan, and xiaochou) reflecting the marriage and family ethics among the people.

Pingju Opera

Applicants: Tianjin City, Hebei Province and Liaoning Province

The Pingju Opera *Flower is a Go-between.*

It is an opera popular in northern China and was created in east Hebei Province.

Pingju Opera is good for singing, the pronunciation is clear, the words are colloquial and the performance has strong live flavours and friendly folk flavours. It is lively and free in form and is best in reflecting the lives of modern people, so it has large audiences in urban and rural areas.

Being good at reflecting real life is a tradition of Pingju Opera. Its performance style absorbed the postures and formulas of Bangzi and Beijing Opera. In terms of singing, acting, reading and fighting, the skills of singing in Pingju Opera are the most outstanding.

Based on the folk music of Tangshan and Lianhualuo, the music of Pingju Opera absorbed the musical elements of errenzhuan in northeastern China, Beijing Opera, Hebei Bangzi and other local operas popular in east Hebei, Beijing and Tianjin. It is lyrical, fluent and naturally full of local flavours.

Wu'an Pingdiao Laozi

Applicant: Wu'an City, Hebei Province

Wu'an Pingdiao Laozi is the general name for Wu'an Pingdiao and Wu'an Laozi which are the two particular local operas from Wu'an City, Hebei Province and they are often performed together so they are generally called

Wu'an Pingdiao Laozi. Pingdiao mainly gives performances of big plays about dynasties and Laozi is good at performing small plays reflecting family plots.

The singing of Pingdiao has an exquisite, loud, sonorous and bright melody and a rough and unrestrained performance. The accompanying musical instruments include the suona. In fighting plays, besides the common percussion instruments there are big gongs, big cymbals, big cha (small cymbals) and battle drums which are called the "four great pieces." Pingdiao has complete roles and most plays have hongsheng, xiaosheng, dan and dalian as leading roles. The fighting style in Pingdiao is particular. It is rough and unrestrained and shows the agile and brave folk wushu spirit. The monologues in the performances are based on the Wu'an dialect and some use the Wu'an dialect completely. The style is honest and simple and has strong local flavours. There are more than 200 traditional plays in Pingdiao.

Laozi has a beautiful, vigorous, low-sound and sweet melody and clear, bright talking combined with singing. It is a humorous and interesting performance with singing while dancing and it is full of local flavours. Wu'an Laozi has complete roles divided into xiaodan, qingyi, xiaosheng, xiaochou and laosheng without strict divisions and some performers can act different roles. The performances are not good at wushu or drama and it combines yangge, gaoqiao and other folk dances and movements in everyday life. Performers sing while dancing and express emotions in narration. The performance is humorous, interesting, lively and free. There are more than 140 traditional plays in Wu'an Laozi.

Yue Opera

Applicants: Shengzhou City, Zhejiang Province and Shanghai City

This is a traditional drama form in China. It is mainly popular in Shanghai, Zhejiang, Jiangsu and Fujian. Yue Opera is good at expressing emotions and singing is the major part. The music is melodious, sweet and touching and the performance is vivid and moving. It is full of local colour from the south of the lower reaches of the Yangtze River. Performers of Yue Opera were all men in the early times and later they were all women.

In the aspect of performance, Yue Opera absorbed the performing styles in stage drama and films to depict factually and meticulously the characters and the psychology of figures on one hand and learned the beautiful dancing postures and performing methods in Kunqu and Beijing Opera on the other hand. This has helped to make the outward actions more exquisite with stronger rhythms. The combination of these two performance aspects formed the particular style of Yue opera i.e. the combination of realistic and free performance.

Stage fine arts are also a characteristic part of Yue Opera. From the early 1930s Yue Opera began to adopt the three-dimensional setting of traditional Chinese painting, colourful lights, acoustics and greasepaint make-up. Dresses are designed based on the plots in the plays. On the basis of inheriting traditions, they learned from the ancient maids paintings. The style of dress is natural and pure and the colour and quality are tender, light and elegant. They made good progress in the style of dresses for traditional operas.

There are many excellent and well-known plays in Yue Opera and they include Liang Shanbo and Zhu Yingtai, A Dream of Red Mansions, The Romance of the West Chamber, The Record of Pipa and The Peacock Flying to the Southeast, etc.

Shanghai Opera

Applicant: Shanghai City

Shanghai Opera is a representative opera in Shanghai and is popular in Shanghai, south Jiangsu and the Hang-Jia-Hu region in Zhejiang. It originated from the field songs and folk ditties on both banks of the Pujiang River and was influenced by Tanci and other folk singing and other spoken arts. Many operas are popular in Shanghai but only Shanghai Opera was created and grew up in Shanghai. It originated from folk songs and customs. The language is vivid, the music is tender, sweet and touching and it is full of the colours of the watery regions in the south of the lower reaches of the Yangtze River.

Shanghai Opera is good at narration and expressing emotions. In order to satisfy the demands of the plots and the figures' emotions, performers artfully make use of rapid or slow speed, changeable rhythms, beats and tunes and short interludes. They also formed a set of formulae.

In the performance of Shanghai Opera, there is no formula for action to set off unreal exaggeration or any gong and drum beat to accompany monologues. The percussion music is simple. In some cases folk music is played quietly and for some plots to set off the atmosphere. Some troupes absorbed the string and wood wind instruments (and copper wind instruments) from western music and have a mixed Chinese and western band. Some troupes are equipped with electronic vocal musical instruments and make use of compound tunes and orchestral music to accompany the performance. They learn from new operas and film music and the incidental music in operas is closely accompanied to the plots. At some recent stage there appeared the application of prelude, interlude and theme music.

Shanghai Opera came from the ordinary people. The words of Shanghai Opera collected many old-style Shanghai life everyday words and common sayings and slang and left abundant materials for folklore scholars to learn about the old customs and social life in Shanghai.

Suzhou Opera

Applicant: Suzhou City, Jiangsu Province

Pingtan, Kunqu and Suzhou Opera were once honoured as the "three flowers" in Suzhou culture. Suzhou Opera is a local opera based on the Suzhou dialect. It originated from Suzhou and has a history of more than 300 years. In early times it was in the form of singing while sitting around on chairs.

The performance of Suzhou Opera is simple, unvarnished and exquisite and pays attention to the inner emotions. The music is sweet and full of local flavours. It is vivid and lively and can be solemn and humorous, tragic and comedic to suit both refined and popular tastes and reflect reality. It is popular with many people because of this.

Due to the influence from Kunqiang, the music of Suzhou Opera is sweet and clear and has strong flavours of the south of the lower reaches of the Yangtze River. The erhu is the major accompanying instrument and there is also the Jiangnan Sizhu (a traditional stringed and woodwind instrument). Some folk ditties popular in Suzhou are often used as interludes.

The roles of Suzhou Opera are basically the same as Kun Opera but are not as strict as that. The role of chou is the leading role followed by the role of dan. In an actual performance only five or seven performers sit around a table and play their own roles. They play instruments while singing. There are five roles of laosheng, xiaosheng, dan, laodan and chou. Each character has singing phases and dialogues. They talk for a while and then sing a song or sing a song and then talk for a while until the whole story is concluded.

The still of the opera highlight *Records of the First of Flower Drunken Return* among the Suzhou Opere masterpieces.

Yangzhou Opera

Applicant: Yangzhou City, Jiangsu Province

Yangzhou Opera is popular in Yangzhou and Zhenjiang in Jiangsu Province plus some places in Anhui Province, Nanjing and Shanghai. It is based on the small-scale flower-drum opera, a folk dance, in Yangzhou and the burning-incense plays by a wizard in northern Jiangsu at the sacrificial ceremony for gods. It absorbed Yangzhou qingqu and local folk ditties and finally came into being as Yangzhou Opera.

The music of Yangzhou Opera is composed of three parts, i.e. the music of the flower-drum opera, the music of the burning-incense plays and Yangzhou qingqu and folk ditties. The music of the flower-drum opera is sound, honest and lively. The music of the burning-incense plays is loud, straightforward and full of local flavours and the music of Yangzhou qingqu and Yangzhou ditties is elegant, sweet and touching. The orchestra of Yangzhou Opera is characterized by brilliant accompaniment, fluent and rapid playing and both normal and flexible performances. It has distinctive colours and unique qualities which are rarely seen among common operas.

The roles of Yangzhou Opera are divided into sheng, dan, jing and chou, but the music for voices is only divided into male and female. The performance of each role comes from Kun Opera and Beijing Opera while it preserves the simple and lively features and strong living flavours of the flower-drum opera. The role of chou is the most outstanding. Yangzhou Opera has always paid attention to the performance of chou and dan. There are many traditional plays about one chou and one dan, hence the comedic style of Yangzhou Opera.

Lu Opera

Applicants: Hebei City and Lu'an City, Anhui Province

Lu Opera is popular in the drainage areas of the Yangtze River and Huaihe River with Hefei as the centre and the areas around Dabieshan Mountain. As Hefei was called Luzhou in ancient times it was named Lu Opera. It has a history of about 200 years and during the Qianlong (1736-1795) and Jiaqing (1796-1820) periods of the Qing Dynasty, there were professional troupes of Lu Opera.

The music of Lu Opera is divided into two kinds i.e. the main tune and florid ornamentation. The main tune music is good at narration and can express emotions and is suitable for reflecting complex dramatic emotions. The florid-ornamentation music is mostly folk ditties with a fixed form and sung repeatedly. It is used for singing small-scale life operas.

The music of Lu Opera has several distinctive features. First, there are many melodies sung in falsetto which are called small voices. Second, when a performer sings some phases on stage the performers on stage and backstage accompany them together. The music is loud and extensive and can set off the plots and exaggerate the stage atmosphere. The local flavour is very strong and the style is bright.

Traditional Lu Opera has no instrumental accompaniment and only gongs and drums are used to play the prelude, interlude and as accompaniment music. In the aspect of performance, Lu Opera has both singing and dancing and is very vivid and lively. After singing a while, performers will dance to the accompaniment of percussion. Their postures are beautiful with various patterns in a new guise. There is plenty of percussion music. Almost every play has a set of scores for gongs and drums and the dancing is performed along with the accompaniment of gongs and drums. Performers often sing while standing and show some small expressions at the same time. After singing for a while, they will perform a dance along with the accompaniment of percussion. The Dances were absorbed from the folk flower-drum opera and land-boat dancing with renewed patterns and beautiful postures.

There are about 200 plays in Lu Opera. Most of them drew materials from historical legends popular among people or folk legends reflecting people's lives. The language is colloquial, fresh and vivid.

Hubei Opera

Applicant: Hubei Province

Hubei Opera, an independent local opera, has a history of about 150 years. It is popular in about 40 counties under seven prefectures of Wuhan, Xiaogan, Huanggang, Jingzhou, Xianning, Yichang and Huangshi.

Hubei Opera has a wide range of themes covering various aspects. It can give performances of small scale life operas, modern operas, large scale royal-court operas and fighting operas with various styles of representation.

The performance of Hubei Opera attaches importance to nature with free formulas and methods and strong local flavours. The monologues of Hubei Opera on stage are completely colloquial in dialect and audiences can hear a familiar dialect. It sounds amiable and natural without big passages of tunes. In the performance of Hubei Opera, the role of dan attaches importance to family life and the music is simple, unvarnished and touching. The role of sheng attaches importance to the adoption of traditional performance formulas and has a wide range of performances. They can perform small-scale folk life operas as well as big-scale operas.

Hubei Opera attaches importance to singing with only a few monologues. In some plays, there are monologues for self introduction but they must be supplemented by librettos. Librettos have distinctive features of narration and the colours of reading. Some singing lines have twenty or thirty words but they can be sung in a breath carefully.

There are 13 professional troupes in Hubei Opera with about 1,500 staff. There are about 500 extant plays including 200 frequently performed.

Jingzhuo Flower-drum Opera

Applicant: Qianjing City, Hubei Province

Jingzhou Flower-drum Opera is one of the major local operas in Hubei Province. Based on the folk dances and singing and talking of the Jianghan Plain during the Daoguang Period (1821-1850) in the Qing Dynasty, it absorbed continuously the plays, tunes and performance styles of other operas and finally developed into a local opera.

Jingzhou Flower-drum Opera is full of strong local colours. The music is melodious and sweet. The performances show the colourful local lives and scenes in the hometown of lakes. It has a strong living folk flavour. Among the people men, women, old and young can sing the flower-drum opera songs when out walking or working. There is even a saying that "after hearing the flower-drum opera a sick person will become well!"

The music of Jingzhou Flower-drum Opera is divided into main-tune and minor-key. In main-tune music, a performer sings with the accompaniment of other performers and gongs and drums traditionally. The music is loud, sonorous and simple. The melody has a wide range and has many steep rises. Men and women use both real voices and falsetto and with the close cooperation of "singing, accompanying and fighting", this is a unique singing style. The minor-key music mostly came from folk songs and various folk singing-and-talking music pieces. The music is short with a lovely melody, agile rhythm and abundant colour. In particular the close combination of music tune and language pronunciation makes singing and reading an integrated and harmonious mass. It is an important factor for Jingzhou Flower-drum Opera to have the strong local style of the Jianghan Plain.

The Huangmei Opera performance

Huangmei Opera

Applicants: Anqing City, Anhui Province, and Huangmei County, Hubei Province

Huangmei Opera, a major local opera in Anhui Province, has a history of more than 200 years. Professional or amateur troupes can be found in Hubei, Jiangxi, Fujian, Zhejiang, Jiangsu, Taiwan and Hong Kong and the opera is widely popular.

Huangmei Opera originated from Huangmei County, Hubei Province and grew up in Anqing, Anhui Province. It is sung in the Anqing dialect. The music is honest, simple and fluent and is mostly bright and lyrical with abundant expressive force. The performance of Huangmei Opera is simple and is famous for realism and liveliness. Huangmei Opera, which came from the common people, suits both refined and popular tastes, entertains people and attracts audiences with its strong living flavour and fresh local colours.

13 Culture

The music of Huangmei Opera is sweet and fresh and is divided into two kinds, florid ornamentation and pingci. Florid ornamentation is often used for small-scale plays and has a strong living and folk-song flavour. Pingci is the principal tune in the original plays and is often used for large-scale narration and expression of emotions. It sounds sweet and melodious. The traditional plays include *Liang Shanbo and Zhu Yingtai* and The *Marriage of a Goddess with a Human*. The gaohu is the major accompanying instrument in Huangmei Opera along with other traditional musical instruments and gongs and drums. The opera is suitable for various plays.

Huangmei Opera developed from lyrical and humorous small-scale plays. Its predecessor is folk songs and ditties. In the course of development it absorbed the cultural traditions from various times, places and people and grew into the Huangmei Opera of today, but its major soul, the quality of folk songs and ditties remains preserved and unchanged. Therefore the language of Huangmei Opera and its indispensable musical quality supplement each other and formed the inner rhythmic beauty of the opera.

Shangluo Flower-drum

Applicant: Shangluo City, Shaanxi Province

Shangluo Flower-drum is popular in the Shangluo region in Shaanxi Province. In the third year of the Guangxu Period (1875-1908) of the Qing Dynasty, Yunyang in Hubei suffered flooding and a large group of victims went to Shangluo and brought there the flower-drum opera popular in Yunyang. Later the flower-drum opera was changed to be sung in the Shangluo dialect. It absorbed many folk ditties from Shangluo and finally formed Shangluo Flower-drum opera.

Shangluo Flower-drum is a folk art of singing and talking while jumping and dancing. The performance is full of jumping and dancing throughout. There are various ways of jumping for the flower-drum, and the postures are vigorous and beautiful, such as hopping, jumping while dodging, bouncing, jumping while swinging and jumping in tread. There is no fixed formula for the various ways of jumping and performers can work freely. The performance is natural, vivid, and interesting.

As to the musical structure of Shangluo Flower-drum, many flower-drum ditties are connected together, or used solely, or only a few tunes are used to represent the plays. They compose the specific flower-drum tunes. The original appearance of folk songs was preserved with few elements of theatrical dramas. There are many tunes and the melody, rhythm and tune are changeable. Some plays are sung with the same tune in various different forms.

Sizhou Opera

Applicants: Suzhou City and Bengbu City, Anhui Province

Sizhou Opera, one of the four great operas in Anhui Province, is popular on both banks of the Huaihe River in Anhui and has a history of more than 200 years.

Sizhou Opera evolved from folk singing-and-talking. Its music combines southern and northern styles and is both sweet and straightforward. In particular the female music is sweet, tender, beautiful and touching. Audiences think it "has the charm of attracting souls."

On the basis of singing-and-talking Sizhou Opera absorbed a lot of performing styles from the land boat dance," the "flower-lantern dance," and the "running donkey." It is not greatly influenced by formulas and the norm of operas and is bright, lively, simple, honest and forceful and it has the strong local flavours of northern Anhui. Performers must pay attention to the coordination of the various body parts such as the hands, eyes, waist, legs and feet.

The music of Sizhou Opera originated from local folk ditties, work songs and the musical pieces in farmers' normal living and working lives, such as driving the cattle to plough a field and the crying of women. It also absorbed the music and tunes of flower-drum, story-telling and other folk arts and made some innovations and development. The music of Sizhou Opera is very free, and the musical accompaniment must follow the singing of the performers which is convenient for performers to play and create. As the musical melody has a close relation with the local dialect, a big jump in tone is frequently seen. In addition to frequent inflexion, one hears fresh, colourful and harmonious singing.

It is worth mentioning that the major stringed instrument in Sizhou Opera developed from a two-stringed local pipa. After several changes of design various alt and median liuqin with three, four, five and six strings have been made. They are used not only in the accompaniment of the opera but also in domestic and foreign orchestras.

Liuqin Opera

Applicant: Tengzhou City, Shandong Province

As its major accompanying musical instrument is liuqin (the instrument is in the shape of a willow (Liu in Chinese) leaf), it is called Liuqin Opera.

Liuqin Opera came into being after the middle of the Qing Dynasty and spread to the border areas of Jiangsu, Shandong, Anhui and Henan provinces. There are two sayings about the origin of the opera. It is said it developed from folk ditties in southern Shandong and was influenced by local Liuzi Opera. It is also said it was spread from Haizhou, Jiangsu.

The music of Liuqin Opera is particular and florid ornamentation and unique lengthened tunes are the major differences which give it

The Liuqin Opera— *Visiting Her Mother's Home*

its distinctive local character. The men's music is rough, straightforward, bright and loud. The women's music is sweet, melodious, colourful and interesting. Singers can play and create at random and change freely. In addition, at the end of the music the women often use falsetto to rise up to ottava alta and the men often add supplementary words for lengthening the tune, which is also part of its unique style.

The performance of Liuqin Opera is rough, straightforward and simple with bright rhythms and strong local flavours. The posture and steps of the performers obviously show the features of folk singing and dancing.

The librettos of Liuqin Opera are colloquial and vivid. They are good at narration and especially the representation of the different figures' psychology. Most of the plays in Liuqin Opera drew materials from historical stories and folk legends to give simple and life-like performances.

Gezai Opera

Applicants: Zhangzhou City and Xiamen City, Fujian Province

Gezai Opera is an opera in the Minnan (southern Fujian) dialect. In the early part of the 20th century Gezai Opera became popular in Taiwan and it soon spread to Xiamen and to the Minnan areas and Southeast Asia where overseas Chinese people lived.

Gezai Opera is the only folk opera created in Taiwan. It is a folk art with distinctive Taiwanese cultural characteristics and is a local opera with the strongest local flavor, widest popular area and best representation among the local operas in Taiwan.

The performance style of Gezai Opera belongs to the pure form of opera. The story plots are narrated by songs and music. Performers use their real voices to sing. The librettos are in the mandarin of the Minnan dialect and are amiable, natural and colloquial. In the music of Gezai Opera there are three ways of singing, solo, antiphonal singing and chorus. In solo, a person sings a music piece till the end. It is the most popular way of singing in Gezai Opera.

Gezai Opera mainly sings about folk stories and attaches importance to loyalty, filial piety, moral integrity and righteousness. Usually there is no fixed script. Today in its performance a Mr. Drama talks about the play and assigns the roles.

In Gezai Opera there are more music pieces and fewer monologues and the rhythm is free. The music and monologues are in Taiwanese style tunes with the combination of Xiamen and Zhangzhou dialect. The librettos can be long or short according to the plots. Among the approximately 100 traditional tunes, there are melodious, loud and sonorous major tunes, folk talking "Taiwan zanian tunes," and various sorrowful crying tunes. In addition it absorbed the folk ditties and some opera music in Taiwan. Its performance, roles, costumes, facial make-up and percussion are all derived from Beijing Opera.

Tea-picking Opera

Applicants: Jiangxi Province and Guangxi Zhuang Autonomous Region

Teak-picking Opera is the general name for the folk singing, dancing, small-scale plays such as tea-picking and flower-lantern in the tea areas in southern, eastern and northern Jiangxi. At first it was the tea-picking songs sung by tea farmers when picking the tea leaves. Later with the combination of folk dances, tea-picking lantern came into being with singing and dancing. For the lantern festival or in the tea-picking season tea farmers often sang improvisations on tea-picking. As tea baskets were used as props it was also called "tea basket lantern." Later, its contents, music and performances became rich and it evolved gradually to the tea-picking opera popular in many rural areas.

The performance of a tea-picking opera was often done by one man and one woman or one man and two women. Later it developed into a group, singing and dancing, of several and even sometimes scores of people. Performers are dressed up in colourful clothes and wear colourful bands on their waists. Men hold whips in their hands to serve as a prop for the shoulder pole, hoe and pole for punting a boat. Women hold flower fans in their hands to serve as the prop for a bamboo basket, umbrella or utensils for holding tea and they sometimes hold paper lanterns and sing while dancing. They often mimic the labour of planting and making tea. Most of the dancing movements in teak-picking opera are simulation of the work in tea-picking and some are a simulation of local life, such as dressing and making up and expressing love between young men and women. In some areas performers sing ditties unrelated to tea-picking as interludes. The specific music and number of music pieces conform to the time and contents of the play. Usually there are two to four such ditties. Some performers add folk legends and local stories. The accompanying instruments in tea-picking opera include the erhu, bamboo flute, suona, big gong and big cymbals. The interludes are mainly played by the suona.

Five-tone Opera

Applicant: Zibo City, Shandong Province

Five-tone Opera, originated from Zhangqiu and Licheng in Shandong and is popular in Jinan, Zibo and neighboring areas in the centre of Shandong Province.

The Still of the Wuyin Opera *Wang Xiao* Show

Five-tone Opera, also called "five-person opera", got its name because a performance troupe was composed of five people. It developed from folk flower-drum and yangge. In the beginning there was no stringed musical instruments used. They only used gongs and drums. Usually four or five people composed a performing troupe. They sang and played gongs and drums. When singing, they did not play any musical accompaniment. A band was composed of four people at the most (clappers, big gong, small gong and small cymbal) and they could all sing. On stage they could sing and down stage they could play gongs and drums. It is the old tradition of Five-tone Opera.

There are many traditional plays in Five-tone Opera, about 160 according to statistics. The librettos in Five-tone Opera have a strong lively flavour and local colours. There are many common words and phrases and they have the features of unwritten folk literature. The performers pronounce a word before using the tune. The music is colloquial, the pronunciation is clear and the melody is changeable. Performers use their real voices to sing. The music for females has a long end sound and melody and is beautiful and unvarnished. It is suitable for expressing various emotions.

As it mostly reflects the images and living conditions of local rural women, it has a strong live flavour and local colour. The dialect is simple and natural. Folk proverbs and vivid metaphors are often used. Five-tone Opera is very popular with local people.

Maoqiang

Applicants: Gaomi City and Jiaozhou City, Shandong Province

Maoqiang is a local opera popular in Weifang, Qingdao and Rizhao and at first it was a local folk ditty. Around 1860, with the influence from Liuqin Opera, women's singing rose up to ottava alta at the end sound. People called it "damao," and later due to the partial tone, it was called Maoqiang.

In the early times there was only percussion as musical accompaniment such as drum, cymbal, and gong. Later due to the influence of Beijing Opera and Bangzi, the jinghu was adopted as the major instrument. Later other instruments were added such as the suona, bamboo flute, sheng, dihu and yangqin. In the aspect of roles, Maoqiang only had sheng, dan and chou at the beginning and later according to the roles in Beijing Opera, its division of roles became complete.

The tune of Maoqiang is simple, unvarnished and natural, the music is sweet, sorrowful and colloquial and is popular with residents in the Shandong Peninsula. The women's tune in Maoqiang is especially developed. It makes people feel sorrowful.

Local ditties are basically the backbone of the music and tunes in Maoqiang. It also absorbed a lot of tunes from Jiaozhou big yangge, Jiaozhou octagon drum, Xihe storytelling, Zhucheng yangge, etc., so it has a lot of local features and a large foundation. The costumes have strong colours and red and green are favourite colours. The librettos make use of many dialects and slang and are colloquial and humorous. Audiences feel very familiar with it.

Quju Opera

Applicant: Henan Province

Quju Opera developed from Henan quyi. At first the performers sang while walking on stilts. Later the stilts were omitted and performers walked onto the dramatic stage. This is a symbolic event in the course of the evolvement from folk singing and dancing to formal "high-stage opera" and is a qualitative change in the development of Quju Opera.

The music of Quju Opera is divided into main-tune and minor-tune. The main-tune music is sweet and melodious with a lot of melody and few words. The accompanying instruments include the sanxian and zheng. The minor-tune music is lively, beautiful, lyrical and fluent with many words and short melodies. It is suitable for expressing emotions and for stage performances. The quhu is the major accompanying instrument and there are other stringed and woodwind instruments. The tunes came from folk life small-scale plays so the librettos are easy to learn. Most of the tunes are sung in real voices and the performances are close to real life, so it spread very fast.

The Quju Opera players performing in Yulin Township, Xuchang County, Henan Province

There are more than 150 tunes in Henan Quju Opera. The music is unvarnished and natural and the melody is sweet and fluent with a strong live flavour. It is good at narration and expressing emotions. The actions and postures in Quju Opera basically preserve the original forms of stilt dancing: performers march forwards and backwards ceaselessly and the chou performers make continuous gags.

There are about 200 traditional plays in Henan Quju Opera. Most of them drew materials from folk stories which reflect family lives or love between men and women. The librettos and monologues are colloquial and full of local interest.

Quzi Opera

Applicant: Gansu Province

Quzi Opera is characterized by a concentrated theme and a small scale. The shortest play only lasts for just over ten minutes on stage.

Quzi Opera is a small-scale folk opera popular in the five provinces and autonomous regions in northwest China. It originated from folk songs during the Ming and Qing dynasties and at the end of the Qing Dynasty and the early part of the Republic of China it formed many local small-scale operas with various styles, such as Dunhuang Quzi Opera, Huating Quzi Opera, etc. The performance of Quzi Opera is divided into two kinds: stage performance and singing while sitting on the ground. The stage performance is commonly known as "colourful singing." It has singing and acting plays and fighting plays, as well as costumes and props. The monologues are read in the local dialect. In a performance the dan figures must dance lightly, lively and vividly and the chou figures must be humorous and bright. Singing while sitting on the ground is commonly called singing without musical accompaniment. It is not restricted by where it can be performed and costumes and props are unnecessary. If a performer has a good voice, accurate tone and many tunes, he or she can sit and sing anywhere. The plays of Quzi Opera cover a very wide range and mostly recount fairy tales, historical legends and society.

As a local opera flourishing for a while in Dunhuang, Dunhuang Quzi Opera had been popular for thousands of years among the people. Even today on festivals there are small-scale performances in this folk art. In Dunhuang Quzi Opera with its unique style, there are songs and tunes from Dunhuang ancient times, which keep the remains of Dunhuang culture passing down continuously in the folk tradition.

Huating Quzi Opera originated earlier. During the Song and Yuan dynasties, it was in the form of cantata. Later with development and time, some folk artists compiled simple singing scripts according to their own styles and formulas in zaju of the Yuan Dynasty and set basic plots, figures and simple and small props. When performers sing without musical accompaniment and do story-telling the audiences are still accustomed to sitting in a circle.

Yangge Opera

Yangge Opera

Applicant: Hebei and Shanxi Provinces

Yangge Opera is a widely popular folk opera in northern China. It originated from the songs farmers sang when working in the fields. It spread to Shanxi, Hebei, Shaanxi, Inner Mongolia and Shandong. Later with the combination of folk dances, acrobatics and wushu, people would hold performances of singing programs with story plots in the first lunar month every year and this form of opera gradually came into being. Yangge Operas in various places were often named after their original or popular places.

At a performance of Yangge Opera, performers hold a fan and make use of the basic method of representation, accompaniment and make-up of Yangge. Singing is a major part while performing is a supplementary part. It reflects many facets of life. Usually there are two performers. The music is divided into folk ditties and songs.

Dingzhou Yangge has its particular features in language, tune, melody and plays. The librettos are colloquial and there are many dialects and slang with a strong local flavour. Both men and women performers use their real voices when singing.

Shuozhou Yangge is a mixed folk art of wushu, dance and opera. Dancing is a major part. It is mainly performed on festivals, birthdays, visiting in-laws and redeeming a vow to gods by invitation.

Fanshi Yangge evolved from folk dances and the stages of evolvement are still preserved. In particular, its music is a combination of various opera tunes. It has an important value for studying the development history of Chinese operas.

Daoqing Opera

Applicants: Shanxi, Shandong, Henan and Gansu Provinces

Daoqiang Opera is a small-scale folk opera popular in the drainage area of the Yellow River. It originated from the "rhyme of sutras" sung by Taoists in the Tang Dynasty (618-907). Later it absorbed the tunes of ci and qu and evolved to the singing of preaching among folk people.

Daoqing Opera evolved from Daoqing singing and talking. For example, Jinbei Singing-and-Talking Daoqing is a quyi with the combination of local dialects. In singing, the lead singer holds a fishing-drum in their arms and bamboo clappers in their hand to beat the rhythm while singing. Another five or six people accompany the lead by singing and music with the bamboo flute, sihu and banhu. It is connected by various qu and has various lyrical and narrative performances. The accompanying instruments in Daoqing Opera include the fishing-drum and bamboo clappers like before as well as stringed and woodwind instruments and percussion to enrich the expressive force. In singing, there is always a vocal accompaniment at the end.

There are four kinds of Daoqing plays. First, there are plays about going up to heaven to become immortal and these have a strong religious content; second, there are plays about cultivation according to religious doctrines and persuading people to do good deeds; third, small-scale plays about everyday life; and fourth, historical stories and plays about legends and legal cases.

Shanxi Daoqing Opera once had professional troupes that were divided into four types: Jinbei, Linxian, Hongdong and Yongji Daoqing. Shaanxi Daoqing originated from shadow plays and there is shadow-play Daoqing in the Guanzhong region. Daoqing Zuoban Opera is performed on a square. Base on Zuoban cantata, it absorbed Jin Opera and shadow play. Gansu Ludong Daoqing shadow play has developed into Long Opera. Henan Daoqing Opera evolved from the combination of the fishing-drum Daoqing and Henan Zhuizi.

Hahaqiang

Applicants: Qingyuan County and Qing County, Hebei Province

Hahaqiang has a history of 300 years. It is a local opera which originated from the folk music in Hebei Province. It is characterized by a simple performance and is based on singing with distinctive features of narration and singing-and-talking.

In the course of spreading, Hahaqiang gradually formed three styles of east, middle and west with different artistic styles and musical features due to the different local dialects and folk art traditions. The eastern style is popular in Wudi, Leling and Ningjin in Shandong and the middle style is popular in Cangzhou and Hengshui in Hebei Province and the western style is popular in Baoding and Langfang. Their monologues are influenced by their respective dialects. The banhu is the major musical instrument, but the bamboo flute in the western style is outstanding with the features of folk wind and percussion instruments.

In the aspect of roles, the locally-born-and-bred Hahaqiang has xiaosheng and xiaodan as the major roles. The tunes of all the roles in Hahaqiang are almost the same. The music is divided into men's and women's tunes. Men and women sing in the same tone with slightly different melodies. The performance of an opera is meticulous, vivid, light-hearted and humorous. Performers are extremely good at representing different actions in an artistic way, such as drawing water, spinning, doing up one's hair, sewing and mending and making shoes. In plays, each role has some comical actions and humorous monologues. So, Hahaqiang is a comic opera.

Er'rentai

Applicants: Hohhot City in Inner Mongolia Autonomous Region, Hequ County in Shanxi Province, and Kangbao County in Hebei Province

This is an opera popular in Inner Mongolia and the northern parts of Shanxi, Shaanxi and Hebei provinces. Most of the plays are performed by one performer of chou and one performer of dan, so it is called "er'rentai" (two-person stage).

The overlord whip, folded fan and handkerchief are the major props for Er'rentai. The most characteristic dance in Er'rentai is "zouchangzi". The two performers move in quick short steps around the stage center with musical accompaniment. The male performer does some wushu actions such as two-kicking feet and three-kicking feet and the female performer echoes such actions by dodging, dropping down like a fish and falling on the ground.

There are two types of performances for full-scale plays. One is singing while dancing and is characterized by lyrical dancing. In dancing, both of the performers hold folded fans. The performer of chou uses the overlord whip and wields the whip in three series of skills of up, middle and down. The dancing posture looks like a dragon circling a pillar and the whip dances up and down quickly. The performer of dan uses a handkerchief. All the dances become quicker and quicker from a slow start and after the climax they stop suddenly. Another is the plot plays with singing as the major part. In some performances there is jumping in and jumping out. This kind of performance is comparatively close to real life and has some invented and exaggerated actions.

The librettos of Errentai attach importance to simple, straightforward narration. The monologues make use of folk slang, cross talk, two-part allegorical sayings and doggerel verse and are full of humorous features and strong local flavours. The music of Errentai is based on yangge ditties from the local folk songs and some musical pieces from Daoqing Opera and has also absorbed the folk ditties from Inner Mongolia and some northern Shaanxi folk songs. It shows a distinctive local colour.

Baizi Opera

Applicant: Haifeng County, Guangdong Province

Baizi Opera is a local opera sung in the Haifeng and Lufeng dialect in Guangdong. After the introduction of Zhengzi Opera into southern Fujian and eastern Guangdong, it combined the folk arts in local areas such as Chaodiao and Quandiao and was sung in local dialects. Local people called Zhongzhou mandarin as "zhengzi" and the local dialect as "baizi", hence the name of Baizi Opera.

Baizi Opera has its own particular way of lengthening a tune with "ai-yi-ai." When a performer is singing others can follow him or her at random. All the lengthened tunes and vocal accompaniment must be ended with "ai-yi-ai."

The monologues of Baizi Opera are read in the Haifeng and Lufeng dialect and are especially liked by local farmers. The music is beautiful and is characterized by connected singing, singing in turns, folk songs and one person singing with others accompanying. The plays are good at love stories. The performance formula is strict but not stiff. Performers dance and sing. It is full of everyday life flavour. Short fighting makes use of southern wushu skills. The stage setting is simple and easy to move.

There are more than 200 traditional plays for singing and acting in Baizi Opera. Some of them originated from legends of the Ming and Qing dynasties and most of them are family and social plays.

Huachao Opera

Applicant: Zijin County, Guangdong Province

Huachao Opera originated from the sacrificial ceremony of "shenchao" in rural areas in Zijin County. It is sung in the Hakka language and is popular in the Hakka areas in east Guangdong Province. Since the Ming and Qing dynasties, the singing and dancing in "shenchao" in Zijin County had been popular with the local people. Later shenchao artists often added some ditties to sing interesting stories after the sacrificial ceremony in order to entertain audiences. Such a performance was humorous and popular with the people compared to the god-fearing and solemn shenchao and was called "huachao."

In the singing of Huachao one person leads and others accompany him or her. The combination of singing and speaking is flexible and free. Performers use their real voices to sing. The monologues are colloquial and have interludes.

Hundreds of traditional plays have been accumulated in its development. The representative plays include *Qiuli Picking Flowers, Selling Groceries, Three Officials Entering a Room, and Transition.* Its monologues are colloquial and often make use of slang, two-part allegorical sayings and puns. The music is mainly divided into shenchao tunes and folk ditties. Sometimes the music of Hakka folk songs is also used. There are only three roles of xiaosheng, xiaodan and xiaochou. Performers sing while dancing and the performance is simple and fresh.

The common figures in Huachao Opera include the countryman, the countrywoman and the rich man. In the old troupes of Huachao Opera there was a saying that "the highest rank of official is only Grade 7". It is a brief introduction to the stage figures. The grass-roots feature of Huachao Opera is represented completely by its performing style and contents.

Caidiao

Applicant: Guangxi Zhuang Autonomous Region

It is one of the local operas in Guangxi Zhuang Autonomous Region. It originated from the singing and dancing and singing and talking in rural areas in Guilin and has a history of nearly 200 years. Caidiao has a distinctive national style and local colour and is mainly based on the local dialect. It is humorous and lively and called the "merry opera". It is very popular with the local people.

The male characters in Caidiao make use of low-posture steps and play with flowery fans in their hands. The female characters make use of moving steps and quick short steps, play with a handkerchief in their hands and sing while dancing and are light-hearted and lively.

The still of the Caidiao Opera *Liu Sanjie* in Guangxi Zhuang Autonomous Region

The fan is the principal article of the "three treasurable pieces" (fan, handkerchief and colourful band). In a performance a fan can be used as an article and a weapon and is called the "all-purpose" prop. As it is deeply rooted among the common people in rural areas and closely combined with local folk ditties, Caidiao formed its humorous content and lively performing style.

Lantern Opera

Applicant: Chongqing and Sichuan Province

This is an opera popular in the northeast and north of Sichuan. Originally it was a "dancing lantern" tradition held at harvest time and the spring festival by farmers. They encircled a lantern and sang while dancing. Later it gradually developed into "Lantern Opera" with story plots.

Lantern Opera is not only a characteristic small-scale folk opera in Chongqing and Sichuan but also one of the important melodies in Sichuan Opera. As it is often performed along with traditional activities such as the Spring Festival, Lantern Festival, shehuo (a fork art performance given on traditional or religious festivals) and qingtan, there are many small-scale, comic and noisy plays.

Chongqing Liangshan Lantern Opera mostly drew materials from interesting rural stories, small family things and stories about common people such as village girls and fishermen. The performance is free, humorous, lively and interesting and has the added folk colour of slang, strong everyday life flavour and the forceful rough flavours of the countryside. Most of the traditional plays are passed down in the oral tradition from older generations. Performers use the local dialects to sing and the librettos are colloquial, natural, vivid and full of living flavours. In addition, Lantern Opera has a distinctive feature of amusement. It has exaggerated plots, outstanding conflicts and is noisy and humorous. Performers make exaggerated actions and different dancing actions and it is very popular with the local people.

Chuanbei (northern Sichuan) Lantern Opera is a small-scale folk singing and dancing opera popular in northern Sichuan and it has a long history. It originated at the end of the Ming Dynasty and is called one of the "three strange flowers" along with Chuanbei Big Puppetry and Chuanbei Shadow Play. It has a distinctive feature in its dancing and there is a saying that "no dancing, no lantern." It absorbed the dancing postures from folk lion-dancing, dragon-dancing, ox lantern, shadow play and puppetry. In particular, the characters of xiaochou and caidan give vivid depictions of figures through funny dancing movements which make audiences laugh.

Flower-lantern Opera

Applicants: Guizhou Province and Yunnan Province

Flower-lantern Opera is an opera which is very popular among the Han people. Its distinctive features are that all the performers' hold fans or handkerchiefs, they sing while dancing and their singing and acting are closely connected. Flower-lantern Opera originated from traditional flower-lantern dancing. It is a local opera which originated at the end of the Qing Dynasty and the early years of the Republic of China. In the course of spreading it formed various singing and performing styles due to the impact from local dialects, folk songs and customs.

Guizhou Flower-lantern Opera at first only had dancing. Later it added small-scale plays to the dancing and with the influences from the exotic operas it developed to the performance of full-scale plays. The performance is characterized by "twisting." Performers use folded fans and handkerchiefs to express their emotions. Guizhou Flower-lantern Opera has its features due to the combination of the local Nuo Opera and some elements of the waving-hand dance. Its sweet and beautiful music, strong local flavours and unique styles shared by lantern opera reflect the humanistic bearing in the drainage area of the Wujiang River.

Yunnan Flower-lantern Opera has the basic action of "bending" and there is a saying that "no bending, no lantern." When watching Yunnan Flower-lantern Opera, audiences see whether performers "bend greatly" – whether the bending of the waist and hips is great, agile and natural. Natural posture is the most important. The feet cannot be stiffened or bent but must be raised up and swung naturally. The hands must be waved naturally along with the feet and should look like dancing willow branches, so the hand posture in "bending step" is called the "willow branch waved by the wind."

Yigougou

Applicant: Linyi County, Shandong Province

Yigougou is one of the rare local operas in China and evolved from yangge tunes. At the end of the Ming Dynasty and the early part of the Qing Dynasty it became popular in Shandong and Hebei and represented the singing-and-talking styles in north-western Shandong and neighboring areas. The music is simple, unvarnished, natural and lively. It uses a tune used by the local labouring people to show unintentionally their thoughts. In north-western Shandong, people described it as a hook that could draw their hearts and souls, hence the name of "Yigougou."

Yigougou opera has a simple and unvarnished performance form and performers are mostly wandering folk artists and usually organize performances in the slack season in spring and winter. Performers work during the day helping with the farm work and weeding and give performances in the evening. They are called the "weeding troupe" by local people. They often organize performances in rural markets and on festivals.

The music of Yigougou is outstanding for both voice and sentiment and is colloquial. At the end of each upper and lower sentence, there is a trill in falsetto with a big jump of seven or eight degrees. The men's voice is straightforward, unrestrained and forceful and the women's voice is sweet, beautiful and moving. Performers use their real voices to pronounce words, use falsetto to lengthen the tune and to sing words without any tune. They talk and read, use a tune without the pronunciation of words and have musical accompaniment. They send words to the audiences' ears and then use a tune for the music. The musical accompaniment and interludes are garish and pleasant and create a harmonious effect. There are about 70 traditional plays for Yigougou opera.

The languages used in Yigougou on stage are the local dialects in Hezhou and Laosheng. Compared to Putonghua it is different in the four tones and the pronunciation of some words is also distinctively different.

Yigougou has particular musical styles and the contents of its plays show strong local colour. It is a typical opera in the system of flower-drum operas.

Tibetan Opera

Applicants: Tibet Autonomous Region and Qinghai Province

Tibetan Opera is an important cultural part of Tibetan social life and is popular in areas with a concentrated Tibetan population, Tibet, Sichuan, Qinghai and Yunnan. This art form has a strong Tibetan Buddhist influence in the aspects of representing styles and content.

Tibetan Opera is a very large opera system. Due to the various natural conditions, customs, cultural traditions and dialects on the Qinghai-Tibet Plateau, it possesses numerous artistic varieties and schools. Tibetan Opera in Tibet is the mother body of Tibetan Opera and it was spread to the Tibetan areas in Qinghai, Gansu, Sichuan and Yunnan by the monks and pilgrims who went to study in the Tibetan temples. In the areas in India and Bhutan where there are Tibetan people there is also Tibetan Opera.

Tibetan Opera originated from the Tibetan religion in the 8th century. In the 17th century it was separated from the religious ceremony in temples and gradually came into being as a live performance style combining such basic formulas as singing, reading, dancing, monologue and acrobatics with singing as the major part. Tibetan Opera has a loud, sonorous and vigorous tune. The tune is fixed by specific people and each sentence has a vocal accompaniment. Tibetan Opera was originally a square opera and the accompanying instruments only included a drum and a cymbal.

Tibetan Opera mainly performs stories about various figures, biographies about gods and Buddha or Buddhist stories. In a performance the make-up is comparatively simple. Besides masks ordinary powder and rouge are used and there is no complex facial make-up.

The Shaton Festival every year is the day when Tibetan opera troupes give performances, so the Shaton Festival is also called the Tibetan Opera Festival. The scripts of Tibetan Opera are also a peak in Tibetan literature. It attaches importance to temperament and artistic conception. A large number of proverbs, ballads and idioms are used and the elite writings of ancient Tibetan literature and language are preserved.

Shannan Menba Opera

Applicant: Tibetan Autonomous Region

The ancient Menyu people mixed with the Tibetan people and other tribes in Menyu for a long time and then came into being as the Menba ethnic group. The Tibetan language is its written language and more than one third of Menba words were borrowed from the Tibetan language.

Menba Opera is an opera of the Menba ethnic group and is popular in the area of the Menba ethnic group on the south-eastern slopes of the Himalayas i.e. the Lebu District in Cuona County and the Shannan Prefecture in Tibet. The scripts of Menba Opera are just Tibetan scripts from Tibetan Opera, so Menba Opera can also be called Menba Tibetan Opera. In the Lebu District during the New Year Festival of the Tibetan lunar calendar, it is recommended that the Menba play, *Lord Noosing,* should be played for seven continuous days and that one section should be performed every day.

The performance of Menba Opera came from the folk dancing, singing and religious artistic performance of the Menba people. Its music originated from the Menba folk song Sama (a drinking song). In addition, it absorbed the singing-and-talking music, ancient songs, sad melodies, and religious music of the Menba ethnic group. The costumes of Menba Opera are based on the everyday clothes of the Menba people and are also influenced by Tibetan dress and adornments.

It is recommended that in Menba Opera there are only six performers and one accompanist playing drum and cymbal. They are all male characters. The six performers act six different roles in a play and any other roles in the play should also be acted by them in turns and it is deemed not necessary for them to change make-up or dress.

Zhuang Opera

Applicant: Guangxi Zhuang Autonomous Region

Zhuang Opera is the general name for all operas in Guangxi Zhuang Autonomous Region and has strong national and local features. According to the different dialects, tunes and performing styles, Zhuang Opera can be divided into northern Zhuang Opera, southern Zhuang Opera and Zhuangshi Opera.

In the aspect of musical accompaniment in Zhuang Opera a horse-bone hu is the major instrument. The tube of the instrument is made from a horse's leg bone and the strings are metal. The tone is clear and bright. The accompanying instruments include the tuhu, gourd hu, erhu, sanxian, vertical bamboo flute and bamboo flute and sometimes the muye assists in the orchestra. The accompanying voice music in Zhuang Opera is in multiple voice parts. Various instruments are tuned up differently and form various harmonic relations in the melody and the playing is very interesting to listen to.

The librettos and monologues in Zhuang Opera are in the dialect of the Zhuang ethnic group and are full of national features. The music comes from the familiar folk songs of the Zhuang people. The librettos of the main tunes preserve the particular metrical structure in the traditional folk songs of the Zhuang ethnic group. Both the southern and northern Zhuang Operas are characterized by setoff words and sentences for almost every song. They play the role of pointing out emotions and are the connecting link between the preceding and the following song. This sets off the atmosphere and intensifies the sense of language.

Dong Opera

Applicant: Liping County, Guizhou Province

The Dong Opera player

Dong Opera is an integrated art form of literature, music and dance of the Dong ethnic group. It has distinctive national styles and is a traditional opera that the Dong people love to see and hear. The actions are simple and unvarnished, the form is simple and the plays are particular.

Dong Opera is a particular traditional art based on the singing-and-talking art of the Dong ethnic group. It absorbed the grand songs of the Dong ethnic group and some singing styles of the Han operas. In the southern villages of the Dong ethnic group there are amateur troupes that go out and give performances in the first and second lunar months every year. In the performance of traditional Dong Opera, performers step onto the stage to the sounds of gongs and cymbals and two performers give antiphonal singing. Positive characters are dressed up in splendid costumes and have light make-up. The chou characters have painted faces and are well liked in plays.

The stage of the Dong Opera is usually about 3 meters long and wide. There is no setting and only a piece of background scene and two pieces of colorful door curtains are hung there. The props on stage include several tables and desks only. The facial make-up has black and white as the basic colours.

The words of the scripts in Dong Opera are vivid with strict rules of rhyming. One play is a long narrative poem. Compared to other operas, Dong Opera is particular in this aspect. In the aspect of the structure of the scripts and methods of representation Dong Opera has distinctive features. A Dong Opera play is always divided into several scenes without any division of acts. During the play the changes of space and time is frequent and is reflected by the performers' stepping on and down from the stage. The scenes are divided meticulously.

The plays of Dong Opera have many figures and are long pieces. A full-scale play needs several days to perform. The antiphonal singing between two performers is the major part in the scripts of Dong Opera and there are few monologues. This is because most of the scripts of Dong Opera are adapted from pipa songs of the Dong ethnic group and pipa songs have long stories, many figures and disconnected plots. Dong Opera has the distinctive mark of the art of singing-and-talking.

Bouyei Opera

Applicant: Ceheng County, Guizhou Province

Bouyei Opera is mainly found in southern and south-western Guizhou where the Bouyei people live. It originated from sacrificial ceremonies and sorcerers' dances in early times. Based in the sorcerers' dances it gradually evolved into the stage art of Bouyei Opera. Folk artists passed their skills down through amateur troupes in villages. On national festivals they put up stages and give performances. Plays are divided into formal and miscellaneous plays; the former are mostly about historical stories popular in Han areas and the latter mostly drew its materials from national folk stories. The monologues in the formal plays are mostly in the Han language and the librettos are in the Bouyei language and the monologues and librettos of miscellaneous plays are in the Bouyei language.

All the performers on stage in Bouyei Opera turn round after three or five steps. In the course of singing they shuttle from opposite directions in lively form and unvarnished style. All the characters in Bouyei Opera wear particular and simple masks carved from wood, bamboo shoot shells or bamboo comb shells. During a performance the characters wear masks and their heads are covered with black gauze. They can look out through the holes in the masks for eyes and perform their skills freely.

The musical instruments include the cattle-bone hu, gourd hu, erhu, bamboo flute, yueqin, baobaoluo, xiaomaluo, chai, cymbal and drum, etc. Some Bouyei troupes also have such instruments as the leyou (a particular bamboo wind instrument of the Bouyei ethnic group) and muye. They are used to set off the stage atmosphere and express the figures' emotions and can be used as interlude music.

The performance of Bouyei Opera has no restrictions on stage size and the stage settings are mostly the Eight-Immortals curtain for getting rid of evils, praying for luck, eliminating calamity, and receiving happiness. The costumes and make-up are simple.

Yi Cuotaiji

Applicant: Weining County, Guizhou Province

Cuotaiji is an old opera existing only in the Weining Yi, Hui and Miao Nationalities Autonomous County in Guizhou Province. Cuotaiji is the transliteration of a Yi word, meaning "the game for people to change to gods and ghosts." Cuotaiji is held from the third to the fifteenth day in the first lunar month every year for getting rid of evil, receiving luck and praying for a good harvest. Performers act as ancestor gods and represent the historical evolvement of migration, farming and breeding offspring of ancestors of the Yi ethnic group by means of dialogues and dancing.

The masks of Cuotaiji are made from alp hardwood such as India azalea and sumac. The craftwork is very simple. The sculpture is mainly characterized by an excessively raised forehead, a fat, straight and long nose, the turned up exterior angle of the eyes and no lips or teeth or ears. It makes people feel elegant, primitive, strange and wild.

It is usually performed by 10 to 17 people. Performers wrap their heads with a white head kerchief in the shape of a taper. The body and limbs are wrapped in cloth to symbolize nudity.

Performances are given at night preferably in a foggy field which gives a mysterious, deep and slightly horrific atmosphere. The torches and lanterns used for lighting are bright and shining and the performers with masks are martial and powerful looking and simulate the labouring, living ancestors. The performance of Cuotaiji is mainly divided into four parts, i.e. offering sacrifice, farming, a happy event and cleaning the village. Farming is the core of the play and reflects the history of migration, farming and breeding offspring of the Yi ethnic group.

In the past hundreds and thousands of years, Cuotaiji grew silently in the deep forests in west Guizhou and has had no impact from the Han culture. It has preserved the strong true qualities of primitive art. It is rare to see such an old opera in China.

Dai Opera

Applicant: Dehong Dai and Jingpo Ethnic Autonomous Prefecture, Yunnan Province

Dai Opera is one of the particular operas of the ethnic minorities in Yunnan and is popular in Dehong Dai and Jingpo Nationalities Autonomous Prefecture in Yunnan Province and some Dai inhabited areas in Baoshan City.

Dai Opera originated from Dai singing and dancing with some figures and plots and Buddhist sutra preaching and singing. Later it absorbed some artistic nutrition from Dian Opera and shadow play and gradually became a complete opera form.

The performance of Dai Opera is mainly singing without monologues. It is accompanied by different facial expressions such as happiness, anger, sadness and joy. Only in some specific plots are there centralized dancing performances. When singing they use the Dai language and librettos have strict rules of rhyming. In the aspect of dressing up, they wear their national costumes with a little make-up.

The music of Dai Opera is an important part of it and is also one of the main reasons that Dai Opera is regarded as a bright pearl in Southeast Asia. It has strong national features, is full of gentle beauty and is not influenced by other opera music. The Dai people believe in Buddhism and the monks read sutras for disciples by singing Buddhist songs which feature reading. It is favoured universally by disciples due to its beautiful poetry, moving rhythm and pleasant singing. These music pieces are mixed with folk songs and form the original basic tunes.

Traditional Dai Opera only uses percussion with the tang drum being the leading instrument. It also uses the big gong, big cymbal, bowl gong, etc. Some also use the percussion style of Dian Opera and the folk musical instruments of the Dai ethnic group such as the elephant-foot drum and gong.

The plays of Dai Opera cover a wide range of themes. Some are small-scaled singing and dancing plays directly reflecting the people's lives and the customs of the Dai ethnic group and some are plays adapted from folk legends and narrative poems of the Dai ethnic group.

Mulian Opera

Applicant: Anhui, Henan and Hunan Provinces

Mulian Opera got its name from its performance of The *Monk Mulian Saved his Mother*. It is one of the oldest operas in China.

During the Wanli Period (1573-1620) of the Ming Dynasty, Zheng Zhizhen (1518-1595), a dramatist in Huizhou, wrote the *Script of Mulian Saved his Mother and Persuaded her to Do Good Deeds* according to the popular adaptation and singing-and-talking story The *Monk Mulian (named Fu Luoka) Saved his Mother from the Nether World.* It is divided into three volumes and 108 scenes. It tells the story about Liu Qing the wife of Fu Xiang. She profaned the gods and was thrown into hell. Her son Fu Luoka was impatient to save his mother. After searching all over hell he finally found his mother. The play absorbed many folk legends and stories and is full of strong local flavours. In the play the teachings of Confucius, Sakyamuni, and Tao are combined together. It is very popular everywhere and

A scene of traditional theatrical piece of Mulian opera "Five Ghosts Seizing Madam Liu", in which the five ghosts have catched Madam Liu.

holds an important position in the development history of Chinese operas.

Mulian Opera combines operas, dance, acrobatics and wushu. It has acrobatics such as sawing off, rubbing, swallowing fire, spitting out smoke and opening belly, dancing actions such as pancha and guncha and boxing skills such as jingang boxing, Wusong picking flowers boxing, five-dragon setting out boxing, etc. Its costumes, props, make-up and performance are particular. As it is deep rooted among the ethnic peoples it still preserves a straightforward and primitive appearance.

Mulian Opera can be found across the whole country. And Beijing Opera, Kun Opera, Shao Opera, Han Oper, Anhui Opera, Xiang Opera, Sichuan Opera, Jiangxi Opera, Fujian Opera, Puxian Opera, Cantonese Opera and Qing Opera of Shanxi and Shaanxi have or had Mulian Opera influences.

Gong-and-drum Mixed Opera

Applicant: Linyi County, Shanxi Province

Gong-and-drum Mixed Opera, one of the oldest operas in Shanxi Province, got its name as it is accompanied by gongs and drums without any stringed instruments. In the first lunar month every year a performance of Gong-and-drum Mixed Opera is given in the Longyan Temple in Linyi County to offer sacrifice to the gods and Buddha.

The band is composed of drums, gongs and the suona. The big drum is the leading instrument and serves as the conductor of the band. Various gong and drum beats are used according to the monologues, singing, marching while observing views and setting up tents for marshals in battles between armies. There are only two simple musical pieces for suona and small drums and cymbals are used at the end of fighting and while arranging a banquet and setting up a tent. There are a few monologues in Gong-and-drum Mixed Opera and gongs sound at the end of each sentence.

Mixed Opera is mostly in the form of recitation. Singing is not accompanied by stringed instruments. There are more monologues and less singing. It is characterized by "not possessing stringed instruments and making pauses in reading and singing by using gong and drum beats." There are nearly 100 traditional plays and they are all fairy tales and historical stories. The actions are comparatively exaggerated and the musical melody has not much variation.

A play of Gong-and-drum Mixed Opera is performed over several scenes and the story is comparatively complex. More than 40 performers are on stage and each play lasts for about four hours. Both the character of solo performers and group performers in battle do boxing movements in their steps, gestures, fighting with knives and spears and there are some fighting skills and formulas. All the characters are men.

The performers of ancient Gong-and-drum Mixed Opera passed down their skills to succeeding generations. Sons learned from fathers. All the skills were taught by fathers to sons. They had to learn carefully and could not invent at random.

Nuo Opera

Applicants: Hebei, Anhui, Hunan and Guizhou Provinces

Ferocious masks, strange costumes, imposing actions, odd language, mysterious scenes and a primitive ceremony add up to the performance of an old opera, Nuo Opera.

Nuo was a sacrificial ceremony in ancient times for getting rid of evils and praying for good luck. Nuo Opera evolved from the primitive Nuo sacrificial ceremony and is a mixture of religious culture and dramatic culture. Nuo Opera is very popular in Anhui, Jiangxi, Hubei, Hunan, Sichuan, Guizhou, Shaanxi, and Hebei provinces.

The Nuo Opera has a long history. It originated from the Nuo sacrificial ceremony of totemic worship in primitive society. The Nuo Dance came into being During the Shang Dynasty. It was originally a fixed sacrificial ceremony for getting ride of evils

Mask worn in the Nuo Opera in Guizhou Province

and pestilence. It used repeated and formula dancing actions in its performance and was often given on fixed festivals. It was derived from primitive dancing styles.

The plays of Nuo Opera can be divided into three types: first, formal plays. They are mostly sung by sorcerers on religious ceremonies. They have a strong religious context and simple plots. The performers wear masks and sing in a sorcerers' style. Second, Nuotang small-scale plays. They are performed on a Nuo altar and a high stage. They have a lighter religious context and a stronger common and comic element. They are often performed at the part of "acting opera" during religious ceremonies. The performance has some formulas and the music has some changes. Third, Waitai plays. They have a higher degree of drama.

Anshun Dixi

Applicant: Anshun City, Guizhou Province

Dixi, commonly called Tiaoshen (sorcerer's dance), is a local opera popular in Anshun City, Guizhou Province.

The performances of Dixi are often given outdoor without a stage that's why it is called Dixi (ground opera). At the center of a space in the front or back of a house or beside a field, a table and two chairs are placed and a flag with the word "marshal" is stuck beside them and that is enough material for the performance.

The performance of Dixi consists of singing and talking accompanied by dancing. The development and running of the plots are pushed forward by monologues. During the conflicts between figures and to show the vehemence of the figures' emotions the performers sing to express the emotions. The tune is unitary and the sound is strong, loud and sonorous. All the characters sing the same tune. The percussion accompaniment includes a bronze gong and a leather drum. Sometimes all the instruments are played together to create the rhythm and atmosphere of fighting in battle.

Anshun Dixi is an old opera. The performers wear black gauze on their heads, battle gowns round their waists and masks on their foreheads. They hold daggers, spears, knives and halberds in their hands, sing at random and dance along with their singing. With the accompaniment of a gong and a drum, one person sings and others accompany him. There are remains of old Yiyang tunes. The dances mainly represent fighting in battle and it is vigorous, straightforward, unvarnished and powerful. The contents of Anshun Dixi opera stories are all about battle.

The masks of Dixi opera possess personality and godship. There are lots of artists engaged in carving masks in Anshun. Before a religious ceremony, the newly bought masks of a troupe for a village performance can be placed anywhere and are viewed as wood carvings. After being granted titles, they are viewed as godlike articles. In a performance of Dixi opera, all the characters wear masks.

Shadow Play

Applicants: Hebei, Shanxi, Liaoning, Zhejiang, Hubei, Guangdong, Shaanxi and Gansu Provinces

Shadow play is a folk style opera. In the play light is shone on engraved figure silhouettes, made from animal hides or paper boards, which perform the stories. In a performance, three to five artists are singing stories in local popular tunes while manipulating the silhouettes behind a white curtain, accompanied by percussion and stringed music.

There are various types of shadow play. The major differences exist in the tunes and plots and the making of the engraved figure silhouettes and performing skills are almost always the same. In order to make the figure silhouettes the hair and blood should be removed from the animal hides first. After being processed to semi-transparency they are engraved and coloured. The carving requires meticulous knife skills in order to produce a vivid sculpture. A figure silhouette is divided into several parts such as the head, the body and the limbs. They are all in profile. A cap is put on the head and the body and limbs are dressed up.

A figure silhouette is manipulated by five bamboo sticks. The artists have nimble fingers and the playing of the silhouettes can make audiences dizzy. They have superb hand skills and can talk, read, fight, sing and control the gongs and drums at the same time. The screen for the shadow play is made from a piece of white gauze one metre wide. After being polished with fish oil the white gauze becomes stiff and transparent. During the performance the figure silhouettes move close to the screen and the hollowed-out figures with their various colours are vivid and touching.

The manipulating skills and singing skills are pivotal for the level of Shadow Play. Some master-hands can manipulate seven or eight figure silhouettes at the same time. In the plays about battles the gong and drum beats are intense, the figure silhouettes fight each other with swords and spears and turn over, up and down. It is very lively. The music and tunes in plays of singing and acting are melodious, beautiful and touching. They can be vehement or touching, showing happiness or sorrow or anger by the voices and words.

Puppetry

Applicants: Liaoning, Zhejiang, Fujian, Hunan, Guangdong, Hainan, Sichuan, Guizhou and Shaanxi Provinces

Traditional puppet show

Puppetry was known as puppet play in ancient times and is an opera where artists manipulate puppets to perform stories.

Chinese puppetry started during the Han Dynasty (206 BC-220 AD) and got a new development and enhancement during the Tang Dynasty (618-907) when puppets could be used to perform singing and dancing operas. In terms of styles it can be divided into string, rod, glove, wire, and puppets.

Besides the level of performance of the artists, the perfect puppet sculptures and setting are also attractive for audiences. In the aspect of sculpture art, importance is attached to the carving and designing of the puppets. Generally speaking, the sculptured string puppets are tall, about 0.68 meters. The key parts are stitched with strings. There are approximately 30 strings at the most and 10 at the least. Several assistant strings should be added according to the requirements for an acrobatic performance. The level of dancing postures and fighting skills of puppets in a performance completely depends on the manipulating skills of the artists and it is the key for the performance of the string puppets. Rod puppets are taller than string puppets. A rod puppet is about 1 meter tall and is set with three manipulating strings. Two strings are used to move the hands and one is used to support the head and body. Glove puppets are the smallest and are only 23 cm tall. Artists use both hands to support the puppets for a performance. The manipulating skill is particular and different from that used for string or rod puppets.

At the present time the performance of puppetry is becoming more and more colourful. Besides the traditional opera programs, there are performances of normal opera, singing and dancing opera, linked series of plays and even advertisements.

Quyi (Chinese Folk Art Forms)

Suzhou Pingtan

(Form of storytelling combined with ballad singing in Suzhou dialect)
Applicant: Jiangsu Province

Suzhou Pingtan is an overall term for Pinghua and Tanci. Pinghua is mostly performed by one narrator on stage. Usually, the content of narration is focused on historical stories focusing on symbols of war and all-conquering heroes. The leading character holds a sanxian (a three-stringed plucked instrument), and the supporting character holds a pipa (four-stringed Chinese lute). Both of them play and sing by themselves.

They tell and sing stories about daily life and love and folk stories. In general, Pinghua and Tanci are good at exquisite talking, accompanied by a smooth tune, with interjections of jokes. Tanci is always sung in the Wu dialect, with the accompaniment of the sanxia and pipa create a sweet sound.

Suzhou Pingtan is an art suiting both refined and popular tastes. It only needs a simple stage. As a rule, one table and one chair is enough. The performance is divided into shuo (storytelling), xue (words or acts meant to amuse), tan (playing the musical instrument), chang (singing) and yan (performance). Shuo (storytelling) is refers to the actor or actress telling stories, including describing the environment and the characters coupled with creating a certain atmosphere. Xue is a joke to attract audience interest in the performance. Tan (playing the musical instrument) and chang (singing) comprise the musical section of PingtanYan (performing) contains "hand" and "type of role". The "hand" shows the action of the hands and facial expressions. The "type of role" is the likeness of character imitated from the story. This can leave a specific impression about the character by visual sense and listening.

Long Pingtan: This is the key style of performance for Pingtan. The story is divided into several dozen or even hundreds of pieces. Each section is called "yihuishu", which is about 10,000 or 20,000 words, and the performance ranges from 40 to 100 minutes.

Medium-length Pingtan: This refers to a story in three or four sections. It is performed by many actors and actresses and lasts two to three hours.

Yangzhou Pinghua (Storytelling in Yangzhou Dialect)

Applicant: Yangzhou City, Jiangsu Province

(See P280)

Fuzhou Pinghua

(Storytelling in Fuzhou Dialect)
Applicant: Fuzhou City, Fujian Province

Fuzhou Pinghua is a unique storytelling style featuring narration in Fuzhou dialect coupled with intonation based on singing without musical accompaniment. It is a sort of Quyi genre, prevailing in the region where the Fuzhou dialect is spoken, namely the east and north of Fujian Province, Taiwan, as well as Southeast Asia where many overseas Chinese live.

Fuzhou Pinghua takes talking as the key part but also including singing. Actors tell stories with singing accompaniment, the latter by beating a cymbal. The singing is usually staged as follows: Firstly, at the beginning of the story, performers often sing about ten sentences as a prologue. The rhythm is relaxed and steady. Secondly, storytellers sing instead of talking when they want to express feelings and narrate details.

The melodies are not confined to the collection of tunes of qu. The tune of recitation is based on Fuzhou dialect. The props include a piece of wood, a folded fan and large cymbals (combined with banzhi and bamboo chopstick) to beat the time. Xingmu, a piece of wood, serves to add vigor and play a role of division. The role of the folded fan is to help strengthen the effect of gestures and facial expression. The folded fan also serves as a prop simulating a knife, gun, club, book, letter and salver. The cymbals look similar to those used in Buddhist rituals.

The traditional repertoire of Fuzhou Pinghua is numerous with rich and colorful features. Its content stems from daily news and anecdotes of the alleyways, which reflects local customs and is imbued with native flavor.

Shandong Dagu

(Musical storytelling accompanied by drum)
Applicant: Shandong Province

Shandong Dagu, which has a history of more than 350 years, is the earliest extant form of songs accompanied by drums in north China. It originated in the villages along the canal through the northwestern part of Shandong Province. At first, it was a free style chant to beating with the broken pieces of the plough and the spade. Later, the instruments became a trestle drum and two pieces of sheet iron or sheet copper coupled with the sanxian and sihu (a traditional Chinese four-stringed fiddle).

Shandong Dagu is mostly performed by one person who sings while standing. Sometimes, there is musical dialogue in antiphonal style performed by two persons. The major instruments include low-foot small drum, big sanxian and crescent plank (also called "pear-flower" plank, pair of brass castanets shaped like plowshares, of which "pear-flower" is a homophone). The singers hold a drumstick in the left hand with the iron sheet (sheet copper) in the right, and sing while beating. The musicians accompany the singing with the sanxian. The content is mainly of medium length which is sung coupled with storytelling. The short piece is only sung without talking.

It has simple coloring and is rich in local features. The melody integrates the talking and singing. It blends narration and expression of emotions. It has a rich repertoire, of which long and medium-length pieces take priority featuring talking as the main part, complemented by singing. Currently, Case by Judge Bao Zheng, Case by Judge Hai Rui and The West Chamber are popular programs.

Xihe Dagu

Applicant: Hejian City, Hebei Province

Xihe Dagu is a typical form of singing accompanied by a drum in the northern China. It is a genre of local Quyi with the largest number of performers and the most popular native art in Hebei Province. It originated from villages of the central part of Hebei and then became popular in Hebei, Henan, Shandong provinces and the northeast region and Beijing and Tianjin. The singer holds a drumstick in the right hand for beating the drum with yuanyanyban (mandarin bamboo clappers) in the left hand, while singing in dialect. The melody is flexible, and the language is popular and rich in expression. The singing and talking receive equal attention. Stories are long, medium and short in length.

The melodies of Xihe Dagu are based on the regional pronunciation of the central area of Hebei Province. It absorbed certain folk ditties and developed into the present form. Additionally, it is harmonious, fluent and vivid. It features a chanting style similar to the tone of folk ways in talking and singing. It is easy to sing and understand.

The programs of Xihe Dagu are traditional items mainly orally accumulated

Xihe Dagu (story-telling with drum accompaniment)

by artists from generation to generation. They are performed in village dialect with local flavor. The programs are mostly of long and medium-length, with clear-cut themes, well-organized plots and vivid language. There are also amusing tricks added, which make it easy to attract audiences.

The repertoire of Xihe Dagu includes over 150 medium and long novels and over 370 pieces of shumao (opening remarks before the programmed episode begins). The content includes wars, historical novels, popular literature, fairy tales and fables.

Dongbei Dagu

Applicant: Shenyang City, Liaoning Province; Heilongjiang Province

Dongbei Dagu is mainly popular in Liaoning, Jilin and Heilongjiang provinces in northeast China. It is a Quyi form of singing accompanied by a drum. It once prevailed in Shenyang which was called Fengtian in the late Qing Dynasty and was called Fengtian Dagu". Originally, it was performed by a singer alone accompanied by a small sanxian, with jieziban (plates that can beat time) tied to the legs; thus, it was also called xianzi shu (storytelling with a three-stringed plucked instrument). Later, it was performed as follows: one actor sang and played dagu and jianban (a kind of percussion instrument consisting of two flat wood or bamboo pieces), while others played a big sanxian and other instruments. They sang and spoke in the northeast dialect.

Dongbei Dagu is usually held at temple fairs, country trade fairs, weddings and funerals. Artists excel in gestures involving hands, eyes, body and footsteps. The talk is complete with rich rhythm and melody. The muted voice is the key characteristic of the melodies. In addition, a natural voice (big voice) is popularly use, while falsetto (small voice) is rare. The libretto belongs to a genre consisting of talking and singing. Besides its natural pattern, the style of singing also absorbs other art features such as Beijing opera, pingju opera (a local opera of north and northeast China), Jingyun dagu and folksongs prevailing in northeast China. Dongbei Dagu gives priority to talking and singing and long stories. The content mainly comes from dramas, novels and legendary stories.

There were more than 200 pieces in the original repertoire of Dongbei Dagu, but currently about 150 remain. The present pieces contain "zidishuduan (brothers' episode)", "sanguoduan (Three Kingdoms episode)" and "caoduan (popular episode)". The material of "zidishuduan (brothers' episode)" draws its subject matter from novels and popular operas of the Ming and Qing dynasties. The libretto boasts elegance and literary grace. There are a few works reflecting life of the Qing Dynasty. "Caoduan (popular episode)" is popular libretto edited and performed by folk artists, its subject matter involves extensive themes.

Muban Dagu

Applicant: Cangxian County, Hebei Province

Muban Dagu, known as Guzi Kuaishu (rhythmic storytelling accompanied by bamboo clappers), is rich in local features. It is the most popular genre of Quyi in the central area of the Shijiazhuang area in Hebei Province. It has developed through drawing on traits of folk songs and the hawking sales patter of peddlers in the central area of Hebei Province. Up to now, it has a history of some 300 years. Initially, it was popular in some counties including Shenze, Wuji and Gaoceng. Later, it spread to all counties of the central area of Hebei Province, Beijing, Tianjin, Shijiazhuang and Baoding. Moreover, Muban Dagu can also be found in Shanxi and Henan provinces.

The libretto of Muban Dagu is easy to understand. The melodies are simple featuring vivid local color. It is performed both in solo and antiphonal singing, which is accompanied by bamboo clappers and a small one-sided drum. Hence, it is comparatively easy to learn. As a result, it is easily promoted and popularized among people.

Cangzhou Muban Dagu is quite rich and colorful in terms of content and pays tribute to heroes, reflects the sufferings of the people, depicts historical stories and rural life. Most of the performers are folk song artists. It has a complete musical structure. There are three different types of rhythm and the speed is flexible, either being lengthened or shortened. Its style of singing is deep and sonorous. It sounds either like talking or singing, as well as speaking and narrating, and features a strong flavor of local life. Usually, the tune at the end is very strong.

Muban Dagu is mainly performed by one artist. The artist holds bamboo clappers in the left hand with a drumstick in the right. During the performance, the artist frequently beats the bamboo clappers and drum while talking and singing. Other persons are specially assigned to play sanxian as accompaniment.

Laoting Dagu

Applicant: Leting County, Hebei Province

Laoting Dagu is a ballad singing art relatively representative in north China, such as in the eastern area of Hebei Province, Beijing, Tianjin and the northeast provinces of Liaoning, Jilin and Heilongjiang.

People in the Laoting area are good at singing and dancing. And Laoting dialect is rich in natural rhythm and melodious tunes combined with drum as an accompaniment to form the basis for Leting Dagu.

He Jianchun (middle), the third generation disciple of Jin Sect of Laoting Dagu is playing the Laoting Dagu.

It has a comparatively simple form of performance, only needing one drum, a piece of bamboo clapper, one sanxian and one performer. On the stage, the singer beats the drum and bamboo clapper, while talking and singing at the same time. The singer describes the scenes and characters of the stories, makes comments about success and loss with various facial expressions and gestures.

Laoting Dagu is endowed with another distinctive feature. It combines talking and singing together. Regarding the singing, it contains "nine melodies and 18 tunes", however, the talking is similar with Pingshu (storytelling) but preformed in Leting dialect without which it would lack its special lingering charm.

Apart from the main form there are also elements of poems, songs and prose. This assisting part mainly appears in the full-length items, playing a role of summary, enlightening, describing and enriching the tales. At the performance of the full-length stories, this kind of form always serves the role of bringing the story to life.

The accompanying instrument is the sanxian. It has diversified timbre and volume. Additionally, it is quite suitable for accompanying the talking and singing. The lyrics have a lingering and fine effect; the climaxes sound impassioned and full of power and grandeur.

Lu'an Dagu

Applicant: Changzhi City, Shanxi Province

Lu'an Dagu, with distinct regional features of northern China, is a form of music played with a small drum and other instruments. It got its name because of its prevalence in the area of ancient Lu'an Mansion (present-day Changzhi County of Shanxi Province). In the reign of Qing Emperor Qianlong, folk artists who lived along the western street of Changzhi County took local dramas and folk operas as the basis for performance. Gradually, they developed a form of storytelling combining singing and talking. Its slow tempo is dictated by pieces of steel plate and a flat drum. It boasts a tight rhythm, vigorous talking and singing and steady performance.

Traditionally, Lu'an Dagu is performed by many artists who respectively hold drum, bamboo clappers, sanxian, erhu (a two stringed fiddle) and dihu (low pitched two-stringed fiddle of the erhu family). These artists talk and sing in a circle in many roles.

On a higher stage, it is usually performed by one artist talking and singing while other performers play the sanxian and erhu as accompaniment. Its melodies and tune are rich and colorful, sounding melodious and reflecting native flavor. The talking and singing alternate, with singing as the main part. It features singing without musical accompaniment, and instruments being played without singing. Lu'an Dagu is rich in diversified forms of beating with unique flavor. It also has a short prelude with flexible changes. Therefore, it is suitable for performances indoors and outdoors and even in an arena.

Jingdong Dagu

Applicant: Baodi District, Tianjin

ingdong Dagu is a ballad singing art in the dialect of the eastern part of Beijing and the areas

to the east of the capital. It is performed in the form of one person singing while standing and beating a drum, and others playing sanxian and dulcimer. It came into being in the mid-Qing Dynasty. It has been popular in Hebei cities such as Langfang, Chengde, Baoding and Tangshan, as well as Huairou County of Beijing and Baodi District of Tianjin.

Jingdong Dagu is good at talking and singing full-length stories. Artists beat drum and use sanxian as accompaniment (later, dulcimer also used). Empty words such as "na", or "a" or often added at the end. Its original tune pattern is relatively simple. However, it has evolved into more than 20 sorts of tune patterns by artists' creation.

Jiaodong Dagu

Applicant: Yantai City, Shandong Provinc

With a history of almost 200 years, this is a folk form of Quyi popular on the Jiaodong Peninsula of Shandong Province. In the past, it was initially performed by blind singers.

In early days, the "tune of the blind" was formed by some simple songs of farming. Later, blind artists of Huangxian County (Longkou City) absorbed native tunes of fishermen's songs and folk songs so as to create new works. The new style has high and sweet tunes, and some narrative forms. As a result, it evolved into a new form of talking and singing with a theme tune and interlude.

The major instruments are sanxian, shugu (drum) and riyueban (sun-moon clappers made from steel plate-according to legend, Shandong artists believed in three 'emperors' consisting of heaven, earth and man and regarded heaven as represented by the sun and the earth by the moon, hence the name sun-moon clappers). Riyueban is a unique instrument which only Jiaodong Dagu uses. Performers often sing combining with the tunes of Beijing Opera. Originally, the melody was evolved from the integration of recitation by local scholars and native ditties of Li Cuilian. Singers were mostly students who failed the imperial civil service examination. Therefore, stories were written by those students themselves, the contents mainly covering historical war stories. Performers hit a small leather drum while beating wooden clappers and singing while unveiling the transcript.

Due to different native dialects and systems inherited by artistic masters and apprentices, Jiaodong Dagu has also formed some distinct styles. The tune of the northern part has a quick, sweet and charming rhythm featuring the village flavor of Shandong Province. In eastern area, the tempo is simple with rich rhythms in the spoken language reflecting folk art. On the other hand, the southern region has tunes featuring a strong flavor of local drama and folk songs.

Heluo Dagu

Applicant: Luoyang City, Henan Province

Based on ballad singing, Heluo dagu is a genre of traditional Chinese music that narrates stories, describes characters, express feelings and reflects social life. It has been passed on through five generations, with a history of more than 100 years. Local people call it "shuoshu (storytelling)". It is often related with storytelling and singing opera in the Luoyang area.

Heluo Dagu is performed by singers who beat a drum with one hand and simultaneously play bamboo clappers with the other, which controls the speed of talking and singing. This is accompanied by specific facial expressions and gestures. In terms of sound, dynamics and speed of the storytelling, the stage atmosphere is remarkably enhanced by the insistent beat of the drum and bamboo clappers.

The melody derives from diversified local drama and opera of Henan Province. They include Bangzi (general term of local opera), Quzi (storytelling), Henan Zhuizi (ballad sing to musical accompaniment) and Luoyang qingshu (storytelling mainly in songs with musical accompaniment). The music encompasses multiple combinations of tunes rather than any stereotyped style. Artists excel in absorbing relative musical elements from rich and colorful local melodies reorganized into new-style music. As a result, they have made Heluo dagu into a performance mode containing storytelling and characterization to become an enriched technique of expression reflecting the western area of Henan Province.

A drum, a folding fan and a Xianzi are the properties of Heluo Dagu

Heluo dagu is a genre of talking and ballad singing in Henan dialect. The Henan dialect is unique in its four tunes of local color affecting the development of its melody.

Wenzhou Guci

Applicant: Rui'an City, Zhejiang Province

Wenzhou Guci (drumbeat lyrics) is popular in Wenzhou City of Zhejiang Province and neighboring areas. It is well known as "Changci" (reciting and singing). It is performed in Wenzhou dialect featuring much local color and a unique style of art. It became popular as early as the mid-Qing Dynasty.

Wenzhou Guci comprises singing and reciting, but the former takes the major part. Its melodies and tune contain the strong savor of folk songs of southern China. The southern style is fine, smooth and soft, the northern sounds rough, bold and unconstrained.

Wenzhou Guci is good at emotive expression and narration. It is simple in language and easily understood. It contains rich folk vocabulary and proverbs. Its musical charm is its natural rhythm and harmonious syllables in the music of storytelling.

The major instrument for performance of Wenzhou Guci consists of flat drum, sanliban (three pieces of bamboo clapper) , niujinqin (a plucked stringed instrument made from tendons of beef) and xiaobaoyue. The sixteen-stringed Niujinqin is a unique instrument as accompaniment, which is the only one in China. The most remarkable feature of performance is when one singer performing, he can play four to six instruments. In addition, the singer can also play various roles (now musical dialogue in antiphonal style by a man and a woman), so he is required to make clear articulation and describe characters carefully. The singer should also accurately express the personalities and gestures of the characters, as well as imitate all kinds of sounds for describing atmosphere.

In subject, Wenzhou Guci mostly derives from folktales and historical stories reflecting family joys and sorrows and love affairs. Wenzhou Guci is a genre reproducing scenes of historical affairs and figures by way of sense of hearing to make association and imagination.

Northern Shaanxi Shuoshu

Applicant: Yan'an City, Shaanxi Province

This is an important style of storytelling in the northwestern region. It has been flourishing mainly in Yan'an and Yulin districts. At first, it was sung by poor, blind people. They used the ditties of Northern Shaanxi for singing and reciting some tales. Later, they absorbed the tunes of Meihu opera, Shaanxi opera, Guanzhongdaoqing opera and Xintianyou (one of the major folk tunes popular in Northern Shaanxi). Thus, Northern Shaanxi Shuoshu has gradually evolved into a form of talking and singing full-length stories.

The performance style of Northern Shaanxi Shuoshu involves one artist singing and beating a drum by himself along with sanxian and pipa. The singing alternates with reciting. It is divided into "sanxian shu" and "pipa shu". Through improvement by various folk artists, it began to be sung by one person playing five kinds of instruments at the same time, including big sanxian, pipa, bangzi (wood clapper), wooden pluck, pieces of wood for beating, small gong and cymbals. It uses popular song words with rich local flavor. Its tune is high pitched and rough, as well as changeable. As a result, its tune has been known as "nine tunes with 18 melodies". It needs only simple props. However, the stage is full of liveliness. The performer begins with the xingmu (small wood block used to strike the table to draw the audience's attention).

Besides special prologue and libretto, artists are not confined to a stereotype performance. Excellent folk artists draw on many tunes such as folk songs, daoqing (chanting folk tales to the accompaniment of percussion instruments), yangge (dance) a popular rural folk dance and Wanwanqiang (local opera) of Northern Shaanxi Province, Shaanxi opera, Meihu opera, Puju opera (indigenous to Shanxi Province), Jinju opera (local opera in Shanxi) and Beijing opera. Through refined integration, it has formed a unique style of libretto.

It is bestowed with a repertoire of more than 200 works. The repertoire is characterized with a strong sense of storytelling, well-organized structure, intricate plots and happy endings.

Fuzhou Chi Yi

Applicant: Fuzhou City, Fujian Province

Fuzhou Chi Yi belongs to a genre of Quyi with singing as the major part. At first, Chi Yi derived from ballads, local ditties collected by folk artists who sang for a living. It came into being in the reign of Ming Emperor Jiaqing. By the Qing Dynasty, some organized bodies of Chi Yi had emerged to perform among the people. With a history of over 400 years, Fuzhou Chi Yi has maintained a repertoire of over 100 works and has spread to overseas Chinese (natives of Fuzhou) through 10 generations.

In terms of melodies, Chi Yi is mostly performed by singers who synchronously sing and play an instrument. On the other hand, it can be also sung on the stage to the accompaniment of music behind the scenes.

Fuzhou Chi Yi is performed in Fuzhou dialect with one or two people playing the erhu or sanxian or diliu. In the traditional performance, there are acrobatic performances included such as paohanchuan (folk dance with one dancer playing the woman passenger carrying a prop boat around her and another as boatman with an oar), caigaoqiao (walking on stilts), taige (a kind of folk amusement with a couple of little boys, who are sitting or standing on a wooden framework which is carried by others, playing their parts in opera stories) and lotus stick play.

The melodies occupy the central position in terms of genre. It plays a role of narrating stories, describing characters and expressing feelings. Chi Yi pays more attention to the popularization of libretto and tune. Additionally, it is featured by sprightly rhythm, short prelude, clear pronunciation and graceful singing tunes. The repertoire is mostly medium-length stories, with sanqu (type of opera popular in the Yuan, Ming and Qing dynasties with tonal patterns modeled on tunes drawn from folk music) as a subsidiary part.

The instruments of Chi Yi comprise xian (string instrument) and wind instrument as the key part; a hexagon-shaped erhu plays the main string music, accompanied by small kuaiban (bamboo clappers) and flat drum. The accompanying instruments include shuangqing, sanxian, pipa, yehu (a kind of two-stringed huqin whose box-type music body is made of half a coconut shell faced with paulownia wood), douguan (a special Chinese bamboo flute) and small suona horn.

Nanping Nanci

Applicant: Nanping City, Fujian Province

Nanping Nanci is a Quyi form popular in Nanping in the northern part of Fujian Province. It is generally said that Nanci from area south of the lower reaches of the Yangtze River was introduced to Nanping from Suzhou in the reign of Qing Emperor Jiaqing, becoming mixed with local folk ditties. The performance mode is one artist as the chief singer and many people respectively holding different instruments sitting around him; they take turns talking and singing according to different roles.

There can be three or five or even more than 10 singers performing. Each plays an instrument such as dulcimer, sanxian, pipa, sheng, sudi flute, kehu (four-stringed bass instrument, tuned and played like cello), big gong and cymbals and yugu (percussion instrument made of bamboo). Kunqu opera takes priority originally chosen as the melodies were sweet and graceful. Later, in order to make the elegant language and words of Kunqu easier to understand, Nanci was gradually changed long into short sentences, one sentence with seven words, becoming adaptable to a wide audience in urban and rural areas.

Since Nanci was introduced to Nanping in the late 18th century, it has passed down through nine generations accumulating deep artistic traditions.

Shaoxing Pinghu Tune

Applicant: Shaoxing City, Zhejiang Province

This a Quyi form of singing and talking prevalent in Shaoxing of Zhejiang Province and neighboring areas. It is famous for its main melody, Pinghu Tune. It is said that this form of art was initially created in the early Ming Dynasty. It is usually performed by one player. The player sings and talks while playing sanxian.

No matter how many people are involved in the performance, there is only

Tashan Central Primary School, Yuecheng District, Shaoxing City are rehearsing folk instrumental ensemble *High Mountain and Flowing Water* with the names of Pinghudiao (Pinghu tunes) as the theme.

one singer playing sanxian, while others are for accompaniment. At the beginning, the introductory song is given priority followed by stories. With excellent skills of talking and singing, the main singer can narrate various stories, create vivid characters and portray sad and sentimental dramas without any gestures or facial expressions. Audiences can lose their sense of reality as they listen and feel they are present at the scene described; then, they return to reality and find it was all the creation of one old man. Both performers and audiences seem to stop breathing by the power of the performance.

According to incomplete statistics, there are more than 130 works in the repertoire. Of these, the introductory song accounts for over 100. At the performance, the introductory song is sung firstly in Shaoxing dialect.

Pinghu Tune boasts elegant language, sweet melodies and rhythm and unique style. It has rich flavor in terms of literature, music and art. Thus, it has inherited and developed the art of singing and talking in Shaoxing prevailing in the area south of the lower reaches of the Yangtze River in the Ming and Qing dynasties.

Lanxi Tanhuang

Applicant: Lanxi City, Zhejiang Province

This is a traditional form of storytelling and singing in Zhejiang Province. It came into being in Lanxi, Jinhua and Quzhou of the central and western areas of Zhejiang Province.

It is endowed with elegant language. Its singing contains clear articulation, with meticulously executed singing and reading. Thus, it has been favored by refined men of letters. Thus singers and players became known as "Mr. Tanhuang", someone wearing a long gown and elegant in manner. Such teams perform only when invited by relatives and friends to add to the fun in festivals or for worship. They never engage in performances for profit.

Xianxiao

Applicant: Gansu Province

"Xianxiao" is a folk art of storytelling accompanied with sanxian (a three-stringed plucked instrument). According to different districts, it is divided into "Liangzhou Xianxiao, Hezhou Xianxiao and Qinghai Xianxiao". Generally, it is performed by blind artists who hold sanxian (a three-stringed plucked instrument) under the arm while singing. Because the stories were about being virtuous and filial, hence it got the name of Xianxiao, literally meaning virtuous and filial.

Performers are mostly blind people, especially congenital blind persons who learned the art from childhood. They have long made a living by singing from door to door, becoming known as "Xiaxian" (sanxian played by blind people). As folk artists, they depend on their hearing and memory.

Xianxiao has a rich repertoire, mostly edited by artists according to story telling down through the generations. These include Guoshu, describing the rise and fall of a country and its heroes, such as Three Kingdoms, Journey to the Western Seas and Case Heard By Judge Bao Zheng. These stories are long and usually performed in tea houses and family homes over a period of several weeks. In order to add effect, sometimes there are two artists playing different roles with sihu and sanxian as accompaniment. The singing, reflecting filial piety and love affairs in daily life, is called "Jiashu".

The music of Liangzhou Xianxiao has maintained many traditional tunes and programs. In addition, it has absorbed the essence of Liangzhou ditties and local folksongs. The language is rooted in Hezhou dialect. It is characterized by humor and is easily understood. The libretto is flexible and changeable.

Henan Zhuizi

Applicant: Hainan Province

With a history of more than 100 years, Henan Zhuizi is a relatively unique form of Quyi. It is prevalent in Henan, Shandong, Anhui provinces, Tianjin and Beijing. The main accompaniment is "Zhuizi Xian" (presently called zhuihu, stringed instrument shaped like sanxian-three-stringed Chinese guitar). It is performed in Henan dialect.

It is normally performed by one singer who treadles wooden clappers while singing. It is also performed by two persons who take different roles for playing and singing. No matter whether in urban parks, rural backyards or temple fairs, there is always a stage arranged with one table with a copper cymbal on it, xingmu and a leather drum. The player of "Zhuizi Xian" sits besides the table and the singer in front with jianban in the left hand and bamboo stick in the right. Along with the drumbeats of "Zhuizi Xian", the player beats the jianban on the downbeat and drum on the upbeat. Another player of sanxian also produces downbeats. Jianban is required to be held neither too high nor too low; it should be kept at the same level as the player's shoulder. When the player needs to beat the cymbals, he can put down jianban and take up a bamboo stick. On the other hand, if there is no drum and cymbals but only a jianban, held in the right hand, the player can make various hand gestures.

At the performance held by professional groups, there is no table set up. After the announcer calls out the item on the program, the performers go onto stage holding jianban. As they beat this, the band begins to play a short prelude. Following this, the players beat jianban and begin to sing. During the qunkou (form of performance in which three or more people sing or talk alternately) and singing by more than two people in succession, jianban can be alternatively beaten by the player's right or left hand; however, the means of exchanging the hand for beating the jianban should be unified and someone is nominated to ensure this.

The performance of Zhuizi pays much attention to posture and gestures graceful and vivid. Additionally, the player is required to perform gestures properly and excellently with both hands and feet.

Henan Zhuizi has retained its simple local coloring and rich life flavor. It has over 200 works of varying length.

Shandong Qinshu

Applicant: Shandong Province

Shandong Qinshu

This is an important genre of Quyi in Shandong Province. It originated from folk ditties from the Heze region in the southwestern part in the mid-Ming Dynasty. Up to the mid-Qing Dynasty, the original accompaniments such as seven-stringed plucked instrument and zither were replaced by dulcimer (also called "hudieqin"), sihu, zither, pipa, jianban and saucer. It is normally played by a large group sitting in a circle. The singing section takes the majority, which include reciting and dialogue arranged by turns.

The singers sit in a splayed manner, while the dulcimer is put in the middle, with other instruments arranged on both sides. In the process of the story, they play different roles, such as sheng (male role in traditional opera), dan (female character) and chou (clown).

Generally, Shandong Qinshu is played by

two to five people. If the latter, there are two or three singers and the others play instruments but also engage in vocal accompaniment. For the traditional performance, its style is steady and easy. The singers are solemn, serious and dignified, they perform the storytelling and depict characters by changeable melodies and skillful cooperation with the accompaniments.

Shandong Qinshu is performed in Shandong dialect. Most works are short and known as an aria, containing 100 to 200 lines performed over 10 to 20 minutes. Owing to short stories and flexible style of performance, the art can always reflect life rapidly.

Luogushu

Applicant: Shanghai Municipality

Luogushu, originally called "Taibaoshu", is a folk form of storytelling and ballad singing of folktales and historical stories, integrating the folk music of Henan, Zhejiang and Jiangsu provinces. It has melodies with rising and falling tones, talking and singing, excellent combination of rhythm, accent and language. It is a rare folk art preserved in a metropolis.

Luogushu takes talking as the major part and singing as a supplement. Originally, it involved a solo performance. The performer sat at a table on which stood a shugu (drum). The artist held a bamboo stick to beat the drum with his right hand, while he had a gong on his left thumb with other four fingers gripping the hammer of the gong for beating. Luogu (gong and drum) sets the tempo for talking and singing, as well as creating an exaggerated atmosphere to draw audience attention. The melody is rich in folk music of the area south of the Yangtze River. Later, its performance style was gradually replaced by the singer standing rather than sitting. In addition, it was also played by two or more people, with instrumental accompaniment. The string instruments, such as pipa and dulcimer, were newly arranged for performance. However, the major performances are often solo accompanied by a band.

Luogushu has both long and medium-length programs. The content derives from folktales, historical novels and family affairs and historical stories.

Shaoxing Lianhua Lao

Applicant: Shaoxing County, Zhejiang Province

Lianhua Lao is a type of Quyi popular in Shaoxing County. Its performance includes prelude in which each verse begins or ends with Lianhua Lao, hence the name, literally, of songs of lotus flowers. It is said to have originated in the late Ming or early Qing period. At that time, singers made up as beggars went singing from door to door. They spread superstitious belief

Shaoxing Lianhua Lao *Xu Wenchang Dunning for Debt*

in ghosts and deities, as well as encouraging charitable deeds. In the past, the performance was normally a duet. One person played the major role in singing while holding a rod from a string of copper cash to beat his shoulders, belly, chest and legs for the tempo, the other speaking out in support. Subsequently, it evolved into a form of talking and singing news, which is coupled with talking, singing and performance.

Its spoken part and libretto are performed in Shaoxing dialect, which is easy to understand and full of humor. The tune is simple, sweet and melodious. The plot teems with life customs, which is especially favored by the people of Shaoxing. In the past, it was normally performed by three people as a team without instrumental accompaniment. One person sang mainly, a second beat a drum and also cooperated with the third person in support of the singer. Consequently, the performance style changed because the responding tune was not suitable for singing the whole program. As a result, it was accompanied by sihu (the traditional Chinese four-stringed fiddle). According to the new style of performance, one person sang mainly, the other play sihu, and the third person beat clappers. The major singer held sanqiaoban (three bamboo or wood boards) in the hand and set the tempo between the "prelude" and "interlude". Sometimes, the major singer engaged in dialogue with the accompanists, or they spoke out in support of him. In recent years, great achievements have been made in terms of performance, tunes and music. Occasionally, some instruments are added, such as pipa, dulcimer, erhu and flute. Moreover, in line with specific conditions, some performances include Shaoju opera, Yueju opera and a few folk ditties. Experiments in two-man performances have been tried. But the original storytelling always remains.

Lanzhou Guzi (Drum Song)

Applicant: Lanzhou City, Gansu Province

As one of the oldest genres of Quyi in China, the Lanzhou Guzi is a popular folk art in the Lanzhou area. As a popular art, a lot of local people can sing while playing the drum. It is performed on occasions, such as marriage celebrations, feasts and leisure times. In rural halls, courtyards, tea houses and pubs, a group of local people like to perform it. At the peak of singing, one person sings, while others chime in. The atmosphere is very joyful.

It is an artistic form with singing as the main content and featuring multiplicity. Some arias contain only talking without singing, while some include both. The main musical instrument used is the sanxian, supported by the dulcimer, banhu (Chinese two-stringed fiddle), erhu, pipa, yueqin (four-stringed moon-shaped Chinese mandolin), xiao (vertical bamboo flute) and flute. It is normally performed by one person. The tune is elegant, beautiful with a broad range, clear and smooth. The singer can incisively and vividly express various feelings like happiness, angry, sorrow and cheerfulness. Meanwhile, the gestures and facial expressions can convey a sense of beauty to audiences.

Lanzhou Guziis is endowed with a wide repertoire. It boasts beautiful melodies, refined style, lingering charm, as well as rich local flavor. Currently, more than 100 works have been collected, mostly folklore, historical stories, classical novels and traditional dramas, which include humorous comments arranged by turns.

Yangzhou Qingqu (Yangzhou Ditty)

Applicant: Yangzhou City, Jiangsu Province

Yangzhou Qingqu originated from ditties in the Yuan Dynasty. On a basis of Sanqu Songs of the period, it absorbed the good qualities of other local music and folk songs in the areas south of the Yangtze River and north of the Huaihe River. Eventually, a peculiar local musical form cane into existence in the middle of the Ming Dynasty. It was popular in Yangzhou and Zhenjiang, Jiangsu Province and Shanghai. It is performed in Yangzhou dialect. Innumerable songs were created and developed during the Ming and Qing dynasties. Its music has a high artistic value. Among the works, the "Five Court Songs" are of strong artistic individuality.

Traditionally the number of performers varied from two to nine people seated while playing traditional Chinese instruments, including the Chinese lute, trichord, yueqin, Sihu, erhu, yangqin and sandalwood board, plates and wine cups. Occasionally, the xiao flute is also used in the performance. Yangzhou Qingqu only exploits music and singing to depict figures and express thoughts and feelings without any makeup, talking and performance. Therefore, it was careful about enunciation. Most singers were men. The method of singing consists of "zhaikou (narrow mouth)" and "kuokou (wide mouth)". The former means the singer imitates the sound of the female, whereas the latter is the true male voice.

Yangzhou Qingqu is a singing form with

13 Culture

Students in Yangzhou Culture and Art School are performing traditional piece of Yangzhou Qingqu (ditty) *Jasmine Flower*.

a long history that preserves many ancient folk songs and has influence on various song forms in some other areas.

"Teaching by oral instruction and demonstration" is the basic way for its transmission.

Jinge Songs

Applicant: Zhangzhou City, Fujian Province

Jinge, a form of singing and playing instruments at the same time, is one of the major folk Quyi in southern Fujian Province. It is popular in an area in central Zhangzhou and neighboring cities in southern Fujian Province like Xiamen, Jinjiang, Longxi and Taiwan and parts of Southeast Asia where overseas Chinese live.

Zhangzhou Jinge songs are one of the five major song genre of Fujian Province. In the late Ming and Qing dynasties, it inherited the Nanci Ditty, Daoqing (a form Taoist Quyi) and folk xiaoxi (small opera). It came from the common people, and used dialect, with sweet melodies of a strong country tinge. Jinge singers were found seen on festivals and celebrations. They sometimes sat to sing or sometimes strolled around. In Zhangzhou, performers always sat to sing, whereas in Xiamen, many performers stood to sing, with some actions to express the feeling.

The traditional instruments used are the yueqin or Chinese lute, vertical end-blown flute, two-stringed or three-stringed instrument, clapper board and twin bells; sometimes a suona is added. In Xiamen, the Muyu (rounded woodblock carved in the shape of a fish, struck with a wooden stick, often used in Buddhist chanting.) is used as a substitute for clapper board. The singing form of Jinge includes solo, antiphonal with two performers, or three or four performers singing and talking.

The tunes are divided in two schools: Tang and Ting. The Tang school was most popular in rural areas. Its tune was boorish and powerful based on folk ballads, with a flexible rhythm involving many changes. Each line is completed by an ending tone. The Ting school was popular in cities, and the tune was elegant with clear enunciation. It adopted the tune of Nanqu and the familiar instruments and fingering methods.

Changde Silk String

Applicant: Changde City, Hunan Province

Changde silk string art is an important branch of Hunan silk string art. Normally, silk string instruments like the yangqin (Chinese hammered dulcimer originally from the Middle East), the Chinese lute, the yueqin and erhu are used in the performance. Changde Silk String got its name from the instruments played and the Changde dialect in art shows understood by southerners and northerners. The Changde people believe their dialect is just like singing. Especially for women, their gentle tone is graceful and restrained, just like a breeze.

The particular traditional performance of Changde Silk String was the solo performer singing and playing. The lone performer played many roles. It is required that the performers should have sweet, crisp and rich voices, using a suitable tune and changeable tone to tell and sing the story, and to build up various figures. In accordance with the requirements of the talking, singing and story-telling, the actors must switch to many roles.

The traditional performance form was scores of performers sitting in a circle, each with a yangqin, drum board, Jinghu (Chinese bowed string musical instrument used primarily in Beijing opera), erhu, three-stringed instrument and Chinese lute. They talk and sing in turn. There are some certain rules about the seating and the instrument positions: "the yangqin to the drum board, the jinghu to the erhu, the three-stringed instrument to the Chinese lute." The main parts of the performance are singing, with a few spoken parts. If there are more roles than performers, doubling up occurs.

Yulin Folk Songs

Applicant: Yulin City, Shaanxi Province

Yulin Folk Songs, involving sitting to sing and play an instrument, was popular in the urban areas in northern part of Yulin, Shaanxi province.

Yulin Folk Songs is an art form between Quyi and folk song, also called Yulin Qingchang Songs (sing without makeup or musical accompaniment). It is said that Yulin Folk Songs were spread south of the Yangtze River by performers starting from the reign of Qing Emperor Kangxi (1662-1722). Normally one performer used antiphonal singing or talking, combining original voice with a falsetto female tone, while playing the yangqin. The percussion instrument was a small porcelain dish. Most arias are lyrical pieces with some narrative story, featuring salient flavors of folk songs from the south. In spreading, it kept the traditional characteristics, coupled with adopting local folk ditties and dialect. Therefore, it became a new art form merging southern and northern characteristics.

It is simple, easy and flexible to sing the ditty without props. Initially, the band would quiet the crowd by playing one or two fixed pieces. Then, the formal performance began, lasting three or four hours.

The words of the Yulin Folk Songs mostly described the delight of urban life. Beside the works about the sorrows of parting and pains of separation, love between the youths, some works about local customs can be detected in Yulin Folk Songs. Some folk stories on everyone's lips, such as Liang Shanbo and Zhu Yingtai, were also adapted. In brief, Yunlin folk songs basically reflected urban life at all levels.

Tianjin Shidiao

Applicant: Tianjin

This is a typical art genre of Tianjin Quyi. Sung in Tianjin dialect, it is easy to understand and its tune is high, bright and clear. The solo is the major form of performance. The repertoires are short. The instruments played include Dasanxian, Sihu, the Jieziban and the yangqin. The melody is very rich, including many ditties from Tianjin folk songs and elsewhere.

Tianjin Shidiao is different from other genre in lyrics, tunes and modes. In lyrics, there are only 50 or 60 lines at most, sometimes only 30, to express the entire contents. There are three speeds: lento, erliu (2/6, which is unique

Tianjin shidiao

Chinese musical speed) and allegro. The tune is bold and unconstrained, fully expressing the personality and feelings of Tianjin people.

Xinjiang Quzi

Applicant: Changji Hui Autonomous Prefecture, Xinjiang Uygur Autonomous Region

This originated form the folk songs of Shaanxi Province, Pingxian from Qinghai Province and Lanzhou drum songs from Gansu Province as well as other folk songs from northwestern China. These were changed under the influence of local ethnic musical art to become Xinjiang Quzi.

Usually people sing in turns while playing the two- or three-stringed fiddle, banhu (a high pitched fiddle with a coconut sound box) and bell. The singing is very rich. During the early period of development, the string instrument included the three-stringed fiddle, Sihu and banhu and the percussion instruments included the Wazi and Feizi. Wazi is also called four sheets wa (tile, made of bamboo), having four sheets, two to a pair with the performer holding one pair in each hand. The Wazi and the feizi are used to control the rhythm, provide atmosphere and enrich the performance effects.

The shows of Xinjiang Quzi were in two original categories: elegant and vulgar. Those based on historical stories, heroes and love are particular in elegant words and expression, whereas folk stories, legends contain wording and phrasing easy to understand. The spoken parts of the present Xinjiang Quzi adopted the dialect of Jimsar County, Changji Hui Autonomous Prefecture as standard pronunciation, which is abstracted and refined, becoming a stage-wise art language.

Xinjiang Quzi, an amalgamation of various musical elements of many ethnic groups, this has high, bright, clear, melodic, sweet and agreeable tunes. With unique rhythm and the vivid mode, it formed its special art style, representing regional characteristics and many ethnic groups. As a rare play genre, it is the only one sung in Chinese in Xinjiang.

Dragon Boat Songs

Applicant: Guangdong Province

This is performed in Guangzhou dialect and is popular in the Pearl River Delta, Hong Kong and Macao. There are two explanations regarding origin. One is that the genre originated from the Double Fifth Festival (Dragon Boat Festival). When People burned joss sticks at the dragon king temple, they sang some songs to pray for elimination of bad things, bring good, and protect the home. Another idea is that beggars sang the auspicious songs with a small gong and a small drum in front of the breast while holding a wood-carved dragon. It is generally believed to have been formed during the late-18th Century.

The contents of the dragon boast songs fall into three categories: Transferred from Buddhism, mainly concerned with the effects of a person's actions that determine his destiny in his next incarnation and the eternal cycle of birth and death; transferred from ballads; and, transferred from wooden fish songs.

The performer holds a wood-carved dragon in his hand and manipulates it by strings like a puppet. At the same time, he beats the small gong and the small drum to control its rhythm. In the performance, one or two people beat drums or gongs to accompany their own singing. The sound is short but strong, an easy way to unleash one's feelings and to tell a story. The stories cover a wide range from fairy tales to current hot political issues. But as few of the artists are highly educated, the songs were passed down mostly by oral teachings.

In the past, the artists always played in the streets and lane. It was common to find them at important ethnic festivals and various celebrations. Dragon Boat Songs is a kind of recitative ballad. It takes the Shunde dialect as its original standard. The tune is simple and deep, with some twists and turns. The sound is short, high, free and easy, with some humorous tinge. Normally, there is no instrument other than gong and drum.

Basin-Beating Song

Applicant: Jingzhou City, Hubei Province

This originated from the ancient custom of beating a basin like a drum and singing to comfort family members at a funeral. The basin-beating song is very popular in Shashi, Jingzhou, Jiangling in the Jinhan Plain. It uses one drum, one pestle, one rectangular table, one screen and burning joss-sticks. The drummer sat in the main position, while the singers, masters and guests sat around tables. The drummer beat the drum to set the rhythm, and the singers followed to sing a tale based on legends, their voices are rising, falling and pausing.

The artists in the Shashi urban area still retain the original pattern, avoiding any unnecessary actions so that the Shashi Basin-Beating Song retains its ancient simplicity. The diameter of the drum used is 60 centimeters while the drumstick is about 40 centimeters long.

The special quality of the music is contributed by the dialect of Shashi and the solo accompaniment of the drummer. The rhythm is downbeat and unaccented at the end of the two-bar-melody, with a caesura in the end bar creating a unique feeling of "suspense". The basin-beating song can be halted any time if the singers and/or audience feel tired.

Hanchuan Shanshu Story-Telling

Applicant: Jingzhou, Hubei Province

Shanshu, by its name, refers to the story-telling of persuade people to do good things. It involves verse and prose, combining singing and talking. It formed during the reign of Qing Emperor Qianlong and has a history of more than 260 years. It used to prevail in Hubei Province, Kaifeng in Henan Province, Leshan in Sichuan Province and the most parts of Hunan Province. Now, only Shanshu artists in Hanchuan in Hubei Province keep it alive.

Shanshu is a narrative form easy to understand and accept, developing into one form of Hanchuan Quyi. Traditionally it was performed by one person, but later evolved into a three-role or a multi-role play. In this case, there are a major narrator and respondent. The first is responsible for the narrative and explanatory parts, the latter for singing parts and some of the spoken parts. The contents of Shanshu cover moral cultivation and exhort one to follow the right way and do good. The major narrator tells the story, the answerer follows him to make some explanation and play various roles.

Hanchuan Shanshu falls into two categories. One is "spot story-telling", which is in a fixed place like tea houses. There are two "spot story-telling" performances all the year round in Hanchuan city and Quezi village, Makou Town. Another is "stage story-telling". It plays from the Spring Festival to the latter half of March in the lunar calendar, on celebrations for birthdays and weddings. Most villages set up the stage and employ rural artists to play Shanshu. What's more, there is a custom that the Shanshu performance should last for three years, three times each year. Old people can recall listening to Shanshu when they were kids.

Dongshan Talking and Singing

Applicant: Dongshan County, Fujian Province

Also called "Chaozhou Songs", this originated from the Chaoshan area using Chaozhou dialect (Min dialect). Most of the narrators and the singers are women. The songbook is a kind of folk literature where, without any accompaniment, the reciter adjusts the rhythm according to the story to increase artistic appeal.

There are two kinds of Dongshan Songbook. One is based on the novels, rewritten into a literature song text. The repertoire includes the *Legend of Sui and Tang Dynasties* and *Xue Gang Revolts against Tang.* Another is rewritten from opera and legend. The repertoire includes *Cui Mingfeng* and *Chen Shimei.* The two forms have their own characteristics. The singers use mellow voices and beautiful words to create audience appeal.

Dongshan Talking and Singing was popular among women before the founding of the PRC in 1949. It was deemed a guidebook for local women. By listening to the stories, they could learn history, understand changing society, gain some common knowledge and learn ways to be good and polite. It is thought to be an honor to sing the songbook and it has been a custom to give it as a gift to brides and to sing it at their wedding ceremony. The art is an oral tradition passed down through the generations. It has a history of more than 600 years as folk oral literature. People love it for its strong local flavor and rich repertoire.

Er'renzhuan

Applicant: Liaoning Province, Jilin Province, Heilongjiang Province

(See P279)

Fengyang Huagu (Flower Drum)

Applicant: Fengyang County, Anhui Province

Fengyang Huagu (Flower Drum) was popular during the Ming and Qing dynasties. It is a folk art form combining song, dance, playing instruments and performance. Normally, the performers consist of one man and one woman. The woman holds a flat drum in her left hand and a thin bamboo stick in her right. She beats the flat drum with the long stick to follow the harmonious rhythm and cooperate with the gong beaten by the male; they sing together while walking. It is popular

Dated back to the early Ming Dynasty in Fengyang County, Anhui Province, Fengyang Flower Drum also called "Small Flower Drum Gong" and "Shuangtiao Drum" is the small drum used in the performance across China, as well as a geme of Chinese folk art.

due to being capable of being performed in the street or on the stage.

The drum prop in Fengyang Huagu is very particular. The earliest huagu was a small waist drum. By the late of the Qing Dynasty, it had been replaced by a small hand drum for convenience sake. The diameter is about 10 centimeters, and the bamboo drum stick is about 50 centimeters long. The drum is also called "Shuangtiao gu (double-stick drum)".

Fengyang Huagu has a fixed style. When playing, the performer firstly beats the huagu to attract the audience. Then the pair sing and dance; after finishing one section, they beat the drum again. The performance has long been very popular in Fengyang. The local people always perform on celebrations and hosting guests to express their happiness. The beating methods, the dance pace, the gestures and the singing also mingle with modern singing and dancing skills. In keeping the traditional strong local flavor, its forms have become more vivid and various, and the atmosphere warmer and happier.

Dazuigu (Comic Dialogue)

Applicant: Xiamen City, Fujian Province

This comic dialogue is performed in the dialect of southern Fujian province, and is popular there as well as in overseas Chinese communities in Southeast Asia. The Dazuigu is also explained as answering only by mouth which attracts the audience by humorous language. It uses lively and humorous proverbs, vulgarity and local slang and attaches importance to the unfolding of plots and roles. It often gives hints foreshadowing later developments or bombards audiences with a series of funny things for comic effect.

The characteristic of Dazuigu is a dialogue form in verse. It makes up the comic story with the vivid and vigorous dialect of Southern Fujian Province to tackle a certain topic. Normally, it attracts the audience with the humorous and funny language and the ingenious skills of using the verse. After refinement it has developed into a debating form between two performers. Once, only one performer was involved imitating two kinds of voices.

Xiaorehun (Small Gong Story-Telling)

Applicant: Hangzhou City, Zhejiang Province

Xiaorehun, a humorous and joking Quyi form, is popular in Zhejiang province, Jiangsu Province and neighboring Shanghai. It is a street singing and telling art. The art originated from the late-Qing Dynasty, starting as news announcing and sales patter.

It is simple to perform. The actor firstly opens a folding wooden frame, and then puts a box on the frame and a shining lantern on the tripod supported by three bamboo pods. A long bench is placed under the lantern. The actor stands on the bench, striking the gong to attract people to gather. Because of the actor's stance he cannot move his feet and legs, relying on his mouth to please the audience.

The performance of the "Xiaorehun" consists of singing and narration in turn. There are two accompanying methods: one uses a gong, the other Sanqiaoban. The latter means three long bamboo or wooden boards, one in the right hand, two in the left. The actor will create all kinds of rhythm with the simple boards. There are a few actors of Xiaorehun who use the three-stringed fiddle and plucked lute.

The contents of the "Xiaorehun" are short jokes and daily stories from life. Most artists make up stories based on the news and are able to extemporize.

Shandong Kuaishu

Applicant: Shandong Province

This is a typical story-telling Quyi form of reciting in verse. It is played in a strong rhythm to recite and narrate. Sing

Shandong Kuaishu (clapper ballad)

in Shandong dialect, it is very plain and powerful. Most Shandong Kuaishu lyrics are seven-character lines with humorous language and vivid scenarios, and performers use exaggerated expressions and speak in quick rhythms. The art form is especially suited to the telling of heroic stories.

The performance is very simple. The actor stands with a small percussion tool in his hands to strike the rhythm. A solo performance is called "dankou" (single mouth), two actors performing are "duikou" (pair of mouths), three actors or above are "qunkou" (group mouths). The percussion instruments are crescent-shaped bronze plates about three centimeters in size. The actor beats the rhythm with one hand, the plates being called a "mandarin duck board".

Shandong Kuaishu combines singing and telling. With the narrative story and flexible performance form, its style is vivid, simple and funny. It has deep roots in the people. The famous actors have appeared over generations, their influence extending over the country.

Wulige'er

Applicant: Zhalute Banner, Ke'erqin Youyi Mid-Banner of Inner Mongolia Autonomous Region, Fuxin Mongolia Autonomous County, Liaoning Province, Qanguo'erluosi Mongolia Autonomous County, Jilin Province

Wulige'er in Mongolian means "story telling". It is a singing and story-telling Quyi form accompanied with the four-string fiddle. Wulige'er has great adaptability and flexibility. Without any stage, props or costume, it is played only with fiddle accompaniment. The accompaniment is called "He'er" in Mongolian. The sound is simple, vigorous, deep and low full of grassland flavor. The musical instrument can be used to represent a sword, gun, horse, or sickle or whip. One actor can play many roles with quick changes.

The performance skills of the Wulige'er involving narrating, singing and actions. The skills of telling include bright rhythm, clear pronunciation and narrating in Mongolian, with some Chinese, local dialect and slang. The skills of singing demand clear enunciation and mellow tune, the light and the heavy, the low and the high, the fast and the slow. The actors use their hands, eyes, bodies, and paces to express shapes, characters and moods.

Wulige'er has short, medium and long repertoires, the latter being the most attractive. It adopts many forms such as eulogizing, satirizing, metaphor, repetition and exaggeration to express various aspects of scientific knowledge and trivia of life.

Wuqin of the Daur Ethnic Group

Applicant: Heilongjiang Province

The Wuqin of the Daur ethnic group, a Quyi form of story-telling, originated and became popular in the compact communities of Daur people in Heilongjiang Province, Inner Mongolia Autonomous Region, and Tacheng, Xinjiang Uygur Autonomous Region.

In the Qing Dynasty, Daur intellectuals wrote and recited narrative poetry in the Man language. Later, folk artists sang and spoke these pieces. Wuqin gradually evolved into an art form of intonating stories.

At first, Wuqin had no instrumental accompaniment. Then, a kind of four-stringed instrument named Huachangsi was added. The melodies became richer. Besides the former recited tune, it also adopted a narrative tune and some ditties. Wuqin has rich contents, including the saga of the hero Morigen, love and marriage, beautiful hometown, fables, fairy tales and legends. The long repertoire is sung over several days, and the short ones can be finished in a few minutes. Wuqin is traditionally performed during festivals and celebrations with the large audience seated cross-legged on the Kang (heated brick bed).

The Daur ethnic group, a nomadic tribe living on fishing, has a spoken but no written language. Therefore, the traditional "Wuqin" is a living fossil of Daur's culture.

Yimakan Story telling of the Hezhe Ethnic Group

Applicant: Heilongjiang Province

This is popular in the compact communities of the Hezhe ethnic group in Heilongjiang Province. According to existing records, it came into being around the late-Qing Dynasty.

The Hezhe ethnic group created many literature styles with salient ethnic features while fishing. Among them, Yimakan story-telling is very popular and much favored by the people. Yimakan is a literature form of telling and singing. It includes ancient hero stories, wars between tribes, and the fishing life of the common people and some improvisation about the modern life of the ethnic group. It not only retains and preserves the ethnic language, coupled with the reflection of their customs and religion, but also records the history of the Hezhen, filling a gap as the group has no written historical documents. It is a living fossil of the ancient history, fishing life, customs and religion.

According to repertoire and performance style, Yimakan is divided into Big Song, and Small Song. The former focuses on talking about heroic and legendary stories such as Morigen (ethnic hero) and the beginning of the world. Small Song focuses on singing short lyric stories.

The Yimakan is a combination form of verse and essay. Telling dominates the performance, supported by singing. The spoken parts must be true, funny, breathtaking and exquisite. The performer can play male and female roles, and the characters of polite letters and martial arts. One actor can perform the whole the play. The Yimakan can be performed anywhere, so Hezhen people do so when hunting in the mountains, fishing in the rivers, and during festivals and celebrations.

Mosukun of the Oroqen Ethnic Group

Applicant: Heilongjiang Province

This is a folk art form of story-telling originating during the late-Qing dynasty and prevalent in the Greater and Lesser Hinggan Mountains where the Oroqen live in Heilongjiang Province. "Mosukun" means "story-telling and singing" in the Oroqen language.

The main characteristic is the exquisite combination of language and musical rhythm, which is to sing one episode, then narrate one episode; this includes long stories, short stories or an episode from the former. The actor sings in good voice and with feeling to move the audience. The tune will change with the contents. Feeling is expressed sometimes high, boorish, straight, sometimes fluent, and sometimes like crying or telling, sometimes reciting or talking, sometimes happy and warm. The performance is not limited by time and the place. The language of the Mosukun is a natural and simple one and the words are full of art, vigor and strong feeling and musical beauty.

The singing and telling art of the Mosukun retains the primitive, simple, and pure style with the strong narration and rich expressiveness. It has a fixed tune but varying tempo. When singing, two tunes are used alternately. In the process, mostly diastole and tremolo are used, as well as some empty words including "nayiye", "xinaye" and "kuyakuyaruo". The rhythm is high, straight, strong and harmonious. The text of the Hero totals 1,900 lines, amounting to more than 100,000 words. It is a rare huge epic in Chinese literature.

Zhangha of the Dai Ethnic Group

Applicant: Xishuangbanna Dai Ethnic Group Autonomous Prefecture of Yunnan Province

Zhangha in Chinese means "can sing" or "people who can sing". Therefore, people in Xishuangbanna call Dai singers "Zhangha". Zhangha of the Dai ethnic group is a kind of Quyi singing art, with Zhangha used to refer to singers and also the performing art.

In Xishuangbanna, people of the Dai ethnic group will invite Zhangha to sing things related to labor, life and love as well as blessings.

Zhangha evolved from the ancient songs. It is performed in the form of solar and antiphon which includes competition. There are two forms of musical accompaniment: one is the use of two-stringed musical instrument caller erhu, which is adopted to accompany mountain and love songs for the young to express what is in their mind; the other is the use of bamboo fluet which is adopted to accompany improvised singing such as blessing songs, prayer songs and story-telling-like songs.

Aites of Kazak Ethnic Group

Applicant: Ili Kazak Autonomous Prefecture, Xinjiang Uygur Autonomous Region

Aites is the symbolic representative of Kazak Quyi music. It is a form of contest in antiphonal singing, and a competition of wisdom, bravery and intelligence of the two parties. Each side creates improvisational songs and words. The traditional programs of Aites mainly reflect the history, culture and feelings of the Kazak ethnic group. The lyrics and tones are full of the strong flavor of the Kazak oral literature and musical culture.

As an antiphonal singing form of competition, there are no specific lyrics or formulaic tones. Normally, one singer sings the question and the other contestant sings the answers. This shows the creative ability of the Kazak people, who are famous for poem and song. The singer plays the dembera or "库布孜"himself without any specific tunes. Singers select some tunes from Kazak folk songs them and play them repeatedly. The Aites is divided into "traditional antiphonal singing" and "Aken antiphonal singing". The latter is normative. The eloquent and knowledgeable is respected by the public and titled "Aken".

The Aites is a very complicated and advanced comprehensive art, which combines various art skills. It requires singers have the ability of improvisation, eloquence and performance skills and musical gift. Since the singing takes place in the form of contest, the singers should be aggressive in order to compete. The song is a flea in the opposite side's ear, but of mutual understanding. The winner will not be arrogant, whereas the loser will not be dispirited. The performances must be held in public places with large audiences. They normally take place with singers from different regions and tribes.

Bayin Singing of the Buyei Ethnic Group

Applicant: Xingyi City, Guizhou Province

Baying singing (eight-sound songs) is a folk Quyi of the Buyei ethnic group passed down from generation to generation. It is also called "Bayin sitting-singing". The performance team consists of eight to 14 people. Each of them play Sheng (male leading role), Dan (female leading role), Jing (character with painted facial make-up), Chou (clown) without makeup. It got its name from the instruments played in the performance: Niutuigu (bones of cow leg), Zutong qin (bamboo tube), Zhixiao (vertical bamboo flute), Yueqin, three-stringed fiddle, Mangluo (gong), gourd and short flute.

The pronunciation of the "Bayin" is "Wanchdi" in the language of Buyei, which means blow, play and sing. In performance, the eight people play and sing in turn. The actor starts to sing and tell the story in the first person, and then explains it in third person. Sometimes the Lelang, Leyou and Muye (the special musical instruments of the Buyei ethnic group) will be added. The male actor usually sings in a high pitch, whereas the woman actor sings in the original tone. This style will create a strong and great contrast in pitch and tone color, adding spice to the performance. The actor sings in the language of the Buyei ethnic group and speaks in Chinese with a small and normal voice. The staff of the instruments team plays different roles. They can play the instrument, and can sing while playing the instrument.

It has two forms: singing with some seats and singing with some opera plots. The rhythm of "Bayin sitting-singing" is a simple, flowing melody. It is performed at festivals and celebrations, weddings and funerals, house-building and birthdays. The contents come from folk oral literature, folk music and telling and singing art. It shows that the Buyei people love life, long for a bump crop, seeking for love, and castigate for the evil.

Aites of Kazak

Wuqiao acrobatics has a long history of more than 2,000 years. One local folk rhyme explains it all: " all the people including the 99-year-old senior ones and the toddlers are good at acrobatics ".

Wuqiao Acrobatic

Applicant: Wuqiao County, Hebei Province

Wuqiao acrobatics has a long history and took shape in the Southern & Northern Dynasties (420-589). It gained a good reputation and prospered after the Yuan Dynasty (1206-1368).

The Wuqiao Acrobatics developed from simple forms into a consummate performing art. In its' early days, Wuqiao Acrobatics consisted of somersaults, juggling and simple martial arts. Later, flying forks, knife playing,plate-spinning,ground hoops, a cloud performance and simple magic was introduced. Some acrobats often performed at home and abroad, so they brought spring-boards and their tamed tigers and bears back to the acrobatic circle. Finally, acrobatics made further progress with an Acrobatic Troupe and director appearing, increasing the quality and enriching the content of the performance.

Wuqiao people are all fond of acrobatics. No matter if they are in the streets or on the field, the dinner table or even the "adobe kang", they can perform somersaults, box, make a human pyramid, and do magic tricks at any time.

Through over two thousand years of changes, the culture of Wuqiao Acrobatics has constantly been developing. Wuqiao Acrobatics has unique rules for its' performance, stage property organization, management and inheritance. The industrial and cultural systems have been integrated and combined. According to statistics, traditional programs have seven main categories, with 486 repertoires; mainly including body skill, prop skill, disguise, animal taming, horsemanship, traditional magic, and buffoonery.

Now the acrobatic troupes from 18 nations of the world all have acrobats from Wuqiao. At present, there are 29 acrobatic troupes in Wuqiao County. The Government of Hebei Province started to host the China Wuqiao International Acrobatics Festival in 1987.

Acrobatics and Sports

Liaocheng Acrobatics

Applicant: Liaocheng City, Shandong Province

Liaocheng is one of the candles of Chinese acrobatics, as well as the hometown of Chinese acrobatics.

Liaocheng acrobatic performances experienced primitive development in the Spring and Autumn and Warring States periods and matured in the Han Dynasty. Acrobatics and circus performances were prevalent in the area of Dong'e in Liaocheng in the Three Kingdoms (220-280), and became a performance based on acrobatics and other arts.

Liaocheng is a city of acrobatics with a long history. which produced more acrobats.

It created an acrobatic cultural system with some characteristics of Qilu.

Liaocheng acrobatics fall into three main categories determined by content: circus, magic and performance. It mainly relies on the skill of your waist and leg, and can be characterized as new, difficult, astonishing, beautiful, dangerous, simple, gallant, and rough. It is known as " heroes of Qilu " and attracts broad citizen participation.

Tianqiao Banner Stunts

Applicant: Beijing City

Banner Stunts are a traditional favorite game in Beijing. Playing Banners Stunt is one of the popular performances in each Beijing temple fair of the Spring Festival. Banner Stunts consist of a pole, umbrella and flag. It is about 10 meters long, more than 60 jin in weight, and has three flags, three umbrellas and a color banner about 5 meters long hanging from it. Banners Stunts are a kind of unique and exciting square art, with banner waving, bell ringing and breathless movement.

Banners are similar to flags with difference sizes. Banner Stunts refers to an over 10 meter pole on which hangs a narrow banner about 0.5 meters wide and 5.5 meters long. On the face of the banner are embroidered words and auspicious designs and blessings. On the back of banner are embroidered the name of the performing team. So it is also called "mark flag". Banner Stunts weighs over 15 kg.

Banner Stunts will train a person in courage, force and skill and needs both intellectual and martial talent. The skill of Chinese tumbling and Qigong is also at the base of practicing Banner Stunts. Banner Stunts are divided into single practice, double practice and team practice which includes more than 50 actions. In the performance, the performer holds the banners on their head or shoulder , with the banners always close to the body and the pole never falling onto the ground. Banners about ten meters high and weight begin waving from the hands, shoulder, head, chin, and back, at the same time that bells are ringing.

Now, Tianqiao Banner Stunts have developed challenging techniques and a wonderful program, including a seven series program, about one hundred routines on the head, shoulder, elbows, hands, knees, and feet.

Diabolo Spinning

Applicant: Beijing

A child is playing diabolo in the forest.

Diabolo Spinning is an interesting Han folk game. It has developed from a court game to a sport, as well as becoming a traditional acrobatics program. Diabolo is made from bamboo and is hollow inside. A Diabolo is simple, small and easy to get. Diabolo Spinning is a representative program to practice the high-level skill of Chinese traditional acrobatics. On holidays, people in the south of china, especially children, like to spin the diabolo, and create interesting poses.

The Diabolo falls into either a single or dual wheel: the single wheel has one wood axis wheel, and the dual wheel has a wood axis on both sides. The wheel is made by glueing several pieces of bamboo together; its edge having several holes that can produce sound. The player's hands will catch two sticks about two feet long, tied together with a cotton string about five feet long . The string reel has one or two circuits on each axis, the players lift one hand and lower their other, constantly shaking the sticks, which creates the wheels to rapidly revolve, and produce a rolling sound.

The Diabolo is first tied to a string attached to two small sticks at the end. The sticks are held up by the Diabolo spinners, as the string is reeled around the Diabolo axis. The Diabolo is rolled again and again as the sticks are manipulated, making the string vibrate. In this way, the Diabolo spins as it is

13 Culture

manipulated from side to side;

When the Diabolo spins fast enough, it produces a humming sound.

Although spinning the Diabolo looks simple, it takes every muscle in the body to manipulate them. One Diabolo generally weighs about 0.2 to 0.3 kg, however, some weigh over 1 kg.

One, playing diabolo, can freely control the exercise depending on his/her physical ability. You don't need any land or much money to spin the Diabolo, and it is suitable for everybody to participate. Spinning the Diabolo is rich and colorful, and includes single spinning or double spinning, which has more people spinning and includes front and back spinning, as well as fancy spinning.

Uygur Darwaz

Applicant: Xinjiang Uygur Autonomous Region

Dawaz is an old traditional acrobatic art of the Uygur ethnic minority. Da means to hang in the air in the Uygur language, and waz means the people who are interested in doing something. Dawaz means walk on a rope in the air.

The performance of Dawaz is mostly held during the festival. Walking on a rope in the air is a breathtaking performance, combining sports and acrobatics. Before the performance, they will first insert a pole over 20 meters high into the ground, tie a rope about 60 meters long around it, like a wrist and bracelet, and on the top of the pole tie another. From the top of the pole, the big rope is taken up, forming an uneven ramp from low to high. Holding a three meters balance bar, the performer walks steadily to the top of the pole, accompanied with the drumbeat. The traditional actor walks barefoot and balances his body by making contact between his feet and the rope.

During this performance, there are sometimes various actions, such as walking sideways, walking backwards, faking a fall and saddling the rope. In the old days, only men are engaged in this acrobatics program, now women also join in.

Ningde Huotong Xianshi (Thread-controlled Puppet Lion)

Applicant: Ningde, Fujian Province

Huotong Xianshi, a unique skill of Chinese folk art, is still preserved in the ancient town of Huotong in Ningde, east of Fujian Province.

Many people have seen "lion dances" before, but few know the secrets of the manipulations nor the expression of the puppet lion created by using threads. That is what we call Ningde Huotong Xianshi. This skill originated from the 39th year of the reign of Jia Jing Emperor in the Ming Dynasty (1368-1644). The original single lion dance has been developed into three lions' dances nowadays. By pulling the threads connecting the head, tail and cheeks of the puppet lion, the puppeteer can manipulate the lion to perform lively actions such as sitting down, getting up, squatting, crawling, shaking its head, etc. It is more amazing that the puppet lion can have a ball in its mouth and spit it out afterwards. Accompanied by constellation of lights, a gorgeous background and music performed by percussion instruments, the Xianshi dance presents a stunning performance to the audience.

The key aspect of the Xianshi performance is threading the puppet lion, which requires carefulness and patience. The ball in the lion's mouth looks small and exquisite. Within this ball, there is another tiny revolving ball, which shines in the darkness, as stars shine in the sky. The puppeteer manipulates the threads, which connect all parts of the lion as a'nervous system', and presents a lively performance to the audience.

Shaolin Kungfu

Applicant: Dengfeng, Henan Province

"Shaolin Kungfu", originated from Buddhism, has been inherited by monks. The ultimate aim of Kungfu is the deep meditation of Buddhism, which includes Buddhism doctrines, martial arts and medical science. The monks of Shaolin Temple try to reach this ultimate aim by practicing both Buddhist meditation and martial arts.

Shaolin Kungfu, focusing on the practice of movements for defence and attack, is presented in different systemized ways, which are deemed as basic units of Kungfu. One systemized way consists of a series of movements. Following the regular pattern of human exercise, the design of the movements and the way of composing them together are based on the Chinese ancient medical science of the human body. It rationally combines two opposing factors together such as movement and the static condition, the Yin and Yang (the two opposing principles in nature), hardness and softness and spirit and form. The most famous principle is "Liu He"(six forms of harmony): the harmony of hands and feet, elbows and knees, shoulders and hip, heart and thought, thought and spirit, spirit and strength.

According to the record of Chinese boxing handed down from generation to generation, there used to be 708 series of Kungfu movements. There are still over 200 series of movements presently preserved and practiced, including Erzhi Zen, Tung Chi Gong, etc.

Wudang Wushu (Martial Arts)

Applicant: Wudangshan Mountain Special Zone, Shiyan, Hubei Province

The history of Chinese Wushu (martial arts) has run a long course from a remote source and was developed into various branches. Based on different ways of practice and styles, it was mainly divided into two big branches: the Northern Branch and the Southern Branch. The Northern Branch originated from the Shaolin Temple, which is located on Songshan Mountain, the famous Holy Mountain of Buddhism. It is also well-known as the Shaolin Branch. The boxing skills developed from the Shaolin Temple are called "Wai Jia Quan" (boxing focusing on the use of external force). The Southern Branch originated from Wudangshan Mountain, the famous Holy Mountain of Taoism. It is well-known as the Wudang Branch. The boxing skill developed from the Wudang Branch is called "Nei Jia Quan"(boxing focusing on the use of internal force).

With a long history, Wudang Wushu boasts a broad scope of martial skills. Zhang Sanfeng, a Taoist priest living in the late part of the Yuan Dynasty and the early Ming Dynasty, created a unique style of martial arts and was honoured as the founder of Wudang Wushu. Zhang Sanfeng cleverly combined the essence of *Yi Jing* (*The Book of Changes*) and the *Dao De Jing* (*The Moral*) with Wushu and created Wudang Wushu, which presents the important aspects of body-building in the forms of Tai Chi (shadow boxing), Xing Yi Quan (boxing strictly following spirit) and Bagua Zhang (boxing with eight trigrams). Thanks to the constant development and innovation from generation to generation, Wudang Wushu has become one of the most famous branches of

Wudang Kungfu

Chinese martial arts. Shaolin Wushu is the most famous in the north as Wudang Wushu enjoys the highest reputation in the south. Wudang Quan (boxing), also named Nei Jia Quan (boxing focusing on the use of internal force), aims to preserve health and protect oneself. It does not only boast the features of skillfully deflecting the attacker and gaining mastery by striking after the enemy has struck, but also is said to extend one's years. Nowadays, Wudang Wushu has been spread to many countries in the world. More and more people have benefited from this sports activity.

Wudang Wushu consists of Tai Chi (shadow-boxing), Xing Yi Quan (boxing strictly following the spirit), Bagua Zhang （boxing with eight trigrams）, Wudang Qigong (breathing exercises) and Wudang Swordsmanship, etc. Owing to its unique style, Wudang Wushu became one of the main branches of Chinese martial arts.

Deeply affected by Taoism, Wudang Wushu took the principle of Yin and Yang (the two opposing principles in nature) and Ba Gua (eight trigrams) as the core of its theories. From which, the skill of coupling hardness with softness and defeating hardness with softness was enhanced.

Hui (Ethnic Group) Heavy Sword Wushu

Applicant: Tianjin

Heavy Sword" was the original name of "Big Sword". With a history of thousands of years in China, it is a traditional weapon used by people in Beijing and Tianjin.

Tianjin Hui Big Swordsmanship, formerly named "Cao's Swordsmanship", was handed down by Mr. Cao Jinzao, the late chivalrous Wushu master in Tianjin. It was improved by his son, Mr. Cao Keming, and has become a set of complete and unique heavy sword skills. The swordsmanship was inherited within the family for over-hundred years. Now it has been handed down to the fifth generation.

Combining harmoniously with Chang Quan (Northern boxing), Zhuang Gong (stake skills), San Shou (confrontational boxing), Xi Yang Quan (western style boxing), Mi Zong Yi (Tantric skills), and Shi Shou Quan (ten movements of hands) and handed down from former generations, the inheritor of Cao's Swordsmanship created "seventy-two forms of boxing", which combines southern boxing, northern leg skills and wrestling together. The movements with the most distinguishing characteristics are "cow wagging its tail", "dragon jumps out of the deep pond" and the "ghost's push".

"Cao's Swordsmanship" absorbed techniques tested during the historical martial exams, such as arrow shooting, horsemanship, etc. Through the difficult practice of wielding stone blocks, the performers integrate all skills with the performance of a heavy sword.

"Cao's Swordsmanship" boasts the feature of combining toughness and softness, movement and gesture, strength and techniques together. The heavy swords are usually played swiftly and quietly. The techniques are skillful and breathtaking.

The sword performed by the Tianjin Hui Ethnic Group Performing Team weighs 80kg at maximum. It is also the heirloom of the Cao's family.

Cangzhou Wushu

Applicant: Cangzhou, Hebei Province

Cangzhou, known as the "South Gate" of Beijing and Tianjin, located in the southeast of Hebei Province, neighbouring on the Bohai Sea in the east and Beijing and Tianjin in the north. In Chinese history, Cangzhou is not only a strategic point, a place businessmen frequently visited, but also an exile destination for prisoners. The local people practiced martial arts for the sake of survival, hence, Wushu became more and more popular. During the reign of Emperor Qianlong of the Qing Dynasty (1736-1795), Cangzhou had become a town of importance in Wushu in north China.

The boxing of Cangzhou was split into various schools, each with unique features. The number of schools of boxing originating or popularly practiced in Cangzhou has reached 52, accounting for 40 percent of the total number of schools of boxing in China. Featuring bravery and unique skills, Cangzhou Wushu attaches importance to the need of actual combat.

Ba Ji Boxing, known as Kai Men (Opening the Door) Ba Ji Boxing in full, is one of the four most famous boxing skills in China. Ba Ji can be divided into Yin and Yang. Ji means that exquisite changes in the boxing may affect movements a while later. Ba Ji Boxing is practiced with strength and fierceness at the beginning, treacherous movements during the course and a quick attack at the end to win the victory. Ba Ji Boxing has been passed down for 11 generations.

Pi Guai Boxing, with sudden movements, looks like a revolving wheel when it is performed. It attaches much importance to speed and strength, so the style of the boxing represents valour and swiftness.

Yanqing Boxing boasts a rich content and comprehensive skills. Its elegant style and proper speed can easily be practised by people at any ages. Yanqing Boxing can benefit people both by keeping your body fit and offering protection. The features are moderate postures accompanied with movements of legs and fists. The combination of true movements and false ones always confuse the enemy.

Tai Chi Boxing

Applicant：Hebei Province and Henan Province

Being one branch of Chinese boxing, Tai Chi Boxing is a series of whole body movements combining three exercises: exercise of body, spirit and breath. The key aspect is to use spirit to instruct movements. The graceful movements are gentle but firm.

Although various styles of Tai Chi Boxing differ in method, gesture and way of breath, all the styles are with slow and connected movements. They also boast similar functions such as limbering up the muscles and joints, harmonizing energy through blood circulation, building up viscera and improving one's health.

There are changes all the time in the world. No matter if natural creatures such as trees and flowers, or things that human beings have created, such as buildings, everything, which looks static, is actually turning old. It is said that only changes are unchangeable. Tai Chi Boxing presents all the changes through different boxing styles. The combinations of moving and static status, gentleness and firmness, quickness and slowness, etc are all in the control of the mind. That is so-called Tai Chi Boxing.

The practice of Tai Chi Boxing requires people to stand still, draw in their jaws, straighten their back and relax their shoulders. Meanwhile, Tai Chi Boxing attaches importance to the exercise of "Qi". The so-called "Qi" is one's spirit. This explains one of the characteristics of Tai Chi as a kind of Kungfu using internal strengthen.

Xingtai Mei Hua Quan

Applicant: Xingtai City, Hebei Province

Mei Hua Quan（Plum Flower Fist Boxing）, also known as the Meihua Pile Boxing or Mei Quan in short, is a style of Kungfu. The Meihua Pile Boxing originated in the late Ming Dynasty, and initially was passed down from one generation to another , not spreading to the outside world until the Qianlong reign of the Qing Dynasty. Guangzong County, known as "Mei Hua Quan town", is currently the home of nearly 10,000 Mei Hua Quan fans.

The pile training methods in Mei Hua Quan are basic, simple and strong yet relaxed and highly adaptable. Originally Meihua was practiced on stumps or platforms. In a square, there would be about one hundred piles, with the lowest ones reaching 1.1 meters. The more complex and difficult the movements would be, the higher the stumps or piles would be. This form of boxing is characterized by five static positions, intermixed with dynamic motions using light rapid footwork and large flowing movements, which are better exercised by more than two people. The simple expansive stature and poise used in Mei Hua Quan releases and strengthens the flow of energy in order to expand and free the mind. The flexible boxing routines and changeable attacking strategy makes it one of the best models of Chinese Kungfu.

Tengpai Battle Array of Shahe

Applicant: Shahe City, Hebei Province

Tengpai Battle Array is an actual combat art of attack and defense used on ancient battlefields in North China. This training has been handed down for several hundred years. It is now only preserved in Shilipu Village, Shahe City, Hebei Province.

The play begins with a rousing symphony commanded by a war drum and accompanied by gongs, cymbals, and small cymbals. The performers are divided into two teams—attack and defense, each with at least four players. The two teams, equipped with forked weapons, broadswords, pikes and crabsticks, fight with each other fiercely. Tengpai soldiers hold a Tengpai in their left hand, and bailiffs in their right hand. During the actual combat, the team formation changes from time to time, sometimes with thousands of people involved in one combat.

Tengpai are made from ordinary tree twigs collected in the Taihang Mountains. The twigs, after being soaked in water for a long time, become tough and taught, and can be used to bind the Tengpai with a tiger painted canvas or cattle hide at the top.

Over the past hundreds of years, the locals have used the practice of the Tengpai Battle Array both as a defense and for entertainment. The ancient and modern dance movements are shown in the performance, which are smooth and beautiful, enjoying high artistic value.

Korean See-Saw and Swinging

Applicant: Yanbian Korean Autonomous Prefecture, Jilin Province

The See-saw Jump is a traditional sport of the Korean ethnic group in Jilin, Heilongjiang and Liaoning provinces. It usually is held during the Lantern Festival, Dragon Boat Festival and Mid-Autumn Festival. See-saw jumping contests are popular among the women of the Korean ethnic group and are usually played by two or four people standing at each side of a five meter long springboard. The board is mounted upon a pivot like a see-saw and two people stand at either end.

Korean girls are riding on a swing.

There are two types, the "threading-out" and the "performance". The "threading-out" refers to two balls of thread that are placed at the sides of the springboard, each linked to the foot of one player. Within a measured amount of time, the winner is the person whom pulls the longer and higher thread out. The "performance" movements are formal exercises where winning depends primarily on the difficulty and posture of the movements. While in the air, the players will either remain in an upright position or perform spins, back flips or other feats of dexterity and courage. With each rebound, the contestants reach higher and higher into the air – a feat that requires perfect timing, skill and courage. Sometimes the players sing while playing.

The Korean people, especially women are particularly expert at swinging. The participants perform acrobatics and exercises of strength and dexterity while using ropes, often quite high above the ground. The thick ropes are tied on horizontal branches of large trees. There are several ways to win the contest: on a high swing, the winner should touch the hanging leaves or flowers of a tree with their foot or teeth; measuring the height with a rope linked to the board; or hanging a ring in front of the swing so the judges can determine which players have touched it most frequently.

Daur Field Hockey

Applicant: Morin Dawa Autonomous Banner, Inner Mongolia Autonomous Region

Field hockey is a traditional sport, the Daur people having a long history of playing it. The stick the Daur people used to play the game was mostly made of oak from local mountains, and hooked at the flat and long bottom, the same as an ice hockey stick. Daur's hockey team has been awarded many times in domestic and international competitions. The Daur inhabited area is the birthplace of modern hockey.

The ball in traditional hockey is made of apricot root, felt or something that can be fired and is as big as a baseball. The original game is almost the same as the modern one. Both sides have 11 members, one of them is the gate keeper, and two are back defenders. If either side hits more balls to the other's gate, they win. A referee will determine the score. On a beautiful spring night, young people would often play the game with a fireball on a spacious playground, which often attracted lots of viewers.

On each festival or happy occasion the Daur people will hold a traditional hockey game with the clan (Mokun) or village as a unit. It is mostly held on a flat grassland or an open place in the village; the size of place has no unified regulations.

Mongolian Wrestling

Applicant: Inner Mongolia Autonomous Region

Boke is the Mongolian word for wrestling. It is one of Mongolia's age-old sports.

The Mongolian way of wrestling is distinguished from other techniques by its rules, methods, uniforms and fields. There is neither a separation of grade (no age or weight distinction) nor a fixed number—as long as the match has an even numbers of participants such as two, four, six, eight, sixteen, thirty-two, sixty-four or one hundred and twenty-eight. All the wrestlers are matched by drawing straws. The judges enjoy high prestige and command universal respect. The game is single-elimination; if a player loses once, he's out. The loser is not allowed to compete again. Half of the people are eliminated with each round.

The wrestlers have distinctive clothing. Wearing loose white trousers underneath their clothes, the wrestler wears embroidered clothes with a variety of animal and flower motifs and a leather-jacket covered with silver or copper nails on the surface. On the back, there is a circle mirror or an "auspicious" shaped Chinese word in the middle. He also wears a three colored (red, blue and yellow) apron and boots. A famous wrestler would wear a colored cloth bracelet - Jiang Ga, which is a symbol of winning during a certain level competition.

The venue is simple, as long as there is a lawn or soft ground, with the audience sitting around, wrestlers can be in the middle to play the game. Before the game, both sides are singing songs, challenging each other with a teasing momentum. After they sing three times, the two wrestlers jump out and do the dance. They then pay tribute to the audience with a mutual salute. Enveloping the other wrestler, fighting with sumo wrestling techniques, a wrestler will circle the group, and begin the Tuixi phase. This phase of the Mongolian-style wrestling uses broad-kicks, tripping, tieing, picking up the other person, and hooking them, and so on with more than 300 actions.

Painting of Emperor Taizu of Song Dynasty Playing the Cuju by Qian Xuan of the Yuan Dynasty

Cuju

Applicant: Zibo City, Shandong Province

In Chinese, cu means "kicking the ball with feet" and ju means "a stuffed ball made of hide." Cuju is the forerunner of today's football and was first used in the game of the same name played in China over 2,300 years ago.

Cuju is believed to have originated in China before the Warring States Period (475-221BC). According to historical records, cuju was a very specializational game in the Western Han Dynasty (206 BC-25 AD). The game of cuju was played on enclosed fields and supervised by judges following prescribed rules. There were 12 players on each side. The winner is judged by the numbers of balls kicked into the other side of the goal. Because of its attacking elements, it was most used in military training.

Methods of playing cuju underwent great changes in the Tang Dynasty (618-907). The level of skill was improved and there were not only large-scale activities, with hundreds of people in the palace playing together, but also small ones, such as within one family. During the Song Dynasty (960-1279), the gate or goal was introduced, encouraging the performance of individual skill.

Up to the Qing Dynasty(1616-1911), the Manchu people combined skating with Cuju, which formed an "Ice Cuju" exercise. After the middle of the Qing Dynasty, with the introduction of Western modern football, the traditional Chinese Cuju was replaced by modern football. In early 2004, FIFA acknowledged China as the birthplace of football and cuju as the true origin of the sport.

Folk Fine Arts

Yangliuqing New Year Woodblock Prints

Applicant: Tianjin City

Yangliuqing New Year Woodblock prints are famous folk New Year Woodblock prints in China. Starting from the early 17th Century, the name derives from Yangliuqing Town, Tianjin, where they were first produced. The art inherited the painting traditions of the Song and Yuan dynasties, absorbed the forms of woodblock prints, industrial fine arts, and drama stage in the Ming Dynasty, and adopted the combination of woodblock overprinting and handicraft painting to create a distinctive style, lively, happy, and lucky with touching themes.

The production of Yangliuqing New Year Woodblock prints is a mix of printing and painting. Artists engrave the lines on a woodblock, print ink on paper, overprint it with single-color blocks two or three times, and paint it with colors. Yangliuqing New Year Woodblock prints have both the charm of knife cutting possessed by woodblock prints and the touch and colors of pen painting, forming an artistic characteristic different from common paintings and other New Year works.

Yangliuqing woodblock New Year Paintings

What is unique is that the artists stand and paint on a door plank to create the works. A row of door planks that can be opened or closed freely are set up in a studio that people call a "painting door." Xuan paper printed with outlines is pasted on it, and a painter stands before the painting door to work carefully.

Maids, babies and fairy tales are frequent themes. The adopted methods include implied meaning and realism. The design is artful and particular; the lines are fluent and clear and full of strong living flavor. For example, in the New Year print Lian Nian You Yu the infant has a typical baby face but a Buddha's body and adopts a posture like wushu action. He holds a cyprinoid in the arms and a lotus flower in the hand. The partial tones of the Chinese words of the objects mean affluent life. It has become a classical work of New Year paintings.

Wuqiang New Year Woodblock Prints

Applicant: Wuqiang County, Hebei Province

Wuqiang is famous for producing New Year paintings. Wuqiang New Year woodblock prints originated from the Song and Yuan dynasties and reached their peak in the second half of the 17th Century and again in the early 19th Century. The prints, involving various brands, have a well-rounded structure, rough lines, brilliant colors, exaggerated decorations and strong features of festivals. It is outstanding genre among folk New Year woodblock prints.

Woodblock printing is one of the four great inventions of ancient China. Inheriting all the traditions of the craft, those of Wuqiang style aim for exaggeration, transformation and bold choices, attach importance to major parts, have distinctive colors and strong contrasts. Each painting has a major color and strong rural flavors. In the early days, when the art was called "raw pen painting", the fact they were entirely hand-made meant production was small and the price high. With the development of woodblock printing, it was both printed and painted, and finally came to be overprinted. There are three procedures: painting, carving and printing.

In the production of Wuqiang New Year woodblock prints, people carve the picture on wood block at first, apply colors, print it on paper, spot-dyeing various colors, so that it is also called woodblock water-printing New Year painting. In terms of woodblock technique, they have relief carving as the main form with some intaglio. The contrast between black and white is adopted to play up the effect of wood carving and charm of cutting. In terms of coloring, bright red and green dominate. The colors are strong and distinctive.

There are dozens of varieties such as door painting, window painting, kang painting, set of scrolls, lantern paintings and calendar paintings. They are also in various forms such as single piece, pairs and several linked pieces.

Taohuawu New Year Woodblock Prints

Applicant: Suzhou City, Jiangsu Province

Taohuawu New Year woodblock prints are folk woodblock paintings with the largest popular coverage area and greatest influence in southern China. Its name derived from Taohuawu in Suzhou, and it has a history of more than 400 years.

Taohuawu New Year woodblock prints are characterized by the fact that they are engraved on wood blocks and printed by traditional water-printing with single color on single block. The structure is well-rounded and colors are bright with a strong sense of decoration. The pictures have clear demarcation between remoteness and nearby objects and clear arrangement of levels. The themes include folk stories, lucky and happy events, god figures, dramatic stories and current affairs. Symbolization, implied meaning and exaggeration are adopted to express people's good wishes. They are popular south of the lower reaches of the Yangtze River and many places in China, and have even spread far to Japan, the UK and Germany.

Taohuawu New Year woodblock prints often adopt decorative exaggerations. The lines are concise and vigorous. Blocks of bright red, peach red, yellow, green, purple (or blue as an alternative), and light ink comprise the basic colors, making the pictures more brilliant, bright and joyful and creating a sense of beauty in decoration and rhythm.

In terms of the extant works, in early times, Taohuawu New Year woodblock prints were elegant, and when treating such themes as maids, scenes and flowers, people often adopted traditional composition forms of standing scroll and volume pages. In terms of management of pictures, one can find influences from academic painting of the Song Dynasty and Jiehua (drawing lines with the aid of ruler in portraying palatial buildings) and literati paintings in the Ming Dynasty. During the 18th Century, there appeared many works imitating the styles of Western copper-plate carving, and such works often adopted focus-perspective and reflected cloth veins, stones, trees, houses and feathers of animals by shades of brightness and darkness.

The contents mainly cover dramatic stories, classical novels and local living customs, such as Wusong Killed a Tiger, White Snake, The Romance of the West Chamber, Picture of Three Beauties, Picture of a Hundred Babies, Wannian Bridge in Gusu, Picture of Chang Men in Suzhou, Picture of Flowers, Picture of Farming and Weaving, Great Celebration on Year of Harvest, Picture of Worshipping Moon, Picture of Playing with Snow, Picture of Chinese Character Shou (Longevity), etc.

Zhangzhou New Year Woodblock Prints

Applicant: Zhangzhou City, Fujian Province

Zhangzhou woodblock New Year Painting

These are mainly popular in Xiangcheng District of Zhangzhou and Minnan (southern Fujian) and Lingnan (south of the Five Ridges in Guangdong and Guangxi), and are also sold to Taiwan, Hong Kong and parts of Southeast Asia. Zhangzhou New Year woodblock prints started from the Song Dynasty and reached the peak during the Ming and Qing dynasties. Various folk activities are the basis for the survival and development of the genre, mainly involving the contents of happiness in welcoming the New Year and warding off evils.

Zhangzhou New Year woodblock prints have a natural structure and exaggerated shapes. They are rough and concise like northern New Year paintings and yet fine and exquisite like southern New Year paintings. They are simple and unvarnished with strong rural charms that convey strong local features. Bright red and green are preferred in coloring with distinctive contrast and strong decorative effect. It is worth mentioning the black-based New Year prints among Zhangzhou New Year woodblock prints, which can be viewed as unique among New Year paintings. Bright red, vermilion, the natural color of paper and black all serve as base colors.

Zhangzhou New Year woodblock prints have special characteristics in artistic skills and craft. The lines on the blocks differ greatly between fat and thin and strong and weak mutually assisting each other. Vigorous black lines are the major type.

Yangjiabu New Year Woodblock Prints

Applicant: Weifang City, Shandong Province

These first appeared in the Ming Dynasty. They are made by hand and in traditional ways. In early development, it was influenced by Yangliuqing New Year woodblock prints, eventually reaching its peak in the Qing Dynasty. In Yangjiabu, there was a flourishing scene of "a hundred painting stores, more than a thousand painting varieties, and more than ten thousand painting blocks", and the products spread across the whole of China.

Yangjiabu New Year woodblock prints have a complete, well-rounded and shapely structure, exaggerated, fat and simple shapes, concise, vigorous and fluent lines, brilliant and vehement colors, and strong contrasts. They are full of decorative qualities and strong life flavors and fully reflect the characters of Chinese northern farmers, being straightforward, bold, unrestrained, forthright, hardworking, humorous, and clearly demarcating love and hate.

The genre attaches importance to the application of colors. Two groups of contrasting colors, i.e. red and green, and yellow and purple, are mainly used to form brilliant and decorative pictures and reflect people's thoughts, wishes, customs and religious beliefs. Red predominates as the happy color.

Yangjiabu New Year woodblock prints have abundant contents such as god figures, door-gods, beauties, boy attendants of fairies, landscapes, flowers, birds, dramatic figures, fairy tales, and legends. There are also works reflecting daily life. But happiness and luck are the major themes.

The production is unique. Craftsmen at first paint the pictures by willow branch carbon sticks or incense ash, called "xiugao" (delineating by carbon pen). On the base of "xiugao", the formal draft and outline draft are completed and pasted on the pear wood for carving, and the blocks of outlines and coloring are carved out respectively. After the New Year paintings are printed, craftsmen apply some colors and do some simple portraying by hand, so that the New Year paintings become natural and vivid.

Gaomi New Year Rubbing-Ash Prints

Applicant: Gaomi City, Shandong Province

These are an old painting type among folk New Year paintings in China. Starting from the second half of the 15th Century, it reached its peak in the Qing Dynasty. Such New Year paintings only appear to exist in Gaomi.

In the course of production, craftsmen

use willow branch carbon sticks to delineate the draft outlines at first, rubbing it on paper to leave the ash draft, hence the name. The faces and hands are then created, followed by application of colors, painting in gold and drawing the outline. At last the key parts are coated with "bright oil" (a kind of glazing oil mixing alcohol and rosin), so that the pictures become dazzling.

Gaomi New Year Rubbing-Ash prints have bright colors, artful and natural structure, images of motion, and bold and fluent lines. Colors take the place of ink; the coloring is strong and brilliant, contrasting colors are frequently used. Demitint technique is used in the major part to harmonize the color contrast and intensify the beauty of the figures. The figures mostly have big heads and ears, but show a well-rounded prettiness with a rich happy and festival atmosphere and elegance. All the figures have one or more pure white "pinked faces"; the artists first paint a pure white face shape, artfully draw the eyes, eyebrows, and the remaining sensory organs, and apply colors and bright oil, so that the figures look elastic, transparent, and tender, and give people a strong sense of flesh. It is the unique artistic effect of New Year Rubbing-Ash prints.

Zhuxianzhen New Year Woodblock Prints

Applicant: Kaifeng City, Henan Province

Zhuxianzhen Town, 10 km south of Kaifeng City, has a history of more than 800 years in producing New Year woodblock prints. The handicraft was born in the Tang Dynasty, became popular during the Song Dynasty and reached its peak in the Ming Dynasty. It is honored as the earliest form of Chinese New Year woodblock prints.

Zhuxianzhen New Year woodblock prints have five features: first, the lines are rough and concise, forms are simple and exaggerated, and thickness alternates with thinness. Second, images are exaggerated; the heads are big while bodies are small and there are both comic effects and a symmetrical and comfortable sense. Third, the structure is well-rounded and symmetrical. Fourth, the colors are bright with strong contrasts; most figures have white faces and red eyelids, which is its particular decorative way; the figures in the New Year prints in some places have red faces as decoration, but the New Year prints of Zhuxianzhen do not decorate figures with red faces and they look natural and harmonious. Among the Chinese traditional folk crafts, people mostly make or paint tigers in yellow or red, but the tigers in the New Year prints of Zhuxianzhen are black. This creative way of not sticking to tradition has won recognition and appraisal from foreign and

One of the special stamps issued by China Post with the Zhuxianzhen woodblock New Year Paintings as content.

domestic fine arts fields. Fifth, there are various door-gods with solemn and elegant bearing. Door-gods are the most frequent subject in Zhuxianzhen New Year woodblock prints.

The prints pay much attention to the coloring. Minerals and plants are used as materials. They are base into dyestuff with pure color. The New Year prints using the dyestuff are bright and vivid and will not fade. Zhuxianzhen New Year prints attach importance to appreciation of the customs of the Chinese. The three primitive colors of blue, yellow and red are mostly used.

Zhuxianzhen New Year prints combine woodblock and hollowed-out block techniques and are printed in colors by water-printing.

Tantou New Year Woodblock Prints

Applicant: Longhui County, Hunan Province

Tantou New Year woodblock prints are the only handicraft New Year woodblock water-printing pictures in Hunan Province, forming a school with strong local characteristics of the southern Chu state. Tantou Town, situated in the southeast of Longhui County, has customs of primitive simplicity and uniqueness. In history, there appeared a paper-making village, engraving village, paper lane and New Year Pictures Street. The handicraft is developed with clear division of work and complementariness.

Over the centuries, Tantou New Year pictures gradually formed their own particular fine arts features: brilliant and moist colors, simple, unvarnished, exaggerated, well-rounded and individual shapes, pure local materials and unique arts, which give the works the artistic effect of relief. Tantou New Year pictures go through more than 20 production procedures from selection of papermaking materials, papermaking, brushing base, engraving block, seven printings and seven paintings by hand. All the procedures from manual papermaking to finished work are done in Tantou and there is a perfect production link, which is rarely seen in the production of New Year pictures across China.

The traditional Tantou New Year woodblock prints have more than 40 varieties classified into three major types of door-gods, luck and dramatic stories. Among the techniques of making the prints, steaming paper, supporting glue and brushing powder are unique in Tantou, and "opening face" is also a particular skill different from other New Year prints. In making the blocks, the main difficulty is to engrave the line block. In this aspect, the technique of "steep knife and standing line" of the Gaofuchang New Year prints workshop is well known. The angle of wielding knife is uniform, the hidden energy is even, the turns and crosses are stable and not disorderly, and all depend on sense and skill.

Foshan New Year Woodblock Prints

Applicant: Foshan City, Guangdong Province

These include door pictures (door-gods), New Year pictures, and god pictures. With strong local flavor and pure and distinctive artistic styles, these prints have become necessary articles on Spring Festival for every family in the Zhujiang Delta. They have some influence in Southeast Asia and other Chinese communities around the world.

Foshan New Year woodblock prints absorbed the elite art of many traditional crafts such as Foshan paper-cuts, copper-chiseled golden flower and wood-carving with gold lacquering, and are overprinted by four color blocks of red, green, yellow and black. They are represented by realistic painting and use of gold powder, so that the pictures are more magnificent, brilliant and vivid. The images are exquisite and well-rounded, the lines are rough and vigorous, and the red color is vehement, bright and symbolizing luck, so Foshan New Year woodblock prints are recognized as "red for ten thousand years."

The prints are classified into three kinds of hand painting, woodblock overprinting, and wood-printing and coloring. They are characterized by rough lines, brilliant colors, concise shapes, well-rounded structure and strong decorative features. The patterns on the clothes of the figures are painted in gold and silver with fluent lines, commonly called "painting flowers", and have distinctive folk charm. They are rarely seen among the New Year pictures in other places and have become the outstanding feature of Foshan New Year pictures. There is good combination of local customs and practices and strong local styles. Foshan New Year pictures show the exquisite artistic features of Guangdong culture in treatment of lines, pattern of shapes, coloring technique and selection of subjects.

Foshan New Year woodblock prints, influenced by the traditional culture south of the Five Ridges, cater to the aesthetic sentiments and living customs of Foshan people, and are mostly folk god pictures, seasonal pictures and depictions of etiquette and custom.

Liangping New Year Woodblock Prints

Applicant: Liangping County, Chongqing City

These prints in Liangping County, Chongqing City, belong to one of the three unique folk fine arts of Liangping (i.e. bamboo curtain, New Year pictures and lantern drama), and have a history of more than 300 years.

Liangping New Year pictures adopt a romantic representational way, bold artistic abstraction, and the themes of getting rid of evils, enjoying a life of comfort, happiness and luck and historical stories. The pictures are well-rounded and concise, shapes are simple, unvarnished and rough, the bearings are vivid, the structure is complete, and the contrasts are strong. As a chromatographic woodblock prints, they have a supreme artistic value.

In regard to painting skills, Liangping New Year woodblock prints not only inherited the traditional water-printed New Year woodblock pictures and the engraving skills of the Sichuan School, but also absorbed the engraving and chromatographic skills of the Anhui and Jinling Schools. They also adopt the focus-perspective of Western paintings, artfully arrange light and shade, and differentiate distance and close-up. The structure is well-rounded and concise, the figures are exaggerated and transformed, the colors have strong contrast, and the shapes are simple, rough and unvarnished.

Liangping New Year woodblock prints pay close attention to coloring. The colors are dignified and composed, and will not fade. After artists paint the drafts, engraving craftsmen paste the drafts firmly on a smooth pear wood block using base sticky-rice paste. They engrave carefully the major outlines according to the drafts, and then engrave various chromatographic blocks according to the outline blocks, one color per block. The lines are even in thickness and are clear, vigorous and have tension.

Mianzhu New Year Woodblock Prints

Applicant: Deyang City, Sichuan Province

Mianzhu County is one of the major production areas of New Year pictures in China.

The production of a New Year picture starts from the drafting by an artist, through the engraving block produced by the engraver, to the printed paper and then painting on the paper. The lines only serve as outlines and the pictures must experience coloring by painters. Besides dyestuff, they also use rock color (mineral color). As this has strong covering ability, the original engraving lines need to be drawn again after being painted over. But in the parts with dyestuff the original lines are still clear and visible and need not be drawn again as the coloring is transparent. The combination of the two ways of coloring forms the integrated artistic characteristics of water-printing and color-painting in Mianzhu New Year pictures.

Mianzhu New Year woodblock prints have unique color treatment. The basic colors include yellowish red, Buddha blue, peach red, and grass green. They also make use of a kind of flat pen called a "mandarin duck pen" to compose three-dimensional special effects for a sense of reality. By use of changes in shade among similar colors, they create a transition from deep to light colors and from light to shade. The created three-dimensional effects intensify the sense of rhythm and decorative sentiments of the pictures.

"Tianshuijiao" is the most representative easy of expression in Mianzhu New Year woodblock prints. When painting "Tianshuijiao", due to the short time needed, artists finish the work without any let-up, depending on their solid skills. The painting style is bold, unrestrained, vigorous and charming. Thanks to its simplicity, rusticity and roughness, "Tianshuijiao" has become the treasure of Mianzhu New Year pictures.

Mianzhu woodblock New Year Paintings—figures in *the Outlaws of the Marsh*

Fengxiang New Year Woodblock Prints

Applicant: Fengxiang County, Shaanxi Province

Fengxiang County, situated in the west of the Guanzhong Plain, is a famous New Year woodblock print production area. The particular Shaanxi Fengxiang New Year woodblock prints are regarded as a "crystallization of oriental wisdom" by foreign collectors and are housed famous museums around the world.

Fengxiang New Year woodblock prints inherited and carried forward the line-making ways of traditional painting art and also absorbed the styles and ways of mural paintings in temples and ancient stone carvings. They mainly involve line carving, the lines vigorous, simple, vivid and natural. The main colors are red, green, yellow and purple, complemented by black lines with strong contrast, living flavor and vivid and well-rounded images. In printing, craftsmen print the sky and earth first, then apply rouge, and add strong colors, and at last overprint the black-line major block. The pictures are harmonious, simple, vivid and unique.

Fengxiang New Year woodblock prints are all made with handicraft engraving blocks, printed by local methods, painted and colored by hand in some parts, and preserve the simple and natural artistic style of ancient New Year pictures. Compared to the New Year pictures of other places, these are rougher, more straightforward and exaggerated. Thickness and thinness are arranged well and the structure is well-rounded. The door-god pictures have powerful and bold shapes and the pictures of customs and practices are close to life. After being painted in gold and silver, the pictures look magnificent. The hands and faces of images become more vivid after being dyed by hand.

Naxi Ethnic Group Dongba Paintings

Applicant: Lijiang City, Yunnan Province

Dongba painting is the most characteristic fine arts heritage of the Naxi ethnic group. When holding ceremonies, Naxi people will paint various Buddhist gods, figures, animals, plants and ghosts and worship and offer sacrifice to them. These various paintings related to religious activities are collectively called Dongba paintings. The art has five artistic qualities of pictographic sutras, i.e.

the form of palm-leaves sutra, beautiful lines, pretty colors, representation of movement, and taking of features.

The painting mode can be classified in two: first, those preserving the original simple painting methods. Such paintings are mostly painted by bamboo pens and use natural dyestuff. There are single lines and colors are applied flat. The shapes have primitive simplicity and are concise, transformed and exaggerated. The lines are rough, fluent, bold, straightforward, and both strong and tender. Second are those that combine Han and Tibetan national painting ways. Such paintings are mostly painted by brush pens and use mineral dyestuff. The traditional painting style of primitive simplicity of Dongba paintings is organically combined with exotic, exquisite and pretty painting styles. Thickness and thinness are arranged in order with proper density. The composition has clear layers. The colors are brilliant, lines are neat and shapes are accurate.

Dongba paintings mainly have wooden pieces, Dongba paper and flax as their materials. The homemade bamboo pens are dipped with pine-fume ink to draw the outlines. After being applied with various natural colors, the pictures are brilliant and colorful and will not fade for hundreds of years. The painting images have a strong sense of primitiveness. They are mostly represented by lines. Primitive colors are often used and are brilliant and dazzling. Many pictures display characters, which preserve the strong features of pictograph characters.

Tibetan Ethnic Group Tangka Paintings

Applicants: Sichuan Province and Tibet Autonomous Region

Tangka is a unique painting art of Tibetan Buddhism lasting more than a thousand years. In Tibetan, "Tangka" means "a cloth scroll painting that can be laid open for appreciation."

There are various classifications for Tangka. In terms of size and hanging method, they can be classified into miniature Tangka and scroll Tangka. In terms of color, they can be classified into colorful, golden, black, red, tinged and light Tangka. In terms of production ways, they can be classified into painting, barbola, embroidery, printing, brocade, and kesi (silk tapestry with cut designs) Tangka. Most Tangka creators are religious personages.

Tibetan Tangka has precise, balanced and well-rounded structure. The arrangement has proper density and is lively and changeable. In terms of painting methods, they mainly involve realistic painting with strong colors and line drawing. Painters draw the drafts according to the measurement standards of figures, and there are strict requirements on the proportions between five organs on the face, head, chest and waist. The coloring attaches importance to contrast, brilliant colors, and magnificent effects, and they use spotted gold and other neutralized colors to dress up the pictures. The last step is drawing lines. One kind of line has uniform thickness and combines strength and tenderness. The other kind has different thicknesses and changes of pause and transition. Some lines are rough and vigorous, and others are mellow and fluent; but they are all vivid.

The colored-drawing Tangka Paintings in Regong, Qinghai Province.

Tangka paintings are mainly religious and include the formation of the world in Tibetan legends, origin of the Tibetan ethnic group, medicine, astronomy, calendar, literature, poetry, drama, and folk stories.

Hengshui Neihua Paintings

Applicant: Hengshui City, Hebei Province

Neihua art is a particular traditional art in China. Artists use glass, crystal ware, and amber as base, and use special thin pens to paint in reverse exquisite pictures of figures, landscape, flowers and birds, and calligraphy works. They are elegant with an exquisite painting style and brilliant colors. It can be said that "there is a place of unique scenery in a small square". Neihua painting is divided into Beijing, Hebei, Shandong and Guangdong schools.

The sources are lyric poems and paintings, calligraphy works, figures and portraits. On base of inheriting the simple, unvarnished, and elegant style of the Beijing School, Hengshui Neihua combined the traditional exquisite and fluent painting style of the Shandong School, introduced the skills of traditional Chinese painting such as light-ink strokes, scraping, dyeing, spotting, drawing outlines, and drawing threads, and brought the skills of Neihua painting into full play. Later oil-painting skills were also introduced to break the traditional and single watercolor painting style and this greatly improved the picture, shape and charm. It is regarded as a heroic undertaking of "combining Chinese and Western styles."

Hebei School Neihua painting is good at figure portraits, especially Baby Playing Picture and Hundred-Son Picture that reflect the artistic features of the Hebei School Neihua-painted snuff bottle. In addition, artists are also good at copying famous paintings of ancient China. The Hebei School Neihua painting is mainly characterized by profound concepts, vivid charm, artful arrangement, elegant and abundant lines and colors, creating a combination of paintings and calligraphy works, and suiting both refined and popular tastes. At present, Hebei School Neihua painting has become an artistic school of the highest level, with most complete varieties, greatest size, quickest development and largest influence among the four great schools in China.

Paper-cuts

Applicants: Hebei, Shanxi, Liaoning, Jiangsu, Zhejiang, Guangdong, Yunnan, and Shaanxi provinces

(See P286)

Guxiu Embroidery

Applicant: Songjiang District, Shanghai City

Guxiu embroidery is a magnificent unique flower among the artworks of Shanghai. The name derived from the family of Gu Mingshi, master of Luxiang Garden in Shanghai County, Songjiang Prefecture during the Ming Dynasty. It is a kind of "painting embroidery" with famous paintings as blueprints and is noted for its exquisite technology, elegant form and supreme artistic qualities.

Through copying ancient famous paintings as drafts, Guxiu embroidery mostly has landscape and figures as its subjects and the thread coloring has the effect similar to traditional Chinese painting. It is good at using demitint and gives a feeling of peacefulness and elegance. Guxiu embroidery inherited the traditional skills of woman's bedroom embroidery in ancient times (referred to as

Suxiu embroidery). The divided thread is thinner than hair, and the stitch is fine and leaves no mark after piercing silk fabric. Guxiu embroidery combines painting and embroidery, and in some parts not suitable for embroidery such as sky, mountains and rocks, people use a painting pen to connect the colors. The work does not lose the features of embroidery and has proper arrangement of void and solidness. These skills had great influences on the development of modern Chinese embroidery.

Guxiu embroidery is different from other kinds of embroidery in the following aspects: first, the subjects are elegant and all the drafts are famous paintings of great masters. Second, it is made completely with silk and the stitch is exquisite and fine, which represent the charm of traditional Chinese paintings and calligraphy works. A silk thread will be divided into 36, 48 and 64 strands. Third, the embroidery skill is peculiar and has great originality. There are a dozen ways of stitching, and the stitch must be flat, equal, pointed, smooth, even, and thin, which is different from other kinds of embroidery that accommodate disordered stitching. Guxiu embroidery is only shown on a single face and the base color is invisible but shows up. It will take at least half a year to make a piece of embroidery work of 0.33 square meters. And the finished work has to be mounted.

Suxiu (Suzhou Embroidery)

Applicant: Suzhou City, Jiangsu Province

(See P287)

Xiangxiu (Hunan Embroidery)

Applicant: Changsha City, Hunan Province

(See P287)

Yuexiu (Guangdong Embroidery)

Applicants: Guangzhou City and Chaozhou City, Guangdong Province

(See P287)

Shuxiu (Sichuan Embroidery)

Applicant: Chengdu City, Sichuan Province

(See P287)

Miaoxiu (Miao Embroidery)

Applicant: Guizhou Province

Miaoxiu refers to the embroidery prevalent among the Miao ethnic group. With particular national styles and artistic skills, it is famous across China for exquisite stitches, elegance, and rich colors. The arrangement of patters is precise, the color contrast strong and the patterns are varied.

Miaoxiu embroidery is woven in five colors and the patterns are mainly regular geometric figures; patterns of flowers and grass are rarely seen. Miao women do not need drafts for embroidery. They count the vertical and horizontal threads on the base cloth and embroider by picking threads, depending completely on their inborn understanding, adept skills and uncommon memory. By means of abundant imagination, they arrange the overall structure, combine artfully all the individual pictures and form well-rounded embroidery with harmonious, beautiful and natural conditions.

Miaoxiu embroidery attaches great importance to symmetry, enrichment and brightness. All the pictures, colors and spaces must be symmetrical; for enrichment, there are no blank spaces; and for brightness, they use colors boldly, red and green being most dazzling.

The patterns on Miao ethnic group embroidery include kylin, dragon and phoenix indicating luck, and common insects, fish, flowers, peaches and pomegranates. The embroidery is divided into flat and protruding embroidery. The former is widely popular and adopted by the Miao groups in Hunan, Guizhou, Yunnan, and Guangxi. The latter needs more layers of paper flowers on the base cloth, so that the embroidered flowers protrude three-dimensionally.

Miaoxiu embroidery is mainly inlaid in collars, fronts of garments, sleeves, handkerchief borders, skirt bottoms and the sides of patrol boats, as well as in making satchels and purses.

Tu Ethnic Group Panxiu (Bowl Embroidery)

Applicant: Huzhu Tu ethnic group Autonomous County, Qinghai Province

Panxiu is a kind of unique embroidery among the Tu ethnic group. It reflects the profound meaning of ancient Tu culture and every women of Tu ethnic group is expected to learn it. The embroidery shows exquisite skills and fine workmanship.

This embroidery has a strong national flavors, a wide range of subjects, rich content and various embroidery methods. These are mainly reflected by exquisite adornments on clothes, as well as headwear, collars, fronts of garments, pigtail tube, waistband, bellyband, shoes and socks, towel used to cover a pillow, pinprick, small bags, Chinese tobacco pipe and bags.

Panxiu embroidery pays attention to the materials. The processing is fine. The black pure cotton cloth is the base material and other materials are pasted on it. Panxiu embroidery is silk thread embroidery and there are seven colors of threads, i.e. red, yellow, green, blue, purple and white. In embroidering all the seven colors are shown and the coordination is harmonious and the colors are bright and dazzling.

The stitches of Panxiu embroidery are particular. In wielding needle, people will arrange two strands of threads with the same color; one is used as bowl thread and the other is used as stitching thread. Panxiu embroidery does not need bamboo framework and people directly use two hands. They hold cloth in left hands and needle in right hands. The thread for boil is hung on right breast and the stitching thread is on the needle. The up stitch is for bowl and the low stitch is for stitching. One needle needs two threads. It takes labor and materials, but the finished work is thick, magnificent, and durable. The design of patterns on Panxiu is artful with strong national styles, including dozens of types such as Taiji picture, figures and Buddha.

Shui Maweixiu (Horse Tail Embroidery)

Applicant: Sandu Shui ethnic group Autonomous County, Guizhou Province

Sandu is the only Shui ethnic group autonomous county in China. Shui Maweixiu is a kind of embroidery made by Shui women for generations with horse tail as an important raw material. The embroidery made by this unique folk traditional handicraft is very exquisite.

Horsetail embroidery, a traditional folk craftwork unique to the Shui Ethnic Group

Maweixiu pays attention to materials and the procedures are complex and numerous. In general, a dozen procedures and more than a month are needed for finishing a piece of embroidery. Among the various embroidery artworks, Maweixiu is unique for its adoption of horse tail. It still uses ancient disordered stitches and pricking stitches. People at first wrap three to five strands of horse tail with pure white silk threads, connect the wrapped horse-tail silk threads without any bursts, embroider their designed patterns on the base cloth with inlaying of each thread, make up the outlines of various exquisite patterns, and color the patterns by various colored silk threads. Finally, they use golden copper pieces for edging, which are shining and dazzling. The end product is exquisite.

Maweixiu has complex skills. The embroidery has the sense of bas-relief with abstract, general and exaggerated shapes. Maweixiu embroidery is mainly used to make binding straps for carrying babies on the back, embroidered shoes with turned-up tops, women's waistband and breast plates, children's caps, small bags, and sheaths. Despite social modernization, the concept of shapes and formulaic symbols is almost unchanged.

Tiaohua (Cross-Stitch)

Applicants: Huangmei County, Hubei Province, and Longhui County, Hunan Province

Tiaohua, also called "cross-stitch", has a long history in China and is popular in particular in the southwest inhabited by ethnic minorities. Huangmei Tiaohua and Huayao Tiaohua are the most famous.

Tiaohua strictly follows vertical and horizontal lines on the base cloth and the cross picking-stitch is most common. Each needle pulls out a diagonal line and two needles make up an inclined cross, which are the basic units for various combinations of patterns. Cross picking-stitch only demands the integrity of the opposite face and the stitch marks on the reverse face are arranged in line. Besides cross picking-stitch, there is dense-stitch spreading patterns, i.e. the threads are spread densely and patterns on the two faces are the same while the colors are different.

Skillful Tiaohua artisans can make up patterns directly without a draft. Modern Tiaohua has made continuous innovations on the base of traditional skills. Several kinds of fiber can be used as material and different embroidery threads can be used such as cotton, hemp, silk and wool. The characteristics of other skills are also absorbed such as other kinds of embroidery, lace, weaving, and mending patterns, enhancing the expressive force.

Tiaohua usually decorates pillows, table cloths and other cloths. Yao ethnic group Tiaohua in Longhui tends to embroider colorful lucky patterns on local home-made dark blue cloth. It is bright, pretty, well-rounded, exquisite and fine. Patterns cover patterns in a unique way. Huangmei Tiaohua in Hubei is different from common embroidery. Embroidery attaches importance to piercing and Tiaohua attaches importance to picking. Huangmei Tiaohua makes use of colored threads. The colorful threads are picked and embroidered by needle on the lattice with the crossing of horizontal and vertical threads on the base cloth to form brilliant patterns with a strong three-dimensional sense.

Qingyang Xiangbao (Perfume Sachets) Embroidery

Applicant: Qingyang City, Gansu Province

Xiangbao (perfume sachets), commonly called "chuchu" in Qingyang, refers to small embroidery sachets in various forms and sizes and with various ancient, mysterious and profound patterns. It is made by embroidering colorful threads on colorful silk. It is filled with the ground powder from traditional Chinese herbal medicines with a strong fragrant scent. It can be used on festivals and for daily use or for appreciation.

It is said that Qingyang Xiangbao embroidery originated from the Yellow Emperor, developed during the Qin, Han, Tang and Song dynasties, and became mature during the Ming and Qing dynasties. It has its particular artistic style and distinctive local features. It is rough, bold, and unrestrained, as well as exquisite and pretty. It is bright, delicate and charming, and pure and elegant. It is both an abstract and a realistic work. The structure of patterns is concise and bright with traditional and ancient meanings. The colors are bright and red and green are the major ones and the transition crosses chromatogram. The embroidery surface is solid and thick and the forms are natural and vivid. The workmanship is exquisite and fine and the stitches are as flat as a picture. The embroidering methods and types are various and changeable.

Exquisite ivory carving

Qingyang Xiangbao embroidery has changeable stitches and pays no attention to perspective or proportion. It demands similarity in spirits instead of shapes. The forms are exaggerated and transformed and heads and bodies are prominent. For the various animal Xiangbao, some have big heads and small bodies with a head but no tail; some have heads and bodies but no feet or legs, and some have long bodies but short hooves and have claws as legs. For example, a shoulder lion-tiger has a bigger head and a smaller body and has claws but no legs. It is not a real image and has no proper proportion, either. It is created completely by the artistic inspiration of the embroidery artisans.

Ivory Carving

Applicants: Chongwen District, Beijing City; and Guangzhou City, Guangdong Province

After thousands of years of development, several comparatively concentrated producing centers of Chinese ivory carving gradually came into being in the middle of the Qing Dynasty, mainly represented by Guangzhou, Suzhou and Beijing. Each center has its particular styles and characteristics in subjects and forms.

Beijing Ivory Carving: It has graceful and noble royal artistic qualities. Ivory carving has always been good at charming and graceful maids in ancient costumes and pretty and touching round-carving flowers.

Guangzhou Ivory Carving: It is slender, exquisite, bright and limpid. It attaches importance to blanching the ivory and color decoration and suits both refined and popular tastes. The works are good at glittering ivory and exquisite carving. The overall arrangement is complex and lively and has no blank space.

Ivory ball is a super decorative artwork of China. It has several layers of hollowing-out and each layer can turn around. It is exquisitely carved and the images are vivid. It is regarded as superlative craftsmanship. The body of the ivory ball is composed of interlinked balls. Each ball is about two mm deep and the space between layers is as thin as a hair and is very exquisite. After being touched lightly, it can revolve freely. All the interlinked balls are hollowed out on a piece of ivory. On each layer there are hollow patterns of chrysanthemum, plum blossom, and sweet-scented osmanthus. They form an appearance like a fishing net with densely-distributed meshes and beautiful round flowers.

Yangzhou Jade Carving

Applicant: Yangzhou City, Jiangsu Province

Yangzhou is an ancient city with a history of more than 2,000 years and is one of the three great jade carving producing areas in China. After such long development, Yangzhou jade carving has formed the basic features of being simple, vigorous, mellow, elegant, graceful, beautiful and exquisite. Yangzhou jade carving is characterized by being dignified and vigorous but not bulky, and exquisitely carved but not fragile. Bottles and burners are the best products with strong national styles and local features.

Yangzhou jade artisans are good at carving large jade ware and combining the art of jade carving and calligraphy. In aspects of shapes and patterns, they make use of the perspective of painting, hollowing out several layers of patterns, and show vivid scenes of story plots.

Yangzhou jade carving started from Yuan and Ming dynasties and reached its peak in the Qing Dynasty. In terms of design and creation, artisans pay attention to the use of the natural beauty of jade, designing subjects according to the colors, giving free play to their skills on base of the shapes, and integrating landscapes, figures, flowers, birds, fish, insects, rare animals and pavilions in endless layers with profound meaning.

Yangzhou jade carving is unique in skills, and the carved-out quoits seem like soybeans and are exquisite, mellow, fine and neat. The works of bottles and burners in Yangzhou jade ware make unconventional innovations on the base of copying bronze ware, creating vessels with unique sentiments and interest. In particular, the product of tower-burner is most representative. The three-legged burner is exquisite, beautiful and hollowed out carefully. The appearance is elegant in the shape of a water chestnut, and is very delicate. It has reasonable proportions, precise structure and five movable circles, so it is also called a "five-ring burner". The head is well-rounded and exquisite and the three legs are vigorous and powerful.

Bronze and Stone Seal Carving

Applicant: Xiling Yinshe, Hangzhou City, Zhejiang Province

Brick carving seal "Lone loon flying amongst red clouds at sunset" by Sun Hengxi, a well-known seal cutting artist from Chaohu, Anhui Province.

Jin means bronze and bronze ware with inscription. Stone refers to stone carving with inscriptions.

Bronze and stone seal carving is an important part of Chinese stone culture. From the unearthing of ancient seals during the Warring States Period (475-221 BC) to the creation of the Chinese Seal for the 2008 Beijing Olympic Games, seal carving art of China has remained strong.

Seal carving art is the perfect combination of calligraphy, the art of composition and the art of knife cutting. A seal comprises an unrestrained and elegant calligraphy conception and beautiful painting composition, as well as the vivid carving charm of knife cutting. It can be said that "the nature abounds in changes even within a very small place".

Over time, Chinese characters have appeared in various forms on the seal faces in an interesting way. The small square of several cm is filled with the passage of time and the vigor of space, remaining attractive for its gentle luster and elegant charm.

Seal carving is an art with close relations with calligraphy. It attaches importance to the composition and the way of carving. Composition is the art of arranging one or more groups of characters on the seal face. It is complex and changeable and is actually an important section of seal carving art. Without superb composition, a seal even with skillful carving cannot be viewed as an excellent work. In particular, a set of works must have changes on all the seals and show the composition skills of the artists. So, designs go through many drafts and forms according to the specific strokes, styles, forms and mutual relationship between the characters.

Xiuyan Jade Carving

Applicant: Xiuyan Manchu Autonomous County, Liaoning Province

Xiuyan jade, called You jade for short, is one of the famous jades in Chinese history. Xiuyan jade carving is good at "su articles" and is listed first among domestic jade carving artworks. Su refers to the ancient vessels copying the burners, bottles, Ding and Xun before the Qin and Han dynasties. They attach importance to balance and steadiness, symmetrical proportions and mellow and smooth appearance. The patterns are simple, unvarnished, elegant and noble and fully represent traditional Chinese aesthetics. Artisans use their skills according to materials, make use of waste materials artfully, cut out flaws, transfer spots to fine jade, and combine skillfully pretty colors, relief, rounding and hollowed-out carving, as well as inlay, which form the craft characteristics of Xiuyan jade carving of su articles.

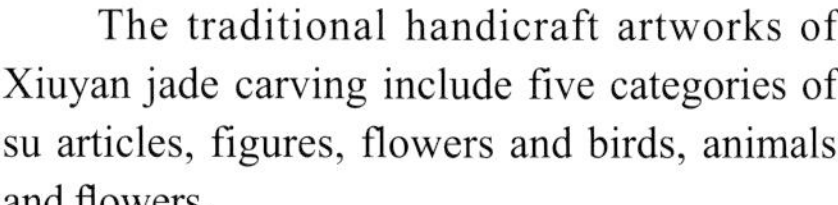

The traditional handicraft artworks of Xiuyan jade carving include five categories of su articles, figures, flowers and birds, animals and flowers.

Xiuyan jade carving is solid, simple, unvarnished and elegant and is precise and uniform and changeable in terms of shapes. In terms of size, there are large pieces with grand momentum and weighing up several hundred tons, and there are also miniscule pieces that are very lovely.

Fuxin Agate Carving

Applicant: Fuxin City, Liaoning Province

Fuxin is the major agate production, processing and distribution area in China, containing more than 50 percent of the country's reserves and with good quality.

The production of a piece of exquisite agate goes through seven processes of selecting material, peeling off, designing, polishing, initial carving, fine carving and pedestal. The skills of drilling and digging out the center, active link, production of shoulder ears, hollowing out an active ball, and decorative carving are unique to Fuxin.

Fuxin agate carving is artful, pretty and elegant. There is bold creativity, artful design and exquisite carving skills. Artisans make full use of the natural pretty colors, veins and sense of quality of agate, and all the represented subjects are vivid, natural and interesting. It is a combination of nature and artificial work. Fuxin is not only good at traditional su articles such as xun, zun and bottles, but also excellent in elegant works with distinctive characters and particular styles. This refers not only to the elegant style and rich cultural contents contained in the works but also expresses the living and aesthetic sentiments of modern people.

Fuxin agate artworks are divided into five major categories of figures, birds and animals, flowers, su articles and water-liner agate. Each piece has a unique shape, pure material, exquisite skill, pretty decoration and vivid images.

Luminous Cup Carving

Applicant: Jiuquan City, Gansu Province

Jiuquan luminous cup is a precious drinking vessel carved out of jade. When filled with wine and put under moonlight, the cup will shine, hence its name.

The exquisite and fine production of Jiuquan luminous cup goes through 28 complex procedures. The luminous cup has following characteristics: 1. Exquisite craftsmanship and a cup wall is as thin as an eggshell; the thinnest place is less than 1 mm and it is smooth and moist from inside to outside. 2. The jade is transparent and limpid. Although named luminous, the cup does not shine for itself. When raising the cup under the bright moonlight, people can see the beautiful moon through the walls and wine with some mysterious colors. 3. The jade stone is rich in metal minerals and some can be attracted by a magnet. The material of the luminous cup, mandarin-duck jade, is flexible and strong.

Liqian jade, the material for producing the luminous cup, is drawn from Qilianshan at an elevation of more than three and four thousand meters. The jade appears dark green. And the cup made of it is lush green and makes people feel cool even in the hot summer.

Jiuquan luminous cup has unique shapes and exquisite modes and is divided into two categories of traditional luminous cups and the luminous cups in the style of the ancients. It is as black as pitch, as white as suet and as green as jade. The patterns are natural. The cup is as thin as paper and shines like a mirror. Both the interior and exterior are smooth. The jade is transparent and bright. And the wine in a cup retains its original flavor for a long time.

Qingtian Stone Carving

Applicant: Qingtian County, Zhejiang Province

Qingtian stone carving refers to a traditional Chinese artwork carved out of Qingtian stone. Qingtian County has always been called the "hometown of Chinese stone carving".

Qingtian stone is as mellow as jade and has richer colors and stranger veins than jade. Nature prints nearly all the colors in Qingtian stone to create a brilliant display containing dark blue, white, yellow, red, brown, purple, green, blue, dark and colored, as well as many wonderful patterns inside the stone, such as landscape, grass and flowers, rosy clouds, animals, fish and insects. There are more than 100 varieties of Qingtian stone.

The art of Qingtian stone carving is characterized artful adoption of the pretty colors, exquisite hollowing out and making use of rich layers. Artisans design according to the natural shapes, qualities, colors and veins. For example, the dark-blue stone containing white can be carved into turned-up lotus leaves and a white pond lily in bud. The dark-brown steatite of light-blue can be carved into an old plum tree branches with blossoms like snow.

"Grape Mountain" is a traditional excellent work of Qingtian stone carving created by the famous artisan Zhang Shikuan. He made great use of colored steatite, splint steatite and other high-quality stones. He carved the yellow and light-blue steatites into strings of well-rounded and glittering grapes, grey steatites into lively squirrels, and dark reddish purple stones into grape vines, leaves and rockworks. He adopted the skills of hollowing out and made the twisted grape vines, clear veins of leaves, and the works vivid.

Quyang Stone Carving

Applicant: Quyang County, Hebei Province

This is the representative of white marble carving. The shapes are vivid, the carving means is mellow and exquisite, and the veins are fluent and free.

The carving craft in Quyang County is good at using such unique skills as peeling waste, scraping and opening face, and in finalizing the design by measuring by the eyes. Works must reach the standard that "lines are straight, planes are flat and curves are lively".

The traditional crafts of Quyang stone carving make use of the unique skill of opening the face to paint the outlines on stones. The nose is carved at first, followed by head to feet. The "inside and outside are moderate and the proportion is harmonious". Quyang stone carving makes use of round, relief and line carving and integrates perspective, dissection, and aesthetics. The works are as smooth as wood carving, as exquisite as ivory carving and as vivid as jade carving. The shapes are beautiful and both appearance and spirits are vivid. The carving mode is exquisite. There are various types of Quyang stone carvings. Some imitate the works of ancient styles and some are figures of modern people and others are articles for building decoration and household decoration.

Quyang stone carving has particular artistic styles. The design is ingenious, shapes are beautiful, veins are clear, hollowed out, and vivid, and the carving way is exquisite, mellow and smooth. Materials include white marble, granite, jade, etc. The colors include white, black, yellow, green, red and grey.

Shoushan Stone Carving

Applicant: Fuzhou City, Fujian Province

Shoushan stone carving is a traditional folk carving art. Shoushan stones produced from Beifeng Peak in northern Fuzhou are used as materials and carved to small works by special skills to delight people. Shoushan stone carving pays attention to sculpture on stones.

In aspect of carving art, Shoushan stone carving pays attention to designing on a base of stone shapes, colors and veins. Artisans design the shape based on stone form and carve on basis of colors, so that the natural colors and forms are integrated with wonderful workmanship. Shoushan stone carving is mostly characterized by use of colors, as there are dozen of brilliant ones in the stones. Artisans should observe the stones before carving. They will look at the appearance and colors for initial designing. After finding other colors after carving, they will think again about the designing. Usually, an excellent work has no joints. The carving of a piece of stone almost retains the original form and is natural.

The carving skills include hollowing out, round, relief, bas relief and inlay. Bas relief is the traditional skill of Shoushan stone carving and can show the profound layers and concepts on the carving surface by exquisite skills. The style is primitive, simple and elegant. In one example, the skill of hollowing out is used to represent the mutual echo of hens inside and outside the coop. Some hens are sticking their heads out from the lattice and calling in a vivid manner. The carving of the bamboo coop gives a full play of the advantages of hollowing out and the skill is very difficult to achieve.

Hui'an Stone Carving

Applicant: Hui'an County, Fujian Province

Hui'an stone carving is a traditional carving art with hard bluestone as materials mainly popular in Hui'an County, Quanzhou Prefecture. The finished works are mostly used in building decoration. Hui'an stone carving has strong national features and distinctive qualities of time. As the representative of southern-school stone carving, it was spread to overseas areas very early and is much favored in Southeast Asia.

Hui'an stone carving integrates Central Plain, Fuji and Zhejiang, and ocean cultures. If "fine horse, autumn wind and northern border" are compared to the bold and unrestrained carving art of northern school, then "apricot blossom, spring rain south of the Yangtze River" can be compared to the important symbols of the stone carving of the southern school that is graceful and exquisite. Dragon pillar and stone lions are representative works.

The southern-school stone lions represented by Hui'an works initiatively changed the northern lion to the form of shaking head and standing tail. It wears a colorful band at the front and holds colorful balls under its feet, portraying a happy and lucky atmosphere and making people feel the joy of festivals. The male and female lions glance to the left and right. The female lion is fondling the playing cub with its front claws, and the male lion has a rolling round stone pearl in its mouth. This is the artistic effect sought by ingenious Hui'an stone carving artisans. Such colorful-ball lions are called southern lions. In materials, southern lions mainly adopt the radish-green rock that is pliable but strong and suitable for exquisite carving.

Shadow carving is the unique skill of Hui'an artisans in modern times. It adopts the theory of black and white imaging. The vivid effect of photography is carved out on the polished black stone, giving full play to the exquisite carving of Hui'an. After being colored, the shadow carving becomes very distinctive.

Three Carving Arts of Huizhou (Wuyuan)

Applicants: Huangshan City, Anhui Province; and Wuyuan County, Jiangxi Province

Ancient Huizhou had jurisdiction over Huangshan City and Wuyuan County. The three carving arts of Huizhou are decorative carving on buildings during the Ming and Qing dynasties and have strong local cultural colors.

The name refers to Hui School brick, stone, and wood carvings. Among them, stone carving had matured as early as the Song and Yuan dynasties and wood and brick carvings developed and reached their peak during the Ming and Qing dynasties. They are found everywhere in tens of thousands of ancient mansions, ancestral temples, memorial archways and gardens in Huizhou.

Brick carving is a building decoration hollowed out exquisitely from hard and smooth caesious bricks abundant in Huizhou. It is widely used on door-towers and makes the buildings elegant and solemn. It is an important part of Hui School architectural art rising. Brick carving is divided into flat, relief and three-dimensional carvings.

Stone carving is widely distributed in urban and rural areas in Huizhou with various types. It is mainly used as decoration for temples' and mansions' porch pillars, door walls, memorial archways, and tombs. It is the art of relief and round carving and enjoys high fame. In terms of carving style, the relief carving is mainly composed of shallow hollowing out and plane carving; the carving method is exquisite, primitive, simple and natural.

Huizhou wood carving adopts the representative ways of round, relief and hollowed out carvings according to the building demands.

Linxia Brick Carving

Applicant: Linxia County, Gansu Province

Linxia County, Linxia Hui ethnic group Autonomous Prefecture is situated in the middle and southwest of Gansu Province. The building brick carving art there has a unique style combining Hui and other nationalities.

Linxia brick carving works are mainly used to decorate temples and mansions. In course of development they absorbed the carving ways of wood, stone and jade carvings, paying close

Brick carving in the Qianheyan Mosque, Linxia County, Gansu Province

attention to integrating traditional Chinese painting, calligraphy, seals and poetry with brick carving. It not only retains the simplicity and conciseness shown by particular materials, but also presents diversified artistic features.

The Hui ethnic group brick carving in Linxia has acquired obvious influences from Islam and formed special trends. As Hui are Muslims, there are no figures in the brick carving.

In terms of production, Linxia brick carving is divided into kneading and carving skills. In the former, artisans mix and make up elaborately the clay and mud, knead them into various sculptures by hands and moulds, and put them into a kiln for firing. Such works are mostly independent; for example, dragon, phoenix and kylin, and are mostly used on ridges of houses. As to carving skill, artisans carve out various patterns with a knife on selected and fired blue bricks. The skill is more complex than kneading and one picture usually is composed of a dozen of or even dozens of blue bricks. It is carved on soft bricks fired in local kilns and is mainly used by wall decoration and stages in buildings.

Tibetan Ethnic Group King Gesar Painted Rock Carving

Applicant: Seda County, Sichuan Province

These are relics of King Gesar culture mainly distributed in the three counties of Seda, Shiqu and Danba in Ganzi Tibetan Autonomous Prefecture, Sichuan Province. Those in Seda County are the most representative.

The painted rock carving of King Gesar is a pioneering work in the history of Tibetan fine arts. It has the large folk hero King Gesar as the core content and integrates exquisite stone carving skills and traditional painting. By means of particular artistic styles, it presents of how King Gesar and his generals brought benefits to the people and fought bravely in battle.

The art uses a natural piece rock as the base for an integrated composition. Numerous pieces of painted rock carvings are combined to compose the organic whole of all the figures in King Gesar. In addition to figures, each piece of rock carving has grassland or forest, snowy mountain or blue sky as backdrop, and shows strong regional characters.

The genre integrates the exquisite stone carving skills with traditional painting. The natural slab-stones are used as materials. People usually keep the natural forms of stones. They draw the outline at first, and then use the carving skills of standing and scraping carving. The lines are natural and fluent like moving clouds and water and the images are natural and vivid. After finishing the carving, they brush the picture surface with white dyestuff and when it is dried they color the carving. They usually use the six colors of red, yellow, blue, white, black and green, and they rarely use demitint. These colors have specific meanings and correspond to the generals supporting King Gesar. Local people can understand this at a glance. The skills are passed down from masters to apprentices or within families and the carvers usually do not inscribe their names on the works.

Chaozhou Wood Carving

Applicant: Chaozhou City, Guangdong Province

Chaozhou wood carving is a folk carving art famous for the several layers of hollowing-out, brilliant and exaggerated styles and exquisite skills. It is mainly used as decoration for buildings, sacrificial articles, furniture and tables. It is usually pasted with pure gold foil after carving, so it is also called Chaozhou gold-lacquer wood carving.

It is divided into wholly-gilded gold lacquering wood carving, colorful carving painted in gold, pure red (or black) lacquering carving, and plain carving with original wood veins; the first is most famous.

Chaozhou wood carving often uses camphor timber as it has the proper tenacity. There are various ways of hollowing out, such

Chaozhou wood carving treasured in the Ancestral Temple of the Chen Family in Guangzhou, Guangdong Province

as relief, deep, round, hollowing out and whole carving. The finished works are exquisite and have rich layers. The composition is often in an "S" shape. Landscapes and pavilions are used to separate the complex and continuous stories into different scenes, so that the figures are numerous but not disordered and the plots are clear. Considering the line of sight of viewers, artisans often exaggerate some parts of the figures on the wood carving placed high on the girders, such as deepened eyes, raised noses and protruding mouths. It is proper for viewers to look up.

Chaozhou wood carving imitates traditional Chinese painting or the drama stage. The stories in different times and space are expressed on the same wood carving surface, and there is a "pathway" for narration (treating the activities of figures by special composition ways).

Ningbo Cinnabar and Gold Lacquer Wood Carving

Applicant: Ningbo City, Zhejiang Province

Ningbo cinnabar and gold lacquer wood carving uses camphor, basswood and gingko timber as raw materials. Relief, rounding and hollowing out skills are used to carve out various figures and patterns of animals and plants. The work is gilded and pasted with spotted mica or shell powders and applied with traditional Chinese grand lacquer. The patterns and shapes are simple and unvarnished, the carving vigorous and the works are brilliant and dazzling.

The genre is mainly characterized by lacquer (i.e. lacquer materials and lacquering skills) instead of carving. As the work relies on gilding and cinnabar lacquer as decoration, the carving is not very exquisite, but the processes of polishing, scraping and filling, coloring, gilding and painting in lacquering are very careful. Such skills create the effects of magnificence and brilliance.

It has well-rounded structures, mainly involves happy and lucky events and folk legends, and has rich and colorful pictures with unique local styles. In terms of wood carving craft, it can be roughly divided into four categories: building carving, cinnabar and gold Buddha figure carving, daily decoration carving and small carving for appreciation. Such exquisite wood carving works can be seen today on wooden buildings in many temples.

Leqing Box Wood Carving

Applicant: Leqing City, Zhejiang Province

Leqing City is located in the southeastern coastline in Zhejiang Province. Leqing box wood carving is a kind of round-carving art for appreciation making use of the natural qualities of box wood, i.e. bright and clean quality, smooth veins, and solemn color. Box wood carving shows milk-yellow. Over time, the color becomes deeper, showing the beauty of primitive simplicity and elegance.

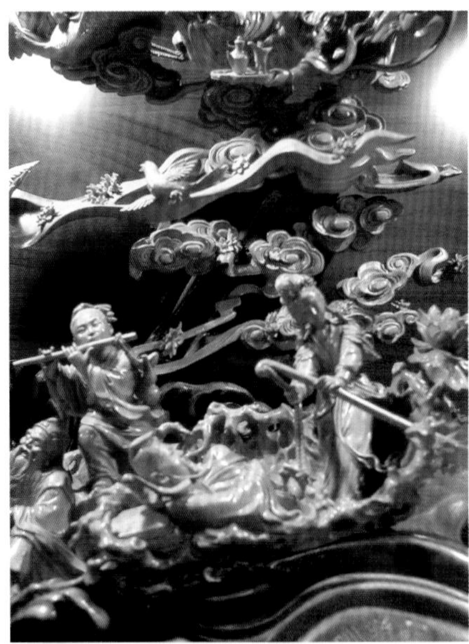

Part of the famous wood carving works *Painting of Celestial Beinings Congratulating on Someone's Birthday*

Box wood is a short evergreen shrub that grows slowly, and that which is 40 to 50 years old can be used for carving. Such timbers have mostly the diameter about 10 to 15 cm and are suitable for carving small-sized figures that are placed on the table for appreciation. Box wood is firm and tenacious with bright and clean surface, smooth veins, proper hardness, and bright yellow color. After being carved and polished exquisitely, it can be compared to ivory carving.

The basic procedures for carving include composing the sculpture according to materials, making a base, rough carving, exquisite carving, and waxing instead of lacquering.

Leqing box wood carving is divided into three types with different sculpting theories, techniques and procedures. First, is the traditional type. The sculptures are mainly single figures but there are also group carving or joint carving. Second, is the root carving type. The natural box root is used as materials and the sculpture is on base of the root. Third, is cleaving carving. The wood blocks that cannot be used for carving figures are cloven and artisans carve them freely and roughly according to the natural veins. The traditional type has clay figure models for drafting. The root carving changes with the occasion and the concept is flexible, so there is no need of clay sculpture as a draft, but the particular shapes of the root should be maintained. Cleaving carving pays attention to the veins.

Dongyang Wood Carving

Applicant: Dongyang City, Zhejiang Province

Dongyang wood carving, also called white wood carving (showing the natural color of timber), has a history of more than 1,000 years from the Tang Dynasty. It is one of the best excellent folk crafts in China and is regarded as a "national treasure."

The traditional type belongs to decorative carving and mainly has plane relief. It has rich layers as well as the basic features of plane decoration. The color is light and a deep lacquer coating is not applied. The natural veins and color of timber are preserved with elegant style. Dongyang wood carving is strict in selecting materials. Basswood, white-peach wood, cinnamomum camphora and gingko wood are the major materials. It is not painted and is often lacquered by natural color and transparent varnish to preserve the natural color of white wood, so that people can appreciate better the superior skills of the carvers. In terms of crafts, it can be divided into two types: carving without paintings and carving with picture drafts. Both pay attention to originality and the qualities of painting and have superb artistic value.

Dongyang wood carving involves many historical stories and folk legends; the design is similar to line drawing of traditional Chinese painting, and the pattern decoration is changeable. It has the scattered perspective or bird's-eye perspective of traditional Chinese painting as the composition feature. Within some planar and spatial range, the contents shown can be freed from the restrictions of Western carving and painting rules such as "big near and small far", "clear scene and misty distant view", so that the contents can be clearly shown.

Li Zhenjiang, a wood carving artisit in Dongyang County, is making a wood carving works.

Zhangzhou Wood Puppet Head Carving

Applicant: Zhangzhou City, Fujian Province

Zhangzhou wood puppet head carving is a special skill in production of puppet props. It is a folk industrial art and mainly distributed in Zhangzhou City, Xiamen City, Quanzhou City and neighboring areas in Fujian Province. The whole model of a Zhangzhou puppet includes head, extremities, costumes, helmets, etc. Puppet head carving only refers to the model of heads.

The most important part of the Zhangzhou glove puppet is the head and the face is crucial. Artisans attach importance to five organs and three bones, i.e. two eyes, one mouth, and two nasal openings and the eyebrow-bone, cheekbone and chin bone. The design depends on the appearance, character, status, experience and quality of the roles. In addition, importance is attached to model, lines and colors to show the spirit of the roles.

Zhangzhou puppet carving also pays attention to the selection of the raw material, cinnamomum camphora, and the mixing of paints in addition to carving skills. The inherited secretly-made paints are especially important. Each color must be applied on each piece dozens of times so that the puppet will not fade or change for a hundred years.

As the carving of the stage figure head for drama, artisans particularly attach importance to the description of figures qualities, exaggerated models, rich expressions and general treatment, which are universal characteristics. This kind of carving has always been inherited by apprentices from masters within families without break until today.

Pingxiang Xiangdong Nuo Drama Masks

Applicant: Pingxiang City, Jiangxi Province

Nuo drama mask is an important part of Nuo culture and is used for ceremonies, dancing and drama. Xiangdong Nuo drama mask is an excellent and traditional folk carving. The masks are simple and exquisite but the procedures for making them are complex.

The carving skills of Pingxiang Xiangdong Nuo drama masks have been inherited since ancient times and most of the products are made of cinnamomum camphora wood. The model of masks inherits the ancient style with unique formality. The images are vivid with exaggerated expressions. The colors include red, yellow, blue, white and black. They create contrast and are harmonious and striking. Nuo drama masks have extremely exquisite decorations that are complex, mysterious and meaningful.

The masks pay attention to the description of the character. Carvers combine exaggeration and realism, use the knife as a pen, integrate relief, hollowing-out, rounding and line carvings according to the requirements of mask characters, and carve out a vivid image of various gods. Although the masks have complex and mysterious religious and folk meanings, they are actually a sculpting art following their own artistic rules and principles.

The expressions and decorations of the masks have specific cultural meanings and implications. The changes of five organs and the decorations are used to represent the different roles while creating endless artistic aesthetic feeling.

Bamboo Carving

Applicants: Shanghai and Hunan Province

Bamboo is a special product of China. Due to the close veins and tough qualities, it is often used as material to be processed in various bamboo artworks after folk artisans carve, engrave, hollow out, cauterize and weave. Bamboo carving is the most common form. Chinese bamboo carving follows traditional Chinese painting, calligraphy, bronze and stone carving, and woodblock prints in terms of art, integrates various art forms, and is accompanied by poems. It has a fresh and elegant style.

bamboo is sawn into tubes. The joints and skin of the tubes are removed to leave a layer of bamboo reed. It is boiled, polished, pressed, glued and inlaid on a wooden base or bamboo pieces, polished, and carved with patterns. The contents include figures, landscapes, flowers and birds and calligraphy works. In the National Palace Museum in Beijing there are many reed-turning bamboo carving works of the 18th Century. The carvings of reed-turning bamboo are mostly made on a very thin reed surface, so intaglio patterns with shallow carving form the majority. It is smooth like ivory. The products mainly include tea leaf pots, vases, reading lamps, photo stands, jewelry boxes, writing cases, pencil vases and fruit plates.

Grandfather together with his grandchild is carving bamboo.

Green-skin-left bamboo carving: the green hard skin of the bamboo surface is left for carving patterns, and then other green hard skins beside the patterns are scrapped off to expose the bamboo muscle as the base. The bamboo green hard skin is as clean as jade. The bamboo muscle has veins. The color of the bamboo skin is light and becomes brighter over time. As time goes by, the color of bamboo muscle becomes deeper and deeper like amber. Such bamboo carving is suitable for fully using the qualities and changes in colors with a natural tinge. Being strong or light depends on the scenes. The products mainly include book ballasts, pencil vases, table screens, and small table articles.

Clay Sculptures

Applicants: Tianjin, and Jiangsu, Henan and Shaanxi Provinces

(See P291)

Tar Monastery Butter Carving

Applicant: Huangzhong County, Qinghai Province

Tar Monastery is the center of Buddhist activities in northwest China. As one of the six great monasteries in China, it enjoys fame in Southeast Asia. Butter carving is a special skill of carving figures and is one of the three unique skills (butter carving, mural paintings and piled-up embroidery) of Tar Monastery. On the fifteenth day of the first lunar month every year, the monastery holds a grand religious conference and butter carvings are viewed as treasures offered to Buddha. Monks will show the butter carvings they have made carefully over a period of three months.

In winter, they will select the milk produced after the grass becomes yellow in autumn, as the butter made of it is pure white and not the usual yellow. The Buddha figures thus made will have faces like the moon and white and smooth skin. The selected butter is soaked in icy water and then kneaded for a long time until all impurities have been removed and the butter becomes smooth. Before sculpting, monks must bathe and undertake a series of religious activities. Then, they will discuss and select the subjects, make drafts, and divide the work between masters and apprentices good at figures, animals, flowers and buildings respectively. They do their respective work from the fifteenth day of the tenth lunar month to the fifteenth day of the first lunar month of the following year.

Painted butter clay is especially good for

large scenes with complex plots. It inherited the treatment of "different time and same place" in Buddhist mural paintings, and can make dozens of plots in the form of linked pictures on a same picture plane within a limited space. The linked pictures are arranged in a crisscross pattern and look complex but not disorderly.

Dengcai (Lanterns)

Applicants: Zhejiang, Fujian, Guangdong, and Qinghai Provinces

These are also called festival lanterns and are often hung on traditional festivals, birthdays, wedding days and other lucky days for a happy atmosphere.

Chinese lanterns are generally called Dengcai. They originated from the Western Han Dynasty some 1,800 years ago. Around the Lantern Festival on the fifteenth day of the first lunar month, people will hang red lanterns implying unity to create a happy atmosphere. Later, lanterns became the symbol of happiness and luck in China. After generations of inheritance and development among lantern artisans, rich varieties and superb skills have emerged. In terms of varieties, there are palace lanterns, gauze lanterns and hanging lanterns. In terms of images, there are figures, landscapes, flowers and birds, dragons and phoenix, and fish and insects. Chinese Dengcai integrates painting, paper-cuts, paper-fastening and embroidery and stitching. They are made of bamboo, wood, vine, wheat stalks, animal horns, metal, and silk produced in various areas. Among the Dengcai produced in ancient China, the palace lanterns and gauze lanterns are the most famous. Dengcai has the major function in lantern arts. With cultural amusement predominant, it combines folk customs, folk amusement and performance and involves various contents.

Many folk lanterns are famous and have been passed down due to the exquisite skill shown and unique artistic styles. Suzhou lanterns have pavilions as the major images. Inside the lanterns there are also patterns of landscape, flowers, birds, figures and animals. And colorful chromatographic paper-cuts are used to show the folk artistic flavors of watery regions in south China. In the Guangdong Xinhui dragon lantern some specially-made candles are burned inside the dragon body to illuminate it. In the dark night, a huge golden dragon flies over the sky and the atmosphere becomes mysterious.

Small and exquisite lotus lamp

Shengzhou Bamboo Weaving

Applicant: Shengzhou City, Zhejiang Province

Shengzhou City is the hometown of bamboo weaving in China. It abounds in bamboo that has good quality for making thin bamboo strips for weaving.

Weaving started from the Warring States Period some 2,000 years ago. During the Ming and Qing dynasties, Shengzhou bamboo weaving workshops could produce very exquisite products. Bamboo woven products became indispensable daily articles and were sold to Hangzhou, Shanghai and Nanjing. In the late 19th Century, bamboo weaving workshops appeared in Shengzhou and mainly produced lifting baskets, examination baskets, perfume baskets, food baskets, shoe baskets and other thin-strips bamboo articles.

Shengzhou bamboo weaving usually takes materials from various local abundant tough green bamboo, such as water bamboo, early bamboo and Mao bamboo. The cloven strip threads are as thin as a hair and the strip slices are as thin as paper. They can be woven to various shapes.

Shengzhou bamboo weaving is famous for exquisite weaving, complex procedures and rich patterns. It is divided into 12 categories of baskets, plates, pots, boxes, bottles, screens, animals, figures, buildings, furniture, lamps, and appliances with more than 6,000 patterns.

Shengzhou bamboo weaving combines thick and thin weaving methods. By the thin method, 150 bamboo threads can be woven in a length of 3.3 cm and they are exquisite and as thin as feather wings. By the thick method, the elasticity of bamboo can be used fully. The strips are inserted and woven artfully. They are bold and unrestrained and neat, refined and simple.

Wild-goose basket is the representative work of Shengzhou bamboo weaving. The head of the wild goose is buried inside the feathers. Its feet are put together and can be used as foundation feet, its wings are raised up and can be used as the basket handle, and its body is open and forms the container.

Painters from the Wutun Art Center, Regong, Qinghai Province are painting the Thangkas.

Regong Art

Applicant: Tongren County, Qinghai Province

Regong art is an important part of Tibetan Buddhist art and got its name as it was developed in Regong (meaning golden valley) in Huangnan Tibetan Autonomous Prefecture, Qinghai Province. Regong art mainly includes painting, as well as painted sculptures, building decorations, wood carvings, piled-up embroidery, etc. The major forms of Tibetan painting are Tangka (scroll cloth paintings) and mural paintings. The subjects involve Previous Life Picture (the stories about reincarnations of Buddha's ancestor in his pre-life), Buddhist legends, historical stories, and folk customs.

Tangka, the transliteration of "scroll paintings", is a kind of art with the largest quantity, widest popularity with Tibetans. Regong Tangka has a well-rounded structure with few blank spaces. The colors are bright, bold and unrestrained and many contrasting colors are used. Pure gold is often used to spot and draw lines.

Mural paintings are large-sized Tibetan paintings on the walls of monasteries and halls. Some are directly painted on the wall and others are painted on canvas, mounted and hung on the wall. Regong mural paintings are realistic with strong colors. Most are sprinkled with powder and gilded. They are splendid and magnificent with strong decorative styles.

Sculptures include clay sculptures, as well as wood, stone and brick carvings. Clay sculpture is also called painted sculpture. Buddha and Bodhisattva figures are applied in gold and Buddha's warrior attendants are painted in various colors. The wood carving surface is gilded or applied with other colors like clay sculpture.

Piled-up embroidery is a Tangka jointed by scattered silk pieces. The small ones are used to decorate halls, and the picture is mostly composed of one major Buddha and two small Buddha figures below. On the picture of the largest ones, the major Buddha is prominent and surrounded by Bodhisattva and attendant gods and various other patterns. The length of huge ones can be more than 100 or even hundreds of meters. They are especially used to "show Buddha" during religious conferences in monasteries.

Traditional Handicraft Skills

Yixing Zisha Ceramic Making Skill

Applicant: Yixing City, Jiangsu Province

This refers to a kind of folk traditional ceramic art located in Dingshu Town of Yixing City, Jiangsu Province. It has developed its own school in industrial arts circles due to its particular raw material, exquisite handicraft skills, simple, unvarnished and natural colors, and sculptures of various shapes.

Zisha is the most famous ceramic of Yixing, being made of zisha mud available in the local area. It is hard, smooth and exquisite, with gentle colors. The ceramics show different colors of azure blue, chestnut, dark liver, pear skin, red-sand purple, crab-apple red, dark gray, and dark green according to changes in compounding methods and kiln temperature. There are various shapes. Importance is attached to the treatment of lines and planes. Some natural objects are copied, such as fruits, melons and flowers. The products include tea ware, flower pots, etc., with the most outstanding achievements in the former.

The raw material is a kind of zisha mud (including purple, red and green mud) with special granule and double air-hole structures. It is a special local product in Yixing. More than a hundred self-made tools are adopted to beat mud pieces, beat tubes (column ware, inlay and connect tubes (square ware) or sculptures (flowery ware), polish surface, carve decorations, and finally finish off.

There are various types of Yixing zisha ceramics, such as pots, cups, dishes, bottles, basins, stationery, elegant playthings, and figure sculptures, etc. Among tea ware, zisha tea pot is the most famous as it retains the original taste of the tea. It is the biggest character of the tea pot. Because its air holes are big and can sop up much water and ventilate the tea well, it can preserve the color, fragrance and taste for a long time.

Purple Stoneware of the Ming and Qing Dynasties ever used in the court, which is collected in the Imperial Palace.

Jieshou Painted Pottery Firing and Manufacturing Skills

Applicant: Jieshou City, Anhui Province

Jieshou painted pottery skills were mainly distributed in 13 villages on the southern bank of the Yinghe River in Jieshou City. The villagers made a living by pottery making and the villages were named after kilns, collectively called the "thirteen kilns."

Jieshou painted pottery has long been connected with the original folk customs in the Huaibei region. After continuous development it has formed the following basic artistic features: "simple shapes, unvarnished, and massive, simple and vivid carving, shiny glazing, and possessing the functions of artwork and practical utensils."

The clay used is from the loess accumulated from flow of the Yellow River. It is easy to sculpt and the pottery fired from the clay has smooth quality and massive body. It has absorbed the shapes of bronze ware and porcelain but looks more unvarnished.

Before the Qing Dynasty, flowers, grass, fish and insects were the major themes. In the middle and later period, there appeared themes of traditional dramatic figures. It absorbed the artistic styles of local folk paper-cutting and wood-block New Year painting with strong local flavors. It also adopted mould-printing, carving, decoration by scraping off and painting.

Jieshou painted pottery absorbed and learned from the tri-colored glazing tomb figures of the Tang Dynasty in regard to glazing. A few drops of colored glazing are sprinkled on a layer of transparent lead glazing. After firing, some parts mixed with others and produced a drifting-cloud-like artistic effect. Jieshou painted pottery also has particular colorants. Besides copper and iron as the major colorants, there is quartz powder, which, in firing, reacts with make-up powder clay to create a deep red look. Contrasted with the white make-up clay, they form the particular style of Jieshou painted pottery, "red background with white decorations."

Shiwan Pottery Sculpture Skills

Applicant: Foshan City, Guangdong Province

Shiwan in Foshan City is an important pottery foundation south of the Five Ridges (area covering Guangdong and Guangxi provinces). Shiwan pottery sculpture skills were developed on a foundation of making pottery for daily use.

Shiwan pottery sculpture has the features of humanism, the local area and ethnic group, and it has particular artistic styles in creation.

The famous ridge adornments with Shiwan ceramic sculptures is on the roof of Ancestral Temple of the Chen Family. Most of the ridge adornments are the figures drawing material froom the historic stories and folk tales, with focus on their contour line and movements.

Shiwan toy pottery sculpture can be divided into five major types according to different shapes, i.e. person, animal, utensil, miniature, and tile ridge pottery sculptures. Represented by human shapes, Shiwan toy pottery sculpture combines both good shape and vivid expression. It absorbed various cultural and artistic elites. A high-level realism is combined with appropriate exaggeration and it shows both living interests and artistic tastes, forming the distinctive local features.

The first characteristic of Shiwan pottery sculpture is vivid shapes. The carving of persons, animals or utensils tries to create artistic and typical sculptures. Each piece of art work has distinctive character and features. Each has reached the artistic realm of "a hundred articles with a hundred different shapes and a thousand persons with a thousand different faces" with few being identical.

The second character of Shiwan pottery sculpture is its simple and vigorous body and glazing. Its body and glazing are both thick and show the elegant and solemn features. At present, there are more than 70 kinds of traditional glazing colors. In addition to the 12 kinds of crystal glazing, innovated first in China in 1963, there are more than 90 kinds of glazing colors. They add colorful artistic aesthetic feeling to Shiwan pottery sculpture. The mixed use of red and white clay in Shiwan has become a major symbol for distinguishing Shiwan pottery sculpture from those produced in other areas at home and abroad.

Li Ethnic Group Primitive Pottery Shaping Skills

Applicant: Hainan Province

Pottery making is one of the important handicraft industries among the Li ethnic group.

Middle-aged and old women in the villages carry out every stage such as digging clay, pounding it into powder, mixing mud pie, kneading, beating clay body, drying pottery utensils, and piling up firewood for firing. Men only do some miscellaneous tasks. This simple and primitive way of making pottery is preserved in Baotu Village, Shilu Town on the bank of the Changhuajiang in Hainan Province. Archaeologists regard it as a living fossil in the history of pottery making.

According to traditional Li custom, before firing the pottery, some skillful woman will pray and drive away ghosts. A young man will then drill the wood for firing, and a female elder will receive the kindling to light the tinder. When the firewood is burned to carbon, women will throw dried straw from all directions onto the pottery to support the fire. After the straw is burned, there will be a thick layer of ash on the pottery.

After more than two hours of firing, the pottery can be removed. Women will at once sprinkle the juice of a local plant on the pottery to increase hardness.

Dai Ethnic Group Slow-wheel Pottery Manufacturing Skills

Applicant: Xishuangbanna Dai Autonomous Prefecture, Yunnan Province

Slow wheel is an important tool for making pottery invented by primitive human beings in the Neolithic Age after they learnt how to knead pottery by hands. This helped produce a wall with even thickness and more beautiful shape. A slow wheel was soon replaced by more advanced quick-wheel technology, making it easier to shape as well as satisfying the demands for volume production. About 4,000 years ago, quick wheel became the most universal tool for making pottery. But in the habitation area of Dai people in Xishuangbanna the ancient manufacturing skills of Neolithic Age have been preserved.

The earthen pottery of the Dai ethnic group is widely used in daily life, production and Buddhist activities. The tools for making pottery include wood pottery bat, pebble, bamboo slips, wooden block, wooden hammer, small winnowing pans of various sizes and decorations. The raw material is abundant local clay. The pottery includes pots, jars, rice steamers and kettles, etc., the earthen pot being the most famous. It is easy to make this by traditional methods to cook delicious food, ensure the water it holds to become cool and tasty, and preserve the best medicinal qualities when boiling medicines. It is favored by local people. The pots are all made by women in the Dai ethnic group.

Dai traditional pottery making process

The pottery is made by hand with a slow wheel, the surface of all articles decorated with lines by wooden bats similar to the pottery decorated with lines of the Neolithic Age unearthed from south China. As to materials, mud is mixed with sand. There are various methods of baking in the open air and closed semi-baking. And there are various shaping methods, such as non-wheel shaping, slow wheel prodded by the toes, and wheel prodded by hands. These technologies fully prove that the pottery production by the Dai ethnic group has completely preserved the manufacturing skills of ancient times.

Uyghur Ethnic Group Earthen Pottery Molding, Firing and Production Skills

Applicant: Xinjiang Uyghur Autonomous Region

The Uyghur ethnic group earthen pottery manufacturing skills are distributed in Kashi and Turfan in the south and east of Xinjiang Uyghur Autonomous Region respectively and have a history of more than 2,000 years. The skills emerged along with the opening of the Silk Road and have been passed down through many generations without any detailed written record.

Earthen pottery is made of river mud that is mixed with the reed catkin on river banks. They are kneaded repeatedly with water, the prepared pottery mud is placed under a self-made wooden axis plate, and people step on the board to make it turn. The two hands above the plate cooperate with the turning mud-denuded body without any blueprint or molding board. What they want to make can all be realized by feel and experiences.

The decorations on Xinjiang earthen pottery can be viewed as seeking of pure beauty by craftsmen. They bring their intelligence to bear in selecting the most distinctive places on the common pottery they touch every day, applying various methods of engraving, printing, painting, turning, and pasting, and show superbly their artistic expressive forces regarding simplicity versus complexity and the abstract versus hard reality. The decorations mainly draw materials from various flowers, branches, leaves, and vines in real life.

The potteries of Uyghur ethnic group are all exaggerated. The particular shaping is mainly represented by various kettles with distinctive Arabian styles. The Abudu kettle is especially strange. It is an article for Uyghur people to wash their hands. Its strangeness is represented by five holes on the two sides of the kettle, which, contrary to appearance, do not penetrate inside so the water will only run out through the spout and not the holes.

Yaozhou Kiln Ceramic Firing and Manufacturing Skills

Applicant: Tongchuan City, Shaanxi Province

Porcelains made in the Yaozhou kilns

Yaozhou Kiln is represented by Huangpu Town in Tongchuan City. During the Song Dynasty Tongchuan was under the jurisdiction of Yaozhou Prefecture, hence the kiln name. The kiln began to fire ceramics from the Tang Dynasty, reached its peak at the end of the Northern Song Dynasty, but was closed during the first half of the 16th Century. The products were mainly for civil use. Yaozhou Kiln also fired black, blue and white glazed porcelain. The outstanding achievement is the decorations including lotus flowers, twisted branches and flowers, wave lines and designs of fish and birds, etc.

The traditional arts and crafts of Yaozhou Kiln are mainly represented by seven aspects of collecting and compounding, components and processing, kneading of the mud, shaping by hand, carving, engraving, cutting, pasting and printing designs by hand, selecting, making and applying glaze, making earthen articles and kiln appliances and putting them in the kiln, and careful control of the temperature, atmosphere and firing degree. The manufacture of one piece goes through 17 procedures. Each procedure has specific technical requirements.

As to the characters of products, during the Tang Dynasty and Five Dynasties, the body was loose and looked gray, the glaze was not limpid and had the feeling of turbid milk; during the Song Dynasty, the celadon body was hard and thin and looked gray-brown or gray-purple, the glaze was glittering and transparent and looked as green as an olive, and the thin glaze was in the color of yellow ginger; in the 12th to the 14th Centuries, the body was crude and looked light gray or gray, and glaze was mostly in the color of yellow ginger and green glaze was rarely seen. The glaze was thin and not smooth.

As to decorative ways, engraving and printing designs are the major methods. In engraving designs, the blade of the knife must be sharp and the lines are fluent and free and easy. In printing designs, the layout is precise and attention is paid to symmetry. There are various types of designs and most are complex and filled with patterns. As to decorative art, the patterns are rich and colorful such as animals, persons, flowers and paintings.

Jingdezhen Porcelain Handicraft Skills

Applicant: Jingdezhen City, Jiangxi Province

Jingdezhen is an old city famous for producing pottery and porcelain. Jingdezhen began to production from the Five Dynasties (907-960) and has always been the "capital of porcelain".

Jingdezhen porcelain has beautiful shapes, various types, rich decorations and unique styles. The porcelain quality is as white as jade, as bright as a mirror, as thin as paper and having the sound like a chime stone. Blue-and-white porcelain, Linglong, powder color, and colored-glazing porcelains are known as the four great famous traditional porcelains in Jingdezhen.

Jingdezhen Porcelain

Jingdezhen blue-and-white and Linglong (exquisite) porcelain were created and developed on the basis of the skills of hollowing out in the early 15th Century. Porcelain craftsmen hollow out the porcelain body with rice-grain spots by a knife blade, known as "mitong" (rice hollow) or linglong eyes. They apply linglong glaze, add blue and white decorations, and then put it in a kiln for firing. It is exquisite, clear, bright, limpid and elegant.

As to Jingdezhen blue-and-white porcelain, the porcelain body is decorated with designs by powder blue after being glazed; it is fired one-off at high temperature. The blue and white reflect each other with joy. It is glittering, translucent and beautiful. The designs are pleasing to both the eye and the mind. Many treasures are collected by museums in the UK and US.

Pink color is a decoration on the glaze. To make it, people draw the outline of designs on white-body porcelain, color the designs, and fire it at a temperature of more than 700 degrees Celsius. It has a gentle color and is exquisite and neat. It has the flavor of traditional Chinese paintings and a sense of bas relief. The paintings are full of strong national features.

With some oxide metals added in the glaze, the porcelain will show some original color after being fired and this is colored glaze.

Thin-body porcelain is as thin as a cicada's wings and as light as gauze.

Longquan Celadon Firing and Manufacturing Skills

Applicant: Longquan City, Zhejiang Province

Longquan is a famous historical and cultural city in Zhejiang Province well known for producing celadon. Longquan Kiln is the largest celadon kiln in China with the longest firing history, widest distribution, best production quality and largest production scale.

Longquan Kiln has a production history of more than 1,600 years. Works are mainly attractive for their glaze color. Glaze is often applied several times and thus is very thick with a strong sense of glass. As to the white-body celadon produced in Longquan Kiln, the body is smooth and exquisite and shows blue in white. The glaze is gentle without chapped pieces, and the bottom looks reddish brown and is commonly called "vermilion bottom." The famous pink-blue glaze and plum-blue glazes produced in Longquan Kiln glitter like green jade and reach the best realm of blue color in ancient China.

Longquan celadon is divided into two types of senior-brother kiln and junior-brother kiln. The main difference is that the celadon produced in the senior-brother kiln has chapped pieces while that produced in junior-brother kiln doest not. Chapped pieces are lines like cracks on surface of celadon and they appear in the course of cooling in the kiln as the expansion of the celadon body is larger than that of glaze. They are naturally a kind of defect, but produce a special decorative effect like gold thread and iron wire.

Celadon produced in the junior-brother kiln has a beautiful shape, thick and solid body, and glittering, pure and jade-green glaze. It is composed of plum green, pink green, bean green, and crab-shell green. The moist pink green looks like pretty jade and glittering plum green looks like emerald. The glaze surface looks like turbid milk and is not transparent, the glaze color is green, gentle and moist, and the glaze is smooth and tender like jade.

Among the celadon produced in the senior-brother kiln "ice-crack line" is the most beautiful. It has unique originality and looks like pieces of transparent ice. The natural cracks look like colliding ice pieces. The cracks are deep and thick and look like fish scale and pieces of plum blossom. Piles of crack pieces have a strong three-dimensional feeling.

Cizhou Kiln Firing and Manufacturing Skills

Applicant: Hebei Province

The site of Cizhou Kiln is in the region of Guantai Town and Fengfeng Mining area in Ci County, Handan City. In ancient times, this area was under jurisdiction of Cizhou Prefecture. Chinese pottery and porcelain reached the peak of development in the Song Dynasty. Cizhou Kiln was the largest folk kiln system in northern China.

Among various types of porcelain produced in Cizhou Kiln, the most famous ones include white ground and black patterns (iron rust patterns), engraved and cut patterns, and black glaze changed in kiln. Its decorative techniques broke through the limitation of the popular solo color of the Five Great Famous Kilns at that time and scores of colorful decorative techniques were adopted. Craftsmen of Cizhou Kiln absorbed the techniques of traditional water-ink paintings and calligraphy works. They created the decorative art of white ground and black painting with the style of water-ink paintings and initiated the colored painting decoration for porcelain in China. The masterly painting skills that finished patterns without any letup make many artistic masters acclaim it as the peak of perfection.

There are two types of body for the porcelain produced in Cizhou Kiln: one is hard, smooth and gray-white body and the other is crude and reddish brown body. The white glaze universally looks milky white and is not transparent. Make-up clay is used and the inside of the porcelain is usually glazed. As to decorative crafts, there are cutting, picking and pearl-field-like patterns in addition to black, brown and green paintings. The decorative themes are abundant such as playing horses, playing bears, fishing children, driving ducks on pond, and lifting up balls. The lines are fluent with bold and unrestrained style and folk living interests. Meanwhile it is frequent to see inscriptions of poems of the Tang Dynasty, ci of the Song Dynasty and folk proverbs and aphorisms as particular decoration.

Cizhou Kiln is also characterized by decoration of various records of the year, inscription of sentences, names and poems and names on articles. The writing style has no fixed rule and is very free. Aphorisms, lucky words and proverbs are frequently seen.

Dehua Porcelain Sculpture Firing and Manufacturing Skills

Applicant: Dehua County, Fujian Province

One type of Dehua porcelain sculpture makes use of high-quality kaolin and is directly sculpted to shape, the other is made by a mud sculpture mould that is filled with the thick liquid or rubbed for shaping. According to the actual requirements they can be glazed and then fired at more than 1,000 degrees Celsius.

In the early Song Dynasty Dehua products were mainly blue and white porcelain. With the continuous enhancement in technology, white-glazed porcelain developed gradually. In the Ming Dynasty, the white glaze looked like suet and jade and a unique "ivory white" was invented, becoming representative of Chinese white porcelain. The decorative crafts mainly include engraving, painting and printing patterns and piling and pasting patterns.

Engraving patterns often has the same position as painting patterns, so they are usually linked. It was a universal decorative technique in firing celadon in Dehua Kiln in the Song Dynasty. Bamboo slips or bamboo pens were used to engrave and paint various patterns on the wet body. Due to the features of bamboo pens, the engraved patterns had distinctive inclined cutting marks. The lines are fluent, bold, unrestrained, vivid and neat.

Porcelains made in the Dehua kiln

Dehua white porcelain is pure white and as smooth as jade, and its glaze surface is smooth and produces a sound like a chime stone. The particularly-made thin-body products are as thin as cicada's wings and extraordinarily exquisite. The folk sculpture craftsmen in Dehua combine sculpture and porcelain and are good at producing white-porcelain Kwan-yin sculptures that have vivid bearing and are regarded as treasures of white porcelain around the world. Dehua white porcelain does not seek for brilliance but for purity, snow white and elegant beauty. The craftsmen have full knowledge about the materials they use and the design orientation shows fully their creative intelligence.

Chengcheng Yaotou Ceramic Firing and Manufacturing Skills

Applicant: Chengcheng County, Shaanxi Province

Chengcheng Yaotou ceramic is fired by local farmers in the slack season and the skills have been passed down for generations. In summer and autumn they produce the body and paint patterns for firing in winter. White, yellow and black are the three major glaze colors and the pattern colors include white, yellow, blue and reddish brown. The products include various household utensils such as bowl, dish, pot, jar, plate and urn and various exquisite toys. They have the shapes of typical traditional folk style.

Yaotou crude porcelain was famous folk porcelain in the history of northern Shaanxi and has a production history of 1,300 years. The site of kiln is also an important place of folk ceramic cultural remains of past dynasties.

Iron rust pattern is the product of Yaotou Kiln during the Song and Yuan dynasties. A paint containing ferric oxide is used to paint flowers and patterns on the porcelain body applied with white make-up clay or black, yellow and green glaze, and then a transparent glaze is applied. It is one of the representative decorations in Yaotou Kiln. The patterns include five, six, seven, eight and nine points plum blossom, chrysanthemum, and butterflies and have the artistic features of water-ink Chinese paintings, being concise, unrestrained, and free.

Chengdi Yaotou crude porcelain is the most famous for black-glazed porcelain that is commonly called "black pearl." The layer of glaze has an even thickness and usually has tear marks (in early times). The glaze is pitch black and shining and small-sized articles look like a string of black pearls.

The Song Brocade Weaving Machine collected in the Suzhou Silk Museum

Songjin (Brocade of Song Dynasty) Weaving Skills

Applicant: Suzhou City, Jiangsu Province

Songjin (brocade is a kind of brocade first developed in the Song Dynasty mainly produced in Suzhou. It has brilliant colors, exquisite patterns, and solid and tender quality. It forms with Nanjing Yunjin, Sichuan Shujin the three famous brocades of China.

Songjin produced in Suzhou is exquisite with elegant artistic style and possesses the traditional styles and features after the Song Dynasty. In the traditional production of Songjin, there are as many as 20-plus procedures from silk reeling, dyeing to weaving products. The silk is characterized by showing patterns through combined longitude and altitude threads. It is produced by hand with a loom. Songjin initiated some particular skills such as connecting knots on the surface latitude threads and newly-polished color. Songjin is smooth, stiff and neat. Patterns are complex and include geometrical designs. There are many layers and colors are pure, clean, simple and elegant. It is suitable for making dresses, adornments and upholstering calligraphy works and paintings. After the Song Dynasty most of the treasures of paintings and calligraphy works are mounted by Songjin.

Songjin is mainly divided into box brocade, big brocade and small brocade, big brocade being most representative. It is thick and massive with exquisite patterns and is mainly woven by gold and silver threads. The product is beautiful and magnificent and suitable for making decoration for various paintings and calligraphy works. Small brocade is soft and solid and is often made of natural silk. The dresses and adornments made of small brocade are elegant and noble and are still very popular. Box brocade is mostly used in works with ancient styles such as folded screen in ancient style and paintings and calligraphy works of masters. The high-grade occasion is ornamented by box brocade to set off the classical atmosphere.

Nanjing Yunjin (Cloud Brocade) Wooden Loom Handicraft Weaving Skills

Applicant: Nanjing City, Jiangsu Province

Nanjing Yunjin (cloud brocade) is a kind of traditional jacquard silk weaving brocade among the brocade crafts in China reflecting elite Chinese silk weaving skills.

Among ancient silk weaving products, jin (brocade) represented the highest skill level. Nanjing Yunjin concentrates all the great achievements of brocade skills of past dynasties and got its name due to its floweriness and brilliance like clouds.

Yunjin is made by an old wooden loom. It is necessary to finish the weaving by a jacquard worker and a weaving worker. The two persons can only produce five to six centimeters every day, and they cannot be replaced by a machine. Yunjin is mainly characterized by different colors. For example, from different observation angles, the flowers on the embroidery can show different colors. As it was used for royal dresses and adornments, great attention was paid to materials regardless of cost and improvements emerged in the course of production.

Yunjin is often woven by gold, silver, and copper threads, long silk, spun silk, and various bird and animal feather and hair. For example, on the embroidery of royal Yunjin, the green was made of peacock feathers. Each pattern on Yunjin has a specific meaning. A piece of brocade of 78 cm wide has 14,000 silk threads on the weaving surface and all the flowers and patterns are organized by shuttling between the 14,000 threads. The whole course from fixing the longitude and latitude to the final production is as complex as computer programming.

Weaving products with adornments represent the skill and style of Yunjin. The patterns have precise and solemn arrangement and concise and general shapes. Large-sized, plump patterns are arranged continuously in four directions in most cases, and sometimes there is only one proper pattern with adornment (such as the dragon robe of the Ming and Qing dynasties and carpets and mats on the kang.

Suzhou Kesi (Silk Tapestry with Cut Designs) Weaving Skills

Applicant: Suzhou City, Jiangsu Province

Kesi (silk tapestry with cut designs) is the prime silk artwork in China. Patterns on the product are shown by colored latitudinal threads as borders of patterns and it has the effect of engraving and hollowing out. It has a three-dimensional sense on both surfaces. It mainly exists in Suzhou and neighboring areas. After the Southern Song Dynasty, Suzhou became a major producing area of kesi characterized by exquisiteness, simplicity, elegance, and showing delicacy amid brilliance. It is regarded as the highest grade in silk products and is the earliest silk product for artistic appreciation.

Kesi is a special silk craft and is different from common silk and brocade. Before weaving kesi, artists paint drafts such as figures, landscapes, fish and insects, birds and animals. Then craftsmen follow the drafts, add the raw silk longitudinal surface, make use of bamboo-leaf-shaped small shuttle on a wooden loom, and weave the product with various colored threads by "passing longitude and returning on latitude." It is an integrative art of painting and silk weaving. A piece of kesi has the same patterns on both surfaces and has the same effect as double-surface embroidery by different approaches. It is similar to carving from points of view of the vertical separation place on painting.

Kesi weaving mainly makes use of an ancient wooden loom and several bamboo shuttles and plectrums and makes the colorful silk threads into a weaving product by cut designs with abundant colors by means of "passing longitude and breaking latitude". This kind of weaving product does not have any differences between positive and reverse surfaces. On the outlines of designs and changes of colors, the surface of weaving seems like be cut by a knife and shows small space or broken marks, hence the name of kesi (cut designs). In course of making a piece of kesi, various skills need to be applied and shuttles need to be changed thousands of times, so the work is especially precious.

Shujin (Sichuan Brocade) Weaving Skills

Applicant: Chengdu City, Sichuan Province

Shujin (Sichuan brocade) is the decorative brocade made in Chengdu. It has a history of more than 2,000 years and can be viewed as the first milestone in Chinese brocade. It is famous for exquisite and meticulous patterns and changeable and abundant colors.

Shujin emerged in the Han Dynasty and is varieties became more abundant after the Tang Dynasty. The patterns are mostly group-flowers, tortoise shell, panes, lotus flowers, pairs of birds, pairs of animals, and flying phoenix, etc. After the Qing Dynasty, due to the impact from brocades made south of the lower reaches of the Yangtze River, Shujin gave birth to yuehua (moon shining), yusi (rain thread), fangfang (pane), and huanhua (washing flower) brocades. Among them, yusi and yuehua brocades with tinged color strips are the most particular. Yusi brocade shows special artistic effects by changes in the width of the longitudinal colored strips and yuehua brocade is characterized by different shades of strips. In course of leading longitude in yuehua brocade, yuezi (a kind of tool for weaving silk product) are arranged according to the number of color strips and longitudinal thread compounds, the order and width of color strips, and the rules of changes in shades of color. After leading a section of the longitude, some yuezi must be changed, called as "change hands by hands". It is a way of leading the longitude particular in Shujin. During the Han and Tang dynasties looms with multiple peddles and footsteps were used frequently, and after the Tang and Song dynasties, bundle jacquard looms were frequently used. Modern Shujin adopts the way of a full-sized longitudinally separated strips.

Wunijing Handicraft Cotton Weaving Skills

Applicant: Shanghai

Wunijing handicraft cotton weaving skills originated from the weaving skills Huangdaopo learned from Yazhou (Hainan Island) and then reformed during the Yuan Dynasty. She invented a set of instruments consisting "cotton gin, gin bow, spinning wheel (three-spindle foot-treadle spinning wheel), and loom", which enhanced the spinning efficiency and offered great advantages. She made use of alternated yarn, color compounds, bundle threads and decoration skills to produce the famous Wunijing quilt and pushed forward the development of cotton weaving skills and the cotton weaving industry along the Songjiang.

Huangdaopo's contributions to cotton weaving are mainly represented by: rolling, the primitive way of removing seeds from cotton by hand was eliminated and the semi-mechanical work of the gin was adopted; fluffing, the original stringed bamboo bow for fluffing cotton was eliminated and a big bow of 1.33m long equipped with a rope was adopted allowing great amplitude of vibration; spinning, the single-spindle hand-operated spinning wheel was changed to three-spindle foot-treadle spinning wheel; and weaving, she developed the jacquard methods for cotton weaving to produce cotton cloth with various patterns. The reforms adopted by Huangdaopo formed the most advanced handicraft cotton weaving skills at the time. Her hometown, Songjiang, suddenly became the largest cotton weaving center in China and Wunijing cotton weaving products won fame "covering the whole world by the dresses and quilts made of it."

Wunijing cotton weaving skills changed the thousands of years of tradition in China with silk and hemp fiber as major materials for cloth.

Tujia Ethnic Group Brocade Weaving Skills

Applicant: Xiangxi Tujia–Miao Autonomous Prefecture, Hunan Province

The Tujia girls make brocade while singing.

Tujia brocade is a handicraft of Tujia ethnic group girls. They use an ancient wooden waist loom and weave the products with cotton yarn longitudinally and colorful silk or cotton thread (also wool in modern times) as latitudinally.

The tools for Tujia brocade are very simple and primitive. But compared to other folk brocades, its particular skills are unique, i.e. the diagonal weaving by longitudinally, latitudinally and diagonally. Three layers of longitude thread are interlaced with that lying latitudinally. After the upper and lower parts are divided into longitudinal lines, the surface longitude is divided in half. The longitudinal line is picked out and the latitudinal one broken, patterns are dug out and woven by picking, so that the latitudinal patterns can change colors at random. It is flexible in a way that cannot be replicated by machine weaving. A particular handicraft feature and brocade surface effect is got to show the potential value and artistic charm of Tujia brocade.

Traditional weaving skills are closely related to the representation of decorative patterns with styles. Due to craft limitations, it is impossible to create too complex, abstract and exquisite natural patterns. The patterns on weaving products only show the arrangement of some rules and color spots.

As to the artistic features of Tujia brocade, importance is attached to representation and creation. The patterns are like natural things in spirit. It has bright, sharp colors, strong contrast, and symmetrical lines. The products are durable. Tujia brocade has brilliant colors. It mainly uses dark blue or black as ground color and brilliant colors are used for harmonious proportion between colors.

Tujia brocade follows the waist diagonal loom (fastening longitudinal threads on the waist). A weaver looks at the reverse surface and weaves the front. It is necessary for the weaver to remember and represent well the patterns and colors. The traditional weaving mode by picking makes the ups and downs of the longitudinal and latitudinal threads become even and the products durable with persistent luster.

Li Ethnic Group Traditional Cotton Weaving Dyeing and Embroidery Skills

Applicant: Hainan Province

Li ethnic group traditional cotton weaving dyeing and embroidery (Lijin) skills combines Li ethnic group cotton weaving, hemp weaving, and printing and dyeing skills.

The living area of the Li ethnic group abounds in weaving raw materials such as silk cotton and wild hemp. Before cotton textiles became popular, those using wild hemp prevailed in the area. People usually strip the bark of collected wild hemp in the rainy season, and after the procedures of soaking and washing, this becomes pieces of hemp. After dyeing, the hemp pieces are twisted into hemp yarn by hand or by spinning wheel, and then woven into cloth.

Women of Li ethnic group use simple tools (crouching loom) to weave Lijin (Li brocade), Limu (Li curtain), Lidan (Li sheet), barreled skirt, decorated cloth and head kerchief with beautiful designs and patterns. Straight lines, parallels, triangles, squares, and circles are used to compose more than a hundred patterns of strange flowers and grass, flying birds, running animals and figures with decorative value and particular national styles.

The patterns on Li ethnic group brocade are mostly embroidered by hands at random without following any painted sketches. Some embroidery pieces are inlaid with gold thread, silver foils, mica pieces, feathers, shells, stringed pearls and copper wires to show brilliance, brightness and elegance. On other embroidery pieces transformed and exaggerated lines are used to embroider exquisite, elegant, particular and brilliant goods.

The Li Brocade in Hainan Province

The Li ethnic group characteristically binds the longitudinal threads before dyeing, and weaving them with colored latitudinal threads, i.e. dyeing before weaving. The designs are both precise and colorful with brilliant and abundant layers to give strong artistic inspiration.

Zhuang Ethnic Group Embroidery Skills

Applicant: Guangxi Zhuang Autonomous Region

People use manual looms equipped with a supporting system, transmission, treadle and jacquard installations to produce Zhuang brocade. Cotton yarns are used as longitudinal threads, various colored velvets are used as latitudinal threads, and Zhuang brocade is woven by means of passing longitudinally and breaking latitudinally. The applied traditional small wooden loom, also called a bamboo-basket loom, is set up with "flowery basket" for jacquard-woven patterns. Usage of the flowery basket is the most distinctive characteristic of the loom for Zhuang brocade.

One of the four great famous brocades in China, it is a national cultural treasure of Guangxi. It is an exquisite artwork woven of cotton or silk threads with vivid patterns, precise structure, brilliant colors, and vehement and bright national styles.

Zhuang people love bright colors. Red, yellow, blue and green are basic colors and others are supplementary ones. The contrast is distinctive and strong. Red is used as background full of a vehement, vivid and joyful atmosphere. Green is used for setting off and has a bright sentiment. The compound of yellow and green is brilliant. A piece of Zhuang brocade is composed of several or even more than ten colors. The proper compound is bright colored, brilliant and unified. The contrast is harmonious, and it is primitive, brilliant and profound.

There are roughly three patterns of designs on Zhuang brocade: first, two-directional or four-directional sequential geometrical patterns are woven, simple and bright. Second, the artisan weaves various geometrical patterns as background and decorates it with patterns of animals and plants to form multiple layers of compound pattern. It is clear and has a sense of bas relief. Third, several kinds of big or small geometrical patterns are combined and squares and circles interlude each other to weave a dense, compound geometric pattern full of rhythm sense and it has the beauty of precision and harmony.

Tibetan Ethnic Group Woolen Bangdian (Apron) and Qiadian (Rug) Weaving Skills

Applicant: Tibet Autonomous Region

Tibetan woolen weaving has a long history, its most famous products including apron and rug.

Bangdian is a special symbol on the costumes of Tibetan women. It is a colorful material with thin horizontal lines for making Tibetan robes. Later it became an adornment tied to the waist of Tibetan women and gradually became symbolic of the Tibetan apron. Tibetan people use bangdian to make women's waistcoats, aprons and satchels or inlaid on Tibetan robes.

The apron has brilliant colors and the weaving is precise, beautiful and natural. People first spin by hand, dye, brush away the hair, weave into strips and then sew to an apron. There are various kinds of apron, the best, called "xiema" in Tibetan language, being woven of 14 to 20 kinds of dyed woolen yarn. A common apron is called "pulu".

The making of bangdian is not simple. The original raw material is top-grade wool. A strip is obtained after the procedures of brushing away the hair, entwine, weaving patterns, coloring up, repeated dyeing by thick liquid, kneading, and drying. Among them, the dyestuff is made by a special Tibetan folk art of rock and plant matter. More than 20 kinds of brilliant colors can be dyed on wool.

Qiadian, i.e. Tibetan rug, is a kind of rug woven by hand of sheep's wool. It is usually about two meters long and one meter wide. The raw material has long fibers with good elasticity. The pattern has unique designs and brilliant colors and it is beautiful and natural. Qiadian has precise structure and brilliant colors. The patterns are mostly dragon, phoenix, deer, flower and grass.

Tibetan Ethnic Group Gyaya Carpet Making Skills

Applicant: Huangzhong County, Qinghai Province

Tibetan carpet is a traditional handicraft textile of the Tibetan ethnic group in Qinghai. Due to historical and geographical reasons, differences exist in knitting skills and pattern designs of Tibetan carpet between Ando and Kangba Tibetan areas. In the latter, many traditional knitting skills have been preserved and in the former, the Tibetan and Han cultures are combined in pattern designs with artful structure, harmonious color and unique style. Jiaya Tibetan carpet belongs to this genre.

The knitting skills contain much traditional folk culture information. It is made by hand knitting. Craftsmen use wool dyed by natural plants such as oak shell, rhubarb, flos sophorae buds and banlangen. After finishing a line, they will fasten all the wool knots and cut off the wreathing wool on a pole by knife. Then the surface of layers of cut-off wool will appear on the carpet. This craft is called as handicraft interlinked knots.

After the whole carpet is out, the craftsmen will trim it with scissors. It is worthy of attention that, in early times, craftsmen had no blueprint to follow. They knitted and wove according to the designed patterns in their minds and the patterns were identical to former designs. Tibetan carpet is made by hand from selecting materials, spinning, dyeing and knitting, so it has bright colors that do not fade and is hard and elastic. On the foundation of traditional knitting ways, the Tibetan ancestors also invented the particular interlinked knots that give the product particular artistic value.

Uyghur Ethnic Group Decorated Carpet and Cloth Weaving and Printing Skills

Applicant: Turpan, Xinjiang Uyghur Autonomous Region

The Uyghur weaving and printing in Xinjiang has a long history and the decorated carpet and printed decorated cloth are the most famous.

According to Uyghur traditional customs, everywhere indoors within sight must be decorated exquisitely, and woolen carpet is one of the traditional artworks for indoor decoration. The printed decorated cloth is characterized by combining handicraft and original printing technique with patterns of national styles. It has the quality of decoration and strong local flavor. There are various kinds of decorated carpet, including pressed, printed, painted and embroidered decorated carpets. There are more than 100 kinds of patterns of fabric for decorated carpet and printed decorated cloth, such as the pattern of Chinese character "寿(longevity)" with the impact of Han culture, Islam, patterns of a hundred antiques, geometrical and flower patterns of Arabian style, patterns of particular daily articles and tools of Uyghur people, patterns of pure kettle and holy niche with Islamic style, and even some patterns popular in ancient Western Region.

Color printing of decorated cloth is the major printing skill of Uyghur ethnic group and is divided into woodblock printing, bandhnu, and wood-mould seal printing. The latter is the most popular with the longest history. A wooden mold is engraved with patterns, dipped into various dyestuff made of natural plants and minerals, and printed as a seal on white handloom cloth. Various wooden molds with different patterns are combined together to print color-printed decorated cloth.

Nantong Indigo Blue Cloth Decoration and Printing Skills

Applicant: Nantong City, Jiangsu Province

he usage of indigo plant coloring matter in China can be traced back to the Spring and Autumn Period and the Warring States Period some 2,500 years ago. Indigo developed to blue printing over a thousand years ago. Indigo blue cloth is a traditional hollowed-out printing skill with resistance of white slurry. Lime and bean powder are mixed to make slurry and cloth is stuck to blue by indigo. The cotton is woven by hand, and the printing procedures include engraving cardboard and scrape-off slurry. Nantong indigo blue cloth decoration and printing skills have been passed till today and are still used to make daily articles by handicraft spinning, weaving and printing.

The most typical patterns for indigo blue cloth are blue ground with white decoration and white ground with blue decoration. As to the former, only one piece of patterned cardboard is necessary and the composed patterns are not connected with each other. As to the latter, usually two pieces of patterned cardboard are used for overprinting. Printing the first pattern cardboard is called "head board". After it is partially dry, people will print the second pattern cardboard that is called "cover board." Cover board covers the connected parts of the first pattern cardboard so that lines are connected together naturally. It is difficult to engrave the board for white ground with blue decoration and it is usually made by master artisans. These traditional skills with intersected blue and white grounds have complex production procedures. Some indigo blue cloth is reversible; so, it is necessary to scrape slurry on the reverse surface aiming at the right surface. After the slurry dries, the cloth is put on a copy table for scraping the slurry on the reverse surface. After dyeing, a reversible indigo blue cloth is made.

All the patterns on Nantong folk indigo blue cloth are carved by hand. Every piece of engraved cardboard seems like a paper-cut artwork with simple, straightforward and bright style. The artistic images are usually highly generalized and exaggerated with strong local characters. The folk indigo blue dyeing skills have basically retained traditional skills of hundreds of years.

Miao Ethnic Group Batik Cloth Dyeing Skills

Applicant: Danzhai County, Guizhou Province

The traditional skills of batik cloth dyeing have been passed down for generations within the Miao ethnic group in Danzhai, Anshun and Zhijin counties in Guizhou Province. The batik dyed by indigo has blue ground and white decoration.

Miao ethnic group batik has two kinds of skills of stippling and painting. In course of production, handloom cloth is soaked in water filtrated through plant ash to take the fats off the fiber so that it is easy to stipple the wax and for coloring up. Yellow wax of proper amount is placed in a small ceramic bowl placed over hot plant ash. After the yellow wax melts, people can use a wax knife to dip wax liquid and stipple it onto the cloth. There is usually no design model. Craftsmen paint according to their ideas and do not use a ruler or compass. The painted parallels, lines and circles are symmetrical. The patterns of painted flowers, birds, insects and fish are vivid. The cloth with stippled decoration is soaked in warm water and then in a prepared indigo dye vat several times. After being dyed, the cloth is washed in the river to rinse off the floating color. Then, it is put into a boiler with clean water. When the water boils, the yellow wax will melt and float on the surface to be recovered for future use. After the wax melts, the white decoration will appear. The batik is then rinsed repeatedly and, when the remaining yellow wax is cleared, the work is finished.

Batik featured an icy pattern that is admired by people. In course of continuous rolling, soaking, and dyeing, the wax on the semi-finished cloth will break and dye liquid sticks in the white cloth following the cracks, so that some natural patterns are left that are hard to paint by hand. Batik with the same design will reveal different icy patterns that seem, like fingerprints, to have no duplicate. They show a sense of fresh and natural beauty.

The Miao batika

Bai Ethnic Group Bandhnu Skills

Applicant: Dali City, Yunnan Province

Bandhnu is an ancient fabric dyeing skill in China. It is mainly produced in Dali and the users are mostly Bai ethnic group.

Bandhnu is divided into two parts, i.e. tying knots and dyeing. Yarn, thread and rope are used to tie, sew, bind, stitch, or nip fabric and then it is dyed. The tied parts of fabric can resist dyeing to maintain the original color and other parts can be dyed evenly. Therefore, tinge and wrinkle marks with uneven depth and abundant layers come into being. The firmer the knots are on the fabric, the better the resistance. Common bandhnu fabrics can be dyed with regular patterns, and exquisite artworks can also be dyed with complex structures and various brilliant colors to represent realistic patterns. They are simple, unvarnished, primitive, novel and fresh. Blue and white are the two major colors to represent the quiet and peaceful atmosphere and create simple and primitive information.

Dali Bai ethnic group bandhnu has a design composed of regular geometrical patterns. The structure is precise and plump. They mostly draw materials from images of animals and plants and dress and adornment patterns of royal members of past dynasties. They are made by hand stitching and soaked in plant dyestuff repeatedly. The products have non-fade brilliant colors.

Dali Bai ethnic group bandhnu uses pure cotton, silk fabric, hemp yarn, spun gold velvet, and corduroy as cloth materials. At present in addition to the traditional indigo kind of blue ground and white decoration, some new kinds of colorful bandhnu have been developed.

Xiangshanbang Traditional Architectural and Building Skills

Applicant: Suzhou City, Jiangsu Province

Xiangshan in Suzhou is situated by Taihu Lake and has a history of more than 2,500 years. In the more than a hundred villages there are large populations and little land. Many architectural craftsmen have been born here, so they are called "Xiangshan craftsmen." Xiangshanbang is a group of architectural craftsmen led by carpenters and integrating various classical architectural types such as plasterer, lacquerer, ash craftsman, sculptor, overlapping-hill craftsman, and painter.

The Imperial Palace and Tian'anmen in Beijing, Suzhou landscape gardens and other world-famous buildings were built up by Suzhou Xiangshanbang people.

Xiangshanbang traditional architectural and building skills are regarded as the outstanding representative of Suzhou-style architecture. It integrates architectural skills and art and is an important school of ancient Chinese architecture. In civil engineering, Xiangshanbang architectural and building skills inherited the models of Chinese traditional architecture and have strong local features. In aspect of architectural decoration, they are good at Suzhou-style wood-carving, brick-carving and colored painting.

The wood carving of Xiangshan craftsmen is excellent. The brick carving is famous around the world for the vigorous and wandering lines, vivid images, elegant style, lucky designs, sentiments suiting both refined and popular tastes, and handsome and free cutting ways. These skills are widely applied and developed in civil buildings in Suzhou.

The architectural technique of "broken-girder hall" in Huqiu, Suzhou, adopted the crafts of Bodhisattva roof, tessellation, pipa hanging and brackets. The two butt-joint girders are very solid and reflect the architectural features of Xiangshanbang: it is a rectangular structure, the components of each part and all the parts are joints of timber, and the rigidity completely depends on combination of tenon and mortise without any nail or iron component. They are exquisite, beautiful and steady.

Hakka Tulou (Stockade) Building Skills

Applicant: Longyan City, Fujian Province

More than 20,000 tulou buildings are distributed over 2,200 square km in Yongding, Longyan City, including nearly 5,000 large-sized buildings of at least three stories and more than 360 round buildings. These round and square grand tulou buildings with various postures and shapes are distributed in order with natural villages as units, integrating harmoniously with the green mountain and river, and comprising a tulou group with majestic vigor, splendor and rarity. The oldest tulou building has a history of 600 years.

Yongding tulou buildings are divided into round and square ones. These encircled buildings are grand, massive, rough, and majestic. In terms of architectural features, the round ones possess distinctive traditional Hakka colors and are the most exquisite. All the ancient structures have encircled buildings

Tu Lou (Earthen Tower), in Yougding, Fujian Province

inside. A building has hundreds of rooms, including halls, storage rooms, wells and bedrooms. Each building has its own defensive system.

Tulou is built up by earth, stone, bamboo, and wood. The main wall is tamped with immature soil. Branches, wood stuff, and bamboo pieces provide stiffening in the walls. Round tulou buildings are still favored today by villagers.

Many of the Yongding Hakka tulou buildings were designed according to the "Eight Diagrams" reflecting traditional Chinese culture. The most typical one is Zhencheng built in Hongkeng Village, Hukeng Town in 1912 and covering 5,000 square meters. It has an overhanging gable roof and post and lintel construction. There are two circles, inner and outer. There is a building inside a building and there is a building outside a building.

Jingdezhen Traditional Porcelain Kiln and Workshop Building Skills

Applicant: Jiangxi Province

Jingdezhen is the earliest porcelain city in China and the kiln and traditional workshop are rare evidence of the development of China's workshop handicraft industry.

An important reason for Jingdezhen to become the center of porcelain is its advantages in natural conditions. It abounds in raw materials. Within its territory run the Changjiang and its branches. It is convenient to transport pine firewood for the kiln, and to set up a water-powered device to crush and pan porcelain clay.

In the Ming Dynasty, Jingdezhen was called the "Capital of Porcelain". Blue and white porcelain became the mainstream in porcelain production in China. In the late 15th Century, doucai porcelain initiated a vogue for painted porcelain. Earlier in the same century, the success in firing copper-red glaze and other uni-color glaze reflected the superb skills of craftsmen of the time.

The particular shapes, structure, materials and functional requirements of the kiln and semi-finished products house resulted in the particular building skills of kiln and workshop. For example, in the 18th Century, Zhen kiln was the most popular kiln in Jingdezhen. The egg-shaped Zhen kiln belongs to the flat-flame kiln style. It integrated the advantages of dragon kiln, steamed-bread kiln, and gourd kiln and became the most outstanding kiln form in ancient China. Laying bricks and repairing kiln is called as Luan kiln, which cannot be found in other places. The semi-finished products house, i.e. workshop, is an important working place and also serves as a living room. It has a compact arrangement. The traditional kiln in Jingdezhen is broad, ventilated, economical, and practical, and serves as storage room, workshop and living place at the same time. It required very high architectural standards.

Dong Ethnic Group Timber Architecture Building Skills

Applicant: Guangxi Zhuang Autonomous Region

The timber architecture of the Dong ethnic group in the Sanjiang is represented by storm-proof bridges and drum towers. They have beautiful appearance and superb techniques. The whole building has tenons and mortises, crossed and joined girders, and standing pillars and connected square woods. There is not a single iron nail and all components are connected together by tenons and mortises. The construction is solid and joints firm. They have a very high craft and artistic value.

The buildings in villages of the Dong ethnic group include some basic constructions: drum tower, temple of grandmother, drama stage, civil house, veranda for drying grains, grain store, village gate, summer house, storm-proof bridge, and the level ground for singing before the drum tower. These ten great constructions comprise a complete complex.

The architects of Dong ethnic group are all local folk craftsmen. Blueprints are not necessary as they keep a mental picture of the structures and only use one tool, a traditional measuring ruler called a craftsman's pole. It is made of a piece of bamboo casually and has the same length as that of the middle pillar of the house. Craftsmen scrape the green skin off the bamboo piece and engrave the lengths and sizes of pillars, short columns, girders and other features with a bamboo pen, and chisel.

Traditional craftsmen of Dong ethnic group also use a set of architectural symbols that have been passed down for generations. There are 26 symbols but only 13 are in common use. Only Dong craftsmen understand these symbols similar to Chinese characters.

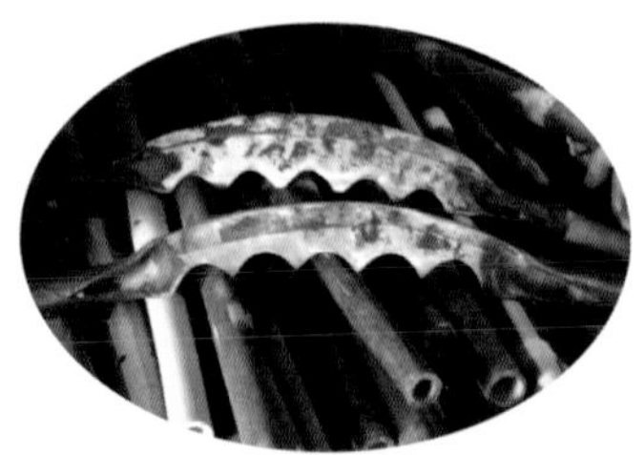

Tools used for more than 100 years to make vertical flute and flute in the flute-making family in Yuping County, Guizhou Province.

Yuping Flute Making Technique

Applicant: Yuping Dong Autonomous County, Guizhou Province

Yuping flute is made of the bamboo produced in Yuping Dong ethnic group Autonomous County, Guizhou Province. Yuping flute is a famous traditional bamboo tube musical instrument in China and is famous for its clear, fresh and beautiful tone color and exquisite engraving. It is a crystallization of many local nationalities' cultural development in Yuping such as Dong, Han, Miao and Tujia and has a high historical, cultural and crafts value.

The technique for making a Yuping flute has a history of more than 400 years. A local produced small fish scale bamboo is the material because it has long and even sections with proper thickness in wall and solid quality. There are three processes for making it, i.e. making foundation, engraving and finishing product. The making procedures are numerous and complex and are all by hand. From felling bamboo to finishing there are 24 procedures for making a vertical flute and 38 procedures for making a tuning flute. The surface of flute is finally engraved with poems and paintings.

As to the technique of making the foundation, pressing flat bamboo and opening holes are the most important part of making a traditional flat vertical flute. The technique of pressing flat bamboo is a unique consummate skill in making flutes in China. It is a procedure to treat the raw bamboo. People bake bamboo material by fire until it is wrought, use iron pincers to press lightly the bamboo tube over its full length to make it become an elliptical flat bamboo, and straighten it by use of a wooden clip. The wind holes on the flute must be opened well, or else the volume, tone and pitch will be adversely affected.

Among the various Yuping flutes, Dragon and Phoenix flute is the most popular one. The male one is fatter and the female one thinner. In playing, the sound of male pipe is vigorous and sonorous and the tone of female one is mellow, indirect and pretty. The cooperation between them seems like a chorus of a couple of lovers and the sound is harmonious and sweet.

Miao Compound Folk Footed House Architectural and Building Skills

Applicant: Leishan County, Guizhou Province

Xijiang at Leishan is the largest ancient village of Miao ethnic group in China. The houses there are mostly built facing stream with their backs to the mountain. Architects often make use of the big inclination of a mountain slope or the side close to a stream, so that the front half of a house can overhang in the air in various styles. The civil houses there are all timber construction without use of a single iron nail. Houses are connected by tenons and mortises and constructed along the contours of the hills. The houses have many stories and appear in the shape of a pyramid.

The building craftsmen in Xijiang confirm the building design according to the landform and building owners' requirements. They use axe, chisel, saw, plane, ink cup and ink thread to build the house on an incline ranging from 30 to 70 degrees. Column and tie construction is the major form, and they became known as "folk footed houses" from front eave columns overhanging (diaojiao).

A side folk footed house is built on a slope with large inclination and the back half stands directly on the ground or rock while the front half is supported by wooden columns made from locally abundant timber. The slope is divided into upper and lower grounds. Longer columns stand on the lower ground and shorter columns stand on the higher ground. The floor of the front half of the house parallels the ground of the back half house to form a side building. Wooden columns, wall and floors are all built up on the rock ridge several meters high. The house frame is six to seven meters high. The last column of each row stands as the same height as the ground of the upper house and forms the hanging columns.

Overlooking the Suspended Wooden Building in the Miao Village

A folk footed house of a Miao compound has flying rafters and turned-up edge. There are corridors on three sides with wood handrails hanging out. Patterns symbolizing luck are engraved on the handrails. The hanging columns are in octagonal or rectangular shape. Various decorations such as ball of silk strips and golden melon are engraved on the bottom of the lower hanging columns.

Suzhou Imperial-Kiln Golden Brick Manufacturing Skills

Applicant: Suzhou City, Jiangsu Province

Golden brick is the well-mannered name for large-sized square brick. According to the records in an ancient book Pave Ground by Golden Brick, golden brick is a fine-stuff square brick especially fired for use in the imperial palace. It had minute granules and dense quality, and makes a sound like metal and stone. The produced golden brick would be transported to Beijing especially for the imperial palace, so it is also called as "Jing brick."

The imperial kiln of golden brick is situated in Yuyao Village, Lumu Town, Xiangcheng District, Suzhou City. For many centuries, villagers there made their lives by firing. The yellow mud at Lumu Town is suitable for producing a brick with exquisite, particular and unique skills, the golden brick produced there is hard, and "striking it can produce sound and there is no hole after being broken", so the Ming Emperor Yongle granted Lumu brick kiln the title of "imperial kiln." All the grounds in Taihe Hall and Zhonghe Hall in the Imperial Palace and Tian'anmen Tower in Beijing were paved by these imperial golden bricks.

The production skills of imperial-kiln golden brick are particular and extraordinarily complex. More than 20 processes are closely linked. The particular materials and strict techniques make the finished imperial-kiln golden bricks appear dark green, smooth, unvarnished and solid. It is as flat as a whetstone and looks like beautiful jade and it is smooth as a mirror and looks like an ink stick. It has high practical and appreciation value. The ground paved by golden bricks is smooth, resisting erosion and becoming brighter over time, and not slippery or humid. It can prevent the underground humidity from rising up and serves as a foil to the grand and majestic imperial palaces.

Among the production processes of modern golden brick, almost all follow the traditional skills of hundreds of years except for polishing and cutting. It takes more than a half year to produce a finished golden brick, so production is limited.

Miao Ethnic Group Pan-Pipes Making Skills

Applicants: Guizhou and Yunnan Provinces

Pan-pipes are a traditional reed pipe musical instrument of the Miao ethnic group. On festivals Miao people hold various and colorful pan-pipes parties, playing and dancing.

The pan-pipes of the Miao ethnic group are composed of cup, pipes, reeds, and resonant pipes. A set of common pan-pipes has six pipes with sound-responding holes open on the outside. They are set up with copper reeds and stuck into a rectangular wood gourd, and each reed represents a tone. A bamboo pipe covers the second and third pipe and serves as the resonant pipe. The pipes of a small set of pan-pipes are more than 10 cm long, but those of larger models can be as long as four or five meters. Some bass pan-pipes have a thin bamboo pipe inside a big bamboo tube. After innovation, the number of pipes increased to more than 20, and each one is set up with a resonant pipe made of thin sheet copper. The diapason can cover two octaves and five more tones. The tone color of pan-pipes is bright and vigorous, and men and women can play the instrument.

In addition to some musical knowledge, a person should possess knowledge of physics and learn mechanical theories before making the instrument. The masters inheriting the production skills of pan-pipes in Miao ethnic group can produce various exquisite and practical pan-pipes only by means of wind box, hammer, brass, axe, chisel, saw, drill, bitter bamboo, tung oil, and lime (or latex that is frequently used today).

Pan-pipes are a symbol of the culture of the Miao ethnic group. Miao people combine libretto, music and dance together when playing them and preserve the originality and primitive simplicity of the history, culture and arts of Miao ethnic group.

Yangcheng Pig Iron Production Skills

Applicant: Yangcheng County, Shanxi Province

Yangcheng County is a remote mountainous area and is an important site of Chinese pig iron metallurgy. Crucible iron-smelting and Lilu (black furnace) iron-smelting are representatives of pig iron metallurgy skills in ancient China.

Yangcheng abounds in iron ore and mines are comparatively close to the surface. In production, the ore should be crushed at first, desulfurization by baking in high temperature, and then put into furnace. Lilu (a black furnace) is a Chinese-style vertical furnace. The inside cavity appears in the shape of curve and has the advantages of ventilation and fluidity. The charcoal burned from local high-quality timber is used as fuel and reducer for smelting. There is a complete set of mature skills for smelting. Craftsmen can well control the furnace situation, duration and degree of heating, and quality of iron and learn well the chemical components and temperature of molten iron by observing fire color and molten iron. The skill for observing molten iron can be regarded as a unique skill. The smelting craftsmen spoon out a little molten iron from the iron exit and observe the color and pattern changes on the surface to determine its quality.

In digging fields and ditches with a walking plough, the blade becomes bright through friction with the soil, so it got the name of plow mirror. It is surprising that Yangcheng plow mirror is made by casting directly raw molten iron, an extremely rare skill in the world.

Yangcheng pig iron production skills include iron-smelting in crucible, iron-smelting in Lilu furnace, and production of plough mirror.

Nanjing Gold Foil Beating Technique

Applicant: Nanjing City, Jiangsu Province

Gold foil beating technique is used to beat gold into excessively thin gold foils often used to decorate Buddha figures or articles. Jinling gold foil production has unique crafts with high requirements on technique. From ancient times it has involved manual beating and is a specific traditional craft in China.

In Longtan and Jiangning, in Nanjing, more than 10 procedures passed down from ancient times are still preserved in the course of producing gold foil. Among the procedures, beating into foil is the most painstaking. A lump of gold must be beaten down to about 0.1micron thickness. Two persons beat it face to face more than 10,000 times. The finished Nanjing gold foil is as thin as cicada's wings and as soft as silk.

The core of gold foil production technique is the secret of Wujin paper that is unique in the world. The gold slice should be wrapped in Wujin paper and be forged to gold foil of 0.12 micron with the size of 15 square centimeters after being beaten for hundreds of thousands of times. It is necessary for thin Wujin paper to be able to resist the repeated striking and high temperature and cannot be broken. Wujin paper is the guarantee for quality of gold foil.

Compared to gold foil, the technique of producing gold thread is even more complex although it is only an accessional product of gold foil. For producing gold thread, the gold foil is pasted on a piece of special paper; yuhuashi stone or agate is used to polish it and then it is cut into threads, and kneaded to round gold thread. There are 12 procedures from making paper to finished gold thread of less than 1 mm diameter. In ancient times, the gold thread would be given to weaving women to make "gold thread cloth" for royal families.

Longquan Precious Sword Forging Skills

Applicant: Longquan City, Zhejiang Province

Longquan precious sword is a representative of ancient Chinese weaponry with a history of more than 2,500 years. The sword produced in Longquan is "extremely exquisite and can cut copper like cutting mud." It is also called "seven-star sword". According to different performances, it can be divided into three types: hard sword (famous for solidity and sharpness), soft sword (famous for flexibility), and traditional wushu sword.

The production of Longquan precious sword passes through 28 procedures such as smelting, forging, shoveling, filing, engraving, inlaying copper, cold forging, quenching, and polishing. In the long course of development, the craftsmen of past generations studied carefully and kept improving until the sword formed its four great traditional features, i.e. firmness and sharpness, mutual assistance between strength and weakness, pressing chill, and exquisite decorative patterns.

The ancient Longquan precious sword was made of pig iron, but, today, it is made of medium-carbon steel along with the technique of quenching. The proper application of quenching makes medium-carbon steel possess the qualities of spring steel. A thin precious sword can be coiled to a circle and tied on waist like a belt. After being untied, the precious sword will straighten out as before.

Within the territory of Longquan, there is a kind of rubbing stone known as "bright stone". The finished sword rubbed by this stone has pressing chill qualities. Longquan precious sword is polished completely by hand. It often takes several days or even several months from superficial to careful and to refined polishing. The finished sword is dazzling.

The sword body is engraved with patterns of seven stars and a flying dragon. Engraving on sword body is also a unique skill of Longquan sword. Craftsmen do not need color pens or blueprint. They use a steel chisel to engrave on the sword body with a width of no more than 3.3 cm, pour in molten copper, and level and polish it. Then a vivid and natural flying dragon pattern appears and will never erode.

Zhang Xiaoquan Scissors Forging Skills

Applicant: Hangzhou City, Zhejiang Province

China's Time-hornored Brand Zhang Xiaoquan Scissor has a brand value of 46 billion Yuan.

In 1663, these scissors were invented in Hangzhou. Zhang Xiaoquan started his business by making traditional scissors for civil use and they possessed 10 great features, i.e. even inlaying of steel, clear demarcation between steel and iron, refined polishing, sharp blade, firm peg, opening and closing well, exquisite mode, novel engraving patterns, being durable, and being cheap with high quality.

Zhang Xiaoquan scissors made by traditional forging technique are all made by hand and each procedure is painstakingly carried out by the craftsman. The scissors are gripped by one hand while the other holds the hammer for continuous beating each day. The craftsman must be most careful when beating the seam and the procedure will not be finished until the scissors shine.

Two specific production skills of the traditional production procedures for Zhang Xiaoquan scissors have been passed down. Firstly, the skill of inlaying steel and forging: the routine of forging scissors by pig iron was changed. They selected good steel from Longquan and Yunhe in Zhejiang and inlaid it on wrought iron. Then, they rubbed it with very fine mud produced particularly in Zhenjiang. After forging many times, the blade of scissors were made and polished by Zhenjiang mud brick. Second, there is the manual engraving skill on the surface of the scissors. Craftsmen engraved the patterns of landscape of the West Lake, flying birds and running animals that are vivid, consummate and exquisite.

New inventions have been made continuously on the basis of inherited traditional skills. The largest scissors are as long as 1.1 meters with the weight of 28.25 kg, while the smallest travel scissors are only 3.3 cm long with the weight of 0.01 kg.

Wuhu Iron Picture Production Skills

Applicant: Wuhu City, Anhui Province

Wuhu has always had a developed iron smelting industry since ancient times with the fame of "iron will become steel naturally after coming to Wuhu". Wuhu iron picture production skills came into being on this foundation. Mild steel is used as raw material for producing iron picture and iron slice and thread are forged and welded to produce various decorative pictures. It is purely made by hand.

The iron picture absorbed the composition of traditional Chinese paintings and the techniques of gold and silver ornaments, paper-cutting, and sculpture. With wrought iron as material, craftsmen forge the iron according to painting drafts. After smelting, forging, welding, drilling, filing, shaping, and lacquering to prevent rust, they set it off against a white background and frame it. The picture retains the original color of iron without coloring and various artworks come into being with exquisite patterns of landscape, figures, flowers, insects and fish, flying birds and running animals. It has both the artistic concept of traditional Chinese paintings and water-ink paintings and strong artistic three-dimensional sense. Black and white are clearly demarcated and it is vigorous and solemn. It has both the romantic charm of traditional Chinese paintings and three-dimensional beauty of sculpture and reflects the softness and ductility and elongation of steel and iron.

There are three types of iron pictures. The first is small-sized scenes. The major themes include pine tree, plum blossom, orchid, bamboo, chrysanthemum, and eagle. Such iron pictures are set in a frame and hung on a white wall. Black and white are clearly demarcated, lines are vigorous, tall and graceful, and the structure is clear. They are most elegant and striking. The second type is colorful lanterns often composed of four to six iron pictures. They are pasted with paper or white silk inside and in the middle a candle can be lit. The third type is a folded screen, mostly landscape scenes simple, unvarnished, elegant and splendid.

Miao Ethnic Group Silver Jewelry Making Skills

Applicants: Guizhou and Hunan Provinces

Silver jewelry is the favorite traditional adornment of the Miao ethnic group. A dressed-up Miao woman can wear about 10 to 15 kg of such jewelry, which is used to show aesthetic judgment and wealth and for warding off evil.

The silver jewelry of Miao ethnic group covers abundant themes in patterns and shapes distinctively reflecting the history, worship of nature, gods and totems. In terms of shape, attention is paid to pure representation of quality and silver is rarely combined with other materials. It is thin and exquisite. The shapes are unchangeable - after being fixed by the ancestors, they form an important symbol of the family branch.

Exquisite silver decorations for Miao girls

The processing of silver jewelry is finished by hand in family workshops. On a foundation of varying requirements, silversmiths make melted silver into slice, bar or thread, make exquisite patterns by pressing and engraving, and weld or knit them into the proper shape. The silver slice requires the most painstaking work. A silver bar must be made into a large, thin slice, the slice is cut into small pieces according to demand, the pieces are put into a mould and pressed with rude patterns, and then they are pasted on a rosinweed board for chiseling the particular patterns. The silversmiths can be regarded as masters of both striking and hammering and sculpture design. They are good at drawing inspiration from the embroidery and batik patterns and pay attention to innovation.

Achang Ethnic Group Husa Knife Making Skills

Applicant: Longchuan County, Yunnan Province

Husa knife, also called as Achang knife, got its name as Husa Township, Longchuan County is the home of the Achang ethnic group.

The Achang have a history of more than 600 years in making such a knife, which is pure and refined, and is so flexible that it can be coiled like a finger, and can cut iron as if cutting through mud. The knife sheath made of wood, hide and silver is also extremely exquisite.

The production of Husa knife goes through 10 processes, i.e. preparing materials, making foundation, making a proof, rubbing, decorating, quenching, polishing, making handle, making a band, and setting up. Among them, the skill of quenching is the most outstanding and after heating treatment the knife blade can reach the premium quality in rigidity and strength. The tools include wooden wind box, furnace made of iron, mud and stone, hammer, pincers, and iron pillow, etc. When making knife, they select the steel produced from Baoshan and Tengchong, put it into furnace for repeated heating, forging, and rubbing to the foundation, and then dipping it in water for quenching. There are high requirements on quenching skill on which depends the final quality of the knife. There is a back knife that is thin and is pliable. It is made by repeated heating by sesame oil after quenching.

There are various types of Husa knife with particular skills. The back knife (long knife) and hidden knife are the most exquisite and typical. The colorful-steel back knife is made of red and white sheet iron and black steel. A piece of red sheet iron and a piece of white sheet iron are piled up. Craftsmen smelt the surface of the sheet iron to form an iron bar. The black steel is added to the back of knife blade. Then, they shape, rub and polish it until the three colors of red, white and black appear on the knife surface, hence the name. Hidden knife is broad and thick with ingenious craftsmanship and different sizes. On the handle are engraved such patterns as "howling ferocious tiger" and "flying swallow welcoming spring".

Bao'an Ethnic Group Waist Dagger Making Skills

Applicant: Jishishan County, Gansu Province

Bao'an waist dagger is a traditional handicraft of the Bao'an ethnic group mainly produced in Dahejia Town, Jiuji Township and neighboring areas in Jishishan Bao'an, Dongxiang and Salar Nationalities Autonomous County, Gansu Province.

The body of the dagger is made of refined iron that is forged repeatedly and quenched with steel. It is firm but not fragile, and pliable but cannot be bent. It can cut both iron and a hair. The shining dagger surface is engraved with symbolic patterns of seven stars, five plum blossoms, a dragon, and a hand with distinctively different styles and modes. The patterns are exquisite and simple, The handle of a waist dagger is often inlaid with a smooth copper slice and bar, firm and pliable yak horn, high-quality colorful plastic, transparent and soft organic glass, silver solder, and celluloid. After polishing, it looks like colorful brocade. The sheath of the waist dagger is often made of iron with a copper hoop, or of uranium with silver hoop. There is a small hole on front face of the sheath stuck with a shining and exquisite

13 Culture

copper nipper which not only makes the sheath more beautiful but prevents the dagger slipping out. On the upper side of the back, a flexible hexagonal object is tied by a copper chain as the belt for hanging on the waist. It can turn around freely.

Shiyangjin is the most beautiful waist dagger. It is inlaid with bright shiyangjin. It is colorful with golden yellow, green, azure blue, dark green, silver white, and peach-red with many plum blossoms. The silver-white knife sheath is covered by three date-red copper hoops and is very brilliant and dazzling. The dagger blade is shining, chilling and very sharp.

Cloisonné Making Skills

Applicant: Beijing

Cloisonné, called enamel in history, is known as "copper-foundation inlaid enamel." It is an enamel artwork combining ceramics and copper and is a famous traditional artwork in Beijing. The craft became mature in the mid-15th Century; in particular, a breakthrough was made in blue glaze. The full-bodied treasure blue like sapphire is noble and elegant and is called jingtai blue (cloisonné).

Various colored enamels are painted on bronzeware to form patterns. Copper, gold or silver threads are inlaid on the surrounds of the patterns and the article fired at high temperature. The making of cloisonné adopted both bronze ware and burning ceramic traditional techniques and drew on the skills of both traditional painting and engraving. It can be viewed as an integration of traditional Chinese crafts. The finished art work is elegant, solemn, simple and vigorous.

The making of cloisonné is the integration of fine arts design, making the base, inlaying threads, spotting the blue glaze, polishing and gilding. The product goes through more than 10 processes. At first, craftsmen create a foundation of purple copper. Then, they paint on it, press thin copper thread flat, inlay, weld and paste the threads to form various patterns according to painted drafts, inlay enamel and glaze of various colors into the patterns, and make the finished product after repeated firing, polishing and gilding.

Juyuanhao Bow and Arrow Making Skills

Applicant: Beijing

Juyuanhao was a royal armory in the Qing Dynasty nearly 300 years ago

The precision of the bow and arrow and many key processes completely depend on the mastery of various skills and the experience of the craftsmen. They use their eyes as a ruler and hands as a measure and they rarely need specific data as reference. For making a bow, they need more than a hundred specific tools and more than 20 natural materials to process manually. After more than 200 procedures lasting three or four months, a traditional Chinese bow emerges.

Bow and arrows made by Juyuanhao Workshop with the traditional process

Juyuanhao bow and arrow making skills inherited the good traditions of Chinese double arch reverse-bend compound bow. The major inside foundation of the bow is made of bamboo. It is pasted with ox horn outside and ox tendon inside and set up with a wooden bow on both ends. The making of a bow is divided into two links, "white work" of making bow and "painting work" of decoration. There are usually two kinds of bow string, ox-hide and cotton thread. Juyuanhao mostly adopted cotton threads. The making of a bow with simple appearance and structure has five major processes, i.e. making the foundation, sticking pegs, spreading ox horn, spreading ox tendon, and setting up the wooden stool, and for subdivision there are 200 procedures. The steps for making arrow mainly include adjusting the pole, striking hide, scraping pole and setting up arrowhead and end feathers.

Juyuanhao had strict requirements on materials for making bow and arrow. For example, the timber must be elm, ox horn must be from a buffalo in the south and longer than 60 cm, and the feather on the arrow must be French goose feather that is hard in blowing.

Ming-Style Furniture Making Skills

Applicant: Suzhou City, Jiangsu Province

Although many places in China produce hardwood Ming-style furniture, those made by master craftsmen south of the lower reaches of the Yangtze River, with Suzhou as the center, win universal recognition.

Ming-style furniture is characterized distinctively by its beautiful shape. It attaches importance to steadiness and lightness, simplicity and interest, and smooth and round lines with turns and changes. The whole size and proportion of the parts in the furniture attach importance to the organic unity of practicability and appreciation of beauty. There is no abuse of decoration. The occasional engravings are mainly lines or small-area exquisite relief, hollowed-out engraving, round engraving and engraving lines. Craftsmen make use of the lines in the timber and various different foot-lines, i.e. wide and narrow, fat and thin, long and short, deep and shallow, concave and protruding lines and planes, to add the changes in lines on furniture and achieve the harmonious and changeable effects.

Ming-style furniture is also characterized by careful selection of materials. It uses precious timbers such as hard red wood, rosewood, jichimu and mesua ferrea, as well as nanmu, walnut, and elm. Due to the careful selection of materials, the furniture has adequate conditions for creating a sense of the reality and beauty of nature and achieves premium artistic effect of firmness, smoothness, purity and cleanness.

Exquisite technique is the third important characteristic of Ming-style furniture. It attaches importance to the contrast and unity of square and round and thickness and thinness. The connection between many components has no seam and is solid and flat. The outlines are fluent and natural. The surface of the furniture is polished and brushed with wax to show the shining and clean effects and the natural beauty of precious timber.

A Round-backed Chair Made of Pea

Mongol Ethnic Group Leleche (All-Purpose Steppe Vehicle) Making Skills

Applicant: Dong Ujimqin Prefecture, Inner Mongolia Autonomous Regio

Lele is the sound the herdsmen make crying out to his livestock. Leleche is also called a Mongolian ox cart as it is often drawn by ox. It suits the natural environment on the northern grasslands and the living customs of Mongolian people. It can still be seen in Dong Ujimqin Prefecture and neighboring areas in Inner Mongolia Autonomous Region.

Leleche is the moving house of the herdsmen. The vehicle body is usually more than four meters long. It can carry a covering and usually accommodates a whole family. Its body is small, but the two wheels are big. It can successfully traverse grassland with flourishing pasture, deep snow, muddy swamp and uneven ground.

Leleche is usually made of birch common on grassland. It is strong and can endure much vibration. The body is light and is not affected by water and damp. The structure is simple, easy to build and repair.

When making the vehicle, craftsmen burn birch or oak until tender and can be bent into an arch. Two or three wooden arches comprise a wheel. The structure can be divided into upper and lower parts. The upper part is compose of two shafts, eight to ten braces, and grooves. The lower part is composed of wheels, rungs and axles. There are usually 15 to 20 rungs. And the diameter of a wheel can be up to 1.5 meters, level with the draft animal's head. The tops of two shafts are tied by a knitted wicker shaped like a rope. It is harnessed onto the horizontal wooden piece on the animal's neck for pulling.

Lhasa Jiami Waterwheel Grain Milling Techniques

Applicant: Tibet Autonomous Region

In the farming areas and some pasturages in Tibet, people use the fall of water between the hills to build a watermill for processing tsamba, flour, and livestock feedstuff. Among them Jiami Quguo is the most famous. Jiami Quguo, meaning Jiami mill, is situated at Nyangrain in the northern suburbs of Lhasa City, the largest mill group in the area. In history, 21 big and small mills have been set up there. Nyangrain has always been an important place for processing tsamba in Lhasa.

A sluice is set up on the head of an aqueduct to control the flow of water. The water runs from high to low wooden troughs and pours into the bottom of the mill to push the wooden wheel connecting the center axes of the millstone. The upper part of the mill is composed of two concentric round stone millstones (with the diameter of about one to 1.2 meters); the two millstones have the same size but the upper one is thin and the lower thick. The millstones are surrounded by tsamba storage pools. Above the millstones is hung a cloth bag holding qingke barley. An exit pipe is set at the bottom of the cloth bag and connected with the millstones. With the turning of the millstones, the barley falls onto the milling surface automatically and evenly through mill holes.

A wooden pole can adjust the width of gap between the two millstones by leverage to produce tsamba of different degrees according to user taste. According to custom, the millstones must turn counter-clockwise.

Lanzhou Yellow River Waterwheel Manufacturing Techniques

Applicant: Lanzhou City, Gansu Province

The Yellow River crosses Lanzhou from west to east. The river surface has a fall of ten to more than twenty meters, producing abundant natural hydro resources.

Lanzhou waterwheel for irrigation stands on the southern bank of the Yellow River. In the peak season, the natural water flow turns the wheel, while, in the low season, cofferdams are used to divide the water into narrow channels that then drive the wheel. The water barrels on the wheel scoop up water and are lifted to 20 meters high. After the barrels reach the top, they pour the water into wood grooves continuously for irrigating the fields. The irrigation installation lifting water automatically to irrigate fields by waterwheel has a history of nearly 500 years.

The radius of a rung is nearly 10 meters for a large one and five meters for small. The center of the rungs is the axis. Surrounding the axes are two layers of parallel rungs. At the end of each layer of rungs there is a scrape board. Between the scrape boards is a movable rectangular water barrel. On two sides of the wheel are built stone dams for fixing the supports of the water-wheel and for gathering and guiding river water to the wheel. A wooden groove is set up horizontally above the waterwheel. Water flow pushes the scrape boards to slowly turn the wheel. The water barrels are filled one by one and are lifted slowly. When they are raised up to the center above the wheel, the mouth of the barrels will tilt down and water will be poured down a wooden groove, run into the aqueduct, and be led to fields.

Exquisite Compass made in Wan'an, Anhui Province

Wan'an Compass Making Skills

Applicant: Xiuning County, Anhui Province

The compass is widely used both by sailors and geomancers to determine a course for the former and geomantic omens for the latter. Since the end of the Yuan Dynasty and early in the Ming Dynasty, Wan'an compass has been the only extant compass made according by traditional means.

Wan'an compass formed its own characteristics in the long production course, with strict requirements on procedures and methods. The making of a compass usually involves six procedures: making the foundation, lath work and polishing, dividing into grids, writing on the compass surface, oiling and setting up the magnetic needle. Of these, the most mysterious procedures are "dividing into grids" and "writing on the compass". The compass craftsmen are required to use a brush pen to write the contents in each in regular script in very small characters according to secret illustrative plates for different types of compass. They must be very careful and cannot make any mistake. The key procedure is the sixth one, "setting up the magnetic needle." They should place a special steel needle on a natural magnet for two weeks for magnetization, determine precisely the center of gravity of the magnetic needle, set up the magnetic needle firmly on the pivot in the round hole, and ensure the needle can freely turn.

The making of a Wan'an compass is full of hardship. Apart from more than 1,000 very small characters distributed densely on the surface of the compass, the spider net-like densely-distributed round and straight cutting lines for dividing the grids take a whole day for one compass, and craftsmen cannot make a mistake, or all their previous efforts is wasted.

Carved Lacquerware Skills

Applicant: Beijing

The crafts of carved lacquerware are the skills of applying natural lacquer on a foundation to some thickness and carving

Carved lacquerware—one of China's traditional arts and crafts

patterns by knife on the piled up plane. Due to various colors, there are different kinds such as "picking out red", "picking out black", "picking out colors" and "picking out rhinoceros color."

It is a very complex course to make a carved lacquerware. The making of a carved lacquerware from design to finished product must pass through several procedures by many craftsmen. Generally speaking, a piece of common carved lacquerware needs at least half a year, top-grade and exquisite carved lacquerware needs around a year, and a precious excellent piece needs even two years.

Beijing carved lacquerware is divided into metal-foundation and non-metal foundation. The former has an interior of enamel and the latter a lacquer interior. Many layers of lacquer must be applied. After the first layer of lacquer is dry, another layer of lacquer is applied. Two layers of lacquer are applied per day. There are scores of layers at least and three or five hundred layers at most. Then craftsmen use their knife as a pen to carve out the relief of landscape, flowers and figures according to designed painting drafts. Red is the major lacquer and yellow, red and black are used as ground color. There are several kinds, i.e. picking out red, picking out yellow, picking out green, picking out colors and picking out rhinoceros color. The procedures of carved lacquer are very complex and mainly include more than ten such as making foundation, burning blue, making bottom, applying lacquer, engraving, and polishing. Each procedure has high requirements on skills.

Pingyao Buffed Lacquerware Lacquering Skills

Applicant: Pingyao County, Shanxi Province

Pingyao buffed lacquerware involves such skills of buffing by the palms and painting in gold and colors. To make a Pingyao buffed lacquerware, people repeatedly lacquer wooden furniture and exquisite utensils and then use palms to buff the surface until it shines; then, paint patterns of landscape, flowers, birds, pavilions or figures from stories. The procedures are meticulous and complex. The appearance is unvarnished and elegant, the structure is refined, lacquer surface is clean, decorative patterns are splendid and magnificent, and the surface is smooth. It is an elaborate work of lacquerware.

Pingyao buffed lacquerware makes use of a natural lacquer seeping from the peeled-off varnish tree widely distributed on the Loess Plateau. Pingyao buffed lacquerware has always been famous for complex procedures with trivial details. Lacquer must be applied with ash five or six times. After applying ash, it will be polished every time when the ash dries until the surface is flat and smooth.

Ink black, rosy-cloud red, apricot, and green-purple are the major ground lacquers for Pingyao buffed lacquerware. The paintings in gold are carved by knife, or inlaid with adornments. The lines are fluent and colors are harmonious. The cutting style of the knife must be like writing style with alternating thickness, proper depth and natural rising and falling. Craftsmen process shells, snails, ivory and colorful stones into various materials for inlaying on the lacquerware according to pattern requirements. Their work depends on vision, meticulousness, sense and repetition and the finished work is brilliant in terms of lacquer surface and shining and touching.

Yangzhou Lacquerware Lacquering Skills

Applicant: Yangzhou City, Jiangsu Province

Yangzhou lacquerware is a special traditional artwork in China. It emerged more than 2,300 years ago and reached a high degree in shape and lacquering skills.

Yangzhou lacquerware is smooth, shining, exquisite, well-balanced, colorful and elegant. The most famous ones include multi-treasure-inlaid lacquerware and shell-inlaid lacquerware.

Multi-treasure-inlaid lacquerware makes use of many precious materials such as emerald, ivory, agate, green jade, white jade, lotus stone, lapis lazuli, and wood-changed stone. According to their natural color, they are carved and inlaid on lacquerware to form a perfect pair without defects and the treasure and lacquerware bring out the best in each other. The finished lacquerware is brilliant, elegant, simple and vigorous.

Shell-inlaid lacquerware is subdivided into polished shell and spotted shell. For the former one, shells of various colors are polished to thin slices, made to various patterns of figures, landscape, pavilions, flowers, birds, insects and fish by special tools, pasted and inlaid on lacquer ground, and lacquered and polished. Its lacquer ground is as shining as a mirror with clear demarcation between black and white. The patterns are orderly in density and the style is elegant and pure. For the latter one, high quality shells such as mussel shells, mica, and night-shining spiral shells are selected carefully, polished to thread as thin as one third of human's hair, cut by special tools to very thin spots, threads and slices, inlaid on lacquer ground, decorated with gold thread and silver slices, lacquered and polished. It is colorful, as brilliant as rosy clouds, and exquisite and fine. The edges of spotted-shell lacquerware are often decorated with exquisite series of patterns continuing in two directions.

Tiantaishan Dried Lacquer Gunny Fetus Skills

Applicant: Tiantai County, Zhejiang Province

Tiantai County abounds in natural raw materials such as Rhus succedanea linn, ramie, and Cinnamomum camphora, etc. Since ancient

Elaborate works collected in the Yangzhou Lacquerware Museum—Advent of Spring mother-of-pearl lacquer screen

times, a handicraft industry has existed there. The dried lacquer gunny fetus skills, with Rhus succedanea linn, ramie, Cinnamomum camphora wood as major materials, appeared before the Eastern Jin Dynasty (317-420).

This craft can show comprehensively the artistic charms of different artists in engraving and painting. The dried lacquer gunny fetus is a special technique for appearance decoration and protection on various products. The handicraft adopts completely natural materials and all the processes are done by hand. It involves 13 kinds of raw materials grown in Tiantai such as Rhus succedanea linn, ramie, colorful stone powder, and tung oil. After being applied by layers of flax and lacquer, it is polished repeatedly, covered with vermilion and other assisting materials, pasted with gold foil; the product is finished after some industrial treatment. Importance is attached to drawing and using materials. The finished product shows comprehensively the artistic charm of sculpture, painting and gilding.

The finished products of dried lacquer gunny fetus are mainly used as decoration and protection for Buddhist sculptures and buildings such as palaces and temples, as well as folk equipment. They are endurable, moth-resistance and shining, and will not crack or transform. The wood-carving Buddha sculptures made by this handicraft can represent the highest achievement. It not only maintains the exquisite veins and fluent lines of wood carving, but also makes the Buddha figure sculptures more vivid.

Fuzhou Bodiless Lacquerware Lacquering Skills

Applicant: Fuzhou City, Fujian Province

Fuzhou bodiless lacquerware, with a history of more than 200 years, is firm and light with elegant shape, brilliant color and exquisite decoration. It has particular national style and strong local characteristics, and it is not easy to break, lose lacquer or fade.

The procedures for making bodiless lacquerware are very complex: make the inside body by mud, gypsum, or wood module, mount it by grass cloth or silk one layer after another with raw lacquer as adhesive, apply it with lacquer ash two times, dry it in the shade and remove the inside body, and this is the embryonic form of bodiless lacquerware. After scores of procedures such as filling ash, lacquering, polishing and drying in the shade, a semi-finished product emerges. At last, it is treated with colorful lacquer and various decorations, and bodiless lacquerware becomes one of the three Chinese handicraft treasures.

Fuzhou bodiless lacquerware is characterized distinctively by "brilliant colors and shining like a mirror". It is favored by people because of the colorful lacquer decoration. The traditional lacquering techniques include black polishing, colored polishing, thin lacquering, gilded colorful lacquering, brocade patterns, gilded red lacquering, silver-inlaid coloring, table flowers, and shell-inlaid lacquering.

Fuzhou bodiless lacquerware makes use of gold and silver powder grinded from gold and silver as concoction on foundation of Chinese traditional red and black lacquer. Generally, the dried lacquer would become black without shining and become difficult to be mixed with other bright colors, but the problem has been solved in this kind of lacquerware. Many lacquers with bright colors such as blue, green and brown are added and they will not fade. Some decorations make use of cut silver thread, cut gold thread, shells and inlaid techniques.

Xiamen Lacquer Line Carving Skills

Applicant: Xiamen City, Fujian Province

Lacquer line carving is a particular folk handicraft work with long history in Xiamen of more than 300 years. It has been passed down through 13 generations of the Cai family. It is exquisite and elegant with vivid images, elegant style and lively paintings.

Lacquer line carving was at first used in decoration of Buddha figures. It is made completely by hand in a very complex way. The procedures developed from the former simple ones of lining, carving and cutting to 10 manual procedures of lining, winding, twisting, piling up, carving and hollowing out. A piece of work will need several months and even years to finish. It is exquisite and elegant with vivid images, elegant style and lively paintings. No two products are alike.

Traditional lacquer line carving includes four aspects of sculpture, foundation make-up, lacquer line decoration, and gilding and coloring. In terms of design, sculpture is the most important, and in terms of special artistic aesthetic feeling, the skill of lacquer line decoration is the key. Aged brick powder is mixed with great lacquer and cooked tung oil and is made into soft and flexible mud pie after repeated pounding, commonly called "lacquer line earth." It is kneaded by hand. On a base, with ground lacquer, a lacquer line is wound, knotted, twisted, piled up and carved to various exquisite relief patterns.

Chengdu Lacquerware Skills

Applicant: Chengdu City, Sichuan Province

Sichuan abounds in raw lacquer and red gems which are the major materials for making lacquerware. As early as the ancient Shu State some 3,000 years ago, lacquerware skills in Chengdu had reached a high level.

Chengdu lacquerware is characterized by natural timber and raw lacquer as major materials and in being made by hand. "No lacquer, no ware". Wood is the foundation and lacquer is the soul. Lacquerware has high requirements on lacquer. Raw lacquer should be filtered through gauze so that it is as clear as oil and reflects like a mirror. There are various kinds and, according to different requirements, craftsmen make up different lacquer materials.

"Carved silver mercerization coloring" is one of the fine and complex skills in traditional Chengdu lacquerware skills. The silver slice as thin as cicada's wings is pasted on a big-square lacquer surface. It is painted with patterns. Craftsmen cut and hollow designs carefully along with the lines of the patterns. In many places lines are as thin as hair and the hollow-out places are as tiny as a needle point. Any careless action would result in waste. After carving and hollowing, according to designs, some mercerization is necessary. Craftsmen use needle point to draw out the lines one after another and the patterns suddenly become shining. According to the designs, some patterns need coloring to show layers and three dimensional sense. After these procedures, lacquer is applied and dried out in the shade. Craftsmen then have their hands stained with clear oil and tile powder (made from two grinding tiles), and polish the decoration surfaces lightly back and forth to clean the cutting marks and any dirt on the surface. This procedure should be repeated three times. Finally, they use gauze to wipe lightly to reveal the full glory of the shining.

Maotai Spirits Distilling Skills

Applicant: Guizhou Province

Guizhou Maotai Spirit, produced only in Huairen Town, Zunyi County, Guizhou Province, is one of the world's three great famous distilled spirits along with Scotch whisky and French Cognac. It is the earliest ancestor of daqu white spirits with the fragrance of fermented soy beans. The quality of Maotai spirit is closely related to the producing place. As Maotai Town is located in a valley with light winds, it is beneficial for the microorganism brewing Maotai spirit to develop.

The water for brewing Maotai spirit is mainly from the Chishuihe. The spirits distilled from the slightly-sweet water without any dissolved impurities are particularly sweet.

The construction of cellar for storing Maotai is also particular. There are strict requirements on the site, direction, space, height, control of temperature and humidity and ventilation, and the form, content and skill of sealing by mud on the mouth of urns. They are all essential to the improvement of finished spirits and fragrance purity.

No fragrances are added to Maotai spirits and its fragrance completely comes naturally from brewing process. It is always kept between 52- and 54-proof, lowest among famous white spirits in China. It is pure, yellowish, glittering, gentle and mellow.

Maotai spirit involves production skills different from other spirits. The production period is seven months. The distilled spirits are stored in the cellar for at least four years and then mixed with aged spirits of various ages up to 40 years.

Luzhou Laojiao Spirits Distilling Skills

Applicant: Luzhou City, Sichuan Province

Luzhou Laojiao spirit is the representative of Chinese white spirits with strong fragrance. It can be divided into tequ, touqu, erqu and sanqu according to different qualities. Luzhou tequ spirits are the best and characterized by strong fragrance, mellowness, sweetness and after-taste.

Luzhou Laojiao spirit got the name from being brewed in aged cellars. These include four aged cellar pools (State-level cultural relic unit under special protection) with a 400-year history in the urban area and more than 300 aged cellar pools aged more than 100 distributed in the urban area and neighboring counties. They are the foundation for the inheritance and development of the brewing skills of Luzhou Laojiao spirits. Wenyongsheng and Tianchengsheng are the most famous among Luzhou aged cellars, the former built in 1729.

Pure wheat is made into daqu for brewing 60-poorf Luzhou daqu spirits. Glutinous kaoliang is used as raw material. The brewing period is 60 days. The production skills involve mixed distilling and mixed distillers' grains and mixing added dregs. "Delamination for returning spirits" and "double wheel bottom" are used to enhance the strong fragrance.

The traditional brewing skills include production and maintenance of the mud cellar, production and supervision of daqu, brewing from original spirits, aged brewing from original spirits, and mixing and appreciation.

Xinghuacun Fen Chiew Spirits Distilling Skills

Applicant: Fenyang City, Shanxi Province

Fen Chiew spirit, produced in Xinghua Village in Fenyang County, is also called Xinghuacun Fen Chiew spirit, and is famous for purity and faint scent, and sweetness.

To brew Fen Chiew spirit, "yibazhua" kaoliang on the Jinzhong Plain is the raw material. Barley and pea are made into fermented sugar. A particular skill of "qingzheng erciqing" is adopted for brewage. The brewed spirit has glittering and transparent liquid, faint scent, and a sweet, mellow and fresh taste. Making qu, fermenting and distilling all require much experience. For many generations these skills have been passed orally from masters to apprentices. They have been developed continuously and still play an important role.

Xinghuacun has Yangshao Cultural Ruins dating back 6,000 years. From unearthed articles, it can be determined that there was brewing activity then. The brewing workshops, ancient wells, steles, tablets and old streets of the Ming and Qing dynasties have been preserved. The traditional skills are still in process of inheritance, a solid foundation for the protection of Fen Chiew traditional brewing skills.

Shaoxing Yellow Wine Distilling Skills

Applicant: Shaoxing City, Zhejiang Province

Shaoxing spirit is one of the outstanding representatives of Chinese huangjiu (yellow wine). Shaoxing has fertile soil, mild climate, sufficient sunshine, clearly-demarcated seasons, and abundant and a high-quality water source of Jian Lake.

For brewing Shaoxing wine, yeast is made in the seventh lunar month, wheat leaven is made in the ninth and lin rice is made in the tenth. Around Daxue, the brewing period lasts for more than 80 days until the following year. Sticky rice is the material. The finished wine passes the procedures of sifting and soaking rice, steaming, cooling, luozuo (adding leaven, lin rice and Jinhu Lake water), major fermentation, opening harrow, pouring later ferment, squeezing wine, clarifying, mixing, boiling, and pouring aged brew (more than three years). The tools for brewing Shaoxing wine are mostly made of wood, bamboo and ceramic products, and a few are made of tin.

Shaoxing yellow wine is the general name for all the yellow wine produced within Shaoxing. Main brands are Yuanhong wine, Jiafan wine, Shanniang wine and Xiangxue wine. They are all fragrant, sweet, pure and orange yellow along with specific tastes.

Yuanhong wine, also named Zhuangyuan Red, got its name as the outside of the jars was painted red in the past. The color is orange yellow and is clear and shining. It has particular fragrance and tastes fresh and a little bitter.

Jiafan wine is the best type of Shaoxing

Winemakers in Shaoxing are making yellow wine.

yellow wine. Jaifan (adding rice) relates to the proportion of raw materials, less water and more rice. Due to great density and mellow quality, the finished wine is deep yellow with red-like amber tones, transparent, glittering and extraordinarily fragrant.

Qingxu Super-Mature Vinegar Distilling Skills

Applicant: Qingxu County, Shanxi Province

Before 700 BCE, Qingxu people began to brew vinegar in jars and urns by means of liquid fermentation. During the Northern Wei Dynasty (386-534) the skills changed to solid fermentation, leading to Qingxu super-mature vinegar distilling skills with specific styles.

The major materials include kaoliang and daqu made of peas and barley. The time for the basic steaming and fermentation is longer than other places. In the course of becoming vinegar, the fermented materials are mixed with proper chaff, rice shell, wheat bran skin and sal. The fermentation takes more than 10 days. With the rise of temperature in the jar, acetic acid bacterium speeds up the growth and breeding. Depending on traditional experience and long-time scientific experiment, brewers can grasp well the rise and fall of temperature to improve the quality of vinegar. The skill with distinctive local characteristics has been passed down for generations in Qingxu. After continuous improvement, a set of superior vinegar distilling skills have come into being.

The production of vinegar produced in Qingxu includes the course of aging. The finished vinegar must be placed in jars for one year for aging and for shining in summer and freezing in winter. That is, depending on natural conditions, workers will expose it to sunlight in summer and remove ice in winter to get rid of the water. After getting rid of about half the water, a jar of new vinegar will become dark purple. It will not go moldy in summer or freeze in winter. And it tastes sweet and sour.

Zhenjiang Hengshun Fragrant Vinegar Distilling Skills

Applicant: Zhenjiang City, Jiangsu Province

Zhenjiang Hengshun fragrant vinegar was invented in 1840 and is one of the four great vinegars in China. Attention is paid to the raw materials, which must be high-quality sticky rice and distillers' grain from Jiangsu and Zhejiang provinces.

The production of Hengshun fragrant vinegar adopts good acetic acid bacterium. The solid fermentation developed its own school. It is divided into three courses of making wine, making unstrained spirits, and pouring vinegar and about 40 big and small processes. It takes around 70 days from preparing sticky rice to finishing the production. The process gives the vinegar five great characteristics in color, fragrance, sourness, mellowness and density.

In course of distilling, the self-made wheat qu is added to the steamed sticky rice to ferment to make high-quality wine liquid. Then, wheat bran skin and rice chaff to solidify it. In proper temperature, the sifted specific acetic acid bacterium is accepted. It is turned over once a day for cooling, ventilation and fermentation. The bacterium will produce a series of biochemical reactions in some 20 days to produce the sour, delicious and fragrant matter such as acetic acid and amino acid. Then, the mature vinegar wine can be sealed off. It is added into a vinegar jar, soaked with water and self-made rice. This is then filtered and boiled and finally poured into ventilated pottery jars, put in open air exposed to gentle breezes, sunshine and rain. It can be placed there for half a year at least and eight years at most. Finally the vinegar with mellow fragrance, gentle sourness and sweetness is created.

Wuyi Yancha (Cliff Tea)

Applicant: Wuyishan City, Fujian Province

Wuyishan range covers an area of 60 square km. It has 36 peaks and 99 famous cliffs. Each cliff produces tea. Oolong produced here is generally called Wuyiyan Tea.

Wuyiyan Tea Garden near the Yunv Peak

Wuyishan City, located in northwest of Fujian Province, is the hometown of Yan Tea (oolong). Cliffs and deep valleys are distributed everywhere. Tea farmers make use of the concave cliffs and stone slits to build up a stone bank and create a "potted-plant-style" tea garden, commonly called "stone foundation". "Each cliff has tea; no cliff, no tea." So, the name of Yan Tea (cliff tea) came into being. Among them, Dahongpao (big red robe) is the most precious and best.

Wuyiyan Tea is favored by people because of its high quality and unique Yangu flower fragrance. And the high quality is the result of an advantageous ecological environment and climate, abundant resources suitable for oolong and unique production skills.

The traditional production involves 10 interrelated and indispensable processes. In the course of production, people choose the tree species most suitable for producing tea, are always strict in picking standards, and apply exquisite and meticulous baking skills. The procedures for baking Yan Tea are: withering, doing blue, killing blue, kneading, and baking. The sun-baked tea blue is placed in a water sifter or swing-blue machine for continuous turning and rubbing of the leaf edges. The rotation speed gradually grows from light to heavy, but the intermission time becomes longer and longer. The course is repeated five to seven times and takes eight to 12 hours. The times and degree of doing blue is differs with the type of tree, climate and degree of sun-baking.

Yan Tea is cooked with water in high temperature and toasted over slow fire. The drinking of Wuyiyan tea is also unique. After boiling water is poured on a second time, the tea starts to exude its full fragrance.

Zigong Well Salt Drilling Skills

Applicant: Zigong City, Sichuan Province

Well salt in Sichuan has a long history. Well salt drilling skills, in fact, are cable drilling skills, also called percussive drilling skills. People make use of the power of man, livestock and machine to break rocks by a drilling bit. It drills into the deep place of the stratum, makes a hole and extracts t rock bits continuously.

Zigong City, regarded as salt capital of China, is the originating place of percussive drilling technique. The technique was born from a shallow well with big mouth during the period from the Eastern Han to the early Song dynasty, transformed to Zhuotong well in the Song Dynasty, and matured to deep well with small mouth from the Ming to Qing dynasties. In 1835, the first deep well with a depth of more than 1,000 meters in the world,

Ancient salt well in Sanghai, Zigong City

Hai Well (1001.42 meters) was drilled. It is an important symbol of mature percussive drilling technique in China and pushed forward the development of well drilling in the world.

In the golden time of the well salt industry, there were 1,711 Zhuotong wells in Zigong City with annual production of more than 4,000 tons. Within Daying County, there are still 41 such ancient salt wells distributed over six square km. The invention of well salt skills resulted in the technique of rope percussive drilling, so that the natural brine deep underground could be exploited.

The percussive drilling technique is especially suitable for the exploitation of low-pressure stratum. As the drilling is slow, any small change in the production stratum under the well can be found in time. This technique will not create the circulation of slurry, so that the production stratum will not be blocked or polluted and the resources under the well can be used effectively.

Qianshan Liansi Paper Making Skills

Applicant: Qianshan County, Jiangxi Province

It is said that Liansi paper was made meticulously by two brothers naming Lian in Shaowu, Fujian after years of study. It got its name as the brothers were listed as numbers three and four (si) in their family.

The production places of Qianshan Liansi paper are distributed around the northern and southern foot of Wuyishan. At its peak, there were more than 2,000 paper troughs. There are 72 processes involved in making Liansi paper and each is exquisite and strict. The raw material must be tender Mao bamboo poles. Around Lixia, when the bamboo is going to grow two pairs of tender leaves, people will fell it. The paper material must be exposed to the sun and rain for several months to bleach naturally. The production period lasts for one year.

Liansi paper is made by hand and workers must depend on their experienc e. The keys for making the paper are: first, water quality; the water for rinsing, soaking, bleaching and washing cannot contain any pollutant and must be local spring water. Second, making up the prescription that is made from "Water insect egg tree."

Qianshan Liansi paper, famed as "longevity paper of a thousand years", was produced as early as the Ming Dynasty. It is as white as jade with even thickness. It will not fade and resist moths and heat. The ink on it is bright and easy to dry. The book printed on the paper is clear and people will feel no eye strain after reading for a long time. When it is used for calligraphy works and painting, the ink will form a tinge and penetrate the paper deeply. It has always been the favorite of domestic and foreign calligraphers and painters.

Bark Paper Making Skills

Applicant: Guizhou Province

Bamboo paper and bark paper made of bamboo and bark respectively are two important varieties in traditional handicraft paper. Guizhou contains many ethnic minorities. The ancient skills of making bamboo and bark paper are still preserved in many places. In particular, the most outstanding are in Xiangzhigou (Buyei ethnic group) in Guiyang City, Xiaotun in Zhenfeng County, and Shiqiao (Miao ethnic group) in Danzhai County.

Take the bamboo paper produced in Xiangzhigou as an example. The 72 processes include felling, breaking and soaking bamboo, steaming, grinding, raising pulp, lifting paper, pressing, and baking and shining. They are exactly the same skills recorded in *Tian Gong Kai Wu* (1637) by Song Yingxing. The finished product is soft and flexible with hidden bamboo lines and faint fragrance.

The white soft paper produced in Xiaotun, Zhenfeng County, was first created in the mid-19th Century. There are more than 1,000 families in the township engaged in the production of bark papermaking. The finished paper is soft, flexible, smooth and tender.

The white-bark paper produced in Danzhai County has bark as the material without any other added material. In the course of production, however, an important assisting material is needed, i.e. "smooth medicine." It can be made from various plants such as rock fir root, wild cotton root, Chinese gooseberry rattan, and glutinous rice leaves. But rock fir root is best. The production of white-bark paper usually passes through more than ten processes. The cotton-fiber-like paper pulp is mixed with water and "smooth medicine". After stirring, lifting, pressing, shining, exposing and wrapping, the finished product emerges. The paper is soft, tender, and smooth with the good water-resistance quality.

Dai and Naxi Ethnic Handicraft Paper-Making Skills

Applicant: Yunnan Province

Naxi ancient books in Dongba language

Naxi ethnic group Dongba paper: The Naxi live in Lijiang and Shangri La in Yunnan Province. Even today, hieroglyphs are preserved. In history, it was controlled by the master of ceremonies Dongba, so it is called Dongba script for recording Dongba sutras. The paper for recording Dongba sutras is called Dongba paper, or white ground paper. The material is a local plant, Adangda. It is Lijiang canescent wikstroemia of the Ruixiang branch. The course of production involves the processes of collecting materials, exposure to the sun, soaking, steaming, washing, pounding materials, pounding again, pouring water on paper, pasting paper and sun exposure again. It is a combination of Chinese papermaking technique with the papermaking methods of the Southwest Asia.

Dai ethnic group lives in Xishuangbanna and Dehong prefecture in Yunnan. The ancient books of the Yuan Dynasty recorded Dai people cut notches in wood for recording. But, in middle of the Ming Dynasty there papermaking was adopted. It is called "mian paper", made of bark with good and fine fiber. The paper is thin, soft and flexible. It is mainly used for making lanterns and writing Buddhist sutras. It is also used for making oil paper umbrellas. Paper is used as the surface of the umbrella and is applied with sesame oil. It is the necessary article for funerals, meaning the dead elders can fly to heaven by the umbrella. Mian paper is essential for monks and living Buddha in temples to write sutras and to learn the Dai language. In the past it was necessary for writing medicinal prescriptions. Monks in Buddhist temples still use mian paper to learn Buddhist sutras.

Tibetan Ethnic Group Paper-Making Skills

Applicant: Tibet Autonomous Region

Tibetan paper uses stellera chamaejasme, gharu-wood, bothrocaryum controversum of Cornaceae, and ericaceous wild camellia tree. The materials with different qualities can produce Tibetan paper with different usage and degrees. The ericaceous material can produce paper with different thickness and it is viewed as top-grade material. The paper made of gharu-wood is thick and suitable for writing sutras and is viewed as medium-grade. The paper made of stellera chamaejasme needs disinfection and is viewed as low-grade material, but the paper can resist moths and be preserved for a long time.

The procedures for making Tibetan paper include peeling off, pounding, steaming, soaking, rinsing, smashing materials, making pulp, and lifting paper. In the course of lifting paper, the gauze sifter fastened by a wooden frame is used as a paper mould and its size can be adjusted at random. The pulp is poured on the sifter. When the water is filtered out, workers must hold the sifter flat, or else the paper will have uneven thickness. After being dried in the sun, the paper is exposed. The standards for good paper are: even thickness, no leakage holes, no dirt or impurity, being soft, white and clean.

Tibetan people cannot only produce the white paper for writing but also dye paper in various colors such as red, yellow, blue, black, purple and green. Making paper of various colors is also an important papermaking technique.

Uyghur Ethnic Group Mulberry Paper Making Skills

Applicant: Turpan, Xinjiang Uyghur Autonomous Region

The Uygur craftsmen making the mulberry paper

Uyghur ethnic group mulberry paper is made of local mulberry bark. The inside bark of mulberry branches is glutinous and the fiber is smooth. It is easy for processing. After peeling off, soaking, boiling, pounding, fermenting, filtering, placing in a mould, sun-drying and roughly polishing, the mulberry paper comes into being. It is square-shaped and the height and length is about 50 cm.

In course of papermaking, the inside white mulberry bark is peeled off and soaked to softness. Ten kg of mulberry bark is mixed with five kg of huyang alkali and boiled in a big iron boiler for two hours. The boiled soft mulberry bark is dragged out, placed on flagstone, and pounded repeatedly by a wooden hammer into a mulberry mud pie. After being stirred evenly, it becomes paper pulp. The paper pulp is scooped out, placed in a mould, and stirred continuously by a wooded stick, so that the pulp can cover the gauze sifter evenly. At last, the mould is dried in the sun. After several hours, the mulberry bark paper is finished. A big boiler of paper pulp can produce 300 pieces of paper of the same size.

The mulberry bark paper made by the traditional skills is yellow. Its fiber is fine and it has tiny impurities. But it is solid, flexible, and soft. It has strong tensile force and will not break. It is non-toxic and has strong force of absorbing water. The ink will not soak into the paper, and good ink will not fade for many years. It can resist moths and be preserved a long time.

Xuan Paper Making Skills

Applicant: Jing County, Anhui Province

Paper-making is one of the four great inventions of ancient China. Xuan paper is the most outstanding representative of traditional handicraft paper products. It heads the four treasures of the study and has a history of more than 1,500 years. Xuan paper got its name from Xuancheng in Anhu, the distribution center for paper made in surrounding areas.

The production Xuan paper takes place in the region of Xiaoling in southwest of Jing County. The climate is mild, and rainfall sufficient. The special karst mountainous region is suitable for the growth of green sandalwood. And the alluvial plain is suitable for the growth of rice haulm. And green sandalwood and rice haulm offer high-quality raw materials for the production of Xuan paper. There are many rivers in Jing County, especially two branches of the Wuxi River on its upper reaches. One is weakly alkaline, suitable for the processing of raw materials, and the other is weakly acidic, suitable for making paper. The people there have made Xuan paper for many generations.

Workers stand beside the paper pulp pool, repeat the actions of scooping water and raising the bamboo curtain, so that the pulp adheres to the bamboo curtain; as the fibers cling to the curtain the water drains off through the seams. The paper film is pressed to get rid of all water and then pasted onto the fire wall for baking. When dragging out paper, a worker's hands will bear the weight of 20 kg. The making of a piece of Xuan paper will pass through 18 processes such as accumulated grass, pressing pulp, dragging from the water, adding glue and pasting. It will take a year from raw material gathering to finished product. Many links in the course have no specific quantity standards to follow and workers have to depend on experience. The skills of making Xuan paper are passed down by masters to apprentices, but it takes five years to thoroughly learn the technique.

Bamboo Paper Making Skills

Applicants: Sichuan and Zhejiang Provinces

Jiajiang County of Sichuan Province and Fuyang City of Zhejiang Province are important producers of bamboo paper.

Jiajiang bamboo paper: The environment in Jiajiang is suitable for growth of bamboo. Handicraft bamboo paper-making started in the Tang Dynasty, became popular during the Ming Dynasty and flourished in the Qing Dynasty. Jiajiang handicraft paper for calligraphy and painting made of tender bamboo is white and soft. It can soak up ink without blurring. The fiber is smooth, and it is soft, flexible and flat. Jiajiang bamboo paper-making retains traditional skills. It is made by the scooping-paper method by hand. There are 15 links and 72 processes from choosing the materials to finished paper. There are strict requirements on materials and the procedures are complex. In particular, in the course of "holding the paper," every tiny action of the workers will influence the quality. A skillful master can hold hundreds of pieces of paper continuously. The fiber arrangement, paper thickness, immersing speed and tensile force is identical.

Fuyang bamboo paper: Fuyang in Zhejiang has always been called a "hometown of local paper". The bamboo paper-making technique started from the Southern Song Dynasty and has been passed down for more than 1,000 years. It uses tender Mao bamboo growing for less than one year. There are 72 processes including making pulp and making paper. A unique set of skills came into being on the basis of inheriting traditional Chinese paper-making skills. For example, the skills of "fermenting by human urine" in making pulp and "waving curtain and flapping billows" in making paper are the unique skills of Fuyang bamboo paper-making and cannot be found in other places.

Huzhou Writing Brush Making Skills

Applicant: Huzhou City, Zhejiang Province

Huzhou writing brush is called Hu brush for short and is outstanding among writing brushes.

There are more than 300 types of brush mainly classified into soft, mixed and hard hair brushes. Take the goat hair brush as an example. Traditionally, only the high-quality goat hair around Hang, Jia and Hu is selected. The goat hair in the region is top grade and sharp, tender, and clean. Workers classify these high-quality brush hairs into more than 40 varieties according to different qualities. There are several sub-classifications under each variety. It is as exquisite as embroidery. The making of a Hu brush has strict requirements on selection of materials. The goat underarm hairs are selected, sun-dried for a long time, and cleaned. Then, the hairs are soaked in water and classified according to whether they are flat or round, bent or straight, long or short, and with or without sharp edge. Usually, they will experience more than 70 procedures such as soaking, pulling, merging and combing.

The water basin phase is the most complex and important procedure. Workers hold a horn comb in one hand and defatted hair in other hand for combing and washing repeatedly in the water basin. They are classified carefully one by one according to different colors, sharpness, and softness. They are made into a knife-head brush in the shape of a knife blade and put in water again for classification. The whole course is very meticulous.

The brush handle of a Hu brush is mainly made of chicken-hair bamboo from the foot of the Lingfengshan in western Zhejiang Province. Its sections are sparse, the pole is straight, and the space inside is small. It is an ideal material for making brush handles.

The Hu brush is also called as Hu awl which is its greatest character. Awl refers to a section of neat and transparent sharp awl on top of the brush. It is made of top-grade goat hairs after nearly a hundred meticulous processes such as soaking, pulling, merging, combing, connecting and combining.

Huizhou She inkstone

She Ink-stone Making Skills

Applicants: Anhui and Jiangxi Provinces

She ink-stone refers to the ink-stone made of the She stone in ancient She prefecture. It is one of the four great famous ink-stones in China.

It has pretty color and is smooth. It is characterized by quick release of ink, not harming brush hairs and not drying the ink water. In terms of engraving decorations, She ink-stone has particular artistic styles. The patterns are simple, vigorous, beautiful and natural, the lines are pretty and firm, the cutting way energetic, and the styles changeable. It is famous particularly for practicability and simplicity. It is not easy to exploit She stone, so it extremely precious. In addition, rosewood, pear wood or wood-body lacquerware is often used to make an ink-stone box engraved with inscriptions.

She ink-stone has many beautiful lines due to combination of various matters. According to different natural lines, it can be divided into such precious varieties as gold star, silver star, gold halo, silver halo, wood grain, and eyebrow grain. She ink-stone is mostly black, but there are other colors such as blue, green, gray, purple, and yellowish. The colors are bright and it is worthy of being appreciated and collected.

The engraving of a She ink-stone has strong local styles. Usually it is in relief. But due to the impact from brick carving, there are some deep carving places. The palaces, pavilions and figures carved by deep cutting on She ink-stone are exquisite with clear delamination. And the opening of ink pool can also echo it. It is very harmonious.

Invention and skills are the most important for making a piece of good ink-stone. The size, color and grains of a stone are natural. Inventors will have their own sense after looking at a stone. They can apply their skills according to different materials and are good at expressing the emotions and concepts by use of the natural grains and colors to reach the effect of unity of nature and man.

Huizhou Ink Making Skills

Applicant: Anhui Province

Huizhou ink is a strange treasure in the Chinese ink-making techniques and is also one of the four great treasures of the study. It got its name as it was produced in ancient Huizhou prefecture. Jixi County of Huangshan City and She County in Anhui Province are the production centers of Huizhou ink.

This is a special ink for traditional calligraphy works and painting and is made of pine fume, tung oil fume, lacquer fume and glue. The finished product is black and moist, firm and shining. It can soak into the paper but does not fade. It can stay on the brush, but is not glutinous. It is fragrant and can resist moths. The opposite face is painted with the calligraphy and painting works of masters. It is elegant and beautiful and is a treasure of calligraphy and painting art.

Huizhou ink with a history of 1,000 years still give off the fragrance.

Huizhou ink is a unique artwork because of the complex production skills that are hard to grasp. The ink mould for pressing ink shape and patterns is engraved on the rare stone nanmu that is as firm as stone. It is very hard to engrave. The details in painting such as window lattice, tree lines, water ripples, and cloth wrinkles are thinner than a hair. This unique skill is hard to learn. Besides ink mould, there are eight procedures for making ink, i.e. spotting fume, mixing materials, pounding base, pressing mould, shining ink, rubbing edge, painting in gold, and boxing. Spotting fume and pounding foundation are the hardest. Spotting fume refers to collecting ashes and fumes [talc] on the top of the bowl of hundreds and thousands of oil lamps. Naked workers run in the high-temperature fume house and are busy moving lamp wicks, adding oil and collecting the ashes. Pounding base refers to pounding mixed fume materials to a base and each piece of ink has to be pounded tens of thousands of times.

Due to the particular prescription and exquisite making skills, Huizhou ink has always been light, clear after grinding the ink, fragrant, as firm as jade, soundless in grinding, as black as lacquer and able to be preserved for long time.

Duan Ink-stone Making Skills

Applicant: Zhaoqing City, Guangdong Province

Among the four great famous ink-stones in China, Duan ink-stone is most celebrated. It is produced in the east of Zhaoqing City (Duan Prefecture in ancient time). The stone is mostly blue-purple, pig liver color and azure blue. In summer or winter, a good Duan ink-stone will show azure and dark green in its heart and stay moist for a long time.

It is precious because the stone is tender, pure, smooth, moist, solid, and firm, and the finished Duan ink-stone can grind out ink only with people's breath and the ink will not damage the brush hair or freeze in winter. The production of a piece of Duan ink-stone will experience more than ten hardships and exquisite procedures such as exploring, excavating, selecting material, preparing uncut stone, designing, carving, and polishing. The ink stone can only be quarried by hand without mechanical operation. The quarrymen of past generations quarried to the deep stratum naturally according to the tendency of the stone chains and started to cut from the cracks. It is rare to get more than 30 to 40 percent of the quarried stone as ink stone material.

The carving of Duan ink-stone is an extremely important procedure. The lines must be clear at a glance and exquisite, and in relief. It is either deep-cutting (high and deep carving) and shallow-cutting (low relief) carving, as well as thin carving and line carving and proper hollowing out.

The procedure of polishing ink-stone usually takes place after boxing. At first it is roughly polished by whetstone with tender river sands to erase cutting cracks and marks, and then it is polished repeatedly by talc and tender sandpaper until it becomes smooth. At last it is soaked in ink. After one or two days it passes the treatment of fading ink. The effect of polishing directly influences the quality and usage of ink-stone.

Jinxing Ink-stone Making Skills

Applicant: Xingzi County, Jiangxi Province

Jinxing ink-stone is a historical famous ink-stone and got its name because there are golden spots of various shapes on the ink-stone such as upwards-slanting eyes, golden circle, golden halo, golden ripples, roe grains, eyebrow grains, etc.

Jinxing ink-stone is made of Song stone produced in Tuoling, Xingzi County. This stone is rare and precious and composed of slight mud rock. It contains sulfide iron crystals in the shapes of various shining golden stars. The big one is like a walnut and the small one is like a grain of rice. They seem like gems inlaid in black jade and like numerous shining stars in the night sky. It is called Jinxing (golden stars) stone. In some stones there is a curve or colorful band, like flying golden dragon in the night sky, and they are more precious.

The stone is smooth and can bear rubbing. It is moist and shining with deliberate lines and natural colors and veins. The finished ink-stone is moist. Dripping water will not dry on it and it will not freeze in winter. It will not produce powder after being ground for a long time and it is soundless. The ink looks like oil and shines. It is not smooth but does not damage the brush. Even in the sultry summer, the ink will not dry and, in severe winter, it continues to allow free writing. So, Jinxing stone has been regarded as the good material for making ink-stone from ancient times.

The production of Jinxing ink-stone goes through five processes of exploiting, selecting material, making foundation, carving and polishing. The procedures from quarry to finishing keep improving. The changes of color and vein in Jinxing stone reflect natural beauty. The shapes and decorations of traditional Jinxing ink-stone are full of local features as they mainly drew materials from local products, landscape and humanistic legends. It is simple, natural, concise, and vivid and a treasure of Chinese folk art.

Carved Block Printing Skills

Applicant: Yangzhou City, Jiangsu Province

Carved block printing is the earliest printing method in China. The extant earliest carved block printing implement is Diamond Sutra of 868 (housed in the British Museum).

The course of carved block printing roughly includes: write down the drawing draft of the original manuscript, paste the draft with the written surface on a block, carve the reverse characters in relief by different cutting knives, eliminate other blank spaces on the block, and make them sunken. The carved characters on the block are about one to two mm higher than the block surface. Wash wood bits out of the carved block with hot water, and the course of carving is concluded. In printing, workers use a column-shaped brush with flat bottom to dip ink, brush evenly on the block surface, cover paper carefully on the block surface, and brush again gently, and as a result the right-side characters or pictures are printed on the paper. Take the paper off the block, and dry it in the shade. A printing worker can print 1,500 to 2,000 pieces of paper per day and a block can be printed 10,000 times continuously.

In some aspects, carved block printing is better than molten type. As to languages like Chinese that has an enormous range of character sets, carved block printing costs less in the period of initial investment. This craft has much more freedom in artistic painting, such as painting of pictures and charts.

At present, this technique is only preserved in Yangzhou. The nearly 300,000 pieces of carved blocks housed in Yangzhou Chinese Carved Block Museum are rarely seen in China.

Wood-block Water-color Print Making Skills

Applicant: Rongbaozhai, Beijing

Wooden board watermark impressing scene in Rongbaozhai, Beijing

This is one of the wood-block printing techniques used to duplicate famous Chinese paintings and calligraphy works. At present, Beijing Rongbaozhai is the most famous and has the highest duplication level.

There are three processes for wood-block water-color printing: delineating, engraving wood-block and printing. At first craftsmen should analyze the school and style of the original work, design in divided spaces according to tiny changes in wetness, shade and color of the writing or painting, and use a brush pen to delineate the original work exactly on a piece of very thin wild goose skin paper. Then, they paste in reverse the engraving drafts on flat pear wood block and engrave meticulously various lines, writing styles and flats by using different knives and cutting ways. At last, they match the materials and colors used in the original work, brush the water-ink and colors onto the engraved wood block according to its artistic style, shade, and rhythm, , and overlap and print all the divided spaces on Xuan paper or painting silk. It is the last and most exquisite procedure and requires that printers not only have great printing skills but also good knowledge of painting, so that they can duplicate the original artistic style by responding to the tiny details and shade changes of the original work. This procedure should be conducted in an environment with humidity above 75 percent, so it is really water printing.

The duplicated art works are characterized by, first, the applied paper and silk have the same color and material as the original work and the copied paintings or calligraphy works look genuine; second, the applied materials will not fade or rot and can be preserved.

Jinling Carved Sutras Printing Skills

Applicant: Nanjing City, Jiangsu Province

Nanjing, called Jinling in ancient times, served as the capital for six ancient dynasties. It has a long history and profound cultural basis, and the Buddhist carved sutras industry also has a long history there. The selection of Jinling carved sutras is strict, the contents are pure, collation is precise, format is alienated, characters are big and easy on the eyes, carving and printing are careful, and paper and ink are fine, and they are customarily called Jinling editions. At present, Nanjing Jinling Carved Sutras Department, situated at No.35, Huaihai Lu, Baixia District in Nanjing City, built in 1866, is a Buddhist cultural organization with the longest history and widest influence on modern Buddhist history in China.

Jinling Carved Sutras Department has preserved the traditional wood-block water-color printing skills of ancient China and the technique mainly includes three links:

Carving block, including drawing draft, setting up draft, and carving;

Printing, including placing block, brushing ink, duplicating on paper, pressing, and taking off paper;

Binding, including pagination, foldout, gathering together with equal size, binding and pressing, counting, uniform of column, stringing paper strips, pasting front and back faces, matching books, cutting books, opening and setting up binding holes, and pasting book titles and labels.

The wood-block water-color printing technique of Jinling carved sutras is a remnant of Chinese ancient wood-block printing that holds an important position in world printing history.

Fan Making Skills

Applicant: Suzhou City, Jiangsu Province

Suzhou fan is a special local product famous for its elegance, exquisiteness and artistic features. It is classified into folded fan, sandalwood fan and silk palace fan. They are generally called Suzhou Elegant Fan. It brings together various consummate skills and includes many crafts such as shaping, mounting, engraving, inlaying and lacquering.

Folded fan have been made since the Southern Song Dynasty. The shapes of fan bone are artistic and colorful and the shapes of the fan head include more than a hundred

Double-faced sandalwood fan

varieties such as round, square, pointed, yulan and bamboo section heads. Polishing, lacquering and inlaying are also involved with various changes and artful designs. Bamboo slice is the major material for fan bone that is made meticulously and divided into more than a hundred varieties. Water-mill fan bone is the top-grade one. The fan face is mounted mostly by cotton-made Xuan paper and is divided into "plain" and "painted" kinds. The painted face is painted by masters. And the plain face can be sub-divided into ancient-style white face, golden face, etc.

It is the first one to make fan of sandalwood in China. It is made of imported sandalwood. Workers pierce an extraordinarily thin steel-wire saw blade through many small pre-opened holes on the thin sandalwood fan, form hundreds and thousands of holes with different sizes and shapes, and make several fan bones into an exquisite picture. After opening the fan, you will smell delicate fragrance and see the vivid picture.

Suzhou silk palace fan is pretty and elegant. The silk face has paintings, calligraphy works, embroidery, or other unique things. The fan handle is hollowed out or painted in colors to show the exquisiteness. The material is plain bamboo, mottled bamboo, ivory, or hawksbill, and is elegant and not vulgar. The shapes of silk palace fan mainly include round, hexagon, oblong, and a shape with round waist. The fan face is often painted with landscape, flowers, birds, and figures, or inscribed with famous poems.

Theater Costumes and Props Making Skills

Applicant: Suzhou City, Jiangsu Province

Theater costumes and props are a unique handicraft in Suzhou and can be traced back to the middle of the Ming Dynasty. It accompanied Kunqu Opera, the most elegant opera in China, for a long time.

Since the Ming and Qing dynasties, Suzhou has always been the major producer of silk and cotton cloth. Suzhou embroidery is also famous around the world for its consummate skills. In the situation, Suzhou theater costumes and props making has incomparable advantages over other places. In the 1830s, the costumes of four great famous dan characters in Beijing Opera in China, i.e. Mei Lanfang, Cheng Yanqiu, Xun Huisheng, and Shang Xiaoyun, were all tailored in Suzhou.

Suzhou today is the only place able to make all of the more than 1,000 articles of six categories of costumes, helmets, boots and shoes, swords and spears, and headwear. There are 378 kinds of costumes, 246 kinds of helmets, 276 kinds of swords and spears and 41 kinds of boots and shoes.

Each variety of Suzhou costumes and props has its own features, all made by hand. Due to different colors and sizes, the embroidery, combining and sewing have to be carefully checked. The selection of each design follows the traditional representation ways and cultural elements. The embroidery colors further show the elegant and pretty features of the watery region in Suzhou.

The sector of Suzhou costumes and props match different cloth materials for characters with different status, age, personality, opera type and troupe styles, such as damask silk, brocade silk, crepe silk, and grass linen. Attention is paid to the selection of threads, thickness and colors. There are complementary crafts such as gold and silver threads and weaving colorful shining pieces. The finished costumes and props are massive and elegant or as thin as cicada's wings. The patterns are vivid and colors are bright. They are full of decorative interests and features of the region south of the lower reaches of the Yangtze River.

Birch Bark Making Skills

Applicant: Inner Mongolia Autonomous Region and Heilongjiang Province

Birch bark making skills are peculiar to northern formerly nomadic hunting nationalities in China and have strong national and regional features. They are mainly distributed in the living areas of the Oroqen, Evenk, and Daur nationalities in northeast of Inner Mongolia Autonomous Region, as well as the Hezhen ethnic group in the ancient drainage area of the Heilongjiang. This broad land grows vast forests of birches, so these nationalities have close relations with birch trees and they have colorful birch bark handicrafts.

In the daily life of these nationalities, birch bark holds some position. Most of the articles for hunting, fishing and milking are made from it. Tableware, brewage ware, vessels, houses, fence, boats, and shrouds are all made of birch bark. In addition, many dresses and adornments of the Evenk ethnic group. are also made of birch bark, such as

About 70 percent of books on Tibetan culture are collected in the Dege Sutra-printing House. In the storeroom of the Sutra-printing house are deposited more than 200,000 pieces of blocks for the sutra, historic books and painting.

Dege Sutra-printing House Tibetan Carved Block Printing Skills

Applicant: Dege County, Sichuan Province

Dege means "good place" in Tibetan. Some 96 percent of the population of Dege County, situated in northwest of Ganzi Prefecture, Sichuan Province, is Tibetan. It was founded in 1729 and is home to Dege Sutra-printing House, well-known as the "Tibetan Cultural Encyclopedia".

Most of the paper used for printing sutras and painting figures in Dege Sutra-printing House is made by traditional handicraft skills using special material, namely, a Tibetan medicine called "ajiaorujiao", i.e. the roots of stellera chamaejasme, containing a slight toxin. Dege paper is yellowish, thick, unsmooth, good at absorbing water, light, long-lived, flexible, not frangible; it can resist moth and mice attack.

Red birch wood is selected as the raw material for a carved block in Dege Sutra-printing House. It is baked by slow fire, left to soak in a livestock dunghill for several months, then boiled, baked dry again, planed flat, and carved with characters or pictures. The carving is very deep. The calligraphy style is beautiful. It is suitable for repeated printing.

The printing course of Dege Sutra-printing House still follows ancient ways. The whole printing course is finished by three people. One is charged with replacing the printing blocks, moving the printed sutra blocks and bringing new sutra ones. The second is in charge of brushing the ink and the third handles the printing.

In Dege Sutra-printing House, traditional skills since the 13th century are retained for making the block, carving, writing, making the ink, making the paper, and printing, and offer an original example difficult to duplicate in world printing culture.

Birch bark cloth making technique is the traditional craftwork of the Ewenqi ethnic group.

cap and shoes. Various birch bark products, especially vessels, are light, practicable and decorated with patterns.

The traditional birch bark processing has four procedures: first, peeling off bark, second, soaking or boiling the bark to become soft, third, tailoring, and fourth, decorating patterns. The decorative ways include pressing and pounding, and cutting and pasting. All the nationalities decorate the birch bark products with patterns symbolizing luck, happiness, peace and harvest. The patterns mostly draw materials from production and daily life, such as imitating-nature designs of flower, grass, tree, peak, insect, fish and cliff. They possess unique national styles.

Li Ethnic Group Tapa Making Skills

Applicant: Baoting Li–Miao Autonomous County, Hainan Province

Tapa is a non-weaving cloth. It has bark as the material and is made by beating. More than 3,000 years ago, people on Hainan Island all used articles made of bark, such as bark dress and bark quilt. At that time, tapa made of trees with thick bark or castor-oil plant was a popular cloth material.

In the Ming Dynasty, there were two ways of using and making local tapa dresses. First, the pure tapa dress. The bark was peeled off, beaten, soaked and sun-dried, and then sewed into a piece of tapa as a loincloth. Second, the outer surface bark was eliminated to get the inside bark. After a complete set of procedures, the fiber of the bark was got and woven to thread to make dress or quilt.

The procedures for making a tapa dress are complex. Cut a horizontal circle on the trunk from up to down, cut another straight line from up to down, peel off the bark by hook knife. Beat the bark with a wooden stick or stone mallet. When the surface peel breaks and becomes rough, peel it off. Beat it horizontally and vertically, and the soft bark fiber appears. Soak it in water for 30 minutes to one hour. Take it out and tread on it. Wash away the gum and leave the fiber. Soak it in water again; dehydrate and sun-dry and it is ready for use. Some broken fiber can be sewed up by bamboo needle and thread of wild fiber crops or banana fiber.

Notwithstanding so many procedures, there are not many tools. Beating tools are the most important. A stone bat is one of the tools and is the symbol of tapa culture.

Hezhen Ethnic Group Fish-skin Making Skills

Applicant: Heilongjiang Province

Tongjiang City of Heilongjiang Province is located on the border between China and Russia and is the major living area of the Hezhe ethnic group, who live in the drainage areas of the Heilongjiang, Songhuajiang and Wusuli rivers. In history Hezhe people lived mainly by fishing and hunting. In early times, their dresses and quilts were made of fish-skin and it is always called the Fish-Skin Tribe.

The dresses of Hezhen ethnic group are mostly made of the skin of bighead fish, sturgeon, and chum salmon. Both dress and adornment materials and sewing threads are made of fish skin. Hezhen people are skillful in kneading fish skin. They scrape away the scales of bighead fish, apply it with oily Esox liver to keep soft and moist, fold it, press it, and cut it to thin threads by knife. As a result, the sewing thread is made.

Hezhen women peel off and dry the fish skin to some degree, then beat it repeatedly by hammer until it becomes soft. In making fish skin thread, they peel off the skin, spread and dry it, cut it to even, apply it with fish liver oil, roll it up, press it with a small wooden board, cut it into thin threads with a sharp knife. One end of the thread should be thin so that it is easy to thread a needle. At last, dye it to various colors by wild flowers. Then they can tailor various clothes according to life demands.

Liuyang Fireworks Production Skills

Applicant: Liuyang City, Hunan Province

Liuyang is a traditional key producing area of Chinese fireworks that are well known around the world for the unique craftsmanship, beautiful shapes, bright colors, loud sound, exquisite decoration and strong traditional style.

Liuyang fireworks began to be produced from 1740. Around 1870, they had become an important handicraft industry and all the households could produce them.

As a traditional handicraft, Liuyang fireworks have complex producing procedures and high technical requirements. The products must experience many procedures such as cutting paper, rolling tubes, pasting red skin, loading bottom mud, filling nitrate, constructing yellow mud, drilling, inserting fuse, etc. At last, they are knitted and wrapped.

The production of Liuyang fireworks adopts traditional handicraft skills and local materials such as paper, nitrate, sulfur, carbon powder, red and white mud, etc. There are 72 processes. With the development of modern science and technology, the ignition of fireworks has changed from traditional manual to remote-control ignition controlled by computer.

There are various Liuyang fireworks. On the foundation of ignition effects, there are mainly 13 categories: ejecting, rotating, rotating and rising up, rocket, spitting pearls, small celebration fireworks, smoke, formative toys, combined fireworks, ascending, rubbing, and celebration fireworks.

Li Ethnic Group Wood-Drilling Skills for Fire

Applicant: Baoting Li–Miao Nationalities Autonomous County, Hainan Province

The skills of getting fire by manual means are still preserved in places of Li ethnic group. Li ethnic group wood-drilling skills for fire are mainly distributed in the living area of the Li ethnic group on Hainan Island.

Li ethnic group wood-drilling for fire has distinctive regional features. The tools comprise two parts: drilling board and drilling pole (or bow wood). Dry and flammable timber is selected as the drilling board. It is cut into a board 35 cm long, seven to ten cm wide, and three to five cm thick. Several small holes are dug out on one side and the bottom of the hole is grooved for ash where spark fells down. The drilling pole (or bow wood) is 50 to 60 cm long and is made of hardwood. It has proper thickness and the diameter is three to five cm. The bottom is a little pointed-like taper. In addition, rush pith, bamboo root fiber and kapok floss are needed as ignitable materials.

It needs skill to make fire and depending on strength alone won't do. The instant spark is invisible. A medium is necessary for making the invisible spark become flourishing fire, i.e. ignitable rush pith, bamboo root fiber and kapok floss. Oxygen must be transported to it at proper time.

In drilling, people tread on the drilling board, insert the drilling pole into the small hole, and knead the pole or bow by both hands, so that the mechanical energy is turned into heat and a spark is produced. The spark fells down along the groove and ignites the material; as soon as a flame appears, people blow on it to encourage the fire to grow.

Kite Making Skills

Applicants: Jiangsu, Shandong and Tibet

Kite originated from China and has a history of more than 2,000 years.

Thin bamboo is used to make the framework of kite. Then, the kite is pasted with paper or silk and tied with a long thread. The traditional Chinese kite skills include binding, pasting, painting and flying. It must be bound symmetrically so that the left and right sides have the same area for wind. It must be pasted flat and tidily. The painted picture must be clear in far sight and realistic close up. When flying a kite, people must adjust the thread angle according to wind power.

Shandong Weifang kite originated from the early of the Ming Dynasty. It has abundant shapes and brilliant colors. It can fly high and stably and is full of local folk flavors. In the course of development it has gradually formed a production and appreciation system with hard-wing kite in the majority, long stringed "centipede" kite as the best, soft-wing kite as the exquisite one, and tube kite as the strange one.

Jiangsu Nantong kite has "hexagonal sparrow hawk" as the most characteristic one. It is a kite combining an oblong and a square with six angles altogether. There are also "seven linked stars" and "nine linked stars" combined by several such kites. The hexagonal kite is as big as several meters high and is equipped with hundreds of big and small mouths and whistles that can create the sound of a large-scale band playing a concert in the sky.

Tibet's Lhasa kite flying skills are represented by fighting and playing in the sky. The tiny changes in loosing and drawing in the thread can make the kite rise and fall, revolve and roll about to left and right quickly. It is characterized by "fighting". The blown-off kite is the loser. Various fighting skills are reflected collectively by inter-twisting threads, so the quality of thread is critical.

Cool-Tea Compounding

Applicants: Guangdong Province, Hong Kong Special Administrative Region, and Macao Special Administrative Region

Cool-tea (herbal tea) is not cool and not even a kind of tea. It is a kind of drink from decocting complex or single local herbal medicine in Guangdong, Hong Kong and Macao. The traditional Chinese herbal medicines with cold medical properties and ability to clear up inner heat are decocted to make a drink to eliminate the summer heat in the human body or to treat such diseases as throat pains due to winter dryness. Cool-tea is a drink with the functions of clearing away heat, detoxifying, producing saliva, stopping thirst, driving away inner heat and eliminating eczema. It is made according to local climate and geographical features. In preventing diseases and healthcare over a long period, it has drawn on the theories of traditional Chinese medicine for guidance and with herbal medicines as the raw materials. It has specific terms to guide people's diet. There is no limitation of dosage or need for physician's guidance.

Argy wormwood leaves and sweet flag are used ass the herbal medicine by the common people to get rid of evils, prevent sunstroke, and relieve heat.

The cool-tea compounding skills are passed down by family inheritance.

Cool-tea can be poured with water directly for drinking. But the ingredients of cool-tea are special compared to tea with the ordinary meaning and mostly have the treatment function, so it is easy for them to play a curative role when boiled. The proper vessels include glass pot, ceramic bowl and tea cup. But in terms of promoting the medical properties, the old-style earthen pottery pot with cover is the best. It will not damage the ingredients, the tea contained in it will not be spoiled, and it has the role of cooling compared to other vessels. The tea water poured out from it is cool and refreshing.

Traditional Chinese Medicine (TCM)

Cognitive Methods of TCM on Human Life and Disease

Applicant: China Academy of Chinese Medical Sciences

In studying disease, TCM, on the basis of Chinese traditional culture, seeks to understand human life phenomena and disease development rules. It has a history of more than 2,000 years since the formation of the *Medical Classic of the Yellow Emperor*.

TCM science has wide content including the theories of yin-yang, five elements (wood, fire, earth, metal, water), visceral symptoms, meridians and collaterals, disease and syndrome, etiology and pathogenesis, syndrome differentiation, therapeutic principles and methods, as well as five-element movements and six kinds of weather (wind, cold, fire, summer heat, dampness, dryness). Understanding of human life and diseases constitutes the core of TCM knowledge, playing a guiding role in terms of health preservation, diagnostic methods, therapies, formulae, Chinese medicinal herbs, acupuncture and moxibustion and clinical practice.

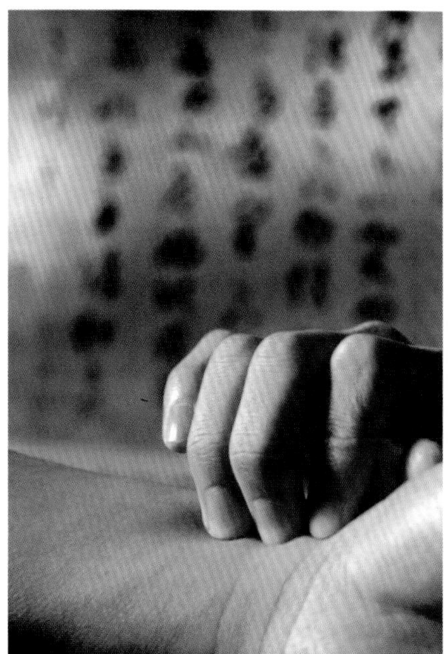

Diagonsis by feeling the pulse in traditional Chinese medicine

TCM applies the principle of the unity of opposites of yin-yang to interpret human life activity and the interdependent relationships between man and nature and man and society. It believes that normality can only be guaranteed by the balance between yin-yang. Hence, if the balance is damaged, disease will occur.

In TCM, the five-element theory is used to explain relations between humans and nature as well as among different parts of body. It is also used to expound the mechanism by which a disease occurs and develops and guide clinical treatment.

Visceral symptoms represent the key life phenomena of the human body. It refers to the physiological functions and pathological changes of five zang organs (heart, liver, spleen, lung, kidney), six fu organs (small intestine, gall bladder, stomach, large intestine, bladder, triple energizer), extraordinary fu organs (brain, marrow, bone, vessel, gall bladder and uterus), essence, qi, blood and body fluid.

Meridians and collaterals are the pathways along which qi and blood circulate through the whole body. The meridian-collateral system is considered as a theoretical basis of diagnosis and treatment. It also provides important guiding principles for the treatment methods of TCM such as acupuncture, moxibustion and Chinese massage.

Treatment based on syndrome differentiation is a process in which doctors analyze and summarize the relevant information gathered from four diagnostic methods (inspection, hearing and smelling, inquiring, pulse-taking and palpation) to determine therapeutic principles.

Diagnostic Methods in TCM

Applicant: China Academy of Chinese Medical Sciences

Diagnostic method is an important component of TCM. It is a basic method for diagnosis and collecting information on the condition of a disease. Diagnostic methods, with the guidance of the theory of TCM, apply "four examinations" to probe the cause, location, nature and state of the disease, with the result of syndrome differentiation leading to diagnosis and determining treatment principles.

Diagnostic methods include inspection, hearing and smelling, inquiring, pulse-taking and palpation, together called the "four examinations", with each being of equal importance. One cannot be a substitute for the other. In clinical practice, doctors should combine the four diagnostic methods to make the correct diagnosis. Tongue inspection and pulse examination fully exhibit traditional characteristics of diagnosing disease in TCM with unique Chinese traditional culture and regional features.

Inspection is centered on three aspects: observing spirit, complexion and tongue. This is because the manifestations of complexion and tongue can reflect the changes of zang-fu functions. Inspection of the tongue, namely, tongue diagnosis, involves observing the changes of the tongue proper and tongue coating so that physicians can know the condition of patients and make prognosis. It is an important part of inspection diagnosis in TCM. Hearing and smelling is a diagnostic method in which doctors make a judgment through examining the changes of patients' voice and the odor of excretions.

Inquiring is a diagnostic method of comprehensively understanding the disease condition. It means to get to know the occurrence and development of a disease, present symptoms, treatment procedure and other information relevant to the disease by asking the patient or those accompanying the patient.

Pulse-taking and Palpation: Pulse-taking speaks for itself, although TCM recognizes more than one pulse, unlike Western medicine. Palpation involves the physician using the hands to touch or press certain parts of the body to detect local coldness, heat, hardness, softness or other abnormal changes to help in making a diagnosis.

The Traditional Chinese Medicine Apparatus used among the common people

TCM Culture of Huqingyutang

Applicant: Huqingyutang Museum of TCM

Huqingyutang, located to the north of the beautiful Wu Hill in Hangzhou City, enjoys a reputation as the "Medicine King south of the Yangtze River". It is the best-preserved Chinese herbal medicine shop in China, and also the most well protected ancient architectural complex of the Qing Dynasty in Hui style.

Founded by a merchant named Hu Xueyan in 1874, Huqingyutang has developed into a drugstore enjoying a similar reputation to Tongrentang. It has formulated its special TCM culture, including many aspects, such as management concepts and medicine processing techniques. The core of its TCM culture is "Avoiding Deception", which was inscribed on a horizontal board and written by Hu Xueyan in person.

Huqingyutang upholds "Avoiding Deception" in management. The slogan aims to tell staff that "All trades, and especially running a pharmacy, should avoid deception. A pharmacy is closely concerned with life." The concept of "Avoiding Deception" is concerned with many aspects. In management, it means "net price", namely, whoever the customers, whether young or old, poor or rich, the choice of materials should be the same. "Be careful and meticulous in the preparation of medicine".

Huqingyutang has also preserved a large collection of ancient formulae and folk remedies. Some old staff outstanding and experienced in manufacturing skills are still alive to provide continuity.

Processing Techniques of Chinese Materia Medica

Applicants: China Academy of Chinese Medical Sciences, China Association of TCM

Processing of Chinese Materia Medica, termed Paozhi in TCM, is the general name for the processing methods of Chinese herbal medicines in the light of their medicinal and therapeutic requirements. It refers to the necessary processes of preparing raw medicinal materials before their application or making them into various dosage forms. Pao means different kinds of processing techniques with fire, while Zhi refers to all kinds of processing techniques.

Processing of Chinese Materia Medica is the centralized reflection and core of traditional pharmacology in TCM. The distinct feature and a great advantage of Chinese herbal medicine is that crude and prepared Chinese herbal pieces have different therapeutic effects. The processing techniques of Chinese herbal pieces are unique to China.

Processing with fire is a major means. The common-used methods include stir-baking and calcination. In stir-baking, carbonizing will attenuate the toxicity in Chinese medicinal herbs and potentiate an astringent action; calcination is generally used to process medicinal materials such as minerals, fossils and shells. After processing, they are easily ground into powder; meanwhile, their efficacy is altered. Due to Chinese herbal medicine having complex constituents, one medicine usually possesses multiple efficacies. When treating a disease, the medicinal efficacy is selected in the light of the disease condition. Thus, processing of Chinese materia medica can modify the nature and efficacy of Chinese herbal medicine to enhance the therapeutic effects and relieve or remove the harmful effects of certain drugs so their curative effects come into full play.

Processing of Chinese materia medica has a long history. Xin Xiu Ben Cao (Newly-Revised Materia Medica) which was completed in the Tang Dynasty is the first national pharmacopoeia in Chinese history, recording the methods of processing of Chinese herbal medicines. It marks the beginning of State protection for the processing techniques of Chinese materia medica. Processing was listed as a separate category in Ben Cao Gang Mu (Compendium of Materia Medica) compiled by Li Shizhen, a great physician and herbalist in the Ming Dynasty. Seventeen fundamental principles of processing of Chinese herbal medicine were listed in *Fundamental Laws of Processing of Chinese Materia Medica* written by Miu Xiyong, also a physician of the Ming Dynasty. Zhang Rui of the Qing Dynasty recorded 232 types of processing methods of Chinese medicinal herbs in detail in *Guidance on Processing of Chinese Materia Medica.*

TCM Culture of Tongrentang

Applicant: Beijing Tongrentang Co., Ltd.

Preparing Chinese traditional medicine

Beijing Tongrentang is a time-honored brand in the TCM industry since it was founded in 1669.

In the 188 years from 1723, when Tongrentang was authorized to provide medicine for the Qing court, to 1911, the company strictly complied with the standards in choosing medicinal materials, using the secret recipes and manufacturing skills of the royal family, thus forming a strict quality control system. Tongrentang's organic cooperation and mutual influence with the Imperial Academy of Medical Science and the royal medicine drugstore of the Qing court contributed to the formulation of its special TCM style and traditional knowledge.

Tongrentang's traditional Chinese medicine and Chinese traditional patent medicine, including those in pill, powder, extract, and pellet form, are famous for use of authentic raw materials, dedicated processing method and rich variety. The market demand for medicine exceed supply, especially the 10 most popular medicines including Bezoars Refreshing Pill (Niu Huang Qing Xin Wan), Major Pill for Activating Collateral Circulation (Da Huo Luo Dan), White Phoenix Bolus of Black-Boned Chicken (Wu Ji Bai Feng Wan), Peaceful Palace Bovine Bezoar Pill (An Gong Niu Huang Wan).

The TCM culture of Tongrentang is mainly represented in the values it cherishes: "Cultivating morality, treating people equally, benefiting mankind and preserving health"; its quality view: "No manpower to be spared, no matter how complicated the procedures of pharmaceutical production, and no material to be reduced, no matter how much the cost"; its management concept: "Keep one's words, focus on harmony between people"; its morality: "Be equally honest with aged and young customers"; and its brand and unique logo. At the same time, Tongrentang's TCM culture is also represented in its special medicine processing skills, the Prescription for pills, powders, extracts and pellets run in the Yue Family and the Catalogue of pills, powders, extracts and pellet of Tongrentang, its pharmaceutical characteristics amalgamating traditional TCM and the traditional royal medicine, summarized as "Special prescription, advanced material, marvelous processing skills and wonderful curative effects".

The brand of Tongrentang is registered under the Madrid and Paris agreements, and is fully protected internationally.

Traditional Methods of Preparation of Formulas of TCM

Applicants: China Academy of Chinese Medical Sciences, China Association of TCM

Preparation of formulae of TCM refers to the processing, under the guidance of TCM theory, of Chinese herbal medicines into certain drugs that can be directly use to prevent and treat disease. The major traditional dosage forms include pills, powders, extracts and pellet. For thousands of years, physicians in different periods have accumulated a wealth of experience in practice for the formation of unique preparation techniques of TCM.

Dating back to the reign of Xia Yu in the Xia Dynasty (2070-1600 BC), the Chinese ancestors discovered the function of wine in the process of wine-brewing and produced medicinal wine. They also found the fermented drug. In the Shang Dynasty, decoction was commonly used. In the Eastern Han Dynasty, pharmaceutical theories and principles have initially taken shape. These established that some Chinese herbal medicines, in terms of their medicinal properties, were suitable for making into pills and some into powders; some needed to be decocted in an appropriate amount of water, some soaked in wine, while some required both processes. The principle was that the kind of dosage form would depend on the medicine's nature. On the basis of existing dosage forms - decoction, pill, powder, extract and wine - Zhang Zhongjing, a famous therapist in the Eastern Han Dynasty (25-220), created ten-plus dosage forms including suppository, enema, medicated liquid, ear-drops, syrup and organo-therapeutic medication. Furthermore, he also gave details of the complete preparation method of each dosage form as well as dosage, administration and indications. Ge Hong(284-364), a well-known medical expert of the Jin Dynasty, developed the skill to make pills with the adhesive property herbal medicines possess and prepared other dosage forms involving lead plasters, wax pills, condensed pills, pastille, lozenge and moxa preparation. Between the 12th and 14th Centuries, coated pills were invented. The new process technique of a pill coated with cinnabar emerged in the Ming Dynasty. Li Shizhen (1518-1593) was a great TCM master at the time and he summed up the methods of preparation of formulae and recorded over 40 types of dosage forms of herbal medicines.

Acupuncture and Moxibustion

Applicants: China Academy of Chinese Medical Sciences, China Association of Acupuncture-Moxibustion

Acupuncture and moxibustion are external therapeutic methods to prevent and treat diseases of the internal organs. Over thousands of years, physicians used a metal needle or a moxa cone and roll to stimulate acupoints or certain parts of the body to dredge the meridians and alleviate disease. On this basis, they founded the unique theory of channels and collaterals, acupoints. The theory has become a branch of Chinese medical science renowned worldwide.

Acupuncture and moxibustion are two different kinds of therapies. Acupuncture is a method to prevent and treat diseases by stimulating the acupoints with metal needles, resulting in clearing the meridians and collaterals and promoting the circulation of blood and qi. Moxibustion utilizes cauterization or heating with a burning moxa cone or roll to acupoints so as to warm the meridians, disperse coldness and relieve pain. Both have the effects of adjusting the functions of the zang-fu organs of the body and promote circulation of qi and blood by stimulating the acupoints of the meridians on the superficial part of the body to prevent and treat diseases. The basic therapeutic principles for acupuncture and moxibustion are to reinforce deficient qi and reduce the excess of evils.

Acupuncture and moxibustion are of the following therapeutic effects:

1. Regulating effects: Acupuncture and moxibustion can restore the normal physiological balance of the body through adjusting excess or deficiency according to the properties of the disease and syndrome.

2. Enhancing immune function: they can both strengthen the body's resistance. Acupoints-stimulating and bloodletting therapies can eliminate pathogenic factors. Both can increase immunity through various ways. For instance, they are able to reinforce movable functions of the reticuloendothelial

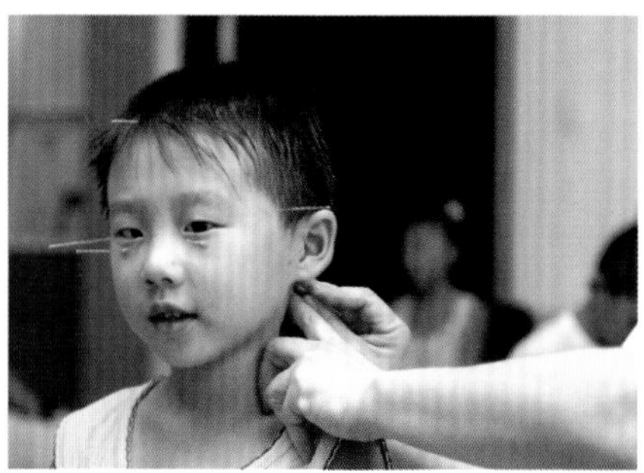

Remarkable curative effect in curing youngsters' short-sighted eyes with the acupuncture, one of therapies of Chinese traditional medicine

system and also have remarkable effects to increase various specific and non-specific antibodies.

3. Promoting blood flow and easing pain: Properly stimulating the acupoints through needling and moxibustion can dredge the channels, increase the flow of blood, promote tissue regeneration and relieve pain.

4. Repairing tissues

Bone-Setting of TCM

Applicant: China Academy of Chinese Medical Sciences

With a history of more than 3,000 years, bone-setting is an important component of TCM. Characterized by be able to heal fractures and dislocated joints quickly without an operation or medicine and at bless cost, it is warmly welcomed by patients.

Bone-setting is a treatment method applied to diseases of the kinetic system, such as fracture and dislocation. Bone-setters treat bone diseases by pulling-manipulation, reduction, alignment, massage, and finally fixing the position with a splint. China was first to adopt splinting in bone-setting.

Bone-setting of TCM has formulated a unique theoretical system and complete treatment principles and methods through long-term treatment practice. It has also accumulated abundant experience. The therapeutics, simple, practical and low-cost, have made a great contribution to the health of the Chinese nation with continuous development while being passed from generation to generation through written records or orally.

Tibetan Medicine

Applicant: Sichuan Province, Tibet, China Medical Association of Minorities

Tibetan medicine is one of the treasures of Chinese traditional culture and an important component of Chinese traditional medical science. With rich content and abundant medical literature, it is a national medical science with a complete system next only to TCM.

Tibet is rich in medical materials, with more than 1,000 kinds of medicinal plants and animals that account for 65-70 percent of the national total. Tibet is home to 400-odd commonly-used medicinal herbs, including Chinese caterpillar fungus, fritillary, gastrodia tuber, salidroside, and snow lotus. There are over 350 kinds of Tibetan medicines mainly composed of medical herbs from Tibet. A large part of these are precious traditional Tibetan patent medicines.

The application of Tibetan medicine is closely related to Tibetan medical practitioners' theoretical system. Tibetan doctors summed up the "Long" (qi), "Chiba" (Fire) and "Peigen" (Water and Earth) symptoms into hot and cold symptoms. Thus, the formulae of Tibetan medicine are divided into the hot- and cold¬-nature types according to their properties. Doctors treat cold symptoms with heat-nature medicine, and vice verse.

Tibetan medicines draw on the materials from the high, cold land, with an average altitude above 3,800 meters. More than 2,000 plants, 159 animals, and 80-odd minerals in the Qinghai-Tibet Plateau can be used. This is the point that other national medicines in the world can't be compared with.

Most Tibetan medicines are combination drugs, which are usually composed by two or more herbal recipes and seldom use only one herb. Most of the prescriptions are composed of more than 25 kinds of herbs and some have 70-80 or even 100 kinds.

Somaratsa (*Yue Wang Yao Zhen*) is the earliest Tibetan medicine classic, which was written in the seventh to eighth centuries. It recorded 780 kinds of Tibetan medicines, including 440 types of plant medicines, 260 types of animal medicines and more than 80 types of mineral-based medicines.

Folk Customs

Spring Festival

Applicant: Ministry of Culture

(See P518)

Tomb Sweeping Festival

Applicant: Ministry of Culture

The Tomb Sweeping Festival, also called Qingming Festival or Pure and Brightness Festival, is an important traditional festival for all Chinese.

It usually falls on April 4-6 in the Gregorian calendar, when nature wakes up to dress the world in green once again. Therefore, the day is also a happy occasion for outdoor activities. In ancient times, the festival was also called the Lunar March Festival, when people held a series of sports activities. It has a history of over 2,000 years.

Among the 24 solar terms in the Chinese lunar calendar, only the clear and bright is both a solar term and a festival. From the perspective of the solar term, it is a token of natural phenomena, indicating fine weather and luxuriant growth. While, it is a festival when people visit the gravesites of their ancestors to clean them and then offer sacrifices such as food and flowers to those who have passed. This is one of the many ways to demonstrate filial piety.

It is the earliest custom of the Tomb Sweeping Festival to clean the gravesite. However, the memorial ceremony in honor of ancestors is not necessarily held on that day, but often on a date close by.

Around the Tomb Sweeping Festival, with rich spring sunshine and rains, the seedlings have high survival rate and grow fast. Therefore, China has long had a custom of planting trees on the festival, so that the festival is often called "Arbor Day".

Dragon Boat Festival

Applicant: Hubei, Hunan and Jiangsu Provinces and Ministry of Culture

As one of the major traditional festivals in China, the Dragon Boat Festival falls on the fifth day of the fifth lunar month (June in the Gregorian calendar).

The festival dates back to the Eastern Zhou Dynasty (770-256 BC) with a number of legends explaining its origin. The best-known story centers on a great patriotic poet named Qu Yuan (1340-278 BC). Born in Zigui, Hubei, which was subject to the State of Chu in the Warring States Period, Qu Yuan had high aspirations when he was young. He eventually held the

Holding dragon boat race to celebrate dragon boat festival

second highest office in the state and resolved to renovate politics, but, later, the King of Chu, believing the aspersions spread by Qu's rivals, banished him from the capital. On the fifth day of the fifth lunar month in 278, Qu Yuan leaped into the river to end his life. The main event of the festival is the Dragon Boat Race, which is said to originate from attempted boat rescue of Qu. At the same time, it is customary to eat zongzi (dumplings made of glutinous rice wrapped in bamboo or reed leaves), which represents the action of local people who threw food into the river to divert the fish from feeding on Qu's body. The wrapping method of the dumplings varies between south and north. The southern people would like to mix the red Chinese dates, earthnut and bacon into the dumplings, paying attention to tasting the light fragrance of the reed leaves, while northern people prefer to use the Chinese dates and preserved fruits as stuffing.

Chinese Valentine's Day

Applicant: Ministry of Culture

The 7th day of the 7th month on the Chinese lunar calendar (usually August in the Gregorian calendar) is the Chinese Valentine's Day, called Qixi (Double Seventh Day) in Chinese. It is also known as "Begging for Needlecraft Festival" or "Daughters' Festival". As a traditional festival full of romance, it was viewed with great importance by girls in ancient times. Besides the Han, such ethnic minorities as Manchu, Korean, Zhuang, Dong, Miao and She also celebrate it.

The festival boasts a long history. A beautiful story widely spread in China describes how the Cowherd and the Weaving Maid will meet on a bridge spanning the Milky Way on that date every year. It occurs on the evening when the Cowherd (a bright star in the constellation Aquila, west of the Milky Way) and the Weaving Maid (the star Vega, east of the Milky Way) appear closer together than at any other time of the year. The Weaving Maid is a beautiful and bright fairy who is good at handicrafts. Hence, girls often present fruit in their courtyard in the hope of being blessed with the handicraft skills of the Weaving Maid as well as a happy marriage. Especially in the past, a good marriage determined a girl's happiness for the whole of her life. Hence, numerous girls, facing the starry sky, prayed for a happy marriage.

Mid-Autumn Festival

Applicant: Ministry of Culture

Mid-Autumn Festival, an important festival second to the Spring Festival among China's traditional festivals, falls on the 15th day of the eighth lunar month. On China's lunar calendar, each year is divided into four seasons, each of which is also divided into three parts, meng (the first month of a season), zhong (the second month of a season) and ji (the last month of a season). Mid-Autumn Festival is also called "Zhong Autumn". The festival originated in the imperial moon-worshipping ceremonies. The ancient emperors had a set of etiquette that they worshipped the sun in spring and the moon in autumn. Subsequently, the nobility and literati began to follow this custom. After the custom spread among the masses, it became a traditional activity. In the Tang Dynasty, people attached more importance to the custom of worshiping the moon; hence, it emerged as a fixed festival, namely the Mid-Autumn Festival.

The myth of "Chang'e Flying to the Moon" is a widely known one about the origin of the Mid-Autumn Festival. In remote antiquity, there were ten suns together rising in the sky, which burned all the crops and plants so that the masses had no means to live. In order to help the common people out of difficulty, Hou Yi shot nine suns down and eradicated the vipers and beasts on the earth so that the people lived and worked in peace and contentment. It was unexpected that the nine suns shot were the sons of the Emperor of Heaven. He angrily caused Hou Yi and his wife Chang'e to be mortals. Xiwangmu, the goddess of the west, sympathized with the couple. She gave the couple two divine pills. But Cheng'e had selfish ideas and stealthily took them. She felt herself becoming light, so light that she flew up in spite of herself, drifting and floating in the air. However, she was afraid of being laughed at by the immortals in the Heaven, and then flew to the moon, becoming the Goddess of the Moon. It was said that the day when Cheng'e flew to the moon was the 15th day of the eighth lunar month. Therefore, the later generations worship the moon on the 15th day of the eighth lunar month.

Mooncake

It is said that on the night of Mid-Autumn the moon is closest to the earth, so the moon looks the biggest and brightest. The round moon symbolizes the reunion of Chinese traditional culture, so the Mid-Autumn Festival is the occasion for the family to reunite, also called the "Family Reunion Festival". In China, various places cherish the habit of enjoying the full moon while eating moon cakes, playing lanterns and enjoy the flower.

Double Ninth Festival

Applicant: Ministry of Culture

The 9th day of the 9th lunar month is the traditional Chongyang Festival, or Double Ninth Festival. It dates back over 2,000 years and usually falls in October in the Gregorian calendar. In 1989, the Chinese Government decided the Double Ninth Festival would be designated as "Seniors' Day". Since then, an autumn trip has been organized each year for seniors in various places to make exchanges and do exercises. The younger generations take their elderly family members to suburban areas.

On this day, people enjoy chrysanthemum, and carry the cornus officinalis and wine to climb mountains for touring and drinking. This day in autumn is the best to climb mountains, as the weather is pleasant, the sky clear and the air crisp. Therefore, climbing mountains has become the important custom of the Double Ninth Festival. Without highlands to climb, the common people living in the plain south of the Yangtze River just make the rice flour cake, on the surface of which a small, colored triangular flag is inserted, showing the meaning of climbing mountains to escape personal misfortune.

The number "9" was thought to be Yang, meaning masculine or positive. The number nine in both month and day, reflected by the Chong in Chongyang, which means "double". The Chinese ancestors considered it an auspicious day worth celebrating.

During the festival, various activities are organized, including ascending mountains, gathering herbs, carrying a spray of dogwood, enjoying the flourishing chrysanthemum, drinking chrysanthemum wine, hunting, willow shooting, flying a kite, kicking a ball, eating Double Ninth Cake, and presenting gifts to one's elders.

Ha Festival of Jing Minority

Applicant: Dongxing City of Guangxi Zhuang Autonomous Region

The Jing mostly reside on the three small islands of Wanwei, Wutou and Shanxin in Dongxing City of Guangxi Zhuang Autonomous Region, located at the extreme southwest of the coastline of China and across the sea from Vietnam. The most representative custom of the ethnic group is the annual Ha Festival.

The Ha Festival is also known as Changha Festival. In the Gin language, the word "Ha" means song and "Chang" means "to sing". Hence, Changha, literally means to sing a song, and has become the singing festival of the Jing, during which, people dance and sing day and night. The date of the Changha Festival varies by region. It is held on June 10 of the lunar calendar on Wanwei and Wutou Islands, but on August 10 on Shanxin Island; some seaside villages hold it on January 25. However, the style and contents of the festival are basically the same.

Before the festival, each family cleans and tidies their home and surrounding area. On the festival, everyone, no matter what age, gathers at the Ha Pavilion to welcome the gods, worship ancestors and sing songs. The Ha Pavilion is a symbolic public construction serving as the fixed site for celebrating the Ha Festival and is the holiest place in Gin villages.

People first get together to go to the sea coast often holding banners and umbrellas, lifting the divine seat and beating drums on the way. Then, they hold a sacrificial ceremony to welcome the gods to the Ha Pavilion to receive people's worship. After returning from the seaside, people perform different kinds of dances, such as the Dance of the Light on the Head. Meanwhile, two girls with sweet voice, beating bamboo clappers and accompanied by a sanxian, begin to sing songs. The Ha Pavilion of each village is the center of the festival entertainment.

Water Splashing Festival of Dai Minority

Applicant: Xishuangbanna Dai Autonomous Prefecture, Yunnan Province

The Water Splashing Festival marks the New Year for the ethnic groups who follow the Dai calendar, such as the Dai, Blang, De'ang and Achang. That of the Dai ethnic group is the grandest and most influential, usually falling in mid-April of the Gregorian calendar. It lasts three to four days, the first two days for sending off the old year and the last two greeting the new.

The festival finds its source in India. It was a kind of ritual of ancient Brahmanism and later was assimilated by Buddhism. Around the 13th century, in this form, it was introduced into the areas inhabited by Dai people in Yunnan via Burma [Myanmar]. With the increasing influence of Buddhism in the Dai-inhabited areas, the festival has

The Dai Water-splashing Festival

been passed down as an ethnic custom for hundreds of years. In this course, Dai people gradually combined it with their ethnic myths and legends, endowing the festival with more magical meaning and ethnic flavor.

On the festival, Dai people, dressed in their holiday best, carry fresh water to clean the local Buddha statues first and then splash water on each other to symbolize auspiciousness and blessing, exorcising evil and bringing happiness; for young people, it also stands for sweet love. The wetter the person becomes, the greater the blessings.

Each year, thousands of foreign and domestic tourists gather in the Dai areas such as Xishuangbanna and Ruili in Yunnan to join in the festival. As time passes, it attracts more tourists and takes on increasingly larger scale.

Westward Moving Festival of the Xibe Minority

Applicant: Chabuzha'er Xibe Autonomous County, Xinjiang Uygur Autonomous Region

On April 18th, 1764 in the Chinese lunar calendar, upon an order issued by Emperor Qianlong, over 4,000 Xibe officials and soldiers, as well as their families, were forced to relocate from Shengjing (today's Shenyang) in northeast China to Xinjiang, far away in the northwest. The Xibe were relocated to the frontier in order to serve as reserve soldiers at a military outpost in case there was an invasion or unrest along the border. In order to commemorate this historical event, Xibe gather on this day to hold various activities. It is also called "Nostalgia Festival".

Activities include picnicking, archery, martial arts contests, singing and dancing. The singing performance recalling the westward migration is a unique part of the festival. It is performed in the style of solo and chorus, with 12 subsections and 400-odd lines of libretto. For over 200 years, it has been enriched so that there are now seven kinds.

Men and women of all ages, all in their best attire sing and dance to joyous rhythms. Girls shimmy their shoulders and boys walk like a duck. In this way, they express their yearning for their hometown and longing for a better life in the future.

Torch Festival of Yi Minority

Applicant: Liangshan Yi Autonomous Prefecture, Sichuan Province; Chuxiong Yi Autonomous Prefecture, Yunnan Province

The Torch Festival is the grandest traditional festival of the Yi especially in the Yi areas of Yunnan, Guizhou and Sichuan provinces. It usually falls on the 24th day of the sixth lunar month and lasts three days. Also called Xinghui Festival, it is New Year in the Yi calendar.

Though there are many explanations on the origin of the festival, they mostly relate to the worship of fire. In the Yi areas, fire worship is extremely prevalent, with a view to eliminating pests to protect the crops.

During the festival, a huge torch is constructed with pines and turpentine in each village; a small torch is placed in front of each household and is lit at night. Meanwhile, holding small torches, groups of villagers walk from house to house and round the edges of the fields and then put the torches and turpentine in the fields, forming a zigzag and charming fire dragons. At last, girls and boys gather many torches into a tower of fire, surrounding which, they sing and dance all through the night.

Each village also holds various social and cultural activities, including singing, dancing, horse racing, bullfighting, wrestling, archery, tug of war, and swinging. Bazaars also spring up.

Munao Singing Party of Jingpo Minority

Applicant: Longchuan County, Yunnan Province

Munao comes from the Jingpo dialect, and means singing and dancing together, prevalent in the compact communities inhabited by the Jingpo ethnic group in the Dehong Dai and Jingpo Autonomous Prefecture in Yunnan Province. The Munao Singing Party is the grandest traditional festival of the Jingpo, during which, tens of thousands of people dance to the same drumbeat. It is the

The Jingpo Singing Party

carnival for the ethnic groups in western China and reputed as the "dance in heaven".

It was originally a grand sacrificial activity held for the Sun God. It is usually held on January 15 of the lunar calendar and in February in the Gregorian calendar, lasting four days. Thousands of people sing and dance to their heart's content. Jingpo boys dance with long swords and girls with handkerchiefs and fans in many different patterns. Though there are many dancers, the change of the team pattern and steps are very orderly, showing an extremely high level of a large collective dance.

Before the celebration, four Munao Pillars are erected in the center of the dance venue; they are used to worship the Sun God and help to direct the dance. There should be lead dancers for keeping order and the accompaniment is provided by large drum bands and other kinds of bands. Based on a stutter step and swinging the shoulder, the movements of dance are easy to learn and feature a unique rhythm. Usually, the elders teach others by personal example as well as verbal instruction; young people are influenced by what they constantly see and hear. In this way, it is passed down from generation to generation, but with appointed inheritors. With such a large number of participants, the festival has an extremely strong ethnic charisma and cohesive force.

March Third Festival of Li Minority

Applicant: Wuzhishan City, Hainan Province

The March Third Festival is the grandest folk traditional festival of the Li People in Hainan Province. It is a wonderful day for the young people as it is the day for love. It falls on the third day of the third lunar month and usually in April in the Gregorian calendar.

During the festival, men and women, old and young, carrying zongzi and cakes, gather from near and far at the Wuzhishan Mountain. In the daytime, boys catch fish that the girls cook. Then, they use the fish as offerings and leave them in front of a special cave for their ancestors. Meanwhile, young men go to hunt in the deep mountains with guns and bows to present a trophy to their sweetheart.

When the night of the festival arrives, the slope and riverside are lit with bonfires. Girls wear seven-colored clothes and bracelets of various styles; boys tie red bands on their waists and carry patterned parasols. They start the festival entertainment, dancing, to lively music, various traditional dances with strong ethnic flavor, including the Bamboo Pole Leaping, Dance with Silver Bell and Two Swords, Betel nut Dance, Firewood Cutting Dance and Hunting Dance.

Songs are heard here and there all night till dawn. The girls and boys sit on their respective sides, pouring out their adoration for each other. If a girl and a boy are harmonized in feeling, they will present tokens to each other: the girl ties the seven-colored waistband she weaves on the boy; and the boy pulls the eardrops on the girl's ears or inserts a hairpin made of deer bone in her hair. They make an appointment of meeting on the festival the next year.

The festival enjoys wide popularity among the Li people. With the changes of times, the content of celebration also increases. However, antiphonal singing, folk sports, ethnic songs and dances and performance of wedding customs are still the basic content.

Fire God Sacrifice of Oroqen Minority

Applicant: Heilongjiang Province

The Oroqen is one of the ethnic minority groups with comparatively small population in China. They have lived in the forest depths of the Heilongjiang River valley in northeast China and lived on hunting for generations. The Greater and Lesser Hinggan Mountains, where the Oroqen live, are the two mountain ranges of the Heilongjiang River valley. This characteristic lifestyle has formed a unique traditional festival, the Gulunmuta Festival.

Gulunmuta in Oroqen means "to worship the fire god". The festival evolved from the ancient ritual of sacrificing to the Fire God. From of old, on festivals or lucky days, Oroqen people would light a fire in front of their houses, burn incense and pray to the Fire God for security. Before the meal, the wine and meat should be thrown into the fire as offerings. Gradually, it became a folk custom that had been passed down for generations.

The festival usually falls in spring. On the occasion, each family, with fine wine, meat and tent and so on, rides to the scheduled venue to take part in various activities. In the daytime, such activities as horse race, archery, shooting, wrestling, singing, dancing, telling story and playing chess and cards. At night, a bonfire is lit. People invite shamans to dance for the worship of deities and ancestors.

King Pan Festival of Yao Minority

Applicant: Guangdong province, Guangxi Zhuang Autonomous Region

The King Pan Festival is a grand occasion for Yao people to worship their ancestor King Pan (Pan Hu). It originated from the Singing Party that falls on October 16 of the lunar calendar (usually the end of November on the Gregorian calendar), a grand festival to worship the ancestors and celebrate a bumper harvest. Nowadays, the event has developed into an entertaining festival to celebrate the harvest, and is also an opportunity

Celebrating the King Pan Festival

for young boys and girls to look for a partner.

During the festival, families slaughter chickens and ducks. All villagers, wearing their best holiday apparel, get together to offer sacrifices to the king first and then sing songs and dance accompanied by yellow-mud drums and tambourines to recall his good deeds. Next, people celebrate the bumper harvest, enjoying themselves to their heart's content. Meanwhile, young people sing antiphonally and take the chance to look for a possible partner for life.

The festival is also known as the Thanksgiving Ceremony to King Pan. The festival is celebrated both within families and within villages; it may be celebrated for three days and nights, even up to a week. The festival ritual mainly includes two parts: one is inviting, redeeming vows to and expressing appreciation to King Pan; the other is entertaining the ancestors and clansmen, with the latter now predominating. The spirits of the Yao ancestors are invited to take part in the entertainment and perform the King Pan Songs, which reflect the myths, history, politics, economy, culture and art, and social life of the Yao people.

Ma Guai Festival of Zhuang Minority

Applicant: Hechi City, Guangxi Zhuang Autonomous Regio

The Ma Guai Festival is prominent in the Hongshui River valleys in the northwest of Guangxi Zhuang Autonomous Region. "Ma Guai" means frog in a local dialect; hence, the festival is also called the Frog Festival. It originates from the frog worship of Zhuang ancestors. The frog is considered the goddess in charge of wind and rain. People pray to it for good weather, bumper harvests and prosperity.

The artistic image of the frog appears widely in paintings, sculptures, tattoo, embroidery, balladry, myths and legends. The main image among the famous cliff drawings of Huashan is also a frog. Many scenes in the drawings depict the sacrificial activities of chiefs and sorcerers of remote ages.

The rituals of the Frog Festival differ slightly between various places. It is held from the first day of the first lunar month to the second day of the second lunar month. The rituals consist of five parts: looking for frøgs, parading the village, offering sacrifices to the frog, burying the frog and checking the auspices. In some areas, people, playing the roles of male and female frog deities, frog generals and other deities with frog masks, perform various dances. In the vivid and quite unique frog dances, most movements and postures imitate those of frogs.

During the festival, people give priority to the activity of offering sacrifices to the frog, beating gongs and drums and singing together.

Yifan Festival of Mulam Minority

Applicant: Luocheng Mulam Autonomous County, Guangxi Zhuang Autonomous Region

The Yifan masks used at the sacrificial ceremony during the Mulao Yifan Festival

Yifan, a transliteration of the Mulam language, literally means "to celebrate bumper harvests and pray for the safety of humans and livestock".

The Mulam is an ethnic group concentrated primarily in Guangxi Zhuang Autonomous Region, South China. In the past, the Mulam worshiped various gods. They had many festivals. Besides October and November, there are festivals almost every month, of which the grandest is the Yifan Festival. Bearing a strong flavor of thanksgiving and well-wishing, it takes place once every three years and occurs on a lucky day after the beginning of winter. The specific date is chosen according to the lunar calendar of that year.

The celebration lasts one to three days and takes place at the public shrine of respective family clans. On the occasion, an ornamental platform is put up in front of the shrine. People tie prepared spikes of sticky rice with plump grains and thick and long stalks with colored thread and hang them on the walls of the shrine to give thanks for a good harvest. A couplet is pasted on the door of the shrine; nine pieces of red, yellow, green and blue papers respectively inscribed with "Feng Shen" (meaning worshipping deities), "Ji Fu" (collecting blessing), "Qing He" (celebrating)" and "Yi Fan" (offering meals in turns)" on the lintel. Meanwhile, three gates are put up with pine branches in front of the shrine. An altar is set up in the shrine, on which, candles and incense are lit and sacrifices offered. The rituals of the festival include inaugurating the altar, inviting the sage, offering sacrifices to the sage, persuading the sage, singing ox songs, uniting armies and sending off the sage, presided over by two persons. One of them, wearing a mask, red gown and sandal, performs dances for inviting and paying respect to the deities; the other, dressed in a slack suit, sings to invite and pay respect to the deities. After the rituals, all the clan have dinner, sing songs and perform dragon and lion dances together, enjoying themselves throughout the night.

Redemption of the Vows of Maonan Minority

Applicant: Huanjiang Maonan Autonomous County, Guangxi Zhuang Autonomous Region

Feitao refers to a traditional sacrificial ritual of Maonan people, in which, singing and dancing are performed at the same time, with straightforward and vigorous movements and melodious rhythm. It is regarded as the "living fossil of Nuoxi Opera".

It derives from the Nuo ritual of sacrificing to heaven, earth and nature and was prevalent in the Ming and Qing dynasties. Feitao (Redemption of Vows) combines the folk activities of the Maonan people, such as oral literature, folk songs, operas, dances, music and percussion instrumental performance. The singing and dancing express the Maonan wish for multiplying in endless succession, good weather, a bumper harvest and a happy life.

Feitao has numerous varieties and rich content. The main contents are the songs, dances, operas, folklore and masks from the Nuo culture, which are performed to pray to the deities for prosperity in producing offspring. In the ritual, the leading vernacular priest (Shigong) incants and sings divine songs. The role of the deity will emerge from the dance. The performance proceeds according to certain procedures. The male performers mostly wear gowns with bright dragon or python designs and decorated with flash pieces; the females wear common clothes except skirts.

Waer Ezu Festival of Qiang Minority

Applicant: Aba Tibetan and Qiang Autonomous Prefecture, Sichuan Province

The Qiang are an old nation in China and are called "the nation in the clouds" because they live next to mountains. Most live in Mao County in Aba Tibetan and Qiang Autonomous Prefecture.

The Waer Ezu is an old celebration of the Qiang, customarily called a "Festival for the Goddess of Song" or "Leading Song Festival". Because women play the main roles, the local people also call it the Qiang Women's Festival. During the festival, all female villagers, young or old, dressed in their best festival attire and silver decorations, go to participate in the activities. On the third day of the fifth lunar month, which usually falls in June in the Gregorian calendar, several pure women are organized to go to the stone tower of the Goddess of Song and Dance-Shalang Sister to worship her with sacrifices such as incense, wax, wine, steamed bun and meat. They pray to the goddess with song and dance, called "leading songs". Returning to the village, they pass the information from one household to another, called "receiving the songs". On the fourth day of the fifth lunar month, women are busy with preparing food for the second day; and the girls are carefully preparing the gifts they have embroidered for their lovers. In the early morning of the following day, old wine is opened for celebration and to pray for prosperity of both people and livestock, as well as a good harvest. The Shalang songs and dances are the main content, performed under the lead of old women. Subsequently, they are imparted to the next generation one by one. The whole festival lasts for three days, during which, all the farming and housework are done by males, showing elements of primitive matriarchal worship.

Guzang Festival of Miao Minority

Applicant: Leishan County, Guizhou Province

Leishan County, lying in the southwest of the Miao and Dong Autonomous Prefecture in Guizhou Province, and is one of the major compact communities inhabited by Miao ethnic group.

The Guzang Festival is a grand ceremony of Miao for ancestor worship held every 12 years. It use to last four years, but now the duration is three years. Customarily, the third year of the festival is regarded as the Guzang Festival. It is a grand sacrificial ceremony of the traditional religion of Miao ethnic group, with magnificent scale and complicated and unique rituals.

The highest-ranking deities in the traditional religion of Miao ethnic group are ancestors, of which, the maple trees and Mother Butterfly which are regarded as the beginning of life, are the foremost. The Miao live in compact communities made up of clans; and that in Leishan County takes the "Gushe", a regional organization made up of kindred clans, as the basic unit, in which, they live and develop. The drum has become the symbol of their ancestral spirit and the core of all rituals and ceremonies during the festival.

Guzang Festival is a worship ceremony for Miao traditional religion.

In the second lunar month in the first year of the festival, the "Zhaolong" (inviting the dragon) ritual is held and presided over by a master. People of all ages gather under the holy maple tree. In the seventh lunar month in the first year of the festival, the "Xinggu" (wakening the drum) ritual is held; in the tenth lunar month in the second year of the festival, the "Yinggu" (welcoming the drum) ritual is held; in the fourth lunar month in the third year of the festival, the "Shenniu" (examining the cattle) ritual is held; and in the tenth lunar month in the fourth year of the festival, a ritual of slaughtering pig to worship the drum is held, called the White Drum Ritual, which is a significant sacrifice that officially ends the festival.

Duan Festival of Shui Minority

Applicant: Sandu Shui Autonomous County, Guizhou Province

The Shui ethnic group mainly lives in Sandu Shui Autonomous County, Guizhou Province. It has a calendar of its own which takes the ninth lunar month as the beginning of the New Year. Equivalent to the Han Spring Festival, the Duan Festival is the grandest traditional festival for the Shui to ring out the old year and welcome the new and celebrate the harvest. It is celebrated after the autumn harvest, generally falling in the period from the eighth to the tenth month of the lunar calendar or from September to November in the Gregorian calendar.

The Duan Festival is celebrated in batches, which are divided on the basis of kindred clans. Though blended with the ethnic geo-culture subsequently, the festival still features strong remnants of the celebration of the kindred clans. It was celebrated by nine batches in ancient times, but that has been reduced to seven now. The festival lasts 49 days, the longest in the world.

Before the festival, Shui people grind rice, make wine and new clothes and prepare various food and fruits for ancestor worship and guests. On New Year's Eve, people hang the bronze drum or bass drum in the courtyard and beat them to their heart's content. In the early morning of the first day of the New Year, each family prepares a vegetarian feast and such sacrifices as fish (Shui take fish as a vegetable dish), new glutinous rice dumplings, new rice, new rice wine, bean curd, peanuts, fruits, candies and vegetables. Among them, the steamed or braised "fish with leek" and "toast fish" are absolutely necessarily sacrifices. A folk saying among Shui goes that it is not a New Year without fish. Each household slaughters chickens and ducks and prepares sumptuous feast for guests who come to pay a New Year call.

Throughout the festival, the Shui villages are immersed in the sea of song and dance. The New Year activities include the solemn ancestor worship, exhibition of the old and mysterious Shui Book and exquisite horsetail embroidery and traditional folk performance of firedrake dance, water dragon dance, grabbing ducks and horse race.

Chabai Song Festival of Bouyei Minority

Applicant: Guizhou Province

The Bouyei man and girl sining in an antiphonal style at the Chabai Song Festival

The Chabai Song Festival is a memorial event of the Bouyei ethnic group in the Xingyi area in southwest Guizhou Province and is usually held in Chabai Ground, Dingxiao Town, Xingyi City from June 21 to 23 on the lunar calendar. It is held for commemorating Chalang and Baimei, a pair of lovers who rid the people of evil and died for love in resistance.

Whenever the festival is approaching, more than 30,000 people from the neighboring counties and Guangxi and Yunnan Provinces come to join the song festival. It usually lasts three days; and the first day is the climax. Before the festival, people wash their clothing, quilts and mosquito nets and hang them all over the village, symbolizing white clouds and cleanliness. In the evening, they drink wine and sing throughout the night with relatives and friends. On the last day of the festival, girls and boys send their love keepsakes with each other and then leave reluctantly.

The song contests constitute the main part of the festival. People compete in the daytime and at night they sing in their own or their friend's or neighbor's house, where sticky rice dyed in five different colors and rice wine are served for the guests. Many people also visit relatives and friends during the festival, eating stewed dishes, in which a cauldron is used to stew pork.

The festival also provides a good opportunity for Bouyei boys and girls to date. Dressed in their best clothes, young people bring their love keepsakes, representing the wish to find a love as strong as Chalang and Baimei. They come to the Chabai Ground to sing antiphonal songs.

Sister Festival of Miao Minority

Applicant: Taijiang County, Guizhou Province

The Sister Festival is held by Miao people in Taijiang County, Shibing County and some parts of Jianhe County in Guizhou Province and is presided over by women, during which, they eat "Sister Rice". The date of the festival varies between areas but customarily falls on February 15 or March 15 of the Chinese lunar calendar. The festival features simple and unique rituals. The most typical and spectacular is the Sister Festival celebrated on the bank of the Qingshui River, Shidong Area, Taijiang County on March 15-17.

The festival centers on young Miao girls. They invite their lovers to sing antiphonal songs, eat "Sister Rice", dance to the accompaniment of reeds and wooden drum, send love keepsakes and make dates. Hence, the festival is reputed as the oldest oriental Valentine's Day.

The Sister Festival in Shidong Area is held during March 13 to 16, following the procedures as before. On the first day, all the girls go to the mountain to pick flowers, grass and leaves for cooking glutinous rice in black, red, yellow, blue and white colors. On the second day, fishes, shrimps, duck, meat and eggs are prepared by one family to feast the boys from other villages. The festival reaches the climax in the last two days. In the daytime, girls, wearing the most beautiful skirts and silver adornments, dance with boys on the reed and drum ground. At night, young people sing love songs antiphonally and flirt. When the young men get ready to leave as the festival is over, the girls will pack the Sister Rice in handkerchiefs and put them in baskets to send to their lovers. In the rice, girls hide a pine needle, Chinese toon or cayenne to show their attitude.

Miao girls in their best celebrating the Sister Festival

Kaquewa Festival of Drung Minority

Applicant: Gongshan Drung and Nu Autonomous County, Yunnan Province

Kaquewa is the New Year Festival of the Drung in Yunnan Province, their only traditional festival.

There is no fixed date for the festival. In the light of the traditional Drung calendar, the celebration is usually held in December of the lunar calendar and lasts three to nine days. The celebratory activities include the invitation through carved wood, dancing, shooting models of quarry, setting fire to pine needles in the fireplace for blessing and drinking wine. Once the date of the festival is confirmed, the host will notify friends and relatives by invitation. The invitations are made of carved wood. The number of jags represents how many days it will take to celebrate the festival. The notified family will prepare gifts and take part in the festival's entertainment. On the first day, hosts and guests drink together and sing in an antiphonal way. At night, all the villagers get together and taste delicious food around the fire. On the second day, a hunting ceremony will be held in some villages. Accompanied by a great din of gongs and drums, people dance and sing in a circle. On the third day, each family burns pine needles in the fireplace to pray for luck and security in the coming year. On the fourth day, all the villagers get together to drink wine and sing and dance until dawn. On the fifth day, people eat and drink together until sunset, which brings the festival to an end. Of all the activities held in the festival, the grandest is stabbing cattle to offer it as sacrifice to the heaven. In 1991, the 10th day of the first month of the Gregorian calendar was decided as the official date for the Kaquewa Festival. The festival is celebrated in various villages in succession. The villages in the upper reaches of the Drung River begin the celebration first, and those in the middle and lower reaches of the river follow in turn. The celebration of the Drung villages along the Drung River lasts about one month.

Fairy Festival of Nu Ethnic Group

Applicant: Gongshan Drung and Nu Autonomous County, Yunnan Province

The Fairy Festival is a traditional festival of the Nu ethnic people living in the Gongshan area of the Nujiang Lisu Autonomous Prefecture in Yunnan Province. The local people call it the Fresh Flower Festival. It takes place on March 15 each lunar year and lasts three days, with activities like sacrificing to the fairy cave and welcoming holy water, praying for blessings by dancing, singing, and holding sports competitions.

On the occasion, every village chooses a cave with stalactites as the fairy cave, where people worship with offerings. The festival coincides with the azalea blooming season, so bundles of flowers are offered to the fairy, too. While worshipping, people light up pine twigs. The emcee does the greetings and chants the scripture while beating a drum. Afterward, all people kowtow to pray to the fairy for safety. After the ceremony, every family will have a feast. Young men and women are dressed up and go to an open ground to hold an archery contest. At the same time, various bazaars will be organized, attracting people from different places. It is said that the fairy was a pretty girl called Ah Rong living in Jiemu village. She invented the bamboo tube cable to link both banks of the Nujiang and channeled a spring from Gongshan. To escape from a forced marriage to the village chief, she hid herself in the cave and became a stone statue. It is said that the day this happened was March 15.

Sama Festival of Dong Ethnic Group

Applicant: Rongjiang County, Guizhou Province

The "Sa" refers to grandmother in the Dong dialect and is also the Grandmother Deity widely worshipped in the areas inhabited by Dongs. She was supposed to bless people security and bring prosperity for both men and animals as well as bumper harvests. The altars have been built in all Dong villages to worship Sama. In spring and autumn as well as on the occasion of collective activities or festivals, people will hold large-scale sacrificial activities and a series of performances such as reed contests, antiphonal songs, dances and Dong Opera and so on at the altars. This is the Sama Festival. The sacrificial activities prevail in the Dong areas in Guizhou, Guangxi and south Hunan. Of the total, the Sama Festival held in Rongjiang boasts the largest scale and most contents.

The festival maintains strong social reliquary of the matriarchal clan. The altar is

13 Culture

usually supervised by a sainted old woman and only the middle and old-aged women and senior men are entitled to take part in the sacrificial rituals. First, the supervisor of the altar makes tea and burns joss sticks piously for Sama. Then, the female host of each family, dressed in their best festival apparel, queues to worship the deity. Each of them drinks a mouth of grandmother tea and inserts a small twig of the evergreen tree in the hair. Subsequently, they follow the old woman who holds a umbrella not completely opened to walk once around the village and come to an appointed place and fervidly dance and sing with Sama. In this way, Dong people pray for security and prosperity. During the festival, most Dong men are willing to look after children and do housework at home. Hence, local people also take Sama Festival as the Dong Women's Festival.

Gelo Mao Dragon Festival

Applicant: Shiqian County, Guizhou Province

The Gelo Mao Dragon Festival reflects the folk worship of the Gelo ethnic group passed down for generations in Shiqian County. It is usually held during the Festival of Lanterns.

It is a kind of folk activity with emphasis on dragon worship, lasting from New Year's Eve to January 16 of the Chinese lunar calendar. Its basic factor includes: "dragon worship" (including telling traditional dragon stories, and worship ceremony), "related totem belief" (including "bamboo king" worship, Panhu worship, folk Buddhist belief and primitive worship and so on), handicraft presentation, games (such as "two dragons grabbing the treasure", "lazy dragon turning over", "one dragon playing with ball", "swan incubating eggs", "hanging upside down", "rhinoceros looking at moon", and so on) as well as reading some religious rituals and singing in the performance of "opening the door of wealth" and "paying respect to the God of Wealth".

Sword-Ladder Climbing Festival of Lisu Minority

Applicant: Lushui County, Yunnan Province

The Sword-Ladder Climbing is the annual traditional sports festival of the Lisu ethnic group; it is held on the eighth day of the second lunar month.

Lisu people come from all over at the Sword Ladder Ground near the banks of the Yangchanghe. When night falls, many piles of firewood are lit. Suddenly, four large piles of firewood are lit in the middle of the ground and the roaring flames reach several meters high. Subsequently, the din of drums and gongs begins and people surround the burning piles hand in hand to dance the brisk sanxian dance. When there are only red charcoals left in the four piles, the emcee announces the beginning of "diving into the sea of flames". Several strong men start their performance. They jump into the piles of red charcoals with bare feet, jumping and rolling. Each of them gives full play to his remarkable skill. On the following day, they insert 36 sharp-edged long swords in two 20-meter long, thick bamboo poles with blade upward. This is called the "sword pole". They climb oblivious to the razor sharp steps of this curious 'ladder'. When they get to the top, they perform extremely difficult actions. Nowadays, this breathtaking traditional sacrificial ritual has become a sports activity in which Lisu men perform their stunts.

Lisu Sword-ladder Climbing Festival—the frightening sword ladder shooting up in the sky

The festival is said to have begun during the Ming Dynasty. The Minister for War, Wangji led armies to the Lisu areas in Yunnan to retake land occupied by foreign forces. He organized the Lisu people to defend their homes. Unfortunately, Wang was maliciously accused by a treacherous court official and murdered on the eighth day of the second lunar month. In order to carry forward his brave and staunch spirit, the Lisu people carried out the activities of diving into the sea of flames and ascending the Ladder of Swords.

Water-drawing Festival and Sowing Festival of Tajik Minority

Applicant: Taxkorgan Tajik Autonomous County, Xinjiang Uyghur Autonomous Region

The Tajik Water-Drawing Festival and Sowing Festival are agricultural festivals in the Taxkorgan Tajik Autonomous County and are held on the first day of every spring planting.

When spring comes, people break the ice and draw the water into the channels to irrigate the land. The Water-Drawing Festival is held to celebrate this. The festival falls in the spring month (March 22 to April 22 in the Gregorian calendar). Led by person in charge of drawing water, people ride the horse and take tools and wheat pancakes to the water-drawing venue. After arriving there, people begin to break the ice to draw water and repair the trenches. After the water is drawn into the trench, people celebrate and then get together nearby to share the wheat pancakes. However, children prefer to play with the water. At last, some entertaining activities such as horse race and holding a sheep in the mouth are held.

On the day following the Water-Drawing Festival, the Sowing Festival begins. All the people of the village gather at the field with farm animals and tools to celebrate the beginning of the spring sowing. Then the wheat seeds taken by each family are gathered. After a sainted person offers prayers, the farmer with the most skill and with most offspring is recommended to take the lead in sowing. It is said that, if such person sow the seeds, there will be a good harvest. So, people invite him to sow the first seed. After finishing the farm work, people visit each other to celebrate the festival, during which, the whole village is filled with harmonious atmosphere of mutual cooperation.

Nadun Festival of Tu Minority

Applicant: Minhe Hui and Tu Autonomous County, Qinghai Province

The Nadun Festival (meaning 'entertainment' and 'carnival' in the Tu language) is a unique folk activity in the ethnic group for celebrating harvests and for recreation.

After the wheat harvest in summer, the Tu people in the Sanchuan area of Minhe Hui and Tu Autonomous County will hold their traditional Nadun Festival. Dressed in festival clothes and wearing old masks, people dance with fans, swords or spears and beat gongs and drums.

The festival usually lasts two months from July 12 to September 15 in the lunar calendar. It's no wonder that some people call it the longest carnival in the world. Local villages celebrate it from east to west in turn; it ends in the central area.

The activities in the Nadun Festival are mainly comprised of dances and drama performances. The first activity is the Huishou Dance, a large-scale dance involving 40 to 50 people who take part in sequence according to seniority. At the front of the dance are the old men in long gowns holding fans, who usually are the organizers of the Nadun festivities and the disciples of Nadun dance. To the rhythm of gongs and drums, people circle the ground in a graceful manner at the same time. The atmosphere is animated and the scene is grand. The following performance is a pantomime Zhuangjiaqi in which, performers wear masks and present the scene that father imparts agricultural technology to the son. It is vivid, exquisite and humorous. The last part is the mask dance The Brave General Who Killed a Tiger, representing the production activities and life of the Tu ancestors, who engaged in animal husbandry, and their spirit of toughly fighting with nature.

Festival of Discharging Water at Dujiang Weirs

Applicant: Dujiangyan City, Sichuan Province

The Festival of Discharging Water at Dujiang Weirs during the Tomb Sweeping Festival is a folk custom in Dujiangyan City, the locus of the Dujiang Weirs, a world cultural heritage site. During the Tomb Sweeping Festival, in order to celebrate the completion of the annual repair of the weirs and the spring plowing and, at the same time, to commemorate Li Bing, the grand ceremonial rituals are held, including both official and folk ones.

In 256 BC, Li Bing built the Dujiang Weirs, which solved the issue concerning flooding of the Minjiang. Thus, a land of abundance came into being on the Chengdu Plain. Hence, the Festival of Discharging Water held before the spring plowing is regarded as a holy festival by local people and given equal importance to the Spring Festival. It completely follows the ancient sacrificial rituals. First, the major emcee, dressed in ancient attire, reads the elegiac address which praises the merits and virtues of Li Bing and his son. Then, an important but unique activity namely discharging water by chopping away the abatises [barricade of tree trunks]. The scene is extremely magnificent. The first step is to tie all the back feet of the trunks in series with thick cables. Then, the back foot of the first log is chopped off and the people on the bank pull the cables forcibly at the same time. The whole structure collapses in an instant. The water gushes down to the Baopingkou Aqueduct and then spreads out to irrigate the plain.

Shoton Festival

Applicant: Tibet Autonomous Region

Before the 17th Century, Shoton in Tibet was a pure religious activity. According to Buddhist regulations and discipline, monks were not allowed to leave temples for many days in the summer. After the ban is removed, monks left the temples and went down the mountain to the nearest village. Common people would prepare yoghurt to give as alms. Lamas not only drank yoghurt to their hearts' content, but also enjoyed themselves with various entertainments.

The traditional Shoton Festival is celebrated at the turn of the sixth month to the beginning of the seventh month in the Tibetan calendar. In Tibetan, 'Shoton' means eating yoghourt. Hence, the festival is also known as the "Yoghourt Festival". The traditional Shoton Festival begins with the Buddha's Portrait Unfolding Ritual; its main contents include the performance of Tibetan Opera and visiting gardens.

The Buddha's Portrait Unfolding Ritual involves the unfolding of a huge Sakyamuni portrait woven with colored silk slowly along the mountain slope behind Drepung Monastery at sunrise. Over 100 monks take part in the ritual, which is accompanied by the dignified and solemn sound of a bugle. The portrait covers 500 square meters, bigger than that of a standard basketball court. When the portrait is unfolded, all the believers pray to it.

From the 17th century, the Shoton Festival was designated as the Festival of Tibetan Opera. During the festival, the main genres of Tibetan Opera from various places in the region gather at Norbu Lingka in Lhasa to perform and compete for several days. The mysterious Tibetan flavor finds full expression in the grandest Buddha's Portrait Unfolding Ritual, the most cheerful performance of Tibetan opera, yak racing and singing and dancing.

Unfolding the giant painting of Buddha during the Shoton (Sour Milk Drinking) Festival of Tibetan Buddhism

Confucius Grand Ceremony

Applicant: Qufu City, Shandong Province

Confucius (551-479 BC) is a great ideologist and educationalist and the founder of Confucianism. This was not only the spiritual foundation for all the previous dynasties in China, but also exerted profound impact on the thought and life of the people.

In order to pay respect to and commemorate the sage, people hold a grand sacrificial ceremony at the Confucius Temple, which has continued interrupted for over 2,000 years.

The Confucius Grand Ceremony is a large and comprehensive activity to commemorate the sage in his hometown of Qufu in eastern China's Shandong Province. This ceremony, originally held on his birthday on August 27 now lasts 15 days from September 26 to October 10 every year.

The ceremony includes four performances: music, singing, dancing and etiquette. The ceremony highlights Confucian ideology and culture, and reflects the unification of art forms and political content. It vividly explains Confucius doctrine of "etiquette"

The most important ritual in the ceremony is the three offerings. The officiating person should tidy his/her clothes and wash the hands first, and then go to the incense burner table to bow and offer incense. When making a bow, the male should put his left hand before his right hand and the female should put her right hand before her left hand. The three offerings refer to first offering, secondary offering and last offering.

The yellow silk and old-style cup are offered in the first offering. After the leading person puts them on the incense burner table, an elegiac address is delivered. Then, all the participants make five bows to the statue of Confucius and read together the Ode to Confucius. All the sacrifices in the secondary and last offerings are incense and wine; they are offered by specific person respectively, following the same procedures as the first offering.

The Sacrificial Ceremonies in the Yellow Emperor's Mausoleum

Applicant: Huangling County, Shaanxi Province

The Yellow Emperor, Xuanyuan, is called the founder of the Chinese nation. His mausoleum lies in Huangling County. There are sacrificial ceremonies performed in memory of Xuanyuan by Chinese both at home and abroad on the Tomb Sweeping Festival. The Yellow Emperor's Mausoleum is known as the "first mausoleum in China".

The Yellow Emperor was great tribal chief towards the end of primitive society in China. He was honored as the ancestor who had initiated Chinese civilization. He invented jade weapons, carts, boats and bows and arrows. Lei Zu, his wife, was good at raising silkworms; Cang Jie, his imperial historian, created the Chinese pictographs; Da Rao, one of his officials, worked out the first "Heavenly Stem and Earthly Branch Calendar"; Ling Lun, his official composer, developed musical instruments.

The sacrificial activities can be classified into official sacrifices and folk sacrifices. The official sacrifice is grand and solemn. On the occasion, a horizontal tablet inscribed with "Ceremony of Official Sacrifices at Yellow Emperor's Mausoleum" is hung on the memorial pavilion. Inside the pavilion, scrolls for condolence are hung. A new couplet is hung on the two pillars. Sacrificial wares, fresh fruits, flowers and candles are placed on the sacrificial desk. The rituals for the sacrifices include playing music, offering floral baskets and wreath, saluting, reading an elegiac address and planting trees, which have taken on certain scale.

The folk sacrifices are held around the Tomb Sweeping Festival and during the Double Ninth Festival; they don't follow fixed patterns and just go with the will and customs of the people. The folk sacrifice not only keeps some of the traditions of the official sacrifice but also displays strong local color, adding drum corps, suona horn band, honor guard and animal sacrifice guard.

Emperor Yan's Mausoleum Ceremony

Applicant: Yanling County, Hunan Province

Also known as the "Mausoleum of the Son of Heaven", Emperor Yan's Mausoleum is located at the foot of Yanlingshan, 15 km southwest of Yanling County, Zhuzhou City, Hunan Province. Emperor Yan is Shennong, a legendary tribal chief in remote ancient times. He was said to teach people to sow seeds and harvest cereal grains, hence the name Shennong ("divine farmer"). He tasted over one hundred herbs and invented medicines, so he was also a "God of Medicine". Moreover, he also benefited people with fire, developed musical instrument and advocated exchange of substance. In a word, Emperor Yan is a god in legend related to inventions in various fields such as agriculture, industry, commerce, medicine and culture. Hence, he has long been respected and worshipped by Chinese.

The memorial ceremony has two types; official and folk, both preserved from ancient times. The sacrifices at Emperor Yan's Mausoleum include literary sacrifice, object sacrifice, fire sacrifice, musical sacrifice and dragon sacrifice, of which, the latter is the most characteristic and original. When it is held, there are also performances of drums which symbolize the 24 solar terms, Shennong gongs and drums and southern and northern lions, fully showing the longstanding culture of Emperor Yan.

It has become a usual practice to hold a large sacrificial activity during the Tomb Sweeping Festival and Double Ninth Festival. Participation in the rituals has become an important way of establishing national identity and expressing expectation for unification of the country and patriotic sentiment for many Chinese.

Sacrificial Ceremony to Genghis Khan

Applicant: Erdos City, Inner Mongolia Autonomous Region

Genghis Khan is an ethnic hero esteemed by Mongolians. He unified the various Mongol tribes in the early 13th century and established the Mongol Khanate, whose territory bestrode Europe and Asia. Hence, he was known as "the proud son of Heaven". After his death in 1227 due to illness, he was secretly buried according to local custom. In order to commemorate this most outstanding leader, the Mongolians built "Eight White House" (eight moveable white Yurts) as The Genghis Khan Mausoleum on the tableland of the northern desert, and collected relics of him and put them into his coffin.

The sacrificial ceremony to Genghis Khan at his mausoleum is the grandest and most solemn activity of its type, divided into normal sacrifice, monthly sacrifice and seasonal sacrifice, all with fixed dates. There are over 60 special sacrificial ceremonies annually, with complete offerings such as a whole sheep, holy wine and various milk foods. The Spring Sacrificial Ceremony held on the 21st day of the third lunar month is the grandest and largest in scale. All the Meng leagues and banners send representatives to the Mausoleum in Ejin Horo Banner.

The sacrifices mainly express people's adoration for heaven, ancestors and heroes. Various kinds of old sacrifices of the Mongolian ethnic group such as animal sacrifice, fire sacrifice, milk sacrifice, wine sacrifice and song sacrifice are represented. Some special precious sacrificial utensils represent Mongolian aesthetic concepts on nature and animals.

The Dalghut is a tribe guarding the Mausoleum for some 800 years. Hence, the sacrificial ceremony to Genghis Khan completely maintains the original rituals held by Mongolian monarchs from the 13th century, which becomes an ethnic cultural heritage with unique style, rich content and profound meaning.

Sacrificing Ceremony for Mazu

Applicant: Putian City in Fujian Province; China Mazu Cultural Exchange Association

Mazu (Lin Mo) was born on the 23rd day of the third lunar month in 960. She was supposed to be able to cross the sea on a mat and rescue drowned people and relieve disasters, thus becoming loved and esteemed by the masses. Unfortunately, Lin Mo died at the young age of 28 when rescuing shipwreck victims on the ninth day of the ninth lunar month in 987. In order to commemorate her, people built a temple for her, now regarded as the Mazu Ancestral Temple. It assumed a certain scale in the Qing Dynasty through expansion.

From the fifth year of the Xuanhe Period during the reign of Song Emperor Huizong to the Qing Dynasty, the emperors endowed titles to Mazu 36 times, establishing her supreme status as a goddess of the sea. The Mazu worship also spread to various places in the world with overseas Chinese, sailors and envoys. The branch temples of Mazu have appeared in 20-odd countries and regions. Statistics show that there are over 5,000 branch temples of Mazu in the world and some 200 million believers.

Meizhou in Southeast China's Fujian Province is the cradle and hometown of Mazu. It has become a "Mecca" for Mazu worshippers both at home and abroad. In recent years, with the rise of "Mazu Culture" and the improvement of the infrastructure on the island, more and more people come to worship and travel. More than one million devotees go to Meizhou to pay homage to Mazu every year.

The sacrificial ceremony to Mazu is held on her birthday, on the 23rd day of the third lunar month, and on the ninth day of the ninth lunar month. The procedures follow those of the Song Dynasty. The rituals are complicated and grand, with strong and bright traditional ethnic culture.

More than 1,000 Mazu temples are scattered throughout the Taiwan islands. Mazu is honored as "Holy Mother" in Taiwan.

The Taihao Fuxi's Fiesta

Applicant: Tianshui City, Gansu Province and Huaiyang County, Henan Province

Tianshui City, Gansu Province, as one of the cultural cradles of ancient China, and also was the first ancestor Fuxi's birthplace.

Fuxi laid the foundation and enlightenment in the development of Chinese civilization. Fuxi is regarded as the founder of the early Chinese civilization and initiator of fishery, animal husbandry and agricultural production. He is the forerunner of the social production and lifestyle in the original period of Chinese nationality. In order to commemorate him, later generations built the Fuxi Temple, and held sacrificial activities every year.

The sacrificial activity of Fuxi Temple began from 1483; in various historical periods, the sacrifice has been on a different scale and with different content. The sacrificial activity lasts from the 15th day to the 17th day of the first lunar month, including the welcoming ritual held on the first day, ceremony held on the second day and sending-off ritual on the third day. There are both folk and official sacrifices.

The mausoleum of Fuxi is located 1.5 km north of downtown Huaiyang County, Henan Province, known as the "first mausoleum under the sun". A sacrificial ceremony to Fuxi is held every year from February 2 to March 3 of the Chinese lunar calendar. Temple fairs are also held during the ceremony. The three days from February 14 to February 16 are the climax of the ceremony.

The Sacrificial Ceremonies for Nvwa

Applicant: She County, Hebei Province

The Emperor Nvwa Palace, 12 km northwest of the Shexian County seat, is located on the cliff of Zhonghuangshan. It was originally built in the Northern Qi Dynasty more than 1,450 years ago, specially used for offering sacrifice to Nvwa. It is the oldest building housing Nvwa across China.

Nvwa's Creating Humans by Kneading Clay and Mending the Sky by Smelting Stone, a famous myth in Chinese history, is widely known. In the myth, she is a goddess with a human head and snake body. Nvwa is the primogenitor of the Chinese nation. During the matriarchal clanship society about 6,500 years ago, people multiplied along the Qingzhanghe near the Emperor Nvwa Palace. Later, they moved to the mountains and set up an altar to offer sacrifice.

Legend has it that the 18th day of the third lunar month is the birthday of Nvwa. Therefore, from the 1st day to 18th day of the third lunar month, people from Shanxi, Hebei, Shandong and Henan Provinces come here on pilgrimage. This gave birth to the Emperor Nvwa Palace temple fair. The sacrificial activities focus on praising Nvwa's virtues of creating human by kneading clay, mending sky by smelting stone, cutting the feet of the huge legendary turtle, setting up four poles, controlling the flood, making people intermarry and making the Sheng and Huang, a reed pipe wind instrument. They can be grouped into civil worship, public worship and pilgrimage. During the temple fair, many Nvwa belief customs are shown, mainly including procreation customs such as opening lock; customs of asking for luck and avoiding the ill luck; customs of worshipping Nvwa such as scattering the flour; marriage customs related to Nvwa.

Sacrificial Ceremonies for Dayu

Applicant: Shaoxing City, Zhejiang Province

Firing a blunderbuss, beating drums, striking the bell, making a libation to Dayu and dancing...On the 5th day of the third lunar month, the birthday of the Dayu, the Chinese people come to the Dayu Mausoleum to commemorate him in these ways.

Dayu is the founder of the first unified dynasty in China's history, as well as a hero in water control in ancient China. His virtues of taking the bull by the horns, showing leadership, being so devoted to public interests as to forget one's own and passing his own door three times without entering in while engaged in controlling floods are gems of Chinese spirit.

Dayu Mausoleum was built on the flanks of Kuajishan in the southeast of Shaoxing City, Zhejiang Province. Yu, who ruled China for 10 years, died at Kuajishan and was buried there in 2062 BC.

Dayu Mausoleum is the center for offering sacrifice to Dayu across China. In past dynasties, the Dayu worship ceremony was grand and exercised great influence. Since Qi, the son of Dayu established the Xia Dynasty in 2,059 BCE, offering sacrifice to Dayu at his mausoleum has been common practice. The Dayu worship ritual initiated by Qi is the embryonic form of the national memorial ceremonies of the Chinese nation. In modern times, the public memorial ceremony is held every five years, while the local memorial ceremony by the people and the descendants every year.

Generally, the memorial ceremony begins at 9:50 am with an implied meaning of the most importance, respect for the Dayu; firing blunderbuss of nine guns symbolizes the immortal achievements of Dayu in controlling the floods and uniting nine states in China; beating a drum 34 times indicates 34 provinces, autonomous regions and municipalities directly under the Central Government cherish the memory of the late sage; striking the bell 13 times shows that 1.3 billion Chinese people cherish the memory of their ancestor. Among the strains of music accompanied by drumbeats, the people participating in the memorial ceremony present the wine preserved for 50 years and bow to the Dayu Mausoleum three times. The one who officiates at sacrificial rites gives the elegiac address before young men and girls in old costumes perform the sacrificial dance, lauding the great achievement of Dayu benefiting later generations and his morality and personal integrity command continued allegiance.

Aobao Worshipping

Applicant: Xilingol League, Inner Mongolia Autonomous Region

Aobao means pile or hill in the Mongolian Language. Aobao Worshipping is one of the grand sacrificial activities held by the Mongolian people. Aobao generally refers to a stone cairn on a high mountain or hill. On the top of this is a pole to which a horn and cloth with religious scriptures are tied. Around the Aobao, stones are placed to be used for burning joss sticks. By the Aobao, branches are inserted in the ground and offerings such as whole sheep, kumiss, butter and cheese are placed. When offering sacrifice to Aobao, the lama lights joss sticks and chants scriptures, while the herders complete three clockwise circles around the Aobao to pray for good fortune. The Mongolian herders, following their ancestors' primitive religion, believe that the majestic mountain is the road to paradise and the home of the god.

Xilingol League is the place where the Aobao Worship is best preserved.

Due to the difference in customs and habits in various areas inhabited by the Mongolian herders, the way of offering sacrifices to the Aobao vary. The worship takes place between the last ten days of the fifth lunar month and the first ten days of the sixth lunar month generally or in July or August in some areas, when the float grass is lush and

Farmers offer sacrifice to the Aobao while walking around the mountain.

13 Culture

flocks and herds are fat. Herders will travel long distances by any means of transport to the place where the Aobao is worshipped.

The ceremony starts before the sunrise. Those who offer sacrifices to the Aobao approach from the southwest, walk a circle around the Aobao clockwise from west to east, bow in salute in front of the incense burner table before putting the stones they have brought onto the Aobao, and decorate the Aobao with willow branches, five-colored hada and colored banners.

Raosanling Festival of the Bai Ethnic Group in Dali

Applicant: Dali Bai Autonomous Prefecture, Yunnan Province

The Raosanling Festival of the Bai ethnic group in Dali is called praying-for-rain gathering by the Bai people. Popular in the Bai-populated villages around Cangshan and Erhai Lake in Dali Bai Autonomous Prefecture, it is the grand gathering integrating song and dance the Bai people hold before the busy season in farming, with a history of more than 1,000 years.

The festival evolved from the activity of praying for rain. Legend has it that Dali often underwent drought long ago, so the people could not grow rice. The Bai people who live on the paddy rice pray for good weather for the crops before growing rice seedlings. This is organized before the season for growing rice seedling comes and the period is the best time for the people to get together, giving birth to this folk custom activity.

During the period from 23rd day to 25th day of the fourth lunar month, the people in Bai-populated villages around Erhai Lake sing while dancing, led by a pair of well-dressed singers, thus beginning the Raosanling activity. They depart from the Buddhist Chongsheng Temple and go to the Shengyuan Temple (home of the god) in Qingdong Village of Xizhou Town along the foot of Cangshan. They conduct religious activities in Shengyuan Temple in daytime, and they sing and dance for revelry in the fields or forests nearby at night. On the second day, they leave Qingdong Village for Jingui Temple (home of the celestial being) in Heyicheng Village by Erhai Lake to offer sacrifices to the King of Erhe River, and then sing and dance at night until dawn to entertain the god and themselves. On the third day, they walk southwards along the west bank of Erhai Lake back to Majiuyi Village near Chongsheng Temple, to pray for a blessing.

Changdian Temple Fair

Applicant: Xuanwu District, Beijing

The temple fair, also known as temple market, was originally a sacrificial activity. In olden times, where there was a temple, a Buddhist rites were performed, drawing pilgrims and, in turn, many merchants to do business; hence, the temple fair formed naturally. In the Ming Dynasty, the Fire God Temple, Lvzhu Temple and Earth God Temple were clustered around a colored glaze plant. During the first lunar month, full of Buddhist ceremonies, peddlers set up their stalls. It became to be known collectively as "Changdian Temple Fair". Changdian is the best place to learn the folk customs, folkways and folk habits in north China represented by Beijing.

With a history of more than 400 years, Changdian Temple Fair began in the reign of Emperor Jiajing of Ming Dynasty and reached its peak in the reign of Emperor Qianlong of the Qing Dynasty. Now the site where Changdian Temple Fair is held during the Spring Festival takes Liulichang as the axis, stretching 1,050 meters from Hepingmen crossing in the north to the Hufangqiao crossroad.

The fair includes the traditional flower fair in old Beijing, exhibition of old pictures on folk customs in old Beijing, unique skill performances in old Tianqiao, performance of Peking Opera and other traditional operas, and special book fair. The temple is full of beautiful things such as sugar-coated haw berries speared onto meter-long sticks, varied kites, pinwheel and other traditional commodities peculiar to Changdian. The artists and clever artisans from various parts of China show their own traditional skills on the streets. Numerous old Chinese trademarks make their appearance on Bolichang Cultural Street, such as .the wooden board watermark of Rongbaozhai. Cultural relic reproduction by Jiguge, pen-making techniques by Lifushou, and old book restoration skills by China Bookstore all attract tourists. Sitting in a bridal sedan chair, jumping across the fire pan and lifting the red veil...The traditional wedding ceremony in old Beijing adds vigor to the temple fair.

Regong Sixth Lunar Month Gathering

Applicant: Tongren County, Qinghai Province

Regong, a place name in the Tibetan language meaning gold valley, is located in Tongren County, Huangnan Tibetan Autonomous Prefecture. Regong Sixth Lunar Month Gathering is a traditional cultural festival peculiar to Tibetan- and Tu-populated villages there, with a history of 1,400 years.

In the sixth lunar month, villages hold a folk activity of offering sacrifices, featuring dense original religious atmosphere and complicated, but rich cultural forms and meanings. It includes offering sacrifice to the god, inviting and welcoming the god, dancing with the god, worshiping the god, praying, sending off the god, military dance performance, god dance performance and dragon dance performance. Dancing plays an important role throughout.

The Sixth Lunar Month Gathering is held from the 17th day to 25th day of the sixth lunar month. It does not begin in all the villages at the same time, but by turns.

Legend has it that the respected god of the mountain comes to the village to be a guest that day, so the hosts must keep their doors open. As long as the god of the mountain is made happy, he blesses the villages. The attendees include all the men and young unmarried girls while others are the audience.

The sainted elder and Master in the village preside over the ceremony. The former represents the will of the people. The latter reports the will of the people to the god and passes back the response. He is also able to foresee good or ill luck, good fortune or misfortune and get rid of the disasters and diseases.

Sixth Lunar Month Gathering is also called Blood Entertainment. The pious people will dedicate their fresh and blood to please the god of the mountain.

Chrysanthemum Fair in Xiaolan

Applicant: Zhongshan City, Guangdong Province

Xiaolan Town, in the central part of the Pearl River Delta, is an important town in Zhongshan City. Its special horticulture makes it a "City of Chrysanthemum".

The chrysanthemum began to be grown in Xiaolan Town in the Southern Song Dynasty. In the Ming Dynasty, the reshaped potted plant emerged. In 1782 and 1791, the larger families jointly held two large-sized chrysanthemum fairs successively. In 1814, another large-sized chrysanthemum fair was held, during which farmers agreed on holding a grand chrysanthemum fair every 60 years in honor of the settling of their ancestor Xianchun.

The residents in Xiaolan Town are good at planting potted chrysanthemum with consummate skills. Various families laid their blooming chrysanthemums together in a competition, the "chrysanthemum examination", and this later developed into the chrysanthemum fair. The time fixed for the fair ranges from several days to a couple of weeks. It includes chrysanthemum viewing, chrysanthemum competition chanting a poem on chrysanthemums, painting chrysanthemums, tasting chrysanthemum tea and chrysanthemum opera. Xiaolan Chrysanthemum Fair is a unique folk traditional integrated flower fair. At present, the 20-day-long chrysanthemum exhibition is held in Xiaolan Town on November 23 to December 12. It is a grand gathering for chrysanthemum culture south of the Qinling Mountain.

Shuagetang Festival of the Yao Ethnic Group

Applicant: Qingyuan City, Guangdong Province

The Shuagetang Songfest

Shuagetang Festival is the grand festival of the Yao people in Liannan Yao Autonomous County and Lianshan Yao Autonomous County in southeast China's Guangdong Province. Shuagetang means celebrating the harvest in Yao language. It is a festival for the young men and girls to sing in antiphonal style and look for friends. It falls on about October 16 every three or five years.

The people from various villages tramp over hill and dale in groups with the figure of their ancestor, the newly harvested Indian corn, sweet potato, cooked glutinous rice pounded into paste, rice wine and fruits, and gather in the Shuagetang Festival village chosen in advance. Firecrackers are set off and ox horns are blown. The young handsome men of the Yao ethnic group who wear their hair in a bun, wrapped with the red cloth and stuck with beautiful feathers, dance the festal long-drum dance. Yao girls wearing costumes embroidered with pretty flowers, flying colored butterflies, beautiful mountains and rivers and floating clouds dance around to choose the men of their heart. Pairs of lovers leave the Shuagetang Festival and express their love by singing in antiphonal style while others drink their fill and watch.

The festival lasts three days. On the first day, the villagers offer sacrifices, and temporarily put the statue of a god in the village; on the second day, the unmarried young men and girls swarm in the Shuagetang Festival, stand face to face to sing in antiphonal style from morning to evening; on the third day, all the villagers return the statue of the god back to the temple. At dusk, the Shuagetang Festival comes to an end to the strains of music accompanied by drumbeats.

Gewei of the Zhuang Ethnic Group

Applicant: Nanning City, Guangxi Zhuang Autonomous Region

"Gewei" (Song Fairs) refers to the festive singing gathering held by the Zhuang. "Gewei" has different titles in Zhuang-populated areas, but they all have the meaning of "gathering on the slope", "singing gathering on the slope" or "joyful festival." It is a time for folk traditional cultural activities and for the young men and girls have social contact.

"Gewei" originated from the sacrificial singing and dancing activity held in the clan society. With social development, this primitive ritual singing and dancing in groups underwent a transition from entertaining the god to entertaining oneself and from focusing on dance to song.

Gewei is mainly held in spring and autumn. That in spring is concentrate between the third and fourth lunar month, especially the 3rd day of the third lunar month, while that in autumn occurs between the eighth and ninth lunar month, especially on the Mid-Autumn Festival.

Gewei varies in size in different areas. People come from all directions to participate in festivities lasting three to five days. In some areas, the Gewei is held at fixed sites such as a fair, while in other areas, it is held on a temporarily selected space not far from the village. Putting up a decorated tent, setting up a song platform, casting pompon, and choosing a mate, creates unique customs and practices.

The young men and girls choose their mate by singing and conduct song competitions. The songs include the meeting song, inviting song, Pan song, new song, love song, pledge-making song, and sending-off songs. The young men and girls in festival attire, carrying gifts and a ball made of strips of silk, sing in antiphonal style.

Slope Gatherings of the Miao in Rongshui County

Applicant: Rongshui Miao Autonomous County, Guangxi Zhuang Autonomous Region

The period from the 3rd to 17th day of the first lunar month is the time for Miao to conduct entertainment, during which people from various villages set out to sing on the mountain slopes. The 18th day of the first lunar month marks the beginning of production, so villagers seal up the sheng (wind pipe instruments) for keeping until the autumn harvest ends. The slope meetings held successively form a complete chain and the locals name them "3rd Slope Gathering" or "17th Slope Gathering" respectively according to the sequence of dates when the gathering is held.

The cultural form of the series of Slope Gatherings of the Miao in Rongshui County is embodied in song, dance and music.

The young men and girls from a wide area, dressed in festive attire and playing the Sheng, gather at Gulong Slope, surrounded by huge crowds of people. In addition to burning joss sticks and setting off firecrackers, they also stage a dragon or lion dance, 芦笙踩堂, horse fighting, bird fighting, horse racing and other activities. Dozens of stallions compete in the horse fighting for hegemony. At last, the owner of the winning horse is a hero in the eyes of the people.

The young men and girls in knots sing the Miao songs in antiphonal style to express their wish for a good life and pursuit of pure love. The Dance on the Slope Gathering is the typical representative of the dances of the Miao ethnic group. Dozens of young women in splendid attire dance in a circle, creating a joyful atmosphere. Sheng is the Miao's favorite folk music instrument. It is certainly used on every slope gathering. The Sheng songs are diversified including guest-welcoming song, seeing-a-visitor-out song, asking-for-road song, and festivity song. The singing is loud and clear.

Nadam Fair

Applicant: Xilingol League, Inner Mongolia Autonomous Region

(See P56)

Uygur Duolong Maxrap

Applicant: Magiti County, Xinjiang Uygur Autonomous Region

Maxrap, meaning a kind of folk entertainment in the Uygur language, integrates traditional music, song, dance and opera of the Uygur ethnic group. With rich content and diversified forms, it has the self-entertainment, performance and multidimensional cultural functions.

Duolong Maxrap refers to the folk Maxrap in circulation in Magiti, Bachu, Awati, and Yeken counties. The aforementioned areas located on the Yarkan River south of Tianshan are called "Duolong". The music and dance in the Maxrap here and all kinds of musical instruments that are used are preceded by "Duolong". Duolong Maxrap comes from the same source as the Maxrap in other areas, but it is notable for its more original perfection and more rustic ethnic

Uygur Duolong Maxrap

13 Culture

character. The areas are far from the main highways, so the Maxrap has experienced little impact from modern civilization.

Duolong Muqam is the first principal part in the Duolong Maxrap. Generally, the overture is sung by a performer without accompaniment, and the singing is melodious. The overture of the Duolong Muqam, like other Uygur Muqam, has most persuasive words and expressions.

Duolong Dance to the Duolang Muqam is the second principal part. What is the biggest difference between Duolong Maxrap and Maxrap in other areas is that both men and women participate; everybody is the audience, as well as the performer gets involved.

Qinhuai Lantern Fair

Applicant: Nanjing City, Jiangsu Province

"Lotus lantern" above the Qinhuaihe River

The Qinhuaihe gestates the ancient civilization of Jinling (present-day Nanjing, capital Jiangsu Province). Over the past 1,000 years, the pomp of the lantern fair on the riverside has had close relations with the development of local society. Qinhuai Lantern Fair, also called "Jinling Lantern Fair", is held around the time of the Lantern Festival.

Qinhuai Lantern Fair has a long history of over 1,500 years. After Zhu Yuanzhang, the founder of the Ming Dynasty, established his capital in Jinling, he made great efforts to promote the event. He not only allowed the people to light 10,000 water lanterns by the Qinhuaihe, but also even earnestly made the riddles written on the lanterns.

During the fair, lanterns are peddled on the streets and all kinds made be seen floating on the river by the Confucius Temple. In light of local custom, people hang the lanterns on the eaves extending over the riverbank from the 13th day of the first lunar month. The 15th day is a time for appreciating the lanterns, which are then launched on the river on the 18th day. At night, thousands of lanterns on both the banks of the river cast a beautiful light on the Qinhuaihe.

As an important folk cultural activity in Nanjing, the Qinhuai Lantern Fair displays paper-cuts, diabolo, rope knotting, carving, shadow play, and singing and dancing, sideshow and other entertainment activities.

Xiushan Festive Lantern

Applicant: Xiushan Tujia– Miao Autonomous County, Chongqing

Xiushan Festive Lantern is so named because the festive lantern art in Xiushan Tujia-Miao Autonomous County, Chongqing City is the most representative. It is a folk cultural phenomenon and folk performance art, integrating religion, folk customs, song, dance, acrobatics and paper binding art. It is popular in Tujia-inhabited areas at the junction of Sichuan, Hunan, Guizhou and Hubei provinces.

Xiushan Festive Lantern is performed from the 2nd to the 15th day of the first lunar month. The performance held after the 16th day is called Thick-Face Lantern. The venues for the Xiushan Festive Lantern performance are wide, such as courtyard, main hall of a building, streets and lanes. Due to the difference in the forms, style and contents of performance by lantern teams in various areas, some activities are conducted in special venues. For example, "Festive Lantern on a small space" needs two or three old-style wooden square desks. Two players performs festive lantern Errenzhuan or Two-Person Performance on the overlapping desks. Festive lantern opera needs a stage with simple settings. It is generally performed on a earth platform or a suspended wooden building in the village.

Xiushan Festive Lantern is performed according to a set of procedures which include setting up the lantern hall, inviting lanterns, jumping lantern and bidding farewell to lanterns. Its performance forms include festive lantern Errenzhuan or Two-Person Performance (single festive lantern performed by two players), double festive lanterns (double lanterns performed by four players), festive lanterns group dance (lanterns group performed by many players) and festive lantern opera.

The festive lantern lyrics, which, with full local flavor, narrate plots and express emotion. Some festive lantern lyrics absorb the original libretto of folk ditties and local operas such as tea-picking opera and flower-drum opera performed by Han people.

Quanfeng Festive Lantern

Applicant: Xiushui County, Jiangxi Province

Quanfeng Festive Lantern is an art performance activity originally held in Quanfeng Town, Xiushui County combining lanterns, opera and dancing. The main feature is the lantern team performance, which has strong folk-custom flavor. Quanfeng Festive Lantern is often held in remote regions and dense forests. At nightfall on the road, the colorful lanterns can be seen parading with loud gong and drum beat. It can be performed any time and anywhere. The villagers welcome and send-off the parade with firecrackers.

The talking and singing use local Quanfeng dialect. The opening of Quanfeng Festive Lantern generally is improvisational funny acting. The festivities are accompanied by percussion instruments such Chinese gong chimes, gong, side drum and cymbals. It is performed to the accompaniment of the huqin, a seven-stringed plucked instrument, flute, and suona horn. The opening, prelude and intermezzo are alike in rhythm. The lyrics include, say, "lei" and "yao".

Quanfeng Festive Lantern performance has three roles: the male character, actress or female character, and clown. The male character pulls a small wagon with both hands; the actress or female character holds a handkerchief in one hand and controls the handlebar in the other. The clown, who wears a hat and glasses, with bean curd painted on the face, exchanges banter with the actress or female. Four colored hexagonal lanterns with flower patterns stand around the stage. The white-craned lantern is in the center of the center, symbolizing luck, longevity and harvest. Quanfeng Festive Lantern performance begins during the Spring Festival and ends with the Lantern Festival. Various lantern teams gathers here.

Taishan Shigandang Customs

Applicant: Tai'an City, Shandong Province

Taishan Shigandang is a geomantic omen. It is generally placed at the entrance of the village, the bank of the river or pond, entrance of the lane and at a road junction. The quadrate stele is embedded into the walls of ancient villages or independently sited, on which the Chinese characters "Shigandang" or "Taishan Shigandang" are carved.

The stone has been apotheosized. It is a typical longstanding folk custom phenomenon with great influence in vast areas. With tangible objects expressing intangible concepts, it aims to help people endure all kinds of disasters and danger, and psychological pressure brought by the delusive gods and spirits, and conquer all kinds of bewilderment and dread.

"Shigandang" custom, centered on Taishan Mountain in Shandong Province, has spread across China (including Taiwan Province and ethnic minorities inhabited areas), Japan and South Korea and overseas Chinese-inhabited areas in Southeast Asia and the rest of the world.

"Taishan Shigandang" custom originated from miraculous stone worship in ancient times. It has gone through many stages of development and decline. Especially starting from the Song and Jin dynasties, the belief was closely combined with the worship of Taishan, the Eastern High Mountain. "Shigandang" then developed into "Taishan Shigandang". Its function also underwent a change from house guarding to "curing disease", "god of the gate", "avoiding evil" and "preventing wind". The myth on "Taishan Shigandang" also has many versions in various areas.

Shehuo Activities

Applicant: Baoji City of Shaanxi Province, Lucheng County of Shanxi Province

Shehuo is a spontaneous traditional folk art performance mainly during the Spring Festival. "She" (society), is the God of Earth", and "Huo" (fire), is the God of Fire, which can drive away evil spirits. Worshipping the God of Earth by singing and dancing aims to pray for good weather for the crops, a bumper harvest, and making the state prosperous and people peaceful.

In China, which is notable for its agricultural culture, the earth is the root of the people preserving their life. Fire is the source for people to cook food and warm themselves, as well as the absolutely necessary condition for survival and development. In remote antiquity, people thought of fire as a spirit, a godly thing with special meaning and so they worshipped it. Earth and fire worship gave birth to the customs of offering sacrifices to the God of Earth and God of Fire. As society underwent some development and people raised their capacity of understanding, entertaining elements were added to the Shehuo ritual, which has developed into the large-scale folk entertainment activity with complicated contents.

Shehuo, based on folklore, narrates a story with a figure or a group of figures. Every figure wears Shehuo facial make-up and Shehuo costumes and holds a staff. When the Shehuo conducts a tour performance, Tanma walks in front, followed by the Shehuo Banner, cannon team, banner team, and Shehuo Team and finally the gong and drum team.

Shehuo may be grouped into posing Shehuo and performance Shehuo in light of its performance ways. The former mainly shows the shapes of the figures and craftwork, while the latter refers to fighting performed in the backyard. Shehuo is often called "mummery". Spectators distinguish the appearance of the actors by the facial make-up.

Ordos Wedding

Applicant: Ordos City, Inner Mongolia Autonomous Region

The Inner Mongolia Autonomous Region is a vast area, so the wedding ceremony of the Mongolians is diversified. The Ordos wedding is the most renowned for distinctive rituals. The Ordos wedding, which has been passed down for more than 700 years, has still kept its old style and flavor. It, featuring unique ethnic flavor, the full breath of life, melodious singing and dancing, expressing the industriousness and bravery of Ordos people in their pursuit of a good life and their virtuous character. The wedding ceremony generally lasts two days, suffused with charming customs and practices of the Mongolian ethnic group from beginning to end.

The Ordos wedding originated from ancient Mongolia and was formed in the Yuan Dynasty. The "Eight White Room" used to offer sacrifice to Genghis Khan is put in the Gander Aobao Yurt in Ordos areas. The Ordos wedding has evolved into a cultural phenomenon integrating etiquette, folk custom and song and dance.

The Ordos wedding takes the bridegroom's family's bringing in the bride as the main thread, condensing the essence of weddings of the Mongolian ethnic group. It contains song and dance with a joyous scene of humor and festivity. The wedding has a series of specific ceremonial procedures, such as presenting the hada for engagement, bringing in the bride while carrying the bow, welcoming the groom with a closed door, offering a sheep and toasting, asking the name and age, separating the bride's hair, mother's blessing, rushing for the cap, baptism by holy fire, lifting the red veil, bride serving tea and the minor and greater visit of a bride to her parents.

Wedding Customs of the Tu Ethnic Group

Applicant: Huzhu Tu Autonomous County, Qinghai Province

The wedding customs of Tu ethnic group in Huzhu Tu Autonomous County are longstanding. The wedding ceremony is held in a complete set of festive song and dance.

The procedures include proposing marriage, engagement, presenting betrothal, the wedding ceremony and the banquet for extending gratitude. The wedding ceremony is very grand.

The day before the wedding ceremony, the bridegroom's family invites two go-betweens called Nashijin to visit the bride's family with gifts, and the clothing and jewelry the bride will wear, and a white ewe (symbolizing chastity and wealth). The go-betweens act as the groom's envoy to welcome the bride and are proficient in singing and dancing. When they arrive outside the bride's house, the family does not open the door immediately, but invites Agu (young girls) to sing Hua'er in antiphonal style with the "Nashijin" and pour water from the top of the door onto them, which is believed to bring good luck. Only when the Agu or the Nashijin can no longer sing are the latter allowed to enter.

The groom dedicates hada to the bride's parents and worships God and Buddha. Then, the visitors are entertained with tea and dinner. During this period, the Agu girls sing the wedding song at the window. Then they rush into the house and draw the groom's side to dance the Anzhao dance in the courtyard until dawn the next day. In the whole process, about 20 varieties of songs and dances are performed. The "Anzhao" is an old folk song and dance form most popular in the Tu areas. A wedding ceremony of Tujia people is a beautiful singing and dancing ceremony.

The wedding songs are beautiful in melody and rich in content involving astronomy, geography, history, religion, mythology and etiquette and custom. They are the most outstanding form expressing the traditional culture of the Tu ethnic group.

Wedding Customs of the Salar

Applicant: Salar Autonomous County in Xunhua County, Qinghai Province

Xunhua is the sole Salar autonomous county in China. The wedding ceremony is an important etiquette activity. For Salar people, the traditional wedding ceremony is generally held in the winter. The procedures for wedding includes having a traditional blind date before engagement, asking a matchmaker to make a proposal to the girl's family, entrusting the matchmaker to send betrothal tea, presenting betrothal gifts, reciting the wedding sutra, accompanying the bride to bridegroom's family on the wedding day and the first visit of a bride to her parents.

The Salar still keep some ancient marriage customs of the primitive Turkic tribe, such as presenting mutton carcasses to the uncle (mother's brother). The wedding ceremony has also preserved many old traditions. For example, Tuiyaoyina is an ethnic dance with ethnic migration, history and traditional education as the main content in the form of a drama. There is a bold and unrestrained wedding eulogy "talking and singing Worohoso".

The wedding customs of the Salar are simple and unsophisticated. The wedding ceremony is always held at dusk in mid-winter. On the wedding day, the bridegroom and his male relatives leave for the bride's home on horses and mules to escort her to the wedding. When they arrive at the bride's home, they do not enter the house but wait in the backyard, listening to the imam reciting the wedding congratulatory message called Nikahe. Then, the elder on the bride's side comes out to pull on the new hat and tie the embroidered waistband for the bridegroom, who is accompanied by a bride's close kin to kneel in front of the imam while the bride also kneels and listen on the corner of the bed in her room. The bride's family also gives a banquet to treat the bridegroom's relatives. The next day, the bride is escorted by two married women of the bride's close kin and other friends to the bridegroom's house.

When bride arrives at the gate of the bridegroom's house, a salute is fired. The men who accompany the bride cluster round her to force their way in. The bridegroom's family closes the door to ask for gifts and only then let the bride get off the horse and walk in. They still cherish the custom whereby the bride squeezes through the half-closed door to reach her groom.

Huji Story-Telling Gathering

Applicant: Huimin County, Shandong Province

Huji is the largest market town in southeastern Huimin County (Wuding Prefecture in olden times), The 2nd, 7th, 12th, 17th, 22nd and 27th days in the lunar calendar are a market day. The 12th day of the first lunar month (between February and March) is the first big market, during which the lantern fair and story-telling festival are held, hence the name Huji Story-Telling Gathering. This originated from the folk art competition. Later, it gradually evolved into the spontaneous folk art exchange activity focusing on the fellowship.

Huji Story-telling Gathering consists of "Qianjie" (literally preceding festival), "Zhengjie" (literally formal festival) and "Pianjie" (literally leaning festival). Before the 12th day of the first lunar month, story-telling artists from afar often come to Huji Town with their musical instruments and bedding several days ahead of schedule so as not to miss the gathering. Some amateur lovers of folk art forms also lodge in the various hostels. On their way to Huji Town, these artists tell story and make a living as a performer. They come to Huji Town before the evening of the 11th day, stay overnight in villagers' homes, and collectively conduct the fellowship activities. This is the "Qianjie".

On the early morning of the 12th day, the story-tellers from various areas come to the market, set up their respective stall, put up their banner and sign, and show their respective skill. At 10 am, as the drumbeats and firecracker sound in unison, the story-telling gathering formally begins. "Zhengjie" (literally formal festival) begins this day and ends on the 16th day of the first lunar month, which is the peak of the story-telling gathering.

During the story-telling gathering, the artists pay a New Year call to each other, learn from each other by exchanging views on skills and formally acknowledge a teacher. Afterwards, the artists also make a living as a performer on the way home.

Majie Story-telling Gathering

Applicant: Baofeng County, Henan Province

Majie Village is located in Yangzhuang Town of Baofeng County. In history, it was a prosperous product-distribution center where merchants gathered. Majie Folk Artists Fair is a grand gathering in the folk art profession with a long history. The original time of the fair is hard to validate.

On the 13th day of the first month, folk artists from across the country carrying drums or musical instruments gather in Majie to demonstrate their skill. The fair lasts three days. Although small, Majie Village is a Mecca in the eyes of artists. The artists engage in story-telling

Storytelling Meeting in Majie

and show their art to make friends, learn from each other by exchanging views and seek to be the best at the Artists Fair. On the hilltops, in the fields and along the riverbank, stages are set up, on which folk artists sing ballads and tell stories to the accompaniment of bamboo clappers or stringed instruments. They perform even if there is no audience. With the sky as the curtain and the field as their stage, the artists perform in all weathers. The stages turn into a sea of folk art performance. Artists use a local accent passed down from generation to generation, releasing and expressing their innermost gladness, sadness and hardship as much as they like.

Medicine Market in Anguo

Applicant: Anguo City, Hebei Province

As early as in the Song Dynasty more than 700 years ago, Anguo City was a famous traditional Chinese medicinal materials distributing center. It reached its peak in the reign of Qing Emperor Daoguang, being known as the "First Medicine Market Under Heaven".

The medicine market's prosperity originated from "Medicine King Temple," located in the south of Anguo City, which is the largest complex in China in honor of the medical sage. Those who participate in the medicine market will pay a formal visit to the temple with reverence. On the 15th day of the first lunar month, personages from pharmaceutical circles and ordinary people offer sacrifices to the medicine king.

Temple fairs are held throughout the year. The spring temple fair lasts five month while autumn temple fair lasts seven months. The official date for spring temple fair falls on the 28th day of the fourth lunar month which is the birthday of the medicine king according to legend. The official date for the autumn temple fair falls on the 15th day of the tenth lunar month which is the fete-day of the king.

In the mid-Qing Dynasty, Anguo Medicine Market had "13 bangs" and "five associations" and at the same time set up the "Anke Hall" serving the businessmen and managing the market. From then on, Anguo has become the largest medicinal material trade center and medicinal material distributing site. From the Ming to Qing Dynasty and even to the Republic of China, the temple fair was hosted by "13 bangs" in turn. On the 1st and 15th day people offer sacrifice near the Temple. The whole county seat is very busy.

The temple fair has its unique worship etiquette, including performing opera, carrying the offerings, presenting the Ding, molding the golden body, hanging the plaque, presenting a gown.

Bronze Drum Custom of Zhuang Ethnic Group

Applicant: Hechi City, Guangxi Zhuang Autonomous Region

The bronze drum is a kind of percussion instrument invented by the ancient Pu and Yue people in south China. With a history of more than 2,700 years, it is distributed most widely in Guangxi. Originally the bronze drum was used for drinking (namely, a kind of jar) and later evolved into the percussion instrument.

The people of ethnic minorities in Guangxi Zhuang Autonomous Region have had the habit of hitting bronze drums while holding festive celebrations or offering sacrifices to the gods or ancestors. The custom has been always followed to this day. When the Zhuang people in Donglan and Tian'e counties celebrate the 3rd Day of the 3rd Lunar Month Festival and Spring Festival, the Yao people in Du'an, Bama and Dahua celebrate Remembering Mother's Kindness Festival, the Yao people in Nandan County hold a funeral or offer sacrifices, and the Miao people in Zhongpu of Nandan County celebrate Spring Festival, they all beat drums to express their feeling of celebration or mourning

The Bronze Drum Festival, the traditional one of the Zhuang in Aidong and Changle Townships of Donglan County, falls on the first, 15th and 30th days of the first lunar month. On those days, the bronze drum teams consisting of the young men from various villages carry the bronze drums onto the top of the neighboring mountain, put them on wooden frameworks, beat the drum for ancestor worshipped and engage in competition. With the big drum versus big drum and small drum versus small drum, a unit of four drums, each is beaten by three people in turn

The competition is held throughout the night until dawn. At the same time, the young men and girls are paired to sing in antiphonal style. After the competition, people have a picnic with foods such as glutinous rice dumpling brought from home and the songs and cheerful talk echo through the valley.

The bronze drum culture is an important component of the culture of the Zhuang ethnic group. Almost every village along the Hongshuihe has a bronze drum. On holidays, funerals and wedding, every family beat the bronze drum.

Couplets on the Doors of the Temple of Manjushri

Couplet Custom

Applicant: Yinglian Society of China

Yinglian refers to couplets hung on the pillars of a hall. It is a kind of literary art form peculiar to China. It started from the Five Dynasties and prospered in the Ming and Qing dynasties, with a history of more than 1,000 years. Yinglian is passed down and widely spread among Chinese, in the areas where the Chinese language is used in the world, and the ethnic groups having a cultural origin with Chinese characters.

Antithetical couplets, using the special function of Chinese language, figures of speech, matched both in sound and sense, level and oblique tones, narrate something, depict a scene and express emotion. They use polished language to express rich meaning. According to function, antithetical couplets may be grouped into Spring Festival couplets, couplets used on weddings, couplet written for birthdays, elegiac couplet, couplet hung for decoration, couplet written to depict a landscape, self-written couplet, couplet in the trade, intercommunicating couplet and couplet expressing all kinds of skills (including comic couplets).

A couplet is a pair of lines of poetry that are usually rhymed. A couplet is comprised of two lines written on vertical strips of red paper in the best calligraphic style one can master. The first (upper) line is posted on the right side of the front door. The second (lower) line is posted on the left side of the front door.

A horizontal scroll bearing an inscription is believed to be the subject of the couplet as well as the core of the couplet. Good horizontal scroll may play a role in adding the touch that brings a work of art to life. The couplet takes the characters as the content and the calligraphy as the carrier. Its products are diversified, including picture frame, woodcarving, carved stone and bamboo carving. There have been many books on couplets and thousands of couplet works. The couplet is widely used. In addition to being hung on the palaces, pavilions, halls, and study rooms, it is used at the festival celebration, inscription present, congratulation, elegiac and mausoleum.

Costume of Women in Luzhi Water Town, Suzhou

Applicant: Suzhou City, Jiangsu Province

The rural women living in Luzhi, Shengpu, Weiting and Lumu towns in Wuxian County, east of Suzhou City, Jiangsu Province, have always preserved the traditional folk custom costume featuring kerchiefs, patchwork jackets and trousers, embroidered shoes. These traditional costumes have the characteristics of water towns south of the lower reaches of the Yangtze River.

The costumes of women in Luzhi Water Town, Suzhou are special in terms of material selection, cutting out, stitching and ornament. The application of patchwork, embroidered borders on a dress, waistband ornament and embroidery craftwork is superb. The combination of the colors does not stick to one pattern.

Women of different ages in Luzhi Water Town have different demands. The young girls like to wrap the head with the red washcloth with the jet black and shining plaint, wear the short jacket button down the front with embroidered borders on a dress, and small lute buttons. A blue pleated apron is tied to the waist. A waist bag is embroidered with all kinds of patterns, the top of the colorized stripe of which is red and green tassels. Under the skirts, they wear Tibet black trousers and wear the embroidered round-mouthed cloth shoes with embroidered borders. For the old women, their costume is dark in color. They wrap the head with the black kerchief, and wear black cloth skirts. For the middle-aged women, the costume is elegant, with a white kerchief, a bob bound with colorized rope, silver adornment vertically on the bob and silver hairpin horizontal.

The shoes of the women resemble a small boat in shape, with no difference in left and right shoes. They are combined with uppers and bottoms. The vamp is embroidered many patterns with bright color and diversified design, hence the name "boat-shaped" embroidered shoes. The shoes are exquisite, solid and economic.

Costume of Women in Hui'an

Applicant: Hui'an County, Fujian Province

Hui'an has a picturesque landscape, in which live female groups with peculiar costume and folk customs.

The whole style of the costume of women in Hui'an was finalized in the Tang Dynasty and matured in the Song Dynasty. At the turn of Ming and Qing dynasties, the costume of women in Hui'an e also underwent marked changes, featuring peculiar style, unique ornaments, harmonized color and flamboyant pattern.

The costume of women in Hui'an features a yellow bamboo hat, silver waistband, blue jacket, and loose black trousers, showing the curved beauty of the stature of women and their graceful and charming bearing.

The bamboo hat is the most outstanding part while the kerchief is also distinctive. The latter is foursquare (66 centimeters) embroidered with white patterns on a blue base, white patterns on green base, and green patterns on a white base. Though the patterns on the kerchiefs are different, they are clear, simple and elegant.

The jacket is so short as to expose their umbilicus. The waistbands are grouped into two categories: The one, woven with colorful plastic bags, has a width ranging from seven to nine centimeters, with the striking color; the other one is made of silver. The trousers are black, which make them appear steady-going and in good taste. In addition, the black trousers make it easy to arrange dress and decorations in other colors.

Women in Hui'an like to wear cabinet earrings, necklaces, finger rings and bracelets. Covered up by the kerchief used to wrap the head, they do not attract attention.

Costumes of Miao Ethnic Group

Applicant: Baoshan City, Yunnan Province

The cross-stitch work, embroidery, brocade, batik, paper-cut and headdress making and other art and crafts of the Miao ethnic group are beautiful and widely known. Of them, their batik craftwork has a history of 1,000 years. There are more than 130 varieties of costumes of Miao ethnic group, which are famous for their flamboyant color.

Costumes of Miao ethnic group vary with gender, age and marital status of the wearers, and they vary in different areas; but they all have retained the traditional style through the ages. Miao women wear a narrow-sleeved and big-collared short gown with buttons down the front and a pleated skirt. In casual times, the women wrap their head with the kerchief, wear a jacket buttoned down the front, long trousers embroidered with chiffon, tie an embroidered apron, and wear a few exquisite silver decorations. The pleated skirt is decorated with embroidery, brocade, batik and cross-stitch. The decorative patterns on the pleated skirt are multi-colored. The color of the costume includes red, blue, yellow, white and black. The costume is made from woven cotton, hemp and hair, which are raw materials produced there. The costume of the Miao men is simple. They wear a short gown buttoned down the front or on the right and felted wool embroidered with patterns, wrap their heads with black cloth and wrap shank with the leggings.

Most of ornaments are the silver ornaments worn on the head, neck, chest and hand. Silver ornaments of the Miao come first on the list of various ethnic groups. The beautiful costumes show the ability and wisdom of the Miao ethnic group, which have still retained the ethnic feature.

Costume of the Hui Ethnic Group

Applicant: Ningxia Hui Autonomous Region

The Hui is one of the Islamic ethnic groups in China. Due to the difference in the region, gender and sects of the Hui people, the costumes have different flavors and features.

The costume of the Hui ethnic group, with vivid ethnic features, includes waistcoat, Masehai socks, and gowns, worship cap, and head-coverings. The waistcoats are made of cloth, silk, thin silk or hemp, which are worn in the four seasons. They can be used as undergarment or outer wear. It is easy to draw the sleeves for cleaning the face, nose, mouth, elbows and feet, and doing work. This wear has the function of preventing cold.

The costume of the Hui ethnic minority is most notable for its head-gear. In areas inhabited by the Hui, men can usually be found wearing a round white or black brimless hat, which is called the "worship hat", while the women often have the habit of wearing a veil or a kerchief. When wearing a head-coverings or a kerchief of various colors, they appear graceful and beautiful.

Muslims favor the colors of black, white and green. The Hui people in China see the white as the cleanest, most joyous color. They also like wearing green and black clothes. Hui Muslims believe that green is the most holy color. The Muslim who pays a pilgrimage to Mecca holds a green banner. The rugs made by Arabian countries which are used for the Muslim to pray have a green background. The imams wear a green hat and green gowns. The young women of the Hui ethnic group also wear green head-coverings and green trousers. The Hui people also like to wear light blue waistcoat, black head-covering and black gown.

Costume of the Yao Ethnic Group

Applicant: Nandan County and Hezhou City, Guangxi Zhuang Autonomous Region

The Yao ethnic group has always been notable for its bright-colored costumes. According to statistics, costumes of the Yao ethnic group have 100 varieties of styles and no less than 100 varieties of headwear.

The Yao people have maintained their own tradition and feature in the custom and habits, especially in dress and personal adornments. Yao women love to embroider various patterns on the front, cuffs and trouser legs of their clothes, plait their hair and arrange it into a bun decorated with colored beads. Men also wear long hair, arrange it in a bun, and then wrap the bun with blue or red kerchiefs, wear collarless, long-sleeved gown buttoned down the front, and white-cloth waistcoat over the gown, and wear long trousers with wide cuffs. Yao boys and girls at the age of 15 or 16 begin wrapping a kerchief, marking their maturity.

The beauty of the costume of the Yao focuses on the composition of cross-stitch patterns. These reflect religion to some extent. The Yao in Xilin County, Guangxi Zhuang Autonomous Region have preserved a religious dress with a history of hundreds of years, on which many patterns of the God of Heaven, God of Mountain, God of Thunder and God of the Sun are embroidered.

Legend has it that the five vertical lines on the white trousers that the Yao men in Nandan County wear are the bloodstain of the ten fingers of their ancestors who, even when wounded, persisted in fighting bravely to safeguard their ethnic dignity. Women wear a pullover "Guantouyi" without collar and buttons, both sides of which are not sewn, with the ends of the fronts joining, and matched with batik skirts. The back is adorned with a square pattern said to be the model of the seal of the Yao King stolen by local officials. In honor of it, it is embroidered on the clothes, and at the same time has become a clan totem.

The Twenty-Four Solar Terms

Applicant: China Agriculture Museum

(See P522)

Nvshu, or Women's Script

Applicant: Jiangyong County, Hunan Province

Nvshu, or women's script, is a single-sex writing system that Chinese scholars believe is the only one of its kind. It was a delicate, graceful script handed down from grandmother to granddaughter, from elderly aunt to adolescent niece, from girlfriend to girlfriend—and never, ever shared with males. Over the past hundreds of years, it has been circulation in Jiangrong County and neighboring areas of south China's Hunan Province, hence another name Jiangrong Nvshu.

The Nvshu characters take the shape of long diamond. With graceful, wispy, unique shape, they are known as "mosquito-shaped characters". All the Nvshu characters consist of four kinds of strokes—dot, vertical stroke, inclined stroke and arc. They may be intoned in the local dialect.

Nvshu differs from Chinese in many respects. For example, the character represents sound, not ideas as in the Chinese ideograms. A Nvshu character resembles a Chinese character, but there is no inevitable connection between them. In addition to being written, Nvshu characters, as the flower pattern, are also embroidered on the clothes or cotton tape, so they are wispy and curved.

The works in Nvshu include the *Third Day Book* (a cloth-bound volume in which her sworn sisters and her mother would record their sorrow at losing a friend and daughter and express best wishes for happiness in the married life that lay ahead, that three days after the wedding the adolescent bride would receive), wedding song, love letters between "sworn cotemporary sisters", complaint song in autobiography, ballad in chronicles, god-praying song in offering sacrifice, letters, translated traditional stories in Chinese and balladry. The works in Nvshu take the complaint as the main content.

Nvshu must be intoned in specific lowering, sorrowful and gentle melodies. Almost all the works in Nvshu are libretto, whose composers are the local intellectuals proficient at Nvshu.

Shuishu

Applicant: Qiannan Miao–Bouyi Autonomous Prefecture, Guizhou Province

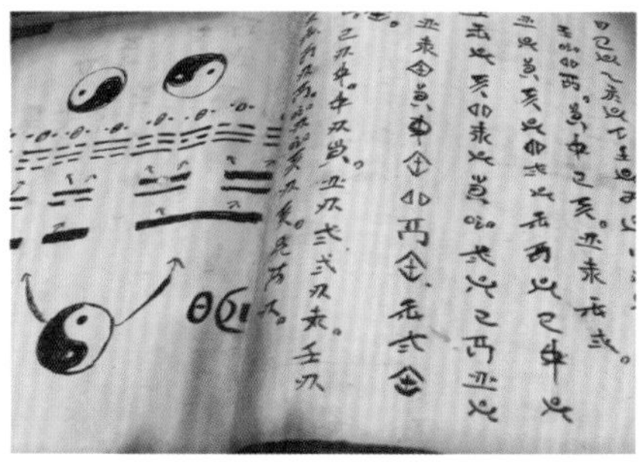

Signboard of fortune-telling by analysing the component parts of a "Shuishu"

"Shuishu" is general term for the unique pictographic characters and books of the Shui ethnic group. It is an ancient writing resembling the inscriptions on bones or tortoise shells and inscriptions on ancient bronze objects. It has recorded the ancient astronomy, folk customs, ethics, philosophy, aesthetics, law and other cultural information of the Shui ethnic group.

The Shuishu characters are grouped into the following three categories in structure: pictographs resembling the inscriptions on bones or tortoise shells and inscriptions on ancient bronze objects; borrowings from Chinese characters, namely the backward writing, mirror writing of Chinese characters or writing by altering the structure of Chinese characters; characters for religious purpose, which are all kinds of secret signs representing the primitive religion of the Shui ethnic group. Shuishu was written from right to left and from top to bottom, without punctuation.

What the Shuishu has recorded mostly are the date, direction, omen of good or ill luck, and methods of warding off evil and ghosts. It has written the month and day in a year, and marked the good or ill luck with the directions put into verse or the omen of things. It is used as the tool of the shamans for practicing the religious ceremonies. In addition to great numbers of contents on primitive religious belief, the Shuishu books also contain the information on celestial phenomena, calendar and ancient writing of the Shui ethnic group which is in urgent need of being deciphered. The information on celestial phenomena and calendar that the Shuishu reflects is the rarest historical and cultural heritage.

Literature

Development of Literature

The earliest achievement in Chinese literature is *Shijing* (Book of Poetry), the first collection of poems in China which was compiled in the 6th century BC. Thereafter, the unvarnished prose in pre-Qin time, the brilliant Fu (poetry in the Han Dynasty) and the Yuefu folksongs (songs of the Han Music Bureau) exemplify the literary features of their respective times. In the Tang Dynasty (618-907), poetry creation reached its peak and thousands of poets including such famous ones as Li Bai and Du Fu had over 50,000 poems handed down. In the Song Dynasty (960-1279), the most outstanding achievements were made in Ci (lyric poetry) and in the Yuan Dynasty (1206-1368) it was Zaju (poetic dramas set to music) that obtained the highest achievements. In the Ming and Qing dynasties (1368-1911), the four full-length novels, namely *The Romance of the Three Kingdoms, Outlaws of the Marsh, Pilgrimage to the West and A Dream of Red Mansions*, were created and still enjoy wide readership owing to their rich cultural and historical contents and special artistic styles and are thus honored as Four Famous Chinese Classics.

Chinese literature in the 20th century reached its peak twice in the period from the 1920s to the 1930s and the period from the 1980s to the 1990s. Starting from the New Cultural Movement, the first peak brought along strong anti-imperialist and anti-feudalist thought from the beginning. Lu Xun, Shen Congwen, Ba Jin, Mao Dun, Lao She and Zhang Ailing became the great masters in the Chinese literary world.

In the 1980s and 1990s, a group of new writers and new works with influence around the world came to exemplify the achievements and flourishing trend of contemporary literature in China. By means of modern Chinese, writers expressed more mature reflection on the life and aesthetic experiences of modern Chinese people. In regard to the group creation level, the contemporary novel writers exceeded their predecessors in the artistic way of thinking and expression.

At present, there are dozens of literary awards in China, among which the authoritative ones include Mao Dun Literature Prize, Lu Xun Literature Prize and Annual Appraisal of Chinese Literature Figures. The Chinese Women Literature Prize, chosen every five years, is a national large-scale literary award covering five categories, namely novels, essays, poetry, recorded literature of actual events, and works on women's artistic theory and translation.

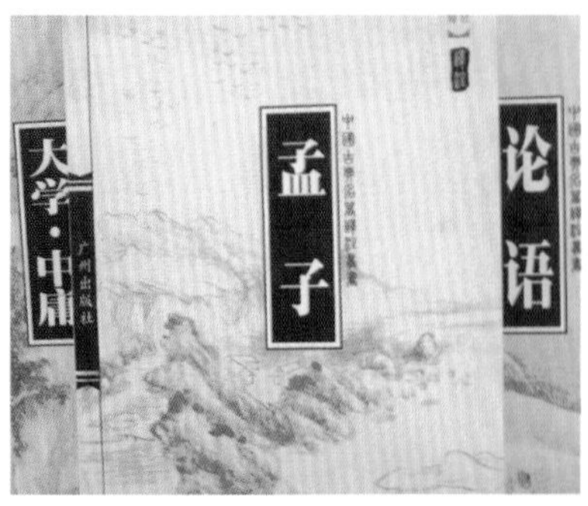

The Four Books and the Five Classics are classics of Confucianism.

The Four Books and the Five Classics

The Four Books and the Five Classics are classics of Confucianism. They recorded in detail the historical materials of politics, military affairs, foreign affairs and culture of the most active time in the development history of Chinese thought and culture, as well as the important philosophical thoughts of Confucius and Mencius that influenced Chinese culture for thousands of years.

The Four Books refer to *Daxue* (The Great Learning), *Zhongyong* (The Center of Harmony), *Lunyu* (The Analects of Confucius), and *Mengzi* (The Book of Mencius). It is said that they were written by Zeng Shen, Zi Si, Confucius and Mencius respectively.

The Five Classics are actually the six classics of Confucianism, namely *Shijing* (The Book of Odes), *Shang Shu* (The Book of History), *Yi Li* (Rites and Ritual), *Yue Jing* (The Book of Music), *Zhou Yi* (Changes of Zhou), and *Chun Qiu* (Spring and Autumn Annals).

Hundred Schools of Thought

In the turbulent Spring and Autumn Period and Warring States Period (770-221 BC), the old slave-owner class declined and a new landlord class arose.

In the great social transformation, new changes emerged continuously in the class-relationship in all states, and representatives of different classes and strata held different opinions on social transformation, hence the appearance of the "Hundred Schools of Thought", mainly including Confucianism, Mohism, Taoism and Legalism. There were politicians, philosophers, eloquent persons and expert scholars. Some of them publicized their theories for rulers to administer their states, such as Confucianism, Legalism and Mohism; and others merely expressed their opinions on politics and society, such as Laozi and Zhuangzi. During this period, the thoughts of people were the most free and boundless and human liberation was the most complete comparing favorably with the golden age of Greek philosophy.

Articles of Hundred Schools

During the Spring and Autumn Period and Warring States Period, the situation of the Hundred Schools of Thought represented philosophy and culture in China. Articles of Hundred Schools are analects and articles on them, and the extant works include *Lunyu* (The Analects of Confucius), *Mengzi* (The Book of Mencius), and *Xunzi* (The Book of Xunzi) of Confucianism; *Mozi* (The Book of Mozi) of Mohism; *Laozi* (The Book of Laozi) and *Zhuang Zi* (The Book of Zhuangzi) of Taoism; *Hanfeizi* (The Book of Han Fei) of Legalism; and *Lushi Chunqiu* (Master Lu's Spring and Autumn) of Eclectics, etc.

Dao De Jing

The *Dao De Jing* (Scripture of the Dao and Its Virtue), also known as *Dao De Zhenjing*, *Lao Zi*, and *Wuqian Yan* (Text in Five Thousand Words), is said to be written by Laozi during the Spring and Autumn Period, which is the important source of philosophic thought of the Taoist School.

The original text was divided into two parts: Part one called *Dejing* (Scripture of Virtue) and *Daojing* (Scripture of the Dao), without the division of chapters. Later it reversed the sequence of the two parts, placing the Dejing first and was divided into 81 sections or chapters. It is the first complete works on philosophy. What can be now seen is the A and B silk scroll Lao Zi excavated in No.3 Mawangdui Han Tomb in Changsha of Hunan Province in 1973, which is the edition of the early years of the Western Han Dynasty (206BC-25AD), placing the Dejing first. The bamboo slip Lao Zi unearthed in the Guodian Chu Tomb in Jingmen of Hubei Province in

1993 is also thought highly by scholars.

The *Dao De Jing* is often ascribed to the doctrine of Taoism. Actually, the Taoist School in philosophy should not be confused with the Taoism in religion. However, *Dao De Jing*, one of the important compositions of the basic doctrines of Taoism, is regarded as the important classics of Taoism, and its writer Lao Zi is viewed as the incarnation of the Supreme Master Lao. So it can be said that the Taoism absorbed the thoughts of Taoist School, which perfects the Taoism.

Lunyu (The Analects of Confucius)

Lunyu is a book of recording the words and deeds of Confucius and his disciples. Written by disciples or descendants of Confucius, it covers various fields such as philosophy, politics, economy, education and literature and is the principal classic of Confucianism. In regard to expression, it shows concise and vivid wording, representing the model of analects. In arrangement, it has no strict stylistic rules and layout; each item constitutes a chapter, each section or chapter is not closely related to each other and is classified in different parts in the rough, and sometimes repeated. The extant Lunyu has 20 sections and 12,000 words in total.

Mengzi (The Book of Mencius)

Mengzi recorded the words and deeds of Mencius and his disciples, including writings by Mencius himself and those by his disciples with the consistent style as a whole. Different from the concise style of *Lunyu*, *The Book of Mencius* is full of lengthy articles, notwithstanding the form of interlocution. All the arguments are composed carefully and the style is imposing with stern words and distinctive color of eloquent persons.

Zhuang Zi (The Book of Zhuang Zi)

This recorded the thoughts of *Zhuang Zi* and his disciples. The extant Book of *Zhuang Zi* has 33 sections divided into interior, exterior and miscellaneous parts. Traditionally, it is usually believed that the *Neipian* (interior part) of the book was written by Zhuang Zi, while the *Waipian* (exterior part) and *Zapian* (miscellaneous part) were written by a combination of Zhuang Zi and his disciples and later scholars. But some people believe that they were mostly written by Zhuang Zi himself at different times, and there were only a few items by later people writing in the name of Zhuang Zi. The *Neipian* (interior part) includes *Qi Wu Lun* (Seeing Things as Equal) and *Xiao Yao You* (A Happy Excursion) representing the most centralized expression of Zhuang Zi's philosophy. He adopted a way of exposition and argumentation different from other schools, namely allegory.

The Book of Changes

Zhuang Zhou Dreaming a Butterfly, Enlightened in Chaos, and Dissecting Cattle by Pao Ding are all excellent allegories. The works of Zhuang Zi can be viewed as a great treasure in the history of Chinese literature, promoting pre-Qin essays to new heights.

Zhou Yi (Changes of Zhou, also called Yi Jing)

Zhou Yi, a book for divination, is a classic of Confucianism with mysterious color in ancient China. It probed the changing rules and the rules of living and the death of all things. It has some resemblance with the working principle of modern computers; the latter one works by various arrangements and combinations of binary digits, 0 and 1, and Yi Jing gives expression of all things by two symbols, Yin and Yang (opposite principles or forces existing in nature and human affair).

As the book was completed very early and words had different meanings with the change of times, it was difficult to comprehend *Yi Jing* as early as during the Spring and Autumn Period and Warring States Period. People in ancient times particularly wrote *Yi Zhuan* (Commentaries on Yi Jing) to unscramble *Yi Jing*. Today, *Zhou Yi* usually refers to the combination of *Yi Jing* and *Yi Zhuan*.

Shang Shu (The Book of History)

Shang Shu is the earliest book of history in China, and the words mean "book of ancient times". The time of its completion is unknown, but it undoubtedly existed in the early times of Zhou Dynasty. It has 28 chapters; in time order, the earliest ones are Yu Shu and Xia Shu, followed by Shang Shu and Zhou Shu. Shang Shu recorded both words and deeds.

Baguwen (Eight-part Essay)

(See P203)

Li Sao (The Poem on Departure)

This is a representative work of Qu Yuan, and is one of the longest lyrics in ancient China. The word of "Li Sao" means "grief on

The Paiting of Xian River Ladies produced according to *Xiang Jun* and *Xiang Furen* in the *Nine Songs* of *Chu Ci (Songs of Chu)*.

• Qu Yuan

Qu Yuan (ca. 339-278 BC), an important politician of the Chu Kingdom in the Warring States Period, was one of the greatest poets in ancient China. His works served as one of the sources of Chinese literature owing to its brilliant words, peculiar imagination, fancy allegories and profound contents. In 1953, the World Peace Council passed a resolution to confirm Qu Yuan as one of the four world celebrities of culture for memorializing in that year as it was the 2,230th anniversary of his death. He passed his life in a vehement and complex political struggle. At last, he committed suicide in the Miluo River in desperation to show his allegiance and love for his country. With profound knowledge, Qu Yuan was familiar with astronomy, geography, ritual and musical systems, the conditions and rise and decline of all past dynasties before the Zhou, and some important historical stories. In his works, he showed strong sentiment of worrying about the country and people and expressed his profound political opinions. As a poet, Qu Yuan is the representative of *Chu Ci*. He left more than 20 famous poems, such as *Li Sao* (The Poem on Departure) and *Tian Wen* (Ask Heaven). His works exerted a great influence on later generations.

departure". It expressed a hidden resentment that he could not carry out his ambition of making the country stronger and saving the people as he had to leave his monarch and the political center.

Li Sao has a character of positive romanticism. The lyric is full of enthusiasm and fancy imagination and creates a figure of a great patriot sacrificing himself for an ideal. The poet spread the wings of his imagination to soar into the heavens, and completely broke the boundary between heaven and the human world and between fable and reality. The magnificent color and wonderful plot come in a continuous stream to create a grand and splendid painting scroll. Li Sao is like a story in some ways. The former part narrates the poet's experience of struggle for almost his entire life, and the latter part works out the plots and illusion of a woman named Xu giving advice, divination, a wizard offering incantations to the gods, and a visionary visit to heaven. The lyric moves in great waves, and gives incisive and vivid expression to the poet's long-time struggle and complex feelings.

Yuefu (Han Music Bureau) Poetry

Emperor Wudi (reigned 140-87 BC) of the Han Dynasty set up a department in charge of music, which was called Yuefu. Its specific tasks included composing music for poems written by literati praising the rulers' merits and virtues to be used and appreciated at grand ceremonies and sacrificial rites held by the court; and collecting ballads and folksongs across the country and composing music for them to amuse the rulers. Later, people also called the poems and songs reserved by Yuefu as "Yuefu", and gave them a general name of Yuefu Poetry or Yuefu Folksongs. Yuefu poetry originating from common people has a strong living flavor and is the soul of the genre. The extant Yuefu folksongs of the Han Dynasty comprise more than 100 pieces, most of which are in five-word verse form. Due to the intentional imitating by later literati, Yuefu poetry became the major poetic form in the Wei and Jin dynasties.

Shi Ji (The Records of the Great Historian)

This is the first historical work in the form of series biographies in China, written by Sima Qian in the Western Han Dynasty. It is also a general historical book composed of Ben Ji (Main Records), Biao (Sheets), Shu or Zhi (Documentation), Shi Jia (Hereditary) and Lie Zhuan (Biographies).

The book contains records from the Yellow Emperor (forefather of the Chinese in legend) to the Han Emperor Wudi, covering the history of more than 3,000 years. There are 130 articles of more than 520,000 words, including 12 pieces of Ben Ji, 10 of Biao, eight of Shu, 30 of Shi Jia and 70 of Lie Zhuan. All these writings show rich historical content, covering thousands of historical figures such as emperors, monarchs, officials, heroes and civilians and involving various fields such as politics, decrees and regulations, culture and thought. The 12 pieces of Bei Ji recorded the words and deeds and achievements of the kings and emperors and grand events. The 10 pieces of Biao list the lineage, historical figures and events in the form of table sheets. The eight pieces of Shu include documentations about ceremonial rites, musicology, metrology, calendar making, grand ceremony of worship of heaven, hydrography and water conservancy, astronomy and astrology, and economy respectively. The 30 pieces of Shi Jia describes the historical stories of the dukes inherited from their forefathers and some famous figures such as Confucius and Chen She, etc. The 70 pieces of Lie Zhuan describes the life of the important historical figures and historical events. Individually speaking, the five styles of writings had appeared or begun to be developed before Sima Qian, but it was he who first compiled the five styles into one book. In regard to the sections and contents of this book, the history of the Qin and Han dynasties occupies the most space, and it provides the complete records from ancient times to the time of the writer.

The longest piece is *Ben Ji of the First Emperor of Qin Dynasty*, with more than 13,000 words, and the shortest one is *Lie Zhuan of Sima Rangju* with only about 700 words. The vivid narration of events and figures in a limited length reaches a very high literary level.

• **Sima Qian**

Sima Qian (ca. 145-87 BC), was a historian and litterateur whose *Shi Ji* (Records of the Great Historian) is viewed as the model of a Chinese historical book. The form of series biographies launched by Sima Qian became the standard form of main historical records in later generations and had a profound influence on the development of the study of history and literature.

At the age of 10, Sima Qian could recite "ancient literatures", and later he mastered classics and historical books and was good at poems and essays. After reaching 20, he traveled to many places, including the middle and lower reaches of the Yangtze River and the Yellow River, the regions inside and outside the Great Wall, places in southwestern China where he served as envoy; he visited many places as an attendant of Emperor Wudi of the Han Dynasty. During his travels, he collected materials and investigated local customs, which was a good foundation for compiling historical books. In the third year of Yuanfeng (108 BC), Sima Qian served as Taishiling, an official involved in astronomy, calendar, keeping records of events, books and archives, and he began to write historical books. He participated in the compilation of the Tai Chu Calendar. During the Tianhan period, a political calamity led him to be punished by castration. He then served as Zhong Shu Ling (official of the Department of the Imperial Secretariat). But his work of compiling historical book was not affected by these matters. Due to suffering from unexpected calamity, he even made a determined effort to finish a work known as the Book of Taishigong. These books were generally named *Shi Ji* by later generations.

Tang Poetry

Tang poetry is the general name for all poems written in the Tang Dynasty when there were most abundant old-style poems from the past dynasties. Hence comes the saying of "Tang poetry, Song Ci, and Yuan dramas".

Tang poetry has neat style of writing and attaches importance to rhyme. In respect of number of words in a verse, it can be divided into five-word and seven-word, and in respect of length, it can be divided into Jueju (a poem of four lines, each containing five or seven characters, with a strict tonal pattern and rhyme scheme), Lushi (a poem of eight lines, each containing five or seven characters, with a strict tonal pattern and rhyme scheme) and Yuefu. Nearly 50,000 poems were handed down during the dynastic reign of nearly 300 years, and about 50 or 60 poets with unique styles emerged. The Four Pre-eminent Poets of the Early Tang Dynasty, namely Wang Bo, Yang Jiong, Lu Zhaolin and Luo Binwang, are the major figures. The period when the dynasty was at its height is also the peak of poetic development, when two great poets emerged, namely Li Bai and Du Fu, along with many others of outstanding achievements. They can be divided into two categories: landscape and pastoral poets represented by Meng Haoran and Wang Wei, and frontier poets among whom Gao Shi and Cen Shen gained the highest achievements, while Wang Changling, Li Qi, Wang Zhihuan were also outstanding. In the Mid-Tang period, the most outstanding poet was Bai Juyi. Late-Tang poetry has a strong, sorrowful feeling and the representative poets are Du Mu and Li Shangyin.

Most of the Tang poems were collected by *The Complete Anthology of Tang Poetry*, and later people collected those outstanding works into *Three Hundred Tang Poems*.

Song Ci (Lyric Poetry)

Ci, originated from folksongs, is a form of poetry also named Song Ci, Quzici, Shiyu, or Changduanju. It sprang up in Liang of the Southern Dynasty during the Southern and Northern Dynasty, came into its own in the Tang Dynasty and reached its peak in the Song Dynasty.

Originally, Ci referred to the words of songs and meant lyrics accompanied by music. Later it was gradually separated from music and became a special poetic form.

Such Ci composers as Yan Shu and Ouyang Xiu in the early Song Dynasty all produced outstanding works, but they did not break away from the influence of the Huajian School. At the time of Liu Yong, slow Ci with large length of over 91 words was created. At the time of Su Shi, the subjects of Ci saw further development and the contents involving meditation on the past and present were covered by his works. In the circle of Ci in the northern and southern Song dynasties, Li Qingzhao, a female Ci composer, occupied a very important position due to her unique style. In the early time of the Southern Song Dynasty, when people were faced with a dangerous situation of a country in turmoil, most of the poetic and Ci works manifested writers' patriotic feelings, represented by Xin Qiji, who was honored as a patriotic Ci composer of the time.

Li Bai

Li Bai (701-762), with a literary name of Taibai, the most outstanding poet at the height of the Tang Dynasty, is one of the great romantic poets after Qu Yuan in Chinese literary history. He was later called a "poetic genius". Li Bai's life was full of frustration and his thoughts were complex. Besides a great talent for poetry, he was also a swordsman, hermit, Taoist and adviser. Notions of Confucianism, Taoism and chivalry were all embodied in his character.

Li Bai's extant works include more than 900 poems, which artistically recount his own life, social reality and the spirit of the Tang Dynasty at its height. As a romantic poet, he brought into play all means of romantic expression and achieved perfect unity between content and form in his poetry. Li Bai's poetry has an intense subjective and self-

Painting of Banquet on Spring Night in Taoli Garden (part)—drawing material from *the Preface to the Banquet on Spring Night in Taoli Garden* by Tang poet Li Bai and describing four literators sitting in the Garden full of peach and plum flowers with candles in hand, drinking and inditing poems.

expressive tendency, and his emotions were always expressed with the momentum of an avalanche. The integrated adoption of extreme exaggeration, apt comparison and profound imagination created a mysterious, splendid and moving artistic conception, resulting in the boldness and elegance expressed in his romantic poems. Just like the lines in his works, "clear water makes lotus come out, and nature removes decoration," his words are bright, lively and meaningful. Li Bai's poems have an extremely profound influence on later generations. Many famous poets of the Mid-Tang period were influenced by his poems.

Du Fu

The poems of Du Fu (712-770) literary name Zi Mei, the exemplary realistic poet in the history of Chinese literature, mirror the social outlook of the once prosperous Tang Dynasty in decline. Du Fu's poems are rich in social content, and have a distinct epochal character and a definitive political inclination. The poetry fervently appeals to the nation and people in the uplifting spirit of self-sacrifice. Du Fu was, therefore, called The Sage of Poetry.

Du Fu wrote more than 1,000 poems throughout his life, the famous ones included *Three Officers, Three Partings, A Song of Chariots, My Thatched Hut is Wrecked by the Autumn Wind, A Song of Fair Ladies and A Spring View*. The distinctive artistic characteristic of Du Fu's poetry is that the poet often hid his subjective feelings behind objective description and let the objects move readers.

Su Shi

Su Shi (1037-1101), literary name Zi Zhan and also named the Dongpo Hermit, was an eminent writer of the Song Dynasty. He was a native of Meishan of Meizhou (in present-day Sichuan Province). He was one of the Eight Great Writers in the Tang and Song Dynasties, and shared the title of "Three Su's" with his father, Su Xun, and his younger brother Su Zhe, also famed writers of the time.

Su Shi was a master of all literary forms, including poetry, lyrics, Fu and prose essays. And he was also good at calligraphy and painting. He was a versatile person rarely seen in Chinese literature history. His prose essays shared fame with Ouyang Xiu and they were called "Ou Su"; his poems shared fame with Huang Tingjian and were called "Su Huang"; his lyrics shared fame with Xin Qiji and were called "Su Xin". He was honored as one of the Four Great Calligraphers in the Northern Song Dynasty with Huang Tingjian, Mi Fu and Cai Xiang; and his paintings launched the Huzhou painting school.

Most of Su Shi's poems were written to express his own feelings and sing the beauty of nature. *Farewell to Lu Yuanhan Posted to Weizhou and Watching Rainstorms at the Hall of Youmei* manifest his artistic achievements in poetry. His *Poem on the Wall of Xilin Temple*, expressing opinions on important national matters, was considered to fully manifest the rationalism of Song Dynasty poetry. The poet gave a sermon by means of artistic figures with rich and interesting contents.

Compared to his poems, Su Shi's lyrics made an even greater impact in terms of creativity. He went beyond merely describing sorrows felt by parting lovers and broadened his canvas to include recollections of the past, travel notes and reasoning, sweeping aside the gentle and restrained style of the lyrics created in the late Tang Dynasty and Five Dynasties period, to establish the powerful and free school of lyricism. *Prelude to a Water Melody* and *Charm of a Maiden Singer* are thought to best represent the style of Su Shi's lyrics. The former one imagines extreme loneliness in heaven and entrusts the poet's hopes in securing eternal happiness in the earthly world. The latter expresses the poet's uplifting sentiments by describing the grand view at the former site of the Red Cliff and praising the mettle of ancient heroes.

Tao Yuanming

Tao Yuanming (365-427), a native of Caisang of Xunyang (present-day southwest of Jiujiang in Jiangxi Province), was born into a family of a downfallen eunuch. He had served as an official for several years, and later abdicated his post and led a reclusive life. His extant works include more than 120 poems and more than 10 essays and Fu. He made rural life the major subject of his creations and, hence, was called a pastoral poet. Many of Tao Yuanming's poems reflect his disgust at the negative side of social reality and a strong love for the quiet and simple life in the countryside. *In Back to Nature*, he compares officialdom to a net and life in official circles to that of a "caged bird" and a "pounded fish" and the recluse's life is likened to "breaking

Portrait of Tao Yuanming

the birdcage" and "returning to nature."

In his most famous work, *Peach Blossom Spring*, Tao Yuanming described an ideal society of Peach Blossom Spring, where life was harmonious and uplifting, there was no chaos caused by war, and everyone earned his or her own living, a utopian society. In Chinese literature history, it is Tao Yuanming who first created a large number of poems with pastoral scenes and life as their subjects. His pastoral poems founded a new school of classic poems and were highly praised by poets of later generations.

Dramas of the Yuan Dynasty

Dramas of the Yuan Dynasty, also named "Yuan Zaju", form a traditional opera prevailing in the period with the general name of "Sanqu Songs" or "Zaju". Sharing the same literary status with Song Ci and Tang Poetry, Dramas of the Yuan Dynasty originated from ballads of the prairie dwellers in north China and were also named "Northern Qu" by later generations.

In its broad meaning, Qu refers to all kinds of music from the Qin and Han dynasties. Later, there was southern and northern Qu, close to lyrics in style and form but where the performer was free to add inserted words outside the melodic form and often adopt oral language. It became every popular after the Yuan and Ming dynasties, hence the name of Yuan Dramas by later generations. Yuan Drama and Tang Dynasty poems enjoyed the same high position in the history of Chinese literature.

Sanqu songs, used to express feelings and self-amusement, almost had no plots, and were contrasted with dramas. The former were only words for singing operatic arias, and the latter were plays for performance with libretto, spoken parts and action. In terms of form, Sanqu songs were close to lyrics, while the former had exoteric and lively words and the latter elegant and implied words. In terms of poetic meter, lyrics had a strict requirement while Sanqu songs were more flexible.

Sanqu Songs

Sanqu songs can be sung accompanied by music. There are various forms, such as performance singing, singing accompanying dancing, and singing accompanied by instruments.

Zaju

The dramas of Zaju were composed of plots, melodies and words, Binbai and Kejie. Kejie, prompt for performance, regulated the performance actions and stage effects, Binbai referred to spoken parts, and the melody and words constituted the parts of singing.

In general, Yuan Zaju plays consisted of four acts, a set of music accompanying one act, so "act" was both the unit of music and the section of the plot. Besides the four acts, there was a prelude and intermission performances.

Six or seven hundred Zaju dramas were created in the Yuan Dynasty, and there are 162 extant. Guan Hanqin, a representative dramatist, created 70 Zaju dramas, including the earthshaking *Dou E Yuan* (Injustice to Dou E), the lively and humorous comedy *Jiu Feng Chen* (Rescue of a Courtesan), the drama based on the legal case *Lu Zhailang* which praised justice and castigated evil, and the historical drama *Dan Dao Hui* (Meeting the Enemies Alone). These dramas with various styles and colors not only showed the abundant, mature and profound Chinese opera but also integrated the strong points of Tang poetry and Song lyrics. They enlarged the functions of poems and lyrics from general intoning to singing accompanied by music, and combined poems and songs closely.

Supernatural Stories

Supernatural stories, referring to fictional accounts of gods and spirits, were created in large numbers during the Wei, Jin and Southern and Northern dynasties, due to prevailing religious and superstitious thoughts. In need of expressing their ideals and hopes, common people made use of their bold imagination and implied means to express their rebellious sentiments and pursuit of ideals. Supernatural stories were about gods and spirits and Taoist magic arts. They mainly adopted unreal stories as subjects and manifested strong romantic color with simple artistic form. The representative work is *Sou Shen Ji* (Records of Spirits) by Gan Bao.

Wen-yen Chinese

Wen-yen Chinese refers to one of the ancient styles of writing of Chinese, which is characterized by concise words, sublime words with deep meaning, elegant words and coordination in rhyme. But in terms of shortcomings, Wen-yen Chinese was hard to comprehend and popularize. A person must receive relevant training before being able to understand the meaning, and it is even harder to write in Wen-yen Chinese. Therefore, after the May 4th Movement of 1919, priority was given to the vernacular understandable by any literate person. Gradually this took the place of Wen-yen Chinese. In modern Chinese society, writing in the vernacular dominates, but considerable attention is still paid to Wen-yen Chinese.

Vernacular

Vernacular refers to a processed written language on a base of modern oral Chinese. Vernacular had a long history in ancient times. As early as the Song Dynasty, there appeared Huaben (scripts for storytelling), and in the Ming and Qing dynasties there appeared some vernacular novels, such as Jin Ping Mei (The Golden Lotus), Outlaws of the Marsh, Pilgrimage to the West, A Dream of Red Mansions, etc., but they were written in the ancient vernacular. At that time, vernacular works only occupied a small part in ancient literary circles and Wen-yen Chinese still formed the mainstream. After the May 4th Movement of 1919, the vernacular became the mainstream and Wen-yen Chinese gradually seceded from the historical stage.

Vernacular is a concept contrary to Wen-yen Chinese. The reform of styles of writing started at the end of the Qing Dynasty included three stages: new style of writing, vernacular and popular Chinese.

Strange Tales from the Liaozhai Studios

Strange Tales from the Liaozhai Studios, also named Liaozhai or The Legends of Fox-fairies, was written by Pu Songling, a famous novelist in the Qing Dynasty. The book includes 491 stories covering a wide range of topics. The book mostly tells stories about fox-fairies, monsters, flower goddesses and spirits to generalize social relationships and reflect the social situation in China in the 17th century.

The content falls into four categories:

1) exposing and satirizing of corrupt officials, despotic landlords and the feudal political system represented by these figures, with the resentment on the social reality. Stories belonging to this category are represented by *The Cricket and Xi Fangping*;

2) severely criticizing the rigid and unjust official examination system. In *Si Wen Lang*, *Kao Bi Si* (Hell Department of Examination), *The Bookworm* and other stories, the author delineated the examiners' fatuity and greed, pointing out the shackling and corrosion of intellectual minds by the examination system;

3) tributes to pure and faithful love between men and women, as well as to those women and poor intellectuals at lower strata who strive for love. Representative stories of this category include *The Crow Head and Xihou*. The work tells many romantic stories about fox-fairies and flower goddesses falling in love with human beings;

and 4) expounding ethics and morals, with valuable educational significance. These include *The Painted Skin* and *The Taoist Priest of Laoshan Strange Tales of Liaozhai*.

The book enjoying a great reputation around the world and has been translated into English, French, German, Spanish and Russian.

Jin Ping Mei (The Golden Lotus)

Jin Ping Mei (The Golden Lotus) is the first novel composed entirely by a scholar. It is thought to have been completed during the reign of Ming Emperor Wanli. The author's name was given as Lanling-xiao-xiao-sheng (a laughing scholar from Lanling). The novel draws its subject matter from a story in Outlaws of the Marsh, which tells how Wu Song kills his wicked sister-in-law to avenge his brother. By describing the rise to wealth and power and the sudden death of a local despot Ximen Qing, the novel portrays an evil world dominated by the decadent ruling class and urban scum, and exposes these people's hideous natures. Ximen Qing lives a rotten life: although he has already a wife and two concubines, he still develops immoral relationships with Meng Yulou, Pan Jinlian and Li Ping'er, later taking them all as concubines. Moreover, he seduces and has an illicit affair with his slave girl, Chunmei. The author also describes how Ximen Qing colluded with prime minister Cai Jing and other ministers to savagely oppress the people. In addition, in terms of art, the author also creates successfully some major characters with vivid description, such as Ximen Qing who is vicious and "looked on the funeral of a person killed by him", Pan Jinlian who is lascivious and shrewish, and Ying Bojue who toadies up to the rich and powerful. The author attaches importance to the structure of the novel and organizes complex plots in neat order. There is also a vivid description of local conditions and customs, which has some value for studying folklore. The language is lively and merry. All these aspects showed the artistic talents of the author.

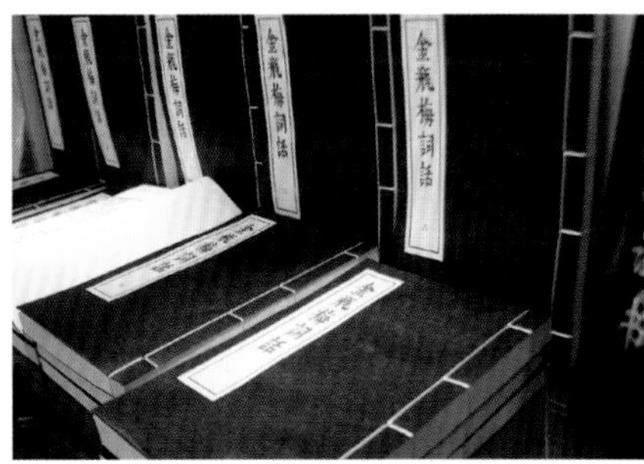

Silk version of the Jin Ping Mei (The Golden Lotus)

Tang Xianzu

The great Ming Dynasty playwright Tang Xianzu (1550-1616), a native of Linchuan (in present-day Jiangxi Province), was born into a family of scholars, and was perspicacious and bookish. He displayed his talents at the age of 12, became a student called a scholar at the age of 14, a successful candidate in the imperial examinations at provincial level at the age of 21, and a successful candidate in the highest imperial examinations at the age of 34. He served in official posts in Nanjing, Zhejiang Province, Guangdong Province and so on. At 48, he abdicated his official post and returned to his hometown.

Tang Xianzu wrote four dramas, namely *The Peony Pavilion, Handan Ji* (*The Tale of Handan*), *Nanke Ji* (*The Tale of Nanke*) and *Zi Chai Ji* (*The Tale of the Violet Hairpin*), and a poem of *The Four Dreams at Yu Ming Tang*. As the four dramas share the theme of dreams and love, they are collectively called "The Four Dreams at Linchuan". *The Peony Pavilion* is the most outstanding of the four, as it depicts a beautiful girl who dies for love and comes to life again also for love.

Guan Hanqing

There is little biographical data on Guan Hanqing, one of the Four Great Playwrights of Yuan Dramas, but he seems to have lived in the period from around 1210 to around 1300, at the end of the Jin and in the early part of the Yuan dynasties. He worked in the capital Da Du (present-day Beijing) and obtained the highest achievements on Zaju. He wrote more than 60 plays, of which 18 have survived completely, including *Dou E Yuan* (Injustice to Dou E).

Guan Hanqing skillfully applied the form of Zaju of the Yuan Dynasty, and obtained outstanding achievements in such aspects as creation of characters, dealing with conflicts in dramas and using dramatic language. In *Dou E Yuan*, Guan Hanqing focused on Dou E, first describing her miserable life, next, developing the conflict between her and a hooligan, then focusing on her oppression and at last describing her struggle for vengeance. In his plays such as *Wang Jiang Ting* (*A Pavilion for Looking at River*), *Bai Yue Ting* (*A Pavilion for Worshiping Moon*), and *Xi Shu Meng* (*A Dream at Xishu*), the excellent descriptions of mentality opened the inner world of people and became the indispensable artistic method of characterization. In 1958, Guan Hanqing was nominated as a "World Cultural Celebrity". An annular mountain on Mercury is named after him.

Dou E Yuan (Injustice to Dou E). The story describes the young widow Dou E from Chuzhou whose husband Cai died two years after marrying. Dou was wrongfully accused by Zhang Lür , literally "The Mule Zhang") of the murder of his father, when Dou E refused to marry Zhang Lür. Before her execution, Dou E swore that her innocence would be proven by the upcoming abnormalities: 1. dripping blood that never drops on the ground; 2. snow in the midst of summer, and 3.a three-year long drought in Chouzhou . And all those, including the eerie "Snow in June" did occur.

Cao Xueqin

Cao Xueqin (ca. 1715-1763) was born into an aristocratic family and experienced a course of a wealthy feudal family going from riches to downfall. The life of luxury in his boyhood acquainted him with the ways of noble families and the ruling class, while poverty in his old age enabled him to observe life more clearly and penetratingly. Based on his own understanding of life and with his progressive ideas, serious attitude and high craftsmanship, he was able to create *A Dream of Red Mansions*. Of its 120 chapters, the first 80 were written by Cao Xueqin, while the last 40 chapters were thought to have been written by another writer, Gao E. Though certain differences can be discerned, in respect of ideological content and artistic achievement, the sequel still basically follows Cao's original plan and makes the novel an integral whole.

Pu Songling

Pu Songling (1640-1715), a native of Zichuan (in present-day Zibo City, Shandong Province) in Shandong Province, is a litterateur of the Qing Dynasty. He is called "Mr. Liaozhai."

He was born into an impoverished landlord-merchant family and was constantly unsuccessful in the imperial examinations notwithstanding his diligent studies. He mastered wide knowledge but did not pass the examination and win the title of "gongsheng" (senior licentiate in feudal China) until he was 71. Through his experiences, he gradually understood that it was very hard for the people with similar status as himself to stand out. His frustrations and indignation drove him to pour out his feelings in the creation of *Strange Tales of Liaozhai*

Four Famous Chinese Classics

The Four Famous Chinese Classics are precious works in Chinese literature. The stories and scenes of the four long-lasting masterpieces have had deep impact on Chinese ideological concepts and value orientation. With a supreme artistic level, the four masterpieces are praised by generations of readers for their meticulous description and profound meanings.

The works are: *The Romance of the Three Kingdoms* by Luo Guanzhong, *Outlaws of the Marsh* by Shi Nai'an, *Pilgrimage to the West* by Wu Cheng'en, and *A Dream of Red Mansions* (also known as *The Legend of Stone*) by Cao Xueqin as the original writer and Gao E who extended the original story.

They are widely known in China, and, today, numerous films and TV plays have drawn material from them. Some contemporary writers have also made new literary creations by means of these famous classics, such as *Shui Zhu San Guo* (Spicy and Hot Three Kingdoms), also popular for a while.

Daiyu Burying the Flowers among the Twelve Beauties in Dream of The Red Mansion.

A Dream of Red Mansions

This is a full-length novel written by Cao Xueqin (ca. 1715-1763). It is viewed as the pinnacle of the Chinese classical full-length novel. Cao Xueqin wrote the first 80 chapters and Gao E added another 40 chapters as a sequel.

A Dream of Red Mansions describes the declining fortunes of a large feudal family. At the heart of the novel is a tragic love story between Jia Baoyu, Lin Daiyu and Xue Baochai. The author, instead of telling the love story superficially, tries to tap the social origins of the tragedy through probing deeply into the characters' mentality and the complicated relationship among them, hence exposing the hypocrisy and cruelty of feudalism and the decadence of the ruling class. The novel goes far beyond the tragic love story to depict a broad swath of society through describing a series of complicated conflicts and struggles, and ultimately predicting the doomed fate of feudal society as a whole.

A Dream of Red Mansions provides a large number of detailed descriptions of everyday life and combines them artfully with the description of many characters. Cao Xueqin attained flawlessness in language. All these aspects have had a deep and wide impact on the creation of novels in later generations. A Dream of Red Mansions reflected high aesthetic quality in many aspects including poetry, drama, painting, architecture, and gardens. In China, it is praised as an encyclopedia for analyzing feudal society. In modern times, it has formed the subject of academic study. The novel has been adapted into popular films and TV plays.

The Romance of the Three Kingdoms

Completed in the period from the end of the Yuan Dynasty to the early Ming Dynasty, *The Romance of the Three Kingdoms* is a long historical novel and can be viewed as the pioneer in the field. Based on folk legends, storytelling scripts and dramas, it was written by Luo Guanzhong. It starts from the uprising of the Yellow Turbans (184) and ends in the unification of the Western Jin Dynasty (266), revealing the history and events of the hundred years with 70 percent of truth and 30 percent of fabrication. The novel describes the struggle between the three kingdoms of Wei, Shu and Wu, and is full of strategies and tricks they adopted, and is honored as complete record of Chinese military and political strategy.

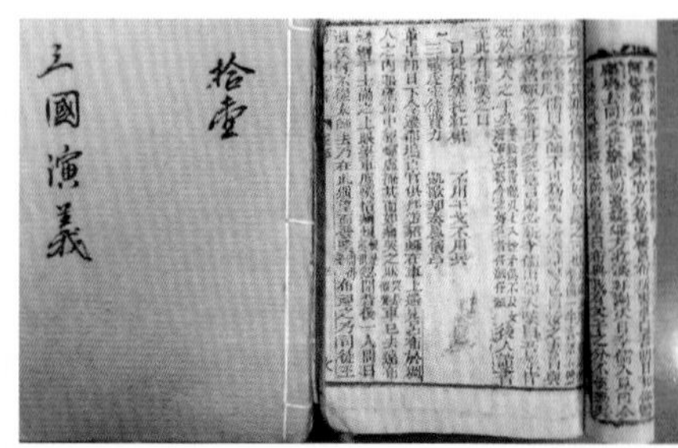

Ancient manuscript of *The Romance of the Three Kingdoms* (cover and *inside*)

Outlaws of the Marsh

Outlaws of the Marsh, completed in the period from the end of the Yuan Dynasty to the early Ming Dynasty by Shi Nai'an, is a novel in chapters written in the vernacular in China. Similar to The Romance of the Three Kingdoms, it was created on a base of folk legends, storytelling scripts and dramas. It is the first novel dealing with the subject matter of peasant uprising in China. Telling how "the government pressed civilians to rebel", it describes the full development of a peasant uprising from its inception, with the rise of a rebel group at Liangshan, down to its defeat, with all the rebels accepting amnesty and surrendering to the government. Its successful portrait of dozens of distinctive characters greatly contributes to the novel's enduring popularity. It places the different characters in different circumstances and reveals their different dispositions and different forms of resistance to oppression through their varying life experiences and status. Its language has a strong colloquial style: succinct, lively, accurate and very expressive. The novel also attained a very high level of artistic achievement in terms of individualization.

Pilgrimage to the West

After the continuous creation, adaptation and spreading by numerous folk artists and writers, *Pilgrimage to the West* was completed by Wu Cheng'en in the mid-Ming Dynasty (16th Century). As the most brilliant Chinese mythological novel, Pilgrimage to the West tells the story of how Xuan Zang, a Buddhist monk of the Tang Dynasty, accepts the duty entrusted by the Emperor, endures countless difficulties imposed by various monsters and demons, and finally gets to the West to obtain the real Buddhist scriptures, assisted by his three disciples: Sun Wukong (Monkey King), Pigsy (pig) and Friar Sha (water monster). Pilgrimage to the West has a strong romantic flavor. The author creates a supernatural world, but the gods and spirits, their magic weapons and even the environment in which they live are all based on reality and reflect some wishes of the people.

The novel has been popular ever since its birth in both China and around the world and has been translated into many languages. The main characters are especially well known, as well as such stories as "Creating a Serious Disturbance in the Heavenly Palace", "Three Battles with the White-Boned Demon", and "Flaming Mountain." It has been adapted into various local operas, as well as films, TV plays, cartoons and caricatures in many versions. In some Asian countries such as Japan there also appear various and numerous artistic works with Sun Wukong in the leading role.

Sun Wukong (Monkey King) in the Peking Opera

• Pizi (Hooligan) Literature

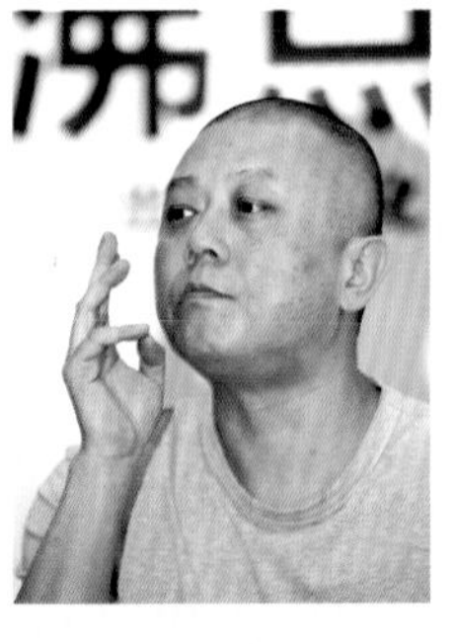

Modern urban tongue, completely unreasonable plots and idle and cynical life of youth are considered as styles of Pizi literature. From the end of the 1980s, it gradually came into being. Wang Shuo is the pioneer of such literature and the language of his novels has been picked up in the daily conversation of young people. Pizi Literature has had a great impact on recent literature, and a younger generation of writers blends such hooligan sentiments into their works to some degree and continues to create classics in the popular vernacular.

Internet Literature

Internet Literature refers to literary works released on the Internet, and the majority of its creators are Internet writers. Starting from My First Close Contact by Pizi Cai, the phrase of Internet Literature became popular and the qualities of freedom, jokes and improvisation have been established. Thereafter, "rongshuxia" became the most successful website of original literature and a group of Internet writers such as Anny Baby and Li Xunhuan appeared. Writing and reading on the net has changed the way literature is now regarded. As it is cheap to write and release works on the Internet, traditional book publishing has been greatly affected. Literal expression has become an everyday deed for many people. Internet Literature has brought vitality to traditional literature. It has lively and free style, the writers are generally young and the contents reflect the time scene instantly. But the creativity of Internet writers is always one-off and the works are usually very short. As they lack artistic pursuit, not many such works can endure the test of time. Meanwhile, as Internet Literature is spread widely, there are problems of plagiarism and copyright violation.

At the beginning, Internet Literature was a kind of non-profit creation, but with the success of some writers, it has gradually become profitable. Internet Literature has aroused an upsurge of writing among the general public, creating some new literary talents. The popular Internet language updates modern speech faster and faster and Internet Literature has become a force in publishing with some profit.

China Federation of Literary and Art Circles (CFLAC)

The China Federation of Literary and Art Circles (CFLAC), established in July 1949, is a non-governmental organization composed of nationwide associations of writers and artists, federations of literary and art circles in the provinces, autonomous regions and municipalities directly under the Central Government. The CFLAC practices a group membership. It now consists of 50 group members, including the China Writers Association (which is administratively independent), China Theatre Association, China Film Association, China Musicians Association, China Artists Association, China Quyi Artists association, China Dancers Association, China Folk Literature and Art Association, China Photographers Association, China Calligraphers Association, China Acrobats Association, China TV Artists Association, 32 federations of literary and art circles in provinces, autonomous regions and municipalities directly under the Central Government, the Literary and Art Federation of the Xinjiang Production and Construction Corps and federations of literary and art circles in six industries (China Coal Mine Federation of Literary and Art Circles, China Railway Federation of Literary and Art Circles, China Petroleum Federation of Literary and Art Circles, China Chemical Industrial Federation of Literary and Art Circles, China Electrical Power Association of Literary and Art Workers, and China Water Conservancy Association of Literary and Art Workers).

The CFLAC undertakes liaison, coordination and service work among various group members and helps them with matters that need overall arrangement. The CFLAC and its national associations publish over 30 national literary and artistic magazines and newspapers, including China Arts Gazette, and operate seven publishing houses for books and audio-video products and a film and television center. The local federations and associations have their own literary and artistic publications. The CFLAC carries out extensive external exchanges and actively encourages and organizes its group members to carry out international culture and art exchanges. Each year, it receives hundreds of foreign writers and artists delegations. At the same time, it organizes and sends an increasing number of Chinese writers and artists to foreign lands, where they carry on lively and vigorous exchanges in various forms with their foreign counterparts, thus furthering mutual friendship and cooperation between Chinese and foreign literary and art circles.

Website: http://www.cflac.org.cn/

China Writers Association

The China Writers Association (CWA) is an independent, central first-grade national people's organization. It was set up on July 23, 1949 in Beiping (present-day Beijing) on the basis of the All-China Association of Literary and Art Workers. It changed into the present name in October 1953. It has 39 group and 6,128 individual members who are all talents in China's literature and art circles. It holds it national congress every five years which elects its national committees. Mao Dun and Ba Jing used to serve as its chairman. Its current chairman is Tie Ning (2006).

In order to strengthen research and exchanges, the China Writers Association set up 11 specialty committees including the Novel Creation Committee, the Children's Literature Committee, the Ethnic Minority Literature Committee, the Reporting Committee, the Film and Television Literature Committee, the Periodical Work Committee, the Work Committee for members form the Departments Under the CPC Central Committee and the Central Government Departments Under the CPC Central Committee, the Committee for Safeguarding Rights and Interests of Writers, the Committee for Exchange Between Chinese Literature and Foreign Literature and the Committee for Exchange of Hong Kong, Macao, Taiwan and Overseas Chinese Literature, respectively in charge of research and exchange for each categories of literature and relative organization and liaison.

In order to promote Contemporary Chinese Literature, the China Writers Association founded five literature prizes, including the Lu Xun Literature Prize, the Mao Dun Literature Prize, the Soong Ching Ling Children's Literature Prize, the National Ethnic Minority Literature Creation Prize, the Youth Literature Prize (Chuang Chung Wen Literature Prize). The Mao Dun Literature Prize is elected through extensive consultation once every four years, and the Soong Ching Ling Children's Literature Prize and National Ethnic Minority Literature Creation Prize once every three years. All these prizes aim at encouraging excellent literature creation and promoting the flourishing development of the socialist literature cause as well as rewarding new writers with excellent achievement.

Website: http://www.chinawriter.org/

Internet Website of Today Writers

The Internet website of Today Writers was launched by the Lu Xun Literature College of Chinese Writers' Association and opened in October 1998.

Website: http://www.jrzj.com.cn

Ba Jin's handprint at the gate of the China Modern Litereture Museum

China Modern Literature Museum

Ba Jin suggested construction of a modern literature museum in 1981 to the warm response of people of various walks of life. The Chinese Writers Association decided to have it built, and the museum was finally founded in May 2000. It collects and shows works of modern writers, their manuscripts, translated versions, letters, diaries, recorded works and other documents and materials of high value for study. They also came from Hong Kong, Macao, Taiwan and overseas sources.

Website: http://www.wxg.org.cn

Chinese Novel Union

The Chinese Novel Union is a national academic group established in Tianjin in 1985, composed of numerous national renowned scholars, professors, novel critics and professional novelists. It attracted much attention after promoting a "ranking of Chinese novels", which played an active role in promoting academic research into the novel. Address: Department of Chinese, Northern Campus of Tianjin Normal University

Website: http://www.zgxsxh.com.cn

Mao Dun Literature Award

The Mao Dun Literature Award is made by the Chinese Writers' Association and was established in 1981 according to Mao Dun's last wish. Mao Dun contributed 250,000 Yuan to help the cause. This award aims at promoting the development of Chinese literature and is one of the highest literature awards in China. The candidate works of this award must be published and released on the Chinese mainland within the appraised year, and created by Chinese writers and must be full-length novels of at least 130,000 Chinese characters.

Lu Xun Literature Award

Lu Xun Literature Award was established to commemorate Lu Xun. encouraging the creation of excellent novellas, short stories, reportage, poems, essays, miscellanies, literary treatises and commentaries, and translations of Chinese and foreign works. It is one of the highest literature awards in China. It is organized by the Chinese Writers' Association covering separate awards for novellas, short stories, essays, poetry and reportage.

Lao She Literature Award

This was established in 1999 jointly by the Beijing Federation of Literature and Art Circles and the Lao She Literature and Art Foundation, aiming at honoring the creations of Beijing writers and excellent works published and released in Beijing. It is held every two or three years. From June 6, 2000, there have been three awards. They categories include full-length novels, novellas, drama scripts, film and TV plays and broadcasting plays. In the third round of awards, a category for newcomers" best works was added. The Lao She Literature Award is the highest award in Beijing literary circles.

Cao Yu Dramatic Literature Award

The Cao Yu Dramatic Literature Award, originally the National Best Play Scripts Award, was held jointly by the Ministry of Culture and Chinese Dramatists' Association from 1980 to conduct national appraisal of excellent scripts. It represents the highest level of Chinese dramatic creations. From 1994, to memorize the great dramatist Cao Yu, it was renamed the Cao Yu Dramatic Literature Award. Currently it is held annually, and, at each time, 10 formal winners and 10 nominated winners will be chosen.

Yao Xueyin Full-Length Historical Novels Award

In 2003, family members of late writer Yao Xueying contributed 500,000 Yuan to establish the Yao Xueyin Full-Length Historical Novels Award Foundation according to his long-cherished wish. It was established to encourage and promote the prosperity and development of full-length historical novels. The awards are organized by the Chinese Literature Foundation of the Chinese Writers' Association.

Important Literature Awards in China

Mao Dun Literature Award, Lu Xun Literature Award, Lao She Literature Award, Cao Yu Dramatic Literature Award

National Best Novellas Award of Chinese Writers' Association

National Best Short Stories Award of Chinese Writers' Association

National Best New Poems (Collections of Poems) Award of Chinese Writers' Association

National Best New Poems of Middle-aged and Young Poets Award

National Best Reportage Award of Chinese Writers' Association

National Best Essay (Collection) and Miscellaneous (Collection) Honorary Award

National Best Essay (Collection) Award

National Best Miscellaneous (Collection) Award

National Best Children Literature Award of Chinese Writers' Association

Film and Television

General Survey of Movie

The Chinese movie sector covers all the films produced by Chinese film practitioners on the mainland and in Hong Kong and Taiwan. From a common cultural resource, they have formed their different development ways under different social systems and cultural and historical backgrounds, creating many different styles and approaches. Together, however, they have created a brilliant movie culture in China and made an important contribution to the development of film art in the world.

Waxwork of the shooting scene of the *Dingjun Mountain*, the first film of China, showed in the China National Film Museum

Movie in China

After the first movie was made in France in 1895, the genre was introduced to China in the following year. According to the records of the newspaper Shen Bao, on August 11, 1896, a French visitor played a short film in a teahouse named "You Yi Cun" in Xuyuan Garden, Shanghai. From 1897 to 1898, several businessmen from the United States, Russia, Italy and Portugal showed commercial films in Tianhua Tea Garden, Qi Yuan Garden, Tongqing Tea Garden, Shengping Teahouse and Paobingchang. Several years later, movies had spread to Beijing. In 1902, a foreigner began to rent Fu Shou Tang (Happiness and Longevity Hall) at Damochang, Qianmen, to show films.

At the beginning, films were called "active shows" or "electro-optic shows" in China. At that time what was shown included were newsreels and short farces. It was in Beijing in 1903 that Chinese entered the industry. A Chinese businessman, Lin Zhu, went to Europe and the United States three times to bring back projectors and films and an showed them in Letian Tea Garden at Damochang. Thereafter, films were shown in Daguanlou Theater at Dazhalan, Wenming Tea Garden in Xidan market, Jixiang Theater in Dong'an market, and Hesheng Theater in Xinfeng market in Xicheng District.

Around 1905, movies had become prevalent in Beijing. At that time, every night films would be played in Daguanlou Theater to a capacity audience. It can be said that the movie had not formally settled in China as an art and entertainment medium until then.

The First Group of Cinemas

In the initial periods, films were shown in rented entertainment places such as teahouses and alehouse, and were often played as interludes between other entertainment programs, which was almost the same with the overseas situation.

In 1905, the first professional cinema of the United States, Nickel Cinema, opened to the public in Pittsburgh. In the next year, there were more than 1,000 cinemas. On December 8 of that year, Quanxian Teahouse in the French concession in Tianjin was renamed Quanxian Electronic Theater as it gave priority to showing American films continuously. It can be called the first cinema in China. According to another popular story, the first professional cinema in China was established by a Spanish businessman in 1908. Having earned some money from showing films, he invested in the construction of a standard cinema with a capacity of 250 at the crossing of Haining Road and Zhapu Road in Hongkou. It was called Hongkou Great Theater. Later, the same person built the larger Victorian Cinema. The first professional cinema in Beijing was Beijing Daguanlou Cinema opened by Ren Qingtai at Dazhalan outside the Qianmen Gate.

The First Film

In 1905, Beijing Fengtai Photo Studio produced an on-the-spot short film of a part of the Peking Opera *Dingjunshan*, which was considered as the first film produced by Chinese. Therefore, this year is recognized as marking the birth of Chinese films.

The initiator of Beijing Fengtai Photo Studio was Ren Qingtai. In 1892, he opened the first photo studio at Liulichang in Beijing. Later he opened Daguanlou Theater at Dazhalan outside Qianmen Gate for playing films. Due to lack of overseas films, Ren Qingtai purchased a France-made hand cinematograph and 14 rolls of film from a firm operated by a German businessman at Dongjiao Minxiang, and tried his hand at film production. In 1905, to celebrate the birthday of Tan Xinpei, a master of Beijing Opera and initiator of the Tan School, Ren Qingtai filmed some representative parts of the opera Dingjunshan with Tan Xinpei in the leading role, such as volunteering for the army, wielding a sword and crossing swords. The film was shot on the outdoor square of Fengtai Photo Studio. The cinematograph was fixed up, actors played before the camera, and natural daylight was used for the shooting. A photographer named Ren Zhonglun took charge of the filming and Ren Qingtai acted as the director. It took three days to produce the film, using three rolls about 600 feet long. It lasted about 10 minutes according to the playing speed at that time. In the following years, Fengtai Photo Studio continued to shoot other opera films, mostly Gong Fu operas using actors good at martial arts. These characters tallied with the needs of silent films.

The First Film Studio

In 1909, an American businessman named Benjamin Blaskey invested to found the Asiatic Film Company in Shanghai, the first film production unit established in China. It produced some short films in Shanghai and Hong Kong, but did not obtain much success. With the outbreak of the Revolution of 1911, the firm could not continue, and then Blaskey transferred the company and all its equipment to Yishir, a manager of Nanyang Insurance Company in Shanghai and another American named Sarfo. In 1913, the new owners produced the first fiction film in China, *A Couple in Adversities*. The company also produced some early important newsreels in China, such as War in Shanghai about *the Revolution of 1911*, which recorded the attack of the revolutionary army on Shanghai Manufacture Bureau and Wusong battery. In 1914, World War I broke out and the import of films from Germany was stopped, so the Asiatic Film Company came to its end as it could not produce films.

Besides it, there was a film production firm run by Chinese, i.e. Huanxian Film Company jointly founded by Zhang Shichuan and his friends in 1916. This firm only produced one film, *Victims of Opium*, and then went bankrupt. Then, the famous Commercial Press began investing to produce films.

Golden Rooster Awards

Cup of the Golden Rooster Awards

Golden Rooster Awards of Chinese Films was founded in 1981, the year of the rooster in the lunar calendar. The awards are organized by the China Film Association, with the aid of film artists, film critics and film entrepreneurs as the appraisal committee. More than 20 categories are involved, such as best feature film, best science film, best fine arts film, best documentary, and best scenarist, best director, best actor, best cinematographic prize, best recording, best fine arts, best music and best director's maiden work.

The appraisal covers two stages, initial and final. The winners will be revealed at the awards ceremony of China Golden Rooster and Hundred Flowers Film Festival. There is a permanent appraisal base in Suzhou City of Jiangsu Province.

Hundred Flowers Awards

The Popular Cinema Hundred Flowers Awards were established in 1962 and are called Hundred Flowers Awards for short. These awards are staged jointly by the China Film Association and China Urban Cinema Development Association. The list of candidates is based on ticket income and votes of a udiences. Nominees are announced in the magazine The Popular Cinema. From 2004, the single voting method via mail was changed to a dual system of mail and mobile phone texting, the latter continuing right up to the last moment for the announcement at the awards ceremony. These awards include five items such as three best feature films awards, two best actor awards and two best actress awards. In the past the awards were held annually, but from 2005, it was changed to even-numbered years. These awards mainly reflect the appraisal and favor of the wide audience and are called "people awards". The name hundred flowers is designed to reflect the beauty of spring and encourage film artists to create more good films favored by common people.

Ornamental Column Awards

Ornamental Column Awards of Chinese Films is the highest honor of Chinese films, and the shape of ornamental column before Tian'anmen Gate in Beijing is adopted. Every year, the Ministry of Broadcast, Film and Television will hold an appraisal on various films completed the year before. The predecessor of these awards was the Best Films Award of the Ministry of Culture, starting from 1957. After a pause for 22 years, the activity was resumed from 1979 and is held annually. In 1985, the Film Bureau under the Ministry of Culture was reorganized into the Ministry of Broadcast, Film and Television, and the original awards were renamed Best Films Awards of the Ministry of Broadcast, Film and Television from 1994.

Shanghai International Film Festival

The Shanghai International Film Festival is the first international film festival in China held in June in Shanghai every year.

It is sponsored jointly by the China State Administration of Radio, Film and Television and the Shanghai People's Government. The festival was first held in 1993 and was recognized by the International Film Producers' Association in 1994. It comprises four major parts: competing for Jin Jue Awards, exhibiting and playing international films, exchanges of international films and the Jin Jue International Film Forum, i.e. appraisal of Asian New Faces Award.

Changchun Film Festival

Changchun Film Festival, established in 1992, is an international State-grade film festival held in Changchun City, Jilin Province every two years. Highlight is the selection of the best Chinese film to win the Golden Deer Cup.

Zhuhai Film Festival

Zhuhai Film Festival, a permanent national film festival, was established in 1994 and is held every two years. It was originally named China Zhuhai Cross-Straits and Hong Kong Film Festival" and is sponsored by Zhuhai People's Government. From the second session in 1996, it changed to the present name. The first session was held in Zhuhai in June 1994.

Aiming at "spreading the excellent national cultural heritage of China and accelerating the development and prosperity of film industries on both sides of the Taiwan Straits and Hong Kong, the festival not only strengthens the exchanges and cooperation in film circles between the mainland, Taiwan, Hong Kong and Macao, but also accepts and appraises all the films with Chinese as major creators beyond the four regions. The festival establishes such awards as best feature film, best scenarist, best director, best actor, best actress, best male supporting role, best female supporting role and best cinematographic prize, etc., and winners will be awarded cups and a cash bonus.

Beijing Student Film Festival

Beijing Student Film Festival is a large-scale cultural activity sponsored jointly by Department of Arts of Beijing Normal University, and China Film Archives. It was established in 1993 and is held from April 20 to May 4 every year. Its authority has been recognized generally by film circles and it is honored as a grand award with international quality. In the past years, many winners have gone on to win various national governmental awards, Golden Rooster Awards, and Hundred Flowers Awards, as well as prizes at international film festivals in Tokyo, Berlin and Spain. Aiming at "enthusiasm of youth, academic taste and cultural consciousness", the festival has a broad and profound impact on education, literature and film and television circles, with the characteristics of "being hosted, watched and appraised by students". The festival also conducts appraisal on video works produced by students, the only one of its type in the country.

Hong Kong International Film Festival

This is the greatest film event in Hong Kong and an allied member of International Film Producers' Association. The festival was established by Hong Kong Urban Council in 1977. From the fourth session, it has been held during Easter from March to April. As an important film production base in Asia, Hong Kong holds this festival to offer opportunities for Hong Kong films to be publicized and for Hong Kong and Asian audiences to see more varied films.

Hong Kong Film Awards

These are important awards in Hong Kong film circles, sharing the honor of three great kinds of awards for highest achievements of Chinese films along with the Taiwan Golden Horse Film Festival and mainland Golden Rooster Awards. They were established in 1982, and the first session was held by the fortnightly magazine Hong Kong City Entertainment.

The awards honor film practitioners making an outstanding contribution to Chinese film and include best actor, best actress, best male supporting role, best female supporting role, best film, best director, best scenarist, and best new face, etc.

Hong Kong Film Critics Society Awards

These awards, sponsored by the Hong Kong Film Critics Society, started in 1995 and the appraisal is held from January to February every year, covering al Chinese films publicly shown in Hong Kong the year before.

Hong Kong Film Golden Bauhinia Awards

Sponsored by Hong Kong Film Critics Association, the Golden Bauhinia Awards were held for the first time in 1996 and are staged at the beginning of every year. Each award is decided by votes of Film Critics Association members. There are not many awards and no technical prizes. Every year, the top 10 Chinese films and foreign films will also be chosen.

Taipei Film Festival

Taipei Film Festival is sponsored by the Taipei municipal government. It started from 1998 and is held every year. It is an important event of film in Taiwan, and from the fourth festival, it began to aim at "city, citizen and student" and consists of three parts: city film exhibition with international cities as subjects, citizen film exhibition with Taipei Film Awards and Taipei Motif Awards as units, and international students film Golden Lion Awards with domestic and foreign students' works as the subjects. In recent years, around the subject of cities, the festival also holds various exhibitions and shows besides showing films.

Golden Horse Film Festival

The festival was launched in 1962. The name of the award (Jin Ma) comes from the names of Jinmen and Mazu and also implies "golden brand".

It is an important film cultural event held once a year in Taiwan, including two parts: competition of Chinese films for the Golden Horse Award and the showing of Taipei Golden Horse international films, when outstanding films of that year from around the world will be screened. In recent years, an international digital short films competition has been included to promote the trend of using digital media as video creation.

Cup of Golden Horse Awards

The First Generation of Chinese Directors

The first generation of Chinese directors generally refers to about a hundred film directors, represented by Zhang Shichuang, Zheng Zhengqiu, Dan Duyu, Yang Xiaozhong and Shao Zuiweng, who were active from the beginning of the 20th century to the end of the 1920s. As the trailblazers of Chinese movies, they created the first batch of feature films despite the extremely crude and rough conditions as well as the absence of previous film experience as a reference. Among those movies, a lot more or less expressed democratic and anti-feudalistic thoughts as a result of the May 4th Movement in 1919, which boosted the birth of a new culture. Nonetheless, the first generation of directors did not understand film well in the terms of artistic skills and expression. They usually approached movies with traditional operatic notions. The shooting followed the method on opera stages, in which the camera generally remained fixed in one position throughout the entire movie. The most prominent of the first generation of Chinese directors were Zhang Shichuang (1889-1953) and Zheng Zhengqiu (1888-1935). Such representative works in China as the first short feature film *A Couple in Adversities*, the first long feature film *Victim of Opium*, the first sound film *The Songstress, Red Peony*, the first Kungfu film *The Burning of Red Lotus Temple*, and the most influential film in early times *Orphan Rescues Grandfather*, are all their creations. However, the artistic pursuits of the two varied: Zhang insisted on the appreciative values in every detail, while Zheng thought movies should not only cater to the taste of the audience, but also influence the audience's artistic taste. His movies are generally more narrative with a compact structure and intense operatic conflicts. *Sister Flowers*, one of his late classic works, is a movie that suits both refined and popular tastes. The performance is simple yet exquisite, while the directing is natural and fluent. It was this combination that enabled the film to run for a record of 60 days as a nonstop feature in Shanghai Xinguang Cinema.

The Still of the film *The Spring River Flows East* directed by Zheng Junli

The Second Generation of Chinese Directors

The second generation of Chinese directors was mainly active during the 1930s and 1940s, though some were still making movies in the 1950s and 1960s and even as late as the 1980s. The directors of this generation included Cheng Bugao, Shen Xiling, Cai Chusheng, Shi Dongshan, Fei Mu, Sun Yu, Yuan Muzhi, Ying Yunwei, Chen Liting, Zheng Junli, Wu Yonggang, Shen Fu, Tang Xiaodan, Zhang Junxiang and Sang Hu. The greatest achievement of this generation is: Chinese movies were liberated from solely being for entertainment purposes, and began to reflect society in a more profound way. The most prominent artistic feature of these movies was their realism. Meanwhile, the directors began their efforts to integrate reality with filming, thus gradually learning the basic rules of film art. Although these directors still had strong "opera ideology", they had begun to follow the internal qualities of operas instead of the outer form, which means that they had gradually broken away from the limits of the stage and started to bring the strong points of filming into full play, although only seeking for dramatic suspense, conflicts and process in the plots. Those with the biggest achievements in this generation included Cai Chusheng, Zheng Junli, Fei Mu, Wu Yonggang, Sang Hu and Tang Xiaodan.

The Third Generation of Chinese Directors

This refers to those directors stepping into the movie circle after the founding of the PRC in 1949. The most representative directors of this period include Cheng Yin, Xie Tieli, Shui Hua, Cui Wei, Ling Zifeng, and Xie Jin, etc. Following the realistic principle, their films endeavored to unveil the nature of life and exhibit contradictions in a profound way. Besides, they also made some beneficial explorations and attained gratifying achievements in demonstrating local and ethnic flavors.

The Fourth Generation of Chinese Directors

The main body of the fourth generation of Chinese directors is composed of graduates from the film academies in the 1960s as well as self-taught talents in the same period. Though they studied in the 1960s, their talents were not brought into the play until 1977 for various historical reasons. With a widened horizon, they assimilated fresh artistic experiences, constantly explored the characteristics of the art form, and formed a link between the preceding and following, endeavoring to reconstruct and develop Chinese films. They proposed that Chinese films should "throw away the walking stick of operas", i.e., break the operatic structure, as well as to pursue the simple, realistic and natural style. They were good at digging beneath the surface of the society and extracting life philosophy from the trivial things in everyday life.

The representatives of this generation include Wu Yigong, Wu Tianming, Zhang Nuanyi, Huang Jianzhong and Teng Wenji. Others like Zheng Dongtian, Xie Fei, and Hu Bingliu all impressed the audience with their works of distinctively different styles.

The Still of the great war film *Assembly* directed by Zheng Junli

• New Year's Day Films

New Year's Day Films refer to the films shown during the New Year Festival or Chinese Spring Festival to celebrate the new year, and this saying comes from Hong Kong kinown as the Oriental Hollywood. From 1980s, at the end of every year, some movie stars in Hong Kong would gather together and produce some jolly and lucky films for audience disregarding their payment. These films are often named after some phrases with the implication of luckiness and good wishes, such as Congratulations on Getting Rich, All's Well, Ends Well, and Blessing, Wealth, Longevity and Happiness, and the contents of the films usually satisfy the following two points: they are comedies, as people seek for relaxation, joy, happiness and luckiness when spending money during New Year festival; and they should accord with the appreciation habits of Chinese people as they are New Year's Films shown in China, i.e. a comparatively satisfactory and happy ending.

The first New Year's Film shown nationwide is *Rumble in the Bronx* played by Jackie Chan in 1995. At that year the nationwide ticket income of the film was only next to the great Hollywood film *True Lies*. Later, such films as *The White-golden Dragon*, *Mr. Nice Guy*, and *Who Am I* continued to intensify the New Year's Films and gradually cultivated the golden time for projecting Chinese films. Furthermore, *Party A, Party B, Be There or Be Square, Sorry Baby*, and *Cell Phone* have pushed the market of New Year's Films to the peak.

The Fifth Generation of Chinese Directors

Mainly referring to Beijing Film Academy graduates of the early 1980s, the fifth generation generally had been involved in social turbulence when young. They accepted professional training in film during the period of initial adoption of reform and opening-up policy and entered the movie industry with innovative enthusiasm. They were keen on new expressive ways and new thoughts, striving to find a new angle for each of their movies. They had a fervent desire to explore the history of China's culture as well as the structure of the national psychology. They were completely innovative in terms of selecting suitable themes, employing narrative ways, portraying figures, using cameras, and dealing with movie frames. Their works were more subjective, symbolic, and implicative. The major representatives of this generation include Chen Kaige, Zhang Yimou, Wu Ziniu, Tian Zhuangzhuang and Huang Jianxin.

Major Film Studios in China

At present the state-owned film studios in China include Changchun Film Studio, Xi'an Film Studio, Fujian Film Studio, Pearl River Film Studio, Xiaoxiang Film Studio, Guangxi Film Studio, Emei Film Studio, Shandong Film and TV Production Center, Tianshan Film Studio, Beijing Forbidden City Film Industry Co., Ltd., Beijing Scientific Education Film Studio, Beijing Youth Film Studio of Beijing Film Academy, Beijing Film Studio, Inner Mongolia Film Studio, August First Film Studio, Yunan Ethnic Film Studio, Central Newsreel and Documentary Film Studio, Agricultural Film Studio of China, Children's Film Studio of China, Shanghai Animation Film Studio, Shanghai Scientific Education Film Studio and Shanghai Film Dubbing Studio.

Changchun Film Studio

Changchun Film Studio, established in 1946, was originally named Northeast Film Studio and the first studio director is Yuan Muzhi. At that time, this studio produced a great number of war newsreels. It is especially worthy to mention that this studio completed the feature film Bridge in May 1949, which is viewed as the first feature film after the founding of the People's Republic of China by film historian. In 1955 Northeast Film Studio renamed to present Changchun Film Studio.

Changchun Film Studio is the first film studio of the People's Republic of China and one of the largest film studios in China. Since its birth, this studio has produced more than 300 artistic films, hundreds of documentary and scientific education films, and hundreds of dubbed films, and it is the film production base with largest scale in China. This studio has offered a great number of artistic fine works with high taste to domestic and foreign audience, such as *Guerilla of the Plain, Heroic Sons and Daughters*, and *The Naval Battle of 1894*, which are applauded by domestic and foreign audience.

This studio is especially good at producing the films with rural and battle subjects. Its works are full of the original and folk flavors and the bold and straightforward styles particularly on black-earth land. This studio has made great contribution to the dubbing of foreign films. People today still remember such excellent films as *Lenin in 1918, Chapaev, and Empress of Sweden*, which are all introduced by this studio.

Address: No.20 Hongqi Avenue, Changchun, Jilin Province

Xi'an Film Studio

Xi'an Film Studio, an integrated film studio, gives priority to production of feature films and also produces scientific education films and documentaries. This studio has made considerable accomplishments in creating feature films and has created many famous films with resounding success, such as *The Thrill of Life, Xi'an Event, River without Buoys, Life (1984), and Wild Mountains*, which are all focus at that time and have won national and international awards. In 1986 the film *The Old Well* directed by Wu Tianming and played by Zhang Yimou as the leading actor won the award on Tokyo Film Festival in Japan and Zhang Yimou won the Best Hero Prize on the Film Festival. It is the first time for Zhang Yimou to show his talents. Another film *Red Sorghum* directed by Zhang Yimou in 1987 won the Golden Bear Award on Berlin Film Festival.

Address: No.70 Dayan Pagoda Xiying Rd., Xi'an City

Tianshan Film Studio

The Tianshan Film Studio was put into production in 1958 and it is the film studio owned by Xinjiang Ugyhur Autonomous Region. Its first work is the documentary Commander-in-Chief Zhu Inspects Xinjiang, its first color documentary is *Xinjiang in Sunshine* produced in 1959, and its first feature film is *Two Generations* produced in 1960. The workers in this studio come from various ethnic groups, including Uyghur, Kazak, Tajik, Uzbek, Tatar, Xibe, Hui, Man and Han ethnic groups. The people from minorities occupy a half of the total number of workers and 80 percent of all creators. The films *Anaerhan, The Guide* and *The Girl not Want to be Actress* won widely favorable comments and various awards including the Outstanding Film Prizes of Ministry of Culture. These films form their special characters by their strong ethnic styles and local customs and favors. This studio spends much time on dubbing films in various ethnic group languages and the number of dubbed films reaches more than 40 every year.

Address: No.17-1 Road, Urumqi, Xinjiang Uygur Autonomous Region

Beijing Film Studio

Beijing Film Studio, established in 1949, is one of the three great film bases in China and has TV program production department. It can independently complete the business from creation of scripts to copy and production. This studio has produced many excellent films such as *New Year's Sacrifice, The Lin Family Shop and Song of Youth*. This studio adapted and produced many traditional dramas such as *Women Generals of the Yang Family, Wild Boar Forest*, and *The Battle of Hongzhou County*. It also produced many films with historical subjects and literary masterpieces subjects such as *Rickshaw Boy, Senior and Junior Mr. Bao, and Border Town*. Meanwhile it also produced a number of films reflecting realistic themes in life. Since 1980s with the cooperation with international film studios, this studio has produced the feature film *The Go Masters* and the 3-D film *Lucky 13*, and helped produce *Marco Polo* and *The Last Emperor*. This studio concentrates a group of excellent artists and technical experts and has the annual production capacity of 30 feature films and more than 200 episodes of TV plays. This studio has produced more than a hundred films which have won national and international awards. This studio has the advantage and tradition of putting Chinese literary masterpieces to screen and has the strength and experience of producing films with international cooperation. More than 50 films cooperated with international parties have won international awards.

Address: No.77 Beisanhuan Zhong Lu, Haidian District, Beijing

August First Film Studio

Established in 1952, the August First Film Studio is the only military film studio in China. Its first military education film is Rivers Attack (1952) and its first color long documentary is *August First Sports Game* in 1953. The first feature film is *Breaking through the Darkness*. Now this studio has become an integrated film studio producing feature films, newsreels, military education films and dubbed films. This studio has produced more than 2,000 various films which cover a wide range of subjects and have abundant contents and various styles, and are favored by officers and soldiers in the army as well as common people. Some of its films have won national and international awards for many times. The large-scale historical battle films produced by this studio have won much applaud. The grand military sequent films of *Turning Point, Decisive Engagement* and *Great Marching* are its representative works.

Address: No.A-1 Liuliqiao Beili, Guanganmenwai Street, Beijing

Shanghai Film Studio

The Shanghai Film Studio, one of the three great film bases in China, renamed to Shanghai Film and Television (Group) Co. in 1996. It has an annual production capacity of 25 films and 350 episodes of TV plays, and developing and printing, and producing and copying 70-million-meter rushes. It is the film studio with the largest scale, the earliest foundation time and the best equipment in south China, and is one of the film groups with the largest scale and the most powerful strength. Before 1949 Shanghai was the major production base of films in China and a series of earliest and most influential film studios at that time such as Asiatic Film Company, Shanghai Film and Drama Company, Great Wall Clip Art Company, Mingxing Film Company, Lianhua Film Company and Yihua Film Company were all founded in Shanghai. Shanghai Film Studio was founded on November 16, 1949 on this base. This studio has produced more than 1,300 films and the films and TV plays produced by it have won national and international awards for more than 500 times. Its representative works include *From Victory to Victory, The Letter with Feathers, Reconnaissance across the Yangtze, The Family (1956), Woman Basketball Player No. 5*, and *My Memories of Old Beijing*.

Address: No.595 North Cao Xi Road, Shanghai

Shanghai Film Dubbing Studio

Founded on the base of the original Dubbing Department of Shanghai Film Studio, Shanghai Film Dubbing Studio is a professional studio dubbing non-Chinese films (domestic or foreign films) into Chinese films. The dubbed films of this studio occupy a majority in the dubbed films market in China today and it can even dub a foreign film perfectly without international sound tapes. It has dubbed nearly a thousand films from scores of countries around the world. Some of the dubbed films almost reach the same appreciation quality as the original films. Besides foreign films, this studio also dubs Cantonese films and films of minorities, and also dubs a few Chinese films into some foreign films such as English, French, and Spanish films. This studio has a group of famous dubbing actors and actresses, such as Qiu Yuefeng and Tong Zirong. Chinese audiences are familiar with and love their voices very much and they are not less famous than those actors and actresses in screen.

Address: 19th Floor, Guangbo Building, No.1376 Hongqiao Lu, Shanghai

Shanghai Animation Film Studio

Shanghai Animation Film Studio is a studio specialized in producing animation films (animation, puppet, clip art and folded paper films). By absorbing the artistic characters of shadow play and paper-cutting, this studio produced successfully the first paper folding film *Pigsy Eats Watermelon*. This studio put the traditional ink-and-wash painting in screen and produced the first ink-and-wash animated film *Baby Tadpoles Look for Their Mother*. It also produced the first folded paper film *A Clever Duck* on base of children handmade paper folding. This studio held animation films exhibitions in 6 cities around China such as Beijign, Shanghai and Hong Kong, which were welcomed by audience. This studio had produced hundreds of animation films.

Address: No. 618 Wanhangdu Lu, Changning District, Shanghai

Agricultural Film Studio of China

The Agricultural Film Studio of China, a specialized studio, was founded in Beijing on June 29, 1949.

This studio has so far produced hundreds of agricultural scientific education films awarded prizes at home and abroad:

Chrysopidae winning the Silver Tassel Prize on the 11th Berlin International Agricultural Films Festival in 1980 and the Silver Tower Prize on the Saragossa International Agricultural Film Festival in Spain in 1981, Blue Blood winning awards on the 12th Berlin Agricultural Film Festival in 1982 and the 13th Belgrade International Scientific Films Festival in Yugoslavia in 1984, Prevention of Desertification winning awards

Beijing Film Academy is a palace to which many young people with a dream of the star look forward.

on the 2nd Nitra International Agricultural Film Festival in Czechoslovakia in 1985 and on the 14th Berlin International Agricultural Film Festival in 1986, and Hibrid Fish winning the award on the 14th Berlin International Agricultural Film Festival in 1986.

Address: No.28 Baishiqiaolu Lu, Beijing

Beijing Film Academy

Beijing Film Academy is a famous higher school specialized in cultivating film professional personnel. Many TV and film directors and stars in China graduated from Beijing Film Academy.

This Academy is the cradle of Chinese film art. Its history can be traced back to the Chinese film higher education i in Jinling University in 1936 when he founded film and broadcasting college. In May 1950 Performance Art Research Institute of Film Bureau under Chinese Central Ministry of Culture was founded and later renamed to Film School in July 1951. In 1952 the Film School and the Film and Broadcasting College of Nanjing Jinling University were combined to a new film school which renamed to Beijing Film School in March 1953 and to Beijing Film Academy on June 1, 1956. In this Academy there are subjects of dramatic, film and TV literature, directing, cinematograph, art design of drama, film and TV, advertisement, digital film and TV technique, performing and animation, etc.

Address: No.4 Xitucheng Lu, Haidian Disrtict, Beijing

Film Production Industry

At present in China there are 36 studios (31 feature film studios, 3 scientific education film studios, 1 newsreel studio and 1 animation film studio), 15 state-owned production units and enterprises, and 21 public institutions (10 of which implement enterprise administration system).

There are 22 state-owned units with Permit for Movie Production (for one film only) (mainly are TV stations and film companies).

There are 187 private enterprises with Permit for Movie Production (for one film only) and ten of them are comparatively very active.

There are 6 public institutions in charge of film scientific research, namely Film Archives, Film Scientific Research Institute, Film Orchestra, Film Scripts Center, production center of Movie Channel, and Film Academy.

Film Distribution Industry

In China there are more than 2,000 state-owned film distribution units, including:

2 units with the right to distribute imported films nationwide (not the right to import), namely national-funded Film Distribution of China Film Group Corporation and Huaxia Film Distribution Co., Ltd. Both can do nationwide distribution of imported films and national films.

31 state-owned production units 10 private distribution companies with the right to distribute homemade films nationwide.

35 film chain companies with the operational right of distribution and projection. Among them, China Film Stellar Film Chain Co., Ltd is organized by China Film Group Corporation and a private company, Century Universal Film Chain Co., Ltd is held by state-owned capitals outside the system, and other film chain companies are all state-owned companies.The 36 film chains include 14 cross-provincial ones, 21 provincial ones and 10 provinces and cities such as Beijing and Shanghai has at least two film chains.

Nearly 500 distribution companies in 7 provinces and autonomous regions in west China such as Tibet which have been approved with the aiding in construction of film chains. The original distribution way is still adopted, i.e. distribution according to administrative levels.

Film Projection Industry

In China there are 6,343 cinemas, most of which are state-owned film enterprises under the administration of all levels of cultural departments (the film projection units in Tibet, Gansu and Ningxia are under the administration of broadcasting, film and TV departments), and some implement the enterprise administration system of public institutions. By the end of 2005, 1,243 cinemas have joined the 36 film chains with 2,668 screens.

The Resting Hall in Show Max Cinema in Beijing

The fill bill of the *Red Sorghum*

There are 16 cinemas with joint ventures from oversea regions, covering 9 provinces and cities, mostly from Hong Kong ventures.

In rural areas there are nearly 30,000 projection teams, owned by state, collective organizations and individuals.

Song of the Fisherman

In March 1935 the film *Song of the Fisherman* written and directed by Cai Chusheng won the honorary award on the Moscow International Film Exhibition in Soviet Union. It is the first time for Chinese films to win award on international film festival. Therefore, Song of the Fisherman became the first Chinese film winning international film award.

Moscow International Film Exhibition is an international film exhibition held by Soviet Union Filmmakers Club to celebrate the 15th anniversary of film nationalization in Soviet Union. Delegates and films from more than 20 countries participated in the activity and nearly a hundred films were sent there. The former three prizes were won by films from Soviet Union, France and the United States respectively. The Chinese film, Song of the Fisherman, was listed as Number 9 and won the formal honorary certification. It was appraised as "excellent and brave try on the realistic description of the life and goodness of Chinese people." The film Song of the Fisherman was produced by Lianhua Film Company in 1934, Cai Chusheng was the scenarist and Wang Renmei and Han Langen played the leading roles. The film tells a miserable story about a fisherman's family.

Red Sorghum

Red Sorghum, the First Chinese Feature Film Winning the Top Award on International Film Festival In 1988 the Chinese film Red Sorghum, directed by Zhang Yimou and played by Gong Li and Jiang Wen, won the top award, Golden Bear Award, on the 38th Berlin International Film Festival. It is the first Chinese film winning the top award on Class A international film festival (competitive not specialized film festival).

Red Sorghum is the first film produced by Zhang Yimou as a director not a cinematographer and is also the maiden film of Gong Li. The film adapted from Mo Yan's novel, Family of Red Sorghum, sets the background in Anti-Japanese War and portrays the life of a group of farmers with primitive simplicity and wilderness and the life course of their brave and bloody struggle against Japanese invaders in 1920s and 1930s in China. This film won eight international awards including the Golden Bear Award on the 38th Berlin Film Festival, the Best Film Award on the 5th Zimbabwe International Film Festival and the Sydney Film Critics Award on the 35th Sydney International Film Festival in Australia. In addition, it also won the Best Feature Film Prize of the 8th Golden Rooster Awards and the Best Feature Film Prize of Hundred Flowers Awards in 1988.

Honored Film: Hibiscus Town

The film Hibiscus Town probes into the origin of the extremely left ideology and thinks over the history of the nation from the portrait of the ups and downs in the lives of some ordinary people in a decade of years around "cultural revolution"and the different distortion and dissimilation on their characters. This film won many national awards such as the Best Feature Film Prize of the 7th Golden Rooster Awards in 1987, and some international awards such as the award on the 26th Karlovy Vary International Film Festival in Czechoslovakia.

Honored Film: Spring Festival

Spring Festival is a tragicomedy reflecting the folk life of common people from a close view. It factually shows a series of conflicts and transformations after the entrance of commercial economy into Chinese families. Setting on the background of Spring Festival, this film portrays some trivial matters happening in Cheng's family on the first day of the first lunar month. It is valuable for the film to make people think: do people possess any more important things beyond brilliant houses, beautiful clothes and delicious food? This film was produced by Beijing Film Studio and Hong Kong United International Pictures in 1990. Huang Jianzhong served as the director and Li Baotian and Zhao Lirong played the leading roles. This film won the Jury Special Award and the Best Actress Prize on the Tokyo International Film Festival in 1991, and the Outstanding Feature Film Award of the Ministry of Broadcasting, Film and Television.

Honored Film: Farewell My Concubine

Adapted from the work of Li Bihua, Farewell My Concubine is the fifth film directed by Chen Kaige. Chen selected the Beijing Opera with the most profound accumulation of Chinese culture and the artists' lives to express his thought and comprehension on the traditional culture, the living conditions of people and the humanity. Its leading Actors and Actress is Leslie Cheung, Zhang Fengyi and Gong Li. This film won the Golden Palm Award on the 46th Cannes International Film Festival in May 1993, the FIPRESCI Award, and the Best Director Award and the Best Film Editing Award on the 38th Asian Pacific Film Exhibition in Japan. The Jury of the International Federation of Film Critics said, "Farewell My Concubine excavates Chinese culture, history and humanity, and the scenes are brilliant and the plots are exquisite."

The film bill of the Farewell My Concubine

Architecture and Gardens

Chinese Architecture

Chinese architecture has a large variety and the traditional architecture is mainly that of Han ethnic group, covering imperial architecture, religious architecture, gardens, local residence, bridges, pavilions, pagoda, and mausoleum, in addition to some characteristic ornamental architecture such as ancient arches, stone tablets and ornamental columns. The modern architecture and sport buildings also have Chinese characters.

City Walls in Beijing

In the history, Beijing was a city surrounded by wall on four sides which was a rectangle of 6,650 meters long from east to west and 5,350 meters long from south to north. The walls on four sides were wrapped by bricks and there were nine city gates, each having a small town outside for defense. On each city gate, there was a high city gate tower of two stories and three eaves. On the fourth floor of the small town outside there was an embrasure watchtower which was built up by huge bricks and was very grand and solid. The extant city gates and towns are only the Zhengyang Gate at the center of the southern walls, the Qianmen Gate (the small town outside of Zhengyang Gate), the watchtower at the southeastern corner and the small town outside of the Desheng Gate.

• Characteristics of Traditional Architecture

Growing and developing in the ancient traditional culture of China, the ancient Chinese architecture has distinctive national cultural characteristics. Different from foreign architecture, ancient Chinese architecture looks simple apparently or even broad-brush, but the entirety and details inside make people have the feeling of complexity and uniqueness. Different types of roofs, steles and couplets have different meanings, symbolizing different social status and meaning. Configurations and functions of ancient Chinese architecture, if necessary, can be easily changed, and rooms within them are easy to be dismantled, rebuilt, or shifted for other uses, as they are all in units of a "space". People's concepts on lives and their requirements on architecture have remained almost unchanged thanks to China having enjoyed such a long history of feudal society. When appraising ancient Chinese architecture, some people think that the traditional Chinese architecture has remained unchanged over thousands of years repeated each other, but one should never neglect the miracle that the architecture have weathered the storms of time and survived till today.

City Walls in Xi'an

Xi'an is the capital of China during the Tang Dynasty (618-907). After losing the status as capital at the end of the Tang Dynasty, Xi'an had stagnated in the urban development for long time. Till the Ming Dynasty (1368-1644), Xi'an, as the political, economic and culture center in northwest China, held an important position in military and communications. The present-day Xi'an City was basically founded in early Ming Dynasty.

In the Ming Dynasty, Xi'an City was built on the enlarged Chang'an City, the imperial city of the Tang Dynasty, and located at the center of present-day Xi'an City. The four avenues of north, south, east and west inside the city presented the shape of cross with the Bell Tower as the center and stretched to a city gate respectively. There was a small town outside of each city gate. This kind of layout was very typical among northern cities and towns. Over hundreds of years, a great number of ancient architecture in the old city has been destroyed, but the city walls have survived almost complete till today, as well as some invaluable ancient architecture complex such as Bell Tower, Drum Tower, the Forest of Steles, Town God Temple, the Mosque, the Laying Dragon Temple, the Guangren Temple, the Dongyue Temple, the Huata Tower in the Baoqing Temple, and a large number of precious traditional residences.

City Walls in Pingyao

Pingyao is the extant and the most complete county survived from the Ming and Qing dynasties in China. Located in Shanxi Province, Pingyao is a famous cultural town with over 2,700 years of history. The present ancient town was enlarged and rebuilt in 1370, the third year of Hongwu Reign. The ancient town covers an area of about 2.25 square km and has the southern avenue as the axis. In accordance with the traditional layout of ancient Chinese cities and towns, temples, official bureaus and watch towers are distributed along both sides of the axis in order. The city tower is at the center of the town, the southern avenue, the east-west avenue, the chenghuang (town god) avenue and the yamen avenue constitute cross-shaped commercial streets. The large scale exceeds ordinary traditional towns and reflects the prosperity in the local area at that time. Other streets and allies also remain the old names of the Ming and Qing dynasties and constitute the street, ally and horse-way system of grid shape or "T" shape. The city walls of Pingyao are in shape of a plane square, like a

♦ Influence on Traditional Chinese Architecture from *Yi Jing* (Changes of Zhou)

The thinking ways of ancient Chinese were influenced by the famous philosophic work, *Yi Jing* (Changes of Zhou) in many aspects. They thought laws would be found on everything if it was set in the background of studies of Yi Jing. So did architecture. For example, why did ancient Chinese architects prefer wooden structures to solid and durable stone materials Technical factors are not included in the reason. It is an expression of social culture. According to Chinese tradition, among the Five Elements, namely Wood, Fire, Earth, Metal and Water, Wood implies spring, green and life and is used to build houses of living people, while Earth, i.e. bricks and stones, implies "this round of life ends to naught and there will be a second birth," and is often used to build mausoleum rooms for dead. Therefore, the Eight Diagrams (formally used in divination), Yin-Yang principle, Five Elements and Fengshui (also known as geomancy with feng meaning wind, and shui water) in ancient Chinese doctrines have various influence on ancient Chinese architecture.

Ancient City Walls in Pingyao, Shanxi Province

turtle shell. There are six city gates, one in the north and south respectively and two in the east and west respectively. It is said that the south gate is the head of the turtle and the two wells outside symbolize the eyes of the turtle. The north gate is the turtle tail and is the lowest place of the town, where all the ponding runs out of the town. Turtle is a kind of animal with longevity and is also symbol of luckiness in ancient China. This legend implies the wish of solidness as a huge rock and existence forever for the Pingyao town.

The Great Wall

The Great Wall is a national defense project in ancient China and is also the most famous city wall in China. It goes from the Yalujiang River in the east to Jiayuguan pass in Gansu Province in the west, passing Liaoning, Hebei, Shanxi, Inner Mongolia, Shaanxi and Ningxia provinces and autonomous regions in north China. Along the undulating mountain ridges and boundless deserts, the Great Wall stretches form more than 12,000 li (i.e. more than 6,000 km), so it is called "Ten Thousand Li Great Wall". In the history, the Great Wall was built up to defense the southern invasion from those nomadic ethnic groups in the north. As early as in the Warring States Period, to the north of Qin, Zhao and Yan states, three of the "Seven Powers in the Warring States Period", was the Hun, mainly pastoral nomadic ethnic group. To prevent the southern invasion by those Hun cavalries, the three states built up the Great Wall of their own at the northern borders. After uniting China, Emperor Qinshihuang (the reign of 221-210 BC) sent 300,000 troops and nearly 2 million civilian people, prisoners of war and criminals to link the walls of Qin, Zhao, and Yan states together to prevent the invasion from the Hun, which is the embryonic form of the Great Wall. In the later dynasties, namely the Han (206 BC-220AD), Northern Wei (384-534), Northern Qi (550-577), Sui (581-618) and Jin (1115-1234) dynasties, the Great Wall was rebuilt and extended. Till the Ming Dynasty, the Han rulers started to build the Great Wall in a large scale to prevent the invasion from the northern Mongolia and the northeastern Nuchen ethnic groups. From 1368, the first year of Hongwu Reign, the construction project of the Great Wall took more than 200 years.

The Forbidden City (Gu Gong)

Lying at the center of Beijing, the Forbidden City, called Gu Gong, meaning past imperial palace, in Chinese, used to be the imperial palace of the Ming and Qing dynasties. The construction of the Forbidden City started in 1407, the 5th year of the Yongle reign of the third emperor of the Ming Dynasty, and was completed 14 years later in 1420. A total of 24 emperors had reigned here during the more than 500 years.

Measuring 961 meters long from south to north and 753 meters wide from east to west, the world's largest, grandest and best preserved ancient imperial palace and palace complex covers a floor space of more than 720,000 square meters, having more than 9,000 buildings with the construction area of about 150,000 square meters. It is the masterpiece of ancient Chinese architecture and the centralized symbolization of the imperial power over the more than 2,000 years of autarchy society in China. The rectangular city is encircled in a 52-meter-wide moat and a city wall which has one grand gate on each side in north, south, east and west. There are four unique and delicate corner towers overlooking the city inside and outside on the four corners. It is a magnificent and closely guarded castle.

Same with the past imperial palaces in China, the general design and construction form of the Forbidden City completely accords with and manifests the requirements of ancient patriarchal clan system and social etiquette, giving prominence to the supreme imperial power. The constructions inside extend to east and west along the city's axis. All the palaces inside are divided into Outer Court and Inner Court. The former one is the place where emperors executed their power, and all significant national activities and rituals were held in the Outer Court. The latter one is the place where the emperors and their wives live, consisting of Qianqinggong (Palace of Celestial Purity), Jiaotaidian (Hall of Celestial and Terrestrial Union), Kunninggong (Palace of Earthly Tranquility), Imperial Garden on the axis and the six palaces in the east and west.

Taihedian (Hall of Supreme Harmony)

Taihedian (Hall of Supreme Harmony) is the highest construction in the Forbidden City and has a construction area of 2,377 square meters. It is the grandest timber framework ever in China. The hip roof of the hall is in form of palace with layers of eaves, i.e. "si-e-chong-wu" in the Yin and Shang dynasties, and is the form of "supreme power". There are the most corner animals and extensions of bracket sets. The dragon and phoenix, symbolizing imperial power, are used as subjects in the engravings on the royal pavements and railings and the colorful paintings in the hall and the designs on caisson ceilings. And the marble Rigui, an ancient timer in the east and the Jialiang, an ancient measuring vessel, as well as the bronze tortoise and bronze crane, are displayed only here. The gilded throne engraved with dragon designs inside the hall is much more the symbol of arbitrary imperial power. Taihedian is the place where emperors held ascending ceremonies and grand celebrations and received the respects from all officials, and when a general was going to go out for a battle, he would also accept the seals

Panorama of the Forbidden City

there. In the Ming Dynasty, the final imperial examination and the New Year's Day banquet offered to officials were also held in Taihedian. The Zhonghedian behind the Taihedian is a square construction with three rooms from south to north and from east to west respectively, surrounded by corridors. It covers a space of 580 square meters. The roof is a pyramidal roof with single eave and the top is made of gilded bronze. It is the place where emperors had a rest when holding the court in the Taihedian.

The Yellow colored glaze tiles of the Forbidden City

• Color of the Forbidden City

The color of the Forbidden City also has profound meaning. Roofs are built with yellow glazed tiles and decorations in the palace are painted yellow, which is especially distinctive in Qianqinggong. This usage comes from the saying of the Five Elements of the ancient classic, Shang Shu. Ancient people believed that the world is composed by the Five Elements, namely Metal, Wood, Water, Fire and Earth, and the Five Elements have relations of being inter-promoting and checking, hence the changeable world. Yellow represents Earth which is the source of everything on earth. And emperors were source of all people, so yellow is frequently used in the imperial palaces.

However, there is one exception in the Forbidden City. Wenyuange, the royal library, has a black glazed tile roof. In the Five Elements, black represents water which can check fire. So black tiles were used in the royal library to imply that water can check fire and fire can be prevented. In Wenyuange there is a complete set of Si Ku Quan Shu (Complete Library in the Four Branches of Literature), including all the most important academic works in ancient China, with 3,505 kinds and 6,304 volumes of books. In addition, in the Wenhuadian, there is a collection of all the archives of central organs and local organs during the over 500 years of the Ming and Qing dynasties, including 74 files and more than 10 million pieces. They are precious historical materials.

Wenshou

Playing the role of avoiding evil, wenshou is a popular decoration of ancient Chinese architecture and is usually placed on the ridge of large-scale constructions. On the main ridges and vertical ridges of ancient official building, imperial palaces, halls and temples, there are various wenshou with different forms and names, and the forms and numbers symbol the different status of the halls and palaces.

Dawen (zhengjiwen), the wenshou on two ends of the main ridges, is usually in form of dragon head with open mouth holding the ridge, and therefore it is also called tunjishou (holding ridge in mouth). At present the largest tunjishou in China is on the roof of Taihedian, consisting of 13 glazed pieces, 3.4 meters high and 4.3 tons of weight. It is the typical work of zhengjiwen in the imperial palaces of the Ming and Qing dynasties in China.

The wenshou on vertical ridges is usually in form of animal head watching out along the ridge and therefore it is also called wangshou (watching) or wuji zoushuo and xianren zoushou. The front one on the eave corner is called qifeng xianren playing the role of fixing the first tile below the vertical ridge. Several xiaoshous (small animals) stand behind the qifeng xianren, which are all called vertical ridge animals. Palaces and halls of different status have different number of xiaoshou. The supreme palace in the Forbidden City is the Taihedian where the number of vertical ridge animals is the largest, 11. Lower palaces have less vertical ridge animals, for example, 9 for Qianqinggong, 7 for Kunninggong and 5 for most of the Six West and East Palaces. Each vertical ridge animal has its own name and implication. From the front to the back, they are dragon: a magic animal in ancient fairytales which can make clouds and rain and is the symbol of emperors in feudal society; phoenix: a king of bird in ancient fairytales, and the male one is called feng, and the female one is called huang, and they are called feng generally. It is the symbol of empress; lion: it was viewed as king of animals by ancient people and is the symbol of power; heaven horse: it is the divine horse; ocean horse: it is also called luolongzi (fallen dragon princess), and the heven horse and ocean horse imply that the power of imperial families can reach heaven and ocean; suanni: a fierce animal in ancient fairytales which can eat tigers and leopards, meaning all animals should submit to it; xiayu: a strange animal in ocean which can also make clouds and rain; xiezhi: a fierce animal with single horn which can distinguish truth from false; douniu: a kind of dragon in ancient fairytales, similar to qiu (small dragon with horns) and chi (hornless dragon); and xingshe: a man image with wings and monkey face and it is the yaweishou. The reduction of the vertical ridge animals starts from the back, i.e. xingshe.

Dougong (Bracket Set)

Dougong, a unique component of ancient Chinese architecture, can enlarge the eaves when used under wudan and can reduce the span of girder if used on two ends of the girder. Ancient craftsmen extended the pillars and girders by layers of bow-shaped short timber to make the wudan stretching out of the house body. These bow-shaped short timbers are called gong, and between two layers of gong is dou, wooden pieces to underlay the gong. Therefore, this kind of component consisting of layers of gong and dou is called dougong. Dou is a kind of 3-D wooden component, and gong is a kind of bow-shaped wooden board. The roof can be extended out by laying gong and dou by turns and rabbeting them together to form a variable roof frame. Dougong, the unique component of ancient Chinese architecture, are distributed evenly on the girders and support the extended eaves.

Huabiao (Ornamental Column)

Huabiao is a kind of huge columns used as symbols and decorations before bridges, palaces, city walls and mausoleums in ancient China. As one of the symbols of China, it is also called shendaozhu, shiwangzhu, biao (表), biao (标) and jie. Those set before mausoleums are also called mubiao (mausoleum columns). Huabiao is usually composed of a foundation, a tortuous dragon column, a plate receiving dew and a couchant animal on it. The two pairs of huabiao in front and at back of Tian'anmen in Beijing are carved from huge white marble with exquisite shapes, and are excellent works of huabiao.

The Temple of Heaven

The Temple of Heaven is located on the east side of the front gate in the south city of Beijing. It is the place where emperors of the Ming and Qing dynasties worshipped and was built in the 18th year (1429) of the Yongle period of the Ming Dynasty. The altar, in a plane round shape, called Huanqiu Hill, was rebuilt in the 17th year (1752) of Emperor Qianlong of the Qing Dynasty. Qiniandian (Hall of Prayer for Good Harvests) was rebuilt in the 16th year (1890) of Emperor Guangxu of the Qing Dynasty.

The Temple of Heaven is very large in area, stretching 1,700 meters from east to west and 1,600 meters from north to south, with two circles of enclosing walls. The southern side had square corner and the north side round ones, symbolizing the place of a round heaven. The Temple of Heaven uses ecological

The Echo Wall of the Temple of Heaven is an ancient architecture with the echo effect still well preserved in China.

artistic technique to give prominence to the theme of "heaven". For example, the density of structures is very small, covered by large tracts of pine and cypress trees, creating a strong atmosphere of solemnity and nobility. Huanqiu is crystal white, setting off the holy, pure, empty and bright "heaven". Its two-layered enclosed walls are only a little more than one meter high before the tall, large round terrace, so as not to block the visual line. The enclosed walls set off the white stone terrace by deep color, and the white stone lattice and star gates on the walls respond to the white stone terrace and help break the monotony of long walls. The 400-meter long and 30-meter wide Danbi Bridge, and the courtyard of Qiniandian Hall, also stand above the surrounding ground, for the same effect. The round Qiniandian is 24 meters in diameter, its three-layered eaved pinnacle covered with green glazed tiles. Under this is a six-meter three-layered, white stone round terrace with a total height of 38 meters. The green roof seemed to merge with the blue sky. All these are designed to create image of the close relationship between man and heaven. The size, color and shape of all buildings in the Temple of Heaven had been deliberated before decision, and the visual effects at the major sights had got particular attention. For example, there is a huge "picture-framework" composed of Quanmen gate of Huangqiongyu and columns of Qinianmen gate, which creates a very good frame-scene effect for viewing Huangqiongyu and Qiniandian.

Shejitan Altar (Altar of Land and Grain)

Located to the west of Wumen of the Forbidden City, Shejitan Altar is the important sacrificial altar and temple where emperors of the Ming and Qing dynasties offered sacrifice to the gods of the land and grain. Sheji is the god of land. She is the god of five earths: green earth in east, red earth in south, white earth in west, black earth in north and yellow earth at center, so the earth of five colors offered from various places of the country was placed on the altar in accordance with their location in the country, symbolizing the national land of five places and expressing the meaning that "the whole world is the land of the emperor". Ji refers to the gold of land in charge of grain growing, i.e. god of agriculture. Offering sacrifice to She and Ji represents the power of ancient emperors governing the people within their reign and also reflects the social quality of viewing agriculture as foundation of nation in ancient China. The square sacrifice altar has two stories. The surrounding altar wall is also square, and green, red, white and black glazed bricks cover the wall on four sides according to the location and direction. On a sunny day, the sacrificial ceremony would be held outdoor, and if on a rainy day, the ceremony would be held indoor. It is on the opposite direction to the Temple of Heaven, and emperors would offer sacrifice to south from north, so the sacrifice hall and the worship hall are to the north of sacrifice altar. So is the zhengmen. In 1914 Shejitan Altar was opened to public as Central Park and later it was renamed to Zhongshan Park.

Taimiao (Royal Ancestral Temple)

Taimiao is the sacrificial construction for ancient emperors to offer sacrifice to their ancestors in China and is also the important symbol of hereditary imperial power in feudal society. The Taimiao in Beijing is the royal ancestral temple of the Ming and Qing dynasties. It is located to at the east side of Tian'anmen and was built in the 18th year (1420) of the Yongle Period of the Ming Dynasty. In the 24th year (1544) of the Jiajing Period in the Ming Dynasty, it was rebuilt to the present scene. It is the only extant Taimiao in the history. Taimiao has two layers of surrounding walls in rectangle, and cypress trees with hundreds of years old are planted between the outer walls. The southern gate is called Jimen. On the axis inside the Jimen are distributed three grand halls, namely front, middle and back halls. All the halls have yellow glazed tile roofs, splendid and grand. The front hall, 11 bays wide and 4 bays deep, has the hip roof of layers of eaves and is the place for emperors to offer sacrifice and worship. The middle hall, 11 bays wide, has the roof of single eave with surrounding halls and is the place for making offerings to spirit tablets of past emperors. The back hall, 9 bays wide, has the hip roof and is the place for making offerings to spirit tablets of emperors long ago which had been moved out from the middle hall. In 1950 it was renamed to Beijing Workers Cultural Palace.

Wenmiao (The Confucian Temple)

Wenmiao, also called the Confucian Temple, is the construction of etiquette for offering sacrifice to founder of Confucianism, Confucius.

In 478 BC, one year after the death of Confucius, the King of the Lu State set Confucius's residence in Qufu, Shandong as a temple. Every year people would offer sacrifice to Confucius and at that time there were only three houses in the temple. Then the Confucian Temple was developed on the base. In 195 BC, Emperor Gaozu of the Han Dynasty, Liu Bang, for the first time offered sacrifice to Confucius with the grand ceremony of offering sacrifice to heaven. With the granting of more and more honors to Confucius, the Confucian Temple in Qufu became larger and larger. Till today there has been a huge architectural complex and the scale and form can even compare to imperial palaces. The Confucian Temple in Qufu and the Confucian Mansion and the Confucian Mausoleum are called "Three Confucian" generally. The Confucian Mansion is the residence of offspring of lineal descent of Confucius, who descended the title of "Yanshenggong" from Confucius, and it is the extant largest mansion in China except the imperial halls and houses of the Ming and Qing dynasties. The Confucian Mausoleum is the mausoleum special for Confucius and his families.

Architecture of Chinese Gardens

Chinese gardens blend the artificial arrangement by artificial hills, fishponds, pavilions, and terraces with the natural scenes of flowers, grass, trees, wind and moon and create an artistic life of harmonious co-existence between man and nature.

The extant royal gardens in the north were mostly built in the Ming (1368-1644) and Qing (1616-1911) dynasties and are the places for feudal emperors to live, play, hold banquet and hunt. They cover broad spaces and have exquisite displays. A lot of materials and manpower had been spent to build them. The private gardens in the south are mostly concentrated in towns at the lower reaches of the Yangtze River where literati would like to gather since long time ago. They are the places for literati to live in seclusion and be close to nature, or for officials and men of wealth to compete in treasures and wealth and amuse themselves. The northern gardens are characterized by grandness and rarity, while the southern gardens are characterized by prettiness and grace.

Temple gardens are another rare treasure in Chinese gardens. They are the gardens affiliated to Buddhist temples, Taoist temples, altars and ancestral temples. The largest one is similar to royal gardens and the smallest one is similar to private gardens. Lying among natural mountains and rivers, these gardens usually integrate with and constitute landscape gardens. The well-known temple gardens include Tanzhe Temple and Jietai Temple in Beijing, Jinci in Taiyuan, Xiyuan in Suzhou, Lingying Temple on West Lake in Hangzhou and Waiba Temple in Chengdu, etc.

Southern Private Gardens

The gardens in Suzhou, Yangzhou, Wuxi, Zhenjiang and Hangzhou are representatives of southern private gardens.

During the Ming and Qing dynasties when the feudal economy and culture developed to its peak in Suzhou, the art of building gardens also developed to mature and with the emergence of a group of garden artists, the activities of building gardens reached the pinnacle. Suzhou gardens make use of the exquisite carvings and fine designs to reflect the profound artistic conception that Chinese culture originates from nature and exceeds nature. Among them, Lion Grove, Zhuozheng Garden, Lingering Garden, Wangshi Garden and the Garden of Canglang Pavilion are listed into World Cultural Heritage by the UNESCO.

The gardens in Yangzhou are mostly those of mansions. At the prosperous time, the gardens were distributed all over the streets and allies in town and in the suburb areas gardens and villas could be seen everywhere along banks of rivers. Till the period of the Emperor Qianlong in the Qing Dynasty, there had appeared the well-known gardens of Slender West Lake with 24 sight spots. At that time the number of gardens in Yangzhou exceeded that of Suzhou and once enjoyed the fame that "Yangzhou Gardens are Number One in the Country". But it is a pity that most of the Yangzhou Gardens were destroyed in battles.

In Hangzhou there is the famous West Lake Gardens. With the West Lake as center, the gardens in the city have different subjects and the best representative one for beauty of Chinese garden-building art is the Most Famous Garden of West Lake, Guozhuang, which was built in 1907.

Jichang Garden

The Jichang Garden lies at the east foot of Huishan Mountain in west Wuxi City, Jiangsu Province. Jichang Garden, also known as Qin Garden, is a famous garden of the Ming Dynasty. The garden is divided into east and west parts. In the east part are mainly ponds with square pavilions and water corridors. In the west part are mainly artificial hills and trees. It is a famous classical garden in south China.

The front door of Jichang Garden faces the Xianghua Bridge of Huishan Temple and the board over the door was inscribed by Emperor Qianlong. To the left of the spacious hall there is a group of yards with unique shapes. In the west, there is a small dooryard, an old vine, and a bended corridor, full of the flavor of southern gardens. There is a huge valley path laid by yellow stones not far away, which is the famous Bayinjian, the masterpiece of Zhang Nanheng and Zhang Shi, masters of piling rockeries. The west end of the Bayinjian is higher than the east end with the dense forest up. A spring runs down with rugged strange stones on both sides. The scenes here are variable.

The success of the Qichang Garden lies is her "natural mountains, beautiful water, concise garden, unsophisticated trees and ingenious scenes." In the Qing Dynasty, Emperors Kang Xi and Qianlong visited this place for many times and inscribed poems there, showing their appreciation particularly.

Zhuozheng Garden

The Zhuozheng Garden in Suzhou, founded in the fourth year (1509) of the period of Zhengde of the Ming Dynasty, is a big garden south of the Yangtze River, covering a space of 4.1 hectares, and was very simple in the initial

The Small Flying Rainbow Bridge (Xiaofeihong), in the middle part of the Humble Administrator's Garden (Zhuozheng Garden) is a covered bridge across the inlet. The Bridge connecting with the Small Pavilion of Quiet Meditation (Xiaocanglang) constitutes a water courtyard, being a relatively independent scenic spot besides the distant, bright scenes inside the Garden.

period. The appearance of the extant garden was formed mainly in the late Qing Dynasty (at the end of the 19th century). The garden is divided into three parts, east, middle and west, the middle being the main part. The middle part is in a horizontal rectangular shape. There are lots of water surfaces which are also long and horizontal. The east and west mountain islands stand out of the water, and the water surface is separated into several blocks by small bridges and dikes. Several small arms stretch out of the pond. The coastline is curved and natural, conveying the meaning of endlessness. Many plots of land are set aside on the southern bank where there is a concentration of structures. The entrance from the residence to the garden opens in the middle part of the southern wall.

In the Zhuozheng Garden, the space of waterscape covers three fifth of the total space and most of the major constructions are by the waterscape. In the garden there are various kinds of flowers and trees, composing many sight spots with appreciation of flowers and forests as subjects.

Wangshi Garden

In 1981 a permanent exhibit was added into New York Metropolitan Museum, Mingxuan, a construction of Chinese classical

Wangshi Garden in Suzhou

garden. The source of the construction is Dianchunyi Small Garden in Wangshi Garden in Suzhou. Located at Kuojiatou Alley in south of Suzhou City, the Wangshi Garden covers a space of 0.4 hectare, less than one sixth of the Zhuozheng Garden. But it presents significance from small appearance with concise distribution. There are many constructions without any view of huddle. The rockeries and ponds are small but not constrained. It is the example of less winning more and manifests the supreme technique of building gardens.

The Wangshi Garden was formally built during the period of Shaoxing (1131-1162) in Southern Song Dynasty, and the extant outlook of the garden was mostly formed in the 60th year of Emperor Qianlong's reign (1795). To the east is the residence of the owner of the garden and the main door of the garden is open at the southeastern corner. The pond is at the center, basically in the square shape. Bank stones are low and near and structures close to water also are low and near to the water surface. This kind of treatment opens the view. There is a very small west yard nearby the garden, with a study in it. The scene is very beautiful when one looks over the waterside pavilion from the door to the west yard. It is called frame view with door as frame. Suzhou gardens pay much attention to the frame view effects. One can find very beautiful scenes from almost every door and broad window. It shows the exquisite method of Chinese classical gardens.

Ge Garden

The Ge Garden was the private garden of Huang Yingtai, a wealthy salt businessman in Yangzhou. It was built in the 23rd year of the Jiaqing period (1818) in the Qing Dynasty and is a private garden of the Qing Dynasty that is preserved well in Yangzhou.

This garden is characterized by piling stones in it. The highest spot at the center of the rockery is 6 meters high. The body of the rockery is piled up by lake stones with exquisite shapes and dense lines. The stones are gray and the rockery is named Xia Hill (summer hill). At the east side of the Building, there is a rockery piled up by yellow stones. The vigorous, straight and forceful shapes of the yellow stones are adopted to make peaks, ridges, chains and caves on the rockery. In the rockery there are stream, valley and cave. The rockery faces west. In the shining of setting sun, the yellow stone surface shows a view of golden autumn, and it is called Qiu Hill (autumn hill). Tou Feng Lou Yu Hall is the place for viewing snow in winter, so some stones with light gray color are piled up in the shade of the wall before the hall, creating a misleading appearance that the snow on the stones have not melted. It is called Dong Hill (winter hill).

The Courtyard of the Shi Family in Tianjin

These three rockeries, along with the Spring Hill—the stalagmite in front of the garden door, compose a mountain scene of spring, summer, autumn and winter. It is the soul of the Ge Garden.

Northern Private Gardens

The northern area is different from the southern area in many aspects such as nature, econmy and culture. In the north, the temperature is very low in winter, the growth of plants is affected by the climate and there are few evergreen trees. In winter except a few kinds of trees such as cypress, most arbors and shrubs withered. Even in spring and summer, the variety of flowers and trees is less than that in the south. Meanwhile the north is different from the south in architectural technique and styles. Although at that time many technicians of garden building in the south were called to the north to build gardens, the different natural conditions, political and cultural backgrounds and architectural forms make the northern private gardens appear unique.

The private gardens in Beijing concentrate along bank of Shichahai Lake and Haidian District in northwestern suburb. Among them, the most famous and largest ones are Tsinghua Garden and Shao Garden.

Tsinghua Garden was the private garden of a royal family member. It covers a space of 80 hectares, located to east of the Summer Palace and to south of the Yuanming Garden. Shao Garden is the private garden of Mi Wanzhong, a famous poet in the Ming Dynasty. It was built up in the period of Wanli (1573-1619) in the Ming Dynasty, located to southeast of the Tsinghua Garden. It is a garden with waterscape as majority. The constructions in it are simple and alienated, imitating the style of traditional scholars' gardens.

Gongwangfu Garden

Gongwangfu Garden, also named Cuijin Garden, is located at Liuyin Street to the west of Shichahai Lake. It is the largest and best preserved garden among the scores of gardens of princes' residences in Beijing, and is also the only prince's residence open to public in name a garden in Beijing. Gongwangfu Garden has exquisite layout and pretty view. It is said that it was the prototype of the Daguan Garden in the Chinese classical literary masterpiece, A Dream of Red Mansions.

Gongwangfu Garden was originally the private residence of He Shen, an important minister during the Qianlong's reign (1736-1795) in the Qing Dynasty. Later it was confiscated by the Qing Court and changed to a prince's residence. The constructions are divided into two parts, mansion and garden. And the mansion is in front of the garden. The garden covers a space of 28,000 square meters with 31 ancient constructions. The later owner of the garden, Prince Gong, Yi Xin, once called hundreds of skillful craftsmen to rebuild the garden, blending the style of southern gardens with the structure of northern constructions and integrating the Chinese and western elements. The layout of the garden is divided into middle, east and west parts. It is elegant, quiet, pretty and exquisite.

In Beijing during the Qing Dynasty, one had to get special approval from emperors before drawing water in private residences. Gongwangfu residence was one of the few royal residences winning the honor. Cuijin Garden, as the garden of the royal residence, has much more and larger constructions put in order compared to ordinary private gardens of officials and scholars. In addition to some huge halls rarely seen in ordinary scholars' gardens, there is even a huge opera tower that was rarely seen in private gardens of officials.

Imperial Gardens of the Ming and Qing Dynasties

The ancient royal gardens in China today are most constructions built up in the Ming and Qing dynasties and concentrate in Beijing.

The imperial gardens of the Ming and Qing dynasties widely absorbed the experience from private gardens in the past dynasties, assembled the souls of ancient and foreign and Chinese gardens, and some directly imitated the structures of private gardens or even rebuilt the private gardens. The gardens in palaces and the surrounding golden and brilliant palaces reflect each other, showing the magnificent air. The imperial palaces for short stays outside re-created successfully the tranquility and seclusion of natural landscape in limited space by relying on natural lands and water or by digging out ponds and piling up rockeries. The Eight Outer Temples in the Imperial Summer Villa of Chengde represent the religious characters of temple gardens in the Ming and Qing dynasties. Emperor Qianlong was fond of landscape in West Lake particularly and migrated the landscape of some natural scenic gardens such as "Qu Yuan Feng He" and "Ping Hu Qiu Yue" in Yuanming Garden.

Royal gardens were usually symbol of imperial power, having the grand scale and magnificent vigor. Looking up the front hill of the Longevity Hill from the Glowing Clouds and Holy Land Archway on bank of the Kunming Lake, the constructions of the Gate that Dispels the Clouds, the Hall that Dispels the Clouds, Hall of Moral Glory and Tower of Buddhist Incense are positioned one after the other with the ascending trend on an axis. The Tower of Buddhist Incense, symbolizing the holy power, is 41 meters high up and has the vigor of ruling all. It is the center and symbol construction in the Summer Palace. The Hall that Dispels the Clouds is at the middle of the axis. The whole architectural complex not only manifests the heaven scene of fairy hills and beautiful towers described in Buddhist sutras, but also reflects the thought that imperial power is granted by gods for maintaining the feudal autarchy.

The Summer Palace

The Summer Palace is a typical represent of royal gardens. Located at northwest of Beijing, it was completed on the 15th year (1750) of Qianlong period in the Qing Dynasty. In the period from the end of the 19th century to the beginning of the 20th century, it was destroyed by Anglo-French Allied Forces and Eight-Power Allied Forces for two times. After rebuilding for two times, it survived today comparatively well. The main body of the Summer Palace consists of Longevity Hill and the Kunming Lake. The Hill stands in the north, stretching horizontally and 60 meters high, while the Lake lies in the south, in a shape of triangle with broadness in north and narrowness in south. The whole garden is divided into four scenic spots: palaces region, front hill and front lake region, west lake region, and back hill and back lake region.

The palaces adopt the strictly symmetrical structure of palaces, but the atmosphere is much more relaxed than that in the Forbidden City and the size of constructions is not comparatively large. Passing the main hall of the palace region, the Hall of Benevolence and Longevity, one can enter the front hill and front lake region by a zigzag and hidden alley. There the atmosphere changes suddenly; there is the flat lake before with a broad and far view to hills far away. The image of the pagoda on Hill of Jade Spring far away is borrowed to the garden, and the rank of the arbors nearby play a role of penetrating scenes and enriching scenic tiers, which strengthen the space feeling of the garden. The body of the Longevity Hill is lack of changes, but the high Tower of Buddhist Incense at the south foot of the hill and the Glaze Tower to the north of the Tower of Buddhist Incense break the figure of the hill. Below the Tower of Buddhist Incense there is a high terrace on southern hill belly instead of hill top, which strengths its close relationship with the Kunming Lake and shows its affinity with the hill. The tower with large size and broad body is the center of the garden. Under the Tower of Buddhist Incense and between the hill foot and the lake bank, ther is a longest corridor in the world, which is 700 meters long from east to west and connects numerous small constructions at the foot of the hill. The Long Corridor turns inside at the axis of the architectural complex of the Tower of Buddhist Incense, and forms a square with the help of protruding bank of the lake.

Yuanming Garden

As the largest royal garden in Beijing in the Qing Dynasty, Yuanming Garden was originally built up in early the 18th century. The construction took 100 years and almost ended at the 14th year of the Jiaqing period (1809). It is the masterpiece of royal gardens in China and is called as Garden of gardens by European people. But in the period from the end of the 19th century to the beginning of the 20th century, Yuanming Garden was destroyed by Anglo-French Allied Forces and Eight-Power Allied Forces for two times. Only the ruins and some blueprints and models are left today.

Before the burning destruction, in the big Yuanming Garden there are some small gardens with too many beautiful scenes. There were more than 120 sight spots with architectural complex as center, and they were absolutely different. The present Yuanming Garden has flat terrain, without any hill or river. But it is desirable that there is a rich groundwater source and the water can emerge with digging 1 meter in depth. These objective conditions decide that the garden can only be built up on flat with dug out ponds and piled up hills to create the environment of landscape garden. The largest water region in it is Fuhai Lake and covers an area of 30 hectares. The small-sized ones are numerous. The brooks with endless circulation of water, like running links, connect those large and small water surfaces together to a complete water system. The earth from digging ponds is piled up to hills, so there are many hills and ponds. All the hills cover one third of the whole area of the garden.

It is also worthy to mention a group of courtyard constructions with European style built up in the period of Emperor Qianlong. This European-style architectural complex was completed in the 25th year (1760) of the period of Qianlong, including six palaces and three courtyards. They are all architecture with the

The Marble Boat in the Summer Palace

Baroque style popular in Europe at that time. They were built up by stone materials with carving decorations outside. It is the first time in Chinese history to blend collectively the Chinese and western architecture and garden culture.

The Imperial Summer Villa of Chengde

Puning Temple, one of the Eight Outer Temples in Chengde, Hebei Province

The Imperial Summer Villa, located in north of Chengde City, Hebei Province, was built up during the period (1703-1790) from the 42nd year of Kangxi's reign to the 55th year of the Qianlong's reign in the Qing Dynasty and was the place for emperors to spend summer every year. The garden can be divided into four parts according to different terrains: hill region, lake region, plain region and palace region. The lake region is the major sight spot of the garden. On the large and small water surfaces there are many islands that are connected together by banks and bridges. The bank line is winding and changeable and every step forward can bring a different scene, full of flavors of southern watery region. In the plain region there are large pieces of grassland and forests, imitating the scene on the grassland of northern frontier. Poplar trees are planted, deer groups are fed, the games of horse racing and wrestling are shown, and some characteristic constructions of northern frontier such as Mongolian tents are built on spaces in forests. In the hill region three valleys stretch to the above-mentioned regions from northwest to southeast. There were originally scores of small gardens temples in the region, most of which survived till today. The construction of the Villa adopts the principle of making the best of occasion. The original terrains are decorated properly to reflect each other and the architectural style is elegant and simple. In addition, a great number of scenes and constructions of the southern China and northern frontier are referred to enrich the scenes in the garden. In the east and north outside of the garden, there are twelve lamaseries with Tibetan and Han styles, called the Eight Outer Temples. Along with the natural scene of Bangchui Peak in east of the garden, they set off the scene of the Villa.

Traditional Residences

Beijing's Siheyuan

Beijing's Siheyuan

From Beijing was formally set as capital (1264) in the Yuan Dynasty, Siheyuan (courtyard with houses on all sides) emerged with the palaces, official bureaus, streets and hutong in Beijing. Being the most typical residence in north China, Beijing's Siheyuan is the outstanding representative of traditional residence of China's Han ethnic group.

The square residence is situated in the north of the compound and faces south, symmetrical along the axis, even between left and right, close to outside and open to inside. Different scales of Siheyuan have greatly different sizes. But both large and small Siheyuan are composed of basic units. The courtyard enclosed by houses on all sides is the basic unit, called as one-entrance Siheyuan. Those with two courtyards are called as two-entrance Siheyuan, with three called as three-entrance Siheyuan, and so on. The large-scale Siheyuan in Beijing, such as prince's residence, can have seven-entrance and nine-entrance courtyards. Beside the main courtyards in the middle, there are east and west crossing courtyards on both sides. They can be called as "a large compound of connecting courtyards".

Siheyuan is the ideal residence for traditional Chinese. There are houses, courtyards, main door, secondary door, covered corridor, private school, guest hall, screen wall, storeroom, and kitchen, and for rich families there are even gardens and rooms for carriages and horses. Siheyuan is a close residence and there is only one door to street outside. With the door closed, the residence is a very private room and is very suitable for a single family. At present a group of Beijing's Siheyuan have been listed as cultural protection units, such as No.87 Xijiao Mingxiang in Xicheng District, No.112 Northern Xinhua Jie in Xicheng District, and Nos.63-65 Dongsi Liutiao in Dongcheng District.

The courtyard in Beijing's Siheyuan is square with moderate scale. In the south of Beijing in summer residences are always exposed to western setting sunshine, so the courtyards are narrow from east to west and long from south to north to reduce sunshine. In the northwest, due to serious sand blown by wind in Gansu and Qinghai, the wall of courtyards is built higher and the residence is called Zhuang Ke (Village Nest). In the northeast, the land is broad and the weather is cold, the courtyards are very wide to accept more sunshine and there is much space inside the wall.

Courtyard Residence in North China

During the Ming and Qing dynasties, the businessmen of Shanxi became the outstanding persons in building up private residence. The large courtyard of Wang's in Lingshou County is called as "No.1 Residence in Sanjin" and has over a hundred large and small courtyards, surpassing that of the large courtyard of Qiao's in Qi County which is well known for the Film Raise the Red Lantern. They are much larger and have much more wooden sculpture adornments than Beijing's Siheyuan. In the northern plain area, all kinds of Siheyuan have almost the same basic form characteristics, such as Confucius's Residence in Qufu, Shandong, the original residence of Zheng Banqian (1693-1765, a famous painter of the Qing Dynasty) in Weifang, Shandong, and the numerous residences of old-style Chinese private bankers in Pingyao, Shanxi. In the wide rural areas, the residences are not as complete as those typical Siheyuan, as they only have courtyards enclosed with two or three houses, such as the Xiangyang (exposed to the sun) rural residences of Manchu in Liaoning and Jilin and Tuweizi in Shanxi and Shaanxi, but they all have the main gate, wall, courtyard, main room and wing room. They can also be viewed as the simple mode of courtyard residence.

Lin Yutang (1895-1976), a famous writer, expressed the reason why Chinese people like courtyard residence from a social psychology. He pointed out, the courtyard residence, like the roof of Chinese architecture, covers the ground, and does not shoot up in the sky like the tower top of Gothic architecture. The largest success of this spirit lies in the offering of a standard for people to weigh whether their lives on the earth are happy and harmonious: the Chinese roof manifests that happiness should be found first at home.

The Southern Tianjing (Small Courtyard) Residence

In southern China a kind of Tianjing residence is very popular. In traditional Chinese architecture, the small courtyard with high wall is called Tianjing, which is frequently seen in the hot and wet regions in the south, as this kind of courtyard residence is beneficial for ventilation.

The southern regions are hot, rainy and wet, and there are many mountain areas and hills. The regions are densely populated but narrow in area, so residences pay attention to sunshine prevention and to ventilation as well as to fire-proofing. Therefore, the small courtyard residence is very popular. Their basic unit takes horizontal, long and square small yard as the core. Surrounded by buildings on all sides, or three sides—left, right and back-sunshine seldom comes in. The narrow and tall small yards play the role of breaking the wind and facilitate ventilation. The principal room faces the small yard and is completely open. All houses drain water out of the small yards, and geomancy calls this "four streams flowing into the hall", containing the meaning of preventing money from flowing out. Corbie gables often appear in the periphery, which is helpful to preventing the spread of fire. Corbie gable, also called fire-sealing gable, is a major molding characteristic of south Chinese architecture. The wall stands above the roof, and the Outline is in the setback type, varied and rich. The wall surface is plastered with lime powder, and the wall top is covered with gray tile wall eaves, so that the white wall and gray tile make it bright, plain and elegant.

Zhejiang's "13-roomed" Residence

Small and medium-sized courtyard houses of south China are mostly composed of one or two courtyards, but various localities have their own rich styles. For example, the "13-roomed" houses in Dongyang and nearby areas of Zhejiang Province, usually consist of three principal rooms and five left and right wing rooms) forming a Sanheyuan (courtyard with houses on three sides). The houses are all buildings. On the ground floor of each building there is a front corridor covered with waist eaves. The three buildings have two-slope roofs. The two tips of the three buildings stand out of the corbie gable; a door is open in the middle of the front wall of the courtyard, and the left and right corridors, which also each have a door, lead to the courtyard. Such layout is highly regulated, simple and clear-cut. The courtyard is wide and open, giving the sense of being comfortable and upright. Dongyang is a famous place for wood-carving. Very exquisite wood-carvings are usually found on the column capitals and eave-porches of residences.

Xitou Sanhuitang in Xiuning County, Anhui Province

The large courtyard houses of wealthy families in the south are comprised of several courtyards. The typical layout consists of left, middle and right routes, with the middle route formed by several courtyards. On the left and right sides separated by vertical courtyards are vertical strip-shaped houses facing the middle route, which are symmetric and concise. The Antai Cuo (coffin shelter) in Taipei is a typical representative of large courtyard residence. As to Taiwan's structures, not only residences but also Confucian temples and monasteries are of the same style as Fujian. The concave curve of the house slope and the height of the two ends of the house ridge are very conspicuous, maintaining the antique style once popular in the central plain. The wood carvings are complicated, the gray plastic beautiful. The overwhelming majority of Taiwan residents moved from the mainland to Taiwan several hundred years ago, and most of them were from Fujian. The close similarity of the architectural style of the two regions sheds light on their Cultural identity.

Free-Style Residence in South China

Free-style residences refer to residences without courtyards, residences whose overall structure and single pattern are both very free. They are mostly distributed in the countryside and small towns in the south, and are mostly used by people of the medium and lower strata.

Free-style residences are mostly small in scale. Special attention is paid to the rational use of space, but the system of discipline rites featuring the elite, the lowly, the upper and lower levels, and the close and distant relationship is not particularly stressed. Its design idea is close to "functionalism". However, they still pursue the beauty of appearance, because they have thrown off the shackle of discipline rites, emancipated the mind, so that their combination is flexible and therefore they are more diversified in form. The molding characteristics of free-style residences are: Most of them are a building linked to both the plain and the roof. A variety of techniques are applied to create a rich space leading to all sides—upper, lower, left and right parts. Their outward side is open and exposed, without any courtyard wall and is integrated with nature. Their style is free, without paying attention to regulation and symmetry. They are constructed in the form either with the slope of the house being small in the front and large at the back; or with the house standing next to top single-storied house; or with the roof partly protruding as the attic; or with an over-hanged attic covered with wrapping eaves at some place on the outer wall; and the plane has various shapes such as a horizontal shape, zigzag shape and other. The inside space is varied and the board is set under the roof to make an attic which is either in the front or back slope, or in the middle. The ground varies with the different elevation of the base. Different rooms vary in height, and one and the same room is allowed not to be in the same plane, or one side and another side of a house not to be on the same floor. All materials used are mostly indigenous and economical products. The roof is covered with small gray tiles or thatch. Walls are set up with small gray bricks, woven fence and plastering lime, planks, riprap stones, riprap rocks or mud; uncolored wood and wall plaster are used according to need, forming a natural contrast between color, texture and quality sense. The naturally exposed wooden structure on the wall, demonstrating the alternate beauty of the structure, gives a kind of pure and artless interest.

Cave Dwelling in Northwest China

A cave dwelling is a special "structure", a useful space formed not by addition, but by subtraction, i.e., subtracting certain things in nature. A great number of cave dwelling residences are preserved in middle-west China, such as Henan, Shanxi, Shaanxi and Gansu Provinces. The Loess there has the depth extending from 100 to 200 meters. With little seepage and a very strong vertical nature, this provides a very good precondition for the development of cave dwellings. At the same time, the natural condition of dry weather, little rain, cold winter and limited timber also creates an opportunity for the development and continuity of cave dwellings which are warm in winter, cool in summer, very economical and require no timber in construction.

There are three kinds—cliff, ground and hoop cave dwellings. The cliff cave dwelling popular in mountainous and hills regions is an earth cave dug horizontally along the vertical earth cliff. Each cave is about 3-4 meters wide and 5-9 meters deep. The straight wall is about 2-3 meters high. The top of the cave is dug into a semi-circular or slotted barrel arch. The various caves can lead to each other through tunnels between them. It is also possible to add another cave upon the cave, and the upper and lower caves can be linked to each other through a passage. The ground cave dwelling in West Henan and South Shaanxi Plains is a square or rectangular pit dug out of the level ground to form a ground yard. Then, a cave is dug horizontally on various walls of the pit, and people go in and out of houses by earth

Cave Dwelling on Loess Platea in Northwest China

stairway. Several or a dozen of families live together. This kind of cave dwelling residence is still preserved in Liquan County near Xi'an in Shaanxi Province. A hoop cave dwelling popular in Jinzhong, Shanxi is not a real cave, but only a cave-shaped house put up with brick or adobe on the level ground modeled after a cave dwelling to create a courtyard. The combination of assembling residences is more flexible and the inside space is varied. The hoop cave dwelling can be a single story house or be a building. If the upper story is also a hoop dwelling, it is called a "dwelling upon a dwelling". If the upper storey is a wooden structured house, it is called a "dwelling upon a house".

Hakka Group Houses

Lingnan Hakka Group houses are a kind of large residence popular among the people called "Hakkas" in Lingnan (places south of the Five Ridges) including Fujian, Guangdong, southern Jiangxi Province and eastern Guangxi Zhuang Autonomous Region.

In Chinese history, there were two large-scale movements of the Han ethnic group, from the Central Plains to south China. They continuously advanced southward, settling in Lingnan areas south of the Five Ridges, which were then still quite backward. The clan lived in compact communities which formed themselves into Hakkas. Hakkas abided by the cultural tradition before their southward movement. They particularly follow the Confucian rites, worship ancestors, treasure clan unity, value their homeland and were patriotic and paid attention to geomancy, to form a special Hakka Culture. Hakkas group houses are the most characteristic expressions of Hakka Culture. In most cases, they embody the original look of the Han Culture in the central plains during the Jin and Tang dynasties. They are in a variety of forms, but mainly fall into some kinds –wu feng lou (five phoenix tower), tu lou (earthen tower), and wei long Wu (a dragon-encircled house). The common characteristics are large size, compact encirclement and a centripetal and symmetrical layout, housing a dozen to several dozen families of the same clan.

Wu Feng Lou (Five Phoenix Tower)

Wu Feng Lou consists of the lower hall, middle hall and main hall, called the three halls, arranged from the front to the back along the axial line of the whole residence. The lower hall is the vestibule, while the middle one is the big hall for clan get-together, and both are single storied. The main hall mostly consists of three to five stories. The center of the ground floor is the ancestral hall, erected with ancestral tablets. Its left, right and upper floors are living rooms for various families. The three halls are separated by a small yard, its left and right sides each having a wing hall which has passage leading to the horizontal house. The so-called horizontal house refers to the strip-shaped long house parallel to the axial line. It also serves as living rooms for various families, the number of floors increasing steadily from the front to the back, and finally, its height is close to that of the main hall. Centered on the main hall, the two horizontal houses look like the wings of a big bird surrounding and protecting the left and right sides. In a stretch manner, it looks like a phoenix spreading its wings, hence is called a "five-phoenix house". The area at the foot of the mountain, low in the front and high at the back, was selected for the Wu Feng Lou. The top of the house has a Chinese hip-and-gable roof. The slope of the house is rather leisurely, while the eave tip is flat and straight, and obviously retains many styles of the Han and Tang dynasties.

Tu Lou (Earthen Tower)

Tu Lou consists of square and round houses. Its characteristic is that the height of the first circle can reach as high as a five-storied house. Inside is a central courtyard. The ancestral hall is generally set up on the ground floor of the house on the axis facing the main door of the courtyard; or, a single-storied house is built within the courtyard to form the second ring or even the third, fourth and fifth ring. The ancestral hall is set up at the center of the central inner ring, which is a place for worshipping ancestors and holding clan grand ceremonies. The mud wall of the outer ring is exceptionally thick, often reaching as much as two meters or more. The first and second floors serve as the kitchen and granary. No window is opened to the outside, or only a very small perforation is allowed. The third floor and above have living rooms with windows, which can also be used for shooting, giving it a strong defensive character.

Yongding Yijinglou is the masterpiece of square house with the greatest vigor and the most outstanding design. The back building has five stories and four-story buildings are on other three sides. The side length is about 45 meters. A Sanheyuan with single-story house is built in the square house, with the ancestral hall on the axis and the small yard before the hall as the center. A front courtyard is built in front of the square house to set off the majesty and the main buildings with strong contrast.

Similar to the square house, the round house is round as a whole anyway. Yongding Chengqilou in Fujian is the representative. There are four circles outside with the diameter of 63 meters. Each circle has its own interior corridors. Within the two circles inside are all single-story houses. The ancestral hall is set up in the core round house.

Wei Long Wu (Dragon-Encircled House)

Wei Long encircled house is a residence construction most popular in Hakka residences in Guangdong. It has grand scale and blends traditional ritual rules, ethnic concepts, Yin-Yang and Five Elements, Feng Shui geography, philosophic ideology and architectural art.

The main body of such house is the main hall, i.e. the constructions on axis are square main halls of two or three halls. The halls are separated by small yards. The upper wide hall is the ancestral hall, the middle hall is the hall for clan get-together, and the lower hall with small depth is the rectangle vestibule. On two sides of the main hall there are supplementary ancestral temples where bright room, secondary room, tip room and end room are separated by allies. On two sides of the main hall are horizontal houses, and a semi-circle encircled house is built in the back to connect with the horizontal house. Inside the semi-circle is the Huatou. There are houses with two horizontal houses with one encircled dragon, or four horizontal houses with two encircled dragons and the largest one have ten horizontal houses with five encircled dragons. This kind of houses is mostly built depending on mountains, with low in front and high in the back. The main hall on axis is set off with magnificence. In front of the door there is a grain level ground with a low wall and semi-circle pond. Wei Long houses present a round shape as a whole, like the Bagua Diagram with Yin and Yang. It has the meaning that sky is round and earth is square.

The Hakka Wei Long Wu (Dragon-Encircled House) in Meixian County, Guangdong Province

Bridges and Architecture

In some cases the combination of bridges with architectural complex or environment can set off some connotation of spiritual culture.

The five stone arched bridges (Jinshui Bridge) in front of the Tian'anmen of the Forbidden City in Beijing face exactly the five gates. The one in the middle is the largest and others are smaller and smaller in order. Along with the Tian'anmen and surrounding environment, the bridges compose the entrance of the palace, which strengthen the vigor of architecture of imperial power. Small bridges are often set up before temples to manifest the importance of the architecture. The bridges in gardens must have close combination with view sights and the requirements for pretty mode are higher. The bridges along with other scenes in the garden create a tranquil and elegant atmosphere. These bridges have surpassed the meaning of practical usage. It is preferred to view them as architectural sketches rather than communication structures.

In terms of materials bridges can be divided into two kinds, stone bridges and wooden bridges. In terms of numbers of stride of the bridges, they can be divided into arched bridges and girder bridges. Arched bridges are mostly stone ones with a few wooden ones which are called "folded girder arched bridges". As to girder bridges, there are flat girder bridges and arm girder bridges; the former ones are made of stones or wood while the latter ones are in wooden structure. Bridge corridors or pavilions can be built on the surface of all kinds of bridges to create a special architecture called as corridor bridges. In short, bridges have various shapes to satisfy different demands in different occasions. Most of bridges have attaching ornamental architecture such as memorial archways at bridge ends. The famous stone arched bridge in front of Qionghua Island in Beihai Lake in Beijing has a large-scale memorial archway on each end. Ornamental columns, sutra columns and small stone towers are often built near bridges, such as Baodai Bridge in Suzhou, Wuli Bridge in Quanzhou and Luoyang Bridge.

Zhaozhou Bridge

Zhaozhou Bridge, the oldest stone arched bridge in China, is also named Anji Bridge and was five li (2.5 km) from present-day Zhao County in Hebei Province. Zhaozhou Bridge was built by the famous craftsman Li Chun during the period of Daye (605-618) in the Sui Dynasty. The river under the bridge is a tiny stream which cannot open for ships, but the river surface is very wide, so the bridge opening must have a large span but need not be high. The flat Zhaozhou Bridge without stairs can represent the style of northern stone arched bridges.

With the length of 64.04 meters, the span of 37.02 meters and the top width of 8.51 meters, Zhaozhou Bridge is the single-opening and open-shoulder stone arched bridge with the largest span and the longest history in the world. As there are two small arches on two shoulders of the arch, it is called open-shoulder. This design can save materials and reduce the weight of the bridge (by 15 percent), as well as increase the sluice area for the river under the bridge. It is an original creation in the history of building bridges in the world.

Zhaozhou Bridge has a history of 1,400 years and has experienced 10 floods, 8 battles and several earthquakes. In particular, in 1966 the 7.6-degree earthquake in Xingtai, over 40 km away, did not destroy the bridge where the earthquake was more than 4 degrees. Mao Yisheng, the famous bridge expert, said, not saying the interior structure, the history of over 1,300 years can explain all. According to records, Zhaozhi Bridge has been rebuilt for 8 times since its construction.

Dr Lee Joseph, the famous English expert on the history of science, in his book Science and Civilization in China once listed 26 items of scientific and technological achievements introduced to Europe from China from the first century to the 18th, of which the 18th item was the circular arc bridge.

Luoyang Bridge

Luoyang Bridge, a cross-ocean girder stone bridge, is located on the Luoyang River in the east suburb of Quanzhou City, Fujian Province and is the starting of bridge raft basis in the world. The Luoyang Bridge was a huge stone bridge across the Luoyang River to connect with the sea built by Cai Xiang as the holder who was the prefect of Quanzhou between the fifth year (1053) of period of Huanghu to the fourth year (1059) of the period of Jiayou in the Northern Song Dynasty. According to historical records, at the beginning, the bridge was 1,200 meters long and 5 meters wide with warrior statues standing on two sides. The building project was very grand and the structure and crafts were superb.

Over 900 years, this bridge has been rebuilt for 17 times. The present bridge is 731.29 meters long, 4.5 meters wide, and 7.3 meters high, with 44 raft-shape piers, 645 railings, 104 stone lions, 1 stone pavilion and 7 stone towers. Nearby the pavilion on the bridge are forests of inscribed steles including "Wan Gu An Lan" and other stone inscriptions. To the north of the bridge are ruins of Zhaohui Temple and Zhenshen Nunnery. To the south is the Caixiang Temple and the famous Song inscription of Records of Wan'an Bridge by Cai Xiang is set there, which is called "three excellence" in calligraphy, article and engravings.

Anping Bridge

Anping Bridge, the longest stone bridge in ancient China, is also called Wuli Bridge and located at Anhai Town, 30 km away from Quanzhou City, Fujian Province. It crosses the beach and connects with Nan'an Shuitou Town on the opposite bank. According to Records of Quanzhou Prefecture, "In the eighth year (1138) of Shaoxing Period of the Song Dynasty Seng Zupai started to build the bridge but could not complete it. In the 21st year (1151), Zhao Lingjin, the prefect, completed it." The project spent 13 years and it is a girder long bridge constructed by granite. After the completion of the Anping Bridge, Zhao Lingjin wrote, "It is 2,255 meters long and more than 5 meters wide, with 362 drainage ways." In the east, west and middle parts of the bridge there are five "rest pavilions". On both sides there are railings and there are also cultural relics such as stone towers and stone general statues, etc. The bridge piers of the Anping Bridge have three kinds: rectangle, semi-boat and boat shapes. The bridge base adopts the method of laying sleepers alternatively on gravels and then the bridge piers were built on the sleepers, widely different from the raft-shape bases of the Luoyang Bridge.

Guangji Bridge

According to historical records the Guangji Bridge is th earliest active stone bridge. Located to east of Chaozhou City, Guangdong Province, the bridge crosses the Hanjiang River and is one of the famous bridges in ancient China. The construction started in the sixth year (1170) of the Gandao Period of the Southern Song Dynasty and took 57 years to complete it. It is 515 meters long and is divided into east and west sections with 18 piers. The middle section is about a hundred meters wide. As the water under the section is rapid, the bridge was not built there and only ferry was possible there. It was called Jizhou Bridge at that time. In the tenth year (1435) of the Xuande Period of the Ming Dynasty 5 piers were added and it was called Guangji Bridge. In the period of Zhengde, another pier was added, and then the total piers were 24. The piers were piled up by granite. In the middle section 18 shuttle boats were connected to form a floating bridge which could open and close. When big boats and wooden crafts passed, the floating boats could be untied for them to pass and later be put to original place. It is the first large active stone bridge in the world. The bridge had been rebuilt for 5 times in the Ming Dynasty and

Guangji Bridge

24 watchtowers of different shapes were built on the piers (which had been destroyed, only seen in the bridge history of China). In the first year (1723) of Yongzheng Period of the Qing Dynasty two iron ox were placed on the stone bridge piers at the two ends of the floating bridge. The four characters "zhen qiao yu shui" (safeguarding the bridge and preventing flood) inscribed on the ox backs had disappeared. In 1958 due to demands of traffic, the shuttle boats were dismantled and it was changed to a bridge straight to two banks. In 1980 an iron ox was made to place on the bridge.

Lugou Bridge

Lugou Bridge, the extant oldest stone linked arch bridge in Beijing, is located in west of Beijing, some 20 km away from the downtown. It crosses the Lugou River (present-day Yongding River), hence its name. The construction of the Lugou Bridge started in the 29th year (1189) of Dading Period of the Jin Dynasty and it has a history of over 800 years. This bridge crosses the Lugou ferry which was the only door of entrance and exit of the city. Lugou Bridge is 266.5 meters long and 9.3 meters wide on the surface. The bridge body was piled up by huge white stones. The piers were built to boat shape with water parting points named "sword of chopping dragon" in front to defend floods. The architectural design of the bridge is advanced and the construction is excellent. The architectural ornaments on the bridge are unique. The railing is 281 watching columns of nearly 1.5 meters high which are connected with the railing board. On each watching column there is a stone lion with small lions in different images on the back of it or hidden in it. So there is an allegorical saying in folk that "the stone lions on the Lugou Bridge are countless." Later according to the survey of archaeological personnel, there are 485 known large and small lions on it.

Yueyang Tower

The Yueyang Tower is on the west bank of Dongting Lake in Yueyang, Hunan Province. As many famous poems and essays in ancient China have mentioned the name of the Yueyang Tower, it has enjoyed a high reputation across the country. The major body of the Yueyang Tower built up in the Song Dynasty had disappeared long ago and modern people can only get knowledge about it from the extant blueprint of Yueyang Tower of the Southern Song Dynasty. The extant Yueyang Tower was rebuilt in the fifth year (1879) of Qing Dynasty Emperor Guangxu's reign, outside of the west city walls of Yueyang, facing the west with back to east, facing Dongting Lake and looking at the Junshan Mountain far away. The plane of the tower is rectangular, its frontage consisting of three rooms, surrounded by corridors. The three stories have three eaves, with a total height of nearly 20 meters. On top of the tower are four sloping helmet-shaped roofs, the upper part of the roofing being convex and the lower part concave. It is China's existing largest helmet-roofed structure, covered with yellow glazed tiles, the wing corner being upturned. The left and right sides before the tower stand parallel with the tower in the shape of "品", with the Sanzui Pavilion and the Xianmei Pavilion serving as a foil.

Chinese Towers and Pavilions

Different from Gothic architecture in Europe, Chinese towers and pavilions are very wide. The inside and outside spaces are connected and penetrated with each other. The corridors are encircled in them for people to look far in them. The horizontal layers of eaves and the circled corridors and railings greatly reduce the tendency of uprising simply of the vertical body shape and make the architecture look back at the ground to respond with nature. The some zigzag house roofing and bended house corners avoid the stiffness and coldness of the mode. Being laid prettily in the nature, the architecture seems to be a part of the heaven and earth, expressing people's infinite thinking of nature. Many poems distinctively express such humanistic spirit to towers and pavilions, such as the classical poem of Li Bai, "Mountains cover the white sun, And oceans drain the golden river; But you widen your view three hundred miles By going up one flight of stairs." This poem expresses the sincere feeling of the poet to climb up the tower and look far away with cleared vision. This connotation can also be found in various meaningful names of the towers and pavilions, such as Wanghai Lou (watching sea tower), Jianshan Lou (Seeing mountain tower), Kanyun Lou (Watching clouds tower), Deyue Lou (Catching moon tower), Yanyu Lou (misty rain tower), Qingfeng Lou (cool breeze tower), Lingyun Ge (reaching clouds pavilion), and Xizhao Ge (evening glow pavilion).

In the history, except those towers and pavilions possessed by temples and palaces, most of the architectures with high fame were built in scenic spots or artificial gardens for tour, such as the three famous southern towers, Huanghe Tower, Tengwang Pavilion and Yueyang Tower. The sites of them are often close to rivers or lakes at the suburb of cities, convenient for people to look far in distant scenes and close to cities. It is easy to "get scenes", the sizes and modes had been thought over and the architecture has a harmonious responding to the nature. Those towers and pavilions also supplement the beauty of nature as the objects for viewing, called as "made scenes".

Huanghe Tower

Huanghe Tower stands on the southern bank of the Yangtze River in Wuchang, Hubei. Legend has it that the tower was initially built during the Three Kingdoms period, although it began to become well known during the Tang Dynasty. This was mainly attributed to poet Cui Hao's verse which reads, "Riding the yellow crane, ancients have gone away, here only the Huanghe Tower remains". The Picture of Huanghe Tower, a Song Dynasty painting, vividly captures its appearance in the Song Dynasty. The Huanghe Tower is built on a platform, under which trees provide pleasant shade from where one can look into the distance and see a vast expanse of misty, rolling water. The central main tower consists of two stories. The plane is of a square form, the left and right sides on the lower floor protruding out, while the verandas on the front and back are linked to the wing-tower. The top of the whole tower is well-arranged, with jagged wing-corners, giving it a magnificent appearance. After the Song Dynasty, Huanghe Tower was repeatedly destroyed and

Huanghe Tower

rebuilt. Reconstructed in the seventh year (1868) of Emperor Tongzhi's reign, it existed only a dozen years or so. The tower, however, no longer consisted of many structures towering above a high platform as shown in the Song picture. Instead, a centralized plane was adopted standing above the city walls. The plane is of an angle cross. There are three stories apparently but six stories actually with a total height of 32 meters. The middle and lower eaves have 12 highly turn-up house corners.

Tengwang Pavilion

Tengwang Pavilion, located by the Ganjiang River on Yangjiang Road in Nanchang City, Jiangxi Province, was initially built up in the fourth year (653) of Yonghui period of the Tang Dynasty. It got its name renown to generations owing to the famous and iridescent essay Prelude of Tengwang Pavilion by Wang Bo, a man of letters in the Tang Dynasty. After Wang Bo, Wang Xu in the Tang Dynasty wrote Ode to Tengwang Pavilion and Wang Zhongshu wrote Record of Tengwang Pavilion, which are called "records of Tengwang Pavilion by three Wangs" in the historical books and became a much-told story.

Over 1,300 odd years, Tengwang Pavilion has been destroyed and rebuilt for 28 times. The extant Tengwang Pavilion was rebuilt by Nanchang People's Government in 1989, the 29th time of rebuilding. It is an architecture imitating the Song style. According to the blueprint painted by Liang Sicheng, the famous Chinese architect, in 1942, and the Song picture Tengwang Pavilion collected in Tianlai Pavilion, the extant one was designed and built up, also getting reference to Model of Architecture, a book of the Song Dynasty. The main body of the tower covers a space of 13,000 square meters, 57.5 meters high with 9 stories. The base is a high dado of 12 meters high, symbolizing ancient city walls. The main architecture has red columns, green tiles, painted ridgepoles, high eaves, and layers of brackets. The vertical face looks like the Chinese character "山" (mountain) uprising to the sky, and the horizontal face looks like a huge kunpeng (legendary fish and bird) opening wings to fly.

Tengwang Pavilion

Pagoda (Bao Ta)

Pagoda is a kind of traditional Chinese architecture. On the vast land of China well-preserved ancient pagodas can be found everywhere.

In fact the prototype and the religious meaning of the pagoda were introduced into China from India. The Chinese word "Ta" is the transliteration of a Sanskrit of India. Its original function in India was a tomb wherein were buried the bones of Sakyamuni. After it was introduced to China, its meaning was expanded. The extant Chinese pagodas are production of combining Chinese and Indian architectural arts. The ancient towers of China have various types. In terms of appearance, the earliest square shape has developed to hexagonal, octagonal, round shapes and other shapes. In terms of materials, there are wooden, brick, stone, iron, bronze, and glaze towers, and even gold, silver and pearl towers. The number of stories of Chinese pagodas is usually odd number from five to thirteen. Most of Chinese Buddhist pagodas are in types of towers and dense eaves. They were built up by combining the prototypes of Indian pagodas and the great number of towers and pavilions in the Han Dynasty of China. It is fair to say they are crystallization of ntional and foreign craftsmen. The extant famous ancient pagodas include Dayan Pagoda in Xi'an, Wooden Pagoda in Ying County, Shanxi Province, Iron Pagoda in Kaifeng, Henan Province, Brick Pagoda of Kaiyuan Temple in Ding County, Hebei Province, Liuhe Pagoda in Hangzhou, and Glaze Pagoda in Fragrant Hills in Beijing. These ancient pagodas reflect the long history and superb architectural art in China, and also set off the beauty of China's landscape.

Dayan Pagoda

Dayan Pagoda, with the full name of "Ji'en Temple Dayan Pagoda", is located in the Ji'en Temple 4km away from downtown of Xi'an City in Shaanxi Province. It was originally built in 652. Legend has it that the first abbot of Ji'en Temple, Master Xuanzang (Tang Sanzang) personally designed and supervised the construction of the pagoda for offering sacrifice and reserving Sanskrit sutras, Buddhist figures and Buddhist relics after he returned back from India. Emperors Gaozong and Taizong of the Tang Dynasty personally wrote down the steles, Datang Sanzang Shengjiao Xu Bei (Stele of Prelude to Holy Religion of Sanzang of the Tang Dynasty) and Shu Sanzang Shengjiao Xu Ji

Dayan Pagoda in Xi'an City, Shaanxi Province

Bei (Recording Stele of Telling Holy Religion of Sanzong). Dayan Pagoda is a brick pagoda in type of towers. It is moer than 64 meters high and side of the pagoda base in 25 meters long. It has 7 stories. The pagoda body is in shape of square cone. The pagoda was built up by linking polished bricks and the brick wall can show prisms which can be used to separate bays, with traditional style of Chinese architecture. Dayan Pagoda is the symbol architecture in Xi'an City. In recent years due to urban environment issues in Xi'an, the pagoda has inclined for more than 1 meter.

Wooden Pagoda in Ying County

The Sakyamuni Pagoda (popular known as Wooden Pagoda in Ying County) in Fogong Temple in Ying County in north Shanxi Province is the extant largest and oldest wooden pagoda in the world. It was originally built up in the second year (1056) of the Qingning Period of the Liao Dynasty and has a history of more than 950 years.

The Wooden Pagoda in Ying County is 67.31 meters high and has nine stories including five clearly-seen ones and four hidden ones. It equals to the height of a building of 20 stories at present. The plane is in octagonal shape and the diameter of the ground floor is 30.27 meters. About 10,000 cubic meters of timbers have been used with the total weight of 7,430 tons. The pagoda has used 54 brackets and it is called "Bracket Museum of Chinese Ancient Architecture". The Wooden Pagoda in Ying County well preserved the architectural style of traditional higher wooden buildings of the Liao Dynasty and reflects the outstanding achievements of Chinese ancient wooden architecture. Meanwhile it is called "a three-dimensional Buddhist sutra" by Buddhist disciples. In the clearly-seen stories inside the pagoda there are statues. On the first ground the statue of Sakyamuni is grand and solemn and the arched roof gives people a feeling of unpredictable heaven. In the walls on the ground floor are six figures of Buddha with proper size and brilliant color. The flying goddesses on both sides of the six Buddhas' heads are lively and vividly and are excellent murals rarely seen. On the second floor, as the light can come in from eight directions, a main Buddha, two Bodhisattvas and two companions stand there vividly. On the third floor, Four-direction Buddha is set up to face four directions. On the fifth floor, the sitting statue of Sakyamuni is set at the center with Eight Great Bodhisattavs sitting in eight directions. It is believed by local monks in Ying County that each story of the pagoda tells a different meaning about Buddhist sutras.

In 2006 Wooden Pagoda in Ying County has been listed into the preliminary list of world heritage recommended by China.

Iron Pagoda in Kaifeng

The Iron Pagoda is located in the Tieta Garden in northeast corner of Kaifeng, Henan Province. As the pagoda body is inlaid with brown glaze bricks, it looks like the color of iron. Hence the name of Iron Pagoda. The pagoda was built up in the first year (1049) of Huangyou period of the Northern Song Dynasty and it is also called Kaibao Temple Pagoda as it is in the Kaibao Temple.

The Iron Pagoda is in equilateral octagonal shape. It is 56.88 meters high and has 13 stories. The each face of the ground floor is 4.16 meters wide and the width reduces gradually upward. The body of the pagoda is covered with colored glaze and the bricks were engraved with vivid designs of more than 50 varieties such as flying goddess, kylin, Bodhisattva, female dancers and lions. With elegant shapes and vivid manners, they can be viewed as masterpiece of brick-carving art of the Song Dynasty. It is astonished to find that these glaze bricks have tenons, mortises, and grooves like timbers cut by axes. According to statistics 28 standard and exquisitely designed brick models have been used on the outer side of the pagoda, which are piled up tightly. Windows are set on the body; the windows in north of the first floor, in south of the second floor, in west of the third floor and in east of the fourth floor are clearly-seen windows and others are hidden windows. 104 bells are hung below the eaves. When wind blows, they will create pleasant sound. There are 168 stairs piled up by bricks inside, up to the top by circling the center of the pagoda.

Three Pagodas in Dali

Three Pagodas in Dali, Yunnan Province

There are three pagodas in Chongsheng Temple in Dali, Yunnan Province. The main pagoda is called Qianxun Pagoda, and the two smaller ones are called South Pagoda and North Pagoda. They are called "Three Pagodas of Chongsheng Temple" generally, or "Three Pagodas in Dali". The three pagodas stand together in the shape of Chinese character "品", and are symbol of the ancient city, Dali.

Qianxun Pagoda is a square brick pagoda with dense eaves. It has 16 stories and the mode seems like that of Xiaoyan Pagoda in Xi'an. It is one of the typical pagoda modes of the Tang Dynasty. The heart of the pagoda is empty. In the ancient time there was a stair in shape of Chinese character "井", by which people could climb up. At four corners of the top, there is a bronze roc respectively. Legend has it that they can beat down the water monsters in the Erhai Lake. Looking far to the east from the pagoda, one can see the whole scene of the Erhai Lake. The South and North smaller pagodas on two sides of the main one are both 42 meters high. They are a pair of octagonal brick pagodas with 10 stairs. The three pagodas compose one integrated mass with grand vigor and the national style of primitive simplicity. There are various sayings about the building time of the three pagodas. It is commonly believed that Qianxun Pagoda was built during the Nanzhao Kingdom period (823-859) of the Tang Dynasty. According to the determination of the time of the timbers of the pagodas the time for building was earlier than the Tang Dynasty. But in terms of the economic basis and technical conditions, it is only possible for the pagoda to be built in the period of Qiyao Kaicheng in late Nanzhao time. The south and north pagodas were added after the completion of the main pagoda, during the Emperor Huizong's reign (1101-1125) of the Song Dynasty.

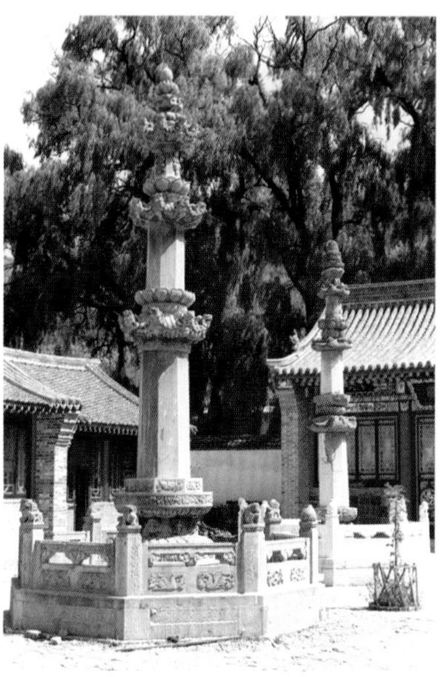

• Sutra Columns

Sutra columns is a kind of new Buddhist architecture emerged in late 7th century, originating from ancient banners and flags.

Due to the introduction of Indian Buddhism and especially the introduction of "True Word" Sect in mid Tang Dynasty, people started to write Buddhist sutras or Buddhist images down on silk banners and flags. To keep them long and well, people changed to engrave them on stone columns.

Dharani sutra is frequently engraved down. So they are called sutra columns. Sutra columns often consist of top, body and base. The principal part is the body, engraved with sutras, and the base and top are engraved with flowers, clouds and Buddha and Bodhisattva figures. Usually they are in shapes of column, hexagon and octagon. The number of sutra columns reached its peak during the Northern and Southern Song (960-1279) of the Five Dynasties. They were usually set along roads and in temples, or along mausoleum path, in tombs or near tombs. The sutra columns in China were mostly made of stones and iron ones are rarely seen. The extant sutra columns are represented by the sutra columns of the Norther Song Dynasty (960-1127) in Zhao County, Hebei Province.

Mausoelum

The mausoleum specifically refers to a type of structure for burying emperors, with the top of the tomb smeared with mud. Born in the prehistoric period and worshipped by primitive ancestors, they achieved refinement through the Confucianism and formed their own types and styles.

Confucianism placed special emphasis on filial piety. Filial piety applied not only during the lifetime of the family elders but also after their death.

After their death, the tomb is their residence in another world, called "yin (negative) residence" to which full, and even more attention, should be paid than when the person occupied the "yang (positive) residence". This was even truer in the case of imperial mausoleums. In ancient hierarchical society, there were, of course, insurmountable differences in rank regarding tomb size. In the size and quantity of palatial halls, houses or utensils, the thickness of the coffin, and the size of the grave, rank should be clearly defined. The more respectable the person, the bigger the tomb and the more graves were set up for them. The most important thing expressing one's rank was the size of the grave, and size has always been a vitally important factor in architectural art. Therefore, the grave of the monarch was particularly high and large, and was called either a "mausoleum" or "imperial tomb". The original meaning of "mausoleum" was a high and big mountain. The graves for other persons, being smaller, were called "graves", "tablets" or "tombs"and referred merely to an earth mound. From the Qin and Han until the Ming and Qing dynasties, the emperors' tombs were always covered with a huge mound. There was a distinguishing feature in the Tang dynasty mausoleum, in that the entire mausoleum district was modeled on the capital city. The design of the mausoleum, like the capital city, was permeated with ritual logic, so as to give prominence to the dignity of the imperial authority. The Ming and Qing dynasties paid still higher attention to, and recorded still greater achievements, in the application of geomancy. Their shape and structure were somewhat different from those witnessed in the Han, Tang and Song dynasties, the Ming Tombs and the East and West Mausoleums of the Qing Dynasty being famous examples.

Qinshihuang Mausoleum

The Mausoleum of First Emperor of the Qin Dynasty is located at Xiahe Village about 5km to the east of Lintong County in Shaanxi Province. It is the first imperial mausoleum in the history of China and is also the large emperor's mausoleum.

The owner of the mausoleum, Qinshihuang, is an unusual figure in Chinese history. In 221 BC. he established the first centralized unitarianism feudal court in Chinese history. He called himself "Shihuangdi" (first emperor). And later people call him "one emperor through the ages". The Qingshihuang Mausoleum is located at the northern foot of the Lishan Mountain in Lintong, Shaanxi Province. The construction of the mausoleum started soon after the emperor ascended his throne. More than 700,000 persons, that is one tenth of all the young labors at that time, were used to build the mausoleum and it lasted for over 40 years. The construction did not finish when the emperor died in 206 BC. The major body of the mausoleum is a three-floor pounded earthen terrace in shape of square taper. The appearance seems like pyramid. The original one was about 120 meters high, but after over 2,000 years of erosion from wind and rain, it is nearly 50 meters high at present. The Qin Mausoleum was originally a mausoleum garden, but now many ground constructions had disappeared. According to archaeological discoveries, its structure and layout completely followed the design of Xianyang City; the ground palace symbolizes the imperial palace and the inner city and outer city symbolize the palace town and outer town of the imperial palace respectively. The whole mausoleum along with the attaching tomb region covers a space of more than 60 square km, wider than the present-day Xi'an City. The Qinshihuang Mausoleum is surrounded by more than 400 accompanied pits and tombs, covering an area of 56.25 square km. In 1974 archaeological staff found three pits containing terracotta warriors and horses outside of the east gate of the mausoleum, which astonished the whole world.

Guanzhong Eighteen Mausoleums

The Tang Dynasty witnessed the second climax in the construction of mausoleums in China, following Qin and Han dynasties. As to the 21 emperors of the Tang Dynasty including Wuzetian, there are so-called Guanzhong 18 mausoleums on the northern bank of the Weishui River in Shaanxi Province except that Emperor Gaozong and Wuzetian were buried together and the last two emperors were buried in Henan and Shandong Provinces.

Tang Dynasty imperial mausoleums are mostly built at the foot of mountains. Tombs were set up in the rocks on naturally isolated mountains, and their great momentum surpassed manually earth-sealed graves. Take Qianling, where Emperor Gaozong is buried together with Wuzetian, for example. Qianling is about 70 meters above the path leading to tombs before the mausoleum, and so is much more magnificent than Qin and Han dynasties grave mounds which generally are only 20-30 meters above the path.

Tang Dynasty tombs inherited and even developed the tradition of Han Dynasty tombs, with doors on four sides, forming a magnificent picture of the superficial characteristics of an imperial residence. Square walls were built around the mausoleum hills, called the inner city. In the middle of the four sides are doors, with an arched gateway. In the four corners are watchtowers. Within the Zhuque (rose finch) Gate, which is the south gate, is a worship hall where grand worship ceremonies were held. Outside the Zhuque Gate is a 3-4 km-long path leading to the tombs. At the southernmost end is a pair of earthen watchtowers, behind which is a door, from which one goes northward to reach the second pair of earthen water towers and the second door, several hundred meters from the Zhuque Door. From there, one goes further to the third pair of earthen water towers in front of the Zhuque Door. In the vast area between the first and second layer of doors are scattered numerous Subordinated tombs. The greatest number of these, 167, is in the Zhaoling Mausoleum of Emperor Taizong. Zhaoling Mausoleum and Zhenling Mausoleum of Emperor Xuanzong have a circumference of 60 km. The scope of the entire mausoleum area is very great, surpassing the walled city of Chang'an. Second comes the Qianling Mausoleum, with a circumference of 40 km, equivalent to Chang'an. And then come various tombs with circumferences ranging from 10-30 km. Among the various tombs, the Qianling Mausoleum is best preserved.

Ming Xiaoling Mausoleum

Ming Xiaoling Mausoleum is the mausoleum of Zhu Yuanzhang (reign in 1368-1398), the first emperor in the Ming Dynasty, and his wife Empress Ma. Ming Xiaoling Mausoleum is located at the Zhongshan Mountain in Nanjing City, Jiangsu Province. It is called the head of Ming mausoleums.

Originally Ming Xiaoling Mausoleum was the site of Linggu Temple. When Zhu

The grand stone archway at the entrance of the Ming Tombs

Yuanzhang selected this geomantic precious land as his mausoleum, the temple was forced to move out and the mausoleum was built there. Xiaoling Mausoleum relies on the whole Zhongshan Mountain as its region and covers a space with a diameter of about 20 to 30 km. It has a very large scale. The Dismounting Lane is the entrance of the Xiaoling Mausoleum. On its horizontal tablet engraves six big characters in regular script, meaning "All the officers dismount here". So all the civil and military officers who visited the mausoleum must dismount the horse and walk on foot. In the northwest of the Square City, the Sacred Way lies at the other side of the Yuhe Bridge. Twelve couples of stone animals are arranged on both sides of the Sacred Way: lion, Xiezhi (a legendary animal), camel, elephant, kylin, horse, four for each kind with two squatting and two standing. The last part of the mausoleum is the Treasure City, in which the huge earthen hillock, called Treasure Top, is round instead of the shape of overturned funnel followed for pasty dynasties after the Qin and Han dynasties. Under the Treasure City lie the tombs of the Emperor and Empress.

Ming Dynasty Tombs

Ming Dynasty tombs are located in two places. One is at the Zhongshan Mountain in Nanjing, and is called Ming Xiaoling Mausoleum of Zhu Yuanzhang. The other is at the foot of Tianshou Mountain in north Changping, Beijing, where 13 emperors after Zhu Di are buried, and called the Ming Tombs. Under the Ming tomb system, grave mounds are changed into round earth mounds, called "baoding". The front axis of the tee is a series of courtyards which emphasizes the in-depth composition of the axis. On both sides of the path leading to the Ming tombs are many stone carvings, called Shixiangsheng, which changed the way of not setting stone sculptures there in the tombs of the Southern Song Dynasty. An additional grand stone archway was built about 1,300 meters outside the entrance, moving the starting-point of the mausoleum area ahead. The stone archway consists of six pillars and five houses, rich in outline, varied in height and size and, with a width of 30 meters, and it is China's largest archway. The huge pillars stand majestically upright in the open countryside, making it look very magnificent.

Changling Mausoleum

The Changling Mausoleum is the tomb of Ming Chengzu, emperor Zhu Di, which is in the center of the Ming Tombs. The three courtyards in the front and at the back of the Changling Tomb are of the same width, and are encircled by high walls. The Lingen Hall, the key structure in the second courtyard, is at the rear. Its shape and structure are the same as the Taihe Hall. The frontal width of Lingen Hall is slightly bigger than that of Taihe hail, but the former's depth is shallower. It is the second largest hall existing in China. Under the hall, there are three layers of stone platforms encircled by stone balustrades. The 32 large pillars inside the hall are all made with super-quality gold filigreed nanmu timber. The largest four pillars are each 1.17 meters in diameter and 12 meters high. The various pillars show the true color of the xylon: deep, elegant and solemn. Originally there were wing-halls on the left and right at front of the hall, but they have long since disappeared. The third courtyard door to the north of the hall is called Neihong Door, similar to gate of the mausoleum. The last construction, looking like a tower, is called square city and soul tower. From the Shijuan Cave below the square city platform, one can climb to the top of the platform on which the soul tower is built. Inside the soul tower a cross juandong is laid, and a big monument engraved with Chinese characters meaning "Mausoleum of Emperor Chengzu of the Ming Dynasty" is erected which serves as a stone-tablet pavilion. Behind the tower is a tee about 250 meters in diameter.

Changling Mausoleum

The Architectural Art of Uygur Ethnic Group

Among Uygur architecture, Islamic architectural achievements are the greatest. Islam originated in Arabia in the seventh century and was gradually introduced into China's Xinjiang during the 10th century (Ming Dynasty) and became popular with the Uygurs. Uygur Islamic architecture includes Salat monastery and holy spirit tomb, and their molding style is quite different from Han structures. The layout of a Salat monastery is free, only requiring that the Salat half must be sited in the west and face east. Believers, while praying before the holy niche in the wall at the back of the Salat hall, also face Masjid al-Haram in Mecca. The holy spirit tomb is also called "mazha", where religious personages making contributions to Islam were buried.

Bangke Building (Tower) inside the Mosque in Xining, Qinghai Province

• Bangke Building (Tower)

Bangke is the transliteration of the Persian word Bānk, meaning "summon" and "awoke". There is another transliteration, Banke, i.e. wakening ritual. The Bangke Building is an architecture particularly of Islam and is the attaching building for Mosque. It is a kind of tower-building standing on two sides of the Salat Hall. The Bangke Building is higher than Mosque and is also called Light Tower, Wakening Building and Minerate, where Akhun climbs up to call believers to do salat and read sutras.

Aitiga Mosque in Kashgar

Kashgar(kashi) a large city in the westernmost part of China, is the first place to accept Islam. Since ancient time it has been a place frequented by merchants, pilgrims and envoys of China and various countries in Mid Asia. Aitiga Mosque within the city was built about 500 years ago, but the existing appearance of the mosque was formed in the latter half of the 19th century. It is China's largest Islamic Salat mosque. Sitting in west and facing east, Aitiga Mosque has its front gate open to the southeast corner. The arch over the gateway is laid up with bricks; the front wall is of a vertical rectangular shape, and the middle is a large pointed arch niche. On the left and right sides of the arch, the courtyard wall is connected to two minarets, on top of which is a small pavilion with a dome. The left courtyard wall is very short, with a fairly sturdy minaret; the right wall is rather long, with a fine, small minaret. A disproportionate balanced composition is thus achieved. On the surface of the courtyard wall there are also pointed arch shallow niches. On the elevation, the constant appearance of many pointed arches and arch tops of various sizes emphasize the unity of molding techniques. The salat hall, sitting in west and facing east, is on the west side of the courtyard, consisting of outer and inner halls. The Outer hall is very long and completely open to the front. The wooden pillar, dense beam and flat-top structure already existed locally in ancient times. The three sides of the inner hall are flanked by the outer halls. There is a door opening in the middle of the front wall with very exquisite gypsum geometric patterns.

Turpan Emin Mosque

The Turpan Emin Mosque, also built in the early part (mid 17th century) of the Qing Dynasty, is located on a vast stretch of tableland. The most attractive point of the whole mosque is a tall brick pagoda, Emin Mosque, towering in one corner adjacent to the mosque. The mosque is 44 meters high and has a tapering shape, leading to a small dome pavilion at the top. The outline of the mosque is perfectly round. The structure was accomplished in one go, and is very simple and unaffected. Uneven floral bricks were laid up exquisitely and distributed in a ring shape on the exterior. There are more than 10 patterns, which are succinct and natural. To the front of the mosque is a tall house wall, its composition resembling ordinary salat mosques with a pointed arch shrine at the center surrounded by small shrines. The shadow inside the shrine and the exposed skies give it an added open and bright atmosphere. The whole mosque, including a big pagoda and house walls, is laid up with ecru bricks instead of glazed bricks and gypsum patterns popular in Xinjiang, hence its simplicity and solemnity.

The vertical and perfectly round tall pagoda and the horizontal salat mosque formed with straight lines achieve a rich contrast between round and square, curve and straight line, high and low, and vertical and level. The front part of the house wall is protruding and slightly elevated appropriately adding some change. The courtyard wall between the house wall and the big pagoda is short, while the other side is relatively long, and although not symmetrical, they are even. The whole Emin Mosque presents a single color and is in perfect coordination with the surrounding loess, reaching a high degree of harmony with the environment.

The Architectural Art of Tibetan Buddhism

Among Tibet's buildings, the achievement of Tibetan Buddhist buildings is the highest. In the seventh century, the Tubo Tsampo Kingdom emerged on the Tibetan Plateau. Along with the development of Tibet's relationship with the inland areas and Southeast Asia, Buddhism

Turpan Emin Mosque

was introduced from India to China.

The two wives of Songsang Gampo, king of Tubo Tsampo, namely, Princess Wencheng of the Tang Dynasty (entered Tibet in 641) and Princess Chizun of Nepal, both worshipped Buddhism. And in particular Princess Wencheng promoted the introduction of Buddhism. Organized personally by Princess Wencheng, the Reshazu Lakang, the first Buddhist structure in Tibet, built in Rosa (present-day Lhasa), is the predecessor of the still existing Jokhang Monastery. In the year 762, Khri-sron-btsan, king of Tubo Tsampo built Tibet's first formal temple, Samye Monastery, and seven Tibetan youths were tonsured to become monks. After the introduction of Buddhism, a primitive religion of Tibet, the Bon religion, was later blended with Buddhism. In addition, due to the strong influence of Tantrism of Indian Buddhism and elements of Hinduism, Tibetan Buddhism developed a very strong mystical color obviously different from Buddhism in the inland areas. In Tibetan Buddhism, commonly called Lamaism, the temple is called a Lama temple, and the dagoba is called a Lama dagoba.

The two wives of Songsang Gampo, king of Tubo Tsampo, namely, Princess Wencheng of the Tang Dynasty (entered Tibet in 641) and Princess Chizun of Nepal, both worshipped Buddhism. And in particular Princess Wencheng promoted the introduction of Buddhism. Organized personally by Princess Wencheng, the Reshazu Lakang, the first Buddhist structure in Tibet, built in Luoxie (present-day Lhasa), is the predecessor of the still existing Gtsug-Khang Monastery. In the year 762, Khri-sron-btsan, king of Tubo Tsampo built Tibet's first formal temple, Bsam-yas Monastery, and seven Tibetan youths were tonsured to become monks. After the introduction of Buddhism, a primitive religion of Tibet, Bon, was later blended with Buddhism. In addition, due to the strong influence of Tantrism of Indian Buddhism and elements of Hinduism, Tibetan Buddhism developed a very strong mystical color obviously different from Buddhism in the inland areas. In Tibetan Buddhism, commonly called Lamaism, the temple is called a Lama temple, and the pagoda is called a Lama pagoda.

Tibetan-type Lama temples can also be divided into those built on level ground and those set up at the foot of mountains, with the latter accounting for the greater part. Flatland temples are often of a semi-regulated and symmetrical form, with the image of the main big hall as the composition center being most outstanding. A free-style layout is used for temples at the foot of mountain areas, which lacks both an overall axis and a pre-determined plan, although they still follow some rules for arrangement. For example, most temples lean against slopes in the north and face flatlands in the south. At the back of the terrace are arranged tall colorful scripture halls and Buddhist halls, and in its outer part are mansions for Living Buddhas. The further outer part is encircled by a large stretch of low small yards in which ordinary monks are living.

Jokhang Monastery

(See P168)

The Jokhang Temple, Lhasa, Tibet

The Potala Palace

In Tibet, there was a kind of government structure called "Zong shan". "Zong" means a local Tibetan administrative unit, equivalent to a county in interior areas. The government center of a "Zong" was mostly constructed on the hill, thus becoming a castle called "Zong shan" (Zong hill). Lhasa's Potala Palace, the greatest building in Tibet, is both the highest "Zong shan" and the temple of the gods of Tibetan Buddhism.

The Potala Palace is built on the Potala Hill. In outward appearance, it consists of 13 stories, 117 meters high, and covers an area of 100,000 square meters. Work to construct the Potala Palace began in the second year (1645) of the reign of Qing Emperor Shunzhi, around the time when the fifth Dalai Lama went to Beijing to have an audience with him. It took 50 years to complete. The outer walls of the central part of the Potala Palace are painted red, earning it the name of the Red Palace. Inside, is the stupa hall containing stupa for the Dalai Lamas of all ages, as well as Buddhist halls. The east and west of the Red Palace are linked to the east and west White Palaces. The east White Palace held the living area of the Dalai Lamas, while the west White Palace provided monks' living rooms. Extending forward from the lower part of the Red Palace is a white terrace linking the East and West White Palaces. In the middle of the Red Palace, there is a concave balcony belt running through the upper and lower parts, along with many gilded copper-tile roofed small halls on the flat-top. A dark brown wall belt runs horizontally on the upper end of the whole palace, making the outline of the structure more distinct. Below the dark brown wall belt of the Red Palace is a white wall belt echoing the wall

The Potala Palace, Lhasa, Tibet

surface of the White Palace. The structure is in tacit agreement with the chevron. The middle part of the front edge, set back a bit along with the hill, is the highest point of the structure right at the peak of the hill. The outer wall is inlaid with stones, its surface clearly inclined and appearing natural and steady. There is no distinct demarcation between the footing of the structures and the hill, man's work and nature being in harmony and tacit agreement.

Xili Tu-Zhao in Hohhot

The Tibetan-Han mixed Lamaist temples in Inner Mongolia are mostly built on flatland which can be represented by the Xili Tu-Zhao in Hohhot. Xili Tu-Zhao was built at the end of the 16th century (latter part of the Ming Dynasty), and it was expanded in the 27th year (1688) of the reign of Qing Emperor Kangxi. Its general plane is fully of a Han style, sitting in north and facing south. Multiple courtyards are arranged in accordance with the symmetrical axial style, and arranged from the front to the back are archways and temple doors. Inside the gate are bell and drum towers, in east and Han-styled Buddhist halls and large scripture halls in west. In the southeast, in front of the large scripture hall, is a Lamaist pagoda, adding much luster to the front courtyard. With regard to single structures, except for the large scripture hall which serves as the heart of the whole temple and is of a Tibetan-Han mixed style and the Lamaist pagoda of Tibetan style, all other structures are of a pure Han style. The protruding golden dharmacakra (wheel of the law) in the center of the parapet wall, dual deer and chin-chuang retain many Tibetan styles. The brick blank walls on both sides of the portico are stuck with peacock blue glazed wall tiles. Tile eaves are used to divide the wall into two sections, the lower section simple, the upper complicated. The roof of the big scripture hall does not use Tibetan-style flat-top; instead, three Han-style Chinese-hip-and gable roofs are strung together from the front to the back, covered by yellow glazed tiles. Together with the bright-colored portico, they present a warm and strong atmosphere, illuminating people with bright colors.

Monasteries of Dai Ethnic Group

The Dai ethnic group, living in the south and southwest of Yunnan, believes in Theravada Buddhism, also called Hinayana Buddhism. The Buddhist monastery and pagoda, among buildings, have gained the highest achievements and possess the most distinguishing features. The Theravada Buddhist monastery is called a miansi temple. There is at least one such temple in almost every Dai village. According to religious discipline, every male must become a monk once during childhood, learning to read and write in the monastery. The Miansi Monastery provides a place not only for religious activities, but also for celebrations, election of leaders and mediation of disputes. Therefore, the Miansi temple is quite different from a Buddhist monastery in Han areas and the Lamaist temples of Tibetan Buddhism. It is not so strict and solemn as the former, nor as magnificent and uninhibited as the latter; rather, it appears closer to the people.

The ManSuman Monastery in Xishuangbanna

The ManSuman Monastery in Ganlanba of Xishuangbanna, Yunnan, located on the east bank of the Lancang River and sitting in west and facing east, is arranged in order from east to west with temple gate, approach porch and Buddhist hall. On the northeast side of the Buddhist hall is a Dai-style Buddhist pagoda; on the other side is a monastic hall, constituting an extremely vivid and beautiful but not symmetrical composition. Temple gate has three rooms and roof has two slopes, high in the middle and low by the side, simple in technique but rich in bodily form. Unlike the Han Buddhist hall which takes longitude as the front, the Buddhist hall, plane and rectangular, takes gable (i.e., short side) as the front. The center of the big hall is covered with two sloping roofs. The four sides surround a single sloping roof, and the whole composition is a two-section roof like a Chinese-hip-and-gable roof. Along each ridge are densely arranged many yellow glazed adornments in shapes of flame and reeled leaves. In the middle of the main ridge there is a small tower. On ridges are ornaments of chi-wen and those in shape of peacocks. A huge statue of Buddha is erected within the hall facing east. On the pillars and girders are colorful paintings called "jinshui" with red bottom and gold color and the designs of plants, pavilions, towers and other ornamental architecture forms.

Storm-Proof Bridges of Dong Ethnic Group

Among the Dong architecture, storm-proof bridges share the same reputation as the drum towers. The storm-proof bridge, also called gallery or pavilion bridge, means building a corridor on the wooden cantilever flat bridge and a bridge tower on the stone bridge pier and bridge abutment. The bridge tower looks very much like a drum tower, but its plane is only in a square or rectangular shape, without a polygonal form. The Dong national district is crisscrossed by streams, so storm-proof bridges can be found almost in every village, and some have more than one. It not only can keep out wind and rain, but also serves as a gateway to the village, and, all the more, is a place for villagers to rest and discuss matters. The largest and most famous storm-proof bridge is the Chengyang Bridge in Ma'an Village, Sanjiang, Guangxi, which spans the Linxi River. This is 78 meters long and consists of two platforms, three piers and five towers. The middle tower is the highest, capped by a hexagonal finial pavilion. The lower part is square, three-eaved; the left and right towers are also square, four-eaved and finial. The outermost two towers are rectangular, four-eaved and with a Chinese-hip-and-gable roof. Under the bridge balustrade there is a long, through split eave covering the four-layer wooden cantilever beam under the bridge.

Qituan Storm-Proof Bridge in ancient Sanjiang Town, Guangxi Zhuang Autonomous Region

• Drum Towers of Dong Ethnic Group

The Dong ethnic group is distributed in the juncture of Hunan, Guangxi and Guizhou. The Dong ethnic group's architectural artistic achievements are mainly manifested in folk public buildings, such as drum towers and storm-proof bridges, containing more folk customs and features.

The Dong's privacy concept is not strong and their houses are all outward-looking without encircling walls and courtyards commonly seen in residences of the Han ethnic group. In Dong villages, there are many contacts between families and village-wide activities, such as song and dance celebrations, discussions of official business, group chats and day-to-day social contacts. All these activities are carried out in the open ground before the drum towers at the village center. The drum tower level ground is also called Lusheng (a weed pipe instrument) level ground, i.e. a stretch of level ground in front of the drum tower, where there is often a simple stage. The drum tower exists in each village, and in some cases, not just one. There are more than 500 drum towers in all. Dong ethnic group drum towers can be divided into two kinds—pagoda type and hall type, with the former accounting for the majority. The Zengchong Drum Tower in Congjiang of Guizhou is typical. It is also a best-shaped pagoda-type drum tower, being octagonal and 11-eaved, and the eave ends slightly upturned. On the top rises a multi-eaved, octagonal finial pavilion. The eave angle is more upturned, and the overall outline is changeable, beautiful in style and about 20 meters high. Dong legend has it that the drum tower was built in accordance with the sample of the "king of cedar", and the overall outline of the Dong ethnic group drum tower really looks like a cedar, embodying the concept of worshipping big trees. Inside, four big pillars stand erect, and benches between the pillars encircle the central fire-pond. A big drum hangs down from the top of the tower, and is beaten whenever something happens. The pagoda-type pagoda is also in a hexagonal or square form in addition to the octagonal.

Modern Chinese Architecture

In the modern time (usually referred to the period 1840-1919), China witnessed unprecedented transformations with the breaking out of "New Culture Movement" and the emergence of such academic ideologies as "making the past serve the present" and "making foreign things serve China". Meanwhile a group of scholars returned back to China with western technologies and ideas that they had studied in the west. In respect of architecture, a special appearance was presented with the complex blending of old and new things and foreign and Chinese things, and a large number of new-type constructions emerged. The so-called new-type means that these constructions offered some unprecedented functions and some new-type building materials as well as relative new structures, construction technologies and equipment were adopted in the constructions. These buildings such as stations, banks, hospitals, schools and new-type residences reflect the aesthetic characters at that time.

Since the 20th century, with the development of modern and contemporary architecture in the west, some "foreign houses" with the same appearance as the buildings in the west at the same time emerged in large numbers in the concessions in various cities. These buildings not only maintain the classical style but also imitate the marks of western architecture during the Renaissance. Some buildings even blend the forms of various ancient western architectures, such as Hongkong and Shanghai Banking Corporation in Bund of Shanghai and the Great Hall of Tsinghua Xuetang (School). By the 1920s and 1930s, Chinese architecture started to turn to "modern architecture". For example, the Shanghai Park Hotel of 24 stories is a typical modern building, similar to western buildings at that same time. From 1930s due to the aggression by Japanese there were endless battles in China and there were few construction activities. The modern Chinese architecture serves as the transition from classical one to contemporary one in China.

Nanjing Road Architecture in Shanghai

Starting from the Bund of Shanghai, Nanjing Road is an arterial road from east to west in Shanghai.

At the beginning along the Nanjing Road were mostly two-story wooden houses of Chinese styles. With the development of the Bund of Shanghai, foreigners started to build up houses along the Nanjing Road. At that time the buildings of foreign style were very simple, two-story brick-wooden structure with the frontage as shops and back as warehouse and upper floor as living rooms. Fuli Company (1848) is a three-story building of brick-wooden structure, appearing early in the Nanjing Road. The City Hall of Shanghai Municipal Council constructed in 1896 and designed by Lester, Johnson and Morriss is the earliest administrative office building with "foreign style". Among the famous "four great companies" in the Nanjing Road, Xianshi Company constructed in 1917 (designed by Lester, Johnson and Morriss and constructed by Gulanji Construction Co.) and Yong'an Company constructed in 1918 (designed by Palmer and Turner Architects and Surveyors and constructed by Xinheji Construction Co.) basically imitated the western classical style. In 1920s and 1930s Xinxin Company constructed in 1926 (designed by Hongda Architects and constructed by Union Building Co.) adopted simple treatment. And the new building of Yong'an Company constructed in 1933 and Daxin Company constructed in 1934 were obviously influenced by western modernization school.

Nanjinglu Commercial Street in Shanghai

Bund Architecture in Shanghai

On November 17,1843, Shanghai formally became a treaty port, opening the prelude of introduction of western architecture into Shanghai. At the beginning foreigners in China lived in the folk residences along the Huangpu River outside of the old town in south Shanghai. At the end of 1940s they moved into concessions in succession and started to operate and construct Bund of Shanghai (also called "Huangpu Beach"). The Bund usually refers to the joining point of the Suzhou River and the Huangpu River, a zone of about 1,500 meters long along the river from the Suzhou River mouth in the north to the east section of Jinling Road in the south. Several arterial latitudinal roads in downtown of Shanghai start from the Bund which can be viewed as the center of Shanghai City. Nearly 30 foreign-style buildings and the roads and greenages in the east, along with the Huangpu River, form the special scene in the Bund.

The buildings in the Bund are mostly in foreign style, experiencing the initial period of modern architecture in the mid 19th century, the prosperity period at the end of 19th century and the early 20th century, and the peak in 1920s and 1930s. Today in the west of the Bund there are still 52 buildings of various styles such as Gothicism, Baroque, Romanesque, Classicism, Renaissance and combination of Chinese and foreign styles. Coming out of different architects with greatly different styles, these buildings have uniform architectural pattern and harmonious architectural outlines, creating a beautiful horizontal line on the west bank of the Huangpu River and enjoying the fame of "international architectural exposition."

Constructions in Concession in Tianjin

The development of constructions in concession in Tianjin experienced two stages.

From 1860 to 1900: it is the initial time for various countries to open their concessions. There were not many buildings and the qualities were not very good. The greater building is the Wanghailou Catholic Church constructed in 1870 at the Sancha River Mouth. Experiencing destruction and rebuilding for several times, it maintains the basic form of European Gothic style. In 1887 Victoria Park was built up to celebrate the fifties birthday of Britain Queen Victoria, and the Gordon Hall constructed in 1889 to the north of the park manifests the architectural way of the United Kingdom in mediaeval times. Astor Hous Hotel constructed in 1890 is the earliest and highest hotel building at that time in Tianjin. Britain Hospital (1897), New Union Church (1898) and Anglican Church (1900) are all major buildings at that time.

After the beginning of the 20th century, with the continuous expansion of Britain and French concessions, the prosperous regions appeared in Zhongjie (present-day North Jiefang Road) and Quanyechang with concentrated buildings. Forty-nine foreign banks were built here, hence the name "Oriental Wallstreet". Most famous of these were the Hong Kong and Shanghai Banking Corporation Limited of Britain and the Chartred Bank of India Australia China of Britain, the City Bank and the Premier Bank of the United States, the Sino-French Industrial Bank and the Banque de l'Indochine of France, the Deutsche Asiatische Bank of Germany, the Yokohama Special Bank Ltd. of Japan, Korean Bank, the Russo Chinese Bank of Russia, the Belgian Bank, the Swiss Bank, the Central Bank, the Continental Bank, the Jincheng Bank, the Yanye Bank and the Zhongnan Bank of China.

Stores and hotels were built mainly in

Tianjin Quan Ye Chang (Mall)

the Quanyechang area. Hotels built after 1922 include National Grand Hotel (1922), Zhejiang Xingye Bank (1925), Huizhong Hotel (1928) and Quanyechang Mall (1928), it has become a downtown of Tianjin City.

Quanyechang Mall in Tianjin

Tianjin Quanyechang Mall is a famous commercial building in modern China. In 1926 Gao Xingqiao, a tycoon in Tianjin, invited a French architect Muller to design the Quanyechang Mall as an integrated mass of shopping, entertainment and recreation. The architectural style was obviously influenced by eclectic architectural form. The principal body is 5 stories with 7 stories for corners. It is a reinforced concrete structure. Above the seventh story there is a high tower, consisting of a two-story hexagonal tower base, a two-story round tower body and the fornical tower top, with some ornaments such as flagpole and lightning rod. The inside shopping space is very high and broad. More than 200 shops, cinemas and dancing halls concentrated in the seven-story Quanyechang Mall. In the past the first and second floors and some parts of the third floor were rented to each shops for selling commodities, cloth, vessels, clocks and watches, jewelries, four treasures of the study, ancient books, antiques and artwork, etc. On the fourth, fifth and sixth floor were theaters, cinemas, tea houses and other entertainment places. Now the operational way and region in the Quanyechang Mall have been enlarged and transformed continuously and it has become a large-scale comprehensive shopping mall in Tianjin.

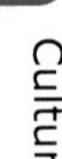

Thirteen Hongs in Guangzhou

During the Ming and Qing dynasties, Guangzhou was the only treaty port in China. Early before the Opium War, there was Thirteen Hongs commodity hall rented and constructed by foreigners in Guangzhou, which is the earliest group of foreign-style buildings in Guangzhou. Thirteen Hongs was a trade group franchise and was established to control and manage foreign trades. The commodity hall of Thirteen Hongs is the building for foreign businessmen to run business and live. The hall was built to south of the avenue of Thirteen Hongs and facing the broad space of the Pearl River. The buildings are not very large, most of which have two stories with out corridors. After the Opium War, Guangzhou opened as a port on July 27, 1843. At that time, the downtown of Guangzhou had come into being along the present-day Yuexiu District where some important official buildings were built. Later on the Changti and Xiti avenues in west along the river were built many large-scale public buildings for commercial, financial and other business offices, most of which were in foreign styles. The Customs Building (1923) and the Post Office were the typical ones.

Shamian in Guangzhou

After the signing of the Treaty of Tianjin in 1858, the British used the burning of Thirteen Hongs in the Second Opium War as an excuse to forcefully select Shamian as its concession. Shamian, located beside Bai E Tan at the mouth of the Pearl River, is an oblong island of about 870 meters long and 290 meters wide. After selected as the concession, Shamian was occupied by Britain and France that auctioned and operated the concession for other countries to rent, and Shamian became the habitat and liberty region for foreigners in Guangzhou. The foreigners built banks along all sides of Shamian as boundary, built bridges as entrances and conducted complete planning. The grid avenues with obvious distinction between primary and secondary divided Shamian to 12 regions of different sizes. All buildings were distributed along avenues and parks were set at center of streets. The boulevard along the river on the north avenue and the park nearby the river on the south avenue formed the natural barrier for Shamian. Various buildings such as consulates, foreign firms, churches and schools concentrated at Shamian which became the exposition place for all countries' buildings in Guangzhou. But the buildings in Shamian usually were small with bad quality and in brick-wooden or brick-stone structures. They were represented by British Consulate, Baohuayi Firm, French Missionary Society, Bank of India and China, HSBC and Lourdes Church.

Ba Da Guan in Qingdao

Ba Da Guan, located in east of Huiquan, Qingdao, covers a space of more than 70 hectares. Ten tranquil and cool avenues cross inside and they are named after the eight famous passes in China, so they are called Ba Da Guan (eight grand passes) generally. Ba Da Guan integrates parks and courtyards, with lush trees and blooming flowers everywhere, and the trees planted along the ten avenues are various kinds. For example, flowering peach trees are planted along Shaoguan Avenue with blooming in spring like pink ribbon; jacarandas are planted along Zhengyangguan Avenue with blooming in summer; pentagonal maples are planted along Juyongguan Avenue with red maple leaves in autumn, adding beauty to the scene; cedars are planted along Zijinguan Avenue with evergreen along the year; and Chinese flowering crabapples are planted along Ningwuguan Avenue From early of spring to end of autumn there is endless blooming and it is honored as "flower avenue". The buildings in Ba Da Guan have special appearances and various styles, enjoying the fame of "international architectural exposition". Huashi Building is the most famous and representative villa in Ba Da Guan. It is said that it was built by a Russian in 1932. As the materials are granite and cobbles, it is named Huashi Building. It is in a typical European castle style, blending the Greek and Roman styles as well as Gothic architectural characteristics.

The Princess Building at Badaguan in Qingdao

Contemporary Chinese Architecture

After the founding of the People's Republic of China in 1949 Chinese architecture entered a new historical stage and the large-scale and planned national economical construction promoted the flourish development of architecture. During this period Chinese architecture experienced the period of restoring ancient ways characterized by adopting big roofs in some parts, the socialist new style period represented by the Ten Major Architectural Projects of the National anniversary celebration, and the period of Guangzhou style integrating modern designing way and national implication. Since 1980s Chinese architecture has gradually tended to be open and compatible and modern Chinese architecture has started to develop in multiple directions.

The National Centre for the Performing Arts

The Great Hall of the People

The Great Hall of the People is located on the western edge of Tian'anmen Square. It was one of the Ten Major Architectural Projects built in Beijing to commemorate the 10th anniversary of the founding of the People's Republic of China in 1959. It is the important place for the State and all people's groups to hold political, foreign affair and social activities. It is also the place for National People's Congress and the Standing Committee to handle official business. The Great Hall of the People, sitting in west and facing east, is 336 meters long from north to south, 206 meters wide from east to west, and 46.5 meters high at the highest point. It covers a space of 150,000 square meters with the construction area of 171,800 square meters. The structure has a solemn, magnificent, brilliant and elegant style as a whole, full of national characteristics and is divided into three main sections: a 10,000-seat auditorium in the middle, a banquet hall where 5,000 people can dine at one time in the north and the offices of the Standing Committee of the National People s Congress in the south. The 10,000-seat Auditorium is the major structure and located at the center. With the structure of no vertical shafts, it has the arched roof and large span. The Banquet Hall is in the north of the second floor and is the place for national leaders to hold grand state banquets and reception.

The Great Hall of the People

The Ethnic Groups Cultural Palace

It is one of the Ten Major Architectural Projects built for celebration of the 10th anniversary (1959) of the foundation of the People's Republic of China and is also a ethnic groups customs exposition with the quality of museum. It was completed and opened to public in September 1959. The Ethnic Groups Cultural Palace has special architectural style with great national flavors. It was listed as one of the palaces of New China by World Architectural History published by the United Kingdom. In 1999 it was selected as "one of the excellent contemporary Chinese architectural arts" on the second conference of the International Union of Architects. In 1994 it was listed at the top of the fifty selected structures in the appraising activity of "my favorite national style structure" in Beijing.

Beijing Workers' Stadium

Beijing Workers' Stadium is one of the Ten Major Architectural Projects for celebration of the 10th anniversary (1959) of the foundation of the People's Republic of China. It covers a space of 350,000 square meters with a construction area of 80,000 square meters. Beijing Workers' Stadium is the largest stadium in China. It is in an oblong concrete frame structure, with the length of 282 meters from south to north and a width of 208 meters from east to west. There are 24 stands with a seating capacity of 65,000. It is a standard professional football playground satisfying the requirements of International Football Federation and can hold comprehensive sports game. In the stadium there are rest rooms for athletes, rest rooms for judges, TV broadcasting hall, press conference hall, news center, internet center, and honored guest rest rooms. In addition there is a stand for disabled persons and 400 seats for journalists with the installations of interfaces to communications and internet. Since 1959 the stadium has held numerous sports games and various large-scale concerts and evening activities. The influential ones include Great Wall Cup Football Invitational Tournament, Kodak Football Game, the first, second, third, fourth, fifth and seventh National Sports Game of the People's Republic of China, the 11th Asian Games, the 6th Far East Pacific Games for the Disabled, and the football game for Guo'an Team in National Football Division A League Matches.

Fragrant Hill Hotel

Built in 1982, Fragrant Hill Hotel is located in Fragrant Hill Park in west suburb of Beijing and was designed by the famous American I.M. Pei Architects. The architecture absorbs the characteristics of Chinese gardens and gives simple treatment to the arrangement of axis, space order and gardens. The whole architecture relies on the hill and has different height in different places with zigzag line and courtyards. The architecture is painted mostly in white with distinct characteristics. The vertical face of the architecture is in shape of castle and the windows are arranged in order. The layout of courtyards in the hotel has the exquisite characteristics of southern gardens and the wide space of northern gardens. The hill stones, lake water, flowers, grass, trees and the major structure with white wall and gray tiles set off each other. The whole architecture not only satisfies the traditional Chinese garden architectural style but also satisfies the function of modern tourism. The hotel won the honorary award of the American Institute of Architects in 1984.

National Grand Theater

National Grand Theater, a modern symbol architecture in Beijing, is located at Chang'an Avenue. It is designed by French architect, Paul Andreu, and is planned to be completed in 2008. It is the largest arched roof architecture in the world and possesses the world top stage and acoustics. The exterior shell is composed of more than 20,000 titanic boards and more than 1,200 pieces of transparent glass. The total construction area is 170,000 square meters. It consists of four theaters: a 2,500-seat opera house for large-scale opera and ballet performances, a 2,000-seat concert hall for large-scale symphonic performances, a 1,200-seat theater for drama performances and even quyi performances, and a 500-seat multifunctional small theater for some small-scale experimental dramas and some local dramas, as well as chamber music and some quyi performances and even fashion show.

The Oriental Pearl TV Tower

Located at Pudong, Shanghai, the construction of the Oriental Pearl TV Tower completed on October 1, 1994. It is 468 meters high, opposite to the "International Architectural Exposition" on the Bund of Shanghai. At the time of completion, it was listed as No.1 highest in Asia and No.3 in the world, only next to the TV towers in Toronto, Canada and in Moscow, Russia. The designers magically set the eleven beautiful spheres of various sizes up from the green grassland to the blue sky with two giant spheres shining like two rubies. On the tower there are ten items of No.1 in the world: the length and weight of the transmission antenna, the over 20,000-square-meter space architectural area, the ascending height of two-double carriage in the elevator inside the tower, and the 3 seven-meter diameter and 92-meter-long slanting stanchions with the 60-degree obliquity. The tower will receive more than 2.8 million person times of tourists around the world every year. The Oriental Pearl Tower is a multifunctional body with sight-seeing, restaurant, shopping, entertainment, pleasure boat, exhibition, historical displays and radio and TV transmissions. It has become a symbol architecture in Shanghai.

Shanghai Jinmao Building

Located at the golden section of Lujiazui financial and commercial region in Pudong, Shanghai, Jinmao Building is on the opposite bank of the famous Bund scenic spot. It is invested and managed by Shanghai Foreign Trade Center Co. Ltd., and designed by SOM Architects in Chicago, the United States. It is 420.5 meters high, the No.1 highest building in China and the No.3 highest one in the world, and covers a space of 23,000 square meters. It has 88 stories on the ground, 3 stories underground, and 6 stories of annex, with the total architectural area of 290,000 square meters. In the building there are offices, Grand Hyatt Hotel, and sightseeing hall. The sightseeing hall is on the 88th story, with the height of 340.1 meters and the area of 1,520 square meters. It is the largest one in China. The adornments in the sightseeing hall are very luxury, all being imported natural marble, with the 3mm-deep wall stone material; the glass screen wall has a broad visual field and one can see all the beautiful scenes of the urban on both banks of the Huangpu River and the mouth of the Yangtze River. Two nonstop elevators with the speed of 9.1 meters per second can take tourists from the underground first floor to the 88th floor.

Commune by the Great Wall

The Communtiy by the Great Wall

Commune by the Great Wall is a private collection of contemporary architecture designed by 12 Asian architects. It was exhibited at the eighth International Architectural Exhibition of the Biennial of Venice in 2002. A special prize to an individual patron of architectural work is awarded to Ms. Zhang Xin, the mastermind of the project, for her "bold personal initiative which emphasizes the role of 12 Asian architects in building privately-owned houses in a definitively contemporary manner." The exhibited model is collected by the Centre Pompidou (Paris) as its first permanent collection from China.

National Stadium

National Stadium or the Bird Nest is the major venue of the 29th Olympic Games in 2008, located in Beijing Olympic Park. It is designed jointly by Herzog and DeMeuron (Swiss), ARUP Engineer Consultant, and China Architecture Design Institute. The principal part of the structure is a series of steel trusses woven around the bowl-like seats areas. Its vertical face and the structure are unified to form a grid structure. The grid is composed of 1.2MX1.2M silver steel girder, like a huge bird's nest woven by metal branches. The space between surface structures will be covered by ETFE film.

During the Olympic Games in 2008, the stadium was used to hold such events as opening ceremony, closing ceremony, track and field events and so on. It has a seating capacity of 91,000, including 11,000 temporary seats. After the Olympic Games, it can also hold special and important sports games, various routine events and non-competitive events, and will become a large-scale special place for Beijing citizens to widely participate in sports and enjoy sports and art entertainments. It will become a symbol of sports and entertainment architecture in China. The stadium has an active arched roof and the construction area is planned to be 150,000 square meters. In it there are 100,000 permanent and temporary seats in total.

National Aquatics Center

During the Beijing 29th Olympic Games in 2008, the National Aquatics Center or the Water Cube was used to hold the events such as swimming, diving, water ballet, and final of water polo. The Water Cube has a construction area of 80,000 square meters with the height of about 30 meters and a seating capacity of 17,000, including 4,000 permanent seats and 13,000 temporary seats. It is the only public structure sealed off by film structures in the world. Its special film wrap is composed of more than 3,000 air pillows ("water bubble") which imitate the air bubble of natural liquid and have different areas. The coverage area reaches 100,000 square meters and the expansion area reaches 260,000 square meters. And the film wrap is more than one layer. The air pillow film at the roof of the Water Cube has 4 layers and the film of walls has 2 to 3 layers.

The Water Cube is one of the symbols of architectures for Beijing 2008 Olympic Games and is the only symbol Olympic gymnasium designated by the government to be constructed by funds donated from Hong Kong, Macao and Taiwan countrymen. At present more than 100,000 persons have donated more than 650 million Yuan, including 60 million Yuan from Taiwan where nearly 1,000 persons donated. After the Olympic Games, it will become a multifunctional large-scale aquatics center offering entertainment, sports, recreation and body training for public. The principal structure is designed to have a life of 100 years.

Society

Life Consumption

General Living Standard

Since entering into the 21st century, China's economy has developed steadily and relatively rapidly, and the people's overall living standard and quality of life has been improved considerably. The gross domestic product (GDP) in 2007 was 24,661.9 billion Yuan, up by 11.4 percent over the previous year. The consumption pattern of society continued to shift from one of basic living to one of modern comfortable living.

The annual per capita net income of rural households was 4,140 Yuan; and the Engel coefficient (proportion of expenditure on food in total household expenditure) was 43.1 percent. The annual per capita disposable income of urban households was 13,786 Yuan; and the Engel coefficient was 36.3 percent. As of the end of 2007, the urban and rural residents' savings deposits reached 17,621.3 billion Yuan, with a year-on-year increase of 5.8 percent. The total retail sales of consumer goods reached 8,921 billion Yuan, with a year-on-year increase of 16.8 percent.

Economic Data

With a large population distributed unevenly and unbalanced economic development, the per-capita living space in rural areas is more than that in cities. The housing conditions and living environment for urban and rural residents have been improved considerably, however. China actively promotes the development of an urban housing security system, which comprises the system of publicly accumulated housing funds, system of affordable and functional housing, and the system of low-rent housing. By the end of 2006, the low-rent housing system for minimum-income families was established in 512 cities out of the 657 cities, accounting for 77.9 percent. In 2008, another 2.5 million households (including 400,000 households provided with low-rent homes by the corresponding government and paying for rent under the relevant criterions) were guaranteed to be provided with low-rent housing. In addition with the previous such households, the number of the households guaranteed to be provided with low-rent housing totaled 3.5 million.

By the end of 2006, per-capita living space in cities reached 27.1 square meters, while it was 30.7 square meters in rural areas. Families and communities began to realize the importance of environmental protection, and the people's living environment was further improved.

Per capita public green area in urban areas stood at 8.98 square meters. The urban public utilities have developed gradually. By the end of 2007, the popularization rate of urban water use and gas use reached 93.8 percent and 87.5 percent. In regard to transport, 94.3 percent of the administrative villages accessed to the highway, there were 44.59 autocycles for every 100 households in rural areas, 37.9 buses for every 10,000 persons in urban areas; the per-capita road area in cities was 11.4 square meters; and there were 4.43 private cars per 100 urban households. In communications, there were 27.8 fixed telephones and 41.6 mobile phones per 100 people. The number of the mobile short messages reached 592.1 billion, increasing 37.8 percent over the same period of the previous year. The entertainment and leisure activities of urban and rural residents have become increasingly diversified. By the end of 2007, the per-capita expenditure for domestic tourism in urban areas reached 906.9 Yuan, and the figure in rural area was 222.5 Yuan.

The pyrotechnic display over the China Millennium Monument

People's Health Level

In making great efforts to improve people's living standard and construct a well-off society in an all-round way, the government continues to take effective measures to help the rural poor shake off poverty. The State attaches great importance to combating natural disasters and carrying out related relief work, making sure that people hit by natural disasters are able to subsist. The State continues to provide special aid to minimum-income urban families whose members either suffer from critical illness or are seriously handicapped and without any financial income.

At present, the general health of the Chinese people is better than that of the average level of middle-income countries, and ranks among the top among developing countries in this respect. According to the News Bulletin on China's Health Development in 2003-2007, the average life expectancy has increased from 71.8 years in 2000 to 73.0 years. The mortality rate of women in childbirth has dropped from 1,500 per 100,000 in 1949 to 36.6 in 2007, and the infant mortality rate from 200 per thousand to 10.7 per thousand. The national public health system has been further strengthened. According to statistics released in 2005, the average life expectancy of Chinese people was 74.09 years, and the birth rate of the total population was 1.72 children per woman.

Gross Amount of Consumption

Since China initiated the reform and opening-up policy in the late 1970s, great changes have occurred in its economy, society, living style and the consumption concept of its people. The varieties of consumer goods have increased constantly. The commodities dominating household consumption underwent change from the 100-Yuan bicycle, sewing machine and watch in those years, to the 1,000-Yuan color TV, refrigerator and washing machine in the later 1980s, and the 10,000-Yuan-cost high-definition large-screen color TV, high-grade household facilities and articles, automobiles and houses. People's consumption conception underwent tremendous development, paying more attention to individuality and enjoyment.

The people have a higher pursuit in terms of food and garments which are usually regarded as living necessities. More and more people have dinner in restaurants. For the constantly updated household appliances with newer and stronger functions replacing the traditional function of making items last as long as possible, people began to pay more attention to brand products, which are thought of as the guarantee of quality and perfect after-service. Consumption by urban residents is developing towards comfortable enjoyment, while consumption by rural residents is developing toward better-off living. China's consumption level is increasingly rising along with the development of the world economy.

Great change has taken place in Chinese consumption level compared with that in the past. China has become the world's third largest auto consumer and the largest mobile phone user. It has established the world's largest fixed telephone network and mobile communications network, and the second largest public Internet. The rural market has become an important "engine" driving the rapid growth of China's total retail sales of consumer goods. According to the National Bureau of Statistics, the total retail sales of consumer goods in 2007 reached 8,921 billion Yuan, with a year-on-year increase of 16.8 percent.

Residents' Income

In the past few years, China's national economy has realized rapid and healthy development, the income of rural and urban residents has maintained rapid growth, people's living standards have improved steadily and people are living a relatively comfortable life. According to statistics, the annual per capita disposable income of urban households was 13,786 Yuan and the annual per capita net income of rural households was 4,140 Yuan. The Engel coefficient was 43.1 percent for rural households and 36.3 percent for urban households. The population in absolute poverty in rural areas (calculated on the basis of annual per-capita net income of 785 Yuan) was 14.79 million at the end of 2007, a decline of 6.69 million over the previous year. The low-income population in rural areas (based on the standard of annual per-capita net income between 786 and 1067 Yuan) was 28.41 million, a decline of 7.09 million.

Residents' Savings

In 1952, residents' savings deposits amounted to 860 million Yuan, growing to 21.06 billion Yuan in 1978. In the 20 years since the start of reform and opening-up, personal savings deposits increased in geometric progression. Between 1979 and 1986, the balance of savings deposits increased 10-fold, reaching 223.85 billion Yuan, this figure rising to 2,151.88 billion Yuan in 1994. In short, within the space of 16 years, savings deposits increased 100-fold. In 2002, the figure was 8,691 billion Yuan, or 411.7 times the 1978 figure. As of the end of December 2007, the figure was 17,253.4 billion Yuan, increasing by 6.8 percent over the previous year. Personal foreign exchange deposits, stocks, bonds, internal stocks, and cash have all grew by a large margin.

Residents' Expenditure

China's urban and rural residents' expenditure for consumption mainly refers to the living expenditures, including eight major varieties, i.e. food, clothing, household facilities, articles and services, medicine and medical services, transportation and communications, recreation, education & cultural services, residence and miscellaneous commodities and services. According to statistics, by the end of 2006, the per capita annual living expenditures of urban residents for consumption reached 8,696.55 Yuan, of which the food consumption totaled 3,111.92 Yuan, clothing consumption 901.78 Yuan, household facilities, articles and services consumption 498.48 Yuan, expenditure for medicine and medical services 620.54 Yuan, expenditure for transportation and communications 1,147.12 Yuan, expenditure for recreation, education and cultural services 1,203.03 Yuan, residence consumption 904.19 Yuan and miscellaneous commodities and services expenditure 309.49 Yuan, respectively, accounting for 35.78 percent, 10.37 percent, 5.73 percent, 7.14 percent, 13.19 percent, 13.83 percent, 10.40 percent and 3.56 percent of the total, respectively.

The per capita annual living expenditures of rural residents for consumption reached 2829 Yuan, of which the food consumption, clothing consumption, household facilities, articles and services consumption, expenditure for medicine and medical services, expenditure for transportation and communications, expenditure for recreation, education and cultural services, residence consumption and expenditure for miscellaneous commodities and services accounted for 43.02 percent, 5.94 percent, 16.58 percent, 4.47 percent, 10.21 percent, 10.79 percent, 6.77 percent and 2.23 percent of the total, respectively.

According to a forecast by the Ministry of Commerce, in addition to motor vehicles, housing and telecommunications service that will continue to secure large sales, catering, tourism, body building, education, culture and holiday and traditional Chinese products and services were likely to grow rapidly in 2006. Consumption of Chinese residents is tending to become brand seeking, environmentally friendly, individualized and fashionable.

During the vocation of China's National Day, tourists went to the southeast Guizhou in an endless stream. The Langde Miao Village attracted numerous visitors with its ancient customs.

Catering Consumption

As China's national economy grows steadily and rapidly, the urban and rural residents' income also increases obviously, thus enhancing their consumption demands. So the catering market takes on the flourishing development momentum and the outside catering consumption expenditure also increases year after year. China's retail sales of catering section reached 1,235.2 billion Yuan in 2007, a year-on-year increase of 19.4 percent; it accounted for 13.8 percent of the total retail sales of consumer goods. It contributed 15.6 percent to or 2.6 percentage points for the growth of the total retail sales of consumer goods. The catering consumption became an important driving force for the steady growth of consumption demand.

Statistics released by the Ministry of Commerce showed that residents' catering consumption accounted for 60 percent of China's catering section retail sales while that for official and business affairs fell to 40 percent. In 2007, China's catering turnover was 225 times that of 1978 when the country began to implement the reform and opening-up policies, with an average annual growth rate of 20.53 percent. It is estimated that the retail sales of the catering section will maintain the rapid growth and exceed 1470 billion Yuan, increasing 19 percent. The per-capita expenditure on catering consumption will reach 1,100 Yuan.

Household Consumption on Major Food

The major food that the urban and rural households purchase includes grain, fresh vegetables, edible vegetable oil, pork, beef and mutton, poultry, fresh eggs, aquatic products, fresh milk, fruits (melon and fruit), nut products, liquor, tea and sugar. According to information released by the State Statistical Bureau, urban household annual per capita consumption on grain, fresh vegetables, edible vegetable oil, pork, beef and mutton, poultry, fresh eggs, aquatic products, fresh milk, fruits, nut products and liquor in 2006 was 75.92 kilograms, 117.56 kilograms, 9.38 kilograms, 20.00 kilograms, 3.78 kilograms, 8.34 kilograms, 10.41 kilograms, 12.95 kilograms, 18.32 kilograms, 60.17 kilograms, 3.03 kilograms and 9.12 kilograms, respectively. Rural household annual per capita consumption on grain (unprocessed food grains), fresh vegetables, edible vegetable oil, pork, beef and mutton, poultry, eggs and egg products, milk and dairy products, aquatic products, fruits and related products, nut products and liquor was 205.62 kilograms, 100.53 kilograms, 5.84 kilograms, 15.46 kilograms, 1.57 kilograms, 3.51 kilograms, 5.00 kilograms, 3.15 kilograms, 5.01 kilograms, 19.09 kilograms, 0.89 kilograms and 9.97 kilograms, respectively.

Green Food

At present, China has formulated the green food authentication system, creating retail stipulations on the standards of agricultural products in regard to producing area environment, production technology, packing and storage and transportation. Green food is divided into Grade A and Grade AA. The latter standard has reached and even exceeded the basic level of organic food set by the International Federation of Organic Agriculture Movements.

Green food refers to that which is pollution-free, of high quality and nutritious. It is produced in a special mode, following the principles of sustainable development, and accredited and permitted by special institutions to use the green food mark. The food similar to green food is called organic food in English-speaking countries, ecological food in non-English-speaking countries such as Finland and Sweden, and natural food in Japan, respectively. On the whole, green food is that in which the production mode avoids or restricts the use of chemical fertilizers, pesticides and other chemical substances.

Green Food Standard

Green Food Standard includes environmental quality standard of the producing area, standard of production technology, product standard, packing standard and other related standards, constituting a standard system of quality control and supervision "from the field to the dinner table."

Firstly, the producing area of the products or raw materials must meet the ecological environmental standard of green food: The area where the main materials of the agricultural primary products or food grow is not subject to any direct industrial pollution, and there is no pollution threat to the water supply area or uptake, ensuring the quality of the air, soil, irrigation water and breeding water in this area meet the standards for green food respectively. Measures will be taken to ensure that the environmental quality in this area will not decline in the future production course.

Secondly, crop planting, livestock and poultry raising, aquiculture and food processing must coincide with green food operating procedures. The technical standard includes two aspects: one is the rules on the use of fertilizer, pesticide, veterinary medicine, aquaculture medicine, food additives and feed additive used for producing green food; second is the operating procedures for crop planting, livestock and poultry raising, aquaculture and food processing formulated according to these rules.

Thirdly, products must be up to the green food sanitary standard, which generally is grouped into three parts: residual pesticides, harmful metals and bacteria.

Fourthly, external packing, storage and transportation must tally with the packing, storage and transportation standard for green food.

• The Mark of Green Food

The mark of green food comprises three parts: the sun shape above, the blade below and the bud in the central, symbolizing the natural ecology. The color of the mark is green, symbolizing life, agriculture and environmental protection. The figure of the mark is round, meaning protection. The mark and background of Grade AA Green Food is green with the impression being white while the mark and background of Grade A Green Food is white with the impression being green. It carries the Chinese characters for "green food" and the English words "Green Food." Nine varieties of food can use this mark. In addition, fertilizers and other products related to growing green food also can use the mark.

The mark of green food serves as a trademark of product quality identification, the private right of which is protected by the Trademark Law of the PRC. If its food passes the authentication by the special institutions, an enterprise is permitted to use this mark.

The longer guaranteed period (shelf life); not bringing about secondary pollution; not doing damage to the original nutrition and flavor; lower packing cost; convenient and safe storage and transportation; enhancing the aesthetic feeling and arousing the appetite. In addition to the basic demands for the packing of products, the packing of green food also accords with the stipulation in the Standard Manual on the Design of Green Food Mark. The brand label must contain the following several contents: name of food; type of product; ingredient sheet; net content and contents of solids; names and addresses of manufacturer and seller; day markings (date of production, guarantee period or preserve period); guide to storage, level of quality; design code of product; special label content.

Grade A Green Food

Grade A green food refers to food that grows in the ecological environment in accordance with the standard, is permitted to use the limited and comparatively safe chemical synthesis substances permitted during the production procedure and is produced and processed according to the specified regulations on production and operation, and whose quality and packing accord with the standards through examination and measurement, and is accredited and permitted by special institutions to use the grade A green food mark.

Grade AA Green Food (equated with "organic food")

Grade AA green food refers to food that grows in the ecological environment in accordance with the standard, does not use any harmful chemical synthesis substances permitted during the production procedure and is produced and processed according to the specified regulations on production and operation, and whose quality and packing accord with the standards through examination and measurement, and is accredited and permitted by special institutions to use the grade AA green food mark.

Garment Consumption

With the largest population in the world, China is a big garment consumer. From January to December in 2007, the accumulative output of garments produced by the garment enterprises above the designated scale reached 20.159 billion pieces, up 14.36 percent compared with 2006, among which 9.456 billion were woven garments and 10.703 billion were knitted ones, increasing 13.13 percent and 15.47 percent respectively.With the marked growth of China's national income, garment consumption has moved beyond basic survival demands to self-satisfying demand. Garments of different qualities, different styles and different prices have undergone corresponding demand. China's garment trend has been directly influenced by international fashion.

The Sun Yat-sen Suit

In the early years of the Republic of China (1912-1949), many Chinese youth who went to Japan to study brought back Japanese-style campus wear to China. This kind of suit which was made through separately cutting the three-piece body and sleeves, following the way of western-style suit, looked solemn and elegant and full of youthful spirit. It had a narrow and low standing collar so that the wearer need not wear a necktie. In the right and left lower parts of the right side of the suit there were two hidden pockets and on the left chest there was a placed pocket. The suit was liked by progressive youth. After improvement, it became the modern Chinese-style typical men's suit—the Sun Yat-sen Suit.

The special feature of the Sun Yat-sen suites lies in the design of collar and pockets. A moderate stand collar and a upturned collar are like the stiff collar of the shirt matching with a Western-style suit. On the front were placed four outer pockets, and the two below were made into the shape of piano pockets by overlapping pieces so as to hold more items, on which the soft covers were added so as to prevent loss of the items in the pockets. In the front part of the trousers there was a hidden-button seam. Two hidden pockets were put in the left and right sides, a small hidden pocket (watch bag) at the front waist of the trousers, and a hidden pocket with soft cover at the right hip of the trousers. The men's dress designed by Sun Yat-sen, the founder of the Republic of China, was considered more practicable than the western-style suit and accorded with Chinese aesthetic judgment and living customs. Although made by adopting western-style cutting, outside materials and color, it showed the symmetrical, solemn characteristics of Chinese-style suit. Since it came into being in 1923, the Sun Yat-sen Suit became men's official dress.

Why it is called the Sun Yat-sen Suit is that it was designed by the head of a western-suit shop according to one that Sun Yat-sen wore. In 1929, the national government officially designated it as the full dress, made improvements and amendments, and, in the process, gave it a political coloring. The turndown collar was changed to the standing collar, showing the idea of examining oneself in three ways and strictly administering the country. The four pockets were said to represent the Four Cardinal Principles cited in the classic Book of Changes and understood by the Chinese as fundamental principles of conduct: propriety, justice, honesty and a sense of shame. The five center-front buttons were said to represent the five powers of the constitution of the Republic of China: administration, legislation judicature, examination and procuratorate.

Qipao

What is called "Qipao" is the long gown that the "Qiren" wear. "Qiren" is the title that the Han people in the Central Plains called the Manchu people. In 1921, it was in vogue when it was a loose-fitting, straight-bottomed, broad-sleeved blue-cloth Qipao with no decorative patterns on the collar, fronts and lower hem, the hem of which reached the ankles. It looked cold and upright. Influenced by the trend of times, Qipao underwent many changes in the length, waist measurement, collar and sleeves.

After the 1930s, the Qipao changed with each passing day. At the beginning, the high collar was very much in vogue, being as high as to reach the cheek. Later, the low collar began to be fashionable. The original sleeves were long enough to cover the wrist, but then became shorter, reaching the mid-forearms, then exposing the elbows, then reaching to the middle part of the upper arm; finally, the Qipao was made with no sleeves at all. Its hem was long enough to reach the feet and then became knee-length.

Apart from the two sides of the hem, the slits were also made on the front with the hem in the shape of arc. Apart from the traditional jacquard brocade, light and thin cotton cloth, hemp cloth and silk with printed pattern were also used as materials. The collar, sleeves and front had decorative but not complicated patterns. China's traditional garments did not give prominence to the waist, but as the women in the 20th century increasingly pursued the curvy figure, the Qipao became the ideal garment to display a sexy female body.

Occupational Garments

Occupational garment refers to the garments indicating the occupation and status of the wearer. In 1978 China initiated the reform and opening-up policies, from when all kinds of occupational garments emerged as the times required. The working personnel of many departments such as police, traffic control, procuratorate, court, post office, bank, revenue, industrial and commercial departments, civil aviation and railway received uniforms designed and made by the State according to the vocation in a unified way. Employees in some industries which could not unify the occupation garment wore the occupational garment that departments made themselves and distributed. Some schools not only purchased the school uniforms for their students, but also ordered the western-style suits for their teachers.

The occupational garment differs from the standardized full dress, which has the function of showing the status, position and power. In general, once the people engaging in some vocation appear in some kind of garment, it is easy for others to recognize them in regard to their vocation. For example, the mail carrier is called the "Messenger in Green", and nurses "Angels in White". Garments indicate the social role of the people which enriches the cultural image of the occupational garments.

Housing Consumption

Housing is a major economic and social problem concerning the national economy and the people's livelihood. And solving the housing problem for the masses is an important aspect of China's program for constructing a harmonious society. The urban housing welfare distribution system has basically come to an end, while the monetization of housing distribution and a market-oriented and socialization supply system has been established. Purchasing a house has become the largest living cost for Chinese.

Welfare Distribution of Houses

Under the planned economic system, China implemented a public-owned housing distribution system of "controlling in a unified way, distributing in a unified way". Most State organs and enterprises and public undertakings built themselves or purchased houses through administrative appropriation, and distributed them as part of employee welfare. For urban residences, welfare distribution of houses was the leading policy to solve housing problems. This system better met the employees' basic housing demand at the lower consumption level of that time. In 1998, the government decided to end the system and push the monetization of housing distribution gradually. It sold 80 percent of urban public-owned houses to the employees, reclaimed parts of the housing fund, thus clearing the relationship between the property and rights of ownership. This measure eased the financial pressure of the government and promoted the development of a real estate industry to drive domestic consumption demand.

On a real estate exhibition

♦ Housing Security System

China's housing security system is one targeted at the different income classes.

The first is the housing accumulation fund system. Almost all salaried classes can benefit from this system, which has several parts: the employee and employer jointly deposit savings; personal income will be exempted from tax for the part of housing accumulation fund; when purchasing, apart from the accumulated amount in the personal account, the person can use the fund as a mortgage loan at an interest rate lower than that of commercial loan.

It is a system combining compulsion and encouragement, helping the common salaried class offset their insufficient purchasing power and realizes their target of purchasing a home early. The housing accumulation fund system is a policy security system, which compulsorily adjusts the consumption structure of employees, thus making them accumulate a part of their income for housing consumption. It is of a social pooling and mutual aid nature, which makes each employee borrow from the accumulation fund collected from society for housing consumption, and enjoy preferential conditions such as the exemption from individual income tax and low-interest loans. This is the most important policy to guarantee the market-oriented house-purchasing of the salaried class.

Second is the semi-market-oriented security system targeted at the low-income group. The government constructed the economically affordable houses and low-rent houses by exempting the fees for assignment, providing land allowance or reducing or remitting the taxations so as to guarantee the housing demand of the low-income group. Under the improved economically affordable system, the Government should make mandatory provisions on how much proportion the economically affordable house must account for among the area of houses that was constructed each year.

Third is the non-market-oriented security way targeted at the needy group. The government established its discount system for the needy who cannot afford to purchase an economically affordable house. For example, when the family with its per capita income lower than a certain level purchases an economically affordable house, the government subsidizes the loan interest. If the family cannot still afford the purchase, the government will provide low-rental housing.

Fourth is the relief way targeted at the poverty-stricken group. The government provides low-rental housing for a few poor families via a rental allowance.

♦ Housing Accumulation Fund System

The housing public accumulation fund refers to long term housing savings deposited by State organs, State-owned enterprises, urban collective enterprises, foreign-funded enterprises, urban private enterprises and other urban enterprises and public undertakings, as well as in-service workers based on the workers' average total wage of the previous year. The security, mutual-aid and long term housing public accumulation fund comes under worker ownership. It can be used to purchase commodity housing, used housing, economically affordable housing, a house that the unit built as permitted by the State and renovated housing. If the worker uses the housing public accumulation fund as a mortgage loan when purchasing houses, the interest will be lower than that of a commercial loan. When the worker terminates his labor relationship with his unit, retires or dies, the balance can be withdrawn.

China's housing accumulation fund system was first set up in Shanghai in 1991. In November 23, 1994, the Ministry of Finance, Housing System Reform Leading Group of the State Council, and People's Bank of China jointly issued *Provisional Regulations on the Establishment of Housing Public Accumulation Fund.*

Economically Affordable Housing

The economically affordable house refers to such housing where the State supports real estate developers to invest in the construction by exempting fees for assignment and reducing or remitting 21 items of taxation. It is a commodity house of social security nature. At the current stage, it is the necessary link in the real estate supply structure as well as a product guaranteeing the housing demand of the medium and low-income households, especially lower middle income households. The market-oriented way is adopted as much as possible to manage economically affordable house, making preparations for the gradual transition from economically affordable housing to common commodity housing.

♦ Housing Distribution System Reform

China's housing distribution system reform went through a number of phases such as pilot house sales (1979-1985), rental allowance (1986-1990) and sale-promoting-renting (1991-1993). In 1994, the Decision of the State Council on Deepening Urban Housing System Reform initiated market-oriented urban housing system reform in an all-round way. This document put forward urban housing system reform as an important part of economic system reform; aims to change the system of unit constructing, distributing, repairing and managing properties to the socialization and specialization operating system; change the way of welfare distribution of housing to wage distribution with priority given to the distribution according to work; establish the economically affordable housing supply system targeted at low and medium-income families as a social security measure, and the commodity housing supply system targeted at high-income families; in the meantime, set up a public housing accumulation fund and a housing finance system.

From 1998, common commodity housing flourished and villas, residential or commercial houses and economically affordable houses came onto the market in succession, and the financial measures on encouraging individuals to purchase houses were implemented successively. Pushing the market-oriented reform of an urban housing system complies with the general demand of the market economy system reform. Meanwhile, monetization of houses is also of realistic significance in stimulating consumption demand, driving economic growth and improving the economic structure.

Low-Rental Housing System

Low-rental housing refers to social security houses the government supplies to urban residents on the lowest living security standard and who have difficulty in obtaining housing via rental allowance or renting in kind.

Housing of Rural Residents

The 1982 Constitution prescribed that "Land in the cities is owned by the State. Land in the rural and suburban areas is owned by collectives except for those portions belonging to the State in accordance with the law." The villagers can apply for a house site only to the collective economic organization but cannot later sell or transfer it. The Land Administration Law of the PRC stipulates that "one household in a rural area can only possess one house site, the area of which shall not exceed the standards prescribed by the provinces, autonomous regions and municipalities directly under the Central Government."

By the end of 2006, the per-capita living space in rural areas reached 30.7 square meters. For a long time, China's rural residents have had the habit of improving their housing conditions and saving money to build a house. In the aspect of housing quality, however, there is a great gap between urban and rural areas. Except a few newly-built rural communities in the developed areas, the houses in rural areas have generally no toilets, tap water, gas pipes and other basic facilities. At present, China has been successively introducing the policies on improving housing in rural areas, which will play an important role in improving the rural outlook, the housing conditions and rural environment.

The household storage furniture attract consumers.

Consumption Boom on Home Decoration

Currently, a consumption boom on home decoration caused by heated house purchasing is still on rise. According to an investigation by China Building Materials Daily, investment in home decoration made by most house purchasers accounts for about 20 percent of the total cost of the house. The investment involves mainly the aspects of kitchen, sanitary wares, living room, bedroom, floor, wall, doors and windows, home appliances, furniture, lights and curtains and so on, with many internationally famed brands of kitchenware, sanitary ware and furniture are now used by Chinese families. In the process of decoration, a large proportion of householders would like to devote much energy and thought to the design, consulting an interior decoration stylist or transferring the decoration project to a creditable decoration company to complete the whole design and construction. Compared with the early period of reform and opening up to the outside world when the common families made simple decorations such as painting the wall, paving the floor and adding sofas, the decoration style and the environmentally-friendly building materials are now most important. For family decoration, more tend to devote much energy and thought to the design.

Automobile Consumption

The ZK6181HG bullet head-shaped bus exhibited by the Yutong Passenger Car Co.,Ltd.

China was once the kingdom of bicycles, but that is changing. With the advent of the 21st Century, the automobile industry began its explosive increase. From 2000 to 2004, the annual output of automobiles rose from 2 to 5 million. In the past five years, automobile consumption increased at an annual speed of 24.2 percent.

In 2007, the output and sales volume of China's automobiles reached 8.8824 million and 8.7915 million respectively and there were 159.8 million automobiles on road. The proportion of the auto consumption of the mainland China in that of the world increased from 4.3 percent in 2001 to 8.6 percent in 2005. In 2008, the sales volume of China's automobiles may surpass 10 million, ranking second in the world.

Currently, among more than 1,000 brand automobiles with various delivery capacities sold in Chinese market, there are 100 kinds with the delivery capacity below 1.0L, and 200 to 300 kinds with a capacity between 1.0L to 1.6L. Of the total, the number of the various types with a capacity of 2.0L reaches over 500, accounting for more than 90 percent of the total. Automobiles with middle and small delivery capacity have become the main weapons for the automobile manufacturers to occupy the market. With respect to the price, middle and small capacity vehicles have remained stable while the price of those of 2.0L or more have declined; a good car can now be purchased for around 100,000 Yuan. The excise collection standard promulgated in April 2006 in China and the continuous rise of oil prices and so on has influenced the concept of middle and senior class consumers. While they pay attention to the brand, quality and equipment, they also attach more importance to the price and use cost instead of blindly buying "brand and status". Most purchasers also pay attention to the vehicle's functions, after-sales service and insurance rate, and so on.

♦ Urban Public Transportation

Although urban public transportation has seen comparatively fast development in recent years, there is still a certain distance with the whole urban development. It is prominent that the contribution rate of public transportation is less than 10 percent. Generally speaking, the severely lagging situation of China's urban public transport construction has not fundamentally changed. According to the Ministry of Construction, the speed of urban public vehicles has become slower, with the average speed being 10 kph. Compared with the situation 10 years ago, journeys take on average 10 minutes more by public vehicles, and 70 percent of residents rate the performance as unsatisfactory. Secondly, investment in public transport has been insufficient, construction of a public network with large transportation capacity has been slow and urban rail transit construction has also advanced slowly. Some relevant investigations show that, in many cities in China, there are too many duplicated services in some areas while the outer suburbs suffer a severe shortage. In addition, insufficient attention has been paid to traffic management.

Currently, the government has issued policy documents stressing that urban public transport is a public product and service that the government should provide and the development of urban public transport should be brought into the public financial system, adhering to the principle of investment mainly by the government. It also requires local governments to realize the strategic meaning of developing public transport and their overall responsibilities so as to sincerely implement a strategy of the "public transport first".

Car Exhibition

Information Consumption

Though telephone communications has experienced more than 100 years of development in China, fixed telephone communications developed extremely slowly due to the factors related to overall social and economic development. On November 18, 1987, the first cellular mobile telephone analog system was set up and put into commercial use in Guangdong Province.

In the mid-1990s, the percentage of fixed phone users was only 10 percent and the digital cellular mobile communication technology became increasingly mature and was put into large-scale use. In 1995, a GSM digital telephone network was officially opened. In 1996, the mobile phone system realized national roaming, and international roaming services also began to be provided. Mobile phone users have started to increase on large scale, and through market competition, the network construction has also proceeded increasingly fast, with the terminal price and network access charge decreasing year by year. The introduction of prepaid business and the cancellation of network access charges ensure further popularization.

According to the statistics of China Internet Network Information Center, by the end of 2007, the total number of internet users of China reached 211 million, and the users with access to the internet broad band reached 163 million. The number of the net users and the population with access to the internet brand band of China all ranked second in the world. The on-line time of the Chinese net users was 16.2 hours on average, and the actual monthly on-line expenses (not including the charge of the intent service) reached 103.6 Yuan. The total scale of the on-line expenses in the whole country surpassed 100 billion Yuan. Moreover, the statistics from the Ministry of Information Industry of China, by the end of 2007, the total number of the telephone users of the country surpassed 900 million, of which, that fixed telephone users was over 365.448 million, with the diffusion rate reaching 27.8 ones per hundred persons; that of the mobile telephone users reached 547.286 million, with the diffusion rate being 41.6 ones per hundred persons. The amount of the mobile phone short messages sent reached 592.1 billion ones. The income of the communication business registered a number of 805.16 billion Yuan. As the largest mobile communication market in the world, China made over one third of the mobile phones in the world, and sold more than 10 percent of the mobile phones in the world.

Consumption by Card

In order to realize the final connection of numerous bank cards and improve the environment of card usage, China Unionpay was set up by more than 80 domestic financial institutes. Now, most of the bank cards have the mark of "Unionpay".

At present, several internationally-famed credit cards such as VISA, MasterCard and AMEX have entered China in an all-round way, and cooperated with domestic financial institutes to issue cards. In hotels, restaurants and marketplaces of many cities in China, international credit cards such as VISA, MasterCard, AMEX, Diners Club and JCB can be used.

At the same time, the payment system of Chinese bank cards has gradually been blended with the international payment and clearing system. The bank cards of China have already been accepted in nearly 20 countries and regions where Chinese residents travel most often for payment of goods and services.

Credit Cards have become an important way of consumption by loan. The consumption volume using bank cards accounted for 10 percent of the total national retail volume of social commodities. In big cities such as Beijing, Shanghai, Guangzhou and Shenzhen, this proportion reached over 30 percent, approaching the level of developed countries, which is 30-50 percemt. The bank card has become the most frequently used non-cash payment tool.

Bank Card

Of various bank cards used by Chinese people, about 95 percent are debit cards, and the other five percent credit cards (including semi-credit cards) widely known and accepted by people in recent years. It was as early as 1978 that the credit card entered into the Chinese market. In 1985, the Zhujiang branch of the Bank of China issued the first RMB credit card. By the end of 2007, there were all together 180 institutions who issued 1.5 billion cards. Of the total, the volume of the debit cards issued amounted to 1.41 billion, a rise of 30.4 percent over the previous year; that of the credit cards issued 90.26 million, increasing 82 percent. In 2007, the consumption volume by bank cards in the whole country accounted for 21.9 percent of the total retail volume of the social commodities, registering an increase of 4.9 percentage points over 2006.

The magic credit cards for females

Online Shopping

From the 1990s, the number of the Chinese netizens increased at an amazing speed of 300 percent, and in 2005, the figure surpassed 100 million. Data issued by the Internet Research and Development Center of China Academy of Science in February 2006, showed there were 22 million internet users shopping online, but the latest research of the investigation and research institute, AC Nielsen, indicated that 63 percent of Chinese Internet users had shopped online at least once

In China, the most favorable online commodity is books, and 56 percent of online shoppers choose to buy books in this way, followed by the electronic products such as DVD, music CD and games software, while small commodities such as clothes, shoes, caps and clothing accessories are also very popular online. The large commodities such as home appliances and luxury products occupy a very small proportion among online commodities. The proportion of buying books online is perhaps the highest in the world, which is mainly because young undergraduates are the main shoppers online. As for sellers, the female online shoppers play more important role, and with their support, clothes, cosmetics, jewelry, food and health-care products, home articles, toys and articles for babies, pets and articles for pets become the staple commodities are frequently traded online.

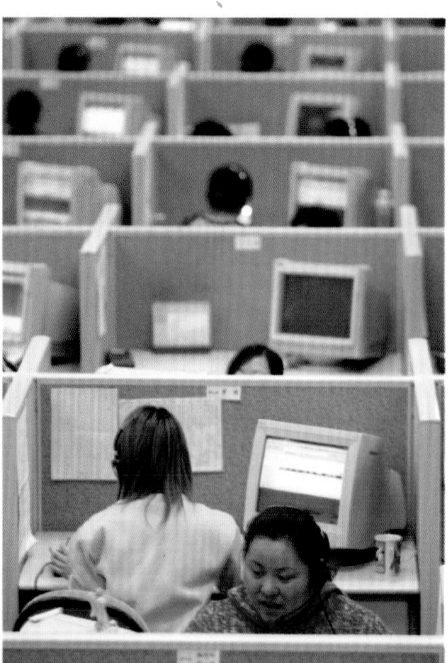
The booking services through Internet and telephone are in the ascendant.

♦ China Consumers' Association

The Association, called CCA for short, was inaugurated on December 26, 1984. It is a national organization legally registered to protect consumers' interests by means of supervision of commodities and services. It also provides reasonable and scientific guidance on consumer activities and seeks to promote healthy development of the socialist market economy. Currently, there are 3,138 consumers' associations at or above county's level covering 31 provinces, autonomous regions and municipalities directly under the Central Government. They have established branches in villages, small towns and urban districts. All kinds of grassroots network organizations, such as supervision points and contact points in village committees, neighborhood committees, industrial administrative departments, colleges and universities and factories and enterprises have amounted to 156,000. More than 100,000 compulsory supervisors and volunteers are working to safeguard consumers' rights.

With assistance of CCA, the Law of Protection of Consumers' Rights and Interests of the PRC went into effect on January 1, 1994 and has had considerable influence.

Website: http://www.seac.gov.cn

Cuisine

Chinese Cuisine

Different geography, climate, resources, products and food habits in accordance combine to form characteristic local cuisines, including "four flavors" and "eight regional cuisines". The "four flavors" refer to the local ones represented by Shandong, Sichuan, Guangdong and Huai Yang (Yangzhou), and the "eight regional cuisines" refer to the ones developed by the aforementioned four flavors, including Shandong cuisine, Sichuan Cuisine, Hunan Cuisine, Guangdong Cuisine, Fujian Cuisine, Jiangsu Cuisine, Zhejiang Cuisine and Anhui Cuisine. Chinese generalize it as "sweet in the south, salty in the north, peppery in the east and sour in the west". From the dishes served at family suppers up to lavish banquets, local famous foods are too numerous to mention one by one, and the delicious foods of all kinds of taste reflect the profound tradition of food culture and the characteristic regional cultures of China.

Lu Cai (Shandong Cuisine)

Lu Cai is one of the most influential and popular cuisines in China. Lu is Shandong Province for short, and Shandong is one of the cradles of Chinese ancient culture. With mountains and rivers meandering in its territory, it boasts vast fertile land, and abundant products. Its grain output currently ranks third in China, and it also has various kinds of high-quality vegetables. Shandong is the location of the hometown of Confucius, and Shandong cuisine incarnates the dining concept of "In his food, he liked to have the rice finely cleaned and the meat, when stewed, cut in small pieces". It stresses the purity of seasonings and is a little salty and fresh. It features freshness, tenderness, aroma and crispness. There are over 30 kinds of common cooking techniques, of which, "bao (quick stir-frying), chao (frying), shao (baking), ta (boiling) and pa (stewing)" are outstanding. In the Ming and Qing dynasties, Shandong cuisine was the main part of imperial meals. The "Feast of Complete Manchu-Han Courses" established in accordance with the national feast of the Qing Dynasty, adopts the whole set of silver dishware, totaling 196 courses, which are delicacies of every kind and as luxurious as possible. As the first cuisine of north China, many basic courses of the high-class feasts prepared for festivals and birthdays and home dishes are developed from Shandong cuisine. Moreover, it also has important influence on the formation of the local cuisines of Beijing, Tianjin and northeast China. The people of Shandong Province are great-hearted and keep open doors, and pay special attention to the principle of treating guests to ensure they go away full and well satisfied. Hence, the dishes will be quite enough, so you will never go hungry when you are a family guest in Shandong.

Jiuzhuan Dachang (Zigzag Great Guts)

Classical Shandong Cuisine

Jiuzhuan Dachang (circulating great guts): rubicund, and the great guts are soft and tender with sour, sweet, fragrant, peppery and salty tastes. This is the traditional dish of Shandong.

Sweet and Sour Yellow River Carp: carp of Yellow River are cooked so that the fish is crisp outside and tender inside; the dish is fragrant and crisp, sour and sweet and a little salty.

Dezhou Stewed Chicken: the chicken skin is bright and ruddy and the meat is fat and tender; when eating it hot, shake the bone and then the meat will part from the bone, sweet-smelling and tasty. It is the traditional flavor of Dezhou.

Chuan Cai (Sichuan Cuisine)

Sichuan Cuisine is a kind of local cuisine that matured in early times, forming part of the culture of ancient Sichuan in Southwestern China. According to ancient books, more than two thousands years ago, there were already such seasonings as brine, rock salt, pepper and ginger and so on. Various bronze and pottery table ware has been found among excavated cultural relics, which show how the great age of the cooking techniques. In the beginning of the 16th century, Sichuan cuisine used the local pepper as seasoning, and inherited the seasoning tradition of "paying much attention to the taste and being attached to pungency" and developed it further. At the turn of the 19th and 20th centuries, it gradually became a system with strong local characteristics. Now, Sichuan Cuisine is widely influential in all places of China and has spread to many countries.

Mentioning Sichuan Cuisine and the tongue-numbing and spicy tastes will come to mind; actually Sichuan Cuisine attaches great importance to seasoning, and abounds in many different tastes, which can be seen from the seasonings such as shallot, ginger, garlic, chili, pepper, Bunge prickly ash, vinegar, bean paste of Pixian County, fermented glutinous wine, sweet and salt and so on. As long as the cooking is skillful, seven flavors such as sour, sweet, bitter, spicy, tongue-numbing, aromatic and salty should be divined. Sichuan enjoys the reputation of a "land of abundance", covering an area of 560,000 square km, with rich cooking materials. Sichuan Cuisine boasts more than 4,000 courses, divided into five such types as feast dishes, refection dishes, home dishes, steamed dishes and characteristic snacks. There are nearly 40 kinds of common cooking techniques, especially being good at sautéing, frying, stir-frying without stewing, dry-frying and home-frying and so on. Most are economic and flavorful home dishes, simple and fresh.

Classical Sichuan Cuisine

Mabo Doufu (Pockmarked Woman's Bean Curd): it is the traditional flavorful dish. It is said that towards the end of the reign of Tongzhi of Qing Dynasty, there was a lady with the family name Chen, who was pockmarked, but she was very good at cooking. Especially the bean curd in her restaurant was tasty with spicy and tongue-numbing flavors and bright red color, which was deeply loved by the masses.

Fish-flavored Pork Shreds: it is red with tender meat. It imitates the seasoning and method of cooking fish, hence its name.

Twice Cooked Pork: it is red and green color, salty with a little sweet and spicy flavor as well as fragrant.

Huai-Yang Cuisine

Huai-Yang Cuisine is the representative flavor in the middle and lower reaches of the Yangtze River and Huaihe River, with the ancient city Yangzhou as the center and cradle. The area abounds in aquatic products, domestic animals, vegetables and venison throughout the whole year. However, Huai-Yang Cuisine adopts few precious delicacies, but only local materials. No matter the materials, the skill of cutting or the seasoning, are all in accordance with propriety, and great stress is placed on the combination of dishes. There are over 1,300 kinds of classical dishes left, showing delicacy and particularity, elegant style and lingering charm.

The materials of Huai-Yang Cuisine are mainly fresh and alive. It stresses strictly the materials and especially duration and degree of heating when cooking. Through adjusting the heating, the characteristics of freshness, fragrance, crispness, tenderness, glutinousness, thinness and ripeness and so on emerge. It is adept at stewing, braising, roasting and boiling, so it can comparatively highlight the original flavor of the materials. When preparing seasoning, it pursues insipidity, and brings the characteristic of the materials into full play when cooking. Not only does Huai-Yang Cuisine feature the freshness, crispness and tenderness of the southern dishes, but also combines the salt taste, color and strong flavor of the northern dishes, thus forming a unique flavor of moderate sweet and salty taste or vice versa. The technique of cutting is exquisite and it pays attention to the effect of filling the plate, which makes it like the elaborate craftwork.

Classical Huai-Yang Cuisine

Xiefen Shizitou (Meatballs with Crab Meat): it is a dish passed down over 1,000 years; "Shizitou" refers to big meatballs. The technique is to cut the rib pork into the megranate grain shape, and add crab meat, crab cream and seasoning and then stew without seasoning.

Duck Triplet: The areas around Yangzhou abound in lake ducks, with fat and delicious meat. As early as in 14th century, the chefs of Yangzhou cooked various dishes with ducks, and later the chef of Yangzhou Restaurant created "duck triplet", which is to fill the wild duck with meat from domestic ducks and pigeons. The domestic duck meat is fat and fresh, the wild duck meat is tight and fragrant and that of the pigeon is loose and tender. The soup is light and fresh, with a little dry flavor. It is a delicious winter food.

Long boiled Dry Soya Milk Film Thread: Boil the soya milk film threads in chicken juice.

Yue Cai (Guangdong Cuisine)

Yue Cai refers to the local cuisine of Guangdong Province, mainly composed of the flavors of Guangzhou, Chaozhou and Dongjiang and represented by that of Guangzhou. It has unique “southland” flavor, famous for broad and rare materials, exquisite ingredients and cooking neatly in accordance with the habits of the eaters. Guangdong Cuisine originated from the coastal area of southern China, in the sub-tropical zone and adjacent to the South China Sea, which is green all four seasons. It abounds in products and delicacies of all kinds, as well as vegetables varying through the four seasons. At the same time, it is also the important trading port to the outside world, so the comparatively developed economy also promotes the development of the food culture with new ideas from home and abroad.

Guangdong Cuisine stresses exquisite preparation and seeks enjoyment, with delicate materials, well-chosen ingredients and beautiful decoration. There are more than 5,000 dishes all together. As for the materials, it adopts a broad range and goes in for live creatures, with cooking techniques including frying, braising, soaking, toasting, soft-frying and stewing without seasoning. It has strict requirements in regard to ingredients, cutting skill, cooking duration, table ware and serving style and so on. For example, the fish should be cooked immediately after being killed to keep its freshness. It attaches importance to both quality and taste, advocating the custom of "nourishing the body" in winter and spring and changing the flavor in accordance with seasons. In summer and autumn, light dishes are favored and in spring and winter, strong ones preferred. The light, fresh, slippery, tender and crisp dishes are preferred and the seasonings are commonly sour, sweet, bitter, spicy, salty or fresh. It pursues the whole effect of the dishes, namely the color, fragrance, taste and shape.

Classical Guangdong Cuisine

Boiled Sliced Chicken: it chooses the pullet or the capon as heavy as 1,500 grams, and the yellow chicken of Qingyuan City is best, with fat and tender meat, short and tasty. When cooking, turn down the flame immediately after putting the chicken into the boiling water. The simmering technique stresses duration and it is best when the chicken is just cooked with a little blood thread on the shank. It is of slippery skin, tender meat and fresh enough flavor.

Soup of the Day: soup is the important part of the Guangdong Cuisine, with the materials changed in accordance with the climate. In the dry and rainless season, the soups such as "dried vegetable and pork lung soup", "white fungus, pawpaw and chop soup", "fig, pachyrhizua angulatus and red pork soup" are adopted to nourish the lung and relieve thirst and benefit the vital energy and lifeblood. In the hot season, the internal heat of the body is ample, so it is wise to select sweet and cool soups, such as "chicken-bone herb and aged chicken soup", "cold melon, red bean and keel soup"; it is cold in winter, so hot soups such as "fresh ginseng and old duck soup" and "aweto and young pigeon soup" are best. It will take three hours to braise the soup.

Braised Whole Shark's Fin in Brown Sauce: the fin is divided into three kinds, with that near the head, near the tail and at the end of the tail. It is cooked neatly, with strong and fragrant flavor. The fin is transparent, tender and tasty, with high content of protein and abundant alimentation. It is the traditional dish of Guangdong Cuisine and sold at high price.

Min Cai (Fujian Cuisine)

Min Cai is Fujian Cuisine for short, originating from Minhou County of Fujian Province represented by the dishes of Fuzhou, Quanzhou and Xiamen and so on. Fujian is mountainous in the north and faces the sea in the south, with the mountainous area abundant in mushrooms, bamboo shoots, white fungus, lotus, stone squama, eel and soft-shelled turtle and so on; in the long shallow sea and beach, there are numerous sea creatures. Hence, the Fujian Cuisine mainly adopts sea food as materials, with beautiful color and light and fresh taste.

It is adept at braising, deep-frying, stir-frying, decocting and stewing, and especially the "flavor pickled with distillers' grains or in wine" is most characteristic. Cutting is important in Fujian cuisine. Everything sliced serves its original aroma and may better show the aroma and texture of food. The chefs of Fujian Province all connect the cooking with

Buddha Jumping over the Wall

the guarantee of the freshness, pure taste and nourishment of the materials and attach importance to soup, which is considered to keep the texture and taste of the original materials. Hence, there are many exquisite soup dishes. Fujian Cuisine is elaborate in the aspects of well-chosen materials, moderate pickle, accurate seasonings, choice soup and proper duration and so on.

Classical Fujian Cuisine

Buddha Jumping over the Wall: at the end of 19th century, this was created by Zheng Chunfa, the famous chef of a restaurant named "Juchunyuan", with a history of over 100 years. It stresses the selection of materials, duration and timing, being elaborately stewed. It tastes flavorful with strong fragrance, and is soft and tender enough to be dissolved immediately in the mouth. It also has abundant nutrition and is the most famous traditional dish of Fuzhou.

Vinasse Chicken: Fujian Cuisine features using the red vinasse to cook various local dishes. The traditional famous dish is to boil the fat hen's meat with water and then bloat it with red vinasse hermetically. It is of light red color and tender meat, with vinasse fragrance and nice taste.

Stir-fried Sea Clam: it takes the sea clam meat as the main material, fried with cooked winter bamboo shoot and mushroom. It boasts unique cutting skill, and the clam meat is savory and the color bright. Color, fragrance and taste all add to it.

Su Cai (Jiangsu Cuisine)

It is the local cuisine of Jiangsu Province on the lower reaches of Yangtze River, with the Huaihe River passing through it. It boasts a developed water system, convenient traffic, rich economy and abundant vegetables and sea and river foods. Hence, it enjoys a reputation of a "land flowing with milk and honey" where famous chefs have gathered since ancient times. The first chef with his name recorded and the first city named after the family name of a chef all came into being in Jiangsu (Xuzhou of today was named Dapengguo in ancient time, which was famous for cooking chicken soup for the Emperor Yao). Some special vegetables were provided for the imperial dynasties.

Jiangsu Cuisine developed from Huai-Yang Cuisine, being composed of Yangzhou Cuisine, Nanjing Cuisine, Suzhou Cuisine and Zhenjiang Cuisine, with wide materials but mainly the river, lake and sea foods. The cutting skill is exquisite and the cooking methods are various, being adept at braising, stewing, simmering and warming. It goes in for the original flavor of the materials, light, fresh and moderate as well as salty with a little sweet flavor. The dishes are elegant, beautiful in both form and quality.

Classical Jiangsu Cuisine

Squirrel-like Mandarin Fish: a famous Jiangsu dish, with exquisite color, fragrance, taste and shape. A ruler-long (about one third of a meter) mandarin fish in the plate holds its head high and the tail up, with the bone removed. After being fried and doused with tomato juice, it is crisp inside and tender outside, properly sweet and sour.

Huai'an Ruandou: it is also called as "Fried Eel without Seasoning". The Jianghuai area (mainly referring to Jiangsu, Anhui, Hubei and Sichuan) abounds in eels, and is adept at cooking eel. Taking the eels as main material, chefs make a feast of 108 courses, called "Long Fish Feast", which was famed in the 18th century. The rich-tasting eel can reduce blood sugar, adjust the functions and cure diabetes, so it is especially suitable for the middle aged and old people. It is tender and flavorful, rich in nourishment.

Dried Bean Curd Boiled in Chicken Broth: it is said that the dish was once tasted by the Emperor Qianlong of Qing Dynasty (1644-1911), and hence became well-known. The cooking method is not complicated: add crucian carp brain, crab cream, lard, shallots and ginger and so on into the chicken broth, and after it boils, put in the bean curd chips, cooked diced meat, shelled dried shrimps and a little sauce into the pan together. When it is boiled, thicken the soup with water chestnut powder and then add a little monosodium glutamate, as well as a little sesame oil or pepper to enrich the flavor.

Zhe Cai (Zhejiang Cuisine)

Zhejiang Province adjoins the sea in the east, boasting the famed Zhoushan Fishery and abundant sea products; while the basin in the middle part teems with vegetables and rice. The world-known Jinhua Ham, Hangzhou Dragon Well Green Tea and Shaoxing Rice Wine are all necessary superior materials of the cuisine.

Zhejiang Cuisine is represented by Shaoxing Cuisine, Hangzhou Cuisine and Ningbo Cuisine and developed through innovation. It uses fragrant lees as seasoning and stresses the cooking skills of stewing, braising and pot-roasting and so on. Ningbo leans against the Zhoushan Islands, boasting abundant marine products, so Ningbo cuisine uses local materials including mainly marine products, which tastes a little salty. Hangzhou Cuisine is light and fresh, basically without spicy seasoning as well as thick oil and red sauce. However, the fragrant soft Dongpo Pork Elbow and the sour and sweet West Lake Vinegar Fish and so on leave a lingering taste. Among the large-scale restaurants of Zhejiang Cuisine in Hangzhou, there is Xihu Louwailou opened during the reign of Daoguang of the Qing Dynasy that is famous for West Lake Vinegar Fish and Shrimp Meat with Dragon Well Tea, and Wangrunxing of Qinghefang in the downtown area known for "imperial cuisine", being good at cooking Grass Carp's Head and Bean Curd Soup called Mulang Bean Curd, Jianer Meat and Pickled Bamboo Shoot. In Shaoxing, the Lanxiang Restaurant has standard Shaoxing Cuisine such as Suoyi Shrimp Ball and Fish in Vinegar. There is Dongfuyuan in Ningbo in eastern Zhejiang Province, with authentic local traditional cuisine such as Yellow Fish Soup with Pickled Vegetable and Soft-shelled Turtle with Rock Candy and so on.

Classical Zhejiang Cuisine

Chicken in Light Soup: it is the most ancient cuisine among Zhejiang dishes, with a history of more than 2,000 years. It is cooked with the Shaoxing special local product Yue chicken which has white and tender meat and loose and crisp bone. It is stewed in light soup, fresh and tasty, and was once a tribute for the imperial palace. Currently, the chefs of Shaoxing add ham, mushroom and bamboo shoot as auxiliary materials, making it tastier.

Lady Song's Fish Soup: it boasts a history of more than 800 years. When cooking, stew the mandarin fish and then get rid of its skin and bone, and then boil it with ham, mushroom and bamboo shoot in chicken soup. The cooked dish is of pleasant color, fresh, tender and smooth, tasting like crab thick soup, so it is also called as "Surpassing Crab Thick Soup".

West Lake Vinegar Fish: It chooses medium grass carp which is better to be starved in clear water to get rid of the earthy flavor. After the grass carp is divided into two pieces, clean it and then boil it in the water, but the duration should be controlled well. When putting it on the plate, the sugar and vinegar juice should be poured on it. The cooked dish is of red bright color and fresh and tender meat, sweet and sour moderately, with a little crab flavor.

Hui Cai (Anhui Cuisine)

It was famed throughout China a hundred years ago, and as the story goes, the restaurants of Anhui cuisine at that time were on a large scale, with the uniform rosewood furniture showing the rich heroic spirit. However, in the fierce competition of the modern catering industry, it quietly declined, and, if one does not travel to the Yellow Mountain, it is difficult to taste the authentic Anhui cuisine elsewhere now.

Anhui lies in the hinterland of eastern

China, boasting mild climate and moderate rainfall and with clear four seasons as well as high-quality grains, oil, vegetables and fruits. The mountainous areas of south Anhui Province and the Dabieshan Mountains abound in tea, bamboo shoots, mushroom, agaric, Chinese chestnut, yam, partridge, and soft-shelled turtle and so on. The areas of Yangtze River, Huaihe River and Chaohu River within the territory of Anhui Province are also important production areas of fresh water fish are the sound material foundation for Anhui cuisine.

There are more than one thousand traditional dishes, featuring simple materials, unique duration, pure flavor and various styles. It pays attention to the oil, color, original flavor and the food nutrition. The cooking techniques of Anhui Cuisine include cutting skill, duration and operating skill. The emphasis in Anhui cuisine is on duration, shown uniquely in elaborate dishes cooked by frying, stewing, smoking and braising. That the diverse dishes use various fire control techniques is the key symbol of the cooking accomplishments of the chefs, as well as the basic means by which the crisp, tender, fragrant and fresh characteristics of Anhui cuisine are formed. The skills of smooth frying, braising in light soup and fresh smoking are highly characteristic.

Classical Anhui Cuisine

Stewed Soft-shell Turtle with Ham: its other name is "Stewed Horse's Hoof Turtle in Light Soup", and it is the most ancient famous traditional dish among Anhui Cuisine. Due to the special environment, the soft-shell turtle produced in Houzhou mountainous area boasts higher quality compared with that of other places. The turtle there has thick meat and a ridged back with big colloid, fat and tender without earth flavor. The dish is braised with the famed "Horse's Hoof Turtle in Sandy Land", which was a tribute for the imperial palace. Some literati in latter generations were also attracted to go to Huizhou to taste it, so it is famed all over the country.

Tunxi Pickled Fresh Mandarin Fish: Tunxi Town of Anhui Province was originally an unknown town, and it became a commodities distribution center after Shanghai became an important foreign trade port after 1840. Immediately after the Double Ninth Festival every year, the famous product, mandarin fish, will be transported to Tunxi to sell. In order to keep the fish fresh, the people invented a method of pickling it in light salt water, braising it with small fire after it is fried in boiled oil. It is especially fresh and tasty.

Fuliji Roast Chicken: the roast chicken of Fuliji of Suxian County of Anhui Province boasts beautiful color and nice taste, fragrant and tender. The meat is fat, but not greasy, and when the meat is cooked, it will separate from the bone and is fragrant when chewed. It was listed as a famous dish for the State banquet. It lays extreme stress on the cooking method, having 12 procedures.

Xiang Cai (Hunan Cuisine)

Xiang Cai refers to Hunan Cuisine. Hunan Province lies in the south of the middle reaches of the Yangtze River, boasting moderate climate, abundant rainfall and rich land. The superior natural condition and rich products provided material foundation for the development of Hunan Cuisine.

Hunan Cuisine attaches great importance to sour and spicy flavor. Due to its geographical position, the climate of Hunan Province is mild and wet, so the people there mostly love to eat red pepper to refresh and get rid of wetness. The dishes with the acid pickled vegetables and red pepper as seasonings are appetizing and refreshing. With respect to the styles of the dishes, there are folk dishes, economical popular dishes as well as substantial banquet and elegant feast dishes. There are also home dishes and disease-curing and body-building food cooked with medicinal herbs. There are more than 800 various local dishes and famous courses of local flavors.

Classical Hunan Cuisine

Dong'an Vinegar Chicken: as early as during the reign of Kaiyuan in the Tang Dynasty (618-907), the people of Dong'an of Hunan Province began to cook Dong'an Chicken. The dish is of graceful sculpting and bright color as well as rich nutrition, featuring fragrant, spicy, tongue-numbing, sour, sweet, crisp and tender.

Steamed Mixed Preserved Meat: "bacon" is one of the important characteristics of Hunan Cuisine, with many kinds of materials such as pork, beef, chicken, fish and duck meat and so on. The dish is steamed with various bacons, with thick fragrance of cured meat and salty and sweet flavor. It is of bright red color, pliable but not greasy with a little thick soup. The tastes of it complement each other with their strong points.

Maoshi Bouilli: it uses the pork with half muscle and half fat as material which should be cut into symmetrical lumps, and then it is braised with sauce, a little sugar and red pepper. It tastes sweet, salty and a little spicy, but not greasy, being of golden color. It got its name because it was deeply loved by Mao Zedong.

Islamic Cuisine

This refers to the typical local cuisine of the ethnic minority groups who believe in

Sautéed Ox Tripe with Coriander

Islam, which derived from the food brought by the ancient Arabs more than 1,000 years ago. The prominent character lies in that the killing of the livestock, processing the food and selecting the materials should adhere to the related dietetic commandments of Islam, and the materials should be selected strictly and the food clean. The meat materials are mainly the beef, mutton, chicken and duck meat. Mutton is a prime ingredient, and the cooking skills include quick-frying, frying, stir-frying and instant-boiling. Vegetable oil, vinegar and sweet flavorings are preferred, and the dishes are fresh, crisp, tender, soft and fragrant. Islamic cuisine has made great contribution to the enrichment of the food customs and cooking skills.

Classical Islamic Cuisine

Complete Mutton Feast: it adopts head, brain, eye, ear, gut, liver, kidney, tongue, tail, hoof, muscle, spinal cord, gut and flank as main materials to cook various dishes and form abundant feast. A famous chef of Tianjin Hongbinlou Restaurant created the Complete Mutton Feast of 128 courses.

Stewed Sheep Belly (Yanbao Sandan): "Sandan" refers to part of the sheep or cattle belly, crisp and pliable with special fragrance. It boils the clean belly and cuts it into five cm long and 1.3 cm wide lumps, and then stir-fries it with cooked chicken oil and adds small shallots and ginger slices, light soup, salt, pepper, vinegar, caraway and balsam. The finished dish is crisp, tender, and fresh with strong caraway fragrance.

Fried Mutton: it must be boiled and stewed before being fried, using more than 20 seasonings such as watery yellow sauce and black sauce, spices and rock candies and so on, and then fried in sesame oil. The cooked dish is crisp outside and tender inside, soft, fat but not greasy with many fragrances. It is better to eat it with wine or sesame seed cakes.

Time-Honored Restaurants of China

In November 2006, the Ministry of Commerce of China publicized the reevaluated list of 430 "time-honored brands of China". The evaluation conditions included: the enterprises should have the property rights or access to the brand, and the it should be established before 1956, have passed-down products, technique or services from various generations, feature vivid excellent traditional culture of China and regional cultures, be of historical value and cultural value, enjoy a good reputation and gain widely recognition and praise of society.

Quanjude

Roast Duck, a famous cuisine

Quanjude Duck was established in 1864, with the original location of its headquarters being on the Qianmen Dajie of Beijing; it moved to Hepingmen Dajie in 1979. With regard to the origin of Quanjude, there was a person called Yang Quanren. After arriving in Beijing in the mid-18th Century, after fleeing from famine in Hebei Province, he sold chickens and ducks in the meat market of Qianmen. As accumulating some capital, he bought a bankrupt dry fruits shop in the meat market in 1864 and opened an oven shop, renaming it as "Quanjude" (namely the present Qianmen Quanjude Duck). He roasted the duck over a naked fire, and called it "Gualu Roasted Duck (duck roasted over fire)". The business soon prospered. After the foundation of New China in 1949, Quanjude increased constantly and gradually formed series of delicacies represented by Quanjude Roasted Duck. In May 1993, on the base of the Peking Quanjude, Qianmen Quanjude and Wangfujing Quanjude, it set up a large scale group enterprise, Beijing Quanjude Toast Duck Group Corporation, and at the same time, it gathered more than 60 member enterprises to establish the Beijing Quanjude Group. The presidents, premiers and leaders in about 200 countries such as the former UN Secretary-General Boutros-Boutros Ghali, the late US President Richard Nixon, British Prime Minister Edward Heath, Japanese premier of Japan Kaifu Toshiki, Singapore's senior minister Lee Kuan Yew, the late Indian Prime Minister Rajiv Gandhi, Cambodia's King Norodom Sihanouk have dined there.

Address of the Hepingmen restaurant: No.14 Building, Qianmen Dajie West, Xuanwu District, Beijing
Website: http://www.quanjude.com.cn/

Fangshan Restaurant

Peking Fangshan Restaurant is a time-honored brand dealing in the dishes of imperial flavors. It was set up in 1925 and now belongs to the subsidiary enterprise of Beijing Quanjude Group. It lies in the ancient building clusters in Beihai Park. When it was founded, it was in the charge of a chef of the imperial kitchen, named "Fangshan", which means imitating the manufacturing methods of the imperial kitchen to cook dishes. The main varieties are the snakes of the palace of the Qing Dynasty and typical local dishes.

There are over 800 kinds of imperial dishes in the restaurant, including the Phoenix Tail Shark's Fin, Fried Shrimps and Chicken Chests. The famous snacks includes Yellow Split Peas Cake, Kidney Bean Roll, Small Steamed Corn Bread and Pancakes with Meat-fillings and so on. Feast of Complete Manchu-Han Courses is of the most imperial characteristic. It adopts precious materials such as the eight treasures from the mountain, eight treasures from the sea, the eight bird treasures and the eight grass treasures and so on and the techniques of the barbecue of Manchu and the stewing of the Han, and so on, which absorbs the quintessence of the southern and northern flavors. The complete Feast of Complete Manchu-Han Courses should be eaten over four or six meals. For years, the restaurant has adhered to the tenet of strictly selecting the materials, exquisitely cooking, graceful color and shape, light flavor and stressing the nutrition.

Address: No.1 Wenjin Jie, Xicheng District (in Beihai Park), Beijing

Bianyi Workshop (Cheap Workshop)

It was set up in 1416 by a southerner, Mr. Wang, in the Mishi Hutong outside Xuanwumen without brand name at first. The owner bought live chickens and ducks and then killed and cleaned them to send to other restaurants or rich families. They did some preliminary processing and roasted ducks and spring chickens in the oven as well. Because they tidied the ducks and chickens cleanly and cooked fragrant, crisp and tasty roasted ducks and spring chickens and sold them at low price, the restaurant became popular. Restaurants and rich families called it the "Bianyi Workshop". It began to set up seats in the shop from the beginning of 20th century. It is adept at frying, stir-frying, baking, stewing, pickling and steaming, and so on. There were more than a hundred kinds of courses, and among the several shops, the business of the Roasted Duck Shop of Bianyi Workshop in Xianyukou Street was the most flourishing. What is uncommon is that the shop has not clung to the traditional roasted duck, but constantly brought forth the new styles, manufacturing the series roasted ducks such as "Flower Crisp Fried Duck" and "Vegetable Crisp Fried Duck". It supplements the singleness of the eating style and taste of Peking Roasted Duck.

Now, it has become a group with 10 timed-honored restaurants and one three-star hotel in Beijing.

Address: No. 15 Yongnei Dongjie Zhongli, Chongwen District, Beijing
Website: http://www.bianyifang.com/

Duyichu

Duyichu Steamed Dumplings Restaurant lies to the east of Qianmen Dajie of Beijing. It was set up by Rui Fu of Shanxi Province in 1738, dealing in cold meat, dishes to go with wine and steamed dumplings. It is said that the Emperor Qianlong liked the steamed dumplings at the small restaurant and inscribed "Duyichu" on a stele to bestow on the shop. Nowadays, the stele is still hung on the center of the shop. The steamed dumplings stress the cooking method: the dumpling coat is made of dough made with boiling water; and the stuffing is of aquatic foods, pork and crab meat. The shape of the dumplings looks like megranate, as well as lotus flower.

Other well-known snacks include "Zha Sanjiao (deep fried triangular snack)", "Fried Spring Roll", and "Buddha Hand" and so on. The stuffing of the "Zha Sanjiao" is frozen pork with soup and is cut into small lumps, and then they are made into the shape of glutinous rice dumplings; it tastes crisp outside and tender inside. The cold dishes include Braised Pork with Iris Ensata Thunb, Steamed Preserved Pork with Distilled Grains Liquor Dregs and fried dishes such as Double Fried Pork and so on, which are all excellent. With the changes of people's life, Duyichu constantly increases some favorable local dishes to satisfy the public from all walks of life with the steamed dumplings. Currently, it belongs to the Beijing Pianyi Workshop Roasted Duck Group Limited Company.

Address: No.36 Qianmen Dajie, Chongwen District, Beijing

Hongbinlou

Hongbinlou Restaurant was set up in 1853, and is a time-honored restaurant of Islamic flavor. It became famed for its unique dishes throughout Beijing, and was praised by the epicures as "the first building of Islamic food in Beijing".

There are over one hundred dishes with the unique point that all the names of the dishes have the Chinese character "yang" (sheep). It is to adhere to the canon of Islam and the living custom of Muslims. The skillful cooking methods include stewing, frying, braising, quick-frying and stir-frying. The main courses are "chopped chicken and shark's fins", "Braised deep-fried Cattle Tail in Brown Sauce", "Cowheel", "Braised Sheep Head in Marmite","Braised Sheep's Ear" and "Fried Kidney" and so on.

Address: No.11 Zhanlanguan Lu, Xicheng District, Beijing
Website: http://www.hongbinlou.com.cn

Fengzeyuan

Fengzeyuan Restaurant is a time-honored brand dealing in Shandong Cuisine. It was built in 1930. There are four yards at its location, Zhushikou, with dark green halls and tile roofs, tidy and spacious. The dining halls boast fine silverware, including the drinking vessels made during the imperial reigns of Kangxi and Qianlong. It employs famous chefs and selects superior materials, featuring unique characteristics. Hence, it became the good place for high-ranking officials and nobles, generals, celebrities and famed personalities of old Beijing. Meanwhile, it added Jiaodong Cuisine to the original single Jinan Cuisine of Shandong flavor, and became the most representative restaurant of Shandong Cuisine in Beijing. Since the foundation of New China in 1949, it has received honored guests from more than 90 countries. Currently, it is the subsidiary enterprise of Beijing Quanjude Group.

The dishes of Fengzeyuan boast elaborate materials and precious manufacturing and pay attention to the cutting skill and duration. It is adept at quick-frying, frying, stewing and steaming, with the courses being of pure and comfortable taste, bright color and favorable shape. Brand dishes include Shark's Fin Stewed in Pot, Braised Sea Cucumber with Scallion, and Diced Chicken with Egg White.

Address: No.83 Xidajie, Zhushikou, Xuanwu District, Beijing

Donglaishun

The founder of Donglaishun was Ding Deshan of Hui ethnic group. In 1903, he sold mutton bean flour and buckwheat cut cakes on a stall in Dong'an Market, adding cakes and porridge later. Due to the increasingly flourishing business, he hung up the signboard of "Donglaishun Porridge", meaning "being from the east of Beijing, all go well" in Chinese. In 1914, the restaurant added fried, roasted and instant-boiled mutton and fried dishes, and renamed "Donglaishun Mutton Restaurant".

Donglaishun cuisines

Donglaishun Restaurant is famed for dealing in instant-boiled mutton, featuring delicate materials, careful processing, complete condiments and vigorous fire and so on. It only adopts the mutton from the high quality gibbed caudala jumbucks in the sheep production area of Silinggele League in Mongolia. The sliced mutton is well known for being thin, even, neat and graceful. A half kilogram of mutton can be cut into 80 to 100 slices, each of which is only 4.5 grams with a length of 20 cm and a width of eight cm, and each slice is folded with clear grain. After being instantly boiled in the dried shrimps and agaric soup, it is delicate and fragrant without smell and oily taste. The condiments contain gingili sauce, rice wine, pickled bean curd, pickled leek flowers, pot-stewed shrimp oil, sauce, capsicum oil and shallot and so on, which are integrated with the fragrance, salt, peppery, pot-stewed, and fresh tastes. In addition with the white peeled sweet garlic and gingili baked cake, it tastes wonderful and unique. Besides the instant-boiled mutton, the restaurant also deals in various Islamic fried dishes, including more than 200 kinds such as the Ganbao Mutton and Yanbao Liji and so on.

In 1996, Donglaishun adopted the chain development road of franchising and established the Donglaishun Chain Headquarters. Currently, there already have over one hundred shops in the country, and Beijing Donglaishun Group Limited Company was established in 2006.

Address of the headquarters of Beijing Donglaishun: Fifth floor of Xindong'an Mansion, No.138 Wangfujing Dajie, Dongcheng District, Beijing
Website: http://www.donglaishun.com

Barbecue Wan

It is the time-honored barbecue restaurant. Its founder was Mr. Wan of the Hui ethnic group in Jingdong Dachang over 300 years ago. At the beginning, he pushed a cart with a charcoal brazier and grill to sell roasted beef along the streets near Xuanwumen. He firstly cut the beef into slices and pickled them, and then roasted them. In the cool autumn and cold winter, it was warming to eat barbecue around the grill. The unique flavor was popular among the masses. With the improvement of managerial style and enlarged fame, many famous celebrities joined the masses in tasting the food.

The beef of Barbecue Wan is selected strictly, with only high-rib, tenderloin and zigai adopted. It also only selects the Xikou Sheep without strong smell, adopting the mutton from high-rib, Shoulder Pole Meat and so on. With respect to the cutting skill, it stresses thin but not loose, symmetrical and tidy slices like the flower in the plate. The wooden materials for toasting the beef are pine branches, smelling fragrant after being burned. The seasonings include sauce, cooking wine, shrimp oil, tomatoes and egg white and so on, and they can be selected according to the customers' taste. Firstly, put the beef slices into mixed juice to pickle; secondly, after the beef is pickled, put shallot slices on the hot grill and then put the tasty beef on top of them; thirdly, add some caraway powder to the roasted beef, so can it be eaten. The beef slices are smooth and tasty, fat but not greasy and thin but not dried, with a special fragrance and tasty flavor. Nowadays, the restaurant also deals in over one hundred Islamic dishes.

Address of the headquarters: No. 102 Xuanwumennei Dajie, Xuanwu District, Beijing

Barbecue Ji

Barbecue Ji Restaurant is located near picturesque Shichahai Sea of Beijing. It is said that, in 1848, Ji Decai of the Hui ethnic group in Tongzhou in eastern Beijing sold roasted mutton on a stall in the Lotus Market near Shichahai and hung up a cloth sign of "Barbecue Ji". After dealing in the business for many years, the family accumulated some wealth and bought a small building to officially operate the restaurant. Nowadays, it becomes the first place for the domestic and foreign guests to enjoy Chinese traditional food.

For more than one hundred years, Barbecue Ji maintained the traditional flavor. It is due to its elaborate processing and exquisite materials that the business keeps flourishing. It selects the mutton of the Xikou Sheep and only adopts that from the back legs and high-ribs. Muscle and moisture is removed before the meat is cut into thin, translucent pieces. The seasonings are complete and carefully selected from fixed places and can be mixed according to the customers' taste. In the hall of the restaurant, there are iron grills under which fragrant pine branches are burned. When eating the barbecue, the people stand around the grill, with one foot stepping on the long wooden stool and the other on the floor. In one hand is held a bowls in which there are seasonings such as sauce,

Barbecue Ji at night

vinegar, ginger powder, cooking wine, pot-stewed shrimp oil, shallot slices and caraway, and using long bamboo chopsticks to dip the sliced mutton into the bowl before putting then on the grill. When cooked, it is better to eat with sweet garlic, cucumber strips and hot ox-tongue cakes as well as wine. Especially in the cool autumn and cold winter, the sweat while eating, feeling comfortable throughout.

Address: No.14 Eastern edge of Qianhai Sea, Di'anmenwai Dajie, Xicheng District, Beijing

Tongchunyuan

The predecessor of Tongchunyuan Hotel is the famed Tongchunyuan Restaurant of Jiangsu Cuisine, opened in 1930 in the prosperous Xidan Commercial District. At the beginning of its operation, it gathered several superior chefs to quickly establish its reputation.

The restaurant is good at cooking fresh products from rivers, with many famous fish and crab dishes. The cooking methods are mainly composed of stir-frying, frying, quick-frying and braising, and the dishes taste fresh, tender, light and a little sweet. The cooked courses keep their original flavor and though crisp and soft but still maintain the original shape. Especially the cooking skills of fish are abundant, such as Dry-fried Herring, Meat Stewed in Soy Sauce, Dry-fried Head and Tail, and Head and Tail in Terrine, Sugar and Vinegar Tile-like Fish, and Spiced Barbecued Fish and so on.

Address: No.14-A Xinjiekouwai Dajie, Xicheng District, Beijing

Quyuan Restaurant

It is a time-honored brand restaurant of Hunan Cuisine in Beijing, with a history of more than 150 years. Before it entered Beijing, it had been of certain scale in the whole country, already owning branches in Kunming and Nanjing, and so on. The authentic Hunan Cuisine won the favor of customers and well-known celebrities from all walks of life often ate there, especially travelers from Hunan Province often gathered. The dishes pay attention to the function of the seasonings as well as the color and are adept at using bacon materials. The flavor features fresh, acid and spicy and soft and tender. The skillful cooking methods include stewing, braising, steaming stir-frying and dry-frying. The characteristic dishes have Dong'anzi Chicken, Sleeve-fish with Liichi, Fried Bacon and Steamed Fish Head with Capsicum and so on. Now, it also deals in Beijing Roasted Duck.

Address: No.145 Fuchengmen Dajie North, Xicheng District, Beijing

Emei Restaurant

It is a time-honored brand restaurant of Sichuan Cuisine in Beijing and was set up in 1950. Before the founder Wu Yusheng came to Beijing, he was already the top-ranking master of Sichuan Cuisine in China. The courses feature elaborate style, stressing color, fragrance, and taste with respect to the cooking methods according to the Chengdu Genre. As for the taste, it is rich, strong and pure. It also lays emphasis on cutting skill and sculpting, adjusting the seasonings.

Kung Bao Chicken (Salted Chicken Cubes with Peanuts) is a famous dish of the restaurant, and has been selling well for 50 years. It is unique as well as common, selecting the chicken from the legs of the young cocks, which is especially tender. The cooking duration is controlled extremely accurately. The diced chicken and pignuts must meet standards with regard to color and shape. It should be cooked when the pan is hot and the oil is warm and the juice should be poured quickly. It should reveal five flavors, sweet, a little acid, light pepper fragrance, salty and fresh and a little tongue-numbing successively. After the dish is eaten, only the red oil can be seen on the plate, without juice.

Address: No. 58 Beilishi Lu, Xicheng District of Beijing

Gongdelin

Shanghai Merits and Virtues (Gong-de-lin) Vegetarian Restaurant was founded in 1922, being the famous Buddhist vegetable restaurant. It was opened by Zhao Yunshao, the apprentice of the Master Gao Weijin of the Changji Temple of Huangshan of Hangzhou City, with the original location at Guizhou Crossing of Beijing Road East. It moved to near Nanjing Road West on Yellow River Road, and began featuring Buddhist ceremonies and Huai-yang Cuisine. The main famous dishes include "Spiced Preserved Bean Curd", "Gongde Ham", "Vegetable Crab Powder", "Asparagus in White Juice" and "Arhat Vegetable", and so on. Besides celebrities from all walks of life of China, it also has received honored guests from other countries.

Beijing Gongdelin Restaurant was built in accordance with the original appearance of the Shanghai restaurant on prosperous Qianmen Dajie South. It is famed for its exquisite dishes, high-quality service, reasonable price and comfortable environment. "Eighteen Arhats" is the characteristic dish there, including more than ten materials such as soybean, egg white, rape, winter bamboo shoot, lotus seed, and currants, and so on. It tastes salty and fresh as well as comparatively light, with rich nutrition and reasonable arrangement.

Address: No.158 Qianmen Dajie South, Chongwen District, Beijing

Old Zhengxing

In 1862, two persons from Wuxi of Jiangsu Province came to Shanghai. They set up a small restaurant mainly dealing in fresh products from rivers and seafood in the Dalu Market of Jiujiang Road, naming it "Zhengxing Restaurant" by adopting the two Chinese characters in their names respectively. Because Shanghai was developing into an important commercial port then and attracting a large number of domestic and foreign enterprises, the city's catering industry flourished in a short time. "Zhengxing Restaurant" got famous for its high-quality food, rational price, exquisite materials and delicacy in the respects of color, fragrance and appearance. Subsequently, several accomplished apprentices went business with the brand of "Zhengxing Restaurant", so Mr. Cai and Mr. Zhuo renamed it as "Old Zhengxing Restaurant" to keep their own reputation. For over a hundred years, the old restaurant has adopted the fresh products from Taihu Lake area as materials, featuring South China flavor and worthwhile Shanghai Cuisine.

In 1956, through the negotiation of the governments of Beijing and Shanghai, the Old Zhengxing Restaurant in the Fourth Street to the east of Xizang Road of Shanghai was asked to move to the Qianmen Dajie of Beijing, being renamed as "Shanghai Old Zhengxing Restaurant", especially dealing in the characteristic dishes of Shanghai. The special peach-shaped birthday cake there has an especially good reputation.

Address of the headquarters of Shanghai Old Zhengxing Restaurant: No. 556 Fuzhou Lu, Shanghai
Website: http://www.laozhengxing-sh.com/
Address of Beijing Old Zhengxing: No. 45 Qianmen Dajie, Beijing

Ma Xiangxing Restaurant

Located on the northwest side of Gulou Square in Nanjing, the restaurant serves genuine Nanjing Cuisine with Islamic flavor. It was founded by Ma Sifa, a Hui from Meng County of Henan Province in 1840. After his son, Ma Shengxiang, succeeded to the restaurant, he renamed it. In the early 20th century, it dealt in Islamic dishes "Niu Bayang" as its characteristic, and later introduced such famous dishes as "Beauty's Liver", "Squirrel-shaped Fish", "Phoenix-Tail-Shaped Shrimp", "Eggs and Shaomai Cakes", "Calabash-shaped Duck with Eight Treasures" and "Lotus-shaped Chicken Pieces".

Address: No.5 Zhongshan Beilu, Gulou District, Nanjing, Jiangsu Province

Taotaoju Restaurant

Taotaoju Restaurant, set up in 1880, features green tea and snacks of Zhejiang and Jiangsu Province and Cantonese dishes.

When drinking tea, the Guangzhou people give priority to "Week Dim Sum", which refers to seasonal varieties changed each week. The variety includes corresponding salted kinds of Chinese pastry and sweet snacks, i.e. four salted kinds of Chinese pastry and four sweet snacks, six salted kinds of Chinese pastry and six sweet snacks or eight salted kinds of Chinese pastry and eight sweet snacks. The shape of dim sum is diversified, including square, round, cuneiform, fancy edge and winding drum. Its colors are coordinated, including yellow, orange, red, and milky white. Each branch tries to be unique in creating novel varieties. It serves hundreds of famous dishes such as oven-roasted duck, grilled chicken and abalone fins in soy sauce, thin-skinned fresh-shrimp-stuffed dumpling, Taotao fragrant scallion chicken, Mapi "bag" and seven-color shelled fresh shrimps.

Address of Guangzhou Taotaoju Restaurant: No.20 Dishifulu, Liwan District, Guangzhou, Guangdong Province

Goubuli Restaurant

Goubuli Bun (steamed stuffed bun) is a traditional snack with flavor famous not only in Tianjin but across the whole country. Its founder was a 14-year-old boy from a peasant family. The stuffed buns made from the half-leavened dough are pleasantly oily and savory without a greasy taste, similar to chrysanthemums in shape and unique in the color, fragrance and taste, so they have long been liked by customers and were even praised by the royalty of the Qing Dynasty. Since it was founded in 1858, the Goubuli Bun Shop has developed into a large-sized group with the Goubuli Hotel, General Goubuli Shop, Goubuli Deep-Frozen Food Distribution Center, Goubuli Fast Food Ltd, Goubuli Materials Circulation Ltd and some 60 franchise chain enterprises.

Address of the General Restaurant of Tianjin Goubuli: No.77 Shandonglu, Heping District, Tianjin
Website: http://www.gblkc.com

China's Tea Culture

Tea was discovered and utilized in China about four or five thousand years ago. The cradle of tea is southwest China. Big wild tea plants of one thousand years ago are still found in Yunnan Province and other areas. Chinese tea drinking saw much develop0ment in the Tang and Song dynasties.

Cha Jing (Classic of Tea), China's and even the world's first treatise on tea, was written in the Tang Dynasty. This book summed-up the knowledge on tea picking, tea processing, tea steeping, the benefit of tea and tea utensils in an all-round way. In the Tang Dynasty, as the tea-drinking tradition spread from south to north China, it also reached neighboring countries.

Emperor Zhu Yuanzhang (1368-1398), who founded the Ming Dynasty, changed the ball tea to leaf tea, and then the tea-drinking custom underwent great changes lasting to this day. As people gained an increasingly deep understanding of tea, they did not depend on picking wild tea leaves, but opened cultivated tea plantations. The technique of processing tea also matured. Because of different processing techniques, six major varieties came into being.

Chinese Cha Dao not only includes judging the quality of tea, but also sets detailed requirements on water and tea sets, time and occasion for tea drinking, steeping and drinking ways and the drinkers. Drinking tea can make people realize the property of tea, and is conducive to keeping health, and grasping the truth of "drinking tea and cultivating oneself".

Famous Chinese Tea

The tea plants originally grew in the virgin forest on the high mountains and with much rainfall in Yunnan, Guizhou, Sichuan and other provinces. Later through artificial planting and replanting, people gradually summed up the tea plants' habits of liking warm, humid and shady environment. General speaking, the temperature the most suitable for the growth of tea plants ranges from 18 to 25 centigrade. Below five centigrade, the tea plants stop growing while above 40 centigrade they are easy to die. Tea plants like the moist habitat featuring high water content both in the air and in the soil. The quality of tea has great relations with the altitude of the place where the tea is produced. Take the world-known Wuyi Yancha (cliff tea) as an example. It is divided into three varieties, i.e. the "Zheng Yancha" produced in the mountaintop, the "Ping Yancha" in mountainside, and the "Zhou Cha" in the flatland and valley. The higher altitude at which the tea is produced, the rarer it is. In addition, the sunshine and soil also play the decisive role in the growth of the tea plants.

China has had the saying that "the famous mountain has produced the famous tea from of old". Take the Chinese famous mountain in the list of "World Heritage" as an example. There are several types of traditional famous tea such as the Wuyi Yancha (cliff tea), Huangshan Maofeng, Lushan Yunwu, Emei Maofeng, Wuling Guzhang Maojian, and Qingcheng Xueya and so on. It is obvious that the high percentage of forest coverage, rich animal and plant resources and healthy environment are conducive to maintaining the exuberant life force of tea plants.

Green Tea

Green Tea

Green tea is the oldest tea, as well as the most widely produced in China. Many provinces and cities are well-known for producing green tea, with Zhejiang, Jiangxi and Anhui provinces as the leader. The spring tea leaves which are plucked during the period from the Waking of Insects to the Pure Brightness Festival (April 5) is the "Mingqian Tea" also called "Tou Tea". The tea leaves are light green in color and taste pure and bitter. Two weeks after the Pure Brightness Festival is the Grain Rain, when the area south of the Yangtze River sees drizzle to moisten the grain, marking the arrival of the second peak of spring tea picking. The tea leaves plucked after the Pure Brightness Festival and before the Grain Rain are called the "Yuqian Tea", and the tea leaves plucked after the Grain Rain, "Yuhou Tea". The price of the spring tea varies according to its picking time. The earlier the tea leaves are picked, the more expensive they are. The green tea plucked in early spring is considered best.

Green tea is the non-fermented tea, which keeps the original savor of tea to a large extent: refreshing and light fragrance and long aftertaste. When drinking, one feels it is light, but after tasting carefully one feel the mouth is full of a faint scent. The green tea is processed through the "steaming green", "pan-frying green" and "drying green" technique, that is to say, the moisture of the fresh tea leaves is removed through steaming, pan-frying and drying in the sun to gain the fragrance of tea. To steep, the green tea does not use the boiling water but that with a temperature ranging from 80 to 90 degrees. Add a little hot water into the cup to steep the green tea for a while, and fill the cup, and steep it for one or two minutes; or, pour the hot water into the cup and then add the tea leaves to it.

West Lake Longjing (Dragon Well Tea)

Hangzhou is one of China's most beautiful cities, having enjoyed the great reputation from old. The West Lake is the most well-known scenic spot in Hangzhou. As early as the Tang Dynasty, the Tianzhu Temple and Lingyin Temple near the West Lake were celebrated for producing tea. Longjing Tea, whose name dated back the Song Dynasty, is produced in the five places in the vicinity of West Lake. It has been famous for its "green color, full-bodied fragrance, sweet flavor and beautiful shape". Longjing tea is the leader among Chinese famous teas.

The Longjing tea-picking period ranges from 190 to 200 days, and the picking totals 22 times from the same plant at intervals of seven to ten days. The quality of the tea depends on the time of the tea-picking. The best Longjing is the "Mingqian Tea" plucked before the Pure Brightness Festival, followed by the "Yuqian Tea" picked after it but before the Grain Rain.

In steeping Longjing tea, one had best use the spring water from the "Hu Pao Quan", luscious and clear, which boasts high water molecule density, large surface tension, and low content of calcium carbonate. It is best to use a transparent glass as the tea settles so as to view and admire the unfolding and up-and-down changes of the tea leaves in the water. The proportion of tea leaves to water is about 1:50. Pour the water of a quarter cup, steep the tea leaves to make them absorb water and fold; when the tea fragrance is detected initially, pour the hot water into the cup, and lift the teapot and water with the force of wrist up and down three times so as to make the tea leaves turn over in the water. The steeping method "phoenix nodding three times" lets the tea leaves touch the water. "Nodding three times" is just like bowing down and saluting guests, which shows respect for the guest and Cha Dao. Longjing tea leaves can be steeped three times. The taste of the second steeping is the best.

Longjing Tea leaves at the West Lake in Hangzhou come into buds.

Huangshan Maofeng

Huangshan Mountain, located in Anhui Province, has been the leader among China's famous mountains from of old. It has overlapping ridges and peaks, among which there are 77 peaks with an elevation of 1,000 meters or above. Huangshan Mountain has a long history of producing tea and the tea made a name for itself in the middle period of the Ming Dynasty. At that time, people liked the Huangshan Mountain's marvelous spectacle "sea of clouds", and named the tea produced in the Huangshan Mountain "Huangshan Yunwu (cloud and mist)". Huangshan Maofeng is green accompanied with a light yellow color, is covered with white hairs and its bud is sharp-pointed, like the peak, hence the name. After being steeped, the tea water is clear, slightly apricot. It tastes mellow, rich and gaudy. After being steeped five or six times, it still contains fragrance. If Huangshan Spring water is used to steep the tea, even when the tea water is left overnight, there is no sediment mark on the cups.

Biluochun (Green Spring Snail Tea)

Biluochun is produced on Dongtingshan Mountain in Wu County of Suzhou City, Jiangsu Province, thence also the name "Dongting Biluochun". It is characterized by its strong fragrance. When the Qing Emperor Qianlong visited the area, a local official served Emperor Qianlong this tea. Before he held the cup and drank, he felt that the full-bodied fragrance assailed the nostrils. After drinking, he acclaimed that this tea deserved its fine reputation. But he disliked its inelegant name and then thought up "Biluochun". Biluochun is green in color, like a trumpet shell in shape, and covered with hairs. It is best to use the glass to drink it. After absorbing the moisture, the tea leaves slowly unfold, floating and sinking, and the silver hairs appear like snowflakes blowing in the wind, which gives not only enjoyment in smell and taste, but has visual aesthetic impact, too.

• Lu Yu

Lu Yu (733-804) is known for writing the *Cha Jing*, and he was also respected as the "Tea Sage", "Tea God" and "Tea Immortal".

Tradition has it that he was born ca. 733 in the Tang Dynasty. Legend has it that a traveling monk found three wild geese protecting a newly-born baby with their wings. He carried the baby back, adopted him and named him Lu Yu (meaning Land Feathers in English). At that time, drinking tea prevailed in Buddhist temples. As a child, Lu Yu followed the monk to pick tea leaves, and learned unconsciously the knowledge of making tea. Later, Lu Yu traveled widely, investigated the producing areas of tea, and learned the methods of picking and processing from farmers, thus accumulating rich knowledge. In 760, he moved to Wuxing of Zhejiang Province, withdrew to the mountains and wrote his classic.

Its publication drew national attention. The emperor even offered him an official position, but he was accustomed to living an idle and free life, i.e. lingering in the tea house and reciting poems with friends.

Mengding Ganlu

Mengding Ganlu is one of the Chinese teas with the longest history, listed as leader among tribute teas as early as the Tang Dynasty. Mengshan Mountain is located in Mingshan County and Ya'an County of Sichuan Province. On the top of the central peak, there is a stretch of flatland where the Mengding Ganlu tea plants grow.

Tradition has is it that, in the Western Han an accomplished monk, Master Ganlu, planted tea trees on top of Mengshan Mountains, thence the name Mengding Ganlu. It has been recommended as an "Immortal Tea".

Mengding Ganlu is tightly curled in shape with many hairs, and light green. After being steeped, the clear tea water produces full-bodied aroma; the second steeping is best.

Taiping Houkui

Taiping Houkui is produced in Houkeng of Taiping County, Anhui Province, a place which is surrounded by hills, boasts picturesque scenery, abundant rainfall, great humidity, much sunshine and fertile soil.

A folk tale recounts the origin of Taiping Houkui. Once upon a time, a mountain villager climbed up to pluck tea leaves. All of a sudden, he smelled a refreshing faint scent and looked around for the source. He found several tea plants growing between the stone crevices on a precipitous cliff, but there is no way to climb up it, so he was unable to pick them. Later, he raised a monkey and when the tea-picking season arrived, he let the monkey climb up the cliff to pick the leaves. The tea leaves are plump with full-bodied aroma. After being processed, the leaves are not messy, warped and bent, but the leader among various teas, hence the name "Houkui (chief of monkeys)".

Taiping Houkui is dark green in color, sharp-pointed at the two ends, flat and straight in the middle and heavy. After being steeped, the clear tea water produces full-bodied aroma. The leaves unfold, floating or sinking.

Taiping Houkui

Xinyang Maojian

Xinyang Maojian is mainly produced in the mountainous area in western Xinyang City of Henan Province, where there are ranging hills, towering peaks, and streams found everywhere. Covered with mists all year around, the area boasts a deep, fertile layer of earth and great humidity. The unique natural conditions are convenient for tea plants to absorb various nutrients so that the characteristics of Xinyang Maojian are formed, such as strong, stout buds, and soft and tender leaves. The finished products are round-bar-shaped with a cutting edge. The tea water is light green, buds and leaves fresh and tender, fragrance full-bodied. They can be steeped four to five times.

Liu'an Guapian

Liu'an Guapian is produced in Liu'an and Jinzhai counties of Anhui Province. The finished tea is shaped like a melon seed, thence the name Guapian (seed). It was long an imperial tribute tea in ancient times. Liu'an Guapian tea is a kind of splinter-shaped green tea processed through the pan-firing green, and the "Guapian" produced in Qiyunshan Mountain in Jinzhai County is of best quality. Qiyunshan Mountain, with lofty ridges and peaks, flourishing forests, mild climate, plentiful rainfall and fertile soil, is suitable for the growth of tea plants. The tea produced in the mountain has a flat shape, strong and stout bud, slightly warped leaf edges, soft leaf and regular size. When steeping, it produces a light aroma, full-bodied savor and sweet aftertaste. The Liu'an Guapian tea leaves differ from other green teas in the picking. The picking season is about the time of the Grain Rain. Until the top buds unfold and the tender leaves ripen, the leaves can be plucked so as to keep the high content of beneficial components in the tea.

Lushan Yunwu Tea

Lushan Yunwu Tea is China's traditional famous tea. Located in northern Jiangxi Province, Lushan Mountain boasts towering and graceful peaks, flourishing forests, upwelling currents and rising mist. With a long growing period, the leaves of the Lushan Yunwu tea plant contain highly beneficial ingredients, more than common tea leaves in the content of tea alkaloid and Vitamin C. With a strong bud and stout leaf, and white hair appearing, Lushan Yunwu Tea is famous for its strong and pervasive fragrance, deep flavor, green and clear tea water.

Black Tea

Black tea is the most produced in the world. It belongs to the fermented tea made from fresh tea leaves by withering, kneading, fermenting and drying. Green tea water is bright green and the black tea water orange red, which is the difference between them on the surface. A more important difference is that black tea is made not through the steaming green or pan-frying green methods, but fermenting, in the course of which a chemical reaction occurs in the tea leaves, reducing the tea polyphenols by 90 percent and promoting the production of new components such as theaflavin and chahongsu. If the proportion of theaflavin to chahongsu element is moderate, the tea water appears red and bright. The green tea keeps the original refreshing savor of tea leaves while the fermented black tea is characterized by its full-bodied and strong aroma.

Chinese Black tea is grouped into three varieties, namely Souchong, Gongfu Black tea and black tea. Souchong is the black tea that appeared earliest in China and was produced in

• Cha Jing (Classic of Tea)

Cha Jing (Classic of Tea) is divided into three sections and ten chapters: first, "the origin of tea" discusses the origin, names, varieties, producing areas and characteristics of tea; second, "the tea utensils" gives the description of the tools by which the tea leaves are plucked and processed, and the methods of application; third, "tea processing" introduces the tea-picking time and requirements, and the six procedures of processing, and groups tea into six grades according to shape and color; fourth, "tea ware" records 20 or 30 varieties of wares used for preparing tea; fifth, "making tea" gives the description of the detailed way that the tea is brewed and judges the water quality of various areas; sixth, "tea drinking" reviews the history of drinking tea and describes the tea-drinking method; seventh, "tea events", a chapter with most contents, compiles documents discussing tea in ancient books and collects 43 historical characters and 48 fames, literary quotations and fables concerning tea from the ancient times to the Tang Dynasty; eighth, "the producing areas", divides the tea-producing area of the country into eight sections, groups the tea leaves produced in each section into four grades, and gives detailed explanations; ninth, "omissions", discusses which wares can be omitted under certain conditions and which procedures can be simplified; tenth, "the diagram", suggests drawing the aforementioned contents into diagrams, putting up them on the wall and often looking at them to maintain proper procedures.

Cha Jing contains the knowledge on tea from picking to processing and to drinking, and puts up the framework of tea culture in an all-round way, being a veritable encyclopedia on tea. Later, it translated into many languages and spread abroad.

the Chong'an area of Fujian Province. Gongfu Black tea is China's specialty developed on the basis of Souchong, as well as the representative of China's black tea s. According to the producing area, it is divided into the several famous varieties, i.e. Anhui Qimen Gongfu, Yunnan Dianhong Gongfu, Jiangxi Ninghong Gongfu, and Fujian Minhong Gongfu.

Zhengshan Souchong

Zhengshan Souchong is a variety of black tea unique to China, which is produced in the high mountains in Chong'an County of Fujian Province. The mountains are known for high temperature, mist, large difference in temperature between day and night reduce the consumption of organic substances in the tea, and stop the condensation of glucide and the forming of fibrin, thus making the tea leaves have natural endoplasm. The leaves are completely fermented and processed through the pan-firing green and baking techniques different from those of Oolong, so this kind of tea has a unique style. The tea bar is tight, round and straight, and the ruby black tea water is clear, dense, with a hint of the fragrance of pine burning smoke and longan soup. It tastes mild without any bitter savor. The leaves in the water are red and unfolded.

Qimen Gongfu Tea

Qimen Gongfu tea has a history of more than 100 years. The tea leaves are plucked about the time of the Pure Brightness Festival. They are processed through the initially making and refining. The newly-plucked tea leaves are made into primary tea first and according to the weight, color and shape, is then classified for refining. The tea is baked in sealed rooms under a low temperature for slow baking so as to let the fragrance of tea leaves emerge.

After being made, the tea water is bright red with full-bodied aroma and long aftertaste. Because the way Qimen Gongfu is processed varies, different Qimen Gongfu produces different tastes, such as sugar aroma, flowery aroma, and fruity aroma, which is internationally known as "Qimen Fragrance".

Oolong Tea

Oolong tea, created in the early Qing Dynasty and also called "Blue Tea", is a half-fermented tea lying between green tea and black tea. In processing Oolong, both the "killing green" technique used in making green tea and the fermentation technique used in processing black tea are adopted, so Oolong has the refreshing flavor of green tea and the full-bodied fragrance of black tea . Even in shape, Oolong maintains the features of green tea and black tea, namely, the light green leaf blade and crimson leaf edge. Oolong is cord-shaped. After being steeped, the leaves are stouter than the green and black tea leaves. With mellow aroma they can be steeped many times.

Oolong tea is mainly produced in Fujian, Guangdong and Taiwan provinces. The famous varieties include Anxi Ti Guanyin, Wuyi Da Hong Pao (Big Red Gown) and Dongding Oolong, which are mainly tasted in the contemporary Chinese Cha Dao. When drinking Oolong tea, small and fine tea utensils are indispensable. It is appropriate to use a small tea pot and cups. Fill three-quarters of the pot with tea leaves and add a little boiling water to wash them; dump this first steeping water, and then fill the tea pot with boiling water again, steeping for two or three minutes, and then serve.

Ti Kuan Yin

Anxi County of Fujian Province is located on the southeastern slope of a mountain, where more than 50 varieties of tea are produced, among which Ti Kuan Yin is the leader.

The tea plant producing Ti Guanyin is delicate in nature, hence "Ti Guanyin is savory to drink but the tea plant is difficult to grow". In the last ten-day period of March, the tea plants sprout, and the tea leaves are plucked in the first part of May; but picking can continue all year-round. The output of the spring tea is largest, while the fragrance of the autumn tea is strongest. The Ti Guanyin tea bar of good quality is curly, tight and heavy with its top like the head of a dragonfly, trunk like the helix in shape and the end like the leg of a frog. The tea bars which produce the clear and melodious sound when being thrown into the tea pot are regarded as top grade.

When steeping the Ti Guanyin, the boiling water is a must to make the tea fragrance throw off fully.

When steeping Ti Guanyin, boiling water is a must, as this can make the tea fragrance spread wide. The just-steeped Ti Guanyin tea produces a sweet-scented fragrance accompanied with a light Chinese chestnut taste, which is the big difference between Ti Guanyin and other varieties of Oolong tea. Ti Guanyin contains more than 30 mineral substances, such as kalium and fluorine, among which the content of selenium is highest. These substances can promote production of immune protein and antibodies, thus boosting body immunity. The tea has a certain curative effect on coronary heart disease. In addition, the fragrance of Ti Guanyin is of great benefit to pleasing the body and mind and keeping in good health.

Wuyi Yancha (Cliff Tea)

(See P428)

Dark Tea

Dark tea belongs to the post-fermented tea and was created absolutely by chance. Historically, the tea leaves produced and processed in Yunnan, Sichuan, Hubei, Hunan and other provinces were transported to western China, a very long journey. Carried in bags on horseback, the tea leaves were affected by damp and dried again, so that great changes took place in their chemical compositions and the tea leaves turned dark after being blown and dried. However, their fragrance assailed the nostrils and soon won a following in the west. Then, people summed up the method of processing dark tea: after killing green and kneading, pile up the tea leaves and drenched them to make them fermented, and then dry them. The dark tea water is yellow like amber. It tastes pure and aromatic.

Unlike green tea, the black tea acts in a diametrically opposite way. It uses the coarse and old tea units consisting of one bud and five or six leaves as the raw material. The green tea leaves are not suitable for being kept for a long time, while the longer the black leaves are kept, the more fragrant they are. Moreover, they are able to bear being steeped many times while the taste of green tea becomes lighter after being steeped two or three times. Pu'er tea and Liupu Tea are rare varieties among black tea.

Pu'er Tea is a kind of ball tea. The supreme charm of Pu'er is that the more antiquated it is, the more fragrant.

Pu'er Tea

Pu'er Tea, a kind of ball tea, is named after Pu'er of Yunnan Province, the distribution center and one of the original producing areas. Pu'er tea, unique to Yunnan Province, was created more than 2,000 years ago. The post-fermentation procedures of tradition Pu'er tea lie in the oxidation after steam pressing and the blowing of the wind, drenching of the rain and drying in the air during transportation. The constant changes of temperature and humidity of the tea leaves creates a biochemical reaction, which is a natural course.

Pu'er tea can be divided into two varieties: one is the tea processed through the simple "drying green", called "raw Pu'er", and the other is the tea made through fermenting caused by the heaping up and drenching, called "ripe Pu'er". The supreme charm of Pu'er is that the older the Pu'er, the more fragrant. Pu'er tea of good quality should be bar-shaped, with orderly grains, while the tea leaves with small and broken grains are degraded products. After being steeped, Pu'er tea water is clear and bright, and an oil droplet-like membrane floats on the surface.

There are some skills in steeping Pu'er tea. First, use a screw driver made from hard wood or hard bamboo to peel the Pu'er tea layer by layer, but avoid producing fanning. Before drinking, the peeled tea leaves should be set aside for two weeks. A teapot with a big body is selected to avoid the quick dissipation of the heat. First, use the boiling water to wash tea leaves so as to arouse the tea properties. You can taste the second steeping, and from then, the steeping time needs to be prolonged gradually. Each time, you should drink half or 60 percent of the tea water. Some tea water needs to be left to steep the tea leaves so that the full fragrance is given off. When the tea water color becomes light and tasteless, the boiling water is poured into the cup, which is drunk again after it is put aside for half an hour. The last steeping tea water contains the essential Pu'er tea.

Yellow Tea

When processing green tea, people found that if the tea leaves were not dried in a timely way, or thoroughly after killing green and being rolled, they would turn yellow, which is the origin of yellow tea. Originally, yellow tea was regarded as green tea of inferior quality. However, some people grew to prefer it. Yellow tea belongs to the fermented tea category, and the course of fermentation is called "Men Huang". After being strictly covered, the leaves turn yellow and then they are dried. Junshan Silver Needles produced in Hunan Province, which is one of China's ten major famous tea areas, belongs to yellow tea.

Junshan Silver Needles

Located by Dongting Lake, Junshan Mountain is surrounded by water and evaporation means the mountain is wreathed by clouds and mist all year around with humid air. The sandy soil on the mountain, deep and fertile, is very suitable for the growth of tea plants. From of old, it got the name of "Tea Island on Dongting Lake". The raw materials of Junshan Silver Needles enjoy stout and straight buds, even size and complete and bright white hairs. They are processed through 11 procedures. The finished products are like silver needles in shape and golden yellow inside. When steeping, put some Junshan Silver Needles leaves into a glass, and pour in boiling water. At this time, the leaves move vertically, falling and coming up to the surface. The water produces a mellow aroma.

Junshan Silver Needles is one of China's ten major famous teas. When steeping, put some Junshan Silver Needles leaves into the glass, and pour the boiling water into it. At this time, the leaves move vertically, falling and coming up to the surface, and at last, stand in a cluster at the bottom of the cup.

White Tea

The white tea is the mildly fermented tea, which only goes through two processes, namely, withering and drying. The finished products which are mostly the buds with the tiny white hairs are like the silver and snow, hence the name. At present, Jianyang, Fuding, Zhenhe, Songxi and other counties of Fujian Province are the main producing areas with undulating hills, mild climate and plentiful rainfall. The hilly country has mostly red and yellow soil, in which the Fuding Big White Tea; Zhenghe Big White Tea; Narcissus; Vegetable Tea are mainly planted.

In general, the white tea is plucked in the unit consisting of one bud and two leaves with the white hairs. The processing method neither destroys the activity of enzymes nor promotes the oxidizing action, and maintains the fragrance of the white tea and refreshing tea water. The White Peony and Pekoe Silver Needle both are top grade. The silvery white haoxin tea between the green leaves is similar to the flower in shape, and after being steeped, the green leaves hold the tender buds as if the bud is in bloom, thence the name "White Peony". The white tea made from the stout buds plucked from the Big White Tea Plants is called "Pekoe Silver Needle." It is white like the silver and similar to the needle in shape, thence the name. This produces a refreshing aroma, light yellow tea water and delicious flavor.

Compressed Teas

The compressed tea is made from the primary tea through compression and steaming at high temperature. According to the shape, it is divided into cake tea, brick tea and ball tea. The tuocha tea in Yunnan is an outstanding example.

Scented Teas

Scented tea is the tea made from the edible dried flowers, with a history of more than 1,000 years. The commonest are jasmine tea and chrysanthemum tea. The former is most popular in north China while the latter has numerous lovers because the chrysanthemum produced in Hangzhou has the good reputation of "tribute chrysanthemum".

Mongolian Tea with Milk

Living in Inner Mongolia and some areas adjoining the province, Mongolians mainly live on beef and mutton, complemented with rice and vegetables. The Mongolians usually have tea three times and one meal a day. To drink salty tea with milk is not only a way of quenching thirst but also a major source of nourishment. Every morning, the first thing that a housewife does is to prepare a pot of salty tea with milk for the whole family. Mongolians like drinking hot tea, so they usually drink it while eating fried rice in the morning and leave the pot on the fire. Every day, Mongolians go out in the early morning and graze the herd for a whole day, so there next meal is after they return home in the evening, but they keep drinking salty tea with milk during the day.

This uses green or black brick tea as its main material and an iron pot as the cooker. Fill the iron pot with 2 to 3 kilograms of water, and then put 50-80 grams of brick tea pieces into the pot once the water boils. After another five minutes, pour milk into the pot with a ratio of 1:5 to water and stir it, and then add a certain amount of salt and boil.

The Three-Course Tea of the Bai Ethnic Minority

The Bai live scattered in southwest China and most of them are distributed in the beautiful Dali area of Yunnan Province. The Three-Course Tea of the Bai ethnic minority is a dramatic tea ceremony. This ceremony was originally held by the senior members of a family to express best wishes to juniors when they were going to pursue studies, learn a skill, start a business or get married. Now, to drink Three-Course Tea has become a conventional ceremony when people of the Bai ethnic minority greet guests.

The first course of tea is called bitter tea, meaning that one will suffer a lot before she/he starts a career. After the water boils, the host takes out a special grit jar for tea making, puts it on a slow fire, and adds leaves. The host will shake the jar to evenly warm the leaves, and immediately add boiling water after the tea leaves in the jar turn yellow and emit a caramel fragrance. The boiling tea water is poured into the tea cup with the amount of half the cup, which is held with both hands and served to the guest. The first course has the color of amber and tastes bitter and acerbic.

The second course of tea is called sweet tea. After serving the first course, the host will empty the pot and repeat the procedure right from the beginning. This time, the host will add brown sugar, a special fan-shaped dairy product, and Chinese cinnamon into the handless cup, and then pour the tea into the cup with an amount of 8/10 cup.

The third course is called aftertaste tea. The brewing procedure is the same as the previous ones, but the materials added in the handless cup are honey, popcorn, Bunge prickly ash, and walnut kernel with a water amount of 6/10 or 7/10 cup. When drinking this course, one should shake the cup to mix up all the materials and then drink while it is hot. One will find a flavor of sweet, sour, bitter, and pungent. One is sure to keep in mind the philosophical theory that bitter comes first, sweet second.

Gongfu Tea of Chaozhou

Tibetan Buttered Tea

Sichuan and Yunnan provinces in southwest China were the main tea producing areas in the ancient times, so someone thought that Tibet, bordering the two provinces, had tea in the Han Dynasty (206 BC-220 AD). A ballad circulated that "the people of Han ethnic group are filled with rice while that of Tibetan ethnic group are filled with tea", and "[Tibetans] would rather go without food for three days, but not do without tea for only one day". It is because the Qinghai-Tibet Plateau lacked vegetables and the local people mostly lived on meat and milk; furthermore, not only is the tea a boon for digestion, but also provides the necessary vitamins for the human body.

Like the people in the Luyu Time of the Tang Dynasty, when the Tibetan people drink tea, they don't make it by pouring water into the cup but boil it with salt. Common families of Tibetan ethnic group have a special bucket for making buttered tea. They pour the boiled tea soup in the bucket and add butter, salt, egg and walnut kernel and so on. Then, they use a wooden stick with a holed disk attached to the bottom to pump up and down until the tea soup and butter are completely mixed, and this produces the fragrant and sweet butteblack tea with long-lingering flavor. Since the people of Tibet live in high and cold areas, buttered tea can quickly blow away the coldness and supply the energy as well as prevent the lips from being dry and cracked.

Gongfu Tea

Gongfu tea is a unique custom of the Chaozhou region of Guangdong Province. It has existed since the Tang Dynasty. It is not just the first line of courtesy, as people of Chaozhou who travel or reside overseas use it as a way of paying respect to their ancestors. "Gongfu" refers to the adept tea-making skills. Authentic Chaozhou Gongfu tea sincerely abides by the old traditions, usually limiting the number of participants including host and guests to four. After the guests are seated, the host starts to work his magic. The Zisha ware teapot should be the first choice for Gongfu tea, and the smaller, the better. The common ones are about as big as a fist, and the cups are even smaller, about half a Ping-Pong ball size. The small and exquisite tea sets are to keep the freshness of the tea, pouring and immediately drinking.

The kind of tea chosen is oolong. Before making tea, the hot water is needed to rinse out the tea pot and warm the tea cups, and then the tea leaves are stuffed into the pot to seven or eight-tenths full. Then, the boiled water is poured into the pot from a high place. The first round is to rinse the tea leaves and the tea should be poured out immediately to add boiled water again until overflowing the pot. The next step is to use the lid of the pot to get rid of the floating foam and cover the lid, pouring the whole pot with boiled water to rinse the foam on it and raise the temperature of the pot body to make the tea smell fragrant quickly. One or two minutes later, it is the time to taste the tea being made for the second round. When pouring tea, it should be done at a low level to keep the warmth of the water and not make foam. One should put all the cups together and pour the water into them one after another quickly without stopping, which is called "Guangong patrols in the cities". It aims to make the tea of each cup have the same flavor, which also shows the host's equal treatment to all the guests. When the thickest tea water is left,

Tea Served in a Set of Cups of Chengdu shows leisure and comfort.

containing the essence of the tea, one should evenly distribute it into each of the cups, and, when coming to the last cup, all the tea is poured out, which is called "Hanxin counts the soldiers". Finally comes the course of tasting the tea, with the order being to watch the color of the tea, smell the fragrance and then sip it gently.

Tea Served in a Set of Cups

Sichuan is the cradle of Chinese tea, as well as the area with a highly developed tea culture of China. Walking in the streets of Sichuan, various kinds of tea houses are seen everywhere. The people of Sichuan loved to drink the tea served in a set of cups which included tea boat, tea lid and tea bowl, mostly the porcelain. The tea boat is the utensil where the tea bowl is put in to insulate the heat. The tea lid is the greatest invention of the people of Sichuan in regard to tasting the tea, with many functions: covering the tea bowl to form a relatively closed space to make the tea leaves smell fragrant; remove the floating tea leaves in the bowl when drinking; pour the tea in the upturned lid to cool it when thirsty and impatient; upturn the lid to put it on the bowl, notifying the waiter to add water when the tea in the bowl is mostly drunk off. The people of Sichuan Province think water boiled in iron and aluminum ware damages the taste of the tea, so they mostly utilize a copper teapot with a long spout. When making tea, the masters in the tea house who specially take charge of adding water for the customers lift high the copper teapot, pouring the water straight into the bowl from a distance, and when the bowl is full, they only shake their arm once to stop the water, without one drop splashing outside. The customers cover the cup with a lid to wait for the tea infused.

Big-bowl Tea

The custom of drinking big-bowl tea prevails mostly in north China, which can be seen on the docks, at the both sides of the streets, on a building site and in workshops and on the farm and so on. Drinking big-bowl tea is a kind of old custom of the Han ethnic group. Hence, since ancient time, selling big-bowl tea was listed as one of 72 industries in China. Though this kind of drinking tea with big bowl is comparatively rough and of "wild flavor", it is natural and needs no special accommodation. It just requires convenient furnishings such as one desk, several farmhouse-style chairs and coarse porcelain bowls. Hence, it is seen in the style of tea stalls or tea pavilions, for the passersby to satisfy their thirst and have a rest. Because the big-bowl tea is close to the life of the masses, it is still very popular nowadays.

Busy in picking tea-leaves

A corner of an elegant tea house

▲ Tea House

Drinking tea is the primary function of tea houses. Besides presenting the art of tea, new varieties are required to be recommended to satisfy the diverse requests of customers. In the winter, tonics are always added to dispel cold for the customers, while, in the summer, something dispelling hotness and cooling will be added, with the cold beverages such as sweetened bean paste, coconut wine, bittern plum water and pawpaw juice and so on, which are can co-exist with tea and not spoil the flavor. The cultublack tea houses attach great importance to their tea sets, and matching different sets for the various teas is the basic method. Some even provide special manufactublack tea sets which could not be seen in the market for the customers to show their deep cultural feeling. The tea houses can be regarded as a vivid miniature of Chinese tea culture and the free life of the people of China.

In order to attract more customers, the tea houses generally hold some entertainment activities. The oldest form which also lasts until now is to invite actors to tell stories. Sichuan boasts many characteristic tea houses. Sitting in the tea house from morning until closing time in the evening, you will not be charged any additional fee. Hence, the tea houses are busy all day long, becoming the sites for people to have a rest, amuse themselves, communicate and do business amid the heat and fragrance of tea.

Tea houses face much competition in modern society, but they still survive as a timeless reflection of Chinese philosophy.

The Art of Wine in China

Chinese wine features the tradition of making wine with corns. The yellow wine, or rice wine, being one of the three main kinds of alcohol beverage (rice wine, grape wine and beer), is very popular. A very important winemaking innovation by the ancient Chinese was the use of yeast. The primitive forms of yeast were molded or germinated crops, mainly wheat and rice. People reformed the molded crops to make distiller's yeast. The yeast contains bacteria that turn starch into sugar and saccharomycete, which facilitate the forming of alcohol. Different kinds of yeast are adopted in different regions, creating much variety.

The basic ingredient for rice wine varies by region. In the north, it is sorghum, millet and glutinous millet, while, in the south, mostly rice (sticky rice being the best choice) is used. The wine's alcohol content is usually around 15-proof, and becomes tastier as time goes by. In many parts of China are families that have the tendency of making their own wines. It demonstrates just how popular the method of using yeast in winemaking is. Some devoted wine drinkers believe that truly delicious wines come not from wineries, but from the hands of skillful common people.

Traditional Chinese white liquor (spirit) is the most characteristic of distilled alcohol. At around the 6th to 8th century, China already had its distilled liquor. Guizhou and Sichuan provinces are the two publicly acclaimed provinces in production of superior grade white wine. Even so, due to differences in natural produce, every region in the north and south use different base ingredients. Nearly every province produces its own unique label with tastes to match local tastes.

Custom of Drinking Wine

"Bottom's up" is a custom practiced widely in both south and north China. When a banquet begins, the host usually delivers a few words of welcome, followed by the first toast. The host first finishes his cup until the last drop, in what we call "finishing first as respect" for the guests. Sometimes, the host will also need to propose toasts to the guests individually in the order of importance. Anyone not returning the favor would be considered disrespectful and would often be subject to punishment in the form of having to consume more drinks. Guests can also propose toasts amongst themselves.

"Marriage Wine Feasts" have long been synonymous with weddings. To prepare for "marriage wine feasts" is the same as preparing for weddings. To drink "marriage wine" means going to attend a wedding. At a wedding banquet, the bride must propose toasts to the parents and guests. The newly weds must also have "arm-crossed wine" to imply a hundred years of happy marriage. On the third day after the wedding, the bride must take the groom back to her parents' home. The bride's family will host a banquet to welcome them; this is called "homecoming wine."

"Month-old wine" or "hundredth-day wine" is popular banquets held for celebration according to Chinese tradition. When the baby is a month or one hundred days old, the parents will put on feast for family and good friends. Most guests will bring gifts or will wrap money inside a small red paper envelope called a "red bag" for the child's family.

Chinese have a custom of preparing birthday feasts for elders in the family. A senior of sixty, seventy, eighty, ninety or even a hundred years can be called "da shou," or "grand longevity." Most times, the banquet is prepared by the sons or daughters, or the grandchildren; attendees include family members and dear friends.

Guizhou Moutai Wine

This is one of the few famous Chinese wines. Guizhou Moutai or Maotai Wine is honored as "the national wine". It is produced in Maotai Town, Renhuai County of Guizhou Province. It has a long history, and is recorded as early as in 135 BC. In 1840, the output of Moutai hit 170 tons, which was rare in the brewing history of Chinese distilled spirit. In 1915, on the Commodities Contest of Myriad Countries in Panama, Moutai Wine won the Golden Medal and diploma, becoming famous internationally.

Wuliangye Wine

This is one of the few famous Chinese wines. Wuliangye Wine belongs to the Highly Flavor Type Spirit, produced by Sichuan Yibin Wuliangye Distillery. Yibin lies in southern Sichuan Province at the junction of the Jinshajiang and Minjiang rivers. It boasts pure water which is suitable to make wine. It is said that as early as over 3,000 years ago, the wine-making industry appeared in Yibin.

The various raw materials and the old fermenting cellar combined to perfect the favorable characteristics of Wuliangye. The present Wuliangye Wine is made from five kinds of high-quality grain namely rice, sticky rice, corn, broomcorn and wheat according to the ingenious prescription. It features "long fragrance, pure taste, mellifluence, refreshing, harmonious flavors and moderation", and is famed for its complete flavor.

Luzhou-flavor Laojiao

This is one of the few famous Chinese wines. Luzhou lies in southern Sichuan at the junction of the Yangtze and Tuojiang rivers, with no extremely cold days in winter. Its mild climate, abundant rainfall and fertile land created good conditions for wine-making. As early as the Eastern Han (25-220), Qujiu Wine was already being made. It is pure with strong fragrance, sweet and refreshing with lingering-flavor.

Xifeng Spirit

Xifeng Spirit is one of the old famous wines in China, produced in Liulin Town, Fengxiang County of Shaanxi Province. Fengxiang was called "Yongxian" in ancient times, which is said to be the place where the phoenixes appeared. There are drinking vessels such as the goblet and Tingjue (an ancient wine vessel with three legs and a loop handle) of the Spring and Autumn Period (770 -476 BC) and the drinking vessels and copper pot of the Warring States Period (475 -221 BC) and so on among unearthed cultural relics.

Xifeng Wine features the unique flavor of "Feng-style" wine, being of moderate strength and harmonious combined taste of sour, sweet, bitter, spicy and fragrant. It blends the advantages of light-flavored and strong-flavored wines, with harmony between fragrance and taste. It belongs to the Daqu Spirit of compound flavor. The features of Xifeng Spirit include: colorless, limpid and transparent, fragrant, sweet and pure with fruity fragrance and lingering aromatic aftertaste. It is extremely liked by drinkers who love ardent spirits.

Xinghua Cun Fen-flavor Spirit

Xinghua Cun Fen-flavor Spirit is the time-honored wine as well as the representative of light flavor spirits as a complement to Guizhou Moutai and Luzhou Laojiao south of the Yangtze River. Its exquisite production technique is honored among the Famous Chinese Wines, and it is famed for its extraordinary color, fragrance and taste. It is produced in Fenyang City of Shanxi Province, and as early as more than 1,500 years ago was already famed throughout China as a product from the former Xinghua Village, a center for wine making and wine culture. Fen-flavor features limpidness, faint scent with elegance, purity, softness, refreshing and lingering aromatic aftertaste.

Passing through the lanes with Nu'erhong Wine

Shaoxing Jiafan Wine

Shaoxing is the old town of wine in China, with worldwide reputation. Shaoxing Wine belongs to rice wine ("Huang" Jiu in Chinese alphabetic writing, and "Huang" meaning "yellow" in color), being the famous traditional wine produced by Zhejiang Shaoxing Distillery. The wine follows the rule that "the older, the more fragrant", so it is also called as "Shaoxing Old Wine". Among famous Shaoxing Wines, the best known is "Jiafan Wine", which has won a State Gold Medal. It is of limpid orange color and strong fragrance, and will not go bad for long time.

♦ China Cuisine Association

The China Cuisine Association was built in 1987, being the national association of the catering industry formally approved by the Ministry of Civil Affairs. It is the nationwide trade organization crossing the departments and system of ownership, composed of enterprises and public service units dealing in catering operations, management and cooking skills, dining hall service, food culture, catering education, cooking theory, and research on nutrition, the trade organizations at all levels, social groups, operations managers, experts, scholars, chefs and service staff of the catering industry on a voluntary basis. Since the foundation of the association, it has actively conducted the work in the aspects of trade organization, trade self-discipline, resource integration, maintaining the rights of enterprises, business coordination, international communication and manpower training and so on, serving society, governments, members and enterprises and so on and playing an active role in promoting the progress and development of the trade.

Website: http://www.ccas.com.cn/Index.html

Traditional Customs

Traditional Festivals

China is a country with many ethnic groups and a long history of 5,000 years. In the constantly developed historical course, many characteristic traditional festivals came into being. In ancient China, most seasons and festivals were related to the increasingly rich astronomical, calendar and mathematical knowledge and especially the solar terms of the lunar calendar had a close relationship with the forming of traditional festivals. In the Han Dynasty, the 24 solar terms dividing a year basically came into being. The solar terms provided the precondition for the formation of festivals with the changes of seasons, and the various folk activities and the sacrificial activities. The traditional festivals were not only an important part of the cultural and recreational life of the masses, but also an opportunity for the trade and cultural exchanges. Almost every festival was a fair trading day as well as a cultural exchange day.

Some grand traditional festivals such as the Spring Festival, the Pure Brightness Festival, the Dragon Boat Festival and the Mid-Autumn Festival are still carried on by the masses. They not only carry on and develop the excellent components of the culture of traditional festivals, but have also introduced new content and forms. However, some small festivals have gradually been forgotten and have disappeared from the daily life.

Spring Festival

The Spring Festival is the most important festival for the Han people, as well as a grandest traditional festival among the common people in China. Apart from the Han, a dozen ethnic minorities such as the Manchu, Mongolian, Yao, Zhuang, Bai, Gaoshan, Hezhen, Hani, Daur, Dong and Li also have the custom of celebrating it.

The Spring Festival originated from the activities of offering sacrifices to gods or ancestors at the end of the year in the Yin and Shang Dynasties. It is the first traditional holiday of the year for Chinese people. On the last day of the old year, people paste couplets on the doors, hang up red lanterns, and also paste the "Fu" character and images of the Fortune God. It falls on the first day of the first lunar month, the beginning of a new year. The Eve of Spring Festival (lunar New Year's Eve), is an important time for family reunions and a sumptuous dinner. Some families stay up all night "seeing the old year out." The next morning, people pay New Year calls on relatives and friends, wishing each other good luck. During Spring Festival, various traditional activities are enjoyed in many parts of China, notably lion dances, dragon lantern dances, land-boat rowing and stilt-walking.

In China's mainland, it is stipulated that "the statutory holiday of Spring Festival" lasts for seven days. No matter how far they are, people will rush home for the festival and family union. People take the festival as the demarcation line between the old and new years.

Spring Festival (setting off firecrackers)

La Yue (the 12th Lunar Month) and Laba Porridge

The 12th lunar month is commonly called "La Yue". In ancient times, once the 12th lunar month came, all the people including both the imperial families and the common ones held a "12th lunar month fete". From the advent of the month, all the activities for the Spring Festival gradually increase.

In many places of China, the eighth day of the 12th lunar month is considered as the beginning of the Spring Festival activities. Since that day, the Buddhists boil this kind of porridge, chanting and worshiping the Buddha to commemorate him on the eighth day of the 12th lunar month every year. They called the porridge "Laba Porridge" and used to give it to the poor people in the hope that they could be blessed by the Buddha. Subsequently, the Buddhist custom gradually spread to the masses, and every family also began to boil "Laba Porridge".

The custom of "eating Laba Porridge" also related to the season. The people thought that in the midwinter, the boiled "Laba Porridge" could nourish, relieve the cold and warm the stomach. The porridge includes eight kinds of main materials and eight kinds of ancillary materials, corresponding to the character "ba" (meaning eight), which implies auspicious. However, due to the vast territory, different products and food habits of various places in China, the materials vary accordingly.

Spring Festival Customs

There is a saying that "no matter rich or not, wash and sweep cleanly to spend the New Year". The people practically spring-clean to ring out the old year and ring in the new. From the 23rd of the 12th lunar month to the New Year's Eve, every family should do thorough cleaning, washing various wares, mending and washing clothes and curtains, sweeping courtyards and whisking away the dust and cobwebs, with no corner left untouched. So, this kind of "sweeping away dust" comes to be associated with clearing away misfortune to make room for a New Year with fresh hope.

The New Year celebration has gone unchanged for several thousand years. Hence, a lot of preparations should be made before it. With the advent of the 12th lunar month, the people begin to purchase various commodities for food, use, wearing, entertainment and decoration as well as those for the relatives, friends and ancestors. All the things concerned with New Year should be properly prepared. For the moment, all the markets are filled with people, with a strong "New Year" flavor.

Spring Festival Foods

In north China, after having the New Year's Eve dinner, the whole family will prepare to make Jiaozi dumplings, which symbolize the alternation of old and new in Chinese culture. Furthermore, the shape of Jiaozi dumpling looks like shoe-shaped gold, so it also symbolizes money and valuables. Some families prefer to eat the dumplings at midnight of New Year's Eve and some on the morning of the first day of the first lunar month, adding more festive atmosphere to the Spring Festival. The usual stuffing of the dumplings includes pork with leek, pork with celery, pork with cabbage, pork with fennel and mutton with carrot and so on. Some families also prepare many new types for fun, specially making some unusual dumplings for good wishes, and the one who eats the special dumpling seems especially lucky and wins warm blessings from everyone.

Southern people are used to eating rice cake and boiling rice dumplings, with the rice cakes meaning "ranking higher year after year" in Chinese (adopting the homophonic tone of "higher" in Chinese) and the rice dumplings symbolizing "reunion" for its round shape. In one word, in order to spend an auspicious and satisfactory New Year, the people also stress good luck in the food.

Staying Up All Night

Staying up all night on New Year's Eve is also an important activity. It is said that this was formerly adopted to guard against the attack of the fierce monster, and the people got together to protect each other and drive it away. Later, although firecrackers had scared off the monster, staying up all night became a custom. In the past, it proceeded with eating the New Year's Eve dinner. At night, the whole family sat around the table, eating and chatting till the deep night. Nowadays, with the development of the TV industry, the form of staying up all night also changed. Generally, after the family finishes the dinner, they will sit around the TV to watch the live Spring Festival Gala Evening. At the 11 or 12 o'clock, thousands of households began to set off firecrackers, extremely noisily. Staying up all night shows not only the attachment for the past but also the expectation for the New Year.

Dumplings at the New Year's Eve

▲ Spring Transportation

In the concept of Chinese, spending the "Spring Festival" means the reunion of the family, so no matter how far the people are away from home, they hope to return for a reunion. Hence, once the Spring Festival comes, railway, road, air and water transportation will experience peak travel. Taking 2006 for example, from January 14 to February 22, the peak season lasted for 40 days, with a flow of hundreds of millions across regions. Totally two billion person/times made the journey.

Paying New Year's Calls

Paying New Year's calls is the necessary ceremony in the Spring Festival. The blessings and greetings such as "Happy New Year" and "Wishing you good fortune" express the wonderful hopes for the New Year.

Generally speaking, people should pay New Year's call on their own family's elders, and in the regions stressing the traditional ceremony, the close kin juniors should kowtow before the elders and give their good wishes to them. The elders will give "gift money" to the juniors with suitable blessing. On the second day of the lunar New Year, the married daughters will pay New Year's call on their parents. Besides the families, the neighbors, colleagues and friends also pay calls to each other. With the modern developments, the form of paying New Year's calls has changed and phoning or sending short messages already becoming normal.

The folk fireworks at the Temple Fair in Zhengzhou

Visiting Temple Fairs

Another grand activity in Spring Festival is temple fairs. In olden times, in order to acknowledge the deities, the people went to the temples to burn joss sticks and worship at the beginning of the New Year, forming characteristic temple fairs. The temple fairs today are mostly the site for commercial trading and cultural entertainment. The people can purchase commodities as well as watch folk performances such as the dragon dance, lion dance, stilt, yangge, land boat and diabolo and so on. Every year, the Changdian Spring Festival Temple Fair, White Cloud Temple Fair, Dongyue Temple Fair of Beijing and the Temple of Town God Fair, Longhua Temple Fair, and Jing'an Temple Fair of Shanghai and so on are very noisy. The colorful folk performance and the characteristic snacks enthrall travelers.

Beijing Longtan Temple Fair

The Lantern Festival

The 15th day of first lunar month is Lantern Festival. It marks the end of the traditional Chinese Spring Festival.

The custom of watching lanterns at the Lantern Festival gradually formed. Later, this activity prevailed in all dynasties, to which was added the dragon dance, lion dance, land boat, stilt and yangge and so on.

Eating rice dumplings is a food custom of Lantern Festival. "Yuanxiao" (rice dumpling) is called "Tangyuan" in the south, because it is round, symbolizing the meaning of reunion. The stuffing of the rice dumplings are generally made with white or brown sugar, sweet-scented osmanthus, nuts and gingili and so on. It is boiled mostly, but some people also fry it.

Guessing the Riddles Written on Lanterns is one of the activities of the Lantern Festival. The riddle written on lanterns is the paronomasia special to China, which hides the identity of the object temporarily, but forms wonderful words with the background and clues related to the object for others to guess. The answer can be a word, short sentence, historical character and so on. The old game is a good way for improving people's ability to understand the language.

Tomb Sweeping Festival

(See P438)

Dragon Boat Festival

(See P438)

Chinese Valentine's Day

(See P439)

Mid-Autumn Festival

(See P439)

Double Ninth Festival

(See P439)

• Lunar Calendar

In ancient times, China depended upon agriculture, and agricultural production relied upon the weather to a great extent. So, industrious and intelligent ancestors of Hua Xia had a thorough understanding of the weather, calendar and climate. On a Chinese traditional calendar each month follows one cycle of the moon, and the intercalation is adopted to make the average length of a year equivalent to the tropical year. The Chinese calendar is a lunisolar calendar, incorporating elements of a lunar calendar with those of a solar calendar. It is used for farming, so it is known as the "agricultural calendar". On the calendar, each year has 12 month, 354 or 355 days, 11 days less than the tropical year. In this regard, seven intercalary months will be inserted every 19 years to harmonize. The arrangement of intercalation depends on the Twenty-Four Solar Terms. The first day of each lunar month is calculated according to the position of the Sun and the Moon, instead of automatically.

正月

春节	初二	初三	初四	破五
初六	人日	初八	初九	初十
十一	十二	十三	十四	元宵
十六	十七	十八	十九	二十
二十一	二十二	二十三	二十四	填仓
二十六	二十七	二十八	送穷日	三十

二月

初一	二月二	初三	初四	初五
初六	初七	初八	初九	初十
十一	十二	十三	十四	十五
十六	十七	十八	十九	二十
二十一	二十二	二十三	二十四	
二十五	二十六	二十七	二十八	
二十九				

三月

初一	初二	初三	初四	初五
初六	初七	初八	初九	初十
十一	十二	十三	十四	十五
十六	十七	十八	十九	二十
二十一	二十二	二十三	二十四	
二十五	二十六	二十七	二十八	
二十九	三十			

四月

初一	初二	初三	初四	初五
初六	初七	初八	初九	初十
十一	十二	十三	十四	十五
十六	十七	十八	十九	二十
二十一	二十二	二十三	二十四	
二十五	二十六	二十七	二十八	
二十九	三十			

五月

初一	初二	初三	初四	端午
初六	初七	初八	初九	初十
十一	十二	雨节	十四	十五
十六	十七	十八	十九	二十
二十一	二十二	二十三	二十四	
二十五	二十六	二十七	二十八	
二十九	三十			

六月

初一	初二	初三	初四	初五
初六	初七	初八	初九	初十
十一	十二	十三	十四	十五
十六	十七	十八	十九	二十
二十一	二十二	二十三	二十四	
二十五	二十六	二十七	二十八	
二十九	三十			

七月

初一	初二	初三	初四	初五
初六	七夕	初八	初九	初十
十一	十二	十三	十四	十五
十六	十七	十八	十九	二十
二十一	二十二	二十三	二十四	
二十五	二十六	二十七	二十八	
二十九	三十			

八月

初一	初二	初三	初四	初五
初六	初七	初八	初九	初十
十一	十二	十三	十四	中秋
十六	十七	十八	十九	二十
二十一	二十二	二十三	二十四	
二十五	二十六	二十七	二十八	
二十九	三十			

九月

初一	初二	初三	初四	初五
初六	初七	初八	重阳	初十
十一	十二	十三	十四	十五
十六	十七	十八	十九	二十
二十一	二十二	二十三	二十四	
二十五	二十六	二十七	二十八	
二十九	三十			

十月

十月一	初二	初三	初四	初五
初六	初七	初八	初九	初十
十一	十二	十三	十四	十五
十六	十七	十八	十九	二十
二十一	二十二	二十三	二十四	
二十五	二十六	二十七	二十八	
二十九	三十			

冬月

初一	初二	初三	初四	初五
初六	初七	初八	初九	初十
十一	十二	十三	十四	十五
十六	十七	十八	十九	二十
二十一	二十二	二十三	二十四	
二十五	二十六	二十七	二十八	
二十九	三十			

腊月

初一	初二	初三	初四	初五
初六	初七	腊八	初九	初十
十一	十二	十三	十四	十五
十六	十七	十八	十九	二十
二十一	二十二	小年	二十四	
二十五	二十六	二十七	二十八	
二十九	除夕			

The Twenty-Four Solar Terms

The Twenty-Four Solar Terms were originated in the Yellow River reaches. As early as the Spring and Autumn Period (722 BC-481 BC), there were four solar terms, i.e. mid-spring, midsummer, mid-autumn and midwinter. Later, they were improved and perfected constantly. In 104 BC, the Twenty-Four Solar Terms were written in the Tai Chu Li created by Deng Ping and others, which defined the astronomical position of every solar term.

"The 24 solar terms" was created mainly on the basis of variations of climate. Simply speaking, there are 24 points on the orbit while the earth goes round the Sun, which are similar to the milestones on the orbit. When it comes to a certain point, the weather will be what it should be. The length of the daylight appeared the longest and the shortest respectively at summer solstice and winter solstice. In spring and autumn, there is a day, respectively, when the length of the day and that of the night are the same, and they are vernal equinox and autumnal equinox. As the Sun is at a different angle to the earth while it goes around the Sun, every season was divided into six solar terms, then the 24 solar terms in total. There are two within one month. Every solar term reflects the variations of climate like four seasons, and temperature. They also reflect the earth's revolution about the Sun, so which day every solar term falls on the Gregorian calendar is basically fixed.

Starting from the Vernal Equinox—0 degree of celestial longitude, the days when the sun travels 15 celestial degrees on the ecliptic longitude are called a solar term. The sun travels 360 degrees each year, so there are twenty-four solar terms. Then, in each month, there were often two solar terms of qi; the first one was generally named 'jieqi' including the Beginning of Spring, the Waking of Insects, the Pure Brightness, the Beginning of Summer, Grain in Ear, The Slight Heat, the Beginning of Autumn, the White Dew, the Cold Dew, the Beginning of Winter, the Great Snow and the Slight Cold, and the other 'zhongqi', including the Rain Water, Spring Equinox, Grain Rain, Grain Ripening, Summer Solstice, Great Heat, Limit of Heat, Autumn Equinox, the Frost's Descent, the Slight Snow, the Winter Solstice and the Great Cold. 'Jieqi' and 'zhongqi' appear by turns, each lasting 15 days. Now, they are called by a joint name “solar terms”.

As far as the names of the 24 solar terms are mentioned, the division of the solar terms gives a full consideration to the change of the season, climate, phenology and other natural phenomena. Some of them reflect the change of seasons such as the Beginning of Spring, the Beginning of Summer, the Beginning of Autumn, and the Beginning of Winter; some embody the turning points of the change in the height of the sun such as the Spring Equinox, the Summer Solstice, the Autumnal Equinox and the Winter Solstice which are divided from the point of view of astronomy.

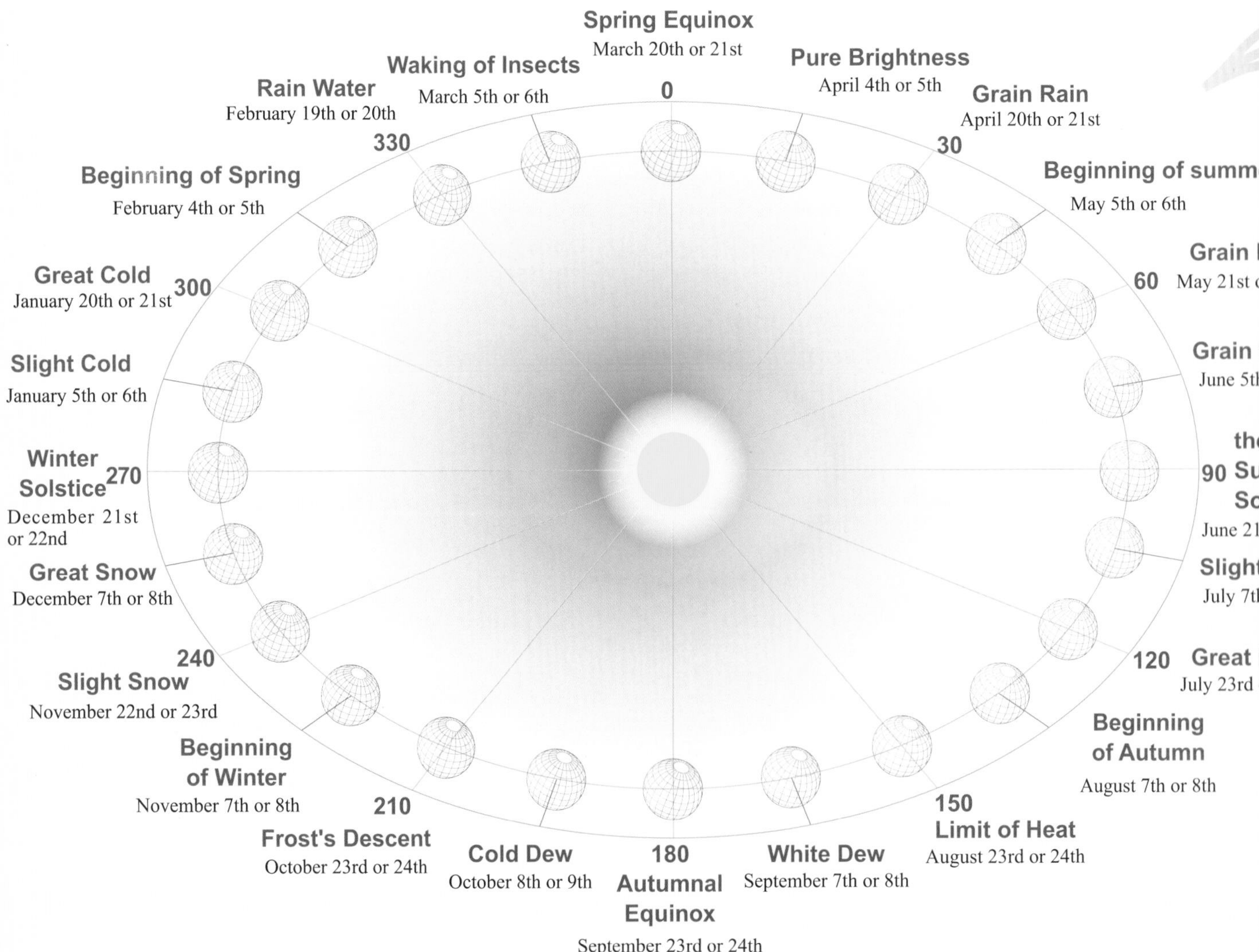

Beginning of Spring

It is the first of 24 solar terms, falling on February 4th or 5th. It means that winter goes, and the spring comes. After the Beginning of Spring, the mercury begins to rise, and the fields turn green.

Rain Water

It falls on February 19th or 20th. During this period, the spring breeze blows, snow melts into water, air is moist and more rain instead of snow, thus the Rain Water. People often said, "During the Start of Spring it becomes warm gradually while during the Rain Water people are busy giving fertilizer to the crop."

Waking of Insects

It falls on March 5th or 6th. This solar term means that the weather turns warm and the thunder rolls, so animals and insects are awakened from hibernation, thus the name Waking of Insects.

Spring Equinox

It falls on March 20th or 21st. The first day of Spring Equinox is the middle day of 90 days of spring, when the length of day and night are approximately equal in both the northern and southern hemispheres, thus the name. After this day, in the northern hemisphere, the sun still continues to follow a higher and higher path through the sky, with the days growing longer and longer. Therefore, the Spring Equinox is the beginning of spring in the northern hemisphere. In most areas of China, the crops living through the winter enter into the growing phase of spring.

Pure Brightness

It falls on April 4th or 5th. It gets warmer, flowers are in bloom, grass and trees sprout new branches and buds, and all plants grow. In this period, the farmers are busy on spring plowing and planting.

Grain Rain

It falls on April 20th or 21st, meaning that a lot of rain will help the five cereals grow. That is to say, the rain moistens the earth so that the five cereals grow. It is the time to plant melons and beans around the Grain Rain, as farmer's saying goes.

Beginning of Summer

It falls on May 5th or 6th, the beginning of the summer. From then on it is summer when the plants are in exuberant growth. Traditionally, the Beginning of Summer is thought to be an important solar term when the mercury rises markedly, hot summer is coming, lighting storms increase, and the crops enter into the booming season.

Grain Fills

It falls on May 21st or 22nd. The crops harvested in summer such as barley and winter wheat are filling out their ears, but not yet ripe, thus the name Grain Fill.

Grain in Ear

It falls on June 5th or 6th. It is the best time to sow the bearded bread crops such as late paddy, millet and broomcorn millet. If the crops are planted after the time of Grain in Ear passes, it is difficult for them to ripen. The Chinese character "mang" also refers to the crops with awn such as wheat and barley, and the "zhong" refers to the seed.

Summer Solstice

It falls on June 21st or 22nd. In the northern hemisphere, the first day of this term is the longest day of the year. This day marks the beginning of the hot season, and from then on everything on earth grows flourishingly. After the Summer Solstice, the Sun moves southward gradually and in the northern hemisphere the day is shorter and shorter while the night is longer and longer.

Slight Heat

It occurs on July 7th or 8th. In this period, it is very hot, but not the hottest, thus the name "Slight Heat". This period is also around the first ten-day period of the hot season.

Great Heat

It occurs on July 23rd or 24th. This is the period when the heat is greatest in the year. This period is also around the second ten-day period of the hot season. In many areas of the Yangtze River reaches, the high temperature of 40 centigrade occurs often. In this solar term, there is a lot of rainfall.

Beginning of Autumn

It occurs on August 7th or 8th. Spring flowers and autumn fruits indicate the sweltering summer days are to end, and cool and comfortable weather will come. Hereafter, the air temperature falls gradually.

Limit of Heat

It falls on August 23rd or 24th. It indicates that the fiery-hot summer is really over. It is a turning point of temperature decrease. It is the symbol of cool weather.

White Dew

It falls on September 7th or 8th. In this period, it is cool at night and water vapor condenses to liquid water.

Autumnal Equinox

It falls on September 23rd or 24th. After the Autumnal Equinox, in the northern hemisphere, the Sun still continues to follow a lower and lower path through the sky, with the days growing shorter and shorter. According to the Autumn Theory of the Chinese lunar calendar, the first day of the Autumnal Equinox is the middle of the 90 days in autumn, thence the name.

Cold Dew

It falls on October 8th or 9th. Dew is more and more and air temperature is much lower. Cold is the gas of dew, and follows the white dew, meaning the climate turns cold while the aqueous vapor coagulates the white dew.

Frost's Descent

It falls on October 23rd or 24th. The celestial longitude is at 210 degrees. The weather is cold, and the frost appears, thence the name Frost's Descent.

Beginning of Winter

It falls on November 7th or 8th. Dong means ending, that is to say, the farm labor is finished, and the reaped grain needs to be stored. After the Beginning, in the middle and lower Yellow River reaches, it freezes. The farmers in various areas begin to enter slack season.

Slight Snow

It falls on November 22nd or 23rd. In this period mercury falls and it begins to snow, but the days featuring the swirling heavy snow do not come yet, thus the name "Slight Snow". Around the Slight Snow, it snows in the Yellow River reaches (two solar terms later for south China), while north China enters into the ice-bound season.

Great Snow

It occurs on December 7th or 8th. Around the Great Snow, in the Yellow River reaches there is the snow cover, while north China is in severe winter featuring a hundred leagues locked in ice and a thousand leagues of whirling snow.

Winter Solstice

It falls on December 21st or 22nd. On the first day of this term, the sunshine almost beats the Tropic of Capricorn. In the northern hemisphere, the day is the shortest day of the year and the longest night. It enters into the coldest days of the year. Astronomically this day marks the beginning of the winter in the northern hemisphere. After the Winter Solstice, the days are longer and longer in northern hemisphere.

Slight Cold

It falls on January 5th or 6th. After the Slight Cold days (first day of this term), it enters into the cold season. In this period, it is cold but not the coldest.

Great Cold

It falls on January 20th or 21st. Around Great cold, it is coldest season of a year. After the Great Cold, the Beginning of Spring is coming. Thus, the Earth goes a single complete cycle around the Sun.

Rat

Rat is the first of the twelve zodiac animals. In the folk-custom culture, people still bestowed an image full of a child's taste on the rat, and regarded it as a creature symbolizing wisdom and intelligence. "Cleverer than the rat" is often used for describing the smartness of a person. The ancients said that the rat boasts five kinds of faculty: running, climbing, and burrowing.

Years of the Rat since the 20th century: 1900, 1912, 1924, 1936, 1948, 1960, 1972, 1984, 1996, 2008.

Characteristics shared by people born in the Year of the Rat are open, optimistic, honest, and simple. They never waste money and are good at making arrangement for family life. However, their ambitions are big, and tend to be too anxious in achieving a success.

Horse

Stout, tall and big, the galloping horse is loved by the Chinese. Besides its prominent looks, the horse's quality is also highly praised. With big ideals, the horse is hardworking and able to endure hardships, busy running about, and loyal and devoted to its master. In Chinese traditional culture, the person of great talent is often likened to a winged steed.

Years of the Horse since the 20th century: 1906, 1918, 1930, 1942, 1954, 1966, 1978, 1990, 2002, (2014).

Characteristics shared by people born in the Year of the Horse are cool, lively, good at making judgement, and talkative. They know clearly what to hate and what to love. Sometimes, however, they give full swing to their inclination, are impatient and tend to give up half way.

Ox

Of the twelve zodiac animals, ox is the largest in size, in contrast with the rat. So in daily life, people use the rat to imply small or little, and the ox big or much. The Ox is the back bone for agricultural cultivation, being the friend of farmers. The custom of whipping the ox at the beginning of spring dates back to early times. In the new year, people pray for a year of abundance, and ox is the most qualified mascot.

Years of the Ox since the 20th century: 1901, 1913, 1925, 1937, 1949, 1961, 1973, 1985, 1997, (2009)

Characteristics shared by people born in the Year of the Ox: People born in the Year of the Ox are straight-forward, honest, diligent and patient. They are stubbon and not romantic.

Ram

The gentle rams stand aloof from worldly affairs. They roam on the hillside in good order, eating the green grass, which is full of a kind and tranquil atmosphere. The Three Rams in the Sunshine, a Chinese traditional auspicious picture, is titled 'Sanyang Kaitai', which is a widely known New Year blessing. The ram can represent beauty. The Chinese character "美" (beautiful) is made up of two characters, "羊" (ram) and "大" (big). Big ram is more beautiful, which actively embodies the ancient people's aesthetic tendency of pragmatism.

Years of the Ram since the 20th century: 1907, 1919, 1931, 1943, 1955, 1967, 1979, 1991, 2003, (2015).

Characteristics shared by people born in the Year of the Ram are soft, mature, good-hearted, gloomy, and very dependent. They are not aggressive enough.

Tiger

Of twelve zodiac animals, the tiger is the most powerful and man-eating one. As the Chinese saying goes, the tiger is the king of beasts. With powerful strength, the tiger becomes the born overlord in the mountain forest. The tiger is also the symbol of a hero. The producers always draw the Chinese character "王" (king) upon the forehead of tiger in the folk fine arts work.

Years of the Tiger since the 20th century: 1902, 1914, 1926, 1938, 1950, 1962, 1974, 1986, 1998, (2010).

Characteristics shared by people born in the Year of the Tiger are warm-hearted, brave, independent, and open-minded. They dare to be adventurous but tend to be rash in action. They are too generous in spending money.

Twelve Zodiac Animals

"Twelve Zodiac Animals" is a way used to mark the year. Each Earthly Branch is also associated with one of the twelve zodiac animals. Zi, the first of the twelve Earthly Branches, represents the rat, in order, Chou the ox, Yin the tiger, Mou the rabbit, Chen the dragon, Si the snake, Wu the horse, Wei

Monkey

The active monkey has been regarded as the smart and clever animal from of old. Of the famous monkey-related stories in China, the Journey to the West is the most famous, which gives a retailed description to the Monkey King—Sun Wukong. Originally he was stubborn and disobedient by nature, and later safeguarded the monk of the Tang Dynasty Xuanzang to go on a pilgrimage for Buddhist scriptures to the west. On the way, he defeats the demons and evils, takes the bull by the horns, and experiences innumerable trials and hardships, and at last reaches the spiritual state of an immortal. The dramas adapted from the novel mainly show the deft and quick actions of the Monkey King.

Years of the Monkey since the 20th century: 1908, 1920, 1932, 1944, 1956, 1968, 1980, 1992, 2004, (2016).

Characteristics shared by people born in the Year of the Monkey are clever, humorous, lively, and good at many arts. Moreover, they maintain good ties with others, and are good at imitating others in terms of actions. However, they chase fame.

Rabbit

Rabbit is a kind of lovely, agile, smart animal. The Chinese ancients considered the rabbit longevity. The myth of the white rabbit grinding medicine means that white can make the elixir of life.

Years of the Rabbit since the 20th century: 1903, 1915, 1927, 1939, 1951, 1963, 1975, 1987, 1999, (2011).

Characteristics shared by people born in the Year of the Rabbit are gracious, prudent, clever, and flexible. They chase after things in vogue. Appearing to be quiet, they are resolute in mind. Sometimes, however, they are too prudish and love to glorify themselves.

the sheep, Shen the monkey, You the rooster, Xu the dog, and Hai the pig. Later there is the saying that the person who is born in the year of some animal is like the animal in some aspects. For example, the person who is born in the year of Rat is like a rat and the person who is born in the year of Ox is like the ox.

Rooster

The rooster is the harbinger of dawn. They sing at daybreak and are never early or late. It is a rooster heralding the break of a day. Roosters can be found everywhere in daily life. It has a better reproductive capacity, with a high survival rate. Without special demands for environment, it can be bred in any place. It is the symbol of a flourishing life force.

Years of the Rooster since the 20th century: 1909, 1921, 1933, 1945, 1957, 1969, 1981, 1993, 2005, (2017).

Characteristics shared by people born in the Year of the Rooster are prudent, good at organizing work and decisive, and have strong sense of economy. However, they are too picky with others.

Dragon

Among twelve zodiac animals, the dragon is the only mythical animal. The Chinese people for generations created the image of the "dragon" and made it one of the zodiac animals with rich connotations and cultural value. The dragon is infinitely resourceful and controls the forces of nature. It can speed across the sky in the heavens, and ride the waves in the sea. In Chinese traditional culture, the dragon is seen as the symbol of power, dignity and honor. The dragon is linked with imperial power, thus becoming a unique proposition of feudal times. The names of the things related to the emperors have the Chinese character "dragon", thus showing their prerogative.

Years of the Dragon since the 20th century: 1904, 1916, 1928, 1940, 1952, 1964, 1976, 1988, 2000, (2012).

Characteristics shared by people born in the Year of the Dragon are powerful, decisive, warm-hearted, aggressive, and attractive to the opposite sex. However, they lack patience and can not carry things through to the end.

Dog

The dog is closely related to the human. In China, some ethnic groups, revering the dog as a totem, thought that their own clans were originated from the dog. Dog, the friend of humans is thought to be the animal that knows man's mind and is very loyal to man. In the ancient times, the Chinese people with lofty ideals cried up a harmonious society featuring hearing roosters crow and dogs bark. The barking of dogs sets off the peace and serenity of well-off society.

Years of the Dog since the 20th century: 1910, 1922, 1934, 1946, 1958, 1970, 1982, 1994, 2006, (2018).

Characteristics shared by people born in the Year of the Dog are honest and loyal. They observe to rules and regulations, boast strong sense of responsibility, work hard, but are not flexible.

Snake

Of the twelve zodiac animals, the snake is also called "small dragon", the snake's outer covering that is shed is called "snake slough", or "dragon robe".

Among the common people, the snake is considered to be crafty, cut-throat and offish, and related to a magical phenomena. In some fairy tales, it is also endowed with the kindhearted quality of trying to repay after getting the favor. The Madame White Snake, a plangent and beautiful story depicting the love between man and snake, is widely known, which expresses the people's ideal of pursuing good love and free living.

Years of the Snake since the 20th century: 1905, 1917, 1929, 1941, 1953, 1965, 1977, 1989, 2001, (2013).

Characteristics shared by people born in the Year of the Snake have a ready wit and are clever, calm, thoughtful, good at aesthetics but often seek to own something and tend to be generous.

Pig

In the eyes of the Chinese people, the pig is simple and honest and behaves discreetly. Every part of the pig is a treasure. It is regarded as the symbol of rich living.

Years of the Pig since the 20th century: 1911, 1923, 1935, 1947, 1959, 1971, 1983, 1995, 2007, (2019).

Characteristics shared by people born in the Year of the Pig are gracious, calm and rational. They are good at economic work, and passionate. However, they never show what is in their mind easily. Sometimes, they are inclined to believe others, and hate to cheat.

Marriage and Family

Marriage and Family

Since China initiated the reform and opening-up policy, great changes have taken place in various aspects such as society, economy and politics. Marriage and family have also changed markedly. As the family planning policy is implemented and the core family structure trend strengthened, China's scale of members household has tended to decrease since 1985. The number of small-sized families with 1 to 3 persons has increased steadily while that of the medium-sized or above families with four persons or above has tended to decrease.

Because the relevant laws and policies are amended and people's ideas are updated constantly, in recent years Chinese people's age at first marriage has been on the rise. Since the early 1980s, the divorce rate has continually increased. As the people's ideas on marriage changed, the remarriage of those who have divorced or been bereft of their spouse has been increasingly understood by society, so that the number of remarriages has increase gradually. Chinese people's concept on marriage and family are undergoing the transformation from traditional to modern and from closed to open. For example, changes have taken place in the concept of choosing a spouse, the position of family members has tended to be equal, and the sexual concept has been diversified. As the economy develops further and people live more freely, the problems concerning marriage and family also appears constantly.

Vision of Love

The word "love" is one introduced into China during the period of the New Culture Movement in the early 20th century and has become the holy base for the marriage. In the course of striving for marriage freedom, the free love has become the basis of China's Marriage Law. Article 2 of the General Principles of Marriage Law stipulated that "a marriage system based on freedom, monogamy and equality between man and woman shall be implemented."

Especially after the 1980s, as China further adopted the reform and opening-up policy, the love of Chinese people underwent a new liberation. Before that time, most of Chinese people were bashful to talk about the word "love", but after 30 years of change, the vision of love of the Chinese people has become diversified. People are more tolerant with the Cross-Age-Group Love, December heartbeat and long-distance love.

Marriage Registration System

China's new Regulations on Marriage Registration came into effect on October 1st, 2003.

From October 1st, Chinese people can get married or divorced as long as the both parties have the ID cards and signed the statement that they have no spouse and that both parties are not lineal relatives by blood, or collateral relatives by blood up to the third degree of kinship, according to the new marriage registration regulations. The procedures such as certification letters from their work units are removed. The new regulations do not draw demands of mandatory premarital health examination, meaning applicants would take it of their own free will. This move greatly simplifies the procedure for divorce. Compared with the Regulation on Administration of Marriage Registration, the new regulations enable people to register marriage in a much easier and more convenient way, shows more respect for individuals' freedom of life and marks that governments will play a role in marriage as a servant rather than an administrator.

◆ The Origin of Chinese Surnames

The Chinese have had surnames long before the period of the Three Emperors and Five Kings (about 5,000 years ago), that is, during the time when recognition was given only to one's mother and not one's father. Hence, the Chinese character for surname is made up of two individual characters — one meaning woman and one meaning to give birth. That is to say, the surnames of the early Chinese followed the maternal line. Before the three dynasties of Xia, Shang and Zhou (2140-256 BC), the people in China were already having surnames (Xing) and clan-names (Shi). The surnames originated from the name of the village in which one lived or the family to which one belonged, while the clan-name was derived from the name of the territory or the title granted, sometimes posthumously, by the emperor to a noble for an achievement. Hence, only nobles had surnames as well as clan-names, while common people had the surname but not clan-names. A man and a woman of the same clan-name could marry each other but they could not if they were of the same surname. This is because the Chinese had discovered, long ago, that marriages of close relatives would be detrimental to future generations.

◆ The Characteristics of China's Surname

The book, *Surnames of a Hundred Families*, which was popular in China during the old days, was written more than 1,000 years ago during the Northern Song Dynasty (960-1127). It recorded 438 surnames, of which 408 were single-syllable surnames and 30 were double-syllable surnames. At present, there are about 300 most commonly used surnames in China.

The surname is generally composed of one character or syllable, among which one character surname is more and the other is less. According to the latest statistics, the people with the surname Li is the most, and the 5 major Chinese surnames are: Li, Wang, Zhang, Liu and Chen. The common two-syllable surnames, or compound surnames, include Ouyang, Zhuge, Sima, Duanmu and Gongsun.

The distribution of Han Chinese surnames has regional disparities. The surnames of Li, Wang, Zhang and Liu are common in northern China, while Chen, Zhao, Huang, Lin and Wu are common among southern people.

Collective wedding

Changes in Wedding

In the past more than 50 years, the changes in the Chinese wedding have characteristics, which are lively summed up: a bed in the 1950s, a bag of candy in the 1960s, three big things in the 1980s, showing off ostentation and extravagance in the star-class hotels in the 1990s, marriage with characteristics to show individuality in the 21st century. These changes from the simple wedding

A pair of young couples are conducting marriage registration.

to diversified wedding forms are closely related with the development of economy and changes in society and politics.

Since the late 1970s, there has appeared the trend of prevalence of "three big things" when people marry. The initial "three big things" referred to the watch, bicycle and sewing machine. According to the general income level of that time, it would take the groom the savings of several years to purchase the three things. Since the late 1980s, with the improvement of people's living standard, "three big things" have also changed to household appliances such as TV, radio-recorder, washing machine, video cassette recorder, and only a few people had too many problems to purchase them. In the early 1990s, in many places of China, hosting a banquet in the restaurant when marrying has come into fashion, and so has the wedding photography and wedding video. Subsequently a new trade—wedding planner has emerged. In the 21st century, people begin to pursue the individualized wedding and some people even put forward the slogan "My Wedding, My Way".

Self-determination in Marriage

Since 1949, China has implemented the new Marriage Law, established the marriage system featuring freedom of marriage, monogamy and equality of men and women, changed the old idea that the only purpose of marriage is the bearing of offspring, and formed the new idea that the people wed for love. Moreover, the rights of women to divorce and remarry have been protected.

The independent name right is an important personal right the women gained after the New China was founded. Traditionally, a Chinese surname is often passed down through the father, and Chinese women always retained their family name even after marriage. In New China, husband and wife have equal name rights. Their children can name after the surname of father or mother. In cities, many children are named after their mother.

Equality of Husband and Wife

In New China, the women can equally participate in the social and economic activities as the men do, thus gaining equal economic income. Women's economic independence gives the women the management and decision-making rights in the major domestic affairs. According to the sample survey, the number of families in which the husband and wife codetermine the major domestic affairs accounted for 58 percent in the urban and rural areas, and the figure still increases constantly.

As the family scale becomes small and the quality of the family members improves, people pay more attention to the quality of marriage. The affection is the important bond to maintain the marriage relation. Affection communication becomes the necessary family function, touching the stability of the family.

Marriage Consultation

In recent years, a new profession—marriage consultant appeared in China. Their main responsibility is to conduct the professional analysis on the marriage situation, mentally lead the people confused about the marriage, help them better know themselves and their spouses so as to solve the marriage problem.

Unmarried Group

There were people who chose not to marry long before. Most of the unmarried were forced to do this for various impersonal reasons. Today, however, the people are unwilling to marry out of their self-conscious, voluntary choice. Most of the unmarried refuse to marry for personal freedom. In their eyes, marriage is the grave of not only the love, but also the freedom and self. Although some people believe that marriage is just a contract, this contract protected by law represents the responsibility, obligation, economic interests and the long and stable cooperative relationship, as well as the restriction on personal freedom. Therefore, these unmarried people are more willing to choose the cohabitation relationship evading the above-mentioned. Another part of unmarried people are those who refuse to enter into the unhappy marriage. Most of them are urban women with high educational degree, high income and high social status. They are the completist in the aspect of affection. The number of "unmarried people" has increased, a challenge to the traditional marriage concept that "a man should get married on coming of age, and so should a girl".

A big family with four generations

♦ Custom of Child-bearing and the Pattern of Providing for the Aged

Chinese traditional family ethic paid more attention to carrying on the ancestral line. It held that marriage aims to multiply the offspring. Because of the lower productivity level, lower average life expectancy and high death rate in ancient times, people wished to maintain a high birth rate. So the early marriage was common in the past in China. According to China's Marriage Law, men and women can marry at the age of 22 and 20 respectively.

Raising children to provide against old age is the Chinese traditional families' pattern of providing for the aged. Parents gave birth to the children and brought up them. In the old age of the parents, their children should show filial piety to their parents and shoulder the obligation to support them.

Chinese people have the tradition of respecting the old and loving the young. Though many young couples do not live with their parents, they maintain close contact with them. Grown-up children have the duty to support and help their parents. The Chinese people attach great importance to relations between family members and relatives, and cherish their parents, children, brothers and sister, uncles, aunts and other relatives.

Upsurge in Divorce

In the past half century, China has undergone an upsurge in divorce three times. The first upsurge in divorce took place in the 1950s, caused mainly by the immense social changes of China. Some marriages arranged by parents broke up and the men and women constituted the new families by free courtship, which led to the disintegration of more than one million families.

In the later 1970s, the second divorce upsurge occurred. After the "Cultural Revolution", the educated youth who went to the countryside for labor returned to the cities for work, which caused some families to dissolve.

The third divorce upsurge occurred in the last several years. According to the statistics by the Ministry of Civil Affairs, 2.098 million couples were registered for divorce in 2007, up 9.7 percent over the previous year. In 1980, only 450,000 couples divorced.

In the past, divorce was been always regarded as an ignominious matter. The divorce parties, especially the woman, were confronted with the great mental and social pressure. According to the statistics released in 2004, however, 30 percent of divorce cases in China were initiated by the women. In Shanghai and other large cities, the rate even exceeded 60 percent.

Marriage certificate

♦ The Law of the PRC on Marriage

Adopted at the Third Session of the Fifth National People's Congress on September 10, 1980, and amended in accordance with the Decision Regarding the Amendment (of the *Marriage Law of the People's Republic of China*) passed at the 21st Session of the Standing Committee of the Ninth National People's Congress on April 28,2001. *The General Principle of the Marriage Law of the People's Republic of China* stipulates that this Law lays the basic principles for marriage and family relations. A marriage system based on freedom, monogamy and equality between man and woman shall be implemented. The lawful rights and interests of women, children and old people shall be protected. Birth control shall be practiced. Marriage arranged by any third party, mercenary marriage and any interference in the freedom of marriage shall be prohibited. Any exaction of money or property by means of marriage shall be prohibited. Bigamy shall be prohibited. No one who has a spouse may cohabit with any other person. Familial violence shall be prohibited. Maltreatment or desertion of any family member shall be prohibited. Husband and wife shall be truthful to and respect each other. Family members shall respect the old, take good care of the underage, and help each other so as to maintain an equal, harmonious and cultured matrimonial and familial relationship.

Trend of Change in Family Structure

First is the family miniaturization and nuclear family trend, which is the important sign of family structure change. Compared with the united family and trunk family with more people and complicated family relations, the small family made up of parents and one or two children has become the main stream of China's contemporary urban and rural family structure. People have had more freedom to choose their own life style, the individuation family life style has been understood and respected more than ever, and various new family types have had their own space for survival. The single-parent family, family of floating population, remarriage family, single-person family, separated family, DINK family, empty nest family which was believed to be the "intentional family", as the new members of the social system, have been accepted and recognized gradually.

The second is the deep changes in family structure, which mainly lies in the shift of family relation in nature from priority given from blood relation to marriage. The proportion of the marriage based on love and freedom increased greatly, and prominence is given to the culture of choosing spouses in the family life, thus weakening the family relation pattern of the past with the blood relation as the core and priority given to the authority of father and husband. The popularization of the concept of equality between man and woman and the improvement of women's social and economic status forces the transformation from the traditional marriage relation pattern featuring "woman following the man" and "superior man and inferior woman" with the personal bondage nature to the modern, democratic and equal relation featuring "equality between man and woman".

The results of "Survey on the Status of the Chinese Women" show that the number of female employed persons accounted for 44.96 percent of China's total, above the world's proportion of 34.5 percent and that the proportion of women's income in families' total increased from 20 percent in the 1950s to 40 percent. In the urban and rural areas, the number of the families in which the husband and wife codetermine the major domestic affairs exceeded 50 percent of the total. The family relation pattern featuring the equality of men and women was popularized to a great extent.

Traditional Mode of Family

Family is the cell of the society. In the old agricultural society, social changes took place slowly, so that the family pattern was single and changed slowly.

In Chinese traditional customs, the large families consisting of grandparents, parents and sons and grandsons, the so-called Four

A collective wedding in Hangzhou

Generations Living Under the Same Roof, were praised highly. The breaking up of the family and living apart was thought to be disgraceful actions. The laws of past dynasties also gave support to the large families. For example, there were such stipulations in the Law of Ming Dynasty and the Law of Qing Dynasty. In these large families, one male, the patriarch (the oldest competent male) has ultimate authority while the junior generations have no right to say and decision.

Core Family

Core family, also called basic family, refers to a household consisting of a marital pair with unmarried children. In today's China, it is the family made up of parents and a child. This family type has become the main stream of contemporary China's society.

Ministry of Civil Affairs

♦ The Ministry of Civil Affairs

The Ministry of Civil Affairs is a department administering social and civil affairs under the State Council. It is in charge of the management of special social and civil affairs, the construction of balanced democratic politics, social aid and welfare, and service for the troops and defense construction. It was founded in May 1978, under the jurisdiction of the State Council of the PRC.

Address: No.147 Beiheyan Dajie, Dongcheng District, Beijing
Website: http://www.mca.gov.cn

14 Society

Increasing old people live a solitary existence.

Compared to the big family with several generations living in one house, nuclear families have the following clear advantages: simple family relation and little dependence upon the relative net decrease in the occurrence of conflicts and disputes in family life; it is easy to form an equal relation and democratic atmosphere in the family, conducive to cultivating the independency of the young people; it satisfies the pursuit of different generations for a different life style. In recent years, a new structure type has appeared in China's nuclear family. After the children marry, they live apart from their parents, but they maintain a close relation with their parents' family, looking after each other in economy. A loose family net has formed.

Empty Nest Family

Empty nest family refers to those families where the old husband and wife live by themselves after their children grow up, get married, and do not live with them. This family type appeared in cities at the beginning. With the development of economy and the improvement of urban housing conditions, different generations have formed their own self-identified life style. Especially the young people who hope to own freer living space. It is the deep reason why the number of "empty nest families" increased rapidly in cities.

In recent several years, as a great number of young laborers flock into the cities from rural areas, the number of empty nest families also increases in rural areas. Almost all the elders in the empty nest families face the same plight: on the one hand, their health is increasingly declining and if there are no people to look after them, they would not be cured in case of their emergent disease. On the other hand, lack of mental comfort and loneliness become the most serious problems that most of them are confronted with.

According to statistics, now China has an aging population of 132 million, accounting for 20 percent of the world's total and equivalent to the sum total of four countries, i.e. Britain, France, Sweden and Norway. In about one third of aging families appeared the "empty nest phenomena". The experts estimated that in the future 50 years, China's aging population will also increase at the speed of 3.2 percent. By then, as the population movement will quicken up and more single parents will step into the aging phase, 90 percent of China's families will become "empty nests". The social problems such as supporting the old and the physical and mental health of the old caused by the "empty nest" will become more serious.

DINK Family

DINK means "double income and no kids". In the late 1980s, this kind of family mode and concept has gradually become the rage in China. There are now at least 600,000 DINK couples in china, mainly in big cities such as Beijing, Shanghai and Guangzhou. This family pattern not only negates the standard family concept of having wife and children, but also the traditional bearing concept of raising children to prevent against old age and carrying on the ancestral line.

The people who choose a DINK family have three marked characteristics: being younger, and having higher educational degrees and higher income. Among the respondents between ages 18 to 34, 10.3 percent of them had chosen the "DINK" family mode, higher than the number of the respondents between ages 35 to 54 with the same choice. Among the couples with different educational degrees, the proportion of couples with college degrees or above choosing the DINK family is highest, reaching 10.3 percent. Among couples whose total monthly income was more than 5,000 Yuan, 13.7 percent of them had opted for a DINK family unit. But among couples whose total monthly income was less than 1,500 Yuan, the number was just 5.5 percent.

One Child

In the late 1970s, China carried out the family planning policy to control the rapid increase in population. Now, thirty years have elapsed. The reform and opening-up policy has made China look brand-new, the family planning policy has also reduced the speed of increase of China's population effectively, and in the meanwhile, 90 million single children have grown up.

In such a short time, there appeared so many singles nationwide, which is a special phenomenon for China's traditional society and even infrequent in the evolutional history of the human. Because the one-child family has only one child, the parents naturally devote all their energies and feelings to the child. Therefore the child is found in a core position in the family and even bears the hope of two generations and three families. The population experts estimated that in the coming 10 years, the number of the one-child families which are made up of singleton and singleton or singleton and non-singleton will reach 10 million at least, and that such families will become the main stream.

▲ Homosexuality

The experts estimate that in China, the most populous country in the world, there are 40 million queers although there is no figure for the queers and people with this pursuit. This means that of 100 persons, there are 2 to 3 or more people who are willing to choose people of the same sex.

For a long time, homosexuality has always been a taboo topic for various reasons, in China. Many people said that they never saw the queers. In order to adapt to the mainstream of culture, half the male queers had had sexual relations with a female. Because of the social and domestic pressure, over 90 percent of grown-up male queers in mainland China were in the state of traditional marriage. After they married, almost all of them not only maintained a sexual life with their own wives, but also kept sexual relations with others of the same sex. Although the actual number of queers does not increase, their life is in the exposed from secret. People also begin to respect and understand homosexuality. In the cities such as Qingdao, Beijing, Dalian, Nanjing, and Harbin, there has appeared the homosexuality health consultation hot line aiming to spread knowledge on venereal disease and AIDS.

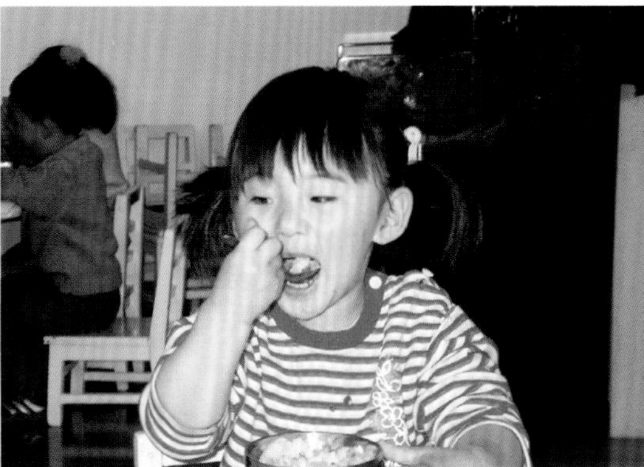
The single child is often regarded as the core of the family.

Healthcare

Survey Data on Health

The recent survey conducted jointly by the Ministry of Health, Ministry of Science and Technology and National Bureau of Statistics of China showed that in the past ten years, the status of diet and nutrition among the urban and rural Chinese population has been improved significantly, the quality of the average diet of the Chinese people has been improved significantly, the growth of Children and teenagers has been steadily improved, the malnutrition prevalence among the Children was significantly decreased, and the prevalence of malnutrition and nutrition deficiency has been continuously decreased. However, in the meantime China is still facing the dual challenges of nutrition deficiency and nutrition imbalance.

The nutrition and health problems in the population should not be ignored. The dietary pattern among the urban residents is not reasonable to a certain extent. Some diseases caused by malnutrition are still quite serious. The prevalence of chronic non-communicable diseases is rising rapidly. For example, the prevalence of both hypertension and diabetes rises to a large extent, the prevalence of being overweight and obesity has been increased markedly, the problem of abnormal blood lipid levels requires close attention, and dietary nutrition and physical activity are closely related to the chronic diseases.

♦ Chinese Center for Disease Control and Prevention

Chinese Center for Disease Control and Prevention (China CDC) is a non-profit government institution working in the fields of disease control and prevention, management of public health technology and provision of services. Its mission is to create a healthy environment, maintain social stability, safeguard State security and promote people's health through the prevention and control of the disease, deformity and injury; and its tenet is to depend on the scientific research. Under the leadership of the Ministry of Health, it exerts the function of the technical management and service, and is committed to strengthen research on strategies and measures for disease control and prevention; it organizes and implements control and prevention plans for different kinds of diseases; carries out public health management for food safety, occupational health, health related product safety, radiation safety, environmental health, health care for women and children and so on; conducts applied scientific research; provides technical guidance, staff training and quality control for disease control and prevention and public health services throughout the country; acts as the national working group for disease prevention, emergency relief, and construction of public health information systems.

Website: http://www.chinacdc.net.cn

Health System

In Beijing, Shanghai, Tianjin, Chongqing and other large cities, general traditional Chinese medicine and hospitals specializing in, for example, cancer, cardio-and cerebra-vascular disorders, ophthalmology, dentistry and infectious diseases can be found. Medium-sized cities throughout China have general and specialized hospitals with modern facilities. Medical treatment, disease prevention, and health-care networks have taken shape at county, township and village levels.

By the end of 2007, there were 315,000 health institutions in China, including 60,000 general hospitals and health centers, 3,007 maternal and child health-care institutions and 1,400 specialized health institutions. General hospitals and health centers in China possessed 3.279 million beds. There were 4.68 million health workers in China, including 2.04 practicing doctors and assistant practicing doctors and 1.47 million registered nurses. China registered 3,540 epidemic disease prevention centers (stations) and 1,925 health monitoring institutions employing 38,000 health workers. There were 39,000 rural health care centers, possessing 675,000 beds and employing 863,000 health care workers. In 2007, about 2.842 billion persons were treated in health institutions (excluding Clinics, health centers, infirmaries and village clinics) and 98.28 million were hospitalized, with the utilization rate of hospital beds being 70.9 percent. In 2007, the residents saw a doctor in health institutions 2.2 times on average in 2007.

Mother and Child Health Care

To ensure the health of mothers and infants and improve the quality of the newborn population, China implemented the Law of the People's Republic of China on Maternal and Infant Health Care on June 1st, 1995. Its general provisions stipulated that this Law is formulated in accordance with the Constitution with a view to ensuring the health of mothers

Children take "sugar balls" to strengthen the immunity against the poliomyelitis.

and infants and improving the quality of the newborn population. The State shall develop the maternal and infant health care undertakings and provide necessary conditions and material aid so as to ensure that mothers and infants receive medical and health care services. The State shall support and assist the maternal and infant health care undertakings in outlying and poverty-stricken areas. People's governments at various levels shall exercise leadership in the work of maternal and infant health care. The undertakings of maternal and infant health care shall be included in the plans for national economic and social development. The Administrative Department of Public Health under the State Council shall be in charge of the work of maternal and infant health care throughout the country, put forth the guiding principles for the work in different areas and at different administrative levels in light of their specific conditions, and exercise supervision and management of the nationwide work of maternal and infant health care. Other relevant departments under the State Council shall, within the scope of their respective functions and duties, cooperate with the administrative department of public health to make a success of the work of maternal and infant health care. The State shall encourage and support education and scientific research in the field of maternal and infant health care, popularize the advanced and practical techniques for maternal and infant health care and disseminate the scientific knowledge in this field. Awards shall be granted to organizations and individuals that have made remarkable achievements in the work of maternal and infant health care or achieved significant results in scientific research of maternal and infant health care.

The death rate of pregnant women fell from 53 per 100,000 in 2000 to 36.6 per 100,000 in 2007. The death rate of children below five years old dropped from 40 per thousand to 18.1 per thousand. The death rate of infant fell from 32 per thousand to 15.3 per thousand. The immunization rate of children reached 87 percent in 2006. The immunization rate of children at the age of one for bcg vaccine, poliomyelitis, and morbilli reached 99 percent.

Prevention and Health Care

"Prevention first" is one of the important principles in all of China's health care work. All administrations have created hygiene and disease-prevention organizations responsible for overall management of these functions, including hygiene and epidemic-prevention stations, and forming a nationwide network of hygiene supervision and control. In order to eliminate or control some serious epidemic and local diseases endangering people's heath, the National People's Congress and State Council issued the Law on the Prevention and Cure of Infectious Diseases, the National Plan for Poliomyelitis Elimination by the Year 1995, and National Outline for IDD Elimination by the Year 2000 and other documents.

Hospital Classification Management

The Ministry of Health has issued the Method of Hospital Classification Management (trial protocol), setting up a hospital accreditation system. It conducts classification management of hospitals in accordance with their functions, tasks, facilities, technical constructions, medical service quality and the comprehensive level of the scientific management. Hospitals are divided into first, second and third level ones according to functions and tasks. First-level hospitals refer to grass-roots hospitals and health centers directly providing prevention, medical treatment, health care and healing services for communities with a certain population; second-level hospitals are regional hospitals offering comprehensive medical care services and taking charge of certain teaching and scientific research tasks for many communities; third-level hospitals refer to those above regional level, providing high-level special medical care services and shouldering the tasks of high-level teaching and scientific research. The examination and approval authority of hospitals at all levels are as follows: the third level top-ranking hospitals are examined and approved by the Ministry of Health; the second and third level A, B and C grade hospitals are examined and approved by the health departments (bureaus) of the provinces, autonomous regions and municipalities directly under the jurisdiction of the Central Government; and the first level A, B and C grade hospitals are examined and approved by the health bureaus of the prefectures (cities).

Plans on Public Health Emergencies

In May 2003, the State Council issued Regulations on Public Health Emergencies, establishing a legal framework for tackling public health crises. Furthering its cooperation with the World Health Organization, the State is planning significant investment in a system to handle all public health crises, improving the responsiveness and capabilities of emergency centers, treatment and hospital information systems.

Community-based Health Network

Reform of medical care and changes in the make-up of society have prompted the spread to most cities of community-based health services whose major role is anti-epidemic work but which also provide treatment and healthcare. These popular organizations are geared to handle at grassroots level problems arising from increased urbanization, an aging population, changes in disease patterns and social strata. Nowadays, a community-based health service network, with community-based health service center as the mainstay and supplemented by other grass-roots medical treatment institutes, has gradually formed in large and medium cities.

Rural Health System

In 2003, China embarked on a new rural cooperative medical care system. Based on major illness health insurance coverage, the system is based on a payment plan by the individual, financial support from the collective, and subsidies from the government. If a farmer who has joined the scheme is hospitalized, incurred costs can be reimbursed according on a sliding scale. Since the conduction of the new rural cooperative medical care experimental units began in 2003, 21 percent of counties (cities and prefectures) of the country, and 163 million farmers have joined the scheme. The system is expected to cover the whole country by 2010.

Meanwhile, China has implemented a medical-aid system for rural areas offering medical aid to poor farmers who are seriously ill. The fund, with special allocations from various levels of government and donations from people from all walks of life, will be used exclusively for medical aid.

The health-care services are provided in farmhouse.

♦ Law of the PRC on Prevention and Treatment of Infectious Diseases

The revised Law of the PRC on the Prevention and Treatment of Infectious Diseases went into force on December 1, 2004. The State shall implement a policy of putting emphasis on prevention, combining prevention with treatment and classified management with respect to infectious diseases, depending on science and the masses. The health administration department under the State Council takes charge of the work; the health administration departments of the local people's governments above the county-level are responsible for all tasks within their administrative districts; the disease prevention and control institutes at all levels undertake monitoring and forecasting of infectious diseases, investigation of the epidemiology, report of the epidemic situation and other prevention and control work; the medical care institutes take charge of the medical treatment and the prevention work of the infectious diseases within their respective spheres of responsibilities; and the medical care institutes of the urban communities and the rural grassroots undertake the corresponding prevention and cure work under the direction of the disease prevention and control institutes.

♦ Law of the PRC on the Prevention and Treatment of Occupational Diseases

The Law of the PRC on the Prevention and Treatment of Occupational Diseases came into force as of May 1, 2002. The "occupational diseases" publicized refer to those caused by contact with dust, radioactive substances and other poisonous and harmful substances in occupational activities. The detailed classifications and catalog of the occupational diseases are regulated, adjusted and publicized by the health administration department and the labor security administration department under the State Council. The prevention and cure of occupational diseases adhere to the policy of putting the emphasis on prevention and combining prevention with treatment, and carry out classified management and comprehensive treatment. Workers enjoy the right of occupational health protection according to the law; the State implements the supervision system of occupational health.

Maternity Leave

The labor department in charge enacted a special labor security system in response under which female employees enjoy the maternity leave.

As early as 1951, the Government Administration Council issued the Regulations on Labor Insurance, making clear provisions for female employees. The Notice Concerning the Regulation on Maternity Leave of Female Employees promulgated by the Government Administration Council again in 1955 set out criteria on maternity leave of female employees of State organs and public service units. The two documents were basically consistent with each other with regard to the items and payment standard, namely: they enjoy 56 days of maternity leave; in the case of dystocia or twin birth, 14 days will be added; and if an abortion occurs within seven months of pregnancy, 30 days or less of maternity leave will be given. The salaries during the maternity period, the examination expenses during pregnancy and pre and ante-natal medical treatment expenses are required to be paid by the employing units.

The Regulations Concerning the Labor Protection of Female Staff and Workers promulgated by the State Council in 1988 amended and improved the system, namely: during pregnancy, maternity leave and nursing period, the basic salary may not be reduced and the labor contract may not be cancelled; the maternity leave shall be prolonged to 90 days from the original 56 days, including 15 days of ante-natal leave. An extra maternity leave of 15 days is granted in case of dystocia; and female staff and workers who have borne more than one child in a single birth shall be granted an extra 15 days for each child.

Blood Donation without Payment

The Chinese government all long has actively accelerated and popularized voluntary blood donation without payment and encouraged healthy people to be frequent voluntary blood donors, and implemented the Law of the PRC on Blood Donation

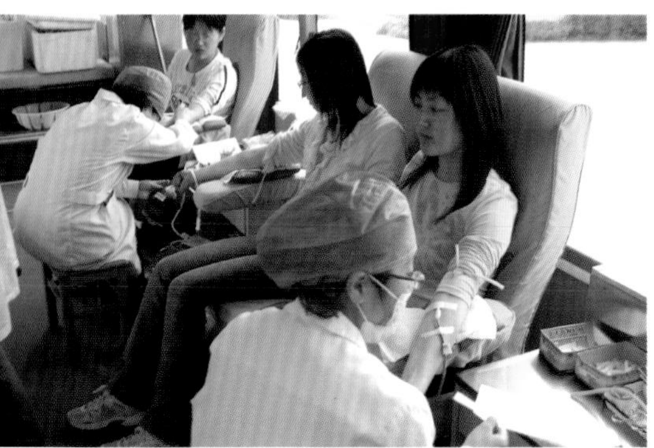

Voluntary blood donation

as of October 1, 1998. In March 2001, the Ministry of Health set forward that, under the condition of guaranteeing blood for clinical use, the blood donation task handled by the Government would gradually be canceled, realizing the transformation from planed ordered blood donation without payment to voluntary donation. In 2003, the proportion of voluntary blood donation without payment increased from 21 percent to 61 percent. The Ministry of Health established the public show system of blood donation without payment and publicized the list of the proportion of the voluntarily donated blood in the total blood for clinical use of the 31 provinces, autonomous regions and municipalities directly under the Central Government. The publicized information showed a continued steady increase everywhere in 2005, basically realizing the stable transition from paid blood donation to that without payment.

Hematopoietic Stem Cell Donation

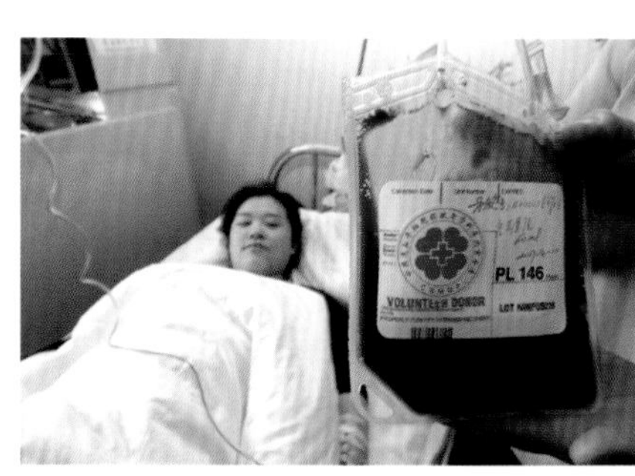

A volunteer is donating the hematopoietic stem cells.

The data bank of Chinese Hematopoietic Stem Cell Donors is also called the "Chinese Marrow Donor Program (CMDP)" (http://www.cmdp.com.cn/). With the approval of the Ministry of Health in 1992, the Red Cross Society of China, in the Red-cross spirit of "humanity, fraternity and devotion", set up the leading group handling the work regarding a data bank of Chinese unrelated marrow donors and established the Chinese Marrow Donor Program, embarking on the work of recruitment and HLA test and so on. Up to 2007, CMDP has established 31 provincial branch registries, capable of providing data on more than 30,000 donors for a matching search. It set up cooperation with about 60 domestic and international hospitals and offered over 6,000 times of search service. More than 2,000 patients found matching donors, and over 800 donors donated their stem cell to patients. In addition, it also provided search service for patients from the US, Canada, Singapore, UK, France, German, Australia, Norway, Japan and Taiwan and Hong Kong, and four of donors donated Hematopoietic stem cells for patients from America and Hong Kong. In 2007, Chinese Marrow Donor Program provided the hematopoietic stem cells to 30-odd overseas persons and signed the co-operative agreement with Japan. This was the fourth international cooperative marrow donor program after those of America, South Korea and Singapore. China is now making efforts to establish a 1 million data bank before 2010.

By May 31, 2008, the Chinese Marrow Donor Program had the data of 782,685 persons, of whom, 970 persons had donated the hematopoietic stem cells.

Prevention and Cure of Severe Acute Respiratory Syndrome (SARS)

SARS refers to the acute disease of the respiratory system caused by the infection of the SARS virus. The main symptoms include fever and the rapid breakdown of the respiratory system, accompanied by chills, muscle aches, headache and anorexia. It spreads through droplets in the air and close contact. From November 2002 to the first half year of 2003, it spread to 32 countries and regions of Asia, America and Europe, infected 8,439 persons in 29 of them and caused 812 deaths. Those cases mainly occurred in the mainland of China, Hong Kong, Taiwan, Singapore and Canada and so on, and 20 percent of the infected cases were scientists and medical personnel. Since China was one of the key areas where SARS emerged, governments at all levels attached great importance to prevention and cure work, carrying out active propaganda and prevention measures. It effectively prevented the large scale expansion of SARS, and won time for researchers to find ways to overcome the disease.

Prevention and Cure of Bird Flu

Bird flu is a kind of severe infectious disease mainly prevailing in chickens, which is also called as real croup or European croup. Once an outbreak occurs, it will kill large numbers of fowls. Since the first outbreak in 2003, it quickly spread worldwide. The Chinese Government took measures to prevent and control the spread of the epidemic situation, and this gained outstanding progress as affirmed by the World Health Organization.

On July 2, 2003, the last three SARS patients got well. Thus, the isolation area was removed. The medical personnels who had worked for it for 193 days were beyond excitement.

Prevention and Control of Acquired Immune Deficiency Syndrome (AIDS)

The evaluation result on the epidemic situation conducted jointly by the Ministry of Health, the United Nations Program on HIV/AIDS and the WHO showed that, Up to October 2007, China had accumulatively 223,501 HIV carriers and people living with AIDS, among which people living with AIDS totaled 62,838. There had 22,205 death reports. The average infection rate was 0.05 percent (0.04 percent-0.07 percent).The government attached great importance to the prevention and control work of AIDS, conducted free treatment and anonymous examination of sufferers and enacted a series of policies and statutes in the aspects of the prevention, control and examination, the treatment of HIV carriers and people living with AIDS and ways to prevent and cure the disease.

It also founded the Chinese Foundation for Prevention of STD and AIDS to raise funds for the prevention and treatment of AIDS. In March 2003, under the support of several State organs, social organizations, news media and international organizations, the fund started a large-scale charity activity, the "121 Combined Action Program" with the theme of "Live and Let Live". In 2005, the fund also launched "121 Combined Action Red Ribbon Love One Yuan Donation Commonweal Education Activity" with the theme of "To resist AIDS, let all of us participate", calling on the people to donate one Yuan each to help the poor HIV carriers and orphans and give them humanistic treatment and care, and through holding the commonweal education activity, to raise public awareness of AIDS, popularize prevention knowledge and effectively check the spread of the disease.

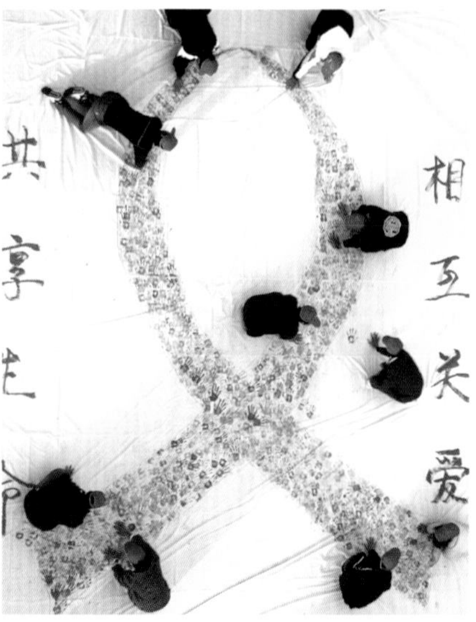

The red ribbon under the sunshine brings care to the AIDS.

Traditional Chinese Medicine

The term Traditional Chinese medicine, or TCM for short, is a general designation for all medicines of different Chinese ethnic groups, including Han, Tibetan, Mongolian and Uygur and so on. Of the Chinese traditional medicines, the Han ethnic group has largest population, earliest characters and comparatively long history, so Han medicine has had the greatest influence in China and throughout much of the world. In the 19th Century, as western medicine was introduced into China and popularized, Han medicine became known as "Traditional Chinese Medicine", so as to differentiate it from "western medicine". TCM is a medical system with unique theoretical style, gradually formed by constant accumulation and repeated summarization in long-term medical treatment and living practice. The report on the world traditional medicines issued by the WHO in 2003 showed that, in China, the traditional Chinese medicines accounted for 40 percent of that provided in health care. The WHO also affirmed the contribution made by traditional Chinese medicine in the aspects of treating and preventing diseases, as well as improving the quality of life.

• TCM History

Chinese medicine originated in the Yellow River basin and was established as a school of science early on. In the process of its development, many good doctors, a lot of important schools and masterpieces emerged.

Records related to medical treatment, hygiene and more than ten illnesses appeared on the oracle bone inscriptions as far back as the Shang Dynasty (ca.1600-1046 BC). In the following Zhou Dynasty (1046-256 BC), the new techniques to diagnose diseases such as observation, auscultation and olfaction, interrogation, and pulse feeling and palpation as well as the drugs, acupuncture and moxibustion and operations and so on were adopted. In the Spring and Autumn Period (770-476 BC), medicine broke away from the bondage of the wizard and began to produce professional doctors. In the Warring States Period (475-221 BC), the new book,

The Medical Classic of the Yellow Emperor, or Huang Di Nei Jing, began to discuss Chinese medicine theories systematically. This is the earliest existing book of its kind. By the time of the Han Dynasty (206 BC-220AD), surgery had reached a comparatively high level. From Wei to the Five Dynasties (220-960), outstanding achievements had been made with regard to pulse feeling and palpation. From the Ming Dynasty (1368-1644), western medicine was introduced into China and the first attempts at combining the two systems occurred.

Basic Theory of TCM

The basic theory of the Chinese medicine attempts to explain the nature of the life cycle and disease changes. It mainly includes five theories: Yin and Yang, the five-elements, how to direct one's strength, internal organs of the body, and channels. It also researches dialectics, explanations as to why diseases occur, how to diagnose and prevent diseases, as well as how to keep the body healthy.

Yin and Yang Theory

The concept of Yin and Yang derived from an ancient philosophical concept. After observing the conflicting phenomenon, ancient people grouped all conflicting ideas into Yin and Yang. They used this concept to explain how things changed. Chinese medicine used Yin and Yang to illustrate the complicated relationship between various things such as the different parts of the human body and living things vs. nature or society. It was believed that the relative balance of Yin and Yang served as the basis to maintain the normal activities of the human body. If such a balance was disturbed, diseases occurred, thus affecting people's health and influencing normal activities of life.

The Theory of the Five Elements

The theory tries to generalize the attribute of various things in the objective world by using the five philosophical categories namely wood, fire, earth, metal and water, and explain the interrelationships and transformational rule by using the dynamic mode of the promoting and restriction relation in five elements. It mainly expounds the functional correlation among the zang-organs and between zang-organs and other organs and tissues as well as the mechanism of the occurrence of the diseases if the balance of the organs is disturbed, and is also used to direct the treatment of the diseases of organs.

Theory of Directing One's Strength

This is also called as five strengths and six climatic factors. The theory of directing one's strength focused on how various components such as astronomy, meteorological phenomena and climate would affect health. The five strengths, namely the strengths of metal, wood, water, fire and earth, refer to the different seasons of the year such as spring, summer, long summer, autumn and winter. People regarded wind, coldness, summer, damp, dryness and fire as the six elements of the climate. This theory tried to predict climatic change and how disease occurred by parameters in astronomy.

Theory of Internal Organs of the Body

This mainly studies the physiological function and pathological changes of the five internal organs (heart, liver, spleen, lung and kidney), six hollow organs (small intestine, large intestine, stomach, urinary bladder, gallbladder and tri-jiao) and extraordinary fu organs (brain, marrow, bone, vessels, gallbladder and uterus).

Theory of Channels (Meridians and Collaterals)

This is closely related to the theory of the internal organs. The meridians and collaterals are the channels for the vital energy and blood to circulate in the body, playing the role of communication between the internal and external and covering the whole body. Under pathological conditions, the function of the channels changes, and corresponding symptoms and physical signs will emerge, through which, internal diseases can be diagnosed.

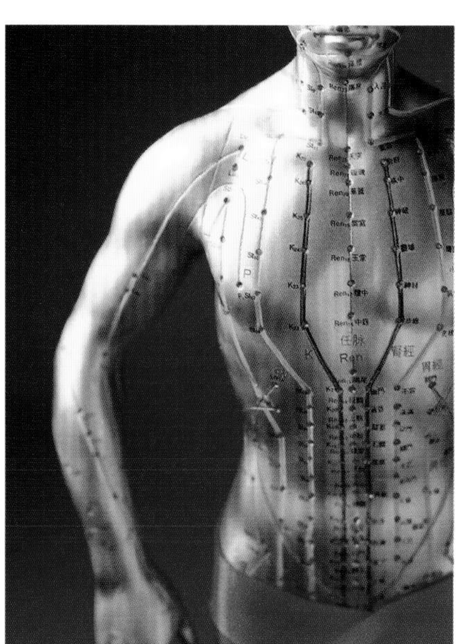

The picture of the body's meridians

Diagnostic Methods in TCM

(See P436)

Massage

Massage therapy of the herbalist doctor

Massage is to apply manipulation on the channels of the human body, thus preventing disease and keeping healthy. The functions include: Firstly, adjust the functions of the internal organs. TCM holds that pathological changes are due to imbalance of internal functions, and massage is to balance the maladjusted functions of the organs. Secondly, dredge the qi and blood of the channels. Qi and blood are the main substances to maintain the life, and the meridians and collaterals are the channels for the qi and blood to circulate, transmit and communicate in the body. Once the qi and blood are out of gear, evils will enter the organs to cause disease, and the channels can also reflect the diseases of the organs. Massage can promote the functions of the channels and the production and operation of qi and blood through the stimulation of manipulation, thus harmonizing the function of the organs to prevent the evils outside and treat the diseases inside. Thirdly, tone up the muscles and deal with arthritis of the bones. For muscles, it can dredge the natural fiber line of flesh; on the blood vessels, it can remove blood stasis and make qi and blood run smoothly. Massage technique is able to directly put right the "wrongly placed muscle and bones". Hence, no matter the disease infected from outside or the internal injuries which could spread outside, as well as the injuries caused by falling down, can be treated by massage.

• History of Chinese Herbal Medicine

Chinese traditional medicine

Dating back to the period around the 22nd century BC to 256 BC (Xia, Shang and Zhou Dynasties), there appeared alcohol medicine and soup medicine. A book, The *Book of Songs* (or Shi Jing) in the Zhou Dynasty is the earliest existing book bearing records of ancient Chinese medicine. Another book, *Nei Jing*, which is the earliest existing book on Chinese medicine theory, proposed theories like "cooling the patient if one has a high temperature and vice versa", "adding the five flavors into the medicine and feeling bitter inside and having diarrhea. These formed the basis of Chinese medicine theory.

The earliest existing book on Chinese herbal medicine, *Shen Nong Ben Cao Jing* (Ben means root and Cao means shoot), was written in the Qin and Han Dynasty based on the work of medical experts who collected lots of ancient materials. The book recorded 365 types of medicine, some of which are still used in contemporary clinics. This book marked a beginning of the establishment of eastern medicine. In the Tang Dynasty, the economy prospered, further promoting medicine development; the Tang government published a book, *Tang Ben Cao*, which is the earliest existing pharmacopeia. This included 850 types of medical herbs and their pictures, which further improved the scale of eastern medicine. In the Ming Dynasty, an expert of herbal medicine Li Shizhen spent 27 years producing the book, *Ben Cao Gang Mu*. This recorded 1,892 types of herbal medicine, making it the greatest book in Chinese history with the most types of herbal medicines.

After the founding of New China in 1949, plenty of research was done in various fields such as botany, identification science, chemistry, pharmacology and clinical medicine, providing a scientific basis to identify the source and authenticity of herbal medicines as well as their functional scheme. Later, a nationwide survey was carried out on the source of the medicine, which helped produced the book, *Zhong Yao Zhi* in 1961. In 1977, the book, *Herbal Medicine Dictionary*, was publicized, which brought the number of recorded herbal medicines to 5,767. In addition, reference books, treatise, newspapers and magazines on Chinese medicine were publicized. There also established institutions on scientific research, teaching and producing of Chinese medicine.

Chinese Herbal Medicine

Chinese herbal medicine aims to prevent, diagnose and treat diseases. It mainly consists of natural medicines and produced ones, namely medicines made from herbal, animal, mineral, some chemical substances and biological substances. The invention and application of Chinese medicine has a history of thousand of years. Yet the word "Chinese medicine" appeared only after western medicine was introduced into China to differentiate them

China enjoys a large territory, various geographical features and different types of climate. These factors have given rise to different ecological environments, which enable it to grow a great variety of herbal plants.

At present, China has cultivated more than 8,000 kinds of herbal medicines, 600 of which are commonly used. This gives China the largest number of herbal medicines in the world. These medicines not only meet domestic demand, but also are exported to 80 countries and regions where they enjoy great fame.

Tibetan Medicine

As part of Chinese medicine, Tibetan medicine prevails in places where Tibetan people live, such as Tibet, Qinghai, Sichuan, and Gansu provinces in China. In India and Nepal in south Asia, it is also a major kind of medicine. Tibetan medicine originated on the Qinghai-Tibet Plateau and manifests the special feature of that region. The Qinghai-Tibet Plateau is located in a frigid zone. The poor transportation long made it difficult to connect with the outside world, thus retaining its special features. With small variety, most of the sources for Tibetan medicines come from cold resistant plants and animals. These plants and animals live in the high mountains where there is lack of oxygen.

In Tibet, Buddhist thought has penetrated all aspects of society and become a strong spiritual force occupying the dominant position, therefore Tibetan medicine possesses a dense Tibetan Buddhism coloring.

Basic Theory of Tibetan Medicine

According to Tibetan theory, there are three factors in the human body, which are "long", "chi ba" and "pei gen". There are seven kinds of substances in the body, the essence of food, blood, flesh, fat, bone, etc. There are three kinds of excreta, urine, feces, and sweat. The three factors decide the changes of the seven substances and three excreta. In normal cases, they co-exist with each other and live in a balanced way. When one or more factors over react or diminish, the body will have disease in "long", "chi ba" and "pei gen". Therefore, patients need to be treated in the above three aspects to regain their health.

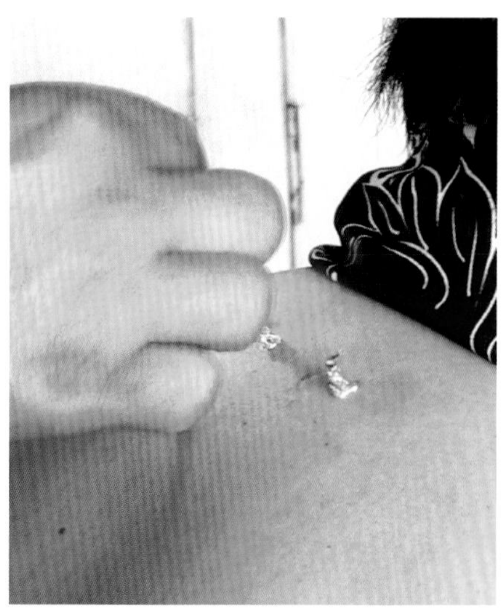

The Tibetan doctor kindled the Tibetan medicine called Zang-Yin-Chen in Chinese to cure arthropathy.

The concept of "long" refers to the power of movement. It is similar to "feng" and "qi" in traditional Han medicine, yet it is a broader idea than that. "Chi ba" is translated as "dan" or "huo", similar to the "hotness" in Han medicine. The main features of "chi ba" is to maintain the body's normal temperature, keep the stomach functioning well, etc; "pei gen" is something like saliva, but more than that, being related to all the liquidation inside the human body.

In Tibetan theory, disease occurs because the "long", "chi ba" and "pei gen" are not in balance, thus affecting health. So, the aim of treatment is to restore harmony if they are overreacting or diminishing.

Medication of Tibetan Medicine

Tibetan medicine uses the ingredient added to medicinal herbs so as to lead them to the diseased position. For example, white sugar is used as the ingredient added to medicinal herbs to cure simple febrile diseases, and brown sugar as the ingredient for cold diseases.

Tibetan doctors often use mugwort wormwood leaves as materials for mugwort moxibustion treatment. Tibetan doctors usually have fixed points for moxibustion.

In Tibetan medicines, applying medicines is a special treatment. It is simple and convenient to apply medicines onto the surface of body so as to cure the internal symptoms. This method was often used among common people. Tibetan medicine holds that the application method has the function of taking a tonic to build up health.

The medicated bath in Tibetan medicine has its special feature. Springs are often applied in this treatment, such as sulfur spring, aluminite spring, spring of dried dung of Trogopterus xanthipes, limestone spring, etc.

The picture of the Divine Husbandman pciking herbal medicines. It is said that the Divine Husbandman is the inventor of the traditional Chinese medicines.

• Shennong Bencao Jing (Shennong Emperor's Classic of Materia Medica)

As a great classic of pharmacology, *Shennong Bencao Jing* was not a product of one person in a single period, and Shennong was only a borrowed name. In the Warring States Period and the Qin and Han Dynasties, many medical scientists collected data on pharmacopeia and hence produced the book.

Shennong Bencao Jing is in four volumes: the first volume is the preface and the other three volumes form the main body. The "Preface" is actually the pandect of pharmacology, talking about the classification of three kinds of medicines, namely, the upper, the middle and lower levels, which is the earliest classification of medicines in China's pharmaceutical history. Moreover, it talks about many aspects of medicines: ingredients with mutual reinforcement and assistance, the harmony of the seven emotions, the properties of drugs and their origins, the identification between the real and the false, the different types of medicament forms, the compatibility and incompatibility in clinical application of drugs, the doses, the time for taking medicine, the conditioning relationship among medicines, and so on. The text part collects 365 kinds of medicines, therein, 252 are plant ones, 67 are animal ones and 46 are mineral ones. More than 170 kinds of diseases are discussed, including diseases of internal medicine, surgery, gynecology, pediatrics and so on.

The book is the earliest extant classic on pharmacology in China. Most of the medicines recorded in it are still in use now, and their efficacy has been proved by long-term clinical practice and modern scientific research. The pharmacological theory and application principles suggested in the book are mostly correct and have a very high scientific value. The book laid a foundation for the pharmacological theory of ancient China, exerted far-reaching influence on the development of pharmacology of later generations, and even now it is still an important reference book for the study of Chinese medicines.

♦ Tongrentang Pharmacy

When we speak of traditional Chinese medicine, most Chinese people will get the name Tongrentang in their mind. Tongrentang is an old pharmacy and has selling traditional Chinese medicine more than 300 years. Yue Xianyang was the founder of Tongrentang; he was born in Ningbo, Zhejiang province. Since Yue's father and grandfather were both physicians, he was influenced by what he constantly saw and heard when he was young. Later, he got to read various pharmacopoeias, and committed himself to researching and making drug recipes. He insisted on making pills with the best raw materials, fine and precise production techniques, thereby bringing about excellent clinical performance for the patients. He took 'curing the sickness to save the patient' as a holy career to serve the patients and benefit the society. Therefore in 1669, Tongrentang came into being.

Tongrentang complies with a set of strict procedures in selecting raw materials and manufacturing drugs. According to the formulation of proven folk recipes, literature proven recipes, ancient secret recipes and effective prescriptions from the imperial physicians, Tongrentang elaborately selected and matched different medicinal materials, studied and experimented the attributes of the materials and drugs time after time, while making many adjustments in terms of the clinical performance for the patients, in order to achieve excellence and perfection through great efforts. Later, *Tongrentang's Medicine List* came forth. From the 6th year of Yongzheng's reign (1728), Tongrentang possessed the privilege of offering TCM for the Qing court for 188 years. Unique recipes, the best raw materials, strict standards and excellent clinical performance brought about a high reputation both in China and abroad for Tongrentang products. Tongrentang's most popular products are Tongren Niuhuang Qingxin Wan, Tongren Dahuoluo Dan, Suhexiang Wan, Guogong Jiu, etc.

Address: No.24 Dashila (Dazhalan), Qianmen, Beijing

Mongolian Medicine

The Mongolian medicine is said to be a traditional medicine that Mongolian people gradually formed over history. It is seen as a summary of the Mongolian people in their struggle against diseases and is the crystallization of wisdom. It is said to be a scientific medicine system with ethnic characteristics. Mongolian medicine has the characteristics of aiming to use small amounts of medicine to treat diseases, with less money, and is convenient and easy.

The Basic Theory of Mongolian Medicine

The Mongolian medicine uses the relations of "he yi", "xi la", and "ba da gan" roots to explain the physiological and pathological phenomenon in the human body. The so-called "he yi" is believed to be the movement power of physiology. The thinking, language, movement of body and internal organs are believed to be directed by it. Abnormality of "he yi" leads to the result that the normal status of the internal organs diminish, manifesting that the mind is abnormal, with sleeplessness and forgetfulness. "Xi la" has the meaning of so-called "hotness". The body temperature, the heat of the organs and spirit are said to be determined by "xi la". Too much "xi la" in manifested in symptoms like bitter taste in the mouth, sourness or anxiety. "Ba da gan" is supposed to be a kind of sticky material in the body, having the nature of coldness. Disorder of "ba da gan" not only shows people with symptoms caused by cold factors, the liquidation also stops and there is more secretion.

Phlebotomy of Mongolian Medicine

For phlebotomy, small veins are cut open for the release of "diseased blood", reaching the aim of treating or preventing disease. The phlebotomy treatment is for treating diseases caused by hotness factors caused by blood or by "xi la", such as the proliferation of wounds, plague, edema and abdominal distension, gout, tuberculosis, etc.

The external treatment which is a mixed way of cupping and phlebotomy. The cup is placed on the diseased part, making it swollen. Then needles are used for stabbing the swollen part, cupping then for sucking out the diseased blood. The movement of vital energy and the state of blood in the human body is improved and the disease is cured. It is said to have the characteristic of effectiveness, short-term period and without pain or danger.

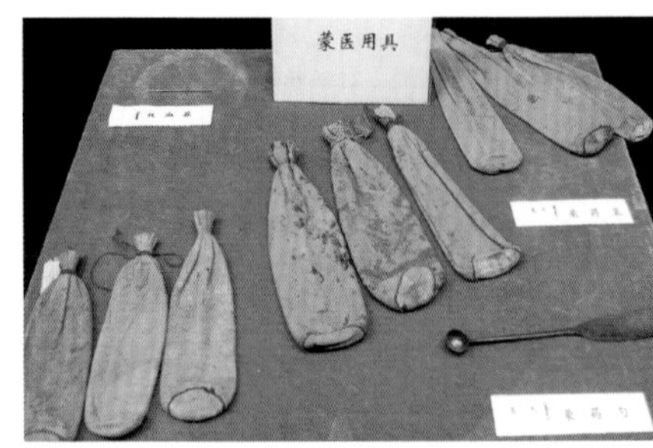

The spoon and bag for Mongolian doctors collected in the Wudang Lamasery in Baotou, Inner Mongolia.

Moxibustion is to cauterize or smoke the points upon the surface of body with moxibustion twigs; it is divided into Mongolian moxibustion, white-mountain thistle moxibustion, Xihe willow moxibustion and warm acupuncture and moxibustion.

This is a dietary treatment. It is said to be make people strong and treat diseases such as shock or pain in the chest or in heart area. Studies find that koumiss is healthy for the body since it contains a great many elements such as sugar, protein, fat, vitamins, amino acid, lactic acid, enzyme, mineral substances, aromatic plants and others.

Mongolian bone setting is a treatment accumulated by medical experts through history which is said to be able to cure disease linked with fracture, joint dislocation, or soft tissue damage. The bone setting treatment is divided into six parts, renovation, fixing, massage, herbal bath, care and recovering. It has the function of releasing the poison and soothing the sinew and quickening the blood.

Uygur Medicine

In the Western Han Dynasty, the Silk Road was established through the western regions, stimulating economic development sand cultural exchange. Eastern and western medicine mingled in Xinjiang, the hinterland of mid-Asia, which stimulated the development of the local ethnic medicine. Therefore, Uygur medicine is one that, based on its own medicine, draws the quintessence of theories and practice from different regions and ethnic minorities to create something unique.

Uygur medicines occupy a large proportion in the treasury of China's traditional medicines. At present, there are 202 varieties of drugs recorded in the national-class pharmacopoeia, including 115 varieties of medicinal materials and 87 varieties of set prescription preparation. In Xinjiang, one of the world's four major areas in which most people enjoy longevity, Uygur medicines are extensively used coming from the snow mountains, desert, grasslands and oases.

The Uygur Style in Making Medicine

According to research, there are about 600 kinds of Uygur medicines in the Xinjiang Uygur Autonomous Region, about 360 of which are commonly used and 160 kinds of which are local products. In Uygur medicine, fragrant herbs and rather poisonous herbs are both used. The most commonly used herbs are musk, ambergris, lilac and amomum cadarmomum.

Hui Medicine

Hui medicine is a mixture of Han medicine and Arab-Islam medicine. It was in the time of great prosperity in the Jin and Yuan period when there was a medical book, *Hui Hui Yao Fang*, which included both Han-style medicines such as bolus, ointment, powder, liquid and Arabic medicines like aromatic compound, collunarium, alcoholic drink mixed with fruit juice, and syrup, etc.

In folk prescriptions of the Hui ethnic group, there is an important characteristic that "medical treatment goes along with dietary treatment" and "diets contain medicinal herbs". It is relative to the Hui people's skill in cooking and fancy in making food with extra care. For instance, the Hui people mix sesame oil and mirabilite together which is said to treat constipation, esophagus inflammation or cancer at an early stage.

Huang Di Nei Jing (Yellow Emperor's Canons of Internal Medicine)

As the first extant theoretical book on Traditional Chinese Medicine, *Huang Di Nei Jing* (*Yellow Emperor's Canons of Internal Medicine*) is thought to be written in the Warring States Period (475-221BC) with basic theories including the Yin-yang and Five Elements theories. It consists of two sections, the *Suwen* (The Book of Plain Questions) and the *Lingshu* (The Vital Axis), containing 81 chapters respectively, covering physiology, pathology, anatomy, diagnosis and treatment of diseases and preventive medicine.

Yin-yang and Five Elements theories are the Chinese philosophical thoughts of ancient times. Though observing all kinds of natural phenomena for a long time, the ancient people thought everything in the world consists of two basic forces, Yin and Yang that not only oppose but also complement each other. According to this theory, Yin and Yang exist between internal and external aspects of every tissue and structure of the human body. When there is a balance between the two, there is no disease; if the balance is disturbed, illness will occur.

Huang Di Nei Jing holds that Yin and Yang is the root, of which everything is produced. The changes of Yin and Yang and four seasons are at the root, through which everything on earth grows, ages and dies. This book brings to light that the physiological and pathological phenomena are related not only to the external environment but also the internal emotional activity of the human body. It always holds that, in discussing the pathology of diseases and healthcare methods, one must take into full account the whole internal and external environment.

This book put forward the thought of preventive medicine. The healthcare methods that the acquainted man adopted must be to acclimatize to cold or hot weather and regulate his own emotions according to the changes of the four seasons. He should not develop excessive happiness and anger and fit in well with the surrounding environment. He should also adjust the change of Yin and Yang to balance it relatively. In this way, illnesses have no way to attack you and then you can prolong your life and it is difficult for to become senile.

Shanghan Zabinglun (Discourse on Fevers and Miscellaneous Illness)

Shanghan Zabinglun (Discourse on Fevers and Miscellaneous Illnesses) is a book mainly specializing in the treatment of infectious diseases and miscellaneous illnesses of internal medicine, penned by Zhang Zhongjing in the late 2nd Century. After being completed, this work was divided into two books called *Shanghanlun* (*Treatise on Febrile Diseases*) and *Jinkui Yailue* (*Summary from the Golden Chest*). It was printed dozens of times through many dynasties and came down to this day. It has always exerted a deep impact on the development of TCM theory and technique on the treatment of acute and chronic infectious diseases, epidemic and miscellaneous illnesses of internal medicine. Zhang Zhongjing was respected as the "Sage of Medicine" by doctors after the Song Dynasty. To praise highly and commemorate his contribution, in the Ming and Qing dynasties people built the Sage of Medicine Temple in Nanyang, Henan Province, his hometown, and offered sacrifices to him. The reason is that other than the contributions he made when the epidemic diseases broke out in the turmoil of war during the Eastern Han Dynasty, the *Shanghan Zabinglun* laid a foundation for the clinical medicine theory of Traditional Chinese Medicine.

Zhenjiu Jiayi Jing (Jiayi Canon on Acupuncture and Moxibustion)

Zhenjiu Jiayi Jing is an exclusive book on Chinese acupuncture and moxibustion with complete system, originally called *Huang Di Sanbu Zhenjiu Jiayi Jing* (*Yellow Emperor's Jiayi Canon on Acupuncture and Moxibustion*) and simply called *Jiayi Jing* (*Jiayi Canon*). The ten-volume book was written by Huangfu Mi (215-282) in the fourth year of Wei Emperor Ganlu's reign (259) and changed into 12-volume book in the Southern and Northern Dynasty. Huangfu Mi was originally a historian. At the age of 50, he was unlucky as to contract arthritis and became deaf, so he commenced studying intensively acupuncture and moxibustion, sorted completely and systemically the theory and clinical practice, the main and collateral channels, points and principle indications. On the basis of the experience summed up by predecessors, he unveiled more than 800 diseases and syndromes suitable for treatment though acupuncture and moxibustion. *Zhenjiu Jiayi Jing* was thought much of by physicians over many dynasties and exerted broad influence on the development of Chinese acupuncture and moxibustion in foreign countries. In the seventh or eighth century, Japan and Korea introduced TCM, and stipulated that *Zhenjiu Jiayi Jing* was used as the teaching material in their medical education.

Maijing (Pulse Classic)

Maijing (The Pulse Classic), compiled by Wang Shuhe (210-285) in the Western Jin Dynasty, is the first extant book specializing in sphygmology in China. It comprises 10 volumes, containing 98 chapters. It categorized pulse tracings into 24 kinds, such

♦ Yong'antang Pharmacy

Yong'antang was established during Emperor Yongle's reign (1403-1421), during the Ming Dynasty, and has a history of more than 580 years. Since its foundation, Yong'antang has abided by the tenet "quality accords with its reputation, while morality brings about wealth". Yong'antang has been making drugs with great seriousness and carefulness: studying the pathology of a disease at first, then probing into the attributes of the medicine. After collecting medicinal materials from all over the country, Yong'antang made them into pills, powders, ointments and small pills for the elderly and troches of the best quality with handpicked first-class ginseng and young pilose antler of deer according to the formulation of the ancient recipes and private recipes from some famous physicians. Meanwhile, Yong'antang set up its own herbal gardens, to plant various fresh herbs. Since the 1930s, Yong'antang has increasingly grown into a pharmacy with more than 1100 self-produced drugs in 16 sections, of which the most popular products are Zixue San, Lingqiao Jiedu Wan and Shenshou Huapi Gao, etc.

Address: No.366 Chaonei Dajie, Dongcheng District, Beijing

as light, heavy, slow, fast, etc., and tells the disease each kind of pulse tracing indicates. The discussion is carried out with reference to the other three ways of diagnosis: looking, listening and asking. Notwithstanding *Maijing* is a book integrating the achievements of the previous generations in sphygmology, its conciseness and convenience for study has earned it an important position in the development of Chinese medicine, and has exerted a great influence both at home and abroad. For example, the Ministry of Imperial Physicians of the Tang Dynasty took it as a compulsory course, and, in the ancient medical education of Japan, it was also regarded as a required course. After the book was completed, it was spread to the Tibetan area, which had a great impact on traditional Tibetan medicine. From Tibet, Chinese sphygmology was spread to India, and then to Arabia and so on. It also exerted some influence on the development of sphygmology of Western Europe.

Qianjin Yaofang (Prescriptions for Emergencies)

Reputed as China's earliest encyclopedia on clinical medicine, *Qianjin Yaofang* was compiled by Sun Simiao (581-682) in 652, totaling 30 volumes. In the volume header, it discusses the *Dayi Jingcheng* and *Dayi Xiye*, thus stressing that an excellent doctor must be provided with the high-minded medical morality and outstanding medical theory and technique. Its contents and scientific values lie in: developing the technique and theory on the diagnosis and treatment of infectious diseases; improving the level of diagnosis and treatment of internal diseases and surgical diseases; laying a foundation for the establishment of department of gynecology and pediatrics with the emphasis placed on the characteristics of women and infants; summing up the drugs with the curative effect over the pathogeny and the fact that treatment aimed at the pathogeny is the most effective method; enriching the theory and technique on acupuncture and moxibustion therapeutics; developing the theory on hygiene; developing the drugs and recipe to prevent and control diseases.

Bencao Gangmu (Compendium of Materia Medica)

Bencao Gangmu is an exclusive book discussing the materia medica of traditional Chinese Medicine, with its content being of naturalistic value. It was compiled by Li Shizhen (1518-1593), a famous physician of the Ming Dynasty, in 1578. It is in 52 volumes, recording 1,892 drugs, including 1,094 from herbs, 443 from animals, 161 from minerals and 194 other drugs. Li unveiled 374 new drugs in his text and included over 1,109 illustrations. The book summarized most of drug information available in the sixteenth century. In order to stress the clinical reference value, the writer annexes 11,096 clinical prescriptions, of which 8,000 are summed up from his experiences. Dr. Joseph Needham, the famous British historian, commented on *Bencao Gangmu*, saying that "beyond question, the greatest scientific achievement of the Ming Dynasty is the *Bencao Gangmu* written by Li Shizhen which reached the limit".

The statue of Li Shizhen, the author of *Compendium of Materia Medica*

Tongren Shuxue Zhenjiu (Illustrated Manual of the Bronze Man Showing Acupuncture and Moxibustion Points)

In the aspect of medical education, the teaching of acupuncture and moxibustion underwent the great reform in the Song Dynasty. Wang Weiyi (987-1067) compiled a book entitled *Tongren Shuxue Tujing* and cast two life-size bronze statues when teaching students acupuncture and moxibustion for practice. This statues exerted great influence on the development of acupuncture and moxibustion in the ages to come.

Furen Daquan Liangfang (Complete Dictionary of Effective Prescriptions for Women)

Furen Daquan Liangfang was finished in 1237, with Chen Ziming as the author. Chen, born in a family of physicians for generations, was good at obstetrics and gynecology. He believed that gynecopathy was the hardest to cure, especially many obstetrical diseases were very dangerous. He compiled the 24-volume *Furen Daquan Liangfang* (*Complete Dictionary of Effective Prescriptions for Women*) based on the merits of other schools of medical theories and the proven recipes in his family.

The book is divided into 10 categories, with a note under each piece of writing, and there are details of cured cases and new prescriptions attached in most parts. The book quotes many kinds of medical books, and expounds such cases in detail as the development of the fetus, diagnosis of pregnancy, hygiene during hygiene, pregnant women's contraindications, special diseases during pregnancy, all kinds of dystocia, puerperal care and diseases after delivery. The book is a summing-up of previous generation's accomplishments and the author's clinical experiences. It has rich contents and forms a complete system both in theory and in practice, having high academic value and practical value as well. It can be regarded as the first sophisticated monographic works on obstetrics and gynecology in China. Its popularization has greatly promoted the development of gynecology of traditional Chinese medicine.

Huihui Yaofang (Hui Medical Preparation)

The writer of and the background to the 36-volume *Huihui Yaofang* (Hui Medical Preparation) are difficult to figure out, but it is certainly a great book on Hui medicine written in the Yuan Dynasty (1206-1368). It is a book containing the essence of Arabian medicine and mature knowledge of the theory on physiology and pathology. Its understanding on hemiplegia, malignant tumor, gynecopathy, artery and vein topped the level of Traditional Chinese Medicine, with unique medicine and therapeutics.

Xiyuan Jilu (Collected Writings on the Washing Away of Wrongs)

The first monographic work on forensic medicine in the world is *Xiyuan Jilu*, written by Song Ci (1186-1249) of the Southern Song Dynasty. It was written in 1247, and is the earliest systematic book on judicial examination in the world. It was some 350 years earlier than the *Report of the Doctor*, the first systemic work on forensic medicine, which was written by Fortunato Fedele in 1598. Later, it was spread abroad, and was translated into English, French, Dutch, German, Korean, Japanese, and Russian as well as other languages.

The major contents of the book include laws on autopsy in the Song Dynasty; methods and caution of autopsy; postmortem phenomena; different kinds of death caused by mechanical asphyxia (suffocation); different kinds of blunt and sharp instrument injuries; traffic accidents in ancient times; death caused by high temperature; poisoning; death from illness; sudden death; corpse exhumation; and so on. All these contents cover the most the central aspects of forensic pathology.

The major achievements include the following: the appearance and distribution of the cadaver (corpse) spasm (instant stiffening of the body); the signs of corruption and the influencing conditions; the relationship between postmortem phenomena (body after death) and postmortem interval (time after death); discovery of postmortem delivery; classification of the ropes for hanging; the characteristics and influencing conditions of the ligature mark of hanging and the characteristics of strangulation and its distinction with suicidal hanging. Other major achievements are: findings in the corpses of drowning and in deaths caused by pressing and stuffing the mouth and the nose with other objects; findings in rose teeth related to suffocation; identification of blood clots before and after death; features of different kinds of knife wounds; injury before death and postmortem injury; the difference between suicide and homicide; determination of a fatal trauma; methods of on-the-spot investigation of different kinds of death; and so on. The book contains theories with regard to examining bodies on the basis of the experience of the period before the Song Dynasty.

♦ Ministry of Health

The Ministry of Health is a governmental department charged with health work throughout the country. The main functions of MHTRC include:

To research and draft laws, regulations, guidelines and policies on health; to research and put forth development plans and strategies on health; to work out technical criterion and health standards, and to supervise the implementation.

To research and put forward regional health planning, integrate and coordinate the health resources allocation throughout the country, to work out development plans and service standards on community health service and to guide the implementation of the health plans.

To research and work out health plans and policies on rural areas and women and children, to direct the implementation of primary health care plans and special techniques in maternal and infant health care.

Carry out the policy of prevention from the start, and to unfold health education for all.

To work out the prevention and treatment plans on serious diseases imperiling people's health; to organize the comprehensive prevention and treatment of enhanced dreaded diseases; to release name lists of quarantines and inspect infectious diseases.

To research and guide the medical institution reform, to work out medical staff professional standards, to set the quality control standards in medical practice and service criterion, and to supervise the implementation.

To supervise and manage the gathering blood and supply of blood to blood centers and plasma collection centers, to ensure the sufficiency and safety of the clinical use of blood in terms of relevant laws and regulations, etc.

Address: No.1 Xizhimenwai Nanlu, Xicheng District, Beijing
Website: http://www.moh.gov.cn

♦ State Food and Drug Administration

The State Food and Drug Administration (SFDA), an organ directly under the State Council, is charged with the comprehensive supervision of the safety management of food, health food and cosmetics, and it's also the final authority on drug regulation. The organ is in charge of the administrative and technical supervision on research, manufacturing, distribution and application of drugs used throughout the country (including raw traditional Chinese medicinal materials, traditional medicines prepared in ready-to-use forms and other prepared Chinese medicines, medicinal chemicals and their preparations, antibiotics, biochemical medicines, biological products, diagnostic aids, radioactivity drugs, narcotics, poisonous substances, psychotropic drugs, medical appliance, sanitation material, medical packing material and so on), and the full inspection and coordination of the management of food, health products and cosmetics. SFDA undertakes the investigation and disposal on serious medical accidents in accordance with the laws and regulations and is responsible for the examination and approval of health products, etc.

Address: Jia-38, Beilishilu, Xicheng District, Beijing
Website: http://www.sfda.gov.cn

♦ State Administration of Traditional Chinese Medicine (SATCM)

Main functions of the SATCM are as follows:

To research and draft guidelines, policies and development strategies on traditional Chinese medical science, integration of traditional Chinese medicine science and traditional Chinese medicine (TCM) , the combining of traditional Chinese and western medicine, the medicine and pharmacies of Chinese Minorities according to national medicine policies, laws and regulations; to draft related laws and regulations and supervise the implementation.

To work out standards of technical position assessment for the medical profession in terms of Chinese medical treatment, health care, medicine and nursing, and standards of vocational qualification for medical professionals in accordance with health technical rules and the specialty of TCM, and supervise the implementation of these standards; to participate in the formulation of the National Essential Drugs List and the standardizing of vocational qualifications for traditional Chinese pharmacists.

To program, direct and coordinate the reform of the structure and operating mechanisms of medical, research and teaching institutions of Chinese medicine; to work out the management specifications and technical standards of traditional Chinese medical and health organizations, and supervise the implementation.

To supervise and direct traditional Chinese medical treatment, prevention, health care, rehabilitation, nursing and clinical drug-use; to conduct vocational qualification systems for the medical profession according to the related regulations.

To research and direct the work concerning the combination of traditional Chinese and western medicine, and draft relative management specifications and technical standards; to supervise, coordinate and manage medical and research institutions combining Chinese and western medicine.

To research and direct the work on the medicine and pharmacies of Chinese minorities including Tibetan medicine, Mongolian medicine and Uighur medicine; to discover, collect, summarize and improve medicines and pharmacies of the Chinese minorities in terms of their theories, skills and drugs; to make and perfect continuously the related system specifications and technical standards; to supervise, coordinate and manage medical and pharmaceutical institutions of the various Chinese minorities. And other functions.

Address: No.13 Baijiazhuang Dongli, Chaoyang District, Beijing
Website: http://www.satcm.gov.cn

Employment

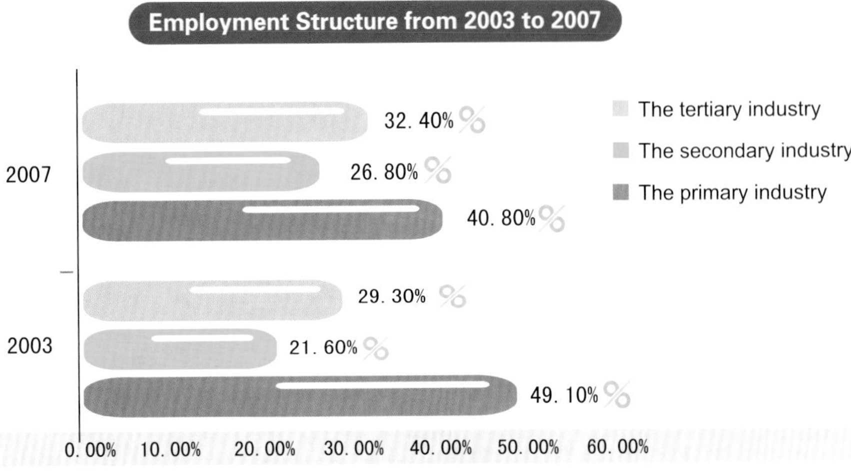

Employment Circumstances

The Chinese Government has explored and drawn on international experiences and adapted them for use in the domestic situation, formulating and implementing a number of proactive employment policies. Currently, China has established a market-oriented employment mechanism; largely solving the problem of surplus enterprise personnel arising over the years under the planned economy; and the course of economic development and economic restructuring, expanding the employment scope continuously. As a result, the employment structure has gradually been optimized; the avenues for employment have been steadily broadened; the forms of employment have become more flexible and the employment situation has been maintained basically stable.

On the principles of mutual respect, equality and mutual benefit, the Chinese Government has actively participated in international labor-related affairs. China has ratified the Convention on the Minimum Age for Admission to Employment, the Convention on Prohibition and Immediate Action for the Elimination of the Worst Forms of Child Labor, the Convention Concerning Equal Remuneration for Men and Women Workers for Work of Equal Value, the Employment Policy Convention, and other international labor-related conventions. In the field of labor and employment, China has carried out remarkably effective exchanges and cooperation with the International Labor Organization, the United Nations Development Program, the World Bank, the Asian Development Bank, and a number of other international organizations and many countries.

Basic Employment Situation

In China, there is a large working-age population, while the average educational level of the people is relatively low, resulting in a very prominent problem in unemployment. This is primarily manifested in the co-existence of the contradiction of the total volume of workforce supply and demand and the contradiction of employment structure, and in the simultaneous appearance of increasing pressure on urban employment and acceleration of the shift of surplus rural laborers to non-agricultural sectors, and in the intertwining of the employment problems of new entrants to the workforce and the reemployment of laid-off workers.

At the end of 2007, the national employment at the year-end stood at 769.90 million persons, a year-on-year rise of 5.90 million persons. Of which, the employment in primary industry reached 314.44 million persons, accounted for 40.8 percent of national employment; that of secondary industry stood at 206.29 million persons, occupied 26.8 percent; that of tertiary industry arrived at 249.17 million persons, occupied 32.4 percent. The employment at the year-end in urban areas valued at 293.50 million persons, increased 10.40 million persons, year-on-year. Of which, the employment at the year-end in various units accounting for 120.24 million persons, rose by 3.09 million persons. The staff and workers at the year-end in urban units standing at 114.27 million persons, growing 2.66 million persons, year-on-year. The new employment in urban areas was 12.04 million persons, 5.15 million laid-off and unemployed workers had found new jobs, of which, 1.53 million so-called "4050" persons which have difficulty in employment are re-employed. The urban registered unemployed persons totaled 8.30 million, and registered urban unemployment rate was 4.0 percent. At the end of the year, 869,000 households without employee had at least one person employed, accounting for 99.9 percent of the total households without employee.

Unemployment and Registered Unemployment Rate

The unemployment rate is the major index used to evaluate the unemployment situation in a country or an area. In recent years, as the employment pressure has been continuously increasing, the Chinese Government has adopted many measures to curb the sharp rise in urban unemployment. Currently, the only official unemployment rate released regularly by the Chinese Government is the urban registered unemployment rate. Urban registered unemployment refers to those who are registered as permanent residents in the urban areas engaged in non-agricultural activities, within the range of working age (from 16 to retiring age), capable to labor, unemployed but desirous to be employed and have registered at the local employment service agencies to apply for a job.

In recent years, there has been a modest rise in the urban registered unemployment rate in China. From 1999 to 2000, the unemployment rate remained at the rate of about 3.1 percent; in 2001, the rate rose to 3.6 percent; by the end of 2002, it was 4 percent. In 2007, the number of new employees in urban areas reached 12.04 million; the urban registered unemployment rate was controlled within 4 percent.

Proactive Employment Policy

China exercises a proactive employment policy, and has established the employment principle of "workers finding their own jobs, employment through market regulation and employment promoted by the government." The government has persisted in promoting employment by way of developing the economy, adjusting the economic structure, deepening

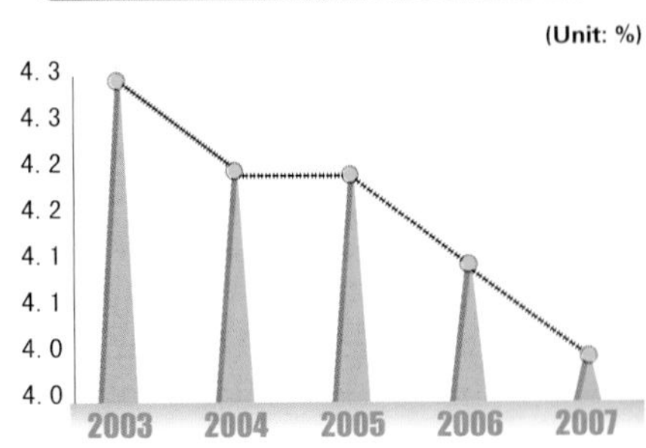

14 Society

reform, coordinating urban and rural economic development, and improving the social security system. It has adopted various effective measures and done everything possible to increase job opportunities, expand the scope of employment, and keep the unemployment rate within a socially tolerable range. Guided by the principle of developing the economy, adjusting the structure and actively creating job opportunities, the government has been working hard to increase employment through developing the economy, expanding the capacity of employment by developing the tertiary sector, developing flexible and diverse forms and increasing the channels for employment. In addition, great efforts have also made to establish a market-oriented employment mechanism, develop and improve the public employment service system and the unemployment insurance system.

Coordination Mechanism of Labor Relations

The Chinese government has made active efforts to promote the establishment of the coordination mechanism of labor relations characterized by "autonomous consultation by employers and employees and regulated by the government according to the relative law" and the system of setting up labor relations through labor contracts. The labor contract system has been fully implemented in rural enterprises of various types. The Chinese government encourages enterprises to continuously strengthen the functions of workers' congresses and trade unions, improve the system of employees' democratic participation, and actively explore and practice the system of conclusion of the collective contract through equal consultation. At present, 30 provinces, autonomous regions and municipalities in China have set up the government-trade union-enterprise tripartite conference system of labor relations coordination at the provincial level, and more than 5,000 tripartite coordination mechanisms have been established. China has also established a system for handling labor disputes, including labor dispute mediation, arbitration and lawsuits, to handle all labor disputes according to law.

Protecting Laborers' Employment Rights

Chinese law stipulates that laborers shall not be discriminated against in employment, regardless of their ethnic community, race, sex, or religious belief. No employing units shall be allowed to recruit juveniles under the age of 16. Any individuals or units recruiting child labor or introducing employment for them shall be strictly combated. Through strengthening the law enforcement and supervision, the Chinese government supervises enterprises to implement the provisions regarding equal employment stipulated by laws and regulations, corrects discriminations against various groups in the labor force market, and prohibits discriminatory employment advertisements from being played or published. Meanwhile, the government also makes efforts to help to improve the rights protection awareness and ability of laborers, and create a good public opinion atmosphere to support and encourage them to protect their employment rights. The Chinese government has been continually perfecting the national, local and trade standards on job safety and hygiene. China promulgated the Occupational Health and Safety Management System in 1999, and the authentication of the system has been fully developed. The Regulation of Industrial Injury Insurance was promulgated in 2003, and has been put into practice since January 1, 2004.

Employment System

With the Chinese economic transformation from the planned economy system to socialist market economy system, the employment system and structure also experienced great changes. The old employment system of the state monopoly for running and distributing was changed step by step into the market-oriented employment system. A new employment mechanism of "laborers finding employment on their own initiative, the market adjusting the demand for employment and the government promoting employment" has been carried out.

China's employment service system mainly includes job-introduction, employment training, unemployment insurance and employment service enterprises. The job-introduction service includes placement registration, recruitment registration, labor market information collection, guidance and consultation for job applicants and employing units, as well as perspective on the employment situation. The employment training includes pre-job training for youth unemployment, women, and the disabled, conversion training for unemployed workers. The unemployment insurance system supplies unemployment compensation, medical subvention, management and aid for reemployment to the unemployed workers. And the employment service enterprises are responsible for setting up various manufacturing and selling points, with the support of the organizing units and preferential policies in terms of investment, taxation and employment, to place the unemployed workers.

At the end of 2007, there were all together 500 overseas employment agencies in China. Through the introduction of those agencies, a total of 105,000 persons were still in employment in Hong Kong, Macao and Taiwan and foreign countries, of which, 65,000 persons went abroad in 2007. At the end of 2007, a total of 210,000 foreigners with employment permits worked in China; and 83,000 with Taiwan, Hong Kong and Macau employment permits worked in mainland China.

Over one-third rural laborers of China have been transferred. The quality of the farmers going out to work has been obviously improved in terms of the legal consciousness, working skills and social ability. This has accelerated the rural economic development, building of the spiritual civilization and elimination of the difference between the rural and urban areas.

Employment of the Rural Workforce

The rural population accounts for a large proportion of China's population, and the government has attached great importance to the employment of the rural workforce. By adhering to the policy of urbanization with Chinese characteristics that enable the big, medium and small cities as well as small towns develop in a coordinated way, the Chinese Government has planned the social and economic development of both urban and rural areas as a whole, adjusted the structure of agriculture and rural economy, expanded the rural employment capacity, and adopted various measures to encourage the surplus rural workforce to transfer to non-agricultural industries, and gradually removed the policies which were not suitable for the urbanization, to guide the rational and orderly flow of the rural workforce.

The Chinese Government has actively adjusted the structure of agriculture and the rural economy, made great efforts to develop agro-industries other than traditional crop cultivation, expanded comprehensive agricultural development to raise the overall returns of agriculture. China has also vigorously promoted the industrialization of agriculture management and developed farm produce processing, sales, storage, transportation and preservation to extend the farm produce-related industrial chain. By

Transfer of the Rural Workforce for Employment Every Year

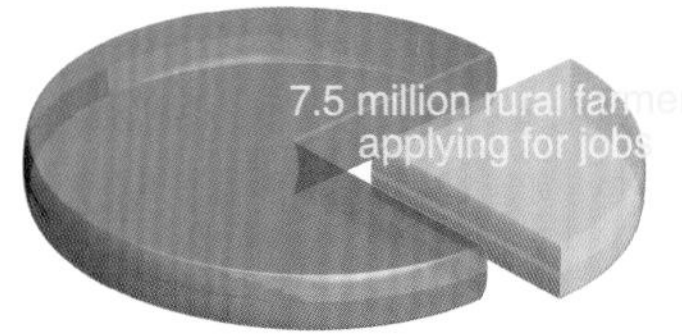

adopting a series of preferential policies in the areas of finance, taxation and credit, the state has helped a group of key and leading enterprises to accelerate their development.

The Chinese Government has taken the development of the township enterprises as an important means to place the surplus rural workforce. During the past two decades, the market competitiveness of township enterprises has been continuously improved through institutional innovation, technological transformation, optimized arrangement and industrial upgrading. At present, township enterprises have attained a considerable size and a considerable economic aggregate. They have become an important force for invigorating the rural economy and increasing farmers' incomes, and have provided employment opportunities for the majority of the surplus rural workforce.

In 2007, the township enterprises in China realized an added value of 6,800 billion Yuan, accounting for 28.25 percent of the GDP; they became the important pillar of the national economy. The employment in township enterprises exceeded 150 million, accounting for 29.13 percent of the rural workforce. The township enterprises contributed 36.3 percent of the income of the farmers.

Training for Employment of Rural Labor Forces

Throughout the 1990s, the number of farmers working away from their native homes increased rapidly at an annual average of five million. To find jobs in places other than their native homes became a major channel for the transfer of the rural workforce. Since the early 1990s, the Chinese Government has adopted the policy of "treating fairly, guiding rationally, and improving administration and service" for farmers working in cities and strengthened guidance and service work in this regard. The government has established effective administrative service systems, such as the labor service cooperation system, employment service system and key monitoring system, aimed at bringing into full play the government's functions in information provision and administrative service. On this basis, great efforts have been made to strengthen the building of public employment service organizations, to set up and improve the labor recruitment information network, to carry out recruitment information surveys and to issue timely analysis and announcement of the recruitment needs of enterprises. The government has worked out the National Plan for Training Rural Migrant Workers, 2003-2010 to improve vocational training for the rural workforce, and plans to provide guiding training and vocational skill training to the 60 million prospective rural migrant laborers in the coming seven years, so as to enhance the overall quality of the rural migrant workers and their employment qualifications.

Safeguarding the Legal Rights and Interests of Rural Migrant Workers

The Chinese Government has gradually improved the administration of labor contracts for rural migrant workers in cities. Any work unit that employs rural workers must, according to law, sign labor contracts with them, in order to clarify the rights and obligations of the respective parties. The government has reorganized the labor market, strengthened supervision over and inspection of the employing units and intermediaries, enhanced management in such areas as wage payment and labor conditions, carried out a special inspection of law enforcement regarding the protection of rural migrant workers' rights and interests, and severely dealt with illegal job agencies and fabrication of false employment information to deceive rural migrant workers, thus effectively safeguarding the rural migrant workers' legitimate rights and interests and the order of the labor market. Active efforts have been made to develop ways to extend social insurance to rural migrant workers, and in the major localities that bring in rural migrant workers, such as Guangdong, Fujian and Beijing, the coverage of social insurance has been extended to include rural migrant workers, also relevant policies and regulations have been worked out and active efforts have been made to provide social insurance to rural migrant workers in cases of work-related injury, medical care and old-age pension.

Making Experiments in Development and Employment of Rural Workforce

The Chinese Government has made experiments in some areas on the development and employment of the rural workforce to explore for specific approaches, means of implementation and policies and measures for the development and employment of the rural workforce in view of different natural and socio-economic conditions. Meanwhile, efforts have been made to set up a relevant socialized service system, and organizational and administrative forms corresponding to various modes of employment, and studies have been carried out on policies, laws and regulations, as well as macro control measures for the government to manage urban and rural employment in a unified way and to promote the employment of the rural workforce. At present, such experimental work, which is characterized by unified planning for employment in both urban and rural areas, rural migrant workers returning home to start their own businesses, training of the rural migrant workforce, and the promotion of western development, is being carried out in 98 counties, and cities in 26 provinces and centrally administered municipalities nationwide.

The surplus labor force in rural areas has the following ways to find a job. The first is to do further exploration on forestry, animal husbandry and aquaculture, while tapping agricultural potentials to develop plant production. The second is to develop township enterprises and tertiary industries in rural areas to use the regional advantages to explore the non-agricultural industries. The third is to develop small-sized towns and cities to enable them to absorb surplus labor forces in rural areas. And the fourth is to direct part of the rural labor force to work in other places, according to needs, in order to meet the requirements of urban economic development.

Women's Employment

(See P34)

Promoting the Employment of Young People

China has a large young population. Every year, a new, million- strong, workforce arises, making young people's employment an increasingly striking problem. Of the registered unemployed people in urban areas, around 70 percent are under the age of 35. To reduce the employment pressure on society, and improve young workers' skills and overall quality, the Chinese Government provides one to three years of work preparation for all junior and senior middle school graduates who have failed to enter schools at higher levels. Vocational guidance is offered in various secondary vocational schools as a required course. To solve the employment problem of graduates from institutions of higher learning, the Chinese Government has adopted measures to promote their employment. These mainly include: in pursuance of the reform

The ikebana training

oriented toward market guidance, government regulation, school recommendation, and the two-way choice of students and employers, graduates from institutions of higher learning are encouraged to go and work at the grassroots level and in areas with tough conditions to strengthen urban communities and rural townships; enterprises and institutions, especially small and medium enterprises and private enterprises and institutions, are urged to hire graduates from institutions of higher learning; graduates from institutions of higher learning are urged to start their own businesses or to get employment in a flexible way, and are offered tax breaks, small loans and training in starting businesses; to establish and improve employment information networks for graduates from institutions of higher learning and to do a better job in employment guidance and services. Meanwhile, guidance is given to institutions of higher learning to readjust their structure of specialties and structure of talent training according to market demand. In Shanghai and some other places, a youth probation program has been implemented, and in line with the principle of "government compensation, public assistance and voluntary participation by enterprises," probation bases for graduates from institutions of higher learning are established in enterprises with the necessary conditions, and graduates who have not found jobs are organized to improve their abilities in practice and enhance their adaptability to their future jobs.

Helping Disabled People to Find Employment

As of April 1, 2006, there are 82.96 million disabled people in China. China has brought into full play the guiding role of the government and general public in promoting the employment of disabled people, and made great efforts to create a favorable environment for disabled people to equally participate in social life. According to China's laws, the state guarantees disabled people's right to work. The government makes the overall plans for the employment of the disabled and creates conditions for this purpose. To guarantee disabled people's legitimate right to employment, the government has strengthened supervision and law enforcement, so as to find and correct in time any employers' infringement of disabled people's legitimate rights and interests in violation of the law and relevant regulations. In line with the principle of combining group and individual employment, China adopts preferential policies as well as supportive and protective measures to promote the employment of disabled people through various channels, at various levels and in various forms. By group employment, it means that the state and the public arrange for the employment of groups of disabled people by running welfare enterprises, recuperation-through-work organizations, massage cure services, and other welfare undertakings. The government encourages the development of welfare enterprises with preferential policies, such as tax reduction and exemption, to enable more disabled people to find employment. By individual employment, it means that employing units hire a certain number of disabled people for suitable posts in proportion to their staff size. Units with disabled employees fewer than the required proportion must pay into an insurance fund for the employment of disabled people. The state has also adopted various preferential policies and supporting measures to encourage self-employment by disabled people in both urban and rural areas and, by way of granting discount-interest, poverty-alleviation loans, helped impoverished disabled people with the ability to work to set up their own businesses or start projects that can increase their incomes. Meanwhile, the government and social organizations actively offer employment services to disabled people, providing them with free vocational guidance, job referral and vocational training.

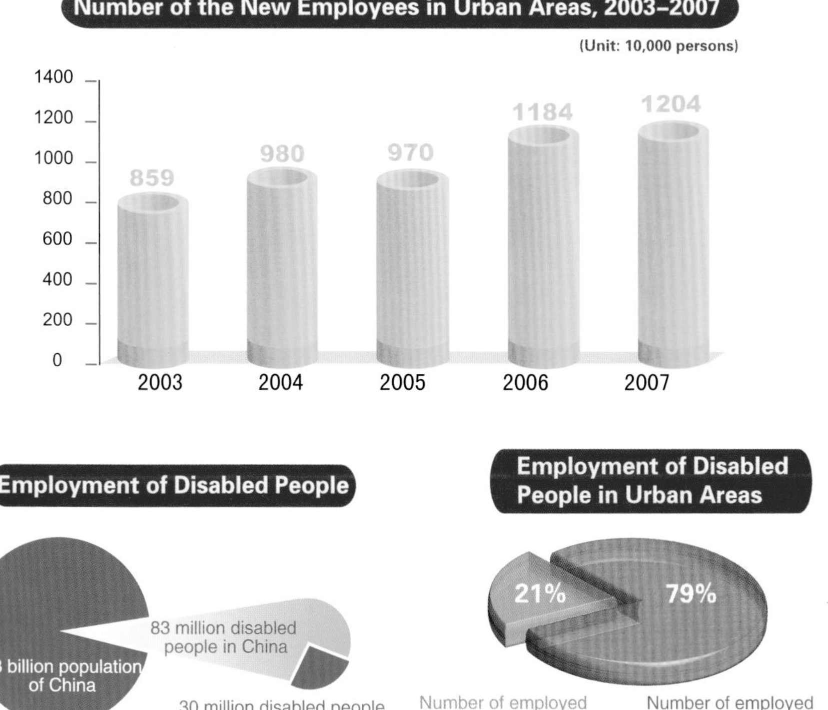

The Employment License for Foreign Employees

The Chinese Government attaches great importance to the administration of the employment of foreigners in China. Various relevant policies and regulations have been adopted to guarantee the labor security of the foreign employees. The reform and opening-up policy of China is developing steady and deeply. Meanwhile, the international economic cooperation also continues to develop in a profound way. More and more foreigners come to China.

Any foreigners seeking employment in China shall meet the following conditions: (1)18 years of age or older and in good health; (2) with professional skills and job experience required for the work of intended employment; (3) with no criminal record; (4) a clearly-defined employer; (5) a valid passport other international travel documents in lieu of the passport; (6) shall hold the Employment License and Residence Certificate after entry.

In China, the labor administration authorities of the people's government in the provinces, autonomous regions and municipalities directly under the Central Government and those at the prefecture and city level with their authorization are responsible for the administration of employment of foreigners. The employer shall apply for the employment permission if it intends to employ foreigners and may do so after obtaining approval and the People's Republic of China Employment License for Foreigners. Besides, it shall fill out the application form for the Employment of Foreigners (hereinafter referred to as the 'Application Form') and submit it to its competent trade authorities at the same level as the labor administrative authorities together with the following documentation: (1) the curriculum vitae of the foreigner to be employed; (2) the letter of intention for employment;(3) the report of the reasons for employment;(4) the credentials of the foreigner required for

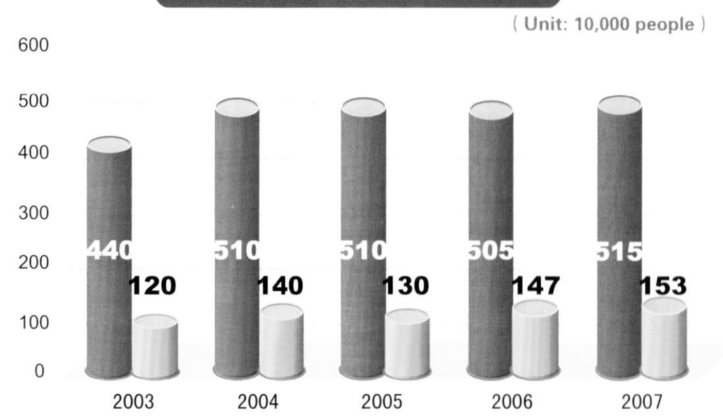

Free business-creation training for laid-off personnel

the performance of the job; (5) the health certificate of the foreigner to be employed; (6) other documents required by regulations. The competent trade authorities shall examine and approve the application in accordance with the relevant laws and decrees. After the approval by them, the employer shall take the Application Form to the labor administrative authorities of the province, autonomous region or municipality directly under the Central Government or the labor administrative authorities at the prefecture and city level, where the said employer is located, for examination and clearance. The labor administration authorities described above shall designate a special body to take up the responsibility of issuing the Employment License.

Establishing a Vocational Training System

At present, Vocational training in China includes pre-employment training, training for people transferred to new occupations, apprentice training and on-the-job training, covering elementary, intermediary, and advanced vocational qualification training for technicians and other types of training to help people adapt to different job requirements.

By developing higher vocational institutions, advanced technical schools, secondary polytechnic schools, technical schools, employment training centers, non-governmental vocational training institutions and enterprise employee training centers, the state endeavors to develop an all-round and multi-level national system of vocational education and training and strengthen training for the new urban workforce, laid-off workers, rural migrant workers and on-the-job employees.

Pre-Employment Training

China has fully adopted the workforce preparation system, and widely established and implemented the system of training the new workforce before employment. Thus, a vocational training network covering both urban and rural areas has been put in place, making it possible for most of the new urban workers to receive work preparation training, and for new rural laborers, especially non-agricultural laborers and rural migrant workers in towns and cities, to be gradually included in the work preparation training program. Each year, some 1 million urban junior and senior middle school graduates who were unable to enter schools for further studies received such training.

Strengthening Labor Skill Training

Since 2002, the state has carried out a widespread skill-enhancement action by implementing the Plan for Strengthening Vocational Training to Improve Employment Qualifications and the National Project for Training Highly Skilled Personnel. Meanwhile, a program for training 500,000 new technicians in three years was also launched. All these were aimed at cultivating rapidly a large number of skilled workers, especially workers with advanced skills, so as to improve the employment qualifications, work competence and job-switching capability of the workforce as a whole. In this process, emphasis was laid on training in new techniques, materials, technology and equipment to meet the urgent needs of enterprises for people with specialized skills and techniques, multi-skilled talents, and people with both the needed knowledge and skills for the development of new and high technology. Of the enterprise employees in China, dozen millions receive job-related skill training.

Technical School

Technical schools are comprehensive vocational training bases mainly engaged in training skilled workers, while offering the middle school graduates three year long training programs. Employment training centers are bases for training the new workforce and laid-off people, technical schools mainly offering teaching in

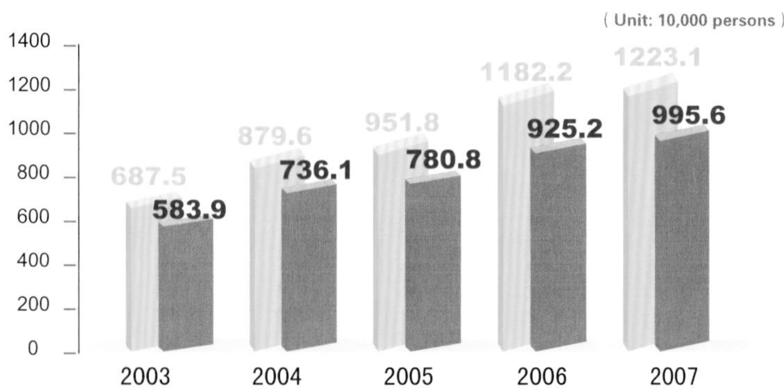

practical skills and helping the trainees to adapt to different job requirements. Currently, the different vocational training system has developed into a multi-level, multi-functional and multi-diversified one, containing elementary, intermediary and advanced levels, coexisting with academic education and vocational qualification certificates education. It covers more than 30 departments and sectors of machinery, electronics, aviation, electric power, petroleum, metallurgy, railway, etc. At present, there were some 2,800 technical schools in China.

Reemployment Service Centers

Reemployment service centers are an important base for training the unemployed. Their training targets the unemployed youth and unemployed workers. The training includes pre-employment training and training for people transferred to new occupations, mainly training the practical skills and job requirement training. The training is flexible, lasting one to three months at the least or six to 12 months at the most. There are some 3,000 employment training centers, of which 20,341 are private training institutions in China.

Vocational Skills Certification

When China adopted the vocational qualification certificate system in 1994, relevant laws and regulations as well as a work system for its application were established initially. In 1999, the Chinese government called upon all social sectors to adopt the system of paying attention both to school diplomas and vocational qualification certificates. In 2000, the framework of the employment permission system was preliminarily set up. At present, China has basically set up a vocational qualification training system at five levels--from elementary-, intermediate- and advanced-grade skilled workers to technicians and senior technicians--that corresponds to the state vocational qualification standards and forms an important part of a life-long learning system for workers. There are some 7,000 vocational skill evaluation organs in China. Some 10 million attended the examination yearly, winning qualification of technician or senior technician.

Vocational Skill Competitions

Skill competitions in China are held at the national, provincial and city levels. The national-level competition is held every other year. Meanwhile, the government, trade unions and enterprises work in close cooperation to hold vocational skill competitions within particular trades or enterprises to enhance the vocational skills of workers and staff members. Since 1995, 10 winners of the "China Grand Skill Award" and 100 "National Technical Experts" have been selected and commended by the state each year.

Social Security

Social Security System

At present, the basic framework of the social security system of China includes 13 programs grouped in three parts in accordance with the fund-raising mode and security goals of various kinds. One part is a security program supported by the national financial budget, which includes social relief, social welfare, and the special care and placement system and community services. The second part is compulsory social insurance, which is enforced by legislation, including old-age insurance, unemployment insurance, medical insurance, work-related injury insurance, maternity insurance and housing insurance. The second part composes the core of the social security system. The funding of this part is undertaken by the State, the employers and the employees. As an important supplementary to the above two parts, business insurance, profit-making as its main aim, composes the third part of the social security system. It is composed of personal insurance, enterprise insurance and mutual aid insurance.

Social Relief

Social relief aims to help people in difficulty and provide assistance to the disadvantaged groups of the society, including those with low income and those who have difficulties in livelihood. Low- income people refer to those who can't achieve the basic living standard by their own labor, such as orphans or long-term job losers. National relief can enable them to obtain a basic living condition.

Special Care and Placement

The special care and placement system is national special care to those who have contributed to the country and its people. They are mainly families of martyrs and servicemen who died on duty or of illnesses, wounded and disabled servicemen, demobilized servicemen and volunteer soldiers. The level of special care and placement shall be above the average living standard of the people in the localities, and also a mechanism for the special care standard to rise gradually with the economic development should be set up.

Social Welfare

Social welfare is aimed at safeguarding a category of people who have no people to depend on, including the aged, orphans, the disabled and people with mental diseases. China is deepening its reform on social welfare undertakings to change the present situation of dealing with all the things itself. It is probing a multi-developmental means in its social welfare undertakings, which features subsidizing by the government, handling by social institutions, shareholding by the enterprises and public institutions, and contracted by the juridical persons. In this way, to make social welfare institutions gradually transform to the mode of being run by the private sectors and subsidized by the State and managed by the juridical persons.

Community Service

This refers to services organized by communities themselves with Government financial aid and legal protection. These services are subject to management by civil administration departments and organized for the retired, the old, the weak, the sick, the disabled, people whose spouses have died, and the empty nesters. The community service features public participation, varied financial supports, and service quality.

14

On March 18, 2008, the workers of the Tuanjiehu Social Security Center of the Chaoyang District of Beijing went to the home of the old people with difficulty in action to fill the application forms of the "Old-age Security for the Aged Residents without Social Security in Both Rural and Urban Areas" and the "New-type Rural Social Old-age Insurance".

Old-age Insurance System

At present, China is trying out the implementation of reform on the basic old-age insurance system for employees in urban areas, which combines the overall social planning with personal accounts. The basic old-age insurance system covers employees in state-owned enterprises, collectively-owned enterprises, shareholding enterprises, private enterprises, Chinese employees in foreign-invested enterprises, persons engaged in individual businesses of industry and commerce and those who are employed in a flexible manner.

The enterprises and the employees jointly pay the premiums of basic old-age insurance. (Because the premiums were paid before taxing, the State pays for part of the premiums.) Generally the premiums paid by the enterprises will not exceed 20 percent of the total wage bill of the enterprise, which includes the part allocated to the personal accounts of the employees. Specific rates will be determined by the people's governments of provinces, autonomous regions and municipalities directly under the Central Government. Individual employees pay eight percent of the total wage bill of the enterprise. A personal account will be set up for every participant of the basic old-age insurance, and the amount of the account shall be 11 percent of the employee's wage bill. A social pooling fund will also be built up. The premiums paid by the employees will flow into his/her personal account completely; the shortfall will be made up by the premiums paid by the enterprise. According to China's actual conditions, such as the economic development, the increase in the wages of the employees, the development of the enterprise annuity system and personal savings insurance, the replacement rate of the basic old-age pensions (the ratio between the old-age pension and the wage level) is about 60 percent. At present, social insurance agencies have commissioned banks to delivered old-age pensions in many towns and cities across China.

Basic Medical Insurance System for Urban Employees

The basic medical insurance program covers all employers and employees in urban areas, including employees and retirees of all government agencies, public institutions, mass organizations, private non-enterprise units and enterprises (including state-owned enterprises, collectively-owned enterprises, foreign-invested enterprises, and private enterprises). The funds for basic medical insurance come mainly from premiums paid by the State, the units and the employees; the premium paid by the employer is about six percent of the total wage bill, while that paid by the employee is two percent of his or her wage. With the development of economy, the premium rate can be adjusted correspondingly. The individuals' premiums and 30 percent of the premiums paid by the employers go to the personal accounts, and the remaining 70 percent of the premiums paid by the employers goes to the social pool program funds. A concrete rate will be set up in accordance to the payment standard in the area, the span employment of the employees and other factors. The basic medical insurance implements a management method of the designation of medical institutions (including Traditional Chinese Medicine hospitals) and pharmacies, allowed to provide services covered by medical insurance. The Ministry of Labor and Social Security, the Ministry of Public Health and the Ministry of Finance and related departments under the State Council have worked together to promulgate a method to examine and improve their qualifications. When choosing the designated medical institutions and pharmacies, the handling agencies should abide by the following principles: choose western hospitals and traditional Chinese medicine hospitals at the same time; take into account the grass-roots hospitals, special hospitals and comprehensive medical organizations; provide convenience for the employees to seek medical treatment. Contracts should also be signed to clarify duties, responsibilities and the rights of both sides. A competitive mechanism should also be established. The employees can choose designated institutions to see the doctors and buy medicines, and can also buy medicine in designated pharmacies with prescriptions.

Industrial Injury Insurance

In order to guarantee the workers who are injured at work or suffer from occupational diseases get medical treatment and economic compensation, and promote the prevention of industrial injury and recovery from the occupational diseases, and lessen the risk of industrial injury assumed by the employing work units, the State stipulates that all enterprises, and individual industrial and commercial entities with employees shall participate in the industrial injury insurance and pay premiums of industrial injury for all employees of their units in accordance with the *Regulations of Industrial Injury Insurance*. The employees of all kinds of enterprises and individual industrial and commercial entities are entitled to enjoy the treatment of industrial injury insurance in line with *Regulations of Industrial Injury Insurance*.

Unemployment Insurance System

In the mid-1980s, China established an unemployment insurance system, providing unemployment benefits and unemployment health insurance subsidies for the laid-off persons, carrying out management and service oriented towards those out of work, and promoting employment and reemployment while bringing unemployment insurance into full play. In January, 1999, the Chinese Government promulgated Regulations on Insurance of Unemployment, which further improved the unemployment insurance system.

♦ Labor Law of the People's Republic of China

The Labor Law of the People's Republic of China were adopted at the Eighth Session of the Standing Committee of the Eighth National People's Congress on July 5, 1994. Laborers shall have the right to be employed on an equal basis, choose occupations, obtain remuneration for their labor, take rest, have holidays and leaves, obtain protection of occupational safety and health, receive training in vocational skills, enjoy social insurance and welfare, and submit applications for settlement of labor disputes, as well as other rights relating to labor as stipulated by law. Laborers shall fulfill their labor tasks, improve their vocational skills, follow rules on occupational safety and health, and observe labor discipline and professional ethics. The employing units shall establish and perfect rules and regulations in accordance with the law in order to ensure that laborers enjoy the right to work and fulfill labor obligations. The State shall take various measures to promote employment, develop vocational education, lay down labor standards, regulate social incomes, perfect the social insurance system, coordinate labor relationships, and gradually raise the living standard of laborers. The State shall advocate the participation of laborers in social voluntary labor and the development of their labor competitions and activities of forwarding rational proposals, encourage and protect the scientific research and technical renovation engaged in by laborers, as well as their inventions and creations; and commend and reward model laborers and advanced workers, etc.

Number of People Participating in the Work-related Injury Insurance Scheme from 2003 to 2007

(Unit: 10,000 people)

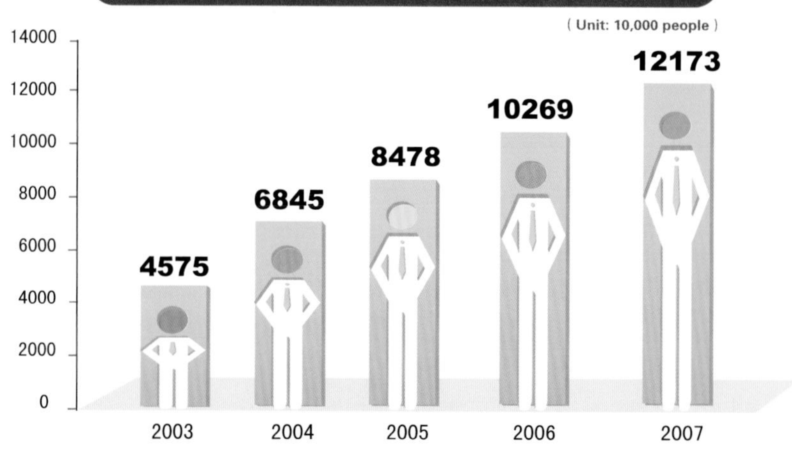

Number of People Participating in the Basic Medical Insurance Scheme from 2003 to 2007

(Unit: 10,000 people)

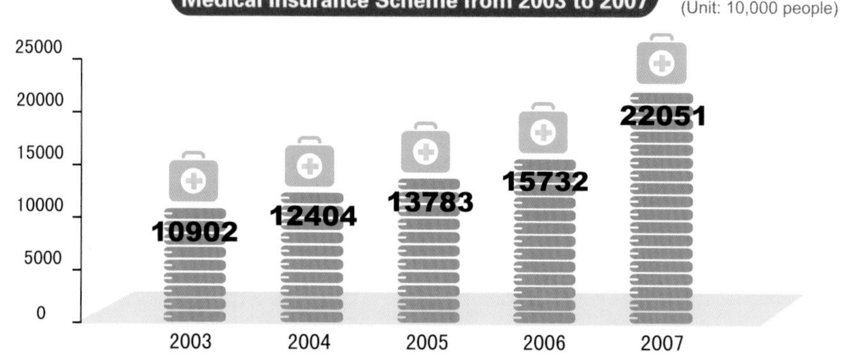

Number of People Participating in the Basic Old-age Insurance Scheme from 2003 to 2007

(Unit: 10,000 people)

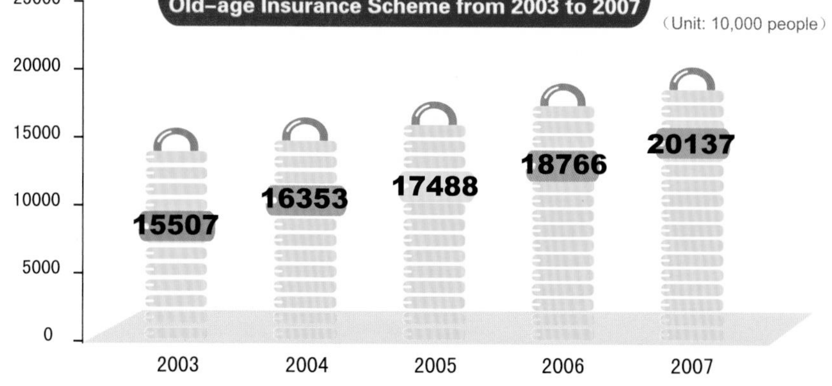

Number of People Participating in the Maternity Insurance Scheme from 2003 to 2007

(Unit: 10,000 people)

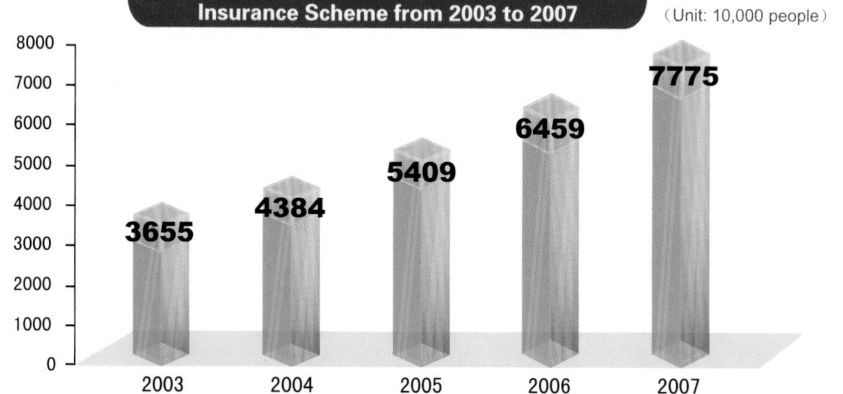

People Buying Basic Medical Insurance at the End of 2007

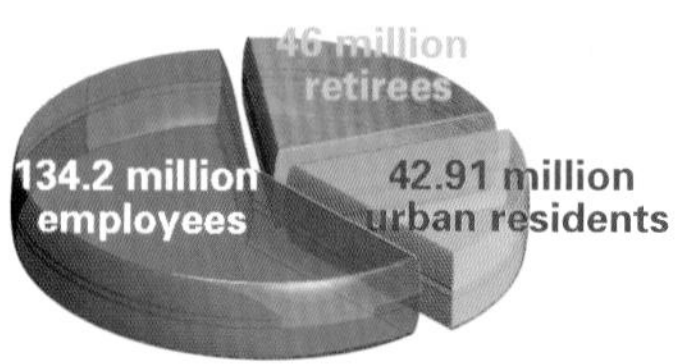

Basic Old-age Insurance for Enterprise Employees

20%

Enterprises pay 20 percent of the total wage bill for establishing the social pool grogram fund.

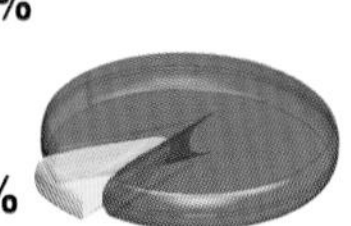

8%

Employees pay 8 percent of their wages as premiums and remit it into their personal accounts.

Basic Medical Insurance for Urban Employees and Residents

6%

The premium paid by the employer is about 6 percent of the total wage bill

2%

The premium paid by the employee is 2 percent of his or her wage

China's Unemployment Insurance System

2%

Employers pay 2 percent of their total wage bill as unemployment insurance premiums.

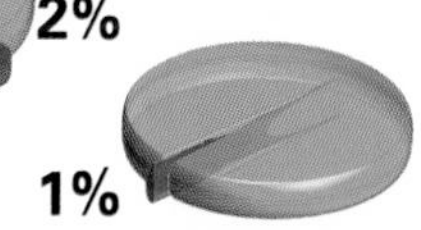

1%

Individuals pay 1 percent of their personal wages as unemployment insurance premiums.

Childbirth Insurance System

In 1994, in order to facilitate the implementation of the Labor Law, the state mapped out the Trial Procedures for Childbirth Insurance for Enterprise Employees. This reformed the childbirth insurance system of the enterprises in the form of social insurance, and standardized the content, standards and format of childbirth insurance.

The essence of the reform of childbirth insurance is to implement unified social arrangement. Funds are raised according to the principle of "collection based on payment, account balance", i.e. the enterprises pay for the childbirth insurance based on a certain proportion of their total salary to the social insurance agencies and establish a childbirth insurance fund. The extracted proportion of the childbirth insurance premium shall be fixed properly by the local people's government according to the birth number within the family plan and fees like childbirth allowance and childbirth medical care expenses, with the upper limit of 1 percent of the total salary. The employees themselves don't pay for the childbirth insurance. The childbirth allowance of the female employees shall be calculated and distributed according to the average monthly salary of the employees of the enterprises in the previous year, and paid by the childbirth insurance fund. The expenses for check-ups, delivery, operation, hospitalization and medicine are paid by the childbirth insurance fund. The medical service and medicine expenses that are beyond the scope and standard of the regulation will be shouldered by the employees themselves.

Minimum Living Standard Security System

The Minimum Living Standard Security System for urban residents is a new social relief system to provide balanced relief to urban poor people in complying with the minimum living standard. Together with the old-age insurance system, guarantee of basic cost of living allowances for the laid-off workers and the unemployment insurance system, they are called the social security system of "three guarantees".

In September, 1997, the State Council issued Notice on Building the System of Minimum Standard of Living for Urban Residents, requiring that the system shall be established in all cities and townships where the County's People's Government is located so as to carry out the work in an all round way. By September, 1999, the system had been established in all cities and townships where the County's People's Government is located. Meanwhile, Regulations on Minimum Subsistence Allowance for Urban Residents issued by the State Council took effect on October 1st, 1999, which incorporated the work into the track of standardized and legalized management.

According to the characteristics of the distribution of the poor people in China at present, the minimum subsistence allowance is mainly oriented to the following three categories of people: first, residents have no source of income or statutory supporters and loose the ability to do labor; second, residents whose average per-capita household income is lower than the local minimum standard of living, if they aren't reemployed during the period when they draw unemployment benefit or after the period of unemployment insurance; third, residents whose average per-capita household income is lower than the local minimum standard of living when the on-work staff and laid-off workers receive their salary or the minimum salary and basic life expenses or the retirees receive their pension.

Minimum Standard of Living for Cities in China

The minimum standard of living is determined by the local authority according to the expenses of life necessities and financial capacity, and adjusted properly in line with the changes of price for life's necessities and the improvement of people's living standard. Due to the great difference in the economic condition and consumption level of various regions of China, the standard for each region also differentiates each, even varying between the cities and counties within a province or autonomous region. For example, the minimum living standard for each person is 390 Yuan per month in Beijing since July 1, 2008, 400 Yuan in Shanghai since April 1, 2008, and only 140 Yuan in Ziyun County, Guizhou Province of southwest China since May, 2008. In general, the residents who have no source of income or statutory supporters and loose the ability to do labor are provided with full relief, another objective under the security system is to provide with relief according to the real balance between the minimum standard and their per-capita household income. The minimum living standard of poor urban residents is basically guaranteed. By the end of August 2007, 22.361 million urban residents of 10.448 million households all together received minimum living standard allowances.

Security System of Minimum Wage

The Labor Laws of the People's Republic of China clearly stipulates in chapter Five, that the State should implement the security system of a minimum wage. As the individual employees attend to their duties at the required working time, they should be paid the minimum remuneration by the enterprises they are employed by. The minimum remuneration does not include overtime wages, allowances for employees serving the middle shift, night shift, and working under special conditions such as high temperature, low temperature, operation in a pit, poisonous and harmful conditions, and other non-monetary incomes in terms of insurance, welfare, food and housing subsidies, which are regulated by the State laws and policies and which enterprises must pay employees.

China has made active efforts to establish a government-trade union-enterprise tripartite coordination mechanism in conformity with its actual conditions, for constituting minimum wage. The standard of a minimum wage is mainly based on income and expenses of local employees with low income, local price level, guardian coefficient, average wage, supply and demand of labor force, labor productivity, and local comprehensive economic benefits. In addition, it also takes into consideration the demand of international competition resulting from introduction of the opening up policy, and endurance capacity of labor cost of enterprises. With the change of the above factors, the standard of a minimum wage should be readjusted in a timely manner; usually it should be regulated one time at most every year.

The security system of a minimum wage is applicable for all domestic enterprises, including state-owned enterprises, collective enterprises, foreign-invested enterprises, and privately-run enterprises. Up to now, the guarantee system of a minimum wage has been established and implemented in 30 provinces, autonomous regions and municipal cities, all except the Tibetan Autonomous Region, including the official promulgation of the standard of a minimum wage.

Poverty Alleviation in Rural Areas

In 1978, in the early part of that year, in which China adopted the reform and opening-up policies, there was a poverty-stricken population of up to 250 million in Chinese rural areas, who suffered with the problem of inadequate food and clothing, accounting for 30.7 percent of the total rural population at that time. Through unremitting efforts for 20-odd years, the Chinese Government and its people have made remarkable achievements in poverty alleviation.

During the 10th Five-Year Plan period, the per-capita net income of the farmers in key counties under the State major poverty alleviation plan increased 35 percent from 1,277 Yuan to 1,723 Yuan, a little higher than that of the national average level in the same period. The per-capita net income of the farmers reached 4,140 Yuan in 2007, increasing 553 Yuan compared with that in 2006. At the end of 2007, the rural poverty-stricken population reduced from the 250 million in 1978 to 21.48 million. The poverty occurrence rate declined from the original 30.7 percent to 2.3 percent.

Poverty Alleviation by Development

In order to further promote poverty alleviation, the Chinese Government has implemented a series of major measures since 1986: such as establishing in particular the institutions of poverty alleviation, allocating special funds, working out preferential policies for deciding counties under the State major poverty alleviation plan, and the principle of poverty alleviation by development. Such great effort has marked the start up of poverty alleviation by development across the country, which is conducted featuring good planning, organizing and a large scale, one new historical time has come into being for the undertaking of poverty alleviation in China.

Under the governments support, poverty alleviation by development refers to encouraging and supporting the masses in poverty-stricken areas on how to be self-dependent, work hard, and enhance their capacity for self-accumulation and self-development in order to change their poverty situations. The poverty alleviation by development refers to reform and adjustment of traditional separate relieves, which belongs to the model of poverty alleviation of "producing blood". Currently, it has become the key and basic part relating to

The agricultural experts give guidance to the vegetable growers.

♦ China Foundation for Poverty Alleviation

The China Foundation for Poverty Alleviation, established in March 1989, subject to the State Council Leading Group Office of Poverty Alleviation and Development, is one non-profit social institution taking charge of the management of donated funds from home and abroad. Its tenet is to improve various conditions relating to production, living and health in poverty-stricken areas and populations, to enhance their living quality and capacity so as to shake off poverty and attain prosperity and sustained development. By the end of 2004, the China Foundation for Poverty Alleviation raised and invested funds for poverty alleviation up of over one billion Yuan, with more than 200 projects, in total, carried out, helping over three million poverty-stricken people shaken by poverty. Presently, the projects of poverty alleviation in the process of implementation mainly include: the projects of poverty alleviation with low-line of credit facility, the project of the New Great Wall, project 120 of Maternal and Infant Health, Project Angel and Disaster Relief and other comprehensive projects.

Website: http://www.fupin.org.cn

♦ The State "Eight Seven" Program for Poverty Alleviation

The State "Eight Seven" Program for Poverty Alleviation was publicized and implemented in 1994, it marked that the development of poverty reduction in China had entered one stage for tackling arduous difficulties. It clearly put forward the task that the problem of inadequate food and clothing in the rural poverty-stricken population should be basically settled in the next seven years, by assembling manpower, material resources, financial power and social resources from all walks of life. It is the first guidelines for the development of poverty alleviation in Chinese history, containing a clear target, object, measure and time limit.

Through various efforts, by the end of 2000, the target of the State "Eight Seven" Program for Poverty Alleviation was basically realized, the poverty-stricken population, who were still suffering the problem of inadequate food and clothing, dropped to 30 million, a decrease of three percent in the rate of poverty occurrence in rural areas. During the implementation of the State "Eight Seven" Program for Poverty Alleviation, the local financial revenue in counties as key targets under the program, experiencing poverty alleviation, has annually increased 12.9 percent, an annual-average increase of 12.8 percent of the annual revenue per capita of rural residents.

♦ Program of Development for Poverty Alleviation in China's Rural Areas (2001-2010)

Entering the 21st century, China has earmarked on a new stage in the development of poverty alleviation. In consideration of the number of poverty-stricken in the population, by the end of 2000, there were 30 million rural residents suffering the problem of inadequate food and clothing across the countryside, more than 60 million people belonging to the population had low income, therefore over 90 million rural residents formed the basic targets of poverty alleviation in the new stage. Meanwhile, due to the poverty-stricken population being distributed widely, living in areas with adverse natural conditions and lagging behind in development, this has further increased the difficulty of poverty alleviation.

In May 2001, the Program of Development for Poverty Alleviation in China's Rural Areas (2001-2010) was promulgated. It is another guideline for poverty reduction following the State "Eight Seven" Program. In the forward of this program, it is said: "to eliminate poverty for realizing the common wealth of the whole nation is the essential requirement of socialism, the obligatory responsibility for the Chinese Communist Party and the people's government". Furthermore, in the first ten years of the new century, the general target for China's poverty alleviation is to settle the problem of inadequate food and clothing for the extremely poverty-stricken people as soon as possible, to further improve the basic conditions of production and living in poverty-stricken areas, to maintain the achievements in the problem of inadequate food and clothing, to gradually change the backward situation relating to society, economy and culture in poverty-stricken areas, so as to create conditions for reaching a moderately prosperous level. By the end of 2005, there were 23.65 million poverty-stricken people across the whole countryside. The target for the Chinese Government is to help the poverty-stricken population achieve a moderately prosperous life by 2020.

policies of poverty alleviation in Chinese rural areas. The Government established in particular the institutions of poverty alleviation, allocated special funds, worked out preferential policies for deciding counties under the State major poverty alleviation plan, and the principle of poverty alleviation by development.

In 2007, the Central Government allocated 14.4 billion Yuan for poverty alleviation, increasing 700 million Yuan over 2006. The whole-village promotion for 20,000 poor villages was launched according to the plan and experimental units combining the whole-village promotion and coordinated development conducted in 21 provinces, autonomous regions and cities. All together one million labour forces in poverty-stricken areas were transferred and trained, of whom, 85 percent realized non-agricultural employment.

NGO Project on Poverty Alleviation

On December 19, 2005, the State Council Leading Group Office of Poverty Alleviation and Development (LGOP), the Asian Development Bank (ADB), the Jiangxi Poverty Alleviation and Development Office (PADO) and the China Foundation for Poverty Alleviation (CFPA) initiated an NGO-Government Partnership in the Village-level Poverty Alleviation Project in the Great Hall of the People of Beijing, China. Following a competitive open tender process, the CFPA entrusted by the LGOP shall select several non-profit NGOs (Non-governmental Organizations) to organize the implementation of the pilot village's poverty alleviation project. The PADO shall allocate directly the project funds to the selected NGOs and audit the use of the funds. In addition, the ADB shall also supervise the special accounts of the NGOs.

The NGOs of China have been participating in the work on poverty alleviation since early times. At present, there are many corresponding projects of poverty alleviation in the different social organizations, such as the China Charity Federation, the Red Cross Society of China, the China Associations of Social workers, the China Youth Development Foundation, the China Children and Teenagers' Fund and the China Women Development Foundation, etc.

Rural Endowment Insurance

China rural endowment insurance, as an important social policy of the Central Government, is a system that ensures a basic standard of living for all the aged rural residents.

In light of the Basic Scheme for Rural Old-Age Insurance (for trial implementation), the residents participating in the rural endowment insurance should be the non-urban population who are not availed to a national supply of commodity grain. Usually, it makes the village the unit for the identification of residents, including the workers of rural enterprises, private enterprises and individual entities as well as migrant rural workers, etc. Others, such as the workers of township enterprises, the teachers of privately run schools, the cadres and workers employed by townships, etc. make the township enterprises or institutional unit the unit for their identification and paying insurance premiums. Usually, the age for paying an insurance premium is from 20 to 60 and the age for drawing a pension is from 60.

Considering that most rural residents of China do not have a fixed income, the rural endowment insurance provides various ways of paying insurance premiums. In general, there are three types as follows: firstly, the premiums are paid regularly by those who have a fixed income or those who are comparatively wealthy, monthly or quarterly by the township enterprises, semiyearly or yearly by the rich, and the amount paid can be a certain share of the participants' income or a fixed amount. Secondly, the premiums are paid irregularly by those who have no fixed income, in most areas. Specifically, more premiums are paid in good year, less in a bad year and later in a year of disaster. The premiums are paid when a better income for the family comes in and vice versa. Thirdly, the premiums are paid by lump sum by those who are at an advanced age. In light of their insurance level at an old age, they can pay by lump sum at present and draw the pension from 60 by regulations.

National Student Loans

On June 28, 1999, the National Rules on Management over Student Loans (for trail implementation) was issued by the State Council, working through the People's Bank of China, the Ministry of Education and the Ministry of Finance. Beginning from September 1st, 1999, the country carried out a pilot system of student loans in the universities of eight cities, including Beijing, Shanghai, etc. Then, the system was promoted to universities throughout the country. The national student loans are the major source of many undergraduate students coming form poor families to help them to finish school. The universities of China usually carry out scholarship systems and help students participate in work-study programs. Along with participation in social practice, the students solve their difficulties on tuition and cost of living.

Public Charity and Welfare Organizations

Experiencing over 20 years development, Public Charity and Welfare Organizations first began to appear in 1981 with the establishment of the China Children and Teenager's Fund. There are more than 700 charity organizations or associations at various levels, including the China Charity Federation. There are more than 70,000 Red Cross societies which are humanitarian social relief organizations, helping refugees in times of conflict and providing assistance to disaster victims. In fact, the registered non-governmental organization in China reached 289,000, including 1,016 grass roots units. Almost all non-governmental organizations are industry associations or non-governmental scientific research institutions that carry out different charity projects as a sideline to their main business.

Currently, the China Charity Federation and the Red Cross Society of China are the best known. Besides these two famous organizations, there are the China Association of Social Workers, China Soong Ching Ling Foundation, China Association for NGO Cooperation, China Youth Development Foundation, China Children and Teenager's Fund, and China Foundation for Poverty Alleviation. Grass roots charity organizations have emerged in both urban and rural areas to raise funds from the local community, and directly serve the masses locally. The establishment of the grass roots community charity organization marks the development of Chinese charity welfare in depth.

The government attaches more importance to non-governmental organization, especially the non-governmental public welfare organizations, and lays great stress on their capacity building, as well as providing policy support for them to lead China's charity cause.

China Charity Federation (CCF)

Currently, as one of the most influential and largest special charity organizations, China Charity Federation develops many programs in various fields: support and care for the senior citizen, orphans assistance, poverty alleviation, rehabilitation for disabled children, special education, disaster relief, and health care. It is the only nationwide united association among all non-governmental organizations in the country, and is entitled to develop association memberships in the country by the social registration and administration department.

Website: http://www.ccf-online.org

Red Cross Society of China

The Red Cross Society of China (RCSC), the only national Red Cross society in the PRC, is a humanitarian social relief organization and a major member of the International Red Cross

Society Activity. RCSC aims to develop the spirits of the Red Cross of humanitarianism, philanthropy, and dedication, protecting human life and health, and promoting peace and progress. Founded in 1904, the RCSC has been involved in assisting wounded soldiers, helping refugees in times of conflict and providing assistance to disaster victims and participating in humanitarian relief activities.

The RCSC was reorganized in August, 1950 and reclaimed its legal membership in the International Federation of Red Cross and Red Crescent Societies in 1952. The RCSC has been contributing much to assisting the government in implementing the Geneva Conventions, supporting State development and improving people's health. Red Cross branches at different state administrative levels were restored or built up. At present, the RCSC has 31 branches at provincial level and branches in the Special Administration Region of Hong Kong and of Macao, and 70,000 grassroots units, claiming a total membership of 20 million people. The RCSC has continued to develop in the humanitarian field, and gained support from the government and all social circles. Its Disaster Preparedness and Disaster Relief network has been initially set up, and the establishment of a computer network has greatly improved its operational capacity and emergency response and relief capabilities. Many serous major disasters have occurred in China. The RCSC carried out relief activities, raised more than 2 billion Yuan in cash and material donations, and contributed to protecting victim's lives and health.

Website: http://www.redcross.org.cn

China Association of Social Workers

Founded in 1991, the China Association of Social Workers is a united, industry-based, non-profit social association approved and registered by the Ministry of Civil Affairs. Over many years, it has shouldered tasks to advocate the idea of social work, popularizing education of social work, integrating social resources, developing social services, strengthening innovation of theory and practice, and optimizing social efficiency.

Website: http://www.cncasw.org/

China Soong Ching Ling Foundation

In honor of PRC honorary president Soong Ching Ling (1893-1981), the Soong Ching Ling Foundation was founded in May 1982. In September, 2005, it was renamed the "China Soong Ching Ling Foundation". It acts as a bridge between friendly associations and individuals at home and abroad. It is a non-profit organization and a juridical association. Its mission is to inherit and develop the unfinished cause that Soong Ching Ling addressed all her life to enhance international friendship, maintain world peace, develop communications across the Taiwan Straits, promote the unity of the motherland, show concern for the nation's future and cultivate the young generation. For over 20 years, in order to practice Soong Ching Ling's commission with deep love, and "create the future", supported by all circles of society, the China Soong Ching Ling Foundation has devoted itself to education and health care for women and children, international friendship and cultural communications, drawing strong support from the people who are enthusiasm for public welfare at home and abroad.

Website: http://www.sclf.org/

China Association for NGO Cooperation

China Association for NGO Cooperation (CANGO) was founded in 1992 with a mission to promote communications and exchanges between Chinese and foreign NGOs, bilateral and multilateral organizations in poverty alleviation, environmental protection and social development, to enhance fundraising for China's poor, remote, and minority-inhabited areas, and to provide technical aid and support the capacity building of grassroots NGOs in China. Currently, CANGO has 115 member organizations across China, and has cooperative relationships with governmental agencies at various levels, colleges and universities, research institutes, and domestic NGOs. Its partnerships with international NGOs and organizations cover various fields: agricultural production, basic living conditions (drinking water for humans and animals), income generation (aquatic production, handicrafts, husbandry), comprehensive community development, medical care and sanitation, aid for poverty, environmental and resources protection, basic and professional education, organ capacity building, practical skills training, emergency disaster relief and reconstruction after disaster, and women's participatory and development (technology training and advancement of women).

Website: http://www.cango.org/

China Youth Development Foundation

China Youth Development Foundation was jointly created by the Chinese Communist Youth League, All-China Youth Federation, All-China Students Federation and China Young Pioneers in March 1989. CYDF is a public-funding organization raising donations from the public in China and other countries and regions. It is expected to help youth to enhance their capacity building and to improve their growth environment through assistance, benefit expression and social advocacy. CYDF has launched nationwide public welfare activities such as "Project Hope", student assistant program, and "Mother River Protection" environmental protection operation to advocate its value outlook of "social responsibility, creative initiative, care for development of young people and aspire to high standards.

Website: http://www.cydf.org.cn/

♦ Guidelines on Philanthropy Development in China (2006-2010)

In November 2005, the Ministry of Civil Affairs and the China Charity Federation convened jointly the first meeting of China philanthropy and published the Guidance Outline on Philanthropy Development in China (2006-2010).

The outline states the overall demands, targets and principles, policy and measures for philanthropy development in China for the next five years. Specifically, China philanthropy shall insist on principles including poverty alleviation, voluntary participation without payment, and being open and just. In terms of operational pattern, the philanthropy shall be propelled by government and shall work through non-profit organizations. The philanthropy shall be supervised, managed and standardized by making policies, laws and regulations, so as to protect the legal rights and interests of charity organizations, donors and beneficiaries. The charity organizations shall fully display a major role in the philanthropy, mobilize the various resources of charity and standardize the use of donated funds and goods. Various voluntary activities should be widely promoted. The plan outlines that in the next several years the culture of charity shall be widely spread. It shall enhance the concept of charity among civilians and the social responsibility of enterprises. Most civilians should identify and participate in philanthropy. Various charity organizations shall be set up in large and medium-sized cities throughout the country and the service stations of charity shall be set up in communities. Finally a noble social environment based on philanthropy will be basically shaped.

At present, the Law for the Promotion for Philanthropy has been listed into a legislative plan of China. With the debut of the Law for the Promotion for Philanthropy, the development of philanthropy in China will enter a new standardized stage.

Project Hope

(See P207)

♦ Regulations on Foundation Administration

In 2004, Chinese Government issued the new Regulations on Foundation Administration. It permits foreigners to set up non-public funding foundations as well as their representative offices in China. To a certain extent, the regulations will standardize and promote the charity activities ran by the international non-government organizations in China.

China Children and Teenager's Fund (CCTF)

Founded on July 28, 1981, China Children and Teenager's Fund is the first nationwide social association serving children and teenager's education and welfare needs by raising funds. It is non-profit, social public welfare organization with independent juridical person status. The mission of the Fund is: to care for, foster and educate children and teenagers, assist the country to develop children and teenager's educational welfare, especially in poverty areas and minority areas.

Since its founding, CCTF has done much in educational welfare It also provided funds and materials for children in areas suffering from natural disasters including earthquake, flood, and fire. CCTF also sponsored the establishment of schools, kindergartens, children welfare institutes, orphanages, children nurseries, and set up children's palaces, children's centers, children activity centers and so on. The "Spring Bud Project" and "Enkon Project", advocated and launched by CCTF, was included in the Central Government's white papers The Situation of Children in China, Poverty Alleviation and Development in China, 2000 China Human Right Development, and 2000-2010 China Children Development Guideline.

Website: http://www.cctf.org.cn/

Spring Bud Project

(See P207)

Enkon Project

In May 2005, CCTF launched a new large-scale social public welfare project "Enkon Project", which aims preventing children from dropping out of school, suffering injury or illness, or becoming involved in crime. Since the Enkon Project started, CCTF has staged a series of large-scale public welfare activities. From 2001, it held the "Enkon Project in the West" and "Enkon Project in the North-East" three times. This involved visits to 10 provinces and regions including Inner Mongolia, Ningxia, Gansu, Tibet, Qinghai, Xinjiang, Guizhou, Yunnan, Sichuan and Chongqing, as well as two old industry bases: Heilongjiang Province and Liaoning Province, to bring material and funds, totaling more than 83.4 million Yuan. With these donations, schools, "Enkon Medical Stations", "Enkon Classrooms", and "Enkon Distance Learning Classrooms" have been set up to improve educational conditions.

China Education Development Foundation

Founded in March, 2006, China Education Development Foundation is a national public funding organization, supported by the Ministry of Education and the Ministry of Finance. After its founding, the Foundation received its first donations totaling 285.7 million Yuan. The aim of the Foundation is to raise donations to regularly hold nationwide activities such as aiding poor students, assisting teachers, improving school facilities, and to solve the special difficulties emerging in reform and development of education in poverty areas.

Website: http://www.cedf.org.cn/

Volunteers

There are three major types in the organized voluntary service in China. They are community volunteers, volunteers and youth volunteers. In addition, there are many individual volunteers in China. They do not participate in voluntary service that is implemented by government or non-government organization but participate in voluntary service as their personal responsibility and social cognition. The voluntary service has been progressing greatly in recent years in China. At present, the problems that need to solve in the development process are as follows: firstly, lack of money is the problem that all the volunteer organizations face and it has been handicapping the volunteers' activities. Therefore, it needs to be solved through tax reform and the second division of wealth in the society. Secondly, there has, as yet, been no law on voluntary service issued by the Central Government yet. Because of a lack of complete laws and regulations, it is impossible to ensure public participation. Thirdly, the volunteers lack the opportunity of training, including the training of professional skills and service philosophy.

Community Volunteers

Community volunteers came into being in 1989. Since then, China has been making vigorous efforts to promote the building of democracy in grass-roots units in urban areas as well as the self-government of communities by practicing self-management, self-service and self-supervision. Meanwhile, China introduced the concept of "community service", originating from the developed countries, and organized the community volunteers with Chinese characteristics. The uniform certification for the community volunteers is made by the Workers Committee of Community Volunteer, governed by the China Association of Social Workers.

At present, there are a total of 75,000 organizations of community volunteers throughout the country, with over 16 million community volunteers. The China Association of Social Workers will enroll a full-time staff of social workers among the community volunteers in order to carry forward the voluntary activities of community.

Volunteer

Volunteering is an activity of voluntary service that was introduced from Hong Kong to China's hinterland. The first organization of volunteering in China's hinterland was the Shenzhen Volunteer Agency. Learning from the experienced service pattern of Hong Kong volunteers, the Shenzhen Volunteer Agency advocates the same ideas, such as "Help others to achieve self-help" and "The rose in her hand, the flavor in mine." At present, most cities of China have established the organizations of volunteers, so as to settle family disputes, give psychological support to juvenile delinquency, protect the environment and help dropouts, etc. In terms of operational pattern, the non-profit organizations ran by non-government organizations enlist and organize activities from society as well as design and implement the items of service. Volunteers are encouraged to participate in the voluntary service in their spare time. Meanwhile, volunteers are also supported by the volunteer organizations in the terms of opportunities and training.

Youth Volunteers

Youth volunteers, initiated by the Chinese Communist Youth League, are the most influential team of voluntary service in China at present. The mission of the youth volunteers is to help people with special difficulties; eradicate poverty and backwardness; wipe out public nuisances and environmental pollution; popularize science and culture; set up the human relations of mutual aid and friendship as well as good social morality. At present, over 60 percent of cities and counties in China have set up youth volunteers associations, with 90,000 voluntary service stations.

Thousands of youth volunteers participate in activities of social public good every year, including poverty alleviation and development in rural areas, community construction in urban areas, large activities, emergency rescues and disaster relief, etc.

The young volunteers in Shanghai accompany the old people in the Social Welfare Institute to enjoy the spring scenery.

Through practicing in the activities of social public good, every youth volunteer fulfills the pledge: I'd like to be an honorable volunteer. I promise: to do the best I can; do not ask for pay; help others; serve society; practice the voluntary spirit; spread advanced culture; and devote my energy to constructing a society with unity and mutual assistance, equality and friendship as well as common development.

The International Cooperation and Development Plan on China Youth Volunteering were carried out in May 2002. The plan is governed by the China Communist Youth League and China Youth Volunteer Association. Through the way of open recruitment, voluntary enrollment and concentrated training, the excellent youth volunteers will be dispatched to work abroad for volunteer service. Up to now, nearly 100 volunteers have been sent to Laos, Burma, Ethiopia and Thailand. The services focus on Chinese teaching, medical and public health, science and technology extension, etc.

China International Rescue Teams

It was in 2003 that China International Rescue Teams first participated in international earthquake relief. Earthquake of 6.2 magnitude occurred in northern areas of Algeria, killing over 2,000 people and injuring over 10,000. China International Rescue Teams, requested by the Algerian Government and dispatched by the Chinese Government, joined 38 teams from more than 20 countries and did outstanding work that earned high praise from local people.

Besides participation in international disaster relief and humanitarian social donation, China actively selected and dispatched volunteers to work in developing countries as well as receiving volunteers from other countries to work in China. For over 20 years, China has dispatched volunteers with advanced technical level and specialties as UN volunteers to develop relief work in 35 developing countries, involving agriculture, water conservancy, medical and health care, engineering design, computer, management and economic system reform.

Regular Social Donation

This program was launched and implemented by the Ministry of the Civil Affairs in the mid-1990's and played a major role in dealing with the aftermath of catastrophic floods in 1998. In recent years, with the enhancement of the citizen's enthusiasm and consciousness, the activities evolved into regular social donation activities, mobilizing urban residents to donate old clothes, quilts, household electrical appliances no longer needed for disaster-stricken and poverty areas. Currently, each community has a receiving station for regular social donation. Many cities set up donations warehouses, where all the donated materials can be strictly sterilized and repaired. The government formulated a series of regulations to manage the activity, including the procedure of receiving the donations, work responsibility, classification standards for the donation materials received, warehouse management system, donation materials adjustment system, and the system of sterilizing, tidying and packing donated materials.

The regular social donation material is not only used for aiding people who have suffered a disaster and helping people living in poverty areas, but also used for under-privileged in the local community. Charity Supermarkets have been established in some cities and communities where poor urban residents can get donated materials at low cost or for free. To date, with some 32,000 social donation receiving stations operating, a social donation service network has been set up initially. In some large and medium-size cities, more than 4,000 "Charity Supermarkets", "Love Heart Supermarkets" have been established, opening a new mode of helping-others among the masses. In some places, a non-governmental organization is expected to take over the regular social donation work. For example, the Shanghai Charity Federation has already been charged with this kind work.

Aiding Disabled People

Through the concern of society, the work of rehabilitation, education, and employment of Chinese disabled has gained great development. Over the past five years, almost 20,000 rehabilitation training service organs at various levels have been set up; as a result, more than 6.3 million disabled people have been able to obtain rehabilitation help to some extent. The school enrollment of disabled children has reached about 80 percent, some 200 special education schools have been established and thousands of regular schools have set up special education classes. There are some 16,000 disabled students enrolled in universities and colleges. More than 2.58 million disabled people received professional education and training, the number of the disabled employed in urban areas reached 4.2 million, and the figure in rural areas totaled 17 million; more than 30,000 disabled welfare enterprises enjoy tax reduction or exemption. Some 7.27 million disabled people enhance their life through poverty alleviation; in addition, some seven million disabled people in urban and rural areas enjoy social security.

In 2006, China's "International Rescue Team" went to Indonesia to participate the rescue work for the Java Earthquake.

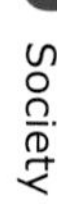

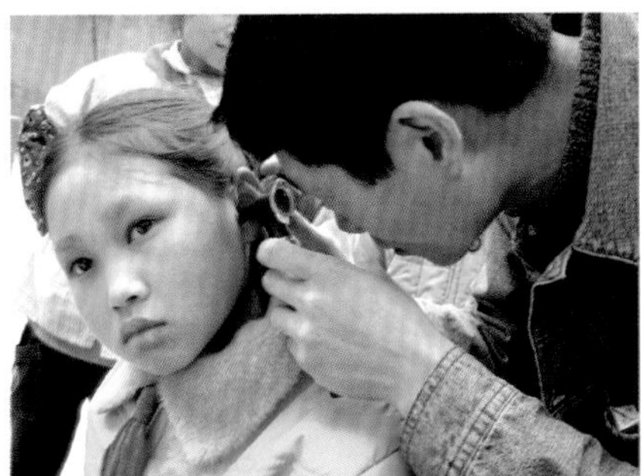
In the Rehabilitation Center For Deaf Children.

Child Social Welfare

At present, child social welfare institutions in China can be classified into three: first, adoptive children social welfare institutions, whose main functions are to adopt orphans, and guarantee their right to education; second, rehabilitative children's social welfare institutions, whose main functions are to implement curing and rehabilitation for disabled children, third, educational social welfare institution, whose main functions are to enhance life and work ability for disabled children. To date, there are 178 various children's social welfare institutions sponsored by the government, and the number of the adopted children has reached 22,000. There are nine SOS children's villages in the country, which adopted more than 1,000 orphans. In addition, nearly 10,000 community children service organizations are set up, such as rehabilitation centers, Children with Mental Retardation training classes and disabled children foster stations. The number of the social organs has exceeded 100. Child social welfare in China has set up a pattern with State-sponsored social organs as the backbone, scattered fostering as the base, urban and rural areas involved in joint social participation for aiding and protecting children with special difficulties.

The Guarantee of Rights and Interests of the Old

The Law of the PRC on Protection of the Rights and Interests of the Elderly was promulgated in August 1996. This regulates that society should carry out measures to prefect the social security system for the old, gradually improve their living standards, their health care, help them take part in the society activities so as to ensure that the later years of life are happy and fulfilling. The rights and interests that the old should enjoy are under State protection, ensuring that they can fully enjoy the achievements of social development. Any act of discrimination, humiliation, maltreatment and abandonment involving the old is strictly prohibited. Governments at all level should bring the old-age career into their socio-economy development plan and gradually allocate more budget. On the other hand, investment in all aspects from society in also encouraged in order to realize coordinated development between an old-age career and overall socio-economic development. At present, over 51,000 welfare institutions help some 800,000 old people.

Starlight Program

(See P33)

Leisure Activity and Entertainment

The Level of Leisure Activity

The leisure activity level is both a symbol of a nation's productive forces and a standard measurement of social civilization. China shortened the working week from six to five days in 1995. In 1999, the government adjusted the holiday structure and started to adopt three Golden Weeks including Labor Day, National Day and Spring Festival. Since the beginning of the 21st century, the State followed a system regulating that a worker has the right to receive salary during the three golden weeks and receive help to rationally schedule their personal time. At present, Chinese people have a total of 114 legal days of rest every year, thus, having much more spare time than before. People in cities spend most of their time in sports and recreations and gaining knowledge. A consumption investigation conducted by Beijing Horizon Research Corporation in Shanghai, Wuhan, Beijing, Guangzhou and Chengdu shows that spending in Beijing on sport and fitness per capita annually was about 888 Yuan, ranking first among the five cities. People's lives are filled with more and more colorful leisure activities.

Tourism

A recent investigation shows that 46.46 percent of interviewees intend to travel in their spare time. Drive travel, self-help travel, village travel, outbound travel, etc are becoming the new fashion for city people.

According to the Bureau of Tourism, 179 million people embarked on tourism on Labor Day in 2007, or 22.7 percent more than 2006. The revenue of tourism in 2007 reached 73.6 billion Yuan, or 25.8 percent than that in 2006. The per-capita expenditure on tourism reached 412 Yuan. China's tourism is in dynamic development.

In addition, more and more people are trying to travel abroad. By June 2008, the China National Tourist Office released data showing there were a total of 92 countries and regions which accepted Chinese citizens to travel. The number of the people who traveled abroad in 2007 was up to 40.95 million, an increase of 18.6 percent over the previous year. Based on this, the China National Tourist Office and institutions of many countries have adopted a marketing method of intensive expansion like "Spring Festival with Chinese Characteristics".

The Tian'anmen Gate Tower, a hot tourist destination

Fitness

Engaging in physical exercises has become popular since 1998. The Chinese concept of fitness has obviously improved.

Many facilities are now available in gyms including running machine, exercise, kickboxing, swordplay, yoga, etc. Some people visit gyms to try and control their weight and keep their figure and some visit for relaxing their spirit and emotions. More and more people are entering gym centers at a fixed time every week. A fitness exercise called "Figure-shape and Slim Body Cares" featuring aerobic exercise, strengthening exercises, heart and lung function adjustment as well as stamina, flexibility and coordinated ability improvement is all the rage.

TV Audience Rating

Since the middle of the 1980s, TV has been generally adopted in Chinese families as a major source of entertainment. Although TV programs in the early period lacked entertainment, they did give viewers some appreciation of life outside China. Now, the range of programs is almost endless. Serials broadcast throughout the country have become a major topic of conversation. The Spring Festival evening party held by CCTV every year also becomes an indispensable part of the celebrations. With the emergence of many varied TV programs since the 1990s, satellite TV programs introduced by the local television stations bring fiercer competition to the audience ratings. Under such circumstances, great efforts have been made to introduce entertainment programs with constant fresh styles so as to attract more audience. An era which deems TV as its primary entertainment is coming. The figure released by

A Survey on National Reading and Book-Purchase showed TV ranked first in terms of the contact rate between audience and media and was the first choice in leisure activities. It is estimated that people in cities and towns spend about three hours and 38 minutes in watching TV every day.

Box Office

In the year 2007, compared to the GDP growth rate of more than 11.4 percent, the box office revenue grew at a remarkably higher speed. Some 402 movies were released into the market, an increase of 21.8 percent from the previous year, when there were 330 movies that came out. The output of digital movies hit a record high of 100, setting a record high. The box office revenue in the domestic market reached 3.327 billion Yuan, rising 30 percent from 2006, and from the overseas market 2.02 billion Yuan. As movies staged on TV added another 1.379 billion Yuan, the overall income of the Chinese movie sector was 6.7 billion Yuan, rising 1.2 billion Yuan from 2006. At the year end, there were 1,425 professional cinemas located around the country, with 3,554 screens.

The Internet changes the leisure style of Chinese people.

E-life

The internet provides entertainment for people in modern society. With a powerful expanding ability and unlimited capacity, it has brought about far-reaching changes affecting recreational activities among millions of Chinese citizens. Surfing on line during spare time, people can read and exchange information, which helps widen their horizons. In recent years, people developed a new liking for reading and writing blogs on line. Especially for those people who do not have experience in writing, it provides a platform for them to express themselves.

Museum Visiting

Talking about museums, common Chinese people no longer regard it as the place for collecting and displaying curios. In recent years, visiting museums has become a new entertainment activity among them. More and more people go to museums on holidays. When there is a large-scale exhibition on show, it is highly likely that the museum is swamped with people. Sometimes, the queue zigzagging from the ticket window even extends out of the hall. There were 2,300 museums in 2005, rising from 711 in 1985. Some 1,600 museums were erected during these years, accompanying the growth of young Chinese. The museum streets, the museum groups and the museum cities were shaped, thanks to the efforts made in this sector. According to some experts, the next five years are expected to be a prime time for the museum building in China.

Collection among Common Chinese

An old saying goes "restoring gold in war times and curios in a prosperous age". Thanks to the rapid socio-economic development, the living standard of Chinese people has been greatly improved. Collection of antiques has become popular among common Chinese people. Young and old, artists and merchants, all like to try their hand at the collecting market. Their collections could be antiques, such as painting and calligraphy works, china, books, furniture, clocks and watches; or common items unique to a special period in history, such as coupons, matchbox pictures, sweet wrappers, coins; or items in fashion, such as modern art pieces, playbills, toys and items once belonging to a celebrity. These items could be collected free of charge or cost their owner a large fortune. Collecting is not only a hobby for Chinese people to amuse them, it is also a way of investment.

Pop Music

Initiated in Japan, karaoke was rapidly well accepted by the Chinese people in the 1990s, soon after entering into the Chinese market. Now it has become a main form of entertainment in China. With the largest market potential, it grew at the fastest speed among its counterparts in the entertainment market during recent years. Before it appeared, the traditional music industry used to rely on releasing albums to make profit. With this new product, it enlarges its market share. Development of karaoke also actively boosts the innovation and progress of pop music and enriches people's ideological life.

A bar street in Gucheng, Lijiang, Yunnan

Bars

As a key media for pop culture in modern society, bars add more fashion to the leisure life of Chinese. Beijing boasts the largest number of bars in China. Shanghai, Guangzhou, Shenzhen, Nanjing and Xi'an are also home to many bars. In tourist destinations such as Tibet, Yunnan and Guangxi, bars, combining distinguishing local features with Western style, have become a common sight. According to a survey carried out among white-collar workers, over 89.8 percent of respondents said they pass time in bars. Some 59.1 were regular bar goers, saying it is a major part of their off- work lives.

Book Bars

Book bars are cultural entertainment resorts. Most of them are retail book shops, providing tables, chairs and even food and beverage for their customers. Accompanied by gentle music, people can take time to enjoy books there. Since it only costs them a little money, from several to dozens of Yuan, many young Chinese are partial to meeting friends in their favorite book bars.

Legal Holidays

In China, legal holidays and commemoration days can be divided into three kinds: the first is the holiday for all civilians to take days off, including the New Year's Day (one day), the Spring Festival (three days), the May Day (one day), the National Day (three days), Qingming Festival (one day) and Dragon Boat Festival (one day); the second is a holiday or commemoration day for special groups of civilians to take days off, including the International Women's Day (half a day for women), the Youth Day (half a day for people aged 14 and above), the Children's Day (one day for children aged 13 and younger) and the Army Day (one day for military personnel on active service); the third is a commemoration day with no break, including the February 7th Strike, the May 30th Movement, July 7th incident, the September 3rd, the day china won the war against Japanese invasion, December 18th incident, Arbor Day, Teacher's Day, Nurses' Day and Reporters' Day.

New Year's Day

The New Year's Day is called Yuan Dan in Chinese, Yuan referring to the initiative and Dan referring to daylight. Yuan Dan, "the initial day", is the first day of the New Year. On September 27th, 1949, on the first national congress of the CPPCC, Common Era was adopted to designate the day. Then the first day of the year was named as Yuan Dan.

International Working Women's Day

International Working Women's Day, also called the U.N. Day for Women's Rights and International Peace or the March 8th holiday, is a holiday for commemorating working women's struggle for peace, democracy, and liberty around the world. After the establishment of the People's Republic of China in December, 1949, the CPC Central Committee designated March 8 as the annual holiday of Chinese women. On that day, all Chinese women can enjoy a half day off to hold all kinds of memorial activities or celebrations.

Tree-planting Day (China Arbor Day)

According to the resolution taken by the sixth session of the Fifth NPC Standing Committee, in February, 1979, the day of March 12 was set as the annual National Tree-planting Day (Arbor Day). On that day, all Chinese citizens are called on to support national forestation and fulfill their obligation by the way of planting memorial trees or memorial forests. Pushed by the government, people fulfill their legal tree-planting obligation, which helps raise public awareness of forestation, ecosystem protection and harmonious development, and enhances social member's sense of responsibility and Concept of legality also.

"I grow with the young tree."

International Labor Day

May 1st, the International Workers' Day, is a working people's holiday throughout the world. In December of 1949 after the establishment of the People's Republic of China, the Government Administration Council of the Central People's Government designated May 1st as the legal Labor Day, with a day off for all the Chinese. On that day, people dress up and happily gather at parks, theaters or squares to hold colorful entertainment activities, also, honoring outstanding workers. On September 18, 1999, the State Council prolonged the holiday to 3 days. Since 2008, it was revised to be one day.

Chinese Youth Day

May 4th was officially proclaimed to be Chinese Youth Day by the Government Administration Council of the Central People's Government in 1949. During the holiday, people around china hold colorful memorial activities, such as implementing all kinds of social volunteer activities or social practice. On that day, many young people hold ceremonies declaring that they have become adults. All youth above 14 years old can enjoy a half day off.

International Children's Day

Children's Day, on June 1st, is a holiday for children all over the world. In 1931, according to a suggestion made by the China Charity Federation, the Chinese government approved every April 4th as Children's day. After the establishment of the People's Republic of China, the Government Administration Council of the Central People's Government decreed June 1st to be Children's Day, aiming at caring for children's growth in a further way. At present, most of the governments worldwide pay high attention to children's future and protect their rights and interests. When the UN Convention on the Rights of Children was approved in 1990, China was one of the signatory countries and co-sponsor countries that raised the draft resolution for the convention. In the same year, china decreed the Law of the People's Republic of China on the Protection of Minors, which plays an active role in guarding children's rights and interests.

On Children's Day, children below 13 years old can enjoy a day off. In some areas, their parents also can have a holiday. As the superstars of June 1st, children with their parents like to go to parks, zoos, or amusement centers. They also love to visit museums like scientific and technological museums or planetariums. Children's places or children's exercise centers hold painting and calligraphy contests, appealing for children to participate. Children all over the country try to make their holiday be a brilliant day.

Army Day

August 1st is the anniversary of the founding of the Chinese People's Liberation Army. It is the Army Day celebrated in the country.

Teacher's Day

On January 21st, 1985, the ninth session of the Sixth NPC Standing Committee formally decided to fix September 10th of every year as the Teacher's Day of the country. The reason for choosing that date had been taken into full consideration. At the beginning of a new academic year, celebrating Teacher's Day can foster a new atmosphere of respecting teachers and prioritizing education, and also establish a harmonious relationship between teachers and students.

Happy Teacher's Day!

The Teacher's Day in the history of the PRC happened on September 10, 1985. Li Xiannian, the chairman of China at that time, extended greetings to all the teachers in china. Tens of thousand of teachers participated in the victory meeting held in the capital Beijing. During the holiday, 11871 province-level excellent teachers collectively or personally were cited as model teachers from 20 provinces and municipalities. From then on, teachers have had their own holiday in china.

National Day

At 3 pm on October 1st, 1949, a grand ceremony inaugurating the People's Republic of China was witnessed by 300,000 people in Beijing's Tiananmen Square. On December 3rd, 1949, the Committee of the Central People's Government approved the Resolution on The National Day of The People's Republic of China, which decreed every October 1st as National Day, also the birthday of the People's Republic of China. The Chinese people of all ethnic groups have warmly celebrated the National Day since 1950. From October 1st, 1949, the National Day celebration activities are endowed with great political significance.

At the eve of the National Day, everywhere is decorated with lanterns, streamers and flowers, full of happiness and auspiciousness.

The annual 7-day national holiday was implemented in 2000 because Chinese enjoy better economic conditions, giving them have more choices of leisure and entertainment activities. More and more people take a trip during the holiday, and some even go abroad for the purpose.

New Year's Day	2	3	4	5
6	7	8	9	10
11	12	13	14	15
16	17	18	19	20
21	22	23	24	25
26	27	28	29	30
31				

1	2	3	4	5
6	7	8	9	10
11	12	13	14	15
16	17	18	19	20
21	22	23	24	25
26	27	28	29	

1	2	3	4	5
6	7	International Working Women's Day	9	10
11	Tree-planting Day	13	14	15
16	17	18	19	20
21	22	23	24	25
26	27	28	29	30
31				

1	2	3	4	5
6	7	8	9	10
11	12	13	14	15
16	17	18	19	20
21	22	23	24	25
26	27	28	29	30

International Labor Day	2	3	Chinese Youth Day	5
6	7	8	9	10
11	12	13	14	15
16	17	18	19	20
21	22	23	24	25
26	27	28	29	30
31				

International Children's Day	2	3	4	5
6	7	8	9	10
11	12	13	14	15
16	17	18	19	20
21	22	23	24	25
26	27	28	29	30

1	2	3	4	5
6	7	8	9	10
11	12	13	14	15
16	17	18	19	20
21	22	23	24	25
26	27	28	29	30
31				

Army Day	2	3	4	5
6	7	8	9	10
11	12	13	14	15
16	17	18	19	20
21	22	23	24	25
26	27	28	29	30
31				

1	2	3	4	5
6	7	8	9	Teacher's Day
11	12	13	14	15
16	17	18	19	20
21	22	23	24	25
26	27	28	29	30

National Day	2	3	4	5
6	7	8	9	10
11	12	13	14	15
16	17	18	19	20
21	22	23	24	25
26	27	28	29	30
31				

1	2	3	4	5
6	7	8	9	10
11	12	13	14	15
16	17	18	19	20
21	22	23	24	25
26	27	28	29	30

1	2	3	4	5
6	7	8	9	10
11	12	13	14	15
16	17	18	19	20
21	22	23	24	25
26	27	28	29	30
31				

Environmental Protection

Environmental Protection in China

The Chinese government believes that environmental protection will have a direct impact on the overall situation of the nation's modernization drive and its long-term development, and considers environmental protection as an undertaking that will not only benefit the present but also future generations. Years ago, it established environmental protection as a basic national policy and sustainable development as an important strategy, and ever since has adhered to the road of a new type of industrialization. While promoting economic growth, it has adopted a whole array of measures to strengthen environmental protection. Especially in recent years, with a scientific outlook on development as the guiding principle, it has focused on preventive measures, comprehensive control and overall progress with breakthroughs at some key points, and worked hard to solve those problems threatening people's health. At the same time, it has continued its efforts for institutional innovation, relied on scientific and technological advances, strengthened the legal system of environmental protection, and brought into full play the initiative of people of all walks of life. Thanks to these efforts, although the amount of resource consumption and pollutants is increasing greatly, the trend toward aggravated environmental pollution and ecological destruction is slowing down; especially, pollution control in some river valleys has seen some positive results, the environmental quality of some cities and regions has improved, the amount of emission of industrial waste products has declined, and the people's awareness of the importance of environmental protection has been enhanced.

Prevention and Control of Industrial Pollution

Prevention and control of industrial pollution is the focal point of China's environmental protection. The strategy in this regard is undergoing a major change compared with the past, moving from control of discharged polluting substances to control of the original source and the whole process from control of the concentration of the pollutants to control of both concentration and total amount of pollutants, from control of source points to comprehensive control of river valleys or entire regions, and from simply addressing the pollution problem of an enterprise to adjusting the overall industrial structure, promoting clean production and developing a cyclical economy. The sulfur dioxide emission amounted to 25.944 million tons in 2006, an increase of 1.8 percent from the previous year; the total discharge amount of COD was 14.313 million tons, an increase of 1.2 percent. When compared with the growth in 2005, the two increases in 2006 fell by 11.3 and 4.4 percentage points respectively. The success in containing pollution proves to be a boon for the readjustment of the industrial structure, and leads to solution of some environmental problems that bring harm to the people.

Treatment of Major Polluted Areas

In recent years, the government has focused its pollution-control efforts on what are known as the "key regions," with marked achievements. The "key regions" refer to the three rivers (Huaihe, Liaohe and Haihe), the three lakes (Taihu, Dianchi and Chaohu), the major State projects (the Three Gorges Project and the South-North Water Diversion Project), the "two control's area" (sulfur dioxide and acid rain), Beijing and the Bohai Sea.

Prevention and Control of Water Pollution in Key Drainage Areas

The drainage area of the aforementioned three rivers and three lakes totals 810,000 square km, traversing 14 provinces (municipalities) with a total population of 360 million. The State formulated and put into

♦ Environmentally-Friendly Society

Environmentally-friendly society refers to a social system featuring coordinated development in economy, society, and environment, which aims at promoting harmonious development. It is based on the sustaining capacity of the environment, conforms to natural law, and initiates an environmental culture and ecological civilization. An environmentally-friendly society comprises environment-friendly technologies, production techniques, individual enterprises and whole industries, schools, and the community. It includes environment-friendly consumption patterns, modes of production, cleaner and low-emission technologies and products. It also includes various development and construction activities harmless to the environment and health, distribution of productive forced conforming to local ecological conditions, industrial structures featuring less-pollution and low-waste, green industries of sustainable development, and a social climate and culture atmosphere in which people are highly aware of environmental protection concepts.

Under the background of sustained and rapid economic growth and increasing pressure on environment, the Fifth Plenary Session of the Sixteenth National Congress of the Communist Party of China held in October 2005 for the first time confirmed the cause of building a resource-saving and environment-friendly society as a strategic duty in the medium and long-term plan of national economy and social development.

practice a plan for the prevention and control of water pollution in key drainage areas for the ninth and 10th Five-Year Plans (2001-2005), under which it set up a system to control the total amount of pollutants. Every enterprise that discharges pollutants is required to reduce its emissions to a certain level, which contributes to the goal of reducing the total amount of pollutants. While improving its pollutant-discharge licensing management method, the State had established a number of key pollution-control projects. By the end of 2005, of the 2,130 water pollution prevention and control projects in key drainage areas in the 10th Five-Year Plan, 1,378 were completed, accounting for 65 percent of the total. In the three-river, three-lake drainage area, 416 sewage treatment plants had been completed or were under construction, with a daily treatment capacity of 20.93 million tons. Over 80 percent of the more than 5,000 former heavy polluters in the drainage area have managed to reach the standard discharge level. Water pollutants in this drainage area have been reduced greatly, and the trend toward deteriorating water environment is now basically under control. Water quality in certain parts of the rivers or lakes has been improved significantly. Since 2002, a special 'infusion' project has been carried out in the severely polluted drainage area of Taihu Lake-that is, the clean river water from Yangtze River is transferred into Taihu Lake, a freshwater lake with its drainage area covering 36,900 square km. This project has greatly improved the water environment of Taihu Lake valley and benefited about 10 million people.

Control of Air Pollution

In 1998, the government approved the delimiting of the acid rain and sulfur dioxide control areas. The "two control's area" covers a total of 1.09 million square km, involving 175 cities or districts in 27 provinces, autonomous regions and municipalities directly under the Central Government. The State readjusted the energy structure by promoting the use of clean fuels and low-sulfur coal, and prohibiting residents in big and medium cities from using coal for household stoves. Compared with 1998, the proportion of cities located within the sulfur dioxide control area achieving the standard annual sulfur dioxide density level in 2005 rose from 32.8 percent to 45.2 percent. The proportion of cities located within the acid rain control area whose sulfur dioxide density surpassed the national third grade level declined from 15.7 percent in 1998 to 4.5 percent in 2005.

Of the 559 cities who air quality was subject to monitoring in 2006, the air quality of 349 cities (62.4 percent) is up to and stays above the Class II standards regarding air quality, and 159 (28.4 percent) the Class III standards; and 51 others (9.1 percent) were found to have Class III bad air quality.

Motor Vehicle Pollution Prevention

Motor vehicle pollution prevention has been carried out in the 1980s, marked by the promulgation and implementation of vehicle emission standards. In 1999, the State Environmental Protection Administration established the control standard of hazardous materials in gasoline. It also established the national Phase I and Phase II emission standards of pollutants in exhaust emissions from compression-ignited (C.I.) engines, including light-duty and heavy-duty motor vehicles (equivalent to the European Standard I, II, respectively). Some cities have launched a clean vehicle campaign to actively promote the use of low-pollution vehicles fueled by natural gas and liquefied petroleum gas. Since July 2000, leaded gasoline has been prohibited throughout China, which has reduced lead emissions by 1,500 tons yearly.

The national Phase II emission standard was introduced on July 1, 2005. Meanwhile, all the vehicles (engines) which meet the national Phase I emission standard are exempted from approval. Fuel with low sulfide is encouraged in China to guarantee the phase III emission standard to be successfully implemented nationwide. In December 2005, with the approval of the State Council, the national emission standard for the third phase (equivalent to the European Standard III) was adopted ahead of schedule in Beijing.

The crowded cars are the large consumers of the gasoline and diesel oil. Furthermore, their tail gas greatly pollutes the air.

On December 6, 2006, the revised standard on unleaded gasoline for motor vehicles was issued. According to the standard, beginning with December 31, 2009, unleaded gasoline with less than 150ppm of sulfur content will have to be supplied. The standard also containis major readjustment of vapor tension and benzene content in summer, which are indicators of environmental protection.

The increasing number of motor vehicles poses a serious threat to urban air environment.

Control of Pollution in the Bohai Sea

In 2001, the Chinese government approved the Action Plan to Bring Back Turquoise Water to the Bohai Sea. By the end of 2005, 166 projects aimed at controlling pollution in the Bohai Sea and protecting the environment were completed, and 70 more were under construction, with the investment totaling 17.5 billion Yuan. Forty-four new urban sewage treatment plants were built, with a total daily treatment capacity of 3.553 million tons. Eighteen new urban garbage treatment plants were established, with a total daily treatment capacity of more than 7,000 tons. In addition, 89 ecologically-friendly agriculture and breeding industry projects were set up, and nine ports and oil-spill response projects built.

Urban Planning and Environment

Considering the capacity of the urban environment and the ability to guarantee resource preservation, many Chinese cities have laid out and implemented general urban planning and planning to fully attain required standards for urban environmental quality based on functional districts, measure the capacity of the atmospheric and water environments, determine city size and the orientation of development in a rational way, adjust the structure and distribution of urban industries, and gradually optimize the division of functional districts. Many large and medium-sized cities have carried out the strategy to phase out secondary industry and promote the tertiary sector; local governments have shut down some enterprises with serious pollution problems, moved some out of the city center through the use of land pricing, and implemented technological transformation and concentrated control of pollution based on the principle of "keeping industry in industrial parks and concentrating on pollution control". Some cities have combined the transformation of old cities with the adjustment of city layout to eradicate change the dirty, disorderly and unsanitary characteristics of old urban areas and improve the living environment. They have made great efforts to adjust the urban energy structure, and actively advocated clean energy and central heating, so as to reduce pollution caused by burning coal. Ready-mixed concrete is introduced in urban construction, and concrete mixing is prohibited in city centers of municipalities directly under the Central Government, the cities directly under provincial governments, some large and medium-sized cities, and tourism cities, so as to reduce dust pollution caused by construction.

Environment and Investment

Governments at all levels in China have taken the construction of urban environmental infrastructure as the focus of financial input, pushing forward the construction of facilities dealing with sewage and waste. In 2006, China built 283 sewage treatment factories; the sewage treatment capacity of such factories rose to 61.22 million cubic meters a day, or an increase of 6.9 percent from the previous year; and the sewage treatment rate in cities and towns rose from 52 percent to 56 percent, a rise of 4 percentage points; the coverage of central heating increased by 5.1 percent to 2.65 billion cubic meters; and the green coverage in the built area registered a one percentage point increase to reach 33.5 percent. The utilization ratio of clean energy in urban areas reaches 40 percent. The environment quality in some important cities and regions has been improved and the trend of ecological deterioration contained.

City Appearance and Environment

The quantitative examination system for comprehensive urban environmental control has been introduced in over 500 Chinese cities. The system gives quantitative standards for the quality of the urban environment, pollution control and construction of urban environmental infrastructure, and thus will help to comprehensively assess the environmental protection work of city governments. Since 1997, the Central Government has started a campaign to build environmental-protection model cities as required by economic development, social progress, facilities amelioration and environmental improvement. At present, more than 100 cities (districts) are building themselves into environmental-protection model cities, among which 56 cities and five districts in municipalities directly under the Central Government have succeeded in meeting the required standards. These model cities enjoy 80 percent of the total number of days a year with air quality reaching or above Grade II, a city sewage treatment rate higher than 70 percent, rate of innocuous disposal of house refuse higher than 80 percent and greenery coverage rate higher than 35 percent—all above the national average. "Azure sky, blue water, green land, tranquility and harmony" have become prominent features of these model cities.

Comprehensive Control of the Rural Environment

In recent years, the government has launched campaigns to build towns and townships with a beautiful environment and ecologically advanced villages, pushing forward the comprehensive control of the rural environment. At present, 178 towns and townships have been awarded the title of "National-level Towns and Townships with a Beautiful Environment". The government is concentrating on the demonstration of comprehensive control of pollution from livestock, poultry and fish breeding, and non-point pollution in Taihu, Dianchi and Chaohu lakes, as well as in the Yangtze, Zhujiang and Yellow river deltas. Some provinces and municipalities have strengthened control of the village environment and improved village infrastructure, and made progress in treating rural sewage and waste and controlling agricultural non-point pollution. In recent years, China has completed more than 800,000 rural drinking water projects, solving difficulties in this regard for 67 million rural residents. The

♦ Water Environment of Three Gorges Reservoir Area

The State has spent more than 187 billion Yuan constructing sewage- and garbage-treatment facilities in the Three Gorges Reservoir Area and its upper stream. It also has had solid wastes removed from the bed of the reservoir to ensure water safety.

Since the Three Gorges Dam began to store water on June, 10, 2003, there have been no significant changes of water quality in the reservoir area. In order to guarantee water environment safety, from 2001 to 2010, about 40 billion Yuan is being used to prevent pollution in the reservoir area and upstream. According to the Prevention Plan of Water Pollution in Three Gorges Reservoir Area and Upper Reaches (2001-2010), by 2010, the water quality should basically meet the second criteria of national surface-water environmental quality with obvious improvement in the ecological environment.

♦ Green Olympics

The environment has been declared the third pillar of the Olympics by the International Olympic Committee (IOC), alongside sport and culture. Recognizing the importance of sport in building a peaceful and better world and in achieving the Millennium Development Goals, the United Nations Environment Program (UNEP) declared 2005 International Year for Sport and Physical Education to promote education, health, development and peace. UNEP has developed an active Sport and Environment Program to promote the links between sport and the environment. The green plans for Beijing are part of a growing commitment by Olympic organizers to put sport at the forefront of environmental planning and awareness.

An agreement aimed at making the summer Olympics of 2008 environmentally-friendly was signed by the United Nations Environment Program (UNEP) and the Beijing Organizing Committee for the Olympic Games (BOCOG). The agreement rests on the ambitious programs of Beijing in areas ranging from air, water and noise pollution up to transport, landscaping and the disposal of solid waste.

A key part of the agreement and one in which UNEP will be actively involved is in the area of public awareness campaigns. In doing so, the UN environmental body hopes to leave a lasting legacy in China and beyond on the links between mass participation events and a healthy environment. The campaigns will also link the importance of the environment generally in delivering sustainable development that benefits current and future generations.

government has started the investigation of soil pollution and demonstration of pollution control throughout the country, and set up a system of testing and controlling the safety of agricultural products; strengthened the environmental safety control of pesticides and chemical fertilizer, popularized high-efficiency, low-toxicity and low-residue pesticides, and prohibited the use of high-toxic and high-residual pesticides in the production of vegetables, fruits, grain, tea and Chinese medicinal herbs; prevented non-point pollution brought about by irrational use of chemical fertilizer, pesticides, farm-use plastic sheeting and wastewater irrigation, so as to ensure the safety of agricultural products; developed and produced new, safe, high-quality and high-efficiency feed, improving the utilization rate of feed and reducing pesticide residues of breeding industry products and discharge of harmful substances; popularized the technique of comprehensively utilizing and treating feces of livestock and poultry, and encouraged the development of eco-agricultural projects that closely integrates breeding industry with crop farming.

Financial Budget for Environmental Protection

During the 10th Five-Year Plan (2001-2005), 111.9 billion Yuan was earmarked from the central budget for environmental protection, of which 108.3 billion Yuan from treasury bonds was used mainly to control dust-storm sources threatening the Beijing-Tianjin area, to protect natural forests, to turn cultivated farmland back into forests or pastures, to control pollution around the Three Gorges Dam area, as well as pollution on the Huaihe, Liaohe and Haihe rivers, Taihu, Dianchi and Chaohu lakes, to industrialize the reuse and recycling of sewage and garbage, and to reclaim waste water. Since 1998, the State has focused treasury bond investment on environmental infrastructure construction, bringing about much social investment. Between 1996 and 2004, China's investment in environmental pollution control reached 952.27 billion Yuan, amounting to one percent of the period's GDP. In 2006, expenditure on environmental protection was formally itemized in State financial budget.

The management and collection of discharge fees have been strengthened by strict separation of their collection and use, and channeling the fees exclusively into the prevention and control of environmental pollution. The collection of sulfur dioxide discharge fees has been expanded to include all related enterprises, public institutions and private businesses, and the rate of such fees per kg has been raised from 0.2 to 0.63 Yuan. The treatment of urban sewage, garbage and hazardous wastes is also charged, so as to channel social capital in a variety of ways into the environmental protection infrastructure construction and operation, and to promote the marketization and industrialization of pollution control. A concession operation system has been established and implemented for the operation of urban sewage and garbage treatment. In some places, the operation of sewage and garbage treatment plants set up by the government has been transferred to enterprises through public bidding/tendering and contracting. In this way, the government has strengthened its role of supervision while the economic returns of the investment in environmental protection have also been augmented.

♦ Development of New-energy Projects in Rural Areas

It is an important approach to protecting and improving the rural ecological environment to develop and popularize new types of energy in rural areas. During the 10th Five-Year Plan (2001-2005), the State spent 3.5 billion Yuan to popularize an ecological model of energy with methane as the pivot. From 2003 to 2006, the State arranged 5.5 billion Yuan State bonds to build 5.73 million methane facilities in 48,000 villages. This helps popularize the use of methane. By the end of 2005, the number of rural households adopting methane reached 22.6 million. So far, more than 2,200 such methane projects have been completed, treating more than 60 million tons of feces. And 137,000 methane pits for purifying domestic sewage and over 500 central heating projects with gas from burning stalks have been built. In addition, 189 million households now use fuel-saving stoves, and solar water heaters cover a total of 28.5 million sq m. Meanwhile, the government has been actively promoting the use of renewable solar, wind and geothermal energy sources.

The rural women in Anshun, Guizhou, clean up the sullage in the river.

State Scientific and Technological Program for Environmental Protection

During the 10th Five-Year Plan (2001-2005), the State has organized and conducted the national key "water pollution control technology and treatment project", carried out research and development of such model programs as lake pollution control and ecological recovery, quality improvement of urban water environment, drinking water safety safeguards and newly developed waste-water treatment projects, thus providing practical technological plans and supportive technological systems for water pollution prevention and control. A batch of environmental monitoring technologies and equipment has been developed, and applied.

The research and development of such

pilot programs as motor-vehicle emission purification, desulphurization of gas discharged by coal-fueled boilers, disposal of solid wastes, clean production of key sectors and other key technologies have been conducted, and a group of high and new technologies and equipment have been developed with independent intellectual property rights.

The "research on countermeasures against significant environmental issues and relevant key supportive technologies" has been listed in the State's key scientific and technological plans; research is underway regarding environmental protection strategy and technological policy, the theory of a cyclical economy and ecological industrial technology, chemicals control technology, and polluted site recovery technology, and a green GDP accounting framework has roughly taken shape.

The government has carried out research on comprehensive ecological system assessment, ecological functional zoning and the recovery and reconstruction of the frail ecological zones in the western part of the country, thus shaping a variety of treatment technology patterns and a mechanism for large-scale demonstration and popularization in those zones.

The country has also completed its survey of alien invasive species, and set up a biodiversity database. It has formulated the State Environment and Health Action Plan, and conducted surveys on environment and health in key areas. It has actively conducted research on global environmental changes, and worked out the *State Assessment Report on Climate Changes*, which provides a scientific basis for the State to formulate policies to cope with global environmental changes and participate in negotiations on relevant international conventions.

Technology of Environmental Pollution Control

During the 10th Five-Year Plan (2001-2005), China has developed 15 key technologies with intellectual property rights in terms of environmental pollution control. Of these, nine have reached the international advanced level including cleaner production of chromic sub-molten salt, quick detection of cyano-bacterial toxin standard sample, algae toxins and toxigenic algae, desulphurization and de-nitrification technology of flue gases by using pulse corona discharge, control of diesel vehicle exhaust fine particle and nitrogen oxide, cleaner production of chromate-free tannery, cleaner production of producing fuel alcohol with self-flocculating yeast, ecological landfill of urban life garbage, analysis and detection of environmental endocrine disruptors and persistent toxic substance, phytoremediation in heavy metal polluted soil. Besides, some other technical achievements have achieved international leading level. Moreover, 12 technologies have been translated into projects or industries, including road-side monitoring of automobile exhausts, automatic monitoring of urban air pollution, control of sulfur dioxide and fine particles from large-sized coal fired power plants, flue gas desulphurization of large and medium-sized coal-fired industrial boilers, and systems of incinerating waste-to-energy technology. The economic benefits (output value) produced by technical achievements have exceeded 1.5 billion Yuan, gaining a profit of 160 million Yuan. Technology-integrated application and comprehensive demonstration in terms of key pollution control, such as ecological restoration of air, soil, urban household garbage, solid and hazardous waste, clean-up of the Bohai Sea and its coastal zone, have made important progress, leading to formation of a batch of high-tech innovation and research bases and industrial bases for environmental protection.

Environmental Protection Industries

After 30 years of development, China's environmental protection industrial sector has developed into a system with various kinds of industries and a certain economic scale. Comprehensive resource utilization and clean technical products have enjoyed rapid development, and the environmental protection service industry has made great progress. Environmental protection products come in great variety and can basically meet the requirements of environmental pollution control, but the technology and reliability of the core products still remain lagging far behind those in some developed countries.

In 2006, China's environmental protection business won 26.9 billion Yuan in sales, a rise of 22.99 percent from the previous year, the profits reached 1.59 billion Yuan, and its assets were valued at 30 billion Yuan.

Environmental Certification System

According to data released by the Environmental Certification Center of SEPA, certification for the Environmental Label has been carried out on 55 kinds of products such as electrical appliances, office equipment, daily necessities and decorative materials. Products of more than 21,000 kinds produced by 1,100-odd enterprises have achieved the Environmental Label. The annual output value of these products has exceeded 90 billion Yuan.

A pre-purchase visit to http://www.cgpn.cn will enable consumers to check whether the product has the Environmental Label.

China is the largest country in the world in terms of the ceramic production and consumption. Sanitation ceramics, including ceramic tiles, used in construction projects gained the certification on September 1st 2006. This is the first time for SEPA to release the environmental protection trade standards for this type of material.

The Measures for the Disclosure of Environmental Information (for Trial Implementation) went into force on May 1, 2008. The Measures requires the environmental protection departments and polluting businesses to make public information on environment for effective protection.

Public Participation in Environmental Legislation

Environmental Impact Assessment Act unveiled in 2002 distinctly stipulated for the first time that experts and the public participate in the environmental impact assessment system. This move ensures that the public can effectively participate in environmental protection in a timely way. In the 2004 revision of the Law on Prevention and Control of Solid Waste-Induced Environmental Pollution, four articles are added on resolution of environmental disputes and environmental civil liabilities, clarifying the defendant's burden of proof in the environmental pollution damage suit. China's environmental legislation has got rid of the mistake of "placing more importance on administration than civil affairs", and turned towards the new phase of "attaching equal importance to administration and civil affairs". The concept that the public participate in environmental protection is also included in the legislative plan by SEPA and increasingly more local People's Congresses and governments.

There are many patterns in public participation in environmental legislation. In September 2004, SEPA carried out open development of its legislation. As a result, the Draft of the Sewage Discharge Regulation adopted the views of the masses. After the Environmental Protection Administrative Permission Hearing Regulation (for Trial Implementation) went into effect, a hearing on environmental administration permission was held for the first time. This is an indication of the direction in which China's legislative processes are moving.

• Environmental Label

The Environmental Label, also called Green Label, is a certificate granted by the quality control department after examination and approval by government departments or public communities in line with correlated environmental standards. It is used to confirm that the whole product life cycle, including the manufacture, usage and waste disposal, complies with environmental requirements, and does little or even no harm to human bodies. It is a kind of certificate trademark, indicating that the product is of good quality and accords with the environmental protection requirements in regard to the manufacturing processes, usage and disposal. It is also an indication that, compared with its counterparts, it has the advantages of smaller side effects, and more economical use of resources. This helps consumers to determine which products are environmental-friendly and convenient when they make their purchase decision. Consumers' choice and market competition can guide the enterprises to readjust their industrial structure conscientiously, adopt cleaner process, and turn out environmentally-friendly products in order to achieve the coordinated development of environmental protection and the economy.

Chinese Environmental Labeling was created under the background of international ecological label movement in 1993 for responding the idea of sustainable development proposed by World Environment and Development Congress held in 1992. Chinese Environmental Labeling Products Certification Commission established in 1994 takes in charge of the implementation and management of Chinese Environmental Labeling.

In February 2006, Public Participation in Environmental Impact Assessment Regulation (for Trial Implementation) was issued by State environmental protection departments. This is the first normative document regarding public participation in the field of environmental protection. It stipulates in detail the range, procedure and organizational form of public participation in environmental impact assessment.

All-China Environmental Award

The award is the first of its kind in the country to award collectives andd individuals who have made contribution to environmental protection. The organizing committee of All-China Environmental Award is composed of 13 departments and social groups including NPC Resources and Environment Committee, Subcommittee of Human Resources and Environment of CPPCC, the Publicity Department of CPC Central Committee, the Ministry of Education, the Ministry of Culture, the Ministry of Civil Affairs, SEPA, State Administration of Radio Film and Television, All-China Federation of Trade Unions, China Communist Youth League, All-China Women's Federation, China Environmental Protection Foundation (CEPF) and Dragon TV. The All-China Environmental Award Office is set up in CEPF.

This is a social award in terms of environmental protection with broad participation. The photos and deeds of the candidates are published in newspapers and magazines from all walks of life. According to the evaluation methods, candidates are not limited by nationality, region, ethnic group and religion. All-China Environmental Award is permanent and granted once a year.

There are no more than five winners each year and 500,000 Yuan is awarded to each. Apart from these winners, there are also four awards of the Green Oriental Award for each prize of All-China Environmental Award. Each winner can receive 50,000 Yuan as a prize. There are no more than 20 winners.

♦ China Association of the Environmental Protection Industry

CAEPI grew out of the China Environmental Protection Industry founded in 1984. Created in 1993, CAEPI is a social group voluntarily organized by registered units, who are engaged in environmental protection R and D, design, manufacture, circulation and service, and experts who follow an environmental protection career. It is a national non-profit organization with a commonalty capacity that carries out cross-regional, cross-sectional and cross-ownership business. By June 2006, CAEPI had 46 group members and some 1,000 corporate members.

CAEPI is composed of 10 professional committees in charge of water pollution control, electric precipitation, exhaust gas purification, bag-type exhaust dust, boiler dust removal and desulphurization, solid waste disposal and utilization, urban life garbage disposal, noise and vibration control, environment monitoring equipment, and vehicle pollution control. Besides, CAEPI also owns 2 branch associations responsible for organic food and ozonosphere protection. All these departments undertake their own professional technical activities.

CAEPI has already launched exchanges with relevant international organizations in more than 30 countries and regions. Cooperation agreements have been signed with some, laying a solid foundation for China to introduce foreign investment, technology and devices, and for China's technology and devices to enter the international market.

Website: http://www.caepi.org.cn

♦ China Environmental Consultative Committee

The China Environmental Consultative Committee is staffed with high-level professionals who are responsible for implementing the investigation and research of problems occurring in environmental protection. They also bear the task of providing consultative suggestions and advice for the mid and long term national environmental development plan, environmental protection laws and regulations, vital economic and technical policies concerning environmental protection, and important guidelines on environmental protection.

Non-governmental Environmental Protection Organization

Non-governmental environmental protection organizations(ENGO) and environmental protection volunteers constitute an important part of public participation. According to a blue paper issued by the All-China Environment Federation in 2006, there were 2,768 non-governmental environmental protection organizations with 224,000 employees in existence by 2005. They have been playing an active role mainly in advocating environmental protection, enhancing the nation's environmental awareness, carrying out social supervision and offering advice. In addition, they also aid the poor, develop the green economy, care about the welfare of disadvantaged groups, safeguard public environmental rights and interests, protect biodiversity, leaving future generations more opportunities for development.

Development of Non-Governmental Environmental Protection Organizations

The First National Conference on Environmental Protection was held in 1973, marking a turning point in the development of China's environmental protection undertakings. In May 1978, the China Environmental Science Society was founded. Many more organizations quickly appeared. A case in point is the foundation of the Saunders' Gull Protection Society in 1991 in Panjin, Liaoning Province. Friends of Nature was founded in 1994.

In 1995, private initiatives were launched to protect the Yunnan snub-nosed monkey and Tibetan antelope. Through various publicity activities, much public awareness and good will was generated towards ENGO. In 1999, Global Village of Beijing (GVB) worked with the Beijing Municipal Government to conduct pilot studies on green communities as the movement began to extend into urban environmental protection, resulting in gradual public understanding and acceptance. The Nujiang hydraulic power work in 2003 and 26°Centigrade air conditioners in 2005 are the actions taken by numerous ENGO, who unanimously work hard together to protect the environment and ecology and achieve proper environmental development. This shows that these organizations have moved from the initial phase of independent to working together with others in a coordinated way. They have also brought more members of the general public into active participation in environmental protection, offering advice for environmental undertakings, launching social supervision, safeguarding public environmental rights and interests and promoting sustainable development.

Types of ENGO

China's ENGO movement is divided into four types. The first are those launched by governmental sectors, such as China Environmental Protection Association, China

♦ Action of "Air Conditioner at 26°Centigrade"

From 2004 to 2005, some non-governmental organizations on environmental protection such as "Global Village of Beijing", World Nature Foundation, China International Non-Governmental Organizations Cooperation Promotion Union and "Friend of Nature" launched the "energy-saving action of air conditioner at 26°Centigrade" for two successive years.

According to statistics, the total charge of air conditioners in Beijing at the midsummer is about 4 to 5 million kilowatt. If the temperature of all the air conditioners is enhanced 1°Centigrade, 6 to 8 percent of the charge will be saved, 110 million Yuan of electric expense will be saved, 160,000 to 250,000 tons of coal for electric generation will be cut down, and 2,400 to 3,500 tons of sulfur dioxide emission will be reduced.

The action proposed to keep the temperature of air conditioners not below 26° Centigrade at the peak of electricity use in summer (from June 26 to September 26), and sent their appeal to governmental organizations, embassies in Beijing, transnational companies, state-owned and non-governmental enterprises and organizations, urban residents, commercial companies, hotels and restaurants.

In 2004 the action was just undertaken in Beijing. On June 26, 2005, some organizations such as "Green Homeland Volunteers", "Hong Kong Friend of Earth" and "Protection International" joined the action, and 9 environmental protection organizations proposed energy-saving again and launched the action of "energy-saving air conditioners at 26°Centigrade". The action in 2005 mainly aimed at the "26°Centigrade alliance" with the governing bodies of public buildings and commercial constructions. The action was supported by more than 50 non-governmental organizations on environmental protection in China and it was expanded across China.

♦ Friends of Nature (FON)

This is the first non-governmental organization initiated by Liang Congjie, Yong Dongping, Liang Xiaoyan and Wang Lixiong. On 5th June 1993, the founders of FON held the first non-governmental environmental seminar called the Linglongyuan Conference. FON was formally founded on 31st March 1994 with Liang Congjie, member of CPPCC and tutor of International Academy of Chinese Culture, serving as its chairman and Professor Yang Dongping, specialist of social culture and education, its vice-chairman. The goal of the organization:conducting mass education in environmental protection, advocating green civilization, promoting green culture with distinct Chinese characteristics, and pushing forward China's environmental protection cause. All fees needed come from membership fees and social donations. Over the past decade, the number of FON members has totaled more than 8,000, of which that of member and group members more than 3,000 and nearly 30, respectively. FON has won more than 15 awards at home and aboard, such as the Asia Environment Award, Earth Award, Panda Award, and Ramon Magsaysay Prize of Philippine. Through the past ten years of foundation and development, FON has grown into an ENGO with fine public confidence and influence. As one of the landmark organizations, FON has made great contributions to China's environmental protection undertakings and social development.

Website: http://www.fon.org.cn

Environmental Protection Foundation, China Environmental Cultural Association, Environmental Science Society, Environmental Industrial Association and Wildlife Conservation Society; The second category are those launched by non-governmental departments spontaneously, such as Friends of Nature, Global Village of Beijing, Environmental protection volunteer groups, network communication organization and other non-governmental organizations engaged in non-profit environmental protection activities. In the third category, a typical example is the Student Environmental Protection Association and its union, formed by numerous university environmental protection associations; the fourth type are international environmental protection organizations in China.

Distribution of ENGO

There have been 2,768 ENGO of all kinds. Of these, 1,382 (49.9 percent) were launched by the government; 202 (7.2 percent) spontaneously by non-governmental organizations; 1116 (40.3 percent) by the Student Environmental Protection Association; and 68 (2.6 percent) by the international environmental protection organizations in Mainland China.

The ENGO are distributed mainly in Beijing, Tianjin, Shanghai, Chongqing and coastal areas in Eastern China; provinces richly endowed with ecological resources including Hunan, Hubei, Sichuan and Yunnan also have many.

A total of 85.8 percent of the ENGO implement membership with a members' congress as the highest authority. The council, executive board, chairman of an executive council, and so on, are chosen through democratic selection.

Environmental Protection Popularization

The Chinese Government has formulated the National Environmental Publicity and Education Action Outline (1996-2010) and National Environmental Publicity and Education Outline (2001-2005). The fourth five-year law-popularization plan started in 2001 regards the popularization of environmental protection laws and regulations as an important part of environmental protection. The annual June 5 World Environment Day is a chance to promote national environmental popularization and education. Green communities, green schools and green families are encouraged. As a result, currently, 2,348 communities have participated in the foundation of green communities, and more than 25,000 middle schools, primary schools, secondary vocational schools and kindergartens have joined in the foundation of green schools. Besides, 100 green families have won praise. Many practices have been unfolded, including protecting "mother" rivers, green promises, daily environmental protection and ecology monitoring, to give adolescents access to eco-environmental moral education and enhance their environmental protection ideology. Green China Forum, China Environment Culture Festival and other activities are held to provide environmental-related training, leading the public to participate in the discussion of environmental issues. Thus, it helps to form a social atmosphere that everybody participates in building a green home.

Publication of Environmental Information

All cities above the prefecture level had achieved the automatic monitoring of urban air quality and issued a daily public report. These cities are organized to monitor water quality for a monthly public report on ten key rivers and weekly report on automatic water quality monitoring. The eastern route for water diverted from south to north is monitored periodically; 113 key environmental protection cities also produce a monthly report on the monitoring of the quality of drinking water resources. A system of quarterly analysis of environmental quality has been set up to make public timely information on environmental quality. Governments and environmental protection departments of all levels

Professor Qu Geping, the major exploiter and founder of China's undertaking of environmental protection, also one of the founders and initial leaders of China's Environmental Protection Administrative Institute

♦ Global Village of Beijing (GVB)

Founded in 1996, Global Village of Beijing (GVB) is a non-governmental, non-profit organization dedicated to environmental education, it has 15 office staff and over 1000 officially-registered volunteers.

GVB's founder and president is Ms. Sheri Liao. Committed to developing environmental education and promoting sustainable development in China, she returned to Beijing to found GVB in 1996.

Since April 1996, GVB has independently produced the Time for the Environment, the only ENGO TV special broadcast weekly by CCTV for five years. It then continued to be broadcast by CCTV and some local TV stations irregularly. The GVB production unit has not only viewed from China's public environmental protection, but also shot and interviewed in scores of countries with a view of grassroots to popularize the international environmental protection experiences. GVB has published a series of books to promote the green lifestyle, such as Citizen Environmental Guide, Children's Environmental Guide, Green Community Guidebook, Collected Songs of Green Voice Environmental Protection cooperated with State Environmental Protection Administration and CDs of the environmental protection education training. GVB also held some large-scale public activities to promote life environmental protection. The achievements made by GVB have attracted widespread concerns of the international society and media. Between 1998 and 2000, GVB served as the first NGO liaison station of China Environmental Protection Foundation, and in 2001, entrusted by UNEP, GVB became China's NGO information liaison. In addition, GVB also acts as a member of World Nature Union Educational Committee and Asia-Pacific Environmental Journalist Association.

Website: www.gvbchina.org.cn

hold periodic press conferences to inform on environmental conditions, important policies and measurements, sudden environmental events and any serious violations. This is a move to safeguard the public's rights to learn the truth of environmental protection and thus promote the public participation in protecting the environment.

Safeguarding Public Environmental Rights and Interests

More than 300 cities at the prefectural level, some 300 cities at the county level and over 600 counties had had access to environmental protection offence reporting hotlines, covering 69.4 percent of the administrative regions above county level. Since 2003, the hotlines have helped environmental protection departments at all levels to handle millions of complaints. Of these, about 97 percent have been solved, with some 80 percent being considered satisfactory. With the continuous improvement of public environmental awareness and requirements of environment quality, the numbers of complaints by letters and visits regarding the encroachment on environmental rights and interests sees an annual increase. Environmental protection departments at all levels coped with more than millions of complaint letters, complaint visits involving hundreds of thousands of people, hundreds of suggestions offered by NPC deputies and hundreds of proposals submitted by members of the CPPCC.

Stockholm Convention

In 2001, a total of 92 countries and the regional economic organizations signed the Stockholm Convention on Persistent Organic Pollutants, POPs for short, which are known for their characteristics of poison and difficulty in decomposition. They can cause cancers, malformation and mutations, and disturb glandular secretion. They can move and be transferred over long distances and accumulate in the eco-system for a long time. Especially if absorbed by a living body, they are difficult to decompose but easy to concentrate and magnify along the food chain. Thus, they cause tremendous harm to human bodies, influencing several generations of human beings. Therefore, the signing and implementation of the Stockholm Convention is a milestone for human society in terms of global environmental protection especially the protection of future generations.

Chinese Regulations on POPs

The State Council issued the Safety Management Regulation on Dangerous Chemical Goods in 2002. It stipulates the production, usage, packaging, delivery, storage, import and export of deliberately-produced dangerous chemicals and the monitoring and management of key dangerous sources. The relevant management measurements and standards are formulated in line with this regulation. Dioxin discharge control standards are implemented in a few industries including waste incineration. The current regulations including Environmental Impact Assessment Act, Cleaner Production Promotion Law and the Regulations on the Administration of Construction Project Environmental Protection serve as the basis of the discharge reduction and control of POPs.

Wastes with POPs have been listed in the dangerous waste list to be managed in accordance with the Law on the Prevention and Control of Solid Waste Induced Environmental Pollution, Measures on the Prevention of Dangerous Chemicals Waste Pollution, and the Technical Policy for Pollution Control of Dangerous Wastes.

The Measures on the Prevention of Dangerous Chemical Waste Pollution implemented in 2005 stipulates the recovery of soil polluted with POPs. The Regulations on the Control of Agricultural Chemicals is applicable for the management of insecticide-type POPs.

Chinese Investigation on POPs

Presently, China has investigated and established data on the production, circulation, usage, import and export of POPs in a systematic and comprehensive way, and identified the potential POPs (dioxin etc.) discharge industries and key enterprises. During a sample survey, China adopted the mode recommended by UN to calculate the discharge of dioxin POPs. Meanwhile, China has made the sample survey of polluted fields and put forward the investigation plan and primary list of abandoned polluted fields. Moreover, it has comprehensively evaluated the organs, regulations, related treatment, disposition and replacement technologies in terms of POPs management.

Implementation of Stockholm Convention

Currently, China has basically finished drawing up the National Executive Plan, listing the requirements in the Stockholm Convention in relevant industry readjustment policies. According to the integrated deployment in implementation, it presents the production methods and technologies that China encourages, limits and bans, and specifies the pollution-control-related standards, environment quality standards, technical guidance rules and specifications that need to be formulated and revised during the 11th Five-Year Plan (2006-2010).

China takes an active role in organizing and implementing demonstration projects that are developed comprehensively in the first three POPs areas including PCBs, insecticides and their by-products. This is a move that has laid a solid foundation for national implementation. Besides, broad bilateral cooperation with Italy, Japan, Canada and America is carried out in terms of ability construction, by-product-type POPs reduction, body exposure risk and insecticide-type POPs elimination.

Recycling Economy

The recycling economy refers to a new production mode and living style focusing on resources utilization and re-use, and optimization of energy. It is of paramount importance to pay attention to recycling resources and the reduction and elimination the pollution at source and implement ecological protection. To maximize efficiency and profit, the utmost efforts should be made to establish a situation featuring reasonable exploitation of resources, economic use of energy, environmental protection and high efficiency.

China has made much headway on cleaner production and energy-saving as well as comprehension utilization in recent years. However, some traditional extensive economic increase patterns featuring high consumption, high exhaust pollution and low efficiency still stand in the way; the rate of resource usage remains low and environmental pollution is still high. In the upcoming 15 years, China will still be in the development stage of accelerating industrialization and urbanization. But the situation regarding resource availability and the environment will become increasingly grim. In this important strategic period, China must grasp the chance to realize the task of building an overall well-off society. By doing this, in accordance with the principle of decreasing, reusing and resource reproduction, it will conduct various effective measures to achieve the target of maximum economic output and minimum waste emission. It also wants to realize the combination of the benefit for economy, environment and society and speed up building a resource-saving and environmental friendly society.

In 2006, China started seven projects including conservation and substitution of petroleum, combined heat and power (CHP) production, surplus heat utilization, building energy efficiency, governmental organization's energy conservation, green lights, energy saving supervising and technological system construction.

China Environmental Monitoring Station

The China Environmental Monitoring Station was established in 1980 and is directly under SEPA. It provides SEPA with technical support, supervision and service for its supervision of and management over environment. The station is responsible for collecting and gathering the national environmental monitoring data accurately and in a timely way, analyzing and evaluating the status of the national environmental quality. It also carries out scientific research to develop and advance the latest technology and methodology of environmental monitoring in the whole nation. It is charged with working out standards for national monitoring technology, and is also responsible for quality guarantee and control of national environmental monitoring system. The station also gives technological guidance and coordination for the national environmental monitoring network.

Website: http://www.cnemc.cn

China Cleaner Production Portal

The China Cleaner Production Portal is sponsored by the China National Cleaner Production Center of the United Nations. It's principle is: To publish guiding documents and important information of SEPA concerning clean production, the recycling economy and the biological industry; provide the network of the China Cleaner Production Center to disseminate information in an all-round way; provide services for the network set up by environmental protection bureaus in provinces and cities, cleaner production centers and cleaner production institutions; introduce theories, working experiences and case research on cleaner production, recycling economy and the ecological industry; enhance public consciousness by providing technological support and popularizing knowledge of cleaner production, the recycling economy and ecological industry; strengthen cooperation with international cleaner production organizations; introduce advanced international technology and experiences of cleaner production, recycling economy and the biological industry; make full use of the advantages of the Internet and use this platform to release hot news and develop discussions in different forums.

Website: http://www.ccpp.org.cn

All China Environmental Federation

This is a non-profit, national society founded on April 26, 2005 by individuals, enterprises, institutions that are keen on the environmental protection undertaking on a voluntary basis.

Its major working scope is: serve as a bridge linking the public and government in accordance with the targets and responsibilities concerning the nation's environment and development; provide advice and suggestions to governments at all levels and environmental monitoring institutes; safeguard the right for environmental protection of the public and the whole society; organize activities of environmental rights protection and legal aid; help the government to put forward the law of environmental right's protection and establish the safeguard system and environmental right center; give aid to citizens, legal person and disadvantaged groups in particular suffering from violation of their environmental rights; organize educational activities and publish public environmental information; carry out research of Chinese environmental NGOs and extensively associate with the other NGOs in the world; and, raise funds through various channels to promote the construction and sound development of NGOs. It also enjoys consultative status with the Economic and Social Council of the United Nations and organizes and takes part in the non-governmental bilateral and multilateral exchanges and cooperation concerning environmental protection.

Website: http://www.acef.com.cn

Online NGO Name List of the Environment

The Chinese Online NGO Name list (Green NGO Directory) was set up on October 11, 2006 in Beijing with the support of the Ford Foundation, with some NGO environmental representatives as consultants.

This project is to build a comprehensive on-line database to introduce the non-governmental organizations involved in environmental protection, provide information interchanges and promote understanding between the environmental protectors, NGOs, and relevant government organizations. It also serves as a platform for researchers, journalists, governmental officers to communicate, and for ordinary people eager to plunge themselves into the environmental protection activities.

The list has its own independent website. It is mainly focusing on practicability, accuracy and objectivity. Up to now, some 100 institutions and organizations have been included in the Green NGO Directory.

Website: http://www.greengo.cn

♦ China Environmental Protection Foundation

China Environmental Protection Foundation, founded in April 1993, is the first foundation in charge of environmental protection in China and non-profit association with independent legal-person qualification. In 2005 it was granted with "special status" by UN Economic and Social Council.

On UN Convention on Environment and Development in June 1992 the UN awarded Professor Qu Geping, the first head of State Environmental Protection Bureau, with UN Award and a bonus of US$ 100 thousand for his participation and leading in Chinese environmental protection cause. Professor Qu Geping proposed to establish China Environmental Protection Foundation on base of the bonus to accelerate the development in environmental protection cause in China. Professor Qu Geping became the first donator and shouldered the director of council. The supreme power organization of the Foundation is the council which is organized by Chinese and international famous personage, representatives devoted to the cause of environmental protection in the society and major donators.

In the light of the principle of "by the people, for the people and benefiting mankind", the Foundation raises money in a wide area and uses the money to award organizations and individuals having made outstanding contribution to environmental protection, to support activities and projects related to environmental protection, to accelerate the exchanges and cooperation in field of environmental protection between China and other countries, and to promote the development of environmental protection in China.

In 2000 the Foundation undertook the first social award on environmental protection in China, "China Environment Award" and launched a series of public welfare activities on environmental protection with "China Green Territory" as the main line in 2001. The project of "China Green Territory" has undertaken promotion activities in 22 provinces, autonomous regions and municipalities in China, and by May 2005, more than 1.8 million person-times of primary and middle-school students have joined the activity, a donation of more than 4 million Yuan has been raised, more than 66.67 hectares of trees have been planted, and the activity has played an active role in improvement and construction of rural environment.

Website: http://www.cepf.org.cn

Target of the Recycling Economy

The overall target of the pilot projects for the recycling economy is: explore and establish models in key industries such as steel, nonferrous metals, chemicals, building materials; set up a group of model enterprises, which succeed in recycling; perfect the re-utilization system to provide an appropriate mechanism for resource recycling exploitation; undertake trials in the development zones and industrial parks; propose ideas on planning, constructing and reforming the industrial parks in accordance with the model of the recycling economy; build a group of sample industrial parks characterized by the recycling economy; explore the road of urban recycling economic development to form many example cities.

The government also started the first pilot enterprises of the recycling economy including 42 enterprises in seven key industries covering steel, nonferrous metals, chemical industry and 17 enterprises of four important fields, 13 industrial parks concentrating on heavy chemical industrialization and agricultural sample districts, 10 provinces and cities in both resource-rich and resource-poor city.

Pilot Areas Conducting the Recycling Economy

On November 1, 2005, a total of 42 enterprises in seven major trades, including iron and steel making, non-ferrous metals and chemical industries, 17 businesses of the four major fields involving recovery and utilization of recycle resources, 13 industrial parks including State and provincial-level development areas, areas where heavy chemical businesses are concentrated and agricultural demonstration areas, and 10 provinces and municipalities which are of the resource type or resource-deficient were chosen as the first group of pilot units for the development of recyclable economy.

In 2006, the State began to undertake seven projects, including the project for economic use of oil and use of oil substitutes, joint production of power and heat, use of used heat, energy conservation in building, energy conservation in government institutions, green illumination, energy conservation monitoring and technical service system.

Achievements of Recycling Economy

Now, more than 5,000 enterprises covering areas such as chemicals, light industry, electrical power, coal, machinery and construction materials have passed the examination of cleaner production and over 12,000 enterprises have received certificates of the ISO14000 environmental management system; more than 18,000 products have achieved environment symbol certification standard. The annual output value has reached about 60 billion Yuan.

Efforts have been made to develop eco-industry in areas where industrial businesses are concentrated. This made it possible for the wastes from the upper-stream businesses to become raw materials for the down-stream enterprises. Thus far, China has set up 17 eco-industrial parks of different types.

The piles of the coal gaugues become the new-type energy-saving building materials. The picture shows the product line of the green bricks of the porous bricks sintered with coal gaugues.

Renewable Energy

This refers to non-fossil energy sources obtained from nature. It includes wind, solar, water, biomass, geothermal and marine energy. China is richly endowed with renewable energy. Further development of renewable energy can effectively reduce the consumption of non-recyclable fossil fuels such as coal, oil and natural gas. It is the new direction of China's energy exploitation.

The government attaches great importance to sustainable development and makes the exploitation and utilization of renewable energy its vital task in the 11th Five-Year Plan (2006-2010). It will adopt a series of important measures to make use of renewable energy.

The first is to set development goals. The total exploitation and utilization of the renewable energy in primary energy consumption will increase 10 percent in 2010. The second is to develop an action plan. Many large-scale hydropower energy bases and wind-power bases producing millions of kilowatts and model solar power generation power stations will be established. The solar water heater will be widely promoted and use of marsh gas will be expanded through rural areas. The government will support biomass energy electrical power generation and biomass liquid fuel. This will really speed up the development process of the industrialization and localization of renewable technology and equipment manufacturing. The third is to provide supporting policies. The government has formulated various policies offering preferential treatment and tax reductions to encourage and stimulate

♦ Extended Producer Responsibility System

This aims to solve environmental problems caused by the increasing amount of electronic waste. This system requires producers to shoulder responsibility for the disposal of the waste from their production. It can stimulate the producers to produce environmental-friendly products by using recycling materials and designs and reducing or eliminating the use of hazardous materials. Pilot areas for the recycling and proper handling of waste and old household electrical appliance and electronic products were set up in Zhejiang Province and Qingdao City in Shandong.

the exploitation and utilization of renewable energy. The fourth is to implement the Law on Renewable Energy, determine the responsibilities and obligations for various social sectors, and introduce the quota system for renewable energy to provide the development and utilization of renewable resources with the best legal guarantees.

Biological Fuel

This refers to the alcohol fuel and biological diesel oil produced by biological resources. It can be a good substitute for gasoline and diesel oil, which abstracted from petroleum. It's of great significance for the development and utilization of the renewable energy.

China has developed large-scale natural alcohol producing technology, laying the solid foundation for developing biological fuel-grain alcohol. By the end of the last century, taking the advantage of relative surplus food, China began to develop bio-fuel alcohol. During the 10th Five-Year Plan (2001-2005), it built factories producing alcohol fuel with the aged grain as its production source in Henan, Anhui, Jilin, Heilongjiang Province respectively, with the total production reached 1.02 million tons annually. Now, the sales of alcohol fuel for vehicles use has expanded in nine provinces. But no more areas have been developed for the production of alcohol fuel recently due to the limitation of food production.

To expand the sources of biological fuel, China has developed its own technology of producing ethanol with sweet sorghum stalks and has set up the pilot areas for the planting of the sweet sorghum and fuel ethanol production in provinces and areas in Heilongjiang, Inner Mongolia, Shandong provinces, Xinjiang and Tianjin. The ethanol production of the pilot project in Heilongjiang Province has reached 5,000 tons annually. This sweet sorghum ethanol, however, has so far failed to enter the transportation and fuel market, and most of production is mixed into low-quality liquor. In addition, China is carrying out research technological development to produce fuel ethanol from cellulose; the test production capacity has reached 600 tons on the annual basis in the enterprises like Fenyuan in Anhui Province.

Prospects for Bio-Fuel

Biological diesel refers to diesel products that are extracted from scrapped plants and animal oil or oil-bearing plants, such as Barbados Nut bark or Chinese pistache. Currently, some Chinese companies' bio-diesel products, produced from recycled restaurant grease, have met the US standard (ASTM-D-6751-03a). With an annual output of 50,000 tons, they provide fuel for transportation companies or construction sites. Moreover, some scientific research centers have already carried out studies on cultivation of superior oil-bearing plants, bio-diesel technology and processing of biological products. In the meantime, they have also conducted small-scale industrial experiments. Thanks to their efforts, the key technologies such as oil-plant cultivation and bio-diesel processing method have been achieved.

According to the experts, sorghum, cassava and sugarcane could provide raw materials for about 30 million tons of denatured fuel ethanol. Other oil-plants could produce at least ten million tons of bio-diesel. And the recycled plant and animal oil could add another five million tons. If waste materials from the agricultural and forestry industry could be finally turned into fuel ethanol or bio-diesel, output could hit more than 100 million tons. Based on these facts, theoretically, China's bio-fuel industry has a bright future.

Wind Power Industry

The utilization of wind power in China dates back to the 1980s and the industry has achieved progress on a certain scale. Since 2003, the Chinese Government has introduced a franchise system to help it develop. Wind power plants with installed capacity over 100,000 kW are put out to tender for franchise approval from the government. It will also offer them suitable sites with richly endowed wind-power resources, the right to use the land, environmental protection, transportation, cable network and purchase contract of electricity at an agreed price. This mechanism has helped launch more large-scale wind power plants and cut the electricity price to a competitive level.

To drive the industry, the government has carried out preparatory work, such as surveys and assessment of wind-power resources and suitable building sites around the country. The Law on Renewable Energy has been approved. According to medium and long term objectives, electricity generated by wind power plants will reach five million kW by 2010 and 30 million kW by 2020 respectively.

Development of Wind Power Industry

The Beijing International Renewable Energy Conference was convened in 2005. It raised not only the public awareness about the importance of renewable resources, but also investor interest in related sectors. Among them, the wind-power industry leads in capital inflows, entering a new mass production phase.

There are 59 wind-power plants distributed among 15 provinces, municipalities directly under the Central Government and autonomous regions. The generating units installed in 2006 reach 1.347 million kW, an increase of 70 percent from the year before. As the 6th largest wind energy market, China boasts 2.604 million kW wind energy generating units. And the figure is to increase by 1.5 million kW in 2007 and 5 million kW in 2010, a goal which is expected to be met ahead of schedule.

China has already mastered key technologies to produce 600 and 750 kW turbine generator units. The home-made 1,200 kW generator unit is in trial operation, while the 1,500 and 2000 kW generator units are under research. China now has the capability to produce key accessories such as casts, fans and electricity generators, which have attracted orders from foreign companies.

♦ Policies on Renewable Energy

The government encourages and supports the renewable source system connected to the power grid. Power grid enterprises should sign a grid-connection contract with the renewable energy-generating enterprise after achieving administrative agreement or reporting for record of the government. It should provide the grid-connected services of the renewable energy after MBO (management buyout.

Government support to set up the stand-alone power systems in the uncovered grid-connected areas is designed to provide power services for local areas. The government encourages the exploration and utilization of clean, efficient biomass liquid fuels and the development of the energy from crops. As long as the gas and the heating power generated from the biomass fuels meets the technical standards for entering the grid system of the urban gas networks and the heat-supply pipe network, they are acceptable.

The government encourages the production and utilization of the biological liquid fuel. Enterprises selling petroleum are required to include biological liquid fuel meeting national standards in their fuel sales system.

The Government also encourages units and individuals to install and use solar water heating systems, solar energy heating and refrigeration systems and grid-connected photovoltaic systems.

World Bank Aid

The World Bank provided a loan of US$86.33 million to help China launch its follow-up project to the 2005 China Renewable Energy Scale-Up Program Phase 1. A total of US$67 million goes to the development of the 100 MW Huitengxile Wind Farm in the Inner Mongolia Autonomous Region, which is currently home to approximately 70 MW of wind generation capacity. An additional US$19.33 million will finance the rehabilitation and development of selected small hydropower projects (not exceeding 10 MW) in Zhejiang Province.

"China's energy demands and its need to decrease air pollution make large-scale renewable energy development an important goal," said Noureddine Berrah, lead energy specialist for China. "The idea behind the program is to increase the commercial, large-scale use of renewable energy sources like wind, small hydropower, and solar energy so that they contribute to meeting the fast-growing electricity demand from homes, farms, and businesses."

Utilizing Imported Recyclable Resources

There are nearly ten thousand businesses engaged in this sector with a total staff of over one million. Since the 1990s, under the supervision of customs and departments responsible for environmental protection or quality control, recyclable solid wastes have been imported by reasonable arrangement. The volume stood at 39.54 million tons in 2005, compared to one million tons on an annual basis in the first few years. The output value hit 100 billion Yuan in that year, efficiently meeting China's growing demand for resources. In 2006 China imported 6.78 million tons of non-ferrous waste, a rise of 3.1 percent from the previous year.

Several hundreds of wind turbine generators are in operation on the Huitengxile Grassland in the central part of Inner Mongolia. The Huitengxile Wind Generators Farm was developed with the loans provided by the World Bank.

Recycling Scrapped Products

Scrapped mechanical or electronic products could be reused after sophisticated processing procedures, such as cleaning, repairing and restoration. With a prolonged life span, products are used more sufficiently. Instead of making a new one, recycling an old product can reduce demand for water, raw materials and cut costs. An example is auto engine recycling. Recycling a motor from a scrapped car could produce an energy saving of 60 percent, along with 70 percent in raw materials and 50 percent of expenditure than producing a new one. Recycling is a newly rising industry providing many job vacancies.

A huge number of machines or appliances are renewed due to the fast growth of the manufacturing industry and upgrading of people's life. The situation lays a basic foundation for the development of the recycling industry. In recent years, the output and ownership of automobile in China has climbed rapidly. Currently, the annual output reaches nearly six million and the car ownership volume tops 30 million. Every year, there will be one million scrapped cars, a huge potential to develop an auto accessory recycling industry.

In recent years, some scientific research centers and enterprises have entered the recycling industry. With the support of relevant government departments, their research has achieved fruitful results, mastering the key technologies and basic theories of recycling. The Academy of Armored Force Engineering established the first equipment recycling laboratory in China. The technologies are protected by patent, such as cleaning, repairing and restoration. Shanghai Volkswagen and other Chinese auto producers have made basic achievements in engine recycling.

Guidelines for the Recycling Industry

The guidelines Guidelines of the 11th Five-Year Plan (2006-2010) were approved at the National People's Congress on March 5, 2006. It mapped out a plan of launching several pilot enterprises for auto engine recycling. At present, the pilot scheme on the reproduction of auto parts is under draft. The government is discussing some preferential policies to encourage more investors to enter the sector. Based on related law and regulations, a measure for administration of recycling accessories from scrapped cars is under discussion. The government also considers building up a system to link accessory recycling with scrapped car collection. The Ministry of Science and Technology has listed key technology research of recycling as major tasks. The State

♦ Medium and Long-Term Development Plan for Recyclable Energy

The Medium and Long-Term Development Plan for Recyclable Energy has a target of raising the proportion of renewable energy to 16 percent. The total installed capacity of hydropower stations is expected to reach 300 million kW, wind-power plants 30 million kW and biomass power plants 30 million kW. The utility of marsh gas is expected to reach 44.3 billion cubic meters. The total installed capacity of solar power farms is expected to hit 1.8 million kW. The solar heating panels are expected to total 300 million square meters. Output of fuel ethanol is expected to be ten million tons and bio-diesel two million tons.

♦ Work Committee for Imported Recyclable Energy

Its aim of to make sure that imported recyclable solid wastes are efficiently used, according to related law, regulations and policies. It helps ease resources shortages in China and promote resource circulation in the international community. It will conduct surveys on renewable resources and recycling economy, providing future references for the government to enact policies, law, regulations and establish criteria. It listens to relevant enterprises and submits their demands and opinions to the government, to protect their rights and interests. It also assists the relevant government departments to build up a Green Corridor to properly transport these special goods, so as to safeguard the international circulation order. It helps related departments regulate this sector, ushering it in an intensive way of development. It helps upgrade the management mode and facilities of pertinent enterprises, by offering consultation, information and training programs. It works to enable them to play a bigger role in building the energy-sufficient and environmentally-friendly society.

The renewable resources imported by the southeast coastal areas in China accounted for 80 percent of China's total. In the picture are the waste paper imported by a paper mill in Ningbo, Zhejiang.

Development and Reform Commission will finance the pilot programs of the recycling industry from the national debt. Meanwhile, the government works to encourage more people to use recycled and recyclable products.

Building an Energy-Efficient Society

(See P71)

Plan of Energy Conservation

The government plans to curb major energy users' consumption by offering long-term supervision and instructions. The chosen 1,000 enterprises are mainly steel or nonferrous metal makers, power plants and construction material producers. It also encourages and supports the development of energy-saving vehicles and agricultural machinery. It gives priority to the development of public transport, while curbing the growth of cars with high fuel consumption. It promotes energy-saving designs in construction of residential houses and public buildings. It also urges to transform existing buildings to an energy-saving style. It encourages the use of energy-saving appliances such as air conditioning, refrigerator and light bulbs in society. It has issued a regulation limiting the lowest indoor temperature of air conditioning in the summer. A new mechanism to save energy combines disseminating information, comprehensive planning, management of electricity demand, energy-saving products certification, administration of energy labling, administration of energy contracts, guarantee of investment and energy-saving agreements on a voluntary basis.

Alternative Energy

Alternative energy mainly refers to substitutions for petroleum, including coal-to-liquid fuel, coal derived alcohol ether and biomass liquid fuel. These products, with raw materials as coal or biomaterial, could be directly used or be added proportionally into finished oil. In addition to its nice combustibility, these products also have a good reputation for less contamination. They are not the temporary choices to meet China's energy demand. However, utility of these products is the strategy to secure sustainable energy utilization in China.

Currently, the coal and chemical industry and deep processing of agricultural products have developed apace. The alternative energy industry has achieved fruitful results in coal liquefaction, alcohol ether and biomass liquid fuel. The alternative liquid fuel sector is flourishing. Pilot enterprises for commercial scale production of coal liquefaction are under construction, with production technologies up to international standard. The output of alcohol ether fuel has risen in line with its widening utilization scale. Homemade dimethyl ether production with IPR protection has entered the industrial experiment phase. Vehicle-use biomass fuel production now totals 700,000 tons on an annual basis. With widening utilization scale, this number is still growing.

Key Sectors for Energy Conservation

China pays attention on the following sectors to save energy.

The first is the manufacturing sector. Some heavy energy users have become the focus of the energy-saving campaign, including steel and non-ferrous metal producers, coal mines, power plants, petroleum and petrochemical companies, building material producers and other enterprises with coal consumption of 10,000 tons or above. These companies are urged to readjust their product composition and improve energy-saving technologies, so as to reduce the energy consumption.

The second is the real estate/construction sector. In this sector, the government attaches importance to building relatively small houses with energy-saving design. It has set a target of building public and new residential buildings with designs that can reduce energy consumption by 50 percent. A stricter criterion of 65 percent has been set for buildings in municipalities directly under the Central Government and other appropriate regions. It has made efforts to transform existing buildings in an energy-saving style. It also promotes the development of energy-saving interior decorating materials.

The third is the transportation sector.

It is accelerating the development of railway and river transportation and prioritizes public transportation and rail traffic. It encourages research on energy-saving vehicles, while speeding up the elimination of obsolete autos, trains and ships. In the meantime, it also encourages research and popularization of alternative clean liquid fuel and vehicles that can use these fuels.

The fourth is the office and residential households. It promotes energy saving facilities and appliances in the public areas, hotels, shopping malls, office buildings and residential households.

The fifth target is the countryside. Replacements of high consumption agriculture equipment and fishing boats are being accelerated. Efforts are also been made to accelerate the upgrading of irrigation facilities. Utilization of marsh gas in rural households is promoted. Facilities are being established in medium and large breeding farms to produce marsh gas. Energy-saving stoves are also being promoted. Small hydropower plants, wind power plants and solar farms are built in suitable areas. The transportation network for marsh gas is also being promoted.

• The One-Watt Plan

The One-Watt Plan is a campaign launched by the International Energy Agency. It aims to propose to member countries' appliance manufacturers and sellers to reduce standby power to less than one watt per device by 2010.

At the first forum held in China on the plan, experts brief on the American 'Energy Star' program, jointly administered by the US Environmental Protection Agency and the Department of Energy. Consumers can identify qualifying products by an Energy Star logo. It saved more than US$12 billion worth of electricity, equivalent to the amount of power generated by one-and-a-half –type installations or more than 50 other hydropower plants. However, in China, only a few major cities have targeted standby power wastage. According to the China Quality Certification Center, daily average leakage of electricity from a Chinese household could light a bulb, from 15 to 30 watt, around the clock. It is a quiet way of energy consumption. In the color television sector, the standby loss level is three watts nowadays. If it could cover all the TV sets, from now to 2011, it could save China a total of six billion Yuan worth of electricity, or 12 billion kWh. A new level of one watt for the standby loss is expected to be reached on March 1, 2009.

• China Green Lights Project

This project focuses on popularizing highly-efficient lighting products and appliances in public areas, hotels, office buildings, stadiums, gyms and residential houses. Efforts are also made to build up the automatic production lines for such products. This project has attracted attention from all walks of life and wins support from the United Nations Development Program and the Global Environment Facility. Electricity used for lighting accounts for about 12 percent of the total. In that case, if one can replace incandescent bulbs with compact fluorescent tubes, able to save 60 to 80 percent of the electricity, energy can be saved by a large margin.

From 1996 to 2005, electricity totaling 59 billion kWh has been saved, which eases the pressure on the transmission system. It also meant that the emission of carbon dioxide and sulfur dioxide were cut by 17 million tons and 530,000 tons respectively.

The lighting products industry flourishes, with optimized product composition. The output of bulbs totaled 10 billion in 2005, first in the world. The proportion of fluorescent tubes to incandescent bulbs was 1 to 1.5 in 2005, compared to 1 to 6.25 in 1995. The export volume of lighting products has continued to grow, with an average annual increase of 20 percent to reach US$8 billion in 2005.

Key Projects for Energy Conservation

The Chinese Government is working on key programs as follows.

The first program focuses on upgrading industrial coal boilers. Efforts are being made to upgrade low-efficient industrial boilers and build centralized coal distribution and processing centers. The industrial boilers available now are being upgraded to an energy-saving level and some obsolete ones replaced.

The second program focuses on linking thermal power plants with other enterprises. The surplus thermal energy will mainly provide heating. It will also be utilized as an industrial heating and power source

The third program focuses on utilizing surplus thermal energy and voltage. Facilities are under construction in high-consuming enterprises such as steel producers, construction material makers and chemical engineering enterprises. They can generate electricity from surplus thermal energy and voltage, as well as recycle combustible gas and low-heat gas.

The fourth program focuses on saving oil and promoting substitutes. Facilities are being upgraded to save oil or use substitution for oil, in power plants, petroleum and petrochemical companies, construction material makers, chemical engineering enterprises and transportation businesses. Efforts are also made to develop coal-to-liquid, alcohol ether, bio-diesel and other alternative fuels.

The fifth program focuses on upgrading electrical machinery. Low-efficiency electrical machinery is being upgraded, as well as equipment links with them. Some medium to large size electrical machinery is being readjusted for higher operating speed.

The sixth program focuses on building up a more energy-saving production system in oil refineries, ethylene producers, synthetic ammonia producers and steel makers.

The seventh program focuses on building energy-saving buildings. New buildings are built according to a 50 percent energy-saving design. Buildings in Beijing, Shanghai, Chongqing and Tianjin, as well as in areas at higher latitude, follow the 65 percent energy saving design. All of them are built under strict supervision.

Activities to Save Energy

Some six provinces, autonomous regions and municipalities directly under the Central Government, including Shanghai and Gansu, have established their energy-saving supervision centers. In Zhejiang, Guangdong, Shangdong and other provinces, energy saving is a contributory factor in examining an official's work. Cities in Zhejiang Province have established energy-saving funds. The local governments of Shangdong, Liaoning and Shenzhen encourage and support the development of energy conservation services, so as to foster a new mechanism of offering related services based on contract. Beijing and Tianjing are implementing the new 65 percent energy-saving standard in construction sectors.

Every summer is the peak time of electricity consumption. In Shanghai,

Installing the solar water heater

♦ Economic Use of Water for the Olympic Venue

The National Aquatics Center, or the Water Cube, is the major water consumer among buildings for Olympic Games. Its water conservation thus arouses much public attention. To enable the water quality to meet the standards of the International Amateur Swimming Federation (FINA), its swimming pools adopt a two-stage filtration system—sand filtration and active carbon. The water will also be sterilized with ozone to help eliminate water's peculiar smell and irritation to human body.

The water is changed by an automatic controller, so as to increase the efficiency of the purifying system and cut consumption of chemicals and energy. In this way, the replenishment volume of water is reduced by 50 percent. In addition, the swimming pools and the swimming amusement parks are built with seepage-free concrete. Besides, other channels of water consumption are well arranged. Waste water from bathing houses is recycled. After a series of purifying courses, such as bio-contact oxidation, filtering, active carbon absorption and sterilization, it will be used to flush the lavatories and garage floor and irrigate the green belts. This method helps save 44,530 tons of water on an annual basis. To reduce the natural evaporation, the green belts are designed to be watered by micro-sprinklers during night, saving five percent of the water consumption.

electricity swallowed by air conditioning units covers 40 percent of its total consumption. According to schedule, the Seasonal Energy Efficiency Ratio (SEER) will reach 3.4 by 2010 in China, rising from the existing level of 2.6. However, Shanghai will only give the green light to manufacturers whose products meet the standard of 3.2 from next year.

In order to cut energy consumption per unit of GDP, Ningxia Hui Autonomous Region will shut down small thermal power plants with installed capacity of 500,000 kW or lower before 2008. Their generating capacity totals three million kW, which means one million tons of coal could be saved. Enterprises are forbidden to build their own power plants. Efforts have also been made to raise the efficiency of thermal plants. Liaoning Province has established a statistical and report system of the energy consumption per unit of GDP, with the aim of strengthening supervision of heavy energy users.

Activities to Save Water

China has taken following actions to save water resources. The government places emphasis on water conservation in rural areas, building rainfall reservoirs. Grass cultivation lands are built with water-saving irrigation systems. High water consumption industries including thermal power plants and metallurgical enterprises are working hard to upgrade their facilities to save water. In cities and towns, installation of water saving equipment is a must. Utility of recycled water is being popularized. Construction of water saving facilities in public areas and residential houses are strengthened. Sea water and water from mines are being utilized. Plans are also carried out to sea water desalination.

Raw Material Conservation

To save raw materials, the following methods have been adopted. The administration of key raw material consumers is strengthened. Technological norms of design, construction and production are strictly formulated, as well as the calculation method of material consumption. Recycled materials are increasingly put into use, raising the utilization ratio of raw material. Adoption of substitutes for wood is promoted, as well as other methods to conserve wood. The packaging of goods is being changed to meet public complaints about excessive packing. Bulk concrete is also promoted.

Using Land Resources in an Efficient Way

To properly use the land resources in an efficient and intensive way, China has adopted the following methods. The area quotas of buildings or infrastructure construction in cities have been readjusted. The system that gives approval to land use has been improved. Efforts are being made to transform land for other use into cultivatable land. Some pilot programs are being carried out for collective constructions in rural areas. It is strictly prohibited to use clay from cultivatable land for brick production. A list has been released of cities that are forbidden to use solid clay bricks. In the meantime, efforts are also being made to promote innovation of building materials.

Strengthening Comprehensive Utilization of Resources

To comprehensively use resources, China has adopted the following activities. It is working to comprehensively utilize associated resources in coal mines, especially gas. It is making efforts to efficiently recycle industrial waste, especially coal ash, coal gangue and organic waste water. It is promoting recycling of renewable resources, including metal, scrapped tires, waste agricultural plastic sheets, obsolete appliances and electronic products. It is actively making use of resources in domestic waste and straws.

• Law of the PRC on Conserving Energy

Thanks to the Law on Conserving Energy, in the past decade, energy consumption per unit of GDP has shrunk significantly. Based on the coal price in 2000, generating every 10,000 Yuan of GDP only consumed 1.43 tons of coal equivalent in 2005, compared to 1.56 tons in 1998. Because the energy consumption drops when producing the same volume of high consuming products, utilization of energy resources is more efficient.

In recent years, the National Development and Reform Commission and the All China Federation of Trade Unions have staged an annual week-long publicity campaign about energy saving. In the meantime, a series of law and regulations, such as the Energy Conservation Management Measures on Key Energy Consumers, the Management Measures on Saving Electricity, the Provisions on the Administration of Energy Conservation for Civil Buildings and the Management Measures on Energy Saving Product Certification were implemented by the National Development and Reform Commission, the Ministry of Construction and the General Administration of Quality Supervision, Inspection and Quarantine. In addition, some medium and long-term plans have been mapped out. Key energy conservation sectors are identified, such as manufacturing and construction, and 10 major energy saving programs are being carried out. Moreover, there are another 70-plus local regulations and rules enacted by more than 20 provinces, autonomous regions and municipalities directly under the Central Government.

♦ Provisions on the Administration of Energy Conservation for Civil Buildings

The Provisions on the Administration of Energy Conservation for Civil Buildings took effect on January 1, 2006. The following actions are included. In the course of planning, design, construction and use of the civil buildings, new materials should be adopted to build the walls, so as to reach the relevant energy-saving standard. Energy consuming facilities should be strictly administered. The enclosure structure should be properly designed for thermal conservation. Heating, refrigeration, lighting, ventilation, water supply, sewage release and channel systems should be upgraded for greater efficiency. Renewable resources should be recycled. While ensuring practical and thermal demands, energy consumption should be cut to a reasonable level.

The government promotes development of following technologies and products:

Technologies and materials that can help build walls and interior surfaces with good thermal insulation properties;

Technologies that can produce windows and doors with good thermal insulation and hermetic properties;

Technologies that combine heating supply with electricity supply and refrigeration, as well as technologies that centralize heating supply;

Technologies and facilities that can control the temperature of the heating system and determine and control thermal conditions in every household.

Technologies and facilities that help utilize solar and geothermal energy;

Energy-saving technologies and products that are utilized in lighting system of construction sites;

Energy-saving technologies and products of air conditioning;

Other technologies and management models with good energy-saving effects.

Strengthened Comprehensive Consumption of Wood Resources

China is relatively poor in forest resources. Its per-capita forest area stands at only 0.132 hectares, which ranking 134th in the world and less than one-quarter of the world average. The per-capita forest capacity is 9.421 cubic meters, ranking 122nd, less than one sixth of the world average. With growing consumption, the gap between supply and demand is widening. It is estimated to reach 140 to 150 million cubic meters by 2015. At present, there are three solutions to narrow the gap—well arranged consumption with proper import, forestation and utilization of wood substitutes.

Wood Saving and Substitution

This refers to rational utilization, protection and recycling of timber and wood products, as well as adopting wood substitutes, in the course of production, circulation, use and other socio-economic activities. It aims to reasonably use wood resources, ease the contradiction between wood supply and demand in China, meet people's needs, protect the forest eco-system and enable people to live in harmony with nature. The government makes efforts to promote the production and use of wood substitutes, limits the use and production of disposable wood products and packing, including excessive wood packing of food, beverages and wines. The utilization of wood resources should be carried out based on protection of the eco-environment.

According to schedule, China will issue a series of laws, regulations and policies for wood saving and adoption of wood substitutes before 2010. Relevant service centers will also be established. All these activities aim to help produce and use wood products or wood substitute products in an efficient and environmentally friendly way. The utilization ratio of wood is expected to top 65 percent and antiseptic treatment cover five percent of total wood output. These efforts will cut the wood consumption by 40-50 million cubic meters on an annual basis, an effective method to narrow the gap between supply and demand.

Seawater Utilization

China's coastal area, particularly the northern coast, is seeing a prominent imbalance between supply and demand of fresh water, and is one of the places suffering from the severest water shortage in the country. At the same time, most of the over 6500 islands larger than 500 square meter in China are not suitable for living and cannot be exploited due to fresh water scarcity.

After more than 40 years' development, China's technology for using seawater has basically matured; the condition of industrialization in this regard is in readiness. This is concretely manifested in following aspects:

Major breakthroughs have been made in key technologies for seawater desalination such as reverse osmosis desalination and distillation. China has completed the Low Temperature and Multiple Effect Seawater Desalination Project with a production capacity of 3,000 cubic meters per day and the Seawater Reverse Osmosis Desalination Project with a production capacity of 5000 cubic meter per day. China owns the intellectual property rights to the two projects. And a demonstration project to achieve 10,000 cubic meters of desalinated seawater per day is being carried out. This shows China has already mastered the technologies for industrialization of seawater desalination.

Seawater once-through cooling technology has been broadly applied, while the seawater cyclic cooling technology is at the industrialization demonstration stage for producing 10,000 cubic meter or over per day. Some related indexes (like corrosion of carbon steel in the use of seawater) have reached advanced world level. Some thermal power plants in coastal areas begin to adopt the technology for seawater desulphurization.

Much progress has been made in the technology for comprehensively utilizing chemical resources in seawater. The sea salt production technology is applied widely. At the same time, intermediate experiments of extracting magnesium, bromine and kalium from seawater with the output of hundreds of tons or thousands of tons have been completed.

A considerable quantity of seawater has been used directly as industrial cooling water by thermal and nuclear power plants. In 2003, 33 billion cubic meter seawater was used in China, and most of the users are the power, petrochemical and chemical industries and so on, with some 90 percent of the total national amount being used by power enterprises.

Seawater desalination is expanding. The capacity for present enterprises reaches 31,000 cubic meter per day. The projects being built and to be built are expected to produce 381,000 cubic meter each day.

The cost of seawater desalination has dropped rapidly. The cost of the main equipment has fallen by nearly 50 percent compared to ten years ago. And that of one ton of desalinated seawater has dropped to about five Yuan.

Sea salt production, a Chinese traditional industry of comprehensively utilizing chemical resources in seawater, has achieved output of 18 million tons a year.

♦ Resource-Saving Enterprises: the China National Building Material Group Corporation (CNBM) and the China National Materials Industry Group

The two enterprises have successfully developed the core technologies which top the national or international level in such fields as float glass, new type non-slurry cement, new building materials, fiberglass, building ceramic and sanitary ware, refractory materials, quartz glass, special concrete, special concrete admixture and composite materials. They own self-dominant intellectual property right (IPR) to these technologies. Of them, the 900t/d ultra large energy-saving floating glass processing line held by CNBM is the largest in the world, and CNBM has the complete IPR. The line adopts the advanced thermal insulation structure and technology. Its technical indices like energy conservation and melting of floating glass melting furnace reach the international advanced level. Energy consumption of the line is 15-20 percent lower than that of domestic 600t/d floating glass processing line; the oxy-fuel firing technology for large alkali-free fiberglass melting kilns, unprecedented in China, enables energy consumption of melting to reach the advanced level in the world. The paper-cover gypsum board project with annual production capacity of 30 million square meters uses 100 percent of industrial wastes as its raw materials, consuming 300,000 tons of industrial gypsum wastes every year. The China Academy of Building Research which has made important achievements in fields like energy saving in architecture, renewable resources, green building and green building materials, plays an important role in energy saving in architecture for the whole society.

China Building Materials Group
Website: http://www.cnbm.com.cn/index.asp
China National Materials Industry Group
Website: http://www.sinoma.cn/

♦ Energy-Saving Enterprise: China Huaneng Group

As one of the largest electricity groups, China Huaneng Group, adopting advanced technologies which are highly-efficient, energy-saving and environmental-friendly, has set many "firsts" in terms of production and technology: the first to introduce the 600 MW supercritical coal-fired generating unit from abroad so as to improve China's technology of thermal generating units in an all-round way; the first to import a complete set of equipment and environmental protection technologies of flue gas desulphurization for large-sized thermal power plants, and installed the earliest and largest equipment of wet flue gas desulphurization in China; the first to use city reclaimed water as makeup water for the cooling water system of its power plants so as to play an exemplary role in water-saving practice in the electricity industry and in advancing the circular economy; the first to introduce the advanced wet bottom boiler and the fly ash re-burning technology from abroad so as to raise the boiler combustion efficiency and the comprehensive use rate of ash and dregs; the first to install the home-made 1 000 MW ultra-supercritical coal-fired generating units, and build the biggest seawater desalination system across the country at the same time. Thanks to technological progress, China Huaneng Group has reached the most advanced level in terms of coal consumption and pollutant discharge among its domestic counterparts.

Website: http://www.chng.com.cn

♦ Energy-Saving Enterprise: Baosteel Group

Baosteel Group, one of the first groups of environmental-friendly enterprises, set a world record in pulverized coal injection (PCI) for blast furnaces, and achieved a water recycling rate of 98 percent. At the same time, it has achieved zero-discharge for coal gas of blast furnaces, converters and coke furnaces, which are all recycled and reused. Baosteel is the first enterprise to release the Annual Environmental Report; furthermore, it also took the lead in releasing the Annual Sustainable Development Report, accepting the supervision of society. In recent years, Baosteel, as a member of the Convention for Construction of Sustainable Development of the Global Economic Alliance, has been making every effort to comprehensively use resources, save energy and reduce consumption to change the image of "high investment, high consumption and severe pollution".

In the workshop of the Shanghai Baosteel Group Corporation

When developing new steel products, it tries to enable downstream users to save resources. At present, the enterprise is working hard to tackle the problem of light-weight automobile steel plate. Through improving the strength of steel sheet and making it thinner to reduce automobile weight, Baosteel expects to finally achieve resource conservation in the automobile industry. In addition, it keeps on developing high efficient steel to cut down unit steel use and prolong its life in an effort to reduce resource consumption of society.

Website: http://www.baosteel.com/

♦ UNIDO International Solar Energy Center for Technology Promotion and Transfer (ISEC-UNIDO)

Solar energy is an important renewable resource. Developing and utilizing solar energy is the radical way for humans to solve the energy problem. The Gansu Natural Energy Research Institute (GNETI), founded in 1978, is a professional research institution devoted to the study and application of solar energy. GNETI has developed a series of solar energy products including solar house, solar cooker, solar water heater and solar drier. In addition, it has set up the Solar Energy Heating and Cooling Technology Experiment and Demonstration Center, the biggest in Asia, and trained over 10,000 people across China in solar energy techniques and more than 600 solar energy talents for 76 developing countries. At the same time, the Institute has actively contributed to the spread and application of techniques in Chinese rural areas.

On March 26, 2006, the United Nations Industrial Development Organization (UNIDO) decided to establish the UNIDO International Solar Energy Center for Technology Promotion and Transfer (ISEC-UNIDO), with GNETI. The move is to help developing countries promote their capability to study solar energy techniques and to produce and apply solar energy products and equipments, to provide personnel training and to take the application and spread of the technique as the major measure to eliminate poverty.

Website:http://www.gneri.org

♦ China Energy Conservation Investment Corporation

China Energy-Saving Investment Corporation, a central enterprise under the State-owned Assets Regulatory Commission of the State Council, is the only state investment corporation in the field of energy saving and environmental protection. The Corporation is devoted to the long-term development of energy-saving and environmental-protection cause in China. CECIC has been making efforts to provide quality public production and services in terms of energy saving and environmental protection. The company sees its task as leading the industrial upgrade of energy saving and environmental protection in China, contributing to and creating value for the Chinese socio-economic sustainable development". Through developing new energies represented by wind power, the company set up energy-saving power plants which can comprehensively utilize resources, like refuse incineration power plant and gangue power plant. CECIC also entered such fields as gas utilization, urban sewage disposal, energy-saving building materials (like new wall materials), green lights and energy saving lamps. At present, the company can save annually 1.3 million tons of coal, reduce carbon dioxide emissions by 300,000 tons per year, dispose of 3.85 million tons of sewage and 1,000 tons of wastes every day. By 2008, the Corporation's capacity in the regard is expected to be improved to a higher level: saving 6.6 million tons of coal annually, reducing carbon dioxide emission of 1 million tons per year, disposing of 6.66 million tons of sewage and 25,000 tons of wastes every day.

Website: http://www.cecic.com.cn

Special Planning of Seawater Utilization

Regional distribution and the key projects concerning the use of seawater during the 11th Five-Year Plan period (2006-2010) have been established. According to this, by 2010, the capacity of seawater desalination is expected to reach 800,000 to 1 million cubic meter per day, and the capacity of direct use of seawater 55 billion cubic meter per year; the nation will actively promote comprehensive use of chemical resources in seawater and make it possible that the contribution rate of seawater utilization to solving the water shortage problems in China's coastal area can reach 16-24 percent. In addition, a number of relatively large-scale demonstration projects in terms of industrialization of seawater desalination and seawater cyclic cooling will be built and put into operation; the technology and equipment will be upgraded continually so as to make the localization rate of equipment for seawater utilization surpass 60 percent. Rules and regulations concerning standards on use of sea water, policy-supporting system, technical service system and supervision system of the use of seawater will take shape and China's use of seawater will join the international competition gradually.

By 2020, the capacity of seawater desalination is expected to reach 2.5 million-3 million cubic meters per day, and the capacity of direct use of seawater 100 billion cubic meters per year. Much progress will be achieved in comprehensive utilization of seawater chemical resources; the contribution rate of seawater utilization to the fight against water shortage in China coastal areas is to reach 26-37 percent. Furthermore, the large-scale industrialization of seawater desalting will be achieved, and the localization rate of equipment for seawater utilization will surpass 90 percent, and some large-scale seawater desalting projects with an output of 200,000-500,000 cubic meters per day will be set up. Consequently, China will realize leap-forward development in the industry and establish a relatively advanced macro-control system as well as an operational mechanism in this regard.

Nuclear and Radiation Environment

In the 10th Five-Year Plan(2001-2005), the government vigorously strengthened the work concerning emergency responses to nuclear and radiation accidents. The State Council approved and promulgated the National Emergency Plan for Environmental Accidents; the State Environmental Protection Administration of China (SEPA) issued the Scheme of the State Environmental Protection Administration of China for Emergency Response to Nuclear and Radiation Accidents and the Scheme for Dealing With Terrorist Nuclear Attacks and Radiation and so on; a number of projects aiming at improving the capacity of emergency response are being built. All these combine to enhance the monitoring and control capacity in case of nuclear and radiation accidents in an all-round way.

A relatively mature legal environment, a unified and coordinated administration system and the stringent and effective supervision combine to effectively ensure the safety of the nuclear and radiation environment. All the nuclear power plants in operation have never been suffered any nuclear accidents of grade III and above, and the waste discharge index stays below the national standard. Radiation monitoring statistics over many years show that radiation in the air, surface water, underground water and soil stays within the natural fluctuating range as a whole.

The government also attaches great importance to international cooperation in supervision and management of the nuclear environment. In 1999, it ratified the Convention on Nuclear Safety. China has taken part in three activities in accordance with the corresponding provision and submitted reports. As far as the supervision and management of radioactive sources concerned, the government has made a solemn promise to the international community that it would abide by the Code of Conduct on the Safety and Safety of Radioactive Sources issued by the International Atomic Energy Agency.

Laws and Regulations on Nuclear Safety and Radiation Environment

On December 1, 2005, the Regulations for Safety and Protection Concerning Radio-Isotopes and Radiation-Emitting Apparatus was put into effect. And on March 1, 2006, the Licensed Management Methods for Safety of Radioactive Isotopic Elements and Ray Devices was put into effect.

The two are only small part of all the regulations of China in this regard. The government, with the aim of ensuring the safety of the nuclear and radiation environment, has formulated and promulgated many administrative regulations and department rules, guidance and technical documents, which are about nuclear facility safety, management of radioactive wastes, control of nuclear materials, supervision and management of civil nuclear pressure-resistant equipments, management of radioactive substances transport and application of nuclear technology. They include four administrative regulations, over 30 rules, 70-odd guides and more than 180 technical documents issued by supervision departments of nuclear safety and other related departments. The Law of the PRC on the Prevention and Control of Radioactive Pollution went into effect on October 1, 2003.

♦ Law of the PRC on the Prevention and Control of Radioactive Pollution

The Law of the PRC on the Prevention and Control of Radioactive Pollution went to force on October 1, 2003. It deals with the prevention and control of radioactive pollution in the cause of site-selection, building, operation and retirement of nuclear facilities, and while developing and applying nuclear techniques and exploiting uranium (thorium) mines and mines associated with radioactivity within the territory of the PRC and other sea areas under her jurisdiction. Other related laws and regulations include the Regulation of Safety and Protection for Radioisotopes and Ray Instruments and the Safety Regulations for Dangerous Chemical Goods.

Nuclear Safety and Radiation Environment Monitored and Controlled According to the Law

While strengthening the legal system, the government has actively integrated the functions of related fields and established monitoring and control system for nuclear safety and radiation environment so as to achieve the integrative management of nuclear safety, the radiation environment and radioactive sources. The National Nuclear Safety Administration, part of SEPA, actively exercises overall and integrative supervision and management of nuclear installations, radiation sources, uranium mines, mines associated with radioactivity and radioactive wastes. SEPA has also established six representative offices in areas with nuclear installations. In addition, the environmental protection departments at provincial level have also set up organs responsible for supervising radiation environment safety. The nuclear safety engineer qualification certification system is initiated to enhance the talent training and introduction for nuclear safety technical backup units. At present, there are about 1,300 people engaged in nuclear and radiation safety supervision.

The No.1 Unit of the Tianwan Nuclear Power Plant in Lian Yungang, Jiangsu Province

As for the supervision of nuclear installation safety, China adopts general international practices and carries out the strict safety license system. In the 10th Five-Year Plan, under the guideline of "safety and quality first", the government fulfilled the goal of "keeping work staff, the public and the environment from being exposed to radiation that is beyond the limits set, and minimizing radiation and its pollution as long as possible". In last decade, China has set up seven nuclear power plants with 15 generating units. During the same period, the capacity of China's nuclear safety supervision saw continuous improvement with the deepening of the work in this regard. As a result, the safe operation of nuclear installations in service is achieved, and the construction quality of ones being built effectively controlled.

Monitoring Network of Radiation Environment

The Chinese Government pays great attention to strengthen the construction of a monitoring network of radiation environment. The project of "National Radiation Environmental Monitoring Network, Emergency Response Technical Center for Nuclear and Radiation Accidents and Radiation Environment Monitoring Technical Center" was basically completed. Thirty-one grade I monitoring sites (in provinces, municipalities directly under the Central Government and autonomous regions) an3/1/2007d two grade monitoring sites (in Baotou and Qingdao) have taken shape, with the equipment basically installed; 24 provinces have monitored routinely the quality of the radiation environment in their key cities; the initial design for the project of building, rebuilding and enlarging urban radioactive waste storages across the country has been completed; the special action on prevention and control of radioactive contamination of uranium mining and metallurgy has been conducted in 14 provinces and autonomous regions. As a result, the monitoring network of radiation environment in China has basically achieved the overall goal of computerized management, standardized technology and methods, modernized equipment and systematic guarantee for quality control. On such a basis, radioactive sources which are discarded or left unused are stored safely.

National Environmental Protection Standards System

National-level environmental protection standards include environmental quality standards, pollutant discharge (control) standards, and standards for certified environmental reference materials, and so on. Local environmental protection standards include environmental quality standards and pollutant discharge standards. In 1973, China promulgated the first national environmental protection standard: the Discharge Standards of Waste Gas, Waste Water and Solid Wastes. By the end of 2005, the State had promulgated 841 national environmental protection standards. The municipalities of Beijing and Shanghai, and the provinces of Shandong and Henan had promulgated over 30 local environmental protection standards.

As for environmental quality standards, the state revised the Environmental Quality Standard for Surface Water; in terms of discharge standards, the state promulgated some important standards for thermal power plants, cement industry, brewing industry, hospital waste disposal, hospital sewage, city sewage, vehicle emission control; as far as technical criteria for environmental protection management is concerned, it formulated a series of environmental impact assessment guidelines, environmental monitoring method standards and technical specification for environmental monitoring, technical specification for environmental engineering and cleaner production standard.

Of the present national environmental protection standards, there are 16 environmental quality standards concerning air, water, soil, noise and vibration, 84 discharge (control) standards for water pollutant, air pollutant, noise and solid waste pollution control, and 251 national certified environmental reference materials of such kinds as water, air, soil and biomass. Additionally, the national standards also include 490 occupational standards and others in terms of prevention and control of nuclear radiation and electromagnetic radiation pollution, measures for monitoring environmental pollutants and dangerous substances, basic criteria for environmental protection, supervision and management of construction projects, cleaner production, products with environmental symbol, environmental-friendly products, technique and policy of preventing and controlling pollution and so on.

Environmental Impact Assessment

Environmental Impact Assessment (EIA) is a legal measure to curb environmental pollution and ecological destruction at source. In 1998, the government promulgated the Regulations on Environmental Management of Construction Projects, which put forth the idea of environmental impact assessment, and required construction projects to design, construct and put into use relevant environmental protection facilities along with the progress of the project itself ("three simultaneousnesses" for short). The Law of the PRC on Environmental Impact Assessment, which came into effect in 2003, extends the EIA practice from construction projects to all development construction plans. The State has also adopted the EIA engineer professional qualification certification system to foster a contingent of professional technicians in this field.

Active Prevention of Environmental Accidents

In 2005, the Chinese Government formulated the National Emergency Plan for Environmental Accidents. And the explicit requirements were brought forward in terms of the receiving, reporting, processing and analyzing of the information about environmental accidents, the alert information monitoring and the accident information release. The State has made nine related environmental emergency plans concerning key drainage areas and sensitive water areas, air, dangerous chemicals (discarded chemicals), nuclear and radiation. At the same time, some emergency plans for environmental accidents had been made and revised including the Emergency Plan for Water Environment in the Sensitive Part of the Yellow River, the Scheme for Dealing With Terrorist Chemical Attacks, the Scheme for Dealing With Terrorist Nuclear Attacks and Radiation, the Emergency Plan for Agricultural Pollution Accidents and the Emergency Plan for the Agricultural Accidents Concerning Major Harmful Living Things and the Invasion of Exotic Pests. In recent years, China has conducted environmental risk checks on 127 key chemical and petrochemical projects distributed in some environmental sensitive areas like areas along rivers, populous regions and natural reserves. China has also conducted overall checks on nearly 50,000 key enterprises.

♦ Nuclear and Radiation Safety Center, MEP

The Nuclear and Radiation Safety Center of MEP was founded in March, 1989. It is the only non-profit public service unit in China engaged in applying the technical safeguards to supervision and management of nuclear and radiation safety. It is charged with the task of providing technical support and safeguards for MEP to independently supervise civil nuclear facilities and radiation-related organizations in the country.

Website: http://www.chinansc.cn/index/index.htm

Management of Industrial Hazardous Wastes

China follows the system of whole-process supervision of industrial hazardous wastes. In 2003, the National Construction Planning for Hazardous Wastes and Medical Wastes Disposal Facilities came into effect. This strengthened various systems including the industrial hazardous waste manifest system and the hazardous waste operation permits system. Solid Wastes Management Centers have been set up in 31 provinces, autonomous regions and municipalities directly under the Central Government.

Environmental Laws and Regulations

Environmental laws rose from six to nine; natural resources laws increased from 10 to 15; administrative regulations on environmental protection climbed from 30 to 50; departmental rules and documents with similar power to laws and regulations surpassed 200; the local environmental rules and regulations promulgated by the local people's congresses and local governments at all levels hit over 1600. All this has happened within the last five years. Environmental protection has increasingly become a legal adjustment lever to the social-economic sustainable development.

Cleaner Production Promotion Law

In June, 2002, China enacted the Cleaner Production Promotion Law, its first law on the cyclical economy. As an environmental law for individual project, it calls on governments at various levels, relevant departments and production and service enterprises to promote and carry out clean production. This marked the beginning not only for the legislation of China's cyclical economy but also for environmental protection in accordance with the law. Clean production shows the

The Qinghai-Tibet Railway (the Golmud-Lhasa Section). A Tibetan woman watches the rail paving in Dung-dkar Village, Lhasa.

♦ Environmental Impact Assessment of the Qinghai-Tibet Railway

EIA of the Qinghai-Tibet Railway is the most special, complicated and the highest standard in Chinese railway history. The impact of the Golmud-Lhasa Section of the Qinghai-Tibet Railway was assessed on the principle of "prevention first, priority on protection, equal importance on development and protection, design conducted alongside with environmental assessment, and environmental management". In the course of the assessment, many plans of the route crossing nature reserves including Hoh Xil, the Chumaerhe River and Suojia were put forward and compared in an effort to minimize interference. While designing bridges and tunnels, the needs of wild animals to cross the railway were fully considered, with 33 wild animal passageways specially added. In order to ensure that wild animals like the Tibetan antelope could get easily across the railway, SEPA, in cooperation with the Qinghai-Tibet Railway Leading Group Office, the State Forestry Administration and the Ministry of Railways and so on, enhanced the tracing and monitoring of the animals using the passageways so as to offer improved solutions in time. For protecting wetlands, it was required to avoid them as much as possible when selecting the route, materials and dump sites. If it was not possible to avoid one, a bridge/aqueduct was the preferred choice. At the same time, the influence on surface runoffs caused by the railway was fully considered. Bridges and culverts were built to enable surface runoffs to supply water to the wetlands.

Data provided by the Shaanxi Institute of Zoology showed 2,911 Tibetan antelopes, who enjoy national first grade protected status, crossed the railway via the passageways in Hoh Xil from June to August, 2004, and 3,450 in 2005; the number rose again in 2006.

15 Environmental Protection

significant change in the pattern of China's pollution treatment from control of the end result to control of the whole process; meanwhile, it also introduces a new legislative concept guiding the industrial structure, product structure and energy structure to be more environment-friendly. Hence, China's environmental legislation further embodies the requirements of sustainable development.

Environmental Impact Assessment Law

When the Environmental Impact Assessment Law was adopted by the Standing Committee of the National People's Congress in October of 2002, the planned environmental impact assessment (EIA) was unveiled. Compared with the micro-EIA, the planned EIA offers a scientific evaluation of the bearing capacity of the planned environmental resources and participates in the major exploitation activities in the regions, drainage areas and sea areas, the distribution of productive forces and resources allocation. It takes society, environment and economy as a whole into consideration so as to bring the scale of the regional economic development under the bearing capacity of the eco-environment. Undoubtedly, the planned EIA plays the most important role when environmental protection is considered into the regional socio-economic development planning.

Catalogue of Toxic Chemicals China Bans or Strictly Restricts

In June of 2005, SEPA and the General Administration of Customs jointly released the Catalogue of Toxic Chemicals under Prohibition or Strict Restriction in China (Batch II), including 7 types of toxic chemicals with potential serious environmental damage into the environmental management of the import and export of toxic chemicals. The Catalogue was then put into effect from July 10th. In December of 2005, the two ministries jointly released the Catalogue of Toxic Chemicals under Strict Restriction in China, pushing the total number of toxic chemicals under relevant environmental protection registration up to 188. This Catalogue was released from January 1st in 2006. In December of 2005, the SEPA, Ministry of Commerce and General Administration of Customs jointly released the Catalogue of Goods Prohibited for Import (Batch VI) and the Catalogue of Goods Prohibited for Export (Batch III), including 20 types of toxic chemicals eliminated and banned by international conventions into the inventory of banned goods for import and export. This Catalogue was put into effect from January 1st of 2006.

Law of the PRC on the Prevention and Control of Environmental Pollution by Solid Waste

On 29th December, 2004, the Law of the PRC on the Prevention and Control of Environmental Pollution by Solid Waste (hereinafter referred to as the Solid Waste Law) was revised. Article 5 of the law stipulates that producers, sellers, importers and users are responsible for the prevention and control of environmental pollution caused by their own pollutant discharges according to law.

In the Solid Waste Law, there are also clear provisions for those prohibited from import, the procedures of examination and approval of imports, category management, environmental standards, inspection and quarantine, as well as the punishment, etc. Based on the Solid Waste Law, China mapped out the Regulations on Waste Imports for Environmental Protection and Management (Temporary) and released the List of Waste Used as Raw Materials under Automatic Import License Category and the List of Waste Used as Raw Materials. Wastes, which are not on the two lists, will be forbidden for import. Moreover, SEPA, teaming up with the General Administration of Quality Supervision, Inspection and Quarantine, formulated the Environmental Protection Control Standard for Imported Solid Wastes as Raw Materials. As China conducts strict management of the import and export of wastes, no overseas report on pollution resulting from China's waste export has occurred. However, China still suffers from pollution caused by illegal import of wastes. Some domestic and foreign enterprises illegally transfer wastes to China in the name of the import of waste and old resources, resulting in severe environmental pollution.

Laws and Regulations for Prevention and Control of Hazardous Wastes

China has promulgated the Regulations on the Administration of Medical Wastes, Measures on Permit for Operation of Hazardous Wastes, Measures on the Management of Duplicated Form for Transferring Hazardous Wastes, etc. It uses these to manage hazardous wastes from beginning to the end and practices the operational license system for those engaged in the collection, storage and disposal of the hazardous wastes.

Regulations on Environmental Protection for Local Areas

The Regulations of Jiangsu Province on Prevention and Control of Yangtze River

China's Regulations on Management Over Collection and Use of Pollution Fees went into force on July 1, 2003. The Regulations stipulate that those who create excessive noise shall pay pollution fees.

Water Pollution was released at the end of 2005. According to this, two responsibility systems will be established in the Yangtze River basin, and they will be listed as one of the environmental protection responsibility goals for the local government in its term of office. One system is for the surface water quality in the environmental functional areas to meet the set standards; the other is for the water quality of the water body which serves as the boundary not only for administrative divisions but also for the upper and lower reaches of Yangtze River. If the gross amount of key water pollutant discharge exceeds the set standard due to ineffective control, the local government will be held responsible. The Regulations of Shanghai Municipality of Environmental Protection, revised in 2005, added the new rules such as the time limits for treatment and the standards of pollutant discharges during the treatment period. In addition, according to this Regulation, those units, whose pollutant discharge did not meet the requirement of the standard, will be limited or stopped production by the relevant environmental protection agencies. Given the requirement of the enforcement of the environmental laws, Fujian, Guangdong and other areas, by the local legislation, formulated some coercive administrative measures, including sealing up and temporarily detaining the illegal commodities.

At the same time, all the province-level areas worked out the administrative penalties for the environmental violations and began to set up administrative responsibility system for environmental protection; awarding system for report on violations of the law on environmental protection is becoming the rule of laws or regulations; and social supervision mechanism for environmental protection is being put in place. When the modes and systems of environmental management improve, and some even have been written into the laws and regulations, China is likely to solve the problem of "low cost for violating the law but high cost for obeying and enforcing" by legislation.

More Effective Measures Taken to Implement the Law on Environmental Protection

China has constantly strengthened checks on the enforcement of environmental legislation, and improved administrative law enforcement. In recent years, the State has conducted checks on the enforcement of laws on environmental protection, and the prevention and control of air pollution, water pollution and solid waste pollution, so as to push forward pollution control in key areas. China's criminal law has special provisions on destruction of environmental resources. The State has promulgated the Interim Regulations on the Punishment of Violations of Environmental Protection Laws or Disciplines, and put in place a responsibility system of administrative law enforcement in the area of environmental protection. For three years in a row, the State has launched special environmental protection campaigns to rectify enterprises that have discharged pollutants in violation of the law and to protect people's health. It has dealt with tens of thousands of environmental law violation cases, and had 16,000 enterprises closed down for having discharged pollutants in violation of the law. More than 10,000 warnings have been issued to environment polluters, obliging them to remedy the problems under government supervision. The State has also conducted special checks on the enforcement of laws regarding mining areas eco-environmental protection and maritime environmental protection, and has dealt with a number of law violations.

♦ Export Policies for Environmental Protection Purpose

In recent years, China has witnessed overheated investment in some high energy-consumption, high pollution and resource-intensive industries. The export of their products has soared. This imposes great pressure on energy, the environment and resources and exerts a negative impact on healthy and stable economic development. Given these facts, the relevant departments employed a series of measures to curtail production capacity gluts, conducting effective consumption control, and at the same time adjusting the corresponding export policies so as to rein in the surging exports of the resource-intensive products that also caused pollution. At present, the policies mainly focus on adjusting the export tax rebates, stopping the processing trade and imposing temporary export taxes on some products. Some 200 varieties of products in more than 30 sectors are included.

Forestation

The Chinese government has set a guideline focusing on ecological construction for the development of forestry, organized large-scale afforestation, strengthened the administration of forest resources, and initiated the compensation system for efforts made to achieve forest ecological efficiency. As a result, the total newly afforested area has reached over 6.67 million hectares every year since 2002. Presently, China has 53.84 million hectares of reserved man-made forest ranking the first in the world. In recent years, although many countries in the world have seen a decline in the forest resources, the total forest area and the amount of forest reserves in China have increased rapidly; the structures in terms of age of stand and the form of forest have become more rationalized, and the quality of forests is improving, achieving a historic turn from a downward to an upward trend. At present, the national forest acreage is 175 million hectares; the forest cover, 18.21 percent; and forest reserves, 12.456 billion cubic meters. The State has given great attention to ecological forest construction. China thus was listed as one of the 15 countries preserving the most area of forests by the UNEP. According to the Research Report on China's Sustainable Development Strategy on Forestry, by 2050, the forest coverage rate is expected to reach 28 percent, with an added area of 110 million hectares of planted forest.

The bird's eye view of the newly-complete forestation project along the Yellow River in spring.

♦ Nationwide Tree-planting Campaign on a Voluntary Basis

China launched the nationwide tree-planting campaign on a voluntary basis many years ago. From the heads of the Central Government, Government's Ministers, Generals of the PLA and the local leaders at various levels to the ordinary people from all walks of life, they always actively take part in the campaign every year. The voluntary tree-planting bases can be found throughout the country and the voluntary tree-planting forms are diversifying, such as planting commemorative trees and forests, building green land according to contract signed, protecting old and rare trees and voluntarily publicizing the forestation campaign. According to statistics, 540 million person-times participated in the voluntary tree-planting activities, with 2.23 billion of newly-planted trees.

Converting Cultivated Land to Forest

The projects of converting farmland to forest is so far the most heavily funded ecological construction project having the strongest policy support, widest-ranging coverage and highest level of participation by the people. It has covered 120 million farmers from over 30 million rural households of more than 1,800 counties in 25 provinces (autonomous regions and the Xinjiang Production and Construction Corps.

Converting farmland to forest is a strategic measure in fundamentally control eroded land and maintain a balanced eco-environment. After the 1998 catastrophic floods in the Yangtze River, Songhuajiang River and Nengjiang River drainage areas, the State Council made the important decision to implement the return of cultivated land to forest starting in 2002. As the practice proved, this project has helped the engineering areas alleviate the degrees of desertification and dust storms by a large margin with a big reduction in the mud flowing into the rivers. Undoubtedly, the returning-farmland-to-forest project is playing a major role in improving the eco-environment and keeping the ecological balance.

The implementation of returning cultivated land to forest extends the coverage of the forestry industry and accelerates the process of greening. The forestation area brought about by the Grain to Green Project takes up more than 60 percent of the national total, while, in many western areas, this proportion is as high as 90 percent or more. If all the cultivated land which has been reforested can successfully turn into forested area, the national forest cover will be over 2 percentage points higher than before.

Natural Forest Conservation Project

Another effective measure of forest protection is the natural forest conservation program, which started in 1998. The program stipulated a nationwide ban on the felling of trees in natural forests. In many areas, the woodchoppers of the past have become today's forest rangers. The natural forest protection project succeeded in securing eight million hectares of public forest for ecological benefits, enabling 93.33 million hectares of forest resources to recover.

Since the Natural Forest Protection Project was implemented in the Greater Higgnan Mountains in 2000, which restricts felling of trees there, the forest coverage rate increases year by year.

Forest Health

A healthy forest, covering the whole forest ecosystem, should have the ability to sustain itself ecologically and perform its multi-service functions in the best way. A healthy forest ecosystem can not only maintain its biodiversity and sustainability, but also satisfy human needs for forests in terms of ecology, society and economy. In terms of the stage development of the forestry industry, a healthy forest can help the forestry industry achieve a transition from a timber-offering sector into a multi-functional one and then toward one that can develop in a sustainable way. This is a prerequisite for China's forestry industry to carry out its development strategy focusing on ecological construction and accomplish the shift from a quantity-oriented one to a quality-oriented one.

Majiang Demonstration Area in Guizhou

This is a demonstration project of China's forest health program involving natural secondary forest and a closed forest area covering 3312.50 hectares; of this, 1888.53 hectares are for forest land-use. The forest coverage rate is 44.31 percent. Great efforts are being made in facilitating the growing of young and medium-age trees on sealed mountains, tending and thinning of the pinus massoniana forest by aerial seeding and cultivating forest mingling broad-leaved and coniferous trees. On forest health side, there is monitoring, prevention, control, inspection and quarantine of diseases and pests and the study of operational technology for forest health. By the thinning of forest, weak trees are removed and the sound preserved. Thus, the standing forest can obtain enhanced ability to resist disease-pest attack, strengthened sustainability and faster growth.

Xinfeng Demonstration Area in Jiangxi

With a total area of 1617.1 hectares, it is mainly aimed at improving the low-benefit coniferous forests and finding a better operational mode for the village-owned forest farm. In addition, lots of work is being done to enhance disease-pest forecasting and actively developing effective measures by ecological, physical, chemical and artificial means to prevent and control forest diseases and pests. Work is also being done on greening the villages, building methane-generating pits and fuel-saving stoves. Industries with unique local characteristics should be given priority to develop, such as the economic forests mainly composed of navel orange trees, so as to increase the income of local farmers.

Foping Demonstration Area in Shaanxi

Covering 7,312 hectares, with forest cover of 79.3 percent, this demonstration area pays close attention to better coordination of community economic development and protection of the habitat of rare wildlife. In the northwestern part of the demonstration area is a habitat and activity corridor for the rare wild animals, the giant panda included. This habitat and corridor covers 5,230 hectares, with half belonging to the demonstration area. It comprises four categories of forest areas, including Health Forest Area, Panda Corridor Construction Area, Recuperation Forest Area, and Health Building Forest Area. Thus, through efforts made in category management, breeding management, the adjustment of forest types and tree species, the original zonal species will be recuperated and effectively protected; and the living environment of the giant panda will be improved a lot.

Lijiang Demonstration Area in Yunnan

The Yulong Snow Mountain in Yunnan Province

Covering 1113.6 hectares, this project is designed to develop a pattern of rational utilization of community forests. By implementing the projects like natural forest protection, restoring cultivated land to forests and national shelterbelt forest construction, the demonstration area works on better forest tending, orchard improvement, forest fire prevention, prevention and treatment of forest diseases and pests, biodiversity protection and forest health monitoring.

Badaling Demonstration Area in Beijing

Covering 546.1 hectares, this contains forest area of 327.8 hectares, open forest area 11.8 hectares, brush area 194.4 hectares, barren hills and wasteland 1.7 hectares and others 10.4 hectares. It focuses on the operation of State-owned forests and the construction of scenic forests and uses sustainable category management to explore forest health management technology and modes on the basis of the China's situation. It employs the forestation pattern of broad-leaved and coniferous trees mingled. In addition, it also promotes the comprehensive technologies of closing off hillsides for forestation to strengthen the study of forest health through various channels. Various measures are used to strengthen the treatment of unhealthy forests and the administration and protection of the healthy ones, such as man-made forestation, improvement of secondary forests, replanting, disease-pest prevention and control, and establishment of disease-pest monitoring and warning system and etc.

The Protection of Pastures

In order to strengthen the eco-construction and planned management of grasslands, the strategic emphasis has been shifted from reaching economic goals to "giving equal importance to ecological, economic and social goals, with ecological goals receiving the priority." As a result, the vegetation coverage has effectively recovered and the eco-environment on the grasslands is improving. There is a continued increase in state investment in pasture protection and construction. From 2000 to 2005, over nine billion Yuan was earmarked for this purpose from the central budget to support the projects of natural pasture vegetation recovery and construction, the building of pasture fences and forage grass seed bases, the halting of herding for vegetation recovery, and grassland eco-construction to control the dust storm sources threatening the Beijing-Tianjin area. These projects have brought about good ecological, economic and social results. By the end of 2005, the acreage of man-made grasslands had added up to 13 million hectares, that of improved pasture to 14 million hectares and that of fenced pasture to 33 million hectares. Twenty percent of the pastures now practice grazing prohibition, grazing land recovery and designated rotation grazing.

Grasslands enjoy better production capacity. When compared with the non-projected areas, the grass coverage, altitude and grass production of the projected grassland area rise by 27 percent, 56 percent and 70 percent respectively. Of these, the grass coverage, altitude and grass production of the land returned to grassland increased by 29 percent, 64 percent and 78 percent respectively.

Land Protection

The Chinese government has set the protection of cultivated land as a basic national policy, and has implemented a strict policy for protecting cultivated land. The State has designated basic farmland conservation area as the key basis for grain security. Meanwhile, a land-use control system has been set up to strictly control the total amount and composition of land used for construction to curb the unjustified appropriation of farmland. The government has also increased the intensity of land development and treatment, drawn up regulations for managing land development and treatment projects, and organized the implementation of the state-invested land development and treatment projects, so as to maintain an overall dynamic balance in farmland and to improve the eco-environment. In the Tenth Five-Year Plan period, 76,000 hectares of land were reclaimed after scientific development and treatment of the land in rural and urban areas, the natural-disaster-damaged land, and the discarded land in industrial and mining areas. A number of new rural areas have emerged with neat layout and sound eco-environment, and the eco-environment of some resources-drained cities and key mining areas has been further improved or restored.

Water and Soil Conservation

The State has organized many special projects to control dust storm sources that threaten the Beijing-Tianjin area, to conserve water and soil for the sustainable use of the water resources in the capital area, to build up silt dams for water and soil conservation on the Loess Plateau, and to prevent and control comprehensively soil erosion in the black earth area in the northeast and in the limestone areas along the Southern and Northern Panjiang rivers on the upper reaches of the Zhujiang River. So far, the key areas of water and soil conservation have been expanded from the upper and middle reaches of the Yangtze and Yellow rivers to the black earth area in the northeast, the upper reaches of the Zhujiang River and the area around Beijing and Tianjin. The construction of national demonstration areas and demonstration projects has resulted in the completion of over 300 water and soil conservation projects each covering over 200 square km, 190 eco-friendly model counties and 1,398 small demonstration drainage areas in terms of water and soil conservation. The State has also started to build the first group of 62 demonstration areas, each no less than 300 square km, and over 50 sci-tech demonstration parks for water and soil conservation. Experimental work for water and soil conservation and ecological restoration has been conducted in 188 counties throughout the country, and overall protection has been carried out by closing off hillsides for afforestation in all key areas covered by water and soil conservation projects, putting some 126,000 square km under such protection. Also, a project for preventing soil erosion is underway in the headwater areas of the Yangtze, Yellow and Lancang rivers. So far, 980 counties in 25 provinces (autonomous regions and municipalities directly under the Central Government) have wholly or partially closed hills or mountains to livestock grazing, which has hastened the recovery of the vegetation in areas totaling more than 600,000 square km. During the Tenth Five-Year Plan period, China succeeded in bringing 240,200 square km of eroded land under comprehensive control of water and soil erosion, improving 11,500 small drainage areas, creating 4.06 million ha of basic farmland, cultivating 15.33 million ha of forests for water and soil conservation, cash fruit and preserving headwaters, building up 7,000 silt dams and 3.5 million small water and soil conservation projects involving silt-blocking dams and slope water works.

In winter and spring every year, Wei Guangcai, a farmer of Minqin County of Gansu Province, and his wife will go to cover up straw grids on the brim of the desert near the Qingtuhu Lake to the east of the village, which can effectively fix the sand hills and hold up the desertification.

Desertification

Desertification is one of the most severe environmental problems in China. The area of desertification, which is 2.62 million square km or about 27 percent of China's land territory, far exceeds the nation's total farmland. It can be found in 498 counties (banners, cities) in 18

♦ State Forestry Administration

The main functions of the ministry is to investigate and formulate guidelines and policies on the construction of the forest ecological environment, protection of forest resources and the afforesting of national land; and, organize the drafting of laws and regulations concerned and supervise the implementation. The ministry also takes charge of formulating a national development strategy of forestry and middle and long term development plan and organizing their implementation; managing forestry funds assigned by the Central Government and overseeing the management and usage of forestry funds. It also has the duty of organizing the plantation of trees and the sealing of a mountain pass; organizing and instructing on preventing and curing the loss of the water and oil with biological measures, such as planting trees and grass and preventing the spreading of sand and controlling sandy land; organizing and coordinating of carrying out international pacts on preventing and curing desertification; instructing on the construction and management of State-owned forestry (tree nursery), forest parks and grass-rooted forestry organizations. It also organizes and instructs on the management of the forest resources, including economic forests, coal forests, tropical forest crops, mangrove and some other kinds of forests for special utilization; organizes the investigation, dynamic monitoring and statistical collection of forestry resources; audits and supervises the utilization of forest resources; organizes the editing of forest cutting limits and supervises its implementation when the cutting limits were approved by the State Council; superintendents the approved cutting and transportation of wood and bamboo; organizes and guides the management of woodland and rights of woodland and makes first trial of the confiscation and engrossing of woodland that should be approved by the State Council according to law. It also has the responsibility of organizing and instructing on the protection and reasonable exploitation of wild plants and animals; determining and adjusting the name list of national-level protected wild plantings and animals; instructing on the construction and management of natural reserves on forest, wild animal habitats and everglade; organizing and coordinating the protection of everglades and the implementation of relevant international pacts of importing and exporting nearly-extinct species and auditing the exporting of national-level protected wild animals, valuable and rare wild plants and implementation of relevant international pacts.

Address: No.18 Hepingli Dongjie, Dongcheng District, Beijing
Website: http://www.forestry.gov.cn

provinces (autonomous region, municipalities directly under the Central Government), including Beijing, Tianjin, Hebei, Shanxi, Inner Mongolia, Liaoning, Jilin, Shandong, Henan, Hainan, Sichuan, Yuannan, Tibet, Shaanxi, Gansu, Qinghai, Ningxia and Xinjiang. Today, although the desertification has been curbed in some areas, it still is expanding at a rate of more than 3,000 square km every year.

Sand Prevention and Control

The Chinese government has promulgated and implemented the Law on Sand Prevention and Control, approved the National Plan for Sand Prevention and Control (2005-2010), and issued the Decision on Further Strengthening the Work of Sand Prevention and Control. It has also organized a number of key relevant projects, achieving a net reduction in the areas suffering from land degradation and desertification. According to the 3rd national monitoring of the desertification situation in the country, success has been made in controlling land deterioration and desertification in the main. The area of deteriorating land decreased from 10,400 square km a year at the end of last century to 3,436 square km a year today, while the area of land suffering from desertification decreased, on the yearly basis, from 3,436 square km to 1,283 square km.

The State Forestry Administration has begun to implement a nationwide sand control program. The program is aimed to get a basic control of desertification by 2010, reduce the area of desertification year by year until 2030 on the basis of the achievements in the previous stage, preliminarily control all the degraded land which the future science and technology can cope with and finally succeed in establishing a complete ecological system in the sand area by 2050.

Prevention and Remedying Desertification Under Local Conditions

Sandy lands in China are mainly distributed in the northwest, the north of the Huabei Plain and the western part of northeast China. Measures of preventing and remedying desertification should be taken in accordance with local conditions and the types of the sandy soil. According to the general strategy of the government, in the area surrounding an oasis in the desert, forest belt and forest nets aiming to protect against the wind and stabilize sand dunes should be built to protect the existing natural vegetation. In the semi-arid sand regions, comprehensive measure, such as planting the forests and grass, bringing small rivers under control, and migration for ecological reasons, should be adopted, on the basis of protecting the existing forests and grass. Furthermore, the sand resources can be moderately explored. For the arctic-alpine sandy area on the Qinghai-Tibet Plateau, comprehensive measures of protecting the existing natural ecological system by sealing a mountain pass should be taken to restore the damaged vegetation and to prohibit irrational development. For the semi-humid area of the Huanghe and Huaihai rivers and humid-sand area in south China, sandy land under the control and resources exploration should be combined. Measures of actively planting forests and grass and developing fast-growing and rich-production commercial forests and economic forest should be taken.

Sandstorms

Sandstorm is a weather phenomenon caused by strong winds. It blows up a large deal of sand and dust, thus forming stale air and lowering visibility to less than 1km. The sand picked up by the storm contains no less than 38 chemical elements. Therefore, the occurrence of a sandstorm will greatly increase the density of the solid-state pollutants in the atmosphere which will bring long-term and potential damage to the environment, soil and agriculture production of the originating place and leeward area. Especially when the limited surface soil which crops rely on is blown away, the impoverished earth will produce much lower output.

Sandstorm Prevention System

The China Meteorological Administration is responsible for monitoring and forecasting of the sandstorm. When omens of sandstorm are detected, timely information should be passed to relevant government departments for action to mitigate the results.

The Ministry of Agriculture is responsible for providing instructions to farming and animal husbandry communities before the occurrence of disasters, conducting self-rescue measures and helping restore production in the disaster area.

MEP is responsible for monitoring atmospheric quality when a sandstorm is occurring and providing information to relevant departments.

The Ministry of Civil Affairs is responsible for organizing disaster prevention and relief and taking part in the investigation of disaster conditions; organizing and distributing funds and materials against the disasters and supervising their usage. It takes charges of the Office of International Disaster Reduction Committee of China and the General Coordinating Office for Disaster Prevention and Reduction.

The Ministry of Health is responsible for coordinating and ascertaining medical materials against the disasters when death and injury occurred in the disaster. It will also assist in resolving the medical resources and prevent the occurrence of plague and diseases and prohibit their spreading and expanding in the disaster area.

The Ministry of Communications is in charge of formulating a preparatory plan of transportation to prevent and reduce disasters, coordinating and ascertaining the vehicles used in the disaster relief efforts.

The Civil Aviation Administration takes charge of working out disaster prevention and reduction emergency plan for civil aviation. It should guarantee the safety of civil aviation in the condition of sandstorm.

The Ministry of Railways takes charge of adopting preparatory plan for emergency handling of preventing and reducing disasters in railway transportation. It should also guarantee the safety of railway transportation in the condition of sandstorm.

Prevention and Treatment of Sandstorm Sources in the Beijing-Tianjin Area

The Sandstorm Prevention and Treatment Project of the Beijing-Tianjin Sandstorm Source Area aims to build up an ecological protection system with high-quality and high-stability and optimize the ecological environment of the capital and its surrounding area, through protecting vegetation, planting trees and grass, converting land for forestry and pasture, bringing small rivers and grasslands under control and moving communities to protect the ecological system, etc. The project includes Damao Banner of Inner Mongolian in the west, Pingquan County of Hebei Province in the east, Dai County of Shanxi Province in the south and Dongwuzhumuqin Banner of Inner Mongolia in the north, thus including some 75 counties, banners, cities and districts in Hebei, Shanxi Provinces, Beijing and Tianjin Municipalities directly under the Central Government and Inner Mongolian Autonomous Region. It covers an area of 458,000 square km in which sandy land was 101,800 square km.

Thus far, the State has invested in the form of State bonds 11.28 billion Yuan in the treatment of 13.1 million hectares of land (including 5.7 million hectares of land where grazing is not allowed). This includes completion of 4.497 million hectares of forested area (including 1.07 hectares re-turned into forests, 1.03 million hectares of forested barren mountains, 0.5 million hectares of land planted with trees by man, 0.53 million hectares of the afforestation area by the plane, 0.1 million hectares of the farmland forestry network), accounting for 52.88 percent of the planned task.

Marine Environment

China has more than 18,000 km of continental coastline and a more than 3 million square km sea area. Offshore waters are divided into four sea areas: Bohai Sea, Huanghai Sea, Donghai Sea and Nanhai Sea. Offshore waters enjoy a diversity of ecological systems, including some typical and representative types, such as estuaries, gulf, offshore everglade, mangrove, coral reef and island. Effective protection of the marine environment has become an important basis for the sustainable socio-economic development of China and the environment. China has fundamentally built up a legal system and administrative law enforcement system on marine environment protection. Efforts have been taken to build up a monitoring network, and adopt and implement different functions in the sea areas and offshore waters, with a view to rationally exploring and protecting marine resources, prevent sea pollution and ecological damage and guarantee sustainable development of the marine economy.

Marine Environment Protection

The government actively carries out pollution prevention and treatment projects on main rivers that empty into the sea and environment protection projects in important sea areas. In 2005, it launched pollution prevention and control work in the Yangtze River and Zhujiang River and their surrounding sea areas, after the same work which had been launched for the Bohai Sea. Synchronous environment surveillance and investigation both in the land and in the sea areas has also been expanded to develop an overall plan.

The government strictly carries out examination and approval regulations in terms of coastal construction projects and waste

THE NATIONAL-LEVEL MARINE NATURE RESERVES LIST

Name of protection zone	Location	Square meter (HM2)	Key objects for protection	Responsible department
Island of Snake-Laotieshan Mountain Nature Reserve	Lushunkou, Liaoning	17000	Pallas pit vipers, migratory birds and ecological environment	SEPA
Yalujiangkou River Mouth Coastal Wetland Nature Reserve	Donggang City, Liaoning	112180	Coastal low beaches, wetland ecosystem environment and waterfowls, Migratory birds	SEPA
Changli Golden Coast Nature Reserve	Changli, Hebei	30000	Natural landscapes and near sea areas	State Oceans Administration
Yancheng National Rare Birds Nature Reserve	Yancheng, Jiangsu	453000	Rare birds like red-crowned cranes and low beach	SEPA
Nanji Islands Ocean Nature Reserve	Pingyang County, Zhejiang	20106	Islands and marine ecosystems, Shellfish, Algae	State Oceans Administration
Woods from submerged forest in Shenhu Bay, Jingjiang, Fujian Nature Reserve	Jingjiang, Fujian	3400	Woods from submerged forest in Vestiges of Coral Reef	State Oceans Administration
Huidong Port Turtle Nature Reserve	Huidong County, Guangdong	800	Turtles spawning and fertility places	Ministry of Agriculture
Neilingding Futian Nature Reserve	Shenzhen Guangdong	858	Macaques, birds and mangrove forest	State Forestry Bureau
Guangdong Zhanjiang Mangrove Forest Nature Reserve	Lianjiang County, Guangdong	11927	Mangrove forest ecological systems	State Forestry Bureau
Shankou National-level Mangrove Forest Nature Reserve	Hepu County, Guangxi	8000	Mangrove forest ecological systems	State Oceans Administration
Beilun Hekou Marine Nature Reserve	Fangcheng, Guangxi	2680	Mangrove forest ecological systems	State Oceans Administration
Hepu Dugong Nature Reserve	Hepu County, Guangxi	86400	Dugong, turtle, dolphin and mangrove forest and so on	SEPA
Dongzhaigang Mangrove Nature Reserve	Qiongshan City, Hainan	3337	Mangrove forest and its ecological environment	State Forestry Bureau
Dazhoudao Marine Ecosystem National Nature Reserve	Wanning County, Hainan	7000	Islands and marine ecosystem and swiftlet and its eco-system	State Oceans Administration
Sanya Coral Reef Nature Reserve	Sanya City, Hainan	8500	Coral reef and its eco-system	State Oceans Administration
Tianjin Ancient Seashore and Wetland National Nature Reserve	Tianjin	21180	Site of the shell bank and oyster beach and the wetland eco-system	State Oceans Administration
Yellow River Delta Nature Reserve	Dongying City, Shandong	153000	Primitive wetland eco-system	State Forestry Bureau
Xiamen Amphioxus Nature Reserve	Xiamen City, Fujian	6300	Amphioxus and its eco-system	State Oceans Administration
Shuangtai Hekou Nature Reserve	Panjin City, Liaoning	80000	Red-crowned crane, white crane and swan and other rare birds	State Forestry Bureau

Comparison of the Inspection of the Administrative Law Enforcement on Marine Ecological Protection (2005-2007)

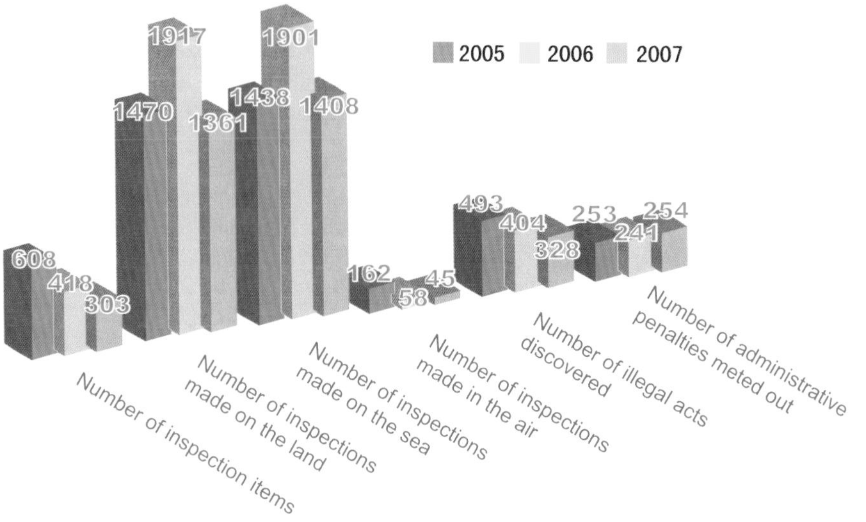

2005 2006 2007

608 418 303 1470 1917 1361 1438 1901 1408 162 58 45 493 404 328 253 241 254

Number of inspection items
Number of inspections made on the land
Number of inspections made on the sea
Number of inspections made in the air
Number of illegal acts discovered
Number of administrative penalties meted out

dumping into the sea. It has also strengthened law enforcement surveillance on dumping and enhanced its monitoring of the marine environment. It has approved the Preparatory Plan for Emergency Handling of Red Tides and the Contingency Plan for Oil-Spills in Offshore Oil Exploration and Exploitation and has also listed them in the management system for State emergency reaction. Management of vessel pollution prevention and dangerous material transportation has been strengthened and an emergency handling system on oil leakage from vessels has been actively promoted. At present, the government has established 29 national marine sanctuaries (covering an area of 25,000 square km) and eight marine special marine reserves, aiming to protect valuable marine resources, including nearly-extinct marine species, typical marine ecological system and marine scenic landforms and historic natural relics. The first stage of the construction of a State Offshore Shelter Belt has been completed. In the engineering area, the forest covering rate increased from 24.5 percent to 35.5 percent. The second stage of the State Offshore Shelter Belt is being built.

Reducing and Controlling Land-sourced Pollutants

The improvement of the environment protection infrastructure is critical to the realization of effective reduction and control of land-sourced pollutants and overall discharges into the sea. In the period of the 10th Five Year Plan (2001-2005), sewage disposal plants in coastal cities increased in its number. Coastal cities, excluding coastal counties, witnessed a growth of second level sewage disposal plants from73 in 2000 to 202 in 2005. The capacity of dealing with sewage water at the second level increased from 5.63 million cubic meters per day in 2000 to 16.23 million cubic meters per day in 2005. The overall rate of sewage treatment reached 56 percent. By the end of 2005, city sewage disposal plant construction projects in coastal prefectural-level and county-level or city administration regions added up to 342; 197 of them were completed, with a daily sewage disposal capacity of 21.86 million cubic meters. 88 harmless refuse disposal plants have been built in 53 of coastal county-level administration areas, with a disposal capacity of 58,373 tons per day and 22.04 million tons per year.

National Action Program Protecting the Marine Environment from Land-Based Activities

It is said that about 60 countries have formulated or are formulating their own National Action Program (NPA) for the Protection of the Marine Environment from Land-based Activities. China is one of the members of the Global Program Action or GPA, and also of some regional projects, such as the Action Plan for the Protection, Management and Development of the Marine and Coastal Environment of the Northwest Pacific Region, the UNEP/GEF Project in the South China Sea and Gulf of Thailand and the UNDP/GEF Yellow Large Marine Ecosystem Project. To fulfill the needs of GPA and guide and improve the marine environment protection all over the country at the national level, the Ministry of Communications, Ministry of Agriculture, Ministry of Construction, Ministry of Water Resources, Ministry of Land and Resources, State Bureau of Oceanic Administration under the Ministry of Land and Resources, State Forestry Bureau, National Tourism Administration, Environment Protection and Afforesting Committee of the PLA and some other relevant departments, under the organization and coordination of MEP, are speeding up the formulation the NPA. China's NPA, in terms of geography, includes 11 coastal provinces, autonomous regions and municipalities directly under the Central Government, which are Liaoning, Hebei, Shandong, Jiangsu, Zhejiang, Fujian, Guangdong, Hainan provinces and Tianjin, Shanghai municipalities directly under the Central Government and Guangxi Zhuang Autonomous Region.

Regulation for the Administration on Prevention and Control of Damage to Marine Environment by Pollution from Marine Construction Projects

Regulation for the Administration on Prevention and Control of Damage to Marine Environment by Pollution from Marine Construction Projects is the first supporting regulation of the Marine Environment Protection Law of the PRC and came into force on November 1, 2006. It makes clear that marine construction projects, such as enclosing the sea, reclaiming land from the sea, building man-made islands in the sea and bridges across the sea, laying pipelines under the sea, must be integrated into legal framework. Strengthening the supervision of marine construction projects will make great significance to protect the marine environment in conformity with the law and maintain the healthy and sustainable development over the marine economy. Furthermore, it will make an end to the situation that China has no operating regulations to protect the marine environment in marine construction projects.

The regulation has eight chapters and 59 articles, including the general principles, assessment on environmental impact, prevention and control of pollution caused by coastal construction projects, management of discharging and dumping of pollutants, prevention and dealing with pollution accidents, surveillance and legal duties, etc.

The Marine Nature Reserve

In July 1988, the government established a new management system for nature reserves, combining the comprehensive administration with classification-based management, it stipulated "various types of Nature Reserves shall be supervised by the following organs, including Ministry of Forestry, Ministry of Agriculture, Ministry of Geology and Mineral Resources, the Ministry of Water Resources, State Oceans Administration People's Republic of China"; in November, the State Council also set out the duties of the State Oceans Administration regarding the selection, planning and management of marine nature reserves. In 1989, under the overall supervision of the State Oceans Administration, the work, concerning investigation and study, site selection and appraisal of building the reserves, was carried out and five areas were chosen: Golden Coast in Lichang, Mangrove Forest in Shankou, Marine Ecology in Dazhoudao Island, Coral Reef in Sanya and Nanji Islands, and in September 1990, the State Council authorized each as a National-Level Nature Reserve. In October 1991, the State Council approved two more, the Tianjing sea coast and wetland, and the submerged forest in Shenhu Bay, Jingjiang, Fujian Province. In the meantime, a number of regional-level nature reserves were also selected by local departments.

Snakes Island-Laotieshan Mountain Nature Reserve

Snakes Island and the Bird Shed in Laotieshan Mountain of Liaoning Province are universally regarded as world wonders. There are not only famous for unique natural scenes and rich resources but also full of natural mysteries. Snakes Island is the only place to find the Pallas pit viper, while Laotieshan Mountain is an inevitable stopping place for birds migrating from north to south, it is said that there are more than 200 species of migrant birds nest here every year, including dozens of species of national first and second class protected birds. In August 1980, these two places were approved as State major nature reserves, and the "Supervision Office of the Snakes Island Nature Reserve in Laotieshan Mountain Liaoning" was set up to oversee management and scientific research.

A bird's eye view of the Laotieshan Mountain

Yancheng Sheyang National Rare Birds Natural Reserve in Jiangsu Province: the hometown of crane.

National-level Rare Birds Nature Reserve in Yancheng City

The National-Level Rare Birds Nature Reserve in Yancheng City, Jiangsu Province, was founded in 1983, and elevated to a National-Level Nature Reserve in 1992. In November of the same year, it was approved as a Biosphere Nature Reserve under the Man and Biosphere Program (MAB) of UNESCO, and included in "the World Nature Reserve Biosphere (WNBR)". In 1996, it was also included in the "Northeast Asian Nature Reserve Crane Species" list.

Yancheng City's Nature Reserve is the biggest coastline nature reserve in China, with a coastline up to 582 km in length and a total area of 453,300 hectares, including the core zone of 17,400 hectares. Its major function is to protect some rare wildlife animals, such as red-crowned cranes, and the ecological environment of low beach wetlands. Every year, thousands of red-crowned cranes winter here, while more than a thousand black-beaked gulls breed, and thousands of river deer living among the low beaches. Yancheng City is also a key place for linking various biological zones of birds, a central place for birds migrating from northeast Asia and Australia, as well as one place for aquatic birds to survive the winter. Every spring and autumn, nearly three million birds migrate through Yancheng City, with more than 200,000 waterfowls living there through the winter. Moreover, this nature reserve is also one of the few areas for endangered animal species in China; it has 29 endangered animal species listed by the World Conservation Union (IUCN). Therefore, Yancheng City Nature Reserve plays an important role in the protection of biological diversity.

Nanji Islands Marine Nature Reserve

Nanji Islands Marine Nature Reserve lies in the coastal area of Zhejiang Province, composed of 23 islands, 14 submerged reefs, 55 Pennsylvania N. Reefs' the biggest island among them is Nanji Island, covering seven square km, with a total area of 20,106 hectares. Thanks to a mild climate, special hydrological and geological conditions, it has formed a unique ecological environment. As it is located in the transitional area between the temperate zone and tropical zone, being influenced by the warm current of the Taiwan Straits and the coastal current of Zhejiang, it is the important gene pool of algae in Chinese seas. There are 403 species of seashells, totaling 20 percent of those seen in China, 174 species of algae, making up 20 percent of Chinese types. In addition to seashells and algae, there are also 368 species of fish, 180 species of shrimp and crab, 55 species of land-sourced seed plants and 55 species vertebrates.

This marine nature reserve is the first relating to maritime ecological system established in China, which has very important value both in science and ecology, and is of significant for the protection of Chinese and global biological diversity. At every summer vocation, there are always thousands of people traveling here, and more and more tourists are attracted. As a result, this nature reserve is not only a base for education and scientific research, but also a good place for marine ecotourism.

Nature Reserve of Woods from Submerged Forest in Shenhu Bay

This is situated in Shenhu Bay, Jinjiang City, Fujian Province, covering 3,100 hectares, with woods from submerged forests and vestiges of oyster reef and metamorphism resulting from marine abrasion as targets for protection. This kind of nature reserve is unique both in China and the world. There are vestiges involving in over 20 kete leerias, which were buried in the littoral ecology inter-tidal zone and underwent more than 7,800 years of exposure to sea water, with a vast region of oyster reefs formed thousands of years ago, typical abrasion terracotta mylonite, scree oil beach rock, and silver sands accumulated in modern times; it also shows metamorphism resulting from marine abrasion during a long evolution in the Paleozoic Era, Mesozoic Era and Cenozoic Era's. The establishment of the reserve offers good conditions for research into various fields related to oceanography, geography, climate and botany of the Paleolithic Era, the geological structure of Taiwan Strait, the rise and fall of sea levels, the movement of geological plates in the Pacific Ocean, and foreign communications history of Gugang Port in Quanzhou.

Nature Reserve of Green Turtles in Huidong Port

The major role for this nature reserve is to protect green turtles. There are now only seven species of turtles existing in the world. In Chinese sea areas, there are five species, such as green turtles, hawksbill turtles, Malayan snail-eating turtle, Olive Ridley turtle and Dermochelys coriacea Linnaeus. Of these five species, the number of green turtles is the biggest, while the other four species are relatively few. About 90 per cent of the Chinese green turtles are located in the South China Sea distributed in coastal provinces from Shandong down. However, their spawning grounds are centered on the islands of the South China Sea, Hainan Province, coastal areas of Guangdong Province and some islands in the eastern part of Fujian Province. In the period between July and September every year, green turtles in groups some ashore to spawn. Green turtles are rare marine animals with an, important economic value, now listed as key wildlife animals under State protection.

Nature Reserve of National-level Mangrove Forest Ecology in Shankou

This is one of the first group (five) of national-level marine-type nature reserves, and was established in September 1990. In 1993, it was included in the Chinese Biosphere Nature Reserve (CBRN) program and ranked as an important wetland in China. In May 1997, it established sister relationship with the Florida's Gulf Nature Reserve on River Mouth Study program, and, in January 2000, it was added to UNESCO's Man and Biosphere program; in 2002, it was listed as a key wetland in the world.

Located in the sub-tropical zone, the reserve is located between the eastern and western parts of Shatian Peninsula, Hepu County, Guangxi Zhuang Autonomous Region, with a coastline totaling 50 km in length, a total area of 8,000 square km, and it is the second national-level nature.

Mangroves are a species of tropical tree that grow in swamps; mangrove forest is also called forest on the sea. It multiplies through viviparity, which is rare in the vegetable kingdom. Seeds grow in the tree, and develop into branches 20-40 centimeters long. The drooping branches reach the earth and take root. The mangrove ecosystem is one of the marine ecosystems with the richest biodiversity and the highest productive force. It is able to regulate torrid temperature and to protect and reinforce dikes with exuberant roots. It not only provides an ideal habitat for marine organism and birds, but also provides them with rich food.

The mangrove forest there is a typical China mainland representative, characterized with healthy growth, unique structure, widely linked, and protected intact. There are 15 species of Mangroves (10 species of true mangroves, Bruguiera, Kandelia candel, Rhizophora stylosa, Aegiceras corniculatum, Aricennia marina, Sonneratia caseolaris, Lumnitzera racemosa Wild, Acanthus ilicifolius, Heritiera littoralis Dryand, Excoecaria agallocha, five kinds of semi-mangroves, Acrostichum aureum, Thespesia populnea (L.) Soland. ex Correa, Pongamia pinnata,Cerbera Manghas L.), 96 species of phyto-planktons, 158 species of benthic diatom, 82 species of fishes, 90 species of shells, 61 species of shrimps and crabs, 132speciess of birds, 258 species of insects, and 26 species of other animals.

♦ State Oceanic Administration

Under the supervision of the Ministry of Land and Resources, the State Oceanic Administration is responsible for supervising and administering the use of sea areas, protection of the oceanic environment, safeguarding oceanic rights and interests according to law, and organizing marine research in science and technology.

Its major functions include: to draw up basic laws, regulations and policies relating to coastlines, islands, inland seas, territorial waters, contiguous zones, continental shelf areas, special economic zone and other sea areas; to map out plans concerning marine functions, marine development, marine scientific and technological plans, as well as strategies for developing marine undertakings; to supervise and administer the use of sea areas (including coastlines); to issue licenses for the use of sea areas, to implement systems concerning the paid use of sea area in accordance with certain regulations, and to manage laying under-water cables and pipelines, to undertake and organize the survey and determine the boundaries of sea areas; to work out plans, criteria and standards relating to protection and recondition for marine environment, to formulate standards of discharging pollutant into seas and systems of controlling total amount of pollutant discharged into seas. In accordance with the State's standards, it will supervise the amount of land-sourced pollutants discharged into oceans, being responsible for preventing environmental pollution from offshore oil exploration, marine dumping, ocean engineering; to administer the investigation, monitoring, surveillance and assessment of the maritime environment; to supervise marine biological diversity and protection of marine eco-system environment; to administer the marine nature reserves and special zones for protection . It examines and approvals the reports of the environmental influence concerning new building or reconstructing, extending seacoasts and marine engineering projects, administer research foreign-related activities involving marine scientific investigation, and supervises, according to law, foreign-related construction of marine facilities, under-water projects and other development activities, and caries out research on policies, measures involving marine rights and interests; puts forward suggestions on coping with issues of boundary line delimitation and right of attribution of islands; safeguards resource rights on the high seas and the international sea bottoms belonging to China; it is responsible for executing relevant conventions and treaties relating to international marine issues. It takes charge of organizing Chinese-foreign cooperation and exchanges, organizing basic and comprehensive investigations of marine topics, tackles major scientific and technological projects and research on high-tech and new technology. It administers public service systems relating to the observation and survey and monitoring of marine, the forecasting and releasing early-warning information of marine disasters, comprehensive information and standard measures. It is also responsible for releasing the forecast and warning of marine disasters and the forecast of marine environment (without weather forecast and warning), managing the investigation concerning polar region and oceans.

Address:No.1 Fuxing Menwai, Xicheng District, Beijing
Website: http://www.soa.gov.cn

Hepu Dugong Nature Reserve

Extending 43 km in length, and covering over 300 square km, Hepu Dugong Nature Reserve is the only national-level reserve for the Dugong. The local sea area in Guangdong Province is the ideal place for the Dugong, with vast seaweed, excellent oceanic environment and underwater slots for their habitat. Dugong is one of the oldest marine animals in the world, and also the only ocean-dwelling vegetarian. It is popularly called "mermaid", as female looks like a person embracing its offspring while feeding them with its breasts emerging from the sea, and is likely to have been the origin of ancient legends about mermaids. It is a first-class endangered rare mammal under State protection. Currently, there are only five species of Dugong in the world, mostly distributed in the southeast of Africa, Malaysia, Philippine, Australia and the northern part of China. They mainly live in shallow sea of the tropical zone, relying on Halodule and Halodule unibervis (Fersk) Asch as staple food. The female normally gives birth every three years.

Sanya Coral Reefs Nature Reserve

Near the sea areas of Hainan Island, there are vast coral reefs and, in order to protect them, in September 1990, the government designated the National-Level Coral Reefs Nature Reserve. The major subjects for protection include Ivanovia cf. manchurica Coral, ahermatypic coral, coral reefs, ecological systems and biological diversity biology. For Ivanovia cf. manchurica Corals, they are produced based on coral worms, tropical marine coelenterates. There are many kinds of coral species in this area; up to now, 115 species of Ivanovia cf. manchurica Coral (including five sub-species) have been found, which respectively belong to 13 families, 33 genus and two sub-genus. Furthermore, in the reef-building process, there are Helioporidae, Tubipora musica, Millepora, various ahermatypic corals, Alcyonacea, and other rich oceanic organisms occupying the same eco-system with the corals and closely relying on each other.

Tianjin Seacoast and Wetland National-level Nature Reserve

In October 1992, this was established as the only national-level marine-type nature reserve in China, based on protection and management for rare vestiges of ancient coastlines involving the Shell Bank, Oyster Beach, wetland natural environment and relevant ecological systems. This is one special area within the administration zone, three different-type geology existing together.

The reserve is located on the Bohai Sea in the eastern part of Tianjin, with a total area of 9,900 hectares. Over 2,000 years ago, this place was many lagoons and the mouth of numerous rivers. At present, there still exist many traces of marine biology. The Shell Bank and Oyster Beach in Tianjin are two important products and vestiges from the time when Bohai Sea was a land area. The Shell Bank is one of three famous shell banks in the world along with one in Louisiana and one in Surinam; the scope of the Oyster Beach can be compared with similar ones north of Bangkok and in Louisiana Bay; but neither of these has oyster deposits as thick as those up to five meters in Tianjin. As a result, this nature reserve has certainly played an important role in research into the Quaternary Period and the ancient environment, and it is one of the typical areas for international cooperation and research in oceanography, geology, geography and wetland ecology.

Management Regulations on Marine Nature Reserves

With the aim of protecting the oceanic natural environment and resources, and in accordance with law, ocean nature reserves involve seashore, river mouth, islands, wetlands and sea areas, including areas laid out for protection. Suitability is determined as follows:

1. Region with a typical oceanic ecosystem;

2. A region with fertile marine biological diversity, or a center for rare and endangered marine biology species;

3. A region with marine natural vestiges with significant value in terms of science and culture;

4. Sea areas, coastlines, islands and wetlands with special value for protection;

5. Other areas needing protection.

The following activities and behavior are prohibited:

1. Activities and behavior without authorization involving the movement, transmission, breakage of boundary tablets and facilities for protection;

2. Illegal fishing, collecting and gathering marine biology;

3. Illegal quarrying, sand digging, tapping mineral resources;

4. Other any behavior concerning damaging subjects of protection, natural environment and resources.

Rank-based System of the Marine Nature Reserve

The National-Level marine Nature Reserves refer to those of significant value in the field of scientific research and protection as well as important influence at home and abroad, which are established under the authorization of the State Council.

Regional-based marine nature reserves are those established by with approval of the government at the level of coastal provinces, autonomous regions, and municipal cities, with great influence in the local areas and special value for scientific research and protection.

Conservation of Biodiversity

China is a country rich in biodiversity. The State has formulated the China Action Plan for Biodiversity Conservation, followed by China's Biodiversity: A Country Study and the Plan for the Protection and Utilization of the Resources of Biological Species.

At present, there are 250 bases for saving and breeding wildlife, over 400 centers for conserving and cultivating wild plant species or preserving wild plant genes, which have artificially produced stable species groups for over 200 kinds of endangered rare animals and about 1,000 types of wild plants. Meanwhile, investigation and collection of key wild plants on the verge of extinction and under State protection have been carried out, and 67 zones have been set up to protect the original habitats of wild agricultural plants. A nationwide investigation has also been carried out on species from abroad, and action has been taken to root out the most harmful and noxious of such species in 100 counties in ten provinces, enhancing public awareness and people's capacity to guard against the intrusion of foreign species.

In August 2003, a national inter-ministerial conference system for biological species resources was established by SEPA together with another 16 ministries and commissions under the State Council, which is responsible for adjusting and improving the conservation of biological species resources. The "State Expert Conservation Committee of Biological Species Resources" was also established with 17 associated experts.

The Rescue Project Concerning Endangered Plants

The government departments concerned attach great importance to effective conservation for biological resources, a number of modern facilities relating to conserving hereditary resources have been built up and put into use. In January 2003, the Chinese Academy of Sciences initiated one rescue project for endangered plants; it planned to have species conserved in 12 botanical gardens to be increased from the present 13,000 to 21,000 within 15 years, and to construct the world biggest botanical garden covering 458 square km. In this project, the capital, for collecting and gathering rare and endangered plants, is more than 300 million Yuan. The genetic pool will be built based on Qinling Mountains, Wuhan, Xishuangbanna and Beijing. Among 189 species of wildlife plant covered in a national investigation of wildlife plants resources, 71 percent had reached the standard for stable survival and development.

Rescue Project Relating to Endangered Wildlife Animals

This has made marked progress, with 250 breeding centers for wildlife established nationwide. The rescue project for seven species, such as panda and red ibis, has attracted much attention. The giant panda is regarded as China's "national treasure" and also as a "living fossil". The number in the wild has reached over 1,500 from 1,100 before, with continuous improvement of their living environment; the number of red ibis has reached more than 560 from seven at tome time. The number of the domesticated Chinese alligator has grown to nearly 10,000, the number of Hainan Elder Deer has risen to over 800 from a virtually-extinct level of 26, and the number of Relict Gulls (Larus relictus) has reached more than 10,000 from 2,000; tigers can be often found in areas of northeast, eastern and southern China; in the global research field of freshwater dolphins, China has played a leading role in the scientific research on white-flag dolphin and helped speed up the artificial propagation of the species. Some wildlife species have been found in wider areas, and new records, breeding grounds or winter homes for species, like black-beaked gulls and black-faced spoonbills, have been constantly discovered. Cupressaceae, which has declared by the International Union for the Conservation of Nature and Natural Resources as an extremely endangered species, while disappeared for over 100 years, has been found again in China. And among 252 species of animals covered by a national investigation, numbers of 55.7 percent of them have increased steadily.

Thanks to unremitting efforts in cracking down on stealing and hunting, with help and support from many international organizations for protecting animals, the Tibetan antelope, for example, has been able to grow in number to the present 70,000 after illegal killing had decimated the species.

Conversation for Wildlife Plants Resources

At present, China has basically confirmed the geographical distribution, ecological environment, vegetation situation, morphological character, value for protection, situation regarding being on the verge of extinction for 191 agricultural wild plant species in the First Batch of List of the Key Wildlife and Wild Plants Under State Special Protection, established census database of agricultural wide plants, image database and information database of GPS/GIS. Meanwhile, the investigation and collection of key wild plants on the verge of extinction and under protection has been carried out, involving wild rice, beans, kindred plants of wild wheat, wild plants with medicinal properties, wild fruit trees, and more than 3,000 resources of wild plants conserved in alien lands; 67 zones have been set up to protect the primordial habitats of agricultural wild plants, great efforts have been made to effectively conserve endangered species and their living environment. And 34 sites of distributing wild rice and two new species of kindred plants of wild wheat have been found.

The northeast tiger is the largest extant catamount, with an average length of 1.8 to 2.8 meters and a 0.9-meter-long tail. Its weight ranges from 227 to 272 kg, with the largest record of over 300 kg.

♦ National-Level Key Laboratory of Satellite Marine Environment Dynamics

The laboratory targets frontier science related to the international marine environment, focusing on environmental scientific issues in coastal waters and adjoining oceans that are now facing China, and makes great efforts on satellite marine environment dynamics, based on pushing forward the development of satellite remote sensing and marine technology of observation and multi-discipline overlapping, so as to carry out research relating to satellite oceanography, marine circulation dynamics and key processes of the offshore environment, and reveal the process, evolution, forecasts and trends of change concerning marine environment dynamics, and establish a theoretical system related to this area in China's adjoining oceans, promote corresponding high-tech and new technology for the observe and survey of marine environment. In this way, it can provide the scientific grounds and technological support for the sustainable development and exploitation as well as safeguarding of marine safety.

It also makes great efforts for the establishment of remote-sensing ground stations of satellite, equipment departments for marine investigation along with database centers and platforms of technological support in marine computer centers. This is designed to improve the level of opening up to the outside for using advanced instruments and equipment in order to enhance the capacity of providing remote sensing of marine satellite and observational data and gradually become an important base for conducting basic research on satellite oceanography and the dynamic process of marine environment.

Website:http://www.soed.org.cn

The black-faced spoonbills wandering on the marsh

Wetland Protection

The wetland refers to swamps, peat bogs and water areas formed under natural, artificial or permanent or temporary conditions, with waters featuring static, flowing, fresh water, half salt water and salt water, including sea areas no less than six meters deep at low tide. China now has 65.94 million hectares of wetland, including 36.20 million hectares of natural wetland; the total area of wetland ranks first in Asia but fourth in the world. China is one of countries with most types of wetland, totaling 28 types in five kinds such as coastal, river, swamp reservoir, and embankment. Since 1992, China entered the *Wetland Ramsar Convention*, it has established 535 various wetland nature reserves, with 40 per cent of natural wetland and containing 33 key animals under State protection. The areas in these nature reserves are low beach within seas, lakes and rivers and wetland adjoining forests; 30 sites, covering 3.43 million hectares, are listed on the international key wetland list. Lalu wetland in Lhasa is a city-natural wetland featuring the highest elevation and biggest area in the world. Thanks to effective protection, its previous withering situation has been reversed, and its space restored to 6.2 square km from less than 6 square km at the end of last century, with more than 95 percent of vegetation coverage based on swamps and meadows.

China's Action on Wetland Protection

In 2006, the nationwide wetland protection project was officially started. In the following five years, the State planned to invest 9 billion Yuan in four key projects, such as wetland conservation, wetland restoration, so as to effectively protect 50 percent of natural wetlands in China. In accordance with the implementation of the National Plan for Wetland Protection Action, initiated in November 2000, China will effective check the trend toward rapid decrease, resulted from human activities, in the overall area of wetlands by 2010, and by 2020, the wetland degenerated or forsaken will be gradually restored.

In 2003, the government promulgated the National Program for Wetland Protection Engineering (2002-2030) proposing that by 2030, China would have 713 wetland nature reserves, including 80 key wetlands reaching international standards, so as to effectively protect over 90 percent of natural wetlands; meanwhile, the engineering of wetland restoration will restore a total of 1.4 million hectares. There will be 53 national-level wetland zones for demonstration, thus establishing a relatively integrated system of protection and rational use, management and construction. At present, there are 10 urban wetland parks.

Yinchuan National Wetland Park

On September 25, 2006, Yichuan National Wetland Park was officially established in Ningxia Hui Autonomous Region. It is the first national-level wetland park in the Yellow River Valley and the middle and western region of China. It is composed of Yuehai wetland and Mingcui Lake wetland. Yuehai wetland park consists of lakes and swamps covering over 2,000 hectares containing 114 species of aquatic plants, 17 species of fish and 107 species of bird. Mingcui Lake wetland covers more than 666.7 hectares, and it is planned to become the world's biggest weed maze featuring the beautiful landscapes of southern China to promote ecological tourism.

Hong Kong Wetland Park

Hong Kong Wetland Park is located in the north of Tin Shui Wai, New Territories, it has an indoor exhibition hall "Wetland Interactive World", with an area of 10,000 square meters, and wetland protection zone covering more than 60 hectares. There is a freshwater swamp, artificial flat, mangrove forest and woodland. It has nearly 190 species of sparrow and other birds, 40 species of dragonfly, over 200 species of butterfly and moth. In design, it shows the theme of protecting the environment, with extensive application of renewable woods, local and recycled materials.

High Mountain Wetland: Maoershan Mountain

Maoershan Mountain is, located in Guilin, Guangxi Zhuang Autonomous Region, and is a rare high mountain wetland in the world. One the one hand it is the origin of the Lijiang, Zijiang and Xunjiang rivers and is a "treasure house" of natural resources and species diversity. Maoershan Mountain is, named as "the First Mountain Peak in South China" covered by primeval forests. Located near the national-level nature reserve of Bajiaotian, this wetland lies at an elevation of about 1,950 meters, surrounded by eight mountain peaks that form a basin covering 240 hectares. This wetland enjoys stable hypsography, is often enveloped in fog, and is thickly covered with mountain forests where moss grows in abundance on the trees. Many streams crisscross the area to create spongy swamplands. Due to the special environment, the mountains and forests here have been severely eroded by strong snows and winds all the year around, therefore the unique forest-type has been gradually formed featuring low trees with thick trunks in a great variety of shapes and postures. The moisture level remains high at around 95 percent all year round, and the annual average rainfall reaches 2,100 millimeters and the annual average temperate is around seven to eight degrees. As a result, after much broken vegetation seeped into soil, because of weak movement of microorganisms with insufficient decomposition, organic substances have accumulated year on year, and the peat soil, 70 to 300 centimeters thick retains the water to create a natural reservoir.

♦ Wetland International-China

Wetland International-China was established on September 26, 1996 in Beijing. It was set up in accordance with the cooperation memorandum signed by the Asia-Pacific Economic Cooperation (APEC) and the Chinese Forestry Ministry in October 1996. The establishment of this body aims at boosting wetland protection and reasonable utilization in China and North-East Asia. Wetland International-China introduces technology and funds, provides personnel training and technology support and develops information exchanges.

Website: www.wetwonder.org

Eco-functional Protection Area

China has established the Eco-Functional Protection Area in regions such as the headwaters of rivers, accumulation areas of important water resources, flood control storage areas of various rivers, sand fixation and wind breaks in sandy regions and other areas of important eco-functional protection. The trial sites of the National Eco-functional Protection Area are established in 18 typical areas, including Dongjiangyuan River, Dongting Lake and Qingling mountain region. Local Eco-functional Protection Areas are established in Inner Mongolia Autonomous Region, Heilongjiang Province, Jiangxi Province, Hubei Province, Hunan Province, Gansu Province and Qinghai Province.

Geothermal Resources

There are 103 Geothermal Fields formally explored in China with the approval of the Reserves Administration Department of the Ministry of Land and Resources. Exploitable geothermal resources are currently estimated at 332.83 million cubic meters on a yearly basis. According to the preliminary valuation, there are some 214 geothermal fields which can produce 500 million cubic meters each year. Estimated by the present level of exploration and utilization, the usable explored geothermal resources total 6.717 million cubic meter, containing 969.28×1015 joule heat.

According to the latest statistics, China leads the world in direct utilization of geothermal resources and the value of this utilization. The direct utilization of geothermal sources has reached 13.76 cubic meters/second producing 10,779 million kWh. The value of the geothermal exploration and utilization is increasing on average by 10 percent each year; however, its proportion in the resources structure is still very small, or less than 0.5 percent. In 2005, the regions with the highest level of the geothermal exploration and utilization included Guangdong Province, Tianjin, Shaanxi Province, Beijing, Yunnan Province, and Shandong Province, Fujian Province and so on.

In 2005, the Ministry of Land and Resources and China Mining Association developed the denomination activity of "Geothermal City in China" and "The homeland of the Hot Springs in China" to promote sustainable utilization model region construction of the geothermal resources, standardize exploration and resource protection and safeguard the environment. Qionghai city in Hainan Province, Xiaotangshan Town in Beijing and Chenzhou City in Hunan Province are named "Homeland of the Hot Spring in China" with official approval.

Dinghushan Mountain National Nature Reserve

Located o the north bank of Xijiang River in Guangdong Province, Dinghushan Mountain Nature Reserve covers an area of 1,133 hectares, mainly to protect evergreen monsoon rain forests of the southern subtropical zone. The natural forest of the region is one of the special natural forest types in the world, and, therefore, of high science and research value. It was established in 1956, the first nature reserve in China. In 1979, it was included in the International Man and Biosphere Reserve Network of UNESCO as a global conservation spot for the research of ecosystems in tropical and subtropical forests. The forest coverage has reached 78 percent. Evergreen broad-leaved forests of the southern subtropical zone with a history of 400 years are well protected. As the top vegetation in the monsoon zone, they are a precious natural heritage. The vegetation is vertically distributed with rich and conspicuous features into several types including monsoon evergreen broad-leaved forests, mountainous evergreen broad-leaved forests and river-side forests.

Huanglong National Nature Reserve

Located in Songpan County, northwest Sichuan Province, the reserve covers a total area of 55,000 hectares. Its main targets for protection are natural scenery and rare wildlife. The Huanglong National Nature Reserve is of great conservation value for its large scale, biodiversity, beautiful scenery, intact ecosystem, high value in science research and aesthetics. It was listed in the World Natural Heritage in 1992 and formally included in the International Man and Biosphere Reserve Network at the end of 2000.Biodiversity is very rich in the reserve. Tall arbors and shrubs, vines, herbs and moss constitute a harmonious picture. In primitive forests, Chinese Larch, spruce, Katsura tree and other rare and endangered plants that only China has are well preserved. In mountain grassy marshlands, there are many precious Chinese medicinal herbs such as Chinese caterpillar fungus and Wujiapi (bark of slender acanthopanax). Therefore, the reserve enjoys a reputation as a kingdom of cold temperate plants. Dense and lush woods and grassland provide favorable conditions for various wild animals to breed. The reserve has more than 30 species of national Class-A and Class-B protected animals including such notable species as giant panda, wildebeest, clouded leopard and golden snub-nosed monkey.

Gaoligongshan Mountain National Nature Reserve

This lies in the west of Yunnan Province covering a total area of 120,000 hectares with forest coverage of 85 percent. It is characterized by its natural landscape of biological and climatic vertical belts, various types of vegetation, and a great variety of plants and animals. In 1992, it was classified as a Class-A reserve of international significance by the World Wildlife Fund (WWF); and it was included in the International Man and Biosphere Reserve Network in 2000. Gaoligong Mountain is surrounded by scores of volcanoes, and therefore the reserve is rich in geothermal resources. There are four score hot springs with marked curative effect on skin diseases and rheumatism. In the Reserve, steam and waterfalls can be seen here and there. Tingminghu Lake on the top of the mountain is a crater lake formed long ago, limpid and transparent. Preliminary research shows that there are more than 1,000 species of higher plants in the reserve. The evergreen broad-leaved forest in the east and west mountain areas is one of the best-preserved forests in Yunnan Province. The evergreen broad-leaved forest here is mainly composed of cupuliferae, camphor trees and camellia. The world-famous "azalea king" is more than five hundred years old and 25 meters high, and Taiwan fiousiana is also more than 1,000 years old, with high and straight trunk The reserve is rich in medicinal, oil, and fibrous plants and has preserved rare medicinal plants in China and the world as a whole.

Changbaishan Mountain National Nature Reserve

Located in the southeast of Jilin Province, this reserve covers an area of 190,781 hectares, with forest coverage of 87.7 percent and a timber storage capacity of 44 million cubic meters. The Changbaishan Mountain National Nature Reserve is the most typical natural composite body in the Eurasian Continent and a rare gene bank of species. It was established in 1960, accepted by the International Man and Biosphere Reserve Network of UNESCO in 1999, and listed as one of the 40 Class-A reserves in China by the World Wildlife Fund (WWF) in 1992.

A varied topography, weather, soil and other natural conditions result in rich biodiversity and vertical zonal distribution of vegetation. Research shows that, 2,277 species of plant from 73 orders and 246 families are distributed in the reserve. It has most of the main timber species, among which Panax ginseng is a national Class-A plant; Panthera spp., Cervus nippon, Mergus squamatus and Gastrodia elata are also under State protection. There are a great variety of wild animals and 1,225 known animal species from 73 orders and 219 families, among which 43 species are under State protection. Some six species are National Class-A protected animals such as leopard, Siberian tiger, sika, sable, golden eagle, and some 37species are National Class-B protected animals including black bear, lynx, otter and goral. All of the animals are of high economic and research value.

♦ Logo of the National Forest Park

The logo of the National Forest Park is made up of the Chinese and English name and pictures of China's National Forest Park, an official symbol possessed by the State Forestry Administration. Some 230 National Forest Parks, including Zhangjiajie in Hunan Province and Shennongjia in Hubei Province, are granted the right to use the Special Symbol of the National Forest Park.

♦ Logo of the Nature Reserve of China

On October 27, 2006, China determined the logo of nature reserves to be one composed of two hands grasped against the backdrop of the Earth. The bright and dark colors of the hands form a mighty turbulent river coming from the horizon. The blue sky in the distance and the nearby green land combine to depict a flourishing and harmonious scene of the natural environment. The two hands symbolize the need to protect nature reserves and the natural environment at large on Earth. They also show the fact that everyone on Earth needs to participate in the protection of the natural environment. "Nature Reserve" in both Chinese and English spread around the rim of the logo. The logo base bears patterns of clouds and water.

♦ Environment Websites

China's Economic Forest Information Website:
www.efic.gov.cn
China's Wildlife Website:
www.wildlife--plant.gov.cn
China's Wetland Website:
www.wetland.gov.cn
China's Nature Reserve Website:
www.naturereserve.gov.cn

The southwest slope of the Changbaishan Mountain.

Scenic Areas and Places of Historical Interest

Thus far, some 677 Scenic and Historic Interest Area titles have been used with government approval, among which, some 187 are dubbed as a "National Key Scenic and Historic Interest Area". National key scenic areas and places of historic interest and a bulk of nature reserve are listed in World Heritage, Man and Biosphere Reserve Network and List of Wetlands of International Importance respectively such as Taishan Mountain, Huangshan Mountain, Emeishan Mountain-Leshan Mountain, Wuyishan Mountain, Lushan Mountain, Wulingyuan, Jiuzhaigou, Huanglong, Qingchengshan Mountain-Dujiangyan, and The Three Parallel Rivers. More than 1,900 forest parks are established, including 627 at national level. China also has 85 National 'Geoparks', among which, eight were initially included in the 'List of Global Geoparks' such as Huangshan in Anhui Province, Lushan in Jiangxi Province, Yuntaishan in Henan Province, Stone Forest in Yunnan Province, Danxiashan in Guangdong Province, Zhangjiajie in Hunan Province, Wudalianchi in Heilongjiang Province and Songshan in Henan Province.

Nature Reserves

Established in recent years, nature reserves represent advanced human civilization. It is a magnificent feat for humankind to protect the ecological environment and nature resources, facing the challenge from the ecological damage. China's nature reserves include nine types such as forest, grassland, wetland, sea, barren desert, wildlife, geological relic and paleontological relic. The government takes the establishment of nature reserves as an important measure to protect the ecological environment. By the end of 2006, China has named 233 national ecological demonstration areas and 2,395 nature reserves, including 265 at the national level. The nature reserves cover a total area of 151.54 million hectares, accounting for 15 percent of national land. Some 85 percent of the land ecological system, some 85 percent of wildlife and 65 percent of the natural plants community are well protected.

Regarding distribution, each province and region has a nature reserve. Guangdong Province, Yunnan Province, Inner Mongolia Autonomous Region, Heilongjiang Province, Sichuan Province, Jiangxi Province, Guizhou Province and Fujian Province have the most. The total number of nature reserves of these eight provinces and regions accounts for 58 percent in the whole country. In terms of area, the nature reserves in the Tibet Autonomous Region, Xinjiang Uygur Autonomous Region, Qinghai Province, Inner Mongolia Autonomous Region, Gansu Province, Sichuan Province and other province in the west are larger; the total area accounts for 77 percent of the whole country. Established in August 2000, the Three River Sources is the most biodiversity-rich nature reserve, with the largest area (about 316,000 square km) and the highest altitude (average height more than 4000 meter). Guangdong Province has 209 nature reserves covering 3.17 million hectares. Some 27 nature reserves are included in the International Man and Biosphere Reserve Network of UNESCO such as Wolong Nature Reserve in Sichuan Province, Changbaishan Mountain Nature Reserve in Jilin Province, Dinghushan Mountain Nature Reserve in Guangdong Province, Baishuijiang River Nature Reserve in Gansu Province and so on.

Sketch Map of Some Nature Reserves

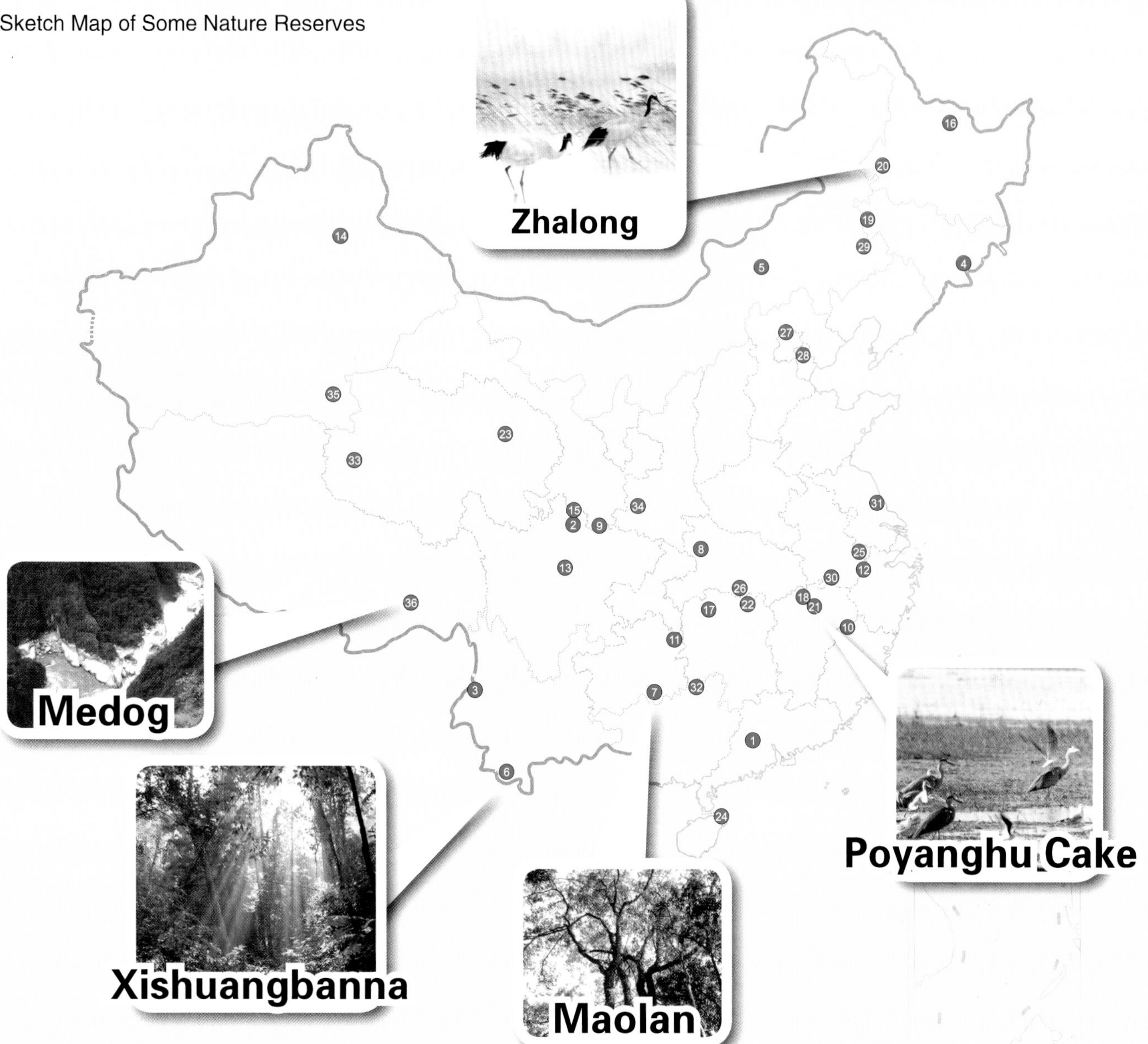

1 Dinghushan Mountain National Nature Reserve
2 Huanglong National Nature Reserve
3 Gaoligongshan Mountain National Nature Reserve
4 Changbaishan Mountain National Nature Reserve
5 Xilinguole National Nature Reserve
6 Xishuangbanna National Nature Reserve
7 Maolan National Nature Reserve
8 Shennongjia National Nature Reserve
9 Baishuijiang National Nature Reserve
10 Wuyishan Mountain National Nature Reserve
11 Fanjingshan Mountain National Nature Reserve
12 Tianmushan Mountain National Nature Reserve
13 Wolong National Nature Reserve
14 Bogeda Peak National Nature Reserve
15 Jiuzhaigou National Nature Reserve
16 Fenglin National Nature Reserve
17 Zhangjiajie Nature Reserve
18 Lushan Mountain Nature Reserve
19 Xianghai Nature Reserve
20 Zhalong Nature Reserve
21 Poyanghu Lake Nature Reserve
22 East Dongtinghu Lake Nature Reserve
23 Qinghaihu Lake Bird Islet Nature Reserve
24 Dongzhaigang Nature Reserve
25 Chinese Alligator Nature Reserve
26 Tian'ezhou White-Flag Dolphin Nature Reserve
27 Songshan Mountain Nature Reserve
28 Paleocoastal Nature Reserve
29 Ke'erqin Nature Reserve
30 Guniujiang Nature Reserve
31 Dafeng David's Deer Nature Reserve
32 Huaping Nature Reserve
33 Hoh Xil Nature Reserve
34 Taibaishan Mountain Nature Reserve
35 Alchin Mountain Nature Reserve
36 Medog Nature Reserve

Xilinguole National Nature Reserve

This lies in the Inner Mongolia Autonomous Region and covers a total area of 10,786 square kilometers. In fact, Xilinguole Grassland attracted great attention from botanists at home and abroad as early as the 1930s.The Xilinguole National Nature Reserve was established in 1985, the first grassland nature reserve in the country, and later joined the International Man and Biosphere Reserve Network. It has abundant wildlife resources. Grassland makes up the main vegetation; there are 625 species of higher plants from 74 families and 291 genera, among which, a majority provide excellent grazing. Spruce, white birth and willows are found here. There are a number of medicinal plants and economic plants such as Chinese thorowax, Scutellaria baicalensis, and polygala tenuifolia. Research has identified many species of floral plants including yellow day lilies and red morningstar lilies. Wildlife in the reserve reflects the feature of fauna of Mongolian Plateau including mammal species such as Mongolian gazelle, wolf and fox, etc., and birds including swans and larks and various insects as well. In addition, there are many lakes of different sizes and shapes with a lot of carps and sandaolin, a local special product of Inner Mongolia. The animal husbandry here develops fast. Xilinguole is home to fine-wool sheep, Mongolian ox and Xilinguole horse.

Xishuangbanna National Nature Reserve

The reserve lies in the south of Yunnan Province. It covers a total area of 241,000 hectares, among which natural forest covers an area of 197,800 hectares and accounts for 81.8 percent of the total. Established in 1958, the reserve was accepted by UNESCO as a member of the International Man and Biosphere Reserve Network in 1993. Its main targets for protection are the tropical forest ecosystem, including marvelous virgin forests, tropical rain forest and monsoon rain forest as well as precious flora and fauna.

Xishuangbanna lies at the northern limit of the tropical rain forests of Southeast Asia. There are two vegetation types of valley and hill rain forests. The abundant flora comprises more than 5,000 species of higher and seed plants, which accounts for 12 percent of the national total. Among them are 58 species of rare and endangered plants under State protection, accounting for 15 percent of the total. The rare plants in the reserve include shorea chinensis, which produces camphol, Gmelina arborea Roxb, which is as valuable as teak, and tetramelaceae the local special product. Here grow ancient tropical plants such as Chinese parashoreas (Parashorea chinensis) and sogo Cycas which have been bypassed in the evolutionary process. In addition, there are over 800 species of medicinal plants and other plants with special use. Xishuangbanna, with its luxuriant forests and varied plant-life, occupies a unique place in China's biota. The reserve boasts 539 species of terrestrial vertebrates accounting for 25 percent of the total in China, 429 species of birds, 36 percent of the total, 47 species of amphibians, 68 species of reptiles and 100 species of fish from 18 families and 54 genera, 40 percent of the total genera, and 27 percent of the total species.

The tropical rain forest in Xishuang Banna

Maolan National Nature Reserve

The reserve lies in the southeast of Libo County, southern Guizhou Province. It covers an area of 20,000 hectares with forest coverage of 91.59 percent. As a subtropical original ancient plant kingdom, it is a karst virgin forest rarely seen in the subtropical zone on the same latitude, and is characterized by its wildness, peculiarity and beauty. Established in 1987, the reserve was included in the International Man and Biosphere Reserve Network of UNESCO in 1996.

Maolan National Nature Reserve is located in the central subtropical zone, and karst in various sizes and shapes is very representative, typical and of scientific importance. Falling leaves pile heavily and the average annual precipitation reaches over 1,700 millimeters in the area. The heavy rainfall and temperate climate provide favorable conditions for the growth of vegetation. High arbors, dense shrubs and various rattans intertwine inextricably. Picturesque stones and rocks due to the hydrologic effect are covered with bryophytes. Many tree roots grow on rocks nakedly and some have already permeated the rocks and become part of them. All these help form the unique doline karst landscape.

Shennongjia National Nature Reserve

The reserve lies in the southwest of the Shennongjia Forest Range, Hubei Province, with a total area of 70,467 hectares. It encompasses three vertical vegetation zones namely subtropical, warm temperate and cold temperate; hence, it is an ideal place for ecological research on biodiversity, typicality and natural transition of vegetation. The reserve was established in 1982, and it was accepted by the International Man and Biosphere Reserve Network of UNESCO in 1990.

A unique geographical location has provided the reserve with opportunities to preserve precious plants surviving from the Quaternary Period. There are 2,062 species of pteridophyte and seed plants. It is known that there are 336 species of terrestrial vertebrate,

The Shennongjia area in Hubei is the most east end distributed with the Sichuan snub-nosed monkeys. Thanks to years of effective protection, the number of the Sichuan snub-nosed monkeys increases to over 1,200 from 501 in 1988.

15

Environmental Protection

200 species of birds, and 30 species of reptiles and 27 orders of insects that approximately account for 81.8 percent of the total. 40 species of animals such as golden monkeys, South China tigers, golden eagles and giant salamanders are under the first-grade State protection. White bears, white monkeys and white toad are found in the Reserve now and then. In addition, Shennongjia is also famous for the sightings of wild, ape-like creatures, a Chinese equivalent of the Himalayan Yeti or Big Foot. Many scientists have been to reserve for investigation.

Baishuijiang National Nature Reserve

The reserve is located in the south of Gansu Province, covering an area of 213,750 hectares. It features verdant and lush forest and a great variety of plants and animals. It was established in 1978 and mainly protects giant pandas, other rare wildlife and their ecosystem. In November 2000, it was formally included in the International Man and Biosphere Reserve Network.

The mild temperature, plenty rain, luxuriant forests and good ecological environment make it an ideal place for the growth of bamboo, giant pandas' favorite food. In Baishuijiang National Nature Reserve, there are altogether 265 species of terrestrial vertebrate, 180 species of birds and over 2,000 species of reptiles. As a colourful wildlife reserve, it is also with great significance in animal geography classification. In addition to pandas, there are other rare and precious animals such as black gibbons, takins, and golden eagles under first-class State protection. Animals under the Second-class state protection include macaques, otters, giant salamanders and gorals.

Wuyishan Mountain National Nature Reserve

This world-famous reserve sits on the highest section of the Wuyishan Mountain Range in Fujian Province. Its total area is 56,527 hectares, and it is a well preserved Mid-Subtropical Forest with the largest area in the same latitude in the world; 95.3 percent of the area is covered by forest. Established in 1979, the reserve joined the International Man and Biosphere Reserve Network in 1986 as the biggest and the most comprehensive extant semi-subtropical forest system in Southeast China. Wuyi Mountain is not only famous for its surprisingly spectacular scenery but also for its rich wildlife resources, making the area an important a rare species database.

The reserve preserves primitive forests with an area of over 20,000 hectares with 30

The Wuyishan Mountain

formations and more than 100 communities. Its vegetation types include evergreen broadleaved forest, coniferous and broad-leaved transitional forest, evergreen and deciduous broadleaved mixed forest, coniferous forest, shrubs and bamboo forest. There are nearly 4,000 plant species, 19 of which, such as ginkgo, Chinese hemlock, Chinese tulip, China cypress and ornament plants, are under first-grade State protection. In addition, there are dozens of rare or local special plant species in Wuyi Mountain National Nature Reserve that have high value in research of plant evolution. There are 57 species of wild animals under State protection. South China tigers, which have not been seen for many years, leopard, white pheasant, macaque, zibet, mandarin duck and pangolin, etc., are officially protected vertebrates seldom seen elsewhere in the world. China has altogether 32 orders of insects and 31 orders with around 5,000 species can be found in the reserve. In addition, there are 64 species of snakes (17 of them vipers), accounting for a third of the total in China.

Fanjingshan Mountain National Nature Reserve

The reserve is located in the northeast of Guizhou Province, with an area of 567 squares kilometers. Fanjing, also a famous mountain for Buddhism in China, is believed to include the best-preserved virgin forests in the subtropical zone. Virgin forests cover an area of about 10,000 hectares and forest coverage reaches 80 percent, especially evergreen broad-leaved forests in the valleys and at the foot of Fanjing Mountain. Established in 1978, Fanjing was classified as a national reserve and joined the International Man and Biosphere Reserve Network in 1986.

The dove tree, a special species of China, is listed in the inventory of plants under first-grade State protection. During spring and summer, dove trees blossom and their flowers look just like doves. And this forms a peculiar and beautiful picture especially in the sunshine. The Chinese tulip tree is also an ornamental plant. In addition, a Guizhou crape myrtle of a thousand years old is found in Fanjing Mountain. It is 30 meters high with a diameter of about two meters.

Tianmushan Mountain National Nature Reserve

Located on the boundary of Lin'an County of Zhejiang Province, this reserve covers a total area of 4,284 hectares. It lies between east longitude of 119° 24′- 119° 28′ and north latitude of 30°18′-30°25′. Tianmushan Mountain is a famous mountain with a long history of close connection with Confucianism, Taoism and Buddhism. The topography and unique Buddhist culture have made Tianmushan Mountain a wonder of the world for its preservation of wildlife and vegetation. Established in 1958 as a tree-felling ban area, it was promoted to be a national reserve in 1986 and included by UNESCO in the International Man and Biosphere Reserve Network in 1996.

It is mild and moist, and vegetation covers many geological ages and biodiversity. The region is one of the sites with the richest subtropical higher plant species in China. There are 2,160 species of higher plants from 246 families and 974 genera, some 1,781 species of seed plants, some 151 species of ferns, some 222 species of mosses and 69 species of mosses. Among them, more than 37 species are named after Tianmu Mountain and 1,200 species of medicinal plants.The ancient pines in Tianmu Mountain, bypassed in the evolutionary process, can top 80 meters and the volume of timber of each can reach over 40 cubic meters. There are only five Tianmu Tiemus (Ostrya rehderiana Chun), which are called a single child of the earth.

Wolong National Nature Reserve

This is located in Aba Tibetan Autonomous Prefecture, Sichuan Province, covering an area of about 700,000 hectares, and its main protection targets are the forest ecosystem and precious animals like giant pandas. Established in 1963, it joined the International Man and Biosphere Reserve Network in 1980.

There are over 50 species of animals and 300 species of birds. The number of giant

On January 1, 2006, the scientific researchers of Sichuan Wolong Research Center gathered the 16 giant pandas born in 2005.

pandas here accounts for about one-tenth of the total, so Wolong National Nature Reserve is also identified as homeland of giant pandas. Besides giant pandas, red pandas, golden pheasants, white-eared pheasants and Chinese monals as well as the stunning Firethroats, golden monkeys and Musk Deer can also be found here. Most of these animals live in temperate coniferous and broadleaved mixed forest between an altitude of 2,200-3,600 meters.

The Wolong National Nature Reserve is the most famous among the 13 giant panda reserve centers established by the Chinese government with the help of the World Wildlife Fund (WWF). It is also the first one of its kind to set up a research center for giant pandas in 1978. Zoologists at home and abroad have made ecological observation of giant pandas including its number, distribution, breeding and population structure.

Bogeda Peak National Nature Reserve

This is located in Fukang City, Xinjiang Uygur Autonomous Region. With a total area of 2,170 square kilometers, it comprises the Tianchi Lake nature reserve and Fukang desert ecological center of the China Academy of Sciences. Its targets for protection include endangered animals, forests, grassland, Tianshan Mountain scenic spots and oases. It is the seventh of its kind in China included in the International Man and Biosphere Reserve Network but also the first in Xinjiang Uygur Autonomous Region.

There are more than 300 species of wild medicinal herbs in the Reserve such as Fritillaria thunbergii, Chinese angelica, Codonopsis pilosula and Saussurea involucrata. The reserve is also a habitat for about a hundred species of rare animals and eight of them such as brown bears, snow leopards and snow cocks are under State protection. Lake Tianchi is especially rich in wild animal resources. According to the record, there are 24 species of animals, 50 species of birds, and six species of reptiles, fish and amphibians respectively. The vertical distribution of animals is obvious, the high and cold area is featured by snow leopards and griffon vultures, the forest area is characterized by red deer and lynx, and while in low area lives badgers and chukars, etc.

Jiuzhaigou National Nature Reserve

This lies in Jiuzhaigou County, northwestern Sichuan Province, in the southern part of Minshan Mountains, approximately 400 kilometers from Chengdu City. Established in 1978, it covers an area of 60,000 hectares with its name stemming from nine Tibetan villages nearby. Luxuriant forests and snow peaks in Jiuzhaigou make it a spectacular gem of nature. Jiuzhaigou is a comprehensive nature reserve, its main protection targets being pandas, other rare wildlife and forest ecosystem. In 1992, it was listed in the World Natural Heritage, and three years later, it was included in the International Man and Biosphere Reserve Network.

Multiple and complex geological changes throughout history have created the unique landscape of the reserve, in which primitive forest covers an area of over 200 hectares. Vertical distribution of the natural vegetation is kept intact. Between the altitude of 2,000-2,400 meters, oaks, birches, poplars and other broadleaved trees and Chinese pines, firs and other conifers grow densely in coniferous and broadleaved mixed forest. Between the altitude of 2,400-3,200 meters, firs and Fragesia denudata grow well in coniferous forest. At the altitude of over 3,200 meters, Korean pines, firs, dragon spruce and other precious tree species as well as medicinal materials such as Cordyceps sinensis and tendril-leaved fritillary bulb grow in the alpine shrub. The reserve is not only rich in plants but also in animal species, among which there are rare species such as giant pandas, golden monkeys, Takins, lesser pandas, otters and swans.

Fenglin National Nature Reserve

The reserve lies in Yichuan City, Heilongjiang Province, covering an area of 18,400 hectares. It was established in 1958, and classified as a national reserve in 1988. In 1997, it joined the International Man and Biosphere Reserve Network. The reserve was established mainly to protect its dense virgin Korean pine (Pinus koraiensis) forests, the last virgin forest in the area.

The diameter of some trees reaches 1.4 meters and the highest tree reaches 37 meters. Tall and straight Korean pine is good construction materials for it is easily processed without being cracked. China's Korean pine is mainly distributed in Lesser Hinggan Mountains and Changbai Mountains, while Korean pine in Fenglin National Nature Reserve accounts for over 80 percent of the total both in terms of number and storage. The Korean pine mixed forest is typical vegetation in the moist Northeast China. The reserve has not only preserved precious Korean pine resources but also become a natural museum and gene bank of species, which provides favorable conditions for scientific research, education and manufacturing activities.

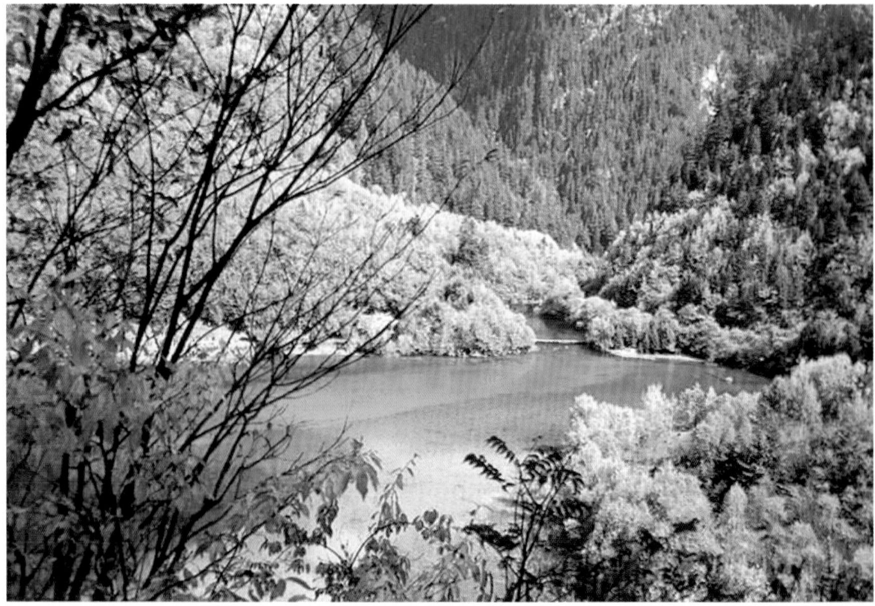

The Jiuzhaigou Valley

15 Environmental Protection

Zhangjiajie Nature Reserve

The Wulingyuan, a national tourist area, is comprised of Zhangjiajie, Suoxiyu Valley and Tianzishan Mountain, with a total area of 369 square km.

Located in the east of Dayong City, Hunan Province, the reserve covers a total area of 13,300 hectares. It is the first national forest park, some 95 percent of which is covered by forests. Belonging to Wuling Mountain Range, the reserve is characterized by 2,000 peaks in fancy shapes being eroded or weathered over so many years. It is a famous scenic spot. Due to its subtropical monsoon damp climate, primitive forests and secondary forests house much rare wildlife. There are more than 500 species of ligneous plants, among them, precious and endemic plants including ginkgo, Chinese tulip, dove tree and Katsura tree, etc. In addition, there are 27 species of beasts, 41 species of birds. Musk deer, civet, blue sheep, giant salamander and other animals are listed under State protection. The Zhangjiajie Nature Reserve is included in World Nature Heritage.

Lushan Mountain Nature Reserve

Located in Jiangxi Province south of Jiujiang City, north of Yangtze River, east of Boyanghu Lake, this reserve covers a total area of 30,466 hectares. The highest peak of Lushan Mountain is 1,474 meters above sea level. Its main protection targets are forest ecosystem, cultural heritage, glacier features and natural landscape. More than 40 species of plants found here are either rare or local special species including Katsura tree, Manglietia fordiana, Chinese tulip and eucommia. Animals under the state protection are leopard, giant salamander, civet, python, pangolin, muntjac, silver pheasant, white crane, and mandarin duck and so on. In addition, there are 26 ancient glacier heritages such as cirque, icehouse and deep valleys. The Lushan Reserve is part of the World Nature Heritage list.

Xianghai Nature Reserve

This is located on the boundaries of Tongyu County of Jilin Province, the center of the Ke'erqin Prairie, with an area of 105,400 hectares. Established in 1981, the main protection targets are rare birds, such as white stork and crane, and elm trees etc. The Reserve was listed as a Wetland of International Importance in 1992, one of the seven wetlands of international importance in China. The main landscape is marshland and desert short forest. The reserve has many lakes and various vegetation types such as reed marsh, Leymus chinensis grassland, shrub with sparse trees, dune with elm trees etc. The natural environment and abundant bio-resources support various types of wildlife, especially, many birds. In the light of preliminary investigation, there are more than 200 species of birds. Every spring, birds, including State protected species such as Grus japonensis, G. Leucogeranus, G. Vipio, G. Grus, Platalea leucorodia, fly here in groups to make it an important breeding place. It is also an important base for protection and research of biodiversity.

Zhalong Nature Reserve

Located in the lower reaches of Wuyu'erhe River, west of Heilongjiang Province, and 30 kilometers from Mudanjiang City, the reserve covers 40,000 square kilometers. Its main protection targets are red-crowned crane and other wild rare birds. It was listed as a Wetland of International Importance in 1992. In the reserve there are wide stretches of marshes and lakes, an ideal inhabit for red-crowned crane and other water fowls. The reserve has 248 species of birds, among which, more than 20 species are under State protection. It is remarkable because of many species of the crane living here. The reserve has six crane species such as red-crowned cranes, white cranes, G. Vipio, Anthropoides virgo, while there are only 15 species in the whole world. In the reserve, there are over 500 red-crowned cranes, accounting for one quarter of the world total. There are also swans, egrets and other rare birds.

Poyanghu Lake Nature Reserve

Located in the north of Jiangxi Province, Poyanghu Lake comprises a triangular collection area of the Ganjiang and Xiushui rivers. There are nine sub-lake areas with Wucheng Town, Yongxiu County, in the center, forming the biggest freshwater lake in China. The Poyanghu Lake Nature Reserve covers a total area of 22,400 hectares. Its protection targets are white cranes, egrets and other rare birds. It was listed as a Wetland of International importance in 1992.

According to related investigation, the Reserve provides shelters for a million birds of 258 species, of which over 40 such as egrets, white cranes, white-crown cranes, great bustards, golden eagles and swans are under first-grade and second-grade State protection. It is known as the world's largest nature reserve for white cranes to live through the winter. Some 95 percent white cranes in the world may fly here to escape winter cold. As a habitat for migratory birds, Poyang Lake becomes an important place for the protection of birds.

East Dongtinghu Lake Nature Reserve

Located on the boundaries of Yueyang City, Hunan Province, the reserve covers an area of 190,300 hectares. It was listed as a Wetland of International Importance in 1992. Its main protection targets are wetland and rare bird species. The reserve is part of Dongting Lake, the second largest freshwater lake in China. Affected by the Yangtze River and Xiang Water System, marshland, swamp, shoal and so on have formed. At the same time, materials brought by floodwaters are deposited, which provide favorable conditions for aquatic wildlife to live and breed. Since the reserve lies in the reproduction area of migratory birds winter and summer, it is rich in species. There are 158 species of migratory birds and 10 species including white cranes under first-grade State protection, 27 species such as swans under the second-grade State protection. Such mammals as white-flag dolphin and black finless porpoise can often be spotted in the lake. The Reserve also boasts 20 fish species of economic value such as Chinese Paddlefish.

Qinghaihu Lake Bird Islet Nature Reserve

The Bird Islet on the Qinghaihu Lake. It is a small island with an area of less than one square km in the Qinghaihu Lake. During the late spring and early summer, 100-odd kinds of birds come here from a great distance. Over 100,000 birds fill the island, whose sounds can be heard several km away.

Located in the northeastern part of the Qinghai Province, this reserve covers an area of 495,200 hectares including the area surrounding the Bird Island of Qinghaihu

Lake. The reserve is one of the important places for the migratory bird to inhabit, breed and live through the winter. It is dry and cold in the Reserve. The winter lasts longer and the summer shorter with big disparity of temperature. The reserve has abundant wetland ecosystem and bio-resources. There are altogether 200 species of birds and beasts in Qinghai hu Lake and lakeside area. As a plateau lake, it is the kingdom of birds. In spring and summer, some 100,000 birds including gulls, cormorants, swans and blank-necked cranes fly in for the summer. Qinghaihu Lake also boasts abundant fish resources, some of which serve as good food for the birds. The reserve was listed as a Wetland of International Importance in 1992.

Dongzhaigang Nature Reserve

The reserve is located in Qiongshan City, Hainan Province. It covers a total area of 3,337.6 hectares, among which mangrove forest accounts for 2,065 hectares. The reserve was listed as a Wetland of International Importance in 1992. It has the largest number of mangrove species in China. In the preservation zone, there are 16 families and 32 species such as Rhizophora stylosa, Kandelia candel, Aegiceras corniculatum and Avicennia marina. Dongzhaigang is therefore an important conservation spot for mangroves. According to statistics, there are 159 species of birds such as egrets and ducks. Dongzhaigang is also a good habitat of marine animals, including fish, shrimps, and shellfish such as sipunculid worm, perch and oyster.

Chinese Alligator Nature Reserve

Located in Xuanzhou City, Anhui Province, the reserve covers an area of 44,300 hectares. Its main protection targets are the Chinese alligator and its habitat. The reserve lies in the temperate zone with four distinct seasons and plenty of rain. It is traversed by the Shuiyang River and Qingyi River and surrounded by many ponds, ditches, gullies and dykes, so is an ideal habitat for Chinese alligators to live and breed. The Chinese alligator and crocodile in the Mississippi are the only two extant crocodilian species living in freshwater in the world, and they are small in number. Chinese alligators are listed as first-grade State protected animals. The Xuanzhou City Government set up a breeding and research center for Chinese alligators, which covers an area of 100 hectares. With over ten years of efforts, artificial propagation has been achieved. More than 4,000 Chinese alligators are living freely in the breeding center, and thus the ancient species gets well preserved.

Tian'ezhou White-Flag Dolphin Nature Reserve

Located in the boundaries of Shisheng City of Hubei Province, the reserve covers an area of 2,000 hectares. Established in 1990 with the provincial government approval, it was promoted to be a national reserve in 1992. The main protection targets are white-flag dolphins and their habitat. The white-flag dolphin, a rare mammal on the verge of extinction in the Yangtze River, is a first-class State protected animal. Tian'ezhou lies in the lower reaches of the Yangtze River with a length of 20.9 kilometers and its surface covers an area of 18-20 square kilometers. The flood season in Tian'ezhou is almost the same as that of the Yangtze River. Tian'ezhu remains unpolluted and the advantageous hydrological conditions, making it ideal for dolphin survival. At present, relocation for the protection of white-flag dolphins is being carried out.

Songshan Mountain Nature Reserve

The reserve is situated at the southern foot of Haituoshan Mountain, Beijing. Covering an area of 4,660 hectares, it mainly protects natural Chinese pine trees (Pinus tabulaeformis) and temperate forest ecosystem as a whole. The reserve claims the only Chinese Pine forest in North China. In addition, the broadleaved forest consists of Chinese lindens, elm trees, birches and other broadleaved trees. There are more than 600 species of seed plants and 70 species of higher animals including some animals under State protection such as leopards and gorals.

Paleocoastal Nature Reserve

Covering an area of 900 hectares, this is located in Jixian County, Tianjin Municipality. It is the first State-level nature reserve with geological sections in China. The reserve has attracted world attention for its complete rock strata, simple construction and Paleozoic fossils, etc. The reserve has been identified as a standard Paleocoastal section. The section is 9,197 meters thick, which demonstrates the history of geological evolution from 1,850 million years to 800 million years ago. In the rock stratum with a geological age of 1,400 million to 1,200 million years ago, microorganisms rarely seen in the world have been discovered. This discovery has greatly moved up the birth date of microorganisms.

Ke'erqin Nature Reserve

The reserve, with an area of 126,987 hectares, lies on the boundaries of Ke'erqin, Inner Mongolia Autonomous Region. The main protection targets are rare birds, wetland and typical natural landscape. Forest, shrub and grassland as well as river, lake and marshland form a complex environment. There are 452 species from 65 families of higher plants and 167 species from 16 orders of birds in the reserve, among which 34 are protected animals. The reserve is also an important reproduction spot for red-crowned cranes, white stocks, great bustards and other rare birds.

Guniujiang Nature Reserve

Mono maples on the Plain of the Horqin Right Middle Banner of the Hinggan League in Inner Mongolia Autonomous Region.

Located on the boundaries of Qimen and Shitai counties in Anhui Province, and west of Huangshan Mountains, the reserve covers an area of 14,821 hectares. Its main protection target is evergreen broadleaved forest in the mid subtropical zone. The reserve preserves relatively intact evergreen broadleaved forest, which is the representative of its kind in Wannan mountainous area. There is a great variety of wildlife in the reserve, including over 500 species of xylophyta such as Chinese tulips under State protection, and over 200 species of higher animals. More than 10 species of animals such as sika and white-necked pheasant are under State protection.

Dafeng David's Deer Nature Reserve

The reserve is located in Dafeng City, Jiangsu Province. Covering an area of 3,000 hectares, it was set up mainly to protect Milu—Père David's deer (Elaphurus davidianus) and its habitat. In August 1986, organized by the Ministry of Forestry and the World Wildlife Fund (WWF), a group of 39 Père David's deer was selected from seven zoological gardens in the United Kingdom, with the deer mainly from the Whipsnade Wild Animal Park. The reserve had 268 Père David's deer after a decade's effort. In addition, 19 more species such as Greater Swan and River Deer are listed as the first-class State protected animals. The reserve also has 95 species listed in Sino-Japan Agreement on Migratory Bird Protection and therefore it is an important place for birds of passage to live through the winter.

Huaping Nature Reserve

Located at the juncture of Longsheng and Lingui counties of Guangxi Zhuang Autonomous Region, the reserve covers an area of 17,400 hectares. The main protection targets are China firs and mid-subtropical evergreen broad-leaved forest. The reserve has a monsoon climate of the subtropical zone. The vegetation here features evergreen broadleaved forest. There are 1,114 species of higher plants and 12 are under State protection. There are more than 1,000 China firs. The reserve boasts 118 species of higher animals and some of them are national protected animals such as rhesus monkeys and musk deer.

Hoh Xil Nature Reserve

Located in the boundaries of Zhiduo County and Qumalai County of Qinghai Province, the reserve covers an area of 4.5 million hectares. It mainly protects indigenous wildlife of the Qinghai-Tibet Plateau and their habitat. A primitive ecosystem is preserved intact in the reserve. There are 202 species of higher plants, and 84 of them are special local plants of the Qinghai-Tibet Plateau. Hoh Xil Nature Reserve is the habitat for rare animals. There are 16 species of mammals and about 30 species of birds. Some 18 species of them are indigenous to the Qinghai-Tibet Plateau. Snow leopards, golden eagles, gorals and yaks are under State protection.

Taibaishan Mountain Nature Reserve

Located at the juncture of Taibai, Mei and Zhouzhi counties of Shaanxi Province, the reserve covers an area of 56,325 hectares, the main protection targets being forest ecosystem and historical remains. The reserve lies in the transitional region of North China, Central China and the Qinghai-Tibet Plateau, which results in an obvious vertical vegetation zone. There are more than 2,000 species of higher plants, and 21 of them such as Katsura tree and Chinese Larch are under the state protection. The reserve has over 270 species of higher animals, over 20 State-protected, including giant panda, takin and leopard. In an alpine region at an altitude of 3,000 meters or more, the glacier heritage of the Quaternary Period is preserved fairly well.

Altun Mountain Nature Reserve

The reserve with an area of 4,500,000 hectares lies in Qarkilik (Ruoqiang) County, Xinjiang Uygur Autonomous Region. It mainly protects the primitive alpine ecosystem and rare animals such as wild asses and wild yaks. Plants are distinguished by their geological location from the Central Asian desert to the Qinghai-Tibet Plateau in light of their species and distribution. There are over 300 species of higher plants and 63 species of higher animals. Some of the animals living in great numbers are under State protection such as wild yak, wild ass, antelope, snow leopard and black-necked crane.

Motuo Nature Reserve

The reserve with an area of 62,620 hectares lies in Motuo County of Tibet Autonomous Region and mainly protects mountain forests and rare plants and animals. The reserve is located in the great canyon of the Yarlung Zangbo River. Its special geological location makes the reserve rich in various mountain forest vegetation types in tropical and cold temperate zones. There are more than 3,000 species of higher plants, which account one-tenth of the total in China. Some 21 species of animals are under State protection. In addition, over 40 indigenous species of plants are named after Motuo. Some 42 species of animals are under State protection including takin, Assamese macaque, tiger and Motuo Zorapteran. Motuo Nature Reserve is an important research center of ecosystems in different climatic zones.

Tibetan antelope

National Nature Reserve

In 2006, SEPA issued the decision that some 22 national nature reserves should be established in 17 provinces and regions including Shanxi Province, Inner Mongolia Autonomous Region, etc. Thus far, 265 have been created with a total area of 91,851 million hectares, accounting for 9.6 percent of the total land area of China.

There are five types of reserves including Forest Reserve, Wetland Reserve, Barren Desert Reserve, Wild-Life Reserve and Paleontological Relic Reserve. They have salient features of sparseness, representative and typical in China's biodiversity conservation. They play an important role in water and soil conservation, creating wind-breaks and sand-fixing, water source conservation, climate adjustment and protecting ecological balance. Among them, Wulushan Mountain Nature Reserve in Shanxi Province is the centralized distribution area for Brown-Eared Pheasant, which is special rare pheasant in China; Tonglinghe River Dolphin Nature Reserve in Anhui Province is the centralized distribution water area for Chinese white-flag dolphin, which is of great significance for protecting this rare breed; Binzhou Shell-Dyke Island and Wetland National Nature Reserve in Shangdong Province is one of the three world largest Shell-Dyke Islands, which is the rare ocean nature heritage with the co-existence of new and old Shell-Dyke Islands; Micangshan Mountain Nature Reserve is the largest in the area and most centralized distribution area of the species of the fungus plant wildwood; Daxueshan Mountain Nature Reserve in Yongde, Yunnan Province, facing the two water systems of Lancangjiang River and Nujiang River, preserves the only existing hog deer groups and the largest group of the black crested gibbon.

Regulatory System on Nature Reserves

The National People's Congress has promulgated a series of laws with respect to nature reserves, namely the Environmental Protection Law, Law on the Protection of Wild Animals, the Forestry Law, Grassland Law,

Fisheries Law and Marine Environmental Protection Law. In 1994, the State Council issued the Regulations on Nature Reserves, the first of its kind in China with special regard to nature reserves. Departments concerned under the State Council also adopted corresponding measures on the management of nature reserves, including the Measures on Management of Nature Reserves for Forestry and Wild Animals, Measures on Management of Nature Reserves for Aquatic Animals and Plants, Measures on Management of Marine Reserves as well as the Measures on Management of the Land of Nature Reserves. Across the country, 24 provinces, such as the Heilongjiang Province, the Inner Mongolia Autonomous Region and the Zhejiang Province, have formulated their administrative regulations concerning nature reserves and 200 or more nature reserves have enacted administrative rules in light of their own conditions. All these laws and regulations have combined to provide a regulatory system for nature reserves and exerted far-reaching influence on their development.

Development-Restricted Zone

Development-restricted zone refers to regions crucial to ecological safety in a wider area or across the country, but handicapped by a weak bearing capacity of resources and environment as well as an unfavorable conditions for economic and population concentration. Under the principle of protection first, appropriate and special development achieved in light of local conditions, the zone is charged with promoting industries with salient features in accordance with the local bearing capacity of resource and environment, to reinforce the administration on ecological restoration and environmental protection, and to guide a rational and orderly flow of surplus population, thus turning itself to an ecological functionary zone of regional or national significance.

Development-Prohibited Zone

The zone is charged with the tasks to carry out mandatory measures to protect the environment under related laws and programs, to curb man-made damage to the natural ecosystem, and to forbid all kinds of development unsuitable to the specific functions of the zone.

Development-prohibited zones include:

243 national nature reserves, covering 89.44 million hectares;

31 world cultural and natural heritages;

187 national landscape parks, covering 9.27 million hectares;

565 national forest parks, covering 11 million hectares;

138 national geology parks, covering 480,000 hectares.

Development-Restricted Zones

Development-restricted zones include:

—the Forest Ecological Functionary Zone in the Greater and Lesser Xing'anling Mountains, which is prohibited from non-protective deforestation and charged with the tasks to plant trees, conserve waters and protect wild animals;

—the Forest Ecological Functionary Zone in the Changbaishan Mountains, which is prohibited from deforestation and charged with the tasks to plant trees, conserve waters and treat soil erosion;

—the Forest Ecological and Biodiversity Functionary Zone in Sichuan and Yunnan Provinces, which is charged with the tasks to maintain biodiversity and the gene pool of rare animals according to the objective of different regions;

—the Biodiversity Functionary Zone in the Qinbashan Mountain Area, which is charged with the tasks to moderately develop waterpower, harness deforestation and protect wild species;

—the Forest Ecological Functionary Zone in the Southeast Border of the Tibetan Plateau, which is charged with the tasks to maintain natural ecosystem;

—the Forest Ecological Functionary Zone in the Altai Mountains in the Xinjiang Uygur Autonomous Region, which is prohibited from non-protective deforestation and charged with the task to properly regenerate forest;

—the Grassland, Meadow and Wetland Ecological Functionary Zone in the Three-River Headwaters in the Qinghai Province, which is charged with the tasks to seal off grassland for seedling cultivation, reduce the amount of livestock breezed in the zone, expand the coverage of wetland, conserve waters, prevent and treat grassland deterioration, as well as guide ecological migration;

—the Tarim River Desert Ecological Functionary Zone in the Xinjiang Uygur Autonomous Region, which is charged with the tasks to make a rational use of surface water and groundwater, adjust the structure of agricultural and livestock breeding industry, as well as reinforce the administration on herb exploitation;

—the Altyn Grassland Desert Ecological Functionary Zone in the Xinjiang Uygur Autonomous Region, which is charged with the tasks to curb the expansion of pastoral area and tourism area, combat poaching activities and curb man-made damages to natural ecosystem;

—the Qiangtang Plateau Desert Ecological Functionary Zone in Northwest Tibet, which is charged with the tasks to conserve desert ecosystem, combat poaching activities and protect wild animals;

—the Three-River Plain Wetland Ecological Functionary Zone in Northeast China, which is charged with the tasks to expand the scope of conservation, slow down the pace of agricultural development and city expansion, as well as improve wetland environment;

—the Costal Wetland Ecological Functionary Zone in North Jiangsu Province, which is charged with the tasks to cease the enclosure of tideland for farming, expand the scope of protection in wetland and conserve the migration channel for birds;

—the Roige Plateau Wetland Ecological Functionary Zone in the Sichuan Province, which is charged with the tasks to cease the enclosure of wetland for farming, prevent overdevelopment, maintain the coverage of wetland and protect rare animals.

Headwaters Zone

The primary functions are to: maintain and enhance the capacity of headwater runoff and capacity of water conservation. The secondary functions are to: maintain biodiversity and conserve water and soil. The State policy is to: energize the ecosystem conservation in glacier plain or wetland that is currently in good and natural condition; energize the conservation of the habitat and the concentration area of rare wildlife; promote a natural restoration of the deteriorating grassland, shrubbery, woods and ecosystem, and; combat soil erosion and

The headstream of the Yellow River in Qinghai

desertification through scientific methods. The major measures are to: designate nature reserves or regions under strict protection, designate fields prohibited from mining, fields prohibited from gathering, fields prohibited from deforestation, fields prohibited from livestock breeding and fields prohibited from soil plowing; seal off grassland for seedling cultivation, convert farming land and pastoral land back to forest, grassland or lake, moderately promote ecological migration; strictly restrict the amount of livestock bred in the zone, turn the extensive cultivation to an intensive one; plant trees, conserve water and soil, and carry out other moderate manual programs under ecological rules; demonstrate the development of eco-industries and promote substitute industry and new economic contributor.

Headwater of the Yangtze River: Mt. Geladaindong, the highest peak of Tanggulha Mountain, with an altitude of 6,621 meters above sea level.

Flood Storage Zone

The primary functions are to: maintain and enhance the capacity to reduce the crest flow of a flood as well as maintain and enhance the capacity to store water. The secondary functions are to: maintain biodiversity, conserve major fishing waters and maintain the purification capacity of waters. The State policy is to: prevent lake and wetland from shrinking or being damaged, energize the conservation of current lakeside areas and beaches, energize the conservation of the ecosystem of wetlands currently in good condition, energize the conservation of the habitats and the concentration areas of rare wildlife; conserve lake outlets to rivers, keep the outlets to rivers in good condition; energize the conservation of lake and wetland converted from farming land, reinforce the administration of lake or wetland converted from farming land, prevent the lake and wetland from being re-converted; tackle water pollution, improve the conditions for water exchange and restore the purification capacity of the water ecosystem. The major measures are to: designate nature reserves or regions under strict protection, develop a comprehensive protection network in nature reserves; convert the farming land back to lake or wetland, promote moderate ecological migration, strictly control the scale of fish breeding in lakes and wetland converted from farming land, adopt administrative measures to forbid fishing activities when there is the need in the lake and wetland converted from cultivated land, regulate the exploitation and utilization of natural resources in the lake or wetland converted from farming land; adjust the structure and layout of agricultural, forestry, livestock breeding and fishery industries, demonstrate and promote the development of eco-tourism, eco-farming and other eco-industries, promote the development of green foods, organic foods and other famous, superior and unique products; run various programs to restore wetland ecosystem, to prevent and treat contamination to agriculture, to prevent and treat pollutions caused by domestic wastes and industrial pollutants in downtown areas.

Major Water Conservancy Zone

The primary functions are to: maintain and enhance the capacity of water conservation, runoff supply and water regulation. The secondary function, however, is decided according to the specific type of zone. For the natural water conservancy zone, the secondary function is to maintain biodiversity, while for the artificial water conservancy zone, it is to conserve water and soil as well as to maintain the water purification capacity. Differentiation also appears between the two zones in terms of major tasks. For the natural water conservancy zone, the major tasks are similar to that of the headwater ecological functionary zone, while for the artificial water conservancy zone, the major tasks are to: energize the conservation of the current surroundings of reservoirs, keep the wetland ecosystem in good condition; restore the grassland, shrubbery, woods and eco-system in reservoirs, prevent and treat soil erosion; harness water pollution, improve the conditions for water exchange and restore the purification capacity of water ecosystem. The two zones are also different from each other concerning their major measures. For the natural water conservancy zone, the major measures are similar to that of the headwater ecological functionary zone. For the artificial water conservancy zone, however, the major measures are to: designate nature reserves and regions under strict protection, designate fields prohibited from mining, fields prohibited from gathering, fields prohibited from deforestation, fields prohibited from soil plowing and fields prohibited from livestock breeding; run programs to restore wetland ecosystem, to prevent and treat contamination to agriculture, and to prevent and treat pollutions caused by domestic wastes and industrial pollutants in downtown areas; run manual eco-programs to convert farming land back to forest or grassland, re-plant trees and treat soil erosion; moderately promote ecological migration; adjust the structure and layout of agricultural, forestry, livestock breeding and fishery industries, demonstrate and promote the development of eco-farming, promote the development of green foods, organic foods, and other famous, superior and unique products.

Windbreak and Sand-Dune Fixation Zone

The primary functions are to create wind breaks, fix sand-dunes and reduce damage from sandstorm. The secondary functions are to maintain biodiversity and conserve water. The State policy is to: conserve lake and wetland in grassland or desert, ensure the supply of water for ecological use; energize the conservation of grassland, shrubbery and woods that are currently in good and natural condition; conserve the habitats and the concentration areas of rare wildlife; restore plants and treat soil desertification through natural and artificial methods. The major measures are to: designate water reserves or nature reserves, designate fields prohibited from livestock breeding, fields prohibited from soil plowing and fields prohibited from harvesting; forbid excessive collection or exploitation of wild herbs, draw rational plans and give encouragements for artificial herb cultivation bases; strictly control the amount of livestock breezed in the zone, establish different systems that forbid livestock breeding, limit livestock breeding or rotate livestock breeding, establish artificial feed cultivation bases, encourage livestock breeding in pens; enclose the deteriorating grasslands or shrubberies to cultivate seedlings, run programs to convert farming land back to forest or grassland, to develop new energy in rural areas and to guide ecological migration; demonstrate and promote the development of eco-tourism, eco-farming and other eco-industries, promote the development of green foods, organic foods and other famous, superior and unique products.

The sand-control straw grids of the sand prevention and control project of Zhongwei, Ningxia.

Major Fishing Waters

The primary function is to maintain biodiversity while the secondary functions are to store flood and improve water quality. The State policy is to: conserve the ecosystem in the spawning grounds, feeding grounds, wintering grounds and migration channels of fish and shrimp, conserve the ecosystem in aquaculture grounds of fish, shrimp, shellfish and aquatic plants, prevent and treat pollutions in fishing waters; conserve the habitat and the concentration area of rare wild aquatic organism; maintain biodiversity in fishing waters. The major measures are to: establish nature reserves to protect rare wild aquatic organism, designate regions prohibited from fishing in these reserves; designate regions prohibited from fishing in the spawning grounds, feeding grounds, wintering grounds and migration channels of fish and shrimp, designate regions prohibited from fishing in aquaculture grounds of fish, shrimp, shellfish and aquatic plants, designate a period when fishing is prohibited in these regions; control the amount of fishing, prevent exhaustion of fishing resources; advocate eco-fishing methods, scientifically define the density of fish bred in the regions, prevent pollution caused by fish breeding; prevent the invasion of exotic species; prevent and treat pollutions caused by agricultural contaminants, industrial pollutants or domestic wastes; forbid exploding fish or poisoning fish, forbid any usage of illegal fishing gears or fishing methods; forbid fishing aquatic fry of significant economic values, work out a quota of fishing amount in accordance with relevant stipulations when there is the need for fishing in designated areas; forbid enclosure of lakes for farming, forbid reclamation in major cultivation bases that breed fry or fish.

Standards for Eco-Industrial Parks

Since September 1, 2006, three standards concerning eco-industrial parks have been put into effect for the first time by SEPA. Since then, the three standards have been applied in the construction, management, inspection and acceptance of eco-industrial parks.

The three standards are the Standard for Sector-Integrated Eco-Industrial Parks (Trial), the Standard for Sector-Specific Eco-Industrial Parks (Trial) and the Standard for Venous Industry Based Eco-Industrial Parks (Trial). The first mentioned has 21 standards in four categories: Economic Development, Reduction and Recycling of Substances, Pollution Control and Park Management. It stipulates the basic qualifications and the primary indices for the inspection and acceptance of sector-integrated eco-industrial parks at national or provincial level. The Standard for Sector-Specific Eco-Industrial Parks has 19 standards and The Standard for Venous Industry Based Eco-Industrial Parks 20 standards.

The three Standards state that an eco-industrial park must hold the basic qualifications as follows: First, the park must properly implement related national and local laws, rules, regulations and policies and not be involved in any activity resulting in severe environmental pollution or severe eco-system violation. Second, the park should meet the national or local environmental standards imposed for environmental functionary zones, with total discharge of pollutants generated inside the park within the required level. Third, a Layout of Eco-Industrial Park Construction should be submitted to SEPA and approved by the local People's Government or local People's Congress.

Eco-Industrial Park Development

In August, 2001, the construction of the Guangxi Guigang National Eco-Industrial (Sugar Refinery) Demonstration Park began with SEPA approval. It was the first eco-industrial park at State level. Later, pilot constructions of eco-industrial parks were carried out by other provinces, autonomous regions and municipalities, including Liaoning Province, Jiangsu Province, Shandong Province, Tianjin Municipality, Xinjiang Uygur Autonomous Region, Inner Mongolia Autonomous Region, Zhejiang Province and Guangdong Province. These parks were engaged either in traditional industries like sugar refining, paper making, chemistry and metallurgy or high-tech industries like electronics, environmental protection, automobile and bio-chemistry. By August, 2006, the construction layout of 19 national ecological demonstration parks had been discussed and passed by SEPA. Thanks to the development, China had accumulated a wealth of experience in the construction and management of eco-industrial parks. In addition to the favorable influence on the transition of industrial parks from status quo to ecology-friendly ones, the three standards have combined to become a boon to the further improvement of eco-industrial park standards and the acceleration of China's development of new industries.

Ecological Conservation in Rural Areas

Eco-farming development is of great significance for the government to coordinate rural development and rural ecological environment. At present, China has some 400 counties involved in the development of eco-farming and more than 500 counties and cities charged with building ecological demonstration areas. These include 102 State-class eco-farming counties and 233 state-class ecological demonstration areas. Geared to achieve a comprehensively improved rural environment, these areas have taken a variety of measures. The National Action Plan for Comfortable Life and Environmental Protection in Rural Areas has been put into trial implementation. The Countermeasures of the Pollution Prevention for Livestock and Poultry Breeding Industry, the Discharge Standard of Pollutants for Livestock and Poultry Breeding Industry and the Technical Standard of Pollution Prevention for Livestock and Poultry Breeding Industry have also entered into effect. All the plans and standards have played a significant role in the legitimizing of rural environmental protection. With a view to keep soil contamination under effective control,

The development of the fishery of the middle and lower reaches of the Yangtze River takes the protection of entironment as the premises.

SEPA has adopted an Environmental Quality Standard for Soils and some other control standards and technical standards. Special investigation has been carried out to evaluate the environmental quality of soils in non-staple food production bases, sewage irrigation areas and organic food production bases. A special program of pollution prevention and treatment has also been carried out in subsequence to a national investigation on the status quo of soil quality. Recent years saw constant improvement in the management and development of the organic foods. Regulations issued include the Measures for the Administration of the Certification for Organic Foods, and the State Norms for Organic Foods. In addition, State norms for standardized agriculture and rules for the implementation of these regulations were issued to treat the polluting source. Efforts were also made to build State organic food production bases.

Establishment of Ecological Villages

China has made great efforts to establish ecological villages geared to help farmers to get rich. A variety of measures are taken to develop rural methane programs and the Clean Village Program. From 2003 to 2006, the State arranged 5.5 billion Yuan State bonds in construction of methane facilities for 5.73 million households in 48,000 villages, and an additional 93.85 million Yuan in construction of 98 large or medium-sized methane projects. In the period of the 10th Five-Year Plan, 9.59 million households turned to adopt methane, a figure which is 5.1 fold the total between 1979 an 2000. By the end of 2006, there were 22.6 million rural households which adopted methane, a figure accounting for 15 percent of the number of rural households which could use the fuel. The Clean Village Program has been implemented in six provinces and municipalities, including Hunan Province, Sichuan Province and Chongqing Municipality. Rural property management has been developed to build various facilities to convert dung, straw and domestic waste and sewage (known as the "Three Wastes") to fuel, manure and feed (known as the "Three Resources"). Thanks to these efforts, rural China now sees clean villages, clean farms and clean water (known as the "Three Cleans").These villages have managed to get rid of their former dirty and messy environment. The polluting sources to agriculture have received due treatment.

Safe Drinking Water Program in Rural Areas

The government is working hard to ensure the supply of safe drinking water in rural areas. By the end of the 10th Five-Year Plan, at least 280 million people in rural areas had gained access to safe drinking water.

The human and livestock drinking water project with an investment of over 600,000 Yuan from the State was completed in Datun of Tenghe Village, Wangdong Town, Rongshui County, Guangxi, solving the water-drinking problem of over 2,000 villagers. In the picture, a villager stands in front of the newly-installed water faucet.

According to the Safe Drinking Water Program in Rural Areas, during the 11th Five-Year Plan (2006-2010), the following measures are expected to be taken:

—improve water quality, such as the high content of fluoride, high content of arsenic, taste of bitterness or saltiness, microbial virus contamination or other contamination, that may seriously damage health; ensure water supply in areas hit by severe water shortage; prioritize the improvement of drinking water quality in areas with sparse population of ethnic minority groups, in areas where people emigrate for the sake of reservoir construction, in areas infected with snail fever and in areas near rural schools;

—effectively protect the source of drinking water; make additional efforts to prevent and treat pollution caused by mining or industrial development; reinforce the overall administration on rural sanitation; guide farmers to use fertilizer and pesticide through scientific methods; provide adequate treatment to waste water, sewage and garbage; reduce contamination to agriculture; create a system to monitor water quality; ensure the safety of the water supplied;

—develop central water supply in places with the potential to conduct the development; encourage separate supply of drinking water and domestic water in light of water quality; reinforce the management on water resources; stabilize the supply of domestic water and industrial water, while putting domestic water first;

—improve the development and management of drinking water projects in rural areas; guarantee the quality of the projects; ascertain the major body in charge of the projects and their major responsibilities; improve the efficiency of the capital used in the projects; facilitate the sound development of the projects; develop the projects mainly with government investment and partially with social aids.

International Environmental Cooperation

As one of the largest countries in the world, China has participated, actively and in a constructive manner, in international environmental cooperation. Since 1994, the year when the United Nations Framework Convention on Climate Change entered into force, China has played a key role in the international negotiations on climate change. While adhering to its principles, China has developed active policies and strategies to ensure the positive progress of negotiations. It has thus effectively defended the rights and interests of itself and other developing countries. After its access to the Kyoto Protocol in May 1998, ratification followed in August 2002.

Multi-lateral Environmental Cooperation

China highly values international environmental cooperation and has participated actively in the environmental activities launched by the UN and other international organizations. In recent years, the government has sent several top delegations to attend the meetings held by the Commission on Sustainable Development of the UN, the meetings held by the World Summit on Sustainable Development and all the preparatory activities to these meetings. Good relationships have been forged between China and the UN Development Program, the World Bank, the Asian Development Bank and other international organizations. Together with the United Nations Environment Programs, China has carried out effective programs in various fields, such as desertification prevention, biodiversity conservation, ozone layer protection, cleaner production, recycling economy, environmental education and training, flood harnessing on the upper and middle reaches of the Yangtze River, the Regional Seas Action Plan and the Global Program of Action for the Protection of the Marine Environment from Land-Based Activities. Meanwhile, China has played an active role in terms of environmental protection and sustainable development within the framework of APEC. It has attended all the APEC ministerial meetings

♦ National Action Plan for Comfortable Life and Environmental Protection in Rural Areas

In October, 2006, SEPA adopted the National Action Plan for Comfortable Life and Environmental Protection in Rural Areas.

According to the overall objectives, by the end of 2020, environmental pollution in rural areas will be effectively harnessed, the dirty and messy rural environment largely changed and the livelihood of rural people significantly improved. Therefore, a safe environment will be in place in the course of building a new socialist countryside and well-off society in an all-round way. According to the objectives of the Action Plan in the 11th Five-Year Plan (2006-2010), by the end of 2010, the dirty and messy rural environment is to be generally changed, rural pollution caused by industrial enterprises effectively curbed and treated, the condition of drinking water largely improved, the pollution of scale animal-or-poultry cultivation generally harnessed, a group of organic food production bases successively established and eco-industries comprehensively developed. By the achievement of these objectives, China will see a further strengthened capacity of for environmental monitoring, greater public awareness of environmental protection and a comprehensively improved rural environment. In an attempt to accomplish the Action Plan, the government decided to build 500 demonstration projects to treat rural pollution caused by industrial enterprises; develop demonstration projects to collect and treat domestic waste and sewage in 10,000 administrative villages, of which 4,000 are in the east China, 3,500 in middle China and 2,500 in west China; build up 500 demonstration projects to prevent and treat rural pollution caused by scale animal-or-poultry cultivation; build 10 demonstration projects to prevent soil contamination and restore contaminated soils; build 600 demonstration projects to treat pollution in the source area of rural drinking water; build 300 organic food production bases; establish 2,000 townships with a beautiful environment and 10,000 ecological villages; strengthen the construction of facilities for environmental monitoring and control.

on environment protection. Thanks to these efforts, China has made much headway in environmental protection that is recognized internationally. Several officials, who are in charge of environmental protection in various governmental departments in China, have respectively won the Sasakawa Prize awarded by the United Nations Environment Programs, the Green Environment Special Award awarded by the World Bank and the Global Environment Leadership Award awarded by the Global Environment Facility. All-China Youth Federation and Zhou Qiang were given the title as Champion of the Earth by the United Nations Environment Programs.

Negotiations on International Conventions and Accomplishment of Relevant Duties

China has signed more than 50 international conventions and protocols in relation to environmental protection. Meanwhile, great efforts are made to accomplish the relevant duties. The conventions and protocols include: the United Nations Framework Convention on Climate Change, Kyoto Protocol, Montreal Protocol on Substances that Deplete the Ozone Layer, Convention on International Prior Informed Consent Procedures for Certain Hazardous Chemicals and Pesticides in International Trade Stockholm Convention on Persistent Organic Pollutants, Convention on Biological Diversity, Cartagena Protocol on Bio-safety and the United Nations Convention to Combat Desertification.

In line with its access to these conventions and protocols, China has released its National Report on Sustainable Development and the Program of Action for Sustainable Development in China in the 21st Century, in which it outlined an action plan in various key domains to promote sustainable development. Subsequent to the approval of the National Program to Gradually Phase Out Substances that Deplete the Ozone Layer, the government has adopted some 100 policies and measures for ozone layer protection. Meanwhile, it has built up many bases to develop and produce ODS substitutes and other products for environmental protection. It has thus managed to keep to its schedule prescribed in the Montreal Protocol to phase out ODS. According to the World Bank, ODS phased out by China accounted for 50 percent of the total by developing countries. In Beijing, the Fifth Conference of the Parties to the Vienna Convention and the 11th Conference of the Parties to the Montreal Protocol were jointly convened. They produced the Beijing Declaration and the Beijing Amendment to the Montreal Protocol respectively.

Regional Environmental Cooperation

China is working hard to address regional environmental problems. As an active participant in regional cooperation, it has spared no efforts to promote and strengthen its cooperation with neighboring countries and those in other regions. China has managed to promote and participate in dozens of regional cooperative programs, including the regular China-Japan-ROK ministerial meeting on the environment, ASEAN-China (10+1) environmental cooperation, ASEAN-China-Japan-ROK (10+3) environmental cooperation, the Acid Deposition Monitoring Network in East Asia, environmental cooperation in Northeast Asia and its related meetings, cooperation in Northeast Asia to monitor and forecast sandstorms as well as cooperation in the Greater Mekong Sub-region. All these programs have combined to exert a favorable influence on the prompt information exchange as well as the overall prevention and reduction of environmental problems in the related regions.

International Cooperation for Sandstorm Prevention

In June 2000, SEPA launched a program to study the influence of sandstorms and dust. With cutting-edge technologies, such as remote sensing, China established a ground dust monitoring network, covering all spots concerned in the Inner Mongolia Autonomous Region, Hebei Province, Shaanxi Province, Beijing Municipality, Xinjiang Uygur Autonomous Region, Shanxi Province as well as some other areas. China has also developed cooperation with Mongolia to monitor and forecast sandstorms. In October 2002, an international symposium was held in Beijing to discuss sandstorm forecasting. Delegates from Japan, ROK and Mongolia

On August 27, 2007, the 2007 International Conference on Ecological Sanitation was held in Ordos of Inner Mongolia Autonomous Region.

15 Environmental Protection

attended the symposium. In December 2003, a senior sandstorm meeting was held in Beijing. Senior officials and the heads of related departments were sent by Japan, ROK, Mongolia and DPRK to attend. Together with the Asian Development Bank, the United Nations Environment Programs and other international organizations, China, Japan, ROK and Mongolia have cooperated in the Technical Assistance for the Prevention and Control of Dust and Sandstorms in Northeast Asia Project. Funded by the Asian Development Bank and the United Nations Environment Programs, the project was launched in April 2003. For the treatment of the sources of the wind and sandstorms in the Beijing-Tianjin area, investment involved also came from various international organizations, foreign governments, and foreign businesses. Projects using the investment totaled some 100.

Acid Deposition Monitoring in East Asia

With the joint efforts of East Asia and the United Nations Environment Programs, the Acid Deposition Monitoring Network in East Asia (EANET) was established, involving China and 12 countries in the sub0region. The EANET is geared to help all the participants to exchange data and technology concerning acid deposition, to raise public awareness on the issue and to provide all participants with references for decision-making. In October 1998, China started its trial implementation of EANET. A sub-center was established, with Chongqing, Xi'an, Xiamen and Zhuhai in charge of monitoring. Since 2002, the government has made a voluntary donation to EANET every year.

Cooperation in Greater Mekong Sub-region for Environmental Protection

China has played an active role in the cooperation in the Greater Mekong Sub-region. It is involved in various activities, including the second-phase Sub-regional Environment Monitoring and Information System, the Poverty Reduction and Environmental Management in Remote GMS Watersheds and the second-phase Sub-regional Strategic Environment Framework. From 24 to 26 May, 2005, Shanghai played a host to the First GMS Environment Ministers Meeting. All these activities have been a boon to the deepening of mutual trust and understanding between countries in the sub-region and exerted far-reaching influence on the sub=regional environmental protection and economic development.

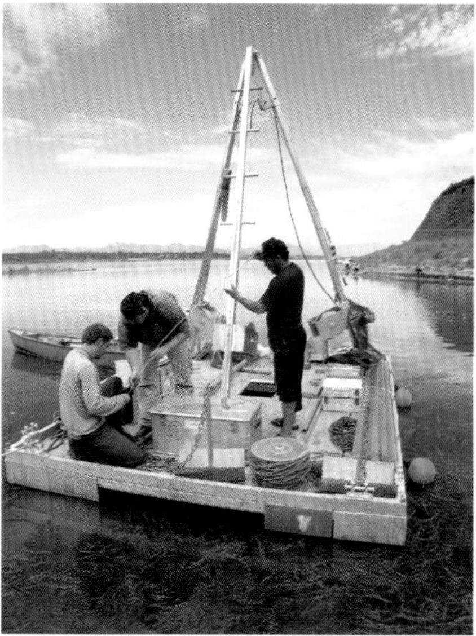

China-German cooperation for reducing and controlling the pollution of the reservoirs

Environmental Cooperation with Other Regions

China has made much headway in its environmental cooperation with other regions. With a purpose to promote environmental cooperation with African countries, it has held a theme program of China's Environmental Protection in Africa. In 2005, China and the United Nations Environment Programs convened the Sino-African Conference on Cooperation in Environmental Protection and the UNEP Sino-African Environmental Protection Center was built in the Republic of Congo. Moreover, the Chinese Government organized a study class on treatment of water pollution and water management in African countries to provide them with instructions in the field of environmental protection. In June 2006, a similar study class concerning Arabian countries was organized in Beijing to provide similar environmental instruction. In July 2006, Beijing witnessed the convention of the APEC study class on ecological environmental management.

Bilateral Environmental Cooperation

China has participated actively in the bilateral environmental cooperation with developed countries, developing countries and neighboring countries. It has signed bilateral cooperation agreements and memoranda concerning environmental protection respectively with 42 countries, including the US, Germany, Japan, Canada, Russia, ROK, India, Mongolia, DPRK, Brazil and South Africa. It has also signed bilateral cooperation agreements and memorandums concerning nuclear safety respectively with 11 countries. China has enjoyed extensive achievements and exchanges with other countries in the fields of environmental policy formulation, pollution treatment, biodiversity conservation, climate change, sustainable production and consumption, potential

♦ China Council for International Cooperation on Environment and Development

In 1992, the United Nations Conference on Environment and Development was convened. Participants proclaimed that a global partnership should be forged in order to achieve sustainable development. Developing countries, driven by the contradiction between environment and development, now feel a pressing need to learn from the developed world. As one of the developing countries, China is benefiting from the model of the developed countries, but still lacks experience concerning environmental protection. Under such a situation, the government approved the establishment of the China Council for International Cooperation on Environment and Development (CCICED), with aid from the Canadian International Development Agency.

A senior consultant to the government, CCICED is charged with the task of facilitating exchange of experiences, policies and theories in relation to environmental development between China and other countries. It also conducts thorough theoretical research on various pressing issues concerning China's environmental development. Meanwhile, it provides professional advice to the government on the formulation of strategic environmental policies. When there is a need, it also helps the government to implement environmental policies or projects for demonstration. CCICED is geared to help China achieve a sustainable development through a coordinated environment and economy. Since its foundation, CCICED has advised the government on the formulation of several policies and has earned a high reputation for this. Through the introduction of new ideas concerning environmental development from overseas, CCICED has made significant contribution to China's sustainable development as well as the view of all-round, balanced and sustainable development.

Website: http://www.cciced.org

The directorate of the World Bank approved to provide a loan of US$128 million to China and a donated fund of US$10 million from the Global Environment Fund for the urban environment project of the Pearl River Delta area.

promotion, demonstration project construction, environmental technology development and environmental industrial development. In addition, under the principle of mutual free aid, China has developed a variety of programs with 13 courtiers or international organizations, such as the EU, Japan, Germany and Canada.

Cooperation between China and Germany has seen significant progress in environmental cooperation since the first initiative in the 1980s. China has played host to the Sino-German Cooperation Conference on Environment in 2000, the First Sino-German Environmental Forum in 2003, the Sino-German (Xiangtan) Cooperation Conference on Environmental Management and Enterprises in October 2004, the Second Sino-German (Qingdao) Environmental Forum in January 2006 as well as the Sino-German (Beijing) Symposium on Chemical Management in July 2006. A Qingdao Initiative was worked out by China and Germany. All these activities show that the Sino-German cooperation is developing soundly. Meanwhile, the German Government has provided great assistance to the China Council for International Cooperation on Environment and Development. Sino-German cooperation has extended from ordinary personnel exchanges to exchanges in the economic, technical and industrial fields. Cooperative programs have been developed in terms of environmental research, technical development, personnel training and exchange, as well as environmental demonstration projects. Thanks to these efforts, China has enjoyed a progressed development in the fields of environmental management, environmental technology and environmental business. At present, China and Germany are consulting with each other over their further cooperation on environment after 2007.

International Cooperation on Nuclear Safety

Nuclear safety, a sensitive issue, has always been a major concern to the Chinese Government. After years of efforts, in 2004, SEPA set up the Division of International Cooperation on Nuclear Safety under its Department of International Cooperation, with a view to strengthen China's cooperation with other countries concerning nuclear issues. In 2005, China took part in the Third Conference of the Parties to the Convention on Nuclear Safety. In the conference, the Chinese Government released a report in which it answered 154 questions of concern to other parties and revealed in detail its latest progress in relation to nuclear safety. China has also made great efforts to prepare for the access to the Joint Convention on the Safety of Spent Fuel Management and Radioactive Waste Management. Meanwhile, it has signed bilateral cooperation agreements and memorandums concerning nuclear safety respectively with 11 countries.

Utilization of Foreign Investments for Environmental Protection

With a view to promote international environmental cooperation, China attaches great importance to the strengthening of exchanges with other countries in the economic and technical fields. It is also aware that great efforts should be made to utilize foreign investments to quicken its pace of environmental protection. China is now working hard to promote environmental protection through diplomatic methods. In addition to bilateral cooperation with the developed countries, it has maintained close ties with various international financial organizations, such as the Global Environment Facility, the World Bank and the Asian Development Bank. Thanks to these efforts, China has collected a wealth of experience from overseas in the use of funding, technical development and managerial skills with regards to environmental protection. It has also enjoyed a strengthened capacity to protect the overall environment across the country. During the 10th Five-Year Plan 2001-2005), China attracted US$500 million or more from overseas, greatly facilitating its environmental protection.

Founded in 1992, the Global Environment Facility is the largest investor in the world in the environmental field, with great achievements made in a variety of activities. As a member country, China has developed close ties with the organization. Although being a developing country, China is among the donors and plays an active role in every fund drive launched by the organization. Meanwhile, the Global Environment Facility has provided great financial and technical assistance to help China protect its environment and fulfill its duties in international conventions. Thanks to this aid, China has embarked on dozens of projects some completed, some under construction and some in preparation.

♦ Award of "Green Chinese Personage of a Year"

This award founded in 2005, is organized by seven ministries and commissions, namely Publicity Department of Central Committee, NPC Environmental Resource Commission, Human, Resource and Environment Commission of National Political Consultation, Ministry of Culture, State Administration of Radio, Film and Television, Central Committee of Communist Youth League, and State Environmental Protection Administration, undertaken by Chinese Environmental Culture Promotion Unity and supported especially by UN Environment Planning Office. Toepfer, the Under-Secretary of UN and Executive Direcotr of Environment Planning Office at that time, presented himself at the conference to grant the award.

"Public Spirit" is the fundamental principle of award of "Green Chinese Personage of a Year". Pan Yue, the initiator of the award and deputy-director of State Environmental Protection Administration said that besides depending on government, the issue of environment in China relies on the enhancement of environmental consciousness in the society and the promotion of public force. The award was established to encourage all the public force in environmental protection including academic circles, media and non-governmental organizations and make contribution to the realization of sustainable development in China. Under the guidance of the spirit, last year the award chose the first initiator of non-governmental organization on environmental protection, the first law scholar in charge of right maintenance against pollution, the first farmer leader as a village leader in environmental protection, the first journalist reporting Yuanmingyuan Garden issue, and the first director of grass-root environmental protection bureau who made the city with the dirtiest air in the world withdrew from the blacklist.

Official Website for election:www.greenchinese.net

▲ Green Chinese Personage of Year 2007 (List)

Professor Zhang Xiaojian from Department of Environmental Science and Engineering, Tsinghua University

As the first home-grown Ph.D. of environmental engineering, he successfully handled the works of emergent water supply such as Wuxi drinking water incident in May 2007 and Qinhuangdao drinking water incident in June 2007. He is called as "master of water treatment" by media.

Journalist Chai Jing from CCTV Column: News Probe

In 2007, she went to Shanxi twice for news investigation. Shanxi: Break Arms to Treat Pollution aroused wide echoes after being broadcast by CCTV.

Huo Daishan, Chairman of "Guards of the Huaihe River" in Zhoukou City, Henan Province

In 2007 he organized the "public monitoring network on contamination of drain mouths on the Huaihe River" at the Shayinghe. He reported the actual information about the water pollution of the Huaihe to the government and public, earning the title "the environmental-protection eyes on the Huaihe" by the public.

One of the winners of the "2007 Green China Annual Characters": Chai Jing, a reporter of the topic *Investigative Journalism* of the CCTV.

Wang Yongchen, Principal of Beijing Green Homeland

In 2007 she organized the action of "ten-year walking along the rivers". She planned to take ten years to finish the journey along the major rivers in the west of Sichuan Province and northwest of Yunnan Province to learn the impact of hydropower exploitation on the environment and lives of common people.

Zhao Xihai, a Retired Worker of Jilin Province Hongshi Forestry Bureau

He once served as a lumberman. In the 18 years after his retirement, he planted 180,000 tree saplings and bred 216,000 seedlings and contributed them to the State.

Liao Sau-tung, Former Director of Hong Kong Environment, Transport and Works Bureau

She actively upholds the "polluter must pay" principle, modified the Regulations on Treatment of Sewage, and promoted air quality control in the Delta of the Pearl River and the harbor area treatment scheme. As a result, the pathogenic microorganism E. coli in Victoria Harbor was reduced by 50 percent.

Shi Zhengrong, President of Jiangsu Wuxi Suntech Power Holdings Co., Ltd.

Under his leadership, the research and development and the conversion rate of industrialization of solar energy continued to lead the world. In March 2007, the photovoltaic system project donated by him was launched formally at the Bird's Nest, main stadium of Beijing Olympic Games.

Feng Xiaoning, a Famous Director

He has long been devoted to the production of films about the environment. In September 2007, his film Qinghai-Tibet Railway, telling the story of three generations of Chinese striving for the realization of the plateau railway, was shown around China.

Zhang Yimou, a Famous Director

He was the general director of the opening and closing ceremonies of the Beijing 2008 Olympic Games. The concept of "Green Olympic Games" became an important theme.

Department of Environmental Impacts Assessment of the Ministry of Environmental Protection(MEP) won the special reward as a group.

Political Parties and Social Organizations

Political Parties

Political Party System

There are nine political parties in China at present. Besides the Communist Party of China (CPC), there are the Revolutionary Committee of the Chinese Kuomintang (founded in 1948), the China Democratic League (1941), the China National Democratic Construction Association (1945), China Association for Promoting Democracy (1945), Chinese Peasants and Workers Democratic Party (in 1930), China Zhi Gong Dang (1925), the Jiusan Society (1945) and the Taiwan Democratic Self-Government League (1947). Since most of these political parties were founded during the War of Resistance Against Japanese Aggression (1937-1945) and the War of Liberation (1946-1949) in the pursuit of national liberation and democracy of the people, they were given the joint name of "democratic parties".

In present-day China, these democratic parties form a political alliance of socialist working people, builders of socialism and patriots who support socialism. Another important force in China's political life is a group of personages without party affiliation, or people who have not joined any political party but have certain public influence coupled with positive contributions. The majority are intellectuals.

The salient characteristics of China's political party system are: multi-party cooperation under the leadership of the CPC, with the CPC holding power and the democratic parties participating fully in State affairs. These democratic parties are close friends of the CPC. They unite and cooperate with the latter in their participation in State affairs, instead of being opposition parties or out-of-power parties. They participate in the exercise of State power, consultation on fundamental State policies and choice of State leaders, administration of State affairs, and the formulation and implementation of State policies, laws and regulations.

The Communist Party of China

The Communist Party of China (CPC) was founded in July 1921.

From 1921 to 1949, the CPC led the Chinese people in their arduous struggle that finally led to the overthrow of the rule of imperialism, feudalism and bureaucratic capitalism with the establishment of the People's Republic of China. After the founding of New China, the CPC, as a party in power, led the Chinese people of all ethnic groups in defending the independence and security of the country, successfully completing the transition from new democracy to socialism and carrying out systematic large-scale socialist construction, thus achieving economic and cultural progress unparalleled in Chinese history.

According to statistics from the Organizational Department of the CPC Central Committee, by the end of 2007, the number of members of the CPC exceeded 74.15 million, accounting for 5.6 percent of the total national population. The number of Party organizations at the grass-roots level reached 3.66 million, including 176,000 grass-roots Party committees, 222,000 general Party committees and 3.265 million Party committees.

The number of female members of the CPC was close to 15.2 million, accounting for 20.4 percent of the total. Party members from ethnic minorities reached 4.8 million, or 6.5 percent of the total. The number of Party members who were officials in government organs, management personnel and professional technology personnel in State-owned enterprises and public institutions was close to 20 million, accounting for 26.5 percent of the total.

Taking the oath on being admitted to the Chinese Communist Party in front of the Party flag

Democratic Parties

Apart from the CPC, there are eight political parties in China at present, given the joint name of "democratic parties". These parties have established cooperation with the CPC at various levels since their founding. All democratic parties responded to the call of the CPC for convening the Chinese People's Political Consultative Conference (CPPCC) from May 1948 to early 1949, and attended the

Eight Democratic Parties (as of April 2007)

Name	Date of foundation	Membership	Chairperson of Central Committee	Parties' publication
Revolutionary Committee of the Chinese Kuomintang	January 1948	600,000	He Luli	Tuanjie Bao (Unity newspaper)
China Democratic League	October 1941	131,000	Jiang Shusheng	Qunyan (Your Say) (magazine)
China Democratic National Construction Association	December 1945	85,000	Cheng Siwei	Jingji Jie (Economic Affairs) (magazine)
China Association for the Promotion of the democracy	December 1945	65,000	Xu Jialu	Minzhu (Democracy) (Monthly)
Chinese Peasants and Workers' Democratic Party	August 1930	More than 70,000	Jiang Zhenghua	Qianjin Luntan (Forum For Advancement) (magazine)
China Zhi Gong Dang	October 1925	17,000	Luo Haocai	China Zhi Gong
Jiusan society	December 1944	74,000	Han Deqi	Minzhu Yu Kexue (Democracy and Science)(magazine)
Taiwan Democratic Self-government	November 1947	More than 1,800	Lin Wenyi	Taiwan Democratic Self-government

First Plenary Session of the Chinese People's Political Consultative Conference in September 1949, at which the Common Program of the CPPCC was enacted and the Central People's Government elected, making contributions to the founding of the People's Republic of China.

After the founding of the PRC, they actively exercised the function of deliberating and deciding on major State policies. Many of their representatives were elected as deputies to people's congresses at different levels and members of the CPPCC committees at different levels. Many members of democratic parties have held leading positions in the standing committees of people's congresses, CPPCC committees and governments at different levels as well as sections of economy, culture, education and science and technology. Adhering to the guideline of "long-term coexistence, mutual supervision, sincere treatment with each other and the sharing of weal and woe", the political parties unite and cooperate with the CPC devotion to building socialism, instead of being opposition parties or out-of-power parties.

The following are eight democratic parties: the Revolutionary Committee of the Chinese Kuomintang (founded in 1948), the China Democratic League (1941), China National Democratic Construction Association (1945), the China Association for Promoting Democracy (1945), the Chinese Peasants and Workers Democratic Party (1930), the China Zhi Gong Dang (1925), Jiusan Society (1945) and the Taiwan Democratic Self-Government League (1947).

On March 6, 2008, the Press Conference of the First Session of the 11th National Committee of the Chinese People's Political Consultative Conference (CPPCC) was held in the Press Conference Room of the People's Great Hall, the theme of which is "the Chairmen of the Central Committees of the Democratic Parties talk about the Multi-Party Cooperation". Wan Gang, Chairman of Central Committee of the China Zhi Gong Dang and the minister of the Ministry of Science and Technology of China aroused much attention.

♦ United Front Work Department of the CPC Central Committee

The United Front Work Department of the CPC Central Committee is the functional department in charge of united front work under the jurisdiction of the CPC Central Committee. The functions of the United Front Work Department are as follows: To investigate and study the theory and important guidelines and policies of the united front, and to organize and carry out the guidelines and policies related top the united front from the Central Committee of the CPC; to report to the CPC Central Committee and put forward opinions and advice on united front work. To connect with the representative personages of democratic parties and the personages without party affiliation, and report their opinions and advice to the CPC Central Committee; to study and carry out the system of multi-party cooperation and political consultation under the leadership of the CPC and the guidelines and policies for democratic parties; to carry out democratic parties' participation in discussions of State affairs and function of democratic supervision; to support and assist democratic parties to strengthen self-construction. To take charge of investigating, study, assorting with inspection of major matters of guideline and policy on relative ethnic minorities and religious works; to connect with the representative personages of ethnic minorities and religious circles; to assist relative sections train and recommend ethnic minorities cadres; to cooperate with relative sections in the fight against hostile forces at home and abroad such as the Dalai clique. To take charge of the development of united front work overseas focusing on the reunification of the motherland; to connect with relative social organizations and representative personages overseas; to deal with the relative works on Taiwan compatriots and their relatives.

Website:http://www.zytzb.org.cn

Revolutionary Committee of the Chinese Kuomintang

The successive chairpersons of the Central Committee of the Revolutionary Committee of the Chinese Kuomintang (RCCK) were Li Jishen, He Xiangning, Zhu Yunshan, Wang Kunlun, Qu Wu, Zhu Xuefan and Li Peiyao. Its present chairwoman is He Luli.

The RCCK draws membership mainly from among personages who once had relations with the Kuomintang, who had historical and social relations with the Kuomintang and who had ties with Taiwan and supported the reunification of the motherland as well as representative personages and intellectuals from the middle and upper levels. The RCCK has its own organizations established in the 30 provinces, autonomous regions and municipalities directly under the Central Government except Tibet and Taiwan. At present, it has a membership of over 60,000.

The RCCK central authorities have established the Unity Press, China Tong He Economic Development Corp., the magazine *Solidarity*, distributed domestically and abroad.

China Democratic League

Founded on March 19, 1941, the China Democratic League (CDL) is mainly made up of senior and middle-level intellectuals engaged in culture and education as well as science and technology. The successive chairpersons of the CDL Central Committee were Huang Yanpei, Zhang Lan, Shen Junru, Yang Mingxuan, Shi Liang, Chu Tunan, Fei Xiaotong, Jiang Shusheng. Its present chairperson is Jiang Shusheng.

The CDL draws its members mainly in medium and large cities, composed mainly of intellectuals engaged in culture and education. The CDL has its own local organizations established in the 30 provinces, autonomous regions and municipalities directly under the Central Government except Tibet and Taiwan. At present, it has a membership of over 140,000.

CDL has established the *Qunyan* Publishing House, the Qunyan Technology Consultation Service Center, Qunyan magazine monthly published at home and abroad, and *Central News*, a publication for internal circulation.

China National Democratic Construction Association (CNDCA)

The China National Democratic Construction Association (CNDCA) was founded in December 16, 1945, and led in succession by Huang Yanpei, Hu Juewen and Sun Qimeng. Its present chairman is Cheng Siwei. The CNDCA draws members mainly in medium and large cities, mainly medium and upper level personages and those from economic circles as well as related specialists and scholars. The CNDCA has its own organizations established in 30 provinces, autonomous regions and municipalities directly under the Central Government except Tibet and Taiwan. At present, it has a membership of over 78,000.

CNDCA has established the Democracy and Construction Press, the magazine *Economical Affairs* as well as *Ming Xun*, a publication for internal circulation.

China Association for Promoting Democracy

Founded in Shanghai on December 30, 1945, the China Association for Promoting Democracy (CAPD) is a political party that draws its membership in medium and large cities, composed mainly of intellectuals engaged in education, culture and publication. The previous chairpersons of the CAPD Central Committee include Ma Xulun, Zhou Jianren, Ye Shengtao and Lei Jieqiong. Its current chairman is Xu Jialu. The CAPD has its own organizations established in 29 provinces, autonomous regions and municipalities directly under the Central Government except Tibet and Taiwan. At present, it has a membership of over 70,000.

The CAPD has established Kaiming Publishing House, Kaiming Culture and Education Audio-Video Publishing House and the magazine *Democracy* which was distributed at home and abroad.

Chinese Peasants and Workers Democratic Party

The party is called CPWDP for short. The successive leaders or chairpersons of the Central Committee were Deng Yanda, Huang Qixiang, Zhang Bojun, Peng Zemin, Ji Fang, Zhou Gucheng and Lu Jiaxi. Its current chairman is Jiang Zhenghua. The CPWDP draws its membership mainly in medium and large cities, composed mainly of representative intellectuals from health and medical circles. It has a membership of over 73,000 and has local organizations in 30 provinces, autonomous regions and municipalities directly under the Central Government, with the exception of Taiwan and Tibet.

The magazine *Forum for Advancement* is the organ of the CPWDP Central Committee.

China Zhi Gong Dang

The China Zhi Gong Dang was founded in October 1925 and led in succession by Chen Qiyou, Huang Dingchen and Dong Yinchu. Its current chairman is Luo Haocai. It draws its membership mainly in medium and large cities, composed mainly of representative personages. Most of them are returned overseas Chinese, relatives of overseas Chinese, and representative individuals and specialists and scholars with overseas connections. So far, the China Zhi Gong Dang has set up local organizations in 17 provinces, autonomous regions and municipalities directly under the Central Government, with a membership of over 18,000.

It has established the *China Zhi Gong* Publishing House and the magazine China Zhi Gong, a publication for internal circulation.

Jiusan Society

The Jiusan Society, officially founded in May 1946, currently has nearly 88,000 members. They are mostly high- and medium-level intellectuals working in science and technology, culture and education, or public health, and 60 percent of them have senior professional titles. So far, the Jiu San Society has set up committees or preparatory committees in 30 provinces, autonomous regions and municipalities directly under the Central Government as well as in 268 cities (counties), except in Taiwan and Tibet. Among the members, there are 104 CPPCC National Committee members, 70 deputies to the National People's Congress, 19 deputy chairpersons of provincial committees of the CPPCC, four vice chairpersons of the provincial people's congress standing committees and four vice governors or vice mayors of municipalities directly under the Central Government. It has 150 academicians of the Chinese Academy of Sciences (members of academician committee) and academicians of the Chinese Academy of Engineering. Many have made brilliant contributions to the Chinese S and T undertakings. Jiusan Society members such as Wang Ganchang, Deng Jiaxian, Zhao Jiuzhang, Chen Fangyun and Cheng Kaijia were warded Medals of Merit for their work on the A and H Bombs and space satellites and Wang Xuan and Huang Kun gained the 2001 National Top Science and Technology Award.

The previous chairmen were Xu Deheng, Zhou Peiyuan and Wu Jieping and its current chairman is Han Qide.

The journals run by the Jiusan Society CC include *Democracy and Science* for public circulation at home and abroad and *Jiu San Central Committee Information* distributed inside the society. It runs a Xueyuan Publishing House and a Xueyuan Audio-Visual Publishing House.

Taiwan Democratic Self-Government League

The Taiwan Democratic Self-Government League (TDSGL), has more than 1,800 members who are most medium and upper levels personages born or with family roots in Taiwan currently residing on the mainland. The successive chairpersons of the Central Committee of the Taiwan Democratic Self-Government League were Xie Xuehong, Cai Xiao, Su Ziheng, Cai Zimin and Zhang Kehui. Its present chairman is Lin Wenyi. At present, the TDGSL has set up local organizations in 12 provinces and municipalities directly under the Central Government.

It has established the Taihai Publishing House and the magazine *Tai Meng*, a bimonthly for internal circulation.

Social Organizations

Chinese People's Association for Friendship with Foreign Countries (CPAFFC)

(See P161)

Website: http://www.cpaffc.org.cn

All-China Federation of Trade Unions (ACFTU)

The All-China Federation of Trade Unions (ACFTU), founded on May 1, 1925, is the leading body of trade union federations at local level and industrial unions at national level. The major social functions are as follows: to protect the legitimate interests and democratic rights of workers and staff members; to mobilize and organize workers and staff members to take part in the construction and reform and accomplish the tasks in the economic and social development; to represent and organize workers and staff members to participate in the democratic management of enterprises; to educate workers and staff members to constantly improve their ideological and moral qualities and raise their scientific and cultural levels. So far, the All-China Federation of Trade Unions has established friendly relations with more than 400 trade unions in over 130 countries and regions as well as a number of international and regional trade union organizations.

By the end of June, 2008, the ACFTU members totaled more than 200 million. The number of grass-roots trade unions reached more than 1.7 million.

Website: http://www.acftu.org/

Communist Youth League of China

The Communist Youth League of China (CYL) is a mass organization of advanced youth led by the CPC. Founded in August 1920, it was originally named the Socialist Youth League of China. In the 3rd National Representation Conference in January 1925, it became the Chinese Communist Youth League. Its national leading body is the National Congress and the Central Committee elected at the Congress. The National Congress takes place every five years. When the National Congress is not in session, the Central Committee implements the resolutions of the Congress and exercises leadership over all the work of the League. The organization plays a role in provincial and sub-provincial local leading organs and fundamental organizations in 31 provinces, autonomous regions and municipalities directly under the Central Government as well as the People's Liberation Army, Chinese People's Armed Police Force, Ministry of Railways, China Civil Aviation, departments directly under the CPC Central Committee, Central Government institutions, Central financial departments and enterprises directly under the Central Government departments concerned.

Website: http://www.ccyl.org.cn/

All-China Women's Federation

Founded on April 3, 1949, the All-China Women's Federation (ACWF) is a mass group of women from various ethnic backgrounds and circles. The ACWF practices an organizational

▲ Logo of All-China Women's Federation

The center of the logo is a stylized Chinese character of "woman". It represents women working in all sectors of society, and also reflects that, along with the reform and opening up of China, the Women's Federation represents and protects women's rights, serves women with heart and soul. There are three "W" in the shape of leaves of a flower around the Chinese Character. The design signifies that the All-China Women's Federation leads women to enhance the spirit of self-esteem, self-confidence, self-reliance, self-improvement, and to devote themselves to the development of the country. It also implies exchanges and friendship with women from all over the world, and world peace. The image of flower signifies the bright future of women's liberation.

system of local women's federations and group members. The local women's federations at various levels are set up according to State administrative divisions. The national leading organization and local leading organizations are elected by the National Women's Congress of China and local women's congress at various levels respectively. The government organs and public institutions set up women committees, and women worker's committees of grass-root trade unions in factories, mines and enterprises, and those at upper levels are all group members of the ACWF. The national or local women's organizations that have registered with the departments of civil affairs and those associations, sodalities and religious organizations working for society and women and organized voluntarily by women from various circles. as well as other mass organizations willing to apply for affiliation with the federations, may become members once approved by the ACWF or local Women's Federations.

The highest power organ of the ACWF is the National Women's Congress convened once every five years. The functions of the ACWF are as follows: to deliberate and decide on the guidelines and tasks of national women's movement; to examine and approve the work report of the ACWF Executive Committee;

The ceremony of joining the Chinese Communist Youth League

to amend the Constitution of the All-China Women's Federation and to elect the ACWF Executive Committee. The ACWF Executive Committee elects and decides the members of national leading organization of the ACWF. The Standing Committee is the leading organ when the Executive Committee is not in session. Under it there is the Secretariat, made up of the First Member and several Members who are elected by the Standing Committee and in charge of the daily work.

Website: http://www.women.org.cn/index.jsp

All-China Federation of Industry and Commerce

(See P72)

China Federation of Literary and Art Circles

The China Federation of Literary and Art Circles (CFLAC), established in July 1949, is composed of nationwide associations of writers and artists, federations of literary and art circles in the provinces, autonomous regions and municipalities directly under the Central Government as well as federations of literary and art circles in various parts of the country. The CFLAC practices a group membership. It now consists of 50 group members, including the China Writers Association, China Theatre Association, China Film Association, China Musicians Association, China Artists Association, China Quyi Artists association, China Dancers Association, China Folk Literature and Art Association, China Photographers Association, China Calligraphers Association, China Acrobats Association, China TV Artists Association, 32 federations of literary and art circles in provinces, autonomous regions and municipalities directly under the Central Government, the Literary and Art Federation of the Xinjiang Production and Construction Corps and federations of literary and art circles in six industries (China Coal Mine Federation of Literary and Art Circles, China Railway Federation of Literary and Art Circles, China Petroleum Federation of Literary and Art Circles, China Chemical Industrial Federation of Literary and Art Circles, China Electrical Power Association of Literary and Art Workers, and China Water Conservancy Association of Literary and Art Workers).

The CFLAC undertakes liaison, coordination and service work among various group members and helps them with matters that need overall arrangement. The CFLAC and its national associations publish over 30 national literary and artistic magazines and newspapers, including China Arts Gazette, and operate seven publishing houses for books and audio-video products and a film and television center. The local federations and associations have their own literary and artistic publications. The CFLAC carries out extensive external exchanges and actively encourages and organizes its group members to carry out international culture and art exchanges. Each year, it receives hundreds of foreign writers and artists delegations. At the same time, it organizes and sends an increasing number of Chinese writers and artists to foreign lands, where they carry on lively and vigorous exchanges in various forms with their foreign counterparts, thus furthering mutual friendship and cooperation between Chinese and foreign literary and art circles.

Website: http://www.cflac.org.cn/

On June 26, 2005, the awarding ceremony of the Third Luxun Literature Awards was held in Shenzhen.

The China Association for Science and Technology decided to designate the general holidays of the third week of september every year as the National Science Popularization Day from 2005. In the picture, the students of the No.5 Middle School of Urumchi are watching the magnetic floating globe.

China Association for Science and Technology

(See P202)

All-China Federation of Returned Overseas Chinese (AFROC)

The All-China Federation of Returned Overseas Chinese (AFROC) was founded in October 1956. It has some 11,000 local Returned Overseas Chinese Federations at various levels.

AFROC is a national mass organization made up of returned overseas Chinese and family members of overseas Chinese. The eighth article of the Law of the PRC on the Protection of the Rights and Interests of Returned Overseas Chinese and the Family Members of Overseas Chinese stipulates: The All-China Federation of Returned Overseas Chinese and local Returned Overseas Chinese Federations shall, in accordance with the law, safeguard lawful rights and interests of the returned overseas Chinese and family members of overseas Chinese on behalf of them. The 23rd article also stipulates: If the lawful rights of Returned overseas Chinese and the family members of overseas Chinese are violated, they have the right to request the relevant competent departments to handle the matter in accordance with the law, or bring a suit in a people's court according to law. Federations of Returned Overseas Chinese will support and assist them.

Website: http://www.chinaql.org/

China Writers Association

(See P462)

China Law Society

The China Law Society was evolved from the China Political Law Society set up in 1953. It adopted its present name in 1980. It is a national social organization and academic organization of Chinese legal academic circle and law circle, with 30 law societies at the level of province, autonomous region and municipality directly under the Central Government, 14 law societies in big cities, 139 in prefecture-level cities or cities, and 43 in counties or county-level cities. It has 16 subject, major and specialty institutions of different fields of law, such as constitution, jurisprudence, civil law and economy law, criminal law, litigation law, administration law, comparative law, ethnic law, military law, marriage law, labor law, police law, prison law, energy sources law, aviation law, and law of both sides of the Taiwan Strait. The China Law Society has over 100,000 members, talents of legal academic circles and law.

In the past 50 years, the China Law Society has been working hard to organize and encourage legal academic personnel and legal personnel to participate in drafting and argumentation for legislation, inquiry for executing the law, reform of the judicatory, teaching law, and publicizing law, as well as undertaking legal research on various subjects. According to the statistics during the recent 20 years, the China Law Society sponsored hundreds of national academic conferences, thousands of regional academic conferences, with tens of thousands of academic papers published and numerous law proposals. The society has carried out much creative work and made a contribution to the forming and implementing of basic guideline and policy of ruling the country according to law and also building a socialist legal system.

Website: http://www.chinalawsociety.com/

China Council for the Promotion of International Trade

The China Council for the Promotion of International Trade (CCPIT), established in May 1952, is a national non-governmental organization engaged in foreign economic and trade activities. It is composed of representative personages, enterprises and associations in the country's economic and trade sectors. The aims of the CCPIT are as follows: to operate and promote foreign trade, to use foreign investment, to introduce advanced foreign technologies, to conduct activities of Sino-foreign economic and technological cooperation in various forms, to promote the development of economic and trade relations between China and other countries and regions around the world, and to promote the mutual understanding and friendship between China and peoples and economic and trade circles of all nations around the world, in line with law and government policies of the PRC. With government approval, CCPIT created the China Chamber of International Commerce (CCOIC) in June 1988.

Currently, CCPIT and CCOIC have established broad economic and trade relations with industrial and commercial circles from over 200 countries and regions, signed cooperation agreements with more than 160 similar organizations in the world and established united chambers of commerce with some countries. CCPIT has 15 overseas offices. At home, it has 49 local branches and more than 600 sub-branches and county-level international commerce chambers, 18 industrial branches in the industries such as machinery, electricity, light industry, weave, agriculture, automobile, petrochemicals, commerce, metallurgy, aviation, space, chemistry, construction materials, supply and marketing cooperatives, construction, grain and foreign-funded enterprise administration, with near 70,000 corporate members. The current president is Wan Jifei.

CCPIT, CCOIC and their affiliated business departments have joined many international organizations including the World Intellectual Property Organization (WIPO), International Association For The Protection Of Intellectual Property (AIPPI), Licensing Executives Society (LES), International Maritime Committee (IMC), Union of International Fairs (UFI), International Federation of Commercial Arbitration Institutions (ICFAI), Pacific Basin Economic Council (PBEC), International Chamber of Commerce (ICC).

Website: http://www.ccpit.com.cn/

All-China Journalists Association

The Association (ACJA for short), set up in 1957, is the national people's organization for China's journalism circles. It practices an organizational system of group members. Those, including national newspaper groups, broadcasting and television groups, newspaper offices, current affairs and political periodicals, State news agencies, State broadcasting stations, State television stations, journalists associations of provinces, autonomous regions and municipalities directly under the Central Government, as well as national journalism organizations and major journalism education and research organizations, which are willing to apply for affiliation with the federations, accept the ACJA Charter and pay members fees, may become members once approved by ACJA . At present, the ACJA has a membership of 213.

The supreme power organ is the National Council, elected for a term of five years. The Standing Council is responsible for executing the resolution of the National Council when the latter is not in session. The Secretariat of the ACJA handles the day-to-day work of the ACJA, and submits the important matters to the Chairman Session or the Standing Council for decision.

Website: http://www.xinhuanet.com/zgjx/

The All-China Journalists' Association, Beijing

China Disabled Persons' Federation

The China Disabled Persons' Federation (CDPF) is a national organization set up to promote the cause of disabled people. It comprises of delegates from various categories of disabilities and workers who work for the disabled. Following the founding of the China Welfare Fund for the Handicapped, the China Association for the Blind and Deaf and the China Secretariat of the UN Decade of Disabled Persons, the federation was set up in March 1988 with headquarters in Beijing. Its aims are to promote humanitarianism, protect the human rights of persons with disabilities, and insure their equal participation in society, contribution to economic growth and social development as well as their equal share in the material and culture achievements of society. Its missions are to represent the common interests of the disabled; coordinate and organize activities related to rehabilitation, education, employment and culture; improve the environment for the disabled to participate in social life; participate in the processes of legislation on disability and of the inspections of the implementation of the laws and regulations so as to protect the lawful rights and interests of persons. As for its active participation in the relevant activities organized by the United Nations, the federation has received the titles and awards such as the United Nations Peace Messenger, the Special Award for UN Decade of Disabled Persons, the UN ESCAP Awards for Outstanding Contributions to the Asian and Pacific Decade of Disabled Persons. In July 1998, the Economic and Social Council of the United Nations decided to give the China Disabled Persons' Federation special consultant status. In December 2003, Deng Pufang, the president of the China Disabled Persons' Federation, was awarded the UN Human Rights Prize. Some other prizes have also awarded to the federation, such as the Paul Harris Humanitarian Award sponsored by the Rotary Club of Los Angeles, the Henry Howard Kessler Award sponsored by Rehabilitation International and a regional award from the Disabled People's International Asia-Pacific

Website: http://www.cdpf.org.cn/cjrzy/fwzn-fwjg-001.htm

China Welfare Fund for the Handicapped

China Welfare Fund for the Handicapped (CWFH) is an independent national non-profit charity organization. It was founded in Beijing on March 15 in 1984.

The governing board of directors of CWFH is composed of over 110 individuals from all walks of society. Mr. Deng Pufang is current President of CWFH. The Secretariat Division acts as CWFH's executive body in charge of its daily activities.

Since its establishment with the banner of humanitarianism, adhering to the principle of 'From the society and for the undertaking for disabled', CWFH has so far raised funds amount to 480 millions RMB yuan, of which 280 millions already used in advancing progress in areas such as rehabilitation, education, employment, culture and sports development for disabled persons and benefiting them practically. For its outstanding achievements, the United Nations presented to CWFH the United Nations Peace Passenger Citation in 1988, and to Mr. Deng Pufang a Special Award for UN Decade of Disabled Persons.

Website: http://www.cwfh.org.cn

▲ Logo of China Disabled Persons' Federation

The image in the center, comprising the letters of C, J and R, indicates "the disabled", which is similar to the logo used by the international community. C, J and R are the first letters of the Chinese Phonetic Alphabets of three Chinese characters, which mean "the handicapped". The logo is the shape of plum blossom, a flower signifying persistence in difficult conditions in Chinese culture. It is used to symbolize the enterprising spirit of disabled people, which are self-esteem, self-confidence, self-reliance and self-improvement. The green color of the background signifies the indomitable power of life. The blossom of the plum implies the prosperous future of the cause of the handicapped and represents the hope of the disabled and their relatives. The edge of the flower is in the shape of five "人", a Chinese character meaning human beings. The linked words imply that the disabled people unite hand in hand and live in a harmonious and mutual aid society where they are treated with understanding and respect. It also indicates that, under the banner of humanism, the people of the whole country and the handicapped comprise a single organism. The golden color of the center and the edge implies the prosperity of the cause of the handicapped. The logo is adopted in the front of the badge of the China Disabled Persons' Federation. The brief name of the China Disabled Persons' Federation is on the badge's back.

The disabled people are making handicrafts in the Hand-in-hand Occupational Rehabilitation Center. The handicrafts are sent as gifts for the Beijing Paralympic Games; some of them enter the commodity market through special institutions.

Administrative Division

General Information

Administrative Division System

China's administrative units are currently based on a three-level system dividing the nation into provinces, counties and townships:

—The country is divided into provinces, autonomous regions and municipalities directly under the Central Government;

—Provinces and autonomous regions are divided into autonomous prefectures, counties, autonomous counties and cities;

—Counties and autonomous counties are divided into townships, ethnic minority townships and towns.

Municipalities directly under the Central Government and other large cities are divided into districts and counties. Autonomous prefectures are divided into counties, autonomous counties, and cities. All autonomous regions, autonomous prefectures and autonomous counties are autonomous areas. According to the Constitution, the State may establish special administrative regions when necessary. The special administrative region is a local administrative area directly under the Central Government.

At present, China is divided into 23 provinces, 5 autonomous regions, 4 municipalities directly under the Central Government and 2 special administrative regions

Municipalities Directly Under the Central Government

China has four municipalities directly under the Central Government—Beijing, Shanghai, Tianjin and Chongqing.

By the end of 2006, China was home to 657 cities. In terms of city planning, the Central Government formulated the policy of controlling the size of large cities, rationally developing the medium-sized cities and actively fostering the small cities. Thanks to that, medium-sized and small cities, with populations of less than 500,000 and 200,000 respectively, have developed apace since the 1980s. As for Large cities which have populations over one million, the government works to build up satellite towns around them.

Beijing Municipality

Beijing, the capital of the PRC, is a municipality directly under the Central Government. It is not only China's political center, but also its cultural, scientific and education center, as well as the key transportation hub. It is situated on the north fringe of the North China Plain, surrounded by mountains to its west, north and east. Its southeastern part is on a plain. Its temperate continental climate produces four distinct seasons—a short spring, a rainy and humid summer, a long and cold winter and a very pleasant autumn.

Beijing, covering an area of 16,807.8 square km, exercises jurisdiction over 16 districts and 2 towns. By the end of 2006, it was home to 15.81 million inhabitants who had lived there for six months or longer. There were 11.976 million people with registered permanent residence. All 56 ethnic groups could be found among the urbanites. In addition to the Han ethnic group, the Hui, Manchu and Mogolian population all exceeded 10,000 people per group. According to the fifth census, the Han ethnic population stood at 13.229 million, accounting for 95.7 percent of the total population. Other ethnic people totaled 590,000, making up the other 4.3 percent.

Based on written history or cultural relics, Beijing's history as a city could date back to 3000-odd years ago. It has been designated as the capital of the dynasties of Liao, Jin, Yuan, Ming and Qing. The United Nations Educational, Scientific and Cultural Organization (UESCO) has listed the Forbidden City, the Great Wall, the site of the discovery of the Peking Man at Zhoukoudian, the Temple

Map of the People's Republic of China

Edition of Administrative Region

GS(2008)1876号 Jun. 2008 Produced by State Bureau of Surveying and Mapping

of Heaven and the Summer Palace as world cultural heritage sites. Richly bestowed with tourism resources, Beijing boasts 200-plus scenic tourist spots, including the Forbidden City, the biggest imperial court in the world; the Heaven Temple, where the emperors of the Ming and Qing dynasties worshipped the heaven; the Winter Palace, the Summer Palace, the Great Wall at Badaling, Mutianyu and Simatai and the Prince Gong's Residence, the biggest courtyard in China. Beijing has cemented a friendly relationship with 124 capitals and major cities in 72 countries. Among them, 27 cities in 24 countries have maintained friendly exchanges with Beijing. Some 137 countries have set up their embassies here. The city is also home to 17 international organizations and regional institutions, 190 foreign news agencies and 7,000 foreign deputy agencies. Foreign students number over 17,000.

Address of City Government: No. 2 Zhengyi Lu, Dongcheng District, Beijing
Website: http://www.beijing.gov.cn

Shanghai Municipality

The urban scene of Shanghai

Shanghai, the biggest city in China, is a municipality directly under the Central Government. It is situated halfway down China's mainland coastline, where the Yangtze River empties into the sea. With such an advantageous location, Shanghai turns out to be an important, comprehensive industrial base and harbor in China. It plays an important role in the national economy. Its major industries include metallurgy, manufacturing, shipbuilding, chemicals, electronics, instruments and meters, textile and other light industries. In addition, its commerce, banking and ocean-going shipping industries are also well developed. At the end of 2006, Shanghai, with a registered permanent residents of 13.681 million, was home to 18.15 million people who had lived there for at least six months. Among them, some 53,000 people, or 0.4 percent of the city's total population, were ethnic minorities. Despite a few unindentified ethnic groups, the Hui ethnic people made up the major part, living together with the other 39 ethnic minority groups.

Shanghai exercises jurisdiction over an area of 6,340.5 square km. The Chongming Island, making up an area of 1,041 square km of Shanghai, is considered the third largest island in China. The North Hemisphere's sub-tropical monsoon climate makes the city enjoy warm and humid weather. There, spring and autumn are relatively short, while winter and summer are comparatively long. The rainy season (May through September) accounts for over 50 percent of the city's precipitation in the year. Shanghai, a city in the area south of the Yangtze River, is famous for its abundant water resources, with rivers and lakes making up 11 percent of the city area. Most of these rivers are tributaries of the Huangpujiang River. The Huangpujiang River, originating from the Taihu Lake, extends some 113km. The river averages 360 meters wide, with the narrowest and widest parts being 300 and 770 meters respectively. The water is fast-moving all year round, making it the major water transportation channel of Shanghai. The handling capacity of the Shanghai Harbor reached 537 million tons in 2006, making the harbor the number one in the world. The container handling capacity reached 21.719 TEU, ranking third in the world.

Shanghai is a city with a long history. It has 13 key cultural relic units under the State-level protection. Some of its cultural heritages date back to the Tang, Song, Yuan, Ming and Qing dynasty. It also preserves some delicate private gardens with unique styles. Since the 1990s, Shanghai has also been famous for its newly erected modern buildings. These buildings combine to create the picturesque scenery that attracts tourists from home and abroad. The Oriental Pearl TV Tower is known as the first building in China and the Shanghai People's Square is dubbed the green lung for the city. They, along with other Chinese or Western style buildings, form a beautiful picture on the bank of the Yangtze River Delta.

Address of City Government: No.19 Gaoan Lu, Shanghai
Website: http://www.shanghai.gov.cn

Tianjin Municipality

Tianjin is situated in the northeastern part of the North China Plain. With a coastal line of 133km, it covers an area of 11,305 square km. Its downtown area is located 50km away from the coast and 120km away from Beijing. Thus Tianjin has kept a good reputation of the key gateway to the capital since ancient times. In addition, it is also an important traffic hub for transportation among North, Northeast and Northwest China. The direct distances from Tianjin to major cities, such as Shenyang in the Northeast, Baotou in the Northwest and Xuzhou and Zhengzhou in areas south of it, are less than 600km away. Tianjin Port, the biggest one of its kind in North China, serves a batch of provinces and municipalities in North China. It extends 30-plus ocean-going shipping lines to over 300 international ports. As the Eurasia Continental Bridge's key access to the sea, Tianjin plays an important role in transportation from the Eurasia interior to the other side of the Pacific Ocean. Lying at such a vantage point, it is highly valued due to its strategic location. In 2006, with permanent registered residents of 9.4888 million, the city was home to 10.75 million people who had resided there for at least half a year. Among them, there were 41 ethnic groups with a population of 220,000.

Tianjin, a city boasting abundant unearthed

The scenery of the Haihe River, Tianjin

relics, is also famous for a batch of historical sites. There are 40-odd cultural relic units under the State-level or city-level protection. The Solitary Joy Temple, a wooden structure dating back to Sui Dynasty, still lies in Jixian County after 1000-plus years. The Great Wall at the Huangyaguan Pass in Jixian County, meanders over 41km through mountains, dubbed Ji Bei Suo Yao, which means the key path to area north of Jixian County. It comprises over 1,000 beacon towers of different styles, creating an imposing picture. The Panshan Mountain, also in Jixian County, enjoys a reputation of the First Mountain in Jingdong (east area of Beijing). It has many sheer and shudderingly attractive precipices and grotesquely shaped rocks and boulders. The artificial buildings perfectly integrate with the natural sceneries. Other relics include the Tianhou Palace (Palace of Heavenly Empress), Confucius Temple, Grand Mercy Monastery, the Great Mosque, the Tianzun Pavilion, the Tiancheng Temple, the Dagu Fort, the Notre Dame des Victories and the Guangdong Guild Hall. A fusion of classicism and modernity, Tianjin is also known as the museum of international architecture. As one of the cities that first opened up to foreign trade in the late Qing Dynasty, Tianjin has concessions of nine countries, where the Western-style buildings feature exotic atmosphere. Actually, the city preserves 1,000-plus distinct Oriental or Western style buildings built in the late 19 century through the early 20th century.

The Yangliuqing's New Year Pictures printed from an engraved wooden plate, Zhang's painted clay figurines, Wei's kites and sculpture Liu's brick sculpture are the four famous fork crafts in Tianjin.

Tianjin by the Bohai Sea in the east is 120 km from Beijing. Known as the "Marine Gate to Beijing", it is cut through by the Haihe River which is formed by north China river system and the Southern and Northern Grand Canals which meet in the city area.

Address of the City Goverment: No.7 Tai'an Dao, Heping District, Tianjin
Website: http://www.tj.gov.cn/

Chongqing Municipality

As a municipality directly under the Central Government, Chongqing is the biggest industrial and commercial center of southwestern China and a land and water traffic hub of the upper reaches of the Yangtze River. It is a comprehensive industrial city, which is well developed in sectors such as steel, chemicals, power generating, auto, manufacturing, ship building, construction material, textile, food stuffs and pharmaceuticals.

Situated in southeast China and the upper reaches of the Yangtze River, it abuts Hubei, Hunan, Guizhou, Sichuan and Shaanxi Provinces. Covering an area of 82,400 square km, it was home to 28.08 million residents who had lived there for at least six months in 2006. Mainly inhabitated by Han ethnic people, the city was also populated by 1.75 million minorities of 49 ethnic groups. The Tu ethnic group makes up the major part of the minority population, making up 1.13 million. It was followed by Miao ethnic group. With a total population of 520,000, the Miao ethnic people are distributed in five autonomous counties in the Qianjiang Development Area and Fuling area.

Thanks to its abundant rivers, the city's exploitable hydropower resources could generate 7.4982 million KW of electricity. In addition, its underground water resources rank among the top 3 in China. It is also richly bestowed with mineral resources, including proven deposites of coal, natural gas, strontium, aluminium, manganese, limestone, marble, spar, gypsum, quartz, mercury, salinastone and another 26 minerals. Among them, the strontium mineral resources rank the first in China and second in the world.

Address of the City Government: Renmin Lu, Yuzhong District, Chongqing
Website: http://www.cq.gov.cn

Hong Kong Special Administrative Region

Hong Kong Special Administrative Region is located at the east of the mouth of the Zhujiang River. Hong Kong has always been a part of Chinese territory since ancient time and was invaded and occupied by the United Kingdom after the Opium War in 1840. According to the Joint Declaration on the Question of Hong Kong Issues signed by the Chinese and UK governments in 1984, China would resume its sovereignty over Hong Kong from July 1, 1997. And Hong Kong Special Administrative Region would be founded formally at the same time. The Chinese Government adopts the basic principles of "one country, two systems", "Hong Kong people administering Hong Kong", and a high degree of autonomy. "One country, two systems" means that in the united country of China, the mainland adopts the system of socialism and Hong Kong preserves the previous capitalist system and way of life which shall remain unchanged for 50 years. "Hong Kong people administering Hong Kong" means Hong Kong people administrate Hong Kong independently and the Central Government will not send officials to hold posts in the government of the Special Administrative Region. A high degree of autonomy means except for the foreign and national defensive affairs administrated by the Central Government, Hong Kong Special Administrative Region enjoys the full powers of administrating local affairs independently including executive, legislative, and independent judicial power including that of final adjudication.

Website: http://www.gov.hk

Macao Special Administrative Region

Macao Special Administrative Region is located at the west of the mouth of the Zhujiang River. Macao has always been a part of Chinese territory since ancient time and was invaded and occupied by Portugal after the Opium War in 1840. According to the Joint Declaration on the Question of Macao signed by the Chinese and Portuguese governments in 1987, China would resume its sovereignty over Macao from December 20, 1999. And Macao Special Administrative Region would be founded formally at the same time. The Chinese Government adopts the basic principles of "one country, two systems", "Macao people administering Macao", and a high degree of autonomy. "One country, two systems" means that in the united country of China, the mainland adopts the system of socialism and Macao preserves the previous capitalist system and way of life which shall remain unchanged for 50 years. "Macao people administering Macao" means Macao people administrate Macao independently and the Central Government will not send officials to hold posts in the government of the Special Administrative Region. A high degree autonomy means except for the foreign and national defensive affairs administrated by the Central Government, Macao Special Administrative Region enjoys the full powers of administrating local affairs independently including executive, legislative, and independent judicial power including that of final adjudication.

Website: http://www.gov.mo

Taiwan Province

Taiwan province lies off the southeastern coast of China, faces the Pacific Ocean on the east, and Fujian Province across the Taiwan Straits on the west. Covering an area of 36,000 square Km, Taiwan includes Taiwan Island, Penghu Islands and 80 other smaller neighboring islands and islets. As early as in the mid-12th century, the Central Government of different periods set up administrative bodies to exercise jurisdiction over Taiwan. During its developments, the Taiwan society has kept the Chinese cultural traditions all along. This basic fact had not changed even during the half century of Japanese occupation which began after the Sino-Japanese War in 1894. After the Chinese people's victory in the war against Japanese aggression in 1945, the Central Government resumed its administrative authority in Taiwan Province.

On the eve of the founding of the People's Republic of China in 1949, the Kuomintang authorities retreated from the mainland to Taiwan. In 1950, the Korean War broke out, and the United States dispatched its Seventh Fleet to invade Taiwan and the Taiwan Straits. In 1954, the government of the United States and the Taiwan authorities signed a Mutual Defense Treaty, resulting in the separation of Taiwan from the mainland.

The Central Government has made unremitting efforts to solve the Taiwan question, and to realize the reunification of the country. In February 1972, when President Richard M. Nixon of the United States visited China, the two sides issued the Sino-US Joint Communique. On January 1, 1979, the United States established official diplomatic relations with China, formally recognizing the government of the People's Republic of China as the sole legitimate government of China and Taiwan as a part of China. At the same time, the United States announced the cessation of "diplomatic relations" with the Taiwan authorities, the annulment of the Mutual Defense Treaty and the withdrawal of all its military personnel from Taiwan. Under such historical conditions, the Chinese government, out of consideration for the interests and future of the whole nation, put forward the principle of "peaceful reunification of the country, and one country, two systems" in accordance with the principle of respecting history and reality, seeking truth from facts and taking into account the interests of both sides. The basic points of this basic principle and the relevant policies are:

China will do its best to achieve peaceful reunification, but will not commit itself to rule out the use of force; will actively promote people-to-people contacts and economic and cultural exchanges between the two sides of the Taiwan Straits, and start direct trade, postal, air and shipping services as soon as possible; achieve reunification through peaceful negotiations and, on the premise of the One-China Principle, any matter can be negotiated. After reunification, the policy of "one country, two systems" will be practiced, with the main body of China (China mainland) continuing with its socialist system, and Taiwan maintaining its capitalist system for a long period of time. After reunification, Taiwan will enjoy a high degree of autonomy, and the Central Government will not send troops or administrative personnel to be stationed in Taiwan. Resolution of the Taiwan question is an internal affair of China, which should be achieved by the Chinese themselves, and there is no call for aid by foreign forces. The afore-mentioned principles and policies embody the basic stand and spirit of adhering to the One-China Principle, and fully respect Taiwan compatriots' wish to govern and administer Taiwan by themselves.

Tucked away at an elevation of 740 meters, the Sun Moon Lake is the only one natural lake on the Taiwan Island, covering an area of 7.73 square km. It has a perimeter of 35 km and an average depth of some 40 meters. A small island called Pearl Island with an elevation of 745 meters divides the lake into two parts. The northern part look like a sun and the southern part like a moon in shape. Thus, it gets the name Sun Moon Lake.

China's Provinces, Autonomous Regions and Municipalities Directly Under the Central Government (2006)

Name	Seat of government	Area(100,000sqkm)	Population(1000,000)
Beijing Municipality	Beijing	1.68	1581
tianjing Municipality	Tianjin	1.13	1075
Hebei Province	Shijiazhuang	19.00	6895
Shanxi Province	Taiyuan	15.60	3375
Inner Mongolia Autonomous Region	Hohhot	119.75	2392
Liaoning Province	Shenyang	14.57	4223
Jilin Province	Changchun	18.70	2723
Heilongjiang Province	Harbin	46.90	3823
Shanghai Municipality	Shanghai	0.62	1815
Jiangsu Province	Nanjing	10.26	7550
Zhejiang Province	Hangzhou	10.18	4980
Anhui Province	Hefei	13.90	6593
Fujian Province	Fuzhou	12.00	3558
Jiangxi Province	Nanchang	16.66	4339
Shandong Province	Jinan	15.30	9309
Henan Province	Zhengzhou	16.70	9820
Hubei Province	Wuhan	18.74	6050
Hunan Province	Changsha	21.00	6768
Guangdong Province	Guangzhou	18.60	9304
Guangxi Zhuang Autonomous Region	Nanning	23.77	4961
Hainan Province	Haikou	3.40	836
Chongqing Municipality	Chongqing	8.20	2808
Sichuan Province	Chengdu	48.80	8169
Guizhou Province	Guiyang	17.00	3955
Yunnan Province	Kunming	39.00	4483
Tibet Autonomous Region	Lhasa	127.49	281
Shaanxi Province	Xi'an	20.50	3735
Gansu Province	Lanzhou	45.00	2606
Qinghai Province	Xining	72.00	548
Ningxia Hui Autonomous Region	Yinchuan	6.28	604
Xinjiang Uygur Autonomous Region	Urumqi	165.58	2050
Hong Kong Special Administrative Region	Hong Kong	0.11	690
Macao Special Administrative Region	Macao	0.00	50.8(in mid 2006)
Taiwan Province		3.60	2288

Northeast China

Heilongjiang Province

The Heilongjiang Province is named after its biggest river, the Heilongjiang River. Located in the northeast of China, it is at the highest latitude and in the northern frontier in this country. It covers an area of 454,000 square km, accounting for 4.7 percent of the total land area of China. There are ten native ethnic minorities living in this province, including Man churian, Korean, Hui, Mongolian, Daur, Xibe, Oroqen, Hezhe, Ewenki, and Kirgiz. In 2006, the population of Heilongjiang is 38.23 million. Heilongjiang Province is an important base of grain, coal, oil, forestry and mechanical industry in China. Its provincial capital is Harbin.

The climate in Heilongjiang Province is a continental monsoon climate, the kind between the temperate and frigid zones, with annual average temperatures of -4 degrees Centigrade to 4 degrees Centigrade. It owns the best soil in China. The total area of its cultivated land and the reserved land resource for cultivation accounts for 10 percent of the total in this country. Per-capita cultivated land and cultivated area run by per-capita are three times the average level of China. There are 11.80 million hectares of cultivated lands in Heilongjiang, with a highest composition of soil organic matter in China. As 60 percent of the soil is black soil, chernozem soil and meadow soil, the cultivated land in Heilongjiang is ranked among the three world-famous main black soil regions. It teems with the crops such as soybean, wheat, corn, potato and rice, and cash crops such as sugar, beet, flax and tobacco, etc. There are 4.33 million hectares of grassland in Heilongjiang, growing high quality and nutritious grass, which is ideal for developing animal husbandry. The Songnen meadow is one of the three largest sheep pastures in the world. The province's forest coverage reaches 41.9 percent of the provincial land, taking first place in China in terms of forested areas, timber reserve and timber output. This makes the province the most important forest area and timber producing area in the country.

Address of the Provincial Government: Zhongshang Lu, Nangang District, Harbin City
Website: http://www.hlj.gov.cn

Jilin Province

Jilin Province lies in the middle of northeast China, which is the center area of northeast Asia combined by Japan, Russia, The Republic of Korea, Korea, Mongolia and Northeast China. The total population of Jilin Province was 27.23 million in 2006 and there are 44 ethnic groups besides the Han ethnic group. Among them the Korean ethnic group, the Manchu ethnic group, the Mongolian ethnic groups, the Hui ethnic group and the Xibe ethnic group also dwell there. The total area of Jilin Province is 187,400 square km, which takes 2 percent of the total of China. Jilin Province has obvious characteristics of a temperate zone territoriality trade wind climate. The provincial capital is Changchun City.

Jilin Province is one of the 6 largest forest areas in China. Changbai Mountain covers thousands km which is named "Changbai immense forest". Forest coverage rate of Jilin Province is 42.4 percent. The culmination of the province is Baiyun Peak of Changbai Mountain, which is 2,691 meters above sea level. The west of the province is grassland, which is located at the center of Songnen grassland. It is the most famous grassland in China, which is named "sheep grass" and also is one of the major bases for commercial cow and fuzz sheep.

Jilin Province is full of mineral resources and there are 136 mineral resources that have been developed, among them 22 mineral resources are ranked top 5 in China. Non-metal mineral resources are the advantage of Jilin Province and the export products are almost all raw materials and products of non-metal mineral resources.

The fertile earthiness of Jilin Province is suitable for the planting of beans, oil, beet, tobacco, hemp, potato, Ginseng, medical materials, fruit and all kinds of crops. The seeding area of Jilin province is 3.959 million hectares. The possession per capita of grain, the commercial rate of grain, the value of export of grain and the exit dose of corn have been ranked No.1 in China for many years. Jilin Province is the largest commercial grain base and it is also famous for corn, soya bean and paddy, etc. The Songliao Plain in Jilin Province is famous for both grain and corn.

Address of the Provincial Government: No.11, Xinfa Lu, Changchun City
Website: http://www.jl.gov.cn

Rime fog of Jilin

Liaoning Province

Liaoning Province is located in the south of Northeast China. North Korea is its neighbor at the southeast separated by the Yalujiang River. The total population of Liaoning Province was 42.71 million in 2006 and consists of the Han ethnic group, the Manchu ethnic group, the Mongolian ethnic group, the Hui ethnic group, the Korean ethnic group and the Xibe ethnic group etc. The length of continent coastal line of Liaoning Province is 2,178 km, which takes 12 percent of the total of China's coastline. The inland and hilly areas in the east are the main forest areas. The slender plain which is the east edge of the inland and hilly area in the west is usually called "Liaoxi corridor", which is the main passage to connect Northeast and Northern China. Liaohe plain, which is located in the middle of the province is the most import agriculture area and base for commercial grain. Liaoning Province belongs to the mainland trade wind climate of north temperature zone, which has four distinct seasons.

There are 115 mineral resources which have been found in Liaoning Province, and the reserves of 64 of them have been verified. Iron, Boron, Magnesium, Diamonds, Talc, Jade and Solvent gray rock are ranked No.1 in China. The Liaohe River oil field is one of the three big oil gas fields in China and the reserves of oil and natural gas make up 15 percent and 10 percent of China's total reserves respectively.

Address of the Provincial Government: No.45 Beiling Dajie, Huanggu District, Shenyang City
Website: http://www.ln.gov.cn

North China

Inner Mongolia Autonomous Region

Inner Mongolia autonomous region is located at the frontier of North China. The total population in the region was 23.9235 million in 2006. It is composed of 49 ethnic groups, such as the Mongolian ethnic group, the Han ethnic group, the Manchurian ethnic group, the Hui ethnic group, the Daur ethnic froup, the Ewenke ethnic group, the Oroqen ethnic group and the Korean ethnic group, etc., among them the total population of the Mongolia ethnic group is 4.2112 million. The total area of earth is 1.183 million square km which is takes up 12.3 percent of the total area of China ranking 3rd largest in China. It borders Mongolia and Russia at the north frontier and the length of frontier is 4,200 km. The Inner Mongolia highland is ranked 2cnd largest among the 4 big highlands in China. Hohhot is its capital.

Inner Mongolia is full of travel resources. It has a rich and colorful national culture, beautiful grassland, the Great Xing'an Mountain virgin forest, the Yellow River, magic echo sand bay, many lakes and hot springs, the tomb of Genghis Khan and Zhaojun, the old great wall, Yin Mountain Wudangzhao, the five tower temple, the Lark temple and the Eastern Han Dynasy fresco, etc.

Address of the Autonomous Region: No.1 Xinhua Dajie, Hohhot Cty
Website: http://www.nmg.gov.cn

Hebei Province

Hebei Province is situated in the north of the North China Plain, with a population of 68.978 million in 2006. It is home to 53 minority ethnic groups including the Mongolian, the Zhuang, the Korean, the Miao and the Tujia ethnic groups, which accounts for 4 percent of the total population, besides the Han ethnic group. Some 6 minority ethnic group autonomous counties have been set up in the province. Hebei encompasses Beijing, the capital of China, and Tianjin, the important trading port, facing the Bohai Sea in the east. Its total area reaches 190,000 square km. As a

The Chengde Summer Resort, also known as Chengde Temporary Imperial Palace, is located in the northern suburb of Chengde City, Hebei Province. It was a place where the Qing emperors had a rest when hunting at the paddock and spent summer as well as another center of political activities. Its construction began in 1730 or the 42nd year during the reign of the Emperor Kangxi and ended in 1790 or the 55th year during the reign of the Emperor Qianlong.

part of the North China Plain, the Hebei Plain accounts for 43.4 percent of the total area of the province, with most of its area under 50 meters above sea level. Hebei enjoys a continental monsoon climate and most of the area has clear-cut seasons. Shijiazhuang is its capital.

So far, a total of 116 varieties of mineral ores have been discovered, of which, deposits of 74 have been surveyed. There are 45 mines whose reserves are among the national top 10. The province boasts two large coalmines at Kailuan and Fengfeng in addition to the North China oil field. The coastal line of Hebei Province stretches 487.3 km and the coastal areas cover 1 million hectares. Such a natural condition is a boon for Hebei to develop ocean petroleum, ocean chemicals, ocean transportation and ocean tour industries. Qinhuangdao is the famous ice-free port in the north of China.

The province is the only one in the country that boasts highlands, mountainous and hilly areas, plains, lakes and a coastline. Across the province, there are 304 ancient ruins and groups of ancient buildings including 58 key relics under state protection. The number of historical and cultural relics in the province ranks first in the country along with Shaanxi Province. The total number of natural and human cultural scenic sites ranks second nationwide. They include the Chengde Summer Resort, Shanhaiguan Pass at the head of the Great Wall, Beidaihe holiday resort and the Eastern and Western Tombs of the emperors of the Qing Dynasty.

Address of the Provincial Government: No.10 Weiming Jie, Shijiazhuang City
Website: http://www.hebei.com.cn

Shanxi Province

Shanxi Province is situated in the middle of the Yellow River valley, its location west of the Taihang Mountains gives the province its name, Shanxi, meaning "west of the mountain." The total population in the region was 33.746 million in 2006. Besides the Han ethnic group it is home to 34 ethnic groups including the Hui, the Manchurian, the Mongolian, the Korean and the Tibetan ethnic group. The population of the minority ethnic groups totaled 67,000, who live in 58 minority ethnic group villages, in which the majority consists of minority ethnic groups. Shanxi province covers an area of 156,000 square km, with forests constituting 20 percent, or about 3.435 million hectares. Taiyuan is its capital.

Shanxi abounds in tourism resources. Famous spots include the Yunguang Caves at Datong City in the north, Wutai Mountain, a sacred Buddhist site in the central part, and the falls at Hukou in the south, the only waterfall on the Yellow River. The province also encompasses the country's largest temple of martial valor—the Guan Yu Shrine at Xiezhou—and one of the four large whispering buildings in China, the Yingying Pagoda of Pujiu Temple in Yongji County. Incomplete statistics show that Shanxi now preserves a total of 31,401 unmovable cultural relics of different kinds. They comprise of 2,639 ruins of ancient monuments, 1,666 ancient graves, 18,118 old buildings and memorial structures of historic interest, 300 grottoes and temples, 360 sites bearing ancient vertebrate fossils, 6,852 sites with stone inscriptions and 1,466 old revolutionary sites and memorial buildings. There are 12,345 painted sculptures in these old buildings as well as a number of memorial structures of historic interest. Altogether there are 26,751 square meters of murals in old temples.

Shanxi abounds in mineral resources. Of the more than 120 kinds of underground minerals so far discovered in the province, 53 have verified reserves. Of them, reserves of coal, bauxite, pearlite, gallium and zeolite rank first in the nation. The province is especially noted as the "kingdom of coal," with verified reserves amounting to 261.2 billion tons, accounting for one-third of the nation's total.

Address of the Provincial Government: No.101 Shifu Dongjie, Taiyuan City
Website: http://www.shanxi.gov.cn

South China

Guangdong Province

Guangdong Province is located in southeast China, with a resident population of 93.04 million in 2006. It is home to 53 ethnic groups out of 56 in the country, accounting for 0.7 percent, among them, the Zhuang, the Yao, the She, the Hui and the Manchurian ethnic groups being the dominant ones. Guangzhou is its capital.

It occupies an area of 178,000 square km. Its many islands add a further 1,600 square km. To the south it meets the warm waters of the South China Sea along a coastline of 3,368 km. The Tropic of Cancer runs through the center of this low latitude province where the Pearl River, at 2,122 km (the third longest in China) meets the sea. The fertile Pearl River Delta is well-known as a land rich in fish and rice. Most areas enjoy a subtropical monsoon climate with adequate rainfall, long summers and warm winters. Guangdong is a green place where plants grow vigorously all year round.

Guangdong boasts rich mineral resources.

The urban scenery of the Binshui area along the Pearl River of Guangzhou

A total of 116 minerals have been discovered, and reserves of 89 minerals have been proven. Among them, 34 kinds of minerals rank among the top 5 in the country, and turf, vericular quartz, kaoline, trachyte, germanium and tellurium rank first in the country. Forests cover 57.5 percent of the province. The province has extensive access to the sea together with a network of interconnected waterways with many reservoirs and fish ponds. It is rich in aquatic products. The main crops are rice, vegetables and fruit. Guangdong boasts 40 forest parks and 30 nature reserves.

Address of the Provincial Government: No.305 Dongfeng Zhonglu, Guangzhou City
Website: http://www.gd.gov.cn

Hainan Province

Hainan Province lies at the southernmost tip of China, with a resident population of 8.3588 million of 2006, of which, the Han, Li, Miao, and Hui ethnic groups are the dominant ethnic groups out of the 37 ethnic groups there. The Li ethnic group first inhabited Hainan Island. The administrative areas of Hainan Province contain island reefs and sea areas of Hainan Island, Xisha Island, Zhongsha Island and South China Sea Islands. Hainan Province covers a land area of 35,000 square km and a sea area of approximately 2 million square km. Hainan Island is China's second largest island after Taiwan, with an area of 33,900 square km. Qiongzhou Strait is 18 km in width between Hainan Island and Leizhou Island of Guangdong Province. The Zengmu Reef of South China Sea is the southernmost tip of China. Haikou is its capital.

A tropical maritime climate prevails in Hainan, making it windy but warm all-year-round with abundant rainfall, clearly divided dry and wet seasons, frequent tropical storms and typhoons, as well as diversified climatic resources.

Distinctive tourism resources abound in Hainan. Sandy beaches make up about 50 to 60 percent of its 1,528-km coastline. The beaches are usually hundreds of or thousands of meters wide, stretching gently into the sea with a slope of five degrees. Located alongside an unruffled sea, with crystal-clear seawater with temperatures between 18 °C and 30°C, plus bright and abundant sunlight, most of its beaches are good for swimming, sunbathing, sand-bathing and wind-bathing almost all year round.

Hainan Island is the largest "tropical treasure" in China, accounting for nearly 42.5 percent of the national tropical land. Thanks to having advantages in light, heat and water, the reproduction rate of the plants there is higher than in temperate zone and subtropical zone, while the farmlands are planted all year round, many crops can be harvested two or three times each year.

Address of the Provincial Government: No.59 Chengfu Lu, Haikou City
Website: http://www.hainan.gov.cn

Guangxi Zhuang Autonomous Region

Guangxi is the only ethnic autonomous region bordering coastal areas. Its coastline extends 1,595 km, with 605 km of islands' coastline. The population in Guangxi totaled 49.61 million in 2006. There are 12 ethnic groups which have lived there for generations, including the Zhuang, Han, Yao, Miao, Dong, Nunao, Maonan, Hui, Jing, Yi, Shui and Gelao. In addition, there are more than 25 smaller ethnic groups in the region. Nanning is its capital.

The mountain peaks and grottoes in Guangxi are typically representative of tropical karst landform, which has well developed. They look as though they have risen straight out of the ground, majestic and grand with unique structures. The most typical and graceful are the limestone moungtain peaks at Guilin and Yangshuo. Guangxi is renowned for its numerous caves with and scenery, winning its reputation "No mountains without caves, and no caves without unique sceneries". According to statistics, there are nearly 100, 000 grottoes in Guangxi. The famous ones are Ludi Yan (Reed Flute Cave), Seven Star Cave in Guilin, Dule Cave in Liuzhou, Yiling Cave in Wuming. On the other hand, Guangxi ethnic autonomous region mainly consists of the Zhuang ethnic group integrated with compact communities of multi-ethnic groups, each ethnic group having its own language, clothing, buildings, living styles, customs, festivals, folk arts, crafts and cooking skills. Therefore their colorful traditional customs and diverse cultures are formed and add much to local tourism. There are many festivals or activities, full of the customs and culture of ethnic minorities, which have attracted many tourists. For example, according to the Chinese lunar calendar, "the third day of the third month" – the Songfests of the Zhuang ethnic minority, "Danu" Festival and "Shuawang" Festival of the Yao ethnic minority, the Flower Mountain festivals of the Miao ethnic minority, the Youth Festival of the Mulam ethnic minority, the Firework-scrambling Festival, and the Oil Camellia cooking festival of the Dong ethnic minority, with its distinctive flavour.

Hills and rivers in Guilin are the most beautiful in China.

Address of the Autonomous Regional Government: No.1 Minle Lu, Nanning City
Website: http://www.gxi.gov.cn

East China

Shandong Province

Shandong Province is located in the coastal areas of east China, near the lower reaches of the Yellow River. It is divided into a peninsula and inland area. The Shandong peninsula lies between the Bohai Sea and Yellow Sea, facing the Liaodong peninsula, with an area of 156,700 square km. It has a warm temperate monsoon pattern climate. In 2006, it has a population of 93.09 million, with 54 ethnic minority groups, including the Han, Hui, Manchurian, Zhuang, Korea, Miao, Tibet, Yi, Yao and Bai. Jinan is its capital.

Shandong Province is a key agricultural region in China. It is honorably called "the granary rich in grain, cotton and edible oil, the home of abundant fruits and aquatic products". It has held a major position nationwide in wheat, cotton, peanut, flue-cured tobacco and fibrous crop production. Meanwhile, it is one of key producing regions of fruits, vegetables, marine products, pods and medicinal materials. Its special products are well known, such as Yantai apples, Laiyang pears, Feicheng peaches and Yueling Chinese dates. Shandong Province is also richly endowed with marine resources, with offing areas accounting for 37 percent of the Bohai Sea and Yellow Sea, the low beaches making up 15 percent nationwide. There are more than 260 species of fish and shrimp inhabiting and migrating in offing areas, including over 40 species of economic fish and hundreds of shellfish species in the shallow seas. Among them, the output of rare marine products, such as prawns, scallops, abalones, stichopus japonicus and echinuses, have all ranked no.1 in the whole country. In addition, Shandong Province has built up many large and middle-sized salt fields; therefore, it is one of the four producing areas of sea salt in China.

Shandong Province has beautiful natural landscapes with numerous cultural and historical relics. It boasts a lot of world-level natural cultural relics, like Taishan Mountain known as "The First One of Five Scared Mountains", the Temple of Confucius, the Mansion of Confucius and the Confucian Woods, Penglai nicknamed "the World Fairyland", Laoshan Mountain named "Holy Land of Taoism", Weifang known as "the World Kite City", Qingdao known as "Beer City", Yantai named "Wine City", Jinan renowned as "City of Spring", and wonderess access to the Yellow River. All these scenic spots are wonderful destinations for tourists.

Address of the Provincial Government: No.1 Qian Jie, Jinan City
Website: http://www.shandong.gov.cn/

Anhui Province

Anhui Province, called "Wan" for short, is located in southeast China, with an area of 139,600 square km, or 1.45 percent of the national territory. It has 1,850 villages and towns, and Hefei is its Provincial Capital. Anhui lies at the transition region between a temperate zone and a semi-tropical zone, enjoying a warm and humid climate with four distinct seasons. The total population in the region was 61.10 million in 2006. Its population is made up mainly of the Han ethnic group. It has 59.484 million Han, accounting for 99.37 percent of its total population, with 376,000 making up the ethnic minority groups, or 0.63 percent. Among the ethnic minority groups, the Hui group is the major one, in addition, there are 52 other ethnic minority groups including Manchurian, Mongolia, Zhuang and She groups. Hefei is its capital.

Anhui is one of the provinces with the richest tourism resources in China. It is fully covered with famous mountains and rivers, therefore the natural landscapes and places of cultural interest enhance each other's beauty. Currently, there are five national-level scenic areas and places of historical interest, such as Huangshan Mountains, Jiuhua Mountain, Tianzhu Mountain, Langye Mountain and Qiyun Mountain, with three national-level natural reserves and 23 State forest parks. In addition, it has three national-level historical and cultural cities, like Huizhou, Shouxian County and Shexian County, with nine national-level cultural units under State protection, including The Central Capital Town of the Ming Dynasty, Fengyang Royal Mausoleum of the Ming Dynasty, and "Ape Man in Hexian County", Xuguo Stone Archway in Shexian County and the Haozhou Flower Theatrical Building to name but a few.

The Huangshan Mountain is a world-famous tourist resort, famous for its towering mountains, green odd pines, absurd stones, sea of clouds and perennial hot springs.

Address of the Provincial Government: No.221 Changjiang Road, Hefei City
Website: http://www.ah.gov.cn

Zhejiang Province

Zhejiang Province lies on the southeast coast of China, and on the northeast it shares a border with Shanghai, the largest city in China. It covers a land area of 101,800 square km. It has a coast line 6,486 km long, the longest in China; and there are 3,061 islands each with an area of 500 square metres, therefore it is the province with the most islands in China. Zhejiang Province has a subtropical and monsoon climate with four distinct seasons with plenty of sunshine and rich resources. In 2006, it has 49.80 million permanent residents. Besides the Han nationality, there are 49 ethnic minorities with a population of about 400,000, including the She minority making up about 200,000 and the Hui minority making up nearly 20,000, who are mainly distributed in southwest region of Zhejiang Province. Zhejiang Province is home to the only She group autonomous county in China-Jingning She autonomous county. Hangzhou is its capital.

Zhejiang Province is one of the birthplaces of Chinese civilization with a long history. About 7,000 to 4,000 years ago, human activity in Zhejiang was quite apparent; more than one hundred heritage sites of the Neolithic Age have been found, which respectively belong to the Hemudu culture (about 6,000 to 7,000 years ago), the Majiabin culture (about 5,000 to 6,000 years ago), and the Liangzhu culture (about 4,000 to 5,000 years ago). Among the plentiful relics unearthed from Yuyao Hemudu Relic, there are varieties of tools and appliances made of bones, stones, pottery and wood, with many ancient paddies, wood components of mortise and tenon with clear structures, colorful lacquer bowls, ancient chirps made of bones which were used to play music. It has been brought to light that Chinese ancestors created an unprecedented historical civilization more than 7,000 years ago. In addition, there are 11 national-level scenic areas and places of historical interest, ranking the first in terms of number in China, such as the West Lake, two rivers with one lake (Fuchun River-Xinan River-Qiandao Lake), Yandang Mountain, Nanci River, Putuo Mountain, Shengsi Islands, Tiantai Mountain, Mogan Mountain, Xuedou Mountain, Shuanglong and Xiandu. In particular, it is worth mentioning the strong tides of the Qiantang River; unique natural scenery in China, which attracts a lot of tourists from home and abroad annually.

Address of the Provincial Government: No.1 Building, the Administration Centre, Hangzhou City
Website: http://www.zhejiang.gov.cn/

Fujian Province

Fujian Province, facing the Taiwan Province across the Taiwan Straits, sits in southeast China on the coast of the East China Sea. Its territory includes 121,400 square Km of land and 136,300 square Km of sea. Its coastline, the second longest in China, stretches 3324 Km. With 1012 islands of different sizes, Fujian possesses 125 ports, including the Fuzhou Port, the Xiamen Port, the Meizhouwan Port and the Sandu'ao Port in Ningde, a city in the northeast of the province. Fujian is a vital navigation hub between the East China Sea and the South China Sea. It is one of the Chinese provinces closest to Southeast Asia, West Asia, East Africa and Oceania. Fuzhou is its capital.

With a temperate subtropical climate, Fujian enjoys abundant rainfall. The population of the province stands at 35.58 million in 2006. According to the fifth national census, Fujian is home to 48 ethnic groups. The Han people makes up the bulk of the population, while the population of the other 47 ethnic groups adds up to 580,000, or 1.67 percent. Among the ethnic minorities, the She ethnic group has the largest population, amounting to some 350,000, or more than half of the total She population in China.

Address of the Provincial Government: Provincial Government Compound, Hualin Lu, Fuzhou City
Website: http://www.fujian.gov.cn/

Jiangsu Province

Jiangsu Province sits at the center of the eastern coast of China, its coastline extending some 1000 Km. Boarding the Yellow Sea in the east, Jiangsu stretches on both banks of the lower reaches of the Yangtze River. With a distinctive monsoon climate, Jiangsu is situated in a transit belt from the subtropics to a warm temperate zone. Generally speaking, the province is warm with moderate rainfalls and clear-cut seasons. Jiangsu has a resident population of 74.745 million in 2006 and it is home to several ethnic groups. In addition to the Han ethnic group, there are 55 other ethnic minority groups with a population of 210,000, or 0.29 percent of the province's total. Nanjing is its capital.

Located in the fertile land of the Yangtze River delta, Jiangsu is mainly made up by the Southern Jiangsu Plain, the Yangtze-Huaihe River Plain, the Yellow-Huaihe River Plain and the East Coastal Jiangsu Plain, as well as the Taihu Lake and the Hongzehu Lake, two of the five largest freshwater lakes in China. Jiangsu is blessed with rich natural resources and a sound economic foundation. It boasts rivers and lakes of different sizes. Broad in tidal land and shallow waters, Jiangsu has 154,000 square Km of fish farms on the east coast. Among them, there are the Lusi Port Fishing Farm and the Haizhouwan Port Fish Farm, two of the four major fish farms in China, which are teeming with yellow-fin tuna, hairtails, pomfrets, shrimps, crabs and aquatic plants. Jiangsu is also a major producer of freshwater crab and eel fry. Within the province, there are some 1.73 million hectares of inland waters. The aquatic farms cover 533,333.33 plus hectares, cultivating 140 types of freshwater fish.

Since ancient times, Jiangsu has been renowned as a tourist resort. Many cities in the province, such as Nanjing, Suzhou, Yangzhou, Zhenjiang, Changshu, Xuzhou and Huai'an, are blessed with a long history and rich in culture. So far, there are 13 national outstanding tourist cities. Among them, the most famous ones include Nanjing, the capital of six dynasties in history, and Suzhou, a city renowned as the "paradise on earth". Jiangsu has three tourism areas, namely the Yangtze River Tourism Area, the Taihu Lake Tourism Area and the Xuhai Tourism Area. In addition, it possesses 20 scenic spots, 23 forest parks, six holiday resorts and 416 historical or cultural sites under state or provincial protection. Suzhou, in particular, boasts nine classic gardens on the UNESCO list of world cultural heritage sites.

Address of the Provincial Government: No. 70, Beijing Xilu, Nanjing City
Website: http://www.jschina.com.cn

Jiangxi Province

Jiangxi Province is an inland province. Covering a total area of 166,900 square Km, it sits in the southeastern part of the country, on the southern bank of the Yangtze River. Jiangxi has plenty of rainfall. The amount of the rain, however, changes as the seasons change. In 2006, Jiangxi had a population of 43.3913 million, of which 99 percent were Han people. The province is home to 38 ethnic groups. In addition to the Han, there are also the Hui, the She, the Zhuang, the Manchu, the Miao, the Yao, the Mongolian, the Dong, the Korean, the Tujia and the Bouyei. Among these ethnic groups, the Hui and the She have the largest population. The She ethnic group is mainly distributed in some 30 She villages, such as the Taiyuan She Village in the Qianshan County, the Zhangping She Village in Guixi and the Yongfeng County.

Abundant in plant resources, Jiangxi boasts 4,000 plus species of seed plant, among which 470 are pteridophytes and more than 100 are bryophytes. A great number of ancient plants with primitive features are found in Jiangxi. Some of them, such as the ginkgo,

Covering an area of 34 square km, Huaxi Village is a well-known village where people live in villa and drive cars.

are reputed as the "living fossil" of plants. The Poyang Lake, located in the province, is recognized as an ideal winter shelter for migratory birds from all over the world. Across Jiangxi, 50.9 percent of its land is covered by forest. There are 250 million cubic meters of timber in storage and 1 billion moso bamboos in reserve. Both of the figures are higher than the other parts of China. With regard to mineral resources, Jiangxi enjoys a noticeable advantage. Among the 150 odd known minerals, some 140 minerals are found here. Among them, the deposits of 89 minerals have been verified, with 33 of them ranking among the top five in the country. In Jiangxi, 4 ferrous metals can be found, including iron, manganese, titanium and vanadium, 13 non-ferrous and precious metals, including copper, lead, zinc, gold and silver, as well as 29 rare and rare-earth minerals, including niobium and tantalum. Attributed to the abundant resources, Jiangxi managed to develop the largest copper mine in Asia and the largest copper smelting base in China. Meanwhile, it has a total water reserve of 141.6 billion cubic meters, with the per capita figure and per hectare figure high above the national average.

Blessed with picturesque sceneries, Jiangxi boasts a great number of historic sites across its territory. Among them, the major tourist resorts include the Lushan Mountain, the Jinggangshan Mountain, the Longhushan Mountain, the Sanqingshan Mountain, the Poyang Lake, Nanchang and Jingdezhen. The Lushan Mountain, in particular, has been listed as a World Cultural Heritage site by UNESCO. The north Jiangxi triangle tourism area, composed of Nanchang, the Lushan Mountain, Jiujiang, the Poyang Lake and the Longhushan Mountain, is one of the 14 major international tour routes in China.

Address of the Provincial Government: No. 69 Beijing Xilu, Nanchang City
Website: http://www.jiangxi.gov.cn

Central China

Located in west Hunan Province, Wulingyuan is 400 km away from Changsha, the capital of Hunan Province. It is a national tourist area comprised of Zhangjiajie, Suoxiyu Valley and Tianzishan Mountain, with 560 scenic spots or more.

Hunan Province

Hunan Province, covering 211,800 square km, had a total population of 67.681 million according to the statistics released in 2006. The province is home to 41 ethnic groups, including the Han, the Tujia, the Miao, the Yao, the Dong, the Bai, the Hui and the Uygur. Folk ethnic minority groups are mainly distributed in the mountainous regions in the west, south or east part of the province. Changsha is its capital.

Sitting in the mid subtropical zone, Hunan has a temperate climate and dense foliage, therefore a suitable habitat for wild animals. Across the country, Hunan ranks among the top in terms of forest coverage, with 34.3 percent of its land forested. As one of the major timber production bases in south China, Hunan has some 564,666.66 hectares of bamboo forest and 8.9 billion moso bamboos, ranking third in China. The economic forest in Hunan mainly includes the tea-oil tree, the tung-oil tree and the tea tree. The Xiangxi Tujia and Miao Autonomous Prefecture is renowned as the "hometown of golden tung oil". The Silver Needle Tea, a white tea produced mainly in the Junshan Mountain on the bank of the Dongtinghu Lake, has gained a good reputation and was designated as a tribute as early as the Tang dynasty (618-907). In 1982, the tea was elected among the top 10 tea products in China. Hunan also has a vast expanse of grassland. Moreover, Hunan enjoys advantages both in the variety and the deposit of metals, thus reputed as the "hometown of non-ferrous metals". So far, the deposits of 37 non-ferrous metals have been verified, with the deposit of antimony ranking the top in the world and that of tungsten, bismuth and monazite the top in China. Major energy sources developed in Hunan include raw coal and electric power. At present, some 3.4 billion tons of coal have been verified in Hunan. In addition, the province has a total water power reserve of 15.3245 million kW.

Hunan boasts 10 major tourism areas and some 100 tourism spots. Among them, the most famous are: the Taohuayuan Valley in Taoyuan County, the Jiuyishan National Forest Park in Ningyuan County, the Suxianling Hill in Chenzhou, the Huiyanfeng Hill in Hengyang, the Mausoleum of Emperor Yandi in Yanling County and the Temple to Quyuan in Miluo. The Hengshan Mountain, the most elegant one of the Five Sacred Mountains in China, is renowned as a summer resort and a sacred Buddhist mountain. Wulingyuan, a tourism spot including Zhangjiajie, Suoxiyu Valley, Tianzishan Mountain and Mengdonghe River, is distinguished for the unique physiognomy, the towering trees, the rare animals, as well as the deep and secluded valleys. With clear brooks and hot springs intersecting each other, Wulingyuan is filled with spectacular hills and grotesque rocks. Zhangjiajie, in particular, is listed as a national forest park and a world geology park.

Address of the Provincial Government: Wu Yi Zhong Lu, Changsha City
Website: http://www.rednet.com.cn

Hubei Province

Hubei Province, also called "E" for short, is situated in central China or in the middle reach of the Yangtze River. It got its name due to its position north of the Dongtinghu Lake. It covers an area of 185,900 square Km, accounting for 1.94 percent of the total area and ranking the 16th in the country. At the end of 2006, Hubei had a population of 56.93 million. It is also home to 50 ethnic groups, including the Han, Tujia, Miao, Hui, Dong, Manchu, Zhuang, and the Mongolian. Minority ethnic groups with over 10,000 people include the Tujia, Miao, Hui, Dong and the Manchu. Wuhan is its capital.

Hubei Province is one of the provinces boasting abundant living resources in China. Over 1,300 tree species have been found. The timber forests account for about 50 percent of all forests in the province. The 'living fossils', Chinese redwood, Chinese dove tree, and ginkgo can be seen in some local areas which are provenance bases for Chinese redwood proliferation in China and even the whole world. Shennongjia virgin forest, dubbed the "Green Treasury", is one of the key virgin forests in China and the only one in the east of China. Its forest coverage rate makes up about 70 percent of the total. There are 350 species of birds, and most of them are also found in south China. Here, migratory birds are the most common. There are 30 rare bird species under state protection including the Reeves's pheasant and the Crimson-bellied tragopan. The rivers and creeks in the mountains in the west of the province are the home to the giant salamander.

Hubei Province is rich in hydro-electric resources, with a usable capacity of 33.4 million kilowatts, ranking fourth in China. Some key hydropower projects have been constructed, such as the projects of Gezhouba Hydropower Station, Geheyan, Hydropower Station, and Danjiangkou Hydropower Station. And now, the Three-gorge Project on the Yangtze River is under construction and is catching the world's attention.

Hubei's tourism resources feature both beautiful landscapes and abounding places of historic and cultural interest. There are many places deserving attention, such as the world famous Three Gorges of the Yangtze River, the Wudangshan Mountain-holy land for Taoism. The key nature reserve of Shennongjia is known as 'Roof of Central China' and 'Green Treasury', in which various rare species have been found and moreover, the 'myth of savage' attracts the most attention.

Address of the Provincial Government: Shuiguohu, Wuchang, Wuhan City
Website: http://www.99sky.com

Henan Province

Henan Province lies in mid-eastern China or the middle-lower reaches of the Yellow River. It got its name because the largest part of the province lies to the south of the Yellow River. Henan covers an area of about 0.167 million square Km. The Yellow River runs for over 700 km through the province. It has a transitional climate between a subtropical and a warm temperate zone. The 4 reasons here are very distinct; rain and high temperatures exist in the same season; the climate is considerably variable. In 2006, the population of Hubei is 93.92million including 51 ethnic groups such as the Han, Hui, Mongolia, Manchu, Zhuang, Miao, Tibet, Uygur, Yi, Korea, Tujia, and the Bai. The Han people account for 98.8 percent of the total population and the other ethnic groups make up the balance at 1.2 percent. Zhengzhou is its capital.

Henan Dengfeng Shaolin Epo Martial Art Institute

As one of the major birthplaces of Chinese civilization, Henan has several epoch-making archeological discoveries, including the Peiligang Culture Site dating back 7,000 years, Yangshao Culture Site of some 6,000 years ago, and Dahe Culture Site of more than 5,000 years ago. In ancient China, more than 20 dynasties established their capitals in Henan. Three of China's seven great ancient capitals are located in Henan: Anyang of the Shang Dynasty, Luoyang of nine dynasties and Kaifeng of seven dynasties. Three of ancient China's four great inventions, the compass, paper-making and gunpowder, were made in Henan. The province is numbered first in the whole country in terms of underground cultural relics and the second in existing cultural relics on the ground. The Yellow River, with numerous ancient relics and scenic attractions, also provides a rich tourist resource to Henan.

Henan has established relations with over 30 countries and regions in the world for scientific and technological exchange and cooperation. The province and its prefectures and cities have also set up sister relations with 30 counterparts in countries such as the United States, Japan, Canada and Italy.

Address of the Provincial Government: No.10 Wei'er Lu, Zhengzhou City
Website: http://www.henanews.org.cn

Southwest China

Yunnan Province

Yunnan Province is the most southwestern province in China, with the Tropic of Cancer running through its southern part. The province has an area of 394,000 square km, accounting for 4.1 percent of the nation's total. Its total population reaches 44.83 million in 2006 and it is home to 25 out of 56 ethnic groups in China. The proportion of the population of ethnic minoring groups in Yunnan is the largest nationwide. The ethnic groups make up 38.07 percent of the province's population. The number of ethnic groups, with a population over 8,000, reaches over 20, including the ethnic groups of the Yi, Bai, and Hani. Kunming is its capital.

Yunnan abounds in natural resources. It is known as the kingdom of plants, animals and home of non-ferrous metals and medicinal herbs. The province not only has more plant species of tropical, subtropical, temperate, and frozen zones than any other province in the

Autumn of Shangri-La, Yunnan.

country, but also has many ancient, derivative plants, as well as species introduced from foreign countries. Among the 30,000 species of plants in China, 18,000 can be found in Yunnan. More than 150 kinds of minerals have been discovered in the province, accounting for 93 percent of the total minerals discovered in China. Some 13 percent of the proven deposits of minerals are the largest of their kind in China. Yunnan ranks first in the country in deposits of zinc, lead, tin, cadmium, indium, thallium, and crocidolite. It has sufficient rainfall and many rivers and lakes. The annual water flow originating in the province is 200 billion cubic meters, three times that of the Yellow River. The rivers flowing into the province from outside add 160 billion cubic meters, which means there are more than 10,000 cubic meters of water per person in the province. This is four times the average in the country. The rich water resources offer abundant hydro-energy, which help Yunnan enjoy its advantage in energy resources.

Yunnan is attractive with its rich tourism resources, including beautiful landscapes, colorful ethnic customs, and a pleasant climate.

Address of the Provincial Government: No.76, Huashan Nan lu, Kunming
Website: http://www.yn.gov.cn/

Guizhou Province

Guizhou Province, a province on the eastern section of the Yunnan-Guizhou Plateau in southwestern China, has an area of more than 176,100 square km. It is well known by the steep hills and deep valleys on the land. The number of the plains over 66.7 million hectares reach over 300. In addition, it has a mean annual temperature of 14 degrees Centigrade to 16 degrees Centigrade. Guiyang is its capital. Its total population reaches 39.553 million in 2006

Guizhou has many kinds of biological resources. Presently, 3,800 kinds of the wild animals are found in Guizhou. Among these wild animals, there are 83 rare species under state protection in which 14 species have been listed as grade one state protected animals, such as the Guizhou Golden Monkey, the South Chinese Tiger, the Francois' Monkey, and the Black-necked Crane (Grus nigricollis). Moreover, it is also one of four major production areas of Traditional Chinese Medicine. Over 3,700 species of medicinal plants are found, accounting for 80 percent of the varieties in China, of which the most renowned ones are the Eucommia ulmoides, gastrodia tuber, Evodia Fruit, and Dendrobium Nobile. It is also home to 70 species of rare plants, among which plants under first-class state protection including athaya argyrophy, Dove Tree, Tree fern are either rare in the world or indemic to China. Besides, Guizhou is considered one of the provinces abounding in mineral resources. Over 110 kinds of minerals have been discovered, in which the proven reserve of 42 kinds rank among the top-ten and 22 kinds among the top three nationwide.

Guizhou, with its peculiar natural sceneries, remarkable national customs, brilliant history, culture and pleasant climate, is famous for its unique, aboriginal, unsophisticated and mysterious landscape. Over 120 scenic spots have been developed and established. Places of historic interest and scenic beauty at national level include the Yellow Fruit Tree Waterfall (Huangguoshu Waterfall), the Anshun Water Cave of Dragon Palace, the Gold-Knit Cave, Hongfeng Lake, Zhibozhang Jiang, Malinhe Gorge, and Chishui Shizhangdng Cave; the four state natural protection zones, Fanjingshan Botanical Garden, Maolan Karst Virgin Forest, Maolan Kast Primitive Forest, Chishui Virgin Forest, Chishui Pristine Forests and Caohai grasslands bird park; as well as many villages with a natural, romantic beauty.

Address of the Provincial Government: No.242 Zhonghua Beilu, Guiyang
Website: http://www.chinaguizhou.gov.cn

Sichuan Province

Sichuan, in China's western hinterland, covers most of the Sichuan Basin. Surrounded by mountains, it has a mild climate. Sichuan covers a vast area of 485,000 square km.

Although it is located in a subtropical zone, it has a complex and diverse climate due to its complicated topography and alternate affection of different monsoonal circulation. The population in Sichuan reaches 81.69 million in 2006. In addition to its majority, the Han people, Sichuan is also inhabited by many ethnic groups including 13 with at least 5,000 people each: the Yi, Tibetan, Qiang, Hui, Mongolian, Lisu, Manchu, Naxi, Bai, Bouyei, Dai, Miao and Tujia. Sichuan has China's second-largest Tibetan-inhabited region as well as the largest region inhabited by the Yi ethnic group and the only region where the Qiang people live in homogeneous communities. The Yi ethnic group, with the largest population of any minority in Sichuan, lives in the Greater and Lesser Liangshan mountains and the Anning River Valley. The Tibetans live in the Garze and Ngawa Tibetan Autonomous Prefectures and the Muli Tibetan Autonomous County in Liangshan Prefecture. The Qiang people, one of China's oldest ethnic groups, live mainly in Maoxian, Wenchuan, Heishui, Songpan and Beichuan on the upper reaches of the Minjiang River. The autonomous region for minority ethnic groups in Sichuan include Ganzi Tibetan Autonomous Prefecture, Garze Tibetan Autonomous Prefecture, Aba Tibetan and Qiang Autonomous Prefecture, Aba Tibetn and Qiang Autonomous Prefecture, Liangshan Yi Autonomous Prefecture, Liangshan Yi Autonomous Prefecture, Beichuan Qiang nationality Autonomous Count, Beichuan Qiang Autonomous County, Erbian Yi Autonomous County, Wobian Yi Autonomous County and Mabian Yi Autonomous County. Chengdu is its capital.

The diversified climate in Sichuan provides a favorable environment for various plants. The forests cover a total area of 7.46 million hectares. It is home to one-fifth of the country's dawn redwoods and Cathaya argyrophylla, two species so old they are regarded as living fossils. It is also rich in animal resources. There are about 1,100 kinds of vertebrates, accounting for 40 percent of the country's total. Among them are 55 kinds of rare animals. The well-known giant pandas inhabit mainly in 36 counties and natural reserves of the four mountain ranges within the territory of Sichuan.

The rich tourism resources in Sichuan are a rare phenomenon in the world. It has three World Cultural and Natural heritages: the Jiuzhaigou Scenic Area, the Huanglong Scenic Area, and Emeishan Mountain with the Leshan Giant Buddha; nine state-class scenic areas, including the Dujiangyan Irrigation System, Qingchengshan Mountain, the Sea of Bamboo in southern Sichuan; 11 national forest parks; 40 nature reserves, 44 provincial-class scenic areas. Almost every variety of tourist resource is available here: plateaus, mountains, ravines, basins, hills, plains, rivers, lakes, hot springs, waterfalls, limestone caves, and even danxia (red bed) land form.

Address of the Provincial Government: No.30 Duyuan Jie, Chengdu City
Website: http://www.sc.gov.cn

Tibet Autonomous Region

Located at the southwest frontier of the People's Republic of China and southwest of the Qinghai-Tibet plateau, the area of Tibet Autonomous Region covers 1.2 million square km., or 12.8 percent of the total national land with a population of 2.81 million in 2006. Most of the Tibetans in China live here, accounting for 45 percent of the total Tibetans in China. Apart from the Tibetan ethnic group, there are also other ethnic groups like the Menba, lhoba, Han, Hui, etc. as well as the Sherpa in Tibet. Among the total population in Tibet, Tibetans make up 2,411,100, or 92.2 percent of the total number, the Hans 155,300, or 5.9 percent and other minorities 49,900, or 1.9 percent. Lhasa is its capital.

With an average elevation of over 4,000 meters, Tibet autonomous region constitutes the major part of Qinghai-Tibet Plateau and is renowned as "the roof of the world". The Himalaya Mountains stretching for 2,400 km at an average of 6,000 meters high above sea level, is situated in the south of Tibet autonomous region, including the highest mountain in the world-Mount Everest at 8848.13 meters above sea level. The Yarlung Zangbo er is the largest river in Tibet and the Yarlung Zangbo River valley dives down 5,382 meters, which is the deepest valley on earth. Compared to other parts of China, Tibet's air is thin with intense sunlight, low temperatures and insufficient rain. The oxygen content per cube meter of air is about 150-170 grams, which equals to 62 to 65.4 percent that of the plain area.

Tibet is both a huge plant kingdom with over 5,000 kinds of higher plants and the largest forest in China which is still completely virgin forest. Special rare animals in Qinghai-Tibet Plateau like antelope, wild yak, wild ass, ovis ammon, etc are listed as national protected animals; Born into China, the white lipped-deer is also a rare animal in the world. Apart from the above, the Black-necked crane and white-eared pheasant are also listed as first-class protected animals.

Lhasa is not only the political, economic, cultural and transportation center of Tibet, but also the center of Buddhism. Jokhang Temple, Ramoche Temple, Potala, Barkhor Street, Norpulingkha and Three Temples (Ganden Monastry, Drepung Monastry, Sera Monastry) have attracted domestic and overseas tourists to Lhasa. And among these places, Jokhang Temple, Potala, Norpulingkha and Three Temples are listed as key historical sites under the state protection.

Address of the Government of the Autonomous Region: Jinzhu Zhonglu, Lhasa
Website: http://www.xizang.gov.cn/index.do

Northwest China

Shaanxi Province

Located on the middle reach of the Yellow River and inner heartland in China, Shaanxi is a province in the grand northwest of China, situated at the junction of east, middle, northwest and southwest of China. Starting from Lianyungang and running west to Rotterdam of Holland, the New Asia-Europe Continent Bridge, an international economic channel connecting Asia and Europe, runs across the middle of Shaanxi. With 205,600 square km of land and a population of 37.35 million in 2006, the Han ethnic group account for 99.4 percent of total population while the Hui, Manchu, Mongolian ethnic groups(amongst others) make up the balance. Xi'an is its capital.

The province has more than 750 species of wild vertebrates, out of which 79 species are well-known rare animals. The animals under national priority protection include the national treasure of giant pandas and 11 other species such as golden monkeys, clouded leopard, etc. 5.93 million hectares of forest are distributed mainly in Qinba Mountain Ranges, the Guanshan Mountain and the Huanglongshan Mountain and the Qiaoshan Mountain, and the forest cover age rate is 28.8 percent. There are over 3,300 species of wild seed plants including 37 species of precious and rare plants and nearly 800 species of medical plants. Medical materials like hippophae rhamnoides, gynostemma pentaphylla, etc are of high

A courtyard in a village of Longxian County, Shaanxi Province on the Lantern Festival

value for exploitation. The output and quality of raw lacquer rank top in the country. Red dates, walnuts and tung oil make up traditional commodities for export.

The 72 emperors' mausoleums in Shaanxi reflect the social-economic and culture situation at that time. There are 10 sites, such as the Huangdi Tomb, the Terra Cotta Warriors and Horses, Famen Temple, Stone Tablets in Xi'an, Museum of Shaanxi History, Xi`an City Wall, etc, ranked top of the nation. The Terra Cotta Warriors and Horses known as the eighth wonder in the world and Mausoleum of the First Qin Emperor are listed as world culture heritage sites by UNESCO.

Address of the Provincial Government: Xinchengnei, Xi'an
Website: http://www.shaanxi.gov.cn

Gansu Province

Situated in the inland of western China on the upper reaches of the Yellow River, Gansu Province faces Shaanxi Province in the east and is bordered on the north by Inner Mongolia Autonomous Region and connects to the People's Republic of Mongolia. It is 1,000 to 3,000 meters above sea level. Among its total population of 26.0625 million (2006) in the 455,000 square km of land, there are 20.515 million Han people, or 91.7 percent of the total number, and 1.856 million consisting of minority populations, taking up 8.3 percent of the total number. Ten minorities with numbers in the thousands are the Hui, Tibetan, Dongxiang, Tu, Manchu, Yugu, Baoan, Mongolia, Sala and Hazak which have inhabited in Gansu for generations. Lanzhou is its capital.

There are about 659 kinds of wild animals living in Gansu, of which 441 are birds. 32 kinds of rare animals are under first-class protection, such as the giant panda, the golden monkey, various antelope, the snow leopard, deer, M.moschiferus and the Bactrian crane. Among the over 4,000 kinds of wild plants, there are 951 kinds of medical materials, ranking second in China.

Address of the Provincial Government: No. 1, Central Square, Lanzhou
Website: http://www.gansu.gov.cn

Ningxia Hui Autonomous Region

As one of the Chinese minority autonomous regions, Ningxia Hui Automonous Region, is located in the middle reaches of the Yellow River in northwest China. The whole area is elevated in the south and low in the north and the highest peak is 3,556 meters above sea level. Among the 5.962 million people in 2006 in the province, the Han group makes up 3.6765 million, or 65.47 percent of the total number, while the minorities make up the other 1.939 million, or 34.53 percent, including 1.9023 million Hui taking up 33.88 percent. Yinchuan is its capital.

With 10.673 million mu of uncultivated farmland, Ningxia is one of the eight provinces whose uncultivated land is in excess of 10 million mu and is one of the ten farming regions with explorable grassland of 45 million mu. The Yellow River irrigation area is over 5.6 million mu made up of the Weining Plain, is one of the four natural irrigation areas in the northwest region. Rich land resources, convenient Yellow River irrigation and sound light and heat conditions all lay solid foundations for agriculture development in Ningxia. A fairly high production level in Yellow River irrigation area helps grow crops such as melons and fruit with high output and quality. The sugar content in water melons, apples and grapes is up 15-20 percent compared to that in the middle China area. Meanwhile, as one of the commodity grain production bases, the rice production per hectare reaches 10,500 kilograms and ranks top in the northwest district. Animal husbandry production takes up 29 percent of agriculture. There are 10,000 hectares of water columns for aquaculture feeding among the total 18.45 million hectares water columns. The production of grass carp, silver carp, crucian carp, carp, river prawn and river crab shows that there is great potential in the development of aquaculture industry. In recent years, the fishing industry developed fairly rapidly and the production of aquaculture per capita ranked top in the northwest region, becoming an important aquaculture supply base in the zone along the Great Wall in the northwest region.

Non-metallic Minerals resources are rich in Ningxia mainly including coal, gypsum, petrol, natural gas, clay, quartz sandstone, barite, etc. The coal has formed a certain production scale with huge reserves and rich types, and the gypsum reserve ranks first in the country.

Address of the Autonomous Regional Government: No. 217 Jiefang West Road, Yinchuan
Website: http://www.nx.gov.cn/default.do

Qinghai Province

Nicknamed "Qing", Qinghai Province is famous for Qinghai Lake-the largest saline inland lake in China. Situated in the northeast of the Qinghai-Tibet plateau in west China, it is the source of the Yangze River, the Yellow River and the Lancang River which is known as "Source of Rivers". Of the total area 250,000 hectares are forests, and the land area ranks No.4 in the country, with grasslands taking up 31.6 million hectares, cultivated land 589,900 hectares, forest 250,000 hectares and remainder consists of mountains, lakes, deserts, the Gobi, glaciers, etc. Owning to natural factors like altitude, land features, latitude, atmospheric circulation, etc, Qinghai has gradually formed a special plateau continental climate featuring long but not cold winters, and short but cool summers. There are 55 minorities with a total population of 5.48 in 2006, among which 2.3506 are minority groups, or 45.5 percent of the total number. Minorities like the Tibetan, Hui, Tu, Sala and the Mongolian have lived here for generations. Among them, the Tu and Sala ethnic groups only live in Qinghai. The proportion of the ethnic group population to the total population in Qinghai Province is as following: Tibet ethnic group–1.89 percent, Hui ethnic group–15.89 percent, Tu ethnic group–3.85 percent, Sala ethnic group–1.85 percent and Mongolia ethnic group–1.71 percent. Xining is its capital.,

Qinghai is one of the largest five farmland areas in China with a grassland area of 31.6 million hectares, or 15 percent of the national usable grassland, this provides a sound foundation for Qinghai to develop the animal husbandry industry. There are over 940 kinds of grasses on this vast and rich grassland and various grass-feeding livestock, such as sheep, yak, camel, goat, etc., which have resistance to low temperatures and are easy to breed. Among these livestock, yaks are the most suitable for the Qinghai-Tibet plateau and the number ranks first throughout the country, accounting for one third of the total yak in the world.

Qinghai Province enjoys spectacular sightseeing unique to the Qinghai-Tibet Plateau. More than 10 tourist attractions are found here, such as the "Bird Kingdom", the bird island of Qinghai Lake, Mengda national nature reserve in Xunhua praised as Xi Shuanbanna in Qinghai-Tibet Plateau, the Tar Monastery in Huangzhong County, Xining's Dongguan Mosque-one of the four major mosques of northwest China, Animaqing Mountain.

Address of the Provincial Government: No.12 Xidajie, Xining
Website: http://www.qh.gov.cn

Xinjiang Uygur Autonomous Region

The Xinjiang Uygur Autonomous Region, also called Western Regions in ancient times, is located in northwestern China. It is the largest in area in all the province-level administrative regions of China, the Xinjiang Uygur Autonomous Region covers an area of 1.66 million square km., or one sixth of China's territory. With a longer border line (5,600 km) than other provinces in China, it borders Mongolia in the northeast, Russia, Kazakhstan, Kirghiziastan and Tajikistan in the west and Afghanistan, Pakistan and India in the southwest. It has a population of 20.50 million in 2006 in the total area of 1.6649 million square km. Among the 47 ethnic groups, 13 have been living here for generations, such as the Uygur, Han, Kazak, Hui, Mongolia, Kirgiz, Tajik, Xibe, Ozbek, Manchu, Daur, Tatar and the Russians. Moreover, Xinjiang is an area where people enjoy a long life span. According to the third population census across China, there are totally 3,765 who are over 100 years old in China among which 865 live in Xinjiang, thus, the Hetian district in Xinjiang is acclaimed to be one of the districts on earth with a long life span by the International Natural Medical Association. Urumqi is its capital.

Address of the Reqional Government: Zhongshan Lu, Shixiaqu, Urumqi
Website: http://www.xj.gov.cn

Most Competitive Chinese Cities in 2007

Ranking	Comprehensive	Brands	Tourism	Living Environment	Talents	Science and Technology	Environment	Capital	Business
1	Hong Kong	Beijing	Beijing	Shenzhen	Hong Kong	Beijing	Weihai	Shanghai	Shanghai
2	Shenzhen	Shanghai	Shanghai	Beijing	Taipei	Shanghai	Wuxi	Beijing	Guangzhou
3	Shanghai	Shenzhen	Shenzhen	Xiamen	Beijing	Taipei	Qingdao	Hong Kong	Beijing
4	Beijing	Guangzhou	Guangzhou	Shanghai	Shanghai	Shenzhen	Suzhou	Shenzhen	Shenzhen
5	Guangzhou	Hangzhou	Hangzhou	Hangzhou	Gaoxiong	Hong Kong	Shaoxing	Taipei	Hangzhou
6	Taipei	Suzhou	Suzhou	Suzhou	Guangzhou	Gaoxiong	Kunming	Guangzhou	Wuxi
7	Wuxi	Xiamen	Nanjing	Kunming	Xinzhu	Taizhong	Yantai	Tianjin	Suzhou
8	Suzhou	Ningbo	Chengdu	Dalian	Taizhong	Tianjin	Hong Kong	Taizhong	Ningbo
9	Foshan	Tianjin	Ningbo	Ningbo	Wuhan	Jilong	Xiamen	Gaoxiong	Xiamen
10	Macao	Nanjing	Xi'an	Shaoxing	Tainan	Xi'an	Yangzhou	Nanjing	Yangzhou

Judicature

Judicial System

The judicial system in general refers to the nature, mission, organizational setup, organization and principles of judicial organs and other regulations and rules for work.

Judicial organs here mean public-security organs (including State security organs) the prosecutors, trial institutions and prison organs responsible for investigation, prosecution, trial and execution of cases. Judicial organizations here refer to lawyers, public notaries, and arbitration organizations. The latter, though not part of the judicial apparatus, are an integral part of the overall judicial system.

The system comprises sub-systems for trial procedures, prosecution, investigation, prison administration, arbitration, lawyers, mediation, public notaries, State compensation and legal assistance

♦ Ministry of Public Security

The Ministry of Public Security is in charge of national public security under the State Council. Its responsibilities and duties are to prevent, break up and investigate crimes; to prevent and combat terrorism; to preserve social order and prevent behavior jeopardizing public security; to manage transportation, firefighting and dangerous articles; to manage registration of households, ID cards, nationality, entry and exit affairs and the affairs relating to foreigners' residence and tourism in China; to maintain security along national borders; to safeguard specially-appointed personnel and key places and facilities; to manage gatherings, parades and demonstrations; to supervise and manage the security supervision of the public information network; to direct and supervise the safeguarding of public order concerning government institutions, social organizations, enterprises, and key construction projects; and to direct the public security of mass security organizations such as Public Order Committee.

Departments of Public Security are set in provinces and autonomous regions. Public Security Bureaus (or Public Security Department Offices) are set in metropolitan areas directly under the Central Government, and also established in cities, prefectures and leagues. Public Security Sub-Bureaus are set in administrative districts under cities, which are directly led by the public security organs at the higher level. Besides, Public Security Bureaus are established in counties, cities and banners, which are led by the people's governments at the corresponding level and the public security organs at the higher level. Local police stations are established under the Public Security Bureaus at the county (or city, district and banner) level, which are directly led and managed by the public security organs at the county (or city, district and banner) level.

The Public Security Bureaus of the Ministry of Railways, Ministry of Communications, General Administration of Civil Aviation of China, and State Forestry Administration and the Smuggling Suppression Bureau of the General Customs Administration are listed in the order of the Ministry of Public Security and subject to the guidance of both competent departments and the ministry.

Address: No.14 Dong Chang'an Jie, Beijing
Website: http://www.mps.gov.cn

Investigation System

his system governs investigations and other mandatory measures taken in accordance with law by public security authorities (including State security organs), people's procuratorates and military security organs in handling cases. It is a preparatory procedure for the investigation authorities to collect evidence and decide whether to prosecute after placing cases on file.

Public security authorities have dual tasks both as an administrative arm and a judicial organ, since they are in charge of maintaining social security, exercising State administration as well as investigating criminals and exercising State jurisdiction.

Acceptance and Establishment of Cases

Public security authorities should immediately accept, inquire about and take note of cases of suspects turned in, reported, accused or brought to the police by citizens or suspects who turn themselves in. efforts will be made to investigate the cases to be handled. Those that meet the necessary conditions should be accepted and filed as a case; for complicated and material cases, an investigation plan and, if necessary, other measures may have to be applied.

Procedures for Criminal Investigations

For criminal cases that have already been filed with the police, investigations should be launched, with a thorough and impartial collection of evidence that may determine whether the suspect is guilty or innocent and, if guilty, whether it is a felony or a misdemeanor. Depending on actual needs, various detective means and measures will be taken including interrogating suspects, questioning witnesses, inspecting, examining, searching and confiscating material and documentary evidences, appraising and ordering the arrest of criminals etc.

Compulsory Measures System

Compulsory measures during an investigation refer to compulsorily depriving of or restricting personal freedom of the suspects and accused, by law, to safeguard the successful launching of an investigation for criminal proceedings. The Criminal Procedure Law provides five types of compulsory measures including summoning for detention, obtaining a guarantor pending trial, residential surveillance, detention and arrest.

Summoning for detention refers to a situation where investigation organs summon criminal suspects who are not detained to be interrogated in a designated place. It differs from summoning to court, because it is compulsory and only applies to suspects.

Obtaining a guarantor pending trial refers to the situation when investigation organs order criminal suspects to provide a guarantor or pay guarantee money so that the suspects won't escape investigation but be on call at any time.

Residential surveillance refers to the situation when investigation organs order criminal suspects not to leave their domicile or designated residence without permission in order to supervise their activities.

Detention refers to the case when investigation organs detain an active criminal or a major suspect and temporarily deprive him of his personal freedom to launch investigation under legal emergency circumstances. The period for detention is generally 10 days, but no more than 14 days, except those major suspects involved in crimes committed in various places, repeated rimes or where the suspect is part of a gang.

Arrest refers to the most serious method that investigation organs detain and investigate the criminal suspects and deprive them of their personal freedom, if there is evidence to support the facts of a crime and the criminal suspect could be sentenced to a punishment of some term of imprisonment, and if such measures as allowing him to obtain a guarantor pending trial or placing him under residential surveillance would be insufficient to prevent the suspect becoming a danger to society. Article 37 of the Constitution provides that freedom of the person of citizens of the PRC is inviolable. No citizen may be arrested except with the approval or by decision of a people's procuratorate or by decision of a people's court, and arrests must be made by a public security organ.

Evidence System

All facts that prove the true circumstances of a case shall be considered as evidence. There are seven categories of evidence: (1) material and documentary evidence; (2) testimony of witnesses; (3) statements of victims; (4) statements and exculpations of the criminal suspects or defendants; (5) expert conclusions; (6) records of inquests and examination; and (7) audio-visual materials. Any such evidence must be verified before it can be used to decide cases.

Investigators must, in accordance with the legally-prescribed process, collect various kinds of evidence that can prove the criminal suspect's or defendant's guilt or innocence and the gravity of his crime. In the decision of all cases, stress shall be laid on evidence; credence shall not be readily given to oral statements. It shall be strictly forbidden to extort confessions by torture and to collect evidence by threat, enticement, deceit or other unlawful means.

Procuratorial System

The inspection system is a general term used to mean the nature, tasks, organization system, organization and activities principles of the State procuratorial organs and related work system.

The people's procuratorates of the PRC are State organs for legal supervision. The PRC establishes the Supreme People's Procuratorate and the people's procuratorates at various local levels, military procuratorates and other special people's procuratorates. The people's procuratorates exercise procuratorial power independently, in accordance with the provisions of the law, and are not subject to interference by any administrative organ, public organization or individual. The Supreme People's Procuratorate is the highest procuratorial organ. The Supreme People's Procuratorate directs the work of the people's procuratorates at various local levels and of the special people's procuratorates. People's procuratorates at higher levels direct the work of those at lower levels. The Supreme People's Procuratorate is responsible to the National People's Congress and its Standing Committee. People's procuratorates at various local levels are responsible to the organs of State power which created them and to the people's procuratorates at higher levels. Special people's

The staff members of the procuratorates handled the prosecutions in the communities.

♦ Supreme People's Procuratorate

The Supreme People's Procuratorate is the highest procuratorial organ of the State. Its main tasks are to direct the work of the local people's procuratorates at the various levels and that of the special people's procuratorates and ensure the unified and correct implementation of State laws. Its main functions and powers are to be responsible and report on its work to the National People's Congress and its Standing Committee; to be supervised by the NPC and its Standing Committee; to propose a bill to the NPC and its Standing Committee according to law; to investigate corruption cases, bribery cases, cases involving infringing citizens' democratic rights, offences on abuse and dereliction of duty, and cases it deems necessary to handle directly; to direct the work of the local people's procuratorates at various levels and that of the special people's procuratorates; to approve the arrest and exercise procuratorial authority in major criminal cases; to direct the local people's procuratorates at various levels and special people's procuratorates to approve the arrest and exercise procuratorial authority in criminal cases; to direct the legal supervision of the local people's procuratorates at various levels and special people's procuratorates in terms of civil and economic trials and administrative suits; to supervise, according to law, whether local people's procuratorates at various levels and the detached procuratorates exercise the penalty and supervision legally; to lodge a protest if some definite error in found in a legally effective verdict or sentence by a people's court at any level; to supervise the decisions made by local people's procuratorates at various levels and special people's procuratorates, and rectify the incorrect decisions; to hear the complaints, claims and accusation; to do research on criminal prevention of the governmental worker, and offer preventive solutions and procuratorial proposals; to be responsible for the legal popularity against duty crimes; to be in charge of the work of procuratorial organs to direct other comprehensive improvement of public order in the procuratorial link; to accept the report of corrupts and bribes; and to direct the reporting work of national procuratorial organs.

Add: No.147 Beiheyan Dajie, Dongcheng District, Beijing
Website: http://www.spp.gov.cn

♦ China Prosecutor Society

The China Prosecutor Society is a nationwide mass organization legal person composed by voluntary public prosecutors from the Supreme People's Procuratorate of the PRC, local people's procuratorates at various levels, military procuratorates and other special people's procuratorates. The legal representative is its Secretary-General. Its predecessor was the China Procuratorate Society which was founded on October 3, 1988. It changed its name on June 27 1996. The Society is based in Beijing.

The academic activities of the China Prosecutor Society include formulating research planning of procuratorial theory, and organizing and harmonizing research activities, holding national research annual meetings of procuratorial theory, seminars and training classes of regional procuratorial theory and business, exchanging research achievements in procuratorial theory and working experience in procuratorial work in order to improve the public prosecutors' professional competence and quality in law enforcement; editing and publishing Chinese Criminal Science (bimonthly magazine, available both domestically and abroad), Chinese Procuratorial Forum (bimonthly, internal distribution), Newsletter of the China Prosecutor Society (internal) and other journals, organizing and promoting cooperation and exchanges between the Society and other academic groups and organizations, and conducting international academic exchanges and friendly connections.

As an initiator and group member of the International League for Prosecutors (ILP), the China Prosecutor Society participates in the annual meetings and all kinds of activities held by ILP. The Society hosted the executive board meeting of the ILP in 1999, and successfully held its annual meeting in 2000.

The sources of the Society's funds are the appropriation of the SPP, governmental subsidies, financial aid or donations from domestic and foreign sources, legal income from conducting various activities, and membership fees.

Address: No. 147 Beiheyan Dajie, Dongcheng District, Beijing

procuratorates include military procuratorates and railway procuratorates. People's procuratorates at various local levels are set corresponding to people's courts at various levels in order to handle cases in accordance with the Criminal Procedure Law of the PRC.

Functions and Powers of the People's Procuratorates

According to the Organic Law of the People's Procuratorates of the People's Republic of China and related laws, the Peoples Procuratorate performs the following duties:

1. Exercise procuratorial authority in case of treason, attempts to split the country and other major crimes that violate State policies, laws, decrees and administrative orders;

2. Investigate cases they deem it necessary to handle directly;

3. Review cases investigated by the public security organs and State security agencies and decide whether to approve arrest and whether to prosecute; supervise the investigation activities to determine whether they conform to the law;

4. Initiate and support public prosecutions of criminal cases; supervise the criminal trials of the people's courts to determine whether they conform to the law.

5. Supervise the verdicts and sentences of the people's courts in criminal cases to determine whether they conform to the law; Supervise the activities of prisons, houses of detention and institutions in charge of reform or rehabilitation through labor to determine whether they conform to the law;

6. Exercise legal supervision over trials of civil and administrative suits by the people's courts.

The people's procuratorates are state organs for legal supervision.

Public Procurators

Public procurators are the procuratorial personnel who exercise the procuratorial authority of the State according to law, including chief procurators, deputy chief procurators, members of procuratorial committees, procurators and assistant procurators of the Procuratorate at various levels.

The functions and duties of public procurators are as follows: (1) to supervise the enforcement of laws; (2) to make public prosecution on behalf of the State; (3) to investigate criminal cases directly accepted by the People's Procuratorates as provided by law; and (4) other functions and duties as provided by law. Chief procurators, deputy chief procurators and members of procuratorial committees shall, in addition to their procuratorial functions and duties, perform other functions and duties commensurate with their posts.

The chief procurators are elected or removed by people's congresses at the corresponding levels of provinces, autonomous regions or municipalities directly under the Central Government. The appointment or removal of the chief procurators of the local People's Procuratorates at the various levels must be reported to the chief procurators of the People's Procuratorates at the next higher level, who shall submit the matter to the standing committee of the people's congress at that level for approval. Deputy chief procurators, members of the procuratorial committees and procurators of the branches of the People's Procuratorates where the chief procurators work shall be appointed or removed by the standing committees of the people's congresses at the corresponding levels of provinces, autonomous regions or municipalities directly under the Central Government. The assistant procurators of the People's Procuratorates shall be appointed or removed by the chief procurators of the procuratorates where they work.

Public procurators are divided into 12 grades: The Procurator-General of the Supreme People's Procuratorate is Procurator-in-Chief. Public procurators from the second grade to the 12th grade are composed of principal public procurators, senior public procurators and public procurators. The grades of the public procurators are determined according to the duties, performance, ability, achievements made and duration of work.

Qualifications for a Public Procurator

A public procurator must possess the following qualifications: (1) to hold Chinese citizenship; (2) to have reached the age of 23; (3) endorse the Constitution of the PRC; (4) possess fine political and professional quality and show exemplary conduct; (5) be in good health; and (6) to have worked for at least two years in the cases of graduates from law specialties of colleges or universities or from non-law specialties of colleges or universities but possessing the professional knowledge of law; to have worked for at least three years in the cases of serving as public procurators in the Supreme People's Procuratorate or People's Procuratorates of the provinces, autonomous regions or municipalities directly under the Central Government; or to have worked for at least one year in the case of graduates with Master's Degree of law or Doctor's Degree of law or non-law Master's Degree or non-law Doctor's degree but possessing the professional knowledge of law; to have worked for at least two years in the case of serving as public procurators in the Supreme People's Procuratorate or People's Procuratorates of the provinces, autonomous regions or municipalities directly under the Central Government.

No public procurators may concurrently be members of the standing committees of the people's congresses, or hold posts in administrative organs, judicial organs, enterprises or institutions, or serve as lawyers. Public procurators who are connected by a marital relationship, or who are directly related by blood, collaterally related within three generations, or closely related by marriage may not, at the same time, hold the posts of procurators in the same People's Procuratorate and chief procurators or deputy chief procurators of the People's Procuratorates at the levels next to each other. Procurators shouldn't serve as process attorneys or defenders with the lawyer capacity within two years after leaving the posts. Procurators also shouldn't serve as process attorneys or defenders of cases handled by the procuratorates where they worked before after leaving their posts. A procurator's spouse and children shouldn't work as process attorneys or defenders of cases handled by the procuratorates where the procurator works.

Participating in International Anti-Corruption Cooperation

The threat of corruption is as a generally-recognized global issue. On October 31 2003, the 58th United Nations General Assembly passed the United Nations Convention against Corruption. Correspondingly, on October 27 2005, it was adopted at the 18th Session of the 10th National People's Congress. Since then, China has formally become one of the signatories of the convention. At present, cases involving judicial assistance handled by China has concerned decades of countries including Thailand, South Korea, Singapore, Russia, Holland, US, Canada and Australia. In the past, cases involving international judicial assistance simply refer to conducting investigation and obtaining evidence, but now they have turned towards sending staff to gather evidence, criminal procedure transfer, and extradition etc. China has signed a bilateral extradition treaty and judicial assistance treaty, respectively, with 20 plus and 49 countries. The Supreme People's Procuratorate has always attached great importance to the cooperation with judicial organs of other countries, and has signed 83 bilateral agreements on cooperation or memorandums of understanding on cooperation with 75 foreign judicial and procuratorial organs.

With the help of relevant foreign organs, China has, so far, successfully arrested more than 70 suspects involved in duty crimes who had absconded to other countries. This helps to play a great deterrent role in preventing corruption crimes, safeguarding national interests and legal sanctity. China is quickening its steps for repatriating suspects and concluding an extradition treaty, and making full use of many ways and channels, including international judicial assistance, Interpol and border regional cooperation, to launch manhunts. Thus there will be increasingly more non-national boundary actions to fight corruption crimes and combat transnational ones.

International Association of Anti-Corruption Authorities

The International Association of Anti-Corruption Authorities is composed of institutions of various countries in the world, which are charged with investigating and bring a lawsuit against bribery and embezzlement crimes. It is an independent, non-governmental, non-political, non-profiting and judiciary international organ. Its goal is to promote implementation of the UN Convention on Anti-Corruption, and promote international cooperation in fight against bribery and corruption. From October 22-25, 2006, the Association held its first annual meeting and conference of its members in China. It was attended by close to 1,000 delegates hailing from 137 countries and regions, and 12 international organizations. They include some 200 officials at and above the vice-ministerial level.

Juridical System

The judicatory system refers to the court system, including the establishment of courts, judges, trial organizations and activities.

The people's courts of the PRC are the judicial organs of the state. The PRC establishes the Supreme People's Court and the people's courts at various local levels, military courts and other special people's courts. Higher People's Courts are established at the level of provinces, autonomous regions and municipalities directly under the Central Government, and at the lower level, the intermediate People's Courts and People's Courts at the grassroots level are established. The Supreme People's Court is the highest judicial organ. The Supreme People's Court supervises the administration of justice by the people's courts at various local levels and by the special people's courts. People's courts at higher levels supervise the administration of justice by those at lower levels. The Supreme People's Court is responsible to the National People's Congress and its Standing Committee. Local people's courts at various levels are responsible to the organs of State power that created them.

Local people's courts at various levels are set up in accordance with the administrative divisions, including People's Courts at the grassroots level, the intermediate People's Courts and the higher People's Courts. People's Courts at the grassroots level include People's Courts of counties and autonomous counties, and People's Courts of cities without administrative districts and administrative districts of cities. People's Courts at the grassroots level establish people's tribunals as detached agencies, but people's tribunals are not trial units. The intermediate People's Courts include the regional intermediate People's Courts in provinces and autonomous regions, the intermediate People's Courts of municipalities directly under the Central

The Supreme People's Court

♦ The Supreme People's Court

The Supreme People's Court is based in Beijing. It is the highest judicial organ and exercises the highest judicial right according to the law. It is responsible to the National People's Congress and its Standing Committee, and supervises the administration of justice by the people's courts at various local levels and by the special people's courts. The Supreme People's Court consists of one president, several vice-presidents, chief judges, associate chief judges of divisions and judges. The term of office of the President is the same as that of the National People's Congress, or five years. The President shall serve no more than two consecutive terms.

Its responsibilities and duties are as follows:

(1) It tries cases of first instance over which it has jurisdiction according to law and cases of first instance it deems that it should try; cases of appeal and protests against the judgments and orders of High People's Courts and special people's courts; and cases of protests filed by the Supreme People's Procuratorate in accordance with the procedures of trial supervision;

(2) Verifying and approving death sentences: Except in the case where death penalty is decided by the Supreme People's Court, all death penalty rulings have to be submitted to the Supreme People's Court for examination and approval.

(3) Supervising the administration of justice by the people's courts at various local levels and by the special people's courts;

(4) Supervising the work of local courts and special courts at every level, overruling wrong judgments they might have made, and deciding interrogations and reviewing cases tried by the lower courts;

(5) Verifying the application of the law against criminals that are not clearly defined in explicit terms in the Specific Provisions of Criminal Law;

(6) Giving judicial explanations of the specific utilization of laws in the judicial process.

Address: No.27 Dongjiaomingxiang, Dongcheng District, Beijing
Website: http://www.court.gov.cn

Government, and the intermediate People's Courts of cities under the jurisdiction of provinces and autonomous regions and autonomous prefectures. Special People's Courts refer to the courts handling special cases set in specific departments according to the actual requirements. China has established military courts, maritime courts, railway courts and other special courts.

Except for the cases involving State secrets, privacy and crimes committed by minors, all cases in the people's courts are heard in public. The accused has the right to defend himself or by entrusting lawyers or relatives, guardians and other citizens. The people's courts exercise judicial power independently, in accordance with the provisions of the law, and are not subject to interference by any administrative organ, public organization or individual.

Higher People's Court

According to the law on court organization, higher people's Courts are set up in provinces, autonomous regions and municipalities directly under the Central Government. Their responsibilities include: (1) trying the following categories of cases: first instance cases subject to its jurisdiction, including criminal, civil and administrative cases of major proportions and complications, as provided for by law; cases of appeal and protests against the first instance made by the intermediate people's courts, and cases put forth by the provincial procuratorate in accordance with the court monitoring procedures; and first-hearing cases transferred by lower courts; (2) supervision: supervising trials by lower courts. For verdicts or judgments passed by lower courts that have been found to contain errors, higher courts are authorized to hear or ask lower courts to retry the case; (3) reviewing cases involving the death penalty: reviewing first-hearing cases involving the death penalty ruled by intermediate courts where the accused renounces the right to appeal. If the death penalty ruling meets no objection, it shall be subject to the Supreme People's Court for examination and approval. In the case where the death penalty is objected, it could be interrogated or retried again.

Intermediate People's Court

Intermediate courts are those set up in provinces and autonomous regions, municipalities directly under the Central Government, cities directly under provinces and autonomous regions, and prefectures. Their responsibilities include: (1) trying the first-hearing cases under their jurisdiction, as prescribed by law. According to the Law on Criminal Procedures, these cases include those involving national security; criminal cases that may involve life imprisonment or the death penalty; criminal cases committed by foreigners or cases involving Chinese citizens violating the lawful rights and interests of foreigners. According to the Law on Civil Procedures, civil cases heard by intermediate courts are major foreign-related cases; cases of major implications within their jurisdictions; and cases that intermediate courts are ordered to hear by the Supreme People's Court. In addition, according to the Law on Administrative Procedures, intermediate courts are authorized to hear the following cases: verification of patent rights; customs handling; suits against administrative actions taken by State Council departments or governments of the provinces, autonomous regions and municipalities directly under the Central Government; other important and complicated cases;

(2) trying cases ruled or protested by the first-instance judgment of the grass-roots people's courts as well as cases protested by people's procuratorates at the provincial, provincial-level city and autonomous regional levels in accordance with the procedure for adjudication supervision.

(3) first-hearing cases transferred by courts at the grassroots level; (4) supervising the performance of courts at the grassroots level within their jurisdiction. They have the power to examine or order courts at the grassroots level to retry verdicts and decisions issued by those courts that have already taken effect but that have been found to contain errors.

For criminal, civil and administrative cases that intermediate courts deem to be of a serious nature, the intermediate court may request that the cases be transferred to superior courts.

The judges of the people's courts at the basic level

18

Judicature

People's Court at the Grassroots Level

Courts at the grassroots level consist of tribunals in counties and autonomous counties, cities without administrative districts or administrative districts of cities. Their responsibilities are: (1) trying cases as courts of first instance, except where otherwise provided for by law; (2) reexamining their incorrect judgments and verdicts that have taken effect according to the judgment supervision procedures; (3) guiding the work of the People's Arbitration Committees.

To facilitate lawsuits, courts at the grassroots level set up tribunals as detached organs, which are not trial units, but have the responsibility to hear general civil and misdemeanors, guide the work of People's Arbitration Committees, publicize laws and regulations, and handle petitions. Their judgments and decisions represent the judgments and decisions of People's Courts at the grassroots level.

Special People's Court

The special People's Courts include the military court, maritime court, railway transport court, forestry court, farm reclamation court and oil court.

The differences between special people's courts and local people's courts are as follows:

(1) Special people's courts are set up according to special organizations or particular range of cases, while local people's courts are set up according to administrative divisions.

(2) Special people's courts have jurisdiction over special cases. It means that the nature of the cases they handle differs from those handled by local people's courts, and the range of cases they handle is specially restricted.

(3) The establishment of special people's courts and the appointment and removal of their personnel differ from those of local people's courts. For example, the President of military courts are not elected in the NPC, but appointed by the Supreme People's Court and Central Military Commission.

The indoor scene of the court session

Military Courts

Military courts are set up based on the military system and the particularity of battle missions. Their role is to try the criminals who jeopardize the State and defense capacity in order to safeguard the national security, maintain the national laws and military order, enforce battle effectiveness, and maintain the legal rights of servicemen and other citizens. The basic responsibilities of military courts are to fight against enemies, punish crimes, protect people and publicize socialist law system.

Military courts are set up at three levels: the PLA Court, Greater Military Region, Services and Arms Courts and grassroots courts. Judicial committees are set up in military courts at various levels. Their duties are to discuss and research important and complicated cases and other issues with regard to trials. Conferences of judicial committees are hosted by the president. Chief procurators of the military procuratorates at the corresponding level can also attend the conferences.

Military courts are limited to handle given criminal cases including criminal cases of military personnel on active service, criminal cases of military personnel on the regular payroll and criminal cases authorized by the Supreme People's Court.

Maritime Courts

Maritime courts are special courts set up to try first-hearing maritime or shipping cases, but not to try criminal and other civil cases. The appeal cases judged or decided by maritime courts are handled by the local higher people's courts.

Maritime courts consist of maritime tribunals, sea-shipping tribunals, research offices and official organs. Maritime courts comprise one president, several vice-presidents, chief judges, associate chief judges of divisions and judges. The presidents of maritime courts are appointed and removed by the corresponding Standing Committee of the local People's Congresses upon the recommendation of the chairmen of the local People's Congresses; vice-presidents, presiding judge and deputy presiding judges, judges and members of the judge committee are appointed and removed in accordance with the submission of the president of the maritime court to the local standing committee of the People's Congress.

Railway Courts

Railway courts consist of intermediate railway courts under Railway Administration and grassroots railway transport courts under Railway Sub-Administration. The trials of intermediate railway courts are supervised by the local higher people's court.

The presidents of railway courts are appointed and removed by the corresponding Standing Committee of the local People's Congresses upon the recommendation of the chairmen of the local People's Congresses. And vice-presidents, presiding judges, deputy presiding judges, and judges are appointed and removed by the local Standing Committee of the NPC upon the recommendation of President.

Railway courts comprise criminal, economic and civil courts. They try the following types of cases: (1) civil and criminal cases along railways; (2) civil and criminal cases of personnel on the regular payroll in the Railway Administration; (3) economic lawsuits directly related to railway departments.

Forest Courts

The responsibilities of forest courts are to protect forests, try cases involving damaging forest resources, cases of terrible responsible accidents and foreign-related cases.

Grassroots forest courts are generally set up where locates the Forestry Bureau, including Timber Waterway Bureau in some given forest areas. Intermediate forest courts are set up in the location of the local (or league) Forest Management Bureau or in areas with vast expanse of national forests.

Open Trials

All court trials should be conducted openly unless otherwise provided for by the law. For cases that, by law, should be open to the public, the court should announce in advance the outline of the case, the name of the litigant, the time and the place of the trial. The entire process should be open to public auditing and to the press. Fixed open trials should be announced ahead of schedule. All trial procedures, except the deliberations of a collegial panel, should be open to the public.

The law provides that the following four types of cases are not open to the public: (1) cases involving State secrets; (2) cases involving personal privacy; (3) cases involving crimes committed by minors; (4) and cases involving divorce and trade secrets upon request by litigants. For the cases that are not open to the public, reasons should be given in court, and the judgment should still be pronounced publicly.

Defense System

The defense system is an important part of the State judicial system which plays extremely important role to guaranteeing the legal rights and interests of the party concerned and promoting judicial fairness.

The accused is entitled to a proper defense. Any accused may, in addition to exercising the right to defend themselves, appoint representatives to defend them, or be defended by a court-designated defender. During the entire criminal prosecution, the accused has the right to defend themselves.

Withdrawal System

The withdrawal system refers to the situation, scope and procedures of withdrawal as determined by the law.

Judicial officers, clerks, interpreters, expert witnesses and inspection personnel shall voluntarily withdraw from a case in any of the following circumstances: where he/she is a party to the case or a near relative of a party or an agent ad litem in the case; he/she is an interested party in the case; or has some other kind of relationship with a party to the case, which might affect the impartiality of the trial. The parties thereto shall be entitled to apply orally or in writing for his withdrawal.

Collegiate System

This refers to the trials of cases conducted by a collegiate panel composed of judges and people's assessors. It is the basic form of trials conducted by people's courts, and the concrete application of democratic centralism in trials.

The Court of Second Instance Being That of Last Instance

This is the system of sentencing cases in China. From a judgment or orders of first instance of a local people's court, a party may appeal to the people's court at the next higher level in accordance with the procedure prescribed by law, and people's procuratorates may present a protest to people's courts at the next higher level in accordance with the procedure prescribed by law. Judgments and orders of second instance become legally effective. Judgments and orders of first instance of the local people's courts at various levels become legally effective judgments and orders if, within the period for appeal, none of the parties has appealed and procuratorates have not protested.

The Supreme People's Court is the highest judicial organ in China. Its judgments and orders of the first and second instances are the last instance.

Judges System

The judge system is prescribed according to the Judges Law of the PRC (revised by the Standing Committee of the NPC in June 2001).

The functions and duties of judges are to take part in a trial as a member of a collegial panel or to try a case alone according to law, and to perform other functions and duties as provided by law.

A judge must possess the following qualifications according to law: (1) be a Chinese citizen; (2) to have reached the age of 23; (3) endorsing the constitution of the PRC; (4) possess fine political and professional quality and show exemplary conduct; (5) to be in good health; and (6) to have worked for at least two years in the cases of graduates from law specialties of colleges or universities or from non-law specialties of colleges or universities but possessing the professional knowledge of law; to have worked for at least three years in the cases of serving as judges in the Supreme People's Court or higher People's courts; or to have worked for at least one year in the case of graduates with Master's Degree of law or Doctor's Degree of law or non-law Master's Degree or non-law Doctor's degree but possessing the professional knowledge of law; to have worked for at least two years in the case of serving as judges in the Supreme People's court or higher People's Courts. No judges may concurrently be members of the standing committees of the People's Congresses, hold posts in administrative organs, procuratorial organs, enterprises or institutions, or serve as lawyers. Judges shouldn't serve as process attorneys or defenders with the lawyer capacity within two years after leaving the posts. Judges also shouldn't serve as process attorneys or defenders of the cases handled by the courts where they worked before after leaving their posts. Judges' spouse and children shouldn't work as process attorneys or defenders of the cases handled by the courts where the judge works.

Judges who are connected by a marital relationship, or who are directly related by blood, collaterally related within three generations, or closely related by marriage may not, at the same time, hold the posts of judges in the same people's court and presidents or vice-presidents of the People's Courts at the levels next to each other.

Judges are divided into 12 grades. The President of the Supreme People's Court is the Chief Justice. Judges from the second grade to the twelfth grade are composed of associate justices, senior Judges and Judges. Grades of judges shall be determined on the basis of their posts, their actual working ability and political integrity, their professional competence, their achievements in judicial work and their seniority. Judges are promoted grade by grade according to the annual appraisal.

Presenting a Petition and Retrial

Presenting a petition refers to the procedure whereby a party and his legal representative present their claim of retrial to the people's court which originally tried the case or superior courts regarding a legally effective judgment, order or arbitration they deem legally flawed. During the period of petition presentation, the execution of the original judgment or order is not suspended. If the petition is reasonable, the judicial committee shall discuss and decide whether to retry upon the recommendation of President of the court.

People's courts retry cases if a petition presented by a party conforms to any of the following conditions: there is new evidence sufficient to overturn the original judgment or order; major evidence was insufficient to prove the facts in the original judgment or order; the application of law in making the original judgment or order was definitely incorrect; people's courts violated legal procedures possibly influencing the correct judgment or order of a case; and the judges in trying the case committed acts of embezzlement, bribery, or malpractice for personal gain, or bent the law in making the judgment. In addition, a party may apply for retrial regarding the mediation documents that have already been legally effective if a party presents evidence to prove that the mediation violates the principles on a voluntary basis, or that the mediation agreements violate the application of law. A party shall apply for retrial within two year after the judgment or order becomes legally effective.

Judicial Committee

The judicial committee, set up within the People's Court, is an organ responsible for the exercise of collective leadership and supervision over the judicial work. Its responsibilities include summarizing judicial practices, and discussing important or complicated cases and other judicial issues. The judicial committee does not handle cases themselves.

Trial Organs

(1) The First Criminal Court serves to hear major criminal cases.

(2) The Second Criminal Court serves to hear and handle petitions presented to the Supreme People's Court by the parties, defendants and their relatives or other citizens regarding a legally effective judgment and order. And it corrects, in time, possible trial mistakes by trial supervision.

(3) The Civil Court serves to try nationwide civil cases.

(4) The Economic Court serves to hear major economic cases.

(5) The Administrative Court hears the administrative cases involving CPC departments.

Jail System

The jail system is stipulated according to the Prison Law of the PRC, adopted and put into force in December 1994 by the Standing Committee of the NPC.

A prison is an organ of the State for executing criminal punishments. Criminal punishments of prisoners sentenced to death penalty with a two-year suspension of execution, life imprisonment, or fixed-term imprisonment are executed in prisons under the Criminal Law and the Criminal Procedure Law. Activities in prison administration, execution of criminal punishments, and education and reform of prisoners conducted according to law by the people's police of a prison are protected by law. People's procuratorates exercise supervision in accordance with the law over the legality of activities conducted by prisons in execution of criminal punishments. The department of judicial administration under the State Council takes charge of the prison work in the whole country.

The human dignity of a prisoner is inviolate, and his personal safety, lawful properties, and rights to defense, petition, complaint and accusation as well as other rights that have not been removed or restricted according to law cannot be violated. A prisoner must strictly observe laws, regulations, and rules and discipline of the prison, subject himself to control, accept education and take part in labor.

Prison Categories

Prisons in China are divided into two categories:

(1) Prisons incarcerating inmates who have been condemned by courts to a fixed-term sentence, life sentence or death penalty with two-year reprieve. Male and female inmates are warded separately, with female wards managed by female law enforcement personnel. Prisons may also be divided into wards for felons and criminals guilty of a misdemeanor according to the criminal character and prison term.

(2) Penitentiaries for juvenile delinquents, criminals of minor age condemned by courts to a fixed-term sentence, life sentence or death penalty with two-year reprieve. They mainly hold criminals younger than 18. China always gives special protection to juveniles, and special protection is also extended to juvenile delinquents, with customized procedures in place to cater to their needs.

The administrative personnel in a prison are the people's police who enjoy the same legal status as public security and traffic police.

Execution of Penalties

This refers to the law enforcement organ implementing court decisions and rulings

Towards the Spring Festival, a policeman and personnels serving a prison sentence are hanging decorative objects in the prison cells.

according to law. Imprisonment in China takes the following forms:

(1) Imprisonment: Criminals are put in prison who have been condemned to death with a two-year reprieve, given a life sentence, a fixed term sentence or a sentence with the remaining term being more than one year. A prison shall give physical examination to the criminals who are handed over for execution of their criminal punishment. A criminal sentenced to life imprisonment or fixed-term imprisonment may, after physical examination, temporarily not be put in prison if he/she is seriously ill and needs to be released on parole for medical treatment, or a pregnant woman or a woman who is breast-feeding her own baby. With respect to a criminal temporarily not put in prison, the decision on temporary housing outside prison shall be made by the people's court which handled the case. With respect to any such criminal whose temporary stay outside prison constitutes a danger to the society, he shall be returned to prison. If a criminal temporarily serves his sentence outside prison, the public security organ in the place of the criminal's residence shall administer the criminal punishment. After the circumstances specified in the preceding paragraph, under which a criminal is temporarily not put in prison, no longer apply, the criminal who has not completed his original term shall be handed over for imprisonment by the public security organ.

(2) Petitions, complaints and accusations: If a prisoner is not satisfied with the effective judgment, he may file a petition. In the course of execution of the criminal punishment, if a prison believes on the basis of a prisoner's petition that the judgment may be wrongfully made, it shall refer the matter to people's procuratorates or a people's court for handling. People's procuratorate or the people's court should notify the prison of the result of its handling within six months from the date of receiving the prison's written recommendation.

(3) Execution outside prison: If a prisoner sentenced to life imprisonment or fixed-term imprisonment serving his sentence in prison complies with the conditions for execution outside prison as provided by the Criminal Procedure Law, he may be permitted to temporarily serve his sentence outside prison. A written recommendation should be made by a prison and submitted for approval to the administrative organ of prisons of the province, autonomous region or municipalities directly under the Central Government. If a prisoner temporarily serves his sentence outside prison, the public security organ in the place of the prisoner's residence takes over administration of the sentence.

(4) Commutation of punishment and release on parole: If a prisoner sentenced to life imprisonment or fixed-term imprisonment has shown true repentance or rendered meritorious service during the term of imprisonment, his sentence may or should be commuted, or he may or should be released on parole on the basis of the result of the assessment made by the prison. A recommendation for commutation of a sentence or release on parole shall be made by a prison to people's courts. People's courts make a ruling thereon.

(5) Release and resettlement: If a prisoner has completed serving his sentence, the prison shall release him as scheduled and issue him with a certificate of release. After a prisoner is released, the public security organ records a residential registration for him on the strength of his certificate of release. With respect to a person released after serving his sentence, the local people's government shall assist him in resettling. If a person released after serving his sentence has lost his ability to work, and has no statutory support or basic source of income, the local people's government shall offer him relief. A person released after serving his sentence shall enjoy rights with other citizens in accordance with the law.

Prison Administration

Prison administration refers to administrative management of the State organ for executing criminal punishments over inmates. Its management activities are as the follows:

Separate custody and separate control: A prison shall practice separate custody and separate control with respect to male adult prisoners, female adult prisoners and juvenile delinquents. In respect of the reform of juvenile delinquents and female prisoners, special consideration shall be given to their physiological and psychological characteristics. A prison shall, with respect to prisoners, carry out separate custody and varied control on the basis of their types of crimes and punishments, terms of sentences and performances of reform. Female prisoners shall be under the direct control of people's policewomen.

Correspondence and meeting with visitors: A prison may, during the service of his sentence, correspond with others, but their correspondence should be examined by the prison. If the prison discovers that the content of a letter presents a hindrance to the reform of the prisoner, the prison may confiscate the letter. Letters from a prisoner to the higher authorities of the prison or to the judicial organs are free from examination. A prisoner may, in accordance with the relevant regulations, meet with relatives and guardians during the term of imprisonment.

Guards: A prison shall set up guard installations in accordance with the need of supervision and control. Under circumstances provided by the law, a prison or the administrative personnel may use restraint implements or weapons.

Lawyer System

The main legislation to define China's lawyer system is the Law of the PRC on Lawyers, passed by the Standing Committee of National People's Congress in May 1996 and revised in October, 2007.

To practice law, a person must acquire a qualification as a lawyer and a practice certificate pursuant to legal requirements. A lawyer has both certain legal rights and obligations. A qualified person can choose not to practice law for a time and retain the qualification; such conduct is called the separation of qualification and practice.

By the end of 2007, China had 130,000 lawyers and 12,428 law firms. The type of law firm has developed from the sole State-owned law firm to multiple types of partnership, State-owned and cooperative firms, among which 71 percent are partnerships.

Lawyer Qualification

To acquire lawyer qualification a person must pass a national uniform judicial examination. Qualification as a lawyer is granted to a person who has undergone four years of legal education or undergraduate education in another major in an institution of higher learning with equivalent professional level, and has passed the bar examination. Within a certain period in regions where it's hard to find applicants with a bachelor degree, upon approval by the judicial administration department under the State Council, and after evaluation and verification in accordance with the prescribed conditions, the requirement can be lowered to persons who have acquired three years legal education in an institution of higher learning and have passed the bar examination.

A person applying to practice law who has acquired undergraduate legal education in an institution of higher learning, who is engaged in professional work such as legal research and teaching, and who has a senior professional title or is of an equivalent professional level, is qualified to be a lawyer, upon approval by the judicial administration department under the State Council after evaluation and verification in accordance with the prescribed conditions.

Law Practice Application

A person applying for law practice must meet the following conditions:

Upholding the Constitution of the People's Republic of China;

Possessing qualification as a lawyer;

Having undergone practice training at a law firm for a full year;

Being a person of good character and conduct.

A person in any one of the following situations cannot be issued a lawyer's practice certificate:

Having no capacity or limited capacity for civil acts;

Having been subjected to criminal punishment, except for a crime of negligence;

Or having been discharged from public employment or having had his lawyer's practice certificate previously revoked.

A lawyer's practice is not subject to regional restriction. A person applying for a lawyer's practice certificate who, upon verification by the judicial administration department of the people's government at or above the level of province, autonomous region or municipality directly under the Central Government, is considered to meet the conditions to be issued a lawyer's practice certificate.

Every lawyer must register the law practice certificate annually, otherwise it becomes invalid. The judicial administrative department of the people's government at or above the level of province, autonomous region or municipality directly under the Central Government supervises and conducts the work of lawyer certificate registration. The judicial administration department can trust its junior offices at regional, city or town level to take charge of the registry work.

A lawyer shall practice in one law firm and not work for two or more firms simultaneously. Any of the active working personnel of a State organ cannot concurrently practice as a lawyer. A lawyer cannot practice while serving as a member of a standing committee of a people's congress at any level.

Law Firms

A law firm is the organization in which lawyers practice and it must meet the following conditions: (1) having its own name, domicile and articles of association; (2) having assets of 100,000 Yuan or more; and (3) having lawyers who conform to the legal provisions.

The Law of the PRC on Lawyers stipulates three types of law firms; law firms under different conditions adopt different operational systems while undertaking their respective relevant obligations, i.e., civil responsibilities. A law firm established with the capital contribution from the State is independent in its practice pursuant to law and undertakes liability for its debts with its entire assets. Lawyers may establish cooperative law firms, which accept liability for their debts with their entire assets. Lawyers may establish partnership firms. The partners accept unlimited and joint and several liability for the debts.

Persons applying to establish a law firm who, after examination and verification by the judicial administration department of the relevant people's government, are considered

A lawyer bringing forth the proofs in the court trail

to meet the conditions provided for in the Law and should be issued a law firm practice certificate. A law firm may establish branch offices but must accept responsibility for any debts they may incur. When lawyers undertake any business, their law firm must accept authorization, sign a written authorization contract with the client(s) and, in accordance with State regulations, collect fees from the parties and truthfully enter them in their accounts.

♦ All-China Lawyers Association

Founded in July, 1986, the All-China Lawyers Association (ACLA) is a social organization with the status of a legal person, a self-disciplining national organization carrying out professional administration over lawyers. All lawyers of the PRC are members of ACLA and the local lawyers associations are group members of ACLA. At present, ACLA has 31 group members, which are lawyers associations of provinces, autonomous regions and municipalities directly under the central government and nearly 110,000 individual members.

Duties of ACLA are as follows:

(1) Assuring that lawyers practice pursuant to the law and protecting lawyers' legal rights and interests;

(2) Summarizing and exchanging lawyers' work experience;

(3) Organizing professional training for lawyers;

(4) Conducting education in, inspection of, and supervision over lawyer's professional ethics and rules of conduct;

(5) Organizing lawyers to develop exchanges with foreign countries;

(6) Mediating disputes arising from lawyers' practice;

(7) Other duties provided for by law.

Led by the Secretary General, the ACLA's executive body is composed of a General Office, Membership Section, Information and Research Section, Training Section and International Section (i.e. China International Lawyers Exchange Centre). The Association also edits and publishes Chinese Lawyers

Address: 5th Floor, Qinglan Plaza, No. 24 Dongsishitiao, Beijing
Website: http://www.acla.org.cn

♦ Chinese Lawyers' Website

http://www.chineselawyer.com.cn

Business of Law Firms

According to the Law of the PRC on Lawyers, in China, A lawyer may engage in the following business:

To accept engagement by citizens, legal persons or other organizations to act as legal counsel;

To accept authorization by a party in a civil or administrative cases to act as agent and participate in the proceedings;

To accept engagement by a criminal suspect in a criminal case to provide him with legal advice and represent him in filing a petition or charge or obtaining a guarantor pending trial; to accept authorization by a criminal suspect or defendant or accept appointment by a People's Court to act for the defense; and to accept authorization by a private prosecutor in a case of private prosecution or by the victim or his close relatives in a case of public prosecution to act as agent and participate in the proceedings;

To represent clients in filing petitions in all types of litigation;

To accept authorization by a party to participate in mediation and arbitration activities;

To accept authorization by a party involved in non-litigation legal matters to provide legal services;

To answer inquiries regarding law and to represent clients in writing litigation documents and other documents regarding legal matters.

Rights of Lawyer

Right to investigate: According to the Law of the PRC on Lawyers, when undertaking legal matters, a lawyer may, with the consent of the relevant units or individuals, address inquiries to such units or individuals.

Right to consult case judicial documents and technical verification material: According to the Criminal Procedure Law of the PRC, defense lawyers may, from the date on which the People's Procuratorate begins to examine a case for prosecution, consult, extract and duplicate the judicial documents pertaining to the current case and the technical verification material; from the date on which the People's Court accepts a case, consult, extract and duplicate the material of the facts of the crime accused in the current case. According to the Law of the PRC on Lawyers, lawyer participating in litigation activities may collect and consult the materials pertaining to the case he is undertaking.

Right to meet and correspond with a person whose personal freedom is restricted: The Law of the PRC on Lawyers stipulates that a lawyer participating in litigation activities may, according to the provisions of procedural laws, meet and correspond with a person whose personal freedom is restricted.

Right to appear in court and participate in litigation: The law stipulates that a lawyer participating in litigation activities may, according to the provisions of procedural laws, appear in court, participate in litigation, and enjoy other rights provided for in the procedure laws.

Right to refuse to defend or to represent a client: According to the law, after accepting authorization, a lawyer shall not, without good reason, refuse to defend or to represent a client. However, if the matter authorized violates the law, the client uses the service provided by the lawyer to engage in illegal activities or the client conceals facts, the lawyer shall have the right to refuse to defend or to represent the client.

Right to be protected: According to the law, in practice activities, a lawyer's right of the person shall not be violated.

Obligations of Lawyers

The obligations of lawyers include:

In his practice, a lawyer must abide by the Constitution and the Law of the PRC on Lawyers, and strictly observe lawyers' professional ethics and practice discipline.

Not to refuse to defend or to represent a client without good reason: According to the law, after accepting authorization, a lawyer shall not, without good reason, refuse to defend or to represent a client.

To provide legal aid: According to the law, a citizen who needs the assistance of lawyers in respect of matters such as livelihood support, work-related injuries, criminal procedure, claims for State compensation or claims for lawful payment of pensions for the disabled or families of a deceased, but cannot afford the legal fees, may obtain legal aid in accordance with State regulations. A lawyer must undertake the duty of legal aid in accordance with State regulations, and provide the recipient with legal services in fulfillment of his duty and responsibility.

To keep secrets: According to the law, a lawyer shall keep confidential secrets of the State and commercial secrets of the parties concerned that come to his knowledge during his practice activities and shall not divulge the private affairs of the parties concerned.

Not to undertake certain cases: According to the law, a lawyer shall not represent both parties involved in the same case. A lawyer who once served as a judge or prosecutor shall not act as agent or defend clients within two years after leaving his post in the People's Court or the People's Procuratorate.

Not to accept authorization privately: According to the law, a lawyer shall not accept authorization privately, charge fees to the client privately, or accept money or things of value from the client;

A lawyer shall not seek the disputed rights and interests of a party or accept money or things of value from the opposing party by taking advantage of providing legal services;

A lawyer shall not meet with a judge, prosecutor, or arbitrator in violation of the regulations;

A lawyer shall not entertain or give gifts to a judge, prosecutor, arbitrator or other relevant working personnel or bribe them, or instigate or induce any other party to bribe them;

A lawyer shall not provide false evidence, conceal facts or intimidate or induce another with a promise of gain to provide false evidence, conceal facts, or obstruct the opposing party's lawful obtaining of evidence;

A lawyer shall not disrupt the order of a court or an arbitration tribunal, or interfere with the normal conduct of litigation or arbitration activities.

Legal Duties of Lawyers

If a lawyer violates any regulations, the judicial administration department may issue a disciplinary warning, impose a penalty of temporary cessation of practice, confiscate any illegal income, or revoke his right to practice accordingly; where the case constitutes a crime, criminal responsibility shall be pursued according to the law.

A law firm that violates any regulations will be ordered to set it right, any illegal income will be confiscated, or a fine imposed, or the firm ordered to cease practice for a period of its certificate of practice is revoked.

If a lawyer practices illegally or causes losses to a party due to his fault, the law firm in which he works bears the liability for compensation. After paying compensation, the law firm may claim recovery from the lawyer. Lawyers and law firms may not be relieved of or limited in the civil liability that they shall bear for losses caused to a party due to illegal practice of law or negligence.

Notary System

Notarization in China is defined as the notary activities on civil legal relationships performed, on behalf of the State, by notary public offices specially appointed by the State. That is to say, the State Notary Department certifies the authenticity and legality, upon application of any party concerned, of legal actions, legal documents and facts in accordance with the law, in order to protect public property, citizens' status, and property rights as well as their lawful interests. Starting from October 1st, 2000, the Ministry of Justice began promoting reform in the public notary system. The public notary offices have gradually shifted from their current State-owned administrative status to a form of partnership and cooperative. New public notary offices will be non-profit public welfare enterprise legal person operating according to market rules and self-disciplinary laws and will bear their own responsibility. The State will not approve of setting up State-owned public notary offices that is of administrative nature.

Notary Websites

Name of website	Website	Owner
China Notaries Association	http://www.chinanotary.org	www.Chinanotary.org
Www.Xjnotary.com	http://www.xjnotary.com/	Notaries Association of Xinjiang Autonomous Region
Notaries Association of Shandong Province	http://www.sdgz.org/index.asp	Notaries Association of Shandong Province
www.tj-notary.org	http://www.tj-notary.org/index.html	Notaries Association of Tianjin Municipality
www.xbgz-china.org	http://www.xbgz-china.org/	Notaries Association of Chongqing Municipality
www.gdnotary.org	http://www.gdnotary.org/index.jsp	Notaries Association of Guangdong Province
www.zjgz.org	http://www.zjgz.org/	Notaries Association of Zhejiang Province

The setting-up of Public Notary Offices:

A notary office shall be set up in municipalities directly under the Central Government, counties (or autonomous counties), and municipalities. With the approval of the judicial administrative authorities of the province, autonomous region and municipality directly under the Central Government, a municipal district may also set up a notary office. A subordinate relationship does not exist between notary offices.

The notary office shall contain positions of director and deputy director assumed by notaries. Notaries shall possess the same qualifications as those of judges and prosecutors.

Scope of Business of Notary Office

A notary office can handle the following items of business:

(1) Give a testimonial in civil legal actions: For example, to give a testimonial to contracts, powers of attorney, wills, donation of property, partition of property and relationship of adoption and the like;

(2) Testifying to facts of civil legal significance: For example, to give a testimonial regarding a person's birth, death, marital status, divorce, family relationship, identity, record of education, and personal experience and the like;

(3) Testify to documents of civil legal significance: For example, to give a testimonial to the authenticity of signatures and seals on documents; to give a testimonial to the conformity of duplicates, abridged versions, translations, and photo-offset copies to the original and the like;

(4) Testify to the effect of execution of documents concerning the claim for repayments of debt: For example, to give a testimonial to the effect of execution of agreements concerning the claim for repayments of money (or articles), and loan contracts concerning the claim for repayments of debt;

(5) Auxiliary business: For example, the preservation of evidence, the safekeeping of wills or other documents, to draft, on behalf of the party concerned, a document of application for a notarized deed;

In practice, notary offices are also responsible for notarizing drawings and lottery results.

The Effect of Notarization

A notarized certificate shall have the following four effects:

1. Evidential effect

The evidential effect of a notarized certificate is also called the evidential ability, referring to its legal qualification as evidence.

2. Executive effect

The executive effect of a notarized certificate refers to its enforceable effect of execution, which, instead of includes all kinds of documents, is currently restricted to documents concerning the claim for repayments of debt and articles in the event that such documents are considered to be unequivocal. As to a notarized creditor's rights document with the effect of enforceable execution, if the debtor fails to perform its duties prescribed in the document, the creditor may file an application with the jurisdictional people's court for execution.

3. Legal effect

The legal effect of a notarized certificate refers to the fact that certain legal actions, such as adoption, and marriage registration between a Chinese citizen and a foreign citizen, are only effective, have legal binding forces, and are protected by the State after they are notarized.

4. Effect outside China

When used outside China, the document has the same inherent legal effect according to international conventions. Where a Chinese citizen or legal person needs to use a notarized certificate outside China, it shall, after notarization, be subject to the certification of the Ministry of Foreign Affairs of the PRC or the Foreign Affairs offices of various provinces, municipalities and autonomous regions or the China-based embassy or consular office of the relevant country in order for it to be acknowledged and to be legally effective in that country.

Notarization Procedures

In accordance with Regulations on Notarization Procedures promulgated by the Ministry of Justice in 2002, Public Notary Offices and any notarizing party concerned shall strictly comply with the following procedures during notarization:

1. Request and acceptance

A citizen or legal person may authorize others to perform a notarization act with the exception of the notarization of a will, adoption relationship and other information closely related to personal matters of the applicant, which shall be performed by the latter himself. Request for notarization shall be filed with the jurisdictional public notary offices, and the public notary offices of the place where the applicant's domicile or habitual residence is located, or where the relevant legal act is committed. Where a notarization is requested, an application form with the applicant's signature or seal shall be filed. Relevant information, such as identification card, authorization letter, documents pending for notarization, ownership evidence or other information related to the notarization matter shall be provided to the notary office. The latter shall make initial performing decisions according to the applicant's request and accept those meeting the requirements.

2. Examination

Examination is an important step when performing notarization. Notary offices shall examine the number and identity of the party concerned, its qualifications for requesting notarization, its capability for civil conduct, its intentions expressed, corresponding rights, whether the acts, facts under request for notarization or the certification materials are authentic and lawful, whether the documents it offers are complete, whether the meanings are clear and whether the signature and seal are complete.

3. Issuance of a notarization certificate

The notary public shall issue a notarization certificate once it considers, upon examination, that the certification materials offered by the applicant meet all the requirements. A notarization certificate shall be made according to the format as required or approved by the Ministry of Justice and contain the following items: (1) a serial number of the notarization certificate; (2) fundamental information of the party concerned; (3) notarized testimonial (4) the signature or seal of the notary as well as the seal of the notary office; (5) the date of issuance. Unless stipulated otherwise in law, the notarization certificate comes into effect as of the date of issuance, and the approval date is the date of issuance.

4. Time period, termination and rejection

A notary office shall perform all notarization acts in time and shall finish within one month after it accepts the notarization request. Where the request concerns a matter involving a major and complicated situation, lack of evidence or the need of power of attorney in investigation, the time period to finish notarization can be accordingly extended, but to no more than six months, with the approval of the director and deputy director of the notary office. The party concerned shall be informed of the reasons of extension. The time for force majeure shall not be included in the aforesaid time period.

A notary office shall terminate a notarization act under any of the following circumstances:

(1) The notarization cannot be finished within six months due to reasons caused by the party concerned;

(2) The party concerned recalls the application before the notarization certificate comes into effect;

(3) The notary act cannot continue to be performed or it is of no significance for it to continue to be performed due to the death of the party concerned (termination of the legal person).

A notary office shall refuse to perform a notarization act when the acts, facts and documents are not authentic or lawful. The party concerned shall be notified in written form of the rejection. If the rejection leads to a lawsuit, the appeal procedure shall be made clear.

5. Special procedures:

This refers to procedures that must be observed for special notary cases, such as notarization for public bidding, lottery drawing and auctioning. For this kind of special notarization, the notary public must be present on the occasion, reading out notarial statement in the public for real and legal cases; and the notarial deed shall be issued to the party concerned.

6. Reconsideration:

This refers to the following case: When the party concerned appeals against the decision made by the notary office to dismiss or refuse to perform a notarization act or to demand discharging notarial deed, it may submit an application to the judicial administrative organ for reconsideration with the legally specified period of time; any who does not obey the decision with regard to the reconsideration may go to the court in the legally specified period of time.

Arbitration System

The arbitration system refers to the legal system under which both parties involved in the civil (business) disputes propose of their own accord to put their disputes to the chosen third party for ruling through a set of procedures, which is charged with the obligation of doing the ruling.

Arbitration is generally a civil action within certain industries. As a private conduct, i.e. a private, instead of national, judging conduct, it is, together with mediation and litigation, one of the mechanisms of resolving civil (commercial) disputes. However, the State conducts supervision over arbitration in accordance with the law. Through the people's court, the State intervenes in the effect of the arbitration agreement, the formulation of arbitration procedures and the execution of the arbitration awards and intervenes, when the party concerned does not execute voluntarily, in accordance with the provisions of the law of the place where the judgment occurs. Therefore, arbitration acts are of judicial nature and comprise an important part of the Chinese judicial system.

The Arbitration Law of the PRC, promulgated on August 31, 1994, has created a uniform arbitration system and adopted fundamental principles, systems and conventions generally used in the international community, which has made it possible for China's arbitration system to meet international standards.

Fundamental Principles of Arbitration

The fundamental principles of arbitration include:

1. Principle of voluntariness

The parties adopting arbitration for dispute settlement must reach an arbitration agreement on a mutually voluntary basis. An arbitration commission cannot accept an application for arbitration submitted by one of the parties in the absence of an arbitration agreement.

2. Principle of independence

Arbitration is conducted in accordance with the law, independent of any intervention by administrative organs, social organizations or individuals, which embodies as follows:

3. Principles of legitimacy and equality

The Arbitration Law prescribes that disputes should be fairly and reasonably settled by arbitration on the basis of facts and in accordance with the relevant provisions of law.

Arbitration Organs

Arbitration organs include:

1. Arbitration Association

The China Arbitration Association is a self-disciplining organization of arbitrators. It conducts supervision over the conduct (any breach of discipline) of arbitration commissions and their members and arbitrators in accordance with its articles of association. Arbitration commissions are members of the China Arbitration Association. The Articles of Association are formulated by a national general meeting of the members. The

Association formulates arbitration rules in accordance with the Arbitration Law and the Civil Procedure Law.

2. Arbitration Commission

Arbitration commissions are permanent arbitration organs and may be established in the municipalities directly under the Central Government, in the municipalities where the people's governments of provinces and autonomous regions are located or, if necessary, in other cities divided into districts. Arbitration commissions cannot be established at each level of the administrative divisions. The people's governments of the aforementioned municipalities and cities organize the relevant departments and the Chamber of Commerce for the formation of an arbitration commission. The establishment of an arbitration commission shall be registered with the judicial administrative department of the relevant province, autonomous region or municipalities directly under the Central Government.

Beijing Arbitration Commission: http://www.bjac.org.cn/
Tianjin Arbitration Commission: http://www.tjac.org.cn/
Shanghai Arbitration Commission: http://web.biz.sh.cn/

Foreign-Related Arbitration

The China International Economic and Trade Arbitration Commission is the only arbitration organ accepting international economic and trade arbitration. With its headquarters in Beijing, it has branches in Shanghai and Shenzhen Special Economic Zone, respectively. In April, 1987, China acceded to the Convention of the Recognition and Enforcement of Foreign Arbitration Awards, i.e. the New York Convention and became an agreement country of the Convention. China's foreign-related arbitration awards may be recognized and executed in over 140 member countries of the Convention.

Before the Arbitration Law was implemented in 1995, all foreign-related arbitration cases in China were accepted by the China International Economic and Trade Arbitration Commission. After the Arbitration Law was promulgated, 95 percent of the parties concerned in foreign-related arbitration cases still filed for acceptance and arbitration awards with the China International Economic and Trade Arbitration Commission, which accepted 8,336 cases from 1995 to 2005, with 6,634 foreign-related cases.

In March, 1999, the Commission set up five arbitration offices in Dalian, Changsha, Chongqing, Chengdu, and Fuzhou for the first time. To date, it has set up, in its local branches, 19 arbitration offices, which act as professional arbitration liaison and publicizing organs of the Commission, providing for the party concerned with arbitration publicizing service, arbitration procedure consultation, and arbitration application transferring service, so as to form an arbitration publicizing network to facilitate the process for the party concerned.

Arbitration Tribunal

An arbitration commission shall not arbitrate a case directly after it accepted it; instead, it forms an arbitration tribunal to exercise arbitration power.

The organizational format of an arbitration tribunal falls into two categories: the collegiate system and the sole system. In the collegiate system, an arbitration tribunal comprises three arbitrators, one of whom presides. In the sole system, an arbitration tribunal comprises one arbitrator.

If the parties agree to form an arbitration tribunal comprising three arbitrators, each party shall select or authorize the chairmen of the arbitration commission to appoint one arbitrator. The third arbitrator shall be the presiding arbitrator and shall be selected jointly by the parties or be nominated by the chairman of the arbitration commission in accordance with a joint mandate given by the parties.

If the parties agree to have one arbitrator to form an arbitration tribunal, the arbitrator shall be selected jointly by the parties or be nominated by the chairman of the arbitration commission in accordance with a joint mandate given by the parties.

Arbitrators

Arbitrators must fulfill one of the following conditions:

1. They have been engaged in arbitration work for at least eight years;

2. They have worked as a lawyer for at least eight years;

3. They have been a judge for at least eight years;

4. They are engaged in legal research or legal teaching and in senior positions; and

5. They have legal knowledge and are engaged in professional work relating to economics and trade, and in senior positions or of the equivalent professional level.

The arbitration commission establishes a list of arbitrators according to different professionals to facilitate the selection of arbitrators by the party concerned.

System of Trial or Arbitration

The system of trial or arbitration is the basic system of the arbitration law, referring to the system in which there will be both arbitration and trial or just one of the two when the parties concerned choose a solution to the dispute.

The system of trail or arbitration reflects respect to the rights of the parties concerned to select dispute-resolving mechanism. It means the following:

1. If the parties concerned have concluded arbitration agreement, the people's court's jurisdiction over the dispute is excluded, which means only an arbitration application may be filed with an arbitration organ and actions may not be submitted to a people's court.

2. Although the arbitration agreement signed by the parties excludes a people's court's jurisdiction over the dispute, the latter may have jurisdiction over disputes which the parties have concluded an arbitration agreement upon under the following circumstances:

A. The arbitration agreement has become invalid;

B. Where the parties agreed on an arbitration agreement. But, if one of the parties initiates an action before a people's court, the other party responds to the action and conducts substantial defense without objecting to the jurisdiction issue, the arbitration agreement shall be considered to have been waived by the party and the people's court shall proceed with the hearing.

Mediation System

Mediation is a consensual process in which a third party (or third parties), works with the disputants, through intervention and persuasive education, to help them reach a mutually acceptable resolution in accordance with the law. The mediation system comprises the following four categories:

(1) People mediation, i.e. civil mediation, an alternative dispute resolution, is the process in which the people's mediation committee mediates civil disputes.

(2) Court mediation is a mediation conducted within a litigation process, in which the people's court mediates civil cases, economical disputes and minor criminal cases. Mediation within a litigation process is compulsory for marriage cases, which is not for other civil cases, where the parties concerned can voluntarily decide whether to accept mediation or not. A court mediation agreement has the same effect as a court written judgment.

(3) Administrative mediation, which comprises the following two categories:

One category is the mediation of general civil disputes conducted by the people's government at the basic level, i.e. government of county and township level, which is an alternative dispute resolution.

The other category is the mediation of specific civil disputes, economic disputes or labor disputes conducted by State administrative organs in accordance with the law, which is also an alternative dispute resolution.

(4) Arbitrational mediation, another alternative dispute resolution, is the mediation of cases that have been accepted for arbitration by an arbitration institution. Arbitration will be conducted if the mediation fails.

People mediation shall following the basic principles of reasonableness and law, voluntariness and equality, and respecting litigation.

People's Mediation Committee

The people's mediation committee is a mass organization that mediates civil disputes. It can be set up in the following forms: (1) a people's mediation committee set up by a villagers committee in rural areas and a residents committee in a urban area (a community); (2) a people's mediation committee set up by a county, a town or a neighborhood; (3) a people's mediation committee set up by an enterprise or an institution according to its needs; and (4) a people's mediation committee set up within a region or within an industry according to needs.

A people's mediation committee can mediate a dispute upon the application filed by the parties concerned. Under circumstances when no application is filed, a people's mediation committee can voluntarily mediate unless the parties concerned have objection. A people's mediation committee shall not charge for civil dispute mediation.

Parties concerned involved in a dispute shall enjoy the following rights during the process of a mediation: (1) Voluntarily deciding whether to accept, reject or terminate a mediation; (2) Requesting that a relevant mediator be withdrawn from his office; (3) Expressing will and proposing reasonable requests without being forced to do so; and (4) Voluntarily reaching a mediation agreement.

The intermediators of the People's Mediation Committee of the Beishan Community of the Xihu District of Hangzhou City are hanging the new badge of People's Mediation in the Intermediation Room.

At present, 860,000 people's mediation committees have been established all over the country. The 6.6 million people's mediators mediate some 6 million civil disputes of various natures each year, with a success rate of over 95 percent. The responsibility of a people's mediation committee is not only to resolve disputes passively, but also to combine prevention and resolution together so as to actively prevent the occurrence and reduce the number of civil disputes, and to prevent the worsening of existing disputes.

People's Mediator

A people's mediator is elected by the masses or appointed, and is engaged in the work of people mediation under the leadership of a people's mediation committee. All members of a people's mediation committee and mediators are referred to as people's mediators. A people's mediation committee of a region where more than one ethic groups reside should include minority members. Woman members should also be included in a people's mediation committee. A people's mediator must be impartial, well connected with the masses, enthusiastic in people mediation and be an adult citizen with certain level of education and legal knowledge of governmental policies. Members of a people's mediation committee of a county, township or neighborhood shall at least finish high school. The term of office of a people's mediator is three years. Re-election, continuance in office and reappointment are allowed.

Mediation Procedure

The following procedures shall be following in the process of people mediation

1. Acceptance of the petition for mediating a dispute;
2. Preparations for mediation;
3. Mediation;
4. Reaching mediation agreement;
5. End of mediation.

Methods of Mediation

The modes of mediation include: direct mediation, public mediation, co-mediation and joint mediation. The methods commonly used are: teaching through concrete actions, arousing sympathy emotionally, and explaining the law with politeness.

Where a dispute resolved by a people's mediation committee is related to civil rights and liabilities, or where the parties concerned request that a mediation agreement in writing be produced this should be complied with. A mediation agreement is not enforceable. If the parties concerned fail to carry out the mediation agreement or retract after a mediation agreement is reached, a people's mediation committee shall, according to various situations, urge the parties concerned to fulfill the agreement, modify the contents of the original agreement or revoke the original agreement, notify the parties concerned to request intervention from local people's government and bring a law suit to a people's court concerning the fulfillment, modification and revocation of the mediation agreement, respectively. In accordance with Provisions of the Supreme People's Court about Several Issues Concerning the Handling of Civil Cases Relating to A People Mediation Agreement, agreement with contents of civil rights and liabilities, reached through mediation by a people's mediation committee, and signed or stamped by both parties concerned is of the nature of a civil contract. Parties concerned shall fulfill their liabilities in accordance with the agreement and shall not modify or revoke the mediation agreement without authorization.

State Compensation System

The Law of the PRC on State Compensation was adopted on May 12, 1994 at the Eighth National People's Congress. Article 2 stipulates: If a State organ or a member of its personnel, when exercising functions and powers in violation of the law, infringes upon the lawful rights and interests of a citizen, legal person or other organization and causes damages the aggrieved person shall have the right to recover damages from the State in accordance with this Law.

The Law stipulates two types of State compensation, i.e. administrative compensation and judicatory (criminal) compensation.

Administrative Compensation

Administrative compensation refers to the system in which if an administrative organ or a member of its personnel, when exercising functions and powers in violation of the law, infringes upon the lawful rights and interests of a citizen, legal person or other organization and causes damages, the state shall be responsible for compensation. Administrative compensation is a major component of the state compensation. In accordance with the Law on State Compensation, a claimant may independently file a claim for compensation with an organ under compensatory obligations and may, in the meantime, file a claim when applying for an administrative reconsideration and instituting an administrative procedure.

When independently filing a claim for compensation, a claimant, first, files it with an organ under compensatory obligations. Only where this organ fails to pay compensation or where the claimant is not satisfied with the amount, may the claimant then apply for a reconsideration with a relevant administrative organ or bring an action in a people's court. Independent claims for compensation with an organ under compensatory obligations are only suitable when both parties have no dispute regarding the illegal nature of the infringement or when the infringement is confirmed to be illegal or is revoked or modified.

Where a claimant files a claim for compensation when applying for administrative reconsideration and instituting an administrative procedure, the relevant organ or a people's court should first confirm the illegal nature of the administrative infringement, and then decide whether or not to pay compensation.

Judicatory (Criminal) Compensation

Judicatory compensation refers to the system in which, if an State organ or a member of its personnel, when exercising functions and powers in violation of the law, infringes upon the lawful rights and interests of a citizen, legal person or other organization and causes damage, the State is responsible for compensation. Criminal compensation is the core of judicatory compensation. The Law on State Compensation has one chapter dedicated to stipulations on criminal compensation system. In addition, it also stipulates State compensation in a situation where a people's court, in the course of a civil or administrative procedure, illegally undertakes compulsory measures, preservative measures or wrongful execution.

Criminal compensation refers to State compensation that occurs under circumstances where organs and their personnel exercising the functions and powers of detection, prosecution, adjudication and administration of prisons infringe the personal or property rights of a citizen when exercising their functions and powers. Where organs and their personnel exercising the functions and powers of detection, prosecution, adjudication and administration of prison infringe upon the lawful rights and interests of a citizen, legal person or other organization when exercising their functions and powers, the organs shall be responsible for fulfilling their compensatory obligations. When compensation is claimed, a claimant shall, first, file the claim with an organ under compensatory obligations. This must, within two months from the date of receipt, decide whether or not to pay compensation; in case of failure to pay within the period specified or where the claimant is not satisfied with the amount, the latter may apply for reconsideration by an organ at the next higher administrative level. Where the organ under compensatory obligations is a people's court, the claimant for compensation may apply to the compensation commission of the people's court at the next higher level. Where the claimant for compensation is not satisfied with the reconsideration decision or failure by the organ for reconsideration to make a decision within the period specified, he or she may apply for a decision of compensation to the compensation commission of the people's court at the same level at the place where the organ for reconsideration is located. An intermediate people's court or the people's court above the intermediate level shall set up a compensation commission consisting of three to seven judges.

Where a people's court, in the course of a civil or administrative procedure, illegally undertakes compulsory measures, preservative measures or wrongfully executes the judgment or award or other legal effective documents and which causes damages, the procedure for the claim of compensation by the claimant shall apply to the provisions of this Law concerning the procedures of criminal compensation.

Methods of Compensation

The main method of State compensation is payment of damages. Where the property can be returned or can be restored to the original state, it shall be returned or made restoration to the original state.

The expenses for compensation are listed in the fiscal budget of governments at all levels and shared by them in accordance with the fiscal management system. Where the claimant claims for State compensation, the organ under compensatory obligations, the organ for reconsideration and the people's court cannot bill the claimant. Taxes must not be levied on the compensation money obtained by a claimant.

The prescription of claim for State compensation by the claimant is two years, calculated from the day on which the act of exercising the functions and powers by the State organ and its personnel was confirmed as unlawful, but the period of custody should be excluded from the limitation of time. Where the claimant for compensation cannot exercise his or her right of claim due to force majeure or other obstacles during the last six months of the prescription of claim for compensation, the limitation of time shall be suspended. The time of prescription of claim for compensation shall resume from the day when the grounds for the suspension are eliminated.

Foreign-Related Compensation

Article 33 of the stipulates: This Law shall be applicable to such cases as claiming by a foreigner, foreign enterprise or organization in the territory of the PRC upon the PRC for State compensation. If the home nation of a foreigner, foreign enterprise or organization does not protect or imposes restrictions upon the rights of claiming for state compensation from it by a Chinese citizen, legal entity or other organization, the PRC shall follow the principle of reciprocity.... This provision not only reflects China's respect for the rights and interests of foreigners, foreign enterprises and organizations, but is also beneficial for China to safeguard its own sovereignty and dignity.

Legal Aid System

Legal aid, also referred to as legal assistance, is a kind of judicial relief system that is adopted by most countries in the world. It is a system in which the State reduces or exempts legal service fees for the disadvantaged group who can hardly safeguard their own basic social rights through usual legal methods due to financial difficulties and other reasons, so as to provide legal security system at all levels in the judicial system. As a State action, this system can help to realize social and judicial justice and to safeguard fundamental rights and interests of the citizens', and therefore is of great significance in China's judicial system.

In China's legislative history, legal aid was fist explicitly written into law when the new Criminal Procedure Law of the PRC was adopted on March 17, 1996, and Law of the PRC on Lawyers on May 15, 1996, and the scope in which Chinese citizens can obtain legal aid was specified. This laid a legal foundation for the formulation of a special statute concerning legal aid in the future. On May 26, 1997, the Legal Aid Center of the Ministry of Justice was officially set up in Beijing.

As of September 1, 2003, the Regulations on Legal Aid, the first statute of its kind in China, were put into effect. This means that a legal aid norm in China is available in the form of administrative regulations, marking the point where the legal aid cause in China is entering into a new stage. The aim of the Regulation is to guarantee that citizens with financial difficulties can access necessary legal service and to promote and standardize the work of legal aid.

Now there are thousands of government legal aid institutions covering the depth of the rural areas and poor families. Some 10,000 people are involved in the work. Governments at various levels have increased financial input

The staff members of the Free Legal Aids of Shenyang Farmer-workers Rights Protection Center help the farmers to get their wages.

in this field and the finances at the Central provincial level are establishing a system for the transfer for legal aid in the poverty-stricken areas. Over the past decade, some 1.6 million people received legal aid service. Recent years saw more social organs, non-governmental organizations and legal institutes of higher level are getting involved in the legal aid work.

Scope of Legal Aid

Those who cannot afford to authorize an agent, due to financial difficulties, for the six kinds of civil and administrative matters that require such agency may apply for legal aid with legal aid institutions. The aforementioned six kinds of matters include: claiming State compensation in accordance with the law; claiming to enjoy social insurance treatment or the lowest living guarantee treatment; claiming pensions and relief fees; claiming alimony and fees for bringing up or living up; claiming wages for labor; and civil rights and interests relating to brave deeds. The Regulations on Legal Aid also stipulates that all provinces, autonomous regions and municipalities directly under the Central Government may formulate supplementary regulations concerning legal aid items other than the aforementioned six matters.

If the accused in a criminal case is blind, deaf, dumb or a minor, or if it is possible for him or her to be sentenced to death but no defender is authorized, the people's court shall appoint a defense in accordance with the law, without having to investigate his or her financial difficulties. That is to say, in these kinds of criminal cases, there are no financial restrictions upon application for legal aid.

There is no national standard for the definition of "financial difficulties". People's governments of various provinces, autonomous regions and municipalities directly under the Central Government shall formulate the standards of financial difficulties of the citizens according to the economic development and the needs of the legal aid cause in their administrative regions. Where the standard of the applicant's residence area is different from that of where the legal aid institution is located, the latter's standard will be followed. Citizens must meet two requirements to be eligible to apply for legal aid, one being that the applicant must provide enough evidence proving that legal aid is needed to safeguard his or her own lawful rights and interests, the other being that the applicant must be unable to pay for the legal services due to financial difficulties.

Structure of Legal Aid Institutions

Currently, the structure of legal aid institutions in China has evolved into four levels:

1. At the State level, the Legal Aid Center of the Ministry of Justice was officially established on May 26, 1997, to guide and coordinate the work in legal aid throughout the country. The Center is mainly responsible for providing guidance to legal aid work and formulating rules and regulations in legal aid that apply to all over the country. Medium-term and long-term development plans and annual working plans are made to coordinate national wide legal aid work and to organize exchange activities with foreign legal aid groups and individuals.

China Legal Aid Foundation was set up on the same day. The foundation recruits, manages and uses legal aid funds to publicize China's legal aid system and to promote judicial justice. Funds come from donations and sponsorships of domestic groups, enterprises, and individuals; interests collected after the funds are deposited into a financial institution; and profit from negotiable securities such as bonds and stocks.

2. At the provincial level, provincial (autonomous regional) legal aid centers shall be established to guide and coordinate the legal aid work in their jurisdiction area.

3. At the regional and city level (including deputy-provincial level), regional and city legal aid centers shall be established to manage and implement local legal aid work.

4. At the county level, county legal aid centers shall be established where conditions are good enough to implement local legal aid work. Where conditions are not good enough, local legal aid work is implemented by the judicial bureau of the county.

Implementing Subjects and Fund Sources in Legal Aid

The three professional implementing subjects in China's legal aid system are lawyers, notaries and grassroots-level legal service people. Lawyers mainly provide litigation legal aid (including criminal defense, criminal agency and civil procedure agency etc.) and non-litigation legal aid. Notaries provide legal aid concerning notary matters. Grassroots-level legal service people provide simple legal aid service such as legal consultation, writing legal documents for others, and assistance in general non-litigation matters.

Legal aid funds in China come from three sources: the government, donations from the society and contribution made by the legal sector (mainly the free service provided).

The State encourages donations for legal aid activities from society. Social groups and institutions are encouraged to provide legal aid to citizens in financial difficulties using their own resources.

Liabilities in Legal Aid

Legal aid service people cannot accept money or things of value from the parties concerned. If any such items are accepted unlawfully, judicial administrative organs will order any illegal income to be returned. If a lawyer accepts money or things of value, a fine of no less than one and no more than three times the amount of the illegal income will be imposed.

If a law firm refuses to accept appointments by legal aid institutions and fails to arrange for its lawyers to handle legal aid cases, the Ministry of Justice renders administrative penalty. A lawyer faces an administrative penalty if he or she refuses to accept a legal aid case without justifiable reason or terminates a legal aid case without authorization. If a legal aid institution or a member of its personnel refuses to provide legal aid for those who meet the requirements, disciplinary measures will be taken against the person directly in charge and others who bear direct responsibilities.

National Judicial Examination

Starting from 2002, one must take a unified national judicial examination to obtain qualification to become a judge, a prosecutor or a lawyer.

Five-year Legislation Plan

The Standing Committee of the 10th National People's Congress formulated a legislative plan aiming at deliberating 76 draft laws in six fields in its five-year tenure. Among the 76 laws listed for drafting in the plan, one is the amendment to the constitution and the other 75 are laws on different issues, 27 of which is to be drafted by the Financial and Economic Affairs Committee. The Agriculture and Rural Affairs Committee is responsible for drafting farmers' cooperative economic organization law and the Budget and Work Committee is to draft financial transfer payment law. All these have made economic legislation a priority. The formulation or revision of these laws is of great significance to the formation of an economic legal system.

China's Police System

China's police system on the whole is divided into three systems: public order police, armed police and judicial police. As they assume different obligations and responsibilities, they are under different leading organs for convenience of administering and commanding. Each police system can be further divided into different police sorts according to different works in charge. Most of the public order police in China are under the leading of the Ministry of Public Security.

Public order police can be further divided into police for criminal cases (cracking criminal cases and arresting criminals, etc.), traffic police (administering traffic and vehicles), domiciliary register police (regional police and administration on residents' domicile), patrolmen (patrol and guarding), and fire police (fire fighting). Other police sorts assuming other important responsibilities can be put under the category of public order police, such as railway police and public order police guarding prisoners under the leadership of judiciary.

China's armed police are under the leading and commanding of the People's Armed Police Force General Headquarters. In terms of their responsibilities, they can be divided into internal security force, border security force, riot squad (special police) and forces guarding gold mines and water and electricity supply.

China's judicial police force is under the leadership of the Supreme People's Court and the Supreme People's Procuratorate and usually carries out such legal affairs as arresting and sending criminals under escort, standing on court and executing sentence.

China's Rank System of Police

Rank system of police is the designation and symbol for differentiating police grades and indicating the status of police, as well as the honor granted to police by the state. Modern rank system of police originated from West Europe. In 1829 France and the United Kingdom created modern police organizations and implemented rank system on police personnel. Therefore, other countries in the world implemented the system one after the other and a universal rank system gradually came into being for police.

Implementation of rank system on police is an important content in the reform of administrative system in Chinese police. On the 26th meeting of the Seventh National People's Congress held on July 1, 1992, Regulations of the PRC on People's Police Rank System. In December 1992 the State Council conferred ranks to people's police, and it is the first time to conferring ranks to people's police since the founding of the People's Republic of China.

The rank system of police includes 13 grades in 5 categories. The first category is Commissioner General and Deputy Commissioner General, approved and conferred by Premier of the State Council; the second category is Commissioner, including 3 grades, and the first and second grades approved and conferred by Premier of the State Council and the third grade approved and conferred by Minister of the Ministry of Public Security; the third category is Supervisor, including 3 grades approved and conferred by Minister of the Ministry of Public Security; the fourth category is Superintendent, including 3 grades approved and conferred by head of Office (Bureau) of Public Security of each province, autonomous region and municipality; and the fifth category is Constable, including 2 grades approved and conferred by director of Department of Politics under Office (Bureau) of Public Security of each province, autonomous region and municipality. The Superintendent and Constable of organs of Ministry of Public Security and other organs directly under it are approved and conferred by director of Department of Politics of Ministry of Public Security.

Tactical performance of special policemen

♦ The Ministry of Justice

The Ministry of Justice takes in charge of the legal work under the leadership of the State Council.

The Ministry of Justice is responsible for the nationwide justice administration within the justice-administrative system of China. Its major responsibilities are:

1. Supervising the reform of offenders and the work of re-education-through-labor;
2. Supervising the practice of lawyers;
3. Supervising the practice of notarization;
4. Supervising training for judicial personnel;
5. Supervising education in jurisprudence;
6. Organizing activities for legal publicity;
7. Foreign-related judicial matters;
8. Conducting legal theory research in the field of justice administration and legal system.

Address: 10 Chaoyangmen Nandajie, Beijing
Website: http://www.legalinfo.gov.cn/

▲ Money Laundering Law

The Law of the PRC on Money Laundering, adopted at the 24th meeting of the Standing Committee of the 10th NPC, came into force on January 1, 2007. Provisions related to legal liabilities stipulate that, where a financial institution does not follow the legal provisions and thus allows money laundering, a fine of 500,000 Yuan up to 5,000, 000 Yuan will be imposed. The goal is to crack down on money-laundering as well as other relevant crimes and to safeguard the financial order and State economic security. The law mainly aims at providing norms for preventing and supervising money laundering, while rules of sanction and cracking down on money laundering crime are set by the criminal law; therefore, this law is restricted to the prevention and supervision of money laundering.

Internet

19 Internet

General Survey of Internet

Key Dates in the Internet Development of China

In 1987, Professor Qian Tianbai of Peking University sent out the first email [to Germany]. At that time, China had no access to the Internet.

In October 1991, the American Walter Toki set out a cooperative plan for bringing China into the Internet network at the Sino-America Annual Meeting of High Energy Physics.

In March 1994, China was given access to the internet network, with the necessary work for access expected to be completed by May.

In January 1995, the Directorate General of Telecommunications of the Ministry of Post and Telecommunications opened Beijing and Shanghai 64K leased lines to the United States, thus beginning to offer Internet access services through the telephone networks, DDN leased lines and X.25 networks.

In May 1995, Zhang Shuxin set up the first Internet service supplier Yinghaiwei, providing Chinese common people with access to the Internet.

During the period from April to July 2000, China's three portal websites i.e. Sohu, Sina and 163 were listed on the NASDAQ Exchange of America.

In the second quarter of 2002, Sohu recorded the first profits to highlight the potential of Internet business in China.

Number of IP Address in China

China has been allocated with 118 million IPv4 addresses. It owns 4.4 percent of such addresses, ranking third in the world behind the United States (59.7 percent) and Japan (6.6 percent). As China's National Internet Registry, CNNIC has an IP address allocation window of 4B rating, largest throughout the world. CNNIC can allocate over 260,000 IP addresses at one time and needing no examination by APNIC.

China's research on IPv6 address assignment is still in its initial stage. The Chinese mainland has been allocated 27 blocks of /32 of IPv6 address. By the end of April 2007, the global top five countries in IPv6 addresses allocated were Germany, France, Japan, Korea and Italy. Japan and Korea in the Asia-Pacific Region are surging ahead in the development of IPv6; the Chinese mainland ranks 15th in the world for the amount of IPv6 addresses.

Number of Chinese Domain Names

So far, CN domain names have accounted to 58.9 percent of China's total domain names, with an annual growth rate of 416.5%. The registration number of ccTLD exceeds that of gTLD in China. Compared with other countries, China's ccTLD number ranks second, to Germany. From the view of per capita resources, there are 70 domain names for every 10,000 Chinese.

Number of Websites in China

So far, every 10,000 persons have 10 websites in China.

China's International Bandwidth

A country's international bandwidth indicates its connection capability with the international Internet. China's international bandwidth has been growing at an annual rate of over 40 percent almost every year. China has an international bandwidth of 312,346Mbps and it is connected with the United States, Russia, France, Britain, Germany, Japan, Korea and Singapore, etc. Every 10,000 Chinese internet users enjoy a bandwidth of 19.3Mbps.

Internet international access can only be conducted by China's operators. In China, Chinanet occupies the majority of the international outlet bandwidth, as high as 155,705Mbps and CNC is next with bandwidth of 122,066Mbps.

IPv4 Address Quantities in Chinese Mainland, Hong Kong, Macao and Taiwan(2007)

Region	Address quantity
Chinese Mainland	118,248,192
Taiwan	18,731,776
Hong Kong	6903808
Macao	146688

IPv6 Address Quantities in Chinese Mainland, Hong Kong, Macao and Taiwan(2007)

Region	Address quantity
Chinese Mainland	27 blocks /32
Taiwan	2308 blocks /32
Hong Kong	9 blocks /32
Macao	2 blocks /32

Domain Names in China(2007)

	Number	Percentage
CN	6149851	67.0%
COM	2301912	25.1%
NET	553372	6.0%
ORG	174304	1.9%
Total	9179439	100.0%

CN domain names in China(2007)

	Number	Percentage
.CN	3620051	58.9%
.COM.CN	2018880	32.8%
.NET.CN	215797	3.5%
.ADM.CN	147121	2.4%
.ORG.CN	103585	1.7%
.GOV.CN	31093	0.5%
.AC.CN	10178	0.1%
.EDU.CN	3139	0.1%
.MIL.CN	7	0.0%
Total	6149851	100.0%

Websites in China(2007)

	Number	Percentage
CN	813357	62.0%
COM	399004	30.4%
NET	85355	6.5%
ORG	13884	1.1%
Total	1311600	100.0%

CN Website Number in China(2007)

	Number	Percentage
.CN	498635	61.3%
.COM.CN	261842	32.2%
.NET.CN	21057	2.6%
.GOV.CN	15334	1.9%
.ORG.CN	8927	1.1%
.ADM.CN	7108	0.8%
.AC.CN	453	0.1%
.MIL.CN	1	0.0%
Total	813357	100.0%

Access Methods of Internet Users in China

Access methods of internet users in China are mainly classified into broadband (including dedicated lines) access, dial-up access and wireless access.

Broadband: Of the total 210 million Internet users, broadband (including dedicated lines) users reach 122 million. The increase in broadband users implies that the access conditions in China have been further improved and therefore more users can enjoy faster speed and more stable connection. ADSL and dedicated lines account for a considerable proportion of broadband users.

Dial-up access: More than 31.60 million users are dial-up users.

Wireless access: Wireless users total 55.64 million at present, and in particular the size of mobile phone users is 44.30 million.

Internet Penetration Rate in China

The Internet penetration rate in China has reached 12.3 percent. By June 2007, the total of Internet users had reached 162 million, next only to the 211 million of United States. The growth rate in the number of internet users in China in that year was 31.7 percent.

Gender Structure of Chinese Internet Users

Female Internet users total 73 million and their male counterparts 89 million. The proportion of female Internet users is 45.1 percent [compared to a population breakdown of 51.5 percent male to 48.5 percent female].

Age Structure of Chinese Internet Users

Age groups of Internet users are inversely proportional to their specific proportion among all users. Of the total 162 million Internet users, 82.94 million are under the age of 25, accounting for 51.2 percent, and those aged up to 30 accounts for 70.6 percent. There are only 1.7 million Internet users among the population aged over 60 years.

According to the level of Internet penetration rate, China's population can be roughly classified into four groups: the first consists of those aged below 18, whose Internet penetration rate is 8.9 percent; the second is the youth group aged 18 to 30, whose rate hits 34.5 percent, indicating that more than one out of three persons access the Internet; the third one is the young and middle-aged group at the age of 31 to 50, and the rate is 10.5 percent, indicating that more than one out of 10 persons accesses the Internet; the fourth includes middle-aged and elderly people at the age of above 50, and the rate is only 1.7 percent, indicating that only about one out of 50 persons accesses the Internet.

Structure of Chinese Internet Users in Terms of Education Level

A large proportion of Chinese Internet users hold high academic degrees. Those with tertiary education total 71.21 million, accounting for 43.9 percent, of which 50 percent have received undergraduate education or higher; thos e with junior secondary education or less amount to 35.43 million.

The structure of Internet users has undergone changes in terms of educational level, with the proportion of these holding higher academic degrees declining and those holding lower degrees gradually increasing.

Structure of Chinese Internet Users in Terms of Profession

The proportion of student users is quite large: up to 36.7 percent. Of the 216 million students, Internet users reach 59.45 million, with an Internet penetration rate up to 27.5 percent, that is, one out of four students is an Internet user. Company employees account for more than 40 million users. Moreover, the number of unemployed and freelancers are also large, exceeding 16 million respectively.

The non-student users, which have larger consumption capacity than student users, are more valuable to Internet firms. As shown in the curve of development, the number of non-student users with larger consumption capacity has been going up steadily, and is close to 103 million at present.

Equipment of Chinese Internet Users for Connection to the Internet

Computers (including desktops and laptops) are the major basic equipment for connection to the Internet. China's computer hosts now amount to 67.10 million. In per capita terms, this represents 0.41 computers because a high proportion of Internet users surf online in Internet cafés and many users don't possess their own computers.

As to the equipment adopted, the desktop unit predominates, but diversification is coming. So far, over 96 percent of Internet users use desktops to access to the Internet. Laptops are now entering Internet users' daily life with about 20 percent of Internet users using them to go online. Another big change is that WAP has become a fashion with 27.3 percent of Internet users using mobile phones to access the Internet.

Home Surfing Equipment in China

The home is the most important site for Internet surfing. According to the experience of Internet developed countries, the higher the Internet development degree the higher the proportion of surfing online at home. For example, the proportion of surfing at home is 97 percent in South Korea and 93 percent in Hong Kong. China is also witnessing an escalating proportion of surfing at home with a current rate of 73 percent.

CNNIC data indicates that the proportion of families connected to the Internet is only 13.0 percent.

International bandwidth of seven backbone Networks in China(2007)

	International bandwidth (Mbps)
CHINANET	155705
CHINA169	122066
CSTNET	17710
CERNET	4796
CMNET	8260
UNINET	3807
CIETNET	2
Total	312346

Internet Access Expenses in China

In China, Internet access expenses are falling year after year. It is no longer the exclusive activity of high earners but is becoming an everyday commodity accessible by ordinary people.

Over 90 percent of the 210 million Chinese Internet users pay their own Internet

Age Structure of China's Internet Users

(2007年)

35.00%
30.00%
25.00%
20.00%
15.00%
10.00%
5.00%
0.00%
8.90%
34.50%
10.50%
1.70%
0-18 years
18-30 years
31-50 years
50 years and over

Hours that the Internet Users Spend on Average Online per Week

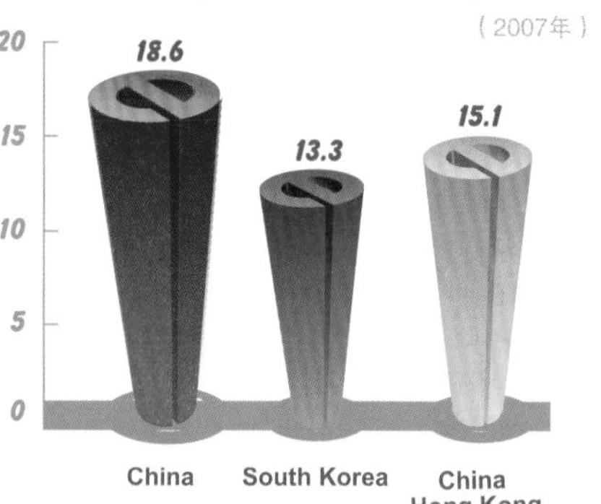

access expenses, 71.7 percent paying in full; only eight percent don't pay by themselves.

Per capita access expenses are now 75.1 Yuan per month. Improving income levels and falling access expenses will certainly promote Internet access. In light of the access expenditure pattern, 44.6 percent of Chinese Internet users, at their own expense, spent less than 50 Yuan per month for access to the Internet.

There is a little difference between student and non-student users. The access expenditure of student users is 63.6 Yuan per month on average and 80.8 Yuan for non-students.

Duration of Surfing Online

Now, the weekly surfing average is 18.6 hours, a little longer than that in South Korea (13.3 hours) and Hong Kong (15.1 hours).

There is difference in online time for different types of Internet users. Compared by gender, male Internet users spend longer time online, averaging 20.6 hours a week, compared to females with 16 hours. Student users have less online time due to having to attend classes than non-student users - 12 hours a week compared to 22.4 hours.

Application of Internet in China

After much development, the functions of the Internet have developed into four aspects at least, i.e. information channel, communications tool, recreation tool and assistance in daily living. Its information channel function is mainly through online news, search engines and blogs; its communication application is represented by email and instant messaging; its typical recreation function takes the forms of online music, online cinema and television, and online games; its role in daily living is demonstrated in such matters as online hunting for a job, online education, online shopping, online travel reservations, online banking and online stock transactions. The Internet is widely used as an information channel, communications tool and recreation tool, but the utilization rate in daily living is still low.

China's Internet Industry

Many indexes on the market of China's Internet industry indicate the industry entered rapid development from 2005 after experiencing ups and downs and adjustments. The market index of a few key fields such as the network advertising surpassed a market penetration rate of five percent. Among various sectors, the network advertising (excluding search engines) and online game fields saw high growth, followed by such services featuring Web2.0 as blog, personal portal/space and Odeo/video as well as new services of the broadband tide such as Witkey, video on demand and live broadcasting and video search engines.

Network Advertising

The annual growth rate of network advertising in China stands between 40 to 50 percent. However, that of overall advertising (including both traditional and network advertising is 15 to 20 percent.

The industry concentration ratio of advertisers tends to fall as the market share of network advertising becomes more widely distributed. The advertising income of vertical websites boasts huge potential in growth. Though network advertising the income of the three major portal websites keeps growing, but their

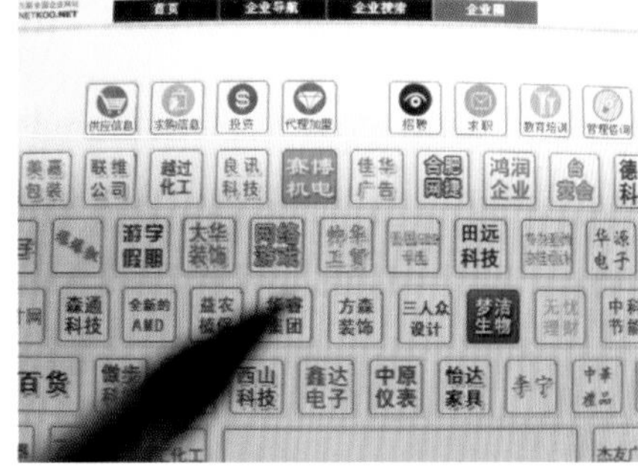

The advertisement positions on the Internet

proportion in the total market scale is decreasing. The income proportion of Sina in that of the overall advertising market has fallen from 41.5 to 20.4 percent, that of Sohu from 18.5 to 13.9 percent and that of 163 to less than 10 percent.

Views of Chinese Internet Users

The internet satisfaction rate of Chinese users is 60.5 percent. Rich content is the most satisfactory factor with an 81.1 percent rating; however, Internet expenditure has only a 24.6 percent approval rate.

Internet users have little trust in the Internet and only 35.1 percent of users claimed to believe what they see; the higher the education level, the less confidence they have.

Computer World

The newspaper *Computer World*, established in 1980, is jointly published by the Electronic Science and Technology Information Research Institute of the Ministry of Information Industry and International Data Corp. It is the first newspaper for the computer and information industry and aims to accelerate the informatization development of various sectors. As the pioneer of Chinese IT, the newspaper has become the largest domestically.

Its domestic unitary issue number: CN 11-0132.

China Information World

China Information World is sponsored by the China Center for Information Industry Development and governed by the Ministry of Information Industry. It is a semi-weekly publication, with 300-odd editions. It issues six major publications namely *News, China Informatization, Network and Communication, Products and Application, Software and Service and Channel and Market* every Monday. Its five regional special publications covering eastern, southern, southwestern, northeastern and northwest China are the most popular professional IT media in regional markets.

Its domestic unitary issue number: CN11-00004

Computer Newspaper

Computer Newspaper, established in 1992, is a weekly sponsored by the Chongqing Association for Science and Technology. Currently, it boasts a circulation of 650,000 copies, ranking first among the newspapers on electronics and computer in China for running years.

Its domestic unitary issue number: CN50-0005

China Internet Weekly

China Internet Weekly focuses on commercial trends and technical revolution, hence forming a distinct style. It is adept in giving forward-looking reports on business ideas and technical trends. It is controlled by the Chinese Academy of Science and published by Science Press every Monday. Its weekly circulation is 150,000. Its core readers are key management people in enterprises and professional specialists.

Its domestic unitary issue number: CN 11-3925

China Internet Network Information Center

China Internet Network Information Center (CNNIC), the state network information center of China, was founded as a non-profit organization on June 3, 1997. As the creator and operator of the infrastructure of the Chinese information society, CNNIC commits itself to "providing service for Internet users and promoting the sound and orderly development of the Internet in China". It takes charge of managing and maintaining the system of Chinese websites, leads the development of Chinese websites, issues authoritative statistical information on China Internet and represents China in the international Internet community.

Address: 1st Floor, No.1 Building of the Software Garden of Chinese Academy of Science, 4 Nansi Jie, Zhongguancun, Beijing
Website: http://www.cnnic.cn

Data Center of the China Internet (DCCI)

DCCI provides an independent platform for uniform market monitoring and audience measurement as well as for professional data collection and research. Through online and offline channels, the center conducts dynamic and accurate monitoring, measuring, statistics, analysis, research and forecasting. Data service products include net measurement, net monitoring and net guidance.

Address: Room 1905, No.16 Building, Jianwai Soho, No.39 Dongsanhuan Zhonglu, Chaoyang District, Beijing
Website: http://www.dcci.com.cn

Internet Society of China

Inaugurated on May 25, 2001, it has more than 70 sponsors, including network access carriers, ISPs, facility manufacturers and research institutes etc. ISC has 200-odd members, most of whom are organizational members. They are legal companies, research institutes, academic associations, universities and other organizations engaged in various activities related with the Internet. There are also some personal members well-known in China Internet community. Its governor is the Ministry of Information Industry.

Address: 9th Floor, East Building A, Tianyin Mansion, No.2-Yi Nan Dajie, Fuxingmen, Beijing
Website: http://www.isc.org.cn

Beijing Digital Imperial Palace was completed. The tourists could appreciate the rare treasures from any orientation and angle of view through remote control.

Utilization Rate of Internet Application in China(2007)

	Utilization rate		Utilization rate
Information		Life assistance	
News	77.3%	Look for jobs	15.2%
Search Engine	74.8%	Online education	24.0%
Blog Writing	19.1%	Online shopping	25.5%
Communication		Online sales	4.3%
Instant message	69.8%	E-journal	3.9%
Email	55.4%	Online banking	20.9%
Entertainment		Stock	14.1%
Online music	68.5%		
Online video	61.1%		
Internet games	47.0%		

The 50 Sub-divided Fields of China Internet Industry and Arrival Size of Users (2006)

(The annual arrival size of users for certain Internet service refers to the total number of the users who utilized the service in the past year.)

50 Sub-divided fields	Arrival Size of users (Unit: million)
Search Engines	122
Portal	121
Email	119
Instant Messengers	119
Download Softwares	117
News	117
Network Security Product Service	116
Software Download	115
Internet Access	114
Online Community/BBS	109
Audio/Music Search Engines	106
Information Technology	104
Blog	101
Music	100
IP Phone Services	100
Online Games	100
Picture/Photography/Album Websites	98
Video on Demand and Live Broadcasting	98
Entertainment Websites	97
C2C Electronic Commerce	93
Network Advertising	93
Online Banking	92
Literature Websites	91
Map Information	90
Game Information	89
Website Navigation	88
Online Recruiting	87
Education Websites	87
Sports Websites	87
Video Search Engines	82
Electronic Payment	82
Health Websites	81
Friend-making Websites	78
Personal Portal and Space	78
Finance	77
Odeo/Video Share	76
Local Portal	76
B2C electronic commerce	74
Cartoons	73
Auto	72
Witkey	72
Online Yellow Pages	68
B2B electronic commerce	67
Women Websites	66
Real Estate	64
Life Service	63
Digital Magazine	63
Domain Name and Hosting Service	62
Traveling Reservations	62
Classified Information	53

Satisfaction Scores of the Internet in China (2007)

Item	Satisfaction score	Item	Satisfaction score
Richness of content	4.07	Propemess	3.26
Speed	3.36	Security	3.01
Facticity of content	3.43	Expenses	2.86
Total satisfaction degree	3.65		

Note: The highest score is set to 5, with 1 the lowest; all scores are average scores.

The 10 Hot Fields in Chinese Internet and the Annual Arrival Rate of Users of Major Websites (2007)

(The annual arrival rate of users refers to the proportion of the total number of the users who utilized the service in the past year in the total size of Internet users in China. The proportion is not more than 100 percent.)

I Portal	
Sina: 55.53%	www.sina.com.cn
163: 51.31%	www.163.com
QQ: 48.02%	www.qq.com
II Blog	
Sina: 32.86%	www.blog.sina.com.cn
Qzone: 19.28%	www.qzone.qq.com
MSN: 15.8%	www.spacemsn.net
Independent blog	
Bokee: 11.66%	www.bokee.com
Blogcn: 11.65%	www.blogcn.com
Anyp: 3.32%	www.anyp.cn
III Instant Messenger	
QQ: 78.73%	www.qq.com
MSN: 34.37%	www.messenger.msn.com
Sina UC: 11.38%	www.uc.sina.com.cn
IV Search Engines	
Baidu: 80.79%	www.baidu.com
Google: 36.38%	www.google.cn
Yahoo: 25.99%	www.yahoo.cn
V Auto Websites	
Sina auto: 16.76%	www.auto.sina.com.cn
Sohu auto: 11.65%	www.auto.sohu.com
Pcauto: 10.67%	www.pcauto.com.cn
Independent auto websites	
Pcauto: 10.67%	www.pcauto.com.cn
China cars: 8.89%	www.chinacars.com
Auto home: 7.94%	www.autohome.com.cn
VI Operators of Oline Games	
QQ: 36.89%	www.game.qq.com
Ourgame: 20%	www.ourgame.com
Shanda: 19.86%	www.shanda.com.cn
Independent operators of oline games	
Ourgame: 20%	www.ourgame.com
Shanda: 19.86%	www.shanda.com.cn
Tiancity: 10.3%	www.tiancity.com
VII Odeo/Video Share	
Tudou: 9.86%	www.tudou.com
Youku: 8.91%	www.youku.com
Mofile: 8.7%	www.mofile.com
VIII C2C Electronic Commerce	
Taobao: 55.29%	www.taobao.com
eBay: 36.51%	www.eachnet.com
Paipai: 20.48%	www.paipai.com
IX Network Advertising	
E-mail advertising: 14.84%	
Advertising on portal websites: 14.39%	
Advertising on news websites: 13.99%	
X Map Service	
Baidu: 32.55%	www.map.baidu.com
Joinmap: 18.95%	www.joinmap.com
Go2map: 10.76%	www.go2map.com
Independent map service provider	
Joinmap: 18.95%	www.joinmap.com
Go2map: 10.76%	www.go2map.com
Hua2: 10.1%	www.hua2.com

19 Internet

E-Government

Introduction to E-Government of China

E-Government of China underwent early slow development and subsequent rapid development. The early development mainly embodied two aspects. Firstly, in the late 1980s, the OA project carried out by the central and local party organizations and government organs established various vertical and horizontal networks for internal information exchanges and work, laying a solid foundation for the utilization of computer technology in the domestic communications network. Secondly, three projects regarding informatization construction were launched at the end of 1993: the Golden Bridge Project, Golden Pass Project and Golden Card Project for promoting for governmental, customs and financial work respectively. Guided by the Central Government, they were implemented to transmit data and information for key industries and departments, becoming E-Government in a preliminary stage.

In the late 1990s, due to the rapid development of the information networking techniques and constant improvement of information infrastructure, E-Government broke of the departmental and regional restrictions, becoming interactive and accessible to Internet.

In January 1999, the information departments in charge of more than 40 ministries (bureaus and offices) jointly launched the "online government project". From then on, E-Government began to develop at a higher level. Many local governments, such as those of Shanghai, Shenzhen, Guangzhou and Tianjin, embarked on the construction of digital cities in which, the building of E-Government was a core element. More professional websites provided governmental services with increasingly richer content and stronger functions.

Governmental Portal Website

This serves as a core platform and a key channel for the government to publicize information on government affairs, serve enterprises and facilitate public participation. It offers the most direct access for the public to the government.

Over 97 percent of central ministries and commissions and more than 92 percent of local governments have websites. Among the local governments, over 91 percent of provincial governments and 95 percent of governments at prefectural or city level have portal websites, as do a large proportion of the governments at county level. The Websites of the governmental websites are classified as gov.

Website of the National People's Congress

Website: http:// www.npc.gov.cn

The website, with English and Chinese versions, run by the General Office, is the major authentic access to legislative and other information on NPC work. The website links the NPC to the local people's congresses and their deputies as well as vast numbers of people, helping the NPC to conduct its work and strengthen the transparency of that work. It focuses on reporting all major missions and activities of the NPC and its standing committee, releasing details of laws, resolutions/decisions and lists of appointments and removals passed by the standing committee.

It introduces the annotation of new laws, juridical questions and answers, special lectures on the Standing Committee, the history of the NPC and the texts of active laws and regulations and provides up-to-date information relevant to the NPC and authoritative law-related knowledge and various legal services. Through the links and e-mail, the website provides a convenient channel for communications and information exchanges.

Website of the National Committee of the Chinese People's Political Consultative Conference (CPPCC)

Website: http:// www.cppcc.gov.cn

The CPPCC is a patriotic united front organization and an important institution of multi-party cooperation and political consultation led by the CPC. The CPPCC National Committee is composed of representatives from the CPC and all the democratic parties as well as dignitaries without party affiliations; representatives of people's organizations, all the ethnic minorities and various sectors of society; representatives of compatriots from Hong Kong Special Administrative Region, Macao Special Administrative Region and Taiwan and of returned overseas Chinese; and specially-invited dignitaries. The main functions are political consultation, democratic supervision and participation in deliberations and administration of State affairs.

The website gives a comprehensive report on the main work and activities of the national committee of the CPPCC and important developments of the local committees of the CPPCC, systematically introduces the composition, work and activities of the CPPCC members. It also introduces the proposals, review reports and reports on special investigations of CPPCC members in an all-round way as well as various conferences and activities of the CPPCC.

The website has simplified and traditional Chinese editions as well as English edition.

Website of the Chinese Government

Website: http:// www.gov.cn

The official web portal of the Central People's Government of the PRC was formally launched on January 1, 2006. Xinhua News Agency takes charge of operational maintenance, content release and updating and technical construction and guarantees. Various regions and departments also provide content guarantees. It now has simplified and traditional Chinese editions as well as an English edition.

The website serves as a comprehensive platform for the State Council and various departments thereof as well as the people's governments of each province, autonomous region and municipality directly under the Central Government to release the information on government affairs and provide online services on the international Internet. It includes four parts concerning information on government affairs, services, mutual exchanges and application. The part of information on government affairs publicizes the major decisions, administrative regulations, official documents and developments of government work. The service part integrates online service items of various regions and departments and provides online services for citizens, enterprises and foreigners. The part of mutual exchanges offers a convenient and efficient channel for exchanges between government and people, facilitates the masses to make suggestions and the government to become acquainted directly with the social situation and public opinions. The application part plays an assistance role with search engines and navigation.

Its simplified and traditional Chinese editions contain 12 first-class topics such as China Today, China Fact File, State Structure, Government Structure, Laws and Regulations, Publication of Government Affairs, Mutual

The online interview at www.gov.cn.

Reaction on Government Affairs, Work Development, Government Construction, Personnel Appointment and Removal, Press Briefings and Online Service. Its English edition has seven topics including China Today, China Fact File, Services for Non-Residents, Business, Official Publications, Laws and Regulations and Special Reports.

Websites of Local Governments

The portal websites of the local people's governments, in line with unified deployment, are comprised of the central websites (namely the governmental websites of the province, autonomous regions and municipalities directly under the Central Government) and sub-websites (namely the governmental websites of the departments of and districts directly under the governments of the province, autonomous regions and municipalities directly under the Central Government).

The major responsibilities of the websites of local governments include: introducing the provincial situation and local information and providing service for investors and tourists; releasing the information on government affairs and promoting social surveillance; integrating information resources of the government system to meet social demand; conducting the online-work and actively promoting the public service. The websites involve various aspects of the work of the local governments such as releasing the business information and related policies and regulations, providing access for the public to make complaints, collecting public opinions, offering leaders' talks, conducting online survey and providing services for downloading tables and online enquiries.

Websites of the Ministries and Com missions of the State Council

Ministry of Foreign Affairs	www.fmprc.gov.cn
National Development and Reform Commission	www.sdpc.gov.cn
Ministry of Education	www.moe.edu.cn
Ministry of Science and Technology	www.most.gov.cn
State Ethnic Affairs Commission	www.seac.gov.cn
Ministry of Public Security	www.mps.gov.cn
Ministry of Supervision	www.mos.gov.cn
Ministry of Civil Affairs	www.mca.gov.cn
Ministry of Justice	www.legalinfo.gov.cn
Ministry of Finance	www.mof.gov.cn
Ministry of Personnel	www.mohrss.gov.cn
Ministry of Land and Resources	www.mlr.gov.cn
Ministry of Housing and Urban-Rural Development	www.mohurd.gov.cn
Ministry of Environmental Protection	www.mep.gov.cn
Ministry of Railways	www.china-mor.gov.cn
Ministry of Communications	www.moc.gov.cn
Ministry of Industry and Information Technology	www.miit.gov.cn
Ministry of Water Resources	www.mwr.gov.cn
Ministry of Agriculture	www.agri.gov.cn
Ministry of Commerce	www.mofcom.gov.cn
Ministry of Culture	www.ccnt.gov.cn
Ministry of Public Health	www.moh.gov.cn
State Family Planning Commission	www.chinapop.gov.cn
People's Bank of China	www.pbc.gov.cn
State Auditing Administration	www.audit.gov.cn

Websites of the Organizations Directly Under the State Council

General Administration of Customs	www.customs.gov.cn
State Administration of Taxation	www.chinatax.gov.cn
State Administration for Industry and Commerce	www.saic.gov.cn
General Administration of Quality Supervision, Inspection and Quarantine	www.aqsiq.gov.cn
State Administration of Radio, Film and Television	www.sarft.gov.cn
General Administration of Press and Publication (National Copyright Administration)	www.ncac.gov.cn
General Administration of Sport	www.sport.gov.cn
National Bureau of Statistics	www.stats.gov.cn
State Food and Drug Administration	www.sda.gov.cn
State Forestry Administration	www.forestry.gov.cn
State Intellectual Property Office	www.sipo.gov.cn
National Tourism Administration	www.cnta.com
Government Offices Administration of the State Council	www.ggj.gov.cn
State Bureau of Religious Affairs	www.sara.gov.cn
Counselors' Office of the State Council	www.counsellor.gov.cn
State Administration of Work Safety	www.chinasafety.gov.cn
Special Organization Directly under the State Council	
State-owned Assets Supervision and Administration Commission	www.sasac.gov.cn

Websites of the Administrative Offices under State Council

Information Office of the State Council	www.scio.gov.cn
Taiwan Affairs Office of the State Council	www.gwytb.gov.cn
Overseas Chinese Affairs Office of the State Council	www.gqb.gov.cn
Hong Kong and Macao Affairs Office of the State Council	www.hmo.gov.cn
Legislative Affairs Office of the State Council	www.chinalaw.gov.cn

Institutions Directly under the State Council

Xinhua News Agency	www.xinhuanet.com
Chinese Academy of Sciences	www.cas.ac.cn
Chinese Academy of Social Sciences	www.cass.net.cn
Chinese Academy of Engineering	www.cae.ac.cn
Development Research Center of the State Council	www.drc.gov.cn
National School of Administration	www.nsa.gov.cn
China Earthquake Administration	www.cea.gov.cn
China Meteorological Administration	www.cma.gov.cn
China Securities Regulatory Commission	www.csrc.gov.cn
China Insurance Regulatory Commission	www.circ.gov.cn
National Council for Social Security Fund	www.ssf.gov.cn
National Natural Science Foundation	www.nsfc.gov.cn
State Electricity Regulatory Commission	www.serc.gov.cn
China Banking Regulatory Commission	www.cbrc.gov.cn

Administrations and Bureaus under the Ministries and Commissions

State Bureau for Letters and Calls	www.gjxfj.gov.cn
State Administration of Grain	www.chinagrain.gov.cn
State Tobacco Monopoly Administration	www.tobacco.gov.cn
State Administration of Foreign Experts Affairs	www.safea.gov.cn
State Oceanic Administration	www.soa.gov.cn
State Bureau of Surveying and Mapping	www.sbsm.gov.cn
State Post Bureau	www.post.gov.cn
State Administration of Cultural Relics	www.sach.gov.cn
State Administration of Traditional Chinese Medicine	www.satcm.gov.cn
State Administration of Foreign Exchange	www.safe.gov.cn
State Archives Administration	www.saac.gov.cn

Websites of People's Organizations

All China Federation of Trade Unions	www.acftu.org
All-China Women's Federation	www.women.org.cn
Chinese Communist Youth League	www.ccyl.org.cn
All China Federation of Industry and Commerce	www.acfic.org.cn

Websites of Local Governments

Beijing	www.beijing.gov.cn
Tianjin	www.tj.gov.cn
Hebei	www.hebei.gov.cn
Shanxi	www.shanxi.gov.cn
Inner Mongolia	www.nmg.gov.cn
Liaoning	www.ln.gov.cn
Jilin	www.jl.gov.cn
Heilongiiang	www.hlj.gov.cn
Shanghai	www.shanghai.gov.cn
Jiangsu	www.jiangsu.gov.cn
Zhejiang	www.zj.gov.cn
Anhui	www.ah.gov.cn
Fujian	www.fujian.gov.cn
Jiangxi	www.jiangxi.gov.cn
Shandong	www.shandong.gov.cn
Henan	www.henan.gov.cn
Hubei	www.hubei.gov.cn
Hunan	www.hunan.gov.cn
Guangdong	www.gd.gov.cn
Guangxi	www.gxzf.gov.cn
Hainan	www.hainan.gov.cn
Chongqing	www.cq.gov.cn
Sichuan	www.sc.gov.cn
Guizhou	www.gz.gov.cn
Yunnan	www.yn.gov.cn
Tibet	www.xizang.gov.cn
Shaanxi	www.shaanxi.gov.cn
Gansu	www.gansu.gov.cn
Qinghai	www.qh.gov.cn
Ningxia	www.nx.gov.cn
Xinjiang	www.xinjiang.gov.cn
Hong Kong	www.gov.hk
Macao	www.gov.mo

Other State Organizations and Social Associations

International Communication Office of the CPC Central Committee	www.idcpc.org.cn
National Library of China	www.nlc.gov.cn
China Machinery Industry Federation	www.mei.gov.cn
China National Light Industry Council	www.clii.com.cn
China Building Material Industry Association	www.bm.cei.gov.cn
China Iron and Steel Association	www.mmi.gov.cn
All-China Federation of Industry & Commerce	www.acfic.org.cn
China National Coal Association	www.chinacoal.gov.cn
China National Textile and Apparel Council	www.ctei.gov.cn
All China Federation of Supply and Marketing Cooperatives	www.chinacoop.gov.cn
China Petroleum and Chemical Industry Association	www.cpcia.org.cn
State Information Center	www.sic.gov.cn
Central Compilation & Translation Bureau	www.cctb.net
All China Federation of Trade Unions	www.acftu.org
Chinese Communist Youth League	www.ccyl.org.cn
All-China Women's Federation	www.women.org.cn
All-China Youth Federation	www.acyf.org.cn
All-China Students' Federation	www.ccyl.org.cn
All-China Federation of Returned Overseas Chinese	www.chinaql.org
All-China Federation of Taiwan Compatriots	www.tailian.org.cn
China Association for Science and Technology	www.cast.org.cn
China Federation of Literary and Art Circles	www.cflac.org.cn
China Disabled Persons' Federation	www.cdpf.org.cn
China Chamber of International Commerce	www.ccpit.org
China Consumers' Association	www.cca.org.cn

Websites of Judicial Organs

The Supreme Court of the People's Republic of China	www.court.gov.cn
Supreme People's Procuratorate of the People's Republic of China	www.spp.gov.cn

19 Internet

Websites of Parties Participating in Politics

Revolutionary Committee of the Chinese Kuomintang	www.gdmg.org.cn
Chinese Democratic League	www.dem-league.org.cn
China Democratic National Construction Association	www.cndca.org.cn
China Association for Promoting Democracy	www.mj.org.cn
Chinese Peasants and Workers Democratic Party	www.ngd.org.cn
China Zhi Gong Dang	www.zg.org.cn
Jiu San Society	www.93.gov.cn
Taiwan Democratic SelfGovernment League	www.taimeng.org.cn

♦ godpp.gov.cn

Website: http:// www.godpp.gov.cn

This is sponsored by the Office of the Spiritual Civilization Steering Committee of the Communist Party of China's Central Committee, aiming to spread civilization and promote a new general mood. Its main channels include: Highlights Today, civilization building, publicity battlefront, leaders' activities, civilization commentary, current events bulletin, theory, social science planning, idea and politics research, System Reform, Literature and Art, News Press, call-board, Civilization Projects, morality building, spiritual cultivation, trust building, For Minor, online hero & model house, Red Tour, Charm Schools, Traditional Festivals, Civilized Supervision, New Countryside, Civilized City, Civilized Units, Civilized Scenic Areas, Information Center, Online Museum, Online exhibition, civilization on pictures, investigation collection, New Book Introduction, Civilization Forum, Civilization Interviews, Multimedia, Website Navigator.

♦ Chinahumanrights.org

Website: http:// www.chinahumanrights.org
http://www.humanrights.cn

This is a special website sponsored by the China Society for Human Rights Studies (CSHRS) and founded in August 1998. It has Chinese and English editions.

Dedicated to spreading information on China's human rights in a balanced and all-round way, it gives a complete, multi-dimensional introduction of China's human rights situation; with a great deal of vivid examples and data, it shows the march of China in building a harmonious society, the improvement of people's living conditions, and human rights guarantees and security provided by society; It conducts tracing reports on hot human rights problems and makes a deep analysis of them; it gives an systemic introduction of Chinese and foreign human rights views and academic achievements; it provides relevant knowledge and information channel for audiences to safeguard human rights according to law.

Electronic Commerce

Introduction to E-Commerce of China

E-Commerce refers to a new commercial operation mode, in which both sides in trade conducted business activities based on Internet explorer/server applications and using electronic data transmission, including online talk and electronic payment, thus realizing online shopping and transactions.

E-Commerce through the Internet may be grouped into three aspects: information services, transactions and payments. Its main content includes electronic business advertising, electronic shopping and transaction, exchange of electronic transaction voucher, electronic payment and settlement, and online after-sales services.

There are two major transaction types, namely, those between enterprise and individual (B to C) and those between enterprises (B to B). Entities participating in e-commerce include customers (individual consumer or enterprise), business (including seller, manufacturer and storage and transport company), banks (including issuing firms and separate admission) and certification center.

With the increase of China's Internet users, online shopping and electronic payment via internet have gradually become popular. E-Commerce has reached a certain scale, with its market shares increasing rapidly. Of them, B2B e-commerce accounts for about 95 percent E-Commerce has ushered in a new investment upsurge.

Electronic Commerce Mode

E-Commerce may be grouped into four varieties of modes, i.e., B2B, B2C, C2C and B2M.

B2B (Business to Business) e-commerce refers to the transaction activities between business (enterprise or companies) using Internet technology or various commercial network platforms. B2B transaction includes the following procedures: issuing supply and demand information, ordering goods and confirming an order, paying, signing and issuing, transmitting and receiving bills, confirming delivery schemes and monitoring delivery processes. In China, the representative B2B service providers include Alibaba and made-in-china.com.

B2C (business to customer) refers to that where the enterprise provides a new shopping environment—online store for consumers through the Internet while consumers conduct online shopping and payment. It is the e-commerce mode to emerge earliest in China, such 8848 online shopping mall. Now, the important B2C online shopping mall includes dangdang.com, Amazon.com.cn, ctrip.com, Elong.com and 139shop.com.

C2C (Consumer To Consumer) commerce platform provides the online transaction service for the buyer and seller. Namely, the seller may provide goods for online auction on one's own initiative while the buyer may voluntarily choose goods for price bidding, thus completing the transaction. The famous C2C websites in China include Taobao.com and EachNet.com.

Compared with B2B, B2C and C2C electronic commerce, B2M (Business to Manager) is a brand-new electronic commerce mode. The client group the B2M is geared to the enterprise, the seller of the products or operator for them, but not the end consumers.

Ordering dishes through palmtop in hotel

Major Websites for Individual Trade

The Mcdonald's Zone on the www.taobao.com, a famous shopping website of China.

Taobao.com

Website: http:// www.taobao.com

Taobao.com is an online C2C (Customer to Customer) individual transaction platform as well as China's largest online auction site, financed by the Alibaba Group.

Since it was founded on May 10, 2003, Taobao.com has become China's leading online shopping website, with its market share reaching about 70 percent. It has more than 30 million registered users. It offers a complete variety of commodities, including auto, computer, clothes, and home decor. It even set up an Internet game equipment trading area.

In regard to security, Taobao.com introduced the real name certification system. The system is divided into individual user and business user certification. They need to submit different information. For certification, the individual user is required to provide identification, while for the business user, the business license is also needed. A user is not allowed to apply for two kinds of certification. Taobao.com also introduced a credit evaluation system, under which users may click and see the past credit appraisal of the sellers.

In order to ensure safe payment between the buyer and seller, Taobao.com introduced the means of payment and delivery of goods, which is called "AliPay", to lower risk. As for goods with a high single price such as computers, mobile phones and jewelry, this transaction method is much safer.

PaiPai.com

Website: http:// www.paipai.com

PaiPai.com, an e-commerce transaction platform run by Tencent, officially went into operation on March 13, 2006. It is one of China's three most influential C2C platforms, alongside EachNet.com and Taobao.com, with more than 25 million registered users and over five million online goods.

At present, it mainly has eight major channels, Internet games, women's street, digital town, sports, books and audio-video products, QQ special area, students, and special offer. The QQ special area also includes QQ pet, QQ show, QQ Gongzi, and other special products and services of Tencent. Paipai.com also has online payment platform—Tenpay.

Dangdang.com

Website: http:// www.dangdang.com

Dangdang.com, went into operation in November 1999, and is the world's largest online Chinese book and audio-video product store, offering approximately 300,000 books and audio-video products for Chinese. It has served six million customers so far.

Dangdang.com spent six years in setting up a colossal S21211 logistics system, with approximately 20,000 square meters of warehouses distributed in Beijing, East China and South China. Its employees use logistics, customer management, financial affairs and other software independently developed by dangdang.com and based on network architecture and wireless technology, to deliver goods to various areas across China and the world via different transportation means such as air, rail and road. In 66 Chinese cities, many express companies provide "delivery to your door, cash on delivery" service for customers of dangdang.com.

EachNet

Website: http:// www.eachnet.com

EachNet is a joint-venture between eBay, the world's largest e-commerce company, and TOM Online, a portal website and a wireless Internet company in China, set up in December 2006.

With US$30 million investment from eBay, EachNet first formed a strategic partnership with the former in the late 1990s. In June 2003, EachNet received an additional investment of US$150 million from eBay, becoming a member of global eBay family. In July 2004, EachNet introduced its new brand "eBay EachNet". In December 2006, eBay cooperated with TOM Online to introduce the online trading platform tailor-made for the Chinese market.

Known as TOM eBay, it has a deep knowledge of Chinese netizens' online shopping habits so that eBay is become almost a pure local C2C enterprise.

Liba.com

Website: http:// www.liba.com

Liba.com, originally called 51tuangou.com, is Shanghai's first group purchase website, mainly geared to family consumption, with branches in Shanghai, Hangzhou and Nanjing.

Founded in 2003, it devotes itself to provide a living and consuming guide for young families and transaction services. At present, it has successfully offered decoration, wedding and auto services to more than 80,000 young families. It has over 1.4 million registered users. Its business covers 14 categories of living and consumption sectors, such as decoration, wedding, baby, auto, food, travel, real estate and financing.

7cv.com

Website: http:// www.7cv.com

7cv.com, founded in 1999 with the support of oversea risk investment, is a large-sized B2C e- commerce company specializing in online shopping.

"7cv Shopping Mall" is a website dealing with sexual well-being products, which include seven categories, i.e., health care products, restorative and Yang-strengthening products, erotic underclothes, cosmetics, personal care products, contraception and pregnancy test products and adult erotica products, totaling 6,000 kinds of commodities. 7cv.com ranks first in online sale volume in all its product lines.

www.7cv.com has over one million registered users and visits of more than 400,000 person times each day. The goods may be ordered online or via telephone, mail, fax and e-mail. Delivery means door-to-door, common mail, EMS, and international distribution. It also provides cash-on-delivery service in China's 1,522 cities.

Joyo

Website: http:// www.amazon.cn

Joyo founded in January 2000, received investment from Tiger Fund, a global famous investment institution in September 2003, becoming the third largest stockholder. In August 2004, Amazon.com (NASDAQ: AMZN) announced its purchase of amazon.cn. At present, amazon.cn deals with more than 300,000 varieties of books and audio-video products. At the same time, its toy/gift, home decor/cosmetic, maternity & baby products, home appliance, clock and watch accouterment, kitchen utensils, IT digital products, and mobile phone stores also contain tens of thousands of products under its new name of Joyo [www.joyo.com].

Joyo is one of the busiest online retailer stores on mainland China in website visits and quantity of daily order. Its business scope also covers Hong Kong, Macao, Taiwan, America, Europe and East Asia.

Major website on B2B Electronic Commerce

Alibaba.com

Website: http:// www.alibaba.com

Alibaba.com, a famous B2B e-commerce brand in China, is an online marketplace and business community, whose operator, Alibaba Group, was listed on the Hong Kong Stock Market in October 2007. It consists of two connected marketplaces:

Its international marketplace (www.alibaba.com) is an online B2B trading market, in which global buyers and importers seek suppliers from China and other manufacturing countries. At present, it forms a community of more than 3.6 million registered users from over 200 countries and regions.

Its China marketplace (www.alibaba.com.cn) is an online B2B trading market geared to China. At present, it has 21 million registered users from China. Its operational headquarters is in Hangzhou. It has 16 sales and service centers in mainland China and branch companies in Hong Kong and the US. The company has more than 3,500 full-time employees. In August 2005, Alibaba.com formed a strategic partnership with the world's largest portal website, Yahoo. The former annexed all the assets of the latter in China, thereby becoming the largest Internet company in China. At present, Alibaba Group has the following operations: B2B (mainly the Alibaba.com), C2C (Taobao.com and 一拍), electronic payment (Alipay.com) and portal website and search (China Yahoo!).

Alibaba, a representative B2B service supplier

Made-in-china.com

Website: http:// www.made-in-china.com

Made-in-China.com provides foreign trade supply and demand information and trade service, thus becoming a B2B platform for Chinese suppliers, manufacturer and exporters and global buyers to do online trading. Buyers may enjoy the following services:

To search China products and make contact with China's suppliers through Chinese Product Directory (http://cn.made-in-china.com/prod/catlist/);

To post purchasing business (http://cn.made-in-china.com/offer/browse/) and place purchasing information on its Business Board;

Adopt the charged trade service (http://cn.made-in-china.com/tradeservice/main/) and effectively carry out the trade exchange with Chinese product suppliers;

Accede to the made-in-china.com (http://cn.made-in-china.com/), read information for free and gain multiple functions.

Made-in-China.com is an e-business platform developed and operated by Focus Technology Co., Ltd. Focus Technology founded in 1996 is one of the new high-tech enterprises earliest specializing in e-commerce development and application.

hc360.com

Website: http:// www.hc360.com

Founded in 1992, www.hc360.com is a leading B2B electronic commerce services provider. In December 2003, it was listed on the Growth Enterprises Market (GEM) in Hong Kong, and became the first listed mainland company in the information services industry and B2B e-commerce services industry.

Relying on the network platform and advanced search technology, it provides a full range of e-commerce services for small and medium-sized enterprises. At present, it has over two million registered enterprise users. Each day, more than 100,000 enterprises issue important information on supply and demand, purchasing, public bidding and agents, with 100,000 business opportunities on average each day.

Hc360.com has extended its service scope to several hundred cities. It has set up branch companies in 17 cities and has agents in around 100. In addition to online trading, hc360.com also provides business advertising via *Yellow Pages of Chinese Industry* covering listings of some 30 industrial sectors, market research and other services. It also provides individualized market research reports geared to different industries according to the Internet information and organizes participation in industrial exhibitions.

Main Travel Reservation Websites

Online Travel Reservation

Online travel reservation is one of the earliest and most mature e-commerce sectors in China. As ctrip.com and Elong, Inc. were listed on the NASDAQ in 2003 and 2004, respectively, this sector began to attract attention.

As the Chinese tourism industry witnesses continuous growth in market scale and number of tourists, there are an increasing number of entrants to the online travel market and new modes are emerging. However, ctrip.com and Elong, Inc. still dominate and have extended their leading role in the sector. Traditional tour enterprises, however, are now entering online travel. In 2005, China Youth Travel Service set up auyou.com while China Travel Service (Hong Kong) Ltd. established mangocity.com in 2006, with their investment both surpassing 100 million Yuan. The ctrip.com and Elong, Inc. have also moved into the offline tourism market.

Online travel attracts great attention. Travel search engines, instant hotel reservations and B2B and B2C tourism electronic commerce platform modes have exerted an impact and absorbed investment of approximately US$10 million over the past year or so.

Travel Search Engine

Before the emergence of travel search engines, users are used to searching for information on airline tickets and hotel price through comprehensive search engines such as Baidu and Google, but without good results. The users need to search among the numerous web pages, thus wasting a lot of time. The travel search engines help users speedily and conveniently acquire needed information and then make reservations on relevant websites by using Chinese full text retrieval technology and integrating nearly 100 Chinese travel websites and relevant Internet information. Travel search engines provide information search service, but not product reservation. Therefore, advertisement fees and reservation commissions are the two major sources of income. The representative operators include www.qunar.com, www.go10000.com and www.soobb.com. At present, various travel search engines mainly offer airline ticket and hotel price comparison services but not many other tourism products.

Instant Hotel Reservations

Instant hotel reservations are a new business mode that professional hotel reservation websites have create using the Internet. Different from the traditional reservation mode, the instant hotel reservation system provides a platform for all cooperating hotels. It sets the ID and password for the hotels issuing relevant information backstage and independently sales rooms. The hotels may change the online price according to the market. Compared with the traditional hotel reservation offices, instant hotel reservation system saves the hotels the fax and telephone fee and precious time, making the hotel directly face the users, thus dispensing with the agents. The traditional hotel reservation offices only show the most simple and basic hotel information, promoting the hotel rooms.

Tabimado, So-Hotel and Hongtel are the representatives of the instant hotel reservation websites. As a new rising operation mode, these websites only accept some commission from the cooperative hotels, about 10 percent of the bargained hotel room price, five percentage points lower than the traditional hotel reservation websites.

B2B and B2C Tourism Electronic Commerce Platform

In July 2003, the Suzhou-based 17u.net went into operation initially as a travel exchange forum. As a growing number of travel agencies established cooperative relations with it, 17u.net gradually became a professional B2B tourism e-commerce websites. At the same time, it began formulating an enterprise membership system, under which they could place their own calling card and portrait on the website that is also used offline. This is a trust guarantee, the first among domestic travel websites. Later, 17u.net set up an online tour store and appraisal system, and charged a membership fee.

After developing the B2B electronic commerce platform geared to travel enterprises, 17u.net also introduced the B2C tourism platform (www.17u.com) geared to individual tourists with the openness of WEB2.0. This platform provides all-round services for tourists, who may leave comments on the website, describing their own experiences of scenic sites and appraisal. Thanks to the participation of tens of thousands of travel agencies, tourist queries may be answered authoritatively and in detail. Tourists, especially self-help travel groups, may book common guest rooms of hotels ranging from five-star hotels to "farmhouses" and scenic area admission tickets. They may also choose from numerous tourism products of small and medium-sized travel agencies via the online tour store. This mode helps develop transactions between travel enterprises and tourists, thus becoming a B2C mode. 17u.com obtains income from its members.

Ctrip.com

Website: http:// www.ctrip.com

Ctrip.com International Ltd., founded in early 1999, is a China's travel company listed on the Nasdaq. With its operational headquarters in Shanghai, it has branches in Beijing, Guangzhou, Shenzhen and Hong Kong. The company also maintains a network of sales offices in about 20 cities in China. It has approximately 7,000 employees.

As an online travel service company, ctrip.com integrates the high-tech industry and the traditional sectors to offer its more than 18 million members travel services including hotel reservation, airplane ticket reservation, tour reservation, business tour management, Octopus business and tour information.

Ctripcom is one of the most famous ones of its kind.

eLong, Inc.

Website: http:// www.elong.com

eLong, Inc. (NASDAQ: LONG) provides one-stop travel services including tourist information and reservations, with its two websites (www.elong.com and www.elong.net) and call center. eLong, Inc. provides reservation service of almost 4,300 hotels in more than 338 cities across China and tens of thousands of overseas hotels. Flight booking services are available in 70 major cities.

Established in 1999, Beijing-based eLong has grown into a company with over 2,000 employees. In October 2004, it was listed on NASDAQ. Expedia, the largest global online travel service company, now owns 52 percent of its stock.

Easytour.com.cn

Website: http:// www.easytour.com.cn

Easytour.com.cn is an online travel service provider, its business lines covering global travel routes service, domestic hotel reservation and conference training service. Beijing Easytour Online Internet Technologies Inc. is a privately-run stock enterprise registered with the Beijing Industrial and Commercial Bureau. At present it has three websites, www.easytour.com.cn, www.outward-bound.com and www.beijingmeeting.com, devoted to travel e-commerce, and research on and popularization of Internet marketing.

Electronic Payment Websites

Introduction to Electronic Payment

Electronic payment refers to the money payment or the transfer of money that the consumers, manufacturers and financial institutions engaging in e-commerce conducted via internet using electronic means. Bank card, credit card and online account are the main online payment tools. At present, there are mainly three kinds of platforms engaging in online payment in China: the first is the gateway payment platform, such as the UnionPay, dominated by the five major commercial banks, whose main advantage is that it has a financial background and is familiar with the operations; the second is the non-independent payment tool relying on the large-sized B2C and C2C websites, such as the Alipay; the third is the third-party payment platform, including online payment, telephone payment, mobile payment and other payment means, which is rapidly booming. With the rapid development of China's Internet and e-commerce, undertakings, electronic payment also develops fast in market scale and number of users.

Alipay

Website: http:// www.alipay.com

Zhejiang Alipay Internet Technology Ltd. is an Internet enterprise providing online payment services sponsored by the Alibaba Group. AliPay users cover the C2C, B2C and B2B fields. AliPay now has more than 58 million users and a daily transaction volume exceeded 250 million Yuan, through more than 1.21 daily transactions.

Alipay was swift in occupying the Internet payment market in the field of B2B,B2C,C2C and other e-business fields with its unique service mode and products. In 2008 there were more than 80 million registered Alipay users.

At present, in addition to Taobao and Alibaba, there are more than 300,000 businesses supporting and using AliPay, covering the virtual game, digital communication equipment, commercial services, airline ticket and other sectors.

The buyer is required to register an Alipay account by transferring money into it by opening an online banking facility, Alipay.com Co., Ltd informs the goods seller of the order and transfers money from the buyer's account to the seller's after receiving confirmation of the buyer's identified delivery of goods and satisfaction.

Tenpay.com

Website: http:// www.tenpay.com

Tenpay.com is an online payment platform founded by Tencent, one of the largest Internet companies in China. Its business scope covers B2B, B2C, and C2C electronic commerce. It provides online payment and liquidation services. For personal customers, Tenpay.com offers online account charge, cash out, payment, transaction management, and other services; for corporate customers, it provides payment liquidation service and QQ marketing resource support with special characteristics.

The process by which users conduct online transactions via tenpay.com is as follows:

1. The buyer or seller needs to open an online banking account.
2. The buyer or seller logs on to www.tenpay.com and open their own Tenpay account.
3. The buyer transfers money into the Tenpay account through the online banking account.
4. The buyer logs on the seller's online store, and chooses goods. After the buyer confirms the quantity and sum of purchased goods, the Tenpay will freeze the money payable on the buyer's account.
5. The buyer may check the state of the transaction in waiting for goods delivery.
6. Tenpay informs the seller of the arrangements for delivery of the goods.
7. The seller delivers the goods according to the buyer's address after receiving the notice.
8. The buyer confirms to Tenpay delivery of the goods and agrees to the transfer of the money to seller.
9. Tenpay transfers the frozen money payable on the buyer's Tenpay account to the seller's Tenpay account.
10. Seller confirms receipt of the money.
11. Buyer and seller make an appraisal of each other.

In the transaction process, Tenpay also provides account charge, payment, transaction management and other added value services for users. Services that it offers to enterprises also include payment clearing and assistant marketing.

99Bill Corporation

Website: http:// www.99bill.com

99Bill Corporation, an independent third-party electronic payment services provider, is the first payment company in China introducing email and mobile number based comprehensive electronic payment services, with tens of millions of registered users.

Basic services include account charge, gathering, payment, account checking, and transaction detail query. Its payment products include Renminbi gateway, wild card gateway, Easyown gateway and other numerous products, supporting multiple end devices, such as PC, mobile phones, IVR, POS and regular telephones. Of them, the Renminbi gateway supports the bank card payment, 99Bill account payment, telephone payment, offline remittance and other payment means. At the same time, 99Bill also provides numerous applied transaction tools for business, including 99Bill button, 99Bill link, many transactions payment and electronic courtesy card, helping them carry out electronic commerce.

99Bill electronic payment platform adopts the internationally advanced application server and database system, with the payment information transmission 128-bit SSL encryption algorithm. The Oracle Corporation, Versign Inc., a digital security company, and ScanAlert, a network security company, provide security services for 99Bill.

E-Bank Online (Beijing) Technology Co., Ltd.

Website: http:// www.chinabank.com.cn

E-Bank Online (Beijing) Technology Co., Ltd is a high-tech enterprise registered in Zhongguancun in June, 2003 with registered capital of 10 million Yuan.

So far, it has signed cooperation agreements with 19 banks such as ICBC, BOC, CMB, ABOC, and CCB, formed a strategic partnership with VISA International, and united Master Card, JBC and other international credit card organizations, thus providing electronic payment services for enterprises and individuals. Its clients include Microsoft China, Kingsoft, Zhejiang Unicom, Jiangsu Unicom, Nokia, Motorola, Sony-Ericsson, NEC, DigitalChina, store.sohu.com, goucctv.com and Elong.com

Experiencing the Internet banking

Online Banking

China's Online Banking Development

The "E-bank Password Card" is a security tool for the E-bank newly launched by Industrial and Commercial Bank of China to prevent the illegal members from stealing the users' password through a false website, Trojan viruses and hackers attacks.

Online banking has emerged with the development of e-commerce and Internet finance. Although fairly new, its convenient and fast service makes it popular with netizens.

Banks offer customers traditional services including opening or closing an account, answering queries, transferring funds among different accounts, credit, online security, investment and financing via the Internet. Customers may safely and conveniently manage their on-demand and fixed deposit accounts, checking, credit card and individual investments online.

Online Banking has two kinds of development mode. One is intangible electronic banking completely relying on the Internet, also called "virtual banking". The other, based on the existing traditional banking, provides the usual business services using the Internet. In fact, online banking in a true sense has not yet emerged in China and current online banking basically belongs to the second mode.

The Industrial and Commercial Bank of China and China Merchants Bank lead the banks in online banking operational capacity, while the China Minsheng Banking Corporation and Pudong Development Bank have good potential in this regard.

China's online banking, still at the elementary development stage, only offers limited products and service varieties, and has many problems in the aspect of safety, supervisory laws and regulations and business modes. Safety still serves as the biggest obstacle to the development of online banking. A survey showed that about 68.1 percent of Internet users who did not use the online banking worried about its safety.

♦ Laws and Regulations Relating to Online Banking

The Electronic Signature Law of the PRC

(Adopted by the Standing Committee of the 10th NPC, went into effect as of April 1, 2005)

Its main contents are:

A reliable electronic signature shall have equal legal force with handwritten signature or seal.

Where a person counterfeits, copies or usurps the electronic signature of another person, which constitutes a crime, his criminal responsibility shall be investigated according to the law; if losses are caused to another person, he shall bear civil responsibility according to law.

Measures for the Administration of Electronic Certification Services

(Adopted by the Ministry of Information Industry came into force on April 1, 2005)

Main contents include:

An electronic certification service institution shall guarantee its provision of the following services: producing, issuing and managing electronic signature certificates; confirming authenticity of the issued electronic signature certificates; providing information search services on the catalogue of electronic signature certificates; and providing information search services on the status of electronic signature certificates.

An electronic certification service institution shall implement the following obligations: guaranteeing that the contents of each electronic signature certificate be integral and accurate within the duration of validity; guaranteeing that each electronic signature dependent be able to prove or know about the contents stated in the electronic signature certificate and other relevant matters; and keeping appropriate custody of the information relating to the electronic certification services.

Several Opinions of the State Council on Accelerating Development of E-Commerce

(Adopted by the State Council and went into force in August 2005)

Main contents: Pushing ahead with the building of online payment system. We shall reinforce the formulation of criterion and technical standard on online payment operations, study the risk prevention measures and strengthen the operation supervision and risk control; we shall actively study the laws and regulations relating to the third-party payment service, lead the commercial banks, China UnionPay and other institutions to establish the safe, shortcut and convenient online payment platform, and make great efforts to popularize the use of online payment tools such as bank card and online banking; we shall further improve online capital clearing system, push forward the standardization of the online payment operations and make them accord with international standard

Websites of China's Banks

Industrial and Commercial Bank of China
www.icbc.com.cn
China Merchants Bank
www.cmbchina.com
China Construction Bank
www.ccb.com
Agricultural Bank of China
www.95599.cn
Bank of China
www.bank-of-china.com
China Minsheng Banking Corp. LTD
www.cmbc.com.cn

Industrial Bank Co. LTD
www.cib.com.cn
Shanghai Pudong Development Bank
www.spdb.com.cn
Shenzhen Development Bank
www.sdb.com.cn
China Everbright Bank
www.cebbank.com
Bank of Communications Online Banking
www.95559.com.cn
Huaxia Bank
www.hxb.com.cn

Search Engines

Introduction to Search Engine

Search engines are widely used by China's Internet users. The operators of the three search engines, Baidu, Google and China Yahoo, basically monopolize the market, with a combined share of 95 percent. The search service most frequently used by Internet users in China is the web page search, and then website navigation. Q&A community function of the knowledge search also attracts many users. Music and image search services are gradually maturing. Video, community, shopping and map search services also have some users.

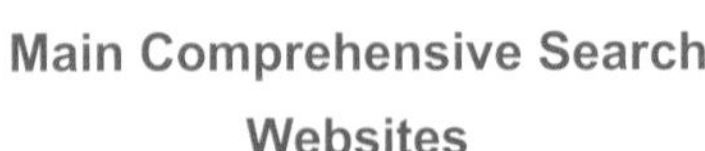

Main Comprehensive Search Websites

Baidu
www.baidu.com
Google
www.google.cn
China Yahoo!
www.yahoo.com.cn
Sogou
www.sogou.com
Soso
www.soso.com

Baidu, the most famous Chinese search engine in the world

Baidu

Website: http:// www.baidu.com

Baidu.com, Inc., is one of the most world-known Chinese language Internet search providers. It was founded in Silicon Valley by Mr. Robin Li and Xu Yong. Baidu.com, Inc. set up its wholly owned subsidiary Baidu Online Network Technology (Beijing) Co., Ltd. in January 2001, a branch company in Shenzhen in October of the same year, and an office in Shanghai in June 2001. On August 5, 2005, Baidu was listed on the NASDAQ.

Baidu, based on its own core technology "hyperlink analysis", provides search services. That is to say, it appraises the quality of the linked website by analyzing the quantity of the linked websites. This ensures that the websites with popular content have a high ranking when the users search. Baidu President Li is the only holder of the "hyperlink analysis" patent. At present, this technology has been widely adopted by various major search engines.

Baidu has the world's largest Chinese web page database. At present, it includes more than two billion Chinese web pages, which is growing at a 10M-speed each day. At the same time, the servers of Baidu distributed across China enable users to search the information from the nearest server and enjoy the fast search transmission speed. Baidu responds to hundreds of millions of search queries from 138 countries each day. And more than 70,000 users set Baidu.com as their Homepage.

The Google.com.cn.

Google

Website: http:// www.google.cn

Google is one of the best known search engines. In addition to web pages, it also offers image, newsgroup, news webpage and movies search services.

Innovative search technology and elegant user interface enable Google to become eminent among the first generation of search engines. Google not only uses the key words or agent search technology, but builds itself on the basis of the advanced PageRank technology, a patent technology ensuring that the most important search results are submitted to the users. PageRank makes an impersonal analysis of the importance of the web pages. The formula that is used to calculate the real value ranking contains 500 million variables and more than two billion terms. PageRank uses the huge internet hyperlink structures to organize and put in order web pages. When webpage A is interlinked to webpage B, Google thinks that "webpage A cast a vote to webpage B'. Google also makes analysis of the voted web pages. With the complicated automatic search methods and structure design, Google is thought to provide the just search results by avoiding any human and affective factors. Google's Chinese name is Gu Ge (pronounced "goo guh"), which was announced by Google in Beijing on April 12, 2006. Google was registered as "Google International LLC" in Chinese Taiwan on February 15.

China Yahoo!

Website: http:// www.yahoo.com.cn

Yahoo (Yahoo!, NASDAQ:YHOO) is a famous portal internet website of the US and one of the creators of the Internet miracle in the late 20th century. Its services include search engine, e-mail and news, and its service scope covers 24 countries and regions. It provides multiple services for more than

500 million independent users in the world. In September 1999, China Yahoo! went into operation. In August 2005, China Yahoo! was purchased by the Alibaba Group. On May 15, 2007, Yahoo! China announced that it had become China Yahoo!.

Yahoo defines its clear development orientation—"in China, Yahoo is just search and search is just Yahoo." Yahoo has more than 2,000 search servers in China which has gathered up to one billion Chinese web pages. At its headquarters in the US, a technical team consisting of most excellent Chinese engineers was set up, giving support to the search operations in China.

Sogou.com

Website: http:// www.sogou.com

Sogou.com is the first third-generation interactive Chinese search engine globally launched by Sohu.com Incorporation on August 3, 2004. Its Website is www.sogou.com.

Its product line consists of page and desktop applications. The page application centers on page search, providing vertical search services for music, pictures, news and maps, and at the same time, establishing a search community among users through the "Speaking Bar"; the desktop application aims to upgrade facilities for users: Sogou's tool bar, Pinyin input and PXP accelerating engine help users search rapidly, input at higher speed and more smoothly enjoy online audio and video live broadcast and on-demand services respectively.

The enterprise officially launched the Sogou Version 3.0 on January 1, 2007, which supported 10 billion retrieved Chinese web pages by right of its independently developed server clustering crawling technique.

Other Sogou search products are also characteristic: the dead link rate of the music search is less than two percent; the picture search has unique function of browsing group of pictures; the news search could timely cover the hot issues; and the map search is capable of national seamless roaming.

The Sogou.com

Soso.com

Website: http:// www.soso.com

Soso.com is a search website under the jurisdiction of Tencent Inc., providing various search services such as pages, pictures, music and commodities. The search results are provided by the search engines of each website. Founded in November, 1998, Tencent Inc. has grown into one of China's largest and most used Internet service portals. On June 16, 2004, Tencent Holdings Ltd. (SEHK 700) went public on the main board of the Hong Kong Stock Exchange.

Tencent's Internet platforms QQ, QQ.com, QQ Games, and PaiPai.com have brought together China's largest Internet community.

3721.com

Website: http:// www.3721.com

3721 Inc. was established in 1998; it provides 3721 "Internet real name" services for accessing the Internet in Chinese, which is an Internet accessing mode of the third generation. It enables Internet users to directly access websites of enterprises on demand and search for relevant on-line information on the enterprises and products by inputting the registered Chinese 3721 Internet real names of the enterprises and products in the browser address line rather than having to remember cumbersome Websites, thus creating more commercial chances for enterprises. Meanwhile, 3721.com unifies the enterprises' names on line and in reality and expands the popularity and influence of the enterprises' brands in reality to the Internet, creating the on-line brands for the enterprises while protecting the brand resources. Over 300,000 enterprises and institutions have registered 3721 Internet real names.

3721 Inc. has set up branches in east, south, central, northwest and southwest China, with the business covering all the cities at and above county level as well as Hong Kong, Taiwan and Macao. It has some 4,000 channel partners.

The 3721 Internet real name business of the company has spread to Japan and Southeast Asia. Moreover, the company has established the strategically cooperative relationship with many world-class IT enterprises.

Fkee.com

Website: http:// www.fkee.com

Fkee.com was established in 2003. Its predecessor Bitower is one of the P2P search service suppliers in China, providing vertical search services such as BT, EMULE, HTTP and video.

Main Website Navigation Websites

3721.com
www.3721.com

Fkee.com
www.fkee.com

Website Navigation 265.com
www.265.com

The websites abounds in such resources as films, TV plays, cartoons, programs, comedies, games, videos and software.

Headquartered in Shenzhen, the enterprise mainly engages in such businesses as P2P search engine, online video search, on-demand films and online TV programs.

Website Navigation 265.com

Website: http:// www.265.com

The 265 Network Technology (Beijing) Corp. runs www.265.com providing Internet navigation services. The corporation was established in 2004, with its headquarters in Beijing and a branch in Xiamen.

The 265 network offers multiple services such as website navigation, comprehensive search, mobile phone navigation and website alliance for the Internet users.

Vertical Search

Vertical search engine is a specialized search engine aiming at some sector and the subdivision and extension of search engines. It needs to integrate some kind of information in the page bank and then give it back to users in a certain form after dealing with the needed data selected by splitting the field directionally. As for the general search engine, such problems as excessive information, inaccurate search results and superficiality exist. However, the new search engine is capable of providing "specialized, accurate and profound" information and relevant service for special demand of special users in special field.

The largest difference between the vertical search engine and common page search engine lies in the minimum unit: that of the latter is the page; and that of the former is the structured data. The vertical search engine first draws out the non-structured page information data to form the special structured information data and then gives it back to the users in the non-structured or structured forms after further processing.

In China, the vertical search engine is mainly applied in searching for enterprise bank, information on supply and demand, shopping, real estate, human resources, map, mp3 and pictures.

Qunar.com

Website: http://www.qunar.com

Qunar.com is a Chinese search engine for tourism. Through integration and issuance of the information on airline tickets, hotels and tourist routes, it compares the price and service of tourist products for customers.

The search channel for airline tickets has the function of searching for domestic and international airline tickets. The users can, at any moment, get information on the price of the latest scheduled flights between any two domestic and foreign cities and the reference about the services such as insurance donation and meeting and seeing off passengers. The information on both connecting and direct scheduled flights is available at the same time enabling users to choose the best scheme in the light of the practical situation.

The search channel for hotels offers updated quoted prices of over 15,000 hotels and provides more convenient and accurate choices for users according to the range of price, star rating, type of management, characteristic facilities, preferential treatment and the surroundings of the hotels they choose.

The preferential search channel can rapidly search for various tourist products provided by various travel agencies and online suppliers, including overseas tourism, suburban tours at promotional rates, domestic and international promotion airline tickets and hotels. Moreover, it provides relevant tourist information of either departure city or arrival city if inputting the name of the departure or arrival city.

So.01hr.com

Website: http://so.01hr.com

This is a human resources search website. When handling the information of each major recruitment websites, it picks up structured data on the name, vacant posts, post descriptions and valid recruiting period of the recruiting employers and then hackles, classifies and compares the data so as to provide more accurate search results for users.

Smarter.com

Website: http:// www.smarter.com

Smarter.com is a leading online comparison shopping service. Its owner is Mezi Media (Shanghai), which takes charge of its operation and maintenance. Mezi Media is a wholly foreign-owned enterprise with the headquarters in Los Angeles and an office in Tokyo.

It aims to help consumers make smarter buying decisions by enabling them to research and compare products, as well as to compare prices and service promises on millions of products available at different stores and look over the remarks and grade of the products and stores.

So far, it has been able to provide 14 channels namely computers, electronics, communication products, office products, cosmetics, sports and outdoors products, automotive products, automobiles, flowers and gardening, gifts and jewelries, books, adult products, movies and individual online stores for commodity search and comparison shopping.

Qihoo.com

Website: http:// www.qihoo.com

Qihoo.com was set up in September 2005. In less than 200 days after its foundation, it gained a joint investment of US$20 million from top domestic and foreign risk investors such as the Sequoia Capital, CDH Investments, IDG, Matrix and Angel Investor Zhou Hongwei. In November of the same year, it again received investment from Highland Capital Partners, Redpoint Ventures, Sequoia Capital, Matrix and IDG.

The PeopleRank search technology and algorithms innovated by Qihoo.com can effectively crawl and identify the contents of high value created by netizens in forums and blogs and present them in a way convenient for reading. The website has become a platform of creation for netizens.

In June 2007, Qihoo.com, joining hands with Discuz! to build You-Marketing, a community integrated marketing platform. It covers 400,000 forums, with a daily flow of 1.6 billion and 130 million users. It categorizes forum users into 20 community life circles so as to help enterprises realize better marketing.

Douban.com

Website: http:// www.douban.com

At Douban.com, users create and share contents on their own, thus forming numerous small circles with common topics and further a huge community of friends. Currently, the book, film and music reviews are the core contents. Hence, a series of recommending mechanisms have come into being.

All the contents, classification, filtration and sequencing at the website are created and decided by netizens. The sequence of some content will rise automatically if it receives a "useful" review. Through the judgments of the public and on the base of the increasingly improved algorithms provided by the website, ordered and useful structures will come into being.

The website makes money mainly from clicks by users and the selling of relevant products of the E-commerce websites.

Isoshu.com

Website: http:// www.isoshu.com

Established in October 2006, Isoshu.com is a supplier of book search services. The website houses large numbers of e-books and sets up a variety of columns such as e-book bag, e-book downloading, free e-books, e-book search, e-book reading, e-book upgrading and e-book on mobile phone.

As a specialized book search engine, the website provides wide categories of books from cartoon, novel, business, lifestyle to religion. It also offers a self-developed application eREAD for faster reading speed and better quality.

Shangsou.com

Website: http:// www.shangsou.com

Shangsou.com is a specialized Chinese business search engine and e-commerce platform, gathering supply and demand information, enterprise information, commodity information and commercial information of 3.5 million enterprises.

Shangsou Network Technology (Beijing) Co., Ltd. is subordinate to China Network Online Media Group. The group engages in investment and management in the Internet network field, mainly investing and holding shares of the network entities such as shangsou.com, liecai.com, 28.com, the online advertising company, 58.com and qiaxing.com.

Mapabc.com

Website: http:// www.mapabc.com

Mapabc is a supplier of basic map services. It provides convenient service guide for travel with digital maps and map publishing technology.

It has become a supplier of basic map services with the highest market occupation rate, fastest response rate and richest map data in China. Several hundred websites including sina.com, google.com, zhongsou.com, xinhuanet.com, alibaba.com and soufun.com choose Mapabc to support their Internet or mobile phone value added businesses. Meanwhile, Mapabc provides those partners with an innovative service mode. There is no need for them to build a map platform on their own. They just need to find the basic map service resources such as the basic maps, yellow page data, transfer routes of public buses and driving routes from the Mapabc.com and then integrate these location-concerned information seamlessly with their search engine or relevant existing contents.

Mapbar.com

Website: http:// www.mapbar.com

Established in 2004, Mapbar engages in location-based service with the maps as the core and is the largest Internet map and wireless map service supplier, with a market occupation rate of over 80 percent. It now has the map data of some 500 cities in China and the data of roads of more than one million km.

Mapbar has navigation map information engine technology with completely independent intellectual property rights and has set up a geospatial comprehensive map service platform in line with the telecom standard, which supports the application of network maps and 2G/3G wireless network maps. The platform can provide location-based services taking the local search, suburban inquiries, transfer routes of public buses and driving navigation through different networks and applicable terminal.

Local Search

This refers to a search confined to a country or region. For example, Baidu.com is a local search engine confined to China and the search results gained from Baidu website are all the pages relating to it.

Furthermore, the local search also confines the search to a regional range and even a city. China Telecom Yellow Page (http:// www.locoso.com) is the most typical website of this kind. In China, the local search refers to the search of a city, providing the search services such as enterprises, maps and life of the city.

Categories of Local Searches

Currently, the domestic local searches in China mainly fall into three categories.

Those of the first category are the yellow page websites represented by China Telecom Yellow Page and Sina enterprise yellow pages. They came into being very early. Preliminarily, they were just the websites providing yellow pages of telephone numbers. Now, they begin to offer the search services concerned life.

Those of the second category are the websites for the search of local life, represented by koubei.com, dianping.com, 58.com and kijiji.cn. They offer the search services relating to people's life such as housing, employment, railway ticket, commodities and catering. Meanwhile, some websites also support the "folk opinions" and provide environment for online communication and share.

Those of the third category provide the local search service by combing the map search technology and local information. The Baidu and Google websites are the pioneers in this regard; and such websites as aibang.com and kooxoo.com develop further in this field, realizing the "close contacts" with people's daily life by dint of search technology.

All the websites of the three categories centered on people's life and commercial activities but differ in emphasis and advantages. With the gradually deepening application of Internet network, the websites of the three categories are blending.

Koubei.com

Website: http:// www.koubei.com

The Koubei.com, one of the largest localization network living communities in China

Koubei.com is one of the largest localized living communities relating to "catering, accommodation and recreation". Established in June 2004, it aims to "be a good guide for people's life". In October 2006, the Alibaba Group formally made strategic investment in the Koubei website.

In Chinese, koubei means public praise. The introduction of neighbors may be more powerful than mass advertisements, and the recommendation of friends and relatives gains much better advertising effects than the market discounts. This is the strength of public praise. In the principle of honesty, koubei.com puts up a communications platform for business people and the masses.

Currently, the two major channels of koubei.com namely the "catering and recreation and house property transaction (lease)" rank first among websites of this kind. The map store and review are two features of the catering and recreation channel; the house property transaction channel provides the information release, inquiry and transaction services on renting and hiring houses and trade of second-hand houses and boasts the improved honesty system in the classified information field in China. The local search is also an important service provided by the website where various living information can be found.

Dianping.com

Website: http://www.dianping.com

Invested by an international venture fund, Dianping.com is a portal of local search and urban consumption as well as one of the most typical web2.0 websites in China. It covers 30-odd major cities such as Shanghai, Beijing and Guangzhou and initiates the mode of consumer reviews. Centering on catering, the website completely covers the urban consumption fields such as shopping, recreation, daily services and activities providing preferences. It engages in such fields as website, publication, added value of mobile phones and catering cooperation.

58.com

Website: http:// www.58.com

58.com is a website with classified information where various living information can be found and released. Opened in 2005, the website has branches in some 100 cities in China, providing services for local users.

At 58.com, various living information on classified advertisement, house rental, jobs, secondhand transfers, dating, housekeeping services, joint driving or tour and secondhand home appliances, computer or mobile phone transaction and ticket service are handled is available.

In March 2006, the website gained investment of US$5 million from Softbank Asia Infrastructure Fund.

Kijiji.cn

Website: http:// www.kijiji.cn

In March 2005, a new type online classified advertisement website, www.kijiji.cn, appeared in China. It is a new business developed by the key enterprising employees of eBay.com, who wish to use this website to create closer contact between people in the same city. It is a website where users living in the same city or same district can gain various living and service information on house renting, job hunting, making friends, large second hand transaction and discussion about the restaurants and hotels in the city. The whole city is a large community on the kijiji.cn, where distance between people becomes close. The website provides free service and convenient pages, and it is a good place for the users to entertain and share various information on the Internet.

The website operates in Beijing, Shanghai, Guangzhou, Nanjing, Hangzhou, Suzhou, Chengdu, Wuhan, Jinan and Zhengzhou with Chinese interface. It will also be opened in many cities in Germany, Canada, Japan, France and Italy.

Kooxoo.com

Website: http:// www.kooxoo.com

This is a specialized search engine for daily living information, covering clothes, catering, accommodation, housing, work, making friends, shopping and so on. It combines on-line search for tickets, housing, jobs and automobiles and WAP products, thus forming a powerful search portal. Meanwhile, it provides an interactive exchange channel for users with such columns as koowa and individual space of web2.0 version.

Currently, the website has such information search columns as job, housing, tickets, automobile, catering, friends, shopping and tourism, covering 200-odd cities. It has an average of 10 million visitor times a day.

52tong.com

Website: http:// www.52tong.com

Established in March 2000, 52tong.com is a new interactive platform providing classified city information and an all-powerful urban life search assistance. It has e-map data and information of 146 large and medium-sized cities, providing services of city search, classified city information, map inquiry, bus inquiry, driving route inquiry and yellow page information of the cities as well as the mobile telephone-based wireless map service. Meanwhile, the website has also developed many mobile phone-based interactive and online products.

Ddmap.com

Website: http:// www.ddmap.com

Ddmap.com provides specialized e-map services such as city map, public bus transfer search and private car and public bus route inquiry, and uses e-maps to show the inquired location.

The website has eight functions of inquiring about public bus or subway transfer, map of any location, public bus or subway route, number of doorplate, key words of combination (such as Huaihai Zhonglu Sichuan cuisine), name of road, crossing and surrounding information (inputting the central location and then its surrounding information).

51ditu.com

Website: http:// www.51ditu.com

51ditu.com is a e-map portal subject to Beijing Lingtu Software Technology Co., Ltd., providing such services as e-map browse, map inquiry, public bus inquiry and travel by car inquiry.

The Beijing Lingtu Software Technology Co., Ltd. is one of the 11 enterprises in China with Class A mapping qualification (including manufacture of navigational e-maps), emphasizing the three major categories of products namely portable navigation, application of network map and solutions for enterprises and governments.

Online Media

Online Media

Online media in China generally falls into three categories: news websites initiated and dominated by governments, such as the peopledaily.com.cn, xinhuanet.com, cctv.com and chinadaily.com.cn; privately-owned news websites, such as sina.com, sohu.com, 163.com, tom.com and China.com; and news websites jointly run by traditional media and commercial enterprises, such as cycnet.com, eastday.com, Qianlong.com and southcn.com.

The application and development of online media have gone through four stages. In the first stage, they basically copied the news and information of the traditional media; in the second stage, they began to independently edit news and carry out interviews; in the third stage, they developed interactive news information services such as setting up forums, electronic listings and communities; and in the fourth stage, they gradually focused on broadband businesses including the short-message business and e-commerce.

Zgjx.cn

Website: http:// www.zgjx.cn

Zgjx.cn is an official website sponsored and governed by the All China Journalists' Association.

This is a national organization, whose predecessor was the Society of Chinese Young Journalists established on November 8, 1937 in Shanghai. In July 1949, 15 national people's organizations including the preparatory committee of All China Journalists' Association and the organizations of workers, youth and women and the democratic parties jointly initiated the Chinese People's Political Consultative Conference. In March 1957, the All China Journalists' Association was formally established in Beijing.

Zgjx.cn mainly reports the news from domestic and foreign press circles and does a good job in protecting the rights of journalists. Currently, there are such columns as important news in domestic and foreign circles, hot subjects, Chinese News Museum, protection of journalists' rights, media blog, checking of press cards, checking of newspapers, researching media development, lecture room and media materials.

News Websites

People's Daily Online

Website: http:// www.people.com.cn

Launched by *People's Daily*, one of the ten major newspapers in the world, people.com.cn is a large online information release platform centering on news and one of the largest news websites in Chinese and many other languages on the Internet. As one of the important news websites in China, it aims to report the world and disseminate China.

The website has several hundred media partners and at the same time, depending on *People's Daily's* rich strength of gathering and editing news, has in its possession websites in simplified Chinese, traditional Chinese, Mongolian, Tibetan, Korean, English, Japanese, French, Spanish, Russian and Arabic, altogether 11 language versions. It releases news around the clock to the world in the first instance and takes part in reporting the grand activities through a multi-media approach including pictures, captions, audio and video broadcasting, forums, blogs, mobile phones, cartoons, RSS and online broadcasting.

Xinhuanet.com

Website: http:// www.xinhuanet.com

Xinhuanet.com is one of the important news websites sponsored by Xinhua News Agency. Its predecessor is the website of Xinhua News Agency, which was renamed xinhuanet.com in March 2000 and adopted the new version and Website in July the same year.

The website boasts 50-odd channels as well as local channels in 31 provinces, autonomous regions and municipalities directly under the Central Government.

The main channels include the news center, Xinhua politics, Xinhua international, summit dynamics, online focus, Xinhua forum, Xinhua finance and economics, Xinhua sports, Xinhua campus, Xinhua military affairs, Xinhua pictures, Xinhua music, Xinhua entertainment, Xinhua real estate, Xinhua subjects, Xinhua views, Xinhua interviews, Xinhua live broadcast, Xinhua auto, Xinhua tourism and Xinhua media.

The website releases news around the clock in such six languages as simplified Chinese, traditional Chinese, English, French, Spanish, Russian and Arabic, covering 200-odd countries and regions.

China.com.cn

Website: http:// www.china.org.cn/ www.china.com.cn

China.com.cn is one of the important news websites under the leadership of the State Council and the management of the China International Publishing Group. Established in 1997, the website releases news in simplified Chinese, traditional Chinese, English, French,

The China.com.cn

German, Japanese, Spanish, Russian, Korean and Arabic, altogether 11 language versions. It covers 200-plus countries and areas in the world.

It operates on the principle of combining local information, on-line subjects, on-line services and media search, introduces China to the world in a timely and all-round way.

Joining hands with the World Bank, China.com.cn established the chinagate.com.cn, which is an important member of the global development portal website. It aims to introduce the Chinese situation, share development experiences, promote international cooperation and try hard to make contributions to the elimination of poverty and promotion of development.

CRI Online

Website: http:// gb.cri.cn

Sponsored by China Radio International, gb.cri.cn is one of the important news websites in China. It operates websites in 43 written languages and audio programs in 48 languages, thus becoming the Chinese website with the most language versions. The website covers 160-odd countries and regions, with daily program broadcasting of 221.5 hours and an average daily audience of 700,000. In addition, through international cooperation, the number of the foreign websites relaying the contents of the gb.cri.cn increases constantly and that of the foreign websites linking to the front pages of the website in different language versions reaches some 15,000.

On July 13, 2005, the website officially launched Inet Radio in Mandarin, English, German and Japanese, consisting of four kinds of programs: information, talks, music and foreign teaching. On July 13, 2006, gb.cri.cn introduced the first video blog in Chinese, English, Japanese and Korean in China. On September 14, 2007, the website formally launched 11 CRI Webcasts in nine languages.

Chinadaily.com.cn

Website: http:// www.chinadaily.com.cn

Sponsored by *China Daily*, this is one of the important comprehensive news media websites combining news information and entertainment services. With daily hits of about nine million, it consists of three major sections: English Portal, World Online, and English Study, including more than 50 sub-sites and over 300 columns.

Chinadaily.com.cn is the largest English portal in China. Complementing the initial online-edition services to all papers affiliated with the China Daily Group, the English Portal, combining the latest information of domestic and foreign authoritative news agencies, feeds up-to-the-minute, accurate and rich news and information to online readers. Contents of English Portal cover all big events of China, which are enriched by editorial and news analysis from unique viewpoints. It also includes Culture, Citylife, News Pictures, News Cartoons, Forum, Olympic, Entertainment and Lifestyle sections.

The World Online, the Chinese-language web page on the China Daily website, reports international affairs in a timely manner, combining the international information in policies, military affairs, extensive reading, humors, entertainment and lifestyle.

The bilingual Language Tips is the English study section, providing a relaxed and solid English learning environment. From the perspectives of listening, speaking, reading and writing, it exclusively sets up the columns such as Audio & Video, Translation Tips, Survival English, Columnist, and Book Channel and at the same time, provides practical services such as Chinese Terms answering readers' questions and the Translation Arena with the real-time remarks of experts.

CCTV.com

Website: http:// www.cctv.com

CCTV.com is the website of China Central Television. Established and put into experimental operation in December 1996, it is one of the earliest websites releasing Chinese information and one of the important news websites in China.

Characterized by audio and video programs and interaction, it is a comprehensive on-line media integrating the news, information, entertainment and service, where the programs on 12 channels such as CCTV1, CCTV 4, CCTV 9 and CCTV 10 and CCTV News can be broadcasted by video at the same time. Moreover, the website also provides the on-line versions of the key columns, special reports, major contests and evenings of the CCTV and various kinds of video streams so as to meet the requirements of different Internet users.

Currently, the main contents of some 400 columns and all contents of 270-odd columns of the CCTV are broadcasted on the website. There are 100-plus interactive on-line living broadcastings for the special programs, evenings and key contests broadcasted on CCTV. The on-line community carries out some 300 on-line interviews annually, supporting over 100,000 on-line users at the same time.

It has channels in English, Spanish and French and Taiwan Channel, broadcasting programs with CDN technology to the world. Its overseas netizens come from more than 150 countries and regions like America, Britain, France, Germany, Spain, Canada, Brazil, Argentina, Australia, Japan, South Korea and Taiwan, China.

China Economic Net

Website: http:// www.ce.cn

The website of the *Economic Daily*, the predecessor of China Economic Net was formally established in September 1999. On July 28, 2003, China Economic Net (www.ce.cn) was officially launched, with versions in simplified Chinese, traditional Chinese, English and German. It is one of the important news websites in China.

Its website in English is committed to providing timely, accurate and in-depth relevant information for people at home and abroad who care for China's economic development. It consists of seven major channels: domestic news, international news, financial and economic news, industrial news, in-depth analysis and market news. Every day, it gives reports on economic trends of China, trend of industrial development, financial market fluctuations, securities business and the behavior of domestic and foreign enterprises on Chinese market.

Its website in German reports on the economic life of China and events in Sino-European communications. It introduces the economic policies of China and development of various sectors and provides timely, practical, extensive and in-depth economic information.

Youth.cn

Website: http:// www.youth.cn
http:// www.cycnet.com

Formally launched on May 4, 1999, Youth.cn is called China Youth Computer Information Network in full. With both Chinese and English versions, it is the largest portal for youth and an important news websites in China.

As the largest comprehensive website tailoring services to youth in China, Youth.cn boasts 400-odd sub-websites on the Chinese Communist Youth League, news, national soul, foundation of Chinese nation, youth forum, campus news agency, entertainment, education and sports and more than 2,000 columns. Of the total, the daxue.youth.cn, daode.youth.cn and the channels of the national soul, foundation of Chinese nation, English corner, youth blog, youth forum, campus news agency and youth on-line broadcasting station have wide influence among youth.

The interview at www.youth.cn

Cnr.cn

Website: http:// www.cnr.cn
http:// www.cnradio.com

Sponsored by China National Radio (CNR), a State radio station, Cnr.cn is the largest audio broadcasting website in China. Its predecessor is the website of China National Radio, registered and launched in August 1998 and formally renamed as "China Radio Website".

Currently, it has 64 specialized channels on news, finance and economy, sports, music, college, autos, tourism, military affairs, nation and Taiwan with 400-odd columns. The total amount of its audio data reached 2TB. The website provides the on-line living broadcasting of the nine sets of programs of the China National Radio and on-demand broadcasting of 270-plus key columns with streaming media audio broadcasting technology.

Chinanews.com

Website: http:// www.chinanews.com

Chinanews.com is sponsored by China News Service, which was initiated by the personnel of Chinese news circles and some domestic and foreign celebrities on September 14, 1952. It is one of the two news agencies in mainland China.

It is the earliest Chinese media on the Internet in Asia, accessing the Internet in Hong Kong in 1995. On January 1, 1999, the headquarters of China News Service in Beijing launched Chinanews.com.

Currently, the website has channels of news center, front page, international, Taiwan, Hong Kong and Macao, Chinese, finance and economy, autos, real estate, culture and entertainment, sports, science and education, pictures and lifestyle as well as such columns as picks from Chinese papers, news Yamato-e and real-time remarks. Meanwhile, it has the English and traditional Chinese versions and picture bank.

The website boasts 30-odd local sub-websites set up by the branches of China News Service at home and abroad in Shanghai, Hong Kong, Tokyo, Chongqing, Jilin, Fujian, Jiangsu and Xinjiang, providing large amount of local news to on-line readers.

Gmw.cn

Website: http:// www.gmw.cn

On January 1, 1998, gmdaily.com.cn sponsored by *Guangming Daily* Press Group was launched, drawing on the rich data of Guangming Daily and its subordinates such as *Life Times* and *China Reading Weekly* and magazines like *Book View, Chinese Book Review Monthly* and Examination as well as the books of the *Guangming Daily* Publishing House.

The Guangming Daily is a time-honored and authoritative news media.

Cyol.net

Website: http:// www.cyol.net

Cyol.net is the website of the *China Youth Daily*, launched on May 15, 2000.

The Beijing China Youth On Line Network Information Technology Co., Ltd, under the control of *China Youth Daily*, takes charge of the news releases, information development, website operation and marketing of Cyol.net. Through several years' development, the website has established a marketing mode based on recruitment club, training club, China Youth Club, the website of pictures and on-line store and characterized by interaction between traditional media and on-line media.

Through 30-odd channels of news, education, studying abroad, touring to study, talents, training, enterprises, books, pictures, store, on-line friends and color, the website provides practical information services for users.

Legaldaily.com.cn

Website: http:// www.legaldaily.com.cn

Online version of the *Legal Daily*, it has news and information, focus on network talks, forums, photographs, legal trends, politics and law, interviews, NPC legislative activities, legal services, legal cases, comments on legal system, blogs, special topics, financial and economic developments, society and law, live broadcasts, law college, judicial examination, global rule of law and other columns.

The *Legal Daily* is a China's only newspaper primarily covering legal developments. It started publication under the name *China Legal Daily* on August 1, 1980 in Beijing and was renamed on January 1, 1988.

The *Legal Daily* has established 33 news bureaus in various provinces, autonomous regions, municipalities directly under the Central Government and some cities specifically designated in the State plan, and established foreign correspondent stations in some parts of Asia, Europe and North America. It also set up printing centers in 20 domestic sites.

China Military Online

Website: http:// www.chinamil.com.cn

The online version of the *PLA Daily* launched on October 1, 1999, is the predecessor of China Military Online, the name it took in 2004.

China Military Online has set up eight news channels including "Chinese Military Affairs", "military affairs hotspot", "International Military Affairs" and "Bilingual News"; it has also introduced some columns with military features, such as Military Salon, Forum on National Defense, White Paper on National Defense, main

The officials and soldiers of the Chinese peacekeeping engineer battalion skimming through the Xinhuanet.com and Chinamil.com.cn.

points of military law and regulations and list of heroes and model personnel in the three arms. China Military Online (English) was unveiled on March 5, 2003.

Chinataiwan.org

Website: http:// www.chinataiwan.org/

Chinataiwan.org, founded in July 1999, is the first non-governmental website on the mainland dealing with Taiwan issues and cross-strait relations.

It provides information in simplified Chinese, traditional Chinese and English. It has 18 Chinese channels with a total of 1,460 columns. The website reports on the Taiwan issue and cross-strait relations developments in an all-round, systemic and authoritative way. It has dozens of experts and scholars who write authoritatively on the major events relating to Taiwan. The website has also established good cooperative relations with the numerous famous media across the straits, and its original news is widely reprinted.

Chinataiwan.org, pursuing the unification of motherland and regarding the cross-strait win-win situation as a happiness and great benefit, wholeheartedly carries out its aim of "passing on cross-straits love, communicating cross-straits public opinion, and serving cross-straits exchange". The website has successfully integrated Taiwan-related information of both sides and built up comments on news, information services, online exchanges and other multi-functional dissemination systems, creating a vital platform for communications and exchanges between cross-straits friends.

China Tibet Online

Website: http://www.tibet.cn

China Tibet Information Center (www.tibet.cn) founded in 2000, introduces Tibet's history and reality to the world in an impersonal and all-round way. It has three versions in Chinese, English and Tibetan.

The website provides the latest Tibet-related information daily in Chinese, English and Tibetan; data release with Tibet-related publications as the base; audio and video sections on news and entertainment; and an interactive section. In addition, it also includes electronic periodicals, Tibet-related website group, Tibetan tourism, Tibetan gallery, classified listings, Tibet yellow pages and other contents.

At present, this website has been linked to more than 3,000 websites globally with the daily click rate of 2.4 million times.

Eastday.com

Website: http:// www.eastday.com

Eastday is a comprehensive news-oriented website jointly set up by Shanghai Jinwin Investment Co Ltd, Shanghai Media & Entertainment Group, Shanghai Media Group, Shanghai Oriental Pearl (Group) Co Ltd, Shanghai Information Investment Inc, Wenhui-Xinmin United Press Group, Jiefang Daily Group, Shanghai Education Television Station, Labor Daily and Youth Daily.

It was launched on May 28, 2000. At present, the website holds stakes in 14 companies including the Shanghai Eastday Chain Administration Co. Ltd., Shanghai Oriental Digital Community Co. Ltd., Shanghai Easttone Ltd., Shanghai East Webtone Data Technology Co. Ltd., Shanghai East Credibility Online Co. Ltd. and *City Herald*.

The website provides 80 channels in three languages – Chinese, English and Japanese. It attracts two million daily users and draws about 20 million page views per day. Adopting more than 1,000 technologies, it provides a network platform for both the website of the Shanghai Municipal Government and World Expo 2010, as well as 1,000 Shanghai-based companies.

Qianlong.com

Website: http:// www.qianlong.com

Qianlong.com was jointly launched on March 7, 2000, by Beijing Daily, Beijing Evening News, Beijing People's Broadcasting Station, Beijing TV, Beijing Youth Daily, Beijing Morning News, Beijing Modern Commercial Daily, Beijing Radio and TV and other major media.

It has developed into a portal website from a specialized news website, providing news, financial and life-related advice and entertainment, as well as other media information, and various value-added services for Beijingers and global users who follow events in Beijing. It owns four major core businesses (4Q)—Qianlong News, Qianlong Wireless, Qianlong Broadband and Qianlong Tech, and has formed an integrated service structure covering broadband, wireless and other various internet fields.

The Qianlong.com

Enorth.com.cn

Website: http:// www.enorth.com.cn

Enorth Netnews Co., Ltd. is a comprehensive network service provider jointly funded by the city's chief news media, including Tianjin People's Broadcasting Station, Tianjin TV Station, Tianjin Broadcasting&TV Guide, and Tianjin Daily and Evening Paper. It was launched on December 18, 2000 and now averages daily page views of 10 million. The two websites of Tianjin TV Station and Tianjin People's Broadcasting Station are both designed and updated by Enorth. It has become a strong media for online publicity for Tianjin.

www.southcn.com

Website: http:// www.southcn.com

This is a member unit of the Nanfang Daily Group officially launched on December 13, 2001.

After many years of rapid development, it has developed into a large comprehensive news-oriented portal website. At present, it can provide news and information services in both Chinese and English. It has set up 30 news and information channels including headline news, international, China, Taiwan, Hong Kong and Macao, society, prefectures (cities) of Guangdong Province, and 13 special information channels including theory, sports, entertainment, rule of law, finance and economics, education, science and technology, IT, real estate, cars, tourism and women's issues. It also has many sub-websites such as English, community, flash and numerous market expanding windows such as mobile phone short messaging, backroom for business, online supermarket, Nanfang bookstore, classified listings, and online Guangdong; It also undertakes the updating of 13 websites, namely, www.pprd.org.cn, www.gd.gov.cn, www.gdgx.southcn.com, www.tongxin.org, gocn.southcn.com, www.gdart.com, www.gdzuoxie.com, www.southphoto.cn, www.gdexpo.com, www.gdass.gov.cn, www.southcn.com/news/gdnews/xcrc/lxgz/, www.wwrp.net and www.nanri.cn.

At present, its daily news information updates reach 3,000, daily click rate over 500,000 times, average daily page views 6.5 million, and daily average host computer visits over one million set times, of which number of the foreign visits accounts for about half.

Wenweipo.com

Website: http://www.wenweipo.com/

Wenweipo.com is a wholly-owned subsidiary of Hong Kong Wen Wei Po Ltd. It is a communications platform between the mainland, Taiwan, Hong Kong and Macao. Every day, it offers instant and comprehensive news and information aimed at Chinese-speaking audiences around the world, linking the three regions across the Taiwan Strait. It has such columns as home, important news, news on Hong Kong, the mainland, Taiwan, international, comments, finance and economics, investing and financing, education, supplement, entertainment, sports, daily news, and real-time news.

Hong Kong *Wen Wei Po Daily News*, which began publication in 1948, is a comprehensive newspaper catering to Hong Kong society. At present, about 15 large sections (60 pages) are published daily in Hong Kong, and delivered to every province, autonomous region and municipality on the mainland each day. With the approval of relevant Taiwan departments, it can now gather news directly through a Taiwan office. Apart from the Hong Kong version, it daily issues nine different overseas versions. *Wen Wei Po Daily News Overseas Edition* has a daily circulation of 400,000.

ifeng.com

Website: http:// www.ifeng.com

Ifeng.com is a comprehensive picture, text, audio and video information website of Phoenix New Media. By joint re-broadcasting of its website and TV station, it covers international news, political developments on the mainland and in Hong Kong, Macao and Taiwan, society, finance and economics, history, military affairs, sport, fashion, entertainment, Buddhism and provides other comprehensive news and information. It provides interactive and communicative space for users with blog services, forum and survey and other Web 2.0 applications. With RSS, TAG, program ordering, individual program list and other custom-made multimedia service, it meets users' individual demands.

Phoenix New Media is a wholly-owned cross-platform internet media of Phoenix TV Media Group, which, with ifeng.com as the flagship, combines three platforms—internet, wireless communications internet and internet video. It is a new media built up by integrating multiple media types, resources, technical platform and spread channels, thus serving Chinese people globally.

Comprehensive Portal Website

Comprehensive Portal Website

Portal website refers to the application system leading to some comprehensive internet information resources and offering relevant information services. Portal websites originally provided search engine and Internet access services. Due to the increasingly intense market competition, they had to rapidly expand various new business types, hoping to attract more internet users, so that their current businesses are all-inclusive, turning them into an "internet supermarket". Now, portal websites mainly provide news, search engine, Internet access, chat room, BBS, free e-mail, multimedia information, e-commerce, online community, online games, free webpage space and other services.

Sina, Sohu, Netease and TOM are China's former four major comprehensive portal websites. In recent years, the homepage of Tencent's QQ has seen rapid development into the front ranks among comprehensive websites. Other famous portal websites include 21cn, china.com, China Yahoo! and MSN CHINA.

The news, science and technology, auto, sports, entertainment and female channels of Sina and Sohu, e-mail services of Netease, Sohu's sogou.com and Sina's iask.sina.com.cn have most users compared with the same channels (services) on other portal websites.

In north and northeast China, most people are subscribers of Sohu; in east China, MSN China has most subscribers; in south and central China, Tencent's QQ.COM has the most users; and in southwest and northwest China, it is split between Tencent's QQ.COM and Netease.

QQ

Website: http:// www.qq.com

QQ.com is an integrated portal website of Tencent, Inc, providing news, search, forum, entertainment, e-mail, network hard drive and other services.

Founded in November 1998, Tencent, Inc. has grown into one of China's largest and most used Internet service portals. On June 16, 2004, Tencent Holdings Limited (SEHK 700) went public on the main board of the Hong Kong Stock Exchange.

Tencent set up its four major Internet platforms QQ, QQ.com, QQ Games, and PaiPai.com, having brought together China's largest Internet community. Tencent's communications and information-sharing services include QQ.com, QQ Instant Messenger, QQ Mail, and search engine SOSO. Linked up with heavily used features such as forums, chat rooms, and QQ Groups, Tencent's Qzone has grown into China's largest personal Internet space. These services foster group interaction and resource sharing. Virtual products such as QQ Show, QQ Pet, QQ Game, and QQ Music/Radio/Live have been successful in providing entertainment and customization options to users. Mobile phone users can take advantage of a number of value-added wireless services. Tencent's PaiPai.com is a C2C on-line shopping platform that seamlessly integrates into Tencent's other community platforms.

The QQ penguins

SINA

Website: http:// www.sina.com.cn

Sina Corp. (NASDAQ: SINA) is a comprehensive portal website providing various information and featuring internet media. It has 40 channels including news, game, e-mail, blog services, podcast, search and chat.

It is a leading online media company and value-added information service (VAS) provider for China and for global Chinese communities. With a branded network of localized web sites targeting Greater China and overseas Chinese, SINA provides services through five major business lines including SINA.com (online news and content), SINA Mobile (mobile value-added services), SINA Community (web 2.0 community-based services and games), SINA.net (search and enterprise services) and SINA E-Commerce (online shopping). Together these business lines provide an array of services including region-focused online portals, MVAS, search and directory, interest-based and community-building channels, free and premium email, blog services, audio and video streaming, online games, classified listings, fee-based services, e-commerce and enterprise e-solutions.

With more than 230 million registered users worldwide and over 700 million daily page views, SINA is the most recognized Internet brand name in China and among Chinese communities globally.

Sohu

Website: http:// www.sohu.com

Sohu.com is a portal website of Sohu.com Inc (NASDAQ:SOHU) with resource navigation as the main business, which is grouped into three parts - news center, and fashion center, including domestic news, international, finance and economics, science and technology, sports, society, comments, military affairs, culture, education and other columns.

On July 12, 2000, Sohu.com Inc. went public on the Nasdaq. Sohu has built one of the most comprehensive matrices of Chinese language web properties and proprietary search engines, consisting of: www.sohu.com, the mass portal and leading online media destination; www.sogou.com, an interactive search engine with over 10 billion retrieved Chinese web pages; www.chinaren.com, the #1 online alumni club; www.focus.cn, a top real estate and home furnishing website; www.17173.com, the #1 games information portal; www.goodfeel.com.cn, a wireless value-added services provider; and www.go2map.com, a leading online mapping service provider. Its average daily page views reach 700 million.

Netease

Website: http:// www.163.com

163.com is the portal website of Netease (NASDAQ: NTES), including news, sports, entertainment, female, tourism, culture, forum, short messaging, digital products, auto, mobile phone, finance and economics, science and technology and other channels. At present, its web pages adopt a two-column structure. Netease reprocesses rather than simply reprinting secondary news. It also issues instant opinions and feedback on the topics at the end of every article, thus increasing interactive effectiveness.

In the development of internet applications, services and other technologies, Netease has always maintained its leading position in domestic circles, and won many firsts in China's internet trade: the first whole text search facility in Chinese, the first to provide large-capacity free e-mail in Chinese, the first capacity free network album, the first free e-card station, the first online virtual community, the first online auction platform, the first 24-hour customer service center, and the first successfully operated and independently developed China-made online games operation.

The cn.yahoo.com

China Yahoo!

Website: http:// www.yahoo.com.cn

China Yahoo! (www.yahoo.com.cn) is a portal search website, including e-mail, Yahoo search, information, knowledge, music, picture, multimedia, shopping, eating, living and enjoying and other channels. Yahoo search includes webpage search, omni search (beta), search ranking, search focus and other columns.

Yahoo! (www.yahoo.com) is the world's No.1 portal search website, with its service scope covering 24 countries and regions. It provides multiple internet services for more than 500 million independent users around the world.

In September 1999, China Yahoo! went into operation. In August 2005, China Yahoo! was purchased by the Alibaba Group. It has been the search engine community and information service provider which has leapt into the top ranks of China's Internet circles.

Other Information Websites

www.rayli.com.cn

Website: http:// www.rayli.com.cn

Rayli Magazine is a media enterprise with print media and internet media as its core business. Its two fashion journals: *Rayli Costume and Cosmetics* and *Rayli YiRenFengShang Magazine*, ranks first and second in China in circulation.

Rayli.com.cn is a continuation of the Rayli Brand on the internet platform, serving female users.

Rayli.com.cn covers various aspects of the life of female in different states. It has 11 channels including 80 sub-columns, with 400 articles being updated daily; Its contents involves costume, cosmetics, household living, catering, travel, pet, entertainment, sex, beauty, health, careers and shopping.

Its daily average page views reach three million, its loyal users 800,000, and simultaneous online users 5,000.

Military Affairs Channel of China.com

Website: http:// military.china.com

The military affairs channel of Chinadotcom Corporation is China's largest military affairs website, including the following columns: Chinese military affairs focus, important news on Chinese military affairs, cross-straits situation, news on international military affairs, special topics of military affairs, armament dynamics and forum.

Chinadotcom Corporation is the leading integrated enterprise solutions company in Asia, with its business scope covering the Asia. It also set up many branch enterprises in other regions in the world. It was listed on NASDAQ in July 1999, the first Chinese Internet company in this regard (NASDAQ: CHINA).

Starting in 1997, Chinadotcom Corporation provided internet formation services on mainland China, with a large number of clients and partners. China.com was officially launched on mainland China in May 1999, and its daily average page views have surpassed 60 million.

China.com provides news, military affairs, sports, science and technology, entertainment, game, finance and economics, education, health, tourism and other information, and at the same time offers e-mail, short messaging, enterprise solution services, friendship, forum, chat room, search engine, search ranking, software unloading and other products and services.

Internet Services

Instant Messaging

Instant Messaging

Instant Messaging (Instant messaging, IM for short) is a terminal service that allows two and more people to instantly send text information and files or conduct voice and video communication through internet.

In the early days of the development of software, namely during 1998-2000, China's instant messaging software regarded the computer as the carrier. Since 2000, with the increasing in instant messaging and mobile communications users, the cross-platform service integrating internet and mobile communication features has become a new tool for communications.

In addition to the most popularized text chat function, file transmission, video, expression chat, voice and other functions are also widespread used.

In the past year, some 86 percent of China's Internet users have continuously used the instant messaging products to conduct online communication. At present, instant messaging tools that are popular in China include Tencent's QQ, MSN, Netease popo.163.com, Sina UC and Yahoo! Messenger.

Tencent's instant messaging products (QQ, TM) account for more than 80 percent shares on China's instant messaging market. MSN Messenger (Live Messenger) is the second in this regard. MSN Messenger (Live Messenger) and QQ are the top two instant messaging tools in terms of user coverage rate.

Tencent's QQ

Website: http://im.qq.com

Tencent's QQ is an instant messaging tool developed by the Tencent. At present, QQ has more than 647.1 million registered accounts and 273.2 million active accounts.

In February 1999, Tencent, as a pure internet-based instant messaging software developer, introduced the first test version of internet-based OICQ, which had more than 200,000 registered users two month later. By the end of 1999, the number of OICQ's average online users has reached 15,000, accounting for over 80 percent of the total Chinese instant messaging market shares. In 2004, Tencent also introduced Tencent Messenger (TM), instant messaging software aimed at business people, emphasizes particularly communications between acquaintances.

Tencent, based on meeting users' entertainment demands, has developed a series of value-added services, such as mobile QQ, QQ show, and QQ game, and first exercises premium registration and QQ flash advertising, thus winning huge profits. In addition, Tencent published RTX in the aspect of enterprise instant messaging business in September 2003, with its enterprise instant messaging strategy taking shape.

MSN

Website: http://messenger.live.cn

MSN Messenger is an instant messaging tool developed by Microsoft. It is globally-popular IM software that has won the favor of many users with its functional advantages.

MSN officially entered China's market in 2005. The MSN China website was launched in May 2005. Shanghai MSN Network Communications Technology Co., Ltd is a limited liability Sino-foreign joint venture co-funded by Microsoft and Shanghai Alliance Investment Co., Ltd., , each of which holds a stake of 50 percent. Contents on the website of MSN China are offered by nine major Chinese partners including Ynet.com, smgbb.com, taobao.com, ccidnet.com, ourgame.com, mop.com, didibaba.com, Englishtown and sensky.com.

Sina UC, UTalk

Website: http://uc.sina.com.cn/

Website of UTalk: http://tech.sina.com.cn

Sina's instant messaging software includes Sina UC and UTalk. Relying on enormous users of sina.com, they also have many users and pay attention to building up entertainment-oriented instant messaging platform.

Sina UC initiated the "video era" in terms of China's IM, building up an interactive entertainment platform for internet users. Sina UC's stereo video chat room leads the instant messaging video sharing in China.

UTalk is another instant voice messaging tool developed by the Sina especially for China's online game users and LAN game users. UTalk supports directly logging on through the UC number and Sina pass, and at the same time conducts relevant promotion cooperation with many online game operation companies and game media.

Popo.163.com

Website: http://popo.163.com

Popo.163.com is the first IM software introduced in China with customized head portrait. Its users may change head portraits at will. Like other IM software, it supports multiple chat modes: text chat, chat room, short messaging, voice and video. As many as 3,000 Chinese characters can be sent at one time. It attracts users by opening popo.163.com's service of sending short message for free.

Sohu's soq.com

Website: http://www.soq.com

Soq.com is an online instant messaging software introduced by Sohu at the end of 2003. Its development time is later than the Netease popo.163.com, and its market is behind Sina UC. However, it is also able to challenge Tencent's QQ with its service of "sending mobile phone short messages for free".

Soq.com is largely identical in IM functions compared with others. It can send short message and files, provide many unique actions, software skins and message windows

The QQ, MSN, Sina UC and POPO are the instant messaging tools frequently used by Chinese people.

with different styles, and reminders to the other side. It can leave word through Soq.com directly on the website of Sohu.

Yahoo! Messenger

Website: http:// cn.messenger.yahoo.com

Yahoo! Messenger developed in 1998, is one of the world's three major instant messaging tools, with several hundred million registered users in the world; as far as the function is concerned, Yahoo! Messenger is largely identical with other China-made instant messaging products, and has no especially conspicuous unique functions. Although it has more users in the US and other regions, it is not too popular in China.

In 2006, Yahoo's and MSN's instant messaging realized integrated e-mail and instant messaging. "Yahoo! Messenger" instant messaging procedure was integrated, so that users may make choice expediently between e-mail and Yahoo! Messenger. Users may simultaneously operate two software procedures in one Internet explorer, without downloading the Yahoo Messenger Software again. Yahoo! Messenger users now enjoy stronger and more value-added service, and can conveniently conduct exchanges with clients, partners and friends who cannot be communicate with. Yahoo! Messenger will be more widely spread and used under the business environment.

GTalk

Website: http://www.google.com

Google, an international search service provider, offered Gmail, a web mail system targeted at individual users in 2004. Gmail has a number of users globally. Later, Google also introduced GTalk, IM software that can support Gmail's online mail test function, and conduct text, voice dialogue and offline voice information recording.

GTalk has also a function leading China's domestic other instant messaging tools: instant messaging dialogue on the webpage. That is to say, while logging on to their Gmail, sending and receiving e-mails, users may realize the function of conducting instant messaging dialogue on the webpage without opening and logging on to GTalk.

In China's instant messaging market, most of users of Gmail are users of Google.

Skype

Website: http://skype.tom.com

Skype is a famous VoIP service provider in Europe. Its entry into China's instant messaging market began with its cooperation with China's portal website TOM Online Inc. In 2004, Skype officially entered into China's market, becoming TOM-Skype that the instant messaging users are familiar with.

Sending Spring Festival blessings through Skype

Skype has always been the top-ranking VoIP service provider in the world, with higher market shares. The number of its registered users has surpassed 80 million, and increased at the speed of six million per month. This is because Skype not only provides computer to computer instant messaging dialogue function, but also realizes computer to fixed telephone or mobile phone communications. However, due to restrictions in China's telecommunications market, it is difficult for Skype to realize computer to fixed telephone or mobile phone communications in an all-round way in a short time and to immediately gain a decisive edge in China's instant messaging market, although it also provides text, voice dialogue and other functions.

Fetion

Website: http://www.fetion.com.cn

China Mobile developed the Fetion, a comprehensive instant messaging tool integrating chat, interactive, entertainment and other functions in the mobile instant messaging field, providing users with a platform for communicating and displaying themselves. Through binding, you can send short messages in groups to your friends joining you. According to survey and search results, about 60 percent of internet users would like to bind mobile phone numbers with Fetion number to use this service.

PICA

Website: http://www.pica.com

PICA instant messaging software developed by pica.com Inc realizes the fusion of traditional Internet, mobile Internet and fixed line. In addition to short message inter-working, PICA also supports multi-media IM, chat room, online customer service and other functions.

PICA pays attention to mobile IM development from the beginning, aimed at mobile internet and its users. PICA, a individualized communication and information platform, supports the basic IM functions such as message mailbox, short messages in group, and mobile chat room, as well as the enlarged businesses such online customer service, information unloading, information service and online games.

PICA supports text, voice, picture, expression signs, video and other multimedia formats; PICA may realize good inter-working with mobile QQ, mobile MSN and other mobile IM tools; in addition, PICA's "touch entry" voice communications also support one to one or group chat. The number of PICA users has witnessed rapid growth. It is reported that at present PICA has approximately two million registered users.

E-Mail Services

E-Mail Services

In China, e-mail services have an Internet penetration rate surpassing 80 percent. As the netizens' basic application, e-mail has an increasingly closer relationship with the users' daily life and has been more frequently used.

E-mail services may be grouped according to audience:

Individual e-mail: grouped into free and premium e-mails;

Enterprise e-mail: e-mail service targeted at enterprises.

Individual E-Mail

Individual e-mail may be grouped into according to whether a fee is paid or not:

Free e-mail refers to the e-mail service that involves access by registration without paying any charge. At present, most of China's e-mail services are free. This creates good user basis for the development of other businesses of the website. Netease, Yahoo and Sina have large numbers of free e-mail users. Netease163 mail is the most widespread used free e-mail product, with 33 percent of total free e-mail users. Netease126 mail and Yahoo! Mail each own 14

The symbol contained in every e-mail address

percent, followed by Sina with 9.2 percent.

Premium e-mail service: Premium e-mail refers to professional grade e-mail services that charge a fee as opposed to free e-mail services supported by advertising. Because free e-mail with good performance may meet the demands of the majority of netizens, there are a few individuals using premium e-mail. Still, the high-end user groups, who have higher performance demands, are relatively stable.

Enterprise E-mail

Enterprise e-mail refers to e-mail service provided for enterprise users. Enterprise employees are allowed to conduct communications on enterprises' internal and external information. The enterprise e-mail regards the domain name of the enterprise website online as its postfix. This not only publicizes the brand and image of these communications, but also conducts unification and safe management It has been an indispensable modern messaging tool in the internet age.

Enterprise e-mail service has wide categories. Enterprises may realize e-mail service through building their own servers. The large enterprises and colleges have their servers, which may provide e-mail service. Enterprises may also use the specialized e-mail service of the provider, namely through outsourcing. These enterprises need not invest more human and material resources, and just enjoy more complicated, all-round e-mail services. This is a good choice for medium and small-sized enterprises

126 Mail

Website: http:// www.126.com

E-mail business is important basic service that Netease pays more attention to developing. In January 1998, Netease first provided such a service in China. In November 2001, it also introduced the virus-killing, anti-spam, large-capacity premium e-mail, being China's largest free e-mail service provider.

Netease has six major e-mail systems: 126.com, 163.com, 188.com, vip.163.com, yeah.net and netease.com, with the total number of users surpassing 190 million. Its free e-mail offers the largest network hard drive.

Netease126.com free e-mail services include: its users may own 3G e-mail storage space, send an e-mail with an attachment up to 20mb, and use the exclusive 280mb network hard drive and innovative Ajax technology. Its maintenance response time limit decreases by 90 percent, and the e-mail may block some 98 percent and 99.8 percent of spam and viruses out of the computer.

Free Email Addresses

www.126.com

mail.163.com

cn.mail.yahoo.com

mail.qq.com

mail.sohu.com

mail.sina.com.cn

Netease Mail

Website: http:// mail.163.com

The 163.com

Netease163 Mail: its users may own 3G e-mail storage space, send an e-mail with an attachment of 20mb, use the exclusive 280mb network hard drive and innovative Ajax technology. Its maintenance responding time limit decreases by 90 percent, and the e-mail may keep some 98 percent and 99.8 percent of spam and viruses out of the computer.

Yahoo! Mail

Website: http:// cn.mail.yahoo.com

Yahoo! is one of the earliest free e-mail service providers in the world. It wins universal praise in the spam and anti-virus level, and its DomainKeys technology is universally recognized as one of globally best spam technologies.

"Lifelong E-mail" that Yahoo! introduced in China has rich functions, which also integrate a large number of practical web functions, such as Yahoo album, music box and music search.

Yahoo! (www.yahoo.com) is the world's No.1 portal search website, with its service scope covering 24 countries and regions. It provides multiple internet services for more than 500 million independent users in the world. In September 1999, China Yahoo! went into operation. In August 2005, China Yahoo! was purchased by the Alibaba Group.

QQ Mail

Website: http:// mail.qq.com

Tencent offers free e-mail service with @qq.com as the suffix. With its convenience and individualization, QQ e-mail is favored by a large number of users. QQ is Tencent's instant messaging tool, so its users may open their e-mail and there are fewer spam. These features enhanced the convenience of QQ.

Founded in November 1998, Tencent, Inc. has grown into one of China's largest and most used Internet service providers. On June 16, 2004, Tencent Holdings Limited (SEHK 700) went public on the main board of the Hong Kong Stock Exchange.

Sohu Mail

Website: http:// mail.sohu.com

Sohu mail features systemic speed, safe and stable service and garbage mails filtering technologies.

Sohu.com Inc. (NASDAQ:SOHU) is China's leading company providing new media, e-commerce, communication and mobile value-added services.

Sina Mail

Website: http:// mail.sina.com.cn

SINA.com offers free e-mail storage space that is as high as 2gb.

SINA Corporation (NASDAQ: SINA) is a leading online media company and value-added information service (VAS) provider. With many regional websites, it provides an array of services including region-focused online portals, MVAS, search and directory, interest-based and community-building channels, free and premium email, blog services, audio and video streaming, online games, classified listings, fee-based services, e-commerce and enterprise e-solutions.

Internet Education

Internet Education in China

The government attaches great importance to Internet education. China has vast territory, but the educational resources have been centralized in coastal areas. Hence, only by developing Internet education can the deficiency in the uneven distribution of educational resources be overcome.

China's Internet education began in the mid-1990s but only entered a stage of rapid growth in recent years, especially in basic education and higher education.

With respect to basic education, more than 4,000 schools form a campus network; some areas also set up educational metropolitan area networks. Furthermore, there are some 300 on-line schools of certain scale. A total of 67 institutions of higher learning have become experimental units approved by the Ministry of Education to develop Internet education.

Internet education is also growing in other fields of pre-school education, E-learning and certification training,

Internet Education Users

With the economic development of China and through State support, Internet education has become an important learning mode for people failing national matriculation or needing teaching guidance or skill training. Recent years have seen the rapid growth of China's Internet education. It is forecast that, in 2010, the number of Internet education users will reach 23.50 million.

▲ Stepping Stones in Internet Education

In 1999, the Ministry of Education formulated the Opinion on the Development of Modern Distance Education; in September, "CERNET", construction of a high-speed trunk network, was authorized, with a view to meeting the requirements of modern distance education.

In July 2000, the Ministry of Education promulgated the *Provisional Methods for Management of Educational Websites and On-line Schools and Several Opinions on Supporting Some Institutions of Higher Learning to Establish Distance Education College and Carry out the Experimental Work of the Modern Distance Education*; by July 31, a total of 31 experimental colleges and universities formed a "modern distance education collaborative group of colleges and universities" to strengthen communications and cooperation and promote the construction and sharing of educational resources; soon after, the ministry increased the number of the experimental colleges and universities from 38 to 45.

The "2003 International Conference of Presidents of Open Universities" was held in Shanghai, showing that modern distance education as a teaching style of vocational training, continued learning and degree education was increasingly being promoted universally.

In June 2004, a total of one billion Yuan was invested by the Central Government to increase the experimental units of distance elementary and secondary education in rural areas; on September 27, the "National Wireless Campus Plan" was launched; some 100 top-ranking universities such as Tsinghua University, Shanghai Jiao Tong University, Fudan University and Tongji University took the lead in arranging the wireless LAN.

The Ministry of Education stipulated that, from 2005, part public courses of the Internet education colleges of 67 institutions of higher learning should hold a national unified examination; the ministry would hold an annual evaluation on the quality of Internet education colleges.

Size of Internet Education Market

China's Internet education market is in the initial stage in general. The elevation in the degree of social informatization, the cognitive degree of Internet education and the approbation degree of the educational background helps accelerate market growth. It is forecast that this market will reach 29.7 billion Yuan, 36 billion Yuan and 44.1 billion Yuan in 2008, 2009 and 2010 respectively.

Internet Education Industry

The Internet education industry mainly consists of content suppliers, software suppliers, hardware suppliers, Internet education operators and Internet education users.

The content suppliers provide teaching contents for the whole Internet education industry, whose quality exerts great influence on the development of the industry. They fall into two categories: those of one category are schools, providing specialized courses; those of the other category are professional content suppliers, providing professional Internet education contents by employing the resources of various schools and training institutions.

The software suppliers provide a teaching platform for Internet education, including the design of software system for educational administration, teaching evaluating and safety management.

The hardware suppliers provide hardware units for Internet education, such as relevant network hardware equipment and network consumer premises equipment.

In addition, on the Internet education industry chain of China, some operators act as both operators and software suppliers, developing the software of Internet education.

Categories of Internet Education

Basic Internet Education refers to elementary and secondary Internet education, customarily called "elementary and secondary Internet schools", or "Internet schools" for short. It is a kind of assistant educational activity without academic certification. Examples of this kind of education include the Beijing No.101 Internet School (www.chinaedu.com), Internet School of Beijing No.4 High School (www.etiantian.com) and Internet School of Huanggang High School (www.huanggao.net).

Higher Internet Education targets those aged over 18, mainly offering specialized courses, courses for promotion from an associate degree to a bachelor's degree and undergraduate courses. If they can pass the relevant examinations, people receiving Internet education can obtain the diplomas acknowledged by the State. Examples of this kind of education include the Online Education of Renmin University of China (www.cmr.com.cn) and Aopeng Distance Education Center (www.openonline.com.cn).

Online Vocational Certification Training targets young students and adults, mainly providing vocational training, tutoring for various examinations and certification training. Examples of this kind of education include New Oriental (www.koolearn.com) and China Accountant Net (www.chinaacc.com).

Enterprise E-learning is a new way for enterprises to train their employees. The enterprises of small scale or non-multiregional enterprises mainly implement training through internal LAN; and the multiregional enterprises mainly through the Internet. APTECH (www.accpbj.cn) is an example of this kind of education.

Internet Education Services include the educational portal, educational network games, educational channel, platform suppliers and content suppliers. They are engaged in providing relevant services for Internet education, without entities and Internet schools. Examples of this kind include 51edu.com (www.51edu.com), Education Online (www.eduol.cn) and Feloo.com (www.feloo.com).

Network Security

Personal Network Security

Personal network security ensures that a personal computer network system consisting of hardware, software and data does not suffer damage, change and divulgence for accidental and vicious reasons and maintains normal operation. Main threats to personal network security come from computer viruses and malware, including spyware, adware, hijacking and Trojan horses.

The computer virus refers to a set of computer instructions or programs designed or planted in the computer programs to damage the computer functions, ruin the data and impact the use of computer; it also can replicate itself.

Malware refers to the software installed in the users' computers or other terminals to infringe upon the legal rights and interests of the users without definite hints for users or users' permission. But it excludes the computer virus stipulated by laws and regulations.

Main Threats to Personal Network Security

Currently, the number of new computer viruses has been increasing rapidly as intercepted by three major domestic antivirus software manufacturers (Rising, Kingsoft and Jiangmin). Most of the new computer viruses are of the Trojan type.

Main reasons for the rapid increase in new computer viruses include the weakness of security in the basic application of the Internet and computer software and hardware and more and more ways and channels being developed for the spread of computer viruses.

Driven by economic benefits, hackers and virus manufacturers tend to become collectivized and industrialized day by day. In particular, the direct economic benefits lead to large numbers of Trojans with a view to intruding into the users' computers to steal personal data, game accounts, bank accounts and QQ password. Moreover, the means of invasion, assault and beguilement become increasingly diversified, imposing a huge threat to the Internet and computer users.

Trojan Industry

With the development and improvement of the virus industrial chain, the personal data stolen by trojans include the QQ password, password of network games, bank accounts and credit card accounts. Anything that can be converted into money is being stolen by hackers. Meanwhile, more and more hacker groups employ computer viruses for illegal profit-gaining behavior such as extortion and assault after being employed.

Trojans represented by password stealing Trojan, hacker backdoor and Trojan downloader have become the money-making tools for most professional virus manufacturers. The tremendous grey industrial chain behind the Trojans has already brought severer tribulation to the whole Internet. Currently, a compartmentalized Trojan industry chain comprises manufacturing and spreading Trojans, stealing account information, dealing in what they steal and laundering money on a third party platform has basically formed in China. Trojans have caused huge economic loss to China's Internet, such as the "online bank Trojan" stealing the password of the bank cards of the Internet users and software attacking network security.

Personal Network Security Products in China

Personal network security products include antivirus software, malicious software removal tools and personal firewalls. Of the total, the antivirus software mainly refers

The anti-virus softwares sold on the digital market.

to the comprehensive antivirus software represented by rising and kaspersky; and the malicious software removal tools are mainly the specialized security software represented by 360 safe. China's personal network security market will continue to expand.

The emergence of specialized security software represented by 360 safe marks the initial specialization of China's antivirus software market. It indicates that personal network security products are becoming further specialized; and the traditional comprehensive antivirus software cannot completely deal with the increasingly rampant malware.

In the Chinese market, the main personal firewall products include those provided by Rising, Tianwang, Norton and Filseclab manufacturers; the major antivirus softwares include those provided by Rising, Kaspersky, Kingsun, Jiangmin and Norton manufacturers; and the malicious software removal tools mainly include 360 safe, Rising Kaka, Super Rabbit and Iparmor.

Rising

Website: http:// www.rising.com.cn

Beijing Rising International Software Co., Ltd. was established in April 1998. Its predecessor, established in 1991, was Beijing Rising Computer Technology Development

Rising anti-irus software

Department. Rising is the earliest specialized enterprise engaged in computer virus prevention and research in China. It is dedicated to research, development, production and sale of computer antivirus products, network security products, and anti-hacker products. Rising possesses all the intellectual property rights and a number of patented technologies for all the products.

Rising has introduced a variety of operating system based antivirus software, firewall software and enterprise antivirus wall, firewall, network security warning system and other hardware products. Rising is the third company in the world and the only one in China to provide a full range of information security products and professional services. Moreover, it also has the only one "telecom-class" calling service center and a service system of "online experts' clinic" in the domestic security industry.

Rising has successfully set up five major network security systems: The Global Computer Virus Monitoring Network, The Global Computer Virus Emergency Response Network, The National Computer Virus Forecast Network, and The National Computer Virus Service Network and The Global Virus Epidemic Situation Monitoring Network.

Kaspersky

Website: http:// www.kaspersky.com.cn

Established in 1997, Kaspersky Lab is a world-famous information security software supplier. Headquartered in Moscow, it has branches in Britain, France, Germany, Holland, Poland, Japan, China, South Korea, Romania and America. It has over 500 partners globally.

Since its entrance into the Chinese market, Kaspersky antivirus software has gained the support of large numbers of Chinese users.

360 Safe

Website: http:// www.360safe.com

This is free software as an auxiliary tool for online security. It has the functions of removing the popular Trojans, clearing odium and system plug-ins, providing international applications and Kaspersky antivirus software, real-time protection for system and repairing system vulnerabilities, and at the same time, has the auxiliary functions of making overall diagnosis for system, popup plug-in immunization and cleaning up usage trails and system restoration. Moreover, it offers an overall diagnosis report on the system for users to find out what's wrong in good time and provides a multi-faceted system security protection for each user.

Daily Life Services

Financial and Economic Category

Introduction to Financial and Economic Websites

China's financial and economic websites are in the stage of rapid growth. Currently, they target individual users, a market of huge potential with the increasing demand of Chinese stock investors for financial and economic information services.

Among Chinese users, netizens aged above 30 account for 35.4 percent; and the users of financial and economic information service occupy 30.9 percent of total netizens. In addition, the groups with high income have more idle funds that can be invested in the capital market.

Main financial and Economic Websites in China

Eastmoney.com
http:// www.eastmoney.com

Business.sohu.com
http:// www. business.sohu.com

Finance.sina.com
http:// www. finance.sina.com.cn

Hexun.com
http:// www. hexun.com

Jrj.com.cn
http:// www.jrj.com.cn

Cnfol.com
http:// www.cnfol.com

Stockstar.com
http:// www.stockstar.com

10jqka.com.cn
http:// www.10jqka.com.cn

Stock.163.com
http:// stock.163.com

Eastmoney.com

Website: http:// www.eastmoney.com

Eastmoney.com is one of the largest financial and economic portals with largest reach in China. It has an average daily reach of over one million.

Launched in March 2004, it provides a wide range of financial and economic data and information covering stocks, funds, futures, bonds, foreign exchange, banking and insurance. It updates over 10,000 pieces of data daily. The stock bar is the most prosperous stock community in China reviewing real-time markets and exchanges.

Business.sohu.com

Website: http:// www. business.sohu.com

The business.sohu.com is a sub-website of sohu.com, including the following contents:

Securities Channel: It provides key news on securities and picks up the most valuable market information and big events among the 100-odd securities media daily. Meanwhile, it offers such contents as the pick of the securities paper and magazines, champion list, map for stock speculation, my stocks and top 10 stock business people.

Financing Channel: It consists of some 10 columns, such as financing programming, banking, insurance, fund, real estate and futures, and many forums, providing financing services for the masses and professional personnel.

Finance.sina.com

Website: http:// www.finance.sina.com.cn

This is the financial and economic channel of sina.com. It provides financial and economic data and information as well as quotes from the global financial market around the clock and covers a wide range of services regarding stocks, bond, fund, futures, entrustment, financing and management for individuals and enterprises.

Hexun.com

Website: http:// www.hexun.com

Established in 1996, hexun.com is one of the earliest professional ICPs.

Centering on finance and economy, the website provides professional business information, unique network community and online financing, commercial and recreational services.

"Business News" gathers global financial and economic data and information and offers online business news for investors and personnel caring for economy.

"Hexun Stocks" is one of the influential platforms for online stock investment and exchanges in China, providing stocks and business data and information, covering stocks, finance and economy, securities, Hong Kong stocks, market, A-shares, stock index and individual shares.

"Hexun Fund" is a famous fund portal in China, offering rich data, rating and information.

"Hexun Foreign Exchange" offers foreign exchange information, reviews, quoted price and financing services.

The commercial white-collars using the lap top computers at Hangzhou Airport

"Hexun Real Estate" is a specialized channel of online real estate information with financial and economic characteristics; its main columns include real estate news, real estate finance and analysis on the value of investment in buildings.

Jrj.com

Website: http:// www.jrj.com.cn

Launched in August 1999, jrj.com is a financial and economic information platform jointly invested by IDG of America and VERTEX of Singapore.

On October 15, 2004, jrj.com (NASDAQ: JRJC) was listed on NASDAQ.

The website provides updated industry developments, information on stock markets, data of listed firms and subjects, media, columns, data and reports on finance and economy.

Cnfol.com

Website: http:// www.cnfol.com

Cnfol.com is one of the fairly influential financial portals in China, with a daily reach of over 10 million. It provides a wide range of services concerning business news, stocks, securities, finance, Hong Kong stocks, market, fund, bond, futures, foreign exchanges, insurance, banking, blogs and stock analysis software for individuals and enterprises.

The stock column of cnfol.com provides stock information around the clock on markets, individual shares, trends, industries, research reports, small and middle enterprises board, B-shares, third market, China concept stock, and a college for stock investors.

Its foreign exchange channel offers foreign exchange information, timely news, analysis and reviews on foreign exchanges and knowledge on foreign exchange speculation.

Stockstar.com

Website: http:// www.stockstar.com

Established in 1996, stockstar.com is a website subject to China Finance Online Co., Ltd. a listed company on NASDAQ. It is the earliest specialized website providing financial services.

Centering on the financial products, it provides specialized and timely financial and economic information through the website, market analysis software, short messaging and WAP.

The contents of the website include securities, funds, financing, gold, Hong Kong stocks, futures and foreign exchanges.

10jqka.com

Website: http:// www.10jqka.com.cn

Established in 1995, Zhejiang Hexin Flush Network Services Co., Ltd. is engaged in research, development and popularity of the software and hardware products with independent intellectual property in the finance and communication sectors. It is a supplier of the online security trade, the Internet security code communication products and the e-commerce software.

At the end of 2003, the company launched the 10jqka.com with IPR.

The Flush Platform is a comprehensive finance and security platform, including the website, real-time market, online trading, information, security analysis tools and comprehensive financing. It provides one-stop financial services consisting of website, software, trade, financing, community and stock speculation by mobile phone.

The exhibition stand of the Tonghs.cn.

Stock.163.com

Website: http:// www.stock.163.com

Stock.163.com is the financial and economic channel of 163.com, with such contents as securities, financing, stocks, stock bar, fund, banking, foreign exchanges, bond, lottery, insurance and gold.

The website features simple, smooth and elegant pages in a two-part structure. The website conducts a second processing of news instead of simple downloads. Often, there are instant reviews and feedbacks on the topic of each article, which strengthens interaction.

Auto Category

Introduction to Auto Websites

The proportion of China's auto consumption in world auto consumption has surpassed Japan, making China the second largest auto consumer after America. This has created a market of people wanting websites related to the auto industry.

The main function of auto websites in China is supply of information. Because the majority of people are interested in picking up information instead of buying autos by this route, domestic auto websites mainly attract people by contents and gain profit through advertisements. The income from network advertisements accounts for some 90 percent of the total.

Currently, the auto websites with large reach include

Chinacars.com
http:// www.chinacars.com

Sina.com
http:// www. auto.sina.com.cn

Autohome.com
http:// www.autohome.com.cn

Che168.com
http:// www.che168.com

PCauto.com
http:// www.pcauto.com.cn

Xcar.com
http:// www.xcar.com

Auto.sohu.com
http:// auto.sohu.com

Autohome.com

Website: http:// www.autohome.com.cn

Autohome.com provides the latest quoted price, pictures, news, market, review and forecasts and shopping guide on autos. It has three characteristic service platforms:

Information Service Platform: Autohome.com is one of the fairly authoritative network media in China. Its main network channels include news, market, review and forecasting and shopping guide.

Data Service Platform: It has a variety of functions of providing product information, dealer community, national quoted price and data investigation, inquiring about dynamic shopping degree and offering user feedback and value added services.

Interactive Service Platform: It offers multi-faceted interactive services and has an auto-home community with over 600,000 registrants and online franchised stores.

CHE168

Website: http:// www.che168.com

Che168.com was launched in May 2004 by Haochen Institution. It is an auto shopping guide and information website centering on database of auto types. The website offers potential auto purchasers in-depth reports on auto products through its four major parts: the auto market conditions, the database containing auto parameter, pictures and panorama, specialized authoritative reviews and interaction between auto purchasers, auto users and auto manufacturers.

PCauto.com.cn

Website: http:// www.pcauto.com.cn

PCauto.com was launched in July 2002. As a professional auto network media, the website takes the information, guide for shopping and use and community as the basic points of consideration and sticks to an original style. It provides netizens with first-hand information on auto quoted prices, shopping guide, review and forecasting, and auto use and play and creates an interactive space for exchanges.

The website has such contents as quoted prices, reviews and forecasting, news, shopping guide, repair, maintenance, security, forum, self-drive tour and recreation on auto as well as auto culture.

The PCauto Reviewing and Forecasting Center depends on a picked test driver and advanced testing instruments.

Xcar.com.cn

Website: http:// www.xcar.com.cn

Launched in August 2002, xcar.com is a specialized auto network media in China. The original articles written from unique angle at xcar.com are frequently adopted by numerous media.

The website boasts a huge auto community, including 121 clubs of auto types of mainstream brands, 32 branches in various provinces, municipalities and regions and 43 forums. With one million registrants, X-car Club is one of the fairly large auto communities, auto forums and auto friend associations.

In response to the demand of users, the website organizes such activities as self-drive tour, group purchase of autos, auto contest, lectures and test driving and selects auto service institutions and auto products suppliers for users. Besides, depending on the network platform, the members of the website organize some 1,000 activities on their own per week, forming an interactive platform based on the network technology.

Real Estate Consultation Category

Real Estate Websites

Recent years have seen rapid development of the real estate industry in China. The number of real estate network media has increased rapidly

Main Real Estate Websites

Soufun.com
Website: http:// www.soufun.com

Focus.cn
Website: http:// www.focus.cn

Goufang.com
Website: http:// www.goufang.com

House.sina.com
Website: http:// www.house.sina.com.cn

Homhow.com
Website: http:// www.homhow.com

and now reaches over 240.

Currently, the real estate network media mainly gain profit through advertisements.

The real estate network media can be divided into the following two categories:

With regard to the business region, they can be divided into the national and local ones;

In respect to business mode, they can be divided into comprehensive ones, those dealing in second-hand houses and those engaged in house decoration.

The main contents of the real estate websites in China include:

Information on house sources: including the information on new houses, second-hand houses, tenements, villas, office buildings and shops.

Relevant news information: including the news on house property, house decoration, house style and building materials.

Relevant content services: such as the information on policies and regulations, loans, evaluation and mobile value added services.

User exchanges: centering on the owner community.

Soufun.com

Website: http:// www.soufun.com

Soufun.com is one of the well-known real estate portals, covering 45 large and medium-sized core cities. It is a real estate website with widest reach in China.

Soufun.com boasts a tremendous owner community and forum as well as over 40,000 active building forums, with over 150,000 notes daily on average. The average monthly number of visitors from unique IP addresses reaches 42 million. The website is fairly influential among the owners and potential owners.

The Sofang.com.

The website has a database of large real estate items, providing details of over 45,000 properties. It offers a rapid and accurate building search channel.

Rent.soufun.com provides some one million pieces of information on tenements and trade of second-hand houses.

Goufang.com

Website: http:// www.goufang.com

Established on July 10, 2006, goufang.com is a large real estate trade service website, headquartered in Dalian. The website has branches in 15 large cities namely Beijing, Shanghai, Guangzhou, Shenzhen, Tianjin, Chongqing, Hangzhou, Ningbo, Chengdu, Wuhan, Changsha, Nanjing, Harbin, Jilin and Shenyang.

The website provides online information on the new buildings, second-hand houses, tenement and building materials for fitment as well as house shopping forum. It offers rapid and accurate building search channel and provides more complete and convenient services for house purchasers.

Homhow.com

Website: http:// www.homhow.com

Established in March 2006, homhow.com is a real estate network video media. Currently, it has set up a huge basic building video information bank, with over 200,000 videos of outdoor scenes. It collects over 98 percent of videos of outdoor scenes of the buildings sold after 2000.

On September 1, 2007, the website launched a platform for second-hand houses and tenement with video style. It contains all the business of taking a look at the new houses, second-hand houses and tenements and provides online maps and a calculator for calculating the loans of the second-hand houses.

In addition, the website has established the largest real estate video broadcasting network and the partnership with various websites on real estate, finance and economy, auto, politics, recreation and IT as well as comprehensive websites. It covers one million netizens.

IT Information Category

Main IT Information Websites

Obtaining information from specialized IT information supplier is a big demand of netizens. Partly due to historical reasons, most well-operated IT information websites hold a number of loyal users, whose publicity helps the IT information websites ward off attacks from the news supermarkets of network portals.

Main IT websites

Yesky.com
Website: http:// www.yesky.com

It168.com
Website: http:// www.it168.com

Zol.com
Website: http:// www.zol.com.cn

Pchome.net
Website: http:// www.pchome.net

Pcpop.com
Website: http:// www.pcpop.com

Yesky.com

Website: http:// www.yesky.com

The Tianji Media Group is an online media group, consisting of four websites namely the chinabyte.com, yesky.com, ctocio.com and mostar.cn and an IT information transmitting website namely the itcpn.net. Facing various IT groups of IT consumption, commerce, franchisers and mobile phones, the group provides the information plus shopping guide and interactive services.

Yesky.com offers IT consumers and fans such services as application and evaluating of IT products, quoted price, shopping guide, software download and interactive community, leading the consumption fashions of the computers, digital products and mobile phones.

IT168

Website: http:// www.it168.com

Established in 1999, it168.com is a website engaged in providing IT products shopping guide information for individuals and enterprises and has branches in Beijing, Shanghai, Guangdong, Shenzhen, Jiangsu and Hubei.

The website has a specific database of users including channel partner, enterprises and individuals and provides a network integrating and marketing platform for IT manufacturers, covering more than 13,000 products such as notebook PC, server, mobile phone, digital camera, MP3, MP4, vidicon, desk computer, switch, router, firewall, laser printer, ink jet printer, projector, copycat, all-in-one printer, CPU, main board, graphic card and LCD.

Zol.com

Website: http:// www.zol.com.cn

Launched in March 1999, zol.com is an IT interactive portal engaged in promoting sales all over the country. Its clients are mainly enterprise and institutional users, individual purchasers and large numbers of IT and IT-related manufacturers and dealers. The websites provides the services in the business fields of IT products, channels and market conditions, market trends, technology application, consumption investigation and e-commerce. It boasts an average daily reach of over 25 million and more than 2.5 million registrants and has influence on over 3.5 million IT purchaser users daily.

PChome.net

Website: http:// www.pchome.net

Established in 1996, pchome.net is a specialized network media providing broadband, digital products and wireless information. It has a digital image club and palmtop equipment club of significant scale in China. The website has the channels of new products, digital products, home appliance, hardware, products, office, enterprises, market, quotation, activities, games, software, download, antivirus, education, community and news.

PCpop.com

Website: http:// www.pcpop.com

Launched in 2000, the pcpop.com is a leading vertical interactive network media of 3C products.

Pcpop.com boasts 30-odd specialized channels, 900-plus sub-channels and the websites of over 25,000 products. It is a network platform offering information, interaction and marketing at the same time. It had 5.32 million registrants by March 2007. It is committed to providing a vigorous channel for the purchase of 3C products and recreation. Its instant quoting system consisting of over 5,000 dealers and several ten thousand products has become an attractive information platform for online shopping and brand popularization.

Health Category

Main Health Websites

More and more people are starting to pay attention to their health situation, and wish to learn more by using the internet. This has made the number of health website users rank first among life service websites.

At present, health websites with more visits include:

39.net Website: http:// www.39.net
Xyxy.net Website: http:// www.xyxy.net

39.net

Website: http:// www.39.net

39.net, launched on March 9, 2000, has many users majoring in medical science, including 3,600 hospital-level enterprise members, and 20,000 qualified doctors; It has established good cooperative relations with nationally-famous professional medicine institutions, having its unique professional resource predominance.

39.net, using professional health information services, online health community, professional health database and medicine and health industry search tool, provides health information service for individuals and enterprises.

It has developed many new professional health services, such as the largest health evaluation center in China and seven health databases having authoritative influence. It has forged strategic cooperation relations with China.com and Netease, respectively, exclusively operating their respective health channel.

Xyxy.net

Website: http:// www.xyxy.net

Xyxy.net, a platform for communications between doctor and patient, is the only medical website set up for patient to conduct online consultation.

In order to help netizens seek medical treatment, the physicians' card channel of this website includes information on thousands of qualified doctors; xyxy community is classified according to different diseases. Each section has a regular number of browsers. It has millions of registered members and thousands of doctor members. There are several thousand interactive consultation posts each day; Medicine search channel handles inquiries about hospitals, doctors, drugs and relevant information for netizens.

Online Recruitment Category

China Online Recruitment

In recent years, as China's online recruitment service modes have improved and the number of users increases rapidly, enterprise interest in recruiting talent through the internet platform has seen an upsurge. Online recruitment shows great development potential, thus impacting on the traditional recruitment market.

Compared with traditional recruitment, online recruitment features rich information, simple operating procedures, effectiveness over a given period of time, and convenience of information transmission, and cheap price. These are the important reasons why users choose online recruitment.

At present, integrated recruitment websites are the main focus, including national and regional ones; at the same time, industry and search recruitment websites also have witnessed good development. Among recruitment websites, 51job.com, ChinaHR.com, and Alliance's Zhaopin.com have large scale.

Foreign investors think highly of China's recruitment market potential. 51job.com was listed on NASDAQ in 2004. In 2006, Japan Recruit purchased 15 percent of shares of 51job for US$110 million; Monster, the world's leading recruitment website acquired 40 percent of the shares of ChinaHR.com for US$ 50 million.

Main Online Recruitment Website

ChinaHR.com
Website: http:// www.chinahr.com

1job.com
Website: http:// www.51job.com

Alliance's zhaopin.com
Website: http:// www.zhaopin.com

job36.com
Website: http:// www.job36.com

tkzp.com
Website: http:// www.tkzp.com

ChinaHR.com

Website: http:// www.chinahr.com

ChinaHR.com, launched in 1997, is China's first recruitment website, and one of the most professional. Its brand and services have been universally recognized by individual job seekers and enterprise human resource department.

In April 2005, ChinaHR.com received strategic investment of US$50 million from Monster.com, the world's leading online recruiting services provider and introduced its management ideas, business mode and products. In May of the same year, ChinaHR.com forged a strategic partnership with the portal website Sina.

Headquartered in Beijing, ChinaHR.com has set up 12 branch companies across China, with its services covering 35 main industries in over 40 cities. It has a human resource service team consisting of some 1,000 professionals. Its main products and services include: online recruitment, talent recruiting treasure, talent SSS, campus recruitment and executive search service. Main achievements:

•daily average visits have exceeded 19.8 million

•more than 15 million individual registered users

•over 13.8 million effective resumes

•more than 1.5 million registered enterprise members

•more than 1.92 million valid jobs offered daily

51job.com

Website: http:// www.51job.com

51job.com (NASDAQ: JOBS), offers a broad array of services in the areas of recruitment solutions, training and assessment, and HR outsourcing services. It has set up service outlet in 26 cities across China, including Hong Kong.

In September 2004, 51job successfully completed its IPO on NASDAQ, being China's first human resource service enterprise listed on there.

Executive search service of 51job first initiated the omni-directional recruitment plan combining the strengths of newspaper, website, executive search, software and campus recruitment. This website has had thousands of individual users and recruited needed talents for 200,000 enterprises.

The professional training and assessment consultant of the 51job custom-tailors various public courses, inner training, actual simulation and professional assessment plan for enterprises.

51job has also introduced a series of human resource outsource services, providing one-stop service and consultation from staff recruiting to dismissing workers for enterprises.

Alliance's Zhaopin.com

Website: http:// www.zhaopin.com

The advertisement of the Zhaopin.com

Founded in 1997, Zhaopin Ltd (www.zhaopin.com) is one of the most professional HR service providers in China. It originally started as a headhunting firm called Alliance Executive Search in 1994.

Headquartered in Beijing, Zhaopin.com has set up branch companies in such cities as Shanghai, Guangzhou, Shenzhen, Tianjin, Xi'an, Chengdu, Nanjing, Wuhan, Changsha, Suzhou, Shenyang, Changchun, Dalian, Jinan, Qingdao, and Zhengzhou, with its business covering more than 50 cities in China.

Zhaopin.com can provide one-stop professional HR services for large companies, as well as fast-growing small and medium-sized enterprises. The services include online recruitment, newspaper recruitment, campus recruitment, headhunting service, human resource outsourcing, corporate training and staff assessment. It also originated the human resources magazine CHO.

Since its establishment, Zhaopin.com has provided professional human resource services for more than 1.13 million customers, covering various industries. It has rich experience in the fields of IT, rapid consumable, industrial manufacturing, pharmaceuticals and healthcare, consultation and financial service.

JOB36

Website: http:// www.job36.com

Job36.com is the industries talents recruitment website, founded in 2002. As the first recruitment website subdividing the industries in China, Job36 has 25 industry recruitment websites. Those with higher fame include:

Tourjob.net: Over 60 percent of five-star hotels in the country are long-term users.

Carjob.com.cn: Over 80 percent of auto production enterprises choose this website when recruiting talents;

Doctorjob.com.cn: The first-choice recruitment website in the field of medical treatment and health.

Tkzp.com

Website: http:// www.tkzp.com

Tkzp.com is the new generation of online recruitment, job-seeking service system. Relying on Content Smart, Match Smart search engines and other vertical search technologies with the independent intellectual property, it integrates a large numbers of job postings online, thus providing the effective information for job seeker and employers in a short time.

Tkzp.com updates tens of thousands of effective job postings each day, while the job seekers use the intellectual search to get their ideal jobs. Job hunting procedures such as search, filling, and resume sending may be completed through one-stop means. Through the Tkzp.com, enterprise recruiters are able to post their job openings to solicit resumes, search for their ideal candidates' resumes, and choose talents.

Photography Category

Main Photograph Websites

There are local photography websites or websites of photography associations in each city across China. Local photography websites are based on medium and small-sized BBS, with the number of online users ranging from a dozen to 100. Although not large in scale, this kind of website predominates.

The national websites which operate with the company as the entity are represented by photo.poco.cn, xiangshu.com, fengniao.com, xitek.com, and photofans.cn. Most of the users of such websites are mainly professional photography enthusiasts. Gain is one of the important indices of whether a website can achieve sustained development. The income of each website mainly comes from the internet advertising.

Dpnet.com.cn

Website: http:// www.dpnet.com.cn

Dpnet.com.cn, founded by Shanghai Dpnet Digital Technology Co., Ltd in 2000, is the professional digital photo information website and Chinese business website, with its columns including industry information, product assessment, photo enjoying, photograph academy, and digital photograph forum.

This website tries to develop itself into a new consuming service platform combining information providing, equipments sale, and digital developing and printing.

Xitek.com

Website: http:// www.xitek.com

Xitek.com, launched on January 18, 2000, is an interactive community, with photography, photography equipment, and pictures as the main theme, concurrently covering music, acoustics, automobile and other themes.

Since its establishment, Xitek.com has accumulated rich content resources: including 2.41318 million pieces of data; more than 867,094 themes and 6,744 updated daily; over 2.575277 million pictures; 21.175543 million posts. This website has more than 256,303 registered users, with the number of peak concurrent online users reaching 6,381 and that of everyday online users 3,529. Its daily page views reach 1.5 million, click mount amounts to 13.5 million, and accumulated page views surpassed 979.897406 million.

Fengniao.com

Website: http:// www.fengniao.com

Fengniao.com is one of China's photograph websites providing information on photography, the photography industry and products. This website has the forum on photography and picture communication, and a platform for equipment trading.

Fengniao.com was founded in 2000, and acquired by CNTE NETWORKS, a world-known internet media in 2004.

As the sole professional photo portal website of CNET (China), Fengniao.com has been the brand among Chinese photo media with the greatest number of visits and is praised highly. Its target audience is distributed throughout China, Hong Kong, Macao, Taiwan and Chinese-inhabited areas in the world, consisting of photography fans, photograph fans, professional photographers, and large numbers of employees of the photo industry and relevant industries.

Photograph Websites with Greater Fame

Dpnet.com.cn
Website: http:// www.dpnet.com.cn

Xitek.com
Website: http:// www.xitek.com

Fengniao.com
Website: http:// www.fengniao.com

Xiangshu.com
Website: http:// www.xiangshu.com

Photofans.cn
Website: http:// www.photofans.cn

POCO
Website: http:// photo.poco.cn

Xiangshu.com

Website: http:// www.xiangshu.com

Xiangshu.com, launched on October 26, 2004, provides online and offline photo information and various value-added services with photo as the theme, one of the photograph websites in China which have witnessed rapid development.

Xiangshu photograph club, a photograph-themed community of Xiangshu.com, covers 50percent of cities in China. Offline activities are very active. Some 10 large photograph activities are held each week on average. The influence of Xiangshu brand grows continually. The number of members of xiangshu.com increases at the speed of 10,000 persons per month.

Photofans.cn

Website: http:// www.photofans.cn

Online Internet Technology Co., Ltd. is a professional internet company in the photograph circle. The professional photograph portal website—photofans.cn operated by the company is one of famous online photograph media in China.

Photofans.cn provides all kinds of information on photography, building China's photography fan community and Chinese photographers' blog homeland. It carries out members' activities, relying on local substations in more than 30 cities across China. Photofans.cn has had more than 100,000 registered members.

Local substations of Photofans.cn are divided and set up at provincial and city levels and are locally managed.

POCO

Website: http:// photo.poco.cn

Poco.cn, founded in 2003, has developed into an individual space service provider with pictures as the core. Headquartered in Guangzhou, the individual interactive entertainment website set up branch companies in Beijing, Shanghai, and Chengdu.

MyPOCO individual Space serves as the core product of POCO. Its 79 million registered users and more than 10 million active users share the most multimedia resources such as photography, foods, pet, tourism, fashion, fad pictures, text, and e-journal in China. It is the original community of fad people.

POCO individual interactive entertainment website has set up the photograph, foods, pet, tourism, mobile phone shooting, individual journal, movies and other individual entertainment interactive channels. All the contents of the website come from original of users the MyPOCO individual space.

Digital Entertainment

Online Games

Online Games Industry in China

China's online games sector began before 1995. During the period, personal edition games achieved some scale, and formed a transition to the network edition game, thus making full preparation for rapid development of China's online game in terms of human resources and technology. From 2001, China entered into the growth period for online game, with some profit potential and wide development space.

In 2005, China's games industry experienced a shift from introduction agency to independent innovation. From then on, the number of online game users, the actual sales income of the publishing market, the number of teams and personnel engaging in independently developing game across China, and the number of developed massive and medium online games are all on the rise. Online games developed by Chinese people themselves are the main stream on the market.

Main Online Game Websites

9you.com
http:// www.9you.com

Netease game
http:// xy2.163.com

Shenda
http:// www.sdo.com

Tiancity.com
http:// www.tiancity.com

The9.com
http:// www.the9.com

Ourgame.com
http:// www.ourgame.com

17game.com
http:// www.17game.com

9you.com

Website: http:// www.9you.com

9you.com is an integrated online game portal website, as well as the first online game operator in China realizing commercial operation of online games services.

In November 2004, three international venture capital funds, including the Carlyle Group, which is the world's largest private fund investment group, China Merchant Fortune Ventures and Sino-Korean Wireless Fund financed by the Government of South Korea, jointly invested US$14 million in 9you.com. With financing and reorganization, Nineyou Information Technology (Shanghai) Co. Ltd. was officially founded. 9you.com's financing has been the largest venture investment in China's games industry since SB Asia Infrastructure Fund, L.P. invested in Shenda.

What 9you.com provides is an interactive online entertainment platform. It integrates game information, global search, massive online game, casual online game, chess and card online game, mobile phone short message, MMS service, electronic greeting card, online game forum, free show (AVATAR), with online chatting, thereby providing multi-platform online entertainment services for professional and non-professional games player at various age levels.

Super Dancer and Super Star that 9you.com has independently developed have been exported to 41 countries and regions in North America, Europe and Southeast Asia, including India, Taiwan and Hong Kong. The number of the website's registered users has exceeded two million, and that of the total online account reached 950,000.

Xy2.163.com

Website: http:// xy2.163.com

In December 2001, Netease first introduced its first independently developed Westward Journey Online, a massively multi-player online role-playing game. In August 2002, it, based on the original product, developed the Westward Journey Online II, which became the first successfully operated China-made online game. In November 2003, Netease introduced the massive Q edition online game Fantasy Westward Journey Online. The number of the concurrent online players of the two games has reached two million. On May 31, 2006, 3Dgame Datanghaoxia (http://dt.163.com/) that Netease independently developed officially began open Beta test, setting the record of 170,000 concurrent online players of the open Beta test; in the first quarter of 2007, 3Dgame Tianxiaer (http://tx2.163.com/) entered the domestic online games market; Westward Journey 3, the updated edition of Westward Journey Online II entered the closed Beta testing phase on May 20, 2007. The operation of other new game products will be put on the agenda successively. At present, Netease games have accounted for most of the domestic online game market shares, becoming the best online game producer in the capacity to independently develop and independently operate.

Netease games have been recognized and liked by a growing number of Chinese players, with more than 200 million registered users and the two million peak concurrent online players.

Shengda Online

Website: http:// www.sdo.com

In November 1999, Shengda was founded and introduced the Online Home Valley, the first graphic online virtual game in China. In September 2001, Shengda began the open Beta test of the Legend of Mir II, a multi-player online role-playing game, thus officially entering into the online games operating market.

In March 2003, SB Asia Infrastructure Fund, L.P. invested US$ 40 million in Shengda. In May 2004, Shengda (NASDAQ: SNDA) was officially listed. Chen Tianqiao, the founder of Shengda created China's new internet legend in 2004.

Games that Shengda operates include multi-player online role-playing games (MMORPG game) and causal games. These games include independently-developed ones and licensed products. The Legend of Mir II has remained the most popular online game in China; In addition, Shengda introduced its independently-developed online games The World of Legend, Poptang (http://bnb.poptang.com/newbnb/bnb04/home/index.htm), Legend of Mir and Magical Land.

Tiancity.com

Website: http:// www.tiancity.com

Tiancity.com is a team of Shanghai Posts & Telecommunications Technology Co., LTD, devoting itself to online entertainment-related business, agent of NEXON of South Korea in mainland China.

In early 2005, tiancity.com was officially licensed to operate the hottest cartoon online game Mabingi, which has entered into the commercial operation phase. On March 17, 2006, tiancity.com joined hands with NEXON to develop the free casual game PopKart, and later introduced the New Talesweaver and PopShot.

PopKart is a casual racing car game developed by NEXON. PopShot (originally called BIGSHOT), developed by another famous development team of NEXON, is a new generation racing cartoon shot online game.

The9.com

Website: http:// www.the9.com

The9.com is the digital online life platform of The9 Computer Technology Consulting (Shanghai) Co., Ltd. It is reported to have more than 14 million registered users.

In July 2002, The9.com obtained the exclusive license to operate the MU, an online game developed by WEBZEN of South Korea,

The World of Warcraft, a network game jointed launched by Coca-Cola and the "Ninth City".

in mainland China. Because this was one of the online games most liked by players on in China in those days, The9.com became the only enterprise able to stand up to Shenda as an equal. In April 2004, The9.com obtained the exclusive license to operate the Blizzard and WOW, the top-ranking games in the world, in China with US$13 million.

On December 15, 2004, The9.com (NASDAQ: NCTY) was officially listed.

So far, products that operated by The9.com include MU, Joyful Journey WestTM, World of Warcraft (WOW), Granado Espada (GE), Soul of the Ultimate NationTM (SUN), Guild Wars, Super Girl World Online and Hellgate: London.

Ourgame.com

Website: http:// www.ourgame.com

The Ourgame Co., Ltd.

Ourgame.com, founded in March 1998, is a online casual and entertainment service provider which mainly operates chess and card games and party-to-party games. At present, it is directly held by the Searainbow Holding Corp (000503), a listed company in China.

Ourgame.com has set up servers in Mainland China, Taiwan, the US, Japan, South Korea and other countries and regions, and planned to introduce the versions in the simplified Chinese, traditional Chinese, English, Japanese and Korean.

17game.com

Website: http:// www.17game.com

17game.com, founded in 2003, signed an agreement with Mgame of South Korea on obtaining the exclusive license to operate party-to-party 3online on Mainland China in December of the same year, making it one of the most popular online games of that year.

In March 2004, 17game.com signed an agreement with CCR and Enet of South Korea on obtaining the exclusive license to operate online game Travia Online in China. Travia Online has gained outstanding achievements, being one of the five online games that are most liked by the Chinese online game users.

In March 2005, 17game.com and China.com officially announced they had forged a strategic partnership and that China.com had made strategic investment in the 17game.com.

Hot Blood Boxing online of Mgame of South Korea that is licensed to this website began open Beta testing on April 20, 2005, and was operated for free in May of the same year. It remains popular.

Games Information

uuu9.com

Website: http:// www.uuu9.com

Uuu9.com, founded in 2003, is a games entertainment portal website focused on providing games information and entertainment services. It has the following main columns:

Warcraft RPG Alliance: China's largest Warcraft RPG map downloading station, which timely updates information on Warcraft and games strategy each day;

Warcraft Electronic Sport: one of China's Warcraft electronic sport stations, which releases the latest international and domestic competition reports, and provides video recording downloading service;

Game Forum: The number of registered users has surpassed one million, and newly increased posts reached 15,000 each day.

U9 entertainment: including funny picture, flash, video, and articles.

U9 Photo: about 100 newest photos are updated each day.

Main Game Information Websites

uuu9.com
http:// www.uuu9.com

Sohu's 17173
http:// www.17173.com

92wy.com
http:// www.92wy.com

Pcgames.com.cn
http:// www.pcgames.com.cn

Tkgame.com
http:// www.tkgame.com

Sina's game information
http:// games.sina.com.cn

Sohu's 17173.com

Website: http:// www.17173.com

Sohu's 17173.com, founded in 2000, is a part of the NetDragon.(China) Websoft Inc. The number domain name of this website has meaning in the following aspects: first, the number 17173 has the harmonic tone of "all go together" in Chinese, showing the group entertainment meaning of online game; second, the numbers are easy to remember.

On November 17, 2003, Sohu.com Inc. officially acquired the online game website17173.com.

17173.com first introduced the online game portal, a new concept, into Mainland China. At present, it has more than 100 games zones and 4.3 million registered users, becoming China's largest online games information and community website. The 17173.com has not only a games special zone, but also online games forum, with more than 200,000 posts per day. Its games player club attracts more than 100,000 game factions, and Gonghui who pitch their camp here.

92wy.com

Website: http:// www.92wy.com

92wy.com, launched in July 2002, is an interactive entertainment portal website based on large-sized community and featuring game and entertainment information.

Interactive entertainment platform that 92wy.com provides includes: Flash fairyland, BT unload, animation, movies, TV, E-show e-journal, and 92wy racing car net.

92wy individual center, highlight of 92wy.com, is the online interactive entertainment platform integrating blogs, album and friends.

PCgames

Website: http:// www.pcgames.com.cn

Pcgames.com.cn, together with PConline (www.pconline.com.cn), PCauto(www.pcauto.com.cn), is one member of Pconline Group.

The predecessor of pcgames.com.cn is the game land channel of the Pconline (www.pconline.com.cn), which was launched in October 2000. Within a year, it rapidly developed into the first professional games website in south China. On December 24, 2003, PCgames (www.pcgames.com.cn) was built independently, including five columns—E-sports, PC games, online game, TV game and animation world.

Tkgame.com

Website: http:// www.tkgame.com

Tkgame.com, launched in January 2004, has seven major sections—TK valuable book, game village, unload center, TK blogs, players' album, game supermarket and TK community, mainly reporting the latest information on online game in the world, such as closed Beta testing account number dispensing, game special zone, game news, game articles, game unload, game pictures, game forum, and game card sales.

TK game valuable book is a electronic strategy software targeted at online game users, introduced in May 2004. Compared with the traditional online game special zone, TK game valuable book has marked dominance in aspects of content and speed; It has also the local search (full text search: rapidly capturing the needed data), automatic update (checking content automatically updating the latest information), Hot Key On (directly opens searched information in the game) and other functions and services that are close to users' demand.

Online Music

China's Online Music Development

The popularization of Internet and broadband, and users' demand for online music make it possible that online music and other broadband entertainment businesses rapidly develop globally. In China, music has also become one of the important internet applications. With the rapid and convenient tuning way, online music has more and more users.

Chinese online music users are very young and with higher educational background. Users below 35 years old are the principal part, and the proportion of users aged 18-24 and 25-30 are highest, accounting for 40.2 percent and 33.6 percent respectively. In addition, users with the medium income are also more.

Computer, MP3 and online audition have been the three main ways of netizens' listening music, accounting for 92.6 percent of the total. The proportion of playing music with computer is most, reaching 44 percent.

China's online music market scale is a far cry from the traditional recording market scale. Pirated music exerted adverse impact on the development of China's online music market; In recent years, the Central Government has strengthened supervision and management in this regard and the mode of reasonable and effective profit distribution among businessmen at various links in the industry chain has emerged, which will have positive impact upon China's online music market.

Music Websites

Fenbei.com
http:// www.fenbei.com

5fad
http:// www.5fad.com

9sky.com
http:// www.9sky.com

Fenbei.com

Website: http:// www.fenbei.com

Fenbei.com (originally called 163888.net), founded on June 18, 2003, is a platform for internet communications with music as the core. It mainly deals with online re-sing music and internet original music, being one of the entertainment websites that were earliest engaged in online music in China.

The website commits itself to packaging and promoting the internet singers. At present, with large numbers of signed singers, it becomes the portal website that has the most song accompaniments, internet friends' uploaded songs and internet original music.

This website successfully developed the K8, online recording software with independent intellectual property rights, thus lowering the threshold of the online music. In 2005 and 2006, fenbei.com (originally called 163888.net) successively gained the investments from the leading international venture fund.

On June 18, 2007, marking the 4th anniversary of its founding, fenbei.com purchased the domain name fenbei.com and completed the updating and re-styling of its website. It has become China's largest digital music interactive platform.

5fad

Website: http:// www.5fad.com

Founded in 2003, Hangzhou-based 5fad.com is China's music copyright operator, and as well as an influential digital culture and entertainment enterprise integrating internet music with traditional entertainment.

5fad.com is devoted to promoting the trend of Chinese music, and at the same time dealing with three platforms for music content, audio-visual production and streaming technology. It has constantly accumulated the monopolistic content resources including song copyright and signed singer from mainland China, Hong Kong and Taiwan.

It is the first original music and digital music website, which collects large numbers of original songs (mp3) and re-sung song (mp3) of internet singers.

9sky.com

Website: http:// www.9sky.com

Established in 1999, 9Sky.com is the largest legal music website in China. With the most comprehensive database, it has more than 750,000 pieces of legal digital, original and re-sung music. It provides the services of listening to, downloading, watching and writing the music and music-related products.

9Sky.com has forged cooperative relations with Universal, EMI, SONY&BMG, Warner Music, Rock and other world-famous record companies. 9Skey is authorized to provide legal music by international Top 4 music company and hundreds of music companies in China..

Its income mainly comes from music distribution and online advertising. Most of expenditure of 9Sky.com goes to pay for copyright, so the aforementioned income contributes little to 9Sky.com.

In June 2007, this website gained US$10 million of venture investment from Asian partners.

Online Video

China Online Video Development

In recent years, the number of users with access to broadband in China has increased swiftly, which lays a solid user foundation for development of the online video industry. Online video-related service also saw rapid development. Different from traditional online video (online movie & TV ordering) mode, online video has the new several characteristics:

In 2006, the MSN Chinese Channel launched the video channel, quietly entering the newwork video market of China.

Broadcast technology: developed from traditional server ordering mode to P2P streaming media technology;

Content source: developed from production by the professional traditional movie & TV institutions to the emergence of large numbers of short video by grass-root individual netizens;

Content category: online video content experienced the development from single movie & TV to sports, entertainment, news and other subdivision;

Showing platform: shifted from the traditional unidirectional ordering platform targeted at the users to podcast featuring users interactive and WEB2.0 sharing.

Video Websites with More Visits

Vnet.cn
http:// www.vnet.cn

Bbvod.net
http:// www.bbvod.net

Mop.com's wideband movie & TV
http:// itv.mop.com

At present, China's online video platform operators are mainly divided into the online movie & TV, traditional portal, TV institutions, P2P streaming media, video sharing, video searching and other varieties. Portal video websites have more visits, followed by TV station, online movie & TV websites.

The business mode of online video industry may be basically grouped into B2B, B2C, and C2C. At present, online video platform operators belong to B2C, while C2C mode is less in China.

Vnet.cn

Website: http:// www.vnet.cn

Vnet.cn is the unified brand of China Telecom's Internet application business. That is to say, China Telecom opens its own users, internet, application platform, marketing channel, customers and other advantaged resources and conducts wide cooperation with SP (content/ application service provider), thus providing content and application services for all the Internet users.

For Internet users, vnet.cn is an Internet application service that China Telecom introduced with the broadband access business. Through vnet.cn portal website, users may enjoy various rich Internet content including movie & TV, game, education, music, finance and economics, internet safety and communications, and application service; At the same time, vnet.cn, as an online payment means, makes it possible for the users to pay the needed charge Internet content online at any time.

The advertisements on the www.vnet.cn under the jurisdiction of China Telecom.

Bbvod.net

Website: http:// www.Bbvod.net

Bbvod.net is an online audio-visual entertainment content service provider, China's earliest premium online audio-visual website, as well as the largest cooperative partner of China Telecom's vnet.cn in the term of wideband content.

Bbvod.net mainly provides video ordering service, and wireless entertainment. Its operated products include the following program types: Bbvod wires, Bbvod theatre, sexual happiness wideband, Bbvod music, king of arts, animation empire, Hong Kong theatre, Hollywood blockbuster.

Mop's wideband movie & TV (itv. mop.com)

Website: http:// itv.mop.com

Itv.mop.com, subject to Mop.com, has P2P internet streaming and media playing technology, thus providing fluent audio-visual entertainment video for its target audience.

Itv.mop.com, relying on its countrywide media partner and its independently developed GDBS internet transmission technology, provides rich and colorful programs for audiences such as direct TV broadcasting, movies, television series, entertainment, arts, music, sports, fashion, and finance and economics.

Mop.com is a famous community website and interactive entertainment portal, including chat room, internet radio station, digital products, game and other columns.

Main Video Sharing Websites

Ku6.com
http:// www.ku6.com

56.com
http:// www.56.com

6rooms.com
http:// www.6rooms.com

Youku.com
http:// www.youku.com

Tudou.com
http:// www.tudou.com

Ku6.com

Website: http:// www.ku6.com

Ku6.com, founded in April 2006, is a video website, on which users who provide content and upload videos take a percentage of the income from advertising. Since its establishment, ku6.com has the revolutionary business concept, namely user generated content (UGC) and User Generated Advertising

(UGA). A transparent trading platform has been set between the video original author and advertising clients. KU6 realizes its own business value through operating this platform.

Ku6.com is positioned to a sharing portal website, consisting of a dozen channels such as information, sports, entertainment, movie & TV, advertising, game, animation. It has more than 2000 members of China original video alliance. Ku6.com pursues the goal of earning money together and making innovation together. It makes itself the video sharing portal with the most uploaded video and most original authors through joint between upper and lower industry chains.

Ku6.com has more than three million registered users in the world, with its daily average number of online users reaching four million, and daily visits exceeding 35 million times.

56.com

Website: http:// www.56.com

56.com, an online video clip sharing and entertainment website, was launched in April 2005. That October, it took the lead in providing the service of recording online and uploading video clips. In two weeks, the number of original videos uploaded exceeded 20,000.

Now 56.com has more than 50 million video works, and over 25 million registered users. The total time length of daily viewed videos exceeds 100 million minutes, making the website one of the hottest online video clip-sharing platforms.

6rooms.com

Website: http:// www.6rooms.com

6rooms.com is a web2.0-based video-sharing website. The website itself does not provide videos, but is the platform onto which they are uploaded. These are mainly originals by users, such as home videos and individual clips. Within six weeks of launch, it had a web traffic level of five million, reaching the scale of a medium-sized website.

6rooms.com is a typical web2.0 website, with users as the core; user-generated content; communications and exchanges between them generated by common interests.

Youku

Website: http:// www.youku.com

Youku.com was launched in June 2006. It welcomes the collection, origination and sharing of micro videos recorded by professionals and amateurs, individuals or organizations.

According to the principal of the youku.com product department, it is the first website in China providing large upload and storage space for micro video for free and having an individual-initiated video arena and grading system. Differing from the accumulation of videos of some websites, Youku mainly uses TOP rankings, classified index of channels, labels, individual-initiated video arena, video club and other effective means, and technology search function and recommended means, to bring into play the force of C2C content aggregation and recommendation.

Tudou.com

Website: http:// www.tudou.com

Tudou.com, an early-developed video sharing platform, was launched in April 2005. It provides a platform for users to be easily post or collect personal audio-visual works.

It provides a personal homepage for each user. On this fixed page, an audience may watch all the programs you have made at an easily remembered fixed address, and allowing free exchange. You may also list friends as links, so that every time you upload a newly-made program, the website informs your friends to download and view. At the same time, you may upload programs onto the given channels and specials; these are co-partners of tudou.com, such as some funny TV columns.

Digital Journals

Development of China's Digital Journals

In China, 2006 was named as "digital journal year" by numerous critics. In the short span of two months early in the year, China's 20 large-sized digital journal issuing platforms were launched, and Acer, Lenovo, IDG, Carlyle Group and other venture capital organizations invested several billion Yuan in various digital journals.

Making a digital journal is not monopoly of young netizens any more. The traditional media have also introduced their respective electronic editions, and enterprises and undertaking units widely use digital journal technology for sample books, antique catalogs, business publications and enterprise publications.

These journals uploaded and disseminated on the internet originally had various names, such as e-journal, interactive journal, digital journal, network magazine, and multimedia journal; They were given the unified appellation—"digital journal" in the Report on 50 Subdivision Fields in China's Internet Industry released at the end of 2006.

Digital Journal Platforms

ZBOX
Website: http:// www.zbox.com.cn

Xplus
Website: http:// www.xplus.com.cn

moker.com.cn
Website: http:// www.moker.com.cn

ZCOM
Website: http:// www.zcom.com

ZBOX

Website: http:// www.zbox.com.cn

Zbox dedicates itself to publishing mainly network books, network magazines and network individual publication. This website focuses on casual lifestyles, fads, music, TV & Movies, game animation, computers, the internet, digital and communications products, auto, real estate and other columns.

Xplus

Website: http:// www.xplus.com.cn

Xplus, a website of the Xplus Beijing Office, was founded in 2003. It not only developed the interface for the "network magazine", but also introduced the internet-based journal sending and subscribing mechanism with its originally created Xplus client software. In 2006, based on the constantly improving Xplus platform, it also introduced the MagA personal network magazine design software as the leading product. At the end of 2006, on the basis of the digital newspaper software Np Maker, Xplus also introduced electronic newspapers.

Moker.com.cn

Website: http:// www.moker.com.cn

Moker.com.cn is a B2C e-journal platform of the Moker Group, providing multimedia e-journal, interactive journal, network magazine and personal DIY works, with contents covering various aspects including fads, politics and economics, management, and literature.

Moker Group, founded in 2005, has set up branch companies in Shanghai, Beijing and Taipei, respectively. Moker specializes in converting TV programs, books, papers, journals, catalogues, guide handbooks and other current documents into high-quality e-journals.

ZCOM

Website: http:// www.zcom.com

ZCOM, founded in early 2004, is one of China's earlier e-journal platform developers, as well as promoter of a new generation of wideband entertainment. With some 200 staff members, Beijing-based ZCOM has branches in Shanghai, Guangzhou, Shenzhen and Xi'an.

Thus far, the number of its registered users has exceeded 30 million, who can be found in China, North America and Southeast Asia, a figure increasing by tens of thousands per day. The website is a journal-reading platform with greater download volumes and more readers.

Basic Web2.0 Application (Friend-making, Blog, Online Community)

Brief Introduction of Web2.0 Application in China

Web2.0 is one of the hottest ideas on the internet since 2003; however, now there is no strict definition of Web2.0. In general, Web2.0 (also called internet2.0) is a general designation for new internet applications. Web1.0 allowed users to get information through the explorer, while Web2.0 pays more attention to interactive exchanges between users and computers. Its users are both the consumers (browsers) and generators of website content.

The typical Web 2.0 websites in China include blogs, online community and video sharing websites, all steadily growing. Especially blog websites have experienced most rapid development with more influence. They include Bokee.com, DoNews IT community (www.donews.com), post.baidu.com, and Sina's blog (blog.sina.com.cn).

Blog Website

Development of China Blog Website

"Blog" is the abbreviation for Web log. In early 2005, blog hosting service began emerging in China. It has been widely popularized and used in various fields such as culture, sport and business. The pure blog writers, and blog readers who only read blogs but do not release their own articles, both contribute to high traffic. At present, the number of blog websites in China is second only to that of network search websites in monthly web traffic.

In 2006, the number of registered blog accounts in China (excluding the number of users of personal blog sites) reached 39 million, up 333 percent over the previous year, while the number of blog readers amounted to 78 million, up 129 percent.

At present, there are about 2,000 blog operators in China, providing blog hosting services, of whom 20 or so are relatively famous. In accordance with the scope of services and their different business background, the websites may be grouped into the following categories: integrated blog, professional blog, blog of integrated portal (such as Sina and Sohu), basic blog and individual blog sites with independent domain name.

Poco.cn

Website: http://: www.poco.cn

Poco.cn is an entertainment website mainly catering to the photo community, and including food, photography, space, e-journal and other functions.

MyPOCO personal space serves as the core product. It is a community including many sections such as photographs, food, pets, tourism, fashion, fad pictures, text, and e-journal. POCO's interactive entertainment website has set up various channels. All the contents of the website come from original of users of MyPOCO personal space.

Bokee.com

Website: http://: www.bokee.com

Bokee.com, originally called blog China (www.blogchina.com), is a knowledge portal website founded by Fang Xingdong, an IT industry critic, in August 2002.

As the second generation internet portal, bokee.com is a neutral, open, humanized, selected information resource-sharing platform. By the end of 2003, it had become the world's first Chinese blog hosting website. It was renamed in July 2005.

Bokee.com provides free professional blog hosting services, having blog community, moblog, Fotolog, video blog, teachers' blog, students' blog, podcast, and other online platforms.

51.com

Website: http://: www.51.com

51.com, launched in 2005, is one of China's larger blog communities. It dedicates itself to provide stable and safe personal space services. Its users may not only enjoy photo storage, diary writing, music upload and other services, but also make friends all over China. Compared with most internet companies, 51.com has relatively few features, but focuses more on ensuring the security of users' data and the authenticity of making friends.

At present, 51.com has had more than 70 million registered users, the number of whom is growing by above 160,000 per day.

Main Blog websites

Poco.cn
http://: www.poco.cn

Bokee.com
http://: www.bokee.com

51.com
http://: www.51.com

QQblog
http://: qzone.qq.com

Sina's blog
http://: blog.sina.com.cn

QQ Zone

Website: http://: qzone.qq.com

QQ zone (Qzone) is a personal space introduced by Tencent, Inc in 2005, providing blog hosting service Users may write a diary, upload photos, and link music on their respective QQ zone, thus showing themselves through many means. They have many ways to personalize their site.

QQ zone offers senior functions to users accomplished in webpage design. They may build their own space through writing various codes. Qzone contains web log, photo album, music box, supernatural flower vine, interactive and other professional dynamic functions, through which one may synthesize one's favorite head photo, varied skins and floaters, and ornaments, and change space decoration

The advertisements of the Bokee.com

style at will. Most services are premium. One who opens a yellow diamond account (10Yuan per month) may freely use all kinds of props. It is reported that the personal space's active accounts have exceeded 57 million.

Founded in November 1998, Tencent, Inc. has grown into China integrated internet service provider in China. Tencent has set up four major Internet platforms QQ, QQ.com, QQ Games, and PaiPai.com, having brought together China's largest Internet community.

Original Literature

Cmfu.com

Website: http://: www.cmfu.com

The predecessor of cmfu.com, founded in May 2002 was the Chinese Magic Fantasy Union. As the largest literature reading and writing platform in China, it has become the country's leading original literature portal website, building up an original literature brand represented by "cmfu.com", and establishing an online electronic publishing mechanism integrating creation, cultivation and distribution, thereby being the most excellent online literature works publishing platform in China.

It now has 70,000 original novels, with their contents covering martial arts, online games, romance, history, military affairs, cliffhanger and horror novel columns.

Readnovel.com

Website: http://: www.readnovei.com

Readnovel.com, launched in May 2004, is praised by literature and novel lovers for its unique style and rich contents. It has millions of visitors recommended by members each day. This website upgrades a number of original novels each day. Its columns include novels, love stories, online games novels, youth literature and martial arts novel.s

Main Original Literature Websites

cmfu.com
http://: www.cmfu.com

Sina's literature
http://: book.sina.com.cns

QQliterature
http://: book.qq.com

eadnovel.com
http://: www.readnovel.com

www.xxsy.net
http://: www.xxsy.net

Xxsy.net

Website: http://: www.xxsy.nett

Xxsy.net, founded by several ardent lovers of martial arts literature in 2001, now has developed into an integrated non-profit reading website containing original, martial arts, love, classical, contemporary, science fiction, and detective stories.

Xxsy.net has more than 20,000 original works, of which dozens of excellent works have been published and issued. There are over 1,000 authors who have signed up with the website, a figure still growing rapidly. It has about 40,000 martial arts, romance and integrated novels, most of which were collected from the internet and uploaded by friends.

Xxsy.net has tens of millions of page views, and five million hits each day. Its regular users have reached six million.

Online Community

Development of China's Online Community

Online community, as the effective carrier and platform for dissemination of netizens opinions, represents the huge value and influence of folk culture with rapid development. There are many newly-built online communities appearing each year, which have highlighted development of China's internet industry. According to CNNIC, China has 1.31 million independent websites, more than 80 percent of which, from portal to trade website, to regional portal to personal sites, have set up an independent community.

Statistics shows that, of websites launched in 2007, 45.3 percent were online communities. The number of the communities launched in 2006 and 2007 accounted for more than 70 percent of the total.

At present, China's online communities mostly cover life, audio-visual, games and casual entertainment themes. The entertainment and casual information attract most browsers. Life and casual lifestyle category ranks first among forum topics, occupying 36.1 percent, followed by the TV, movie and music category, accounting for 31.6 percent.

Mop

Website: http://: www.mop.com

Mop.com is an influential online forum in simplified Chinese founded in October 1997. In 2004, it was purchased by DUDU.com through an equity buy-out. In December 2005, mop.com officially released a statement that it acquired Donews. It is said to have more than 11 million registered id numbers.

Many influential posts have appeared on mop.com, which has created many popular network terms such as BT, YY, 874, 253, TJJTDS, 011 and 110.

Mop.com animation entertainment information is also popular.

Main Online Community Websites

Mop
http://: www.mop.com

zhanzuo.com
http://: www.zhanzuo.com

Tianya virtual community
http://: www.tianya.cn

xiaonei.com
http://: www.xiaonei.com

Teein
http://: www.teein.com

daqi.com
http://: www.daqi.com

xici.net
http://: www.xici.net

ChinaRencommunity
http://: club.chinaren.com

The Mop.com

Zhanzuo.com

Website: http://: www.zhanzuo.com

Zhanzuo.com is called the most in-vogue individualization online community of college students. Pursuing the principle of reality and frankness, it encourages college students to register their real name, and upload real photos and personal information. It differs from the traditional college students' BBS in paying more attention to the individual.

Zhanzuo.com is a more interactive universities campus SNS website, encouraging students to show themselves, share and exchange, creating more opportunities in life.

Tianya Virtual Community

Website: http://: www.tianya.cn

Tianya virtual community (www.tianya.

cn), founded in March 1999, is operated by the Hainan Tianya Online Network S&T Co., Ltd. Since its launch, Tianya Community has been praised for its open, free, loose, and rich features. After many years of development, it has grown into a large online humanistic community with 300 public sections and 210,000 bloggers with three BBS.

Major Page: This includes Tianya tittle-tattle, emotion world, Guantian Tea House, economics forum, poems, totaling 54 sections. Of them, Guantian Tea House, Tianya tittle-tattle, fad information, photo zone, entertainment, emotion world and other section have 150 hits each day.

City Page: There are 120 discussion pages divided according to 40 provinces and prefectures, including the Hong Kong, Macao, Taiwan and overseas edition.

Tianya Bieyuan: This includes literature, fad, emotion, entertainment, women, audio-visual, interests, parties, special, and other, belonging to 10 categories and 81 sections.

Occupational Exchange: This includes real estate, accountancy, police world, migrant workers and other sections, totaling 20.

Universities campus: This includes youth talk, quail-roost, schoolboys' night talk, after graduation, campus photo, examination service station, totaling 16.

Tianya Wangshi: This includes Tianya network publication, watch tower, Tianya Residents' Committee, Tianya Wedding Hall, Tianya rosary, Tianxiang Bet Room, and Tianya bourse, totaling 13.

Xiaonei.com

Website: http://: www.xiaonei.com

Xiaonei.com (Xiaonei means 'Inside the Campus' in Chinese), launched in December 2005, is the earliest campus SNS community in the country. Xiaonei.com was acquired by Oak Pacific Interactive in October 2006. 5Q.com which is also owned by Oak Pacific Interactive was merged with it.

Xiaonei.com only allows users who have a university IP address or the e-mail of a university website to register, so as to ensure everyone is an on-campus college student. Registered users may post their own photos, write logs, and leave comments on the website. This website encourages college student users to register with their real name, and upload real photos, thus letting them experience the pleasure of real life on the internet.

At present, xiaonei.com has opened service for 2,000 universities, 1,800 senior schools and 546 companies. Since the launch of xiaonei.com, websites of the same type have come to the fore. Compared with xiaonei.com, these friend-making websites targeting college students have yet to make great breakthroughs in regard to function and page layout.

Teein

Website: http://: www.teein.com

Teein.com, founded in October 2004, is a Chinese syndication portal based on the Chinese community search engine, which provides unified solutions for original contents and marketing resources.

Since its launch, it has dedicated itself to clearing up, classifying and indexing Chinese original contents using its independently developed community search technology, thus providing one-stop Chinese community browse and search services for netizens. At present, this website attracts millions of loyal users. Teein.com also operates the first alliance of Chinese communities, providing web traffic and advertising services for more than 100,000 Chinese community websites.

Daqi.com

Website: http://: www.daqi.com

ChinaBBS.com, predecessor of daqi.com was launched in November 2004 and officially renamed in March 2006. Daqi.com received venture capital investment from IDG Technology Venture Investment (IDGVC Partners) and WI Harper Group. At present, it is the capital elite topic portal, as well as the community marketing and consulting services provider in China with greatest fame.

Daqi.com devotes itself to providing the hottest information on internet topics and consumer trends for new-era netizens. Since its launch, daqi.com has had 150 million users, covering more than 100,000 Chinese active communities. It selects the hottest information to ensure good service to people in big cities.

Since its establishment, daqi.com has accumulated an integrated database on Chinese communities, thus taking the lead in providing community marketing and consulting services for many known partners in the world on the Chinese market.

Xici.net

Website: http://: www.xici.net

Xici hutong is not a hutong, but a website. It is an online community with the strongest focus on the humanities in China, attracting great numbers of loyal users at various age levels who are engaged in different vocations and have varied interests and fancies. It has 50 million daily page views and 12,000 peak online users.

This website has set up various bardian?? sections, in which internet friends may freely build a home, to make friends. Its numerous sections such as "comments", "Wang Xiaopo Running Dog Alliance", and "journalists' home", not only have great influence on the internet, but haves attracted much attention in the real world..

Xici.net includes the following sections: fads, digital products, journalism, auto, travel, real estate, IT, life, media, humanity, literature, economics, entertainment, sport, art, emotions, academies, education, games and animation.

ChinaRen Community

Website: http://: club.chinaren.com

ChinaRen community, launched in 1999 and bought by Sohu.com, is one of China's larger student communities. After many years of constant development, it has 60 million registered users, eight million classes (including more than four million on-campus classes), and 40 million daily average page views.

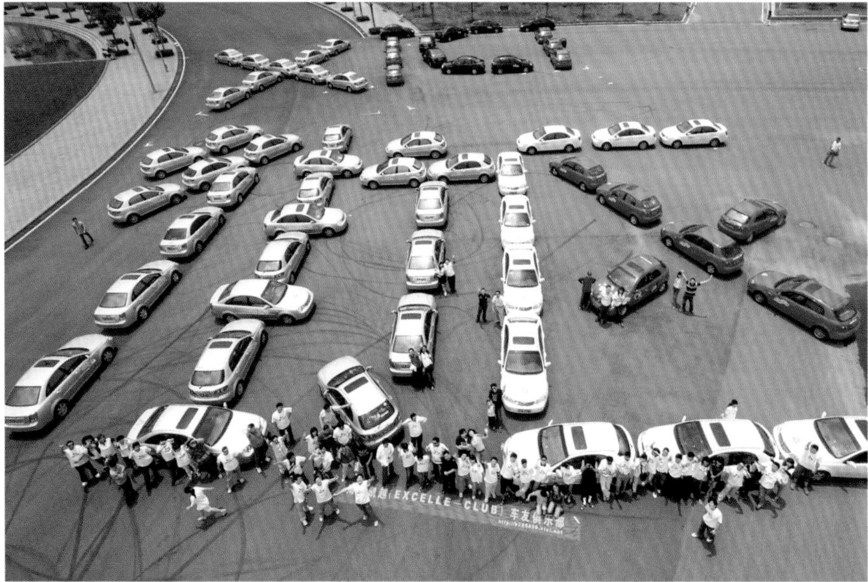

The 63 Kaiyue cars of the Xici Hutong Kaiyue Car Friends Club formed the Xici Block map to celebrate that the number of Kaiyue cars reached 400.

Witkey

Witkey main websites

witkey.com
http://: www.witkey.com

Task China
http://: www.taskcn.com

witkey China
http://: www.vikecn.com

zhubajie.com
http://: www.zhubajie.com

Witkeysky.com
http://: www.witkeysky.com

Development of China's Witkey

Witkey is one of the 171 new Chinese words published by the Ministry of Education of China in August 2007.

Witkey is the combination of English words "wit" and "key". According to the definition of witkey by Liu Feng, who initially brought up the concept, witkeyers are those who turn their own wit, knowledge, capability, and experience into actual interests through the internet. They solve the issues on science, technology, work, life, and learning on the internet, thus converting their knowledge, wit, experience, and skills into an economic value. Witkey mode is mainly used to settle issues in science, technology, work, life and learning, showing the new concept of rewarding according to labor and putting people first.

Witkeyers may find and finish jobs (tasks) on a witkey platform to reap reward. While helping others, they also make profit themselves.

Witkey and witkeyers first became popular all over China in September 2006, because of reportage by CCTV. The current witkey modes include rewards in cumulative scoring and cash, knowledge sales and witkey map (witmap). Witmap refers to the formation of a search engine by integrating the four important properties—people's geographical location, specialties or interests, linking mode, and witkey space (not excluding other secondary properties such as age, occupation and gender) through internet.

Witkey.com

Website: http://: www.witkey.com

Witkey.com is an international website for realzing exhibition and promotion of innovative products of enterprise through the participation and interaction of users and providing service for innovation of enterprises through holding online innovative product fairs, conducting rewarded activity and survey for innovative products, and releasing reports on innovative products data analysis. Witkey.com was launched by Beijing Zhongke Witkey S&T Co., Ltd in July 2005.

Witkey.com, as the flagship of witkey mode, has always held a leading edge. In July 2005, it first put forward the witkey mode concept of turning knowledge, wit, and experience into wealth through the internet. This concept attracted a great response in China.

Task China

Website: http://: www.taskcn.com

Task China is a famous witkey website whose one million real-name witkeyers offer services in demand by netizens.

All the witkeyers who participate in witkey tasks pass the duplex real name authentication (telephone number and ID card), so as to ensure the credibility of both sides of the trade. At present, Task China divides the tasks into design, hatch, procedure, animation, labor service, website, contributors and other categories. Users may post their own rewarded tasks on the corresponding sub-categories, and also participate in bidding for rewarded tasks posted by other users.

Witkeyers and clients conduct the most direct trade for reward here, thus showing their own talents and excellent human relations.

Witkey China

Website: http://: www.vikecn.com

Vikecn.com is a professional witkey mode website, as well as one of the portal websites leading the witkey industry. Witkey China provides the following rewarded projects (tasks): LOGO design, Flash production, website design, procedural design, names for new-born babies, advertising messages, translation, planning and labor services.

Every day, witkeyers from various areas conduct exchange here, and each member may post their articles, show their strong suit, add photo albums undertake or put out projects for reward and own the second-class domain name of witkey China.

Zhubajie.com

Website: http://: www.zhubajie.com

Zhubajie.com is one of the true and safe witkey platforms in China, a witkey work bidding platform for reward in cash, as well as web2.0-based website. Witkeyers living all over the world may convert their knowledge, wit and originality into profit through zhubajie.com. Now zhubajie.com has more than 500,000 witkeyers, who provide online creative work service for various institutions, enterprises, social organizations and individuals.

It is independently operated by Chongqing Yiaoke S&T Development Co. Ltd.

Witkeysky.com

Website: http://: www.witkeysky.com

Witkeysky.com, launched on September 30, 2006, is a witkey information website designed for witkeyers. The sections of this website include: witkey design tutorial channels, rewarded tasks hall, witkey website navigation, witkey site listing, witkey experience exchange, information on witkey, general witkey software download!

It has become one of the famous witkey information platforms in China, with approximately 30,000 registered members.

Friendship

Development of China's Friend-Making Websites

In China, casual friend-making is popular with young people due to its early development and new concept, and takes the lead among online friend-making websites; Online marriage friend-making website entered into the rapid development phase, with the market penetration rate being raised rapidly; online business friend-making website are in the early days of development.

Casual friend-making and marriage friend-making websites have witnessed rapid development, and casual friend-making websites will be greatly impacted by marriage websites.

Wangyou.com

Website: http://: www.wangyou.com

Wangyou.com is a company providing internet, wireless value-added and TV & Radio services.

WangYou.com is an original entertainment interactive website, targeted at young users aged 13-35, as well as based-Web 2.0 entertainment internet platform.

It has four channels—UGC, information, interactive, basic categories. Since its launch in 2002, the website has attracted more than five million registered users, and its daily hits exceed 15 million.

At present, original works of internet friends of WangYou.com have been broadcast by 35 radio stations across China, covering 400 million people.

360quan.com

Website: http://: www.360quan.com

360quan.com is an online interactive community tailored for urban youth, with stress on fashion and other aspects of life for the young. The website not only provides a variety of interactive services such as albums, videos and blogs, but also encourages personality and diversity and attaches importance to sharing.

Integrated Friend-making Websites

wangyou.com
http://: www.wangyou.com

360quan.com
http://: www.360quan.com

9158.com
http://: www.9158.com

ipart.cn
http://: www.ipart.cn

love.qq.com
http://: love.qq.com

Websites for Dating and Making Friends

Love21cn.msn.com
http://: love21cn.msn.com.cn

Jiayuan.com
http://: www.jiayuan.com

Marry5.com
http://: www.marry5.com

Tianji.com
http://: www.tianji.com

Formally launched on February 15, 2007, 360quan.com became the "fastest growing Web 2.0 website in China" and one of the five major social network communities within four months.

9158.com

Website: http://: www.9158.com

9158.com is a large website providing a platform for making friends. Over 100 kinds of recreational activities with different themes are available. The activities are held both online and offline in different cities and regions.

The website features multi-part video. It adopts multi-part h.264 video compression technology and self-developed 9158Sound(TM) audio encoding and decoding algorithm to create MP3 quality in sound. Hence, its video and audio qualities reach a high level. Over 50,000 users can be on-line at the client-side at the same time.

Ipart.cn

Website: http://: www.ipart.cn

Established in March 2005, ipart.cn is a warm friend-making community loved by girls; the average age of the staff is 24. Sticking to the concept of "originality and innovation", the blog website features unique connotations and operating mode, and, through the network information platform, provides mass Internet and mobile phone users with various Internet services such as suite, diary and pets. More than half of the users are females ranging in age from 20 to 30 in large cities such as Beijing, Shanghai, Shenzhen and Guangzhou.

Love21cn.msn.com

Website: http://: love21cn.msn.com.cn

This is a channel of cn.msn.com helping people to find love.

Launched in May 2005, it is a portal website tailored to white collar users and giving reports around the clock mainly on fashion, entertainment, life and services. Its contents are provided by nine partners including the Beijing Youth Daily Group, smgbb.cn, taobao.com, ccidnet.com, ourgame.com, mop.com, didibaba.com, Englishtown and sensky.com.

Jiayuan.com

Website: http://: www.jiayuan.com

This is a matchmaking website. Through the network platform and offline activities, the website providing serious dating services for singles in mainland China, Hong Kong, Macao and Taiwan as well as other countries and regions.

The website was officially launched on October 8, 2003. By October 2007, it had 9.57 million members and helped 870,000 people to wed, a tribute to the hard work of its founder Mrs. Gong Haiyan.

It is the first dating website in China establishing minimum educational standards for its candidate members and requiring they should have received at least a college education. Undergraduates total 48 percent of membership and there are 33 percent with a masters or doctorate degree.

Marry5.com

Website: http://: www.marry5.com

Marry5.com is a matchmaking website run by Shenzhen Haotian Investment Co., Ltd.

Depending on self-developed Web IM, the website serves as an online instant messenger and offline messenger, helps users realize seamless instant communication between the website and mobile phone, and between mobile phones, and provides a "marry 5 soft nothings" voice communication product. Members, through their ID number, can safely enjoy voice services such as chatting on the phone and instant messaging.

The website has established local operating institutions in 22 large and medium-sized cities throughout China, providing various offline dating services for members.

Tianji.com

Website: http://: www.tianji.com

Tianji.com is a social networking platform specially serving professional personnel that has gained international investment.

According to the website, "there are no pictures of beautiful girls and boys appearing on the website constantly because it is not that kind of website; it only meets the requirements of young people for dating. It is targeted at professional personnel such as white collar workers to meet their needs in commerce and occupation. Efforts are made to help the`m to establish, manage and expand their interpersonal relationship net in a more effective way, which is no doubt the most valuable wealth in their whole occupational career".

The "jiayuan.com", the largest matchmaking website in China, held the 10,000 collective wedding.

Chapter Laws and Regulations

Laws

Brief Introduction of the Electronic Signature Law of the PRC

The Electronic Signature Law of the PRC was adopted at the 11th Meeting of the Standing Committee of the Tenth National People's Congress on August 28, 2004 and went into effect on April 1, 2005. It is the first law on informatization with real meaning in China.

The law stipulates that a reliable electronic signature has equal legal force with a handwritten signature or seal and sets forth requirements for electronic verification services.

The law defines the electronic signature as the data in electronic form contained in and attached to a data message to be used for confirming the identity of the signatory and for showing that the latter recognizes what is in the message. The electronic signature refers to the signature "signed" with an electronic cipher comprised of symbols and codes so as to replace the handwritten signature or seal. Adopting the standardized program and scientific method, it can validate whether the original text of the document has been changed in the process of transmission. Hence, it is not a digital image of the handwritten signature.

The promulgation and implementation of the Electronic Signature Law plays an extremely important role in developing e-government affairs and e-commerce. It solves the problems concerning the identification of the identity of participants in these fields and an affirmation of their behavior. The stipulation that a reliable electronic signature has equal legal force with a handwritten signature or seal is one of the key guarantees for the network environment.

Brief Introduction of the Decision of the Standing Committee of the NPC on Preserving Computer Network Security

The Decision of the Standing Committee of the NPC on Preserving Computer Network Security was adopted at the 19th Meeting of the Standing Committee of the Ninth National People's Congress on December 28, 2000.

The Decision stipulates that anyone who commits any of the following acts, which constitutes a crime, shall be investigated for criminal responsibility in accordance with the relevant provisions in the Criminal Law:

Invading the computer data system of State affairs, national defense or the sophisticated realms of science and technology;

Intentionally inventing and spreading destructive programs such as computer viruses to attack and damage a computer system and communications network;

In violation of State regulations, disconnecting the computer network or the communications service without authorization, thus making it impossible for them to operate normally.

Making use of the computer network to spread rumors, libels or publicize or disseminate other harmful information for purpose of whipping up attempts to subvert State power and overthrowing the socialist system, or to split the country and undermine State unification;

Stealing or divulging State secrets, intelligence or military secrets via a computer network;

Making use of the computer network to stir up ethnic hostility or discrimination, and thus undermining national unity;

Making use of the computer network to form cult organizations or contact members of cult organizations, thus obstructing the implementation of State laws and administrative regulations.

Making use of the computer network to sell shoddy products or create false publicity on commodities or services;

Making use of the computer network to jeopardize another person's business credibility and commodity reputation;

Making use of the computer network to infringe another person's intellectual property rights;

Making use of the computer network to fabricate and spread false information affecting the exchange of securities and futures or other information which disrupts the financial order;

Establishing pornographic web sites or web pages on a computer network, providing services for connecting pornographic web sites, or spreading pornographic books and periodicals, movies, audiovisual material or pictures.

Making use of the computer network to humiliate another person or to libel another person by fabrications;

In violation of the law, intercepting, tampering with or deleting other persons' emails or other data, thus infringing on citizens' freedom and privacy of correspondence; or

Making use of the computer network to commit theft, fraud or blackmail.

Brief Introduction of the Measures for the Administration of Internet Information Services

The Measures for the Administration of Internet Information Services (hereinafter referred to as Measures) was adopted at the 31st Executive Meeting of the State Council on September 20, 2000 and went into effect on October 1. It is regarded as the "fundamental law" on the management of the contents of the Internet in China. The promulgation of the Measures provides the legal basis and reference for the formulation of the network regulations such as the Provisions on the Administration of Internet Electronic Messaging Services, Interim Provisions on the Administration of

After the Electronic Signature Law went into force, the seal wilted its power in front of the computer.

Internet Culture, Interim Provisions on the Administration of Internet Publication and Interim Provisions on the Administration of Internet Websites' Engaging in News Publication Services.

The Measures stipulate that the term "Internet information services" means the service activity of providing information services through the Internet to online subscribers. Internet information services are divided into commercial and non-commercial services. The term "commercial Internet information services" means service activities such as compensated provision to online subscribers through the Internet of information services or website production, etc. The term "non-commercial Internet information services" means the service activity of non-compensated provision to online subscribers through the Internet of information that is in the public domain and openly accessible. It also prescribes that the State subjects commercial Internet information services to a permit system and non-commercial Internet information services to a record-filing system and the conditions that shall be met in order to engage in the provision of commercial Internet information services and the examination and approval procedures concerned in a way of enumeration. There are also other provisions on the obligation of the Internet information service providers that engage in the provision of such services as news, publishing or electronic bulletin board services in recording and keeping copies for investigation and on the punishment standards for those who illegally engage in Internet information services and the authority and responsibility of the supervising and administrating departments as well as the nine bans on information that Internet information service providers may not produce, reproduce, disseminate or broadcast.

Brief Introduction of the Regulations on Protection of the Right of Communication through Information Network

The Regulations on Protection of the Right of Communication through Information Networks was adopted at the 135th Executive Meeting of the State Council on May 10, 2006 and went into effect on July 1. The Regulations were formulated in accordance with the 58th article of the Copyright Law of the PRC (Article 58 Measures for the protection of computer software and the right of communication of information on network shall be established separately by the State Council.) The Copyright Law regulates the protection of the right of communication of information on network; and the Regulations have specific provisions on the protection of the right. Since China has acceded into the Berne Convention and TRIPS Agreement, the citizens of other countries which have also acceded into the Berne Convention and TRIPS Agreement can also enjoy the following protection in accordance with the Copyright Law of the PRC and the Regulations.

Administrative Regulations

Brief Introduction of the Regulations on the Administration of Business Sites of Internet Access

In order to meet the huge demand of netizens accessing the Internet at Internet bars and supervise those network bars with jumbled and disordered management and constant accidents, the State Council promulgated the Regulations on the Administration of Business Sites of Internet Access, which came into effect as of November 15, 2002.

The Regulations prescribe the jurisdiction of examining, approving and managing network bars and strengthen the requirements on the responsibilities and management of operators.

They stipulate that an operating entity may not accept any minors to enter its business site and display prominent signs prohibiting minors from entering at the entrance of its business site.

The Regulations also stress network security. Emphasis is laid on supervision over Internet users touching and spreading harmful information. They prescribe that neither an operating entity nor an Internet user can make use of a business site of Internet Access Services to produce, download, reproduce, consult, promulgate, spread or use through other forms the harmful information and not conduct the acts that endanger the security of information or networks such as producing or spreading computer viruses and hacking.

Protection Measures for the Right Owners

In line with the characteristics of the right of communication of information on networks, the Regulations on Protection of the Right of Communication through Information Networks stipulate the protection measures for rightful owners mainly from the following aspects:

The first is to protect the right of communication of information on a network. It is stipulated that any organization or person that makes any other person's works, performances, sound recordings or video recordings available to the public through information network shall obtain permission from and pay remuneration to the right owner unless otherwise provided for in the laws or administrative regulations.

The second is to protect the technological measures adopted for protecting the right of communication of information on network. The Regulations prescribe that any organization or person shall not intentionally circumvent or sabotage technological measures; nor shall it or he intentionally manufacture, import or offer to the public any device or part used primarily for circumventing or sabotaging technological measures; nor shall it or he intentionally provide other with any technical service designed to circumvent or sabotage technological measures, except that permissible under the laws and administrative regulations.

The third is to protect the electronic rights management information used for making out the authorized ascription of or conditions for the use of the works. The Regulations not only forbids the behaviors that intentionally remove or alter the electronic rights management information or that make available to the public, through information networks, works, performances, sound recordings or video recordings of which one knows or has reasonable grounds to know the rights management information has been removed or altered without permission from the rightful owners.

The fourth is to establish simple "notifying and removing" procedures for dealing with tortuous dissensions.

Notifying and Removing Procedures for Dealing with Tortuous Dissension

The dissensions of impinging on the right of the communication of information on networks generally involve a small amount of money, making it unnecessary to solve them through administrative or judicatory procedures. Hence, referring to the international common practice, the Regulations establish the simple "notifying and removing" procedures:

Where a rightful owner believes that a work, performance, sound recording or video recording involved in the service provided by a network service provider of information storage space, searching or linking services has infringed his/her right of communication through an information network, or that his/her electronic right management information on such work has been removed or altered, he/she may notify the network service provider in writing, requesting it to remove, or disconnect the link to, the work, performance, sound recording or video recording; the network service provider, upon receipt of the notification from a rightful owner, should promptly remove or disconnect the aforesaid link, and, at the same time communicate the notification to the subscriber who provides the work, performance, sound recording or video recording. And that is the end of the matter. In addition, in line with the principle on the reciprocity of rights and obligations, the Regulations also stipulate that if the abuse of notification by the rightful owner brings damage to subscribers, the former is liable for the damage.

Restrictions on the Rightful Owner's Right of the Communication of Information on A Network

The Regulations on Protection of the Right of Communication through Information Networks, based on the relevant provisions of the Copyright Law and under the premise of not being lower than the lowest requirements of the relevant international conventions, provide reasonable restrictions on the right of the communication of information on networks. The provisions in this regard are in line with the relevant requirements of the Internet Convention.

The first is reasonable use. Combining the features of network environment, the Regulations spread the "reasonable uses" prescribed in the Copyright Law to the network environment, regulating that for the purposes of classroom teaching and performing official duties by a State organ, another person's work may be made available through the information network without permission from, and without payment of any remuneration to the copyright owners. In addition, giving considerations to that China's libraries and archives and so on have purchased a number of digital works and made legal digitalization for some damaged and lost works or those whose existing storage format has become obsolete, the Regulations prescribe that those institutions may make available to their service recipients through an information network in order to bring the digital works into play.

The second is legal permission. In order to develop the public welfare cause, the Regulations, giving consideration to China's factual conditions, prescribe two kinds of legal permissions. The first kind of permission is for the development of education. It is stipulated that for the purpose of implementing the nine-year compulsory educational program or the national educational plan through an information network, extracts of published works, short literary works, musical works, single works of fine art, or photographic works may be used for preparing courseware or a distant educational establishment that has prepared or legitimately obtained the courseware may make them accessible to the registered students through information network, without permission from the copyright owners, provided that the latter are paid a remuneration. The second kind is for poverty alleviation. It is prescribed that, in order to alleviate poverty, a published work of a Chinese citizen, legal entity or any other organization and any work that meets the cultural needs may be made available free of charge to people in rural areas through an information network. The network service provider shall, before making available of these works, make public the works involved and the authors thereof and the standard of remuneration to be paid, and shall not seek any financial benefit directly or indirectly from this.

Provisions on the Legal Responsibilities of Network Service Providers

Network service providers include the network information service providers and network access service providers, who are the bridge between the rightful owners and work users.

In order to promote the development of the network industry, it is necessary to reduce the cost and risk of the network service provider providing a work through the information network. Moreover, the service provider has no subjective fault in providing the tortuous works for service recipients. Hence, the Regulations on Protection of the Right of Communication through Information Networks, based on effective practice, prescribe four conditions under which the network service providers are not liable for damage:

The first condition is that the provider of an automatic access service at the direction of its subscribers, or one providing service for automatic transmission, does not alter the transmitted works and prevents those other than designated recipients from receiving them.

The second condition is that a network service provider that provides the service of automatic storage for work obtained from another network service provider in order to improve the efficiency of network transmission, and automatically provides it to its subscribers, does not alter the automatically stored work and influence the monitoring and control of the website providing the work and conducts disposal according to the relevant procedures of the website who provides the work.

The third condition is that a network service provider provides subscribers with network storage space, if it clearly indicates that this is so provided and does not alter the stored works; or does not know or has no reasonable grounds to know that the works infringes any other persons' rights; or does not seek financial benefits directly from the infringement; or promptly removes the works alleged of infringement by the right owner upon receipt of notification.

The fourth condition is that a network service provider who provides searching or linking service to its subscribers, disconnects the link to infringing works on receipt of the rightful owner's notification. However, where it knows or has reasonable grounds to know that the linked works infringe another person's right, it is jointly liable for the infringement.

♦ Brief Introduction of the Administration of China Internet Domain Names Procedures

The Procedures for the Administration of China Internet Domain Names was adopted at the eighth ministerial conference of the Ministry of Information Industry on September 28, 2004 and went into effect on December 20.

It is stipulated that the Ministry of Information Industry is responsible for the administration of China's Internet domain names; establishment of domain name root servers and domain name root server operators within the PRC shall be approved by the Ministry; and establishment of domain name registration administrators and domain name registration service providers within the PRC shall be approved by it.

Other provisions include: registration of domain names follow the principle of "first come, first served"; in order to protect State and public interests, domain name registration administrators may provide necessary protection for certain pre-reserved characters, and implement the same after submitting them to the Ministry of Information Industry for record filing, and name registration administrators and domain name registration service providers shall not pre-reserve domain names or do so in a disguised form; domain name registration administrators and domain name registration service providers shall not in the course of providing domain name registration services represent any real or potential domain name holder; domain name registration applicants shall submit true, accurate and complete domain name registration information and sign a client registration agreement with the domain name registration service provider. Once a domain name has been registered, the domain name registration applicant becomes the holder of that domain name; and domain name registration administrators may designate a neutral domain name dispute resolution institution to resolve disputes.

♦ Brief Introduction of the Measures for Administration of E-mail Service on Internet

With the rapid popularization and development of Internet in China, junk e-mails occupy large amount of network resources and often become the tools of transmitting a virus, threatening Internet information security and infringing on the legal rights and interests of e-mail users. The anti-junk mail situation becomes increasingly serious. In order to regulate E-mail service on Internet, safeguard the legitimate rights of users and promote the sound development of the Internet, the Ministry of Information Industry formulated the Measures for Administration of E-mail Service on the Internet (the No.38 Decree of the Ministry of Information Industry), which came into effect on March 30, 2006.

It is stipulated that no organization or individual can, without explicit agreement of the receiver of Internet E-mail, send Internet E-mail containing the content of business advertisement thereto, or not provide a clear indication by use of the word "advertisement" or "AD" in front of the message title. Anyone who sends e-mail in violation of the regulations shall be punished correspondingly.

The Measures prescribe that the provider of E-mail service close anonymous transmission function of E-mail server.

Meanwhile, the Measures set forth the implementation of market access management for e-mail services for the first time. All providers must obtain a business license for value added telecommunication services or go through recording formalities. The State shall register the IP address of the server. The providers of Internet access services and other providers of telecommunication services shall not provide Internet access service for any organizations or individuals that have not obtained a business license for value added telecommunication business or have not gone through the appropriate recording formalities for non-operational Internet information services to carry out E-mail service on the Internet.

♦ Brief Introduction of the Measures for the Administration of Electronic Certification Services

The Measures for the Administration of Electronic Certification Services was formulated under the authorization of the Electronic Signature Law of the PRC and is a ministerial regulation implemented for supplementation of the latter. It has important legal effect and function and promulgated as the order of the Ministry of Information Industry on February 8, 2005.

The Measures focus on the electronic certification service institution and make specific provisions mainly on its establishment, the standards required and the relevant supervision over and administration of it.

The Measures consist of eight chapters and 43 articles, including the general provisions, electronic certification service institutions, the suspension and termination of the electronic certification service, electronic signature certificates, supervision and administration, penalty provisions and supplementary articles. It mainly lays stipulations on the issuance and administration of the "Permit for Electronic Certification Services", the standard for the electronic certification service, the disposal of supervision over and administration of the electronic certification service, the format of the electronic signature certificates and the security guarantee measures for it, the supervision and administration and penalties for the violation of the laws and regulations.

♦ Brief Introduction of the Administration of Internet News Information Services Provisions

The Press Office of the State Council and Ministry of Information Industry jointly promulgated the Provisions for the Administration of Internet News Information Services, which is an important regulation on standardizing the Internet news information services.

The Provisions clearly stipulate that Internet news information services include the publication of news information, provisions of electronic bulletin board services for current and political affairs and distribution of communications of current and political affairs to the public through the Internet. According to the Provisions, Internet news information service units are divided into the following three types: Internet news information service units that are established by press work units and that publish news information beyond the scope of what has been published or released by the press work unit and that provides electronic bulletin board services on current and political affairs and distributes communications of current and political affairs to the public; an Internet news information service unit that is established by a non-press work unit and that republishes news information, provides electronic bulletin board services on current and political affairs and distributes communications of current and political affairs to the public; and an Internet news information service unit that is established by a press work unit and that publishes news information published or released by the press work unit. Of these, the first two types are subject to examination and approval by the Press Office of the State Council; establishment of an Internet news information service unit specified as the third type should be filed with the Press Office of the State Council or with the press office of the province, autonomous region or municipality directly under the Central Government.

♦ Brief Introduction of the Regulations on Administration of Internet-based Audio-Video Program Services

The Regulations on Administration of Internet-based Audio-Video Program Services were promulgated upon approval by the State Administration of Radio, Film and Television and the Ministry of Information Industry and took effect on January 31, 2008.

It is stipulated that the department in charge of radio, film and television operations under the State Council, as the industrial authority for Internet-based audio-video program services, is responsible for supervision and administration of Internet-based audio-video program services, overall planning of industrial development and management, content creation and safety monitoring in the area of Internet-based audio-video program services. The department implements supervision and administration of Internet-based audio-video program services as required according to administrative responsibilities of the telecommunications industry.

Other provisions include: operators of Internet-based audio-video program services must obtain a License for Spreading Audio-Video Programs over Information Networks issued by radio, film and television authorities or complete record-filing procedures as required in these Regulations; programs that fall in the category of films and TV shows and other programs used for Internet-based audio-video program services must comply with the government's administrative regulations for radio, film and TV programs. Audio/video news programs that fall in the category of political news and current events broadcast by Internet-based audio-video program service providers must be those produced and broadcast by a prefecture or higher level city's radio or TV station and those posted on a website of a Central Government-affiliated news unit.

Sports

General Introduction

Introduction to Sports Development in China

China enjoys a long tradition of various sports activities. Since the introduction of modern events to China at the turn of the 20th century, the physical culture in the country has been brought in line with the world. Unfortunately, little improvement was made in the semi-colonial and semi-feudal nation. It was only after the founding of the P.R.C. in 1949 when the Chinese Government began to attach great importance to the development of sports. Rapid progress has since been made with tremendous input.

Chinese athletes have made enviable achievements since March 1959, when Rong Guotuan claimed China's first ever world title at the 25th World Table Tennis Championships in Germany. From 2001 to 2005, China won 493 world champions, and set 98 world records. In Salt Lake City 2002, China broke the gold medal jinx in the Winter Games. And in 2004 Athens Summer Olympics, it hit a new high with 32 gold. In 2008, Beijing successfully hosted the 29th Olympiad. This stimulates the further development of mass sports and competitive sports.

At present, there are more than 10 professional sports universities and colleges in China, which have produced over 100,000 graduates; 30-plus research institutions of sports science; and thousands of amateur training schools and secondary sports schools with an enrollment of 300,000 students. In addition, over the past 50 years, we have built more than 500 thousand sports venues, published some 2,700 sports-related books. With an established national competition system, China has organized National Games, National Juvenile Games, Traditional Sports Games of National Minorities, National Workers' Games, National Military Games, National City Games, and National Farmers' Games. More than 200 nationwide games of individual event are held every year, and many more at other levels.

Traditional Sports

China's cultural background features stability and uniqueness, thanks to its long history and profound social environment. It exerts great influence on China's traditional sports, which take on the characteristics of an agricultural society. Chinese people have been accustomed to live in a peaceful and harmonious way, and are not inclined to take part in competitive sports involving much risk or confrontation. Therefore, instead of competitive sports, what dominate Chinese traditional sports are those for health-building and self-cultivation. Originating in the pre-historic era, these activities, including qigong, martial arts, and shadow boxing, aim at obtaining a metaphysical experience through the regulation of breathing patterns. They boast high values in strengthening and improving physical, metabolic and mental functions. These sports are fully integrated into the stable social structure, slow life pace, and Chinese way of thinking, and represent the highest level of physical culture and sports of an agricultural society.

Constrution of Sports Teams

In 1949, the Chinese government urged development of physical culture for better health of the citizens. On November 15, 1949, the Central Commission for Physical Culture and Sports was set up, which issued "Decision on Improving Students' Health in Educational Institutions at all levels" (1951), "General Outline of Physical Education in Middle and Primary Schools" (1956), and "Sports System to Strengthen Labor and Defense Capabilities" (1954). In 1951, China formed the first national team of 58 athletes, selected from national basketball and volleyball games. By 1956, other events, such as athletics (1953), table tennis, swimming, badminton (1954) and gymnastics (1955), etc., have also formed national teams.

In 1954, the central government initiated "the mass participation for more popular and frequent sports activities". Two years later, China issued "Provisional Regulations on Athletic Competition System of the P.R.C.", "Rule on the Grading System of Athletes and Referees of the P.R.C. (Draft)", and the grading system of athletes in athletics, swimming and other 14 events, etc. Finally in 1959, the first National Games was convened, marking the overall development of China's physical culture and sports.

Training System of Competitive Sports

China's achievements in competitive sports are attributed to the ever-improving nation-wide training system, featuring amateur youth sports schools and grass-roots

In order to carry forward the Olympic spirit and commemorate the International Olympic Day, the disabled athlete Li Chenggang successfully swam across the Yangtze River.

sports clubs as the foundation, provincial and regional teams as the main force, and national teams as the lead. Such a system keeps some 20,000 athletes each year, forming a competitive force in international games. Meanwhile, to further speed up the development of competitive sports, China has adopted international management models. Today, China is a member of 110 international, 128 Asian and Pan-Pacific sports organizations.

Sports Events Practiced in China

Sports practiced in China include: archery, athletics, badminton, baseball, basketball, boxing, canoe/kayak, cycling (including mountain cycling), equestrian dressage, fencing, soccer, gymnastics (including rhythmic gymnastics), handball, hockey, judo. Modern pentathlon, rowing, shooting, swimming (including diving, synchronized swimming, polo), softball, table tennis, tennis (including soft tennis), volleyball (including beach volleyball), weightlifting, wrestling, sailing (including dinghy), speed skating, short track speed skating, figure skating, ice hockey, alpine skiing, cross-country skiing, ski jumping, Nordic combined, freestyle skiing, winter biathlon, bobsleigh, luge, curling, bowling, bocce, golf, snooker, sepak takraw, chess, Chinese chess. I-go, bridge, marine modeling, aero modeling, parachuting, dynamic parachuting, paragliding, gliding, hang gliding, hot air balloon, mountain climbing, rock-climbing, car racing, car modeling, motoring, motorboating, boarding, fin swimming, radio sports, Chinese wrestling, martial arts, acrobatics, triathlon, taekwondo, roller skating, skateboarding, fishing, pigeon sport, dragon dancing, lion dancing, dragon boat racing, kite flying, gateball, shuttlecock ball sport, qigong, body building, aerobatics, sports dancing.

Mode of Development

In 1903, regular schools in China set up course of gymnastics in their curriculum, with national education concept as the guiding principle for developing physical culture. Around the 1920s, from a pragmatic view, China's physical education completed the transition from the German and Japanese model to the Anglo-American model. To compete in the Olympics, China put forward the guideline of "popularization and promotion" in the 1950s, to ease the conflict between mass participation and the improvement of competitive sports. After reform and opening up in the late 1970s, China made clear its strategy of "overall development of physical culture and sports with competitive sports as the lead", and designed a mode of development featuring "institutionalised popular sports system, and national competitive sports system", to catch up with international level. During the 1990s, China further stressed the principle of "coordinated development of all events", emphasizing the dual progress in the Olympic Games and the Whole Nation Health Building Campaign. Propelled by such strategies, China's sports system gradually transformed from a traditional model to a modern one.

The national men's volleyball team training in the Training Bureau of the General Administration of Sport of China

♦ "Olympic Glorious Program"

"Olympic Glorious Program" was initiated in 1994, and issued in the year after. The program ensures by law the status of Olympic events in China's competitive sports, and puts forward the objectives for China's basic athletic and performance capability in these events. According to statistics, China is highly competitive in about 60 events, and potentially competitive in another 70, of 26 major items. They comprise the main force of China's athletic sports in world arena. The program outlines the distribution of competitive and potentially competitive events according to the medal winning prospects at the Olympics. The National Games, whose event setting is based on the Olympic strategy, should give priority to competitive events in its planning and operation. The National City Games, on the other hand, should continue to train and select promising young athletes for the Olympic Games, focusing children and teenagers. At the same time, they are expected to provide participating cities with guidance in developing competitive events with relatively weak foundations. "Olympic Glorious Program" focuses Olympic events in event distribution, particularly the events of high gold prospects.

The Three-Tier Training System

The present three-tier training system can be divided vertically as follows: senior training in national teams, and teams of provinces, municipalities, autonomous regions and the P.L.A.; intermediate training in sports schools, schools affiliated to sports colleges, and amateur youth training centers; and basic training in traditional sports project schools, middle schools and primary schools. The system can also be divided horizontally as follows: professional training, including national teams and outstanding provincial teams; and amateur training, embracing the intermediate and basic level mentioned above. The inter-related, three-dimensional network corresponds with the Nationwide System, featuring streamlined concept, organization and training.

At present, amateur training of individual provinces, municipalities and autonomous regions shoulders more responsibility in nurturing young athletes. According to statistics, some 80,000 people are involved in intermediate training at nearly 2,000 sports schools, covering all items in China's competitive sports; 4.7 million students are engaged in basic training at 24,000 traditional sports project schools; and over 20,000 students in regular regional and county-level amateur sports schools.

China and Olympics

At the beginning of the 20th century, school sports meet stepped out of schoolyards to a higher level. Inter-school games evolved into regional games in North China, Central China and East China, etc., and finally into the first National Games in 1910, resembling the form of the Olympics. In September, 1911, China, Japan and Philippines initiated the Far-East Games, a hallmark in China's stride toward the international arena. The 1924 National Games was reformed according to international practice, and started the era when Chinese people began to manage and organize sports events on their own. In 1932, Liu Changchun became the first Chinese athlete participating in the 10th Olympic Games in Los Angeles.

After the founding of P.R.C, China took part in the 15th Olympic Games held in Helsinki, 1952. In 1958, in order to maintain national unity, China ended its relationship with international sports organizations that attempted to create "two Chinas", however, Chinese people did not give up their Olympic dream, but continued to nurture athletes, host games, and establish competitive sports systems. In 1984, China returned to the Olympic Games arena in Los Angeles, with the first gold medal won by a Chinese shooter Xu Haifeng. This first Olympic gold collected by a Chinese was thus called "a break through zero" for half of the century—an event that aroused global awareness of China's athletic ability. And the subsequent 24th, 25th, 26th, 27th, 28th and 29th Games further presented the whole world the development of China's Olympics events.

Influence of Olympics on China's Physical Culture

China's participation of Olympics exerts a big influence on its development of physical culture.

First, it enhanced health-building and sports awareness of the Chinese people, and promoted the expansion of popular sports.

Second, it improved athletic capability, and brought China to the forefront of competitive sports.

Third, it promoted China's participation in international sports affairs, and enhanced its influence in global arena.

Fourth, it initiated the establishment of sports science research institutions from nothing, building a sports science system with Chinese characteristics.

Fifth, it facilitated the modernization of traditional Chinese sports, including martial arts, go, and dragon boat racing, etc. Some traditional health-building methods have also caught the attention of researchers throughout the world.

Sixth, it accelerated the construction of sports venues, greatly improving the infrastructure of sports activities.

Seventh, it served as a driving force of cultural development, constructing a network of sports publishing.

Eighth, it promoted the industrialization process of physical culture, and the development of related industries.

The Olympic Games speeded up the development of China's physical culture, which in turn contributed to the popularization of Olympics.

The Olympic Badge

To commend China's contribution, IOC has successively awarded gold, silver and bronze Olympic badges to 12 Chinese leaders and sports celebrities for their promotion of world sports. Wan Li was the 15th recipient of the gold badge; Rong Gaotang, Zhong Shitong, Huang Zhong, Li Menghua etc. were awarded the silver badges; and weight lifter Chen Jingkai got a bronze one. On April 28, 1986, Juan Antonio Samaranch, IOC President, conferred the Olympic Cup to the Chinese Olympic Committee, to commend China's contribution to the improvement of sports facilities in developing countries, especially in Asia.

Successful Bid for 2008 Olympics

As the most populous country in the world, China's hosting of the Olympic Games best represents the extensiveness and mass participation of the event. When the first National Games was held at the beginning of the 19th century, some people proposed that China should bid to host the Olympic Games at the earliest possible time. In February, 1991, Beijing bade for the 27th 2000 Olympics. And then on September 23, 1993, the 101th IOC plenary session was convened in Monte Carlo and announced that Sydney had a narrow win with 45 votes against Beijing's 43 votes. On April 7, 1999, Beijing made its second bid for the 29th Olympic Games, with the motto "New Beijing, Great Olympics". On June 20th the following year, it underlined the themes of "Green Olympics, a Hi-Tech Olympics, and a People's Olympics" in its official bidding application. On August 28, 2000, IOC decided upon the shortlist of five bidding cities, including Beijing. And in January 2001, China delivered its bidding report to IOC. Altogether 58 training venues and 37 competition venues are required to host the 2008 Games, including 32 in Beijing, and 5 in other cities. With sustained support and efforts of the Chinese government and officials, Beijing was highly regarded by the IOC appraisal team, which observed that a successful bid would be a unique heritage to China and sports alike. On July 13 the same year, IOC President Juan Antonio Samaranch declared Beijing as the host for the 2008 summer Olympic Games. By then, China has realized its century-old Olympic dream.

Olympic Day Run

Celebrated each year on June 23, Olympic Day commemorates the founding of the IOC. Chinese Olympic Committee held the first Olympic Day Run in 1987, which has now become a popular activity among the Chinese. The year 2006 marked the 20th anniversary

Celebrating the success of Beijing's bidding for 2008 Olympic Games

Citizens participating in the long-distance running on the Olympic Day

of the IOC, and at 9:00 AM, on June 24, led by several Olympic champions and world titlists, nearly 60,000 runners participated in the spectacular Olympic Day Run in 8 cities, namely Beijing, Tianjin, Shanghai, Shenyang (Liaoning Province), Yinchuan (Ninxia Hui Nationality Autonomous Region), Wuxi (Jiangsu Province), Pingdingshan (Henan Province) and Suining (Sichuan Province).

♦ The First Olympic Gold of Hong Kong SAR

At the 26th Atlantic Olympic Games, Li Lishan claimed a gold medal in women's sailboard event, the first Olympic gold for Hong Kong. At the 1998 Asian Games, Li once again won the champion in IMCO sailboard, the first gold at the Asian Games after Hong Kong's return to China. Li was selected as one of the top ten figures of Hong Kong SAR during 1988-1998 as a tribute to her outstanding performance.

♦ Beijing Olympic Mascots

Beijing unveiled its mascots for the coming 2008 Olympics—five Fuwas based on fish, giant panda, the Olympic flame, Tibetan antelope and Beijing swallow, respectively named Beibei, Jingjing, Huanhuan, Yingying and Nini. The five syllables together sound identical to "Beijing Huanying Ni", which means "Beijing welcomes you". These lovely Fuwas draw inspiration from the Olympic rings, the landscapes in China and the animals popular with the Chinese people. Each of the mascots represents prosperity, happiness, passion, health and good luck. They will carry good wishes and hospitality to every corner of the world, and invite friends from both home and abroad to the 2008 Beijing Olympics.

International Sports Exchange

The Chinese government has always been supportive of the popularization and promotion of Olympic works, actively engaging itself in sports exchanges throughout the globe. Currently, about 30,000 Chinese are involved in over 2000 international sports competitions and exchanges. Besides, China also successfully hosted the 11th Asian Games, 3rd Asian Winter Games, 1st East Asian Games, 6th Far East and South Pacific Games for the Disabled, and other multi-sport games and international competitions. China is also active in aiding other members of the IOC, helping building over 50 stadiums and gymnasiums in more than 30 countries and regions.

The Anti-Doping Work

Sports circles in China knew little about doping before the 1980s. However, this "international nuisance" began to find its way into China as the nation's exchanges with the outside world expanded and sports competition became tenser, especially because of adverse influences brought along by the commercialization of sports.

China has acceded to the International Olympic Charter against Doping in Sport, the Lausanne Declaration on Doping in Sport, and the Sydney Communiqué. On May 19, 1989, the State Physical Culture and Sports Commission promulgated Provisional Regulations on Doping Control in National Sports Events. In December the same year, China Doping Control Center passed the IOC accreditation and officially went into operation. These marked a new beginning of an all-round anti-doping drive in China.

Laws on Anti-Doping

In the past dozen of years, China has made unprecedented achievements in its anti-doping efforts, and the legal system on anti-doping has been improved. Article 34 of the Law of P.R.C. on Physical Culture and Sports (enacted on October 1, 1995) stipulates that "the principle of fair competition shall be followed in sports competitions. Organizers of competitions, athletes, coaches and referees shall abide by sportsmanship, and may not practice fraud or engage in malpractice for selfish ends." With regards to the doping issue, article 34 provides that "use of banned drugs and methods is strictly prohibited in sports activities. Institutions in charge of testing banned drugs shall conduct strict examination of the banned drugs and methods." As for legal liabilities, article 50 maintains that "whoever resorts to banned drugs or methods in sports activities shall be punished by the relevant

The members of the delegation of the Australian Olympic Committee visited the China Doping Control Center.

public sports organization in accordance with the provisions of its articles of association; State functionaries who are held directly responsible shall be subject to administrative sanctions in accordance with law." The foregoing lends legal basis and judicial support to China's anti-doping campaign.

Legal Documents on Anti-Doping

Based on Law on Physical Culture and Sports, the authorities concerned has formulated and issued 30 legal documents in the past decade, which form the core of China's legal system on anti-doping. Other existing laws and regulations have also given legal support to the campaign in either direct or indirect ways. With regards to the regulation of medicines, Chinese government has issued a number of decrees on the basis of the Law of the People's Republic of China on Pharmaceutical Administration (1984) to strengthen supervision over medicines and their circulation. Especially, the making of the regulations on supervising and administering anesthetics, psychoactive drugs, ephedrine, prescribed and non-prescribed medicines has provided important legal grounds for controlling the medicinal source of doping. The "Criminal Law of the People's Republic of China" (revised in 1997) imposes severe punishment for crimes involving heroin, methylamphetamine, morphine, cannabis, cocaine, and other medicines banned by IOC.

On March 1, 2004, the State Council promulgated Anti Doping Regulations. For 16 years consecutively, China's doping labs have been certified by IOC and World Anti Doping Agency. Its quality management system of doping control has also been certified by international authority concerned, a sign of meeting the international standard. Advanced anti-doping system helped assure China's "zero positive case" at the past two Olympic Games. This was highly appreciated by the world, and has laid a solid foundation for doping control at the 2008 Beijing Olympics.

Changes in Sports Development

Convened every four years, the National Games is a nation-wide, multi-sport event of the largest scale in China. To fully implement the strategic guideline of "holding National Games in preparation for the Olympics", China has shifted its time to the year following the Olympics since the 8th National Games in 1997. Gradually, some adjustments were also made in event setting to follow the Olympic Games, along with corresponding reforms in athlete exchange and scoring method.

To form a competition market, institutions in charge of sports affairs promoted professionalism in some individual events, starting from the reform of soccer games. For instance, soccer matches adopted host and guest round robin system, while basketball matches adopted trans-year host and guest system. As a result of improved athletic skills and better organization, sports games attract more and more audience year on year.

The authority concerned also drew on the experience of other countries in hosting big events, and began to mobilize market mechanism instead of government investment alone. The 21st Universiade in 2001 held in China combined multi-channel funding with government input, advertising revenue, and issuing of sports lottery, etc. The last item alone collected 90 million RMB, and ticket sales gained an extra 21 million RMB. It was the first time for China to achieve balance of payment with moderate gains in hosting international sports events.

Sports Goods Industry

The Whole People Health-Building Campaign directly stimulates sports goods industry in China. In recent years, China's market of sports utilities has been expanding at an annual rate of 50 percent, and in 2005, the total sales reached US$50 billion. With a huge market and great demands for sporting equipment, Guangdong, Fujian and the Yangtze River Delta have emerged as the three manufacturing bases of sports goods, accommodating over 10,000 specialized enterprises. The city of Jinjiang in Fujian alone has more than 3,000 shoe manufacturing factories and 2,000 related enterprises. Such a manufacturing scale not only meets domestic demand, but also enables export. Currently, 65 percent of sports utilities in the world are made in China, including 50 percent of health-building equipment. These statistics have shown that China's once-labour-intensive sports goods industry is already a main force in the electro-mechanical production of modern health-building equipment.

Sports Entertainment Industry

With sports industrialization and socialization comes the sports entertainment industry, growing out of nothing and from small to large. As time went by, snooker and bowling clubs, golf courts, taekwondo and martial arts gyms, fencing halls, shooting ranges, and gymnasiums have become part of the life of some well-off Chinese.

The world is surprised at Chinese people's extraordinary love for sports, especially for golf, bowling and snooker, traditionally exclusive games for the rich in the West. Surveys estimate that within a few years, there will be more than 3,000 gyms for health-building purposes in Shanghai, the city with the highest level of marketization in China, and over 1,000 gyms in Beijing. Moreover, many of these gyms are nation-wide chain clubs, and are bound for further development in the coming years.

Professionalization of Sports

Sponsored by a multinational tobacco company, professional football league in China started in 1994, in 12 cities, including Beijing, Shanghai, Guangzhou, Chengdu, Dalian, and Shenyang, etc. This marked the beginning of sports professionalism in China.

Subsequently, basketball, volleyball, table tennis and the game of go also joined the professionalism trend, yielding unexpected progress. Entity reform took place in professional associations, and sports clubs were formed. Professional league has produced a market of scale, gradually attracting social capital to the football market, and improving the overall environment for sports development. The value for the second five-year contract approached 100 million RMB between IMG, operator of League A, and Chinese Football Association (CFA). The value for the six-year contract stood at 300 million RMB between ISL and CFA. By then, commercial operation has primarily taken shape. Professionalism speeds up the formation of sports market and industrial structure; and club operation now ranges from ticket selling, advertising, player transfer, commercial games, TV broadcasting and trade dealing.

Meanwhile, some Chinese athletes have joined professional leagues of other countries. The most eminent one is Yao Ming, who established himself in Huston Rockets in 2002 at the age of 22, and is expected to become a top center in NBA. Prior to Yao, Chinese soccer player Yang Chen and Fan Zhiyi also played in the German Bundesliga and England Primere League, respectively.

Breakthroughs (2006)

On February 23, 2006, Han Xiaopeng came from nowhere to win the gold medal in men's aerial freestyle skiing with two flawless jumps at Turin Winter Olympics. This was China's first ever Olympic gold medal in snow events, and also the first won by a man athlete.

On the evening of October 18, 2006, China won the first women's team title at the world gymnastics championships in Aarhus, Denmark. This was the first women's team champion in its 53-year history. The men's team also claimed gold at the championships.

On July 11, 2006, Liu Xiang broke the 13-year old world record set by British sprinter Colin Jackson in men's 110m hurdles, with his 12.88 seconds at Athletissima', a Super Grand Prix meeting in Lausanne, Switzerland, which is part of the IAAF World Athletics Tour.

At Doha Asian Games from December 1-15, 2006, China ranked the first on the medal tally with 165 gold medals, the seventh time in succession in the past 24 years.

On January 27, 2006, Chinese pair Zheng Jie and Yan Zi won women's double champion at the Australia Open, China's first title in the Grand Slams. Then on July 10, they again claimed gold at the Wimbledon Open.

♦ The 11th Five-Year Plan on Physical Culture and Sports

In its "11th Five-Year Plan on Physical Culture and Sports", the Chinese government brings forward the overall objectives for 2006-2010: on the opportunity of hosting 2008 Olympics, expand popular sports, and improve athletic skills, so as to meet the ever-increasing public demand for physical culture and sports. During the eleventh five-year plan period, a whole-people fitness system with Chinese characteristics will be established, with the objectives of improving the health condition of Chinese people, and creating a sound atmosphere for health-building. More efforts will be made in the construction of sports facilities in urban and rural residence communities; apart from the existing "Whole-People Fitness Paths Project" and aiding projects, more emphasis shall be given to the health-building campaign among Chinese farmers, to make standard public sports venues and facilities available in 1/6 of the administrative villages by 2010. In terms of competitive sports, China shall further enhance the overall athletic capability and international competitiveness, strengthen national teams at all levels, and optimize event setting and distribution. China will continue to rank among the tops on the gold medal tally in summer events both at Asian Games and Olympic Games, and at the same time improve its records in winter games.

Sports History

Ancient Sports

Ancient sports in China originated from the daily activities of prehistoric mankind, evolving in the historical development of the Chinese nationality over thousands of years. Pre-Qin years (prior to 221 BC) witnessed the germination of ancient sports, while Qin, Han, and the Three Kingdoms Period (221 BC-265 AD) saw its development, and it reached the climax during the West Jin, East Jin, Northern and Southern Dynasties, Sui, Tang, and the Five Dynasties (265-960). By Song, Liao, Jin, and Yuan Dynasties (1206-1368), ancient sports had flourished in China.

Chinese ancestors have left rich practical experience and abundant theoretical works in the pursuit of longevity, health-building, skill-training, and entertainment.

Baixi (A Hundred Acrobatics)

Baixi, also called Juedixi or Juedi, is an ancient form of gymnastics, incorporating ancient Chinese culture, art, and sports. It involves dancing, music, acrobatics, conjuring and wrestling. Many items of Baixi belong to sports events: rope skill is handstand on a tight rope; Yuangan is a sports of strength; Nongwanjian is a game of conjuring balls or knives; Kangding (lifting metal tripods), Zhuanshi (revolving rocks) are games for Hercules. Horseback riding and Juedi (wrestling) are even more typical athletic events. Unearthed relics with Juedi patterns attest to its popularity among all Chinese nationalities during the Qin and Han Dynasties (221 BC.-220 AD). On the murals of No.2 Late East Han (25-220) cemetery in County Mi, Hennan Province, Juedi patterns are found, which resemble Japanese sumo.

Sports Murals

Sports scenes are often depicted in the murals of ancient temples and cemeteries, including Juedi, Jiqiu (ball hitting), go, arrow shooting, spear arts, martial arts, and swimming, etc. For instance, in the mural in No. 345 cave of the Mogao Caves in Dunhuang, Gansu Province, one can find a squatting man shooting arrows, a traditional sport in the Five Dynasties (907-960). A painting in the Hall of White Robe of Shaolin Temple, Henan, portrays a group of Shaolin monks practicing martial arts in the Qing Dynasty (1616-1911). A mural in the Potala Palace in Tibet depicts a swimming scene in the Qing Dynasty.

Bingxi (Games on Ice)

Bingxi refers to all the games played on ice. It flourished in the Ming and Qing Dynasties, featuring speed skating, sledding, and arrow shooting on ice, etc.

Ancient Acrobatics

Ancient Acrobatics are traditional sports with strong ethnic characteristics, featuring handstand, jujitsu, and somersault. With the development of society, acrobatics have improved both in terms of quantity and artistic performance, constituting an important component of ancient Chinese sports.

Murals in the Shaolinsi Temple

• Jing Wu Athletic Association

Jing Wu Athletic Association, founded in Shanghai by Huo Yuanjia, in 1910 at the end of the Qing Dynasty, was one of the largest sports organizations in modern China with big international influence. Martial arts were its main activities, together with soccer, basketball, table tennis, gymnastics, weightlifting, horseback riding, roller staking, shooting, boxing and wrestling, etc. The association organized a series of activities: training sessions conducted by guest martial art masters from various schools of the North and the South; demonstration sports schools set up in affiliation to the association; discovery, systemization, research, and publication of works related to martial arts. Besides, branches of Jing Wu were established in South East Asia in the 1920s, and spread to Europe and America. The association has also published dozens of books on martial arts, including *The Book of Jing Wu* and *Anecdotes of Jing Wu*, related films were shot, with the purpose of popularizing this traditional Chinese sport.

Ancient Horsemanship

Horse racing, horseback acrobatics, and circus are the major forms of ancient horsemanship. During the Ming and Qing Dynasties, such competitions and performances became very popular, a proof of the sophistication of China's horsemanship sports.

Modern Sports (1860-1949)

The years between 1860 and 1949 served as a transitional period in China's sports history. After the Opium War in 1840, the closed-door feudal China was reduced to a semi-colonial, semi-feudal country. Unprecedented changes occurred with the incoming western cultures. On the one hand, sports systems and events were introduced through western education, and gradually became the mainstream over dozens of years. On the other hand, traditional sports featuring martial arts conceded the dominant position, though they still enjoyed mass popularity. Introduced modern sports and traditional Chinese sports comprised the major part of modern sports in China, and laid a sound foundation for its future development.

With social development and the influence of the Olympics, state-fund schools began to carry out various modern sports events and competitions; and the games branched out of the Church to public schools and society at large. Cities, provinces and regions also joined the trend, with National Games, regional games, and provincial and city games emerging one after another. These games, interrelate with each other, are convened regularly, which promoted the formation of an athletic competition system. The participation in the Olympics further standardized domestic games, and played a key role in the promotion of modern Chinese games.

Regional Games

The ever-increasing influence of the Olympic Games results in regional games at all levels in North, Central and East China, etc. The one in North China was the earliest and the best developed.

North China has an early start in modern sports, with relatively high athletic capabilities and mass participation. Regional games evolved from the games in Beijing and Tianjin in particular. As early as 1910, Beijing branch of the Young Men's Christian Association organized the Interuniversitary Sports Alliance involving Tsinghua University, Xiehe College and Yanjing University (now Peking University). Two years later, it organized a small sports meeting in Beijing, and co-established the Beijing Athletic Federation together with Beijing Normal University and Huiwen College. The year 1913 saw the first North China Games, and the following year saw the second Games, with the participation of some 20 universities from Tianjin, Tangshan, Baoding, Henan and Shanxi. The newly established North China Sports Confederation decided to host the annual event in different cities every year, and 18 regional games had been held during the 20 plus years, until turbulence picked up in 1934. North China Games was the largest regional games during that period, with the longest history, most extensive participation, highest athletic competitiveness and biggest influence. It exerted a positive influence on the development of physical culture and sports in North China and the whole nation at large. Outstanding performances and distinguished athletes at these games shall be recorded in the modern sports history of China.

Provincial and Municipal Games

From 1904 to 1908, Guangdong and Fujian hosted the first provincial and municipal games. After the 2nd Far Eastern Championship Games in Shanghai in 1915, various provinces and cities began to organize similar games, including Beijing, Tianjin, Fujian, Hong Kong, Hunan, Sichuan, and Anhui, etc. Hunan Province, in particular, held 17 standard provincial games between 1905 and 1948. Other provinces like Shandong, Jiangsu and Zhejiang also joined the trend in the late 1920s, with more and more people taking part in the games.

National Games, regional games, provincial and municipal games basically form an integrated system of competitive sports in modern China, and have laid a sound foundation for China's achievements at the Olympic Games.

Far Eastern Championship Games

The Far Eastern Championship Games, originally named the Olympic Games for the Far East, was an international regional event, and the earliest trans-continental games in the world. It was initiated by the Philippines, China and Japan at the beginning of the 20th century, while India, Indonesia and Vietnam joined in the last two Games. Due to the low athletic levels of West, South, Southeast, and Northeast Asia at that time, the Far East Championship Games represented the highest competitiveness of Asia, and was regarded the predecessor of today's Asian Games. The Far Eastern Sports Association and the Far Eastern Championship Games were officially recognized by the IOC in 1920. For better coordination with the Olympic Games, the Far Eastern Championship Games was held every 3 years starting from 1927, and every 4 years from 1930 up to now. Its event setting, rules, scoring and measuring systems were also standardized according to those of the Olympics. By then, competitive sports in Asia has been streamlined to meet the Olympic standard.

Among all the events China took part in at the past 10 Far Eastern Championship Games, we dominated the football pitch, winning 9 champions in streak at the 2nd-10th Games. It was a sign that China was once a football giant in Asia in the 1920s and 1930s. After football there is volleyball, in which China has claimed 5 titles, and then one gold for basketball, swimming, tennis and baseball each. However, China failed to overwhelm Japan and the Philippines in other events. Three Games out of the ten thus convened (the 2nd in 1915, 5th in 1921, and 8th in 1927) were held in Shanghai, which propelled China's early efforts to realize its Olympic dream.

Early Experiences of Olympic Activities

Missionaries poured into China after the mid of the 19th century. Apart of religious activities, they were mostly engaged in education, and set up batches of mission schools. By the end of the century, more than 2,000 such school had been established. In 1890, St. John's College in Shanghai organized a sports meeting mainly of athletics events, and was followed by other schools. In 1896, St. John's College organized a series of soccer tournaments, and held inter-school matches with Nan Yang Public School. Around 1896, basketball was introduced to the mission schools in Beijing and Tianjin through the Young Men's Christian Association, and competitions were held. Around 1900, most mission schools in Beijing, Tianjin, Shanghai, Guangdong, Fujian, Wuhan, and Yantai had extra-curricular sports activities, such as football, baseball, tennis, basketball, volleyball, squash, and athletics, etc., as well as inter-school matches. Some public and private schools also initiated athletics and ball games under such influence.

Modern schools flourished at the beginning of the 20th century, with an increase in inter-school games. More events are included, with athletics, basketball, volleyball, tennis, baseball, softball, table tennis and gymnastics as the main constitution. Later, provincial and regional games appeared on the horizon. Just before the Chinese Bourgeois Democratic Revolution in 1911, sports games had been held in provinces and municipalities like Hunan, Sichuan, Guangdong, Zhejiang, and Tianjin, which greatly promoted Olympic events in China.

♦ The Law of the Republic of China on Physical Culture and Sport Issued in 1929

The Law on Physical Culture and Sport consists of 13 articles. It was officially issued on April 16, 1929, and was the first law specially promulgated for sports affairs in China. In August, 1932, Kuomingtang government held the national conference on physical culture and sport in Nanjing, at which the Implementing Plan for National Sports was passed. Some of these articles drew upon the ones in the West. The plan put forward a series of specific measures and policies as for the development of national sports, and at the same time, provided detailed notation and explanation for The Law on Physical Culture and Sport. The promulgation of the Implementing Plan plays a considerable role in standardizing the works of national sports.

Early Spread of Olympic Education

The Chinese learned about the Olympics originally through the Games itself. In 1904, some of the Chinese newspapers reported on the 3rd Olympic Games held in St. Louis, USA. However, the influence of these reports was limited, due to the small scale of the Games, and the lack of knowledge of modern sports among the public.

In 1908, several newspapers gave pre-game reports on the 4th London Olympics, weeks before this incomparable pageant was celebrated. Some proposed that China should bid for the Games at the earliest possible time. An article in *Tianjin Youth* Daily posed three questions:

When will China send an athlete to the Olympics?

When will China send a delegation to the Olympics?

When will China host an Olympic Games?

More articles on this subject appeared in newspapers and magazines thereafter. And the wish of participation was conducive to the further spread and development of Olympic Games in China.

Early Relationship between the IOC and China

It dates back to the Far Eastern Championship Games (originally named the Olympic Games for the Far East) when China and the IOC first established contacts. In September, 1911, the Philippines, China and Japan initiated the Far Eastern Amateur Athletic Association, or the Far Eastern Athletic Federation (FEAF). The FEAF decided to hold the Olympic Games for the Far East ever other year in different cities in the region. E.S. Brown, one of the initiators, reported the Games to the IOC, which sent China official invitation to the 1916 Olympics and IOC Conference. However, the plan failed when WWI broke out. In 1920, IOC officially recognized the Federation and the Games, and the FEAF became the first regional sports association in contact with the IOC. Through these Games, China had a chance to establish its relationship with the IOC.

The First Chinese IOC Member

In 1922, Wang Zhengting, initiator and sponsor of the Far Eastern Championship Games, was elected IOC member. As the president of the 2nd, 5th, and 8th Games, Wang was the first IOC member from China, and the second from the Far East. Thus, China has established relations with the IOC, a sign of mutual recognition and acceptance.

Accession to the Olympic Family

In August 1924, All-China Sports Federation (ACSF) was established in Shanghai, the first national sports association composed of Chinese only. ACSF not only took over the organization of all events originally sponsored by the foreigners of the Young Men's Christian Association. It also started other regional games, individual event games and training classes. Moreover, ACSF branches were set up one after another throughout China. After 1927, ACSF acceded to eight international sports federations (athletics, swimming, gymnastics, tennis, weightlifting, boxing, football and basketball) and organizations.

The IOC fully recognized ACSF as the Chinese Olympics Committee in 1931, and China became a member of the Olympic family. Henceforward, China has established closer relations with the IOC, and has been actively engaged in its activities. The establishment of ACSF promoted competitive sports both at national and regional levels, and enhanced international exchange in sports. It has played a significant role in China's participation in international events and its progress in Olympic events, which is a sign of spontaneous acceptance of the Olympic Games by the Chinese people.

The First Olympic Bid

China's first Olympic bid was made in 1945. At the 2nd conference of the ACSF board of trustees in Chongqing, Wang Zhengting, the first Chinese IOC member, and Dong Shouyi proposed that China bid for hosting the 1952 Olympic Games, which was agreed upon unanimously. However, the proposal was ignored and remained a scrap of paper, due to the historical conditions in old China, and the way of proposing which fell short of the IOC requirement.

Kong Xiangxi

Kong Xiangxi (1880-1967), former IOC member. In 1901, he went to Yale University and got his degree there. Kong became an adviser of Yan Xishan, the governor of Shanxi after the revolution in 1911. In 1924 he moved to Guangzhou and was named finance minister. He later took up the enterprise ministry in the National Government of Wuhan (led by Wang Jingwei) in 1927. After the Wuhan government was incorporated into the one in Nanjing, he continued his career as cabinet minister, and also served as the president of the Central Bank as well as the Bank of China. In 1939, at the recommendation of Wang Zhengting, Kong was named IOC member, which he resigned in August 1955. He had stayed in USA since 1948 until he died in 1967.

Wang Zhengting

Wang Zhengting (1882-1961) was China's first IOC member. He studied in USA after graduating from Peiyang University in Tianjin, and got his doctoral degree at Yale University in 1910. After the 1911 revolt in Wuchang, Wang was appointed vice speaker of the Senate in Nanjing, and vice minister of Commerce of the Kuomingtang. He also served as minister of foreign affairs, where he was acting premier, and president of Peking University from 1921 to the 1940s. As a result of his involvement in the Young Men's Christian Association, Wang panned out as one of the leaders in China's modern sports, and occupied key positions in national sports associations, and the organization of important national and international events. As one of the initiators of the Far Eastern Athletic Federation, and one of the sponsors of the Far Eastern Championship Games, Wang was the president of the 2nd, 5th, and 8th Games. In 1922, he was officially elected IOC member, the first from China, and the second from the Far East. In 1924, Wang was elected honorary president of the newly-founded ACSF, and in 1933, chairman of board of ACSF. He led the Chinese delegation to the 11th and 14th Olympics in 1936 and 1948 respectively. Wang moved to Hong Kong SAR and lived there until he died in 1961. Though chiefly known as a key figure in China's politics, Wang Zhengting also made considerable contribution to the spread of Olympic events in China.

Dong Shouyi

Dong Shouyi (1895-1978), former IOC member. He graduated from Tongzhou Xiehe College in Beijing, where he was known for his keenness on sports, especially basketball. In 1923, Dong became secretary in charge of sports of Tianjin Youth Association, and a part-time PE teacher at Nankai Middle school, where he trained an excellent basketball team. Dong went to USA the same year to study at the Department of Sports at Springfield University. When he returned in 1925, he was appointed director of sports of Tianjin Youth Association. In 1936, Dong Shouyi participated in the 11th Olympic Games as the coach of Chinese basketball team. He also visited Denmark, Sweden, Germany, Czechoslovakia, Austria, Hungary and Italy, etc. on inspection and exchange programs. In 1947, he was elected IOC member, and the next year, director-general of the Chinese delegation to the 14th Olympic Games. After the founding of New China in 1949, Dong was actively engaged in the development of Olympic events in China, as well as the resumption of China's legal status in the IOC. Besides, Dong Shouyi served as chairman of Chinese Basketball Association, vice president of the 4th committee of ACSF, and the director of technical department of the State Commission of Physical Culture and Sports, etc. He died in 1978 in Beijing.

Debut at the Olympics

The 10th Los Angeles Olympic Games in 1932 took place just around Japanese September 18th invasion. On the initiation of officials and celebrities in the sports circle, and the sponsorship of General Zhang Xueliang, ACSF intended to dispatch two athletes, Liu Changchun and Yu Xiwei to the Olympics. But finally only Liu made the trip. Yet he was not in form, due to disrupted training under the Japanese aggression, and the 21-day journey on the Pacific. Liu, who ranked fifth and sixth after the first rounds of the men's 100m and 200m races, failed to qualify in both events. China's one-man-debut at the Olympics was depressing, but opened a new chapter in the Olympic history. Athletes like Liu Changchun and Zhang Xueliang are remembered for their contribution to China's progress in the Olympic arena.

♦ China's Participation in the Olympics from 1932 to 1948

In 1932, China sent a delegation of three to the 10th Olympics, including one leader, one coach (Song Junfu), and one athlete (Liu Changchun). Liu took part in men's 100m and 200m sprints, but was eliminated at the preliminaries of both events.

In 1936, 69 Chinese athletes (excluding nine-people martial arts performing troop, and a 32-people observation team) competed at the 11th Olympics in Berlin. All the Chinese athletes were eliminated in the preliminaries in athletics, swimming, weightlifting, basketball, football, cycling and boxing, except for Fu Baolu, who managed into the finals of men's pole jump.

The 14th Summer Olympics were held in London, in 1948. China sent a delegation of 53 to Britain, including 33 athletes competing in five sports, namely athletics, swimming, basketball, football and cycling. However, none of them achieved good results.

Liu Changchun

Liu Changchun (1909-1983), was once known as "the fly man of China". At the 5th National Games in 1933, he claimed gold in the 200 m with 22'1", and broke the national record in the 100 m with 10'7", which was not broken until 25 years after. In 1932, Liu was the first person, and the only athlete in the delegation from the Republic of China to take part in the Olympic Games. Four years later he also appeared at the 11th Olympics.

China's Participation at Berlin Olympic Games

The 11th Olympics was held in 1936, in Berlin, the capital of Germany. China applied for nearly 30 competition events, and a 140-plus-member delegation was sent, consisting of 69 competitors, while others were demonstrators of traditional martial arts, observers and clerks.

It was a pity that the Chinese men's football team was eliminated by the team of Britain, 0:2, after the first round. During the Olympics, the 11 martial arts demonstrators gave several awesome performances of double-sword, dual-fighting, and shadow boxing, etc., which astounded the European spectators and won tremendous applause. Regrettably, none managed to make it to the finals except Fu Baolu, who finished with 3.80m in the pole vault. It is worth mentioning that the Berlin Games saw the first Chinese journalist to cover the Olympic Games, who was Feng Youzhen, head of Nanchang branch of China's news agency.

China's Participation at the 14th London Olympic Games

Disrupted by WWII, the 12th and 13th Olympics were not convened as scheduled. The 14th Olympics was held in London in 1948, among debris and desperation three years after the war. China sent 33 male athletes for five events, namely basketball, football, athletics, swimming and cycling, but none reached the finals. What is more, national economy was shattered by the civil war, and could not sponsor the national teams. Therefore, the delegation had to borrow money to come back home, thanks to the overseas Chinese there.

Introduction of Modern Weightlifting into China

Modern weightlifting, practiced with barbells, originally appeared in Europe at the end of the 18th century. But at that time, there were no uniform rules, and the game was often practiced with a variety of equipment. When weightlifting was listed as one of the events at the 1st Olympics in 1896, China organized a qualifying trial in Shanghai. Shen Liang, Wang Shaoji and Weng Kangting panned out as the first batch of Chinese weightlifters to the Olympics.

Their best personal records: Shen Liang, 270 kg in the 60 kg lightweight class; Wang Shaoji, 275 kg in the 60 kg lightweight class; Weng Kangting, 297.5 kg in the 82.5 kg light heavyweight class. Wang and Shen's records were actually among the top six compared with those at the previous ten Games. However, due to intensified competition at the 11th Games, and their inadequate preparation, they underperformed in Berlin.

♦ China National Amateur Athletic Federation

When the 4th Far Eastern Championship Games was held in 1919 in the Philippines, officials and celebrities in the sports circle in China proposed the establishment of a national sports federation. In 1921, representatives of sports federations throughout China gathered in Shanghai, and founded a temporary management team, composed of 3 foreigners. On April 3, 1922, the federation put forward its principle: organizing sports activities, unifying standards of amateur games in China, improvement of amateur athletic capability, and selection of athletes by regional federations for international games, etc. As an unofficial organization, China National Amateur Athletic Federation aimed at advancing amateur sports. Before the establishment of ACSF in 1924, it had played a key role in promoting physical culture and sports in China.

♦ China Young Men's Christian Association

Young Men's Christian Associations appeared in China in the 1870s. Composed of young Christian believers, it features religious promotion, as well as the moral, intellectual and physical education of the youth. After 1908, a delegation of secretaries in charge of sports affairs from American Young Men's Christian Association came to China, and took posts in the associations in Beijing, Shanghai, Changsha, and Tianjin, etc., some of them even acted as PE professors or deans in Chinese universities. They were conducive to the early spread of Olympic events in China, through bringing in western events like basketball and volleyball, organizing standardized competitions, setting up venues, and training athletes.

♦ The First Chinese Champion in Race Walk

One Sunday in December, 1928, the Chinese athlete Zhou Yuyu won the Walk Race of Nations with 2h 37m 24s, becoming the first ever Chinese champion in this time-honoured event. Twenty athletes out of a total of some 200 were from China. The route was the same with those at previous games, from Wangjiasha on Nanjing Road, in the east, via Jing'an Temple, Beixinjing, Hami Road, Hengshan Road, and Yan'an Road, all the way to the stand of Paoma Hall (now west to the People's Square), stretching 27 km and 453 m in total.

♦ The First Baseball Team

In 1873, the Manchu Government of the Qing Dynasty sent 30 young Chinese to pursue studies in America, including Zhan Tianyou, who later became a well-known railway engineer. During their stay in USA, they were fond of baseball and set up a China Baseball Team. Its skillful pitchers earned many awards for Yale University. In 1887, the team beat the best team in San Francisco by 10 points. And in the same year, baseball was introduced to China with the return of these students.

♦ The First Chinese Overseas Student of Sports

Wu Yunrui

In 1924, the department of education of Jiangsu Province planned to send one student to America to pursue further studies in sports. Finally, Wu Yunrui was selected as the first government-funded overseas student of this kind, since the previous ones were self-sponsored or sent by churches or the Young Men's Christian Association.

Wu Yunrui (1892-1976) was born in the County of Yin in Jiangsu Province. He graduated from the department of sports at Nanjing Normal University in 1918, and got his bachelor's degree at Southeast University in 1924. As a government-funded overseas student, he first went to Chicago University, majoring in anatomy and hygienics, and later transferred to the department of sports at Columbia Normal University. Wu also conducted research in the principles of sports under the supervision of Professor Williams, dean of the sports department at Columbia University, and flagship of sports theories in America. After Wu obtained his master's degree, he went to Europe on a 6-month inspection tour. When he returned to China, Wu Yunrui successively served as the professor or department dean of China's Central University, Northeast University, and Beijing Normal University, etc. Wu spend 58 years in PE, and was the first Chinese researcher in the field of biomechanics. His works, including Sport Studies, Human Kinematics and Dynamics, Teaching Methodology of Sports, and Basics of Athletics, were popular textbooks at that time for sports majors.

♦ The First National Games

In October 1910, in order to increase its influence, Shanghai branch of the Young Men's Christian Association initiated the first National Interuniversitary Sports Meeting, which was recognized in retrospect the first National Games by the government after the Chinese Bourgeois Democratic Revolution in 1911.

The presidents, clerks, and referees at that National Games were all foreigners, who used English as the only working language for documentation, addresses, and adjudication. Not only did the foreigners speak English, the Games' brochures were also printed in English, and even Chinese athletes used English for sports jargons. The Games was rather a small occasion, with little equipment, and only four events, namely athletics, football, tennis and basketball. However, it already took the shape of big modern games, and served as a prototype for subsequent events. By 1948, seven National Games had been convened in China.

♦ The First Bodybuilding Contest

In 1944, the Modern Stadium, Shanghai Sports Institute, and Shanghai Young Man's Christian Association co-hosted the Shanghai Men's Bodybuilding Contest, the first of its type in China.

The contest adopted the form and rules of Mr. America: some 20 competitors were divided into three groups—A (tall), B (medium height) and C (short). All of them were required to present their physiques from three different angles (from under, side and back) with various poses.

♦ The First Woman Doctor of Sport Studies

Professor Zhang Huilan (1898-1996) at Shanghai Sports Institute is the first women doctor of sport studies in China.

After graduating from Normal University of Sports affiliated to Shanghai Young Women's Christian Association, Zhang Huilan pursued further studies in America, majoring in sports teaching. In 1923, Zhang returned to China and lectured at her former university. From 1925 to 1926, and from 1938 to 1946, she went to America again to study and research in sport studies, biology and public health. Zhang Huilan got her BaS, MaS and PhD in the State University of Wisconsin, MIT, and the State University of Iowa. In 1946, Zhang Huilan returned to China and took the post of dean of the department of sports in Jinling Women's University the next year, and then professor at Shanghai Sports Institute, where she also served as the dean and head of the research center of anatomy. For the past half century, Zhang has devoted herself to sports teaching in China, and has produced batches of graduate students as well as teachers. On June 4, 1987, UNESCO conferred on her in Paris a distinguished medal and certificate for her contribution to sport studies. Hence, she has been remembered as a Chinese pioneer in the field.

♦ The First Boxing Champion

Chen Hanqiang (1891-1959) was born in Guangdong, and moved to Sydney, Australia as a child. He was the first Chinese to win a boxing champion overseas. In 1919, he claimed a gold medal in Australian Boxing Tournament in the 126 pd division, which astounded the whole nation. He fought in more than 300 matches—87 of them were over 20 rounds, which was rare at that time. At the end of the 1920s, Chen returned to China, and coached in Shanghai Jingwu Sports Association. He then moved to HK in 1957 at the age of 64, and died there two years later.

♦ The Earliest Sports Textbook

Hubei Military Studies is the earliest existing sports textbook, published in 1900, the 26th year of the reign of Emperor Guangxu. This bound edition consisted of six volumes and was one of the textbooks at Hubei Military School, founded by Zhang Zhidong. The book consists of two parts, German military exercises, and Japanese school exercises. The first part includes five volumes: bare-handed exercises, exercises with spears, exercises with other equipment, steeplechase, and principles of exercises. This part was co-translated by hired Germany military officials and Chinese teachers. The second part includes 201 chapters in 4 events, featuring regular exercises in Japanese middle schools and normal universities, such as dumbbell exercises, loop and pole exercises, club exercises, and exercises with wooden rings.

Contemporary Sports

In 2006, in order to commemorate the 35th anniversary of the establishment of the Sino-American table tennis diplomatic relationship, in response to the invitation of the Chinese Table Tennis Association, the American table tennis delegation came to Shanghai to review the beautiful past events with the Shanghai athletes who had ever joined the Sino-American diplomacy during its visit to China.

Ping Pong Diplomacy

After the 31st World Table Tennis Championships in 1971, the Chinese government attached great importance to the re-opening of Sino-US relations. Chinese Table Tennis Association invited American team to China, which marked the beginning of mutual understanding, and laid a solid foundation for bilateral exchange and the establishment of diplomatic relations. In 1972, the Chinese table tennis team visited America on the invitation of National Committee on US-China Relations, and American Table Tennis Association. The contact between ping pong players played a significant role in improving bilateral relations and promoting friendly exchange. Therefore, it was known as the "ping pong diplomacy".

The "ping pong diplomacy" solved this political and diplomatic issue which had global effect. As former IOC president Samaranch put it in his congratulatory letter to the 25th anniversary of the ping pong diplomacy in 1997, it is conducive to the development of Sino-US relations, and is a vivid epitome of the active role of sports in promoting peace, friendship and mutual understanding.

The People's Republic of China and the IOC

After the founding of New China in 1949, the All-China Sports Promotion Association was renamed All-China Sports Federation (ACSF), which continued to serve as the Chinese Olympics Committee. At the 16th Olympic Games in Melbourne, a cluster of people in the IOC allowed the Taiwan authority to participate in the Olympics, and created the Two China problem with such terms as "Peking China" and "Formosa China". The Holy Games was used as an international political instrument, which was aroused strong protests and rejection of the Games by the Chinese Committee.

Under such situations, ACSF and the associations of events involved announced in August, 1958, that they would have nothing to do with IOC and 9 international organizations before they had corrected their mistakes. Besides, Chinese IOC member Dong Shouyi refused to work with Brundage, who committed the mistake. Since then, the normal relation between China and the IOC had been suspended for 21 years.

The Mode of Olympics

Officials and celebrities made sustained efforts in searching for appropriate ways of solving the Taiwan problem. On November 26, 1979, after reaching consensus of all members, leaders of the IOC declared in IOC HQ in Lausanne, Switzerland, that the official name of Olympics Committee of the PRC as Chinese Olympics Committee (COC), sited in Beijing. And the one in Chinese Taipei is Chinese Taipei Olympic Committee, whose new association flag, anthem and emblem should be approved of by the IOC. This is the well-known Olympic Mode. Following this mode, other international sports associations re-acknowledged China's legal status, while at the meantime, allowing Taiwan to have a place as a regional branch of China in international sports associations. Thus, China regained its full status in the IOC, and resumed the normal relations with the IOC. China, which has one fourth of the world population, is actively engaged in the Olympic Games, which has greatly promoted the Games. It is not only conducive to the development of physical culture and sports in China, and cross-straits sports exchange, but also to the healthy development of international Olympic movement.

Xu Heng

Xu Heng(1912-) graduated from State University of Jinan, and received his bachelor degree in law. He was already a versatile athlete of various events during these years. At the 9th Far Eastern Olympic Games in Tokyo in 1930, he was a member of the champion volleyball team; and four years later at the 10th Games, a member of the champion soccer team. In 1940, he titled in pool in the 50m and 100m freestyle, at Hong Kong Swimming Tournament. And in 1948 at Hong Kong Water Polo Tournament, Xu again claimed gold. From 1950 onward, he acted as head of the swimming, volleyball and basketball associations of HK, and vice secretary of Taiwan Sports Promotion Association, etc. He was appointed IOC member in 1970, and left the post in 1988. Xu Heng was the president of Chinese Taipei Olympic Committee from 1973 to 1974, and he retired in 1987. Now, he is the vice president of Asian Amateur Swimming Federation, and honorary member of the IOC.

He Zhenliang

He Zhengliang(1929-) graduated from Electrical Engineering department from Fudan University in 1950. He had always been a lover of sports, especially table tennis, tennis and swimming. In 1952, He was a delegate member to the 15th Olympic Games in Helsinki, Finland. In his life-time work in sports, He served as Secretary General of the NOC (1982-1986), Vice-President (1986-1989), then President (1989-1994), now Honorary President; Advisor to the National Sports Federation of China (1997-); President of the Chinese Athletics Association (1992-1996) and of the Chinese Rowing Association from 1986;

He Zhenliang made the last statement for Beijing's bidding for the Olympic Games in 2001.

President of the Asian Rowing Association (1990-1994). In terms of international sports organizations, He Zhenliang is the honorary chairman of China's Olympic Committee, advisor of the Beijing Organizing Committee for the Games of the XXIX Olympiad (BOCOG). He was elected a member of the International Olympic Committee in 1981, a member of the Executive Committee of the International Olympic Committee in 1985 and vice-chairman of the International Olympic Committee in 1989; Member of the Executive Board (1985-1989, 1994-1998, 1999-2003). As a Chinese IOC member, he acted as a bridge connecting Chinese sport with the rest of the world, and had done a lot of work in the resumption of China's legal status in the IOC.

Lu Shengrong

Lu Shengrong (1940-) graduated from the English department of Beijing Foreign Studies University, and was later associate professor of linguistics. She was fond of a variety of events, including windsurfer, skating, badminton, athletics, softball, and table tennis, etc. She worked at the international department of the All-China Women's Federation, and foreign affairs office of State Physical Culture and Sports Commission, and General Administration of Sport of China. From 1980-1988, she was the director of foreign affairs office of the China National Badminton Association, and chief secretary of the Asian Badminton Association. During that period, Lu was elected as vice chairwoman of the China National Badminton Association and the International Badminton Association. In 1993, she was elected chairwoman and the latter and its council, in 1995, member of the IOC's Women's Rights Group; and in 1997, member of the 2004 IOC Coordination Committee.

Wu Jingguo

Wu Jingguo (1946-), graduated from British Institute of Science and Technology and the University of Liverpool. He was keen on basketball, tennis, swimming, and golf, etc. In his early years, Wu worked as an architect with Milton Keynes Corporation in Britain, but later moved back to Taiwan, and acted as the manager for several technological research and construction companies, as well as university professor. In 1966, he was the captain of the runner-up basket-ball team in Taiwan, the East Sea University. And as the leader of the women's basketball team of Chinese Taipei, he participated in the Asian Women's Basketball Championships, and the 10th World Women's Basketball Championships. In 1982, Wu was appointed member of the executive board of the International Amateur Boxing Association, and four years later, member of the women's rights committee of the International Basketball Federation. In 1988, Wu Jingguo was elected IOC member, and since 1989, served as members of Commission for the International Olympic Academy, Commission for the International Olympic Culture, and IOC Coordination Committee.

The 26th World Table Tennis Championships

According to the charter of the International Table Tennis Association, its member can either be a nation or a region, and thus Taiwan has maintained its status as a regional organisation in the ITTA. Therefore, when suspending its relations with other eight international sports associations out of nine in all, China was still in normal contact with the ITTA. In 1961, Beijing hosted the 26th World Table Tennis Championships, the first ever international sports events held in China since 1949. Altogether 242 players from 32 countries and regions took part in the championships. Chinese players not only won the champion of men's team event, runner-up of women's team event, but also harvested two gold medals in men's and women's single (Zhuang Zedong and Qiu Zhonghui), four silver medals and eight third places. These championships heralded the coming of a "Chinese Era" in the event of table tennis.

Games of the New Emerging Forces

The first Games of the New Emerging Forces was held in Jakarta, from November 10-20, 1963. In all, 2404 athletes from 48 countries and regions took part in the Games, which included athletics, cycling, archery, swimming and diving, gymnastics, judo, wrestling, weightlifting, fencing, boxing, football, basketball, volleyball, table tennis, badminton, tennis, polo, sailing, and hockey.

China sent a delegation of 229 athletes to the event, ranking the first on the medal tally with 66 gold, 56 silver and 46 bronze medals. They also set two world records in weightlifting and archery. A group of young athletes panned out, displaying tremendous potential in some competitive events, including weightlifting, table tennis, archery, gymnastics, and athletics. Though China's performance at the first Games of the New Emerging Forces still lagged behind advanced international levels, it was a starting point for unprecedented progress. New China's debut in the international arena attests to the sound athletic capability of the nation.

♦ The Nationwide Fitness Plan

On June 20, 1995, China promulgated the epoch-making Nationwide Fitness Plan, which aims at improving the health condition of the Chinese people, especially of the young. It recommends every one to do participate in at least one sports activity every day, learn at least two ways of health-building, and have one physical check-up every year. The plan is expected to rouse people's health awareness, and to make regular exercises a part of life, in order to promote the Nationwide Fitness Campaign.

In the past ten years, the mass sport has been more and more popular among the Chinese people. Public health awareness has been raised; about 37 percent of the people are involved in regular exercises, more than most developing countries; people's life expectancy rose to 71.8 years, reaching the level of moderately development countries. According to the fifth national census of sports venues, there were 859,080 stadiums and gymnasiums in China, up by 38 percent over 1995.

Since 1995, about 300 million people take part in the activities during the Nationwide Fitness Week every year. Some 140 ethnic sports events have been revived and systemized, while sports for the disabled have also developed considerably.

Legislation Related to Sports

The Law of the People's Republic of China on Physical Culture and Sport (The Law on Physical Culture and Sport) was promulgated by the State Council on August 29, 1995, and effective on October 1 the same year. As the first basic law of authorities concerned since 1994, it specifies the responsibility and obligation of the government and the sports administrative bodies in developing China's physical culture and sport, and also clarifies people's rights in participating in sports activities.

The promulgation of the law sped up China's legislation work related to sports. Supporting laws and regulations were formulated one after another, based on the Law on Physical Culture and Sport. From February, 2002 to January, 2004, three administrative laws were issued, namely Regulations on the Protection of Olympic Symbols, Rules Regarding Public Recreational Facilities, and Anti-Doping Regulations. Meanwhile, regional laws and regulations on sports also flourished.

The Regulations on the Protection of Olympic Symbols was issued after Beijing won the 2008 Olympic bid. In its bidding report, Beijing commits itself to the protection, through laws and regulations, of the rights and interests related to the Olympic Games, according to the requirement of the IOC, including Olympic symbols. The promulgation of the regulations has checked the torts for Olympic symbols. Within one year, over 400 such cases were looked into. These measures were highly appreciated by the IOC and the international community.

The Insurance Scheme

Since 1998, the All-China Sports Fund has paid invalidity insurance premium for 1,400 athletes in national teams. Ordinary athletes can get proceeds up to 300,000 Yuan in case of death or invalidity, while world champions can get up to 600,000 Yuan. Meanwhile, every athlete is entitled to up to 200,000 Yuan of proceeds in case of accidental injuries when they are not training or competing in a game. The period of insurance lasts for the athletes' stay in the national teams.

In the first half of 1998, the All-China Sports Fund and Insurance Companies worked out some key documents regarding "invalidity insurance for athletes in national teams", a new type of insurance. They include Invalidity Grading Criteria for Athletes in National Teams, Details Rules of Invalidity Grading Criteria for Athletes in National Teams, and Trial Methods for the Implementation of Invalidity Insurance for Athletes in National Teams. In 2001, the General Administration of Sport of China shifted the commercial mode to the mutual aid mode. While designating 12 provinces and municipalities for trial implementation, it kept amending and improving the existing invalidity grading criteria, and carried out classified payment according to individual events. In 2002, the mutual aid validity insurance was adopted in China.

The sports facilities in urban areas

On March 7, 2004, China Insurance Brokers Ltd. for Sports was founded in Beijing, the first company specializing in sports insurance in China. It is expected to deal with all insurance brokerage ratified by the China Insurance Regulatory Commission, mainly with athlete insurance, game insurance, and sports insurance consultancy, etc.

Construction of Sports Facilities

Thanks to the Nationwide Fitness Plan, which covers a period of 15 years, the environment and facilities of public sports are being improved. Sports venues equipped with various facilities have been set up in urban communities, residential areas, parks, and on squares, lawns, and roadside. At present, there are about 616,000 stadiums and gymnasiums in China, most of which are open to the public. In recent years, General Administration of Sport has put 60 percent of the government gains from public welfare fund of sports lottery into public health-building activities, or 750 million RMB in total. At the same time, 146 million RMB of fund goes to the construction of sports facilities in economically backward western regions and Three Gorges area along the Yangtze River, benefiting 36 counties and cities.

In 2005, over 37 percent of the Chinese were engaged in regular exercises. In economically developed areas, the penetration rate of public sports facilities reached 100 percent in the residential communities in municipalities and province capitals, 80 percent in other cities, and 25 percent in villages, towns, and rural areas; in western China and economically underdeveloped regions, 80 percent in the residential areas of province capitals, 60 percent in other cities, and 15 percent in villages, towns, and rural areas. The number of coaches and PE teaching staff reached 350,000. And sports coaching centers and stations were available in over 70 percent of urban communities, 70 percent of counties, and 50 percent of villages and towns. Besides, some 3,000 sports clubs for young people were established, sponsored by the public welfare fund from sports lotteries.

Multi-Sport Competitions

Competition is a means of promoting athletic activities. China has organized various big multi-sport competitions, including national university games, middle school games, games of traditional ethnic events, farmers' games, and games of the disabled. According to the requirements put forward by the Nationwide Fitness Plan, (that sports activities should be popular, interesting, scientific, health-beneficial, and embrace ethnicity), large public games and competitions have been reformed, underlying the characteristics of each participant, and the promotion of Nationwide Fitness Campaign.

The National Physique Monitoring

As one of the measures to implement the core issues of the Nationwide Fitness Plan and the Law on Physical Culture and Sport, the National Physique Monitoring was initiated to get hold of the health condition of Chinese people as well as its trend of development. The one in 2000 was the first of its kind, with the largest coverage since 1949. A whole year was spent from April 2000, in collecting data from a sample of over 500,000 people aged between 3 to 68 years old. The data basically could reflect Chinese people's constitution at the turn of the century.

It has been institutionalized that a national physique monitoring should be carried out every five years. And besides, several documents have been the basis of physique monitoring and scientific exercises for different age groups, such as Criteria of Civil Constitution, Criteria of Students' Constitutional Health, and Criteria of Sports Exercises for the Public.

Activities of the Nationwide Fitness Week

♦ Nationwide Fitness Week

Every year since 1995, General Administration of Sport has observed 11 Nationwide Fitness Weeks in the week of June 10th every year. From 2001 onward, nation-wide demonstration activities have been organized, targeting children, women, farmers, workers and senior citizens. To meet the demand of different groups of people, and give them scientific guidance, sports administrative authorities have systemized, recommended and created health-building methods within 10 years. Public exercises, such as the popular set exercises to radio music, have greatly enriched people's cultural life.

Sports Activities for the Public

In the past, sports activities were usually large events organized by the employers mainly through administrative management. But since reform and opening up, this phenomenon has gradually faded out. At the end of the 1980s, residential communities became the major organizers of sports activities, which was inevitable due to the changes of social structure. Such changes also resulted in the System of PE Social Instructors.

The Nationwide Fitness Campaign exerted tremendous impact on people's way of life and thinking. In some bid and medium-sized cities, it has become a fashion to pay for better health, as a new way of improving life quality. Some newly-introduced events are especially popular among the young people, such as rock-climbing, equestrian, bungee, bowling, skateboarding, women's boxing, sand ball, taekwondo, and golf, etc.

Public Sports Organizations

With further reform in physical culture and sports, it has been universally acknowledged that "people's sports should be by the people and for the people". According to a research in 26 provinces, autonomous regions and municipalities, there were 530,000 sports associations below the provincial level, with 213,000 member groups, and 8.665 million individual members. There were 137,000 sports coaching stations in Chinese cities, villages and towns; over 11.8 million people were engaged in regular exercises. A network of public sports for mass participation has been formed in China. It is based on sports organizations, supported by grass roots coaching centers, sports venues and facilities, and guided by PE instructors.

Sports Population

Sports population refers to the group of people in a certain region, who are engaged in regular sports, or are closely involved in sports activities during a certain period of time. According to international practice, Chinese scholars have defined "sports population" as people who do exercises of medium intensity at least 3 times a week, and 30 minutes each time.

Currently, the age distribution of China's sports population is as follows: 33.4 percent of those aged between 16-25; 14.4 percent, between 26-35; 12.8 percent, between 36-45; 15.3 percent, between 46-55; 21.7 percent, between 56-65; and 22.2 percent of those above 65. The result shows a saddle-like distribution, higher rates at both ends, and low at the middle.

The top 10 events for China's sports population are: 1. long-distance walking or running; 2. badminton; 3. swimming; 4. football, basketball and volleyball; 5. table tennis; 6. gymnastics; 7. mountain-climbing; 8. dancing; 9. snooker and bowling; and 10. rope-skipping.

Timetable for Public Sports Activities

According to research, most people do exercises before 8:00 A.M., constituting 79.80 percent of the total; 48.6 percent in the evening; while only few do exercises in the forenoon or in the afternoon. Preference to the time prior to 8:00 A.M. is attributed to the choice of venues. The top 3 favorites are parks, vacant lands in communities, and the streets. Table 13 shows that these places are least crowded in the morning, and thus most available for sports activities. Besides, it also has something to do with people's habit, especially senior citizens' habit of "early to bed and early to rise".

Distribution of Venues in Beijing

	Nunber	Percentage	No.
Total	381	100.00	
Public venues of sports commission	31	8.10	6
Venues in schools	38	10.00	5
Venues of enterprises and public Institutions	43	11.30	4
Parks	87	22.80	1
In the streets	64	16.80	3
Venues in residential communities	76	19.90	2
River side and lake shore	22	5.80	7
Others	20	5.20	8

Community Sports

The way of sports participation witnessed tremendous change in the past ten years, with more and more urban Chinese taking part in sports activities organized by residential communities, instead of employers.

In recent years, with public welfare funds from sports lotteries, authorities concerned at all levels have built a lot of fitness paths, communities sports clubs, morning and evening exercises venues and squares (activity centers). Up to now, in more than 90 percent of urban residential communities, a five-in-one health-building pattern has been formed: family activities, activities at morning and evening exercise venues, competitions in public institutions within the community, individual event competitions at community-level, and comprehensive community games. Huanghuamen Community in Dongcheng District established the first "demonstration community of sports life" in Beijing. Health-building has thus become part of people's daily life, as important as food, clothing, lodging, and traveling. Again in Beijing, Tianqiao Community set up a sports club, providing nearby residents with sports venues and services. What is more, good equipment and low prices have attracted people from other communities, and the club has truly become a club by the people and for the people.

Sports for the Working People

As part of the public fitness campaign, various forms of exercises are practiced among people from all walks of life, including government, enterprises, and other organizations. They aim at improving working people's physiological health so that they can better adjust to different environments and prevent occupational diseases. Such activities mainly feature popular sports, varying according to different natures of occupations. And they include pre-work exercises, exercises during the breaks, small-scale competitions, and annual sports meeting, etc.

Sports for Senior Citizens

China's increase rate of its elderly population is rare in the world. With the improvement of people's living standard, it has become a trend for the elderly in China to participate in sports and recreational activities. At present, over 58 million of them are engaged in regular exercises. Since 2001, China has begun senior citizens' health-building campaign, to attract more of them to join the trend. And in recent years, it also implemented the Nationwide Fitness Plan, which sped up the construction of public sports venues and facilities for the elderly. Now more than 30,000 health-building projects have been completed. And by the end of 2005, all governments above county level, 70 percent of urban communities and 50 percent of rural villages and towns had established sports associations for the elderly, with proper organization and guidance.

With the ever increasing popularity of sports among the elderly, China is also expanding exchange in sports for senior citizens with other countries, including tennis, gate ball, martial arts, and shadow boxing, etc. Chinese have done a good job in international long-distance running competitions for the elderly.

Sports for Women

More elder Chinese women than young ones are engaged in regular sports activities, and the overall participation rate is 27.15 percent. The events are relatively limited, mainly jogging, running and ball games, but more events are found among elder women, including qigong, shadow boxing, and dancing, etc.

The choice of activities for Chinese women is closely related to their physiological characteristics: young and elderly women do sports for health-building and recreation, while middle-aged women do sports for molding temperament.

Sports for the Young

China attaches great importance to the improvement of young people's health conditions, and conducts regular research and monitoring on their constitution. To ensure students' health, China promulgated the State Athletic Fitness Standard, and the Rules of School Physical Education. These two have made it a rule and routine that students do regular sports. According to the statistics in the past two decades, nearly one billion students have reached the State Athletic Fitness Standard. A national middle school sports meet will be convened every three years, while a national interuniversitary sports meet, every four years, with the objective to better P.E. in Chinese schools. In addition, the government fully taps the existing sports venues, P.E. staff and other resources to meet the increasing demand in this fast developing society. Starting from 2000, China has set up 2,134 youth clubs with some 500 million yuan from public welfare fund of sports lottery. Hence, a network of off-campus sports activities for students has been basically established in China.

College Physical Education Syllabus

In 1961, the ministry of education formulated and promulgated the first nationwide College Physical Education Syllabus, which was edited later in 1979. It rules that P.E. is one of the fundamental courses, one subject to tests and inspections. Grades are given according to students' athletic performance, learning attitude, and mastery of sports knowledge and skills.

Nantong Sports and Exhibition Center, the first gymnasium with moveable cover in China

Children Roller-skating Team in training

Sports for Children

China pays a good deal of attention to physical education in kindergartens and primary schools. Activities range from sports homework, morning exercises, and outdoor activities, to sports games, walking and children's sports performances, etc. Some of the most popular events among Chinese children are tug-and-war, springboard, swing, shuttlecock kicking, rope skipping, football, and kite flying, etc. There are numerous part-time youth sports schools and other PE institutions for traditional events. Nation-wide games for children are held annually, including age-group swimming tournament for children, summer camp swimming competition for primary school students, youth table tennis tournament, youth badminton tournament, and youth gymnastics competition.

Social Sports Coaching Center

Social sports coaching center is one of the leading organizations of community sports. It promotes mass participation, leads and organizes the implementation of the Nationwide Fitness Plan. Its main function is to improve the rules and policies of community sports organizations, to formulate outlines for the development of community sports. Also the center engages core sports staff in practical studies, community service, and the improvement of residents' cultural level, etc.

Social Sports Instructors

Social sports instructors are organizers of community sports activities. Their work involves imparting basic sports knowledge and skills, providing guidance to sports exercises, and managing the organization of activities. It is of non-service nature, and is for public services targeting a broad range of people. Social sports instructors organize community residents to participate in sports activities, provide people with guidance on health-building, and help them form a rational concept of sports consumption and investment.

Social sports instructors are the main force in the promotion of public sports, and the implementation of the Nationwide Fitness Plan. By the end of 2004, there had been over 430,000 social sports instructors at all levels throughout China. Thus a team of PE workers had been formed basically, with sports administrative staff as the lead, sports cadres in social organizations, towns, villages and districts as the backbone, and social sports instructors as the main body.

Grade System of Social Sports Instructors

It is one of the policies of China's social sports management, enacted by State Physical Culture and Sports Commission on December 4, 1993, and implemented on June 10, in the following year. The 19-item system aims to strengthen the construction and management of a team of social sports instructors. They are divided into four grades according to skill evaluation, namely the 3rd grade, 2nd grade, 1st grade, and the national grade. The system specifies their range of work, responsibilities, qualification, application procedures, promotion requirements, approval authority, making and awarding of certificates, and ways of reward and punishment, etc. The implementation of the system plays a significant role in the promotion of extensive and regular sports among the Chinese people.

♦ Locomotive Sports Association of China

In November, 1988, at the second MINEPS (International Conference of Ministers and Senior Officials Responsible for Physical Education and Sport) of the UNESCO, the Locomotive Sports Association of China was granted the Award for Distinguished Services to Physical Education and Sport. Thus, the association became the first Chinese organization to receive this biannual award.

The Locomotive Sports Association of China was founded in 1952 as the earliest professional association of sports within a certain industry. It is in charge of sports work of 3.2 million railway workers and their relatives, as well as nearly one million students in railway schools. It composes 57 sub-associations at bureau-level, 208 ones at branch-level, and thousands of regional or grass-root organizations. Besides, the Locomotive Sports Association of China specially established sports associations for senior citizens and 16 individual event associations, including athletics, swimming, etc. About 1.38 million people in the railway industry are involved in regular exercises, among which 906 are professional sports workers.

The Locomotive Sports Association of China has set up 19 stadiums and gymnasiums (8 of them can accommodate over 2,000 people), over160 ground track fields, 4,345 basketball courts, 1,206 volleyball courts, and several thousand venues for other ball games as well as sports complexes.

Public Health-Building Goes Hand in Hand with the Olympics

To synchronize the development of mass sports and athletic sports, the General Administration of Sport plans to carry out a series of activities throughout China, from 2007 to the Beijing Olympics. The focus will be the promotion of public health-building in the Olympic background.

Among all the activities, some are directly administered by the General Administration of Sport, such as the national New Year mountain-climbing campaign, the nationwide Fitness week, community public health-building with the Olympics, fitness project for farmers, etc. These are enriched by provincial, regional, and municipal games, individual event sports associations, and special activities organized by sports associations of various industries.

These activities before the upcoming 2008 Olympic Games improve people's constitution, and help them lead a healthy life. At the same time, they facilitate the coordinated development of China's mass sports and athletic sports, and create a nationwide fitness environment for the successful convening of the Olympics.

Students doing exercises to radio music

♦ Set Exercises to Radio Music

Set exercises to radio music is a good form of popularizing sports. On November 24, 1951, the illustrations of the first set were publicized. Then China National Radio began to broadcast relevant programs on December 1st, followed by local radio stations. Every day, when music came from the loudspeakers, hundreds of thousands of people began doing the exercises, an unprecedented scene in China.

On March 1, 1954, governments at all levels made it a policy that workers should do the set exercises during the break. Then the first set exercises to radio music for teenagers, and the one for children, were publicized in 1954 and 1955 respectively. The 2nd to the 8th set exercises for adult came out in 1954, 1957, 1963, 1971, 1981, 1990 and 1997 respectively, with only a few changes. The eighth set in current use is composed of eight sections, while the first one consisted of 10 sections.

Sports in Rural Areas

China's rural population accounts for over 80 percent of the total. Before 1949, people in rural areas mainly practiced traditional folk sports like wushu, wrestling, equestrian, and dragon boat racing, etc. Since the founding of New China, rural sport has been incorporated into the state work plan on sports. Sports in rural areas are mainly organized into voluntary teams, like martial arts troops and ball game teams. Some of the most representative activities are the martial arts performance in Wuqiao of Hebei, and Dengfeng of Henan, wrestling and horsemanship competitions at the Nadam Fair in Inner Mongolia, and swimming in Dongguan, Guangdong. In 1986, the National Famers' Sports Association was founded in Beijing, and organized the first National Farmers' Games two years later in the capital. By 2006, all together five such games had been held.

Farmers' Swimming Competition

On August 10, 1987, the first National Farmers' Competition was opened in Jiaozhou, Shandong Province, marking the first one of its kind since 1949. Hence, Chinese farmers' swimming records have been noted down in the country's sports history.

In all, 112 contestants participated in 19 events at the competition. They were from 10 provinces, municipalities and autonomous regions, namely Guangdong, Guangxi, Fujian, Jiangxi, Jiangsu Anhui, Henan, Hebei, Shandong and Shanghai.

Military Sports

Military sports refer to the basic trainings for better mastery of practical military skills. They include bare-handed exercises, boxing, exercises with equipment, cross country, climbing, obstacle running, obstacle swimming, skiing, military pentathlon, and marine pentathlon, etc. Different armies and arms also have particularly designed events in accordance with their own characteristics, missions and local environment. These events include rolling wheel, spiral staircase, and swing log, etc.

Sports for the Disabled

Sports for the disabled is one part of China's efforts in improving the life of the disabled, and is also one of the means of full integration into society for the disabled people.

Since the founding of China Sports Association for the Disabled, many others have been established, like China Sports Association for the Mentally Handicapped, China Sports Association for the Deaf, and many others at provincial, regional or municipal levels. Public welfare institutions, residential communities, and special schools for the disabled have organized various forms of activities for mass participation. Nearly 300 sports training centers for the disabled have been set up, receiving some 10,000 people. Besides, over 200,000 amateur disabled athletes have participated in all levels of sports meetings and trials. Now the number of full time officials in charge of sports for the disabled has increased from 10 to 50, and nearly 100 qualified coaches and judges are now dealing with related training and competition organization. Up till now, six National Games for the Disabled have been held, along with nearly 40 national individual event competitions. The number of events has increased from four in the 1980s to the current 14, and the number of disabled athletes has also exceeded 10,000.

The establishment of the associations mentioned above weaves a whole network of sports activities for the disabled in China. These organizations are now promoting rehabilitation and health-building activities in a planned way, for the 82.96 million disabled people in China.

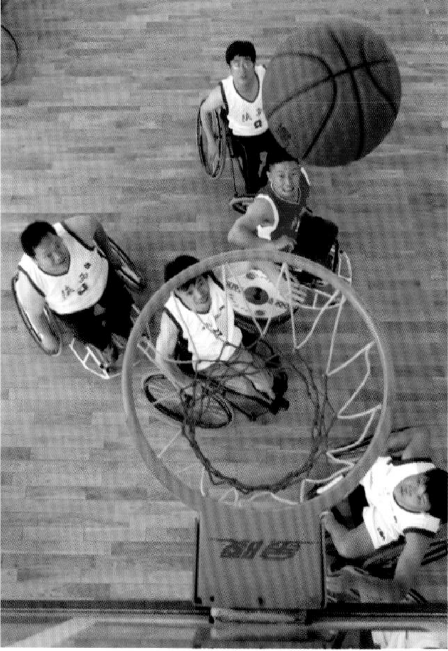

The training of the wheelchair basketball

International Sports Events for the Disabled

China Sports Association for the Disabled has acceded to many international sports organizations for the disabled, such as IPC, ISOD, IBSA, CP-ISRA, CISS, ISMWSF, SOI, and FESPIC, etc.

From 1984 onward, China has put on outstanding performance at 6 Summer Paralympics, 2 Winter Paralympics, 7 Far East and South Pacific Games for the Disabled, and many international individual event competitions. In particular, Chinese athletes claimed 63 gold, 46 silver, and 32 bronze medals at the 2004 Paralympics in Athens, ranking the first both on the gold medal tally and the total medal tally. Then at the 9th Far East and South Pacific Games for the Disabled, the Chinese delegation won 199 gold, 72 silver and 36 bronze medals.

As the host of the 2008 Paralympics, China will take part in all the 18 events. China is making big strides in promoting sports undertakings for the disabled, and the government is also giving increasing support to the course. Now, the establishment of a state-level sports training base for the disabled people is underway.

Selection of Disabled Athletes

China selects its athletes to participate in international events for the disabled through fair competition. At present, a competition system has been formed, featuring the National Games for the Disabled every four years, annual individual event tournaments and preliminary rounds, local games every four years in provinces, municipalities and autonomous regions, as well as regular games in some cities and areas where conditions allow.

Disabled people can apply at local disabled person's federation or sports bureau, as long as they love and excel in sports, and meet the basic criteria for disability. Then they may go through tryouts at different levels, and the qualified ones will join competitions for the disabled on behalf of their own regions. Athletes who pan out at national games can take part in international games.

Special Olympic Games

The Special Olympic Games are designed for the mentally-challenged people, with the objective to improve their constitution and increase their confidence through sports activities, so that they may overcome difficulties and make more contributions to society. The first Special Olympic Games was held in Chicago, USA, in 1968. And China made its debut at the 7th Special Olympics, convened in South Bend, Indiana, USA, from July 30 to August 8, 1987. This first Chinese delegation was made up of 23 athletes with their IQ below 70. They had been selected from the national Special Olympics. To our delight, Chinese athletes won 18 gold, 20 silver and 13 bronze medals at the Games.

The team match of the wheelchair sword play at the Seventh National Sports Meeting for the Disabled in 2006.

Special Olympic Games in China

There are more than 60 million disabled people in China, including 11.82 million mentally-challenged people. These people belong to a disadvantaged group with special needs. China has formulated constructive laws and policies to ensure their equal status and opportunities in taking part in social life. In 1985, Special Olympics China (SOC) was established, which joined SOI in the same year. For over a decade, Special Olympics in China have registered remarkable achievement, with the support of government of all levels, various social organizations and the efforts of sports workers. Now over 20 provinces, municipalities and autonomous regions have set up sports organizations for the mentally-challenged. In 1987, 1991, 1995, 1999, and 2005, China took part in the Special Olympic Games, and hosted the first Asia-Pacific Special Olympics in Shanghai in 1996, as well as two National Special Olympics (NSO).

SOC's goals for the next five years are:

— Increase the number of participants of NSO to 500,000 from the current 50,000, and make Special Olympics nation-wide;

— Establish 6-8 national and 30 provincial Special Olympics training bases;

— Set up 5,000 community Special Olympics centers;

— Develop certain events in accordance with the national condition, and increase the number of events to 10 from 6.

The SOI highly appreciated the progress of SOC in the past 10 years. And in May, 2002, it came to China to raise funds for the future development of Special Olympics in China.

Events for the Disabled

Now 11 sports for the disabled are very popular in China, including track and field, swimming, weightlifting, shooting, judo, wheelchair basketball, sitting volleyball, table tennis, badminton, wheelchair tennis, and goalball by the blind. In addition, wheelchair fencing, archery and boccia are also being practiced.

Sports for Ethnic Minorities

Traditional sports for China's ethnic minorities display various spectra. Ethnic sports form an inalienable part of China's religious ceremonies, celebrations of harvest, weddings and funerals, as well as numerous holidays. Some of the existing ones are the Mongolian wrestling, Uygur "girl's chase", Korean swing, Hui people's cricket, Dai people's bamboo pole dance, Miaos' "knife ladder climbing", Gaoshan people's back basket ball game, and Qiangs' pole exercise, etc. All of them come from the wisdom of China's ethnic minorities, and represent each nationality's characteristics, ideology and ethnic awareness.

Traditional Sports Games of Ethnic Minorities

In recent years, various kinds of sports games for national minorities are organized at different levels, which greatly boost the development of ethnic sports. The quadrennial National Ethnic Sports Meet is growing both in scale and in the range of events. Meanwhile, the formulation of a good deal of rules for these events has laid a solid foundation for the promotion and exchange of ethnic sports, and systemized their future development.

Characteristics of Traditional Sports of Ethnic Minorities

Traditional: Since its beginning, sports of ethnic minorities has always born a close relationship with each nationality's political, economic, cultural, religious background and its social customs, handed from generation to generation. These events have been passed on, tested, systemized, and developed, before they became traditional events with relatively stable content, form, time and place.

Regional: China's 55 ethnic minorities, though comprise only a small population, are widely distributed. Their distinctive ideology, economics, cultures, and customs lead to sports events of all forms with ethnic characteristics. According to incomplete statistics, there are over 230 traditional sports of national minorities in China, and over 150 events in Guangxi Province alone.

Ethnical: Each nationality has its own customs. Sometimes, traditional sports are integrated into local festivals, wedding customs and sacrificial ceremonies; sometimes, they are included by these activities; and at other times, they run through various ethnic customs.

Entertaining: Most of the traditional sports of ethnic minorities are for health-building, performance, or entertainment. They are mainly practiced during the leisure time, to add festive atmosphere to harvest ceremonies, entertainment, and other traditional festivals, etc.

Cultural exchange: Chinese ethnic minorities are fond of singing, dancing and sports. The mutual influence between traditional sports and culture attributes to the artistic and athletic values of their sports events. Thus, they are a good combination of health-building, temperament-molding, and aesthetic cultivation.

Paomashi, an entertaining and competitive event in the equestrian competition of the ethnic sports meet

Lu Shengrong

Women Administrators of Sports

While outstanding women athletes are panning out in China, some Chinese women also distinguish themselves as members of the Olympic management team. In 1993, Ms. Lu Shengrong was elected the first ever woman president of International Badminton Federation in its 59 years of history. This is also the first time for a Chinese woman to be the president of an international individual event federation of the Olympics. In 1996, Lu was elected IOC member as one of the ten females in the committee, and was directly involved in its highest level of decision making. In 1996, China's world table tennis champion Deng Yaping became IOC member. At present, about 20 Chinese women have their posts in some 30 administrative setups of the Olympics. Their contribution to world Olympics proves that women are also up to the senior management work, and outlines a bright future for achieving gender equality in the realm of sports as well as in other areas.

First Chinese Woman to Win the Olympic Badge

On May 11, 1993, Zhang Caizhen was awarded the silver Olympic Badge, becoming the first Chinese woman to receive it.

Cross-Straits Athletes—Competing in the Same Arena

In February 1984, the 14th Winter Olympics was held in Sarajevo, Yugoslavia. China sent 37 athletes to participate in 26 individual events of 5 sports, namely speed skating, figure skating, alpine skiing, cross-country skiing, winter biathlon, bobsleigh and luge. At the same time, Chinese Taipei also sent 14 athletes to take part in skiing, winter biathlon, bobsleigh and luge. Though they failed to win a medal, the Games was memorable since it marked the first time that the athletes from both sides of the Taiwan Straits met at the Winter Olympics.

The First Olympic Medal

After the founding of New China in 1949, China's legal status in the IOC remained a pending issue. Therefore, China did not send any delegation to the Olympics from 1956 to 1979, though during that period, Yang Chuanguang from Chinese Taipei won a decathlon silver medal at the 1960 Olympics in Rome. He was the first ever Chinese athlete to win an Olympic medal. Eight years later, Ji Zheng, also from Chinese Taipei, claimed a bronze medal in women's 80m hurdles in Mexico City, becoming the first Chinese woman to stand on the Olympic podium.

The First World Champion

At the 25th World Table tennis Championships in March, 1959, Rong Guotuan beat Richard Miles from USA, and prevailed over Hungarian Ferenc Sido to win men's singles final. He thus became the first world champion from China.

Rong Guotuan (1937-1968) was born in Hong Kong. He had been fond of table tennis as a child, and played for the Hong Kong Federation of Trade Unions at the age of 15. Five years later, he was enrolled into Guangzhou Physical Education Institute, and then selected to play for Guangdong Province in 1958. In the same year, Rong, who won the men's singles at the National Championships, became a member of the national team. Rong Guotuan adopted and developed the traditional Chinese skills in table tennis—backhand block with forehand attack, and created some new techniques, such as serving spin or non-spin, and pushing spin or non-spin, etc. He used various techniques and some unique skills in matches, out of which came out the Chinese tactics of short court drive. Hence, Chinese players added "change" to their original focus of "speed, accuracy, and strength". Then at the 26th World Table tennis Championships in 1961, Rong Guotuan, as one of the Chinese delegates, again made considerable contribution to China's first ever men's teams title.

The First World Record

On June 7, 1956, the Sino-Soviet Weightlifting Friendly Match was held in Shanghai. The 20-year-old Chen Jingkai broke world clean and jerk record of 132.5 kilograms in the bantamweight class by lifting 133 kilograms. He was the first Chinese to set a world record.

Chen Jingkai (1935-) was fond of sports as a boy, and started weightlifting in 1955. His made remarkable progress in clean and jerk, from 95 kg to 130 kg within one year. After Chen set the world record, he altogether broke 8 world records in the bantamweight and the lightweight division. In August, 1957, Chen Jingkai lifted 139.5 kg, and broke the world record the fourth time for bantamweight division at the 3rd International Youth Festival-Friendly Match in Moscow. Meanwhile, he overwhelmed his USSR rival with a total of 322.5 kg, and became the champion. Later, Chen Jingkai became the coach of China's weightlifting team, and was awarded the gold badges of International Weightlifting Federation and Asian Weightlifting Federation.

Sports Documentary Film

In 1983, the fifth National Games was held in Shanghai. To give a faithful account of this pageant, the Central Newsreel and Documentary Film Studio produced a sports documentary called *Come on, Chinese Athletes* (camera: Shen Jie, Director: Mu Tie, Advisor: Wu Chongyuan). The film fully recorded the exciting and memorable moment when Zhu Jianhua surmounted 2.38 metres, setting a new world record. It is the first Chinese sports documentary to be kept at the IOC headquarter.

In 1984, the film won the second prize at the 40th Torino International Sports Film Festival.

♦ The Olympic Cup

The Olympic Cup was created by Pierre de Coubertin, and awarded every year by the IOC to institutions and groups which have made special contribution to the Olympics. The award is symbolic in that the receiver gets a bronze medal and a certificate; while the cup is kept in the IOC headquarter, in Lausanne, Switzerland.

On February 11 and 12 in Lausanne, the IOC executive committee decided to confer on Chinese Olympic Committee the Olympic Cup, to commend China's aid to some African countries in the construction of sports facilities. This was the first time China got this award.

Major Events

The National Games

The National Games is the most premier sports event of China which is held at a 4 year interval. There had been 7 games between 1910 and 1948. And since the first National Games of New China in 1959, altogether 10 Games have been convened. To do a better job at the Olympics, the National Games was held a year after the Olympics instead of before it, starting from the 7th Games. Apart from the Olympic events, competitive events also include polo, acrobatics, motorboat, martial arts, Chinese chess, chess, go, motoring, radio sport, parachuting, aero modeling, and gliding, etc.

The 1st National Games

Time: September 13 to October 3, 1959

Venue: Beijing

Altogether 10,658 athletes from 28 provinces, municipalities and autonomous regions, and PLA participated in the Games. They were only 21 years old on average. During the Games, 7 athletes broke 4 world records in swimming, parachuting, shooting and aero modeling, 664 athletes broke 844 national records in 106 individual events, and 99 athletes in motoring and radio sport surpassed the best records of 16th Olympics champion and socialist countries' radio sports competition for 44 times.

World records broken at the 1st Games:

Swimming: Mu Xiangxiong, men's 100m breaststroke, 1'11"1;

Airplane parachuting: Guo Xin'e, Mei Yan, Zhang Jingwen, women's 1000m group accuracy landing, 5.11m;

Shooting: Chen Rong, women's 50m and 100m small bore free rifle (30 shots prone), 589;

Aero modeling: Zhao Jiazhen, Wang Yongxi, piston-engine radio-control aero model plane flying height, 1,260m.

The 2nd National Games

Time: September 11 to 28, 1965

Venue: Beijing

Altogether 7,395 athletes took part in 22 sports: football, basketball, volleyball, table tennis, tennis, badminton, water polo, athletics, cycling, gymnastics, weightlifting, fencing, swimming, diving, wrestling, archery, shooting, motoring, radio transmitting and receiving, airplane parachuting, aero modeling, and marine modeling. wushu was an event for performance at the Games.

During the Games, 24 people bettered 9 world records 10 times, and 331 people broke 130 national records on 469 occasions.

The 3rd National Games

Time: September 12 to 28, 1975

Venue: Beijing

It was held in Beijing from September 12 to 28, 1975.

28 sports: football, basketball, volleyball, table tennis, badminton, tennis, baseball, softball, handball, athletics, gymnastics, acrobatics, swimming, diving, water polo, boating (rowing, kayaking, and canoeing), weightlifting, shooting, archery, fencing, wushu, cycling (road cycling and track cycling), Chinese wrestling, chess (go, Chinese chess and chess), hockey, speed skating, figure skating, and skiing. Events for performance included equestrians, swing, springboard, wrestling for ethnic minorities, airplane parachuting, aero modeling, marine modeling, motor boating, motor racing, and children's sports. In all, 12,497 athletes from 31 teams participated in the Games, including those from Taiwan.

One team, four athletes broke three world records six times at the Games, and another two records were equaled; 49 teams and 83 athletes set 62 national records 197 times; and 4 teams and 36 athletes broke 58 records of the national youth 144 times.

The 4th National Games

Time: September 15 to 30, 1979

Venue: Beijing

34 sports: football, basketball, volleyball, table tennis, badminton, tennis, handball, baseball, softball, athletics, gymnastics, acrobatics, weightlifting, swimming, diving, water polo, boating (rowing, kayaking, and canoeing), wushu, archery, chess (go, Chinese chess and chess), fencing, cycling (road cycling and track cycling), wrestling (Chinese, freestyle, and classic style), speed skating, figure skating, hockey, skiing, shooting, motoring, parachuting, aero modeling, marine modeling, motor boating, and scuba diving. Group callisthenics was included as a performance event. In all, 3,824 athletes competed at the Games.

Five athletes smashed five world records, 2 people set 3 world records of the youth, 3 people equaled 3 world records; 12 athletes rewrote 8 Asian records for 24 times; 36 teams and 204 people broke 102 national records for 376 times, and 2 teams and 6 people broke 5 records of the national youth for 10 times.

The 5th National Games

Time: September 18 to October 1, 1983

Venue: Shanghai

It was held in Shanghai from September 18 to October 1, 1983.

25 sports: football, basketball, volleyball, table tennis, badminton, tennis, handball, hockey, track and field, gymnastics, rhythmic gymnastics, weightlifting, swimming, diving, water polo, sailing, dinghy, archery, shooting, fencing, cycling, wrestling, judo, wushu performance, rowing, canoeing, and one event for performance. Among these, rhythmic gymnastics, judo, dinghy, and field hockey were newly added events. Altogether 8,943 athletes from 31 teams competed at the Games, including 29 provinces, municipalities and autonomous regions, the PLA and the Locomotive Sports Association.

The 5th Games saw the birth of 2 world records set by 2 people; 4 people equaled 3 world records 5 times, and set one world record of the youth; 7 people broke 9 Asian records 12 times; 64 people and 38 teams broke 60 national records on 142 occasions.

The 6th National Games

Time: November 20 to December 5, 1987

Venue: Guangzhou

There were 44 competition sports and 3 performance sports. The competition events included football, basketball, volleyball, table tennis, tennis, badminton, handball, hockey, softball, baseball, track and field, swimming, diving, water polo, synchronized swimming, weightlifting, gymnastics, rhythmic gymnastics, fencing, judo, international wrestling, Chinese wrestling, acrobatics, go, Chinese chess, chess, equestrians, modern pentathlon, wushu, shooting, archery, rowing, canoeing, sailing, dinghy, fin swimming, marine, modeling, aero modeling, cycling, boarding, motor cross, radio direction finding, and parachuting. Performance events included golf, bowling and bridge. Some 12,400 athletes from 37 teams (of provinces, municipalities, autonomous regions, the PLA, and sports associations of various industries) participated at the Games.

At the Games, 10 athletes and 2 teams broke 15 world records for 17 times, 3 people matched 3 world records, and 2 people surpassed 2 world records; 48 Asian records or bests were set or surpassed; 85 national records or bests were created.

The 7th National Games

Time: September 4 to 15, 1993

Venue: Beijing

It was held in Beijing from September 4 to 15, 1993.

There were 43 sports at the 7th National

Games. Twenty six of them were competed in Beijing, including athletics, swimming, gymnastics, rhythmic gymnastics, weightlifting, fencing, judo, international wrestling, boxing, modern pentathlon, equestrians, Chinese wrestling, go, speed skating, short-track speed skating, cycling, marine modeling, radio direction finding, parachuting, soccer, basketball, table tennis, tennis, handball, hockey, and softball. Fifteen sports were hosted in Sichuan, including diving, water polo, synchronized swimming, acrobatics, shooting, archery, rowing, canoeing, fin swimming, boarding, aero modeling, volleyball, badminton, baseball, and wushu. Two events were held in Qinhuangdao, namely sailing and dinghy. Altogether 7,481 athletes participated in the Games.

The 7th National Games embraced 4 new world records set by 4 Chinese; 18 people and 4 teams surpassed 21 world records for 43 times, 4 people tied 3 world records for 4 times; 54 athletes and 1 team bettered 34 Asian records on 93 occasions, 61 people and 3 teams broke 66 Asian records 143 times; and 130 athletes and 14 teams broke 117 national records 273 times.

The 8th National Games

Time: October 12 to 24, 1997

Venue: Shanghai

It was held in Shanghai from October 12 to 24, 1997.

The 8th National Games was of the largest scale in the late 20th century. Some 20,000 people (including 7,647 athletes) from 46 teams (all provinces, municipalities, autonomous regions, Hong Kong SAR, the PLA, and 13 professional athletic associations) took part in it. It was the first time for Hong Kong delegation, composed of 257 members, to be present at the National Games. There were 319 events in 28 sports, awarding a total of 327 gold medals in football, basketball, volleyball (including beach volleyball), table tennis, badminton, tennis, handball, hockey, baseball, softball, athletics, swimming (including diving, water polo, and synchronized swimming), gymnastics (including rhythmic gymnastics), weightlifting, shooting, archery, fencing, judo, wrestling, boxing, cycling, boating, canoeing, sailing (including dinghy), modern pentathlon, equestrians, speed skating, short track, and wushu. All of them were official competition events at the Olympic Games except wushu.

At the Games, 179 people surpassed 41 world records for 659 times. Among them, 16 athletes surpassed 7 world records of Olympic events for 19 times, 4 people tied 3 world records on 4 occasions; 100 athletes and 3 teams bettered 55 Asian records 367 times; and 88 athletes and 6 teams broke 66 national records 142 times.

The 9th National Games

Time: November 11 to 25, 2001

Venue: Guangzhou

It was held in Guangzhou from November 11 to 25, 2001.

Guangdong hosted the finals of 27 sports, including athletics, swimming, gymnastics, rhythmic gymnastics, weightlifting, fencing, judo, international wrestling, boxing, modern pentathlon, equestrians, Chinese wrestling, go, speed skating, short track, cycling, parachuting, football, basketball, table tennis, tennis, handball, hockey, softball, diving, water polo, synchronized swimming, acrobatics, shooting, archery, boating, canoeing, volleyball, badminton, baseball, wushu, and sailing. In all, 12,314 athletes from 45 teams competed in the preliminaries, and 8,608 of them appeared in the finals.

The 9th National Games witnessed the creation of 7 world records by 24 athletes 35 times; 6 people and 1 team bettered 6 Asian records 7 times, 28 people surpassed the Asian records 41 times; and 32 athletes and 4 teams rewrote 37 national records 52 times.

The 10th National Games

Time: October 12 to 23, 2005

Venue: Nanjing

It was held in Nanjing, Jiangsu from October 12 to 23, 2005.

Following the dramatic breakthrough at Athens Olympics in 2004, the 10th National Games was the largest multi-sport game with the highest athletic level during the preparation of Beijing Olympics. The Games featured 357 events of 32 sports, and attracted almost 10,000 athletes, the biggest number of participants in history.

At the 10th National Games, 15 Chinese surpassed 6 world records 21 times, 7 people equaled 6 world records 7 times; 5 people broke 5 Asian records 6 times; and 1 team and 19 athletes bettered 19 national records 25 times.

On October 12, 2005, the opening ceremony of the 10th National Games was launched in Nanjing Olympic Sports Center.

The National Winter Games

The National Winter Games is the largest multi-sport winter event in China. The first four National Games consisted of both summer and winter sports, but in 1983, State Physical Culture and Sports Commission decided to separate winter sports from the National Games, and hence the National Winter Games. It fell in the year of the Summer Games, and though held for the first time as a separate event, the one in 1983 was still called the 5th National Winter Games to correspond to the Summer Games.

The 1st National Winter Games

The 1st National Winter Games was hosted in Harbin from February 10 to 20, 1959, but the skiing events were held in Jilin, from February 1 to 5. Altogether 224 athletes took part in 40 events of 5 competition sports, namely, speed skating (20 events), figure skating (2 events), ice hockey (1 event), alpine skiing (8 events), and cross-country skiing (9 events).

The 3rd National Winter Games

On-the-rink events were competed in Harbin from January 16 to 26, 1976, while one-snow events were hosted in Shangzhi County, also in Heilongjiang Province, from February 18 to 23. All the events had preliminaries, and each sport had youth divisions. In all, 972 athletes took part in 67 events of 5 sports (excluding medals for individual events of figure skating), namely, speed skating (30 events), figure skating (8 events), ice hockey (adult group, and youth group), alpine skiing (11 events), and cross-country skiing (16 events).

The 4th National Winter Games

The 4th National Winter Games was held in 1979 in three different places. Skiing events were competed in Shangzhi County, Heilongjiang, from February 15 to 20, speed skating events were held in Tianchi, Urumchi, Xinjiang, from March 4 to 9, and ice hockey and figure skating events were hosted in Beijing from Sepetember 8th to 17th. There were preliminaries only for ice hockey and figure skating. In all, 477 athletes contended in 60 events of 5 sports: speed skating (20 events), figure skating (9 events), ice hockey (1 event), alpine skiing (14 events), and cross-country skiing (16 events).

The 5th National Winter Games

The 5th National Winter Games was held in Harbin from March 12 to 23, 1983. On-snow events were convened in Yabuli Ski Resort in Heilongjiang, from February 20 to 28. All the events at the Games had preliminaries, except for the ones of on-snow events, which were cancelled due to snow condition. Altogether 603 athletes from 7 ethnic nationalities (Han, Man, Hui, Mongolian, Korean, Uygur, Daur, and Kazakh) competed in 49 events of 7 sports: figure skating (4 events), speed skating (20 events), short track skating (4 events), ice hockey (1 event), alpine skiing (8 events), cross-country skiing (8 events), and winter biathlon (4 men's events). Among them, short track and winter biathlon appeared at the Games for the first time. There was team award for speed skating only.

The 6th National Winter Games

The 6th National Winter Games was held in the city of Changchun, Jilin, from March 8 to 16, 1987. Alpine skiing and ski jumping were competed before that from February 3 to 10, and cross-country skiing and winter biathlon were hosted in Changbaishan Skiing Resort from February 13 to 20. All the events had preliminaries. Altogether 575 athletes competed in 46 events of 8 sports, namely, speed skating (10 events), short track (10 events), figure skating (4 events), ice hockey (1 event), alpine skiing (8 events), cross-country skiing (8 events), winter biathlon (4 men's events), and ski jumping (1 event). Among all the 47 gold medals awarded, 21 went to on-snow events, while the other 26 went to on-the-rink events. Li Jinyan from Jilin set a world record of 5'30"58 in women's 3000m short track.

The 7th National Winter Games

The 7th National Winter Games was convened in Harbin from February 2 to 9, 1991, which gathered together 691 athletes. The delegate of Zhongshan from Guangdong Province was the first team from South China to join the event. The Games had 57 events of 8 sports: speed skating, figure skating, ice hockey, alpine skiing, cross-country skiing, winter biathlon, and ski jumping; and one sport for performance: freestyle skiing (2 events). Wang Xiulan smashed a world record with her 48"52 in 500m short track.

The 8th National Winter Games

The National Winter Games was held from January 14 to 24, 1995 in the city of Jilin, Jilin Province. 579 athletes from 33 teams eyed gold in 58 events. Zhang Yanmei from Jilin and Wang Chunlu from Changchun respectively broke the world records for women's 500m and 1000m short track. Li Jiajun outshone all the other medalists by winning 6 champions in men's short track events, individual all-round, and 5000m relay.

The 9th National Winter Games

Changchun in Jilin Province hosted the 9th National Winter Games from January 10 to 19, 1999, gathering together 1,168 athletes from 30 teams to contend in 62 events. Hong Kong participated in the event for the first time. The Games was remarkable in the application of high technology, featuring the use of the Internet, man-made snow, and blood test for skiing and skating events.

The 10th National Winter Games

In January, 2003, the 10th National Winter Games was held in Harbin, Heilongjiang. The joining of Hong Kong and Macao made the event a winter pageant with the largest number of teams (38) and athletes (nearly 4,000) and best facilities in national history. There were 74 events in 10 sports, also the largest in number since the Games was first held, including speed skating (20 events), short track (14 events), figure skating (8 events), ice hockey (2 events), alpine skiing (6 events), cross-country skiing (8 events), freestyle skiing (6 events), winter biathlon (6 events), and curling (2 events). It was curling's debut as an official competition sport at the Games.

The National Sports Meeting

Like the National Games and the City Games, the National Sports Meeting is one of the three major multi-sport events in China. It has been organized every four years since the third games, comprising non-Olympic events only. The National Sports Meet aims to popularize non-Olympic events in China, improve athletic capacity, meet people's increasing demand for sports activities, and promote the coordinated development of mass sports and athletic sports. The previous three Sports Meetings proved effective in propelling the nationwide fitness campaign, and promoting mass participation of sports.

All the events at the Sports Meeting are popular among the Chinese, carrying rich cultural and entertaining elements. The participants boast high athletic skills, including many world champions. There is no gold medal tally so that team ranking will fade out of people's focus, while attention will be given to skills and performance. Apart from competition, there are also many interactive theme activities, which highlight the purpose and characteristics of the event.

The 1st National Sports Meeting

The first National Sports Meeting was held in Ningbo, Zhejiang Province, in May, 2000. This 10-day event, which involved nearly 10,000 athletes, judges and other staff members, was the first time for China to have such a multi-sport game of non-Olympic events. They included snooker, golf, bowling, gate ball, fin swimming, marine modeling, aero modeling, motor boating, sports dancing, aerobatics, bodybuilding, acrobatics, Chinese wrestling, go, Chinese chess, chess and bridge. The choice of events emphasized both athletic skills and mass participation, with much importance attached to performance and entertainment.

The 2nd National Sports Meeting

The city of Mianyang in Sichuan Province hosted the 2nd National Sports Meeting in May 2002. The 22 events included snooker, golf, bowling, gate ball, fin swimming, marine modeling, aero modeling, motor boating, sports dancing, aerobatics, bodybuilding, acrobatics, Chinese wrestling, go, Chinese chess, chess, bridge, rock-climbing, parachuting, dragon boat racing, roller skating, orienteering, and

The roller skating match of the Second National Sports Meeting on May 27, 2002

dragon and lion dancing. Athletes came from 32 provinces, municipalities and autonomous regions, the PLA, and cities like Ningbo, Dalian, Xiamen, Shenzhen, and Mianyang, etc. Nine professional sports associations also sent their delegates, such as the aeronautics, petrochemistry, electronics, power, and banking industries, so did sports colleges in Beijing, Wuhan and Xi'an. The total number of participants amounted to 13,000.

The 3rd National Sports Meeting

The 3rd National Sports Meeting lasted from May 20 to 30, 2006, in Suzhou, a thriving tourist destination of historic and cultural relics in China. The games included 28 events, namely acrobatics, fin swimming, aero modeling, marine modeling, golf, snooker, go, chess, Chinese chess, bodybuilding, bowling, bridge, gate ball, dragon and lion dancing, roller skating, Chinese wrestling, sports dancing, aerobatics, rock-climbing, orienteering, dragon boat racing, boarding, radio direction finding, parachuting, tug-of-war, bocce, squash, and open water swimming (official competition event at 2008 Beijing Olympics).

Altogether 4,085 athletes from 55 teams contended in 268 events of 28 sports, more than the two previous games. They came from 31 provinces, municipalities, autonomous regions, Hong Kong, Macao, Taiwan, and 16 professional sports associations. Five people and one team broke 11 world records for 16 times; four people and three teams bettered 5 Asian records for 11 times; and sixteen people and five teams broke 16 national records for 27 times.

National Games for the Disabled

There have been 6 National Games for the Disabled since 1984. Starting from the third Games, it has been listed as one of the major sports events approved by the State Council, and held quadrennially. At the same time, Law of the People's Republic of China on the Protection of Disabled Persons lent legal force to the Games.

The 1st National Games for the Disabled

The first National Games for the Disabled held in Hefei, Anhui Province in October, 1984 attracted the participation of thirty delegations from 29 provinces, autonomous regions, municipalities and HK SAR of over 1,500 athletes, coaches and judges. It was a great event in the history of Chinese Sports as much as an overall test of the disabled athletes. There were four big items–athletics, swimming, table tennis and wheel chair basketball.

The 2nd National Games for the Disabled

From August 23 to September 1, 1987, the second National Games for the Disabled was held in Tangshan, Hebei. It was a milestone in the sports history of the disabled. 32 delegations from 29 provinces, autonomous regions, municipalities, HK and Macao participated and 900 athletes competed in five sports, or athletics, swimming, wheel chair basketball, wheel chair driving and table tennis. They broke 6 world records and created 197 national records, marking a new high for the sports.

The 3rd National Games for the Disabled

The 3rd National Games for the Disabled was held in Guangzhou, Guangdong province from March 18 to 23, 1992. It was a record event with its number of participants or results. It was also the first such large sports meeting after Law of PRC on the Protection of Disabled Persons went into force. Thirty three delegations from 30 provinces, autonomous regions, municipalities, HK SAR and Macao SAR and the host city Guangzhou participated. In a spirit of equality, involvement, independence and advancement, 1,153 athletes went for six sports, including athletics, swimming, wheel chair basketball, weight lifting, shooting and table tennis and achieved amazing results: 27 world records broken by 20 people 42 times and 238 national records broken by 136 people.

The 4th National Games for the Disabled

The fourth National Games for the Disabled was held in Dalian, Liaoning province from May 10 to 15. 34 delegations from 30 provinces, autonomous regions, municipalities, HK and Macao and the host city Dalian participated. Over 1,200 athletes competed in eight big items, including athletics, swimming, wheel chair basketball, weight lifting, shooting, table tennis, gate ball for the blind and judo for the blind. The tenet of the games is equality, involvement, independence and progress. Between the third and the fourth Games, China released Outline of the Undertakings of China's Disabled persons in the Ninth Five Year Plan, Outline of National Sports Program, Outline of the Preparation for the 2008 Olympics and Sports Law. State Council Member Li Tieying and Peng Peiyun were the honorary chairpersons of the games. Athletes made great results on the meeting and were well prepared for the 10th Paralympic Games to be held in Atlanta, U.S.A.

The 5th National Games for the Disabled

The 5th National Games for the Disabled was held in Shanghai from May 6 to 14, 2000. 34 delegations from 31 provinces, autonomous regions, municipalities, Xinjiang Production and Construction Army Corps, HK SAR and Macao SAR were involved. Over 1,800 athletes competed in 11 sports, including athletics, swimming, wheel chair basketball, weight lifting, shooting, table tennis, gate ball for the blind and judo for the blind, badminton, wheel chair tennis and seat volleyball. Intelligence challenged people participated for the first time. This Games was a good preparation for the 11th Paralympic Games held in Sydney in October, 2000.

The 6th National Games for the Disabled

The 6th National Games for the Disabled unveiled on September 16, 2004 in Nanjing, the capital city of Jiangsu. The number of events and athletes surpassed all previous Games, marking a big stride in China's development of sports for the disabled in the past two decades.

When the first National Games for the Disabled was held 19 years ago, only about 800 athletes competed in four sports, namely track and field, swimming, table tennis, and wheelchair basketball. But the 6th Games gathered the biggest number of athletes, up to 2,300 people in 14 sports, such as track and field, swimming, blind judo, wheelchair basketball, sitting basketball, and newly added events like wheelchair shooting, cycling, archery and deaf basketball. The new event setting and competition rules were in line with those of the Paralympics.

National Paralympics Games

Games	Time	Place	Number of athletes	Events	Records
1	October 7-14, 1984	Hefei, Anhui	Over 500	Track and field, swimming, table tennis	2 new world records
2	August 23-September 1, 1987	Tangshan, Hebei	Over 1000	Track and field, swimming, table tennis, wheelchair basketball	6 new world records set by 8 athletes
3	March 18-23, 1992	Guangzhou, Guangdong	Over 1100	Track and field, swimming, table tennis, shooting, weightlifting	20 people broke 27 world records for 42 times
4	May 10-15, 1996	Dalian, Liaoning	Over 1100	Track and field, swimming, table tennis, shooting, weightlifting, blind judo, blind gate ball	75 people broke 105 world records; 2 people tied world records
5	May 6-14, 2000	Shanghai	Over 1200	Track and field, swimming, table tennis, shooting, weightlifting, blind judo, basketball, blind gate ball, sitting volleyball, badminton, wheelchair tennis, wheelchair dart (for performance)	53 people broke 46 world records for 87 times; 253 people broke 196 Games records for 471 times
6	September 17-23, 2004	Nanjing, Jiangsu	Over2229	track and field, swimming, blind judo, wheelchair basketball, sitting basketball, wheelchair shooting, cycling, archery and deaf basketball	79 people broke 95 world records; 3 people tied three world records; and 260 people broke447 national records

National Traditional Ethnic Sports Games

National Traditional Ethnic Sports Games evolved from the Sports Performance and Competition Festival of National Minorities in 1953. It is now co-hosted by State Commission of Ethnic Affairs and State Physical Culture and Sports Commission, organized by different regions every four years.

The 1st National Traditional Ethnic Sports Games

From November 8 to 12, 1953, the Sports Performance and Competition Festival of National Minorities, or the first National Traditional Ethnic Sports Games, was celebrated in Tianjin. The Games included 395 athletes from 13 ethnic nationalities joined the Games, including Man, Mongolian, Hui, Tibetan, Miao, Korean, Naxi, and Han, etc., and 120,000 spectators from all over China. The Games included competitions, performances and invitational performances. The competitions consisted of weightlifting, boxing, wrestling and archery. The performances comprised 22 varieties of martial arts competition and 9 kinds of equitation and the invitational performances included aerobatics, polo, Mongolian wrestling, etc. Among all these, Uygur Dawazi (tight-rope walking), Mongolian wrestling, Korean spring board, Hui martial arts and Mongolian military equitation were the most impressive. During the Games, 10 weightlifters created national records.

The 2nd National Traditional Ethnic Sports Games

The 2nd National Traditional Ethnic Sports Games was held in the city of Hohhot in the Inner Mongolia Autonomous Region from September 2 to 8, 1982. In all 863 athletes and coaches, including 593 athletes from ethnic minorities, from the country's 56 ethnic groups took part in the competitions of the Games. Apart from competitions, the 68 performances also witnessed the participation of 800 athletes from 46 ethnic minority groups, attracting an audience of 800,000 people to the Games. During the Games, there was also an exhibition featuring traditional sports of ethnic minorities, and a grand party attracting 12,000 people. The Games consisted of competition and performance events. The two competitions were archery and Chinese wrestling. A total of 24 athletes of 5 nationalities from Inner Mongolia, Xinjiang, Tibet and Qinghai contended in the archery event, while 58 amateurs of 13 nationalities from 15 provinces, municipalities and autonomous regions competed in the four divisions of Chinese wrestling event. Besides, over 800 athletes of 46 ethnic minorities participated in the 68 performance events, including Dai's peacock boxing, Bai's overlord whip, Gaoshan's back basket ball game, Hui's bullfighting, Korean's swinging, Li's bamboo pole jumping, Zhuang's lion dancing, Uygur Dawazi, Kazakstan Diaoyang (sheep snatching on horseback), Mongolian camel racing and horse racing, and Daur Boyiko (similar to modern hockey), etc.

The 3rd National Traditional Ethnic Sports Games

The 3rd National Traditional Ethnic Minorities Sports Games was held in Urumqi, the capital city of Xinjiang Uygur Autonomous Region from August 10 to 17, 1986, much larger than the last two ones in scale. IOC member He Zhenliang, vice minister of State Physical Culture and Sports Commission, presented the organizing committee with a bronze dove on behalf of the IOC. It was also the first time to have a Games badge, flag and emblem, marking the systemization of the Games. In all 1,097 athletes, coaches, and staff from all the nation's ethnic groups took part in the competitions and performances, together with over 2,000 observers, special guests, journalists, friends from Hong Kong, Macao and abroad. The Games included 7 competitions and 115 performances. Apart from archery and wrestling in the previous Games, 5 more events were added to the competitions, namely horse racing, Diaoyang (Snatching the sheep on horseback), crossbow-firing, firework-catching, and swinging.

The 4th National Traditional Ethnic Sports Games

The 4th National Traditional Ethnic Sports Games was held in Nanning, the capital city of Southwest China's Guangxi Zhuang Autonomous Region from November 10 to 17, 1991. The horseracing event of the Games is held in Hohhot, hosted by the Inner Mongolia Autonomous Region. Altogether, 3,000 people, including athletes, coaches, and staff from all the ethnic groups, as well as observers and journalists from home and abroad, took part in the competitions and 120 performances. The Games also witnessed the participation of Taiwan for the first time in its 30-year history, which sent a dragon boat racing team and an ethnic singing and dancing troop.

All the events fell into two categories. The 9 competition events awarded 34 gold medals in dragon boat racing, firework-catching, swinging, crossbow-firing, pearl ball, cricket, wrestling, equitation, and martial arts. The 120 performances had 114 awards. The Fourth National Traditional

Ethnic Sports Games not only surpassed the previous Games in terms of the number of events, but also developed scientific and systemized general rules, competition and judging rules,

The 5th National Traditional Ethnic Sports Games

The 5th National Traditional Ethnic Sports Games was held in Kunming, the capital city of Southeast China's Yunnan Province, from November 5 to 12, 1995. The Games was larger than any of the last 4 ones as far as scale and the number of events was concerned. More than 9,000 people from 55 ethnic minorities participated in the Games and the Games had 11 competitions and 129 exhibition ones. Shaolingmin ethnic team from Taiwan took part in the dragon boat racing. The 11 competition events awarded 65 gold medals in firework-catching, pearl ball, cricket, shuttlecock kicking, wrestling, swinging, martial arts, crossbow-firing, dragon boat racing, horse racing, and top-whipping. Besides, first, second and third places were awarded in the 129 performance events.

The 6th National Traditional Ethnic Sports Games

The 6th National Traditional Ethnic Sports Games was held in Beijing from September 24 to 30, 1999. A venue was also set up in the Tibet Autonomous Region and some of the events were held there from August 18 to 28. It was the last multi-sport meeting in China in the 20th century. The Games was significant in the sense of its time and place. The year 1999 was not only the last year before the coming millennium, but also marked the 50th anniversary of the founding of the People's Republic of China, and 40th anniversary of the democratic reformation of Tibet Autonomous region, one of the two venues of the Games. About 6,000 athletes and coaches from the nation's all ethnic groups took part in the 13 competitions and 112 performances. The competitions comprised firework-catching, pearl ball, cricket, shuttlecock kicking, Cuqiu, swinging, martial art, crossbow-firing, dragon boat racing, top-whipping, Yajia (Tibetan tug-of-war, using the neck to pull the rope), ethnic wrestling, and horseback events. Among them, crossbow-firing, top-whipping, Yajia, and part of the horseback events and performances were held in Lhasa.

The 7th National Traditional Ethnic Sports Games

The 7th National Traditional Ethnic Sports Games was held from September 6-13, 2003 in Yinchuan, capital of Ningxia Hui Autonomous Region. In all, 2,591 athletes of 34 teams (of provinces, municipalities, autonomous regions, and the PLA) from 46 ethnic minorities took part in the 14 competitions and 126 performances. This Games integrated ethnic features, athletic skills, and entertainment elements. The performance events were warmly received by the spectators.

The dragon boat venue on the Shahu Lake in Ningxia at the 7th National Traditional Ethnic Sports Games on September 9, 2003

National City Games

The National City Games is a quadrennial nationwide gala, with the objective of promoting sports in urban areas, and selecting young promising athletes. It was first held in 1988, and the previous 5 Games were hosted by the provincial government of Shandong, Hebei, Jiangsu, Shaanxi, and Henan, respectively.

The 1st National City Games

The 1st National City Games was held in Jinan and Zibo, Shandong Province from October 23 to November 2, 1988. The Games comprised 169 events in 12 sports, including track and field, swimming, weightlifting, shooting, wrestling, judo, soccer, basketball, volleyball, badminton, table tennis, and gymnastics. Altogether 2,332 athletes from 42 delegations took part in 12 competitions, rewriting 1 world record, 1 world youth record, 3 Asian Records, 4 national records, 4 national junior records and leveling 1 national record and 1 national junior record. The 17-year-old Cui Yingzi from Shenyang surpassed the world record for women's 5,000m walking race, shedding light on a bright future of China's sports.

The 2nd National City Games

The 2nd National City Games was co-hosted by Shijiazhuang and Tangshan, Hebei Province from September 20 to 28, 1991. Competitions were held in 170 events of 16 sports, including track and field, swimming, weightlifting, shooting, wrestling, judo, soccer, basketball, volleyball, badminton, table tennis, gymnastics, diving, archery, fencing, and boating. In all, 2,928 athletes from 96 delegations took part in the 16 competitions and 4 Asian records, 4 national records and 15 national junior records were beaten.

The 3rd National City Games

The 3rd National City Games was held in 6 cities of Nanjing, Changzhou, Wuxi, Suzhou, Yangzhou and Zhenjiang of Jiangsu Province from October 22 to 30, 1995. The Games had 16 competitions, comprising of 202 items in track and field, swimming, weightlifting, shooting, wrestling, judo, soccer, basketball, volleyball, badminton, table tennis, gymnastics, diving, archery, fencing, and boating. Altogether 3,352 athletes from 50 cities across the country took part in the competition, smashing 6 world junior records, 5 Asian junior records, 8 national records and 31 national junior records.

The 4th National City Games

The 4th City Games was held in Xi'an, Shaanxi Province from September 11 to 20, 1999. The Games consisted of 220 events in 16 competitions, including soccer, basketball, volleyball, table tennis, badminton, track and field, swimming, diving, gymnastics, weightlifting, shooting, archery, fencing, judo, international wrestling, and boating. It witnessed the participation of 7,000 people from 53 cities across the country.

National Farmers' Games

The National Farmers' Games is the only regularly held sports gala solely for Chinese farmers. This quadrennial event is co-hosted by China's Ministry of Agriculture, General Administration of Sport of China, and Farmers' Sports Association. There have been 5 Games since 1988 when it was first held. Apart from competition sports like track and field, basketball, table tennis and swimming, there are also events carrying rural characteristics and ethnic traditions, such as martial art, Chinese wrestling, Chinese chess, bicycle carrying race, militia triathlon, tug-of-war, shuttlecock kicking, dragon and lion dancing, dragon boat racing, and kite flying, etc. Some interesting varieties are also incorporated into track and field and swimming, which are easy to be practiced and popularized in rural areas.

National University Games

The quadrennial National University Games is co-hosted by China's Ministry of Education, General Administration of Sport of China, All-China Students' Federation, and Federation of University Sports of China. The have been 7 Games since 1982.

There are 6 to 8 events at the National University Games. Track and field, swimming, basketball, soccer and table tennis are regular events, while 1 to 2 other popular events can be added, like martial arts, aerobatics, badminton and tennis, etc.

The 5th National City Games

The 5th National City Games was launched grandly in Changsha, Hunan Province on October 18, 2003.

The 5th National City Games was held in Changsha, capital of Hunan Province from October 18 to 27, 2003. Nineteen of the events were competed in Hunan, while the games for sailing and cycling, etc. were hosted outside Hunan. Altogether 78 teams joined the Games, including Hong Kong SAR, Macao SAR, Taipei and Tainan of Taiwan province. It was the first time for athletes from China's mainland, Hong Kong, Macao and Taiwan to compete together. The Fifth City Games added ten more Olympic sports to its traditional 16 sports. It attracted more than 7,000 athletes to participate. The team of Guangzhou, Nanjing and Shenyang ranked at the top of the gold medal tally. During the ten-day competition, 4 athletes broke 5 world records 8 times and 6 new Asian records were created by 8 athletes. Also, 11 people and 13 teams rewrote 16 world junior records 34 times, 9 people and 1 team tied 9 world junior records 13 times; 8 people bettered 6 Asian records 12 times; 2 set 2 national records, 7 people and 1 team matched 7 national records 8 times; and another 14 broke 12 national junior records 19 times. Many promising young athletes emerged onto the horizon, laying a solid foundation for the preparation of 2008 Beijing Olympics.

Summer Olympic Games

The 22nd Summer Olympics in Moscow was boycotted by 63 countries due to Soviet Union's breach of the international law by invading Afghanistan. Though China was fully prepared for the Games, the COC announced on April 24, 1980, to boycott it for the sake of world peace. With the restoration of Chinese Olympic Committee's legal seat in the IOC and of the Chinese Sports Delegation's right to participate in the Olympics, Chinese athletes were sent to Los Angeles in 1984 for the 23rd Olympic Games.

China has been a traditional power in men's gymnastics, diving, table tennis, women's walking race, shooting, and women's swimming, etc.

The 15th Olympic Games in Helsinki

The 15th Summer Olympics was held in July 1952, in Helsinki, Finland. Yet due to the hostility against New China, and the deliberate attempt to create "Two Chinas", the IOC decided not to invite China. The decision was strongly opposed by All-China Sports Federation, which finally made the IOC compromise.

Delayed for formal competitions, the Chinese athletes arrived at the Olympic Village five days before the closing ceremony. Only Wu Chuanyu had the chance to contend in the swimming event. Though due to jet lag and others, he did not make it to the finals, Wu became the first New China athlete to compete in the history.

The debut was a tortuous one, but the hoisted red five-starred national flag marked China's legal status in Olympic arena. Meanwhile, Chinese people expressed their love for peace and the wish to strengthen friendship with other peoples.

The 23rd Summer Olympics in Los Angeles

The Chinese sports delegation consisted of 353 people (225 athletes) to the 23rd L.A. Olympics in 1984.This was different from 52 years ago when only one athlete, Liu Changchun, represented China to attend the Olympic Games also held in the city. This was China's first full participation in Olympic Summer Games and the first important step taken by China in the sports world. The Olympic Committee of Chinese Taipei also sent 67 athletes, the first time Chinese from both sides of the Straits met at the Olympics.

The 24th Summer Olympics in Seoul

China sent a delegation of 445 to the 24th Seoul Olympics in 1988, including 300 contestants. Chinese athletes competed in all the 23 other sports except field hockey and equestrians.

The 15 gold medals at the 23rd Games was remarkable, but non-representative, because some sporting powers, including the Soviet Union, did not show up. Their medal tally in Seoul, though less glorious than it was four years before, represented no mean effort considering the unprecedentedly high performance attained by the Seoul Games. Attracting athletes of 160 countries and regions from both east and west, the Games was of the highest standard since the 1976 Olympics in Montreal.

Nevertheless, the bright side should not be overlooked, as some young athletes panned out at the Games. Two teenager divers, Xu Yanmei and Gao Min, brought home a gold medal each for their elegant performances in the women's platform and springboard events respectively. China also claimed two gold medals in table tennis: Chen Jing in women's singles and Chen Longcan/Wei Qingguang in men's doubles. On the total medal tally, China got 5 gold, 11 silver and 12 bronze medals.

The 25th Summer Olympics in Barcelona

The 25th Olympic Games was held in Barcelona in 1992 on a larger scale than ever before-with the participation of 10,251 athletes from 172 countries and areas. The Chinese sports delegation, composed of 380 members, including 250 athletes, took part in 23 sports. Besides, 37 athletes from Chinese Taipei competed in baseball, shooting, judo, and track and field, etc. China placed fourth in medal standing with 16 gold, 22 silver and 16 bronze—an achievement that was indicative of China's new progress.

Gao Min, in the women's 3-meter platform event of the Seoul Olympics

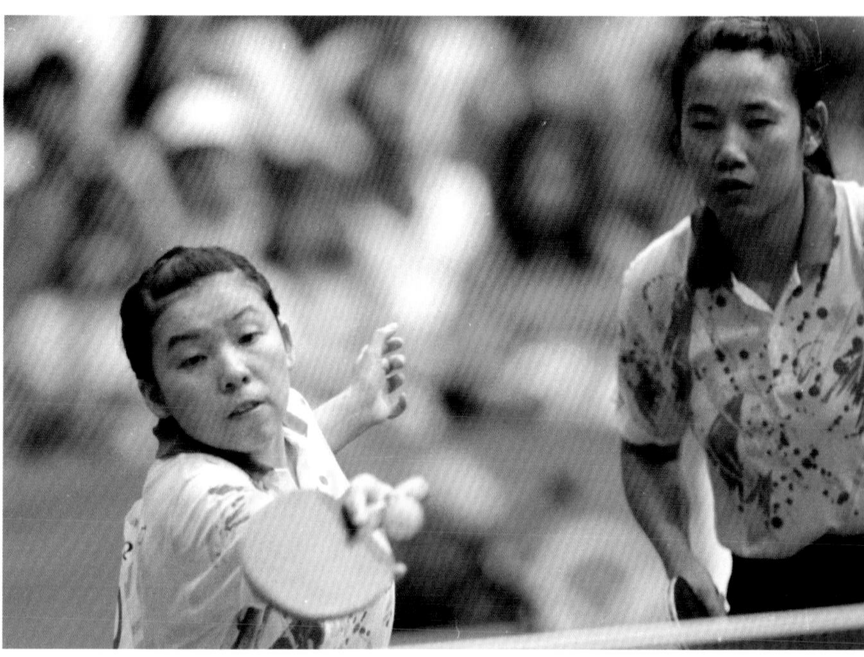

The 25th Olympic Games was held in Barcelona from July 25 to August 9, 1992. China placed fourth in medal standing with 16 gold, 22 silver and 16 bronze. In the picture are Deng Yaping and Qiao Hong (right) on this Olympic Games.

Achievements at the 25th Olympics Games

China led the world in diving, wrapping 3 gold out of the 4 in total. The 14-year-old Fu Mingxia from Hubei, and the "diving queen" Gao Min each won a gold. In men's events, the 16-year-old Sun Shuwei titled in 10-meter platform with 677.31 points. In women's swimming, China also had good news. Zhuang Yong led all the way in 100m freestyle, and became China's first champion in swimming. It was followed by Qian Hong in 100m butterfly; Lin Li in 200m individual medley; and Yang Wenyi in 50m freestyle. Woman shooter Zhang Shan beat all men opponents in skeet, claiming another gold medal.

In table tennis, men's doubles, women's doubles and women's singles were won by Wang Tao/Lu Lin, Deng Yaping/Qiao Hong and Deng Yaping respectively. Deng thus became the only Chinese to win two gold medals in Spain. In gymnastics, Li Xiaoshuang was arguably the champion of men's floor exercises with his astounding "three saltos tucked". In addition, the 15-year-old Lu Li titled in women's high and low bars with the first full score in gymnastics at the Games.

The 26th Summer Olympics in Atlanta

The Olympic Games held in Atlanta, the United States, in August 1996 saw a large gathering of athletes. China sent a delegation of 495 to the Games, including 309 athletes (199 women athletes), ranking the 12th in all the participating countries. The Chinese team was very young, 21.7 years old on average, and 85 percent of the athletes had never taken part in the Olympics before.

The centennial Atlanta Olympics, a large gathering of athletes from 197 countries and regions, saw the fiercest competition in the 20th century. China collected 16 gold, 22 silver and 12 bronze medals, ranking fourth both in gold medals tally and in the total number of medals won.

Achievements at the 26th Olympics

China made a good start on the first day in Atlanta by winning two gold and two silver, ranking at the top of the medal tally. Sun Fuming took the first gold in the +72kg heavyweight judo after toppling Rodríguez from Cuba.

In men's 59kg category weightlifting, China's Tang Lingsheng came out of nowhere among all the competitors. He not only emerged the winner but also set a world record. In the pool, 18-year-old diver Fu Mingxia proved her superiority in both women's 3m springboard and 10m platform diving and rose as the first dual-Olympic-champion in diving. Wang

Junxia, nicknamed as "Oriental Deer", a fleet-footed distance runner, won the gold in the women's 5000m and the silver in the 10,000m, a pride for China and the whole Asia.

In table tennis, Kong Linghui and Liu Guoliang's debut in men's double won them a title. China rookie marksman Yang Ling shot a gold in men's 10m running target. In men's gymnastics, 23-year-old Li Xiaoshuang managed to beat Russia's Nemov to win the most-valued all-around gold medal for China.

The 27th Summer Olympics in Sydney

Altogether 11,116 athletes from 199 delegations participated in the Sydney Olympic Games in September, 2000. China's 284 athletes took part in 166 events of 24 sports.

Hong Kong SAR, for the first time, sent a delegation of 59 under the designation of Chinese Hong Kong. Taipei also sent 55 athletes and 22 coaches, harvesting one silver and four bronze. China was awarded 28 gold, 16 silver and 15 bronze medals, a historical breakthrough into the First Group. By then, Chinese athletes had won over 80 gold medals at the Olympics.

♦ Achievements of Chinese Taipei Athletes at the Olympiad

At the Rome Olympiad in 1960, Yang Chuan-Kwang from Chinese Taipei won the silver in the decathlon, being the first Chinese to win an Olympic medal.

At the Mexico Olympiad in 1968, Chi Cheng (female) from Chinese Taipei won a bronze at the 80-meter hurdles, being the first Chinese woman to win an Olympic medal and also the only Asian woman to win a medal at the Olympiad.

At the Los Angles Olympiad in 1984, athletes from Chinese Taipei won two bronze medals, with Chai Wenyi winning a bronze and the Taiwan Nine Team winning a bronze during the demonstration match.

At the Barcelona Olympiad in 1992, the Taiwan Nine Team won a silver.

At the Athens Olympiad in 2004, Chen Shih Hsin and Chu Mu Yen, both from Taiwan, won two gold at the Taekwondo items. In addition, the Taiwan athelets won two silver at the Taekwondo and Men's Archery Team Competitions and the bronze at the Women's Archery Team Competition. This was the best achievement of the Chinese Taipei atheletes at the Olympiad.

♦ Achievements of Hong Kong Athletes at the Olympiad

At the 26th Atlanta Olympic Games in 1996, Hong Kong woman windsurfer Lee Lai Shan won a gold medal, being the first gold Hong Kong athletes had won in history.

Achievements at the 27th Olympics

China enjoyed a more remarkable lead in her strong sports at the 27th Games. Among the 28 gold medals, 20 came from the five sports: table tennis, badminton, women's weightlifting, diving and shooting. And China's table tennis team and diving team were acknowledged as "dream teams". The former got 4 gold, and broke 2 records, while the latter wrapped 5 gold out of the total 8. Women weightlifters breezed into the finals and picked all the 4 champions with clear win. The underperformed shooting team also claimed 3 gold. Three Chinese athletes set eight world records, 12 times, and a further six athletes set 11 Olympic records.

The 28th Summer Olympics in Athens

The 28th Olympic Games was held in Athens of Greece in August 2004. China sent a delegation of 633 people, 407 athletes (including 269 women and 138 men) of which took part in all games of 26 sports except baseball and equestrian skills. A total of 11,099 athletes from 201 countries and regions across the world took part in the Games.

Heartening breakthroughs were made in track and field, canoeing, and tennis. Liu Xiang made history when he struck gold in the men's 110m hurdles final in a world record-equaling time of 12"91. Meng Guanliang and Yang Wenjun demonstrated perfect teamwork in the men's C2 500m canoe, China's first gold in water sports. Another Chinese pair Li Ting and Sun Tiantian won China's first gold medal in the women's doubles in tennis. It is worth to note that 36 medals out of the 63 were reaped by young athletes, accounting for 57.1 percent of the total. Among all the gold medalists, 10 were teenagers. It proved the growth of young Chinese athletes, and the nation's increased overall strength in competitive sports.

On August 28, 2004, Hu Jia finished first in the final of the men's 10m platform with 748.08 points at the Athens Olympics.

♦ "Ice Break" of Swimming in Olympics

Some weak sports for China saw an unprecedented come-around at the 24th Games. No Chinese swimmers reached the finals for Group B in L.A., while 3 silver and 1 bronze medals were snatched at the 24th Games, 7 Asian bests created, and 10 national records bettered. The heartening achievements, a breakthrough of zero medals, helped open a new era in China's swimming history. Chinese women rowers sprang a surprise by taking a silver and a bronze medals in the coxed fours and coxed eights respectively. Before that, no Asian athletes had ever entered the finals. In addition, the number of Chinese athletes in track and field witnessed a big increase, and notably, woman shot-putter Li Meisu gained a bronze—the only track and field medal for Asia at the Games.

♦ The First Olympic Gold

On July 29, 1984, Xu Haifeng's victory in the 50 meter free pistol shooting final earned the world's most populous nation its first Olympic gold medal, with the prize awarded him by IOC President Samaranch himself. He solemnly announced that Chinese athlete won the first gold medal in that Olympics and he felt honored to award this medal by himself.

The breakthrough was followed by more gold medals won by Chinese athletes. Wu Xiaoxuan was the first Chinese woman to win an Olympic title, in small-bore standard rifle, 581. Li Ning won three gold medals in floor exercises, pommel horse and rings, respectively, two silver medals and one bronze medal to become the athlete with the most medals in the Games.

At the end of the event, China earned 15 gold, eight silver and nine bronze medals and placed fourth in medal standing, a testimony to its athletic ability. The L.A. Games was a milestone in China's Olympic journey.

The 29th Summer Olympics in Beijing

On August 8, 2008, the 29th Olympic Games opened in Beijing. More than 10,000 athletes from 204 countries and regions broke 38 world records and 85 Olympic Games records and many countries and regions won their first ever gold medals and medals in the Olympic Games.

The Chinese delegation had 1,099 members, including 639 athletes taking part in all 28 sports categories. China had the largest number of athletes and participated in the most categories in its history. A total of 469 athletes participated in the Olympic Games for the first time. The Chinese delegation had 28 foreign coaches from 16 countries, involving 17 sports categories. A breakthrough in such sports as men's fencing and women's hockey was realized after the invitation of foreign coaches, reflecting China's further connection with the international community and the tendency of learning and using advanced international experience.

China topped the medals table for the first time with 51 gold, 21 silver and 28 bronze medals; overall, China jumped to No.2, next only next to the United States and ahead of Russia Olympic medals.

As the host, China made great efforts to run the Beijing Olympic Games with local characteristics and high standards. Thanks to outstanding venues and excellent organization and services, China won favorable comment from the big Olympic family and the international community.

The Propitious-clouds torch of the 29th Beijing Olympics

The gold medal inlaid with jade of the 29th Beijing Olympics

The 29th Beijing Olympics mascot Fuwas

Records of Gold Medals on the 29th Olympic Games

In the 29th Olympic Games, the Chinese delegation spared no efforts to succeed. It not only maintained its high level of success in such traditional strong areas as diving, table tennis, women's weightlifting, gymnastics, shooting, and badminton, but also made breakthroughs in many comparatively laggard sports such as fencing, windsurfing, hockey, rhythmic gymnastics, beach volleyball, and synchronized swimming. It won gold medals for the first time in sailing, archery, rowing, boxing, and trampoline. This enabled it to compile its best Olympic record ever of 100 medals comprising 51 gold, 21 silver and 28 bronze medals.

List of Gold Medals of the Chinese Delegation in Beijing 2008 Olympic Games

Date	Name	Sport	Performance [times or points]
August 24	Zhang Xiaoping	Boxing	
August 24	Zou Shiming	Boxing	
August 23	Ma Lin	Table Tennis	
August 23	Meng Guanliang /Yang Wenjun	Canoeing (Flatwater)	1:41.025
August 22	Zhang Yining	Table Tennis	
August 21	Chen Ruolin	Diving	447.70
August 20	Wu Jingyu	Taekwondo	
August 20	Yin Jian	Sailing	39
August 19	He Chong	Diving	572.90
August 19	Lu Chunlong	Gymnastics Trampoline	41.00
August 19	Zou Kai	Gymnastics	16.200
August 19	Li Xiaopeng	Gymnastics	16.450
August 18	Wang Hao/Wang Liqin/Ma Lin	Table Tennis	
August 18	He Wenna	Gymnastics Trampoline	37.80
August 18	He Kexin	Gymnastics	16.725
August 18	Chen Yibing	Gymnastics	16.600
August 17	Guo Jingjing	Diving	415.35
August 17	Lin Dan	Badminton	
August 17	Wang Nan/Zhang Yining/Guo Yue	Table Tennis	
August 17	Xiao Qin	Gymnastics	15.875
August 17	Zou Kai	Gymnastics	16.050
August 17	Wang Jiao	Wrestling	
August 17	Tang Bin, Jin Ziwei, Xi Aihua, Zhang Yangyang	Rowing	6:16.06
August 17	Qiu Jian	Shooting	1272.5
August 16	Zhang Ning	Badminton	
August 15	Du Jing/Yu Yang	Badminton	
August 15	Lu Yong	Weightlifting	394
August 15	Tong Wen	Judo	
August 15	Cao Lei	Weightlifting	282
August 14	Yang Xiuli	Judo	
August 14	Zhang Juanjuan	Archery	
August 14	Yang Wei	Gymnastics	94.575
August 14	Du Li	Shooting	690.3
August 14	Liu Zige	Swimming	2:04.18
August 13	Liu Chunhong	Weightlifting	286
August 13	Wang Feng/Qin Kai	Diving	469.08
August 13	Chen Ying	Shooting	793.4
August 13	Cheng Fei, Yang Yilin, He Kexin, Li Shanshan, Deng Linlin, Jiang Yuyuan	Gymnastics	188.900
August 12	Liao Hui	Weightlifting	348
August 12	Zhong Man	Fencing	
August 12	Wang Xin/Chen Ruolin	Diving	363.54
August 12	Chen Yibing, Huang Xu, Li Xiaopeng, Xiao Qin, Yang Wei, Zou Kai	Gymnastics	286.125
August 11	Zhang Xiangxiang	Weightlifting	319
August 11	Chen Yanqing	Weightlifting	244
August 11	Lin Yue/Huo Liang	Diving	468.18
August 10	Long Qingquan	Weightlifting	292
August 10	Xian Dongmei	Judo	
August 10	Guo Jingjing/Wu Minxia	Diving	343.50
August 10	Guo Wenjun	Shooting	482.6
August 9	Pang Wei	Shooting	688.2
August 9	Chen Xiexia	Weightlifting	212kg

The Winter Games

The Winter Games is organized by the IOC, and first held in France, in 1924. There have been 19 Games up till 2002. China has participated in every Winter Games, since the 13th Games in 1980, in Lake Placid, USA. At the 16th Games, Ye Qiaobo and Li Yan made a breakthrough by winning 3 silver medals in speed skating and short track events.

The 13th Winter Games

In February, 1980, China made its debut at the Lake Placid Winter Olympic Games, sending 28 athletes. None of them managed to reach the top six, but they were the pioneers in China's progress in catching up with winter sporting powers.

The 14th Winter Games

In 1984, the Winter Games took place in Sarajevo, Yugoslavia. Thirty-seven Chinese athletes took part in 5 sports, namely speed skating, figure skating, cross-country skiing, alpine skiing, and modern biathlon. China ranked the 23rd with a total of five points. Chinese Taipei also sent 14 athletes to the Games—the first reunion for athletes from both sides of the Straits at the Winter Games.

The 15th Winter Games

The 15th Winter Olympics was held in Calgary, Canada. Since China failed to qualify for the ice hockey event, had a late start in alpine skiing, ski jumping, and modern biathlon, and had no bobsleighing or luge team, the 20 athletes only competed in speed skating, figure skating, and cross-country skiing. Chinese Taipei's 13 athletes contended in skiing, figure skating, luge and bobsleighing, etc. The best result for the team of China and Chinese Taipei were only 14th and 15th respectively, but some sparkles should not be neglected. Short-track speed skater Li Yan claimed gold medal in the women's 1,000m, though it was only a demonstration sport.

The 16th Winter Games

In February 1992, China sent 33 athletes to the Albertville Winter Olympic Games in France. Twelve years' of hard work led China to a breakthrough on the medal standing: 3 silver, and 2 fourth places. Despite her injuries, Ye Qiaobo clinched the country's first winter Olympics medal, a silver, in the women's 500m speed skating. Ye then took her second silver in the women's 1,000m speed skating. Nine athletes from Chinese Taipei competed at the Games.

The 17th Winter Games

A total of 27 Chinese athletes, including 19 women, competed in the Lillehammer Winter Olympic Games from February 17 to 27, 1994. They participated in speed skating, short track, figure skating, winter biathlon, and freestyle skiing. Chinese athletes were basically in form, taking home three medals, ranking the 18th in terms of total score. Zhang Yanmei settled for a silver in women's 500m short-track speed skating. Veteran Ye Qiaobo struggled for a bronze medal in the women's 1,000m speed skating. And 17-year-old Chen Lu emerged as the third-place finisher in the women's figure skating, winning China's first medal in Olympic figure skating. Three athletes from Chinese Taipei competed in two-seat bobsleighing, making the 35th in all the 43 teams.

The 18th Winter Games

The 18th Winter Olympics was held in Nagano, Japan, from February 7 to 22, 1998. Chinese athletes achieved remarkable results, especially in short track events, in which they reaped at least one medal for each of the 6 events. Yang Yang got two silver medals in women's 500m and 1000m short-track speed skating, after finishing the second place in women's 3000m short-track speed skating relay. Yang has won more medals at the Winter Games than any other Chinese athlete. Li Jiajun got a silver medal in men's 1,000m short-track speed skating, becoming the first Chinese male medalist. Seventeen-year-old An Yulong also finished second in men's 500m short-track speed skating. Faced with fierce competition from Canada and Italy, An and his teammates also managed a bronze in men's 5000m short-track speed skating relay. Besides, Chen Lu took home another bronze medal in figure skating. The 18th Winter Games was the last one in the 20th century, and China wrapped it up with 6 silver and 2 bronze. In recent years, China has made headway in speed skating and short track. It got 13 champions in all at international tournaments, laying a solid foundation for a gold medal at the Winter Games.

The 19th Winter Games

The 19th Olympic Winter Games was held in Salt Lake City, 2002. China collected two gold metals, two silver medals and four bronze. Yang Yang triumphed in women's 500m short-track speed skating, bringing China its first gold medal at the Winter Olympics. Later, she added one more gold medal for her team in the 1000m short-track speed skating finals.

The 20th Winter Games

Turin in Italy hosted the 20th Winter Games, from February 10 to 26, 2006. The Games encompassed 84 items of 15 events in 7 sports. China took part in skating, skiing, and winter biathlon, competing in 47 items of 9 events, namely speed skating, figure skating, short track, freestyle skiing, cross-country, alpine skiing, ski jump, snowboard, and biathlon. It was China's debut in ski jumping and snowboarding at the Games.

At this Olympics, the Chinese team won two gold medals, four silver medals and five bronze medals, China's best performance in history. Most remarkably, Chinese athlete Han Xiaopeng won the title of men's freestyle skiing aerials, which was China's first gold medal in a snow event and he became the first Chinese male gold-medal winner at a winter Olympics. Women's 500-meter short track skater Wang Meng seized another gold medal for China.

Chinese athlete Liu Yan in the short program match of the women's figure skating at the Torino Olympic Winter Games on February 21, 2006

China at Paralympics

The 1984 Paralympics Games of New York, the United States, saw China's participation in the games for the first time ever. For the past six Paralympics, a total of 415 Chinese athletes appeared on the competition fields, winning 143 gold medals, 118 silver medals, and 85 bronze medals, breaking world records for 104 times. In the Athens Paralympics 2004, China got 63 gold medals, ranking first among the gold winners, which marked a significant breakthrough in the history of Paralympics.

The 7th Paralympics

In June 1984, the Chinese delegation comprising 24 athletes with disabilities appeared for the first time at the 7th Paralympics Games held in New York, the United States. Ping Yali, a blind from Beijing, won a gold medal for B2 long jump, thus saying goodbye to a Non-gold history in China's Paralympics Games. China won 2 gold, 13 silver and 9 bronze medals at last, with 9 of the athletes breaking world records.

The 8th Paralympics

In October 1988, the Chinese delegation including 43 athletes participated at the 8th Paralympics Games in Seoul, South Korea. They competed in four sports (Athletics swimming, table tennis, and shooting) and took 17 gold, 17 silver and 10 bronze medals, with 11 of them breaking a total of 9 world records.

The 9th Paralympics

In September 1992, when the 9th Paralympics Games were held in Barcelona, Spain, China sent a delegation of 34 athletes to the games, and took home 11 gold, 7 silver and 7 bronze medals, ranking 11th in the list of gold winners, 18th for the number of medals. As many as 8 people broke 7 world records for 14 times, and 11 of the athletes breaking the Paralympics records 21 times.

The 10th Paralympics

In August 1996, China sent 37 athletes to attend the 10th Paralympics Games held in Atlanta, the United States. They got 16 gold, 13 silver and 10 bronze medals, ranking the 9th for the number of medals won, the first time among top ten. And 10 of the athletes broke 11 world records for 16 times.

The 11th Paralympics

In October 2000, China sent a delegation of 122 athletes to the 11th Paralympics Games held in Sydney, Australia. They grasped 34 gold, 22 silver, and 16 bronze medals, ranking the 6th in the list of gold winners. 15 of them broke world records for 25 times, the most splendid chapter in the history of China's participation in the Paralympics.

The 12th Paralympics

In September 2004, the 12th Paralympics Games were held in Athens, Greece. The Chinese delegation, made up of 200 handicapped athletes went all out to compete and won 63 gold, 46 silver, and 32 bronze medals (a total of 141) in the 11 sports and 284 events. Both the number of gold medals and number of medals exceeded those of any other countries or regions.

The 13th Paralympics

The 13th Paralympics was held in Beijing from September 6 to 17 in 2008. More than 4,000 athletes with a disability from 147 countries and regions participated in the games of 20 events. The sailing was held in Qingdao and equestrian was held in Hong Kong.

The Chinese delegation sent 547 people to participate in the Paralympics Games, the largest number of Chinese delegation since its first participation into the Paralympics Games and the largest number of delegation in the Beijing Paralympics. It included 332 athletes and 68 percent of them participated in the Paralympics for the first time. The youngest athlete was 15 years old.

Chinese athletes participated in the games of all the 20 events and won 89 golden, 70 silver and 52 copper medals totaling at 211. China was listed as No.1 in both golden medal and medal lists.

China's Records at the Paralympics

Games	Venue	Time	Number of Chinese Athletes	Gold	Silver	Bronze	Remarks
7th	New York, USA	1984.6	24	2	13	9	9 people broke world records
8th	Seoul, South Korea	1988.10	43	17	17	10	11 people broke world records
9th	Barcelona, Spain	1992.9	24	11	7	7	14 people broke world records; 21 people bettered Games' records
10th	Atlanta, USA	1996.8	37	16	13	10	10 people rewrote 11 world records 16 times
11th	Sydney, Australia	2000.10	87	34	22	16	15 people rewrote 15 world records 25 times; 4 people bettered 4 Games' records
12th	Athens, Greece	2004.9	200	63	46	32	
13th	Beijing, China	2008.9	332	89	70	52	

Universiade

The Universiade is an international multi-sport event which is called "Mini-Olympics", organized for university athletes by the International University Sports Federation (FISU). It is exclusively for university students or those who have graduated no more than two years, aged between 17 and 28. The Universiade was first held in 1959, known as World University Games then.

Chinese athletes took part in some events of track and field in 1959, but did not compete in the 2nd to 8th Games. In 1957, China was officially recognised as FISU member, and hence has participated in every Universiade starting from the 9th one. By 2005, there had been 23 Games, and the 21st Universiade was held in Beijing.

The 9th Universiade

On August 17, 1977, China made her debut at the 9th Universiade in Sofia, Bulgaria. The delegation of 51 strove for 1 silver and 3 bronze in women's basketball, women's volleyball, men's gymnastics, and track and field, ranking the 21st on the medal tally.

The 19th Universiade

The 1997 Summer Universiade took place in Catania of Sicily, Italy, from August 19 to 31. Over 6,000 sportsmen from 160 countries contended in athletics, swimming, diving, tennis, fencing, football, basketball, volleyball, water polo, and gymnastics (including rhythmic gymnastics). The top three on the medal tally were USA (20 gold, 19 silver, and 22 bronze), Ukraine (17 gold, 6 silver, and 4 bronze), and Japan (14 gold, 8 silver, and 11 bronze). Chinese athletes took part in all the 10 sports except swimming and water polo, ranking the 5th on the medal tally with 10 gold, 9 silver, and 7 bronze medals.

The 20th Universiade

The 1999 Summer Universiade, also known as the XX Summer Universiade, took place in Palma de Mallorca, Spain from July 3rd to 13th. The Games encompassed 12 sports, namely athletics, swimming, judo, sailing, diving, tennis, fencing, football, basketball, volleyball, water polo, and gymnastics, attracting 5,776 athletes from 114 countries. Finally, USA outshone all the other components with 30 gold, 19 silver and 15 bronze, followed by Russia (14 gold, 18 silver, and 12 bronze), and Cuba (12 gold, 3 silver, and 12 bronze). Japan ranked the fourth with 11 gold, 13 silver, and 17 bronze. The 174 Chinese athletes competed in all the sports except sailing, football and water polo, finishing the 5th with 9 gold, 6 silver, and 10 bronze.

The 21st Universiade

Beijing hosted the 21st Universiade from August 20 to September 1st, 2001, receiving 6,800 athletes, coaches and officials from 169 countries and regions.

It was China's first time to organize international multi-sport games, yet turned out to be the largest Universiade by then in terms of numbers of participating countries, regions and athletes. This Universiade awarded 171 gold in 168 events of 12 sports. Twenty-one Universiade records were rewritten by 20 people and 3 teams, in swimming and athletics, 1 Universiade record was set. China occupied the top place on the medal tally with 54 gold, 25 silver and 24 bronze medals. It also pocketed all the gold medals in diving and table tennis, showing invincible domination in the two sports.

The 22nd Universiade

The 22nd Universiade was opened in Daegu, South Korea, on the evening of August 21, 2003. Over 6,600 athletes, coaches and officials from 174 countries appeared at the games, a record high in the number of participating countries and regions. In the competition of 13 sports, 26 athletes (teams) broke 21 Universiade records. China's Wu Minxia, together with other 4 athletes, bagged four gold medals each. American archerists broke one world record and equaled another.

China again topped the gold medal tally with 41 gold, 27 silver, and 13 bronze medals in 12 sports. Russia (26 gold, 22 silver, and 34 bronze) and Korea (26 gold, 11 silver, and 15 bronze) tied the second, followed by Ukraine (23 gold, 15 silver, and 17 bronze), and Japan (13 gold, 11 silver, and 20 bronze). Chinese Taipei ranked the 11th with 3 gold, 3 silver, and 5 bronze medals, the best result in history.

The 23rd Universiade

From August 11 to 21, 2005, the 23rd Universiade was celebrated in İzmir, the second largest port in Turkey. Over 110 countries and regions joined the games, competing in 196 events of 15 sports, including athletics, swimming, football, and basketball, etc. Altogether 201 Chinese participated in 148 events, in accordance with the development of each sport among Chinese university students. Finally, it found the second place on the gold medal tally with 21 gold, 16 silver, and 12 bronze medals.

Chinese Athletes at the Universiade

China's first gold at the Universiade: on September 8, 1979, at the 10th Universiade in Mexico City, Mexico, 17-year-old Chen Xiaoxia toppled USSR'S Kalinina, the world champion in 1978, to seize a gold in women's platform diving with 444.7 points.

China's first champion in big balls: at the 11th games in 1981, Chinese women's volleyball team smashed Cuba in the final, 15:13, 15:8, and 15:9.

China's first gold in athletics: also in Bucharest, Romania, 1981, Zou Zhenxian's 17.32m in men's triple jump rewrote two records: the Asia record set by himself, and the Universiade record by former USSR's Viktor Sanyeyev, in 1970, Turin, Italy.

China's first champion in women's football: on July 17, 1993, China made history by beating world champion USA in women's football final, 2:1, at the 17th Universiade in Hamilton, Canada.

On February 24, 1985, at the 12th Winter Universiade, Zhang Shubing snatched China's first gold in figure skating at the games, with his perfect 2 Lutz + 2 Toeloop, and 5 kinds of 3Sth.

Asian Games

The Asian Games, also called the Asiad, is a multi-sport event held every four years among athletes from all over Asia. Since 1951 when the Games was first held, Asia has made headway in sports, and finally emerged as a strong force in international arena. China also made remarkable contribution to this development trend.

In September, 1973, Olympic Council of Asia (OCA) officially accepted All-China Sports Federation as its member. Since its debut in 1974, China has participated in the 7th to 13th Asiad, and successfully held the 11th Asiad in Beijing, 1990.

China has secured a place in the top three on the medal tally since the first time it participated in Asian Games. It topped the medal standing from 1878 Asiad, Bangkok. Since the 1982 Games in New Delhi, the Asian Games are dominated by the People's Republic of China. The 16th Games will be held in Guangzhou, China in 2010.

The 1st Asian Games

The 1st Asian Games was held in New Delhi, India, in 1951, with 489 participants from 11 countries, including Japan, India, Iran, and Singapore, etc. Competitions started in six sports, namely athletics, swimming, football, cycling, basketball, and weightlifting, etc. Korea did not show up due to the Korean War, while Japan was in with its accession into UN. All-China Sports Federation was invited to send observers to the Games, led by Wu Xueqian.

The 7th Asian Games

The 7th Asian Games were held from September 1 to 16, 1974 in Tehran, Iran. Altogether 2,363 athletes from 25 countries participated in the Asiad, including Japan, Iran, China, South Korea, North Korea, India, Thailand, Indonesia, Mongolia, Pakistan, Sri Lanka, Singapore, and the Philippines, etc. Fencing, gymnastics and women's basketball were added to the existing disciplines: athletics, swimming, shooting, cycling, weightlifting, wrestling, boxing, table tennis, men's basketball, volleyball, football, tennis, badminton, and field hockey. One world record was broken, and 55 Asian Games records rewritten.

The 8th Asian Games

The 8th Asian Games opened on December 9, 1978, attracting 2,879 athletes from 25 countries and regions (Japan, China, Korea, DPRK, Thailand, Indonesia, Pakistan, the Philippines, Singapore, Malaysia, Mongolia, Lebanon, and Saudi Arabia, etc.). The Games encompassed athletics, swimming, football, tennis, basketball, volleyball, table tennis, cycling, boxing, wrestling, weightlifting, fencing, shooting, gymnastics, field hockey, badminton, archery, bowling, sailing and dinghy, etc. Altogether 66 Asiad records were bettered.

The 9th Asian Games

The 9th Asiad was held on November 19, 1982, in its birth place, New Delhi, India. The competing countries/NOCs grew to 33 (China, Japan, Korea, DPRK, India, Indonesia, Iran, Pakistan, Mongolia, and the Philippines, etc.), and participants to 3,345. Competitions set off in athletics, swimming, football, tennis, basketball, volleyball, cycling, boxing, wrestling, weightlifting, fencing, shooting, gymnastics, hockey, badminton, archery, bowling, sailing, and dinghy. A world record of archery was tied and best record of that year in field and track was created.

The Olympic Council of Asia (OCA) was founded that year and took the overall responsibility of the Asiad.

The 10th Asian Games

Seoul, the capital of South Korea, hosted the 10th Asiad. The 10th Asiad, with the participation of 3,345 athletes from 27 countries and regions, including China, Korea, Japan, Iran, India, the Philippines, Thailand, Pakistan, Indonesia, Hong Kong of China, Qatar, Lebanon, Bahrein Islands, Malaysia and Jordan, etc. The events were composed of athletics, swimming, archery, badminton, basketball, bowling, boxing, cycling, equestrian, fencing, football, golf, gymnastics, handball, hockey, judo, sailing and dinghy, shooting, table tennis, taekwondo, tennis, volleyball, weightlifting, wrestling and wushu. More than 200 athletes bettered the Asiad records. In archery in particular, two world records were broken, and another two equaled.

The 11th Asian Games

The 11th Asian Games was held from September 22 to October 7, 1990 in Beijing, China. A total number of 4,684 athletes, coming from from 37 countries and regions (China, Korea, Japan, DPRK, Iran, Pakistan, Indonesia, Qatar, Thailand, Malaysia, India, Mongolia, the Philippines, Saudi Arabia, Oman, and Chinese Taipei, etc.), competing in athletics, swimming, archery, badminton, basketball, boxing, canoe/kayak, Kabaddi, cycling, fencing, football, golf, gymnastics, handball, hockey, judo, sailing and dinghy, sepak takraw, shooting, soft tennis, table tennis, tennis, volleyball, weightlifting, wrestling, wushu and boat race. Four world records and 42 Asian records were broken and 98 Asiad records rewritten.

China's Achievements at the Asian Games

Year	Games	Place	Medal	Gold	Ranking
1974	7th	Teheran	106	33	3
1978	8th	Bangkok	151	51	2
1982	9th	New Delhi	153	61	1
1986	10th	Seoul	222	94	1
1990	11th	Beijing	341	183	1
1994	12th	Hiroshima	289	125	1
1998	13th	Bangkok	274	129	1
2002	14th	Busan	308	150	1
2006	15th	Doha	316	165	1

The 12th Asian Games

The 1994 Asian Games was held from October 2 to 16, 1994 in Hiroshima, Japan. There were about 7,000 athletes from 42 countries and regions, including China, Japan, Korea, Kazakhstan, Uzbekistan, Iran, Chinese Taipei, India, Malaysia, Qatar, Indonesia, Saudi Arabia, the Philippines, and Kuwait, etc. Altogether 25 world records were set at the Games. Events at the Games were athletics, swimming, archery, badminton, baseball, basketball, bowling, boxing, canoe/kayak, cycling, equestrian, fencing, football, golf, gymnastic, handball, hockey, judo, Kabaddi, Karate, modern pentathlon, sailing and dinghy, sepak takraw, shooting, soft tennis, softball, table tennis, Taekwondo, tennis, volleyball, weightlifting, wrestling, wushu and boat race.

The 13th Asian Games

The 13th Asian Games were held from December 6 to 20, 1998 in Bangkok, Thailand. 9,699 athletes from 41 countries and regions participated, which were China, Korea, Japan, Thailand, Kazakstan, Chinese Taipei, Iran, DPRK, India, Uzbekistan, Indonesia, Malaysia, Hong Kong SAR, Kuwait, Sri Lanka, Pakistan, Singapore, Qatar, Mongolia, etc. Events at the Games included athletics, archery, badminton, baseball, basketball, billiards, bowling, boxing, canoe/kayak, cycling, equestrian, fencing, football, golf, gymnastic, handball, hockey, judo, Kabaddi, Karate, sailing and dinghy, sepak takraw, shooting, soft tennis, softball, swimming, table tennis, Taekwondo, tennis, volleyball, weightlifting, wrestling, Wushu, and boat race.

The 14th Asian Games

The 14th Asian Games were held in Pusan, South Korea from September 29 to October 14, 2002. A total number of 6,714 athletes competed, coming from 44 countries and regions which were Nepal, Korea, East Timor,

On October 5, 2002, in the team final of the table tennis event at the 14th Asian Games held in Pusan, the Chinese table tennis team beat South Korean team 3:0 and claimed the title. In the picture is Wang Liqin in the competition.

Laos, Lebanon, Macao, Malaysia, Maldives, Mongolia, Myanmar, Bahrain, Bangladesh, Vietnam, Bhutan, Brunei, Saudi Arabia, Sri Lanka, Syria, Singapore, United Arab Emirates, Afghanistan, Yemen, Oman, Jordan, Uzbekistan, Iran, India, Indonesia , Japan, DPRK, China, Chinese Taipei, Kazakhstan, Qatar, Cambodia, Kuwait, Kyrgyzstan, Tajikistan, Thailand, Turkmenistan, Pakistan, Palestine, Philippines, and Hong Kong SAR.

Events at the Games: athletics, aquatics, archery, badminton, baseball, basketball, billiards, body building, bowling, boxing, canoe/kayak, cycling, equestrian, fencing, football, golf, gymnastic, handball, hockey, judo, Kabaddi, Karate, modern pentathlon, boat race, rugby, sailing and dinghy, sepak takraw, shooting, soft tennis, softball, squash, table tennis, Taekwondo, tennis, volleyball, weightlifting, wrestling, and Wushu.

The 15th Asian Games

The 15th Asian Games was held in Doha, Qatar from December 1 to 15, 2006. Doha was the first city in the gulf region and only the second in West Asia after Tehran in 1974 to host the Games. There were 46 disciplines from 39 events scheduled to be contested.

Events at the Games: athletics, aquatics, archery, badminton, baseball, basketball, billiards, body building, bowling, boxing, canoe/kayak, cycling, equestrian, fencing, field hockey, football, golf, gymnastic, handball, judo, Kabaddi, Karate, rowing, rugby, sailing, sepak takraw, shooting, soft tennis, softball, squash, table tennis, Taekwondo, tennis, volleyball, weightlifting, wrestling, Wushu, chess, and triathlon. The last two were newly added events.

Doha received more athletes than any of the previous Asiads, altogether 11,000 from 45 countries and regions. China swept 165 gold, 39 percent of the total. The most valued gold medal came from women's weightlifting: 27-year-old Chen Yanqing from Suzhou defied all opponents in 58kg category, breaking three world records in snatch, jerk, and total. Besides, Mu Shuangshuang crowned women's +75kg weightlifting champion, creating a new world record in snatch.

Medals Won in the 7th-15th Asian Games

Games	Ranking	Country	Gold	Silver	Bronze
7th	1	Japan	75	49	53
	2	Iran	36	28	17
	3	China	33	45	28
8th	1	Japan	70	59	49
	2	China	51	55	45
	3	South Korea	18	20	31
9th	1	China	61	51	41
	2	Japan	57	52	44
	3	South Korea	28	28	37
10th	1	China	94	82	46
	2	South Korea	93	55	76
	3	Japan	58	76	77
11th	1	China	183	107	51
	2	South Korea	54	54	73
	3	Japan	38	60	76
12th	1	China	125	93	58
	2	Japan	64	75	79
	3	South Korea	63	56	64
13th	1	China	129	78	67
	2	South Korea	65	46	53
	3	Japan	52	61	68
14th	1	China	150	84	74
	2	South Korea	96	80	84
	3	Japan	44	73	72
15th	1	China	165	88	63
	2	South Korea	58	53	82
	3	Japan	50	71	77

On January 27, 2007, the Chinese men's ice hockey team (in white) beat China's Macao team 26:0 at the 6th Asian Winter Games held in Changchun.

Asian Winter Games

Asian Winter Games was a multi-sport event for Asia, initiated by the OCA. There have been five Games since 1986.

The 1st Asian Winter Games

Sapporo, Japan was given the privilege of hosting the 1st Winter Asian Games on March 1 to 8, 1986. Up to 300 athletes from 7 countries and regions (China, DPRK, Hong Kong SAR, India, Mongolia, Korea, and Japan) participated in 5 sports, namely skating, skiing, winter biathlon, curling, and ice hockey.

The 2nd Asian Winter Games

The 2nd Asian Winter Games were held from March 9 to 14, 1990 in Sapporo, Japan. It saw nearly 1,000 athletes from 10 countries and regions participating in the games, much more than the previous one. Events from only five sports were held, including skating, skiing, biathlon, curling, and ice hockey. Japan topped the medal tally with 18 gold, 16 silver and 13 bronze medals, followed by China's 9 gold, 9 silver, and 8 bronze. South Korea took home 6 gold, 7 silver, and 8 bronze medals, while DPRK, 1 silver, 4 bronze, and Mongolia, 4 bronze.

The 3rd Asian Winter Games

The 3rd Asian Winter Games were held from February 4 to 11, 1996 in Harbin, China. It was the first time for China to host multi-sport winter event on such a scale. There were 17 countries and regions participating in the Games. Five sports were held, namely skating, skiing, biathlon, curling, and ice hockey. China ranked first on both gold medal and total medal tally, with 15 gold, 7 silver, and 15 bronze medals. Kazakhstan came to the second, winning 14 gold, 9 silver and 8 bronze. The 3rd place went to Japan, 8 gold, 14 silver medals, and 10 bronze. Korea ranked 4th with 8 gold, 10 silver, and 8 bronze medals, followed by Uzbekistan's 1 silver and 1 bronze.

The 4th Asian Winter Games

The 4th Asian Winter Games were held from January 30 to February 6, 1999 in the mountainous northern province of Kangwon, South Korea. Altogether 798 athletes from 21 countries and regions competed in five sports, namely skating, skiing, biathlon, curling, and ice hockey. China outshone all other teams with 15 gold, 10 silver and 11 bronze medals. Korea, as the host country, ranked second with 11 gold and 10 silver medals, followed by Kazakhstan. The former winter sporting power Japan dropped to the fourth place.

The 5th Asian Winter Games

The 5th Asian Winter Games took place from February 1 to 8, 2003 in Aomori Prefecture, Japan. About 1,200 people (1,043 athletes) from 29 countries and regions took part in the event. This Winter Asiad offered 51 events in 5 sports, namely skating, skiing, biathlon, curling, and ice hockey. Japan, the host country, grabbed 24 gold, 23 silver and 20 bronze to occupy the first place on the medal tally, followed by Korea's 10 gold, 8 silver, and 10 bronze. China took home 9 gold, 11 silver and 13 bronze, and Kazakhstan, 7 gold, 7 silver and 6 bronze medals.

East Asian Games

The idea of having East Asian Games was initiated at the 1st council meeting of national Olympic committees in the region on September 15th, 1991, in order to enhance sports and cultural communication in East Asia. In November the same year, it was approved as a quadrennial event. Since the 1st Games held in Shanghai in 1993, China has occupied the 1st place on both gold medal and total medal tally at all the four Games thus convened.

Medals Won in the 1st-4th East Asian Games

Games	Ranking	Country	Gold	Silver	Bronze	Total
1st	1	China	105	74	34	213
	2	Japan	25	37	55	117
	3	South Korea	23	28	40	91
	4	North Korea	10	20	24	54
	5	Chinese Taipei	6	5	19	30
	6	Hong Kong SAR	1	2	8	11
	7	Mongolia	0	1	16	17
	8	Macao SAR	0	0	1	1
	Total		170	167	197	534
2nd	1	China	62	59	64	185
	2	Japan	47	53	53	153
	3	South Korea	45	38	51	134
	4	Kazakstan	24	12	22	58
	5	Chinese Taipei	8	22	19	49
	6	Mongolia	3	2	19	24
	7	Hong Kong SAR	1	2	2	5
	8	Guam	0	0	1	1
	9	Macao SAR	0	0	1	1
	Total		190	188	232	610
3rd	1	China	85	48	58	191
	2	Japan	61	65	65	191
	3	South Korea	34	46	32	112
	4	Kazakstan	13	18	26	57
	5	Chinese Taipei	6	16	31	53
	6	Hong Kong SAR	3	1	3	7
	7	Mongolia	1	2	7	10
	8	Macao SAR	1	0	3	4
	9	Guam	0	0	1	1
	Total		204	196	226	626
4th	1	China	127	63	33	223
	2	Japan	46	56	77	179
	3	South Korea	32	48	65	145
	4	Chinese Taipei	12	34	26	72
	5	Macao SAR	11	16	17	44
	6	North Korea	6	10	20	36
	7	Hong Kong SAR	2	2	9	13
	8	Mongolia	1	1	6	8
	9	Guam	0	0	1	1
	Total		237	230	254	721

China's Records at the FESPIC Games

Games	Time	Venue	Number of Athletes	Medals			Records			Ranking
				Gold	Silver	Bronze	Person	Event	Time	
1	June 1-3, 1975	Oita, Japan	-	-	-	-	-	-	-	-
2	November 20-26, 1979	Parramatta, Australia	-	-	-	-	-	-	-	-
3	October 31-November 7, 1982	Sha Tin, Hong Kong SAR	15	6	12	7	-	-	-	-
4	August 31-September 7, 1986	Solo, Indonesia	23	64	21	3	-	-	-	1
5	September 15-20, 1989	Kobe, Japan	57	99	32	8	14	14	14	1
6	September 4-10, 1994	Beijing, China	422	298	238	148	27	36	52	1
7	January 7-17, 1999	Bangkok, Thailand	195	205	90	45	13	17	17	1
8	October 26-November 1, 2002	Pusan, South Korea	206	191	90	50	17	16	16	1
	Total		918	863	483	261	71	83	99	

The 1st East Asian Games

The 1st East Asian Games: May 9-18, 1993. Shanghai, China.

12 Sports: athletics, swimming, soccer, basketball, badminton, gymnastics, weightlifting, judo, boating, boxing, bowling, and martial arts.

Demonstration sport: soft tennis.

Participating countries and regions: China, Japan, Korea, DPRK, Chinese Taipei, Hong Kong SAR, Mongolia, and Macao

The 2nd East Asian Games

The 2nd East Asian Games: May 10-19, 1997. Pusan, Korea.

13 Sports: athletics, aquatic sports, basketball, badminton, boxing, soccer, gymnastics, judo, soft tennis, taekwondo, weightlifting, wrestling, and martial arts.

Participating countries/regions: China, Japan, Korea, Kazakhstan, Chinese Taipei, Hong Kong SAR, Mongolia, Guam, and Macao

The 3rd East Asian Games

The 3rd East Asian Games: May 19-27, 2001. Osaka, Japan.

15 Sports: athletics, aquatic sports, basketball, bowling, boxing, football, gymnastics, handball, judo, soft tennis, taekwondo, volleyball, weightlifting, wrestling, and wushu, etc.

Demonstration sports: hockey and boat race.

Participating countries/regions: China, Japan, Korea, Kazakhstan, Chinese Taipei, Hong Kong SAR, Mongolia, Guam, Macao, and Australia (unofficial member)

The 4th East Asian Games

Macao hosted the 4th East Asian Games, which started on October 29, 2005. It was the first time for the region to have such an international multi-sport event. During the 9 days, nearly 2,000 athletes (from China, Guam, Hong Kong SAR, Japan, Korea, Macao, Mongolia, DPRK, and Chinese Taipei) competed in 234 events of 17 sports. One world record in women's weightlifting was broken, 6 Asian records in swimming were bettered 8 times, and 12 Games records in athletics were rewritten 17 times. China, Japan and Korea once again occupied the top three places on the medal tally, with 127, 46, and 32 gold medals respectively.

As the host, Macao ranked fifth on the gold medal standing with 11 gold, 16 silver and 17 bronze, its best records at the East Asian Games.

The 5th Games will be held in Hong Kong SAR in 2009.

On November 5, 2005, the twin sisters Jiang Wenwen and Jiang Tingting won the silver gold in the final of the duet free routine of the women's synchronized swimming at the East Asian Games.

World Championships and Games for the Disabled

World Championships and Games for the Disabled was held in Assen, Netherlands, from July 14 to 26, 1990. about 2,000 athletes from 49 countries and regions participated in the Games. Nine Chinese sportspeople competed in athletics and swimming. Zhao Xueen (high jump and long jump), Wu Hongping (discus throw), Zhao Jihong (long jump) strove for four gold. China also bagged four silver and four bronze medals.

Far East and South Pacific Games for the Disabled (FESPIC Games)

A sitting volleyball match between the Chinese team and South Korean Team at the Seventh Far East and South Pacific Games for the Disabled in January 1990

The quadrennial FESPIC Games is administered by the Fareast and South Pacific Games Federation for the Disabled. It is the largest international multi-sport event for the disabled only after the Paralympics. From the first one held in Japan in June 1975, there have been 9 Games. China acceded to the FESPIC in 1983, and sent delegation to the Games starting from the third one, and ranked first on the gold medal tally for six times in a roll.

From September 4 to 10, 1994, the 6th FESPIC Games was held in Beijing. In all, 2,097 athletes from 40 some countries and regions competed in 14 sports, namely athletics, swimming, table tennis, badminton, wheelchair basketball, wheelchair tennis, sitting volleyball, boccia, gateball, fencing, judo, weightlifting, shooting, and archery. China's 422 athletes altogether pocketed 298 gold medals.

Asia-Africa Table Tennis Friendship Invitational

The Asia-Africa Table Tennis Friendship Invitational is an inter-continental tournament, initiated by table tennis associations of China, DPRK, Egypt, Japan, Mauritius, and Nepal, etc. In November 1971, 51 Asian and African countries and regions came to Beijing for the event. The tournament included 10 events, such as team, singles, doubles, mixed doubles, youth divisions, and veteran divisions. China titled in women's team, women's singles, and men's doubles. At the high-level meeting of the founding nations later, the tournament was expanded into the Asian-African-Latin American Table-Tennis Friendship Invitational.

World Table Tennis Championships

The World Table Tennis Championships are held under the authority of International Table Tennis Federation (ITTF). The first one was held in London, UK in 1926, consisting of a mixed doubles competition and a single, a doubles and a team competition for both men and women. Since the 24th Championships in Stockholm, Sweden, 1957, the event has been held biannually. China has competed in every game since the 20th in 1953. At the 25th Championships in 1959, Rong Guotuan was crowned in men's singles as the first ever Chinese world champion of table tennis.

Altogether 313 gold medals had been awarded during the 46 championships from 1926 to 2001, among which 89.5 champions were under the names of the Chinese. As a traditional power in table tennis, China won both the men's and women's team event for 10 times, at 28th, 33rd, 34th, 36th, 37th, 39th, 43rd, 44th and 46th Championships. Most spectacularly, it swept all the seven gold at the 36th, 43rd and 46th Championships. By the 47th one in 2003, China had won 13 gold in men's team event, 12 in men's singles, 11 in men's doubles, 14 in women's team event, 15 in women's singles, 15 in women's doubles (one in collaboration with a player from DPRK), and 14 in mixed doubles.

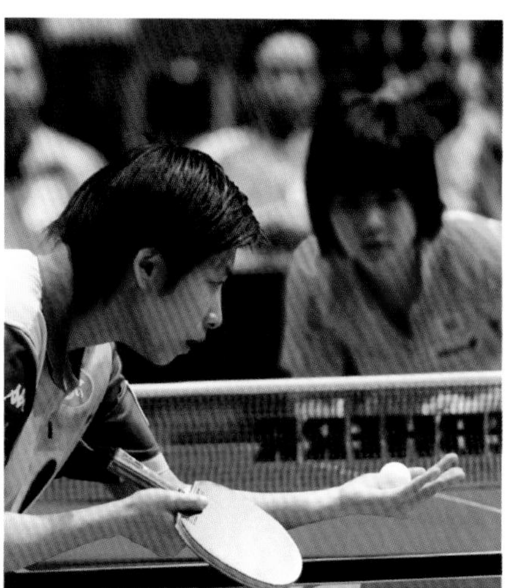
On April 29, 2006, the Hong Kong, China beat Japan 3:2 and marched into the final in the women's team semifinal at the 48th World Table Tennis Championship. In the picture, Lin Ling is competing with Ai Fukuhara.

▲ The 1st China International Table Tennis Open Championships

The Table Tennis Grand Prix, composed of a series of international open championships, is one of the four major international events of table tennis, together with World Championships, World Cup, and Olympic table tennis competition starting from the 24th Games.

The 1st China International Table Tennis Open Championship was held in Guangzhou from June 11 to 14, 1988. China pocketed six gold but in women's doubles. Jiang Jialiang, Chen Longcan, Teng Yi, and Wei Jingguang titled in men's team event, while Dai Lili, He Zhili, Jiao Zhimin and Li Huifen triumphed in women's team competition. Xu Zengcai, a long-time training partner, surprised the world by winning men's singles, whereas He Zhili defied all opponents in women's singles. The young pair, Lin Zhigang and Liu Wei titled in mixed doubles.

Table Tennis World Cup

Table Tennis World Cup is co-organized by the ITTF and International Management Group (IMG). This annual tournament started in 1980. All the participants are top seeds on the ITTF list, or champions of the continent or the hosting country. Each team is allowed to send no more than two players. By now, the Table Tennis World Cup only has competitions in men's singles.

The first tournament was held in Hong Kong SAR, from August 29 to 31, 1980. Guo Yuehua and Li Zhenshi panned out as the champion and runner-up among all the 16 contestants. Chinese players altogether had titled 11 times out of all the 21 tournaments held by the year 2000.

At the 2006 Paris Table Tennis World Cup, Chinese players occupied the top three places. No.3 seed Ma Lin beat his teammate Wang Hao with 4:3, to win his fourth title of the tournament.

Gymnastics World Cup

Gymnastics World Cup, first held in 1975, is organized by the International Gymnastics Federation (FIG). After the second World Cup in 1977, it became an annual event, but later turned into a quadrennial game in 1982. Then since 1998, the World Cup has been reformed into a series of matches. At the 1982 games in Zagreb, in former Yugoslavia, Li Ning from China bagged six gold medals in individual all-around, floor exercise, pommel horse, rings, vault, and horizontal bar.

The 7th Gymnastics World Cup was held in Beijing in August, 1986, China's first time to organise such international gymnastics tournament. This sporting pageant was highly appreciated by spectators from home and abroad. After three days of fierce competition among 36 athletes from 13 countries, USSR ranked at the top of the medal tally with 11 gold, followed by China's 4 gold, and Democratic Germany's 1 gold.

Veteran Li Ning once again demonstrated his outstanding skills by claiming three gold in men's all-around, floor exercise, and pommel horse, added by bronze medal in rings. In particular, he was the only man athlete to get a 10 in pommel horse. Besides, Xu Zhiqiang from China titled in parallel bars and got the third place in pommel horse.

Volleyball World Cup

The World Cup is a quadrennial volleyball competition for both men and women, organized by the International Volleyball Federation (IVF). It was born in 1965 (men) in Warsaw, Poland, and 1973 (women) in USSR. Since 1991, the game has been held one year prior to the Olympics as an international qualification event, allowing top three teams into the Olympic Games. Chinese women's volleyball team became the champion for the first time at the 3rd Women's World Cup in 1981, and defended the title four years later.

The 11th World Women's Volleyball Championship

The World Women's Volleyball Championship is another event coordinated by the IVF. Beijing saw the games from August 22 to September 1 in 1990. The USSR, China, and USA panned out from all the 16 teams to occupy the top three places.

World Military Pentathlon Championships (WMPC)

The International Military Sports Council (CISM) initiated the Championships in 1950. China for the first time joined in the event at the 31st WMPC in Denmark in 1983. in 1999, Beijing hosted the 46th Championships. China, as the host country, not only wrapped five gold in men's and women's team event, men's and women's individual all-around, and women's obstacle relay, but also set four world records in team events' total scores, women's individual total, and women's 500m obstacle run. Two years later at the 48th WMPC, China again swept gold in team and individual all-around competitions, added by two gold medals in men's 8,000m and women's 4,000 cross-country. Thus China became the only one to title six consecutive times in a roll in men's team event at the WMPC.

The 1st FIFA World Championships of Women's Football

Guangzhou hosted the first FIFA World Championships of Women's Football, from November 16 to 30, 1991. The 12 teams from all continents were first divided into 3 groups, and the qualified 8 teams in the preliminaries went into the second round. China, Norway, Denmark and New Zealand were put in Group A, USA, Sweden, Brazil and Japan, Group B, and Germany, Italy, Nigeria and Chinese Taipei, Group C. China failed to reach the semi-final after a 0:1 defeat by Sweden, and ranked 5th place. USA claimed championship by beating Norway in the final, 2:1.

ISF World Gymnasiade

ISF World Gymnasiade is sponsored by International Schoolsport Federation (ISF), solely for students under 17 years old. The Gymnasiade was initiated in 1974 as a biannual event, but has been held every four years since 1990. Up till now there have been 12 Gymnasiades. The 11th ISF World Gymnasiade was held in Shanghai, China from October 13 to 19, 1998. Over 1,300 young people from 28 countries and regions competed in the games. The top three on the gold medal standing went to China (41 gold), Italy (13 gold) and France (10 gold). China's gymnast Xing Aowei took six gold medals, and thus became the king at this Gymnasiade.

Beijing International Marathon

The Beijing International Marathon (BIM) is organized by the Chinese Athletics Association (CAA). Since it was first held in 1981 and annually after that, BIM has become a very famous and traditional international race. Recorded officially by the Association of International Marathons and Road Races, the BIM is the highest-level marathon in China.

The Beijing International Marathon began at the Tian'anmen (Gate of Heavenly Peace) on October 15, 2006. In the picture, the players passed the Tian'anmen.

On February 8th, 1982, the International Association of Athletics Federations (IAAF) sanctioned and approved the BIM as one of the top marathons in the world. The course stretched 42.195km from Tian'anmen Square all the way to the Olympic Centre. Champions of the men's group and women's groups can get US$20,000 and US$15,000 respectively.

The 1st BIM was held on September 17, 1981 at Tian'anmen Square. Altogether 75 runners from 12 countries (Australia, Canada, Finland, Italy, Japan, Kenyan, Norway, DPRK, Sweden, Tanzania, USA, and China) set out, and 62 of them finished the course.

Women's event was included at the 9th BIM in 1989, and later half marathon and 5kg marathon were added to the event in 1998. The best record for men is 2h'07m'35s, and 2h'19m'38s for women.

At the 10th BIM in 2006, Kenya's James Kwambi Kipsang won the men's event, 2h'10m'36s. China's Sun Weiwei stayed in the leading pack throughout the grueling race to title in the women's event with 2h'34m'41s.

Beijing International Wushu Invitational

Beijing International Wushu Invitational Tournament is sponsored by Chinese Wushu Association, and hosted by Beijing Wushu Institute. Since it began in 1994, the Beijing International Wushu Invitational Tournament has become a pageant for wushu practitioners to build friendships and exchange tricks of the trade. And there had been six of them by 2005. The 6th tournament, opened on August 21, 2005, attracted over 400 Wushu practitioners from 49 teams, a record high in history. They had been selected from 20 some countries and regions in Europe, Americas, Africa and Asia. All the contestants were divided into five age groups, competing in 50 events, including set, freestyle and traditional forms; bare-handed and weapon sparring, shadowboxing, sword forms, and collective performances, etc.

Sports Events

Sports Events

Since the founding of the People's Republic of China in 1949, China has worked hard to develop its sports programs on a large scale, including 29 official Olympic events. The 50 some sports associations thus established have laid a solid foundation for the improvement of athletic capabilities. As early as 1954, all the swimming records set before 1949 had been rewritten, so had been most records in athletics. At the National Games, Chinese athletes broke world records over 30 times in athletics, swimming, shooting, weightlifting, archery, parachuting, and aero modeling, etc., and bettered national records over 2,000 times.

On December 7, 2006, Taibei, China beat Japan 8:7 and won the gold medal in the baseball round robin of the 15th Doha Asian Games.

Baseball

Baseball had a late start in China, and is not yet well-known to most Chinese.

It was first included as a competition event at the 1st National Games in 1959. China began international exchange in baseball after Aichi Gakuin University (Japan) team came for a visit in September, 1975. Four years later, The Chinese Baseball Association was founded, followed by the establishment of provincial and municipal branch associations.

At present, there are several baseball teams of universities, sports institutes, and enterprises, in addition to some seven or eight provincial and municipal teams. Annual national competitions are held, but they lag behind in terms of athletic skills. China's national baseball teams competed in Asian Championships for several times, ranking 4th or 5th place. In 1990 China hosted baseball performance event at the 11th Asian Games, and one year later, the Asian Baseball Championships.

Taiwan of China has become a power in baseball especially since the 1970s. Young players from Taiwan have achieved a streak of enviable results in international tournaments. Starting from the 1980s, their adult team has also emerged as one of the top five teams, ranking 3rd at 23rd Olympics in 1984, and 2nd at 16th Asia Baseball Championship in 1990.

Baseball for the Youth

In recent years, the Chinese Baseball Association has been promoting the sport extensively in primary schools, high schools, and universities. To spot and groom young talents on campus, the CBA streamlined a system with special baseball schools at all levels from primary schools to universities. Besides, the University Baseball League is gaining ground, attracting more than 50 universities.

The 1980s saw rapid development of baseball as a sport in China. At the 3rd World U12 Soft Baseball Championship in 1985, China managed to become the runner-up, and titled four times in 1986, 1989, 1993 and 1999. Besides, China's youth baseball team took the third prize at the 1st AA World Baseball Championship in 1989, sponsored by the IBF. And it was the runner-up at the 18th World Youth Soft Baseball Championship in Japan, 2000.

Professionalization of Baseball in China

Baseball touched home in China in September 2002, when the Chinese Baseball Association (CBA) signed a six-year contract extending to 2008 Olympics, with Dynasty Sports Marketing LTD. The contract covers the Chinese Baseball League, national team, Youth League, University League, and a selection plan of young baseball players, called Swing for the Wall.

In May, 2002, in collaboration with Positive baseball Limited (PBL), the Chinese Baseball Association established four teams, namely Beijing, Tianjin, Shanghai, and Guangdong. In March, 2003, Tom Mccarthy was appointed vice president of CBA, the first ever American official in Chinese sports associations. The Chinese Baseball League was launched in April, 2003. The 3-month professional baseball league is comprised of 48 regular games and 5 finals. The four seasons of league matches thus competed have popularized baseball, arousing international attention. Many well-known sports product manufacturers from USA, Japan and Korea embarked on Chinese market in the light of China's rapid development of the sport.

♦ Chinese Baseball Association (CBA)

The Chinese Baseball and Softball Association was founded in 1979. It acceded into the International Federation of Amateur Baseball in August, 1981, and the Asian Baseball Federation four years later. In 1986, CBA was separated as an individual association, headquartered in Beijing.

CBA holds national league and national tournament annually, together with other events like national championships, league grand finals, youth championships, university games, etc. By the end of 2000, there had been 12 teams affiliated to CBA, with over 300 professional players. In 2001, CBA promoted the professionalization of baseball in China, by setting up baseball clubs.

Address: No.5 Tiyuguan Lu, Beijing
Website: http://www.baseball.sport.org.cn

Sailing

Sailing as a sport was introduced to China in the 1950s, and became an official competition event in Qingdao, China's port city, in 1954. Since the 1st China Sailing Championship in 1980, annual national competitions have been held. Now China practices 470-two person dinghy, Finn-single dinghy, women's single-handed dinghy-Europe, Laser-men's one person dinghy, and U15 OP dinghy (unlimited for man or woman, singles, under age of 15). Annual sailing events in China include national tournament, national championship, national youth tournament, national OP tournament, and China Open.

In 1981, China for the first time sent a team to the East-Asia Sailing Competition in

Japan, and the 1st Asian Sailing Tournament in India. Three years later, China joined the ISF. At the 6th Asian Sailing Tournament in Hong Kong, 1991, China got 2 gold, 2 silver, and 1 bronze medals. And three years later, at the 1st World Sailing Tournament held in France, China's best result in all events was the 8th place. And at the 10th Asian OP Sailing Tournament in 1999, China titled in the team event.

Currently, there are sailing competition venues in Qinghuangdao, Qingdao, Haikou and Xiamen, etc. All the facilities for the 2008 Olympics have been approved of by the ISF, the first approval of all the 28 individual sports.

China Club Challenge Match

The China Club Challenge Match was initiated by the ISF, China Amateur Sailing Club, and Boat and Yacht Club. The annual league promotes sailing as a sport in China by creating opportunities to have official games between amateur clubs exclusively.

The China Club Challenge Match offers a good platform for amateur sailors. Participating teams go through dozens of competitions in seven rounds all the way up to the final. The champion club has its name engraved on the 5kg-sterling-silver cup, and automatically becomes the host of the next tournament.

♦ China Sailboat and Sailboard Sport Association

China Sailboat and Sailboard Sport Association was founded on May 11, 1981, derived from the Chinese Marine Sport Association (established in 1964). China is the founding member of the Asian Sailboard Federation, set up in December, 1983. And on November 24, 1983, the association was officially accepted by the ISF, as the only legal organization to represent China. As a nation-wide public sports organization, it is an independent legal entity, and is recognised by COC as a national sports association.

China Sailboat and Sailboard Sport Association organizes regular national sailing tournaments, championships, junior tournaments, OP sailing tournaments, China Open, Funboard tournaments, and championship for distinguished sailboard athletes.

Address: No.3 Longtan Zhonglu, Chongwen District, Beijing
Website: Http://www.sailboarding.sport.org.cn

Sailboard

Sailboard as a sport in China started in 1976. The State Sports Commission organized nation-wide sailboard training in 1980, and accepted the sport as an official competition event. In 1984, China took part in the sailboard competition at the 23rd Olympic Games, the debut at international events. At the 11th World Windsurfer Championships, Zhang Xiaodong panned out as China's first world sailboard champion by winning two gold medals. At the 10th Asiad in 1986, Qi Jianguo won the first gold in sailboard at the Games. Three years later, Li Ke and Zhang Xiaodong claimed gold and silver respectively in Lechner A-390 at the 12th World Women's Sailboard Championships. Li Lishan from Hong Kong SAR became China's first Olympic gold medalist in the sport. She titled at the 26th Atlantic Games in 1996.

Hosting International Sailboard Events

China's progress in sailboard and its sound natural waters have called the attention of the world. Therefore, the Chinese Sailing Association has been commissioned to host various inter-continental and international events. In 1996, the Asian-Pacific Sailboard Championship was held in Shantou, Guangdong Province. Over 180 participants of 19 countries and regions from six continents competed in four classes, namely IFC, ICC, ISC, and IMC. This was the first time to have four classes of events at one tournament in the world.

Promoting Sailboard as a Sport in China

In 1979, China produced its first dinghy, and the next year, the first national training session was completed. After that, China saw quick development of the sport, with the establishment of 20 provincial or municipal professional teams and dozens of grassroots training centres. At present, there are four major national events held annually, namely National Mistral Tournament, National Funboard Tournament, National Championship, and Junior National Championship. Sailboard is also a competition event at the quadrennial National Games, as well as at the Asiad, and Olympics.

Achievements at the Olympics of Chinese Sailboard Team

Year	Venue	Name	Event	Result
1992	Barcelona, Spain	Zhang Xiaodong	Women's sailboard	Runner-up
1996	Atlanta, USA	Li Lishan(Hong Kong SAR)	Women's sailboard	Champion
2000	Sydney, Australia	Zhou Yuanguo	Men's sailboard	Fifth
2004	Athens, Greece	Yin Jian	Women's sailboard	Runner-up

♦ The First Chinese World Champion of Sailboard

On December 29, 1984, at the 11th World Windsurfer Championships, 20-year-old Zhang Xiaodong defied all opponents to win the women's long-distance class, also called marathon on the sea. This was China's first time to title in major world sailboard tournaments.

Zhang Xiaodong (1964-) was selected after graduating from senior middle school to be trained for the national team in December 1981, and at 17, started to learn wind-surfing. One week after her victory in the long-distance event at the 11th World Windsurfer Championships, Zhang again claimed gold in Olympic course, and ranked the 3rd place in women's all-around, as well as the fourth place in women's obstacles.

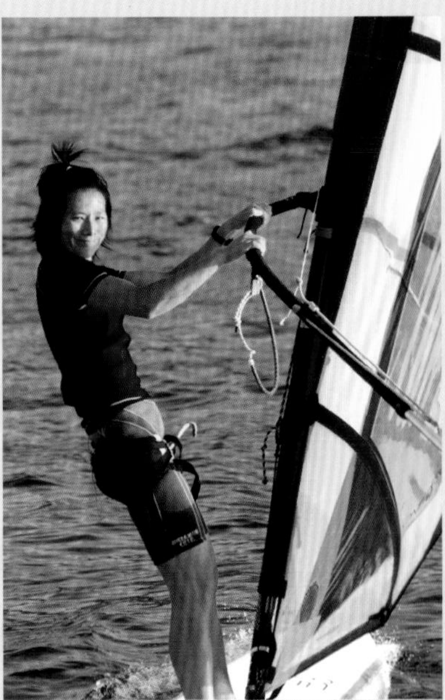

On December 29, 2003, the 2003 National Windsurfing Tournament and the 2004 Asian Windsurfing Tournament were held in the maritime space of the Longcheer Yacht Club of Daya Bay. Hong Kong player Li Lishan led the women's group.

♦ The First Chinese Olympic Champion in Sailboard

Li Lishan (1970-), born in Hong Kong SAR, is one of the best women sailors in Hong Kong. She was the runner-up in her 1983 debut in a regional competition, and strove to be the champion in 1988's Hong Kong Open. In 1989, she entered the Hong Kong Sports Academy to receive regular sailing training. One year later, she collected a silver in the 11th Asian Games held in Beijing. Then in 1993, she claimed the title in the World Sailing Championships. At the 1996 Atlanta Olympics, Li grasped the women's sailboard (Mistral) gold, becoming the first HK athlete to win a Olympic gold.

Fencing

Fencing originated in Europe, and has been included as an official competition ever since the first Olympic Games. In the late 1950s, the sport was introduced into China from the former Soviet Union. Starting from 1973, China has made much headway in this traditional European sport. At the 23rd Olympics in 1984, Luan Jujie toppled all the opponents and strove for a gold in women's foil. This was the first time for Asian fencers to title at the Olympics. At the 27th Games, Chinese men's foil team and women's epee team won a silver and a bronze medal respectively in the team events.

With such a solid foundation, China witnessed rapid development in fencing. It not only leads Asia in the sport, but has also increased its international influence. At the 15th Doha Asiad in December 2006, 7 gold in fencing out of the total 12 went to Chinese fencers. Chinese women's epee team and men's sabre team beat defending champion Korea in the finals, and women's sabre team also titled in the team event.

Encouraged by such achievements, fencing in China has been prospering. Currently, there are over 2,000 professional athletes in China, and some 1,000 amateur fencers. In May, 1974, China acceded into the International Fencing Federation (IFF).

World Wheelchair Fencing Championships

From September 30 to October 7, 2006, the quadrennial World Wheelchair Fencing Championship was held in Turin, Italy. Altogether 139 athletes from 17 countries and regions participated in the competition.

On October 2, 2006, Chinese disabled player Ye Ruyi won over the Italian player Pellegrini in the men's fencing final of the World Fencing Tournament held in Torino, Italy.

China sent nine fencers to the championships, pocketing 4 gold, 6 silver, and 3 bronze. Zhang Lei, Ye Ruyi, and Zhang Wenxin claimed three gold in men's foil A, men's sabre A, and women's foil A, respectively. Paralympics gold medalist Zhang Lei led Zhang Chong, Hu Daoliang and Ye Ruyi to title in men's foil team event. Hong Kong SAR also sent its team, which took home 4 gold in individual events, and 2 gold medals in team events, ranking on the top of the medal tally.

China competed in wheelchair fencing at the Far East and South Pacific Games for the Disabled (FESPIC Games) held in Beijing, in 1994. Then the sport was revived first in Shanghai in 2001, and then in Jiangsu the following year. China quickly caught up with other countries in the world in the event. In 2002, it participated in wheelchair fencing at 8th FESPIC Games; the next year, at the 6th National Games for the Disabled, wheelchair fencing was officially included as a competition event. In 2004, Zhang Lei, Zhang Chong and Hu Daoliang strove for a gold medal in the team event at Athens Paralympics. And by 2005 National Championship, six provinces and cities had been practicing the game, namely Shanghai, Jiangsu, Yunnan, Beijing, Shandong, and Guangzhou.

World Fencing Championships

The 2006 World Fencing Championship was held in Turin, Italy. The event took place from September 29 to October 7, 2006. China took part in both men's and women's individual and team events in foil, epee, and sabre. This was a young team, and most of the athletes were below 25 years old, while fencing relies much on experience. In men's individual epee, Wang Lei from China beat Portuguese Joaquim Videira, 6:5, making a good start for the Chinese team. On the women's side, after toppling world No.2 Hungary in the quarter final, China thrashed world No.1 France in the final of epee team event, 45:26, the first gold in this event at the Championships. Finally, China ranked third on the gold medal tally, with 2 gold and 1 bronze, a record high in all the tournaments thus competed. The two gold are most worth noting, marking two "firsts": one was China's first gold in men's event, and the other was China's first gold in team event.

♦ China's First Fencing Champion

Since fencing officially became a competition sport at the 1896 Olympics, it had been dominated by Europeans, until the 23rd Games in L.A., when Luan Jujie from China defied all Europeans to become the first Asian champion of the game.

Jujie Luan (1958-) was born in Nanjing, Jiangsu Province. As a child, she loved volleyball, badminton, and track and field, especially high jump, but later was persuaded to join the fencing team. Surprisingly, she turned out to be a national runner-up within 4 months of training, and then national champion three years later. At 29th World Youth Fencing Tournament, she strove for a silver medal despite arm injury. She was the first Asian medalist since the game was first held. And then she won champion in women's foil individual at the 8th Asiad, and runner-up at 36th World Fencing Championship in 1981. At the 6th International Women's Fencing Tournament held in Germany in 1983, Luan Jujie beat a strong field in the individual foil event to become the first Asian fencer to win an international competition. She was also the first ever Asian Olympic fencing champion breaking the monopoly of Olympic fencing champion by Europeans, when she took the women's individual foil title in Los Angeles in 1984. Two years later at the 10th Asiad, she led her teammates all the way to the women's foil team champion.

Dong Zhaozhi

Dong Zhaozhi (1973-), men's fencing athletes.

Dong Zhaozhi is known for his swiftness, determination and fierceness in attacks. He is one of the "three musketeers" in men's foil team, together with Wang Haibin and Ye Chong.

Achievements:

1994 Asian Games—1st foil individual; 2nd foil team

1995 Asian Championships—1st foil team; 2nd foil individual

1995 World Military Games—1st foil team

1996 World Team Cup—1st foil

1999 World Military Games—1st foil individual/team

1999 World Championships—2nd foil team
2000 Olympic Games—2nd foil team
2000 World Cup—3rd foil individual
2001 World University Games—1st foil individual
2004 World Cup Foil Grand Prix—1st foil individual

Wang Haibin

Wang Haibin (1973-), men's fencing athletes.

Wang Haibin is one of the "three musketeers" in men's foil team, together with Dong Zhaozhi and Ye Chong. He got the 9th place at the 1992 Barcelona Olympics. And in 1999, the three musketeers made a breakthrough in China's men's foil by winning the second place in the team event at the World Championships. At 2000 Olympic in Sydney, he again narrowly missed the champion in foil team. Two years later at Pusan Asian Games, Wang snatched the title of the men's individual foil, which was previously tailored for Korea's Sydney Olympic gold medalist Kim Sang-hun. Trailing Kim Sang-hun 8-11 with two minutes to go, Wang was awarded a penalty point and scored six kills to win over the SouthKorean 15-11. Later, he also helped China to win a gold in men's foil team event.

Wang Lei

Wang Lei (1981-), men's fencing athletes.

Wang Lei began his fencing career at Shanghai Jing'an District Sports School. Then he was sent to Shanghai Institute of Sports Technique in February 1994, and had been trained there until he was selected into the national fencing team in 1998.

Achievements:

2000 World Cup (France)—3rd epee individual
2001 World Junior Championships—2nd epee individual
2001 National Games—1st epee team; 3rd epee individual
2002 Asian Games—2nd epee individual
2004 World Cup (Spain)—7th epee individual
2004 Olympic Games—2nd epee individual

Wu Hanxiong

Wu Hanxiong (1981-), men's fencing athletes.

Wu Hanxiong began his formal training in Guangzhou Stadium in 1991, and entered Guangzhou Weilun Sports School in May, the same year. In 1997, he was selected into Guangdong Provincial Fencing Team, and then into the national team a year later. Wu who is from Wuhan is known for his quick-mind, flexible strategies, and attacks on opponent's errors.

Achievements:

2001 Asian Championships—1st foil team
2001 World University Games—1st foil team
2002 World Championships—3rd foil individual
2002 Asian Games—3rd foil individual
2002 World Cup—2nd foil individual
2003 World Championships—2nd foil team
2003 World Cup—2nd foil individual
2004 World Cup—3rd foil individual/team in Portugal; 3rd team in Shanghai, in France, and 2nd team in Spain

Tan Xue

Tan Xue (1984-), women's fencing athletes.

Tan Xue began athletics training in 1994 as a hurdler, but then switched to fencing by the end of 1998, at Tianjin Sports School. Within one year of formal training, she established herself as national champion. At 2002 World Championships, she titled in women's sabre individual, the first Chinese champion at the tournament. At the 2003 Championships, Tan missed the gold by only one point. Tan Xue is a left-handed fencer, known for her good individual physical and mental quality. She excels in swiftness, explosive force, and agility. Her attacks are highly effective, while her counter-attacks are initiated in a variety of ways. In recent years, Tan has almost swept clean all the national champions.

♦ Chinese Fencing Association

Chinese Fencing Association (CFA) was established in Beijing in 1873. It is a nationwide amateur sports organization directed by All-China Sports Federation. At the IFA meeting in Monte Carlo, Monaco, convened on May 17, 1974, China officially acceded into the IFA.

Address: No.5 Old Shanxi Jie, Shijingshan District, Beijing
Website: http://www.fencing.sport.org.cn

Weightlifting

Weightlifting has been a traditional sport in China, but the modern sport, as a competition event, was not introduced into China until the beginning of the 20th century. At the National Games in 1936, weightlifting was only for performance, but was later included as a competition event at the 1948 Games. The People's Republic of China held its first major weightlifting competition in 1952. At the 1990 World Weightlifting Championships in Hungary, China ranked second in terms of total score, by winning three gold medals. Most spectacularly, at the first World University Weightlifting Championships in 1998, China pocketed all the gold. From 1949 to 1998, Chinese athletes won 287 world champions, and bettered world records 458 times. At the 27th Olympic Games in 2000, China claimed five gold medals, and rewrote world records 12 times.

From March 3 to 5, 2006, the IWF held a grand centennial ceremony and election in Istanbul. IOC president Jacques Rogge, IWF president Aján, and other IWF officials were present at the ceremony. Ma Wenguang from China was elected vice president of the IWF, Wang Yan was elected IWF science and research commissioner, and Ding Meiyuan and Liu Chunhong were awarded best centennial weightlifters.

Men's Weightlifting

On June 7, 1956, in a weightlifting competition held in Shanghai Luwan Stadium, the yound athlete Chen Jingkai managed a lift of 133kg in bantamweight category to become the first Chinese to break the world record. For a long period of time since then, many Chinese weightlifters demonstrated high athletic capabilities in lightweight divisions. And a batch of them broke world records and titled in various international tournaments.

At the 33rd World Weightlifting Championships on November 3rd, 1979, Chinese athletes got one gold, one silver, and two bronze medals. Wu Shude not only claimed a gold in 52kg snatch, as China's first champion in men's weightlifting, but also set two junior world records in snatch and total. Wu was an outstanding weightlifter after Chen Jingkai, winning titles and rewriting world records in subsequent tournaments. His contemporaries, including Chen Weiqiang and He Zhuoqiang, also staged high performances in international events. Chen broke another record in men's 56kg clean and jerk at the 33rd Championships.

Weightlifting was China's dominating event from the 1950s to 1980s.

Achievements of Weightlifting at the Olympics

At the 23rd L.A. Olympics, China harvested several gold medals in weightlifting on July 28, 1984. Zeng Guoqiang hoisted 235kg in men's 52kg division to claim a gold medal. Wu Shude titled in men's 56kg category with the total score of 267.5. So did Chen Weiqiang in men's 60kg group with 285kg total, and Yao Jingyuan in men's 67.5kg class with a total result of 320kg.

Since then, weightlifting has become China's "gold mine" at the Olympic Games. On September 12th, 1988, China gained one silver and four bronze at the 24th Olympics in Seoul. And four years later in Barcelona, it got two silver and two bronze medals. On July 20, at 1996 Atlanta Olympics, Tang Lingsheng and Zhan Xugang strove for two gold medals in men's 59kg and 70kg category respectively. China's weightlifting saw the biggest harvest at the 29th Beijing Olympic Games. Five gold medals came from weightlifting out of the total 51 that China took home: four gold medal from men's event, and four gold medals from women's events.

World Weightlifting Championships

Apart from the Olympic Games, China also achieved remarkable results in men's events at World Weightlifting Championships. Boosted by the four Olympic gold medals in Los Angeles, Chinese weightlifters bagged ten gold medals at the 58th World Championship, in the same year.

Achievements at the World Weightlifting Championships

Year	Event	Gold
1986	60th Championship	1 gold
1989	62nd Championship	3 gold
1990	63rd Championship	3 gold
1991	64th Championship	4 gold
1993	65th Championship	1 gold
1995	67th Championship	5 gold
1997	68th Championship	8 gold
1998	69th Championship	1 gold
1999	70th Championship	2 gold
2002	72nd Championship	7 gold

Women's Weightlifting

China has led the world in women's weightlifting since the sport started in the mid 1980s. At the first World Women's Weightlifting Championship, held on October 30th, 1987, China topped the medal tally with an amazing total of 22 gold, 4 silver and 1 bronze.

On December 2 of the following year, the 2nd Championship (also the 1st Asian Women's Weightlifting Championship), China pocked 26 gold in 9 classes, and nine people broke 21 world records. And at subsequent Championships, China has maintained its dominance in the event.

Chinese women weightlifting team claimed four gold medals in Sydney, 2000, at which women's weightlifting was officially included as a competition event at the Olympics.

At the 2006 World Weightlifting Championship in San Domingo, Chinese women's weightlifting team, known as the Dream Team, swept all the gold in five categories, except for the 69kg and +75kg. Two athletes bettered five world records.

The game's superstar was Yang Lian from China, the only one to rewrite three world records in snatch, clean and jerk and total. Besides, rookie Qiu Hongxia broke two world records in clean and jerk and total of women's 53kg division.

Weightlifting Reserve

Whenever a world weightlifting championship is held, about or more than half of the gold medals are won by the Chinese. This is especially true with the women's team. This has much to do with the reserve force and the mode of training in China.

China's men's team failed to achieve what the Chinese felt satisfactory performance in 1988 and 1992 but won excellent achievement in other years. Chinese weightlifters always emerged as good winners in Olympic Games, with Zhan Xuegang winning gold medals at the -70kg class in the Atlanta Olympic Games and -77kg class in the Sidney Olympic Games. The success of the men's team promoted the fast growth of the weightlifting program. Liaoning, Shandong, Hunan, Fujian, Guangdong and Guangxi all boast successful training system and good reserve force.

Chen Jingkai

Chen Jingkai (1935-),man weightlifter. As the first Chinese athlete to set a world record, he altogether broke world records in clean and jerk on 9 occasions during his career life: 56kg class (133kg, 135kg, 135.5kg, in 1956; 139.5kg, 140.5kg, in 1957), 60kg class (148kg in 1959, 148.5kg in 1961, 151kg in 1963, 151.5kg in 1964). After he retired as an athlete, Chen acted as the president of CWA from 1979 to 1996, and is Honorary President for Life of Asian Weightlifting Federation. He was awarded gold badge of the IWF in 1980, silver badge of the International Bodybuilding Federation in 1985, and Olympic bronze badge of the IOC in 1987. Chen Jingkai was included into the World Weightlifting Hall of Fame in 1994.

Cai Wenyi

Cai Wenyi (1956-), man weightlifter. He won a bronze in men's weightlifting 60kg class total (272.5kg) at the 23rd Olympic Games in Los Angeles, the only Olympic medal of official competition events for Taiwan. In the same year, Cai titled in snatch (125kg) at the 58th World Weightlifting Championships. During his thirteen years of career life, Cai Wenyi altogether broke the Taiwan record on 40 occasions.

♦ China's First Weightlifting World Champion

In November 1979, Thessaloniki, the second largest city in Greece, hosted the 33rd World Weightlifting Championship, which attracted participants from 39 countries. China's first-ever world champion in weightlifting was born on November 2nd, when Wu Shude hoisted 110kg in his third attempt in men's 52kg class, defying USSR's world record holder A. Voronin, the "invincible" 21st Olympic gold medalist.

Wu Shude (1959-) bettered junior weightlifting world record six times before he titled at the World Championship and rewrote world snatch records three times later:

1980 National Championships, —WR in 52kg snatch (112kg)

1981 Asian Championships—WR in 56kg snatch (126.5kg)

1983 National Games, Shanghai—WR snatch (128kg)

From 1978 to 1983, Wu's average progress in snatch was an astounding 3.75kg every year.

♦ China's First Olympic Champion in Weightlifting

The weightlifting competitions for the 23rd L.A. Olympics were held from July 30th to August 8th, 1984. China sent 10 weightlifters to the Games, namely Zhou Peishun, Zeng Guoqiang, Wu Shude, Lai Runming, Wang Guoduo, Chen Weiqiang, Yao Jingyuan, Ma Jianping, Li Shunzhu, and Ma Wenguang, headed by two coaches, Huang Qianghui, and Zhao Qingkui. Faced with the fierce competition from Romania and Japan, Chinese weightlifters met the challenge, and made a clean sweep in lightweight classes by claiming 4 gold and 2 silver medals. This was China's first time to title in weightlifting at the Olympic Games.

The four gold medalists were:

Zeng Guoqiang: 52kg class, 235kg

Wu Shude: 56kg class, 267.5kg

Chen Weiqiang: 60kg class, 282.5kg

Yao Jingyuan: 67.5kg class, 320kg

Chen Weiqiang

Chen Weiqiang (1958 -), man weightlifter. He began weightlifting training in a spare-time sports school in Guangdong Gymnasium in 1972, and joined the Guangdong provincial team two years later.

Achievements:

1977 Asian Championships & China-Pakistan Dual Competition - Thrice breaking world youth records for 52kg C&J and total

1978 China-West Germany Dual Competition - World youth record in 56kg C&J

1979 National Qualification Tournament & World Championships - Twice breaking WRs in 56kg (151.5kg & 153kg)

1982 Asian Games–1st 60kg snatch & total

1984 World Championships–1st snatch, total

1984 Los Angeles Olympic Games–1st 60kg total

Yao Jingyuan

Yao Jingyuan (1958-), man weightlifter. He was known as a "power boy" at the tender age of 13. He began weightlifting training in 1973 and was soon selected by the Liaoning provincial team. Yao joined the national team for intensified training in 1979.

During his career life, Yao Jingyuan altogether broke the Asian record 16 times, and thus was also known as a "Powerman with small hands".

Achievements:

1979 World Championships–3rd 67.5kg C&J (172.5kg)

1982 Asian Championships–1st 67.5kg total

1983 National Games–Three ARs in 67.5kg snatch (140kg), C&J (177.5kg) & total (317.5kg)

1984 World Championships–1st 67.5kg C&J & total

1984 Los Angeles Olympic Games–1st 67.5kg total

1985 World Championships–3rd 67.5kg snatch & total

1986 Seoul Asian Games–1st 675.kg

1987 National Games–3rd 67.5kg (breaking ARs on several occasions)

Zeng Guoqiang

Zeng Guoqiang (1965-),man weightlifter. He took up weightlifting in a local spare-time sports school in 1976, and was chosen by the national team in 1983

His achievements included:

1983 World Youth Championships–1st 52kg

1984 Los Angels Olympic Games–1st 52kg

1984 World Championships–1st 52kg C&J & total

1984 Asian Championships–1st 52kg snatch, C&J & total

1985 World Championships–2nd 52kg C&J & total

He Zhuoqiang

At the 6th National Games held in November, 1987, 20-year-old He Zhuoqiang from Guangdong rewrote two world records in men's 56kg class: 117.5kg in snatch, and 265kg total. He thus became the first Chinese to set a total record in weightlifting, the first-ever weightlifter to break two world records in one competition, and the first to hold all the three world records in one class.

He Zhuoqiang (1967-) started formal training at the age of 13 in local youth sports school, and entered Guangdong provincial weightlifting team the next year.

Achievements:

1985 National Weightlifting Championship-1st 52kg snatch/total, AR in C&J (141.5kg)

1986 12th World Youth Weightlifting Championship-1st 52kg snatch (115kg)/C&J (137.5kg)/total (252.5kg), WR in snatch (11tkg), AR in total (252.5kg)

1986 10th Asian Games, 1st 52kg

1987 19th Asian Weightlifting Championship, 1st snatch/C&J/total, WR in snatch (116.5kg)

1987 World Weightlifting Championship, 1st 52kg C&J (147.5kg), 2nd snatch (112.5kg), 2nd total (260kg), WR in C&J (153kg)

1987 6th National Games – WR in 52kg snatch (117.5kg)/WR in total (265kg)

1987 China-Japan Weightlifting Competition-surpassed WR in 52kg snatch (118kg)

Honour:

1987 Awarded International Mater Athlete

1987 Awarded National Sports Medal of Honour by the State Physical Culture and Sports Commission

Tang Lingsheng

Tang Lingsheng (1971-), man weightlifter. He took up weightlifting in a local spare-time sports school at age 12. The young athlete was taken on by the Guangxi sports team in 1985, and began systematic weightlifting training two years later. His personal best was a title in men's 59kg class at 26th Olympic, 1996-China's first Olympic gold in 12 years. The Chinese Hercules was also known as "Crane" because of his outstanding power.

Xing Fen

Xing Fen (1973-), the famous woman weightlifter from China. Her achievements include:

1988 2nd World Women's Championships-1st/WR in 44kg snatch (70.5kg)/C&J (87.5kg)/total (147.5kg)

1989 3rd World Women's Championships-1st in 44kg snatch/C&K/total, WR in snatch (72.5kg)/C&J (92.5kg)/total (160kg, 165kg)

1990 11th Asian Games–1st in 44kg

1991 5th World Women's Championships-1st in 44kg snatch/C&K/total, WR in C&J (93.5kg, 95kg)

1992 5th Asian Women's Championships-1st in 44kg snatch/C&K/total, WR in snatch (75.5kg, 77.5kg)/C&J (100.5kg, 102.5kg)/total (177.5kg, 180kg)

1997 10th Asian Women's Championships-WR in 46kg C&J (105.5kg)

Zhang Guozheng

On August 18, 2004, Chinese player Zhang Guozheng titled the men's 69kg weightlifting at the Athens Olympics with a total grade of 347.5 kg.

Zhang Guozheng (1974-), man weightlifter. The -69kg final of the Athen Olympic Games was held on August 18, 2004, and Chinese weightlifter Zhang Guozheng won the champion with a total of 347.5 kg.

Sports career:

2002 Asian Games–1st 69kg snatch/C&J/total

2002/2003 World Championships–1st 69kg snatch/C&J/total

2003 Asian Championships–1st 69kg snatch/C&J/total

Records:

2003 Asian Championships–69kg C&J, 197.5kg (WR)

Zhan Xugang

Zhan Xugang (1974-), man weightlifter. He began to receive weightlifting training in Kaihua Sports School at the age of 10. He entered national team in January, 1994.

Achievements:

1993 National Games – Breaking Asia Records(AR) in 70kg snatch

1993 Asian Youth Championships – 1st 70kg snatch, C&J & total

1994 World Youth Championships – 1st 70kg snatch, C&J & total (WR of 183kg in snatch)

1995 World Championships – 1st 70kg total

1996 Asian Championships – WR in 70kg snatch (160.5kg)

1996 Atlanta Olympic Games – 1st 70kg, three WRs in snatch, C&J & total

1999 Asian Men's Championships – WR in 77kg C&J (206kg)

2000 Sydney Olympic Games – 1st 77kg class

Honour:

1993 – Selected an outstanding weightlifter of Asia

Chen Xiaomin

Chen Xiaomin (1977-), woman weightlifter. She entered the Guangdong provincial team in 1991, and joined the national team a year later. Her achievements included:

1993 National Games – 1st 54kg (surpassing three ARs on six occasions)

1993 World Women's Championships – 1st 54kg snatch, C&J & total (three WRs)

1994 National Championships – 1st 59kg

1994 Hiroshima Asian Games – 1st 59kg (equalling WR with 97.5kg in snatch and breaking WRs with 122.5kg in C&J and 220kg in two-lift total)

1995 World Women's Championships – 1st 59kg snatch, C&J & total (92.5kg, 122.5kg & 215kg, rewriting WR in C&J with 123.5kg), 1st team

1996 Asian Championships – 1st 59kg total (207.5kg)

1996 Warsaw World Women's Championships – 1st 59kg snatch (97.5kg) & total (207.5kg), breaking WR in snatch (99kg); 2nd C&J (110kg)

1997 Asian Women's Championships – 1st 64kg snatch, C&J & total (breaking WR in snatch with 107.5kg)

2000 Sydney Olympic Games – 1st 63kg class

Yang Xia

Yang Xia (1977-), woman weightlifter. She was the champion of women's 53kg class at 1998 Bangkok Asian Games. In 2000, she titled in 53kg total at Sydney Olympic Games, and her successful 100kg attempt bettered the world record in snatch by 2kg.

Chen Yanqing

Chen Yanqing (1979-), woman weightlifter.

Chen Yanqing began weightlifting training with Cao Xinmin, the famous coach in 1990. She was recruited into the weightlifting team in Suzhou of Jiangsu province, which is a strong team in China. At the age of fifteen, she began to make achievements in weightlifting. She got the 4th at China Championships and in the same year she won the title at the Asian Youth Women's Weightlifting Championships. She started to reap all the championship of China, world and Asia. At the Athens Olympic Games, Chen Yanqing got the title of the 58kg class with total of 237.5kg (107.5kg of snatch and 130kg of clean and jerk). In the 58 class competition on December 3, 2006, she rewrote all the three records in snatch, clean and jerk, and total. Her 251kg total bettered the world record by 10kg, which was set by her countrywoman Gu Wei the year before.

Ding Meiyuan

Ding Meiyua (1979-), woman weightlifter. She began weightlifting training at the age of 12 in Dalian Sports School. She later joined the Liaoning provincial team and then the national team. Her achievements included:

1997 Capetown World Cup – 1st +75 kg (240kg)

1998 Bangkok Asian Games – 1st +75kg (270kg)

1998 Hungary World Cup – 1st +75kg (285kg)

1999 Athens World Championships – 1st +75kg

2000 Asian Championships – 1st +75kg

2000 Sydney Olympic Games – 1st +75kg total

2003 World Championships – 1st +75kg snatch (137.5kg), C&J(162.5kg) & total (300kg) (Surpassing WRs on two occasions)

Lin Weining

Lin Weining (1977-), woman weightlifter. She entered Changyi Sports School at the age of 10, and took up Wushu in Weifang Sports School in 1991. But the next year, she switched to weightlifting, and finally joined the Shandong provincial weightlifting team in 1996. Her personal best was a title in women's 69kg class at 2000 Sydney Olympic Games, on September 19. Lin hoisted more weight than the Hungarian athlete, who actually weighed heavier than her. This was quite rare in China's Olympic history.

Achievements:

1999 National Championships – 2nd 69kg

1999 World Women's Youth Championships– 1st 69kg snatch, C&J & total, breaking WR in snatch (137.5kg)

On September 19, 2000, Lin Weining titled the women's 69kg weightlifting at the 27th Sydney Olympics.

1999 Asian Championships – 1st 69kg snatch, C&J & total, breaking WRs in C&J (142.5kg) and total (252.5kg)

2000 National Championships – 2nd 69kg total (252.5kg)

2000 Sydney Olympic Games – 1st 69kg

Tang Gonghong

Tang Gonghong (1979-), woman weightlifter. Hard life during childhood imbued her with determination and toughness. At the age of 11, she was already a strong woman with the weight of 62kg. Tang's sporting career began in 1994, at Shandong Weihai Sports Training Base, and entered National Team in 1998. Due to some reasons, Tang Gonghong did not compete at 2000 Sydney Olympics, but she had never given up her Olympic dream. At 2001 National Games, She toppled Sydney Olympic champion Ding Meiyuan to claim a gold, and broke five national records. Then at 2002 Asian Games and the subsequent 2004 World Championships, Tang rewrote world records in clean and jerk, and bettered the world record total by 2.5kg.

Shi Zhiyong

Shi Zhiyong(1980-) began formal training at the age of nine in Fujian Longyan Sports School, and was selected into Fujian Provincial Sports School in 1993.

Achievements:

1997 World Youth Championships – 1st 59kg snatch/C&J/total

1997 National Games – 2nd 59kg total

1999 National Championships – 1st 62kg snatch/C&J/total

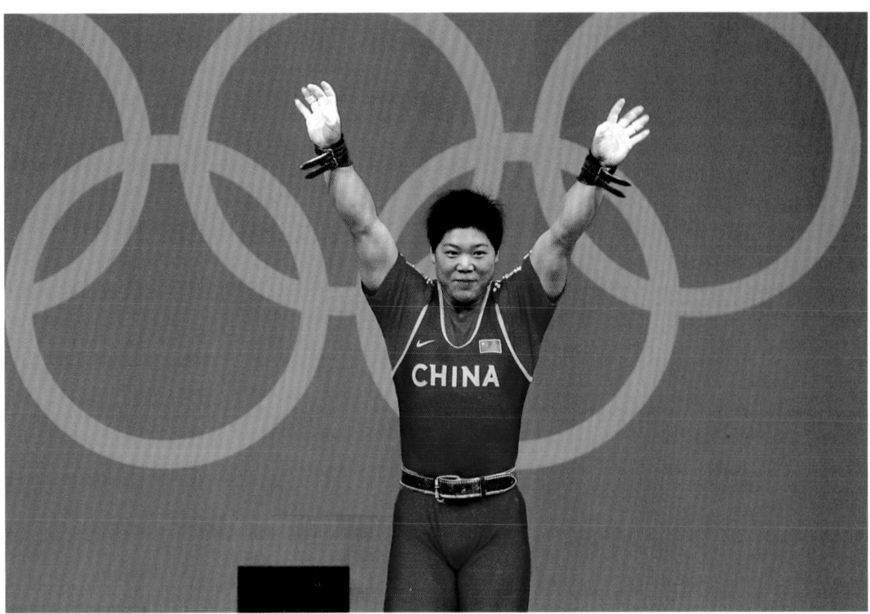

On August 19, 2004, Chinese player Liu Chunhong won the gold medal in the women's 69kg snatch at the 28th Athens Olympics and chalked up the world record with a grade of 122.5 kg.

1999 World Youth Championships – 1st 62kg snatch/total; 2nd C&J

1999 World Championships – 1st 62kg snatch

2000 Asian Championships – 1st 62kg total

2003 World Championships – 2nd 62kg snatch/total; 3rd C&J

Records:

1999 National Championships – 62kg total, 322.5kg (NR)

1999 World Youth Championships – 62kg snatch, 150kg (WR)

1999 National Inter-city Games – 62kg snatch/total, 152.5kg/327.5kg (NRs)

2000 Asian Championships – 62kg snatch, 152.5kg (WR)

2000 World Championships for University Students – 62kg snatch, 153kg (WR)

2004 Olympic Games – 62kg snatch, 152.5kg (OR)

Liu Chunhong

Liu Chunhong (1985-), woman weightlifter. Liu switched to weightlifting from judo, Yantai Sports School, and had been trained there until she was selected into the national team in January, 2002. At the age of 15, Liu Chunhong beat Chinese ace weightlifter Lin Weining to become a champion. After that, she soon emerged as an invincible hoister and record breaker in women's 69kg class in the world. In her leisure time, Liu enjoyed music and cartoon drawing. Several impressive cartoon figures hung in her bedroom were done by Liu herself.

Achievements:

2001 National Games – 1st 69kg snatch/C&J/total

2002 Asian Games – 1st 69kg total

2003 World Championships – 1st 69kg snatch/C&J/total

2003/2004 Asian Championships – 1st 69kg snatch/C&J/total

Records:

2001 National Games – 69kg snatch/C&J/total, 122.5kg/155kg/277.5kg (NRs)

2002 Asian Games – 69kg snatch/C&J/total, 115.5kg/148kg/262.5kg (WRs)

2003 Asian Championships – 69kg snatch/total, 117.5kg/265kg (WRs)

2003 World Championships – 69kg snatch/C&J/total, 120kg/150kg/270kg (WRs)

2004 Olympic Games – 69kg snatch/C&J/total, 122.5kg/153.0kg/275.0kg (JWR,WR,OR)

♦ Chinese Weightlifting Association (CWA)

Chinese Weightlifting Association was founded in 1956, headquartered in Beijing. China joined International Weightlifting Federation in 1936, and gained official membership in 1955. Huang Qianghui, then vice president of CWA was elected vice president of Asian Weightlifting Federation in 1982. CWA regularly organizes a variety of competitions, including National Weightlifting Championships, National Youth/Juvenile Weightlifting Championships, and National Weightlifting Champion Competitions, etc.

Address: No.14 Tiantandongli, middle section A, Beijing
Website: http://www.cwa.org.cn

Basketball

The first time China sent its basketball team to play in an international game is in the 1st Far East Games held in Manila, Philippines, 1913, from February 1 to February 8. It marks the start of international era in the basketball history of China. In the 5th Far East Games held in Shanghai, 1921, from May 30 to June 4, China wrested the championship from Japan and the Philippines. It is the first time that China won a championship in the modern history of basketball.

In 1984, the Chinese team played in the Los Angeles Olympics; it received a bronze medal in women's game and ranked the 10th in the men's game. In the 25th Olympic Games held in Barcelona, China grabbed a silver medal in the women's game and topped the record the women basketball team previously put down in the Olympic Games. In the 1996 Atlanta Olympics, the Chinese men basketball team ranked the 8th; it was the best record of the men's team in the Olympics.

In 1995, the Chinese Basketball Association (CBA) formally took shape.

In February, 1997, Zheng Haixia was selected by the Los Angeles Sparks (16th pick overall) in the second round of the WNBA Draft. She is the first Chinese basketball player that went overseas to play in world's top basketball league. In March 2001, Wang Zhizhi, previously a player in the Bayi team in China, signed the contract with the Dallas Mavericks, and became the first Asian player in NBA. In 2002, Yao Ming ranked the first in the NBA Draft, and started his career as a NBA player in the Houston Rockets.

National Basketball Events

The National Basketball Events in China include: the basketball game in the National Games, the CBA league (the premier league and the second division), the National Men's Basketball Club Tournament, the WCBA league (the premier league and the second division), the Men's National Basketball Youth Tournament, the Men's National Basketball Youth League, the Men's and Women's National Basketball Youth League, the Men's and Women's National Sports School Basketball Game, the Men's and Women's National Traditional Sports Project School Basketball Game (aged 13-14), the Men's and Women's National Basketball Game for Teenagers in 2nd Division, the National Enterprise Basketball Game, and the National Club Cup Basketball Game.

The Chinese Women's Basketball Team

The basketball game in the 9th Asian Games was held from the November 19 to the December 4, 1982, in New Deli, India. In the game, the Chinese women's basketball team wrested the championship from the South Korean team by a final match of 75:67.

In the 9th Women's Basketball World Championships from July 24 to August 6, 1983, in San Paulo, Brazil, the Chinese women's basketball team made their debut and occupied the 3rd place in the ranking. It is an important step for China's basketball game on its way towards the world's top. It is also by far the best performance of the Chinese women's team in international games. In the game, Song Xiaobo, one of the players, scored 134 points on her own, and was selected to be a member in the best team of Women's World Basketball Series A.

During the May 5-16, 1984, the qualifying competitions of the women's basketball game of the 23rd Olympics were held in Havana, Cuba. The Chinese women's basketball team was ranked No.1 and was qualified to play in the Olympic basketball game. On July 29, the game was held in Los Angeles. It was the first time the team played in the Olympics, but they won a bronze medal. Now, the Chinese women's basketball team ranked the 10th internationally.

The Chinese Men's Basketball Team

When the Chinese men's basketball team was having its first experience in the Basketball Asian Championships in 1975, they beat South Korea and Japan separately by 97:78 and 80:59, and won the championship. Ever since 1978, the team had nailed its dominance in Asia for 14 years. Now, the Chinese men's basketball team ranked the 11th internationally.

The Men's Basketball World Championship

From 1950 on, the Men's Basketball World Championships began to be held periodically, usually by an interval of 4 years. The participation qualifying standards were varied by time. At the 8th game in 1978, the qualified parties were: the top three in the previous Olympic Games, the top three in the previous World Championship, the champion or the pre-dominant team in Europe, America, Asia, Africa and Australia, and the teams on invitation. There would be in total 14 teams in 3 groups competing for the preliminary round. The top 2 teams in each group will join the previous World Championships winner and the team from the host country in single round-robin system to play for the final.

In 1977, the Chinese men's basketball team won the 9th Asian Championship, and got the qualification to play in the 8th Men's Basketball World Championships with 13 other major teams in the world. From the of October 1-14, 1978, the Chinese team represented Asia to join the 8th World Championships held in Manila, Philippines. It was their first time in the World Championships games, but they got the 11th place.

The CBA League

By the end of 1994, China initiated some reforms on the Chinese basketball competition schedule. The previous "fixed spot" game was replaced by a "host/guest" system. When the system was put in trial in the basketball games among the top eight teams in 1995, it received a great success. Thus, from the end of 1995, the schedule of Chinese Basketball League was changed to a cross-year host/guest league system. In other words, the CBA league took shape. This reform has pushed the Chinese basketball game into a new age.

In the end of 2001, the Chinese women's basketball game learnt from the men's, and adopted the same host/guest schedule. In other words, the WCBA league took shape.

A Decade of CBA

From the 1995-1996 game season to the 2004-2005 game season, the CBA league has accumulated a decade of history. The host/guest CBA Top Eight Games held from 5th February to April l9, 1995, marks the start of the commercialization of Chinese basketball. In the following season of 1995-1996, or the first cross-year host/guest league season, Chinese basketball has changed a new face with even more exciting and fierce games.

International Management Group, the world renowned sports management and marketing firm, has become the closest partner of the CBA Premier League Series A, bringing great amounts of funds to the league. The season of 1995-1996, the premier league series A was commercially named for the first time, after the tobacco brand 555. In the same season, the Zhejiang Zhongxin team hired the first foreign player in the history of CBA. In the same season, the 1st CBA All-Star Game was held in Beijing.

In the season of 1996-1997, all the 12 participating teams in the premier league founded a club of their own. It was also in the same season that CBA All-Star game was expanded to a CBA All-Star Weekend, which aimed to satisfy the fans and put them in the utmost position.

Previous Records of the Chinese Men Basketball Team in Major Events (1990-2004)

Year	Event	Rank	Coach
1990	11th Asian Games	Champion	Sun Bang
	11th Asian Championship	14th	Wang Changyou
1991	16th Asian Championship	Champion	Jiang Xingquan
1992	25th Olympic Games	12th	Jiang Xingquan
1993	17th Asian Championship	Champion	Jiang Xingquan
1994	12th Asian Games	Champion	Jiang Xingquan
	12th World Championship	8th	
1995	18th Asian Championship	Champion	Jiang Xingquan
1996	26th Olympic Games	8th	Gong Luming
1997	19th Asian Championship	3rd	Zhang Bin
1998	13th Asian Games	Champion	Wang Fei
1999	20th Asian Championship	Champion	Jiang Xingquan
2000	27th Olympic Games	10th	Jiang Xingquan
2001	21st Asian Championship	Champion	Wang Fei
2002	14th World Championship	12th	Wang Fei
	14th Asian Games	2nd	
2003	22nd Asian Championship	Champion	Jiang Xingquan
2004	28th Olympic Games	8th	Delmer W. Harris

Previous Records of the Chinese Women's Basketball Team in Major Events (1990-2004)

Year	Event	Rank
1990	13th Asian Championship	champion
	11th Asian Games	2nd place
	11th World Championship	9th place
1992	14th Asian Championship	champion
	25th Olympic Games	2nd place
1994	15th Asian Championship	champion
	12th Asian Games	3rd place
	12th World Championship	2nd place
1995	14th Asian Championship	champion
1996	26th Olympic Games	9th place
1998	13th Asian Games	2nd place
	13th World Championship	12th place
2001	19th Asian Championship	champion
2002	14th World Championship	6th place
	14th Asian Games	champion
2004	28th Olympic Games	9th place

In the season of 1997-1998, the Sichuan Pandas hired the first foreign coach in CBA league. It was also the first time that the All-Star Game was transformed into a Sino-Foreign Star Game.

In the 10th season, or the season of 2004-2005, the Chinese Basketball Association made a series of adjustments and changes on the structure, schedule and promoting strategies of the league. For the first time, promotion and relegation were eliminated from the system, and the participating teams were divided separately into the south and north regions. Both region would produce a champion in the end.

♦ The First Foreign Basketball Player in CBA League

In the season of 95-96, the Zhejiang Zhongxin Club hired Savinkov from Kazakhstan to play in the league. He is the first foreign basketball player in CBA league.

♦ The First Chinese Basketball Player in NBA

In 2001, Wang Zhizhi, previously a player in the Bayi Rockets, signed the contract with the Dallas Mavericks, and became the first Chinese player in NBA.

Mou Zuoyun

Mou Zuoyun (1913-) was the first batch of Chinese basketball coach. He had represented China to play in the basketball game in the 11th Olympic Games in Berlin, 1936. He was the coach of the Chinese team, and the vice department chief of the former National Ball Games Department. He also worked on various positions in the Chinese Basketball Association and the Asian Basketball Association. In 1996, he was recognized as the "Lifetime Honorable Member" of the International Basketball Federation for his 44 years work in the Technical Committee in FIBA. There were only 8 people in the world graced by this honor, and he was the only one in Asia.

Qian Chenghai

Qian Chenghai (1934-2008) was famous basketball player and senior coach. Counting from 1972, his 15 years working as the coach of the Chinese men's basketball team has proved to be very fruitful. After numerous trials and practices, he developed his own strategies for the Chinese team to play. He made good use of the flexibility of Chinese players and trained them intensively on cornering, speed attack and jump-shot. Those techniques were proved to be very useful in the international events. In 1980s, he was selected to be the one of "the Best Ten Coaches" in China.

Yang Boyong

Yang Boyong (1935-) is a famous basketball player and coach. During his coaching, the Chinese women's basketball team won the 3rd place in the 9th World Championships games in 1983 and a bronze medal in the 23rd Olympic Games in 1984. He emphasized on the importance of "muscularity", or physical constitution, of female players. He had led the Chinese women's basketball team to the world. Li Yaguang, the coach of the women's team after him, was also appointed by him.

Jiang Xingquan

Jiang Xingquan (1940-), basketball player and coach. He was a former player in the Liaoning Team from 1960 to 1970. He was selected in the National Youth Team in 1963. He coached an played in the Liaoning Team from 1970 to 1973. In a game against the Yugoslavia in 1971, he scored 32 points by himself. He was the coach of the Liaoning Team from 1973 to 1976 and the head coach from 1976 to 1990. He led the team to win the champion of the CBA Premier League, the National Championship, the CBA Cup and the Club Cup each twice. He head coached the National Youth Team several times during 1985 and 1990 and led the team to win the championship of the Japan International Invitational Competition and the Asian Youth Cup in 1985. He was the head coach of the National Team during 1991 and 1995. Under his coach, the team won four Asian championships and the 8th position in the 1994 World Championships. He was the vice director in the Sports Committee of Liaoning Province in 1995. He was selected to be the vice president of Chinese Basketball Association in 1996. In 1999, he returned to head coach the National Team and led the team to win the 20th Asian Championships and the ticket to the 2000 Olympic Games. In 2003, he became the head coach of the National Team once again and led the team to win the 22nd Asian Championships and the ticket to the 2004 Olympic Games. In 2004, he was appointed to be the technical consultant of Chinese men's basketball.

Jiang Xingquan

Li Yaguang

Li Yaguang (1958-)used to be one of the best defenders in Chinese basketball history when he was a player. He was also known for his accurate shots and his tireless performance. On January 3rd, 1991, Li started to coach the Chinese women's basketball team, which was then in a very gloomy state. But he lifted the team to win the title of the Asian Championship. In the following Barcelona Olympics, Li Yaguang led the team to win the 2nd place, although it was not the best record of the women's team in history. In the 1994 World University Games, the Chinese team under his coach finally claimed a championship.

Song Xiaobo

Song Xiaobo (1958-), elite basketball player. Former team leader of the Chinese Women's Basketball Team.

Song became a player in the National Team since 17 and made herself known in the 6th Asian Basketball Championships games in 1976. She was selected to be the best player and elite player for several times in her over 100 international games held in 30 countries and regions. She's an all-rounded player who excels in breaking in, multi-angel jump shot and baseline driving. She can both be a defender and an attacker. In 1979 and 1983, she represented the Beijing Team to win the 4th and 5th National Games. In 1983, she won the 3rd place in the 9th Women's World Basketball Championships games with the Chinese National Team and was selected to be in the World's Best Team of Women's Basketball. She was also selected to be the 3rd Best Scorer. In 1985, she played in the 9th Asian Championships. In the games against South Korea and Japan, she scored 35

♦ The North Star Program

The North Star Program aimed to nurture CBA into a world-class professional basketball league in ten years' time, to transform CBA into the largest basketball market besides NBA, and to make basketball the "first sports" in China. The season of 2004-2005 is a trial season for the CBA Premier League Series A games. Relegation and promotion were eliminated for the first time. In the season of 2005-2006, all the participating 15 teams in CBA league were professionalized club teams, with their own brand and registered capitals. The games were operated in a commercial way. Thus, it is also called the first CBA Professional League.

By statistics, the growing rate of the fans in the season of 2005-2006 has reached 41 percent. The average number of fans in the playoffs reached 5071, which capped the previous record in history. Also, the public influential power of CBA league as a brand has also been increasing. It has gradually become the best brand of Chinese professional sports leagues. The total income of the league has increased by 17 million Yuan compared with the previous season, exhibiting a great prospective.

points on her own and contributed greatly to the championship of the Chinese team in the Championships games.

Cong Xuedi

Cong Xuedi (1963-), female basketball player and coach.

Cong was a player in the Shanghai Youth Team, the Shanghai Team and the National Team from 1981 to 1993. She had won the 2nd place in the WCBA Premier League in 1984 and 1985. She was selected to be in the National Best Team and won the "Best Scorer Award" in the same years. She was the 3rd, the 6th and the 2nd in the 23rd, the 24th and the 25th Olympic Games and was once selected to be the "Best Rear Guard" in the Olympic qualifying competitions. She won the championship of the Asian Championships in 1986, 1990 and 1992. She was the 5th in the 10th World Championships games, and the champion of the 10th Asian Games and the 1993 Asian Games. She was selected to be in the Best Team for several times in the duration. She started a basketball club in 1993 and head coached the Shanghai Women's Team from 1995 to 2002. Under her coaching, the team won the championship of the 1996 WCBA Second Division League and returned to the Premier League, which the team left long ago. She also led the team to win the 3rd in the 1997 National Games, and the 6th and 9th in the 1998 and 1999 WCBA Premier League.

Cong is know her good control over the ball, excellent driving and passing and accurate long-range shots. She's also a good team organizer.

The most memorable game for Cong is the semi-final against Cuba in the 25th Olympic Games. In the 22 minutes Cong was playing, she had three foul shots and one jump shot, averaging a field goal percentage of 63%. Finally, China won over Cuba by 39 points in the game.

Zheng Haixia

Zheng Haixia (1967-), female basketball player and National elite center player.

Zheng was selected in the Wuhan Army Basketball Team. Because of her height and agility, she was soon selected into the National Women's Youth Team. In 1983, she entered the National Team. She won the Women's Asian Youth Championships with the National Youth Team in 1982 and 1984. In 1983, she won the championship of the 5th National Games with the Liberation Army Team and the 3rd place in the World Championships with the National Team. She also won the bronze medal in the 23rd Olympic Games in 1984, the 5th position in the 10th World Championships games and the championship of the 10th Asian Games. She's good in running and bouncing, and is a great threat in the lower posts. She's also the major scorer in the National Team and was selected to be in the National Best Team in various events. In 1984, she was awarded as the Best Young Player in the Olympic qualifying games, and won the "Best Scorer Award" and "Best Rebound Award" in the 6th "Baltic Sea Cup" Women's International Basketball Games in 1985. In 1986, she won the "Best Center Player" award in the preliminary games in the 10th World Championship, and the "Best Scorer" title in the final. She was also awarded as the Woman Pace-setter and the New Long March Pace-setter.

Gong Xiaobin

Gong Xiaobin (1969-), basketball player and coach.

Gong used to play in the Shandong Youth Team, the Shangdong Team, the National Youth Team and the National Team during 1985 and 1999. In the duration, he had won the Asian Championships for many times and was selected to be a player in the Asian All-Star Team. He won the 4th position in the 1997 National Games and the 8th position in the 1994 World Championships and the 1996 Olympic Games. He was also formerly the MVP and the "Scoring King" of the CBA Premier League Series A. He had won the Best Technique Award and been selected in the CBA Best Team for several times.

He started to coach the Shandong Kingston Men's Basketball Team in 2003, and led the team to the 6th position in the 2003-2004 CBA Premier League Series A.

Gong is known for his powerful bounce, fast speed and all-rounded techniques. When talking his experience in playing basketball, he said, "it depends on how well you can put your potentials into performance in the game."

Hu Weidong

Hu Weidong(1970-), basketball player and elite rear guard.

He began his career in 1987, playing sequentially for the Jiangsu Youth Team, the Jiangsu Team, the National Youth Team and the National Team. In the duration, he had won the 3rd position in the 1993 World University Games, the championship of the 1993 East Asian Games, the championship of the 1994 and 1998 Asian Games, the championship of the 1995 and 1999 Asian Championships and the 3rd place in the 1997 Asian Championships. He won the MVP title of the CBA Premier League Series A games in the season of 1995-1996 and 1996-1997. He was also the "Scoring King", "Three-Pointer King" and "Stealing King" of the 1995-1996, 1996-1997 and the 1999-2000 CBA games. He was also selected to be a member in the CBA Premier League Series A Best Team for several times.

Hu is an agile and all-rounded player. He excels in three-point shots, quick stealing and breaking-in.

The 5th of September 1999 was a happy day for Hu. It was the day China played against Korea in Asian Championships games. When the game was only 6 minutes to the finish, the Koreans began to score by consecutive three-point shots and reduced the gap on the scoring board to 4 points by a 40:44. The atmosphere became very tense. It was at this critical moment that Hu played his magic and nailed China's success by 4 three-point shots in 2 minutes. The Chinese Team won over Korea by a final score of 63:45 and collected the Asian Championships title, which had been lost for two years, and the ticket to the Olympic Games in its pocket.

Li Xin

Li Xin (1970-), basketball player and coach. She is a former player in the Shenyang Army Youth Team, Shenyang Army Team, National Youth Team and National Team during 1980 and 1997. In 2003, Li began to coach the Bayi Team. In 2004, she coached and played in the Bayi Team. She is a regular champion in the CBA league, the National Games and the Asian Games. Former "Scoring Queen" in the Asian Championships games. Li won the 2nd place in the Olympics and the World Championships separately in 1992 and 1994 and the championship in 1993 East Asian Games. She had begun to study in the International Business department in the School of Business and Administration of the Renmin's University of China (previously known as the People's University of China) since the end of 1997. She was the head coach of the Beijing Aoshen Olympian in late 1997 and led the team to win the 1998 CBA Premier League Series B Championships and the Asian Club Cup Championships.

On December 14, 2006, Chinese women's basketball team gained another gold medal at the 15th Doha Asian Games.

Li Xin is known for her accurate jump shots, powerful bounce, fast speed and strong driving.

In the 1994 World Basketball Championships game against Cuba, Li Xin had a very impressive performance. Especially in the last minute, she made use of her speed and power to fast break in to the low post, shot 2 points, caused her opponent to foul, and got the two fouled shots, too. She made her contributions to the winning of the game and the team's 2nd place in the finals.

When talking about playing basketball, Li said, "Every player should try to be the inspiration of the field."

Mengke Bateer

Bateer (1975-), basketball player and coach.

Bateer started his career in Inner Mongolian Youth Team in 1986. He was selected into the National Youth Team in 1991, and the National Team in 1993.

His major achievements include: champion of the 1992 Asian Youth Championships games; champion of the 1993 Asian Championships; 8th position in the 1996 Atlanta Olympic Games; champion of the 1998 Bangkok Asian Games; champion of the Asian Championships games in 1999, 2001 and 2003; the final champion of NBA 2003.

Wang Zhizhi

Wang Zhizhi (1977-), basketball player.

Wang was selected to be in the National Special-Figured Teenager Basketball Team in 1993. In the same year, he became a member of the National Men's Youth Team and the Bayi Team. He entered the National Team in 1996 and won the CBA Premier League championship in 1995-1996. He won the 8th position in the 1996 Olympic Games and the championship of the 1997 National Games. He was the champion of the 13th Asian Games and the Asian Championships in 1998. He was rewarded as the World's Best Center Player and Best Blocking Player in the 1995 Men's World Championships games, and was selected to be in the Best Team. He won the title of Best Defender and "Blocking King" in 1999 CBA Premier League Series A games, and was selected to be the "Best Center Player in Asia 1999". He was the first picked Asian player in formal NBA Draft and joined the NBA league in 2001.

Sui Feifei

Sui Feifei (1979-), female basketball player.

She won the Asian Championships in 1996, the National Women's Basketball Club League under Twenties in 1999, and the East Asian Games in 2001. She won the 2nd place in World University Games in 2001, and the 6th in World Championships in 2002. She was the champion of the 14th Asian Games of 2000. She also won the championship of the WCBA league in 2002, 2003 and 2004.

Yao Ming

Yao Ming (1980-), basketball player. Now he is the No. 11 in the Houston Rockets in NBA, playing center. He's the tallest player in NBA league now, with a height of 2.29m (7'6").

Yao Ming was selected into the Chinese National Team in 1997, the Chinese All Star Basketball Team in 1998, and the Asian All Star Team in February, 2000. In 2002, he went to play in the NBA. He was a member in the NBA All-Star Team in three consecutive years of 2003, 2004 and 2005.

In 1997, Yao Ming won the Asian Youth Championship. In 1999, he won the Asian Championship. In March, 2000, he won three awards for rebound, dunk and rejections for his performance in the CBA Premier League Series A of the season 1999-2000. In the same month, he was selected into the All-Star Team of CBA Premier League Series A. In February, 2000, he was selected into the Asian All-Star Team. It's also in the same year that he was awarded as "the Most Promising Player in the Globe" by ESPN. On the December 17, 2002, Yao had 5 rejections and 8 rebounds in the game against Miami Heat, and created his personal record in NBA. It's also in the same year that Yao was ranked the first in the NBA Draft and was selected to be in the Best Team of the World Championship. He won the championship in the CBA Premier League Series A in 2002, too.

He was ranked the 7th in field goal percentage, the 15th in average rebounds per game, and the 13th in blocked shots per game in the 2004 NBA playoffs. In the 03-04 season, he was ranked the 7th in field goal percentage, the 13th in blocked shots, and the 15th in average rebounds per game among all the NBA players. In 2004, he was consecutively selected to be the starting centre of the Western Team in the NBA All-Star Game. On February 23, 2004, Yao created his personal career record by scoring 41 points and having 7 assists in a game. On the December 7, 2003, he had his personal rebounding record by having 20 rebounds in a game. On the November 12, 2003, he had his personal rejection record by blocking 7 shots in a game. He was selected to be in NBA All-Rookie First Team of the year by averaging 13.5 points, 8.2 rebounds and 1.74 blockings per game. During the 6 games he played from the November 10-22, 2002, he scored 31 shots out of 35 and updated a NBA record by the 88.6percent field goal percentage in 6 consecutive games in NBA history. He was also the top pick of the 2002 NBA Draft. In 2005, Yao Ming was voted as the starting center representing the Western Conference at the NBA All-Star consecutively for the third time. The ballots he's gained made a record high in NBA history. On March 11, 2005, he grabbed 22 rebounds (career-high, including 9 offensive rebounds) in a game with the Suns. In 2004-05 season, his field goal rate is the 3rd highest and block ranks 11th among all the NBA players. On March 6, 2006, he gained 32 points and 13 rebounds, upgrading his average statistics to 20 point/10 rebounds for the first time in 4 years.

Yao Ming, at a match of NBA Regular Season on December 15, 2006

Yi Jianlian

Yi Jianlian (1987-), basketball player.

Yi won the championship in the 2002 Asian Youth Championships games and the 2nd place in the 2003 CBA Premier League Series A games. In 2004, he won the championship in the CBA Premier League Series A games and the 8th place in the Athens Olympic Games. Now he serves in the New Jersy Nets of the United States.

♦ Chinese Basketball Association

The Chinese Basketball Association (CBA) was founded in May, 1956. It won its legal position in Asian Amateur Federation in 1975. In 1976, the International Amateur Basketball Federation recognized CBA's legal position in the organization, and acknowledged that CBA is the sole legal basketball organization that can represent China in the world. The administration center of basketball, a sub-division of CBA, takes the responsibility of promoting the sport in China. After the introduction of some reforms in 1994, the first CBA league was launched the following year, with 12 teams participating. By 2000, there were 43 men's teams, and 42 women's teams registered under CBA. The total member of players had reached 998. The advent of the With CBA league represented a giant step in the development of professional basketball in China. In 1989, the first basketball club, sponsored by Anshan Steel Company, was founded in Shenyang. By 2000, the members of professional basketball clubs registered under CBA had reached 29.

Address: No.5 Tiyuguan Lu, Beijing
Website: http://www.cba.gov.cn

♦ Chinese University Basketball Association

CUBA, the Chinese University Basketball Association, was founded in 1985. Before the CUBA league was launched in 1998, it had already done a lot of work in promoting the sport on campus. When the CUBA league was held for the first time, it drew 617 teams form 26 provinces and cities. During the 2000-2001season, CUBA activities enjoyed even greater popularity on campus. Many famous universities have begun to put huge effort into succeeding in this new league. Compared with NCAA, the National Collegiate Athletic Association, which has been in existence for 63 years, the CUBA is still very much in its infancy. However, at its current rate of development, the future leaves bright for this new basketball association in China.

Softball

Softball was first introduced to China in the early 20th Century. After the Philippine women's softball team gave a performance in the Far East Games held in Shanghai in 1915, softball gradually began to be played in the church schools of Shanghai, Beijing, Tianjin and etc. In the 3rd National Games of the Old China in 1924, the women's softball was listed as a performance program for the first time. And it was officially included in the game list in the 5th National Games of the Old China in 1933.

After the founding of the New China in 1949, the women's softball teams from 21 provinces and municipalities took part in the 1st National Games in 1959. The women's softball was officially listed as a game item for eight times during the ten times of National Games except in the 2nd and the 5th Games. The Chinese Softball Association was founded in 1974, and China became a regular member of the International Softball Association in November of 1979. The Chinese women's softball team won the bronze medal and the silver medal respectively in the World Championships of 1990 and 1994. It got the second place in the 26th Atlanta Olympic Games in 1996, and won the fourth place respectively in the 27th and the 28th Olympic Games.

The 7th Junior Women's World Championship was held in Nanjing, the capital city of Jingsu Province of China from October.12 to 21 in 2003, and the junior teams from 14 countries and regions took part in the championship. From August 27 to September 5 in 2006, XI Women's World Championship was held in Beijing, which was the highest level of international softball games hosted by China.

Softball Players

Now there are 11 softball teams, namely Beijing, Tianjin, Shanghai, Liaoning, Jiangsu, Guangdong, Henan, Hunan, Sichuan, Gansu, and PLA, with a total number of about 300 professional players. Besides, there are around 1,000 youth amateurs. The Chinese women's softball team began to attend the international competitions in the early 1980s, and by the end of 2005, they had won the second place at the Olympic Games once, the fourth place twice; and the second place twice in the World Champion, once the third place, twice the fourth place; and the first place in the Asian Champion for three times; and the championship in the Asian Games for three times, and once the second place.

The physical condition of Chinese softball players is very good. Their heights range from 1.68m to 1.70m, and the pitchers are from 1.77m to 1.80m in height. The standard shows that the new generation of players exceeds the previous generations in height. In terms of physical quality, they are fast in pitching speed and strong in power. According to the statistics provided by the speed measuring instrument, there are at least 3 or 4 pitchers whose pitching speed has reached 100km per hour, and another 4 or 5 pitchers with 96-98km per hour of pitching speed. The former has been close to the world advanced level.

♦ Chinese Softball Association

The Chinese Softball Association was once attached to the Chinese Baseball & Softball Association. It began to be an independent one from 1986, with its headquarters in Beijing. The Chinese Softball Association is a member of the Individual Sports Association under the All-China Sports Federation, and is a mass organization of Chinese softball. In November, 1971, China became a member of the International Softball Federation (ISF). In August, 1982, the Chinese Baseball & Softball Association joined the International Association of Amateur Baseball & Softball. The Asian Softball Federation accepted the Chinese Softball Association as its member in 1986. He Huixian, the chairman of the Chinese Softball Association, is now the vice chairman of the ISF.

Tenets of the Chinese Softball Federation: to organize international competitions; to organize all kinds of national competitions and trainings at all levels; to make an initial draft for the system of management and competition as well as the class standard on the skills of players, coaches and referees; to manage the training of coaches, referees and players; to select and recommend the coaches and players for the national team and be responsible for organizing the national team to participate all competitions both at home and abroad; to organize activities of exchanging experience and academic studies.

Address: No.2 Tiyuguan Lu, Chongwen District, Beijing
Website: http://www.softball.sport.cn

Previous records of Chinese Women's Softball Team

Time	Venue	Game	Ranking
1986	New Zealand	the 6th Women's Softball World Championship	2nd place
1990	United States	the 7th Women's Softball World Championship	3rd place
1994	Canada	the 8th Women's Softball World Championship	2nd place
1996	United States	softball game of the 26th Olympic Games	2nd place
1998	Japan	the 9th World Championship	4th place
2000	Australia	softball game of the 27th Olympic Games	4th place
2002	Canada	the 10th World Championship	4th place
2004	Greece	softball game of the 28th Olympic Games	4th place

Women's Softball World Championship

The modern softball originated from the USA. It's a group game developing from baseball, and was officially named as softball in 1932. The International Softball Association was founded in September 1952. In 1965, the first Women's Softball World Championship was held in Australia, which is the highest level of competition for the women's softball teams in the world.

The 6th Women's Softball World Championship was held in Auckland from January 17 to January 27 in 1986. A total number of 12 teams participated in the 71 rounds of fierce competitions which lasted 10 days, and finally the American team won the champion. It was the first time for the Chinese team to participate in the world championship. They won six rounds consecutively within less than 24 hours and got the second place of the championship. The Chinese team member, Li Hong, was selected to be a member of the World Star team; Liu Xuqing, another member of Chinese team won the "Optimum Defense Prize"; Ren Yanlu got the "Homer Prize" and "Score Prize"; Li Chunlan was the prizewinner of "Optimum Pitcher"; Shi Minyue and Hua Jie got the consolation prize.

The 11th Women's Softball World Championship

After ten days of competition, the 11th Women's Softball World Championship which is also the first testing match for the Beijing 2008 Olympic Games completed on the softball field in Fengtai District of Beijing on September 5, 2006.The Chinese women's softball team got the fourth place, and the US team won the champion in the final against the Japanese team with the score of 3:0 by pitching homer twice. It was the sixth time for the US team to won the champion in the World Championship.

The 11th Women's Softball World Championship involved a total number of 16 teams, however, the Columbian team quitted for some incidents, so the rest 15 teams are respectively from China, England, South Africa, DPRK, Japan, Tapei of China, New Zealand, Canada, the US, Italy, Botswana, Australia, Greece, Venezuela and Holland. After fierce competition, the Chinese team got the fourth place and the Australian team the third.

What's worth mentioning, as it is the qualifying match for the 2008 Olympic Games, the first three winners including the US, Japan and Australia are qualified to participate in the women's softball competition of the 2008 Olympic Games. The Canadian team got another qualification through an extra match. China, as the host nation, is naturally qualified to participate in the Olympic Games.

On September 4, 2006, the Chinese and Australian team competed for the third place at the 11th World Women's Softball Tournament.

Li Minkuan

Li Minkuan (1937-), softball coach. In 1975, he took up the post as the head coach of Beijing women's softball team, which won the national champion under his guidance. Then He led the Chinese women's softball team to win the second place of the World Championship in 1986, the champion of the 4th Asian Women's Softball Championship in 1987 and the second place of Women's Softball at the 26th Olympic Games in 1996. He was once the head coach of the Chinese women's softball team, the head coach of the national softball team, the vice chairman of the Chinese Softball Federation and the vice chairman of the Asian Softball Federation. In 2000, he was conferred the certificate of "International Softball Federation Hall of Fame".

Li Nianmin

Li Nianmin (1957-), Softball Player. In 1976, she was chosen to play in the Beijing softball team and played the role of key pitcher for many times in the national softball team. She is a pitcher who never loses the game in the competition against the most powerful teams in the world. In the competition against Japan, she got the pitching rate of 46 percent and the pitching speed of 103km/h, over 10km/h faster than the fastest female pitcher of Japan and nearly the same speed with the Japanese fastest male pitcher.

Previous records of Chinese Junior Women's Softball Team

Time	Venue	Games	Ranking
1981	Canada	1st Junior Women's World Championship	2nd place
1985	New Zealand	2nd Junior Women's World Championship	1st place
1987	United States	3rd Junior Women's World Championship	2nd place
1991	Australia	4th Junior Women's World Championship	3rd place
1995	Canada	5th Junior Women's World Championship	6th place
1999	Taipei, China	6th Junior Women's World Championship	4th place
2003	Nanjing, China	7th Junior Women's World Championship	4th place

Large-scale International Softball Championships Hosted by China

Time	Venue	Games
October, 1999	Shanghai	Asian Softball Championship
October, 2003	Nanjing	Junior Women's World Championship
August, 2006	Beijing	Women's Softball World Championship
August, 2008	Beijing	Olympic Games
October, 2008	Nanjing	College Students' Softball World Championship

Equestrianism

Modern Chinese equestrian sport was based on the traditional sports and military training of the nation.

The equestrian performance was first started in the 1st Ethnic Games in 1953. Equestrianism was listed as a formal event in the 1st National Games in 1959, which involved over 300 riders and 400 horses from 13 teams, and became the first large-scale equestrian event since the founding of the People's Republic of China.

The equestrianism developed at the end of the 1970s. In 1979, the Chinese Equestrian Association was founded, and it was accepted as a member of the International Equestrian Federation in 1982. Since 1984, the Chinese Equestrian Association has been holding the National Equestrian Championship annually which gives priority to the field jumping obstacle riding, accompanied by speed horse racing. Then dressage and Three-day Event were added. And the three equestrian items gradually developed in China. China has held the "Inner Mongolia International Equestrian Invitation Game" consecutively for five times since 1992. In the 1st Asian Championship held in the South Korea in 1997, Zhang Ke, an excellent Chinese equestrian, won the champion of the B-class field jumping obstacle riding.

Although at present China has around 10 million horses, accounting 1/6 of the total

On April 9, 2005, Beijing Tongshun Racecourse, the largest professional racecourse in China, formally resumed the open competition.

number of the world, they haven't reached the professional standard required by the modern equestrian games, so the Chinese Equestrian Association still introduced the ex-service horses from Hong Kong. The Hong Kong Equestrian Federation provided several batches of horses within several years. In recent years, the Chinese Equestrian Association has welcomed many visitors from the international equestrian organizations of different countries and regions, such as France, the United States, Italy, Australia, England, Hong Kong and Macao, to China. It plays a positive role in the development of the Chinese equestrian games.

The First National Equestrian and Polo Game

From August 27 to September 16 in 1959, the equestrian and polo game of the 1st National Games of China was held in Huhhot, the capital of Inner Mongolia. It was the first national equestrian game held since 1949, which involved 226 players and 293 horses from 13 different parts, namely Hebei, Shandong, Shanxi, Jiangsu, Jilin, Xinjiang, Heilongjiang, Guizhou, Qinghai, Inner Mongolia and the PLA. The total score of the Inner Mongolian team including men and women ranked No.1 in horse racing; the Inner Mongolian team also won the 1st place in men's jumping obstacles and polo games; and the Guizhou team ranked No.1 in women's jumping obstacles.

♦ The Chinese Equestrian Association

The Chinese Equestrian Association, founded in 1979, is the most authoritative administration for all games involving horses and the sole legal organization which can, on behalf of China, participate in all international sports on horsebacks as well as the International Federation and the International Speed Horse Racing Organization. It is a mass sports organization and non-profit. It is a professional group voluntarily set up by professional personnel, coaches and managerial personnel of equestrianism, with its headquarters in Beijing.

The Chinese Equestrian Association often holds competitions such as the National Equestrian Championship, the National Equestrian Elite Competition, the Open Tournament of "the Chinese Equestrianism Cup" Club Speed Horse Racing, the Open Tournament of "China Cup" Speed Horse Racing and etc.

Address: No.153 Laoshaoxi Dajie, Shijingshan District, Beijing
Website: http://www.equestrian.sport.org.cn

Volleyball

The Early Development of the Chinese Volleyball

Volleyball was introduced into China in 1905. It first started in several middle schools in Guangzhou and Hong Kong, and then gradually developed to Shanghai, Beijing and etc. At that time, volleyball which was less associated with competitions was mainly used for get-together and entertaining.

In 1913, China first participated in the volleyball competition of the 1st Far East Games held in Philippines, which, in the historic records, was the earliest international volleyball game China participated in. China's participation aroused the attention and interest in volleyball of people. Afterwards, volleyball competitions developed in large scale. At the 2nd National Games of 1914, men's volleyball was officially listed in the competition.

The Chinese men's volleyball made remarkable achievements in the early period. In the 2nd Far East Games held in Shanghai in 1915, the Chinese men's volleyball team won the champion only on the occasion that they participated in the competition for the second time. By 1934, the Chinese men's volleyball had got the first place for five times in the total number of ten competitions of the Far East Games.

Compared with the men's volleyball, the Chinese women's volleyball started relatively late. It first appeared at the sports meeting of the Guangdong Province in 1921, and was officially listed in competitions of the National Games in 1930. Since 1923, the Chinese women's volleyball team participated in the Far East Games for five times and ranked the second in each.

China has a twenty-four years history of volleyball played by nine people in each team. Within the 24 years, volleyball-playing skills with the Chinese characteristics were gradually developed, with the Chinese players summing up a lot of tactics in high quality, such as "quick attack", "double quick-attack" and so on, which greatly promoted the development of the Chinese volleyball.

Modern Development of the Chinese Volleyball

After the founding of the Peoples' Republic of China in 1949, volleyball was popularized as a key sport and gradually became one of the well-received and fast-developing games all over the country. In July, 1950, the All-China Sports Federation introduced the game rules and techniques of six-man volleyball. In August the first men's volleyball team of the new China—a

On September 30, 2006, Chinese men's volleyball team held the open training classes.

delegation of the Chinese students, was formed. It participated in the volleyball competition of the 2nd World Students' Conference held in Prague. From then on, the six-man volleyball began to develop in China.

In May 1951, China held the national basketball and volleyball games in Beijing, which was the first national volleyball game since 1949. In the same year, the Chinese Junior Men's Volleyball team participated in the 11th Berlin College Students' Winter Games and the 3rd World Youth Get-together. In 1953, the Chinese Junior Women's Volleyball team participated in the volleyball competition of the 1st International Youth Friendship Games held in Bucharest, the capital of Romania.

The Chinese Volleyball Association was founded in 1953 and was officially accepted by the International Volleyball Federation as a member in 1954. In August of 1956, the Chinese men's volleyball team and the women's team participated in the Paris 3rd Men's World Championship and the 2nd Women's World Championship respectively. The former ranked the 9th place and the later the 6th.

In 1964, Premier Zhou Enlai personally invited Omatsu Hirofumi, titled "Devil Coach" which reflected his strict style of training, to visit China with the Japanese women volleyball team. He also trained the Chinese women's volleyball team.

The Splendid Period of the Chinese Volleyball

In the 3rd Volleyball World Cup held in Japan in 1981, the Chinese women's volleyball team, for the first time ever, China snatched the world title after winning all the seven competitions it participated in. Thereafter, it also won the titles of the Volleyball World Championship in 1982, the Los Angeles Olympic Games in 1984, the Volleyball World Cup in 1985 and the Volleyball World Championship in 1986. This is what we called "Five Consecutive Titles" the whole nation is still proud of till today.

At the same time, the Chinese men's volleyball also made tremendous breakthrough, not only creating many new tactics such as "forward flight", "back flight" and etc, but also becoming an insurmountable team in Asia. It ranked before the 8th place many times in a series of world competitions, with the 5th as its success.

The Current State of the Chinese Volleyball

From the late 1980s, the performance of the Chinese volleyball, both men's and women's, went down to the bottom. The men's volleyball lost the qualifications to participate in the Los Angeles Olympic Games, the Seoul Olympic Games and the Volleyball World Cup in a row, and their performance was not good enough in several Asian Volleyball Championships. The women's volleyball fell to the places of 7th and the 8th respectively at the Olympic Games of 1992 and the Volleyball World Championship in 1994.

The competition rules of the Chinese volleyball went through reforms in 1995, and the 1st National Volleyball League was held a year later. The reform and professionalization refreshed the Chinese volleyball. The women's volleyball team won the champion of the Asian Volleyball Championship, ranked the 3rd place in the Volleyball World Cup and got the first place at the 1996 Atlanta Olympic Games as well as "Competitions Among Six Outstanding Teams" at the end of that year. The men's volleyball team regained the champion of the Asian Volleyball Championship in 1997. It also got the first place in the Asian Games in 1998, so did the women' volleyball team.

After reorganization, the Chinese women's volleyball quickly demonstrated its powerfulness. Led by the new coach, Chen Zhonghe, it won 11 competitions consecutively in the 2003 Volleyball World Cup and regained the world champion after 17 years. The achievement again stimulated the Chinese passion for the women's volleyball team as well as the volleyball games. At 2004 Athens Olympic Games, the Chinese women's volleyball team smoothly went through all competitions and beat the powerful Russian team with 3:2 in the finals, the first time to win the Olympic Champion after 20 years.

Now the Chinese women's volleyball team is in the run-in time when elder players are being replaced by the younger, and the men's is gradually seeking the steady development in ups and downs. And both aim at the Beijing 2008 Olympic Games.

Becoming a Member of the International Volleyball Federation

In 1953, the Chinese Volleyball Association was founded. It was officially acknowledged and accepted as a member of the International Volleyball Federation on January 11, 1954. In August 1956 the 3rd Men's Volleyball World Championship and the 2nd Women's Volleyball World Championship, organized by the International Volleyball Federation, was held in Paris. The Chinese men's and women's volleyball teams were officially invited to participate in the competition, so in February 1956, the national volleyball team of both Men's and Women's were formed through selecting organized by the Chinese Volleyball Association.

The Chinese Women's Volleyball Team

The Chinese women's volleyball team persists in the style of "Quick, Comprehensive and versatile" with its own characteristics. It's the appropriate style that puts the Chinese women's volleyball team on the world top list in recent 30 years. The old Chinese women's volleyball team was good at both attacking and defending. It had Lang Ping, one of the three world top spikers, Zhang Rongfang titled "Strange Volleyball-player", Liang Yan and Yang Xiaojun who were good at quick attack and blocking, the world top setter Yang Xilan, and also Zhen Meizhu with the excellent defense skills. The new women's volleyball team now inherited the old team's combatant sprit and excellent tactics. Feng Kun has been the world top second transmitter who is superior in blocking, just as Yang Xilan of the old team. Zhao Ruirui, Liu Yanan and Zhang Ping are all world top co-spikers, but they all have their own merits: Zhao Ruirui who is the tallest is good at blocking, Liu Yanan's is a good master of all skills and the attacking tactics of Zhang Ping are awesome to others. Although it lacks super attackers like Lang Ping, the Chinese women's volleyball team has its own strong points, as it also has Yang Hao, Wang Lina and Zhang Yuehong who have versatile tactics, the most excellent second setter in the world, Zhou Suhong, and the best liberal player Zhang Na. From the above, we can get a rough idea of the comprehensive tactics and strength of both the old and the new women's volleyball team.

Now, eleven of the twelve players of the Chinese women's volleyball team are taller than 1.80m. Zhao Ruirui, the tallest player, stands at 1.97m, over 13cm taller than Lang Ping who was the tallest of the old team and whose height could only rank the 5th in the new team.

The Volleyball League

The volleyball league, just like the leagues of both basketball and foot, is one of the three leagues which marked the Chinese sports' achievement concerning the orientation towards professionalization. It has been 10 years since we began to hold the national volleyball leagues. Within the 10 years, in order to expand the scale and improve the quality of the leagues, the organization committee adopted many measures including: hosting the leagues by clubs; implementing the double-host-double-guest game rule, carrying out the single-host-single-

On August 28, 2004, the Chinese team won over the Russia team 3:2 in the final of the women's volleyball at the Athens Olympics, retaining the Olympic gold medal after an interval of 20 years. In the picture, the Chinese members kissed the gold medals.

guest game rule, increasing the numbers of teams participating the competitions, prolonging the game cycle, accepting the college teams to participate in the competitions and etc. The number of teams participating in the national volleyball league increased from 24 to 32 during the competition season of 2005-2006, including not only those teams which are at the edge of the league but the college volleyball teams such as Bei Hang University, Nan Kai University and etc. After the expansion, the league lasts eight months, with around 220 matches. In terms of scale, the Chinese volleyball league ranks the second in the world, just following the Italian International Professional League which accepts the volleyball teams from all round the world.

At the 1st league in 1996, there were only 110 thousand on-the-sport spectators, with an average of 500 for each match. However, at the 10th, the total number had reached 510 thousand.

The First Time to Participate in the Volleyball World Championship

From August 30 to September 12, 1956, the 3rd Men's Volleyball World Championship and the 2nd Women's Volleyball World Championship were held in Paris, the capital of France. There were 24 men's teams and 17 women's. It was the first time for the China to participate the championship, where the men's team got the 9th place and the women's 6th.

Deng Ruozeng

Deng Ruozheng (1936-) was once the player and the advanced coach of the Chinese men's volleyball team. In 1955, he was selected to play in Sichuan volleyball team and was selected into the state volleyball training team in 1959. Afterwards, he attended the international competitions for many times. He was titled "Master Sportsman" in 1958. The team he played in had a series of good records: the 8th place in the volleyball competitions of Europe, Asia and America in 1959, the 9th place of the 5th Men's Volleyball World Championship in 1962, the winner at the Games of the New Emerging Forces in 1963, the 9th place of the Men's Volleyball World Championship in 1966 and the title of the Asian Games of the New Emerging Forces in the same year. From 1979, he began to act as the coach of the Chinese women's volleyball team. He got the title of "National Coach" in 1980. His close cooperation with the head coach Yuan Weimin helped the Chinese women's volleyball team won the champions at the 3rd Volleyball World Cup in 1981, the 9th Women's Volleyball World Championship and the Women's Volleyball Competition of the 9th Asian Games in 1983. It also won the title of the women's volleyball at the 23rd Olympic Games in 1984, making his dream of "Three Consecutive Titles" come true. In the same year, he began to act as the head coach. In 1985, the Chinese women's volleyball team won the champion of the 4th Volleyball World Cup, and he was awarded the title of "Best Coach".

Yuan Weimin

Yuan Weimin (1939-), volleyball coach. In August, 1981, the Chinese women's volleyball team won the title in the 3rd Women's Volleyball World Cup held in Japan. Yuan Weimin was awarded the title of "The Best Coach". He was the first Chinese coach to have such an honor.

In the early 1960s, Yuan Weimn was an excellent setter of the Chinese men's volleyball team and played over 200 international matches. He was appointed coach of the Chinese women's volleyball team in 1976. From then on, he began to dedicate himself to training the team. He learnt from practice as well as others and created a way of development with his own characteristics. His technical and tactic thoughts, training principles, methods of managing the team, ways of scientifically dealing with the problems emerging from the substitution of the old members by the new, transmission work relying on a good master of minds and thoughts of the players, directing methods and so on, have created precious treasures for the development of the Chinese and world volleyball. His composed and competent direction in face of whatever matches demonstrate the talent and quality of an excellent coach.

Chen Yuxin

The eleven referees of the International Volleyball Federation are the most excellent referees selected from over 900 international referees all over the world by the IVF in 1987 to act as the first referees in the four great international volleyball competitions, namely the Olympic Games, the World Volleyball Championships, the Volleyball World Cup and the Junior World Championships. Chen Yuxin, the Chinese referee, topped the eleven referees of the IVF.

Chen Yuxin was born in Jiangsu Province. In the 1960s, he was a volleyball player. After he retired due to injuries, he went to study in Beijing Sport Institute (today's Beijing Sport University). He worked as professional volleyball referee after graduation. On Mar.7th, 1976, he went to Japan to take the examinations for the international referee candidates. He got the first place in the exams of both theories and practice. Then he acted as the law-executor of the Volleyball World Cup, the World Volleyball Championships and many intercontinental competitions hosted by the IVF. He enjoyed a good reputation all over the world because of his fairness, preciseness and diligence. In August of 1984, he went onto the first referee's platform of the men's volleyball competition at the 23rd Olympic Games.

Sun Jinfang

Sun Jinfang (1955-), volleyball player. In the 3rd Women's Volleyball World Cup, Sun Jinfang won three prizes: "the Best Player", "the Excellent Player" and "the Best Setter", which she richly deserved. It was the first time for the Chinese player to win "the Best Player" and "the Best Setter". Sun Jinfang's consummate skills and tenacious spirits greatly impressed the fans both at home and abroad.

Sun Jinfang was selected to play in the women's volleyball team II of the Jiangsu Province where she received the setter-oriented training. In 1976, she was selected into the state team, and she began to act as captain in 1978, going through more comprehensive and stricter training. She was the inspiration of the Chinese women's volleyball team, as she was quick-witted, smart and confident. She was good at understanding and carrying out the coach's tactic thoughts and arranging the way of attacking in accordance with the unpredictable conditions in the court and the tactics of every team member. She also had tacit cooperation with the attacker. Besides, she could dump with the left hand out of expectation. Under her organization and direction, the Chinese women's volleyball team created varieties of quick attack tactics, giving full play to the unique and variable style of Chinese tactics and skills in some major international competitions. In 1982, she retired after playing hard with injury and finally finishing wonderfully the Women's Volleyball World Championship.

Sun Jinfang, the current director of the Tennis Management Center of the General Administration of Sport of China

Lang Ping

Lang Ping (1960-), Volleyball Player. In 1976, Lang Ping was selected into the Beijing women's volleyball team I headed by Yuan Weimin. She was selected into the state women's volleyball team and played as the key attacker. She had the advantaged physical conditions: 1.84m in height, good flexibility and strong bouncing capability. She was well known for her fierce attacking in the world. Many sports fans called her "Metal Lang". She was also acknowledged as one of the "World Top Spikers". In 1982, she participated in the 3rd Women's Volleyball World Cup held in Japan, where her team won the world title for the first time. It was also the first world title for the three major ball games of China. Lang Ping was one of "Three Key Attackers" in the world women's volleyball in the 1980s. After she retired, she twice acted as the head coach of the Chinese women's volleyball team and made great contribution to the re-rise of the Chinese women's volleyball team.

Lai Yawen

Lai Yawen (1970-), volleyball player. She started her sportsman career in 1982, and was selected into the state women's volleyball team in 1989. She retired in 1998. She has been serving as coach of the Chinese women's volleyball team since 1999.

Major records: the 5th of the Volleyball World Cup in 1999; the 5th place at the Sydney Olympic Games; the champions of the Asian Volleyball championships in 1999, 2001 and 2003; the champion of Women's Volleyball World Grand Champions Cup; the 2nd place of the World Women's Volleyball Grand Prix in 2001; the 4th place of the World Volleyball Championship in 2002; the champion of the Busan Asian Games in 2002; the 2nd place of the World Women's Volleyball Grand Prix in 2002; the champion of the Women's Volleyball World Cup in 2003; the champion of the World Women's Volleyball Grand Prix in 2003.

Zhang Yuehong

Zhang Yuehong (1975-), volleyball player. From 1989, she began to play volleyball in the Shenyang School of Physical Education, and was selected into the state women's volleyball team in 2000.

Major records: the champion in the finals of the World Women's Volleyball Grand Prix in 2001; the 4th place of the Women's Volleyball World Championship in 2002; the champion of the World Women's Volleyball Grand Prix in 2003; the champion of the Asian Volleyball Championship in 2003; the champion of the Women's Volleyball World Cup in 2003.

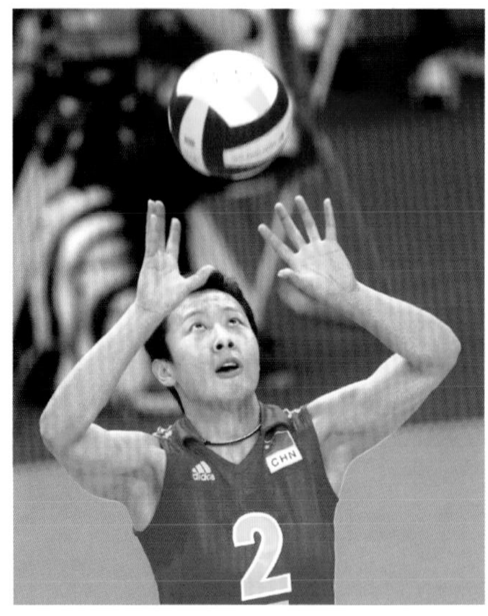

Feng Kun in the competition of the Group A of the group match of the women's volleyball at the 15th Daoda Asian Games on December 6, 2006

Feng Kun

Feng Kun (1979-), volleyball player.

Feng Kun is the key setter of the Chinese women's volleyball team. She played the core role in the tactics of "quickness and changeability". She was twice titled as the "Best Setter" at the Volleyball World Cup in 2003 and the 12th Asian Volleyball Championship. She is nicknamed "Panda". Now she is the captain of the Chinese women's volleyball team. She is not only good at passing but also very calm in face of difficulties. She is the tallest setter in the history of the Chinese women's volleyball. She is also good at blocking. As a matter of fact, Feng Kun liked attacking very much. She practiced setting because she was short when she just began to play volleyball. Till now, she has a strong sense of attack. Once chances come, she would attack the opponents by surprise, which made it hard for the opponents to guard against.

Zhao Ruirui

Zhao Ruirui (1981-), volleyball player. She started to play basketball in the Youngster's School of Physical Education in Jiangsu Province when she was 11 years old. In 1999, she was selected into the state women's volleyball team.

She was the tallest among the players of the Chinese women's volleyball team. According to the statistics on skills about the 2003 Volleyball World Cup, she ranked the first, the second and the sixth in terms of spiking, blocking and scoring respectively. Standing at 196cm in height, she has the very high spiking point and is also good at quick playing and blocking. The serious injury in 2002 nearly damaged her sportsman career; however, she has been making great progress and become No.1 score-maker in the team.

♦ "Three Consecutive Titles" of the Women's Volleyball Team

"Three Consecutive Titles", that is, consecutively winning the titles of Volleyball World Cup, World Volleyball Championships and the Olympic Games, is the highest reputation for volleyball games in the world. On August 7, 1984, girls of the Chinese women's volleyball team made their dreams of "Three Consecutive Titles" come true at the 23rd Olympic Games.

It was the new team which was reorganized in 1982 that won the gold medal of the Olympic Games. The team members average 22 years' old, three years younger than the old members. Their average height is 1.29m, 2cm higher than that of the old team. The new team consists of the coaches Yuan Weimin and Deng Ruozeng and the team members including Zhang Rongfang(the captain), Lang Ping, Hou Yuzhu, Yang Xiaojun, Ying Qin, Li Yanjun, Jiang Ying, Su Huijuan, Yang Xilan, Zhu Ling, Liang Yan and Zhen Meizhu.

♦ The "Five Consecutive Titles" of the Women' Volleyball Team

Every Chinese who have experienced the 1980s can never forget the day, November 6, 1981, when the Chinese women's volleyball team beat the Japanese women's volleyball team with 3:2 at the 3rd Women's Volleyball World Cup held in Osaka, Japan.

The Chinese women's volleyball team, led by the coach Yuan Weimin, won the title again in the World Volleyball Championship held in Peru in 1982.

In the volleyball finals of the 23rd Olympic Games in August, 1984, the Chinese women's volleyball team won the title after beating the Japanese and American teams with the same score 3:0, achieving the "Three Consecutive Titles" in the world matches.

From 1985 on, many members of the old team retired and Lang Ping, "World No.1 Spiker", began to act as the captain. She led the team to participate in the 4th Volleyball World Cup held in Japan where it got the world title after winning all the competitions.

Two years later, the Chinese women's volleyball team won the title of the 14th World Volleyball Championship without those world famous players in the past, creating the wonder of "Five Consecutive Titles" for the team.

Beach Volleyball

Beach volleyball appeared in China a bit late. It started in the late 1980s and early 1990s when several national and international beach volleyball invitation games, including 4-man and 2-man competition rule, were unofficially organized by the journal of "Chinese Volleyball". After it was officially confirmed to the on the list of games by the International Olympic Committee in 1993, the Chinese Volleyball Association began to hold the official national beach volleyball competitions. In 1997, the Chinese team participated in the World Beach Volleyball Championship for the first time.

History of the Chinese Beach Volleyball

— In 1994, the beach volleyball was included in the official games and listed in the competitions of the National Games.

— In 1997, it first appeared in the 8th National Games.

— In the 13th Asian Games in 1998, the Chinese players, Li Hua and Gu Hongyu won the title of men's beach volleyball.

— The National Circuit started in 1994, and the National Championships and the National Titles in 2000. It has been hosting the competitions on behalf of the International Volleyball Federation and the Asian Volleyball Federation for many years. There are over 10 provinces which have held the national and international beach volleyball competitions.

— In 2000, two pair of players, Chi Rong and Xiong Zi, Zhang Jingkun and Tian Jia, successfully passed the qualification competition and went into the finals of the Olympic Games, where they ranked the 9th and the 19th respectively.

At the 1st Asian Beach Volleyball Championship held in Guangdong Province of China, the Chinese women players won the first and second place.

— From 1998, China hosted the Women's Beach Volleyball Circuits of the International Volleyball Federation for five successive years in Dalian, Lianing Province and Maoming, Guangdong Province.

— In the World Beach Volleyball Championship in 2001, the Chinese players, Chi Rong and Xiong Zi, Tianjia and Wang Fei, ranked the 5th and the 17th. It was the best result the Chinese beach volleyball got in the world highest level of individual events.

— In the beach volleyball competition of the Friendly Games in 2001, Chi Rong and Xiong Zi participated on behalf of China, and got the 6th place. It was the best result the Chinese beach volleyball got in the world comprehensive games.

♦ The Chinese Volleyball Association

The Chinese Volleyball Association (CVA) is a mass sports organization responsible for the volleyball games. It is a national non-government and non-profit organization with corporate capacity. The CVA is the sole legitimate organization that represents China in the International and Asian Volleyball Federations.

In 1996, the CVA began to hold beach volleyball and soft volleyball games. The events organized by the CVA at home are the National Men's Volleyball Championships, the National Women's Volleyball Championships, the National Junior Volleyball Championships, the National Volleyball League of B-level, the National Volleyball League of A-level, the National Volleyball Championships, the National Volleyball League, the International Women's Volleyball Game of China and etc. Of all, the National Volleyball League and the International Women's Volleyball Game of China have become the traditional competition event held in China.

The headquarter of CVA is in Beijing.

Address: 5th Floor, Weitu Plaza, C3 Longtan Lu, Chongwen District, Beijing
Website: http://www.volleyball.org.cn

The Chinese Beach Volleyball Team

Major records of the Chinese women's beach volleyball team: In the World Beach Volleyball Championship in 2001, the Chinese women players ranked 3rd and 5th. In the 14th Asian Games in 2002, women players won both the title and the 2nd place, and men players ranked 3rd and 5th. In the World Circuits of 2003, women players won titles in both Indonesia and Italy. It was the first time for the Chinese national flag to rise and the national anthem to be played in the international beach volleyball court. In that year, three pairs of Chinese players ranked 5th, 14th and 34th respectively among the 194 pairs of players all over the world. In 2004, two pairs of women players were qualified to participate in the finals at the Olympic Games, and got the 9th and the 19th place respectively. In 2005, the best pair of players ranked 3rd in the world. In recent three years, the ranks of Chinese women players on the world annual lists kept staying within the top ten. In the Doha 2006 Asian Games, the Chinese players made a historic breakthrough, with men players ranking 1st and 2nd, and women plays winning the title.

On the recent rand list of the world beach volleyball teams, the Chinese women's teams occupy the 2nd and the 3rd, and the men's team the 6th.

On May 6, 2007, the first match of the 2007 Beach Volleyball Tour of the International Volleyball Federation and the First Points Race in China began in Shanghai. Chinese athletes Wang Jie and Tian Jia won the championship. In the picture is Tian Jia.

Tian Jia

Tian Jia (1981-), beach volleyball player. She began to play volleyball in 1995. In 1998, she was selected into the PLA beach volleyball team. She began to play in the state beach volleyball team in 2003.

Major records: the 19th place in the beach volleyball competition of the Sydney 2000 Olympic Games; the champion in the beach volleyball competition of 2002 Busan Asian Games; the champion in Indonesia at the World Women's Beach Volleyball Circuit in 2003; the champion in Italy at the World Women's Beach Volleyball Circuit in 2003 (ranking 2nd in the world).

Wang Fei

Wang Fei (1981-), beach volleyball player. She is on the left in the court and wears No.2 sports suit. She began to play volleyball in 1995. She was selected into the PLA beach volleyball team in 1998 and into the state beach volleyball team in 2003.

Major records: the 19th place in the beach volleyball competition of the Sydney 2000 Olympic Games; the champion in the beach volleyball competition of 2002 Busan Asian Games; the 5th place in Norway at the World Women's Beach Volleyball Circuit in 2003; the 5th place in China at the World Women's Beach Volleyball Circuit in 2003; the champion in Indonesia at the World Women's Beach Volleyball Circuit in 2003; the champion in Italy at the World Women's Beach Volleyball Circuit in 2003 (ranking 5th in the world).

Canoe/Kayak

As early as 2000 years ago, the Chinese started the "dragon boat competition", a sport very similar to canoeing. The modern canoe/ kayak game was introduced to China around 1930. The British first founded a "Boating Federation" in Shanghai. Then the Russians launched a "Water Club" in the Northeast Region. At that time, the Canoeing games were only for the entertainment of the foreigners in China. When the new China was established, the government paid great attention to the development of the sport. At the end of 1952, China made the first canoe of its own. In the 1954 Beijing Water Sports Games, the men's 1000m canoeing game and the women's 500m canoeing game were introduced. The sport had been forced to stop during the Culture Revolution in China and didn't return to view until 1972. In 1974, China joined the International Canoe Federation and canoeing was listed to be an official sport in the 3rd National Games in China. In the same year, China began to compete in World Championships games for canoeing. From that point on, canoeing began to develop quickly in China. In recent years, China took great effort in learning from the overseas strong forces for their techniques and training methods. By these techniques and methods, the Chinese athletes made fast improvement. Some of their performances could be ranked as the world tops. Canoeing began to have some unprecedented developments in the athlete number, game size and publicity.

China is now strong in the women's K1 500m, women's Kayak 1000m, women's K4 500m, men's C1 and C2 500m and men's C1 1000m.

The Development of Canoe/ Kayak Sports in China

The Canoeing sports in China began in the 50s of the last century. By the end of the last century, China was still positioned in the middle of the world in this sport. Although in some games, China used to rank the 3rd and 4th in the World Championship, or 4th and 5th in the Olympic Games, its overall performance cannot be listed as one of the world tops.

To reduce the gap between China and the strong forces in the world, the Chinese Canoeing Team hired foreign coaches to help with the training in 2002. The advanced training concepts and methods brought by the foreign coaches and the diligence and hard-working of the Chinese athletes had soon resulted in an overall improvement in performance of the Chinese Canoeing Team. In the 2004 Athens Olympic Games, Chinese athletes Meng Guanliang and Yang Wenjun won a gold medal in the Men's C2 500m Final. It was the first medal from Canoe/ Kayak that China ever won in the Olympic Games.

Experienced in the Athens Olympic Games, the Chinese Canoeing Team hired another foreign coach to prepare for the 2008 Beijing Olympics. The coach, Joseph, was the former head coach in Germany and had led the German team to win 17 Olympic gold medals. With even more hard works, the Chinese athletes stepped onto a higher platform in canoeing. In the late 2006 Canoe World Cup, the Chinese team won 6 gold, 13 silver, and 9 bronze medals out of the 27 finals. It was the best performance of the Chinese Team in the World Cup so far.

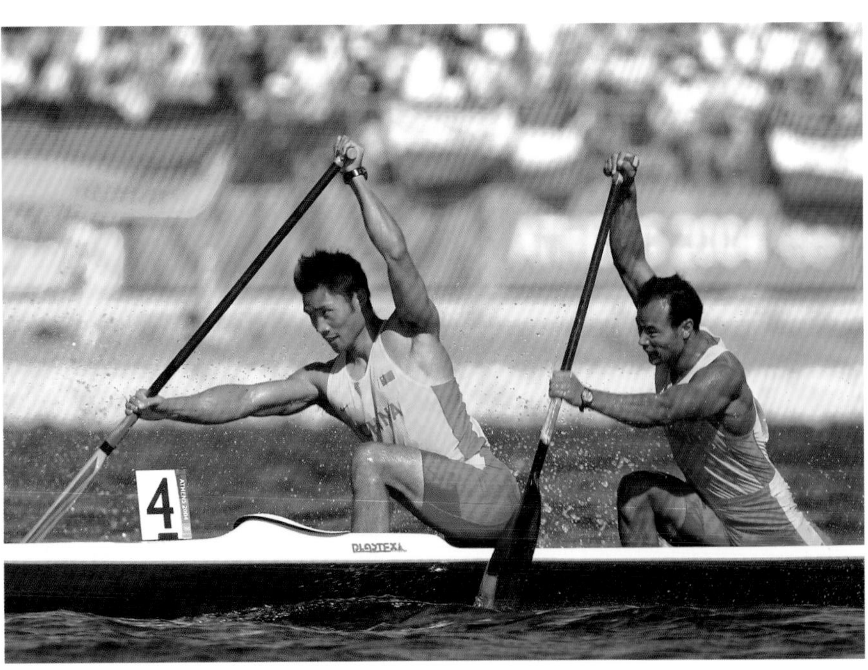

On August 28, 2004, Chinese players Meng Guanliang and Yang Wenjun won the gold medals in the men's 500m kayak doubles at the Anthens Olympics.

The First Canoe/Kayak World Champion

The 2004 World Cup finals ended in Duisburg Germany on the 27th, in which the Chinese athletes claimed championships in two Olympic events. In the Men's C2 500m final, Meng Guanliang and Yang Wenjun beat the Polish World Championships winner and won the title by a time of 1'42"920. This is the first world championship Chinese male canoeing athletes ever won. In the following Women's K2 500m final, Chinese athletes Xu Linpei and Zhong Hongyan claimed gold by a performance of 1'45"817. In the same day, the Chinese team also won the 2nd and 3rd in the Women's K4 500m final. By now, the Chinese team had achieved to win 3 gold, 2 silver and 1 bronze medals in the three-day event.

Meng Guanliang

Meng Guanliang (1977-), canoe/kayak athelete. was born in 1977. Meng entered the Shao Xing Amateur Sports School to practice canoeing in 1994. In the same year, he entered the professional team and became a member of the National Team a year later.

Meng, known for his strong arms, won gold medals of the Men's C1 500m and C1 1000m in the 8th National Games. In the 1998 National Championships games, he claimed titles in the C1 200m, C1 500m, C1 1000m, C1 5000m and Men's All-Around games. In the same year, he won a bronze medal in the Men's C2 500m and a gold medal in C1 1000m in the Bangkok Asian Games. In 1999, Meng won the championships of the Men's All-Around and C1 5000m games in the National Championship. A year later, he claimed championship in the C1 500m game of the National Tournament. In 2001, Meng remained to be the winner of the C1 500m game in the National Games. He won two gold medals separately in C1 500m and C1 2000m in the 2002 Busan Asian Games. A year later, he won the championship of the National Spring Championships C1 2000m game and the National Tournament C1 500m and C1 2000m games. In year 2004, Meng and Yang Wenjun cooperated to compete in the Men's C2 500m game of the Athens Olympic Games and won a gold medal. It was the first medal from Canoe/Kayak of the Chinese people in the China's Olympic history.

Yang Wenjun

Yang Wenjun (1983-), canoe/kayak athelete. He was selected by the Polish coach of the Province Team into the National Team.

Yang won the championship of the Men's C2 500m and C2 1000m games in the 2002 Asian Games. A year later, he was ranked the 7th in the C1 1000m game in the World Championship. In 2004, he and Meng Guanliang won the gold medal in the C2 500m game of the Athens Olympic Games by 1'40"278. It was the first Olympic gold medal in the history of Chinese Canoeing. In the 2006 Doha Asian Games, he won the championship of the Men's C1 500m.

♦ Chinese Canoeing Association

The Chinese Canoeing Association, a national non-governmental organization based in Beijing, was originally affiliated to the Chinese Boating Sports Association. In 1981, it became an independent organization. It is a member of the All-China Sports Federation. In 1974, the International Canoeing Association formally accepted China as its member.

Regular events held by the Chinese Canoeing Association include: the National Canoe/Kayak Championship, the National Youth Canoe/Kayak Tournament and the National Canoe/Kayak Tournament.

Address: C3, Longtan Road, Chongwen District, Beijing
Website: http://www.canoe.sport.org.cn

Major Achievements of the National Canoe/Kayak Team

The 2002 Pusan Asian Games	
Champion in Women's K1 500m	Zhong Hongyan
Champion in Women's K2 500m	Zhong Hongyan, Xu Linpei
Champion in Men's C1 500m	Meng Guanliang
Champion in Men's C1 1000m	Meng Guanliang
Champion in Men's C2 500m	Wang Bing, Yang Wenjun
Champion in Men's C2 1000m	Wang Bing, Yang Wenjun
Champion in Men's K4 1000m	Lin Yongjing, Liu Haitao, Song Zhongbo, Wan Wenjie
Champion in Men's K1 1000m	Liu Haitao
The 2004 German World Cup	
Champion in Women's K2 500m	Xu Linpei, Zhong Hongyan
Champion in Men's C2 500m	Meng Guanliang, Yang Wenjun
Women's k-4 1000m	GaoYi, Zhang Jinmei, Xu Linbei, Xu Yaping
The 2004 Athens Olympic Games 2004	
Champion in the Men's Flatwater C2 500m	Meng Guanliang, Yang Wenjun
9th in the Men's Flatwater C2 1000m	Meng Guanliang, Yang Wenjun
9th in the Men's Flatwater C1 500m	Wang Bing
4th in the Women's Flatwater K2 500m	Xu Linpei, Zhong Hongyan
9th in the Women's Flatwater K1 500m	Li Ting
7th in the Women's Flatwater K4 500m	Xu Linpei, Zhong Hongyan, He Jing, Gao Yi

Table Tennis

Table tennis is considered as China's national ball game.

In the recent fifty years, China has been among the top powers of world table tennis. Even if it encounters some difficulties sometimes, China National Table Tennis Team can always find the most effective way to solve the problems as soon as possible. Several generations of excellent Chinese table tennis players created many classic matches and invincible legends. The level of performance and influence of table tennis in China is incomparable.

In 1959, Rong Guotuan won men's single title at the 25th World Table Tennis Championships (WTTC), which was the first championship that China had ever won in any sports competition since the establishment of People's Republic of China (PRC). In 1961, Beijing, the capital of China, hosted the 26th WTTC, which was the first international sports event held in the PRC. In 1972, China launched "ping pong (another term for table tennis) diplomacy", which defroze Sino-US relations... There is never a country, except China, whose development has been connected so closely with a sport. As China's national ball game, table tennis has been bouncing with the pulse of the new China.

Debut of Table Tennis in China

Table tennis was introduced into China around the year of 1904, when a man called Wang Daoping who was the owner of a stationer in Shanghai, bought ten sets of table tennis equipment from Japan, including the tables, nets, balls and rackets with holes. However, nobody in Shanghai knew what they were at that time. Therefore, in order to let people know what they were used for, Wang set up a table to demonstrate how to play table tennis by himself, and told the audience how people played table tennis in Japan. From then on, Chinese began to play table tennis.

Development of Table Tennis in China

In October 1952, the first China national table tennis competition was held in Beijing. The competitors included sixty-two players from the Sports Federation of the Railway System and the six administrative regions of China, namely South China, North China, Northeast China, Southwest China, Northwest China and East China. At about the same time the Table Tennis Association under All-China Sports Federation was admitted to the International Table Tennis Federation (ITTF).

The scene of the 48th Shanghai World Table Tennis Championship

From then on table tennis has quickly risen in popularity among Chinese people all over the country, and a number of national competitions have been held every year.

Since its foundation in 1952 China National Table Tennis Team has experienced a process from failure to victory and from the bottom to the top of the world. It has made excellent performances in the WTTC and other international competitions. Through competitions and friendly visits, it has helped strengthen the friendship between China and other nations and promote the development of table tennis across the world.

It has been fifty years since China National Table Tennis Team was founded in 1952. The team won 125.5 world champions, including China's first world champion, China's first women's world champion, China's first team world champion, three clean sweeps of gold medals at the WTTC, and two clean sweeps of gold medals in the table tennis events at the Olympic Games.

Cultivation System of Table Tennis Players in China

Behind the glamorous achievements of China Table Tennis Team lies China's special cultivation system of table tennis players, which together with the great efforts made by the players maintains China's dominance of the sport. Thanks to the cultivation system, the sport of table tennis enjoys a mass foundation in China and abundant talented young players, who, however, will be quickly replaced by a younger generation.

Table tennis is considered as China's "national ball game", which demonstrates its strong popularity in China. Since the 1960s, China National Table Tennis Team has adopted a training regime of highly concentration, with the high-level players of different styles across China converging in the national squad, forming "a little world of table tennis". The national squad provides good training, living and boarding conditions, and sufficient services in medical care and logistics. Through simulative competitions, the core Chinese players are fighting against the world top players everyday, which enable them to practice with a focus. As a result, sometimes even the inexperienced young Chinese players can surprisingly defeat the world-level players. When preparing for a world major tournament, the members that are not going to attend the competition, even if they are the former champions, will make every effort to help the competitors.

Techniques Innovation

In the 1960s Chinese Table Tennis Team conquered Japanese pen-hold offensive play and European handshake defensive play by its pen-hold close-table fast attack and "fast, precise, harsh and changeable" techniques, representing the highest level of table tennis play in the world. Later Japanese invented loop, and the Europeans created new handshake offensive play combining Chinese fast attack and Japanese loop, reviving the European table tennis. In face of the revival of Europe, Chinese table tennis team on the one hand began to improve the performance of racket; and on the other hand added "spin" to the original style characterized by "fast, precise, harsh and changeable", integrating the five elements of speed, strength, spin, trajectory and point of fall. These improvements made Chinese players more invulnerable to the handshake offensive play, recapturing the dominance of table tennis in terms of techniques. The clean sweep of the champions at the 36th WTTC in 1981 was the best reward for the technique innovation. After that Chinese team no longer stick to pen-hold fast attack as the mainstream play, instead, it allowed the handshake loop develop itself, which led to a boom of talented table tennis players. The late 1990s witnessed a new climax of Chinese table tennis.

As for personal technique innovations, Chinese table tennis team also gave an outstanding performance. According to the incomplete statistics, in the recent 100 years, there have been 46 most outstanding innovations in terms of table tennis techniques and equipment in the world, among which 27 are from China, taking up 58.7 percent of the total.

♦ The Latest Rankings of Table Tennis Championships

On January 3, 2007 the ITTF published the latest world ranking list in 2007. The top three on the ranking list for both men and women are all Chinese. On the men's list, Wang Liqin maintained the world No.1 place with Ma Lin and Wanghao in the second and third places respectively. As for the women's rankings, Zhang Yining was on the top, and Wang Nan made a breakthrough to the second place because of her performance in the Asian Games. Guo Yan was down to the third place.

China's Performance in Table Tennis Competitions

From 1926 till now, China has won 89.5 gold medals at WTTC out of a total of 314 WTTC gold medals, ranking the first on the gold medal tally. Following China, Hungary ranks the second with 68.5 gold medals; and Japan is in the third place with 47 gold medals. Since 1980 there have been 38 champions of Table Tennis World Cup, among which China has won 21, more than any other country. Since 1988 when table tennis was first concluded in the Olympic Games, there have been 16 championships of table tennis at the Olympic Games. China with 13 champions is on the top of gold medal tally. Up till now, China has captured 124.5 gold medals of table tennis in total at World Cup, World Championships and Olympic Games. There are 45 male players and 41 female players in China's national squad who won one or more gold medals in the three major world competitions, among which Liu Guoliang (male) has won 11 gold medals, and Deng Yaping (female) has won 18, creating unprecedented records. Indeed, the China's National Table Tennis Team that has cultivated more than 80 world champions is a star-dudded team.

China's advantage is demonstrated by its great number of championships and world-level players as well as the three clean sweeps of gold medals at WTTC, namely the 36th in Novisad, the 43rd in Tianjin and the 46th in Osaka.

Chinese Table Tennis Club Super League

China owns the largest number of world champions and fans of the table tennis sport in the world. Chinese Table Tennis Club Super League was established with the goal of becoming the top-class league in the world just as NBA in the US. The present Chinese Super League is still lagged behind by the table tennis league match in Germany, which is the best in

The 15th round competition of the Table Tennis Club Super League held in Tieling City, Liaoning Province on August 6, 2005.

the world, in the operation and management of clubs and market promotion. However, its competitive level exceeded that of the German league match from the very beginning, and is even paralleled to that of many world tournaments, because of China's abundance in active world champions and amateur players that are as skillful as the world champions.

Chinese Table Tennis Club Super League has become one of the top-class table tennis events in the world, attracting many famous paddlers from outside China. Therefore, the Super League is more than a competition between Chinese paddlers. However, the world-class players who attend the Super League are convenient to know more about the training and skills of Chinese paddlers. In some world events, they become "the lions in the way" of Chinese competitors winning the gold medals. The most obvious example was in the men's singles final at 2004 Athens Olympic Games, Korean player Rye Seung-min defeated Chinese player Wang Hao depending on the experience from attending Chinese Super League.

Popularity of Table Tennis Sport in China

Chinese Table Tennis Club League Match began in 1995, and has developed into three levels now. The Super League is on the highest level with 12 men's and 12 women's teams being registered. It adopts the host-guest system. Besides the paddlers on the national squad, some international paddlers also attend the teams registered in the Super League, which makes the competition more attractive to the audience. Besides the Super League, there are even more teams contending the Premier League series A and B. More than 50 men's and 50 women's teams are registered. In order to broaden the market of table tennis competition, and increase the influence of table tennis, Chinese Table Tennis Association (CTTA) in cooperation with CCTV held CCTV Cup China Table Tennis Tournament in 1996, which was later developed into Ericsson Chinese Table Tennis Tournament, International Table Tennis

The "table tennis' zone" on the campus

Tournament and International Junior Table Tennis Tournament (under 17), which reveals the top performances of junior paddlers. These tournaments have entertained a large number of audiences with brilliant competitions, and at the same time have made them know more about the sport.

A pyramid of talented paddlers in China is constructed as follows: the top layer is the national squads, containing about 100 paddlers; the second layer is nearly 2000 adult professionals and junior amateurs registered in CTTA; the third layer contains more than 30 thousand junior paddlers that are under training of amateur sports schools and major sports schools; the bottom layer contains about 10 million people who regularly play table tennis.

First Swaythling Cup

China National Table Tennis Team won its first Swaythling Cup on the 26th WTTC, which delegations of 32 different countries and regions attended, after winning all its rivals, namely Czechoslovakia, West Germany, Ecuador, Mongolia, Ghana, Nepal, Burma, Hungary and Japan. It was China's first gold medal of men's team in table tennis as well.

♦ The First Table Tennis Grand Slam Winner in the World

A Grand Slam of table tennis is earned by a player who wins an Olympic Games gold medal, world championship title and World Cup of Table Tennis gold medal. The first table tennis Grand Slam winner is Swede Jan-Ove Waldner. The first Chinese female Grand Slam winner is Deng Yaping, and the fist Chinese male Grand Slam winner is Liu Guoliang.

First Marcel Corbillon Cup

The 28th WTTC were held in Ljubljana, Yugoslavia from April 15-25, 1965, with contenders from 48 countries and regions. Chinese delegation with 38 members won 5 gold medals in total. It was the first time that China won this title for women's team. And Lin Huiqing and Zheng Minzhi won the title for women's doubles, which was also unprecedented for China.

First WTTC Held in China

In April 1961 the 26th WTTC were held in Beijing, the capital of China. It was the first time for China to hold WTTC.

The Japanese team who obtained six championships in the last championships claimed that they had invented "a secret weapon"— loop; and that in spite of its progress the Chinese team couldn't constitute a threat on Japan. In face of the challenges from the powerful athletes from across the world the young Chinese players gained consistent victories and eventually captured three titles in men's team event, men's individual event and women's individual event, handling their powers of close-table fast attack and flexible techniques and tactics.

First Zdenek Haydusek Prize

The 31st WTTC were held in Nagoya, Japan from March 28 to April 7, 1971, with contenders from 52 countries and regions. Chinese team of 34 members captured four titles. Zhang Xielin and Lin Huiqing won the Zdenek Hayduek Prize in the mixed doubles event. It was the first time that China has ever won a mixed doubles title.

First Clean Sweep of Championships

From April 14-16, 1981 in the 36th WTTC in Novisad, Yugoslavia, with 62 teams from countries and regions in five continents, the Chinese team containing 19 players had an unprecedented clean sweep of all seven championships and five individual silver medals.

In the team finals on April 20, China won both women's and men's team titles with Chinese women's team defeating South Korea, 3:0, and Chinese men's team defeating Hungary, 5:2. In the five all-Chinese individual finals, Guo Yuehua won the men's individual title, Tong Ling won the women's individual title, Li Zhengte and Cai Zhenhua won the men's double title, Zhang Deying and Cao Yanhua won the women's double title, and Xie Saike and Huang Junqun won the mixed double title.

The St. Bride Vase Forever in China

The ITTF prescribes that every country that wins the title of men's singles at World Table Tennis Champions three times in a row, or wins that of women's singles four times in a row, will be awarded with a copy of St. Bride Vase or that of G. Geist Prize, and can keep it forever.

The famous Chinese paddler Zhuang Zedong won the St. Bride Vase in the 26th, 27th and 28th WTTC, so the ITTF awarded him with a copy of St. Bride Vase on 1st September 1973.

First Table Tennis Referee

Table tennis entered the Seoul Olympic Games in 1988. Chinese Gu Koufeng was appointed to work there as the only representative of Chinese table tennis referees. She began to work as a table tennis referee when she was 18, and there were three "first-times" in her career, which were one of the earliest Chinese international table tennis referees, the first female table tennis referee in China who was appointed to work abroad, and the first Chinese table tennis referee that worked at the Olympic Games.

First Table Tennis Champion at the Olympic Games

There have been numerous famous table tennis players in these years. Among the 100 gold medals of Summer Olympic Games China has captured, 16 are of table tennis events. Who are China's first champions in table tennis events at the Olympic Games? Please remember their names: Chen Longcan and Wei Qingguang. They won the trophy of men's doubles at 1988 Seoul Olympic Games. In the final they lost the first game, but finally defeat their Yugoslavian rivals, and seized the precious gold medal, which was China's first gold medal of Olympic Games and one of the five gold medals that China won at 1988 Olympic Games.

China National Junior Table Tennis Open

In order to explore more talented players, State Physical Culture and Sports Commission (PCSC) held National Junior Table Tennis Open in Zhengzhou, Henan from April 4-12, 1987. Every Chinese born in 1974 and whose residence was registered in China could attend the competition. The tournament received warmly welcome all over China because it was considered as an important attempt of reforming the competition system. 685 juniors from 28 provinces, municipalities and autonomous regions, except Tibet, took part in the competition at their own expenses.

Table Tennis as an Olympic Sport

Table tennis was introduced as an Olympic sport at the 24th Olympics in 1988. The table tennis events at the Olympics include men's singles, women's singles, men's doubles and women's doubles. The ITTF Olympic Commission, made up of the president and vice-president of the ITTF and the president of the table tennis federation of the host nation, is responsible for the management of table tennis competitions at the Olympics. From the 24th to the 27th Olympics China has won 13 gold medals, including 2 at the 24th Olympics, 3 at the 25th, 4 at 26th and 4 at the 27th.

Overseas Chinese Table Tennis Players

The outflow of talented Chinese table tennis players dates back to the 1970s. In 1978 the PCSC appointed the former national squad member Diao Wenyuan to coach in Italy. In 1980 the former world champion Liang Geliang was sent to Germany with a contract time of two years. And he went to Germany at his own expense in 1985. After that more and more Chinese table tennis players went to work abroad, generally including three kinds of player: the former world champions, the former national squad members without any world titles and the vocational players in the provincial and city teams.

According to incomplete statistics, the number of Chinese overseas players has exceeded 220, among which 21 are former world champions, taking up 10 percent of total. These players have become an important force in the international competitions. At the 43rd WTTC in 1995, Chinese overseas table tennis players took up 3 places in the top 32 male paddlers, and 9 places in the top 32 female paddlers. At the 2004 Athens Olympics, the number reached 6 and 11 respectively.

In today's world where China is playing a leading part in the table tennis sport, Chinese overseas players serve as a bridge connecting China and the other places of the world, and inspire the Chinese national squad to give more and more brilliant performances. They have brought the sport to the whole world, improving its development. The popularity of table tennis in many countries and regions comes in part from their efforts. Nowadays, they are reputed as "overseas mission".

Fu Qifang

Fu Qifang (1923-1968), table tennis player. He began to play table tennis ever since he was a pupil. In 1952 Fu attended the 19th WTTC in Bombay, India on behalf of Hong Kong.

Fu Qifang was originally a chopper, and was converted into an offensive player after going to Hong Kong. His three best skills are smash after service, feint play and short ball. He has made efforts to study the table tennis techniques, forming his own opinions. Since 1958 he began to hold the post as coach of Chinese National Men's Team. As the coach of Rong Guotuan, who is a famous table tennis player, he made use of his own ideas to constructed Rong, resulting in Rong's winning the gold medal of men' singles at the 25th WTTC in Dortmund, which was the first world champion that Chinese had ever won in an international competition. After that, at the 26th WTTC in Beijing in 1961, he led Chinese team to smash Japan's secret weapon—loops by fast attacks, and won the final at 5:3, claiming the title of men's team at WTTC and winning Swaythling Cup for the first time. Under his construction, China successively won the gold medals of men's singles and men's team at the 26th, 27th and 28th WTTC.

Qiu Zhonghui

Qiu Zhonghui (1935-), table tennis player. She played in the national squad from 1952 to 1963, and won the title of women's singles at the 26th WTTC in 1961, becoming the first female world champion in China. Before her, the winners of G. Geist Prize were from either Europe or Japan. After retirement she worked as the coach of the national women's squad before she was selected the vice-president of CTTA. She started her own business in 1994, opening a table tennis shop named after her own name.

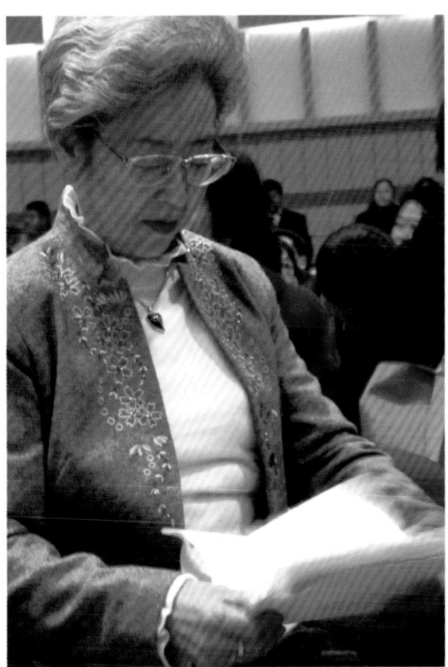

Qiu Zhonghui

Rong Guotuan

Rong Guotuan (1937-1968), table tennis player. He came back from Hong Kong to Canton province in 1957, and entered Cantonese Table Tennis Team in the next year. In 1958 he captured the title of men's singles at the National Table Tennis Championships, and was selected for the national squad. He won the gold medal of men's singles at the 25th WTTC in 1959, becoming the first world champion in China. He won the gold medal of men's team at the 26th WTTC in 1961. In 1963 he began to coach the Chinese Women's Table Tennis Team, which won the title of women's team at the 28th WTTC under his instruction. In memorial of Rong's great contribution to the table tennis in China his bronze statue was set up in Zhuhai, Canton province in 1987.

Xu Yinsheng

Xu Yinsheng(1938-), table tennis player and Chinese sports leader. He comes from Suzhou, Jiangsu province. He was picked for Shanghai Table Tennis Team of Middle School Students in 1955 when he was studying at Shanghai Daguang Middle School. In 1956 he began to study at Shanghai Sports Institute, and was selected for Shanghai City Table Tennis Team. Two years later, he entered National Training Team.

He is a right-handed penholder and especially good at close-table fast attack. His all-around techniques, flexible tactics and changeable path of the stroke won him the title of "star of wisdom". He was one of the key players of Chinese National Team in the 26th, 27th and 28th WTTC when it won the title of men's team. He won the bronze medal of men's singles at the 26th WTTC, the silver medal of men's doubles (with Zhuang Zedong) at the 27th WTTC and the gold medal of men's doubles (with Zhuang Zedong) at the 28th WTTC. Since 1971 he led the national squad to attend the WTTC for several times as coach or head coach. He was selected the vice-president of ITTF Asia Office and a member of ITTF Umpires and Referees Committee in 1975, and president of ITTF in 1997. He has been the president of CTTA since 1979, making great contributions to the development of Chinese competitive sports. The International Olympic Committee awarded him with the Silver Olympic Order in 1991.

On April 2, 2006, the Chinese and Japanese table tennis veterans gathered at CCTV. In the picture is Zhang Xielin performing playing skills.

Zhang Xielin

Zhang Xielin (1940-), table tennis player and coach. At the 27th WTTC in 1963, Japan intended to regain the Swaythling Cup from China depending on its newly invented "loop". But Chinese player Zhang Xielin shattered Japanese's dream. He is a penholder, and masters perfect attacking skills, especially good at attacking with low and high-spin chops. He defeated both of his rivals in the men's team final against Japan with help of the unique features of long pimpled rubber. He confused his rivals with unexpected high-spin strikes, and occasionally harsh smashes. Zhang won four games in a row losing only 33 points, which meant that he only lost 8.25 points per game. Therefore, he got a title of "magician".

Zhuang Zedong

On July 23, 2005, the 18th "Zhuang Zedong Cup" Youth and Children Table Tennis Invitational Tournament was launched at Luohu Gymnasium in Shenzhen. Zhuang Zedong had the serve for it.

Zhuang Zedong (1940-), table tennis player. He became a key player of China National Table Tennis Team in 1961. He adopts a typical Asian style of pen-hold fast attack, characterized by forehand and backhand drive with high speed and stability. He was one of the key players of Chinese men's team when it won the title of men's team at the 26th, 27th, 28th and 31st WTTC. Zhuang, who is a three-time world men's singles champion, is the first Chinese that wins three WTTC titles in a row. On September 1, 1973 the ITTF awarded him with a copy of St. Bride Vase. He worked as chairman of the PCSC of the PRC from 1974 to 1976.

Li Furong

Li Furong(1942-), table tennis player and coach. He received table tennis training for the sports officials in Shanghai in 1957 when he was studying at Shanghai Gonghe Middle School. In 1958 he was selected for Shanghai City Team and entered Chinese Youth Table Tennis Team in November. In 1960 he entered the national squad. He is a penholder whose particular skills are fast attacks, unpredicted services, swift and fierce attacks and flexible footwork. He won four gold medals of men's team, men's singles, men's doubles and mixed doubles in the national tale tennis competitions in 1961. Since 1961 he has taken part in the WTTC for five times, serving as one of the key players of Chinese men's team when it won the Swaythling Cup at the 26th, 27th, 28th and 31st WTTC, and won three silver medals of men's singles and three bronze medals of men's doubles in a row. At the 26th WTTC he won the silver medal of mixed doubles with Han Yuzhen. In 1973 Li was designated as the coach of Chinese national men's team before he was promoted to be the head coach. Since 1979 he has been the vice-president of CTTA. And at the same time he worked as a member of the Ranking Committee of the ITTF and honorary secretary-general of Asian Table Tennis Federation.

Zheng Minzhi

Zheng Minzhi (1945-), table tennis player. She has loved table tennis ever since she was a little girl. She was selected for Shanghai City Team in 1958 and for the national squad in 1960. She is a hand-shake chopper, who is good at defending and sudden drive. At the 28th WTTC in 1965 the Chinese women's team made up of Zheng Minzhi, Lin Huiqing and Li Henan claimed the title of women's team, and Zheng won the gold medal of women's doubles with Lin Huiqing. She was one of the key players of Chinese team that won the silver medal of women's team at the 31st WTTC in 1971 and the 32nd WTTC in 1973. She won the gold medal of women's doubles with Liu Huiqing and the silver medal of women's singles at the 31st WTTC. She began to work as the coach of Chinese table tennis team in 1974. She came back to Shanghai and established Minzhi Sports Culture Exchange Center to provide financial support to junior table tennis events. Minzhi Cup Primary and Middle School Table Tennis Championships have been held annually since 1994, becoming one of the major events for primary and middle school students in Shanghai in summer vacations.

Liang Geliang

Liang Geliang (1950-), table tennis player. He is a handshaker, who is good at both defending and attacking with forehand inward pimpled rubber and backhand outward pimpled rubber. His unprecedented skills combine chop with attack and back-court with close-table stroke. At the 31st WTTC in 1971 Liang Geliang served as a secret weapon in the men's team competitions against the powerful rivals such as Hungary and Sweden. In the competition against Hungary Liang Geliang smashed after service and rush to defense, defeating his rival at 17:21. In the following competition against Sweden, he played the first game and won at 2:0, and won another game at 2:1. His triumphs made a good foundation for China to enter the final and beat Japan finally.

Ge Xin'ai

Ge Xin'ai (1953-), table tennis player. She is a penholder, and most of the time a chopper. If there is an opportunity, she can drive to attack. In the preliminary phase of the 33rd WTTC in 1975 Ge didn't attend any competition. She showed up for the first time in the semifinal against Japan, which left an impression as a unique and untraditional player. Not until she defeated two key players in the final against Korea, winning the important two points for China's gainning Marcel Corbillon Cup, did people realize that she was the secret weapon of China to beat Korea. At that time her coach was Zhang Xielin, who used to be the secret weapon of Chinese Men's Team.

Zhang Deying

Zhang Deying(1953-), table tennis player. She began to receive table tennis training in Shanghai Amateur Sports School in 1964. She attended the National Junior Table Tennis Championships on behalf of Shanghai as one of the key player of Shanghai team who won the team title. She was selected for the national squad in 1975. She is a pen-holder whose particular skills are fast attack, half-volley with attack, flexible path of stroke, high speed and high service. She was one of the key players in Chinese women's team who won the title of women's team at the 34th, 35th and 36th WTTC. She won the gold medal of women's doubles with Zhang Li at the 35th WTTC. At the 37th WTTC she won the first place of women's doubles with Cao Yanhua and the third place of women's singles. After retirement she coached Shanghai City Table Tennis Team. In 1986 she went to America for further study, studying sports psychology in University of California, Los Angeles, at the same time working as a coach in South California. In 1998 she came back to Shanghai establishing Zhang Deying Table Tennis Training Center in Luwan district of Shanghai.

Lu Yuansheng

Lu Yuansheng (1954-), table tennis player. He is a handshaker and a tough player. He often slows the pace of a game by steady defense, and defeats his flurried rivals. At the 33rd WTTC in 1975 Lu methodically fought against Dragutin Surbek. As Surbek's loops were more and more spinning, Lu's chops were steadier and steadier. Lu won the first game at 21:10. In the second game, Surbek had built up a commanding lead by loop drives before Lu found his range and caught up point by point using chop-and-attack and changing the placement of the ball and the pace of strikes. Finally, Lu won the second game at 21:19, winning the competition. His success got China a precious point of regaining the title.

Chen Xinhua

Chen Xinhua (1960-), table tennis player. He is a handshaker and an offensive player. His particular skills include steady and changeable chops of high spin which can attack on both sides. In the men's team final against Sweden at the 38th WTTC in 1985 Chen defeated Lindh at 2:0 in the first set. When China was taking the lead by 4:0 Chen defeated Jan-Ove Waldner making the biggest contribution to China's triumph. He won all his 12 competitions in the men's team event.

Cai Zhenhua

Cai Zhenhua (1961-), table tennis player and coast. Since 1985 he had coached the Italian national squad for 4 years, and went back to China in 1989. He was designated as head coach of Chinese national men's team in 1991, and as chief coach in 1997.

Cai won the gold medals of men's team at the 1979 WTTC and at the 5th Asian Championships in 1980. In 1981 he won the gold medal of men's doubles with Li Teshi, the silver medal of men's singles and the gold medal of men's team. He won the second place in men's singles event and the first place in the men's team event at the 37th WTTC in 1983. At the 38th WTTC in 1985 he won the champion of mixed doubles with Cao Yanhua.

Under his instruction Chinese national team has achieved great accomplishment. China won the champion of men's doubles at the Barcelona Olympics in 1992, the gold medals of men's singles and men's doubles at the Atlanta Olympics in 1996, the title of men's team at the 44th WTTC in 1997, the gold medal of singles at the 1998 Women's World Cup, the gold medals and silver medals of four events at the 1998 ITTF Pro Tour. China had a clean sweep of the four gold medals of table tennis events at the Sydney Olympics in 2000. At the 46th WTTC in 2001 China seized all the seven champions. It also won the champions in Men's World Cup and Women's World Cup in 2002, four gold medals at the 47th WTTC in 2003, the champion of Men's World Cup and four gold medals of the ITTF Pro Tour in 2003, the gold and silver medals at the 8th Women's World Cup in 2003 and the champions of men's team and women's team at the Katar WTTC in 2004.

Cao Yanhua

Cao Yanhua (1962-), table tennis player. She entered Shanghai Youth Sports School in 1973, was selected for Shanghai City Team in 1977, and for the national squad in the same year. She is a pen-hold looper whose particular skills are fast attack, accelerated loop with high speed, brilliant placement and high spin. She acts calm in competitions, and adopts a flexible style combining fierceness and agility. She won a gold medal of mixed doubles in France in 1977. In 1978 she won the gold medal of women's doubles and the silver medal of women's singles at Scandinavian Championships in 1978. She was one of the key players of Chinese national team who won the title of women's team at the 35th, 36th and 37th WTTC. She won the silver medal of women's singles at the 36th WTTC, and the gold medal of women's singles and the bronze medals of women's doubles and mixed doubles at the 37th WTTC. She seized the first places of women's singles, women's doubles with Dai Lili and mixed doubles with Xie Saike at the 9th Asian Games in 1982. She won the titles of women's singles, mixed doubles with Cai Zhenhua, and the second place of women's doubles with Ni Xialian at the 38th WTTC in 1985. In 1997 she started Cao Yanhua Table Tennis Training Center in Shanghai.

Tong Ling

Tong Ling (1962-), table tennis player. She is a world champion and world-class table tennis player. She began to receive table tennis training in Zigong Amateur Sports School in 1971, entered Beijing Military Table Tennis Team in 1975, and was selected for the National Training Team in 1977. She was a handshaker whose particular skills are stable chops. Her style is mainly defensive, blended with attacks. She won the gold medals of women's singles and mixed doubles (with Huang Liang) and the silver medal of women's doubles (with Ge Xin'ai) at Scandinavian Championships in 1978. In the next year she won the third place of women's singles at the 35th WTTC. She was one of the key players of Chinese women's team when it won the title of women's team at the 36th WTTC in 1981 and the 37th WTTC in 1983. She also won the gold medal of women's singles and the silver medals of women's doubles (with Pu Qijuan) and mixed doubles (with Chen Xinhua) at the 36th WTTC, and the silver medal of the mixed doubles (with Chen Xinhua) and the bronze medal of women's doubles (with Pu Qijuan) at the 37th WTTC. She won the bronze medals of women's singles and women's doubles at the 5th ATTC in 1980, and the gold medal of mixed doubles and silver medals of women's singles and women's doubles at the 6th ATTC in 1982. She won the silver medal of women's singles at the 1st Asian Cup in 1983 and the gold medal of women's singles at the 2nd Asian Cup in 1984. She won three silver medals of women's singles, women's doubles and mixed doubles at the 9th Asian Games. She was credited with the title of "Master of Sports" in 1980 and the title of "International Master of Sports" in 1985. She was awarded with the "Honor Award of Sports" by the Physical Culture and Sports Commission (PCSC) of the PRC for four times.

Ni Xialian

Ni Xialian (1963-), table tennis player. She began to receive table tennis training as early as in the primary school in 1972. In spite of her below-average height of 1.56 meters, she is a diligent player. She won the first place in the table tennis competition of pupils in Shanghai in 1975. She entered Shanghai Amateur Sports School in 1976, and was selected for Shanghai City Team in 1978 after winning the first place in the table tennis event of the World Middle School Games in the same year. In 1929 she was selected for the national squad. She is a left-handed penholder, using long pimpled rubber. Her particular skills include unexpected path of the stroke, thus, she is described as "a unique ball player". She was one of the key players of Chinese women's team when it won the title of women's team at the 37th WTTC in 1983, at which she won the gold medal of mixed doubles with Guo Yuehua and the third place of women's doubles with Cao Yanhua. She won the silver medal of women's doubles with Cao Yanhua at the 38th WTTC. After her retirement in 1987 she moved to Europe. Since then she has attended the international table tennis events on behalf of the European countries.

He Zhili

He Zhili (1964-), table tennis player. She learnt table tennis during primary school. In 1977 she entered Luwan District Amateur Sports School to receive table tennis training, and was selected for the national squad in 1978. She is a right-handed handshaker, who is calm and quick in response. She is able to control the attacks effectively. Once left behind she can always get back to win. She was one of the key players of Chinese women's team that won the gold medal of women's team at the 7th

Asian Table Tennis Championships (ATTC) in 1984, at which she won the gold medal of women's singles and the silver medal of mixed doubles. She was one of the key players of Chinese women's team that won the title of women's team at the 38th WTTC in 1985. At the 10th Asian Games in 1986 she won the silver medal in women's team as a key player, and the silver medals of women's singles and women's doubles. At the 39th WTTC in 1987 she won the title of women's singles and the bronze medal of women's doubles. At the 9th ATTC in 1988 she won the gold medal of women's singles and the bronze medal of women's doubles. After marrying to a Japanese named Koyama Hideyuki in 1989 she changed her name to Koyama Chire. She attended the 12th Asian Games in 1994 on behalf of Japan, claiming the title of women's singles.

Wang Tao

Wang Tao (1967-), table tennis player. He is a left-handed handshaker using forehand inward pimpled rubber and backhand raw pimpled rubber. He is especially good at fast attack combining with loop.

Wang Tao won the gold medal of mixed doubles and the silver medal of men's doubles at the 41st WTTC, the champions of men's doubles and mixed doubles at the 42nd WTTC, the gold medals of men's team, men's doubles and mixed doubles at the 43rd WTTC, the title at the 2nd World Team Cup, the gold medal of men's doubles at the 25th Olympics, the silver medal of men's singles at the 13th WTTC, the championship in 1994 World Stars Tournament Grand Finals and the silver medals of men's singles and men's doubles at the 26th Olympics. Wang is famous for his advantage in doubles. And when the rivals tried their best to avoid his backhand attack that is considered the fastest in the world, Wang had improved the techniques of forehand loop drive and backhand loop bringing. He is able to keep a cool mind in competitions and is sensitive to his rival's weakness. Besides, the flexible tactics and close-table and fast play are also his advantages.

Chen Jing

Chen Jing (1968-), table tennis player. She entered the national squad in 1985. She won the gold medals of women's team at the 39th WTTC in 1987 and the 40th WTTC in 1989, and the gold medal of women's singles and the silver medal of women's doubles at the 24th Olympics in 1988. Later she moved to Taiwan province, and attended the international events on behalf of Chinese Taipei Table Tennis Team, including 5 WTTC and 2 Olympics, winning a silver medal and a bronze medal of women's singles at the Olympics and two silver medals of women's team and women's singles at WTTC.

Ma Wenge

Ma Wenge (1968-), table tennis player. He's a right-handed handshaker, using inward pimpled rubber on both sides of the racket. His particular skills include loops combining with attacks.

Ma won the gold medal of men's singles at the 10th World Cup, the gold medal at the 2nd World Team Cup, the third place of men's singles at the 25th Olympics, the gold medal of men's singles at the 13th World Cup, the silver medals of men's team and men's doubles at the 42nd WTTC and the gold medal of men's team at the 43rd WTTC. Despite of his handshake grip, he masters the characteristics of Chinese traditional pen-hold fast attack. In 1989 Chinese men's team fell to the bottom because it lost its four-time Swaythling Cup and St. Bride Vase and didn't gain any gold medal at the 40th WTTC. However, Ma won the gold medal of men's singles at the 10th World Cup in the same year, relighting China's flame of hope. In preparation of the 43rd WTTC he gave up the opportunity of attending the World Stars Tournament that provided high prizes in order to take treatment. At a result, he defeated Kim Taek Soo, Yoo Nam Kyu, Jan-Ove Waldner, Jorgen Persson, and etc, making great contributions to China's triumph.

Qiao Hong

Qiao Hong (1968-), table tennis player. In 1980 she entered Hubei Provincial Team. In December 1987 she was selected for the national squad. Qiao Hong is a right-handed hand-shaker with a cool mind and an overall grasp of techniques and capable of both-sided loop drive and fast attack. Besides her powerful service, her backhand half volley or fast bringing can effectively hold down her rival's attack. Her special skills also include forehand drive and smash with high accuracy rate and pendulum speed, which is effective in dealing with all kinds of attacks. The experts considered Qiao as Asia's most successful representative of the masculinization of female handshake both-sided loop drive.

Qiao Hong won the gold medals of women's singles, of women's doubles with Deng Yaping, and of women's team at the 40th WTTC in 1989. She won the gold medal of women's team at the 1st World Cup in 1990 and at the 2nd World Cup in 1991. She won the silver medal of women's singles and the gold medal of women's doubles with Deng Yaping at the 25th Olympics in Barcelona, Spain in 1992. In August 1995 she won the gold medal of women's team at the 4th World Team Cup in Atlanta. In 1996 she won the gold medal of women's doubles with Deng Yaping at the 26th Olympics in Atlanta.

Ding Song

Ding Song (1971-), table tennis player. He is an offensive-and-defensive handshaker who uses forehand inward pimpled rubber and backhand outward pimpled rubber.

Ding, who won the gold medal of mixed doubles at the 1994 CTTA Cup and the third place in the National Championships, was one of the key players of Chinese Men's Team that won the Swaythling Cup at the 43rd WTTC. Endowed with a quick mind and a sense of the ball, he is flexible in strike, forceful in attack and unique in style. He has developed the skills of chop and smash into a new level, forming the three features of his skills, which are high-quality service, changeable and steady forehand and backhand chop and fast attack. His unique play style of chop-and-attack once made the world-class paddlers puzzled despair. His outstanding performance at the 43rd WTTC made him famous, becoming another talented Chinese chopper embodying the international table tennis trend of "faster, spinner, harsher".

Deng Yaping

Deng Yaping (1973-), table tennis player. She is the only table tennis player in the world who won two successive gold medals at the Olympics, and who won four gold medals at the Olympics. At the Atlanta Olympics in 1996 President of International Olympic Committee Juan Antonio Samaranch personally presented her the prize.

The 25th Olympic Games was held in Barcelona, Spain. Chinese table tennis athlete Deng Yaping won the gold medal of the women's singles at the Olympics.

Deng Yaping won the gold medal of women's doubles and the silver medal of women's singles at the National Table Tennis Championships in 1988, the championship of women's doubles at the 40th WTTC in 1989, the gold medal of women's singles at the 41st WTTC in 1991, the gold medals of women's singles and women's doubles at the 25th Olympics in 1992, the gold medals of women's singles and women's doubles at the Atlanta Olympics in 1996. She is credited as "Queen of Ping Pong" and "Small Giant".

She worked as a member of the IOC Ethics Commission and Sport and Environment Commission in 2002 and now as a staff member of the Marketing Department of the Beijing Organizing Committee for the 2008 Olympic Games.

Kong Linghui

Kong Linghui (1975-), table tennis player. As a Grand Slam winner he has been among the top players in the ITTF ranking in terms of men's singles in recent years.

Kong has adopted a style combining typically traditional pen-hold fast attack with European handshake offensive play. His particular skills include loop on both sides of the racket, which is steady, fierce, highly competitive and combined with fast attack. His forehand loop drive is especially forceful. With a good sense of ball and a comprehensive grasp of techniques, he is able to impart high speed to the ball, and change the placement during rallies.

Kong's main achievements include: 1st singles and doubles (with Liu Guoliang) at the 1996 CTTA Cup, 1st doubles (with Liu Guoliang) in 1996 Atlanta Olympic Games, 1st singles in the first WTTC Pro Tour in 1996, 1st doubles (with Liu Guoliang) and team and 2nd mixed doubles (with Deng Yaping)at 1997 WTTC, 1st singles in 1997 ITTF Pro Tour, 2nd team at the 45th WTTC in 2000, 1st team in 2000 World Men's Table Tennis Club Championships, 1st singles, 2nd doubles in 2000 Sydney Olympic Games, 1st team in the 47th WTTC in 2004 and 1st doubles at the 48th WTTC in 2005.

Kong Linghui won the gold medal of the men's singles of the table tennis at the 2000 Sydney Olympics.

Liu Guoliang

Liu Guoliang (1976-), table tennis player and coach. He began to play table tennis at the age of 6. He entered the National Youth Team when he was 13, and was granted special admission to the national squad in 1991. He is a right-handed penholder with techniques of close-table fast attack on both sides and excellent service combining with such reformed pen-hold skills as service on the reverse of the racket.

He seized the championships of doubles (with Kong Linghui) and singles at 1996 Olympics. He is the first Chinese winner of "Grand Slum". After 1996 World Cup he captured the first place on the ITTF ranking. After his retirement in 2002 Liu took the post as a coach of Chinese National Table Tennis Team.

Li Jun

Li Jun (1976-), table tennis player. She started to play table tennis at the age of 6.

Li is a right-handed handshaker, whose particular skills include forehand and backhand loop with high spin and speed as well as fast attack. She won the champion of women's team and the runner-up of men's singles at the 13th Asian Cup in 1996. In 1997, she won the champion of women's team, the silver medal of women's doubles (with Wang Nan) and the bronze medal of women's singles at the 44th WTTC, the single silver medal at World Cup, the silver medals of singles and doubles (with Wang Chen) at Australian Open, the first place of women's singles and the third place of women's doubles (with Wang Nan) at China Grand Prix and the champion of women's singles in the ITTF Pro Tour Grand Finals. In 1999, she won the champion of women's doubles (with Wang Nan) at the ITTF Pro Tour, the champion of women's singles at the Ericsson China Open Challenge Finals, the silver medal of women's singles in the Asia-Top 12, the gold medal of women's doubles at the 45th WTTC. In 2000, she won the gold medal of women's singles at the World Cup and the silver medal of women's team at the World Club Cup, the gold medal of women's doubles and silver medal of women's singles at the Olympics, the champion of women's team at the 45th WTTC and the second place of women's singles at the Japan Open. In 2001, she won the gold medals of women's team and women's doubles at the 46th WTTC and the team champion at the World Women's Club Championships in 2001.

Wang Nan

Wang Nan (1978-), table tennis player. She began playing table tennis when she was seven years old. Her ITTF rank kept progressing year by year, from the 5th in 1996, the 3rd in 1997, the 3rd in 1998 to the world No.1 from 1999 to 2001.

She is a left-handed hand-shaker with particular skills of high-spin loop with good point of fall combined with fast attack. As a cool player she can skillfully adjust the striking rhythm. She uses TSP blade and Tianjin 729 rubber on both sides.

Wang won the single title in 2001 ITTF Pro Tour Grand Finals in January 2002. In 2004 she won the team champion at the 47th WTTC in Doha from the 1st to the 7th March, the gold medal of doubles at the Athens Olympics and the double title of ITTF Pro Grand. In 2005 she won the second place of singles at 2005 Qatar Open, the double title (with Zhang Yining) at the 48th WTTC. In 2006 she captured the double titles of Qatar Open and Kuwait Open, the single title of Asian Cup and the team title at Bremen WTTC.

Wang Liqin

Wang Liqin (1978-), table tennis player. He began playing table tennis at the age of nine, and was picked for Shanghai city team in 1991, for the Chinese National Youth team in 1993 and for the National Team in 1995. He is a right-handed hand-shaker using racket with inward pimpled rubbers on both sides. His style is probably best described as a strong both-sided looper who is also good at

On April 30, 2006, Wang Liqin in the semifinal of the men's team semi-final of the World Table Tennis Championship

fast attack. His above average height allows him additional leverage for acceleration and momentum, creating more powerful shots. He has a comprehensive grasp of skills, especially his aggressive pivot attack.

In 1995, Wang won the team and single silver medals at the 1995 National Table Tennis Championships. In 1996, he captured the team and single titles at the National Club Championships, and the double title at the ITTF Pro Tour Grand Finals. In 1997, he won the bronze medal of mixed doubles at the WTTC and the second place of singles in the World Star Tournament Grand Finals. In 1998, he won the team and mixed double gold medals at the Asian Games and the gold medals of singles, mixed doubles and team at the Asian Championships. In 1999, he won the second place of doubles and the third place of mixed doubles at the 45th ITTF and the single and team championships in the ITTF Pro Tour Grand Finals, rank increasing from the 8th to the 1st. In 2000 he captured the double gold medal with Yan Sen after defeating his teammates Liu Guoliang and Kong Linghui in the 27th Olympics in September and the championships of singles and doubles (with Yan Sen) in the ITTF Pro Tour Grand Finals.

Ma Lin

Ma Lin (1980-), table tennis player. He began to learn table tennis in 1986.

Ma Lin won the single title at China National Junior Tournament in 1995, the single title and the team title at China National Junior Tournament in 1996, the men's double champion in the ITTF Pro Tour Grand Finals in 1999, the champion of men's singles at the World Cup in 2000, the champion of men's team at 2000 World Club Cup, the champion of men's singles in the ITTF Pro Tour Grand Finals in 2001, the champion of men's team and the third place of men's singles at the 46th WTTC in 2001, the champion of men's doubles in the ITTF Pro Tour Grand Finals in 2002, the champion of mixed doubles (with Wang Nan) at the 47th WTTC in 2003, the champion of men's singles at 2003 World Cup, the champion of men's doubles (with Chen Qi) in 2003 ITTF Pro Tour Grand Finals and the champion of men's team at the 47th WTTC in 2004.

Zhang Yining

Zhang Yining (1982-), table tennis player. She started to play table tennis at the age of 6. She is a right-handed handshaker using inward pimpled rubber on both sides of the racket, with particular skills of loop and fast attack and a harsh play style. She has taken the place of Wang Nan as the leading role of Chinese Women's Table Tennis Team.

Zhang Yining successfully defended the

On August 22, 2004, Chinese player Zhang Yining won the 20th gold medal of the Chinese Olympic delegation in the women's singles table tennis competition at the Athens Olympics.

champion of women's doubles (with Wang Nan) and captured the gold medal of women's singles at Athens Olympics in 2004. At the 48th WTTC in 2005 she seized the champion of women's singles, achieving the Grand Slam containing three champions in the WTTC, the Olympics and the World Cup.

Wang Hao

Wang Hao (1983-), table tennis player. He is a right-handed handshaker using forehand inward pimpled rubber and backhand long pimpled rubber and adopting the style of chop-and-attack. Chinese men's team lost Swaythling Cup at two successive WTTC. After Cai Zhenhua held the post as head coach of men's team, he recalled Wang Hao who was then playing in a Spanish table tennis club, to attend the men's team event at the 2nd World Team Cup in 1991. Before the final between China and Sweden began, Chinese coach Lu

The Chinese Table Tennis Team went to Jinzhou of Liaoning Province to make preparations for the World Table Tennis Championships. Picture shows Wang Hao.

Yuansheng suddenly found that Lindh of the Swede team was very exciting at the table. According to Lu's observation, Cai changed the arrangement of the lineup within two minutes, making Wang Hao the third key player instead of the first key player, aiming at Lindh. Sweden's lineup arrangement was exactly the same as China had expected. As a result China defeated Sweden at 3:0, winning the title of men's team. For Chinese men's team that was in the bottom, the victory contained an "epochal meaning".

The Current ITTF Members in the CTTA

Chairman of the ITTF Technical Committee: Yao Zhenxu

Full member of the ITTF Equipment Committee: Yu Bin

Member of the ITTF Rules Committee: Yang Shu'an

Full member of the ITTF Sports Science Committee: Zhang Xiaopeng

♦ Chinese Table Tennis Association

Chinese Table Tennis Association (CTTA) was admitted to the ITTF in March 1953, embodying the international recognition of Chinese table tennis, which gained the membership in its corresponding international federation at an earlier time than many other sports in China after the PRC was founded. In the same year, CTTA sent a team to attend the 20th WTTC held in Bucharest, the capital of Romania, which was the first WTTC that a Chinese team competed in.

Since its admission in 1953 the CTTA has been a persistent supporter of the ITTF. And at the same time it has designated many table tennis coaches and technique personnel to work in the countries and regions where table tennis is less popular, and has provided these places with much equipment, making great contributions to the popularity and development of the sport across the world. China has held WTTC twice, respectively in Beijing in 1961 and in Tianjin in 1995. Besides, the CTTA held Men's World Cup for four times, in 1985, in 1988, in 1993 and in 1998 respectively; and hosted the 2nd Women's World Cup in Shanghai in 1997.

Address: No.4 Tiyuguan Road, Chongwen District, Beijing.
Website: http://www.ctta.cn

Field Hockey

Although field hockey has always been a popular sport in the Tahurs in China's Inner Mongolia autonomous region, the modern field hockey games did not start to develop in China until the mid-1970s. In 1975, China sent a team of 4 coaches to visit and study field hockey games in Pakistan. In 1976, field hockey was introduced into the sports school in the Inner Mongolia autonomous region Morin Dawa Tahur and Beijing on trial. In 1978, China held the first national field hockey competition. In the same year, the State Physical Culture and Sports Commission (PCSC) formed a Chinese Youth Field hockey Team on the basis of Morin Dawa Tahur Field hockey Team. The team played several friendship matches with the visiting Pakistan Youth Team in Beijing, Shanghai, Shenyang and Harbin. Later on, a National Team was shaped on the basis of the Morin Dawa Tahur Team, and a Pakistan coach was hired to help with the training. Field hockey began to develop steadily in China.

As a formal competition sport in Olympic Games and Asian Games, field hockey has received attentions and supports from the government and the China State General Sports Administration. Field hockey was listed to be a formal game in the National Games in China since the 5th National Games in 1983. Now, there are 5 men's team and 8 women's team in the Premier League under Chinese Field Field hockey Association. Regular events held by the Chinese Field Field hockey Association include: the National Field hockey League, the National Field hockey Champions Trophy, the Youth Field hockey Championships and the Middle School Field hockey Championships; among which, the National Field hockey League has the highest reputation.

On November 26, 2005, the 13th Woman Champion Cup of the Intemational Hockey Federation was formally launched in Canberra, Australia. The Chinese team won the first fight.

On December 14, 2006, Chinese team won the second place in the hockey final at the 15th Doha Asian Games.

The Chinese Women's Field Hockey Team

The Chinese Women's Field hockey Team is a new star in world field hockey teams. The Korean head coach Kim Chang-Back has led the team to a series of success and break-through in 2002. After claiming championship in the first Field hockey Champions Trophy games in Macau, they went on to grab the 3rd position in the World Cup. In the Busan Asian Games, they won the well-reputed Korean team and made a leap to be the winner.

The Chinese Women's Field hockey Team is a diligent team that excels in basic skills. In the 2002 Champions Trophy games, they exhibited their steady defending and quick attacks, and made several unstoppable goals by sudden shootings from their opponents' defensive line. The major scoring way of the team is short corners. Chen Zhaoxia, one of the veterans in the team, is known for short corners.

According to the new lease by the International Field hockey Federation, the Chinese Women's Field hockey Team ranked the 5th in the world.

Achievements of the Chinese Field Hockey Team in 2006

In 2006, the Chinese Women's Field hockey Teams had three big events, namely, the Champions Trophy games in Netherlands, the World Cup in Madrid, and the Doha Asian Games, in which they won the 2nd, the 10th and the championship separately.

The Men's Field hockey Team made a break-through in the Doha Asian Games by winning the silver medal. This first step will surely win them more attention. Before the game, the Chinese Men's Field hockey Team was ranked the 19th in the world, and never made to the World Cup. To win over the world 7th Indian Team and the world 5th Pakistan Team in the Doha Games was undoubtedly a great improvement for the Chinese Men's Field hockey Team.

♦ Chinese Field Hockey Association

The Chinese Field Hockey Association, a national and non-government organization based in Beijing, was founded in 1981. It is a member of the All-China Sports Federation and was accepted as a formal member of the International Hockey Federation in 1980.

Objectives of the Chinese Field Hockey Association are: to increase public participation and interests in field hockey; to formulate regulations on field hockey games; to organize national games, host international games and assist Chinese teams' participation in international games in other countries; to organize training of field hockey teams, and launch training programs for coaches and judges; to select players and coaches for national teams and to assist research programs.

Address: No. 2 Tiyuguan Lu, Beijing
Website: http://www.hockey.sport.org.cn

Boxing

The Chinese boxers completed a historical break-through by holding two gold medals and three bronze medals in their arms as the 2006 Doha Asian Games drew curtain.

Boxing in China had a very uneven development. In 1959, it was no longer recognized as a kind of sport, and didn't get its place back until 1986. By then, China was almost 30 years behind the European and American strong forces in techniques and training methods. Chinese boxers were ignorant of the advanced techniques and training methods overseas, and didn't even own the most basic facilities. In March 1986, boxing was finally re-validated as a sport in China. In January, 1987, the first boxing competition after its re-validation was held in Beijing. In April of the same year, the Chinese Boxing Association (CBA) was founded, and the first National Boxing Championship was held in May in Nanjing. In June, 1987, the Chinese Boxing Association was accepted by the International Amateur Boxing Association (AIBA) as its 159th member.

After years of hard work, the Chinese boxer Bai Chongguang finally won the first gold medal in history for China in the 1990 Beijing Asian Games. This medal had greatly encouraged the Chinese boxing community. In 2002, China decided to focus on the light-weight games. Young boxers such as the 48kg Zou Shiming and the 60kg Hu Qing were selected into the National Team. Four years later, Hu Qing won the championship in the 10th National Games and Zou Shiming won a bronze medal in the Olympic Games and a gold medal in the World Championship. China finally had its first world champion boxer.

There are 41 professional boxing teams in China now, involving a number of 1400 athletes. There also many back-up talents in local provinces and cities. Some amateur sport schools had formed boxing teams of their own.

The Performance of Chinese Boxing

Chinese boxing is ranked in the upper-middle in Asia, and lower-middle in the world. However, it has a great potential in lightweight games where swiftness and agility are the keys. 8 boxers from the Chinese boxing team participated in the 2002 Busan Asian Games, but they didn't get any gold medals except 3 bronze. In the 2004 Athens Olympics, Zou Shiming won the 48kg bronze medal. It is the best record that Chinese boxers ever achieved in the Olympic Games. On Novermber 20, 2005, Zou Shiming won his Hungarian opponent at the 13th World Senior Boxing Championships held in Mianyang, Sichuan, and grabbed the championship of the men's 48kg event. He was the first boxing world champion in China.

The Chinese boxers made a break-through to in the World Professional Boxing Championships held in Chengdu on the April 15, 2006. Wu Zhiyu from Yu'nan and Zhang Xiyan from Heilongjiang beat their world-renowned opponents respectively and grabbed a continental golden belt and a world golden belt. It was the first time Chinese boxers competed for the WBC golden belts and they won. The crowns had re-lit the Chinese's passions towards boxing.

On April 15, 2006, the Chinese boxer Zhang Xiyan beat the American boxer and won the WIBA world women's lightweight gold belt in the World Professional Boxing Championship of the World Boxing Council held in Chengdu on April 15, 2006.

The Start of Professional Boxing

Representatives from the World Boxing Association (WBA), the World Boxing Council (WBC), the World Boxing Organization (WBO) and International Boxing Federation (IBF) have formally authorized the Beijing Oriental Dawn Sports and Culture Communication Limited Corporation to promote the professional boxing events of their organizations in China.

Although the professional boxing had a late start in China, it held a great potential to develop and received attentions from the international boxing organizations. Now, there are several corporations in China promoting professional boxing events. The united authorization from the four biggest international boxing federations would help to regulate and standardize Chinese boxing events and make it more international. It is also a signal that Chinese boxing is quickly catching up with the global development.

World Boxing League

The first game in the 8th qualifying competition of the China WBA/PABA World Professional Boxing Championship was held in Shanghai, of December 24, 2005. Four countries joined the game, including China, Korea, Philippines and Thailand.

This is the first WBA World Professional Boxing event that is held in Shanghai with Chinese boxers. It is also a milestone for Chinese boxing to go international. The rules in the 8th Golden Belt competition were specially adapted by the WBA for the international professional boxing in China. All the golden belt winners in the competition would be qualified to challenge the boxing champion in Asia or the World. The game also acts as an opening of the 2006 Chinese Professional Boxing League.

The game marks the start of the professional b oxing in China, and the internationalization of Chinese professional boxing. It is a milestone in the development of Chinese boxing.

Zou Shiming

Zou Shiming (1981-), boxer. He started his career in Zunyi Sports School in 1996, when he was 15. He was selected into the National Team in Novermber, 1999.

He was the champion in the 2003 National Boxing Champion 48kg game and the runner-up in the 12th World Amateur Boxing Championships 48kg game of 2003. He won the 2nd place in the 48kg game in the 22nd Asian Boxing Championship, or the qualifying competition of the Athens Olympic Games, in 2004.

On November 20, 2005, Chinese athlete Zou Shiming won the gold medal of the 48kg class boxing at the 13th World Boxing Championship.

♦ The Chinese Boxing Association

The Chinese Boxing Association (CBA), a national non-government nonprofit organization based in Beijing, was founded in April 1987. It is a member the All-China Sports Federation. In June 1987, the Chinese Boxing Association became a formal member of the International Amateur Boxing Association.

Major tasks of the association are: to organize national and international competitions; to set up a national training system; to select and recommend players for the national boxing team; to organize research programs and to study and formulate rules of boxing competitions.

Main events organized by the Chinese Boxing Association include: the boxing games in the National Games, the National Boxing Tournament, the National Boxing Championship, the National Boxing Elite Games, the National Youth Boxing Tournament, the National Teenager Boxing Tournament, the Chinese Amateur Boxing Competition and various other national boxing events approved by the State Physical Culture and Sports Commission.

Address: A14, Middle district of Tiantandongli, Beijing
Website: http://www.sport.org.cn/quanji

▲ Three visits of Ali to China

In December, 1979, Muhammad Ali, the American Boxing King of the world, paid his first visit to China on invitation. In 1985, Ali visited China again and in 1986, visited China for the third time.

Judo

Judo has made a quick development in China since its introduction in the 1970s. Judo, especially the women's events, are the major events for China to win Olympic gold medals.

Judo is still a new sport in China. It used to be listed as a kind of introductory course for wrestling after 1949, and there were only exhibition games. In 1979, two judo coach training classes have been opened in Beijing with teachers invited from the Japanese judo community. In 1980, the Seikei University judo team and Japanese university judo team came from Japan to visit and play judo games in China. In the same year, the Chinese judo team visited Japan. With the increasing communications between China and the world, Chinese judo had been developing very quickly. In September, 1980, the first National Judo Championship was held in Qinhuangdao. From then on, there is a nation-wide judo game every year.

In April 1981, the young athlete from the Chinese judo team made their debut in international games, and won two 3rd in the Yugoslav Cup Invitation Games. In the 2006 Doha Asian Games, the Chinese team grabbed five titles including women's 48kg, 57kg, 63kg, 78kg above, and the open category.

The First Chinese Judo World Champion

In October, 1986, Gao Fenglian won a gold medal in the 72kg above event in the 4th Women's World Judo Championships that was held in Vaeshartelt, Holland. She was the first judo world champion from China.

Gao Fenglian, who was from Inner Mongolia and who was 22 by then, with a height of 1.86m and a weight of 116kg, was also the runner-up in the 72kg above event and 3rd in the open category event of the 3rd Women's World Judo Championships in 1984.

Zhuang Xiaoyan

Zhuang Xiaoyan (1969-), female athlete of the Chinese judo team. She entered the Amateur Sport School in Shenyang to join the training of triathlon at 14 and set the city's teenager record. She entered the Liaoning Judo Team in 1984, and the National Team in 1986.

The achievements of Zhuang include: several champions of nation-wide open category competitions; the gold medalist of the 72kg above judo event of the 25th Barcelona Olympic Games in 1992 which brought China the first Olympic gold medal from judo and the sole champion that won 5 consecutive judo games. She's been nicknamed as "Tiger" or "Open Category Queen".

The Judo World Champions

Year	Name	Event	Game
1986	Gao Fenglian	Women's 72kg above	The 4th Women's World Judo Championship
1987	Gao Fenglian	Women's 72kg above	The 5th Women's World Judo Championship
1987	Gao Fenglian	Women's Open Category	The 5th Women's World Judo Championship
1987	Li Zhongyun	Women's 48kg	The 5th Women's World Judo Championship
1989	Gao Fenglian	Women's 72kg above	The 6th Women's World Judo Championship
1991	Zhuang Xiaoyan	Women's Open Category	The 7th Women's World Judo Championship
1992	Zhuang Xiaoyan	Women's 72kg above	The 25th Olympic Games
1993	Leng Chunhui	Women's 72kg	The 1993 Women's World Judo Championship
1996	Sun Fuming	Women's 72kg above	The 26th Olympic Games
2000	Tang Lin	Women's 78kg	The 27th Olympic Games
2000	Yuan Hua	Women's 78kg above	The 27th Olympic Games
2004	Xian Dongmei	Women's 52kg	The 28th Olympic Games

Sun Fuming

Sun Fuming (1974-), Chinese female judo athlete. Began shot-put and weightlifting training at the age of 13. Entered the Liaoning provincial judo team the following year. She was chosen by the national team for intensified training in 1995 in preparation for the 1996 Olympics.

Her major achievements include: champion of the open category event in the 1995 World Championships games; 2nd place in the open category event in the 1995 Fukuoka International Women's Judo Tournament; winner of the 72kg above event in 1996 Rome International Competition Division; gold-medalist of the 26th Olympic Games in 72kg above event; champion of the open category in 2000 Asian Championships; champion of the 78kg above in 2002 Busan Asian Games; and winner of the 78kg above event in the 2003 Osaka World Championships.

Yuan Hua

Yuan Hua (1974-), Chinese female judo athlete.

Yuan entered the Liaoning Sport School to be trained on judo in 1988, and the National Team in 1996.

Her achievements include: champion of women's 78kg above judo game in 13th Asian Games in 1998; champion of women's 78kg above and open category judo games in the 1999 World University Games; gold-medalist of the 27th Olympic Games in women's 78kg above in 2000; winner of the women's 78kg above game of the 2001 Beijing World University Games.

Xian Dongmei

Xian Dongmei (1975-), Chinese female judo athlete. She entered the Guangdong Sports School to practice wrestling in 1989, and began to practice judo in Guangdong Sports School in 1990. She entered the National Team in 1993.

Her major achievements include: runner-up in the 1995 Asian Championships; champion of the 21st World University Games in 2001; runner-up in the 14th Asian Games in 2002; champion of French Super A 2004; runner-up in the 2004 Asian Championships; and the individual events champion in the 2004 Germany World Cup games.

On August 15, 2004, Chinese athlete Xian Dongmei won the first gold medal of the Chinese judo team at the Athens Olympics.

Tang Lin

Tang Lin (1976-), Chinese female judo athlete.

Tang's achievements include: the 2nd place in the 72kg above event of the 1996 Asian Championships; champion of 78kg in the 13th Asian Games held in Bangkok, Thailand, December of 1998; gold-medalist of the 2000 Sydney Olympic Games in women's judo 78kg event, September 2000.

The Records of Chinese Judo Team in Olympic Games

2004	Athens	1 gold 1 silver 3 bronze
2000	Sydney	2 gold 1 silver 1 bronze
1996	Atlanta	1 gold 1 bronze
1992	Barcelona	1 silver 2 bronze

♦ Chinese Judo Association

The Chinese Judo Association is the only legal association that can represent China to participate in any international judo organizations. It joined the International Judo Federation. on January 1, 1983.

The regular events held by the Chinese Judo Association include: Men's National Judo Tournament, Women's National Judo Tournament, Men's National Youth Judo Tournament, Women's National Youth Judo Tournament, Men's National Teenager Judo Tournament, Women's National Teenager Judo Tournament, Men's National Judo Championships and Women's National Judo Championship.

Address: A14 Tiantandongli Zhongqu, Beijing
Website: http://www.judo.sport.org.cn

Rowing

Rowing, being one of the most important sports in the Olympic Games, has not entered China for long. China only had its first rowing contest untill November 5 to 15, 1956, in Hangzhou, with merely two events in the game. From that time on, rowing has stepped over a harsh road for its development in China, and did not play an important role in the competitive sports arena of China until 1980s. In the Games of the New Emerging Forces held in 1966, Chinese National Rowing Team won all the gold medals of three rowing events (single sculls, double sculls and quadruple sculls). China joined the International Rowing Federation in 1973, and has been sending its rowing team to the World Rowing Championships since 1975.

On December 6, 2006, the Chinese team comprised of Mu Suli, Yu Chengxi, Cheng Ran and Gao Yanhua titled the women's quadruple sculls at the 15th Doha Asian Games.

Up to now, there are 22 provinces, autonomous regions and municipalities, as well as the Chinese People's Liberation Army and the sport associations of all industries that have started the sport of rowing; from which the first, second and third echelon of the rowing team have been formed gradually, with new stars coming forth one after another.

Development of Rowing Sport in China

In the past years, Chinese rowing athletes has achieved outstanding successes in international contests. China rowing team has won two silver and two bronze in the Olympics Games held from 1984 to 1996, with several times being ranked in the top 6. Also,I, it has reaped almost all the gold in the quadrennial Asian Games and biennial Asian Championships, with six World Rowing Championships titles already on its head. In the four Olympics Games it participated in, China rowing team has won two silver and two bronze with several times being ranked in the top 6. It has also won six titles in the World Rowing Championships it took part in.

The First Gold Medal in Rowing

On the August 7, 1988, Zeng Meiyun, Zhang Huajie, Lin Zhiai and Liang Sanmei in the Chinese Women's Rowing Team won the gold medal by a performance of 6'51"47 in the Women's Four Coxless 2000m game of the World Lightweight Rowing Championships in Milan, Italy. It was the first rowing gold medal of China in World Championship.

The First Rowing Game in Asian Games

From November 4-19 to December 4, 1982, the 9th Asian Games was held in New Deli, India. In this Asian Games, rowing first became a formal competition game. China was previously ranked the 3rd and the 2nd in the 7th and 8th Asian Games, but in New Deli, it climbed up to be the No.1 in total gold medal numbers. Among which, rowing had won the Chinese team 4 gold.

The remarkable thing is that ever since 1982, the Chinese Rowing Team had grabbed all the rowing gold medals in the Asian Games except two gold medals in the 1986 and 1994 Asian Games. In other words, China scored best in rowing according to the performances in Asian Games. In the 2006 Doha Asian Games, the Chinese team won 3 gold and two 4th out of the 5 rowing events.

On August 27, 2006, the World Rowing Championship was launched in Eton, Britain. The Chinese team won the women's lightweight double sculls. In the picture are Yan Shimin and Xu Dongxiang.

Records of the Chinese Rowing Team (2006)

Event	Performance	Rank	Name	From	Game	Date	Venue
Women's lightweight single Sculls	7:57.46	3	Xu Dongxiang	Zhejiang	German Station, World Cup	25-27 May, 2006	Munich
Women's lightweight double Sculls	7:11.36	1	Xu Dongxiang	Zhejiang	German Station, World Cup	25-27 May, 2006	Munich
			Yu Hua	Beijing			
Women's lightweight double Sculls	6:49.77	1	Xu Dongxiang	Zhejiang	Poland Station, World Cup	15-17 June, 2006	Poznan
			Yan Shimin				
Women's lightweight double Sculls	6:52.78	2	Fan Xuefei	Zhejiang	Poland Station, World Cup	15-17 June, 2006	Poznan
			Chen Haixia	Guangdong			
Women's lightweight single Sculls	8:15.28	1	Yu Hua	Beijing	Poland Station, World Cup	15-17 June, 2006	Poznan
Women's quadruple sculls (Open site)	6:16.60	2	Tang Bin	Liaoning	Poland Station, World Cup	15-17 June, 2006	Poznan
			Xi Aihua	Shandong			
			Jin Ziwei	Jiangxi			
			Feng Guixin	Jiangxi			
Women's eight with coxswain (Open site)	6:08.00	2	Yu Fei	Beijing	Poland Station, World Cup	15-17 June, 2006	Poznan
			Luo Xiuhua	Sichuan			
			Cheng Ran	Shandong			
			Mu Suli	Henan			
			Wu You	Jiangxi			
			Yan Xiaoxia	Liaoning			
			Gao Yanhua	Fujian			
			Yang Cuiping	Shanxi			
			Zheng Na	Beijing			

Liang Sanmei

Liang Sanmei (1968-), rowing athlete. She was the winner of Lightweight Double Sculls in the 1986 National Rowing Championship. She won the Women's Lightweight Double Sculls in the 14th World University Games in 1987, and cooperated with Lin Zhiai, Zhang Huajie and Zeng Meilan to win the Women's Four Coxless 2000m game in the 1988 World Lightweight Rowing Championship, which was the first rowing gold medal of China in the World Championships games. In 1989, she remained to be the winner of the Women's Lightweight Four Coxless game in the 15th World Championships and won the title for the third time in 1991.

♦ Chinese Rowing Association

The Chinese Rowing Association, founded in May 1981, is a national non-governmental organization based in Beijing. It is a member of the All-China Sports Federation. In 1973, China became a formal member of the International Rowing Federation.

Regular events held by the Chinese Rowing Association include: the National Rowing Championship, the National Youth Rowing Tournament, the National Teenager Rowing Tournament and National Rowing Tournament.

Address: C3, Longtan Xilu, Chongwen District, Beijng
Website: http://rowing.sport.org.cn

Shooting

China is half a century later than the American and European countries in Shooting Sports. The first national shooting competition was held in 1956. Right now, there are over 330 regular shooting training units in the country and more than 1,500 elite shooting athletes being trained. There are 35 registered teams for national shooting competition under the Chinese Shooting Association, more than 1200 shooting coaches, within which more than 400 are beyond provincial ranks, and 800 are on the preparation line to become provincial coaches. There are 167 national referees, of which 55 are international referees. Since the Chinese Shooting Association regained its seat in the International Shooting Federation in 1979, shooting in China had fastened its step to join the international development, and became active in Asian and World competitions. Shooting has won China 14 Olympic gold medals, 113 world champions and 117 world records in 50 years. It has become a true strength in China's competitive sports.

Popularity of Shooting

In 1952, shooting has been listed as one of three sports for popularization by the central government. The major form for the commons to practice shooting sport is to join shooting games organized for the common people. Every year, more than 100 thousand of people will join the activity. Based on this, sports authorities organized various shooting competitions for the delegation teams of different provinces, municipal cities and autonomous regions. Right now, there are more than 190 sports middle schools of city level in China that have shooting majors, accommodating more than 2,500 students practicing shooting and more than 900 amateur shooting coaches.

Development of Shooting

China entered the first division in shooting by 7 gold medals in the 46th World Shooting Championships. In the 27th World Shooting Championships, China was ranked the No.1 in team performance with 13 gold medals, and won a trophy that had only been traveling in the hands of America and European countries for decades. It is the first time for China and Asia to win this honor. In the 48th World Shooting Championships, China won 17 gold, 18 silver and 11 bronze. It secured the second position in the medal list by 46 medals. In this Championships games, China broke 12 world records and equaled a world record for 2 times. In the 27th Olympic Games, China won 3 gold medals, and was ranked the first among all the participating countries in gold medal and total medal. In the 14th Busan Asian Games, the national team of China won 27 gold, 16 silver and 7 bronze, ranking the first among all the participating countries and regions by a total of 50 medals. It broke 3 world records, equaled one, and broke 11 Asian records.

In 2006, China reaped 5 gold, 5 silver and 2 bronze in the 15 Olympic events in the World Shooting Championships in August, and secured its top position in Asia by a total of 27 gold in the Doha Asian Games in December. But the most important achievements of China Shooting Team was 7 tickets to the 2008 Beijing Olympic Games, which has increased China's seats in the Olympic Games to 24.

China is pre-dominantly strong in pistol, running target and rifle, but relatively weak in clay-shooting and prone positions.

♦ First Skeet World Champion Team

In the 42nd World Shooting Championships, China sent a team of 3 athletes, namely Wu Lanying, Feng Meimei and Shao Weiping. It was the first time China sent its skeet team to play in World Championships, and the team won the title in Women's Team Skeet by a performance of 383 hits. It was China's first skeet world champion team. In the game, Wu Lanying, a member in the team, also grabbed an individual title from her Italian component, whom was also a world record setter, and became the first athlete in China that holds a individual title in World Shooting Championships.

♦ China's First World Record in Shooting

The 43rd World Shooting Championship was held in Venezuela from November 1st to 13th, 1982. Over 1000 athletes from 55 countries joined the games, in which, Chinese athletes participated in 5 Men's events and 7 Women's events. It is the first time China joined multiple events in the World Championships. In the end, China won 1 gold, 3 silver and 6 bronze.

In the games, the Chinese women's skeet team, consisted of Wu Lanying, Feng Meimei and Shao Weiping, won the Women's Skeet Team Title by a performance of 436 hits, breaking the previous world record of 417 hits set by USSR. Feng Meimei won the 2nd place in individual games by a performance of 194 hits and broke the world record of 192 hits set by Italy. China finally had its first two entries in the shooting world records.

Rifle

Rifle shooting has been listed as an official game since the 1st National Games of China in 1959. Chen Rong, who broke the world record by 589 points in the Women's Small-Bore Rifle 60 Shot Prone Position, was the first Chinese player that broke a world record in shooting. In the 1994 National Shooting Championships, Zhao Bi broke the world record of Women's Small-Bore Rifle 60 Shot again, by a record of 595 points. In the 46th World Shooting Championships in 1994, Li Wenjie grabbed the championship of Men's Rifle Prone Position, and became the first rifle shooting world champion in China.

Clay-shooting

Clay-shooting has a relatively late start in China. Shotgun 100 Target was first listed to be an official event in the 1962 National Shooting Championships. Shotgun 200 Target was listed to be an official event in the 1st

Games of the New Emerging Forces in 1963. In the 1973 National Shooting Games, skeet and shooting trap were both added into the official game schedule. Wu Lanying, who won the titles of Women's Individual and Team Skeet in the 1981 World Champions, began Chinese clay-shooting's journey to "gold medals" in world-class competitions. Zhang Shan, also a member from the Chinese national team, grabbed a gold medal for China from the hands of competitors from all over the world in the 1992 Barcelona Olympic Games, by a perfect performance of 200 out of 200. Li Bo, another member in the national team, won the championship of Men's individual Skeet and Shooting Trap by a performance of 189 hits in the 2000 Clay-Shooting World Cup final.

In the 2006 World Cup competition Qingyuan Station in Guangzhou, the Chinese team delivered a great show that was rarely seen in recent years. In the games, Qu Rirong, gold medalist of Men's Skeet, had 124 hits; Shi Hongyan had 74 hits in Women's Skeet; Chen Li also had 74 hits in the Women's Shooting Trap. Their performances had been recognized by the International Shooting Federation as the new world records.

Pistol

Pistol Shooting was first listed as an official competition event in the 1st National Games in 1959. In the same year, Zhang Hong refreshed the previous world record of 566 points set by the USSR athlete in the Small-Bore Free Pistol 50m 60 Shot Slow Fire by a new world record of 567 points. He was the first man that breaks a world record in the Chinese shooting history.

Running Target

China has listed running deer as an official competition event ever since the 1st National Games in 1959. In the 2nd National Games in 1965, Han Ruichang broke the world record of Men's Individual Running Deer 50 Single Shot by a performance of 293 points. In the 5th National Games in 1983, China added the Team's 50m Running Target Standard Speed and Team's 50m Running Target Mixed Speed in the official game list. In the 7th National Games in 1993, the 10m Running Target 30+30 event was also added in the game. In the 8th National Games in 1998, Women's 10m Running Target 20+20 was listed as an official game as well. In the 3 World Shooting Championships held in 1990, 1994 and 1998, China won 6 gold medals in total. In the 1984 23rd Olympic Games, Li Yuwei grabbed the title of Men's 50m Running Target and became the first running target world champion in China.

Dong Xiangyi

Dong Xiangyi (1951-), male shooting athlete. Dong created a world record in the Small-Bore Pistol Slow Acceleration Individual event in the 1975 All-Army Games. In the same year, she broke the world record of Small-Bore Pistol Slow Acceleration for two times in the 3rd National Games in China. In 1977, she again broke the world records for two times. In her 1978 visit to Romania, she broke the world record of Small-Bore Pistol Slow Acceleration one more time, by a record of 593 points. She was the champion of the team event in the 23rd Shooting Championships held by the International Military Sports Council. She had broken the world record in the team events for 7 times and the individual events for 6 times. She was awarded the "Sports Star" medal by the International Military Sports Council in 1984.

Wu Lanying

Wu Lanying (1955-), the first female clay-shooting athlete in China.

She won the championship of Women's Skeet in both team and individual events in the 1981 World Shooting Championships. In the 1984 Sino-Italy Friendship Competition, she broke a world record. In the 1990 World Shooting Championships, she broke the world record of the Women's Skeet Team event again. She was the winner of the team event of the 43rd World Shooting Championships in 1982. She got this title again in 1983 and 1989. In the 11th Asian Games in 1990, she grabbed a gold medal and set a new world record in Skeet 200 Hit Team event.

Feng Meimei

Feng Meimei (1957-), female shooting athlete. She is a world champion and a world record setter.

In the 1981 National Shooting Competition regional games, she broke the skeet world record by a record of 194 hits. She had won the world title for 3 times with her teammate Wu Lanying and Shao Weiping. She won the gold medal in Women's Team Skeet in the World Championships in 1981 and grabbed this gold medal again in 1982 with a new world record of 436 hits. She also broke the Individual Skeet world record by 194 hits in the 1982 World Championships. In 1983, she again won the championship in Women's Team Skeet of the World Championships, and was ranked the 3rd in individual event. She won the title of Women's Team Skeet with Shao Weiping and Liu Ling in the 1986 World Championships. In 1987, she won the Women's Individual Skeet title by 192 hits in the World Championships. In 1989, she won the team title again with Wu Lanying and Zhang Shan in the World Championships.

Wu Xiaoxuan

Wu Xiaoxuan (1957-), female shooting athlete. She was selected into the National Team in 1981. In 1980, she won the Air Rifle championship in the 4th Asian Championships. In 1982, she grabbed the title in Air Rifle in the 9th Asian Games, and reset the Asian record by a performance of 584 points. In the 1984 23rd Olympic Games, she was the gold-medalist in the Women's Small-Bore Rifle 3×20 and the bronze-medalist in Women's Air Rifle. She's the first female athlete in China that wins an Olympic gold medal.

Xu Haifeng

Xu Haifeng (1957-), male shooting athlete. He was selected into the Anhui Team in 1982 and the National Team in 1984. In the shooting training center, he worked as both an assistant coach and an athlete. He retired from the National Team in 1995 and began to coach the Women's National Team in pistol shooting. Later, he began to be the deputy coach of the National Shooting Team. In March, 2003, he became the head coach of the National Shooting Team. He was the first Olympic gold-medalist in China and in Chinese Olympic history. It's him who entered the first entry for China in the book of Olympic gold medal history.

In the 23rd Los Angeles Olympic Games in 1984, he won the first gold medal of that Olympic Games—the gold medal in Men's Free Pistol, by a performance of 566 points, and became the first Olympic gold-medalist in China. In the 24th Seoul Olympic Games in 1998, he won the 2nd place in Men's Air Pistol. In the 11th Asian Games in Beijing, 1990, he grabbed the championship of Men's Individual Free Pistol 60 Shot Slow Fire and the championship of Men's Team Free Pistol 60 Shot Slow Fire with his teammates. In the 46th World Championships in Milan, July, 1994, he cooperated with his teammates and won the Men's Team 10m Air Pistol championship. In the 12th Asian Games in Hiroshima, September, 1994, he won the title of Men's Team Pistol Slow Fire with his teammates.

Under his coach, Li Duihong and Tao Luna in the Chinese National Team won the title of Women's 25m Pistol 30+30 in the 1996 Atlanta Olympic Games and the title of Women's 10m Air Pistol 40 Shot in the 2000 Sydney Olympic Games separately.

Wang Yifu

Wang Yifu (1960-), male shooting athlete. Wang entered the Liaoning Amateur Sports School to study shooting in 1977. He was selected into the Liaoning Team in 1978, and the National Team in 1979. He was reassigned

Wang Yifu won the final of the men's shooting 10m air pistol at Athens Olympics.

to the Shooting and Archery Administrative Centre of the State Physical Culture and Sports Commission in 1994. He enrolled in the School of Business and Administration in Tsinghua University in December, 2000. From 1984 to 2004, he participated in 6 Olympic Games, and was honored as the "6-time Olympic Veteran". In the 25th Barcelona Olympic Games in 1992 and the 28th Athens Olympic Games in 2004, he won the title of Men's Air Pistol. Now, he worked as the vice captain, coach and athlete in the national team.

The achievements of Wang include: bronze medal in Men's Free Pistol Slow Fire of the 23rd Los Angeles Olympic Games in 1984; 7th position in the 24th Seoul Olympic Games in 1988; gold medal in the Men's Air Pistol and silver medal in Men's Free Pistol Slow Fire of the 25th Barcelona Olympic Games in 1992; silver medal in Men's 10m Air Pistol of the 26th Atlanta Olympic Games in 1996; silver medal in the Men's 10m Air Pistol of the 27th Sydney Olympic Games in 2000; gold medal in the Men's 10m Air Pistol in the 28th Athens Olympic Games in 2004.

Gao E

Gao E (1962-), female shooting athlete. She began to receive professional training in July, 1979 and entered the National Team in October 1980.

She was the champion of Shooting Trap Individual event in the 1986 World Shooting Championships; the champion of Shooting Trap Team event in 1994 World Cup; the champion in Shooting Trap in the 1995 World Cup; the champion in Shooting Trap Individual and Team events in the 1996 World Cup; winner of the Shooting Trap Team event in the 1998 and 1999 World Championships; bronze-medalist of the Shooting Trap Individual event in 2000 Sydney Olympic Games; runner-up in the Shooting Trap Team event in the 2001 World Championships; champion of the Shooting Trap Individual event in the 2002 and 2003 World Cup final; winner of the Shooting Trap Individual event in the 2004 World Cup Athens Station.

Gao created a new world record of 210 hits with her teammates in the 1998 World Shooting Championships, and equaled this world record in the 2004 Asian Countries Championships in Malaysia, 2004.

Li Yuwei

Li Yuwei (1965-), shooting athlete. His story with shooting begins with an ordinary rifle. When he was a boy, the rifle owned by his brother-in-law fascinated him. He always followed his brother-in-law to shoot birds in the forest. Later, he received the rifle from his brother-in-law as a gift and began his initial trying-outs in shooting.

In 1979, the 14-year-old Li Yuwei entered Shenyang Land Sports School by his outstanding performance in rifle shooting. He received professional running target training and developed an even stronger interest in shooting. After two years of practive, he possessed all the qualities that a top shooter should possess: patience, steadiness, fast-reaction and quick-decision. In the first national competition he participated in 1981, he shot 572 points. In October the same year, he joined the National Teenager and Youth Individual Shooting Championships with Liaoning Team, and won the championship by 388 points in the 50m Running Target Mixed Speed. He was the "Boy Champion".

In the 23rd Olympic Games in 1984, he won the title of Men's Running Target by a performance of 587 points.

Zhang Shan

Zhan Shan (1968-), female shooting athlete. She entered the Amateur Sports School In Nanchong to play basketball in 1976, and switched to skeet shooting in Sichuan Shooting Team in 1984. In 1989, she was selected in the National Team. She enrolled in the Faculty of Economics in Sichuan University in September, 1993, and launched "Zhang Shan Shooting Club" in 1995. In February, 1998, she entered the National Team again.

In the Barcelona Olympics, the 23-year-old Zhang Shan beat all the male athletes in the mixed skeet game by a performance of 223 hits and won the title. She's the first woman that grabbed the title in a mixed game in Olympics. From the Atlanta Olympic Games on, women's events and men's events were separated. Thus, she is the first and also the last female winner in the mixed skeet event.

In September 1989, she cooperated with Wu Lanying and Feng Meimei and won the team skeet championship in the

Zhang Shan won the gold medal of skeet at the 25th Olympics in 1992.

World Shooting Championships. She also won herself a world title in individual event by a performance of 191 hits + 23 hits. She was the runner-up in the Women's Individual Skeet event of the 45th World Shooting Championships in 1990 and the winner of Women's Individual and Team Skeet events of the 11th Asian Games. In the 25th Barcelona Olympic Games held in July, 1992, she won the title in the mixed skeet game by 223 hits. In July, 1998, she participated in the World Championships games in Barcelona, and won the title in the Women's Skeet Team event with her teammates, breaking the previous world record of 205 hits by a performance of 213 hits. She was also ranked the 2nd in individual skeet event by a performance of 96 hits.

Li Duihong

Li Duihong (1970-), shooting athlete. She entered the Daqing Amateur Sports School to learn shooting when she was 12, and entered the National Team in 1987.

Li was the Women's Small-Bore Sport Pistol champion in the 1982 Havana Shooting World Cup. Other achievements of hers include: a silver medal in the Women's Sport Pistol in the 25th Barcelona Olympic Games in 1992; championship and record-setter in the Women's Sport Pistol, runner-up in the Women's Military Pistol High Speed, and runner-up in the team events of the previous two events in the 32nd Shooting Championships held by the International Military Sports Council in Norway, 1993; champion and record-setter in the Women's 25m Sport Pistol in the 26th Atlanta Olympic Games in 1996; champion in the team and individual events of Women's Sport Pistol Slow Fire in the Shooting Championships held by the International Military Sports Council in 2001; winner of the Women's 25m Sport Pistol Team event in the 2002 World Shooting Championships.

Tan Zongliang

Tan Zongliang (1971-), Shooting athlete. He began to receive professional training in Shandong Sports and Competition School in December, 1998. He entered the National Team in 1993.

He was the champion of the Free Pistol Slow Fire team event in the 27th World Championships in 1998. He won the titles of Free Pistol Slow Fire in both the team and individual events in the 28th World Championships in 2002. In the World Cup final in 2002, he was crowned the champion in the Free Pistol Slow Fire. He was also the winner in the Air Pistol Individual event in the 2002 World Cup in America and the 2003 World Cup in Germany. He won the titles of Air Pistol in both the individual and team events in the 2002 Busan Asian Games.

On December 3, 2006, Tan Zongliang won the gold medal of the men's shooting 10m air pistol at the 15th Doha Asian Games.

Tan broke the world record of air pistol team event by 1757 points in the 2000 Asian Championships in Malaysia. He also broke the national record of air pistol in China by a record of 593 points in the 2003 Asia-Africa Games in India.

Jia Zhanbo

Jia Zhanbo (1974-), male shooting athlete. He entered the Xinyang Sports School in Henan Province to study shooting in 1988, and entered the Henan Team in 1990. In 1997, 1998 and 2003, he was selected into the National Team.

Jia was the champion of Men's Rifle 60 Shot Prone Position in the 8th National Games in 1997. He was also the champion in the Rifle 60 Shot Prone Position team event, and the 2nd in the Rifle 60 Shot Prone Position individual event. In the 2004 Olympics, he won a gold medal in the Rifle 3×40 event.

Tao Luna

Tao Luna (1974-), female shooting athlete. She entered the National Team in 1997. In the end of 1997, she won the title in the World Cup final, and renewed her championship in 1998. She was also the winner of Women's 10m Air Pistol in the 2000 Sydney Olympics. She has been selected to be the best female shooter in two consecutive years by the International Shooting Federation.

Tao Luna is fast yet steady. She majors in air pistol. Her top performances before 1998 was all in air pistol. However, her performance in pistol, which used to be her minor focus, is improving very fast in recent years. Now, she is competitive in both events.

She equaled the world record of 390 points in Women's Air Pistol in the 2000 Sydney Olympics and created a new world record of 695.9 points in Women's Pistol in the 2002 World Cup final in Munich, Germany.

Tao Luna won the first gold medal of the Chinese team in the women's shooting 10m air pistol competition with 488.2 rings at the 27th Summer Olympic Games held in Sydney, Australia in September 2000.

Chen Ying

Chen Ying (1977-), female shooting athlete. Since selected by Xu Haifeng to enter the National Team in March, 2001, Chen has been improving drastically. In the 9th National Games in 2001, she won over several Olympic champions and world champions such as Tao Luna and Li Duihong, and won two titles in Women's Air Pistol and Sport Pistol. She also won several gold medals for China in the 2003 and 2004 Asia-Africa Games and Shooting World Cup.

Cai Yalin

Cai Yalin (1977–), male shooting athlete. Initially a fan in martial arts, he was recommended to learn shooting in Chengde Sports School by a manager of a sports complex. In the end of 1997, he entered the National Team.

In the 1998 Bangkok Asian Games, he

Cai Yalin titled the men's air rifle with 696.4 rings at the Sydney Olympics.

grabbed the title of Men's Individual 10m Air Rifle and the 2nd place in the Men's 10m Air Rifle Team event. He was also the champion and record-setter of Air Rifle in the 1998 National Shooting Tournaments. It was also in 1998 that he got the 7th place in the World Shooting Championships and a ticket to the Olympic Games. In 2000, he reaped a gold medal in Men's 10m Air Rifle in 2000 Sydney Olympic Games, and reset the world record of 695.7 points to 696.4 points. In 2002 Busan Asian Games, he grabbed two gold medals in the team events and broke a world record and an Asian record with his teammates. Especially in Men's 10m Air Rifle, he cooperated with Li Jie and Zhangfu and created a new world record of 1788 points. They won a gold medal for such excellent performance. The previous world record was 1785, created by the Russian team. In Men's 50m Free Rifle, he cooperated with Yao Ye and Qiu Jian and rewrote the Asian record to 3472 points. This also brought them a gold medal in the Busan Asian Games.

On August 14, 2004, Du Li titled the women's shooting 10m air rifle at the Athens Olympics with 502 rings.

Li Jie

Li Jie (1979-), male shooting athlete. In his first endeavor in the Asian Games in 2002, he won two gold medals. In the 48th World Championships in July, 2002, he was ranked the 2nd in the Men's 10m Air Rifle and got a ticket to the 2004 Olympic Games. He won the championship in the World Cup Final in August the same year. In October, he played in the 14th Busan Asian Games, and grabbed a title and broke the previous world record of 699.1 points in the individual event of Men's 10m Air Rifle by a total record of 700.8. He also won the title and reset the previous world record of 1785 points to 1788 points in the team event of Men's 10m Air Rifle with his teammates Zhang Fu and Cai Yalin. He won a silver medal in the Men's 10m Air Rifle in the 2004 Athens Olympic Games.

Yang Ling in the shooting competition at the 2000 Sydney Olympics

Yang Ling

Yang Ling (1979-), male shooting athlete. He began his career when he was 14, studying shooting in Beijing Amateur Sports School. He entered Beijing 2nd Sports School in 1988 and the Beijing Team in 1989. He was selected into the National Team in 1993, of which the coach was Cai Tianxiang. The world records created by Yang Ling were still the unsurpassable targets of many shooting athletes in China.

He ranked the third in Men's Individual 10m Running Target by a performance of 673.1 points, and grabbed the 2nd place in the Men's Team 10m Running Target with Shu Qingquan and Xiao Jun in the Shooting World Cup held in Beijing, May 1994. In July the same year, he grabbed the title of Men's Team 50m Standard Speed with his teammates by a record of 1759 points. In the Men's 10m Running Target event in the Shooting World Cup that was held in Milan on June13, 1996, he broke two world records by the 586 points in the qualification game and the 687.9 points in total, and finally won the title. In the 10m Running Target event of the 26th Atlanta Olympic Games which was held on July 26, 1996, he won the championship again, by a record of 685.5 points. In July, 1998, he participated in the Shooting World Cup in Barcelona, and won the 2nd place in Men's Team Running Target with his teammates, by a performance of 1143. He was also the champion of Men's Running Target in the 2000 Asian Championships in Malaysia and the 2000 Shooting World Cup Milan Station.

Ren Jie

Ren Jie (1980-), female shooting athlete in China. She entered the Baoding Sports School in November, 1994, and the National Team in 1997.

Ren was the champion in the team event of Air Pistol 40 Shot in the 13th Asian Games in 1998, the champion of Air Pistol 40 Shot in the 2001 World Cup Final, and the champion of Sport Pistil 60 Shot in the 2002 World Cup. She won in the team event of Air Pistol 40 Shot in the 2002 Asian Games, and was the runner-up in the 10m Air Pistol event in the 2004 World Cup. She created a world record of 493.5 points in the 1999 World Cup in Germany.

Du Li

Du Li (1982-), female shooting athlete. Du entered Zibo Sport School in Shandong Province in 1996, and joined the National Team in 2002.

She was the runner-up in Women's Air Rifle and the champion in the Women's Air Rifle Team event in the 2002 World Championships. She won two titles in the team event and individual event of Women's 3×20 and one title in the team event of Women's Air Rifle in the 2002 Busan Asian Games. She grabbed the gold medal in the individual event of Women's Air Rifle in the 2003 World Cup in Croatia, and a 2nd place in the 2003 World Cup Final. She was also the silver-medalist in the individual event of Women's Air Rifle in the 2002 World Cup in Thailand.

Du created a world record of 1192 points in the team event of Women's Air Rifle in the

2002 World Championships in Finland. She broke her own world record by 1194 points in the 2002 Busan Asian Games. In the 2003 World Cup games in Croatia, she created a new world record of 504.9 points in the individual event of Women's Air Rifle.

Zhu Qinan

Zhu Qinan (1984-), male shooting athlete. Zhu is the champion of Men's 10M Air Rifle in the 2004 Athens Olympic Games.

He began amateur training in shooting in the Wenzhou Sports School in 1999, under of the coach of You Xiuxia and Tang Gongxi. He entered the Zhejiang Shooting Team in February, 2002, under the coach of Zhu Xiaobo. He entered the National Team on December 14, 2003, under the coach of Chang Jingchun.

The main achiements of Zhu Qinan include: title of Men's 10m Air Rifle in Team Round the 2003 National Shooting Tournament; title of Men's Air Rifle in 2003 National Shooting Championships; title of Men's Individual 10m Air Rifle in the 5th City Games in Changsha, 2003; title of Men's 10m Air Rifle in the 2004 Shooting World Cup in Thailand; title of Men's Individual 10m Air Rifle in the 10 Asian Championships in 2004, Kuala Lumpur; title of Men's 10m Air Rifle in the 2004 Athens Olympic Games, with a new Olympic record of 599 points and a new world record of 702.7 points in the final.

♦ Chinese Shooting Association

The Chinese Shooting Association (CSA), founded in 1956, is a national non-governmental organization based in Beijing. It is a member of the All-China Sports Federation. In 1979, the CSA became a formal member of the International Shooting Sport Federation.

Regular events held by the CSA include: National Shooting Championships, National Team Shooting Championships (rifle), National Team Shooting Championships (pistol), National Team Shooting Championships (running target), National Team Shooting Championships (clay-shooting), National Shooting Championships (rifle and running target), National Shooting Championships (pistol and clay-shooting), and National Youth Shooting Competitions.

Address: A3 Futian Temple, Shijingshan District, Beijing

Website: http://www.shooting.sport.org.cn

Archery

Archery has a long history in China and enjoys a great popularity, especially in the ethic minorities. Every year, the ethnic minorities in China would celebrate their festivals by archery competitions of their own traditions, such as the competitions held by the Tibetans in Qinghai on the shooting-distance, bow-stretching and precision, and the traditional archery-on-horse and precision competitions in the Nadamu Games in Inner Mongolia. However, modern archery had a late start in China. From 1949 to 1955, archery remained to be an exhibition game and only quitted to be so in 1956. It was not until 1959 that there were archery competitions under international rules. From then on, archery began to progress in 25 provinces, autonomous regions and municipal cities.

In 1961, Zhao Suxia from Shanghai first broke a world record of archery. During 1961 and 1994, Chinese archery athletes had broken 46 world records in total, in which the world-renowned female athlete Li Shulan had contributed 11 for individual events and 6 for team events. By far, she is the one that owns the most world records in Chinese sports history. Chinese archery experienced a steady development. Ma Xiangjun is the first archery world champion in China for her championship in 1987. In the 2000 World Championships in Beijing, the Chinese Women's Archery Team won the first and by far the only team gold medal, but they only ranked the rd in the 2002 Asian Games. In the 2004 Olympics, the Chinese team had a close lose to the Koreans by a difference of 1 point, and got the silver medal.

The First Archery World Champion in China

In July 1981, Zhao Suxia, the 19-year-old female archer from Shanghai, created the world record of 270 in the Single Round 50m event and became the first female archer that breaks the world record in China.

The Daur people of Mongolian ethnic group in Altay, Xinjiang, held the traditional archery competition to celebrate the New Year's Day.

Li Shulan

Li Shulan (1944-), a well-known archer in China. Li entered the China People's Liberation Army Sports School in 1960 and started to study archery in March the same year.

Li became a national champion in 1962. In a national archery event in 1963, she had broken 5 world records for 5 times. In same year, she won an individual championship and a team championship in the 1st Games of the Emerging Forces held in Jakarta, and created a world record. During 1963 and 1966, she had broken the world records of individual events for 11 times, and the world records of team events for 6 times with her teammates. She had the most world records among Chinese archers and Chinese athletes.

In the competition she participated from 1962 to 1966, she had many consecutive championships and a dozen of national records.

Meng Fanai

Meng Fanai (1955-), a well-known archer in China. She entered the Beijing Sports School in 1971 and began to practice archery the second year of her admission.

In the national competition in March, 1978, she broke the women's world team record by 3,780 points with teammates Song Shuxian and Huang Shuyan. In the archery competition on the June 17, 1979, Japan, she broke the previous Women's Single Round 70m world record of 319 points by shooting 321 points. Since 1978, she had won various championships in nation-wide competitions and broke dozens of national records. She also won the individual Single Round championship in the 1st Asian Archery Championships in 1980. In the 31th World Championships, in which the Chinese team made their debut, Meng won the individual 70m championship and the 3 in the women's team event with her teammates Fu Hong and Kong Yaping by a point of 7,433. She was also the winner of the women's Double Round 50m event in the Asia-Pacific Archery Championships in 1982.

Li Lingjuan

Li Lingjuan (1966-), female archer. She started learning archery in 1982 and won the National Teenager Championship in the same year. In 1983, she grabbed 3 gold medals in the 5th National Games and shocked the Chinese archery community. Three months after the National Games, she went abroad for the first time, to join the 2 Asia-Pacific Archery Championships. She won Kim Jin-ho, the well-known individual Double Round champion of the 1979 and 1983 World Championships from

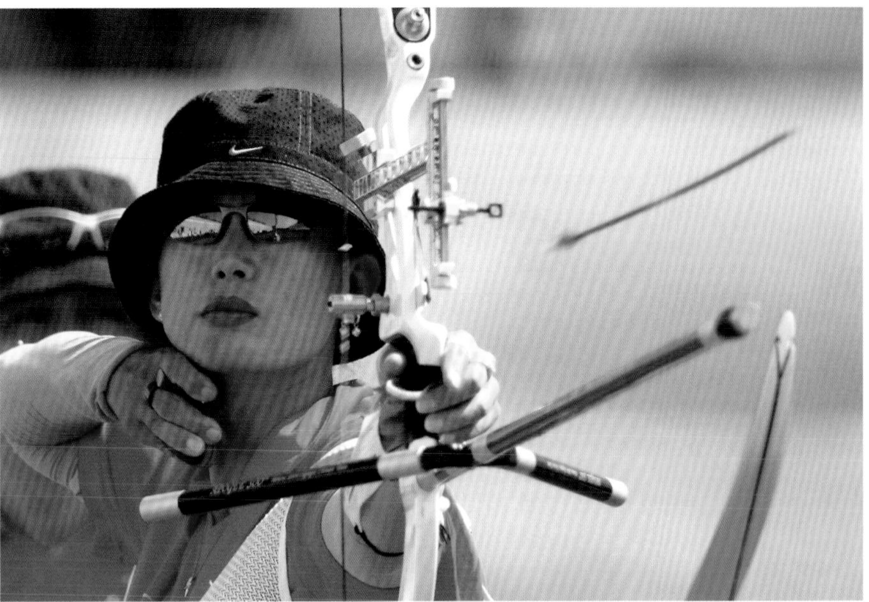

He Ying in semifinal of the archery women's team competition at the Athens Olympics on August 20, 2004

South Korea, and shocked the Asian archery community. The president of the International Archery Federation complimented her as "the youngest champion".

In the 23rd Olympic Games in 1984, the 18-year-old Li Lingjuan made her debut in international arenas by winning a silver medal in Women's individual Double Round and breaking the Olympic records of all the 5 events he participated in. She has broken the most Olympic records among female archers. She shot 694 points in Double Round 30m event, updating the previous Olympic record of 690 points created by the Russian archer in 1980, and was written into the history of Olympics.

He Ying

He Ying (1977-), a well-known archer in China. She started archery training at 14. She participated in 4 national games, the 1996 Atlanta Olympic Games, the 2000 Sydney Olympic Games and the 2004 Athens Olympic Games. She had also broken the world record of women's Single Round 60m.

In 1990, she was in Siping Army Sports School on archery training under the coach of Tian Wenlan. She entered the Jilin Team in 1992, under the coach of Wang Jianxin. She was selected into the National Team in May, 1993, still under the coach of Wang Jianxin.

He Ying was the 3rd of the individual elimination events in the 7th National Games in 1993, and the champion of team event in the 1994 Hiroshima Asian Games, the 2nd in the National Championships in Guangxi in 1995 and of the individual elimination events in the 1996 Atlanta Olympic Games, the 2nd of the team elimination events in 1998 Asian Games in Thailand, the 2nd of the team elimination events in 1999 World Championships, the champion of the team elimination events in 2001 World Championships and the individual elimination events in the 9th National Games of the same year, the winner of the individual events in the 2002 National Championships, the 2nd of the team elimination events in 2003 Asian Championships in Myanmar and the silver-medalist of the team events in 2004 Athens Olympic Games.

♦ Chinese Archery Association

The Chinese Archery Association, a national non-governmental organization based in Beijing, was established in 1964. It is the only legal organization that can represent China in international archery organizations. It joined the International Archery Federation in 1967 and resumed its legal seat in International Archery Federation in 1979. In 1978, it joined the Asian Archery Federation.

Regular events held by the Chinese Archery Association include: National Archery Competition for Talented Archers, National Archery Target Competition, National Indoor Archery Tournament, National Youth and Teenager Archery Competition, National Archery Tournament and Beijing International Archery Tournament.

Address: A 3 Futian Temple, Shijingshan District, Beijing
Website: http://archery.sport.org.cn

Handball

Modern handball was played as introductory sport among sport colleges since its introduction into China. This situation didn't change until 1956, when the trial teaching of 11-a-side handball was carried out in Beijing Sport College. In the 1st National Games in 1959, handball was included as an official game. After 1960, 7-A-side handball started to find its way in China and, in 1964 and 1965, two National Championships games for 7-a-side handball were held respectively in Hefei,An Hui and Shenyang, Liaoning. National handball competitions took place every year after 1974. In 1977, China became one of the first member countries of Asian Handball Federation. Two years later, China joined International Handball Federation. In the last few years, handball has been growing considerably in China and China has become a strong force in Asia.

Chinese men's handball team won the gold medal in the 1982 Asian Games. The women's handball team claimed bronze in 1984 Los Angeles Olympic Games and occupied the fifth place in 1996 Atlanta Olympic Games. It was also in 1996 that the Chinese men's handball team beat Korea to qualify into the Handball World Championships.

However, due to various reasons, team sports in China have run into difficulty these years. Sloping down of performance can be seen in a variety of team ball games, and handball is no exception. Today, because of the serious scarcity of fresh blood, the performance of China is very unstable.

The First Female Handball Referees with International Class A Certificate

From April 13-18, 1984, the International Handball Federation held an International

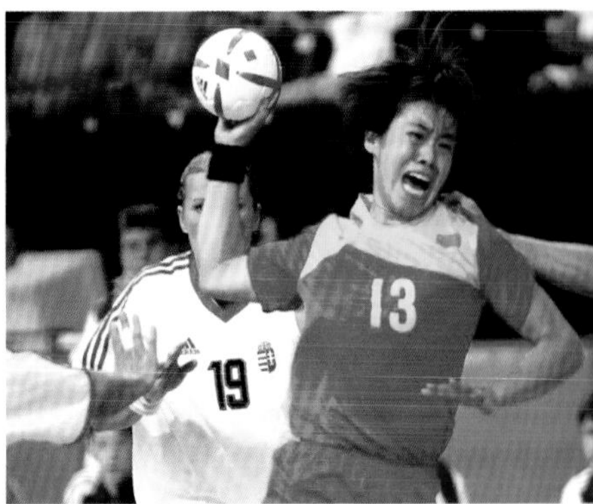

Chinese player shooting in the women's handball group match at the Athens Olympics on August 15, 2004

Class A Certificate course for handball referees, which was presided by Karl Wang, president of the Referees Committee of the International Handball Federation, and Elias, the vice president. 22 referees holding international Class B certificate from Korea, Japan, India, Kuwait and China took the exam. 7 out of 8 from China passed to become the first handball referees with international Class A certificate at home. Among them, Ren Jun and Wang Zhiguang are the only two female referees holding Class A Certificate.

In 1985, they were both invited by the IHF to participate in the World Youth Handball Championships in South Korea. It was the first time that Chinese referees were assigned to umpire international games. They even refereed 28 men's games, besides numerous women's.

The First Olympic Handball Medal

China women's handball team claimed bronze in the 23rd Olympic Games, China's first handball medal in Olympics. Every match in the finals was a new encounter to the girls, who had never been faced with any of their rivals except South Korea. In the first match against America on August 1, they were defeated by 23:25. Only one day after, they were confronted with West Germany, a tough team consisted of picked players from clubs all over the country. The West Germany players were good at positional attack and defense; they never hesitated to take advantage of their height (average 1.75m) to give long shots. The defenders of West Germany, 1.80 meters in average, were very hard to break down. China players, nevertheless, managed to launch attacks using tactics such as fast strike back, position-shifting and double-act; finally, they grabbed a narrow win. They continued their invincible way by defeating Austria, one of the top teams in Europe, and drawing with South Korea, which had defeated China twice before, before they were outscored by the most favored Yugoslavia and received their bronze medal.

♦ Chinese Handball Association (CHA)

Chinese Handball Association (CHA) was founded in the city of Baoding, North China's Hebei Province, in September 1979. Headquatered in Beijing, the CHA is one of the individual sport associations under China National Sports Confederation. It's a national non-governmental organization. The CHA became a member of Asian Handball Federation in 1976, and was granted the membership of the International Handball Federation in August, 1980.

The CHA is responsible for organizing various handball events, including the National Youth Handball Tournament, the National Women's Handball Tournament, the National Men's Handball Tournament and the National Handball League for College Students, the National Schools Handball League and the National Amateur Schools Handball League.

Address: No.5 Tiyuguan Road, Chongwen District, Beijing
Website: http://www.handball.sport.org.cn

Chinese Wrestling

Chinese wresting is an ethnic sport with a long history, which can be traced back to 2,000 years ago, according to records in historical materials and relics. It's a cultural heritage of China. Towards the closing of the Qing Dynasty, China reached its peak in wrestling skills. After thousands of years' evolution, it has become more and more popular today. To promote this traditional sport, the State Physical Culture and Sports Commission listed Chinese wrestling as an national competitive sport and stipulated that the handball tournament should be held once a year.

It was listed as an official competitive sport in the 1st National Ethnic Sports Performance and Contest, which was held in Tianjin, 1953. In 1956, Beijing hosted the National Wrestling Competition. It's the first individual wrestling event in China, with 96 players from 21 provinces, autonomous regions and municipalities were involved. Today, Chinese wrestling has become a major event in National Games.

China has three national wrestling teams: men's Greece-Roman, men's freestyle and women's freestyle.

Freestyle Wrestling

Men's freestyle wrestling started nearly a century before women's. In men's freestyle, experience, physical constitution and fitness, as well as skills and tactics, are all key factors that can affect the result of a match. Consequently, it's much fiercer than women's. While Russia is taking the lead in men's freestyle wresting, China is quite weak. In the World Wrestling Championships that was held in Guangzhou from the end of September to the start of October, only several Chinese men players advanced to the third round.

China started to promote women's freestyle wrestling before Japan in the early 1990s. China women's freestyle wrestling team, drawing on men's training style and working hard, soon made their mark in the World Wrestling Championships and started to snatch gold medals. After the Atlanta Olympics Games, however, a lot of teams were dismissed and good players quitted because of the dim prospect of advancing to the Sydney Olympics. With only one college team survived, China's position in women's freestyle wresting declined, and was exceeded by Japan not long after. In Athens Olympics, 2004, women's freestyle wresting made its debut in the Olympics. Wang Xu won the 72 kg gold medal out of the four gold medals in all. In World Wrestling Championships that was held in Guangzhou, 2006, Jing Ruixue claimed gold in women's 67 kg category, China's only gold medal in this event.

Greece-Roman Wresting

In the early 1990s, China Greece-Roman wresting team attached much importance to the fostering of young players and there emerged a bunch of excellent new players. Among them are Sheng Zetian, Hu Hongguo and Li Daxin. Thus China has improved a lot in this sport. In Barcelona Olympics, 1992, Sheng Zetian won the first Greece-Roman wresting medal for China. He continued to win two bronze medals in the next two Olympics.

World Wresting Championships (2005)

From September 26 to October 2, 2005, the World Wresting Championship was held in Budapest, Hungary. Over 700 players from 85 countries and regions took part in it. The 20 players from China competed in all the categories of men's freestyle and Greece-Roman, and 6 out of 7 women's freestyle categories. Ren Xueceng and Meng Lili clinched gold in 48 and 67 kg categories respectively, while Su Lihui and Jing Ruixue took the silver medals in 55 and 63 kilos. Wen Juling ranked third in the 51 kg category and Wang Jiao fifth in the 72 kg category. China's women players finished second with a team total of 52, 9 points below Japan. Qu Lei made a breakthrough for China by winning the fifth place in men's freestyle 120 kg category. Overall, China ranked third with 2 gold medals, 2 silver medals and 1 bronze medal, the best result of Chinese players in World Wresting Championships.

This result indicates that China's wrestling is in a relatively high level. Players have reached a stable state not only in terms of skills and strategies, but also psychologically. This is especially true for women's freestyle wrestling, in which China is among the top teams.

World Wrestling Championships (2006)

The 27th World Wrestling Championships opened on September 25, 2006, in Tianhe Stadium of Guangzhou, Guangdong Province. Chinese player Li Yanyan won the Greece-Roman 66 kg championship, a historic breakthrough for China.

It is the largest and of the highest rank ever hosted by China before Beijing Olympics, 2008. It covered three types of wrestling: men's freestyle, men's Greece-Roman and women's freestyle. With each involving 7 categories, there are 21 gold medals in all.

China Women's Wrestling Team

Since 1990s, China women's wresting team has been playing an active part in international stage and it has won over ten titles in World Wresting Championships. When women's wrestling was included in the Olympic program, it's predicted that China women's wresting team might win an Olympic gold medal before men's. Sure enough, Chinese girl Wang Xu snatched gold in Athens Olympic Games. Famous players of this team includes: Ren Xueceng and Meng Lili, two World Wresting Championships gold medalists, Wang Xu, the Athens Olympic champion, Jing Ruixue and Su Lizhen, both good players in their respective categories.

♦ Chinese Wrestling Association

Founded in 1953, Chinese Wrestling Association (CWA) became a member of the International Wrestling Federation in 1954. To fight against the scheme for "two Chinas", Chinese Wrestling Association discontinued its relations with the International Wrestling Federation in 1958. In 1979, the International Wrestling Federation restored China's membership in the federation. The association acquired the membership of Asian Amateur Wrestling Federation in 1974. It is in charge of regularly holding national wrestling events include: the National Freestyle Wresting Tournament, the National Greece-Roman Wrestling Tournament, the National Youth Freestyle Wresting Tournament, the National Youth Greece-Roman Wrestling Tournament, and the National Greece-Roman Wrestling Tournament for Teenagers, the National Freestyle Wrestling Tournament for Teenagers, the National Chinese Wrestling Tournament and the National Greece-Roman and Freestyle Championship.

Address: A14 Tiantandongli, Zhongqu, Beijing
Website: http://www.wrestling.sport.org.cn

Sheng Zetian (the first on the right) won the bronze medal of the 58kg classic-style wrestling at the Sydney Olympics on September 27, 2000.

Sheng Zetian

Sheng Zetian (1971-), was bronze medal winner of the 1992, 1996 and 2000 Olympic Games and chief coach of the Chinese Men's Classic-style Wrestling Team.

He came to Huaibei city of middle China's Anhui province at 6. Influenced by his father and two elder brothers, all martial arts practitioners, Sheng Zetian had been obsessed by martial arts since 6. He began with rudimental martial arts and kept practicing until 14, when he began to learn Chinese wrestling in Huaibei Amateur Sport School. He was transferred to Anhui provincial Sport Team to improve his skills in 1986. In February 1987, he was admitted to Shanghai Sport College, where he started to learn Greece-Roman wrestling. After graduation in 1996, he stayed in the college as a teacher and coach. In 26th, 27th and 28th Olympics, he won three bronze medals, For this reason, he was rated as the best man wrestler in China.

Wang Xu

Wang Xu (1985-) is a 72 kg wrestler. She started her wrestling career in Athletics Sport

On August 23, 2004, Wang Xu won the championship of the women's 72kg class freestyle wrestling at the Athens Olympics.

School of Beijing Sport University, 1999. Her coach was Xu Kuiyuan then. Three years later, when she was chosen to be a member of the national team, Xu Kuiyuan was still her coach.

In the first year after she became a national team member, she won a title in Asian Wresting Championships. A year later, she won a gold medal in the National Wresting Tournament, a silver medal in World Wrestling Championships and another gold medal in the National Wresting Championship. The next year, she succeeded in defending her Championships in the National Wresting Tournament and the National Wresting Championship.

In 2004, she won the title the third time in the National Wresting Tournament; then in Athens, she beat the Russian player 7:2 to snatch gold in the women's freestyle, China's first Olympic wrestling gold medal. What was worth mentioning is that the Japan player she defeated in the quarter-final is a 5 times gold medalist in World Wresting Championships.

Taekwondo

In 2006, the Hainan Team conducted the acrobatic performance in the First National Taekwondo Tournament.

The State Physical Culture and Sports Commission held the fist National Taekwondo Competition in Kunming, Yunnan Province, 1994. Since then, various types of Taekwondo competitions have been taking place in different areas each year. The Commission also held courses for coaches and referees, in which Taekwondo experts from home and abroad were invited to give lectures and on-site guidance and conduct seminars. China became a member of the International Taekwondo Federation in November 1995. Then the national Taekwondo team was organized. In the 12th World Taekwondo Championships in Philippine, they did very well. Out of the eight Taekwondo gold medals, China gained two: Chen Zhong, the veteran, won the 67 kg plus title, while Luo Wei snatched another gold medal in the 67 kg category. So far, China has won three Olympic Taekwondo gold medals, a great success to China Taekwondo Team, which was not organized until 1995.

Being more and more popular in China, Taekwondo has become a major sport for China to claim gold medals in a variety of individual or comprehensive events. China Taekwondo team has won 3 Olympic gold medals and 7 titles in World Taekwondo Championships. In the World Taekwondo Championship, 2003, China women's Taekwondo team scored second. Today, there are about 1,000 Taekwondo clubs promoting this sport, and millions of people are involved.

National Public Taekwondo Championships

The first National Public Taekwondo Championships closed in a series of splendid stunt performances. The days between August 1-4, 2006, is very special, for it's the first time Chinese Taekwondo Association set up a public competition. To prepare for the first Pinshi World Taekwondo Championships, the Chinese Taekwondo Association held three courses for public Taekwondo coaches. The courses also aimed to pick players for the national children team, teenagers' team, youth team and adult team based on their performance in the Championships matches. These courses and matches are very useful: they make the national team better prepared for the upcoming World Taekwondo Championships, make public coaches well trained, and provide more useful information to ordinary Taekwondo practitioners.

Over 1000 people, mostly children and teenagers, from 79 teams participated in this competition. The majority of the participants are boys, who do not have much experience. In their eyes, Taekwondo is "a lot of fun". They volunteered to start practicing and volunteered to get enlisted in this competition.

Chen Shixin

Chen Shixin (1978-), Taekwondo player, M.A. in Sport Psychology in Taipei Sport College.

On August 27, 2004, in the early morning, she outscored Labrada of Cuba 5:4 to win the women's under-49kg flyweight gold, the first-ever Olympic gold medal for Taiwan.

Chen Zhong

Chen Zhong (1982-), a Taekwondo player, did not attract much attention when she made her Olympic debut, but sweep into the final and outscored her Russian rival Ivanova 8-3 with her irresistible attack to take the first Olympic Taekwondo gold medal for China.

Chen Zhong had been playing basketball for four years in Jiaozuo Basketball Amateur School until 1995, when she was admitted to Beijing Sport College. She spent most of her time in the training hall.

Chen Zhong won the first gold medal of the Chinese team in the women's over 67kg class taekwondo at the Athens Olympics on August 26, 2004.

One main reason why she turned from basketball to Taekwondo is that she looked forward to the free boarding life. But when she started the real Taekwondo career, her life was, far from free, unbelievably hard. Her relentless hard working earned her two gold medals in 2000 and 2004 Olympic Games.

Luo Wei

Luo Wei (1983-), Taekwondo player. She started her Taekwondo training in 1999 in Beijing Shichahai Sport School. In the same year, she was chosen to be a member of Beijing city team and her coach then was Yao Qiang. Three years later, she became a member of the national Taekwondo team and her coach was Chen Liren.

She was a 67 kg silver medalist in the National Taekwondo Championships even before she was chosen into the national team. As a national team member, she won a lot of medals: the 72 kg title in the National Taekwondo Tournament and, later, the 67 kg bronze medal in Pusan Asian Games, 2002, the 72 kg title in World Taekwondo Championship, 2003, the 72 kg gold medal in the National Taekwondo Tournament, 2004, and the 67 kg gold medal in the Athens Olympic Games (China's 29th medal in Athens).

Wu Jingyu

Wu Jingyu (1987-), Taekwondo player. She started her training of Taekwondo at 12, and, different from most of the Taekwondo player in China, she received professional training from the very start. She is a versatile player with marked individuality. She is good at quick attack and famous for her beautiful movements of battle and flight.

Wu Jingyu won a title in the World Youth Taekwondo Championships in 2004, a historic breakthrough for China. She continued to win a gold medal in World University Games, a silver medal in the Asian Championships, 2006 and in the same year, a gold medal in China Opens of International Taekwondo Tournament.

♦ Chinese Taekwondo Association

Chinese Taekwondo Association, founded on November 26, 1995, became a member of World Taekwondo Federation (WTF) in 1996.

Events held: the National Taekwondo Tournament, the National Youth Taekwondo Tournament; the National Taekwondo Championship.

Address: A14 Tiantandongli, Zhongqu, Beijing
Website: http://www.taekwondo.org.cn

Gymnastics

In 1953, a sports game of field and track, gymnastics and cycling was held in Beijing. It is the first time China included gymnastics in a national sports game. There are horizontal bar, parallel bars, floor exercise and vaulting box in the Men's event, and parallel bars, floor exercise and vaulting box in the Women's event. Only 8 teams participated in the game, with a total of 68 gymnasts. The performances and techniques were quite poor back then. In the same year, the USSR gymnastics team paid China a visit, and promoted the development of gymnastics in China in a sense. From then on, China began to organize gymnastics teams in provinces and cities, and began to train gymnasts with plans and purposes. In 1954, a 13-city track and field, gymnastics sports game was held in Dalian. It was the first gymnastics game in China that followed the modern convention of 6 events in Men's game and 4 events in Women's game. In the National Gymnastics Test Competition in 1955, gymnastics became an independent competition sport for the first time. From then on, an annual nation-wide gymnastics event would be held, with increasing participants and improving performance each year. It was also in 1955 that the Chinese Gymnastics Association was founded, and joined the International Gymnastics Federation. According to the international rules and regulation of gymnastics and the actual situation in China, China made its own rules and regulations in gymnastics and set up its own hierarchy of referees and gymnasts. In the same year, 8 male and female gymnasts were awarded the title of Master of Sports in the national gymnastics competition held in Tianjin.

The Booming Years of Gymnastics in China

Gymnastics had a big leap in China in the 1980s of the 20th century. In August, 1980, the Chinese Gymnastics team won over the US and Japan in the International Gymnastics Invitation Games in the US, and won the championships in the Men's and Women's team competitions. The team grabbed 9 gold medals in the end. In the same year, the Chinese gymnast Li yuejiu won the championship in parallel bars and Huang Yubin shared the championship in rings together with a Russian gymnast in the Gymnastics World Cup games in Toronto. In the 21st World Gymnastics Championships in November 1981, the Chinese Women's Team won the 2nd place in team competition and the Men's team 3rd in the team competition. In the 6th World Cup games in October 1982, Li Ning grabbed the championship of Men's all-around, and reaped 5 gold medals in other individual events. He was awarded as the World's Second Best Athlete. In the 22nd World Gymnastics Championships in 1983, the Chinese Men's Team beat the Russian team, who was the dominating team back then, and won the titles of team competition, floor exercise and parallel bars. This has shocked the gymnastics world. In the 23rd Los Angeles Olympic Games in 1984, China won a silver in Men's team competition and a bronze in Women's team competition. In the 1984 Olympics, Li Ning won 3 gold medals from floor exercise, pommel horse and rings; Lou Yun won a gold medal in vault; and Ma Yanhong won a gold medal in uneven bars. In November the same year, the International Gymnastics Federation first announced four innovated drills named after Chinese gymnasts. From 1986 to 1992, Chinese Men's Team had won 3 silver medals in team competition out of 5 world-class games; Chinese Women's Team had won 3 gold medals in uneven bars; and the Chinese national team had won 16 gold medals in total.

The 7th Gymnastics World Cup

In August 1986, the 7th Gymnastics World Cup was held in Beijing. It was the first time that Beijing held a world-class gymnastic competition. 36 gymnasts from 13 countries competed for 3 days. In the end, Russia won 11 gold medals, China 4 and the Democratic Germany 1. The exciting performances in the games were very impressive.

Li Ning, the well-known Chinese gymnast, delivered a outstanding performance in the games. He won 3 gold medals in Men's all-around, floor exercise and pommel horse and 1 bronze medal in rings. His performance in pommel horse won him the only full mark out of all the male gymnasts. Xu Zhiqiang, another Chinese gymnast, won the championship in parallel bars, and a 3rd place in pommel horse.

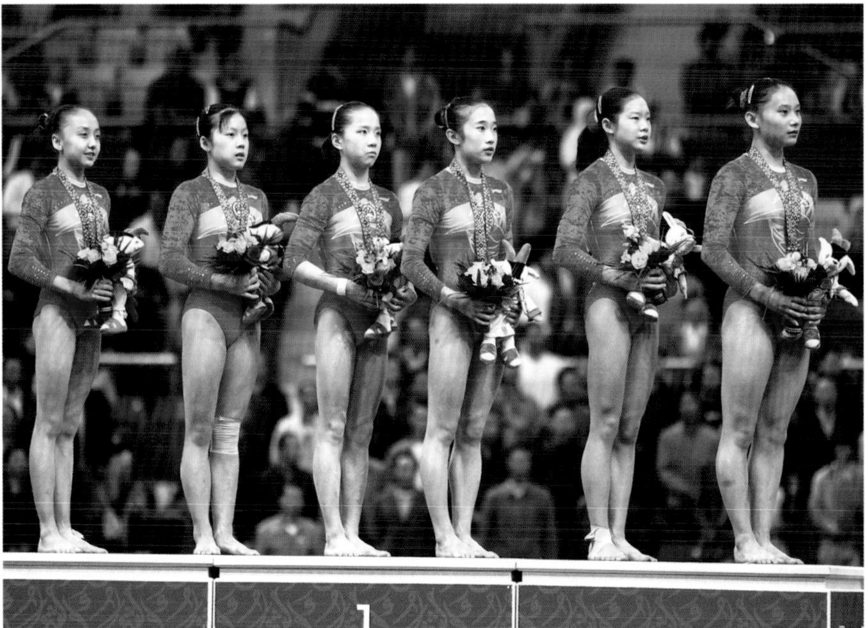

China won the women's gymnastics team final at the 15th Doha Asian Games on December 3, 2006. North Korea and Japan won the second and third place respectively.

Floor Exercise

In the 1980 Hardford Gymnastics Championships in the US, Li Yuejiu completed a backward double flip 720-degree turn, which is a movement of high degree of difficulty and which appears for the first time. Li got the 1st position in the event and became the first floor exercise world champion in China. In the 1984 Olympic Games, Li Ning won the 1st Olympic gold medal in floor exercise for China. The drills named after Chinese gymnasts in floor exercise include "Liu Yuejiu".

Pommel Horse

Pommel Horse was listed as a competition event in the 1st Olympic Games in 1896. Modern Pommel Horse was introduced in China in the mid 19 centuries. In the 1st National Games in China in 1959, it was included in the official events. In 1980, Tong Fei won the title in Pommel Horse in the Hartford Gymnastics Championships in U.S.A, and became the first Pommel Horse world champion in China. The drills named after Chinese gymnasts in Pommel Horse first emerged in 1985, they include "Tongfei" and "Wang Chongsheng". In the 7th World Cup in Beijing in 1986, Li Ning was given full mark in Pommel Horse event. During 1990 and 2000, Chinese gymnasts have harvested three championships in World Gymnastics Championships and World Cup games.

Parallel Bars

In the 1950s of the last century, talented gymnasts in Japan, Italy, Russia, the US and China had some new technique innovations in parallel bars. Chinese gymnasts were good masters of support swing and twirl drills, and improved greatly in rising drills. In the 1980 Hartford Gymnastics Championships, Cai Huanzong won the first world championship in parallel bars for China. In the World Championships of the same year, Li Yuejiu was crowned the champion. The drills named after Chinese gymnasts in parallel bars include: "Li Ning".

Horizontal Bar

Horizontal Bar was listed as an official event in the 1st National Games in 1959. In the 6th World Cup in 1982, Li Ning grabbed a gold medal in horizontal bar, and became the first horizontal bar world champion in China. Li Chunyang won the championships in horizontal bar in the 25th World Gymnastics Championships in 1989 and the 26rd World Gymnastics Championships in 1991. The drills named after Chinese gymnasts in horizontal bar include: "Lou Yun"and "Xiao Ruizhi".

Rings

Modern Rings games began in China in the 1950s. In the National Gymnastics Games in 1965, Liao Runtuan, the all-around champion, completed the drills of piked press handstand with straight arms and backwards roll. In the 8th Asian Games in 1978, Huang Yubin won the first Asian championship in rings for China by a score of 19.15 points. In the 1980 World Cup events, Huang shared the championship in rings together with the Russian gymnast. Li Ning won the championship of rings in the 23rd Olympic Games in 1984 and the 23rd World Championships in 1985. The drills named after Chinese gymnasts in rings include: "Li Ning".

Vault

Vault was listed as an official event in the 1st National Games in 1959. In the 6th World Cup in 1982, Li Ning grabbed a gold medal in vault, and became the first vault world champion in China. Lou Yun won the championships in vault in the 24th World Gymnastics Championships in 1987, the 23rd Olympic Games in 1984 and the 24th Olympic Games in 1988. The drills named after Chinese gymnasts in vault include: "Zou Limin".

Uneven Bars

Uneven Bars was listed as an official event in the 1st National Games in 1959. Qi Yufang was the first national champion of uneven bars in China. She won by a score of 19.05 points. In the 20th World Gymnastics Championships in 1979, Ma Yangong shared the world championship together with a Democratic Germany gymnast in uneven bars and became the first world champion of uneven bars in China. In the 23rd Olympic Games in 1984, Ma won the championship of uneven bars again. The drills named after Chinese gymnasts include: "Li Lizheng", "Mo Huilan" and "Wu Jiani".

Balance Beam

Chinese gymnasts are quite strong in Balance Beam. In the 3rd International Gymnastics Invitation Games, which was held in France in 1980 with 12 participating countries, Jiang Wei, the 12-year-old Chinese female gymnast, won the championship in Balance Beam. In the 8th World Cup in 1990, Yang Bo won the championship in Balance Beam and became the first Balance Beam world champion in China. In the 27th Olympic Games in 2000, Liu Xuan grabbed the title of Balance Beam.

Performance in Asian Games

Gymnastics was not listed as an official event until the 7th Teheran Asian Games in 1974, which was also the first Asian Games China participated in. In the 32 years from 1974 to 2006, China had won a total of 102 medals in gymnastics in Asian Games. This number has fully demonstrated China's dominance in gymnastics in Asia. From the 1974 Teheran Asian Games to the 2006 Doha Asian Games, China participated in for 9 times, reaping an average of 11 gold medals each time. It is an amazing achievement for Chinese gymnastics team.

Major Events of Gymnastics in 2006

The first gold medal of the 39th World Gymnastics Championship was awarded on October 18, 2006. Chinese team had stepped out of the failure in the 2004 Olympic Games completely and performed excellently in the Men's team competition: they won the championship by a performance of 277.775 points. It was the 7th time that the Chinese Men's Team won this title.

In the Women's team competition final of the 39th World Gymnastics Championships on 19th October, 2006, China grabbed the gold medal from the US, who was ranked the No.1 in preliminary events, by a total score of 182.200 points. It was the first time that the Chinese Women's team won a gold medal in team competition.

In the Men's Individual All-around Final event of the 39th World Gymnastics Championships, which was held on October 20, 2006, Yang Wei swept the previous champion Hiroyuki Tomita and won his first all-around world championship. He scored 94.400 points.

On October 21, 2006, China exhibited its strong dominance in gymnastics in the World Championships events. Cheng Fei and Xiao Qin won themselves a consecutive championship in vault and pommel horse respectively. The young gymnast, Chen Xiaobing, had also brought people some surprises. He beat several famous gymnasts in the Men's Rings and won the gold medal. Later in the day, Yang Wei and Cheng Fei won the championships in Parallel Bars and Floor Exercise respectively. China had won 8 gold medals out of 14 in this World Championships in Denmark up to the point.

In the 2006 Doha Asian Games, which was held in December, 18 gold medals from 14 events of Men's and Women's Gymnastics were awarded. China had won 11 of them, with 6 more silver medals.

♦ The first Gymnastics World Cup for Chinese Athletes

The 5th Gymnastics World Cup held in Toronto in October, 1980 was the debut show of the Chinese gymnasts. In the games, Li Yuejiu won the championship in parallel bars, the 2nd place in floor exercise and the 3rd place in individual all-around; Zhu Zheng won the 3rd place in Women's uneven bars.

♦ The First World Gymnastics Championship for Chinese Gymnasts

The 14th World Gymnastics Championship was held in Moscow from July 6 to 10 in 1958. 196 gymnasts from 22 countries and regions joined the games, including China. It was the first World Gymnastics Championship for Chinese gymnasts. In the games, they won the 11th place in the men's team competition and the 7th place in women's team competition.

♦ The First Olympic Championship in Men's Gymnastics Team Competition

In the men's team competition final event of Sydney Olympic Games on September 18, 2000, China won the championship by a total score of 231.919 points. It was China's first Olympic championship in men's gymnastics team competition. The team members were: Yang Wei, Xing Aowei, Zheng Lihui, Li Xiaopeng, Xiao Junfeng and Huang Xu.

♦ The First Championship in Gymnastics Team Competition in World Championships

In the 22nd World Gymnastics Championships in Budapest, Hungary, October 1983, the Chinese men's team had a close winning of 0.10 points over the Russian team in men's team competition, who was the dominating team in gymnastics in recent years. The team was under the coach of Zhang Jian, Gao Jian and Yang Mingming. Its members were Tong Fei, Li Ning, Lou Yun, Li Yuejiu, Li Xiaoping and Xu Zhiqiang. It was the first championship in gymnastics team competition in World Championships.

♦ The First Gymnastics World Champion

The first gymnastics world champion in China is the Muslim gymnastic Ma Yanhong, who was still in the army back then.

In December 1979, the 20th World Gymnastics Championship was held in Fort Worth, US. Over 330 gymnasts from 33 countries joined the game. Ma Yanhong, only 15 years old back then, shared the world championship in uneven bars together with the gymnast from the Democratic Germany and became the first gymnastics world champion in China. In the game, Ma selected drills with high degree of difficulty for selected drills, in which a rare multi-C drill was included. She also innovated a "Backhip circle turn 180-degree body bunch-up forward airspring", making the whole drills neatly organized and intricately difficult.

Ma was born in Beijing. She went to the Amateur Sports School to learn gymnastics when she was 8, and later joined the "Ba Yi" Gymnastics Team of the People's Liberation Army. In the International Invitation Games in Shanghai, 1978, she won the championship in uneven bars by a score of 9.95 points; in the same year, she became the champion of uneven bars in the 8th Asian Games. After she became the first gymnastics world champion in China, she won the title of uneven bars again in the 23rd Olympic Games.

▲ Drills Named After Chinese Athletes

According to the International Gymnastics Federation, an innovated drill which has never appeared in previous world-class games would be named after its performer or the country of the performer, such as "Thomas","Tsukahara"and "Comăneci", to encourage more innovations and developments in drills and techniques.

In November, 1984, in the reedited gymnastics rule and regulations for 1985 by the International Gymnastics Federation, drills named after the Chinese gymnasts appeared: "Li Ning" (Rings), "Li Ning"(Parallel Bars), "Li Yuejiu"(Floor Exercise) and "Tong Fei"(Pommel Horse). They were the first batch of drills that were named after the Chinese gymnasts.

On September 18, 2000, the Chinese team won the men's gymnastics team gold at the Sydney Olympics. This was the first gold medal gained by the Chinese gymnastics team since it participated in Olympic Games 16 years ago.

Li Yuejiu

Li Yuejiu (1957-), male gymnast. He entered the Liaoning team at 12, and won his first all-around title in the World Middle School Games in 1974. In 1978, he claimed gold in the floor exercise in the Bangkok Asian Games. In May, 1980, he reaped the championship of floor exercise by a score of 10 points, the full mark. It is the first 10 marks in Chinese Gymnastics History.

The 21st World Gymnastics Championships which was held in Moscow, December 1981, was the second World Championships China ever participated in. In the games, Li Yuejiu won the championship of floor exercise by a unique drill of his own, the 720-degree Spin, and became the first Chinese winner in World Gymnastics Championships. This medal changed the history of Chinese Gymnastics. Two years later, he changed the history of Chinese Gymnastics again by winning a gold medal in team competition of the World Championships events in Budapest with his teammates. In the 1984 Olympic Games, the 27-year-old Li led the Chinese team to win a silver medal in team competition.

Li Yuejiu used to be the icon of Chinese gymnasts of that age. Up to his retirement, he had won 171 medals in competitions home and abroad, out of which 82 medals are gold. He's the gymnast that had won the most number of medals in China. He's depicted as "the explorer of beauty" by some writers, as the great combination of technique and power in him made up the slight imperfections of his figure. The drill "Straddled 3/2 salto sideway, 1/4 twist to rollforeward" performed by him in floor exercise had been named after him as "Li Yuejiu" by the International Gymnastics Federation. It was the first drill in Gymnastics that was named after a Chinese gymnast.

Huang Yubin

Huang Yubin (1958-), male gymnast and coach.

He was the champion of all-around and rings in the 1978 National Gymnastics Competition. In the International Gymnastics Invitation Games held in Shanghai, June, 1978, he was the champion in team competition, individual all-around, parallel bars and horizontal bar, the 2nd in floor exercise and the 3rd in pommel horse; in the 8th Asian Games in December 1978, he won the championships in team event and rings; in the 1980 World Cup, he won a gold medal in rings and a bronze medal in parallel bars; in the 12th Tokyo International Invitation Games in April 1981, he was the winner of the rings event; in the 22nd World Championships, he won the team event.

He was the head coach of the National Team from 1989 to 2003.

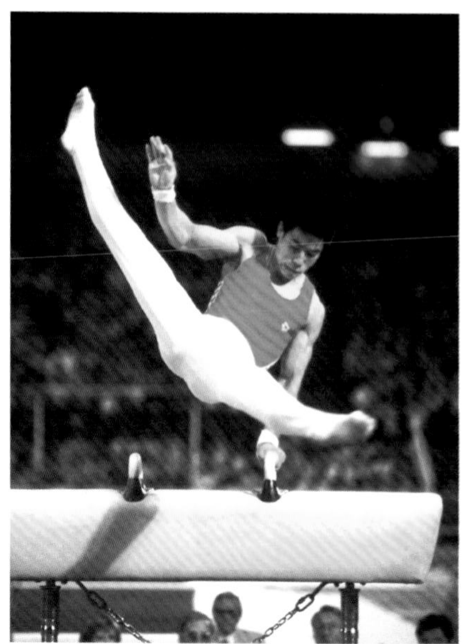

Li Ning titled the pommel horse event with 19.95 points at the 23rd Los Angeles on August 4, 1984.

Li Ning

Li Ning (1963-), male gymnast. He began to practice gymnastics when he was 7 and entered the national team when he was 17. He retired from the national team at 26. In 1981, he grabbed the titles of men's floor exercise, pommel horse and rings in the World University Games. In the 6th Gymnastics World Cup in 1982, he reaped 6 gold medals out of the 7 men's events, created a legend in world gymnastics history, and was honored as the "Prince of Gymnastics". In China, everyone knows the name of Li Ning. He was the greatest athlete in China several decades ago, and he was selected to be one of the World's Best 50 Gymnasts.

In the 23rd Los Angeles Olympic Games in 1984, Li Ning won 3 gold, 2 silver and 1 bronze. The medals won by him almost took up 1/5 of the total medals won by the Chinese delegation team. He was also the athlete that had won the most number of medals in that Olympic Games. In the 17 years of his career, Li Ning had won 106 gold medals in gymnastics competitions home and abroad. The drills innovated by him, "Piked press handstand with straight arms" and "Grand swing 180-degree turn handstand", were named by the International Gymnastics Federation as "Li Ning"(Rings) and "Li Ning" (parallel bars).

He was accepted to be a member in the International Olympic Committee in 1987, and became the only representative in Asia. He retired after the 1988 Seoul Olympic Games, and started his endeavor in business. The clothes brand "Li Ning" after his name was the sponsor for many sports activities. In 2000, his name was listed as a Gymnastics Famous Personnel edited by the International Gymnastics Federation. He became the first Chinese there.

Ma Yanhong

Ma Yanhong (1963-), female gymnast. Ma began to practice gymnastics at 8. She was selected into the "Ba Yi" Team of the People's Liberation Army in 1975. In 1978, she entered the National Team. In the same year, she won two consecutive championships in the uneven bars events of the Shanghai International Invitation Games and the 8th Asian Games. In the 20th World Gymnastics Championships in 1979, she delivered a set of difficult, innovative and beautiful drills and shared the uneven bars championship with the gymnast from the Democratic Germany. She's the first gymnastic world champion in China. In the 21st World Gymnastics Championships in 1981, she won the 2nd place in uneven bars and the 4th place in individual all-around. In the 23rd Los Angeles Olympic Games in 1984, Ma performed an innovated set drill of her own and won the championship of uneven bars. She retired from the field after the Los Angeles Olympic Games and went to Britain to coach in gymnastics.

Lou Yun

Lou Yun (1964-), male gymnast. Lou entered the national team in 1977. He was the main power in the national team that won the 22nd World Championships team competition in 1983. He was also the winner of parallel bars and the 3rd in the all-around and vault events in the 1983 World Championships. He remained to be the main power in the national team at the 23rd Olympic Games in 1984. In the games, he won a silver medal in team competition, a gold in vault, and another silver in floor exercise. He was called the "King of Vault". In the 24th Olympic Games in 1988, he was the gold-medalist in vault and the bronze-medalist in floor exercise. He's the first male athlete in China that had two consecutive Olympic championships in gymnastics. He was selected to be the one of the Elite Gymnasts in the World by "World Gymnastics" in 1983 and 1984. He was selected to be one of Best 10 Gymnasts by the International Sports Journal Federation.

Li Xiaoshuang

Li Xiaoshuang (1973-), male gymnast. Li began to receive gymnastics trainings in 1980, when he was in primary school, and was selected into the National Team in

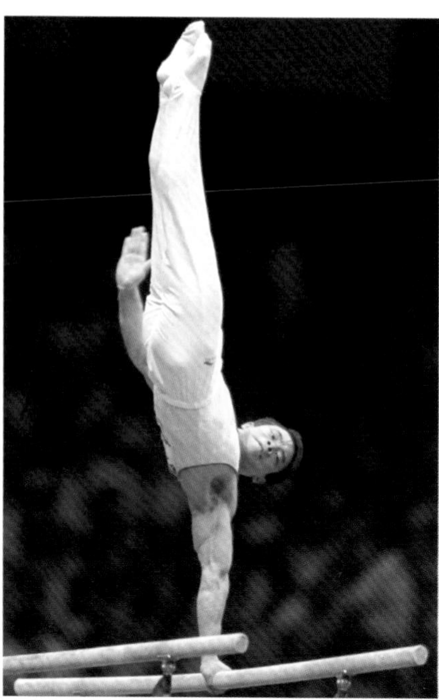

Li Xiaoshuang won the men's individual competition at the 26th Olympic Games held in Atlanta, America in 1996.

1989.Li had a strong power and were good at drills with high degrees of difficulty. He was strong in floor exercise, vault and rings. In the 11th Asian Games in Beijing, 1990, Li won the gold medal in floor exercise, and was the main power in grabbing the championship of the Men's team competition. In the 1991 National Gymnastics Tournaments, he was the champion of all-around, floor exercise and vault and the runner-up of parallel bars. In the 26th World Gymnastics Championships of the same year, he played an important role in winning a silver medal in Men's team event for China. In the 25th Olympic Games in 1992, he won a gold medal in floor exercise by an excellent drill of "Triple Back Flips Bunched-up", a bronze medal in rings, and the 5th place in individual all-around. In the games, he also won a silver medal in team competition for China with his teammates. In the World Championships in 1995, he won the first Men's Individual All-Around championship for China. He also contributed greatly to China's consecutive championship in the team competition. He won a runner-up in the floor exercise as well. In the 26 Atlanta Olympic Games on July 22, 1996, he cooperated with his teammates and won a silver medal in team competition for China. On July 24, he claimed gold in Men's Individual All-Around event, which was the first Olympic gold medal of Chinese male gymnasts in all-around event. On July 28, he won a silver medal in the Men's Floor Exercise event.

Huang Xu

Huang Xu (1979-), male gymnast. Huang entered the Nantong Amateur Sports School when he was 5, and was selected into the Jiangsu Team in February, 1989. He was selected into the National Team in1993. The 1997 World Championships in Lausanne is the first world-class competition Huang ever joined. He cooperated with his teammates and won a gold medal in team event in the game.

Huang is an all-around gymnast. He's known for his large and rhythmic movements. His drills are of high degree and are well standardized. He's especially strong in parallel bars and pommel horse. He had claimed titles in nation-wide competitions for many times.

Yang Wei

Yang Wei (1980-), male gymnast. Yang is a major and all-around gymnast in the Chinese Men's Gymnastic Team. He's especially strong in floor exercise and rings. He is agile and neat in his drills, strong in power, and has a good control of tempo. His jumps and flips are always very light and steady.

Yang won 5 titles in the National Children Competitions in 1993. In the 1998 Bangkok Asian Games, he won the championships of team competition and floor exercise, and a 2nd place in all-around. He won a title in team competition in the World Gymnastics Championships in Tianjin, 1999. In the 2000 Sydney Olympics, he claimed gold in the team competition, and silver in the individual all-around event. He was also the champion of team event and all-around event in the 2002 Busan Asian Games. In 2003, he won a gold medal in the team competition and a silver medal in the all-around event in the World Championships.

Chinese athlete Yang Wei won the gold medal of the gymnastics men's competition with 95.500 points at the 15th Doha Asian Games on December 4, 2006.

Li Xiaopeng

Li Xiaopeng (1981-), male gymnast. He began to practice gymnastics in Changsha Sports School in Hunan Province when he was 6. He entered the Hunan Gymnastics Team at 12, and the National Team at 15.

The achievements of Li include: champion in team competition and parallel bars and 3rd in floor exercise in the 1997 World Gymnastics Championships; champion in floor exercise and parallel bars in the 1998 World Cup Final in Japan; champion in team competition and parallel bars and 3rd in vault in the 1998 Bangkok Asian Games; champion in floor exercise and 3rd in horizontal bar in the Cottbus International Gymnastics Competition in Germany, 1999; champion of team competition and vault in the 1999 World Gymnastics Championships in Tianjin; champion of team competition and parallel bars in 2000 Sydney Olympic Games; winner of team competition, parallel bars and all-around in the 37th World Gymnastics Championships in 2003.

Xing Aowei

Xing Aowei (1982-), male gymnast. He entered the Yantai Amateur Sports School in Shandong Province when he was 5, and was selected into the Shandong Team when he was 8. At 12, he entered the National Team.

Xing was the champion in team event and pommel horse in the 1998 Bangkok Asian Games, the champion in pommel horse in the 1999 World Cup series, and the champion in team event in the 1999 World Championships. He was a gold-medalist in team event in the 2000 Sydney Olympics and the 2002 Asian Games. In 2003, he claimed gold again in team event in the World Championships.

Teng Haibin

Teng Haibin (1985-), male gymnast. Teng began to practice gymnastics in Beijing Shishahai Sports School. He entered the Beijing Gymnastics Team in 1996, and the National Team in 1998.

In 2000, Teng won the titles of all-around, floor exercise, horizontal bar and parallel bars in the National Teenager and Youth Championships. In the same year, he won the championships in parallel bars, pommel horse and floor exercise in the International Gymnastic Invitation Games in France. In 2002, he was the winner of team event, horizontal bar and pommel horse in the Busan Asian Games. In the 36th World Gymnastics Championships of the same year, he was ranked the 4th in the pommel horse event. In the 36th World Gymnastics Championships in 2003, he claimed championship in the team event and pommel horse.

The best performance of his so far is the championship in team event, individual all-around and parallel bars in the 2006 World Gymnastics Championships.

♦ Chinese Gymnastics Association

The Chinese Gymnastics Association (CGA) was founded in 1954. It is a mass sports organization with corporate capacity.

The CGA is a member of the All-China Sports Federation and is recognized by the Chinese Olympic Committee as a national sport association. It joined the International Gymnastics Federation in October, 1978.

Regular events held by the CGA include: National Gymnastics Tournament, National Gymnastics Championships, National Teenager and Youth Gymnastics Championships and National Children and Teenager Gymnastics Championships.

Address: No 5 Tiyuguan Lu, Beijing
Website: http://www.cga.net.cn

Cheng Fei

Cheng Fei (1988-), male gymnast. She has a unique drill in vault, named "Yurchenko 1/2 on to layout front with a 1 1/2 twist". This drill has never been performed by anyone in the world except her. It has not been classified in the degree of difficulty list of the gymnastics. It is the absolute "intellectual property" owned by Cheng.

Cheng won the title of vault in the Japan Junior Gymnastics Tournament in 2003. In the Asian Gymnastics Championships of the same year, she won the championships of team event, vault and floor exercise. In 2004, she claimed gold in the balance beam and floor exercise in the National Gymnastics Tournament. In 2005, she won a bronze medal in vault in the Gymnastics World Cup Ghent Station. She was also the champion of vault in the 38th World Championships in Melbourne, 2005 (the first female world champion of vault in China).

Rhythmic Gymnastics

Rhythmic Gymnastics is a new female competitive sport. It was originated from Europe, and received world-wide popularity in the 40s and 50s of the last century. In 1984, it was listed as an Olympic event, but only individual all-around event was included. In 1996, the team event was added in. In the 50s of the last century, China began to learn the basic techniques of rhythmic gymnastics from Russia. Rhythmic gymnastics practice was first launched in China in 1981. In the 1987 World Championships, China was ranked the 3rd in the all-around team event and the 2nd in the individual events. Also, China was ranked the 5th in team event in the 1996 Olympic Games and the 6th in team event in the 2004 Olympic Games.

China's Performance in Rhythmic Gymnastics in Asia

China has been in the leading position of rhythmic gymnastics in Asia since the 1990s. Especially in the period from 1992 to 1995, China had reaped almost all the gold medals in rhythmic gymnastics of the Continental Championships events. It becomes relatively less dominating after 1997, but the medals were still wrestled between the hands of Japan and China. Now, countries in Mid-Asia had been gradually recovered from their political despairs, and would pose challenges to China together with North Korea, South Korea and Malaysia.

China's Performance in Rhythmic Gymnastics in the World

China is strong in team event, and used to list the team event as the potential medal event in Olympic Games. In the 26th Atlanta Olympic Games, China, as the only non-European team, beat several strong European teams in the final, and ascended to the 5th from the 8th in the qualification games. Although China missed the ticket to Olympic Games in 1999 due to various reasons, China had improved its techniques in rhythmic gymnastics. In the preparation for the next Olympic Games, the Chinese Rhythmic gymnastics Team faces a critical moment of member shift, but it is still promising to stay in the second division of the rhythmic gymnastics teams.

Zhong Ling

Zhong Ling (1983-), rhythmic gymnast. She entered the Beijing Sport University in October, 1993. She was selected into the national team in December, 1996. She became the first batch of members in the national team of rhythmic gymnastics when it was officially established in December, 2002.

In the World Rhythmic gymnastics Championships in Spain, 2001, Zhong Ling exhibited four drills that were later named after her. Zhong Ling had grown from a promising gymnast to the leading character in China's rhythmic gymnastics now.

Achievements of hers include: 7th place in the 1998 World Championships (Spain); all-around champion in the 2000 National Championships; runner-up in hoop, 3rd place in ball, 4th place in all-around in the 2001 World University Games; all-around champion in the 9th National Games; champion in team competition, individual all-around, rope, clubs, ball and hoop events of the 2002 National Tournaments; champion in team competition and individual all-around event of the 2002 Asian Games; 8th place in individual all-around in the 2003 World Championships; all-around champion in the 2004 National Championships.

♦ China Student Aerobics and Rhythmic Gymnastics Association

China Student Aerobics And Rhythmic Gymnastics Association (CSARA) was founded in 1992 under the Ministry of Education. It focuses to promote aerobatic gymnastics, rhythmic gymnastics, cheer leading, sports dance, street dance and body-shaping in the Chinese campuses, nurture professional trainers, train and verify the qualification of referees, and organize events and international exchanges. CSARA organize competitions in aerobatic gymnastics, rhythmic gymnastics, cheerleading, sports dance, street dance and body-shaping annually, and is one of the popular organizations among the national sports organizations. It has divisions in 30 provinces nation-wide with more than 500 member groups.

The international partners of CSARA include: US All-Star Federation for Cheer and Dance Teams, Japanese Amateur Fitness Association, Korean Aerobatic Gymnastics Association, International All Star Cheerleading Association, Asian Cheerleading Association.

Events organized by the association include: China Student Health and Vigor Competition, China All Star Cheerleading Championships, China Student Sport Dance Championships, China All Star Body Shaping Championships, China Student Rhythmic gymnastics Championships and China All Star Street Dance Championships.

Address: Level 2, Block D, Guangdong Sports Univeristy458, Mid Guangzhou Avenue, Guangzhou, Guangdong
Website:http://www.csara.cn

The Chinese Rhythmic Gymnastics Team won the 6th place in the rhythmic gymnastics collective event at the Athens Olympics in August 2004.

Trampoline

Trampoline had a late start in China and was not listed as an official sport event until 1997. China national trampoline team was founded in 2002. However, trampoline had a rapid development in China because of Chinese's solid skills in gymnastics. From December 10 to 22, 1998, 8 athletes of the Chinese national trampoline team took part in the World Cup Series in Danmark and France. It is the debut show of the Chinese trampoline team in the world.

In October 1999, China sent its team to play in the World Age Group Competition for the first time, in which, Huang Shanshan finished second in the woman's 13-14 age-group to win the first international trampoline medal for China. Since 2000, trampoline has stepped into a stable and rapid development, thus achieving more successes in international competitions. In 2003, China national trampoline team, while participating in its first world championships, pulled off the silver of the team event. At the Athens 2004 Olympic Games, China national trampoline team reaped a bronze medal of individual event.

In the 24th Trampoline World Championships held in Eindhoven, Netherlands, September 2005, more than 40 countries joined the competition and made it even more rigorous than the Athens Olympic Games. However, the Chinese Trampoline Team pulled off four gold in man' trampoline team, woman's trampoline team, man's tumbling and man's tumbling team respectively. This had shaken the 40 years of monopoly of the European countries, thus expanding the influence of China in the international trampoline community.

Huang Shanshan

Huang Shanshan (1986-), female trampolinist.

Huang Shanshan finished second in woman's individual event while representing China National Team to take part in the World Junior Trampoline Championships held in Sydney in January 2001. In August of the same year, she won the woman's 15-16 at the World Age Group Competition held in Danmark. In 2003, she reaped the silver of the woman's individual event at the World Cup held in France, and pulled off the silver of the team event and took the eighth place in the individual event at the World Championships. In 2004, Huang Shanshan won the bronze of woman's individual event in the Athens Olympic Games, which is the first ever Olympic medal won by Chinese trampolinists in trampoline.

Acrobatics

China held its first national exhibition game of sports acrobatics in 1956, joined the International Federation of Sports Acrobatics in 1979, and first sent its team to play in the World Championships of Sports Acrobatics in 1980. Acrobatics, since its introduction to China, has been a strong sport of the Chinese. By 2002, Chinese athletes pulled off a total of 214 gold medals in international and Asian games. However, in recent years, Chinese sports acrobatics is at a low ebb, with a decreasing number of gold medals every year. Its rank has also dropped from the 1st to the 3rd.

World Championships of Acrobatics

International Federation of Sports Acrobatics held the first biennial World Championships of Sports Acrobatics in 1974. China, after joined the International Federation of Sports Acrobatics in 1979, first sent its team to play in the 4th World Championships of Sports Acrobatics in 1980.

The Chinese team's first participation in the international games had the Chinese national flag raised in the field for 11 times. Out of the 7 events in the All-Around game, they won 5 events including woman's single, man's pair, woman's pair, mixed pair and woman's trios, and was ranked the 3rd. Together with the individual events, the team won a total of 11 bronze.

Zhu Haiying

Zhu Haiying (1977-), female athlete of sports acrobatics.

Zhu Haiying, in cooperation with Yu Jie, won three bronze of mixed pairs all-around, mixed pairs routine I and II at the 1st Junior World Championships of Sports Acrobatics held in 1989, reaped the gold of mixed pairs all-around at the 8th World Cup held in 1991, cooperated with Li Zhi to pull off three gold of mixed pairs all-around, mixed pairs routine I and II at 10th World Championships of Sports Acrobatics held in 1992, and, in cooperation with Li Zhi, crowned three champions of the mixed pairs all-around, mixed pairs routine I and II at the 9th World Cup held in 1993. She was thus honored with the title of master of sport of international class in 1992.

♦ Chinese Trampoline and Acrobatic Gymnastics Association

The Chinese Trampoline and Acrobatic Gymnastics Association was originally a branch of the Chinese Gymnastics Association and became an independent organization in 1979. As a national non-governmental organization, it has its headquarter in Beijing. There are four committees, namely the Coaches Committee, the Judges Committee, the Research Committee and the Secretariat under the Association. Tasks of the association include: to study and work out development plan and policies for acrobatic gymnastics; to establish elite acrobatic teams and train youth athletes; to select and recommend athletes and coaches for the Chinese national team; to organize training of coaches, athletes and judges on a national scale; to study and work out competition systems and plans, as well as judging rules; to organize and supervise national games; to organize international games hosted in China; to work out technical standards on the evaluation of athletes and judges; to conduct research programs; to organize outbound visits and assist Chinese teams' participation in international games and to promote international exchanges and cooperation.

Website: http://acrobatics.sport.org.cn

Track and Field

Athletics was introduced to China by the missionary at the beginning of this century. It was held primarily only among church schools and later extended to public and private schools at all levels. China has been holding large-scale national athletics sports meeting almost every year since 1953.Due to the widespread of sports games among the public, the gap between Chinese athletic skills and those on international level was narrowed. In 1956, Zheng Fengrong, a female high jumper, broke the world record of 1.76m with a jump of 1.77m. Ten other events were among world's top 10 in 1960s. In 1983, Zhu Jianhua, a male high jumper, broke his own world record of 2.37m with a jump of 2.38 m at the 5th National Games held in Shanghai. In 1990s, with the advent of Ma Family Army, a series of women's middle and long distance running world records were created. Wang Junxia even won the title of "Asian Deer". However, the athletics performances suffer in recent years. There is still a visible gap between Chinese runners and those of the world top performers.

Events in which Chinese athletics players have stood out internationally include: Men's High Jump, Long Jump & Triple Jump; Women's High Jump, Pole Vault, Long Jump, Triple Jump, Middle-Long Distance Running, Shot Put, Javelin Throw, Discus Throw and Race Walk.

China's athletics skill as a whole is gradually on the move. In terms of total points, the rank rose from No.20 with 25 points in 2003 World Championships to No.17 with 31 points in 2004 Olympics and to No.9 with 43 points in 2005 World Championships.

The Holding of International Track and Field Competitions

In recent two years, China was a successful sponsor of 2005 Asian Cross Country Championships, 2006 IAAF World Junior Championships, 2006 Asian Marathon Championships, 2006 IAAF Summer Council Meeting and the IAAF Race Walking Challenge (an annual event). In August 2006, IAAF World Youth Championships which was held in Beijing attracted a record number of 182 countries and regions, over 2200 players and more than 300 officials from international organizations.

Moreover, China has many active candidates for posts in international sports organizations. Up to now, the number of job holders in international organizations has increased from 7 in 8 seats in 2001 to 10 in 15 seats. Their working scope is expanding, covering key areas like council, technical department, referee department and medical department.

International Communication

In 2006, Chinese Athletics Association (CAA) expanded communication with other countries. China Sprint Team was sent to Michael Johnson's training camp in Baylor

University, USA. Middle and Long-distance team was sent to the University of Arizona for the training with the coach, Li Li. Some hammer throwers received short training in Russia and several race walker and middle and long distance runners would get one week training in Spain.

CAA also invited Donald Quarrie, Jamaican sprint legend, to hold training camps and clinics twice. Among those who came to China for training camps and clinics also included Sergei Andrei, an Olympic Champion and famous race walker in Russia and Alexei Markov, a famous coach. Losa, an Italian long distance coach and Li Li, a middle and long distance coach in Arizona University, USA also came to china to share with their training experience.

In addition, athletics powers like USA, Canada, France, England and Russia have signed bilateral exchange visits agreement, according to which, bilateral competitions will be held annually before 2008. It is disclosed that there will be more athletic exchange and training programs in 2007 such as US middle and long-distance training camp, Russian throw programs, which are expected to give the athletes more chances to improve their skills.

Athletic Skills

According to the statistics of December 20, 2006, 78 Chinese athletes were among top 50 in 24 events, 10 for men, 14 for women; 31 athletes were among top 20 in 12 events, 4 for men and 8 for women; 16 among top 10 in 8 events, 3 for men, 5 for women; 4 among top 3 in 4 events, 3 for men and 1 for women. Only two events were No.1 in ranking. Both of them were from men's events: 110 hurdles and 20 km race walk.

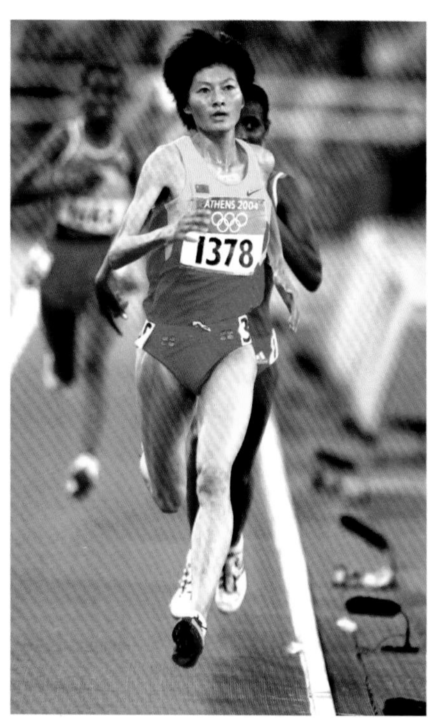

On August 27, 2004, Xing Huina titled the women's 10,000 metres event at the Athens Olympics.

Sprint

Men's sprint is tier-2 in Asia. Women's sprint tops Asia. .

Chinese women were gold holders of 100m in 1990, 1994 and 1998 Asian Games, of 200m in Asia Games 1994 and of 400m in 1990 and 1994 Asian Games.

By June 2006, the national record of women's 100m is 10.79, 200m 22.01 and 400m 49.81.

By June 2006, the national record of men's 100m is 10.17, 200m 20.54 and 400m 45.25.

Middle and Long-Distance Running

After 1990s, the rise of Ma Family Army brings all hopes on women's middle and long-distance running. At World Athletics Championships in Stuttgart, the players from Ma Family Army swept 3 gold medals in middle and long-distance running. At the 7th and 8th National Games, they work wonders twice by setting and breaking multiple world records. All this made the event a flagship of China's athletics in mid-1990s.

By June 2006, the national record of women's 800m is 1:55.54, 1500m 3:50.46, 3000m 8:06.11, 5000m 14:28.09 and 10,000m 29:31.78.

By June 2006, the national record of men's 800m is 1:46.44, 1500m 3:36.49, 3000m 7:56.19, 5000m 13:25.14, 10,000m 28:10.08.

Marathon

From 1950 onwards, Marathon gained more popularity and was listed as official national event. Marathon is a part of each National Games. In recent years, China hosted Beijing International Marathon Invitational Tournament which becomes an important stop of World Marathon and boots the performance of Chinese runners. .

On October 19, 2003, Sun Yingjie won the race with 2:19:39 which is the best record Chinese woman has ever created in the history of marathon and the best in Asia. Her success is a signal that Chinese women marathon runners are in a leading position now.

The best record for Chinese male marathon athletes is 2:9:39, one that was created by Hu Gangjun in 1997 Beijing International Marathon. Hu is also the first Chinese man to finish first in the race and run within 2:10.

At 2005 Beijing International Relay Marathon, Chinese women's team won a silver with 2:19:36

Ma Family Army in the women's 1,500 meters event

• Ma Family Army

Ma Family Army is an epithet given to a group of long-distance champions which brought China gold medals of Olympic Games, World Championships and World Cup. The coach was Ma Junren who led the team to create a legend in the history of Chinese Athletics.

Ma Junren, a famous coach of women's middle and long-distance running, led his athletes to break a great number of world records. Until now, the world record holders of women's 5000m and 10,000m are still Chinese. Ma Family Army got this name since after the summer of 1993. In mid-Aug, 1993, the Chinese athletes coached by Ma Junren swept the board by winning the gold of women's 10,000m, 1500m and gold, silver and bronze of 3000m at Stuttgart World Athletics Championships held in Germany. In September 1993, Wang Junxia, age 20, won the 10,000m with 41 seconds faster than the seven years'world record formerly created. Subsequently, Qu Yunxia and Wang Junxia stunned the world by breaking the 13-year world record of 1500m. In the 3000m heat, five Ma Family Army members, namely Wang Junxia, Qu Yunxia, Zhang Linli, Zhang Lirong and Ma Liyan all broke the 9-year world record and did it again in the final.

Steeplechase

The distance of steeplechase was designated as 3000m at the 7th Olympic Games in 1920. It was not until 1956 that China made Men's 3000m Steeplechase as an event of National Games. Women's 3000m Steeplechase lagged far behind other countries. By June 2006, the national record of Men's 3000 Steeplechase is 8:10.46 and Women's 9:50.88.

Hurdles

It was around 1900 that hurdles found its way to China via Europe and USA. Men's 120 Yard Hurdles became one of the events in the National Games in 1910 and was changed into Men's 110m Hurdles in 1926. It was in 1933 that Men's 400m Hurdles and Women's 80 Hurdles entered into national competition. Before 1950s, only a small number of people got into the game with poor techniques. The national record of Men's 110m hurdles is 15.7 and Men's 400m national record is 57.9. After the founding of the People's Republic of China, the hurdles took an impressively positive turn. Many excellent athletes mushroomed, claiming titles in many national and international tournaments. The Chinese men's 110 hurdles record reached 13.8 in 1960 and rose to 13.5 in 1965. In the same period, women's 80m hurdles was 10.7. Both records hit world level. Since the initiation of Women's 100m hurdles in China, things went very well. The national record by June 2006 is 13.64. Men's 400m hurdles is 49.03, women's 400m hurdles 53.96.

At the IAAF Super Grand Prix in Lausanne, SWI, Liu Xiang finished first in 110m in 12.88, rewriting national and world record.

Relays

Men's 4×100m Relay, 4×400m Relay and Women's 4×100m Relay, 4×400m Relay were set as official events at the 1st National Games in 1959. Women's 4×200m Relay was changed to 4×400m Relay at the 3rd National Games in 1975. By June 2006, the national record of Men's 4×100m Relay is 38.81, 4×400m Relay 3:04.35, 4×800 Relay 8:16.2. The national record of Women's 4×100m Relay is 42.23, 4×400m Relay 3:24.28, 4×800 Relay 7:26.0.

Race Walk

Race walk started early almost in tandem with world powers. It is blessed with a strong foundation. Among the world's top 3 athletics events, the record of race walk stands out. In fact, Chinese athletes created many spectacular records in world race walk from 1980s to early 1990s. At 1985 World Cup, Yan Hong and Xu Yongjiu finished first and second. Among the top 7, 4 were Chinese. The gold medals also went to Chinese race walkers at 1992 and 2000 Olympic Games.

Li Zewen won the event at the 17th Word Cup in April 1995, becoming the first Chinese man to win in international competition of race walk.

By June 2006, the national record of Men's 10,000m Race Walk is 40:11.15, 20km 1:17:41. 20,000m 1:18:03.3, 50km 3:36.06, 50,000m 4:02.51. The national record of Women's 5km Race Walk is 21:39, 5,000m 20:37.7, 10km race walk 41:16, 10,000m 41:37:9, 20km 1:26:22, 20,000m 1:29:32.4.

The First Female Marathon Champion

Zhao Youfeng is the first Chinese woman to win marathon in the international competition. She was a student in Nanjing Institute of Physical Education. In 1986, she was sent to Aichi University of Education, Japan and became a student of Professor Takeuchi Shinya. Takeuchi is a famous sports physiologist of Aichi Athletic Association. By studying vital capacity, he guided his students to set 800m and 1,500m Asian records. So it was a turning point in Zhao Youfeng's athletics career to be trained by him.

On March 6, 1983, Zhao took part in Women's Marathon in Nagoya, Japan. Initially, she was not noticed by any expert as so many excellent athletes were there. When the race began, Zhao ran closely behind Berskens, the famous player from Netherland. At 30km, she felt her pace was still very relaxing and subconsciously realized that she might be able to win. At 35km, Zhao sped up. Her competitor was suddenly left behind. Ultimately, Zhao got the gold with 2:27:56 which was faster than the best score created by Japan 5 weeks ago and far better than best national record—2:32:11 that Xiao Hongyan from Shandong set at 1987 National Games.

The First Chinese Woman Athletics World Champion

In September 1983, the 22-year old Chinese athlete Xu Yongjiu finished first in Women's 10km Race walk with 45:13.4 at World Cup in Bergen, Norway, becoming the first Chinese woman champion in athletics.

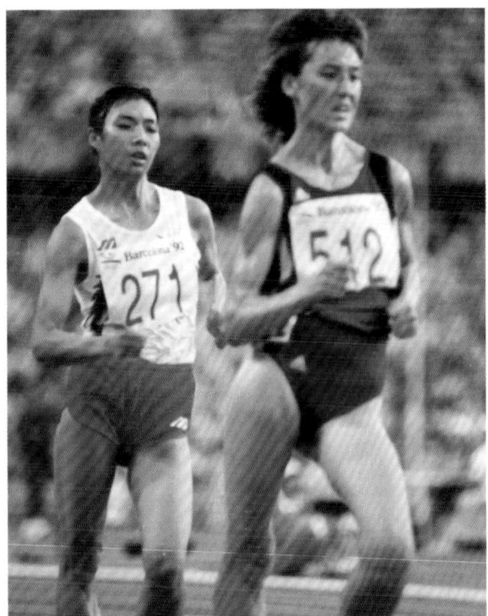

Chen Yueling won the first Olympic gold medal in athletics in the women's 10km walking race at the 25th Barcelona Olympics in 1992. In the picture is Chen Yueling (left) in competition.

Born in a Village in Jin County, Dalian City, Yu Yongjiu was able to withstand hardships ever since she was a young girl. She was a middle and long-distance runner and switched to race walk under the guidance of Coach Wang Kui. Despite her lackluster physical conditions, the undaunted spirit led her to be armed with outstanding rack walk techniques with highly frequent and small steps. In 1981, she set the first national record with 26:24.6 and raised the bar to 26:24 in the same year. In 1983, she finished first at the 5th National Games. In September, she and other Chinese women race walk team players got the 10km group title at 1981 World Cup. She was the fastest runner of this event that year. In May 1984, she set a 5km race walk world record with 21:41.

Olympic Athletics Medal Standing

Date	Medal	Athlete	Event
1984	Bronze	Zhu Jianhua	Men's High Jump
1988	Bronze	Li Meisu	Women's Shot Put
1992	Gold	Chen Yueling	Women's 10km Race Walk
1992	Silver	Huang Zhihong	Women's Shot Put
1992	Bronze	Li Chunxiu	Women's 10km Race Walk
1992	Bronze	Qu Yunxia	Women's 1500m
1996	Gold	Wang Junxia	Women's 5000m
1996	Silver	Wang Junxia	Women's 10000m
1996	Silver	Sui Xinmei	Women's Shot Put
1996	Bronze	Wang Yan	Women's 10km Race Walk
2000	Gold	Wang Liping	Women's 20km Race Walk
2004	Gold	Liu Xiang	Men's 110m Hurdles
2004	Gold	Xing Huina	Women's 10000m

Athletics World Records Held by Chinese runners

World records (men)			
Event	Record	Athlete	Place & Date
110m Hurdles	12.88	Liu Xiang	Lausanne July 12,2006
World records (women)			
Event	Record	Athlete	Place & Date
1500m	3:50.4	Qu Yunxia	Beijing Nov.11,1993
3000m	8:06.11	Wang Junxia	Beijing Sept.13,1993
5000m	14:28.09	Jiang Bo	Shanghai Oct.23,1997
10000m	29:31.78	Wang Junxia	Beijing Sept.8,1993
20km Race Walk	1:26:22	Wang Yan	Guangzhou Nov.19,2001
Marathon Relay	2:11:41	Chinese team	Beijing Feb.28,1998
Olympic records (women)			
Event	Record	Athlete	Place & Date
20km Race Walk	1:29:05	Wang Liping	Sydney Sept.28,2000
World championships records (women)			
Event	Record	Athlete	Place & Date
3000m	8:28.71	Qu Yunxia	Stuttgart Aug.16,1993
World junior records (men)			
Event	Record	Athlete	Place & Date
110m Hurdles	13.12	Liu Xiang	Lausanne July 2,2002
World junior records (women)			
Event	Record	Athlete	Place & Date
800m	1:57.18	Wang Yuan	Beijing Sept.8,1993
1500m	3:51.34	Lang Yinglai	Shanghai Oct.18,1997
10000m	30:31.55	Xing Huina	Paris Aug.23,2003
Javelin Throw	63.93	Xue Juan	Changsha Oct.27,2003
10km Race Walk	41:57	Gao Hongmiao	Beijing Sept.8,1993

The First World Group Champion in Women's Race Walk

At Race Walk World Cup held in Bergen, Norway, Chinese women race walk team consisting Xu Yongjiu, Yan Hong from Liaoning Province, Guan Pinghe from Shandong and Yu Heping from Jilin took the 10km race walk group title with a point of 132, becoming the first Chinese world group champion of women's race walk.

They were 17.5 years old on average and with only short systematic training. This is also their first time to participate in such an important international competition. However, they beat world powers like the Soviet Union, Australia and Sweden en route to the Cup.

High Jump

Since high jump was introduced to China in the early 1900s, it embarked on a slow track. After the founding of the People's Republic of China, it took off and became a relatively common event in athletics. The athletes' skills improved rapidly. In 1950s, some players even jumped as high as 2 meters. 1960s and 1980s was the heyday of China's high jump. Chinese men and women broke records for many times. In recent years, the skills suffered setbacks but remained strong in Asia. By June 2006, the national record of men's jump is 2:39 and women's 1.97.

Pole Vault

Pole Vault was a late comer with slow development. The national record before liberation is 4.15m which was replaced by 4.35m in 1956. In 1965, Hu Zurong jumped over 4.58m with a metal pole. Afterwards, Chinese athletes began to use nylon pole. In 1974, Cai Changxi became the first Chinese man to go beyond 5.00m with a jump of 5.01m. In 1990, Liang Xueren set Asian and national record with a jump of 5.62m.

As China adopted the event early, Chinese remained world record holders before 1995. Cai Weiyan set new Asian and national record with a jump of 4.32m, the world's second best that year.

By June 2006, the national record of pole vault is 5.70 for men and 4.53 for women.

Shot Put

China's shot put, especially women's shot put, is quite strong. Chinese female athletes have won international championships many times. It is also a traditionally strong athletics event for China. Women's Shot Put has been our strength. Li Meisu placed fifth at Los Angles Olympic Games and third at Seoul Olympic Games. At Barcelona and Atlanta Olympic Games, Huang Zhihong and Sui Xinmei both won a silve medal.

By June 2006, the national record of shot put is 20.15m for men and 21.76m for women.

Discus Throw

Modern Discus throw was introduced to China in early 1920s. Men's discus throw became an official event of national Games initially. In 1933, women's discus throw also joined in the sports meeting. After the founding of People's Republic of China, discus throw, women's discus throw in particular, experienced rapid development. Chinese players triumphed in international tournaments. In recent years, however, the Chinese skills slid down. A visible gap remains between China and EU and US. In Women's Discus Throw Final of the Asian Games Doha 2006, Chinese player Song Aimin won the event with a distance of 63.52m. Another Chinese player Ma Xuejun finished second with 62.43m. In Men's Discus Throw Final, Chinese player Wu Tao placed first with 60.76m. In Women's Discus Throw of the Universiade 2006, Li Qiumei, a 27-year old Chinese athlete won the gold with 61.66m. Another Chinese player Li Yanfeng took the second spot with 60.50m.

By June 2006, the national record of discus throw is 65.16m for men and 71.68m for women.

Hammer Throw

Hammer throw matches have been held in China since 1930s. But no official record was made since the weight of the hammer throw was not uniform. After the founding of People's Republic of China, hammer throw took off. In 1965, the men's national record was 63.50 which narrowed the gap with the world record, 71.74. In recent years, Chinese women's hammer throw stood out. Together with shot put and discus throw, it became one of world-class events of China's athletics.

At the 9 IAAF World Cup in Athletics held in Madrid 2002, Chinese player Gu Yuan finished first in hammer throw after beating famous players including Kuzenkova from Russia and Moreno from Cuba. In 2003, she

▲ The First Chinese Woman to Throw Farther Than 21m

On the afternoon of March 25, 1988, Li Meisu, a famous thrower from Hebei Province, created the best record of Asian women's shot put with 21.08 and thus became the first Asian female player who crossed the threshold of 21 meters. Her success meant that Chinese women's shot put topped the world. At the 24th Olympic Games in Seoul on Oct 1, 1988, Li Meisu competed with 11 other world's strong women throwers. At her 5th throw, the yellow shot drew a beautiful parabola in the air and fell down 21 meters away. The score board showed 21.06m. Finally, she came unluckily in third with only 1 cm from the silver winner Neimke.This was the only medal China got at that Olympics.

20 Sports

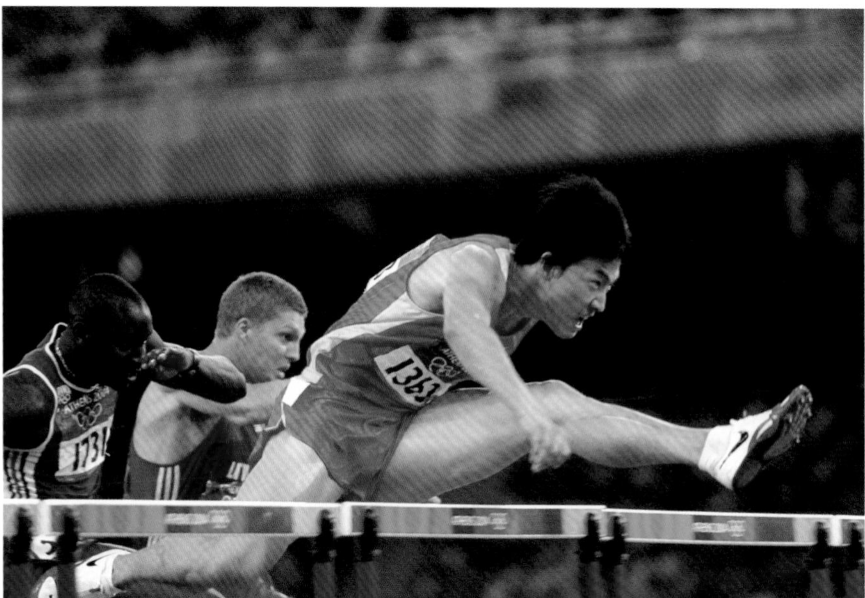

On August 27, 2004, Liu Xiang won the championship in the men's 110m hurdles final with a grade of 12.91 seconds at the Athens Olympics. He was the first Chinese man to win an Olympic gold medal in athletics.

threw a distance of 72.03m in Shanghai and became the first to throw farther than 72m. In July 2004, she created her personal best by throwing 72.35m. In 2004, Zhang Wenxiu finished 7th with 72.03m in Athens Olympics, the best ranking Chinese female throwers has ever got in Olympic Game. She was the youngest among the top 8. At a national competition held in Changsha in June 2005, Zhang claimed the gold with 73.24, thus pushing the bar farther than 73m.

By June 2006, the national record of hammer throw is 77.04m for men and 73.24 for women.

Javelin Throw

In China, men's javelin throw and women's were included as official events of national sports meeting in 1924 and 1931 respectively. But it was not until 1950s that the skills took a posive turn. By June 2006, javelin throw national record is 84.29 for men and 63.92m for women.

Long Jump

The skill level of long jump was very poor before the founding of PRC. The national record was 6.91m for men and 5.06m for women. After liberation, long jump improved a lot. In 1965, a Chinese woman made a jump of 6.44m, world's fourth best. In 1986, a Chinese male jumper, made it to 8.23m, placing 9th worldwide. At the end of 20th century, Huang Geng and Yao Weili held Asian and national men's and women's long jump record of 8.38m and 7.09m respectively.

By June 2006, the national record is 8.40m for men and 7.01m for women.

Triple Jump

Triple jump has a long history in China. The first competition was held in 1923. In 1936, Wang Shilin set a national record with a jump of 14.36m. In 1981, Zhou Zhenxian created an Asian record with 17.34m. At the 11th Asian Games held in Beijing in 1990, Chen Yanping won the title with 17.51m and 17.36m.

By June 2006, the national record of long jump is 17.34m for men and 14.72m for women.

Heptathlon and Decathlon

Ma Miaolan broke national and Asian Women's Heptathlon with a point of 6750 at the 7th National Games, ranking among world top 3 that year. At 1995 Asian Championships, Liu Bo finished second with a point of 5512.

2006 IAAF Decathlon Challenge came to an end in Sturm Graz, Austria. Qi Haifeng, a young Chinese athlete, finished fourth with a point of 8290, breaking his own national record in men's decathlon.

By June 2006, the national record of men's decathlon is 8,126 and women's Heptathlon record is 6,570.

Hu Hongfei

Hu Hongfei (1925-), track and field coach. He has long been committed to athletics. He once served as vice president of Shanghai Athletic Association. He began his coaching career in 1958 and turned out Zhu Jianhua, a three-time setter of high jump world record (2.37m, 2.38m, and 2.39m). Hu was credited as state-level coach in 1981. He was also a winner of National Sports Medal of Honor for several times. In 1984, he was awarded China's Best Coach. His training was bold and unique. He proposed the guiding principle of taking speed as the key and striking a balance between the speed and skills. On the skill front, he proposed the combination of run-up and take-off, which is enshrined in one of his works Zhu Jianhua's Run-up and Take-off Techniques.

Huang Jian

Huang Jian (1927-), track and field coach. He graduated from Moscow Institute of Physical Education, USSR, in 1950. Since 1953, he began to serve as coach and head coach of national athletic team and produced Zheng Fengrong, Ni Zhiqin, Zheng Dazhen, Yang Wenqin and other excellent high jumpers, of whom, Zheng Fengrong and Ni Zhiqin were high jump world record breakers. He began to work as vice president of CAA in 1984. He was awarded Sports Medal of Honor by the State Physical Culture and Sports Commission in 1978 and was twice credited as excellent coach by Asian Athletics Association. He was given Excellent Athletic Staff by IAAF in 1987 and Excellent Coach In 40-year history of PBRC in 1988.

Wang Kui

Wang Kui (1931-), track and field coach. He is the vice president of China Race Walk Association, state-level coach and coach of Liaoning Provincial race walk team. He did teaching after graduation from Liaoning Institute of Physical Education in 1961. From 1973 to 1977, he served as a middle and long-distance coach. When he formed Liaoning race walk team in 1978, he turned out world class race walkers like Chen Yueling, Jin Bingjie and Wang Yan. He was a multiple-time winner of Sports Honor Prize by the State Physical Culture and Sports Commission since 1984. He was granted IAAF Medal in 1987. In 1989, he was credited as one of 40 amazing coaches in China

Yang Chuanguang

Yang Chuanguang (1933-), is a Gaoshan minority. He graduated from California University, USA in 1964. He won men's decathlon at the 2nd Asian Games in 1952 with a score of 5454. At the 16th Olympic Games 1956, he placed eighth. He took the title of the same event with Asian best score of 7107 at the 3rd Asian Games in 1958. In early 1960, he broke decathlon world record with a point of 8426 and got a silver medal at the 17th Olympic Games with a score of 8334, the first time Chinese has ever got a medal at Olympic Games. At the IAAF International Decathlon held in University of Saint Anthony, Califonia, USA in April 1963, he set a world record of 9,121 (8,009 according to 1985 score calculator). In the same year, he was accredited as World's Best . Since late 1960s, he coached Taiwan Athletics Team and led Taiwan team to attend the 11th Asian Games 1990.

Lou Dapeng

Lou Dapeng (1936-) traveled to England when young, came back in 1953 and graduated from Machinery Department, Beijing Steel Institute. He was an excellent hurdler in University and broke 200m low hurdle national record with 25.2. He taught in PE Teaching and Research office of Beijing Steel Institute between 1959 and 1966 and was transferred to the State Physical Culture and Sports Commission later. Since 1980s, he served as vice president of Asian Athletic Association and director of race walk and technical commission, IAAF counselor and vice president of General Association of Asian Sports Federation. He was awarded Elder Medal by IAAF and Sports Medal of Honor by State Sports Commission and a member of Chinese Olympic Working Group

Zheng Fengrong

Zheng Fengrong (1937-), track and field athletes. She is the first Chinese athlete to break athletics world record. On November 17, 1957, she jumped over 1.77m at Beijing Athletics Games, breaking 1.76m world record that American athlete Michael Daniel had held.

When she was 14, Zheng became women's high jump champion in her hometown and then that of the whole province. On October 21, 1987, she and her coach Huang Jian received IAAF 75th Anniversary Souvenir Golden Medal, which was given to those elder coaches and athletes who have contributed to athletics.

Chen Jiaquan

Chen Jiaquan (1938-), track and field athletes. He was a six-time breaker of 100m national record. In the Performance Competition finals of the 2nd National Games held in Sichuan on October 24, 1965, he tied 100m world record that Germany runner created in 1960. In 1973, he was included in Encyclopedia of Sports published by France. In 1977, Athletics Encyclopedia of UK listed his grade of 10 seconds. Later, he served as a coach for state athletics team.

Ni Zhiqin

Ni Zhiqin (1942-), track and field athletes. He is the first Chinese athlete to break high jump world record. In 1970, he jumped over 2.29m, shattering the world record of 2.28m, one that was held by Brumel from USSR.

He was chosen into Fujian athletics team in 1958. In 1960, he jumped over 1.95m for which he won the title of excellent . In September 1960, he broke national record with a jump of 2.05m for the first time. In 1963, he jumped over 2.20m which was the second best among the world's high jumpers that year. In 1996, he finished first with 2.27m at Asian New Forces Games. On November 11, 1970, Ni Zhiqin became the world's best high jumper with 2.29m at an athletics competition in Changsha, Hunan.

Ji Zheng

Ji Zheng (1944-), track and field athletes. She graduated from California University, USA.

She went to study in USA after taking the title of pentathlon in 1963.

At the 19th Olympic Games 1968, she claimed a bronze in 80m hurdles, becoming the first Chinese woman to get an Olympic medal. As a twice participant of Asian Games, she took the title of long jump with a jump of 5.59m in 1966 and 100m sprint in 11.6 in 1970. She broke world record 7 times: 6.2 in 50m hurdle, 10.0 in 100 yards, 11.0 in 100m, 22.4 in 200m, 22.7 in 200 yards, 22.6 in 200 yards and 12.8 in 100m. She enjoyed the reputation as Oriental Antelope and was voted World's Best Female Athlete in 1970 by International Journalist Association.

In 1987, she was awarded IAAF Medal of Honor. She also served as athletics coach at University of Redlands, the director general and president of Taiwan Athletics Association, China.

Ma Junren

Ma Junren (1944-), track and field coach. As a famous middle and long-distance running coach, he produced many world-class athletes such as Wang Junxia, Qu Yunxia, Zhang Linli, Zhang Lirong, Ma Liyan, Liu Dong and Jiang Bo. Initially they swept 800m, 1500m, 3000m, and 10,000m gold medals and broke 4 World Junior Championship records at the 4th IAAF World Youth Athletics Championships 1992. At the 4th IAAF World Championship in Athletics held in Stuttgart in 1993, they finished first in Women's 1500m, 3000m, 10, 000m and nailed all the prizes of women's 3000m. At the 7th National Games, 3 of them broke 1500m, 3000m and 10,000m world records five times. At the 5th Marathon World Cup, his students claimed the top four places and group championship. Their excellent track record stunned the whole world and contributed a lot to the development of China's athletics. Chinese Athletics Association awarded Ma "The Best Track Coach of the Country" in November, 1993.

Zou Zhenxian

Zou Zhenxian (1955-), a triple jumper, received the gold medal on the podium of the Sports Ground in Bucharest on July 22, 1981 when he was 26 years old. This is the first time Chinese athletics has ever got a gold medal at Universiade acclaimed as Small Olympic Games.

He is the first to jump over 17m in Asia. Zou set an Asian record with a jump of 17.02m at Asian Athletics Championships. In 1981, he took the title of triple jump at Universiade with a jump of 17.32m which did not only go far beyond his 17.05m Asian Record but also broke the 17.27m Universiad record Saneyev from USSR has created 8 years ago at Torino, Italy in 1970.

Li Meisu

Li Meisu (1959-) had been engaged in shot put training for 13 years between 1976 and 1989 since joining national athletics team in 1976. In 1996, she resumed training and competitions with 21.76m being her personal best. She was a participant of 3 Olympic Games, 2 World Championships and 2 World Indoor Championships. At the 23rd Olympic Games in 1984, she took the fourth place with 17.96m. She finished third at the 24th Olympic Games in 1988. Li was a 26 times breaker of national and Asian records and the first to throw farther than 21m in China. In 1996, she took the title of shot put with 19.39m at National Athletics Championships, ranking world's 10th of that year. Li Meisu was also a participant of the 26th Olympic Games.

Zhu Jianhua

Zhu Jianhua (1963-), track and field athletes.

The 17-year-old Zhu Jianhua broke Asian record for the first time at the 4th Asian Athletics Championships with a jump of 2.30m in 1980, and broke Asian records three times at Beijing International Athletics Invitational Tournament, Shanghai Athletics Contest and the 9th Asian Games in 1982 and rewrote world records twice in 1983. In 1984, he broke world record the third time with 2.39m. In Los Angles Olympic Games in 1984, he got a bronze. He was a household name in early 1980s.

Huang Zhihong

Huang Zhihong (1965-) is the first woman shot put world champion in Asia. She went to Zhejiang Sports School in 1978 and was chosen into national team in 1979. She was a champion of women's shot put at the 10th Asian Games in 1986, twice breaker of Asian records in 1988. She ranked world's No.6 with 21.28m. In 1989, she finished second with 20.25m at the 2nd World Indoor Athletics Championships, first with 20.56m at the 15th Universiad and first with 20.73m at the 5th World Cup in Athletics. She had been ranking world's top 5 for many years. In 1990, she ranked 2nd with 21.52m. Huang was the twice gold holder of shot put at the 3rd and 4th World Cup in Athletics in 1991 and 1992, the silver holder at the 25th Olympic Games in 1992 and the gold medalist at 1994 World Cup. She placed third at the 5th IAAF World Athletics Championships in May 1995. She was the only Asian athlete who got medals in Olympic Games, IAAF World Athletics Championships and World Cup.

Sui Xinmei

Sui Xinmei (1965-) is an outstanding women's shot put athlete of Shanghai. After graduation from Shanghai Sports Institute, she joined Shanghai athletics team where her performance took off. She won at the 11th and 12th Asian Games in 1990 and 1994 with 20.55m (a new Asian Games record) and 20.45m respectively. In 1991, she won at World Indoor Athletics Championships with 20.54m, a new record for the championships. At the Friendly Sports Meeting held in Sintisburg in July 1994, she took the gold with 20.15m. She threw over 20.45m at the Asian Games, the world's third best that year. In 1995, she finished 5th at the 5th IAAF World Athletics Championships and 1st in Asian Athletics Championship in Jakarta. Her personal best 19.79m ranked No.6 that year. At the 26th Olympic Games in 1966, she finished second with 19.88m which ranked No.3 worldwide that year. She was awarded Sports Medal of Honor by the State Physical Culture and Sports Commission.

Tian Yumei

Tian Yumei (1965-), a famous female sprinter, is a multiple champion of National Athletics Championships and National Athletics Championship Tournament. She was a silver medalist at the 6th World Athletics Championship in 1992 and a member of 4× 100m group champion. At the 7th National Games in 1993, she got a silver of women's 100m with 11.24. She was awarded Sports Medal of Honor by the State Physical Culture and Sports Commission.

Wang Xiuting

Wang Xiuting (1965-), female track and field athletes.

At the 10th Asian Games held in Seoul in 1986, she took the title of women's 10,000m and broke Asian Games record with 32:47.77. She placed 8th with 31:48.88 at the 2nd World Athletics Championships 1987. At the 6th National Games in 1987, she finished first in 5000m and 10,000m and also held 3000m, 5000m, and 10,000m Asian records with 8:50.68, 15:23.58 and 31:27.0 respectively. She finished first in women's 10,000m with 31:40.23 at the 24th Olympic Games in 1988. In February, 1989, she worked with his teammates to win at the 7th Yokohama International Women's Road Marathon Relay. She won the group champion and her individual champion at the 7th Cross Country Championships in September, 1989. She won the title of women's 10,000m at the 11th Asian Games in 1990 and got a silver of the same event at the 3rd World Athletics Championships.

Xu Demei

Xu Demei (1965-) finished first in women's long jump with a jump of 6.36m at National Athletics Championships in 1981, second at the 9th Asian Games in 1982 and first at World Youth Athletics Championships. After joining national athletics team in 1983, she began to be trained in triple jump and set women's triple jump world record at 14.54m in 1990. In 1992, she reset Asian record at 14.55m, the world's second best that year. At the 6th World Cup in Athletics in 1992, she took the title of the event, her first champion in this event which was also listed as an official event at international competitions for the first time. She was awarded Sports Medal of Honor by the State Physical Culture and Sports Commission.

Yan Hong

Yan Hong (1966-), female track and field athletes.

She claimed the title of 5km race walk at the 5th National Sports Meeting in 1983. Yan set a 5km world record with 21:40.3 at Norway International Invitational Tournament in 1984. A week later, she set a 10km world record at Denmark Race Walking Open. Both records were acknowledged by IAAF. She was a main runner of 10km race walk group champion and got her individual championship at 1985 IAAF World Race Walking Cup. At the 2nd World Athletics Championships, she finished third in 10km race walk with 44:42. At 1989 IAAF World Race Walking Cup, she was again the main runner of silver medal group.

Chen Yueling

Chen Yueling (1968-), female track and field athletes. During her primary and middle school years, she loved middle and long-distance running and began to take up race walk.

In October 1987, Chen took the title of 10,000m at the 6th National Games and broke world record. She was also the silver holder of women's 5000m at the event. She claimed the gold of 10km race walk in world cup, at the 11th Asian Games 1990 and at the 25th Olympic Games 1992. In 1993, she was awarded Souvenir Golden Medal by Asian Athletic Association.

The sports with its boundless clamor made her a respected figure in USA.US Art Co., Ltd made her two bronze of her height, one for USA and one for her hometown-Tieling.

Xiao Yehua

Xiao Yehua (1971-), is an excellent female sprinter and a multiple champion of national competitions. She broke 100m national record with 11.23 at Shijiazhuang Elite Contest and clinched women's 4×100m relay championship with her teammates. She was awarded Sports Medal of Honor by the State Physical Culture and Sports Commission.

Qu Yunxia

Qu Yunxia (1972-) is a middle and long-distance runner. She broke 1500m Asian record with 4:07.71 at the 16th Univeria in 1991 and claimed 800m and 1500m gold medals at Asian Athletics Championships. At the 25th Olympic Games in 1992, she got a 1500m bronze with 3:57.08 and set a new Asian record. She is the first Asian athlete to run 1500m within 4 minutes and said goodbye to the history of zero medal for China's middle and long-distance event at international competitions. In 1993, she created a 1500m world record of 3:50.46 at the 7th National Games, took the title of 3000m at the 4th IAAF Athletics Championships in August and was awarded 1993 World's Best Athlete in November. At the 12th Asian Games in 1994, she finished first in 800m with 1:59.85 and 1500m with 4:12.48 .

Zhao Yongsheng

Zhao Yongsheng (1972-), male track and field athletes. He took the title of 50km with 41:20 at the 17th World Race Walking Cup in Beijing in April, 1995, the world best in that year.

Cai Weiyan

Cai Weiyan (1973-), female pole-vaulter. She took athletics skill and gymnastics as a start and sprint later on. It was not until 1987 that she started her pole vault training. She broke women's pole vault world record with a vault of 4.07 on April 28, 1995 and Asian record with 4.25m in May 1996. In 1996, she took the title of pole vault at Athletics Grand Prix on September 30, set Asian record twice with a vault of 4.26m and 4.32m respectively and made another Asian record with 4.33m at Shenzhen International Pole Vault Invitational Tournament.

Li Zewen

Li Zewen (1973-), male track and field athletes. He claimed the title of 20km race walk at the 17th World Race Walking Cup in 1995 and became the first Chinese male athletics world champion. In the same

Li Zewen in the men's 20km walking race

August, he took the fifth place in 20km race walk with 1:21:39 at the 5th IAAF World Athletics Championships in Gothenburg. In 1997, he placed 4th in 20km walk race at the 18th World Race Walking Cup.

Liu Dong

Liu Dong (1973-), a female middle-distance runner, took the title of 1500m with 4:05.14 at the 4th IAAF World Youth Athletics Championships in 1992, and made the same achievement with 4:00.50 at the 4th IAAF World Athletics Championships in August and set an 800m Asian record with 1:55.54 at the 7th National Games in September.

Sun Caiyun

Sun Caiyun (1973-), a female pole-vaulter, jumped over 4.05m in May 1992, with which she won the National Athletics Championships and the vault was acknowledged as the first female pole vault world record by International Amateur Athletics Association in January 1995. She broke this record herself with 4.08m in National Athletics Championships. In November of the same year, she broke the world record of 4.22m with 4.23m in the International Female Pole Vault Invitational Tournament held in Shenzhen. She broke female pole vault indoor world record 8 times, 5 times in 1995 (4.10m, 4.11m, 4.12m, 4.13m and 4.15m) and 3 times in 1996 (4.21m、4.27m and 4.28m). At National Athletics Championships in May 1996, she set an Asian record with a vault of 4.25m.

Wang Junxia

Wang Junxia (1973-), track and field athletes.

At the 4th World Athletics Championships in Stuttgart in 1993, Wang took the 10,000m title. She claimed individual and group champion at Marathon World Cup held in Spain in 1993. At the 7th National Games in 1993, she finished first 3000m and broke 3000m world record twice (8:12.11, 8:06.11) in tryout and final. In the meantime, she broke

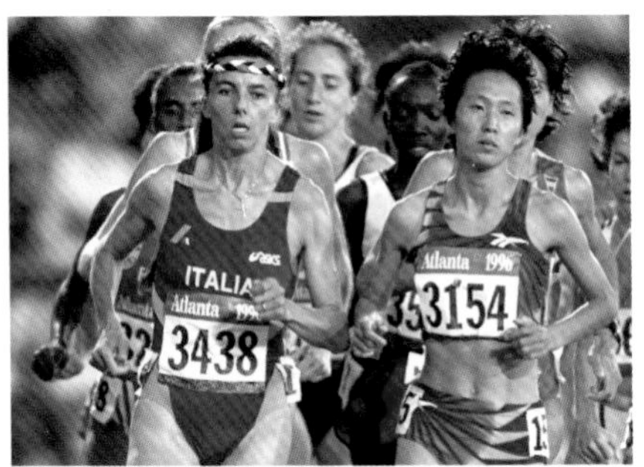

Wang Junxia won the championship of the 5,000m race event at the 1996 Atlanta Olympics.

women's 10,000m world record with 29:31.78 and thus became the first won to run 10,000m within 30 minutes. At present, she is still the event's world record holder. At 1996 Olympic Games, she finished first in 5000m title and second in 10,000m, becoming the first Chinese runner win a gold medal in long-distance running at Olympic Games. As a result, she was credited as Oriental Deer.

In 1994, she was awarded Jesse Owens Prize in New York, USA. It was the first time Chinese was given such an honor.

Wang Liping

On September 28, 2000, Wang Liping (in the middle) titled the women's 20km walking race at the Olympics.

Wang Liping (1976-), female track and field athletes. She got professional training in Liaoning Marine Sports Schoolin 1991 and was chosen into national athletics team in 1995 and into national team in 2002.

She is the champion of 20km race walk at 2000 Sydney Olympic Games.

Huang Xiaoxiao

Huang Xiaoxiao (1983-), female track and field athletes.

She is the champion of women's 400m hurdles and women's 4×400m relay at 2003 Asian Athletics Championships. She broke 400m hurdles world youth record with 55.15 at the 9th National Games in Guangdong and set 400m hurdles Asian Championships record with 55.66 in 2003 Manila Asian Athletics Championships.

Liu Xiang

Liu Xiang (1983-), tops the latest 110m hurdles rankings. His world's highest rank is 7.

On July 11, 2006, Liu Xiang finished first with 12.88 at IAAF Super Grand Prix in Lausanne. On Sept.16, 2006, he placed second with 13.03 at Athens World Cup in Athletics. On July 5, 2005, he won the event with 13.05 at IAAF Grand Prix in Lausanne. On Sept.17, 2005, he took the first spot in 13.05 at IAAF Golden Grand Prix in Shanghai. On August 27, 2004, he claimed the gold medal with 12.91 at the 28th Olympic Games in Athens, the first athletics gold Chinese man has ever got at Olympic Games.

He set a 110m hurdles world youth record and Asian record with 13.12 at 2002 IAAF Grand Prix in Lausanne, 60m hurdles record with 7.51 at 2003 IAAF Word Indoor Championships in Vienna and 110m hurdles Asian record with 13.06 at 2004 IAAF Grand Prix in Osaka. He set 110m hurdles Olympic Games record with 12.91 at 2004 Athens Olympic Games and 110m hurdles world record with 12.88 at 2006 IAAF Super Grand Prix in Lausanne.

Qi Haifeng

Qi Haifeng (1983-), scored over 8000 points in three competitions since 2001 Universiade, becoming the first

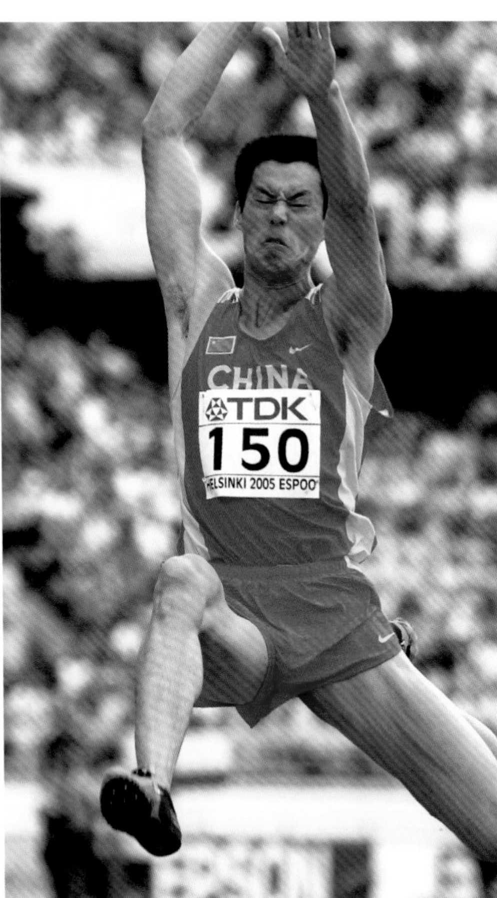

Qi Haifeng in the long jump competition of the men's decathlon of the World Athletic Championship on August 9, 2005

Chinese athlete to break 8,000 points in decathlon. He is very tough and stands out in running and jump events. His advent pushed Chinese men's decathlon a big step further in international sporting community. He won men's decathlon at 2001 National Athletics Championships and at Universiade. He finished first at 2002 National Athletics Championships, breaking his own Asian youth record and national record of 8,021 points with a score of 8,030. He placed seventh at 2003 IAAF Athletics Championships. It is the first time that Chinese athlete was ever among top 8 of this event over 40 years. At 2006 Asian Athletics Men's Decathlon Competition, he finished first with a score of 8,041.

♦ Chinese Athletics Association

CAA, short for Chinese Athletics Association, was founded in 1954 and was affliated to IAAF in 1978. The main events under its auspices include: National Athletics Championships, National Athletics Championship Contest, National Indoor Athletics Championships, National Marathon Championships, National Marathon Championship Contest, Beijing International Marathon, National Race Walk Championships, National Championship Contest, and National Cross Country Championships.

Address: No.2 Jia Longtan Lu, Beijing
Website: http://www.athletics.org.cn

Shi Dongpeng

Shi Dongpeng (1984-), track and field athletes. He placed second with 13.29 at 2005 Shijiazhuang National Athletics Championships, the second with 13.36 at 2005 Macao East Asian Games, the second with 13.39 at 2006 Shijiazhuang National Athletics Championships, the first with 13.40 at 2003 Shanghai National Athletics Championships, the first at 2005 Yixing National Athletics Championships and the third with 13.40 at 2005 Shanghai IAAF Golden Grand Prix.

Xing Huina

Xing Huina (1984-) , track and field athletes.

She placed third in 10,000m at 2002 Pusan Asian Games and the seventh in 10,000m at 2003 World Athletics Championships and set 10,000m world youth record in 30:31.55 at 2003 Paris World Athletics Championships.

Triathlon

Triathlon came to China in 1987 and caught on soon in Sanya, Beijing and Ningbo. On January 13, 1989, the State Physical Culture and Sports Commission listed it as an official competition event, released the regulations and held referee training. In February 1990, China Triathlon Association was founded in Beijing, which demonstrated that the competition and training of triathlon was standardized.

The first professional triathlon team appeared in 1993 and 8 other professional teams represented by Bayi, Chengdu Military Zone, Jiangsu, Shanghai, Shandong and Gansu triathlon team were in place in 2004. In 1996, a triathlon player Wang Dan finished first at Asian Triathlon Championships and was crowned Asia's First Female Triathloner. 2000 Asian Triathlon Championship was held in Xuzhou, the first time that the event was held in China. In 2002, General Administration of Sport of China incorporated triathlon into National Games, thus turning the event from being amateurish to professional.

At present, 5 large triathlon competitions are annually held in China, attracting the participation of amateurs and professionals nationwide. Li Zhihe from Hong Kong, China finished second in men's triathlon and Chinese female player Wang Hongni finished first in women's triathlon with 1:59:27 at 2006 Doha Asian Games.

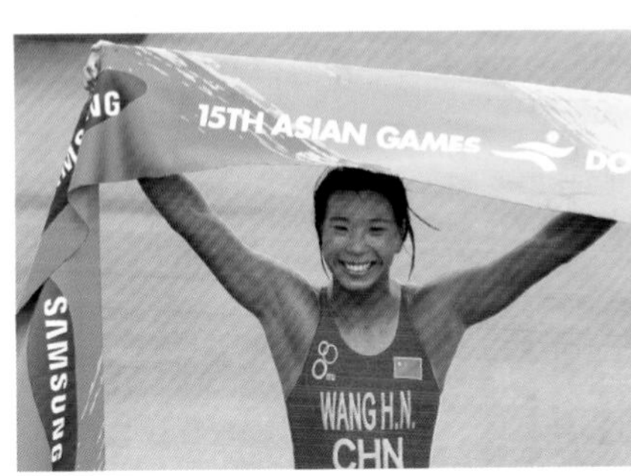

Wang Hongni finished first in women's triathlon at the 15th Doha Asian Games on December 8, 2006.

♦ China Triathlon Sports Association

CTSA, short for China Triathlon Sports Association, was founded on January 16, 1990 and was affiliated to International Triathlon Sports Association in the same year. The main events under its auspices include National Triathlon Championships and National Triathlon Championship Contest.

Address: No.153, Laoshan Xijie, Shijingshan District, Beijing
Website: http://www.triathlon.sport.org.cn

Tennis

Tennis, unlike other events, has a rather long history in China. The first National Tennis Performance Contest was held in Tianjin in 1953. Chinese Tennis Association was founded in the same year. In early 1955, a temporary national team was established in Beijing. Tennis was listed as annual national event in 1956. The scale was bigger on an annual basis since then. It was also since then that Chinese athletes began to participate in international competitions. As the tennis skills of Chinese athletes improved, efforts were made to tailor-make them to International tennis competitions. In 1992, China began to hold national tennis tour with over ten stops all year round. In 1993, Beijing sponsored Saloon Tennis Open, the first professional tennis tour ever held in China. Since then, China opened its gate to international professional tennis competitions with men's and women's professionals landing in China one after another. In 2005, Chinese fans had two Golden Weeks as China Open and Tennis Master Cup were held in Beijing and Shanghai respectively.

Evolution of Tennis Skills

Li Fang is the first Chinese athlete to attend four tennis open events. In 1992, she went to the third round in Australian Open, the best performance Chinese athlete has ever achieved in the conquest of grand slam. The achievement lasted for 12 years. In 1994, she found her way to the second round in French Open, also the best for Chinese athlete in the same event. Such a record was maintained for 10 years.

Yi Jingqian advanced to the third round of Australian Open in 2000. At the Tashkent Open in Uzbekistan, Li Na and Li Ting took women's doubles, the first title for women's doubles Chinese athletes have ever won in WTA.

The failure of Chinese tennis team at 2002 Pusan Asian Games gave Chinese tennis community a chance for reflection. They recognized the importance of professional system and mapped out a strategic guideline, namely, focus on women and find a breakthrough in women's doubles. In 2004, women's single battled to the second round at Australian Open early that year; women's doubles finished first in the youth category; women's single made a history by placing among top 16 at French Open and women's double won the gold medal at Athens Olympic Games. In 2005, Chinese tennis took a positive turn. The former strategic guideline took shape after adjustment. On January 27, 2006, Zheng Jie and Yanzi beat top seeds Lisa Raymond of USA and Australian Samantha Stosur en route to the first champion for China in women's doubles of the adult category at one of the four grand slams.

The First World Tennis Champion

Tennis event was included in the 10th Far East Games held between 1913 and 1914. Apart from the First Far East Games, China took part in the following nine games but only took the title at the 8th Games by Lin Baohua and Qiu Feihai, the first tennis championship Chinese men and women have ever won in international competitions.

The First Tennis Players Participating in Olympic Games

At the 24th Olympic Games, the tennis event was added. Liu Shuhua and Ma Keqin were the only two Chinese athletes to participate.

Liu Shuhua (1962-), 1.9 meters, is the tallest tennis player in China. Ma Keqin, born on February 24, 1962, is China's No.1 tough server. Both born in Tianjin, they cooperate smoothly with each other on the tennis court. They took the men's doubles at 1983 Kuala Lumpur Rafael Cup, Japan Lawn Tennis Championships and Japan Hokkaido Open and Latin America Coffee Cup.

The First Time to Hold International Tennis Tournament

From October 13 to 19, 1980, Marlboro Guanzhou Tennis Elite Tournament was held in Guanzhou, the first large international tennis tournament China has ever held.

The event was launched by China Tennis Association and IMG Tennis, cosponsored by Philip Morris and Guangdong Sporting Service Co., Ltd. As it was also funded by Marlboro, it was named 1980 Marlboro Guanzhou Tennis Elite Tournament. It was part of 95 grand prixes involved in "Volvo International Tennis Tournament" and the first leg of Asian tour. It would be later held in other places like Tokyo, Hong Kong, Taipei, Bangkok and India. The prize of the whole Volvo could be as high as 14 million USD.

There were 37 male players from 15 countries including USA, Australia, India, France, UK, Netherland, Columbia, West Germany, Mexico, Chile, Zimbabwe, Bolivia, Sweden, Austria and China.

The First Time to Win Asian Women's Tennis Group Champion

Chinese female tennis team composed of Li Xinyi, Zhong Ni, Duan Lilan and Pu Xiu won the women's team champion by beating DPRK's team by 2:1 under unfavorable conditions at the 10th Asian Games in 1986. Li Xinyi also claimed the title of women's singles, ending the no tennis gold history of China at Asian Games.

The First Olympics Tennis Gold Medal

No one would have imagined that Chinese athletes could advance to the finals of women's doubles at Olympic Games. And no one could even have imagined that Li Ting and Sun Tiantian, two unrenowned Chinese pair, could beat Spain's Conchita Martinez and Virginia Ruano Pascual, the No.2 seeds. However, they did it by 2:0 and took the first Olympics tennis gold medal, the greatest achievement Chinese tennis players have ever achieved in international competitions. As then-China's No.1 women's pair, Li Ting and Sun Tiantian made the following achievements: gold medal at 2004 Athens Olympic Games, 2003 Vienna Tennis Tournament, Bell Challenge, Thailand Open and silver medals at 2004 Indian Open and 2003 Tashkent Open. They also advanced to top 16 at Australia Open and Wimbledon Open in 2004.

Li Ting

Li Ting (1980-), female tennis player, is primarily versed in baseline with good basic techniques, a clear mind and a strong sense of team spirit in doubles.

She won women's doubles at the 21st Universiad doubles in 2001, six legs of 2003 ITF and three legs of WTA. She was among top 16 doubles players of the Australian Open.

Chinese tennis players Li Ting and Sun Tiantian won the women's doubles final at the Athens Olympics on August 22, 2004.

▲ 2006 China Open

2006 China Open was held between September 11 and 26, 2006. The events included: ATP Men's Singles, ATP Men's Doubles, SE WTA Women's Singles, SE WTA Women's doubles and ITF. Over 300 world professionals participated. The prize money was US$1.085 million, US$500,000 for ATP and US$585,000 for SEWTA.

At the women's singles final, No.2 seed Russian player Kuznetsova defeated Mauresmo to win with a score line of 6:4 and 6:0.

In women's doubles final, Pascual and Suarez beat Chakvetadze and Elena (RUS) in two straight sets with a score line of 6:2 and 6:4.

In men's singles final, 21-year-old player Baghdadis from Cyprus triumphed over Ancic Mario, a new tennis star from Croatia, to win his first ATP championship in his professional career.

2005 China Open Men's Singles Champion: Nadal Women's Singles Champion: Kirilenko

2004 China Open Men's Singles Champion: Safin Women's Singles Champion: Serena Williams.

She was trained in Wuhan Gym, sent to US Nick Tennis School for six months and chosen into national team in 1997.

On behalf of China, Li Ting is a participant of Bangkok Asian Games, Sydney Olympic Games and each Confederations Cup and many other international professional tournaments including the four opens. She won the doubles at 2004 Olympic Games and reached top 16 of doubles at the 2004 Australian Open.

Sun Tiantian

Sun Tiantian (1981-), female tennis player, has 88 as her highest world singles ranking and 18 as her highest doubles ranking.

She finished first in singles and second in doubles at 2000 National Tennis Circuit. She got a silver at 2001 ITF Women's Circuit at Shengzhen stop and advanced to top 4 at 2001 WTA (Shanghai Qiwei Open). She won two 2001 ITF Women's Circuit singles tournaments, two 2002 ITF Women's Circuit singles tournaments at Vietnam and Beijing legs, one 2003 ITF Women's Circuit singles tournament, 3 legs of 2003 WTA Circuit, seven legs of 2003 ITF Women's Circuit. She advanced to top 16 of doubles at 2004 Australian Open, top

16 of mixed doubles at 2004 Wimbledon Open and top 32 of doubles (with Li Ting) at 2004 French Open.

She is strong in baseline serve with good basic techniques and all-round play. She also has an outstanding physique. She is very hard-working in practice. She claims to be found of hard court and football.

Li Na

Li Na (1982-), female tennis player, is a right hand bat holder and became a professionals in 1999. Her current world singles ranking is 22 with the highest being 20.

In 1999, Li Na got the women's singles title at the second, third and fourth legs of ITF Challenge, two of which she got as a non-seed player. In addition, she won seven successive doubles tournament. In 2001, she finished first in singles, doubles (with Li Ting) and mixed doubles (with Zhu Benqiang) at Beijing Universiade, becoming the most shining star at the event. In 2002, the world 308-ranked player Li Na took the singles title at the ITF tournament in Midland, USA without losing a single battle in all eight matches. She went through the qualifying by defeating the No.1 seed and 5 other players with higher world ranking en route to her 13th ITF singles. Her world ranking rose to 33 in May, 2005. In 2006, she took a surprising turn by defeating world N0.9-ranked Swedish Schnyder, her first time to win top 10 world-ranked players and also the first Chinese player advancing to top four in red clay courts. In 2006, she made a history by being the first Chinese women to reach a quarterfinal at Wimbledon Open, one of the four grand slams.

Zheng Jie

Zheng Jie (1983-), female tennis player, ranks 30 currently with the highest world singles ranking 27 and doubles ranking 3.

Zheng Jie finished first in women's singles and second in women's doubles at 2000 ITF Women's Circuit (Hangzhou). She was two successive stops winner of women's singles and eight legs winner of women's doubles at the 2002 ITF Women's Circuit. She finished first in one stop (USA) women's and 8 legs women's doubles at 2003 ITF Women's Circuit. She advanced to top 8 of doubles at 2004 Australian Open and top 16 of singles at 2004 French Open and top 16 of doubles (with Yan Zi) at 2004 Wimbledon Open.

In 2006, Zheng Jie took the women's singles title at Doha Asian Games.

On January 27, 2006, Zheng Jie and Yan Zi won the first championship for China in women's doubles of the adult category at one of the four grand slams at the Australian Open.

Peng Shuai

Peng Shuai (1986-), female tennis player, is a right hand bat holder and became a professional in 2003. Her current world singles ranking is 38 with the highest singles ranking being 31 and the highest doubles ranking 47.

She practiced tennis since 8 and was believed to be a rare potential star. In June 2002, Chinese Tennis Association sent her through an agent to the tennis school established by former famous female tennis player, Chris Evert for a one year. She thus became the first Chinese female tennis player to be packaged by CTA and foreign agency into international professionals. Due to her reception of advanced training concept, she was believed to be a Chinese player whose style is closest to that of European and the US players. She has strong serve and forehand. She is also physically stronger than other Chinese players.

Chinese Tennis Association

CTA stands for Chinese Tennis Association which was founded in 1953 and was affiliated to ITF in July 1981.

Address: No.9, Tiyuguan Street, Beijing.
Website: http://www.tennis.org.cn

Modern Pentathlon

Pentathlon is a comprehensive event consisting of shooting, fencing, swimming, horsemanship and cross country run. In a one-day event, the players need to finish air pistol shooting in a distance of 10.20m, fencing, 200m free style swimming and horesmanship with 12 obstacles and end in a 3,000m cross country run. The one with the hig, hest score is the winner.

The event started late in China in 1981. At present, there are only 95 registered pentathlon players nationwide. Despite all this, pentathlon evolved rapidly in China in recent years. Men's team finished fourth at Asian Games. In recent years, the overall skill rose to Asia's top. At 2000 Asian Championships, China took five of the six titles with one man and one woman qualifying for Olympic Games. At 2006 Asian Championships, Chinese players finished first in men's singles and took the first two places in women's singles.

At 2005 Pentathlon Championships, Qian Zhenhua got his singles title, breaking the domination of European players of the event. At 2006 Pentathlon World Cup, Chinese men's team finished first in group and individual event. At 2006 Pentathlon Championships, Chinese men's team got a bronze in relay, breaking the Europeans-dominating history.

The Track Record of Pentathlon (2006)

The 3-day Pentathlon Egypt Leg of World Cup came to a stop in Cairo on September 17, 2006. Chinese men's team composed of Cao Zhongrong, Qian Zhenhua, Liu Yang and Liu Yanli took the group title with outstanding performance. Cao Zhongrong won his singles with 5464 points followed by Liu Yang with 5404.

At the 10th National Games in 2006, men's singles, women's singles and men's relay were included. The accumulating score of shooting, fencing, swimming, horsemanship and cross country run were the final score of individuals or teams. Shooting, fencing and swimming are Chinese traditional strong events blessed with excellent coaches. Many players can even challenge professionals in the three events. The two disadvantages of Chinese players which are sportsmanship and weak physique also begin to change. There are 5 Chinese men with a total score exceeding 5500 and 9 women 5300. All of the scores are among world's best. Men's highest 5784 and women's highest 5768 even top the world.

Chinese Modern Pentathlon Association

Chinese Modern Pentathlon Association was founded in 1981 and was orgigionally affiliated to China Winter Games Association. It joined International Modern Pentathlon Union and International Biathlon Union in 1979. In 1984, it became a member of Asian Modern Pentathlon Union. The association regularly holds National Women's Modern Pentathlon Championship, Men's Singles Training Match and National Modern Championships.

Website: http://modernpentathlon.sport.org.cn

Swimming

At 1992 Barcelona Olympic Games, Chines women swimmers, Zhuang Yong, Lin Li, Qian Hong, Yang Wenyi and Yang Xiaohong, also renowned as Five Golden Flowers, stunned the world by winning 4 gold and one silver. At 1994 Rome World Swimming Championships, Ten Small Flowers under the leadership of Le Jingyi swept the board by winning 12 gold and breaking many world records. However, Chinese swimming team took a negative turn ever since.

At Athens Olympic Games, Luo Xuejuan finished first in women's breaststroke.

At 2006 Doha Asian Games, Chinese team got 13 gold medals in 19 women's events.

Only three gold went to Chinese men's team at this event. At the 8th FINA World Swimming Championships in 2006, Chinese team took five gold, one silver and six bronze with the total medals excedding that of 2002 Moscow Short Course Swimming Championships. Chinese men's team made full breakthrough by reaching 13 finals and claiming a precious gold medal, the first gold Chinese men have ever got at international competitions in 10 years.

Current Strength of Chinese Swimming Team

Women's events stand out in Chinese swimming. 100m and 200m breaststroke and 200m freestyle are world-class. 100m freestyle, 100m breaststroke, 100m backstroke as well as 200m and 400m individual medley are also very strong.

Womne's 200m freestyle and 4×200m freestyle relay are also traditional strength of China.

An increasing number of Chinese swimmers are world-class. In 2002, only 26 (17 women and 9 men) advanced to world's top 50. Up to 2003, 64 (44 women and 20 men) advance to world's top 50.

The First Chinese Woman to Set World Swimming Record

In April 1988, the 3rd Asian Swimming Championship was held in Tianhe natatorium, Guangzhou. 16-year old Yang Wenyi set a word record in 50m freestyle final with 24.98, 0.3 seconds faster that the orginal world record. She became the first woman to break world record in China and in Asian swimming history.

The new record was approved at FINA executive meeting held in Amsterdam, Netherland from May 16 to 19, 1989. It was the first time that FINA had approved world record set by Chinese swimmers since China assumed its legitimate rights since 1980.

Chinese Women's World Records

Event	Name	Performance	Date	Venue
50m Backstroke	Li Hui	0:26.83	Dec 2, 2001	Shanghai
200m Butterfly	Yang Yu	2:04.04	Jan.18, 2004	Berlin
4×100 Freestyle Relay	Chinese team	3:34.55	April 19, 1997	Gothenburg
4×100 Freestyle Relay	Chinese team	7:46.30	April 3, 2002	Moscow

The First Olympics Swimming Medal

On September 19, 1988, Chinese swimmers said good bye to the no medal history at Olympics. 16-year-old Zhuang Yong finished second in 100m freestyle final with 44.47, thus gaining the first medal for Chinese swimmers at Olympic Games. Swimming had been a weak sport for China. Her success broke through the zero medal record in China's swimming history. Her 55.47 was a new start for Chinese swimming.

The First Olympics Gold Medal

At the 25th Summer Olympic Games in Barcelona, Spain in 1992, Zhuang Yong from Shanghai,won the first Olympics gold for China.

The First World Record Setter of Men's Breaststroke

Swimming Performance Tournament in celebration of International Labor Day by Guangzhou city was held on May 1, 1957. Qi Lieyun finished first in men's 100m breaststroke in a time of 1:11.6, breaking the 1:12.7 world record held by V.Svozil from Czechoslovakia,

Olympics Aquatics Gold Board

Time	Venue	Medal	Name	Event
2000	Sydeny Olympic Games	5 gold	Xiong Ni	Men's Individual Springboard and Men's Synchronized Springboard
			Xiao Hailiang	Men's Synchronized Springboard
			Tian Liang	Men's Individual Platform
			Fu Mingxia	Women's Individual Springboard
			Li Na and Sang Xue	Women's Synchronized Platform
1996	Athlanta Olympic Games	4 gold	Xiong Ni	Men's Individual Springboard
			Fu Mingxia	Women's Individual Springboard
			Fu Mingxia	Women's Individual Platform
			Le Jingyi	Women's 100m Freestyle
1992	Barcelona Olympic Games	7 gold	Sun Shuwei	Men's Individual Platform
			Fu Mingxia	Women's Individual Platform
			Gao Min	Women's Individual Springboard
			Yang Wenyi	Women's 50m Freestyle
			Zhuang Yong	Women's 100m Freestyle
			Qian Hong	Women's 100m Butterfly
			Lin Li	Women's 200m Individual Medley
1988	Seoul Olympic Games	2 gold	Xu Yanmei	Women's Individual Platform
			Gao Min	Women's Individual Springboard
1984	Los Angles Olympic Games	1 gold	Zhou Jihong	Women's Individual Platform

China's 50m National Swimming Records (By September 7, 2006)

Event	Women		Men	
50m Freestyle	24.51	LeJingyi	22.33	Jiang Chengji
100m Freestyle	54.01	LeJingyi	49.56	Chen Zuo
200m Freestyle	1:56.89	Lu Bin	1:48.10	Zhang Lin
400m Freestyle	4:05.00	Chen Yan	3:48.94	Zhang Lin
800m Freestyle	8:25.36	Chen Hua	8:04.10	Zhang Lin
1500m Freestyl	16:13.01	Chen Hua	15:00.27	Zhang Lin
50m Backstroke	28.31	Gao Chang	25.18	Ouyang Kunpeng
100m Backstroke	1:00.16	He Cihong	54.09	Ouyang Kunpeng
200m Backstroke	2:07.40	He Cihong	1:57.91	Ouyang Kunpeng
50m Breaststroke	30.64	Luo Xuejuan	27.83	Zeng Qiliang
100m Breaststroke	1:06.64	Luo Xuejuan	1:01.66	Zeng Qiliang
200m Breaststroke	2:22.99	Qi Hui	2:13.68	Lai Zhongjian
50m Butterfly	26.30	Zhou Yafei	23.86	Zhou Jiawei
100m Butterfly	58.32	Zhou Yafei	52.70	Zhou Jiawei
200m Butterfly	2:06.77	Liu Limin	1:55.78	Wu Peng
200m Individual Medley	2:09.72	Wu Yanyan	2:00.59	Qu Jingyu
400m Individual Medley	4:34.79	Chen Yan	4:15.38	Wu Peng
4×100m Freestyle Relay	3:37.91		3:20.52	
4×200m Freestyle Relay	7:55.97		7:21.74	
4×100m Medley Relay	3:59.89		3:39.29	

becoming the first Chinese man to set men's 100m breaststroke world record.

Qi Lieyun liked swimming when he was a child. He got enrolled by Guangzhou Sports School and transferred to Beijing Sports College before he attended the national swimming team in 1956. Technically, he developed his own unique style-Gaohangshi (lifting the upper body higher when pushing water).

Freestyle Swimming

Short-distance freestyle swimming has long been China's strength. Chinese players once claimed 3 gold medals at Olympics and are unrivaled in Asia. At 2006 Doha Asian Games, Chinese women's team took 13 swimming titles with 4 coming from freestyle events. At present, Chinese team is blessed with group advantage in freestyle.

Backstroke

At the first FINA Short Course World Championships in 1993, He Cihong finished first in women's 200m breaststroke with 2:06.09, breaking world record and becoming the first breaststroke world champion in China. At the 7th FINA World Championships in 1994, she finished first in 100m breaststroke in a world-record breaking time of 1:00.16. At the 3rd FINA Short Course World Championships, Lu Donghua and Chen Yanji finished first in women's 100m and 200m breaststroke respectively.

Breaststroke

The breaststroke event has seen many talents in China. As early as 40 years ago, Wei Lieyun and Mu Xiangxiong broke breaststroke world records many times. Later, Lin Li, Wang Xiaohong and Dai Guohong went for gold at international tournaments. China has rich experience and unique method in breaststroke training. Luo Xuejuan and Qi Hui are two flagships of this event, the former leading 100m and the latter mainly engaged in 200m.

Butterfly Swimming

China has since 2004 lagged behind other countries in butterfly swimming. But China has many butterfly swimmers. At the 2008 Olympic Games, Liu Zige won the 200m butterfly swimming champion with 2:04.18, breaking the world record in the field. The runner-up was also Chinese.

Individual Medley

Women's Individual Medley was the gold mine of Chinese swimming. Four swimmers once got 12 such titles and turned out many China's best.

At the 6th IFNA World Championships in 1991, Li Li finished first in 400m individual medley at the first-day's event and change the Chinese swimming history of zero champions. Several days later, she took the 200m individual medley title, becoming the indisputable Queen of Individual Medley at this event.

Dai Guohong and Lu Bin are second generation world-class individual medley swimmers following Lin Li. Early at the first IFNA Short Course Championships in 1993, 16-year-lod Dai Guohong became the Queen of Individual Medley. At the 7th IFNA World Championships in July 1994, Dai took 400m individual medley title for the second time. Another famous player Lu Bin finished first in 200m individual medley.

At the 8th IFNA World Championships in 1998, Chinese outstanding swimmers took 3 gold medals two of which came from medley events. They also won 200m and 400m individual medley titles at three consecutive world championships, the first three Consecutive champions Chinese swimmers have ever won at international tournaments.

Relay Swimming

Chinese women's team won 7 relay swimming gold medals at IFNA World Championships and IFNA Short Course Championships in 1994, 1995 and 1997, breaking three world records.

At 2003 IFNA World Championships, Chinese women's team finished first in 4×100m medley relay with 3:59.89.

At 2004 Athens Olympic Games, Chinese team finished second in 4×200m freestyle final with 7:55.97.

Synchronized Swimming

Synchronized swimming had a short history in China. Since 1983, people were sent abroad to learn about the event. In April 1983, the first national synchronized swimming traning class was held in Chengdu. In August 1984, the First Naional Synchronized Swimming Championship was held in Beijing.

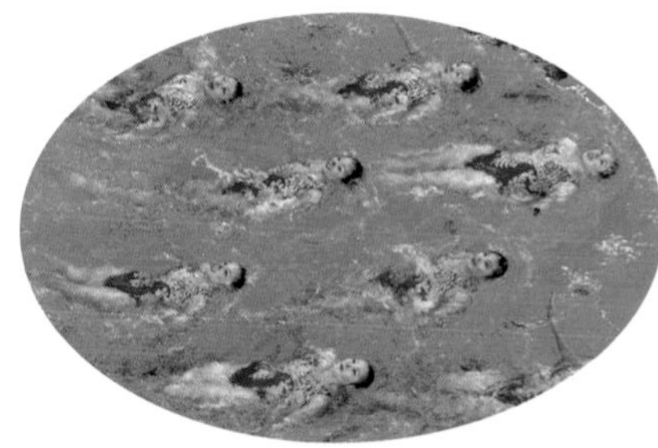

On December 9, 2006, the Chinese team finished first in the synchronized swimming team final with 96.584 points at the 15th Doha Asian Games.

In 1987, it was listed as an official event at the 6th National Games. After many years of learning, skills of Chinese athletes were greatly enhanced. At 2000 Sydney Olympic Games, Chinese players finished seventh in doubles.

The reason why Chinese synchronized swimming could win over audiences and referees lies in the efforts to explore the combination of western and domestic styles, invite foreign choreographers and build up talent pool. At national tournament, 8 provincial and municipal professional teams represented by Beijing, Shanghai, Sichuan, Guangdong and Jiangsu team with nealy 200 participants.

At 2006 Doha Asian Games, Chinese swimmers swept doubles and team titles, a breakthrough in the synchronized swimming non-gold history. At 2006 Asian Swimming Championships, Chinese synchronized swimming team took all the 6 title. At the 11th IFNA World Cup, Chinese team finished fifth.

Lin Li

Lin Li

Lin Li (1970-), woman swimmer. She took the title of 400m individual medley, becoming the first world champion in Chinese swimming at the 4th World Swimming Championships held in Perth, Australia on Jan.7, 1991. Since then, she became famous abroad. She also finished first in 200m individual medley.

At 1992 Barcelona Olympic Games, she became the leader of the 5 Golden Flowers. She finished first in 200m individual medley, becoming the first Chinese woman to break world record at Olympics. She also finished second in 400m individual medley and 200m breaststroke, taking the most medals among Chinese swimmers at the Olympics.

At Atlanta in 1996, the then 26-year-old Lin Li, a coach, reappeared at Olympics arena and took the third spot in 200m individual medley. In the meantime, she set a record as the oldest swimmer in Chinese swimming team and the only who was involved in 3 successive Olympics.

Qian Hong

Qian Hong (1971-), woman swimmer. Butterfly swimming, an event once affiliated to breaststroke, involves pushing water backwards with both hands and plunging into water with the aid of waist. It looks like a dancing butterfly and thus the swimmers are called "Water Butterfly". In her 13-year career, Qian Hong took 30 national titles and 51 world titles, a majority of which were from butterfly swimming. In 1991 and 1992, she claimed 100m breaststroke title at the 6th FINA World Swimming Championships and the 25th Olympic Games held in Barcelona. For a long time, she was named "water butterfly" and a verified Queen of Butterfly Swimming.

At 1992 Barcelona Olympic Games, Qian Hong had no advantages over those world tops. When it came to the 50m at 100m butterfly final, she was already behind two swimmers. At this critical moment, she made a bold decision, shortening time for inhale with 5 pulls and one inhale. Ultimately, she broke 100m butterfly Olympics record and claimed the gold. She was also the first Chinese woman to swim within one minute.

Yang Wenyi

Yang Wenyi (1972-), woman swimmer. She was tall and thin with 1.78m and 62 kilos. Her father was a sports collector, her mother a baseball and her brother a member of national youth fencing team. In 1978, she started learning swimming in swimming class of Shanghai sports club at age 6 and broke national youth records 18 times. She was mainly engaged in 100m, 200m breaststroke and 200m mixed. In 1984, she was chosen into Shanghai municipal swimming team. In 1986, she was chosen into national assembled swimming team. In 1987, she finished in 50m freestyle and 100m breaststroke at the 6th National Games with a score of Asia's best. At the 3rd Asian Swimming Championships in April 1988, the 16-year-old Yang finished in 50m freestyle, breaking world record with 24.98. She also finished first in 100m breaststroke with an Asian best performance of 1:3.08 and worked together with her teammates to claim two gold medals at 4×100m medley relay and 4×100m freestyle relay. At the 24th Olympic Games Women's 50m Freestyle Final in the same year, Yang Wenyi had a fierce battle with Christine Otto from Democratic Germany Republic, the heroin at this Olympics. As she started late, she was 1 meter behind Otto at 25 meters and placed second at 45 meters. Ultimately, the 1.88m tall Otto finished fist by touching the finishing line 0.15 second earlier than her. Yang Wenyi finished second in a time of 25.64. At the 25th Olympic Games Swimming Event in 1992, she took the 50m freestyle title and broke the Olympics record.

Zhuang Yong

Zhuang Yong gained the gold medal of the women's 100m freestyle swimming at the 25th Olympics in 1992.

Zhuang Yong (1972-), woman swimmer. She was originally named Zhuang Yong (with "yong" referring to "reciting" in Chinese) which was changed to Yong (referring to "swim") as she liked swimming. She started swimming at age 7 and received professional training at age 9 and broke national junior record at age 12. She got three gold and three silver medals at the first FINA World Youth Championships in 1985 and was chosen into the national team in 1986. She finished first in four events and second in one event and broke Asian records twice at the 6th National Games. In 1988, she finished first in women's 4 ×100m freestyle and second in 100m and 200m freestyle at Asian Swimming Championships. At the 24th Olympic Games 1988, she finished second in 100m freestyle, the first medal Chinese swimmers have ever got at Olympics. In 1989, her world ranking in 100m freestyle stood in the second place. In 1991, she won 50m freestyle at the 6th FINA World Championships. At the 25th Olympic Games in 1992, she finished first in 100m freestyle, second in 50m freestyle and 4×100m freestyle. The gold medal she got was the first gold for Chinese delegation and also the first Olympics gold for the swimming team. It was a new chapter in the history of Chinese swimming.

Jiang Chengji

Jiang Chengji (1975-), man swimmer. He was the 100m butterfly Asian record holder in of 53.80. He finished fourth in 50m freestyle at 1996 Olympic Games, the best score that Chinese men have ever got at Olympics.

At 1996 Atlanta Olympic Games, he broke 50m freestyle Asian record with 22.33 and 100m butterfly Asian record with 53.20, the best two scores ever achieved by Asian men at this Olympics although he finished in fourth. It is also the first time Chinese men have ever reached Olympics finals.

Chen Hua

Chen Hua (1982-) , woman swinnmer. She won 400m, 800m freestyle and 4×200m freestyle relay at 1998 Bangkok Asian Games, 400m and 800m freestyle at 1999 IFNA Short Course Paris and Glasgow tournaments, 800m freestyle at 2000 Short Course Championships with a third spot in 400m freestyle, 800m freestyle at Shanghai leg of 2001 IFNA Short Course World Cup, 800m freestyle at 2002 IFNA World Championships with a silver in 400m freestyle, 800m freestyle at 2002 Pusan Asian Games and 800m freestyle at 2004 National Swimming Championships.

Chen Hua set a 400m freestyle Asian record with 4:12.31 at 1998 Pusan Asian Games, an 800m freestyle world record in 8:15.15 at 2001 IFNA Short Course World Cup Shang Stop and 1500m freestyle Asian record with 16:13.01 at 2002 National Swimming Championships.

Luo Xuejuan

Luo Xuejuan (1984-), woman swimmer. She took three gold medals in 2005 World Championshis and claimed two successive championship of 100m breaststroke world cup. In 100m breaststroke, she has hardly been defeated in recent years, becoming a leader of Chinese swimming.

She finished first in 50m and 100m breaststroke at 2001 World Championships, 100m breaststroke at the 14th Asian Games in 2002, 50m and 100m breaststroke and 4×100 medley relay at 2003 Barcelona Championships and 100m breaststroke at 2004 Athenes Olympic Games.

She set 100m breaststroke Asian and national record of 1:06.96 at the 9th Naitional Games held in Guangdong, 2001, another Asian and national record of 1:06.80 at the 10th FINA Swimming Championships Barcelona 2003 and an Olympics record with 1:06.64 at 2004 Athens Olympic Games.

On August 16, 2004, Luo Xuejuan finished first and chalked up the Olympic record in the women's 100m breast stroke final at the Athens Olympics.

Qi Hui

Qi Hui (1985-) , woman swimmer. She finished first in 200m breaststroke at 1999 FINA Edmonton Short Course World Cup; 50m,100m and 200m breaststroke at 1999 Rio Short Course World Cup; 50m,100m and 200m breaststroke at Sweden leg of 2001 World Cup Short Course Swimming Meet; 100m and 200m breaststroke at France Leg of 2001 World Cup Short Course Swimming Meet; 100m and 200m breaststroke and 200m medley at Shanghai leg of 2002 Short Course World Cup 200m medley, 400m meley and 200m breaststroke at 2006 World Short Course Championships.

In 200m breastroke, Qi Hui set an Olympics record with 2:24.21 at 2000 Sydney Olympic Games, a world record of 2:22.99 at 2001 Hangzhou Naitonal Swimming Championship Contest, a world record of 2:19.25 at 2001 Paris World Cup Short Course Swimming and a world record of 2:18.86 at 2002 Shanghai World Short Course Cup.

Wu Peng

Wu Peng (1987-), man swimmer. He finished first in 200m butterfly at the 9th National Games in 2001, at 2002 Pusan Asian Games and at 2006 Shanghai World Short Course Championships.

Diving

Diving is a traditionally strong event for China. Chinese diving team has made splendid achievements, bringing home countless honors. It enjoys the reputation of China's Dream Team. At Athens Olympics, the team took six gold, two silver and one bronze medals in all eight events, ranking No.1 in terms of total gold medals and total medals. It was an oversliding victory and a record number of gold medals that Chinese single team has ever got in one Olympics. It made history by pushing the number of swimming gold medals to a total of 20 in Chinese conquest of Olympics.

Chinse diving team is full of legendary players represented by the veterans Zhou Jihong, Gao Min, Xiong Ni and Fu Mingxia and the current divers like Guo Jingjing and Hu Jia. They are all super stars and created legends one after another.

The First Time to Become an Asian Diving Giant

The 7th Asian Games was held in Tehran, Iran from Sept.1 to 16, 1974. 2363 players from 25 countries and regions participated in 16 events. The Chinese athletes take part in this competition for the first time. 7 divers swept the board by winning all four gold medals in men's and women's spring board and platform events, two silver and two bronze medals. 15-year-old Li Kongzheng finished first in men's platform with dives at difficult levels from 2.7to 2.9. Zhong Shaozhen took two women's titles. Xie Caiming took men's springboard title. The achievement was a sign that China had became an Asian diving power.

On August 14, 2004, Chinese athletes Tian Liang (left) and Yang Jinghui won the championship of the men's synchronized 10 meter platform event with 383.88 points at the 28th Athens Olympics.

The First Time to Participate in IFNA Diving World Cup

The 2nd IFNA Diving World Cup was held in Mexico City from June 12 to 14, 1981. 18 divers from 8 coutries were involved. Chinese divers participated for the first time and achieved stunning results. Shi Meiqin, Li Hongping and Chen Xiaoxia finished first in women's springboard, men's platform and women's platform.

The First Team Title at World Cup

The 3rd IFNA Diving World Cup was held in Houston, USA from April 27 to May 1, 1983. Over 60 players from 18 countries and regions participated. 8 Chinese divers, namely, Li Hongping, Tong Hui, Li Kongzheng, Tan Liangde, Li Yihua, Peng Yuanchun, Chen Xiaoxia and Zhou Jihong, defeated with concerted efforts US team which swpet all diving titles at the 4th IFNA World Championships. They took the title of men's and women's total score and women's team title.

At this tournament, Chinese diving team got four gold, two silver and two bronze medals in all 7 events, becoming a world diving power.

The First Olympics Diving Champion

At the 23rd Olympic Games in 1984, Zhou Jihong finished first in women's platform with a score of 435.51, becoming the first Olympics diving champion of China.

Zhou Jihong was born in Wuhan city. She went to learn gymnastics at 12. In the same Autumn, she joined Hubei diving team and began platform training. Four year later in 1981, she took the national platform title. In 1982, 17-year-old Zhou Jihong was chosen into the national diving team. She participated in the 4th IFNA World Championships the same year and finished third. In April 1983, she captured a gold medal at the 3rd IFNA Diving World Cup. At 1984 Olympic Games, Zhou Jihong, age 19, took the women's platform title with calm, consistent, beautiful and smooth difficult dives, winning the first Olympics diving platform for China.

The First Diving World Champion

In 1979, Chinese divers participated in the 10th Universiad held in Mexico City, the first international tournament Chinese players have ever attended. Chen Xiaoxia, aged 17, defeated all the powers including Russian legend Karenina en route to the women's platform title, becoming the first diving world champion.

Chen Xiaoxia was born in Guangzhou City, Guangdong Province. She went to learn diving at Guangzhou Yuexiushan Amateur School at the age of 12. Due to her industrious learning, she quickly mastered 5237 or Back $1\frac{1}{2}$ Som., $3\frac{1}{2}$ Twists. After 1979 when she became the first diving world champion in China, she beat world powers like USA, Mexico and Canada in 1980. In the same year, she finished first in platform at Martigny World Diving Championships held in London. In 1981, she finished first at the 2nd IFNA World Cup and the 11th Universiade. In 1982, she won the International Diving Invitational by defeating many famous divers from Canada, US, Mexico and other countries. In 1983, she was the leading diver of Chinese diving team and women's diving team when they took the men's and women's team title and women's team title at the 3rd IFNA Diving World Cup.

Xu Yiming

Xu Yiming, man diver, and the head coach of Chinese national diving team. He led the athletes to participate in several Olympics, championships and world cup, the three biggest events in diving, and won 16 times. He was crowned Father of Modern Diving Technical Skills. Since 1984, he was a four times successive member of FINA Technical Diving Committee as an established diving power.

FINA held a grand awarding ceremony in the International Swimming Hall of Fame located in Fort Lauderdale, Florida, a dynamic shrine dedicated to the memory and recognition of the famous persons in the second weekend of May 2003. Mr.Xu Yiming, former head of Chinese diving team, received the prize from Thomas, president of FINA Technical Diving Committee and left his foot and hand mark in the hall which also recognized his extraordinary achievement and contribution to diving.

Shi Meiqin

Shi Meiqin (1962-), woman diver.

She started gymnastics at Shanghai Sports Palace and was chosen into Shanghai diving team in 1972 and into national team in 1975. She was blessed with flexible, beautiful and mature skills. In 1978, she won at the 8th Asian Games in springboard. In 1979, she finished third in springboard at the 10th Universiade. In 1980, she won at Martigny World Diving Invitational tournament held in UK in individual springboard. In 1981, she claimed the individual springboard title at the 2nd World Diving Cup. In 1983, she won at the 10th Universiad in individual springboard. In 1984, she was the winner of individual springboard at the 2nd Asian Swimming Championships. In 1978 and 1981, she got Sports Medal of Honor given by the State Physical Culture and Sports Commission. She also served as a coach of Shanghai team.

Gao Min

Gao Min (1970-), woman diver.

She has great talent in diving and climbed to the top of her diving career at the age of 16. In 1986, she won at the first International Diving Competitions held in Rostock, East Germany. Since then, she swept all the individual springboard titles totaling 70 at continental diving tournament, world tournament, world championships, world cup and the Olympics until 1992 when she quit diving. She became the verified Queen of Springboard Divers with her high techniques and stability surpassing all other competitors. She was voted by *Swimming World* magazine world best diver successively in 1987, 1988 and 1989. During this period, there was a classic saying that it was a sad thing for a female diver to be in the same era with Gao Min.

Xiong Ni

Xiong Ni (1974-), man diver.

In 1987, he won platform gold at World Diving Invitational tournaments held in Democratic Germany Republic, Canada and Mexico. In 1988, he finished first in platform at the 3rd Asian Swimming Championships held in Guangzhou, came in second at the 24th Olympics held in Seoul and took springboard and platform titles at International Diving Tournament Sweden Cup. In 1989, he was the triple winner in the 6th session of World Cup diving championships for platform diving, the men's group event and the men and women mixed event. In 1992, he was the bronze medalist at the Barcelona Olympic Games for platform diving. Between 1991 and 1995, he won multiple platform and springboard gold and silver medals. In 1996, he was the gold medalist at the 26th Olympics in springboard. In 2000, he won the springboard two person event in the World Cup, partnered by Xiao Hailiang, gold medal at the Sydney Olympic Games in the men's springboard synchronised event, with Xiao Hailiang, and gold medal in the men's 3 meters boards individual.

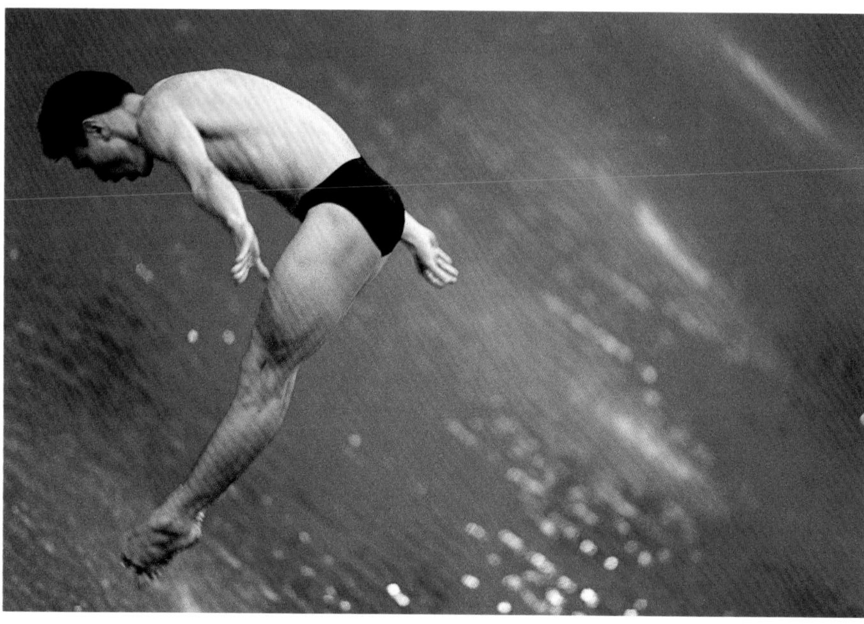

On September 26, 2000, Xiong Ni titled the men's 3-meter springboard event at 2000 Sydney Olympics.

In 1989, he was voted by Swimming World magazine world best diving athlete of 1989.

Sun Shuwei

Sun Shuwei (1976-), man diver. He became national champion at age 13, Asian champion at age 14 and world champion at age 15. Olympic champion could be the top for a professional. He was only 16 years old was he climbed the top. The legend happened at the 25th Olympic Games held in Barcelona in 1992. His last dive got 99.960 points, the highest score ever in world diving community.

In 1992, he was the gold medalist at the 25th Olympic Games held in Barcelona in platform diving, the first time Chinese men has ever won a diving gold at Olympics. He also became the first Chinese man to claim three men's platform titles in grand pix. In 1991, he was voted world best male platform diver and became the youngest male ever voted by *Swimming World* magazine.

Fu Mingxia

Fu Mingxia (1978-), woman diver. She became a world champion in 1990 when she was 12 years old. At 1992 Barcelona Olympic Games, she took the 10m platform title,

At 1992 Barcelona Olympic Games, Fu Mingxia took the 10m platform title, becoming the youngest Olympics champion. At 1996 Atlanta Olympic Games, she took platform and springboard titles, renowned as the "Diving Queen" after Gamin.

becoming the youngest Olympics champion. The title was one of China's successive three titles in platform diving. She is also the first Chinese athlete to take three successive gold medals at Olympics.

At the 6th FINA World Swimming Championships held in Perth, 1991, she defeated all famous players en route to the platform title with a score of 426.50, becoming the youngest world champion ever written into Guinness World Records in the modern world swimming history. At 1992 Barcelona Olympic Games, she finished first in platform. At the 7th FINA World Swimming Championships held in Rome in 1994, she claimed the platform title with a score of 434.04. At 1996 Atlanta Olympic Games, she took springboard and platform titles. At 2000 Sydney Olympic Games, she finished first in springboard.

Fu Mingxia was renowned as Diving Queen. She was voted by *Swimming World* magazine (USA) world excellent diving in 1990 and 1991.

Tian Liang

Tian Liang (1979-), man diver.

In 1995, he won men's synchronized platform at FINA World Diving Grand Prix held in USA and finished first in men's synchronized, group and mixed group at the 9th World Diving Cup. In 1997, he was the winner at the 10th World Diving Cup in mixed event. In 1999, he won at New Zealand World Cup in individual and synchronized events. In 2000, he finished first at World Cup in individual and synchronized platform. He was also the winner of men's platform at 2000 Sydney Olympic Games. In 2001, he won the gold at FINA World Championships in individual and synchronized event. In 2002, he made the same achievement at World Diving Cup. In 2003, he finished third at World Championships in platform diving. In 2004, he won at the 14th World Diving Cup in individual and synchronized platform diving.

Peng Bo

Peng Bo (1981-), man diver.

In 2001, he won at the 9th FINA World Swimming Championships in synchronized springboard. In 2002, he finished second in individual springboard and first in synchronized springboard at the 13th World Diving Cup. In the same year, he also won at Pusan Asian Games in synchronized springboard. In 2003, he finished second in springboard at the 10th FINA World Swimming Championships and first in 1 meter individual springboard at World Soldiers Games. In 2004, he finished first in synchronized springboard and third in individual springboard at the 14th FINA World Diving Cup.

Guo Jingjing

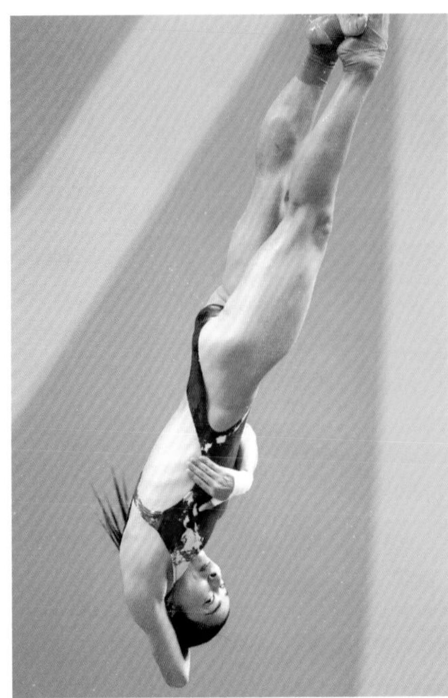

On August 26, 2004, Guo Jingjing won the championship of the women's 3-meter springboard event.

Guo Jingjing (1981-), woman diver. She was the winner of individual and synchronized springboard in 2004 and at 2001, 2003 and 2005 FINA World Swimming Championships. She finished first in individual springboard at 2004 Olympics.

Hu Jia

Hu Jia (1983-), man diver.

In 2000, he was the winner of men's individual platform at the FINA Diving Grand Prix Finals and finished first in individual platform and second in synchronized platform at Sydney Olympic Games. In 2001, he won at the 9th FINA World Swimming Championships in synchronized platform. In 2002, he won at the 13th World Diving Cup in men's team event. In 2003, he finished third in synchronized platform at the 10th FINA World Swimming Championships. In 2004, he won the Shanghai leg of World Diving Championship Circuit and finished second in individual platform at the 14th World Diving Cup.

On August 28, 2004, Hu Jia finished first in the final of the men's 10-meter platform with 748.08 points at the Athens Olympics.

Wu Minxia

Wu Minxia (1985-), woman swinner.

In 2001, she was the winner of synchronized springboard at FINA World Diving Championships. In 2004, she finished first in synchronized springboard and second in individual springboard. In 2006, she won at World Diving Championships in individual springboard.

Lao Lishi

Lao Lishi (1987-), woman diver.

In 2002, she finished first at the Spain and Canada legs of FINA Diving Grand Prix in women's platform. She also won synchronized platform at the USA leg of 2002 FINA Diving Grand Prix. In the same year, she took the individual and synchronized platform at World Diving Cup and the individual platform title at Pusan Asian Games. In 2003, she won at the Australia and Zhuhai legs of FINA Diving Grand Prix in individual and synchronized platform events. She also finished first in individual platform and second in synchronized platform at FINA Swimming Championships. In 2004, she finished first at the 14th FINA Swimming World Cup in synchronized platform.

Li Ting

Li Ting (1987-), woman diver.

In 2001, she won at Moscow leg of FINA Diving Grand Prix in individual platform diving. In 2002, she was the winner at World Diving Cup in synchronized platform. In 2004, she finished first in synchronized platform diving at Canada leg of FINA Diving Grand Prix, at World Diving Cup and at USA leg of FINA Diving Grand Prix.

Seven Gold at 2004 Athens Olympic Games

Name	Event
Luo Xuejuan	Women's 100m Breaststroke
Guo Jingjing	Women's Individual Springboard
Guo Jingjing, Wu Minxia	Women's Synchronized Springboard
Peng Bo	Men's Individual Springboard
Hu Jia	Men's Individual Platform
Tian Liang, Yang Jinghui	Men's Synchronized Platform
Lao Lishi, Li Ting	Women's Synchronized Platform

♦ China Swimming Association

China Swimming Association, founded in 1956, is headquartered in Beijing. It was affiliated to FINA in April 1952. In 1958, it discontinued its relations with FINA in an attempt to defeat the "two Chinas" conspiracy. In July 1980, it was given the legitimate seat by FINA. The main events under the auspices of this association include: National Spring Division Swimming Test Tournament, National Youth and Children Category Indoor Short Course Swimming Tournament, National Championship Contest, National Summer Division Swimming Test Tournament, National Youth and Children Category Division Swimming Tournament, National Swimming Championships, National Synchronized Swimming Championship Contest, National Synchronized Swimming Championships, National Diving Championship Contest, National Diving Championships, National Water Polo Championships and National Youth Water Polo Tournament.

Address: No.4 Stadium Road, Chongwen District, Beijing.
Website: http://swimming.sport.org.cn

Water Polo

Water Polo was introduced to Hong Kong, Guangdong Province and coastal cities via Europe and USA in 1920s. Since then, the event caught on in China. At the fifth Guangdong Province Water Sports Games in 1931, water polo was listed as an event. It was the earliest official water polo competition held in China. After the founding of the People's Republic of China, the event was given dued attention by the state. Coaches and athletes absorbed the advanced techniques from world powers and developed a method featuring fast counterattack with alternate cuts, thus greatly enhancing the level of skills. Chinese Men's Water Polo Team had an impressive record in Asia. In late 1970s and early 1980s, the team took the water polo Asian title four times. After the dismemberment of the Soviet Union, former republic nations of the Soviet Union in central Asia brought excellent players, changing the dynamics of water polo in Asia. At that time, Chinese team hovered around the second or third place. In recent years, Chinese water polo was given renewed attention. In 2006, it recaptured the title in Asian Championships and returned to the dominant position.

Badminton

Modern badminton was introduced to China around 1920s. It was primarily seen in youth councils and church universities in Shanghai, Guangzhou, Tianjin and Beijing. In 1954, the returning Chinese Indonesians represented by Wang Wenjiao and Chen Fushou brought back the hope and techniques for Chinese badminton, fully speeding up the development of the event. In 1956, Chinese Badminton Association was founded under whose auspices National Badminton Tournament was held annually. The badminton competition was standardized ever since. In mid-1960s, Chinese team rose as a leader. It defeated Indonesian team, the world champion in 1963 and 1964. In 1965, it crushed all major powers in northern Europe. As a result, it was renowned Uncrowned King due to the fact that China could not participate in World Championships as it had not been a member of International Badminton Federation, IBF.

After 1980s, Chinese badminton entered into a second heyday. The Chinese players were involved in all kinds of world competitions and made great achievements. The Chinese Men's team won Thomas Cup in 1986, 1988 and 1990. At Uber Cup held in Kuala Lumpur, 1984, the Chinese women players claimed the Uber Cup. Afterwards, the women's team won the title of Uber Cup five times with overriding advantage. 1980s was the heyday of Chinese badminton and was crowned Chinese Era.

Chinese Women Badminton

The Chinese women badminton started in 1950 and advanced to world level in 1960s. The women players represented by Chen Wangniang, Liang Xiaomu and Liang Qiuxia learned men's techniques and defeated world champions with quick offense and flexible skills. In 1980s, like men's team, the Chinese women team was fully exposed to the world. The Chinese women team represented by Zhang Ailing, Han Meiping and Li Lingwei ushered in a heyday of techniques and strategies in World women badminton with their full-blown and changeable tactics as well as their initiative and quick offense.

Chinese Badminton Team

There may be only a dozen famous players in Chinese badminton team. However, the whole team has over a hundred players. At present, the team can be divided into No.1, No.2 and No.3 team respectively as the national team, the national youth team and the national junior team. By attending national tournaments, top players that meet age requirement may all join national youth and junior team and gain the opportunity to attend international tournament. Through internal selections, they may also have the chance to be part of the national team and participate in international tournaments-adult category. Within the national team, a could rise or fall among No.1, No.2 and No.3 team in light of their records in the competitions which determine rise or fall. Through the program, the Chinese badminton team established a solid foundation. Due to the existence of No.2 and No.3 team, it is fair to say that all good youth in China are pocketed by the national team for further extensive training.

Apart from the ladder team arrangement, the number of coaches is also extraordinary. Men's singles, women's singles, men's doubles, women's doubles and mixed doubles all have head and assistant coaches, which is rare in other ball teams.

On March 15, 2004, Lin Dan won the championship of the men's singles of All England Open (Badminton).

The Latest IBF World Rankings (2006)

Event	Ranking	Name
Men Singles	1	Lin Dan CHN
	4	Chen Hong CHN
Women Singles	1	Xie Xingfang CHN
	2	Zhang Ning CHN
	5	Wang Chen HKG
Men's Doubles	4	Fu Haifeng/Cai Yun CHN
Women's Doubles	1	Yang Wei/Zhang Jiewen CHN
	2	Wei Yili/Zhao Tingting CHN
	3	Gao Ling/Huang Sui CHN
Mixed Doubles	1	Zhang Jun/Gaoling CHN
	3	Chen Qiqiu/Zhao Tingting CHN

The First Time to Participate in All England Open Badminton Championships

All England Open Badminton Championships is one of the world's oldest and most prestigious unofficial world badminton tournaments. It was initiated by England Badminton Association in 1899. It was primarily participated by players from local associations and later was expanded to the whole England. After the founding of IBF, the old tournament gained great support and evolved to a world-wide competition. It was held in London at the last week of March annually. Five single events were included. In March 1982, the Chinese badminton team took part in it for the first time with Zhang Ailing winning the women singles title and Li Ying and Wu Dixi the women doubles title.

World Mixed Team Badminton Championships

IBF is the main sponsor of this event. The champion cup was donated by Indonesian Badminton Association as "Sudirman Cup". In 1988, IBF decided to hold world mixed team badminton championships every two years. It was followed by the World Championships in the same place and at the same time. In 1989, the first Sudirman Cup was held. Since 1995, the Chinese team was the successive winner of the fourth straight to the ninth tournaments.

Winning Thomas Cup for the First Time

The Thomas Cup is the top men's international team competition in world badminton. In 1939, Thomas, the then-president of IBF, donated 1700 pounds to build a 28-feet tall golden cup for the men's international team competition in world badminton and gave it to IBF as the prize cup. The tournament was interrupted by World War II. It was not until 1949 that IBF named the golden cup after Thomas for its contribution to badminton event and decided to hold Thomas Cup every three years. From May 10-21, 1982, the Chinese men's badminton team attended the 12th Men's International Team Competition in World Badminton held in London, UK and took the cup, the symbol for the highest level of men's world badminton team.

Winning Uber Cup for the First Time

Uber Cup is the top women's international team competition in world badminton. Mrs. H.S. Uber, the former championship of All England in 1930, finished first in women's singles, women's doubles and mixed doubles 12 times. After witnessing the grand event of Thomas Cup, she donated a prize cup for women's team event. The move was endorsed by IBF and the first Uber Cup was held in 1956. From May 7 to 18, 1984, the 10th Uber Cup was held in Kuala Lumpur, Malaysia and China sent the women's team to the event for the first time.

Li Lingwei, Han Aiping, Zhang Ailing, Qian Ping, Wu Jianqiu, Xu Rong, Lin Ying and Wu Dixi made impressively quick victories with their extraordinary playing flair and flexible footsteps. In the five round battles with Japan, Indonesia, Danmark, South Korea and England, they won in 5:0 and undisputedly took the cup.

The First Badminton Olympics Gold Medal

At Atlanta Olympics in 1996, Ge Fei and Gu Jun, women's doubles pair, won the first badminton Olympics gold for China.

The First Time to Sweep All Titles of World Badminton Championships

Considering that All England World Badminton Championships could not meet the increasing need of world badminton campaign, BWF decided to hold the first World Badminton Championships held in Malmo, Sweden in 1977. As a follow-up, the tournament would be held every three years. No team event would be involved at the championships as there were already Thomas Cupa and Uber Cup in place.

From May 17 to 24, 1987, the 5th Word Badminton Championship was held in Beijing, China for the first time with 226 players from 37 countries and regions participated. It was the highest level event with the largest number of countries and regions. In the event, the Chinese badminton team swept all 5 titles. Yang Yang took men's singles, Han Aiping women's singles, Li Yongbo and Tian Bingyi men's doubles, Lin Ying and Guan Weizhen women's doubles and Wang Pengren and Shi Fangjing mixed doubles. It was unprecedented in the history of World Badminton Championships with five titles all falling into the hands of the same Country.

Chen Fushou

Chen Fushou (1932-), badminton coach. He joined Indonesian national team in 1953 and in Chinese national team in 1954 after returning to the motherland. At the 6th World Youth Festival held in 1957, he finished first in men's singles, men's doubles and mixed doubles. In 1972, he assumed the coach of the national team and led the Chinese women team to place first at the 10th and 11th Uber Cup. In 1986, he was awarded Contribution Award by IBF.

▲ The Sweeping of All Three Cups

On May 16, 2005, China took the Sudirman Cup without losing a single point with three 5:0 in the team competitions and two 3:0 in the semi-final and the final. Thus China becomes the only country which has ever taken Sudirman Cup, Thomas Cup and Uber Cup in world history.

On May 15, 2005, the final of the Ninth Sudirman Cup was held in Beijing Capital Indoor Stadium. China won the championship for the fifth time and became a country winning the gold cups of the three major team competitions of the Sudirman Cup, Thomas Cup and Uber Cup.

Tang Xianhu

Tang Xianhu (1942-), badminton player and coach. He was the champion of the mixed doubles event at the 8th Asian Games in 1978 and men's singles and men's team events at the 2nd National Games in 1965 and at the 3rd National Games in 1975. In 1979, he discontinued his sports life and became a coach in late 1981 and the men's doubles coach of the Chinese badminton national team in July 2002.

Han Jian

Han Jian (1956-), man badminton player. He has techniques with focus on defense, assault while defending and the ability to do a protracted battle. He was renowned as typical "Niupitang" (a kind of candy that is very sticky). He was also very calm and many other established players failed to adjust to his techniques. With great flexibility and stamina, he could always calmly drag his opponent to a failure.

In 1979, Han Jian took the men's team title with his teammates at the first IBF World Cup and men's singles at the 2nd IBF International Championships. In 1981, he won at the first World Badminton Cup in men's singles event. In 1983 and 1984, he was the winner at World Badminton Cup in men's singles event. At the 4th IBF International Championships in June 1985, he defeated Robert Frost, then recognized king of world badminton, and became the first Chinese male to win men's singles world championships. In the same year, he defeated many famous players en route to the men's title at IBF Grand Prix Final.

Li Yongbo

Li Yongbo (1962-), man badminton player and coach. As an athlete, Li Yongbo was a leading of Chinese men's team to win three successive Thomas Cup tournaments from Jan.1978 to 1992. He also finished first at 1988 World Cup and 1987 and 1989 World Championships. From 1992 to now, he has been coach, deputy head coach and head coach of the national team. Under his leadership, the great achievements that have been made include: four Sudirman Cup titles (1995, 1997, 1999 and 2001), four Uber Cup titles (1998, 2000, 2002 and 2004), one Thomas Cup title (2004).

Tian Bingyi

Tian Bingyi (1963-), man badminton player and coach. He won the Thomas Cup in 1986. At the 5th World Badminton Championships in 1987, he took men's doubles together with Li Yongbo. At the Olympics Badminton Performance Contest held in Seoul in 1988, he finished first in men's doubles with Li Yongbo. In 1988 and 1990, he was a member of the Chinese men's team to take the Thomas Cup. After quitting as a , he served as a coach of the Chinese badminton team.

Tian Bingyi, the coach of the women's doubles badminton

Yang Yang

Yang Yang (1963-), man badminton player. He started badminton training at the age of 12 and was chosen into the national team in 1983. His techniques were characterized by flexible footsteps, multiple placements of shuttle and powerful jumping strike. In 1984, he attended the 13th Thomas Cup on behalf of the national team and won all five matches as the third men's singles . In 1987, he was the winner of successive world championships and international open tournaments. In 1990, he made great contribution to the winning of Thomas Cup. Therefore, he was crowned King of the Four Kings in world badminton.

After saying good bye to his athlete career, Yang Yang was engaged in men's singles coaching in Malaysia. In 1994, he quit the job and converted to business in 1994. He opened his sports products cooperation, badminton club and badminton school in Malaysia, Australia and Shenzhen. After leaving the court, his life was still badminton-related.

Li Lingwei

Li Lingwei (1964-), woman badminton player and coach. At 1983 World Championships, Li Lingwei got her first women's singles title. Afterwards, the multitude of her achievements consolidated her position as the best among women players. She had full skills and the ability to both attack and defense. Her strike and razer-sharp shot were then the best among women players.

For Chinese women singles players, her major advantage was her calmness. She had extraordinary tactics. Even though she might fall behind her competitors by a large margin, she could remain calm, change her tactics and defeat the competitors.

She took thirteen world titles altogether, three Uber Cup, six women's singles (two at world championships and four at world cup) and four women's doubles titles (one at world championships and three at world cup). In addition, she won two women's singles titls and one women's doubles title at All England and three women's singles titles and three women's doubles titles at grand prix.

Ye Zhaoying

Ye Zhaoying (1974-), woman badminton player. Her excellent techniques included rare razor-sharp shot, tough smashes, backcourt defense and flexible net plays. Her play was typically offensive. On September 1, 1998, she topped IBF world women singles rankings

She is a with the best track record among Chinese women. For many years, her top position in women singles has remained unchanged with standout world ranking. She has ideal physical condition with good intuitiveness and excellent offensive skills. At age 15, she was chosen into the national team. At 1992 Uber Cup, the 18-year-old Ye Zhaoying won at the fifth game 2:1 (the previous four games were all tied in 2:2) in the final with great strength, thus ensuring the fifth title of Uber Cup for the Chinese team.

She won in women's singles at 1995 and 1997 International Championships, at 1997 All England, at 1997 IBF International Grand Prix Final and 1997 Singapore Open. She was also the leading to claim mixed team title at 1995 and 1997 Sudirman Cup.

Ye Zhaoying won the bronze medal of the women's singles badminton at the 2000 Sydney Olympics.

Zhang Ning

Zhang Ning (1975-),woman badminton player. In 1994, she finished first at French Open in women's singles and second at Uber Cup. In 1996, she won in women's singles at Sweden Open, Asian Cup and World Cup. In the same year, she placed second at Uber Cup. In 1998, she took the first place in women's singles at Malaysia Open, Denmark Classics and the Grand Prix Final and finished second at Bangkok Asian Games in women's team event. In 2001, she finished first in women's singles at Singapore Open and Asian Championships. In 2003, she claimed the women's singles title at Sweden Open, Singapore Open, German Open and Hong Kong Open and World Championships.

Zhang Jun

Zhang Jun (1977-), man badminton player. In 1998, he finished first in men's doubles along with Zhang Wei at Switzerland Open. In 1996, he won at the 6th Sudirman Cup in men's team event. In 2000, he took the mixed doubles title along with Gao Ling at Sydney Olympics. In 2001, he took the men's doubles title at IBF World Superior Gand Prix. In the same year, he finished third in men's doubles with Zhang Wei and mixed doubles with Gao Ling at World Badminton Grand Prix. He also won at 2001 World Badminton Championships in mixed doubles event with Gao Ling. In 2002, he placed third at England Open in mixed doubles event along with Gao Ling.

Chen Hong

Chen Hong (1979-), man badminton player. In 1999, he finished first in men's singles at Sweden Open. In 2000, he took the men's singles title at Netherland Open. In 2001, he placed third at World Championships and Grand Prix Final. In 2002, he finished first in men's singles at England, Denmark and Singapore Open. In 2003, he took the second place at England Open and the first place at Singapore, Indonesia and Malaysia Open in men's singles. In 2004, he claimed a silver medal in men's singles at Korea Open. He took the men's singles title at 2004 Thomas Cup.

Gao Ling

Gao Ling (1979-), woman badminton player. In 2000, she finished first in mixed doubles at Thailand Open and first in mixed doubles along with Zhang Jun and third in women's doubles at Sydney Olympic Games. In 2001, she won the title in women's doubles and mixed doubles at England Open, Japan Open, Asian Championships and World Champions. She won at the 7th Sudirman Cup in women's team event in 2001. In 2002, she took the women's doubles title at South Korea, England, China and Indonesia Open. In 2003, she finished first in women's doubles and mixed doubles at Japan and England Open. She was also the winner of women's doubles event at World Championships, Indonesia, Hong Kong and China Open. In 2004, she finished first in women's doubles at Switzerland and England Open.

Huang Sui

Huang Sui (1981-), woman badminton player. In 1998, she finished second in women's doubles at World Championships, Sweden Open and England Open. In 1999, she won at the 6th Sudirman Cup in women's team and women's doubles events. In 2001, she finished first in women's team and women's doubles at the 7th Sudirman, England Open, Japan Open and Asian Championships. She was also the winner of women's doubles event at 2001 World Championships. In 2002, she finished first at South Korea, China, England and Indonesia Open in women's doubles event. In 2003, she claimed the same title at Japan, England, Indonesia, Hong Kong and China Open. In 2003, she won at World Championships in women's doubles and placed second at Singapore and Malaysia Open. In 2004, she claimed the women's doubles title at Switzerland and England Open.

On August 19, 2004, Zhang Ning titled the women's singles badmintion event at the Athens Olympics.

Gong Ruina

Gong Ruina (1981-), woman badminton player. In 1998, she finished first in women's singles and second in women's doubles along with Huang Sui at World Youth Championships. In 1999, she placed second in women's singles at South Korea, Malaysia, Thailand and China Open and first in Sweden Open. In 2000, she won the silver at Switzerland Open. In 2001, she took the second spot at Japan Open and the first spot at World Championships, England and Malaysia Open in women's singles. In 2002, she finished first in women's singles at England, South Korea, Denmark, China and Singapore Open and Pusan Asian Games. In 2003, she finished second in women's singles at World Championships, Hong Kong Open and Chinese Open and first at Denmark Open. In 2004, she took the women's singles title at Sweden and England Open and second at Japan Open.

♦ Chinese Badminton Association

China Badminton Association (CBA) was founded in 1957. Since the 1970s, it has kept frequent communications with Asia, Europe, America and Australia. In April 1977, CBA held the first Asia badminton coach training class. Entrusted by Asia Badminton Federation, it sponsored the third Asia Badminton Championships in Beijing in May, 1978. In June 1978, it became the host of the first World Cup and the first World Badminton Championships held in Hangzhou, Zhejiang Province.

CBA was affiliated to Asia badminton federation in 1974, to International Badminton Federation in 1981, and to IFBA in 1987. The major events under its auspices include: National Youth Championships, National Badminton Championships, National Adolescent (age 12-13) Badminton Tournament, National Adolescent (age 14-15) Badminton Tournament, National Youth and Adolescent Badminton Tournament and National Badminton Doubles Championship Contest.

Address: C No.3, Longtan Lu, Chongwen District, Beijing
Website: http://www.cba.org.cn

Xie Xingfang

Xie Xingfang (1981-), woman badminton player. She placed second at world rankings in April, 2006. She is very tall and flexible with long hands. With attrition war as her main technique, she takes great advantage of her height and strong will to grip her opponent. The movements are not graceful yet effective.

In 2000, she finished first at Asian Championships in women's singles. In 2002, she placed among top 4 in women's singles at China, Denmark, Singapore and Malaysia Open. In 2004, she won at Uber Cup, China Open, German Open, Denmark and India Open. In 2005, she claimed women's singles title at German and England Open and World Championships. She was also a leading of women's team to win 2005 Sudirman Cup. She was the winner at 2005 World Cup and 2006 England Open.

Xie Xingfang won champion at the 2006 England Open on January 22, 2006.

Lin Dan

Lin Dan (1983-),badminton player. In 2000, he finished first at Asian Youth Championships in men's team and men's singles events and placed first in team event and third in men's singles at World Youth Championships. In 2001, he claimed the men's singles title at Netherland Open and Germany Youth Open. In the same year, he finished first in team event and second in men's singles event at Asian Championships. He was also a silver medalist at 2001 Denmark open in men's singles. In 2002, he won at Korea Open in men's singles. In 2003, he finished second at Japan Open and first at Denmark Open, German Open, Hong Kong Open and China Open in men's singles. In 2004, he took the men's singles title at Sweden Open and England Open and won the Thomas Cup.

Cycling

China has the largest amount of bicycles but is not a power in the cycling event. Despite its dominant position in the quantity of bicycles worldwide, its cycling skills still lag far behind other countries.

In 1959, China built the first standard cycling track in Beijing. In August 1959, the first Chinese cycling track tournament was held to celebrate the establishment of the track.

At the 2nd National Games held in 1965, road and track races were listed as the main events. At men's 100km team event, Shanghai team finished first with 2:18:8.7. Zhang Lihua, a cycler from Beijing, set a national record in 1km track with 1:11.4, the first performance that was close to world level. Among the other events that top Asia include women's 1km track. There are some other events that are close to world level.

In 1978, China sent players to attend the Universiade, the 8th Asian Games and Asian Championships. In August 1978, Union Cycling Federation (UCI) accepted China as one member of World Amateur Cycling Federation. Since then, the Chinese cycling officially said hello to the world cycling community. In 1980, the first women cycling team was sent to attend World Women Cycling Championships held in France.

At the 11th Asian Games in 1990, Chinese cycling team swept all the titles of women's events. Zhou Meiling broke world record in 1km time trial event with 1:13.899, becoming the first Chinese to break world cycling record.

On July 15, 2006, the 5th Tour of Qinghai Lake International Cycling Race was launched.

The Track Record of the Chinese Cycling Team

The Women's 500m Time Trial Event has been strength of the Chinese cycling team and is the only event that Chinese cyclers could top the world. It has been a key event in which the Chinese team could get medals at Olympics and World Championships. In 2000, Jiang Cuihua claimed a bronze medal in the event at Sydney Olympic Games where it was listed as an official event. In 2002, Jiang Yonghua broke the world record in 500m Time Trial Event at World Cup Final. In 2004, Jiang finished second in the same event at Athens Olympic Games.

In 2006, the Chinese cycling team made new breakthrough at the 15th Asian Games. Among the 17 race and track events, they claimed 6 gold, 4 silver and 2 bronze medals in 11 events, topping the gold medal chart. They still stand out in women's short-distance track events.

Tour of China

In 1995, China held the first Tour of China. Although only two such events were sponsored, the event was a milestone in Chinese tour event. Thereafter, many other tours followed suit. At present, the brand-name events include: Tour of South China Sea, Tour of Qinghai Lake, Tour of Beijing, Tour of Hainan Island and Tour of Shanghai Chongming Island. In China, road race has a large room for development boosted by the increasing number of official events.

In recent years, Tour of Qinghai Lake (TDQL), attracts the participation of many professionals and becomes on of the most important cycling events in Asia. However, the five-year-old TDQL is still hard to compare with Tour De France which has been existed for over a hundred years. TDQL learns from Tour De France to expand its influence with the radiation effect of sports games and enhance the brand image of the event. With several years' efforts, it has risen to 2.3 HC from 2.5 HC as fastest growing cycling event around the world.

Professional Development of Cycling Event

At present, Chinese Cycling Association (CCA) has taken professional development as major means of achieve breakthrough in Chinese road race event. Initial achievements have been made.

In the Calendar New Year of 2005, Chinese Marco Polo Team was founded in Zhouhai. Since then, Chinese cycling has embarked on a road of professional development with cyclers involved in different forms. In March 2006, Giant's women professional team was born. It is also the first women cycling professional team in Asia.

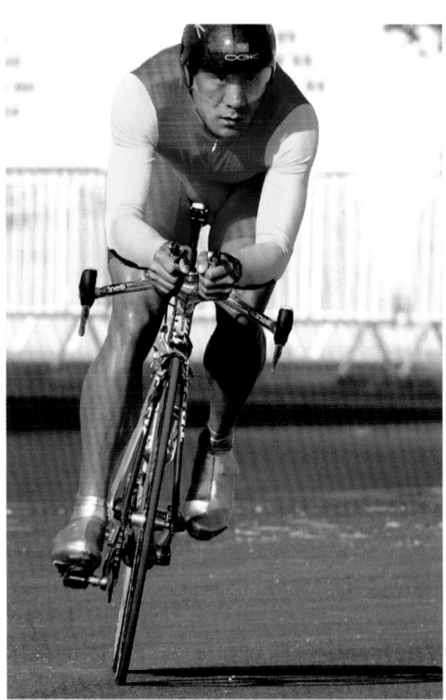

On December 5, 2006, Song Baoqing titled the road cycling men's time trial event at the 15th Doha Asian Games.

Among the 8 members of the team, 6 are from mainland China, one from Canada and one from HK China. After the founding of the team, they often go to Europe for training and tournaments at which they make great achievements.

Transfer of Foreign Transfer in Chinese Cycling Event

With an in-depth understanding of world cycling event, "Transfer of Foreign Transfer" has become a development trend for Chinese cycling event. From Tour de France, we can see that every professional team is composed of players from many different countries. In addition, the cycling event witnesses the highest skills in Europe where there are world's top teams and events. At present, however, China does not have the environment to produce professional tournaments and professional teams. Therefore, Chinese Cycling Association must build on external forces to truly improve itself.

Since 2004, CCA has expressed the intention to UCI which is also willing to offer such help and recommend some cycling teams to be registered in China. For example, Marco Polo Team from Netherland is registered in Asia and becomes Chinese Marco Polo team, an inter-continental team. Since 2005, 20 excellent Chinese players have joined European professional teams.

The First National Cycling Tournament

From October 2-7, 1953, national athletics, gymnastics and cycling meetings were held in Beijing. The participants included 44 from 10 units in 6 administrative zones-Inner Mongolia, Railway, Overseas Chinese from Myanmar and PLA. In the athletics field, 24 men took part in 1500m, 5000m and 10,000m events and 20 women in 1,500m, 3,000m and 5,000m events.

The First Asian Cycling Champion

From December 4-11, 1983, the 11th Asian Cycling Championship was held in Philippines 149 players from 10 countries and regions participated. The Chinese men's road team consisting of Liu Fu, Han Shuxiang, Lifei and Zhang Zhonglu finished first in 100km Men's Time Trial Event.

The First Time to Break Asian Cycling Record

At the 11th Asian Cycling Championships held in December 1983, Lu Yue, a female Chinese athlete, finished first in 1,000m Women's Time Trial Event and 3,000m Women's Individual Pursuit and broke the Asian records of these two events respectively with 1:18.68 and 4:16.57. It is also the first time for Chinese cyclers to break Asian records.

The Best Track Record of Mountain Bike (2006)

The women's cross-country event in the 23 and below category was held at 2006 UCI Mountain Bike and Trials World Championships held in Rotorua, New Zealand. Ren Cheng Yuan and Liu Ying, two Chinese young players and also the first time participants of World Championships, finished first and second with 1:31:17 and 1:32:56 respectively after battling established names. This is also the best track record since mountain bike started as an event in China a decade ago.

Jiang Yonghua

Jiang Yonghua won the silver medal of the women's cycling track 500m time trial at the Athens Olympics.

Jiang Yonghua (1973-), woman cyclist. In 2002, she finished first in Women's 500m Time Trial Event at UCI Track Cycling World Cup Final and first in Women's 500m Time Trial Event at Asian Games. In 2003, she placed fifth in Women's 500m Time Trial Event at UCI Track Cycling World Cup. In 2004, she took the second place in the same event at UCI Track World Championships.

In 2001, she set national and Asian record in Women's 500m Time Trial Event at the 9th National Games. In 2002, she set a world record of 34.000 in the same event at UCI Track Cycling World Cup.

Ma Yanping

Ma Yanping (1977-), woman cyclist. She won in Women's Cross-Country at 1998 Bangkok Asian Games, 1999 Mountain Bike Asian Championships, 2002 Pusan Asian Games and 2003 Mountain Bike Asian Championships.

Li Meifang

Li Meifang (1978-),woman cyclist. In 2001, she finished first in Women's 120km Event at UCIB World Championships held in Qingdao. In 2002, she took the title of Women's 24km Road Time Trial at Pusan Asian Games and Asian Championships. In 2003, she finished first at Asian Cycling Championships held in South Korea in Women's 24km Road Time Trail Event, Women's 3km Track Individual and Mass Pursuit events. In 2004, she placed first at Asian Cycling Championships in Women's Time Trial Event and Women's 3km Individual Pursuit and fifth at UCI World Championships in Women's 25km Points Race.

♦ Chinese Cycling Association

Chinese Cycling Association was founded in 1953 and headquartered in Beijing. In 1954, UCI recognized China's legitimate seat. CCA was affiliated to Asian Cycling Association in 1962. It held the first Qingzang Plateau World Road Cycling Tournament in 2000. Currently the events under its auspieces include: CCA Cup, Mountain Bike Sub-station Tournament, National Road Championships, National Track Championships and National Youth Cycling Championships.

Address:No.15 laoshan Rd West, Shijingshan District, Beijing
Website: http://www.chncycling.com

Football

In 1954, football teams were gradually established in some provinces and professional football training was started ever since. Two teams of excellent youth footballers were sent by the Chinese government to Spain for further training. In January 1955, Chinese Football Association (CFA) was founded. National League-Division 1 Group A and League-Division 1 Group B have been held since 1956. Upgrade and degrade method was adopted along with the system for graded athletes and referees. In addition, CFA holds National Football Championships and National Youth Championships.

In 1977, CFA held the World Football Invitational Tournament for the first time in Chinese football history. Later the event was renamed as China Great Wall Cup World Football Championships. In 1979, FIFA resumed the legitimate seat for CFA.

In 1983, China successfully held Guangzhou World Women's Football Invitational. The tournament did not only Propel the evolution of Chinese Women's football event but also laid

Historical Results at Asian Cup

Asian Cup	Time	Venue	Champion	China's ranking
6th Asian Cup	1976	Iran	Iran	3rd place
7th Asian Cup	1980	Kuwait	Kuwait	Eliminated in group games
8th Asian Cup	1984	Singapore	Saudi Arabia	2nd place
9th Asian Cup	1988	Qatar	Saudi Arabia	4th place
10th Asian Cup	1992	Japan	Japan	3rd place
11th Asian Cup	1996	United Arab Emirates	Saudi Arabia	5th place
12th Asian Cup	2000	Lebanon	Japan	4th place
13th Asian Cup	2004	China	Japan	2nd place
14th Asian Cup	2007	Indonesia, Thailand, Malaysia, Vietnam	Iraq	5th place

the foundation for the First Women's Football World Cup held in Guangzhou in November 1991, contributing to the world women's football. Currently, Chinese football is still a mediocre performer worldwide and has an elusive record even in Asia.

By December 2006, FIFA ranking is 84 for Chinese men's football team and 9 for Chinese women's football team.

The First National Football Tournament

From December 1-9, 1951, National Football Tournament was held in Tianjin, the first time that China held national football tournament. The 8 teams that participated were from Northeast, Eastern China, Northern China, Mid-South, Northwest, Southwest, PLA and Railway. As a result, the Northeast Team finished first.

The Earliest Football Organization

The earliest football organization in China was the South China Football Club founded in Hong Kong, 1908.

In 1904, a Chinese football team was organized voluntarily by several schools in Hong Kong. In 1908, it changed its name to the South China Football Club with Liu Zhubo from Yucai Bookstore as the first chairman and only 40 members. In 1909, the club was removed to Wanzai College where Yang Xi, the head of the College was crowned the chairman. As the club was better equipped, the club was renamed South China Athletic Association in 1916 and became a household name ever since.

South China football team attended the first 7 Far East Games on behalf of China and claimed 6 crowns with the exception of the first event. With many years of battle, the team produced a great number of world-renowned players such as Mo Qing, Tang Fuxiang, Guo Baogeng, Liang Yutang and Feng Ping. Of them, Li Huitang stood out and was crowned "King of Asia".

▲ Major Events of Chinese Football

In 1931, CFA became a member of FIFA.

In 1954, CFA joined AFC as one of its founders

In 1976, Chinese men's football team finished 4th at Asian Cup.

In 1982, Chinese men's football team advanced to the continental elimination match in the preliminary competition of the FIFA World Cup.

In 1984, Chinese men's football team finished second at Asian Cup.

In 1996, Chinese women's football team placed second at Atlanta Olympic Games.

In 1999, Chinese women's football team finished second at Women's World Cup.

In 2002, Chinese men's football team advanced to the final competition of the FIFA World Cup.

In 2004, Chinese men's football team took the second place at CFA-sponsored Asian Cup.

The First Time to Be Qualified for FIFA World Cup in 2001

Football as the world's No.1 game is particularly favored by Chinese people. Top Asian and Challenge the World has been the undying dream for the Chinese. Coached by Bora Milutinovic from Yugoslavia, Chinese men's football team gained the ticket to 2002 FIFA World Cup. Along with Beijing's successful bidding of 2008 Olympic Games and China's accession to WTO, it became the most exciting news of the year in China.

Women's Football

In February 1981, Middle School Girl's Football Invitational Tournament was first held in Beijing. In May 1981, the first Women's Football Tournament was held in Guangdong Province and another invitational tournament attracting six teams from five provinces was held in Henan. At the end of 1982, the State Physical Culture and Sports Commission listed women's football as part of national competition plan and held the First National Women's Championships, an annual event held since 1983. In 1985, women's football was listed as an official event at the 6th National Games with its large population base and high potentiality. In 1989, National Youth Women's Championship was added to promote the further development of women's football among young people.

Chinese women's football started its communication with the outside world from 1983. From November 8-27, 1983, the first World Women's Invitational Tournament was held in Guangzhou for the first time in Chinese history, thus unveiling the communication with other countries. In 1984, the tournament was held in Xi'an. In July 1986, Chinese women's team made its first debut in Europe. During its presence at two international invitationals held in Venice and Toronto, it claimed the third and the first spot respectively. In December 1986, Chinese women's football team won the first Asian Women's Championships held in Hong Kong, the first continental event the team has ever attended.

The women's team was credited as Asian excellent team consecutively in 1995, 1996 and 1997.

The First National Women's Invitational Tournament

Sponsored by Sports Press, People's Sports Publishing House, New Sports magazine, China Sports magazine and editorial department of Football World magazine, National Women's Invitational Tournament was held in Beijing from August 8-14, 1982. The participants were ten teams from Shanghai, Shaanxi, Yunnan, Hebei, Beijing, Jilin, Liaoning, Shanxi, Shandong and Tianjin. Shaanxi team won. It was a good start in the history of Chinese women's football.

The Track Record of Women's Football

With the joint efforts of Asian Sports Federation, China Organizing Committee and Asian Football Confederation and approved by Asian Olympics executive committee, women's football was listed as an official event of Asian Games.

In 1991, the first World Women's Championship was held in China, laying the first cornerstone for FIFA women's football. Chinese team placed 5th at the championships and 4th at the second FIFA Women's World Cup in 1995. At the 17th Universiade 1993, women's football was list as an event for the first time. Chinese team placed first. With the efforts of FIFA and Atlanta Olympic Organizing Committee, women's football was approved as an official event of Olympic Games at the 101st Plenary Meeting of IOC held in Morocco on September 20, 1993. It was a sign that football was more extended with more women going for the game and women's football could be better promoted worldwide. At the 26th Olympic Games in July 1996, Chinese women's football team finished second at the newly-added event. The women's team was the seven times winner of Asian Women's Championships, four times participant of FIFA Women's World Cup on behalf of Asia and three times participant of Olympic Games.

IMG Promotes the Reform of Chinese Football

In the process of Chinese football reform, IMG plays an important role. As a follow-up to the successful launching of professional league in China, IMG succeeded in packaging another important event-CFA (Chinese Football Association) Cup National Football Championships. Additionally, it also plays an important part in many other events. With its capital and experience, IMB is of extreme importance to the marketization of China's sports.

Chinese Football Association Premier League (Group A)

On April 17, 1994, Chinese football embarked on the road of professionalization. On this day, the first round of Marlboro Cup National Football Premier League (Group A) after being re-packaged was held in Chengdu. Altogether 150,000 audiences in 6 venues watched the first round with Chengdu and Yanjie topping other places by attracting over 40,000 audiences each. It symbolized that Chinese football was beginning to be professional.

In a span of 10 years between 1994 and 2004, professional league became the No.1 sports in China in terms of size and influence. During ten years, the professional league was a great success in attracting audience and creating prevalence of football in local areas and media. During this period, a total number of 127 clubs joined the league with the number of leagues totaling 3042 and the number of audience 46.95 million. A competition system was basically established on all levels.

On July 4, 2004, the Chinese women's football team prepared for the Olympics Games at Hebei Xianghe National Football Training Base.

▲ Chinese Fans

Before the professional league with home and visiting matches was adopted, the turnout rate for domestic football tournaments was below 30 percent. Since the league was put in place in 1994, however, the audience reached 2.176 million or 20,000 for each match and 60 percent for turnout rate. In 1995, Sichuan football team went for the King's Cup held in Philippine on behalf of China. 108 fans from Sichuan Province went on a charter plane to cheer for the team, the first time Chinese fans went aboard for cheering. In the same year, Premier League-Group A witnessed more intense competitions. The number of audience soared to 3.14 million, 1 million more than that of 1994. It was also the first time that the game was broadcast live to over 50 countries and regions. In 1996, the number of audience made another breakthrough, climbing to 3.2085 million with 24,300 for each match, a level that was close to that of the countries where football was very strong.

As football caught on, it found its way into almost every corner of the country. Premier league-Group A grabbed the attention of all sides. Watching and talking about football became a fashion. Fan associations mushroomed in the major venues of the league such as Shenyang, Chengdu, Beijing and Dalian. Most of these associations played a positive role in enlivening the games, serving as a bridge between social communities and football community, preventing field violence, developing football market and reaching out to masses.

The Rules for Chinese Super League

Chinese Super League adopts the double round rating under which each club plays each of the other club twice, as home and guest team respectfully. One club has to play 28 games altogether. It is ruled that 3 points go to the club which win the game within 90 minutes with the losing party gaining nothing and 1 point goes to each of the clubs when they are at tie.

The First Bunch of Footballs to Join Foreign Teams

On March 2, 1988, Liu Haiguang and Jia Xiuquan joined the football team of Guerrilla Sports Club in light of the cooperation agreement between China and Yugoslavia. They were the first two players to become members of foreign clubs. It was also the first time the club took in foreigns.

The First FIFA Women's of the Year

Sun Qingmei, the No.8 of Chinese women's football team, shot in three goals with her strong physique, courage and dexterous skills at the first FIFA World Women's Championships held in 1988 and was crowned FIFA Women's of the Year.

In world's football history, there was only FIFA of the Year. Of the first two women to gain the honor, one was the No.14 in Norway's women team and the other was Sun Qingmei. She was also the first Chinese woman to receive this honor.

Li Huitang

Li Huitang (1905-1979) was a star in early Chinese football games. In 1920s and 1930s, he was claimed Football King of Asia. He was the 3 times participant of national Games, 4 times of Far East Games and two times of Olympic Games. He was seen on the field pitch of Asia, Australia and Europe. He was credited by the English as Oriental Football King and nicknamed Oriental Standard Footballer by Japanese.

In 1923, the 18-year-old made an expedition to Australia as a member of South China Football Team. In a match with a strong Australian team called New South Wales, Li stood out and shot in three goals. As a result, he was crowned General with Accurate Shooting and won a gold medal of Australia. In 1947, he became a coach. Since 1954, he had been General Secretary of Asian Football Confederation for 12 years. In 1965, he was the only Asian in FIFA and the first Chinese to claim the highest honor in the world's football. His whole life was closely linked with football. He died in Hong Kong on July 4, 1979 at age 74.

Li Fenglou

Li Fenglou (1911-1988), the first football coach for Chinese national team.

Li Fenglou loved sports and football ever since he was a child. When he was a young man, he joined the famous football teams in northern China such as Beihua, Beining and Zixing where he participated in domestic and international competitions and enjoyed good reputation. From 1934 when he graduated from Furen University to 1952, he had been engaged in physical education in school. In 1952, national football team was established and he was entrusted the job of coaching. In 1955, he left national team and served as vice president and later president of Chinese Football Association. He was also involved in designing the judging, and referee rules for Chinese football and co-wrote the first Judging Laws of Football Competitions. As the president of Chinese Football Association, he became the chief editor of Football World magazine after its initiation.

Xu Fang

Xu Fang (1947-1996), was the predecessor of Chinese Premier League-Group A, who died an untimely death. In the football community, Xu Fang is a respectable name, although he could not witness the further professional development of Chinese football himself. As the vice president of Chinese Football Association who was mainly responsible for the development and foreign affairs, he succeeded in raising US$1.2 million for the association with his rich experience in international communication and negotiation in 1993. The funding saved the money-hungry Chinese football reform. It was said that the reform of professional football could be delayed indefinitely if it were not for this sum of money. In terms of foreign affairs, his work was recognized by Asian countries. He was elected the first vice president of Asian Football Association, a post ensuring that the voice of Chinese football could be heard in Asia. Regretfully, he died of heart attack due to overtiredness at age 49, a great loss for Chinese football.

Fan Zhiyi

Fan Zhiyi (1969-), football player. He was transferred to England Crystal Palace football club on September15, 1998.

He was twice winner of Best of Asian Games in 1994. In 1995, he claimed the title of Chinese Footballer of the Year, Golden Shoe Award and the membership of Asian Star Team by Asian Football Confederation. He was also the champion in Chinese Super League, the silver medalist of CFA Cup and Best of the Year. In 1996, he was appointed captain of the national team, the captain of Asian First Eleven. He was the only guard who was crowned the best of the pitch in Asian Football Championships, China's Football of the Year, Silver Shoe Award, the runner-up in Chinese League and Best of the Year. In 1997, he was the runner-up in Chinese Super League, the captain of Asian All-star, Best of the pitch. In September 1998, he joined Crystal Palace and became the first Chinese to play for English professional football team. In the Washington Cup, the Crystal Palace tied Brighton in a visiting match with him on the pitch. He scored his first goal for the team at home in Selhurst Park.

Sun Wen won both the Golden Boot and the Golden Ball of the Women's World Cup due to her excellent performance at the 1999 Women's World Cup. In the picture, Sun attended the awarding ceremony of the FIFA Best Player.

▲ Golden Ball Award and Golden Boot Award of China

Golden Ball Award and Golden Boot Award were designed by Sports Magazine to improve the athletic skills of Chinese football. The first Golden Ball Award or China's best football award was granted to Jia Xiuquan. The Golden Boot Award or China's best football shooter was given to Huang Dexing, the striker of Nanjing Football Team, who scored 27 goals at official games in 1984.

The two awards were manufactured and bequeathed by Dalian Glass Product Manufacturing Company. They were the world's most precious manufacturing product made from high lead crystal glass and colored with rare earth, making it golden color, each 40cm high and 4kilos heavy. One was shaped like a ball and the other boot.

Sun Wen

Sun Wen (1973-) is the spiritual symbol of Chinese women's football team renowned as Strong Rose. She was the former captain of Chinese women's team. She is 1.63m, forward and the No.9 in the national team.

In October 1995, she won at the 10th Asian Women's Football Championships held in Kuala Lumpur, Malaysia, the fifth win of the event for Chinese women's team. In 1996, she was the runner-up at the 26th Olympic Games held in Atlanta, USA. In December 1998, she won at the 13th Asian Games Football Event. In June 1999, she was the runner-up of the 3rd FIFA Women's World Cup.

She won Chinese Football Golden Boot in 1994 and the Bronze Boot at the 2nd FIFA Women's World Cup in 1995. From June-July 1999, she was voted the Best by FIFA at the 3rd FIFA Women's World Cup held in USA where she also won both the Golden Boot and the Golden Ball. In July 1999, she was chosen into Team of All-star at the 3rd FIFA Women's World Cup. In August 1999, she was voted Asian Best in July. In January 2000, she won the Golden Boot and the Golden Ball at 1999 FIFA Women's World Cup held in Brussels, Belgium.

Yang Chen

Yang Chen (1974-), football player. He is now plays in Shenzhen Jianlibao team. He was the captain of 1996 Chinese National Olympic Football Team and played in Beijing Guoan.

In 1998/99 season, he was loaned to Frankfurt where he shot in 8 balls in 23 competitions. On Sept.8, 1998, he became the first Chinese to kick in a goal at the third round of Bundesliga. In 2002/03 season, he was transferred to FC St. Pauli. In 2003, he came back and joined Shenzhen Jianlibao football club.

Yang Chen in the sixth round competition of the Chinese Football Association Super League

On April 9, 2007, the Manchester City, as a visiting team beat the Fulham 3:1 in the 33rd round of the England Football Super League.

Li Tie

Li Tie (1977-), football player. He is now serving the Chengdu Blades Football Club. He was crowned China's Football of the Year in 2001.

He started professional training with Zhang Yin in 1985 and went to study in Brazil when he was chosen as member of Chinese Jianlibao Youth Team. In January 1997, he was chosen into the national football team and attended FIFA U-20 World Championships on behalf of China Jianlibao Team. He was voted China's Football of the Year in December 2001 and joined Everton in the summer of 2002.

♦ Chinese Football Association

Chinese Football Association was founded in January 1955 and headquartered in Beijing. In 1952, it became a member of AFC where Chen Chengda, Xu Fang and Zhang Jilong served as vice president. Affiliated to FIFA in 1931, it severed its relations with the organization in 1950s in an effort to crush the Two China Conspiracy. In October 1979, FIFA Executive Committee decided to give CFA its legitimate seat. The association published Football World magazine in 1980 and issued Chinese Football newspaper in 1994. It held an annual campaign to grant awards such as Best Team, Best Coach, Golden Ball, Golden Whistle and Golden Boot to recognize the achievements made in football event. The annual events held under its auspices include: National Football Club Championships, Women's Youth National Championships, National Youth Elite Grand Prix, CFA U-17 National Championships, CFA U-19 National Championships, CFA U-21 National Olympic Youth Tournament.National Second Division for men's football teams, Male Youth National League, Women's Youth National League, Women's National League, CFA Cup, Chinese Premier League-Group A and Chinese League 2.

Address: C-3 Longtan Lu, Chongwen District, Beijing
Website: http://www.fa.org.cn

Sun Jihai

Sun Jihai (1977-), football player. He is now serving Sheffield United, an England team.

He received training in a district-wide amateur sports school in 1984 and joined Wanda Football Team in early 1996 and was chosen into the national team in the same year. In February 1998, he was chosen into the best team of Chinese football and joined Crystal Palace of the English First Division in August and was credited as the Asian Footballer of the Year in July. In early 2002, he was transferred to Man City for £350,000.

Ma Xiaoxu

Ma Xiaoxu (1988-), is an outstanding representative of excellent women's footballers mushrooming worldwide in recent years. With the comprehensive skills and the superb physical counteraction ability, she distinguishes herself from traditional Chinese women footballers. Her male-style in much resemblance with that of Rooney, a football icon in England, gives her an epithet Female Rooney in the football community.

2006 is a fruitful year for her. On behalf of Chinese women's football team and Chinese women's youth team, she claimed two gold medals and one silver medal at AFC Women's Asian Cup, Asian Women's Youth Cup and Women's Youth World Championships. Meanwhile, she won the Golden Ball and Golden Boot in these three events. Among the AFC awards in 2006, she was voted Asian Young Footballer of the Year and broke the monopoly held by male footballers in the category of AFC Best Youth, becoming the first woman to receive such an honor. In the meantime, she wrote a legend with her flair in Asian football community.

Events in Olympic Winter Games

In 1980, Chinese sports delegation made its debut at Lake Placid Olympic Winter Games, USA, with 28 athletes participated, but no one gained a medal. It was not until 1992 when Ye Qiaobo and Li Yan took 3 gold in speed skating and short track speed skating at Albertville, France that the spell of no medal was broken. At Salt Lake City 2002, Yang Yang claimed two titles, the first time Chinese players have ever got a gold medal in Olympic Winter Games. Chinese players have participated in 8 Olympic Winter Games over 26 years. When the fire of the 26th Olympic Winter Games extinguished in Torino, Italy, Chinese players was a guaranteed member of the Olympic Winter Games Gold Medal Club.

Ice Hockey

Ice hockey has had a history of over 60 years in China. The first ice hockey event was held at the first North China Ice Sports Performance Meeting held in Beijing, 1935. In 1953, the first Ice Sports Meeting was held in Harbin where five teams were participated. Afterwards, ice hockey teams of all forms were founded one after another in provinces and cities in East and North China. Since 1955, National Ice Hockey Tournament was held annually. From 1956 and onwards, Chinese ice hockey team began their journey at international tournaments. At the C Group of World Ice Hockey Championships held in Beijing 1981, the Chinese team finished second and rose to B group. The Chinese team got a gold medal at the first Asian Winter Games held in Japan, 1986. Limited by the condition of season and training, Chinese skills are still mediocre. Comparatively speaking, however, women gain an upper hand of men. The Chinese women's ice hockey team was six times participant of World Championships and twice participant of Olympic Winter Games. Its best track record was No.4 at World Championships.

♦ Chinese Ice Hockey Association

Chinese Ice Hockey Association was founded and affiliated to International Ice Hockey Federation in 1957. Since 1986, the events held under its auspices include: National Ice Hockey League Division 1, National Ice Hockey Championships, National Ice Hockey League, National Women Ice Hockey Championships, National Youth Ice Hockey Championships, Goup A of National Ice Hockey League and Group B of National Ice Hockey League.

Address: No.56, South Street, Zhongguancun, Haidian District, Beijing
Website: http://icehockey.sport.org.cn

Skating

In the late 1890s, Skating was introduced to China from Europe. Speed skating gradually caught on among civilians in Northern China. The first skating tournament was held in Beijing 1935. An increasing number of youth began to be involved since then. The masses ice sports gained momentum in cities such as Harbin, Changchun, Qiqihar and Jilin. In February 1953, the first National Ice Games was held in Harbin where a bunch of skating records were set. In 1959, Yang Jucheng finished second in 500m with 42.4 (a tie with the first) at the 53rd World Men's Speed Skating Championships. In 1961, Liu Fengrong finished fourth in all-round event at World Women's Speed Skating Championships. At World Men's and Women's Championships, Wang Jinyu and Luo Zhihuan both broke world men's all-round record. Luo Zhihuan finished first in 1500m with 2:09.2, setting a record for the Championships. In 1980, Chinese speed skating team participated in the 13th Olympic Winter Games held in Lake Placid, USA.

At present, places where speed skating was very popular include: Heilongjiang, Jilin, PLA, Inner Mongolia, Liaoning and Xinjiang.

On February 15, 2006, the Torino Winter Olympics entered the fifth day. Wang Meng (in the middle) won the gold medal with 44.345 seconds in the women's 500-meter short track skating.

Speed Skating

Chinese speed skating event had a glorious past. Early in 1963, Luo Zhihuan took the title of men's 1500m at the World Speed Skating Championships held in Karuizawa Nagano, Japan. Wang Xiuli, (born in 1963), grabbed the lead in women's 1500m at the World Women's Speed Skating Championships held in Ottawa, Canada, the first Chinese woman champion in speed skating.

In 1992, Ye Qiaobo took two silver medals at the 11th Olympic Winter Games held in France, breaking the spell of no medal for China at the event. Later, she claimed all-round and a single event's title at World Short Track Speed Skating Championships. Women's middle and short distance event have been the strength of Chinese speeding skating and are currently above world's average level. Wang Manli and Wang Beixing are excellent players falling into this category. Women's long distance is above world's average. Men's events fall far behind world's level. At Torino 2006, Wang Manli and Ren Hui finished second and third.

National speed skating tournaments include: National Ice Games, National Excellent players Test Competition, Level-1 Athlete Speed Skating Tournament, National Speed Skating Tournament, National Speed Skating Championship Tournament, National Youth Tournament and National Short Track Speed Skating Tournament.

The First Participation in Speed Skating World Championships-Ladies

The 15th Speed Skating World Championships-Ladies was held in Imatra, Finland on February 9, 1957. The participants were 25 skaters from 8 countries, Canada, China, Czech, Finland, Germany Democratic Republic, Poland, Sweden and Soviet Union. As a participant for the first time, China sent out three skaters. The best track record was from 1000m speed skating, placing 18th.

The First Speed Skating World Champion

From February 21-24, 1963, Chinese men's and women's speed skating teams participated in the 57th Speed Skating World Championships-Ladies & Men held in Karuizawa, Nagono, Japan. Among the 84 skaters from 18 countries,

Luo Zhihuan finished first in men's 1500m with 2:9.2, the first champion Chinese speed skaters have got since they participated World Championships in 1957.

The First Best World Performance

From February 1-8, 1962, the Chinese men's and women's speed skating teams visited Soviet Union. They had a competition against Soviet Union Skating Team in Irkutsk on February 3-4. During the event, Wang Jinyu from China tied the world's best in men's all-round at a point of 185.620 at plain ice stadium. It was also the first time that Chinese speed skater has ever created men's all-round best world score.

The First to Be Punished Due to Doping

At Calgary Olympic Winter Games in 1988, the urine sample of Chinese speed skater Wang Xiuli was tested positive. She was disqualified and became the first Chinese whose Olympic score was cancelled due to doping in Chinese sports history.

Prior to the event, Wang Xiuli took some medicines given by the team doctor to prevent cold as she could not adapt herself to the local weather. It turned out that those medicines contained Methylstanazolum tested in her urine sample. Therefore she was proved to take stimulin. As a result, she had to face the cancellation of her bronze medal of 1500m with tears in her eyes. Subsequent investigation proved that it was an accident. The traditional Chinese medicine Huarongweixiong contained performance enhancer element. As it happened at a time when the management and use of medicine was still inferior in China, neither the nor the coach should be accountable. Later, Wang Xiuli, after being suspended for 15 months, returned to Calgary and took the title of women's 1500m speed skating at World Championships, thus clearing the stigma attached to her.

Short Track Speed Skating

Short Track Speed Skating was introduced to China in 1981 and listed as an official event of Olympics in 1992.

At Calgary Olympic Winter Games in 1988, Short Track Speed Skating became part of performance events. Li Yan took the title of 1000m and broke world records of 1000m and 1500m. In 1995, Chinese team claimed the title of Women's 3000m Relay at World Championships. In 1996, Li Jiajun finished first in 1000m at World Championships, claiming the first men's title in the event. In 1997, Yang Yang became the first all-round champion of China at World Championships held in Nagano, Japan. In a span of 6 years from 1997 to 2002, she went on a winning streak on the all-round event. At the 19th Olympic Winter Games in Salt Lake City in 2002, Yang Yang finished first in 500m and 1000m, saying goodbye to the no gold history of China at Olympic Winter Games.

After over 20 years efforts, Chinese speed skating team is now home to 23 excellent players at Olympic Winter Games, World Championships and World Cup rankings who have broken world records 20 times and claimed 103 world titles. At Olympic Winter Games, they have captured 2 gold, 9 silver and 4 bronze.

The First World Champion of Short Track Speed Skating

At World Short Track Speed Skating Championships held in Australia, 1991, Chinese Zhang Yanmei finished first in 500m with 47.08, taking the first gold among Chinese at world's official tournaments.

Wang Jinyu

Wang Jinyu (1939-) started skating at age 15 and became a speed skater of Harbin city in 1958. In the same year, he set 1500m, 5000m and 10,000m national records and won the all-round title at national tournaments. On behalf of China, he participated in 6-country speed skating tournament held in Aima Ata, Soviet Union. He had sound basic training and strong physique with high explosive force in leg muscles, fast speed and stamina in the latter part of the track. He was also blessed with big slide, mature techniques and balanced track record in 4 indices. In 1962, he set a 5000m plain ice stadium world record in Irkutsk, Soviet Union, and was granted Best by ISU. In 1963, Chinese players broke men's and women's speed skating all-round world records at World Championships held in Karui Zawa, Japan.

Luo Zhihuan

Luo Zhihuan (1940-) started skating at age 13 and went to Qiqihar Amateur Sports School in 1957. In 1959, he finished first in 5000m and 10,000m at National Games. He trained with his brain and developed a unique and fabulous curve technique. At the 57th World Speed Skating Championships-Men's, 1963, he set a new 1500m World Championships record in 2:09.2, becoming the first speed skating champion in China.

In 1985, he was appointed coach of the women's national team.

Wang Xiuli

Wang Xiuli (1964-), woman skater. In 1983, she finished first in 1,000m speed skating and third in allround at the 5th National Winter Games. At China-Japan Dual Meet, she broke 3,000m national record and created her personal best in 5,000m.

In February 1990, Wang Xiuli finished first in 1,500m at World Speed Skating Championships-Ladies, held in Calgary, Canada, becoming the first women's speed skating champion in China.

Ye Qiaobo

Ye Qiaobo (1964-), woman skater. She finished first in 500m, 1,000m and all-round with 42.34, 22.21 and 163.185 points respectively at World Short Track Speed Skating Championships in 1991. In 1992, she placed second in 500m and 1,000m with 40.51 and 1:21.92 at the 16th Olympic Winter

National Record of Speed Skating

Event	Record	Record holder	Tournament	Date	Place
Men					
500m	34.59	Yu Fengtong	World Championships Sprint Distance	January 2005	Salt Lake City
1000m	1:09.09	Yu Fengtong	World Championships Sprint Distance	January 2005	Salt Lake City
1500m	1:47.13	Gao Xuefeng	Essent ISU World Cup Speed Skating	November 2005	Salt Lake City
5000m	6:37.27	Gao Xuefeng	Essent ISU World Cup Speed Skating	November 2005	Salt Lake City
10000m	13:55.75	Gao Xuefeng	Essent ISU World Cup Speed Skating	November 2004	Heerenveen (NED)
Short Track All-round	139.850	Yu Fengtong	World Championships Sprint Distance	January 2005	Salt Lake City
All-round	159.179	Gao Xuefeng	National Championship Tournament and Preliminary for the tenth National Games	December 2004	Harbin
Women					
500m	37.28	Wang Manli	Essent ISU World Cup Speed Skating	November 2005	Salt Lake City
1000m	1:14.62	Wang Beixing	Essent ISU World Cup Speed Skating	November 2005	Salt Lake City
1500m	1:55.71	Wang Fei	Essent ISU World Cup Speed Skating	November 2005	Salt Lake City
3000m	4:03.86	Wang Fei	Essent ISU World Cup Speed Skating	November 2005	Salt Lake City
5000m	7:08.63	Wang Fei	Essent ISU World Cup Speed Skating	December 2005	Heerenveen
Short Track All-round	151.060	Wang Beixing	World Championships Sprint Distance	January 2005	Salt Lake City
All-round	166.884	Wang Fei	National Championship Tournament	January 14-15, 2006	Harbin

On October 22, 2006, Ye Qiaobo (the second on the left) in the torch passing activity of the 15th Doha Asian Games in Beijing

Games. In the same year, she took the title of 500m with 40.09 at World Speed Skating Championships, Ladies and the titles of 1000m, 1000m and all-round with 1:23.79, 1:25.16 and 167.260 points at World Short Track Speed Skating Championships-Ladies. In 1993, she won in 500m with 40.41 at World Speed Skating Championships-Ladies and in two 500m champion and all-round with 40.23. 40.26 and 165.925 points at World Short Track Speed Skating Championships-Ladies.

In 1990, she was awarded with the honor of World-class Master Athlete.

Zhao Hongbo

Zhao Hongbo (1973-), pair figure skater.

In pair figure skating, Zhao Hongbo finished fifth at Nagano Olympic Winter Games in 1998, second at 1999 World Championships, second at 2000 World Championships, first at 2000 World Figue Skating Grand Prix final, third at 2001 World Championships, third at 2002 Olympic Winter Games, first at 2002 World Championships, first at 2003 World Championships and first at 2004 World Championships. The record is written as follows: His maximum score is 196.08 points with 68.76 for short program and 130.08 for free skating.

Li Jiajun

Li Jiajun (1975-) man skater. He finished first in ISU World Cup held in Netherland in 1996 as the first time to attend international tournament and took other medals in international ice rink. In 1999, he placed first in 500m and third in 1,500m at Sophie World Championships, becoming the first Chinese man to win in short track speed skating all-round. In 2001, he won in 500m and 1,000m at ISU World Cup held in South Korea and took the all-round title the second time. At Nagano 1998, Li Jiajun captured a silver medal, becoming the first Chinese man to win a medal at Olympic Winter Games. Unfortunately, he missed his touch with the gold medal after losing to Kim Dong-sung, an outstanding skater in South Korea, by a margin of 0.053 seconds. In addition, he finished third in 5000m relay with his teammates. In 1999, he won the all-round and 500m at three legs of World Short Track Speed Skating Championships.

At Olympic Winter Games in Salt Lake City in 2002, he finished second in 1500m and third in 5000m relay with his teammates. In January 2003, he swept 6 gold medals at the 10th National Winter Games, becoming one of the top gold-winning players. At the subsequent short track speed skating competition at Asian Winter Games, he added a gold medal and a silver medal for Chinese delegation.

Yang Yang

Yang Yang (1975-) woman skater.

Among the world's short track speed skaters worldwide, Yang Yang is undoubtedly an established name. Of the over 20 international tournaments, she reached finals 18 times and captured 12 gold medals. At present, she is still the world record holder of 1,000m in women's short track speed skating. At Salt Lake City Olympic Winter Games in 2002, she took the titles of 500m and 1,000m in women's short track speed skating, saying goodbye to the no gold history of China at Olympic Winter Games.

Chen Lu

Chen Lu (1976-) is the most successful individual figure skater. In 1994, she claimed the first medal for China at the 17th Olympic Winter Games. In 1995, she became the first champion in the event at World Figure Skating Championships. In 1998, she took another figure skating medal for China at the 18th Olympic Winter Games, becoming the first Asian figure skater to win medals at two consecutive Olympics Winter Games. Due to a successful interpretation of Butterfly Lover Violin Concerto, she was crowned Butterfly on Icy Rink.

Yang Yang

Yang Yang (1977-), woman skater.She finished second in 500m, 1,000m and 3,000m relay at the 18th Olympic Winter Games in Nagano in 1998. The heroes in her heart are American speed skating legend Janson and Bonnie Blair. From 1994 to 2001, she participated in 8 World Championships and took 11 medals in individual events. Her only world title came from 1,500m at ISU World Championships held in Sophie, 1999. But as a member of relay team, she took 5 world titles. Her personal best of all-round came in 1999-2000 season, placing third.

Wang Chunlu

Wang Chunlu (1978-), woman skater. She finished in first 500m, 1,000m and 3,000m relay and second in all-round as a first time participant of World Championships in 1995. Since then, she has been among the top skaters of the world. Up to now, she has taken into her hands 4 gold medals, 2 silver medals and 1 bronze medal at World Olympics and Olympic Winter Games. At Nagano 1998, she did not perform well in 500m and 1,000m but finished second in 3,000m relay along with her team members. One month later, she finished first in 500m and second in 1,500m and all-round at World Championships held in Vienna. In 2001, she took another two gold medals at ISU World Cup held in South Korea. As a relay member, she took 5 world titles with her teammates. Her strength is 500m in which she finished first

On February 12, 2006, Li Jiajun (in the middle) won the bronze medal of the men's 1,500m short track skating event at the Torino Olympic Winter Games.

three times at World Championships and two times in World Cup.

Before she converted to short track training, she had received six years' speed skating training. After finishing her school years in Jilin Sports Institute, she quit skating and began coaching. She hopes that she could learn English in Brigham Young University in Utah, USA. Of all the cities she has been to, she likes Salt Lake City best for its cleanness and serenity.

Shen Xue

Shen Xue (1978-), pair figure skater.

Shen Xue/Zhao Hongbo, No.1 figure skating pair in China, has been among top three at the three latest World Championships. They finished second in 1999 and 2000 and third in 2001. They placed third at Salt Lake City, 2002, the best performance Chinese pair has ever made at Olympic Winter Games. They are also the pair that could probably seize a gold medal in figure skating after Cheng Lu. They also won the first champion in pair figure skating for China in the World Championships in 2002.

They started figure skating as a couple in August 1992. At present, they have been together for 10 years. What distinguish their skills are their highly difficult moves. But due to the lack of artistic touch, they always failed to get a gold medal. To make up for the deficiency, they went for furter training in Europe and invited foreign experts to give them guidance on artistic interpretation. Their Quadruple Throw is the most difficult move in pair figure skating around the world.

Shen Xue and Zhao Hongbo finished first again in the pairs skating of the World Figure Skating Championship.

Li Chengjiang

Li Chengjiang (1979-), figure skater. His parents were both state speed skating legend. His mother was a speed skating coach. He started speed skating training at age 4 and converted to figure skating at age 5 until 12. Later, he resumed speed skating and began to participate in competition. But one year later, he came back to figure skating until now.

He is an excellent individual figure skating man after Guo Zhengxin. He took the national title in 1998. In 2000, he stunned the world by placing fifth as a first time participant of World Championships, also the best record Chinese men's figure skating players have ever got. In 2001, he advanced to top eight and finished seventh at World Championships. In 2000, he succeeded in completing two difficult quadruple for the first time and placed third at the famous HNK Cup held in Japan. In 2001, he battled Japanese and American established names en route to the gold with his successful completion of two kinds of highly difficult quadruple throws at Four Continents Figure Skating Championships (without European s). In August 2001, Li Chengjiang won a national champion once again at the 9th National Games.

Figure Skating

Chinese figure skating started late but developed very fast. Its rise in world skating community in recent years could trace back to Chen Lu, an individual women skater, who took the first World Championships title for China in 1995 and quit after placing third at 1994 and 1998 Olympic Winter Games. As a follow-up, Shen Xue and Zhao Hongbo, the No.1 pair in China, stepped up with difficult skills and pushed the overall skills of Chinese pairs to a new level. After they took the third spot at Olympic Winter Games Salt Lake City 2002, and then won two World Championships in 2002 and 2003 respectively with their classic *Turandot*. At Olympic Winter Games Torino 2006 which was concluded not long ago, 3 Chinese pairs finished second, third and fourth at a time when they all suffered injuries.

If the first gold in figure skating claimed by Chen Lu in 1995 was regarded as a talent-creating-history tale, the overall rising skills in Pairs and Individual Men would rank China among the powers.

The First World Champion in Figure Skating

In 1995, Chen Lu took the title of Individual Women at World Championships, the first such title Chinese players have ever got.

The Track Record of Chinese Skating Team (2006)

On March 23, 2006, Pang Qing/Dong Jian and Zhan Dan/Zhang Hao finished first and second at World Figure Skating Championships held in Calgary, Canada. As the No.4 winner in Torino Olympic Winter Games in 2006, Pang Qing and Dong Jian reset their personal best of 123.48 at Torino by winning 65.71 points for technical element, 60.51 points for program component and 124.22 points for free skating. They finished first with a total number of 189.20 points, winning their first World Championships title in their professional career.

The First ISU Referee

In September 1984, Yang Jiasheng, Chinese figure skating referee, passed the ISU referee promotion test held in London and was appointed as a referee for World Championships and Olympic Winter Games.

▲ Ice Dancing

Ice Dancing has a high demand for coaches that are in extremely short supply in China. In 1980s when the event first appeared, all Chinese coaches didn't start as ice dancing coaches. Later, many foreign coaches were invited to teach and give guidance. But as each training class did not last long, the expected result was not achieved. Even now, a majority of coaches haven't got the teaching requirements which, to certain extent, have restricted the development of the event. Zhang Weina and Cao Xianming placed 17th at 2003 World Championships, setting their personal best in the event.

♦ Chinese Skating Association

Chinese Skating Association was founded in 1980 and was affiliated to ISU in the name of Chinese Winter Games Association. The regular tournaments under its auspices include: National Speed Skating Champion Tournaments, National Speed Skating Championships, National Youth Speed Skating Championships, National Adolescent Speed Skating Championships, National Short Track Speed Skating Champion Tournament, National Short Track Speed Skating Championships, National Youth and Adolescent Championships, National Figure Skating Champion Tournament and National Figure Skating Championships.

Address: No.56 Nanjie, Zhongguancun, Haidian District, Beijing

Website: http://skating.sport.org.cn

> **♦ Chinese Ski Association**
>
> Founded in 1981, CSA joined the International Ski Federation in May the same year. It regularly hosts national championships for alpine, freestyle, cross-country skiing and ski jumping as well as national try-outs for alpine skiing and ski jumping.
>
> Address: No.56, Zhongguancun Nanjie, Haidian District, Beijing.
> Website: http://www.skiing.org.cn

Skiing

Geographical limitations and social restrictions have greatly slowed down modern skiing activities in China, which wasn't introduced to China until the 1920s from Russia and Japan. The first national competition was held in 1957, opening a whole new chapter of modern skiing in the People's Republic. It was carried out in some narrow regions, mainly the Northeast. Due to geographical and economic hindrance, it didn't make much progress over the years, and was mostly confined to athletic skiing. China's participation in the 13th Winter Olympics in 1980 marked the beginning of the modernization of this game in the ancient country, but it wasn't until the end of the millennium did recreational skiing take the first steps to become popular. So far, Chinese athletes have taken home an Olympic silver medal and many World Cup championships in aerial acrobatics, and female players have done well in biathlon, but other than that, China still has a long way to go before it could catch up with other countries in many skiing events.

The good news is that this sport in China has been growing on an unprecedented fast track as a result of successful major international skiing events held in this country lately, including Vasaloppet China, World Cup Cross-Country Short-Track Skiing, etc. Here are some statistics. A decade ago, there were only 10 skiing places prepared for around 20,000 people, but today this figure has jumped to over 200 with an additional 20 to 30 new resorts each year.

Alpine Skiing

Alpine skiing has just started in China. Two skiers, one male and one female, were qualified for the Torino Winter Olympics in 2006, the second time Chinese athletes ever appeared in skiing competitions at the winter Olympics since 1980. With rising living standards in recent years, the Chinese public has demonstrated tremendous enthusiasm for skiing, and many amateur skiers closely follow every prestigious international event, which in turn provides a great driving force for this industry in China.

Cross-Country Skiing

Cross-country skiing is a traditional sport for Chinese athletes. Since it has a lower threshold than alpine skiing, it currently boasts the largest numbers of teams, sports schools as well as participants nationwide.

China won its first gold medal for skiing in Asian games in 4-person cross-country relay, and produced silver medalists in individual cross-country skiing both at the Asian Winter Games and the Winter Universiade.

Freestyle Skiing

Freestyle skiing has three events for both men and women, altogether six, but only aerial acrobatics is officially carried out in China, for it depends on flexibility, subtlety and skills. With China's outstanding record in gymnastics, it is most suitable for the Chinese public. Athletic performance has been improving so fast ever since it was introduced in 1989 that it is currently the trump card of the Chinese skiing team where female skiers are world-class. Able to sweep away top four at the Asian Winter Games, championships at the World Cup, and even gold medals at the Olympics, the Chinese team is admired and closely observed by foreign peers for their extremely high degrees of difficulty, fast improvement, beautiful body positions and a huge reservoir of talented skiers. With rising training conditions, better equipments and an unlimited number of talents, this is the brightest star among China's skiing sports.

In 1997, Guo Dandan seized the championship in the second leg of the World Cup Freestyle Skiing Series in Australia, the first world No. 1 for Chinese skiers. At the 1998 Nagano Winter Olympic Games, Xu Nannan finished second in freestyle aerial skiing with 186.97 points. In that same year at the World Cup Freestyle Skiing Series in Canada, Ji Xiao'ou topped the game with 200.21 points, the first in history to have ever exceeded the 200-point milestone in women's freestyle aerial acrobatics. At the 2006 Torino Winter Olympics, Han Xiaopeng ended China's zero gold medal history in snow events at this most prestigious international sports affair. Another Chinese skier Li Nina also brought home a silver medal.

Yu Shumei

Yu Shumei (1977-), a Gold medalist at the 1996 Asian Winter Games both in women's biathlon 4×7.5 km relay and in women's cross-country 4x5 km skiing relay; gold medalist at the 1st Biathlon World Championship (mountain running and rifle shooting) 6 km the same year, the first world winner among Chinese snow sports athletes.

Xu Nannan

Xu Nannan (1979-), female skier.

Unlike ice-related games, Chinese athletes lag behind other countries in snow sports. Xu Nannan, however, is a world-renowned freestyle aerial acrobat, claiming silver at the 18th Winter Olympics. She was in the first place in preliminaries, but unfortunately the goddess of victory wasn't on her side in the finals.

Freestyle aerial skiing is a perfect match for Chinese athletes who are famous for their achievements in high degrees of difficulty and masterful skills. Xu Nannan had been an acrobat before taking up this sport. As a result, she managed to improve her performance in a fast pace. At three world championships from 1997 to 2001, Xu finished ninth, eighth to seventh respectively. Meanwhile, she took home a hard-won silver medal at the 1998 Nagano Winter Olympics, a milestone of China's snow sports.

Xu is a distinguished skier for her spot-on body positions and firm landing. Her degree of difficulty ranks among top 10 in the world. Ever since her debut in 1996, she has grabbed one gold and seven silver at a series of World Cup, Winter Olympics and Asian Winter Games. During the 2002 World Cup Tournament, she took the second spot in USA and Canada in tandem. It's truly a great achievement.

On February 22, 2006, Xu Nannan won the fourth place in the women's aerial skill competition at the Torino Olympic Winter Games.

Han Xiaopeng

Han Xiaopeng (1982-) is a gold medalist at the 2006 Torino Winter Olympic Games, silver medalist at the 2005 Australia and Czech World Cup, and third place at the World Cup Finals in Italy the same year.

Modern Biathlon

Biathlon is a sport combining shooting and cross-country skiing. In China, it is traditionally carried out by a PLA athlete team. A national competition was held in 1980 for men's biathlon. It was 1988 for women, but they have made fast progress. The Chinese team is one of the best worldwide. Only a few in China are familiar with biathlon, so it is an "exclusive" sport of the PLA skiing team.

In 2001, Yu Shumei won the gold medal at the World Cup for women's biathlon 12.5 km with 36:46.7, the first time for a Chinese athlete at this event.

Curling

Most Chinese got to meet curling 8 years ago on TV when the Nagano Winter Olympics curling game was on. This exotic, highly competitive and beautiful sport quickly captured the interest of a vast number of Chinese audience and sports fans. But due to its particular requirements, today it is still a mystery for many. Actually, curling was introduced to China in 1995, and the first professional team was formed in 2001. There wasn't any special training venue for curling at that point, so the team had to train at night on common rinks. Today, Team China has fast become one of the strongest in Asia Pacific. In November 2006, the Chinese women's team claimed the first at the Asia Pacific Curling Championship in Japan.

On January 20, 2006, the final of the 2006 Pacific Youth Curling Championship was held in the Curling Sports Center in Huairong, Beijing. Both the men's and women's teams of China won the championship and gained the participation qualification of the 2006 World Youth Curling Championship.

Non-Olympic Events

Karate

Karate can trace its origin to the Chinese Shaolin shadowboxing and the Japanese Okinawa shadowboxing. Incorporating countless traditional Chinese martial arts and cultures, it was originally named as Tang hand and was popular in Okinawa islands. At present, Chinese karate is gaining momentum and finding its way into many other provinces and cities such as Shanghai, Beijing, Hubei, Henan and Jiangsu. Among these places, Shanghai is where it gains the most rapid development. There are also dozens of karate shops in Beijing. An increasing number of people are involved, ushering in another fashion trend for body-building.

Karate has been popular among the public and has not gained government support. In 2006, it took a positive turn. To better develop karate and enhance the competitive skills, General Administration of Sport of China founded Chinese Karate Association in May 2006.

Squash

Squash is not a member of the Olympic family. Hong Kong was the first in China to welcome it. Now it's a "hip" sport there as evidenced by nearly 700 squash courts catering to more than 900,000 people. As living standards rise in the mainland, squash has also won over many with its unique style. Aiming to popularize this sport, with the permission of the State Administration of Sports, the Small Ball Sports Management Center of the SAS and World Squash Federation jointly launched the first National Squash Training Class from April 3-5, 1999 when Chairmen of the WSF and Asian Squash Federation plus a group of senior professional coaches came to China to teach the trainees, demonstrating their passion to reach out to the Chinese public. From October 25-29 of the same year, the first China Open was held at Haigeng Sports Training Base in Kunming, Yunnan, gathering all first-class players across the nation. These successful events have made a great start for squash to sweep over China in the future.

In 1999, the Chinese Squash Association was founded, and it was officially affiliated to the WSF. The association will update its agenda in the near future to host more world-class squash competitions and promotional events.

Sanshou

Not a part of the Olympics, Sanshou is a combat sport of Wushu. It was added to the textbooks of sports colleges across the country in 1949, and was included in the World Wushu Championships in 1991. In 1955 at the same event, Chinese fighters won the championships for 52 kg, 60 kg and 65 kg.

On October 30, 2005 at the 4th East Asian Games, all of China's six athletes, both men and women, won in all 7 categories, adding 6 high notes to the national team's victory song.

At the 2006 Asian Games, Xu Yanfei finished first for Men's 70 kg, Zhao Guangyong for 65 kg, Ma Chao for 60 kg, and Li Teng for 56 kg.

Kendo

Kendo is not an Olympic game. In 1996, Godi, a Swiss man who was studying Chinese medicine in Beijing, himself being 3-dan and later upgrading to 5-dan in 2001, founded the Beijing Kendo Association, a start for mainland Chinese to engage in such a sport. Soon Shanghai, Guangzhou, Chongqing, Wenzhou, Yantai, Yanbian and other cities followed suit and formed their own clubs. The number of Kendo fans has been climbing gradually to 1,500-2,000 in 2006.

China Kendo Competitions

There is a national-level competition called the Asian Invitational Kendo Tournament hosted by Hong Kong Kendo Association (under the IKF) since 2000. Kendoists from Beijing and Shanghai have been participating in this event ever since it was first launched. Early invitations were sent out to Japanese athletes, but recently years have seen an increasing number of Chinese contestants as well. At the sixth Tournament in February 2006, 47 kendoists were from Beijing (30 of them Chinese), and its Team A won the second place in men's team. There are also more and more players from Shanghai and Guangzhou. On the eve of the Tournament, a grade advancement examination was held for 1-dan to 4-dan, a golden opportunity for kendo fans from the mainland and other Asian countries.

Golf

On November 25, 2005, the VOLVO China Open entered the second round. In the picture is Zhang Lianwei in competition.

Golf was officially accepted in China in 1984 when the government began training the first group of professional golf players. One year later, the China Golf Association was founded. In January 1986, the Yat-sen Cup International Invitational Tournament for professional and amateur players was held on Yat-sen Hot Spring Golf Links in Guangdong, the first international golf competition in China. 68 golfers accepted the invitation, including 17 world-class pros from the Philippines, Singapore and Hong Kong. After a 36-hole match in 2 days, the person with the best individual scores 36 holes (146) was Raymon Brobin from the Philippines. Deng Shuquan from China finished fifth with 36 holes (154). Golf has grown to be a popular game in China today.

Volvo China Open

Launched in 1995, the Volvo China Open has a prestigious position in the 20-year history of golf in China as it helped this sport enjoy an unprecedented growth in popularity.

Skyrocketing economy plus the upcoming 2008 Beijing Olympics have made the most populous country a hotspot for international investment, including world golf tournament sponsors flocking to China, hosting as many as 6 tournaments each with above $1 million in prize money in 2005 alone.

However, there were only less than 10 golf courses in 1995, with most players from foreign countries. There were altogether 11 Chinese pros, men and women combined. One of the largest sports sponsors, Volvo joined hands with the China Golf Association in creating a true professional world golf tournament, Volvo China Open, a milestone that speeded up the development of golf competitions in this country. It is rather like an infant compared to the British Open or US Open, but it is the fastest growing professional tournament in Asia. In 2004 on its 10th anniversary, Volvo China Open successfully transformed itself into a top international event by making it into the PGA European Tour with prize money exceeding one million US dollars.

Golf Tournaments

The achievements of Volvo China Open over the past 11 years have laid a firm foundation for future development of this sport in China, attracting many world-class golf tournaments as well as multinational sponsors.

In 2005, China hosted the largest number of European Tours after Europe, prompting BBC to claim in its report *International Business Eyeing Sports in China* that China would hold 5 European Golf Tournaments that year, more than those in England and Scotland combined. The vast Chinese potential has indeed captured the heart of world golf, with the US Tour closely following its European and Asian counterparts landing on this fast emerging market.

Zhang Lianwei

Zhang Lianwei (1965-), golf player.

In 1994, Zhang Lianwei, an amateur at that time, outperformed himself in claiming the silver medal in golf at the Hiroshima Asian Games.

On April 10, 1995, after becoming a pro only five months ago, Zhang took home the title of the Volvo Open, leg 1 of the 1st China Tour, the first international championship he claimed in his pro career. At the following 1st Volvo China Open, he placed third with an outstanding performance of 282 (-6) in 4 rounds.

Zhang began to shine in the next two years at Asian Volvo tournaments. In 1995, he won the Volvo Thailand Masters and Malaysia Masters, and defended his position at both events the next year. The next five years witnessed his rise in Asia as he cleaved his way through the Japan Tour, Asia Tour, European Tour and Canada Tour.

In February 2003, Zhang landed his biggest victory to date by defeating South African world-class golf Ernie Els in the final round at the Caltex Masters in Singapore, becoming the first Chinese to have won the title of a European Tour.

In 2004, Zhang became the first mainland Chinese golf to have been invited to the US Masters for his outstanding performance at Asian tournaments.

Model Ships

The sport of marine model was introduced to China in the 1930s. The Chinese team took part in the World Model Ship Building Championship for the first time in 1981, and surprised everyone by taking home one gold medal. The Chinese Marine Model Association was founded in March 1986, after which Chinese athletes have undergone fast improvement in their skills, and have made stellar achievements in world competitions.

China leads the world in marine modeling. Although it started late, its modelers are now highly competitive. By the end of 2005, Chinese players have won 124 world championships with 77 times breaking World records that they now hold six of them among all 11 in the world.

Achievements of the Chinese Model Ship Building Team

From June 8 to 14, 1987, the fifth World Model Ship Building Championship was held in Schwerin, East Germany. During the fierce competition of 8 categories of the motor boat adult group, Chinese athletes won 7 gold medals, 4 silver and 2 bronze, with 7 people resetting world records 9 times in 6 categories, the biggest victory for Chinese builders at international games. Furthermore, China took all top three positions in F1-V3.5 and F1-E+1 kg, which was described by the chairman of NAVIGA as "the first time in world marine modeling history, a Chinese miracle!"

The 14th World Model Ship Building Motor Boat Championship was held in Germany from July 13 to 23, 2006, where the Chinese team took part in 5 categories. After 10 days of cruel race, Zhou Jianming from Shanghai become the world champion of three categories, F1-E<1kg (below 1 kg, triangle course, electronic boat), F1-V3.5 (3.5 ml. triangle course) and F1-V7.5 (7.5 ml., triangle course) while shattering the previous F1-E<1kg

WR. Qiu Weiqiang from Guangdong finished first in F3-E (electronic under-water oars) and second in F3-V (internal combustion engine). Wu Yuheng won the gold medal in F1-E<1kg junior group while breaking its world junior record. Chen Qichao from Zhejiang claimed the top spot in F3-V and F3-E junior groups.

The October 16, 2006 was the 20th anniversary of the establishment of China Aviation Museum. A number of Chinese and foreign superiors in aeromodelling gathered there to join the aeromodelling flight for celebration.

♦ Chinese Marine Model Association

The Chinese Marine Model Association (CMMA) is a public organization for Chinese model ship building fans, a group member of the All China Sports Federation. Registered at the national community management authorities in 1992, it is the only legitimate representative of China in Vienna-based NAVIGA. It aims to promote the development of Chinese model ship building and strengthen its ties with international organizations as well as foreign marine model associations.

Since it was founded in 1986, CMMA has trained more than 500 qualified athletes, over 200 qualified referees and above 100 qualified coaches. It is also in contact with 2,000 fans across the country. The association annually sends out a team for world championships, and with China it organizes national championships and biennial junior contests. Over the past decade, Chinese builders broke world records 77 times and won 121 world championships. The number of gold medals they have taken home is one of the largest among all Chinese sports.

Address: A-14, Tiantan Dongli Zhongqu, Chongwen District, Beijing

Hu Shenggao

Hu Shenggao (1956-) renewed the A3 WR three times in 1981 at the national Model Ship Building Category Contests and the second National Model Ship Building Championships. He broke the WR in F1-V15 in 1987 at the 6th National Games, and did it again at the 6th World Championships in 1989 while taking home the title. In 1993, he becomes the winner (11.2 seconds) of F1-V15 at the 8th World Championships.

Pu Haiqing

Pu Haiching (1958-) rewrote the WR in F1-V5 at the National Model Ship Building Category Contests in 1983. In 1984 at the National Model Ship Building Championships, he broke the WR in F1-V6.5, and did it again at the 5th World Model Ship Championships in 1987 as the winner. He kept the first position two years later at the 6th Championships, and won F1-V6.5 and F1-V15 at the 7th Championships in 1991. At the 7th National Games, he again updated the WR in F1-V6.5 in 10.07 seconds.

Zhou Jianming

Zhou Jianming (1959-) is a three-time champion in F1-V3.5 from the 4th to 6th World Model Ship Championships from 1985 to 1989. He has reset world records 6 times since 1983.

Lu Weifeng

Lu Weifeng (1970-) won the F3-V and F3-E races at the 6th World Model Ship Building Championships in 1989 while upsetting both world records. He is also the winner of F3-V at the 8th World Model Ship Building Championships in 1993.

Aeromodeling

The first Chinese aeromodeling contest was held in Hong Kong in 1940. After 1949, this sport became quickly popular across the country. Starting from 1956, every year a national competition was launched while Wang Gong first shattered the previous WR in 1959. The sport of model ship building was popularized in China in 1954 and the 1st national model ship competition was held in Beijing in 1958.

In 1980, NAVIGA accepted China as one of its members. In October, Chinese athletes shattered previous World records in two categories, and they have been making marvelous achievements ever since while updating world records time after time.

China's model aircraft sport is also becoming increasingly competitive. From 1978 till now, 58 Chinese builders have renewed world records 59 times in 31 categories with 24 gold medals at world competitions.

During international aeromodeling games that China has participated in, the famous Han Xinping with his teammates have made 5 consecutive wins in control line stunt flying, both individual and team.

♦ Aero Sports Federation of China

The Aero Sports Federation of China (ASFC) was founded in August 1964, consisting of 12 branches including committees of flight, ballooning, parachuting, aeromodeling, hang gliding and paragliding, flight simulation, general aeronautics, etc.

The ASFC is a national public sports organization assuming the functions of a juristic person. It is a member of the All China Sports Federation in charge of managing and regulating national aero sports, and is the only legitimate representative of China in FAI and all the international events it sponsors.

Address: A-14, Tiantan Dongli, Zhongqu, Chongwen District, Beijing

First Chinese World Champion in Model Aeronautics

On September 13, 1984, the World Control Line Aeromodeling Championship was held in the suburbs of Boston, USA. Colorful F2B control line scale model aircrafts from 24 countries were competing with each other against the deep-blue sky where they had to complete 16 dazzling stunts within 7 minutes. One model with red and white spots and stripes immediately attracted all the attentions when it perfectly finished one difficult yet vigorous move one after another at the hands of its controller Zhu Younan. Finally, with the aircraft's consistent, natural and skillful performance, Zhu comfortably sat on the throne that had been occupied by American athletes for so many years, becoming the first Chinese to have ever claimed No. 1 at world aeromodeling events.

First Chinese Team Gold Medal at the World Aeromodeling Championships

From October 1 to 4, 1983, the 21st World Free Flight Aeromodeling Championship was held in Goulburn, Australia with 137 players from 18 countries. The Chinese team, composed of Lu Jifa, Zhang Wenyi and Wang Guocai, claimed the top prize in F1B-International Rubber Band Model Aircraft team, the first time the Chinese team became No. 1 at the World Aeromodeling Championships.

Zhu Younan

Zhu Younan (1961-), the Chinese aeromodeling athlete. In 1984, he interrupted the Americans' 11-year winning streak in F2B control line stunt flying at the World Control Line Aeromodeling Championships, the first Chinese to have won an international top prize. In 1990, he and his teammates together claimed the first place in F2B international control line team stunt flying at the World Control Line Aeromodeling Championships. He was awarded the Master of Sports in 1982, World Master of Sports in 1986, and also won Sports Medal of Honor.

Parachuting

Private skydivers emerged in China as early as the 1940s. The ASFC Parachuting Committee was founded in August 1964, and the PRC was officially listed as a member in FAI when Chinese athletes began competing in a series of world events organized by the federation. With concerted efforts by all skydivers from several generations, the Chinese team's performance has been greatly improved, boasting stellar achievements at international competitions. By the end of 2001, 12 people had rewritten World records 7 times in 4 categories, and 22 had won gold medals 17 times in 8 categories, demonstrating China's leading position in parachuting in the world.

The First Parachuting WR

From September 17 to 24, 1958, the National Gliding and Parachuting Competitions were held in Beijing with 17 divers from two teams, Beijing and China People's Aviation Clubs. He Jianhua, Di Guifang and Cui Xiuying from Chinese Team together scored an average 9.81 meters from the bull's-eye in women's 1,000 meters team skydiving, more than one third shorter than the previous WR of 14.94 meters held by USSR athletes set in 1956. This is the first WR for China's parachutists.

The First Women's All Round Parachuting World Champion

From September 3 to 11, 1983, the 2nd Parachuting World Cup was held in Siena, Italy with 19 athletes from 8 countries, China, East Germany, Argentina, Australia, Belgium, Switzerland, Italy and Yugoslavia. Yang Zhelin won the gold medal in men's stunt, and Li Rongrong finished the first in women's all round individual, the first Chinese world champion in women's all round parachuting.

Jia Chengxiang

Jia Chengxiang (1935-) joined the national team in 1956, renewed the 1,500 meter men's group accuracy landing in 1963, and broke the WR in 1,000 meters team accuracy landing and all-round parachuting twice in 1964 and 1965. He was the Chinese representative on the FAI Parachuting Committee from 1979 to 1995, and was awarded the Leonardo Da Vinci Parachuting Diploma in 1994 by the committee.

He Jianhua

He Jianhua (1938-) reset the WR six times in accuracy landing and all-round parachuting, starting from 1958 when he reset the WR of 1,000 meters group accuracy landing at the 1st National Gliding and Parachuting Competitions, the first time for a Chinese diver.

Mei Yan

Mei Yan (1939-) reset 6 world records 8 times from 1959 to 1965 in 600 meters 3-person accuracy and all-round, 1,000 meters 3-person accuracy and all-round, 1,500 meters 3-person accuracy and all-round and 7-person accuracy landing, breaking most parachuting world records among Chinese athletes during the 1960s.

Chen Li

Chen Li (1962-) broke the world record in 4-way sequential at the Canopy Formation World Cup in 1983, and won the title in 1984 at the World Canopy Formation Championship. In 1986, he rewrote the record 3 times at the 6th National Games in 1987.

Li Rongrong

Li Rongrong (1963-) joined the national team in 1979, became the first Chinese world parachuting champion at the 2nd World Cup in 1983 as the gold medalist in women's all round parachuting, and updated the WR in individual stunt at the 19th World Parachuting Championship in 1988. From 1979 to 1987, she won 28 gold medals in 4 categories at both international and domestic parachuting competitions.

Motorcycling

The sport of motorcycling started in China in 1952. With inadequate sponsorship and promotion by motorcycle manufacturers, it didn't make much progress. But in the mid to late 1950s, clubs sprouted in many major cities, laying a solid foundation for its bright future to come. The first National Motorcycle Competition was held in Beijing in 1958. Half a century later, the Chinese Zongshen Team surprised the International Motorcycling Federation by winning the annual title of the EWC in 2002. In 2004, Zongshen, officially representing China, joined the WSBK.

On May 1, 2005, the MOTOGP held the third round at Shanghai International Circuit in China.

The number of group members registered at the Chinese Motor Sports Association, including associations and clubs, has now grown above 46 with over 180 pros and more than 1,000 amateurs in 22 teams. The Chinese motorcycling community is happy to see that its members are organized and the competitions have been developing steadily.

The two top motorcycling events in China today are the national road race and national cross-country race.

The MotoGP Chinese Grand Prix

MotoGP (World Motorcycling Championship) is the top motorcycling event in the world with a vast audience base due to its huge popularity. With the largest volume of motorbike manufactured, China also boasts a great number of fans across the country. MotoGP in China definitely offers the Chinese motorcycling community a golden opportunity to learn from the far more advanced sport in foreign countries.

Ever since the MotoGP Chinese Grand Prix landed on China in May 2005, it has enjoyed an unprecedented growth in popularity. With its time-honored history, world-class operation, the charisma of star racers and the suspenseful and thrilling races, MotoGP has become a hot topic for Chinese audience and racing fans.

Sepak Takraw

Included in the Asian Games in 1982 as a performance sport, Sepak Takraw became a medal event at the 1990 Asian Games. This sport had been relatively unknown in China until 1987 when a team of Asian Sepak Takraw Association came to visit. The fantastic performance opened the eyes of the Chinese audience and greatly helped this game spread in this country. China began training ST and introducing this healthy sport to the public.

So fat, ST has been played in 8 provinces, and there have been 5 national events. The Chinese team has done so well in Pool B of the International Sepak Takraw Competition that even the chairman of the Asian ST Association was amazed by the fast growth of this sport in China. At the 2006 Doha Asian Games, the Chinese team won three bronze medals in women's team, individual group and doubles.

On December 2, 2006, the women's sepak takraw group match of the 15th Doha Asian Games

On September 4, 2005, the "Red River Cup" China Circuit Championship launched the Shanghai round. In the picture is the scene of China Production Car Race 2000cc.

Automobile Sports

Auto racing in China started from the 1st Hong Kong – Beijing Rally Racing in 1985. Today there are many categories widely popular across the country, including rallying, cross-country, circuit, drag, stunt, karting, etc. Beijing, Shanghai, Shenyang, Shenzhen, Beihai and other places have all build their own karting circuits. In October 1996, the first Chinese F1 circuit was constructed in Zhuhai.

During 2006, apart from local events hosted by provincial associations and clubs, there were 57 national and international races organized by the Federation Automobile Sports of China (FASC), including 12 rallies, 25 circuit races and 20 circuit cross-country races. Statistically speaking, auto sports in China have made much progress with the number of domestic events of various types rising and national championships developing steadily.

China Rally Championship

The China Rally Championship (CRC), the most significant event of the FASC, continued to grow in prestige and popularity during the year of 2006, when it was successfully held in 4 locations, Jinshan in Shanghai, Liupanshui in Guizhou, Kaiyang in Guizhou, and Longyou in Zhejiang, some of which saw over 100 cars registered with no less than 10 high-caliber foreign teams. All these have made the CRC a true international racing event. In 2006, the format of the National Short-Track Rally Championship underwent reforms, and 4 legs of series and 2 national events were held throughout the year with 284 new participants as local clubs became more capable of organizing competitions which ensured a better future for auto sports in China.

China Circuit Championship

As the major category at the China Circuit Championship (CCC), the production car 1600cc group has always had fierce competitions. Eight out of the ten teams are corporate-sponsored, which bodes well for business growth in the future. The production car 2000cc group takes the form of open racing, and has attracted many outstanding racers from Hong Kong, Macau and Taiwan, improving the sport of circuit racing on the whole. A highlight of China's auto sports is of high interests of the automobile industry in the CCC, which indicates that the championship will continue to perfect itself.

China Karting Championship

In 2006, the FASC made some further changes to the administration of kart racing as it transformed the China Karting Championship into a new type of event that integrates teaching and training with competition, and provided support in terms of incentive policies, funds and racing cars. The federation held 19 training classes, teaching competitions and championship during the year for nearly 200 young racers.

China Circuit Cross-Country Championship

The China Circuit Cross-Country Championship has gradually become a widely respected brand. 2006 saw 11 championships that were 10 leg races and the finals. 1134 racers in 98 teams, including 3 from Hong Kong, joined the championship. It was truly remarkable in terms of land coverage, participants and the number of races held.

China Cross-Country Championship

Born in 2005, the China Cross-Country Championship is undoubtedly the most prestigious domestic event for cross-country sports. Even with strict limitations by the FASC on the numbers of cars and the years a racer must have completed in racing before registering, there were still 77 cars qualified for the race. Successful championships will absolutely help this sport drive onto a fast track in the future.

International Events

China successfully held many a major international competition during 2006 which further popularized auto sports in China. 12 were launched in Beijing, Shanghai, Nanning, Zhuhai and Longyou, and the F1 China Grand Prix graced the Shanghai International Circuit with its presence during the National holidays as all auto sports fans throughout the region celebrated this grand occasion. It was highly recommended by the FIA for its perfect organization and the effective work by competent referees. The Chinese leg of the FOA Asia-Pacific Rally Championship in Longyou was widely acclaimed, and following the F1 Grand Prix in April, the A1 GP Beijing Road Race was also a success that won extensive media coverage.

The 1st China-ASEAN International Touring Assembly passed through 6 ASEAN countries in 21 days with a total length over 10,000 km, strengthening the ties between China and its Southeast Asian neighbors. The Hohhot-Ulaanbaatar International Touring Assembly was also a success in consolidating the friendship between China and Mongolia. It's worth noting that the China-ASEAN International Touring Assembly involved more countries and covered longer roads than any other Chinese-organized auto races over recent years.

China's Performance in Auto Sports

Chinese racers have been steadily improving their performance as they take part in more and more world competitions. At the 2006 Dakar Rally, Xu Lang from the Paladin Team did a nice job finishing 19th in the race. He was also remarkable in placing 22nd in the Australia leg of the WRC. As a registered racer at the FIA Asia-Pacific Rally Championship, Fan Fan raced in all of the legs. After steadily finishing the 2005-2006 season, China's A1 team continues to grow in the 2006-2007 season as well.

The fan base of auto sports in China keeps expanding. By the end of 2006, there were 88 group members registered at the FASC with 1,252 new registered racers including 314 in rally, 280 in circuit, and 658 in cross-country. Registered teams accounted for 144, including 34 in rally, 17 in circuit, and 92 in cross-country.

Many racing clubs organize events to showcase their strength. A lot of Chinese clubs seek to create a bright future by building their websites and providing all kinds of services to boost their popularity. The growth of these clubs will, without a doubt, cultivate a huge fan base to keep the auto sports in China young and vigorous.

Racing Referee

There are no professional racing referees in China. All of them are employed part-time by competition organizers. As a series of regulations such as the Management Measures on Automobile Sports Referees, Standards for Ranking Automobile Sports Coaches, Management Measures on Ranking Automobile Sports Athletes, and Standards for Ranking Automobile Sports Athletes were being enforced, the training and management of referees, coaches and athletes was greatly improved, laying a solid foundation for future development of auto sports in China.

Throughout 2006, the FASC opened 23 training sessions in rally driving and navigation for 370 junior racers, and one training session in rallying for 19 junior referees.

Mountaineering

Home to extensive mountainous areas, including Mt. Qomolangma at the boarders between the Tibetan Plateau and Nepal, China is the perfect place for mountaineering. The Chinese Mountaineering Association was officially founded in June 1958, and the first National Rock Climbing Invitational was held at Beijing Huairou Mountaineering Base in 1987 with 40 athletes in 12 teams, including the national team, geology colleges from Xinjiang, Tibet, Qinghai, Chengdu and Wuhan, Huochetou Sports Association, and, as special guests, the Japanese Nagano Mountaineering Association and Hong Kong Rock Climbing Team. It has been held annually ever since.

On May 2, 1964, Xu Jing, Wang Fuzhou, Zhang Junyan, Wu Zongyue, Chen San, Migmar Zhaxi, Dorjê, Yun Deng, Soinam Dorjê and Cheng Tianliang, altogether 10 climbers, mounted the Shishapangma with an altitude of 8,012 meters, the last virgin summit above 8,000 meters. The human conquest of mountains over this milestone was officially closed, and a new chapter with even higher marks began.

First Ascent Up Vinson Massif

On the early morning of December 2, 1988, Li Zhixin and Wang Yongfeng of the China-US Joint Mountaineering Expedition ascended Mt. Vinson, the highest summit in Antarctica within the shortest period in their times.

Mt. Vinson is located on the Ellsworth Mountains on Antarctica. Its highest peak is 5,140 meters, and the second-highest 5,110 meters. Although it is far lower than Mt. Everest in terms of absolute height, its vertical climbing distance exceeds 3,500 meters, only 300 meters shorter than the distance in the Mt. Everest case from the 5,154-meter high base camp to the utmost point. The expedition had 6 members, but all four Americans failed. However, it only took Li Zhixin seven hours two minutes to go from Camp III to the summit, faster than anyone else who succeeded before him.

First Ascent of Mt. Qomolangma via the North Ridge

Chinese climbers made the first climbing via the North Ridge of Mt. Qomolangma in 1960.

The team made 3 marches beforehand to get used to the local conditions. On the morning of May 24, Wang Fuzhou, Ginbu, Qu Yinhua and Liu Lianman proceeded from 8,500-meter high camp and determined to make the attempt. Shortly after they departed, the "Second Step" described by British mountaineers as insurmountable appeared in their sight. Here is a rocky slope with an average angle of 60 to 70 degrees where a 5-meter high stonewall must be climbed. After more than a dozen of failed attempts, these four decided to build a human ladder when Liu Lianman managed to uplift three teammates one after another with his shoulders. Five hours later, they ascended the wall. However, when they reached the 8,700-meter mark in the evening, Liu was physically too drained to go any further. After 19 excruciating hours, at 4:20 on the morning of May 25, Wang Fuzhou, Gingbu and Qu Yinhua finally climbed the 8,848.13-meter high Mt. Everest, becoming the first climbers to have ever succeeded via the North Ridge.

♦ Chinese Mountaineering Association

Founded in 1958, the CMA joined the Union International Alpine Associations in 1985 and the Union of Asian Alpine Associations in 1994. The CMA regularly organizes the National Rock Climbing Championship, National Ice Climbing Championship, National Rock Climbing Classics, International Rock Climbing Invitational, International Rock Climb Classics, etc., among which the national rock climbing and ice climbing championships have become a tradition for the Chinese alpine community.

Address: No.5, Tiyuguan Jie, Beijing.
Website: http://cmasports.sport.org.cn

Wang Fuzhou (right in front) and mountaineering athletes

The First Woman to Reach the Summit of Mt. Qomolangma from the North Ridge

On May 27, 1975, a Chinese team including 10 women ascended Mt. Qomolangma for the second time since 1960. Unfazed by the abominable weather that defeated three attempts and killed the leader Wu Zongyue, Phantog and 8 men managed to reach the summit during the fourth try. Phantog thus became the first female climber who's literally ever been to the top of the world.

Born a serf in Tibet, Phantog spent her childhood working on a farmland and shepherding for her master. After 1951, she became the first generation of farm workers. After joining the Chinese Mountaineering Team in 1959, she ascended Mt. Muztagata the same year and Kongur Tiube in 1961, both breaking world records in women's mountaineering. She was already 37 years old with 3 children when she became the first woman to reach Mt. Qomolangma via the North Ridge in 1975. The State Physical Culture and Sports Commission awarded her the top national honor for her outstanding achievements, and conferred upon her 3 Sports Medal of Honor over the years.

The First Chinese Mountains Open to Foreign Climbers

In 1980, the Chinese government for the first time removed the restrictions on eight mountains accepting foreign climbers who would pay a certain amount of money to climb them. These are: Mount Everest (on the border between China and Nepal), Shishapangma (Tibet), Mount Muztagata (Xinjiang), Kongur Tagh (Xinjiang), Kongur Tiube (Xinjiang), Mount Bogda (Xinjiang), the Gongga Shan (Sichuan), and the Amne Machin Shan (Qinghai).

Wang Fuzhou

Wang Fuzhou (1935-), mountaineer. On May 25, 1960, Wang Fuzhou, Gingbu and Qu Yinhua ascended the 8,848.13-meter high Mt. Qomolangma up the northeast ridge, the first climbers to make it from the north face.

Wang Fuzhou graduated from Petroleum Geological Prospecting Department of Beijing Geology College. Selected into the Chinese Mountaineering Team the same year, he climbed the 7,134-meter high Mount Lenin in the former Soviet Union in 1958, Mount Muztagata (7,546) in Xinjiang in 1959, then Shishapangma (8,012) in 1964. He founded the China International Sports Travel Company in 1985, and was appointed the chairman of the Chinese Mountaineering Association in 1992.

Aero Sports

The Aero Sports Federation of China was founded in 1964, governing aero sports such as gliding, parachuting, flight and hot air ballooning. In 1996, China hosted an international stunt flying competition for the first time. At the Air Show China 1998, the Bayi Stunt Flying Team completed its first tight-V formation in F-7E fighters at 850 km per hour. The distance between wings was 5 meters, and only 1 meter between heights. In 1999 in Zhangjiajie, Hunan, Chinese pilots made a Guinness World Record by flying through the Tianmen Cave, a natural cave for the first time.

Radio Sports

China's amateur radio sports mainly include amateur broadcasting station communications, radio direction finding, Radio Speed Communications, and Wireless Engineering Contest.

The history of radio dates back to the 19th century when Marconi invented telegram. But it wasn't a popular sport until 1992 when amateur radio activities were resumed. Radio sports are highly competitive in mainland China, with speed communications, radio direction finding, model aeronautics all becoming medal games. Fans from communist countries during the Cold War often got together and competed with each other in these sports, and China was extremely hard to beat. Some categories even saw their throne permanently occupied by the Chinese, who, by the way, broke many world records in speed communications.

Latest statistics show that the current number of registered amateur fans is above 20,000 with more than 9,000 in Beijing.

Radio direction finding was first introduced to China in the 1960s, and China won their first gold medal in this category at an international event in 1988. The following years saw 11 gold medals by the Chinese team at the World Championship.

♦ Chinese Radio Sports Association

The Chinese Radio Sports Association (CRSA) is a public organization for all amateur radio sports fans in China and the only representative of China in the International Amateur Radio Union (IARU).

Under the guidance of IARU rules and Chinese radio management regulations, the CRSA aims to extensively promote radio sports across the country. Whether sitting at home transmitting signals with broadcasting stations or taking interest in radio direction finding, or passionately exploring electronic wireless engineering, thousands of fans all over China are devoting their time and energy in these fascinating sports.

The CRSA currently has nearly 10,000 members, and, with permission from state radio authorities, has set up over 1000 amateur broadcasting stations.

Address: A-14, Tiantan Dongli Zhongqu, Chongwen District, Beijing
Website:http://www.crsa.org.cn

On November 1, 2005, 50 athletes from 16 countries such as Britain, Italy, Japan and China joined the Shanghai round competition of the World Park Directional Elite Circuit.

Cross-Country Orienteering

Ever since it came to China in 1979, cross-country orienteering has been on a fast track over the years, a fun sport widely popular due to its challenges, techniques and educational values. Orienteering in all forms can be found in China right now, and seminars, training classes of cross-country orienteering are emerging everywhere, not only reaching out to the vast population within this country, but also eagerly learning advanced foreign technologies and international rules as the entire community Hong Kong started early in orienteering and is enthusiastic about it. The Hong Kong Cross-Country Orienteering Championship is held every December.

By the end of 1982, the Orienteering Association of Hong Kong officially became a member of the International Orienteering Federation and qualified for international competitions. In 1984 at the biennial Asia-Pacific Cross-Country Orienteering Championship in New Zealand, HK athletes finished first in men's middle age group B (H35B), and fourth in women's junior group B (D21B).

The Orienteering Association of China is in charge of organizing the annual National Cross-Country Orienteering Championship and the World Ranking Event. This sport itself is on the list of student sports competitions approved by the Chinese Ministry of Education, while every year the China Student Orienteering organizes the National Student Cross-Country Orienteering Championship and Student Classics.

On average, every week in 2004 had a cross-country orienteering contest going on in mainland China which, despite being disorganized and unregulated, truly demonstrates that this sport is winning hearts and minds of the Chinese population.

Water Skiing

Water skiing started taking off much later in China than in developed countries. It indeed was introduced to this country in the 1950s, but few people took a part in it. After much hardship, it became an official competition sport in the 1980s. The 1st National Championship was held in 1983. The Chinese Water Ski Association was founded in 1986 and joined the International Water Ski Federation the same year, after which Chinese athletes began participating in international contests. In the Singapore leg of the 2004 Water Ski World Cup, the 17-year-old Chen Lili won the gold medal, the first time for Chinese or even Asian athletes to have stood on the highest level of the medal podium at international events. So far, Chinese Team has won over 50 world championships and above 60 Asian gold medals. The number of frequent skiers in China is nearly 40,000, most in major coastal cities.

Motor Boat

Chinese powerboat racing officially started in 1956. A national team was formed the same year and took part in the 2nd International Water Sports Games in Bulgaria the next year where Chinese athletes took home 1 gold, 3 silver and 3 bronze.

Ever since the early 1980s, every year China sends out teams to World Championships and finished second three times. In 2002, Peng Linwu from Jiangxi claimed title of the O-125 Powerboat World Championship in Finland, winning the first gold medal for Chinese powerboat racers at world championships.

At the O-125 Powerboat World Championship and International Powerboat Classics in 2006, Shi Haiwen grabbed the first prize in the O-125 category also known as the "F1 on Water". Chinese players won gold and silver in O-350 and occupied all top three in OSY400.

Every year, there are a series of races including national championship and finals. Chinese players take part in categories such as water motorcycle, OA (250 ml.), OB (350 ml.), OSY-400 (400 ml.), etc. The length of an OB boat stretches to 3.80 meters with a speed up to 160 km per hour.

F1 Powerboat World Championship China Grand Prix

The venue of the Shanghai Round of the 2004F1 Motorboat Competition

China successfully held the F1 Powerboat World Championship China Grand Prix in Hangzhou in 1995, then in Shanghai in 2004. Seeing this, the UIM decided to organize one or two such events in China every year starting from 2006.

The F1 Powerboat World Championship China Grand Prix is the most prestigious, marketable powerboat event in China. Substantive media coverage led by CCTV effectively weaved competitions, promotions and corporate profits together with the participation of target audience. The GP has huge commercial potential to its stable and smooth management. Based on intensive races and promo events, it takes full advantage of publicity campaigns to enhance the image of itself and its business partners.

The 2004 0-125 Class Motorboat World Championship and International Motorboat Elite Championship was held at the Daminghu Lake, Jinan, Shandong Province.

20 Sports

Chinese Motorboat Association

The Chinese Motorboat Association joined the UIM on December 11, 1986, and regularly organizes the National Motorboat Championship.

The CMA successfully co-sponsored three F1 Powerboat World Championships in 1995, 1996 and 1997. More than one million people went to watch the competitions.

Address: C-3, Longtan Lu, Chongwen District, Beijing
Website: http://motoboat.sport.org.cn

In October 2004, the 12th World Fin Swimming Championship was held in Shanghai. The Chinese team gained 12 gold medals.

Water Motorcycling

Water motorcycling is a thrilling new water sport spectacular to watch, widely popular throughout the world. Ever since this sport kicked off in the 1990s in China, its market has been expanding in a fast pace. Currently there are more than 10,000 water motorbikes nationwide, and the number is growing at 30 percent annually in coastal and riverside areas. Starting from 1995, the World Water Motorcycling Finals have been held 5 times. In June 1999, China hosted the 1st National Water Motorcycling Classics, an event extensively covered by the media and closely followed by the public. Chinese riders also did well at the 1999 World Water Motorcycling Finals in the United States.

Gliding

Gliding officially began in China in 1953 and came to a climax in 1960. At that time, except Tibetan Autonomous Region, Ningxia Hui Autonomous Region and Taiwan province, there were altogether 85 aero clubs established in China, which represented the flourish and popularization of this sport. In 1981, Gliding was included as a formal event by the Physical Culture and Sports Commission of the PRC and the first National Gliding Championship was held in Shenyang. Since 1982, the aero training base in Datong, Shanxi province, which has superior field and updraft, sponsors the National Gliding Championship every year. Sometimes there were more than 20 gliders participating in the game, and the competition was extremely furious. General Administration of Sport of China has also held the International Gliding Invitational Tournament for many times in the flying school in Anyang, Henan province, and the aero training bases in Jiayuguan, Gansu province and Datong, Shanxi province, which not only enhances the exchanges in this sport, but also improves its skill level.

At the end of 1980s, paragliding was introduced to China. It is interesting, safe, easy to learn and doesn't have high requirement of strength, so more and more aero-sports lovers are fascinated with this sport. At present, there are more than 50 paragliding clubs in China, and the registered paragliding athletes in the Aero-sports Association reached more than one thousand.

Paragliding Record

The highest: In 1988, the French adventurer Jean-Marc Boivin started from the top of Mt. Everest and ascended by paraglider to the height of 9,000 meters. The record of the Chinese is 4,000 meters.

The longest: The longest distance achieved by a paraglider is 337 km. and the longest record created by the Chinese is 120 km.

The longest in time: The longest paragliding time is 17 hours, and the Chinese record is 7 hours.

The age record of the athletes: The oldest paragliding athlete is 85 years old, while the youngest 4. The oldest Chinese paragliding athlete is 64, while the youngest 16.

Fin Swimming

Since 1979, China's diving events are gradually turned to the fin swimming events announced by World Underwater Federation. China achieved a breakthough in this sport during the 1980s. In the national competition held in 1983, Qiu Yadi, an athlete from Guangdong province, broke the world record on the 50m breath-hold diving by 15"8. In the 12th World Fin Swimming Championships in 2006, the Chinese team won 11 of the total 12 gold medals in women's events, and created 11 world records; meanwhile, the men's team also won their first gold medal, realizing the historical breakthrough. The Chinese team won half of the total 24 gold medals, ranking first in the medal tally.

The Chinese fin swimming team altogether takes part in the World Championships 9 times and 3 times in the World Games, and won 106 and 15 gold medals respectively. According to some statistics, in the past 20 years or so, 53 Chinese athletes broke the world records 136 times. For all those years, Chinese team keeps its leading position in the world. Among the 24 fin swimming events, Chinese hold the world records of 15, especially women's events.

Zheng Shiyu

Zheng Shiyu(1969-), who won the title of 100m breath-hold diving in the 4th World Fin Swimming Championships, is the first Chinese world champion in this event. During 1987-1992, she rewrote the world records 23 times in the world and national competitions. In 1992, the World Underwater Federation bestowed her "Make a Difference" Award.

Cheng Chao

Cheng Chao (1975-), the winner of 3 individual champion titles and 1 team title in the 5th World Fin Swimming Championships in 1990, while in 1992, the 6th World Championships, she took 5 titles and created a new record on 800m breath-hold diving. In more than10 years as a swimmer, she broke the world records 10 times and gained world titles 11 times.

• Sports Activities and Events for Athletes With Visual or Mobility Impairment

Mobility impairment could be divided into three categories: amputation and other disabilities, spinal cord injury and cerebral palsy.

People with amputation and other disabilities could participate in sports activities such as: Weightlifting, Gymnastics, Board Games, Athletics, Swimming, Archery,Shooting, Wheelchair Basketball, Table Tennis, Wheelchair Tennis, Volleyball, etc.

Those listed as events are: Athletics, Swimming, Weightlifting, Archery, Wheelchair Basketball, Wheelchair Fencing, Wheelchair Tenni,Shooting and Wheelchair Volleyball.

People with spinal cord injury could participate in such sports activities as: Gymnastics, Board Games, Athletics, Swimming, Weightlifting, Archery, Shooting, Wheelchair Basketball, Wheelchair Table Tennis, and Wheelchair Dancing.

Those listed as events are: Athletics, Swimming, Weightlifting, Archery, Shooting, Wheelchair Basketball, Wheelchair Fencing, Wheelchair Table Tennis, Wheelchair Tennis and Wheelchair Rugby.

People with cerebral palsy could participate in such sports activities as: Gymnastics, Board Games, Athletics, Table Tennis, Shooting, Boccia, Football, Wheelchair Tennis, and Wheelchair Rugby.

Those listed as events are: Athletics, Swimming, Table Tennis, Boccia, Football, Wheelchair Tennis, and Wheelchair Rugby.

People with visual impairment could participate in sports activities such as: Gymnastics, Board Games, Athletics, Swimming, Goal ball for the Blind, Table Tennis for the Blind, Judo, and Football for the Blind.

Those listed as events are: Athletics, Goal ball for the Blind, Judo, and Football for the Blind.

• Sport Activities and Events for Deaf People

Currently, China is home to 20.57 million people with hearing dysfunction, or 34.3 percent of the total disabled.

People with deafness can share all kinds of sport activities with normal people. The events include: Basketball, Volleyball, Football, Table Tennis, Tennis, Water ball, Swimming, Cycling, Gymnastics, Wrestling, Judo, Shooting for men in summer games and Basketball, Volleyball, Table Tennis, Athletics, Swimming, Cycling, Gymnastics, Shooting for women.

For winter games, events like Downhill, Giant Slalom,Special Slalom, Ski Jumping and 15 km Ski, 3×10 km Relay Ski go to men and events represented by Downhill, Giant Slalom,Special Slalom, 5km Ski and 3×5 km Relay Ski come to women.

• Sport Activities and Events for Mentally Defective Persons

Events for people with mental defectiveness can be divided into events and national outreach programs.

The official events fall into two categories: summer and winter. The summer and winter Olympic Games are alternately held every four years.

Official summer events include: Aquatics, Golf, Athletics, Gymnastics, Weight Lifting, Bowling, Skidding of Wheel, Cycling, Soft Ball, Equestrian, Tennis, Football, and Volleyball. Events with a large population base include: Boccia, Badminton, Table Tennis, Hand Ball, and Sailing.

Official winter events include: Alpine Skiing, Cross Country Skiing, Ice Hockey, Speed Skating, and Figure Skating. Events with a large population base include: snowshoe walking.

Shen Jiliang

Shen Jiliang (1951-), table tennis at the level TT7, won two bronze in 100m free style swimming and 100m backstroke swimming at the New York Paralympics in June 1984. In August 1986, at the 4th FESPIC Games held in Solo, Indonesia, he won gold medals in 100m free style and 100m backstroke swimming, and men's singles of table tennis. In 1989, he won a gold medal in the men's singles of table tennis at the 5th FESPIC Games held in Kobe, Japan. At the Sixth FESPIC Games held in Beijing, he claimed one silver and one gold medal. In 1999, he finished first in men's singles of table tennis at the 7th FESPIC Games in Bangkok, Thailand.

The judge informed the athlete with dumb show that there was still a lap left in the deaf men's 400m race.

Ping Yali

Ping Yali (1961-), Visual Impairment B12, won the first gold medal for China at the 7th Paralympics held in New York, U.S.A in 1984. She finished first in sprint, long jump, and 400m running at the first and second NGD in 1984 and 1988 respectively, first in sprint, long jump and 400m running at the third and fourth FESPIC Games (Far East & South Pacific Games for the Disabled) respectively in 1982 and 1986 respectively. She currently works as Senior Chiropractor.

Zhao Tiliang

Zhao Tiliang (1962-), Mobility Impairment A4, works in Tongxian Disabled Persons Federation. His strength was high jump. He won the silver medal at the 3rd FESPIC Games held in Hong Kong SAR in October, 1982. He finished first with a new world record of 1.82m in high jump, and second in Javelin Throw, at the NGD held in Guangzhou in March 1993. He won the gold medal at the 9th Paralympics held in Barcelona, Spain in September 1992. He was voted national excellent athlete in 1992. In September 1994, he claimed the first place with a new world record at the 6th FESPIC Games.

Lin Haiyan

Lin Haiyan (1972-), Mobility Impairment SH1B, won the gold medal in shooting at the 6th FESPIC Games held in Beijing in September 1994. In 1998, she attended the World Shooting Championship for the Disabled held in Spain and won a gold medal, breaking the world record for air pistol consists of 40 shots. In January 1999, she finished first at the 7th FESPIC Games held in Bangkok, Thailand, 1999. In 2000, at the 11th Sidney Paralympics, she took a second place and broke the world record in air pistol. In 2005, she won the first place at the NGD in shooting and broke two world records.

Wang Juan

Wang Juan (1975-), Mobility Impairment T44, won three gold medals and broke two world records at the 7th FESPIC Games in 1999. In August 1999, she claimed the first place in 100m running and broke the world record at World Star Games for the Disabled. In 2000, she took home two bronze medals in 100m and 200m running at the Eleventh Chinese National Games for the Disabled. In 2004, she was the silver medalist in long jump at the 12th Olympics held in Athens.

Wu Bin

Wu Bin (1978-), swimmer at the level S12. In October 2002, at the 8th FESPIC Games held in Pusan, South Korea, he finished first in 50m free style, and second in 100m breaststroke, 100m free style, 200m medley, 4×100m medley relay and 4×100m free style relay. In 2003, at the World Blind People Games held in Quebec, Canada, he took a gold medal in 50m free style, and three bronze respectively in 100m breaststroke, 4×100m medley relay and 4×100m free style relay.

Li Yansong

Li Yansong (1982-), Visual Impairment T12, was strong in athletics. In July 2002, he finished third in 400m running at the 3rd World Championships for the Disabled held in France. He finished first in 200m, 400m and 4×100m at the 8th Far South Games for the Disabled and broke national record several times at the 4th and 5th NGD. In 2004, he finished first in 4×100m relay, second in 400m running, fourth in 200m running and fifth in 100m at the Athens Paralympics.

♦ China Sports Association for the Disabled

China Sports Association for the Disabled, a public sports organization under the leadership of All-China Sports Confederation (ACSF), was founded in Tianjin on October 21, 1983. Its major tasks include: helping all the disabled persons and encouraging them to take part in sports exercises so as to improve their health, enrich their life and make them more confident towards life and join those without disabilities to contribute to the building of a modernized society. Since its birth, the association has been affiliated to International Association of the Disabled (ISOD), Cerebral Palsy—International Sports and Recreation Association (CP-ISRA), International Blind Sports Association (IBSA),International Sports Mandeville Games Federation (ISMGF) and FESPIC.

♦ China Sports Association for the Deaf Persons

Founded in Beijing on Dec.10, 1986, China Sports Association for the Deaf Persons is a mass sports organization led by All-China Sports Federation. The main task of the Association is to mobilize and organize the deaf to engage in sports, which can promote rehabilitation, enhance health and their technical skills. The Association also encourages the deaf to gain the courage and have faith in life, take active part in the material and spiritual building of a socialist society and contribute to the modernization drive. The Association joined the International Committee of Sports for the Deaf after it was born, host the National Deaf Basketball Games and led the deaf to attend the NGD. In 1989, the Chinese deaf athletes took part in table tennis matches at the 16th World Deaf Games, the first time that Chinese deaf attended the world games.

♦ China Sports Association of the Mentally Retarded People

Founded on June 17, 1986, China Sports Association of Mentally Retarded People is a mass sports organization under the auspices of All-China Sports Confederation (ACSF). Its main tasks include: organizing sports activities for mentally retarded people to help them improve their health and intelligence, encourage them to become more confident in face of challenges and contribute to the society. After its initiation, it was affiliated to Special Olympics International (SOI).

Mass Sports

Mass sports have been a hot spot of Chinese people's consumption now. More and more people take part in the traditional Chinese sports, such as setting-up exercises, shadowboxing, wushu, dance and swordplay, while other sports like bowling became prevalent among ordinary citizens from the well-offs very quickly. In some cities, the price of 2.5 yuan for one game does bring lots of people to join in. Even some typical Western sports like billiards have gained ground in China rapidly. At the crossings of the village fairs, billiard tables setting in the open air is a commonplace, and the local youths love this sport very much.

While the government focuses on winning more gold medals in the Olympics, the mass sports are mainly decided by the market. The privately run and foreign sponsored sports are developing together with the state-run sports. Different from those traditional sports such as Ping-Pong, radio exercises and swimming, new sports like body building, motoring, extreme sports and outward bound training are all run under the circumstances of market economy, initiated and popularized by commercial clubs. Currently, the top 5 hottest sports are bodybuilding, swimming, billiards, tennis and bowling, and other popular sports include badminton, taekwondo, motoring and shooting.

Group Callisthenics

At the beginning of the 20th century, group calisthenics had appeared in some provinces and cities, but the scale was relatively small, and the form simple, which only limited to setting-up exercises, human pyramid and Chinese character forming, etc. In 1959, at the opening ceremony of the 1st National Games, a large scale group calisthenics *Celebrating Together* was performed by 7,823 people, which was the first time in the history that calisthenics was performed with several parts under one consolidated themes, and all directed by music. *Celebrating Together*, symbolizing that Chinese group calisthenics had developed from one or several single performances. It entered a new stage of the designing, organizing and training of Chinese large scale group calisthenics, making it systematic from theory to practice and organization to training..

In November 1987, at the opening ceremony of the 6th National Games, China's first nighttime group calisthenics *Reaching the Clouds* was successfully performed. The background composed of lanterns holding by 8,000 people was a rare scene, which perfectly matched the performances of fire dragon and torch dance. *Reaching the Clouds* created a resplendent visual effect that could hardly be realized in daytime. As a milestone, it greatly expanded the scope of China's group calisthenics.

Bowling

Bowling was set up as an event in 1984 in China. After more than ten year's development, the level has been improved greatly. At present, there are nearly a thousand registered bowling athletes in China. In recent years, Chinese athletes gained good grades many times in international matches, but the highest grade that Chinese team got in the Asian Games is the fourth. Now, the Bowling Association of China has adopted the athletes ranking system and holds the International Open Tournaments, National Championships, National Youth Championships and National Elite Games, so as to accelerate the development of this sport.

Bowling has kept growing in China for nearly 20 years, and now it has entered the stage of steady development. We have great improvement in both the popularization and achievements. In the World Women's Bowling Championship in 2005, the Chinese team won one gold medal, one silver medal, one fourth, two fifths, and two sixths. Yang Huiling became the first Chinese world bowling champion, which greatly encouraged all the Chinese bowling players. In the bowling events, Asia has the world-class level, while Chinese team is only in the upper middle.

Winter Swimming

Winter swimming is quite popular in China, and most provinces and cities have their own winter swimming association. According to statistics, the number of people participating in winter swimming is at least 700,000 to 800,000. Chinese Swimming Association was established in 1995, and now it has 162 member organizations and more than 200,000 members. From those northern cities like Mudanjiang, Fushun, and Dalian to those southern provinces like Anhui and Zhejiang, winter swimming enjoys great popularity. The National Winter Swimming Championship sponsored by the Winter Swimming Committee will be held in 2007 for the ninth time, with nearly 2500 athletes joining in. While the International Winter Swimming Games held in Dalian has entered its third consecutive year. More and more young people at 20s and 30s take part in this sport, and the youngest athlete in the National Championship is only 6.

The 2007 Harbin International Invitational Tournament has 31 delegations from Russia, France and China with more than 400 athletes. The athletes are divided into 9 teams, which are young men's team, young women's team, middle-aged team, the first aged team, the second aged team, the aged performing team and will compete in 25m breast stroke against the current and 25m freestyle swimming. The oldest Chinese athlete is Che Shuqi from Beijing delegation, who is 80, and the oldest foreign athlete is Mr. Sam of 68 from France, who joined the Harbin Tournament for the first time. The youngest athlete is the 8-year-old Daniel from Russia.

Car Modelling

The sports of Car Modelling starts late in China, but develops rapidly. The National Youth's Car Modelling Championship has been held for 20 consecutive years. In the 4th Kyosho World Vehicle Model Competitions held in Beijing in the January 2002, Chinese Lin Yuqing and Liu Jiarong made their way among 150 contestants from 24 countries, and won the second place of the competition of the 1/10 gas engine motorhome.

Since Car Modelling Association of China was established in 1996, it actively communicates with international vehicle organizations and officially joined the International Federation of Model Auto Racing in 2003.

The National Car Modelling Championship represents the highest level of the Car Modelling competition in China, and all the models taking part in are remote controlled. In recent years, Chinese athletes have achieved profound improvement in the event, and have won a second place in the international tournament.

Multi-bowls

This sport was introduced to China in 1984. In last over ten years, the level of multi-bowls of China improves rapidly, and the number of participants keeps increasing. In some provinces and cities, the sport has more than ten thousand enthusiasts. At present, China's multi-bowls events have five individual events, including bocce, boule, petangue, Lawn ball and shuffle ball.

In the 5th World Bocce Championship hold in 1991, Chinese men's team got the second place, while in the 1992 World Bocce Clubs Championship, the first place. In 1998, Chinese women's boule team took part in the World Championship for the first time, winning one silver medal. Then in 2001, the women's team won the second place in the World Championship and the sixth place in the World Games Boule event. In August 2002, Chinese team won two bronze medals respectively in consecutive throwing and individual game, and broke the Asian record two times in the World Women's Boule Championship. In the 2006 World Women's Bocce Championship, China realized a historical breakthrough—winning three titles in the six events and ranking first in the medal tally, which showed that China's team had become one of the strongest team of the world.

The multi-bowls sports has developed in China over 20 years and won more than 50 medals in various international competitions. China represents the highest level of Asia in this sport.

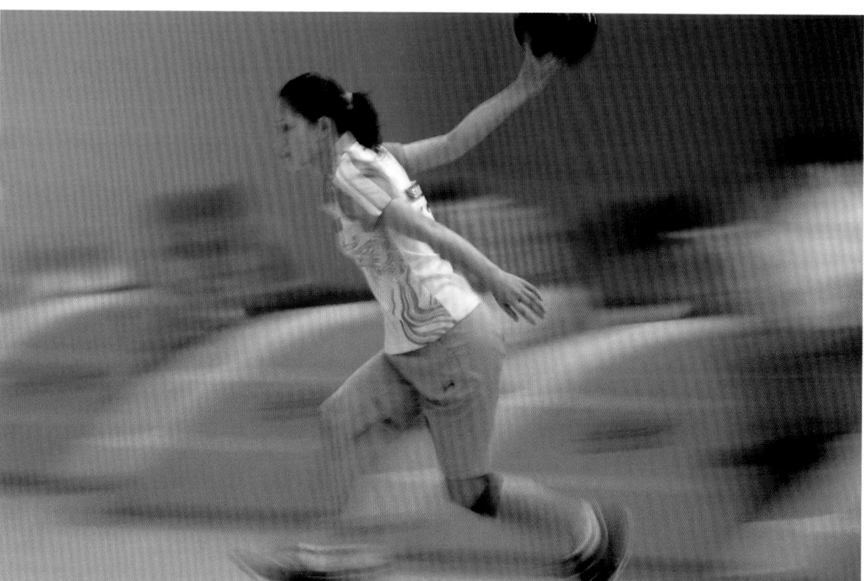

Yang Suiling in the bowling competition at the 15th Doha Asian Games on December 10, 2006

Angling

Since 1950s, some European countries began to list angling as an official sports event. The International Federation of Sport Fly Fishing was established in 1952. In 1980s, China began to hold angling competitions in the cities like Wuxi, Chongqing and Shanghai. China Angling Association was set up in 1983, and since 1985, the national angling competition is held every year.

In 2006, the 3rd World Fly Fishing Championship held in Taiwan Province drew 265 angling masters from 41 countries. At both side of the Taiwan Strait, there were altogether 66 Chinese competitors joined the game, among whom 54 athletes from Taiwan gained all the titles in boat angling, lake angling, long distance angling, while the title of rock fishing was gained by the Japanese team.

Dart

Originating from bars, the sport of dart has a history of hundreds of years and is popular all over the world as it can serve the purpose of exercise, competition as well as entertainment. But in China, this sport is still a newcomer. In 1999, General Administration of Sport of China included dart as one of the 94 official events, and holds the national dart games for six consecutive years ever since.

Dart will be a popular sport of China in the 21st century. Currently, many people are enthusiastic about this sport, and many competitions have the record of more than 10 thousand people signing up. In Beijing, Shanghai, Qingdao, Guangdong, Shandong, Shenyang and many other cities or provinces, lots of dart games are initiated by the citizens themselves. Peking University and Tsinghua University set dart as elective and hold intercollegiate dart games. The national open darts championship "Dart King" which is held every year has become the highest level dart competition of China. Now, with the support of the world top games, this sport, which is simple and has no weather and age limitations, will prevail in China in the future.

Extreme Sports

Since the extreme sports was first introduced to China in 1990s, the number of people engaging in rock climbing, benji jumping, skateboarding and other extreme sports increases by about 20 percent annually.

Among the aquatic sports, water skiing, canoeing, drifting, motorboating and water motorcycling develop fast in China, especially drifting. At present, china has more than 150 commercial drifting centers, and explorative drifting activities organized by the enthusiasts are much more. The land extreme sports are even more popular in all the Chinese cities. The land sports refer to roller skating, skateboarding, BMX (bicycle motocross). According to the field, they can also be grouped as street course competition and U-shaped ramps competition. Among the youths, especially the teenagers, playing extreme sports has become a fashion and the symbol of urban life. The air extreme sports mainly refer to rock climbing. In order to cater for the requirement of the modern urban life, this sport which needs specialty, stamina and suitable place has been rapidly popularized and has become a mass sport. Now there are more than 50 climbing walls in China, and many rock-climbing teams are very famous, such as the Mountaineering Association of Peking University and the rock climbing team "Snow" from China University of Geosciences.

Bodybuilding

Bodybuilding has been developed in China for more than 20 years. Along with the level of the sport continually improves, Chinese bodybuilders have made big progress in the world bodybuilding competitions in many levels and events. From November 23-28, 2005, the 59th World Bodybuilding Championship sponsored by the International Federation of Bodybuilding & Fitness, was held in Shanghai, China. Over 300 top bodybuilders from more than 80 countries and areas took part in this world-class bodybuilding competition. Chinese athlete Qian Jicheng won the title of Men's 60kg, which was a historical breakthrough, becoming China's first bodybuilding champion. This success greatly encouraged all the Chinese bodybuilders.

In 1986, Chinese Weightlifting Association set up the Bodybuilding Committee as one of its branches. China entered the International Federation of Bodybuilding & Fitness in November 1985. Now, almost all the provinces, autonomous regions and municipalities directly under the Central Government have developed this sport. Bodybuilding clubs and gymnasiums are more than ten thousand all over the country and the number of bodybuilding participants and enthusiasts is over ten million. Bodybuilding has been written into the college physical education textbook. Currently, national championship, miss fitness contest and the bodybuilding clubs qualifying are held every year. Now, china has two international class bodybuilding umpires and 35 national class ones.

On November 27, 2005, Qian Jicheng won the 60kg class gold medal at the 59th World Bodybuilding Championship, which was the first gold medal in the championship gained by Chinese player.

At 01:26 on July 30, 2001 (18:26 on July 29 in Britain), Zhang Jian arrived at the Strait of Dover in France successfully, becoming the first Chinese crossing over English Channel alone.

▲ Zhang Jian

Zhang Jian (1964-) crossed the 29.5-km-wide Qiongzhou Straits in 1988 with nine hours, 19 minutes and 2.64 seconds. Hence known as "China' s No.1 Man Who Crosses the Qiongzhou Straits." In August 2000, without any aid, he crossed the Bohai Straits, covering 123.58 km, with 50 hours and 22 seconds. He thus created the man' s world record in crossing the widest sea straits.

First Women Bodybuilding Champions

On November 28-30, 1986, at the 4th "Strong Man" Bodybuilding Invitational Tournament, women's events were included into formal competitions for the first time. According to the rules of world bodybuilding competitions, 57 women bodybuilders wearing bikini, fully present their strong muscles, balanced proportion of figures and clear features. This is a huge progress in the history of China's bodybuilding sport, which represents that Chinese woman bodybuilders are making great improvement in competing with other countries.

World Top Professional Bodybuilding Stars Performed in China for the First Time

In December 1988, in order to celebrate the magazine *China Sports'* 30th anniversary, top professional bodybuilding stars from the US, Britain, Netherland and Canada came to China give a performance. This was not only the first time world professional bodybuilding stars came to China, but also the first time the International Federation of Bodybuilding & Fitness sent high level bodybuilders to its 127th member country China. More than ten thousand spectators enjoyed the marvelous performance of Mr. Universe and Miss Olympic in the Capital Stadium. With the exciting music, their flexible body, perfect posture and rakish movements all symbolized the highest level of bodybuilding. All the spectators enjoyed their beauty with great interest. Later, the bodybuilding stars went to Wuhan, Guangzhou and Xi'an for a performing tour.

Callisthenics

Since November 1997, China Aerobic Association consecutively attended all the competitions organized by the three major international callisthenics organizations. From January 27 to February 4, 1999, China invited foreign experts to give lectures to "athletic calisthenics referees and coaches training course". And at the same year, the national championship for the first time adopted the international rules, which symbolized that China's athletic callisthenics had been geared to international standards.

In the 2002 World Championship, Chinese team achieved a small success, both team event and individual event ranking before 8. At the last day of the 7th World Games held in Duisburg in Germany in 2005, Chinese callisthenics athletes won their first gold medal by a set of perfect performance.

Dance Sport

This kind of ballroom dancing was introduced to China in 1930s, first popular in Shanghai, later in Tianjin and Guangzhou and other big cities, and gradually becomes a common social dance. Since 1980s, the international standard dance entered a new era of development. The foreign experts and outstanding dancers came to China for lecturing, performing, communicating and training in succession. The international standard dance rapidly spread from Beijing, Guangzhou to other places. In 1989, Chinese Dancers Association formally set up "China Ballroom Dance Federation", and later renamed as "China Ballroom Dancing Society". The first National International Standard Dance Championship was held in 1987, and holds every year since then.

In 1991, Chinese Dance Sport Federation was established, and in accord with the international rules, constituted China's first draft of the rules for dance sport. Thirty provinces, autonomous regions and municipalities under the central government set up their dance sport association, and the first National Competitive Dance Championship was held. Chinese Dance Sport Federation consecutively joined in World Dance & Dance Sport Council (WDDSC) and the International Dance Sport Federation (IDSF). At the end of 1993, Chinese Dance Sport Federation held the World Competitive Dance Championship, which is China's first world open game acknowledged by WDDSC and IDSF.

At the same time, some colleges such as the social dance department of Beijing Dance Academy has set up the major of international standard dance, while Beijing Sport University also has dance sport course. Along with dance sport gradually brought into the course of colleges, its science research, training and competition level will be further improved.

On June 3, 2006, the Chinese team won the gold medal, bronze medal and the second place in team in the Six-person Team Exercise Competition of the Ninth World Bodybuilding Championship.

Roller Skating

The sport of roller skating starts late in China, although it was introduced to China in 19th century, but only as an amusement and confined to several coastal cities. Not until the early 1980s was the formal competition held in China. The first National Roller Skating Championship was held in Beijing in October 1983, and the events included speed skating and figure skating.

Chinese Roller Skating Association was formally established in 1980 and joined in the International Roller Sports Federation the same year. In 1986, it became a member of Confederation of Asian Roller Sports. Presently, Chinese Roller Skating Association is in charge of four events: figure skating, speed skating, roller hockey and skateboarding, among which speed skating can fully represent the competitiveness of roller sports. A series of competitions sponsored by Chinese Roller Skating Association brought the "roller sports heat" to the whole country, such as National Speed Skating Championship, National Road Skating Championship, National Figure Skating Championship and Free Skating Open. In order to make the games complying with the international standard, all the road skating competitions adopt the rules of international championships. At present, the number of roller skating participants in China is no less than 10 million. China's level of figure skating keeps ahead in Asia.

Hot Air Balloon

In September 1982, the chief editor of Forbes magazine M. L. Forbes visited China's Xi'an, Luoyang and Beijing with his hot air balloon. At the foot of Badaling Great Wall, he drove the hot air balloon in person to give a performance. This was the first hot air balloon flying in China mainland since the PRC founded in 1949. Forbes gave his hot air balloon "China-US friendship" to China as a gift. In 1983, the first group of hot air balloon drivers began to fly, which meant that China's hot air balloon sport started. In the following several years, HGQ-1and RQ-1 hot air balloons, which were designed and produced by China itself, passed the test-fly. Since then on, China possessed the ability of producing hot air balloon, which greatly accelerate the development of this sport. Now, China has 120 registered hot air balloons.

The Aero Sports Federation of China has successfully held Beijing International Hot Air Balloon Invitational Tournament for 3 times, the theme of which was to fly across the Great Wall. Besides, it also successfully organized the adventuring fly over the Huanghai Sea and Qiongzhou Strait and the large scale hot air balloon performance on the Shanghai Film Festival. Since 1983, the Aero Sports Federation of China organizes Chinese hot air balloon team and hot air airship team to participate in the 7th, 10th and 12th World Hot Air Balloon Championship and the First World Hot Air Airship Championship, and have visited the US, France, India, Switzerland, Japan, Poland, Korea, Luxemburg and many other countries.

On July 3, 2005, the Second Zhongkun Cup Xinjiang Fire Balloon International Invitational Tournament was held in Khotan, Kashgar, Artux and Akasu, which was the largest fire balloon competition in China, attended by 60 fire balloons from six countries including China.

Croquet

The Croquet has been introduced to China for only twenty years, but it develops very fast. Now, more than 5 million people take part in this sport, and the number of croquet teams is more than 40,000, as well as nearly 10000 pieces of standard croquet fields. The speed of development is so rare compare to other countries. Along with the increasing of the croquet participants, China's croquet sport has entered a new stage.

The First China Croquet Championship was held in 1986. In the same year, China took part in the First World Croquet Championship. After contesting with the several strong teams, China entered the semi-final, which was also the first time that Chinese team participated in the international croquet games. China Croquet Association was established in 1987, and later, Beijing, Shanghai and the Inner Mongolia set up their croquet association in succession. Now, China Croquet association has 54 member organizations. In September 1989, China entered the World Croquet Federation, and then in May 1991, joined the Asia Croquet Federation. China Croquet Association organizes many national games every year, such as National Croquet Game for the Elders, National Croquet Championship, National Youth's Croquet Game, National Cities' Croquet Game, National Villages and Towns Croquet Game, National Enterprises' Croquet Game and National Hundred Cities' Croquet Game.

In 2006, Chinese croquet team got a historical breakthrough, winning the third place in the World Croquet Championship, which is the first metal that Chinese croquet team won in the international croquet games.

Every year, over 3 million people experience diving in Hainan.

Non-Professional Diving

Like most newly rising sports, non-professional diving is under fast development. The first 8 diving clubs were established in China in 1989, which symbolized that diving has entered China. After the first several years of slow launching, with the improvement of the Chinese citizens' consumption level, since

1999, the development of non-professional diving began to speed up. PADI, NAUI, SSI and other international diving training organizations entered Chinese diving market in succession. The number of participants and diving clubs has notable increase. According to the statistics announced by Chinese Underwater Sports Association in 2006, in 2005, the newly established diving clubs is more than ten and the total number has reached 102. Currently, China's registered diving clubs have over one million members.

Bridge

Bridge, a brain sport originated in Europe and America, was officially introduced into China in the 1930s. However, the game didn't experience real development in China until in 1980s. With the establishment of Chinese Contract Bridge Association in 1980, local bridge associations are established across the country, and a variety of bridge tournaments are held and training classes opened.

China has its national bridge teams, including men's team and women's team. Chinese Contract Bridge Association is responsible for organizing national teams to participate in international and regional bridge tournaments. In recent years, China's performance in this game is increasingly improved, and the national teams have made remarkable achievements in international and regional competitions. The women's team, as the strongest team in Asian and Pacific region and one of the strongest ones in the world, took its third runner-up title in the World Bridge Championship in 2003. The men's team, a strong team in Asian and Pacific region and above average level in the world, won the championship in IOC Bridge Grand Prix, which is also its best performance up to now.

The Chinese national bridge teams are posing a great challenge to strong powers in Europe and America. At the same time, various bridge competitions are being carried out in China, including the CCBA Championship Tournament attended by provincial teams, the National Bridge Club Championship attended by professional club teams, the National Bridge Championship with free registration and the quasi-professional National Class-A Club Championship, all held annually.

The First Bridge Masters

Bridge world master titles fall into 3 categories: World Master, World Life Master and World Grand Master. The world grand master is the most advanced level. A bridge is granted a relevant title when he/she accumulates certain master points and position points. A world master title demands 15 master points only and a life master title requires 50 master points and 5 position points. A grand master has to earn 200 master points and 10 position points, besides a world champion title.

In 1982, the 1 World Bridge Championship was held in Biarritz, France, in which the Chinese teams ranking 28 in the team event, with every earning 2.5 master points. Wang Junren and Lu Yulin got a rank and relevant master points in men's double event, becoming the first world masters of China.

Women's Bridge Team of China

From November 11 to 18, the 29 Far East Bridge Championship was held in Penang, Malaysia. Since champions of this event would be entitled to attend the Venice Cup Bridge Championships, the 9 attending teams, respectively from Japan, Indonesia, Malaysia, Thailand, Australia, New Zealand, China, Hong Kong and Chinese Taipei, all sent their best players, aiming to grasp this opportunity to get to the throne of bridge world.

The women's team of China, with a short history of less than 2 years, was composed of 6 players: Gu Ling and Zhang Yalan from Guangdong, Zhu Xiaoyin and Sun Ming from Beijing, and Lu Qin and Li Manling from Shanghai. Their average age was only 28. From the very beginning of the match, the Chinese team and Chinese Taipei team were taking the lead all the time. The final game eventually went on between these two teams. After fierce competition, the Chinese team defeated its opponent 20:10 VP, claiming women's title of Far East Bridge Championship for the first time. This means that the team had reached the top level in Asia and was striding for a position in the world.

Rock Climbing

Rock climbing is an extreme sport with a combination of skill, adventure and visual impact. Since its introduction into China in 1987, it has drawn the attention of young people with its unique charm. With its development for about two decades, this fashionable sport has already begun to exert its influence in China. It has developed a fixed group of enthusiasts and the group is expanding with an unprecedented speed.

The development of rock climbing in China mainland, Hong Kong and Chinese Taipei are almost at the same level, that is, the average level in Asia. With a history of more than ten years, the development of rock climbing has achieved a considerable scale in China, especially in the past couple of years. Beginning from 1997, more than two national or international tournaments are held in China annually. In August 1998, an international rock climbing invitational tournament was held in Huashan, which is the most advanced of its kind ever held in China. In September 1999, China hosted the 8 Asian Rock Climbing Championship, the second time it undertook such a task.

In order to popularizing and promoting rock climbing in China, Chinese Mountaineering Association has made great efforts to hold a variety of tournaments, including big events like World Cup, Asian Championship, Asian Cup, Asian Juniors Championship and National Championship. This has helped to improve Chinese athletes' performance greatly.

In 2005, in the 1 Asian Indoor Games held in Thailand, Chen Xiaojie, an athlete from PLA Institute of Physical Education, won the gold medal in speed competition of rock climbing, the first gold medal China has won in international rock climbing tournaments.

Billiards

With adoption of the policy of reform and opening up to the outside world in the 1980s, people's living standard in China has been greatly improved, leading to the spontaneous rise and rapid spread of billiards across the country. At present, there are about 60 million billiards enthusiasts in China, and the TV audience of snooker games amounts to 50 million.

In 1986, Chinese Billiards & Snooker Association (CBSA) emerged as the times required. From then on, snooker is not only an entertainment for ordinary people, but also an athletic sport included in annual national sports competition. This shows that snooker has developed into a more advanced stage in China. A variety of matches are held by China Billiards & Snooker Association and other local associations. The earliest is the National Snooker Championship, started in 1981 and held annually. Then is the National Snooker Elites Tournament, started in1990 and held annually. In 1995, another annual match was added to the list—the National CBSA Cup Tournament.

In the meantime, more and more international snooker tournaments were held in China. From 1988 to 1992, CBSA consecutively hosted "Kent Cup" World Snooker Tournament, attended by the best professional snooker players in the world. In 1996, the International Professional Snooker Invitational Tournament was held in Guangzhou, the first time for this tournament in China.

In the 2006 Doha Asian Games, the Chinese billiards team won three gold medals in men's single, double and team events.

The Chinese team finished first in the final of the Snooker Team Competition at the 15th Doha Asian Games.

♦ Chinese Go Association

Established in 1962, the Chinese Go Association is a non-profit specialized organization, which is composed of management staff, professional players, amateur players and local go associations at various levels. It aims to proactively develop friendly relationship with international go associations and that of other countries, and enhance the friendly exchange among countries through go game.

Address: No.80 Tiantan Donglu, Beijing
Website: http://www.weiqi.org.cn

Ding Junhui

Ding Junhui (1987-), keeps the status of snooker skyrocketing in China, the champion of two international snooker tournaments, one of which is the prestigious United Kingdom Snooker Championship.

In 2005, when the 18-year old Ding defeated Stephen Hendry in World Snooker China Open, more than 110 million people were watching the match on TV. It was the sports program with the biggest audience in 2005. In September, Ding won the championship of All-England Open, the first foreigner other than people from England, Scotland, Ireland and Northern Ireland to do so in this classic tournament. Naturally, he became the most convincing spokesman of China's snooker in the world.

♦ China Billiards & Snooker Association (CBSA)

China Billiards & Snooker Association (CBSA) was established in 1986,with its headquarter in Beijing. It is composed of four specialized committees respectively in charge of training, competition, promotion and publicity. It became a member of International Billiards and Snooker Federation in 1988. CBSA often organizes various matches, including National Billiards Championship, National Snooker Championship, National Snooker Elites Tournament, National Snooker Competition, National South-North Confrontation and other national games.

Address: No.5 Tiyuguan Lu, Beijing
Website: http://billiards.sport.org.cn/

Go (Weiqi)

With many enthusiasts, go has solid foundation for development in China. Since the founding of PRC, amateur games at all levels have been held across the country, and the great number of go enthusiasts forms a solid basis for the development of this sport.

The year 1999 has great significance in China's go history. It is the year in which the first National Go Level A Team Competition was started, and go began to climb out of the low tide in China. Since then, the development of go in China has been oriented onto a professionalized track. Attracted by national competition of China, the famous South Korean Lee Changho, nicknamed "stone Buddha", joined in as a super foreign , which shocked the international go community. In March 2005, Chang Hao, the leading of Shanghai Mobile team, the champion team of the previous year, defeated South Korean players and claimed the world championship which had been won by foreign players in the previous five years. With a short history of merely a few years, the National Go Level A Team Competition has produced fruitful results.

There are around 10 million go enthusiasts in China, but professional players haven't been in existence for a long time. The biggest contribution of the National Go Level A Team Competition is to have provided a platform for professional players to show their talent. The twelve professional teams in the league almost have all the top players in China.

The First Female 9-dan Go (*weiqi*) in the World

From June 12 to 25, 1988, the National Go Ranking Match was held in Beijing. Among the 197 players, 39 were promoted to a higher rank. Rei Naiwei, a female from Shanghai, was honored the 9-dan band, becoming the first female 9-dan go in the world.

Born in Shanghai, Rei Naiwei started learning go at the age of 11 and was recruited by the national team at 17. From 1982 to 1985, she consecutively won the runner-up title for four years. In 1986 and 1987, she defeated all her opponents in women's individual matches (which means 12 consecutive victories) and won the championship twice. In 2000, in the 43rd National Master Competition of South Korea, Rei defeated the famous South Korean master Cho Hoonhyun 2 to 1 and won the championship, becoming the first foreigner to win the national championship in the go history of South Korea.

National Go Ranking Match

From March 18 to April 1, 1982, the 1st National Go Ranking Match was held in Beijing. One hundred and thirty-three players from 16 provinces and municipalities participated in this match. Among the ten higher-ranking players announced by the State Physical Culture and Sports Commission, all attended the match except the three 9-dan players. After 12 rounds of fierce competition, 114 players were officially ranked, among whom 20 got a ranking higher than 5-dan.

The First Generation of National Gos

In 1964, the go competition of National Board Games began on April 26 in Hangzhou. Fifty-six players from 17 provinces, municipalities and autonomous regions attended the competition which lasted for 29 days. What's most exciting was that all the top three contestants were young players, with an average age of only 19.7. The champion, the runner-up and the third-place winner were Chen Zude, Wu Songsheng and Shen Guosun.

A native of Shanghai, the champion Chen Zude, enlightened by his father at 6, became a student of go master Gu Shuiru at seven and got instructions from another great , Liu Lihuai. In

1963 and 1965, Chen defeated Japanese 9-dan players for twice. During his 9 visits to Japan, he played more than 200 games with famous Japanese players which he mostly won. In 1963, he adopted the "bridge shape" layout—called "Chinese stream" in Japan—and achieved great success. In 1979, he ranked second in the 1st World Amateur Championship. Chen is now the vice chairman of China Weiqi Association.

Nie Weiping

Nei Weiping giving a lecture.

Nie Weiping (1952-), Go game player, In 1985, the heated first China-Japan Go Ring Contest was on. After the Japanese Kobayashi Koichi defeated Ma Xiaochun, the Chinese delegate was in an extremely unfavorable situation. Three great players in the Japanese delegation, namely Kobayashi Koichi, Masao Kato and Fujisawa Hideyuki, hadn't lost a game, whereas the Chinese delegation only had its leading , Nie Weiping. But Nie defeated his three opponents single-handedly like a tornado, helping the Chinese delegate to win the match eventually.

To liken Nie to a tornado is no exaggeration. In 1973, he swept the championships in the 1st Guoshou Tournament, the third and fourth National Games plus the 1st World Amateur Championship. During his visit to Japan in 1976, he defeated Ishida Yoshio, the champion of Honinbo match, and made great contribution to China's first victory in its exchange with Japanese go community. Nie thus got two nicknames from Japanese go community: "tornado Nie" and "go weirdo". Nie played an important role in go development of China, now at an equivalent level with that of Japan. After leading Chinese team to win three consecutive victories in China-Japan Go Ring Contest, he was crowned the title of "go sage". Now, Nie has been working as the head coach of Chinese go team for over a decade, with a new generation of players pursuing his dream.

Ma Xiaochun

Ma Xiaochun (1964-), Go game player, a 9-dan. He started learning go at the age of 9. He was recruited by a sports school at 10 and joined the national training team at 12. He won the championship in the 6th Tong Yong Cup and the 8th Fujitsu Cup. He is the winner of 5th and 7th China-Japan Meijin Match, 7th, 8th and 9th China-Japan Tengen (Tianyuan) Match. He won the 2nd Bawang Cup champion, the 2nd Friendship Cup champion, five National Go Individual champions, two New Sports Cup champions and two Guoshou Titles. Ma also won the 1st and 8th-10th Tianyuan titles, Mingren (Meijin) titles (including in 1998) in 10 consecutive years, two Strongest Top Ten champions, and CCTV Cup champions in 1991, 1992, 1994 and 1995. He also won the 3rd and 5th-6th Qiwang titles, 1st and 2nd Da Guoshou champions. He was also the runner-up in the 7th Tong Yong Cup and the 9th Fujitsu Cup, and won the third place in the 10th Fujitsu Cup. He won 1995 Longshan Contest and 1995 Rongguan Cup titles, 2nd National Mixed Pair champion. He won the second place in the 3rd World Go Open and the 3rd World Qiwang. In 1982, Ma became a 7-dan , advanced to 9-dan two years later. He is also the author of several books, among which are Thirty-six Strategies and Go and Know-how in Go Game.

Chang Hao

On January 24, 2007, Chang Hao (right) beat Lee Changho 2-0 and won the championship at the 11th "Samsung Cup" World I-go Open.

Chang Hao (1976-), a 9-dan go, started learning go at 6 and was recruited into Shanghai go team at 8. At the age of 10, he entered the national training team.

He won the titles of the 1st and 3rd National Children Go Competition, the 5th World Youth Contest and the 12th World Amateur Go Tournament champion. In 1994, he won two straight games in China-Korea New Pro Confrontation. In the 10th China-Japan Go Ring Contest, he helped the Chinese team to win with his five straight victories. He won the championship of the 10th and 11th Tianyuan Cup, the 1st Robust Cup and the 3rd NEC Cup and won the second place in the 11th Fujitsu Cup. In 1999, he won the titles of Robust Cup, Tianyuan Cup, CCTV Cup and the 1st Qisheng Contest in a row. He became a 1-dan in 1986 and was advanced to 8-dan in 1997. In 1999, he was further advanced to 9-dan.

Chinese Chess

As a cultural heritage, Chinese chess has a long history and large number of enthusiasts in China. Even children know the basic rules for moving chess pieces, and one can find people playing the game almost anywhere. After the founding of PRC, the game is included as an official event in sports competitions. Since the first National Chinese Chess Championship was held in 1956, the development of Chinese chess has been oriented to a right direction. Professional teams were established across the country, and the overall skills of players improved a lot. In 1960, after winning a national champion title, a 15-year old named Hu Ronghua devoted himself to the study of chess skills and improved it to a much higher level. He himself became a "remarkable master".

Domestically, the individual and team tournaments are held annually, plus Wuyang Cup and Yinli Cup, also held annually. Besides domestic games, there are Asian Cup and World Cup for this game. China is naturally the strongest power in Chinese chess, and General Administration of Sport of China lists the game as a sport to be promoted worldwide.

The First Big Chessboard

The first big chessboard in China was invented by Xie Xiaxun. At that time, a Chinese chess game would always attract such a big audience that the players were affected and the spectators' view blocked. Thus Xie Xiaxun invented a big chessboard to explain chess skills to enthusiasts. The first big chessboard was made of iron sheet, and chess pieces were made of glass with light installed in them. Such a chessboard was inconvenient to use, because it was hard to move around with electric wires connected to the pieces. Thus Xie substituted glass pieces with lead pieces. The board was about 3.3 meters long and 2 meters wide, and a chess piece was about 0.3 meter in diameter.

The invention of big chessboard pushed this game to a new stage of development. The Shanghai Office of International Chess Association at that time was interested in the big board and made a similar one for international chess so that open performance could be staged.

Hu Ronghua

Hu Ronghua(1945-), a Chinese chess master, started learning to play the game at the age of 8. Aged 15, He won the National Chinese Chess championship for the first time in 1960, thus creating the record for the youngest champion in this brain sport. He is the only winning ten consecutive victories in national championships and winning fourteen national individual titles, and also the only who dominated the game for over 40 years. He

Hu Ronghua in the National Chinese A-class Tournament on April 29, 2006

became the most outstanding Chinese chess talent in this century.

When Chinese team won the championship in 6 Asian Cups between 1980 and 1990 and the 1st World Chinese Chess Championship in 1990, Hu Ronghua was one of the leading players. In 1984, he won the title in the 1st Qixing Cup International Chinese Chese Invitational Tournament. He is also the champion of the 5th and 6th Asian City Chinese Chess Masters Tournament held in 1991 and 1993. He won the titles of Chinese chess Master and Grand Master respectively in 1982 and 1988.

Hu is good at playing blind chess and can play with several opponents at the same time. He is so skilled at this game and has such a strong memory that he can deal with 14 opponents simultaneously. While performing blind chess in Macao in 1977, he defeated all his opponents, which was viewed as an impossible task. He is considered a super talent in Chinese chess community.

Lu Qin

Lu Qin (1962-), Grand Master of Chinese Chess. Beginning from 8, he started learning to play Chinese chess from his uncle. Besides his tenacious style and nice layout, he impresses people by his incisive play and sharp reaction.

Lu ranked first in the National Junior Chinese chess Championships in 1978 and the second Asian City Chinese Chess Masters Tournament in 1985. In 1990 and 1995, he won the championship for both men's individual and team competition of the first and fourth World Chinese Chess Championship. He was granted the titles of Chinese chess Master and Grand Master respectively in 1986 and 1989.

▲ The First English Version of Chinese Chess Manual

Gleenrein, a Dane working at China Customs in the 1920s, is an enthusiast of Chinese chess. Versed in chess and Chinese chess, he was an enthusiastic advocator of the popularization of Chinese chess across the world. In 1916, he translated *qi xing ju hui* (7-star constellation), the most complicated puzzle in Chinese chess, into English and published it as a book titled *Seven-star Constellation in Chinese Chess* in the US and Europe. In order to facilitate the reading of English natives, he substituted chess pieces with ones similar to international chess pieces in shape. It was the first English version of Chinese chess manual.

Chess

China first began to hold national chess competitions in 1957, and didn't have any exchange activities with other countries until 1958. In 1975, Chinese Chess Association became an official member of FIDE (Federation Internationale des Echecs). In 1977, Chinese chess team participated in Asian Team Championship. In 1986, the national chess training team came into being. The training team was a cradle for top-notch chess players of China. A group of world-level master players cultivated here greatly enhanced the country's overall performance in this game, especially women's games which produced a great number of first-class talents.

In 1991, Xie Jun claimed a world title, breaking the monopoly of women's championship by Soviet Union (41 years) and European players (64 years) and becoming the 7th female champion in the history of chess. In 1988, Chinese women's team won the title in Olympic Team Championship, which showed that they had occupied the leading position in the world. In 2000 and 2002, women's team consecutively won the world team championship, thus making three victories in a row. Among the dozen of top womens shown on FIDE's score tally, six are Chineses. In the five years from 1998, FIDE altogether organized 8 women's world tournaments and all the titles were claimed by Chinese players.

At present, there are altogether 15 female Grand Masters and 15 male Grand Masters.

The First Title of Asian Chess Team Championship

From October 18 to 19, the 5th Asian Chess Team Championship was held in New Delhi, India, with 10 national teams attending from China, Philippines, Pakistan, Malaysia, New Zealand, Bengal, Kuwait, Bahrain and Brunei Darussalam. In this tournament, Chinese players snatched the title from Philippine team, the long-time defending championship. This means that women's team of China had reached the top level of Asia and was striding for a strong position in the world.

Ye Jiangchuan

Ye Jiangchuan (1960-), a chess Grand Master, born in 1960, currently is the head coach of Chinese national chess teams.

Ye's professional career is a mirror of China's development in chess. In 1981, he participated in the National Chess Championship and won the title, after which he claimed the title in 1984, 1986, 1987, 1989, 1994 and 1996, becoming a with the most national champion titles. Beginning from him, Chinese chess players began to demonstrate their talents in world arena. In the 1980s, he not only made remarkable achievements in individual events, but also won 3 Asian team championships with his teammates, thus winning a position for China in world chess community.

Despite his tight schedule, Ye undertook

♦ Chinese Chess Association

In November 1962, Chinese Chess Association was established, in charge of both Chinese chess and chess games. In March 1986, Chinese Chess Association was established as an independent organization for chess game. It is a mass organization in sports industry with legal status, responsible for the establishment and administration of national chess teams at various levels. It's also the only legal organization to join FIDE on behalf of China.

Chinese Chess Association has a training base in Yongchuan, Chongqiong and many high level reserve talent bases in Wenzhou, Qingdao, Shanghai, Chenghai of Guangdong, Wuxi, Ji'nan, Handan, Suzhou, Tianjin, etc. In Beijing, the association and the High School Affiliated to Renmin University work together to build the national junior chess team.

Chinese Chess Association holds about 60 domestic and international games annually, including professional events like National Individual Championship and Team Championship and amateur events like National College Chess Championship and Li Chengzhi Cup Children's National Chess Championship. Li Zhicheng Cup has been held for 12 years, with an annual attendance of more than 1,000.

Address: No. 80 Tiantan Donglu, Beijing.
Website: http://chess.sport.org.cn/

the task of coaching Xie Jun, helping her to win women's world champion for four times. In the meantime, he kept improving his skills. In 1993, he was granted the chess grandmaster title by FIDE, after which he won the championship twice in Chen Zhennan Cup Beijing Chess Grandmaster Match in 1995 and 1999. He has encountered all the best male players in the world, drawing Garry Kasparov and Anatoly Karpov to a tie, and defeating Swedish Viktor Korchnoi and British Nigel Short, both of whom are world runners-up.

In July 1999, his total score reached 2620, the first time a Chinese male exceeded the record of 2600. At present, with his score ranking around 20th in FIDE's list, he is no doubt in the list of world super players.

Liu Shilan

Liu Shilan (1962-) is the first chess Grand Master of China and also the first female Grand Master in Asia. In the regional competition of World Chess Championship in 1981, Liu won the title with a remarkable performance after defeating all her 14 opponents, which won her the ticket to the Championship. In the Championship, she ranked the third place with a performance of 7 victories, 7 ties and 3 losses. After this event, she became one of the world's top eight players and was granted the Grand Master title.

Xie Jun

Xie Jun (1970-) is the first world chess champion. On October 29, 1991, Xie defeated Maya Chiburdanidze, a famous Soviet Union, and won the women's world chess title, becoming the first world chess champion in China. It was also the first time after 1950 that the title was claimed by a from a country other than Soviet Union. Two years later, she successfully defended the title and became an unshakable "chess queen". Xie demonstrated her outstanding skills and strong mind in the game, and all the other players were impressed by her unique charm.

In October 1991, Xie Jun won the women's world championship for the first time, winning a match against Maya Chiburdanidze, who had held the title since 1978, by a score of 8.5:6.5. In November 1993 she successfully defended her title against Nana Ioseliani (winning their match 8.5:2.5) before losing her defending match to Hungarian Zsuzsa Polgar 4.5:8.5 in February 1996. In the Women's World Chess Championship held in Kazan, Russia and Shenyang, China, she defeated Alisa Galliamova (5 victories, 7 ties, 3 losses) and won her title back at the turning of the century.

Xie Jun in the competition

Zhu Chen

Zhu Chen in the competition

Zhu Chen (1976-), a female chess Grand Master. She started learning to play chess at an early age. In 1988 Zhu became the first Chinese to win an international chess competition when she won the "Children and Peace" World Girls Under-12 Championship in Romania. In the same year, Zhu entered the national team for further improvement. In the Olympic Team Championship held in 2000, she won the title of Best Female , the first time a Chinese won the title. In the World Chess Championship 2001, she put on an outstanding performance and defeated Russian Alexandra Kosteniuk, becoming the 9th women's world champion. At the same time, she broke a world record — to become the first female with the titles of World Girls Championship, World Junior Girls Championship and Women's World Chess Championship.

Now as a graduate student of School of Humanities and Social Sciences of Tsinghua University, the 26-year-old Zhu Chen owns the titles of male Grand Master and female Grand Master, her total score reaching 2,497. In April 2002, she defeated world champion Igor Ponomarev in the FIDE Chess Championship, thus becoming the first female world championship to win a male counterpart still in active status.

Xu Yuhua

Xu Yuhua (1976-) , a female chess Grand Master, with a total score of 2,487, ranks the 9th among women players in the world.

Major titles: champion of Regional Championship in 1993, women's champion

Shen Yongju, an old person in Shanghai, set a world record that his young pigeon returned in two days after flying 1,500 km away.

Racing Pigeon

Chinese Racing Pigeon Association was established in 1984, the same year FCI (Federation Colombophile Internationale) was born. At present, thirty-one provinces, municipalities and autonomous regions and two industrial sport associations have established their own racing pigeon associations, with members exceeding three-hundred thousand. Chinese Racing Pigeon Association became a member of FCI in January 1997, and began to organize national teams to attend world championships and world ranking tournaments. The association sends its delegation to attend FCF convention in every odd year.

In recent 10 years, pigeon racing has been developing rapidly with a strong momentum in China. From 1997 to 1999, Chinese Racing Pigeon Association sponsored three International Racing Pigeon Exhibitions in Beijing and Tianjin, attracting exhibitors from a dozen of countries and regions in Europe and America. In 2000, the association successfully hosted World Racing Pigeon Championship and Ranking Tournament, with 1,059 attendant pigeons from 17 countries and regions around the world.

In the meantime, Chinese pigeon athletes have presented outstanding performance in international events. In Thailand round of World Racing Pigeon Ranking Tournament unveiled in Bangkok on November 29, 2000, a pigeon breeded by Jia Chenggang from Sichuan, a member of Chinese Racing Pigeon Association, won the championship and got US$3,900 prize bonus. On August 18, 2002, when the World Racing Pigeon Championship was held in Lille, the fourth largest city of France, a Chinese pigeon athlete won the title. On October 4, 2003, in the Tianjin round of World Racing Pigeon Ranking Tournament, Chinese pigeon athletes won a decisive victory, sweeping the first three places in individual events and overall ranking.

of Huangzhuang Cup National Chess Championship in 1998, champion of Asian Chess Championship in 1998, women's champion of World Cup Chess Championship and women's champion of the 34th Olympic Chess Championship in 2000, champion of World Chess Championship, Moscow and champion of Regional Championship in 2001, champion of World Chess Championship and women's champion of the 35th Olympic Chess Championship in 2002, women's champion of the 36th Olympic Chess Championship in 2004.

Zhao Xue

Zhao Xue (1985-), a chess Grand Master, was born in 1985 and started learning to play chess at the age of 8. She participated in the national summer camp competition at 9 and won the third place in junior women's event. She entered the national training team at 10 and was enrolled by the national team at 14. In Women's Selection Competition of the 35th Olympic Team Championship, Zhao won the title with a difference of 5 scores over the runner-up, and got her first ticket to the Olympic Championship. After Xie Jun, Zhu Chen and Xu Yuhua, Zhao Xue is another outstanding female of China.

Major titles: champion of World Girls Under-12 Championship in 1997, champion of World Girls Under-14 Championship in 1999, champion of World Junior Girls Chess Championship in 2002, leading of champion team in two consecutive Olympic Team Championships

Folk Sports

Traditional Chinese folk sports include wushu, shadowboxing, qigong, Chinese wrestling, Chinese chess, go, etc.

Wushu is a traditional folk sport practiced for physical training and self-defense. It's practiced in various types of set exercises, either barehanded or with weapons. Taijiquan (shadowboxing) is a kind of barehanded exercises involving three aspects: regulation of the body, regulation of the mind and regulation of respiration. It's full of graceful and natural body movements. The key to this exercise is to control body movement with the mind.

Qigong is a unique health-building exercise in which practitioners, by controlling the mind and regulating the breath, can keep fit, live long, overcome diseases and strengthen physiological functions.

Colorful sports activities are organized in areas inhabited by minority peoples. These include Mongolian-style wrestling and horsemanship, Tibetan yak races, Korean people's springboard and swing, and the crossbow of the Miaos, which are all both entertaining and competitive.

Wushu

Wushu is an invaluable cultural legacy accumulated by Chinese people through long-time social practice, and is the most important traditional sport. *Wushu*, also called *wuyi* or *kungfu*, has many different schools and styles. Traditionally, a *wushu* school was named after its founder or the region, mountain or river where it originated or developed, or according to its technical features. Today, *wushu* generally falls into five categories: *quanshu* (barehanded exercises), *qixie* (exercises with weapons), *duilian* (dual combats), group performances, and combats using offensive and defensive skills.

In 1957, *wushu* was listed as sport event for the first time in China. In 1960, a national *wushu* tournament was held. Following that, a national *wushu* championship and national archery championship were respectively held in 1963 and 1964. Beginning from 1979, *wushu* competition and performance developed to a new stage, with national *wushu* performance contests and national *wushu* conventions held annually. In the national championship held in 1982, events for both male and female athletes were increased to 16, including group events, *changquan* (northern boxing), *taijiquan* (shadowboxing), *nanquan* (southern boxing), broad-sword play, double-edged sword play, spear play, cudgel play, traditional *quanshu* (category 1), traditional *quanshu* (category 2), traditional *quanshu* (category 3), traditional *quanshu* (category 4), traditional single weapon, traditional double weapon, traditional soft weapon, dual combats (in 1984, traditional *quanshu* and traditional weapon were renamed as "other *quanshu*" and "other weapon"). Every *wushu* event would attract many enthusiasts, including foreigners who are interested in this game.

The Origin of the Word "Wushu"

The word "*wushu*" first appeared in a poem by Yan Yannian in Southern and Northern Dynasties, but it referred to military in a general sense at that time. Literally translated, "wu" is military, fighting and strength; "shu" is skill, method and art. In its modern sense, "*wushu*" means the same as "*wuyi*", referring to the art of fighting for health-building and self-defense, practiced in many forms, including individual exercises, dual combat, set exercises, offensive and defensive combat, performance, competition, etc. Viewed as a cultural heritage, *wushu* was once called "guoshu", meaning national art. After the founding of PRC, it resumed its original name.

Over one hundred community residents doing boxing exercises at Guanqian Jie, Suzhou

On December 14, 2006, Zhao Guangyong finished first in the men's 65kg class boxing of martial arts at the 15th Doha Asian Games.

Set Exercises

Set exercises, composed of body movements of various styles, demonstrate philosophical thinking and high aesthetic value in combining offense with defense. It includes *quanshu*, *qixie*, *duilian* and group exercises. *Quanshu* in turn includes barehanded exercises like *changquan* (northern boxing), *taijiquan* (shadowboxing), and *nanquan* (southern boxing), *qiexie* includes weapon exercises like broad-sword play, double-edged sword play, spear play and cudgel play, and dual combats includes barehanded combats, combats with weapons and barehanded against weapons. Besides these, there are group performances in which group of athletes practice *wushu*, either barehanded or with weapons.

From 1982, *wushu* began to be promoted in a planned and systematic manner to the outside world. In 1985, the first International Wushu Invitational Tournament was held in Xi'an. In 1987, Asian Wushu Federation was established in Yokohama, Japan, and first Asian Wushu Championship was held, which has been held for five times up to now. In 1989, entrusted by Asian Wushu Federation, Chinese Wushu Association designed seven set exercises, which were later adopted by international events. From 1990 on, many comprehensive sports events, like Asian Games, Southeast Asian Games, East Asian Games, listed *wushu* as an official competition event. In October 1990, International Wushu Federation was established in Beijing, which organized 6 World Wushu Championships in China, Malaysia, the United States, Italy, Hong Kong and Armenia. At present, International Wushu Federation has 86 member federations from 5 continents which also organize various *wushu* competitions regularly.

Sanda Exercises

Sanda, also called Xiangbo or Shoubo in ancient times, is a barehanded dual combat practiced on a platform. In May 1979, the first sanda performance was given in the first World Wushu Convention held in Nanning, Guangxi. In October 1980, the State Physical Culture and Sports Commission constituted Rules for Sanda Competition and held the National Sanda Invitational Tournament in Beijing. In 1989, sanda was approved as an official competition event. In 1991, it became an official competition event in World Wushu Championship. In 1993, the 7th National Games listed it as an official competition event, and in 1998 it was listed as official competition event in the 13th Asian Games. In 2002, the first World Cup Wushu Sanshou Competition was held in Shanghai.

Wushu Competition Rules

In order to enhance the development of wushu through competition, a scoring system was first put into trial in a wushu convention held in Beijing from November 1 to 7, to differentiate athletes' performance by a more specific standard. This practice had its defects, but it did push *wushu* competitions a step forward. In 1957, China listed *wushu* as an official competition event for the first time. In 1958, Chinese Wushu Association invited some wushu experts and drafted the first *Wushu Competition Rules*, which was approved and promulgated by the State Physical Culture and Sports Commission in 1959. From then on, *wushu* competitions had rules to follow, which was a great progress.

With the guidance of competition rules, many *wushu* tournaments were held, including National Junior Wushu Championships and the first National Games Wushu Competition. The National Games Wushu Competition had two categories: competition events and performance events. Competition events included four events, namely *changquan*, *taijiquan*, long weapon exercise and short weapon exercise, in which the first 8 individuals or teams were awarded. As to performance events, individuals or teams were given a score but not a ranking, and the excellent ones were granted relevant award. That was a significant result of *wushu* reform.

Wushu Athletes Ranking Standards

In order to enhance the development of *wushu* and improve athletes' performance, the State Physical Culture and Sports Commission promulgated *Wushu Athletes Ranking Standards (Trial Version)* in February 1985. It was the first of its kind in the history of Chinese *wushu* and had great significance for the improvement of *wushu* skills. According to the standards, *wushu* athletes are classified into 5 levels: *Wuying* level (super warrior), 1st-grade warrior, 2nd-grade warrior, 3rd-grade warrior and *Wutong* level (petty warrior).

The First Wushu Team of China Performing in the Olympics

In 1936, the first *wushu* team of China came to the 11th Olympics held in Hamburg for a performance, which was the debut that Chinese *wushu* made in Europe.

Although in that Olympics, the grades of Chinese team were very disappointing, but the *wushu* performance was ardently welcomed. Because there were many programs for show, the Chinese *wushu* performance was only arranged for 15 minutes. But just in such a short time, the *wushu* team of China had won furious applause of all the audiences time and time again. Especially at last, the performance of "seizing the spear with bare hands" deeply attracted the audiences. As soon as the athletes

The 4th International Martial Art Invitational Tournament was held in Beijing Ditan Gymnasium in 2002.

stepped down the stage, they were encircled by cameras at once. The audiences were so enthusiastic that the athletes couldn't get out of the stadium. In order to satisfy people's interests, the Olympics arranged a special *wushu* performance in the Hamburg Theatre the next day. Later, the *wushu* team was invited to Frankfurt, Wiesbaden and other cities for performance, which were all warmly welcomed and praised.

The First China International Wushu Festival

As an ethical culture of China, *wushu* not only widely fancied by the Chinese, but also loved by people all over the world. In order to benefit all the human being and add luster to the international sports family, the Chinese *Wushu* Association, Chinese *Wushu* Research Institute, Sports Commission of Zhejiang Province, Sports Commission of Shenzhen and the Shenzhen *Wushu* International Development Center together held the First China International *Wushu* Festival on October 11-20, 1988.

Over 500 athletes form 33 countries and regions attended the festival. The festival was held both in Hangzhou and Shenzhen. The opening ceremony and the 3rd International *Wushu* (set exercises) Invitational Tournament were held in Hangzhou, while the International *Sanda* Arena Contest, awarding prize and the closing ceremony were in Shenzhen. With the largest scale, most participants and richest activities, this *wushu* festival was an international *wushu* pageant.

At the 3rd International *Wushu* (set exercises) Invitational Tournament, both the men's and women's individual all-around winner are Chinese athletes. Meanwhile, the level of foreign athletes prominently improved, and they won 4 golden medals. In the finals of the 7 levels of the International *Sanda* Arena Contest, Chinese athletes won 5 golden medals and the other 2 were taken by foreign athletes.

The First Wushu School Recruiting Overseas Students

Donglin *Wushu* School was located next to the Shaolin Temple which is called "the most famous temple under the sun". It is a modern comprehensive *wushu* school and also the first *wushu* school recruiting overseas students.

The school covers an area of 43*mu*, with performing lobby, practice room, the corridor of 18 bronze warriors and overseas student apartment inside. The emblem of Donglin *Wushu* School is the green olive leaves surrounding a man's figure which is like a "W". It is not only beautiful, but also has many deep meanings. The most notable "W" is the first letter of "*wushu*", which represents that Shaolin *wushu* is the essence of Chinese *wushu*. The "W" looks like a man sitting with two palms together, which means that the Shaolin *wushu* originates from the Buddhist temple; meanwhile it has the implication of practising or fighting hand to hand. The green olive leaves mean the world peace.

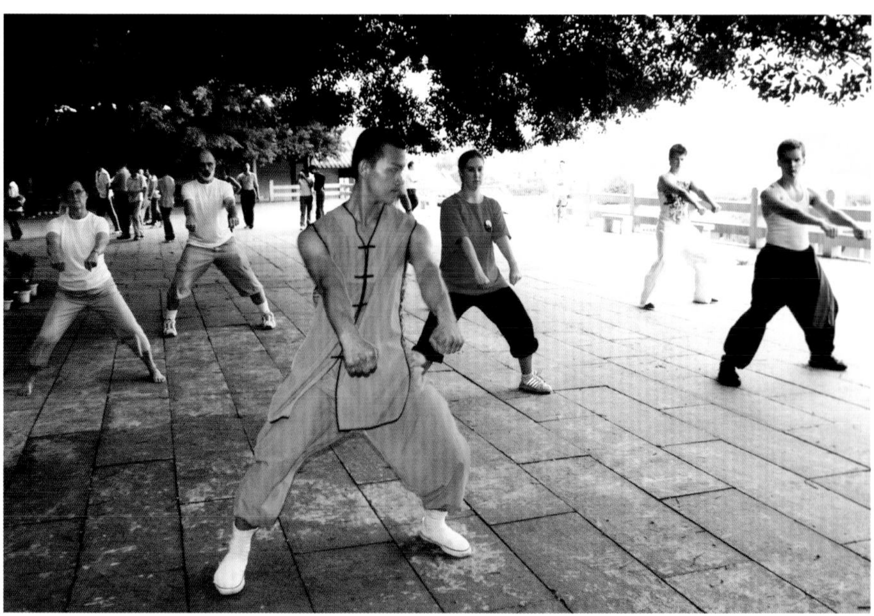

Canadian chinese martial art lovers are learning and practicing in the Quanzhou South Shaolin Temple in Fujian.

Chinese Wushu Walking Toward the World

Today, the Chinese traditional sports culture increasingly shows its enchantment to people all over the world. They appreciates the magic power of Chinese *wushu*, so more and more overseas *wushu* fans come to China to explore its profoundness. The two famous *wushu* towns, Dengfeng in Zhengzhou and Wenxian in Jiaozuo are respectively renowned by the Shaolin boxing and Shadowboxing. Many foreigners travel a long way here to visit the masters and learn their feat. Since 1979, China has sent *wushu* delegations overseas for hundreds of times and chooses hundreds of *wushu* coaches to teach overseas. Meanwhile, China also actively organizes all kinds of *wushu* contests, *wushu* festivals and *wushu* training courses. We can say, Chinese *wushu* is walking toward the world.

In 1985, the preparatory committee of the International *Wushu* Federation was established in Xi'an, and the International *Wushu* Federation was formally set up during the 1990 Beijing Asia Games, and was accepted as a member organization of the International Gymnastics Federation. Later, all the continents also established their *wushu* organizations in succession. Chinese *wushu* has become a formal event in the Asia Games, East Asia Games and Southeast Asia Games. In 1999, the International *Wushu* Federation was recognized by the International Olympic Committee and became a member of the Olympic family, which certainly will contribute to the communication between the Western and Chinese sports culture.

Zhao Changjun

Zhao Changjun (1960-), a *wushu* athlete, was born in Kaifeng, Henan province. He began to learn *wushu* in 1967 and was chosen to the *wushu* team of Shanxi province in 1971. He was good at cudgel play, *changquan* and *Ditanquan*. He has solid basic skills and his movements are the perfect combination of speed and power. Zhao won the second place in individual all-around in the National *Wushu* Competition held in 1978, and the titles of cudgel play and individual *Quan*, and the second place of free-style *Quan* and first category changquan. In the 4th National Games in 1979, he gained the title in free-style *Quan*. In 1980, he got three second places respectively in cudgel play, free-style *Quan*, and traditional *Quan*. Since 1974, he visited and performed in Japan, Britain, Mozambique, Australia, Malta, Luxemburg, Italy, Belgium, France, Rumania and many other countries.

From 1978 to 1987, with his perfect command of *wushu* and strong willpower, he won the *wushu* all-around champion ten times in the international and national competitions, and won 54 golden medals, becoming the only "ten consecutive all-around *wushu* champions" of China.

Liang Rihao

Liang Rihao (1968-), a wushu athlete of Hong Kong, China was born in Zhaoqing, Guangdong province. Liang entered the wushu team of Guangxi Province from the Zhaoqing armature sports school in 1979 and entered the wushu team of Guangdong Province in 1984. He moved to Hong Kong in 1989. He won the title of Nanquan in the Second Asia Wushu Championship in 1989, the second place in the 11th Asia Games in 1990, the title in the First World Wushu Championship in 1991, the second place in the 3rd Asia Wushu Championship in 1992, the second place in the First East Asia Games in 1993, the second place in the 12th Asia Games in 1994, the title in the 3rd World Wushu Championship in 1995 and the second place in the 4th World Wushu Championship in 1997.

Rope Skipping

Rope skipping is a popular folk sport of China, which has a broad foundation among the masses. Many governmental units and enterprises set rope skipping as an event of the employee sports meetings. Rope skipping is also a good event for middle and primary school pupils, and many schools hold various rope skipping contests. Rope skipping can greatly improve the strength of muscles, the harmoniousness and cleverness of the whole body and the development of bones of the teenagers. The adults and elders can exercise their cardiac muscle, increase the vital capacity, improve the enginery of respiratory system and nervous system and lose weight through rope skipping, so as to be healthier.

Tug-of-war

Tug-of-war is a traditional event fancied by all ethnic groups of China, which has a long history. The formats of tug-of-war are various, which can be between two people, two groups of people, or bare hands, using instruments and so on. Tug-of-war is not limited by time and field, so it is easy to develop. This sport can not only develop strength, but also can exercise willpower. Whenever in holidays, tug-of-war are played all over the country.

Tug-of-war is listed as a formal event by the General Administration of Sports of China in 1997, and the rules for the games were drafted in 2003. A number of referees and coaches were brought up, which laid a solid foundation to the improvement and healthy development of this sport. Chinese Tug-of-War Association was set up in 2005. From then on, this sport got onto the track of standardization. Tug-of-war as a sport event has widely spread to the whole world. In order to promote this sport, China actively develops the communication with other countries. We took part in the competitions and training course in Britain, the US, South Africa, Netherlands and other countries. Meanwhile, athletes from Japan and Britain are invited to China. Through those activities, Chinese athletes learned the advanced experiences and technologies, which greatly energized China's tug-of-war sport.

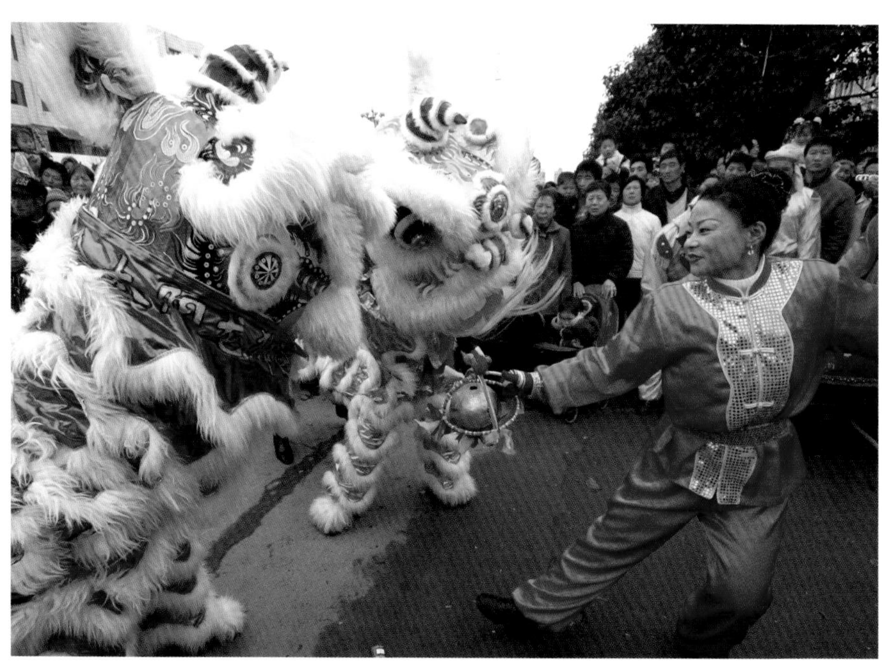

Lion dance is a traditional festive activity of China.

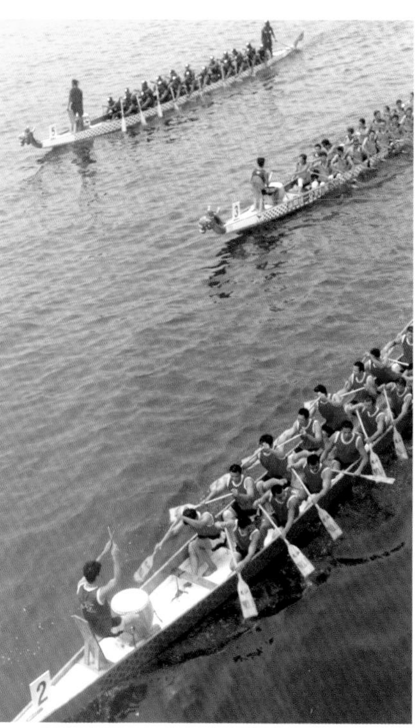

In 2005, 17 dragon boat teams including those from America and Philippines participated in Shenyang International Dragon Boat Tournament.

Lion Dance

(See P348)

Dragon Boat

The dragon boat refers to the boats with dragons painting on it or of the shape of dragon. The dragon boat race is a traditional Chinese water sports event, which has a history of more than two thousand years. The race is often held in festivals and each boat has many people paddling together. The dragon boat race is a common place in China, and has formed the "Dragon Boat Festival" which celebrates every year. The size of the dragon boats are various according to different areas. The contest is to race the same distance and the place is decided by the time they need to arrive the destination.

Dragon boat has a long history, and when it is introduced to other countries, it wins the favor of their people and becomes an international race. In 1983, China sent their team to participate the International Dragon Boat Race, and won both the two titles. The International Dagon Boat Race was held in Hong Kong in 1984, with the participants coming from the US, Germany, Japan, Britain, New Zealand, Singapore, Thailand, Malaysia, Australia, Macao, Hong Kong, all together 16 teams, and China gained the title again.

Sports Institutions

General Administration of Sport of China

The main function of the General Administration of Sport of China is to research and draw out the policies, regulations and development programs for the sports undertakings of the country, while supervising its conduction; guide and push forward the sports system reform; constitute the sports development strategy and draw the middle and long term development plan; coordinate the sports development of different areas; push forward the nationwide fitness plan; instruct the masses sports activities; put the state exercise standard into practice and guarantee people's physical quality; plan the overall athletic sports development and research on the balance of the national competitions and events setting; organize the anti-doping work; manage the foreign affairs and enhance the communication and cooperation in sports with Hong Kong SAR, Macao and Taiwan as well as many other countries; organize and participate in the important international competitions.

Address: No.11 Stadium Road, Chongwen District, Beijing
Website: http://www.sport.gov.cn/

All-China Sports Federation

The first Congress of the All-China's Sports Federation was held on October 26 to 27, 1949, in Beijing. It made a decision to reorganize Chinese Sports Association into All-China's Sports Federation, and locate its headquarter in Beijing. Later, all the provinces, autonomous regions and municipalities directly under the central government set up their local branches. The All-China's Sports Federation was recognized by the International Olympic Committee in 1954 as the representative of Chinese Olympic Committee. The federation has 152 member organizations, including the branch federations of all the provinces, autonomous regions and the municipalities directly under the central government (the membership of Taiwan is kept), 122 national individual events sports associations, and the sports industries' associations.

Address: No.2 Stadium Road, Chongwen District, Beijing
Website: http://www.sport.org.cn

Chinese Olympic Committe

With the goal of developing Olympic sports, Chinese Olympic Committee is a mass and nonprofit organization, which participates in the international Olympic affairs on behalf of China. Among the Asian Olympic Council and all the Olympic committees of different countries and areas, only Chinese Olympic Committee has the right of representing China's Olympic sports.

According to the Olympic Charter of the International Olympic Committee, within the limit of nonprofit activities, Chinese Olympic Committee has the right to use the name of "Olympic" and the Olympic emblem, flag, aphorism and theme song, while it also should fulfill the duty of protecting the abovementioned name, emblem, flag, aphorism and theme song from illegal use.

Chinese Olympic Committee is made up by the directors of the associations of those individual Olympic events and the representatives of other mass sports organizations. The conference of the committee of the whole has the highest power. The main task of Chinese Olympic Committee is to coordinate the development of every Olympic event, select and organize athletes to take part in the Olympics and Winter Olympics, Asian Games and Asian Winter Games.

Besides, Chinese Olympic Committee and Chinese Taipei Olympic Committee are both the members of Olympic council of Asia (joining in respectively in 1973 and 1982).

Address: No.2 Stadium Road, Chongwen District, Beijing
Website: http://www.olympic.cn

Chinese Olympic Committee and General Administration of Sport of China

Hong Kong Olympic Committee

Hong Kong Amateur Sports Association & Olympic Committee was established in 1950 and reorganized to Hong Kong Olympic Committee in 1951. On March 8, 1999, it renamed as the Sports Federation & Olympic Committee of Hong Kong, China. The Hong Kong Olympic Committee is the member of International Olympic Committee, Olympic Council of Asia and Chinese Olympic Committee, which is responsible for arranging Hong Kong athletes to take part in Olympics, Asian Games, East Asian Games, Pacific Games, National Games and other competitions. The Federation has 72 member associations, which are the mouthpiece of Hong Kong sports circle.

Those member associations of the Sports Federation & Olympic Committee of Hong Kong are all members of international Associations or Asian Associations of the relative events and present themselves in the conferences of those international or Asian associations on behalf of Hong Kong.

Since 1952, Hong Kong athletes participated in all the Olympics except in 1980. The events they joined in including track and field, boxing, bicycling, canoeing, jujitsu, sailing boat, swimming, shooting, swordplay, hockey, sailboarding and so on. At the 1996 Atlanta Olympics, Hong Kong athlete Li Lishan grasped the women's sailboard (Mistral) gold, becoming the first HK athlete to win an Olympic gold.

Address: 2nd Floor, Sports House, 1 Stadium Path, So Kon Po, Causeway Bay, Hong Kong
Website: http://www.hkolympic.org

Macao Olympic Committee

Macao Olympic Committee was established on October 20, 1987, based on the rules made by the International Olympic Committee. The function of Macao Olympic Committee is to develop and maintain Olympic sports and other mass sports, inspire youth's interests toward sports and sports spirit, plan and prepare the training, together with other relative organizations, select athletes capable of representing Macao to participate in the Olympics and other Games sponsored by International Olympic Committee or Olympic Council of Asia, and cooperate with personal and public organizations and promote good sports policies.

Macao Olympic Committee had 20 member organizations in 1996.

Address: Sports Road, Taipa, Macao

Chinese Taipei Olympic Committee

Chinese Taipei Olympic Committee was set up in 1960 and acknowledged by the International Olympic Committee in the same year. When Chinese Olympic Committee resumed its legal seat in the International Olympic Committee, the Sports Association in Taiwan was renamed as Chinese Taipei Olympic Committee, and its membership is kept. It was divided into two organizations in 1989, one of which is the General Sports Committee of Taiwan, in charge of the 23 sports associations of individual events and coordinating the sports activities and competitions within Taiwan. The other was Chinese Taipei Olympic Committee, located in Taipei, which is responsible for participating in Olympics, Asian Games and other international or Asian competitions and conferences.

China Sports Foundation

China Sports Foundation was established on April 1,1994, which is made up of celebrities of the sports circle and entrepreneurs home and abroad. Locating in Beijing, this Foundation is a nonprofit organization, which is responsible for managing the fund donated by social bodies, enterprises, business associations and individuals in China and abroad.

The principle of the foundation is to promote the mass sports, provide service to the athletic sports training, raise fund, strictly manage and scientifically use the fund. In recent years, through great efforts, and with the support from social bodies and celebrities, a number of funds have been raised, and the foundation has become an important institution of China's sports undertaking. In order to provide good service, especially for the athletes participating in the 2008 Olympics, the foundation has set up "National Outstanding Athletes Mutual Insurance Fund", "National Outstanding Athletes Scholarship and Stipend", "2008 Olympics Outstanding Athletes and Coaches Encouragement Fund", "National Teams' Retired Athletes and Coaches Fund " and many other funds. All the works concerning the sports fund are carried out smoothly, especially the National Outstanding Athletes Mutual Insurance Fund, which has covered all the outstanding sports team of the country. Presently, the fund has paid several millions of injuries and deformities compensation, and the athletes benefited from it including Sang Lan, Wang Zexiu, Zhu Gang, Yuan Ying and other hundreds of athletes. This fund relieved the outstanding athletes' worry about their injuries and diseases caused by challenging physiological limits.

In 2004, the members of the delegation of the Australian Olympic Committee visited the China Doping Control Center.

Address: A-11D the Eastern Ginza, Dongzhimenwai Street, Beijin

Website: http://www.tyjjh.org.cn

China Doping Control Center

China Doping Control Center was established on July 14, 1987 and passed the qualification test of the International Olympic Committee's Medical Commission, getting the international testing qualification. Now, China Doping Control Center is an A grade international testing lab.

China Doping Control Center is located in the beautiful Beijing Olympic Sports Center. It has 18 professional technicians, most of whom have a doctor or master degree, and several prestigious managers. This center has all the modern testing equipments required by the International Olympic Committee, and was appointed to be the backup testing lab of the 2000 Sydney Olympics. The level of the testing technology of this center comes out top of the 29 labs recognized by the IOC.

Along with the development of the technology, the doping test is very difficult and highly required now. To testify 1ml. urine containing 2 nano-gram (1nano-gram equals to 1/1,000,000,000gram) dope is like to put a spoon of sugar to the water of five standard swimming pools (50m×25m), and then randomly take a small bottle of the water for testing. In the past over 10 years, every year there are labs failing to pass the reexamination, so being degraded or disqualified. But until now, China Doping Control Center passed smoothly in every year's reexamination and it is also the only Asian lab qualified for 14 consecutive years.

Address：No.1 Anding Lu, Chaoyang Disgtrict, Beijing

Hong Kong Sports Association for the Mentally Handicapped

The principle of Hong Kong Sports Association for the Mentally Handicapped is to develop, promote and organize sports activities for the mentally challenged people, so as to help them fully develop their potential and participate in the social activities. The association held many sports trainings and competitions in 2004, with the participants over 25,000 person-times. With the development of many years, the training program of this association has gradually enhanced from popularization sports activities to cultivating outstanding athletes.

In 2004, their mentally handicapped athletes took part in many international competitions, so as to enhance their sports skill. The Hong Kong team won 3 silver medals and 8 bronze medals in the 3rd World Swimming Championship for the Mentally Handicapped which was held in Hong Kong for the first time in January. Later, the Hong Kong team participated in the 2004 World Games sponsored by the International Sports Federation for Persons with an Intellectual Disability in July in Sweden. They won 7 golden medals, 12 silver medals and 7 bronze medals in the track and field events, swimming and pingpong.

Address:Unit No.2, LG/F, Lek Yuen Community Hall, Shatin, N.T., Hong Kong

Website:http://www.hksam.org.hk

Federation of University Sports of China

Founded in 1975 and joining the International University Sports Federation in the same year, Federation of University Sports of China is a group member of All-China Sports Federation and a member country of International University Sports Federation. It is a nationwide non-profit social organization composed of the students of higher institutions, sports teachers and other sports workers across the country out of their own free will. The university sports associations and student sports associations of all the provinces, autonomous regions and municipalities of China are all its members. During the international exchange of university sports, Federation of University Sports of China performs the governmental functions on behalf of China and conducts the organization and administration of the national university sports games.

Address: North Huizhong, Datun Rd. Chaoyang District, Beijing

Website: http://www.fusc.org.cn

China Sports Association of the Elder

Today, China is becoming an aging society with a population of the elders as much as 143 million. With the increasing population of the elders and the demission and retirement of many elder cadres and workers, the Association was established.

A mass sports organization under the administration of All-China Sports

Federation, China Sports Association of the Elder adopts a membership system and takes in individual members. It also sets up grass-root organizations in residential districts, large factories, mines, enterprises and governmental bodies so as to organize the members for activities and administrations.

By the end of 2005, all the administrative regions above the county level, 70 percent of the urban neighborhoods and 50 percent of the towns had established sports associations of the elder. Over 30 kinds of sports activities had been conducted for the elders, and climbing, running, Wushu, Fit Ball, balloon volleyball were among the common games with great population among the elders.

With the unremitting efforts of the whole society and the sports associations of the elder at all levels, China's elder sports working have made remarkable achievements. By the end of 2005, over 58 million elders had become the regular sports participants, which made them the backbone of sports in both rural and urban regions of China.

China Farmer Sports Association

China Farmer Sports Association was founded in September 1986.

Mission Statements: to mobilize, organize and guide the mass farmers to connduct mass sports activities, so as to improve their physical fitness and make contributions to the improvement of the quality of the whole nation; to organize farmer sports games at the national level so as to make constant progress in the sports technology; depending on the social power, to promote the construction of sports facilities in the rural area and to promote the socialization of sports; to explore, regulate, research and gradually spread the folk traditional sports in China's rural area, and to make proposals of the sports activities for national competition; to organize international exchange of farmer sports and to hold international farmer sports games.

The guidelines for developing farmer sports: geared to the vast rural area, to develop mass sports activities widely, and to combine popularization and development so as to improve the physical fitness of the farmers at large.

China Farmer Sports Association has held China Farmer Sports for five times successfully and has conducted the program of "Mass Farmer Physical Exercises" in the countryside nationwide. Through the colorful and various sports activities, the Association has made it possible for the mass farmers to devote themselves into the construction of New Countryside with robust physique and had made great contributions to the economic prosperity and social stability in the rural area.

Address: No. 20, Maizidian Street, Chaoyang Distrct, Beijing

Physical Education

Beijing Xiannongtan Athletics Technology School

Beijing Xiannongtan Athletics Technology School is situated in time-honored Xiannongtan. In 1956 Beijing Sports Undertakings Unit, the predecessor of Xiannongtan Athletics Technology School, was established there and has developed into the cradle of China's athletics sports. It has trained many world champions, such as Zhuang Zedong, Lang Ping, Zhang Jinjing, Zhang Yining, etc. as well as some famous coaches like Bai Jinshen, Ma Yuan'an and so on. Currently, the School boasts of nearly 300 athletes and over 60 excellent coaches, of whom 4 are national coaches and 16 are senior coaches. And there are six excellent sports teams in the School, namely Beijing Pingpong Team, Beijing Gym Team, Beijing Track and Field Team, Beijing Women's Football Team, Beijing Tennis team, and Beijing Weight-Lifting Team.

Beijing Xiannongtan Athletics Technology School covers an area of 168,000 m^2, with 70,000 m^2 being the venues for training and competition of the athletes. Large sports competitions like the football game of the 11th Asian Games, the men's football game and women's football final match of the 21st University Sports Games were held there.

Address; No. 11, Xiannongtan Street, Xuanwu Distirct, Beijing

Beijing Sport University

Beijing Sport University was founded in November 1953 and covers an area of over 250,000 m^2. It offers 12 undergraduate programs, namely Physical Education, Sports Training, Sports Sociology, Kinesiology, Chinese Traditional Sports, Public Administration (Sports Administration), Journalism (Sports Journalism), Applied Psychology (Sports Psychology), English (International Sports), Acting (Sports Arts), Sports Rehabilitation and Health, and Sports Industrial Management. Now the University has 17 indoor training stadiums, 21 outdoor training venues, a library with a collection of 700,000 books, and a publishing house specialized in sports books, the only one in the institutions of higher education across the country. Currently, the University has an enrollment of 15,000 students, including over 200 international students.

Emblem of Beijing Sport University

During the past half century, the University has always maintained high level of sports technology. Since 1980, students of the University have won more than 50 championships in world sports games, more than 80 championships in Asian sports contests, and broken over 30 Asian records. The University has always attached great importance to international cooperation and exchange. It has established interscholastic relations with 39 universities of 18 countries and regions, including Russian State Academy Of Physical Education And Sports, Indiana University of the USA, Cologne P. E. Institute of Germany, Japan Sports University and so on. In addition, it has carried out exchanges with many international and non-governmental sports organizations. Two medals of IOC have been awarded to people from the University.

Address: North Street, Zhongguancun, Haidian District, Beijing
Website: http://www/bsu.edu.cn

Shanghai University of Sport

As the earliest institution of higher learning in sports after 1949, Shanghai University of Sport was founded in November 1952. Ever since its foundation, the University has trained over 23,000 students, including 107 doctoral students, 730 postgraduates, 11,402 graduates, 8866 students of adult education program, and 2,035 students with associate diplomas.

The coaches and students of the University have made great achievements in large sports games both at home and abroad. Among them, 12 students and 7 coaches have been awarded the "Honorary Medal of National Sports" for 14 times and 11 times respectively. During the period from 1994 to 2004, the students of the University had won 14 world championships, 3 world junior championships, 31 Asian championships and over 200 national championships, and 3 students had broken 3 world records and 2 had broken 7 Asian records.

The University offers 12 undergraduate programs, namely Physical Education, Sports Training, Sports Sociology, Chinese Traditional Sports, Dance Choreography, Kinesiology,

Applied Psychology, English, Journalism, Public Administration, Marketing, Information Management and Information System. It also conducts many international academic exchange activities and has established cooperation and exchange with 20 universities in 10 countries and regions including USA, South Korea, Japan, Germany, Finland, Australia and so on.

Address: No. 399, Changhai Lu, Yangpu District, Shanghai
Website: http://www.sus.edu.cn

Wuhan Institute of Physical Education

Wuhan Institute of Physical Education is situated by the Donghu Lake, the famous scenery spot in Wuchang District, Wuhan City, and it covers an area of 556,110 m^2. The Institute focuses on the sports disciplines with athletics sports as its specialty. Currently, it has an enrollment of over 7,100, and the quality of its athletics training is among the best in the sports institutes and universities nationwide. After the long-term development, the Institute has developed a group of sporting events with great competitive edge, with boating, taekwondo, boxing, *Wushu*, and wrestling as its representative ones. It has been established as the National Base for High-quality Racing Boat and Kayaking Boat Athletes, National *Sanda* Training Bases for Teenager Athletes, National Water Sports Training Base for Teenager Athletes and National Training Base for Talents of *Wushu* schools.

Since the initiation of reform and opening up, the Institute has established cooperation and exchanges with 20 educational and sports institutions, including Ball University of USA, Springfield College of USA, University of Delaware in the USA, University of Hawaii, Ukraine University of Physical Culture, Japan Shaolin Boxing Association, Bulgaria Hanlin Institute, Hanoi Sports Committee of Vietnam, Minxin Institute of Technology in Taiwan, Taiwan Canoe Association, Hong Kong Sports Institute, etc., with regular exchange of visits, lectures and competitions.

Address: No.461 Luoyu Lu, Hongshan District, Wuhan, Hubei Province
Website: http://www.wipe.edu.cn

Chengdu Sport University

Chengdu Sport University is a comprehensive sports institution of higher education focusing on the undergraduate and graduate education. It offers the most undergraduate and graduate programs among all the sports institutions and universities in China. Currently, the University has an enrollment of over 5,000 and consists of Faculty of Physical Education, Faculty of Athletic Sports, Faculty of Sports Iatrology, Faculty of *Wushu*, Faculty of Sports Humanities and Social Science, Graduate Student Faculty, Adult Education Department, and the affliated Athletics Sports School, Secondary Sports School and Chengdu Basketball School under the administration of Chinese Basketball Association. In recent years, the University has made great achievements in many sports events, e.g. *Wushu*, artistic gymnastics taekwondo, soft tennis, basketball and so on, and has won over 30 gold medals in national sports games. More than 40 people have taken part in international sports competitions on behalf of China and won over 10 medals.

In Recent years, the University has carried out more and more international exchanges. It has established cooperation with many universities in the USA, Canada, Germany, Austria, South Korea, etc., and has expert and scholar exchanges for academic purposes with more than 20 countries. The University also offers all kinds of programs for international students.

Address: No. 2, Tiyuan Lu, Chengdu, Sichuan Province
Website: http://www.cdsu.edu.cn

Xi'an Physical Education Universit

Founded in 1954, Xi'an Physical Education University is the only sports institution of higher education in northwest China with an area of 696 *mu* and an enrollment of over 6,000. It consists of a graduate school offering graduate programs of Physical Education Training, Kinesiology, Sports Humanities and Sociology, Applied Psychology and Chinese Traditional Sports, and the National Training Base of Taekwondo, the National Judo Training Center for Coaches at Intermediate and Higher Level, China Multi-bowls Training Center, Physical Condition Test Center, and the training centers for the amateur athletes of track and field, basketball, football, pingpong, tennis, *Wushu*, gymnastics, artistic gymnastics, calisthenics, etc.

The University attaches great importance to training and competition. In recent years, it has made great achievements in athletics sports and has won over 70 gold medals in national and international contests, with especially remarkable achievements in sports events like taekwondo, Sanda, set exercises, track and field, gymnastics, calisthenics, artistic gymnastics, trampolining, multi-bowls and so on. The University has established cooperation and exchange with Osaka University of Health and Sports Science, University of California at Northridge, Kenyatta University of Kenya, and Macau Polytechnic Institute, and it has established academic exchange and friendly contacts with over 20 countries and regions.

Address: No. 65, Hanguang Lu, Xi'an City, Shaanxi Province
Website: http://www.xaipe.edu.cn

Sports Facilities

Stadium & Gymnasium

Currently, China has more the 850 thousand stadiums and gymnasiums, averagely 6.58 for every 10 thousand persons and 1.03m^2 sports field for each person. China's accumulated investment in building gymnasiums and stadiums has been 191.45 billion yuan, and keeps increasing by 20 percent annually.

Contemporary Sports Constructions Written into the World Architecture History

Seven contemporary sports constructions of China are included by the authoritative architecture publication *World Architectural History* for the first time. This book, published in Britain in 1988, records 43 Chinese constructions built after 1940, including Beijing Capital Stadium, Beijing Workers Gymnasium, Beijing Workers' Stadium, Shanghai Gymnasium, Shanghai Swimming Pool, Nanjing Wutaishan Gymnasium and Changchun Gymnasium.

The First Large Comprehensive Stadium

Built in 1959, Beijing Workers' Stadium is the first large comprehensive stadium in China. It covers an area of 350,000 square meters with a total floor area of 120,000 square meters. The Stadium consists of a central sports venue and over 10 training venues of basketball, volleyball, football, tennis, and track and field surrounding it, a natatorium, two outdoor swimming pools, a diving pool, a man-made lake and Beijing Workers Gymnasium.

The central sports venue can hold 80,000 audiences. There are two layers of stands, with a windshield shelter of 12.70 meters wide above the upper layer. There is a 400-meter plastic cement track and a football playground that is 104 meters long and 69 meters wide with natural lawn.

Workers Gymnasium is oval shaped with a total floor area of 38,000 square meters, the truss of which is 94 meters wide. With the design of cable suspension being adopted, the construction is made up of concentric rings, outer girder and 288 two-layer suspended cables. The stands can hold 15,000 spectators. The venue for competition is a circle whose diameter is about 40 meters. When part of the mobile stand is removed, it can turn into a rectangular venue.

Capital Stadium

Capital Stadium is a comprehensive and multi-functional stadium which is responsible for providing venues for national and international sports competitions, performance and training, and large assemblies and theatrical performances as well. It covers an area of 7 hectares with a total floor area of 40,000 square meters. The Stadium is 122 meters long from east to west, 107 meters wide from north to south and 28 meters high. The roof is constructed in the structure of flat-plate two-way space steel truss with a width of 99 meters.

The competition hall of the Stadium can be used for many sports events, e.g. Pingpong, badminton, volleyball, basketball, gymnastics, ice hockey, figure skating, etc. The competition venue is 88 meters long and 40 meters wide. It is composed of 21 mobile floors, each being 30 meters long and 3.5 meters wide. Under the floors is the skating rink. By operating the machine, the floors will be removed to the eastern and western areas and lowed layer by layer to the warehouse of floors.

After the mobile floors are removed, we can see the water-polished-stone floor. If we splash water on it, the low-temperature ammonia liquid pipe inside the stone can refrigerate the water and make it ice up all the year through. It can keep a certain temperature of the ice as well. Even if in hot summer, people can enjoy the ice hockey matches and skating performances. Around the competition venue are the stands which can hold 18,000 spectators. There are 18 entrances and exits for the spectators who can be evacuated within 5 minutes.

Beijing International Tennis Center

Established in 1989, Beijing International Tennis Center consists of 9 tennis courts of international standards. There are two tennis stadiums, which has 8 inner tennis courts and can accommodate 4,000 audiences and one outdoor stadium, which has 1 outdoor tennis court and can accommodate 5,000 audience.

Ever since its establishment, Beijing International Tennis Center has held many tennis games, including that of the Asian Games in Beijing, Davis Cup international Game, China Open, Salon International Open, Beijing Open, China Open Tournament and Nokia International Women Open, etc. players registered at the center for game include the world's No. One Coria, the world's No. two Zhang Depei, and other famous Players like Woodford and Larsson, etc. The complete facilities of the center and considerate service from its working stuff have won much praise from International Tennis Federation and players from various countries.

Beijing University Students' Gymnasium

Beijing University Students' Gymnasium is a modern sports complex affiliated to the Capital Institute of Physical Education. Built for the Asian Games as a basketball stadium, Beijing University Students' Gymnasium has held a series of both national and international games, including the basketball game of Asian Games, International Volleyball Games, etc. The gymnasium is completed in September in 1988, and can hold volleyball game, wrestling game, evening show, etc.

Beijing University Students' Gymnasium is of whole-frame structure, square-shaped and white color. With a floor area of 12,000 square meters, the 32-meter-high gymnasium can accommodate 4078 audiences. There are four huge octagonal columns with a height of 28 meters at the four corners of the gymnasium, which look splendid and eminent, symbolizing that physical exercises can make people healthy, strong, intelligent and bring people endless vitality. The four white ridges spread from the center of the roof to the four directions just as four flying dragons, which is of typical Chinese style and makes the gymnasium quite unique and spectacular.

Beijing Shooting Gallery

Located in the Futian Temple in the western suburb of Beijing, Beijing Shooting Gallery is situated at the foot of the picturesque Cuiwei Mountain. It enjoys fresh air, elegant environment and is a quite place in the boisterous city.

The Main Shooting Stadium of Beijing Shooting Gallery has a floor area of 3,187 square meters, which consists of two layers. The lower layer is the shooting area, which allows 96 to shoot at the same time; the upper layer has a grandstand which can hold 800 audiences. There are also places for coaches and players to rest.

Shanghai Gymnasium

Established and put into use in 1975, Shanghai Gymnasium is one of the large-scale gymnasiums in China. With round shape and a height of 33 meters, the main structure of the gymnasium has a span length of roof of 110 meters, and can accommodate 18,000 audiences.

There are natatoriums, badminton courts, Ping-Pong stadiums, volleyball courts, outdoor tennis courts, outdoor three-person basketball courts and squares for exercises, which can satisfy various demands from the citizens.

The gymnasium is surrounded by trees and forms together with the stadium which can hold 80,000 people a new attraction of tourism of Shanghai. The gymnasium is of superb location and convenient transportation, with access to subway, light rail, many bus lines and tour lines which lead to tour spots in all districts and counties as well as neighboring provinces and cities.

The Workers' Gymnasium in construction before the 2008 Beijing Olympic Games

Shanghai Stadium

Shanghai Stadium is by now a sports complex with the largest scale and the most advanced facilities in China, as well as one of the landmark buildings in Shanghai. With a floor area of 170,000 square meters, Shanghai Stadium has a saddle-shaped contour, the world's longest cantilevered steel truss roof structure with fabric canopy and the longest cantilevered truss is of 73.5 meters, which are all of the advanced international level. There are the evergreen soccer filed and plastic track-and-filed venues which fit the international standard.

Shanghai Stadium consists of a platform of 500 seats, a reporters' platform of 300 seats, and 100 sets of luxury boxes. The stadium can hold 56,000 spectators to watch the game or 4,300 spectators to watch large-scale variety show.

Shanghai Stadium was entitled as "the Best Sports Complex in Shanghai" in 1998.

Kunming Sports Training Base

Located in the southern suburb of Kunming city of Yunnan province in China, Kumming Sports Training Base, or Haigeng Base has an area of 407,412 square meters. The base has been put into use since 1975.

Kumming Sports Training Base is of high altitude, with an annual average barometric pressure of 81.5 MD. Compared with the places of zero altitude, it lacks 17 percent oxygen. The annual average temperature is 15.5 centigrade, and the annual temperature difference is 12.1 centigrade. With an annual rainfall of about 1,000 mms, Kumming Sports Training Base is neither cold in winter nor hot in summer, and has the ideal natural conditions for training in highland.

Kumming Sports Training Base is up to now one of the most comprehensive training bases with most functions and of the largest scale in China. There are 16 football fields with turf (including 4 simple ones), 2 standard track-and-field standard charcoal fields, 2 standard softball fields, 2 softball-training fields, 17 tennis courts with illumination (5 indoor soft plastic standard tennis courts, 6 indoor sand standard tennis courts, 6 outdoor hard plastic standard tennis courts), 1 standard natatorium for all-day training and 1 standard diving stadium for all-day training, 2 indoor basketball/volleyball courts, and 1 outdoor beach volleyball court for training.

After its establishment, Kumming Sports Training Base has organized 30 large-scale games, which include Davis Cup of tennis in 1984, 1999 and 2000, the group round game of World Cup of World's Youth in 1992, the invitational tournament of International Women Football in 1993 and the FIFA—Coca Cola coach training program in 1985, etc.

A sports training base at Haigen, Dianchi in Kunming, Yunnan

Anyang Aero Sports School

Established in 1955, Anyang Aero Sports School is up to now the largest aero club of Aero Sports Federation of China largest aero physical education training and game center. It undertakes the following responsibilities: the training and competition of parachuting, gliding, light aeroplanes, helicopters, hot air balloons on both national and international level; aero performance, flying training, and the popularization of science and technology about aero, etc.

Anyang Aero Sports School has the comprehensive capability to organize large–scale world level aero games. With an airport of 2.4 square kilometers, it has rich land and space resources. Anyang Aero Sports School has complete training facilities and plenty of various aero vehicles including Cessna planes, helicopters, sailplanes, hot air balloons, etc. Besides, it has a teaching stuff with rich experiences, facilities for the maintenance and repair of planes as well as advanced teaching facilities including electronically teaching devices, photographing devices and translation devices, etc. The school has trained hundreds of pilots of helicopters, sailplanes etc. for Japan, Hong Kong, Taiwan etc.

Anyang Aero Sports School has in recent years organized many national and international games such as the 4th Parachute Championship, the 1st Asia-Pacific Parachute Championship, etc.

Yabuli Snow Sports Training Base

Yabuli Skiing Site is up to now the largest skiing site in China, as well as the largest training center for snow sports.

Yabuli Skiing Site is established in 1980, and consists of 5 sites for training and competing, including Alpine Skiing site, free-style skiing site, ski jumping site and Biathlon site and 2 skiing sites for tourists. The skiing sites is divided into two areas: one is Yabuli Skiing Site for Competition, which is mainly used to hold national and international games, as well as to be used by skiers of and above middle level; the other is the Skiing Site of Fengche Village, which is for skiers of different levels and to organize common competitive ski games.

Ever since its establishment, Yabuli Skiing Site has held in succession some large-scale trans-continental games, including the 4th Asian Teenagers' Alpine Skiing Championship, the 3rd Asian Winter Games and a dozen of games on the national and provincial level. The training base of National Polar Scientific Exploration Office (Originally the National Office for Scientific Exploration in South Pole) is also situated here. Ever since its establishment in 1984 till now, the training base has received and trained 15 groups of personnel before their expedition in South Pole. Besides, two of its staff has gone to South Pole Station to be in charge of the administration of affairs of the station.

National Olympic Sports Center

National Olympic Sports Center, located at Olympic Village, Beijing, is an integrated sports center as well as the national sports center and the important training base for national teams. It is also called Olympic Center. The Olympic Center Gymnasium is a multifunctional gymnasium with a seating-capacity of 5,748 and the total construction area of 25,300 square meters. It is the largest newly-constructed gymnasium for Asian Games and is called "Asian No.1 Gymnasium". The Yingdong Natatorium and the Integrated Gymnasium in the National Olympic Sports

National Stadium

Center have a similar appearance; silver gray roof and high tower. In addition, there is a modern ground track field, tennis court, green hockey stadium, softball field, throwing field, martial art museum, baseball field, mini-Golf field, and fishing garden, and many sports gyms, including the Sports Museum.

Guangdong Olympic Center Stadium

Located in the south of Guangdong Olympic Center, Guangdong Olympic Center Stadium covers a space of 300,000 square meters with a seating-capacity of 80,012. The construction of the stadium started on December 31, 1998 and completed on September 22, 2001. It has held the opening ceremony of the Ninth National Sports Game and the track and field in November 2001. After the Ninth National Sports Game, the stadium has held many important games such as international football invitational tournament of China vs. Brazil, Four-Nation Women's Football Tournament, and the third stage of National Women's Football Premier League, etc.

National Stadium

(See P494)

National Gymnasium

During the Beijing 29th Olympic Games in 2008, the National Gymnasium will hold gymnastics (excluding rhythmic gymnastics) and handball events. After the Olympic Games, the National Gymnasium will become a civil sports center integrating collective sports games and art entertainment as the top grade sports installation in Beijing. This project is mainly composed of the principal structure of the gymnasium, a contiguous warm-up gymnasium and the relevant outdoor environment. It covers a space of 6.87 hectares in total with the construction area of 80,900 square meters and a seating capacity of 18,000. The design of the gymnasium originates from Chinese folding fans and fully manifests the Olympic concepts of "Green Olympics", "High-tech Olympics", and "People's Olympics" and the principle of "running an economical Olympic Games".

Olympic Village

The Olympic Village, built for Beijing 2008 Olympic Games, has a construction area of 360,000 square meters and 110,000 square meters of temporary construction facilities, including residences, apartments and attaching facilities. During the Olympic Games it will serve as the apartments for athletes and coaches. After the Games, the athletes apartments will be changed to houses for sale or renting, the rest space for waiters and waitresses will be changed to public space for residents, restaurants, entertainment center and shopping center will be changed to attaching houses for entertainment and conferences, the integrated clinic will be changed to a kindergarten, and the training region for athletes will be changed to an international school.

National Aquatics Center

(See P494)

National Conference Center

With the construction area of 230,000 square meters, the National Conference Center consists of several conference and exhibition halls. In principle, the exhibition halls will be used as the fields for four games, namely table tennis, fencing & modern pentathlon, wrestling and badminton. Some conference rooms will serve for International Broadcasting Center and Major Press Center. The conference center will be equipped with the advanced international intelligent integrative wiring system, computer internet system, digital program control switch system, satellite cable TV system, background music and emergency broadcasting system, multimedia TV conference system, digital conference system, video-on-demand system, building automatic system, central air conditioner system, auto office system, auto fire protection system, security protection supervision system and integrated management system.

After the Olympic Games, the conference center will hold various conferences, exhibitions, performances and other commercial or public welfare activities as an important conference and exhibition center in Beijing. It can attract national and international enterprises and organizations to organize conferences and tourism there.

Olympic Park

Beijing Olympic Park, located to the north of the North Sihuan Zhonglu in Beijing, to the south bank of the Qinghe River in the north, the North Sihuan Zhonglu in the south, the Anillu and Beichen Donglu in the east and Lincuilu and Beichen Xilu in the west, is a large-scale place for concentrated construction of sports facilities for Beijing 2008 Olympic Games. The subject of the forest park is designed as "axis to nature". The park is planned to cover a space of 1,135 hectares. It is the largest city park in Beijing at present. After the Olympic Games, it will become a natural scene tourist region for Beijing citizens. The "major hill and major lake" in south of the park is the symbol of the forest park. The major hill is laid by 3.98 million cubic meters of earth hillock, responding to the Yanshan

National Aquatics Center

Mountain chain far away, a barrier in northwest Beijing. It not only accords with the tradition of Chinese garden architecture, but also brings out the best in each other with the surrounding environment. The major lake, Olympic Lake, and the scenic riverway compose the "dragon-shaped" water system in the park, and the water surface of 122 hectares surpasses a half the Kunming Lake.

Olympic Rowing-Canoeing Park

Olympic Rowing-Canoeing Park is located in the northeast of Xiangyazha, Chaobaihe, Mapo Town, Shunyi District in Beijing. The park covers a space of 302.7 hectares, neighboring at Olympic Equestrian Center (also called Beijing Village Racecourse). During the Olympic Games in 2008, the games of rowing and canoeing will be held there. The two games will use one field with 30,000 seats including 10,000 stands. The kayak-slalom will have an individual field without permanent seats but 15,000 temporary seats. After the construction, the park will become the largest and best equipped aquatic sports center, as well as an important heritage from Beijing 2008 Olympic Games.

Qingdao International Sailing Ship Center

Qingdao International Sailing Ship Center will be the field for the sailing ship event of the 29th Olympic Games. Located on the coast of Fushan Bay, i.e. the relocation of Beihai Ship Building Plant, the center covers a space of 45 hectares and the space for Olympic Games is about 30 hectares. It includes land project and aquatic project; the former one mainly includes Administrative Center, Athletes Apartments, Athletes Center, Media Center, and Logistics and Support Center as well as the environment and attaching facilities, and the latter one mainly includes Main Breakwater, Secondary Breakwater, Jetty Wharf, Olympic Memorial Wall Wharf, Bank Revetment Transformation and other supporting facilities. The harbor area encircled by Olympic Memorial Wall Wharf, Secondary Breakwater and Jetty Wharf is about 15.5 hectares and the harbor water area encircled by Main Breakwater and Jetty Wharf is about 7.5 hectares. In addition some temporary constructions and facilities will be added during the games to satisfy better the demands of the sailing ship games. For example, a temporary measuring hall will be built up on the Jetty Wharf, and a pontoon dock will be built up on the west side of Olympic Memorial Wall Wharf for spectators to use as parking lot.

The berth area of Qingdao International Sailing Ship Center

Hong Kong Olympic Equestrian Venues

Hong Kong Olympic Equestrian Venues

The two Olympic equestrian venues in Hong Kong are located at the suburb with beautiful scenes, only a 20-minute-drive from the downtown. The Hong Kong Sports Institute, neighboring Shatin equestrian ground, and the Penfold Park at the center of the equestrian ground are the major venues for full-dress pas game and ground steeplechase. In addition, the venues for point-to-point are in Beas River Country Club of Hong Kong Equestrian Federation and the Hong Kong Golf Club.

The major venue in the Hong Kong Sports Institute has a full-day 100m×80m sand major venue with a seating capacity of 19,000, where the full-dress pas game and ground steeplechase will be held. The air-conditioned buildings on both sides of the venue will be used as administrative headquarters, guest reception and dormitory for people caring horses. Beside the major venue, there is a 90m×45m sand warm-up ground, separated from the major venue by covered examiners (for going out of venue). On the east and west of the major venue, there are two 100m×50m training ground, the one for ground steeplechase being 90m×40m and the one for full-dress pas being 60m×20m. In the Hong Kong Sports Institute there is an indoor gymnasium which will be changed to indoor training ground. The training facilities in Penfolk Park include 4 full-dress pas sand training grounds. A 800m point-to-point training route will be built in the park, and there is a completed 1,000m full-day raceway. The grass training raceway on riverbank in Shatin Equestrian Federation club will also be used as equestrian training. The venue for point-to-point is to north of the Shatin major venue. The point-to-point parts of three games will be held in Beas River Country Club of Hong Kong Equestrian Federation and the Hong Kong Golf Club nearby.

▲ China Sports Museum

Situated in the Beijing Olympic Sports Center, China Sports Museum is the first museum of professional level which collects, displays, studies and popularize relics and documents relative to sports. Completed in September 1990, it was inaugurated by the Chairman of International Olympic Committee and Mr. Huo Yingdong on September 22, the same day as the opening of the 11th Asian Games.

China Sports Museum has a floor area of 7,100 square meters, and a display area of 5100 square meters. It has collected more than 4,700 pieces of sports relics and above 5,000 pictures of precious sports relics, and is an important channel to popularize and study Chinese sports culture and to understand the sporting of China. The exhibition consists of five parts: the ancient China, modern China, the sports achievements of People's Republic of China, Olympic Games and ethnic sports. Through observing these collections, one can have a comparatively complete understanding of the development of China's sports career.

China Sports Museum also hold various temporary exhibitions, such as the 11th Asian Game Stamps Exhibition (which is the largest stamp exhibition on a specific subject in Asia and exhibited more than 207 sets, or 1,374 frames of stamps from 30countires and areas in the world), the Tournament Exhibition Exalting the Spirit of Beijing Asian Games, Chinese Athletes at Baseline, An Open China Looks Forward to the Olympic Games, etc. Every year the museum receives more than 200,000 person/times.

China Sports Museum also carries out cooperation and communication with the sports circle and museum circle from many countries and areas including North America, Europe, Japan, South Korea, Hong Kong and Taiwan, etc.

Address: Jia-3 Anding Lu, Chaoyang District, Beijing

Comprehensive Sports Information

Sports Economy

China's modern sports market started at 1980s. In August 1994, the State Physical Culture and Sports Commission set up the sports industry office, and then Sports Lottery Management Center, Sports Fundraising Center and Sports Equipments Center. By the year 1998, the operating income of the country's sports management bodies was about 180 million yuan, and the income from running all kinds of games was about 100 million yuan. 18 thousands sports enterprises were registered in Beijing, Shanghai, Shenzhen, Hubei and Anhui, and the sports lottery were issued more than 6.2 billion yuan. Chinese Olympic Committee Commercial Emblem was put to use on March 28, 2001. Meanwhile, Measures of Recruiting Sponsors for Chinese Olympic Committee (2001-2004) and Measures of Implementing the Plan of Licensed Chinese Olympic Committee Commercial Emblem (2001-2004) were issued. Chinese Olympic Committee Commercial Emblem officially in use meant that the market developing of Chinese Olympic Committee followed the international practice and got onto the track of standardization.

Sports Industries

Since China adopted the policy of reform and opening-up, the sports industry entered the stage of profound and rapid development, and has formed an industrial structure of taking sports service as foundation, with sports goods production and distribution developing together. China has preliminary built up the sports market system on the basis of four major trades, which are bodybuilding and relaxation, competition and performance, sports training and sports agency.

The consumption of sports goods is heated in recent years. The total production value of China's sports industry averagely increases 49.3 billion yuan each year. In 2000, the export value of China's sports goods reached 7 billion dollars. The proportion of the sports equipments taking in the domestic market are increasing year by year and the operating area keeps expanding.

Since in 1994, China's football took the lead to be professionalized and market-oriented, every year about 5 million people buying tickets to watch the games on the spot, earning an average annual production value nearly 700 million yuan. During the 2001-2002 seasons, the 194 games of CBA (Chinese Basketball Association) professional basketball league received 746,500 person-time spectators, the box-office rate reaching 87 percent. With sports competition performances as the leader, the sports sponsor, TV rebroadcast, sports media, sports advertisement, sports lottery and other relative industries are brought along.

The 2007 International Trade Show for Brands in Sports, Fashion and Lifestyle in Asia was held in Beijing. In the picture is the exhibition stand for Italian ski boot and gloves.

▲ Sports Goods Exhibitions

China has become a major production base of sports goods in the world, with its output taking up 65 percent of the world market. A significant indicator of the achievements in this respect is China Sport Show. In 2004, China Sport Show covered a display area of 100,000 m^2, as large as ISPO, the largest sports goods exhibition in the world.

Starting from 1993, China Sport Show is held every two years. The exhibits are mainly sports wear and casual wear, sports venue facilities including facilities for sports, fitness, rehabilitation, training, competition and leisure sports, apparatus and instruments specially designed for sports, electronic timing equipment, etc., sports goods for children, sports books and magazines, patent products for sports technology, designated products for sports lottery and so on.

Sports Goods

Sports goods includes sports instruments, sports clothing, sports foods and so on. Since 1980s, along with the fast development of the mass sports and the historical improvement of the level of the athletic sports, the production and consumption of sports goods are also notably increased.

China's famous brand includes: Lining sports goods, Dengyaping sports goods, Shenzhou sports goods, Doubel Red Xi sports goods and so on. Presently, over 270 international sports brand have opened more than 5,000 branches in China. By the end of 2004, China has about 700 large sports goods markets, 1,200 sports department stores, 600 sports equipment stores, 160 local sports goods agencies and 3 sports ecommerce enterprises.

Now, the turnover of China's sports goods market is between 30-40 billion yuan and the production has reached a relatively large scale. There are 3,372 sports goods enterprises in China, among which 17 have more than 20 million yuan production value. China has become the world largest production base of sports goods, and over 2/3 of the sports goods are produced in China. The export value of sports good in 1998 is 4.598 billion dollars in1999, 5.387 billion dollars, and the number in 2000 reached 7 billion dollar. Sports industry has become a major foreign exchange earner of China.

The fitness activities bring all-round and sustainable business chances for sports articles.

Sports Market

With China's accession to WTO and the successful bid for 2008 Olympic Games in Beijing, sports industry and sports economy has become a new focus of economic development in China, which brings new vitality to China's sports goods market. Ever since 2000, China's sports goods market has been developing at an annual growth rate of over 10 percent. By 2004, the total value of the market had reached US$4.2 billion. Meanwhile, China has become the largest sports goods production base, and 60 percent of the sports goods in world market come from China. In 2004, China's total export value of sports goods reached US$5.4billion. It is estimated that the total value of China's sports goods market will have reached US$6.2 billion by 2008. China is also encouraging people to take part in sports activities. Currently, 400 million Chinese people regularly engage in physical exercises, and this number keeps increasing, which produces great demands to China's sports goods market.

Sports Goods Retailing

In general, there are the following 4 models of retailing in China's sports goods market:

Mono Brand Chain Store: Now it is one of the major selling methods in China's sports goods retailing, Nike, Adidas and Lining being the significant examples. Currently, Nike has 1,200 chain stores taking up 10 percent of the market share, and there are 10 more Nike stores every week. Adidas takes up 9.3 percent of the market share, only second to Nike. It has 1,300 chain stores in 250 cities in China, and this number is planned to reach 4,000 in 2008. Lining, the No.1 domestic sports goods producer, takes up 8.7 percent, ranking third in China market. It has 2,500 chain stores and plans to open another 1,500 by 2008.

Specialty Chain Store: In this kind of stores, there are products of many brands including private brands. It sells a complete series of sports goods, with self-run as the major business type. Decathlon and Quest Sports are good examples of this kind in China. Decathlon is a French sports goods retailer. It entered Chinese market in 2003 and has 5 chain stores in China now.

Store-in-Store: This kind of companies usually rent a certain space, e.g. one floor, in department stores and supermarkets and bring in name brands of sports goods in and abroad. Each brand rents a certain space within and opens a specialty store. And each brand manages their store independently without interference from other stores. The income of sports city comes in two ways, partly from the rent paid by each brand and partly from the commission paid according to the commission agreements with the brands, i.e. if the monthly or annual turnover of a brand reaches a certain amount, a certain proportion of the turnover will be paid to the sports city as commission. This model of retailing is at advantage in that it creates a collective effect and provides consumers with wide choices in a single fixed area.

Other Models of Retailing: Other Models of retailing including sales in department stores, supermarkets, outlet stores and gray markets. They are not specialized sports goods stores but sell some sports goods in a small scale.

Olympic Stamps

In memory of Chinese sports delegation participated in the Winter Olympics in 1980, the Ministry of Posts and Telecommunications issued a set of stamps on the winter sports. This set of stamps The 13th Winter Olympics contains 4 copypieces, and the designs are respectively the emblem of the Olympics, speed skating, figure skating and skiing. On November 26 the same year, in order to celebrate that China resumed its seat in IOC, the Ministry of Posts and Telecommunications issued another set of stamps One Year Anniversary of Coming Back the IOC, which contains 5 copypieces, of which the designs are respectively shooting, gymnastics, diving, volleyball and toxophily, with the athletes' dynamic images under the background of the five Olympic rings, which mean that China's sports teams have walked onto the shinning Olympic road.

In July, 1984, the Ministry of Posts and Telecommunications issued a series of postal souvenirs, including a set of stamps The 23rd Olympic Games, which contains 6 copypieces and a sheetlet, a stamp set FDC containing 3 copypieces, a set of commemorative stamped postcards In Memory of China Being Awarded the Gold Medal in the 23rd Olympics containing 16 copypieces, a set of two commemorative envelopes respectively with a gold coin and a silver coin inlaid, two postcards and so on. In July 1992, in order to commemorate the achievements Chinese sports delegation made in the 25th Barcelona Olympics, the Ministry of Posts and Telecommunications issued a set of commemorative stamps, which contained 4 copypieces and a sheetlet. The designs on the stamps are respectively basketball, weightlifting, diving and Gymnastics, while the design of the sheetlet is marathon. In 1996, in memory of the 100th anniversary of the modern Olympics, another piece of commemorative stamp was issued, the design of which is the statue of ancient Greek discobolus.

The First Miniature Sheet Pingpong Stamp

The first miniature sheet pingpong stamp was issued in 1961 in China, when the 26th World Pingpong Championship was held in Beijing. Except issuing a set with four copypieces, a miniature sheet was also issued. This is the only miniature sheet pingpong stamp of the world.

The First Set of Sports Stamps

The first set of sports stamp in China's history was issued in January 1952, which is called *Radio Exercises*. It has 40 designs to reflect the 10 basic movements of the radio exercises, and each design is a copypiece, so this set of stamps has 40 copypieces, which is the most among all the sports stamps of the world.

The First Set of Chinese Ancient Sports Stamps

On December 20, 1986, the first set of Chinese ancient sports stamps was issued, which is a favorite of the stamp collectors and sports enthusiasts. This is the first set of stamps reflecting Chinese ancient sports after the foundation of PRC. Ancient Chinese Sports contains 4 copypieces, respectively represents toxophily, Chuiwan, Weiqi (Go), Cuju (ancient Chinese Football). The general style of the design imitates the effect of the rubbings of the paintings of the Han Dynasty, which are bold, unconstrained in artistic style.

Lu Enchun, the leader of the National Gymnastics Team in 1950s and the judge of the 23rd Olympics came to the Dongsi Olympic Community, bringing over one hundred Olympic judge's clothes, badges and souvenirs collected himself.

The First National Sports Stamps Exhibition

From July 28 to August 12, 1984, the first national sports stamps exhibition was held in Beijing. 305 frames, 3,660 stamp mounting papers and over 20,000 copypieces were displayed in this exhibition, which are from 24 provinces, autonomous regions and municipalities directly under the central government, People's Liberation Army, unites directly under the State Physical Culture and Sports Commission, 138 individual collectors and 4 organizations. During the exhibition, the award of best design of sports stamps was chosen through public appraisal.

Licensed Olympic Postcards

On March 2, 1996, Beijing Jianguomen Post and Telecommunication Office and Beijing Stamp Company are authorized to use the emblem and mascot of the 1996 Atlanta Olympics, which are the first in China. They issued the appointed commemorative postal souvenirs—a set of sports postcards coded BT-PI, containing 32 pieces. So the mascot "IZZY" came to China in spring. This set of postcards with the pictures of "IZZY" is the first licensed Olympic postcards issued in China. The pictures of this set of postcards contain the Olympic emblem, the mascot "IZZY" and the 31 events of the Olympics. The whole set has 32 pieces, and the total circulation is 320,000 sets with code on them. The colors of the pictures are relative to the certain event it represents. The events signs and emblem of 1996 Atlanta Olympics are printed on the back of the postcards, which emphasize the commemorative theme of the postcards.

The First Silver Commemorative Coin

On March 26, 1984, people's bank of China decided to issues silver commemorative coins to commemorate China's participation in the 23rd Olympics and the 14th Winter Olympics. The commemorative coins have three kinds, which respectively with the pictures of women's volleyballs, men's jumpers and the skating athletes. The par values of the coins are ten yuan and five yuan. This was the first time that China issued commemorative coins for Olympics.

Sports Lottery

The Sports Lottery Management Center of the General Administration of Sports of China was established in 1994, and all the provinces, autonomous regions and municipalities directly under the central government set up their branch management center in succession, so the national distribution network for publicly issuing lotteries was formed. From then on, China's sports lottery industry got onto the track of standardization, featuring the consolidated issue, printing, distribution and management, so the real Chinese sports lottery came into existence. At present, China's sports lotteries include Spot Sports Lottery, Traditional Lottery, Twice Drawing Lottery, Computer Lottery, Double Lottery, Number Lottery and so on.

Since 1994 until now, China's sports lottery experienced a fast development. Now, it plays a more and more important role in raising sports fund. Its distribution system and production structure all meet the international requirements. Since the sports lotteries realized the consolidated issuing in 1994, 50,000 selling ends are located all over the country by the end of 2004 and the accumulated sales value is over 91.7 billion yuan. Through the sports lottery, more than 30.3 billion yuan sports fund are raised, which strongly support the sports course and other public welfare undertakings. The sports lottery has become an important capital source of the development of the sports.

The sports lottery also contributes a lot to the construction of the 2008 Beijing Olympic

Buy sports lotteries

Gymnasiums and Stadiums. The sports lottery will raise 2.75 billion yuan for the Beijing Olympics within 8 years. Until the end of 2006, it has provided 2.05 billion yuan to the Special Fund for Olympics.

The Earliest Sports Lottery

The earliest sports lottery of China was issued in 1984, which was for the Beijing International Marathon Race. The lottery ticket was made in the traditional way, and the specification was 12.5cm multiplying 7cm. In the face of the ticket, there was an abstract picture of seven athletes running side by side. The issuing of this lottery was to raise funds for the Beijing International Marathon Race, and the issuing time was from October 10, 12:00 at the noon to October 13, 1984, and the time of announcing the winning tickets was October 14, 10:00 in the morning, 1984.

The lottery issued for the 1984 Beijing International Marathon Race was the earliest sports lottery of China. Because they were only issued in Beijing in a quite limited time, and the amount issued was only 50,000, they were very hard to collect and quite rare.

Sports Collection

The sports collection history of China has three stages.

The first the stage is before the year 1949. In this period of time, Sports collection is not common in China, and the collections are mainly Chinese chesses, stone locks, engineries and so on. In 1936, a few people joined in the 11th Olympic Games and took back some souvenirs such as ties, ornaments and badges. From then on, China began to have real sports collections.

The second stage is from 1929 to 1982. In 1952, China issued sports stamps for the first time and the philately activities of new China began. In 1959, the first National Games was hold and issued souvenirs for collection. In 1980, after issuing the sports gold and silver commemorative coins, the sports commemorative coins in currency were issued, which were fancied by the people very much. Besides, other sports collections, such as tickets, key chains and cards appeared in successions, which expanded the domain of sports collection further.

The third stage is from 1983 to now. Along with the improvement of people's living standard, the sports collection heat was aroused in China. In 1984, in order to celebrate the historical breakthrough of winning the first golden medal in the Olympics by the Chinese sports delegations, the first National Sports Stamps Exhibition was held in Beijing, which greatly inspired the zest of the sports collection enthusiasts all over the country.

Mountaineering athletes set out towards the top of the mountain on the 17th Taishan International Climbing Festival.

Sports Media

China's sports media mainly includes TV, newspapers, magazine, websites and broadcasting, and TV plays the most important role among them.

— Sports TV station: includes CCTV Sports channel and the sports programs of others provincial TV stations. China's central TV station began to broadcast TV sports news since 1958 and rebroadcasted Sports competitions at the end of the same year. In 1959, a special program named *Sports Enthusiasts* was set up, later it was renamed as *Sports View*. CCTV-5 is the sports channel, which reports the sports news, living broadcasts or rebroadcasts all the major international and national competitions.

— Sports newspapers and magazines: China's first national sports newspaper started its publication on September 1, 1958. Now, the main sports newspapers and magazines of China include *China Sports, Sports Reference, Sports Weekly, Football News, Sports Salon* and so on.

The Beijing Olympics will raise a battle on the TV Medias of the whole world. The TV stations from all over the world have begun to contend. The NBC (National Broadcasting Company) has bought the live broadcasting right of the 2008 Beijing Olympics in 1996. Besides NBC, Star Group Limited, FR2, NHK and other medias all have the rebroadcasting right of the 2008 Olympics. The participation of international Medias is a great challenge for Chinese TV sports media.

New Sports

The *New Sports* started publication on July 1, 1950, Chairman Mao inscribed the title of the magazine in person, and the three characters are used until today. *New Sports* is the earliest national comprehensive sports journal, with the largest circulation of its kind. The first issue's cover is red, with the images of the famous ancient Greek Olympic Discobolus. The first published 10,000 copies were sold out at once, so another 5,000 were added. *New Sports* is the good teacher and helpful friend of the sports workers and sports enthusiasts, and its circulation has been more than 1 million.

The First Sports Encyclopedia

In January, 1983, under the requirement of State Physical Culture and Sports Commission, *China Sports Encyclopedia* was officially published, which was the first sports encyclopedia of China.

The encyclopedia has altogether 763 entries, 1.2 million words, 1,222 pictures and some appendixes, taking page spaces for 1.5 million words. The book comprehensively and systematically introduces the basic subjects of sports, sports history, China's modern sports undertakings, the mass sports activities, sports events, international sports organizations, international competitions, the basic sports situations of other countries altogether seven big groups, concerning sports philosophy, history, sociology, pedagogy, aesthetics and other subjects. It is also an authoritative sports reference book, which can serves as a tool for the sports enthusiasts and workers doing deep researches. *China Sports Encyclopedia* has been collected by the International Olympic Museum located in Lausanne.

The First Sports Dictionary

In January 1984, Shanghai Lexicographical Works Press published a sports dictionary, which is the first comprehensive middle sized sports dictionary of China. The whole book has 5,220 entries, which were divided into sports theories, sports events, ancient sports, folk sports, competitions, famous athletes, sports organizations, sports institutions, gymnasiums and stadiums, works, newspapers and magazines and other nine groups. It also has 23 different kinds of appendixes, which include the world records and the national records of some sports events, statistics on the champions of the international and domestic competitions and so on. The appendixes have about more than 400,000 words.

The First English Sports Magazine

The first English sports magazine of China is *China Sports*, which was established in April 1957. Its publication was stopped from 1966 to 1978, and when the publication of this magazine was resumed in January 1979, it became a bimonthly, and then changed into a monthly in 1980. The main contents of *China Sports* include reporting the mass sports activities of China, such as the characteristic folks sports and minorities' sports, the achievements that the Chinese athletes got in the various domestic and international competitions, the training experiences of the coaches and the athletes, the long history of Chinese *wushu* and some other effective ways of doing exercises, knowledge about medical treatment and sports history and the friendly communication between China and other countries through sports affairs.

Currently, *China Sports* has set up exchanging relationship with more than 60 magazines of the world, and was published in more than 130 countries and areas. More and more articles and the pictures of *China Sports* were cited or transshipped by foreign newspapers and magazines. The *World Sports Communication* of Britain once took eight pages to publish the materials from *China Sports*. Some departmental publications of the IOC also transshipped or cited the point of view of some articles from this magazine.

The Earliest Modern Sports Publication

The magazine *Sports Circle* was started in 1909, which was the earliest modern sports magazine of China. *Sports Circle* was edited by Xu Yibing, the famous modern sports expert and the headmaster of Chinese Gymnastics School, and published by China Publishing Group. The magazine was in the book size of 24, letterpress printing, published aperiodically and stopped its publication at the 10th issue. The *Sports Circle* resumed publication in March 1918 and became a monthly. The guideline of this magazine is to introduce modern sports, advocate warrior spirit, research on the modern sports events and attack the weak ethos of whole society at the time.

The First National Sports Publishing House

People's Sports Publishing House is the only national publishing house on sports, which was established in January 1954.

The main task of the publishing house is to propagandize China's guideline and policy on sports, introduce sports knowledge and various exercising methods, introduce sports training experiences and sports S&T research, present traditional physical culture, present advanced overseas sports technologies, publish textbooks of sports academies and physical education textbooks for primary, middle school and college students, publish books on rules of different events and introduce Chinese traditional physical exercises abroad. Meanwhile, People's Sports Publishing House is also responsible for the publication of *Sports Science* and more than 20 other sports journals.

Attending the International Olympic Film Festival

Produced by the Central Newsreel and Documentary Film Studio, two colored documentaries *World Women's Volleyball Star Game and Sports Elite of Our Nation* took part in the First International Olympic Film Festival held in Tunisia on April 22-26, 1987. This Festival was sponsored by the International Federation of Sport Cinema and Television (FICTS) and Tunisian Olympic Committee, aiming to spread the Olympic spirits, record and narrate history of Olympic Games. China is one of the founding countries of FICTS.

Titan Sports Media

As the most influential sports media group of China, *Titan Sports* Media was established in 1988. It possesses one newspaper, *Titan Sports*, which publishes more 5 million copies a week, and five other magazines, including Soccer *Weekly, All Sports, Dunk Shot, Golf Masters* and *Outdoors*. In addition, Titan Sports Media has its own website, broadcasting station, TV program, wireless increment service and two other branch companies.

Sports Festivals

Holding sports festival is an effective way to develop popular sports. The content, name and form of sports festivals are various in different areas.

— Beijing Sports Festival: Initiating in 1997, Beijing Sports Festival is held every two years. Its main content includes: ten thousands citizens climbing the hills, ten thousands citizens bicycling, demonstrating ways of exercise for the masses, bodybuilding exercises performing and primary and middle school pupils skateboarding. The festival lasts one month every time.

— Shandong Weifang Kite Festival: This festival is held every year since 1986. The International Kite Federation was established in Weifang in 1989.

— Asian Sports Festival: Asian Sports Festival was held in Shenyang in 1998, and the 18 events of this festival included billiards, croquet, water polo, bowling, shadowboxing, bicycling around the city, chess, etc.

— Taishan International Mountaineering Festival: since 1987, Taishang International & National Mountaineering Festival is held in early September every year.

— Harbin Ice and Snow Festival: Harbin is called "ice city", which is one of the origins of the ice and snow culture. The first Harbin Ice and Snow Festival was held on Jan. 5th, 1985, and is held every year since then. The main activities of the festival include ice-made lights garden party, snow sculpture garden party and international ice sculpture and snow sculpture contest. Besides, there are also winter swimming, ice hockey, skating, skiing and langlauf competitions during the festival.

— Yueyang International Dragon Boat Festival: With the Miluo River and Dongting Lake, Hunan Province is the hometown of dragon boat racing custom, so the festival held in this place is of much significance in spreading the local culture. Since the First International Dagon Boat Festival on Jun. 16th, 1991, it is held every year here.

Sports Information Websites

Almost all the major websites of China have their sports information column. The government has established official sports information website, which is responsible for the spreading and communicating of sports information. In 1996, the CCTV.com set up a branch CCTV Sports Programs; the 163.com Sports Channel was established in 1997, and sina.com also has a column called Competition Storm. Xinhua Sports Database is a professional sports information website. Other sports websites includes Chinese Chess (cchess.com), World of Sports (osports.cn), Yahoo Sports (sports.yahoo.com.cn) and China Sports on Web (sportschina.com).

Index

1

1 Percent Sample Census (2005) P30
10jqka.com P676
10th Asian Games P726
10th Five-Year Plan (2001-2005) P69
10th National Games P714
10th National Winter Games P715
10th Paralympics P724
111 Project (Program of Introducing Overseas Talents in Disciplines to Universities) P229
11th Asian Games P726
11th Five-Year Plan (2006-2010) P70
11th Five-Year Plan on Physical Culture and Sports P698
11th Paralympics P724
11th Women's Softball World Championship P744
11th World Women's Volleyball Championship P730
126 Mail P672
12th Asian Games P726
12th Paralympics P724
13th Asian Games P726
13th Paralympics P724
13th Winter Games P723
14th Asian Games P726
14th Winter Games P723
15th Asian Games P727
15th Olympic Games in Helsinki P719
15th Winter Games P723
16th Winter Games P723
17game.com P681
17th Winter Games P723
18th Winter Games P723
19th Universiade P724
19th Winter Games P723
1st Asian Games P725
1st Asian Winter Games P727
1st China International Table Tennis Open Championships P729
1st East Asian Games P728
1st FIFA World Championships of Women's Football P730
1st National City Games P718
1st National Games P713
1st National Games for the Disabled P716
1st National Sports Meeting P715
1st National Traditional Ethnic Sports Games P717
1st National Winter Games P714

2

2006 China Open P789
20th Universiade P725
20th Winter Games P723
21st Universiade P725
22nd Universiade P725
23rd Summer Olympics in Los Angeles P719
23rd Universiade P725
24th Summer Olympics in Seoul P720
25th Summer Olympics in Barcelona P720
26th Summer Olympics in Atlanta P720
26th World Table Tennis Championships P705
27th Summer Olympics in Sydney P721
28th Summer Olympics in Athens P721
29th Summer Olympics in Beijing P722
2nd Asian Winter Games P727
2nd East Asian Games P728
2nd National City Games P718
2nd National Games P713
2nd National Games for the Disabled P716
2nd National Sports Meeting P715
2nd National Traditional Ethnic Sports Games P717

3

360 Safe P674
360quan.com P688
3721.com P661
39.net P678
3rd Asian Winter Games P727
3rd East Asian Games P728
3rd National City Games P718
3rd National Games P713
3rd National Games for the Disabled P716
3rd National Sports Meeting P716
3rd National Traditional Ethnic Sports Games P717
3rd National Winter Games P715

4

4th Asian Winter Games P727
4th East Asian Games P728
4th National City Games P719
4th National Games P713
4th National Games for the Disabled P716
4th National Traditional Ethnic Sports Games P717
4th National Winter Games P715

5

51.com P685
51ditu.com P664
51job.com P678
52tong.com P664
56.com P684
58.com P663
5fad P682
5th Asian Winter Games P727
5th National City Games P719
5th National Games P713
5th National Games for the Disabled P716
5th National Traditional Ethnic Sports Games P718
5th National Winter Games P715

6

6rooms.com P684
6th National Games P713
6th National Games for the Disabled P716
6th National Traditional Ethnic Sports Games P718
6th National Winter Games P715

7

7cv.com P655
7th Asian Games P725
7th Gymnastics World Cup P774
7th National Games P713
7th National Traditional Ethnic Sports Games P718
7th National Winter Games P715
7th Paralympics P724

8

863 Program P196
8th Asian Games P726
8th National Games P714

8th National Winter Games P715
8th Paralympics P724

9.com P681
9158.com P689
92wy.com P682
973 Program P196
99Bill Corporation P658
9sky.com P682
9th Asian Games P726
9th National Games P714
9th National Winter Games P715
9th Paralympics P724
9th Universiade P724
9you.com P680

A Decade of CBA P739
A Dream of Red Mansions P462
A Leadership and Administration System for National Defense P135
A New Security Concept P134
Abundant Folk Paper Cuts P286
Acceptance and Establishment of Cases P631
Access Methods of Internet Users in China P649
Accession to the Olympic Family P701
Achang Ethnic Group P51
Achang Ethnic Group Husa Knife Making Skills P422
Achievements at the 25th Olympics Games P720
Achievements at the 26th Olympics P720
Achievements at the 27th Olympics P721
Achievements of Chinese Taipei Athletes at the Olympiad P721
Achievements of Hong Kong Athletes at the Olympiad P721
Achievements of Recycling Economy P568
Achievements of the Chinese Field Hockey Team in 2006 P760
Achievements of the Chinese Model Ship Building Team P813
Achievements of Weightlifting at the Olympics P734
Acid Deposition Monitoring in East Asia P605
Acrobatics P780
Action of "Air Conditioner at 26°Centigrade" P564
Active Prevention of Environmental Accidents P578
Active Service P139
Active Troops of the PLA P137
Activities of Commercial Satellites P89
Activities to Save Energy P572
Activities to Save Water P573
Acupuncture and Moxibustion P437
ADB-Financed Railway Projects P93
Administration System for Military Service Work P139
Administration System of Militia Force P141
Administrative Compensation P644
Administrative Division System P615
Administrative System P66
Adopting the Principle of Independence and Self-management P182
Adult Education P212
Aero Sports P818
Aero Sports Federation of China P814
Aeromodeling P814
Aerospace Industry P85
Affairs for Entering to China and Admission P227
AFS Exchanges and Activities in China P221
AFS Intercultural Programs in China P220
After-School Education P207
Age Structure of Chinese Internet Users P649
Agencies and Special Commission Directly Under the State Council P66
Agreements on Disarmament and Confidence-Building Measures between China and Relevant Countries P149
Agricultural Bank of China P101
Agricultural Development Bank of China P103
Agricultural Film Studio of China P469
Agricultural Industrialization P75
Aiding Disabled People P553
Aid-Study System P208
Aigita Mosque in Kashgar P488
Air China Limited P95
Aites of Kazak Ethnic Group P393
Aitiga Mosque of Kashi (Kashgar) P178
Alibaba.com P656
Alipay P657
All China Environmental Federation P567
All-China Environmental Award P563
All-China Federation of Industry and Commerce P72 (P612)
All-China Federation of Returned Overseas Chinese (AFROC) P612
All-China Federation of Trade Unions (ACFTU) P611
All-China Journalists Association P613
All-China Lawyers Association P640
All-China Sports Federation P836
All-China Women's Federation P611
Alliance's Zhaopin.com P679
All Religions Are Equal P182
Alpha Magnetic Spectrometer Experiment P198
Alpine Skiing P811
Alternative Energy P571
Altun Mountain Nature Reserve P599
Ancient Acrobatics P699
Ancient Bells Museum at the Great Bell Temple P306
Ancient Horsemanship P699
Ancient Pottery Civilization Museum P316
Ancient Song of Miao People P320
Ancient Sports P699
Angling P824
Anhui Museum P300
Anhui Opera P366
Anhui Province P623
Animals P13
Annual Review of the Chinese Government Scholarship P223
Anping Bridge P482
Ansai Waist Drum Dance P350
Anshun Dixi P382
Anti-dumping Policies and Procedures P126
Anti-Doping Work P697
Anyang Aero Sports School P841
Aobao Worshipping P448
Application Approach and Time for the Chinese Government Scholarships P223
Application Documents for Chinese Government Scholarships P222
Application of Internet in China P650
Applications for Short-term Course and Visa Application P226
Applications for Study in China of Non-Government Scholarship Students P225
Aquatic Products P12
Arbitration Organs P642
Arbitration System P642
Arbitration Tribunal P643
Arbitrators P643
Archery P769
Architectural Art of Tibetan Buddhism P488
Architectural Art of Uygur Ethnic Group P488
Architecture of Chinese Gardens P476
Army Day P557
Army Emblem of the PLA P137
Army Flag of the PLA P137
Art of Quyi P279
Art of Suona Horn P337
Art of Wine in China P517
Articles of Hundred Schools P456
Asia-Africa Table Tennis Friendship Invitational P729
Asian Games P725
Asian Winter Games P727
Athletic Skills P781
Attending the International Olympic Film Festival P848
August First Film Studio P469
Autohome.com P676
Automobile Consumption P501
Automobile Industry P84
Automobile Sports P816

Autonomous Areas for Ethnic Minority Groups P58
Autumnal Equinox P523
Award of "Green Chinese Personage of a Year" P606

B

B2B and B2C Tourism Electronic Commerce Platform P657
Ba Da Guan in Qingdao P492
Baba Mosque of Langzhong City P177
Background of the Policies on the Population P32
Backstroke P792
Badaling Demonstration Area in Beijing P581
Badminton P797
Baguwen (Eight-part Essay) P203 (P457)
Bai Ethnic Group P44
Bai Ethnic Group Bandhnu Skills P418
Baidu P660
Baishuijiang National Nature Reserve P595
Baixi (A Hundred Acrobatics) P699
Baizi Opera P377
Balance Beam P775
Baling Opera P367
Ballads of Liu Sanjie P325
Bamboo and Rattan Weaving P295
Bamboo Carving P409
Bamboo Paper Making Skills P430
Bangke Building (Tower) P488
Banhu P263
Bank Card P502
Bank of China P100
Bank of Communications P103
Banpo Museum in Xi'an P314
Banruo (Prajna) Temple of Shenyang City P169
Banruo (Prajna)Temple of Changchun City P169
Bantou Tunes P340
Bao'an Ethnic Group Waist Dagger Making Skills P422
Barbecue Ji P508
Barbecue Wan P508
Bark Paper Making Skills P429
Bars P556
Baseball P731
Baseball for the Youth P731
Basic Education P205
Basic Employment Situation P540
Basic Forms of foreign Direct investment P131
Basic Framework of the State-owned Asset Management System P72
Basic Medical Insurance System for Urban Employees P546
Basic Theory of Mongolian Medicine P536
Basic Theory of TCM P533
Basic Theory of Tibetan Medicine P535
Basin-Beating Song P390
Basketball P738
Bawu P262
Bayin Singing of the Buyei Ethnic Group P393
Bbvod.net P683
Beach Volleyball P749
Becoming a Member of the International Volleyball Federation P746
Beginning of Autumn P523
Beginning of Spring P523
Beginning of Summer P523
Beginning of Winter P523
Beijing Ancient Observatory P307
Beijing Capital International Airport P96
Beijing Film Academy P470
Beijing Film Studio P469
Beijing International Marathon P730
Beijing International Tennis Center P840
Beijing International Wushu Invitational P730
Beijing Jiaotong University P234
Beijing Language and Culture University P233
Beijing Municipality P615
Beijing Natural History Museum P305
Beijing Normal University P233
Beijing Olympic Mascots P697
Beijing Opera P274 (P366)
Beijing Opera: A Fork in a Road P276
Beijing Opera: Autumn River P276
Beijing Opera: Chisang Town P277
Beijing Opera: Conqueror Xiang Yu Bids Farewell to His Concubine P276
Beijing Opera: Create Serious Disturbance in the Heavenly Palace P278
Beijing Opera: Dragon and Phoenix Is a Good Omen P278
Beijing Opera: Empty-City Strategy P277
Beijing Opera: Entering the Palace for the Second Time P276
Beijing Opera: Gathering of Heroes P278
Beijing Opera: Have the Aid of East Wind P277
Beijing Opera: Hongniang P277
Beijing Opera: Mu Guiying Takes Command P277
Beijing Opera: Qin Xianglian P277
Beijing Opera: Suo Lin Nang P277
Beijing Opera: The Drunken Concubine P276
Beijing Opera: White Snake P277
Beijing Opera: Wild Boar Forest P278
Beijing Opera: Xu Ce Runs in the City P277
Beijing Opera: Yang Silang Visits His Mother P278
Beijing Opera: Yu Tangchun P276
Beijing Opera: Zhaojun Goes to the Border Area P277
Beijing Oriental University P215
Beijing People's Art Theater P283
Beijing Planetarium P307
Beijing Shooting Gallery P840
Beijing Sport University P838
Beijing Student Film Festival P466
Beijing Summit of the Forum on China-Africa Cooperation P162
Beijing Symphony Orchestra P270
Beijing University Students' Gymnasium P840
Beijing Workers' Stadium P493
Beijing Xiannongtan Athletics Technology School P838
Beijing's Siheyuan P479
Beilu Bangzi P363
Bencao Gangmu (Compendium of Materia Medica) P538
Best Track Record of Mountain Bike (2006) P802
Bianyi Workshop (Cheap Workshop) P507
Bianzhong (Chime Bells) P266
Big-bowl Tea P516
Bilateral Cooperation on the Space Project P87
Bilateral Environmental Cooperation P605
Bilateral Governmental Cooperation Programs P220
Bilateral Investment Protection Agreement P132
Bilateral Taxation Agreement P133
Billiards P827
Biluochun (Green Spring Snail Tea) P511
Bingxi (Games on Ice) P699
Biological Fuel P569
Biotechnology P190
Birch Bark Making Skills P433
Black Tea P512
Blang Ethnic Group P48
Blood Donation without Payment P532
Bodybuilding P824
Bogeda Peak National Nature Reserve P596
Bokee.com P685
Bonan Ethnic Group P53
Bone-Setting of TCM P438
Book Bars P556
Booming Years of Gymnastics in China P774
Border and Coastal Defense System P141
Border Trade P123
Bouyei Ethnic Group P42
Bouyei Opera P380
Boxing P760
Bowling P823
Box Office P555
Breakthroughs (2006) P698
Breaststroke P792
Bridge P827
Bridges and Architecture P482
Brief History of Beijing Opera P274
Brief History of China's Protection for Intangible Cultural Heritage P317
Brief History of Chinese Kites P294
Brief History of Folk Music P260
Brief Introduction P77
Brief Introduction of the Administration of China Internet Domain Names Procedures P692

Brief Introduction of the Administration of Internet News Information Services Provisions P693
Brief Introduction of the Measures for Administration of E-mail Service on Internet P693
Brief Introduction of the Measures for the Administration of Electronic Certification Services P693
Brief Introduction of the Regulations on Administration of Internet-based Audio-Video Program Services P693
Brief Introduction of the Regulations on Protection of the Right of Communication through Information Network P691
Brief Introduction of the Decision of the Standing Committee of the NPC on Preserving Computer Network Security P690
Brief Introduction of the Electronic Signature Law of the PRC P690
Brief Introduction of the Measures for the Administration of Internet Information Services P690
Brief Introduction of the Regulations on the Administration of Business Sites of Internet Access P691
Brief Introduction of Web2.0 Application in China P685
Bronze and Stone Seal Carving P405
Bronze Drum Custom of Zhuang Ethnic Group P453
Bronze Drum Dance P353
Bronze Inscriptions P247
Bronze Ware P284
Brush P256
Bu Luo Tuo P320
Buddhism in China P164
Buddhist Association of China P174
Buddhist Painting in China P173
Buddhist Sculpture P173
Building an Energy-Efficient Society P71 (P571)
Building Border and Coastal Defense P141
Building Legal System on Non-Proliferation Export Control P155
Bund Architecture in Shanghai P491
Burning Books and Burying Confucian Scholars Alive P21
Business of Law Firms P640
Business.sohu.com P675
Butter Sculptures P294
Butterfly Lovers P322
Butterfly Swimming P792

C

Cai Lun and the Art of Paper-making P23
Cai Weiyan P786
Cai Wenyi P735
Cai Yalin P767
Cai Zhenhua P756
Caidiao P378
Calligraphy P246
Callisthenics P825
Cangzhou Wushu P396
Canoe/Kayak P750
Cantonese Opera P367
Cao Xueqin P461
Cao Yanhua P756
Cao Yu Dramatic Literature Award P464
Capital P2
Capital Markets' Opening Up P109
Capital Museum P297
Capital Stadium P840
Car Modelling P823
Carved Block Printing Skills P432
Carved Lacquerware Skills P424
Carving P289
Catalogue of Toxic Chemicals China Bans or Strictly Restricts P579
Categories of Internet Education P673
Categories of Local Searches P663
Catering Consumption P496
Catholic Churches in Beijing P179
Catholicism in China P178
Cave Dwelling in Northwest China P480
CBA League P739
CCTV.com P665
Central Academy of Drama P283
Central Conservatory of Music P232
Central Experimentary Huaju Opera Troupe P283
Central Military Commission (CMC) P135
Cha Jing (Classic of Tea) P512
Chabai Song Festival of Bouyei Minority P443
Cham of Tashilhungpo Monastery in Xigaze P352
Champion P782
Chang Hao P829
Changbaishan Mountain National Nature Reserve P591
Changchun Film Festival P466
Changchun Film Studio P468
Changde Silk String P389
Changdian Temple Fair P449
Changes in Sports Development P698
Changes in Wedding P526
Changes of the Telecommunication P127
Changjiang New Mileage Plan P37
Changling Mausoleum P487
Chaohu Folk Song P329
Chaohu Lake P7
Chaozhou Music P341
Chaozhou Opera P359
Chaozhou Wood Carving P407
Characteristics of China's Surname P526
Characteristics of Traditional Architecture P472
Characteristics of Traditional Sports of Ethnic Minorities P711
CHE168 P676
Chen Fushou P798
Chen Hong P800
Chen Hua P793
Chen Jiaquan P785
Chen Jing P757
Chen Jingkai P735
Chen Li P815
Chen Lu P809
Chen Shixin P773
Chen Weiqiang P736
Chen Xiaomin P737
Chen Xinhua P756
Chen Yanqing P737
Chen Ying P767
Chen Yueling P786
Chen Yuxin P747
Chen Zhong P773
Cheng Chao P820
Cheng Fei P778
Chengcheng Yaotou Ceramic Firing and Manufacturing Skills P414
Chengdu Lacquerware Skills P426
Chengdu Shuangliu International Airport P98
Chengdu Sport University P839
Chenxiangge Pavilion P169
Chess P830
Child Social Welfare P554
Childbirth Insurance System P548
China Academic Degrees and Graduate Education Development Center (CDGDC) P212
China Academy of Launch Vehicle Technology (CALT) P86
China Adult Education Association (CAEA) P214
China and APEC P163
China and Olympics P696
China and Shanghai Cooperation Organization P163
China and the UN P162
China and the WTO P163
China Association for NGO Cooperation P551
China Association for Promoting Democracy P610
China Association for Science and Technology (CAST) P202 (P612)
China Association of Automobile Manufacturers P85
China Association of Enterprises with Foreign Investment P133
China Association of Social Workers P551
China Association of the Environmental Protection Industry P563
China at Paralympics P724
China Banking Association P100
China Banking Regulatory Commission P100
China Billiards & Snooker Association (CBSA) P828
China Calligraphers Association P252

China Central Audio-Visual Education Center P218
China Central Radio and Television University P217
China Charity Federation (CCF) P550
China Children and Teenager's Fund (CCTF) P552
China Christian Council P182
China Circuit Championship P816
China Circuit Cross-Country Championship P816
China Cleaner Production Portal P567
China Club Challenge Match P732
China Construction Bank P101
China Consumers' Association P502
China Council for International Cooperation on Environment and Development P605
China Council for the Promotion of International Trade P613
China Cross-Country Championship P816
China Cuisine Association P518
China Democratic League P610
China Development Bank P102
China Disabled Persons' Federation P614
China Doping Control Center P837
China Eastern Airline Holding Company(MU) P95
China Economic Net P665
China Education and Research Network P217
China Education Development Foundation P213
China Education Satellite Broad Band Transmission Network Platform P218
China Education Television P217
China Educational Associations for International Exchange P221
China Energy Conservation Investment Corporation P576
China Environmental Consultative Committee P563
China Environmental Monitoring Station P567
China Environmental Protection Foundation P567
China Europe International Business School (CEIBS) P230
China Everbright Bank P103
China Export and Credit Insurance Corporation P112
China Farmer Sports Association P838
China Federation of Literary and Art Circles (CFLAC) P463
China Foundation for Poverty Alleviation P549
China Future Association P108
China Green Lights Project P572
China Information World P650
China Insurance (Holdings) Co.,Ltd. P111
China Insurance Regulatory Commission P112
China Intangible Cultural Heritage Protection Center P320
China International Rescue Teams P553
China International Science and Technology Cooperation Award P194
China Internet Network Information Center P650
China Internet Weekly P650
China Karting Championship P816
China Kendo Competitions P812
China Law Society P613
China Life Insurance (Group) Company P111
China Machinery Industry Federation P84
China Makes Effort to Ban Chemical Weapons P153
China Merchants Bank P102
China Military Online P666
China Minsheng Bank P101
China Modern Literature Museum P464 (P308)
China National Amateur Athletic Federation P702
China National Art Academy P259
China National Children's Art Troupe P283
China National Democratic Construction Association (CNDCA) P610
China National Huaju Opera Troupe P282
China National Institute for Educational Research P206
China National Junior Table Tennis Open P753
China National Museum of Fine Arts P305
China National Nuclear Corporation P83
China National Offshore Oil Corporation P81
China National Petroleum Corporation P81
China National Silk Museum P309
China National Space Administration (China's Space Institution) P145
China National Symphony Orchestra P271
China National Youth's Art Theater P282
China Nuclear Engineering and Construction Group Corporation P83
China Online Recruitment P678
China Online Video Development P683
China Pacific Insurance (Group) Co., Ltd. P112
China Patent Information Center P120
China Petrochemical Corporation P81
China Philharmonic Orchestra P271
China Ping An Insurance (Group) Co., Ltd. P111
China Prosecutor Society P633
China Provides Educational Aid to Developing Countries P220
China Rally Championship P816
China Sailboat and Sailboard Sport Association P732
China Scholarship Council P224
China Securities Regulatory Commission P109
China Soong Ching Ling Foundation P551
China Southern Air Holding Company (CZ) P95
China Sports Association for the Deaf Persons P822
China Sports Association for the Disabled P822
China Sports Association of the Elder P837
China Sports Association of the Mentally Retarded People P822
China Sports Foundation P837
China Sports Museum P843 (P306)
China Student Aerobics and Rhythmic Gymnastics Association P779
China Swimming Association P797
China Tea Museum P309
China Tibet Online P667
China Triathlon Sports Association P788
China UnionPay P100
China University of Mining and Technology P232
China University of Political Science and Law P233
China Welfare Fund for the Handicapped P614
China Women's Wresting Team P772
China Writers Association P463 (P612)
China Yahoo! P660 (P669)
China Young Men's Christian Association P702
China Youth Development Foundation P551
China Zhi Gong Dang P610
China.com.cn P664
China/UNESCO-The Great Wall Fellowship P224
China-Aerospace Science and Industry Corporation P86
Chinadaily.com.cn P665
China-EU Student Exchange Scholarships Program P228
ChinaHR.com P678
Chinahumanrights.org P654
Chinanews.com P666
ChinaRen Community P687
China's 10 Most Important Developments in Science and Technology in 2006 P192
China's Accession to International Conventions for the Protection of IPR P118
China's Action on Wetland Protection P590
China's Action Plan on IPR Protection in 2006 P120
China's Active Participation in UN Peacekeeping Operations P150
China's Armed Forces P137
China's Basic Position on Issues Related to Arms Control, Disarmament and Non-proliferation P150
China's Commitments to the WTO on Opening Its Securities Market P109
China's Defense Expenditure P142
China's Efforts in Banning Biological Weapons P153
China's First Fencing Champion P733
China's First Olympic Champion in Weightlifting P735
China's First Privately-Run Railway P93
China's First Weightlifting World Champion P735
China's First World Record in Shooting P764
China's Fulfilling International Obligations of Non-Proliferation P152
China's Intangible Cultural Heritages P320

China's International Balance of Payment Statistics P104
China's International Bandwidth P648
China's International Military Exchanges and Cooperation P147
China's International Scientific and Technological Cooperation Plan P92
China's Internet Industry P650
China's Large-scale Reduction of Military Personnel P136
China's Measures in Promoting International Arms Control and Disarmament P150
China's Museum of Stamps P306
China's Museum of the Three Gorges of the Yangtze River P313
China's National Defense Education P146
China's National Defense Policy P134
China's Online Banking Development P659
China's Online Music Development P682
China's Participation at Berlin Olympic Games P702
China's Participation at the 14th London Olympic Games P702
China's Participation in the Olympics from 1932 to 1948 P702
China's Performance in Auto Sports P817
China's Performance in Rhythmic Gymnastics in Asia P779
China's Performance in Rhythmic Gymnastics in the World P779
China's Performance in Table Tennis Competitions P752
China's Police System P647
China's Policy and Measures on Nuclear Disarmament Issue P151
China's Policy and Position on Banning Biological Weapons P153
China's Policy and Position on Banning Chemical Weapons P153
China's Position on Nuclear Disarmament Issue P151
China's Position on Prevention of Proliferation of Weapons of Mass Destruction (WMD) P153
China's Positive Participation in Other International Multilateral Arms Control Processes P151
China's Promotion on Conclusion of a Multilateral Treaty on Mutual No-First-Use of Nuclear Weapons P155
China's Rank System of Police P647
China's Support to Building Nuclear-Weapon-Free Zones P155
China's Support to Comprehensive Nuclear Test Ban Treaty P153
China's Tea Culture P510
Chinataiwan.org P667
Chinese P242
Chinese Academy of Agricultural Sciences P189
Chinese Academy of Forestry P189
Chinese Academy of Medical Sciences P189
Chinese Academy of Sciences P189
Chinese Academy of Social Sciences P199
Chinese Alligator Nature Reserve P598
Chinese Archery Association P770
Chinese Architecture P472
Chinese Artists' Association P256
Chinese Athletes P775
Chinese Athletes at the Universiade P725
Chinese Athletics Association P788
Chinese Aviation Museum P307
Chinese Badminton Association P800
Chinese Badminton Team P797
Chinese Baseball Association (CBA) P731
Chinese Basketball Association P743
Chinese Beach Volleyball Team P749
Chinese Boxing Association P761
Chinese Buddhist Academies P172
Chinese Canoeing Association P751
Chinese Catholic Organization P180
Chinese Center for Disease Control and Prevention P530
Chinese Characters P243
Chinese Characters and Chinese Seal Cutting P245
Chinese Characters and Names P245
Chinese Characters and Couplets P245
Chinese Chess P829
Chinese Chess Association P830
Chinese Cloisonné P285
Chinese Cuisine P503
Chinese Culture Research Fellowship Scheme P224
Chinese Cycling Association P803
Chinese Dramatists Association P272
Chinese Engineering Science and Technology Guanghua Award P195
Chinese Equestrian Association P745
Chinese Fans P804
Chinese Fencing Association P734
Chinese Field Hockey Association P760
Chinese Football Association P806
Chinese Football Association Premier League (Group A) P804
Chinese Go Association P828
Chinese Government Scholarships P223
Chinese Guqin Art P336
Chinese Gymnastics Association P778
Chinese Handball Association (CHA) P771
Chinese Herbal Medicine P535
Chinese Ice Hockey Association P807
Chinese Investigation on POPs P566
Chinese Judo Association P763
Chinese Knots P295
Chinese Language Proficiency Certificate P229
Chinese Laws Must Be Observed P184
Chinese Lawyers' Website P640
Chinese Marine Model Association P814
Chinese Men's Basketball Team P739
Chinese Modern Pentathlon Association P791
Chinese Motorboat Association P820
Chinese Mountaineering Association P817
Chinese Musicians Association P271
Chinese Novel Union P464
Chinese Nuclear Power Research and Design Institute P83
Chinese Olympic Committe P836
Chinese Peasants and Workers Democratic Party P610
Chinese People's Armed Police Force P138
Chinese People's Association for Friendship with Foreign Countries (CPAFFC) P161 (P611)
Chinese People's Institute of Foreign Affairs P161
Chinese People's Liberation Army P137
Chinese People's Political Consultative Conference (CPPCC) P65
Chinese Pinyin P242
Chinese PLA Military Academy of Sciences P146
Chinese Proficiency Test (HSK) P228
Chinese Proficiency Test (HSK) Overseas Exam Sites Distribution P229
Chinese Radio Sports Association P818
Chinese Regulations on POPs P566
Chinese Religion P164
Chinese Rowing Association P764
Chinese Shooting Association P769
Chinese Skating Association P810
Chinese Ski Association P811
Chinese Softball Association P743
Chinese Table Tennis Association P759
Chinese Table Tennis Club Super League P752
Chinese Taekwondo Association P773
Chinese Taipei Olympic Committee P837
Chinese Tennis Association P790
Chinese Towers and Pavilions P483
Chinese Trampoline and Acrobatic Gymnastics Association P780
Chinese University Basketball Association P743
Chinese Valentine's Day P439 (P520)
Chinese Volleyball Association P749
Chinese Weightlifting Association (CWA) P738
Chinese Women Badminton P797
Chinese Women's Basketball Team P738
Chinese Women's Field Hockey Team P760
Chinese Women's Volleyball Team P746
Chinese Wrestling P771
Chinese Wrestling Association P772
Chinese Wushu Walking Toward the World P834
Chinese Youth Day P556
Chinese-Funded Insurance Companies' Overseas Investment P111
Choice of Higher Learning Institutions and Specialty P224
Chongqing Municipality P617
Chongqing Museum P302

Chongshan Temple P169
Chongsheng Temple P172
Chrysanthemum Fair in Xiaolan P449
Chu Ci (Songs of Chu) P267
Chuan Cai (Sichuan Cuisine) P503
Chuanjiang Haozi P333
Chuida Music P341
Chunhui Program P221
Ci'en Temple P169
CITIC Industrial Bank P102
City Appearance and Environment P560
City Walls in Beijing P472
City Walls in Pingyao P472
City Walls in Xi'an P472
Cizhou Kiln Firing and Manufacturing Skills P413
Classical Anhui Cuisine P506
Classical Fujian Cuisine P505
Classical Guangdong Cuisine P504
Classical Huai-Yang Cuisine P504
Classical Hunan Cuisine P506
Classical Islamic Cuisine P506
Classical Jiangsu Cuisine P505
Classical Lists of Beijing Opera Items P276
Classical Shandong Cuisine P503
Classical Sichuan Cuisine P503
Classical Zhejiang Cuisine P505
Classification of Overseas Students P222
Classified Management of the Import of Electromechanical Products P126
Clay Figurine Master Zhang P293
Clay Sculptures P291 (P409)
Clay-shooting P764
Clean Energy Sources P78
Cleaner Production Promotion Law P578
Cliff Painting P253
Cloisonné Making Skills P423
Cmfu.com P686
Cnfol.com P675
Cnr.cn P666
Coal Industry P80
Coexistence of Diverse Economic Elements P72
Cognitive Methods of TCM on Human Life and Disease P435
Cold Dew P523
Collection among Common Chinese P555
College Physical Education Syllabus P708
Collegiate System P637
Color of the Forbidden City P474
Colored Painting (Gongbi) and Water-Ink Painting (Xieyi) P253
Colored Sculptures in the Jin Temple P292
Combating the Illicit Trade in Small Arms and Light Weapons (SALW) P157
Commission of Science, Technology and Industry for National Defense (COSTIND) P143
Commonly Used Chinese Characters P245
Commune by the Great Wall P494
Communist Party of China P608
Communist Youth League of China P611
Community Service P545
Community Sports P707
Community Volunteers P552
Community-based Health Network P531
Compass P186
Composition of Ethnic Groups P38
Comprehensive Control of the Rural Environment P560
Comprehensive Portal Website P668
Compressed Teas P514
Compulsory Education in Ethnic Autonomous Areas P61
Compulsory Measures System P632
Computer Newspaper P650
Computer World P650
Computers Research Progress P191
Concise History of China P16
Conducting Exchanges and Cooperation on Non-Proliferation P154
Confucianism (Confucian School) P19
Confucius (Kong Zi) P19
Confucius Grand Ceremony P446
Confucius Institute P229
Cong Xuedi P741
Congress of Workers and Staff P68
Conservation of Biodiversity P588
Constitution of the PRC P65
Construction of Sports Facilities P706
Constrution of Sports Teams P694
Construction Project of Fast Growing and High Yield Timber Forest Bases P11
Constructions in Concession in Tianjin P491
Consumption Boom on Home Decoration P500
Consumption by Card P502
Contemporary Chinese Architecture P493
Contemporary Development of Symphonic Music P270
Contemporary Drama P282
Contemporary Sports Constructions Written into the World Architecture History P839
Contention of a Hundred Schools of Thought P19
Control of Air Pollution P559
Control of Pollution in the Bohai Sea P559
Conversation for Wildlife Plants Resources P589
Converting Cultivated Land to Forest P580
Cool-Tea Compounding P435
Cooperation in Greater Mekong Sub-region for Environmental Protection P605
Cooperation in International Finance P108
Cooperation in Space with the United Nations P88
Cooperation with Overseas Partners in Information and Communication P91
Cooperation with the Other International Space Organizations P88
Coordination Mechanism of Labor Relations P541
Copyright Administrative Management System P115
Copyright Agency of China (CAC) P120
Copyright Law P120
Copyright Protection Center of China P120
Copyright Trade P115
Corban Festival P56
Core Family P528
Costume of the Hui Ethnic Group P455
Costume of the Yao Ethnic Group P455
Costume of Women in Hui'an P454
Costume of Women in Luzhi Water Town, Suzhou P454
Costumes of Miao Ethnic Group P454
Couplet Custom P454
Court of Second Instance Being That of Last Instance P637
Courtyard Residence in North China P479
Cracking Down on Copyright Infringement and Piracy P114
CRI Online P665
Croquet P826
Cross-Country Orienteering P819
Cross-Country Skiing P811
Cross-Straits Athletes—Competing in the Same Arena P712
Ctrip.com P657
Cuju P398
Cultivatable Land P12
Cultivation System of Table Tennis Players in China P751
Cultural Institutions in Ethnic Autonomous Areas P63
Cultural Palace of the Ethnic Groups P308
Cultural Treasures in the Palace P297
Curling P812
Current ITTF Members in the CTTA P759
Current State of the Chinese Volleyball P746
Current Strength of Chinese Swimming Team P791
Cursive Script P248
Custom of Child-bearing and the Pattern of Providing for the Aged P527
Custom of Drinking Wine P517
Customs Examination System P117
Customs Laws and Regulations P129
Customs Protection Mechanism P117
Cycling P801
Cyol.net P666

D

Dabei Temple P168
Dafeng David's Deer Nature Reserve P598
Dagu and Gushu P280
Dai and Naxi Ethnic Handicraft Paper-Making Skills P429
Dai Ethnic Group P45

Dai Ethnic Group Slow-wheel Pottery Manufacturing Skills P412
Dai Opera P380
Dalai Lama P166
Dalian University of Technology P236
Daming Temple of Yangzhou City P170
Dance Sport P825
Dangdang.com P655
Dangtu Folk Song P328
Danxian P279
Danzhou Tunes P331
Dao De Jing P456
Daoqing Opera P377
Dapingdiao P365
Daqi.com P687
Dark Tea P513
Dart P824
Data Center of the China Internet (DCCI) P651
Daur Ethnic Group P49
Daur Field Hockey P397
Daur Lurigele Dance P354
Daxian Opera P369
Daya Bay Nuclear Power Plant P82
Dayan Pagoda P484
Dazuigu (Comic Dialogue) P391
Ddmap.com P664
De'ang Ethnic Group P53
Debut at the Olympics P702
Debut of Table Tennis in China P751
Defense System P637
Dege Sutra-printing House Tibetan Carved Block Printing Skills P433
Dehua Porcelain Sculpture Firing and Manufacturing Skills P414
Democratic Parties P608
Deng Ruozeng P747
Deng Yaping P757
Dengcai (Lanterns) P410
Department of WTO Affairs, Ministry of Commerce P128
Derung Ethnic Group P54
Desertification P582
Developing Relations with Multinational Export Control Mechanisms P154
Development of a Wind Power Industry P569
Development of Canoe/Kayak Sports in China P750
Development of China Blog Website P685
Development of China's Digital Journals P684
Development of China's Friend-Making Websites P688
Development of China's Online Community P686
Development of China's Witkey P688
Development of Chinese Cartoons P258
Development of Chinese Oil Painting P258
Development of Education P203
Development of Educational Undertakings P60
Development of Ethnic Autonomous Areas P60
Development of Lacquer Ware P285
Development of Literature P456
Development of Modern Lian Huan Hua (Linked Serial Pictures) P258
Development of New-energy Projects in Rural Areas P561
Development of Non-Governmental Environmental Protection Organizations P564
Development of Rowing Sport in China P763
Development of Shooting P764
Development of Table Tennis in China P751
Development-Prohibited Zone P600
Development-Restricted Zone P600
Development-Restricted Zones P600
Diabolo Spinning P394
Diagnostic Methods in TCM P436 (P534)
Dianping.com P663
Dictionaries P244
Difference between Volunteer Military Service System and Mercenary Military Service System P138
Digital Journal Platforms P684
Ding Junhui P828
Ding Meiyuan P737
Ding Song P757
Dinghushan Mountain National Nature Reserve P591
Dingling Museum P307
DINK Family P529
Diplomatic Relations P160
Disabled Population P36
Disabled Receiving Higher Education P208
Discharge from Active Service and Resettlements P140
Discus Throw P783
Distance Education for Primary and Middle Schools in Rural Areas P216
Distinguished International Students Scholarship Scheme P224
Distribution of ENGO P565
Distribution of Ethnic Groups P38
Diving P794
Dog P525
Dong Ethnic Group P43
Dong Ethnic Group Timber Architecture Building Skills P419
Dong Grand Song P334
Dong Opera P380
Dong Shouyi P701
Dong Xiangyi P765
Dong Zhaozhi P733
Dongbei Dagu P384
Dongbula P264
Dongda Mosque of Kaifeng City P178
Dongguan Mosque of Xining City P177
Dongguantou Church P180
Donglaishun P508
Dongshan Talking and Singing P391
Dongtinghu Lake P7
Dongxiang Ethnic Group P47
Dongyang Wood Carving P408
Dongzhaigang Nature Reserve P598
Douban.com P662
Double Ninth Festival P439 (P520)
Dough Sculpture P293
Dougong (Bracket Set) P474
Dpnet.com.cn P679
Dragon P525
Dragon Boat P835
Dragon Boat Festival P438 (P520)
Dragon Boat Songs P390
Dragon Dance P348
Dramas of the Yuan Dynasty P460
Drills Named After Chinese Athletes P776
Drum P267
Drum Towers of Dong Ethnic Group P490
Du Fu P459
Du Li P768
Duan Festival of Shui Minority P443
Duan Ink-stone Making Skills P431
Dule Temple P168
Dunhuang Murals P173 (P254)
Duo Yun Xuan P259
Duration of Surfing Online P650
Duyichu P507

E

EachNet P655
Eagle Dance of the Tajik Ethnic Group P357
Earliest Football Organization P803
Earliest Modern Sports Publication P848
Earliest Sports Lottery P847
Earliest Sports Textbook P703
Early Development of the Chinese Volleyball P745
Early Drama P281
Early Experiences of Olympic Activities P700
Early Relationship between the IOC and China P701
Early Spread of Olympic Education P701
East Asian Games P728
East China Normal University P239
East Dongtinghu Lake Nature Reserve P597
Eastday.com P667
Eastern Church P179
Eastern Jin Dynasty (317-420) P24
Eastmoney.com P675
Easytour.com.cn P657
E-Bank Online (Beijing) Technology Co., Ltd. P658
Eco-functional Protection Area P590
Eco-Industrial Park Development P602
Ecological Conservation in Rural Areas P602

Ecological Construction and Environmental Protection in Ethnic Autonomous Areas P61
Economic and Technological Development Zones P128
Economic Construction Objective P71
Economic Data P495
Economic Development P59
Economic Growth Rate P69
Economic Restructuring P70
Economic Use of Water for the Olympic Venue P573
Economically Affordable Housing P500
Edible Plants P13
Education for Illiteracy P212
Education for Overseas Students in China P222
Education for Women P35
Education in Modern China P204
Education System P205
Educational Management System P204
Educational System (Basic Education) P206
Effect of Notarization P641
Eight Eccentric Painters of Yangzhou P255
Electronic Commerce Mode P654
Electronic Signature Law of the PRC P659
E-life P555
eLong, Inc. P657
E-Mail Services P671
Emblem of Intangible Cultural Heritage P319
Embroidery P287
Emei Restaurant P509
Emeishan Mountain P171
Emperor Qin Shihuang (259-210 BC) P21
Emperor Yan's Mausoleum Ceremony P447
Employment Circumstances P540
Employment License for Foreign Employees P543
Employment of the Rural Workforce P541
Employment System P541
Empty Nest Family P529
Energy Industry P84
Energy Minerals P10
Energy-Saving Enterprise: Baosteel Group P575
Energy-Saving Enterprise: China Huaneng Group P575
Enkon Project P552
Enlistment into Active Service in Peacetime P140
Enorth.com.cn P667
Enterprise E-mail P672
Entrance Examination and Assessment P226
Entrance Examination for Post-Graduate Students P209
Entrance Examination for Universities and Colleges P209
Environment and Investment P560
Environment Protecting Plants P15
Environment Websites P592
Environmental Certification System P562
Environmental Cooperation with Other Regions P605
Environmental Impact Assessment P578
Environmental Impact Assessment Law P579
Environmental Impact Assessment of the Qinghai-Tibet Railway P578
Environmental Label P563
Environmental Laws and Regulations P578
Environmental Protection in China P558
Environmental Protection Industries P562
Environmental Protection Popularization P565
Environmentally-Friendly Society P558
Epic of Janggar P326
Epic of Manas P326
Equality and Unity Among Ethnic Groups P58
Equality of Husband and Wife P527
Equestrianism P744
Equipment of Chinese Internet Users for Connection to the Internet P649
Erhu P262
Er'rentai P377
Er'renzhuan P279 (391)
Establishing a Vocational Training System P544
Establishing Representative Office in China P133
Establishment of Ecological Villages P603
Ethnic Autonomous Areas Encouraged to Open Wider to the Outside World P62
Ethnic Autonomous Regions and Autonomous Organs P67
Ethnic Groups Cultural Palace P493
Ethnic Minority Education P215
Ethnic Publication P62
Ethnic Regional Autonomy P58
European Galileo Project P198
Events for the Disabled P711
Events in Olympic Winter Games P807
Evidence System P632
Evolution of Calligraphy P246
Evolution of Chinese Characters P243
Evolution of Tennis Skills P788
Ewenki Ethnic Group P52
Examination for Obtaining Certificate P210
Exchange Rate System P104
Exchanges and Cooperation with Foreign Countries in Science, Technology and Industry for National Defense P143
Exchanges between the Overseas Students P220
Execution of Penalties P638
Exhibition of Cultural Treasures of the Palace P296
Expenses for Self-Supporting Overseas Students P226
Export Credit Insurance P111
Export Policies for Environmental Protection Purpose P580
Export Processing Zone P128
Export-Import Bank of China P102
Extended Producer Responsibility System P568
Exterior and Interior Rivers P4
Extreme Sports P824

F

F1 Powerboat World Championship China Grand Prix P819
Fairy Festival of Nu Ethnic Group P444
Famen Temple P173
Famous Chinese Tea P510
Fan Making Skills P432
Fan Zhiyi P805
Fangshan Restaurant P507
Fanjingshan Mountain National Nature Reserve P595
Far East and South Pacific Games for the Disabled (FESPIC Games) P729
Far Eastern Championship Games P700
Farmers' Swimming Competition P709
Fast-Breaking Festival P56
Fayuan Temple P168
Feature of Chinese Buddhism P164
Fencing P733
Federation of University Sports of China P837
Fenbei.com P682
Feng Kun P748
Feng Meimei P765
Fenglin National Nature Reserve P596
Fengniao.com P679
Fengxiang New Year Woodblock Prints P401
Fengxiang Painted Clay Figurines P292
Fengyang Huagu (Flower Drum) P391
Fengzeyuan P508
Festival of Discharging Water at Dujiang Weirs P446
Fetion P671
Field Hockey P760
Fifth Generation of Chinese Directors P468
Fifty Years in China's Space Industry P144
Fifty-Six Ethnic Groups P38
Figure Painting P252
Figure Skating P810
Film Distribution Industry P470
Film Production Industry P470
Film Projection Industry P470
Fin Swimming P820
Finance.sina.com P675
Financial Budget for Environmental Protection P561
Financial Reform P99
Financial Sector's Opening Up P106
Financial Support for Ethnic Autonomous Areas P61
Financial Support for the Foreign-invested Enterprises P131
Financial System P99

Fire God Sacrifice of Oroqen Minority P441
Firewood Gathering Dance of Li Ethnic Group P355
First Archery World Champion in China P769
First Ascent of Mt. Qomolangma via the North Ridge P817
First Asian Cycling Champion P802
First Ascent Up Vinson Massif P817
First Badminton Olympics Gold Medal P798
First Baseball Team P703
First Best World Performance P808
First Big Chessboard P829
First Bodybuilding Contest P703
First Boxing Champion P703
First Bridge Masters P827
First Bunch of Footballs to Join Foreign Teams P805
First Canoe/Kayak World Champion P750
First Championship in Gymnastics Team Competition in World Championships P775
First China International Wushu Festival P834
First Chinese Basketball Player in NBA P740
First Chinese Champion in Race Walk P703
First Chinese IOC Member P701
First Chinese Judo World Champion P762
First Chinese Mountains Open to Foreign Climbers P818
First Chinese Olympic Champion in Sailboard P733
First Chinese Overseas Student of Sports P703
First Chinese Team Gold Medal at the World Aeromodeling Championships P814
First Chinese Woman Athletics World Champion P782
First Chinese Woman to Win the Olympic Badge P712
First Chinese Woman to Set World Swimming Record P791
First Chinese Woman to Throw Farther Than 21m P783
First Chinese World Champion in Model Aeronautics P814
First Chinese World Champion of Sailboard P732
First Clean Sweep of Championships P753
First Diving World Champion P794
First Female 9-dan Go (weiqi) in the World P828
First English Sports Magazine P848
First English Version of Chinese Chess Manual P830
First Foreign Basketball Player in CBA League P848
First Female Handball Referees with International Class A Certificate P770
First Female Marathon Champion P782
First FIFA Women's of the Year P805
First Film P465
First Film Studio P465
First Foreign Basketball Player in CBA League P739
First Generation of Chinese Directors P467
First Generation of National Gos P828
First Gold Medal in Rowing P763
First Group of Cinemas P465
First Gymnastics World Champion P776
first Gymnastics World Cup for Chinese Athletes P775
First ISU Referee P810
First Large Comprehensive Stadium P839
First Marcel Corbillon Cup P753
First Miniature Sheet Pingpong Stamp P845
First National Cycling Tournament P802
First National Equestrian and Polo Game P745
First National Football Tournament P803
First National Games P703
First National Sports Publishing House P848
First National Sports Stamps Exhibition P846
First National Women's Invitational Tournament P804
First Olympic Bid P701
First Olympic Championship in Men's Gymnastics Team Competition P775
First Olympic Gold P721
First Olympic Gold of Hong Kong SAR P697
First Olympic Handball Medal P771
First Olympic Medal P712
First Olympics Diving Champion P794
First Olympics Gold Medal P791
First Olympics Swimming Medal P791
First Olympics Tennis Gold Medal P789
First Parachuting WR P815
First Participation in Speed Skating World Championships-Ladies P807
First Rowing Game in Asian Games P763
First Set of Chinese Ancient Sports Stamps P845
First Set of Sports Stamps P845
First Set of Chinese Ancient Sports Stamps P846
The First Silver Commemorative Coin P846
First Skeet World Champion Team P764
First Speed Skating World Champion P807
First Sports Dictionary P848
First Sports Encyclopedia P847
First Swaythling Cup P753
First Table Tennis Champion at the Olympic Games P753
First Table Tennis Grand Slam Winner in the World P753
First Table Tennis Referee P753
First Team Title at World Cup P794
First Tennis Players Participating in Olympic Games P789
First Time to Be Qualified for FIFA World Cup in 2001 P803
First Time to Become an Asian Diving Giant P794
First Time to Break Asian Cycling Record P802
First Time to Hold International Tennis Tournament P789
First Time to Participate in All England Open Badminton Championships P798
First Time to Participate in IFNA Diving World Cup P794
First Time to Participate in the Volleyball World Championship P747
First Time to Sweep All Titles of World Badminton Championships P798
First Time to Win Asian Women's Tennis Group Champion P789
First Title of Asian Chess Team Championship P830
First to Be Punished Due to Doping P808
First Woman Doctor of Sport Studies P703
First Woman to Reach the Summit of Mt. Qomolangma from the North Ridge P818
First Women Bodybuilding Champions P825
First Women's All Round Parachuting World Champion P815
First World Champion P712
First World Champion in Figure Skating P810
First World Champion of Short Track Speed Skating P808
First World Group Champion in Women's Race Walk P783
First World Gymnastics Championship for Chinese Gymnasts P775
First World Record P712
First World Record Setter of Men's Breaststroke P791
First World Tennis Champion P789
First WTTC Held in China P753
First Wushu School Recruiting Overseas Students P834
First Wushu Team of China Performing in the Olympics P833
First Zdenek Haydusek Prize P753
Fitness P555
Five Dynasties and Ten States (907-960) P26
Five Principles of Peaceful Coexistence P158
Five-tone Opera P375
Five-year Legislation Plan P646
Five-Year Plans P69
Fkee.com P661
Flood Storage Zone P601
Floor Exercise P774
Flower Lane Church in Fuzhou City P181
Flower-and-Bird Painting P253
Flower-lantern Opera P378
Flowery Drum Lantern Dance P349
Flute P261
Folk Chinese New Year Painting P294
Folk Customs of Ethnic Groups P59
Folk Musical Instruments P260
Folk Musical Instruments of Hui Ethnic Group P344

Folk Song of the Lisu Ethnic Group P331
Folk Song of the She Ethnic Group P329
Folk Song of the Yugur Ethnic Group P332
Folk Song Region with Hunting Culture P269
Folk Song Region with Primitive Culture P268
Folk Songs P268
Folk Sports P832
Folklore of Gengcun Village P323
Folklore of Wujiagou Village P324
Folklore of Xiabaoping Township P324
Football 803
Foping Demonstration Area in Shaanxi P581
Forbidden City (Gu Gong) P473
Forbidding or Restricting Import of Commodities P126
Foreign Exchange Management System P104
Foreign Policy P158
Foreign Taxation in China P74
Foreign Trade Law P129
Foreign-Funded Banks P107
Foreign-Related Arbitration P643
Foreign-Related Civil and Commercial Laws P129
Foreign-Related Compensation P645
Foreign-related Economic Laws and Regulations P129
Forest Courts P636
Forest Health P581
Forest Resources P11
Forestation P580
Forms of Private Enterprise Organization P73
Foshan New Year Woodblock Prints P400 (P295)
Four Books and the Five Classics P456
Four Famous Chinese Classics P462
Four Great Inventions of Ancient China P186
Four Great Painters of the Yuan Dynasty and Chinese Landscape Painting P255
Four Phases of Renminbi Exchange Rate Reform P105
Four Treasures of the Study P256
Fourth Generation of Chinese Directors P468
Fragrant Hill Hotel P493
Free Email Addresses P672
Freedom of Religious Belief P182
Freedom of Religious Belief of Ethnic Minorities P59
Free-Style Residence in South China P480
Freestyle Skiing P811
Freestyle Swimming P792
Freestyle Wrestling P771
Friends of Nature (FON) P564
From "Shanghai Five" to Shanghai Cooperation Organization P147
Frost's Descent P523
Fu Mingxia P795
Fu Qifang P754
Fudan University P236
Fujian Museum P300
Fujian Province P624
Full Market Economy Status P126
Functions and Powers of the People's Procuratorates P633
Functions and Powers of the State Council P66
Fundamental Principles of Arbitration P642
Furen Daquan Liangfang (Complete Dictionary of Effective Prescriptions for Women) P538
Furniture P288
Fuxin Agate Carving P405
Fuzhou Bodiless Lacquerware Lacquering Skills P426
Fuzhou Chi Yi P386
Fuzhou Pinghua P383

Games of the New Emerging Forces P705
Gansu Museum P303
Gansu Province P629
Gao E P766
Gao Ling P800
Gao Min P795
Gaohu P262
Gaojia Opera P371
Gaoligongshan Mountain National Nature Reserve P591
Gaomi Clay Figurines P292
Gaomi New Year Rubbing-Ash Prints P399
Gaoqiang P359
Gaoshan Ethnic Group P46
Garment Consumption P498
Ge Garden P477
Ge Hong P175
Ge Xin'ai P755
Gelo Mao Dragon Festival P445
Gelo Ethnic Group P51
Gender Structure of Chinese Internet Users P649
General Administration of Civil Aviation P98
General Administration of Customs P128
General Administration of Press and Publication P121
General Administration of Sport of China P836
General Armaments Department P136
General Headquarters of the Chinese People's Liberation Army P135
General Higher Education P209
General Level of Tariff P125
General Living Standard P495
General Logistics Department P136
General Political Department P136
General Situation of Agriculture P75
General Situation of Foreign Trade P122
General Staff Headquarters P135
General Survey P99
General Survey of China's Intangible Cultural Heritage P317
General Survey of Economic and Technological Development Zones P128
General Survey of Movie P465
Geographic Location P3
Geological Museum of China P305
Geospace Double Star Exploration Program P198
Geothermal Resources P591
Germplasm Resources P15
Gewei of the Zhuang Ethnic Group P450
Gezai Opera P375
Giant Stone Buddha at Leshan P291
Gliding P820
Global Change Program P198
Global Village of Beijing (GVB) P565
Gmw.cn P666
Go (Weiqi) P828
Goal and Guiding Principle of Protecting of Intangible Cultural Heritages P318
godpp.gov.cn P654
Golden Ball Award and Golden Boot Award of China P805
Golden Horse Film Festival P467
Golden Rooster Awards P466
Golf P813
Golf Tournaments P813
Gong P267
Gong Ruina P800
Gong Xiaobin P741
Gong-and-drum Mixed Opera P381
Gongdelin P509
Gongfu Tea P515
Gongwangfu Garden P477
Google P660
Goubuli Restaurant P510
Goufang.com P677
Gourd Panpipe Dance of Yi Ethnic Group P356
Governmental Portal Website P652
Grade A Green Food P497
Grade AA Green Food (equated with "organic food") P498
Grade System of Social Sports Instructors P709
Graduate Education and Academic Degrees System P210
Grain Fills P523
Grain in Ear P523
Grain Rain P523
Grand Canal P6
Grapheme of Chinese Characters P244
Grassland Folk Song Region P269
Grassland Resources P10
Great Ci'en Temple P172
Great Cold P523
Great Hall of the People P493

Great Heat P523
Great Snow P523
Great Wall P473
Great Xingshan Temple P172
Greater Publicity for Laws and Regulations on Export Control and Education for Enterprises P156
Greater Seal Script P247
Greece-Roman Wresting P771
Green Chinese Personage of Year 2007 (List) P607
Green Food P497
Green Food Standard P497
Green Olympics P560
Green Tea P510
Gross Amount of Consumption P496
Group Callisthenics P822
GTalk P671
Gu Kaizhi and Scroll Painting P253
Guan Hanqing P461
Guanfu Classic Art Museum P316
Guangchang Meng Opera P361
Guangdong Hanyue Music P341
Guangdong Museum P301
Guangdong Music P340
Guangdong Olympic Center Stadium P842
Guangdong Province P621
Guangji Bridge P482
Guangji Temple P168
Guangjiao Temple (Mahatma Temple) P170
Guangxi Ethnic Relics Center P312
Guangxi Zhuang Autonomous Region P622
Guangxiao Temple P171
Guangzhou Baiyun International Airport P97
Guanzhong Eighteen Mausoleums P486
Guanzi P261
Guarantee of Rights and Interests of the Old P554
Guaranteeing the Rights of Foreign Rights Holders P118
Gui Opera P368
Guidelines for the Recycling Industry P570
Guidelines on Philanthropy Development in China (2006-2010) P551
Guizhou Moutai Wine P517
Guizhou Museum P302
Guizhou Province P627
Guniujiang Nature Reserve P598
Gunpowder P186
Guo Jingjing P796
Guoqing Temple P171
Guozhuang Dance P352
Guqin P264
Guxiu Embroidery P402
Guyuyan Folk Stories P324
Guzang Festival of Miao Minority P443
Gymnastics P773
Gymnastics World Cup P730

H

Ha Festival of Jing Minority P439
Hahaqiang P377
Haidian Christian Church in Beijing P181
Haier Group P73
Haihe River P6
Hainan Province P621
Haizhou Wuda Gongdiao Music P338
Hakka Group Houses P481
Hakka Tulou (Stockade) Building Skills P418
Hammer Throw P783
Handball P770
Han Dynasty (206BC-220 AD) P22
Han Ethnic Group P39
Han Folk Song Region P269
Han Jian P799
Han Opera P366
Han Xiaopeng P811
Hanchuan Shanshu Story-Telling P390
Handiao Erhuang P366
Handiao Guangguang P362
Handling Aberrant Behavior According to the Law P185
Hangzhou Xiaoshan International Airport P98
Hani Ethnic Group P44
Hani Multi-Voice-Part Folk Song P335
Hanshan Temple P170
Harbin Institute of Technology P237
hc360.com P656
He Jianhua P815
He Ying P770
He Zhenliang P704
He Zhili P756
He Zhuoqiang P736
Headwaters Zone P600
Health Level of the Children P35
Health System P530
Hebei Bangzi P364
Hebei Museum P298
Hebei Province P620
Heilongjiang Museum P299
Heilongjiang Province P619
Heilongjiang River P5
Hejian Song Poem P325
Helping Disabled People to Find Employment P543
Heluo Dagu P385
Hematopoietic Stem Cell Donation P532
Henan Museum P301
Henan Opera P364
Henan Province P626
Henan Zhuizi P387
Hengshui Neihua Paintings P402
Heptathlon and Decathlon P784
Hepu Dugong Nature Reserve P588
Hequ Folk Song P328
Heroic Epic of King Gesar P326
Hexi Baojuan P323
Hexun.com P675
Hezhen Ethnic Group P55
Hezhen Ethnic Group Fish-skin Making Skills P434
High Energy Physics Research Program P198
High Jump P783
High Mountain Wetland: Maoershan Mountain P590
High Technology Industry P91
Higher Education for Adults P213
Higher Education System P210
Higher People's Court P635
Highways P93
History and Status Quo of China's Exchange Rate System P104
History of Chinese Herbal Medicine P534
History of the Chinese Beach Volleyball P749
Hoh Xil Nature Reserve P599
Holding of International Track and Field Competitions P780
Home Surfing Equipment in China P649
Homhow.com P677
Homosexuality P529
Hong Kong Film Awards P466
Hong Kong Film Critics Society Awards P467
Hong Kong Film Golden Bauhinia Awards P467
Hong Kong International Film Festival P466
Hong Kong Museum P304
Hong Kong Olympic Committee P836
Hong Kong Olympic Equestrian Venues P843
Hong Kong Space Museum P314
Hong Kong Special Administrative Region P617
Hong Kong Sports Association for the Mentally Handicapped P837
Hong Kong Wetland Park P590
Hongbinlou P508
Hongqiao International Airport P97
Hongzehu Lake P7
Honored Film: Farewell My Concubine P471
Honored Film: Hibiscus Town P471
Honored Film: Spring Festival P471
Honoring Commitment to International Arms Control and Non-Proliferation P150
Hoomii of the Mongolian People P328
Hope Group P73
Horizontal Bar P774
Horse P524
Horse Stepping on a Swallow P284
Horse-head Stringed Instrument Music of Mongolia P337
Hospital Classification Management P531
Hosting International Sailboard Events P732
Hot Air Balloon P826
Housangyu Village Church P180
Household Consumption on Major Food P497

Household Registration System P33
Housing Accumulation Fund System P499
Housing Consumption P499
Housing Distribution System Reform P500
Housing of Rural Residents P500
Housing Security System P499
HSK Winner Scholarship Scheme P224
Hu Hongfei P784
Hu Jia P796
Hu Ronghua P829
Hu Shenggao P814
Hu Weidong P741
Hua Luogen Mathematics Award P195
Huabiao (Ornamental Column) P474
Huachao Opera P377
Hua'er P332
Huai Su P251
Huaibang P365
Huaihe River P6
Huai-Yang Cuisine P503
Huang Di Nei Jing (Yellow Emperor's Canons of Internal Medicine) P537
Huang Jian P784
Huang Kun P200
Huang Shanshan P780
Huang Sui P800
Huang Xiaoxiao P787
Huang Xu P778
Huang Yubin P776
Huang Zhihong P785
Huanghe Tower P483
Huanglong National Nature Reserve P591
Huangmei Opera P374
Huangshan Maofeng P511
Huaping Nature Reserve P599
Huashan Mountain P175
Huashi Mosque of Beijing P177
Huayan Temple P169
Huazhong University of Science and Technology P238
Hubei Museum P301
Hubei Opera P373
Hubei Province P625
Hui (Ethnic Group) Heavy Sword Wushu P396
Hui Cai (Anhui Cuisine) P505
Hui Ethnic Group P39
Hui Medicine P537
Hui'an Stone Carving P406
Huihui Yaofang (Hui Medical Preparation) P538
Huishan Clay Figurines P292
Huizhou Ink Making Skills P431
Huji Story-Telling Gathering P453
Hulusi P262
Human Brain Project P198
Human Genome Project P198
Hunan Museum P301
Hunan Province P625
Hundred Flowers Awards P466
Hundred Schools of Thought P456
Huqin P262
Huqing Yutang Museum of Traditional Chinese Medicine P310
Hurdles P782
Huzhou Writing Brush Making Skills P430

I

Ice Break of Swimming in Olympics P721
Ice Dancing P810
Ice Hockey P807
ifeng.com P668
IMG Promotes the Reform of Chinese Football P804
Imperial Civil Examination System P203
Imperial Gardens of the Ming and Qing Dynasties P478
Imperial Painting Academy of the Song Dynasty P254
Imperial Summer Villa of Chengde P479
Implementation of 9-Year Compulsory Education P205
Implementation of Stockholm Convention P566
Implementation of the Commitments Made for the Entry into the WTO P124
Implementing Subjects and Fund Sources in Legal Aid P646
Import and Export of the Agriculture P75
Important Achievements Plan P76
Important Literature Awards in China P464
Important Progress in Aviation Industry for Civil Use P144
Improved Transport Conditions in Ethnic Minorities Areas P61
Increased Grain Output P77
Independent Colleges P215
Independently Developing Ethnic Culture P60
Individual E-Mail P671
Individual Medley P792
Industrial and Commercial Bank of China P101
Industrial Bank P103
Industrial Injury Insurance P546
Industrial Policies P72
Industrial Policies P133
Influence of Olympics on China's Physical Culture P696
Influence on Traditional Chinese Architecture from Yi Jing (Changes of Zhou) P472
Information Consumption P501
Information Industry P90
Information Products Export P91
Ink P256
Ink Stone P257
Inland Aquatic Resources P13
Inner Mongolia Autonomous Region P620
Inner Mongolia Museum P298
Inner Mongolia Pasturing Area P10
Inscriptions on Tortoise Shells and Animal Bones P247
Instant Hotel Reservations P656
Instant Messaging P670
Insurance Industry P110
Insurance Scheme P706
Insurance Sector's Opening Up P111
Intangible Cultural Heritage P317
Intangible Cultural Heritage in China P319
Intangible Cultural Heritage List P318
Integrated Friend-making Websites P689
Intellectual Property Right Protection P113
Intellectual Property Rights Protection for Audio and Video Products P115
Intermediate People's Court P635
International Association of Anti-Corruption Authorities P634
International Children's Day P556
International Class A Certificate P770
International Communication P780
International Contracted Projects P124
International Cooperation P320
International Cooperation for Sandstorm Prevention P604
International Cooperation on Nuclear Safety P606
International Cooperation on Piracy P116
International Economic and Trade Treaties and Customs P126
International Environmental Cooperation P603
International Events P816
International Exchange on IPR P118
International Exchanges and Cooperation P220
International Exchanges and Cooperation in Non-traditional Security Fields P148
International Friendship Museum P306
International Labor Day P556
International Military Academic Exchanges P147
International Religious Exchanges P184
International Sports Events for the Disabled P710
International Sports Exchange P697
International Working Women's Day P556
Internet Access Expenses in China P649
Internet Development P91
Internet Education in China P672
Internet Education Industry P673
Internet Education Users P673
Internet Literature P463
Internet Penetration Rate in China P649
Internet Society of China P651
Internet Website of Today Writers P463
Introduction of Modern Weightlifting into China P702
Introduction to Auto Websites P676
Introduction to Chinese Drama P272
Introduction to E-Commerce of China P654
Introduction to E-Government of China P652

Introduction to Electronic Payment P657
Introduction to Financial and Economic Websites P675
Introduction to Search Engine P660
Introduction to Sports Development in China P694
Invention of Gunpowder P27
Investigation System P631
Investment in China (2006) P130
Ipart.cn P689
Iron Pagoda in Kaifeng P485
ISF World Gymnasiade P730
Islam in China P177
Islamic Association of China P178
Islamic Cuisine P506
Islands P3
Isoshu.com P662
IT168 P677
Ivory Carving P404

J

Jade Buddha Temple P170
Jade Production P285
Jade Ware P284
Jail System P638
Javelin Throw P784
Ji Zheng P785
Jia Chengxiang P815
Jia Zhanbo P767
Jianchuan Museum P316
Jiang Chengji P793
Jiang Xingquan P740
Jiang Yonghua P802
Jiangnan Sizhu P338
Jiangsu Province P624
Jiangxi Museum P300
Jiangxi Province P624
Jiangzhou Drum Music P343
Jianzhen P167
Jiaodong Dagu P385
Jiayuan.com P689
Jichang Garden P476
Jieshou Painted Pottery Firing and Manufacturing Skills P411
Jile Temple P169
Jilin Museum P299
Jilin Province P619
Jilin University P237
Jin Opera P363
Jin Ping Mei (The Golden Lotus) P461
Jin Yilian P200
Jing Ethnic Group P55
Jing Music at Beijing Zhihuasi Temple P345
Jing Wu Athletic Association P699
Jing'an Temple P169
Jingci Temple of Hangzhou City P170
Jingdezhen Ceramics Museum P311
Jingdezhen Porcelain P288
Jingdezhen Porcelain Handicraft Skills P413
Jingdezhen Traditional Porcelain Kiln and Workshop Building Skills P419
Jingdong Dagu P385
Jinge Songs P389
Jinghe Opera P367
Jingpo Ethnic Group P47
Jingxi Taiping Drum Dance P348
Jingxing Lahua P348
Jingzhou Miao Geteng P333
Jingzhuo Flower-drum Opera P373
Jinling Carved Sutras Printing Skills P432
Jinling Xiehe Divinity School P181
Jino Bass Drum Dance P356
Jino Ethnic Group P54
Jinxing Ink-stone Making Skills P431
Jiuhua Mountain P171
Jiusan Society P610
Jiuzhaigou National Nature Reserve P596
Jizhong Sheng and Pipe Music P343
JOB36 P679
Joint Development P132
Jokhang Monastery P168 (P489)
Joyo P655
Jrj.com P675
Judges System P637
Judicatory (Criminal) Compensation P645
Judicial and Administrative Guarantees and Supervision P183
Judicial Committee P637
Judicial Protection of Intellectual Property Rights P117
Judicial System P631
Judo P762
Junshan Silver Needles P514
Juridical System P634
Juyuanhao Bow and Arrow Making Skills P423

K

Kaiyuan Temple P171
Kaquewa Festival of Drung Minority P444
Karate P812
Ka-Si-Da-Wen Dance P355
Kaspersky P674
Kazak Ethnic Group P44
Ke Dao Narrative Poetry P321
Ke'erqin Nature Reserve P598
Kendo P812
Key Dates in the Internet Development of China P648
Key Projects for Energy Conservation P572
Key Sectors for Energy Conservation P571
Kharchin and Eastern Inner Mongolia Folklore P324
Kijiji.cn P663
King Pan Festival of Yao Minority P441
Kirgiz Ethnic Group P48
Kite Making Skills P435
Knife Money of the Qi State P18
Kong Linghui P758
Kong Xiangxi P701
Konghou P266
Kooxoo.com P663
Korean Ethnic Group P42
Korean Nongle Dance P353
Korean See-Saw and Swinging P397
Koubei.com P663
Ku6.com P683
Kuaiban and Kuaishu P281
Kunming Sports Training Base P841
Kunqu Opera P358
Kwan-yin Temple of Jilin City P169

L

La Yue (the 12th Lunar Month) and Laba Porridge P519
Labor Law of the People's Republic of China P546
Lacquer Ware P285
Lahu Ethnic Group P46
Lai Yawen P748
Laiziluogu at Liangping P341
Lama P166
Lancangjiang River P6
Land Boundary P3
Land Protection P582
Landscape Painting P253
Lang Ping P748
Language Policy P242
Language Used in Teaching P225
Lantern Festival P520
Lantern Opera P378
Lantian Puhua Water Fair Music P344
Lanxi Tanhuang P387
Lanzhou Guzi (Drum Song) P388
Lanzhou Taiping Drum Dance P351
Lanzhou University P239
Lanzhou Yellow River Waterwheel Manufacturing Techniques P424
Lao Lishi P796
Lao She Literature Award P464
Lao Zi P175 (P20)
Laoting Dagu P384
Larenbu and Jimensuo P327
Latest Rankings of Table Tennis Championships P752

Launching Vehicles P85
Law Firms P639
Law of the PRC on Conserving Energy P573
Law of the PRC on Marriage P528
Law of the PRC on Prevention and Treatment of Infectious Diseases P531
Law of the PRC on the Prevention and Control of Environmental Pollution by Solid Waste P579
Law of the PRC on the Prevention and Control of Radioactive Pollution P577
Law of the PRC on the Prevention and Treatment of Occupational Diseases P531
Law of the Republic of China on Physical Culture and Sport Issued in 1929 P700
Law Practice Application P639
Laws and Regulations for Prevention and Control of Hazardous Wastes P579
Laws and Regulations Governing Health Quarantine P129
Laws and Regulations Governing Inspection of Imported and Exported Commodities P129
Laws and Regulations Governing Quarantine of Animals and Plants P129
Laws and Regulations on Copyright Protection P114
Laws and Regulations on Foreign Exchange Control P129
Laws and Regulations on Nuclear Safety and Radiation Environment P576
Laws and Regulations on Privately-Run Education P214
Laws and Regulations on Supervision and Management on Foreign-Funded Bank P107
Laws and Regulations on the Protection of Intellectual Property Rights P119
Laws and Regulations on Trademark Protection P113
Laws and Regulations Relating to Online Banking P659
Laws Concerning Foreign Investment P132
Laws on Anti-Doping P697
Lawyer Qualification P639
Lawyer System P639
Layout Designs of Integrated Circuits P120
Leading Bodies of Armed Services P136
Legal Aid System P645
Legal Documents on Anti-Doping P697
Legal Duties of Lawyers P641
Legal Holidays P556
Legal Protection P208
Legal System P64
Legaldaily.com.cn P666
Legalist School P21
Legend of Ashima P327
Legend of Meng Jiangnv P322
Legend of the White Snake P321
Legislation on Intangible Cultural Heritage Protection P319
Legislation Related to Sports P706
Lenovo Group P91
Leqing Box Wood Carving P408
Lesser Seal Script P247
Level of Leisure Activity P554
Lhasa Jiami Waterwheel Grain Milling Techniques P424
Lhoba Ethnic Group P54
Li Bai P459
Li Chengjiang P810
Li Duihong P767
Li Ethnic Group P45
Li Ethnic Group Primitive Pottery Shaping Skills P411
Li Ethnic Group Tapa Making Skills P434
Li Ethnic Group Traditional Cotton Weaving Dyeing and Embroidery Skills P416
Li Ethnic Group Wood-Drilling Skills for Fire P434
Li Fenglou P805
Li Furong P755
Li Huitang P805
Li Jiajun P809
Li Jie P768
Li Jun P758
Li Lingjuan P769
Li Lingwei P799
Li Meifang P803
Li Meisu P785
Li Minkuan P744
Li Na P790
Li Nianmin P744
Li Ning P777
Li Rongrong P815
Li Sao (The Poem on Departure) P457
Li Shulan P769
Li Tie P806
Li Ting P789
Li Ting P796
Li Xiaopeng P778
Li Xiaoshuang P777
Li Xin P741
Li Yaguang P740
Li Yansong P822
Li Yongbo P799
Li Yuejiu P776
Li Yuwei P766
Li Zewen P786
Li Zhensheng P201
Liabilities in Legal Aid P646
Liang Geliang P755
Liang Rihao P835
Liang Sanmei P764
Liangping New Year Woodblock Prints P401
Liaocheng Acrobatics P394
Liaohe River P6
Liaoning Museum P298
Liaoning Province P620
Liaoning Wind and Percussion Ensemble P338
Liaozhai Liqu P333
liba.com P655
Licensed Olympic Postcards P846
Lijiang Demonstration Area in Yunnan P581
Limit of Heat P523
Lin Dan P801
Lin Haiyan P821
Lin Li P792
Lin Weining P737
Ling'ao Nuclear Power Plant P82
Lingguang Temple P168
Lingqiu Luoluoqiang P369
Lingyanshan Temple P170
Lingyin Temple of Hangzhou City P170
Linji Temple P168
Linxia Brick Carving P407
Lion Dance P348 (P835)
Lishui Boatmen Haozi P336
List of Arms Control, Disarmament and Non-Proliferation Treaties That China Has Joined P152
List of Gold Medals of the Chinese Delegation in Beijing 2008 Olympic Games P722
Lisu Ethnic Group P45
Lisu Song-Dance Achi-Mugua P356
Liu Changchun P702
Liu Chunhong P738
Liu Dong P787
Liu Dongsheng P201
Liu Gongquan P251
Liu Guoliang P758
Liu Shilan P831
Liu Xiang P787
Liu'an Guapian P512
Liuqin P263
Liuqin Opera P374
Liurong Temple P171
Liuyang Fireworks Production Skills P434
Liuzi Opera P369
Living Buddha P166
Liyuan Opera P358
Local Operas P273
Local People's Congresses and Local People's Governments P67
Local Search P663
Locomotive Sports Association of China P709
Logo of All-China Women's Federation P611
Logo of China Disabled Persons' Federation P614
Logo of the National Forest Park P592
Logo of the Nature Reserve of China P592
Long Jump P784
Longchang Temple of Jurong County P170
Longmen Grottoes P291
Longquan Celadon Firing and Manufacturing Skills P413
Longquan Precious Sword Forging Skills P42
Longzhuang Church P180
Lou Dapeng P784

Index

Lou Yun P777
Love21cn.msn.com P689
Low-Rental Housing System P500
Lu Cai (Shandong Cuisine) P503
Lu Opera P373
Lu Qin P830
Lu Shengrong P705
Lu Weifeng P814
Lu Xun Literature Award P464
Lu Yu P511
Lu Yuansheng P756
Lu'an Dagu P384
Luantan P368
Lugou Bridge P483
Luminous Cup Carving P405
Lunar Calendar P521
Lunyu (The Analects of Confucius) P457
Luo Wei P773
Luo Xuejuan P793
Luo Zhihuan P808
Luochuan Biegu Drum Dance P351
Luogushu P388
Luohan Temple (Arhat Temple) P172
Luoyang Bridge P482
Lushan Mountain Nature Reserve P597
Lushan Yunwu Tea P512
Luzhou Laojiao Spirits Distilling Skills P427
Luzhou-flavor Laojiao P517

Ma Family Army P781
Ma Guai Festival of Zhuang Minority P442
Ma Junren P785
Ma Lin P759
Ma Wenge P757
Ma Xiangxing Restaurant P510
Ma Xiaochun P829
Ma Xiaoxu P806
Ma Yanhong P777
Ma Yanping P802
Macao Museum P304
Macao Olympic Committee P836
Macao Special Administrative Region P617
Machinery Manufacturing Industry P84
Made-in-china.com P656
Maijing (Pulse Classic) P537
Maijishan Grottoes P291
Main Comprehensive Search Websites P660
Main Datum of the Fifth National Census (2000) P30
Main Financial and Economic Websites in China P675
Main Game Information Website P681
Main Health Websites P678
Main IT Information Websites P677
Main IT websites P677
Main Online Community Websites P686
Main Online Game Websites P680
Main Online Recruitment Website P678
Main Original Literature Websites P686
Main Photograph Websites P679
Main Real Estate Websites P677
Main Threats to Personal Network Security P674
Main Video Sharing Websites P683
Main Website Navigation Websites P661
Mainland Coastline P3
Maintain Low-level Defense Expenditure P142
Majiang Demonstration Area in Guizhou P581
Majie Story-telling Gathering P453
Major Breakthroughs in Space Technologies for Civil Use P143
Major Ethnic Festivals P56
Major Events of Chinese Football P803
Major Events of Gymnastics in 2006 P775
Major Film Studios in China P468
Major Fishing Waters P602
Major Goal of Spaceflight P86
Major Rare Animals P14
Major Schools of Beijing Opera P275
Major Water Conservancy Zone P601
Making Experiments in Development and Employment of Rural Workforce P542
Making of Chinese Kites P294
Management of Industrial Hazardous Wastes P578
Management on the Foreign-funded Banks P106
Management Regulations on Marine Nature Reserves P588
Manchu Ethnic Group P43
Mandarin and Dialects P243
Man-made Satellites P85 (P145)
Manned Spacecraft P85
Manned Spaceflight P145
ManSuman Monastery in Xishuangbanna P490
Manual Weaving P295
Mao Dun Literature Award P464
Maolan National Nature Reserve P594
Maolin Museum P314
Maonan Ethnic Group P50
Maoqiang P375
Maotai Spirits Distilling Skills P426
Mapabc.com P662
Mapbar.com P663
Marathon P781
March Third Festival of Li Minority P441
Marine Aquatic Resources P12
Marine Environment P584
Marine Environment Protection P584
Marine Nature Reserve P585
Marine Resources P12
Maritime Courts P636
Mark of Green Food P497
Marriage and Family P526
Marriage Consultation P527
Marriage Registration System P526
Marry5.com P689
Mass Sports P822
Massage P534
Masterpieces of Oral and Intangible Heritage of Humanity P318
Material Technological Research Progress P191
Maternity Leave P532
Matouqin (Horse-Head Fiddle) P263
Mausoelum P486
Mawangdui Han Tombs P312
Mawangdui Han Tombs Relics Display Hall in Changsha P312
Measures for the Administration of Electronic Certification Services P659
Mediation Procedure P644
Mediation System P643
Medication of Tibetan Medicine P535
Medicinal Plants P15
Medicine Market in Anguo P453
Medium and Long-Term Development Plan for Recyclable Energy P570
Mei Lanfang P275
Mei Yan P815
Meizhou Hakka Mountain Song P330
Men's Basketball World Championship P739
Mencius (Meng Zi) P20
Meng Fanai P769
Meng Guanliang P750
Mengding Ganlu P511
Mengke Bateer P742
Mengxi Bitan (Dream Pool Essays) P27
Mengzi (The Book of Mencius) P457
Men's Weightlifting P734
Metallic Minerals P9
Methods of Compensation P645
Methods of Mediation P644
Mi Fu P251
Mianzhu New Year Woodblock Prints P401 (P295)
Miao Compound Folk Footed House Architectural and Building Skills P420
Miao Ethnic Group P41
Miao Ethnic Group Batik Cloth Dyeing Skills P418
Miao Ethnic Group Pan-Pipes Making Skills P420
Miao Ethnic Group Silver Jewelry Making Skills P422
Miaoxiu (Miao Embroidery) P403
Mid-Autumn Festival P439 (P520)
Middle and Long-Distance Running P781
Military Affairs Channel of China.Com P669
Military Area Commands P136
Military Courts P636
Military Museum of the Chinese People's Revolution P305

Military Rank System of the PLA P137
Military Service System of China P139
Military Sports P710
Military System P67
Military Training on Basic Militia Force P141
Militia Force P138
Min Cai (Fujian Cuisine) P504
Min Enze P201
Min Opera P370
Mineral Resources P9
Ming Dynasty (1368-1644) P28
Ming Dynasty Style Furniture P288
Ming Dynasty Tombs P487
Ming Xiaoling Mausoleum P486
Ming-Style Furniture Making Skills P423
Minimum Living Standard Security System P548
Minimum Standard of Living for Cities in China P548
Ministry of Agriculture P75
Ministry of Civil Affairs P528
Ministry of Commerce P123
Ministry of Communications P94
Ministry of Education P206
Ministry of Foreign Affairs P160
Ministry of Health P539
Ministry of Justice P647
Ministry of National Defense P135
Ministry of Public Security P631
Ministry of Railways P94
Ministry of Science and Technology P202
Minxi Han Opera P367
Mode of Development P695
Mode of Olympics P704
Model Ships P813
Modern Biathlon P812
Modern Chinese Architecture P491
Modern Chinese Music P270
Modern Cloisonné P285
Modern Development of the Chinese Volleyball P745
Modern Distance Education P216
Modern Distance Education in Peking University P218
Modern Distance Education in Zhejiang University P218
Modern Drama P281
Modern Folk Songs P269
Modern Pentathlon P790
Modern Sports (1860-1949) P699
Modern Symphonic Music P270
Mogao Grottoes P291
Mohist School P21
Moinba Ethnic Group P55
Moker.com.cn P684
Monasteries of Dai Ethnic group P490
Money Laundering Law P647
Mongol Andai Dance P354
Mongol Ethnic Group Leleche (All-Purpose Steppe Vehicle) Making Skills P424
Mongolian Ethnic Group P39
Mongolian Medicine P536
Mongolian Sihu Music P337
Mongolian Tea with Milk P514
Mongolian Wrestling P397
Monitoring Network of Radiation Environment P577
Monkey P524
Monsoon Climate P8
Mop P686
Mop's wideband movie & TV (itv.mop.com) P683
More Effective Measures Taken to Implement the Law on Environmental Protection P580
Moslem Pilgrims P177
"Most" of Qinghai-Tibet Railway P94
"Most" of the Three Gorges Project P79
Mosukun of the Oroqen Ethnic Group P392
Mother and Child Health Care P530
MotoGP Chinese Grand Prix P815
Motor Boat P819
Motor Vehicle Pollution Prevention P559
Motorcycling P815
Motuo Nature Reserve P599
Mou Zuoyun P740
Mountaineering P817
Moveable Type P27
Movie in China P465
MSN P670
Mu Pa Mi Pa Poetry Legend P321
Muban Dagu P384
Mudong Mountain Song P334
Mulam Ethnic Group P49
Mulian Opera P381
Multi-bowls P823
Multilateral Cooperation in the Space Project P88
Multi-lateral Environmental Cooperation P603
Multi-Party Cooperation System and Political Consultative Conference System P65
Multi-Sport Competitions P706
Munao Singing Party of Jingpo Minority P440
Municipalities Directly Under the Central Government P615
Museum of Chinese Science and Technology P305
Museum of Guangxi Zhuang Autonomous Region P301
Museum of Medical History in the Shanghai College of Traditional Chinese Medicine P309
Museum of Ningxia Hui Autonomous Region P304
Museum of Ocean Transportation History in Quanzhou P311
Museum of the Former Site of Ancient Tonglushan Copper Mine P312
Museum of the Hemudu Site P310
Museum of Xinjiang Uygur Autonomous Region P304
Museum Visiting P555
Museums P296
Music Copyright Society of China P121
Music Websites P682
Mutual Confidence and Cooperation between China and ASEAN P148

N

Nadam Fair P56 (P450)
Nadun Festival of Tu Minority P445
Nanhua Temple P171
Nanji Islands Marine Nature Reserve P586
Nanjing Gold Foil Beating Technique P421
Nanjing Road Architecture in Shanghai P491
Nanjing University P238
Nanjing Yunjin (Cloud Brocade) Wooden Loom Handicraft Weaving Skills P415
Nankai University P238
Nano Technological Research Progress P190
Nanping Nanci P386
Nantong Indigo Blue Cloth Decoration and Printing Skills P417
Nanxi Haozi P334
Nanyang Museum of Han Dynasty Stone Carving P311
Nanyin Music P346
Napo Zhuang Folk Song P335
National Action Plan for Comfortable Life and Environmental Protection in Rural Areas P604
National Action Program Protecting the Marine Environment from Land-Based Activities P585
National Anthem of the People's Republic of China P1
National Aquatics Center P494 (P842)
National Basketball Events P738
National City Games P718
National Conference Center P842
National Copyright Administration P121
National Day P2
National Day P557
National Day of Assisting Disabled Persons P36
National Defense Education for the Whole People P146
National Defense Policy P134
National Defense University P146
National Development and Reform Commission P71
National Emblem of the People's Republic of China P1
National Environmental Protection Standards System P577
National Farmers' Games P719
National Flag of the People's Republic of China P1

National Games P713
National Games for the Disabled P716
National Go Ranking Match P828
National Grand Theater P494
National Gymnasium P842
National Intangible Cultural Heritage List P320
National Judicial Examination P646
National Key Technologies Research and Development Program P196
National Museum of China P296
National Natural Science Foundation of China P202
National Nature Reserve P599
National Olympic Sports Center P841
National People's Congress P64
National Physique Monitoring P706
National Population and Family Planning Commission of China P31
National Program to Apply Research Fruits to Production P92
National Public Taekwondo Championships P773
National Sports Meeting P715
National Stadium P494 (P842)
National Student Loans P550
National Teaching Experimental Demonstration Centers of Higher Institutions P210
National Technical Invention Award P195
National Traditional Ethnic Sports Games P717
National University Games P719
National University of Defense Technology P146
National Winter Games P714
National-Level Key Laboratory of Satellite Marine Environment Dynamics P589
National-level Rare Birds Nature Reserve in Yancheng City P586
Nationwide Fitness Plan P705
Nationwide Fitness Week P707
Nationwide Tree-planting Campaign on a Voluntary Basis P580
Natural Forest Conservation Project P581
Natural Resources of China P9
Nature Reserve of Green Turtles in Huidong Port P587
Nature Reserve of National-level Mangrove Forest Ecology in Shankou P587
Nature Reserve of Woods from Submerged Forest in Shenhu Bay P586
Nature Reserves P592
Naxi Ethnic Group P47
Naxi Ethnic Group Dongba Paintings P401
Necessary Preparations P227
Negotiations on International Conventions and Accomplishment of Relevant Duties P604
Netease P669
Netease Mail P672
Network Advertising P650
New and Hi-tech Development Zone P92
New Energy Resources P84
New Investment Forms P132
New Regulation on Network Copyright Protection P116
New Sports P847
New Varieties of Plants P116
New Year Wood Block Paintings P294
New Year's Day P556
New Year's Day Films P468
NGO Project on Poverty Alleviation P550
Ni Xialian P756
Ni Zhiqin P785
Nie Weiping P829
Nine-Year Compulsory Education P36
Ningbo Cinnabar and Gold Lacquer Wood Carving P408
Ningde Huotong Xianshi (Thread-controlled Puppet Lion) P395
Ninghai Pingdiao P360
Ningxia Hui Autonomous Region P629
Niujie Mosque of Beijing P177
Non-governmental Environmental Protection Organization P564
Non-Metallic Minerals P9
Non-Olympic Events P812
Non-Professional Diving P826
Non-Proliferation Export Control Organs P156
Non-Public Ownership Economic Sector P73
Non-Tariff Measures and Import-Export Licensing Procedures P125
Normal Education P219
North Star Program P740
Northeast Forestry University P240
Northern and Southern Dynasties (420-589) P24
Northern Church P179
Northern Private Gardens P477
Northern Shaanxi Shuoshu P386
Northern Sichuan Weeding Drum-Gong Singing P334
Notarization Procedures P642
Notary System P641
Notifying and Removing Procedures for Dealing with Tortuous Dissension P691
Nu Ethnic Group P52
Nuclear and Radiation Environment P576
Nuclear and Radiation Safety Center, MEP P578
Nuclear Power Industry P80
Nuclear Safety and Radiation Environment Monitored and Controlled According to the Law P577
Nujiang River P6
Number of Chinese Characters P244
Number of Chinese Domain Names P648
Number of IP Address in China P648
Number of Websites in China P648
Nuo Opera P381
Nuowu Dance P349
Nvshu, or Women's Script P455

O

Obligations of Lawyers P640
Occupational Garments P498
Official Conservatory in the Han Dynasty P265
Official Script P248
Offshore Aquatic Resources P13
Old Zhengxing P509
Old-age Insurance System P546
Olympic Badge P696
Olympic Cup P712
Olympic Day Run P696
Olympic Glorious Program P695
Olympic Park P842
Olympic Rowing-Canoeing Park P843
Olympic Stamps P845
Olympic Village P842
One Child P529
One-Watt Plan P572
Online Games Industry in China P680
Online Media P664
Online NGO Name List of the Environment P567
Online Shopping P502
Online Travel Reservation P656
Oolong Tea P513
Open Dramatic World P282
Open Trials P636
Opening-up of the Service Field P133
Opening-up of Commerce P127
Opening-up Pattern P127
Opening-up the Telecom Industry P126
Operational Procedures for Reorganization of Foreign Banks' Branches P108
Opium War P28
Ordos Wedding P452
Organisms Resources P13
Organizational Setup of the State P65
Organs of Self-Government of Ethnic Autonomous Areas P58
Oriental Pearl TV Tower P494
Origin of Chinese Surnames P526
Origin of the Word "Wushu" P832
Ornamental Column Awards P466
Oroqen Ethnic Group P54
Ourgame.com P681
Outlaws of the Marsh P462
Outlays for Education P205
Outline of China's Space Science Plan in the 10th Five-Year Plan Period P88
Outline of Ethnic Education P215
Outline of Lakes P7
Outline of Rivers P4
Outline of Scientific and Technical Awards P194
Ouyang Xun P250
Overseas Chinese Table Tennis Players P754
Overseas Investment P124
Ox P524

P

Pagoda (Bao Ta) P484
PaiPai.com P655
Pairing Off More Developed Areas and Ethnic Autonomous Areas for Aid P62
Palace Museum P296
Paleocoastal Nature Reserve P598
Panchen Lama P166
Pandas P14
Paper P257
Paper-Cuts P286 (P402)
Papermaking P186
Parachuting P815
Paragliding Record P820
Parallel Bars P774
Participating in International Anti-Corruption Cooperation P634
Patent Application and Granting P113
Patent Examination System P113
Paying New Year's Calls P520
PCauto.com.cn P676
PCgames P682
PChome.net P678
PCpop.com P678
Peacock Dance of Dai Ethnic Group P354
Pearl River P5
Peking Man P16
Peking University P230
Peng Bo P796
Peng Shuai P790
People's Bank of China P100
People's Court at the Grassroots Level P636
People's Daily Online P664
People's Education Press P211
People's Health Level P495
People's Mediation Committee P644
People's Mediator P644
People's Republic of China (founded in 1949) P29
People's Republic of China and the IOC P704
Percussion and Wind Music in Hebei Province P342
Performance in Asian Games P775
Performance of Chinese Boxing P761
Performances of Beijing Opera P275
Performances of Quyi P279
Personal Network Security P673
Personal Network Security Products in China P674
Petroleum and Natural Gas Industry P80
Philosophical Taoism (Daojia) and Religious Taoism (Daojiao) P20
Phlebotomy of Mongolian Medicine P536
Photofans.cn P680
PICA P671
PICC Property and Casualty Co.,Ltd. P111
Pig P525
Pilgrimage to the West P462
Pilot Areas Conducting the Recycling Economy P568
Ping Pong Diplomacy P704
Ping Yali P821
Pingju Opera P371
Pingshu P280
Pingxiang Xiangdong Nuo Drama Masks P409
Pingyao Buffed Lacquerware Lacquering Skills P425
Pipa P264
Pipa of Dong Ethnic Group P265
Pipa Song of the Dong Ethnic Group P335
Pistol P765
Pizi (Hooligan) Literature P463
PLA Participates in Cooperation in Non-traditional Security Fields P149
Plan of Energy Conservation P571
Plan of Revitalizing Trade through Science and Technology P92
Plans on Public Health Emergencies P531
Plants P13
Plants of Industrial Utilization P15
Plaque P250
POCO P680
Poco.cn P685
Pole Vault P783
Policies Concerning Encouraging Foreign Businessmen to Invest in Central and Western Parts of the Country P131
Policies Concerning Encouraging Foreign Businessmen to Invest in the Old Industrial Bases of Northeast China P131
Policies of Ethnic Education P216
Policies on Ethnic Groups P58
Policies on International Space Exchanges P89
Policies on Population P32
Policies on Renewable Energy P569
Policies on the Equality between Men and Women P34
Policies on the Foreign Investment P130
Political Deputies of the Religious Circle P183
Political Party System P608
Pommel Horse P774
Pop Music P555
Popo.163.com P670
Popularity of Shooting P764
Popularity of Table Tennis Sport in China P752
Popularizing the Concept of Market Economy P126
Population Density P30
Population Distribution P31
Population Forecast P32
Population Growth Rate P30
Population Structure P31
Population Target P32
Porcelain P288
Ports P95
Post-Doctorate System P211
Posts and Telecommunications P89
Potala Palace P489
Poverty Alleviation by Development P549
Poverty Alleviation in Rural Areas P548
Power Grid Construction P77
Power Industry P77
Poyanghu Lake P7
Poyanghu Lake Nature Reserve P597
Prairie Fire Program P76
Precipitation P8
Pre-Employment Training P544
Prehistoric World and Slave Society (1.7 million years ago-476 BC) P16
Preparatory Education in Chinese for International Students in China P227
Pre-School Education (Early Childhood Education) P205
Presenting a Petition and Retrial P637
President of State P66
Prevention and Control of Acquired Immune Deficiency Syndrome (AIDS) P533
Prevention and Control of Industrial Pollution P558
Prevention and Control of Water Pollution in Key Drainage Areas P558
Prevention and Cure of Bird Flu P532
Prevention and Cure of Severe Acute Respiratory Syndrome (SARS) P532
Prevention and Health Care P531
Prevention and Remedying Desertification Under Local Conditions P583
Prevention and Treatment of Sandstorm Sources in the Beijing-Tianjin Area P584
Prevention of Weaponization of and Arms Race in Outer Space (PAROS) P157
Primary and Secondary Education P205
Primitive Sculpture P289
Princess Wencheng P165
Principle of Establishing Diplomatic Relations P159
Print Hand P249
Printing P187
Prints P255
Prison Administration P638
Prison Categories P638
Private Education P214
Private Museums P316
Proactive Employment Policy P540
Procedures for Criminal Investigations P631
Processing Techniques of Chinese Materia Medica P436
Processing Trade P123
Procuratorial System P632
Professional Development of Cycling Event P802

Professional Drama Troupes P281
Professionalization of Baseball in China P731
Professionalization of Sports P698
Program of Development for Poverty Alleviation in China's Rural Areas (2001-2010) P549
Progress of Renminbi Exchange Rate Reform P104
Project 211 P210
Project Hope P207 (P551)
Project on Converting Cultivated Land to Forest P11
Promoting Sailboard as a Sport in China P732
Promoting the Employment of Young People P542
Promoting the Important Role of the UN in Field of Non-Proliferation P154
Pronunciation of Chinese P242
Prospects for Bio-Fuel P569
Protecting Aliens' Exchanges With Respect to Religion P184
Protecting Laborers' Employment Rights P541
Protecting Well-known Trademark P114
Protection for the Children in Need P36
Protection Measures for the Right Owners P691
Protection of Children's Rights and Interests P35
Protection of New Varieties of Agriculture and Forestry Plants P116
Protection of Pastures P582
Protection of the Pandas P14
Protection on Cultural Treasures of the Palace P297
Protestantism in China P180
Provincial and Municipal Games P700
Provisions on Foreign Investment P124
Provisions on the Administration of Energy Conservation for Civil Buildings P574
Provisions on the Legal Responsibilities of Network Service Providers P692
Pu Haiqing P814
Pu Songling P461
Public Charity and Welfare Organizations P550
Public Health-Building Goes Hand in Hand with the Olympics P709
Public Participation in Environmental Legislation P562
Public Procurators P633
Public Sports Organizations P707
Publication of Environmental Information P565
Pudong International Airport P97
Pu'er Tea P514
Pumi Ethnic Group P51
Puning Temple P169
Puppetry P382
Pure Brightness P523
Putuo Mountain P171
Puxian Opera P358
Puzhou Bangzi P363

Q

Qi Haifeng P787
Qi Hui P794
Qi Min Yao Shu (Essential Techniques for the Peasantry) P25
Qian Chenghai P740
Qian Hong P793
Qiang Ethnic Group P49
Qiang Flute Performance and Manufacture P336
Qianjin Yaofang (Prescriptions for Emergencies) P538
Qianling Museum P314
Qianlong.com P667
Qianming Temple P172
Qianshan Liansi Paper Making Skills P428
Qianshan Mountain Temple Music P345
Qiao Hong P757
Qihoo.com P662
Qimen Gongfu Tea P513
Qin Dynasty (221-206 BC) P21
Qin Great Wall P22
Qin Terracotta Army Museum P313
Qing P266
Qing Dynasty (1616-1911) P28
Qing Dynasty Style Furniture P288
Qingchengshan Mountain P175
Qingdao Catholic Church P178
Qingdao Christian Church P180
Qingdao International Sailing Ship Center P843
Qinghai Museum P303
Qinghai Pasturing Area P10
Qinghai Province P629
Qinghaihu Lake P7
Qinghaihu Lake Bird Islet Nature Reserve P597
Qinghai-Tibet Railway P94
Qinglinsi Conundrum P327
Qingtian Stone Carving P406
Qingxu Super-Mature Vinegar Distilling Skills P427
Qingyang Melody P359
Qingyang Xiangbao (Perfume Sachets) Embroidery P404
Qingyun Temple P171
Qingzhou Statuary P174
Qinhuai Lantern Fair P451
Qinqiang P362
Qinshan Nuclear Power Plant P82
Qinshihuang Mausoleum P486
Qipao P498
Qiu Zhonghui P754
Qixia Temple P170
QQ P668
QQ Mail P672
QQ Zone P685
Qu Yuan P457
Qu Yunxia P786
Qualification of applicants for the Chinese Government Scholarship P222
Qualifications for a Public Procurator P634
Quality of Population P30
Quanfeng Festive Lantern P451
Quanjude P507
Quanyechang Mall in Tianjin P492
Quanzhou Beiguan Music P347
Quanzhou Breast Clapping Dance P350
Quju Opera P376
Qunar.com P662
Quyang Stone Carving P406
Quyuan Restaurant P509
Quzi Opera P376

Raba Dance P352
Rabbit P525
Race Walk P782
Racing Pigeon P831
Racing Referee P817
Radio and Television Universities P217
Radio Sports P818
Railway Courts P636
Railways P93
Rain Water P523
Ram P524
Rank-based System of the Marine Nature Reserve P588
Raosanling Festival of the Bai Ethnic Group in Dali P449
Rapid Growth in Shipbuilding Industry for Civil Use P144
Rat P524
Raw Material Conservation P573
Readnovel.com P686
Real Estate Websites P676
Realistic Play Writers P282
Reasons for the Ageing Trend P33
Records of Gold Medals on the 29th Olympic Games P722
Recycling Economy P566
Recycling Scrapped Products P570
Red Cross Society of China P550
Red Sorghum P471
Redemption of the Vows of Maonan Minority P442
Reducing and Controlling Land-sourced Pollutants P585
Reed Panpipe Dance of Miao Ethnic Group P353
Reemployment Service Centers P545
Reform of the State-owned Enterprises P72
Regional Environmental Cooperation P604
Regional Games P700
Regional Policies P130

Regional Security Cooperation P147
Registration Procedures of Religious Activities P183
Regong Art P410
Regong Sixth Lunar Month Gathering P449
Regular Script P248
Regular Social Donation P553
Regulation for the Administration on Prevention and Control of Damage to Marine Environment by Pollution from Marine Construction Projects P585
Regulations on Environmental Protection for Local Areas P579
Regulations on Foundation Administration P552
Regulatory System on Nature Reserves P599
Related Laws and Regulations P119
Relations between China and the Surrounding Countries P161
Relations between China and the World's Economy P124
Relations with ASEAN P162
Relations with Developing Countries P162
Relations with the Vatican P185
Relay Swimming P792
Relays P782
Relic Hall of Chinese Buddhism Books P307
Religion Is Separated from Political Power P182
Religions Should Abide by the Laws P182
Ren Jie P768
Renaming the Guangzhou Commodities Trade Fair P125
Renewable Energy P568
Renmin University P231
Renminbi P105
Republic of China (1912-1949) P29
Requirements for Foreign-Funded Banks P107
Rescue Project Concerning Endangered Plants P588
Rescue Project Relating to Endangered Wildlife Animals P589
Research and Development Institutions Subject to Enterprises P188
Research and Development Institutions Subject to Higher Schools P188
Research Institute of Buddhism Culture of China P172
Reserve Force P138
Reserve Force Building P141
Reserve Service P140
Resettlement Policy on Officers and Civil Cadres Transferred to Civilian Work and Discharged Conscripts P140
Residents' Expenditure P496
Residents' Income P496
Residents' Savings P496
Resource-Saving Enterprises: the China National Building Material Group Corporation (CNBM) and the China National Materials Industry Group P575
Respecting and Protecting Freedom of Religious Belief of Minorities P182
Respecting Freedom of Religious Belief of Foreigners in China P184
Restrictions on the Rightful Owner's Right of the Communication of Information on a Network P692
Revolution of 1911 P29
Revolutionary Committee of the Chinese Kuomintang P609
Rhythmic Gymnastics P779
Rice Technological Research Progress P191
Rifle P764
Rights of Lawyer P640
Rigorous Implementation of Laws and Regulations on Non-Proliferation Export Control P155
Rings P775
Rising P674
RMB Business Conducted by the Foreign-Funded Banks P107
RMB Exchange Rate Regime P105
Rock Climbing P827
Roles in Beijing Opera P274
Roller Skating P825
Romance of the Three Kingdoms P462
Rong Bao Zhai P259
Rong Guotuan P754
Rooster P525
Rope Skipping P835
Rowing P763
Ruan P264
Rules for Chinese Super League P805
Rules on Management of Foreign Trade Operators P129
Rules on Management of Imported and Exported Commodities P129
Running Script P248
Running Target P765
Rural Compulsory Education P207
Rural Endowment Insurance P550
Rural Health System P531
Russian Ethnic Group P52

Sacrificial Ceremonies for Dayu P448
Sacrificial Ceremonies for Nvwa P448
Sacrificial Ceremonies in the Yellow Emperor's Mausoleum P447
Sacrificial Ceremony to Genghis Khan P447
Sacrificing Ceremony for Mazu P447
Safe Drinking Water Program in Rural Areas P603
Safeguarding Public Environmental Rights and Interests P566
Safeguarding the Legal Rights and Interests of Rural Migrant Workers P542
Sailboard P732
Sailing P731
Salar Ethnic Group P50
Salvaging Intangible Cultural Heritage P319
Sama Festival of Dong Ethnic Group P444
Same Origin of Calligraphy and Painting P246
Sand Prevention and Control P583
Sanda Exercises P833
Sandstorm Prevention System P583
Sandstorms P583
Sangzhi Folk Song P330
Sanqu Songs P460
Sanshou P812
Sanxingdui Museum P313
Sanya Coral Reefs Nature Reserve P588
Satellite Navigation and Positioning P86
Satellite Remote-sensing P86
Satellite Telecommunications and Broadcasting P86
Scenic Areas and Places of Historical Interest P592
Scented Teas P514
Scholarships for International Student P223
Schools of Beijing Opera P275
Scientific and Technical Bodies P188
Scientific and Technical Cooperation between China and Foreign Countries P197
Scientific and Technical Progress Award P195
Scientific and Technological Innovation and Incubation System P92
Scientific Research Institution for Copyright P115
Scope of Business of Notary Office P641
Scope of Legal Aid P646
Se P265
Seawater Utilization P574
Second Generation of Chinese Directors P467
Securities Market P108
Security System of Minimum Wage P548
Selection of Disabled Athletes P710
Self-determination in Marriage P527
Self-Government Regulations and Separate Regulations P59
Self-Management System of the Urban Residents P68
Self-Management System of Villagers P68
Self-Taught Higher Education Examination P214
Semi-Agriculture and Semi-Pasturing Folk Song Region P268
Semi-official and Folk Science and Technology Cooperation P197
Sepak Takraw P815
Serious Investigation on Suspected Cases of Illegal Export P156
Service Trade P123
Set Exercises P833
Set Exercises to Radio Music P709
Settlement on the Chemical Weapons Japan

Abandoned in China P154
Seven Towers Temple P170
Several Opinions of the State Council on Accelerating Development of E-Commerce P659
Shaanxi Geological Museum P314
Shaanxi History Museum P303
Shaanxi Province P628
Shadow Play P382
Shamian in Guangzhou P492
Shandong Airlines Group Co., Ltd.(SC) P96
Shandong Dagu P383
Shandong Jinan Dough Sculptures P293
Shandong Kuaishu P391
Shandong Langzhuang Dough Sculptures P293
Shandong Museum P300
Shandong Province P622
Shandong Qinshu P387
Shandong University P235
Shang Dynasty (1600-1046 BC) P17
Shang Shu (The Book of History) P457
Shangdang Bangzi P364
Shangdang Bayinhui Music P343
Shanghai Airlines Co., Ltd. (FM) P96
Shanghai Animation Film Studio P469
Shanghai Community Church P181
Shanghai Film Dubbing Studio P469
Shanghai Film Studio P469
Shanghai Gymnasium P840
Shanghai International Film Festival P466
Shanghai Jiaotong University P241
Shanghai Jinmao Building P494
Shanghai Municipality P616
Shanghai Museum P299
Shanghai Museum of Natural Sciences P309
Shanghai Old Cathedral P179
Shanghai Opera P372
Shanghai People's Art Theater P283
Shanghai Pudong Development Bank P102
Shanghai Stadium P841
Shanghai Stock Exchange P110
Shanghai Symphony Orchestra P271
Shanghai Theater Academy P283
Shanghai University of Finance and Economics P241
Shanghai University of Sport P838
Shanghan Zabinglun (Discourse on Fevers and Miscellaneous Illness) P537
Shangluo Flower-drum P374
Shangsou.com P662
Shannan Chamgocho Dance P356
Shannan Menba Opera P379
Shanxi Dough Sculptures P293
Shanxi Museum P298
Shanxi Province P621
Shaolin Kungfu P395
Shaolin Temple P171
Shaoxing Jiafan Wine P518
Shaoxing Lianhua Lao P388
Shaoxing Pinghu Tune P386
Shaoxing Yellow Wine Distilling Skills P427
She Ethnic Group P46
She Ink-stone Making Skills P431
Shehuo Activities P452
Shejitan Altar (Altar of Land and Grain) P475
Shen Jiliang P821
Shen Xue P810
Shen Xue Ren Gallery P259
Sheng P260
Shengda Online P681
Sheng Zetian P772
Shengzhou Bamboo Weaving P410
Shengzhou Wind and Percussion Music P339
Shennong Bencao Jing (Shennong Emperor's Classic of Materia Medica) P535
Shennongjia National Nature Reserve P594
Shenyang Palace Museum P308
Shenzhen Baoan International Airport P97
Shenzhen Development Bank P101
Shenzhen Stock Exchange P110
Shi Dongpeng P788
Shi Ji (The Records of the Great Historian) P458
Shi Jing (The Book of Poetry) P265
Shi Meiqin P795
Shi Zhiyong P737
Shifan Music P339
Shijiazhuang Sixian P369
Shiwan Pottery Sculpture Skills P411
Shizhu Tujia Luo'er Tune P331
Shooting P764
Short Track Speed Skating P808
Short-term Courses for Foreigners P227
Short-term Scholarship for Foreign Teachers of Chinese Language P225
Shot Put P783
Shoton Festival P446
Shouning Beilu Opera P370
Shoushan Stone Carving P406
Shuagetang Festival of the Yao Ethnic Group P450
Shui Ethnic Group P47
Shui Maweixiu (Horse Tail Embroidery) P403
Shuishu P455
Shujin (Sichuan Brocade) Weaving Skills P415
Shuxiu (Sichuan Embroidery) P287 (P403)
Sichuan Airlines Co., Ltd. (3U) P96
Sichuan Dazu Stone Carvings P174
Sichuan Museum P302
Sichuan Opera P361
Sichuan Province P627
Sichuan University P236
Significance of Safeguarding Intangible Cultural Heritage P317
Significant Scientific and Technical Achievements P190
Signing of Relevant Agreements between China and India P148
Sihai Pots Museum P316
Silk Painting P253
Silk Road P23
Silk Road on the Sea P23
Sima Qian P458
Simuwu Rectangular Ding Tripod P284
SINA P668
Sina Mail P672
Sina UC, UTalk P670
Sino-African Education Minister Forum P229
Sino-European Relations P161
Sino-foreign Cooperation Enterprise P132
Sino-foreign Joint Venture Enterprise P131
Sino-Japanese Relations P160
Sino-Russian Relations P160
Sino-US Relations P160
Siping Opera P361
Sipingdiao P371
Sister Festival of Miao Minority P444
Six-syllable Prayer P166
Size of Internet Education Market P673
Sizhou Opera P374
Skating P807
Skiing P811
Skype P671
Slight Cold P523
Slight Heat P523
Slight Snow P523
Slope Gatherings of the Miao in Rongshui County P450
Smarter.com P662
Snake P525
Snakes Island-Laotieshan Mountain Nature Reserve P586
So.01hr.com P662
Social Relief P545
Social Security System P545
Social Sports Coaching Center P708
Social Sports Instructors P708
Social Welfare P545
Softball P743
Softball Players P743
Sogou.com P661
Sohu P669
Sohu Mail P672
Sohu's 17173.com P682
Sohu's soq.com P670
Song Ci (Lyric Poetry) P459
Song Dynasty (960-1279) P26
Song of the Bashan Back-Carriers P331
Song of the Fisherman P471
Song Xiaobo P740
Songjin (Brocade of Song Dynasty) Weaving Skills P414
Songshan Mountain Nature Reserve P598
Songtsan Gampo P165
Soso.com P661
Soufun.com P677

Southern Private Gardens P476
Southern Putuo Temple P171
Southern Tianjin (Small Courtyard) Residence P479
Southwestern Shandong Guchuiyue P339
Space Science P87
Spark Program P76 (P197)
Special Arrangements for Tibet P60
Special Care and Placement P545
Special Care for Ethnic Minorities P62
Special Education P208
Special Olympic Games P710
Special Olympic Games in China P710
Special People's Court P636
Special Planning of Seawater Utilization P576
Speed Skating P807
Sphere of Application of HSK P228
Splendid Period of the Chinese Volleyball P745
Spoken and Written Languages of the Ethnic Groups P59
Sports Activities and Events for Athletes With Visual or Mobility Impairment P821
Sport Activities and Events for Deaf People P821
Sport Activities and Events for Mentally Defective Persons P821
Sports Activities for the Public P707
Sports Collection P847
Sports Documentary Film P712
Sports Economy P844
Sports Entertainment Industry P698
Sports Events P731
Sports Events Practiced in China P695
Sports Festivals P848
Sports for Children P708
Sports for Ethnic Minorities P711
Sports for Senior Citizens P707
Sports for the Disabled P710
Sports for the Working People P707
Sports for the Young P708
Sports for Women P708
Sports Goods P844
Sports Goods Exhibitions P844
Sports Goods Industry P698
Sports Goods Retailing P845
Sports in Rural Areas P709
Sports Industries P844
Sports Information Websites P848
Sports Lottery P846
Sports Market P845
Sports Media P847
Sports Murals P699
Sports Population P707
Spread of Chinese P245
Spring and Autumn Period (770-476 BC) P18
Spring Bud Project P207 (P552)
Spring Equinox P523
Spring Festival P56 (P438、P518)
Spring Festival Customs P519
Spring Festival Foods P519
Spring Moon Light on the Flowers by the River P264
Spring Transportation P520
Sprint P781
Squash P812
St. Bride Vase Forever in China P753
St. Michael's Church P180
Stadium & Gymnasium P839
Standards for Eco-Industrial Parks P602
Starlight Program P32 (P554)
Start of Professional Boxing P761
State Administration for Religious Affairs P185
State Administration of Foreign Exchange P105
State Administration of Taxation P74
State Administration of Traditional Chinese Medicine (SATCM) P539
State Administration of Work Safety P78
State Compensation System P644
State Council P66
State Council Office for West Region Development P70
State "Eight Seven" Program for Poverty Alleviation P549
State Ethnic Affairs Commission P63
State Food and Drug Administration P539
State Forestry Administration P583
State Intellectual Property Office P121
State Oceanic Administration P587
State Postal Bureau P90
State Power Grid Corporation of China P78
State Protects Normal Religious Activities P182
State Science and Technology Programs P196
State Scientific and Technological Program for Environmental Protection P561
State Spark Awards P195
State Supreme Science and Technology Award P194
State Trade and Authorized Operation P122
State Yangtze Scholar Award Program (Cheung Kong Scholars Program) P211
State-owned Assets Supervision and Administration Commission P71
State-owned Banks Getting Listed P99
Staying Up All Night P519
Steeplechase P781
Stepping Stones in Internet Education P673
Stilt Dance P350
Stock.163.com P676
Stockholm Convention P566
Stockstar.com P675
Stone Carving P290
Stone Horse Stepping on a Hun Soldier P290
Stone Lion P290
Storm-Proof Bridges of Dong Ethnic Group P490
Story of Dong Yong and the Seventh Fairy Maiden P322
Story Song of She People P327
Strange Tales from the Liaozhai Studios P460
Strategic Consultation and Dialogue P147
Straw Weaving P295
Strengthened Comprehensive Consumption of Wood Resources P574
Strengthening Comprehensive Utilization of Resources P573
Strengthening Labor Skill Training P544
Structure of Chinese Internet Users in Terms of Education Level P649
Structure of Chinese Internet Users in Terms of Profession P649
Structure of Legal Aid Institutions P646
Study of the Ethnic Ancient Classics P63
Studying Abroad P221
Su Cai (Jiangsu Cuisine) P505
Su Shi P459
Subjects of the National Adult College Entrance Examination (NACEE) P213
Successful Bid for 2008 Olympics P696
Sui Dynasty (581-618) P25
Sui Feifei P742
Sui Xinmei P785
Suizhou Zeng Houyi Tomb Relics Display Hall P311
Summer Olympic Games P719
Summer Palace P478
Summer Solstice P523
Sun Caiyun P787
Sun Fuming P762
Sun Jihai P806
Sun Jinfang P747
Sun Shuwei P795
Sun Tiantian P789
Sun Wen P806
Sun Wu P18
Sun Yat-sen P29
Sun Yat-sen Suit P498
Sun Yat-sen University P239
Sunlight P8
Super Rice Popularization Project P77
Supreme People's Court P635
Supernatural Stories P460
Supervision and Management Standard on Chinese-Funded Banks and Foreign-Funded Banks P107
Supreme People's Procuratorate P632
Survey Data on Health P530
Sutra Columns P485
Suxiu (Suzhou Embroidery) P287 (P403)
Suzhou Imperial-Kiln Golden Brick Manufacturing Skills P420
Suzhou Kesi (Silk Tapestry with Cut Designs) Weaving Skills P415
Suzhou Opera P372
Suzhou Pingtan P383
Suzhou Steles Museum P309

Sweeping of All Three Cups P798
Swimming P791
Sword Pole Festival of Lisu Minority P445
Symphony Orchestra of the China National Opera House P270
Synchronized Swimming P792
Syntax of Chinese Language P243
System and Principles on Non-Proliferation Export Control P156
System for IPR Protection P118
System of Civil Aviation P95
System of Civil Officers P139
System of Education Master Degree (EMD) P219
System of Social Sciences P198
System of Trial or Arbitration P643

T

Table Tennis P751
Table Tennis as an Olympic Sport P754
Table Tennis World Cup P729
Taekwondo P773
Tai Chi Boxing P396
Taibaishan Mountain Nature Reserve P599
Taihao Fuxi's Fiesta P448
Taihedian (Hall of Supreme Harmony) P473
Taihu Lake P7
Taimiao (Royal Ancestral Temple) P475
Taining Meilin Opera P367
Taipei Film Festival P467
Taipei Insect Science Museum P315
Taipei Palace Museum P315
Taiping Houkui P512
Taiqing Palace of Laoshan Mountain P176
Taiqing Palace of Shenyang City P176
Taishan Shigandang Customs P451
Taiwan Democratic Self-Government League P610
Taiwan Museum of Natural Science P315
Taiwan Province P617
Tajik Ethnic Group P50
Taking the Market Economy Road P126
Tale of Monk Jigong P323
Tale of Xishi P322
Tan Xue P734
Tan Zhenshan's Folk Stories P325
Tan Zongliang P767
Tanbu'er P265
Tang Dynasty (618-907) P26
Tang Gonghong P737
Tang Lin P762
Tang Lingsheng P736
Tang Poetry P458
Tang Xianhu P799
Tang Xianzu P461
Tangka Paintings P173
Tantou New Year Woodblock Prints P400
Tao Luna P767
Tao Yuanming P459
Taobao.com P655
Taohuawu New Year Woodblock Prints P399 (P295)
Taoism (Taoist School) P20
Taoism in China P175
Taoist Association of China P176
Taoist Music of Xuanmiaoguan Taoist Temple P346
Taoist Temple of Maoshan Mountain P176
Taotaoju Restaurant P510
Tar Monastery P168
Tar Monastery Butter Carving P409
Target of the Recycling Economy P568
Tariff Laws and Regulations P129
Task China P688
Tatar Ethnic Group P53
Taxation Policies P74
TCM Culture of Huqingyutang P436
TCM Culture of Tongrentang P437
TCM History P533
Tea House P516
Tea Served in a Set of Cups P516
Teachers P218
Teacher's Day P557
Teachers' Law of the PRC P219
Teaching Chinese as a Foreign Language P228
Teaching Materials for Primary and Middle Schools P206
Tea-picking Opera P375
Technical School P544
Technical Trade P197
Techniques Innovation P752
Technological Trade P123
Technology Development in the Present Age P188
Technology Development Today P187
Technology of Environmental Pollution Control P562
Teein P687
Temperature P8
Temperature Zones P8
Temple of Heaven P474
Tencent's QQ P670
Teng Haibin P778
Tengpai Battle Array of Shahe P397
Tengwang Pavilion P484
Tennis P788
Tenpay.com P658
Terracotta Warriors P290
The "Five Consecutive Titles" of the Women' Volleyball Team P748
Theater Costumes and Props Making Skills P433
Theism and Atheism Should Respect Each Other P182
Themes of Previous National Day of Assisting Disabled Persons P36
Theory of Channels (Meridians and Collaterals) P534
Theory of Directing One's Strength P534
Theory of Internal Organs of the Body P534
Theory of the Five Elements P533
Third Generation of Chinese Directors P467
Thirteen Hongs in Guangzhou P492
Three Carving Arts of Huizhou (Wuyuan) P407
Three Consecutive Titles of the Women's Volleyball Team P748
Three Gorges Project P79
Three Gorges Project Construction Committee P79
Three Gorges Transport Hub Situation (2006) P79
Three Industrial Sectors P72
Three Kingdoms (220-280) P24
Three Pagodas in Dali P485
Three visits of Ali to China P761
Three-Course Tea of the Bai Ethnic Minority P515
Three-North and Yangtze River Valley Key Forest System Construction Project P11
Three-Self Patriotic Movement Committee of the Protestant Churches of China P182
Three-Tier Training System P695
Ti Kuan Yin P513
Tian Bingyi P799
Tian Jia P749
Tian Liang P796
Tian Yumei P786
Tiancity.com P681
Tian'ezhou White-Flag Dolphin Nature Reserve P598
Tianji.com P689
Tianjin Folklore Museum P308
Tianjin Historical Museum P298
Tianjin Municipality P616
Tianjin Natural History Museum P308
Tianjin Seacoast and Wetland National-level Nature Reserve P588
Tianjin Shidiao P389
Tianjin University P235
Tianjin Xikai Church P179
Tianmushan Mountain National Nature Reserve P595
Tianqiao Banner Stunts P394
Tianshan Film Studio P469
Tiantaishan Dried Lacquer Gunny Fetus Skills P425
Tianwan Nuclear Power Plant P82
Tianya Virtual Community P686
Tiaohua (Cross-Stitch) P404
Tibet Autonomous Region P628
Tibet Museum P303
Tibet Pasturing Area P10
Tibetan Antelopes P14

Tibetan Buddhism P165
Tibetan Buttered Tea P515
Tibetan Ethnic Group P40
Tibetan Ethnic Group Gyaya Carpet Making Skills P417
Tibetan Ethnic Group King Gesar Painted Rock Carving P407
Tibetan Ethnic Group Paper-Making Skills P429
Tibetan Ethnic Group Tangka Paintings P402
Tibetan Ethnic Group Woolen Bangdian (Apron) and Qiadian (Rug) Weaving Skills P417
Tibetan Folk Song Region P268
Tibetan Lagzhas P333
Tibetan Medicine P535
Tibetan New Year P56
Tibetan Opera P379
Tiger P524
Time-Honored Restaurants of China P507
Timetable for Public Sports Activities P707
Titan Sports Media P848
Tkgame.com P682
Tkzp.com P679
Tobacco Case Dance of Yi Ethnic Group P356
Tomb Sweeping Festival P438 (P520)
Tong Ling P756
Tongchunyuan P509
Tongji University P237
Tongren Shuxue Zhenjiu (Illustrated Manual of the Bronze Man Showing Acupuncture and Moxibustion Points) P538
Tongrentang Pharmacy P536
Tooth and Horn Carving P289
Top 10 Items of Progress in Science and Technology in 2007 P192
Top 10 Scientific and Technoloical Achievements for 2005 P192
Top 100 Chain Enterprises P127
Topography P3
Torch Festival of Yi Minority P440
Torch Program P196
Tour of China P801
Tourism P554
Township Enterprises P75
Track and Field P780
Track Record of Chinese Skating Team (2006) P810
Track Record of Pentathlon (2006) P790
Track Record of the Chinese Cycling Team P801
Track Record of Women's Football P804
Trade Friction P126
Trademark Law P120
Trademark Registration From Overseas P114
Trademarks Registration P114
Traditional Artware P284
Traditional Chinese Medicine P533
Traditional Chinese Painting P252
Traditional Festivals P518
Traditional Methods of Preparation of Formulas of TCM P437
Traditional Mode of Family P528
Traditional Sports P694
Traditional Sports Games of Ethnic Minorities P711
Training for Employment of Rural Labor Forces P542
Training System of Competitive Sports P694
Trampoline P779
Transfer of Foreign Transfer in Chinese Cycling Event P802
Transfer Service for Chinese Government Full-Scholarship Students P225
Transmitter of Intangible Cultural Heritage P319
Travel Search Engine P656
Treatment of Major Polluted Areas P558
Tree-planting Day (China Arbor Day) P556
Trend of Aging Population P33
Trend of Change in Family Structure P528
Trial Organs P637
Triathlon P788
Triple Jump P784
Trojan Industry P674
Tsinghua MBA Program P212
Tsinghua University P231
Tu Ethnic Group P48
Tu Ethnic Group Panxiu (Bowl Embroidery) P403
Tu Lou (Earthen Tower) P481
Tubo Kingdom P165
Tudou.com P684
Tug-of-war P835
Tujia Daliuzi P342
Tujia Ethnic Group P44
Tujia Ethnic Group Brocade Weaving Skills P416
Tujia Hand Wielding Dance P351
Tujia Sayeryo Dance P352
Tune of Four-Season Production P326
Turpan Emin Mosque P488
TV Audience Rating P555
Twelve Copper Drum Melodies P343
Twelve Zodiac Animals P524
Twenty-Four Solar Terms P522 (P455)
Types of Autonomous Areas for Ethnic Minority Groups P58
Types of ENGO P564
Types of Facial Make-up in Beijing Opera P274

U

Ulabun Biographical Singing and Talking P323
Undertakings for the Disabled P36
Unemployment and Registered Unemployment Rate P540
Unemployment Insurance System P546
Uneven Bars P775
UNIDO International Solar Energy Center for Technology Promotion and Transfer (ISEC-UNIDO) P575
United Front Work Department of the CPC Central Committee P609
Universal Convention on the Protection of Plant Varieties P120
Universiade P724
University of International Business and Economics P231
University of Science and Technology of China P232
Unmarried Group P527
Upsurge in Divorce P527
Urban Planning and Environment P559
Urban Public Transportation P501
Urtiin Duu or "Long Song" of the Mongolian People P328
Use of Defense Expenditure P142
Use of the Chinese Language P242
Using Land Resources in an Efficient Way P573
Usual Subjects in Traditional Chinese Paintings P252
Utilization of Foreign Investments for Environmental Protection P606
Utilizing Imported Recyclable Resources P570
uuu9.com P681
Uyghur Ethnic Group Decorated Carpet and Cloth Weaving and Printing Skills P417
Uyghur Ethnic Group Earthen Pottery Molding, Firing and Production Skills P412
Uyghur Ethnic Group Mulberry Paper Making Skills P429
Uygur Darwaz P395
Uygur Duolong Maxrap P450
Uygur Ethnic Group P40
Uygur Medicine P536
Uygur Style in Making Medicine P536
Uzbek Ethnic Group P52

V

Va Ethnic Group P45
Vault P775
Vernacular P460
Vertical Search P661
Video Websites with More Visits P683

Views of Chinese Internet Users P650
Visa Application and Registration in China P225
Vision of Love P526
Visiting Temple Fairs P520
Vnet.cn P683
Vocational Education P209
Vocational Skill Competitions P545
Vocational Skills Certification P545
Vocational Training for the Disabled P208
Volleyball P745
Volleyball League P746
Volleyball World Cup P730
Volunteer P552
Volunteers P552
Volvo China Open P813

W

Waer Ezu Festival of Qiang Minority P442
Waking of Insects P523
Wan'an Compass Making Skills P424
Wanbang P365
Wang Chunlu P809
Wang Fei P749
Wang Fuzhou P818
Wang Haibin P734
Wang Hao P759
Wang Jinyu P808
Wang Juan P822
Wang Junxia P787
Wang Kui P784
Wang Lei P734
Wang Liping P787
Wang Liqin P758
Wang Nan P758
Wang Tao P757
Wang Xianzhi P250
Wang Xiuli P808
Wang Xiuting P786
Wang Xizhi P249
Wang Xu P772
Wang Xuan P200
Wang Yifu P765
Wang Yongzhi P201
Wang Zhengting P701
Wang Zhizhi P742
Wangshi Garden P476
Wangyou.com P688
Wanwan Melody P371
Warring States Period (475 -221 BC) P19
Water and Soil Conservation P582
Water Environment of Three Gorges Reservoir Area P560
Water motorcycling P820
Water Polo P797
Water Skiing P819
Water Splashing Festival of Dai Minority P440
Water-drawing Festival and Sowing Festival of Tajik Minority P445
Waterpower Resources P12
Wax Printing P286
Website Navigation 265.com P661
Website of the Chinese Government P652
Website of the National Committee of the Chinese People's Political Consultative Conference (CPPCC) P652
Website of the National People's Congress P652
Websites for Dating and Making Friends P689
Websites of China's Banks P659
Websites of Local Governments P653
Websites of the Ministries and Commissions of the State Council P66
Wedding customs of the Salar P452
Wedding Customs of the Tu Ethnic Group P452
Wei Long Wu (Dragon-Encircled House) P481
Weifeng Gong and Drum in South Shanxi Province P342
Weightlifting P734
Weightlifting Reserve P735
Welfare Distribution of Houses P499
Wenmiao (The Confucian Temple) P475
Wenshou P474
Wenshu Temple P171
Wenshui Guzi P344
Wenweipo.com P668
Wen-yen Chinese P460
Wenzhou Guci P385
West Lake Longjing (Dragon Well Tea) P511
Western Church P180
Western Jin Dynasty (265-317) P24
Western Region Development P70
Western Zhou Dynasty (1046 to 771 BC) P18
Westward Moving Festival of the Xibe Minority P440
Wetland International-China P590
Wetland Protection P590
White Cloud Temple P176
White Dew P523
White Horse Temple P171
White Tea P514
Wholly Foreign Owned Enterprise P132
Wild Animal and Plant Protection and Natural Reserve Construction Project P11
Wild Animal DNA Bank P191
Wind Power Industry P569
Wind Power Resources P12
Windbreak and Sand-Dune Fixation Zone P601
Winning Thomas Cup for the First Time P798
Winning Uber Cup for the First Time P798
Winter Games P723
Winter Solstice P523
Winter Swimming P823
Withdrawal System P637
Witkey China P688
Witkey main websites P688
Witkey.com P688
Witkeysky.com P688
Wolong National Nature Reserve P595
Women Administrators of Sports P712
Women Participating in the Political Affairs P35
Women's Bridge Team of China P827
Women's Employment P34 (P542)
Women's Football P803
Women's Softball World Championship P743
Women's Weightlifting P735
Wood Carving P289
Wood Saving and Substitution P574
Wood-block Water-color Print Making Skills P432
Wooden Drum Dance P353
Wooden Pagoda in Ying County P484
Word-formation of Chinese Characters P244
Work Committee for Imported Recyclable Energy P570
World Bank Aid P570
World Boxing League P761
World Championships and Games for the Disabled P729
World Championships of Acrobatics P780
World Fencing Championships P733
World Military Pentathlon Championships (WMPC) P730
World Mixed Team Badminton Championships P798
World Table Tennis Championships P729
World Top Professional Bodybuilding Stars Performed in China for the First Time P825
World Weightlifting Championships P735
World Wheelchair Fencing Championships P733
World Wresting Championships (2005) P771
World Wresting Championships (2006) P772
Writing Utensils in the Study P257
WTO Notification and Consultation Bureau P127
Wu Ballad P325
Wu Bin P822
Wu Changshuo P252
Wu Daozi, Sage in Chinese Painting P254
Wu Feng Lou (Five Phoenix Tower) P481
Wu Hanxiong P734
Wu Jingguo P705
Wu Jingyu P773
Wu Lanying P765
Wu Mengchao P201
Wu Minxia P796
Wu Peng P794
Wu Wenjun P200
Wu Xiaoxuan P765
Wu Zhengyi P202
Wu'an Pingdiao Laozi P371
Wudang Wushu (Martial Arts) P395
Wudangshan Mountain Taoist Music P346

Wuhan Institute of Physical Education P839
Wuhan University P234
Wuhu Iron Picture Production Skills P422
Wuliangye Wine P517
Wulige'er P392
Wunijing Handicraft Cotton Weaving Skills P415
Wuqiang New Year Woodblock Prints P398 (P295)
Wuqiao Acrobatic P394
Wuqin of the Daur Ethnic Group P392
Wushu P832
Wushu Athletes Ranking Standards P833
Wushu Competition Rules P833
Wutaishan Mountain P169
Wutaishan Mountain Buddhist Music P345
Wutu Dance of Tu Ethnic Group P357
Wuyi Yancha (Cliff Tea) P428 (P513)
Wuyishan Mountain National Nature Reserve P595
www.rayli.com.cn P669
www.southcn.com P667

X

Xcar.com.cn P676
Xia Dynasty (2070 -1600 BC) P17
Xiamen Airlines Ltd. (MF) P96
Xiamen Lacquer Line Carving Skills P426
Xiamen Overseas Chinese Museum P310
Xiamen University P237
Xian Dongmei P762
Xi'an Drum Music P344
Xi'an Film Studio P468
Xi'an Jiaotong University P239
Xi'an Physical Education University P839
Xi'an Stele Forest P249
Xi'an Translation University P215
Xiang Cai (Hunan Cuisine) P506
Xiang Opera P361
Xianghai Nature Reserve P597
Xiangji Temple P173
Xiangshanbang Traditional Architectural and Building Skills P418
Xiangsheng P279
Xiangshu.com P680
Xiangxi Drum Dance of Miao Ethnic Group P354
Xiangxi Maogusi Dance Drama of Tujia Ethnic Group P355
Xiangxiu (Hunan Embroidery) P287 (P403)
Xianxiao P387
Xianzi Dance P352
Xiao P261
Xiao Yehua P786
Xiaonei.com P687
Xiaorehun (Small Gong Story-Telling) P391
Xibe Ethnic Group P51
Xici.net P687
Xie Jun P831
Xie Xingfang P801
Xifeng Spirit P517
Xihe Dagu P383
Xihuangsi Temple P168
Xili Tu-Zhao in Hohhot P489
Xilinguole National Nature Reserve P594
Xinchang Melody P360
Xinfeng Demonstration Area in Jiangxi P581
Xing Aowei P778
Xing Fen P736
Xing Huina P788
Xingguo Mountain Song P329
Xinghua Cun Fen-flavor Spirit P518
Xinghuacun Fen Chiew Spirits Distilling Skills P427
Xingshan Folk Song P329
Xingtai Mei Hua Quan P396
Xinhuanet.com P664
Xinjiang Folk Song Region P268
Xinjiang Pasturing Area P10
Xinjiang Quzi P390
Xinjiang Uygur Autonomous Region P630
Xinjiang Uygur Muqam Art P347
Xinyang Maojian P512
Xiong Ni P795
Xiqin Opera P370
Xishuangbanna National Nature Reserve P594
Xitek.com P679
Xiushan Festive Lantern P451
Xiuyan Jade Carving P405
Xiyuan Jilu (Collected Writings on the Washing Away of Wrongs) P538
Xplus P684
Xu Demei P786
Xu Fang P805
Xu Haifeng P765
Xu Heng P704
Xu Nannan P811
Xu Yiming P794
Xu Yinsheng P754
Xu Yuhua P831
Xuan Paper Making Skills P430
Xuankong Temple P169
Xuanzang (Tang Seng) P167
Xuanzhong Temple P169
Xun P260
xxsy.net P686
Xy2.163.com P680
Xyxy.net P678

Y

Yabuli Snow Sports Training Base P841
Yahoo! Mail P672
Yahoo! Messenger P671
Yan Hong P786
Yan Zhenqing P250
Yanbei Shuahai'er P369
Yang Boyong P740
Yang Chen P806
Yang Chuanguang P784
Yang Ling P768
Yang Liwei P88
Yang Wei P778
Yang Wenjun P751
Yang Wenyi P793
Yang Xia P737
Yang Yang P799
Yang Yang P809
Yang Yang P809
Yangcheng Pig Iron Production Skills P420
Yangge P348
Yangge Opera P376
Yangjiabu New Year Woodblock Prints P399
Yangliuqing New Year Woodblock Prints P398 (P295)
Yangqin (Dulcimer) P266
Yangtze River P4
Yangzhou Jade Carving P404
Yangzhou Lacquerware Lacquering Skills P425
Yangzhou Opera P373
Yangzhou Pinghua (Storytelling in Yangzhou Dialect) P280 (P383)
Yangzhou Qingqu (Yangzhou Ditty) P388
Yao Ethnic Group P43
Yao Jingyuan P736
Yao Ming P742
Yao Xueyin Full-Length Historical Novels Award P464
Yaozhou Kiln Ceramic Firing and Manufacturing Skills P412
Yarlung Zangbo River P5
Yazhou Folk Song P330
Ye Duzheng P201
Ye Jiangchuan P830
Ye Qiaobo P808
Ye Zhaoying P799
Yellow River P4
Yellow Tea P514
Yesky.com P677
Yi Cuotaiji P380
Yi Ethnic Group P41
Yi Jianlian P742
Yi Seaweed Singing P335
Yichang Sizhu P340
Yicheng Flowery Drum Dance P350
Yidu Zhenjiao Mosque P178
Yifan Festival of Mulam Minority P442
Yigougou P378
Yihuang Opera P368

Yimakan Story telling of the Hezhe Ethnic Group P392
Yin and Yang Theory P533
Yin Ruins P17
Yinchuan National Wetland Park P590
Yingge P349
Yixing Baccaro Teapot P289
Yixing Zisha Ceramic Making Skill P411
Yiyang Melody P359
Yong'an Daqiang Opera P360
Yong'antang Pharmacy P537
Yonghegong Lamasery P167
Yongle Palace in Shanxi Province P176
Yongle Palace Mural P254
Yongxin Shield Dance P350
Youku P684
Youth Volunteers P552
Youth.cn P666
Yu Shumei P811
Yuan Dynasty (1206-1368) P27
Yuan Hua P762
Yuan Longping P199
Yuan Weimin P747
Yuanming Garden P478
Yuanming Schoolroom P170
Yuantong Temple P172
Yue Cai (Guangdong Cuisine) P504
Yue Melody P365
Yue Opera P372
Yuefu (Han Music Bureau) Poetry P458
Yuelushan Temple P171
Yuexiu (Guangdong Embroidery) P287 (P403)
Yueyang Tower P483
Yugur Ethnic Group P53
Yuhang Rolling Lantern Dance P351
Yulin Folk Songs P389
Yungang Grottoes P291
Yunnan Museum P302
Yunnan Province P626
Yuping Flute Making Technique P419

Zaju P460
ZBOX P684
ZCOM P684
Zeng Guoqiang P736
Zeng Houyi Bells P266
Zgjx.cn P664
Zhalong Nature Reserve P597
Zhan Xugang P737
Zhang Deying P755
Zhang Guozheng P736
Zhang Heng and Armillary Sphere P23
Zhang Jian P824
Zhang Jun P800
Zhang Lianwei P813
Zhang Ning P799
Zhang Shan P766
Zhang Xiaoquan Scissors Forging Skills P421
Zhang Xielin P755
Zhang Yining P759
Zhang Yuehong P748
Zhang Zeduan and the Qingming Festival by the Riverside P254
Zhangha of the Dai Ethnic Group P393
Zhangjiajie Nature Reserve P597
Zhangzhou New Year Woodblock Prints P399
Zhangzhou Wood Puppet Head Carving P409
Zhanshan Temple P171
Zhanzuo.com P686
Zhao Changjun P834
Zhao Hongbo P809
Zhao Mengfu P251
Zhao Ruirui P748
Zhao Tiliang P821
Zhao Xue P832
Zhao Yongsheng P786
Zhaozhou Bridge P482
Zhe Cai (Zhejiang Cuisine) P505
Zhe Pama and Zhe Mima P321
Zhejiang Museum P299
Zhejiang Province P623
Zhejiang University P234
Zhejiang's "13-roomed" Residence P480
Zheng Fengrong P784
Zheng Haixia P741
Zheng He's Voyage to Southeast Asia and the Indian Ocean P28
Zheng Jie P790
Zheng Minzhi P755
Zheng Shiyu P820
Zheng Xie P251
Zhengshan Souchong P513
Zhengzi Opera P362
Zhenjiang Hengshun Fragrant Vinegar Distilling Skills P428
Zhenjiu Jiayi Jing (Jiayi Canon on Acupuncture and Moxibustion) P537
Zhijiang Folk Wind and Percussion Music P340
Zhong Ling P779
Zhongshan Xianshui Song P330
Zhou Dance P355
Zhou Jianming P814
Zhou Yi (Changes of Zhou, also called Yi Jing) P457
Zhoushan Gong and Drum Music P339
Zhu Chen P831
Zhu Haiying P780
Zhuhai Film Festival P466
Zhu Jianhua P785
Zhu Qinan P769
Zhu Younan P815
Zhuang Ethnic Group P41
Zhuang Ethnic Group Embroidery Skills P416
Zhuang Opera P379
Zhuang Xiaoyan P762
Zhuang Yong P793
Zhuang Zedong P755
Zhuang Zi P175 (P20)
Zhuang Zi (The Book of Zhuang Zi) P457
Zhubajie.com P688
Zhuihu P263
Zhuozheng Garden P476
Zhuxianzhen New Year Woodblock Prints P400 (P295)
Zigong Dinosaur Museum P313
Zigong Salt History Museum P313
Zigong Well Salt Drilling Skills P428
Ziyang Folk Song P332
Zol.com P677
Zou Shiming P761
Zou Zhenxian P785
Zouma Town Folklore P324
Zu Chongzhi and π P25
Zuoquan Blossom Tune P328

Sources of Data: Except for those otherwise indicated, all the data in this book is drawn from State Statistics Bureau sources: China Statistics Yearbook (all past years) and 2007 Statistics Communiqué on the National Economy and Social Development; and relevant departments and commissions.

图书在版编目（CIP）数据

中国辞典=China Encyclopedia：英文 /《中国辞典》编写组.
—北京：五洲传播出版社，2008.11
ISBN 978-7-5085-1385-0

Ⅰ.中… Ⅱ.中… Ⅲ.中国—概况—英文 Ⅳ. D61

中国版本图书馆CIP数据核字（2008）第089202号

中国辞典

出版发行：五洲传播出版社
地址：北京市海淀区北小马厂6号华天大厦24层
邮编：100038
电话：(86-10) 58891280/58880274
网址：www.cicc.org.cn

开本：210mm × 285mm 1/16
印张：57.5
版次：2008年11月第一版第一次印刷
印刷：北京华联印刷有限公司
印数：3000
书号：ISBN 978-7-5085-1385-0
定价：1280.00元